D1796693

THE DICTIONARY OF CLASSICAL HEBREW

Volume IV

ל—י

The Dictionary of Classical Hebrew

David J.A. Clines
Editor

Philip R. Davies J. Cheryl Exum John W. Rogerson
Consulting Editors

Volume IV

ל—י

John Elwolde
Executive Editor

Frank Gosling, David Stec,
with
Anne Lee
Research Associates

Published under the auspices of
The Society for Old Testament Study

and with the support of
The University of Sheffield

The Dictionary of Classical Hebrew

David J.A. Clines
Editor

Volume IV

ל—י

John Elwolde
Executive Editor

Sheffield
Sheffield Academic Press

1998

Published by Sheffield Academic Press Ltd
The Mansion House, Kingfield Road, Sheffield
England

Typeset by the Hebrew Dictionary Project
University of Sheffield
and
Printed on acid-free paper in Great Britain
by Bookcraft
Midsomer Norton, Somerset

British Library Cataloguing in Publication Data

Dictionary of Classical Hebrew. – Vol. 4: Yodh–Lamedh
I. Clines, David J. A.
492.43

ISBN 1 85075 681 3

CONTENTS

PREFACE

With this volume, the Dictionary of Classical Hebrew reaches the half-way mark. Four volumes have been completed, and another four remain to be written. If all goes according to plan, the complete Dictionary will be in the hands of scholars and students by the end of the year 2004. This fourth volume, the largest of all, has been compiled in the space of eighteen months, and it is hoped that the future volumes will appear at similar intervals.

When the first volume was published, in 1993, the Editor estimated the length of the articles of the dictionary proper in the subsequent volumes; five years later, it is interesting to compare the reality with the estimates.

vol. no.	estimated no. of pages of articles	actual number of pages of articles	actual number of total pages
1	372	372	475
2	533	518	660
3	407	308	424
4	483	512	642

It will be seen that the Dictionary proper has been kept close to the original targets, and we remain eager to maintain the uniformity of treatment and length throughout the entire work. The growing number of published texts from Qumran has made a noticeable difference in the size of the dictionary proper compared with what was originally envisaged. The Bibliography also has increased the size of each volume—but in so doing has added, we believe, significant extra value to the Dictionary.

This volume is expected to be the longest of the set of eight. Not only does it cover more than 1200 words, it also treats fourteen words occurring more than 1000 times: יהוה *Yahweh*, ישראל *Israel*, יום *day*, יד *hand*, ידע *know*, יצא *go out*, ישב *sit, dwell*, כל *all*, כי *for*, כ *as*, ל *to*, לא *not*, לפני *before*, and לקח *take*. For all these high-frequency words, as for the others in the Dictionary, we have considered and registered every occurrence—with the exceptions only of ל *to*, occurring over 26,000 times, לא *not* (c. 6500 times) and כ *as* (c. 3200 times).

Readers may be surprised to learn that every one of the references cited in the Dictionary has been looked up by hand in the Hebrew Bible or its relevant Classical Hebrew source. When there are so many printed and electronic concordances and other resources available, this may seem an antiquated way of working, but there are four reasons why we have maintained this pattern. The first is that our system of establishing the verbs of which a noun is the subject or object, and the nouns that are the subject or object of a verb, requires us to consider, for each occurrence, a much longer stretch of text than any concordance will show; for instance, sometimes the subject of a verb appears many verses or sentences before the verb itself. Secondly, we take account of, and register in the appropriate places, all the emendations mentioned in the critical apparatus to the *Biblia hebraica stuttgartensia*, and there is no convenient way of knowing whether such an emendation exists short of looking up each text. Thirdly, in our citations from the biblical texts we note pausal forms of words when they differ from the normal forms, and we can identify those forms only by inspecting the text of *Biblia hebraica stuttgartensia*. Fourthly, we want the satisfaction of assuring ourselves and our readers that everything written in our Dictionary has passed through the mind of a living Hebraist. We may not be infallible, and we certainly do not have the time to linger over every debatable point, but we regard it as a special merit of this Dictionary that it has not been generated automatically or mechanically.

In this fourth phase of the research, it is the Editor's pleasant duty to record his thanks for the excellent work of John Elwolde as Executive Editor, of David Stec and of Frank Gosling as full-time Research Associates, of Anne Lee as a part-time Research Associate, and of other participants in the work whose names are recorded below.

In broad terms, the key authors of this volume have been David Stec, who was responsible for Lamedh and the first half of Yodh, and Frank Gosling, who was responsible for Kaph and the second half of Yodh. Anne Lee drafted the articles on יהוה *Yahweh* and ירד *go down*, Rosemarie Kossov those on יהודה *Judah* and יצא *go out*, and James Harding those on ישׂראל *Israel* and ילד

give birth. John Rogerson very kindly exceeded his responsibility as a Consulting Editor by undertaking the entries for the prepositions כ *as* and ל *to*, as well as checking the Arabic transcriptions in the Bibliography. We are grateful to Carl Follingstad for his comments on an early draft of כי *for*. John Elwolde organized and supervised the work of writing the articles, updated the list of Qumran sources, and compiled the Bibliography on the basis of materials gathered by Kate Dove Davis, Anne Lee and Duncan Burns. Duncan Burns finalized the frequency indexes, while Anne Lee and Rosemarie Kossov helped in the preparation of the English–Hebrew index. A special debt of thanks is owed to John Jarick, who at short notice generously devoted himself to a week of proof-reading. David Clines edited the entire volume and proofread it in its final three sets of proofs.

It should be recorded that the whole of this volume, as of the previous three volumes, has not only been composed, but also typeset, by the researchers involved in the project. The accuracy, consistency and attractiveness of the text owes much to the vigilance and skill of the researchers as they have followed detailed and rigorous rules for the composition of their articles.

Thanks are due to those who have funded the work of this volume. The work of one Research Associate and of the part-time staff was supported by the Department of Biblical Studies in the University of Sheffield. Another Research Associate was largely supported by a major grant from the British Academy. Sheffield Academic Press, the publisher of the Dictionary, sustained one post and part of another.

The reception the Dictionary has received from the scholarly public has been extraordinarily positive and enthusiastic. There have indeed been some criticisms of the policies of the Dictionary, as is inevitable when matters of academic judgment are involved. But in general the Dictionary team have been much encouraged by the approbation their work has received, and purchasers of the Dictionary may also regard the scholarly reviews as enhancing the value of their investment in it.

DJAC
Sheffield, 7 July, 1998

INTRODUCTION

Readers are referred to the Introductions in previous volumes for details of the principles and procedures of this Dictionary. No substantive changes have been made in this volume, but there are a few points we would draw to the attention of readers of the Dictionary.

1. *Articles on Nouns and Articles on Verbs*

It may be worth repeating something said in the Introduction to Volume 2 on this matter. It is a principle of the Dictionary that, in the case of nouns, the verbs of which they are the subjects and objects are recorded, and, in the case of verbs, the nouns that they have as subjects and objects. If readers compare entries for verbs and nouns—for example, for the combination אָב *father* and בוא *come*—they might well expect to find the same data in both places, and, not finding it, might think there is an error in the Dictionary. They might well think, that is, that there should be as many places where אָב *father* is the subject of בוא *come* as where בוא *come* has אָב *father* as its subject. That is not the case, however, and it is not an error. Such a discrepancy occurs for this reason: when we are looking for the subject of *come*, we go back as many verses as it takes to find it. But when we are looking for the verbs of which *father* is the subject, we do not always go beyond the verse in which the noun occurs. Thus in the article on אָב *father* there are five places cited where it is the subject of בוא *come*, whereas in the article on בוא *come* there are eleven places cited where אָב *father* is the subject. To include every verb of which David (for example) is the subject, even verbs many verses later than the occurrence of the name David, would extend the work and the size of the Dictionary unreasonably. The rule of thumb the Dictionary user may find useful is this: entries on verbs are fuller than those on nouns.

2. *Organization of Subjects and Objects*

Users of the Dictionary will be familiar with its practice of showing, for every verb, the nouns that are its subjects and objects, and, for every noun, the verbs of which it is the subject or object. Some users, however, have been a little mystified about how the sections listing those subjects and objects have been organized, and it may be helpful to say here that it is by a principle of association. A good example of the principle can be seen in the article on יהוה *Yahweh*, where an outline of the structure appears at the beginning of the article. In that case, because there are of course very many verbs of which יהוה is the subject, our categorization has been explicit in the outline, showing that we review the verbs in these groups: states and attributes, movement, communication, perception, general activities, beneficial activities, hostile activities.

A similar principle is in operation for other articles. Thus in articles on nouns, the verbs of which the noun is the subject are commonly arranged with verbs for being at the beginning, then verbs for movement, then verbs for speaking, and so on. In the case of articles on verbs, the subjects are commonly arranged with words for persons at the beginning, then words for things, and words for abstracts at the end. No two words can be treated exactly alike, and the authors of each article have been free to arrange the words in the sequence that they feel makes best logical sense.

We could, of course, have arranged words within the sections Subject and Object alphabetically, so that if the reader had wished to find, for example, where יהוה *Yahweh* was the subject of אמר *say*, one could have found a list of references very readily. But we thought that many other readers would also welcome finding close together all the verbs for Yahweh's communication, whether אמר *say* or דבר *speak* or צוה *command* or ענה *answer*. For that added benefit, the principle of alphabetization had to be sacrificed, but we decided it was worth it.

3. *Gendered Language*

From the beginning, we were clear that in the *Dictionary of Classical Hebrew* we should strive to use gender-inclusive language in English as far as possible (cf. Volume 1, p. 16), translating אָדָם, for example, as *human*, *humankind* and the like, and reserving *man* for the gendered Hebrew nouns such as אִישׁ and

גֶּבֶר. Increasingly, we have been taking care to find suitable equivalents for traditional translations such as *workman* and *ploughman* and *watchman* (in this volume they will usually be *artisan, plougher* and *sentry*), so as not to imply that only males may fulfil such occupations (even if in the world of Classical Hebrew that may have been typically the case).

In this volume, we have taken a further step, in eliminating gendered forms in English where modern practice favours the use of an unmarked form. Thus, for example, both נָבִיא and נְבִיאָה are now translated *prophet*, since *prophetess* is now almost an archaic form, and one that perpetuates the idea, no longer defensible, that prophets are, normally and properly speaking, male. But to indicate that in Hebrew the feminine form is marked, as it no longer is in English, we write נְבִיאָה *prophet* (fem.), both to signify that fact and at the same time to suggest that the appropriate English term for a female prophet is—*prophet*. The same goes for quite a few other words; thus רֹעֶה is *shepherd* and רֹעָה is *shepherd* (fem.), not *shepherdess*, while מוֹאָבִי is *Moabite* and מוֹאָבִיָּה is *Moabite* (fem.), not *Moabitess*.

These were cases where English offers gender-marked forms corresponding to the Hebrew but where we feel that the marked forms in English should now be abandoned. What of cases where Hebrew marks gender but English does not? There is no problem about how we should translate or gloss, for example, אֹפֶה and אֹפָה; they are both *baker*. But as dictionary makers we can hardly ignore the fact that אֹפָה is only a *female* baker. In such cases we have glossed אֹפֶה as *baker* and אֹפָה as *baker* (fem.).

There would seem to be less difficulty with words that are in English both gender-marked and gender-specific, and that are not due for retirement. A מֶלֶךְ and a *king* can only be males and a מַלְכָּה and a *queen* can only be females, and it seems to us that no inappropriate implication is conveyed by the retention of the traditional terms. So too a כֶּבֶשׂ is a male sheep, a *ram*, and a כִּבְשָׂה is a female sheep, a *ewe*.

A שִׁפְחָה remains a *female servant*, since there is no corresponding male form. It might seem that we should similarly gloss עֶבֶד as *male servant* or *manservant* (it would be interesting to think of the Ebed Yhwh as the *manservant of the LORD*); and so we would if there were only the singulars to consider. But in the plural, we supposed that in principle נְבִאִים *prophets* and אֲנָשִׁים

men and perhaps also עֲבָדִים *servants* can include women as well as men. If we glossed עֶבֶד as *male servant* we would mean that it is only ever used of males, whether in singular or plural, just as שִׁפְחָה is only ever used of females; and we did not think that was the case.

As will be evident to anyone who has spent more than a few minutes thinking about it, the whole matter is very complicated, and we cannot pretend to have solved the problems definitively. But the foregoing are, rightly or wrongly, our provisional decisions.

4. *Exhaustive Treatment*

In this volume every word beginning with Yodh, Kaph and Lamedh has been treated exhaustively—with the exception only of the very common words or particles כ *like,* כי *for,* ל *to* and לא *not.* That is to say, for every word this Dictionary cites every place it occurs in Classical Hebrew texts, and every occurrence has been analysed according to the principles of the Dictionary. That applies even for high-frequency words like יהוה *Yahweh,* which occurs over 7000 times.

The Sources

a. *Qumran and Related Texts*

The following list and bibliography replaces those of Volume 1, pp. 34-45, 51-54, Volume 2, pp. 15-31, and Volume 3, pp. 11-27. The second list of Dead Sea Scrolls published in Volume 1 (pp. 45-51), which correlates the sigla used in the Dictionary with numbers assigned to documents, will be replaced in the final volume of the Dictionary.

Qumran and Related Non-Biblical Texts in Cave and Number Order

In this list, which is intended to include all known non-biblical texts in Hebrew, published and unpublished, from Qumran and related sites, there appear, in the five columns, the following:

(1) The number by which the texts are known (in the case of four major Qumran texts from Cave 1 and several minor Cave 4 texts, no number is assigned).

(2) The abbreviated title used in the Dictionary.

(3) Short title or description of the text (titles are capitalized, whereas mere descriptions, such as 'sapiential', are shown in lower case).

(4) A reference to the edition of the text that has been the standard for this Dictionary.

(5) A reference to the page numbers of the translation of the text (or part of it) by F. García Martínez; but occasionally the reference is to another English translation, notably that of M. Wise, M. Abegg, and E. Cook (WAC). For the third column in particular, we have also made use of the latest translation of the Dead Sea Scrolls by G. Vermes.

As far as we can tell, all published texts—that is, texts that have been printed in transcription, with or without translation and technical notes—have been read for the Dictionary and incorporated in it. As further texts are published, information relating to them will be included in updated lists in future volumes of the Dictionary.

No.	Siglum	Name / Description	Edition	Translation
Cave 1				
	1QH	Thanksgiving Hymns (*Hodayot*)	Licht	317-61
	1QM	War Scroll (includes 1Q33: two fragments of 1QM, col. 19)	DSS, II, 96-140	95-115
	1QpHab	Habakkuk *pesher*	Horgan, 1-9	197-202
	1QS	Community Rule	DSS, I, 6-51	3-19
1Q14	1QpMic	Micah *pesher*	DJD, I, 77-80	193-94
1Q15	1QpZeph	Zephaniah *pesher*	DJD, I, 80	202
1Q16	1QpPs	Psalms *pesher*	DJD, I, 81-82	206
1Q17	1QJub^{a}	Jubilees	DJD, I, 82-83	245
1Q18	1QJub^{b}	Jubilees	DJD, I, 83-84	245
1Q19	1QNoah	Book of Noah	DJD, I, 84-86, 152	263
1Q22	1QDM	Words of Moses/*Dibre Mosheh*	DJD, I, 91-97	276-77
1Q25		prophetic	DJD, I, 100-101	
1Q26		sapiential	DJD, I, 101-102	388^{WAC}
1Q27	1QMyst	wisdom text mentioning *razim*	DJD, I, 102-107	399-400
1Q28a	1QSa	Community Rule	DSS, I, 110-17	126-28
1Q28b	1QSb	Community Rule	DSS, I, 122-31	432-33
1Q29		Liturgy of the Three Tongues of Fire	DJD, I, 130-32	277-78
1Q30		liturgical	DJD, I, 132-33	438
1Q31		liturgical	DJD, I, 133-34	438
1Q34	1QLitPr	Festival Prayers	DJD, I, 152-55	411
1Q35	1QH^{b}	two fragments of 1QH	DJD, I, 136-38	361-62
1Q36		Hymns	DJD, I, 138-41	
1Q37-40		hymnic	DJD, I, 141-43	438
1Q41-50		unidentified	DJD, I, 144-45	
1Q51		Eternal Fragment	DSS, II, 216	
1Q52-62		unidentified	DJD, I, 146-47	
1Q69		unidentified	DJD, I, 148	
Cave 2				
2Q19	2QJub^{a}	Jubilees	DJD, III, 77-78	244
2Q20	2QJub^{b}	Jubilees	DJD, III, 78-79	245
2Q21	2QapMoses	perh. Moses Apocryphon	DJD, III, 79-81	281
2Q22	2QapDavid	perh. David Apocryphon	DJD, III, 81-82	224
2Q23	2QapProph	Apocryphal prophecy	DJD, III, 82-84	
2Q25	2QJuridical	juridical	DSS, II, 218	86
2Q27		unidentified	DJD, III, 91	
2Q28	2QVerdict	Verdict Fragment	DSS, II, 223	
2Q29–33		unidentified	DJD, III, 92-93	

Cave 3

3Q4	3QpIsa	Isaiah *pesher*	DJD, III, 95-96	185
3Q5	3QJub	Jubilees	DJD, III, 96-98	244
3Q6	3QHymn	Hymn	DJD, III, 98	401
3Q7	3QTJud	Testament of Judah	DJD, III, 99	265
3Q8		Angel of Peace	DJD, III, 100	
3Q9		perh. sectarian	DJD, III, 100-101	
3Q10-11		unidentified	DJD, III, 101-102	
3Q15	3QTr	Copper Scroll	DJD, III, 284-302	461-63

Cave 4

4Q158	4QBibPar	Biblical Paraphrase	DJD, V, 1-6	219-22
4Q159	4QOrd[a]	Ordinances	DSS, I, 150-57	86-87
4Q160	4QVisSam	Vision of Samuel	DJD, V, 9-11	284
4Q161	4QpIsa[a]	Isaiah *pesher*	DJD, V, 11-15	185-86
4Q162	4QpIsa[b]	Isaiah *pesher*	DJD, V, 15-17	186-87
4Q163	4QpIsa[c]	Isaiah *pesher*	DJD, V, 17-27	187-90
4Q164	4QpIsa[d]	Isaiah *pesher*	DJD, V, 27-28	190-91
4Q165	4QpIsa[e]	Isaiah *pesher*	DJD, V, 28-30	191
4Q166	4QpHos[a]	Hosea *pesher*	DJD, V, 31-32	191-92
4Q167	4QpHos[b]	Hosea *pesher*	DJD, V, 32-36	192-93
4Q168	4QpMic	Micah *pesher*	DJD, V, 36	194-95
4Q169	4QpNah	Nahum *pesher*	DJD, V, 37-42	195-97
4Q170	4QpZeph	Zephaniah *pesher*	DJD, V, 42	203
4Q171	4QpPs[a]	Psalms *pesher*	DJD, V, 42-50	203-206
4Q172	4QpUnid	unidentified *pesher*	DJD, V, 50-51	
4Q173	4QpPs[b]	Psalms *pesher*	DJD, V, 51-53	206-207
4Q174	4QMidrEschat[a]	eschatological	Steudel, 23-29	136-37
4Q175	4QTestim	Testimonia	DJD, V, 57-60	137-38
4Q176	4QTanḥ	Consolations	DJD, V, 60-67	208-209
4Q176a	4QJub[i]	Jubilees 23 (=4Q176 fr. 19-21)	Kister, *RQ* 12 (1987)	244
4Q177	4QMidrEschat[b]	eschatological	Steudel, 71-76	209-11
4Q178		unidentified	DJD, V, 74-75	
4Q179	4QapLam[a]	Lamentation on Jerusalem	DJD, V, 75-77	401-402
4Q180	4QAges[a]	Ages of Creation/ Wicked and Holy	DSS, II, 206-10	211-12
4Q181	4QAges[b]	Ages of Creation/ Wicked and Holy	DSS, II, 208-12	212-13
4Q182	4QCat	Catena	DJD, V, 80-81	213
4Q183		historical	DJD, V, 81-82	213
4Q184	4QWiles	Wiles of the Wicked Woman	DJD, V, 82-85	379-80
4Q185		Eulogy on Wisdom	DJD, V, 85-87	380-82

4Q186	4QCrypt	horoscopes	DJD, V, 88-91	456
4Q200	4QTobit^{e}	Tobit	DJD, XIX, 63-76	297-99
4Q215	4QTNaph	Testament of Naphtali	DJD, XXII, 78-81	270-71
4Q215a	4QTime	Time of Righteousness	WA, III, 7-8	271
4Q216	4QJub^{a}	Jubilees 1-2	DJD, XIII, 5-22	238-40
4Q217	4QJub^{b}	Jubilees (perh. 1-2)	DJD, XIII, 24-33	
4Q218	4QJub^{c}	Jubilees 2	DJD, XIII, 37-38	242
4Q219	4QJub^{d}	Jubilees 21-22	DJD, XIII, 42-53	242-43
4Q220	4QJub^{e}	Jubilees 21	DJD, XIII, 57-61	
4Q221	4QJub^{f}	Jubilees 21-23, 33, 37-39	DJD, XIII, 66-85	243-44 (fr. 1)
4Q222	4QJub^{g}	Jubilees 25, 27, 48	DJD, XIII, 89-94	
4Q223-24	4QJub^{h}	Jubilees 32, 34-40	DJD, XIII, 101-40	
4Q225	4QpsJub^{a}	Pseudo-Jubilees /	DJD, XIII, 143-55	262-63^{WAC}
		Genesis and Exodus Paraphrase		
4Q226	4QpsJub^{b}	Pseudo-Jubilees	DJD, XIII, 159-69	263-64^{WAC}
4Q227	4QpsJub^{c}	Pseudo-Jubilees /	DJD, XIII, 172-75	245 (fr. 2)
		Enoch and the Watchers		
4Q228	4QCitJub	Text with a Citation of Jubilees	DJD, XIII, 178-85	
4Q229		pseudepigraphon in Mishnaic Hebrew		
4Q230		Catalogue of Spirits		
4Q231		Catalogue of Spirits		
4Q232		perh. New Jerusalem		
4Q233		place names		
4Q234		exercise on Genesis 27.20-21		
4Q239		*pesher* on the true Israel		
4Q240		perh. commentary on Song of Songs		
4Q241		fragments citing Lamentations		
4Q247	4QApocWeeks	*pesher* on Apocalypse of Weeks	Milik, *Enoch*, 256	
4Q248	4QActs	Acts of a Greek King	WA, III, 33	271^{WAC}
4Q249-50	4QMSM	*Midrash Sepher Mosheh*		
4Q251	4QHalakhah^{a}	halakhic	WA, III, 34-40	272-74^{WAC}
4Q252	4QCommGenA	Commentary on Genesis	DJD, XXII, 193-207	212-15
4Q253	4QCommGenB	Commentary on Genesis	DJD, XXII, 210-12	215
4Q253a	4QCommMal	Commentary on Malachi	DJD, XXII, 214-15	215
4Q254	4QCommGenC	Commentary on Genesis	DJD, XXII, 220-36	215-16
4Q254a	4QCommGenD	Commentary on Genesis	DJD, XXII, 234-36	216
4Q255	4QS^{a}	Community Rule	WA, III, 41-42	20
4Q256	4QS^{b}	Community Rule	DSS, I, 60-67 21 (fr. 5)	
4Q257	4QS^{c}	Community Rule	WA, III, 48-50	21-22 (fr. 1)
4Q258	4QS^{d}	Community Rule	DSS, I, 72-83 22 (fr. 1.1)	
4Q259	4QS^{e}	Community Rule	WA, III, 58-61	26-27
4Q260	4QS^{f}	Community Rule	WA, III, 62-64	29-30
4Q261	4QS^{g}	Community Rule	WA, III, 65-67	30-31

4Q262	4QS[h]	Community Rule	WA, III, 68-69	31
4Q263	4QS[i]	Community Rule	DSS, I, 100-101	31
4Q264	4QS[j]	Community Rule	DSS, I, 102-103	31-32
4Q265	4QSD	Community Rule and Damascus Document	WA, III, 72-78	279-81[WAC]
4Q266	4QD[a]	Damascus Document	DJD, XVIII, 31-93	48-57
4Q267	4QD[b]	Damascus Document	DJD, XVIII, 96-113	60-62
4Q268	4QD[c]	Damascus Document	DJD, XVIII, 119-21	47-48
4Q269	4QD[d]	Damascus Document	DJD, XVIII, 125-36	67-69
4Q270	4QD[e]	Damascus Document	DJD, XVIII, 141-68	62-67
4Q271	4QD[f]	Damascus Document	DJD, XVIII, 173-83	57-60
4Q272	4QD[g]	Damascus Document	DJD, XVIII, 188-91	69-70
4Q273	4QD[h]	Damascus Document	DJD, XVIII, 194-98	70
4Q274	4QTohA	Purification Rules	WA, III, 79-82	88-89
4Q275	4QTohB[a]	Purification/Initiation Rules	WA, III, 83-84	89
4Q276	4QTohB[b]	Purification Rules	WA, III, 85	89
4Q277	4QTohB[c]	Purification Rules	WA, III, 86-87	89-90
4Q278	4QTohC	Purification Rules	WA, III, 88	90
4Q279	4QTohD	Purification Rules	WA, III, 89	286[WAC]
4Q280	4QBer[f]	Curse on Melchiresha	WA, III, 91	434
4Q281-83		Purification Rules		
4Q284	4QNidd	Menstrual Impurity	WA, III, 92-95	290[WAC]
4Q284a	4QLeqeṭ	Gleaning	WA, III, 96	90
4Q285	4QM[g]	perh. War Scroll (fr. 1=11QBer)	WA, II, 223-27	292-94[WAC]
4Q286	4QBer[a]	Blessings and Curses	WA, III, 97-106	434-35
4Q287	4QBer[b]	Blessings	WA, III, 107-111	435-36
4Q288	4QBer[c]	Blessings and Curses	WA, III, 112-13	289[WAC]
4Q289	4QBer[d]	Blessings and Curses	WA, III, 114	289[WAC]
4Q290	4QBer[e]			
4Q291	4QPrayers[a]		WA, III, 115-16	
4Q292	4QPrayers[b]		WA, III, 117	
4Q293	4QPrayers[c]		WA, III, 118	
4Q294–97		rules and prayers		
4Q298	4QCryptA	Words of the *Maskil*	DJD, XX, 19-30	382
4Q299	4QMyst[a]	wisdom text mentioning *razim*	DJD, XX, 34-97	400 (fr. 3a2-b)
4Q300	4QMyst[b]	wisdom text mentioning *razim*	DJD, XX, 100-112	400-401
4Q301	4QMyst[c]	perh. related to foregoing	DJD, XX, 114-23	401
4Q302	4QAdmonPar	Admonitory Parable	DJD, XX, 129-49	296[WAC] (fr. 2.2; 3.2)
4Q303	4QCreatA	Meditation on Creation	DJD, XX, 152-53	
4Q304	4QCreatB	Meditation on Creation	DJD, XX, 155	
4Q305	4QCreatC	Meditation on Creation	DJD, XX, 157-58	

4Q306	4QErr	Men of People who Err	WA, III, 122-23	
4Q307		sapiential		
4Q308		sapiential		
4Q311		unidentified		
4Q312		Hebrew text in cursive Phoenician		
4Q313		unidentified, cryptic		
4Q316		unidentified		
4Q317	4QAstrCrypt	Phases of Moon (cryptic)	Milik, *Enoch*, 68-69	302-303[WAC]
4Q319	4QOtot	Heavenly Concordances	WA, I, 96-101	27-29
4Q320	4QMishA	Priestly Calendar	WA, I, 60-67 452-54	
4Q321	4QMishB[a]	Priestly Calendar	WA, I, 68-73 454-55	
4Q321a	4QMishB[b]	Priestly Calendar	WA, I, 74-76 312[WAC]	
4Q322	4QMishC[a]	Priestly Calendar	WA, I, 77-78 314[WAC]	
4Q323	4QMishC[b]	Priestly Calendar	WA, I, 79-81 315[WAC]	
4Q324	4QMishC[c]	Priestly Calendar	WA, I, 81-82 315[WAC]	
4Q324a	4QMishC[d]	Priestly Calendar	WA, I, 82-84 316[WAC]	
4Q324b	4QMishC[e]	Priestly Calendar	WA, I, 84-85 316[WAC]	
4Q324c	4QMishC[f]	Priestly Calendar		
4Q325	4QMishD	Priestly Calendar	WA, I, 86-87 317-18[WAC]	
4Q326	4QMishE[a]	Priestly Calendar	WA, I, 88	318[WAC]
4Q327	4QMishE[b]	Priestly Calendar	WA, I, 89-91 455	
4Q328	4QMishF[a]	Priestly Calendar	WA, I, 92	320[WAC]
4Q329	4QMishF[b]	Priestly Calendar	WA, I, 93-95 321[WAC]	
4Q329a	4QMishG	Priestly Calendar	WA, I, 94	322[WAC]
4Q330	4QMishH	Priestly Calendar	WA, I, 95	322[WAC]
4Q331		historical		
4Q332		historical		
4Q333		historical		
4Q334	4QOrdo	Liturgical Calendar	WA, III, 124-25	323[WAC]
4Q335–336		astronomical		
4Q337		calendar		
4Q338		genealogical		
4Q340	4QNetin	List of Nethinim	DJD, XIX, 82	
4Q341	4QNames	List of Proper Names	Naveh, *IEJ* 36 (1986)	
4Q344		Debt Acknowledgment		
4Q348		act regarding ownership		
4Q349		sale of property		
4Q356		account of money		
4Q360		writing exercise		
4Q362		cryptic		
4Q363		cryptic		
4Q363a		cryptic		
4Q364	4QRP[b]	Reworked Pentateuch	DJD, XIII, 205-54	325-26[WAC]

4Q365	4QRP[c]	Reworked Pentateuch	DJD, XIII, 263-318	222-23
4Q365a		perh. shorter version of Temple Scroll	DJD, XIII, 322-33	223-24 (fr. 2)
4Q366	4QRP[d]	Reworked Pentateuch	DJD, XIII, 337-43	
4Q367	4QRP[e]	Reworked Pentateuch	DJD, XIII, 347-51	
4Q368	4QapPent	Pentateuch Apocryphon	WA, III, 135-39	
4Q369	4QPrEnosh	perh. Prayers of Enosh and Enoch	DJD, XIII, 354-62	329-30[WAC]
4Q370	4QAdmon	Admonition on the Flood	DJD, XIX, 90-97	224-25
4Q371	4QapJoseph[a]	Joseph Apocryphon	WA, III, 140-44	
4Q372	4QapJoseph[b]	Joseph Apocryphon	WA, III, 145-53	225-26
4Q373	4QapJoseph[c]	Joseph Apocryphon	WA, III, 154	226
4Q374	4QDiscourse	Discourse on the Exodus / Conquest Tradition	DJD, XIX, 100-110	278 (Col.2.2)
4Q375	4QapMos[a]	Moses Apocryphon	DJD, XIX, 113-18	278
4Q376	4QapMos[b]	Moses Apocryphon (1.1-2 = 1Q29 1)	DJD, XIX, 123-29	279
4Q377	4QapMos[c]	Moses Apocryphon	WA, III, 164-66	338[WAC]
4Q378	4QapJoshua[a]	Joshua Apocryphon	DJD, XXII, 242-37	282, 340-41[WAC]
4Q379	4QapJoshua[b]	Joshua Apocryphon	DJD, XXII, 264-88	283
4Q380	4QapPs[a]	Non-Canonical Psalms	Schuller, 241-65	311-12
4Q381	4QapPs[b]	Non-Canonical Psalms	Schuller, 71-240	312-16
4Q382	4QparaKings	Elijah Apocryphon	DJD, XIII, 364-416	348[WAC] (fr. 1, 2, 9, 31, 104)
4Q383	4QapJerA	Jeremiah Apocryphon		
4Q384	4QapJerB	perh. Jeremiah Apocryphon	DJD, XIX, 140-52	350[WAC] (fr. 7, 9)
4Q385	4QpsEzek[a]	Pseudo-Ezekiel, Pseudo-Moses, Apocryphal Jeremiah	WA, III, 228-44	350-52[WAC]
4Q386	4QpsEzek[b]	Pseudo-Ezekiel	WA, III, 245-47	287
4Q387	4QpsEzek[c]	Pseudo-Ezekiel	WA, III, 248-51	353-54[WAC]
4Q388	4QpsEzek[d]	Pseudo-Ezekiel, Pseudo-Moses	WA, III, 252-58	
4Q389	4QpsMos[d]	Pseudo-Ezekiel, Pseudo-Moses, Apocryphal Jeremiah	WA, III, 259-63	354-55[WAC]
4Q390	4QpsMos[e]	Pseudo-Moses	WA, III, 264-66	280-81
4Q391	4QpsEzek[e]	Pseudo-Ezekiel	DJD, XIX, 156-93	
4Q392		liturgical	WA, II, 38-39	438
4Q393	4QConfess	Communal Confession	WA, III, 267-70	357[WAC]
4Q394-99	4QMMT	Halakhic Composition	DJD, X, 44-63	77-85
4Q400	4QShirShabb[a]	Songs of the Sabbath Sacrifice	Newsom, 85-123	419-20
4Q401	4QShirShabb[b]	Songs of the Sabbath Sacrifice	Newsom, 125-46	420

4Q402	4QShirShabb[c]	Songs of the Sabbath Sacrifice	Newsom, 147-66	420-21
4Q403	4QShirShabb[d]	Songs of the Sabbath Sacrifice	Newsom, 185-247	421-24
4Q404	4QShirShabb[e]	Songs of the Sabbath Sacrifice	Newsom, 249-55	424-25
4Q405	4QShirShabb[f]	Songs of the Sabbath Sacrifice	Newsom, 257-354	426-30
4Q406	4QShirShabb[g]	Songs of the Sabbath Sacrifice	Newsom, 255-57	
4Q407	4QShirShabb[h]	Songs of the Sabbath Sacrifice	Newsom, 259-60	
4Q408		sapiential	WA, II, 240-43	377[WAC]
4Q409	4QLiturgy	liturgical	WA, III, 297-98	402
4Q410		sapiential	WA, II, 40	380[WAC]
4Q411	4QsapHymn	Sapiential Hymn	DJD, XX, 160-62	
4Q412	4QsapDidA	Sapiential-Didactic Work	DJD, XX, 164-67	379[WAC] (fr. 1)
4Q413	4QdivProv	On Divine Providence	DJD, XX, 169-71	382-83
4Q414	4QBapt	Baptismal Hymn	WA, III, 299-307	439
4Q415		sapiential	WA, II, 44-53	380-82WAC (fr. 6, 9)
4Q416		sapiential/Children of Salvation	WA, II, 54-62	383-85
4Q417		sapiential	WA, II, 63-76	385-87
4Q418		sapiential/Children of Salvation	WA, II, 77-154	388-93
4Q419		sapiential	WA, II, 155-58	393
4Q420	4QWays[a]	Ways of Righteousness	DJD, XX, 174-82	390[WAC] (fr. 1a2-b)
4Q421	4QWays[b]	Ways of Righteousness	DJD, XX, 185-201	390[WAC] (fr. 1a2-b)
4Q422	4QParGenEx	Paraphrase of Genesis and Exodus	DJD, XIII, 421-41	391-93[WAC]
4Q423		sapiential	WA, II, 166-73	388[WAC]
4Q423a		sapiential	WA, II, 166	
4Q424		sapiential/Sons of Righteousness	WA, II, 174-76	393-94
4Q425	4QsapDidB	Sapiential-Didactic Work	DJD, XX, 204-10	
4Q426	4QsapHymnA	Sapiential Hymnic Work	DJD 20, 212-24	
4Q427	4QHod[a]	*Hodayot*/Hymns	WA, II, 254-61	362-66
4Q428	4QHod[b]	*Hodayot*/Hymns	WA, II, 262-74	367
4Q429	4QHod[c]	*Hodayot*/Hymns	WA, II, 275-78	367-69
4Q430	4QHod[d]	*Hodayot*/Hymns	WA, II, 279	369
4Q431	4QHod[e]	*Hodayot*/Hymns	WA, II, 280	369
4Q432	4QHod[f]	*Hodayot*/Hymns	WA, II, 281-84	
4Q433	4QpsHod[a]	*Hodayot*-like	WA, III, 308	
4Q434	4QBark[a]	Bless, my soul	WA, III, 309-313	436, 439
4Q435	4QBark[b]	Bless, my soul	WA, III, 314-15	
4Q436	4QBark[c]	Bless, my soul	WA, III, 316-17	437
4Q437	4QBark[d]	Bless, my soul	WA, III, 318-22	396-97[WAC]
4Q438	4QBark[e]	Bless, my soul	WA, III, 323-25	

4Q439	4QBark^{f}	perh. Bless, my soul	WA, III, 327-28	397^{WAC}
4Q440	4QpsHod^{b}	*Hodayot*-like	WA, III, 329-30	
4Q441		prayer/hymn		
4Q442	4QPrayer^{b}	prayer/hymn	WA, III, 331	
4Q443	4QPrayer^{c}	prayer/hymn	WA, III, 332-34	398^{WAC}
4Q444	4QPrayer^{d}	prayer/Meditation of Sage	WA, III, 335-36	398-99^{WAC}
4Q445		poetic fragments		
4Q446	4QPoet^{b}	poetic fragments	WA, III, 337	
4Q447		poetic fragments		
4Q448	4QJonathan	Paean for King Jonathan, Psalms 135, 154	Eshel, Eshel,Yardeni, *IEJ* 42 (1992)	399-400^{WAC}
4Q449	4QPrayer^{e}	prayer/hymn	WA, III, 338	
4Q450		prayer/hymn		
4Q451	4QPrayer^{g}	prayer/hymn	WA, III, 339	
4Q452		prayer/hymn		
4Q453	4QPrayer^{i}	prayer/hymn	WA, III, 340	
4Q454-56		prayers/hymns		
4Q457	4QPrayer^{m}	prayer/hymn	WA, III, 341-42	
4Q458	4QNarrA	Tree of Evil	WA, II, 287-91	228
4Q459	4QPseud^{a}	pseudepigraphic	WA, III, 343	
4Q460	4QPseud^{b}	pseudepigraphic	WA, III, 344-47	
4Q461	4QNarrB	narrative	WA, III, 348-49	
4Q462	4QNarrC	Return from Exile and Restoration of Jerusalem	DJD, XIX, 198-209	226-27 (fr. 1)
4Q463	4QNarrD	Israel's Restoration	DJD, XIX, 211-14	
4Q464	4QPatr	Exposition on the Patriarchs	DJD, XIX, 217-30	402^{WAC}
4Q464^{a}	4QNarrE	perh. Interpretation of Exodus	DJD, XIX, 231-32	
4Q464^{b}		unidentified	DJD, XIX, 233-34	
4Q465		unidentified		
4Q466-68		apocryphon		
4Q469		apocryphon	WA, III, 359-60	
4Q470	4QZedek	Michael and Zedekiah	DJD, XIX, 237-43	403^{WAC}
4Q471	4QM^{h}	Texts perhaps related to War or Temple Scroll, prayer of Michael, polemical text	WA, II, 294-96	404-405^{WAC}
4Q472		sapiential		
4Q473	4QTwoWays	Deuteronomic admonitions	DJD, XXII, 291-94	405^{WAC}
4Q474		sapiential	WA, III, 362	
4Q475		sapiential		
4Q476		sapiential	WA, II, 297-98	
4Q477	4QRebukes	offences and punishments	WA, III, 363-64	90-91
4Q478	4QFest	Fragment Mentioning Festivals	DJD, XXII, 295-96	
4Q479	4QDescDavid	David's Descendants	DJD, XXII, 297-99	

4Q480	4QNarrF	fragment mentioning God's miracles	DJD, XXII, 301-302	
4Q481	4QMixedKinds	Text Mentioning Mixed Kinds	DJD, XXII, 303-304	
4Q481a	4QapElisée	Elisha Apocryphon	DJD, XXII, 306-309	
4Q481b	4QNarrG	Restoration of Israel	DJD, XXII, 311-12	
4Q481c	4QPrMercy	Prayer for Mercy	DJD, XXII, 313-14	
4Q481d	4QRedInk	includes words in red ink	DJD, XXII, 315-19	
4Q481e	4QNarrH	perh. consequences of failure to attend to words of God	DJD, XXII, 321-22	
4Q482		perh. Jubilees	DJD, VII, 1-2	
4Q483		perh. Jubilees	DJD, VII, 2	
4Q484	4QTJud	Testament of Judah	DJD, VII, 3	
4Q485	4QProph	prophetic or sapiential	DJD, VII, 4	
4Q486	4QSap[a]	sapiential	DJD, VII, 4-5	
4Q487	4QSap[b]	sapiential	DJD, VII, 5-10	
4Q491	4QM[a]	War Scroll	DSS, II, 142-66	115-19
4Q492	4QM[b]	War Scroll	DSS, II, 168-70	120
4Q493	4QM[c]	War Scroll	DSS, II, 172	120-21
4Q494	4QM[d]	War Scroll	DSS, II, 174	121
4Q495	4QM[e]	War Scroll	DSS, II, 176	121
4Q496	4QM[f]	War Scroll	DSS, II, 178-96	121-23
4Q497	4QM[g]	War Scroll	DSS, II, 198-202	
4Q498	4QHymnSap	hymnic or sapiential	DJD, VII, 73-74	
4Q499	4QHymnPr	hymns and prayers	DJD, VII, 74-79	
4Q500	4QBen	Benediction	DJD, VII, 78-79	402
4Q501	4QapLam[b]	Lamentation	DJD, VII, 79-80	403
4Q502	4QRitMar	Marriage Rite	DJD, VII, 81-105	440-41
4Q503	4QPrQuot	Daily Prayers	DJD, VII, 105-36	407-10
4Q504	4QDibHam[a]	Words of the Luminaries	DJD, VII, 137-68	414-17
4Q505	4QDibHam[b]	Words of the Luminaries	DJD, VII, 168-70	418
4Q506	4QDibHam[c]	Words of the Luminaries	DJD, VII, 170-75	418
4Q507	4QPrFêtes[a]	Festival Prayers	DJD, VII, 175-77	411-12
4Q508	4QPrFêtes[b]	Festival Prayers	DJD, VII, 177-84	412
4Q509	4QPrFêtes[c]	Festival Prayers	DJD, VII, 184-215	412-13
4Q510	4QShir[a]	Songs of the Sage	DJD, VII, 215-19	371
4Q511	4QShir[b]	Songs of the Sage	DJD, VII, 219-62	371-76
4Q512	4QRitPur	Ritual of Purification	DJD, VII, 262-86	441-42
4Q513	4QOrd[b]	Ordinances	DSS, I, 158-75	91
4Q514	4QOrd[c]	Ordinances	DSS, I, 178-79	91-92
4Q515–520		unidentified	DJD, VII, 299-312	
4Q521	4QapMes	Messianic Apocalypse	Puech, *RQ* 15 (1992)	394-95
4Q522	4QSela	perh. Joshua Apocryphon/ Rock of Zion	EW, 90-91; Puech, *RB* 99 (1992)	227-28

4Q523		Hebrew fragment B		
4Q524		halakhic		
4Q525	4QBéat	Beatitudes	WA, II, 185-203	395
4Q526		Hebrew fragment C		
4Q527		Hebrew fragment D		
4Q528		Hebrew fragment E		
	4QAcademyFr	Academy Fragments	AHL, 368	
	4QpsHod^{c}	*Hodayot*-like	WA, III, 369-70	446-47^{WAC}
	4QpsHistA	pseudo-historical	WA, III, 371	
	4QpsHistB	pseudo-historical	WA, III, 372	
	4QHymn	hymnic	WA, III, 373	
	4QSl*	perh. apocryphon	WA, III, 374	
	4QS^{z}	Community Rule	WA, III, 375-76	
	4QUnidA	unidentified	WA, III, 377	
	4QUnidC	unidentified	WA, III, 378	
	4QUnidD	unidentified	WA, III, 379	
	4QUnidE	unidentified	WA, III, 380	
	4QUnidF	unidentified	WA, III, 381	
Cave 5				
5Q9	5QTopon	toponyms	DJD, III, 179-80	
5Q10	5QapMal	Malachi *pesher* or apocryphon	DJD, III, 180	203
5Q11	5QS	Community Rule	DSS, I, 106-107	32
5Q12	5QD	Damascus Document	DJD, III, 181	70-71
5Q13	5QRègle	similar to Community Rule and Damascus Document	DSS, I, 134-43	73
5Q14		liturgical curses	DJD, III, 183-84	403
5Q16-25		unidentified	DJD, III, 193-97	
Cave 6				
6Q9	6QapSamKgs	Samuel and Kings Apocryphon	DJD, III, 119-23	284
6Q10	6QProph	prophetic	DJD, III, 123-25	
6Q11	6QAllegory	Allegory of the Vine	DJD, III, 125-26	403
6Q12	6QapProph	apocryphal prophecy	DJD, III, 126	
6Q13	6QPriestProph	priestly prophecy	DJD, III, 126-27	
6Q15	6QD	Damascus Document	DJD, III, 128-31	71
6Q16	6QBen	blessings	DJD, III, 131-32	437
6Q17	6QCal	calendar	DJD, III, 132-33	
6Q18	6QHymn	Hymn	DJD, III, 133-36	403
6Q20	6QDeut	perh. Deuteronomy-related	DJD, III, 136-37	228
6Q21	6QfrProph	unidentified	DJD, III, 137	
6Q22		unidentified	DJD, III, 137	
6Q24–25		unidentified	DJD, III, 138	

6Q26		account or contract	DJD, III, 139	
6Q27–31		unidentified	DJD, III, 139-41	
6QX1–2		unidentified		
Cave 8				
8Q3	8QPhyl	phylactery	DJD, III, 149-57	
8Q5	8QHymn	liturgical poem	DJD, III, 161-63	404
Cave 9				
9Q1		unidentified	DJD, III, 163	
Cave 10				
10Q1		ostracon	DJD, III, 164	
Cave 11				
11Q5	11QPs[a]	apocryphal compositions (Cols. 18-19, 22, 24, 26-28)	DJD, IV, 39-40, 43, 45, 47-49, 53-93	304-10
11Q11	11QPsAp[a]	Apocryphal Psalms	Puech, *RQ* 14 (1990)	376
11Q12	11QJub	Jubilees; fragments of Temple Scroll, MS A	van der Woude, *Fragmente;* Milik, *Bib* 54 (1973)	241-42
11Q13	11QMelch	Melchizedek	Puech, *RQ* 12 (1987), 488-92	139–40
11Q14	11QBer	blessings (= 4Q285, fr. 1)	van der Woude, *Segensspruch*	124
11Q15	11QHymn[a]	*Hodayot*-like	van der Ploeg, *RQ* 12 (1985), 11	404
11Q16	11QHymn[b]	*Hodayot*-like	van der Ploeg, *RQ* 12 (1985), 12	
11Q17	11QShirShabb	Songs of the Sabbath Sacrifice	Newsom, 361-87	430-31
11Q19-20	11QT	Temple Scroll, MSS A-B	Qimron, *Temple Scroll*	154-84
11Q21–23		unidentified		
Masada				
MasShirShabb		Songs of the Sabbath Sacrifice	Newsom, 67-84	
MasJub		Jubilees fragment mentioning Mastemah	Talmon, 171-72	
MasUnid1		unidentified	Talmon, 173-76	
MasUnid2		unidentified	Talmon, 176-77	
Murabba'at				
Mur 6		hymn	DJD, II, 86	
Mur 7		contract	DJD, II, 86	
Mur 22		deed of sale	DJD, II, 118-19	

Mur 24		farming contracts	DJD, II, 122-34	
Mur 29		deed of sale	DJD, II, 140-44	
Mur 30		deed of sale	DJD, II, 144-48	
Mur 42	MurEpBeth-Mashiko	Bar-Kokhba correspondence	DJD, II, 155-59	Pardee, 124
Mur 43	MurEpBarC[a]	Bar-Kokhba correspondence	DJD, II, 159-61	Pardee, 130
Mur 44	MurEpBarC[b]	Bar-Kokhba correspondence	DJD, II, 161-63	Pardee, 132
Mur 45		Bar-Kokhba correspondence	DJD, II, 163-64	Pardee, 134
Mur 46	MurEpJon-athan	Bar-Kokhba correspondence	DJD, II, 164-66	Pardee, 136
Mur 47		Bar-Kokhba correspondence	DJD, II, 166-67	Pardee, 137
Mur 48		Bar-Kokhba correspondence	DJD, II, 167-68	Pardee, 138

Naḥal Ḥever

5/6 ḤevBA 44	deed of sale	Nebe, 156	
5/6 ḤevBA 45	contract	AHL, 407	Yadin, 178
5/6 ḤevBA 45 fr. 1–2		AHL, 407	Yadin, 178
5/6 ḤevBA 46	contract	AHL, 410	Yadin, 180
5/6 ḤevEp 1	Bar-Kokhba correspondence	AHL, 420	
5/6 ḤevEp 5	Bar-Kokhba correspondence	AHL, 421	
5/6 ḤevEp 12	Bar-Kokhba correspondence	AHL, 422	
5/6 ḤevEp 12 fr.	Bar-Kokhba correspondence	AHL, 422	

Cairo Genizah

CD	Damascus Document	Qimron, 'Text of CDC'	33-47
GnzPs	apocryphal psalms	AHL, 54-57	

Bibliography

Academy of the Hebrew Language (The Historical Dictionary of the Hebrew Language), *Materials for the Dictionary. Series I. 200 B.C.E.—300 C.E.* (Jerusalem: The Academy of the Hebrew Language, 1988)

AHL, *see* Academy of the Hebrew Language

Allegro, John M., with the collaboration of Arnold A. Anderson, *Qumrân Cave 4, I (4Q158–4Q186)* (Discoveries in the Judaean Desert of Jordan, 5; Oxford: Clarendon Press, 1968)

Attridge, Harold, Torleif Elgvin, Jozef Milik, Saul Olyan, John Strugnell, Emanuel Tov, James VanderKam and Sidnie White, in consultation with James VanderKam, *Qumran Cave 4; VIII: Parabiblical Texts, Part 1* (Discoveries in the Judaean Desert, 13; Oxford: Clarendon Press, 1994)

Baillet, M., *Qumrân Grotte 4 (4Q482–4Q520)* (Discoveries in the Judaean Desert, 7; Oxford: Clarendon Press, 1982)

—, J.T. Milik and R. de Vaux, *Les 'petites grottes' de Qumrân* (Discoveries in the Judaean Desert of Jordan, 3; Oxford: Clarendon Press, 1962)

Barthélemy, D. and J.T. Milik, with contributions by R. de Vaux, G.M. Crowfoot, H.J. Plenderleith and G.L. Harding, *Qumran Cave I* (Discoveries in the Judaean Desert, 1; Oxford: Clarendon Press, 1955)

Baumgarten, Joseph, on the basis of transcriptions by Józef T. Milik, with contributions by Stephen Pfann and Ada Yardeni, *Qumran Cave 4.* XIII. *The Damascus Document (4Q266–273)* (Discoveries in the Judaean Desert, 18; Oxford: Clarendon Press, 1996)

Benoit, P., J.T. Milik and R. de Vaux, with contributions by G.M. Crowfoot, E. Crowfoot and A. Grohmann, *Les grottes de Murabba'ât* (Discoveries in the Judaean Desert, 2; Oxford: Clarendon Press, 1961)

Brooke, George, John Collins, Torleif Elgvin, Peter Flint, Jonas Greenfield, Erik Larson, Carol Newsom, Émile Puech, Lawrence H. Schiffman, Michael Stone, and Julio Trebolle Barrera, in consultation with James VanderKam, *Qumran Cave 4.* XVII. *Parabiblical Texts, Part 3* (Discoveries in the Judaean Desert, 22; Oxford: Clarendon Press, 1996)

Broshi, Magen, Esther Eshel, Joseph Fitzmyer, Erik Larson, Carol Newsom, Lawrence Schiffman, Mark Smith, Michael Stone, John Strugnell and Ada Yardeni, in consultation with James VanderKam, *Qumran Cave 4.* XIV. *Parabiblical Texts, Part 2* (Discoveries in the Judaean Desert, 19; Oxford: Clarendon Press, 1995)

Charlesworth, James H. (ed.), *Rule of the Community and Related Documents* (The Dead Sea Scrolls: Hebrew, Aramaic, and Greek Texts with English Translations, 1; Tübingen/Louisville: J.C.B. Mohr [Paul Siebeck]/Westminster John Knox Press, 1994)

—*Damascus Document, War Scroll, and Related Documents* (The Dead Sea Scrolls: Hebrew, Aramaic, and Greek Texts with English Translations, 2; Tübingen/Louisville: J.C.B. Mohr [Paul Siebeck]/Westminster John Knox Press, 1995)

DJD, I, *see* Barthélemy, D. and J.T. Milik

DJD, II, *see* Benoit, P., J.T. Milik and R. de Vaux

DJD, III, *see* Baillet, M., J.T. Milik and R. de Vaux

DJD, IV, *see* Sanders, J.A.

DJD, V, *see* Allegro, J.M.

DJD, VII, *see* Baillet, M.

DJD, X, *see* Qimron, Elisha and John Strugnell

DJD, XIII, *see* Attridge, Harold, Torleif Elgvin, Jozéf Milik, *et al.*

DJD, XVIII, *see* Baumgarten, Joseph M. (1996)

DJD, XIX, *see* Broshi, Magen, Esther Eshel, Joseph Fitzmyer, *et al.*

DJD, XX, *see* Elgvin, Torleif, Menachem Kister, Timothy Lim, *et al.*

DJD, XXII, *see* Brooke, George, John Collins, Torleif Elgvin, *et al.*

DSS, I, see Charlesworth, James H. (1994)

DSS, II, see Charlesworth, James H. (1995)

Eisenman, Robert H. and Michael Wise, *The Dead Sea Scrolls Uncovered* (Shaftesbury, Dorset: Element, 1992)

Elgvin, Torleif, Menachem Kister, Timothy Lim, Bilhah Nitzan, Stephen Pfann, Elisha Qimron, Lawrence H. Schiffman, and Annette Steudel, in consultation with Joseph A.

Fitzmyer, *Qumran Cave 4. XV. Sapiential Texts, Part 1* (Discoveries in the Judaean Desert, 20; Oxford: Clarendon Press, 1977)

Eshel, Esther and Hanan Eshel and Ada Yardeni, 'A Qumran Composition Containing Part of Ps 154 and a Prayer for the Welfare of King Jonathan and his Kingdom', *IEJ* 42 (1992), pp. 199-229

EW, *see* Eisenman, Robert H. and Michael Wise

García Martínez, Florentino, *The Dead Sea Scrolls Translated: The Qumran Texts in English* (tr. Wilfred G.E. Watson; Leiden: E.J. Brill, 1994)

Horgan, Maurya P., *Pesharim: Qumran Interpretations of Biblical Books* (The Catholic Biblical Quarterly Monograph Series, 8; Washington, DC: The Catholic Biblical Association of America, 1979)

Kister, M., 'Newly Identified Fragments of the Book of Jubilees: Jub. 23:21-23, 30-31', *Revue de Qumran* 12 (1985–87), pp. 529-36

Licht, J., *The Thanksgiving Scroll* (Jerusalem: The Bialik Institute, 1957)

Milik, Józef T., 'A propos de 11QJub', *Biblica* 54 (1973), pp. 77-78

—with the collaboration of Matthew Black, *The Books of Enoch: Aramaic Fragments of Qumrân Cave 4* (Oxford: Clarendon Press, 1976)

Naveh, Joseph, 'A Medical Document or a Writing Exercise? The So-called 4Q Therapeia', *Israel Exploration Journal* 36 (1986), pp. 52-55

Nebe, G.W., 'Die hebräische Sprache der Naḥal Ḥever Dokumente 5/6Ḥev 44–46', in *The Hebrew of the Dead Sea Scrolls and Ben Sira: Proceedings of a Symposium held at Leiden University, 11–14 December 1995* (ed. T. Muraoka and J.F. Elwolde; Studies on the Texts of the Desert of Judah, 26; Leiden: E.J. Brill, 1997), pp. 150–57

Newsom, Carol, *Songs of the Sabbath Sacrifice: A Critical Edition* (Harvard Semitic Studies, 27; Atlanta, GA: Scholars Press, 1985)

Pardee, Dennis, *Handbook of Ancient Hebrew Letters: A Study Edition* (SBL Sources for Biblical Study, 15; Chico, CA: Scholars Press, 1982)

Ploeg, J. van der, 'Les manuscrits de la grotte XI de Qumran', *Revue de Qumran* 12 (1985), pp. 3-15

Puech, Émile, 'Notes sur le manuscrit de 11QMelkîsédeq', *Revue de Qumran* 12 (1987), pp. 483-513

—'*11QPsAp*[a]: Un rituel d'exorcismes. Essai de reconstruction', *Revue de Qumran* 14 (1990), pp. 377-408

—'Un apocalypse messianique (4Q521)', *Revue de Qumran* 15 (1992), pp. 475-519

—'La pierre de Sion et l'autel des holocaustes d'après un manuscrit hébreu de la grotte 4', *Revue Biblique* 99 (1992), pp. 676-96

Qimron, Elisha, 'The Text of CDC', in *The Damascus Document Reconsidered* (ed. Magen Broshi; Jerusalem: The Israel Exploration Society/The Shrine of the Book, Israel Museum, 1992), pp. 9-49

—and John Strugnell, in consultation with Y. Sussmann and with contributions by Y. Sussmann and A. Yardeni, *Qumran Cave 4. V. Miqṣat Ma'aśe ha-Torah* (Discoveries in the Judaean Desert, 10; Oxford: Clarendon Press, 1994)

—*The Temple Scroll: A Critical Edition with Extensive Reconstructions* (Bibliography by Florentino García Martínez; Judean Desert Studies; Beer Sheva: Ben Gurion University of the Negev Press/Israel Exploration Society, 1996)

Richter, Hans-Peter, 'A Preliminary Concordance to the Hebrew and Aramaic Fragments from Qumrân Caves II–X' (5 vols., unpublished, printed in Göttingen, 1988, and distributed by Hartmut Stegemann on behalf of John Strugnell)

Sanders, J.A., *The Psalms Scroll of Qumrân Cave 11* (Discoveries in the Judaean Desert of Jordan, 4; Oxford: Clarendon Press, 1965)

Schuller, Eileen, *Non-Canonical Psalms from Qumran: A Pseudepigraphic Collection* (Harvard Semitic Studies, 28; Atlanta: Scholars Press, 1986)

Steudel, Annette, *Der Midrasch zur Eschatologie aus der Qumrangemeinde (4QMidrEschat$^{a.b}$): Materielle Rekonstruktion, Textbestand, Gattung und traditionsgeschichtliche Einordnung des durch 4Q174 ('Florilegium') und 4Q177 ('Catena A') repräsenterten Werkes aus den Qumranfunden* (Studies on the Texts of the Desert of Judah, 13; Leiden: E.J. Brill, 1994)

Talmon, Shemaryahu, 'Hebrew Written Fragments from Masada', *Dead Sea Discoveries* 3 (1996), pp. 168-77

Vermes, Geza, *The Complete Dead Sea Scrolls in English* (London: Allen Lane/Penguin, 1997)

WA, *see* Wacholder, Ben Zion and Martin G. Abegg

WAC, *see* Wise, Michael, Martin G. Abegg and Edward Cook

Wacholder, Ben Zion and Martin G. Abegg (and, for Fascicle 4, James Bowley), *A Preliminary Edition of the Unpublished Dead Sea Scrolls: The Hebrew and Aramaic Texts from Cave Four Based on a Reconstruction of the Original Transcriptions of Jozef T. Milik, John Strugnell and Jean Starcky*, Fascicles 1–4 (Washington, DC: Biblical Archaeology Society, 1991–96)

Wise, Michael, Martin G. Abegg and Edward Cook, *The Dead Sea Scrolls: A New Translation* (London: HarperCollins, 1996)

Woude, Adam van der, 'Ein neuer Segensspruch aus Qumran (11QBer)', in *Bibel und Qumran: Beiträge zur Erforschung der Beziehungen zwischen Bibel- und Qumranwissenschaft: Hans Bardtke zum 22.8.1966* (ed. S. Wagner; Berlin: Evangelische Haupt-Bibelgesellschaft, 1968)

—'Fragmente des Buches Jubiläen aus Qumran Höhle XI (11QJub)', in *Tradition und Glaube: Das frühe Christentum in seiner Umwelt: Festgabe für Karl Georg Kuhn zum 65. Geburtstag* (ed. Gert Jeremias, Heinz-Wolfgang Kuhn, and Hartmut Stegemann; Göttingen: Vandenhoeck & Ruprecht, 1971), pp. 140-46

Yadin, Yigael, *Bar-Kokhba: The Rediscovery of the Legendary Hero of the Last Jewish Revolt against Imperial Rome* (London: Weidenfeld and Nicolson, 1971)

b. *Inscriptions*

The following texts are supplementary to those listed in Volume 3, pp. 28-32.

City of David add. ost. 1
J. Naveh, *On Sherd and Papyrus* (Jerusalem: Magnes Press, 1992), pp. 50-53

City of David add. ost. 2
J. Naveh (1992), pp. 55-56

WORDS BEGINNING WITH YODH, KAPH AND LAMEDH IN ORDER OF FREQUENCY

In these tables are listed all the words beginning with Yodh, Kaph, and Lamedh, in descending order of their frequency of occurrence in the corpus of classical Hebrew. Including proper names, there are 625 words beginning with Yodh, 361 with Kaph, and 188 with Lamedh, 1174 in all. Words that are conjectured, and for which therefore no occurrence statistics are noted in the Dictionary, are of course absent from this list. Words for which the lemma form is reconstructed (for example, when only plural forms are attested and the presumed singular form is therefore shown within square brackets) are included, without their square brackets.

In the first column, a number ranks the words in order of frequency. Following the Hebrew word itself, and (in the case of homonyms) a roman numeral to distinguish one word from another spelled alike, five columns of figures follow. They record in turn the number of occurrences of the word in the four corpora of texts that comprise Classical Hebrew—the Masoretic text of the Hebrew Bible (MT), Ben Sira (Si), the Dead Sea Scrolls (Qumran and related texts) (Q) and the Hebrew inscriptions (Inscr)—and the total number of occurrences. It is this total that determines a word's position in the table. In the next column the part of speech is noted, and a simple gloss follows, to identify the word in question.

Words Beginning with Yodh

י

Rank	Lemma		MT	Si	Q	Inscr	Total	Type	Gloss
1	יהוה		6828	66	181	32	7107	prnm	*Yahweh*
2	יִשְׂרָאֵל		2512	21	354	22	2909	prnm	*Israel*
3	יוֹם	I	2268	53	525	15	2861	nm	*day*
4	יָד	I	1634	52	379	6	2071	nf	*hand*
5	ידע	I	957	28	261	5	1251	vb	*know*
6	יצא		1067	20	156	1	1244	vb	*go out*
7	ישׁב		1085	20	82	1	1188	vb	*sit*
8	יְהוּדָה		806	3	59	13	881	prnm	*Judah*
9	יְרוּשָׁלַםִ		641	2	29	5	677	pln	*Jerusalem*
10	ילד		499	7	39		545	vb	*give birth*
11	ירא		378	13	62		453	vb	*fear*
12	יָם		392	2	35		429	nm	*sea*
13	ירד		379	8	31	2	420	vb	*go down*
14	יַעֲקֹב		350	6	39		395	prnm	*Jacob*
15	ירשׁ	I	230	5	32		267	vb	*take possession*
16	יסף		215	5	40		260	vb	*add*
17	ישׁע		205	7	37	3	252	vb	*save*
18	יכל		207	4	19	1	231	vb	*be able*
19	יְהוֹשֻׁעַ		218	1	1	4	224	prnm	*J(eh)oshua*
20	יוֹסֵף		210	1	6	3	220	prnm	*Joseph*
21	יַחַד		45	1	168		214	n[m]	*unity*
22	יַיִן		141	17	17	31	206	nm	*wine*
23	יֵשׁ		138	43	22		203	part	*(there) is*
24	יַרְדֵּן	I	181		3		184	pln	*Jordan*
25	יָמִין	I	139	3	26	1	169	nf	*right (side)*
26	ידה	I	110	17	40		167	vb	*praise*
27	יָשָׁר		118	1	31		150	adj	*straight (one)*
28	יִרְמְיָהוּ		127	1	7	12	147	prnm	*Jeremiah*

Rank	Lemma		MT	Si	Q	Inscr	Total	Type	Gloss
29	יוֹאָב		145				145	prnm	*Joab*
30	יִצְחָק		112	2	13		127	prnm	*Isaac*
31	יטב		114	8	2	1	125	vb	*be good*
32	יתר		105	1	18		124	vb	*exceed*
33	יַחְדָּו		98	4	6		108	adv	*together*
34	יָרָבְעָם		104	1		3	108	prnm	*Jeroboam*
35	יְהוֹנָתָן		82		16	7	105	prnm	*J(eh)onathan*
36	יְשׁוּעָה		78	1	22		101	nf	*salvation*
37	יֶתֶר	I	96	1	1	2	100	nm	*remnant*
38	יַעַן	I	96		3		99	prep	*because*
39	יכח		59	1	37		97	vb	*contend*
40	יֶלֶד		89	2	4		95	nm	*child*
41	יצר		63	11	19		93	vb	*form*
42	יעץ		80	4	7		91	vb	*advise*
43	יְהוּדִי	I	82		1	4	87	gent	*Jewish*
44	יְהוֹשָׁפָט		84				84	prnm	*Jehoshaphat*
45	יצב		48	7	27		82	vb	*stand*
46	יֵצֶר	I	9	2	65		76	nm	*formation*
47	ירה	III	45		30		75	vb	*teach*
47	יוֹמָם		52		21		73	adv	*by day*
48	יְאֹר		65	2	3		70	pln	*Nile*
49	יִשְׁמָעֵאל		48		1	20	69	prnm	*Ishmael*
50	יסר	I	44	4	19		67	vb	*discipline*
51	יבשׁ	I	60		5		65	vb	*be dry*
52	יצק		55	3	6		64	vb	*pour out*
53	יַעַר	I	57		5		62	nm	*forest*
54	יסד	I	43	2	16		61	vb	*establish*
55	יְרִיחוֹ		58		3		61	pln	*Jericho*
56	יֵהוּא		57			1	58	prnm	*Jehu*
57	יִרְאָה		44	8	5		57	nf	*fear*
58	יְשַׁעְיָהוּ		39	1	5	12	57	prnm	*Isaiah*
59	יָהּ		50	1	4	1	56	prnm	*Yah*
60	יֹאשִׁיָּהוּ		53	2			55	prnm	*Josiah*
61	יְרִיעָה		54		1		55	nf	*curtain*

Words Beginning with Yodh

Rank	Lemma		MT	Si	Q	Inscr	Total	Type	Gloss
62	יוֹבֵל	I	27		25		52	nm	*ram*
63	יֵשַׁע		36	2	11	3	52	nm	*salvation*
64	יְהוֹיָדָע		51				51	prnm	*Jehoiada*
65	יוֹנָתָן		42		3	3	48	prnm	*Jonathan*
66	יחל	I	41		7		48	vb	*wait*
67	יִשָּׂשכָר		43		5		48	prnm	*Issachar*
68	יָתוֹם		42	2	4		48	nm	*orphan*
69	יוֹאָשׁ		47				47	prnm	*Joash*
70	יֵשׁוּעַ	I	27	2	18		47	prnm	*Jeshua*
71	יעד		29		17		46	vb	*appoint*
72	יָפֶה		42		4		46	adj	*fair*
73	יִשַׁי		41	1	4		46	prnm	*Jesse*
74	יָקָר	I	36	1	7		44	adj	*precious*
75	יְבוּסִי		41		2		43	gent	*Jebusite*
76	יְסוֹד		20	1	22		43	nm	*foundation*
77	יפע		8	2	32		42	vb	*shine forth*
78	ירה	I	32		6		38	vb	*throw*
79	יְהוֹיָקִים		37				37	prnm	*Jehoiakim*
80	ישׁר		25	1	11		37	vb	*be straight*
81	יְדַעְיָה		11		13	12	36	prnm	*Jedaiah*
82	יִצְהָר	I	23	1	12		36	nm	*fresh oil*
83	יְמָנִי		33		2		35	adj	*right*
84	ינק		31		4		35	vb	*suck*
85	יָרֵךְ		34		1		35	nf	*thigh*
86	יגע		26	2	6		34	vb	*be weary*
87	יהב		33		1		34	vb	*give*
88	יִזְרְעֶאל	II	34				34	pln	*Jezreel*
89	יוֹנָה	I	33		6		33	nf	*dove*
90	יצת		30	3			33	vb	*kindle*
91	ידע	II	30	1	1		32	vb	*be quiet*
92	יָגוֹן		14		16		30	n[m]	*grief*
93	יְהוֹרָם		29			1	30	prnm	*Jehoram*
94	יוֹחָנָן		24	1	3	2	30	prnm	*Johanan*
95	יָרֵחַ		27	2	1		30	nm	*moon*

Rank	Lemma	MT	Si	Q	Inscr	Total	Type	Gloss
96	יְרֵכָה	28		1	1	30	nf	*flank*
97	ילל	27		2		29	vb	*howl*
98	יעל	23	3	3		29	vb	*profit*
99	יִפְתָּח I	29				29	prnm	*Jephthah*
100	יֳפִי	19	2	5		26	nm	*beauty*
101	יֶרַח I	12		4	9	25	nm	*month*
102	יֹשֶׁר	14	4	7		25	nm	*uprightness*
103	יָתֵד	24		1		25	nf	*peg*
104	יבל	18	1	5		24	vb	*bring*
105	יוֹתָם	24				24	prnm	*Jotham*
106	יָשָׁן	8	1		14	23	adj	*old*
107	יְהוֹחָנָן	9		2	11	22	prnm	*Jehohanan*
108	יוֹאֵל	19			3	22	prnm	*Joel*
109	ינה	19		3		22	vb	*oppress*
110	יָבֵשׁ II	21				21	pln	*Jabesh*
111	יְהוֹאָחָז	20			1	21	prnm	*Jehoahaz*
112	יאל I	19		1		20	vb	*be pleased*
113	יוֹרָם	20				20	prnm	*Joram*
114	יחשׂ	20				20	vb	*register*
115	יַבָּשָׁה	14		5		19	nf	*dry land*
116	יְהוֹסֵף	1		15	3	19	prnm	*J(eh)oseph*
117	יוֹנָה II	19				19	prnm	*Jonah*
118	יָחִיד	12		7		19	adj	*only*
119	ישׁן I	16	1	2		19	vb	*sleep*
120	יבשׁ II	18				18	vb	*be ashamed*
121	יְגִיַע	16	1	1		18	nm	*toil, product*
122	יְחֶזְקֵאל	3	1	14		18	prnm	*Ezekiel*
123	יַאֲזַנְיָה	5			12	17	prnm	*Jaazaniah*
124	יְדוּתוּן	17				17	prnm	*Jeduthun*
125	יְהוֹאָשׁ	17				17	prnm	*Jehoash*
126	יוֹתֵר	9	5	2	1	17	nm	*surplus*
127	יצג	16	1			17	vb	*place*
128	יֶקֶב	16		1		17	nm	*wine-vat*
129	יְקָר	17				17	nm	*preciousness*

Words Beginning with Yodh

Rank	Lemma		MT	Si	Q	Inscr	Total	Type	Gloss
130	יִרְמְיָה		17				17	prnm	*Jeremiah*
131	יָדִיד		8		8		16	adj	*beloved*
132	יוֹיָרִיב		5		11		16	prnm	*Joiarib*
133	יְפֻנֶּה		16				16	prnm	*Jephunneh*
134	יְקַמְיָה		3			13	16	prnm	*Jekamiah*
135	יְבוּל		13	1	1		15	nm	*produce*
136	יְהֻד		1			14	15	pln	*Jehud*
137	יָוָן		12		3		15	prnm	*Javan*
138	יְרֻבַּעַל		14			1	15	prnm	*Jerubbaal*
139	ידע	III	14				14	vb	*care*
140	יִדְּעֹנִי		11		3		14	nm	*familiar spirit*
141	יְחִיאֵל		14				14	prnm	*Jehiel*
142	יָכִין		8		6		14	prnm	*Jachin*
143	יקשׁ		8	6			14	vb	*trap*
144	יְרֻשָּׁה		14				14	nf	*possession*
145	יָאִיר		12			1	13	prnm	*Jair*
146	יָבֵשׁ	I	9	2	2		13	adj	*dry*
147	יִזְרְעֵאלִי		13				13	gent	*Jezreelite*
148	יָלִיד		13				13	adj	*born*
149	יַעְזֵיר		13				13	pln	*Jazer*
150	יְעִיאֵל		13				13	prnm	*Jeiel*
151	יפה		7	5	1		13	vb	*be beautiful*
152	יֶפֶת		11		2		13	prnm	*Japheth*
153	יְשִׁימוֹן		13				13	nm	*desert*
154	יחד		3	1	8		12	vb	*be united*
155	יִסּוֹר		1	1	10		12	n[m]	*reprover*
156	יקר		11	1			12	vb	*be precious*
157	יֹתֶרֶת		11		1		12	nf	*appendage*
158	יוֹאָח		11				11	prnm	*Joah*
159	יוֹזָבָד		11				11	prnm	*Jozabad*
160	יָצוּעַ	I	5	3	3		11	nm	*couch*
161	יָקִים		2		9		11	prnm	*Jakim*
162	יקץ		11				11	vb	*awake*
163	יְהוֹיָכִין		10				10	prnm	*Jehoiachin*

Rank	Lemma		MT	Si	Q	Inscr	Total	Type	Gloss
164	יקד		8	1	1		10	vb	*be kindled*
165	יְרֹחָם		10				10	prnm	*Jeroham*
166	יֶרֶק		6		4		10	nm	*grass*
167	יִתְרוֹן		10				10	nm	*profit*
168	ידע	IV	8	1			9	vb	*punish*
169	יְהוֹנָדָב		8			1	9	prnm	*Jehonadab*
170	יַהַץ		9				9	pln	*Jahaz*
171	יוֹבָב		9				9	prnm	*Jobab*
172	יֶלֶק		9				9	nm	*locust*
173	יָע		9				9	nm	*fire-shovel*
174	יְעוּשׁ		9				9	prnm	*Jeush*
175	יִצְהָר	II	9				9	prnm	*Izhar*
176	יְרַחְמְאֵל		8			1	9	prnm	*Jerahmeel*
177	יָשֵׁן	I	9				9	adj	*asleep*
178	יֶתֶר	III	9				9	prnm	*Jether*
179	יִתְרוֹ		9				9	prnm	*Jethro*
180	יָבִין		8				8	prnm	*Jabin*
181	יגה	I	8				8	vb	*be grieved*
182	ידה	II	6	1	1		8	vb	*throw*
183	יְהוֹצָדָק		8				8	prnm	*Jehozadak*
184	יוֹנָדָב		8				8	prnm	*Jonadab*
185	יַחַת		8				8	prnm	*Jahath*
186	יְכָנְיָה		7			1	8	prnm	*Jeconiah*
187	יַעֲנָה	I	8				8	nf	*desert*
188	יַעֲנָה	II	8				8	nf	*greed*
189	יעף	I	8				8	vb	*be weary*
190	יָפֵחַ	II	8				8	nm	*witness*
191	יקע		8				8	vb	*be dislocated*
192	יְרִימוֹת		7			1	8	prnm	*Jerimoth*
193	יִשְׁמְעֵאלִי		8				8	gent	*Ishmaelite*
194	יאשׁ		6	1			7	vb	*despair*
195	יַבֹּק		7				7	pln	*Jabbok*
196	יגר		7				7	vb	*fear*
197	יַד	III	7				7	n[m]	*love*

Words Beginning with Yodh

Rank	Lemma		MT	Si	Q	Inscr	Total	Type	Gloss
198	יַדּוּעַ		3			4	7	prnm	*Jaddua*
199	יצע		4	1	2		7	vb	*extend*
200	יָצִת					7	7	pln	*Jazith*
201	יְקוּם		3	1	3		7	nm	*living form*
202	יֶרֶד		7				7	prnm	*Jared*
203	יַרְמוּת		7				7	pln	*Jarmuth*
204	יֵרָקוֹן		6		1		7	nm	*rust*
205	יֶשֶׁבְאָב		1		6		7	prnm	*Jeshebeab*
206	ישׁט		3	4			7	vb	*extend*
207	יֶתֶר	II	6	1			7	nm	*cord*
208	יאל	II	4	1	1		6	vb	*be foolish*
209	יָד	II	4		2		6	n[f]	*penis*
210	יְדִיעֲאֵל		6				6	prnm	*Jediael*
211	יְהוּכַל		1			6	6	prnm	*Jehucal*
212	יַחֲזִיאֵל		6				6	prnm	*Jahaziel*
213	יחל	II	4	1	1		6	vb	*be desperate*
214	יחם		6				6	vb	*be hot*
215	יִלּוֹד		6				6	adj	*born*
216	יָמִין	II	6				6	prnm	*Jamin*
217	יָעֵל	II	6				6	prnf	*Jael*
218	יָקְטָן		6				6	prnm	*Joktan*
219	יָרוּם		6				6	adj	*exalted*
220	ירם		6				6	vb	*be high*
221	יְרֵמוֹת		6				6	prnm	*Jeremoth*
222	יִשִּׁיָּה		6				6	prnm	*Isshiah*
223	יָשִׁישׁ		4	2			6	adj	*aged (one)*
224	ישׁן	II	3	2	1		6	vb	*be old*
225	יָאוּשׁ					5	5	prnm	*Jaush*
226	יְבֶמֶת		5				5	nf	*sister-in-law*
227	יִדּוֹ		2			3	5	prnm	*Iddo*
228	ידע	V	4	1			5	vb	*sweat*
229	יְהוֹחַיִל					5	5	prnm	*Jehohail*
230	יוּבַל	I	1		4		5	n[m]	*stream*
231	יוֹיָדָע		5				5	prnm	*Joiada*

Rank	Lemma		MT	Si	Q	Inscr	Total	Type	Gloss
232	יוֹרֶה	I	3		2		5	n[m]	*early rain*
233	יָחֵף		5				5	adj	*barefoot*
234	יְלָלָה		5				5	nf	*howling*
235	ימן		5				5	vb	*go right*
236	יִמְנָה		5				5	prnm	*Imnah*
237	יָרָק		5				5	nm	*herbage*
238	יִשְׂרְאֵלִי		5				5	gent	*Israelite*
239	יִשְׁעִי		5				5	prnm	*Ishi*
240	יְשֻׁרוּן		4	1			5	prnm	*Jeshurun*
241	יָתֵר			3	2		5	adv	*more*
242	יאב		1		3		4	vb	*be willing*
243	יְבוּס		4				4	pln	*Jebus*
244	יִגְאָל		3			1	4	prnm	*Igal*
245	יְהוֹאָב					4	4	prnm	*Jehoab*
246	יְהוּדִי	II	4				4	prnm	*Jehudi*
247	יְהוֹזָבָד		4				4	prnm	*Jehozabad*
248	יוֹאָחָז		4				4	prnm	*Joahaz*
249	יוֹיָקִים		4				4	prnm	*Joiakim*
250	יוֹצָדָק		4				4	prnm	*Jozadak*
251	יַחַשׂ		1		3		4	n[m]	*registration*
252	יַלְדָּה		3		1		4	nf	*girl*
253	יְמִינִי	I	4				4	gent	*Benjaminite*
254	יַעְלָם		4				4	prnm	*Jalam*
255	יָעֵף		4				4	adj	*weary*
256	יָפוֹ		4				4	pln	*Joppa*
257	יָפִיעַ	I	4				4	prnm	*Japhia*
258	יִצְהָרִי		4				4	gent	*Izharite*
259	יָקוּשׁ		3		1		4	n[m]	*(game) hunter*
260	יָקְשָׁן		4				4	prnm	*Jokshan*
261	ירק		3			1	4	vb	*spit*
262	יִשְׂחָק		4				4	prnm	*Isaac*
263	יִשְׁבַּעַל		4				4	prnm	*Ishbaal*
264	יָשׁוּב	I	3			1	4	prnm	*Jashub*
265	יִשְׁוִי	I	4				4	prnm	*Isvi*

Rank	Lemma		MT	Si	Q	Inscr	Total	Type	Gloss
266	ישׁם		4				4	vb	*be desolate*
267	יַתִּיר		4				4	pln	*Jattir*
268	יִבְחָר		3				3	prnm	*Ibhar*
269	יָבָל	I	2	1			3	n[m]	*stream*
270	יִבְלְעָם		3				3	pln	*Ibleam*
271	יבם	I	3				3	vb	*marry sister-in-law*
272	יָבֵשׁ	III	3				3	prnm	*Jabesh*
273	יָגֵעַ		3				3	adj	*weary*
274	יָגָר				3		3	n[m]	*cairn*
275	ידע	VI	3				3	vb	*seek*
276	יְהוֹעַדָּן		2			1	3	prnf	*Jehoaddan*
277	יְהוֹעַז					3	3	prnm	*Jehoaz*
278	יְהוֹעֶזֶר					3	3	prnm	*Jehoezer*
279	יְהוֹקִם					3	3	prn[m]	*Jehokim*
280	יְהוֹשַׁבְעַת		3				3	prnf	*Jehoshabeath*
281	יָהֲלֹם		3				3	n[m]	*onyx*
282	יוֹבָנָה					3	3	prn[m]	*Jobanah*
283	יוֹכִן					3	3	prn[m]	*Jochin*
284	יוֹם	II	3				3	nm	*wind*
285	יוֹעֶזֶר		1			2	3	prnm	*Joezer*
286	יִזְרַחְיָה		3				3	prnm	*Izrahiah*
287	יַחְצְאֵל		3				3	prnm	*Jahzeel*
288	יָטְבָתָה		3				3	pln	*Jotbathah*
289	יְטוּר		3				3	prnm	*Jetur*
290	יַלְדוּת		3				3	nf	*youth*
291	יָנוֹחַ		3				3	pln	*Janoah*
292	יַנְשׁוּף		3				3	nm	*screech*
293	יַעְבֵּץ	II	3				3	prnm	*Jabez*
294	יַפְלֵט		3				3	prnm	*Japhlet*
295	יָצִיעַ		3				3	nm & f	*terrace*
296	יֵצֶר	II	3				3	prnm	*Jezer*
297	יָקְנְעָם		3				3	pln	*Jokneam*
298	ירה	II	3				3	vb	*water*

Rank	Lemma		MT	Si	Q	Inscr	Total	Type	Gloss
299	יָרִיב	I	3				3	n[m]	*adversary*
300	יָרִיב	II	3				3	prnm	*Jarib*
301	יְרִיָּהוּ		3				3	prnm	*Jeriah*
302	יְרַקְרַק		3				3	adj	*greenish*
303	יְרֵשָׁה		2		1		3	nf	*possession*
304	יָשָׁבְעָם		3				3	prnm	*Jashobeam*
305	יָשְׁפֵה		3				3	nm	*jasper*
306	יִשְׁרָה		2		1		3	nf	*uprightness*
307	יִתְרִי		3				3	gent	*Ithrite*
308	יִתְרָן		3				3	prnm	*Ithran*
309	יַאֲזָן					2	2	prnm	*Jaazan*
310	יָבָם		2				2	nm	*husband's brother*
311	יַבְנְאֵל		2				2	pln	*Jabneel*
312	יַבֶּשֶׁת		2				2	nf	*dry land*
313	יגב		2				2	vb	*farm*
314	יָגְבְּהָה		2				2	pln	*Jogbehah*
315	יִגְדַּלְיָהוּ		1			1	2	prnm	*Igdaliah*
316	יָגִיעַ		1	1			2	adj	*weary*
317	יָגָע		1		1		2	n[m]	*gain*
318	יָדֶה		2				2	n[m]	*voice*
319	יְדָיָה		2				2	prnm	*Jedaiah*
320	יְדָנְיָהוּ					2	2	prnm	*Jedoniah*
321	ידע	VII	2				2	vb	*leave*
322	ידע	VIII	2				2	vb	*call*
323	ידע	IX	2				2	vb	*tear down*
324	ידע	X	2				2	vb	*leave alone*
325	ידע	XI	2				2	vb	*wrap up*
326	יָדָע		2				2	prnm	*Jada*
327	יָהוּ					2	2	prnm	*Yahu*
328	יְהוֹאָח					2	2	prnm	*Jehoah*
329	יְהוֹבָנָה					2	2	prn[m]	*Jehobanah*
330	יְהוֹזָרָח					2	2	prnm	*Jehozarah*
331	יְהוֹיָרִיב		2				2	prnm	*Jehoiarib*
332	יְהוֹעַדָּה		2				2	prnm	*Jehoaddah*

Rank	Lemma		MT	Si	Q	Inscr	Total	Type	Gloss
333	יָהִיר		2				2	adj	*proud*
334	יְהַלֶּלְאֵל		2				2	prnm	*Jehallelel*
335	יוֹחָא		2				2	prnm	*Joha*
336	יוֹכֶבֶד		2				2	prnf	*Jochebed*
337	יָוֵן		2				2	n[m]	*mire*
338	יוֹסֵי				1	1	2	prnm	*Jose*
339	יוֹעִלְיָהוּ					2	2	prnm	*Joiliah*
340	יוֹעָשׁ		2				2	prnm	*Joash*
341	יוֹעָשָׂה					2	2	prnm	*Joasah*
342	יוֹקִים		1			1	2	prnm	*Jokim*
343	יוֹשָׁפָט		2				2	prnm	*Joshaphat*
344	יְזַנְיָהוּ		2				2	prnm	*Jezaniah*
345	יִזְרְעֶאל	I	2				2	prnm	*Jezreel*
346	יֶחְדְּיָהוּ		2				2	prnm	*Jehdeiah*
347	יַחְזְיָה		1			1	2	prnm	*Jahazeiah*
348	יְחִיאֵלִי		2				2	prnm	*Jehieli*
349	יַחְלְאֵל		2				2	prnm	*Jahleel*
350	יַחְמוּר		2				2	n[m]	*roebuck*
351	יַחְמַלְיָהוּ					2	2	prn[m]	*Jahmaliah*
352	יֻטָּה		2				2	pln	*Juttah*
353	יטשׁ		2				2	vb	*clash*
354	יְכָלְיָהוּ		2				2	prnf	*Jecoliah*
355	יַלֶּפֶת		2				2	nf	*scab*
356	יְמוּאֵל		2				2	prnm	*Jemuel*
357	יָמִין	IV	2				2	n[m]	*oath*
358	ימר		2				2	vb	*exchange*
359	יסד	II	2				2	vb	*plot*
360	יסר	II	2				2	vb	*be strong*
361	יַעְדָּה		2				2	prnm	*Jadah*
362	יַעֲזִיָּהוּ		2				2	prnm	*Jaaziah*
363	יָעֵל	I	2				2	nm	*mountain goat*
364	יַעְרָה		2				2	prnm	*Jarah*
365	יַעֲשִׂיאֵל		2				2	prnm	*Jaasiel*
366	יִפְעָה	I	2				2	nf	*splendour*

Rank	Lemma		MT	Si	Q	Inscr	Total	Type	Gloss
367	יִפְעָה	II	2				2	nf	*arrogance*
368	יצה		2				2	vb	*order*
369	יְצֻרִים		1		1		2	nm	*bodily members*
370	יְקֹד		2				2	nm	*conflagration*
371	יְקָהָה		2				2	nf	*obedience*
372	יקח		2				2	vb	*be shameless*
373	יָקְמְעָם		2				2	pln	*Jokmeam*
374	יְקַמְעָם		2				2	prnm	*Jekameam*
375	יָקְתְאֵל		2				2	pln	*Joktheel*
376	ירא	II	2				2	vb	*drink deeply (of)*
377	יִרְאִיָּה		2				2	prnm	*Irijah*
378	יָרֵב		2				2	adj	*great*
379	ירה	IV	2				2	vb	*be led*
380	יָרוֹק		1		1		2	nm	*green plants*
381	יְרוּשָׁא		2				2	prnf	*Jerusha*
382	יֶרַח	II	2				2	prnm	*Jerah*
383	יְרַחְמְאֵלִי		2				2	gent	*Jerahmeelite*
384	יַרְחָע		2				2	prnm	*Jarha*
385	ירט		2				2	vb	*be precipitate*
386	יְרֵמַי		1			1	2	prnm	*Jeremai*
387	יָרֹת					2	2	pln	*Jaroth*
388	יִשְׁאָל		1			1	2	prnm	*Ishal*
389	יִשְׁבָּק		2				2	prnm	*Ishbak*
390	יָשְׁבְּקָשָׁה		2				2	prnm	*Joshbekashah*
391	יִשְׁוָה		2				2	prnm	*Ishvah*
392	יָתֻם					2	2	pln	*Jathum*
393	יִתְרָא		1		1		2	prnm	*Ithra*
394	יִתְרָה		2				2	nf	*abundance*
395	יִתְרְעָם		2				2	prnm	*Ithream*
396	יְתֵת		2				2	prnm	*Jetheth*
397	יאה		1				1	vb	*befit*
398	יַאֲחַץ					1	1	prnm	*Jaahaz*
399	יָאִרִי		1				1	gent	*Jairite*
400	יְאָתְרַי		1				1	prnm	*Jeatherai*

Words Beginning with Yodh

Rank	Lemma		MT	Si	Q	Inscr	Total	Type	Gloss
401	יבב		1				1	vb	*cry aloud*
402	יָבָל	II	1				1	prnm	*Jabal*
403	יַבֶּלֶת		1				1	nf	*running sore*
404	יַבְנֵה		1				1	pln	*Jabneh*
405	יִבְנְיָה		1				1	prnm	*Ibneiah*
406	יִבְנִיָּה		1				1	prnm	*Ibnijah*
407	יְבֶרֶכְיָהוּ		1				1	prnm	*Jeberechiah*
408	יִבְשָׂם		1				1	prnm	*Ibsam*
409	יָגֵב		1				1	n[m]	*field*
410	יגה	II	1				1	vb	*remove*
411	יָגוֹעַ		1				1	adj	*toiling*
412	יָגוּר		1				1	pln	*Jagur*
413	יְגִיעָה		1				1	nf	*wearying*
414	יָגְלִי		1				1	prnm	*Jogli*
415	יַד		1				1	n[m]	*love*
416	יִדְאֲלָה		1				1	pln	*Idalah*
417	יִדְבָּשׁ		1				1	prnm	*Idbash*
418	יְדִדוּת		1				1	nf	*loved one*
419	יָדוֹן		1				1	prnm	*Jadon*
420	יַדַּי		1				1	prnm	*Jaddai*
421	יְדִידָה		1				1	prnf	*Jedidah*
422	יְדִידְיָהּ		1				1	prnm	*Jedidiah*
423	יְדִידֹת		1				1	nfpl	*love*
424	יִדְלָף		1				1	prnm	*Jidlaph*
425	יַדָּע				1		1	adj	*expert*
426	יְהָב		1				1	n[m]	*burden*
427	יהד		1				1	vb	*be a Jew*
428	יָהְדַּי		1				1	prnm	*Jahdai*
429	יְהוֹאֵל					1	1	prnm	*Jehoel*
430	יְהוֹבַעַל					1	1	prn[m]	*Jehobaal*
431	יְהוּדִית	I	1				1	prnf	*Judith*
432	יְהוֹחַי					1	1	prnm	*Jehohai*
433	יְהוֹיִשְׁמַע					1	1	prnf	*Jehoishma*
434	יְהוֹמָלָךְ					1	1	prnm	*Jehomalach*

Rank	Lemma		MT	Si	Q	Inscr	Total	Type	Gloss
435	יְהוֹעֲלִי					1	1	prn[m]	*Jehoale*
436	יְהוֹעָנָה					1	1	prn[m]	*Jehoanah*
437	יוֹאָמָן					1	1	prn[m]	*Joaman*
438	יוֹאֹר					1	1	prn[m]	*Joor*
439	יוֹב		1				1	prnm	*Job*
440	יוּבַל	II	1				1	prnm	*Jubal*
441	יוֹד				1		1	n[m]	*yodh*
442	יוּדָן					1	1	prnm	*Judan*
443	יוֹזָכָר		1				1	prnm	*Jozacar*
444	יוֹזָן					1	1	prnm	*Jozan*
445	יוֹיָכִין		1				1	prnm	*Joiachin*
446	יוֹיָשָׁע					1	1	prn[m]	*Joiasha*
447	יוּכַל		1				1	prnm	*Jucal*
448	יְוָנִי		1				1	gent	*Greek*
449	יוֹסִפְיָה		1				1	prnm	*Josiphiah*
450	יוֹסְתֵר					1	1	prnm	*Joster*
451	יוֹעֵאלָה		1				1	prnm	*Joelah*
452	יוֹעֵד		1				1	prnm	*Joed*
453	יוֹרָה		1				1	prnm	*Jorah*
454	יוֹרַי		1				1	prnm	*Jorai*
455	יוּשַׁב חֶסֶד		1				1	prnm	*Jushab-hesed*
456	יוֹשִׁבְיָה		1				1	prnm	*Joshibiah*
457	יוֹשָׁה		1				1	prnm	*Joshah*
458	יוֹשַׁוְיָה		1				1	prnm	*Joshaviah*
459	יְזֶבֶל					1	1	prn[f]	*Jezebel*
460	יְזִיאֵל		1				1	prnm	*Jeziel*
461	יִזִּיָּה		1				1	prnm	*Izziah*
462	יָזִיז		1				1	prnm	*Jaziz*
463	יִזְלִיאָה		1				1	prnm	*Izliah*
464	יזן		1				1	vb	*be on heat*
465	יֶזַע		1				1	n[m]	*sweat*
466	יִזְרָח		1				1	gent	*Izrahite*
467	יְחֻבָּה		1				1	prnm	*Jehubbah*
468	יַחְדּוֹ		1				1	prnm	*Jahdo*

Rank	Lemma		MT	Si	Q	Inscr	Total	Type	Gloss
469	יַחְדִּיאֵל		1				1	prnm	*Jahdiel*
470	יְחוֹעֵלִי					1	1	prn[m]	*Jehoeli*
471	יַחֲזָא					1	1	prn[m]	*Jahaza*
472	יֹחָזָק					1	1	prn[m]	*Johazak*
473	יַחְזֵרָה		1				1	prnm	*Jahzerah*
474	יְחִי					1	1	prn[m]	*Jehi*
475	יְחִיָּה		1				1	prnm	*Jehiah*
476	יָחִיל		1				1	n[m]	*waiting*
477	יַחְלְאֵלִי		1				1	gent	*Jahleelite*
478	יַחְמַי		1				1	prnm	*Jahmai*
479	יֹחָמָל					1	1	prn[m]	*Johamal*
480	יחן			1			1	vb	*dwell*
481	יֹחָן					1	1	prn[m]	*Johan*
482	יֹחָנֶה				1		1	prnm	*Jannes*
483	יְחָנֵּנִי					1	1	prn[m]	*Jehonneni*
484	יַחְצְאֵלִי		1				1	gent	*Jahzeelite*
485	יָטְבָּה		1				1	pln	*Jotbah*
486	יְישׁוֹר				1		1	n[m]	*uprightness*
487	יכה		1				1	vb	*crouch*
488	יָכִינִי		1				1	gent	*Jachinite*
489	ילהּ		1				1	vb	*be anxious*
490	יָלוֹן		1				1	prnm	*Jalon*
491	יְלֵל		1				1	n[m]	*howling*
492	יַלְקוּט		1				1	n[m]	*pouch*
493	יְמִימָה		1				1	prnf	*Jemimah*
494	יָמִין	III	1				1	adj	*propitious*
495	יָמִינִי		1				1	gent	*Jaminite*
496	יַמְלֵךְ		1				1	prnm	*Jamlech*
497	יֵמִם		1				1	n[m]	*hot spring(s)*
498	יִמְנָע		1				1	prnm	*Imna*
499	יִמְרָה		1				1	prnm	*Imrah*
500	ימשׁ		1				1	vb	*touch*
501	יָנוּם		1				1	pln	*Janum*
502	יְנִיקָה		1				1	nf	*shoot*

Rank	Lemma	MT	Si	Q	Inscr	Total	Type	Gloss
503	יְסֵד	1				1	nm	*establishment*
504	יְסוּדָה	1				1	nf	*foundation*
505	יָסוּר	1				1	n[m]	*one who departs*
506	יִסְכָּה	1				1	prnf	*Iscah*
507	יִסְמַכְיָהוּ	1				1	prnm	*Ismachiah*
508	יָסֹף				1	1	prnm	*Jasoph*
509	יַעְבֵּץ I	1				1	pln	*Jabez*
510	יֶעְדּוֹ	1				1	prnm	*Iddo*
511	יעה	1				1	vb	*sweep together*
512	יְעוּאֵל	1				1	prnm	*Jeuel*
513	יְעוּץ	1				1	prnm	*Jeuz*
514	יעז	1				1	vb	*insult*
515	יַעֲזִיאֵל	1				1	prnm	*Jaaziel*
516	יעט	1				1	vb	*cover*
517	יָעִיר	1				1	prnm	*Jair*
518	יַעְכָּן	1				1	prnm	*Jachan*
519	יַעֲלָה	1				1	nf	*wild she-goat*
520	יַעְלָה	2				1	prnm	*Jaalah*
521	יָעֵן I	1				1	n[m]	*ostrich*
522	יָעֵן II	1				1	n[m]	*bedouin*
523	יַעַן II	1				1	pln	*Jaan*
524	יַעְנַי	1				1	prnm	*Janai*
525	יעף II	1				1	vb	*be swift*
526	יְעָף I	1				1	nm	*weariness*
527	יְעָף II	1				1	nm	*flying*
528	יַעֲפּוּר			1		1	pln	*Jaapur*
529	יַעֲקֹבָה	1				1	prnm	*Jaakobah*
530	יַעֲקָן	1				1	prnm	*Jaakan*
531	יַעַר II	1				1	nm	*honeycomb*
532	יַעַר III	1				1	pln	*Jaar*
533	יַעֲרָה I	1				1	nf	*honeycomb*
534	יַעֲרָה II	1				1	nf	*kid*
535	יַעֲרֵי אֹרְגִים	1				1	prnm	*Jaare-oregim*
536	יַעֲרֶשְׁיָה	1				1	prnm	*Jareshiah*

Rank	Lemma		MT	Si	Q	Inscr	Total	Type	Gloss
537	יַעַשׂ					1	1	prnm	*Jaas*
538	יַעֲשָׂו		1				1	prnm	*Jaasu*
539	יִפְדְיָה		1				1	prnm	*Iphdeiah*
540	יָפֵחַ	I	1				1	adj	*breathing out*
541	יְפֵה־פִיָּה		1				1	adj	*handsome*
542	יְפוּת				1		1	nf	*harmony*
543	יפח		1				1	vb	*breathe*
544	יָפְטַר					1	1	prnm	*Jophtar*
545	יְפָיָהוּ				1		1	prnm	*Jephaiah*
546	יָפִיעַ	II	1				1	pln	*Japhia*
547	יְפֵיפִיָּה		1				1	adj	*handsome*
548	יַפְלֵטִי		1				1	gent	*Japhletite*
549	יָפְקַד					1	1	prm	*Jophkad*
550	יפר		1				1	vb	*be many*
551	יִפְרַעְיוֹ					1	1	prn[m]	*Iphraio*
552	יִפְתָּח	II	1				1	pln	*Iphtah*
553	יָצוּר			1			1	nm	*creature*
554	יִצְהָר		1				1	prnm	*Izhar*
555	יָצִיא		1				1	adj	*coming out*
556	יְצִיאָה				1		1	nf	*outlet*
557	יְצֻקָה		1				1	nf	*casting*
558	יצר				1		1	nm	*inclination*
559	יִצְרִי	I	1				1	gent	*Jezerite*
560	יִצְרִי	II	1				1	prnm	*Izri*
561	יְקַבְצְאֵל		1				1	pln	*Jekabzeel*
562	יָקְדְעָם		1				1	pln	*Jokdeam*
563	יָקֶה		1				1	prnm	*Jakeh*
564	יָקוּד		1				1	nm	*hearth*
565	יָקוֹט		1				1	nm	*gossamer*
566	יָקוֹשׁ		1				1	n[m]	*(game) hunter*
567	יְקוּתִיאֵל		1				1	prnm	*Jekuthiel*
568	יְקִימְיָהוּ					1	1	prnm	*Jakimiah*
569	יַקִּיר		1				1	adj	*precious*
570	יָקָר	I	1				1	adj	*split*

Rank	Lemma		MT	Si	Q	Inscr	Total	Type	Gloss
571	יִרְאוֹן		1				1	pln	*Iron*
572	יִרְאִוִּיָּהוּ					1	1	prnm	*Irivvijah*
573	יְרֻבֶּשֶׁת		1				1	prnm	*Jerubbesheth*
574	ירד	II	1				1	vb	*appear*
575	יַרְדֵּן	II	1				1	nm	*river*
576	ירה		1				1	vb	*be terrified*
577	יְרוּאֵל		1				1	pln	*Jeruel*
578	יָרוֹחַ		1				1	prnm	*Jaroah*
579	יְרִיאֵל		1				1	prnm	*Jeriel*
580	יְרִיבַי		1				1	prnm	*Jeribai*
581	יְרִידָה				1		1	nf	*descent*
582	יְרִיעוֹת		1				1	prnm	*Jerioth*
583	ירע		1				1	vb	*tremble*
584	יִרְפְּאֵל		1				1	pln	*Irpeel*
585	יַרְקוֹן		1				1	pln	*Jarkon*
586	יָרְקְעָם		1				1	prnm	*Jorkeam*
587	ירשׁ	II	1				1	vb	*press*
588	יְשִׂימִאֵל		1				1	prnm	*Jesimiel*
589	יְשַׂרְאֵלָה		1				1	prnm	*Jesharelah*
590	יֹשֵׁב בַּשֶּׁבֶת		1				1	prnm	*Josheb-basshebeth*
591	יִשְׁבָּח		1				1	prnm	*Ishbah*
592	יִשְׁבִּי		1				1	prnm	*Ishbi*
593	יָשֻׁבִי לֶחֶם		1				1	prnm	*Jashubi-lehem*
594	יָשׁוּב	II				1	1	pln	*Jashub*
595	יָשׁוּבִי		1				1	gent	*Jashubite*
596	יְשׁוֹחָיָה		1				1	prnm	*Jeshohaiah*
597	יִשְׁוִי	II	1				1	gent	*Ishvite*
598	יֵשׁוּעַ	II	1				1	pln	*Jeshua*
599	יְשׁוּר				1		1	nm	*uprightness*
600	יֶשַׁח		1				1	nm	*dysentery*
601	יָשִׁיב		1				1	prnm	*Jashib*
602	יְשִׁיבָה			1			1	nf	*sitting*
603	יִשִּׁיָּהוּ		1				1	prnm	*Isshiah*
604	יְשִׁימָה		1				1	nf	*desolation*

Rank	Lemma		MT	Si	Q	Inscr	Total	Type	Gloss
605	יְשִׁישַׁי		1				1	prnm	*Jeshishai*
606	יִשְׁמָא		1				1	prnm	*Ishma*
607	יִשְׁמַעְיָה		1				1	prnm	*Ishmaiah*
608	יִשְׁמַעְיָהוּ		1				1	prnm	*Ishmaiah*
609	יִשְׁמְרַי		1				1	prnm	*Ishmerai*
610	יָשֵׁן	II	1				1	prnm	*Jashen*
611	יְשָׁנָה		1				1	pln	*Jeshanah*
612	יְשֵׁנָה			1			1	nf	*sleep*
613	יֵשַׁע		1				1	nm	*salvation*
614	יֵשֻׁעָא					1	1	prnm	*Jeshua*
615	יִשְׁפָּה		1				1	prnm	*Ispah*
616	יִשְׁפָּט					1	1	prnm	*Ishpat*
617	יִשְׁפָּן		1				1	prnm	*Ishpan*
618	יֵשֶׁר		1				1	prnm	*Jesher*
619	יָשֵׁשׁ		1				1	adj	*aged (one)*
620	יָתוּר		1				1	n[m]	*outcrop*
621	יִתְלָה		1				1	pln	*Jethlah*
622	יִתְמָה		1				1	prnm	*Ithmah*
623	יֹתֵן					1	1	prnm	*Jothen*
624	יַתְנִיאֵל		1				1	prnm	*Jathniel*
625	יִתְנָן		1				1	pln	*Ithnan*

כ

Rank	Lemma		MT	Si	Q	Inscr	Total	Type	Gloss
1	כֹּל	I	5408	143	2540	15	8106	nm	*all*
2	כִּי	I	4488	151	898	10	5547	conj	*for*
3	כְּ		2471	153	550	17	3191	prep	*as*
4	כֹּהֵן		752	4	181	21	958	nm	*priest*
5	כֵּן	I	565	56	97	1	719	adv	*thus*
6	כֹּה		582				582	adv	*thus*

Rank	Lemma		MT	Si	Q	Inscr	Total	Type	Gloss
7	כָּבוֹד		199	32	315		546	nm & f	*glory*
8	כֶּסֶף	I	403	4	49	6	462	nm	*silver*
9	כְּלִי		324	7	65		396	nm	*vessel*
10	כרת		288	6	53		347	vb	*cut*
11	כון		217	15	101		333	vb	*be upright*
12	כלה		206	6	37		249	vb	*be complete*
13	כתב		225	1	13	6	245	vb	*write*
14	כֹּחַ	I	125	11	94		230	nm	*strength*
15	כַּף	I	192	2	17		211	nf	*hand*
16	כבד		113	22	56	1	192	vb	*be heavy*
17	כסה		156	6	19		181	vb	*cover*
18	כְּמוֹ		140	7	17		164	prep	*as*
19	כִּסֵּא		135	4	21		160	nm	*throne*
20	כפר		101	3	50		154	vb	*cover*
21	כֶּבֶשׂ		107	1	23		131	nm	*ram*
22	כָּנָף		109	1	19		129	nf	*wing*
23	כֶּרֶם	I	91	1	4	10	106	nm	*vineyard*
24	כִּכָּר	II	55		47		102	nf	*talent*
25	כְּרוּב	I	91		5		96	nm	*cherub*
26	כשל		62	7	24		93	vb	*stumble*
27	כְּנַעַן	II	84		5		89	pln	*Canaan*
28	כבס		48		30		78	vb	*wash*
29	כְּנַעֲנִי	I	73		3		76	gent	*Canaanite*
30	כְּסִיל	I	70	5	1		76	nm	*fool*
31	כַּשְׂדִּי		69		1	1	71	gent	*Chaldaean*
32	כָּלָה		22	2	46		70	nf	*end*
33	כָּתֵף	I	67			1	68	nf	*side*
34	כעס		54	1	3		58	vb	*be angry*
35	כול		37	7	8	4	56	vb	*contain*
36	כנע		36	4	15		55	vb	*be humble*
37	כָּזָב		31	5	18		54	nm	*lie*
38	כִּתִּי		8		35	11	54	gent	*Kittite*
39	כּוֹכָב		37	2	12		51	nm	*star*
40	כָּכָה		37	3	11		51	adv	*thus*

Rank	Lemma		MT	Si	Q	Inscr	Total	Type	Gloss
41	כָּבֵד	I	41	5	4		50	adj	*heavy*
42	כלם	I	38	5	1		44	vb	*humiliate*
43	כֶּלֶב	I	32	3	2	5	42	nm	*dog*
44	כִּנּוֹר		42				42	nm	*lyre*
45	כִּלְיָה		31		10		41	nf	*kidney*
46	כחד		32		5		37	vb	*hide*
47	כָּלֵב	I	34	2		1	37	prnm	*Caleb*
48	כרע		36		1		37	vb	*bow*
49	כּוֹס	I	31		5		36	nf	*cup*
50	כְּפִיר		31	1	4		36	nm	*young lion*
51	כַּלָּה		34		1		35	nf	*bride*
52	כְּלִמָּה	I	30		4		34	nf	*insult*
53	כִּיּוֹר		23		10		33	nm	*bowl*
54	כּוּשׁ	I	30		2		32	prnm	*Cush*
55	כֻּתֹּנֶת		29	1	2		32	nf	*tunic*
56	כבה		24	2	2		28	vb	*be extinguished*
57	כִּפֻּר		8		20		28	nm	*atonement*
58	כַּפֹּרֶת		26		2		28	nf	*cover*
59	כהן		23	3	1		27	vb	*be priest*
60	כְּהֻנָּה		14	1	12		27	nf	*priesthood*
61	כחשׁ		22	2	2		26	vb	*deny*
62	כַּעַס		21	1	4		26	nm	*anger*
63	כְּתָב		17	4	4		25	nm	*writing*
64	כּוּשִׁי	I	24				24	gent	*Cushite*
65	כֹּתֶרֶת		24				24	nf	*capital*
66	כּוּר		9	2	11		22	nm	*smelting-pot*
67	כָּלִיל	I	15	3	4		22	adj	*whole*
68	כזב		16	1	4		21	vb	*lie*
69	כרה	I	15	1	4		20	vb	*dig*
70	כתת		17		3		20	vb	*crush*
71	כַּד		18			1	19	nf	*jar*
72	כֹּפֶר	I	13		6		19	nm	*ransom*
73	כלא		17		1		18	vb	*restrain*
74	כְּפִי		11	1	6		18	prep	*in accordance with*

Rank	Lemma		MT	Si	Q	Inscr	Total	Type	Gloss
75	כַּפְתּוֹר	I	18				18	nm	*knob*
76	כָּבֵד	II	14		3		17	nm	*liver*
77	כבשׁ		14		2		16	vb	*subdue*
78	כּוֹרֶשׁ		16				16	prnm	*Cyrus*
79	כנס		11		4		15	vb	*gather*
80	כֶּשֶׂב		13		1		14	nm	*sheep*
81	כִּכָּר	I	13				13	nf	*district*
82	כֵּן	IV	13				13	nm	*stand*
83	כַּר	I	13				13	nm	*ram*
84	כַּרְמֶל	I	13				13	nm	*orchard*
85	כֶּתֶם		9	1	3		13	nm	*gold*
86	כְּאֵב		6	4	2		12	nm	*pain*
87	כַּחַשׁ		6	2	4		12	nm	*lie*
88	כֶּרַע		9		3		12	n[f]	*leg*
89	כַּבִּיר		10		1		11	adj	*strong*
90	כְּבָר	I	9		2		11	adv	*already*
91	כֶּלֶב	II	8			3	11	nm	*servant*
92	כֶּסֶל	II	7	1	3		11	nm	*thigh*
93	כאב		8	2			10	vb	*hurt*
94	כְּבָר	II	8		2		10	pln	*Chebar*
95	כּוֹסִבָא				10		10	prnm	*Cosiba*
96	כִּידוֹן		9	1			10	nm	*javelin*
97	כֶּלֶא	I	10				10	nm	*confinement*
98	כְּמוֹשׁ		8			2	10	prnm	*Chemosh*
99	כֵּן	III	10				10	nm	*right*
100	כְּנַעַן	I	9		1		10	prnm	*Canaan*
101	כֹּר		8		2		10	nm	*cor*
102	כַּרְמִי	I	8			2	10	prnm	*Carmi*
103	כְּרֵתִי		10				10	gent	*Cherethite*
104	כִּלְאַיִם		4		5		9	nmdu	*two kinds*
105	כְּסוּת		8		1		9	nf	*covering*
106	כְּפוֹר	I	9				9	nm	*bowl*
107	כַּרְמֶל	II	7		2		9	pln	*Carmel*
108	כִּבְשָׂה		8				8	nf	*ewe*

Rank	Lemma		MT	Si	Q	Inscr	Total	Type	Gloss
109	כהה	I	8				8	vb	*be dim*
110	כֵּהֶה		7		1		8	adj	*dim*
111	כִּיס		5	2	1		8	nm	*bag*
112	כֵּן	V	7	1			8	n[m]	*louse*
113	כנה		4	3	1		8	vb	*name*
114	כִּנֶּרֶת		7				7	pln	*Chinnereth*
115	כֶּסֶל	I	6		1		7	nm	*stupidity*
116	כפל		5		2		7	vb	*double*
117	כַּרְמְלִי		7				7	gent	*Carmelite*
118	כַּשְׂדִּים		7				7	pln	*Chaldaea*
119	כשף		6		1		7	vb	*practise sorcery*
120	כֹּבֶד		4		2		6	nm	*heaviness*
121	כִּבְשָׁן		4	1	1		6	nm	*furnace*
122	כּוֹבַע		6				6	nm	*helmet*
123	כסף	I	6				6	vb	*long for*
124	כפף		5	1			6	vb	*bend*
125	כֶּשֶׁף		6				6	nm	*sorcery*
126	כָּתִית		5		1		6	adj	*beaten*
127	כאה		3		2		5	vb	*be discouraged*
128	כְּדָרְלָעֹמֶר		5				5	prnm	*Chedorlaomer*
129	כִּידֹן				5		5	nm	*(Spanish) sword*
130	כְּלוּב	I	3	2			5	nm	*basket*
131	כֵּן	VI	5				5	n[m]	*position*
132	כָּנְיָהוּ		3			2	5	prnm	*Coniah*
133	כְּנַעֲנָה		5				5	prnm	*Chenanah*
134	כְּסִיל	II	4		1		5	prnm	*Orion*
135	כְּפוֹר	II	3	2			5	nm	*hoar frost*
136	כרה	II	4		1		5	vb	*purchase*
137	כֹּרֵם		5				5	nm	*vinedresser*
138	כֶּבֶל		2		2		4	nm	*fetter*
139	כּוּשַׁן רִשְׁעָתַיִם		4				4	prnm	*Cushan-rishathaim*
140	כָּחְלִת				4		4	pln	*Cohlith*
141	כמר		4				4	vb	*be agitated*

Rank	Lemma		MT	Si	Q	Inscr	Total	Type	Gloss
142	כֵּן	II	3		1		4	adj	*right, correct*
143	כַּעַשׂ		4				4	nm	*vexation*
144	כַּף	II	4				4	nf	*skirt*
145	כָּפִיס		1		3		4	nm	*beam*
146	כְּפִירָה		4				4	pln	*Chephirah*
147	כֶּפֶל		3	1			4	nm	*double*
148	כְּרִיתוּת		4				4	nf	*divorce*
149	כשׁר		3	1			4	vb	*be proper*
150	כתר	II	4				4	vb	*surround*
151	כֶּתֶר		3		1		4	nm	*crown*
152	כְּבוּדָּה		3				3	nf	*glory*
153	כבר		2		1		3	vb	*be great*
154	כִּבְרָה	II	3				3	nf	*stretch (of land)*
155	כוה		2	1			3	vb	*burn*
156	כּוּמָז		2	1			3	nm	*ornament*
157	כּוֹס	II	3				3	nm	*tawny owl*
158	כִּיּוּן	I	1		2		3	prnm	*Kivvun*
159	כִּיּוּן	II	1		2		3	n[m]	*pedestal*
160	כִּימָה		3				3	nf	*Pleiades*
161	כִּלָּיוֹן		2		1		3	nm	*destruction*
162	כִּלְיוֹן		3				3	prnm	*Chilion*
163	כָּלִיל	II		1	2		3	n[m]	*crown*
164	כַּלְכֹּל		2			1	3	prnm	*Calcol*
165	כַּלְנֵה		3				3	pln	*Calneh*
166	כִּמְהָם	I	3				3	prnm	*Chimham*
167	כַּמֹּן		3				3	nm	*cummin*
168	כֹּמֶר		3				3	nm	*priest*
169	כָּנַנְיָהוּ		3				3	prnm	*Conaniah*
170	כְּנַעֲנִי	II	3				3	nm	*trader*
171	כִּסְלֵו		2		1		3	prn[m]	*Chislev*
172	כסם		2		1		3	vb	*clip*
173	כֻּסֶּמֶת		3				3	nf	*spelt*
174	כִּפָּה		3				3	nf	*branch*
175	כֹּפֶר	IV	3				3	nm	*henna*

Rank	Lemma		MT	Si	Q	Inscr	Total	Type	Gloss
176	כַּפְתּוֹר	II	3				3	pln	*Caphtor*
177	כַּפְתֹּרִי		3				3	gent	*Caphtorite*
178	כַּרְכְּמִישׁ		3				3	pln	*Carchemish*
179	כַּרְמִיל		3				3	nm	*crimson*
180	כַּרְמֶל	III	3				3	nm	*fresh ears*
181	כרר		3				3	vb	*turn*
182	כְּרֻתוֹת		3				3	nf	*beam*
183	כִּשָּׁלוֹן		1	1	1		3	nm	*stumbling*
184	כֹּשֶׁר				3		3	n[m]	*propriety*
185	כִּשְׁרוֹן		3				3	nm	*skill*
186	כֹּתֶל		1		2		3	n[m]	*wall*
187	כאף			2			2	vb	*bend*
188	כאר	II	1		1		2	vb	*be repulsive*
189	כָּבוּל		2				2	pln	*Cabul*
190	כָּבִיר		2				2	nm	*braided article*
191	כַּבְלוּלָה				2		2	prn[f]	*Cablulah*
192	כַּדּוּר		2				2	nm	*ball, skein*
193	כַּדְכֹּד		2				2	nm	*agate*
194	כְּוִיָּה		2				2	nf	*burn*
195	כַּוָּן		2				2	nm	*cake*
196	כּוֹס	III			2		2	n[m]	*purse*
197	כּוּשִׁי	II	2				2	prnm	*Cushi*
198	כּוּת		2				2	pln	*Cuth*
199	כֹּזֵבָא		1		1		2	pln	*Cozeba*
200	כָּזְבִּי		2				2	prnf	*Cozbi*
201	כֹּחַ	II	1		1		2	n[m]	*lizard*
202	כֶּחָשׁ		1		1		2	adj	*untruthful*
203	כִּיּוּר				2		2	n[m]	*pannelling*
204	כִּיר		1		1		2	nm	*cooking-furnace*
205	כָּלֵב	II	2				2	pln	*Caleb*
206	כְּלוּא		2				2	nm	*confinement*
207	כְּלוּב	II	2				2	prnm	*Chelub*
208	כֶּלַח	I	2				2	nm	*old age*
209	כֶּלַח	III	2				2	pln	*Calah*

Rank	Lemma		MT	Si	Q	Inscr	Total	Type	Gloss
210	כָּל־חֹזֶה		2				2	prnm	*Col-hozeh*
211	כלל		2				2	vb	*perfect*
212	כִּנָּם		2				2	n[m]	*vermin*
213	כְּנַנְיָהוּ		2				2	prnm	*Chenaniah*
214	כְּנֶסֶת				2		2	nf	*congregation*
215	כֶּסֶא		2				2	nm	*full moon*
216	כָּסוּי		2				2	nm	*covering*
217	כסח		2				2	vb	*cut off*
218	כֹּסֵלָא					2	2	prnm	*Choselah*
219	כִּסְלָה		2				2	nf	*stupidity,*
220	כַּסְלֻחִי		2				2	gent	*Casluhite*
221	כָּסִפְיָא		2				2	pln	*Casiphia*
222	כֶּסֶת		2				2	nf	*band*
223	כער		2				2	vb	*be dark*
224	כֵּף	I	2				2	nm	*rock*
225	כפה		1		1		2	vb	*subdue*
226	כַּפָּה		1		1		2	nf	*(palm) branch*
227	כָּפָן		2				2	nm	*hunger*
228	כָּפָר		1		1		2	nm	*village*
229	כַּר	II	2				2	nm	*pasture*
230	כרה	III	2				2	vb	*feast*
231	כְּרוּב	II	2				2	pln	*Cherub*
232	כָּרִי		2				2	gent	*Carite*
233	כְּרִית		2				2	pln	*Cherith*
234	כַּרְכֹּב		2				2	nm	*edge*
235	כְּרָן		2				2	prnm	*Cheran*
236	כָּרֵשׂ		1	1			2	nf	*stomach*
237	כְּתֹבֶת		1		1		2	nf	*writing*
238	כָּתֵף	II	2				2	n[m]	*weapon*
239	כָּאוֹר				1		1	adj	*repulsive*
240	כאר	I	1				1	vb	*bind*
241	כְּבֵדֻת		1				1	nf	*heaviness,*
242	כִּבָה			1			1	nf	*dimness*
243	כַּבּוֹן		1				1	pln	*Cabbon*

Words Beginning with Kaph

Rank	Lemma		MT	Si	Q	Inscr	Total	Type	Gloss
244	כִּבּוּס				1		1	n[m]	*washing*
245	כְּבָרָה	I	1				1	nf	*sieve*
246	כֶּבֶשׁ		1				1	nm	*footstool*
247	כדם		1				1	nf	*bind*
248	כהה	II	1				1	vb	*rebuke*
249	כהה	III			1		1	vb	*be blunt*
250	כֵּהָה		1				1	nf	*lessening*
251	כּוּב		1				1	pln	*Cub*
252	כּוֹכָבָה				1		1	pln	*Cochaba*
253	כּוּן		1				1	pln	*Cun*
254	כּוֹנְנָה				1		1	nf	*bowl*
255	כור		1				1	vb	*bind*
256	כּוֹר עָשָׁן		1				1	pln	*Chor-ashan*
257	כּוּשָׁן		1				1	pln	*Cushan*
258	כּוֹשָׁרוֹת		1				1	nf	*prosperity*
259	כְּזִיב	I	1				1	pln	*Chezib*
260	כְּזִיב	II	1				1	n[m]	*menopause*
261	כֹּחַ	III	1				1	nm	*suppuration*
262	כחל		1				1	vb	*paint (eyes)*
263	כָּחֹל					1	1	adj	*blue*
264	כֹּחֵל					1	1	pln	*Cohel*
265	כחס				1		1	vb	*lie*
266	כִּי	II	1				1	nm	*vulture*
267	כִּי	III	1				1	nm	*burn*
268	כִּיד	I	1				1	n[m]	*misfortune*
269	כִּיד	II	1				1	n[m]	*cup*
270	כִּידוֹד		1				1	nm	*spark*
271	כִּידוֹר		1				1	n[m]	*attack*
272	כִּידֹן		1				1	nm	*Chidon*
273	כִּילַי		1				1	nm	*villain*
274	כֵּילָף		1				1	nf	*crowbar*
275	כִּירְגָּר				1			n[m]	*cistern*
276	כִּישׁוֹר		1				1	n[m]	*spindle*
277	כֹּל	II	1				1	n[m]	*mallow*

Rank	Lemma		MT	Si	Q	Inscr	Total	Type	Gloss
278	כֹּל	III	1				1	n[m]	*measure*
279	כְּלָא		1				1	nm	*all*
280	כִּלְאָב		1				1	prnm	*Chileab*
281	כְּלָאָה				1		1	nf	*fold*
282	כָּלְבִּי		1				1	gent	*Calebite*
283	כָּלֶה		1				1	adj	*longing*
284	כְּלֻהִי		1				1	prnm	*Cheluhi*
285	כְּלוּבַי		1				1	prnm	*Chelubai*
286	כְּלוּהוּ		1				1	prnm	*Cheluhi*
287	כְּלוּלֹת		1				1	nfpl	*betrothal*
288	כֵּלַי		1				1	nm	*villain*
289	כְּלִיא		1				1	nm	*confinement*
290	כְּלִילָה		1					nf	*crown*
291	כַּלְכֹּלְיָהוּ					1	1	prnm	*Calcoliah*
292	כְּלָל	I			1		1	n[m]	*total*
293	כְּלָל	II	1				1	prnm	*Chelal*
294	כלם	II	1				1	vb	*speak*
295	כָּלֶם					1	1	prnm	*Chalem*
296	כִּלְמַד		1				1	pln	*Chilmad*
297	כְּלִמָּה	II	1				1	nf	*speech*
298	כְּלִמּוּת		1				1	nf	*disgrace*
299	כמהּ		1				1	vb	*long for*
300	כִּמְהָם	II	1				1	pln	*Chimham*
301	כמס		1				1	vb	*store up*
302	כַּמְרִיר			1			1	n[m]	*darkness*
303	כָּן				1		1	adv	*here*
304	כַּנָּא				1		1	n[f]	*base*
305	כַּנָּה		1				1	nf	*stock*
306	כַּנֵּה		1				1	pln	*Canneh*
307	כְּנָנִי		1				1	prnm	*Chenani*
308	כְּנַנְיָה		1				1	prnm	*Chenaniah*
309	כִּנְעָה		1				1	nf	*bundle*
310	כִּנְעָן		1				1	nm	*trader*
311	כנף		1				1	vb	*hide*

Words Beginning with Kaph

Rank	Lemma		MT	Si	Q	Inscr	Total	Type	Gloss
312	כְּנָת		1				1	nm	*associate*
313	כֹּסֵא					1	1	prnm	*Choseh*
314	כֵּסְיָהּ		1				1	nf	*great throne, rump*
315	כְּסִיל	III	1				1	pln	*Chesil*
316	כְּסִילוּת		1				1	nf	*stupidity*
317	כסל		1				1	vb	*be foolish*
318	כְּסָלוֹן		1				1	pln	*Chesalon*
319	כִּסְלוֹן		1				1	prnm	*Chislon*
320	כִּסְלֹת תָּבוֹר		1				1	pln	*Chisloth-tabor*
321	כסס		1				1	vb	*reckon*
322	כסף	II	1				1	vb	*be ashamed*
323	כֶּסֶף	II	1				1	n[m]	*disappointment*
324	כֶּסֶף	III	1				1	n[m]	*food*
325	כָּסֵר					1	1	pln	*Caser*
326	כִּפָּא				1		1	pln	*Kippa*
327	כְּפִיר	II	1				1	nm	*copper vessel*
328	כְּפִירִים		1				1	pln	*Chephirim*
329	כפן		1				1	vb	*be hungry*
330	כֹּפֶר	II	1				1	nm	*bitumen*
331	כֹּפֶר	III	1				1	nm	*village*
332	כְּפַר הָעַמֹּנִי		1				1	pln	*Chephar-ammoni*
333	כֹּפְרִי	I			1		1	adj	*tarred*
334	כפשׁ		1				1	vb	*bend*
335	כַּר	III	1				1	nm	*saddle-basket*
336	כרבל		1				1	vb	*wrap*
337	כרה	IV	1				1	vb	*bind*
338	כרה	V	1				1	vb	*be short*
339	כָּרָה		1				1	nf	*cistern*
340	כֵּרָה		1				1	nf	*feast*
341	כִּרְכּוּר				1		1	n[m]	*circuit*
342	כַּרְכֹּם		1				1	nm	*saffron*
343	כַּרְכַּס		1				1	prnm	*Carcas*
344	כִּרְכָּרָה		1				1	nf	*dromedary*
345	כֶּרֶם	II	1				1	pln	*Cherem*

Rank	Lemma		MT	Si	Q	Inscr	Total	Type	Gloss
346	כַּרְמִי	II	1				1	gent	*Carmite*
347	כרסם		1				1	vb	*tear*
348	כַּרְפַּס		1				1	n[m]	*linen*
349	כַּרְשֹׁן					1	1	prnm	*Carshon*
350	כַּרְשְׁנָא		1				1	prnm	*Carshena*
351	כִּשְׂבָּה		1				1	nf	*ewe*
352	כֶּשֶׂד		1				1	prnm	*Chesed*
353	כשה		1				1	vb	*be sated*
354	כָּשַׁי					1	1	prnm	*Cashai*
355	כַּשִּׁיל		1				1	nm	*axe*
356	כַּשָּׁף		1				1	nm	*sorcerer*
357	כִּתְלִישׁ		1				1	pln	*Chitlish*
358	כתם		1				1	vb	*be stained*
359	כתר	I	1				1	vb	*be patient with*
360	כתר	III	1				1	vb	*be crowned*
361	כתשׁ		1				1	vb	*pound*

ל

Rank	Lemma		MT	Si	Q	Inscr	Total	Type	Gloss
1	לְ		4360	640	6000	926	26253	prep	*to*
2	לֹא	I	5196	173	1092	9	6470	part	*no(t)*
3	לִפְנֵי		1103	40	251	2	1396	prep	*before*
4	לקח		965	16	91	7	1079	vb	*take*
5	לֵב		599	58	166	1	824	nm	*heart*
6	לֵבָב		252	9	96	1	358	nm	*heart*
7	לֶחֶם	I	297	12	40	6	355	nm & f	*bread*
8	לֵוִי	II	296		36	2	334	gent	*Levite*
9	לְמַעַן		272	10	51		333	prep	*for the sake of*
10	לַיְלָה		227	1	57		285	nm	*night*
11	לָכֵן		200	2			202	adv	*therefore*

Words Beginning with Lamedh

Rank	Lemma		MT	Si	Q	Inscr	Total	Type	Gloss
12	לָשׁוֹן		117	15	62		194	nf	*tongue*
13	לָמָּה		178	10	2		190	adv	*why?*
14	לחם	I	171	2	10		183	vb	*fight*
15	לְבַד		156	2	18		176	adv	*alone*
16	לבשׁ		112	6	13		131	vb	*dress*
17	לכד		121	2	6		129	vb	*capture*
18	למד		86	10	26		122	vb	*learn*
19	לֵוִי	I	58	1	23	5	87	prnm	*Levi*
20	לְבָנוֹן		71	2	7		80	pln	*Lebanon*
21	לין		71	4	1	2	78	vb	*lodge*
22	לָבָן	II	54		3		57	prnm	*Laban*
23	ליץ		28	11	17		56	vb	*scorn*
24	לוּחַ		43		5		48	nm	*tablet*
25	לִשְׁכָּה		47				47	nf	*chamber*
26	לְאֹם		38		6		44	nm	*nation*
27	לְעֻמַּת		31	2	10		43	prep	*close by*
28	לקט		37		5		42	vb	*gather*
29	לֵאָה	I	34		2		36	prnf	*Leah*
30	לוֹט	II	33	1			34	prnm	*Lot*
31	לְבוּשׁ		31		2		33	nm	*garment*
32	לָבָן	I	29		4		33	adj	*white*
33	לְפָנִים	I	21	3	7		31	adv	*formerly*
34	לְבוֹנָה	I	21	1	7		29	nf	*frankincense*
35	לֹא	II	27				27	part	*indeed*
36	לֶהָבָה		20	2	5		27	nf	*flame, point*
37	לָכִישׁ		24			1	25	pln	*Lachish*
38	לוה	II	12	1	10		23	vb	*accompany*
39	לְחִי	I	20	1	2		23	nf	*jaw*
40	לוּ		22				22	conj	*if*
41	לעג		18	2	1		21	vb	*deride*
42	לאה	I	19	1			20	vb	*be weary*
43	לַהַב		12		8		20	nm	*flame*
44	לחץ		19		1		20	vb	*squeeze*
45	לִבְנָה		18				18	pln	*Libnah*

Rank	Lemma		MT	Si	Q	Inscr	Total	Type	Gloss
46	לוה	I	14	3	1		18	vb	*borrow*
47	לְפִי		16	1	1		18	prep	*according to*
48	לון	I	14		3		17	vb	*murmur*
49	לֶקַח	I	9	3	4		16	nm	*teaching*
50	לְבֵנָה		12		3		15	nf	*brick*
51	לוּלֵא		14				14	conj	*unless*
52	לַעֲנָה		8	1	5		14	nf	*wormwood*
53	לַפִּיד		13		1		14	nm	*torch*
54	לַחַץ		12		1		13	nm	*oppression*
55	לֻלָאָה		13				13	nf	*loop*
56	לָבִיא		11		1		12	n[m]	*lion* (fem.)
57	להט	I	10	2			12	vb	*blaze*
58	לִמֻּד		6	1	5		12	adj	*taught*
59	לֶמֶךְ		11		1		12	prnm	*Lamech*
60	לוז		5	1	4		10	vb	*depart*
61	לַעַג		8		2		10	n[m]	*derision,*
62	לַח		6		3		9	adj	*moist*
63	לָצוֹן		3		6		9	n[m]	*scorning*
64	לֹג		5			3	8	nm	*log*
65	לוּז	II	8				8	pln	*Luz*
66	לחך		6		2		8	vb	*lick*
67	לַיִל		8				8	nm	*night*
68	לְבוֹא חֲמָת		7				7	pln	*Lebo-hamath*
69	לוֹטָן		7				7	prnm	*Lotan*
70	לִוְיָתָן		6		1		7	nm	*Leviathan*
71	לָט		7				7	n[m]	*secrecy*
72	לַעְדָּן		7				7	prnm	*Ladan*
73	לקק		7				7	vb	*lick*
74	לבן	I	5		1		6	vb	*be white*
75	לַהַב				6		6	n[m]	*point*
76	לוּד		5		1		6	prnm	*Lud*
77	לחם	II	6				6	vb	*eat*
78	לַחַשׁ	I	5	1			6	n[m]	*whisper*
79	לטשׁ		5	1			6	vb	*sharpen*

Words Beginning with Lamedh

Rank	Lemma		MT	Si	Q	Inscr	Total	Type	Gloss
80	לבט		3		2		5	vb	*ruin*
81	לְבִיָּה		4		1		5	nf	*lion* (fem.)
82	לִבְנִי	I	5				5	prnm	*Libni*
83	לוּשׁ		5				5	vb	*knead*
84	לְחִי	II	5				5	pln	*Lehi*
85	לֹד		4				4	pln	*Lod*
86	לֵדָה		4				4	nf	*birth*
87	לַהַט	II	4				4	n[m]	*enchantment*
88	לוּבִי		4				4	gent	*Libyan*
89	לוט		4				4	vb	*wrap*
90	לֵחָה				4		4	nf	*liquid*
91	לַיִשׁ	II	4				4	pln	*Laish*
92	לֹא רֻחָמָה		3				3	prnf	*Lo-ruhamah*
93	לבב	I	3				3	vb	*think*
94	לְבִבָה		3				3	nf	*cake*
95	לְבוֹנָה	II	3				3	pln	*Lebonah*
96	לבן	II	3				3	vb	*make bricks*
97	לְבָנָה	I	3				3	nf	*moon*
98	להה		1	2			3	vb	*be mad*
99	לוֹ דְבָר		3				3	pln	*Lo-debar*
100	לוּדִי		3				3	gent	*Lydian*
101	לוּחִית		2		1		3	pln	*Luhith*
102	לחשׁ		3				3	vb	*whisper*
103	לֹיָה		3				3	nf	*spiral (border)*
104	לַיִשׁ	I	3				3	nm	*lion*
105	לפת		3				3	vb	*twist*
106	לֶקֶט		2		1		3	n[m]	*gleaning*
107	לֶקֶשׁ		2			1	3	n[m]	*crop*
108	לֹא עַמִּי		2				2	prnm	*Lo-ammi*
109	לבב	II	2				2	vb	*bake*
110	לְבָנָה	II	2				2	prnm	*Lebanah*
111	לִבְנֶה		2				2	n[m]	*storax*
112	לִבְנִי	II	2				2	gent	*Libnite*
113	לְהָבִי		2				2	gent	*Lehabite*

Rank	Lemma		MT	Si	Q	Inscr	Total	Type	Gloss
114	לַהַט	I	1		1		2	n[m]	*flame, blade*
115	להם		2				2	vb	*swallow*
116	לָהֵן		2				2	conj	*therefore*
117	לוֹחֵשׁ		2				2	prnm	*Hallohesh*
118	לִוְיָה		2				2	nf	*garland*
119	לֵחַ		1	1			2	nm	*moisture*
120	לְחוּם	I	2				2	nm	*flesh*
121	לְחֶם	II		2			2	n[m]	*war*
122	לֹט		2				2	n[m]	*myrrh*
123	לְטָאָה		1		1		2	nf	*lizard*
124	לִילִית		1		1		2	prnf	*Lilith*
125	לַיִשׁ	III	2				2	prnm	*Laish*
126	לְמוּאֵל		2				2	prnm	*Lemuel*
127	לעב		1	1			2	vb	*deride*
128	לָעִיר		2				2	pln	*Lair*
129	לעע	I	2				2	vb	*be rash*
130	לעע	II	1	1			2	vb	*swallow*
131	לְפָנִים	II	2				2	nm	*predecessors*
132	לֶקַח	II		2			2	nm	*acquisition*
133	לָשָׁד		2				2	nm	*cake*
134	לֶשֶׁם	I	2				2	n[m]	*jacinth*
135	לֶשֶׁם	II	2				2	pln	*Leshem*
136	לשׁן		2				2	vb	*slander*
137	לֶתֶךְ		1		1		2	n[m]	*lethech*
138	לָאֵל		1				1	prnm	*Lael*
139	לְאֻמִּים		1				1	prnm	*Leummim*
140	לָבֶא		1				1	n[m]	*lion*
141	לְבָאָה		1				1	nf	*lion* (fem.)
142	לְבָאוֹת		1				1	pln	*Lebaoth*
143	לַבָּה		1				1	nf	*flame*
144	לִבָּה		1				1	nf	*spirit*
145	לְבִיָּא		1				1	nf	*lion* (fem.)
146	לָבָן	III	1				1	pln	*Laban*
147	לַבֵּן		1				1	prn[m]	*Labben*

Words Beginning with Lamedh

Rank	Lemma		MT	Si	Q	Inscr	Total	Type	Gloss
148	לֹבֶן			1			1	n[m]	*whiteness*
149	לְגוֹס				1		1	prn[m]	*Legos*
150	לִדְבִר		1				1	pln	*Lidbir*
151	להב				1		1	vb	*blaze*
152	לַהַג		1				1	n[m]	*study*
153	לַהַד		1				1	prnm	*Lahad*
154	להה		1				1	vb	*languish*
155	להט	II	1				1	vb	*devour*
156	לַהֲקָה		1				1	nf	*seniority*
157	לוּב				1		1	prnm	*Libya*
158	לוֹז				1		1	n[m]	*perversity*
159	לוּז	I	1				1	nm	*almond (tree)*
160	לוֹט	I	1				1	nm	*covering*
161	לוּל		1				1	n[m]	*step*
162	לוּלָב				1		1	n[m]	*lulab*
163	לָזוּת		1				1	nf	*perversity*
164	לְחוּם	II	1				1	n[m]	*warfare*
165	לָחֶם		1				1	n[m]	*warrior*
166	לַחְמִי		1				1	prnm	*Lahmi*
167	לַחְמָס		1				1	pln	*Lahmas*
168	לַחַשׁ	II				1	1	prn[m]	*Lahash*
169	לְטוּשִׁים		1				1	prnm	*Letushim*
170	לַיְשָׁה		1				1	pln	*Laishah*
171	לֶכֶד		1				1	n[m]	*capture*
172	לֵכָה		1				1	pln	*Lecah*
173	לְכוּשִׁי				1		1	adj	*pine*
174	לָמֶד				1		1	n[m]	*lamedh*
175	לֹעַ		1				1	n[m]	*throat*
176	לָעֵג		1				1	adj	*mocking*
177	לַעְדָּה		1				1	prnm	*Laadah*
178	לעז		1				1	vb	*speak a foreign language*
179	לעט		1				1	vb	*swallow*
180	לַפִּידוֹת		1				1	prnm	*Lappidoth*

Rank	Lemma	MT	Si	Q	Inscr	Total	Type	Gloss
181	לִפְנַי	1				1	adj	*front*
182	לפף	1				1	vb	*cling*
183	לָקָה		1			1	nf	*trap*
184	לַקּוּם	1				1	pln	*Lakkum*
185	לִקְחִי	1				1	prnm	*Likhi*
186	לקשׁ	1				1	vb	*glean*
187	לֶשַׁע	1				1	pln	*Lasha*
188	לַשָּׁרוֹן	1				1	pln	*Lasharon*

ABBREVIATIONS AND SIGNS

TEXTS

Gn Ex Lv Nm Dt Jos Jg 1 S 2 S 1 K 2 K Is Jr Ezk Ho Jl Am Ob Jon Mc Na Hb Zp Hg Zc Ml Ps Jb Pr Ru Ca Ec Lm Est Dn Ezr Ne 1 C 2 C

Si $\text{Si}_{(M)}$ (Sirach from Masada)

SIGNS

+ = the following is used in association with the preceding

:: = the following is used in contrast or opposition to the preceding

|| = the following is used in parallel to the preceding, or, the following text is parallel to the preceding

§ = section

† = not all these occurrences are listed in this article

* (at the beginning of an article) = see the Bibliography for discussion of the existence of this word

* (elsewhere in an article) = see the Bibliography for further semantic studies

⇒ = the following are related words

ABBREVIATIONS

abs. = absolute
add. = additional (inscription)
adj. = adjective
adv. = adverb
AHL = Academy of the Hebrew Language
Akk. = Akkadian
alw. = always
anat. = anatomical
app. = apposition
appar. = apparently
Arab. = Arabic
Aram. = Aramaic
architect. = architectural
assoc. = associated, association
BCE = before the Common Era
BHS = *Biblia hebraica stuttgartensia*
CE = Common Era
cent. = century
coll. = miscellaneous collocations
conj. = conjunction
corrupt. = corruption
cpl = common plural
cs = common singular
cstr. = construct
del. = delete
der. = derivands, derivatives, i.e. morphologically related forms
descr. = describing, description
design. = designation, designating
du. = dual
em., *see* if em., or em.
emph. = emphatic
encl. = enclitic
erased = erased reading
esp. = especially
Eth. = Ethiopic
EW = Eisenman and Wise
f., fem. = feminine

fpl = feminine plural
fr. = fragment
freq. = frequently
fs = feminine singular
gent. = gentilic
Gnz = Genizah fragment, manuscript
graf. = graffito
Heb. = Hebrew
hi. = hiphil
HN = Horbury and Noy
ho. = hophal
hothp. = hothpael
htp. = hithpael
htpal. = hithpalel
htpalp. = hithpalpel
htpo. = hithpoel
htpol. = hithpolal, hithpolel
I = inscription
ident. = to be identified
if em. = the foregoing results from an emendation
impf. = imperfect
impv. = imperative
inf. = infinitive
ins. = insert
inscr. = inscription
intens. = intensive
interj. = interjection
intrans. = intransitive
interrog. = interrogative
Kh. = Khirbet
Kt = ketiv
L = Codex Leningradensis B19 A, text of *BHS*
lit. = literally
m., masc. = masculine
mg = marginal, sublinear, supralinear reading
MH = Mishnaic Hebrew
mod. = modern
mpl = masculine plural
ms = manuscript; (in morphology) masculine singular
MT = Masoretic Text
n. = noun
ni. = niphal
nom. cl. = noun clause
ntp. = nithpael
nu. = nuphal (ni. mixed with pu.)
obj. = object
oft. = often
or em. = the foregoing will not be the case if the following emendation is accepted
orig. = originally
OSA = Old South Arabic
ost. = ostracon
part. = particle
pass. = passive
PC = Preliminary Concordance (Richter)
perh. = perhaps
pf. = perfect
Phoen. = Phoenician
pi. = piel
pilp. = pilpel
pl., plur. = plural
pl.n. = place name
po. = poel, poal,
pol. = polal, polel
polp. = polpal
prep. = preposition
pr.n. = personal name
prob. = probably
pron. = pronoun
pronom. = pronominal
ptc. = participle
pu. = pual
pulp. = pulpal
Q = Qumran
Qr = qere
ref. = reference
Sam = Samaritan
Seb = Sebir (supposed reading)
sf. = suffix
sg. = singular
Si = Ben Sira

sim. = similar, similarly
sing. = singular
specif. = specifically
subj. = subject
syn. = synonym
Syr. = Syriac
T. = Tel, Tell
t = times
TiqSof = tiqqun soferim
trans. = transitive
Ug. = Ugaritic
usu. = usually
var. = variant
vb. = verb
W. = Wadi
WA = Wacholder and Abegg
Y. = Yhwh

OTHER ABBREVIATIONS

Other abbreviations will be found in The Sources and in the Bibliography

י

יאב $_{1.0.3}$ vb. **be willing—Qal** $_{1.0.3}$ Pf. יָאַבְתִּי—**desire, long (for),** <SUBJ> worshipper Ps 119$_{131}$ (11QPs^{a} תאבתי *I long,* from תאב) 4QBark^{d} 2.1$_{14}$ (יאבתי[י]). <PREP> לְ *for,* + מִצְוָה *commandment* Ps 119$_{131}$. <COLL> יאב + inf. of עבד *serve* 4QBark^{d} 5$_{3}$ ([י]אבת[י]).*

יאה $_{1}$ vb. **befit—Qal** $_{1}$ Pf. יָאָתָה—**befit,** <SUBJ> impersonal Jr 10$_{7}$. <PREP> לְ introducing object, + מֶלֶךְ *king* (Y.) Jr 10$_{7}$.

יְאוֹר, see יְאֹר *Nile.*

[יָאוּשׁ] $_{0.0.0.5}$ pr.n.m. **Jaush**—I יאש (unless יֹאָשׁ *Joash*)—
1. recipient of letters, appar. commander of Lachish, <APP> אָדוֹן *lord* Lachish ost. 2$_{1}$ 3$_{2}$ ([אד[ני יאו[ש]) 6$_{1}$. <PREP> לְ of direction, *to,* + נגד hi. *declare* Lachish ost. 3$_{2}$ (להג[ד] ל[אד[ני יאו[ש]]); אֶל *to* Lachish ost. 2$_{1}$ 6$_{1}$.

2. father of Nathan, <CSTR> בן יאש *son of Jaush* Seal 530 (T. Beit Mirsim?, 7th/6th cent.).

3. son of Elishama, <APP> בֵּן *son* Seal 566 (T. Beit Mirsim?, 7th/6th cent.).

4. son of Pedaiah, <APP> בֵּן *son* Seal 567 ([ב]ן; T. Beit Mirsim?, 7th/6th cent.).*

[יַאֲזַן] $_{0.0.0.2}$ pr.n.m. **Jaazan, 1.** son of Zephaniah ([צפנ]יהו), <APP> בֵּן *son* Arad ost. 59$_{5}$. **2.** appar. father of Shemaiah, Seal 662 (T. Beit Mirsim?, 7th/6th cent.).

יַאֲזַנְיָה $_{5.\ 0.0.12}$ pr.n.m. **Jaazaniah**—יַאֲזַנְיָהוּ—**1.** son of a Maacathite, army captain supporting Gedaliah, <SUBJ> בוא *come* 2 K 25$_{23}$||Jr 40$_{8(mss)}$ (L יְזַנְיָהוּ *Jezaniah*). <APP> בֵּן *son* 2 K 25$_{23}$||Jr 40$_{8(mss)}$.

2. Rechabite, son of Jeremiah, son of Habazziniah, <OBJ> לקח *take* Jr 35$_{3}$. <APP> בֵּן *son* Jr 35$_{3}$.

3. son of Shaphan, elder, <SUBJ> עמד *stand* Ezk 8$_{11}$. <APP> בֵּן *son* Ezk 8$_{11}$.

4. son of Azzur, official, <OBJ> ראה *see* Ezk 11$_{1}$. <APP> בֵּן *son* Ezk 11$_{1}$, שַׂר *prince* Ezk 11$_{1}$. **5.** son of Tob-shalom, <APP> בֵּן Lachish ost. 1$_{2}$. **6.** father of Hagab, <CSTR> בן יאזניהו *son of Jaazaniah* Lachish ost. 1$_{3}$.

7. son of Benaiah, <APP> בֵּן *son* Arad ost. 39$_{9}$. **8.** father of Honan, <CSTR> בן יאזניה Seal 21. **9.** servant of king, <APP> עֶבֶד *servant* Seal 69 (T. en-Naṣbeh, 8th/7th cent.). <PREP> לְ of possession, *(belonging) to, of* Seal 69 (T. en-Naṣbeh, 8th/7th cent.).

10. son of Giddel, <APP> בֵּן *son* Seal 241 ([ב]ן; 7th/6th cent.). <PREP> לְ of possession, *(belonging) to, of* Seal 241 (ליאזניה; others ליאזניה[ו]; 7th/6th cent.).

11. appar. son of Maabadiah, <PREP> לְ of possession, *(belonging) to, of* Seal 722 (7th cent.).

12. father of Shemaiah, <CSTR> בן יאזנ[ה] *son of Jaazaniah* Seal 805 (City of David, 7th/6th cent.).

13. son of Maaseiah, <APP> בֵּן *son* Seal 848 (יאזניה[ו] [ב]ן; City of David, 7th/6th cent.). <PREP> לְ of possession, *(belonging) to, of* Seal 848 ([ליאזניה[ו]; City of David, 7th/6th cent.).

14. <APP> בֵּן *son* Ḥorvat 'Uza jar inscr. 2$_{5}$. **15.** <PREP> לְ of possession, *(belonging) to, of* Ḥorvat 'Uza jar inscr. 2$_{7}$. **16.** <APP> בֵּן *son* Ḥorvat 'Uza jar inscr. 2$_{7}$.

→ אזן *hear* + יה *Y.*

[יַאֲחַץ] $_{0.0.0.1}$ pr.n.m. **Jaahaz,** in list of names, Arad ost. 58$_{4}$.

יָאִיר $_{12.0.0.1}$ pr.n.m. **Jair**—I יאר—**1.** son of Manasseh, <SUBJ> הלך *go* Nm 32$_{41}$, לכד *capture* Nm 32$_{41}$, לקח *take* Dt 3$_{14}$. <CSTR> חַוֹּת יָאִיר *tent villages of Jair* 1 K 4$_{13}$. <APP> בֵּן *son* Nm 32$_{41}$ Dt 3$_{14}$ 1 K 4$_{13}$.

2. Israelite, son of Segub, <OBJ> ילד hi. *beget* 1 C 2$_{22}$. <PREP> לְ of possession, *(belonging) to, of,* + היה *be* 1 C 2$_{22}$.

3. Gileadite and judge, <SUBJ> קום *rise* Jg 10$_{3}$, שׁפט *judge* Jg 10$_{3}$, מות *die* Jg 10$_{5}$, קבר ni. *be buried* Jg 10$_{5}$. <ADJ> גִּלְעָדִי *Gileadite* Jg 10$_{3}$. <PREP> לְ of possession, *(belonging) to, of,* + היה *be* Jg 10$_3$.

4. father of Mordecai, <CSTR> בֶּן יָאִיר *son of Jair* Est 2$_5$. <APP> בֵּן *son* Est 2$_5$.

5. Lachish inscr. 31$_5$, <CSTR> [ב]ן יאר *son of Jair* Lachish inscr. 31$_5$ (others יגר *Jagur*). **6.** perh. father of Zechariah, Weight 54.

7. in pl.n. חַוֹּת יָאִיר **Havvoth-jair,** lit. 'tent villages of Jair', in Argob region of Bashan, <CSTR> חַוֹּת יָאִיר *Havvoth-jair* Nm 32$_{41}$ Dt 3$_{14}$ Jos 13$_{30}$ Jg 10$_4$ 2 K 15$_{25}$ (if em. וְאֶת־הָאַרְיֵה *and with Arieh* to חַוֹּת יָאִיר *Havvoth-jair*) 1 C 2$_{23}$.

⇒ אור hi. *enlighten;* יָאִרִי *Jairite.*

יָאִרִי, see יָאִרִי *Jairite.*

יאל I $_{19.0.1}$ vb. **be pleased—Hi.** $_{19.0.1}$ Pf. הוֹאִיל, הוֹאַלְתָּ, הוֹאַלְנוּ, הוֹאַלְתִּי (Q הואלתה); impf. יֹאֵל; + waw וַיּוֹאֶל (וַיֹּאֶל); impv. הוֹאֶל (הוֹאֶל־), הוֹאִילוּ—**be pleased, willing, undertake** to do something; **be determined** to do, i.e. **persist** in doing (Jos 17$_{12}$ Jg 1$_{27.35}$ Ho 5$_{11}$), <SUBJ> Y. 1 S 12$_{22}$ 2 S 7$_{29}$‖1 C 17$_{27}$ Jb 6$_9$ Is 38$_{20}$ (if ins. הוֹאִיל *he was pleased*) 1QH 16$_8$, Amorite(s) Jg 1$_{35}$, Canaanite(s) Jos 17$_{12}$ Jg 1$_{27}$, Ephraim Ho 5$_{11}$, Israel(ites) Jos 7$_7$, Abraham Gn 18$_{27.31}$, David 1 S 17$_{39}$ (or em. וַיֹּאֶל *and he was willing* to וַיֵּלֶא *and he was [too] weary* or וַיֵּאַל *and he was unable*),* Elisha 2 K 6$_3$, Gehazi 2 K 5$_{23}$, Moses Ex 2$_{21}$ Dt 1$_5$, אָדָם *human being* 4Q185 1.2$_{13}$, אִישׁ *man* Jg 19$_6$, לֵוִי *Levite* Jg 17$_{11}$, friends of Job Jb 6$_{28}$.

<COLL> יאל hi. with other verb, **1.** pf. or impf. of יאל, before inf. of ישׁב *dwell* Ex 2$_{21}$ Jos 17$_{12}$ Jg 1$_{27.35}$ 17$_{11}$, הלך *go* 1 S 17$_{39}$ (or em.), דבר pi. *speak* Gn 18$_{27.31}$, ברך pi. *bless* 1 C 17$_{27}$, עשׂה *make* 1 S 12$_{22}$ 1QH 16$_8$ ([לעש]ות), ישׁע hi. *save* Is 38$_{20}$ (if em.; see Subj.).

2. pf. or impf. of יאל, before pf. or impf. of ישׁב *dwell* Jos 7$_7$, הלך *go* Ho 5$_{11}$, באר pi. *explain* Dt 1$_5$, דכא pi. *crush* Jb 6$_9$.

3. impv. of יאל, before impv. of לין *lodge* Jg 19$_6$, הלך *go* 1 K 6$_3$, פנה *turn* Jb 6$_{28}$, ברך pi. *bless* 2 S 7$_{29}$, לקח *take* 2 K 5$_{23}$.*

יאל II $_{4.1.1}$ vb. **be foolish—Ni.** $_{4.1.1}$ Pf. נוֹאֲלוּ, נוֹאַלְנוּ; + waw וְנֹאֲלוּ; ptc. Si, Q נואל—**be foolish, become a fool,** <SUBJ> Aaron Nm 12$_{11}$ (‖ חטא *sin*), Miriam Nm 12$_{11}$, אִישׁ *man* 4QMyst[a] 6.2$_{13}$, שַׂר *prince* Is 19$_{13}$ (1QIsa[a] נאולו perh. from אול *be foolish;* ‖ נשׁא ni. *be deluded*), בַּד *diviner* Jr 50$_{36}$ (‖ חתת *be shattered*), inhabitants of Jerusalem Jr 5$_4$, חָכָם *wise one* Si 37$_{19(Bmg, D)}$, לְבִיָּא *lion* (fem.) Ezk 19$_5$ (if em. נוֹחֲלָה *she waited* to נוֹאֲלָה *she was foolish*). <PREP> לְ of direction, *to(wards),* + נֶפֶשׁ *soul,* i.e. self Si 37$_{19(Bmg, D)}$.

<SYN> נשׁא ni. *be deluded,* חתת *be shattered,* חטא *sin.**

יֹאֵל, see יוֹאֵל *Joel.*

יְאֹר $_{65.2.3}$ pl.n. **Nile**—יְאוֹר; + article הַיְאֹר, בַּיְאֹר (בַּיְאוֹר), כַּיְאֹר (כָּאֹר Am 8$_8$); + ה- of direction הַיְאֹרָה; cstr. כִּיאֹר (כִּיאוֹר); sf. יְאֹרִי; pl. יְאֹרִים; + article הַיְאֹרִים, בַּיְאֹרִים; cstr. יְאֹרֵי (Q יאורי); sf. יְאֹרֶיךָ, יְאֹרָיו, יְאֹרֵיהֶם—**1.** the river **Nile** (Gn 41$_{1+5t}$ Ex 1$_{22}$ 2$_{3.5.5}$ 4$_{9.9}$ 7$_{15+13t}$ 8$_{5.7}$ 17$_5$ Is 19$_{7.7.7.8}$ 23$_3$ [‖ שִׁיחוֹר *Shihor*] 23$_{10}$ Jr 46$_{7.8}$ [both + נָהָר *river*] Ezk 29$_{3.9}$ [both §2, if em.; see Nom. Cl.] Am 8$_{8.8}$ 9$_{5.5}$ Zc 10$_{11}$ [+ יָם *sea*] Si 39$_{22}$ [‖ נָהָר *river*] 47$_{14}$ 4QParGenEx 3$_3$).

2. pl. **(Nile-)streams,** i.e. the **branches** and **canals** of the lower Nile (Ex 7$_{19}$ 8$_1$ [both ‖ נָהָר *river,* אֲגַם *pool*] 2 K 19$_{24}$‖Is 37$_{25}$ Is 7$_{18}$ 19$_6$ [+ נָהָר *river*] Ezk 29$_{3.3}$ [if em.; see Nom. Cl.] 29$_{4.4.5.9}$ [if em.; see Nom. Cl.] 29$_{10}$ 30$_{12}$ Na 3$_8$ Ps 78$_{44}$ [+ נֹזֵל *stream*] 4QpNah 3.3$_9$).

3. other **river, stream** (Is 33$_{21}$ perh. 4QapPs[b] 14 [אור ותיה; + אָפִיק *channel,* אֲגַם *pool*] 4QBer[a] 5$_{10}$); Tigris (Dn 12$_{5.5.6.7}$).

4. channel, i.e. **gallery,** of mine (Jb 28$_{10}$).

<SUBJ> חרב *be dried up* Is 19$_6$, באשׁ *stink* Ex 7$_{18.21}$, שׁרץ *swarm* with frogs Ex 7$_{28}$.

<NOM CL> לִי יְאֹרִי *my Nile is mine* Ezk 29$_3$ (or em. יְאֹרִי to יְאֹרִים *the Nile-streams*) 29$_9$ (יְאֹר *the Nile;* or em. יְאֹרִים), היאורים הם גדו[ל]י מנשה *the Nile-streams are the great ones of Manasseh* 4QpNah 3.3$_9$.

<OBJ> נכה hi. *strike* Ex 7$_{25}$ 17$_5$, עשׂה *make* Ezk 29$_3$ (if em. עֲשִׂיתִנִי *I have made myself* to עֲשִׂיתִים *I have made them*), חרב hi. *dry up* 2 K 19$_{24}$‖Is 37$_{25}$, נתן *give,* i.e. make, dry ground Ezk 30$_{12}$, הפך *turn* into blood Ps 78$_{44}$, בקע pi. *cut* Jb 28$_{10}$, שׂוך *hedge in* perh. 4QapPs[b] 14 (אור ותיה).

<CSTR> יְאוֹר מִצְרַיִם *the Nile of Egypt* Am 8_8 9_5 (יְאֹר), יְאֹרֵי *the streams of* Is 7_{18}, יְאֹרֵי מָצוֹר *streams of Egypt* Is 19_6 2 K 19_{24}||Is 37_{25}, יאורי מצולות *streams of the deeps* 4QBer^a 5_{10}; שְׂפַת הַיְאֹר *bank of the Nile* Gn $41_{3.17}$ Ex 2_3 7_{15} Dn $12_{5.5}$, יַד *side of* Ex 2_5, פִּי יְאוֹר *mouth*, or *bank*, *of the Nile* Is 19_7, סְבִיבֹת הַיְאֹר *circuits of*, i.e. around, *the Nile* Ex 7_{24} (+ חפר *dig*), מֵימֵי *water of* Ex 4_9 7_{24} Dn $12_{6.7}$, מְצוּלוֹת יְאֹר *depths of the Nile* Zc 10_{11}, מִזְרַע יְאוֹר *place of sowing of*, i.e. by, *the Nile* Is 19_7, קְצִיר *harvest of* Is 23_3, דְּגַת יְאֹרֶיךָ *fish of your streams* Ezk $29_{4.4.5}$, קְצֵה יְאֹרֵי *end of the streams of* Is 7_{18}, מְקוֹם ... יְאֹרִים *place of ... streams* Is 33_{21}, כֹּל יְאֹרֵי *all the streams of* 2 K 19_{24}||Is 37_{25}.

<APP> נָהָר *river* Is 33_{21} (unless del. נְהָרִים *rivers*), נַחַל *wadi* 4QBer^a 5_{10}.

<ADJ> רָחָב *wide* Is 33_{21} (רַחֲבֵי־יָדָיִם *wide of both hands*, i.e. on both sides).

<PREP> לְ of direction, *to*, + שׁלך hi. *throw* 4QParGen Ex 3_3 ([וישליכו ... ליוא[ר]).

בְּ of place, *in(to)*, *by* Ex $7_{17.18.20.20.21}$ 4QpsEzek^a 34_4, + שׁאר ni. *remain* Ex $8_{5.7}$, ישׁב *sit* Na 3_8, שׁלך hi. *cast* Is 19_8.

כְּ *as*, + עבר *pass*, i.e. overflow Is 23_{10}, צוף hi. *overflow* Si 39_{22} 47_{14}, עלה *go up* Jr $46_{7.8}$ Am 8_8 9_5, שׁקע ni. *sink* Am 8_8 9_5.

מִן of direction, *from* Ex $7_{18.21}$, + עלה *go up* Gn $41_{2.3.18}$, לקח *take* Ex 4_9.

עַל *over*, + נטה *stretch* hand Ex 7_{19} 8_1, *beside, at* Is 19_7 (or del. עַל יְאוֹר), + עמד *stand* Gn 41_1, רחץ *wash* (intrans.) Ex 2_5; אֶל *against* Ezk 29_{10}.

בְּתוֹךְ *among*, + רבץ *lie* Ezk 29_3, עלה hi. *bring up* Ezk 29_4.

ה- of direction, + שׁלך hi. *cast* Ex 1_{22}.

<SYN> §1 שִׁיחוֹר *Shihor*, נָהָר *river*; §2 נָהָר *river*, אֲגַם *pool*.*

יָאִרִי 1 gent. **Jairite,** descendant of Jair, <SUBJ> היה *be* 2 S 20_{26}. <APP> עִירָא הַיָּאִרִי *Ira the Jairite* 2 S 20_{26}.

⇒ יָאִיר *Jair*.

יאשׁ 6.1 vb. **despair—Ni.** 5 + waw וְנוֹאַשׁ; ptc. נוֹאָשׁ (נֹאָשׁ)—**1. despair (of),** <SUBJ> Saul 1 S 27_1. <PREP> מִן *of*, + David 1 S 27_1 (וְנוֹאַשׁ מִמֶּנִּי שָׁאוּל לְבַקְשֵׁנִי *and Saul will despair of me to seek me*, i.e. of seeking me). <COLL> + adverb, עוֹד *again* 1 S 27_1.

2. ptc. as noun, **despairing one,** <CSTR> אִמְרֵי נֹאָשׁ *words of a despairing one* Jb 6_{26}.

3. ptc. as interjection, **desperate!, it is hopeless!,** <COLL> after אמר *say* Is 57_{10} Jr 2_{25} 18_{12}.

Also 4QTanḥ 8_{13} (ו[נ]ואשׁ).

Pi. 1 inf. יַאֵשׁ—**cause to despair,** <SUBJ> Koheleth Ec 2_{20}. <OBJ> לֵב *heart* Ec 2_{20}. <PREP> עַל *on account of*, + עָמָל *toil* Ec 2_{20}.

Pu. 0.1 Ptc. Si מיואשׁ—**be in despair,** <SUBJ> Solomon Si 47_{23} (וישכב שלמה מיואש *and Solomon lay down in despair*).

[יָאֵשׁ], see יָאוּשׁ *Jaush*.

יֹאָשׁ, see יוֹאָשׁ *Joash*.

יֹאשִׁיָּה, see יֹאשִׁיָּהוּ *Josiah*.

יֹאשִׁיָּהוּ 53.2 pr.n.m. **Josiah**—יֹאשִׁיָּה, יאוֹשִׁיָּהוּ—**1.** king of Judah, son of Jedidah, successor of Amon, and father of Jehoahaz, Eliakim (Jehoiakim), and Mattaniah (Zedekiah), <SUBJ> מלך *reign* 2 K 21_{26} 22_1||2 C 34_1 Jr 1_2, הלך *go* 2 K 23_{29}, בוא *come* 2 C 35_{22}, יצא *go out* 2 C 35_{20}, שׁוב *go back* 2 K 23_{19}, פנה *turn* (intrans.) 2 K 23_{16}, סבב hi. *turn* (trans.) 2 C 35_{22}, שׁלח *send* 2 K 23_{16}, קרא *meet* 2 K 23_{29}||2 C 35_{20}, עמד hi. *cause to stand* 2 C 35_1, אמר *say* 2 K 23_{16} 2 C 35_1, ראה *see* 2 K 23_{16}, שׁמע *listen* 2 C 35_{22}, חפשׂ htp. *disguise oneself* 2 C 35_{22}, לקח *take* 2 K 23_{16}, סור hi. *remove* 2 K 23_{19} 2 C 34_{33}, בער pi. *remove* 2 K 23_{24}, שׂרף *burn* 2 K $23_{16.19}$, טמא pi. *defile* 2 K 23_{16}, עשׂה *do* 2 K $23_{16.19.28}$ 2 C $35_{1.18}$, כון hi. *prepare* 2 C 35_{20}, לחם ni. *fight* 2 C 35_{22}, זבח *slay* 2 K 23_{19}, עבד hi. *cause to serve* 2 C 34_{33}, רום hi. *raise*, i.e. contribute 2 C 35_7.

<NOM CL> יֹאשִׁיָּהוּ בְנוֹ *Josiah was his son* 1 C 3_{14}, יֹאשִׁיָּהוּ שְׁמוֹ *Josiah is his name* 1 K 13_2, בֶּן־שְׁמֹנֶה שָׁנָה יֹאשִׁיָּהוּ *Josiah was a son of eight years*, i.e. was eight years old 2 K 22_1||2 C 34_1.

<OBJ> מלך hi. *make king* 2 K 21_{24}||2 C 33_{25}, ראה *see* 2 K 23_{29}, מות hi. *kill* 2 K 23_{29}, בוא hi. *bring* 2 K 23_{29}, רכב hi. *cause to ride* 2 K 23_{29}, קבר *bury* 2 K 23_{29}.

<CSTR> בֶּן־יֹאשִׁיָּהוּ *son of Josiah* 2 K 23_{30}||2 C 36_1 2 K

23_{34} Jr $1_{3.3}$ $22_{11.18}$ 25_1 26_1 27_1 (יאוֹשִׁיָּהוּ) 35_1 $36_{1.9}$ 37_1 45_1 46_2, בְּנֵי *sons of* 1 C 3_{15}, דִּבְרֵי *deeds of* 2 K 23_{28}||2 C 35_{26}, יְמֵי *days of* Jr 1_2 3_6 36_2 Zp 1_1, מַלְכוּת *reign of* 2 C 35_{19}, מִצְוַת *command of* 2 C 35_{16}, שם יאשיהו *name of Josiah* Si 49_1.

<APP> אָב *father* 2 K 23_{34} Jr 22_{11}, בֵּן *son* 2 K 21_{24}||2 C 33_{25} 2 K 21_{26} Jr 1_2 25_3 Zp 1_1, מֶלֶךְ *king* 2 K $22_{3.23.29}$ Jr 1_2 3_6 25_3 Zp 1_1 2 C $35_{16.23}$.

<PREP> לְ of possession, *(belonging) to, of* 2 K $22_{3.23}$ Jr 25_3; introducing object, + ירה hi. *shoot* 2 C 35_{23}.

כְּ *like*, + היה *be* 2 K 23_{24}.

אֶל *to*, + אמר *say* 2 K 23_{16}, שׁלח *send* 2 C 35_{20}.

עַל *for*, + אבל htp. *mourn* 2 C 35_{24}, קנן po. *make lamentation* 2 C 35_{25}; *concerning*, + אמר *speak* 2 C 35_{25}.

לְבַד *apart from*, + שׁחת hi. *act corruptly* Si 4_4.

לִפְנֵי *before*, + היה *be* 2 K 23_{24}.

אַחֲרֵי *after*, + קום *arise* 2 K 23_{24}.

תַּחַת *in place of*, + מלך *reign* Jr 22_{11}, hi. *make king* 2 K 23_{34}.

2. son of Zephaniah, <CSTR> בֵּית יֹאשִׁיָּה *house of Josiah* Zc 6_{10}. <APP> בֵּן *son* Zc 6_{10}.

יאתון, see אִיתוֹן *entrance*.

יְאָתְרַי, 1 pr.n.m. **Jeatherai,** Levite, descendant of Gershom, perh. ident. with Ethni at 1 C 6_{26}, <NOM CL> יְאָתְרַי בְּנוֹ *Jeatherai was his son* 1 C 6_6 (or em. אֶתְנִי *Ethni*).

יבב 1 vb. **cry aloud—Pi.** 1 + waw 3fs וַתְּיַבֵּב—**cry aloud,** perh. **lament,** <SUBJ> אֵם *mother* Jg 5_{28} (or em. וַתַּבֵּט *and she looked*, i.e. נבט hi.; + שׁקף ni. *look down*). <PREP> בְּעַד *through*, + אֶשְׁנָב *window* Jg 5_{28} (or em.; see Subj.).

יְבוּל 13.1.1 n.m. **produce**—cstr. יְבוּל; sf. יְבוּלָהּ (יְבֻלָהּ), יְבוּלָם—**produce** of the soil; perh. **possessions** (Jb 20_{28}; or em.; see Subj.), <SUBJ> גלה *depart* Jb 20_{28} (or em. יְבוּל to יָבָל *flood*). <NOM CL> אֵין יְבוּל בַּגְּפָנִים *there is no produce on the vines* Hb 3_{17}. <OBJ> נתן *give* Lv $26_{4.20}$ (both || פְּרִי *fruit*) Dt 11_{17} Ezk 34_{27} (|| פְּרִי, טַל *dew*) Ps 67_7 78_{46} (|| יְגִיעַ *product of labour*) Ps 85_{13} (|| טוֹב *goodness*), כלא *withhold* Hg 1_{10} (+ טַל) Zc 8_{12} (|| פְּרִי), שׁלק hi. *burn* Si 43_{21}, אכל *devour* Dt 32_{22} (+ אֶרֶץ *land*), שׁחת hi. *destroy* Jg 6_4. <CSTR> יְבוּל הָאָרֶץ *produce of the land* Jg 6_4, בֵּיתוֹ *of his house* Jb 20_{28} (or em.; see Subj.), יבול הרים *produce of the mountains* Si 43_{21}; עֵץ יְבוּלָם *trees of their produce* Ps 105_{33} (if em. גְּבוּלָם *of their boundary*), כול יבולה *all its produce* 4QRitMar 9_6.

<SYN> פְּרִי *fruit*, טַל *dew*, יְגִיעַ *product of labour*, טוֹב *goodness*.*

⇒ יבל *bring*.

יְבוּס 4 pl.n. **Jebus,** former name of Jerusalem, <SUBJ> היה *be* Jos 18_{28} (if em. הַיְבוּסִי *the Jebusites*; + הִיא יְרוּשָׁלַםִ *that is Jerusalem*). <NOM CL> הִיא יְבוּס *that is Jebus* 1 C 11_1 (+ יְרוּשָׁלַםִ *Jerusalem*). <CSTR> יֹשְׁבֵי יְבוּס *inhabitants of Jebus* 1 C 11_5. <PREP> עִם *with*, i.e. near Jg 19_{11}; עַד־נֹכַח *as far as in front of*, + בוא *come* Jg 19_{10} (+ הִיא יְרוּשָׁלָםִ *that is Jerusalem*).

⇒ יְבוּסִי *Jebusite*.

יְבוּסִי 41.0.2 gent. **Jebusite**—יְבֻסִי—belonging to Jebus, **1.** as collective sing. noun **Jebusites,** <SUBJ> היה *be* Jos 18_{28} (or em. יְבוּס *Jebus*), ישׁב *dwell* Nm 13_{29} Jos 15_{63} Jg 1_{21}, שׁמע *hear* Jos 9_1, קבץ htp. *gather* (intrans.) Jos 9_1, לחם ni. *fight* Jos 9_1 24_{11}.

<NOM CL> הַיְבוּסִי בָּהָר *the Jebusites (who) were in the hill-country* Jos 11_3, שָׁם הַיְבוּסִי *the Jebusites were there* 1 C 11_4 4QSela 8.2_9 ([היבוסי]).

<OBJ> ילד *beget* Gn 10_{16}||1 C 1_{14}, נתן *give* Gn 15_{21} Jos 24_{11}, ירשׁ hi. *dispossess* Jos 3_{10} 15_{63} Jg 1_{21}, גרשׁ *expel* Ex 34_{11} 11QT 2_4 ([גורש ... היבוסי]), pi. *expel* Ex 33_2, נשׁל *clear away* Dt 7_1, נכה hi. *strike* Jos 12_8 2 S 5_8||1 C 11_6, חרם hi. *destroy* Dt 20_{17}=11QT 22_{15}.

<CSTR> מְקוֹם ... הַיְבוּסִי *place of ... the Jebusites* Ex 3_8, אֶרֶץ *land of* Ex 3_{17} 13_5 Ne 9_8, עִיר *city of* Jg 19_{11}, כֶּתֶף *shoulder*, i.e. slope, *of* Jos 15_8 (+ הִיא יְרוּשָׁלַםִ *that is Jerusalem*) 18_{16}.

<APP> גּוֹי *nation* Dt 7_1, אֶרֶץ *land* Gn 15_{21}, מֶלֶךְ *king* Jos 9_1 11_3 12_8, בַּעַל *lord* Jos 24_{11}, יֹשֵׁב *inhabitant* Jos 15_{63} Jg 1_{21} 2 S 5_6||1 C 11_4.

<PREP> לְ of possession, *(belonging) to, of* Ezr 9_1; כְּ *as* Zc 9_7; מִן partitive, *from among*, + יתר ni. *remain* 1 K 9_{20}||2 C 8_7; אֶל *to*, + הלך *go* 2 S 5_6, בוא hi. *bring* Ex 23_{23}, שׁלח *send* Jos 11_3; בְּקֶרֶב *among*, + ישׁב *dwell* Jg 3_5.

2. as sing. noun, a particular **Jebusite,** <CSTR> ... גֹּרֶן הַיְבוּסִי *threshing floor of ... the Jebusite* 2 S $24_{16.18}$||1 C $21_{15.18}$ 1 C 21_{28} 2 C 3_1. <APP> הָאֲרַוְנָה *Araunah* 2 S $24_{16\,(Qr).18\,(Qr)}$||1 C $21_{15.18}$ 1 C 21_{28} 2 C 3_1 (1 C, 2 C all four אָרְנָן *Ornan*).

Also 4QapMos^c 1.1$_8$ ([הי]בו[ס]י).

→ יְבוּס *Jebus*.

יבושה, see יַבָּשָׁה *dry land*.

יִבְחָר 3 pr.n.m. **Ibhar,** son of David, <SUBJ> ילד ni. *be born* 1 C 3_6. <NOM CL> ... אֵלֶּה שְׁמוֹת הַיִּלֹּדִים לוֹ בִּירוּשָׁלָם ... יִבְחָר *these are the names of those born to him in Jerusalem ... Ibhar* 2 S 5_{15}, var. 1 C 14_5.

→ י״ Y. + בחר *choose*.

יָבִין 8 pr.n.m. **Jabin, 1.** king of Hazor, defeated by Joshua, <SUBJ> שׁמע *hear* Jos 11_1, שׁלח *send* Jos 11_1. <APP> מֶלֶךְ *king* Jos 11_1.

2. king of Hazor, defeated by Deborah and Barak, <SUBJ> מלך *reign* Jg 4_2, לחץ *oppress* Jg 4_2. <OBJ> כנע hi. *subdue* Jg 4_{23}, כרת hi. *cut off* Jg 4_{24}. <CSTR> יַד יָבִין *hand of Jabin* Jg 4_2, צָבָא *army of* Jg 4_7. <APP> מֶלֶךְ *king* Jg $4_{2.17.23.24.24}$. <PREP> כְּ *as* Ps 83_{10} (עֲשֵׂה־לָהֶם ... כְּיָבִין *do to them ... as [to] Jabin*); עַל *upon, against,* + הלך *go* Jg 4_{24}, בֵּין *between* Jg 4_{17} (+ בַּיִת *house* of Heber).

→ (?) בין *understand*.

יָבֵישׁ, see יָבֵשׁ II, III *Jabesh*.

יבל 18.1.5 vb. **bring—Qal** 0.1.4—Ptc. Q יובל (Si יבלי, Q יובלי)—perh. ptc. as noun, **channel** (unless יוּבַל *stream* in 1QIsa^a and 1QH and יָבָל stream in Si),* <SUBJ> היה *be* 1QIsa^a 30_{25}. <CSTR> יובלי מים *streams of water* Si 50_8 (יבלי) 1QIsa^a 30_{25} 44_4 (MT יִבְלֵי *streams of* in both). <PREP> לְ of direction, *to,* + שׁלח *send* 1QH 8_7 (ליובל[ו]); אֶל *to,* + שׁלח *send* 1QH 8_{10}; עַל *beside,* + שׁלח pi. *send* roots Jr 17_8 (if em. יוּבַל *stream;* + מַיִם *water*), צמח *grow* 1QIsa^a 44_4, יצא *go out* Si 50_8.

Also perh. 6QProph 15_2 (וּבלות[י]; unless ובלות, from בלה *be worn out*).

Hi. 7.0.1 Impf. יוֹבִילֵנִי (יַבְלֵנִי), יוֹבִילוּ (יַבִלוּ), יוֹבִלוּן, אוֹבִילֵם, (יַבְלוּהָ); impv. Q הובל—**bring, carry, lead,** <SUBJ> Y. Jr 31_9 (+ בוא *come*, הלך hi. *lead*), Assyrians Ho 10_6 (if em.; see Ho. Subj.), Ephraim Ho 12_2 (if em.; see Ho. Subj.), מֶלֶךְ *king* Ps 68_{30}, בַּת *daughter* Zp 3_{10}, בְּתוּלָה *young woman* Ps 45_{16} (if em.; see Ho. Subj.), רֵעָה *companion* Ps 45_{16} (if em.; see Ho. Subj.), עָתָר *suppliant* Zp 3_{10}, סָבִיב pl. *those around* Ps 76_{12}, רֶגֶל *foot* Is 23_7, מִי *who?* Ps 60_{11}=108_{11} (|| נחה *lead*); subj. not specified, 4Q417 1.1$_{18}$.

<OBJ> Tarshish Is 23_7, עַם *people* Jr 31_9, בַּת *daughter* Ps 45_{16} (if em.; see Ho. Subj.), שְׁאֵרִית *remnant* Jr 31_9, worshipper Ps 60_{11}=108_{11}, עֵגֶל *calf* Ho 10_6 (if em.; see Ho. Subj.), שֶׁמֶן *oil* Ho 12_2 (if em.; see Ho. Subj.), מִנְחָה *offering* Zp 3_{10}, שַׁי *gift* Ps 68_{30} 76_{12}.

<PREP> לְ of direction, *to,* + Y. Ps 68_{30}, מוֹרָא *fear,* i.e. one to be feared Ps 76_{12} (or em. לַמּוֹרָא to לַנּוֹרָא *to the one to be feared,* i.e. ירא ni. ptc.), חיה pi. ptc. *one who keeps alive* 4Q417 1.1$_{18}$, Assyria Ho 10_6 (if em.; see Ho. Subj.), Egypt Ho 12_2 (if em.; see Ho. Subj.); בְּ of accompaniment, *with,* + תַּחֲנוּן *supplication* Jr 31_9 (or em. בְּתַחֲנוּנִים *with supplications* to בְּתַנְחוּמִים *with consolations*), שִׂמְחָה *joy* Ps 45_{16} (if em.; see Ho. Subj.), גִּיל *rejoicing* Ps 45_{16} (if em.; see Ho. Subj.); מִן of cause, *on account of,* + הֵיכָל *temple* Ps 68_{30} (or em. מֵהֵיכָלֶךָ to יְמַהֲרוּ לָךְ *they shall hasten to you*).

<COLL> + inf. of purpose, גור *sojourn* Is 23_7; + noun used adverbially, עִיר *(to) city* Ps 60_{11}=108_{11}, מִנְחָה *(as) tribute* Ho 10_6 (if em.; see Ho. Subj.).

<SYN> נחה *lead.*

Ho. 11 Impf. יוּבַל (יוּבָל), 3fs תּוּבַל, אוּבַל, יוּבָלוּ, תּוּבַלְנָה, תּוּבָלוּן—**be brought, be carried, be led,** appar. to safety (Jb 21_{30}; or em.; see Subj.), <SUBJ> Israelites Is 55_{12} (+ יצא *go out*), Job Jb 10_{19}, בַּת *daughter* Ps 45_{15}, בְּתוּלָה *young woman* Ps 45_{16} (or em. תּוֹבֵלְנָה *they lead*), רֵעָה *companion* Ps 45_{16} (or em.; see above), רַע *evil one* Jb 21_{30} (or em. יוּבָלוּ *they are led* to יִנָּצֵל *he is delivered,* i.e. נצל ni., or יוּכַל *he prevails,* i.e. יכל) 21_{32}, שֶׂה *sheep* Is 53_7, עֶגְלָה *heifer* Ho 10_6 (or em. עֶגְלוֹת *heifers* to עֵגֶל *calf,* and יוּבַל *it shall be brought* to יוֹבִילוּ *they shall bring*), כֶּבֶשׂ *ram* Jr 11_{19}, שֶׁמֶן *oil* Ho 12_2 (or em. יוּבַל to יוֹבִילוּ), שַׁי *gift* Is 18_7.

<PREP> לְ of direction, *to,* + י״ *Y.* Is 18_7, Assyria Ho

10$_{6}$ (or em.; see Subj.), Egypt Ho 12$_{2}$ (or em.; see Subj.), מֶלֶךְ *king* Ps 45$_{15}$, טֶבַח *slaughter* Is 53$_{7}$, קֶבֶר *grave* Jb 10$_{19}$ 21$_{32}$; of time, *in, on,* + יוֹם *day* Jb 21$_{30}$ (or em.; see Subj.); of accompaniment, *with, in,* + רִקְמָה *many-coloured material* Ps 45$_{15}$; בְּ of accompaniment, *with, in,* + שָׁלוֹם *peace* Is 55$_{12}$, שִׂמְחָה *joy* Ps 45$_{16}$ (or em.; see Subj.), גִּיל *rejoicing* Ps 45$_{16}$ (or em.; see Subj.); מִן of direction, *from,* + בֶּטֶן *womb* Jb 10$_{19}$.

<COLL> + inf. of purpose of טבח *slaughter* Jr 11$_{19}$; + noun used adverbially, מִנְחָה *(as) offering* Ho 10$_{6}$ (or em.; see Subj.).*

→ יָבָל *stream,* יוּבַל *stream,* יְבוּל *produce.*

[יָבָל] I 2.1 n.[m.] **stream**—pl. cstr. יִבְלֵי—**stream, flood** (Jb 20$_{28}$, if em.; see Subj.), <SUBJ> היה *be* Is 30$_{25}$, סבב *surround* Ps 18$_{5}$ (if em.; see Cstr.), גלל *roll,* i.e. sweep away Jb 20$_{28}$ (if em. יְבוּל *produce* to יָבָל *flood,* and יִגֶל *it departs,* i.e. גלה *be removed,* to יָגֹל *it sweeps away,* i.e. גלל *roll*). <CSTR> יִבְלֵי־מָיִם *streams of water* Is 30$_{25}$ 44$_{4}$ (both יובלי in 1QIsa^{a}, i.e. יוּבַל *stream* or יוֹבֵל *channel,* i.e. ptc. of יבל *bring*) Ps 18$_{5}$ (if em. חֶבְלֵי שְׁאוֹל *cords of Sheol* to יִבְלֵי מַיִם) Si 50$_{8}$. <APP> פֶּלֶג *channel* Is 30$_{25}$. <PREP> עַל *beside,* + צמח *grow* Is 44$_{4}$, יצא *go out* Si 50$_{8}$.

→ יבל *bring.*

יָבָל II 1 pr.n.m. **Jabal,** son of Lamech and Adah, <SUBJ> היה *be* Gn 4$_{20}$ (+ אֲבִי יֹשֵׁב אֹהֶל וּמִקְנֶה *the ancestor of those who dwell in tents and [keep] cattle*). <OBJ> ילד *give birth to* Gn 4$_{20}$.

יִבְלְעָם 3 pl.n. **Ibleam,** town in territory of Issachar allocated to Manasseh, appar. ident. with Bileam at 1 C 6$_{55}$, perh. Kh. Bel'ame, 26 km N of Shechem, <SUBJ> היה *be* Jos 17$_{11}$. <OBJ> נתן *give* Jos 21$_{25}$ (if em. גַּת־רִמּוֹן *Gath-rimmon*). <CSTR> יֹשְׁבֵי יִבְלְעָם *inhabitants of Ibleam* Jg 1$_{27}$. <PREP> בְּ of place, *in,* + נכה hi. *strike* 2 K 15$_{10}$ (if em. קָבָל־עָם *before the people* to בְּיִבְלְעָם); אֵת *with, near to* 2 K 9$_{27}$ (מַעֲלֵה־גוּר אֲשֶׁר אֶת־יִבְלְעָם *the ascent of Gur, which is near Ibleam*).

יַבֶּלֶת 1 n.f. **running sore,** or perh. **wart,** in animal, <OBJ> קרב hi. *bring near,* i.e. offer Lv 22$_{22}$. <APP> אֵלֶּה *these* Lv 22$_{22}$. <PREP> מִן partitive, *(some) of,* + נתן *give,* i.e. place Lv 22$_{22}$.

יבם I 3 vb. **marry sister-in-law—Pi.** 3 + waw וְיִבְּמָהּ; impv. יַבֵּם; inf. יַבְּמִי—**marry sister-in-law** of deceased brother, **perform brother-in-law's duty** to widow, <SUBJ> Onan Gn 38$_{8}$ (+ הָקֵם זֶרַע לְאָחִיךָ *raise up descendants for your brother*), יָבָם *husband's brother* Dt 25$_{5}$ (+ וּלְקָחָהּ לוֹ לְאִשָּׁה *and he shall take her to himself as a wife*) 25$_{7}$ (+ לְהָקִים לְאָחִיו שֵׁם *to raise up for his brother a name*). <OBJ> אִשָּׁה *wife* Gn 38$_{8}$ Dt 25$_{5}$, יְבֵמֶת *sister-in-law* Dt 25$_{7}$.*

→ יָבָם *husband's brother,* יְבֵמֶת *sister-in-law.*

* **יבם** II vb. **create—Qal, create,** אָדֹן יָבַם סִינַי בְּקֹדֶשׁ (or בְּקָדְשׁוֹ) *the Lord created Sinai as (his) sanctuary* Ps 68$_{18}$ (if em. אֲדֹנָי בָם סִינַי בַּקֹּדֶשׁ *my Lord is among them [at] Sinai, in holiness*).

[יָבָם] 2 n.m. **husband's brother**—sf. יְבָמִי, יְבָמָהּ—<SUBJ> בוא *come* Dt 25$_{5}$, אבה *be willing* Dt 25$_{7}$, מאן pi. *refuse* Dt 25$_{7}$, קום hi. *raise up* Dt 25$_{7}$.*

→ יבם *marry sister-in-law.*

[יְבֵמֶת] 5 n.f. **sister-in-law**—sf. יְבִמְתּוֹ, יְבִמְתֵּךְ—specif. wife (widow) of brother (Dt 25$_{7.7.9}$), of husband's brother (Ru 1$_{15.15}$), <SUBJ> עלה *go up* Dt 25$_{7}$, נגשׁ ni. *draw near* Dt 25$_{9}$, שׁוב *go back* Ru 1$_{15}$, אמר *say* Dt 25$_{7.9}$, ענה *answer* Dt 25$_{9}$, חלץ *take off* Dt 25$_{9}$, ירק *spit* Dt 25$_{9}$. <OBJ> לקח *take* Dt 25$_{7}$, יבם pi. *marry sister-in-law* Dt 25$_{7}$. <PREP> אַחֲרֵי *after,* + שׁוב *go back* Ru 1$_{15}$.*

→ יבם *marry sister-in-law.*

יַבְנְאֵל 2 pl.n. **Jabneel, 1.** town on northern border of Judah, perh. ident. with Jabneh at 2 C 26$_{6}$, Yebna 21 km S of Jaffa. <COLL> יַבְנְאֵל used adverbially, *to Jabneel,* + יצא *go out* Jos 15$_{11}$.

2. town on southern border of Naphtali, perh. Kh. Yemmā, 11 km SSW of Tiberias, <PREP> מִן of direction, *from,* + היה *be* Jos 19$_{33}$.

→ בנה *build* + אֵל *God.*

יַבְנֵה 1 pl.n. **Jabneh,** Philistine town, perh. ident. with Jabneel (Jos 15_{11}), <CSTR> חוֹמַת יַבְנֵה *wall of Jabneh* 2 C 26_6.

→ בנה *build.*

יִבְנְיָה 1 pr.n.m. **Ibneiah,** Benjaminite, son of Jeroham, <NOM CL> מִבְּנֵי בִנְיָמִן ... יִבְנְיָה *of the sons of Benjamin were ... Ibneiah* 1 C 9_8. <APP> בֵּן *son* 1 C 9_8.

→ בנה *build* + יה Y.

יִבְנִיָּה 1 pr.n.m. **Ibnijah,** Benjaminite, father of Reuel, <CSTR> בֶּן־יִבְנִיָּה *son of Ibnijah* 1 C 9_8.

→ בנה *build* + יה Y.

יְבֻסִי, see יְבוּסִי *Jebusite.*

יַבֹּק 7 pl.n. **Jabbok,** eastern tributary of Jordan, Wādi ez-Zerqā, entering Jordan 1 km N of Adam and 37 km N of the Dead Sea, <CSTR> מַעֲבַר יַבֹּק *ford of the Jabbok* Gn 32_{23} (Sam הַיַּבֹּק), נַחַל *wadi of* Dt 2_{37} (Sam הַיַּבֹּק). <APP> נַחַל *wadi* Dt 3_{16} Jos 12_2. <PREP> מִן of direction, *from*, + לקח *take* Nm 21_{26} (if em. מִיָּדוֹ *from his hand* to מִיַּבֹּק *from Jabbok*); עַד *unto*, + ירשׁ *possess* Nm 21_{24} Jg 11_{22}, נתן *give* Dt 3_{16}, לקח *take* Jg 11_{13}, משׁל *rule* Jos 12_2. <COLL> Jabbok + Arnon Nm $21_{24.26}$ (if em.; see Prep.) Dt 3_{16} Jos 12_2 Jg $11_{13.22}$, Gilead Dt 3_{16} Jos 12_2, Jordan Jg 11_{13}.

יְבֶרֶכְיָהוּ 1 pr.n.m. **Jeberechiah**—Q יברכיה—**1.** father of Zechariah, <CSTR> בֶּן יְבֶרֶכְיָהוּ *son of Jeberechiah* Is 8_2 (1QIsa[a] יברכיה).

2. Lachish inscr. 31_2, <CSTR> [ב]ן יברכ[יהו] *son of Jeberechiah* Lachish inscr. 31_2 (others [ ]ן יברכ[ ]).

→ ברך *bless* + יה Y.

יִבְשָׂם 1 pr.n.m. **Ibsam,** Issacharite, son of Tola, <NOM CL> בְּנֵי תוֹלָע ... יִבְשָׂם *the sons of Tola were ... Ibsam* 1 C 7_2.

יבשׁ I 60.0.5 vb. **be dry—Qal** 42.0.3 Pf. יָבֵשׁ, יָבְשָׁה, יָבְשׁוּ (יָבֵשׁוּ); impf. ייבַשׁ (יִיבָשׁ, יִבַשׁ), 3fs תִּיבַשׁ (תִּיבָשׁ), אִיבָשׁ, יָבֵשׁוּ; + waw וְיָבֵשׁ, וְיָבֵשׁוּ; וַיִּיבַשׁ (וַיִּיבָשׁ, וַיִּבַשׁ), 3fs וַתִּיבַשׁ, וַיִּיבָשׁוּ; inf. abs. יָבוֹשׁ (יָבֹשׁ); cstr. יְבֹשׁ, יְבֹשֶׁת—**be dry, dried up, wither.**

<SUBJ> רֹזֵן *ruler* Is 40_{24}, שֹׁפֵט *judge* Is 40_{24}, יֹשֵׁב *inhabitant* 2 K 19_{26}||Is 37_{27} (if em. in 2 K וַיֵּבֹשׁוּ and in Is וָבֹשׁוּ *and they were ashamed* to וַיִּיבָשׁוּ *and they have withered*), עזב ptc. *one who abandons* Y. Jr 17_{13} (if em. יֵבֹשׁוּ *will be put to shame* to יִיבָשׁוּ *will wither*), worshipper Ps 102_{12}, תָּמִים *blameless one* Ps 37_{19} (if em. לֹא־יֵבֹשׁוּ *they will not be put to shame* to לֹא־יִיבָשׁוּ *they will not wither*), חזק hi. ptc. *one who grasps* evil 4Q418 69.2_8 ([ו]יבשו), דָּגָה *fish* 1QIsa[a] 50_2, יָד *hand* 1 K 13_4, זְרוֹעַ *arm* Zc $11_{17.11}$, רֹאשׁ *head*, i.e. top Am 1_2, עֶצֶם *bone* Ezk 37_{11}, עוֹר *skin* Lm 4_8, לֵב *heart* Ps 102_5, לֶחֶם *bread* Jos $9_{5.12}$, חָצִיר *grass* Is 15_6 $40_{7.8}$ Ps 90_6 129_6 (or del.), עֵשֶׂב *grass* Jr 12_4, אָחוּ *reed* Jb 8_{12}, גֹּמֶא *reed* Jb 8_{12}, perh. צִיץ *blossom* 4Q185 1.1_{11}, עֵץ *tree* Jl 1_{12} 1QH 8_{20} (צ[ע]י), רִמּוֹן *pomegranate* Jl 1_{12}, תָּמָר *palm* Jl 1_{12}, תַּפּוּחַ *apple* Jl 1_{12}, תְּבוּאָה *produce* Jr 12_{13} (if em. וּבֹשׁוּ מִתְּבוּאֹתֵיכֶם *and they will be ashamed of your produce* to וְיָבְשׁוּ־תְבוּאֹתֵיכֶם *and your produce will wither*), גֶּפֶן *vine* Ezk $17_{9.10.10.10}$, קִיקָיוֹן *castor oil plant* Jon 4_7, קָצִיר *branch(es)* Is 27_{11}, מַטֶּה *stem* Ezk 19_{12}, טָרָף *fresh leaf* Ezk 17_9, שֹׁרֶשׁ *root* Ezk 9_{16} Jb 18_{16}, מִזְרָע *place of sowing* Is 19_7, נָוֶה *pasture* Jr 23_{10}, חֶלְקָה *field* Am 4_7, מַיִם *water* Gn 8_7 Jr 50_{38} Jb 12_{15}, נָהָר *river* Is 19_5 Jb 14_{11}, נַחַל *wadi* 1 K 17_7, אָפִיק *channel* Jl 1_{20}, מָקוֹר *fountain* Ho 13_{15} (if em. יֵבוֹשׁ appar. *it will be ashamed* to יִבַשׁ *it will be dry*), אֶרֶץ *earth* Gn 8_{14}, כֹּחַ *strength* Ps 22_{16} (or em. חֵךְ *palate*).

<PREP> לְ of time, *at, in*, + עֶרֶב *evening* Ps 90_6; בְּ of time, *on*, + יוֹם *day* Gn 8_{14}, עֵת *time* Ps 37_{19} (if em.; see Subj.); כְּ *as*, + חֶרֶשׂ *potsherd* Ps 22_{16}, עֵשֶׂב *grass* Ps 102_{12}, עֵץ *tree* Lm 4_8 (if del. הָיָה *it has become*); מִן of cause, *on account of*, + רָעָה *evil* Jr 12_4, מאין מים *lack of water* Is 50_2 (1QIsa[a]); עַל *upon*, + עֲרוּגָה *garden bed* Ezk 17_{10}; מֵעַל *from upon*, + אֶרֶץ *earth* Gn 8_7; מִפְּנֵי *because of*, + אָלָה *curse* Jr 23_{10}; לִפְנֵי *before*, + חָצִיר *grass* Jb 8_{12}.

<COLL> יבשׁ || חרב *be dry* Is 19_5 Jb 14_{11}, נשׁת ni. *be dried up* Is 19_5, נבל *wither* Is $40_{7.8}$, מלל *wither* Jb 18_{16}, po. *wither* Ps 90_6, כהה *be dim* Zc 11_{17}, אבד *perish* Ezk 37_{11}, כלה *come to an end* Is 15_6, נדף ni. *be driven away* Is 19_7, בזז pu. *be plundered* Jr 50_{38}, אבל *mourn* Jr 12_4 23_{10} Am 1_2.

+ צפד *shrivel* Lm 4$_{8}$, גזר ni. *be cut off* Ezk 37$_{11}$, אמל pulal *languish* Jl 1$_{12}$, דבק ho. *be caused to adhere* Ps 22$_{16}$, נכה ho. *be struck* Ps 102$_{5}$.

:: היה *be* Is 15$_{6}$, קום *rise*, i.e. remain Is 40$_{8}$.

<SYN> חרב *be dry*, נשׁת ni. *be dried up*, נבל *wither*, מלל *wither*, כהה *be dim*, אבד *perish*, כלה *come to an end*, נדף ni. *be driven away*, בזז pu. *be plundered*, אבל *mourn*.

<ANT> היה *be*, קום *rise*.

Pi. 3.0.2 Impf. 3fs תְּיַבֵּשׁ (תְּיַבֶּשׁ־); + waw Q ויבש; וַיְבַּשֵׁהוּ; impv. Q יבש—**make dry, dry up, make wither,** <SUBJ> Y. Na 1$_{4}$ (or em.; see Hi. Subj.) 11QPs^{a} 24$_{12}$, רַחַשׁ *worm* 4QD^{a} 6.1$_{8}$, שַׁלְהֶבֶת *flame* Jb 15$_{30}$, רוּחַ *spirit* Pr 17$_{22}$. <OBJ> יֹנֶקֶת *shoot* Jb 15$_{30}$, פֶּרַח *flower* 4QD^{a} 6.1$_{8}$, שֹׁרֶשׁ *root* 11QPs^{a} 24$_{12}$, יָם *sea* Na 1$_{4}$ (or em.; see Hi. Subj.), גֶּרֶם *bone* Pr 17$_{22}$. <PREP> מִן of direction, *from*, + worshipper 11QPs^{a} 24$_{12}$. <COLL> יבשׁ pi. || חרב hi. *dry up* Na 1$_{4}$, קוץ hi. *sever* 4QD^{a} 6.1$_{8}$; + אמל pulal *languish* Na 1$_{4}$; :: נצץ *blossom* 11QPs^{a} 24$_{12}$.

<SYN> חרב hi. *dry up*, קוץ hi. *sever*.

Hi. 16 Pf. הוֹבִישׁ (הֹבִישׁ), הוֹבִישָׁה, הוֹבַשְׁתְּ, הוֹשַׁבְתִּי; impf. אוֹבִישׁ; + waw וְהֹבִישׁוּ, וְהֹבַשְׁתִּי—**1. make dry, dry up, make wither,** <SUBJ> Y. Jos 2$_{10}$ 4$_{23.23}$ 5$_{1}$ Is 42$_{15.15}$ 44$_{27}$ Jr 51$_{36}$ Ezk 17$_{24}$ Na 1$_{4}$ (if em. וַיַּבְּשֵׁהוּ *and he dried it* [i.e. pi.] to וַיֹּבִשֵׁהוּ *and he dried it*) Ps 74$_{15}$ (or em. הוֹבַשְׁתָּ *you dried up* to הֲשִׁיבֹתָ *you have turned*, i.e. שׁוב hi.), רוּחַ *wind* Ezk 19$_{12}$ Ho 13$_{15}$ (if em. יֵבוֹשׁ appar. *it will be ashamed* to יוֹבִישׁ *it will dry up*).

<OBJ> עֵשֶׂב *grass* Is 42$_{15}$, עֵץ *tree* Ezk 17$_{24}$, גֶּפֶן *vine* Ezk 19$_{12}$, מַיִם *water* Jos 2$_{10}$ 4$_{23}$ 5$_{1}$, יָם *sea* Jos 4$_{23}$ Na 1$_{4}$ (if em.; see Subj.), נָהָר *river* Is 44$_{27}$ Ps 74$_{15}$ (or em.; see Subj.), אֲגַם *pool* Is 42$_{15}$, מָקוֹר *fountain* Jr 51$_{36}$ Ho 13$_{15}$ (if em.; see Subj.).

<PREP> מִפְּנֵי *from before*, + Israelites Jos 2$_{10}$ 4$_{23.23}$, בֵּן *son* of Israel Jos 5$_{1}$.

<COLL> יבשׁ hi. || חרב hi. *dry up* Is 42$_{15}$ Jr 51$_{36}$; + חרב *be dry* Is 44$_{27}$; :: פרח hi. *make flourish* Ezk 17$_{24}$.

2. intrans. **be dry, dry up, wither** (Jl 1$_{10.12.12.17}$ perh. בושׁ hi. *be ashamed*), <SUBJ> תִּירוֹשׁ *new wine* Jl 1$_{10}$, גֶּפֶן *vine* Jl 1$_{12}$, דָּגָן *grain* Jl 1$_{17}$, שָׂשׂוֹן *joy* Jl 1$_{12}$, מְצוּלָה *depth* Zc 10$_{11}$. <PREP> מִן *from among*, + בֵּן *son* Jl 1$_{12}$. <COLL> יבשׁ hi. || אמל pulal *languish* Jl 1$_{10}$, שׁדד pu. *be destroyed* Jl 1$_{10.12}$.*

→ יָבֵשׁ *dry*, יַבָּשָׁה *dry land*, יַבֶּשֶׁת *dry land*, יָבֵשׁ II, III *Jabesh*.

*** יבשׁ II** $_{18}$ vb. **be ashamed—Hi.** $_{17}$ Pf. הוֹבִישׁ (הֹבִישׁ), הוֹבִישָׁה, הֹבַשְׁתְּ, הוֹבִישׁוּ (הֹבִשׁוּ)—or perh. בושׁ hi. *be ashamed*, or יבשׁ hi. *be dry*—**1. be ashamed,** Jr 8$_{9}$ (|| חתת *be shattered*, לכד ni. *be captured*) 8$_{12}$ Jl 1$_{11}$ (|| ילל hi. *wail*) Is 30$_{5(Qr)}$ Jr 10$_{14}$=51$_{17}$ (+ בער ni. *be brutish*).

2. be put to shame, Jr 2$_{26}$ 6$_{15}$ 46$_{24}$ (|| נתן ni. *be given*) 48$_{1}$ (|| לכד ni. *be captured*) 48$_{20}$ (+ חתת *be shattered*) 50$_{2}$ (|| לכד ni., חתת) Jl 1$_{10}$ (|| שׁדד pu. *be destroyed*) 1$_{12}$ (both || אמל pulal *languish*) 1$_{12.17}$.

3. act shamefully, Ho 2$_{7}$ (|| זנה *prostitute oneself*).

4. put to shame, 2 S 19$_{6}$.

<SUBJ> Bel Jr 50$_{2}$, בֵּן *son* of Israel Jr 2$_{26}$ (if em. בֵּית *house of* to בְּנֵי *sons of*), בַּת *daughter* Jr 46$_{24}$, מֶלֶךְ *king* Jr 2$_{26}$ 2 S 19$_{6}$, שַׂר *prince* Jr 2$_{26}$, כֹּהֵן *priest* Jr 2$_{26}$, נָבִיא *prophet* Jr 2$_{26}$, חָכָם *wise one* Jr 8$_{9.12}$, אִכָּר *farmer* Jl 1$_{11}$, יֹשֵׁב *inhabitant* Jr 6$_{15}$, צרף ptc. *refiner, goldsmith* Jr 10$_{14}$=51$_{17}$, הרה ptc. *one who conceives* Ho 2$_{7}$, בַּיִת *house* Jr 2$_{26}$ (or em.; see above), Kiriathaim Jr 48$_{1}$ (or del. הֹבִישָׁה), Moab Jr 48$_{20}$, גֶּפֶן *vine* Jl 1$_{12}$, דָּגָן *grain* Jl 1$_{17}$, תִּירוֹשׁ *new wine* Jl 1$_{10}$, שָׂשׂוֹן *joy* Jl 1$_{12}$, כֹּל *all* Is 30$_{5(Qr)}$ (Kt באשׁ hi. *stink*; or em. כֹּל *all* to כָּל־הַבָּא *any who comes*).

<OBJ> פָּנִים *face* 1 S 19$_{6}$.

<PREP> מִן *from among*, + בֵּן *son* Jl 1$_{12}$; of cause, *on account of*, + פֶּסֶל *image* Jr 10$_{14}$=51$_{17}$; עַל *on account of*, + עַם *people* Is 30$_{5(Qr)}$.

<COLL> יבשׁ hi. + noun used adverbially, הַיּוֹם *today* 1 S 19$_{6}$.

<SYN> §1 חתת *be shattered*, לכד ni. *be captured*, ילל hi. *wail*; §2 נתן ni. *be given*, לכד ni. *be captured*, חתת *be shattered*, שׁדד pu. *be destroyed*, אמל pulal *languish*; §3 זנה *prostitute oneself*.

יָבֵשׁ I $_{9.2.2}$ adj. **dry**—יְבֵשָׁה; pl. יְבֵשִׁים, יְבֵשׁוֹת—**1.** used attributively of עֶצֶם *bone* Ezk 37$_{4}$, עֵנָב *grape* Nm 6$_{3}$ (:: לַח *moist*), עֵץ *tree* Is 56$_{3}$ Ezk 17$_{24}$ 21$_{3}$ (both :: לַח) Si 6$_{3}$ 1QH 3$_{30}$ 8$_{19}$ ([עֵץ]), קַשׁ *stubble* Na 1$_{10}$ Jb 13$_{25}$, מַעְיָן *spring* Si 14$_{10}$.

2. in nom. cl., used predicatively of נֶפֶשׁ *soul, self* Nm 11$_{6}$, עֶצֶם *bone* Ezk 37$_{2}$ (הִנֵּה יְבֵשׁוֹת מְאֹד *behold [the bones* *were] very dry*).

<ANT> לַח *moist*.* → יבשׁ I *be dry*.

יָבֵשׁ II $_{21}$ pl.n. **Jabesh**—יָבֵישׁ; + ה- of direction יָבֵ֫שָׁה (יָבֵ֫ישָׁה)—(except 1 S 11$_{1.3.5.9.10}$) יָבֵשׁ גִּלְעָד **Jabesh-gilead,** town in Transjordan, perh. T. el-Maqlūb, on Wādi el-Yābis, 35 km SSE of southern tip of Sea of Galilee, <SUBJ> שׁמע *hear* 1 C 10$_{11}$. <CSTR> זִקְנֵי יָבֵישׁ *elders of Jabesh* 1 S 11$_{3}$, אַנְשֵׁי *men of* 1 S 11$_{1.5.9.10}$, אַנְשֵׁי יָבֵישׁ גִּלְעָד *men of Jabesh-gilead* 1 S 11$_{9}$(mss (L אִישׁ *men of*) 2 S 2$_{4.5}$, בַּעֲלֵי *lords of* 2 S 21$_{12}$, יוֹשְׁבֵי יָבֵישׁ גִּלְעָד *inhabitants of Jabesh-gilead* Jg 21$_{9.10}$ (both יָבֵשׁ גִּלְעָד) 21$_{12}$ 1 S 31$_{11}$‖1 C 10$_{11}$ (1 C if ins. יֹשְׁבֵי), נְשֵׁי *women of* Jg 21$_{14}$ (יָבֵשׁ גִּלְעָד), כֹּל יָבֵישׁ גִּלְעָד *all Jabesh-gilead* 1 C 10$_{11}$ (or em.; see above). <PREP> בְּ of place, *in*, + קבר *bury* 1 S 31$_{13}$‖1 C 10$_{12}$; מִן of direction, *from*, + בוא *come* Jg 21$_{8}$; עַל *against*, + חנה *encamp* 1 S 11$_{1}$; ה- of direction, + בוא *come* 1 S 31$_{12}$, hi. *bring* 1 C 10$_{12}$.*

→ יבשׁ I *be dry*.

יָבֵשׁ III $_{3}$ pr.n.m. **Jabesh**—יָבֵישׁ—father of Shallum, <CSTR> בֶּן־יָבֵשׁ *son of Jabesh* 2 K 15$_{10.13.14}$ (both יָבֵישׁ).

Also Lachish ost. 19$_{5}$ (others עבשׁ *Abash*; others ערשׁ *Arash*). → יבשׁ I *be dry*.

יַבָּשָׁה $_{14.0.5}$ n.f. **dry land**—Q יבושה—<SUBJ> ראה ni. *appear* Gn 1$_{9}$. <OBJ> עשׂה *make* Jon 1$_{9}$ (:: יָם *sea*). <CSTR> רקוע יבשה *expanse of dry land* 1QH 3$_{31}$=4QHod^{b} 3$_{6}$ (רקיע). <PREP> לְ *into*, + הפך *turn*, i.e. change Ps 66$_{6}$ (:: יָם *sea*); *as*, + חשׁב *reckon* Jb 41$_{24}$ (if em. לְשֵׂיבָה *as a grey-haired one* to לַיַּבָּשָׁה); introducing object, + קרא *call*, i.e. name Gn 1$_{10}$ (+ אֶרֶץ *earth*; :: יָם); בְּ of place, *in*, *on* 1QH 17$_{4}$, + הלך *go* Ex 14$_{29}$ 15$_{19}$ (both + יָם), בוא *come* Ex 14$_{16.22}$ (both + יָם), עבר *pass over* Jos 4$_{22}$ Ne 9$_{11}$ (+ יָם) 4QapJoshua^{b} 12$_{3}$ (ע]ברו]), נזל *flow* 1QH 8$_{4}$; אֶל *to*, + שׁוב *go back* 4QM^{g} 4$_{5}$, hi. *bring back* Jon 1$_{13}$, קיא *vomit* Jon 2$_{11}$; עַל *upon*, + יצק *pour* Is 44$_{3}$ (‖ צָמֵא *thirsty place*). <COLL> הַיַּבָּשָׁה used adverbially, *upon the dry land*, + שׁפך *pour* Ex 4$_{9}$.

<SYN> צָמֵא *thirsty place*.

<ANT> יָם *sea*.*

→ יבשׁ I *be dry*.

יַבֶּ֫שֶׁת $_{2}$ n.f. **dry land**—יַבֶּשֶׁת—<OBJ> יצר *form* Ps 95$_{5}$ (+ יָם *sea*). <PREP> בְּ of place, *on*, + היה *be* Ex 4$_{9}$.*

→ יבשׁ I *be dry*.

יִגְאָל $_{3.0.0.1}$ pr.n.m. **Igal, 1.** Issacharite, son of Joseph, one of the twelve spies, <NOM CL> לְמַטֵּה יִשָּׂשכָר יִגְאָל *of the tribe of Issachar was Igal* Nm 13$_{7}$. <APP> בֶּן *son* Nm 13$_{7}$.

2. one of David's warriors, son of Nathan, appar. ident. with Joel at 1 C 11$_{38}$, <NOM CL> יִגְאָל ... מִצֹּבָה *Igal (who was) ... from Zobah* 2 S 23$_{36}$. <APP> בֶּן *son* 2 S 23$_{36}$.

3. son of Shemaiah (or of Shecaniah, if em.) and descendant of Zerubbabel, <NOM CL> בְּנֵי שְׁמַעְיָה ... יִגְאָל *the sons of Shemaiah were ... Igal* 1 C 3$_{22}$ (or del. בְּנֵי שְׁמַעְיָה to read בְּנֵי שְׁכַנְיָה ... יִגְאָל *the sons of Shecaniah were ... Igal*).

4. son of Zichri, <APP> בֶּן *son* Seal 309 (6th/5th cent.). <PREP> לְ *(belonging) to, of* Seal 309 (6th/5th cent.).

→ *'' Y.* + גאל *redeem*.

יגב $_{2}$ vb. **farm—Qal** $_{2}$ Ptc. יֹגְבִים—ptc. used as noun, **farmer,** <OBJ> נתן *give* Jr 39$_{10}$ (if em. וִיגֵבִים *and fields* to וְיֹגְבִים *and farmers*). <PREP> לְ *as*, + שׁאר hi. *leave* 2 K 25$_{12}$‖Jr 52$_{16}$ (2 K Kt mss לגבים *as diggers*, from גוב *dig*; ‖ כֹּרֵם *vinedresser*).

<SYN> כֹּרֵם *vinedresser*.

→ יָגֵב *field*.

[יָגֵב] $_{1}$ n.[m.] **field**—pl. יְגֵבִים—<OBJ> נתן *give* Jr 39$_{10}$ (or em. וִיגֵבִים *and fields* to וְיֹגְבִים *and farmers*; ‖ כֶּרֶם *vineyard*).

<SYN> כֶּרֶם *vineyard*.

→ יגב *farm*.

יָגְבְּהָה $_{2}$ pl.n. **Jogbehah**—L יָגְבֳּהָה; mss יָגְבְּהָה, Sam. יָגְבְּחָה—town in Gad, perh. Kh. el-Ǧubēha, 11 km NW of Amman, <OBJ> בנה *build* Nm 32$_{35}$. <PREP> לְ *(with respect) to* Jg 8$_{11}$.

→ גבה *be high*.

יָגְבְּהָה, see יָגְבֳּהָה *Jogbehah.*

יִגְדַּלְיָהוּ $_{1.0.0.1}$ pr.n.m. **Igdaliah, 1.** father of Hanan, <CSTR> בֶּן־יִגְדַּלְיָהוּ *son of Igdaliah* Jr 35$_{4}$.

2. appar. father of Jehoazar, Seal 421 (7th cent.).

→ גדל *be great* + יה *Y.*

יגה I $_{8}$ vb. **be grieved—Ni.** $_{2}$ Ptc. נוּגֵי, נוּגוֹת—**be grieved,** <SUBJ> בְּתוּלָה *young woman* Lm 1$_{4}$; subj. not specified, Zp 3$_{18}$ (or em.; see Coll.). <COLL> נוּגֵי מִמּוֹעֵד perh. *ones grieved because of a festival* Zp 3$_{18}$ (or em. כְּיוֹם/כִּימֵי מוֹעֵד *as on the day/days of festival,* or כִּימֵי מֵעַד/עַד *as in days of old*).

Pi. $_{1}$ + waw וַיַּגֶּה—**grieve,** <SUBJ> Y. Lm 3$_{33}$ (or em. וַיֹּגֶה, i.e. hi.; || ענה pi. *afflict,* + דכא pi. *crush*). <OBJ> בֵּן *son* of man Lm 3$_{33}$ (or em.; see subj.).

<SYN> ענה pi. *afflict.*

Hi. $_{5}$ Pf. הוֹגָה (הוֹגָהּ); impf. תּוֹגְיוּן; ptc. מוֹגַיִךְ—**grieve, cause to suffer,** <SUBJ> Y. Lm 1$_{5.12}$ (or em. הוֹנַנִי *he has oppressed me,* i.e. ינה hi.) 3$_{32.33}$ (if em.; see Pi. Subj.), friends of Job Jb 19$_{2}$ (+ דכא pi. *crush*); subj. not specified, Is 51$_{23}$. <OBJ> בֵּן *son* of man Lm 3$_{33}$ (if em.; see Pi. Subj.), Jerusalem/Zion Lm 1$_{5}$ Is 51$_{23}$, נֶפֶשׁ *soul, person* Jb 19$_{2}$, רוּחַ *spirit* 4QTobit^{e} 2$_{1}$ ([תוגה רוחה]), מַכְאֹב *pain* Lm 1$_{12}$ (מַכְאֹבִי ... אֲשֶׁר הוֹגָה י׳ *my pain, which Y. has caused*; or em.; see Subj.). <PREP> בְּ of time, *in, on,* + יוֹם *day* Lm 1$_{5}$; עַל *on account of,* + רֹב *multitude* of transgressions Lm 1$_{5}$. <COLL> יגה hi. + adverb, עַד־אָנָה *how long?* Jb 19$_{2}$.*

→ יָגוֹן *grief,* תּוּגָה *grief.*

יגה II $_{1}$ vb. **remove—Hi.** $_{1}$ Pf. הָגָה—**remove,** 2 S 20$_{13}$ (or em. הוּגָה *he was removed,* i.e. ho., or הֻטָּה *he was removed,* i.e. נטה ho., or הֻסַר *he was removed,* i.e. סור ho.), <SUBJ> אִישׁ *man* 2 S 20$_{13}$ (+ סבב hi. *bring round*). <OBJ> Amasa 2 S 20$_{13}$ (if em. הָגָה *he removed* to הֹגָהוּ). <PREP> מִן of direction, *from,* + מְסִלָּה *highway* 2 S 20$_{13}$.

Ho. be removed, see Hi.

יָגוֹן $_{14.0.16}$ n.[m.] **grief**—cstr. Q יגון; sf. Q יגוני, Q יגוננו, יְגוֹנָם—**grief, sorrow,** <SUBJ> נוס *flee* Is 35$_{10}$=51$_{11}$ (|| אֲנָחָה *sighing*; :: שָׂשׂוֹן *joy,* שִׂמְחָה *gladness*) 4QHod^{a} 7,2$_{3}$ (+ אֵבֶל *mourning*), עלה *go up* Jr 8$_{18}$ (if em.; see Prep.), סבב pol. *encircle* 1QH 5$_{34}$.

<NOM CL> יָגוֹן בְּלִבְּבִי *grief is in my heart* Ps 31$_{3}$, אין יגון *there is no grief* 1QH 11$_{26}$ (|| אֲנָחָה *sighing*).

<OBJ> ראה *see* Jr 20$_{18}$ (|| עָמָל *toil*) 4QBark^{d} 2.2$_{7}$, זכר *remember* 4QPrFêtes^{c} 12.3$_{6}$ ([תז]כור), יסף *add* Jr 45$_{3}$ (+ מַכְאֹב *pain*), מצא *find* Ps 116$_{3}$ (|| צָרָה *distress*), דין *vindicate* 1QH 5$_{13}$.

<CSTR> יגון זקנינו ונכבד[ינו] *grief of our elders and honourable ones* 4QPrFêtes^{c} 16.4$_{4}$, יגון אשמה *grief of guilt* 1QH 11$_{20}$; לב יגון *heart of grief* 4QPrFêtes^{b} 39$_{1}$, יגון *bed of grief* 4QTohA 1.1$_{1}$, אבל *mourning of* 1QS 4$_{13}$ 1QH 2$_{5}$ ([יגו]ן; =4QHod^{f} 3$_{4}$ אב]ל [י]גוני] *mourning of my grief*) 11$_{22}$ ([יגו]ן), הגו יגון *meditation of* 1QH 11$_{22}$.

<PREP> לְ of possession, *of, (belonging) to* 1QH 11$_{20}$; בְּ of accompaniment, *with, in,* + חיה *live* 4QPrFêtes^{b} 39$_{1}$, כלה *come to an end* Ps 31$_{11}$ (|| אֲנָחָה), ירד hi. *bring down* Gn 42$_{38}$ 44$_{31}$, אסף ni. *be gathered* 4Q418 88$_{7}$, עזב ni. *be forsaken* 1QH 8$_{27}$ ([בי]גון); מִן *from,* + שׂמח pi. *cause to rejoice* Jr 31$_{13}$ 4QPrFêtes^{c} 3.1$_{3}$ ([שמחת]נו), הפך ni. *be turned* Est 9$_{22}$ (|| אֵבֶל *mourning*; :: שִׂמְחָה *gladness*), נחם pi. *comfort* 1QH 11$_{32}$; of cause, *on account of,* + שׁחח *be bowed down* Ps 107$_{39}$ (|| רָעָה *evil,* עֹצֶר *oppression*); עַל *upon* Jr 8$_{18}$ (or em. מַבְלִיגִיתִי עָלַי יָגוֹן appar. *my cheerfulness is upon grief* to מִבְּלִי גֵהֹת עָלָה יָגוֹן *grief without healing has gone up*). <COLL> יָגוֹן תִּמָּלֵאִי *you will be filled with sorrow* Ezk 23$_{33}$ (|| שִׁכָּרוֹן *drunkenness*).]

Also 4Q418 200$_{1}$ 4QHod^{a} 3.1$_{14}$ ([י]גון).

<SYN> אֲנָחָה *sighing,* עָמָל *toil,* צָרָה *distress,* אֵבֶל *mourning,* רָעָה *evil,* עֹצֶר *oppression,* שִׁכָּרוֹן *drunkenness.*

<ANT> שָׂשׂוֹן *joy,* שִׂמְחָה *gladness.*

→ יגה *be grieved.*

יָגוֹעַ $_{1}$ adj. **toiling,** used predicatively of אֲנִי *I* Ps 88$_{16 (mss)}$ (L גֹּוֵעַ *expiring*; || עָנִי *afflicted*).

<SYN> עָנִי *afflicted.*

→ יגע *be weary.*

יָגוֹר, see יגר *fear.*

יָגוּר $_{1}$ pl.n. **Jagur,** town in south of Judah towards border with Edom, perh. Kh. el-Ġarra, 18 km E of Beer sheba, perh. ident. with Gur-baal (2 C 26$_7$), <SUBJ> היה *be* Jos 15$_{21}$. <PREP> מִן *from* Arad ost. 42$_1$ (מ[ן]גור).

[יָגִיעַ] 1.1 adj. **weary**—pl. cstr. יְגִיעֵי—**1. concerned (for),** אם תכשל יגיע אליך *if you stumble, (he is) concerned for you* Si 37$_{12(B)}$ (but prob. נגע hi. *reach out* to). **2.** as noun, **weary one,** <SUBJ> נוח *rest* Jb 3$_{17}$. <CSTR> יְגִיעֵי כֹחַ *those weary of strength,* i.e. whose strength is weary Jb 3$_{17}$.*

→ יגע *be weary.*

[יְגִיעַ] 16.1.1 n.m. **toil, product**—cstr. יְגִיעַ; sf. יְגִיעֲךָ, (יְגִיעֶךָ), יְגִיעוֹ, יְגִיעָהּ, יְגִיעֲכֶם, יגיענו Q, יְגִיעָם; pl. sf. יְגִיעַי—**1. toil, labour,** Gn 31$_{42}$ (|| עֳנִי *affliction*) Is 55$_2$ (|| כֶּסֶף *silver*) Jb 39$_{11.16}$.

2. product of labour, property, Dt 28$_{33}$ (+ פְּרִי *fruit*) Is 45$_{14}$ (or em.; see Cstr.; || סַחַר *merchandise*) Jr 3$_{24}$ (+ צֹאן *flock,* בָּקָר *herd,* בֵּן *son,* בַּת *daughter*) 20$_5$ (|| חֹסֶן *wealth,* יְקָר *preciousness,* אוֹצָר *treasure*) Ezk 23$_{29}$ Ho 12$_9$ Hg 1$_{11}$ (+ אֲשֶׁר תּוֹצִיא הָאֲדָמָה *what the land brings forth,* דָּגָן *grain,* תִּירוֹשׁ *new wine,* יִצְהָר *fresh oil,* אָדָם *human being,* בְּהֵמָה *beast*) Ps 78$_{46}$ (|| יְבוּל *produce*) 109$_{11}$ (+ כָּל־אֲשֶׁר־לוֹ *all that he has*) 128$_2$ Jb 10$_3$ Ne 5$_{13}$ (|| בַּיִת *house*) Lm 5$_5$ (if em.; see Subj.) Si 14$_{15}$ (|| חַיִל *wealth*).

<SUBJ> היה *be* Is 45$_{14}$ (or em.; see Cstr.), עבר *pass* Is 45$_{14}$ (or em.; see Cstr.), מצא *find* Ho 12$_9$, נוח ho. *be placed,* i.e. given Lm 5$_5$ (if em. יָגַעְנוּ *we are weary* to יְגִעֵנוּ *the product of our labour*). <NOM CL> לְרִיק יְגִיעָהּ *her labour is in vain* Jb 39$_{16}$.

<OBJ> ראה *see* Gn 31$_{42}$, אכל *eat* Dt 28$_{33}$ Jr 3$_{24}$ Ps 129$_2$, עזב *leave* Jb 39$_{11}$ Si 14$_{15}$, נתן *give* Ps 78$_{46}$ Jr 20$_5$ 4QapLam[b] 1$_1$ (|| נַחֲלָה *inheritance*), לקח *take* Ezk 23$_{29}$, בזז *plunder* Ps 109$_{11}$, שׁקל *weigh,* i.e. pay Is 55$_2$, שׁוב hi. *give back* Jb 20$_{18}$ (if em. יָגָע *[his] gain* to יְגִיעוֹ *the product of his labour*), בלע *swallow* Jb 20$_{18}$ (if em.; see above).

<CSTR> יְגִיעַ אֲבוֹתֵינוּ *(product of) the labour of our fathers* Jr 3$_{24}$, כַּפַּיִם *of the hands* Hg 1$_{11}$, כַּפַּי *of my hands* Gn 31$_{42}$, כַּפֶּיךָ *of your hands* Ps 128$_2$ Jb 10$_3$, מִצְרַיִם *of Egypt* Is 45$_{14}$ (or em. יֹגְעֵי *labourers of*), כָּל־יְגִיעַ *all the product of labour of* Hg 1$_{11}$, כָּל־יְגִיעַי *all the product of my labours* Ho 12$_9$ (or em. כָּל־יְגִיעָיו *all the products of his labours*), כָּל־יְגִיעֲךָ *all the product of your labour* Dt 28$_{33}$, כָּל־יְגִיעֵךְ *all the product of your* (f.) *labour* Ezk 23$_{29}$.

<PREP> מִן of direction, *from,* + נער pi. *shake* Ne 5$_{13}$; עַל *against,* + קרא *call* drought Hg 1$_{11}$.

<SYN> §1 עֳנִי *affliction,* כֶּסֶף *silver;* §2 סַחַר *merchandise,* חֹסֶן *wealth,* חַיִל *wealth,* יְקָר *preciousness,* אוֹצָר *treasure,* נַחֲלָה *inheritance,* יְבוּל *produce,* בַּיִת *house.**

→ יגע *be weary.*

[יְגִיעָה] 1 n.f. **wearying**—cstr. יְגִעַת—<NOM CL> לַהַג הַרְבֵּה יְגִעַת בָּשָׂר *much study is a wearying of the flesh* Ec 12$_{12}$. <CSTR> יְגִעַת בָּשָׂר *wearying of the flesh* Ec 12$_{12}$.*

→ יגע *be weary.*

*[יגל] vb. **be afraid—Qal,** <SUBJ> כֹּמֶר *priest* (of foreign god) Ho 10$_5$ (if em. יָגִילוּ *they rejoiced,* i.e. גיל to יָגֻ[ו]לוּ *they will be afraid*). <PREP> עַל *on account of,* + כָּבוֹד *glory* Ho 10$_5$ (if em.; see Subj.).

יָגְלִי 1 pr.n.m. **Jogli,** Danite, father of Bukki, <CSTR> בֶּן־יָגְלִי *son of Jogli* Nm 34$_{22}$ (or em. יִגְלִי *Jigli*).

→ י׳ Y. + גלה *reveal.*

*[יגן] vb. **beat, Ni. be downcast,** <SUBJ> worshipper Ps 77$_7$ (if em. נְגִינָתִי *my song* to נוּגַנְתִּי *I am downcast*). <PREP> בְּ of time, *in,* + לַיְלָה *night* Ps 77$_7$ (if em.; see Subj.).

יגע 27.2.6 vb. **be weary—Qal** 20.2.4 Pf. יָגְעָה, יָגַעְתָּ (יגעתה), יָגַעְתִּי, (יָגַעְתְּ), יָגַעְנוּ; impf. יִיגַע, 2ms תִּיגַע, אִיגַע, יִיגְעוּ (יִגְעוּ, יִיגָעוּ); ptc. Si יגע—**1. be weary, weary oneself,** 2 S 23$_{10}$ Is 40$_{28}$ (|| יעף *be weary*) 40$_{30}$ (|| יעף, כשׁל ni. *stumble;* :: חלף hi. *renew* strength) 40$_{31}$ (|| יעף; :: רוץ *run*) 43$_{22}$ 57$_{10}$ Jr 45$_3$ Ps 6$_7$ 69$_4$ Si 11$_{11}$ (:: רוץ) 4Q417 2.1$_{23}$ 4Q418 69.2$_{11}$.

<SUBJ> Y. Is 40$_{28}$, Israel Is 43$_{22}$, Baruch Jr 45$_3$, נַעַר *lad* Is 40$_{30}$, קוה ptc. *one who waits* Is 40$_{31}$, worshipper Ps 6$_7$ 69$_4$ (+ קָרְאִי because of *my crying*), יָד *hand* 2 S 23$_{10}$; subj. not specified, Si 11$_{11}$ (יֵשׁ ... יגע *there is one ... who is weary*) 4Q417 2.1$_{23}$ 4Q418 69.2$_{11}$. <PREP> בְּ of cause, *because of,* + Y. Is 43$_{22}$, אֲנָחָה *sighing* Jr 45$_3$ Ps 6$_7$, רֹב *greatness,* i.e. length, of way Is 57$_{10}$, עַוְלָה *unrighteousness* 4Q417 2.1$_{23}$, בִּינָה *understanding* 4Q418 69.2$_{11}$ (בְּ perh. *for [the sake of]*).

2. toil, labour (for), Jos 24$_{13}$ (+ בנה *build*) Is 47$_{12}$ (or del.) 47$_{15}$ 49$_{4}$ (+ כלה pi. *spend* strength) 62$_{8}$ 65$_{23}$ (|| ילד *give birth*) Jr 51$_{58}$ Hb 2$_{13}$ (both || יעף *weary oneself*) Jb 9$_{9}$ Pr 23$_{4}$ (+ חדל *leave off*) Lm 5$_{5}$ (or em.; see Subj.; :: נוח ho. *be given rest*) Si 34$_{4}$ 4Q418 69.2$_{13}$.

<SUBJ> Israel(ites) Jos 24$_{13}$ 65$_{23}$ Pr 23$_{4}$ Lm 5$_{5}$ (or em. יָגַעְנוּ *we have toiled* to יְנִעֵנוּ *he causes us to wander*, i.e. נוע hi., or יְגִעֵנוּ *the product of our labour*), Jerusalem Is 62$_{8}$, עַם *people* Jr 51$_{58}$ Hb 2$_{13}$, Job Jb 9$_{29}$, בַּת *daughter* of Chaldaeans Is 47$_{12}$ (or del.) 47$_{15}$, עֶבֶד *servant* Is 49$_{4}$, עָנִי *poor one* Si 34$_{4}$; subj. not specified, 4Q418 69.2$_{13}$.

<OBJ> סֹחֵר *merchant* Is 47$_{15}$. <PREP> לְ *for (the purpose of)*, + רִיק *vanity* Is 49$_{4}$ 65$_{23}$; of benefit, *for*, + חֶסֶר *need* Si 34$_{4}$; בְּ of price, *(in exchange) for*, + אֶרֶץ *land* Jos 24$_{13}$, תִּירוֹשׁ *new wine* Is 62$_{8}$, סֹחֵר *merchant* Is 47$_{15(mss)}$ (בַּאֲשֶׁר *for whom*); of instrument, *by (means of), with*, + כֶּשֶׁף *sorcery* Is 47$_{12}$ (or del.), פְּעֻלָּה *deed* 4Q418 69.2$_{13}$; מִן of time, *since*, + נְעוּרִים *youth* Is 47$_{12}$ (or del.); בְּדֵי *(in exchange) for*, + רִיק *vanity* Jr 51$_{58}$, אֵשׁ *fire* Hb 2$_{13}$. <COLL> יגע + noun used adverbially, הֶבֶל *vanity*, i.e. in vain Jb 9$_{29}$; + inf. of purpose, עשׁר hi. *gain riches* Pr 23$_{4}$.

3. ptc. as noun, **labourer,** <SUBJ> היה *be* Is 45$_{14}$ (if em.; see Cstr.), עבר *pass* Is 45$_{14}$ (if em.; see Cstr.). <CSTR> יְגִעֵי מִצְרַיִם *labourers of Egypt* Is 45$_{14}$ (if em. יְגִיעַ *product of*).

Also perh. 4Q418 112$_{2}$ ([יגען]; others [ ]ותען) 206$_{5}$.

<SYN> §1 יעף *be weary*, כשׁל ni. *stumble*; יעף *weary oneself*.

<ANT> §1 חלף hi. *renew* strength, רוץ *run*; נוח ho. *be given rest*.

Pi. 3 Impf. 3ms יְיַגַּע, 3fs תְּיַגְּעֶנּוּ, 2ms תְּיַגַּע—**1. make weary,** <SUBJ> עָמָל *toil* Ec 10$_{15}$. <OBJ> כְּסִיל *fool* Ec 10$_{15}$.

2. cause to toil, <SUBJ> Joshua Jos 7$_{3}$. <OBJ> עַם *people* Jos 7$_{3}$. <COLL> יגע pi. + adverb, שָׁמָּה *there* Jos 7$_{3}$.

3. perh. **torture,** וְיַגַּע בַּצִּנּוֹר וְאֶת־הַפִּסְחִים וְאֶת־הַעִוְרִים perh. *and tortures with a pike/dagger both the lame and the blind* 2 S 5$_{8}$ (unless נגע בְּ *reach* channel or *strike with* pike; or em. בְּצִנּוֹרוֹ אֶת־ torture/strike the blind *with his pike/dagger*).*

Hi. 4.0.2 Pf. הוֹגַעְתַּנִי, הוֹגַעְתִּיךָ, הוֹגַעְתֶּם, הוֹגַעְנוּ; inf. Q לוגיע—**make weary, cause to toil,** <SUBJ> Y. Is 43$_{23}$ (|| עבד hi. *cause to labour*), Israel Is 43$_{24}$ (|| עבד hi.) 4QDibHam[a] 1.5$_{19}$ ([הו]גענו; || עבד hi.), כֹּהֵן *priest* Ml 2$_{17.17}$, נטף hi. ptc. *teacher* of lies 1QpHab 10$_{11}$.

<OBJ> Y. Is 43$_{24}$ Ml 2$_{17.17}$ (or em. הוֹגַעְנוּ *we have wearied [him]* to הוֹגַעֲנֻהוּ *we have wearied him*) 4QDibHam[a] 1.5$_{19}$ ([הו]גענו), Israel Is 43$_{23}$, רַב pl. *many* 1QpHab 10$_{11}$. <PREP> בְּ of instrument, *by (means of), with*, + לְבוֹנָה *frankincense* Is 43$_{23}$, עָוֺן *iniquity* Is 43$_{24}$ 4QDibHam[a] 1.5$_{19}$ ([הו]גענו), עֲבוֹדָה *service* 1QpHab 10$_{11}$, דָּבָר *word* Ml 2$_{17}$. <COLL> יגע hi. + adverb, בַּמָּה *how?* Ml 2$_{17}$.

Also 4Q418 46$_{2}$.

<SYN> עבד hi. *cause to labour*.*

⇒ יָגֵעַ *weary*, יְגִיעַ *toil, product*, יָגָע *gain*, יָגֵעַ *weary*, יָגוֹעַ *toiling*, יְגִיעָה *wearying*.

יָגָע 1.0.1 n.[m.] **gain,** i.e. product of labour, <OBJ> שׁוב hi. *give back* Jb 20$_{18}$ (or em. יְגִיעוֹ *the product of his labour*) 4QapPent 10.2$_{5}$, בלע *swallow* Jb 20$_{18}$ (or em.; see above).*

⇒ יגע *be weary*.

יָגֵעַ 3 adj. **weary**—pl. יְגֵעִים—**weary** (Dt 25$_{18}$ 2 S 17$_{2}$), **wearisome** (Ec 1$_{8}$), **troubled** (Ps 88$_{16}$ [if em.]), used predicatively of אֲנִי *I* Ps 88$_{16}$ (if em. גֹּוֵעַ *expiring* to יָגֵעַ *troubled*), אַתָּה *you* Dt 25$_{18}$ (|| עָיֵף *faint*), הוּא *he* 2 S 17$_{2}$ (|| רְפֵה *weak*), דָּבָר *word* Ec 1$_{8}$.

<SYN> עָיֵף *faint*, רָפֶה *weak*.*

⇒ יגע *be weary*.

יגר 7 vb. **fear—Qal** 7 Pf. יָגֹרְתִּי, יָגֹרְתָּ; ptc. יָגוֹר—**fear, be afraid,** <SUBJ> Coniah Jr 22$_{25}$, Ebed-melech Jr 39$_{17}$, Job Jb 3$_{25}$ (+ פחד *fear*) 9$_{28}$, Moses Dt 9$_{19}$, Israel Dt 28$_{60}$, בֵּן *son* Jr 22$_{25}$, מֶלֶךְ *king* Jr 22$_{25}$, worshipper Ps 119$_{60}$, כּוּשִׁי *Ethiopian* Jr 39$_{17}$. <OBJ> חֶרְפָּה *fear* Ps 119$_{39}$, עַצֶּבֶת *pain* Jb 9$_{28}$, אֲשֶׁר *that which* Jb 3$_{25}$. <PREP> מִפְּנֵי *(on account) of*, + אִישׁ *man* Jr 39$_{17}$, אַף *anger* Dt 9$_{19}$, חֵמָה *wrath* Dt 9$_{19}$, מַדְוֶה *sickness*, אֲשֶׁר *those who* Jr 22$_{25}$.

⇒ see also גור III *fear*.

[יָגֻר] pr.n.[m.] **Jagur,** Lachish inscr. 31$_{5}$ (יגר; others יאר *Jair*).

[יָגָר] 0.0.3 n.[m.] **cairn,** <NOM CL> יגר של גי הסככא *the cairn of the valley of Sekaka* 3QTr 4$_{13}$, יגר שבמגזת הכוהן הגדול *the cairn that is at the ford of the high priest* 3QTr 6$_{14}$, יגר של פי צוק הקדרוה *the cairn of the mouth of the gorge of Kidron* 3QTr 8$_{8}$. <PREP> בְּ of place, *in* 3QTr 4$_{13}$ 6$_{14}$ 8$_{8}$.

יָד I 1634.52.379.6 n.f. (sometimes m.) **hand**—cstr. יַד (Si יוד, Q ייד); sf. יָדִי, יָדְךָ (יָדְכָה, יָדֶךָ) יָדֵךְ, יָדוֹ, יָדָהּ, יָדֵנוּ, יֶדְכֶם, יֶדְכֶן, יָדָם (Q ידמה), Q ידן; du. יָדַיִם (יָדָיִם); cstr. יְדֵי (Q יידי); sf. יָדַי (יָדָי), יָדֶיךָ, יָדַיִךְ (יָדַיִךְ), יָדָיו (יָדֵיהוּ), יָדֶיהָ, יְדֵיכֶם, יְדֵיהֶם (Q ידיהמה), יְדֵיהֶן; pl. יָדוֹת (יָדֹת); cstr. יְדוֹת; sf. יְדֹתָיו, יְדֹתֶיהָ, יְדוֹתָם.

1. hand, a. of human being (e.g. Gn 3$_{22}$ Ex 4$_{2}$ Lv 21$_{19}$ Nm 22$_{23}$ Dt 9$_{15}$ Jos 8$_{18}$ Jg 6$_{21}$ 1 S 14$_{27}$ 2 S 21$_{20}$ 1 K 13$_{4}$ Is 2$_{8}$ Ezk 47$_{3}$ Pr 30$_{28}$ Est 3$_{10}$), of image (1 S 5$_{4}$), of personified object (Hb 3$_{10}$ [unless יָדָה *voice*] Pr 14$_{1}$); also **wrist, forearm** (Gn 24$_{22}$ Ezk 16$_{11}$ 23$_{42}$), perh. **arm*** (Ec 7$_{26}$), **upper arm** (Jr 38$_{12}$), but distinctions not alw. clear.; perh. specif. **left hand*** (e.g. Jg 3$_{21}$ 5$_{26}$ 2 S 20$_{9.10}$ Ps 26$_{10}$ 138$_{7}$ 139$_{10}$).

b. of Y. (e.g. Ex 9$_{3}$ 14$_{31}$ Nm 11$_{23}$ 14$_{30}$ Jos 4$_{24}$ Jg 2$_{15}$ 1 S 5$_{6}$ 1 K 18$_{46}$ 2 K 3$_{15}$ Is 19$_{19}$ 64$_{7}$ Jr 1$_{9}$ Ezk 1$_{3}$ 13$_{9}$ 20$_{5}$ Am 1$_{8}$ Zc 2$_{13}$ Jb 10$_{8}$ Pr 21$_{1}$ Ru 1$_{13}$ Ezr 7$_{6}$ Si 43$_{12}$ 1QS 3$_{16}$ 1QM 1$_{14}$ 4QD^{a} 11$_{9}$).

2. perh. **penis** (Is 57$_{8}$ [or em.; see יָד III *love*] 57$_{10}$ Jr 5$_{31}$ [unless §4a] 50$_{15}$ 1QS 7$_{13}$=4QD^{a} 10.2$_{11}$), unless יָד II *penis*.

3. hand as representing the person (e.g. Gn 9$_{5}$ 31$_{29}$ 33$_{19}$ 2 S 3$_{12}$ 2 K 9$_{7}$), nation, tribe (e.g. Jg 4$_{24}$ Ps 106$_{41}$ 2 C 34$_{9}$), animal (e.g. Gn 9$_{5}$ 1 S 17$_{37}$), object (e.g. Ps 141$_{9}$); also בְּיַד **in the possession of** (e.g. Gn 35$_{4}$ 44$_{16}$ Ex 21$_{16}$ 22$_{3}$ 1 S 9$_{8}$ Ec 5$_{13}$), **by means of** (e.g. Ex 9$_{35}$ 35$_{29}$ Lv 8$_{36}$ 26$_{46}$ Nm 4$_{37}$ 9$_{23}$ Jos 14$_{2}$ 22$_{9}$ Jg 3$_{4}$ 1 S 28$_{15.17}$ 2 S 10$_{2}$ 1 K 8$_{53}$ 2 K 17$_{13}$ 2 K 19$_{23}$||Is 37$_{24}$ Ho 12$_{11}$ Hg 1$_{1}$ Ml 1$_{1}$ Est 1$_{12}$ 1 C 5$_{41}$ 11$_{3}$ 16$_{7}$ 2 C 34$_{14}$ Si 48$_{20}$ Lachish ost. 9$_{7}$).

4a. hand as **(sphere of) power, rule, control** (e.g. Gn 16$_{6}$ Ex 4$_{21}$ Dt 12$_{7}$ 2 K 8$_{20.22}$ Is 47$_{14}$ Jr 18$_{21}$ Ezk 27$_{15.21}$ 35$_{5}$ Ho 13$_{14}$ Ps 22$_{21}$ 49$_{16}$ 63$_{11}$ 89$_{49}$ Jb 2$_{6}$ 5$_{20}$ 8$_{4}$ Pr 18$_{21}$ Dn 11$_{16}$ 1 C 29$_{12}$ Si 6$_{2}$ 8$_{1}$ 15$_{14}$ 1QS 2$_{6}$ 3$_{16}$ 4QJub^{d} 21$_{22}$ 4Q418 4Q418 81$_{10}$),* **grip,** i.e. hold on power (e.g. 1 K 2$_{46}$), **authority** (e.g. Gn 41$_{35}$), **charge, custody, command** (e.g. Gn 39$_{6}$ Nm 4$_{28}$ 31$_{49}$ 1 S 17$_{22}$ 2 S 18$_{2}$ 1 K 14$_{27}$ ||2 C 12$_{10}$ Jr 5$_{31}$ Est 2$_{3.8.14}$ Ezr 1$_{8}$ 1 C 6$_{16}$ 26$_{28}$ 29$_{8}$ 2 C 23$_{18}$ 26$_{11.13}$), pl. **directions** (Ezr 3$_{10}$ 1 C 25$_{2.3.6}$).

4b. hand as **power, strength, force** (e.g. Nm 20$_{20}$ Dt 32$_{36}$ 34$_{12}$ Jos 8$_{20}$ 2 S 17$_{2}$ 2 K 19$_{26}$||Is 37$_{27}$ Is 28$_{2}$ Jr 16$_{21}$ Dn 12$_{7}$), i.e. act of power (Ex 14$_{31}$ Ps 78$_{42}$), **courage** (e.g. 2 S 4$_{1}$).

5. sleight of hand, theft (Si 41$_{19}$).

6. bounty (1 K 10$_{13}$ Est 1$_{7}$ 2$_{18}$ 1 C 29$_{14.16}$).

7a. side,* of gate (1 S 4$_{18}$ 2 S 18$_{4}$ Pr 8$_{3}$), of way (1 S 4$_{13[Qr]}$ 2 S 15$_{2}$ Ezk 48$_{1}$ [or em.; see Prep.] Ps 140$_{6}$), of city (Ne 7$_{4}$), of land (e.g. Gn 34$_{21}$ Nm 34$_{3}$ Jos 15$_{46}$ Jg 18$_{10}$ Is 22$_{18}$ 1 C 4$_{40}$ 2 C 21$_{16}$), of river (Ex 2$_{5}$ Nm 13$_{29}$ Dt 2$_{37}$ Jg 11$_{26}$ Jr 46$_{6}$ Dn 10$_{4}$), of sea (Ps 104$_{25}$), of rock (Ps 141$_{6}$), of pipes of lamp (Zc 4$_{12}$), of buried treasure (3Q Tr 12$_{2}$), of battle formation (1QM 8$_{2}$ 9$_{7}$), of person, i.e. position next to person (e.g. Nm 2$_{17}$ 1 S 19$_{3}$ 2 S 14$_{30}$ 15$_{18}$ Jr 6$_{3}$ [unless §14] Ne 3$_{2+13t}$ 2 C 7$_{6}$), position next in authority (e.g. Ne 13$_{13}$ 1 C 18$_{17}$ 23$_{28}$ 2 C 17$_{15.16.18}$); **latrine** outside camp (Dt 23$_{13}$ 1QM 7$_{7}$ 11QT 46$_{13}$); **region, direction** (Nm 24$_{24}$).

7b. in compound prepositions, **beside,** (1) לְיַד (e.g. 1 S 19$_{3}$ Ps 140$_{6}$ Pr 8$_{3}$); (2) בְּיַד (e.g. 2 C 7$_{6}$); (3) אֶל־יַד (e.g. 2 S 14$_{30}$ 18$_{4}$); (4) עַל־יְדֵי ,עַל־יַד (e.g. Ex 2$_{5}$ Jg 11$_{26}$ 2 S 15$_{2}$ Jr 46$_{6}$ Jb 1$_{14}$ Dn 10$_{4}$ Ne 3$_{2}$ 2 C 21$_{16}$ Si 14$_{25}$).

8. pl. **(fractional) parts, portions,* divisions** (Gn 47$_{24}$ 2 S 19$_{44}$ 2 K 11$_{7}$ Ne 11$_{1}$ 11QT 58$_{8}$), **times (greater)** (Gn 43$_{34}$).

9. monument (1 S 15$_{12}$ 2 S 18$_{18}$ Is 56$_{5}$ [unless both §15] 1 C 18$_{3}$ perh. Ezk 21$_{24}$ [unless יָד = **signpost**] 3QTr 10$_{12}$).*

10. **tenon, peg,*** in boards of tabernacle (Ex 26$_{17}$).

11. **axletree*** of wheel (1 K 7$_{32.33}$).

12. **stay, support** of stand (1 K 7$_{35.36}$). **arm rest*** of throne (1 K 10$_{19.19}$||2 C 8$_{18.18}$).

13. **handle** of pot (Is 45$_9$ 4QMMT B$_{22}$), **hilt** of sword (1QM 5$_{14}$).

14. perh. **flock** (Jr 6$_3$).*

15. perh. **descendant*** (2 S 18$_{18}$ Is 56$_5$ Jb 20$_{10}$).

16. perh. **signal** for order of battle (1QM 8$_{5.7.12}$ 17$_{11}$).

<SUBJ> היה *be* Gn 27$_{23}$ 37$_{27}$ 47$_{24}$ Ex 9$_3$ 17$_{12}$ (+ אֱמוּנָה *steadiness*) Dt 2$_{15}$ 13$_{10}$ 17$_{7.7}$ 23$_{13}$ Jos 2$_{19}$ 8$_{20}$ Jg 2$_{15}$ 1 S 5$_9$ 7$_{13}$ 12$_{15}$ 18$_{17.17.21}$ 24$_{13.14}$ 2 S 24$_{17}$||1 C 21$_{17}$ 1 K 18$_{46}$ 2 K 3$_{15}$ 15$_{19}$ Jr 26$_{24}$ Ezk 1$_3$ 3$_{22}$ 13$_9$ 33$_{22}$ 37$_1$ 40$_1$ Ps 80$_{18}$ 119$_{173}$ Ezr 8$_{31}$ 9$_2$ 1 C 4$_{10}$ 2 C 30$_{12}$ Si 4$_{31}$ 11QT 58$_8$, ישׁב *dwell* Ne 11$_1$, אזל *go* Dt 32$_{36}$, עלה *go up* Zc 14$_{13}$, יצא *go out* Ru 1$_{13}$, נגשׁ hi. *bring near* Si 32$_{12(Bmg)}$, משׁשׁ *feel* 4QapLam^a 1.2$_{12}$ (unless ימשׁו from מושׁ *feel*), אחז *hold* Gn 25$_{26}$ Dt 32$_{41}$ 2 S 20$_9$, דבק *cling* 2 S 23$_{10}$, נגע *touch* Ex 19$_{13}$ 1 S 6$_9$ Jb 19$_{21}$ Dn 10$_{10}$, hi. *reach.*, i.e. afford Lv 5$_7$, נשׂג hi. *reach*, i.e. afford Lv 5$_{7(Sam).11}$ 14$_{21.22.30.31.32}$ 25$_{26.47.49}$ 27$_8$ Nm 6$_{21}$ Ezk 46$_7$ Si 32$_{12(B)}$ 1QS 7$_8$ 4QD^a 6.2$_{12}$ ([ה]ידה) 4Q418 126.2$_{13}$, נשׁק *kiss* Jb 31$_{27}$, נטה *stretch out* Is 45$_{12}$ Si 43$_{12}$, pass. *be stretched out* Is 5$_{25}$ 9$_{11.16.20}$ 10$_4$ 14$_{26.27}$ Jr 21$_5$, שׁלח pass. *be stretched out* Ezk 2$_9$, נגר ni. *be poured*, i.e. stretched out Ps 77$_3$, ישׁט ho. *be stretched out* Si 4$_{31(C)}$, פתח *open* Si 51$_{19(B)}$, pass. *be open* Si 4$_{32(A)}$, קפץ pass. *be clenched* Si 4$_{31(A)}$, קפד pass. *be clenched* Si 4$_{31(C)}$, הלך *go* Jg 4$_{24}$, נחת *go down* Ps 38$_3$, שׁוב *go back* Ex 4$_7$ 1 K 13$_{6.6}$, hi. *take back* Jb 20$_{10}$ (unless יָד III *love*; or em. יָדָיו *his hands* to וִילָדָיו *and his children*), בוא hi. *bring* Lv 7$_{30}$, סור *turn aside* 1 S 6$_3$, נחה hi. *lead* Ps 139$_{10}$, מצא *find* Lv 12$_8$ 25$_{28}$ Jg 9$_{33}$ 1 S 10$_7$ 23$_{17}$ 25$_8$ Is 10$_{10.14}$ Ps 21$_9$ Jb 31$_{25}$ Ec 9$_{10}$, לקח *take* Am 9$_2$ Si 4$_{31(A)}$, נשׂא *take* Si 4$_{31(C)}$, ni. *be lifted up* 1QM 18$_1$ (בה[נ]שא).

נוח *rest* Is 25$_{10}$, נפל *fall* Ezk 8$_1$, hi. *bring down* 1QM 16$_8$, אסר pass. *be bound* 2 S 3$_{34}$, רפה *be weak* 2 S 4$_1$ Is 13$_7$ Jr 6$_{24}$ 50$_{43}$ Ezk 7$_{17}$ 21$_{12}$ Zp 3$_{16}$ Ne 6$_9$ 2 C 15$_7$ 1QpHab 7$_{11}$, חול *whirl* or *be weak* Lm 4$_6$ (unless יָד III *love*; or em. יְלָדִים *children* and/or חלה *be weak*), דלל *be brought low* 4QapLam^a 1.2$_6$, יגע *be weary* 2 S 23$_{10}$, קצר *be short* Nm 11$_{23}$ Is 50$_2$ Is 59$_1$, פוג *be numb* Ps 77$_3$, כבד *be heavy* Jg 1$_{35}$ 1 S 5$_{6.11}$ Ps 32$_4$ Jb 23$_2$, קשׁה *be hard* 1 S 5$_7$, חזק *be strong* Jg 7$_{11}$ 2 S 2$_7$ 16$_{21}$ 2 K 14$_5$ Ezk 22$_{14}$ Zc 8$_{9.13}$ 4QapJoshua^a 4$_{11}$ ([ת]חזקנה), hi. *hold* Ne 4$_{11}$, עזז *be strong* Jg 3$_{10}$ 6$_2$ Ps 89$_{14}$, רשׁה *be powerful* 1QM 12$_4$ 4QM^a 1$_3$, משׁל *rule* Pr 12$_{24}$, יבשׁ *dry up*, i.e. wither 1 K 13$_6$, צרע pu. *be leprous* Ex 4$_6$, זור *be strange* 4QShir^b 18.2$_{10}$, בהל ni. *be terrified* Ezk 7$_{27}$, רום *be high* Ex 14$_8$ Nm 15$_{30}$=4QMMT B$_{70}$ ([ביד רמה]) 33$_3$ Dt 32$_{27}$ Is 26$_{11}$ Mc 5$_8$ 1QS 5$_{12}$ 8$_{17.22}$ 9$_1$ 4QOrd^a 2$_6$ 4QpPs^a 3.4$_{15}$ 4QCat 1$_3$ CD 8$_8$=19$_{21}$ 10$_3$ (all except Dt בְּיָד רָמָה *with a high hand*, i.e. intentionally, aggressively),* ירשׁ hi. *dispossess*, i.e. destroy Ex 15$_9$, כנע hi. *subdue* 1QM 1$_{14}$, נגף *strike* 4QM^a 1$_4$.

כון ni. *be established* Ps 89$_{22}$, pol. *establish* Ex 15$_{17}$ Ps 119$_{73}$, יסד *found* Is 48$_{13}$, pi. Zc 4$_9$, שׁמר *keep* 2 K 11$_7$ 11QT 58$_8$, ישׁע hi. *save* Jg 7$_2$ 1 S 25$_{26.33}$ Is 59$_1$ 1QS 6$_{27}$ (ה[ו]שיעה) 4QapPs^a 1.2$_4$ CD 9$_{9.10}$, עזר *help* 4QMidr Eschat^b 11$_{14}$, רפא *heal* Jb 5$_{18}$, עשׂה *do, make* Is 31$_7$ 41$_{20}$ 56$_2$ 66$_2$ 119$_{73}$ Jb 5$_{12}$ 10$_8$ 12$_9$ Pr 21$_{25}$ Ec 2$_{11}$ 9$_{10}$ 4QParGenEx 9$_1$ 11QPs^a 28$_4$ GnzPs 2$_{14}$, יצר *form* Ps 95$_5$, עצב pi. *shape* Jb 10$_8$, שׁלב pu. *be joined* Ex 26$_{17}$||36$_{22}$, יצק ho. *be poured*, i.e. cast 1 K 7$_{33}$, מוט *shake* Lv 25$_{35}$, שׁמט hi. *release* Dt 15$_3$, נדח ni. *be pushed* Dt 19$_5$, חלל hi. *begin* 1QM 9$_1$, מלא *be full* Is 1$_{15}$ Ezk 10$_{12}$, בצע pi. *complete* Zc 4$_9$, חלק pi. *apportion* Is 34$_{17}$, עשׁר hi. *make rich* Pr 10$_4$, ידע ni. *be known* Is 66$_{14}$ (unless יָד III *love*), נטף *drip* Ca 5$_5$, חלל po. *pierce* Jb 26$_{13}$, שׁפך *shed* blood Dt 21$_6$=11QT 63$_5$ Dt 21$_7$ Pr 6$_{17}$, בלע pi. *destroy* Lm 2$_8$, בשׁל pi. *boil* Lm 4$_{10}$, שׁטף pass. *be rinsed* 4QTohB^c 1$_{11}$ (... שט[ו]פות [י]דיו), מאן pi. *refuse* Pr 21$_{25}$.

<NOM CL> הַיָּדַיִם יְדֵי עֵשָׂו *the hands are the hands of Esau* Gn 27$_{22}$, יָדָיו גְּלִילֵי זָהָב *his hands are rods of gold* Ca 5$_{14}$, אֲסוּרִים יָדֶיהָ *her hands are fetters* Ec 7$_{26}$ (unless יָד III *love*), יְדֵי מֹשֶׁה כְּבֵדִים *the hands of Moses were heavy* Ex 17$_{12}$, יְדֵיהֶם *their hands*, i.e. they have hands Ps 115$_7$, עֶשֶׂר־יָדוֹת לִי *I have ten portions* 2 S 19$_{44}$, יָד לְפֶה *hand to the mouth*, i.e. put your hand to your mouth Pr 30$_{32}$, יָדְךָ בְּעֹרֶף אֹיְבֶיךָ *your hand shall be on the neck of your enemies* Gn 49$_8$, יָדוֹ בַכֹּל *his hand is against everyone* Gn 16$_{12}$, יְדוֹת הָאוֹפַנִּים בַּמְּכוֹנָה *the axletrees of the wheels were in*, i.e. part of, *the stands* 1 K 7$_{32}$, יְדֹתֶיהָ ... מִמֶּנָּה *its stays were ... from*, i.e. of one piece with, *it* 1 K 7$_{35}$, יָדוֹת מִזֶּה וּמִזֶּה *there were arm rests on either side* 1 K 10$_{19}$||2 C 9$_{18}$, מאת אל יד מלחמה *from God is a hand of war* 1QM 4$_3$, יָד

תַּחַת יָד *a hand for a hand* Ex 21$_{24}$, sim. Dt 19$_{21}$=11QT 61$_{12}$ (בְּיָד), יָדָם עִם־דָּוִד *their hand is with David* 1 S 22$_{17}$, הִנֵּה יָדִי עִמָּךְ *behold, my hand is with you* 2 S 3$_{12}$, יד אל הגדולה עמהמה *the great hand of God is with them* 4QMidrEschat^{b} 11$_{14}$, עם אביונים יד גבורתכה *the hand of your might*, i.e. your mighty hand, *is with the poor* 1QM 13$_{14}$, הֲיַד יוֹאָב אִתָּךְ *is the hand of Joab with you?* 2 S 14$_{19}$, יַד־אֱלֹהֵינוּ עַל־כָּל־מְבַקְשָׁיו *the hand of our God is upon all who seek him* Ezr 8$_{22}$, יָדַיִךְ עַל־רֹאשֵׁךְ *your hands shall be on your head* Jr 2$_{37}$, יָדָיו עַל־חֲלָצָיו *his hands are on his loins* Jr 30$_{6}$, ידך על פיך *your hand shall be upon your mouth* Si 5$_{12(A)}$, יַד־י״ עָלַי חֲזָקָה *the hand of Y. was strong upon me* Ezk 3$_{14}$, ידי על כול בוזי *my hand is against all those who despise me* 1QH 4$_{22}$, יְדֵי אָדָם מִתַּחַת כַּנְפֵיהֶם *hands of a human being were under their wings* Ezk 1$_{8(Qr)}$, אֵין יָדוֹ מַשֶּׂגֶת *his hand does not reach*, i.e. afford Lv 14$_{21}$, אֵין־יָדַיִם לוֹ the pot *has no handles* Is 45$_{9}$, זֹאת הַיָּד הַנְּטוּיָה *this is the hand that is stretched out* Is 14$_{26}$, יָדְךָ זֹּאת *this is your hand* Ps 109$_{27}$.

<OBJ> שׁלח *send*, i.e. stretch out Gn 3$_{33}$ 8$_{9}$ 19$_{10}$ 22$_{10.12}$ 37$_{22}$ Ex 3$_{20}$ 4$_{4.4}$ 9$_{15}$ 22$_{7.10}$ 24$_{11}$ Dt 25$_{11}$ Jg 3$_{21}$ 5$_{26}$ 15$_{15}$ 1 S 17$_{49}$ 22$_{17}$ 24$_{7.11}$ 26$_{9.11.23}$ 2 S 1$_{14}$ 15$_{5}$ 18$_{12}$ 24$_{16}$||1 C 21$_{15}$ 1 K 13$_{4.4}$ 2 K 6$_{7}$ Jr 1$_{9}$ Ezk 10$_{7}$ Ps 55$_{21}$ 125$_{3}$ 138$_{7}$ 144$_{7}$ Jb 1$_{11.12}$ 2$_{5}$ 28$_{9}$ 30$_{24}$ Ca 5$_{4}$ Est 2$_{21}$ 3$_{6}$ 6$_{2}$ 8$_{7}$ 9$_{2.10.15.16}$ Dn 11$_{42}$ Ne 13$_{21}$ 1 C 13$_{9.10}$ Si 15$_{16}$ 1QM 17$_{13}$ 1QS 6$_{5.5}$ 1QSa 2$_{18}$ ([ישלח]) 2$_{20}$ ([וישלח]) 2$_{20}$ (ישל[ח]) 4QpHos^{b} 2$_{3}$ 4QpPs^{a} 1.2$_{17}$ 4QCommGenA 3$_{7}$ 4QD^{f} 2$_{4}$ 4QapJoseph^{a} 2$_{2}$ 4QapPs^{b} 29$_{4}$ 4Q418 2.3$_{4}$ 33$_{3}$ (ת[ש]לח) 96$_{3}$ 4QM^{c} 1$_{8}$, pi. *send*, i.e. stretch out Pr 31$_{19.20}$, נטה *stretch out* Ex 7$_{5.19}$ 8$_{1.2.13}$ 9$_{22}$ 10$_{12.21.22}$ 14$_{16.21.26.27}$ Jos 8$_{19.26}$ Is 5$_{25}$ 23$_{11}$ Jr 51$_{25}$ Ezk 6$_{14}$ 14$_{9.13}$ 16$_{27}$ 25$_{7.13.16}$ 35$_{3}$ Zp 1$_{4}$ 2$_{13}$ Jb 15$_{25}$ Pr 1$_{24}$ Si 46$_{2}$ 48$_{18}$ 1QM 8$_{8}$, hi. Is 31$_{3}$ Jr 6$_{12}$ 15$_{6}$, ישׁט hi. *stretch out* Si 7$_{32}$ (הו[ש]יט) 34$_{14(B).18}$, משׁך *stretch out* Ho 7$_{5}$, הדה *stretch out* Is 11$_{8}$ (or em. יָדוֹ הָדָה *he stretched out his hand* to יְדַהְדֵּהַ *he will roll stones*), ארך hi. *stretch out* Si 33$_{7(Bmg)}$, רוץ hi. *hasten (to stretch out)* Ps 68$_{32}$, פרשׂ pi. *spread* Is 25$_{11}$ 65$_{2}$ Ps 77$_{3}$ (if ins. פֵּרַשְׂתִּי *I spread*) 143$_{6}$ Lm 1$_{10}$.

בוא hi. *bring* Ex 4$_{6.6}$, יצא hi. *bring out* Ex 4$_{6.7}$ 1QS 7$_{13.15}$=4QD^{a} 10.2$_{11.13}$, שׁוב hi. *bring back* Gn 38$_{29}$ Ex 4$_{7.7}$ Jos 8$_{26}$ 1 S 14$_{27}$ 2 S 8$_{3}$ (or em. לְהָשִׁיב *to turn* to לְהַצִּיב *to set up* his monument, i.e. נצב hi.) Is 1$_{25}$ 14$_{27}$ Jr 6$_{9}$ Ezk 18$_{8.17}$ 20$_{22}$ 38$_{12}$ Am 1$_{8}$ Zc 13$_{7}$ Ps 74$_{11}$ 81$_{15}$ Lm 2$_{8}$ 1QH 8$_{24}$ 18$_{9}$ CD 19$_{9}$, הפך *turn* 1 K 22$_{34}$||2 C 18$_{33}$ 2 K 9$_{23}$ Lm 3$_{3}$ (unless יָד III *love*), נוף hi. *wave* 2 K 5$_{11}$ Is 11$_{15}$ 13$_{2}$ Zc 2$_{13}$ Jb 31$_{21}$ Si 12$_{18}$ 33$_{3}$ 37$_{7(B)}$ 47$_{4}$ 1QH 8$_{22.33}$ 1QM 17$_{9}$, pol. *shake* Is 10$_{32}$, נוע hi. *shake* Zp 2$_{15}$, מחא pi. *clap* Ezk 25$_{6}$, נוד hi. *cause to wander* Ps 36$_{12}$, קרב *approach* Dt 2$_{37}$, אוץ hi. *hasten* 4Q417 1.2$_{1}$, יסף hi. *add* Is 11$_{11}$ (unless יָד III *love* or שֵׁנִית יָדוֹ = add *the repeated action of his hand*, i.e. cstr.; or em.),* נשׂא *raise* Ex 6$_{8}$ Lv 9$_{22}$ Nm 14$_{30}$ Dt 32$_{40}$ 2 S 18$_{28}$ 20$_{21}$ Is 11$_{11}$ (if em. שֵׁנִית add *a second time* or add *the repeated action of* his hand, to שְׂאֵת again *raise*) 49$_{22}$ Ezk 20$_{5+5t}$ 36$_{7}$ 44$_{12}$ 47$_{14}$ Hb 3$_{10}$ Ps 10$_{12}$ 28$_{2}$ 106$_{26}$ 134$_{2}$ Ne 9$_{15}$ Si 50$_{20}$, רום hi. *raise* Gn 14$_{22}$ 41$_{44}$ Ex 17$_{11}$ Nm 20$_{11}$ 1 K 11$_{26.27}$ 1QM 15$_{13}$ 16$_{6}$ 17$_{12}$ 1QS 10$_{15}$ CD 11$_{6}$ 20$_{30}$, קום pol. *raise* 4QBark^{c} 1.1$_{1}$, שׁנה pi. *raise* Is 11$_{11}$ (if em. שֵׁנִית add *a second time* or add *the repeated action of* his hand, to שַׁנּוֹת again *raise*), נוח hi. *rest*, i.e. lower Ex 17$_{11}$ Ec 7$_{18}$ 11$_{6}$, רפה pi. *weaken* Jr 38$_{4.4}$ Ezr 4$_{4}$ Lachish ost. 6$_{6}$, hi. *let drop* Jos 10$_{6}$ 2 S 24$_{16}$||1 C 21$_{15}$, שׁקט hi. *make quiet*, i.e. limp Lachish ost. 6$_{7}$ (ל[הש]קט), אסף *gather*, i.e. withdraw 1 S 14$_{19}$, חזק pi. *strengthen* Jg 9$_{24}$ 1 S 23$_{16}$ Is 35$_{3}$ Jr 23$_{14}$ Ezk 13$_{22}$ Jb 4$_{3}$ Ezr 1$_{6}$ 6$_{22}$ Ne 2$_{18}$ 6$_{9}$ 1QM 7$_{12}$ 16$_{14}$ 4QM^{a} 10.2$_{14}$, hi. *grasp* Gn 21$_{18}$ Ezk 16$_{49}$ Zc 14$_{13}$, תמך *grasp* Gn 48$_{17}$.

שׂים *place* Gn 24$_{2.9}$ 47$_{29}$ Jg 18$_{19}$ 2 S 13$_{19}$ 2 K 11$_{16}$||2 C 23$_{15}$ 2 K 13$_{16}$ Ezk 39$_{21}$ Mc 7$_{16}$ Ps 89$_{26}$ Jb 21$_{5}$ 40$_{4}$ Si 5$_{12(C)}$, שׁית *place* Gn 48$_{17}$ Ex 23$_{1}$ Jb 9$_{33}$ Si 34$_{14(Bmg)}$, נתן *give, place* Gn 38$_{28}$ Ex 7$_{4}$ 2 K 10$_{15.15}$ Is 56$_{5}$ Jr 50$_{15}$ Ezk 17$_{18}$ Lm 5$_{6}$ 1 C 29$_{24}$ 2 C 30$_{8}$ 1QM 1$_{17}$ 4QRitPur 21.8$_{1}$ ([י]דו), סמך *lay* Ex 29$_{10.15.19}$ Lv 1$_{4}$ 3$_{2.8.13}$ 4$_{4.15.24.29.33}$ 8$_{14.18.22}$ 16$_{21}$ 24$_{14}$ Nm 8$_{10.12}$ 27$_{18.23}$ Dt 34$_{9}$ Am 5$_{19}$ Ps 37$_{24}$ 2 C 29$_{23}$ 1QM 12$_{11}$ 19$_{3}$ 1QDM 4$_{9}$ (יד[יו]) 11QT 15$_{18}$ ([ידיהמה]), חלל pi. *profane*, i.e. place 1QM 16$_{8}$, שׂכל pi. *lay crosswise* Gn 48$_{14}$, נשׂג hi. *cause to reach*, i.e. place 1 S 14$_{26}$, פקד hi. *deposit* Si 42$_{7(B)}$, רכב hi. *cause to ride* upon, i.e. grasp, bow 2 K 13$_{16.16}$, נצב hi. *erect* monument 1 S 15$_{12}$ 2 S 8$_{3}$ (if em.; see above) 1 C 18$_{3}$, חבק *fold* Ec 4$_{5}$, טמן *hide* Pr 19$_{24}$ 26$_{15}$, שׁמר *keep* Is 56$_{2}$, מצא *find* Ps 76$_{6}$, ראה *see* Ex 14$_{31}$ Dt 11$_{2}$, hi. *show* Dt 3$_{24}$, חזה *see* Is 57$_{8}$ (or em.; see יָד III *love*), שׁמע *hear of* 1 K 8$_{42}$, זכר *remember* Dt 7$_{19}$ Ps 78$_{42}$, ידע *know* Jos 4$_{24}$ Ps 95$_{7}$ (if ins. ידע), hi. *cause to know* Jr 16$_{21}$ 4QM^{a} 11.1$_{23}$, קרא *call*, i.e. name

2 S 18$_{18}$, למד pi. *teach* 2 S 22$_{35}$||Ps 18$_{35}$ Ps 144$_{1}$ 4QapJoseph^{b} 2$_{4}$ ([ל]מד]) 4QM^{a} 8$_{4}$ ([ידי]ם]), נגד hi. *tell of* Ne 2$_{18}$, כתב *write on* Is 44$_{5}$, אדר hi. *make glorious* Si 33$_{7(B)}$, רעה *graze* portion Jr 6$_{3}$, עשׂה *do* Ex 14$_{31}$ (הַיָּד הַגְּדֹלָה אֲשֶׁר עָשָׂה י׳ *the great act of power that Y. did*) 2 S 19$_{25}$ (if ins. וְלֹא עָשָׂה יָדָיו *and he had not done*, i.e. manicured, *his hands*) 4Q 185 1.3$_{13}$, *make* 4QMMT B$_{22}$, קלל hi. *make light* 1 S 6$_{5}$.

מלא pi. *fill* 4QShirShabb^{b} 22$_{2}$, i.e. consecrate Ex 28$_{41}$ 29$_{9.9.29.33.35}$ 32$_{29}$ Lv 8$_{33}$ 16$_{32}$ 21$_{10}$ Nm 3$_{3}$ Jg 17$_{5.12}$ 1 K 13$_{33}$ 43$_{26}$ 1 C 29$_{5}$ 2 C 13$_{9}$ 29$_{31}$ Si 45$_{15}$ 11QT 15$_{16}$ 35$_{7}$,* *draw* bow 2 K 9$_{24}$, רחץ *wash* Ex 30$_{19.21}$ 40$_{31}$ Dt 21$_{6}$ =11QT 63$_{5}$ 11QT 26$_{10}$, שׁטף *rinse* Lv 15$_{11}$, פתח *open* Dt 15$_{8.11}$ Ps 104$_{28}$ 145$_{16}$ Si 51$_{19}$ (11QPs^{a} [Sanders] [פתח]תי]), קפץ *close* Dt 15$_{7}$ 4Q417 1.1$_{24}$ 1.2$_{4}$ 4Q418 88$_{5}$ 4Q419 8.2$_{7}$, נתר hi. *loosen* Jb 6$_{9}$, קצץ pi. *cut off* 2 S 4$_{12}$, ברא pi. *cut out* signpost Ezk 21$_{24}$, כור *dig*, i.e. pierce Ps 22$_{17(mss)}$ (L כָּאֲרִי יָדַי appar. *like a lion, my hands*), נפץ pi. *shatter* Dn 12$_{7}$ (or em. כְּכַלּוֹת נַפֵּץ יַד *when he has accomplished the shattering of the power of* to כִּכְלוֹת יַד נֹפֵץ *when the power of the one who shatters comes to an end*), כלה *come to an end* Dn 12$_{7}$ (if em.; see above), דבק *adhere to* Si 13$_{1}$, תקע *blow*, i.e. sound, signal 1QM 8$_{5.7}$ 17$_{11}$, רוע hi. *blow*, i.e. sound, signal 1QM 8$_{12}$, רתק *bind* 11QMelch 3$_{6}$ ([יר]תקו ידי]ן]).

<CSTR> יַד־י׳ *hand of Y.* Ex 9$_{3}$ 16$_{3}$ Nm 11$_{23}$ Jos 4$_{24}$ 22$_{31}$ Jg 2$_{15}$ 1 S 5$_{6.9}$ 7$_{13}$ 12$_{15}$ 2 S 24$_{14}$||1 C 21$_{13}$ 1 K 18$_{46}$ Is 19$_{16}$ 25$_{10}$ 40$_{2}$ 41$_{20}$ 51$_{17}$ 59$_{1}$ 62$_{3}$ 66$_{14}$ Jr 25$_{17}$ 51$_{7}$ Ezk 1$_{3}$ 3$_{14.22}$ 33$_{22}$ 37$_{1}$ 40$_{1}$ Ps 75$_{9}$ Jb 12$_{9}$ Pr 21$_{1}$ Ru 1$_{13}$ Ezr 7$_{6.28}$ 1 C 28$_{18}$ 2 C 29$_{25}$ 4QpsEzek^{b} 1.3$_{1}$, אֲדֹנָי *of my Lord* Ezk 8$_{1}$, אלהים *of God* Si 10$_{4.5}$ 4QpPs^{a} 1.1$_{16}$ (אל[והי]ם), הָאֱלֹהִים *of God* 1 S 5$_{11}$ Ec 2$_{24}$ 9$_{1}$ 2 C 30$_{12}$, *of the gods* 1 S 4$_{8}$, אֱלֹהַי *of my God* Ezr 7$_{28}$ Ne 2$_{8.18}$, אֱלֹהָיו *of his God* Ezr 7$_{6.9}$, אֱלֹהֵינוּ *of our God* Ezr 8$_{18.22.31}$, אֱלוֹהַּ *of God* Jb 19$_{21}$, אֵל *of God* Jb 27$_{11}$ Si 43$_{12(B, M)}$ (Bmg לא a hand has *not*) 1QM 1$_{14}$ 18$_{1}$ 4QM^{a} 1$_{4}$, יד אל *hand of the God of* 1QM 18$_{3}$, יְדֵי אֲבִיר *hands of the mighty one of* Jacob Gn 49$_{24}$.

יַד *hand of, charge of*, + pr.n. Aaron Ex 29$_{9}$ Ps 77$_{21}$ 1 C 24$_{19}$, Abishai 2 S 10$_{10}$||1 C 19$_{11}$ 2 S 18$_{2}$, Absalom 2 S 16$_{8}$ 18$_{18}$ 3QTr 10$_{12}$, Ahab 1 K 18$_{9}$, Ahijah 1 K 12$_{15}$||2 C 10$_{15}$ 1 K 14$_{18}$ 15$_{29}$, Ahikam Jr 26$_{24}$, Asaph 1 C 16$_{7}$ 25$_{2}$, Azariah Arad ost. 16$_{6}$ (יד א[זריהו]), Benaiah 1 K 2$_{25}$, Ben-hadad 2 K 13$_{3}$ 13$_{25}$, Conaniah 2 C 31$_{13}$, Cushanrishathaim Jg 3$_{8}$, David 1 S 16$_{20}$ 2 S 3$_{8.18}$ 21$_{22}$||1 C 20$_{8}$ 1QM 11$_{2}$, Elasah Jr 29$_{3}$, Elijah 1 K 17$_{16}$ 2 K 9$_{36}$ 10$_{10}$, Elisha Arad ost. 24$_{15}$, Esau Gn 32$_{12}$, Ezekiel CD 3$_{21}$ 19$_{12}$, Gedaliah Jr 41$_{9}$ (or em. בְּיַד־גְּדַלְיָהוּ *by the hand of Gedaliah* to בּוֹר גָּדוֹל *a large cistern*), Gemariah Jr 29$_{3}$, Haggai Hg 1$_{1.3}$ 2$_{1}$, Hananiah 2 C 26$_{11}$, Hazael 2 K 13$_{3}$, Hegai Est 2$_{3.8}$, Isaiah Is 20$_{2}$ Si 48$_{20}$ CD 4$_{13}$, Ithamar Ex 38$_{21}$ Nm 4$_{28.33}$ 7$_{8}$, Ittai 2 S 18$_{2}$, Jabin Jg 4$_{2}$, Jacob Gn 27$_{17}$ 4QJub^{h} 35$_{16}$, Jehiel 1 C 29$_{8}$, Jehoahaz 2 K 13$_{25}$, Jehu 1 K 16$_{7.12}$, Jeiel 2 C 26$_{11(Qr)}$ (Kt Jeuel), Jeremiah Jr 37$_{2}$ 50$_{1}$ Si 49$_{7}$, Jeroboam 2 K 14$_{27}$, Jezebel 2 K 9$_{7}$, Joab 2 S 14$_{19}$ 18$_{2}$ 20$_{10}$, Jonah 2 K 14$_{25}$, Joseph Gn 39$_{6.22}$ 41$_{42}$, Joshua Jg 2$_{23}$ 1 K 16$_{34}$ 4QapJoshua^{a} 22.1$_{2}$, Maaseiah 2 C 26$_{11}$, Malachi Ml 1$_{1}$, Malchiah Arad ost. 24$_{13}$ (ד[י]), Meremoth Ezr 8$_{33}$, Mithredath Ezr 1$_{8}$, Moses Ex 9$_{35}$ 34$_{29}$ 35$_{29}$ Lv 8$_{36}$ 10$_{11}$ 26$_{46}$ Nm 4$_{37.45.49}$ 9$_{23}$ 10$_{13}$ 15$_{23}$ 17$_{5}$ 27$_{23}$ 33$_{1}$ 36$_{13}$ Jos 14$_{2}$ 20$_{2}$ 21$_{2.8}$ Jg 3$_{4}$ 1 K 8$_{53.56}$ Ps 77$_{21}$ Ne 8$_{14}$ 9$_{14}$ 10$_{30}$ 2 C 33$_{8}$ 34$_{14}$ 35$_{6}$ 1QM 10$_{6}$ 1QH 17$_{12}$ 1QS 1$_{3}$ 8$_{15}$ 4QD^{a} 1c$_{2}$ ([מושׁ]ה]) 11$_{1}$ 4QapJoshua^{a} 22.1$_{3}$ 4QapPs^{b} 69$_{5}$ ([משׁה]) 4QparaKings 104$_{7}$ 4Q418 184$_{1}$ 4Q419 1$_{2}$ 4Q423 11$_{1}$ ([מ]שׁה]) 4QDibHam^{a} 1.5$_{14}$ 4$_{8}$ ([מושׁ]ה]) CD 5$_{21}$, Nabal 1 S 25$_{39}$, Naomi Ru 4$_{5.9}$, Nathan 2 S 12$_{35}$, Nebuchadnezzar, Nebuchadrezzar Jr 21$_{7}$ 22$_{25}$ 27$_{6}$ 29$_{21}$ 32$_{28}$ 44$_{30}$ 46$_{26}$ Ezk 30$_{10}$ 1 C 5$_{41}$ CD 1$_{6}$, Nebuzaradan Jr 39$_{11}$, Samuel 1 C 11$_{3}$, Saul 1 S 23$_{12.17}$ 27$_{1}$ 2 S 12$_{7}$ Ps 18$_{1}$, Sennacherib 2 C 32$_{22}$, Shaashgaz Est 2$_{14}$, Shelemiah Lachish ost. 9$_{7}$, Shelomith 1 C 26$_{28}$, Shimei 2 C 31$_{13}$, Shishak 2 C 12$_{5.7}$, Simeon Mur 24 2$_{2}$ 4$_{2}$ ([שמעו]ן]) 5$_{2}$ 6$_{2}$ ([י]ד) ([שמעון]) 9$_{2}$ ([שמעו]ן]), Sisera 1 S 12$_{9}$, Solomon 1 K 2$_{46}$ 10$_{13}$ 11$_{31}$, Uriah 2 S 11$_{14}$, Zechariah CD 19$_{7}$, Zerubbabel Zc 4$_{10}$.

יְדֵי *hands of, directions of*, + pr.n. David Ezr 3$_{10}$, Elijah 2 K 3$_{11}$, Esau Gn 27$_{22.23}$, Jeduthun 1 C 25$_{3}$, Moses Ex 17$_{12}$, Nathan Ḥorvat 'Uza jar inscr. 1$_{2}$, Zerubbabel Zc 4$_{9}$.

יַד *hand of*, + Adullamite Gn 38$_{20}$, Amorite Gn 48$_{22}$ Dt 1$_{27}$ Jos 7$_{7}$, Aram(aeans) 2 K 13$_{5}$, Chaldaeans Jr 23$_{14}$ 32$_{4.24.25.29.43}$ 38$_{18}$ 43$_{3}$, Egypt(ians) Ex 3$_{8}$ 14$_{30}$ 18$_{9.10.10}$ Jg 6$_{9}$ 1 S 10$_{18}$ 2 S 23$_{21}$||1 C 11$_{23}$ 4QBibPar 14.1$_{5(mg)}$, Ephraim Ezk 37$_{19}$ 2 C 34$_{9}$, Ethiopians 2 C 21$_{16}$, Gershonite 1 C 29$_{8}$, Gibeonites 2 S 21$_{9}$, Gittite 2 S 18$_{2}$, Ishmaelite

Gn 39$_{1}$, Israel Jos 10$_{30.32}$ 11$_{8}$ Jg 3$_{20}$ 11$_{21}$ 1 S 14$_{12.37}$ Ezk 25$_{14}$ (or em.; see Prep.) 4QD^{f} 14.2$_{13}$, Judah 2 K 8$_{20.22}$ ||2 C 21$_{8.18}$, Kittite Arad ost. 17$_{9}$, Manasseh 2 C 34$_{9}$, Midian Jg 6$_{1.2}$ 8$_{22}$ 9$_{17}$, Moab 2 K 3$_{10.13}$, Philistine(s) Jg 10$_{7}$ 13$_{1.5}$ 15$_{12}$ 1 S 7$_{3.8.14}$ 9$_{16}$ 12$_{9}$ 17$_{37}$ 18$_{17.21.25}$ 28$_{19.19}$ 2 S 3$_{18}$ 8$_{1}$||1 C 18$_{1}$, Shilonite 1 K 12$_{15}$||2 C 10$_{15}$ 1 K 15$_{29}$, Tishbite 2 K 9$_{36}$, גּוֹיִם *of the nations* Ps 106$_{41}$ 1QpHab 5$_{3}$ (הגוים) 4QapJoseph^{b} 1$_{4.16}$ (both הגוים) 3$_{10}$ 11QT 57$_{7}$ (הגואים), כָּל־הַמַּמְלָכוֹת *of all the kingdoms* 1 S 10$_{18}$.

יַד אִישׁ *hand of a man* Gn 9$_{5}$ Lv 16$_{21}$ 1 S 12$_{4}$ Ezk 40$_{5}$ (הָאִישׁ) Est 6$_{9}$ 1QS 6$_{19}$ (האיש) 11QT 26$_{13}$ CD 11$_{19}$, הָאֲנָשִׁים *of the men* Jr 38$_{16}$ 39$_{17}$ Ezk 21$_{36}$ (אֲנָשִׁים), יְדֵי אַנְשֵׁי *hands of the men of* Jr 38$_{4}$, יַד אָדָם *hand of a human being* Gn 9$_{5}$ (הָאָדָם) 2 S 24$_{14}$||1 C 21$_{13}$ Ezk 10$_{8}$ 4Q423 13$_{4}$ (האדם), כָּל־אָדָם *of every human being* Jb 37$_{7}$ (or em.; see Prep.), יְדֵי אָדָם *hands of a human being* Ezk 1$_{8(Qr)}$ 10$_{21}$ 2 C 32$_{19}$ (הָאָדָם) 11QT 59$_{3}$, יַד אִשָּׁה *hand of a woman* Nm 5$_{25}$ (הָאִשָּׁה) Jg 4$_{9}$, אִשְׁתּוֹ *of his wife* Gn 19$_{10}$, יְדֵי נָשִׁים *hands of the women* Lm 4$_{10}$, יַד אָבִי *hand of my father* 1 S 19$_{3}$ 23$_{17}$, אָבִיו *of his father* Gn 48$_{17}$ 2 K 13$_{25}$, אֲבוֹתַי *of my fathers* 2 C 32$_{15}$, יְדֵי אֲבִיהֶם *hands*, i.e. directions, *of their father* 1 C 25$_{3.6}$, יַד ... בֶּן־ *hand of the son of* Ex 38$_{21}$ Lv 22$_{25}$ Nm 7$_{8}$ 2 S 18$_{2}$ 1 K 2$_{25}$ 16$_{7.12}$ (בֶּן־) 2 K 13$_{3.25}$ 14$_{25.27}$ Is 20$_{2}$ Jr 26$_{14}$ 29$_{3}$ Ezr 8$_{33}$ Arad ost. 24$_{13}$ (ב[י]ד) 24$_{15}$ CD 4$_{13}$, בִּנְךָ *of your son* 2 S 16$_{8}$ (בְּנֶךָ) 1 K 11$_{12}$, בְּנוֹ *of his son* 1 S 16$_{20}$ 1 K 11$_{35}$, בָּנָיו *of his sons* Gn 30$_{35}$ Ex 29$_{9}$, בְּנָהּ *of her son* Gn 27$_{17}$, בְּנֵי *of the sons of* Gn 33$_{19}$ Jos 9$_{26}$ Jg 4$_{24}$ 10$_{7}$ Ezk 23$_{9}$ Jl 4$_{8}$ Ps 144$_{7.11}$ 1 C 23$_{28}$ 2 C 13$_{8}$ 1QM 1$_{1}$ 4QapJoseph^{b} 1$_{15}$, שְׁתֵּי בְנֹתָיו *of his two daughters* Gn 19$_{16}$, אָחִי *of my brother* Gn 32$_{12}$, אָחִיו *of his brother* 2 S 10$_{10}$||1 C 19$_{11}$ 2 C 31$_{13}$, אֶחָיו *of his brothers* 1 C 16$_{7}$ 26$_{28}$ Si 50$_{12}$, יְדֵי ... אָחִיו *hands of ... his brother* Gn 27$_{23}$, אֲחֹתוֹ *of his sister* Gn 24$_{30}$.

יַד פַּרְעֹה *hand of Pharaoh* Gn 41$_{35}$ Ex 18$_{10}$ Dt 7$_{8}$ 2 K 17$_{7}$, הַמֶּלֶךְ *of the king* 1 S 23$_{20}$ 1 K 10$_{13}$ 13$_{6}$ 22$_{6.12}$||2 C 18$_{5.11}$ 1 K 22$_{15}$ Est 1$_{7}$ 2$_{18}$ Ne 11$_{24}$ 1 C 18$_{17}$ 2 C 30$_{6}$, מֶלֶךְ *of the king of* Dt 7$_{8}$ Jg 3$_{8}$ 4$_{2}$ 1 S 12$_{9}$ 1 K 22$_{3}$ 2 K 13$_{3}$ 17$_{7}$ 18$_{30.33}$||Is 36$_{15.18}$ 2 K 19$_{10}$||Is 37$_{10}$ Jr 20$_{4}$ 21$_{7.10}$ 22$_{25}$ 27$_{6}$ 29$_{21}$ 32$_{3.4.28.36}$ 34$_{2}$ 37$_{17}$ 38$_{23}$ 44$_{30}$ 46$_{26}$ Ezk 30$_{25}$ 2 C 28$_{5.5}$ 32$_{22}$ CD 1$_{6}$, מלכינו *of our kings* 1QM 11$_{3}$, מַלְכֵי *of the kings of* Ezr 9$_{7}$, שְׁנֵי מַלְכֵי *of the two kings of* Dt 3$_{8}$, מַלְכּוֹ *of his king* Zc 11$_{6}$, יד מלכיה[ם] *hand of their kings* 4QparaKings 10$_{4}$, יְדֵי הַמֶּלֶךְ *hands*, i.e. directions, *of the king* 1 C 25$_{2.6}$, יד שר *hand of a prince* 1QSb 4$_{24}$, יַד שַׂר *hand of the commander of* 1 S 12$_{9}$ 1QS 3$_{20}$ CD 5$_{18}$, שָׂרֵי *of the commanders of* 1 K 14$_{27}$||2 C 12$_{10}$, הַשָּׂרִים וְהַסְּגָנִים *of the princes and the rulers* Ezr 9$_{2}$, רַב *of the captain of* the bodyguards Jr 39$_{11}$, אֵיל *of the leader of* Ezk 31$_{11}$, גִּבּוֹר *of a warrior* Ps 127$_{4}$, אֲדֹנִים *of a master* Is 19$_{4}$, אֲדֹנִי *of my lord* 1 S 30$_{15}$, אֲדוֹנֵיהֶם *of their masters* Ps 123$_{2}$ 4QapJoshua^{a} 19.2$_{5}$ (אדונ[יהם]), גְּבִרְתָּהּ *of her mistress* Ps 123$_{2}$, [ ]י[ד משיח] *hand of the anointed one* 4QapMes 9$_{3}$, יד משיחיכה *hand of your anointed ones* 1QM 11$_{7}$, משיחו *of his anointed one* CD 2$_{12}$ (or em. מחישי *of the anointed ones of*), יד ... משרת *hand of the minister of* 4QapJoshua^{a} 22.1$_{2}$.

יַד ... עֶבֶד *hand of ... the servant of* Ne 10$_{30}$, עַבְדִּי *of my servant* 2 S 3$_{18}$, עַבְדְּךָ *of your servant* Jg 15$_{18}$ 1 K 8$_{53}$ (עַבְדֶּךָ) Ne 9$_{14}$ (עַבְדֶּךָ) 1QM 11$_{2}$ (עבדכה) 4QDibHam^{a} 1.5$_{14}$ (עבדכה), עַבְדּוֹ *of his servant* 1 K 8$_{56}$ 14$_{18}$ 15$_{29}$ 2 K 9$_{36}$ 10$_{10}$ 14$_{25}$, עֲבָדַי *of my servants* 2 K 17$_{13}$ Ezk 38$_{17}$ 4QpsMos^{e} 2.1$_{4}$ (ד[י]), עֲבָדֶיךָ *of your servants* Is 37$_{24}$ 2 C 34$_{16}$, כול עבדיך *of all your servants* 4QPrayers^{b} 2$_{4}$, עֲבָדָיו *of his servants* Gn 32$_{17}$ 2 S 10$_{2}$ 21$_{22}$||1 C 20$_{8}$ 1 K 15$_{18}$ 2 K 21$_{10}$ 24$_{2}$ Jr 46$_{26}$ Dn 9$_{10}$ Ezr 9$_{11}$ 2 C 8$_{18}$, כָּל־עֲבָדָיו *of all his servants* 2 K 17$_{23}$ 1QS 1$_{3}$ (כול), סְרִיס *of the eunuch of* Est 2$_{3.14}$, הַסָּרִיסִים *of the eunuchs* Est 1$_{12.15}$, הַגִּזְבָּר *of the treasurer* Ezr 1$_{8}$.

יַד רֵעֵהוּ *hand of his friend* Gn 38$_{20}$ Zc 11$_{6}$ (or em. רֵעֵהוּ to רֹעֵהוּ *of his shepherd*) 14$_{13.13}$, עֲמִיתֶךָ *of your neighbour* Lv 25$_{14}$, רֹעֵהוּ *of his shepherd* Zc 11$_{6}$ (if em.; see above), הָרֹעִים *of the shepherds* Ex 2$_{19}$, הַכֹּהֵן *of the priest* Ex 38$_{21}$ Nm 5$_{18}$ 7$_{8}$ Ezr 8$_{33}$, הַכֹּהֲנִים *of the priests* 2 C 23$_{18}$, כוהניו *of his priests* 4Q419 1$_{3}$, הַלֵּוִי *of the Levite* Jg 17$_{12}$, הַלְוִיִּם *of the Levites* 2 C 23$_{18}$ 24$_{11}$ 30$_{16}$, הַנָּבִיא *of the prophet* 2 S 12$_{35}$ 1 K 14$_{18}$ 16$_{7.12}$ 2 K 14$_{25}$ Jr 37$_{2}$ 50$_{1}$ Hg 1$_{1.3}$ 2$_{1}$ CD 3$_{21}$ 4$_{13}$ 19$_{7}$, הַנְּבִיאִים *of the prophets* 1 S 28$_{15}$ (הַנְּבִאִם) 2 K 17$_{13.23}$ 2 K 21$_{10}$ 24$_{2}$ Ho 12$_{11}$ Zc 7$_{7.12}$ Dn 9$_{10}$ Ezr 9$_{11}$ 1QS 1$_{3}$ 4QPrayers^{b} 2$_{4}$ 4QpsMos^{e} 2.1$_{4}$ (ד[י]), נְבִיאֵי *of the prophets of* Ezk 38$_{17}$, כָּל־נְבִיאֵי *of all the prophets of* 2 K 17$_{13(Qr)}$ (Kt נביאו *his* every *prophet*, ms נְבִיאָיו all *his prophets*, mss נָבִיא every *prophet*), נְבִיאֶיךָ *of your prophets* Ne 9$_{30}$, נְבִיאָיו *of his prophets* 2 C 29$_{25}$, הָעֵדִים *of the witnesses* Dt 17$_{7}$, יד מלאך *hand of the angel of* 1QS 3$_{20}$,

מלאכי *of the angels of* 4QMyst^{a} 35$_{2}$ ([מלאכן]) 4Qps Ezek^{c} 3.3$_{4}$, כול מלאכי *of all the angels of* 1QS 4$_{9}$ perh. CD 2$_{6}$ (ב׳), הַמַּלְאָכִים *of the messengers* 1 S 11$_{7}$ 2 K 19$_{14}$ ||Is 37$_{14}$ 27$_{3}$ (מַלְאָכִים), מַלְאָכֶיךָ *of your messengers* 2 K 19$_{23}$, מַלְאָכָיו *of his messengers* 2 C 36$_{15}$, הָרָצִים *of the runners*, i.e. couriers Est 3$_{13}$ 8$_{10}$, בחירו *of his chosen one* 1Qp Hab 5$_{4}$.

יַד הָעֲרֵלִים *hand of the uncircumcised* Jg 15$_{18}$, זָרִים *of foreigners* Ezk 7$_{21}$ (הַזָּרִים) 11$_{9}$ 28$_{10}$ 30$_{12}$, עָנִי וְאֶבְיוֹן *of the afflicted and poor* Ezk 16$_{49}$ CD 14$_{14}$, עני ואביון וגר *of the afflicted and poor and the sojourner* CD 6$_{21}$, יד אביונים *hand of the poor* 1QM 11$_{13}$, אביוני *of the poor of* 1QM 11$_{9}$, כורעי *of the prostrate of* 1QM 11$_{13}$, ידי נופלי[ם] *hands of those falling* 4QBark^{c} 1.1$_{1}$, יַד מְאַהֲבֶיהָ *hand of her lovers* Ezk 23$_{9}$, יד ידידיכה *hand of your beloved ones* 4QPrayer^{g} 1$_{2}$, יַד שֹׁמֵר *hand of the keeper* 1 S 17$_{22}$ Est 2$_{8}$ (שֹׁמֵר), הַצֹּפֶה *of the sentry* Ezk 33$_{6}$, הַשּׁוֹטֵר *of the officer* 2 C 26$_{11}$, הַסּוֹפֵר *of the secretary* 2 C 26$_{11}$, יְדֵי מוֹנֶה *hands of one who counts* Jr 33$_{13}$, יַד הַקֹּנֶה *hand of the one who purchases* Lv 25$_{28}$, הַנֹּדֵר *of the one who vows* Lv 27$_{8}$, עֹשֵׂי *of those who do* 2 K 22$_{5}$||2 C 34$_{10}$ (עֹשֵׂה *one who does*) 2 K 22$_{9}$||2 C 34$_{17}$ (עוֹשֵׂי), יְדֵי עֹשֵׂי *hands of those who do* 2 K 12$_{12(Qr)}$ (Kt יד *hand of*) Est 3$_{9}$, יַד חָרָשִׁים *hand of the artisans* 1 C 29$_{5}$, יְדֵי־חָרָשׁ *hands of an artisan* Jr 10$_{3}$, יְדֵי צוֹרֵף *hands of a goldsmith* Jr 10$_{9}$, יד המבקר *hand of the overseer* CD 14$_{13}$, יַד ... הַמְּפֻקָּדִים *hand of ... the overseers* 2 K 22$_{9}$||2 C 34$_{17}$, הַיּוֹצֵר *of the potter* Jr 18$_{4.6}$, יְדֵי יוֹצֵר *hands of the potter* Lm 4$_{2}$, יַד גֵּר וְתוֹשָׁב *hand of the sojourner and inhabitant* Lv 25$_{47}$, יָקוּשׁ *of the fowler* Pr 6$_{5}$ (mss מִפַּח *from the snare of*), ידי רופא *hands of the doctor* Si 38$_{15(Bmg)}$, יד כול משכילכה *hand of all your instructors* 4Q418 81$_{17}$, צדיקים *of the righteous* 11QPs^{a} 18$_{9}$, יַד חָרוּצִים *hand of the diligent* Pr 10$_{4}$ 12$_{24}$, כְּסִיל *of a fool* Pr 17$_{16}$ 26$_{6}$, שִׁכּוֹר *of a drunkard* Pr 26$_{9}$, יד בוטא *hand of one who speaks impetuously* Si 5$_{13}$ (A יוד בוטא, C יד בוטה), עצל *of a slothful one* 4Q424 1$_{6}$.

יַד רָעִים *hand of the evil ones* Jr 15$_{21}$ Ezk 30$_{12}$, מְרֵעִים *of evildoers* Jr 20$_{13}$ Jb 8$_{20}$, כל מרעים *of all evildoers* GnzPs 3$_{25}$, יְדֵי מְרֵעִים *hands of evildoers* Jr 23$_{14}$, יַד רָשָׁע *hand of the wicked one* Ps 71$_{4}$ Jb 9$_{24}$ 4QM^{a} 25$_{2}$, רְשָׁעִים *of wicked ones* Ps 36$_{12}$ 82$_{4}$ 97$_{10}$ 4QJonathan 1$_{9}$ ([יד רשעים]), יד ר[שעי] *hand of the wicked ones of* 4QpPs^{a} 3.4$_{21}$, יְדֵי רָשָׁע *hands of the wicked one* Ezk 13$_{22}$ Ps 140$_{5}$, רְשָׁעִים *of wicked ones* Jb 16$_{11}$, יד חלכאים *hand of the wicked ones* 1QH 4$_{25}$, בליעל *of Belial* 4QMidrEschat^{b} 11$_{12}$ CD 8$_{2}$=19$_{14}$ 11Q Melch 2$_{13}$ ([יד]) 2$_{25}$ ([י]ד), יַד אוֹיֵב *hand of the enemy* Lv 26$_{25}$ Ps 31$_{9.16}$ 106$_{10}$ Lm 2$_{7}$, אֹיְבֵי *of the enemies of* 1 S 20$_{16}$, אֹיְבָיו *of his enemies* 2 S 18$_{19}$ Jr 44$_{30}$ 1QpHab 9$_{10}$ (אויביו), אֹיְבֵינוּ *of our enemies* 1 S 12$_{10}$, אֹיְבֵיכֶם *of your enemies* 1 S 12$_{11}$ 4QpsEzek^{c} 1$_{7}$ (אי[בי]כם), כָּל־אֹיְבֵיכֶם *of all your enemies* 2 K 17$_{39}$, אֹיְבֵיהֶם *of their enemies* Jg 2$_{14}$ (אוֹיְבֵיהֶם) 2$_{18}$ 2 K 21$_{14}$ Jr 20$_{5}$ 21$_{7}$ 34$_{20.21}$ Ne 9$_{28}$ 4QpsMos^{e} 1$_{8}$ 11QT 59$_{11}$ (אויביהמה), כָּל־אֹיְבֵיהֶם *of all their enemies* Jg 8$_{34}$ 2 S 3$_{18}$, צָר *of the adversary* Ps 78$_{61}$ 107$_{2}$ Jb 6$_{23}$ Lm 1$_{7}$ (צָר), יד צרים *hand of adversaries* 4QJonathan 1$_{9}$, יַד צָרֵיהֶם *hand of their adversaries* Ezk 39$_{23}$ Ne 9$_{27.27}$.

יַד עָרִיצִים *hand of the terrible ones* Jb 6$_{23}$ 4QBark^{a} 1.2$_{5}$, עריצי *of the terrible ones of* 4QpPs^{a} 1.2$_{19}$ 3.4$_{10}$ (עריצ[י]), שׂוֹנֵא *of the one who hates* Ps 106$_{10}$, שונאיו *of those who hate him* 11QT 59$_{18}$, כָּל־הַקָּמִים *of all those who rise up* 2 S 18$_{31}$, גֹּאֵל *of the avenger of* blood Nm 35$_{25}$ Dt 19$_{12}$ Jos 20$_{9}$, נוקמי *of the avengers of* 4QBer^{f} 1$_{3}$, כול נוקמי *of all the avengers of* 1QS 2$_{6}$, כול משלמי *of all those who recompense* 1QS 2$_{6}$, מַכֵּהוּ *of the one who strikes him* Dt 25$_{11}$, שֹׁסִים *of plunderers* Jg 2$_{14}$ 2 K 17$_{20}$, שֹׁסֵהוּ *of the one plundering him* 1 S 14$_{48}$, שֹׁסֵיהֶם *of ones plundering them* Jg 2$_{16}$, חותפו *of the one who snatches him away* Si 15$_{14}$, עוֹשֵׁק *of the oppressor* Jr 21$_{12}$, עֹשְׁקֵיהֶם *of their oppressors* Ec 4$_{1}$, עָשׁוֹק *of the oppressor* Jr 22$_{3}$ (or em. עֹשְׁקוֹ *of his oppressor*), כָּל־לֹחֲצֵיכֶם *of all your oppressors* Jg 6$_{9}$, הָעֹבְדִים *of those who enslave* Ezk 34$_{27}$, מוֹגַיִךְ *of your tormentors* Is 51$_{23}$, הוֹרֵג *of the slayer* Ezk 21$_{16}$, מְחַלְלֶיךָ *of those who pierce you* Ezk 28$_{9}$, מְבַקְשֵׁי *of those who seek* Jr 19$_{7}$ 21$_{7}$ 22$_{25}$ 34$_{20.21}$ 44$_{30}$ 46$_{26}$ Si 51$_{3}$ 11QT 59$_{18}$, זעירים *of inferiors* Si 11$_{6}$, חָזָק *of a strong one* Jr 31$_{11}$ Jb 5$_{15}$ 1QH 2$_{35}$, גדולו *of his great one* 4QpIsa^{a} 8$_{8}$, אדירים *of mighty ones* 1QH 2$_{35}$, יַד חַיִל *hand of the army of* Jr 34$_{21}$ 38$_{3}$ 1QpHab 9$_{6}$, המחזיקים *of those who hold* 4QpsEzek^{c} 3.2$_{5}$, נכבדי[ו] *of his honoured ones* 4Q419 6$_{1}$, יד ראשי *hand of the heads of* 1QSa 1$_{23}$.

יַד הָעָם *hand of the people* Jr 26$_{24}$, כָּל־הָעָם *of all the people* Dt 13$_{10}$ 17$_{7}$ 1 S 13$_{22}$, עַם *of the people of* Jr 46$_{24}$ Dn 12$_{7}$ Ezr 4$_{4}$, עַמֵּי *of the peoples of* Ne 9$_{30}$, עַמִּי *of my people* Ezk 25$_{14}$ (or em.; see Prep.) 4QapJoseph^{b} 2$_{8}$, יְדֵי כָל־הָעָם *hands of all the people* Jr 38$_{4}$, יְדֵי עַם *hands of the people of* Ezk 7$_{27}$, יד זר[ים] *hand of strangers* 11QPs^{a} 18$_{15}$, יד רוחי

hand of the spirits of 4QPrayer^{d} 24 11QMelch 2_{13} (כול [רו]חי), יְדֵי אֲשֶׁר *hand of those who* Jr 22_{25} Ezk $23_{28.28}$, יְדֵי לֹא־אוּכַל קוּם *the hands of those whom I cannot withstand* Lm 1_{14} (or em. יְדֵי to יָדוֹ *his hand*), יַד כֹּל *hand of everyone* 2 C 32_{22} 4Q418 102_{3} (כול).

יד גבורת *hand of the might of* 1QM 3_{8}, יד גבורתו *hand of his might* 4QShirShabb^{d} 1.1_{39} 4QPrQuot 1.3_{5} (גבורת[ו]), יד גבורתכה *hand of your might* 1QM $13_{12.14}$ 18_{11}, ידי גבורת *hands of the might of* 1QH fr. 48_{4}, יד חסידכה *hand of your loyal one* 1QM 18_{11}, נאמנך *of your faithful one* GnzPs 2_{11}, ידי נאמנו *hands of his faithful one* GnzPs 4_{6}.

יַד־יְמִין *right hand of* 2 S 20_{9}, יַד יְמִינִי *my right hand* Jr 22_{24} Ps 73_{23}, יַד יְמִינְךָ *your right hand* Ezk 39_{3} Ps 121_{5} (יְמִינֶךָ), יַד־יְמִינוֹ *his right hand* Gn 48_{17} Jg 3_{15} 20_{16}, יְמִינָם *their right hand* Jg 7_{20}, יַד שְׂמֹאולֶךָ *your left hand* Ezk 39_{3}, יַד שְׂמֹאלוֹ *his left hand* Jg 3_{21} 1QS 7_{15} (שמאולו), יַד־שְׂמֹאולָם *their left hand* Jg 7_{20}.

יַד הָאֲרִי *hand of the lion* 1 S 17_{37}, הַדֹּב *of the bear* 1 S 17_{37}, כָּל־חַיָּה *of every beast* Gn 9_{5}, יַד בֵּית *hand of the house of* Jg 13_{5}, יד כול אוט *hand of every storehouse* of human beings 4Q418 126.2_{2}, יַד־תִּשְׁלָח *hand of (the one whom) you will send* Ex 4_{13}, יַד־מִי *hand of whom?* 1 S 12_{3}, יַד אֶחָד *hand of one of* Jg 17_{5}, יַד כֹּל *hand of everyone* Gn 16_{12} 4QparaKings 31_{2} (כול) 4Q418 81_{7} (כול), יַד־כֻּלָּם *hand of all of them* Jg 7_{16}, יְדֵי כָל־אֲשֶׁר *hands of all who* 2 S 16_{21}, יְדֵי פָח *hands of the trap*, i.e. snares Ps 141_{9}, יד הכידן *hand*, i.e. hilt, *of Spanish sword* 1QM 5_{14}.

יַד הַיְאֹר *side of the Nile* Ex 2_{5}, הַיַּרְדֵּן *of the Jordan* Nm 13_{29}, כִּתִּים *of the Kittim* Nm 24_{24}, הַנָּהָר *of the river* Dn 10_{4}, נְהַר *of the river of* Jr 46_{6}, נַחַל *of the wadi of* Dt 2_{37}, אַשְׁדּוֹד *of Ashdod* Jos 15_{46}, דֶּרֶךְ *of the way of* 1 S $4_{13(Qr)}$ 2 S 15_{2} Ezk 48_{1} (or em. דֶּרֶךְ to הַיָּם *of the sea*; or em. אֶל־יַד *to the side of* to מִן־הַיָּם *from the sea* by way of), מַעְגָּל *of the way* Ps 140_{6}, הַשַּׁעַר *of the gate* 1 S 4_{18} 2 S 18_{4}, שְׁעָרִים *of the gates* Pr 8_{3}, יַד שְׁנֵי צַנְתְּרוֹת *side of the two pipes of* Zc 4_{12}, יד החרף *side of the catapult* 4QM^{c} 1_{5}.

יְדֵי אֱדוֹם *side(s) of Edom* Nm 34_{3}, אַרְנוֹן *of the Arnon* Jg 11_{26}, סֶלַע *of the rock* Ps 141_{6}, ידות כ[לים] *handles of vessels* 4QMMT B_{22}, יְדֵי כְלֵי *side of the instruments of* 2 C 29_{27}, יְדֵי־בְנֵי *side of the sons of* 1 C 7_{29}, יְדוֹת הָאוֹפַנִּים *axletrees of the wheels* 1 K 7_{32}.

יַד לָשׁוֹן *power of the tongue* Pr 18_{21}, לֶהָבָה *of the flame* Is 47_{14}, יְדֵי חָרֶב *power of the sword* Jr 18_{21} Ezk 35_{5} Ps 63_{11} Jb 5_{20} (all three חָרֶב) 4QapPs^{b} 31_{7}, יַד־עֲוֹנֵנוּ *power of our iniquities* Is 64_{6}, פִּשְׁעָם *of their transgression* Jb 8_{4}, אשמה *of guilt* 4QShir^{b} 20.1_{3}, שְׁאוֹל *of Sheol* Ho 13_{14} Jb 17_{16} (יְדֵי שְׁאֹל; if em. בַּדֵּי *bars of* to בִּידֵי *into the power of*) Ps 49_{16} 89_{49} Si 51_{2}, עָמָל *of misery* Jb 20_{22} (if em. עָמֵל *of a sufferer*), כֶּלֶב *of the dog* Ps 22_{21}, יד אסון *hand of danger* Si $41_{9(Bmg)}$ (B ידי *hands of*), יד נפשך *hand of your soul*, i.e. control of your desire Si 6_{2}, בשר *of flesh* 1QH 15_{12}, יצרו *of his inclination* Si 15_{14}, ייד פשעיכה *power of your transgressions* 4QJub^{d} 21_{22}, יְדֵי־שִׁיר *charge of the song of* 1 C 6_{16}, יד המערכה *side of the battle formation* 1QM 8_{2} 16_{6}, יד מלחמה *power of war* 1QM 4_{3}, ידי מלחמה *sides*, i.e. flanks, *of battle* 1QM 9_{7}, perh. *signal of*, i.e. for, *battle* 1QM 8_{12}, יידי התקרב *signal of*, i.e. for, *confrontation* 1QM 17_{11}, ידי סדר *signal of*, i.e. for, *the order* of battle 1QM 8_{5}, מפשע *of*, i.e. for, *advance* 1QM 8_{7}, יד כולמ[ה] *hand of all of them* 1QMyst 1_{9}.

חכמי ידים *those who are wise of*, i.e. skilful with their, *hands* Si 9_{17}, רְפֵה יָדַיִם *(one) weak of strength* 2 S 17_{2}, קִצְרֵי־יָד *(ones) short of strength* 2 K 19_{26}||Is 37_{2}, טְהָר־יָדַיִם *pure one of hands*, i.e. whose hands are pure Jb 17_{9}, בֹּר יָדַי *cleanness of my hands* 2 S 22_{21}||Ps 18_{21}.

זְרֹעֵי יָדָיו *arms of his hands*, i.e. his arms Gn 49_{24} (or em. גִּידֵי זְרֹעָיו *sinews of his arms*), כַּפּוֹת הַיָּדַיִם *palms of the hand* 2 K 9_{35}, יָדָיו *of his hands* 1 S 5_{4}, אֶצְבְּעֹת יָדָיו *fingers of his hands* 2 S 21_{20} 4QCrypt 1.3_{4} (אצבעות) 2.1_{4}, בֹּהֶן יָדָם *thumb of their hand* Ex 29_{20} Lv 8_{24}, יָדוֹ *of his hand* Lv 8_{23} $14_{14.17.25.28}$, [אצבעות י]דיהא *fingers of her hands* 4QJub^{g} 25_{11}, בְּהֹנוֹת יְדֵיהֶם *the thumbs of his hands* Jg 1_{6}, יְדֵיהֶם *of their hands* Jg 1_{7}, אַצִּלוֹת יָדֶיךָ *joints of your hands*, i.e. your armpits Jr 38_{12}, אַצִּילֵי יָדַי *joints of my hands* Ezk 13_{18} (or em. יָד or יָדַיִם *of [your/their] hands*), חִבֻּק יָדַיִם *folding of the hands* Pr 6_{10} 24_{33}.

שִׁפְלוּת יָדַיִם *sinking of hands*, i.e. negligence Ec 10_{18}, שפול ידים *sinking of hands*, i.e. negligence 1QS 4_{9}, רִפְיוֹן יָדַיִם *weakness of hands* Jr 47_{3} Si 25_{23}, חֶזְקַת הַיָּד *grasping of the hand* Is 8_{11}, חֹזֶק יָד *strength of hand* Ex $13_{3.9.16}$, חזוק ידים *strength of hands* 1QS 10_{26}, [כו]ח יד *strength of the hand of* 4QPrQuot 1.3_{5}, כֹּחַ יָדִי *strength of my hand* Is 10_{13}, כוח ידכה *strength of your hand* 1QM 11_{1} 1QH 4_{35} 4Q418 88_{4}, כֹּחַ יְדֵיהֶם *strength of their hands* Jb 30_{2}, עוז

ידו *strength of his hand* 4QHod^{a} 7.1$_{16}$, אל ידנו *power of our hand* 4QapLam^{a} 1$_{2}$, עֹצֶם יָדְךָ *power of your hand* Jb 30$_{21}$ Pr 3$_{27(Qr)}$ (Kt ידיך), עצום ידינו *power of our hands* 1QM 11$_{5}$, אֵל יָדִי *power of my hand* Gn 31$_{29}$ Si 5$_{1}$, יָדְךָ *of your hand* Dt 28$_{32}$ Si 14$_{11}$, יָדֵינוּ *of our hand* Ne 5$_{5}$, יָדָם *of their hand* Mc 2$_{1}$, עֹצֶם יָדִי *might of my hand* Dt 8$_{17}$, גבורת ידכה *might of your hand* 1QM 11$_{11}$, ארך ידכה *length of your hand*, i.e. your ability 4QTobit^{e} 2$_{6}$, מֶמְשֶׁלֶת יָדוֹ *rule of his hand* Jr 34$_{1}$, חכמת ידים *wisdom*, i.e. skill, *of hands* 4Q418 81$_{15}$ 137$_{2}$ (חכ[מת]), ידיכה *of your hands* 4Q418 81$_{19}$ 102$_{3}$ (with erasure of ידים *of hands*) 139$_{2}$ (חוכמת), ידיו *of his hands* 4Q424 3$_{7}$.

עִצְּבוֹן יָדֵינוּ *toil of our hands* Gn 5$_{29}$, מעשה ידים *work of hands* 4QapJoshua^{a} 15.1$_{2}$, מַעֲשֵׂה יָדְךָ *work of your hand* Dt 2$_{7}$ (יָדֶךָ) 14$_{29}$ 28$_{12}$ (יָדֶךָ) 30$_{9}$ (יָדֶךָ) Is 64$_{7}$, יְדֵי *of the hands of* Dt 4$_{28}$ 27$_{15}$ 2 K 19$_{18}$||Is 37$_{19}$ Jr 10$_{3.9}$ Ps 115$_{4}$ 135$_{15}$ Ca 7$_{2}$ Lm 4$_{2}$ 2 C 32$_{19}$, יָדַי *of my hands* Is 19$_{25}$ 29$_{23}$ 60$_{21}$, יָדֶיךָ *of your hands* Dt 16$_{15}$ 24$_{19}$ Mc 5$_{12}$ Ps 102$_{26}$ 143$_{5}$ Jb 14$_{15}$ Ec 5$_{5}$, יָדָיו *of his hands* Ps 19$_{2}$ 28$_{5}$ Jb 1$_{10}$ 34$_{19}$, יָדֵינוּ *of our hands* Ho 14$_{4}$ Ps 90$_{17}$, יְדֵיכֶם *of your* (pl.) *hands* Dt 31$_{29}$ Jr 25$_{6.7}$ Hg 2$_{17}$, יְדֵיהֶם *of their hands* 2 K 22$_{17}$||2 C 34$_{25}$ (מַעֲשֵׂי *works of*) Is 65$_{22}$ Jr 25$_{14}$ 32$_{30}$ Hg 2$_{14}$ Ps 28$_{4}$ Lm 3$_{64}$ GnzPs 2$_{20}$, יָדָיו *of his hands* 1 K 16$_{7}$ Is 2$_{8}$ 5$_{12}$ 17$_{8}$, מעשי ידי *works of the hands of* 4QDibHam^{c} 13$_{14}$ (מ[עשי]) 11QT 59$_{3}$, מַעֲשֵׂי יָדֶיךָ *works of your hands* Ps 8$_{7}$ 92$_{5}$ 138$_{8}$ 1QLitPr 3.2$_{7}$ 4QDibHam^{a} 7$_{4}$ (ידיכה), מַעֲשֵׂי יָדָיו *works of his hands* Ps 111$_{7}$, מַעֲשֵׂי יְדֵיכֶם *works of your hands* Jr 44$_{8}$, מַעֲשֵׂי יְדֵיהֶם *works of their hands* Jr 1$_{16}$, פֹּעַל יָדַי *work of my hands* Is 45$_{11}$, פֹּעַל יָדָיו *deed of his hands* Dt 33$_{11}$ Si 14$_{19}$, אָרְבּוֹת יָדָיו *skill of his hands* Is 25$_{11}$, השיגת ידך *attainment of your hand* Si 14$_{13}$, משפטי ידו *judgments of his hand(s)* 4QShir^{b} 10$_{12}$ (if em. יוד *yodh*, appar. in ref. to י).*

תרומת יד *offering of the hand* Si 7$_{32}$, תְּרוּמַת יָדְךָ *offering of your hand* Dt 12$_{17}$, יֶדְכֶם *of your* (pl.) *hand* Dt 12$_{6.11}$ (תְּרֻמַת), נִדְבַת יָדְךָ *freewill offering of your hand* Dt 16$_{10}$, מַתְּנַת יָדוֹ *gift of his hand* Dt 16$_{17}$, מַתַּת יָדוֹ *gift of his hand* Ezk 46$_{5.11}$, תְּשׂוּמֶת יָד *placing of the hand*, i.e. security Lv 5$_{21}$, משלוח יד *outstretching of hand of* 1QM 1$_{1}$, ידיכה *of your hands* 4Q418 87$_{13}$, משלח ידי *outstretching of my hand* 1QS 10$_{13}$, מִשְׁלַח יָדְךָ *outstretching of your hand* Dt 12$_{18}$ 15$_{10}$ 23$_{21}$ (יָדֶךָ) 28$_{8}$ (יָדֶךָ) 28$_{20}$ (יָדְךָ), יֶדְכֶם *of your* (pl.) *hand* Dt 12$_{7}$, מִשְׁלוֹחַ יָדָם *outstretching of their hand* Is 11$_{14}$, תְּנוּפַת יַד *waving of the hand of* Is 19$_{16}$, מֹעַל יְדֵיהֶם *lifting of their hands* Ne 8$_{6}$, שאת יד *lifting up of the hand of* 1QM 18$_{3}$, משוב יד *return of the hand of* 4QShirShabb^{d} 1.1$_{39}$, גְּמוּל יָדָיו *recompense of his hands* Jg 9$_{16}$ Is 3$_{11}$, יְדֵי *of the hands of* Pr 12$_{14}$, פְּרִי יָדֶיהָ *fruit of her hands* Pr 31$_{31}$, תִּגְרַת יָדְךָ *hostility of your hand* Ps 39$_{11}$, חֲמַס יְדֵיכֶם *violence of your hands* Ps 58$_{3}$, מלחמות ידיכה *wars of your hands* 1QM 11$_{8}$, מפקד יד *deposit of the hand* Si 42$_{7(Bmg)}$, כָּל־בַּעַל מַשֵּׁה יָדוֹ perh. *every possessor of a pledge of*, i.e. under, *their control* Dt 15$_{2}$ (or ins. מַשֵּׁה אֶת־ every possessor of *a pledge* is to release the pledge under their control) 11QMelch 2$_{3}$ (יד),* מַשָּׁא כָּל־יָד *debt of every hand*, i.e. person Ne 10$_{32}$, נחלת ידו *inheritance of his hand* 4QTanḥ 18$_{1}$.

שֶׁבֶר יָד *fracture of the hand* Lv 21$_{19}$, אֶבֶן יָד *stone of*, i.e. in, *the hand* Nm 35$_{17}$, כְּלִי עֵץ יָד *weapon of wood of*, i.e. in, *the hand* Nm 35$_{18}$, מַקֵּל יָד *staff of the hand* Ezk 39$_{9}$, צֵל יָדִי *shadow of my hand* Is 51$_{16}$, יָדוֹ *of his hand* Is 49$_{2}$, תַּבְנִית יָד *form of a hand* Ezk 8$_{3}$, תַּבְנִית יַד *form of a hand of* Ezk 10$_{8}$, דְּמוּת יְדֵי *likeness of the hands of* Ezk 10$_{21}$, יוצר יד *form of*, i.e. thing formed by, *hand* 1QS 11$_{22}$, חַיַּת יָדֵךְ *life*, i.e. vigour, *of your hand* Is 57$_{10}$ (or em. דֵּי חַיָּתֵךְ *sufficiency of your life*), צֹאן יָדוֹ *the flock of his hand* Ps 95$_{7}$ (unless יָד III *love*; or em. צֹאן מַרְעִיתוֹ דְּעוּ יָדוֹ *the flock of his pasturing; know his power*), סְחֹרַת יָדֵךְ *merchandise of your rule*, i.e. under your control Ezk 27$_{15}$, סֹחֲרֵי *merchants of* Ezk 27$_{21}$.

רַחֲבַת־יָדַיִם *wide of both hands*, i.e. on both sides Gn 34$_{21}$ Jg 18$_{10}$ Is 22$_{18}$ 33$_{21}$ Ne 7$_{4}$ 1 C 4$_{40}$, רְחַב *wide of* Ps 104$_{25}$, עמק ידת perh. *valley of sides* Ophel ost.$_{2.3}$ (others read ידת in both as יהו[שפט] *of Jehoshaphat*; others ירת *of Jereth*), מקום היד *place of the latrine* 1QM 7$_{7}$ 11QT 46$_{13}$ (יד), מקום ידים *place of hands* Si 42$_{6}$.

שְׁתֵּי יָדָיו *his two hands* Lv 16$_{21(Qr)}$, יָדַי *my two hands* Dt 9$_{15.17}$ (יָדָי), שְׁתֵּי יָדוֹת *two tenons/divisions* Ex 26$_{17}$||36$_{22}$ (יָדֹת) 2 K 11$_{7}$ (הַיָּדוֹת) 11QT 58$_{8}$ (הידות), שְׁתֵּי יְדֹתָיו *its two tenons* Ex 26$_{19.19}$||36$_{24.24}$, כָּל־הַיָּד *all the strength* Dt 34$_{12}$, כָּל־יַד *every side of* Dt 2$_{37}$, *all the strength of* Jb 20$_{22}$, כָּל־יָדַיִם *every pair of hands* Jr 48$_{37}$ Ezk 7$_{17}$ 21$_{12}$.

<APP> אִשָּׁה *woman*, i.e. each one Ex 26$_{17}$, אֶחָד *(each)*

one Ex 36$_{22}$, לוּחַ plate 1 K 7$_{36}$, קוֹל sound 1QM 8$_{5.7.12}$, תרועה trumpet blast 1QM 17$_{11}$.

<ADJ> חָזָק *strong* Ex 3$_{19}$ 6$_{1.1}$ 13$_{9}$ 32$_{11}$ Nm 20$_{20}$ Dt 3$_{24}$ 4$_{34}$ 5$_{15}$ 6$_{21}$ 7$_{8.19}$ 9$_{26}$ 11$_{2}$ 26$_{8}$ 34$_{12}$ 1 K 8$_{42}$ Jr 32$_{21}$, Ezk 20$_{33.34}$ Ps 136$_{12}$ Dn 9$_{15}$ Ne 1$_{10}$ 2 C 6$_{32}$ 1QH 2$_{35}$, רָפֶה *weak* Is 35$_{3}$ Jb 4$_{3}$ Si 42$_{6(B)}$ 4QM^{a} 8$_{4}$ ([ידי]ם), גָּדוֹל *great* Ex 14$_{31}$ 1QM 1$_{14}$ 18$_{1}$ 4QMidrEschat^{b} 11$_{14}$, רַב pl. *many* Si 42$_{6(M)}$, טוֹב *good* Ezr 7$_{9}$ 8$_{18}$ Ne 2$_{8}$, יְמָנִי *right* Ex 29$_{20}$ Lv 8$_{23.24}$ 14$_{14.17.25.28}$, אֶחָד *one* Ne 4$_{11}$.

<PREP> לְ *(in)to* Pr 11$_{21}$ 16$_{5}$, + בוא *come* 1QM 8$_{2}$, אנה pi. *allow to come* Ex 21$_{13}$, תקע ni. *be struck*, i.e. stand surety for Jb 17$_{3}$.

לְ *at* (לְיַד perh. as compound prep. *beside*) 1 S 4$_{13}$ (if em.; see Coll.) Ne 11$_{24}$ 1 C 18$_{17}$ 23$_{28}$ 1QM 8$_{4}$ perh. 4Q M^{c} 1$_{5}$, + עמד *stand* 1 S 19$_{3}$ 1QM 16$_{6}$, שִׁית *place* Ps 140$_{6}$, רנן *cry out* Pr 8$_{3}$; *for*, i.e. to receive (tenons), + עָשָׂה *make* Ex 26$_{19.19}$||36$_{24.24}$; *for, with respect to* Dt 34$_{12}$; appar. *by (means of)*, + ברך pi. *bless* 1QSb 3$_{28}$; *for (one who acts with)* 4QS^{d} 3.1$_{2}$ (=1QS 9$_{1}$ ביד *with* a high *hand*).

בְּ of place, *in(to), at* (distinction from בְּ of instrument not alw. clear; sometimes בְּיַד perh. as compound prep. *beside, in the power of*, etc.; at 1 S 21$_{14}$ Is 64$_{66}$ Ezk 37$_{19}$ Jb 9$_{4}$ 15$_{23}$ 27$_{11}$ בְּיַד is perh. a variant of בְּעַד *for, because of, on behalf of, for the sake of*),* Gn 16$_{6}$ 24$_{10}$ 35$_{4}$ 38$_{18}$ 39$_{23}$ 40$_{11}$ 43$_{26}$ Ex 4$_{2}$ 7$_{17}$ 12$_{11}$ 17$_{9}$ 32$_{15}$ 34$_{29}$ Nm 4$_{28.33}$ 7$_{8}$ 22$_{7.29}$ 31$_{6.49}$ Dt 10$_{3}$ 33$_{3}$ (or em. בְּיָדֶךָ *in your hand* to בֵּרַךְ *he blessed*) Jos 8$_{18.18}$ 9$_{25}$ Jg 6$_{21}$ 7$_{19}$ 8$_{6.15}$ 14$_{6}$ 1 S 2$_{13}$ 4$_{18}$ (if em.; see below) 14$_{27.43}$ 17$_{40.50.57}$ 19$_{9}$ 22$_{6}$ 24$_{12.12}$ 26$_{18}$ 2 S 20$_{10}$ 23$_{21}$||1 C 11$_{23}$ 2 K 11$_{8.11}$||2 C 23$_{7.10}$ Is 6$_{6}$ 10$_{5}$ (or em. בְּיוֹם *in the day of*) Jr 18$_{6.6}$ 21$_{4}$ 26$_{14}$ 38$_{5}$ 41$_{5}$ 51$_{7}$ Ezk 2$_{9}$ 8$_{11}$ 9$_{1.2}$ 23$_{37.45}$ 28$_{9}$ 37$_{19}$ 40$_{3.5}$ 47$_{3}$ Ho 12$_{8}$ Am 7$_{7}$ Zc 2$_{5}$ 4$_{10.12}$ 8$_{4}$ Ps 26$_{10}$ 31$_{16}$ 75$_{9}$ 95$_{4}$ 127$_{4}$ 149$_{6}$ Jb 1$_{12}$ 2$_{6}$ 11$_{14}$ 12$_{10}$ 21$_{5}$ Pr 17$_{16}$ 18$_{21}$ 21$_{1}$ Ec 5$_{13}$ 9$_{1}$ (perh. בְּיַד = *from* God)* Est 5$_{2}$ Dn 11$_{16}$ 1 C 29$_{12}$ 2 C 13$_{8}$ 20$_{6}$ 26$_{19}$ Si 5$_{13}$ 10$_{4.5}$ 38$_{13}$ 50$_{13}$ 1QH 5$_{4}$ (י[ד]כה) 11$_{7}$ 15$_{12.13}$ fr. 2$_{7}$ fr. 6$_{13}$ fr. 13$_{4}$ 1QM 5$_{6}$ 7$_{14}$ 18$_{13}$ 1QS 3$_{16.20.20}$ 10$_{16}$ 11$_{2}$ perh. 1Q26 2$_{4}$ 1QSb 1$_{5}$ 4$_{23}$ 3QTr 12$_{2}$ perh. 4QpIsa^{a} 8$_{20.24}$ perh. 4QpUnid 3$_{1}$ 4QTobit^{e} 5$_{2}$ perh. 8$_{3}$ 4QD^{a} 11$_{9}$ 4Q Myst^{a} 21$_{2}$ 31$_{4}$ 35$_{2}$ 77$_{2}$ 4QMyst^{b} 11$_{2}$ 4QapJoseph^{b} 1$_{15.18}$ perh. 4QapPs^{b} 102$_{2}$ perh. 4QparaKings 124$_{2}$ 4Qps Ezek^{b} 1.3$_{1}$ 4QpsEzek^{c} 1$_{7}$ 4Q416 3$_{2}$ 4Q418 81$_{10}$ perh. 88$_{7}$ perh. 91$_{17}$ 126.2$_{12}$ 172$_{13}$ (ב[י]דכה) perh. 223$_{1}$ 4Q423 5$_{4}$ perh. 4QPrayer^{d} 2$_{4}$ perh. 4QM^{a} 25$_{2}$ 4QDibHam^{a} 3.2$_{19}$ perh. 4QShir^{b} 18.2$_{10}$ 20.1$_{3}$ 42$_{8}$ 11QPs^{a} 19$_{3}$ 11QT 26$_{6}$ (בי[די]) GnzPs 3$_{22}$.

+ היה *be* Lv 25$_{28}$ Nm 5$_{18}$ 2 S 8$_{10}$ Is 62$_{3}$ Ezk 13$_{21}$ 37$_{17.19}$ 1QM 7$_{12}$, ידע *know* 1QH 15$_{12}$, עמד *stand* CD 5$_{18}$, קום *rise* 1 S 24$_{21}$, נפל *fall* Jg 15$_{18}$ 2 S 21$_{22.22}$||1 C 20$_{8.8}$ 2 S 24$_{14.14}$||1 C 21$_{13.13}$ Lm 1$_{7}$ Si 6$_{2}$ 8$_{1}$ 4QJub^{h} 36$_{9}$ (ביד[ו יפול]), הלך htp. *go* 1QMyst 1$_{9}$, בוא *come* Gn 32$_{14}$, hi. *bring* Jb 12$_{6}$, ירד *go down* 1 S 23$_{6}$ Jb 17$_{16}$ (if em.; see Cstr.), hi. *bring down* Gn 43$_{22}$, עלה *go up* Pr 26$_{19}$ 2 C 24$_{13}$, hi. *bring up* Jg 16$_{18}$, נוח hi. *bring down* Is 28$_{2}$, שמט ni. *be brought down* Ps 141$_{6}$, שׁוב hi. *bring back* Gn 43$_{12.21}$.

נתן *give, place* Gn 30$_{35}$ 32$_{17}$ 39$_{4.8.22}$ 40$_{13}$ Ex 5$_{21}$ 10$_{25}$ 23$_{31}$ Lv 26$_{25}$ Nm 21$_{2.34}$ Dt 1$_{27}$ 2$_{24.30}$ 3$_{2.3}$ 7$_{24}$ 19$_{12}$ 20$_{13}$ =11QT 62$_{9}$ Dt 21$_{10}$=11QT 63$_{10}$ Dt 24$_{1.3}$ Jos 2$_{24}$ 6$_{2}$ 7$_{7}$ 8$_{1.7}$ 8$_{18}$ 10$_{8.19.30.32}$ 11$_{8}$ 21$_{44}$ 24$_{8.11}$ Jg 1$_{2.4}$ 2$_{14}$ Jg 2$_{23}$ 3$_{10.28}$ 4$_{7.14}$ 6$_{1}$ 7$_{2.7.9.14.15.16}$ 8$_{3.7}$ 9$_{29}$ 11$_{21.30.32}$ 12$_{3}$ 13$_{1}$ 15$_{12.13.18}$ 16$_{23.24}$ 18$_{10}$ 20$_{28}$ 1 S 14$_{10.12.37}$ 17$_{47}$ 21$_{4}$ 23$_{4.14}$ 24$_{5.11}$ 26$_{23}$ 28$_{19.19}$ 30$_{23}$ 2 S 5$_{19.19}$||1 C 14$_{10.10}$ 2 S 10$_{10}$||1 C 19$_{11}$ 2 S 16$_{8}$ 21$_{9}$ 1 K 15$_{18}$ 18$_{9}$ 20$_{13.28}$ 22$_{6.12}$||2 C 18$_{5.11}$ 1 K 22$_{15}$ 2 K 3$_{10.13.18}$ 17$_{20}$ 21$_{14}$ Is 22$_{21}$ 47$_{6}$ Jr 20$_{4.5}$ 21$_{7.7.7}$ 22$_{25.25.25.25}$ 26$_{24}$ 27$_{6.8}$ (if em.; see below) 29$_{21}$ 32$_{3.28.28}$ 34$_{2.20.20.21.21.21}$ 38$_{16.19}$ 43$_{3}$ 44$_{30.30.30}$ 46$_{26.26.26}$ Ezk 7$_{21}$ 11$_{9}$ 16$_{39}$ 21$_{16.36}$ 23$_{9.9.28.28.31}$ 30$_{24.25}$ 31$_{11}$ 39$_{23}$ Ps 10$_{14}$ 78$_{61}$ 106$_{41}$ Lm 1$_{14}$ Dn 1$_{2}$ Ezr 10$_{19}$ Ne 9$_{24.27.30}$ 1 C 22$_{18}$ 2 C 13$_{16}$ 16$_{8}$ 24$_{24}$ 25$_{20}$ 28$_{5.9}$ 36$_{17}$ Si 15$_{14}$ 45$_{5(Bmg)}$ 1QpHab 5$_{4}$ 9$_{10}$ 1QS 2$_{6}$ 4QpPs^{a} 3.4$_{10}$ 4QJub^{d} 21$_{22}$ 4QBer^{f} 1$_{3}$ ([יתנכה]) 4Qap Joseph^{b} 1$_{4}$ 2$_{8}$ 4QparaKings 31$_{2}$ 4QpsMos^{e} 1$_{8}$ 4QBark^{a} 1.2$_{5}$ 4QPrayer^{g} 1$_{2}$ 4QNarrB 1$_{2}$ 6QapSamKings 33$_{2}$ CD 1$_{6}$ Arad ost. 17$_{9}$, ni. *be given* Gn 9$_{2}$ 2 K 18$_{30}$||Is 36$_{15}$ 2 K 19$_{10}$||Is 37$_{10}$ 2 C 18$_{14}$ Jr 21$_{10}$ 32$_{4.24.24.25.36.43}$ 34$_{3}$ 37$_{17}$ 38$_{3.18}$ 39$_{17}$ 46$_{24}$ Jb 9$_{24}$ Dn 11$_{11}$ Ezr 9$_{7}$ 1 C 5$_{20}$ 2 C 28$_{5}$ Si 11$_{6(B).6}$ 1QpHab 4$_{8}$ 9$_{6}$ 4QpIsa^{a} 8$_{8}$ (ינת[נו]) 4QpPs^{a} 1.2$_{19}$ 4QJub^{h} 35$_{16}$, מגן pi. *deliver* Gn 14$_{20}$, סגר pi. *deliver* 1 S 17$_{46}$ 24$_{19}$ 26$_{8}$, hi. *deliver* Jos 20$_{5}$ 1 S 23$_{11.12.20}$ 30$_{15}$ Ps 31$_{9}$ Lm 2$_{7}$ 1QM 11$_{2.13.13}$, סכר pi. *deliver* Is 19$_{4}$, שׁלח pi. *send* 2 S 18$_{2.2.2}$ Jb 8$_{4}$.

שׂים *place* Ex 4$_{21}$ Jg 4$_{21}$ 1 K 20$_{6}$ Is 51$_{23}$ 2 C 23$_{18}$ Si 45$_{5(B)}$, מכר *sell* Jg 2$_{14}$ 3$_{8}$ 4$_{2.9}$ 10$_{7.7}$ 1 S 12$_{9.9.9}$ Jl 4$_{8}$, נכר pi. appar. *alienate* 1 S 23$_{7}$, לקח *take* Gn 22$_{6}$ 43$_{12.15}$ Ex 4$_{17.20}$ 7$_{15}$ 15$_{20}$ 17$_{5}$ 34$_{4}$ Nm 25$_{7}$ Dt 1$_{25}$ Jos 9$_{11}$ Jg 7$_{8}$ (or em. וַיִּקְחוּ אֶת־צֵדָה הָעָם בְּיָדָם *and the people took provisions in* their hand to וַיִּקַּח אֶת־כַּדֵּי הָעָם מִיָּדָם *and he took the jars of the people from their hand*, or צֵדַת הָעָם כְּ/בְּיָדָם and they they took *provisions of* [i.e. for] *the people as sufficient for them*) 9$_{48}$ 1 S 16$_2$ 17$_{40}$ 21$_9$ 1 K 14$_3$ 17$_{11}$ 2 K 4$_{29}$ 5$_5$ 8$_{8.9}$ 9$_1$ 19$_{14}$||Is 37$_{14}$ Jr 36$_{14.14}$ 38$_{10.11}$ 43$_9$ Pr 7$_{20}$, נשׂא *lift* Ec 5$_{14}$, עזב *leave* Gn 39$_{6.12.13}$ Ps 37$_{33}$ Ne 9$_{28}$ 2 C 12$_5$ 1QH fr. 6$_{13}$ 4QpPs^a 1.2$_{15}$ 4QJub^h 39$_9$ ([ויעזב ... ב]ידה) 4QapJoseph^b 1$_{16}$ 4QparaKings 104$_4$ 4QpsEzek^c 3.3$_4$ ([ועזבתי]) 4QHod^b 55$_1$ ([עזבת]ם) 4QapMes 9$_3$ (ב[י]ד), פקד *commit* 1Q26 1$_7$, hi. Ps 31$_6$ 4Q424 1$_6$, חלף hi. *renew* Jg 29$_{20}$, מצא *find* 1 S 12$_5$, ni. *be found* Gn 44$_{16.17}$ Ex 21$_{16}$ 22$_3$ 1 S 9$_8$ 13$_{22}$ 4QMMT C$_9$ ([י]מצא), hi. *cause to find*, i.e. deliver up 2 S 3$_8$ Zc 11$_{6.6}$, נגשׁ hi. *bring near* 1 S 14$_{34}$, חבא hi. *hide* Is 49$_2$, כסה pi. *cover* Is 51$_{16}$, חזק hi. *hold* Jg 7$_{20.20}$ 1QM 6$_{15}$, *strengthen* 2 K 15$_{19}$, תפשׂ pi. *hold* Pr 30$_{28}$, צור *bind* Dt 14$_{25}$.

צלח *prosper* Is 53$_{10}$, hi. *cause to prosper* Gn 39$_3$ Dn 8$_{25}$, כון ni. *be established* 1 K 2$_{46}$ Jb 15$_{23}$ (or em. בְּיָדוֹ to פִּידוֹ/בִּידוֹ *his ruin*, or לְאֵיד *for calamity*) 2 C 17$_5$, שׁלף pass. *be drawn* Nm 22$_{23.31}$ Jos 5$_{13}$ 1 C 21$_{16}$, פתח pass. *be open* Ne 6$_5$, מוג hi. *cause to melt* Is 64$_6$ (mss pol.; 1QIsa^a מגד *give*), הלל htpol. *feign madness* 1 S 21$_{14}$, שׁחת ni. *be spoilt* Jr 18$_4$, חצצר hi. *sound trumpet* 2 C 7$_{6(Kt)}$, בקשׁ pi. *require* Si 20$_{4(Bmg)}$.

בְּ of instrument, agent, *by (means of), with, through, at* (בְּיַד sometimes as compound prep. *by means of, with*) Ex 16$_3$ Nm 4$_{37.45}$ 9$_{23}$ 10$_{13}$ Jos 22$_9$ Ml 1$_1$ Est 1$_{12.15}$ 1 C 11$_3$ 24$_{19}$ 29$_5$ 2 C 26$_{11}$ 29$_{25.25}$ 33$_8$ 34$_{14}$ 35$_6$ Si 49$_7$ 1QS 4$_{12}$ 1QSb 4$_{24}$ 4QapJoshua^a 22.1$_{2.3}$ perh. 4QpPs^a 1.1$_{16}$ 3.4$_{15}$ 4Q418 184$_1$ 4Q419 1$_{2.3}$ perh. 6$_1$ perh. 4Q423 11$_1$ perh. 13$_4$ perh. CD 2$_6$ (בי) 5$_{21}$ 8$_2$=19$_{14}$, + היה *be* 1 K 16$_7$ Hg 1$_{1.3}$ 2$_1$, שׁלח *send* Gn 38$_{20}$ Ex 4$_{13}$ Jg 3$_{15}$ 1 S 16$_{20}$ 2 S 11$_{14}$ 12$_{35}$ 15$_{36}$ 1 K 2$_{25}$ 2 K 17$_{13}$ Jr 29$_3$ Zc 7$_{12}$ Pr 26$_6$ Est 8$_{10}$ 2 C 8$_{18}$ 36$_{15}$ 11QT 26$_{13}$ CD 11$_{19}$ Arad ost. 16$_6$ ([ב]י[ד]) 24$_{13}$ ([בי]ד), pi. Ex 6$_1$ Lv 16$_{21}$ 1 S 11$_7$ Jr 27$_3$, ni. *be sent* Est 3$_{13}$, הלך *go* Ex 3$_{19}$, בוא hi. *bring* 2 C 24$_{11}$, יצא *go out* Ex 14$_8$ Nm 33$_{1.3}$, hi. *bring out* Ex 13$_9$ 32$_{11}$ Dt 5$_{15}$ 6$_{21}$ 7$_8$ 9$_{26}$ 26$_8$ 1 K 10$_{29}$||2 C 1$_{17}$ Jr 32$_{21}$ Ps 136$_{12}$ Dn 9$_{15}$, גרשׁ pi. *expel* Ex 6$_1$, עבר *transgress* 1QS 8$_{22}$ CD 10$_3$, שׁוב hi. *bring back* word Lachish ost. 9$_7$, קבץ pi. *gather* Ezk 20$_{34}$, נחה *lead* Ps 77$_{21}$, תעה hi. *lead astray* 1QH 4$_{25}$, קרא *meet* Nm 20$_{20}$, נפל *fall* 1 C 5$_{10}$, hi. *cause to fall* 1 S 18$_{25}$ Jr 19$_7$ 1QM 11$_9$, ספה ni. *be swept away* 1 S 27$_1$, סור *turn aside* 1QS 8$_{17}$, hi. *remove* Jb 34$_{20}$, הרס *tear down* Pr 14$_1$, כלה pi. *destroy* 1QpHab 5$_3$, שׁמד hi. *destroy* 4QapJoseph^b 3$_{10}$, גלה hi. *exile* 1 C 5$_{41}$, לקח *take* Dt 4$_{34}$ 2 S 23$_6$, תפשׂ ni. *be seized* Jr 38$_{23}$ 11QT 57$_{7.11}$, חתר *dig* Ezk 12$_7$, שׂרג htp. *be fastened* Lm 1$_{14}$, נתך *pour out* 2 C 12$_7$, טוה *spin* Ex 35$_{25}$, נגן pi. *play stringed instrument* 1 S 16$_{16.23}$ 18$_{10}$ 19$_9$.

דבר pi. *speak* Ex 9$_{35}$ Lv 10$_{11}$ Nm 17$_5$ 27$_{23}$ Jos 20$_2$ 1 S 28$_{17}$ 1 K 8$_{53.56}$ 12$_{15}$||2 C 10$_{15}$ 1 K 14$_{18}$ 15$_{29}$ 16$_{12.34}$ 17$_{16}$ 2 K 9$_{36}$ 10$_{10}$ 14$_{25}$ 17$_{23}$ 21$_{10}$ 24$_2$ Is 20$_2$ Jr 37$_2$ 50$_1$ Ezk 38$_{17}$ 1QM 10$_6$ (ד[בר]תה) 1QH 17$_{12}$ ([ד]ברתה) 4QPrayers^b 2$_4$ ([דבר]תה) CD 4$_{13}$, צוה pi. *command* Ex 35$_{29}$ Lv 8$_{36}$ Nm 15$_{23}$ 36$_{13}$ Jos 14$_2$ 21$_{2.8}$ Jg 3$_4$ Jr 39$_{11}$ Ezr 9$_{11}$ Ne 8$_{14}$ 9$_{14}$ 1QS 1$_{3.3}$ 8$_{15}$ 4QD^a 1c$_2$ 4QpsMos^e 2.1$_4$ ([בי]ד) 4QDibHam^a 1.5$_{14}$ 4$_8$ ([צו]יתה), אמר *say* 4QD^a 11$_1$ CD 19$_{12}$, קרא *proclaim* Zc 7$_7$, נגד hi. *tell* 1QM 11$_7$, ספר pi. *relate* 1QpHab 2$_9$, ענה *answer* 1 S 28$_{15}$, ידע hi. *make known* CD 2$_{12}$, קום hi. *promise* CD 3$_{21}$, ידה hi. *give thanks* 1 C 16$_7$, חרף pi. *revile* 2 K 19$_{23}$||Is 37$_{24}$, עוד hi. *warn* 2 K 17$_{13}$ Ne 9$_{30}$, דמה pi. *use similitudes* Ho 12$_{11}$, נתן *give, place* Lv 26$_{46}$ Ezk 25$_{14}$ (or em. בְּיַד to בְּעַד *for the sake of*) Dn 9$_{10}$ 1QpHab 5$_4$ 104$_7$, ni. *be given* Ne 10$_{30}$, כתב *write* Ezk 37$_{20}$ 1QS 6$_{20}$ CD 9$_{18}$, pass. *be written* CD 19$_7$, שׁקל *weigh* perh. 4Q418 123.2$_6$ ([בי]דה).

פקד *visit*, i.e. punish 1QS 2$_6$, *appoint* Nm 4$_{49}$, מלך *rule* Ezk 20$_{33}$, עשׂה *do* Nm 15$_{30}$ Ne 4$_{11}$ 1QS 5$_{12}$ 9$_1$ (=4QS^d 3.1$_2$ ליד *for [one who acts with]*) 4QOrd^a 2$_6$, מלא pi. *fulfil* 1 K 8$_{15.24}$||2 C 6$_{4.15}$ Jr 44$_{25}$, עמד hi. *establish* 4QapPs^b 69$_5$, פתח *open* 1QH 8$_{21}$, נחם pi. *comfort* 2 S 10$_2$, שׁחח *recline* 1QS 7$_{15}$, לקק *lap* Jg 7$_6$, נכה hi. *strike* Nm 35$_{21}$ Jr 41$_9$ (or em.; see Cstr.), קטף *pluck* Dt 23$_{26}$, ישׁע hi. *save* Jg 6$_{36.37}$ 2 S 3$_{18}$ 2 K 14$_{27}$ Si 48$_{20}$ 1QM 11$_3$, פדה *redeem* Ne 1$_{10}$, ריב *contend* Dt 33$_7$ (if em.; see Coll.), לחם ni. *fight* Jr 21$_5$, פרץ *break through* 1 C 14$_{11}$, פרע *let go* 4QCat 1$_3$ CD 8$_8$=19$_{21}$, תלה ni. *be hanged* Lm 5$_{12}$, תמם *consume* Jr 27$_8$ (or em. תֻּמִּי *my consuming* to תִּתִּי *my giving*), שׁבת hi. *bring to an end* Ezk 30$_{10}$, שׁמם hi. *devastate* Ezk 30$_{12}$, מות *die* Jos 20$_9$ Jr 11$_{21}$ Ezk 28$_{10}$.

בְּ of price, *(in exchange) for* Dt 19$_{21}$=11QT 61$_{12}$; of cause, *on account of*, + עמד *stand* Si 46$_4$.

בְּ introducing object, + אחז *hold* Ps 73$_{23}$, חזק hi. *seize* Gn 19$_{16.16.16}$, *hold, strengthen* Jg 16$_{26}$ Is 42$_6$ 51$_{18}$ Jr 31$_{32}$

Jb 8_{20} perh. 4QMyst^{a} 56_{3} (חזיק[י]ו) 4QBark^{c} 1.1_{9} CD 6_{21} 14_{14}, תמך *support* Ex 17_{12}, פרשׂ pi. *spread* Lm 1_{17}, חתם *seal* Jb 37_{7} (or em. בְּיַד to בְּעַד *around*, or בַּדֵּי *the limbs of*); דבק בְּ *cling to* Dt 13_{18} 11QT 55_{11}; ירה בְּ hi. *teach concerning* Jb 27_{11}; שׂמח בְּ *rejoice in* 1QM 13_{12}.

כְּ *as, like*, + היה *be* Gn 27_{23}; *according to* Est 1_{7}, + נתן *give* 1 K 10_{13} Est 2_{18} Ezr 7_{6} Ne 2_{8}, בוא *come* Ezr 7_{9}, hi. *bring* Ezr 8_{18}, חזק htp. *strengthen oneself* Ezr 7_{28}.

מִן of direction, *from* (מִיַּד sometimes perh. as compound prep. *from*) Nm 24_{24} 1 S 25_{39} Hb 3_{4} Ps 17_{14} (if em.; see Coll.) Ec 2_{24} 4_{1} 1 C 28_{19} 2 C $30_{6.16}$ 31_{13} 35_{11} 1QS 11_{10} perh. 1QDM 46_{1} perh. 1Q25 7_{2} perh. 4Q CommGenC 3_{3} 4QPrEnosh 3_{3} 4Q418 126.2_{2} 4QHod^{a} 14_{3} 4QJonathan 1_{9} 11QPs^{a} 18_{8} perh. 4QPrFêtes^{c} 56_{1}, + היה *be* Is 50_{11} Ml 1_{9} 1QH 14_{27} 4Q418 102_{3}, ברח *flee* Jb 27_{22}, יצא hi. *bring out* 4QpsEzek^{c} 3.2_{5} ([א]וציא), לקח *take* Gn 4_{11} 21_{30} 33_{10} 48_{22} Ex 29_{25} 32_{4} Nm 5_{25} 21_{26} (or em. מִיָּדוֹ *from his hand* to מִיַּבֹּק *from Jabbok*) Dt 3_{8} 26_{4} Jg 7_{8} (if em.; see above) 13_{23} 1 S 10_{4} $12_{3.4}$ 25_{35} 2 S 8_{1}||1 C 18_{1} 1 K $11_{34.35}$ 22_{3} 2 K $5_{20.24}$ $13_{25.25}$ Is 40_{2} 51_{22} Jr $25_{15.17.28}$ Ml 2_{13} Jb 35_{7} 1QS 5_{16} 4QD^{e} 4_{7} 4QD^{f} 4.2_{13} 4Qps Ezek^{a} 13.2_{4} 4Q418 81_{11} 97_{2} 4QRedInk 3_{4}, קבל pi. *receive* Si 50_{12}, רצה *accept* Ml $1_{10.13}$, אסף *gather* 2 C 34_{9}, גזל *seize* 2 S 23_{21}||1 C 11_{23}, קרב hi. *bring near*, i.e. offer Lv 22_{25}, שׁלך hi. *throw* Ex 32_{19} Jg 15_{17}, נפל hi. *cause to fall* Ezk 30_{22} 39_{3}, נכה hi. *strike* Ezk 39_{3}, שׁמר *keep* Ps 140_{5} 141_{9}, יסף hi. *add* 4Q418 811_{17}, בקשׁ pi. *require* Gn 31_{29} 43_{9} 1 S 20_{16} 2 S 4_{11} Is 1_{12} Ezk $3_{18.20}$ 33_{8} Si $20_{4(B)}$, דרשׁ *require* Gn $9_{5.5.5}$ Ezk 33_{6} 34_{10} 4QD^{a} 7.3_{4} 4QapJoseph^{b} 3_{11} 4Q418 81_{7} 11QT 53_{11}.

נצל hi. *deliver* Gn $32_{12.12}$ $37_{21.22}$ Ex 2_{19} 3_{8} $18_{9.10.10}$ Nm 35_{25} Dt 25_{11} 32_{39} Jos 9_{26} 22_{31} 24_{10} Jg $6_{9.9}$ 8_{34} 9_{17} 1 S $7_{3.14}$ $10_{18.18}$ $12_{10.11}$ 14_{48} $17_{37.37.37}$ 2 S 12_{7} 2 K 17_{39} 18_{29}. $18_{33.34.35.35}$||Is $36_{18.19.20.20}$ Is 43_{13} 47_{14} Jr 15_{21} 20_{13} 21_{12} 22_{3} 42_{11} Ezk $13_{21.23}$ 34_{27} Ho 2_{12} Zc 11_{6} Ps $18_{1.1}$ 22_{21} 31_{16} 82_{4} 97_{10} $144_{7.11}$ Jb 10_{7} Dn $8_{4.7}$ 2 C 25_{15} 32_{13+7t} Si 51_{2} 4QpPs^{a} 3.4_{21} (צילם[י]ו) 4QJonathan 1_{9} ([מציל ... מיד]) 11Q Melch 2_{25} ([יצי]ל[מה מי]ד) GnzPs 3_{25}, ni. *deliver oneself* Pr 6_{5} (or em. מִיָּד to מִצַּיָּד *from the hunter*, or מִמָּצוֹד *from the net*) 6_{5} (mss מִפַּח *from the snare of*) 11QMelch 2_{13} ([וינצ[ל]ו]), פרק *deliver* Lm 5_{6}, פצה *deliver* 4QTobit^{e} 6_{7}, ישׁע hi. *save* Ex 14_{30} Jg $2_{16.18}$ 8_{22} 10_{12} 12_{2} 13_{5} 1 S 7_{8} 9_{16} 2 S $3_{18.18}$ 2 K 19_{19}||Is 37_{20} Ps $106_{10.10}$ Jb 5_{15} Ne 9_{27} 2 C $32_{22.22}$ 4QapJoseph^{b} 1_{16} 11QT $59_{11.18.18}$, גאל *redeem* Ps 107_{2} 11QPs^{a} 18_{19}, פדה *redeem* Dt 7_{8} Ho 13_{14} Ps 49_{16} Jb 5_{20} 6_{23} 1QH 2_{35} 4QpPs^{a} 1.2_{19}, קנה *purchase* Gn 33_{19} 39_{1} Lv 25_{14} Ru $4_{5.9}$, שׁפט *judge*, i.e. deliver 1 S 24_{16} 2 S $18_{19.31}$, מלט pi. *deliver* Ps 89_{49} Jb 6_{23}, ni. *escape* 1 S 27_{1} Jr 32_{4} 34_{3} $38_{18.23}$ Dn 11_{41} 2 C 16_{7}, פלט pi. *deliver* Ps 71_{4}, קרע *tear* 1 K $11_{12.31}$, כרת hi. *cut off* Mc 5_{11}, גזר ni. *be cut off* Ps 88_{6} (unless יָד III *love*) 4QD^{a} 10.1_{10}, עזר *help* Si 51_{3} 1QH 2_{35} 4QMidrEschat^{b} 11_{12}, שׁלח pi. *send* 1 K 20_{42}, נקם *take vengeance* 4QAdmonPar 3.2_{6}, ni. *take vengeance* 2 K 9_{7}, קדשׁ hi. *consecrate* Jg 17_{3}, אכל *eat* 2 S 13_{5}, ברה *eat* 2 S $13_{6.10}$, שׁתה *drink* Is 51_{17}.

מִן of instrument, agent, *by (means of), with, through* (מִידֵי perh. as compound preposition *by [means of], with, through*), + פזז *be made supple* Gn 49_{24}.

מִן partitive, *(some) of, from* (the bounty of) 1 C 29_{16}, + נתן *give* 1 C 29_{14}.

אֶל *to(wards), (in)to, at* (אֶל־יַד sometimes perh. as compound prep. *beside*) 2 S 14_{30} Ezk 48_{1} (or em. אֶל־יַד to מִן־הַיָּם *from the sea*) Ps $123_{2.2}$ 4QapJoshua^{a} 19.2_{5}, + עמד *stand* 2 S 18_{4}, שׁוב *go back* Est 2_{14}, קרב *draw near* 1QS 6_{19} (hi. *bring near* corrected to qal), קבץ *gather* Est 2_{3}, לקח ni. *be taken* Est 2_{8}.

אֶל *upon*, + נתן *give*, i.e. place Ezk 23_{42}.

עַל *upon, over, (in)to, at, under (the command of)* Gn $24_{22.30}$ 38_{30} (עַל־יְדֵי, עַל־יַד sometimes perh. as compound prep. *beside*) Ex $13_{9.16}$ 17_{16} Dt 9_{15} Jos 15_{46} Jg 11_{26} 19_{27} 1 S 4_{18} (if em.; see below) Jr 22_{24} 40_{4} 48_{37} Ps 121_{5} Ne 13_{13} 1 C 7_{29} $25_{2.3.6.6}$ 26_{28} 2 C $17_{15.16.18}$ 21_{16} $26_{11.13}$ 29_{27} 31_{15} 1QH fr. 48_{4} 4QapPs^{b} 18_{3} Ḥorvat ‘Uza jar inscr. $1_{2.6}$ ([י]די), + היה *be* Nm 34_{3} Dn 10_{4}, ישׁב *dwell* Nm 13_{29}, עמד *stand* 2 S 15_{2}, hi. *appoint* 1 C 6_{16}, הלך *go* Ex 2_{5}, בוא hi. *bring* 2 K 10_{24}, יצא hi. *bring out* Ezr 1_{8} 1QSa 1_{23}, ירד hi. *let down* Gn 24_{18}, עלה *go up* 1 S 14_{13}, שׁוב hi. *bring back* 1QM 9_{7}, נסע *set out* Nm 2_{17}, עבר *pass* 2 S 15_{18} Jr 33_{13}, נטשׁ *leave* 1 S 17_{22}, כשׁל *stumble* Jr 46_{6}, נפל *fall* Jr 46_{6}, שׁען ni. *lean* 2 K 5_{18} $7_{2.17}$, perh. ירט *thrust* Jb 16_{11} (unless רטה *wring out*), שׂים *place* Gn 24_{47} 2 K 13_{16} Est 6_{9}, שׁית *place* Gn 46_{4}, נתן *give, place* Gn 41_{42} 42_{37} 2 K $12_{12.16}$ 22_{5}||2 C 34_{10} Ezk 16_{11} 1 C 29_{8} CD 14_{13}, ni. *be given* 2 K $22_{7.9}$||2 C 34_{17} 2 C 34_{16}, יצק *pour* 2 K 3_{11}, נגר hi.

pour, i.e. deliver Jr 18$_{21}$ Ezk 35$_{5}$ Ps 63$_{11}$, סגר htpo. *be delivered* Si 38$_{15(Bmg)}$, נטה *stretch*, i.e. pitch, tent Si 14$_{25}$, שׁקל *weigh* Est 3$_{9}$ Ezr 8$_{26}$, ni. *be weighed* Ezr 8$_{33}$, קבץ *gather* Pr 13$_{11}$, פקד hi. *commit* 1 K 14$_{27}$||2 C 12$_{10}$ Arad ost. 24$_{15}$ (הבקידם, appar. error for הפקידם), לבשׁ hi. *put on* Gn 27$_{16}$, קשׁר *bind* Gn 38$_{28}$ Dt 6$_{8}$ 11$_{18}$, פתח pi. *engrave* 1 K 7$_{36}$, בנה *build* Ne 3$_{2.2}$, חזק hi. *repair* Ne 3$_{4+11t}$, רעה *graze* Jb 1$_{14}$.

עַל *according to*, + רדה *rule* Jr 5$_{31}$ (unless רדה *run* beside),* הלל pi. *praise* Ezr 3$_{10}$.

עַל *by means of* (or עַל־יַד as compound preposition, *by means of*) Mur 24 2$_{2}$ 4$_{2}$ (ע[ל יד]) 5$_{2}$ 6$_{2}$ ([על י]ד) 9$_{2}$ ([על]), + פרה *be fruitful* Si 41$_{9(Bmg)}$, ראה *see* GnzPs 2$_{11}$, כבד hi. *glorify* GnzPs 4$_{6}$.

עַל *against*, + עלה *go up* Zc 14$_{13}$.

עַל נבט hi. *look towards* Si 30$_{30}$, בושׁ עַל *be ashamed of* Si 41$_{19}$.

מֵעַל *from upon*, + סור hi. *remove* Gn 41$_{42}$ Est 3$_{10}$, שׁלך hi. *throw* Dt 9$_{17}$, מסס *melt* Jg 15$_{14}$.

בַּעַד *behind* 1 S 4$_{18}$ (or em. בְּעַד יַד to בְּיַד *beside*, or עַל־יַד *beside*).

לְמַעַן *for the sake of*, + בוא *come* 2 C 6$_{32}$.

מִפְּנֵי *because of*, + ישׁב *sit* Jr 15$_{17}$ (unless יָד III *love*).

אֵצֶל *beside*, + עמד *stand* 1 K 10$_{19}$||2 C 9$_{18}$.

בֵּין *between* Zc 13$_{6}$ (בֵּין יָדֶיךָ *between your hands*, i.e. perh. on your back).*

תַּחַת *under* 1 S 21$_{4.9}$ Is 3$_{6}$ 3QTr 10$_{12}$, + ענה htp. *submit oneself* Gn 16$_{9}$, כנע ni. *be subdued* Jg 3$_{20}$ Ps 106$_{42}$, צבר *heap up* Gn 41$_{35}$, מות *die* Ex 21$_{20}$.

תַּחַת *(in exchange) for* Ex 21$_{24}$.

אֶל־תַּחַת *under* 1 S 21$_{5}$ (אֵין לֶחֶם חֹל אֶל־תַּחַת יָדִי *there is no common bread on hand*).

מִתַּחַת *from under*, + יצא *go out* 2 K 13$_{5}$, עלה hi. *bring up* 2 K 17$_{7}$, נצל hi. *deliver* Ex 18$_{10}$, פשׁע *rebel* 2 K 8$_{20.22}$ ||2 C 21$_{8.18}$ 2 C 21$_{10}$.

<COLL> || כַּף *hand* Jr 15$_{21}$ Ps 18$_{1}$ 71$_{4}$ Pr 10$_{4}$ 31$_{20}$ 11QT 59$_{11}$; + כַּף Ex 4$_{4}$ Pr 31$_{19}$; || זְרוֹעַ *arm* Dt 4$_{34}$ 5$_{15}$ 7$_{19}$ 11$_{2}$ 26$_{8}$ 1 K 8$_{42}$||2 C 6$_{32}$ Jr 21$_{5}$ 32$_{21}$ Ezk 20$_{33.34}$ Ps 136$_{12}$ Si 33$_{7(B)}$; + זְרוֹעַ Ps 89$_{22}$; || יָמִין *right hand* Is 48$_{13}$ Ps 21$_{9}$ 74$_{11}$ 89$_{14.26}$ 139$_{10}$ Si 33$_{7(B)}$; + יָמִין Jg 5$_{26}$ Ps 26$_{10}$ 138$_{7}$; || אֶצְבַּע *finger* Ps 144$_{1}$ Ca 5$_{5}$ 11QPs^{a} 28$_{4}$; + אֶצְבַּע Is 2$_{8}$ 17$_{8}$; אֶגְרֹף *fist* CD 11$_{6}$.

|| רֶגֶל *foot* Gn 41$_{44}$ Ex 12$_{11}$ 21$_{24}$ 29$_{20}$ 30$_{19.21}$ 40$_{31}$ Lv 8$_{23.24}$ 14$_{14.17.25.28}$ 21$_{19}$ Dt 19$_{21}$ Jg 1$_{6.7}$ 1 S 14$_{13}$ 2 S 4$_{12}$ 21$_{20}$ Ps 22$_{17}$ 115$_{7}$ 1QS 10$_{13}$ 11QT 26$_{10}$; + רֶגֶל 2 S 3$_{34}$ 2 K 9$_{35}$ Ezk 25$_{6}$ Ps 36$_{12}$ Pr 6$_{17}$; || בֶּרֶךְ *knee* Is 35$_{3}$ Ezk 21$_{12}$ Si 25$_{23}$; כָּנָף *wing* Ezk 10$_{12}$.

|| אַף *nose* Gn 24$_{47}$; אֹזֶן *ear* Gn 35$_{4}$ Lv 14$_{14.17.25.28}$ Is 59$_{1}$; עַיִן *eye* Ex 13$_{9.16}$ 21$_{24}$ Dt 6$_{8}$ 11$_{18}$ 19$_{21}$ 21$_{6}$=11QT 63$_{5}$; + עַיִן Pr 6$_{17}$; || שֵׁן *tooth* Ex 21$_{24}$ Dt 19$_{21}$; + פֶּה *mouth* 1 K 8$_{15.24}$||2 C 6$_{4.15}$ Jr 44$_{25}$; לָשׁוֹן *tongue* Pr 6$_{17}$; צַוָּאר *neck* Gn 27$_{16}$; || ראשׁ *head* Ezk 23$_{42}$ Si 12$_{18}$; + גֻּלְגֹּלֶת *skull* 2 K 9$_{35}$.

+ מָתְנַיִם *loins* Ex 12$_{11}$; || גַּב *back* Ezk 10$_{12}$, *rim* 1 K 7$_{33}$; לֵב *heart* Ezk 21$_{12}$ 22$_{14}$; + לֵב Pr 6$_{17}$; || לֵבָב *heart* Dt 15$_{7}$ Is 13$_{7}$; קוֹל *voice* Gn 27$_{22}$ Hb 3$_{10}$; נֶפֶשׁ *soul*, i.e. life Dt 19$_{21}$; רוּחַ *spirit* Ezk 21$_{12}$; אַף *anger* Jr 21$_{5}$; חֵמָה *anger* Jr 21$_{5}$ Ezk 20$_{33.34}$; קֶצֶף *anger* Jr 21$_{5}$; גְּבוּרָה *might* Jr 16$_{21}$; כֹּחַ *strength* Ex 32$_{11}$ Ne 1$_{10}$ 1QH 11$_{7}$; גֹּדֶל *greatness* Dt 3$_{24}$ 9$_{26}$ 11$_{2}$; שֵׁם *name* 1 K 8$_{42}$||2 C 6$_{32}$ Is 56$_{5}$ (יָד וָשֵׁם); מַסָּה *testing* Dt 4$_{34}$ 7$_{19}$.

|| נֵס *ensign* Is 49$_{22}$; אוֹת *sign* Dt 4$_{34}$ 7$_{19}$ 11$_{2}$ 26$_{8}$ 34$_{12}$; מוֹפֵת *wonder* Dt 4$_{34}$ 7$_{19}$ 26$_{8}$ 34$_{12}$; מוֹרָא *fear* Dt 4$_{34}$ 26$_{8}$ 34$_{12}$ Jr 32$_{21}$; מוּסָר *discipline* Dt 11$_{2}$; עֵצָה *counsel* Is 14$_{26}$; מַעֲשֶׂה *deed* Dt 11$_{2}$; מַחֲשָׁבָה *thought* 1QH 11$_{7}$; + שְׁבִי *captivity* Ezr 9$_{7}$; בִּזָּה *plunder* Ezr 9$_{7}$; בֹּשֶׁת *shame* Ezr 9$_{7}$; || מִלְחָמָה *war* Dt 4$_{34}$; חִשּׁוּק *spoke* 1 K 7$_{33}$; חִשּׁוּר *hub* 1 K 7$_{33}$; מִסְגֶּרֶת *border* 1 K 7$_{35.36}$; + חֶרֶב *sword* Jr 19$_{7}$ Ps 22$_{21}$ Ezr 9$_{7}$; || עַם *people* Nm 20$_{20}$.

שְׁתֵּי יָדָיו *his two hands* Lv 16$_{21(Qr)}$, שְׁתֵּי יָדַי *my two hands* Dt 9$_{15.17}$ (יָדַי), שְׁתֵּי יָדוֹת *two tenons/divisions* Ex 26$_{17}$||36$_{22}$ (יָדֹת) 2 K 11$_{7}$ (הַיָּדוֹת) 58$_{8}$ (הידות), שְׁתֵּי יְדֹתָיו *its two tenons* Ex 26$_{19.19}$||36$_{24.24}$, אַרְבַּע הַיָּדֹת *four parts*, i.e. four fifths Gn 47$_{24}$, תֵּשַׁע הַיָּדוֹת *nine parts*, i.e. nine tenths Ne 11$_{1}$, עֶשֶׂר־יָדוֹת *ten portions* 2 S 19$_{44}$, *ten times* Dn 1$_{20}$, וַתֵּרֶב ... חָמֵשׁ יָדוֹת *it was greater ... (by) five times* Gn 43$_{34}$.

יָד עַל־כֵּס יָהּ perh. *a hand upon the throne of Y.* Ex 17$_{16}$ (Sam כִּסֵּא upon *the throne of* war).

יָדָיו רָב לוֹ appar. *(with) his hands he contended for him* Dt 33$_{7}$ (or em. יָדֶיךָ יָרֶב לוֹ *[with] your hands let him contend for him*, or יָדֶיךָ רִיב לוֹ *[with] your hands contend for him*, or בְּיָדָיו רָב *with his hands he contends*), יָדַיִם נוּס *strength to flee* Jos 8$_{20}$, אִטֵּר יַד־יְמִינוֹ *shut in respect of his right hand*, i.e. left-handed Jg 3$_{15}$ 20$_{16}$, וַיִּמְצָאֵם עֶשֶׂר יָדוֹת

עַל כָּל־הַחַרְטֻמִּים *and he found them ten times above*, i.e. better than, *all the magicians* Dn 1$_{20}$, נכאה רגלים או ידים *one crippled with respect to legs or hands* 1QSa 2$_{6}$.

יָד used adverbially, (1) *with the hand*, + פלט pi. *deliver* Ps 17$_{14}$ (or em. מְמִתִים *from men* to הֲמִיתֵם *put them to death*, or הַתִּימֵם *consume them*, or em. מְמִתִים יָדְךָ to מְמִתִים מִיָּדְךָ *death is from your hand*), מות hi. *put to death* Ps 17$_{14}$ (if em.), תמם hi. *consume* Ps 17$_{14}$ (if em.), ירשׁ hi. *drive out* Ps 44$_{3}$.

(2) *at the side*, + ישׁב *sit* 1 S 4$_{13}$(Qr) (or em. לְיַד *beside*).

(3) יָד לְיָד *a hand to a hand*, i.e. surely, + נקה ni. *be innocent*, i.e. unpunished Pr 11$_{21}$ 16$_{5}$.

(4) בְּאֶפֶס יָד *without a hand*, + שׁבר ni. *be broken* Dn 8$_{25}$.

Also 4QMidrEschat[b] 11$_{13}$ 4QD[g] 1.2$_{17}$ perh. 4Qap Joseph[b] 6$_{3}$ 4QapPs[a] 3$_{1}$ 4Q393 3$_{3}$ 4QPatr 6$_{2.3}$ perh. 4Q 417 14$_{5}$ perh. 21$_{3}$ 4Q418 126.2$_{15}$ 204$_{1}$ 247$_{2}$ 4Q423 10$_{1}$ 4Q 469 1$_{2}$ perh. 4QDescDavid 1$_{2}$ ([ ]ידכ) 4QM[c] 1$_{3}$ 4QRit Mar 99$_{1}$ 4QDibHam[a] 8$_{12}$ 5Q25 1$_{2}$.

<SYN> כַּף *hand*, זְרוֹעַ *arm*, יָמִין *right hand*, אֶצְבַּע *finger*, רֶגֶל *foot*, בֶּרֶךְ *knee*, כָּנָף *wing*, אַף *nose*, אֹזֶן *ear*, עַיִן *eye*, שֵׁן *tooth*, רֹאשׁ *head*, גַּב *back, rim*, לֵב *heart*, לֵבָב *heart*, נֶפֶשׁ *soul*, רוּחַ *spirit*, אַף *anger*, חֵמָה *wrath*, קֶצֶף *anger*, גְּבוּרָה *might*, כֹּחַ *strength*, גֹּדֶל *greatness*, שֵׁם *name*, מַסָּה *testing*, נֵס *ensign*, אוֹת *sign*, מוֹפֵת *wonder*, מוֹרָא *fear*, מוּסָר *discipline*, עֵצָה *counsel*, מַעֲשֶׂה *deed*, מִלְחָמָה *war*, חִשּׁוּק *spoke*, חִשּׁוּר *hub*, מִסְגֶּרֶת *border*, עַם *people*.*

* [יָד] II 4.0.2 n.[f.] **penis**, <SUBJ> ינק ni. *be emptied*, i.e. ejaculate 1QIsa[a] 65$_{3}$ (וינקו ידים על האבנים *and penises empty themselves into the vaginas* [אָבְנַיִם]; MT וּמְקַטְּרִים עַל־הַלְּבֵנִים *and burning incense on tiles*). <OBJ> חזה *see* Is 57$_{8}$, נתן *give* Jr 50$_{15}$, יצא hi. *take out* 1QS 7$_{13}$. <CSTR> חַיַּת יָדֵךְ *life of your penis*, i.e. your sexual vigour Is 57$_{10}$ (or em. דֵּי חַיָּתֵךְ *sufficiency of your life*). <PREP> עַל *by means of*, + רדה *rule* Jr 5$_{31}$.

[יָד] III 7 n.[m.] **love**—cstr. יַד; sf. יָדוֹ, יָדְךָ; pl. sf. יָדָיו, יָדֶיהָ—**1. love, desire,** <SUBJ> ידע ni. *be known* Is 66$_{14}$ (+ זַעַם *indignation*). <NOM CL> אֲסוּרִים יָדֶיהָ *bonds are her love(s)* Ec 7$_{26}$ (or em. יַדָּהּ in same sense). <OBJ> הפך *turn* Lm 3$_{3}$ (or em. יָדוֹ *his love/hand* to יַדּוֹ, i.e. יַד *love*), יסף hi. *add* Is 11$_{11}$ (or em. יָדוֹ to יַדּוֹ). <CSTR> יַד י׳ *love of Y.* Is 66$_{14}$, יַד חֲזוּת *love of (the) sight (of them)* Is 57$_{8}$ (if em. יָד חָזִית *you saw [their] hand/penis*), צֹאן יָדוֹ *the flock of his love* Ps 95$_{7}$ (or em. יָדוֹ to יַדּוֹ). <PREP> מִן of direction, *from*, + גזר ni. *be cut off* Ps 88$_{6}$ (or em. מִיָּדְךָ *from your love/hand* to מִיַּדְּךָ in same sense); מִיַּדָּם *for the love of them*, i.e. for their sake Ps 16$_{4}$ (בַּל־אַסִּיךְ נִסְכֵּיהֶם מִיַּדָּם *I will not pour out their libations for their sake*; if em. מִדָּם *of blood*); מִפְּנֵי *away from*, + ישׁב *sit* Jr 15$_{17}$ (or em. יָדְךָ *your love/hand* to יַדְּךָ in same sense; + זַעַם *indignation*).

2. loved one, <SUBJ> שׁוב hi. *take back* Jb 20$_{10}$ (unless יָד I, §15 *descendant*; or em. וְיָדָיו *and his loved ones/his hands* to וְיַדָּיו in same sense; or em. וִילָדָיו *and his children*; + בֵּן *son*), חול *whirl* or *be weak* Lm 4$_{6}$ (if em. יָדַיִם *both hands* to יַדִּים/יָדִים *loved ones*; or em. יְלָדִים *children* and/or חלה *be weak*).*

⇒ יַד *love*, יְדִדוּת *loved one*, יָדִיד *beloved*, יְדִידֹת *love*, יְדִידָה *Jedidah*, יְדִידְיָהּ *Jedidiah*, מֵידָד *Medad*.

[יַד] 1 n.[m.] **love**—cstr. יַד—(perh. all occurences are יָד III *love*) **1. love, desire,** <SUBJ> ידע ni. *be known* Is 66$_{14}$ (+ זַעַם *indignation*). <NOM CL> אֲסוּרִים יַדָּהּ *bonds are her love(s)* Ec 7$_{26}$ (if em. יָדֶיהָ in same sense). <OBJ> הפך *turn* Lm 3$_{3}$ (if em. יָדוֹ *his love/hand* to יַדּוֹ), יסף hi. *add* Is 11$_{11}$ (if em. יָדוֹ to יַדּוֹ). <CSTR> יַד י׳ *love of Y.* Is 66$_{14}$, יַד חֲזוּת *love of (the) sight (of them)* Is 57$_{8}$ (if em. יָד חָזִית *you saw [their] hand /penis*), צֹאן יַדּוֹ *the flock of his love* Ps 95$_{7}$ (if em. יָדוֹ to יַדּוֹ). <PREP> מִן of direction, *from*, + גזר ni. *be cut off* Ps 88$_{6}$ (if em. מִיָּדְךָ *from your love/hand* to מִיַּדְּךָ in same sense); מִיַּדָּם *for the love of them*, i.e. for their sake Ps 16$_{4}$ (בַּל־אַסִּיךְ נִסְכֵּיהֶם מִיַּדָּם *I will not pour out their libations for their sake*; if em. מִדָּם *of blood*); מִפְּנֵי *away from*, + ישׁב *sit* Jr 15$_{17}$ (if em. יָדְךָ *your love/hand* to יַדְּךָ in same sense; + זַעַם *indignation*).

2. loved one, <SUBJ> שׁוב hi. *take back* Jb 20$_{10}$ (unless יָד I, §15 *descendant*; if em. וְיָדָיו *and his loved ones/his hands* to וְיַדָּיו in same sense; if em. וִילָדָיו *and his children*; + בֵּן *son*), חול *whirl* or *be weak* Lm 4$_{6}$ (if em. יָדַיִם *both hands* to יַדִּים *loved ones*; or em. יְלָדִים *children* and /or חלה *be weak*).*

⇒ יָד III *love*, יְדִדוּת *loved one*, יָדִיד *beloved*, יְדִידֹת *love*,

יְדִידָה *Jedidah,* יְדִידְיָה *Jedidiah,* מֵידָד *Medad.*

יִדְאֲלָה 1 pl.n. **Idalah,** town in territory of Zebulun, perh. Kh. el-Ḥuwwāra, 16 km NNW of Megiddo, <SUBJ> היה *be* Jos 19$_{15}$ (+ תּוֹצָאָה *outgoing*).

יִדְבָּשׁ 1 pr.n.m. **Idbash,** Judahite, <NOM CL> אֵלֶּה אֲבִי עֵיטָם ... יִדְבָּשׁ appar. *and these were the father of Etam ... Idbash* 1 C 4$_3$ (or em. אֲבִי *father of* to בְּנֵי *sons of*).
→ (?) דְּבַשׁ *honey*.

[ידד], see ידה II, *throw*.

[יְדִדוּת] 1 n.f. **loved one**—cstr. יְדִדוּת—<OBJ> נתן *give* Jr 12$_7$. <CSTR> יְדִדוּת נַפְשִׁי *loved one of my soul* Jr 12$_7$ (+ בַּיִת *house*, נַחֲלָה *heritage*).
→ יָד III *love*.

ידה I $_{110.17.40}$ vb. **praise—Hi.** $_{99.17.39}$ Pf. Si הוֹדִיתִי, הוֹדִינוּ; impf. אוֹדֶה, יוֹדֶה (יְהוֹדֶה, יוֹדְךָ, יוֹדֻךָ), 3fs Q תודה (תּוֹדֶךָּ), יוֹדוּ (אֲהוֹדֶנּוּ, אוֹדֶנּוּ, אוֹדֶךָּ, Q אודכה, Si או[ו]דיך, אוֹדְךָ), (יְהוֹדוּךָ, יוֹדוּךָ), נוֹדֶה (Q נודך); + waw וְהוֹדוּ; impv. הוֹדוּ (הֹדוּ); ptc. מוֹדֶה, מוֹדִים; inf. הודאה, הֹדוֹת (הוֹדוֹת, הוֹדֹת)—**give praise, praise** (used transitively, without לְ of direction at Gn 29$_{35}$ 49$_8$ Jb 40$_{14}$ 2 S 22$_{50}$ 1 K 8$_{33.35}$ ||2 C 6$_{24.26}$ Is 38$_{15}$ [if em.] 38$_{18.19}$ Jr 33$_{11}$ Ps 7$_{18}$ 9$_2$ 28$_7$ 30$_{10.13}$ 35$_{18}$ 42$_6$||42$_{12}$||43$_5$ 43$_4$ 44$_9$ 45$_{18}$ 49$_{19}$ 52$_{11}$ 54$_8$ 57$_{10}$ ||108$_4$ 67$_{4.4.6.6}$ 71$_{22}$ 74$_{19}$ [if em.] 76$_{11}$ 86$_{12}$ 88$_{11}$ 89$_6$ 99$_3$ 109$_{30}$ 111$_1$ 118$_{19.21.28}$ 119$_7$ 138$_{1.2.4}$ 139$_{14}$ 142$_8$ 145$_{10}$ Si 51$_{1.12}$ 1QS 11$_{15}$ 11QPs^a 19$_{1.2.2}$); sometimes perh. **give thanks, thank** (e.g. Is 38$_{19}$ Ps 49$_{19}$) or **acclaim** (e.g. Ps 6$_6$ 30$_5$=97$_{12}$ 71$_{22}$ 106$_{47}$||1 C 16$_{35}$) or **lead worship, act as choir, orchestra** (e.g. Ne 11$_{17}$ 12$_{24}$ 1 C 16$_4$ 23$_{20}$ 25$_3$ 2 C 31$_2$); also **confess** sin (Ps 32$_5$ Pr 28$_{13}$ 1QS 1$_{24}$).*

<SUBJ> ׳י Y. Jb 40$_{14}$, אֵל *god* 4QShirShabb^d 1.1$_{38.38}$, Asaph 1 C 16$_7$, David 2 S 22$_{50}$||Ps 18$_{50}$ 1 C 29$_{13}$, Heman 1 C 16$_{41}$, Hezekiah Is 38$_{15}$ (if em. אֶדַּדֶּה כָל־שְׁנוֹתַי עַל־מַר נַפְשִׁי *I shall go all my years in bitterness of soul* to אוֹדְכָה *I shall praise you,* despite bitterness of soul), Jeduthun 1 C 16$_{41}$ 25$_3$, Joshua 4QTestim$_{21}$, Leah Gn 29$_{35}$, Sheol Is 38$_{18}$.

worshipper (first person sing.) Ps 7$_{18}$ 9$_2$ 28$_7$ 30$_{13}$ 32$_5$ 35$_{18}$ 42$_6$||42$_{12}$||43$_5$ Ps 43$_4$ 52$_{11}$ 54$_8$ 57$_{10}$||108$_4$ 71$_{22}$ 86$_{12}$ 109$_{30}$ 111$_1$ 118$_{19.21.28}$ 119$_{7.62}$ 138$_{1.2}$ 139$_{14}$ Si 51$_{1.12}$ 1QH 2$_{20.31}$ 3$_{19.37}$ 4$_5$ 5$_{5.20}$ 7$_{6.26}$ ([א]ודכה) 7$_{34}$ (אודכ[ה]) 8$_4$ ([אוֹ]דכה=4QHod^b 7$_{11}$ א[וד]כה) 11$_{3.15}$ 4QShir^b 28$_2$ (אודכ[ה]), (not first person sing.) Ps 44$_9$ 75$_{2.2}$ 92$_2$ 105$_1$ ||1 C 16$_8$ Ps 106$_1$ 106$_{47}$||1 C 16$_{35}$ Ps 118$_{1.29}$ 136$_{1.2.3.26}$ 1 C 16$_{34}$ Si 51$_{12(13t)}$ 1QLitPr 3.1$_6$ 4QapPs^b 50$_5$ 4QDibHam^a 1.6$_{15}$ 1.7$_4$ 4QPrFêtes^b 1$_2$.

עַם *people* 1 K 8$_{33.35}$||2 C 6$_{24.26}$ Ps 45$_{18}$ 67$_{4.4.6.6}$ 79$_{13}$ 99$_3$, קָהָל *assembly* 1 C 29$_{13}$, עֵדָה *congregation* 11QPs^a 122$_4$, שֵׁבֶט *tribe* Ps 122$_4$, שְׁאָר *remnant* 1 C 16$_{41}$, צֹאן *flock* Ps 79$_{13}$.

יוֹשֶׁבֶת *inhabitant* of Zion Is 12$_4$, אִישׁ *man* Ps 49$_{19(ms)}$, בֵּן *son* Ezr 3$_{11}$ 2 C 7$_3$ 4QTobit^e 6$_7$, אָח *brother* Gn 49$_8$ 1 C 16$_7$, צֶאֱצָא *offspring* perh. 1QH fr. 10$_8$ ([הוד]ות), מֶלֶךְ *king* Ps 138$_4$ 4QShirShabb^d 1.1$_4$ ([מ]לכ[ין]), כֹּהֵן *priest* Ezr 3$_{11}$ 2 C 31$_2$, לֵוִי *Levite* Ezr 3$_{11}$ 1 C 16$_4$ (מִן־הַלְוִיִּם *some of the Levites*) 23$_{30}$ (בְּנֵי־לֵוִי *sons of Levi*) 2 C 31$_2$, מְשׁוֹרֵר *singer* Ne 12$_{46}$ (if em. וְאָסָף מִקֶּדֶם רָאשֵׁי הַמְשֹׁרְרִים וְשִׁיר *and Asaph of old; heads of the singers and song of* to אָסָף רֹאשׁ הַמְשֹׁרְרִים וּפְקֻדָּם לְשִׁיר *Asaph was head of the singers and their appointment, for song[s] of* praise) 2 C 5$_{13}$ 20$_{21}$, עבר ptc. *one who enters* the covenant 1QS 1$_{24}$, הלל pi. ptc. *one who praises* 2 C 20$_{21}$, מְחַצֵּר *trumpeter* 2 C 5$_{13}$, מַשְׂכִּיל *instructor* 1QS 11$_{15}$.

צַדִּיק *righteous one* Ps 33$_2$ 97$_{12}$ 140$_{14}$, חָסִיד *loyal one* Ps 30$_5$ 107$_{8.15.21.31}$ (if em. in all four חַסְדּוֹ *[for] his loyalty* to חֲסִדָיו *his loyal ones*), גאל pass. ptc. *one who is redeemed* Ps 107$_{1.8.15.21.31}$ (or em. all four), מוט pol. ptc. *one who slips* 11QPs^a 19$_2$ (מוטטי), חַי *living being* Is 38$_{19}$ 11QPs^a 19$_2$, לָשׁוֹן *tongue* 4QRitPur 28$_2$ ([לשונ]י), נֶפֶשׁ *soul* Ps 74$_{19(ms)}$ (נֶפֶשׁ תּוֹדֶךָ *a soul that praises you*; or em. L נֶפֶשׁ תּוֹרֶךָ *the soul of your dove* to מוֹדֶךָ soul of *one who praises you* or חֲסִידֶךָ *one loyal to you* or תּוֹרֶךָ *taught by you* or נַפְשׁוֹת דַּךְ *souls of one crushed*)* 142$_8$ 11QPs^a 19$_8$, רוּחַ *spirit* 4QShirShabb^d 1.1$_{38.43}$ ([להוד]ות), קוֹל *voice* Jr 33$_{11}$, מַעֲשֶׂה *deed*, i.e. created being, Ps 145$_{10}$, רִמָּה *worm* 11QPs^a 19$_1$.

רְפָאִים *Rephaim* Ps 88$_{11}$, מִי *who?* Ps 6$_6$, עָפָר *dust* Ps 30$_{10}$, שָׁמַיִם *sky* Ps 89$_6$, אֶרֶץ *earth* Ps 100$_4$, אֲדָמָה *earth* Ps 76$_{11}$ (if em. חֲמַת אָדָם תּוֹדֶךָּ *the anger/family of humankind will praise you* to חָמְתָה אֲדָמָה when *the earth saw*, it praised you; or em. אֱדֹם the anger of *Edom*, i.e. wrathful Edom, will praise you, or חֲמַת אֲרָם *Hamath of Aram* will praise you; and/or em. תּוֹדֶךָּ to תּוּרַד earth/anger /family/Hamath *will be brought down* or to תָּדֹךְ [from דכך] or תָּדֹךְ *you crush* the anger of humankind);* subj. not specified, Pr 28_{13} 4QShirShabbd 1.1_{20}.

<OBJ> י׳ *Y.* Gn 29_{35} 2 S 22_{50}||Ps 18_{50} Is $12_{1.4}$ 38_{15} (if em.) $38_{18.19}$ Jr 33_{11} Ps 7_{18} 9_2 28_7 $30_{10.13}$ 35_{18} 45_{18} 52_{11} $57_{10(mss)}$||108_4 71_{22} 74_{19} (if em. תּוֹרֶךָ *your dove*) 76_{11} (or em.) 88_{11} 109_{30} 111_1 $118_{19.21}$ 119_7 $138_{1.4}$ 139_{14} 145_{10} Si $51_{1.22}$ perh. Ps 49_{19}, אֲדֹנָי *Adonai* Ps 57_{10} 86_{12} 1QH $2_{20.31}$ $3_{19.37}$ 4_5 $5_{5.20}$ (אודכה corrected to ברוך אתה *blessed are you*) $7_{6.26}$ ([אודכה אדוני]) 7_{34} 8_4 ([או]דכה אדוני); =4QHodb 7_{11} (או[ד]כה), אֵל *God* Ps 118_{28} 1QH $11_{3.15}$, אֱלֹהִים *God* Ps 42_6||42_{12}||43_5 43_4 $67_{4.4.6.6}$ perh. 4QapPsb 50_5 ([אלהים]) 4QShirb 28_2 ([אודכ]ה), Job Jb 40_{14}, Judah Gn 49_8, שֵׁם *name* 1 K $8_{33.35}$||2 C $6_{24.26}$ Is 25_1 Ps 44_9 54_8 99_3 138_2 140_{14} 142_8 Si 51_{12}, אֱמוּנָה *trustworthiness* Ps 89_6, perh. אֱמֶת *truth* Ps 71_{22} (but see Coll.), חֶסֶד *loyalty* 11QPsa 19_8, צְדָקָה *righteousness* 1QS 11_{15}, פֶּלֶא *wonder* Ps 89_6, יְשׁוּעָה *salvation* Ps 42_6||42_{12}||43_5 (if em. Ps 42_6; see Coll.), פֶּשַׁע *transgression* Ps $32_{5(mss)}$ Pr 28_{13}.

<PREP> לְ of direction, *to*, + י׳ *Y.* Is 12_4||Ps 105_1||1 C 16_8 Ps 6_6 32_5 33_2 92_2 100_4 106_1 $107_{1.8.15.21.31}$ $118_{1.29}$ 119_{62} 136_1 Ezr 3_{11} 1 C $16_{4.7.34.41}$ 23_{30} 25_3 2 C 5_{13} $7_{3.6}$ 20_{21} Si 51_{12} 11QPsa $19_{1.2.2}$, אֲדֹנָי *Adonai* Ps 75_2 79_{13} 136_2, אֵל *God* Ps 136_{26} Si 51_{12} 1QS 11_{15} 4QShirShabbd 1.1_4 4QsapDidB 4.24 4QRitMar 2_2 9_{10} 4QPrQuot 1.3_8 4QShirb 8_{10} ([מ]ודים [ל]אל), אֱלֹהִים *God* Ps 136_2 Ne 12_{46} 1 C 29_{13} Si 51_1 4QTobite 6_7 ([אלהים]) 4QShirShabbd 1.1_{20}, מֶלֶךְ *king* Si 51_{12} 4QShirShabbd 1.1_{38} (למ[ל]ך), שֹׁמֵר *keeper* Si 51_{12}, יוֹצֵר *creator* Si 51_{12}, גֹּאֵל *redeemer* Si 51_{12}, בֹּנֶה *builder* Si 51_{12}, אָבִיר *strong one* Si 51_{12}, בחר ptc. *one who chooses* Si $51_{12.12}$, קבץ pi. ptc. *one who gathers* Si 51_{12} (הו[דו]), צמח hi. ptc. *one who makes prosper* Si 51_{12}, מָגֵן *shield* Si 51_{12}, שֵׁם *name* Ps 106_{47}||1 C 16_{35} Ps 122_4 1QLitPr 3.1_6 4QDibHama 1.6_{15} (ל[שם]) 4QPrFêtesb 1_2 ([לש]מכו[ה]), צוּר *rock* Si 51_{12}; לְעוֹלָם *forever* Ps 30_{13} 44_9 45_{18} 52_{11} 79_{13} 1QLitPr 3.1_6 4QPrFêtesb 1_2 ([לעולם]); introducing object, + זֵכֶר *remembrance*, i.e. name, of holiness Ps 30_5=97_{12}, כָּבוֹד *glory* 4QShirShabbd 1.1_{38}.

בְּ of place, *in, among*, + Sheol Ps 6_6, עַם *people* Ps 57_{10}||108_4, גּוֹי *nation* 2 S 22_{50}||Ps 18_{50}, בַּיִת *house* 1 K 8_{33}||2 C 6_{24}, שַׁעַר *gate* 2 C 31_2, קָהָל *assembly* Ps 35_{18} 89_6, עֵדָה *congregation* Ps 111_1, סוֹד *council* Ps 111_1; of instrument, *by (means of), with*, + לֵב *heart* Ps 9_2 86_{12} 111_1 (לֵבָב) 138_1, פֶּה *mouth* Ps 109_{30}, לָשׁוֹן *tongue* Si 51_{22}, יָד *hand* 1 C 16_7, כִּנּוֹר *lyre* Ps 33_2 43_4, כְּלִי *(musical) instrument* Ps 71_{22}, תְּהִלָּה *praise* 4QTestim$_{21}$; of accompaniment, *with, in (a state of)*, + יֹשֶׁר *uprightness* Ps 119_7, צֶדֶק *righteousness* Ps $7_{18(mss)}$, רִנָּה *cry* 11QPsa 19_8, הוֹדָה *thanksgiving* 4QShirShabbd 1.1_4 (הו[ד]ות); introducing object, + אֱמֶת *truth* 4QShirShabbd 1.1_{38}.

כְּ *as*, + Hezekiah Is 38_{19}; *in accordance with*, + צֶדֶק *righteousness* Ps 7_{18} (mss בְּ of accompaniment).

מִן of instrument, *by (means of), with*, + שִׁיר *song* Ps 28_7 (or em. לֵב *heart*, with מִן perh. of direction, *from*).

עַל *on account of, for*, + מִשְׁפָּט *judgment* Ps 119_{62}, חֶסֶד *loyalty* Ps 138_2, אֱמֶת *truth* Ps 138_2, פֶּשַׁע *sin* Ps 32_5, כֹּל *all* 4QsapDidB 4.24 (כו[ל]); *against*, + psalmist Ps $32_{5(mss)}$; *despite*, + מַר *bitterness* of soul Is 38_{15} (if em.; see subj.).

לִפְנֵי *before*, + אֵל *God* 4QBerd 1_6 (להוד[ות]).

אַחֲרֵי *after*, | כֹּהֵן *priest* 1QS 1_{24}, לֵוִי *Levite* 1QS 1_{24}.

<COLL> with adverb or noun used adverbially, עוֹד *again* Ps 42_6||42_{12}||43_5, מְאֹד *exceedingly* Ps 109_{30}, הַיּוֹם *today* Is 38_{19}, הַפַּעַם *this time* Gn 29_{35}, עוֹלָם *eternity*, i.e. forever 4QShirShabbd 1.1_{43} (להוד[ות עולמי ע]ולמים *to give praise forever and ever*), יוֹדוּ לַי׳ חַסְדּוֹ *let them give praise to Y. for his loyalty* Ps $107_{1.8.15.21.31}$ (or em. חֲסִדָיו let *his loyal ones* give praise), אֹדְכָה כָל־שְׁנוֹתַי *I shall praise you all my years* Is 38_{15} (if em.; see Subj.), ... אוֹדְךָ אֲמִתְּךָ perh. *I shall praise you ... for your truth* Ps 71_{22}, עוֹד אוֹדֶנּוּ יְשׁוּעוֹת פָּנָיו *I shall praise him again for the salvations of his face*, i.e. saving presence Ps 42_6 (or em. יְשׁוּעַת פָּנַי וֵאלֹהָי I shall again praise him [who is] *the salvation of my face and my God*, as ||42_{12}||43_5).

הוֹדוּ לַי׳ כִּי־טוֹב כִּי לְעוֹלָם חַסְדּוֹ *give praise to Y. for he is good, for his faithful love is forever* Ps 106_1 107_1 $118_{1.29}$ 136_1 1 C 16_{34} 2 C $20_{21(mss)}$ Si 51_{12}, var. Jr 33_{11} (הוֹדוּ אֶת־י׳ צְבָאוֹת כִּי־טוֹב י׳ *praise Y. of hosts, for Y. is good*) Ezr 3_{11} 1 C 16_{41} (lacks כִּי־טוֹב) 2 C $7_{3.6}$ (all four הוֹדוֹת *to give /giving praise*), הודו ל ... כי לעולם חסדו *praise ... for his faithful love is forever* Si $51_{12(13t)}$.

ידה hi. || זמר pi. *praise* 2 S 22_{50}||Ps 18_{50} Ps 7_{18} 33_2 57_{10}

||108$_4$ 71$_{22}$ 92$_2$ 138$_1$ (+) Ps 30$_{5.13}$, הלל pi. *praise* Is 38$_{18}$ Ps 35$_{18}$ 109$_{30}$ Ezr 3$_{11}$ 1 C 16$_4$ 23$_{30}$ 25$_3$ 29$_{13}$ 2 C 5$_{13}$ 31$_2$ Si 51$_{1.12}$ (+) Ps 44$_9$, שׁבח htp. *praise* 4QRitMar 9$_{10}$ (+), ברך pi. *bless* Ps 100$_4$ 145$_{10}$ Si 51$_{12}$, זכר hi. *invoke* 1 C 16$_4$, רום pol. *elevate* Ps 118$_{28}$, פלל htp. *pray* 1 K 8$_{33.35}$||2 C 6$_{24.26}$, חנן htp. *seek favour* 1 K 8$_{33}$||2 C 6$_{24}$, קרא *call* Is 12$_4$||Ps 105$_1$||1 C 16$_8$, שׁרת pi. *minister* 2 C 31$_2$.

ידה hi. + ספר pi. *relate* praise Ps 79$_{13}$ 11QPs^a 19$_1$, שׁוב *repent* 1 K 8$_{35}$||2 C 6$_{26}$, ידע hi. *make known* Is 12$_4$||Ps 105$_1$||1 C 16$_8$, זכר hi. *cause to be remembered* Is 12$_4$||1 C 16$_8$ Ps 45$_{18}$, רום pol. *elevate* Is 25$_1$, נגד hi. *tell* Ps 30$_{10}$ 11QPs^a 19$_8$, כבד pi. *honour* Ps 86$_{12}$, שׂמח *rejoice* Ps 97$_{12}$, שׁבח htp. *praise* Ps 106$_{47}$||1 C 16$_{35}$, כרע *bow* 2 C 7$_3$, שׁחה htpal. *prostrate oneself* Gn 49$_8$ 2 C 7$_3$,

ידה hi. :: כסה pi. *cover*, i.e. conceal, sin Pr 28$_{13}$.

Also perh. 4QMyst^b 23$_3$ (מודה[ ]) 4QShirShabb^b 37$_1$ 4QPrayer^b 1$_1$ 4QHymnic 1$_3$ perh. 4QRitMar 7$_2$ ([ ]הודו[ן]) 13$_2$ ([ ]הודו[ ]) 4QDibHam^a 4$_{21}$ perh. 4QShir^a 12$_1$ ([ ]מודה).

<SYN> זמר pi. *praise*, הלל pi. *praise*, ברך pi. *bless*, זכר hi. *invoke*, רום pol. *elevate*, פלל htp. *pray*, חנן htp. *seek favour*, קרא *call*, שׁרת pi. *minister*.

<ANT> כסה pi. *cover*.

Htp. 11.0.1 + waw וַיִּתְוַדּוּ, וָאֶתְוַדֶּה, וְהִתְוַדּוּ, וְהִתְוַדָּה; ptc. מִתְוַדֶּה, מִתְוַדִּים; inf. הִתְוַדֹּתוֹ—**confess (sin),** <SUBJ> Aaron Lv 16$_{21}$, Daniel Dn 9$_{4.20}$, Ezra Ezr 10$_1$, Nehemiah Ne 1$_6$, אִישׁ *man* Nm 5$_7$, אִשָּׁה *woman* Nm 5$_7$, נֶפֶשׁ *soul* Lv 5$_5$, זֶרַע *seed* of Israel Ne 9$_{2.3}$, לֵוִי *Levite* 2 C 30$_{22}$, שׁוב hi. ptc. *one who makes restitution* CD 11$_{13}$ (if em. והתורה appar. *and the law* to והתודה *and he shall confess*), חזק hi. ptc. *one who holds* CD 20$_{28}$, שׁאר ni. ptc. *remnant* Lv 26$_{40}$; subj. not specified, CD 15$_4$. <OBJ> עָוֹן *sin* Lv 16$_{21}$ 26$_{40.40}$ Ne 9$_2$, פֶּשַׁע *sin* Lv 16$_{21}$, חַטָּאת *sin* Lv 26$_{40(Gnz)}$ Nm 5$_7$ Dn 9$_{20.20}$, אֲשֶׁר *that which*, i.e. the sin that Lv 5$_5$. <PREP> לְ of direction, *to*, + Y. Ne 9$_3$ 2 C 30$_{22}$, כֹּהֵן *priest* CD 9$_{13}$ (if em.; see Subj.); introducing object, + חַטָּאת *sin* Lv 16$_{21}$; עַל *on account of, for*, + חַטָּאת *sin* Ne 1$_6$ 9$_2$, עָוֹן *sin* Ne 9$_2$; *(standing) over*, + שָׂעִיר *goat* Lv 16$_{21}$; לִפְנֵי *before*, + אֵל *God* CD 20$_{28}$. <COLL> || פלל htp. *pray* Dn 9$_{4.20}$ Ezr 10$_1$, דבר pi. *speak* Dn 9$_{20}$, שׁחה htpal. *bow down* Ne 9$_3$; + נפל htp. *prostrate oneself* Ezr 10$_1$, בכה *weep* Ezr 10$_1$. <SYN> פלל htp. *pray*, דבר pi. *speak*, שׁחה htpal. *bow down*.*

⇒ הוֹדָאָה *(song of) thanksgiving*, הוֹדָה *thanksgiving*, הֻיְּדוֹת *songs of praise*, תּוֹדָה *thanksgiving*.

ידה II 6.1.1 vb. **throw—Qal** 1.1.1 Impv. יְדוּ; ptc. Si יודי—**1. shoot (arrow),** <SUBJ> דרך ptc. *one who treads*, i.e. bends, bow Jr 50$_{14}$ (mss ירה *throw*; + חֵץ *arrow*). <PREP> אֶל *at, towards*, + Babylon Jr 50$_{14}$.

2. perh. **throw,** <OBJ> בָּשָׂר *flesh* 4QErr 1$_4$ (והודים perh. error for והיודים).

3. ptc. as noun, **one who casts** lots, <CSTR> יודי גורל *casters of a lot* Si 14$_{15}$ (perh. from ידד *cast [lot]*).

Pi. 5 Impf. יַדּוּ; + waw וַיַּדּוּ; inf. יַדּוֹת—**throw** stone (Lm 3$_{53}$), **cast** lots (Jl 4$_3$ Ob$_{11}$ Na 3$_{10}$ [all three perh. ידד Qal), appar. **throw down, cut off** horn of enemy (Zc 2$_4$), <SUBJ> אוֹיֵב *enemy* Lm 3$_{53}$, appar. enemy of Nineveh Na 3$_{10}$ (4QpNah ירה *throw*), גּוֹי *nation* Jl 4$_3$, נָכְרִי *foreigner* Ob$_{11}$, חָרָשׁ *artisan* Zc 2$_4$. <OBJ> גּוֹרָל *lot* Jl 4$_3$ Ob$_{11}$ Na 3$_{10}$, קֶרֶן *horn* Zc 2$_4$, אֶבֶן *stone* Lm 3$_{53}$. <PREP> בְּ of place, *at* (inhabitant of) Jerusalem Lm 3$_{53}$; עַל *over, for*, + Jerusalem Ob$_{11}$, כבד ni. ptc. *honoured citizen* Na 3$_{10}$, עַם *people* Jl 4$_3$ (if em. אֶל in same sense).*

* **[יָדֶה]** 2 n.[m.] **voice**—cstr. יְדֵי; sf. יָדֵיהוּ—נָתַן תְּהוֹם קוֹלוֹ רוֹם יָדֵיהוּ נָשָׂא *the deep makes its voice heard, high up it raises its voice* Hb 3$_{10}$ (unless יָד *hand*), בְּדֵי שֹׁפָר יֹאמַר הֶאָח *at the sound of the trumpet he says, Aha* Jb 39$_{25}$ (unless דַּי *sufficiency*).

יִדּוֹ 2.0.0.3 pr.n.m. **Iddo, 1.** Manassite, son of Zechariah, <NOM CL> לַחֲצִי הַמְנַשֶּׁה גִּלְעָדָה יִדּוֹ *to the half (tribe) of Manasseh in Gilead was Iddo* 1 C 27$_{21}$ (or em. יַדַּי *Jaddai*). <APP> בֵּן *son* 1 C 27$_{21}$ (or em.; see Nom. Cl.).

2. member of Nebo family, husband of foreign wife, <NOM CL> מִבְּנֵי נְבוֹ ... ידו *of the sons of Nebo were ... Iddo* Ezr 10$_{43(Kt)}$ (Qr יַדַּי *Jaddai*).

3. T. en-Naṣbeh inscr. 5. **4.** father of Azaliah, <CSTR> בן ידו *son of Iddo* Seal 752 (7th cent.). **5.** Seal 860 (7th cent.), <NOM CL> ידו אשר [ע]ל הבית *Iddo, who is over the house* Seal 860 (7th cent.). <PREP> of possession, *of, (belonging) to* Seal 860 (ל[ידו]; 7th cent.).*

יָדוֹן 1 pr.n.m. **Jadon,** Meronothite and repairer of walls of Jerusalem, <SUBJ> חזק hi. *strengthen*, i.e. repair Ne 3_{7}. <APP> אִישׁ *man* Ne 3_{7}, מֵרֹנֹתִי *Meronothite* Ne 3_{7}.
→ דין *judge.*

יַדּוּעַ 3.0.0.4 pr.n.m. **Jaddua, 1.** leader and co-signatory with Nehemiah, <NOM CL> רָאשֵׁי הָעָם ... יַדּוּעַ *the chiefs of the people were ... Jaddua* Ne 10_{22}.

2. high priest, son of Jonathan (or em. יוֹנָתָן *Jonathan* to יוֹחָנָן *Johanan*), <OBJ> ילד hi. *beget* Ne 12_{11}. <CSTR> יְמֵי ... יַדּוּעַ *days of ... Jaddua* Ne 12_{22}.

3. Stamp/Coin 50 (4th cent.). **4.** Frey 1285_{19}. **5.** Frey 1285_{27}. **6.** Frey 1286_{15}.

7. perh. father of Shallum, <CSTR> בן ידע *son of Jaddua* Lachish ost. 3_{20} (but prob. יָדָע *Jada*).
→ ידע *know.*

יְדוּתוּן 17 pr.n.m. **Jeduthun**—יְדִיתוּן, יְדֻתוּן (1 C 16_{38}; Kt Ps 39_{1} 77_{1} Ne 11_{7})—**1.** Levite, musician and singer, and king's seer, perh. ident. with Ethan at 1 C $15_{17.19}$, Ne 11_{17} 1 C 9_{16} $16_{38.41.42}$ (both + Heman) 16_{42} 25_{1} (+ Asaph, Heman) $25_{3.3.3.6}$ 2 C 5_{12} 29_{14} 2 C 35_{15} (all four + Asaph, Heman).

2. in Psalm titles, perh. ident. with §1, Ps 39_{1} 62_{1} 77_{1}. <NOM CL> עִמָּהֶם ... וִידוּתוּן *with them were ... and Jeduthun* 1 C 16_{42}, עַל יְדֵי הַמֶּלֶךְ ... וִיוּדתוּן *under the hands*, i.e. direction, *of the king were ... and Jeduthun* 1 C 25_{6}. <CSTR> בֶּן־יְדוּתוּן *son of Jeduthun* Ne $11_{17(Qr)}$||1 C 9_{16} (Ne Kt ידיתון) 1 C $16_{38(Qr\ mss)}$ (יְדִיתוּן), בְּנֵי *sons of* 1 C $16_{41.42}$ 25_{1} (בְּנֵי ...) 25_{3} 2 C 29_{14}, יְדֵי ... *hands*, i.e. charge, *of* ... 1 C 25_{3}, מִצְוַת ... *commandment of* ... 2 C 35_{15} (וִידֻתוּן). <APP> אָב *father* 1 C 25_{3}, חֹזֶה *seer* 2 C 35_{15}. <PREP> לְ of possession, *(belonging) to*, 1 C 25_{3} 2 C 5_{12} (+ Heman, Asaph), Ps 39_{1} $62_{1(mss)}$ (both perh. לְ *according to*); עַל *according to* Ps 62_{1} 77_{1}.
→ ידה *give thanks.*

יַדַּי 1 pr.n.m. **Jaddai, 1.** member of Nebo family, husband of foreign wife, <NOM CL> מִבְּנֵי נְבוֹ ... יַדַּי *of the sons of Nebo were ... Jaddai* Ezr $10_{43(Qr)}$ (Kt ידו *Iddo*).

2. Manassite, son of Zechariah, <NOM CL> לַחֲצִי הַמְנַשֶּׁה גִּלְעָדָה יַדַּי *to the half (tribe) of Manasseh in Gilead was Jaddai* 1 C 27_{21} (if em. יִדּוֹ *Iddo*). <APP> בֵּן *son* 1 C 27_{21} (if em.; see Nom. Cl.).*

[יָדִיד] 8.0.8 adj. **beloved**—cstr. יְדִיד; sf. יְדִידִי, יְדִידוֹ; pl. Q ידידים, יְדִידוֹת; sf. יְדִידֶיךָ (Q ידידיכה), 2fs Q ידידיך, mss יְדִידָיו—**1.** as adj. **beloved,** used predicatively of בֵּן *son* 4Q474 1_{3} ([ידי]ד), מִשְׁכָּן *dwelling place* Ps 84_{2} מַה־יְּדִידוֹת מִשְׁכְּנוֹתֶיךָ *how beloved are your dwelling places*).
2. as noun, **beloved (one),** <SUBJ> שׁכן *dwell* 4QSela 8.2_{8}, חלץ ni. *be delivered* Ps 60_{7}||Ps 108_{7}, שִׁיר *sing* 4Q Hod[a] 7.1_{11}, זמר pi. *praise* 4QHod[a] 7.1_{11}, לוה ni. *join oneself* 11QPs[a] 22_{7} (+ בֵּן *son*). <CSTR> יְדִיד י׳ *beloved of Y.* Dt 33_{12} (Sam יד יד י׳; or em. יְדִד יָהּ *beloved of Yah*) 4Q Sela 8.2_{8}, ידיד המלך *beloved one of the king* 4QM[h] 6_{6}; יד ידידיכה *hand of your beloved ones* 4QPrayers[g] 1_{2}. <APP> לֵוִי *Levi* 4QapJoshua[b] 1_{2}. <PREP> לְ of direction, *to* perh. 4QNarrA 1_{1}, + נתן *give* Ps 127_{2}; *for, on behalf of*, + שִׁיר *sing* Is 5_{1} (+ דּוֹד *beloved*); of possession, *(belonging) to, of* Jr 11_{15} (or em. לִידִידִי to לִידִידָתִי *to my beloved* [fem.], or לִי דוּדַיִךְ *to me are your baskets*), + היה *be* Is 5_{1}.
Also 4QNarrA 1_{2}.*
→ יַד III *love.*

יְדִידָה 1 pr.n.f. **Jedidah,** mother of Josiah and daugher of Adaiah, <NOM CL> שֵׁם אִמּוֹ יְדִידָה *the name of his mother was Jedidah* 2 K 22_{1}. <APP> בַּת *daughter* 2 K 22_{1}.*
→ יַד III *love.*

יְדִידוֹת, see יְדִידֹת *love.*

יְדִידְיָהּ 1 pr.n.m. **Jedidiah,** name given to Solomon, 'beloved of Yah', <OBJ> קרא *call*, i.e. name 2 S 12_{25}.
→ יָדִיד *beloved* + י׳ *Y.*

יְדִידֹת 1 n.f. pl. **love**—mss יְדִידוֹת; mss יְדִידָת—<CSTR> שִׁיר יְדִידֹת *song of love* Ps 45_{1}.*
→ יַד III *love.*

יְדִידָת, see יְדִידֹת *love.*

יְדָיָה 2 pr.n.m. **Jedaiah**—mss יְדָיָהוּ—**1.** son of Harumaph, and repairer of walls of Jerusalem, <SUBJ> חזק

hi. *strengthen*, i.e. repair Ne 3₁₀. <APP> בֵּן *son* Ne 3₁₀.

2. Simeonite, son of Shimri, <CSTR> בֶּן־יְדָיָה *son of Jedaiah* 1 C 4₃₇.

⇒ יה *Y.*

יְדִיעֲאֵל 6 pr.n.m. **Jediael, 1.** son of Benjamin, <NOM CL> בְּנֵי בִנְיָמִן ... וִידִיעֲאֵל *the sons of Benjamin were ... and Jediael* 1 C 7₇₍mss₎ (L lacks בְּנֵי). <CSTR> בְּנֵי יְדִיעֲאֵל *sons of Jediael* 1 C 7₁₀ (Seb בֵּן *son of*) 7₁₁.

2. son of Shimri, and soldier in David's army, <NOM CL> גִּבּוֹרֵי הַחֲיָלִים ... יְדִיעֲאֵל *the mighty men of the armies were ... Jediael* 1 C 11₄₅. <APP> בֵּן *son* 1 C 11₄₅.

3. Manassite chief who defected to David, perh. ident. with §2, <SUBJ> נפל *fall* 1 C 12₂₁. <APP> רֹאשׁ *head*, i.e. chief 1 C 12₂₁.

4. Korahite gatekeeper, son of Meshelemiah, <NOM CL> יְדִיעֲאֵל הַשֵּׁנִי *Jediael was the second (son)* 1 C 26₂.

⇒ ידע *know* + אֵל *God.*

יְדִיתוּן, see יְדוּתוּן *Jeduthun.*

[יְדַלְיָהוּ] pr.n.m. **Jedaliah,** appar. son of Hanan, Seal 49 (others [ידעיה[ו; Jerusalem, 8th/7th cent.).

⇒ דלה *draw water* + יה *Y.*

יִדְלָף 1 pr.n.m. **Jidlaph,** son of Nahor and Milcah, <OBJ> ילד *bear* Gn 22₂₂.

[יְדָנְיָהוּ] 0.0.0.2 pr.n.m. **Jedoniah, 1.** son of Shebaniah (([שב[ניהו), <APP> בֵּן *son* Arad ost. 27₄. **2.** son of Nethaniah, <APP> בֵּן *son* Seal 870 (7th cent.). PREP> לְ of possession, *of, (belonging) to,* Seal 870 (7th cent.).

⇒ יה *Y.* + דין *judge.*

ידע I 957.28.261.5 vb. **know.**

Qal 822.24.204.5 Pf. יָדַע (יָדֵע, יָדְעוֹ, Q ידעהו, יְדָעָהּ, יְדַעְתּוֹ, יְדַעְתַּנִי, יְדַעְתָּה (יָדַעְתָּה) יָדַעְתְּ, יְדָעָה, (יְדָעָנוּ, יְדַעְתִּיךָ, Q ידעתיכה, (יָדַעְתִּי) יָדַעְתִּי, (יָדַעַתְּ) יָדַעַתְּ, (יְדַעְתֶּם, (יָדֵעוּ) יָדְעוּ, (יְדַעְתִּין, יְדַעְתִּים, יְדַעְתִּיהָ, ידעתיו, Q ידעתיכהו, יְדַעְתֶּם, (יְדָעוּם, יְדָעֻהוּ, יְדָעוּךָ mss, יְדָעוּךָ, יְדָעוּנִי, יְדָעוּן, Q ידענוכה, יְדַעֲנוּךָ, (יָדַעְנוּ) יְדַעְנוּ, יְדַעְתֶּן, (ידעתמה Q) (יְדַעֲנוּם); impf. יֵדַע (יֵדָע, יֵיְדַע, יְדָעֵנוּ, יֵדָעֵם), 2ms תֵּדַע (תֵּדָע), תֵּדְעִי (תֵּדָעִי), תֵּדְעִין, (אֵדַע) אֵדָע, אֵדְעָה, אֵדָעָה, (אֵדָעֵךְ), יֵדְעוּ (יֵדְעוּן, Q ידעוכה), תֵּדְעוּ (תֵּדָעוּ), תֵּדְעוּן, (תֵּדָעוּהָ), נֵדַע (נֵדָע, נֵדְעָה, נֵדָעָה, נֵדָעֵנוּ); + waw וְיָדַעְתָּ, וְיָדַעַתְּ, וְיָדַעְתִּי, וְיָדְעוּ, וִידַעְתֶּם, וִידַעְתֶּן, וִידַעְנוּ, וְיָדַעְנוּ; וַיֵּדַע, 2ms וַתֵּדַע (וַתֵּדָעֵהוּ), וָאֵדַע (וָאֵדְעָה, וָאֵדָעָה), וַיֵּדְעוּ, וַנֵּדָעֵם; impv. דַּע (דָּע, דְּעֵה, דָּעֵהוּ), דְּעִי, דְּעוּ; ptc. יֹדֵעַ (יוֹדֵעַ, Q יודיע, יוֹדְעוֹ, יֹדְעֵנוּ), יֹדַעַת, יֹדְעִים (יוֹדְעִים, Q יודעין), sf. יֹדְעֵי, יְדָעֵי, יוֹדְעֶיךָ (יֹדְעֶיךָ, Q יודעיכה), יְדָעָיו, Q יודעיו), יֹדְעֵי, (יוֹדְעֵי), Q ידעות; ptc. pass. cstr. יְדוּעַ (Q ידע), יְדוּעִים, (יְדֻעִים); inf. abs. יָדֹעַ (יָדוֹעַ); inf. cstr. דַּעַת (דַּעְתִּי, דַּעְתְּךָ, דַּעְתּוֹ, דַּעְתָּהּ, L דַּעְתָּהּ)—**1. know, realize, be aware, have knowledge (of), a.** with object (e.g. Gn 9₂₄ 27₂ 30₂₆ Ex 3₇ Nm 10₃₁ 20₁₄ Dt 29₁₅ 34₆ 1 K 2₅.₄₄ Jr 8₇ Jb 38₃₃ 4Q417 2.1₆); sometimes **acknowledge** (e.g. Is 59₁₂ Jr 3₁₃ 14₂₀ Ps 51₅); sometimes perh. specif. legally **recognize** (authority of)* (e.g. Gn 18₁₉ Ex 33₁₂ Dt 9₂₄ 1 S 2₁₂ 3₇ 2 S 7₂₀ Is 19₂₁ Jr 2₈ 22₁₆ 24₇ 31₃₄ Ho 2₂₂ 4₁ 5₄ 8₂ 13₄ Am 3₂ Ps 14₄ 36₁₁ Dn 11₃₂ 1 C 28₉ 1QS 5₁₉), but in some of these refs. and others (e.g. Dt 34₁₀ Jr 12₃) perh. **choose.***

b. used absolutely (e.g. Gn 4$_{9}$ 18$_{21}$ 28$_{16}$ 48$_{19}$ Lv 5$_{1.3.4.17.18}$ Dt 29$_{3}$ Jos 22$_{22}$ 1 S 17$_{55}$ 26$_{12}$ 2 S 3$_{26}$ 1 K 1$_{18}$ 23$_{2}$ 2 K 2$_{3}$ 4$_{39}$ Is 1$_{3}$ 40$_{21}$ 44$_{9}$ 45$_{20}$ 58$_{3}$ Jr 5$_{1}$ 14$_{18}$ 41$_{4}$ Ho 8$_{4}$ Ps 73$_{11.22}$ Jb 34$_{2}$ Ca 1$_{8}$ Ec 8$_{17}$ Ne 4$_{5}$ Si 35$_{8}$ 1QS 6$_{25}$).

c. before conjunction and subordinate clause (e.g. Gn 19$_{33.35}$ 47$_{6}$ 2 S 12$_{22[Qr]}$), or subordinate clause without conjunction (e.g. Nm 22$_{6}$).

d. before indirect question (e.g. Gn 21$_{26}$ 43$_{22}$ 47$_{6[Sam]}$ Ex 10$_{26}$ 16$_{15}$ 32$_{1.23}$ 33$_{5}$ Nm 22$_{19}$ Jos 2$_{4.5}$ Jg 18$_{14}$ 1 S 14$_{38}$ 22$_{3}$ 25$_{11.17}$ 2 S 18$_{29}$ 24$_{13}$ Jr 2$_{23}$ 36$_{19}$ 44$_{28}$ Ezk 17$_{12}$ Jl 2$_{14}$ Jon 1$_{7}$ 3$_{9}$ Zc 4$_{5.13}$ Ps 39$_{5.7}$ 74$_{9}$ Jb 34$_{4}$ Pr 4$_{19}$ 27$_{1}$ Ec 2$_{19}$ 3$_{21}$ 6$_{12}$ 8$_{7}$ 11$_{2.5.6}$ Est 2$_{11}$ 4$_{14}$ Dn 10$_{20}$ Ne 2$_{16}$ 1 C 12$_{33}$ 2 C 20$_{12}$ 32$_{13}$ Si 8$_{18}$ 9$_{11}$ 4QMyst^{b} 1a.2-b$_{1}$ 8$_{6}$ ([ת]דעו) 4Q416 2.3$_{15}$ 4Q417 1.1$_{8.11}$).

e. know (that), realize (that), be aware (that), (1) before כִּי *that* (sometimes also with object, e.g. יָדַעְתָּ אֶת־אָבִיךָ וְאֶת־אֲנָשָׁיו כִּי גִבֹּרִים הֵמָּה *you know your father and his men, that they are mighty men,* i.e. you know that your father and his men are mighty 2 S 17$_{8}$), Gn 3$_{5.7}$ 8$_{11}$ 12$_{11}$ 15$_{8.13}$ 20$_{6.7}$ 22$_{12}$ 24$_{14}$ 31$_{6.32}$ 33$_{13}$ 38$_{9.16}$ 42$_{23.33.34}$ 43$_{7}$ 44$_{15.27}$ Ex 3$_{19}$ 4$_{14}$ 6$_{7}$ 7$_{5.17}$ 8$_{6.18}$ 9$_{14.29.30}$ 10$_{2.7}$ 14$_{4.18}$ 16$_{6.12}$ 18$_{11}$ 23$_{9.46}$ 31$_{13}$ 32$_{22}$ 34$_{29}$ Lv 23$_{43}$ Nm 16$_{28.30}$ 22$_{34}$ Dt 3$_{19}$ 4$_{35.39}$ 7$_{9}$ 8$_{5}$ 9$_{3.6}$ 11$_{2}$ 20$_{20}$ 29$_{5}$ 31$_{29}$ Jos 2$_{9}$ 3$_{7.10}$ 4$_{24}$ 8$_{14}$ 22$_{31}$ 23$_{13.14}$ Jg 6$_{37}$ 13$_{16.21}$ 14$_{4}$ 15$_{11}$ 16$_{20}$ 17$_{13}$ 18$_{14}$ 20$_{34}$ 1 S 3$_{13.20}$ 4$_{6}$ 6$_{9}$ 12$_{17}$ 14$_{3}$ 17$_{46.47}$ 18$_{28}$ 20$_{3.7.9.30.33}$ 22$_{17.22}$ 23$_{9}$ 24$_{12.21}$ 26$_{4}$ 28$_{1.14}$ 29$_{9}$ 2 S 1$_{5.10}$ 2$_{26}$ 3$_{37.38}$ 5$_{12}$||1 C 14$_{2}$ 2 S 11$_{16}$ 14$_{1.22}$ 17$_{8.10}$ 19$_{7.21.23}$ 1 K 2$_{15.37.42}$ 5$_{17.20}$ 8$_{43}$||2 C 6$_{33}$ 1 K 8$_{60}$ 14$_{2}$ 17$_{24}$ 18$_{37}$ 20$_{7.13.28}$ 22$_{3}$ 2 K 2$_{3.5}$ 4$_{1.9}$ 5$_{7.8.15}$ 7$_{12}$ 10$_{10}$ 19$_{19}$||Is 37$_{20}$ Is 41$_{20}$ 41$_{23}$ 44$_{3}$ 45$_{6}$ 48$_{4}$ 49$_{23.26}$ 50$_{7}$ 60$_{16}$ Jr 2$_{19}$ 3$_{13}$ 10$_{23}$ 11$_{19}$ 13$_{12}$ 16$_{21}$ 24$_{7}$ 26$_{15}$ 32$_{8}$ 40$_{14}$ 42$_{19.22}$ 44$_{15.29}$ Ezk 2$_{5}$ 6$_{7.10.13.14}$ 7$_{4.9.27}$ 10$_{20}$ 11$_{10.12}$ 12$_{15.16.20}$ 13$_{9.14.21.23}$ 14$_{8.23}$ 15$_{7}$ 16$_{62}$ 17$_{21.24}$ 20$_{12.20.38.42.44}$ 21$_{10}$ 22$_{16.22}$ 23$_{49}$ 24$_{24.27}$ 25$_{5.7.11.17}$ 26$_{6}$ 28$_{22.23.24.26}$ 29$_{6.9.16.21}$ 30$_{8.19.25.26}$ 32$_{15}$ 33$_{29.33}$ 34$_{27.30}$ 35$_{4.9.12.15}$ 36$_{11.23.36.38}$ 37$_{6.13.14.28}$ 38$_{23}$ 39$_{6.7.22.23.28}$ Ho 2$_{10.22(mss)}$ 11$_{3}$ Jl 2$_{27}$ 4$_{17}$ Jon 1$_{10.12}$ 4$_{2}$ Zc 2$_{13.15}$ 4$_{9}$ 6$_{15}$ Ml 2$_{4}$ Ps 4$_{4}$ 20$_{7}$ 41$_{12}$ 46$_{11}$ 56$_{10}$ 50$_{14}$ 83$_{19}$ 94$_{11}$ 100$_{3}$ 109$_{27}$ 119$_{75.152}$ (unless ידע II *be quiet*) 135$_{5}$ 140$_{13}$ Jb 5$_{24.25}$ 8$_{9}$ 9$_{2.28}$ 10$_{13}$ 11$_{6}$ 12$_{9}$ 13$_{18}$ 15$_{23}$ 19$_{6}$ 42$_{2}$ Pr 7$_{23}$ 9$_{18}$ 28$_{22}$ Ru 3$_{11}$ Ec 3$_{12.14}$ 11$_{9}$ Ne 6$_{16}$ 9$_{10}$ 1 C 29$_{17}$ 2 C 13$_{5}$ 25$_{16}$ 33$_{13}$ Si 9$_{13}$ 33$_{5}$ 34$_{13}$ (Bmg) 36$_{22(B)}$ 46$_{6}$ ([דע]ת) 46$_{10}$ 1QH 2$_{22.33}$ 3$_{20}$ 4$_{30}$ 6$_{6}$ 9$_{14}$ (כ[י]) 11$_{7.17}$ ([כי]) 13$_{18}$ ([כיא]) 15$_{12.13.22.23.25}$ 16$_{4.10.11}$ 18$_{21}$ fr 1$_{9}$ 1QS 10$_{16}$ 1QDM 1$_{11}$ ([כי]) 4QMidrEschat^{a} 4$_{4}$ ([י]דע) 4QJub^{a} 1$_{5}$ ([יד]עו) 1$_{6}$ (ידע[ו כי]) 1$_{28}$ ([כי]) 4QJub^{f} 37$_{14}$ (יד[ע ... כי]) 4QJub^{h} 37$_{23}$ 4QMyst^{a} 7$_{23}$ ([י]דע) 4QapPs^{b} 13$_{2}$ (כ[י]) 4QparaKings 9$_{5}$ ([היד]עתה) 4QpsEzek^{a} 2$_{4}$ 4QpsEzek^{b} 1.2$_{1}$ 4QpsMos^{d} 1.2$_{6}$ ([כ]י) 4QpsEzek^{e} 65$_{5}$ 4QM^{h} 1$_{4}$ CD 1$_{8}$ GnzPs 2$_{14.18}$ Lachish ost. 4$_{10}$ Arad ost. 40$_{13}$ ([כי]).

(2) before אֲשֶׁר *that,* Ex 11$_{7}$ Ezk 20$_{26}$ Ec 7$_{22}$ 8$_{12}$ Est 4$_{11}$ 2 C 2$_{7}$ 1QH 6$_{7}$ ([יד]עתי) 1QJub^{b} 35$_{9}$ (י[וד]ע) 4QTobit^{e} 4$_{3}$ 4QD^{f} 3$_{7}$ 4QapJoshua^{b} 6$_{2}$.

(3) before -שֶׁ *that,* Jb 19$_{29}$ Ec 1$_{17}$ 2$_{14}$ 9$_{5}$ Si 34$_{16}$ 4QMMT B$_{68}$ ([שעל]) B$_{80}$ C$_{8}$ (י[ודעים שלוא]).

(4) without conjunction, Ps 9$_{21}$ Jb 19$_{25}$ 30$_{23}$ Si 34$_{15}$ 37$_{12}$.

2. know, be familiar with, experience something (e.g. Ex 23$_{9}$ Nm 14$_{31.34}$ Dt 7$_{15}$ Jg 3$_{1}$ 1 K 9$_{27}$||2 C 8$_{18}$ Is 42$_{16}$ 47$_{8}$ Zp 3$_{5}$ Jb 20$_{20}$ Ec 8$_{5}$ 2 C 12$_{8}$).

3. know, be acquainted with a person (e.g. Gn 29$_{5}$ Ex 1$_{8}$ Dt 22$_{2}$ 1 S 10$_{11}$ 2 S 17$_{8}$ 1 K 5$_{17}$ 2 K 9$_{11}$ Is 29$_{15}$ Jb 42$_{11}$ 4Q416 2.3$_{5}$), nation (e.g. Dt 9$_{2}$ 28$_{33}$ 2 S 22$_{44}$||Ps 18$_{44}$), God (e.g. Ex 5$_{2}$ 33$_{13}$ Jg 2$_{10}$ 1 S 2$_{12}$ 3$_{7}$ Is 19$_{21}$ 45$_{5}$ Jr 2$_{8}$ 31$_{34}$ Ho 2$_{22}$ Ps 36$_{11}$ 79$_{6}$ Jb 18$_{21}$ Pr 3$_{6}$ Dn 11$_{32}$ 1 C 28$_{9}$ Si 16$_{15}$ 4QHod^{a} 7.2$_{12}$ GnzPs 3$_{19}$), other gods (Dt 11$_{28}$ 13$_{3.7.14}$ 28$_{64}$ 29$_{25}$ 32$_{17}$ Jr 7$_{9}$ 19$_{4}$ 44$_{3}$ Dn 11$_{38}$); of God knowing humans (e.g. Ex 33$_{12.17}$ Dt 34$_{10}$ 2 S 7$_{20}$||1 C 17$_{18}$ Jr 12$_{3}$ Ho 5$_{3}$ Jb 11$_{11}$), birds (Ps 50$_{11}$); of animal knowing owner (Is 1$_{3}$).

4. know a person **carnally, have sexual relations (with)** (e.g. Gn 4$_{1}$ 19$_{8}$ 38$_{26}$ Nm 31$_{17}$ Jg 11$_{39}$ 19$_{25}$ 21$_{11}$ 1 S 1$_{19}$ 1 K 1$_{4}$1 1QSa 1$_{10}$); of male homosexual relations (Gn 19$_{5}$ Jg 19$_{22}$).

5. know, recognize, learn, perceive, understand (e.g. Gn 3$_{5}$ Dt 1$_{39}$ Jos 3$_{4}$ 2 S 19$_{36}$ Is 6$_{9}$ 29$_{24}$ 32$_{4}$ 42$_{25}$ Jr 17$_{9}$ Ho 14$_{10}$ Mc 3$_{1}$ Ps 73$_{16}$ Jb 11$_{8}$ 42$_{3}$ Est 1$_{13}$).

6. know (how) to do, **be skilful in, be knowledgeable about** (e.g. Gn 25$_{27}$ Ex 36$_{1}$ 1 S 16$_{16}$ 1 K 5$_{20}$ Is 7$_{15.16}$ 8$_{4}$ 29$_{11.12}$ 47$_{11}$ 50$_{4}$ Jr 1$_{6}$ 4$_{22}$ Am 5$_{16}$ Jb 32$_{22}$ Ec 4$_{13.17}$ 6$_{8}$ 2 C 2$_{6.7.13}$ Si 47$_{5}$ 4QBer^{a} 7.1$_{6}$ Lachish ost. 3$_{8}$).

7. know, find out, discover (e.g. Dt 8$_{2}$ 2 S 24$_{2}$||1 C 21$_{2}$ Ru 3$_{4}$ Est 2$_{11}$ 4$_{1}$ 2 C 32$_{31}$); before כִּי *that* (Ne 13$_{10}$); before indirect question (Gn 24$_{21}$ Ex 2$_{4}$ Dt 13$_{4}$=11QT 54$_{12}$ Jg 3$_{4}$ 18$_{5}$ Ru 3$_{18}$ Est 4$_{5}$ Si 37$_{8}$).

8. pay attention to, be concerned about something

(e.g. Gn 39$_{6}$), someone (e.g. Dt 33$_{9}$), one's self (e.g. Jb 9$_{21}$); before indirect question (e.g. Gn 39$_{8}$).

<SUBJ> Y. Gn 3$_{5.5}$ 18$_{19}$ (unless ידע III *care*) 18$_{21}$ (unless ידע IV *punish*) 20$_{6}$ Ex 2$_{25}$ (unless ידע III; or em. וַיֵּדַע אֱלֹהִים *and God knew* to וַיִּוָּדַע אֲלֵיהֶם *and he made himself known to them*) 3$_{7}$ (unless ידע X *leave alone*) 3$_{19}$ 4$_{14}$ 33$_{5.12.17}$ Dt 2$_{7}$ 8$_{2}$ 9$_{24(Sam)}$ 11$_{2}$ 13$_{4}$=11QT 54$_{12}$ Dt 31$_{21}$ 31$_{27}$ 34$_{10}$ Jos 22$_{22}$ Jg 3$_{4}$ 2 S 7$_{20}$‖1 C 17$_{18}$ 1 K 8$_{39.39}$‖2 C 6$_{30.30}$ 2 K 19$_{27}$‖Is 37$_{28}$ Is 41$_{22.23}$ appar. 44$_{8}$ (or del.) 48$_{4.8}$ 58$_{3}$ Jr 1$_{5}$ (unless ידע III) 12$_{3}$ 15$_{15.15}$ 17$_{16}$ 18$_{23}$ 29$_{11.23(Qr)}$ 48$_{30}$ Ezk 11$_{5}$ 37$_{3}$ Ho 5$_{3}$ 8$_{4}$ 13$_{5}$ (unless ידע III; or em. רעה *tend*) Am 3$_{2}$ Na 1$_{7}$ (unless both ידע III) Am 5$_{12}$ Ps 1$_{6}$ 31$_{8}$ (unless both ידע III) 37$_{18}$ 40$_{10}$ 44$_{22}$ 50$_{11}$ 69$_{6.20}$ 73$_{11}$ 94$_{11}$ 103$_{14}$ 138$_{6}$ (unless ידע II *reduce to submission*) 139$_{1.2}$ (unless ידע III *care*) 139$_{4.23.23}$ 142$_{4}$ 144$_{3}$ (unless ידע III) Jb 11$_{11}$ 22$_{13}$ 23$_{10}$ (unless ידע III) 28$_{23}$ 31$_{6}$ 35$_{15}$ (unless ידע II *be humiliated*) appar. 42$_{2(Kt)}$ Ne 9$_{10}$ Si 42$_{18(M)}$ perh. 1QH 1$_{7.28}$ 7$_{13.16}$ 9$_{12.30}$ 10$_{19}$ 1QM 18$_{10}$ 1QS 4$_{25}$ 4QAges^{a} 2.2$_{10}$ 4QPrFêtes^{b} 2$_{4.5}$ (דעת[י]) CD 2$_{7.9}$.

אֱלֹהִים *god* Ps 82$_{5}$ (or del.), מַלְאָךְ *angel* Gn 22$_{12}$ 1QH fr. 1$_{3}$ ([מלאכי]) 11QPs^{a} 26$_{12}$.

Israel(ites) Ex 10$_{2}$ 23$_{9}$ Dt 4$_{35.39}$ 7$_{9.15}$ 8$_{3.5}$ 9$_{2.3.6}$ 11$_{28}$ 13$_{3.7}$ =11QT 54$_{10.21}$ Dt 13$_{14}$=11QT 55$_{4}$ Dt 18$_{21}$=11QT 61$_{2}$ Dt 20$_{20}$ 22$_{2}$=11QT 64$_{15}$ Dt 28$_{33.36.64}$ 29$_{5,15.25}$ 32$_{17}$ Jos 3$_{7.10}$ 22$_{22}$ 23$_{13.13.14}$ Jg 3$_{1}$ 1 S 3$_{20}$ 2 S 3$_{37}$ 11$_{20}$ 17$_{10}$ 1 K 8$_{38}$‖2 C 6$_{29}$ 1 K 20$_{28}$ 2 K 5$_{7}$ Is 1$_{3}$ 5$_{19}$ 40$_{21.28}$ 41$_{20.26}$ 42$_{25}$ 43$_{10.19}$ 44$_{18}$ 45$_{6}$ 48$_{6.7.8}$ 55$_{5}$ 59$_{8.12}$ Jr 2$_{19.23}$ 3$_{13}$ 5$_{1.4}$ 7$_{9}$ 9$_{2.5}$ 13$_{12.12}$ 14$_{20}$ 15$_{14}$ 16$_{13.21}$ 19$_{4}$ Ezk 14$_{23}$ 15$_{7}$ 19$_{7}$ (unless ידע II *be humiliated*, or IV *punish*, or IX *tear down*; or em. יֵדַע אַלְמְנוֹתָיו *and he knew his widows* to וַיָּרַע אַרְמְנוֹתֵיהֶם *and he shattered their fortresses*) 20$_{12.38}$ 34$_{27.30}$ Ho 6$_{3}$ (unless ידע II *be submissive*, or VI *seek*, or del.) Ho 2$_{22}$ (or em.; see Obj.) 5$_{4}$ 7$_{9.9}$ (unless ידע XI *wrap up*) 9$_{7}$ (unless ידע II *be humiliated*, or IV *be punished*) Ho 8$_{2}$ Jl 4$_{17}$ Zc 2$_{13}$ 4$_{9}$ 6$_{15}$ 7$_{14}$ Ps 78$_{3}$ Ne 4$_{5}$ 2 C 12$_{8}$ 13$_{5}$ 20$_{12}$ Si 33$_{5}$ 1QM 10$_{16}$ 1QDM 1$_{11}$ 4QpsMos^{e} 2.1$_{6}$ CD 1$_{8}$.

Ephraim Is 9$_{8}$ (unless ידע II *be humiliated*) Ho 5$_{4}$ 11$_{3}$ 13$_{4}$, Jacob Ezk 39$_{28}$, specif. Judah Jr 17$_{4}$ 2 C 23$_{13}$, יְהוּדִי *Jew* Jr 44$_{3}$.

Ammonites Ezk 25$_{5.7}$, Aram(aeans) 2 K 7$_{12}$, Edom(ites) Ezk 25$_{14}$ 35$_{15}$, Egypt(ians) Ex 7$_{5}$ 14$_{4.18}$ Is 19$_{21}$ Ezk 29$_{16}$ 30$_{19.25.26}$ 32$_{15}$, Midianite Nm 10$_{31}$, Moab(ites) Ezk 25$_{11}$, Philistines 1 S 4$_{6}$ 6$_{9}$ Ezk 25$_{17}$, Sidonians Ezk 28$_{22.23}$, Ziphites 1 S 23$_{22.23}$, Babylon Jr 50$_{24}$, Zion Is 49$_{23}$ 60$_{16}$, עִיר *city* Ezk 22$_{16}$.

עַם *people* Ex 32$_{1.23}$ Jos 3$_{4}$ 4$_{24}$ 1 S 12$_{17}$ 14$_{3}$ 2 S 3$_{37}$ 1 K 8$_{38.43.43}$‖2 C 6$_{29.33.33}$ 1 K 6$_{60}$ 18$_{37}$ 2 K 10$_{10}$ Is 6$_{9}$ 9$_{8}$ (unless ידע II *be humiliated*) 51$_{7}$ 52$_{6}$ Jr 4$_{22.22}$ 8$_{7}$ 9$_{15}$ 26$_{15.15}$ 42$_{22.22}$ 44$_{15.29}$ Ezk 7$_{27}$ 12$_{20}$ 24$_{24.27}$ 33$_{33}$ Mc 6$_{5}$ Ps 89$_{16}$ Est 4$_{11}$ Dn 11$_{32}$ Si 33$_{5}$ 4QD^{a} 2.1$_{3}$ 4QVisSam 1.2$_{5}$, לְאֹם *people* 1QH 6$_{12}$, גּוֹי *nation* 2 K 17$_{26.26}$ Is 55$_{5}$ Jr 10$_{25}$ Ezk 12$_{16}$ 36$_{23.36}$ 37$_{28}$ 38$_{16.23}$ 39$_{7.23}$ Mc 4$_{12}$ Ps 9$_{21}$ 79$_{6}$ 147$_{20}$ (or em. יְדָעוּם *they knew them* to יִדְּעֵם *he taught them*, i.e. hi.) Ne 6$_{16}$ Si 46$_{6}$ ([דע]ת) 1QH 6$_{12}$, עֵדָה *congregation* Nm 16$_{28.30}$ Jr 6$_{18}$ (or em. דְּעִי עֵדָה *know, O congregation* to דְּעוּ דֵעָה *know knowledge*, or רֹעֵי עֶדְרֵיהֶם *shepherds of their flocks*), סוֹד *assembly* 1QH 2$_{33}$ ([יד]עו), קָהָל *assembly* 1 S 17$_{47}$, מַמְלָכָה *kingdom* 2 K 19$_{19}$‖Is 37$_{20}$, בַּיִת *house* of Israel Jr 5$_{15}$ Ezk 11$_{10.12}$ 12$_{15}$ 14$_{8}$ 17$_{12.21}$ 20$_{42.44}$ 22$_{22}$ 28$_{24.26}$ 29$_{21}$ 36$_{38}$ 37$_{13.14}$ 39$_{22.28}$, יֹשֵׁב *inhabitant* Is 9$_{8}$ (unless ידע II *be humiliated*) Ezk 29$_{6.9}$ 33$_{29}$ 39$_{6}$ Ps 91$_{14}$ (unless ידע VIII *call*) GnzPs 2$_{18}$.

Abigail 1 S 25$_{17}$, Abimelech Gn 20$_{7}$ 21$_{26}$, Abner 1 S 17$_{55}$ 2 S 2$_{26}$ 3$_{25.25}$, Abra(ha)m Gn 12$_{11}$ 15$_{8.13.13}$ Is 63$_{16}$ CD 16$_{6}$, Absalom 2 S 17$_{8}$, Achish 1 S 28$_{2}$ 29$_{9}$, Adam Gn 4$_{25}$, Agur Pr 30$_{3.18}$, Ahab 1 K 20$_{13}$, Ahimaaz 2 S 18$_{29}$, Balaam Nm 22$_{19.34}$, Balak Nm 22$_{6}$, Barzillai 2 S 19$_{36}$, Bathsheba 1 K 2$_{15}$, Ben Sira Si 51$_{15(11QPs^{a})}$, Bezalel Ex 36$_{1}$, Bildad Jb 8$_{9}$, Boaz Ru 4$_{4}$, Cain Gn 4$_{9.17}$, Coniah Jr 22$_{28}$, Cyrus Is 45$_{3.4}$ (unless ידע II *be submissive*) 45$_{5}$, Daniel Dn 9$_{25}$ 10$_{20}$, David 1 S 20$_{39}$ 22$_{3.22}$ 23$_{9}$ 26$_{4}$ 28$_{1.1}$ 2 S 3$_{26}$ 5$_{12}$‖1 C 14$_{2}$ 2 S 19$_{23}$ 24$_{13}$ 1 K 1$_{11}$ 2$_{32}$ 1 C 21$_{2}$ 29$_{17}$, Eli 1 S 3$_{13}$, Eliab 1 S 17$_{28}$, Elihu Jb 32$_{22}$ 34$_{4}$ 36$_{26}$ 37$_{5}$, Elisha 2 K 2$_{3.3.5.5}$ 4$_{1}$ 8$_{12}$, Elkanah 1 S 1$_{19}$, Ezekiel Ezk 10$_{20}$, Gedaliah Jr 40$_{14.14}$, Gideon Jg 6$_{37}$, Gog Ezk 38$_{14}$ (or em. תֵּדָע *you will know* to תֵּעֹר *you will stir yourself*, i.e. עור ni.), Hathach Est 4$_{5}$, Hiram 1 K 5$_{17.20}$, Hobab Nm 10$_{31}$, Immanuel Is 7$_{15}$, Isaac Gn 27$_{2}$ 1QJub^{b} 35$_{9}$ (י[וד]ע) 35$_{10}$ ([יודע]) 4QJub^{h} 35$_{13}$ ([יוד]ע), Jacob Gn 29$_{5}$ 31$_{32}$ 4QJub^{f} 37$_{14}$ ([יד]ע) 4QJub^{h} 37$_{23}$, Jeremiah Jr 1$_{6}$ 6$_{27}$ 10$_{23}$ 11$_{18.19}$ 32$_{8}$ 33$_{3}$, Jeroboam 2 C 13$_{5}$, Jethro Ex 18$_{11}$, Joab 2 S 11$_{16}$ 14$_{1}$ 19$_{7}$, Job Jb 5$_{24.25.27}$ 8$_{9}$ 9$_{2.21.28}$ 10$_{13}$ 11$_{6.8}$ 13$_{2.18}$ 15$_{9}$ 19$_{25}$ 20$_{4}$ 21$_{27}$ 23$_{3}$ (unless ידע VIII *call*) 23$_{5}$ 30$_{23}$ 34$_{33}$ 36$_{26}$ 37$_{5.15.16}$ 38$_{4.5.18.21.33}$ (or em. הֲיָדַעְתָּ *do you know?* to הֲיָעַדְתָּ *have you appointed?*, i.e. יעד, or הֲיִדַּעְתָּ *have you made known?*, i.e. pi.) 39$_{1.2}$ 42$_{2(Qr).3}$, Johanan Jr 42$_{22.22}$, Jonah Jon 1$_{12}$ 4$_{2}$, Jonathan 1 S 20$_{3.7.9.9.33.39}$, Joseph Gn 47$_{6}$ 4QapJoseph[b] 1$_{10}$ ([ד]ע]י), Joshua Jos 14$_{6}$, Judah Gn 38$_{16.26}$ 44$_{15.27}$, Koheleth Ec 1$_{17.17}$ 2$_{14}$ 3$_{12.14}$ 7$_{25}$ (or em.; see below) 7$_{25}$ 8$_{12.16}$, Laban Gn 30$_{26.29}$, Leah Gn 31$_{6}$, Levi 4QTestim$_{16}$, Lot Gn 19$_{33.35}$, Magog Ezk 39$_{6}$, Malchiah Arad ost. 40$_{9}$, Manasseh 2 C 33$_{13}$, Manoah Jg 13$_{21.22}$, Micah Jg 17$_{13}$, Mordecai Est 2$_{11}$ 4$_{1}$, Moses Ex 9$_{30}$ 32$_{22}$ 33$_{13}$ 34$_{29}$ Nm 11$_{16}$ Dt 2$_{7}$ 9$_{24}$ 31$_{29}$, Naaman 2 K 5$_{8.15}$, Nabal 1 S 25$_{11}$, Nehemiah Ne 13$_{10}$, Noah Gn 8$_{11}$ 9$_{24}$ 4QCommGenA 2$_{5}$ 4QCommGenC 3$_{4}$ ([נוח]), Obadiah 1 K 18$_{12}$, Oholah and Oholibah Ezk 23$_{49}$, Oholiab Ex 36$_{1}$, Onan Gn 38$_{9}$, Phinehas Jos 22$_{31}$, Rachel Gn 31$_{6}$, Ruth Ru 2$_{11}$, Samson Jg 15$_{11}$ 16$_{20}$, Samuel 1 S 3$_{7}$, Saul 1 S 18$_{28}$ 20$_{30}$ 23$_{17}$ 24$_{21}$ 28$_{9.14}$, Shimei 1 K 2$_{37.37.42.42.44}$, Solomon 1 K 2$_{5.9.44}$ 1 C 28$_{9}$ 2 C 2$_{7}$, Tobiah 4QTobit[e] 4$_{3}$, Zechariah Zc 4$_{5.13}$.

אָדָם *human being* Gn 3$_{22}$ 4$_{1}$ Jon 4$_{11}$ Pr 28$_{2}$ (or em. יֹדֵעַ כֵּן יַאֲרִיךְ *[who] knows, thus it will last long* to יִדְעָכוּן *they will be extinguished*) Ec 8$_{7}$ 9$_{1.12}$ 10$_{14}$, אֱנוֹשׁ *human being* Jb 14$_{21}$ 28$_{13}$, אִישׁ *man* Gn 3$_{7}$ 19$_{5}$ 24$_{16.21}$ 25$_{27}$ 42$_{33.34}$ 43$_{22}$ Ex 16$_{15}$ 36$_{1}$ Dt 33$_{9}$ 34$_{6}$ Jg 18$_{5}$ 19$_{22.25}$ 1 S 16$_{16}$ 21$_{3}$ 2 S 15$_{11}$ 1QIsa[a] 53$_{3}$ 1 K 5$_{20}$ 9$_{27}$ Jr 36$_{19}$ 38$_{24}$ 40$_{15}$ 41$_{4}$ 44$_{15}$ Jon 1$_{7.10}$ Ps 39$_{7}$ 92$_{7}$ Jb 37$_{7}$ (unless ידע II *be quiet*) Pr 28$_{22}$ 2 C 2$_{6.12.13}$ Si 40$_{29}$ 47$_{5}$ 1QS 5$_{11}$ 6$_{25}$ 8$_{18}$ 4QParGenEx 3$_{7}$ (א[נשי]) 4Q417 1.1$_{8}$ 4Q424 3$_{7}$ 4QsapHymnA 1.2$_{5}$ CD 16$_{11}$ ([י]דענה), גֶּבֶר *man* 4QMyst[a] 8$_{5}$ ([גב]ר), אִשָּׁה *woman, wife* Gn 3$_{7}$ Nm 31$_{17.35}$ Jos 2$_{4.5}$ Jg 21$_{11}$ 1 S 25$_{17}$ 1 K 17$_{24}$ 2 K 4$_{9}$ Jr 44$_{15.29}$ Pr 9$_{13}$ (unless ידע II) 4QD[f] 3$_{11.11}$ (both [אשה]) 3$_{14}$ ([נשים]).

אָב *father* Gn 48$_{19.19}$ Dt 8$_{3.15}$ 28$_{36.64}$ Jg 14$_{4}$ 1 S 2$_{12}$ 20$_{3.3}$ 23$_{17}$ 24$_{12}$ 1 K 2$_{32}$ Jr 16$_{13}$ 19$_{4}$ 44$_{3}$ Dn 11$_{38}$ 1QH 9$_{35}$ 4QDibHam[a] 1.2$_{10}$, חֹתֵן *father-in-law* Nm 10$_{31}$, אֵם *mother* Jg 14$_{4}$ Ho 2$_{10}$, בֵּן *son* Gn 43$_{7.7}$ Nm 10$_{31}$ 22$_{6}$ 32$_{23}$ Dt 13$_{9}$ 11$_{2}$ 31$_{13}$ 33$_{9}$ Jos 22$_{31}$ Jg 30$_{34}$ 1 S 16$_{18}$ 2 S 3$_{25.25}$ 14$_{1}$ 2 S 14$_{1}$ 1 K 2$_{5.9}$ 2 K 4$_{39}$ Jr 2$_{15(mss)}$ (unless ידע II *cause to be submissive*; L יִרְעוּךְ appar. *they have fed upon*, i.e. devastated, *you*) Jr 42$_{22.22}$ Ezk 2$_{5}$ 20$_{20.26}$ Ps 44 78$_{6}$ Pr 3$_{6}$ 4$_{1}$ 23$_{35}$ (unless ידע III *care*) 24$_{12.14}$ (unless ידע VI *seek*; or em. דֵּעָה *know* to דֵּעָה *knowledge*) 30$_{3.18}$ 1 C 12$_{33.33}$ 28$_{9}$ 2 C 2$_{11.13}$ Si 7$_{3}$ (אל תדע *do not know*; appar. error for אל תזרע *do not sow*) 7$_{20(A)}$ (unless ידע II *reduce to submission* or IV *punish*) 8$_{18}$ 9$_{11.13}$ 12$_{1}$ (תדיע; unless ידע V hi. *cause to sweat*) 12$_{11}$ 34$_{13(Bmg)}$ (B זכור *remember*) 34$_{15.16}$ 37$_{8.12}$ 1QH 12$_{22}$ ([בני]) 1QS 4$_{26}$ 4Q417 2.1$_{18}$ 11QpsAp[a] 2$_{8}$ ([בני]), of Israel Ex 6$_{7}$ 11$_{7}$ 16$_{6.12.15}$ 29$_{46}$ 31$_{13}$ Nm 14$_{34}$ 4QpsEzek[a] 2$_{4}$ perh. 4QpsEzek[b] 1.2$_{1}$ 4QpsMos[d] 1.2$_{6}$, of Zion Jl 2$_{27}$, בַּת *daughter* Gn 19$_{8}$ Jg 11$_{39}$ Ezk 13$_{21.23}$ 26$_{6}$ Zc 2$_{15}$ Ru 3$_{4.18}$, אָח *brother* Gn 29$_{5}$ 42$_{23}$ 44$_{15.27}$ Jg 18$_{14.14}$ 1 S 17$_{28}$ Jr 31$_{34}$, אָחוֹת *sister* Ex 2$_{4}$.

מֶלֶךְ *king* Ex 1$_{8}$ Nm 20$_{14}$ Jos 8$_{14}$ 2 S 3$_{25}$ 24$_{2}$ 1 K 1$_{4.18}$ 20$_{13.22}$ Jr 19$_{4}$ Ezk 7$_{27}$ 32$_{9}$ Ec 4$_{13}$ Dn 2$_{3}$ Arad ost. 40$_{13}$, פַּרְעֹה *Pharaoh* Ex 5$_{2}$ 7$_{17}$ 8$_{6.18}$ 9$_{14.29}$ 10$_{7}$ Ezk 32$_{9}$ Si 16$_{15}$, שַׂר *prince* Jr 26$_{15.15}$ 42$_{22.22}$, נָשִׂיא *prince* Ezk 7$_{27}$, אָדוֹן *lord* Gn 33$_{13}$ 39$_{6.8}$ 42$_{33.34}$ 2 S 14$_{20}$ 1 K 1$_{11.18}$ Lachish ost. 2$_{6}$, זָקֵן *elder* Jos 23$_{13.13.14}$ 24$_{31}$ 1 K 20$_{7}$, ראשׁ *head*, i.e. leader Jos 23$_{13.13.14}$ Mc 3$_{1}$, קָצִין *ruler* Mc 3$_{1}$, שֹׁטֵר *officer* Jos 23$_{13.13.14}$, שפט ptc. *one who judges* Jos 23$_{13.13.14}$ GnzPs 1$_{2}$, דַּיָּן *judge* GnzPs 1$_{2}$, פִּנָּה *corner*, i.e. ruler 1 S 14$_{38}$, סָגָן *official* Ne 2$_{16}$, גִּבּוֹר *warrior* perh. 4QM[h] 1$_{4}$ ([גבור]יכם), עֶבֶד *servant* Gn 24$_{14}$ 1 S 22$_{15}$ 2 S 3$_{38}$ 14$_{22}$ 19$_{21}$ 1 K 9$_{27}$||2 C 8$_{18}$ 1 K 22$_{3}$ 2 K 5$_{8}$ 9$_{11}$ Est 4$_{11}$ 2 C 2$_{7}$ Lachish ost. 3$_{8}$ 4$_{10}$ 1QH 13$_{18}$, יֶלֶד *youth* Dn 1$_{4}$, טַף *children* Nm 14$_{31}$ (or em. וְיָדְעוּ *and they shall know* to וְיִרְעוּ *and they shall tend*, i.e. רעה, or וְיָרְשׁוּ *and they shall possess*) 31$_{18}$, נַעַר *lad* 1 S 20$_{39}$ 2 S 1$_{5.10}$ Is 7$_{16}$ 8$_{4}$ Pr 7$_{23}$, בָּחוּר *young man* Ec 11$_{9}$, נַעֲרָה *young woman* Jg 21$_{12}$, בְּתוּלָה *young woman* Jg 21$_{12}$, זוֹנָה *prostitute* Ezk 16$_{62}$, זָרָה *foreign woman* Pr 5$_{6}$ (unless ידע II *be quiet*), רֵעַ *neighbour* Jr 31$_{34}$ Jon 1$_{7}$, friends of Job Jb 15$_{9}$ 19$_{6.29}$, female lover Ca 6$_{12}$.

כֹּהֵן *priest* Jos 22$_{31}$ 1 S 22$_{17}$ Jr 6$_{15}$ 8$_{12}$ 14$_{18}$ (unless ידע II *be quiet*) Ml 2$_{4}$, נָבִיא *prophet* Jr 6$_{15}$ 8$_{12}$ 14$_{18}$ (unless ידע II) Ezk 13$_{9.14}$ 2 C 25$_{16}$, יָרֵא *one who fears* Y. Ps 119$_{79(Kt)}$, worshipper 2 S 22$_{44}$||Ps 18$_{44}$ Ps 20$_{7}$ 35$_{11.15}$ (unless ידע II) 39$_{5}$ 41$_{12}$ 46$_{11}$ 51$_{5}$ 56$_{10}$ 71$_{15}$ 73$_{16.22}$ 81$_{6}$ 101$_{4}$ 119$_{75.125.152}$ (unless ידע II) 135$_{5}$ 140$_{13(Qr)}$ 1QH 1$_{21}$ 3$_{20}$ 4$_{30}$ 5$_{3}$ 6$_{6.7}$ ([יד]עתי) 9$_{9.14}$ 11$_{7.17.20}$ 13$_{18.20}$ (אדע[ה]) 14$_{12.17}$ 15$_{12.13.22.23.25}$ ([ידעת]י) 16$_{4.6.10.11}$ 18$_{21}$ fr. 1$_{9}$ 3$_{14}$ 4$_{16}$ 6$_{6}$ 4QHod[a] 7.2$_{12}$ 4Q PrQuot 51$_{14}$ 4QDibHam[a] 4$_{5}$ GnzPs 3$_{5}$, מַשְׂכִּיל *instructor* 1QH 12$_{11}$ 1QS 10$_{16}$.

צַדִּיק *righteous one* Pr 12$_{10}$ (unless ידע III *care*) Pr 29$_{7}$, מָשִׁיחַ *anointed one* Is 45$_{4}$ (unless ידע II *be submissive*), חָכָם *wise one* Is 19$_{12}$ (or em. hi. *make known*) Jb 34$_{4}$ Ec 8$_{17}$ Est 1$_{13}$, בין ni. ptc. *understanding one* Ho 14$_{10}$, שמע ptc. *one who hears* CD 9$_{12}$, חשׂך ptc. *one who restrains* words Pr 17$_{27}$, אֵין לֵב *(one who has) no understanding* 4QapPs[b]

1$_{2}$, חֵרֵשׁ *deaf one* 4QMMT B$_{54}$ ([י]דע).

רָשָׁע *wicked one* Jb 15$_{23}$ 20$_{20}$ 21$_{14.19}$ (unless ידע II *be quiet*) Pr 4$_{19}$, חָנֵף *profane one* Jb 20$_{20}$ (unless ידע II *be quiet* or IV *punish*), פעל ptc. *one who does* evil Ps 14$_{4}$‖53$_{5}$ (unless ידע II), זֵד *presumptuous one* 11QPs^{a} 18$_{13}$, עָדִין *voluptuous one* Is 47$_{8.11.11}$, נֹאֵף *adulterer* Jb 24$_{16}$, רֹצֵחַ *murderer* Jb 24$_{16}$, חשב ptc. *one who devises* evil Ps 35$_{8}$, אצר ptc. *one who treasures* violence Am 3$_{10}$ (unless ידע III *care*), עַוָּל *unjust one* Zp 3$_{5}$, עָרִיץ *terrible one* 1QH 2$_{22}$, אוֹיֵב *enemy* Ps 83$_{19}$ Ne 6$_{16}$, שׂנא pi. ptc. *one who hates* Ps 83$_{19}$, שֹׂטֵן *adversary* Ps 109$_{27}$, תעה ptc. *one who goes astray* Is 29$_{24}$, מהר ni. ptc. *hasty one* Is 32$_{4}$, כְּסִיל *fool* Ec 4$_{17}$ 10$_{15}$, חֲסַר *one lacking* sense Pr 7$_{23}$ 9$_{18}$, פֶּתִי *simple one* Pr 9$_{18}$.

מצא ptc. *one who finds* CD 9$_{15}$, נשׂא ptc. *one who carries* Is 45$_{20}$, תפשׂ ptc. *one who holds* Jr 2$_{8}$, סמך ptc. *one who supports* Ezk 30$_{8}$, נצר ptc. *one who keeps* Pr 24$_{12}$, שׁמר ptc. *one who keeps* Ec 8$_{5}$, עשׁר htp. ptc. *rich one* Si 11$_{19}$, עָנִי *poor one* appar. Zc 11$_{11}$ (or em. כֵּן עֲנִיֵּי *so the poor ones of* to כְּנַעֲנֵי *the traders of* the sheep knew) Ec 6$_{8}$, גָּדוֹל *great one* Jr 5$_{5}$ 31$_{34}$, קָטָן *small one* Jr 31$_{34}$ קָרוֹב *near one* Is 33$_{13}$, צפה ptc. *sentry* Is 56$_{10}$, עִוֵּר *blind one* Is 42$_{16.16}$, יָפֶה *beautiful one* Ca 1$_{8}$, עֵד *witness* Is 44$_{9}$, חַי *living one* Ec 9$_{5}$, מֵת *dead one* Ec 9$_{5}$, דּוֹר *generation* Lv 23$_{43}$ Jg 2$_{10}$ 3$_{2.3}$ Ps 78$_{6}$ 95$_{10}$ 4QJub^{a} 1$_{5}$ ([יד]עו) 1$_{6}$, שְׁאֵרִית *remnant* Jr 42$_{19.19}$ 44$_{28}$.

שָׂפָה *lip* Pr 10$_{32}$ (unless ידע V *sweat* or VI *seek*; or em. hi. *make known* or נבע hi. *pour*; mss רעה *feed*), פֶּה *mouth* Pr 10$_{32}$, לֵב *heart* Dt 29$_{3}$ Jr 24$_{7}$ Pr 14$_{10}$ Ec 7$_{22.25}$ (or em. וְלִבִּי לָדַעַת וְלָתוּר *and my heart to know and search out* to נָתוֹן לִבִּי לָתוּר *to set my heart to search out*) 8$_{5}$, לֵבָב *heart* 1 K 2$_{44}$, נֶפֶשׁ *soul* Ps 139$_{14}$ (or em. נַפְשִׁי יֹדַעַת appar. *my soul knows* to יָדַעְתָּ נַפְשִׁי *you care for my soul*, i.e. ידע III), רוּחַ *spirit* of flesh 4Q417 2.1$_{18}$, בָּשָׂר *flesh* Is 49$_{26}$ Ezk 21$_{10}$, עֶצֶם *bone* Ezk 37$_{6}$, זֶרַע *seed*, i.e. descendants Jr 22$_{28}$ Si 46$_{10}$ 1QLitPr 3.2$_{3}$, נֵפֶל *miscarriage* Ec 6$_{5}$, מַעֲשֶׂה *work*, i.e. creature 1QH 4$_{32}$.

שׁוֹר *ox* Is 1$_{3}$, חֲמוֹר *ass* Is 1$_{3}$, כֶּלֶב *dog* Is 56$_{11}$, חֲסִידָה *stork* Jr 8$_{7}$, עַיִט *bird of prey* Jb 28$_{7}$, עֵץ *tree* Ezk 17$_{24}$.

שַׁעַר *gate* Ru 3$_{11}$, הַר *mountain* Ezk 6$_{7.10.13.14}$ 35$_{4.9.12.15}$ 36$_{11}$ Jb 9$_{5}$ (unless ידע II *be quiet*), גִּבְעָה *hill* Ezk 6$_{7.10.13.14}$, גַּיְא *valley* Ezk 6$_{7.10.13.14}$, אָפִיק *channel* Ezk 6$_{7.10.13.14}$, אֶרֶץ *earth* 1 S 17$_{46}$ Hb 2$_{14}$ Ps 100$_{3}$, appar. אֲדָמָה *land* Ezk 7$_{4}$ (lacking in ms) 7$_{9}$, אֶפֶס *end* of earth Si 36$_{22(B)}$ (וידעו; Bmg ויראו *and they will see*), שֶׁמֶשׁ *sun* Ps 104$_{19}$ (or em. יָדַע *it* [the sun] *knew* to יִדַּע *he caused* the sun *to know*, i.e. pi.).

שְׁנַיִם *two* Gn 3$_{7}$, הוּא *he* 1QH fr 3$_{7}$ 4QShir^{b} 48.2$_{7}$, אַתֶּם *you* 4QMMT B$_{68.80}$ ([א]תם) C$_{8}$ (י[ודעים]), אֲשֶׁר *one who* Is 29$_{12.12}$ CD 14$_{10}$ (א[ש]ר), מִי *who?* 2 S 12$_{22}$ Is 29$_{15}$ Jr 17$_{9}$ Jl 2$_{14}$ Jon 3$_{9}$ Ps 90$_{11}$ Jb 12$_{9}$ Pr 24$_{22}$ Ec 2$_{19}$ 3$_{21}$ 6$_{12}$ 8$_{1}$ Est 4$_{14}$ Si 16$_{21}$ 4QShir^{b} 2.2$_{6}$, כֹּל *everyone* Jr 31$_{34}$ 1QH 1$_{31}$ 15$_{20}$ fr. 5$_{9}$ 1QS 5$_{19}$ 4QJub^{a} 1$_{28}$ ([כל]) 4QDiscourse 2.2$_{8}$ GnzPs 2$_{14}$ 3$_{19}$.

Subj. not specified, Lv 5$_{1.3.4.17.18}$ Nm 24$_{16}$ 1 S 10$_{11}$ 26$_{12}$ 1 K 14$_{2}$ Is 29$_{11}$ 50$_{4.7}$ 51$_{7}$ Jr 9$_{23}$ 15$_{12(mss)}$ (הֲיֵדַע *can one know?*; unless ידע II *reduce to submission*; L הֲיָרֹעַ *can one break?*) Jr 48$_{17}$ Ezk 28$_{19}$ Am 5$_{16}$ Ps 9$_{11}$ 36$_{11}$ 59$_{14}$ 67$_{3}$ 74$_{9}$ 87$_{4}$ 119$_{79(Qr)}$ 140$_{13(Kt)}$ Jb 18$_{21}$ 19$_{13}$ 24$_{1}$ 29$_{16}$ 34$_{2}$ 42$_{11}$ Pr 1$_{2}$ 14$_{7}$ (or em. בַּל־יָדַעְתָּ *you have not known* to כְּלֵי־דַעַת *vessels of knowledge*, or בַּל־תַּדִּח *you shall not thrust aside*, i.e. נדח hi.; unless ידע V *flow with* or X *leave*) 27$_{1.23.23}$ 30$_{4}$ Ec 9$_{11}$ 11$_{2.5.5.6}$ Est 1$_{13}$ Ne 10$_{29}$ Si 35$_{8}$ 1QH 11$_{14}$ 14$_{15}$ fr. 10$_{6}$ 1QM 13$_{3}$ 1QSa 1$_{10.28}$ 4QAges^{b} 2$_{5}$ 4QD^{e} 2.2$_{19}$ 4QCryptA 1.1$_{3}$ ([י]דעים) 3.2$_{4.6}$ (יו[דעי]) 3.2$_{10}$ 4QMyst^{b} 6$_{3}$ (יודע[י]) 4QapPs^{b} 31$_{6}$ 4QShirShabb^{a} 2$_{9}$ (ידע[י]) 3.2$_{5}$ 4QShirShabb^{b} 17$_{4}$ (יו[ד]עי) 4QShirShabb^{f} 3.2$_{9}$ 8$_{3}$ 4QBer^{a} 7.1$_{6}$ 4Q416 2.3$_{5.9.15}$ 4Q417 1.1$_{11}$ 2.1$_{6.8.13}$ 11$_{1}$ (יוד[עי]) 4Q418 81$_{15}$ 4QShir^{b} 2.1$_{2}$ 4QBéat 14.2$_{15}$ MasShirShabb 1$_{4}$ 2$_{26}$ CD 1$_{1}$.

<OBJ> Y. Ex 5$_{2}$ 33$_{13}$ Jg 2$_{10}$ 1 S 2$_{12}$ 3$_{7}$ Is 19$_{21}$ 45$_{4}$ (unless ידע II *be submissive*) 45$_{5}$ Jr 2$_{8}$ 4$_{22}$ 9$_{2.5.23}$ 10$_{25}$ 24$_{7}$ 31$_{34.34}$ Ezk 38$_{16}$ Ho 2$_{22}$ (or em. וְיָדַעַתְּ אֶת־י׳ *and you shall know Y.* to וּבְדַעַת י׳ *and in the knowledge of Y.*; mss כִּי אֲנִי י׳ *that I am Y.*) 5$_{4}$ 8$_{2}$ Ps 36$_{11}$ 79$_{6}$ 87$_{4}$ Jb 18$_{21}$ 24$_{1}$ Pr 3$_{6}$ Dn 11$_{32}$ 1 C 28$_{9}$ Si 16$_{15}$ 1QH 1$_{31}$ 12$_{11.22}$ 14$_{15}$ 1QM 13$_{3}$ 1QLitPr 3.2$_{3}$ 4QD^{a} 2.1$_{3}$ 4QDiscourse 2.2$_{9}$ 4QHod^{a} 7.2$_{12}$ 4QPseud^{a} 1$_{2}$ GnzPs 3$_{19}$, אֱלֹהִים *god* Dt 11$_{28}$ 13$_{3.7}$=11QT 54$_{10.21}$ Dt 13$_{14}$=11QT 55$_{4}$ Dt 28$_{64}$ 29$_{25}$ 32$_{17}$ Jr 7$_{9}$ 44$_{3}$ Ho 13$_{4}$ (אֱלֹהִים זוּלָתִי לֹא תֵדָע *you know no God except me*) Dn 11$_{38}$.

Israel(ites) Dt 9$_{24}$ Is 55$_{5}$ 63$_{16}$ Jr 2$_{16(mss)}$ Ho 13$_{5}$ (or em.; see Subj.; unless ידע III *care*) Am 3$_{2}$ (unless ידע III), Ephraim Ho 5$_{3}$, עַם *people* Dt 9$_{2}$ 28$_{33}$ 2 S 22$_{44}$‖Ps 18$_{44}$ Is 29$_{15}$, גּוֹי *nation* Dt 28$_{36}$ Is 55$_{5}$ Jr 9$_{15}$ Zc 7$_{14}$ Ru 2$_{11}$.

Abner 2 S 3$_{25}$, Abraham Gn 18$_{19}$ (unless ידע III), David

1 K 5$_{17}$, Eve Gn 4$_{1}$, Hannah 1 S 1$_{19}$, Jeremiah Jr 1$_{5}$ (unless ידע III) 12$_{3}$, Job Jb 19$_{13}$, Joseph Ex 1$_{8}$, Laban Gn 29$_{5}$, Moses Ex 33$_{12.17}$ Dt 34$_{10}$, Saul 1 S 10$_{11}$, Tamar Gn 38$_{26}$.

אָדָם *human being* Ps 144$_{3}$ (unless ידע III *care*), מַת *man* Jb 11$_{11}$, אִישׁ *man* Gn 19$_{5.8}$ Nm 31$_{17}$ Jg 11$_{39}$ 19$_{22}$ 21$_{12}$ 2 S 17$_{8}$ 2 K 9$_{11}$ 4Q416 2.3$_{5}$, אִשָּׁה *woman* Gn 4$_{1.17.25}$ 1 S 1$_{19}$ 1QSa 1$_{10}$, אָב *father* 2 S 17$_{8}$ 1 K 5$_{17}$, אֵם *mother* 4QTestim$_{16}$, בֵּן *son* Gn 29$_{5}$ Dt 9$_{2}$ 33$_{9}$ 2 S 3$_{25}$, פִּלֶגֶשׁ *secondary wife* Jg 19$_{25}$, אָח *brother* Dt 22$_{2}$=11QT 64$_{15}$, אַלְמָנָה *widow* Ezk 19$_{7}$ (unless ידע II *be humiliated* or IV *punish*; or em.; see Subj.), נַעֲרָה *young woman* Gn 24$_{16}$ 1 K 1$_{4}$, מֶלֶךְ *king* Ezk 28$_{19}$, עֶבֶד *servant* 2 S 7$_{20}$||1 C 17$_{18}$, גָּבֹהַּ *proud one* Ps 138$_{6}$ (unless ידע II *reduce to submission*), חסה ptc. *one who seeks refuge* Na 1$_{7}$ (unless ידע III *care*), עבד ptc. *one who serves* Si 7$_{20(A)}$ (unless ידע II or IV *punish*), קֹנֶה *purchaser* Is 1$_{3}$, worshipper 1QH 9$_{30.35}$.

יָד *hand* Dt 11$_{2}$ Jos 4$_{24}$, זְרוֹעַ *arm* Dt 11$_{2}$, שָׂפָה *lip* Pr 14$_{7}$ (unless ידע V *flow with*, or X *leave alone*; or em.; see Subj.), specif. *language* Ps 81$_{6}$, לָשׁוֹן *tongue*, i.e. language Jr 5$_{15}$, עֹרֶף *neck* Dt 31$_{27}$, פָּנִים *face* Pr 27$_{23}$, לֵב *heart* Jr 17$_{9}$, לֵבָב *heart* 1 K 8$_{39.39}$||2 C 6$_{30.30}$ Ps 139$_{23}$, נֶפֶשׁ *soul* Ex 23$_{9}$ Pr 12$_{10}$ Jb 9$_{21}$ (unless ידע III *care [for]* soul in both), רוּחַ *spirit* 4QMyst^{c} 4$_{2}$ ([ידע]ו), שֵׁם *name* 1 K 8$_{43}$||2 C 6$_{33}$ Is 52$_{6}$ Jr 48$_{17}$ Ps 9$_{11}$ 91$_{14}$ (unless ידע VIII *call*).

עוֹף *birds* Ps 50$_{11}$, לֶחֶם *bread* Gn 39$_{6}$, מָן *manna* Dt 8$_{3.3.15}$, מִשְׁכָּב *bed* Nm 31$_{18.35}$ Jg 21$_{11}$, קְבוּרָה *grave* Dt 34$_{6}$, אֵבוּס *crib* Is 1$_{3}$, perh. חרשׁ pass. ptc. *furrow* Si 7$_{3}$ (אל תדע חרושי perh. *do not know the furrows of*, but אל תדע appar. error for אל תזרע *do not sow*), עֵץ *wood* Dt 28$_{64}$, בַּרְזֶל *iron* Jr 15$_{12(mss)}$ (unless ידע II *reduce to submission*), אֶבֶן *stone* Dt 28$_{64}$, צוּר *rock* Is 44$_{8}$ (or del.), אֶרֶץ *land* Nm 14$_{31}$ (or em.; see Subj.) Jr 15$_{14}$ 16$_{13}$ 17$_{4}$ 22$_{28}$ Ezk 32$_{9}$ 4QapJoseph^{b} 1$_{10}$ (י[דע]), יָם *sea* 1 K 9$_{27}$||2 C 8$_{18}$, מָקוֹם *place* 1 S 23$_{22}$ Jb 28$_{23}$ Ru 3$_{4}$, שֶׁמֶשׁ perh. *sun* Ec 6$_{5}$.

דֶּרֶךְ *way* Jos 3$_{4}$ Is 42$_{16}$ 59$_{8}$ Jr 5$_{4.5}$ 6$_{27}$ Ps 1$_{6}$ (unless ידע III *care*) 67$_{3}$ 95$_{10}$ Jb 21$_{14}$ 23$_{10}$ (unless ידע III) 28$_{13}$ (if em. עֶרְכָּהּ *its value* to דַּרְכָּהּ *its way*) 4QCryptA 3.2$_{6}$ (יו[דעי] הדרך), נָתִיב *path* Jb 28$_{7}$ GnzPs 3$_{5}$, נְתִיבָה *path* Is 42$_{16}$ Ps 142$_{4}$, דַּעַת *knowledge* Nm 24$_{16}$ Pr 17$_{27}$ 30$_{3}$ Ec 1$_{17}$ Dn 1$_{4}$ Si 42$_{18(M, Yadin)}$ (דע[ת]) 4QapJoshua^{a} 26$_{1}$ (יוד[ע]), דֵּעָה *knowledge* Jr 6$_{18}$ (if em.; see Subj.), מוּסָר *discipline* Dt 11$_{2}$ Pr 1$_{2}$, חָכְמָה *wisdom* Pr 1$_{2}$ 24$_{14}$ (or em.; see Subj.; unless ידע VI *seek*) Ec 1$_{17}$ 7$_{25}$ (or em.; see Subj.) 8$_{16}$ appar. Si 51$_{15(11QPs^a)}$ perh. 4Q417 2.1$_{6}$ 11QPs^{a} 18$_{13}$, בִּינָה *understanding* Is 29$_{24}$ Jb 38$_{4}$ Pr 4$_{1}$ 1 C 12$_{33}$ 2 C 2$_{11.12}$ 4QapPs^{b} 31$_{6}$ 4Q417 11$_{1}$ (יוד[עי בינה]), שֶׂכֶל *insight* 2 C 2$_{11}$, צֶדֶק *righteousness* Is 51$_{7}$ CD 1$_{1}$ 4QD^{a} 2.2$_{19}$ 4QShir^{b} 2.1$_{2}$ ([צדק]), צְדָקָה pl. *righteous acts* Mc 6$_{5}$, תֻּמָּה *integrity* Jb 31$_{6}$, יֹשֶׁר *uprightness* 4QShir^{b} 2.2$_{9}$, רָז *mystery* 1QMyst 1.1$_{3}$=4QMyst^{b} 3$_{3}$ 4QShirShabb^{f} 3.2$_{9}$ 4Q418 177$_{7a}$, סתר ni. *hidden thing* 1QS 5$_{11}$ 4QPrFêtes^{b} 2$_{4}$, יְשׁוּעָה *salvation* Ps 67$_{3}$, רָצוֹן *acceptance* Pr 10$_{32}$ (or em.; see Subj.; unless ידע V *sweat* or VI *seek*), כָּבוֹד *glory* Hb 2$_{14}$ 1QH 6$_{12}$ 15$_{20}$ fr. 10$_{3}$, שָׁלוֹ *prosperity* Jb 20$_{20}$ (if em. שָׁלֵו perh. *ease*; unless ידע IV *punish*) 4QParGenEx 2$_{9}$, טוֹב *good* 1QS 4$_{26}$ 4Q423 1.1$_{7}$, *good* and evil Gn 3$_{5.22}$ Dt 1$_{39}$ 1QSa 1$_{10}$ ([טוב] ורע),* שָׁלוֹם *peace* Est 2$_{11}$, אַהֲבָה *love* Ec 9$_{1}$, מַעֲשֶׂה *deed* 4QD^{f} 3$_{11}$ ([מעשה]).

דִּין *judgment* Pr 29$_{7}$ Est 1$_{13}$, דָּת *law* Est 1$_{13}$, מִשְׁפָּט *justice, ordinance* 2 K 17$_{26.26}$ Jr 8$_{7}$ Mc 3$_{1}$ Ps 147$_{20}$ Ec 8$_{5}$ (or em.; see Subj.) 4Q418 221$_{4}$ CD 9$_{15}$, חֻקָּה *statute* Jb 38$_{33}$ (or em.; see Subj.), בְּרִית *covenant* 1QH fr. 7$_{7}$ 1QS 5$_{19}$, עֲבוֹדָה *service* Gn 30$_{26}$ 2 C 12$_{8}$, מַעֲשֶׂה *work* Jos 24$_{31}$ Jg 2$_{10}$ Jb 37$_{7}$ (unless ידע II *be quiet*) Ec 11$_{5}$ 1QH 1$_{7}$ 11QpsAp^{a} 2$_{8}$ ([מעשי]) CD 2$_{7}$, פְּעֻלָּה *recompense* 1QS 4$_{25}$, תְּרוּעָה *shout* Ps 89$_{16}$ (יוֹדְעֵי תְרוּעָה *those who know the festal shout*), מִלְחָמָה *war* Jg 3$_{1.2}$ Si 47$_{5}$.

דָּבָר *word, matter* Dt 18$_{21}$=11QT 61$_{2}$ Jos 14$_{6}$ 1 S 20$_{39}$ 21$_{3}$ 22$_{15}$ 2 S 15$_{11}$ Ec 8$_{5}$ 1QH 1$_{28}$ perh. 4Q185 1.3$_{13}$ 11QMelch 3$_{2}$ (דב[רי]ם) Lachish ost. 2$_{6}$, מִלָּה *word* Ps 139$_{4}$ Jb 23$_{5}$, מוֹצָא *utterance* of lips Jr 17$_{16}$, שִׂיחַ *talk* 2 K 9$_{11}$, שְׁבוּעָה *oath* CD 16$_{11}$ ([י]דענה), עֵצָה *counsel* Jr 18$_{23}$, סוֹד *counsel* Si 40$_{29(B)}$, יֵצֶר *purpose, inclination* Dt 31$_{21}$ 1QH 7$_{13.16}$ 11$_{20}$ 1QJub^{b} 35$_{9}$ (י[וד]ע) 4QPrFêtes^{b} 2$_{5}$ ([י]דעת), *form* Ps 10$_{14}$, מַחֲשָׁבָה *thought* Jr 29$_{11}$ Mc 4$_{12}$ Ps 94$_{11}$ Jb 21$_{27}$ 4QAges^{a} 1.2$_{10}$ (מחשב[ותיהם]) 4QShir^{b} 42$_{7}$, שַׂרְעַפִּים *thoughts* Ps 139$_{23}$, מְזִמָּה *device* Jb 21$_{27}$ 1QH 9$_{12}$, אֱמֶת *truth* 1QH 6$_{12}$ 4Q417 2.1$_{6}$, עָוֶל *injustice* 4Q417 2.1$_{6}$, מַעֲלָה *what goes up* into mind Ezk 11$_{5}$, תַּעֲלֻמָה *secret* Ps 44$_{22}$, עֵדָה *testimony* Ps 119$_{79.125}$, סֵפֶר *book* Is 29$_{11.12.12}$, מִכְתָּב *letter* Arad ost. 40$_{9}$ ([המכתבם]), פֵּשֶׁר *interpretation* Ec 8$_{1}$, חֲלוֹם *dream* Dn 2$_{3}$.

מַכְאֹב *pain* Ex 3$_{7}$ (unless ידע X *leave alone*) 2 C 6$_{29}$, חֳלִי *sickness* Dt 7$_{15}$ 1QIsa^{a} 53$_{3}$, מַדְוֶה *sickness* Dt 7$_{15}$, נֶגַע *afflic-*

tion 1 K 8_{38}||2 C 6_{29} 1QH 10_{19}, תְּלָאָה *hardship* Nm 20_{14}, יִסּוּר *suffering* Si $40_{29(Bmg, M)}$, שְׁכוֹל *bereavement* Is 47_8, נְהִי *lamentation* Am 5_{16}, שׁוֹאָה *devastation* Is 47_{11} Ps 35_8, פִּיד *ruin* Pr 24_{22}, נְקָמָה *vengeance* Ezk 25_{14}, בֹּשֶׁת *shame* Zp 3_5 Ps 69_{20}, כְּלִמָּה *shame* Ps 69_{20} Pr 9_{13} (if em. מָה *what* to כְּלִמָּה; unless ידע II *be quiet*), חֶרְפָּה *reproach* P s69_{20}, חַטָּאת *sin* Nm 32_{23}, פֶּשַׁע *transgression* Ps 51_5, עָוֹן *iniquity* Is 59_{12} Jr 3_{13}, רֶשַׁע *wickedness* Jr 14_{20} Ec 7_{25}, רַע *evil* Gn $3_{5.22}$ Dt 1_{39} Ps 101_4, רֹעַ *evil* 1 S 17_{28}, רָעָה *evil* 1 K 2_{44}, זָדוֹן *presumptuousness* 1 S 17_{28}, תַּהְפֻּכָה *perversity* Pr 10_{32} (unless ידע V *sweat* or VI *seek*; or em.; see Subj.), עֶבְרָה *arrogance* Jr 48_{30}, תְּנוּאָה *opposition* Nm 14_{34}, מְרִי *rebellion* Dt 31_{27}, שִׂנְאָה *hatred* Ec 9_1, הוֹלֵל *madness* Ec 1_{17}, הוֹלֵלוֹת *madness* Ec $1_{17(mss)}$ 7_{25}, סִכְלוּת *folly* Ec 1_{17} 7_{25}.

חֲדָשָׁה *new thing* Is 43_{19} $48_{6.7}$, נצר pass. ptc. *hidden thing* Is $48_{6.7}$, בצר pass. ptc. *fortified*, i.e. inaccessible, *thing* Jr 33_3, גְּבוּרָה *might* Is 33_{13} GnzPs 2_{14}, כֹּחַ *strength* 1QH 15_{20} 4QDibHam[a] 2.2_{10}, עֹז *strength* Ps 90_{11}, גָּדוֹל *great thing* Jr 33_3, גֹּדֶל *greatness* Dt 11_2, פלא ni. ptc. *wonderful thing* Jb 42_3, שָׂבְעָה *satiety* Is 56_{11}, נַחֲלָה *inheritance* 4Q416 2.3_9.

עֵת *time* Jb $39_{1.2}$ Ec 8_5 9_{12} Est 1_{13}, מוֹעֵד *season* Jr 8_7, יוֹם *day* Gn 27_2 Ps 37_{18}, שָׁנָה *year* CD 2_9, אַחֲרִית *end* Is 41_{22} Si 12_{11}, עוֹלָם *eternity* 4QShirShabb[f] 8_3 ([ע]ולמים) MasShir Shabb 2_{26}, שַׁחַר *dawn* Is 47_{11} (or em. שַׁחְרָהּ *its dawn* to שַׁחֲרָהּ *to control it*, or שַׁחֲדָהּ *to bribe it*), מִסְפָּר *number* 2 S 24_2||1 C 21_2, סְפֹרָה *number* Ps 71_{15},* עֵרֶךְ *value* Jb 28_{13} (or em. דֶּרֶךְ *way*), הֶבְדֵּל *difference* 4QMyst[b] 6_1 ([י]דעו ההבו[דל]), אַרְבַּע *four* Pr 30_{18}.

הלך inf. *going* Dt 2_7, מוֹצָא *going out* 2 S 3_{25}, בוא inf. *coming in* 1 K 2_{44} 2 K 19_{27}||Is 37_{28}, יצא inf. *going out* 1 K 3_7 2 K 19_{27} ||Is 37_{28}, מָבוֹא *coming in* 2 S $3_{25(Kt)}$ Ps 104_{19} (or em.; see Subj.), מוּבָא *coming in* 2 S $3_{25(Qr)}$, ישׁב inf. *sitting* Ps 139_2 (unless ידע III *care*), חנה inf. *encamping* Nm 10_{31}, נשׂא inf. *bearing* Jr 15_{15}, צַיִד *hunting* Gn 25_{27}.

אֲשֶׁר *that which, how (it is that)* Gn 9_{24} 30_{29} Dt 8_2 29_{15} 1 S $28_{2.9}$ 2 S 11_{20} 1 K $2_{5.9}$ 20_{22} 2 K 8_{12} Ps 35_{11} 4QComm GenA 2_5 4QCommGenC 1_3 ([אש]ר) 11QPs[a] 26_{12}, מַה אֲשֶׁר *that which* 1QMyst 1.1_4=4QMyst[b] 3_3, מַה־שֶׁ- *that which* Ec 10_{14}, כֹּל *everything* 2 C 32_{31}, כָּל־אֲשֶׁר *everything that* 2 S 3_{25} 14_{20} Ec 4_1 1QJub[b] 35_{10} ([יודע ... כול אשר]) 4QD[f] 3_6, כֹּל *everything* 4QPrFêtes[c] 5.2_4, כֻּלָּה *all of it*, i.e. of the preceding Jb 38_{18}, מָה *what?* Jb 11_8 15_9 22_{13} 34_{33} Pr 9_{13} (or em. כְּלִמָּה *shame*), מְאוּמָה *anything* Gn 39_6 1 S 20_{39} 21_3 Ec 9_5, זֶה *this* Ps 56_{10} Pr 24_{12}, זֹאת *this* 1 S 20_3 Ps 73_{16} Jb 20_4, אֵלֶּה *these* Ho 14_{10} 1QH 1_{21} 5_3 1QM 10_{16} 4QPr Quot 7.4_7 ([א]לה) 4QDibHam[a] 4_5.

<PREP> לְ in ref. to subj. of ידע, + Job Jb 5_{27}, יָפֶה *beautiful one* Ca 1_8.

לְ of benefit, *for*, + נֶפֶשׁ *soul* Pr 24_{14} (unless ידע VI *seek*; or em.; see Subj.).

לְ of direction, *to*, + דּוֹר *generation* 4QDibHam[a] 1.2_{10}.

לְ *with respect to*, + מִשְׁכָּב *lying down* Jg 21_{12}.

לְ introducing object, + אִוֶּלֶת *folly* Ps 69_6, מוֹעֵד *appointed time* 1QM 18_{10}, מְזִמָּה *plan* 1QH fr. 3_7 (למ[זמתו]).

בְּ of place, *in, among*, + עַם *people* Ezk 28_{19}, גּוֹי *nation* Ps 67_3, בֶּטֶן *womb* Jr 1_5 (unless ידע III *care*), אֶרֶץ *land* Ho 13_5 (unless ידע III *care*; or em.; see Subj.) Ps 67_3, מִדְבָּר *desert* Ho 13_5 (unless ידע III; or em.; see Subj.), דֶּרֶךְ *way* Pr 3_6, דָּבָר *word* 1QLitPr 3.2_3 ([בכ]ול דברך).

בְּ of time, *in, on*, + יוֹם *day* 1 S 22_{22} 2 S 3_{37} Is 19_{21}.

בְּ of instrument, *by (means of)* Gn 24_{14}, רוּחַ *spirit* 1QH 12_{11} 13_{18} fr. 3_{14}, רֹב *greatness* of goodness 1QH 14_{17}, בִּינָה *insight* 1QH 15_{12}, זֹאת *this* Gn 42_{33}.

בְּ of accompaniment, *with*, + לֵבָב *heart* Jos 23_{14}, נֶפֶשׁ *soul* Jos 23_{14}, אֱמֶת *reality* Si $7_{20(A)}$ (unless ידע II *reduce to submission* or IV *punish*), אֱמוּנָה *faithfulness* 1QM 13_3.

בְּ *concerning*, + דָּבָר *word* Jr 38_{24}, בִּינָה *understanding* 4QShirShabb[b] 17_4 (יו[ד]עי).

בְּ introducing object, + דֶּרֶךְ *way* GnzPs 1_2, צָרָה *distress* Ps 31_8 (unless ידע III *care*), פֶּשַׁע *transgresssion* Jb 35_{15} (if em. פַּשׁ perh. *folly* to פֶּשַׁע; unless ידע II *be humiliated*), כֹּחַ *strength* 1QH 4_{32}, כָּבוֹד *glory* 1QH fr. 5_9 4Q417 2.1_{13}, רָז *mystery* 1QH fr. 1_4, אוֹת *sign* 4QPrQuot 51_{14} (נאותו[ת]), נַחֲלָה *inheritance* 4Q417 2.1_{18} (בנחל[ת]), אֱמֶת *truth* 1QH 9_9, עֵצָה *counsel* 1QS 8_{18}, רֹב *abundance* 1QH 4_{32}, כֹּל *all* 1QH fr. 1_3, אֵלֶּה *these* 1QH 16_6.

ידע בְּשֵׁם *know by name* Ex $33_{12.17}$.

כְּ *according to*, + דַּעַת *knowledge* Jb 13_2

מִן of direction, *from*, + מֶרְחָק *distance* Ps 138_6 (unless ידע II *reduce to submission*), עֵדָה *testimony* Ps 119_{152} (unless ידע II *be quiet*).

מִן of time, *since*, + אָב *father*, i.e. since before conception 1QH 9_{30}, נְעוּרִים *youth* Si $51_{15(11QPs^a)}$, אֶתְמוֹל *yester-*

day 1 S 10_{11}, עַד *perpetuity* Jb 20_{4}.

מִן partitive, *(some) of, from among,* + מִשְׁפָּחָה *family* Am 3_{2} (unless ידע III *care*), מַחֲבֹא *hiding place* 1 S 23_{23}.

מִן of agent, *by (means of),* + בִּינָה *insight* 1QH 1_{21} 14_{12} 1QM 10_{16}.

עַל *to* 1 K 18_{12} (עַל אֲשֶׁר לֹא־אֵדָע *to [a place] that I do not know*).

עַל *about, concerning,* + מִפְלָשׂ *swaying* Jb 37_{16} (or em. עֶלֶם do you know *the secret of* the swaying of clouds?).*

עַד *unto,* + דּוֹר *generation* 4QParGenEx 3_{7} ([דו]רות).

עִם *with,* + לֵבָב *heart* Dt 8_{5}.

אֵת *with,* + Joseph Gn $39_{6.8}$.

עַד *unto,* + יוֹם *day* Dt 34_{6}.

בֵּין *(the difference) between* 4Q418 78_{1}, + Elihu Jb 34_{4}, חָכָם *wise one* Jb 34_{4}, טוֹב *good* 2 S 19_{36} (+ לְרָע *and evil*) 4QMyst^{b} 3_{2} (בין ט[וב ובין רע ובין שקר לאמת *between good and evil, and between falsehood and truth*) 4QAdmon 1.2_{4} ([בין טוב לרע]) 4Q417 2.1_{8} ([טו]ב ל[רע] *good and evil*) 2.1_{17} ([טו]ב לרע), צַדִּיק *righteous one* 4QPrFêtes^{b} 1_{1} (לדע[ת]; + רָשָׁע *evil one*).

<COLL> ידע || נכר hi. *recognize* Dt 33_{9} Is 63_{16} 1QH 7_{13} 4QapPs^{b} 13_{2}; + נכר hi. 4QTestim$_{16}$; || חשׁב pi. *consider* Ps 144_{3}; + שׁית לֵב *place heart,* i.e. consider Pr 27_{23}; || שׂים *place (heart),* i.e. consider Is 41_{20}.

בין *understand* Is 6_{9} Ho 14_{10} Ps 82_{5} Jb 14_{21} 15_{9} Pr 24_{12} 4QpsMos^{e} 2.1_{6}; + בין Is 32_{4} 43_{10} Ps 92_{7} 139_{2} Jb 23_{5} Pr 29_{7} CD 1_{8}; || בין hi. *understand* Jb 28_{23} Pr 1_{2} 28_{2} Dn 1_{4} Ne 10_{29} 4QapPs^{b} 1_{2}; + בין hi. Is 40_{21} Mc 4_{12}; || בין ni. *be intelligent* Ec 9_{11} 1Q Sa 1_{28}; + בין ni. Jr 4_{22}; || בין htpol. *understand* Is 1_{3} 44_{18}; + בין htpol. *understand* Jb 11_{11} 38_{18} 4QMyst^{a} 8_{5}; || שׂכל hi. *understand* Is 41_{20} Dn 9_{25}; + שׂכל hi. Jr 9_{23} Dn 1_{4}.

|| למד *learn* Is 29_{24}; + למד Pr 30_{3}; || בקשׁ pi. *seek* Ec 7_{25}; + בקשׁ pi. *seek* Jr 5_{1}; חקר *search* Ps $139_{1.23}$; || תור *search out* Ec 7_{25}; + בחן *test* Jr 6_{27} 12_{3}.

|| ראה *see* Lv 5_{1} Dt 11_{2} 29_{3} 1 S 12_{17} 14_{38} $23_{22.23}$ 24_{12} 25_{17} 26_{12} 2 S 24_{13} 1 K $20_{7.22}$ 2 K 5_{7} Is 29_{15} 41_{20} 44_{9} 58_{3} Jr 2_{19} 5_{1} 12_{3} Ec 6_{5} Ne 4_{5}; + ראה Ex 2_{25} Dt 33_{9} Jr 2_{23} Ps 31_{8} 138_{6} Jb 11_{11} Ec 8_{16}; + ראה ho. *be shown* Dt 4_{35}; :: ראה *see* Is 6_{9}; + חזה *see* Nm 24_{16}; שׁזף *see* Jb 28_{7}; + גלה ni. *be revealed* 1 S 3_{7}.

|| שׁמע *hear* Nm 24_{16} Dt 9_{2} 29_{3} Is 33_{13} $40_{21.28}$ 48_{8} Jr 6_{18} 4QMyst^{a} 8_{5}; + שׁמע Jr 5_{15} Ps 78_{3} Jb 5_{27} Pr 4_{1}; || חרשׁ hi. *be silent* Si 35_{8}.

|| שׁמר *observe* Jb 39_{1}; + פתח appar. pi. (of ear) *be opened* Is 48_{8}; פלס pi. *weigh out* Pr 5_{6}; אמן hi. *believe* Is 43_{10}; || שׁרת pi. *serve* 1QM 13_{3}; + עבד *serve* 1 C 28_{9}; + קרא בְּשֵׁם *call upon name* Jr 10_{25} Ps 79_{6}; שׁוב אֶל־לֵבָב hi. *lay to heart* Dt 4_{39}.

+ נגד ho. *be told* Is 40_{21}; || קוץ hi. *awake* 1 S 26_{12}; + חשׁק *cling* Ps 91_{14}; קדשׁ hi. *consecrate* Jr 1_{5}; || פעל *do* Jb 11_{8}; + עלל htp. *deal wantonly with* Jg 19_{25}; || חלה *be sick* Pr 23_{35}; + זָכוּר *mindful* Ps 103_{14}; יֵשׁ דֵּעָה *there is knowledge* Ps 73_{11}.

:: כחד ni. *be hidden* Ho 5_{3}; :: מאס *despise* Jb 9_{21}.

+ adverb or noun used adverbially, עוֹד *again* Gn 4_{25} Ec 4_{13}, מְאֹד *much* Ps 139_{14} (or em.; see Subj.) Jb 35_{15} (unless ידע II, *be humiliated*), אָז *then* 4QMyst^{b} 1a.2-b_{1} 4Q416 2.$3_{9.15}$ 4Q417 2.$1_{6.8.13}$, עַתָּה *now* Jg 17_{13} 18_{14} 1 K 1_{18}, לְפָנִים *formerly* Jb 42_{11}, *firstly* Si 37_{8}, תְּמוֹל שִׁלְשׁוֹם *yesterday and the day before* Ru 2_{11}, כֵּן *thus* 1 S 23_{17} Zc 11_{11} (or em. כֵּן עֲנִיֵּי *so the poor ones of* to כְּנַעֲנִי *the traders of* the sheep knew), אֵיכָה *how?* Dt 18_{21} Ps 73_{11}, בַּמָּה *how?* Gn 15_{8}, הַיּוֹם *today* Dt 1_{39} 4_{39} 9_{3} 2 S 19_{7} 2 K $2_{3.5}$, פָּנִים אֶל־פָּנִים *face to face* Dt 34_{10}.

ידע *know (how to)* + inf. cstr. of עשׂה *do* Gn 36_{1} Am 3_{10} (unless ידע III *care*) Ec 4_{17} 2 C 2_{13} 4QMMT B_{54} (יד[ע]), יטב hi. *do good* Jr 4_{22}, נגן pi. *play* 1 S $16_{16(mss).18}$, כרת *cut* 1 K 5_{20} 2 C 2_{7}, פתח pi. *engrave* 2 C $2_{6.13}$, חשׁב *devise* 2 C 2_{13}, ירא *fear* 1 K 8_{43}||2 C 6_{33}, קרא *call* Is 8_{4}, *read* Lachish ost. 3_{8}, הלל *praise* 4QBer^{a} 1.7_{6} (כל ידעי עולמים להל[ל] *all those who know how to praise eternally*), שׁחר pi. *avert* Is 47_{11} (if em.; see Obj.), שׁחד *bribe* Is 47_{11} (if em.; see Obj.), עות perh. *help* Is 50_{4} (or em. עות to רעה *feed*, ענה *answer*, or עוה pi. *turn*), בין hi. *understand* Is 56_{10} (if em. יָדְעוּ *they have* no *knowledge* to יָדְעוּ לְהָבִין *they do* not *know how to understand*) 56_{11}, כלם ni. *be ashamed* Jr 6_{15} (if em. hi. in same sense) 8_{12}, זהר ni. *be warned* Ec 4_{13}, הלך *go* Ec 6_{8} 10_{15}.

+ inf. abs. of מאס *refuse* Is $7_{15.16}$, בחר *choose* Is $7_{15.16}$.

inf. abs. + finite form of ידע Gn 15_{13} 43_{7} Jos 23_{13} 1 S $20_{3.9}$ 28_{1} 1 K $2_{37.42}$ Jr 13_{12} 26_{15} 40_{14} $42_{19.22}$ Pr 27_{23}.

אִישׁ יֹדֵעַ מְנַגֵּן בַּכִּנּוֹר *a man skilful in playing the lyre* 1 S 16_{16}, לֹא יָדַעְתִּי אֲכַנֶּה *I do not know how to give flattering* titles Jb 32$_{22}$, תדיע למי תטיב *you should know for whom you do good* Si 12$_{1}$ (unless ידע V hi. *cause to sweat;* or em. אם תטיב דע *if you do good, know*), לֹא־יָדַע בֵּין־יְמִינוֹ לִשְׂמֹאלוֹ *he does not know (the difference) between his right and his left* Jon 4$_{11}$, מְקוֹם לֹא־יָדַע־אֵל *the place of one who does not know God* Jb 18$_{21}$, רִב לֹא־יָדַעְתִּי *the cause of one whom I did not know* Jb 29$_{16}$.

יֹדְעֵי/יוֹדְעֵי *ones knowing, those who know,* followed by noun(s), אֱלֹהִים *God* Dn 11$_{32}$, שֵׁם *name* Jr 48$_{17}$ Ps 9$_{11}$, דֶּרֶךְ *way* 4QCryptA 3.2$_{6}$ ([יו]דעי), טוֹב וָרָע *good and evil* Gn 3$_{5}$, דָּת וָדִין *law and judgment* Est 1$_{13}$, דַּעַת *knowledge* Dn 1$_{4}$, בִּינָה *understanding* 1 C 12$_{33}$, צֶדֶק *righteousness* Is 51$_{7}$ 4QShir^{b} 2.1$_{2}$ ([צדק]), עֵדָה *testimony* Ps 119$_{79(Qr)}$, תְּרוּעָה *shout* Ps 89$_{16}$, נְהִי *lamentation* Am 5$_{16}$, יָם *sea* 1 K 9$_{27}$||2 C 8$_{18}$, עֵת *time* Est 1$_{13}$.

9. pass. **a. be known,** <SUBJ> impersonal MurEpBeth-Mashiko$_{2}$. <PREP> לְ of direction, *to*, + Jeshua MurEp Beth-Mashiko$_{2}$.

b. be well known or perh. **be experienced, be proved,** <SUBJ> אִישׁ *man* Dt 1$_{13.15}$ (or em. וִידֻעִים *and well known* to וְיַדְּעִים *and expert*), חָדָשׁ *new (friend)* Si 9$_{10}$ (ידו[ע]יך appar. *known to you*). <COLL> || בִּין ni. *be intelligent* Dt 1$_{13}$; + חָכָם *wise* Dt 1$_{13.15}$.

10. pass. ptc. as noun, **a. one who is known,** <CSTR> יְדוּעַ חֹלִי *one who is known of,* i.e. by, *sickness* Is 53$_{3}$ (unless ידע II pass. *be humbled* or IV pass. *be punished;* 1Q Isa^{a} יודע *knowing*). **b. one who is well known** or perh. **one who is experienced,** <CSTR> כול ... הנבונים והידעים *all ... the intelligent ones and the well-known ones* 1QSa 1$_{28}$ (unless יָדַע *expert*).

Also 1QH fr. 7$_{6}$ perh. fr. 46$_{2}$ 1QM 11$_{15}$ 1QMyst 1.2$_{11}$ 2QapDavid 2$_{1}$ ([י]ידעתן) 4Q185 1.2$_{7.15}$ 4QJub^{b} 12$_{4}$ 4Q CitJub 1.1$_{3}$ 4QD^{d} 13$_{1}$ 4QMyst^{a} 4$_{4}$ ([י]דע) 68$_{4}$ 70$_{2}$ 4QapJoseph^{b} 1$_{13}$ ([י]ידעת) 4QapJoshua^{a} 13.1$_{6}$ 4QpsMos^{e} 2.2$_{6}$ 4QShirShabb^{b} 35$_{1}$ 4QsapDidA 4$_{4}$ 4QBapt 16$_{2}$ 4Q415 12$_{3}$ 23$_{1}$ 4Q416 2.1$_{17}$ 17$_{3}$ 4Q418 83$_{1}$ 140$_{4}$ perh. 222$_{4}$ 4QWays^{b} 5$_{2}$ 4QNarrA 1$_{4}$ 4QHymnPr 3$_{3}$ 4QRitMar 28$_{2}$ 4QPrQuot 7.4$_{1}$ 4QDibHam^{a} 8$_{10}$ 6QapSamKings 36$_{2}$ (ידע[ון/ת]).

<SYN> §§1-8 נכר hi. *recognize,* חשב pi. *consider,* בין *understand,* hi. *understand,* htpol. *understand, be intelligent,* שׂכל hi. *understand,* למד *learn,* תור *search out,* בקשׁ pi. *seek,* ראה *see,* שׁמע *hear,* שׁמר *observe,* שׁרת pi. *serve,* חרשׁ hi. *be silent* שִׂים *place (heart),* i.e. consider, קוץ hi. *awake,* פעל *do,* חלה *be sick;* §9 בין ni. *be intelligent.*

<ANT> §§1-8, ראה *see,* כחד ni. *be hidden,* מאס *despise.*

Ni. 40.3.8 Pf. נוֹדַע, נוֹדַעְתִּי, נוֹדְעוּ, Q נודענו; impf. יִוָּדַע (יִוָּדֵעַ), 3fs תִּוָּדַע, תִּוָּדְעִי, Si אודע; + waw וְנוֹדַע (וְנוֹדְעָה), וְנוֹדַעְתִּי (וְנוֹדָעְתִּי); וָאִוָּדַע, וַיִּוָּדַע; ptc. נוֹדָע, Si נודעת; inf. הִוָּדְעִי—**1. be known, made known** (e.g. Gn 41$_{31}$ Lv 4$_{14}$ Dt 21$_{1}$ 2 S 17$_{19}$ Is 61$_{9}$ Na 3$_{17}$ Zc 14$_{7}$ Ps 48$_{4}$ 79$_{10}$ 88$_{13}$ Est 2$_{22}$ Ne 4$_{9}$ Si 12$_{8}$ 1QH 1$_{23}$); before כִּי *that* Gn 41$_{21}$ Ex 21$_{36}$ 33$_{16}$ 1 K 18$_{36}$ Ru 3$_{14}$ 1QMyst 1.1$_{8}$ 11QPs^{a} 18$_{4}$; before indirect question, Dt 21$_{1}$ 1 S 6$_{3}$ Na 3$_{17}$.

2. make oneself known (e.g. Ex 6$_{3}$ Is 19$_{21}$ Ezk 20$_{5.9}$ 35$_{11}$ 38$_{23}$ Ps 9$_{17}$ Ru 3$_{3}$).*

3. be found out, discovered (e.g. Jg 16$_{9}$ 1 S 22$_{6}$ Pr 10$_{9}$).

4. perh. **be made to know** (Jr 31$_{19}$).

<SUBJ> Y. Ex 2$_{25}$ (if em.; see Prep.) 6$_{3}$ Is 19$_{21}$ Ezk 20$_{5.9}$ 35$_{11}$ 38$_{23}$ Hb 3$_{2}$ (if em. hi. *make known*) Ps 9$_{17}$ 48$_{4}$ 76$_{2}$ 4Q apPs^{b} 48$_{7}$.

Ephraim Jr 31$_{19}$ (unless ידע IV ni. *be punished;* or em. יסר ni. *be disciplined*), David 1 S 22$_{6}$ (unless ידע VII ni. *take leave;* or em. יעד ni. *meet*), אִישׁ *man* 1 S 22$_{6}$, בַּעַל *husband* Pr 31$_{23}$, בֵּן *son* Si 16$_{17}$, בַּת *daughter* Ru 3$_{3}$, זֶרַע *seed,* i.e. descendants Is 61$_{9}$, צֶאֱצָא *offspring* Is 61$_{9}$, אֹהֵב *friend* Si 12$_{8}$, נָבִיא *prophet* Jr 28$_{9}$, עקשׁ pi. ptc. *one who perverts* his ways Pr 10$_{9}$ (unless II ni. *be made submissive* or IV ni. *be punished* or V ni. *be made to sweat;* or em. רעע ni. *be hurt*).

יָד *hand* Is 66$_{14}$, חַטָּאת *sin* Lv 4$_{14}$, חָכְמָה *wisdom* Pr 14$_{33}$ (unless ידע II ni. *be made submissive* or V ni. *it is caused to sweat;* or em. תִּוָּדַע *it makes itself known* to אִוֶּלֶת *folly,* or תֵּרוֹעַ *it is hurt*) Si 4$_{24}$ 11QPs^{a}18$_{4}$, תְּבוּנָה *understanding* Si 4$_{24}$, כֹּחַ *strength* Jg 16$_{9}$ (unless ידע II ni. *be made submissive*), כַּעַס *anger* Pr 12$_{16}$ (unless ידע II ni. *be made quiet;* or em. hi. *make* anger *known*), צְדָקָה *righteousness* Ps 88$_{13}$, appar. נְקָמָה *vengeance* Ps 79$_{10}$.

דָּבָר *matter* Ex 2$_{14}$ 2 S 17$_{19}$ Est 2$_{22}$, מָקוֹם *place* Na 3$_{17}$, שָׂבָע *plenty* Gn 41$_{31}$, פֶּלֶא *wonder* Ps 88$_{13}$, יוֹם *day* Zc 14$_{7}$, נֵצֶר *shoot* 1QH 8$_{11}$, מָה *what?* 1QH 1$_{23}$, מִי *who?* CD 9$_{11}$, כֹּל *anything* 1QH 1$_{8}$ 10$_{9}$.

Subj. not specified, Gn 41$_{21}$ Ex 21$_{36}$ 33$_{16}$ Dt 21$_{1}$ 1 S 6$_{3}$ (unless ידע II ni. *be granted rest*) 1 K 18$_{36}$ Ezk 36$_{32}$ Ps 74$_{5}$

(unless ידע IX *tear down;* or em. גדע *hew*) Ru 3_{14} Ec 6_{10} Ne 4_{9} 1QH fr. 10_{6} 1QMyst 1.1_{8}.

<PREP> לְ of benefit, *to, for,* + Philistines 1 S 6_{3} (unless ידע II ni. *be granted rest*).

לְ of direction, *to,* + Egypt Is 19_{21}, Israelites Ne 4_{9}, בַּיִת *house* of Israel Ezk 36_{32}, Abraham Ex 6_{3}, Isaac Ex 6_{3}, Jacob Ex 6_{3}, Mordecai Est 2_{22}, אָדָם *human being* 11QPs[a] 18_{4}, אִישׁ *man* Ru 3_{3}, זֶרַע *seed,* i.e. descendants Ezk 20_{5}.

לְ of agent, *by,* + Y. Zc 14_{7}.

לְ *in, before,* + עַיִן *eye* Ezk 20_{9} 38_{23} Ps 79_{10}.

לְ *as,* + מִשְׂגָּב *refuge* Is 48_{4}.

בְּ of place, time, *in, among, during,* + Judah Ps 76_{2} 4QapPs[b] 48_{7} ([יהו]דה), גּוֹי *nation* Is 61_{9} Ezk 35_{11} (or em. בָּם *among them* to בְּךָ *among you,* i.e. Edomite[s]) Ps $79_{10(Qr)}$, עַם *people* Si 16_{17}, יַחַד *community* 1QH fr 10_{6}, אֶרֶץ *land* Gn 41_{31} Ezk 20_{5} 35_{11} (or em.) Ps 88_{13}, הַר *mountain* Ezk 35_{11} (or em.), חֹשֶׁךְ *darkness* Ps 88_{13}, שַׁעַר *gate* Pr 31_{23}, טוֹבָה *prosperity* Si 12_{8}, יוֹם *day* Pr 12_{16} (unless ידע II ni. *be made quiet*); of instrument, *by (means of), through,* + אֹמֶר *speech* Si 4_{24}, מַעֲנֶה *answer* Si 4_{24}; of cause, *on account of* Ex 33_{16} (בַּמֶּה *how?*).

בְּלֹא *without,* + רָצוֹן *will* 1QH 1_{8} 10_{9}.

כְּ *as when* Ps 74_{5} (unless ידע IX *tear down;* or em. גדע *hew*).

מִן *by (means of),* + זֶה *this* 1QMyst 1.1_{8}.

אֶל *to,* + Israelites Ezk 20_{9}, בֵּן *son* of Israel Ex 2_{25} (if em. וַיֵּדַע אֱלֹהִים *and God knew* to וַיִּוָּדַע אֲלֵיהֶם *and he made himself known to them*).

מִפְּנֵי *on account of,* + רָעָב *famine* Gn 41_{31}.

אֵת *with,* i.e. among, + עֶבֶד *servant* Is 66_{14}.

בְּקֶרֶב *among, within,* + כְּסִיל *fool* Pr 14_{33} (unless ידע II ni. *be made submissive* or V ni. *be caused to sweat*), שָׁנָה *year* Hb 3_{2} (if em. hi. *make known*).

בְּתוֹךְ *among,* + עַם *people* Is 61_{9}.

<COLL> ידע ni. ‖ ספר pu. *be told* 1QH 1_{23}, חשב ni. *be considered* 1QH 8_{11}; נוֹדַע אֲשֶׁר הוּא אָדָם *it is known what a human being is* Ec 6_{10}.

<SYN> ספר pu. *be told,* חשב ni. *be considered.*

Pi. 1 Pf. Qr יִדַּעְתָּ (Kt ידעתה)—**1. cause to know,** with double object, <SUBJ> Y. Ps 104_{19} (if em. יָדַע *it* [the sun] *knew* to יִדַּע *he caused* the sun *to know*), Job Jb 38_{12}. <OBJ> (1) recipient of knowledge, שַׁחַר *dawn* Jb 38_{12}, שֶׁמֶשׁ *sun* Ps 104_{19} (if em.); (2) contents of knowledge, מָקוֹם *place* Jb 38_{12}, מָבוֹא *place of setting* Ps 104_{19} (if em.).

2. make known, <SUBJ> Job 38_{33} (if em. הֲיָדַעְתָּ *do you know?* to הֲיִדַּעְתָּ *have you made known?*). <OBJ> חֻקָּה *statute* Jb 38_{33} (if em.).

Pu. 7 Ptc. מְיֻדָּעִי, מְיֻדָּעַי (מְיֻדָּעָי) מְיֻדָּעָיו; fs Kt מידעת—**1. be made known,** <SUBJ> זֹאת *this* Is $12_{5(Kt)}$. <PREP> בְּ of place, *in,* + אֶרֶץ *land* Is $12_{5(Kt)}$. **2.** as noun, **acquaintance, intimate friend; kinsman** (Ru $2_{1[Kt]}$), <SUBJ> חרף pi. *reproach* Ps 55_{14}, גדל hi. *act mightily* Ps 55_{14}, שׁכח *forget* Jb 19_{14} (unless subj. is גָּרֵי בֵיתִי *the guests in my house*), חדל *cease* Jb 19_{14}. <NOM CL> מְיֻדָּעַי מַחְשָׁךְ *my intimate friends are (in) a dark place* Ps 88_{19}, לְנָעֳמִי מידע אִישָׁהּ *Naomi had a kinsman of her husband's* Ru $2_{1(Kt)}$ (Qr מוֹדַע *kinsman*). <OBJ> נכה hi. *strike* 2 K 10_{11}, רחק hi. *make distant* Ps 88_{9}. <APP> אִישׁ *man* Ru 2_{1}. <PREP> לְ of direction, possession, *to, of,* + היה *be* Ps 31_{12}. <COLL> ‖ אַלּוּף *companion* Ps 55_{14}, שָׁכֵן *neighbour* Ps 31_{12}, קָרוֹב *near one,* i.e. kin Jb 19_{14}, כֹּהֵן *priest* 2 K 10_{11}, גָּדוֹל *great one* 2 K 10_{11}; + אֹהֵב *lover* Ps 88_{19}, רֵעַ *friend* Ps 88_{19}, שׁאר ni. ptc. *one who remains* 2 K 10_{11}, אֱנוֹשׁ כְּעֶרְכִּי *a person like myself* Ps 55_{14}.

<SYN> אַלּוּף *companion,* שָׁכֵן *neighbour,* קָרוֹב *near one,* i.e. kin, כֹּהֵן *priest,* גָּדוֹל *great one.*

Po. 1 Pf. יוֹדַעְתִּי—**cause to know,** i.e. direct (to a place), <SUBJ> David 1 S 21_{3} (unless ידע VII *say farewell;* or em. יעד ni. *make appointment*). <OBJ> נַעַר *lad* 1 S 21_{3}. <PREP> אֶל *at,* + מָקוֹם *place* 1 S 21_{3}.

Hi. 71.1.49 Pf. הוֹדִיעַ (הוֹדִיעַנִי, Q הודיעו, הודעו), הוֹדַעְתָּ, הוֹדַעְתִּי (הוֹדַעְתַּנִי, הודעתם Q, הודעתי Q, הוֹדַעְתָּ), הוֹדִיעוּ (הוֹדַעְתִּיךָ); impf. יוֹדִיעַ (יֹדַע, יוֹדִיעֵנוּ, יודיעהו Q, אוֹדִיעָה) אוֹדִיעַ, (יודיעה), 2ms תּוֹדִיעַ (תּוֹדִיעֵנִי, Q תודיענו), נוֹדִיעָה, (יוֹדִיעֵם) יֹדִיעוּ, (אוֹדִיעֵם, אוֹדִיעֲךָ; + waw וְהוֹדַעְתָּ (וְהוֹדַעְתָּה, וְהוֹדַעְתֶּם, וְהוֹדַעְתָּם), וְהוֹדַעְתִּי; וַיֹּדַע (Q ויודע, Q וידיעהו); impv. הוֹדַע (הוֹדִיעֵנִי, הֹדִיעֵנִי, הוֹדִיעֵנוּ), (הוֹדִעֻנוּ) הוֹדִיעוּ (הוֹדִיעֵם; ptc. מוֹדִיעֲךָ, מוֹדִיעָם, מוֹדִיעִים; inf. הוֹדִיעַ (הֹדִיעַ, הוֹדִיעֵנִי, הוֹדִיעֲךָ) (Q הודיעכה), Q הודיעו, הוֹדִיעָם)—**cause to know, make known, declare (to), teach**; with בֵּין perh. **distinguish*** (Ezk 22_{26} CD 6_{17} 12_{20}); before indirect question (1 S 6_{2} 28_{15} 1 K 1_{27} Is 19_{12} [if em.; see Subj.] Ps 39_{5} Jb 10_{2} 37_{19}).

<SUBJ> Y. Gn 41_{39} Ex $33_{12.13}$ Nm 16_{5} 1 S 16_{3} 2 S 7_{21}

‖1 C 17$_{19}$ Is 5$_5$ 64$_1$ Jr 11$_{18}$ 16$_{21.21}$ Ezk 20$_{11}$ 39$_7$ Ho 5$_9$ Hb 3$_2$ (or em. תּוֹדִיעַ *you make known* to תִּוָּדַע *you make yourself known*, i.e. ni.) Ps 16$_{11}$ 25$_{4.14}$ 39$_5$ 51$_8$ 77$_{15}$ 78$_5$ 90$_{12}$ 98$_2$ 103$_7$ 106$_8$ 143$_8$ 147$_{20}$ (if em. יְדָעוּם *they knew them* to יִדָּעֵם *he taught them*) Jb 10$_2$ 13$_{23}$ Ne 9$_{14}$ Si 38$_5$ 1QpHab 7$_{2.4}$ 1QH 4$_{27.28}$ 7$_{27}$ 10$_{5.14}$ 11$_{9.16}$ 1QLitPr 3.2$_7$ 4QapMos^c 2.2$_8$ 4QapPs^b 15$_8$ 4Q418 201$_1$ 4QPrQuot 51$_9$ ([הוד]עתנו) 51$_{13}$ ([ה]ודיענו) 76$_2$ ([אל]) 4QDibHam^a 4$_{14}$ (הודי[ענו]) 11QPs^a 19$_2$ CD 1$_{11}$ 2$_{12}$.

Israel Dt 4$_9$, יַחַד *community* 11QPs^a 18$_2$, Shuhite Jb 26$_3$, Baruch Samaria-Sebaste ost. 1101$_2$ (הדעם; others הרעם; others הפעם *this once*), Bildad Jb 26$_3$, Ezra Ne 8$_{12}$, Gabriel Dn 8$_{19}$, Gideon Jg 8$_{16}$ (unless ידע II hi. *make submissive*, or IV hi. *punish*; or em. דוש *thresh* or רעע hi. *hurt*), Job 37$_{19}$ 38$_3$ 40$_7$ 42$_4$, Moses Ex 18$_{16.20}$, Nehemiah Ne 8$_{12}$, Samuel 1 S 10$_8$ 28$_{15}$ 4QVisSam 1$_5$ ([הו]דיעני), אִישׁ *man* 1 S 14$_{12}$ Is 40$_{13}$ CD 9$_{22}$ 13$_{15}$ 15$_{10}$ 4QD^e 7.1$_{16}$ (אי[ש]), אָב *father* Is 38$_{19}$, בֵּן *son* perh. 4QapJoseph^b 1$_{13}$ (וידעיו), of Israel Jos 4$_{22}$, of man Ezk 16$_2$ 20$_4$ 22$_2$ 43$_{11}$, מֶלֶךְ *king* 1 K 1$_{27}$, אָדוֹן *lord* 1 K 1$_{27}$, תִּרְשָׁתָא *governor* Ne 8$_{12}$, סֹפֵר *scribe* Ne 8$_{12}$, כֹּהֵן *priest* 1 S 6$_2$ Ezk 22$_{26}$ 44$_{23}$ Ne 8$_{12}$, לֵוִי *Levite* Ne 8$_{12}$, קֹסֵם *diviner* 1 S 6$_2$, מְשֹׁרֵר *singer* 2 C 23$_{13}$, מְבַקֵּר *examiner* CD 15$_{14}$ (ויודיעה[ו]), מַשְׂכִּיל *instructor* 4QD^a 1$_5$ ([משכיל]), חָכָם *wise one* Is 19$_{12}$ (or em. וְיֵדְעוּ *and they shall know* to וְיֹדִעוּ *and let them make known*) Pr 22$_{19.21}$, חָסִיד *righteous one* 11QPs^a 18$_{12}$, צַדִּיק *righteous one* 11QPs^a 18$_{12}$, אֱוִיל *fool* Pr 12$_{16}$ (if em. יִוָּדַע *it is made known* to יוֹדִיעַ *he makes known*), הבר ptc. *one who divides the heavens*, i.e. astrologer Is 47$_{13(Qr)}$, חָסִיד *loyal one* Ps 145$_{12}$, worshipper Is 12$_4$ Ps 32$_5$ 89$_2$ 105$_1$‖1 C 16$_8$ 4QapPs^b 15$_8$ (אודי[עך]), רֵעַ *neighbour* CD 9$_{17}$, שָׂפָה *lip* Pr 10$_{32}$ (if em. יֵדְעוּן *they know* to יוֹדִעוּן *they make known*), פֶּה *mouth* Pr 10$_{32}$ (if em.; see above), חָכְמָה *wisdom* Pr 1$_{23}$ 11QPs^a 18$_{3.4}$, מַעֲשֶׂה *work* Ps 145$_{12}$, מִי *who?* Is 40$_{14}$, שָׁנָה *year* Jb 32$_7$, אֶחָד *one* CD 9$_{19}$, אֵלֶּה *these* 1QH 13$_{13}$, כֹּל *everyone* CD 6$_{17}$; subj. not specified, Pr 9$_9$ Samaria-Sebaste ost. 1101$_2$ (הדעם; others הרעם; others הפעם *this once*) 1QH 1$_{29}$ 4QHod^a 7.1$_{16}$ CD 12$_{20}$.

<OBJ> (1) recipient of knowledge, Y. Is 40$_{13.14}$ Ps 32$_5$ Jb 38$_3$ 40$_7$ 42$_4$ 4QapPs^b 15$_8$ ([אודי]עך), Israel(ites) Is 5$_5$ Jr 16$_{21}$ Ezk 20$_{11}$ Ps 147$_{20}$ (if em.; see Subj.), עַם *people* Ex 18$_{16}$ 44$_{23}$, בַּיִת *house* Ezk 43$_{11}$, Philistines 1 S 6$_2$, Jerusalem Ezk 16$_2$, עִיר *city* Ezk 22$_2$, Daniel Dn 8$_{19}$, Eli 4QVisSam 1$_5$ ([הו]דיעני), Elihu Jb 37$_{19}$, Habakkuk 1QpHab 7$_2$ Jeremiah Jr 11$_{18}$, Job Jb 10$_2$ 13$_{23}$, Jonathan 1 S 14$_{12}$, Joseph Gn 41$_{39}$, Moses Ex 33$_{13}$, Samuel 1 S 16$_3$, Saul 1 S 28$_{15}$, אֱנוֹשׁ *human being* Si 38$_5$, אָדָם *human being* 1QH 10$_5$, אִישׁ *man* Jg 8$_{16}$ (unless ידע II *be quiet* or IV *punish*; or em.; see Subj.), בֵּן *son* Jos 4$_{22}$ 1QH 11$_9$ 4QD^a 1$_5$ (ב[נ]י), זֶרַע *seed*, i.e. descendants 1QLitPr 3.2$_7$, זָקֵן *elder* Ezk 20$_4$, עֶבֶד *servant* 2 S 7$_{21}$, פֶּתִי *simple one* Pr 1$_{23}$, קָרִיא *one called* CD 2$_{12}$, שׁוּב ptc. *one who repents* CD 15$_{10.14}$ (ויודיעה[ו]), נשׂא ptc. *one who bears* armour 1 S 14$_{12}$, ירא ptc. *one who fears* Ps 25$_{14}$, מוֹרֶה *teacher* 1QpHab 7$_4$, worshipper Ps 16$_{11}$ 25$_4$ 39$_5$ 51$_8$ 143$_8$ 1QH 4$_{27}$ 7$_{27}$ 10$_{14}$ 11$_{16}$ 4QapPs^b 15$_8$ 4QPrQuot 51$_9$ ([הוד]עתנו) 51$_{13}$ ([ה]ודיענו) 76$_2$ 4QDibHam^a 4$_{14}$ (הודי[ענו]), יָד *hand* 4QM^a 11.1$_{23}$; object not specified, Pr 22$_{19.21}$.

(2) contents of knowledge, קָדוֹשׁ *holy one* Nm 16$_5$, יָד *hand*, i.e. power Jr 16$_{21}$, שֵׁם *name* Is 64$_1$ Ezk 39$_7$, צוּרָה *form* Ezk 43$_{11}$, תּוֹרָה *law* Ex 18$_{16}$ 43$_{11}$ Ps 78$_5$, חֹק *statute* Ex 18$_{16}$ 43$_{11}$, מִשְׁפָּט *ordinance* Ezk 20$_{11}$ Ps 147$_{20}$ (if em.; see Subj.) CD 15$_{10}$, יִסּוּר *regulation* 1QLitPr 3.2$_7$, עֵצָה *counsel* perh. Is 40$_{13}$, סוֹד *counsel* 1QH 10$_5$ 11$_{16}$, מַחֲשָׁבָה *thought* 4QD^a 1$_5$ ([מח]שבות), דָּבָר *word, matter* Pr 1$_{23}$ perh. 4QapJoseph^b 1$_{13}$ (וידעיו [דברי]) CD 9$_{17}$, אֹמֶר *word* Pr 22$_{21}$, מַרְאֶה *vision* 4QVisSam 1$_5$ ([הו]דיעני), עֵדוּת *testimony* Ps 78$_5$, בְּרִית *covenant* Ps 25$_{14}$, מִסְפָּר *number* 4QMidrEschat^b 10$_{12}$, שַׁבָּת *sabbath* Ne 9$_{14}$, חָכְמָה *wisdom* Ps 51$_8$ Jb 32$_7$, תּוּשִׁיָּה *sound wisdom* Jb 26$_3$, שֵׂכֶל *insight* 1QH 10$_{14}$ ([שכ]לכה), אֱמֶת *truth* 1QH 6$_{12}$, קֹשְׁטְ *truth* Pr 22$_{21}$, אֱמוּנָה *faithfulness* Ps 89$_2$, אמן ni. ptc. fem. *certainty* Ho 5$_9$, חֶסֶד *loyalty* 11QPs^a 19$_2$, רָז *mystery* 1QpHab 7$_4$, סתר hi. ptc. *hidden thing* 5QRègle 1$_{11}$ ([להו]דיע נסתר[ות]), רָצוֹן *acceptance* Pr 10$_{32}$ (if em.; see Subj.), דֶּרֶךְ *way* Ex 18$_{20}$ 33$_{13}$ Is 40$_{14}$ Ps 103$_7$ 143$_8$, אֹרַח *path* Ps 16$_{11}$ 25$_4$, כֹּחַ *strength* Si 38$_5$, עֹז *strength* Ps 77$_{15}$ 4QHod^a 7.1$_{16}$ 11QPs^a 18$_{4.12}$, גְּבוּרָה *might* Jr 16$_{21}$ Ps 106$_8$ 145$_{12}$ 1QH 4$_{28}$ fr. 7$_6$, גְּדוּלָּה *greatness* 1 C 17$_{19}$, כָּבוֹד *glory* 1QH 1$_{29}$ 13$_{13}$ 11QPs^a 18$_3$, מַעֲשֶׂה *deed* Ex 18$_{20}$, פֹּעַל *deed* Hb 3$_2$ (or em.; see Subj.), עֲלִילָה *deed* Is 12$_4$ Ps 103$_7$ 105$_1$‖1 C 16$_8$, יֶשַׁע *salvation* 11QPs^a 18$_2$, יְשׁוּעָה *salvation* Ps 98$_2$, דָּבָר *thing* Dt 4$_9$ 1 S 14$_{12}$ Ne 8$_{12}$, חַטָּאת *sin* Ps 32$_5$ Jb 13$_{23}$, פֶּשַׁע *transgression* Jb 13$_{23}$, תַּהְפֻּכָה *perversity* Pr 10$_{32}$ (if em.; see Subj.), תּוֹעֵבָה

abomination Ezk 16$_{2}$ 20$_{4}$ 22$_{2}$, כַּעַס *vexation* Pr 12$_{16}$ (if em.; see Subj.), קֵץ *end* Ps 39$_{5}$, גֶּמֶר *completion* of age 1QpHab 7$_{2}$, זֹאת *this* Gn 41$_{39}$, אֵלֶּה *these* perh. 1Q36 1$_{4}$, אֲשֶׁר *the one who, that which* Ex 33$_{12}$ Nm 16$_{5}$ 1 S 10$_{8}$ 16$_{3}$ Is 5$_{5}$ Dn 8$_{19}$ 4Q 419 1$_{4}$ CD 1$_{11}$; object not specified, CD 9$_{22}$ 15$_{14}$ (ויוד[יעה]ו) 4QD^{e} 7.1$_{16}$.

<PREP> לְ of direction, *to* (or as introducing object), + Moses Ps 103$_{7}$, Noah 4QCommGenB 1$_{4}$ ([לנו]ח), Saul 1 S 10$_{8}$, עַם *people* Ex 18$_{20}$ Ne 8$_{12}$, בֵּן *son* Dt 4$_{9}$ Is 38$_{19}$ Ps 78$_{5}$, of Israel Ps 103$_{7}$, of man Ps 145$_{12}$, צַר *adversary* Is 64$_{1}$, דּוֹר *generation* Ps 89$_{2}$ 4QCommGenD 3$_{4}$ CD 1$_{11}$, צַדִּיק *righteous one* Pr 9$_{9}$, מְבַקֵּר *examiner* CD 9$_{17.19.22}$ 13$_{15}$, כֹּהֵן *priest* 4QD^{e} 7.1$_{16}$, פֶּתִי *simple one* 11QPs^{a} 18$_{4}$, מוט pol. ptc. *one who slips* 11QPs^{a} 19$_{2}$ (מוטטי), חַי *living one* 1QH 4$_{28}$ 11QPs^{a} 19$_{2}$, מַעֲשֶׂה *creature* 1QH 13$_{13}$ ([למעשי]ך).

לְ *at*, חֹדֶשׁ *month* Is 47$_{13}$.

לְ *before*, + עַיִן *eye* CD 9$_{17}$.

בְּ of place, *among*, + Bethel 5QRègle 2$_{6}$ ([הו]דעתה), עַם *people* Is 12$_{4}$ Ps 77$_{15}$ 105$_{1}$||1 C 16$_{8}$, סתם pass. ptc. *closed place* Ps 51$_{8}$; of time, *in, on*, + יוֹם *day* Pr 12$_{16}$ (if em.; see Subj.); בְּ of instrument, *by (means of), with*, + יָד *hand* CD 2$_{12}$, פֶּה *mouth* Ps 89$_{2}$, בַּרְקָן *brier* Jg 8$_{16}$ (unless ידע II *be quiet* or IV *punish*; or em.; see Subj.), קוֹץ *thorn* Jg 8$_{16}$, כֹּחַ *strength* 4QM^{a} 11.1$_{23}$; of accompaniment, + יכח hi. inf. *reproof* CD 9$_{17}$.

בְּ of place, *in, at*, + פַּעַם *time* Jr 16$_{21}$; introducing object, + סוֹד *counsel* 1QH 10$_{5}$ 11$_{9}$, רָז *mystery* 1QH 4$_{27}$ 7$_{27}$, מַחֲשָׁבָה *thought* 4QPrQuot 51$_{13}$ ([ה]ודיענו), תְּהִלָּה *psalm* 4QPrQuot 51$_{9}$ ([הוד]עתנו).

מִן partitive, *(some) of*, + אֲשֶׁר *that which* Is 47$_{13}$.

אֶל *concerning*, + אֱמֶת *faithfulness* Is 38$_{19}$.

בֵּין (make known difference) *between*, + טָמֵא *impure* and pure Ezk 22$_{26}$, קָדוֹשׁ *holy* and profane CD 6$_{17}$ 12$_{20}$.

בְּתוֹךְ *among*, + עַם *people* Ezk 39$_{7}$.

בְּקֶרֶב *among*, + שָׁנָה *year* Hb 3$_{2}$ (or em.; see Subj.).

<COLL> || גלה pi. *reveal* Ps 98$_{2}$, למד pi. *teach* Is 40$_{14}$ Ps 25$_{4}$, נבע hi. *pour out* Pr 1$_{23}$, בדל hi. *distinguish* Ezk 22$_{26}$ CD 6$_{17}$ 12$_{20}$, ספר pi. *tell* 1QH 1$_{29}$ 11QPs^{a} 18$_{3}$, שׂכל hi. *instruct* 1QH 11$_{9}$ 11QPs^{a} 18$_{4}$.

+ ראה hi. *show* Jr 11$_{18}$, דבר pi. *speak* Jb 32$_{7}$, זהר hi. *teach* Ex 18$_{20}$, צוה pi. *command* Ne 9$_{14}$, חיה pi. *revive* Hb 3$_{2}$, נתן *give* Ezk 20$_{11}$ Pr 9$_{9}$.

:: כסה pi. *cover* Ps 32$_{5}$.

+ adverb or noun used adverbially, כֵּן *so* Ps 90$_{12}$, הַיּוֹם *today* Pr 22$_{19}$.

+ infinitive of היה *be* Pr 22$_{19}$, מנה *count* Ps 90$_{12}$, הלל pi. *praise* 2 C 23$_{13}$.

בֵּין־הַטָּמֵא לְטָהוֹר לֹא הוֹדִיעוּ *they have not taught (the difference) between the unclean and the clean* Ezk 22$_{26}$, var. 44$_{23}$.

Also 1Q36 21$_{1}$ 4QD^{a} 1$_{19}$ 4QMyst^{b} 8$_{4a}$ 4Q418 135$_{2}$ 4Q RP^{b} 15$_{3}$ perh. 4QPrayer^{b} 1$_{2}$ ([ ]דיעני).

<SYN> גלה pi. *reveal*, למד pi. *teach*, נבע hi. *pour out*, ספר pi. *tell*, שׂכל hi. *instruct*, בדל hi. *distinguish*.

<ANT> כסה pi. *cover*.

Ho. 3 Pf. הוּדַע; ptc. Qr מוּדַעַת—**be made known,** <SUBJ> חַטָּאת *sin* Lv 4$_{23.28}$, זֹאת *this* Is 12$_{5(Qr)}$, impersonal Ex 21$_{29}$ (if em. הוּעַד *warning has been made* to הוּדַע *it has been made known*).* <PREP> בְּ of place, *in*, + אֶרֶץ *land* Is 12$_{5(Qr)}$; *to*, + בַּעַל *owner* Ex 21$_{29}$ (if em.; see Subj.); אֶל *to*, + נָשִׂיא *prince* Lv 4$_{23}$, עַם *people* Lv 4$_{28}$.

Htp. 2 Impf. אֶתְוַדָּע; inf. הִתְוַדַּע—**make oneself known,** <SUBJ> Y. Nm 12$_{6}$, Joseph Gn 45$_{1}$ <OBJ> אָח *brother* Gn 45$_{1}$. <PREP> אֶל *to*, + נָבִיא *prophet* Nm 12$_{6}$.

Also Lachish ost. 6$_{7}$ ([ ]ידע; others ה[ע]יר *the city*).*

→ דֵּעַ *knowledge*, דֵּעָה *knowledge*, דַּעַת *knowledge*, יַדָּע *expert*, מַדָּע *knowledge*, מוֹדָע *kinsman*, מֹדַעַת *kin*, יִדְּעֹנִי *familiar spirit*, מַדּוּעַ *why?*, אֲבִידָע *Abida*, אֶלְיָדָע *Eliada*, בְּעֶלְיָדָע *Beeliada*, דְּעוּאֵל *Deuel*, יַדּוּעַ *Jaddua*, יְדִיעֲאֵל *Jediael*, יָדָע *Jada*, יְדַעְיָה *Jedaiah*, יְהוֹיָדָע *Jehoida*, שְׁמִידָע *Shemida*.

* ידע II 30.1.1 vb. **be quiet** (unless ידע I *know*)—**Qal** 22.1 Pf. יָדַע, יָדְעָה, יָדַעְתָּ (יְדַעְתֻּנִי, Q ידעתם), יָדַעְתִּי, יָדְעוּ (יֵדְעוּ, mss יְדָעוּךָ); impf. יֵדַע (יֵדַע, יֵידַע), 3fs תֵּדַע, 2ms תֵּדַע, יֵדְעוּ, נֵדְעָה; + waw וַיֵּדַע, וַיֵּדְעוּ; ptc. pass. cstr. יְדוּעַ; inf. דַּעַת—**1. be quiet, be at rest;** also **be submissive** (e.g. Jb 21$_{19}$), <SUBJ> Israel Ho 6$_{3}$, אִישׁ *man* Jb 37$_{7}$, אִשָּׁה foolish *woman* Pr 9$_{13}$, זָרָה *foreign woman* Pr 5$_{6}$, כֹּהֵן *priest* Jr 14$_{18}$, נָבִיא *prophet* Jr 14$_{18}$, רָשָׁע *wicked one* Jb 21$_{19}$, חָנֵף *profane one* Jb 20$_{20}$, worshipper Ps 35$_{15}$ 119$_{152}$, הַר *mountain* Jb 9$_{5}$. <PREP> מִן of direction, *from*, + מַעֲשֶׂה *work* Jb 37$_{7}$ (if em. אַנְשֵׁי מַעֲשֵׂהוּ appar. *men of his work* to אֱנוֹשׁ מִמַּעֲשֵׂהוּ *man from his work*); of cause, *on account of*,

+ עֵדָה *testimony* Ps 119$_{152}$. <COLL> בַּל־יָדְעָה מָּה *she is not still at all* Pr 9$_{13}$.

2. be humiliated, humbled, reduced to submission, <SUBJ> Israel Ho 9$_7$, Ephraim Is 9$_8$, עַם *people* Is 8$_9$ (if em. רֹעוּ *be broken* to דְּעוּ *be reduced to submission*) 9$_8$, יֹשֵׁב *inhabitant* Is 9$_8$, אַלְמָנָה *widow* Ezk 19$_7$, perh. רַע *evil one* Jb 35$_{15}$, פעל ptc. *one who does* evil Ps 14$_4$||53$_5$, שָׂרִיד *survivor* Jb 20$_{26(mss)}$ (L יֵרַע *it feeds on* what is left [שָׂרִיד] in his tent). <PREP> בְּ of place, *in*, + אֹהֶל *tent* Jb 20$_{26(mss)}$; of instrument, *by (means of), with*, + פַּשׁ perh. *folly* Jb 35$_{15}$. <COLL> + adverb מְאֹד *much* Jb 35$_{15}$.

3. be submissive (as devotee) to, <SUBJ> Cyrus Is 45$_4$, מָשִׁיחַ *anointed one* Is 45$_4$. <OBJ> Y. Is 45$_4$.

4. cause to be submissive, reduce to submission, humiliate, <SUBJ> Y. Ps 138$_6$ (or em. יֵדָע to יְיַדַּע, i.e. pi.) 4QapPs^b 31$_5$, בֵּן *son* Jr 2$_{15(mss)}$ (L יִרְעוּךְ appar. *they have fed upon*, i.e. devastated, *you*) Si 7$_{20(A)}$, שָׂפָה *lip* Pr 10$_{21}$ (if em. יִרְעוּ *they feed* to יֵדְעוּ *they reduce to submission*); subj. not specified, Jr 15$_{12(mss)}$ (הֲיֵדַע *can one reduce to submission?*; L הֲיָרֹעַ *can one break?*, i.e. רעע).

<OBJ> Israel Jr 2$_{16(mss)}$, גָּבֹהַּ *proud one* Ps 138$_6$ (or em.; see Qal), עבד ptc. *one who serves* Si 7$_{20(A)}$, צֹרֵר *adversary* 4QapPs^b 31$_5$, רַב pl. *many* Pr 10$_{21}$ (if em.; see Subj.), בַּרְזֶל *iron* Jr 15$_{12(mss)}$. <PREP> בְּ of accompaniment, *with*, + אֱמֶת *reality* Si 7$_{20(A)}$; מִן of direction, *from*, + מֶרְחָק *distance* Ps 138$_6$. <COLL> יֵדְעוּךְ קָדְקֹד appar. *they have made you submissive (with respect to your) crown* Jr 2$_{16(mss)}$.

5. pass. ptc. as noun, **one who is humbled,** <CSTR> יְדוּעַ חֳלִי *one who is humbled of*, i.e. by, *sickness* Is 53$_3$.*

Ni. $_6$ Pf. נוֹדַע; impf. יִוָּדַע (יִוָּדֵעַ), 3fs תִּוָּדֵעַ; + waw וְנוֹדַע; inf. הִוָּדְעִי—**1. be made quiet, be made submissive, be weakened,** <SUBJ> Ephraim Jr 31$_{19}$, עקשׁ pi. ptc. *one who perverts* his ways Pr 10$_9$, כֹּחַ *strength* Jg 16$_9$, חָכְמָה *wisdom* Pr 14$_{33}$, כַּעַס *vexation* Pr 12$_{16}$. <PREP> בְּ of time, *in, on*, + יוֹם *day* Pr 12$_{16}$; בְּקֶרֶב *among, within*, + כְּסִיל *fool* Pr 14$_{33}$.

2. be granted rest, <SUBJ> impersonal 1 S 6$_3$. <PREP> לְ of benefit, *to, for*, + Philistines 1 S 6$_3$.

Pi., see Qal, §4.

Hi. $_1$ + waw וַיֹּדַע—**make submissive, humiliate,** <SUBJ> Gideon Jg 8 $_{16}$. <OBJ> אִישׁ *man* 8$_{16}$.

<PREP> בְּ of instrument, *by (means of), with*, + בַּרְקָן *brier* 8$_{16}$, קוֹץ *thorn* 8$_{16}$.

⇒ דַּעַת IV *humiliation*.

* ידע III $_{14}$ vb. **care** (unless ידע I *know*)—**Qal** $_{14}$ Pf. יָדַע, יָדַעְתָּ, יְדַעְתִּי, יְדַעְתִּיךָ (יְדַעְתִּיו), יָדְעוּ; impf. אֵדַע; + waw וַיֵּדַע, וַתֵּדָעֵהוּ; ptc. יוֹדֵעַ (יֹדֵעַ)—**care, care about, care for,** <SUBJ> Y. Gn 18$_{19}$ Ex 2$_{25}$ (+ ראה) Jr 1$_5$ (+ קדשׁ hi. *consecrate*) Ho 13$_5$ Am 3$_2$ Na 1$_7$ Ps 1$_6$ 31$_8$ (+ ראה) 139$_2$ (+ בין *understand*) 139$_{14}$ (if em.; see Obj.) 144$_3$ (|| חשׁב pi. *consider*) Jb 23$_{10}$, Job Jb 9$_{21}$, בֵּן *son* Pr 23$_{35}$ (|| חלה *be sick*), צַדִּיק *righteous one* Pr 12$_{10}$, אצר ptc. *one who treasures* violence Am 3$_{10}$, גֹּרֶן *threshing floor* Ho 9$_2$ (if em. לֹא יִרְעֵם *it shall not feed them* to לֹא יֵדָעֵם *it shall not care for them*), יֶקֶב *wine vat* Ho 9$_2$ (if em.; see above). <OBJ> Israel Ho 9$_2$ (if em.; see Subj.) 13$_5$ Am 3$_2$, Abraham Gn 19$_{19}$, Jeremiah Jr 1$_4$, אָדָם *human being* Ps 144$_3$, חסה ptc. *one who seeks refuge* Na 1$_7$, נֶפֶשׁ *soul* Ps 139$_{14}$ (if em. נַפְשִׁי יֹדַעַת appar. *my soul knows* to יָדַעְתָּ נַפְשִׁי *you care for my soul*) Jb 9$_{21}$ Pr 12$_{10}$, דֶּרֶךְ *way* Ps 1$_6$ Jb 23$_{10}$, ישׁב inf. *sitting* Ps 139$_2$. <PREP> בְּ of place, + בֶּטֶן *womb* Jr 1$_5$, אֶרֶץ *land* Ho 13$_5$, מִדְבָּר *desert* Ho 13$_5$; בְּ introducing object, + צָרָה *distress* Ps 31$_8$; מִן partitive, *from among*, + מִשְׁפָּחָה *family* Am 3$_2$. <COLL> + infinitive, עשׂה *do* Am 3$_{10}$; + adverb, מְאֹד *much* Ps 139$_{14}$ (if em.; see Obj.).

<SYN> חלה *be sick*, חשׁב pi. *consider*.

* ידע IV $_{8.1}$ vb. **punish** (unless ידע I *know*)—**Qal** $_{5.1}$ Pf. יָדַע; impf. 3fs Si תדע, אֵדְעָה, יֵדְעוּ; + waw וַיֵּדַע; ptc. pass. cstr. יְדוּעַ—**1. punish,** <SUBJ> Y. Gn 18$_{21}$, Israel (as lion) Ezk 19$_7$, בֵּן *son* Si 7$_{20(A)}$. <OBJ> אַלְמָנָה *widow* Ezk 19$_7$, עבד ptc. *one who serves* Si 7$_{20(A)}$. <PREP> בְּ of accompaniment, *with*, + אֱמֶת *reality* Si 7$_{20(A)}$.

2. be punished, <SUBJ> Israel Ho 9$_7$, חָנֵף *profane one* Jb 20$_{20}$.

3. pass. ptc. as noun, **one who is punished,** <CSTR> יְדוּעַ חֳלִי *one who is punished of*, i.e. by, *sickness* Is 53$_3$.

Ni. $_2$ Impf. יִוָּדֵעַ; inf. הִוָּדְעִי—**be punished,** <SUBJ> Ephraim Jr 31$_{19}$, עקשׁ pi. ptc. *one who perverts* his ways Pr 10$_9$.

Hi. $_1$ + waw וַיֹּדַע—**punish,** <SUBJ> Gideon Jg 8$_{16}$. <OBJ> אִישׁ *man* 8$_{16}$. <PREP> בְּ of instrument, *by (means of), with*, + בַּרְקָן *brier* 8$_{16}$, קוֹץ *thorn* 8$_{16}$.

ידע V 4.1 vb. **sweat** (unless ידע I *know*)—**Qal** 2 Pf. יָדַ֫עְתָּ; impf. יֵדְעוּן; inf. דַּעְתּוֹ—**sweat, flow with,** <SUBJ> שָׂפָה *lip* Pr 10$_{32}$; subj. not specified, Pr 14$_{7}$. <OBJ> רָצוֹן *acceptance* Pr 10$_{32}$, שָׂפָה *lip* Pr 14$_{7}$ (בַּל־יָדַעְתָּ שִׂפְתֵי־דָעַת *you will surely flow with lips of knowledge*).

Ni. 2 Impf. יִוָּדַע, 3fs תִּוָּדַע—**be caused to sweat,** <SUBJ> עִקֵּשׁ pi. ptc. *one who perverts* his ways Pr 10$_{9}$, חָכְמָה *wisdom* Pr 14$_{33}$. <PREP> בְּקֶרֶב *among, within,* + כְּסִיל *fool* Pr 14$_{33}$.

Hi. 0.1 Impf. 2ms Si תדיע—**cause to sweat,** i.e. **vex,** <SUBJ> בֵּן *son* Si 12$_{1}$. <OBJ> טוֹב *good one* Si 12$_{1}$.*

⇒ דַּעַת VI *sweat*.

***ידע VI** 3 vb. **seek** (unless ידע I *know*)—**Qal** 4 Impf. נֵדְעָה, יֵדְעוּן; impv. דְּעֶה—(unless דעה I *ask, desire*) **seek, ask for, desire,** <SUBJ> Israel Ho 6$_{3}$ (or del.; + רדף *pursue*), בֵּן *son* Pr 24$_{14}$, שָׂפָה *lip* Pr 10$_{32}$. <OBJ> רָצוֹן *acceptance* Pr 10$_{32}$, חָכְמָה *wisdom* Pr 24$_{14}$. <PREP> לְ of benefit, *for,* + נֶפֶשׁ *soul* Pr 24$_{14}$.

***ידע VII** 2 vb. **leave** (unless ידע I *know*)—**Po.** 1 Pf. יוֹדַ֫עְתִּי—**bid farewell, leave,** <SUBJ> David 1 S 21$_{3}$. <OBJ> נַעַר *lad* 1 S 21$_{3}$. <PREP> אֶל say farewell (bidding to meet) *at,* + מָקוֹם *place* 1 S 21$_{3}$.

Ni. 1 Pf. נוֹדַע—**take leave,** <SUBJ> David 1 S 22$_{6}$, אִישׁ *man* 1 S 22$_{6}$.

***ידע VIII** 2 vb. **call** (unless ידע I *know*)—**Qal** 2 Pf. יָדַע, יָדַ֫עְתִּי—**call (upon),** <SUBJ> Job Jb 23$_{3}$, ישׁב ptc. *one who dwells* Ps 91$_{14}$ (+ חשׁק *cling to*). <OBJ> שֵׁם *name* Ps 91$_{14}$.

***ידע IX** 2 vb. **tear down** (unless ידע I *know*)—**Qal** 1 + waw וַיֵּדַע—(unless דעה II *pull down*) **tear down, destroy,** <SUBJ> Israel (as lion) Ezk 19$_{7}$ (|| חרב hi. *lay waste*), צֹרֵר *enemy* Ps 74$_{5}$ (if em. יִוָּדַע כִּמֵבִיא לְמַעְלָה בִּסְבָךְ־עֵץ קַרְדֻּמּוֹת perh. *it is torn down as [when] one brings axes upwards in a thicket of trees* to יָדְעוּ כִּמְבִיאֵי קַרְדֻּמּוֹת לְמוֹ עָלֶה בִּסְבַךְ־עֵץ *they tear down as men bringing axes to the foliage in a thicket of trees*). <OBJ> אַרְמוֹן *fortress* Ezk 19$_{7}$ (if em. אַלְמְנוֹתָיו appar. *his widows* to אַרְמְנוֹתֵיהֶם *their fortresses*). <PREP> כְּ *as,* + בוא hi. ptc. *one who brings* Ps 74$_{5}$ (if em.; see Subj.).

<SYN> חרב hi. *lay waste.*

Ni. 1 Impf. יִוָּדַע—**be torn down,** <SUBJ> temple Ps 74$_{5}$ (or em.; see Qal Subj.). <PREP> כְּ *as when* Ps 74$_{5}$ (or em.; see Qal Subj.).

***ידע X** 2 vb. **leave alone** (unless ידע I *know*)—**Qal** 2 Pf. יָדַ֫עְתִּי, יָדַ֫עְתָּ—**leave alone, neglect; let off, exempt** (Jb 33$_{24}$), <SUBJ> '' *Y.* Ex 3$_{7}$, אֵל *God* Jb 33$_{24}$ (if rd. פְּ־דָעֵהוּ *then exempt him;* unless פְּדָעֵהוּ = פְּדֵהוּ *redeem him;* or em. דְּפָעֵהוּ *push him back;* mss פְּרָעֵהוּ *release him*); subj. not specified, Pr 14$_{7}$. <OBJ> שָׂפָה *lip* Pr 14$_{7}$, מַכְאֹב *pain* Ex 3$_{7}$, אָדָם *human being* Jb 33$_{24}$. <PREP> מִן privative, *from, so as not to,* + ירד inf. *going down* to the pit.

***ידע XI** 2 vb. **wrap up** (unless ידע I *know*)—**Qal** 2 Pf. יָדַע—**wrap up,** <SUBJ> appar. אֹפֶה *baker* Ho 7$_{9.9}$. <OBJ> עֻגָה *cake* (in ref. to Ephraim) Ho 7$_{9.9}$.

***[ידע] XII** vb. **reconcile—Ni. be reconciled,** <SUBJ> שְׁנַיִם *two* Am 3$_{3}$ (if em. נוֹעָדוּ *they have made an appointment* to נוֹדְעוּ *they have been reconciled*).

***[ידע] XIII deposit—Hi. place,** <SUBJ> '' *Y.* 1 K 8$_{12}$ (if ins. שֶׁמֶשׁ הוֹדִיעַ בַּשָּׁמַיִם *he placed the sun in the heavens;* others הֵכִין, i.e. כון hi. *place* or הוֹעִיד, i.e. יעד hi. *place*). <OBJ> שֶׁמֶשׁ *sun* 1 K 8$_{12}$ (if em.). <PREP> בְּ of place, *in* 1 K 8$_{12}$ (if em.).

Ho. be placed, deposited, <SUBJ> דּוּד *basket* Jr 24$_{1}$ (if em. מוּעָדִים appar. *placed*, i.e. יעד ho., to מוּדָעִים *placed*). <PREP> לִפְנֵי *before,* + הֵיכָל *temple* Jr 24$_{1}$ (if em.; see Subj.).*

יָדָע 2 pr.n.m. **Jada, 1.** Judahite, son of Onam, <NOM CL> בְּנֵי־אוֹנָם שַׁמַּי וְיָדָע *the sons of Onam were Shammai and Jada* 1 C 2$_{28}$. <CSTR> בְּנֵי יָדָע *sons of Jada* 1 C 2$_{32}$. <APP> אָח *brother* 1 C 2$_{32}$.

2. father of Shallum, <CSTR> בן ידע *son of Jada* Lachish ost. 3$_{20}$ (unless Jaddua; see יַדּוּעַ, §7).

⇒ ידע I *know.*

***[יָדָע]** 0.0.1 adj. **expert**—pl. Q וידעים—**1.** used attributively of אִישׁ *man* Dt 1$_{13.15}$ (if em. וִידֻעִים *and well known* to וְיָדְעִים *and expert*). **2.** as noun, **expert,** <CSTR> ... כול הנבונים והידעים *all ... the intelligent ones and the experts* 1Q Sa 1_{28} (unless = ידעים *well-known ones*).

⇒ ידע I *know*.

יִדְּעֹנִי, see יִדְּעֹנִי *familiar spirit.*

יְדַעְיָה 11.0.13.12 pr.n.m. **Jedaiah**—I ידעיהו (§§6-13, 17), ידעיו (§§14-16)—**1.** priest in David's time, ancestor of priestly family, <NOM CL> מִן־הַכֹּהֲנִים יְדַעְיָה *of the priests was Jedaiah* 1 C 9_{10}. <CSTR> בְּנֵי יְדַעְיָה *sons of Jedaiah* Ezr 2_{36}‖Ne 7_{39}. <PREP> לְ of direction, *to,* + יצא *go out* 1 C 24_7.

2. head of post-exilic priestly family, <SUBJ> עלה *go up* Ne 12_6. <NOM CL> מִן־הַכֹּהֲנִים יְדַעְיָה *of the priests was Jedaiah* Ne 11_{10}. <APP> בֵּן *son* Ne 11_{10}. <PREP> לְ of possession, *of, (belonging) to* Ne 12_{19}.

3. appar. head of another post-exilic priestly family, <SUBJ> עלה *go up* Ne 12_7. <PREP> לְ of possession, *of, (belonging) to* Ne 12_{21}.

4. exile returned from Babylon, <PREP> מֵאֵת *from,* + לקח *take* Zc 6_{10}. <PREP> לְ of possession, *of, (belonging) to,* + היה *be* Zc 6_{14}.

5. member of Bani family, husband of foreign wife, Ezr 10_{29} (if em. וַעֲדָיָה *and Adaiah* to וִידַעְיָה *and Jedaiah*).

6. Arad ost. 31_7.

7. father of Tanhum, <CSTR> בן ידעיהו *son of Jedaiah* Arad ost. 39_4.

8. father of Gealiah, <CSTR> בן ידעיהו *son of Jedaiah* Arad ost. 39_5.

9. appar. son of Hanan, Seal 49 ([ו]ידעיה; others ידליהו *Jedaliah*; Jerusalem, 8th/7th cent.).

10. appar. son of Cushi, Seal 494 (7th cent.).

11. son of Carmi, <APP> בֵּן *son* Seal 568 (T. Beit Mirsim?, 7th/6th cent.). <PREP> לְ of possession, *of, (belonging) to,* Seal 568 (T. Beit Mirsim?, 7th/6th cent.).

12. son of Shual, <APP> בֵּן *son* Seal 569 (T. Beit Mirsim?, 7th/6th cent.). <PREP> לְ of possession, *of, (belonging) to,* Seal 569 (T. Beit Mirsim?, 7th/6th cent.).

13. son of Meshullam, <APP> בֵּן *son* Seal 812 (City of David, 7th/6th cent.). PREP> לְ of possession, *of, (belonging) to,* Seal 812 (City of David, 7th/6th cent.).

14. Samaria ost. 1_8.

15. <PREP> לְ of possession, *of, (belonging) to,* Samaria ost. 42_2.

16. <PREP> לְ of possession, *of, (belonging) to,* Samaria ost. 48_1.

17. father of Abda, <CSTR> בן ידעיהו *son of Jedaiah* Bulla 927 Seal 928 (7th/6th cent.).

18. name of priestly course (derived from §1) and its period of office, <NOM CL> השלישי י[דעיה] *the third is Jedaiah* 4QOtot 1.7_{19}, [ב]שנית ידעיה *in the second (year) is Jedaiah* 4QMishFa 1_3. <CSTR> [ביא]ת ידעיה *arrival of Jedaiah* 4QMishCa 1_2. <PREP> בְּ of time, *in, at, during* 4QMis A 1.1_6 ([בידע]ה) 1.2_{10} 1.3_{13} 4.3_3 ([ב]ידעו[יה]) 4.3_9 4Q MishhBa 1.2_2 (both ביד[עיה]) 1.3_6 $2.2_{2.4}$ ([בידע]יה) 4Q MishCa 3_3; עַל *according to* 4QMishD $1_{2.4}$.

Also 4QOtot 1.8_2 2_3 ([יד]עיה) 9.1_2 ([יד]עיה) 4QMish Fb 2_1.

⇒ ידע I *know* + ׳י *Y.*

ידעיהו, see יְדַעְיָה *Jedaiah.*

ידעיו, see יְדַעְיָה *Jedaiah.*

יִדְּעֹנִי 11.0.3 n.m. **familiar spirit**—יִדְּעוֹנִי; pl. יִדְּעֹנִים (Q ידעונים)—**familiar spirit,** perh. sometimes **medium, necromancer,** i.e. one who consults a familiar spirit (e.g. 1 S $28_{3.9}$ 2 K 21_6‖2 C 33_6 2 K 23_{24}), <SUBJ> היה *be* Lv 20_{27}, צפף pilp. *chirp* Is 8_{19}. <OBJ> שׁאל *ask* Dt 18_{11}=11QT 60_{19}, סור hi. *remove* 1 S 28_3, בער pi. *remove* 2 K 23_{24}, כרת hi. *cut off* 1 S 28_9, עשׂה perh. *appoint* 2 K 21_6‖2 C 33_6. <CSTR> משפט ... הידעוני *judgment of,* i.e. against, ... *the necromancer* CD 12_3. <PREP> בְּ of instrument, *by (means of), with,* + טמא *be unclean* Lv 19_{31}; introducing object, + דרשׁ *inquire of* 4QDe 2.1_{10}; אֶל *to,* + פנה *turn* Lv 19_{31} 20_2; דרשׁ אֶל *inquire of* Is 8_{19} 19_3. <COLL> ‖ אוֹב *ghost* Lv 19_{31} $20_{6.27}$ Dt 18_{11}=11QT 60_{19} 1 S $28_{3.9}$ 2 K 21_6‖2 C 33_6 2 K 23_{24} Is 8_{19} 19_3 4QDe 2.1_{10} CD 12_3, אִטִּי *ghost* Is 19_3, גִּלּוּל *image* 2 K 23_{24}, אֱלִיל *image* Is 19_3, תְּרָפִים *teraphim* 2 K 23_{24}, שִׁקּוּץ *abomination* 2 K 23_{24}; + קסם *practise divination* Dt 18_{11}=11QT 60_{19}, נחשׁ pi. *practise divination* Dt 18_{11}=11QT 60_{19} 2 K 21_6‖2 C 33_6, ענן po. *practise soothsaying* Dt 18_{11}=11QT 60_{19} 2 K 21_6‖2 C 33_6, כשׁף pi. *practise* *sorcery* Dt 18$_{11}$=11QT 60$_{19}$ 2 C 33$_{6}$, חבר *cast* spell Dt 18$_{11}$ =11QT 60$_{19}$, עבר hi. *make* child *pass* into fire Dt 18$_{11}$ 2 K 21$_{6}$||2 C 33$_{6}$, דרשׁ ptc. *one who inquires* of dead Dt 18$_{11}$.

<SYN> אוֹב *ghost*, אִטִּי *ghost*, גִּלּוּל *image*, אֱלִיל *image*, תְּרָפִים *teraphim*, שִׁקּוּץ *abomination*.

⇒ ידע I *know*.

יָהּ 50.1.4.1 pr.n.m. **Yah,** form of divine name יהוה *Yahweh*, <SUBJ> שׁכן *dwell* Ps 68$_{19}$, ראה *see* Ps 94$_{7}$, יסר pi. *discipline* Ps 94$_{12}$ 118$_{18}$, למד pi. *teach* Ps 94$_{12}$, שׁקט hi. *give quietness* Ps 94$_{12}$, נתן *give* Ps 118$_{18}$, שׁמר *keep*, i.e. mark, iniquities Ps 130$_{3}$ (Gnz, mss יהוה Y.), בחר *choose* Ps 135$_{4}$, נקה pi. *acquit*. Kh. Beit Lei graf. 6$_{1}$ (נקה יה; others פקד יה *Yah has visited*; others המוריה *Moriah*) 6$_{2}$ (others נוה יה *habitation of Yah*).

<NOM CL> הוא יה *he is Yah* 4QAdmonPar 1.1$_{8}$, עָזִּי וְזִמְרָת יָהּ *Yah is my strength and (my) song* (or *[my] refuge*, from זִמְרָה III) Ex 15$_{2}$ (mss, Sam זִמְרָתִי *my refuge*) Is 12$_{2}$ (mss, 1QIsa[a] זִמְרָתִי; or del. יָהּ) Ps 118$_{14}$ (ms זִמְרָתִי; or in all three em. זִמְרָת to סִתְרָתִי *my hiding place* and/or del. יָהּ), ענה *answer* Ps 118$_{5}$.

<OBJ> ראה *see* Is 38$_{11.11}$ (or em. יָהּ יָהּ to יהוה *Y.*), הלל pi. *praise* Ps 102$_{19}$ 104$_{35}$ (lacking in ms) Ps 105$_{45}$ 106$_{1}$ (lacking in mss) 106$_{48}$ 111$_{1}$ 112$_{1}$ 113$_{1.9}$ 115$_{17.18.19}$ 117$_{2}$ 135$_{1.3.21}$ 146$_{1.10}$ 147$_{1.20}$ 148$_{1.14}$ 149$_{1.9}$ 150$_{1}$ (lacking in mss) 150$_{6.6}$ Si 51$_{12}$, ידה hi. *give thanks to* Ps 118$_{19}$, קרא *call to* Ps 118$_{5}$.

<CSTR> שִׁבְטֵי־יָהּ *tribes of Yah* Ps 122$_{4}$, כֵּס יָהּ perh. *throne of Yah* Ex 17$_{16}$ (Sam כִּסֵּא *throne*; or em. כֵּס to נֵס *banner of*, or כִּסֵּא *throne of*), מַעַלְלֵי־יָהּ *deeds of Yah* Ps 77$_{12}$, מַעֲשֵׂי יָהּ *deeds of Yah* Ps 118$_{17}$ (Gnz, mss מַעֲשֵׂה *deed of*), מֶרְחַבְיָהּ *broad place of Yah* Ps 118$_{5(mss)}$, שַׁלְהֶבֶתְיָה *flame of Yah* Ca 8$_{6}$ (or em. שַׁלְהֲבֹתֶיהָ שַׁלְהֶבֶת־יָהּ *its flames are flames of Yah*), נוה יה *habitation of Yah* Kh. Beit Lei graf. 6$_{2}$ (others נקה יה *Yah has acquitted*).

<APP> יהוה *Y.* Is 12$_{2}$ 26$_{4}$ (or in both del. יָהּ) Kh. Beit Lei graf. 6$_{2}$, אֱלֹהִים *God* Ps 68$_{19}$, חֲסִין *strong (one)* Ps 89$_{9}$ (or em. חֲסִין יָהּ *[a] strong [one], O Yah* to חָסְנְךָ *your stronghold*, or יֶחֱסַן your faithfulness *is strong*), אֲדֹנָי *Adonai* Ps 130$_{3}$.

<PREP> בְּ *in* Is 26$_{4}$ (בְּיָהּ יהוה צוּר עוֹלָמִים appar. *in Yah Y. is a rock of eternity*; or del. בְּיָהּ) Ps 68$_{5}$ (בְּיָהּ appar. *in Yah* is his name; or em. כִּי יָהּ *for Yah* is his name).

<COLL> הַלְלוּ יָהּ, הַלְלוּ־יָהּ, הַלְלוּיָהּ *praise Yah* Ps 104$_{35.45}$ 106$_{1.48}$ 111$_{1}$ 112$_{1}$ 113$_{1.9}$ 115$_{18}$ 116$_{19}$ 117$_{2}$ 135$_{1.3.21}$ 146$_{1.10}$ 147$_{20}$ 148$_{1.14}$ 149$_{1.9}$ 150$_{1.6}$ Si 51$_{12}$ 4QJonathan 1$_{1}$ 4QPrayer[i] 1$_{2}$ 2$_{3}$; as name of type of psalm, 11QPs[a] 28$_{3}$ (הלליה לדויד בן ישי *a hallelujah of David the son of Jesse*).

יָהּ + אֵל *God* Ex 15$_{2}$ Is 12$_{2}$ Ps 150$_{1}$, אֱלֹהִים *God* Ex 15$_{2}$ Ps 68$_{5}$ 94$_{7}$ 146$_{10}$ 147$_{1}$, יהוה *Y.* Ex 17$_{16}$ Is 26$_{4}$ Ps 104$_{35}$ 106$_{1.48}$ 111$_{1}$ 112$_{1}$ 113$_{1}$ 117$_{2}$ 135$_{1.3.21}$ 146$_{1.10}$ 148$_{1}$ 149$_{1}$ Kh. Beit Lei graf. 6$_{2}$, אֲדֹנָי *Adonai* Ps 130$_{3}$.*

⇒ יהוה *Yhwh*, יָהוּ *Yahu*.

יהב 33.0.1 vb. **give—Qal** 33.0.1 Impv. הָבָה (הָֽבָה), הָבִי, הָבוּ (הָֽבוּ)—**1. give** (Gn 29$_{21}$ 30$_{1}$ 47$_{15.16}$ Jg 1$_{15}$ 20$_{7}$ 1 S 14$_{41}$ 2 S 16$_{20}$ Zc 11$_{12}$ Ps 60$_{13}$ 108$_{13}$ Jb 6$_{22}$ Pr 30$_{15.15}$ Ru 3$_{15}$), **ascribe** (Dt 32$_{3}$ Ps 29$_{1.1.2}$ 96$_{7.7.8}$||1 C 16$_{28.28.29}$ 4QHod[a] 7.1$_{13}$), **set aside** (Dt 1$_{13}$ Jos 18$_{4}$), **place** (2 S 11$_{15}$, or em.; see Subj.).

<SUBJ> Y. 1 S 14$_{41}$ Ps 60$_{13}$, Egyptians Gn 47$_{16}$, Israelites Dt 1$_{13}$ 32$_{3}$ Jos 18$_{4}$, מִשְׁפָּחָה *family* Ps 96$_{7.7.8}$||1 C 16$_{28.28.29}$, Ahithophel 2 S 16$_{20}$, Caleb Jg 1$_{15}$, Jacob Gn 30$_{1}$, Joab 2 S 11$_{15}$ (or em. הָבוּ *place* to הָבֵא *bring*, i.e. בוא hi.), Joseph Gn 47$_{15}$, Laban Gn 29$_{21}$, Ruth Ru 3$_{15}$, בֵּן *son* of Israel Jg 20$_{7}$, of gods Ps 29$_{1.1.2}$, appar. עָנִי *poor one* Zc 11$_{12}$ (or em. כֵּן עֲנִיֵּי *so the poor ones of* to לִכְנַעֲנִיֵּי *to the traders* of the sheep), כְּנַעֲנִי *trader* Zc 11$_{12}$ (if em.; see above), friends of Job Jb 6$_{22}$ (+ שׁחד *bribe*), worshipper 4QHod[a] 7.1$_{13}$; subj. not specified, Pr 30$_{15.15}$ (or em. בָּנוֹת הַב הַב *daughters; give, give* to בְּנוֹת הַב הַב *daughters of give, give*, i.e. of greed, or בְּנוֹת הַבְהַב *daughters of desire*).

<OBJ> Uriah 2 S 11$_{15}$, אִישׁ *man* Dt 1$_{13}$ Jos 18$_{4}$, אִשָּׁה *wife* Gn 29$_{21}$, בֵּן *son* Gn 30$_{1}$, תָּמִים appar. *perfect one* 1 S 14$_{41}$ (or em. הָבָה תָמִים *give a perfect one* to הָבָה אוּרִים וְאִם יֶשְׁנוֹ בְּעַמְּךָ יִשְׂרָאֵל הָבָה תֻמִּים if this guilt is in me or in Jonathan my son, *give Urim, but if it is in your people Israel, give Thummim*), מִקְנֶה *cattle* Gn 47$_{16}$, לֶחֶם *bread* Gn 47$_{15}$, מִטְפַּחַת *cloak* Ru 3$_{15}$, דָּבָר *word* Jg 20$_{7}$, עֵצָה *counsel* Jg 20$_{7}$ 2 S 16$_{20}$, עֶזְרָה *help* Ps 60$_{13}$ 108$_{13}$, שָׂכָר *wages* Zc 11$_{12}$, בְּרָכָה *blessing*, i.e. gift Jg 1$_{15}$, גֹּדֶל *greatness* Dt 32$_{3}$, עֹז *strength* Ps 29$_{1}$ 96$_{7}$||1 C 16$_{28}$, כָּבוֹד *glory*

Ps 29$_{1.2}$ 96$_{7.8}$||1 C 16$_{28.29}$.

<PREP> לְ in ref. to subj. of יהב, + Israelites Dt 1$_{13}$ Jos 18$_4$ Jg 20$_7$, Ahithophel 2 S 16$_{20}$; of direction, *to*, + Y. Dt 32$_3$ Ps 29$_{1.1.2}$ 96$_{7.7.8}$||1 C 16$_{28.28.29}$ 4QHod^a 7.1$_{13}$, Egyptians Gn 47$_{15}$, Achsah Jg 1$_{15}$, Job Jb 6$_{22}$, Rachel Gn 30$_1$, בַּת *daughter* Jg 1$_{15}$, worshipper Ps 60$_{13}$ 108$_{13}$; of possession, *of, (belonging) to*, + שֵׁבֶט *tribe* Jos 18$_4$; *according to*, + שֵׁבֶט *tribe* Dt 1$_{13}$; אֶל־מוּל *before*, + פָּנִים *front* of battle 2 S 11$_{15}$. <COLL> + adverb, הֲלֹם *here* Jg 20$_7$.

2. as interjection, **come!, come on!, a.** with impf. 1cs of בוא *come* Gn 38$_{16}$. **b.** with cohortative or impf. 1cpl of לבן *make bricks* Gn 11$_3$, בנה *build* Gn 11$_4$, ירד *go down* Gn 11$_7$, חכם htp. *make oneself wise* Ex 1$_{10}$.

→ הַבְהָב *gift*, יְהָב *burden*.

[יְהָב] 1 n.[m.] **burden**—sf. יְהָבְךָ—**burden,** i.e. matter of concern, perh. **lot,** i.e. portion in life, <OBJ> שׁלך hi. *cast* Ps 55$_{23}$.

→ יהב *give*.

יהד 1 vb. **be a Jew—Htp.** 1 Ptc. מִתְיַהֲדִים—**become a Jew,** perh. **declare oneself to be a Jew,** <SUBJ> רַב pl. *many* Est 8$_{17}$ (רַבִּים מֵעַמֵּי הָאָרֶץ מִתְיַהֲדִים *many of the peoples of the land became Jews*).

→ יְהוּדָה *Judah*, יְהֻד *Jehud*, יְהוּדִי I *Jewish*, II *Jehudi*, יְהוּדִית *Judith*.

יְהֻד 1.0.0.14 pl.n. **Jehud**—I יהוד—**1.** town in Dan, perh, El-Yehūdīye, 13 km ESE of Jaffa, <SUBJ> היה *be* Jos 19$_{45}$.

2. shortened form of יְהוּדָה *Judah*, as name of territory, Stamp/Coins 1 (יהד) 2 (יהוד) 3 (יהוד; others ליהועזר *[belonging] to Jehoezer*; all three 5th/4th cent.) 4 (יהד; 3rd/2nd cent.) 5 (יהוד; 4th cent.) 8 9 10 (all three יהוד; all three 5th/4th cent.) 11 (יהוד; 5th cent.) 13 (יהוד; 5th/4th cent.) 14 (יהוד; 5th/4th cent.) 15 (לזבדיו ט יהד *[belonging] to Zebadiah, T. Jehud*; others עזבק צדקיה *Azbuk [son of] Zedekiah*; others יהועזר פחוא *Jehoezer, governor*; others יהועזר פחרא *Jehoezer, potter*) 41 42 (both יהד; both 4th cent.) 45 (יהד; 3rd cent.), <CSTR> פקד יהד perh. *overseer of Jehud* Stamp/Coin 12 (6th cent.), הרי יהד *mountains of Jehud* Kh. Beit Lei graf. 5 (others יהודה *Judah*; את יהוה *Y., you* are my God).

→ יהד *be Jewish*.

[יָהְדַי] 1 pr.n.m. **Jahdai**—יָהְדָּי, mss יַהְדַּי—descendant of Caleb, <OBJ> ילד hi. *beget* 1 C 2$_{46}$ (if em. גָּזֵז *Gazez*). <CSTR> בְּנֵי יָהְדָּי *sons of Jahdai* 1 C 2$_{47}$.

[יָהוּ] 0.0.0.2 pr.n.m. **Yahu,** alternative form of divine names יהוה *Yhwh* and יָהּ *Yah*, <SUBJ> נתן *give* Kuntillet 'Ajrud add. inscr. 2. <PREP> לְ of agent/instrument, *by (means of)*, + ברך pass. *be blessed* Kuntillet 'Ajrud inscr. C1. <COLL> בְּקֶרֶב שֹׁנִים חַי־יָהוּ *among exalted ones, Yahu lives* Hb 3$_2$ (if em. בְּקֶרֶב שָׁנִים חַיֵּיהוּ *through the years, revive it*).*

→ יהוה *Yhwh*, יָהּ *Yah*.

יֵהוּא 57.0.0.1 pr.n.m. **Jehu, 1.** king of Israel, son of Nimshi, <SUBJ> אמר *say* 2 K 9$_{5.11.15.18.19.22.24.27.31}$ 10$_{1.5.13.18.20.21.23.24.25}$, נגד hi. *tell* 2 K 9$_{11}$, ברך pi. *bless* 2 K 10$_{13}$, זכר *remember* 2 K 9$_{24}$, כתב *write* 2 K 10$_{1.5}$, עמד *stand* 2 K 10$_5$, קום *rise* 2 K 10$_{11}$, הלך *go* 2 K 9$_{16}$ 10$_{11.13.31}$, בוא *come* 2 K 9$_{30.31}$ 10$_{11.13.23}$, hi. *bring* 2 K 10$_{24}$, יצא *go out* 2 K 9$_{11}$ 10$_5$, עלה hi. *bring up* 2 K 10$_{13}$, רכב *ride* 2 K 9$_{16}$, נהג *drive* 2 K 9$_{20}$, רדף *pursue* 2 K 9$_{27}$, שׁלח *send* 2 K 10$_{1.21}$, בקשׁ pi. *seek* 2 C 22$_8$, מצא *find* 2 K 10$_{13}$ 2 C 22$_8$, קבץ pi. *gather* 2 K 10$_{18}$, סור *turn aside* 2 K 10$_{29.31}$, שׁפט ni. *execute judgment* 2 C 22$_8$, מלך *reign* 2 K 9$_{13}$ 10$_{36}$, עבד *serve* 2 K 10$_{18}$, אכל *eat* 2 K 9$_{31}$, שׁתה *drink* 2 K 9$_{31}$, נשׂא *lift* 2 K 9$_{31}$, מלא pi. *fill*, i.e. draw, bow 2 K 9$_{24}$, קשׁר *conspire* 2 K 10$_5$, htp. 2 K 9$_{14}$, נכה hi. *strike* 2 K 9$_{5.24}$ 10$_{11.13}$, הרג *kill* 2 K 10$_5$, מות hi. *kill* 1 K 19$_{17}$, שׁמד hi. *destroy* 2 K 10$_{13.28}$, כרת hi. *cut off* 2 C 22$_7$, כלה pi. *finish* 2 K 10$_{25}$, עשׂה *do* 2 K 10$_{5.19.25.30.34}$, טוב hi. *do well* 2 K 10$_{30}$, שׂים *place* 2 K 10$_{24}$, שׁמר *keep* 2 K 10$_{31}$, שׁכב *lie down* 2 K 10$_{35}$.

<OBJ> ראה *see* 2 K 9$_{2.22}$, קרא *meet* 2 K 9$_{17.21}$ 10$_{13}$, מצא *find* 2 K 9$_{21}$, קום hi. *cause to rise* 2 K 9$_2$, בוא hi. *bring* 2 K 8$_2$, משׁח *anoint* 1 K 19$_{16}$ 2 K 9$_{2.5.11}$ 2 C 22$_7$, קבר *bury* 2 K 10$_{35}$.

<CSTR> בֶּן־יֵהוּא *son of Jehu* 2 K 13$_1$ 14$_8$||2 C 25$_{17}$, בֵּית יֵהוּא *house of Jehu* Ho 1$_4$, שִׁפְעַת *multitude of* 2 K 9$_{17}$, חֶרֶב *sword of* 1 K 19$_{17}$, מִנְהַג *driving of* 2 K 9$_{20}$, דִּבְרֵי *deeds of*

2 K 10$_{34}$. <APP> בֵּן *son* 1 K 19$_{16}$ 2 K 9$_{2.14.20}$ 2 C 22$_{7}$. <PREP> לְ of direction, *to,* + אמר *say* 2 K 9$_{11}$, נגד hi. *tell* 2 K 9$_{31}$; of benefit, *for,* + ישׁב *sit* 2 K 10$_{30}$; of possession, *of, (belonging) to* 2 K 10$_{5.18}$ 12$_{2}$; אֶל *to,* + אמר *say* 2 K 10$_{30}$, דבר pi. *speak* 2 K 15$_{12}$, בוא *come* 2 K 9$_{11}$, hi. *bring* 2 C 22$_{9}$, יצא *go out* 2 C 22$_{7}$, עלה hi. *bring up* 2 K 10$_{13}$, שׁלח *send* 2 K 10$_{2}$, קרא *call,* i.e. summon 2 K 10$_{18}$, שׁקף hi. *look down* 2 K 9$_{31}$; אֵת *with,* + הלך *go* 2 K 10$_{13}$; אֶל־אַחֲרֵי *behind,* + סבב *turn* 2 K 9$_{18.19}$; תַּחַת *under,* + שׂים *place* 2 K 9$_{11}$; *instead of,* + מלך *reign* 2 K 10$_{35}$. <COLL> יֵהוּא as vocative 2 K 9$_{22}$; Jehu addressed as Zimri 2 K 9$_{31}$.

2. son of Hanani, prophet in time of Baasha and Jehoshaphat, <SUBJ> יצא *go out* 2 C 19$_{2}$, אמר *say* 2 C 19$_{2}$. <CSTR> דִּבְרֵי יֵהוּא *words of Jehu* 2 C 20$_{34}$. <APP> בֵּן *son* 1 K 16$_{1.7}$ 2 C 19$_{2}$ 20$_{34}$, נָבִיא *prophet* 1 K 16$_{7}$ (mss lack הַנָּבִיא) 16$_{12}$, חֹזֶה *seer* 2 C 19$_{2}$. <PREP> אֶל *to,* + היה *be* 1 K 16$_{1}$; בְּיַד *by means of,* + היה *be* 1 K 16$_{7}$, דבר pi. *speak* 1 K 16$_{12}$.

3. Judahite, son of Obed and father of Azariah, <SUBJ> ילד hi. *beget* 1 C 2$_{38}$. <OBJ> ילד hi. *beget* 1 C 2$_{38}$.

4. one of David's warriors, <APP> עַנְּתֹתִי *one from Anathoth* 1 C 12$_{3}$.

5. Simeonite, son of Joshibiah, <APP> בֵּן *son* 1 C 4$_{35}$ (or em. וְהוּא *and he* [Joel] was the son of Joshibiah).

6. son of Meshammesh, <APP> בֵּן *son* Seal 570 (T. Beit Mirsim?. 7th/6th cent.).

7. Seal 910 (ייהו; others אבן[י]יהו *Abijah;* 7th cent.).

⇒ ׳י Y. + הוּא *he.*

יֵהוּא, see הוה *be.*

[יְהוֹאָב] 0.0.0.4 pr.n.m. **Jehoab, 1.** son of Heldai, <APP> בֵּן *son* Arad ost. 39$_{10}$. **2.** Arad ost. 49$_{3}$. **3.** Arad ost. 59$_{1}$, <APP> בֵּן *son* Arad ost. 59$_{1}$. **4.** father of Amariah, <CSTR> בן יהואב *son of Jehoab* Seal 531 (T. Beit Mirsim?, 7th/6th cent.). **5.** father of Elishama, <CSTR> בן יהואב *son of Jehoab* Seal 810 (others יהואר *Jehoar;* City of David, 7th/6th cent.). **6.** appar. father of Ahimelech, Seal 890 (others יהואר *Jehoar;* 7th cent.).

⇒ ׳י Y. + אָב *father.*

[יְהוֹאָח] 0.0.0.2 pr.n.m. **Jehoah,** son of Eliaz, <APP> בֵּן *son* Seal 573 ([בן] יה[ו]אח; T. Beit Mirsim?, 7th/6th cent.). <PREP> לְ of possession, *of, (belonging) to* Seal 571 572 ([ל]יהואח) 573 (ליה[ו]אח; all three T. Beit Mirsim?, 7th/6th cent.).

⇒ ׳י Y. + אָח *brother.*

יְהוֹאָחָז 20.0.0.1 pr.n.m. **Jehoahaz**—יוֹאָחָז—**1.** king of Israel, son of Jehu, ident. with Joahaz at 2 K 14$_{1}$, <SUBJ> מלך *reign* 2 K 10$_{35}$ 13$_{1}$, הלך *go* 2 K 13$_{1}$, סור *turn aside* 2 K 13$_{1}$, עשׂה *do* 2 K 13$_{1.8}$, חלה pi. *entreat* 2 K 13$_{4}$, שׁכב *lie down* 2 K 13$_{9}$. <OBJ> קבר *bury* 2 K 13$_{9}$. <CSTR> בֶּן־יְהוֹאָחָז *son of Jehoahaz* 2 K 13$_{10}$ 14$_{8.17}$||2 C 25$_{17.25}$, יַד יְהוֹאָחָז *hand of Jehoahaz* 2 K 13$_{25}$, דִּבְרֵי *deeds of* 2 K 13$_{8}$, יְמֵי *days of* 2 K 13$_{22}$. <APP> אָב *father* 2 K 13$_{25}$, בֵּן *son* 2 K 10$_{35}$ 13$_{1.25}$ 14$_{8}$||2 C 25$_{17}$. <PREP> לְ of benefit, *to, for,* + שׁאר hi. *leave* 2 K 13$_{7}$; אֶל *to,* + שׁמע *listen* 2 K 13$_{4}$; תַּחַת *instead of,* + מלך *reign* 2 K 13$_{9}$.

2. king of Judah, son of Josiah, ident. with Joahaz at 2 C 36$_{2.4}$, appar. ident. with Johanan at 1 C 3$_{15}$, <SUBJ> בוא *come* 2 K 23$_{34}$, מלך *reign* 2 K 23$_{31}$ (||2 C 36$_{2}$ יוֹאָחָז *Joahaz*), עשׂה *do* 2 K 23$_{31}$, מות *die* 2 K 23$_{34}$. <NOM CL> בֶּן־שָׁלוֹשׁ וְעֶשְׂרִים שָׁנָה יְהוֹאָחָז *Jehoahaz was a son of twenty-three years,* i.e. twenty-three years old 2 K 23$_{31}$. <OBJ> לקח *take* 2 K 23$_{30}$||2 C 36$_{1}$ 2 K 23$_{34}$ (||2 C 36$_{4}$ יוֹאָחָז *Joahaz*), משׁח *anoint* 2 K 23$_{30}$, מלך hi. *make king* 2 K 23$_{30}$ ||2 C 36$_{1}$, אסר *imprison* 2 K 23$_{31}$. <APP> בֵּן *son* 2 K 23$_{30}$.

3. king of Judah, appar. ident. with Ahaziah, son of Jehoram, at 2 K 8$_{24}$||2 C 22$_{1}$ 2 K 8$_{25.26}$||2 C 22$_{2}$ 2 K 8$_{29}$ 9$_{16.21.23.23.27}$||2 C 22$_{8}$ 2 K 9$_{29}$ 10$_{13.13}$ 11$_{1}$||2 C 22$_{10}$ 2 K 11$_{2.2}$||2 C 22$_{11}$ 2 K 12$_{19}$ 13$_{1}$ 14$_{13}$ 1 C 3$_{11}$ 2 C 20$_{37}$ 22$_{1+10t}$, <SUBJ> שׁאר ni. *remain* 2 C 21$_{17}$ (ms אֲחַזְיָהוּ *Ahaziah*). <CSTR> בֶּן־יְהוֹאָחָז *son of Jehoahaz* 2 C 25$_{23}$ (||2 K 14$_{13}$ אֲחַזְיָהוּ *Ahaziah*). <APP> קָטֹן *small one,* i.e. youngest, of sons 2 C 21$_{17}$.

4. son of a king, <APP> בֵּן *son* Seal 252 (7th/6th cent.). <PREP> לְ of possession, *of, (belonging) to* Seal 252 (7th/6th cent.).

⇒ ׳י Y. + אחז *hold.*

[יְהוֹאֵל] 0.0.0.1 pr.n.m. **Jehoel,** appar. son of Miamun, <PREP> לְ of possession, *of, (belonging) to* Seal 256

(Lachish, 7th cent.).
⇒ י״ *Y.* + אֵל *God.*

[יְהוֹאָר] pr.n.m. **Jehoar, 1.** father of Elishama, <CSTR> בן יהואר *son of Jehoab* Seal 810 (others יהואב *Jehoab* City of David, 7th/6th cent.). **2.** appar. father of Ahimelech, Seal 890 (others יהואב *Jehoab*; 7th cent.).
⇒ י״ *Y.* + ארה *pluck.*

יְהוֹאָשׁ 17 pr.n.m. **Jehoash, 1.** king of Judah, son of Ahaziah and Zibiah, ident. with Joash at 2 K 11_{2}||2 C 22_{11} 2 K $12_{20.21}$ $13_{1.10}$ $14_{1.3.17}$||2 C 25_{25} 2 K 14_{23} 1 C 3_{11} 2 C $24_{1.2.4.22.24}$ 25_{23}, <SUBJ> אמר *say* 2 K $12_{5.8}$, קרא *call,* i.e. summon 2 K 12_{8}, מלך *reign* 2 K $12_{1.2}$, עשׂה *do* 2 K 12_{3} (||2 C 24_{2} יוֹאָשׁ *Joash*), לקח *take* 2 K 12_{19}, שׁלח *send* 2 K 12_{19}. <NOM CL> בֶּן־שֶׁבַע שָׁנִים יְהוֹאָשׁ *Jehoash was a son of seven years,* i.e. seven years old 2 K 12_{1} (||2 C 24_{1} יֹאָשׁ *Joash*). <OBJ> ירה hi. *teach* 2 K 12_{3}. <CSTR> בֶּן־ יְהוֹאָשׁ *son of Jehoash* 2 K 14_{13} (||2 C 25_{23} יוֹאָשׁ *Joash*). <APP> בֵּן *son* 2 K 14_{13} (or del.), מֶלֶךְ *king* 2 K $12_{7.8.19}$ 14_{13} (if transfer מֶלֶךְ־יְהוּדָה *king of Judah*). <PREP> לְ of possession, *of, (belonging) to* 2 K 12_{7}.

2. king of Israel, son of Jehoahaz, ident. with Joash at 2 K $13_{9.12.13.13.14.25}$ $14_{1.23.27}$ Ho 1_{1} Am 1_{1} 2 C $25_{17.18.21.23.25}$, <SUBJ> אמר *say* 2 K 14_{9} (||2 C 25_{18} יוֹאָשׁ *Joash*), מלך *reign* 2 K 13_{10}, הלך *go* 2 K 14_{8}, בוא *come* 2 K 14_{13}, עלה *go up* 2 K 14_{11} (||2 C 25_{21} יוֹאָשׁ), שׁלח *send* 2 K 14_{9}, שׁוב *go back* 2 K 13_{25} 14_{13}, סור *turn aside* 2 K 13_{10}, עשׂה *do* 2 K 13_{10} 14_{15}, לקח *take* 2 K 13_{25} 14_{13}, תפשׂ *seize* 2 K 14_{13} (||2 C 25_{23} יוֹאָשׁ), פרץ *break down* 2 K 14_{13}, ראה htp. *look at one another* 2 K $14_{8.11}$, לחם ni. *fight* 2 K 14_{15}, שׁכב *lie down* 2 K 14_{16}, קבר ni. *be buried* 2 K 14_{16}. <CSTR> דִּבְרֵי יְהוֹאָשׁ *deeds of Jehoash* 2 K 14_{15}, מוֹת *death of* 2 K 14_{17} (||2 C 25_{25} יוֹאָשׁ *Joash*). <APP> בֵּן *son* 2 K $13_{10.25}$ $14_{8.17}$, מֶלֶךְ *king* 2 K $14_{9.11.13.17}$. <PREP> אֶל *to,* + שׁלח *send* 2 K 14_{8} (||2 C 25_{17} יוֹאָשׁ *Joash*); תַּחַת *instead of,* + מלך *reign* 2 K 14_{16}.*
⇒ י״ *Y.*

[יְהוֹבָנָה] 0.0.0.2 pr.n.[m.] **Jehobanah**—יהבנה—**1.** perh. ident. with יובנה *Jobanah* on Seals 197, 457 and 788; Seals 488 (Ramat Raḥel, 8th cent.) 771 (Beth-Shemesh, 8th cent.). **2.** Lachish inscr. 27 (יהו[בנה]). **3.** Lachish inscr. 28 ([י]הובנה; others [נ]ריהו בן *Neriah son*).
<PREP> לְ of possession, *of, (belonging) to* Lachish inscr. 27 (ליהו[בנה]) Lachish inscr. 28 (לי[הובנה]; others לנ[ריהו בן] *to Neriah son*) <COLL> מנחם ויהבנה *Menahem and Jehobanah* Seal 488 (Ramat Raḥel, 8th cent.) Seal 771 (Beth-Shemesh, 8th cent.).
⇒ י״ *Y.* + בנה *build.*

[יְהוֹבַעַל] 0.0.0.1 pr.n.[m.] **Jehobaal,** Seal 857.
⇒ י״ *Y.* + בעל *be lord.*

יהוד, see יְהֻד *Jehud.*

יְהוּדָה 806.3.59.13 pr.n.m. **Judah**—I יהדה, Q יאודה—**1.** fourth son of Jacob and Leah, father of Er, Onan, and Shelah (mother, Bath-shua) and of Perez and Zerah (mother, Tamar) (Gn 29_{35} 35_{23} 37_{26} $38_{1.2.6.7.8.11.12.12.15.20.22.23.24.24.26}$ $43_{3.8}$ $44_{14.16.18}$ $46_{12.28}$ $49_{8.9}$ Ex 1_{2} Nm $26_{19.20}$ Ru 4_{12} Ne 11_{24} 1 C $2_{3.4}$ $4_{1.21}$ 5_{2} 9_{4}).

<SUBJ> חיה *live* Gn 43_{8}, צדק *be righteous* Gn 44_{16}, גבר *be strong* 1 C 5_{2}, נחם ni. *be consoled* Gn 38_{12}, מות *die* Gn 43_{8}, הלך *go* Gn 43_{8} 4QJub^{h} 41_{10} ([יהו]דה), בוא *come* Gn 38_{2} 44_{14} 46_{28} Ex 1_{2}, יצא *go out* 4QJub^{h} 38_{5} (ויצאו] [יהודה]), נגשׁ *approach* Gn 44_{18}, קום *arise* Gn 43_{8}, עלה *go up* Gn 38_{12} 4QJub^{h} 41_{8} ([עלה יהודה]), ירד *go down* Gn 38_{1}, נתן *give* Gn 38_{26}, יסף *do again* Gn 38_{26}, לקח *take* Gn $38_{2.6.20}$, שׁלח *send* Gn 38_{20}, נטה *extend,* i.e. pitch, tent Gn 38_{1}, אמר *say* Gn 37_{26} $38_{8.11.23.24.26}$ $43_{3.8.8}$ $44_{16.18}$, דבר pi. *speak* Gn 44_{16}, ירה hi. *point* way (Sam ראה ni. *appear*; or em. קרא ni. *meet*), ראה *see* Gn $38_{2.15}$, נכר hi. *recognize* Gn 38_{26}, ידע *know* Gn 38_{26}, כסה pi. *cover,* i.e. conceal Gn 37_{26}, הרג *kill* Gn 37_{26}.

<NOM CL> בְּנֵי לֵאָה ... יְהוּדָה וְיִשָּׂשכָר *the sons of Leah were ... Judah and Issachar* Gn 35_{23}.

<OBJ> קרא *call* Gn 29_{35}, ידה hi. *praise* Gn 49_{8} (יְהוּדָה אַתָּה יוֹדוּךָ אַחֶיךָ *O Judah, your brothers will praise you*), שׁלח *send* Gn 46_{28}. <CSTR> אֵשֶׁת־יְהוּדָה *wife of Judah* Gn 38_{12}, בְּכוֹר יְהוּדָה *firstborn of Judah* Gn 38_{7} 1 C 2_{3}, בֶּן־ *son of* Ne 11_{24} 1 C 4_{21} 9_{4} 4QSela 8.2_{3} ([יה]ודה), בְּנֵי *sons of* Gn 46_{12} Nm $26_{19.20}$ (בְּנֵי־) 1 C $2_{3.4}$ 4_{1}. <APP> בֵּן *son* 4Q Sela 8.2_{3} ([יהודה בן]) 11QT 39_{12}.

<PREP> לְ of direction, *to*, + נגד ho. *be told* Gn 38$_{24}$; perh. of benefit, *to, for*, + ילד *give birth* Ru 4$_{12}$; introducing object, + כעס hi. *anger* 4QapJoseph^{b} 1$_{14}$; בְּ of place, *among*, + עוד hi. *testify* Gn 43$_{3}$; מִן of comparison, *(more) than*, + צדק *be righteous* Gn 38$_{26}$; אֶל *to*, + שׁוב *go back* Gn 38$_{22}$; אֵת *with*, + שׁלח *send* Gn 43$_{8}$. <COLL> in list of sons of Israel (i.e. Jacob), 1 C 2$_{1}$.

2. people and nation claiming Judah as eponymous ancestor; territory of people of Judah.

<SUBJ> היה *be* Ps 114$_{2}$ 2 C 11$_{12}$, הלך *go* Jg 1$_{10}$ (or em. Caleb) 1$_{17}$ Jr 3$_{8}$, בוא *come* 2 S 19$_{16}$ Ho 4$_{15}$, 2 C 20$_{24}$, שׁוב *go back* Jr 3$_{10}$, עלה *go up* Jg 1$_{2.4}$ 20$_{18}$ (if ins. עלה) Ho 4$_{15}$, נוס *flee* 2 K 14$_{12}$||2 C 25$_{22}$, עמד *stand* Dt 27$_{12}$ Jos 18$_{5}$ 2 C 20$_{17}$, יצב htp. *stand* 2 C 20$_{17}$, נפל *fall* 2 K 14$_{10}$||2 C 25$_{19}$ Is 3$_{8}$, כשׁל *stumble* Ho 5$_{5}$ (or del.), פנה *turn* 2 C 13$_{14}$, מצא *find* Lm 1$_{3}$, אמר *say* Jg 1$_{3}$ Ne 4$_{4}$, שׁבע ni. *swear* Ho 4$_{15}$, שׁמע *hear* 2 C 20$_{20}$, ראה *see* Jr 3$_{7}$ Ho 5$_{13}$ (or ins. בֵּית *house of* Judah) 2 C 20$_{17}$, אבל *mourn* Jr 14$_{2}$, ירא *fear* Jr 3$_{8}$, עשׂה *do* evil 1 K 14$_{22}$ (or del. יְהוּדָה) 21$_{16}$ 2 C 33$_{9}$, שׁמר *keep* 2 K 17$_{19}$, לכד *capture* Jg 1$_{18}$ (or em. ירשׁ hi. *possess*), ישׁב *dwell* 1 K 5$_{5}$ (or del. Judah) Jr 31$_{24}$ Jl 4$_{20}$ Lm 1$_{3}$, חרשׁ *plough* Ho 10$_{11}$ (or del. Judah), רבה hi. *increase* Ho 8$_{14}$ (or del.), צרר *oppress* Is 11$_{13}$, אשׁם *be guilty* Ho 4$_{15}$, בגד *betray* Jr 3$_{8.11}$ Ml 2$_{11}$, זנה *prostitute oneself* Jr 3$_{8}$, חלל pi. *profane* Ml 2$_{11}$, נכה hi. *strike* Jg 1$_{17}$, נגף ni. *be struck*, i.e. routed 2 K 14$_{12}$||2 C 25$_{22}$, גלה *be exiled* 2 K 25$_{21}$||Jr 52$_{27}$ Lm 1$_{3}$, ho. Jr 13$_{19}$, פוץ ni. *be scattered* Jr 40$_{15}$, קבץ ni. *be gathered* Jr 40$_{15}$ 2 C 20$_{4}$, ישׁע ni. *be saved* Jr 33$_{16}$, לחם ni. *fight* Zc 14$_{14}$ (or del.) 2 C 20$_{17}$.

<NOM CL> יְהוּדָה וְיִשְׂרָאֵל רַבִּים *Judah and Israel were many* 1 K 4$_{20}$ (or del. Judah), יְהוּדָה בַתְּחִלָּה *Judah is (at) first* Jg 20$_{18}$ (or ins. עלה *go up*, with Judah as subj.), וִיהוּדָה אַרְבַּע מֵאוֹת וְשִׁבְעִים אֶלֶף *and Judah were four hundred and seventy thousand* 1 C 21$_{5}$, גּוּר אַרְיֵה יְהוּדָה *Judah is a lion's cub* Gn 49$_{9}$, לֹא־אַלְמָן יִשְׂרָאֵל וִיהוּדָה *Israel and Judah are not widowed* Jr 51$_{5}$, עַל גְּבוּל רְאוּבֵן ... יְהוּדָה אֶחָד *on the border of Reuben ... was Judah, one (tribe)* Ezk 48$_{7}$, יְהוּדָה וְאֶרֶץ יִשְׂרָאֵל הֵמָּה רֹכְלָיִךְ *Judah and the land of Israel were your merchants* Ezk 27$_{17}$ (or em. וְאֶרֶץ *and the land of* to וּבְנֵי *and the sons of*), יְהוּדָה מְחֹקְקִי *Judah is my sceptre* Ps 60$_{9}$.

<OBJ> מצא *find* 2 C 25$_{5}$, נחל *inherit* Zc 2$_{16}$ (or em. hi. *cause* Judah *to inherit*), עמד hi. *position* 2 C 25$_{5}$, רדף *pursue* Lm 1$_{3}$, נשׂג hi. *overtake* Lm 1$_{3}$, קבץ *gather* 2 C 25$_{5}$, זרה pi. *scatter* Zc 2$_{2.4}$, סור hi. *remove* 2 K 23$_{27}$, גלה hi. *exile* 1 C 5$_{41}$, תעה hi. *lead astray* 2 C 33$_{9}$, נדח hi. *lead astray* 2 C 21$_{11}$, זנה hi. *prostitute* 2 C 21$_{13}$, חטא hi. *cause to sin* 2 K 21$_{11.16}$ Jr 32$_{35}$, זעק hi. *summon* 2 S 20$_{5}$, מנה *count* 2 S 24$_{1}$, פקד *muster* 2 C 25$_{5}$, שׁחת hi. *destroy* 2 K 8$_{19}$, מאס *reject* Jr 14$_{19}$, קנא pi. *envy* Is 11$_{13}$, כנע hi. *humble* 2 C 28$_{19}$, דרך *tread*, i.e. draw, Judah as a bow Zc 9$_{13}$, טהר pi. *purify* 2 C 34$_{3.5}$, רשׁע hi. *condemn* CD 20$_{27}$.

<CSTR> בֵּית יְהוּדָה *house of Judah* 2 S 2$_{4.7.10.11}$ 12$_{8}$ 1 K 12$_{21}$||2 C 11$_{1}$ 1 K 12$_{21.23}$ 2 K 19$_{30}$||Is 37$_{31}$ Is 22$_{21}$ Jr 3$_{18}$ 5$_{11}$ 11$_{10.17}$ 12$_{14}$ 13$_{11}$ 31$_{27.31}$ 33$_{14}$ 36$_{3}$ 8$_{17}$ 9$_{9}$ 25$_{3.8.12}$ Ezk 4$_{6}$ Ho 1$_{7}$ 5$_{12.13}$ (if ins. בֵּית) 5$_{14}$=4QpHos^{b} 2$_{2}$ ([בית יהודה]) 12$_{1}$ Mc 1$_{5}$ (if em. בָּמוֹת *high places* to בֵּית *house of*) Zp 2$_{7}$ Zc 8$_{13.15.19}$ 10$_{3.6}$ 12$_{4}$ Ne 4$_{10}$ (כָּל־) 1 C 28$_{4}$ 2 C 11$_{1}$ 19$_{11}$ 22$_{10}$ CD 4$_{11}$ 1QpHab 8$_{1}$ 4QpPs^{a} 1.2$_{13}$ 4QMidrEschat^{a} 2$_{15}$ 4$_{1}$ ([בית י]הודה).

בְּנֵי(־)יְהוּדָה *sons of Judah* Nm 1$_{26}$ 2$_{3}$ 10$_{14}$ Jos 14$_{6}$ 15$_{1+5t}$ 18$_{11.14}$ 19$_{1.9}$ 21$_{9}$ Jg 1$_{8.9.16}$ 2 S 1$_{18}$ 21$_{2}$ Jr 7$_{30}$ 32$_{30.32}$ 50$_{4.33}$ Ho 2$_{2}$ Jl 4$_{6.8.19}$ Ob$_{12}$ Dn 1$_{6}$ Ezr 3$_{9}$ Ne 11$_{4.4.25}$ 13$_{16}$ 1 C 2$_{10}$ 4$_{27}$ 6$_{50}$ 9$_{3}$ 12$_{17.25}$ 2 C 13$_{18}$ 25$_{12}$ 28$_{10}$ 31$_{6}$ 1QM 1$_{2}$ 4Qps Ezek^{a} 16.2$_{7}$ 4QPrFêtes^{c} 183$_{7}$ ([יה]ודה)11QT 24$_{11}$ 44$_{7.11}$, בַּת *daughter of* Lm 1$_{15}$ 2$_{5}$, בְּנוֹת *daughters of* Ps 48$_{12}$ 97$_{8}$, אִישׁ *man of* Jg 15$_{10}$ 1 S 11$_{8}$ 15$_{4}$ 2 S 19$_{15.17.42.43.44.44}$ 20$_{2.4}$ 2 K 23$_{2}$ 24$_{9}$ Is 5$_{3.7}$ Jr 4$_{3.4}$ 11$_{2.9}$ 17$_{25}$ 18$_{11}$ 32$_{32}$ 35$_{13}$ 36$_{31}$ 44$_{26.27}$ Dn 9$_{7}$ 2 C 13$_{15.15}$ 20$_{27}$ 34$_{30}$, אַנְשֵׁי *men of* 1 S 17$_{52}$ 2 S 2$_{4}$ 1 K 1$_{9}$ Ezr 10$_{9}$, יֹשְׁבֵי *inhabitants of* Ezr 4$_{6}$, אַלְפֵי *clans of* 1 S 23$_{23}$ Zc 12$_{5.6}$ (if em. אַלֻּפֵי *chiefs of* in both) Mc 5$_{1}$, צאצאי *offspring of* 4QMidrEshat^{b} 10$_{12}$.

קְהַל יהודה *assembly of Judah* 2 C 20$_{5}$ 30$_{25}$, מַחֲנֵה *camp of* Nm 2$_{3.9}$, צְבָא *army of* 1 K 2$_{32}$, אָהֳלֵי *tents of* Zc 12$_{7}$, שֵׁבֶט *tribe of* Jos 7$_{16}$ 1 K 12$_{20}$ 2 K 17$_{18}$ Ps 78$_{68}$ 4QComm GenA 5$_{1}$ 4QDibHam^{a} 1.4$_{6}$ (יאודה), מַטֵּה *tribe of* Ex 31$_{2}$ 35$_{30}$ 38$_{22}$ Nm 1$_{27}$ 7$_{12}$ 13$_{6}$ 34 Jos 7$_{1.18}$ 21$_{4}$ Si 45$_{25}$ 11QT 23$_{10}$ 24$_{10}$, מִשְׁפַּחַת *family of* Jos 7$_{17}$ Jg 17$_{7}$, מִשְׁפְּחֹת *families of* Nm 26$_{22}$, מַחְלְקוֹת *divisions of* Ne 11$_{36}$, עַם *people of* 2 S 19$_{41}$ 2 K 14$_{21}$ Jr 25$_{1.2}$ 26$_{18}$ Ezr 4$_{4}$ 2 C 26$_{1}$, שְׁאֵרִית *remnant of* Jr 40$_{15}$ 42$_{15.19}$ 43$_{5}$ 44$_{12.14.28}$, גָּלוּת *diaspora of* Jr 24$_{5}$ 28$_{4}$ 29$_{22}$ 40$_{1}$, שְׁבוּת *captivity of* Jr 33$_{7}$ Jl 4$_{1}$, נְפֻצוֹת *scattered ones of* Is 11$_{12}$.

מֶלֶךְ(־)יְהוּדָה *king of Judah* 1 K 12$_{23.27.27}$ 15$_{9.17.25.28.33}$

16$_{8.10.15.23.29}$ 22$_{2.10.29.52}$ 2 K 1$_{17}$ 3$_{1.7.9.14}$ 8$_{16.16}$ 8$_{25.29}$ 9$_{16.21.27}$ 10$_{13}$ 12$_{19}$ 13$_{1.10.12}$ 14$_{1+6t}$ 15$_{1+6t}$ 16$_{1}$ 17$_{1}$ 18$_{1.14.14.16}$ 21$_{11}$ 22$_{16.18}$ 24$_{12}$ 25$_{27.27}$ Is 7$_{1}$ 37$_{10}$ 38$_{9}$ Jr 1$_{2.3.3}$ 15$_{4}$ 21$_{7.11}$ 22$_{1+5t}$ 22$_{1.6}$ 24$_{1.8}$ 25$_{1.3}$ 26$_{1.18.19}$ 27$_{1+5t}$ 32$_{1.2.3.4}$ 34$_{2.4.6.21}$ 35$_{1}$ 36$_{1+5t}$ 37$_{7}$ 38$_{22}$ 39$_{1.4}$ 44$_{30}$ 45$_{1}$ 46$_{2.34}$ 51$_{59}$ 52$_{31.31}$ Am 1$_{1}$ Zp 1$_{1}$ Zc 14$_{5}$ Pr 25$_{1}$ Est 2$_{6}$ Dn 1$_{1.2}$ 1 C 4$_{41}$ 5$_{17}$ 2 C 11$_{3}$ 16$_{1.7}$ 18$_{3.9.28}$ 19$_{1}$ 20$_{35}$ 21$_{12}$ 22$_{1.6}$ 25$_{17.18.21.23.25}$ 30$_{24}$ 32$_{8.9.23}$ 34$_{24.26}$ 35$_{21}$ 4QApocWeeks 1$_{4}$ 4QapPs[b] 31$_{4}$ ([מ]לך) 33$_{8}$ 4QMMT C$_{19}$ ([יהוד[ה) Arad ost. 40$_{13}$ ([יהוד[ה), מַלְכֵי *kings of* 1 S 27$_{6}$ 1 K 14$_{29}$ 15$_{7.23}$ 22$_{46}$ 2 K 8$_{23}$ 12$_{19.20}$ 14$_{18}$ 15$_{6.36}$ 16$_{19}$ 18$_{5}$ 20$_{20}$ 21$_{17.25}$ 23$_{5.11.12.22.28}$ 24$_{5}$ Is 1$_{1}$ Jr 1$_{18}$ 8$_{1}$ 17$_{19.20}$ 19$_{3.4.13}$ 20$_{5}$ 33$_{4}$ 44$_{9}$ Ho 1$_{1}$ Mc 1$_{1}$ 1 C 9$_{1}$ 2 C 25$_{26}$ 27$_{7}$ 28$_{26}$ 32$_{32}$ 34$_{11}$ 35$_{27}$ 36$_{8}$ Si 49$_{4}$, שָׂרֵי *princes of* Jr 24$_{1}$ 26$_{10}$ 29$_{2}$ 34$_{19}$ 52$_{2}$ Ho 5$_{10}$ Ps 68$_{28}$ Ne 12$_{31.32}$ 2 C 12$_{5}$ 22$_{8}$ 24$_{17}$ CD 8$_{3}$ 19$_{15}$, חֹרֵי *nobles of* Jr 27$_{20}$ 39$_{6}$ Ne 6$_{17}$ 13$_{17}$, פַּחַת *governor of* Hg 1$_{1.14}$ 2$_{2.21}$, זִקְנֵי *elders of* 1 S 30$_{26}$ 2 S 19$_{12}$ 2 K 23$_{1}$ Ezk 8$_{1}$ 2 C 34$_{29}$, פתאי יהודה *simple ones of Judah* 1QpHab 12$_{4}$, מרשיעי יהודה *ones who condemn Judah* CD 20$_{27}$.

אֶרֶץ יְהוּדָה *land of Judah* Dt 34$_{2}$ 1 S 22$_{5}$ 30$_{16}$ 2 K 23$_{24}$ 25$_{22}$ Is 26$_{1}$ Jr 31$_{23}$ 37$_{1}$ 39$_{10}$ 40$_{12}$ 43$_{4}$ 44$_{9.14.28}$ Am 7$_{12}$ Zc 2$_{4}$ Ru 1$_{7}$ Ne 5$_{14}$ 1 C 6$_{40}$ 2 C 9$_{11}$ 15$_{8}$ 17$_{2}$ 1QpZeph 1$_{5}$ CD 4$_{3}$ 6$_{5}$, אַרְצוֹת *territories of* 2 C 11$_{23}$, אַדְמַת *land of* Is 19$_{17}$, גְּבוּל *boundary of* Ezk 48$_{8.22}$, מַלְכוּת *kingdom of* 2 C 11$_{17}$, הַר *hill country of* Jos 11$_{21}$ 20$_{7}$ 21$_{11}$ 2 C 21$_{11}$ (הָרֵי) 27$_{4}$ Kh. Beit Lei graf. 5$_{2}$ (הרי יהודה; others הו יהוה את *he is; you are Y.* or הרי יהד לו *the hill country of Jehud is his*), מִדְבַּר *steppe of* Jg 1$_{16}$ Ps 63$_{1}$, נֶגֶב *Negev of* 1 S 27$_{10}$ 2 S 24$_{7}$, בֵּית לֶחֶם *Bethlehem of* Jg 17$_{7.8.9}$ 19$_{1.2.18.18}$ 1 S 17$_{12}$ Ru 1$_{1.2}$, אֲפִיקֵי *channels of* Jl 4$_{18}$, מֵי *waters of* Is 48$_{1}$, בָּמוֹת *high places of* Mc 1$_{5}$, עֵץ *tree of* Ezk 37$_{19}$, עִיר *city of* 2 C 25$_{28}$, עָרֵי *cities of* 2 S 2$_{1}$ 1 K 12$_{17}$ 2 K 18$_{13}$ 23$_{5.8}$ Is 36$_{1}$ 40$_{9}$ 44$_{26}$ Jr 1$_{15}$ 4$_{16}$ 7$_{17.44}$ 9$_{10}$ 10$_{22}$ 11$_{6.12}$ 17$_{26}$ 25$_{18}$ 26$_{2}$ 32$_{44}$ 33$_{10.13}$ 34$_{7.7.22}$ 36$_{9}$ 40$_{5}$ 44$_{2.6.17.21}$ Zc 1$_{12}$ Ps 69$_{36}$ Lm 5$_{11}$ Ne 11$_{3.20}$ 2 C 10$_{17}$ 14$_{4}$ 17$_{2.7.9.13}$ 19$_{5}$ 20$_{4}$ 23$_{2}$ 24$_{5}$ 25$_{13}$ 31$_{1.6}$ 1QM 12$_{13}$ 19$_{5}$ ([יהו[דה) 1QpHab 12$_{9}$, מִבְצְרֵי *fortifications of* Lm 2$_{2}$, שַׁעַר *gate of* Ezk 48$_{31}$ 11QT 39$_{16}$ 40$_{15}$ 44$_{4.7}$, חומ[ו]ת יהודה *walls of Judah* 11QMelch 3$_{9}$.

מִנְחַת יְהוּדָה *cereal offering of Judah* Ml 3$_{4}$, מָסָךְ *screen of* Is 22$_{8}$, עֲצַת *counsel of* Jr 19$_{7}$, יַד־ *hand*, i.e. rule, *of* 2 K 8$_{20.22}$‖2 C 21$_{8.10}$, קוֹל *voice of* Dt 33$_{7}$, שִׂמְחַת *joy of* Ne 12$_{44}$, גְּאוֹן *pride of* Jr 13$_{9}$, כבוד *glory of* 4QpNah 3$_{4}$, חַטַּאת *sin of* Jr 17$_{1}$ 50$_{20}$, פִּשְׁעֵי *sins of* Am 2$_{4}$, צָרֵי *enemies of* Ezr 4$_{1}$, צֹרְרֵי *oppressors of* Is 11$_{13}$.

כָּל־יְהוּדָה *all Judah* 1 S 18$_{16}$ 2 S 5$_{5}$ 1 K 15$_{22}$ 2 K 15$_{37}$ (mss) 22$_{13}$ Jr 7$_{2}$ 17$_{20}$ 20$_{4}$ 26$_{19}$ 36$_{6}$ 40$_{15}$ 44$_{11.24.26}$ Ne 13$_{12}$ 2 C 15$_{2.9.15}$ 16$_{6}$ 17$_{5.19}$ 20$_{3.13.15.18}$ 23$_{8}$ 25$_{5}$ 30$_{6}$ 31$_{1.20}$ 32$_{9.33}$ 34$_{9}$ 35$_{18.24}$.

<APP> אָחוֹת *sister* Jr 3$_{7.8.10}$, עַם Jr 30$_{3}$ (or del. Judah), אֶחָד *one (tribe)* Ezk 48$_{7}$.

<PREP> לְ of possession, *of, (belonging) to* Nm 1$_{7}$ 1 S 17$_{1}$ 30$_{14}$ 2 S 3$_{8}$ (or del.) 1 K 19$_{3}$ Ezr 1$_{5.8}$ 1 C 13$_{6}$ 27$_{18}$ 2 C 12$_{4}$ 16$_{11}$ 17$_{14}$ 25$_{21}$ 28$_{18.25}$, + שׁאר ni. *remain* Si 48$_{15}$; of direction, *to* Dt 33$_{7}$, + הלך *go* 2 C 11$_{14}$, בוא *come* 2 C 20$_{22}$, שׁוב *go back* Ezr 2$_{1}$‖Ne 7$_{6}$, hi. *take back*, i.e. restore, city 2 K 14$_{22}$‖2 C 26$_{2}$ 2 K 14$_{28}$ (or del. לִיהוּדָה), אמר *say*, 2 K 18$_{22}$‖Is 36$_{7}$‖2 C 32$_{12}$ 2 C 14$_{3.6}$ 33$_{16}$, נתן *give*, i.e. allow Jr 40$_{11}$; of benefit, *to, for*, + עשׂה *do* Ho 6$_{4}$ (or em. Israel), perh. שׁית appar. *be appointed* Ho 6$_{11}$; introducing obj., + גאל *redeem* 4QapPs[b] 24$_{5}$.

בְּ of place, *in(to), among, through(out)* Jg 18$_{12}$ 1 S 23$_{3}$ 1 K 12$_{32}$ Zc 9$_{7}$ 14$_{21}$ Ezr 1$_{2.3}$ Ne 6$_{18}$ 2 C 2$_{6}$ 11$_{10}$ 21$_{3}$ 33$_{14}$ 36$_{23}$, + היה *be* 2 C 12$_{12}$, שׁאר ni. *remain* 2 C 34$_{21}$, ישׁב *dwell* 2 C 30$_{25}$, חנה *encamp* Jg 15$_{9}$, מצא ni. *be found* 4QD[a] 5.1$_{10}$ ([נמ[צא), בנה *build* 2 C 11$_{5}$ 14$_{5}$ 17$_{12}$, בוא come 2 C 32$_{1}$, סבב *go around* 2 C 23$_{2}$, חלף *pass* Is 8$_{8}$, עבר hi. *cause* voice *to pass* Ezr 10$_{7}$, נתן *give* Ezr 9$_{9}$ 2 C 24$_{9}$, פרע hi. *loosen*, i.e. behave without restraint 2 C 28$_{19}$, נגד hi. *tell* Jr 4$_{5}$, שׁמע hi. *proclaim* Jr 5$_{20}$, למד pi. *teach* 2 C 17$_{9}$, ידע ni. *be known* Ps 76$_{2}$ 4QapPs[b] 48$_{7}$ ([יהו[דה), ראה *see* Ne 13$_{15}$, נשׂא *raise* 4QapElisée 3$_{5}$ (נ]שא]); *in charge of, over* Ne 6$_{7}$, + מלך *rule* 1 K 14$_{21}$, משׁל *rule* Jr 22$_{30}$; partitive, *(some) of, from (among)*, + הרג *kill* 2 C 28$_{6}$, נכה hi. *strike* 2 C 28$_{17}$; *against*, + היה *be* 2 K 24$_{3.20}$‖Jr 52$_{3}$, עלה *go up* Is 7$_{6}$ 2 C 21$_{17}$, לחם ni. *fight* Jg 10$_{9}$, פגע *strike* against, i.e. touch Jos 19$_{34}$ (or del. בִּיהוּדָה), עוד hi. *testify* against, i.e. warn 2 K 17$_{13}$, שׁלח pi. *send (away)* 2 K 24$_{2}$ Am 2$_{5}$, hi. 2 K 15$_{37}$, חרה *burn* 2 K 23$_{26}$; of accompaniment, *with*, + היה *be* 2 C 30$_{12}$; בחר בְּ *choose* 1 C 28$_{4}$.

מִן of direction, *from*, + בוא *come* 1 K 13$_{1.12.14.21}$ 2 K 23$_{17}$, hi. *bring* 2 C 24$_{6}$, סור *depart* Gn 49$_{10}$, hi. *remove* Is 3$_{1}$ 2 C 17$_{6}$, יצא hi. *take out* Is 65$_{9}$; of possession, *of, (belonging) to* Jg 15$_{11}$ Ne 1$_{2}$ 2 C 14$_{7}$; of comparison, *more (than)*, + צדק pi. *make* soul *righteous* Jr 3$_{11}$.

עַל *in charge of, over* 1 K 1_{35}, + קום hi. *establish* throne 2 S 3_{10}, + מלך *rule* 2 S 5_{5} 1 K 22_{41} 2 K 9_{29} 2 C 13_{1} 20_{31}, hi. *make king* 2 C $36_{4.10}$; *against* Is 9_{20} 2 C 28_{9}, + היה *be* Zc 12_{2} (or del. עַל, leaving יְהוּדָה as subj. of היה) 2 C 24_{18} 29_{8} 32_{25}, בוא hi. *bring* 2 K 21_{12}, עלה *go up* 1 K 15_{17} ||2 C 16_{1}, נטה *extend* hand Zp 1_{4}; *to*, + שׁלח *send* word 2 C 30_{1}; *for (the sake of)*, + בוא hi. *bring* sacrifice 2 C 29_{21} (or em. Israel), perh. פקד *visit* against, i.e. punish Jr 9_{25}; perh. of comparison, *(more) than*, + גדל *be great* Zc 12_{7}; *concerning*, + חזה *see* vision Is 1_{1} 2_{1}, דבר pi. *speak* Jr 36_{2}; שׁוּף עַל *look upon* 4QapPs^{b} 17_{2}; מֵעַל *from*, + סור *depart* Is 7_{17} CD $7_{12.13}$ 14_{1}.

אֶל *to(wards)*, + בוא *come* Ne 2_{7}, שׁלח pi. *send (away)* Ne 2_{5}; *against*, + בוא *come* Ezk 21_{25} (if em. אֶת appar. object-marker) 2 C 24_{23}, hi. *bring* Jr 35_{17}; *concerning* + דבר pi. *speak* Jr 30_{4} (or del. וְאֶל־יְהוּדָה).

אֶת *with*, + היה *be* Jg 1_{19}, עלה *go up* Jg 1_{3}.

עִם *with* 2 C 20_{17}; *against* Ho 12_{3} (or em. Israel)

עַד *unto*, + בוא *come* Mc 1_{9}.

לִפְנֵי *in front of*, + היה *be* 2 C 13_{13} + נגף *strike* 2 C 13_{15} 14_{11}; מִפְּנֵי *from (before)*, + נוס *flee* 2 C 13_{16}.

מִתּוֹךְ *from (among)*, + כרת hi. *cut off* Jr 44_{7}.

בֵּין *between*, + פרר hi. *frustrate* brotherhood between Judah and Israel Zc 11_{14}.

סָבִיב *around* 2 C 17_{10}.

<COLL> יְהוּדָה *O Judah* Jr 2_{28}=11_{13} 2 C $20_{17.20}$.

Judah + Israel Ex 35_{30} Jos $7_{1.16}$ 11_{21} Jg 10_{9} 19_{1} 20_{18} 1 S 11_{8} 17_{52} 18_{16} 2 S 2_{10} 3_{10} 5_{5} 11_{11} 12_{8} $19_{12.41.42.43.44}$ 20_{2} 21_{2} $24_{1.9}$ 1 K 1_{35} 2_{32} 4_{20} 5_{5} $12_{17.20.21}$ 14_{21} $15_{9.17.25.33}$ $16_{8.23.29}$ $22_{2.10.29.41.52}$ 2 K $3_{1.9}$ $8_{16.25}$ 9_{21} $13_{1.10.12}$ $14_{1.9.11.12.13.15.17.23.28}$ $15_{1.8.17.23.27.32}$ $17_{1.13.18.19}$ $18_{1.5}$ 21_{12} 22_{18} $23_{22.27}$ Is 5_{7} 7_{1} 11_{12} 48_{1} Jr $3_{8.11.18}$ 5_{11} 9_{25} $11_{10.17}$ 12_{14} 13_{11} 19_{3} 23_{6} 24_{5} 27_{21} 30_{3} 30_{4} $31_{23.27.31}$ $32_{30.32}$ $33_{4.7.14}$ 34_{2} $35_{13.17}$ 36_{2} 37_{7} 42_{15} $44_{2.7.11}$ $50_{4.20.33}$ 51_{5} Ezk 9_{9} 25_{3} 27_{17} $37_{16.19}$ 48_{31} Ho 1_{1} 2_{2} 4_{15} 5_{5} 8_{14} 12_{1} Am 1_{1} Mc 1_{5} 5_{1} Zc 2_{2} 8_{13} 11_{14} Ml 2_{11} Ps 76_{2} 114_{2} Lm 2_{5} Dn 9_{7} Ezr 1_{3} 4_{1} Ne $11_{3.20}$ 1 C 2_{1} 5_{17} 9_{1} 13_{6} 21_{5} 28_{4} 2 C 10_{17} $11_{1.3}$ $13_{15.16.18}$ 15_{9} $16_{1.11}$ $18_{3.9.28}$ 20_{35} 21_{13} 23_{2} $24_{5.6.9}$ $25_{17.18.21.22.23.25}$ 25_{26} 27_{7} $28_{19.26}$ $30_{1.6.25}$ $31_{1.6}$ 32_{32} $33_{9.16}$ $34_{9.21.26}$ $35_{18.27}$ 36_{8}.

Judah + Jerusalem Jos 15_{63} Jg 1_{8} 2 S 5_{5} 20_{2} 1 K $12_{21.27}$ 14_{21} 2 K 12_{19} 14_{13} 18_{22} 19_{10} $21_{12.16}$ $23_{1.2.5.24.27}$ 24_{20} Is 1_{1} 2_{1} $3_{1.8}$ 5_{3} 7_{1} Is 22_{21} 36_{7} 37_{10} 40_{9} 44_{26} Jr $1_{3.15}$ $4_{3.4.5.16}$ $7_{17.34}$ 8_{1} 9_{10} $11_{2.6.9.12.13}$ 13_{9} 14_{2} 15_{4} $17_{19.20.25.26}$ 18_{11} $19_{3.7.13}$ $24_{1.8}$ $25_{2.18}$ $27_{3.18.20.21}$ 29_{2} $32_{2.32.44}$ $33_{10.13.16}$ $34_{6.7.19}$ $35_{13.17}$ $36_{9.31}$ 39_{1} 40_{1} $44_{2.6.9.17.21}$ 52_{3} Ezk 21_{25} Jl $4_{1.6.20}$ Am 2_{5} Mc $1_{1.5.9}$ Zp 1_{4} Zc 1_{12} $2_{2.16}$ 8_{15} 12_{2}.

Judah + Ephraim Dt 34_{2} Jo 20_{7} Jg 10_{9} 17_{8} $19_{1.18}$ 2 K 14_{13} Is 7_{17} 9_{20} 11_{13} Ezk $37_{16.19}$ Ho $5_{5.12.13}$ 6_{4} 10_{11} 12_{1} Zc 9_{13} Ps 60_{9} 108_{9} 1 C 9_{3} 2 C $15_{8.9}$ 17_{2} $25_{10.23}$ 30_{1} 31_{1} 34_{9}.

Judah + Benjamin Dt 27_{12} Jo 18_{11} 21_{4} Jg 10_{9} 20_{18} 1 K $12_{21.23}$ 15_{22} Jr 17_{26} 32_{44} 33_{13} Ezk 48_{22} Ps 68_{28} Ezr 1_{5} 4_{1} 10_{9} Ne $11_{4.36}$ 12_{34} 1 C 6_{50} $9_{3.4}$ 12_{17} 2 C $11_{1.3.10.12}$ 14_{7} $15_{2.8.9}$ 25_{5} 31_{1} 34_{9}.

3. Benjaminite, deputy military governor of Jerusalem, son of Hassenuah (or em. הַסְּנָאָה *Hassenaah*), <NOM CL> יְהוּדָה בֶן־הַסְּנוּאָה עַל־הָעִיר מִשְׁנֶה *Judah son of Hassenuah was over the city (as) second-in-command* Ne 11_{9}.

4. Levite, husband of non-Jewish wife, <NOM CL> מִן־הַלְוִיִּם ... יְהוּדָה *from the Levites was ... Judah* Ezr 10_{23}.

5. post-exilic Levitical singer, <NOM CL> יְהוּדָה ... עַל־הֻיְּדוֹת *Judah ... was in charge of praise* Ne 12_{8} (or em. Judah to Hodaviah and/or הֻיְּדוֹת to הוֹדוֹת *praising* or הוֹדָיוֹת *songs of praise*). <APP> לֵוִי *Levite* Ne 12_{8}.

6. appar. priest at dedication of walls of Jerusalem, <SUBJ> הלך *go* Ne 12_{34} (or em. וּמִבְּנֵי *and from the sons of* the priests, to מִבְּנֵי Judah ..., *of the sons of* the priests, was with trumpets [12_{35}]).

7. Levite musician at dedication of walls of Jerusalem, <NOM CL> יְהוּדָה ... בִּכְלֵי־שִׁיר *Judah ... was with instruments of song* Ne 12_{36}. <APP> אָח *brother* 12_{36}.

8. high priest at time of Aristobulus II, <APP> כֹּהֵן *priest* Aristobulus Coins 28 29, חָבֵר *companion* Aristobulus Coins 28 29.

9. appar. priest, son of Josek/Joseph, <APP> בֵּן *son* Bene Ḥezir tomb inscr. <PREP> לְ of possession, *of, (belonging) to* Bene Ḥezir tomb inscr.

10. husband of Salome, <CSTR> אשת יהודה Frey 1295.

11. scribe, son of Eleazar, <APP> סֹפֵר *scribe* Frey 1308A 1308B, בַּר *son* Frey 1308B.

12. rabbi, <APP> רַבִּי *rabbi* Frey 1410.

13. <CSTR> בן יהודא *son of Judah* Frey $1285_{3(AHL)}$ (Frey חדא *Hadda*).

14. Coins 46 51 52 ([י]הדה; all three 3rd cent.).

15. father of Alma, <CSTR> בן יהודה *son of Judah* 5/6ḤevBA 44$_{4.14.22.30}$.

16. son of Joseph, <APP> בֵּן *son* 5/6ḤevBA 44$_{31}$, עֵד *witness* 5/6ḤevBA 44$_{31}$.

17. father of Eleazar, <CSTR> בן יהודה *son of Judah* 5/6ḤevBA 44$_{32}$.

18. son of Rabba, party to land tenancy agreement, <SUBJ> היה *be* Mur 24 5$_{4}$ (א[שאה] ... הודה[י]), אמר *say* Mur 24 5$_{4}$ (הודה[י]), חכר *rent* Mur 24 5$_{4}$ (הודה[י]), מדד *measure* Mur 24 5$_{4}$ (הודה[י]). <APP> בֵּן *son* Mur 24 5$_{4}$ (הודה[י]). <PREP> לְ of possession, *of, (belonging) to* Mur 24 5$_{4}$ (הודה[י]); קוּם עַל pi. *oblige* Mur 24 5$_{4}$ (הודה ... [י] [ו]ק[ים] [עלי]).

19. father of Judah, <CSTR> בר יהודה *son of Judah* Mur 29 2$_{10}$.

20. son of Judah, signatory to deed of sale, <SUBJ> חתם *seal* Mur 29 2$_{10}$. <APP> בַּר *son* Mur 29 2$_{10}$.

21. father of Jacob, <CSTR> בן יהודה *son of Judah* Mur EpBeth-Mashiko$_{4.10}$.

Also 1Q25 3$_{2}$ 4QpHos[b] 25$_{1}$ (both הודה[י]) 4QapLam[a] 1$_{3}$ 4QapJoseph[b] 1$_{9}$ 4QapJoshua[b] 1$_{3}$ ([י]הודה) 4Qpara Kings 38$_{1}$ (יה[ו]דה) 4QNarrA 14$_{3}$ 4QPseud[b] 1$_{5}$ (הודה[י]) 4QSela 1.1$_{10}$ (הודה[י]).*

⇒ ידה *be Jewish;* בַּעֲלֵי יְהוּדָה *Baale-jehudah.*

יְהוּדִי I $_{82.0.1.4}$ gent. **Jewish**—fem. יְהוּדִית, יְהֻדִיָּה; pl. יְהוּדִים (Kt יהודיים, I יהדים, abbreviated as יה, ידי, יהו, יהד)—**1. Judaean, Jewish,** used attributively of אִישׁ *man* Jr 43$_{9}$ Zc 8$_{23}$ Est 2$_{5}$ 4QMishC[d] 5$_{1}$.

2. as plural noun, **Judaeans, Jews,** <SUBJ> היה *be* 2 K 25$_{25}$ Jr 41$_{3}$ Est 8$_{13}$ (+ עָתוּד *ready*) 9$_{20.27}$, שׁאר ni. *remain* Ne 1$_{2}$, מצא ni. *be found* Est 4$_{16}$, ישׁב *sit* Jr 32$_{12}$, *dwell* Jr 44$_{1}$ Est 9$_{19}$ Ne 4$_{6}$, hi. *marry* Ne 23$_{23}$, עמד *stand* Est 8$_{11}$ 9$_{16}$, נוח *rest* Est 9$_{16.18.22}$, שׁלח *send*, i.e. stretch, hand Est 9$_{2.15.16}$, אמר *say* Ne 4$_{6}$, חשׁב *plan* Ne 6$_{6}$, שׁמע *hear* Jr 40$_{11}$, בוא *come* Jr 40$_{12}$ Ne 4$_{6}$, שׁוב *go back* Jr 40$_{12}$, נדח ni. *be driven* Jr 40$_{12}$, נפל *fall* Jr 38$_{19}$, אסף *gather* Jr 40$_{12}$, קהל ni. *be gathered* Est 8$_{11}$ 9$_{2.15.16.18}$, מכר ni. *sell oneself* Ne 5$_{8}$, עזב *leave*, i.e. restore Ne 3$_{34}$, חיה pi. *revive* Ne 3$_{34}$, זבח *sacrifice* Ne 3$_{34}$, נכה hi. *strike* Est 9$_{5}$, הרג *kill* Est 8$_{11}$ 9$_{6.12.15.16}$, אבד pi. *destroy* Est 8$_{11}$ 9$_{6.12}$, שׁמד hi. *destroy* Est 8$_{11}$, חלל hi. *begin* Est 9$_{23}$, כלה pi. *finish* Ne 3$_{34}$, קבל pi. *receive*, i.e. undertake Est 9$_{23.27}$, עשׂה *do* Est 9$_{5+9t}$ Ne 3$_{34}$, עלל htp. *deal wantonly* Jr 38$_{19}$, שׁלט *have power* Est 9$_{1}$, מרד *rebel* Ne 6$_{6}$.

<NOM CL> הַיְּהוּדִים אֲשֶׁר־בְּמוֹאָב *the Jews who were in Moab* Jr 40$_{11}$, sim. Est 3$_{6}$ 8$_{5}$ 8$_{11}$ 9$_{15.16.18.20}$, הַיְּהוּדִים וְהַסְּגָנִים מֵאָה וַחֲמִשִּׁים אִישׁ *the Jews and the officials were a hundred and fifty persons* Ne 5$_{17}$.

<OBJ> ראה *see* Ne 13$_{23}$, נשׂא *lift*, i.e. assist Est 9$_{3}$, קנה *purchase* Ne 5$_{8}$, דאג *fear* Jr 38$_{19}$, צור *show hostility to* Est 8$_{11}$, כנס *gather* Est 4$_{16}$, נשׁל pi. *clear out* 2 K 16$_{6}$, גלה hi. *exile* Jr 52$_{30}$, המם *discomfit* Est 9$_{24}$, נכה hi. *strike* 2 K 25$_{25}$ Jr 41$_{3}$, הרג *kill* Est 3$_{13}$, אבד pi. *destroy* Est 3$_{13}$ 4$_{7}$ 8$_{5}$ 9$_{24}$, שׁמד hi. *destroy* Est 3$_{6.13}$.

<CSTR> צֹרֵר הַיְּהוּדִים *enemy of the Jews* Est 3$_{10}$ 8$_{1(Qr)}$ (Kt היהודיים) 9$_{10.24}$ (כָּל־הַיְּהוּדִים *of all the Jews*), אֹיְבֵי *enemies of* Est 9$_{1}$, ... עֵינֵי *eyes*, i.e. sight, *of* ... Jr 32$_{12}$, זֶרַע *seed of* Est 6$_{13}$, פַּחַד *fear of* Est 8$_{17}$, שְׁאָר *remainder of* Est 9$_{16}$, חבר היהודים *community of the Jews* Alexander Jannaeus Coins 12 ([היהודים]) 13 (חב יה) 14 (יהדים) 17 (היה) Hyrcanus II Coins 18 (היהדים) 18A (הידי) 19 20 (החבר היהדים) 22 (חב היהו) 23 (החבר הידי) appar. 28 29 (היהד) 30 ([ה[יהדים]; all thirteen 1st cent.), כָּל־הַיְּהוּדִים *all the Jews* Jr 32$_{12}$ 40$_{11.12}$ 41$_{3}$ 44$_{1}$ Est 3$_{6.13}$ 4$_{13.16}$ 9$_{20.24.30}$.

<APP> עַם *people* Est 3$_{6}$, אָח *brother* Ne 5$_{1.8}$, נֶפֶשׁ *soul*, i.e. person Jr 52$_{30}$, פְּרָזִי *hamlet-dweller* Est 9$_{19(Qr)}$ (Kt פרוזי), פְּלֵיטָה *survivors* Ne 1$_{2}$.

<ADJ> אֲמֵלָל *feeble* Ne 3$_{34}$.

<PREP> לְ of direction, *to*, + נגד hi. *tell* Ne 2$_{16}$, נתן *give*, i.e. allow Est 8$_{11}$, ni. *be given*, i.e. allowed Est 9$_{13}$; of possession, *of, (belonging) to* Est 4$_{3}$ 8$_{17}$ 10$_{3}$, + היה *be* Est 8$_{16}$; of benefit, *to, for*, + עמד *stand*, i.e. arise Est 4$_{14}$, הפך ni. *be turned* Est 9$_{22}$; בְּ of price, *(in exchange) for*, + שׁקל *weigh* Est 4$_{7}$; *against*, + שׁלח *send*, i.e. stretch, hand Est 8$_{7}$; שׁלט בְּ *have power over* Est 9$_{1}$; מִן of comparison, *(more) than*, + מלט ni. *escape* Est 4$_{13}$; אֶל *to*, + היה *be* Ne 5$_{1}$, שׁלח *send* Est 9$_{20.30}$, כתב *write* Est 9$_{23}$, ni. *be written* Est 8$_{9}$; *concerning*, + היה *be* Jr 44$_{1}$, צוה pi. *command* Est 8$_{9}$ (or em. אֶל to עַל *concerning*); עַל *upon*, + קבל pi. *take (obligation)*, + יְהוּדִי *Jew* Est 9$_{27}$, זֶרַע *seed*, i.e. descendants Est 9$_{27}$, לוה ni. ptc. *one who joins* Est 9$_{27}$; *concerning*, + כתב *write* Est 8$_{8}$, צוה pi. *command* Est 8$_{9}$ (if em.;

see above), שׁאל *ask* Ne 1$_{2}$; *against*, + חשׁב *devise* Est 8$_{3}$ 9$_{24.25}$ Ne 4$_{6}$ (if em. תָּשׁוּבוּ *you shall return* to חָשְׁבוּ *they devised*), *at*, or introducing object, + לעג hi. *mock* Ne 3$_{33}$; מִתּוֹךְ *from among*, + עבר *pass* Est 9$_{28}$.

3. as sing. noun, a particular **Jew, a.** masc., <SUBJ> ישׁב *sit* Est 5$_{13}$ 6$_{10}$, קום pi. *impose obligation* Est 9$_{31}$. <NOM CL> הוּא יְהוּדִי *he* (Mordecai) *was a Jew* Est 3$_{4}$, הַיְּהוּדִי מִשְׁנֶה לַמֶּלֶךְ ... וְגָדוֹל לַיְּהוּדִים Mordecai *the Jew was second (in rank) to the king ... and a great one of*, i.e. among, *the Jews* Est 10$_{3}$. <OBJ> ראה *see* Est 5$_{13}$. <CSTR> בַּת ... יְהוּדִי *daughter of ... the Jew* Est 9$_{29}$. <APP> Aha Samaria ost. 51$_{3}$ ([י]היהד), Mordecai Est 5$_{13}$ 6$_{10}$ 8$_{7}$ 9$_{29.31}$ 10$_{3}$, אָח *brother* Jr 34$_{9}$. <PREP> לְ of direction, *to*, + אמר *say* Est 8$_{7}$; of benefit, *to, for*, + עשׂה *do* Est 6$_{10}$; בְּ of instrument, *by (means of), with*, + עבד *work* Jr 34$_{9}$.

b. fem., <SUBJ> ילד *bear* 1 C 4$_{18}$. <APP> אִשָּׁה *wife* 1 C 4$_{18}$.

4. יְהוּדִית as adverb, **in Judaean,** i.e. Hebrew, the language of Judah, with דבר pi. *speak* 2 K 18$_{26}$||Is 36$_{11}$ (:: אֲרָמִית *in Aramaic*) Ne 13$_{24}$ (:: אַשְׁדּוֹדִית *in Ashdodite*), קרא *call* 2 K 18$_{28}$||Is 36$_{13}$||2 C 32$_{18}$.

⇒ יהד *be a Jew.*

יְהוּדִי II 4 pr.n.m. **Jehudi,** court official of Jehoakim, son of Nethaniah, <SUBJ> קרא *read* Jr 36$_{21.23}$, לקח *take* Jr 36$_{21}$. <OBJ> שׁלח *send* Jr 36$_{14.21}$. <APP> בֵּן *son* Jr 36$_{14}$.*

⇒ יהד *be a Jew.*

יְהוּדִית I 1 pr.n.f. **Judith,** wife of Esau, daughter of Beeri the Hittite, <SUBJ> היה *be* Gn 26$_{34}$ (+ מֹרָה *bitterness* of spirit). <OBJ> לקח *take* as wife Gn 26$_{34}$. <APP> בַּת *daughter* Gn 26$_{34}$.*

⇒ יהד *be a Jew.*

יְהוּדִית II, see יְהוּדִי *Jewish.*

יהוה 6828.66.181.32 pr.n.m. **Yhwh**—L יְהוָה (Qr שְׁמָא), sometimes יְהוָֹה (Qr אֲדֹנָי) (Gn 3$_{14}$ 9$_{26}$ Ex 3$_{2}$ 13$_{3.9.15}$ 14$_{1.8}$ Lv 25$_{17}$ Dt 31$_{27}$ 32$_{9}$ 33$_{12.13}$ 1 K 3$_{5}$ 16$_{33}$ Jr 2$_{37}$ 3$_{13.21.22.25}$ 4$_{3.8}$ 5$_{2.3.9.15.18.22.29}$ 6$_{9}$ 8$_{13}$ 30$_{10}$ 36$_{8}$ Ezk 33$_{23}$ 44$_{5}$ Na 1$_{3}$ Ps 15$_{1}$ 40$_{5}$ 47$_{6}$ 100$_{5}$ 116$_{5.6}$ Pr 1$_{29}$);* אֲדֹנָי יְהוִה, rarely אֲדֹנָי יֱהוִה (Qr אֲדֹנָי אֱלֹהִים) (Gn 15$_{2.8}$ Jg 16$_{28}$); יְהוִה אֲדֹנָי (Hb 3$_{19}$ Ps 109$_{21}$ 141$_{8}$), לֵיהוִה אֲדֹנָי (Ps 68$_{21}$), יְהוִה אֲדֹנָי (Ps 140$_{8}$), with Qr אֱלֹהִים אֲדֹנָי; prefixed forms מֵיְהוָה (Qr מֵשְׁמָא), מֵיהוָה rarely (1 S 24$_{7}$ 26$_{11}$ 1 K 21$_{3}$ Is 29$_{15}$); לַיהוָה, כַּיהוָה, וַיהוָה, הַיהוָה, (בַּיהוָֹה Jr 3$_{23}$) בַּיהוָה (Ex 13$_{12}$ Lv 23$_{34}$ Ezk 46$_{13}$ לַיהוָֹה; Ps 68$_{21}$ לֵיהוִה אֲדֹנָי), with Qr, appar., despite absence of holem, וַאדֹנָי, הַאדֹנָי, בַּאדֹנָי, כַּאדֹנָי, לַאדֹנָי; also לָמָּה יְהוָה (not לָמָּה), שֶׁיֱהוָה, הֲ־לַיְהוָה; Si ייי, יי, י׳י; Q ····; cstr. יהוה—not in Ca, Ec, or Est.

<SUBJ> **1.** Verbs of states and attributes, היה *be* Gn 26$_{28}$ (+ עִם *with*) 28$_{21}$ (+ לֵאלֹהִים *as God*) 39$_{2.21}$ (both + אֵת *with*) Ex 4$_{11}$ (+ עִם) 6$_{6}$ (+ לֵאלֹהִים) Lv 11$_{45}$ 22$_{33}$ 25$_{38}$ (all three + לֵאלֹהִים) Nm 14$_{43}$ (+ עִם) 15$_{41}$ Dt 26$_{17}$ (both + לֵאלֹהִים) 31$_{8}$ (+ עִם) 33$_{7}$ (+ עֵזֶר *help*) Jos 1$_{17.17}$ (both + עִם) 6$_{27}$ Jg 1$_{19}$ (both + אֵת) 2$_{18}$ (+ עִם) 11$_{10}$ (+ שֹׁמֵעַ *witness*) 1 S 3$_{19}$ 17$_{37}$ 18$_{12}$ 20$_{13.13}$ (all five + עִם) 1 S 20$_{42.42}$ (+ בֵּין *between*) 24$_{16}$ (+ לְדַיָּן *as a judge*) 1 S 28$_{16}$ (+ סָר *adversary*) 2 S 7$_{24}$ ||1 C 17$_{22}$ (+ לֵאלֹהִים) 2 S 14$_{17}$ (+ עִם) 2 S 22$_{19}$||Ps 18$_{19}$ (+ [לְ]מִשְׁעָן *[as] a support*) 1 K 1$_{37.37}$ (both + עִם) 8$_{57.57}$ (both + עִם) 1 K 10$_{9}$||2 C 9$_{8}$ (+ ברך pass. *be blessed*) 2 K 18$_{7}$ (+ עִם) Is 12$_{2}$ (+ לִישׁוּעָה *as deliverance*) 28$_{5}$ (+ לַעֲטֶרֶת *as a crown*, לִצְפִירָה *as a diadem*, לְרוּחַ מִשְׁפָּט ... וְלִגְבוּרָה *as a spirit of judgment ... and of valour*) 33$_{2}$ (+ יְשׁוּעָה *salvation*, זְרוֹעַ *arm* [or em. עֶזְרָה *help*]) 55$_{6}$ (+ קָרוֹב *near*) 60$_{19.20}$ (both + לְאוֹר *as light*) 63$_{7}$ (+ לְמוֹשִׁיעַ *as a deliverer*) Jr 15$_{16}$ (+ כְּמַיִם *as water*) 17$_{7}$ (+

מִבְטָח *security*) 30$_{21}$ 31$_{1.33}$ (all three + לֵאלֹהִים) 42$_5$ (+ לְעֵד *as a witness*) Ezk 14$_{11}$ 34$_{24}$ (both + לֵאלֹהִים) 36$_{10}$ (+ שָׁם *there*) 36$_{23}$ (+ לֵאלֹהִים) Am 5$_{14}$ (+ אֵת) Mc 1$_2$ (+ לְעֵד) Zc 2$_9$ (+ חוֹמַת אֵשׁ *wall of fire*) 2$_9$ (+ לְכָבוֹד *as glory*) 14$_9$ (+ לְמֶלֶךְ *as a king*) 14$_9$ (+ אֶחָד *unique*) Ps 9$_{10}$ (+ מִשְׂגָּב *stronghold*) 30$_{11}$ (+ עֹזֵר *helper*) 31$_2$ (+ לְצוּר־מָעוֹז *as a rock of stronghold;* לְבֵית מְצוּדוֹת *as a house of strongholds*) 71$_1$ (+ לְצוּר מָעוֹן *as a rock of habitation*) 94$_{22}$ (+ מִשְׂגָּב) 99$_8$ (+ אֵל נֹשֵׂא *a forgiving God*) 124$_{1.2}$ (both + לָנוּ *for us*) Pr 3$_{26}$ (+ בְּכִסְלֶךָ *as your confidence* or *at your side*) Lm 2$_{5(mss)}$ (+ כְּאוֹיֵב *as an enemy*) 1 C 22$_{11.16}$ 2 C 17$_3$ 19$_{11}$ (all four + עִם) Si 50$_{22}$ (+ בשלום *in peace*) Kuntillet ʿAjrud inscr. 2.2 (+ עִם).

טוב *be good* Ps 106$_1$||1 C 16$_{34}$ Ps 107$_1$ 118$_{1.29}$ 119$_{65}$ 136$_1$ Ezr 3$_{11}$ 2 C 5$_{13}$ 7$_3$, אדר *be exalted* Ex 15$_{11}$ (Sam נֶאְדָּרִי *my exalted one*), גבה *be exalted* Is 5$_{16}$, hi. *make high* Ezk 17$_{24}$, *arise* Ps 113$_5$, שׂגב ni. *be exalted* Is 2$_{11.17}$ 33$_5$, pi. *exalt* Is 9$_{10}$ Ps 107$_{31}$, רום *be exalted* Is 30$_{18}$ Ps 21$_{14}$ 99$_2$ 113$_4$ 138$_6$ 4QapPs^b 33$_2$, pol. *raise* 1 S 2$_7$ Ps 9$_{14}$ Si 11$_{12}$, hi. *raise* 1 S 2$_8$=Ps 113$_5$ 1 S 2$_{10}$ Ps 3$_4$ 27$_4$ 37$_{34}$ 92$_{10}$ 148$_{14}$ Lm 2$_{17}$ Si 47$_{11}$ GnzPs 3$_{20}$, גדל *be great* 2 S 7$_{22}$ Ml 1$_5$ Ps 35$_{27}$ =40$_{17}$ 104$_1$, הלל pu. *be praiseworthy* 2 S 22$_4$||Ps 18$_4$ (or em. מְהֻלָּל *worthy of praise* to מִמְּהֹלְלַי *because of those who mock me* or מְחֹלָל *wounded*) Ps 48$_2$ =96$_4$||1 C 16$_{25}$ Ps 145$_3$, כבד *be honoured* Is 66$_5$, ni. Ex 14$_{4.18}$ Is 24$_{23}$ (if em. כָּבוֹד *glory*) 26$_{15}$ Ezk 28$_{22}$ 39$_{13}$, hi. *make* heart *unresponsive* Ex 10$_1$, *make* chain *heavy* Lm 2$_{22}$, קנא pi. *be zealous* Jl 2$_{18}$ 4QapPent 2$_6$, ירא ni. *be feared* Ex 15$_{11}$ Zp 2$_{11}$ (or em. ראה ni. *appear*) Ps 47$_3$ 89$_7$ 96$_4$||1 C 16$_{25}$ Ps 130$_{3(mss)}$, ערץ ni. *be terrible* Ps 89$_7$.

ברך pass. *be blessed* Gn 9$_{26}$ (or em. בָּרוּךְ *one blessed of* Y. or בָּרֵךְ *bless*, O Y.) 24$_{27}$ 18$_{10}$ 1 S 25$_{32.39}$ 2 S 18$_{28}$ 1 K 1$_{48}$ 5$_{21}$||2 C 2$_{11}$ 1 K 8$_{15}$||2 C 6$_4$ 1 K 8$_{56}$ Zc 11$_5$ Ps 28$_6$ 31$_{22}$ 41$_{14}$=72$_{18}$=89$_{53}$=106$_{48}$=1 C 16$_{36}$ Ps 119$_{12}$ 124$_6$ 135$_{21}$ 144$_1$ Ru 2$_{20(ms)}$ 4$_{14}$ Ezr 7$_{27}$ 1 C 29$_{10}$ Si 51$_{30}$ 4QJub^g 25$_{12}$ 4QapJoshua^b 22.2$_5$ GnzPs 2$_{2.6}$ 3$_{10}$ 4$_{13.16}$ En-Gedi cave inscr.$_4$ (יהו[ה]; others יהון as part of pr.n.), pi. *bless* Gn 22$_{16}$ 24$_{1.35}$ 26$_{12}$ 27$_{27}$ 30$_{27.30}$ 39$_5$ Ex 20$_{11}$ Nm 6$_{24}$ Dt 2$_7$ 7$_{12.12}$ 14$_{24}$ 15$_{4.4.6.10.14.18}$ 16$_{15}$ 23$_{21}$ 24$_{19}$ 26$_{14}$ 28$_{8.12}$ 30$_{16}$ 33$_{11}$ Jos 17$_{14}$ Jg 13$_{24}$ 2 S 6$_{11}$||1 C 13$_{14}$ 2 S 6$_{12}$ 7$_{29}$||1 C 17$_{27}$ Is 19$_{25}$ Is 61$_9$ Jr 31$_{23}$ Ps 5$_{13}$ 29$_{11}$ 107$_{31}$ 109$_{27}$ 115$_{12.12.12.13}$ 128$_5$ 134$_3$ Jb 42$_{12}$ Pr 3$_{33}$ (mss יְבֹרַךְ the abode *will be blessed*) Ru 2$_4$ 1 C 17$_{27}$ 2 C 31$_{10}$ Si 36$_9$ ([ב]רך) 4QTestim$_{19}$ 4QpsJub^a 2.2$_{10}$ 4QpsJub^b 7$_2$ Ketef Hinnom inscr. 1$_{15}$ 2$_6$ Kuntillet ʿAjrud inscr. E2.2, pu. *be blessed* 1 C 17$_{27}$, אמן ni. *be faithful* Is 49$_7$ 4Q408 1$_6$.

2. Verbs of movement, הלך *go* Gn 18$_{33}$ Ex 13$_{21}$ Nm 14$_{14}$ Dt 1$_{30}$ 20$_4$ 23$_{15}$ (htp.) 31$_{6.8}$ Is 52$_{12}$ Zc 9$_{14}$, hi. *lead* Dt 8$_{2.14}$ Is 48$_{20}$ Jr 2$_{6.17}$, *cause to go* Ex 14$_{21}$= 4QRP^c 6a.1$_{13}$ Dt 28$_{36}$ Ps 125$_5$ Jb 12$_9$, *cause* rivers *to flow* Ezk 32$_{14}$.

בוא *come* Dt 33$_2$ 1 S 3$_{10}$ 4$_3$ Is 3$_{14}$ 13$_5$ 19$_1$ 40$_{10}$ perh. 59$_{19.20}$ 66$_{15}$ Ezk 44$_2$ Ho 6$_3$ Zc 2$_{14}$ 14$_5$ Ps 96$_{13}$ 96$_{13}$=98$_9$ =1 C 16$_{33}$ Ps 143$_1$, hi. *bring* Gn 2$_{19.22}$ 18$_{19}$ Ex 6$_7$ 13$_{5.11}$ 15$_{17}$ Lv 18$_3$ Nm 14$_{3.8.16}$ Dt 4$_{38}$ 6$_{10.23}$ 7$_1$ 8$_7$ 9$_{4.28}$ 11$_{29}$ 26$_9$ 29$_{26}$ (unless אַף *anger* is subject) 30$_5$ 33$_7$ Jos 23$_{15}$ 24$_7$ 2 S 7$_{18}$||1 C 17$_{16}$ 2 S 17$_{14}$ 1 K 9$_9$||2 C 7$_{22}$ 2 K 22$_{19}$||2 C 34$_{27}$ Is 7$_{17}$ 23$_8$ 48$_{14}$ (if em. אהב *love*) Jr 3$_{14}$ 5$_{15}$ 23$_{12}$ 25$_9$ 28$_4$ 45$_5$ 48$_{44}$ 49$_{5.32.37}$ Ezk 5$_{17}$ 11$_8$ 16$_8$ 20$_{7.12.42}$ 36$_{23}$ 40$_1$ Zc 13$_8$ Jb 42$_{11}$ Lm 2$_{22}$ Dn 9$_{14}$ 2 C 33$_{11}$ Si 45$_{19}$, *cause* sun *to set* Am 8$_9$, *bring about* Jr 40$_2$ Lm 1$_{20}$, בכר *bring about quickly* Lachish ost. 2$_5$ (others עכר *discomfit*), אתה *come* Dt 33$_2$, אנה *allow to come* Ps 88$_2$ (if em. ענה pi. *afflict*) Si 15$_{13(A)}$.

יצא *go out* Jg 4$_{14}$ 5$_4$ 2 S 5$_{24}$ Is 26$_{21}$ 42$_{13}$ Mc 1$_3$ Zc 14$_3$, hi. *take out* Gn 15$_{4.7}$ Ex 6$_{6.7}$ 7$_5$ 12$_{51}$ 13$_{3.9.14}$ 13$_{16}$=11QT 54$_{16}$ 16$_6$ 18$_1$ 20$_2$||Dt 5$_6$ Ex 29$_{46}$ Lv 19$_{36}$ 22$_{33}$ 25$_{38}$ 26$_{13}$ Nm 15$_{41}$ 20$_{16}$ Dt 1$_{27}$ 4$_{20.35}$ 5$_{15}$ 6$_{12.21.22}$ 7$_{8.19}$ 8$_{14.14}$ 9$_{26.28.28}$ 13$_{6.11}$ 16$_1$ 26$_8$ 29$_{24}$ Jg 2$_{12}$ 2 S 22$_{19}$||Ps 18$_{19}$ 1 K 8$_{21.53}$ 9$_9$ ||2 C 7$_{22}$ Is 43$_{17}$ Jr 31$_{32}$ 50$_{25}$ 51$_{10}$ Ezk 11$_8$ 20$_{7.7.12.20.38}$ 21$_{10}$ 37$_1$ Mc 7$_9$ Zc 5$_4$ Ps 26$_{15}$ 31$_2$ 107$_{13.28}$ 135$_6$ 142$_6$ 143$_{11}$ Jb 12$_9$ Dn 9$_{15(mss)}$ Ne 9$_{7.7}$.

שׁוב *go back* Nm 10$_{36}$ Dt 13$_{18}$ 23$_{15}$ 30$_{3.3.9}$ Jos 7$_{26}$ 24$_{20}$ 2 K 23$_{26}$ Is 52$_8$ 63$_{17}$ Jr 29$_{14}$ 30$_3$ Jl 2$_{14}$ Am 4$_{10}$ Zc 1$_{3.16}$ Ps 6$_5$ 7$_7$ (or em. יֹשֵׁב *sit*) 90$_{13}$ 132$_{11}$ Dn 9$_{16(mss)}$ 2 C 30$_6$, *restore* from exile Jr 48$_{47}$ 49$_{39(Kt)}$ Zp 2$_7$ Ps 14$_7$ 85$_2$ 126$_{1.4}$ Jb 42$_{10}$, appar. *do repeatedly* Lm 2$_{22}$, hi. *take back* Gn 28$_{13}$ Ex 15$_{19}$ Dt 28$_{68}$ 1 S 25$_{39}$ 2 S 15$_8$ 16$_8$ 1 K 2$_{32.44}$ 2 K 20$_{11}$ Is 44$_{24}$ 66$_{15}$ Jr 27$_{22}$ 28$_6$ 29$_{14}$ 30$_3$ 31$_{18}$ 32$_{44}$ 34$_{22}$ 49$_{6.39(Qr)}$ Na 2$_3$ Zc 10$_6$ (if em. יֹשֵׁב hi. *accommodate*) 13$_7$ Ps 80$_{20}$ 81$_{11}$ Ru 1$_{21}$ Lm 5$_{21}$, *remove* Ezk 20$_{20}$ Ps 85$_2$ (mss שׁבת hi. *cause to cease*) 132$_8$=2 C 6$_{42}$ Pr 24$_{18}$ Lm 2$_{2(mss)}$ 2$_8$, *repay* 1 S 26$_{23}$ 2 S 16$_{12}$ 22$_{21.25}$||Ps 18$_{21.25}$ Ho 12$_3$ Ps 54$_{6(mss)}$ (Kt שׁוב qal) Lm 3$_{64}$, pol. *restore* Ps 23$_1$, סור *depart* Jg 16$_{20}$ 1 S 18$_{12}$ 28$_{16}$, hi. *remove* Ex 8$_{4.27}$ 10$_{17}$ 14$_{25}$ (Sam אסר *lock* wheel) Dt 7$_{15}$ Nm 21$_7$ 2 K 17$_{18.23}$ 24$_3$ Is 3$_1$ 25$_8$ Ezk 36$_{23}$

Zp 3_{15} Jb $12_{9.9}$ 2 C 30_9, pol. *divert* Lm 2_{22}, הפך *turn* Ex 10_{19} Zp 3_8 Lm 2_{22}, *transform* Dt 23_6 Am 5_8 Ps 30_{11} 41_4, פנה *turn* Dt 9_{26} Jg 6_{14} 1 K 8_{28}||2 C 6_{19} 2 K 13_{23} Ml 2_{13} Ps 69_{17} 102_{17}, pi. *clear away* Zp 3_{15}, סבב hi. *cause to turn* 1 K 18_{37} Ezr 6_{22} 1 C 10_{14}, עוד pol. *restore* Ps 146_9 147_6, שׁנה *change (oneself)* Ml 3_6, pi. *change* ways Si 36_{11}.

קרב *approach* Ps 69_{17} Lm 3_{55}, hi. *bring near* Nm $16_{5.5}$ Jr 30_{21}, קדם pi. *approach* Ps 17_{13} 21_2, פגשׁ *meet* Ex 4_{24}, קרא *meet* Nm $23_{3.16(Sam)}$, קרה ni. *meet* Ex 3_{18} Nm $23_{3.16}$, hi. *grant success* Gn 24_{12} 27_{20}, רדף pi. *pursue* Na 1_7 (or em. הדף *push*) Lm 3_{64}, עבר *pass* Ex $12_{12.23}$ 34_6 Dt 9_3 31_3 1 K 19_{11} Ezk 16_8 Mc 2_{13}, hi. *cause to pass* Jos $7_{7.7}$ 2 S 12_{13} 24_{10} Ezk 37_1 Zc 13_2 Ps $119_{33.33}$ Si 47_2 4QActs 1_5, htp. *be angry* Dt 3_{26} Ps 78_{21}, פסח *pass over* Ex $12_{23.27}$ 31_5, רחק *be distant* Ps 22_{20} 38_{22}, pi. *distance* Is 6_{12} 26_{15}, hi. *make distant* Ps $88_{2.15}$ 103_8, חלץ *withdraw* Ho 5_6, pi. *deliver* 2 S 22_{19}||Ps 18_{19} Ps 6_5 140_2, דרך *tread* Am 4_{13} Lm $1_{15(mss)}$, *bend* bow Lm $2_{2(mss).22}$, hi. *cause to tread* Is 48_{17} Hb 3_{19} Ps 25_8 107_6 119_{33}, צעד *march* Jg 5_4, פשׂע *march* Is 27_3, רכב *ride* Is 19_1 Hb 3_8.

עלה *go up* Ps 47_6, ni. *be exalted* Ps 97_9, hi. *take up* Lv 11_{45} Dt 20_1 28_{61} Jos 24_{17} Jg 6_{13} 1 S 2_6 12_6 2 K 2_1 $17_{7.36}$ Jr 2_6 $16_{14.15}$ $23_{7.8}$ 27_{22} 30_{17} Ezk $37_{6.13}$ Ho 12_{14} Am 4_{10} 9_7 Jon 2_7 Ps 30_4 40_2 81_{11} 135_6 2 C 36_{16}, קום *arise* Nm 10_{35} Is $2_{19.21}$ 14_{22} 28_{21} Zp 3_8 Ps 3_8 7_7 9_{20} 10_{12} 12_6 17_{13} 102_{13} 132_8=2 C 6_{41}, hi. *raise* Dt 8_{18} 9_5 18_{15} 28_9 Jg $2_{16.18}$ $3_{9.15}$ 1 S 1_{23} 2_8=Ps 113_5 2 S 7_{25} 1 K 2_4 8_{20}||2 C 6_{10} 1 K 11_{14} 12_{15}||2 C 10_{15} 1 K 14_{14} 15_4 Is 44_{24} Jr $23_{4.5}$ 29_{15} Ho 6_1 Am 2_{11} 6_{14} Ps 41_{11} $110_{5(mss)}$, *establish* Ex 6_3 Jr 28_6 33_{14} Ezk 16_{62} Ps 40_2 78_4 107_{28} 119_{33} Ne 9_7 Si 50_{22}, גאה *arise* Ex $15_{1.21}$ (in both גָּאֹה גָּאָה *he has indeed arisen*; Sam גּוֹי גָּאָה *a nation has arisen*), נצב ni. *stand* Gn 28_{13} Is 3_{13}, hi. *set up* Pr 15_{25} Lm 2_{22}, יצב htp. *stand* Ex 34_5 1 S 3_{10}, עמד *stand* Nm 12_5 Ps 10_1 109_{30}, hi. *establish* 1 K 15_4 Ps 30_8 105_7||1 C 16_{14} Ps 107_{24} 148_5 (or em. qal *arise*, of wind) 4QapJoshua[a] 11_1 ([ה]עמיד) 4QConfess 2_6.

ירד *go down* Gn 11_5 Ex $19_{11.18.20}$ 34_5 Nm 11_{25} 12_5 Jg 5_{13} (if em. רדה pi. *rule*; or em. עַם י׳ *people*; *Y.* to עַם י׳ *the people of Y.* went down/will rule) Is 31_4 $63_{17.17}$ Mc 1_3 Ps 144_5 Ne 9_7, hi. *take down* 1 S 2_6 Jr 49_{16}||Ob$_4$ Jl 2_{23}, נחת hi. *take down* Jl 4_{11}, נפל hi. *cause to fall* Gn 2_{21} 1 S 3_{19} Jr 3_{12} Ps $106_{25.25}$, רפה pi. *cause to drop* Jb 12_9, hi. *abandon* Dt $31_{6.8}$ Ps 138_8 1 C 28_{20} Si 51_{10}, *apportion* Is 34_{16}, רבץ hi. *allow to lie down* Ezk 34_{15} Ps 23_1, ישׁב *sit*, perh. specif. *be enthroned* 1 S 4_4 2 S 6_2||1 C 13_6 2 K 19_{15} ||Is 37_{16} Ps 7_7 (if em. שׁוב *go back*) $29_{10.10}$ 99_1 102_{13}=Lm 5_{19} Ps 113_5 4QapPs[b] 76_{12}, *dwell* Ex 15_{17} Ps $9_{8.12}$, hi. *accommodate* 1 S 2_8=Ps 113_5 1 K 2_{24} Ezk 36_{11} Ho 11_{11} 12_{10} Zc 10_6 (or em. שׁוב hi. *take back*) Ps 4_9 107_{31} 113_5 Lm 2_{22}, שׁכן *dwell* Nm 35_{34} 1 K 8_{12}||2 C 6_1 Is 8_{18} 33_5 Jl $4_{17.21}$ Zc 2_{14} Ps 68_{17} 135_{21} 1 C 23_{25}, perh. Dt $33_{12.12}$ (unless Benjamin is subj. in both) 11QT 45_{14} 51_7, pi. *establish* Gn 3_{23} Dt 14_{23} $16_{2.6.11}$ 26_2.

נהג *lead* Is 63_7, נחה *lead* Gn 24_{27} Ex 15_{11} Is 58_{11} Ps 5_9 27_{11}, hi. Gn 24_{48} Ex 13_{21} Dt 32_{12} Ps 23_1 31_2 107_{28} Jb 12_9 (or em. נוח hi. *leave*) Ne 9_7, נהל pi. *lead* Ex 15_{11} (Sam נחל pi. *cause to inherit*) Ps 23_1 31_2 2 C 32_{22}.

שׁלח *send* Gn $24_{7.40}$ Ex 3_{15} 7_{16} Nm $16_{28.29}$ 20_{16} Dt 9_{23} 34_{11} Jg 6_8 1 S $12_{8.11}$ $15_{1.18.20}$ 2 S $12_{1.25}$ 22_{14}||Ps 18_{14} 2 S 24_{12}||1 C 21_{12} 2 K $2_{2.4.6}$ 1QIsa[a] 9_7 (MT אֲדֹנָי) Is 19_{20} 48_{16} 61_1 Jr 1_9 14_{15} $16_{16.16}$ 19_{14} 23_{32} $25_{4.9.17}$ $26_{12.15}$ 27_{15} $28_{9.15}$ $29_{9.19}$ $42_{5.21}$ $43_{1.2}$ Ezk 13_6 Jl 2_{19} Hg 1_{12} Zc 1_{10} $2_{13.15}$ 4_9 6_{15} 7_{12} Ps 105_7 107_{19} 110_2 135_6 $144_{5.5}$ 2 C 24_{19} 25_{15} 32_{21} 36_{15} 4QparaKings 11_1, pi. *send away* Gn 3_{23} 19_{13} Nm 21_6 Dt 7_{20} 28_{20} 1 S 20_{22} 2 K 17_{25} $24_{2.2}$ Is 10_{16} Jr 8_{17} 48_{12} 49_{37} Ezk 5_{17} 28_{23} 39_6 Ps 81_{11} 104_{24} Jb 12_9, hi. 2 K 15_{37} 24_{20}||Jr 52_3.

נהג pi. *drive away* Dt 4_{27} 28_{37}, *make* wind *blow* Ex 10_{13}, נשׁל *drive away* Dt $7_{1.22}$, גרשׁ pi. *expel* Gn 3_{23} Jos 24_{18}, ירשׁ hi. *dispossess* Dt 4_{35} $9_{4.5}$ 11_{23} 18_{12} Jos $23_{5.9.13}$ Jg 2_{23} $11_{23.24}$ 1 S 2_7 1 K 14_{24} 21_{26} 2 K 16_3||2 C 28_3 2 K 17_8 21_2||2 C 33_2 Zc $9_{4(mss)}$ 2 C 28_5 29_8, נדח hi. *banish* Dt 30_1 Jr 8_3 16_{15} 23_8 27_{15} 29_{14} 46_{28}, מושׁ appar. *remove* Zc 3_9 (or em. hi. *remove*).

שׁלך hi. *throw* Dt 29_{27} Jos 10_{11} 2 K 13_{23} 17_{20} Na 3_5 Ps 71_5 Lm $2_{1(mss)}$ Ne 9_7, ירה *throw* Ex 15_3, רמה *throw* Ex $15_{1.21}$, קלע pi. *sling* 1 S 25_{29}, טול pilp. *hurl* or perh. *shake* Is 22_{17}, hi. *send* wind Jon 1_4, נוף hi. *brandish* Is 11_{15} 19_{16}, נער pi. *shake off* Ex 14_{27}, *shake* someone *free* Si 11_{12}, הדף *push* Dt 9_4 (Sam דוף hi. *push*) Jos 23_5 Jr 46_{15} Na 1_7 (if em. רדף pi. *pursue*) Pr 10_3, *overthrow* Gn 19_{25} Dt 29_{22} Jr 20_{16} Am 4_{11}, זרה pi. *scatter* 1 K 14_{15} Jr 31_{10} 49_{32} Ezk 12_{15} 20_{20} 30_{26} Ps 106_{25}, *sift* or *measure* Ps 139_1, פוץ hi. *scatter* Gn $11_{8.9}$ Dt 4_{27} 28_{65} 30_3 2 S 22_{14}||Ps 18_{14}

Is 24_{1} Jr 30_{11} Ezk 12_{15} 20_{20} 30_{26} Ps 144_{5}.

נטה *extend* hand Ex 7_{5} 15_{11} Is 5_{25} 23_{11} Jr 6_{12} 15_{6} 51_{25} Ezk 6_{14} 14_{9} 25_{7} Zp 2_{11} 4QpIsa[b] 2_{8}, heavens Is 42_{5} 44_{24} 51_{13} Zc 12_{1} Ps 104_{1}, loyalty Gn 39_{21}, line Lm 2_{8}, light Ps 4_{7} (if em. נשׂא *raise*), hi. *turn* towards worshipper Ps 40_{2}, *incline* ear 2 K 19_{16}||Is 37_{17} Ps 31_{2}=71_{1} 86_{1} 88_{2} 116_{2}, human heart 1 K 8_{57} Ps 119_{33} 141_{3} Pr 21_{1}, *extend* arm Is 31_{3}, *direct* favour Ezr 7_{27}, *tilt* heavens Ps 144_{5}, פרשׂ pi. *stretch out* hands perh. Is 25_{10}, garment Ezk 16_{8}, Zion Zc 2_{10} (or em. כנס *gather*), רקע *extend* earth Is 42_{5} 44_{24}, שׁטח *enlarge* nations Jb 12_{9}, קרם *cover with* skin Ezk 37_{6}.

נתן *give* Gn $15_{2.2.7}$ 24_{35} 28_{13} 29_{33} 39_{21} Ex $6_{3.7.7}$ 9_{23} 11_{3} $12_{23.25.36}$ $13_{5.11}$ $16_{8.9.15.29.29}$ 20_{12}||Dt 5_{16} Ex $36_{1.2}$ Lv 25_{38} Nm 11_{18} 14_{8} $32_{7.9}$ Dt $1_{8.20.25.27}$ $2_{12.29.30}$ $3_{3.18.20}$ $4_{1.21.35.40}$ 5_{22} $6_{10.22.23}$ $7_{2.16}$ 8_{10} $9_{6.10.11}$ 10_{4} $11_{9.13.13.17.21.31}$ $12_{1.9.21}$ $13_{13.18}$ $15_{4.7}$ $16_{5.17.18.20}$ $17_{2.14}$ $18_{9.14}$ $19_{1.2.8.8.10.14}$ $20_{13.14.16}$ 21_{1} Dt $21_{10.23}$ 24_{4} $25_{15.19}$ $26_{1.2.3.10.11.14}$ $27_{2.3}$ $28_{8.11.12.52.53.65}$ 29_{3} 30_{20} Jos $1_{11.13.15}$ $2_{9.14.24}$ 6_{16} 7_{7} 8_{7} $10_{19.30.32}$ 11_{8} 18_{3} $21_{43.43.44}$ $23_{13.15}$ Jg 1_{4} $2_{14.23}$ $3_{10.28}$ 4_{14} $6_{1.13}$ 7_{15} 8_{7} $11_{21.32}$ 12_{3} 13_{1} 1 S $1_{11.27}$ 2_{10} $12_{17.18}$ $14_{10.12}$ 15_{28} 17_{47} 24_{11} 26_{23} $28_{17.19.19}$ $30_{23.23}$ 2 S 4_{8} 16_{8} 1 K 1_{48} 5_{21}||2 C 2_{11} 1 K 5_{26} 8_{56} 13_{26} 14_{15} 15_{4} 17_{14} 22_{12}||2 C 18_{11} 1 K 22_{15} 2 K $3_{10.13.18}$ 5_{1} 8_{19}||2 C 21_{7} 2 K 13_{5} 17_{20} 1QIsa[a] 7_{14} (MT אֲדֹנָי) Is 8_{18} 34_{2} 40_{28} $42_{5.8}$ $43_{3.3}$ 50_{4} 61_{8} Jr 5_{24} 8_{13} 15_{9} 17_{10} 21_{7} 25_{5} 25_{30}||Jl 4_{16}||Am 1_{2} Jr 25_{31} 27_{8} (if em. תֻּמִּי *my completing* to תִּתִּי *my giving*) 30_{3} 34_{17} 45_{5} 46_{26} Ezk 7_{9} 11_{8} 16_{19} $20_{7.12.12.20.42}$ 25_{7} $29_{20.21}$ $36_{23.23.23}$ Ho $9_{14.14.14}$ Jl $2_{11.23}$ Am 4_{6} Zp 3_{5} Hg 2_{9} Zc 10_{1} Ps $21_{2.2}$ 27_{11} 29_{11} 37_{4} 55_{23} 84_{12} $85_{8.13}$ 99_{6} $104_{24.2}$ 106_{40} $115_{1.16}$ 121_{2} 127_{1} 135_{6} 140_{9} 146_{5} 148_{5} Jb 1_{21} Pr 2_{6} 3_{33} Ru $1_{6.9}$ $4_{12.13}$ Lm $1_{14(mss)}$ 3_{64} Dn 9_{10} Ezr 1_{2}=2 C 36_{23} Ezr $7_{6.27}$ 9_{8} Ne $9_{7.7.7.7.7}$ 1 C $22_{12.18}$ 28_{5} $29_{18.25}$ 2 C 1_{9} 2_{10} 13_{5} 16_{8} 24_{24} 25_{9} 32_{24} 36_{16} Si $45_{19.25}$ 47_{11} 50_{22} 51_{22} 4QJub[g] 25_{12} 4QapJoshua[a] 11_{1} 12_{3} 4QConfess 2_{6}.

נתן *place* Lv 26_{46} Nm $11_{25.29}$ Dt $1_{8.21}$ $2_{33.36}$ $7_{15.23}$ 11_{25} 21_{8}=11QT 63_{7} 23_{15} 26_{19} $28_{1.48}$ 30_{7} 31_{5} Jos 10_{12} 22_{25} Jg 11_{9} 1 S 12_{13} 2 S 24_{16}||1 C 21_{14} 1 K 5_{17} 10_{9}||2 C 9_{8} 1 K 22_{23} ||2 C 18_{22} Is 43_{16} Jr $31_{33.35}$ Ezk 7_{4} 11_{21} 14_{8} 15_{7} 16_{43} 22_{31} $25_{14.17}$ 30_{25} 32_{8} 32_{32} (or em. נָתַתִּי *I placed* to נָתַן Pharaoh *placed*) $36_{23.23.23}$ $37_{6.6.14}$ Jl 2_{27} Jon 1_{14} Zc 3_{9} Ps 4_{7} 8_{2} (or em. נִתַּן your glory *is placed* or נָתְנָה the earth *has given*) 33_{6} 40_{2} 1 C 14_{17} 2 C 20_{22}, *cause to be* Nm $5_{21.21}$ Dt $28_{7.13.24.25}$ Is 3_{1} 42_{6} Jr 15_{20} 19_{12} 29_{26} $34_{17.17.22}$ 51_{25} Ezk 5_{13} 6_{14} 15_{8} 26_{21} 30_{12} 32_{15} 33_{29} 35_{9} Jl $2_{17.19}$ Ps 106_{40} 124_{6} Ru 4_{11} 1 C 17_{20} 2 C 30_{7}.

שׂים *place* Gn 2_{8} 4_{15} Ex 4_{11} $8_{8.18}$ 9_{5} $15_{26.26}$ Nm 6_{26} $23_{5.12.16}$ Dt 7_{15} 10_{22} $12_{5.21}$ 14_{21} Jos 24_{7} Jg 7_{22} 1 K 10_{9} 14_{21} ||2 C 12_{13} Is 51_{15} Jr 5_{22} 21_{10} 49_{38} Ezk 15_{7} 16_{14} Ps 78_{4} 85_{13} Pr 8_{22} Si 36_{11}, *cause to be* Ex 4_{11} 14_{21} 15_{25} Is 14_{23} 25_{1} 41_{14} $49_{1.1}$ 51_{3} Jr $25_{9.12}$ 29_{22} Ezk 35_{4} Mc 4_{6} Na 3_{5} Hb 1_{12} 3_{19} Zp 2_{11} Hg 2_{23} Zc 10_{3} Ml 1_{2} Ps 46_{9} $107_{31.31.31}$ Lm 2_{22} Ne 9_{7}, *perform* signs Ex 10_{2}, שׁית *place* Ps 8_{2} 9_{21} 12_{6} 21_{2} 88_{2} 139_{4} 141_{3}, *cause to be* Jr 51_{39} Ps 21_{2} 88_{2}, *perform* signs Ex 10_{1}, שׁוה pi. *place* Ps 21_{2}.

נוח hi. *place* Gn 2_{15} Is 14_{1} Ezk 37_{14}, *leave* Jg 2_{23} 3_{1} Jr 14_{9} 27_{11} Jb 12_{9} (if em. נחה hi. *lead*) Ps 119_{108}, *cause to rest* Is 30_{32} 37_{1}, *secure rest* Dt 3_{20} 12_{10} 25_{19} Jos $1_{13.15}$ 21_{44} 22_{4} 23_{1} 2 S 7_{1}||1 C 17_{1} 1 K 5_{18} Is 14_{3} 1 C 22_{18} 23_{25} 2 C $14_{5.6}$ 15_{15}, *permit* Ps 105_{7}||1 C 16_{14}, *vent* anger Ezk 21_{22}.

מצא *find* Jr 23_{11} Ps 17_{1} Ne 9_{7}, ni. *let oneself be found* Is 55_{6} Jr 29_{14} 1 C 28_{9} 2 C $15_{2.4.15}$, hi. *give* Zc 11_{6}, אצל (perh. hi.) *withhold* Nm 11_{25} (Sam נצל hi. *take away*) Ps 119_{41} (if em. נצל hi. *take away*), חשׂך *withhold* 1 S 25_{39}, מנע *withhold* Nm 24_{11} 1 S $25_{26.34}$ Ps 21_{2} 84_{12}, כלא *withhold* Ps 40_{12}, לקח *take* Gn $2_{15.21.22}$ 24_{7} Ex 6_{6} Dt 4_{20} 30_{4} 1 K 19_{4} 2 K $2_{3.5}$ Jr 3_{14} 15_{15} Ezk 36_{23} Am 7_{15} Jon 4_{3} Jb 1_{21} 12_{9} 4QparaKings 9_{5}, *accept* Ml 2_{13} Ps 6_{10}, לכד *take* Jos 7_{14}, נחל *take as a possession* Zc 2_{15}, pi. *cause to inherit* Ex $15_{11(Sam)}$, hi. *give as an inheritance* Dt 12_{10} 19_{3}, מכר *sell* Jg 2_{14} 3_{8} $4_{2.9}$ 10_{7} 1 S 12_{9} Ezk 30_{12}.

אסף *gather* 2 K 22_{19}||2 C 34_{27} Jr 8_{13} Mc 4_{6} Zp $1_{2.3.3}$ (if em. סוף hi. in all three) 3_{8} Ps 26_{8} 27_{10}, *remove* Jr 16_{5} Ps 85_{2} 104_{24}, חוק *gather* foundations of earth Pr 8_{22} (unless חקק *engrave*, i.e. establish; or em. חזק pi. *strengthen*), כנס pi. *gather* Ezk 39_{28} Ps 33_{6} 147_{2}, קבץ *gather* Zp 3_{8}, pi. *gather* Dt $30_{3.4}$ Is $56_{8.8}$ Jr 23_{2} 31_{10} Ezk 36_{23} Mc $4_{6.12}$ Ps 106_{47}.

נשׂא *raise* Nm 6_{26} Dt 28_{49} 2 K 9_{25} Is 10_{26} Ps 4_{7} (נָסָה; ms נָשָׂא; or em. נָסְעָה light *has set out* or נָטֵה *extend* light) Jb 42_{9} Si 11_{12}, specif. *raise* hand to swear Ex 6_{7} Ezk $20_{5.5.5.12.20.42}$ 44_{12} Ps 106_{25} Ne 9_{7}, *carry* Dt 1_{31}, *bear consequences of* Jr 44_{22} Ps 32_{5}, *forgive* sin Ex 34_{6} Nm 14_{18} Jos 24_{19} Ps 85_{2}, ni. *rise* Ps 7_{7}, pi. *exalt* 2 S 5_{12} Is 63_{7}, זקף *raise* Ps 145_{14} 146_{8}, נטל pi. *raise* Is 63_{7}.

שׁמר *keep* Gn 28_{13} Nm 6_{24} Dt $7_{9.12}$ Jos 24_{17} 1 S 30_{23} 2 S

22$_{22}$||Ps 18$_{22}$ 1 K 8$_{23.25}$||2 C 6$_{14.16}$ Jr 5$_{24}$ 31$_{10}$ Ps 12$_{8}$ 34$_{20}$ 41$_{3}$ 86$_{1}$ 97$_{10}$ 116$_{6}$ 121$_{5.7.7.8}$ 127$_{1}$ 140$_{5}$ 141$_{8}$ (mss אֱלֹהִים *God*) 145$_{20}$ 146$_{5.9}$ Pr 2$_{6}$ 3$_{26}$ Ne 1$_{5}$ 1 C 29$_{18}$ Ketef Hinnom inscr. 1$_{15}$ 2$_{6}$ Kuntillet ʿAjrud inscr. 2.2, נצר *keep* Ex 34$_{6}$ Is 27$_{3}$ Ps 12$_{8}$ 31$_{24}$ 140$_{2.5}$ Pr 2$_{6}$ 20$_{27}$ (if em. נֵר י׳ *lamp of* Y. to נֹצֵר י׳ *Y. keeps*).

כסה pi. *cover* Is 29$_{10}$ 51$_{15}$ Ps 85$_{2}$, חפף *cover* Dt 33$_{12}$ (or em. עָלָיו *above/beside him;* to עֶלְיוֹן *Elyon* or עַל *Al* covers), גנן *cover,* i.e. protect Is 31$_{5.5}$ Zc 9$_{15}$ 12$_{8}$, סכך *cover,* i.e. protect Ps 91$_{2}$ (hi.) 140$_{8}$, צור *enclose* Ps 139$_{4}$, נקף hi. *surround* Lm 2$_{22}$, עטר *surround* Ps 5$_{13}$, pi. *crown* Ps 8$_{2}$ 103$_{2}$ Si 45$_{25}$, חבא hi. *conceal* Is 49$_{1}$, סתר ni. *hide oneself* Ps 89$_{47}$, hi. *conceal* Is 8$_{17}$ 49$_{1}$ Jr 36$_{26}$ Ezk 39$_{29}$ Mc 3$_{4}$ Ps 13$_{2}$ 22$_{24}$ 27$_{4}$ 30$_{8}$ 31$_{18}$ 69$_{17}$ 88$_{15}$ 104$_{24}$ 143$_{7}$, צפן *conceal* Ps 27$_{4}$ 31$_{18}$, *store* Ps 31$_{18}$ Pr 2$_{6}$, עלם hi. *conceal* 2 K 4$_{27}$ Ps 10$_{1}$ Lm 3$_{55}$, גלה *uncover* ear 1 S 9$_{15}$ 2 S 7$_{27}$, ni. *be revealed* 1 S 3$_{21}$ Is 22$_{14}$, pi. *uncover* Nm 22$_{31}$ Na 3$_{5}$ Ps 98$_{2}$ Jb 12$_{9}$, hi. *(take into) exile* 2 K 17$_{11}$ Jr 29$_{14}$ Ezk 39$_{28}$ 1 C 5$_{41}$.

מלא *fill* Ps 110$_{6(mss)}$, pi. *fill* Ex 35$_{30}$ Is 33$_{5}$ Jr 15$_{16}$ 23$_{24}$ Ps 17$_{14}$ 81$_{11}$ 83$_{17}$ 107$_{8}$ 110$_{6(mss)}$ (if em. מָלֵא גְוִיּוֹת *full of corpses* to בְּגְוִיּוֹת מִלֵּא גֵאָיוֹת *he has filled valleys with corpses*), *fulfil* 1 K 8$_{15}$||2 C 6$_{4}$ Ps 20$_{6}$, יתר hi. *make abundant* Dt 28$_{11}$ 30$_{9}$, *leave over* Is 1$_{9}$ Ezk 12$_{16}$ 39$_{28}$, רחב *broaden* Dt 12$_{20}$, hi. *broaden* Gn 26$_{22}$ Dt 19$_{8}$ Ps 119$_{31}$, רבה hi. *multiply* Gn 22$_{16}$ Dt 1$_{10}$ 7$_{12}$ 13$_{18}$ 30$_{5}$ Jr 46$_{15}$ (or em. הִרְבָּה *he multiplied* to רַהַב הָרַב *the great Rahab* or וַהֲמוֹנֵךְ *and your multitude*) Ezk 36$_{11.23.23}$ Ho 12$_{10}$ Lm 2$_{5(mss)}$ 1 C 27$_{23}$, חסר pi. *diminish* Ps 8$_{2}$, מעט hi. *diminish* Jr 10$_{24}$ Ps 107$_{31}$, קצר pi. *shorten* Ps 102$_{23}$ (or em. קָצְרוּ my days *were shortened*), גלל pilp. *roll* Babylon Jr 51$_{25}$.

פתח *open* Gn 29$_{31}$ Nm 22$_{28}$ Dt 28$_{12}$ Is 45$_{1}$ 50$_{5}$ Jr 50$_{25}$ Ezk 33$_{22}$ 37$_{13}$ Ps 104$_{24}$ 4QapJoseph[b] 3$_{7}$, pi. *ungird* Is 45$_{1}$, *loosen* Ps 30$_{11}$ 116$_{16}$ Jb 12$_{9}$, פקח *open* eyes 2 K 6$_{17.17.20.20}$ 19$_{16}$||Is 37$_{17}$ Zc 12$_{4}$ Ps 146$_{8}$.

שׂתם *shut out* prayer Lm 2$_{22}$ (mss סתם *shut up*), סגר *shut* Gn 2$_{21}$ 7$_{16}$ 1 S 1$_{5.6}$ Jb 12$_{9}$ 11QPsAp[a] 4$_{8}$, pi. *hand* someone *over* 1 S 17$_{46}$ 24$_{19}$ 2 S 18$_{28}$, hi. *hand* someone *over* Dt 32$_{30}$, *hand* city *over* Am 6$_{8}$ Lm 2$_{7(mss)}$, סכר pi. *hand* Egyptians *over* Is 19$_{4}$, עצם pi. *shut* eyes Is 29$_{10}$.

חלק *apportion* Dt 4$_{19}$, בדל hi. *separate* Lv 20$_{24}$ Dt 10$_{8}$ 29$_{20}$ 1 K 8$_{53}$ Is 56$_{3}$ Si 36$_{11}$ 11QPsAp[a] 1$_{11}$ ([יהוה]) 11QT 51$_{7}$, פלה hi. *separate* Ex 9$_{4}$ 11$_{7}$ Ps 4$_{4}$, בלל *mix* Gn 11$_{9}$ Ps 92$_{11}$ (if em. בַּלֹּתִי appar. *I have mixed* to בַּלֹּתַנִי *you have mixed*, i.e. anointed), מסך *mix* Is 19$_{14}$, אסר *bind* wheel Ex 14$_{25(Sam)}$, Belial 11QPsAp[a] 4$_{8}$ (ך[יאסר]), *fasten* belt Jb 12$_{9}$, דבק hi. *cause to cling* Dt 28$_{21}$ Jr 13$_{11}$, חשׂף *expose* Is 52$_{10}$, ערה pi. *expose* Is 3$_{17}$ (1QIsa[a] אדוני) Zp 2$_{11}$ (or del. ערה pi.), *pour out* Ps 141$_{8}$ (mss אֱלֹהִים *God*), עוה pi. *twist* Is 24$_{1}$ Lm 2$_{22}$.

3. Verbs of communication, אמר *say* Gn 2$_{16.18}$ 3$_{9.9.13.14.14.14.22}$ 4$_{6.9.15}$ 6$_{3.7}$ 7$_{1}$ (Sam, mss אֱלֹהִים *God*) 8$_{21}$ 11$_{6}$ 12$_{1.7}$ 13$_{14}$ 14$_{1}$ 15$_{4.4.7.8.8.18}$ 17$_{1}$ 18$_{13.14.17.20.26.26.26.26.26.26}$ 21$_{1}$ 24$_{7.12}$ 25$_{23}$ 26$_{2.24}$ 28$_{13}$ 31$_{3}$ 32$_{10.10}$ Ex 3$_{7.16}$ 4$_{2.2.4.6.6.11.14.19.21.22.27}$ 5$_{1}$ 6$_{1.10.26.29}$ 7$_{1.8.14}$ (Sam דבר pi. *speak* in both) 7$_{16.17.19.26.26}$ (Sam דבר pi.) 8$_{1.12.16.16.23}$ 9$_{1.1.5.8.13.13.22}$ 10$_{1.3.12.21}$ 11$_{1.4.9}$ 12$_{1.43}$ 13$_{1}$ 14$_{15}$ Ex 14$_{26}$ 16$_{4.11.28}$ 17$_{5.14}$ 19$_{9.10.21.24}$ 20$_{22}$ 24$_{12}$ 30$_{34}$ 31$_{12.12}$ 32$_{9.33}$ 33$_{5.17.21}$ 34$_{1.27}$ 35$_{4}$ Lv 5$_{20}$ 7$_{22.28}$ 10$_{8}$ 11$_{1}$ 12$_{1}$ 13$_{1}$ 14$_{1.33}$ 15$_{1}$ 16$_{2}$ 17$_{1.2}$ 18$_{1}$ 19$_{1}$ 20$_{1}$ 21$_{1.16}$ 22$_{1.17.26}$ 23$_{1.9.23.26.33}$ 24$_{1.13}$ 25$_{1}$ 27$_{1}$ Nm 1$_{1.48}$ 2$_{1}$ 3$_{5.11.14.40.44}$ 4$_{1.17.21}$ 5$_{1.5.11}$ 6$_{1.22}$ 7$_{4.4.11}$ 8$_{1.5.23}$ 9$_{1.9}$ 10$_{1.29}$ 11$_{16.23}$ 12$_{4.5.14}$ 13$_{1}$ 14$_{11.20.26.40}$ 15$_{1.17.35.37.37}$ 16$_{20.23}$ 17$_{1.9.16.25}$ 18$_{1.20}$ 20$_{12}$ 20$_{23}$ 21$_{8.16.34}$ 23$_{16}$ 25$_{4.10.16}$ 26$_{1.65}$ 27$_{6.12.18}$ 28$_{1}$ 31$_{1.25}$ 33$_{50}$ 34$_{1.16}$ 35$_{1.9}$ 36$_{6}$ Dt 1$_{6.34.37.42}$ 2$_{2.2.9.17.31}$ 3$_{2.26}$ 4$_{10}$ 5$_{27.28}$ 9$_{12.13.13.23.25}$ 10$_{1.11}$ 17$_{16}$ 18$_{17}$ 31$_{2.3.14.16}$ 32$_{19.36.48}$ 34$_{4}$ Jos 1$_{1.1}$ 3$_{7}$ 4$_{1.1.15.15}$ 5$_{2.9}$ 6$_{2}$ 7$_{10.13}$ 8$_{1.18}$ 10$_{8}$ 11$_{6.9}$ 13$_{1}$ 20$_{1}$ 24$_{2}$ Jg 1$_{2}$ 2$_{20}$ 6$_{8.14.16.23.25}$ 7$_{2.4.5.7.9}$ 10$_{10}$ 20$_{18.23.28}$ 1 S 2$_{27}$ 3$_{11}$ 8$_{7.22}$ 9$_{15}$ 10$_{18.22}$ 15$_{2.18}$ 16$_{1.2.7.12}$ 23$_{2.11.12}$ 24$_{5}$ 2 S 2$_{1.1}$ 3$_{18}$ 5$_{2}$||1 C 11$_{2}$ 2 S 5$_{19}$||1 C 14$_{10}$ 2 S 5$_{23}$ 7$_{5.8}$||1 C 17$_{4.7}$ 2 S 7$_{27}$ 12$_{7.11}$ 16$_{10.11}$ 21$_{1}$ 24$_{12.16}$||1 C 21$_{10.15}$ 1 K 1$_{36}$ 2$_{4}$ 8$_{12.15.18.25}$||2 C 6$_{1.4.8.16}$ 1 K 9$_{3}$||2 C 7$_{12}$ 1 K 11$_{2.11.31}$ 12$_{24}$||2 C 11$_{4}$ 1 K 13$_{2.21}$ 14$_{5.7.8}$ 17$_{14}$ 19$_{9.11.15}$ 20$_{13.14.28.42}$ 21$_{19.19.23}$ 22$_{11}$||2 C 18$_{10}$ 1 K 22$_{14}$ 22$_{17.20.21.21}$||2 C 18$_{16.19.20.20}$ 2 K 1$_{4.6.16}$ 2$_{21}$ 3$_{16.17}$ 4$_{43}$ 7$_{1}$ 8$_{19}$||2 C 21$_{7}$ 2 K 8$_{3}$ 9$_{6.12}$ 10$_{30}$ 14$_{6}$ ||2 C 25$_{4}$ 2 K 15$_{12}$ 17$_{12.35}$ 2 K 18$_{25}$||Is 36$_{10}$ 2 K 18$_{25}$||Is 37$_{6}$ 2 K 19$_{6.20.32}$||Is 37$_{6.21.33}$ 2 K 20$_{1.5}$||Is 38$_{1.5}$ 2 K 20$_{17}$||Is 39$_{6}$ 2 K 21$_{4}$||2 C 33$_{4}$ 2 K 21$_{7.12}$ 22$_{15.16.18}$||2 C 34$_{23.24.26}$ 2 K 23$_{27}$ Is 1$_{11.18}$ 3$_{16}$ 1QIsa[a] 6$_{11}$ (MT אֲדֹנָי) Is 7$_{3.7.10}$ 8$_{1.3.11}$ 10$_{24}$ 14$_{24}$ 16$_{14}$ 18$_{4}$ 19$_{25}$ 20$_{2.3}$ 1QIsa[a] 21$_{16}$ (MT אֲדֹנָי) Is 22$_{14.15}$ 23$_{11}$ 28$_{16}$ 29$_{22}$ 30$_{15}$ 31$_{4}$ 33$_{10}$ 41$_{13.21}$ 42$_{5}$ (1QIsa[a] האלוהים *God*) 43$_{1.14.15}$ 44$_{2.6.6.24}$ 45$_{1.11.13.14.19}$ 48$_{17.22}$ 49$_{1.5.5.7.8.22.25}$ 50$_{1}$ 51$_{22}$ 52$_{3.4}$ 54$_{1.8.10}$ 56$_{1.4}$ 57$_{19}$ 58$_{9}$ 59$_{21.21}$ 63$_{7}$ 65$_{7.8.13.25}$ 66$_{1.9.12.20.21.23}$ Jr 1$_{7.9.12.14}$ 2$_{2.5}$ 3$_{6.11}$ 4$_{3.10.27}$ 5$_{14}$ 6$_{6.9.15.16.21.22}$ 7$_{3.20.21}$ 8$_{4.12}$ 9$_{6.12.14.16.22}$ 10$_{2.18}$ 11$_{3.6.9.11.21.22}$

12_{14} $13_{1.6.9.12.13}$ $14_{10.11.14.15}$ $15_{2.11.19}$ $16_{3.5.9}$ $17_{5.19.21}$ $18_{11.13}$ $19_{1.3.11.15}$ 20_{4} $21_{4.8.12}$ $22_{1.3.6.11.18.30}$ $23_{2.15.16.38}$ $24_{3.5.8}$ $25_{8.15.27.28.32}$ $26_{2.4.18}$ $27_{2.4.16.19.21}$ $28_{2.11.13.14.16}$ $29_{4.8.10.16.17.21.25.25.31.32}$ $30_{2.2.3.5.12.18}$ $31_{2.15.16.23.35.37}$ $32_{3.14.15.25.28.36.42}$ $33_{2.4.10.11.12.13.17.20.25}$ $34_{2.2.4}$ $35_{13.17.18.19}$ $36_{29.30}$ $37_{7.9}$ $38_{2.3.17}$ 39_{16} $42_{9.15.18}$ $43_{2.10}$ $44_{2.7.11.25.25.26.30}$ $45_{2.4}$ 46_{25} 47_{2} $48_{1.8.40}$ $49_{1.2.7.12.18.28.35}$ $50_{18.33}$ $51_{1.33.36.58}$ Ezk 2_{4} $3_{11.22.27}$ 4_{13} $5_{5.7.8}$ $6_{3.11}$ $7_{2.5}$ $9_{4.9}$ $11_{5.7.16.17}$ $12_{10.19.23.28}$ $13_{3.8.13.18.20}$ $14_{6.21}$ 15_{6} $16_{3.36.59}$ $17_{3.9.19.22}$ $20_{3.5.5.5.7.12.12.20.30.39}$ $21_{3.8.29.31.33}$ $22_{3.19.28}$ $23_{22.28.32.35.36.46}$ $24_{3.6.9.21}$ $25_{3.6.8.12.13.15.16}$ $26_{3.7.15.19}$ 27_{3} $28_{2.6.12.22.25}$ $29_{3.8.13.19}$ $30_{2.6.10.13.22}$ $31_{10.15}$ $32_{3.11}$ $33_{25.27}$ $34_{2.10.11.17.20}$ $35_{3.14}$ $36_{2.3.4.5.6.7.13.22.33.37}$ $37_{1.3.5.6.9.9.12.19.21}$ $38_{3.10.14.17}$ $39_{1.17.25}$ 43_{18} $44_{2.5.6.9}$ $45_{9.18}$ $46_{1.16}$ 47_{13} Ho $1_{2.4}$ 3_{1} Jl 2_{19} 3_{5} Am $1_{3.5.6.8.9.11.13.15}$ $2_{1.3.4.6}$ $3_{11.12}$ $5_{3.4.16.17.27}$ $7_{3.6.8.15.17}$ $8_{1.2}$ 9_{15} Ob_{1} Jon 2_{11} $4_{4.10}$ Mc 2_{3} 3_{5} 6_{1} Na 1_{12} Hb 2_{2} Zp 3_{20} Hg $1_{2.2.5.7.8}$ $2_{6.7.9.11}$ Zc $1_{3.3.4.14.16.17}$ 2_{12} 3_{2} (or ins. מַלְאַךְ *messenger* of Y.) 3_{7} 4_{6} $6_{12.12}$ $7_{9.9.13}$ $8_{2.3.4.6.7.9.14.14.19.20.23}$ $11_{4.13.15}$ 13_{8} Ml $1_{4.6.8.9}$ (or del. in both) $1_{10.11.13.13.14}$ $2_{2.4.8.16.16}$ $3_{1.5.7.10.11.12.13.17.19.21}$ Ps 2_{7} 12_{6} 105_{7}||1 C 16_{14} 106_{34} 107_{24} Jb $1_{7.8.12}$ $2_{2.3.6}$ 40_{1} 42_{7} Lm 3_{55} Ne 9_{7} 1 C $21_{9.11.27.28}$ 27_{23} 2 C 1_{25} 20_{15} 21_{12} 32_{24} 4QBibPar 1_{16} 7_{3} 4QapPent 4_{4} ([יאמר יהו]ה) 4QAdmon 1.1_{1} (י[ה]וה) 1.1_{2} 4QDiscourse 9_{3} 4QpsEzek^{a} 2_{3}=4QpsEzek^{d} 8_{6} 4QpsEzek^{a} 2_{9} 3_{4} 12_{4} 4QpsEzek^{b} 1.2_{3} 4QpsEzek^{d} 8_{6} 4QpsEzek^{e} 36_{4} ([לאמר]), hi. *proclaim* Dt 26_{18}.

דבר pi. *speak* Gn 12_{4} 16_{13} $18_{19.33}$ 21_{1} $24_{7.51}$ Ex 4_{30} 6_{2} (Sam)* $6_{10.13.28.29.29}$ $7_{13.22}$ $8_{11.15}$ $9_{12.35}$ 12_{25} 13_{1} 14_{1} $16_{11.23}$ 19_{8} $24_{3.7}$ 25_{1} $30_{11.17.22}$ 31_{1} $32_{7.26.27}$ $33_{1.11}$ 34_{32} 40_{1} Lv 1_{1} 4_{1} $5_{14.20}$ $6_{1.12.17}$ $7_{22.28}$ 8_{1} $10_{3.8.11}$ 11_{1} 12_{1} 13_{1} $14_{1.33}$ 15_{1} 16_{1} 18_{1} 19_{1} $20_{1.16}$ $22_{1.17.26}$ $23_{1.9.23.26.33}$ $24_{1.13}$ 25_{1} 27_{1} Nm $1_{1.48}$ 2_{1} $3_{1.5.11.14.44}$ $4_{1.17.21}$ $5_{1.4.5.11}$ $6_{1.22}$ $8_{1.5.23}$ $9_{1.9}$ $10_{1.29}$ 11_{25} $12_{2.2.6}$ 13_{1} $14_{26.35}$ $15_{1.17.22}$ $16_{20.23}$ $17_{1.5.9.16}$ $18_{8.25}$ 19_{1} 20_{7} $22_{8.19}$ $23_{17.26}$ 24_{13} $25_{10.16}$ 26_{52} $27_{6.23}$ 28_{1} $31_{1.25}$ 32_{31} 33_{50} $34_{1.16}$ $35_{1.9}$ Dt $1_{6.11}$ $2_{1.17}$ $4_{12.15}$ $5_{4.22.27}$ $6_{3.19}$ $9_{3.10.28}$ $10_{4.9}$ 12_{20} 15_{6} $18_{21.22}$ 19_{8} $26_{18.19}$ 27_{3} 32_{48} Jos 4_{8} 11_{23} $14_{6.10.10.12.12}$ 20_{1} 21_{45} 22_{4} $23_{5.10.14.15}$ 24_{27} Jg 2_{15} 6_{27} 1 S 3_{9} 15_{16} 16_{4} 25_{30} 28_{17} 2 S 7_{19} $7_{25.25.28}$||1 C $17_{23.23.26}$ 2 S 7_{29} 1 K $2_{4.24.27}$ $5_{19.26}$ $8_{15.20.20}$||2 C $6_{4.10.10}$ 1 K 8_{25}||2 C 6_{16} 1 K $8_{53.56.56}$ 12_{15}||2 C 10_{15} 1 K $13_{3.26}$ $14_{13.18}$ 15_{29} $16_{12.34}$ 17_{16} 21_{23} $22_{23.28}$||2 C $18_{22.27}$ 2 K $10_{10.10.17}$ $14_{25.27}$ 15_{12} 17_{23} 19_{21}||Is 37_{22} 2 K 20_{9}||Is 38_{7} 2 K 21_{10}||2 C 33_{10} 2 K 22_{19}||2 C 34_{27} 2 K $24_{2.13}$ Is 1_{2} 7_{10} 8_{5} $16_{13.14}$ 20_{2} 21_{17} 22_{25} 24_{3} 25_{8} $45_{19.19}$ Jr $7_{13.13}$ 10_{1} 11_{17} 13_{15} 16_{10} $23_{17.35.37}$ $26_{13.19}$ 27_{13} 30_{4} 31_{20} 33_{14} $34_{5.13.17}$ $36_{4.7}$ 37_{2} $40_{2.3}$ $42_{19.20}$ 46_{13} 50_{1} $51_{12.62}$ Ezk $5_{13.15.17}$ 6_{10} $12_{25.25.25.28}$ 13_{7} $17_{21.24}$ $21_{22.37}$ $22_{14.28.34}$ 24_{14} $26_{5.14}$ 28_{10} 30_{12} 34_{24} 36_{36} 37_{14} $39_{5.8}$ Ho 1_{2} (or em. דִּבֶּר־י׳ *Y. spoke to* דְּבַר־י׳ *word of Y.*) 12_{10} Jl 4_{8} Am $3_{1.8}$ Ob_{18} Ps 50_{1} $85_{9.9}$ 99_{6} Jb $42_{7.9}$ Ne 9_{7} 1 C 21_{9} 22_{1} 2 C 6_{17} 11_{2} 23_{3} $4QTestim_{1}$ 4QJub^{a} 1_{1} 4QapJoshua^{a} 11_{1} 4QpsEzek^{a} 1_{1} 4QpsEzek^{e} 36_{4} 11QT 61_{3}.

צוה pi. *command* Gn 2_{16} 7_{5} 28_{13} Ex 4_{28} 6_{13} $7_{6.10.20}$ $12_{28.50}$ $16_{16.32.34}$ 19_{7} 34_{4} $35_{1.4.10.29}$ $36_{1.5}$ 38_{22} $39_{1.5.7.21.26.31.32.42.43}$ $40_{16.19.21.23.25.27.29.32}$ Lv $7_{36.38}$ $8_{4.5.9.13.17.29.34.36}$ $9_{6.7.10}$ 10_{15} 16_{34} 17_{2} 24_{23} 27_{34} Nm $1_{19.54}$ $2_{33.34}$ $3_{42.51}$ 4_{49} $8_{3.20.22}$ $9_{5.8}$ $15_{23.23.36}$ 17_{26} Nm 19_{2} 20_{27} 26_{4} $27_{11.22}$ $30_{1.2.17}$ $31_{7.21.31.41.47}$ $34_{13.29}$ $36_{2.2}$ (if em. וַאדֹנִי צֻוָּה בי׳ *and my lord was commanded by Y.* to וְאֹתָנוּ צִוָּה י׳ *and Y. commanded us*) $32_{6.10.13}$ Dt $1_{3.19.21.41}$ 2_{37} $4_{5.14.23}$ $5_{12.15.16.32.33}$ $6_{1.17.20.24.25}$ 9_{16} 10_{5} 11_{25} 13_{6}=11QT 54_{16} 20_{17} $26_{13.14.16}$ $28_{8.45.69}$ 34_{9} Jos 4_{10} 8_{27} 9_{24} 10_{40} $11_{15.15.20}$ $14_{2.5}$ 17_{4} $21_{2.8}$ 23_{16} Jg 3_{4} 4_{6} 1 S $13_{13.14}$ 2 S 5_{25} 17_{14} 24_{19} 1 K 8_{57} $11_{9.10}$ 13_{21} 15_{5} 2 K 14_{6}||2 C 25_{4} 2 K $17_{15.34.35}$ 18_{6} Is 23_{11} Jr 13_{5} 23_{32} 26_{8} 29_{23} 34_{22} 47_{7} 50_{21} Ezk 37_{9} Am 6_{11} Na 1_{14} Zc 1_{4} Ps 7_{7} 42_{9} 71_{1} 78_{4} 105_{7}||1 C 16_{14} 119_{137} 133_{3} 148_{5} Lm 1_{17} 2_{17} Ne $1_{5.5}$ $8_{1.14}$ 9_{7} 1 C 16_{40} 24_{19}, *appoint* 1 S 13_{14} 25_{30} 2 S 6_{21} 1 C 22_{12} (or em. וִיצַוְּךָ *and may he appoint you* to וְיֵצֶר רַךְ *and a gentle disposition* or וְיֵצֶר יַצִּיב *and may he establish a disposition*) 22_{13} 4QapMos^{c} 2.2_{5} ([מצו]ה).

ענה *answer* 1 S 7_{9} 8_{18} 9_{15} 23_{4} 28_{6} 2 S 22_{42}||Ps 18_{42} 1 K $18_{37.37}$ Is 41_{17} 58_{9} Jr $23_{35.37}$ 42_{4} Ho 2_{23} Jl 2_{19} Jon 2_{3} Mc 3_{4} Hb 2_{2} Zc 1_{13} 10_{6} 13_{8} Ps 3_{5} 13_{4} $20_{2.7}$ 27_{7} 34_{5} $69_{17.17}$ $86_{1.6}$ $99_{6.8}$ 119_{145} 120_{1} $143_{1.7}$ Jb 38_{1} $40_{1.6}$ 1 C 21_{26}, *testify against* Ru 1_{21}, ni. *be moved to answer* Ezk $14_{4.7}$, עתר ni. *answer* prayer Gn 25_{21} 2 S 24_{25}.

קרא *call* Gn 3_{9} $19_{3.20}$ 34_{5} 35_{30} Lv 1_{1} 17_{1} Nm 12_{5} 1 S $3_{4.6.8.8.10}$ 2 K $3_{10.13}$ 8_{1} Is 22_{12} 42_{6} 45_{3} 49_{1} 54_{6} 65_{15} Jr $1_{8.15}$ 7_{13} 11_{16} 20_{3} 25_{29} 34_{17} Ezk 36_{23} 38_{21} Jl 3_{5} Am 5_{8} 7_{4} 9_{5} Hg 1_{9} Zc $7_{7.13}$ Ps 50_{1} 105_{7} Ps 147_{2} Lm $1_{15(mss).20}$ 2_{20}.

חוה pi. *declare* Hb 3_{2} (if em. חיה pi. *revive it*), נאם *declare* 1 S $2_{30.30}$, נגד hi. *declare* 1 S 23_{11} 2 S 7_{11} 2 K 4_{27} Is 43_{12} 45_{19} Jr 42_{3} Am 4_{13}, דמה pi. *speak in parables* Ho 12_{11} (or em. אֲדַמֶּה *I speak in parables* to מַרְאָה I have increased *visions*), שאל *ask* Dt 10_{12} Ps 40_{6} Arad ost. 18_{2}, יעץ *advise* Is 14_{27} $19_{12.17}$ 23_{9} Jr 49_{20} 50_{45} Ps 16_{7}, ni. *con-*

sult together Is 40$_{13}$, גער *rebuke* Na 1$_{3}$ Zc 3$_{2.2}$, יכח hi. *reprove* Ps 6$_{2}$=38$_{2}$ 105$_{7}$||1 C 16$_{14}$ Pr 3$_{12}$, *appoint* Gn 24$_{44}$, htp. *argue* Mc 6$_{2}$, ענה *sing* Jr 25$_{30}$, רוע *shout* Is 42$_{13}$, צרח hi. *roar* Is 42$_{13}$, שׁאג *roar* Jr 25$_{30}$||Jl 4$_{16}$||Am 1$_{2}$ Jr 25$_{30.30}$ Ho 11$_{10.10}$, תקע *sound* ram's horn Zc 9$_{14}$.

שׁבע ni. *swear* Gn 22$_{16}$ 24$_{7}$ Ex 13$_{5.11}$ Nm 14$_{16}$ Dt 1$_{8.34}$ 2$_{14}$ 4$_{21}$ 6$_{10.18}$ 7$_{8.12.12}$ 8$_{1}$ 9$_{5}$ 11$_{9.21}$ 13$_{18}$ 19$_{8}$ 26$_{3.14}$ 28$_{9.11}$ 30$_{20}$ Jos 5$_{6.6}$ 21$_{43.44}$ Jg 2$_{15}$ 2 S 3$_{9}$ Is 14$_{24}$ 62$_{8}$ Jr 22$_{5}$ 49$_{13}$ 51$_{14}$ Ezk 16$_{8}$ Am 4$_{2}$ 6$_{8}$ 8$_{7}$ Ps 89$_{50(mss)}$ 110$_{4}$ 132$_{11}$ 4QapJoshua^{a} 11$_{1}$, hi. *adjure* 11QPsAp^{a} 2$_{4}$ נדר *vow* Nm 30$_{3.4}$.

כתב *write* Dt 5$_{22}$ 10$_{4}$ Jr 31$_{33}$, פתח pi. *engrave* Zc 3$_{9}$, חקק *engrave*, i.e. draw, circle Pr 8$_{22}$, i.e. establish, foundations of earth Pr 8$_{22}$ (unless חוק *gather;* or em. חזק pi. *strengthen*), זרה pi. *measure* or *sift* Ps 139$_{3}$, תכן *weigh* Pr 16$_{2}$ 21$_{2}$, ספר *count* Ps 87$_{6}$, מנה *count* Ps 147$_{2}$, pi. *appoint* Jon 2$_{1}$ 4$_{6}$.

4. Verbs of perception, ראה *see* Gn 2$_{19}$ 6$_{5}$ 11$_{5}$ 29$_{31.32}$ Ex 3$_{4}$ (Sam אלהים *God*) 4$_{31}$ 5$_{21}$ 12$_{23}$ Dt 23$_{15}$ 26$_{7}$ 32$_{19.36}$ 1 S 1$_{11.11}$ 16$_{7}$ 2 S 16$_{12}$ 2 K 9$_{26}$ 13$_{4}$ 14$_{26}$ 19$_{16}$||Is 37$_{17}$ Is 59$_{15}$ 63$_{7}$ Jr 7$_{11}$ 12$_{3}$ 20$_{12}$ 23$_{24}$ 46$_{5}$ Ezk 8$_{12}$ 9$_{9}$ 16$_{8}$ Ps 9$_{14}$ 14$_{2}$ 33$_{13}$ 35$_{22}$ 59$_{4}$ 106$_{40}$ 113$_{5}$ 119$_{151.156}$ 138$_{6}$ 142$_{2}$ Pr 24$_{18}$ Lm 1$_{9.11.20}$ 2$_{20}$ 3$_{50.59.59}$ Ne 9$_{7}$ 1 C 17$_{17}$ (or em. hi. *show*) 21$_{15}$ 2 C 12$_{7}$ 24$_{22}$ 4QNarrB 1$_{10}$, *provide* Gn 22$_{14}$ (or em. ni. *appear*) 22$_{14}$ (if em. ni.) Si 45$_{19}$, ni. *appear* Gn 12$_{7.7}$ 17$_{1}$ 18$_{1}$ 22$_{14}$ (if em.) 22$_{14}$ (or em.) 26$_{2.24}$ Ex 3$_{16}$ 4$_{1.5}$ 6$_{3}$ Lv 9$_{4}$ Nm 14$_{14}$ Dt 31$_{15}$ 1 S 3$_{21}$ 1 K 3$_{5}$ 9$_{2}$||2 C 7$_{12}$ 1 K 9$_{2}$ 11$_{9}$ Jr 31$_{3}$ Zp 2$_{11}$ (if em. ירא ni. *be feared*) Zc 9$_{14}$ Ps 102$_{17}$ 2 C 3$_{1}$, hi. *show* Ex 15$_{25}$ Nm 8$_{4}$ 23$_{3}$ Dt 3$_{24}$ 4$_{35}$ 5$_{24}$ 34$_{1}$ Jos 5$_{6}$ Jg 13$_{23}$ 2 K 8$_{10.13}$ Is 30$_{30}$ Jr 11$_{18}$ 24$_{1}$ 38$_{21}$ Ezk 11$_{25}$ Am 7$_{1.4}$ 8$_{1}$ Hb 1$_{2}$ Zc 2$_{3.17}$ Ps 25$_{8}$ 85$_{8}$ 1 C 17$_{17}$ (if em. qal) Lachish ost. 5$_{7}$ 6$_{1}$ 4QapPs^{a} 1.1$_{9}$, חזה *see* Si 15$_{18}$, שׁעה *gaze*, i.e. regard with favour Gn 4$_{4.4}$, hi. *divert gaze* Ps 39$_{13}$, נבט hi. *look* Is 63$_{7}$ 64$_{8}$ 66$_{2}$ Hb 1$_{2}$ (or em. תַּבִּיט *you look* to אַבִּיט *I* [Habakkuk] *look*) Ps 13$_{4}$ 33$_{13}$ 102$_{20}$ 104$_{31}$ 142$_{2}$ Lm 1$_{11}$ 2$_{20}$ 3$_{61}$ 4$_{16}$ 5$_{1}$, שׁקף hi. *look down* Ex 14$_{24}$ Dt 26$_{14}$ Ps 14$_{2}$ 102$_{20}$ Lm 3$_{50}$, שׁקד *keep watch* Jr 31$_{28.28}$ Dn 9$_{14}$, צפה *keep watch* Gn 31$_{49}$ Si 46$_{6}$.

שׁמע *hear* Gn 16$_{11}$ 29$_{33}$ Ex 6$_{3}$ 16$_{7.8.12}$ Nm 11$_{1}$ 12$_{2}$ 20$_{16}$ 21$_{3}$ Dt 1$_{34.45}$ 3$_{26}$ 5$_{28}$ 9$_{19}$ 10$_{10}$ 23$_{6}$ 26$_{7}$ 33$_{7}$ Jos 10$_{14}$ 2 S 22$_{7}$ ||Ps 18$_{7}$ 1 K 8$_{28}$||2 C 6$_{19}$ 1 K 17$_{22}$ 2 K 13$_{4}$ 19$_{4.4.16.16}$||Is 37$_{4.4.17.17}$ 2 K 22$_{19}$||2 C 34$_{27}$ Jr 18$_{19}$ Ezk 35$_{11}$ Jon 2$_{3}$ Hb 1$_{2}$ Ml 3$_{16}$ Ps 4$_{4}$ 5$_{4}$ 6$_{9.10}$ 10$_{17}$ 17$_{1}$ 22$_{24}$ 27$_{7}$ 28$_{6}$ 30$_{11}$ 34$_{7.18}$ 39$_{13}$ =102$_{2}$ 40$_{2}$ 55$_{17}$ 69$_{34}$ 78$_{21}$ 84$_{9}$ 106$_{40}$ 116$_{1}$ 119$_{145}$ 130$_{2(mss)}$ 143$_{1}$ 145$_{18}$ Pr 15$_{29}$ Lm 3$_{55.59}$ Dn 9$_{18(mss)}$ Ne 9$_{7}$ 2 C 30$_{20}$ Si 51$_{11}$, hi. *cause to hear* Dt 4$_{35}$ Jg 13$_{23}$ Is 30$_{30}$ 43$_{12}$ Jr 49$_{2}$ Ps 143$_{7}$ Lachish ost. 2$_{2}$ 3$_{3}$ 4$_{1}$ 5$_{1}$ ([יהוה]) 8$_{1}$ ([י]הוה) 9$_{1}$, *make heard* Is 62$_{11}$ Ezk 36$_{15}$, אזן hi. *hear* Ps 5$_{2}$ 17$_{1}$ 39$_{13}$ 86$_{6}$ 140$_{7}$ 141$_{1}$ 143$_{1}$ Si 51$_{11}$, קשׁב hi. *attend* Jr 18$_{19}$ Ml 3$_{16}$ Ps 17$_{1}$ 86$_{6}$ 142$_{6}$, appar. *cause to attend* Ps 10$_{17}$, כרה *dig* ears, i.e. cause to hear Ps 40$_{6}$, חרשׁ *be deaf* Ps 35$_{22}$, hi. *be silent* Zp 3$_{17}$ (or em. חדשׁ pi. *renew*), חשׁה *be silent* Is 64$_{11}$.

ידע *know* Dt 2$_{7}$ 8$_{2}$ 13$_{4}$ 34$_{10}$ Jos 22$_{22}$ Jr 12$_{3}$ 15$_{15.15}$ 18$_{23}$ 29$_{11.23}$ 48$_{30}$ Na 1$_{7}$ Ps 1$_{6}$ 37$_{18}$ 40$_{10}$ 69$_{17}$ 94$_{11}$ 103$_{13}$ 138$_{6}$ 139$_{1.1.4}$ 142$_{2}$ 144$_{3}$ Ne 9$_{7}$, ni. *make oneself known* Ex 6$_{3}$ Is 19$_{21}$ Ezk 20$_{5.7}$ 35$_{11}$ Hb 3$_{2}$ (if em. hi.) Ps 9$_{17}$, hi. *make known* Nm 16$_{5}$ 2 S 7$_{20}$||1 C 17$_{19}$ Ezk 39$_{7}$ Hb 3$_{2}$ (or em. ni.) Ps 98$_{2}$ 103$_{6}$, *cause to know* Dt 8$_{3}$ Jr 11$_{18}$ Ezk 20$_{7}$ Ps 25$_{4}$ 39$_{5}$ 143$_{8}$ Ne 9$_{7}$, htp. *make oneself known* Nm 12$_{6}$ Ezk 38$_{23}$, סכן hi. *know* Ps 139$_{1}$, בין *understand* Ps 5$_{2}$ 139$_{1}$ 1 C 28$_{9}$, hi. *cause to understand* Ps 119$_{33.65.108.137.169}$, ירה hi. *teach* Ex 4$_{11}$ Is 2$_{3}$||Mc 4$_{2}$ Ps 25$_{12}$ 27$_{11}$ 86$_{11}$ 119$_{33.89}$, *show* Ex 15$_{25}$ (Sam ראה hi. *show*), למד pi. *teach* Is 48$_{17}$ Ps 25$_{4.8}$ 119$_{12.64.65.65.108.108.169}$ 143$_{9}$ 144$_{1}$, זמם *plan* Jr 51$_{12}$ Zc 1$_{6}$ Lm 2$_{17}$, חשׁב *think* Gn 15$_{6}$ Jr 29$_{11}$ 49$_{20}$ 50$_{45}$ Ps 32$_{2}$ 40$_{18}$ $_{(mss)}$ 119$_{108(mss)}$ Lm 2$_{8}$, pi. *consider* Ps 144$_{3}$.

זכר *remember* Ex 6$_{3}$ Dt 9$_{26}$ 1 S 1$_{11.19}$ 2 K 20$_{3}$||Is 38$_{3}$ 63$_{7}$ 64$_{8}$ Jr 14$_{10}$||Ho 8$_{13}$ Jr 14$_{20}$ 15$_{15}$ 31$_{20.20.34}$ 44$_{21}$ Hb 3$_{2}$ Ps 8$_{2}$ 9$_{12}$ 25$_{6.7.7}$ 79$_{5}$ 88$_{2}$ 89$_{47.51(mss)}$ 105$_{7}$||1 C 16$_{14}$ (if em. זִכְרוּ *remember*, with worshipper as subj., as Ps 105$_{7[mss]}$) 106$_{4.40}$ 115$_{12}$ 119$_{41}$ 132$_{1}$ 137$_{7}$ Lm 2$_{1(mss)}$ 5$_{1}$ Ne 1$_{5}$ 2 C 6$_{42}$ 4QapPs^{a} 1.1$_{9}$ (ו[זכ]ר), hi. *cause to be mentioned* Is 49$_{1}$, שׁכח *forget* 1 S 1$_{11}$ Ps 9$_{12}$ 13$_{2}$ Lm 5$_{19}$, pi. *cause to be forgotten* Lm 2$_{6}$.

פקד *pay attention to* Gn 21$_{1}$ Ex 4$_{31}$ 1 S 2$_{21}$ Is 23$_{17}$ Jr 15$_{15}$ 27$_{22}$ 32$_{5}$ (or del. פקד in both) Zp 2$_{7}$ Ps 8$_{2}$ 17$_{1}$ 106$_{4}$ Ru 1$_{6}$ 4QapPs^{a} 1.1$_{9}$, *punish* sin Jr 14$_{10}$=Ho 8$_{13}$, sinner Jr 50$_{31}$ (mss פְּקֻדָּתֶךָ *your punishment*) Ps 59$_{6}$, *extend* punishment Ex 34$_{6}$||Nm 14$_{18}$ Dt 5$_{9}$ Is 24$_{21}$ 26$_{13.21}$ 27$_{1}$ Jr 5$_{9.29}$ 9$_{8.24}$ Jr 21$_{14}$ 23$_{2}$ 25$_{12}$ 27$_{8}$ 29$_{32}$ 44$_{29}$ 51$_{52}$ Ho 2$_{15}$ 12$_{3}$ Zc 10$_{3}$, *appoint* Nm 27$_{16}$ Ezr 1$_{2}$=2 C 36$_{23}$, pi. *muster* Is 13$_{4}$.

בקשׁ pi. *seek* Ex 4$_{24}$ Jos 22$_{23}$ Jg 14$_{4}$ 1 S 13$_{14}$ 20$_{16}$ Ps 119$_{174}$ Si 5$_{3}$ 20$_{4}$, דרשׁ *seek* Dt 11$_{12}$ 23$_{22.22}$ Ezk 20$_{40}$ Mc 6$_{8}$ Ps 9$_{12}$ 2 C 24$_{22}$, ni. *be consulted* Ezk 20$_{3.31.31}$, תור *search out* Ezk 20$_{5}$, חקר *search* Jr 17$_{10}$ Ps 139$_{1}$.

בחר *choose* Nm 16$_{5.7}$ Dt 4$_{35}$ 7$_{6.7}$ 10$_{15}$ 12$_{5.11.14.18.21.26}$ 14$_{2.23.24.25.29}$ 15$_{20}$ 16$_{2.6.7.10.11.15.16}$ 17$_{8.10.15}$ 18$_{5.6}$ 21$_{5}$ 31$_{11}$ 1 S 10$_{24}$ 16$_{8.9.10}$ 2 S 6$_{21}$ 16$_{18}$ 1 K 14$_{21}$||2 C 12$_{13}$ Is 14$_{1}$ 43$_{11}$ 44$_{2}$ Jr 33$_{24}$ Ezk 20$_{5}$ Hg 2$_{23}$ Zc 1$_{17}$ 2$_{16}$ 3$_{2}$ Ps 33$_{12}$ 47$_{3}$ 132$_{13}$ Ne 9$_{7}$ 1 C 15$_{2}$ 28$_{4.4.5.10}$ 2 C 29$_{11}$ 4QapPs^{a} 1.1$_{3}$ 4QConfess 2$_{6}$, שפת *appoint* Is 26$_{12}$.

5. Verbs of general activities, יכל *be able* Nm 14$_{16}$ Dt 9$_{28}$ Jr 18$_{6}$ 44$_{22}$, *prevail* Jr 20$_{7}$, פלא hi. *act exceptionally* Dt 28$_{59}$ Is 28$_{29}$ Jl 2$_{26}$ Si 50$_{22}$, יסף *add* Dt 5$_{22}$ Is 26$_{15.15}$ Jr 45$_{3}$, hi. *add* Gn 30$_{24}$ Dt 1$_{11}$ 2 S 24$_{3}$||1 C 21$_{3}$ Ps 115$_{14}$ Jb 42$_{10}$, *do again* Jos 23$_{13}$ 1 S 3$_{6.8.21}$ 20$_{13}$ Is 7$_{10}$ 8$_{5}$ Ru 1$_{17}$ Lm 4$_{16}$, עצר *restrain* Gn 16$_{2}$ 20$_{18}$ Dt 11$_{17}$ Jb 12$_{9}$, נוא hi. *frustrate* Ps 33$_{10}$, פרר hi. *frustrate* Is 44$_{24}$ Jr 14$_{20}$ Ps 33$_{10}$.

חוש *be quick* Ps 40$_{14}$||70$_{2}$ 141$_{1}$, hi. *cause to hurry* Is 60$_{22}$, צלח *rush* Am 5$_{6}$, אחר pi. *stay behind* Dt 7$_{9}$ Ps 70$_{6}$ (mss, ||40$_{18}$ אֱלֹהַי *my God*), קוה pi. *wait* Is 5$_{7}$, חכה pi. *wait* Is 30$_{18}$, חלל hi. *begin* Dt 3$_{24}$ 2 K 10$_{32}$ 15$_{37}$ Jr 25$_{29}$, חדש pi. *renew* Zp 3$_{17}$ (if em. חרש *be silent*) Ps 104$_{24}$ Lm 5$_{21}$, בצע pi. *complete* Lm 2$_{17}$, תמם *complete* Jr 27$_{8}$ (or em. תִּתִּי *my giving*), כלה pi. *cease* Gn 18$_{33}$, *destroy* Dt 28$_{21}$ Jos 24$_{20}$ Jr 5$_{3}$ 49$_{37}$ Ezk 20$_{12}$ 22$_{31}$ Si 45$_{19}$, *use up*, i.e. vent, anger Ezk 20$_{7.20}$ Lm 4$_{11}$, חדל *cease* Am 7$_{5}$, שבת *cease* Ex 31$_{17}$, hi. *cause to cease* Jr 48$_{35}$ Ps 46$_{9}$ 85$_{2(mss)}$ 119$_{108}$ (mss חשב *think*) Ru 4$_{14}$, פרע *refrain* Ezk 24$_{14}$, אפק htp. *restrain oneself* Is 64$_{11}$.

עשה *do, perform, exercise* Gn 21$_{1}$ 24$_{12}$ 28$_{13}$ 32$_{10}$ Ex 8$_{9.20.27}$ 9$_{5.6}$ 12$_{12}$ 13$_{8}$ 14$_{13.31}$ 15$_{11}$ 18$_{8.9}$ 32$_{14}$ Nm 14$_{28.35}$ 33$_{4}$ Dt 1$_{30}$ 3$_{21.21}$ 4$_{3.34}$ 5$_{9}$ 7$_{18.19}$ 11$_{2.4.7}$ 24$_{9}$ 29$_{1.23}$ 31$_{4.4}$ Jos 3$_{5}$ 4$_{23}$ 9$_{9}$ 10$_{25}$ 23$_{3}$ 24$_{17.31}$ Jg 2$_{7.10}$ 11$_{36}$ 1 S 3$_{18}$ 11$_{13}$ 12$_{6.7.16}$ 14$_{6}$ 19$_{5}$ 20$_{13}$ 25$_{28.30}$ 28$_{17.18}$ 2 S 2$_{6}$ 7$_{20.25}$||1 C 17$_{19.23}$ 2 S 10$_{12}$||1 C 19$_{13}$ 2 S 23$_{10.12}$ 1 K 8$_{59}$ 8$_{66}$||2 C 7$_{10}$ 1 K 9$_{8}$||2 C 7$_{21}$ 2 K 10$_{10}$ 19$_{31}$||Is 37$_{32}$ 2 K 20$_{9}$||Is 38$_{7}$ Is 10$_{23}$ 12$_{5}$ 25$_{1}$ 28$_{21}$ 44$_{23}$ 45$_{7}$ 63$_{7.17}$ Jr 5$_{19}$ 9$_{23}$ 14$_{7}$ 18$_{6.23}$ 19$_{12}$ 21$_{2}$ 22$_{8}$ 28$_{6}$ 29$_{32}$ 32$_{17}$ 40$_{3}$ 51$_{12}$ Ezk 5$_{15}$ 6$_{10}$ 11$_{8}$ 12$_{25}$ 14$_{23.23}$ 17$_{24}$ 20$_{7.12.20.44}$ 22$_{14.14}$ 24$_{14}$ 25$_{11.17}$ 28$_{22.26}$ 30$_{19}$ 35$_{11}$ 36$_{32.36}$ 37$_{14}$ Jl 2$_{21.26}$ Am 3$_{6.7}$ 5$_{8}$ 9$_{12}$ Jon 1$_{14}$ Mc 7$_{9}$ Zp 3$_{5}$ Zc 1$_{6}$ Ps 9$_{17}$ 37$_{5}$ 40$_{6}$ 72$_{18}$ 78$_{4}$ 86$_{9(mss)}$ 86$_{17}$ 88$_{10}$ 98$_{1}$ 103$_{6.8}$ 105$_{4}$||1 C 16$_{11}$ Ps 109$_{21.27}$ 119$_{65.75.108.126(ms)}$ 126$_{2}$ 135$_{6}$ 140$_{13}$ 145$_{18}$ 146$_{5}$ Ru 1$_{8.17}$ Lm 1$_{20}$ 2$_{17}$ Dn 9$_{14}$ Ne 9$_{7}$ Si 50$_{22}$ GnzPs 3$_{18}$.

עשה *make* Gn 2$_{4}$ 3$_{1.21}$ Ex 20$_{11}$ 31$_{17}$ Dt 26$_{19}$ 32$_{6}$ Jg 21$_{15}$ 1 S 12$_{22}$ 2 S 7$_{11}$ 1 K 2$_{24}$ 2 K 7$_{2.19}$ 19$_{15}$||Is 37$_{16}$ Is 25$_{6}$ 44$_{2.24}$ 45$_{7.18}$ 51$_{13}$ 54$_{5}$ 66$_{22}$ Jr 14$_{22}$ 32$_{17}$ 33$_{2}$ 38$_{16}$ Ezk 35$_{15}$ 36$_{23}$ Am 4$_{13}$ Jon 1$_{9}$ Zc 10$_{1}$ Ps 52$_{11}$ (if ins. 'י *Y.*) 86$_{9(mss)}$ 95$_{6}$ 96$_{7}$ 100$_{3}$ 104$_{16.24}$ 111$_{2}$ 115$_{15}$ 118$_{24}$ 121$_{2}$=124$_{8}$ 134$_{3}$ 135$_{6}$ 146$_{5}$ Pr 8$_{22}$ (or em. עָשְׂתָה the earth *made*) 20$_{12}$ 22$_{2}$ Dn 9$_{15(mss)}$ Ne 9$_{6.7}$ 2 C 2$_{11}$ Si 43$_{5(B)}$ 50$_{22}$ 11QPsAp^{a} 1$_{11}$ ([יהוה ... עשה]) 2$_{4}$, specif. *make an end* (כָּלָה) *of, destroy* Jr 5$_{18}$ 30$_{11.11}$ 46$_{28.28}$ Ezk 11$_{13}$ 20$_{12}$ Na 1$_{7.9}$ Zp 1$_{18}$, *prepare* for blood, or *cause to be* like blood Ezk 35$_{6}$, appar. *appoint* 1 S 12$_{6}$, פעל *do* Dt 32$_{27}$ Is 26$_{12}$ Ps 31$_{18}$, *make* Ex 15$_{17}$ Pr 16$_{4}$, עבד *work* Is 28$_{21}$.

כון hi. *establish* 1 S 13$_{13}$ 2 S 5$_{12}$||1 C 14$_{2}$ 1 K 2$_{24}$ Jr 33$_{2}$ Ps 10$_{17}$ (ms בין hi. *understand* their heart; or em. הֶגְיוֹן *music* of their heart) 11$_{4}$ (if ins. כון hi.) 103$_{19}$ Pr 8$_{22}$ 16$_{9}$ 1 C 29$_{18}$ 2 C 17$_{5}$ Si 47$_{11}$, *prepare* Zp 1$_{7}$, pol. *establish* Dt 32$_{6}$ 2 S 7$_{24}$ Ps 7$_{10}$ 8$_{2}$ 9$_{8}$ 24$_{1}$ 40$_{2}$ 119$_{89}$ Pr 3$_{19}$, יסד *establish* Is 51$_{13}$ Am 9$_{5}$ Zc 12$_{1}$ Ps 24$_{1}$ Pr 3$_{19}$, pi. Is 14$_{32}$ Ps 8$_{2}$ 119$_{151}$.

ערב *guarantee* Ps 119$_{108}$, כול pilp. *sustain* Ps 55$_{23}$, סמך *support* Ps 3$_{6}$ 37$_{17.24}$ 119$_{108}$ 145$_{14}$, סעד *sustain* Ps 41$_{4}$ 119$_{108}$, חיה pi. *let live* Dt 6$_{24}$ Ps 41$_{3}$ 119$_{33.33.75.89.107.149.151.156.159}$ 143$_{11}$ Ne 9$_{6}$, *revive* 1 S 2$_{6}$ Ho 6$_{1}$ Hb 3$_{2}$ (or em. חוה pi. *declare*) Ps 30$_{4}$, hi. *let live* Jos 14$_{10}$, שאר hi. *leave* Jr 50$_{20}$ Jl 2$_{14}$ Ezr 9$_{8}$.

ברא *create* Nm 16$_{30}$ Is 4$_{5}$ 42$_{5}$ 43$_{1.15}$ 45$_{7.7.8.18.18}$ Jr 31$_{22}$ Am 4$_{13}$ Ps 89$_{47}$ 4QsapHymn 1.2$_{11}$ ([יהו]ה ברא) 1.2$_{12.13}$ GnzPs 2$_{18}$, קנה *create* Gn 14$_{22}$ Ex 15$_{16}$ Dt 32$_{6}$ Ps 139$_{4}$ Pr 8$_{22}$, יצר *form* Gn 2$_{7.19}$ Is 42$_{6}$ 43$_{1}$ 44$_{2.24}$ 45$_{7.11.18}$ 49$_{5}$ 64$_{7}$ Jr 33$_{2}$ Am 4$_{13}$ 7$_{1}$ (or em. יוֹצֵר *forming* to יֵצֶר *form* or יוֹצֵא *going out*, with גֹּבַי *locusts* as subj.) Zc 12$_{1}$ Ps 104$_{24}$, סכך *weave* worshipper in womb Ps 139$_{4}$.

קיץ hi. *awake* Ps 59$_{6}$, ריח hi. *smell* Gn 8$_{21}$ 1 S 26$_{19}$, נפח *breathe* Gn 2$_{7}$, שחק *laugh* Ps 59$_{9}$, שרק *whistle* Is 7$_{18}$, נפש ni. *refresh oneself* Ex 31$_{17}$, שתה *drink* Ps 110$_{5(Gnz, mss)}$, לבש *be clothed* Ps 93$_{1.1}$ 104$_{1}$, hi. *clothe* Gn 3$_{21}$, עטה *wrap oneself* Ps 104$_{1}$, צנף *wind around oneself* Is 22$_{17.17}$, אזר pi. *gird* another Ps 30$_{11}$, *envelop* Is 45$_{5}$, htp. *gird oneself* Ps 93$_{1}$.

יגע *be weary* Is 40$_{28}$, hi. *make weary* Ml 2$_{17}$, יעף *be weary* Is 40$_{28}$, לאה ni. *be weary* Jr 15$_{6}$, עצב htp. *be troubled* Gn 6$_{6}$, חזק *be strong* or *outwit* Jr 20$_{7}$, pi. *strengthen* Jg 3$_{12}$ 16$_{28}$, specif. *harden* heart Ex 9$_{12}$ 10$_{20.27}$ 11$_{10}$ 14$_{4.8}$ Jos 11$_{20}$, hi. *strengthen* Ezk 30$_{25}$, *grasp* Is 41$_{13}$ 42$_{6}$ 45$_{1}$ Jr

31_{32}, חלץ hi. *strengthen* Is 58_{11} (MT יַחֲלִיץ; or em. חלף hi. *renew* strength; 1QIsa[a] יחליצו bones *will be strong*; 1QIsa[b] יחלצו ni. bones *will be strong*), אמץ pi. *strengthen* Pr 8_{22}, *harden* heart Dt 2_{30}, קשה hi. *harden* spirit Dt 2_{30}, heart Si 16_{15}, קשח hi. *harden* heart Is 63_{17}.

זרע *sow* Jr 31_{27}, נטע *plant* Gn 2_8 Ex 15_{17} Nm 24_6 Jr 11_{17} 31_{28} Ezk 36_{36} Ps 104_{16}, צמח hi. *cause to sprout* Gn 2_9 Is 61_{11} Jr 33_{14} Ezk 29_{21}, פרח hi. *cause to bud* Ezk 17_{24}, חבט *beat out* Is 27_{12}, רעה *pasture* Ezk 34_{15} Ho 4_{16} Ps 23_1, עטה *grasp* or *delouse* Is 22_{17}.

בנה *build* Jr 31_{28} Ezk 36_{36} Am 9_5 Ps 102_{17} 127_1 147_2 Lm 2_{22} 1 C 17_{10}, *fashion* rib Gn 2_{22}, גדר *build wall* Lm 2_{22}, *block* way Lm 2_{22}, שחה hi. *take* wall *down* Is 25_{10}, פלס pi. *make* path *level* Pr 5_{21}, ישר pi. *make* way *smooth* Pr 3_5, hi. Ps 5_9, עות pi. *make* way *crooked* Ps 146_9, טאטא pilp. *sweep* Is 14_{23}.

נזל hi. *cause to flow* Is 48_{20}, צוף *cause to flow over* Dt 11_4, יצק *pour* Is $44_{2.2}$, נגר hi. *pour* Ps 75_9, נסך *pour* Is 29_{10}, שפך *pour* Is $4?_{21}$ Jr 14_{15} Ezk 9_8 $20_{7.12.20}$ $22_{22.31}$ 39_{29} Jl $2_{27.27}$ Am 5_8 9_5 Zp 3_8 Ps 69_{17} 79_5 107_{31} Jb 12_9 Lm 2_2 (mss) 4_{11}, זרק *sprinkle* water Ezk 36_{23}, שקע hi. *cause waters to sink* Ezk 32_{14}, יבשׁ hi. *dry* Jos 2_{10} $4_{23.23}$ 5_1 Ezk 17_{24} Na 1_3 (if em. pi. *dry*), חרב hi. *dry* Is 11_{15} (if em. חרם hi. *destroy*) Na 1_3.

רעם hi. *thunder* 1 S 7_{10} 2 S 22_{14}||Ps 18_{14} Ps 29_3 4Q Admon 1.1_3, ברק *flash* lightning Ps 144_5, מטר hi. *cause to rain* Gn 2_5 19_{24} Ex 9_{23} Ps 11_5, חשך hi. *darken* Jr 13_{16} Am 5_8 8_9 Ps 105_{28}, קדר hi. *darken* Ezk 32_8, עוב hi. *cloud* or *scorn* Lm $2_{1(\text{mss})}$.

אור hi. *give light* Ex 13_{21} Ps 118_{27}, *make* face *shine*, i.e. show favour Nm 6_{25} Ps 31_{15} 80_{20} Ketef Hinnom inscr. 1_{17} ([י]אר) 2_8 (יה[ו]ה), *enlighten* eyes, i.e. revive Ps 13_4 Pr 29_{13}, יפע hi. *shine* Dt 33_2 Ps 94_1, זרח *shine* Dt 33_2 Is 60_2, נגה hi. *enlighten* 2 S 22_{29}||Ps 18_{29}.

6. Verbs of beneficial activities, פאר pi. *beautify* Ps 149_4, htp. *be glorified* Is 44_{23}, אדר hi. *make glorious* Is 42_{21}, קדשׁ *be holy* 4QPrayer[c] 1_5 (ק[ודש] ... [··]··), pi. *sanctify* Ex 20_{11} 31_{13} Lv 20_8 $21_{8.15.23}$ $22_{9.16.32}$ Dt 1_{11} Ezk 20_{12} 36_{23} 37_{28}, ni. *sanctify oneself* Nm 20_{13} Ezk 28_{22} 36_{23}, hi. *sanctify* Jr 12_3 Zp 1_7 2 C 36_{14}, htp. *sanctify oneself* Ezk 38_{23}, ברר *purify* Ezk 20_{38}, טהר pi. *purify* Ezk 36_{23} 4Q Admon 1.2_2, צדק *justify* 4QAdmon 1.2_2, מול *circumcise* heart Dt 30_6, משח *anoint* 1 S 10_1 15_{17} Is 61_1 2 C 22_7.

יטב hi. *do good* Nm $10_{32.32}$ Dt 30_5 Jos 24_{20} Jg 17_{13} 1 S 25_{31} Ezk 36_{11} Zp 1_{12} Ps 119_{65} 125_4 Kuntillet ‘Ajrud inscr. D2_2, שׁלם hi. *cause to be at peace* Pr 16_7, יחל pi. *cause to hope* Ps 119_{41} (or em. יִחַלְתָּנִי to יִחֲלְתִּי *I* [worshipper] *have hoped*), צלח hi. *cause to prosper* Gn $24_{21.40.42.56}$ $39_{3.23}$ Ps 118_{25}, עשׁר hi. *enrich* 1 S 2_7.

שׁקה hi. *cause to drink* Is 27_3, רוה pi. *refresh* Jr 31_{14} Ps 21_2 (if em. חדה pi. *make joyful*) Lm 2_{22} (hi.), שׂבע pi. *satisfy* Ps 90_{13}, hi. *satisfy* Is 58_{11} Ps 103_2 107 Lm 2_{22}.

גמל *repay* 2 S 22_{21}||Ps 18_{21} Is $63_{7.7}$ Ps 103_8, *deal generously* Ps 13_6 116_7, סלח *forgive* Nm $30_{6.9.13}$ Dt 29_{19} 2 K $5_{18.18}$ Jr 31_{34} 50_{20} Am 7_2 Ps 25_{11} 103_2 Dn $9_{18(\text{mss})}$, כפר pi. *atone* Dt 21_8=11QT 63_7 2 K 24_4 Jr 18_{23} Ezk 16_{63} 2 C 30_{18}.

מלט pi. *rescue* Jr $39_{18.18}$ Ps 116_4, hi. Is 31_5 Ps 41_2 107_{19} Si 51_{11}, פלט pi. *rescue* 2 S 22_2||Ps 18_3 Ps 17_{13} 22_9 31_2 =71_1 $37_{40.40}$ 144_1, נתר hi. *release* Ps 146_7, פצה *release* Ps 144_5, דלה *draw up*, i.e. rescue Ps 30_2, נצל hi. *rescue* Gn 32_{10} Ex 6_6 12_{27} $18_{8.9.10}$ Dt 23_{15} Jg 8_{34} 1 S 7_3 12_{11} $17_{37.37}$ 26_{24} 2 S 22_1||Ps 18_1 2 K 17_{39} $18_{30.30.32.35}$||Is $36_{15.15.18.20}$ Is 19_{20} 31_5 Jr 1_{19} 15_{20} 20_{13} 39_{17} 42_{11} Ezk $13_{21.23}$ 34_{27} Zc 11_6 Ps 7_2 22_9 31_2=71_1 31_{15} $34_{5.18.20}$ 35_{10} 40_{14} $86_{12(\text{mss})}$ 91_2 97_{10} 106_{40} 107_6 109_{21} $119_{151.169}$ 120_2 142_6 143_9 144_5 (or em. פְּצֵנִי וְהַצִּילֵנִי *set me free and deliver me* to הַמְשֵׁנִי *draw me out*) 2 C 32_{11} Si 51_8 4QapPs[a] 2_4, *take away* word of truth Ps 119_{41} (or em. תְּאַצֵל do not *withhold*).

גאל *redeem* Ex 6_6 15_{11} Is 43_{14} $44_{6.23.24}$ 47_4 $48_{17.20}$ $49_{7.26}$ 54_8 perh. 59_{20} 60_{16} 63_7 Jr 31_{11} Mc 4_{10} Ps 19_{15} 69_{17} 103_2 107_2 119_{151} Lm $3_{58(\text{mss})}$ Si 51_8, פדה *redeem* Dt 7_8 9_{26} 13_6 =11QT 54_{16} Dt 15_{15} 21_8=11QT 63_7 Dt 24_{18} 2 S 4_9 1 K 1_{29} Is 29_{22} Jr 31_{11} Ps 26_8 31_6 34_{23} 55_{17} 69_{17} 130_7 Ne 1_5 1 C 11_{14} 17_{20} Si 51_{11} perh. Kh. Beit Lei graf. 5_2 (see Nom. Cl.).

ישׁע hi. *save* Ex 14_{30} Jg 2_{18} 1 S 4_3 7_8 $14_{6.23}$ 17_{47} 2 S $8_{6.14}$ ||1 C $18_{6.13}$ 2 K 6_{27} 14_{27} 19_{19}||Is 37_{20} Is 33_{22} 38_{20} $43_{3.12}$ 49_{26} 60_{16} Jr 15_{20} 17_{14} $30_{10.11}$ 31_7 42_{11} Ezk 36_{23} Hb 1_2 Zc 9_{16} 10_6 12_7 Ps 6_5 7_2 12_2 $20_{7.10}$ 31_{15} $34_{7.19}$ 36_7 37_{40} 55_{17} 71_1 $106_{4.47}$ $107_{13.19}$ $109_{26.30}$ 116_6 118_{25} $119_{89.145}$ 145_{18} Pr 20_{22} 2 C 32_{22} Lachish ost. 8_4 Kh. Beit Lei graf. 7 ([י]הוה).

עזר *help* 1 S 7_{12} Is $41_{13.14}$ $50_{7.9}$ Ps 30_{11} 37_{40} 86_{17} 109_{26} 118_{13} 119_{75} 2 C $14_{10.10}$ 18_{31} 32_8, נקה pi. *leave unpunished*

Ex 20$_7$||Dt 5$_{11}$ Ex 34$_{6.6}$||Nm 14$_{18.18}$ Jr 30$_{11.11}$ 46$_{28.28}$ Na 1$_{3.3}$ Ps 99$_8$, פוק hi. *promote* Ps 140$_9$, שׂגא hi. *make great* Jb 12$_9$, גדל pi. *magnify* Jos 4$_{14}$ 1 C 29$_{25}$ 2 C 1$_1$, *bring up* Si 50$_{22}$, hi. *magnify* 1 S 12$_{24}$ Is 28$_{29}$ 42$_{21}$, *act mightily* Jl 2$_{21}$ Ps 126$_{2.3}$ GnzPs 3$_{18}$, htp. *display greatness* Ezk 38$_{23}$, גבר pi. *make mighty* Zc 10$_{6.12}$ (or em. וְגִבַּרְתִּים *and I shall make them mighty* to וּגְבֻרָתָם *and their strength* is in Y.), htp. *display might* Is 42$_{13}$.

חמל *pity* Jr 13$_{14}$ Ezk 7$_{4.9}$ Jl 2$_{18}$ Zc 11$_6$ Lm 2$_{17.20}$ 2 C 36$_{15.16}$, רחם pi. *pity* Dt 13$_{18}$ 30$_3$ 2 K 13$_{23}$ Is 14$_1$ 30$_{18}$ 49$_{13}$ 54$_{10}$ 55$_7$ Jr 13$_{14}$ 31$_{20}$ Zc 1$_{12.17}$ (if em. נחם pi. *comfort*) 10$_6$ Ps 102$_{13}$ 103$_{13}$, חוס *pity* Jr 13$_{14}$ Ezk 24$_{14}$ Jl 2$_{17}$, נחם ni. *be sorry* Gn 6$_6$ Ex 32$_{14}$ Jg 2$_{18}$ 1 S 15$_{28.28.35}$ 2 S 24$_{16}$||1 C 21$_{15}$ Is 1$_{24}$ Jr 15$_6$ 20$_{16}$ 26$_{13.19}$ Ezk 24$_{14}$ Jl 2$_{13.14}$ Am 7$_{3.6}$ Ps 90$_{13}$ 106$_{40}$ 110$_4$, pi. *comfort* Is 12$_1$ 49$_{13}$ 51$_{3.3}$ 52$_9$ Zc 1$_{17}$ (or em. רחם pi. *pity*) Ps 86$_{17}$ 119$_{75}$, htp. *pity* Dt 32$_{36}$=Ps 135$_{14}$, חנן *be gracious* Nm 6$_{25}$ 2 S 12$_{22}$ 2 K 13$_{23}$ Is 30$_{18}$ 33$_2$ Am 5$_{15}$ Ps 6$_3$ 9$_{14}$ 26$_8$ 27$_7$ 30$_{11}$ 31$_{10}$ 41$_{5.11}$ 59$_6$ 86$_{3(mss)}$ 123$_3$ 4QapPs^a 2$_5$.

אבה *be willing* Dt 10$_{10}$ 23$_6$ 29$_{19}$ 2 K 8$_{19}$||2 C 21$_7$ 2 K 24$_4$, יאל hi. *be willing* 1 S 12$_{22}$ 2 S 7$_{29}$||1 C 17$_{27}$, חפץ *desire* Nm 14$_8$ Jg 13$_{23}$ 1 S 2$_{25}$ 2 S 22$_{19}$||Ps 18$_{19}$ 1 K 10$_9$||2 C 9$_8$ Is 42$_{21}$ 53$_{10}$ 62$_4$ Jr 9$_{23}$ Ezk 18$_{23.23.32}$ 33$_{11}$ Ml 2$_{17}$ Ps 22$_9$ 35$_{27}$ 37$_{24}$ 40$_6$ 135$_6$ Pr 21$_1$, אוה pi. *desire* Ps 132$_{13}$, רצה *desire* Dt 33$_{11}$ 2 S 24$_{23}$ Jr 14$_{10}$||Ho 8$_{13}$ Ezk 20$_{40}$ 43$_{27}$ Mc 6$_7$ Ps 40$_{14}$ 85$_2$ 119$_{108}$ 147$_{11}$ 149$_4$ Pr 16$_7$ 1 C 28$_4$ perh. Kh. Beit Lei graf. 5$_1$ (see Nom. Cl.).

חשק *love* Dt 7$_7$ 10$_{15}$, אהב *love* Dt 4$_{35}$ 7$_{12}$ 10$_{15}$ 23$_6$ 2 S 12$_{24}$ 1 K 10$_9$ Is 43$_3$ 48$_{14}$ (or em. אֲהֵבוֹ *has loved him* to הֱבִיאוֹ *has brought him*) 61$_8$ Ml 1$_{2.2.2}$ 2$_{11}$ Ps 11$_7$ 33$_4$ 37$_{28}$ 47$_3$ 87$_2$ 97$_{10}$ (if em. אֹהֲבֵי י׳ שִׂנְאוּ רָע *those who love Y. hate evil* to אֹהֵב י׳ שֹׂנְאֵי רָע *Y. loves those who hate evil*) 146$_8$ Pr 3$_{12}$ 15$_9$ 2 C 2$_{10}$, חבב *love* peoples Dt 33$_2$ (unless חֹבֵב = *pure one* of the peoples, or em. חִבֵּב *he loved* or חֲבַב /חֲבִב *beloved of* the nations).

גיל *rejoice* Zp 3$_{17}$, שׂישׂ *rejoice* Dt 28$_{63.63}$ 30$_{9.9}$ Zp 3$_{17}$, שׂמח *rejoice* Ps 104$_{31}$, pi. *make joyful* Ps 30$_2$ 90$_{13}$ 92$_2$ Lm 2$_{17}$ Ezr 6$_{22}$ 2 C 20$_{27}$ 4QapPs^a ([לשׂ]מח), חדה *make joyful* Ps 21$_2$ (or em. תְּרַוֵּהוּ *you saturate him*), רקד hi. *cause to skip* with joy Ps 29$_6$.

רפא *heal* Ex 15$_{26}$= 4QRP^c 6a.2$_{14}$ ([יהוה רופ]אכה) 2 K 20$_8$ Is 19$_{22.22}$ 30$_{26}$ Jr 17$_{14}$ 30$_{17}$ Ho 6$_1$ Ps 6$_3$ 30$_3$ 41$_5$ 103$_2$ 147$_2$ 2 C 30$_{20}$, חבשׁ *bind up* Is 30$_{26}$ Ho 6$_1$ Ps 147$_2$ (pi.).

7. Verbs of hostile activities, דין *judge* Dt 32$_{36}$ 1 S 2$_{10}$ Is 3$_{13}$ Ps 7$_9$ 9$_8$=96$_{10}$ 35$_{24}$ 110$_{5(mss)}$ 135$_{14}$ perh. 11QPsAp^a 2$_4$ ([וידי]ן), שׁפט *judge* Gn 16$_5$ Ex 5$_{21}$ Jg 11$_{27}$ 1 S 24$_{13}$ 2 S 18$_{19.31}$ Is 33$_{22}$ Jr 11$_{20}$ Ezk 11$_{10}$ 18$_{30}$ 35$_{11}$ Ps 7$_9$ 9$_8$=96$_{13}$ =98$_9$ Ps 96$_{13}$=98$_9$=1 C 16$_{33}$ Ps 26$_1$ Lm 3$_{59}$ 4QAdmon 1.1$_3$ 4QapPs^b 76$_{12}$ 11QPsAp^a 2$_{10}$ ([וישפו]ט), ni. *contend* Is 66$_{16}$ Jr 25$_{31}$ Ezk 20$_{36.36}$ Ps 96$_{13}$=98$_9$, ריב *contend* Dt 33$_7$ 1 S 25$_{39}$ Is 3$_8$ Jr 2$_{9.9}$ 50$_{34.34}$ Am 7$_4$ (or em. לָרִב בָּאֵשׁ *to contend with fire* to לַהֶבֶת אֵשׁ *flame of fire*) Mc 7$_9$ Ps 35$_1$ 103$_8$ 119$_{151}$ Pr 22$_{23}$ Lm 3$_{58(mss)}$, רשׁע hi. *condemn* Ps 37$_{33}$, עוד hi. *witness* Ml 2$_{14}$, *warn* 2 K 17$_{13}$.

מלך *rule* Ex 15$_{18}$ Is 24$_{23}$ Ezk 20$_{33}$ Mc 4$_7$ Zp 3$_{15}$ (if em. מֶלֶךְ *king* of Israel to יִמְלֹךְ *he will rule over* Israel) Ps 93$_1$ 96$_{10}$ 97$_1$ 99$_1$ 146$_{10}$ 1 C 16$_{31}$, hi. *cause to rule* 1 K 3$_7$ 1 C 28$_4$ 2 C 1$_9$, משׁל *rule* Jg 8$_{23}$ Is 63$_{17}$ 1 C 29$_{11}$ 2 C 20$_6$ 4QNarrC 1$_7$, hi. *cause to rule* Ps 8$_2$, רדה *rule* Jg 5$_{13}$ (pi.; or em. ירד *go down* and/or עַם י׳ *people; Y.* to עַם י׳ *the people of Y.* will rule/went down) Ps 144$_{1(ms)}$, בעל *be lord* Jr 3$_{14}$ 31$_{32}$ (or em. בחל *reject* or געל *abhor* in both), *marry* Is 54$_5$ (or em. בַּעַל Y. is your *lord*).

בחן *test* Jr 11$_{20}$ 12$_3$ 17$_{10}$ 20$_{12}$ Zc 13$_8$ Ps 11$_5$ 26$_2$ Pr 17$_3$, נסה pi. *test* Ex 15$_{25}$ Dt 8$_{2.14}$ 13$_4$ Jg 3$_1$ Ps 26$_2$, צרף *refine* Zc 13$_8$ Ps 17$_1$ 26$_2$, יסר *discipline* Is 8$_{11}$ (or em. pi.; 1QIsa^a סור hi. *cause to turn aside*), pi. *discipline* Dt 4$_{35}$ 8$_5$ Jr 10$_{24}$ 30$_{11}$ 31$_{18}$ 46$_{28}$ Ps 6$_2$=38$_2$.

לחם *fight* Ps 35$_1$, ni. Ex 14$_{14}$ Ex 14$_{25}$ Dt 1$_{30}$ 3$_{22}$ Jos 10$_{14.42}$ 23$_{3.10}$ Is 30$_{32}$ 31$_4$ Zc 14$_{3.3}$ 2 C 20$_{29}$ 32$_8$ Si 4$_{28}$, נגע pi. *strike* Gn 12$_{17}$ 2 K 15$_5$||2 C 26$_{20}$ Am 9$_5$ Ps 104$_{31}$ 144$_5$, hi. *throw* to ground Is 25$_{10}$ Ezk 13$_{14}$ Lm 2$_{2(mss)}$, נגף *strike* Ex 12$_{23.27}$ 32$_{35}$ Jg 20$_{35}$ 1 S 4$_3$ 25$_{38}$ 26$_{10}$ 2 S 12$_{15}$ Is 19$_{22.22}$ Zc 14$_{12.18}$ 2 C 13$_{20}$ 14$_{11}$ 21$_{14.18}$, נכה hi. *strike* Ex 7$_{25}$ 12$_{12.29}$ Nm 11$_{33}$ 32$_4$ 33$_4$ Dt 28$_{22.27.28.35}$ 1 S 5$_9$ 6$_{19}$ 2 S 5$_{24}$ 1 K 14$_{15}$ 2 K 6$_{18}$ Is 5$_{25}$ 11$_{15}$ Jr 5$_3$ Ezk 21$_{22}$ 32$_{15}$ Ho 6$_1$ Am 3$_{15}$ 4$_9$ Hg 2$_{17}$ Zc 9$_{4(mss)}$ 12$_{4.4}$ 13$_7$ (if em. הַךְ *strike*, with sword as subj., to הַכֵּה אַכֶּה *I shall surely strike*) Ps 69$_{17}$ 135$_{6.6}$ 4QpIsa^b 2$_8$.

הרג *kill* Ex 13$_{15}$ Am 4$_{10}$ Ps 135$_6$ Lm 2$_{2(mss).20}$, מות *die* Hb 1$_{12(TiqSof)}$, hi. *kill* Gn 38$_7$=1 C 2$_3$ Ex 4$_{24}$ Dt 9$_{28}$ Jg 13$_{23}$ 1 S 2$_{6.26}$ 1 K 17$_{20}$ Is 65$_{15}$ 1 C 10$_{14}$, טבח *slaughter* Lm 2$_{20}$, שׁחט *slaughter* Nm 14$_{16}$.

אבד pi. *destroy* Dt 11$_4$ Is 26$_{13}$ Jr 12$_{17}$ 51$_{55}$ Lm 2$_9$ (or del. אבד pi.), hi. *destroy* Dt 7$_{9}$ 8$_{20}$ Jos 7$_{7}$ 1 S 12$_{15}$ (if ins. אבד hi.) Jr 31$_{28}$ 49$_{38}$ Ezk 25$_{7}$ Ob$_{8}$ Mc 5$_{9}$ Zp 2$_{11}$ Ps 143$_{11}$ Jb 12$_{9}$ 11QPsAp^{a} 5$_{2}$ ([יהו]ה יאביד), דמם hi. *destroy* Jr 8$_{14}$, חבל pi. *destroy* Is 13$_{5}$ Jr 14$_{20}$ (if em. נבל pi. *consider invalid*), חרם hi. *destroy* Jos 11$_{20}$ Is 11$_{15}$ (unless חרם hi. *divide*; or em. חרב hi. *dry*) 34$_{2}$ Jr 25$_{9}$, שחת pi. *destroy* Gn 13$_{10}$ Lm 2$_{5(mss)}$ (or em. hi.) 2$_{5(mss)}$, hi. *destroy* Gn 19$_{14}$ Dt 9$_{26}$ 10$_{10}$ 2 K 8$_{19}$||2 C 21$_{7}$ 2 K 13$_{23}$ Jr 13$_{14}$ 15$_{6}$ Ezk 9$_{8}$ Lm 2$_{5(mss)}$ (if em. pi.) 2$_{8}$, צמת hi. *destroy* Ps 94$_{23}$ 143$_{11}$, שמד hi. *destroy* Dt 1$_{27}$ 2$_{21}$ 4$_{3}$ 6$_{15}$ 7$_{4.23}$ 9$_{3.8.19.20.25}$ 28$_{48}$ 31$_{3.4}$ Jos 11$_{20}$ 23$_{15}$ 2 K 21$_{10}$||2 C 33$_{9}$ Is 26$_{13}$ Ezk 14$_{9}$ 25$_{7}$ Am 9$_{8.8.8}$ Ps 145$_{20}$ Lm 3$_{64}$, סוף hi. *make an end*, i.e. destroy Jr 8$_{13}$ (or em. אֲסִיפֵם *I shall destroy them* to אֲסִפָם *their harvest*) Zp 1$_{2.3.3}$, בלע pi. *devour* Is 25$_{6.8}$ (or em. pu. *be devoured*, with מָוֶת *death* as subj.) Ps 21$_{10}$ Lm 2$_{2(mss).5(mss)}$, אכל *eat*, i.e. destroy Am 5$_{6}$ Si 45$_{19}$, hi. *feed* Dt 8$_{3.14}$ Ezk 16$_{19}$ Ps 81$_{11}$, רעב hi. *allow to hunger* Dt 8$_{3}$ Pr 10$_{3}$, רזה appar. *make lean* Zp 2$_{11}$ (or em. pi. in same sense).

מחה *erase* Dt 29$_{19}$ 2 K 14$_{27}$ Is 25$_{8}$ Jr 18$_{23}$ (or em. תִּמַּח *let it not be erased*) Si 5$_{6}$, בלק *devastate* Is 24$_{1}$, בקק *devastate* Is 24$_{1}$, שדד *devastate* Jr 25$_{36}$ 47$_{4}$ 51$_{55}$, שמם hi. *devastate* Ezk 14$_{8}$ 20$_{26}$ 30$_{12}$, גרס hi. *crush* Lm 2$_{22}$ (or em. גרש pi. *expel*), דכא pi. *crush* Is 53$_{10}$, בלה pi. *wear out* Lm 2$_{22}$, קבע *despoil* Pr 22$_{23}$ (or em. עקב *betray*), טמא pi. *defile* Ezk 20$_{26}$, חלל pi. *profane* Lm 2$_{2(mss)}$ Ezk 39$_{7}$ (hi.).

כרת *cut* perh. Is 18$_{5}$, *make* covenant Gn 15$_{18}$ Ex 24$_{8}$ 34$_{10.27}$ Dt 4$_{23}$ 5$_{2.3}$ 9$_{9}$ 28$_{69}$ 29$_{11.24}$ 31$_{16}$ 1 K 8$_{9}$||2 C 5$_{10}$ 1 K 8$_{21}$||2 C 6$_{11}$ 2 K 17$_{15.35.38}$ Is 54$_{17}$ 61$_{8}$ Jr 11$_{9}$ 31$_{31.32.33}$ 32$_{36}$ 34$_{13}$ Ezk 34$_{24}$ 37$_{21}$ Ho 2$_{18}$ Hg 2$_{4}$ Ps 89$_{2}$ 105$_{7}$||1 C 16$_{14}$ Ne 9$_{7}$ 2 C 7$_{12}$ 21$_{7}$ 4QapJoshua^{a} 14$_{4}$, hi. *cut off* Lv 17$_{1}$ 20$_{1}$ 26$_{13}$ Dt 12$_{29}$ 19$_{1}$ 1 S 2$_{30}$ 7$_{8}$||1 C 17$_{7}$ 20$_{15}$ 1 K 9$_{3}$ 14$_{7.14}$ 2 K 9$_{6}$ Is 9$_{13}$ 14$_{22}$ Jr 51$_{62}$ Ezk 14$_{8}$ 21$_{8}$ 25$_{7.13.16}$ 29$_{8}$ 30$_{13}$ 35$_{6}$ Am 1$_{5.8}$ 2$_{3}$ Mc 5$_{9}$ Na 1$_{14}$ 2$_{14}$ Zp 1$_{3}$ 3$_{5}$ Zc 9$_{1}$ 13$_{2}$ Ml 2$_{12}$ Ps 12$_{4}$ 34$_{17}$ 109$_{15}$ (mss יִכָּרֵת *let* their memorial *be cut off*).

קצה pi. *cut off* 2 K 10$_{32}$, קצץ pi. *cut off* Ps 46$_{9}$ 129$_{4}$, סעף pi. *cut off* branches Is 10$_{33}$, טרף *tear* Ho 6$_{1}$, קרע *tear* 1 S 15$_{28}$ 28$_{17}$ Is 63$_{17}$ Ezk 13$_{21}$, נתק *tear off* ring Jr 22$_{24}$, pi. *tear apart* Jr 30$_{8}$ Ps 107$_{13}$, hi. *drag away* Jr 12$_{3}$, שפח pi. *tear apart* Lm 2$_{22}$, הרס *tear down* Jr 31$_{28}$ Ezk 13$_{14}$ Ml 1$_{4}$ Jb 12$_{9}$ Lm 2$_{2(mss)}$ 2$_{17}$, נסח *tear down* Pr 15$_{25}$, נתץ *break down* Jr 31$_{28}$ Ps 58$_{7}$, גדע *hew down* Lm 2$_{2(mss)}$, Ps 107$_{15}$ (pi.), נתש *uproot* Dt 29$_{27}$ 1 K 14$_{15}$ Jr 12$_{17.17}$ 31$_{28}$, בקע *split open* Is 48$_{20}$ Ne 9$_{7}$, מחץ *smash* Dt 33$_{11}$ Ps 110$_{5(mss).5(mss)}$, שבר *break* Is 14$_{5}$ Jr 28$_{4}$ 30$_{8}$ 48$_{38}$ Ezk 34$_{27}$ Ps 105$_{7}$ Lm 1$_{15(mss)}$, pi. *shatter* Ps 29$_{5}$ 46$_{9}$ 107$_{15}$ Lm 2$_{9}$ (or del. שבר pi.) 2$_{22}$ perh. 2QapDavid 1$_{1}$ ([שברו י]הוה) perh. 4QapJoseph^{c} 1$_{6}$, נפץ pi. *shatter* Jr 13$_{14}$, פתת perh. *shatter* Nimrud ivory inscr. 1$_{1}$ ([י]הוה; others [י]), חיל hi. *convulse* steppe Ps 29$_{8}$, פרץ *break out* against Ex 19$_{22}$ 2 S 5$_{20}$ 6$_{8}$||1 C 13$_{11}$ 1 C 15$_{13}$ 2 C 20$_{37}$.

יצת hi. *kindle* Is 27$_{3}$ (if em. צות hi. *kindle*) Jr 11$_{16}$ 21$_{14}$ Lm 4$_{11}$, בער *burn* Lm 2$_{2(mss)}$, pi. Ezk 21$_{4}$, hi. Na 2$_{14}$, שרף *burn* Lv 10$_{6}$ Ps 46$_{9}$.

נקם *avenge* 1 S 24$_{13}$ Na 1$_{2.2}$, ni. Is 1$_{24}$ Jr 15$_{15}$ 46$_{10}$, גמר *avenge* Ps 138$_{8}$, שלם pi. *repay* Dt 7$_{9.9}$ 1 S 24$_{20}$ 2 S 3$_{39}$ 2 K 9$_{26}$ Is 66$_{6}$ Jr 32$_{18}$ 51$_{24.56}$ Ps 31$_{24}$ Pr 19$_{17}$ 25$_{22}$ Ru 2$_{12}$ Arad ost. 21$_{4}$, hi. *perform* Is 44$_{24}$, סלף pi. *bring to ruin* Jb 12$_{9}$ Pr 22$_{12}$, עכר *bring calamity upon* Jos 7$_{25}$, אבל hi. *cause to mourn* Lm 2$_{8}$, חלה *make sick* Dt 29$_{21}$, שכר hi. *make drunk* Jr 51$_{39}$, רעה hi. *hurt* Mc 4$_{6}$, רעע hi. *hurt* Jos 24$_{20}$ 1 K 17$_{20}$ Jr 25$_{29}$ 31$_{28}$ Zp 1$_{12}$, פגע hi. *let* iniquity *hurt* Is 53$_{6}$, חמס *treat violently* Lm 2$_{5(mss)}$, רגע *disturb* Is 51$_{15}$ Jr 31$_{35}$ 50$_{34}$, חתת hi. *terrify* Jr 49$_{37}$, *shatter* 1 S 2$_{10}$ (if em. ni. *be shattered*, of Y.'s enemies), המם *discomfit* Ex 14$_{24}$ Dt 7$_{23}$ (if em. הום *discomfit*) Jos 10$_{10}$ Jg 4$_{15}$ 1 S 7$_{10}$ 2 S 22$_{14}$ Ps 144$_{5}$, יגה hi. *torment* Lm 1$_{5.12}$, הלל po. *make foolish* Is 44$_{24}$ Jb 12$_{9}$, סכל pi. *make foolish* 2 S 15$_{31}$ Is 44$_{24}$ (יְשַׂכֵּל), סלה *treat as worthless* Ps 119$_{108}$, pi. *throw away* Lm 1$_{15(mss)}$, בוש hi. *shame* Ps 119$_{31.108}$.

דבר hi. *subdue* Ps 47$_{3}$, כנע hi. *humble* Dt 9$_{3}$ Ps 81$_{11}$ 2 C 28$_{19}$, רדד *subdue* Is 45$_{1}$ Ps 144$_{1}$ (ms רדה *rule*), ענה pi. *afflict* Dt 8$_{2.3.14}$ 2 K 17$_{20}$ Is 64$_{11}$ Ps 88$_{2}$ (or em. אנה pi. *allow to come*) 90$_{13}$ 119$_{75}$, *break* Ps 102$_{23}$ (or em. pu. my strength *was broken*), כרע hi. *make low* Ps 17$_{13}$, שפל hi. *make low* 1 S 2$_{7}$ Is 25$_{10.10}$ (or del.) Ezk 17$_{24}$ Ps 113$_{5}$ 147$_{6}$ GnzPs 3$_{20}$, כפש hi. *tread* into dust Lm 2$_{22}$.

עשן *be angry* Ps 80$_{5}$, קצף *be angry* Dt 1$_{34}$ 9$_{19}$ Jos 22$_{18}$ Is 64$_{8}$ Zc 1$_{2}$ Lm 5$_{21}$, אנף *be angry* 1 K 8$_{46}$||2 C 6$_{36}$ Is 12$_{1}$ Ps 79$_{5}$, htp. *be angry* Dt 1$_{37}$ 4$_{21}$ 9$_{8.20}$ 1 K 11$_{9}$ 2 K 17$_{18}$ Si 45$_{19}$, חרה *be angry* Hb 3$_{8}$, נטר *keep* anger Jr 3$_{12}$ Na 1$_{2}$ Ps 103$_{8}$, רגז *shake* with anger Is 28$_{21}$, hi. *cause to shake* Is 23$_{11}$ Jr 50$_{34}$, זעם *be indignant* Is 66$_{14}$ (or em. וְזָעַם *and he shall be indignant* to וְזַעְמוֹ *and his indignation*) Na 1$_{6}$ (if em. לִפְנֵי זַעְמוֹ *before his indignation* to זֹעֵם הוּא *he is in-*

dignant) Zc 1_{12} Ml 1_4, *curse* Nm 23_8, ארר pi. *curse* Gn 5_{29}.

שׂנא *hate* Dt 9_{28} 12_{31} 16_{22} Is 61_8 Am 6_8 Zc 8_{17} Ml 1_2 Pr 6_{16} Si $15_{13(A)}$, געל *abhor* Lv 26_{44} Jr 3_{14} 31_{32} (if em. בעל *be lord* in both), תעב pi. *abhor* Am 6_8 (מְתָאֵב) Ps 5_7 106_{40}, שׁקץ pi. *abominate* Ps 22_{24}, נאץ *despise* Dt 32_{19} Jr 14_{20} Lm 2_6, בזה *despise* Ps 22_{24} 69_{34} 102_{17}, נאר pi. *repudiate* Lm $2_{7(mss)}$, בחל *reject* Jr 3_{14} 31_{32} (if em. בעל *be lord* in both), זנח *reject* Zc 10_6 Ps 88_{15} Lm $2_{7(mss)}$ $3_{31(mss)}$, hi. 1 C 28_9, מאס *reject* 1 S $15_{23.26}$ 2 K 17_{20} Jr 2_{37} 6_{30} 7_{29} 31_{37} 33_{24} Lm 5_{21}, מאן *refuse* Nm 22_{13}, לעג *mock* Ps 59_9, ליץ hi. *scorn* Pr 3_{33}, נבל pi. *consider invalid* Jr 14_{20} (or em. חבל pi. *destroy)* Na 3_6, עלל po. *act severely* Ex 10_2 (htp.) Lm $1_{20.20}$ 2_{20}, שׁקר pi. *act falsely* 1 S 15_{28}, עקב *betray* Pr 22_{23} (if em. קבע *despoil)*, נשׁא hi. *deceive* Jr $4_{10.10}$, פתה pi. *deceive* Jr 20_7 Ezk 14_9, תעה hi. *cause to err* Is 63_{17} Ps 107_{31} Jb $12_{9.9}$, סוך pilp. *provoke* Is 9_{10}, סות hi. *incite* 1 S 26_{19} 2 S 24_1, עור *rouse oneself* Ps 7_7 59_4, ni. *be roused* Zc 2_{17}, pol. *stir up* Is 10_{26}, hi. *stir up* Is 42_{13} $50_{4.4}$ Jr 51_{11} Hg 1_{14} Ezr 1_1=2 C 36_{22} 2 C 21_{16}.

נטשׁ *abandon* Jg 6_{13} 1 S 12_{22} 1 K 8_{57} Jr 7_{29} 23_{33} Ps 94_{14}, עזב *abandon* Gn 24_{27} 28_{13} Dt $31_{6.8}$ 1 K 8_{57} Is 49_{14} Ezk 8_{12} 9_9 Ps 9_{11} $37_{28.33}$ 38_{22} 71_5 94_{14} Ru 2_{20} (unless Boaz is subj.) Lm 5_{19} 1 C 28_{20} 2 C 15_2 24_{20}.

<NOM CL> אֱלֹהֵי עוֹלָם י׳ בּוֹרֵא קְצוֹת הָאָרֶץ *Y. is God of eternity, creator of the ends of the earth* Is 40_{28}, י׳ אֱלֹהֵיכֶם הוּא אֱלֹהֵי הָאֱלֹהִים וַאֲדֹנֵי הָאֲדֹנִים *Y., your God, is God of gods and Lord of lords* Dt 10_{17}, אַתָּה י׳ אֱלֹהִים לְבַדֶּךָ *you alone, O Y., are God* 2 K 19_{19}.

י׳ (...) אֱלֹהִים *Y. (...) is God* Jos 22_{34} 2 S 7_{26}||1 C 17_{24} 1 K $18_{21.37}$, י׳ (...) הוּא (הָ)אֱלֹהִים *Y. (...) is God* Dt $4_{35.39}$ Jos 2_{11} 1 K 8_{60} $18_{39.39}$ Ps 100_3 2 C 33_{13}, י׳ אַתָּה־הוּא הָאֱלֹהִים *O Y., you are God* 2 S 7_{28}||1 C 17_{26}, י׳ ... אֵל אֱלֹהֶיךָ *Y., your God, is ... God* Dt 4_{31}, י׳ אֱלֹהִים אֱמֶת *Y. is God (in) truth* Jr 10_{10}, י׳ אֱלֹהֶיךָ הוּא הָאֱלֹהִים הָאֵל הַנֶּאֱמָן *Y., your God, is God, the faithful God* Dt 7_9, י׳ אֱלֹהֵי הָרִים *Y. is a God of the mountains* 1 K 20_{14}, י׳ אֱלֹהֵי מִשְׁפָּט *Y. is God of judgment* Is 30_{18}, י׳ אֱלֹהַי אַתָּה *O Y., you are my God* Is 25_1, י׳ אֱלֹהָי *Y. is my God* Zc 13_9, י׳ אֱלֹהֵינוּ *Y. is our God* 2 C 13_{10}, י׳ אֱלֹהָיו *Y. is his God* Ps 33_{12} 144_{15}.

י׳ אלהי כל הארץ הו יהוה את אלהי ירשלם *Y. is God of all the land; O Y., you are the God of Jerusalem* Kh. Beit Lei graf. 5 (others rd. הרי יהד לו *Y.* is God of all the land, *the mountains of Judah are his*, the God of Jerusalem; or הרי יהודה לאלהי *the mountains of Judah belong to the God of* Jerusalem; or [אני] י׳ אלהיכה ארצה ערי יהדה וגאלתי ירשלם *I am Y. your God; I am pleased with the towns of Judah and I have redeemed Jerusalem)*.

אַתָּה י׳ אֵל־רַחוּם וְחַנּוּן אֶרֶךְ אַפַּיִם וְרַב־חֶסֶד *you, O Y., are a God merciful and gracious, slow to anger and great of mercy* Ps $86_{15(mss)}$, י׳ קַנָּא שְׁמוֹ אֵל קַנָּא הוּא *Y., whose name is zealous, is a zealous God* Ex 34_{14}, אָנֹכִי י׳ אֱלֹהֶיךָ אֵל קַנָּא *I, Y., your God, am a zealous God* Ex 20_5||Dt 5_9, י׳ אֵל קַנָּא אֱלֹהֶיךָ *Y., your God, is a zealous God* Dt 6_{15}, י׳ אֵל *Y. is God* Ps 118_{27}, י׳ אֵל גָּדוֹל *Y. is a great God* Ps 95_3 (+ וּמֶלֶךְ גָּדוֹל *and a great king*; or del. גָּדוֹל), י׳ אֵל דֵּעוֹת *Y. is a God of knowledge* 1 S 2_3, י׳ אֵל גְּמֻלוֹת *Y. is a God of retribution* Jr 51_{56}, י׳ אֵל קַנּוֹא וְנֹקֵם *Y. is a zealous and avenging God* Na 1_2.

י׳ אֱלֹהֵינוּ י׳ אֶחָד *Y., our God, is one Y.* or *Y., our God, Y. is one*, or *Y. is our God, Y. is one*, or *Y. is our God, Y. alone* Dt 6_4.

י׳ שֹׁפְטֵנוּ י׳ מְחֹקְקֵנוּ י׳ מַלְכֵּנוּ *Y. is our judge, Y. is our lawgiver, Y. is our king* Is 33_{22}, י׳ שופט *Y. is judge* throughout all the world GnzPs 3_{20}, י׳ מֶלֶךְ עוֹלָם *Y. is king of eternity* Ps 10_{16}, י׳ ... מֶלֶךְ גָּדוֹל *Y. ... is a great king* Ps 47_3, י׳ ... מַלְכְּכֶם *Y. ... is your king* 1 S 12_{12}, מִי זֶה מֶלֶךְ הַכָּבוֹד י׳ ... י׳ *who is the king of glory? (The king of glory is) Y., ... Y.* Ps 24_8, י׳ ... הוּא מֶלֶךְ הַכָּבוֹד *Y. ... is the king of glory* Ps 24_{10}.

י׳ אִישׁ מִלְחָמָה *Y. is a man of war* Ex 15_3 (Sam י׳ גִּבּוֹר בְּמִלְחָמָה *Y. is a mighty one in war)*, אַתָּה י׳ אָבִינוּ *you, O Y., are our father* Is 63_{16}, י׳ אָבִינוּ אָתָּה *O Y., you are our father* Is 64_7, י׳ עֵד *Y. is (a) witness* 1 S 12_5, י׳ רֹעִי *Y. is my shepherd* Ps 23_1.

י׳ חֶלְקִי *Y. is my portion* Ps 119_{57} Lm 3_{24}, י׳ הוּא נַחֲלָתוֹ *Y. is his inheritance* Dt 10_9 18_2, י׳ ... הוּא נַחֲלָתָם *Y. ... is their inheritance* Jos 13_{33}, י׳ מְנָת־חֶלְקִי וְכוֹסִי *Y. is the portion of my share*, i.e. my chosen portion, *and my cup* Ps 16_5.

י׳ מַחֲסֶה *Y. is a refuge* Jl 4_{16}, אַתָּה י׳ מַחְסִי *you, O Y., are my refuge* Ps 91_9 (or em. מַחְסֶךָ you have made Y. *your refuge)*, י׳ מַחְסֵהוּ *Y. is his refuge* Ps 14_6, י׳ סַלְעִי וּמְצוּדָתִי וּמְפַלְטִי *Y. is my rock and my stronghold and my deliverer*

2 S 22$_{2}$||Ps 18$_{3}$ (+ אֵלִי צוּרִי אֶחֱסֶה־בּוֹ מָגִנִּי וְקֶרֶן־יִשְׁעִי מִשְׂגַּבִּי *my God, my rock in whom I take refuge, my shield and the horn of my salvation, my secure height*), ״ מָעוֹז־חַיַּי *Y. is the stronghold of my life* Ps 27$_{1}$, ״ צִלְּךָ *Y. is your shade* Ps 121$_{5}$, ״ אוֹר לִי *Y. is a light for me* Mc 7$_{8}$, ״ אוֹרִי וְיִשְׁעִי *Y. is my light and my salvation* Ps 27$_{1}$, שֶׁמֶשׁ וּמָגֵן ״ *Y. is sun and shield* Ps 84$_{12}$, אַתָּה ״ מָגֵן בַּעֲדִי כְּבוֹדִי *you, O Y., are a shield around me, my glory* Ps 3$_{4}$, ״ נִסִּי *Y. is my standard* Ex 17$_{15}$.

עָזִּי ״ עֻזִּי וּמָגִנִּי *Y. is my strength and my shield* Ps 28$_{7}$, וְזִמְרָת יָהּ ״ *Yah, Y., is my strength and (my) song* or *(my) refuge* Is 12$_{2}$ (mss, 1QIsa[a] זִמְרָתִי *my song/refuge*), ״ ... חֵילִי *Y. ... is my strength* Hb 3$_{19}$, ״ עֹז־לָמוֹ *Y. is a strength for them* Ps 28$_{8}$ (mss לְעַמּוֹ *for his people*), לוּלֵי ״ עֶזְרָתָה לִּי *if Y. had not been a help for me* Ps 94$_{17}$, ״ עֶזְרֶךָ *Y. is your help* Dt 33$_{29}$ (if em. מָגֵן *shield of* your help to ״; or em. מָגִנּוֹ *his shield* is your help).

״ אֱלֹהֵי הַצְּבָאוֹת ״ זִכְרוֹ *Y., the God of hosts, Y. is his memorial*, i.e. name Ho 12$_{6}$, ״ (...) שְׁמוֹ *Y. (...) is his name* Ex 15$_{3}$ Is 51$_{15}$ 54$_{5}$ Jr 10$_{16}$ 32$_{18}$ 33$_{2}$ 46$_{18}$ 48$_{15}$ 50$_{34}$ 51$_{19.57}$ Am 4$_{13}$ 5$_{8}$ 9$_{6}$, שְׁמִי ״ *my name is Y.* Jr 16$_{21}$, שִׁמְךָ ״ *your name is Y.* Ps 83$_{19}$, ״ שָׁלוֹם *Y. is peace* Jg 6$_{24}$, ״ צִדְקֵנוּ *Y. is our righteousness* Jr 23$_{6}$ 33$_{16}$, ״ אֱלֹהֶיךָ אֵשׁ *Y., your God, is a fire* Dt 4$_{24}$, ״ אֱלֹהֶיךָ הוּא־הָעֹבֵר לְפָנֶיךָ אֵשׁ אֹכְלָה *Y., your God, is the one who passes before you, a devouring fire* Dt 9$_{3}$.

חַי ״ *(as) Y. is alive* Jg 8$_{7}$ 1 S 14$_{39}$ 19$_{6}$ 20$_{3.21}$ 25$_{26.34}$ 26$_{10.16}$ 28$_{10}$ 29$_{6}$ 2 S 4$_{9}$ 12$_{5}$ 14$_{11}$ 15$_{21}$ 22$_{47}$||Ps 18$_{47}$ 1 K 1$_{29}$ 2$_{24}$ 17$_{1.12}$ 18$_{10.15}$ 22$_{14}$||2 C 18$_{13}$ 2 K 2$_{2.4.6}$ 3$_{14}$ 4$_{30}$ 5$_{16.20}$ Jr 4$_{2}$ 5$_{2}$ 12$_{16}$ 16$_{14.15}$ 23$_{7.8}$ 38$_{16}$ 44$_{26}$ (חַי ... ״) Ho 4$_{15}$ Ru 3$_{13}$ Lachish ost. 3$_{9}$ (חיהוה) 6$_{12}$ 12$_{3}$ Arad ost. 21$_{5}$ (חיה[וה]).

קָדוֹשׁ קָדוֹשׁ קָדוֹשׁ ״ צְבָאוֹת *holy, holy, holy is Y. of hosts* Is 6$_{3}$, קָדוֹשׁ ״ *Y. is holy* Ps 99$_{9}$, קָדוֹשׁ אֲנִי ״ *I, Y., am holy* Lv 19$_{2}$ 20$_{26}$ 21$_{8}$, אֲנִי ״ קָדוֹשׁ בְּיִשְׂרָאֵל *I, Y., am holy in Israel* Ezk 39$_{7}$.

רחום ״ *Y. is merciful* Si 5$_{6}$ רַחוּם וְחַנּוּן ״ *Y. is merciful and gracious* Ps 103$_{8}$, חַנּוּן וְרַחוּם ״ *Y. is gracious and merciful* Ps 111$_{4}$ 145$_{8}$ 2 C 30$_{9}$ (חַנּוּן וְרַחוּם with pronoun in ref. to Y. Ex 22$_{26}$ [חַנּוּן only] Jl 2$_{13}$ Jon 4$_{2}$ Ne 9$_{17}$), ״ אֶרֶךְ אַפַּיִם *Y. is slow to anger* Nm 14$_{18}$ (+ וְרַב־חֶסֶד *and great of mercy*) Na 1$_{3}$ (+ וּגְדָל־כֹּחַ *and great of power*) Ps 103$_{8}$ (+ וְרַב־חֶסֶד) 145$_{8}$ (+ וּגְדָל־חָסֶד *and great of mercy*) (אֶרֶךְ אַפַּיִם וְרַב־חֶסֶד with pronoun in ref. to Y. Jl 2$_{13}$ Jon 4$_{2}$), ״ ארך אפים הוא *Y. is slow to anger* Si 5$_{4(C)}$, חַנּוּן ״ וְצַדִּיק *Y. is gracious and righteous* Ps 116$_{5}$.

״ צַדִּיק *Y. is righteous* Zp 3$_{5}$ Ps 129$_{4}$, ״ הַצַּדִּיק *Y. is in the right* Ex 9$_{27}$, צַדִּיק (...) ״ *Y. (...) is righteous* Ps 11$_{7}$ 145$_{17}$ Lm 1$_{18}$ Dn 9$_{14}$ 2 C 12$_{6}$, צַדִּיק אַתָּה ״ *you are righteous, O Y.* Jr 12$_{1}$ 119$_{137}$, צַדִּיק אַתָּה ... ״ *O Y., ... you are righteous* Ezr 9$_{15}$, חָסִיד ... ״ *Y. is ... loyal* Ps 145$_{17}$ (with pronoun in ref. to Y. Jr 3$_{12}$), יָשָׁר (...) ״ *Y. (...) is upright* Ps 92$_{16}$, טוֹב ״ *Y. is good* Jr 33$_{11}$ Na 1$_{7}$ (+ לְמָעוֹז *as a refuge*; or em. לְמְחַכֵּי־לוֹ מָעוֹז Y. is good, *a refuge to those who wait for him*) Ps 25$_{8}$ (+ וְיָשָׁר *and upright*) 34$_{9}$ 86$_{5(mss)}$ (+ וְסַלָּח וְרַב־חֶסֶד *and forgiving and great of mercy*) 100$_{5}$ 119$_{65}$ 135$_{3}$ 145$_{9}$ Lm 3$_{25}$.

גָּדוֹל ״ *Y. is great* Ps 48$_{2}$=96$_{4}$||1 C 16$_{25}$ Ps 135$_{5}$ 145$_{3}$ Si 43$_{5(B)}$ (גדיל), גָּדוֹל ... ״ *Y. is great* Ps 99$_{2}$, גָּדוֹל ״ מִכָּל־הָאֱלֹהִים *Y. is greater than all the gods* Ex 18$_{11}$, אַתָּה ״ עֶלְיוֹן עַל־כָּל־הָאָרֶץ *you, O Y., are supreme over all the earth* Ps 97$_{9}$ (״ lacking in ms), אַדִּיר (...) ״ *Y. (...) is majestic* Is 33$_{21}$ Ps 93$_{4}$.

אֲנִי ״ רִאשׁוֹן *I, Y., am (the) first* Is 41$_{4}$, קָרוֹב (...) ״ *Y. (...) is near* Ps 34$_{19}$ 119$_{51}$ 145$_{18}$, רָחוֹק ״ מֵרְשָׁעִים *Y. is far from the wicked* Pr 15$_{29}$.

״ שָׁמָּה *Y. is there* Ezk 48$_{35}$, אַיֵּה ״ *where is Y.?* Jr 2$_{6.8}$ Mc 7$_{10}$ (if em. אַיּוֹ *where is he?*), אַיֵּה ״ אֱלֹהֵי אֵלִיָּהוּ *where is Y., the God of Elijah?* 2 K 2$_{14}$.

״ לִי בְּעֹזְרָי *Y. is for me, among those who help me* Ps 118$_{6}$ (if ins. בְּעֹזְרָי) 118$_{7}$.

״ בְּסֹמְכֵי נַפְשִׁי *Y. is among those who uphold my life* Ps 54$_{6(mss)}$, ״ בְּהֵיכַל קָדְשׁוֹ *Y. is in the temple of his holiness* Hb 2$_{20}$ Ps 11$_{4}$, לֹא בָרוּחַ ״ *Y. was not in the wind* 1 K 19$_{11}$, לֹא בָרַעַשׁ ״ *Y. was not in the earthquake* 1 K 19$_{11}$, לֹא בָאֵשׁ ״ *Y. was not in the fire* 1 K 19$_{12}$, יֵשׁ ״ בַּמָּקוֹם הַזֶּה *Y. is in this place* Gn 28$_{16}$, הַ״ אֵין בְּצִיּוֹן *is Y. not in Zion?* Jr 8$_{19}$.

אַתָּה בְקִרְבֵּנוּ ״ *you are among us, O Y.* Jr 14$_{7}$, הֲיֵשׁ ״ בְּקִרְבֵּנוּ אִם־אָיִן *is Y. among us or not?* Ex 17$_{7}$, הֲלוֹא ״ בְּקִרְבֵּנוּ *is not Y. among us?* Mc 3$_{11}$, בְּקִרְבֵּךְ (...) ״ *Y. (...) is among you* Zp 3$_{15.17}$ (L בְּקִרְבֵּךְ), אֵין ״ בְּקִרְבְּכֶם *Y. is not among you* Nm 14$_{42}$, ״ אֱלֹהֶיךָ בְּקִרְבֶּךָ אֵל גָּדוֹל *Y., your God, is among you, a great God* or *Y., your God among you, is a great God* Dt 7$_{21}$.

בְּתוֹכֵנוּ ״ *Y. is among us* Jos 22$_{31}$, בְּתוֹכָם ״ *Y. is among them* Nm 16$_3$.

הֲלוֹא אַתָּה מִקֶּדֶם י׳ *are you not from of old, O Y.?* Hb 1$_{12}$.

י׳ עַל־יְמִינְךָ *Y. is at your right hand* Ps 110$_{5(mss)}$.

י׳ אוֹתִי *Y. is with me* Jos 14$_{12}$ (mss אִתִּי) Jr 20$_{11}$ (+ כְּגִבּוֹר *as a mighty one*), י׳ אִתָּנוּ *Y. is with us* Nm 14$_9$, י׳ אִתּוֹ *Y. was with him* Gn 39$_{3.23}$, אֲנִי י׳ אֱלֹהֵיהֶם אִתָּם *I, Y., their God, am with them* Ezk 34$_{30}$.

אֵין עִם־י׳ אֱלֹהֵינוּ עַוְלָה *there is no injustice with Y., our God* 2 C 19$_7$, אֵין י׳ עִם־יִשְׂרָאֵל *Y. is not with Israel* 2 C 25$_7$, י׳ עִם־דָּוִד *Y. was with David* 1 S 18$_{28}$, יֵשׁ י׳ עִמָּנוּ *Y. is with us* Jg 6$_{13}$, י׳ עִמָּנוּ *Y. is with us* 2 C 32$_8$, עִמָּנוּ (...) י׳ *Y. (...) is with us* Ps 46$_{8.12}$, עִמְּךָ (...) י׳ *Y. (...) is with you* Dt 2$_7$ 20$_1$ (both עִמָּךְ) Jos 1$_9$ Jg 6$_{12}$ 2 S 7$_3$ (עִמָּךְ) 1 C 28$_{20}$ (עִמָּךְ), י׳ עִמָּכֶם *may Y. be with you* Ex 10$_{10}$ Ru 2$_4$, *Y. is with you* 2 C 15$_2$, *Y. will be with you* 2 C 20$_{17}$, הֲלֹא י׳ ... עִמָּכֶם *is not Y. ... with you?* 1 C 22$_{18}$, עִמּוֹ (...) י׳ *Y. (...) is with him* Nm 23$_{21}$ 1 S 16$_{18}$, *Y. (...) was with him* 1 S 18$_{14}$ 2 S 5$_{10}$||1 C 11$_9$ 1 C 9$_{20}$ 2 C 1$_1$ 15$_9$, *may Y. be with him* 2 C 36$_{23}$ (ms אֱלֹהָיו may *his God* be with him), י׳ עִמָּם *Y. is with them* Jg 1$_{22}$ Zc 10$_5$.

י׳ בֵּינִי וּבֵינְךָ *may Y. be between me and you* 1 S 20$_{23}$.

י׳ סָבִיב לְעַמּוֹ *Y. is round about his people* Ps 125$_2$.

אָנֹכִי אָנֹכִי י׳ *I, I am Y.* Is 43$_{11}$, אָנֹכִי י׳ *I am Y.* Is 44$_{24}$, אָנֹכִי י׳ אֱלֹהֶיךָ *I am Y., your* (masc. sg.) *God* (but here and in some of the following, perh. י׳ is in app. with אָנֹכִי or אֲנִי, *I, Y., am*, etc.) Ex 20$_2$||Dt 5$_6$ Is 51$_{15}$ Ho 12$_{10}$ 13$_4$ Ps 81$_{11}$.

אֲנִי י׳ רִאשׁוֹן וְאֶת־אַחֲרֹנִים אֲנִי־הוּא *I am Y., the first and with the last; I am he* Is 41$_4$, אֲנִי (...) י׳ *I am (...) Y.* Gn 15$_7$ 28$_{13}$ Ex 6$_{2.6.7.8.29}$ 7$_{5.17}$ 8$_{18}$ 10$_2$ (Sam אֲנִי אֱלֹהֵיכֶם *I am your God*) 12$_{12}$ 14$_{4.18}$ 15$_{26}$ Lv 11$_{45}$ 18$_{5.6.21}$ 19$_{12.14.16.18.28.30.32.37}$ 20$_8$ 21$_{12.15.23}$ 22$_{2.3.8.9.16.30.31.32.33}$ 26$_{2.45}$ Nm 3$_{13.41.45}$ 35$_{34}$ 1 K 20$_{13.28}$ Is 42$_8$ 43$_{15}$ 45$_{5.6.19.21}$ 49$_{23.26}$ Jr 24$_7$ Ezk 6$_{7.10.13.14}$ 7$_{4.9.27}$ 11$_{10.12}$ 12$_{15.16.20}$ 13$_{9.14.21.23}$ 14$_8$ 15$_7$ 16$_{62}$ 20$_{26.38.42.44}$ 22$_{16}$ 23$_{49}$ 24$_{24.27}$ 25$_{5.7.11.17}$ 26$_6$ 28$_{22.23.24}$ 29$_{6.9.16.21}$ 30$_{8.19.25.26}$ 32$_{15}$ 33$_{29}$ 34$_{27}$ 35$_{4.9.12.15}$ 36$_{11.23.38}$ 37$_{6.13}$ 38$_{23}$ 39$_6$ Ml 3$_6$ 4QpsEzek[a] 2$_4$=4QpsEzek[d] 8$_6$ 4QpsEzek[b] 1.2$_1$, אֲנִי י׳ אֱלֹהֵי כָּל־בָּשָׂר *I am Y., the God of all flesh* Jr 32$_{27}$, אֲנִי י׳ אֱלֹהֶיךָ *I am Y., your* (sg.) *God* Is 41$_{13}$ 43$_3$ 48$_{17}$, אֲנִי י׳ אֱלֹהֵיכֶם *I am Y., your* (pl.) *God* Ex 6$_7$ 16$_{12}$ 29$_{46}$ Lv 11$_{44}$ 18$_{2.4.30}$ 19$_{3.4.10.25.31.34.36}$ 20$_{7.24}$ 23$_{22.43}$ 24$_{22}$ 25$_{17.38.55}$ 26$_1$ 26$_{13}$ Nm 10$_{10}$ 15$_{41.41}$ Dt 29$_5$ Jg 6$_{10}$ Ezk 20$_{5.7.19.20}$ Jl 2$_{27}$ 4$_{17}$, אֲנִי י׳ אֱלֹהֵיהֶם *I am Y., their God* Ex 10$_7$ 29$_{46}$ Lv 26$_{44}$ Ezk 28$_{26}$ 39$_{22.28}$ Zc 10$_6$.

אַתָּה הוּא י׳ *you are Y.* Ne 9$_7$ 4QConfess 2$_6$, אתה י[הוה] *you are Y.* 4QPrayer[c] 1$_7$, אַתָּה־הוּא י׳ לְבַדֶּךָ *you alone are Y.* Ne 9$_6$, אַתָּה י׳ לְבַדֶּךָ *you alone are Y.* Is 37$_{20}$, הֲלֹא אַתָּה־הוּא י׳ *are you not he, O Y.?* Jr 14$_{22}$, אַתָּה י׳ אֱלֹהָי *you are Y., my God* Jr 31$_{18}$, י׳ אֱלֹהֵינוּ אַתָּה *you are Y., our God* 2 C 14$_{10}$, אַתָּה י׳ אֱלֹהֵינוּ *you are Y., our God* Jr 3$_{22}$.

הוּא י׳ *it is Y.* 1 S 3$_{18}$ 11QPsAp[a] 2$_4$, הוּא י׳ אֱלֹהֵינוּ *he is Y., our God* Ps 105$_7$||1 C 16$_{14}$, זֶה י׳ *this is Y.* Is 25$_9$, מִי י׳ *who is Y.?* Ex 5$_2$ Pr 30$_9$.

<OBJ> perh. 4QapJoshua[b] 3.1$_2$ 4QpsEzek[a] 12$_3$ 4Q408 6$_1$ (א]ת י׳]) 4Q474 1$_4$ (unless prep. אֵת *with* in all four); קדם pi. *approach* Mc 6$_{6.6}$ Ps 88$_{14}$, סבב po. *surround* Ps 7$_7$, מצא *find* Ho 5$_6$, שׁית *place* Ps 16$_8$, שׂים *cause to be* Ps 40$_5$ 91$_9$ (if em. מַחְסִי you, O Y., are *my refuge* to מַחְסֶךָ you have made Y. *your refuge*), נתן *give (to)* Is 27$_3$ 4QapPent 9$_4$.

עבד *serve* Ex 10$_{7.8.11.24.26.26}$ 12$_{31}$ 23$_{25}$ Dt 6$_{13}$ 10$_{12.20}$ 11$_{13}$ 13$_5$=11QT 54$_{13}$ 28$_{47}$ Jos 22$_5$ 24$_{14.14.15.15.18.19.21.22.24.31}$ Jg 2$_7$ 10$_6$ 1 S 7$_{3.4}$ 12$_{14.20.24}$ 2 S 15$_8$ Jr 30$_9$ Ezk 20$_{40}$ Zp 3$_9$ Ps 2$_{11}$ 100$_2$ 102$_{23}$ 2 C 30$_8$ 33$_{16}$ 34$_{33}$ 35$_3$, שׁרת pi. *minister (to)* Dt 10$_8$ 17$_{12}$ 1 S 2$_{11}$ Is 56$_6$ Ezk 40$_{46}$ 45$_4$ Jl 1$_9$ 2$_{17}$ 1 C 15$_2$ 23$_{13}$ 2 C 29$_{11}$.

בקשׁ pi. *seek* Ex 33$_7$ Dt 4$_{29}$ Is 45$_{19}$ 51$_1$ Jr 50$_4$ Ho 3$_5$ 5$_6$ 7$_{10}$ Zp 1$_6$ 2$_3$ Zc 8$_{21.22}$ Ps 40$_{14}$||70$_2$ 105$_3$||1 C 16$_{10}$ (or em. מְבַקֵּשׁ רְצוֹנוֹ *one who seeks his desire*, as 4QPs[e]) Pr 28$_5$ 2 C 11$_{16}$ 15$_{4.15}$ 20$_4$, דרשׁ *seek* Gn 25$_{22}$ 1 K 22$_8$||2 C 18$_7$ 2 K 3$_{11}$ 8$_8$ 22$_{13}$||2 C 34$_{21}$ 2 K 22$_{18}$ Is 9$_{12}$ 31$_1$ 55$_5$ Jr 10$_{21}$ 21$_2$ Ezk 20$_{1.3}$ Ho 10$_{12}$ Am 5$_6$ Zp 1$_6$ Ps 9$_{11}$ 22$_{27}$ 34$_{5.11}$ 105$_4$||1 C 16$_{11}$ Ps 34$_{11}$ 119$_1$ Lm 3$_{25}$ 1 C 28$_{9.9}$ 2 C 12$_{14}$ 14$_{3.6.6}$ 15$_{2.12}$ 16$_{12}$ 22$_9$ 26$_5$ 30$_{19}$, פקד *seek* Is 26$_{16}$, שׁחר pi. *seek* Is 26$_8$ Ho 6$_3$ (if em. כְּשַׁחַר נָכוֹן *as established as the dawn* to כְּשַׁחֲרֵנוּ כֵּן *as [soon as] we seek him, then*).

אהב *love* Dt 6$_5$ 10$_{12}$ 11$_{1.13.22}$ 13$_4$ 19$_9$ 30$_{6.16.20}$ Jos 22$_5$ 23$_{11}$ 1 K 3$_3$ Ps 31$_{24}$ 97$_{10}$ (or em. אֹהֲבֵי י׳ שִׂנְאוּ רָע *those who love Y. hate evil* to אֹהֵב י׳ שֹׂנְאֵי רָע *Y. loves those who hate evil*) 116$_1$ (if em. אָהַבְתִּי י׳ *I love Y.*) 145$_{20}$ Ne 1$_5$ 11QT 54$_{12}$, רחם *love* Ps 18$_2$ (or em. אֲרוֹמִמְךָ *I shall exalt you*), אוה pi. *desire* Is 26$_8$, בחר *choose* Jos 24$_{22}$, קוה *await* Lm 3$_{25}$, pi. Is 26$_8$ 40$_{31}$ 49$_{23}$ Ps 25$_4$ 37$_9$ 40$_2$ 69$_7$ 130$_5$.

·ברך pi. *bless* Gn 24$_{48}$ Dt 8$_{10}$ 12$_{7}$ Jg 5$_{2.9}$ Ps 16$_{7}$ 26$_{12}$ 34$_{2}$ 68$_{27}$ (mss אֲדֹנָי) 103$_{1.2.20.21.22.22}$ 104$_{1.35}$ 134$_{1.2}$ 135$_{19.19.19.19}$ 145$_{10}$ Ne 8$_{6}$ 9$_{5}$ 1 C 29$_{10.20}$ 2 C 20$_{26}$ 31$_{8}$ Si 45$_{25}$, *curse* Ps 10$_{3}$ (or em. מְהַלֵּל *the one who boasts*) Si 50$_{22}$ 4QpsEzek[a] 2$_{8}$, רום pol. *exalt* Is 25$_{1}$ Ps 18$_{2}$ (if em. אֶרְחָמְךָ *I shall love you* to אֲרֹמִמְךָ *I shall exalt you*) 30$_{2}$ 99$_{5.9}$ 107$_{31}$ Pr 3$_{9}$ Si 51$_{10}$, כבד pi. *honour* Is 24$_{15}$ Ps 22$_{24}$ 4QapPent 9$_{2}$, קדשׁ hi. *sanctify* Is 8$_{13}$ (+ וְהוּא מוֹרַאֲכֶם וְהוּא מַעֲרִצְכֶם *and he is the one you are to revere and he is the one you are to dread*) Pr 3$_{7}$.

הלל pi. *praise* Is 62$_{9}$ 64$_{8}$ Jr 20$_{13}$ Ps 22$_{24.27}$ 69$_{34}$ 107$_{31}$ 109$_{30}$ 117$_{1}$ 119$_{159.174}$ 146$_{1.2}$ 148$_{1.1.1.1.1.1.1.7}$ Ezr 3$_{10}$ (mss לַי׳ or אֶל־י׳ give praise *to Y.*) Ne 5$_{13}$ 4QapJoseph[b] 1$_{26}$ 34 ([יהוה]), זמר pi. *praise* Is 12$_{5}$ Ps 30$_{11}$ 57$_{10(mss)}$=108$_{4}$, שׁבח pi. *praise* Ps 117$_{1}$ 147$_{12}$, ידה hi. *give thanks to* Gn 29$_{35}$ 2 S 22$_{50}$||Ps 18$_{50}$=57$_{10(mss)}$=108$_{4}$ Is 12$_{1}$ Jr 33$_{11}$ Ps 7$_{18}$ 9$_{2}$ 28$_{7}$ 30$_{9.13}$ 86$_{12(mss)}$ 88$_{10}$ 109$_{30}$ 111$_{1}$ 138$_{4}$ 139$_{4}$ 145$_{10}$ Si 51$_{22}$.

ירא *fear* Ex 14$_{31}$ Dt 6$_{2.13.24}$ 10$_{12.20}$ 13$_{5}$=11QT 54$_{13}$ 14$_{23}$ 17$_{19}$ 28$_{58}$ 31$_{12.13}$ Jos 4$_{24}$ 22$_{25}$ 24$_{14}$ 1 S 12$_{14.18.24}$ 2 S 6$_{9}$ 1 K 18$_{3.12}$ 2 K 4$_{1}$ 17$_{25.28.32.33.34.36.39.41}$ Is 50$_{10}$ Jr 5$_{22.24}$ 10$_{6}$ 26$_{19}$ Ho 10$_{3}$ Jon 1$_{9.16}$ Ml 3$_{16}$ Ps 15$_{4}$ 22$_{24}$ 25$_{12.14}$ 31$_{18}$ 33$_{18}$ 34$_{8.10.10}$ 85$_{9}$ 103$_{8.13.17}$ 112$_{1}$ 115$_{11}$=135$_{20}$ 115$_{13}$ 118$_{4}$ 119$_{33.65.75}$ 128$_{1.4}$ 145$_{18}$ 147$_{11}$ Pr 14$_{2}$ 24$_{21}$.

ראה *see* 1 K 22$_{19}$||2 C 18$_{18}$ Is 6$_{5}$, שׂכל hi. *understand* Jr 9$_{22}$, ידע *know* Ex 5$_{2}$ Jg 2$_{10}$ 1 S 2$_{12}$ 3$_{7}$ Is 11$_{9}$ (דֵּעָה אֶת־י׳ *knowledge of Y.*) 19$_{21}$ Jr 9$_{2.5.22}$ 31$_{34.34}$ Ho 2$_{22}$ 5$_{4}$ 6$_{3}$ Ps 79$_{5}$ Pr 3$_{5}$ GnzPs 3$_{19}$, hi. *inform* Is 40$_{13.13}$ Ps 25$_{14}$, בין hi. *explain (to)* Is 40$_{13}$, למד pi. *teach* Is 40$_{13.13}$, קרא *call (upon)* 2 S 22$_{4.7}$||Ps 18$_{4.7}$ Is 55$_{5}$ Ps 14$_{4}$ 31$_{18}$ 86$_{6}$ 88$_{10}$ 119$_{145}$ 130$_{1}$ 141$_{1}$ 145$_{18.18}$ Lm 3$_{55}$, עוד hi. *call as witness* Si 46$_{19}$, אמר hi. *proclaim* Dt 26$_{17}$, ענה *answer* Jb 1$_{7.9}$ 2$_{2.4}$ 40$_{3}$ 42$_{1}$.

זכר *remember* Dt 8$_{18}$ 2 S 14$_{11}$ Jr 51$_{50}$ Jon 2$_{8}$ Si 51$_{10}$, hi. *cause to be remembered* Is 62$_{6}$, שׁכח *forget* Dt 6$_{12}$ 8$_{11.14.19.19}$ Jg 3$_{7}$ 8$_{34}$ 1 S 12$_{9}$ Is 51$_{13}$ Jr 3$_{21}$ 13$_{25}$ Ezk 22$_{12}$, מאס *reject* Nm 11$_{20}$, עזב *abandon* Jos 24$_{16.20}$ Jg 2$_{12.13}$ 10$_{6}$ 1 S 12$_{10}$ 1 K 9$_{9}$||2 C 7$_{22}$ 2 K 21$_{22}$ Is 1$_{4.28}$ 65$_{11}$ Jr 2$_{17.19}$ 16$_{11.11}$ 17$_{13.13}$ Ho 4$_{10}$ 1 C 28$_{9}$ 2 C 13$_{10.11}$ 15$_{2}$ 21$_{10}$ 24$_{20.24}$ 28$_{6}$ 29$_{6}$, נטשׁ *abandon* Jr 15$_{6}$.

כעס hi. *enrage* Dt 9$_{18}$ 31$_{29}$ Jg 2$_{12}$ 1 K 14$_{15}$ 15$_{30}$ 16$_{7.13.26.33}$ 22$_{54}$ 2 K 17$_{17}$ 21$_{6}$||2 C 33$_{6}$ Jr 7$_{19}$ 11$_{17}$ 25$_{7}$ 32$_{30}$ 2 C 28$_{25}$, קצף hi. *enrage* Dt 9$_{7.8.22}$, קנא pi. *enrage* 1 K 14$_{22}$, נסה pi. *test* Ex 17$_{2.7}$ Dt 6$_{16}$ Is 7$_{12}$, ריב *strive (with)* Nm 20$_{13}$, מרה *rebel (against)* Jr 4$_{17}$, שׂנא pi. *hate* Ps 81$_{16}$ 139$_{21}$ 2 C 19$_{2}$, נאץ pi. *despise* Nm 16$_{30}$ Ps 10$_{3}$, בזה *despise* Pr 14$_{2}$, חרף pi. *revile* Ps 74$_{18}$, גדף pi. *blaspheme (against)* Nm 15$_{30}$.

<CSTR> צְבָאוֹת י׳ *Y. of hosts* 1 S 1$_{11}$ 4$_{4}$ 17$_{45}$ 2 S 5$_{10(Q)}$||1 C 11$_{9}$ 2 S 6$_{2.18}$||1 C 16$_{2}$ 2 S 7$_{8.26}$||1 C 17$_{7.24}$ 2 S 7$_{27}$ 1 K 18$_{15}$ 2 K 3$_{14}$ 19$_{31(Qr)}$||Is 37$_{32}$ Is 1$_{9.24}$ 3$_{1.15}$ 5$_{7.9.16.24}$ 6$_{3.5}$ 8$_{13.18}$ 9$_{6.10.18}$ 10$_{16.23.24.26.33}$ 13$_{4.13}$ 14$_{22.24.27}$ 17$_{3}$ 18$_{7}$ 19$_{4.12.16.17.18.25}$ 21$_{10}$ 22$_{5.12.14.14.15.25}$ 23$_{9}$ 24$_{23}$ 25$_{6}$ 28$_{5.22.29}$ 29$_{6}$ 31$_{4}$ 37$_{16}$ 39$_{5}$ 44$_{6}$ 47$_{4}$ 48$_{2}$ 51$_{15}$ 54$_{5}$ Jr 2$_{22}$ 6$_{6.9}$ 7$_{3.21}$ 8$_{3}$ 9$_{6.14.16}$ 10$_{16}$ 11$_{17.20.22}$ 16$_{9}$ 19$_{3.11.15}$ 20$_{12}$ 23$_{36}$ 25$_{27.28.29.32}$ 26$_{18}$ 27$_{4.18.19.21}$ 28$_{2.14}$ 29$_{4.8.17.21.25}$ 31$_{23}$ 32$_{14.15.18}$ 33$_{11.12}$ 35$_{13.18.19}$ 39$_{16}$ 42$_{15.18}$ 43$_{10}$ 44$_{2.11.25}$ 46$_{10.10.18.25}$ 48$_{1.15}$ 49$_{5.7.35}$ 50$_{18.25.31.33.34}$ 51$_{5.14.19.33.57.58}$ Am 5$_{8(mss)}$ 9$_{5}$ (הַצ׳) Mc 4$_{4}$ Na 2$_{14}$ 3$_{5}$ Hb 2$_{13}$ Zp 2$_{9}$ (or del.) 2$_{10}$ 3$_{9.12}$ Hg 1$_{2.5.7.9.14}$ 2$_{4.6.7.8.9.9.11.23.23}$ Zc 1$_{3.3.3.4.6.12.14.16.17}$ 2$_{9.10.10.13.14.15}$ 3$_{7.9.10}$ 4$_{6.9}$ 5$_{4}$ 6$_{12.15}$ 7$_{3.4.9.12.12.13}$ 8$_{1.2.3(mss).3.4.6.6.7.9.9.11.14.14.18.19.20.21.22.23}$ 9$_{15}$ 10$_{3}$ 12$_{5}$ 13$_{2.7}$ 14$_{16.17.21.21}$ Ml 1$_{4.6.8.9}$ (or del. both) 1$_{10.11.13.14}$ 2$_{2.4.7.8.12.16}$ 3$_{1.5.7.10.11.12.14.17.19.21}$ Ps 24$_{10}$ 46$_{8.12}$ 48$_{9}$ 59$_{6}$ (if del. אֱלֹהִים) 69$_{7}$ 80$_{5.20}$ (if del. אֱלֹהִים in both) 84$_{2.4.9}$ (if del. אֱלֹהִים) 84$_{13}$ 4QpsEzek[a] 2$_{8}$ 12$_{3}$.

התמן י׳ *Y. of Teman* Kuntillet ʿAjrud add. inscr. 1 inscr. E2.2, שׁמרן י׳ *Y. of Samaria* Kuntillet ʿAjrud inscr. E1.

שֵׁם י׳ *name of Y.* Gn 4$_{26}$ 12$_{8}$ 13$_{4}$ 16$_{13}$ 21$_{33}$ 26$_{25}$ Ex 20$_{7}$||Dt 5$_{11}$ Ex 33$_{19}$ 34$_{5}$ Lv 24$_{16}$ Nm 36$_{2}$ (if em. וַאדֹנִי צֻוָּה בַי׳ *and my lord was commanded by Y.* to וַאדֹנִי צִוָּה בְשֵׁם י׳ *and my lord commanded in the name of Y.*) Dt 18$_{5.7.22}$ 21$_{5}$ 28$_{10}$ 32$_{3}$ Jos 9$_{9}$ 1 S 17$_{45}$ 20$_{42}$ 2 S 6$_{2}$ 6$_{18}$||1 C16$_{2}$ 1 K 3$_{2}$ 5$_{17}$ 5$_{19}$||2 C 2$_{3}$ 8$_{17.20}$||2 C 6$_{7.10}$ 1 K 10$_{1}$ 18$_{24.32}$ 22$_{16.19}$||2 C 18$_{15.18}$ 2 K 2$_{24}$ 5$_{11}$ Is 18$_{7}$ 24$_{15}$ 30$_{27}$ 48$_{1}$ 50$_{10}$ 56$_{6}$ 59$_{19}$ 60$_{9}$ Jr 3$_{17}$ 11$_{21}$ 26$_{9.16.20}$ 44$_{16}$ Jl 2$_{26}$ 3$_{5}$ Am 6$_{10}$ Mc 4$_{5}$ 5$_{3}$ Zc 13$_{3}$ Ps 7$_{18}$ 20$_{8}$ 102$_{16.22}$ 113$_{1}$=135$_{1}$ 113$_{2.3}$ 116$_{4.13.17}$ 118$_{10.11.12.26}$ 122$_{4}$ 124$_{8}$ 129$_{8}$ 148$_{5.13}$ Jb 1$_{21}$ Pr 18$_{10}$ 1 C 21$_{19}$ 22$_{7.19}$ 2 C 1$_{18}$ 33$_{18}$ Si 50$_{20}$ 51$_{12.30}$ 4QErr 2$_{5}$ 4QapPs[a] 1.1$_{5.8}$ ([שׁ]ם) 11QPsAp[a] 1$_{2}$ ([יהוה]) 1$_{3}$ 4$_{4}$ (י[הוה]) 11QT 61$_{3}$.

כְּבוֹד י׳ *glory of Y.* Ex 16$_{7.10}$ 24$_{16.17}$ 40$_{34.35}$ Lv 9$_{6.23}$ Nm 14$_{10.21}$ 16$_{19}$ 17$_{7}$ 20$_{6}$ 1 K 8$_{11}$||2 C 5$_{14}$ Is 35$_{2}$ 40$_{5}$ 58$_{8}$ 60$_{1}$ Ezk 1$_{28}$ 3$_{12.23}$ 10$_{4.4.18}$ 11$_{23}$ 43$_{4.5}$ 44$_{4}$ Hb 2$_{14}$ Ps 104$_{31}$ 138$_{5}$ 2 C 7$_{1.2}$ Si 42$_{16}$ 4QJub[a] 1$_{2}$ ([כ]בוד י[הוה]), גְּאוּת *majesty of* Is 26$_{10}$, גְּאוֹן *pride of* Is 24$_{14}$, נֹעַם־ *beauty of* Ps 27$_{4}$, תְּמֻנַת *form of* Nm 12$_{8}$.

תְּהִלַּת י׳ *praise of Y.* Ps 145_{21}, תְּהִלֹּת *praiseworthy deeds of* Is 60_6 63_7 Ps 78_4 (תְּהִלּוֹת), קִנְאַת *zeal of* 2 K 19_{31}||Is 37_{32} Is 9_6, רצון *will of* Si 48_5, חֵפֶץ *pleasure of* Is 53_{10}, חֶדְוַת *joy of* Ne 8_{10}, חֶמְלַת *compassion of* Gn 19_{16}, רחמי *mercy of* Si 51_8, טוּב *goodness of* Jr 31_{12} Ps 27_{13}, צִדְקַת *righteousness of* Dt 33_{21}, צִדְקוֹת *righteous acts of* Jg 5_{11} 1 S 12_7 Mc 6_5 (or em. צִדְקוֹתָי *my righteous acts*).

יְשׁוּעַת י׳ *salvation of,* i.e. from, *Y.* Ex 14_{13} 2 C 20_{17}, תְּשׁוּעַת *salvation of,* i.e. from Lm 3_{26}, אַהֲבַת *love of,* i.e. from Dt 7_8 (Sam mss אַהֲבוֹת *deeds of love* by Y.) Ho 3_1 (or em. אַהֲבָתִי *my love*), חֶסֶד *loyalty of* 1 S 20_{14} Ps 33_5 103_{17}, חַסְדֵי *deeds of loyalty of* Is 63_7 Ps 89_2 (or em. חֲסָדֶיךָ *your deeds of loyalty*) 107_{43} Lm 3_{22}, בִּרְכַּת *blessing of* Gn 39_5 Dt 12_{15} 16_{17} 33_{23} Ps 29_8 Pr 10_{22} Si 4_{13} 50_{20}, [מ]תן י׳] *gift of* Si 11_{17}, אֱמֶת־י׳ *constancy of Y.* Ps 117_2.

חכמת י׳ *wisdom of Y.* Si $15_{18(B).18}$ 36_8, מַחְשְׁבוֹת *thoughts of* Jr 51_{29} Mc 4_{12}, עֲצַת *counsel of* Is 19_{17} Jr 49_{20} 50_{45} Ps 33_{11} Pr 19_{21} Ezr $10_{3(mss)}$, סוֹד *counsel of* Ps 25_{14}, *council of* Jr 23_{18}

דֶּרֶךְ י׳ *way of Y.* Gn 18_{19} Jg 2_{22} 2 K 21_{22} Is 40_3 Jr $5_{4.5}$ Ezk $18_{25(mss).25(mss)}$ $33_{17(mss).20(mss)}$ Pr 10_{29}, דַּרְכֵי *ways of* Ho 14_{10} 2 S 22_{22}||Ps 18_{22} Ps 138_5 2 C 17_6, אָרְחוֹת *paths of* Ps 25_{10}.

מַעֲשֵׂה י׳ *deed of Y.* Ex 34_{10} Dt 11_7 Jos 24_{31} Jg 2_7 Jr 51_{10} Ps $107_{24(mss)}$ $111_{1(mss)}$, מַעֲשֵׂי *deeds of* Ps 107_{24} 111_1 Si $11_{4(A)}$ 43_2, פֹּעַל *deed of* Is 5_{12}, מִפְעֲלוֹת *deeds of* Ps 46_9, פְּעֻלֹּת *deeds of* Ps 28_5, מִפְעַל *deed of* Pr 16_9 (if em. מאֹזְנֵי מִשְׁפָּט לַי׳ *balances of judgment* belong *to Y.* to מאֹזְנַיִם מִפְעַל *balances are the work of Y.*), (...) גְּבוּרוֹת י׳ *mighty deeds of Y.* Ps 71_{16} (גְּבֻרוֹת) 106_2 4Q Admon 1.2_7 4QM[a] 8.14 11QapPs[a]2 2_5, נפלאות י׳ *miracles of Y.* Si $42_{17(B)}$, עֹז *strength of* Mc 5_3, כֹּחַ *strength of* Nm $14_{17(mss)}$.

אַף י׳ *anger of Y.* Ex 4_{14} Nm $11_{10.33}$ 12_9 $25_{3.4}$ $32_{10.13.14}$ Dt 6_{15} 7_4 11_{17} $29_{19.26}$ Jos 7_1 23_{16} Jg $2_{14.20}$ 3_8 10_7 2 S 6_7 ||1 C 13_{10} 2 S 24_1 2 K 13_3 24_{20}||Jr 52_3 Is 5_{25} Jr 4_8 12_{13} 23_{20} 25_{37} 30_{24} 51_{45} Zp $2_{2.2.3}$ Ps 106_{40} Lm 2_{21} 1 C 12_{12} 2 C 28_{11} 4QpIsa[b] 2_8 11QPsAp[a] 3_{11} ([יהוה]), חֲמַת *anger of* 2 K 22_{13}||2 C 34_{21} Is 51_{20} Jr 6_{11} 2 C 28_9 36_{16}, קֶצֶף *anger of* Jr 50_{13} 2 C 29_8 32_{26}, עֶבְרַת *anger of* Is 9_{18} 13_{13} Ezk 7_{19} Zp 1_{18}, זַעַף *anger of* Mc 7_9, נִקְמַת *vengeance of* Nm 31_3 Jr $50_{15.28}$ 51_{11}.

יִרְאַת י׳ *fear of,* i.e. towards, *Y.* Is $11_{2.3}$ 33_6 Ps 19_{10} (or em. אִמְרַת י׳ *word of Y.*) 34_{12} 111_{10}=Pr 1_7=9_{10} Pr 1_{29} 2_5 8_{13} 10_{27} $14_{26.27}$ $15_{16.33}$ 16_6 19_{23} 22_4 23_{17} 31_{30} 2 C 19_9 Si $10_{22(B)}$ 16_2 $40_{26(B)}$ 50_{29}, פַּחַד *fear of,* i.e. from, 1 S 11_7 Is $2_{10.19.21}$ 2 C 14_{13} 17_{10} 19_7, מְהוּמַת־ *panic of,* i.e. from Zc 14_{13}.

תּוֹעֲבַת י׳ *abomination (in the sight) of Y.* Dt 7_{25} 12_{31} 17_1 18_{12} 22_5 23_{19} 25_{16} 27_{15} Pr 3_{32} $11_{1.20}$ 12_{22} $15_{8.9.26}$ 16_5 17_{15} $20_{10.23}$, אַשְׁמַת *sin of,* i.e. against 2 C 28_{13}.

רוּחַ י׳ *spirit of Y.* Jg 3_{10} 6_{34} 11_{29} 13_{25} $14_{6.19}$ 15_{14} 1 S 10_6 $16_{13.14}$ 19_9 2 S 23_2 1 K 18_{12} 22_{24}||2 C 18_{23} 2 K 2_{16} Is 11_2 $40_{7.13}$ 59_{11} 61_1 (רוּחַ ... י׳) 63_{14} Ezk 11_5 37_1 Mc 2_7 3_8 2 C 20_{14}, *wind of,* i.e. from Ho 13_{15}, נִשְׁמַת *breath of* Is 30_{33}, עֲנַן *cloud of* Ex 40_{38} Nm 10_{34}, אוֹר *light of* Is 2_5, צֶמַח *seedling* or *radiance of* Is 4_2, נֵר *lamp of* Pr 20_{27} (or em. נֹצֵר י׳ *Y. keeps*), אֵשׁ *fire of,* i.e. from Nm $11_{1.3}$ 1 K 18_{38}, סַעֲרַת *whirlwind of* Jr 23_{19} 30_{23}, תַּרְדֵּמַת *deep sleep of,* i.e. from 1 S 26_{12}.

יַד י׳ *hand, power of Y.* Ex 9_3 16_3 Nm 11_{23} Dt 2_{15} Jos 4_{24} 22_{31} Jg 2_{15} 1 S $5_{6.9}$ 7_{13} 12_{15} 2 S 24_{14}||1 C 21_{13} 1 K 18_{46} 2 K 3_{15} Is 19_{16} 25_{10} 40_2 41_{20} 51_{17} 59_1 62_3 66_{14} Jr 25_{17} 51_7 Ezk 1_3 $3_{14.22}$ 8_1 (יַד ... י׳) 33_{22} 37_1 40_1 Ps 75_9 Jb 12_9 (mss אֱלוֹהַּ *God*) Pr 21_1 Ru 1_{13} Ezr $7_{6.28}$ 1 C 28_{19} 2 C 29_{25} (or em. בְּיַד־י׳ *by Y.* to בְּדָוִיד הָיָה the commandment *was from David*) 4QpsEzek[b] 1.3_1, יְמִין *right hand of* Hb 2_{16} Ps $118_{15.16.16}$, זְרוֹעַ *arm of* Is 51_9 53_1, רגלי *feet of* perh. 4QpsEzek[e] 36_1.

פְּנֵי י׳ *face,* i.e. favour or presence, *of Y.* Ex 32_{11} 1 S 13_{12} 26_{20} 2 S 21_1 1 K $13_{6.6}$ 2 K 13_4 Jr 26_{19} Zc 7_2 $8_{21.22}$ Ps 34_{17} Jb 1_{12} 2_7 Lm $2_{19(mss)}$ 4_{16} 9_{13} 1 C 12_{24} 2 C 33_{12}, אָזְנֵי *ears,* i.e. hearing, *of* Nm $11_{1.18}$ 1 S 8_{21}.

עֵין י׳ *eye of Y.* Ps 33_{18} (ms עֵינֵי י׳ *eyes of Y.*) Si 11_{12}, עֵינֵי *eyes of* Gn 6_8 $38_{7.10}$||1 C $2_{3.3}$ (if ins.) Lv 10_{19} Nm 24_1 32_{13} Dt 4_{25} 6_{18} 9_{18} 11_{12} $12_{25.28}$ 13_{19} 17_2 21_9 Jg 2_{11} $3_{7.12.12}$ 4_1 6_1 10_6 13_1 1 S 12_{17} 15_{19} 26_{24} 2 S 11_{27} 15_{25} 1 K 11_6 14_{22} 15_5 15_{11}||2 C 14_1 1 K $15_{26.34}$ $16_{7.19.25.30}$ $21_{20.25}$ 22_{43} ||2 C 20_{32} 1 K 22_{23} 2 K $3_{2.18}$ 8_{18}||2 C 21_6 2 K 8_{27} 12_3||2 C 24_2 2 K $13_{2.11}$ 14_3||2 C 25_2 2 K 14_{24} 15_3||2 C 26_4 2 K $15_{9.18.24.28}$ 15_{34}||2 C 27_2 2 K 16_2||2 C 28_1 2 K $17_{2.17}$ 18_3||2 C 29_2 2 K $21_{2.6}$||2 C $33_{2.6}$ 2 K 21_{16} 21_{20}||2 C 33_{22} 2 K 22_2 ||2 C 34_2 2 K $23_{32.37}$ 24_9||2 C 36_9 2 K 24_{19}||Jr 52_2||2 C 36_{12} Is 49_5 Am 9_8 (עֵינֵי ... י׳) Zc 4_{10} Ml 2_{17} Ps $33_{18(ms)}$

34_{16} 116_{15} Pr 5_{21} 15_{3} 22_{12} 2 C 22_{4} 25_{15} 29_{6} 36_{5} Si 11_{21} 46_{20} 4QJonathan 1_{7} ([עיני ה']).

פִּי י' *mouth*, i.e. command, *of Y.* Ex 17_{1} Lv 24_{12} Nm $3_{16.39.51}$ $4_{37.41.45.49}$ $9_{18.18.20.20.23.23.23}$ Nm 10_{10} 13_{3} 14_{41} 21_{18} 24_{13} $33_{2.38}$ 36_{5} Dt $1_{26.43}$ 8_{3} 9_{23} 34_{5} Jos 9_{14} 15_{13} 17_{4} 19_{50} 21_{3} 22_{9} 1 S $12_{14.15}$ 1 K $13_{21.26}$ 2 K 24_{3} Is 1_{20} 40_{5} 58_{14} 62_{2} Jr 9_{11} 23_{16} Mc 4_{4} 1 C 12_{24} 2 C 36_{12} 4QapPent 9_{2} 4QpsEzek^{a} 3_{9}.

מִצְוַת י' *commandment of Y.* Jos 22_{3} 1 S 13_{13} Ne 10_{30} 4QapMos^{c} 2.2_{5} (מצ[ות י]הוה), מִצְוֹת *commandments of* Lv $4_{2.13.22.27}$ 5_{17} Nm 15_{39} Dt 4_{2} 6_{17} 8_{6} 10_{13} $11_{25.28}$ $28_{9.13}$ 30_{16} (if ins.) Jg 2_{17} 3_{4} 1 K 18_{18} 2 K $17_{16.19}$ Ps 19_{9} Ezr 7_{11} 1 C 28_{8} 2 C 24_{20} 4QapMos^{a} 1.2_{8} ([מצוות]), קוֹל *voice, sound of* Gn 3_{8} Ex 15_{26} Dt 5_{25} 8_{20} 13_{19} 15_{5} 18_{16} 26_{14} 27_{10} $28_{1.2.15.45.62}$ $30_{8.10}$ Jos 5_{6} 1 S 12_{15} $15_{19.20.22.24}$ 28_{18} 1 K 20_{36} 2 K 18_{12} Is 30_{31} 66_{6} Jr 3_{25} 7_{28} 26_{13} 38_{20} $42_{6.6.13.21}$ $43_{4.7}$ 44_{23} Mc 6_{9} Hg 1_{12} Zc 6_{15} Ps $29_{3.4.4.5.7.8.9}$ 106_{25} Dn 9_{10}.

תּוֹרַת י' *law of Y.* Ex 13_{9} 2 K 10_{31} Is 5_{24} 30_{9} Jr 8_{8} Am 2_{4} Ps 1_{2} 19_{8} 119_{1} Ezr 7_{10} Ne 9_{3} 1 C 16_{40} 22_{12} 2 C 12_{12} 17_{9} $31_{3.4}$ 34_{14} 35_{26} 4QpIsa^{b} 2_{7}, חֹק *statute of* Ps 2_{7}, פִּקּוּדֵי *precepts of* Ps 19_{9}, עֵדוּת *testimony of* Ps 19_{8}, מִשְׁפַּט *judgment of*, i.e. from 2 C 19_{8} Jr 8_{7} Ps 19_{10}, רִיב *lawsuit of* Mc 6_{2}, מוּסַר *discipline of* Dt 11_{2} Pr 3_{11}, גַּעֲרַת *rebuke of*, i.e. from 2 S 22_{16}.

בְּרִית י' *covenant of Y.* Nm 10_{33} 14_{44} Dt 4_{23} 10_{8} $29_{11.24}$ $31_{9.25.26}$ Jos $3_{3.17}$ $4_{5.18}$ 6_{8} 7_{15} 8_{33} 23_{16} 1 S $4_{3.4.5}$ 20_{8} 1 K $3_{15(mss)}$ 6_{19} $8_{1.6}$||2 C $5_{2.7}$ 1 K 8_{21}||2 C 6_{11} Jr 3_{16} 22_{9} 1 C $15_{25.26.28.29}$ 16_{37} 17_{1} 22_{19} $28_{2.18}$, שְׁבֻעַת *oath of* Ex 22_{10} 2 S 21_{7} 1 K 2_{43}, מְאֵרַת *curse of* Pr 3_{33}.

דְּבַר י' *word of Y.* Gn $15_{1.4}$ Ex $9_{20.21}$ Nm 15_{31} Dt 5_{5} Jos $8_{8.27}$ 1 S $3_{1.7.21}$ $15_{10.13.23.26}$ 2 S 7_{4} 12_{9} 24_{11} 1 K 2_{27} 6_{11} $12_{24.24}$ $13_{1.2.5.9.17.18.20.26.32}$ 14_{18} 15_{29} $16_{1.7.12.34}$ $7_{1.5.8}$ $17_{16.24}$ $18_{1.31}$ 19_{9} 20_{35} $21_{3.28}$ $22_{5.19}$||2 C $18_{4.18}$ 1 K 22_{38} 2 K 1_{17} 3_{12} 4_{44} $7_{1.16}$ $9_{26.36}$ $10_{10.17}$ 14_{25} 15_{12} 20_{4}||Is 38_{4} 2 K $20_{16.19}$||Is $39_{5.8}$ 2 K 23_{16} 24_{2} Is 1_{10} 2_{3}||Mc 4_{2} Is $28_{13.14}$ 66_{5} Jr $1_{2.4.11.13}$ $2_{1.4.31}$ 6_{10} 7_{2} 8_{9} 9_{19} $13_{2.3.8}$ 14_{1} 16_{1} $17_{14.20}$ 18_{1} 19_{3} 20_{8} 21_{11} $22_{2.29}$ 24_{4} 25_{3} 27_{18} 28_{12} $29_{20.30}$ 31_{10} $32_{6.8.8.26}$ $33_{1.19.23}$ $34_{4.12}$ 35_{12} 36_{27} 37_{6} 39_{15} $42_{7.15}$ 43_{8} $44_{24.26}$ 46_{1} 47_{1} 49_{34} Ezk 1_{3} 3_{16} $6_{1.3}$ (דְּבַר ... י') 7_{1} 11_{14} $12_{1.8.17.21.26}$ $13_{1.2}$ $14_{2.12}$ 15_{1} $16_{1.35}$ $17_{1.11}$ 18_{1} 20_{2} $21_{1.3.6.13.23}$ $22_{1.17.23}$ 23_{1} $24_{1.15.20}$ $25_{1.3}$ (דְּבַר ... י') 26_{1} 27_{1} $28_{1.11.20}$ $29_{1.17}$ $30_{1.20}$ 31_{1} $32_{1.17}$ $33_{1.23}$ $34_{1.7.9}$ 35_{1} $36_{1.4}$ (דְּבַר ... י') 36_{16} $37_{4.15}$ 38_{1} Ho 1_{1} 4_{1} Jl 1_{1} Am 7_{16} 8_{12} Jon 1_{1} $3_{1.3}$ Mc 1_{1} Zp 1_{1} 2_{5} Hg $1_{1.3}$ $2_{1.10.20}$ Zc $1_{1.7}$ $4_{6.8}$ 6_{9} $7_{4.8}$ $8_{1.18}$ 9_{1} 11_{11} 12_{1} Ml 1_{1} Ps $33_{4.6}$ Dn 9_{2} Ezr 1_{1}=2 C 36_{22} 1 C 10_{13} $11_{3.10}$ 15_{15} 22_{8} 2 C 12_{7} 19_{11} 30_{12} 34_{21} 35_{6} 36_{21} 4QJub^{a} Prologue.

דִּבְרֵי י' *words of Y.* Ex 4_{28} $24_{3.4}$ Nm 11_{24} Jos 3_{9} 1 S 8_{10} 15_{1} Jr 23_{36} (דִּבְרֵי ... י') $36_{4.6.8.11}$ 37_{2} 43_{1} Ezk 11_{25} Ho 1_{2} (if em. דִּבֶּר־י' *Y. spoke*) Am 8_{11} Zc 7_{1} 2 C 11_{4} 29_{15} 4Q185 1.2_{3} 4QAdmon 1.2_{9} ([דברן י יהוה]), אִמְרַת *word of* 2 S 22_{31}||Ps 18_{31} Ps 105_{19}, אִמֲרוֹת *words of* Ps 12_{7}, אִמְרֵי *words of* Jos 24_{27}, מַשָּׂא *oracle of* Jr $23_{33.34.36.38.38.38}$, מַלְאֲכוּת *message of* Hg 1_{13}.

נְאֻם י' *utterance of Y.* Gn 22_{16} Nm 14_{28} 2 K 9_{26} 19_{33}||Is 37_{34} 2 K 22_{19}||2 C 34_{27} Is $14_{22.22.23}$ $17_{3.6}$ 22_{25} 30_{1} 31_{9} 41_{14} $43_{10.12}$ 49_{18} $52_{5.5}$ 54_{17} 55_{8} 59_{20} $66_{2.17.22}$ Jr $1_{8.15.19}$ $2_{3.9.12}$ 2_{29} $3_{1.10.12.12.13.14.16.20}$ $4_{1.9.17}$ $5_{9.11.15.18.22.29}$ 6_{12} $7_{11.13.19.30}$ (L נְאוּם; mss נְאֻם) 7_{32} $8_{1.3.13.17}$ $9_{2.5.8.21.23.24}$ 12_{17} $13_{11.14.25}$ $15_{3.6.9.20}$ $16_{5.11.14.16}$ 17_{24} 18_{6} $19_{6.12}$ $21_{7.10.13.14}$ $22_{5.16.24}$ $23_{1.2.4.5.7.11.12.23.24.24.28.29.30.31.32.32.33}$ $25_{7.9.12.29.31}$ $27_{8.11.15.22}$ 28_{4} $29_{9.11.14.14.19.19.23.32}$ $30_{3.8.10.11.17.21}$ $31_{1.14.16.17.20.27.28.31.32.33.34.36.37.38}$ $32_{5.30.44}$ 33_{14} $34_{5.17.22}$ 35_{13} $39_{17.18}$ 42_{11} 44_{29} 45_{5} $46_{5.23.26.28}$ $48_{12.25.30.35.38.43.44.47}$ $49_{2.6.13}$ 49_{16}||Ob 4 Jr $49_{26.30.31.32.37.38.39}$ $50_{4.10.20.21.30.35.40}$ $51_{24.25.26.39.48.52.53}$ Ezk $13_{6.7}$ 16_{58} 37_{14} Ho $2_{15.18.23}$ 11_{11} Jl 2_{12} Am $2_{11.16}$ $3_{10.15}$ $4_{3.6.8.9.10.11}$ $6_{8.14}$ $9_{7.8.12.13}$ Mc 4_{8} 5_{9} Na 2_{14} 3_{5} Zp $1_{2.3.10}$ 2_{9} 3_{8} Hg $1_{9.13}$ $2_{4.4.4.8.9.14.23.23.23}$ Zc $1_{3.4.16}$ 2_{12} $3_{9.10}$ 5_{4} $8_{6.11.17}$ 10_{12} 11_{6} 12_{1} $13_{2.7.8}$ Ml 1_{2} Ps 110_{1}.

נְאֻם ... י' *utterance ... of Y.* Is 1_{24} 3_{15} Is 19_{4} 56_{8} Jr $2_{19.22}$ 49_{5} 50_{31} Ezk 5_{11} $11_{8.21}$ $12_{25.28}$ $13_{8.16}$ $14_{11.14.16.18.20.23}$ 15_{8} $16_{8.14.19.23.30.43.48.63}$ 17_{16} $18_{3.23.30.32}$ $20_{3.31.33.36.40.44}$ $21_{12.18}$ $22_{12.31.34}$ 24_{14} 25_{14} $26_{5.14.21}$ 28_{10} 29_{20} 30_{6} 31_{18} $32_{8.14.16.31.32}$ 33_{11} $34_{8.15.30.31}$ $35_{6.12}$ $36_{14.15.23.32}$ $38_{18.21}$ $39_{5.8.10.13.20.29}$ $43_{19.27}$ $44_{12.15.27}$ $45_{9.15}$ 47_{23} 48_{29} Am 3_{13} 4_{5} $8_{3.9.11}$.

בְּרוּךְ י' *one blessed of Y.* Gn 9_{26} (if em. בָּרוּךְ *blessed* be Y.) 24_{31} 26_{29}, מְבֹרֶכֶת *(land) blessed of* Dt 33_{13}, בְּרוּכֵי *those blessed of* Is 65_{23}, יְדִיד *one beloved of* Dt 33_{12} 4QSela 8.2_{8} ([יהו]ה), בְּחִיר *one chosen of*, i.e. by 2 S 21_{6}, מְשִׁיחַ *one anointed of*, i.e. by 1 S $24_{7.7.11}$ $26_{9.11.16.23}$ 2 S $1_{14.16}$ 19_{22} Lm 4_{20}, קְדוֹשׁ *holy one of* Ps 106_{16}, פְּדוּיֵי *those redeemed of*, i.e. by Is 35_{10} ||51_{11}, גְּאוּלֵי *those redeemed of*, i.e. by Is 62_{12} Ps 107_{2}, לִמּוּדֵי *disciples of* Is 54_{13}.

מַלְאַךְ י׳ *messenger* or *angel of Y.* Gn $16_{7.9.10.11}$ $22_{11.15}$ Ex 3_{2} Nm $22_{22.23.24.25.26.27.31.32.34.35}$ Jg $2_{1.4}$ 5_{23} $6_{11.12.21.21.22.22}$ $13_{3.13.15.16.16.17.18.20.21.21}$ 2 S 24_{16}||1 C 21_{15} 1 K 19_{7} 2 K $1_{3.15}$ 19_{35}||Is 37_{36} Hg 1_{13} Zc $1_{11.12}$ $3_{1.2}$ (if ins. מַלְאַךְ) $3_{5.6}$ 12_{8} Ml 2_{7} Ps 34_{8} $35_{5.6}$ 1 C $21_{12.16.18.30}$ 4QpsEzek^{e} 52_{5}.

עֶבֶד י׳ *servant of Y.* Dt 34_{5} Jos $1_{1.13.15}$ $8_{31.33}$ 11_{12} $12_{6.6}$ 13_{8} 14_{7} 18_{7} $22_{2.4.5}$ 24_{29} Jg 2_{8} 2 K 18_{12} Is 42_{19} Ps 18_{1} 36_{1} 2 C 1_{3} 24_{6} Seal 272 (8th cent.)$_{2.4}$, עַבְדֵי *servants of* 2 K 9_{7} 10_{23} Is 54_{17} Ps 113_{1}=134_{1}=135_{1} 11QPsAp^{a} 2_{12} (יהו[ה]), מְשָׁרְתֵי *ministers of* Jl 1_{9} 2_{17}, נְבִיאֵי *prophets of* 1 K $18_{4.13.13}$, כֹּהֵן *priest of* 1 S 14_{3}, כֹּהֲנֵי *priests of* 1 S $22_{17.17.21}$ Is 61_{6} 2 C 13_{9}.

דֹּרְשֵׁי י׳ *seekers of Y.* Ps 34_{11}, מְבַקְשֵׁי *seekers of* Is 51_{1} Ps 105_{3}||1 C 16_{10} (or em. מְבַקֵּשׁ רְצוֹנוֹ *one who seeks his desire*, as 4QPs^{e}) Pr 28_{5}, קֹוֵי *those who wait of*, i.e. for Is 40_{31} Ps 37_{9}, אֹהֲבֵי *lovers of* Ps 97_{10} (or em. אֹהֲבֵי י׳ שִׂנְאוּ רָע *lovers of Y. hate evil* to אֹהֵב י׳ שֹׂנְאֵי רָע *Y. loves those who hate evil*), נְזִיר *consecrated one of* Si 46_{13}, יְרֵא *fearer of* Is 50_{10} Ps 25_{12} $128_{1.4}$ Pr 14_{2} Si 15_{1} 16_{4} 26_{3} 35_{16} 36_{1}, יִרְאֵי *fearers of* Ml 3_{16} Ps 15_{4} 22_{24} 115_{11}=135_{20} 115_{13} (or em. יְרֵאָיו *those who fear him*) 118_{4} Si 35_{16}, מַלְוֵה *one who lends of*, i.e. to Pr 19_{17} Si $32_{13(mg)}$.

עַם י׳ *people of Y.* Nm 11_{29} 17_{6} Jg $5_{11.13}$ 1 S 2_{21} 2 S 1_{12} 6_{21} 2 K 9_{6} Ezk 36_{20} Zp 2_{10}, עֵדֶר *flock of* Jr 13_{17}, קְהַל *assembly of* Nm 16_{3} 20_{4} Dt $23_{2.3.3.4.4.9}$ Mc 2_{5} 1 C 28_{8}, עֲדַת *congregation of* Nm 27_{17} 31_{16} Jos $22_{16.17}$ 4QapMos^{c} 2.2_{3}, צְבָא *army of* Jos $5_{14.15}$, צִבְאוֹת *armies of* Ex 12_{41}.

אֹיְבֵי י׳ *enemies of Y.* 1 S 30_{26} 2 S 12_{14} Ps 37_{20} 4QapJoshua^{b} 3.1_{4} (או]יבי]), מְשַׂנְאֵי, שֹׂנְאֵי *haters of* 2 C 19_{2}, מְשַׂנְאֵי י׳ *haters of* Ps 81_{16}, עֹזְבֵי *abandoners of* Is 1_{28} 65_{11}, זְעוּם *one cursed of*, i.e. by Pr 22_{14}, חַלְלֵי *slain of* Is 66_{16} Jr 25_{33}.

אֲחֻזַּת י׳ *possession of Y.* Jos 22_{19}, נַחֲלַת *inheritance of* 1 S 26_{19} 2 S 20_{19} 21_{3} Ps 127_{3}, חֵלֶק *portion of* Dt 32_{9}, מַלְכוּת *dominion of* 1 C 28_{5}, מַמְלֶכֶת *kingdom of* 2 C 13_{8}.

אַדְמַת י׳ *land of Y.* Is 14_{2}, אֶרֶץ *land of* Ho 9_{3}, שְׁמֵי *heavens of* Lm 3_{66}, הַר *mountain of* Gn 22_{14} Nm 10_{33} Is 2_{3}||Mc 4_{2} Is 30_{29} Zc 8_{3} Ps 24_{3} 4QJub^{a} 1_{2}, עִיר *city of* Is 60_{14} Ps 48_{9} 101_{8}, מַטָּע *plantation of* Is 61_{3}, כֶּרֶם *vineyard of* Is 5_{7}, גַּן *garden of* Gn 13_{10}, עֲצֵי *trees of* Ps 104_{16}.

בֵּית י׳ *house of Y.* Ex 23_{19}||34_{26} Dt 23_{19} Jos 6_{24} Jg 19_{18} 1 S $1_{7.24}$ 3_{15} 2 S 12_{20} 1 K 3_{1} 6_{37} $7_{12.40}$ 7_{45}||2 C 4_{16} 1 K 7_{48} 7_{51}||2 C 5_{1} 1 K 7_{51} 8_{10}||2 C 5_{13} 1 K $8_{11.63}$ 8_{64}||2 C 7_{7} 1 K 9_{1}||2 C 7_{11} 1 K 9_{10}||2 C 8_{1} 1 K 9_{15} $10_{5.12}$||2 C $9_{4.11}$ 1 K 12_{27} $14_{26.28}$||2 C $12_{9.11}$ 1 K 15_{15} 15_{18}||2 C 16_{2} 2 K $11_{3.4.4.7.10}$ $11_{13.15.18}$||2 C $23_{12.14.18}$ 2 K 11_{19}||2 C 23_{20} 2 K $12_{5.5.10.10.11.12}$ 12_{12}||2 C 24_{12} 2 K $12_{13.14.14.15.17.19}$ 14_{14} 15_{35}||2 C 27_{3} 2 K $16_{8.14.18}$ 18_{15} $19_{1.14}$||Is $37_{1.14}$ 2 K 20_{5} 20_{8}||Is 38_{22} 2 K $21_{4.5}$||2 C $33_{4.5}$ 2 K $22_{3.4}$ $22_{5.5.8.9}$||2 C $34_{10.10.15.17}$ 2 K $23_{2.2}$||2 C $34_{30.30}$ 2 K $23_{6.7.11.12.24}$ 24_{13}||2 C 36_{10} 2 K $25_{9.13.13.16}$||Jr $52_{13.17.17.20}$ Is 2_{2}||Mc 4_{1} Is 38_{20} Is 66_{20} Jr 7_{2} 17_{26} 19_{14} $20_{1.2}$ $26_{2.2.8.9.10}$ $27_{16.18.21}$ $28_{1.3.5.6}$ 29_{26} 33_{11} $35_{2.4}$ $36_{5.6.8.10.10}$ 38_{14} 41_{5} 51_{51} Ezk $8_{14.16}$ 10_{19} 11_{1} $44_{4.5}$ Ho 8_{1} 9_{4} Jl 1_{14} 4_{18} Hg $1_{2.14.17}$ Zc 7_{3} 8_{9} 11_{13} $14_{20.21}$ Ps 23_{6} 27_{4} 92_{14} 116_{19} 118_{26} $122_{1.9}$ 134_{1}=135_{2} Lm 2_{7} Ezr 1_{1}=2 C 36_{22} Ezr $1_{5.7}$ 2_{68} $3_{8.11}$ $6_{22(mss)}$ 7_{27} 8_{29} Ne 10_{36} 1 C $6_{16.17}$ 9_{23} $22_{1.11.14}$ $23_{4.24.28.32}$ 24_{19} 25_{6} $26_{12.22.27}$ $28_{12.13.13}$ 29_{8} 2 C 3_{1} $7_{2.2.11}$ $8_{16.16}$ $20_{5.28}$ $23_{5.6.18.19}$ $24_{4.7.8.12.14.14.18.21}$ $26_{19.21}$ $28_{21.24}$ $29_{3.5.15.16.16.17.18.20.25.31.35}$ 30_{1} $31_{10.11.16}$ 33_{15} $34_{8.14}$ 35_{2} $36_{7.14.18}$ Arad ost. 18_{9} Ivory pomegranate inscr. (בי]ת יהו[ה).

נוה ... י׳ *habitation of ... Y.* Kh. Beit Lei graf. 6_{2} (others נקה ... י׳ *Y. has left unpunished*), הֵיכַל *temple of* 1 S 1_{9} 3_{3} 2 K 18_{16} 23_{4} 24_{13} Jr $7_{4.4.4}$ 24_{1} Ezk $8_{16.16}$ Hg $2_{15.18}$ Zc $6_{12.13.14.15}$ Ezr $3_{6.10}$ 2 C 26_{16} 27_{2} 29_{16}, מִקְדַּשׁ *sanctuary of* Ex $15_{17(mss, Sam)}$= 4QMidrEschat^{a} 3_{3} Nm 19_{20} Jos 24_{26} Ezk 48_{10} Lm $2_{20(mss)}$ 1 C 22_{19}, מִשְׁכַּן *tabernacle of* Lv 17_{4} Nm $16_{9.28}$ 19_{13} $31_{30.47}$ Jos 22_{19} 1 C 16_{39} 21_{29} 2 C 1_{6} 29_{6}, אֹהֶל *tent of* 1 K $2_{28.29.30}$, אוּלָם *porch of* 2 C 15_{8} 29_{17} 30_{15}, שַׁעַר *gate of* Jr 26_{10} (mss שַׁעַר בֵּית י׳), חַצְרוֹת *courts of* Ps 84_{3}, אוֹצַר *treasury of* Jos 6_{19}, מַחֲנֵה *camp of* 1 C 9_{19}, מַחֲנוֹת *camp(s) of* 2 C 31_{2}.

כִּסֵּא י׳ *throne of Y.* Jr 3_{17} 1 C 29_{23}, אֲרוֹן *ark of* Jos 3_{13} $4_{5.11}$ $6_{6.7.11.12.13.13}$ 7_{6} 1 S 4_{6} $5_{3.4}$ $6_{1.2.8.11.15.18.19.21}$ $7_{1.1}$ 2 S $6_{9.10.11.13.15.16.17}$ 1 K 2_{26} 8_{4} 1 C 15_{2} (mss אֲרוֹן אֱלֹהִים *ark of God*) $15_{3.12.14}$ 16_{4} 2 C 8_{11} 15_{8}, שֻׁלְחַן *table of* Ml 1_{7}, מִזְבַּח *altar of* Lv 17_{6} Dt $12_{27.27}$ 16_{21} 26_{4} 27_{6} Jos 9_{27} $22_{19.28.29}$ 1 K 8_{22}||2 C 6_{12} 1 K 8_{54} 18_{30} 23_{9} Ml 2_{13} Ne 10_{35} 2 C 8_{12} $29_{19.21}$ 35_{16} 11QT 21_{10}, חֶרֶב *sword of* 1 C 21_{12}, סֵפֶר *scroll of* Is 34_{16}, קֹדֶשׁ *holy thing of* Lv 19_{8} Is 58_{13} Ml 2_{11}, קָדְשֵׁי *holy things of* Lv 5_{15}, מִשְׁחַת *ointment of* Lv 10_{7}, כְּלֵי *vessels of* Is 52_{11}, [···]· קשת *bow of Y.* perh. 4QpsEzek^{e} 36_{3}.

זֶבַח י׳ *sacrifice of*, i.e. to, *Y.* Zp 1_{8}, מִנְחַת *offering of*, i.e.

to 1 S 2_{17}, תְּרוּמַת *offering of*, i.e. to Ex $30_{14.15}$ $35_{5.21.24}$ Nm $18_{26.28.28.29}$ $31_{29.41}$ 2 C 31_{14}, קָרְבַּן *offering of*, i.e. to Nm $9_{7.13}$ 31_{50}, עֹלוֹת *burnt offerings of*, i.e. to 2 C 23_{18}, אִשֵּׁי *fire offerings of*, i.e. to Lv $2_{3.10}$ 4_{35} 5_{12} 6_{11} $7_{30.35}$ $10_{12.13}$ $21_{6.21}$ 24_{9} Dt 18_{1} Jos 13_{14} Si $45_{21.22}$ 50_{13}.

עֲבֹדַת י״ *service of*, i.e. due to, *Y.* Nm 8_{11} Jos 22_{27} 2 C 35_{16}, כְּהֻנַּת *priesthood of* Jos 18_{7}, מִשְׁמֶרֶת *observation (of statutes) of* Lv 8_{35} Nm $9_{19.23}$ 1 K 2_{3} 2 C 13_{11} 23_{6}, מְלֶאכֶת *business (on behalf) of* Jr 48_{10} 1 C 26_{30}, מִלְחֲמֹת *wars (on behalf) of* Nm 21_{14} 1 S 18_{17} 25_{28} Si 46_{3} (מלחמות), עֶזְרַת to the *aid of* Jg $5_{23.23}$, שִׁיר *song of* Ps 137_{4} 2 C 7_{6} 29_{27}.

יוֹם י״ *day of Y.* Is 13_{6}||Jl 1_{15} Is 13_{9} Ezk 13_{5} Jl $2_{1.11}$ 4_{14} Am $5_{18.18.20}$ Ob$_{15}$ Zp $1_{7.14.14}$ Ml 3_{23}, שַׁבְּתֹת *sabbaths of* Lv 23_{38}, חַג *feast of* Ex 10_{9} Lv 23_{39} Jg 21_{19} Ho 9_{5}, מוֹעֲדֵי *appointed times of* Lv $23_{2.4.37}$=11QT 29_{2} ([מועדי יהוה]) Lv 23_{37} Ezr 3_{5}.

<APP> י״ *Y.* Ex 34_{6} Jr 50_{7} (or del. י״ or em. to הוֹי *alas* and move to next verse) Ho 12_{6}, יָהּ *Yah* Is 12_{2} 26_{4}, Kh. Beit Lei graf. 6.

אֲדֹנָי *(my) Lord* or *Adonai* preceding י״ Gn $15_{2.8}$ Dt 3_{24} 9_{26} Jos 7_{7} Jg 6_{22} 2 S $7_{18.19.19.20}$ (mss אֲדֹנָי אֱלֹהִים) 7_{22} (mss י״ אֱלֹהִים *Y., God*) $7_{25(mss)}$ (L י״ אֱלֹהִים) $7_{28.29}$ 1 K 2_{26} (mss י״ אֱלֹהִים in all three) 8_{53} Is 3_{15} 7_{7} 10_{23} (mss lack י״) 10_{24} $22_{5.12.14.15}$ 25_{8} $28_{16.22}$ 30_{15} 40_{10} 48_{16} 1QIsa^{a} 49_{7} (MT lacks אֲדֹנָי) Is 49_{22} (1QIsa^{a} lacks אֲדֹנָי) $50_{4.5}$ (1QIsa^{a} אדני אלוהים) $50_{7.9}$ 52_{4} (1QIsa^{a} lacks אֲדֹנָי) 56_{8} 61_{1} (1QIsa^{a} lacks אֲדֹנָי) 61_{11} (1QIsa^{a} י״ אלוהים) $65_{13.15}$ Jr 1_{6} $2_{19.22}$ 4_{10} 7_{20} 14_{13} $32_{17.25}$ 44_{26} $46_{10.10}$ 49_{5} $50_{25.31}$ Ezk 2_{4} $3_{11.27}$ 4_{14} $5_{5.7.8.11}$ $6_{3.3.11}$ $7_{2.5}$ 8_{1} 9_{8} $11_{7.8.13.16.17.21}$ $12_{10.19.23.25.28.28}$ $13_{3.8.8.9.13.16.18.20}$ $14_{6.11.14.16.18.20.21.23}$ $15_{6.8}$ $16_{3.8.14.19.23.30.36.43.48.59.63}$ $17_{3.9.16.19.22}$ $18_{3.23.30.32}$ $20_{3.3.5.30.31.33.36.39.40.44}$ $21_{3.5.12.18.29.31.33}$ $22_{3.12.19.28.31}$ $23_{22.28.32.34.35.46.49}$ $24_{3.6.9.14.21.24}$ $25_{3.3.6.8.12.13.14.15.16}$ $26_{3.5.7.14.15.19.21}$ 27_{3} $28_{2.6.10.12.22.24.25}$ $29_{3.8.13.16.19.20}$ $30_{2.6.10.13.22}$ $31_{10.15.18}$ $32_{3.8.11.14.16.31.32}$ $33_{11.25.27}$ $34_{2.8.10.11.15.17.20.30.31}$ $35_{3.6.11.14}$ $36_{2.3.4.4.5.6.7.13.14.15.22.23.32.33.37}$ $37_{3.5.9.12.19.21}$ $38_{3.10.14.17.18.21}$ $39_{1.5.8.10.13.17.20.25.29}$ $43_{18.19.27}$ $44_{6.9.12.15.27}$ $45_{9.9.15.18}$ $46_{1.16}$ $47_{13.23}$ 48_{29} Am 1_{8} (or del. אֲדֹנָי) $3_{7.8.11.13}$ $4_{2.5}$ 5_{3} 6_{8} $7_{1.2.4.4.5.6}$ $8_{1.3.9.11}$ $9_{5.8}$ (or em. עֵינֵי אֲדֹנָי י״ *the eyes of my Lord, Y.* to עֵינַי *my eyes*) Ob$_{1}$ Mc 1_{2} (1QpMic has [י]הוה [אדני יהי]ה *Y., my Lord, will be* for MT וִיהִי אֲדֹנָי י״ *let my Lord, Y., be*) Zc 9_{14} 69_{7} 71_{5} (or em. אֲדֹנָי י״ *my Lord; Y.*) 71_{16} (or del. אֲדֹנָי or י״) 73_{28}.

(Mss lack אֲדֹנָי at 1 K 2_{26} Is 22_{15} 28_{22} 48_{16} Ezk 2_{4} 7_{5} $11_{7.8.16}$ $12_{10.19.28}$ $13_{8.9.18}$ $14_{6.11.16.18}$ $16_{8.19.30.43}$ 17_{9} $18_{3.32}$ $20_{3.31.36.44}$ 21_{3} 22_{12} $23_{28.32.49}$ 24_{24} 25_{16} 26_{15} 27_{3} 28_{24} $29_{8.13.16.20}$ 30_{6} 32_{3} 33_{25} 34_{11} 35_{3} $36_{4.13.14.22.23.37}$ $37_{5.19}$ $39_{8.10.13.29}$ $43_{18.19}$ 44_{6} 45_{18} 46_{16} Am 3_{13} 6_{8} $7_{1.6}$ 8_{1} Mc 1_{2} Ps 73_{28}; or del. אֲדֹנָי at Ezk 4_{14} $26_{3.5.7.14.19.21}$ $28_{2.6.10.12.22.25}$ 29_{3} Zc 9_{14}; or del. אֲדֹנָי י״ at Is 3_{15} Ezk 21_{5} Am 7_{4}.)

אֲדֹנָי following י״ Am 5_{16} (י״ ... אֲדֹנָי) Hb 3_{19} Ps 68_{21} 109_{21} 140_{8} 141_{8} (or del. אֲדֹנָי; mss אֱלֹהִים אֲדֹנָי).

הָאָדֹן *the Lord* Ex 23_{17} (Sam ארון *ark of* Y.) 34_{23} (Sam הארון *the ark of* Y.), הָאָדוֹן *the Lord* Is 1_{24} 3_{1} 10_{16} (mss lack הָאָדוֹן) 10_{33} 19_{4} (or del. הָאָדוֹן), י״ אֲדֹנֵינוּ *Y., our Lord* Ps $8_{2.10}$ Ne 10_{30}, אֲדֹנַיִךְ י״ *your* (fem. sg.) *Lord, Y.* Is 51_{22}, י״ אֲדוֹן כָּל־הָאָרֶץ *Y., Lord of all the earth* Jos 3_{13}.

אֵל *God* Ex 20_{5}||Dt 5_{9} Ex 34_{6} Nm 23_{8} Jos $22_{22.22}$ Is 42_{5} Jr 10_{2} (if em. אֶל־ *concerning*) Ps 31_{6} 39_{13} (if em. אֶל־ be deaf *to*) 50_{1} 85_{9} (or. em. הָאֵל י״ *God Y.* to הֲלֹא י״ hear what *Y.* will say, *is it not* that) 89_{7} 143_{1} (if em. אֶל־ listen *to*) 143_{7} (if em. אַל־ *do not* conceal) Ne 1_{5} 4QpsJub^{a} 2.2_{10}, perh. Ps 10_{12} 18_{3};* אֵל עוֹלָם *God of eternity* Gn 21_{33}, אֵל־נְקָמוֹת *God of vengeance* Ps 94_{1}, אֵל עֶלְיוֹן *God Most High* Gn 14_{22} (or del. י״) 4QJub^{d} 21_{21} ([יהו]ה), עֶלְיוֹן *Most High* Ps 7_{18} 47_{3}, אלוהי אלים *God of gods* 11QPsAp^{a} 1_{11}.

אֱלֹהִים *God*, following י״ Gn $2_{4.5.7.8.9.15.16.18.19.21.22}$ $3_{1.8.8.9.13.14.21.22.23}$ Ex 9_{30} 19_{22} 24_{2} (if ins. אֱלֹהִים in both) 1 S 6_{20} 2 S $7_{22(mss).25}$ 1QIsa^{a} 61_{11} (MT אֲדֹנָי י״) Ps 72_{18} 84_{12} Dn $9_{2(mss)}$ Ne 8_{6} 9_{7} 1 C $17_{16.17}$ $22_{1.19}$ 28_{20} 29_{1} 2 C 1_{9} $6_{41.41.42}$ 26_{18} 4QBibPar 1_{18} 4QJub^{g} 25_{12} (אלוה[ים]) 4QapPent 9_{4} 4QapJoshua^{a} 12_{3} (אלוה[ים]) 4QapPs^{b} 24_{4}; preceding י״ Jos $22_{22.22}$ Jr 23_{36} Ps 50_{1} 68_{27} (mss אֱלֹהִים אֲדֹנָי *God, my Lord*) 1 C 13_{6} 2 C 30_{19}.

אֱלֹהַי *my God* Nm 22_{18} Dt 18_{16} 26_{14} Jos $14_{8.9}$ 2 S 24_{24} 1 K 3_{7} 5_{18} 5_{19}||2 C 2_{3} 8_{28}||2 C 6_{19} 1 K 17_{21} Jr 31_{18} Jon 2_{7} Hb 1_{12} (or em. אֱלֹהַי קְדֹשִׁי *my God, my holy one* to אֱלֹהֵי קָדְשִׁי *God of my holiness*) Zc 11_{4} (or em. אֵלַי *to me*) 14_{5} Ps $7_{2.4}$ 13_{4} 18_{29} $30_{3.13}$ 35_{24} 40_{6} 84_{4} $86_{12(mss)}$ 88_{2} (if em. אֱלֹהֵי יְשׁוּעָתִי *God of my salvation* to אֱלֹהַי שִׁוַּעְתִּי *my God, I cry*) 104_{1} 109_{26} Dn $9_{4.20}$ Ezr 7_{28} 9_{5} 1 C 21_{17} 22_{7} 28_{20} 2QapMoses 1_{5} ([יהוה אלוהי]ם) 4QapJoseph^{b} 1_{26} 4QPrayer^{c} 1_{5} (··[··] *[Y]*.).

אֱלֹהֵינוּ *our God* Ex 3_{18} 5_3 $8_{6.22.23}$ $10_{25.26}$ Dt $1_{6.19.20.25.41}$ $2_{29.33.36.37}$ 3_3 4_7 $5_{2.24.25.27.27}$ $6_{4.20.24.25}$ $29_{14.17}$ Jos 18_6 $22_{19.29}$ $24_{17.24}$ Jg 11_{24} 1 S 2_2 7_8 1 K $8_{57.59.61.65}$ 2 K 18_{22}||Is 36_7 2 K 19_{19}||Is 37_{20} Is 26_{13} Jr $3_{22.23.25.25}$ $5_{19.24}$ 8_{14} 14_{22} 16_{10} 23_{36} 26_{16} 31_6 37_3 $42_{6.6.20}$ (or del.) $42_{20.20}$ 43_2 50_{28} 51_{10} Mc 4_5 7_{17} Ps 20_8 94_{23} $99_{5.8.9.9}$ 105_7||1 C 16_{14} Ps 106_{47} 113_5 122_9 123_2 Dn $9_{10.13.14.15(mss)}$ Ezr 9_8 Ne 10_{35} 1 C 13_2 15_{13} 29_{16} 2 C 13_{11} $14_{6.10}$ 19_7 29_6 $32_{8.11}$ 2QapDavid 1_1 ([י]הוה אלהינ[ו]) 4QapJoseph[c] 1_6 GnzPs 2_8.

אֱלֹהֶיךָ *your* (masc. sg.) *God* Gn 27_{20} Ex $13_{5(Sam, mss)}$ $13_{11(mss)}$ 15_{26} $20_{2.5.7}$||Dt $5_{6.9.11}$ Ex 20_{10} 20_{12}||Dt 5_{16} Ex 23_{19} $34_{24.26}$ Dt $1_{21.31}$ $2_{7.7.30}$ $4_{3.19.21.23.24.25.29.30.31.40}$ $5_{12.14.15.15.16}$ $6_{2.5.10.13.15.15}$ $7_{1.2.6.6.9.12.16.18.19.19.20.21.22.23.25}$ $8_{5.6.7.10.11.14.18.19}$ $9_{3.4.5.6.7}$ $10_{9.12.12.12.20.22}$ $11_{1.12.12.29}$ $12_{7.9.18.18.18.20.21.27.27.28.29.31}$ 13_6 Dt 13_{11}=11QT[b] 55_7 ([יהוה] אלוהיכה) Dt 13_{13} 13_{17}=11QT 55_9 (אלוהיכה) Dt 13_{19} 13_{19}=11QT 55_{14} (אלוהיכה) Dt 14_2=11QT $48_{7.10}$ (both אלוהיכה) Dt $14_{21.23.23.24.24.25.26.29}$ $15_{4.5.6.7.10.14.15.18.19.20.21}$ $16_{1.1.2.5.6.7.8.10.10.11.11.15.15.16.17.18.19.20.21.22}$ $17_{1.1.2.2.8.12.14.15.19}$ $18_{5.9.12}$ 18_{13}=11QT 60_{21} $18_{14.15.16}$ $19_{1.1.2.3.8.9.10.14}$ $20_{1.4.13.14.16.17}$ $21_{1.5.10.23}$ 22_5 $23_{6.6.6.15.19.19.21.22.22.24}$ $24_{4.9.13.18.19}$ $25_{15.16.19.19}$ $26_{1.2.2.3.4.5.10.10.11.13.16.19}$ $27_{2.3.5.6.6.7.9.10}$ $28_{1.1.2.8.9.11.13.15.45.47.52.53.58.62}$ $29_{11.11}$ $30_{1.2.3.3.4.5.6.6.7.8.10.10.16}$ (if ins.) $30_{16.16.20}$ $31_{3.6.11}$ Jos $1_{9.17}$ $9_{9.24}$ Jg 6_{26} 1 S 12_{19} 13_{13} $15_{15.21.30}$ 25_{29} 2 S $14_{11.17}$ 18_{28} 2 S $24_{3.23}$ 1 K 1_{17} 2_3 18_{10} $19_{4.4}$||Is $37_{4.4}$ Is 7_{11} 43_3 48_{17} 51_{15} 55_5 Jr 40_2 $42_{2.3.5}$ Ho 12_{10} 13_4 14_2 Am 9_{15} 1 C 11_2 $22_{11.12}$ 2 C 16_7 4QapMos[a] 1.1_2 (אלוהיכה) 4QapJoshua[a] 3.1_8 ([יהו]ה אלוהיך) 11QT 53_8 54_{16} 63_8 (all three אלוהיכה) Lachish ost. 6_{12}.

אֱלֹהַיִךְ *your* (fem. sg.) *God* Is 60_9 Jr $2_{17.19}$ 3_{13} Mc 7_{10} Zp 3_{17}.

אֱלֹהֵיכֶם *your* (pl.) *God* Ex 6_7 8_{24} $10_{8.16.17}$ $12_{24(ms)}$ 16_{12} 23_{25} 29_{46} Lv 11_{44} $18_{2.4.30}$ $19_{2.3.4.10.25.31.34.36}$ $20_{7.24}$ $23_{22.28.40.43}$ 24_{22} $25_{17.38.55}$ $26_{1.13}$ Nm 10_{10} $15_{41.41}$ Dt $1_{10.26.30.32}$ $3_{18.20.21.22}$ $4_{2.4.23}$ $5_{32.33}$ $6_{1.16}$ 8_{20} $9_{16.23}$ 10_{17} $11_{1.13.22.25.31}$ $12_{4.5.7.10.11.12}$ $13_{4.4}$ 13_5=11QT 54_{13} (אלוהיכמה) Dt 13_6 14_1=11QT 48_8 (אלוהיכמה) 20_{17} $29_{5.9}$ $31_{12.26}$ Jos $1_{11.13.15}$ 2_{11} $3_{3.9}$ $4_{5.23.23.24}$ 8_7 10_{19} $22_{3.4.5}$ $23_{3.3.5.8.10.11.13.13.15.15.16}$ Jg 6_{10} 1 S $12_{12.14}$ 1 K 10_9||2 C 9_8 1 K $13_{6.21}$ 17_{12} 2 K 17_{39} 23_{21} Is 41_4 Jr 13_{16} 26_{13} $42_{4.13.20.21}$ Ezk $20_{5.7.19.20}$ Jl 1_{14} $2_{13.14.23.26.27}$ 4_{17} Zc 6_{15} Ps 76_{12} Ne 9_5 1 C 22_{18} 28_8 29_{20} 2 C 9_8 20_{20} 28_{10} $30_{8.9}$ 35_3 4QapPent 9_2 4QapJoshua[a] 11_1 (אלהיכ[מה]).

אֱלֹהָיו *his God* Ex 32_{11} Lv 4_{22} Nm 23_{21} Dt 18_7 1 S 30_6 1 K 5_{17} 11_4 $15_{3.4}$ 17_{20} 2 K 5_{11} Jr 7_{28} Jon 2_2 Mc 5_3 Ps 146_5 Ezr 7_{10} 2 C 1_1 $14_{1.10}$ 15_9 26_{16} 27_6 28_5 31_{20} 33_{12} 34_8 $36_{12.23}$.

אֱלֹהֵיהֶם *their God* Ex 10_7 29_{46} Lv 26_{44} Jg 3_7 8_{34} 1 S 12_9 1 K 9_9 2 K $17_{7.9.14.16.19}$ 18_{12} Jr 3_{21} 22_9 30_9 $43_{1.1}$ 50_4 Ezk 28_{26} 34_{30} $39_{22.28}$ Ho 1_7 3_5 5_4 7_{10} Hg $1_{12.12.14}$ Zc 9_{16} 10_6 12_5 Ne $9_{3.3.4}$ 2 C 31_6 33_{17} 34_{33} 4QNarrB 1_9 (אלוהיהמה).

אֱלֹהֵי (...) יִשְׂרָאֵל *God of (...) Israel* Ex 5_1 32_{27} 34_{23} Jos $7_{13.19.20}$ 8_{30} $9_{18.19}$ $10_{40.42}$ $13_{14.33}$ 14_{14} 22_{24} $24_{2.23}$ Jg 4_6 $5_{3.5}$ 6_8 $11_{21.23}$ 21_3 1 S 2_{30} 10_{18} 14_{41} 20_{12} $23_{10.11}$ 25_{34} 2 S 7_{27} 12_7 1 K $1_{30.48}$ 8_{15}||2 C 6_4 1 K $8_{17.20.23.25}$||2 C $6_{7.10.14.16}$ 1 K $11_{9.31}$ $14_{7.13}$ 15_{30} 18_{36} 22_{54} 2 K 9_6 10_{31} 14_{25} 18_5 $19_{15.20}$||Is $37_{16.21}$ 2 K 21_{12} $22_{15.18}$||2 C $34_{23.26}$ Is 17_6 $21_{10.17}$ 24_{15} Is 45_3 Jr $7_{3.21}$ 9_{14} 11_3 13_{12} 16_9 $19_{3.15}$ 21_4 23_2 24_5 $25_{15.27}$ $27_{4.21}$ $28_{2.14}$ $29_{4.8.21.25}$ 30_2 31_{23} $32_{14.15.36}$ 33_4 $34_{2.13}$ $35_{13.17.18.19}$ 37_7 38_{17} 39_{16} $42_{9.15.18}$ 43_{10} $44_{2.7.11.25}$ 45_2 46_{25} 48_1 50_{18} 51_{33} Ezk 44_2 Zp 2_9 Ml 2_{16} Ps 41_{14}=72_{18}=106_{48}=1 C 16_{36} Ps 59_6 Ru 2_{12} Ezr 1_3 $4_{1.3}$ $6_{21.22(mss)}$ 7_6 9_{15} 1 C $15_{12.14}$ 16_4 17_{24} (or del.) 22_6 23_{25} 24_{19} 28_4 $29_{10.18}$ 2 C 2_{11} 6_{17} 11_{16} 13_5 $15_{4.13}$ $16_{13.26.33}$ $17_{1.14}$ 20_{19} 29_{10} $30_{1.5.6}$ 32_{17} $33_{16.18}$ 36_{13} Si 50_{22} 4QapJoshua[b] 22.2_5 ([י]שראל) 4QSela 8.2_5 GnzPs 2_6 3_{10} 4_{16}, אֱלֹהֵי מַעַרְכוֹת יִשְׂרָאֵל *God of the ranks of Israel* 1 S 17_{45}.

אֱלֹהֵי אַבְרָהָם *God of Abraham* Gn 28_{13} (+ אָבִיךָ Abraham, *your father*) Ex $3_{15.16}$ 4_5 1 K 18_{36} 1 C 29_{18} 2 C 30_6, אֱלֹהֵי (...) יִצְחָק *God of (...) Isaac* Gn 28_{13} Ex $3_{15.16}$ 4_5 1 K 18_{36} 1 C 29_{18} 2 C 30_6, אֱלֹהֵי (...) יַעֲקֹב *God of (...) Jacob* Ex $3_{15.16}$ 4_5, אֱלֹהֵי אֵלִיָּהוּ *God of Elijah* 2 K 2_{14}, אֱלֹהֵי דָּוִד *God of David* 2 K 20_5||Is 38_5 2 C 21_{12} (דָּוִיד), אֱלֹהֵי שֵׁם *God of Shem* Gn 9_{26}.

אֱלֹהֵי אָבִי אַבְרָהָם *God of my father Abraham* Gn 32_{10}, אֱלֹהֵי אָבִי יִצְחָק *God of my father Isaac* Gn 32_{10}, אֱלֹהֵי אֲבֹתֵינוּ *God of our fathers* Dt 26_7 Ezr 7_{27} 2 C 20_6 4QapMos[c] 2.2_5 (אלוהי אבותינו), אֱלֹהֵי אֲבֹתֶיךָ *God of your* (sg.) *fathers* Dt 1_{21} 6_3 12_1 27_3, אֱלֹהֵי אֲבֹתֵיכֶם *God of your* (pl.) *fathers* Ex $3_{15.16}$ Dt 1_{11} 4_1 Jos 18_3 Ezr 8_{28} 10_{11} 2 C 13_{12} 28_9 29_5 11QT 54_{12} (אלוהי אבותיכמה), אֱלֹהֵי אֲבֹתָיו *God of his fathers* 2 K 21_{22} 2 C 21_{10} 28_5 30_{19}, אֱלֹהֵי אֲבֹתָם *God of their fathers* Ex 4_5 Dt 29_{24} Jg 2_{12} 2 C 28_6, אֱלֹהֵי אֲבוֹתֵיהֶם *God of their fathers* 1 C 29_{20} 2 C 7_{22} 11_{16} 13_{18} 14_3 15_{12} 19_4 $24_{18.24}$ $30_{7.22}$ 34_{33} 36_{15}.

אֱלֹהֵי אֲדֹנִי הַמֶּלֶךְ *God of my lord the king* 1 K 1_{36}, אֱלֹהֵי אֲדֹנִי אַבְרָהָם *God of my master Abraham* $24_{12.27.42.48}$, אֱלֹהֵי הָעִבְרִים *God of the Hebrews* Ex 3_{18} (הָעִבְרִיִּים) 7_{16} $9_{1.13}$ 10_{3}.

אֱלֹהֵי צְבָאוֹת *God of hosts* 2 S 5_{10} 1 K $19_{10.14}$ Jr 5_{14} 15_{16} 35_{17} 38_{17} 44_{7} Ho 12_{6} Am 3_{13} (both הַצְּבָאוֹת) Am 4_{13} $5_{14.15.16}$ 6_{8} Ps 59_{6} $80_{5.20}$ 84_{9} (all four אֱלֹהִים צְבָאוֹת; or del. אֱלֹהִים) 89_{9}.

אֱלֹהֵי הַשָּׁמַיִם *God of heaven* Gn $24_{3.7}$ Jon 1_{9} Ezr 1_{2}=2 C 36_{23} Ne 1_{5}, אֱלֹהֵי הָאָרֶץ *God of the earth* Gn 24_{3}, אֱלֹהֵי הָרוּחֹת לְכָל־בָּשָׂר כָּל־בָּשָׂר *God of all flesh* Jr 32_{27}, *God of the spirits of all flesh* Nm 27_{17}, אֱלֹהֵי יְשׁוּעָתִי *God of my salvation* Ps 88_{2} (or em. אֱלֹהַי שִׁוַּעְתִּי *my God, I cry*).

קָדוֹשׁ *holy one* Is 10_{20} 30_{15} $43_{3.14.15}$ 45_{11} 48_{17} 49_{7} Jr 50_{29} Hb 1_{12} (or em. אֱלֹהַי קְדֹשִׁי Y., *my God, my holy one* to אֱלֹהֵי קָדְשִׁי *God of my holiness*), מֶלֶךְ *king* Is 6_{5} 43_{15} 44_{6} Zp 3_{15} (or em. יִמְלֹךְ *he will rule*) Zc $14_{16.17}$ Ps 84_{3} 98_{6}, גֹּאֵל my *redeemer* Ps 19_{15}, אֲבִיר יַעֲקֹב *mighty one of Jacob* Is 49_{26} 60_{16}, אֲבִיר יִשְׂרָאֵל *mighty one of Israel* Is 1_{24}, עִזּוּז *mighty one* Ps 24_{8}, גִּבּוֹר *mighty one* Ps $24_{8.8}$.

שֵׁם *name* Ex 6_{3} Dt 28_{58}, מִקְוֶה *hope* Jr 17_{13} 50_{7}, חֶסֶד my *loyalty* Ps 144_{1} (or em. חָסְנִי *my stronghold* or סַלְעִי *my rock*), חֹזֶק my *strength* Ps 18_{2}, עֹז *strength* Jr 16_{19} Ps 140_{8}, מָעוֹז my *refuge* Jr 16_{19}, מָנוֹס my *refuge* Jr 16_{19}, מִשְׂגָּב my *refuge* Ps 144_{1}, מְצוּדָה my *fortress* Ps 144_{1}, צוּר my *rock* Ps 19_{15} 144_{1}, מָגֵן *shield* Dt 33_{29} (or em. מָגֵן Y., *the shield of* your help, to מָגֵן י׳ *the shield of Y.* is your help, or מָגִנּוֹ *his shield* is your help) Ps 144_{1}, נָוֶה *dwelling place* or *pasture* Jr 50_{7}, הֵיכָל *palace* Jon 2_{3}, מָקוֹר *source* of living water Jr 17_{13}.

אָנֹכִי *I* Ex 4_{11}, אֲנִי *I* (some refs. under Nom. Cl. may also be app.) Ex 31_{13} Nm 14_{35} Is 27_{3} $41_{4.17}$ 42_{6} $45_{3.7.8}$ $60_{16.22}$ 61_{8} Jr 9_{23} 17_{10} Ezk $5_{13.15.17}$ 12_{25} $14_{4.7.9}$ $17_{21.24.24}$ 20_{12} $21_{4.10.22.37}$ $22_{14.22}$ 24_{14} 26_{14} 30_{12} $34_{24.24}$ $36_{36.36}$ $37_{14.28}$ 39_{7} 11QT 45_{14} 51_{7} 53_{8}.

אַתָּה *you* (some refs. under Nom. Cl. may also be app.) Nm $14_{14.14}$ 2 S 7_{24}||1 C 17_{22} 2 S 7_{27} $7_{28.29}$||1 C $17_{26.27}$ 1 K 3_{7} 8_{53} 18_{37} Is 63_{16} Jr $12_{1.3}$ 15_{15} 18_{23} Jon 1_{14} Ps 3_{4} 4_{9} $6_{4(Qr)}$ 12_{8} 22_{20} $40_{6.10.12}$ 41_{11} $59_{6.9}$ 71_{5} $86_{5(mss)}$ $86_{15(mss)}$ 86_{17} 91_{9} (or em. אַתָּה י׳ מַחְסֶךָ *you* have made *Y. your refuge*) 92_{9} 97_{9} 102_{13}=Lm 5_{19} Ps $109_{21.27}$ $119_{12.137.151}$ 132_{8}=2 C 6_{41} 1 C 29_{10} GnzPs $2_{2.18}$ 4_{13} perh. Kh. Beit Lei graf. 5_{2} (see Nom. Cl.), הוּא *himself* Dt $31_{3.6.8}$ 1QIsa[a] 7_{14}; אַיּוֹ י׳ *where is he, Y.?* Mc 7_{10} (or em. אַיֵּה י׳ *where is Y.?*).

<ADJ> י׳ + טוֹב *good* 2 C 30_{18} Si 45_{25}.

<PREP> לְ of possession, *of, (belonging) to* Ex 9_{29} $12_{11.14.27.42.42.48}$ 13_{6} $16_{23.25}$ 17_{16} 20_{10} 28_{36}||39_{30} $29_{18.18}$ 29_{25}||Lv 8_{28} Ex 29_{28} 29_{41}||Nm 28_{8} Ex $30_{10.13.20.37}$ 31_{15} 32_{5} 35_{2} Lv $1_{9.13.14.17}$ $2_{2.9.11.16}$ $3_{5.6.11.16}$ 4_{31} $6_{8.15}$ $7_{5.20.21}$ 8_{21} $16_{8.9}$ 17_{6} 19_{24} 22_{27} $23_{3.6.12.13.17.18.18.20.34.41}$ 24_{7} $25_{2.4}$ $27_{21.23.26.28.30.30.32}$ Nm 6_{17} $8_{12.13}$ $9_{10.14}$ $15_{3.3.14.19.24}$ 18_{17} $28_{6.16.24}$ $29_{2.6.12}$ $31_{28.38.39.40}$ Dt 5_{14} 7_{6} 10_{14} 13_{17} $14_{1.2.21}$ 15_{2} $16_{1.8.10}$ 26_{19} 27_{9} 29_{28} Jos $6_{17.19}$ 22_{24} 1 S 1_{3} 2_{8} 3_{20} 14_{6} 15_{22} 1 K 2_{27} 18_{22} 22_{7}||2 C 18_{6} 2 K 3_{11} 11_{17}||2 C 23_{16} 2 K 13_{17} 23_{21} Is 2_{12} $19_{19.20}$ 22_{5} 23_{18} 27_{3} 1QIsa[a] 28_{2} (MT אֲדֹנָי) $34_{2.6.6.8}$ $44_{5.5}$ Is 58_{5} 61_{2} Jr 2_{3} 5_{10} 12_{12} 25_{31} 31_{40} $46_{10.10}$ 47_{6} 50_{25} 51_{6} Ezk 30_{3} 43_{24} $45_{1.23}$ $46_{12.13.14}$ 48_{14} Ho 4_{1} 12_{3} Jl 2_{14} Jon 2_{10} Mc 6_{2} Hg $2_{8.8}$ Zc $14_{20.21}$ Ps 3_{9} 22_{29} 24_{1} 33_{12} 68_{21} 89_{19} $100_{3(Qr)}$ 115_{16} 118_{20} $119_{89.126}$ (ms י׳, for לַי׳, as subj.) Jb 12_{9} Pr 16_{11} (or em. מֹאזְנֵי מִשְׁפָּט לַי׳ *balances of judgment belong to Y.* to מֹאזְנַיִם מִפְּעַל י׳ *balances are the work of Y.*) 21_{31} Ezr $8_{28.28.35}$ 1 C 25_{7} $29_{1.11.11}$ (if ins. לְךָ *to you*) $29_{11.16}$ 2 C 25_{9} 26_{17} 28_{9} 29_{32} $30_{1.5}$ $35_{1.3}$ 4QpsEzek[a] 5_{4} 11QT 8_{11} ([ליהוה]) 13_{13} $14_{7.8}$ $16_{4.10}$ (ל[יהוה]) 17_{7} ([ליהוה]) $17_{12.13.16}$ (ל[יה]וה) $18_{13.14}$ 19_{11} (ליהו[ה]) 19_{16} 11QT[b] 20_{10} 11QT 22_{8} ([ל]יהוה) 23_{3} (ליה[וה]) 23_{17} $24_{5.7}$ 25_{5} (all three [ליהוה]) 25_{13} $26_{4.5}$ 28_{2} (all three [ליהוה]) 28_{6} $48_{7.8.10}$ 55_{9} Kuntillet ʿAjrud add. inscr. 1, + היה *be* Nm 31_{37} (+ מֶכֶס *tax*) Jg 11_{31} (+ יצא ptc. *one who goes out*) Is 55_{13} (+ הֲדַס *myrtle*) Ob$_{21}$ (+ מְלוּכָה *kingship*) Ml 3_{3} (+ בֵּן *son* of Levi), בכר pu. *belong as firstborn* Lv 27_{26}, נתן *cause to be(long)* 1 C 17_{20}.

לְ of direction, *to(wards)* Ezk 42_{13} Zc 9_{1} (or em. עֵין אָדָם *the eye of humankind* is towards Y., to עָווּ אֲרָם *Aram has sinned* against Y.) Ps 69_{14}, + יבל ho. *be brought* Is 18_{7}, שׁאל pass. *be lent* 1 S 1_{28} 2_{20}, hi. *lend* 1 S 1_{28}, שׁוב hi. *take back*, i.e. repay 1 S $6_{8.17}$ Ps 116_{12}, ho. *be taken back*, i.e. be repaid Nm 5_{8}, גמל *repay* Dt 32_{6}, שׁלם pi. *repay* vow Ps 76_{12} $116_{14.18}$, לקח *take* Gn 15_{8} Ex 35_{5}, בוא *come* Zc 14_{1}, hi. *bring* Gn 4_{3} Ex $35_{22.29}$ Lv 2_{8} $5_{6.7.15.25.29}$ 19_{21} Nm 15_{25} 18_{13} 31_{54} Is 66_{20} 2 C 24_{9} 32_{23}, נתן *give* Ex 30_{12} Lv 22_{22} 23_{38} 27_{9} Nm 15_{21} $18_{6.12}$ Jos 7_{19} 1 S 1_{11} Jr 13_{16} Ezr 10_{11} 2 C 9_{8} 30_{8} 11QT 39_{8} ([נתן]), חרם hi. *dedicate* Lv 27_{28} Mc 4_{13}, עבר hi. *transfer*, i.e. dedicate Ex

13$_{12}$, יהב *ascribe* glory, etc. Ps 29$_{1.1.2}$ 96$_{7.7.8}$||1 C 16$_{28.28.29}$, שׂים *place*, i.e. ascribe, glory Jos 7$_{19}$ Is 42$_{12}$, perh. פרשׂ pi. *extend* soul Ps 143$_{1}$.

רוץ *run* Si 11$_{21}$, קדד *bow down* 1 C 29$_{20}$, שׁחה htpal. *bow down* Gn 24$_{26.48.52}$ 1 S 1$_{28}$ 15$_{25.30.31}$ Is 27$_{13}$ Jr 7$_{2}$ Zp 2$_{11}$ Zc 14$_{16.17}$ Ps 29$_{2}$=96$_{9}$||1 C 16$_{29}$ Ps 97$_{5}$ Ne 8$_{6}$ 9$_{3.6}$ 1 C 29$_{20}$ 2 C 7$_{3}$ 20$_{18}$, עלה *go up* 1 S 1$_{3}$, hi. *take up*, i.e. present, offering Dt 27$_{6}$ Jos 8$_{31}$ Jg 13$_{16.19}$ 1 S 6$_{14}$ 7$_{9}$ 2 S 24$_{24}$ Ezr 3$_{3.6}$ 1 C 16$_{40}$ 23$_{31}$ 29$_{21}$ 2 C 1$_{6}$ 8$_{12}$, קרב hi. *present* offering Lv 1$_{2.3}$ 2$_{1.11.12.14}$ 3$_{3=9}$ 3$_{14}$ 4$_{3}$ 6$_{13.14}$ 7$_{11.14.25.29.35.38}$ 17$_{4}$ 22$_{18.21.22.24}$ Lv 23$_{8}$||Nm 28$_{19}$ Lv 23$_{16.25.27.36.36.37}$ 27$_{9.11}$ Nm 6$_{14.16}$ 15$_{4.7.10.13}$ 18$_{15}$ 28$_{3.11.13.15.26.27}$ 29$_{8.13.36}$ Ezk 46$_{4}$ 2 C 35$_{12}$ 11QT 15$_{5}$, נגשׁ hi. *present* offering Ml 2$_{12}$, נשׂא *raise*, i.e. present 1 C 21$_{24}$, רום hi. *raise*, i.e. present Lv 22$_{15}$ Nm 18$_{19.24}$ 31$_{52}$ Ezk 48$_{9}$ 11QT 20$_{14}$, זבח *offer in sacrifice* Ex 3$_{18}$ 5$_{3.17}$ 8$_{4.22.23.24.25}$ 13$_{15}$ 22$_{19}$ 24$_{5}$ Lv 19$_{5}$ 22$_{29}$ Dt 15$_{21}$ 16$_{2}$ 17$_{1}$ Jg 2$_{5}$ 1 S 1$_{21}$ 6$_{15}$ 15$_{15.21}$ 16$_{2.5}$ 1 K 8$_{63}$ Jon 1$_{16}$ 2$_{8}$ Ml 1$_{14}$ (mss לַאדֹנָי *to my Lord*) Ps 54$_{8}$ 116$_{17}$ 1 C 29$_{21}$ 2 C 11$_{16}$ 15$_{11}$ 30$_{22}$ 33$_{17}$, עשׂה *offer* sacrifice Ex 10$_{25}$ Lv 17$_{9}$ Nm 29$_{39}$ 2 K 5$_{17}$ perh. Nm 15$_{8}$, ni. *be offered* 2 K 23$_{23}$, נדב htp. *volunteer* offering Ezr 3$_{5}$ 1 C 29$_{9}$ 2 C 17$_{6}$, קטר hi. *offer* sacrifice *in smoke* 2 C 13$_{11}$, נסך hi. *offer in libation* Nm 28$_{7}$ 2 S 23$_{16}$||1 C 11$_{18}$ Ho 9$_{4}$.

אמר *say* Ps 16$_{2}$ 27$_{8}$ 91$_{2}$ 140$_{7}$, דבר pi. *speak* Jos 10$_{12}$ 2 S 22$_{1}$||Ps 18$_{1}$, נגד hi. *declare* Dt 26$_{3}$, עתר hi. *pray* Gn 25$_{21}$ Ex 10$_{17}$, פלל htp. *pray* Dn 9$_{4}$, נדר *vow* Nm 6$_{21}$ 21$_{2}$ Dt 12$_{11}$ 23$_{22.24}$ Jg 11$_{30}$ 2 S 15$_{7}$ Is 19$_{21}$ Ps 76$_{12}$, פלא hi. *make explicit* vow Lv 27$_{2}$, שׁבע ni. *swear* Is 19$_{18}$ Zp 1$_{5}$ Ps 132$_{2}$ 2 C 15$_{14}$, קרא *call* Ps 141$_{1}$ 4QapPs[b] 24$_{8}$, צעק *cry* 2 C 13$_{14}$, רוע hi. *shout* Ps 98$_{4}$ 100$_{1}$, שׁיר *sing* Ex 15$_{1.1.21}$ Jg 5$_{3}$ Is 42$_{10}$||Ps 33$_{3}$||149$_{1}$ Jr 20$_{13}$ Ps 7$_{1}$ 13$_{6}$ 27$_{6}$ 33$_{2}$ 96$_{1}$ 96$_{1}$||1 C 16$_{23}$ Ps 96$_{2}$ 98$_{1}$ 104$_{33}$ 105$_{1}$||1 C 16$_{8}$ Ps 149$_{1}$, pol. 2 C 20$_{21}$, ענה *sing* Ps 147$_{7}$ Ezr 3$_{11}$, רנן pi. *sing joyfully* Ps 95$_{1}$, זמר pi. *sing (praise)* Jg 5$_{3}$ Ps 9$_{12}$ 27$_{6}$ 30$_{5}$ 33$_{2}$ 98$_{4}$ 101$_{1}$ 105$_{1}$ ||1 C 16$_{8}$ 4QapPs[b] 31$_{1}$ (לְ[יהו]ה), הלל pi. *give praise* Ezr 3$_{10(mss)}$ (L אֶת־י״ praise *Y.*) 3$_{11.11}$ 1 C 16$_{4.36}$ 23$_{5.5(mss).30}$ 25$_{3}$ 2 C 5$_{13}$ 20$_{19}$ 29$_{30}$ 30$_{21.21}$, ידה hi. *give praise* Is 12$_{4}$||Ps 105$_{1}$||1 C 16$_{8}$ Ps 6$_{5}$ 33$_{2}$ 92$_{2}$ 100$_{3}$ 106$_{1}$ 107$_{1.8.15.21.31}$ 118$_{1.29}$ 119$_{55}$ 136$_{1}$ Ezr 3$_{11}$ 1 C 16$_{4.7.34.41}$ 23$_{30}$ 25$_{3}$ 2 C 5$_{13}$ 7$_{3.6}$ 20$_{21}$ Si 51$_{12}$, *confess* sin Ps 32$_{5}$, htp. *give thanks* 2 C 30$_{22}$.

לְ of benefit, *to, for, on behalf of* Ex 32$_{26}$ 2 K 10$_{16}$ Jg 7$_{18.20}$, + עשׂה *do* Dt 12$_{4.31}$, *make* name Ne 9$_{7}$, שׂים *place*, i.e. make, name 1 C 17$_{20}$ (לְךָ *for you*; ||2 S 7$_{22}$ לוֹ *for himself*, i.e. אֱלֹהִים *God*), בנה *build* Gn 8$_{20}$ 12$_{7.8}$ 13$_{18}$ Dt 27$_{5}$ Jos 8$_{30}$ Jg 6$_{24.26}$ 1 S 7$_{17}$ 14$_{35.35}$ 2 S 24$_{21.25}$||1 C 21$_{22.26}$ 1 K 6$_{1.2}$ 9$_{25}$ Ezr 1$_{2}$=2 C 36$_{23}$ Ezr 4$_{1.3}$ 1 C 22$_{5.6}$ 28$_{10}$ (if ins. לְ) 29$_{16}$ 2 C 2$_{11}$ 4QSela 8.2$_{5}$, ni. *be built* Jr 31$_{38}$, כהן pi. *serve as priest* 2 C 11$_{14}$, שׁרת pi. *minister* 2 C 13$_{10}$, משׁח *anoint* perh. 1 C 29$_{22}$, מלא pi. *fill* hand, i.e. consecrate oneself Ex 32$_{29}$ 1 C 29$_{5}$ 2 C 29$_{31}$, קדשׁ hi. *consecrate* Lv 22$_{3}$ 27$_{14.16.22}$ Dt 15$_{19}$ Jg 17$_{3.3}$ 2 S 8$_{11}$||1 C 18$_{11}$ 2 C 2$_{3}$ 30$_{17}$, pu. *be consecrated* 2 C 31$_{6}$, נזר hi. *live as Nazirite* Nm 6$_{2.5.6.12}$, מול ni. *circumcise oneself* Jr 4$_{4}$, קנא pi. *be zealous* 1 K 19$_{10.14}$, חגג *celebrate (festival)* Dt 16$_{15}$, שׁפט *judge* 2 C 19$_{6}$, מצא *find* place Ps 132$_{5}$, קום hi. *raise* altar 2 S 24$_{18}$||1 C 21$_{18}$, ירד *go down* Jg 5$_{13}$ (if em. עָם י״ יְרַד־לִי *people; Y. will rule for me* to עַם י״ יָרַד־לוֹ *the people of Y. came down for him*).

לְ of agent, *by*, + תכן ni. *be measured* 1 S 2$_{3(Qr)}$, בחר ni. *be chosen* Pr 21$_{3}$, ברך pass. *be blessed* Jg 17$_{2}$ 1 S 23$_{21}$ 2 S 2$_{5}$ 15$_{13}$ Ps 115$_{15}$ Ru 2$_{20}$ (mss י״ blessed be *Y.*) 3$_{10}$, ידע ni. *be known* Zc 14$_{7}$; of instrument, *by (means of)*, + ברך pass. *be blessed* Kh. el-Qom tomb inscr. 3$_{2}$, pi. *bless* Arad ost. 16$_{2}$ 21$_{2}$ (לְ[יהו]ה) 40$_{3}$ (ברכת[ך ליהו]ה) Kuntillet ʿAjrud inscr. E1 2.2; introducing object, + דרשׁ *seek* Ezr 6$_{21}$ 1 C 22$_{19}$ 2 C 15$_{13}$ 20$_{3}$, ברך pi. *bless* 1 C 29$_{20}$, גדל pi. *magnify* Ps 34$_{4}$, זכר hi. *invoke* 1 C 16$_{4}$, חרף pi. *reproach* 2 C 32$_{17}$; of comparison, *with*, + ערך ni. *be comparable* Ps 89$_{7}$, דמה *be comparable* Ps 89$_{7}$.

לְ wait *for* Ps 130$_{6(Gnz, mss)}$ (נַפְשִׁי לַי״ perh. *my soul waits for Y.*), + חכה *wait* Is 30$_{18}$, pi. *wait* Is 8$_{17}$ Na 1$_{7}$ (if ins. לִמְחַכֵּי־לוֹ Y. is good *to those who wait for him*) Zp 3$_{8}$ Ps 33$_{20}$, יחל pi. *wait* Ps 31$_{25}$ 33$_{22}$, hi. *wait* 2 K 6$_{33}$ Ps 37$_{7}$ (if em. חיל htpol. *wait*) 38$_{16}$ Lm 3$_{24}$, קוה pi. *wait* Is 8$_{17}$ 25$_{9}$ 33$_{2}$ Pr 20$_{22}$, דום *wait* Ps 37$_{7}$ (if em. דמם *be silent* before).

לְ *against* Gn 13$_{13}$ 2 C 28$_{10}$, + חטא *sin* Ex 10$_{16}$ Nm 32$_{23}$ Dt 1$_{41}$ 9$_{16}$ 20$_{18}$ Jos 7$_{20}$ 1 S 7$_{6}$ 12$_{23}$ 14$_{33.34}$ 2 S 12$_{13}$ 2 K 17$_{7}$ Is 42$_{24}$ Jr 3$_{25}$ 8$_{14}$ 16$_{10}$ 40$_{3}$ 44$_{23}$ 50$_{7.14}$ (or del.) Mc 7$_{9}$ Zp 1$_{17}$ Ps 41$_{5}$ Dn 9$_{8}$ Ne 1$_{5}$, חבל *act corruptly* Ne 1$_{5}$, אשׁם *trespass* Lv 5$_{19}$ 2 C 19$_{10}$.

לְ *before*, + כחשׁ pi. *cower* Ps 81$_{16}$, יקע hi. *impale* Nm 25$_{4}$ 2 S 21$_{6}$, ערך *array* sacrifice Ho 9$_{4(mss)}$, perh. words Ps 5$_{4}$, דמם *be silent* Ps 37$_{7}$ (or em. דום *wait* for).

עָרֵב לְ *be pleasing to* Ho 9$_4$ Ml 3$_4$, יטב לְ *be pleasing to* Ps 69$_{32}$, אבה לְ *accede to* Ps 81$_{11}$, שׁמע לְ *listen to* Ps 81$_{11}$, אמן לְ hi. *trust in* Dt 9$_{23}$, כרת לְ *make* covenant *with* 2 C 29$_{10}$, שׂכל לְ hi. perh. *be skilful in the service of* 2 C 30$_{22}$, קרא לְ *name* Ho 2$_{18}$ (if em. תִּקְרְאִי *you will call* to תִּקְרָא לִי *she will name me*), קָדֹשׁ לְ *holy to* Nm 6$_8$ Ne 8$_9$.

בְּ of place, *in* perh. 11QPsAp^a A$_3$, + חסה *take refuge* 2 S 22$_{31}$||Ps 18$_{31}$ Na 1$_7$ Ps 2$_{11}$ 7$_2$ 11$_1$ 31$_2$=71$_1$ 31$_{18}$ 34$_{9.23}$ 37$_{40}$ 64$_{11}$ 118$_8$ (4QPs^b בטח *trust* in) 118$_9$ 141$_8$ (mss אֱלֹהִים *God*) 144$_1$ Si 51$_8$; partitive, *(some) of* Jos 22$_{25.27}$ (both חֵלֶק בַּי׳ *a portion in Y.*).

בְּ *against*, + דבר pi. *speak* Nm 21$_7$, ענה *testify* 1 S 12$_3$, פשׁע *sin* Is 59$_{13}$ Jr 3$_{13}$, בגד *betray* Jr 3$_{20}$ 5$_{11}$ Ho 5$_7$, מעל *be unfaithful* Lv 5$_{21}$ Nm 5$_6$ 31$_{16}$ (if em. מסר *transmit* treachery) Jos 22$_{22}$ (מַעַל בַּי׳ *treachery against Y.*) 22$_{31}$ 1 C 10$_{13}$ 2 C 12$_2$ (lacking in ||1 K 14$_{25}$) 26$_{16}$ 28$_{19.22}$ 30$_7$, כחשׁ pi. *be unfaithful* Is 59$_{13}$ Jr 5$_{12}$, מרד *rebel* Nm 14$_9$ Jos 22$_{16.18.19.29}$, מרה hi. *rebel* Ezk 20$_{7.12.20}$, גרה htp. *fight* Jr 50$_{24}$.

בְּ of instrument, *by (means of), with, through*, + שׁבע ni. *swear* Gn 22$_{16}$ Jos 2$_{12}$ 9$_{18.19}$ Jg 21$_7$ 1 S 24$_{22}$ 28$_{10}$ 2 S 19$_8$ 1 K 1$_{17.30}$ 2$_{8.23}$, hi. *adjure* Gn 24$_3$ 1 K 2$_{42}$, חזק htp. *strengthen oneself* 1 S 30$_6$, ישׁע hi. *save* Ho 1$_7$, גבר pi. *make mighty* Zc 10$_{12}$ (or em. וְגִבַּרְתִּים בַּי׳ *and I shall make them mighty through Y.* to וּגְבֻרָתָם בַּי׳ *and their strength is on account of Y.*); of cause, *on account of* Jr 3$_{23}$ Zc 12$_5$, perh. Is 45$_{24}$ Zc 10$_{12}$ (if em.), + היה *be* Pr 22$_{19}$, רום *be high* 1 S 2$_1$ (mss אֱלֹהִים *God*), צדק *be (held) righteous* Is 45$_{25}$, הלל htp. *boast* Is 45$_{25}$, יסף *add*, i.e. increase, joy Is 29$_{19}$; of agent, *by*, + צוה pu. *be commanded* Nm 36$_2$ (or em. וַאדֹנִי צֻוָּה בַּי׳ *and my lord was commanded by Y.* to וְאֹתָנוּ צִוָּה י׳ *and Y. commanded us* or וַאדֹנִי צִוָּה בְּשֵׁם י׳ *and my lord commanded in the name of Y.*), ישׁע ni. *be saved* Dt 33$_{29}$ Is 45$_{17}$.

בְּ + אמן hi. *trust in* Gn 15$_6$ Ex 14$_{31}$ Dt 1$_{32}$ 2 K 17$_{14}$ 2 C 20$_{20}$, בטח *trust in* 2 K 18$_5$ Is 26$_4$ perh. 26$_4$ (if כִּי בְּיָהּ י׳ צוּר עוֹלָמִים = *indeed in Yah, Y., a rock of eternity*; or del. בְּיָהּ) Jr 17$_7$ Zp 3$_2$ Ps 9$_{11}$ 21$_8$ 26$_1$ 28$_7$ 32$_{10}$ 37$_3$ 40$_4$ perh. 56$_{11}$ 84$_{13}$ 112$_7$ 115$_{9.10.11}$ 4QPs^b 118$_8$ (MT חסה *take refuge*) 125$_1$ 143$_7$ Pr 16$_{20}$ 29$_{25}$ Si 35$_{24}$ GnzPs 3$_{18}$.

בְּ + גיל *rejoice in* Is 41$_{16}$ Jl 2$_{23}$ Zc 10$_7$ Ps 35$_9$, עלץ *rejoice in* 1 S 2$_1$, שׂמח *rejoice in* Jl 2$_{23}$ Ps 32$_{11}$=97$_{12}$ 33$_{20}$ 40$_{14}$ ||70$_2$ 64$_{11}$ 104$_{34}$, שׂישׂ *rejoice in* Is 61$_{10}$ Ps 40$_{14}$||70$_2$, הלל htp. *glory in* Ps 34$_3$, עלז *rejoice in* Hb 3$_{18}$, רנן pi. perh. *exult in* Ps 33$_1$.

שׁאל בְּ *ask (of)* Jg 1$_1$ 20$_{23.27}$ 1 S 10$_{22}$ 22$_{10}$ (mss אֱלֹהִים *God*) 23$_4$ 28$_6$ 30$_8$ 2 S 2$_1$ 5$_{19.23}$, דבק בְּ *cling to* Dt 4$_4$ (הַדְּבֵקִים בַּי׳ *those clinging to Y.*) 10$_{20}$ 11$_{22}$ 13$_5$=11QT 54$_{13}$ Dt 30$_{20}$ Jos 22$_5$ 23$_8$ 2 K 18$_6$, חזק hi. *hold onto* 11QPs Ap^a 1$_{11}$ ([ביהוה]), צפה בְּ pi. *look out (for)* Mc 7$_7$, פגע בְּ *plead with* Jr 27$_{18}$, דרשׁ בְּ *seek* 1 C 10$_{14}$ 2 C 34$_{26}$, perh. שׁית בְּ *place*, i.e. cause to be Ps 73$_{28}$.

כְּ *as* Ex 8$_6$ 15$_{11.11}$ Dt 4$_7$ 1 S 2$_2$ 7$_{22}$||1 C 17$_{20}$ 1 K 8$_{23}$||2 C 6$_{14}$ Jr 10$_6$ Ps 35$_{10}$ 86$_{8(mss)}$ 113$_5$.

מִן of direction, *from* Jg 14$_4$ Is 30$_1$ Ps 37$_{23}$ (if em. גֶּבֶר כּוֹנָנוּ the steps of *a man are established* by Y., i.e. מִן of agent, to גֶּבֶר כּוֹנְנוּ from Y. are the steps of *a man; he establishes him*) 37$_{39}$ Pr 16$_{1.33}$ 19$_{14}$ 20$_{24}$ 29$_{26}$ Lm 3$_{18}$ 1 C 13$_2$ 2 C 26$_{18}$ Si 11$_{14.15.15}$, + שׁאל *ask* 1 S 1$_{20}$ Zc 10$_1$ Ps 21$_2$, בקשׁ pi. *ask* 2 C 20$_4$, סור *depart* Jr 17$_5$, יצא *go out* Gn 24$_{50}$, פוק hi. *take out*, i.e. obtain, favour Pr 8$_{35}$ 12$_2$ 18$_{22}$ Si 4$_{12}$, מצא *find*, i.e. receive, vision Lm 2$_9$, glory Si 4$_{13}$, recompense Si 12$_2$, חָלִילָה לִּי מֵי׳ *may it not be to me from Y.*, i.e. may Y. prevent me 1 S 24$_7$ 26$_{11}$ 1 K 21$_3$.

מִן of cause, *on account of*, + היה *be* 1 K 2$_{15}$, גור *fear* Ps 22$_{24}$ 33$_8$, ירא *fear* 33$_8$, perh. חשׁך hi. *be dark* 139$_4$; *in the estimation of*, + היה *be* innocent Nm 32$_{22}$, פלא ni. *be wonderful*, i.e. too difficult Gn 18$_{14}$; כחד מִן ni. *be concealed from* Ps 139$_4$, סתר מִן ni. *be concealed from* Is 40$_{27}$, עמק מִן hi. *make deep*, i.e. conceal, from Is 29$_{15}$, אַלְמָן מִן *widowed from*, i.e. bereft of Jr 51$_5$.

מֵאַחֲרֵי *(away) from*, + שׁוב *depart* Nm 14$_{43}$ Jos 22$_{16.18.23.29}$, סור *depart* 1 S 12$_{20}$ 2 C 25$_{27}$ 34$_{33}$, סוג ni. *depart* Zp 1$_6$, נדח hi. *push* 2 K 17$_{21(Qr)}$, זנה *prostitute oneself* from, i.e. be unfaithful to Ho 1$_{2.2}$.

מֵאֵת *from (with)* Gn 19$_{24}$ 1 S 16$_{14}$ 2 K 6$_{33}$ 20$_9$||Is 38$_7$ Jr 37$_{17}$ Mc 5$_6$ Hb 2$_{13}$ (=1QpHab 10$_7$ מֵעִם *from*) Ps 109$_{20}$, + היה *be*, i.e. come Jos 11$_{20}$ Zc 7$_{12}$ Ps 118$_{23}$ Ezr 9$_8$, specif. of word of Y. Jr 7$_1$ 11$_1$ 18$_1$ 21$_1$ 26$_1$ 27$_1$ 30$_1$ 32$_1$ 34$_{1.8.12}$ 35$_1$ 36$_1$ 40$_1$, יצא *go out* Nm 16$_{35}$ Ezk 33$_{29}$, ירד *go down* Mc 1$_{12}$, נסע *set out* Nm 11$_{31}$, נשׂא *raise*, i.e. obtain, blessing Ps 24$_5$, שׁמע *hear* Is 21$_{10}$ 28$_{22}$ Jr 49$_{14}$=Ob$_1$, שׁאל *ask* Ps 27$_4$.

מֵעַל *from (upon)*, + נדח hi. *lead astray* Dt 13$_{11}$=11QT^b

20$_7$ ([ה]דיחכה [מעל יהוה]), רחק *be distant* Ezk 11$_{15}$, סור *depart* Nm 31$_{16}$ (if em. לִמְסָר־מַעַל בַּ׳ *to transmit treachery against Y.* to לָסוּר מֵעַל י׳ *to depart from Y.*).

מֵעִם *from (with)* Is 8$_{18}$ 1QpHab 10$_7$ (=Hb 2$_{13}$ מֵאֵת *from*) Ps 121$_2$, + היה *be* 1 K 2$_{33}$ 12$_{15}$ Ru 2$_{12}$, שׁאל *ask* Dt 18$_{16}$ Is 7$_{11}$, פנה *turn* (of heart) Dt 29$_{17}$, נטה *turn* (of heart) 1 K 11$_9$, יצא *go out* Is 28$_{29}$; *by*, + פקד ni. *be punished* Is 29$_6$; perh. innocent *in the sight of* 2 S 3$_{28}$.

אֶל of direction, *to(wards)* 1 K 8$_{59}$ 14$_{13}$ Ezk 40$_{46}$ Hg 2$_{17}$ Ps 25$_{15}$ 123$_2$ 141$_8$ (mss אֱלֹהִים *God*), + לוה ni. *join oneself* Is 56$_3$ Jr 50$_5$ Zc 2$_{15}$, קהל ni. *be assembled* Jg 20$_1$, בוא *come* (of prayer) Jon 2$_3$ Ps 102$_2$, רגז *come trembling* Mc 7$_{17}$ (or del. ׳י), פחד *come fearfully* Ho 3$_5$, נגשׁ *approach* Ex 19$_{22}$ 24$_2$ (both ni.) Ps 34$_5$ (if em. נבט hi. *look*), הרס *break through* Ex 19$_{21}$, עלה *go up* Ex 19$_{24}$ 24$_1$ 32$_{30}$ Jg 21$_{5.5.8}$ Jr 31$_6$, שׁוב *go back* Ex 5$_{22}$ 19$_8$ 32$_{31}$ Dt 30$_{10}$ 1 S 7$_3$ 2 K 23$_{25}$ Is 55$_7$ Ho 6$_1$ 7$_{10}$ 14$_3$ Jl 2$_{13}$ Hg 2$_{17}$ (if em. וְאֵין־אֶתְכֶם appar. *and you were not to* וְלֹא שַׁבְתֶּם *and you did not return*) Zc 1$_3$ Ps 22$_{28}$ 2 C 30$_6$ 36$_{13}$, hi. *take back* Lm 5$_{21}$ 2 C 19$_4$ 24$_{19}$ 4QNarrB 1$_9$, קרב hi. *bring* chosen person *near* Nm 16$_5$ (or em. וְהִקְרִיב *and he will bring [him] near* to וְהַקָּרוֹב *and the one who is near* to Y.; Sam יַקְרִיב *he will bring [him] near*).

שׁלח *send* Jr 42$_{6.9.20}$ (or del. ׳י), נטה hi. *turn* heart Jos 24$_{23}$, כון hi. *direct* heart 1 S 7$_3$, נשׂא *raise* soul, etc. Ps 25$_1$ (or em. אֵלֶיךָ ... אֶשָּׂא *I raise* my soul *to you* to אֵלֶיךָ קִוִּתִי ... אֶשָּׂא אֶל־ ... *I wait for you ..., I raise* my soul *to* my God) 143$_7$ Lm 2$_{18(mss)}$ 2QapMoses 1$_5$ ([יהוה] ... אשׂ[א] ... [אליך]), גלל *roll*, i.e. entrust, oneself Ps 22$_9$ (or em. גלה pi. *reveal* or גיל *live* for Y.), way Ps 37$_{5(mss)}$, deeds Pr 16$_3$ (or em. in both גלה pi. *reveal*).

אמר *say* Gn 4$_{13}$ Ex 4$_{10}$ 19$_{23}$ 33$_{12}$ Nm 11$_{11}$ 14$_{13}$ 16$_{15}$ Jg 10$_{15}$ 1 S 14$_{41}$ 2 S 24$_{10.17}$ Ho 14$_3$, דבר pi. *speak* Nm 27$_{15}$ 2 S 7$_{19}$, הלל pi. *give praise* Ezr 3$_{10(mss)}$, חנן htp. *pray* Dt 3$_{23}$ Ps 30$_{9(mss)}$ 142$_2$, עתר *pray* Ex 8$_{26}$ 10$_{18}$ Jg 13$_8$, hi. Ex 8$_{4.25}$ 9$_{28}$, פלל htp. *pray* Nm 11$_2$ 21$_7$ Dt 9$_{26}$ 1 S 1$_{10(mss).26}$ 7$_5$ 8$_6$ 12$_{19}$ 2 S 7$_{27}$ 1 K 8$_{44.54}$ 2 K 4$_{33}$ 6$_{18}$ 20$_2$||Is 38$_2$||2 C 32$_{24}$ Is 37$_{15}$ Jr 29$_7$ 32$_{16}$ 37$_3$ 42$_{2.4.20}$ Jon 2$_2$ 4$_2$, פרשׂ *spread out* hands, i.e. pray Ex 9$_{29.33}$ Ezr 9$_5$, pi. Ps 143$_6$, שׁטח pi. *spread out* hands, i.e. pray Ps 88$_{10}$, רום hi. *raise* hand, i.e. swear Gn 14$_{22}$ (or del. ׳י), פצה *open* mouth Jg 11$_{35.36}$, נגד hi. *declare* Ex 19$_9$.

קרא *call* Dt 15$_9$ 24$_{15}$ Jg 15$_{18}$ 16$_{28}$ 1 S 12$_{17.18}$ 1 K 17$_{20.21}$ 2 K 20$_{11}$ Jl 1$_{19}$ Jon 1$_{14}$ 2$_3$ Ps 3$_5$ 4$_4$ 28$_1$ 30$_9$ 86$_{3(mss)}$ 99$_6$ 120$_1$ 1 C 21$_{26}$ 2 C 14$_{10}$, זעק *cry* Jg 3$_{9.15}$ 6$_{6.7}$ 10$_{10}$=1 S 12$_{10}$ 1 S 7$_{8.9}$ 12$_8$ 15$_{11}$ Jl 1$_{14}$ Mc 3$_4$ Ps 107$_{13=19}$ 142$_{2.6}$ Ne 9$_4$ 4QapPs^a 2$_4$ ([ויזעקו אל]) 4QNarrC 1$_{12}$, צעק *cry* Ex 8$_8$ 14$_{10.15}$ 15$_{25}$ 17$_4$ Nm 12$_{13}$ 20$_{16}$ Dt 26$_7$ Jos 24$_7$ Jg 4$_3$ Is 19$_{20}$ Ps 107$_{6=28}$ Lm 2$_{18(mss)}$, hi. *summon* 1 S 10$_{17}$, שׁוע pi. *cry* 2 S 18$_{42(ms)}$ Ps 22$_{24}$ 30$_3$ 88$_{14}$.

קשׁב hi. *attend* Zc 1$_4$, שׁמע *hear* Ezk 20$_7$, נבט hi. *look* Ps 34$_5$ 2QapMoses 1$_5$ ([יהוה]), שׁעה *look* 2 S 22$_{42}$ (ms, ||Ps 18$_{42}$ שׁוע על pi. *cry to*), נתן *give*, i.e. turn, face Dn 9$_{3(mss)}$,

אֶל *for*, + יחל pi. *wait* Ps 130$_7$ 131$_3$, קוה pi. *wait* Ps 25$_1$ (if em. אֵלֶיךָ ... אֶשָּׂא *I raise* my soul *to you* to אֵלֶיךָ קִוִּתִי ... אֶשָּׂא אֶל־ ... *I wait for you ..., I raise* my soul *to* my God) 27$_{14.14}$ 37$_{34}$, שׂבר pi. *wait* Ps 104$_{24}$; *against* Is 3$_8$, + דבר pi. *speak* Is 32$_6$=4QpIsa^c 26$_2$ ([לדבר אל י׳]) Jr 28$_{16}$ (or del.), זיד *be presumptuous* Jr 50$_{29}$, חשׁב pi. *plan* Na 1$_9$; *by*, + זכר ni. *be remembered* Ps 109$_{14}$ (or del. אֶל־י׳); *in the opinion of* 1 K 14$_{13}$; perh. *with*, + כסה pi. *hide (oneself)* Ps 143$_9$ (unless כסה pi. *reveal* to; ms נוס *flee* to; ms חסה *take refuge* in; or em. pu. *be covered* by or כִּסְלָה/כְּסוּת with you is my *covering/confidence*).

ערך אֶל *draw comparisons with* Ps 40$_6$ (אֵין עֲרֹךְ אֵלֶיךָ *there is none to compare with you*); בטח אֶל *trust in* 2 K 18$_{22}$||Is 36$_7$ Ps 4$_6$ 31$_7$ 86$_2$ Pr 3$_5$, hi. *cause to trust in* 2 K 18$_{30}$||Is 36$_{15}$.

עִם *with* Ps 39$_{13}$, + הלך htp. *go* Si 44$_{16}$; *(belonging) to* Ps 130$_{3(mss)}$ 130$_{7.7}$ Jb 12$_9$; + היה *be* Ex 34$_{28}$; *towards, in the service of*, + היה *be* wholehearted Dt 18$_{13}$=11QT 60$_{21}$ 1 K 8$_{61}$ 11$_4$ 15$_{3.14}$; *in the presence of*, + גדל *grow up* 1 S 2$_{21.26}$, טוב *be good* 1 S 2$_{26}$; *against*, + מרה hi. *rebel* Dt 9$_{7.24}$ 31$_{27}$, לחם ni. *fight* 2 C 13$_{12}$.

אֵת *with* Is 49$_4$; *by means of*, + קנה *acquire* Gn 4$_1$; *in the care of*, + צרר pass. *be bound* 1 S 25$_{29}$.

עַל *upon* Ps 16$_2$ (אֲדֹנָי אַתָּה טוֹבָתִי בַּל־עָלֶיךָ appar. *you are my Lord; my goodness is not upon you* Ps 16$_2$ [unless בַּל affirmative, my goodness is *indeed* upon you; or em. כֻּלָּהּ עָלֶיךָ as for my goodness, *all of it is on account of you* or בַּל־בִּלְעָדֶיךָ *does not exist apart from you*, or אֲדֹנָי אַתָּה טוֹבָתִי : בְּלִיַּעַל כָּל־ *you are my Lord, my goodness. Worthless are all* the holy ones), + סמך ni. *lean* Ps 71$_5$, שׁען ni. *lean* 2 C 13$_{18}$ 16$_{7.8}$ Is 10$_{20}$ Mc 3$_{11}$.

עַל *against* Ex $16_{7.8}$, + דבר pi. *speak* Dt 13_{6}=11QT 54_{16} Jr 29_{32} 2 C 32_{16}, לון hi. *murmur* Ex 16_{8}, יעד ni. *be assembled* Nm 16_{11} 27_{3}, perh. יצב htp. *position oneself* Ps 2_{2}, יסד ni. *be based* or *conspire* Ps 2_{2}, חשב *plan* evil Na 1_{11}, חפא pi. perh. *do secretly* 2 K 17_{9}, נצה hi. *struggle* Nm 26_{9}, גדל hi. *magnify oneself* Jr $48_{25.42}$ Ezk 35_{12}, זעף *be angry* Pr 19_{3}.

עַל *to(wards)*, + גלל *roll*, i.e. entrust, way Ps 37_{5} (or em. גלה pi. *reveal*; mss אֶל *to*), פלל htp. *pray* 1 S 1_{10} (mss אֶל), שוע pi. *cry* Ps 18_{42} (||2 S 22_{42} שעה אֶל *look towards*), שוב *go back* 2 C 15_{4} 30_{9}, שלך hi. *throw* cares Ps 55_{23}, לוה ni. *attach oneself* Is 56_{6}.

עַל *in the presence of*, + יצב htp. *position oneself* Jb 1_{6} 2_{1}; עַל *beside*, + שכן *dwell* Dt 33_{12} (or em. עָלָיו *above /beside him* to עֶלְיוֹן *Elyon* or עָל *Al*); ערב עַל *be pleasing to* Ps 104_{33}, ענג עַל htp. *delight in* Is 58_{14} Ps 37_{4}, בטח עַל *trust in* Ps 31_{15} 37_{5} Pr 28_{25}, שִׂבְרוֹ עַל *his hope is in* Y. Ps 146_{5}.

לִפְנֵי *in the presence of* (sometimes perh. *by*) Gn $10_{9.9}$ Ex $28_{29.38}$ 29_{23}||Lv 8_{26} Ex 29_{42} 30_{16} Lv 16_{18} Nm 18_{19} 32_{22} Dt 24_{13} 2 S 6_{21} 1 K 8_{64} 9_{25} 2 K 16_{14} Ezk 41_{22} Hg 2_{14} Ps 96_{5} 141_{1} Ezr 9_{15} 1 C 23_{31} 11QT 15_{12} ([ל]פני) 15_{13} 20_{9} ([לפני יהוה]) 21_{16} 11QT[b] 22_{6} 11QT 24_{9} 25_{4} ([ל]פני) 25_{7} ([לפני יהוה]) 34_{14}, + היה *be* Nm 15_{15} 16_{16} 2 S 7_{29}||1 C 17_{27} Ps 19_{15}, חיה *live* Hosea 6_{1}, אמן ni. *be faithful* Ne 9_{7}, כון ni. *be established* 2 S 7_{26}||1 C 17_{24} 1 K 2_{45}, hi. *establish* ways 2 C 27_{6}, צדק *be justified* Ps 143_{1}, זכר ni. *be remembered* Nm 10_{9}, ארר pass. *be cursed* Jos 6_{26} 1 S 26_{19}, עצר ni. *be detained* 1 S 21_{8}, שבר ni. *be broken*, i.e. scatter 2 C 14_{12}, pi. *shatter* rocks 1 K 19_{11}, טהר *be pure* Lv 16_{30}, רצה ni. *be acceptable* 4QJub[d] 21_{20} ([נרצית לפני יהו]ה), כנע ni. *be humble* 2 C 34_{27}, כבש ni. *be subdued* Nm 32_{22} 1 C 22_{18}, חלץ ni. *be equipped* for war Nm 32_{20}, כתב ni. *be written* Ml 3_{16}.

הלך pi. *go* Ps 85_{13}, htp. Gn 24_{40} 2 K 20_{3}||Is $38_{3}$$116_{9}$, בוא *come* Ex $28_{30.35}$ 34_{34} Lv 15_{14} Ezk 46_{9} Ps 88_{2} 100_{2} 119_{169} Lm 1_{20} 1 C 16_{29}, hi. *bring* Lv 4_{4} 14_{23} Nm 7_{3} 15_{25}, עבר *pass* Nm $32_{21.27.29.32}$ Jos 4_{13}, קרב *approach* Ex 16_{9} Lv 16_{1} Ps 119_{169}, hi. *present* Lv $3_{1.7.12}$ 6_{7} 9_{2} $10_{1.19}$ 12_{7} Nm 3_{4} 8_{10} 16_{17} 17_{3} 26_{61} 27_{5} Ezk 43_{24}, עמד *stand* Gn 18_{22} Lv 9_{5} Dt 4_{10} 10_{8} 18_{7} 19_{17} 29_{14} 1 S 6_{20} 1 K 19_{11} 22_{21}||2 C 18_{20} Ezr 9_{15} 2 C 20_{13}, hi. *position* Lv 14_{11} 16_{7} Nm $5_{16.18.30}$, ho. *be positioned* Lv 16_{10} (or em. hi.), יצב htp. *stand* 1 S 10_{19}, נצב ni. *stand* Dt 29_{9}, שים *place* Lv 24_{6} Nm 16_{7}, נוח hi. *place* Ex 16_{33} Nm 17_{22} Dt 26_{10} 1 S 10_{25}, נתן *give*, i.e. place Lv 4_{7} 16_{13} Nm 16_{7}, יצק hi. *place* Jos 7_{23}.

נפל *fall* 2 C 20_{18}, specif. be offered (of supplication) Jr 36_{7}, hi. *present* supplication Jr 42_{9} Dn 9_{20}, htp. *bow down* Dt $9_{18.25}$, שחה htpal. *bow down* Dt 26_{10} 1 S 1_{19} Ezk 46_{3} Ps $86_{9(mss)}$, ברך *kneel* Ps 95_{6} (or em. בכה *weep*), שרת pi. *minister* 11QT 15_{15} ([שרת לפני יהוה]), עלה hi. *take up* Ex 40_{25}, *offer* Jg 20_{26} 2 S 6_{17}, נשא *raise* Ex $28_{12.30}$ Jos 6_{8}, ירה *cast* lot Jos 18_{6}, שלך hi. *cast* lot Jos $18_{8.10}$, שפך *pour* 1 S 1_{15} 7_{6} Ps 102_{1} 142_{2}, ערך *array* Ex 27_{21}||Lv 24_{3} Lv $24_{4.8}$.

עשׂה *do* Dt 6_{25} 1 K 8_{65} 2 C 31_{20} 11QPsAp[a] 2_{9} (עושים] לפני יהו]ה) 11QT 53_{8} (לפני אני י׳) 55_{14} 63_{8}, אמר *say* Ex 6_{30} Dt $26_{5.13}$, דבר pi. *speak* Ex 6_{12} Jg 11_{11}, נגד hi. *declare* Ps 142_{2}, קרא *call* fast Jr 36_{9}, רנן pi. *exult* Ps 96_{12}=98_{9}, עלז *exult* Ps 96_{12}, שמח *rejoice* Lv 23_{40} Dt $12_{12.18}$ 16_{11} 27_{7} Ps 96_{12} 11QT 21_{8} ([לפ[ני]) 11QT[b] 23_{9} ([לפני יהוה]), גיל *rejoice* Ps 96_{12}, רוע hi. *shout* Ps 98_{6}, רעם *thunder* in praise Ps 96_{12}=98_{9}, מחא *strike*, i.e. clap, hand Ps 98_{9}, שפט ni. *enter judgment* 1 S 12_{7}, שאל *ask* Nm 27_{21}, פרש *extend* document 2 K 19_{14}||Is 37_{14}, פרק pi. *tear* mountains 1 K 19_{11}, בכה *weep* Dt 1_{45} Jg 20_{23} 2 K 22_{19}||2 C 34_{27} Ps 95_{6} (if em. ברך *kneel*), שחק pi. *play*, i.e. dance 2 S $6_{5.21}$ Pr 8_{22}, כרר pilp. *dance* or *clap* 2 S $6_{14.16}$, פזז *leap* 2 S 6_{16}, אכל *eat* Dt $12_{7.18}$ $14_{23.26}$ 15_{20} Ezk 44_{3} 1 C 29_{22} 11QT 21_{3} 22_{14}, שתה *drink* 1 C 29_{22}, ישב *sit* Jg 20_{26} 2 S 7_{18}||1 C 17_{16}, *dwell* Is 23_{18}.

נחל pi. *assign* territory Jos 19_{51}, מלך hi. *make king* 1 S 11_{15}, כרת *cut*, i.e. make, covenant 1 S 23_{18} 2 S 5_{3}||1 C 11_{3} 2 K 23_{3}||2 C 34_{31}, עבד *serve*, i.e. perform, divine service Jos 22_{27}, ברך pi. *bless* Gn 27_{7}, חנן htp. *pray* 1 K 8_{59}, פלל htp. *pray* 1 S 1_{12} 2 K 19_{15} Ne 1_{5} 2QapMoses 1_{4} GnzPs 2_{7} 3_{11} 4_{17}, סמך *rest* hands on head Lv 4_{15}, שחט *slaughter* Ex 29_{11} Lv $1_{5.11}$ $4_{4.15.24}$, ni. *be slaughtered* 6_{18}, זבח *sacrifice* Lv 9_{4} 1 S 11_{15} 1 K 8_{62}||2 C 7_{4}, קטר hi. *burn (in sacrifice)* Ex 29_{25} 30_{8} $40_{27(Sam)}$ Nm 17_{5} 1 C 23_{13} 2 C 2_{3}, נוף hi. *wave* sacrifice Ex 29_{24} 29_{26}||Lv 8_{29} Lv 7_{30} 8_{27} 9_{21} 10_{15} $14_{12.24}$ $23_{11.20}$ Nm 5_{25} 6_{20} $8_{11.21}$, כפר pi. *atone* Lv 5_{26} 10_{17} $14_{18.29.31}$ $15_{15.30}$ 19_{22} 23_{28} Nm 15_{28} 31_{50} 11QT 22_{16}, נזה hi. *sprinkle* Lv $4_{6.17}$ $14_{16.27}$, יקע hi. *impale*

2 S 21_{9}, שׁסף *cut up* 1 S 15_{33}, גוע *expire* Nm 20_{3}, מות *die* Lv 10_{2} Nm 3_{4} 14_{37}.

מִלִּפְנֵי *from (the presence of)* 2 C 19_{2} 4QpsEzek[a] 16.1_{2}, + בוא *come* Jon 1_{3}, ברח *flee* Jon $1_{3.10}$, יצא *go out* Gn 4_{16} Lv 9_{24} 10_{2} Nm 17_{11} Ps 17_{1}, hi. *bring out* Nm 17_{24}, לקח *take* Lv 16_{12} Nm 20_{9}, סור ho. *be removed* 1 S 21_{7}; *in the presence of* 1 C 29_{11} 1QpHab 13_{1} (=Hb 2_{20} מִפְּנֵי), + כנע ni. *be humble* 2 C 33_{23}, חיל *tremble* Ps $96_{9(mss)}$ (L מִפְּנֵי *in the presence of*), פחד *tremble* 11QPsAp[a] 2_{10} ([יפחדון]), מסס ni. *be melted* Ps 97_{5}, רנן pi. *exalt* 1 C 16_{33}.

מִפְּנֵי *in the presence of* Hb 2_{20} (=1QpHab 13_{1} מִלִּפְנֵי *in the presence of*) Zp 1_{7} Zc 2_{17} (all three הַס מִפְּנֵי *silence*, i.e. be silent, *in the presence of*), + כנע ni. *be humble* 2 K 22_{19}, הלך *go* mournfully Ml 3_{14}, חיל *tremble* Jr 5_{22} Ps 96_{9} (mss מִלִּפְנֵי), נזל *flow* Jg $5_{5.5}$; *from (the presence of)*, + חבא htp. *hide oneself* Gn 3_{8}; perh. *on account of*, + היה *be* Is 26_{17} Jr 23_{9}, ירא *fear* Ex 9_{30} Hg 1_{12}, נתץ ni. *be torn down* Jr 4_{26}.

אֶת־פְּנֵי *in the presence of* Gn 19_{13}, + היה *be* 1 S 2_{17} (+ גָּדוֹל *great*), ראה ni. *appear* $34_{23.24}$ Dt $16_{16.16}$ 31_{11} 1 S 1_{22}, עמד *stand* Gn 19_{27}, שׁרת pi. *minister* 1 S 2_{18}; אֶל־פְּנֵי *in the presence of*, + ראה ni. *appear* Ex 23_{17} (Sam אֶת־פְּנֵי אֲרוֹן *in the presence of the ark* of Y.).

נֶגֶד *in the presence of* 1 S 16_{6} Ps 69_{17} (or em. נֶגְדְּךָ *in your presence* to נֶגֶד *in the presence of* my enemies) 119_{166} Pr 15_{11}, + היה *be* Ps 109_{15}, צעק *cry* Ps 88_{2} (or em. צָעַקְתִּי *I cried* to צַעֲקָתִי *my cry*); לְנֶגֶד *against* or *in comparison with* Pr 21_{30}; נֹכַח *in the presence of* Jg 18_{6}.

עַד *(un)to*, + בוא *come* Ex $22_{8(Sam)}$=4QBibPar 10_{11}, שׁוב *go back* Dt 4_{30} 30_{2} Is 19_{22} Ho 14_{2} Jl 2_{12} Am $4_{6.8.9.10.11}$ Lm 3_{40} 4QapMos[a] 1.1_{2}.

אַחַר *after*, + היה *be*, i.e. follow 1 S 12_{14} (mss אַחֲרֵי), הלך *go* 2 K 23_{3} 4QapMos[c] 2.2_{5}; אַחֲרֵי *after*, + הלך *go* Dt 13_{5}=11QT 54_{13} Ho 11_{10} 2 C 34_{31}, מלא pi. *follow wholeheartedly* Nm 32_{12} Dt 1_{36} Jos $14_{8.9.14}$ 1 K 11_{6} Si 46_{10}, שׁאר hi. *leave* blessing Jl 2_{14}, נהה ni. perh. *cling* to 1 S 7_{2},

תַּחַת *under*, + דושׁ ni. *be trampled* (of Moab) Is 25_{10} (unless תַּחְתָּיו = *in its* [Moab's] *place*), רדד *subdue* people Ps $144_{1(mss)}$ (L תַּחְתָּי *under me*; ms רדה *rule*), מסס ni. *be melted* (of mountains) Mc 1_{3}.

בֵּין *between*, + היה *be* as a sign between Y. and house of Jacob Ezk 20_{20}, עמד *stand* between Y. and Israel Dt 5_{5}, כרת *cut*, i.e. make, covenant between Y. and Joash 2 K 11_{17}.

אֵצֶל *beside*, + היה Pr 8_{22}.

סְבִיבֵי *around* Ps 97_{1}, + להט pi. *burn* adversaries Ps $97_{1(mss)}$.

בִּלְעֲדֵי *apart from* Is 45_{5} Ps 16_{2} (if em. בַּל־עָלֶיךָ my goodness *is not upon you* to בַּל־בִּלְעָדֶיךָ my goodness *does not exist apart from you*); מִבַּלְעֲדֵי *apart from* 2 S 22_{32} ||Ps 18_{32} Is 43_{11}; *without the consent of*, + עלה *go up* 2 K 18_{25}||Is 36_{10}; זוּלַת *apart from* 2 S 7_{22}||1 C 17_{20} $45_{5.21}$, בעל *be lord* Is 26_{13} (or ins. ידע *know* no one apart from Y.), ידע *know* Is 26_{13} (if em.) Ho 13_{4}.

לְמַעַן *on account of*, + קום *arise* Is 49_{7}, שׁחה htpal. *bow down* Is 49_{7}, רוץ *run* Is 55_{5}, perh. קרא *call* Is 55_{5}, אור hi. *let* face *shine* Dn $9_{17(mss)}$; בַּעֲבוּר *on account of*, + קרא *call*, i.e. name 2 S 12_{25}.

<COLL> י׳ *O Y.* Gn $15_{2.8}$ $24_{12.42}$ Gn 32_{10} 49_{18} Ex $15_{6.6.11.16.17.17(mss, Sam)}$ 32_{11} Nm $10_{35.36}$ $14_{14.14}$ Dt 9_{26} 21_{8} =11QT 63_{7} 26_{10} Jos 7_{7} Jg $5_{4.31}$ 6_{22} 16_{28} 21_{3} $23_{10.11}$ 2 S 7_{18} ||1 C 17_{16} 2 S 7_{19} (unless בְּעֵינֶיךָ אֲדֹנָי י׳ = *in the eyes of my Lord, Y.*)* $7_{19.20.22.24.25.28.29}$||1 C $17_{17.19.20.22.23.26.27}$ 2 S 7_{29} 15_{31} 22_{29} 22_{50}||Ps 18_{50}=$57_{10(mss)}$=108_{4} 2 S 2_{17} 24_{10} 1 K 3_{7} $8_{23.25.28}$||2 C $6_{14.16.19}$ 1 K 8_{53} $17_{20.21}$ $18_{36.37.37}$ 19_{4} 2 K 6_{17} 19_{15} $19_{16.16.17.19}$||Is $37_{17.17.18.20}$ 2 K 20_{3}||Is 38_{3} 1QIsa[a] 6_{11} Is 12_{1} $26_{4.11.12.13.15.16.17}$ 33_{2} $63_{16.17}$ $64_{7.8.11}$ Jr 1_{6} 4_{10} 5_{3} $10_{6.23.24}$ 11_{5} $12_{1.3}$ $14_{9.13.20}$ $15_{15.16}$ 16_{19} $17_{3.14}$ $18_{19.23}$ 20_{7} 31_{7} (or em. הוֹשַׁע י׳ *save, O Y.* to הוֹשִׁיעַ י׳ *Y. has saved*) $32_{17.25}$ 51_{62} Ezk 4_{14} 9_{8} 11_{13} 37_{3} Ho 9_{14} Jl 1_{19} 2_{17} 4_{11} Am $7_{2.5}$ Jon $1_{14.14}$ 2_{7} $4_{2.3}$ Hb $1_{2.12.12}$ $3_{2.2.8}$ Zc 1_{12} Ps $3_{2.8}$ $4_{7.9}$ $5_{2.4}$ (or del.) $5_{9.13}$ 6_{2}=38_{2} $6_{3.3.4.5}$ $7_{2.4.7.9}$ $8_{2.10}$ $9_{11.14.20.21}$ $10_{1.12}$ $12_{2.8}$ $13_{2.4}$ 15_{1} $17_{1.13.14}$ $18_{16.50}$ 19_{15} 20_{10} 21_{2} (+ מָאֵד *Great One*, if em. מְאֹד *exceedingly*)* 21_{14} 22_{20} $25_{1.4.6.7.11}$ $26_{1.2.6.8}$ $27_{7.8.11}$ 28_{1} $30_{2.3.8.9.11.11.13}$ 31_{2}=71_{1} $31_{6.10.15.18}$ 33_{22} $35_{1.10.24}$ $36_{6.7}$ $38_{16.22}$ 39_{5} 39_{13}=102_{2} $40_{6.10.12.14}$ 40_{14} ||70_{2} $41_{5.11}$ 54_{8} 58_{7} 59_{4} (mss אֱלֹהַי *O my God*, ms אֲדֹנָי *O Adonai*) 59_{9} $69_{7.14.17}$ 70_{6} (mss אֱלֹהַי) $71_{5.16}$ 79_{5} $80_{5.20}$ 83_{17} $84_{2.4.13}$ $85_{2.8}$ $86_{3(mss).5(mss).6.8(mss).9(mss).11.12(mss).15(mss).17}$ $88_{2.10.14.15}$ $89_{6.9.16.47.50(mss).51(mss).52}$ 91_{9} (or em. מַחְסִי you, O Y., are *my refuge* to מַחְסֶךָ you have made Y. *your refuge*) $92_{5.6.9.10.16}$ $93_{3.5}$ $94_{1.3.5.18}$ $97_{8.9}$ 99_{8} 101_{1} 102_{13}=Lm 5_{19} Ps 104_{1} $106_{4.47}$ $109_{21.26.27}$ 110_{2} (if em. יִשְׁלַח Y. *will send* to שְׁלַח *send*, O Y.) 115_{1} $116_{4.16}$ $118_{25.25}$

119$_{12.31.41.52.55.64.65.75.89.107.108.126(ms).145.149.151.156.159.169.174}$ 120$_{2}$ 123$_{3}$ 125$_{4}$ 130$_{1.2(mss).3(mss)}$ 131$_{1}$ 132$_{1}$ 132$_{8}$=2 C 6$_{41}$ Ps 135$_{13.13}$ 137$_{7}$ 138$_{4.8}$ 139$_{1.4.21}$ 140$_{2.5.7.8.9}$ 141$_{1.3.8}$ (mss אֱלֹהִים *O God*) 142$_{6}$ 143$_{1.7.9.11}$ 144$_{3.5}$ 145$_{10}$ Lm 1$_{9.11.20}$ 2$_{20}$ 3$_{55.58(mss).59.61.64}$ 5$_{21}$ Dn 9$_{8.15(mss).16(mss).17(mss)}$ (if em. לְמַעַן *for the sake of* Y., to לְמַעַנְךָ *for your sake*, O Y.) 9$_{19(mss).19(mss)}$ Ne 1$_{5}$ 1 C 21$_{17}$ 29$_{10.11.11.16.18}$ 2 C 1$_{9}$ 6$_{17.41.42}$ 14$_{10.10}$ 20$_{6}$ 4QTestim$_{19}$ 2QapMoses 1$_{5}$ ([יהוה]) 4QapPs^{b} 33$_{2}$ 4QpsEzek^{a} 2$_{9}$ 4QpsEzek^{b} 1.2$_{2}$ 4Q408 1$_{6}$ 4QPseud^{b} 5.1$_{9}$ GnzPs 2$_{6.8.14.18}$ perh. Kh. Beit Lei graf. 5$_{2}$ (see Nom. Cl.).

י״ indicated by scribal dots ···· 4QTestim$_{1.19}$ 4QActs 1$_{5}$ 4QErr 2$_{5}$ 4QparaKings 9$_{5}$ 4QpsEzek^{e} 36$_{1.3}$ ([···]·) 36$_{4}$ 52$_{5}$ 55$_{2}$ 58$_{3}$ (....) 65$_{5}$ 4QPrayer^{c} 1$_{5}$ (··[··]) 4QNarrC 1$_{7.12}$ (·· ··); written in palaeo-Hebrew, e.g. 4QPs^{a} 2$_{4.12.24.24}$ 3$_{14.15}$ 4$_{7.10}$ 2$_{1}$ 3$_{1}$.

י״ *by Y.!* 1 S 20$_{12}$.

י״ יֵחַתּוּ מְרִיבָיו *as for Y., those who strive against him will be shattered* 1 S 2$_{10(Qr)}$ (or em. יָחֵת *Y. shatters*), י״ כמה גב[ור] *As for Y., how mighty* 4QapPs^{b} 1$_{2}$, י״ עֵינָיו מְשֹׁטְטוֹת בְּכָל־הָאָרֶץ *as for Y., his eyes range through the whole earth* 2 C 16$_{9}$, י״ בַּשָּׁמַיִם כִּסְאוֹ *as for Y., his throne is in the heavens* Ps 11$_{4}$ (mss הֵכִין כִּסְאוֹ Y. *has established his throne* in the heavens), בְּאָזְנָי י״ צְבָאוֹת *in my ears, Y. of hosts* Is 5$_{9}$, י״ ... לְבַד־בְּךָ נַזְכִּיר שְׁמֶךָ perh. *O Y. ..., you alone, we mention your name*, i.e. we mention only your name Is 26$_{13}$ (or em. לְבַדְּךָ *you alone* [and] your name do we mention).

י״ identified by other names, titles, and descriptions (see also Nom. Cl. and App.), יָהּ *Yah* Ex 17$_{16}$ Ps 89$_{9}$ 104$_{35}$ 106$_{48}$ 111$_{1}$ 112$_{2}$ 113$_{1}$ 118$_{4.4}$ 122$_{4}$ 130$_{3}$ 135$_{1.21}$ 146$_{1.10}$ 148$_{1}$ 149$_{1}$, אֲדֹנָי *(my) Lord* Ex 4$_{10}$ 15$_{17}$ Jg 13$_{8}$ 16$_{28}$ Is 3$_{17}$ 49$_{14}$ Am 7$_{8}$ Mc 1$_{2}$ Ps 16$_{2}$ 30$_{9}$ (mss י״) 35$_{22}$ 135$_{3}$ Lm 2$_{20.20}$ (mss י״), אֲדֹנֵי הָאֲדֹנִים *lord of lords* Dt 10$_{17}$ Ps 136$_{1}$, אֲדֹנָי אֱלֹהָי *Adonai, my God* Ps 38$_{16}$, אֲדֹנֵינוּ *our Lord* Ps 135$_{5}$, אֲדוֹן כָּל־הָאָרֶץ *lord of all the earth* Ps 97$_{5}$, אֲבִיר יַעֲקֹב *mighty one of Jacob* Ps 132$_{2.5}$, בַּעַל חֵמָה *lord of anger* Na 1$_{2}$, קָדוֹשׁ *holy one* Is 49$_{7}$ Pr 9$_{10}$, רִאשׁוֹן *(the) first* Is 44$_{6}$, אַחֲרוֹן *(the) last* Is 44$_{6}$.

מֶלֶךְ *king* Nm 23$_{21}$ Jr 46$_{18}$ 48$_{15}$ 51$_{57}$ Ps 29$_{10}$, מַלְכָּהּ *her king* Jr 8$_{19}$, מֶלֶךְ הַגּוֹיִם *king of the nations* Jr 10$_{6}$, מֶלֶךְ הַכָּבוֹד *king of glory* Ps 24$_{8.9}$, מֶלֶךְ יַעֲקֹב *king of Jacob* Is 41$_{21}$, מֶלֶךְ עוֹלָם *king of eternity* Jr 10$_{10}$, מֹשִׁעִי *my saviour* 2 S 22$_{2}$, גֹּאֵל *redeemer* Is 41$_{14}$ Jr 50$_{34}$, שֹׁמְרֶךָ *your guardian* Ps 121$_{2}$, שׁוֹמֵר יִשְׂרָאֵל *guardian of Israel* Ps 121$_{2}$, גִּבּוֹר *warrior* Zp 3$_{17}$, שׁוֹדֵד *devastator* Jr 51$_{56}$, דֹּב *bear* Lm 2$_{22}$, אֲרִי *lion* Lm 2$_{22}$.

טוֹבָתִי *my good(ness)* Ps 16$_{2}$, חֶלְקִי *my portion* Ps 142$_{6}$, עֵזֶר *help* Ps 33$_{20}$ 115$_{9.10.11}$, אֱיָלוּתִי *my help* or *my strength* Ps 22$_{20}$, קֶרֶן יִשְׁעִי *horn of my salvation* 2 S 22$_{2}$||Ps 18$_{3}$, מָגֵן *shield* 2 S 22$_{2}$ 22$_{31}$||Ps 18$_{31}$ Ps 33$_{20}$ 115$_{9.10.11}$ 119$_{108}$ Pr 2$_{6}$, חֶרֶב *sword* Dt 33$_{29}$.

צוּר *rock* Dt 32$_{30}$ 2 S 22$_{2.32.47}$||Ps 18$_{3.32.47}$ Hb 1$_{12}$ Ps 28$_{1}$ 94$_{22}$ 95$_{1}$, סַלְעִי *my rock* Ps 31$_{2}$=71$_{1}$, מַחְסִי *my refuge* Ps 91$_{9}$ 142$_{6}$, מְנוּסִי *my refuge* 2 S 22$_{2}$, סִתְרִי *my hiding-place* Ps 119$_{108}$, מָעוֹז *stronghold* Jl 4$_{16}$ Ps 28$_{8}$ 31$_{2}$ 37$_{39}$, מְצוּדָתִי *my stronghold* Ps 31$_{2}$||71$_{1}$ 91$_{2}$, מִשְׂגַּבִּי *my stronghold* 2 S 22$_{2}$||Ps 18$_{3}$.

אֵל *God* Nm 12$_{13}$ 2 S 22$_{31}$||Ps 18$_{31}$ Is 12$_{2}$ 31$_{3}$ 43$_{12}$ Jon 4$_{2}$ Ps 10$_{12}$, אֵל־הַכָּבוֹד *God of glory* Ps 29$_{3}$, אֵל־חָי *living God* Ps 42$_{9(mss)}$ (L אֵל חַיָּי *God of my life*) Ps 84$_{3}$, אֵל קָדוֹשׁ *holy God* Is 5$_{16}$, אֵל קַנָּא *zealous God* Ex 34$_{14}$ Dt 4$_{24}$ 6$_{15}$ Jos 24$_{19}$ (קַנּוֹא), אֵל גָּדוֹל *great God* Dt 7$_{21}$ Jr 32$_{18}$ (+ הַגִּבּוֹר *mighty*), אֵלִי *my God* Ps 140$_{7}$, אֵל רֳאִי *God of seeing* Gn 16$_{13}$, אֵל יַעֲקֹב *God of Jacob* Ps 146$_{5}$, אֵלִם *gods* Ex 15$_{11}$, אֵל שַׁדַּי *El-Shaddai* Gn 17$_{1}$ Ex 6$_{3}$, שַׁדַּי *Shaddai* Ru 1$_{21}$, עֶלְיוֹן *Elyon* 2 S 22$_{14}$||Ps 18$_{14}$ Ps 21$_{8}$ 83$_{19}$ 91$_{9}$ 92$_{2}$, אֱלוֹהַּ *God* Ps 18$_{32}$,

אֱלֹהִים *God* Ex 3$_{4}$ 6$_{2}$ (Sam י״) 19$_{3}$ Lv 26$_{45}$ Jg 16$_{28}$ 1 S 4$_{4}$ 2 S 6$_{7}$ 7$_{22}$||1 C 17$_{20}$ 2 S 22$_{2}$ 22$_{47}$||Ps 18$_{47}$ 1 K 3$_{5}$ 8$_{23}$||2 C 6$_{14}$ 1 K 18$_{24.24.36}$ 2 K 1$_{3.6.16}$ 4$_{27}$ 8$_{8}$ 17$_{33}$ 19$_{15}$||Is 37$_{16}$ 2 K 23$_{16}$ Is 45$_{18}$ Jr 23$_{24.24}$ 24$_{7}$ 50$_{35}$ Ho 4$_{1}$ 13$_{4}$ Jl 2$_{17}$ Am 4$_{11}$ Ml 3$_{14}$ Ps 14$_{2}$ 47$_{6}$ 48$_{9}$ 55$_{17}$ 56$_{11}$ 58$_{7}$ 69$_{14}$ 70$_{2}$ 73$_{28}$ 86$_{9(mss)}$ Ezr 1$_{3}$ 2 C 5$_{14}$ 10$_{15}$ 11$_{2}$ 13$_{12}$ 17$_{3}$ 18$_{13.31}$ 20$_{6.15.29}$ 23$_{3}$ 24$_{7.9}$ 26$_{5.5.5}$ 28$_{24.24}$ 30$_{12.14.16}$ 32$_{17}$ 33$_{12}$.

אֱלֹהִים חַי *living God* 2 K 19$_{4.16}$||Is 37$_{4.17}$, אֱלֹהִים חַיִּים *living God* Jr 10$_{10}$, אֱלֹהֵי הָאֱלֹהִים *God of gods* Ps 136$_{1}$, אֱלֹהֵי־צְבָאוֹת *God of hosts* Am 5$_{20}$, אֱלֹהֵי יִשְׂרָאֵל *God of Israel* 2 S 23$_{2}$ Is 41$_{17}$ 48$_{1.2}$ 52$_{12}$ Ezk 10$_{19}$ Ps 69$_{7}$ Ezr 8$_{35}$, אֱלֹהֵי הָעִבְרִים *God of the Hebrews* Ex 5$_{3}$, אֱלֹהֵי אַבְרָהָם *God of Abraham* Gn 26$_{24}$, אֱלֹהֵי יַעֲקֹב *God of Jacob* Is 2$_{3}$||Mc 4$_{2}$ Ps 20$_{2}$ 46$_{8.12}$ 84$_{9}$, אֱלֹהֵי כָל־הָאָרֶץ *God of all the earth* Is 54$_{5}$, אֱלֹהֵי מָרוֹם *God of height* Mc 6$_{6}$, אֱלֹהֵי יִשְׁעִי *God of my salvation* Mc 7$_{7}$ Hb 3$_{18}$ Ps 18$_{47}$, אֱלֹהֵי יִשְׁעוֹ *God of his salvation* Ps 24$_{5}$, אֱלֹהֵי הַמִּשְׁפָּט *the God of judgment* Ml 2$_{17}$.

אֱלֹהַי *my God* 2 S 22$_{7.22}$||Ps 18$_{7.22}$ Is 40$_{27}$ 49$_{4.5}$ 61$_{10}$ Mc 7$_{7}$ Ps 3$_{8}$ 31$_{15}$ 91$_{2}$ 94$_{22}$ 104$_{33}$=146$_{2}$ 143$_{9}$ Pr 30$_{9}$, אֱלֹהֵינוּ *our God* Dt 32$_{3}$ Jg 10$_{10}$ 2 S 22$_{32}$||Ps 18$_{32}$ Is 1$_{10}$ 25$_{9}$ 35$_{2}$ 40$_{3}$ Is 52$_{10}$ 55$_{7}$ 59$_{13}$ 61$_{2.6}$ Ps 40$_{4}$ 48$_{2.9}$ 92$_{14}$ 95$_{6}$ 116$_{5}$ 135$_{2}$ 147$_{7}$ Dn 9$_{15(mss)}$ 1 C 28$_{2.8}$, אֱלֹהֶיךָ *your* (masc. sg.) *God* Lv 18$_{21}$ 19$_{12.14.32}$ 25$_{17}$ Dt 26$_{17}$ Mc 6$_{8}$ 2 C 9$_{8}$, אֱלֹהַיִךְ *your* (fem. sg.) *God* Is 51$_{20}$ 51$_{22}$ 54$_{6}$ 60$_{19}$ 62$_{3}$ 66$_{9}$ Ps 146$_{10}$ 147$_{12}$, אֱלֹהֵיכֶם *your* (pl.) *God* Nm 10$_{10}$ Jos 24$_{27}$ 1 S 10$_{19}$ Ezk 34$_{31}$, אֱלֹהָיו *his God* 2 C 33$_{18}$ Is 50$_{10}$ Jr 51$_{5}$, אֱלֹהֶיהָ *her God* Zp 3$_{2}$, אֱלֹהֵיהֶם *their God* Lv 21$_{6}$ Jr 5$_{4.5}$.

נֵצַח יִשְׂרָאֵל *glory of Israel* 1 S 15$_{28}$, קְדוֹשׁ יִשְׂרָאֵל *holy one of Israel* Is 1$_{4}$ 5$_{24}$ 29$_{19}$ 31$_{1}$ 41$_{14.16.20}$ 47$_{4}$ 54$_{5}$ 55$_{5}$ 60$_{9.14}$ Jr 50$_{29}$ Ps 89$_{19}$, מִקְוֵה יִשְׂרָאֵל *hope of Israel* Jr 14$_{7}$, חֵלֶק יַעֲקֹב *portion of Jacob* Jr 10$_{16}$ 51$_{19}$.

״ associated or contrasted with other deities and their images, אֵל *god* Ex 15$_{11}$ 34$_{14}$ Dt 3$_{24}$ 32$_{12}$ 2 S 22$_{32}$ Is 43$_{10}$ 45$_{21}$, אֱלֹהִים *god(s)* Ex 22$_{19}$ Lv 19$_{4}$ Dt 4$_{34}$ 8$_{19}$ 10$_{17}$ 11$_{28}$ 12$_{31.31}$ 28$_{64}$ 29$_{17.24.24}$ Jos 23$_{16}$ 24$_{14.15.15.16.20.23}$ Jg 2$_{12.12}$ 6$_{10}$ 10$_{6.6.6.6.6}$ 11$_{24}$ 1 S 7$_{3}$ 26$_{19}$ 1 K 9$_{9}$||2 C 7$_{22}$ 1 K 11$_{9}$ 18$_{24}$ 20$_{28}$ 2 K 1$_{3.6.16}$ 5$_{17}$ 17$_{7.35}$ 18$_{30.35}$||Is 36$_{18.20}$ Is 44$_{6}$ 45$_{5.21}$ Jr 22$_{9}$ Ho 3$_{1}$ Mc 4$_{5}$ Ps 95$_{3}$ 96$_{4}$ 97$_{9}$ 135$_{5}$ Jb 1$_{6}$ 2$_{1}$ Pr 2$_{5}$ 2 C 13$_{9}$ 33$_{15}$, אֱלֹהָיו *his god* Ezr 1$_{7}$, אֱלֹהֵי אֲבֹתָיו *gods of his fathers* 2 C 28$_{25}$, אֱלֹהֵי הָעַמִּים *gods of the peoples* Ps 96$_{5}$||1 C 16$_{25}$, אֱלֹהֵי גּוֹיֵ הָאֲרָצוֹת *gods of the nations of the lands* 2 C 32$_{17}$, צְבָא הַשָּׁמַיִם *the host of heaven* 1 K 22$_{19}$||2 C 18$_{18}$ 2 K 17$_{16}$ 21$_{5}$||2 C 33$_{5}$ 2 K 23$_{4}$ Zp 1$_{5}$, אֱלִילִם *images* Lv 26$_{1}$ Is 19$_{1}$ Ps 96$_{5}$||1 C 16$_{26}$, עָצָב pl. *image* 2 C 24$_{18}$.

בַּעַל *Baal* Jg 2$_{11.13}$ 3$_{7}$ 10$_{6.10}$ 1 S 7$_{4}$ 12$_{10}$ 1 K 16$_{13}$ 18$_{18.21.22}$ 22$_{54}$ 2 K 3$_{2}$ 10$_{23.23.23}$ 17$_{16}$ 23$_{4}$ Jr 11$_{17}$ 12$_{16}$ Ho 2$_{18}$ 2 C 17$_{3}$ 24$_{7}$, בַּעַל זְבוּב *Baal-zebub* 2 K 1$_{3.6.16}$, אֲשֵׁרָה *Asherah* Jg 3$_{7}$ 1 K 14$_{15}$ 16$_{33}$ 17$_{16}$ 2 K 21$_{7}$ 23$_{4.6.7}$ 2 C 24$_{18}$, עַשְׁתֹּרֶת *Ashtoreth* 1 K 11$_{4}$ 2 K 23$_{12}$, עַשְׁתָּרוֹת *Ashtaroth* Jg 2$_{13}$ 10$_{6}$ 1 S 7$_{3.4}$ 12$_{10}$, דָּגוֹן *Dagon* 1 S 5$_{3.4}$, כְּמוֹשׁ *Chemosh* Jg 11$_{24}$ 2 K 23$_{12}$, מִלְכֹּם *Milcom* 1 K 11$_{4}$ 2 K 23$_{12}$ Zp 1$_{5}$ (מַלְכָּם), שֶׁמֶשׁ *sun* 2 K 23$_{11.11}$, מַסֵּכָה *molten image* 2 K 17$_{16}$, סֶמֶל *image* 2 C 33$_{15}$, עֵגֶל *calf* 2 K 17$_{16}$, תּוֹעֵבָה *abomination* 2 C 34$_{33}$.

״ associated with human beings, מֹשֶׁה *Moses* Ex 14$_{31}$, דָּוִד *David* Jr 30$_{9}$ Ho 3$_{5}$, שְׁמוּאֵל *Samuel* 1 S 12$_{18}$, חִזְקִיָּהוּ *Hezekiah* 2 C 32$_{23}$, אָדָם *human being* 1 S 16$_{7}$ 2 S 24$_{14}$||1 C 21$_{13}$ Is 31$_{3}$ 1 C 29$_{1}$, הָעָם *the people* 2 S 16$_{18}$, עַמּוֹ *his people* 1 C 22$_{18}$, כָּל־אִישׁ יִשְׂרָאֵל *all the men of Israel* 2 S 16$_{18}$, בְּנֵי־יַעֲקֹב *sons of Jacob* Ml 3$_{6}$, מֶלֶךְ *king* 1 C 29$_{20}$, מֶלֶךְ אֲרָם *king of Aram* 2 C 16$_{7}$, עַבְדּוֹ *his servant* Is 50$_{10}$, מְשִׁיחוֹ *his anointed one* 1 S 12$_{3.5}$ Ps 2$_{2}$, מוֹשִׁיעַ *saviour* Is 43$_{11}$ Ho 13$_{4}$, יַד אֲדוֹנֵיהֶם *the hand of their master* Ps 123$_{2}$, יַד גְּבִרְתָּהּ *the hand of her mistress* Ps 123$_{2}$.

״ associated with other expressions: רוּחוֹ *his spirit* Is 48$_{16}$, מוֹרָא *fear*, i.e. object of reverence Ps 76$_{12}$ (or em. נוֹרָא *feared one*), צֶדֶק *righteousness* Is 51$_{1}$ Zp 2$_{3}$, עֲנָוָה *humility* Zp 2$_{3}$, דִּבְרֵי קָדְשׁוֹ *his words of holiness* Jr 23$_{9}$, טוּבוֹ *his bounty* Ho 3$_{5}$, אֲרוֹן עֻזֶּךָ *ark of your strength* Ps 132$_{8}$ =2 C 6$_{41}$, הֵיכָלוֹ *his temple* Jr 50$_{28}$ 51$_{11}$, מַחֲנֵהוּ *his camp* 2 C 14$_{12}$.

Also Si 45$_{2(Bmg)}$ (B אלהים *God*) 46$_{17(B)}$ 4QBibPar 4$_{8}$ 2Q30 1$_{1}$ 4QapJoseph^{b} 2$_{2}$ 4$_{4}$ 4QapJoshua^{b} 14$_{1}$ 4QapPs^{b} 86$_{2}$ 4QparaKings 53$_{1}$ (יהו[ה]) 4QpsEzek^{a} 12$_{2}$ 4QpsEzek^{e} 55$_{2}$ 65$_{5}$ 4QConfess 7$_{1}$ 4Q408 6$_{1}$ 4QsapHymn 1.2$_{2.17}$ 4QNarrF 1.2$_{2}$ 8QHymn 2$_{3}$ Ketef Hinnom inscr. 1$_{12}$, Mount Gerizim Stone inscr. 3, perh. 4QpsEzek^{e} 58$_{3}$.*

⇒ (association with ״ not alw. certain) יָהּ *Yah*, יָהוּ *Yahu*, אֲבִיָּה (אֲבִיָּהוּ, אֲבִי, אֲבִיו) *Abijah*, אֲבִיהוּא *Abihu*, אֲבִיָּם *Abijam*, אֲבַרְיָהוּ *Abariah*, אֲדֹנִיָּה (אֲדֹנִיָּהוּ, אֲדֹנִיו, אֲדֹנִי) *Adonijah*, אוּרִיאֵל *Uriel*, אוּרִיָּה (אוּרִיָּהוּ, אוּרִיו) *Uriah*, אֲזַנְיָה *Azaniah*, אֲחַזְיָהוּ (אֲחַזְיָה) *Ahaziah*, אֲחִיָּה (אֲחִיָּהוּ, אֲחִיו) *Ahijah*, אַיָּה *Aiah*, אֵלִיָּהוּ (אֵלִיָּה) *Elijah*, אֱלִיהוּא (אֱלִיהוּ) *Elihu*, אֲמַצְיָהוּ (אֲמַצְיָה) *Amaziah*, אֲמַרְיָה (אֲמַרְיָהוּ, אֲמַרְיוֹ) *Amariah*, אֲנָיָהוּ *Oniah*, אֲצַלְיָהוּ *Azaliah*, אֲשִׁיָּהוּ (אֲשִׁיָּה) *Ashiah*, בֵּדְיָה *Bedeiah*, בְּדָיָהוּ (בְּדָיוֹ) *Bedaiah*, בְּנָיָהוּ (בְּנָיָה) *Benaiah*, בְּסוֹדְיָה *Besodeiah*, בַּעֲדְיָהוּ *Baadiah*, בְּעַלְיָה *Bealiah*, בַּעֲשֵׂיָה *Baaseiah*, בַּקְבֻּקְיָה *Bakbukiah*, בֻּקִּיָּהוּ *Bukkiah*, בְּרָאיָה *Beraiah*, בֶּרֶכְיָה (בֶּרֶכְיָהוּ) *Berechiah*, בִּתְיָה *Bithiah*, גְּאַלְיָהוּ *Gealiah*, גַּדִּיָּהוּ (גַּדִּיוֹ) *Gaddiah*, גְּדַלְיָהוּ (גְּדַלְיָה, גְּדָלָה) *Gedaliah*, גְּמַלְיָהוּ *Gemaliah*, גְּמַרְיָהוּ (גְּמַרְיָה) *Gemariah*, גְּרִיָּהוּ *Gerijah*, דֹּדָוָהוּ *Dodavahu*, דֹּדִיָּהוּ *Dodiah*, דְּלָיָהוּ (דְּלָיָה, דְּלִיו, דְּלָה) *Delaiah*, דֶּלֶתְיָהוּ *Delethiah*, דְּמַלְיָהוּ *Domliah*, דַּרְשִׁיָּהוּ *Darshiah*, הִגְלָנְיָה *Higlaniah*, הוֹדַוְיָה (הוֹדַוְיָהוּ, הֹדַיְוָהוּ) *Hodaviah*, הוֹדִיָּה (הוֹדִיָּהוּ) *Hodiah*, הוֹשַׁעְיָה (הוֹשַׁעְיָהוּ) *Hoshaiah*, הִצִּלְיָהוּ *Hizziliah*, וַנְיָה *Vaniah*, זְבַדְיָה (זְבַדְיָהוּ, זְבַדְיוֹ) *Zebadiah*, זְכַרְיָה (זְכַרְיָהוּ, זְכַרְיוֹ) *Zechariah*, זְמַרְיָה (זְמַרְיָהוּ) *Zemariah*, זְרַחְיָה *Zerahiah*, זְרָיָהוּ *Zeraiah*, חֲבַיָּה *Habaiah*,

חֲבַצִּנְיָה *Habazziniah,* חַגִּיָּה *Haggiah,* חִוְהְיָהוּ (others חִוַּיָהוּ) *Hivvahiah,* חִזְקִיָּהוּ (יְחִזְקִיָּה, יְחִזְקִיָּהוּ, הִזְקִיָּה) *Hezekiah,* חַיָּהוּ *Haiah,* חֲכַלְיָה *Hacaliah,* חַלִּיו *Hallio,* חֶלֶצְיָהוּ *Heleziah,* חִלְקִיָּהוּ (חִלְקִיָּה) *Hilkiah,* חַנִּיָּהוּ *Hanniah,* חֲנַנְיָה (חֲנַנְיָהוּ) *Hananiah,* חֲסַדְיָה (חֲסַדְיָהוּ) *Hasadiah,* חָפְפִּיו *Haphaphiah,* חֲשַׁבְיָה (חֲשַׁבְיָהוּ) *Hashabiah,* חֲשַׁבְנְיָה *Hashabniah,* טוֹבִיָּה (טוֹבִיָּהוּ) *Tobiah,* טְבַלְיָהוּ *Tebaliah,* טוֹב אֲדֹנִיָּה *Tob-adonijah,* יַאֲזַנְיָהוּ (יַאֲזַנְיָה) *Jaazaniah,* יֹאשִׁיָּהוּ (יֹאשִׁיָּה) *Josiah,* יִבְנְיָה *Ibnijah,* יְבֶרֶכְיָהוּ *Jeberechiah,* יִגְדַּלְיָהוּ *Igdaliah,* יְדִידְיָה *Jedidiah,* יְדָיָה (יְדָיָהוּ) *Jedaiah,* יְדַלְיָהוּ *Jedaliah,* יְדַנְיָהוּ (יְדַנְיָה) *Jedoniah,* יְדַעְיָה (יְדַעְיָהוּ, יְדַעְיוֹ) *Jedaiah,* יֵהוּא *Jehu,* יְהוֹאָב *Jehoab,* יְהוֹאָח *Jehoah,* יְהוֹאָחָז (יוֹאָחָז) *J(eh)oahaz,* יְהוֹאֵל *Jehoel,* יְהוֹאָר *Jehoar,* יְהוֹאָשׁ *Jehoash,* יְהוֹבָנָה *Jehobanah,* יְהוֹבַעַל *Jehobaal,* יְהוֹזָבָד *Jehozabad,* יְהוֹזָרָח *Jehozarah,* יְהוֹחַי *Jehohai,* יְהוֹחַיִל *Jehohail,* יְהוֹחָנָן *Jehohanan,* יְהוֹיָדָע *Jehoiada,* יְהוֹיָכִין *Jehoiachin,* יְהוֹיַעֲמֹד *Jehojaamod,* יְהוֹיָקִים *Jehoiakim,* יְהוֹיָרִיב *Jehoiarib,* יְהוֹיִשְׁמַע *Jehoishma,* יְהוּכַל *Jehucal,* יְהוֹמָלָךְ *Jehomalach,* יְהוֹנָדָב *Jehonadab,* יְהוֹנָתָן *J(eh)onathan,* יְהוֹסֵף *J(eh)oseph,* יְהוֹעַדָּה *Jehoaddah,* יְהוֹעַדָּן *Jehoaddan,* יְהוֹעַז *Jehoaz,* יְהוֹעֶזֶר *Jehoezer,* יְהוֹעֲלֵי *Jehoale,* יְהוֹעָנָה *Jehoanah,* יְהוֹצָדָק *Jehozadak,* יְהוֹקִם *Jehokim,* יְהוֹרָם *Jehoram,* יְהוֹשֶׁבַע *Jehosheba,* יְהוֹשַׁבְעַת *Jehoshabeath,* יְהוֹשֻׁעַ *J(eh)oshua,* יְהוֹשָׁפָט *Jehoshaphat,* יוֹאָב *Joab,* יוֹאָח *Joah,* יוֹאָחָז *Joahaz,* יוֹאֵל *Joel,* יוֹאָמָן *Joaman,* יוֹאֹר *Joor,* יוֹאָשׁ *Joash,* יוֹבָנָה *Jobanah,* יוֹזָבָד *Jozabad,* יוֹזָכָר *Jozacar,* יוֹזָן *Jozan,* יוֹחָנָן *Johanan,* יוֹיָדָע *Joiada,* יוֹיָכִין *Joiachin,* יוֹיָקִים *Joiakim,* יוֹיָרִיב *Joiarib,* יוֹיָשָׁע *Joiasha,* יוֹכֶבֶד *Jochebed,* יוּכַל *Jucal,* יוֹכִן *Jochin,* יוֹנָדָב *Jonadad,* יוֹנָתָן *Jonathan,* יוֹסֵף *Joseph,* יוֹסִפְיָה *Josiphiah,* יוֹסְתֵּר *Joster,* יוֹעֵד *Joed,* יוֹעֶזֶר *Joezer,* יוֹעִלְיָהוּ *Joiliah,* יוֹעָשׁ *Joash,* יוֹעָשָׂה *Joasah,* יוֹצָדָק *Jozadak,* יוֹקִים *Jokim,* יוֹרַי *Jorai,* יוֹרָם *Joram,* יוֹשִׁבְיָה *Joshibiah,* יוֹשַׁוְיָה *Joshaviah,* יוֹשָׁפָט *Joshaphat,* יוֹתָם *Jotham,* יִזִּיָּה *Izziah,* יְזַנְיָה (יְזַנְיָהוּ) *Jezaniah,* יִזְרַחְיָה *Izrahiah,* יֶחְדְּיָהוּ *Jehdeiah,* יַחְזְיָה *Jahzeiah,* יְחִיָּה *Jehiah,* יַחְמַלְיָהוּ *Jahmaliah,* יְכָלְיָהוּ (יְכָלְיָה) *Jecoliah,* יְכָנְיָה (יְכָנְיָהוּ, יְכוֹנְיָה) *Jeconiah,* יְכִילְיָה *Jeciliah,* יִסְמַכְיָהוּ *Ismachiah,* יַעֲזִיָּהוּ *Jaaziah,* יַעֲרֶשְׁיָה *Jaareshiah,* יִפְדְיָה *Iphdeiah,* יְפָיָהוּ *Jephaiah,* יִפְרַעְיוֹ *Iphraio,* יְקַמְיָה *Jekamiah,* יִרְאִוִּיָּהוּ *Irivvijah,* יִרְאִיָּיה *Irijah,* יִרְמְיָהוּ (יִרְמְיָה) *Jeremiah,* יְשׁוֹחָיָה *Jeshohaiah,* יִשִּׁיָּה (יִשִּׁיָּהוּ) *Isshiah,* יִשְׁמַעְיָה (יִשְׁמַעְיָהוּ) *Ishmaiah,* יְשַׁעְיָהוּ (יְשַׁעְיָה) *Isaiah, Jeshaiah,* כְּנַנְיָהוּ (כְּנַנְיָה) *Chenaniah,* כַּלְכֹּלְיָהוּ *Calcoliah,* כְּנַנְיָהוּ (כּוֹנַנְיָהוּ) *Conaniah,* מִבְטַחְיָהוּ *Mibtahiah,* מַחְסֵיָה *Mahseiah,* מִיכָיָהוּ (מִכָיְהוּ, מִיכָיָה, מִיכָיְהוּ) *Micaiah,* מְלַטְיָה *Melatiah,* מִלְיָהוּ *Milaiah,* מַלְכִּיָּה (מַלְכִּיָּהוּ) *Malchiah, Malchijah,* מַעֲבַדְיָה *Maabadiah,* מַעַזְיָה (מַעַזְיָהוּ) *Maaziah,* מַעֲשֵׂיָהוּ (מַעֲשַׂי, מַעֲשֵׂיָה) *Maaseiah,* מִקְנֵיָהוּ (מִקְנֵיוֹ) *Mikneiah,* מְרָיָה *Meraiah,* מְרָנִיוֹ *Meraniah,* מְשֶׁלֶמְיָהוּ (מְשֶׁלֶמְיָה) *Meshelemiah,* מַתַּנְיָהוּ (מַתַּנְיָה) *Mattaniah,* מַתִּתְיָהוּ (מַתִּתְיָה) *Mattithiah,* נְדַבְיָה (נְדַבְיָהוּ) *Nedabiah,* נוֹעַדְיָה *Noadiah,* נְחֶמְיָה (נְחֶמְיָהוּ) *Nehemiah,* נְכָנְיָהוּ *Nechoniah,* נְעַרְיָה *Neariah,* נֵרִיָּהוּ (נֵרִיָּה) *Neriah,* נְתַבְיָהוּ *Nethabiah,* נְתַנְיָהוּ (נְתַנְיָה) *Nethaniah,* סְבַכְיָהוּ *Sebachiah,* סְדַרְיָהוּ *Sedariah,* סְמַכְיָהוּ (סְמַכְיָה, סְמַכְיוֹ) *Semachiah,* סְעַגְיָהוּ *Seagiah,* סְעַדְיָהוּ (סְעַדְיָה) *Seadiah,* סְעַרְיָהוּ *Seariah,* עֹבַדְיָה (עֹבַדְיָהוּ, עֹבַדְיוֹ, עֹבַדְאִיוֹ) *Obadiah,* עֲבִיּוֹ *Abijah,* עֶגְלְיוֹ *Egliah,* עֲדָיָה (עֲדָיָהוּ) *Adaiah,* עֻזִּיָּא *Uzzia,* עֻזִּיָּהוּ (עֻזִּיָּה, עֻזִּיּוֹ) *Uzziah,* עֲזַרְיָהוּ (עֲזַרְיָה, עֲזַרְיוֹ) *Azariah,* עֲלָיָהוּ (עֲלָיָה, עֲלָיוֹ) *Alaiah,* עֲמַדְיָהוּ *Amadiah,* עֲמַלְיָהוּ *Amaliah,* עִמָּנוּיָהוּ (עִמָּנְיָהוּ) *Immanuiah,* עֲמַסְיָה *Amasiah,* עֲנָיָה (עֲנָיוֹ) *Anaiah,* עֲנַנְיָה (עֲנַנְיָהוּ) *Ananiah,* עַנְתֹתִיָּה *Anathothijah,* עֲשָׂיָה (עֲשָׂיָהוּ) *Asaiah,* עֲשַׁנְיָהוּ *Ashanijah,* עֲתָיָה (עֲתָיָהוּ) *Athaiah,* עַתְלָי *Athlai,* עֲתַלְיָהוּ (עֲתַלְיָה) *Athaliah,* פְּדָיָה (פְּדָיָהוּ, פְּדָיוֹ) *Pedaiah,* פְּטָיָהוּ *Petaiah,* פְּלָאיָה (פְּלָאיָהוּ) *Pelaiah,* פְּלַטְיָה (פְּלַטְיָהוּ) *Pelatiah,* פְּלָיָה *Pelaiah,* פְּלַלְיָה *Pelaliah,* פְּנָיָה *Penaiah,* פְּקַדְיוֹ *Pekadiah,* פְּקַחְיָה (פְּקַחִי) *Pekahiah,* צִבְיָא *Zibia,* צִבְיָה *Zibiah,* צִדְקִיָּהוּ (צִדְקִיָּה) *Zedekiah,* צְפַנְיָה (צְפַנְיָהוּ) *Zephaniah,* צְרוּיָה (צְרְיָה) *Zeruiah,* קוֹלָיָה (קוֹלָיָהוּ, קֹלָיָהוּ, קֹלָיוֹ) *Kolaiah,* קוּשָׁיָהוּ *Kushaiah,* קֵלָיָה *Kelaiah,* קְנָיוֹ *Kenaiah,* רְאָיָה *Reaiah,* רַבִּיָּהוּ (רַבִּיָּה) *Rabbijah,* רְחַבְיָהוּ (רְחַבְיָה) *Rehabiah,* רַמְיָה *Ramiah,* רְמַלְיָהוּ *Remaliah,* רְעֵלָיָה *Reelaiah,* רַעַמְיָה *Raamiah,* רְפָיָה (רְפָיָהוּ) *Rephaiah,* שָׂכְיָה *Sachiah,* שְׁבַנְיָה (שְׁבַנְיָהוּ, שְׁבַנְיוֹ) *Shebaniah,* שְׁכַנְיָה (שְׁכַנְיָהוּ) *Shecaniah,* שֶׁלֶמְיָהוּ (שֶׁלֶמְיָה) *Shelemiah,* שְׁמַעְיָהוּ (שְׁמַעְיָה, שְׁמַעְיוֹ, שְׁמָיָה) *Shemaiah,* שְׁמַרְיָהוּ (שְׁמַרְיָה, שְׁמַרְיוֹ) *Shemariah,* שְׁנָיוֹ *Shenaiah,* שְׁעַרְיָה (שְׁעַרְיָהוּ) *Sheariah,* שְׁפַטְיָה (שְׁפַטְיָהוּ) *Shephatiah,* שְׁכַנְיָה *Shekaniah,* שֵׁרֵבְיָה *Sherebiah,* שְׂרָיָה (שְׂרָיָהוּ, סְרָיָה) *Seraiah,* תִּירְיָא (תִּרְיָהוּ) *Tiriah,* תְּנָיָהוּ *Tenaiah.*

יְהוֹזָבָד 4 pr.n.m. **Jehozabad, 1.** conspirator against Joash, son of Shomer (2 K 12_{22}) and appar. of Shimrith, a Moabite woman (2 C 24_{26}), <SUBJ> נכה hi. *strike* 2 K 12_{22}, קשׁר htp. *conspire* 2 C 24_{26}. <APP> בֵּן *son* 2 K 12_{22}

||2 C 24_{26}, עֶבֶד *servant* 2 K 12_{22}.

2. son of Obed-edom, <NOM CL> יְהוֹזָבָד הַשֵּׁנִי *Jehozabad was the second (son)* 1 C 26_4. <APP> בֵּן *son* 1 C 26_4.

3. Benjaminite, military commander at time of Jehoshaphat, <NOM CL> עַל־יָדוֹ יְהוֹזָבָד *beside him was Jehozabad* 2 C 17_{18}. <PREP> עִם *with* 2 C 17_{18}.

⇒ ״ *Y.* + זבד *endow.*

[יְהוֹזָרָח] 0.0.0.2 pr.n.m. **Jehozarah, 1.** son of Hilkiah, <APP> בֵּן *son* Seal 321 (Hebron 8th/7th cent.), עֶבֶד *servant* Seal 321 (Hebron 8th/7th cent.). <PREP> לְ of possession, *of, (belonging) to* Seal 321 (Hebron 8th/7th cent.). **2.** father of Mattan, <CSTR> ב[ן] יהוזרח *son of Jehozarah* Seal 618 (T. Beit Mirsim?, 7th/6th cent.).

⇒ ״ *Y.* + זרח *arise.*

[יְהוֹחַי] 0.0.0.1 pr.n.m. **Jehohai,** father of Jehucal, <CSTR> בן יהוחי *son of Jehohai* Seal 253 (Lachish, 7th cent.).

⇒ ״ *Y.* + חיה *live.*

[יְהוֹחַיִל] 0.0.0.5 pr.n.m. **Jehohail**—I יהוחל—**1.** father of Elzachar, <CSTR> בן יהוחיל *son of Jehohail* Seal 42 (Palestine).

2. appar. son of Shahar, Seals 198 199 (both Ramat Raḥel) 396 (Lachish) Jar Stamp 951 (T. Beit Mirsim?, all four 8th cent.).*

⇒ ״ *Y.* + חַיִל *power.*

יְהוֹחָנָן 9.0.2.11 pr.n.m. **Jehohanan, 1.** high priest or member of high priestly family, son of Eliashib, <CSTR> לִשְׁכַּת יְהוֹחָנָן *chamber of Jehohanan* Ezr 10_6. <APP> בֵּן *son* Ezr 10_6 (mss יְהוֹנָתָן *Jehonathan*).

2. member of Bebai family, husband of non-Israelite wife, <NOM CL> ... מִבְּנֵי בֵבָי יְהוֹחָנָן *of the sons of Bebai were Jehohanan ...* Ezr 10_{28}.

3. son of Tobiah, official in Samaria and opponent of Nehemiah, <SUBJ> לקח *take (in marriage)* Ne 6_{18}. <APP> בֵּן *son* Ne 6_{18}.

4. priest and head of Amariah family at time of Joiakim, <NOM CL> לַאֲמַרְיָה יְהוֹחָנָן *(belonging) to Amariah was Jehohanan* Ne 12_{13}.

5. Levite musician at dedication of Nehemiah's wall, <SUBJ> עמד *stand* Ne 12_{42}.

6. Korahite gatekeeper, son of Meshelemiah, <NOM CL> יְהוֹחָנָן הַשִּׁשִּׁי *Jehohanan was the sixth (son)* 1 C 26_3.

7. military commander at time of Jehoshaphat, <NOM CL> עַל־יָדוֹ יְהוֹחָנָן *beside him was Jehohanan* 2 C 17_{15}. <APP> שַׂר *commander* 2 C 17_{15}. <PREP> עִם *with* 2 C 17_{15}.

8. father of the military commander Ishmael, at time of Jehoiada, <CSTR> בֶּן־יְהוֹחָנָן *son of Jehohanan* 2 C 23_1.

9. Ephraimite, father of Azariah, <CSTR> בֶּן־יְהוֹחָנָן *son of Jehohanan* 2 C 28_{12}.

10. father of Shemaah, <CSTR> בר יהוחנן *son of Jehohanan* Mur 29 1_2 2_{12}.

11. Frey 1285_{11}, <CSTR> בן יהוחנן *son of Jehohanan* Frey 1285_{11}.

12. high priest, <APP> כֹּהֵן *priest* Hyrcanus I Coins 26 27 Hyrcanus II Coins 18 18A 19 20 20A 21 22 23 24 25 ([יהוחנ]ן הכהן) (יהוחנן הכ[ה]ן), ראשׁ *head,* i.e. chief, of community of Jews Hyrcanus II Coins 22 23.

13. son of Mahanaim and party to lease transaction, <SUBJ> חכר hi. *let* 5/6ḤevBA 44_{25} (יהונת[ן]). <APP> בֵּן *son* 5/6ḤevBA $44_{6.18}$ 5/6ḤevBA 45 fr. 2_1, פַּרְנָס *administrator* 5/6ḤevBA 44_6 5/6ḤevBA 45 fr. 2_1. <PREP> מִן of direction, *from,* + חכר *rent* 5/6ḤevBA $44_{6.18}$ 5/6ḤevBA 45 fr. 2_1.

14. son of Baajan and commander at time of Bar Cochba, <APP> בַּר *son* 5/6ḤevEp 12_2 (ליהו[נ]תן ב[ר]). <PREP> לְ of direction, *to* 5/6ḤevEp 1_2 5/6ḤevEp 12_2 (ליהו[נ]תן).

⇒ ״ *Y.* + חנן *be gracious.*

יְהוֹיָדָע 51 pr.n.m. **Jehoiada, 1.** father of Benaiah, in the time of David, <CSTR> בֶּן־יְהוֹיָדָע *son of Jehoiada* 2 S 8_{18}||1 C 18_{17} 2 S 20_{23} $23_{20.22}$||1 C $11_{22.24}$ 1 K $1_{8.26.32.36.38.44}$ $2_{25.29.34.35.46}$ 4_4 1 C $27_{5.34(mss)}$. <APP> נָגִיד *prince* 1 C 12_{28} (הַנָּגִיד לְאַהֲרֹן *the prince of Aaron*). <PREP> עִם *with* 1 C 12_{28}.

2. king's counsellor, son of Benaiah, in the time of David, perh. ident. with §1 (mss בְּנָיָהוּ בֶּן־יְהוֹיָדָע *Benaiah the son of Jehoiada*), <NOM CL> אַחֲרֵי אֲחִיתֹפֶל יְהוֹיָדָע *after Ahithophel was Jehoiada* 1 C 27_{34}. <APP> בֵּן *son* 1 C 27_{34}.

3. high priest at time of Joash (Jehoash), husband of Jehoshabeath, leader of the coup against Athaliah, <SUBJ> אמר *say* 2 K 11$_{4.15}$||2 C 23$_{14}$ 2 C 23$_{1.11}$, צוה pi. *command* 2 K 11$_{4.9}$||2 C 23$_{8}$ 2 K 11$_{15}$, ראה hi. *show* 2 K 11$_{4}$, ירה hi. *teach* 2 K 12$_{3}$, בוא hi. *bring* 2 K 11$_{4}$, יצא hi. *bring out* 2 C 23$_{14}$, ירד hi. *bring down* 2 C 23$_{18}$, שׁלח *send* 2 K 11$_{4}$, פטר *set free* 2 C 23$_{8}$, עמד hi. *cause to stand* 2 C 23$_{9.18}$, נתן *give, place* 2 K 12$_{8.10}$ 2 C 23$_{9}$ 24$_{12}$, שׂים *place* 2 C 23$_{18}$, לקח *take* 2 K 11$_{4}$||2 C 23$_{1}$ 2 K 12$_{8.10}$ 2 C 23$_{18}$, נשׂא *lift*, i.e. take 2 C 24$_{3}$, דרשׁ *require* 2 C 24$_{6}$, כרת *cut*, i.e. make, covenant 2 K 11$_{4.17}$||2 C 23$_{16}$, שׁבע hi. *cause to swear* 2 K 11$_{4}$, משׁח *anoint* 2 C 23$_{11}$, חזק pi. *strengthen*, i.e. repair 2 K 12$_{8}$, htp. *take courage* 2 C 23$_{1}$, נקב *bore hole* 2 K 12$_{10}$, עשׂה *do* 2 C 24$_{22}$, זקן *be old* 2 C 24$_{15}$, שׂבע *be satisfied*, i.e. full, of years 2 C 24$_{15}$, מות *die* 2 C 24$_{15}$. <CSTR> בֶּן־יְהוֹיָדָע *son of Jehoiada* 2 C 24$_{20.25}$ (if em. בְּנֵי *sons of* to בֶּן־ *son of*), אֵשֶׁת יְהוֹיָדָע *wife of Jehoiada* 2 C 22$_{11}$, יְמֵי *days of* 2 C 24$_{2.14}$, מוֹת *death of* 2 C 24$_{17}$. <APP> אָב *father* 2 C 24$_{22}$, בֵּן *son* 2 C 24$_{15}$, כֹּהֵן *priest* 2 K 11$_{9.9}$ ||2 C 23$_{8.8}$ 2 K 11$_{15}$ 12$_{3}$||2 C 24$_{2}$ 2 K 12$_{8.10}$ 2 C 22$_{11}$ 23$_{9.14}$ 24$_{20.25}$. <PREP> לְ of direction, *to*, + אמר *say* 2 C 24$_{6}$, קרא *call*, i.e. summon 2 K 12$_{8}$||2 C 24$_{6}$; אֶל *to*, + בוא *come* 2 K 11$_{9}$, אמר *say* 2 K 12$_{8}$; לִפְנֵי *before*, + בוא hi. *bring* 2 C 24$_{14}$.

4. priest at time of Jeremiah, <APP> כֹּהֵן *priest* Jr 29$_{26}$. <PREP> תַּחַת *instead of*, + נתן *give*, i.e. make, priest Jr 29$_{26}$.

⇒ ״ Y. + ידע *know*.

יְהוֹיָכִין 10 pr.n.m. **Jehoiachin**—יְהוֹיָכִן—king of Judah, son of Jehoiakim and Nehushta, ident. with יוֹיָכִין *Joiachin* at Ezk 1$_{2}$, יְכָנְיָהוּ (יְכָנְיָה ,יְכוֹנְיָה) *Jeconiah* at Jr 24$_{1}$ 27$_{20}$ 28$_{4}$ 29$_{2}$ Est 2$_{6}$ 1 C 3$_{16.17}$, and כָּנְיָהוּ *Coniah* at Jr 22$_{24.28}$ 37$_{1}$.

<SUBJ> יצא *go out* 2 K 24$_{12}$, מלך *reign* 2 K 24$_{6.8}$||2 C 36$_{8.9}$ 2 K 24$_{12}$, עשׂה *do* 2 K 24$_{8}$||2 C 36$_{9}$, אכל *eat* 2 K 25$_{27}$ ||Jr 52$_{31}$. <NOM CL> בֶּן־שְׁמֹנֶה עֶשְׂרֵה שָׁנָה יְהוֹיָכִין *Jehoiachin was a son of eighteen years*, i.e. was eighteen years old 2 K 24$_{8}$||2 C 36$_{9}$ (שְׁמֹנֶה שָׁנִים *eight years*).

<OBJ> בוא hi. *bring* 2 C 36$_{9}$, יצא hi. *bring out* 2 K 25$_{27}$ ||Jr 52$_{31}$ (2 K if ins. וַיֹּצֵא אֹתוֹ *and he brought him out*), לקח *take* 2 K 24$_{12}$, גלה hi. *exile* 2 K 24$_{15}$. <CSTR> רֹאשׁ יְהוֹיָכִין *head of Jehoiachin* 2 K 25$_{27}$||Jr 52$_{31}$, גָּלוּת *exile of* 2 K 25$_{27}$||Jr 52$_{31}$ (יְהוֹיָכִן). <APP> בֵּן *son* 2 K 24$_{6}$||2 C 36$_{8}$, מֶלֶךְ *king* 2 K 24$_{12}$ 25$_{27.27}$||Jr 52$_{31.31}$.

<PREP> לְ of direction, *to*, + נתן ni. *be given* 2 K 25$_{27}$ ||Jr 52$_{31}$; אֵת *with* 2 K 25$_{27}$||Jr 52$_{31}$, + דבר pi. *speak* 2 K 25$_{27}$||Jr 52$_{31}$; תַּחַת *instead of*, + מלך hi. *make king* 2 K 24$_{15}$.

⇒ ״ Y. + כון *be established*.

[יְהוֹיַעֲמֹד] pr.n.[m.] **Jehojaamod**, <CSTR> בן יהויעמד *son of Jehojaamod* Frey 1285$_{4}$ (others [יוסי בן דרן [*Jose son of ...*; others יהוסף נזר *Joseph the Nazirite*).

⇒ ״ + עמד *stand*.

יְהוֹיָקִים 37 pr.n.m. **Jehoiakim, 1.** king of Judah, originally named אֶלְיָקִים *Eliakim* (2 K 23$_{34}$), son of Josiah and Zebidah, <SUBJ> היה *be* 2 K 24$_{1}$, אמר *say* Jr 36$_{29}$, שׁמע *hear* Jr 26$_{21}$ 36$_{30}$, שׁוב *go back*, i.e. do again 2 K 24$_{1}$, שׁלח *send* Jr 26$_{22}$, שׁלך hi. *cast* Jr 26$_{23}$, מלך *reign* 2 K 23$_{36}$ ||2 C 36$_{5}$, נתן *give* 2 K 23$_{35}$, ערך hi. *tax* 2 K 23$_{35}$, נגשׂ *exact* 2 K 23$_{35}$, עשׂה *do* 2 K 23$_{36}$||2 C 36$_{5}$ 2 K 24$_{5}$||2 C 36$_{8}$ 2 K 24$_{19}$||Jr 52$_{2}$, מרד *rebel* 2 K 24$_{1}$, נכה hi. *strike* Jr 26$_{23}$, שׂרף *burn* Jr 36$_{28.29.32}$, שׁכב *lie down* 2 K 24$_{6}$, קבר ni. *be buried* Jr 22$_{18}$.

<NOM CL> בֶּן־עֶשְׂרִים וְחָמֵשׁ שָׁנָה יְהוֹיָקִים *Jehoiakim was a son of twenty-five years*, i.e. twenty-five years old 2 K 23$_{36}$||2 C 36$_{5}$, הַשֵּׁנִי יְהוֹיָקִים *the second (son) was Jehoiakim* 1 C 3$_{15}$. <OBJ> נתן *give* Dn 1$_{2}$, סחב *drag* Jr 22$_{18}$, שׁלך hi. *cast* Jr 22$_{18}$. <CSTR> בֶּן־יְהוֹיָקִים *son of Jehoiakim* Jr 22$_{24}$ 24$_{1}$ 27$_{20}$ 28$_{4}$ 37$_{1}$, בְּנֵי *sons of* 1 C 3$_{16}$, דִּבְרֵי יְהוֹיָקִים *deeds of Jehoiakim* 2 K 24$_{5}$||2 C 36$_{8}$, מַלְכוּת *reign of* Jr 26$_{1}$ Dn 1$_{1}$, מַמְלֶכֶת *reign of* Jr 27$_{1}$ (mss לְצִדְקִיָּהוּ *of Zedekiah*), יְמֵי *days of* Jr 1$_{3}$ 35$_{1}$. <APP> בֵּן *son* Jr 1$_{3}$ 22$_{18}$ 25$_{1}$ 26$_{1}$ 27$_{1}$ (mss צִדְקִיָּהוּ *Zedekiah*) 35$_{1}$ 36$_{1.9}$ 45$_{1}$ 46$_{2}$, מֶלֶךְ *king* Jr 1$_{3}$ 22$_{18}$ 25$_{1}$ 26$_{1.21.22.23}$ 27$_{1}$ (mss צִדְקִיָּהוּ) 35$_{1}$ 36$_{1.9.28.29.30.32}$ 45$_{1}$ 46$_{2}$ Dn 1$_{2}$.

<PREP> לְ of possession, *of, (belonging) to* Jr 25$_{1}$ 36$_{1.9}$ 45$_{1}$ 46$_{2}$, + היה *be* Jr 36$_{30}$, ספד לְ *mourn for* Jr 22$_{18}$; אֶל *to*, + בוא hi. *bring* Jr 26$_{23}$; *concerning, against*, + אמר *say* Jr 22$_{18}$, דבר pi. *speak* Jr 36$_{30}$; עַל *upon, concerning, against*, + אמר *say* Jr 36$_{29.30}$, בוא hi. *bring* Jr 36$_{30}$, מצא ni. *be found* 2 C 36$_{8}$, פקד *visit* Jr 36$_{30}$; תַּחַת *instead of*, + מלך

reign 2 K 24_{6}||2 C 36_{8}. <COLL> וַיַּסֵּב אֶת־שְׁמוֹ יְהוֹיָקִים *and he changed his name (to) Jehoiakim* 2 K 23_{34}||2 C 36_{4}.

2. high priest, ident. with יוֹיָקִים *Joiakim* at Ne 11_{10} (if em.) $12_{10.10.12.26}$, <CSTR> בֶּן־יְהוֹיָקִין *son of Jehoiakim* 1 C 9_{10} (if em. וִיהוֹיָרִיב *and Jehoiarib* to בֶּן־יְהוֹיָקִים יְהוֹיָרִיב *son of Jehoiakim, Jehoiarib*).

3. Lachish inscr. 31_{3} ([י]הוי[קם]; others [ ]בגי[ ]).

⇒ ״ *Y.* + קום hi. *raise up.*

יְהוֹיָרִיב 2 pr.n.m. **Jehoiarib, 1.** head of priestly family at time of David, <PREP> לְ of direction, *to,* + יצא *go out* 1 C 24_{7}.

2. postexilic family of priests, prob. claiming §1 as eponymous ancestor, ident. with יוֹיָרִיב *Joiarib* at Ne 11_{10}, <NOM CL> מִן־הַכֹּהֲנִים ... יְהוֹיָרִיב *of the priests were ... Jehoiarib* 1 C 9_{10}. <APP> בֵּן *son* 1 C 9_{10} (if em. וִיהוֹיָרִיב וְיָכִין: וַעֲזַרְיָה *and Jehoiarib and Jachin and Azariah* to יְהוֹיָרִיב בֶּן־עֲזַרְיָה *Jehoiarib son of Azariah*).

⇒ ״ *Y.* + ריב *strive.*

[יְהוֹיִשְׁמַע] 0.0.0.1 pr.n.f. **Jehoishma,** daughter of Shoshashrizar (others Shanshashrizar), <APP> בַּת *daughter* Seal 226 (7th cent.). <PREP> לְ of possession, *of, (belonging) to* Seal 226 (7th cent.).

⇒ ״ *Y.* + שׁמע *hear.*

יְהוּכַל 1.0.0.6 pr.n.m. **Jehucal, 1.** court official of Zedekiah, son of Shelemiah, ident. with יוּכַל *Jucal* at Jr 38_{1}, <OBJ> שׁלח *send* Jr 37_{3}. <APP> בֵּן *son* Jr 37_{3}.

2. Arad ost. 21_{1}, <SUBJ> שׁלח *send* Arad ost. 21_{1}, ברך pi. *bless* Arad ost. 21_{1}. <APP> בֵּן *son* Arad ost. 21_{1}.

3. father of Mikneiah, <CSTR> בן יהוכל *son of Jehucal* Seal 162 (others יהומלך *Jehomalach*; Palestine, 7th cent.).

4. son of Jehohai, <APP> בֵּן *son* Seal 253 (Lachish, 7th cent.). <PREP> לְ of possession, *of, (belonging) to* Seal 253 (Lachish, 7th cent.).

5. appar. father of Raphti, Seals 452 (T. Sandahannah) 453 (T. eṣ-Ṣafi; both 8th cent.).

6. father of Joel, <CSTR> בן יהוכל *son of Jehucal* Seal 869 (8th cent.).

⇒ ״ *Y.* + יכל *be able.*

[יְהוֹמָלָךְ] 0.0.0.1 pr.n.m. **Jehomalach, 1.** father of Mikneiah, <CSTR> בן יהומלך *son of Jehomalach* Seal 162 (others יהוכל *Jehucal*; Palestine, 7th cent.).

2. Ḥorvat 'Uza ost. 3.

⇒ ״ *Y.* + מלך *reign.*

יְהוֹנָדָב 8.0.0.1 pr.n.m. **Jehonadab, 1.** son of David's brother Shimeah, friend of Amnon, ident. with יוֹנָדָב *Jonadab* at 2 S $13_{3.3.32.35}$, and perh. ident. with יְהוֹנָתָן *Jonathan* at 2 S 21_{21}||1 C 20_{7}, <SUBJ> אמר *say* 2 S 13_{5}.

2. son of Rechab and founder of the Rechabite community, ident. with יוֹנָדָב *Jonadab* at Jr $35_{6.10.19}$, <SUBJ> אמר *say* 2 K 10_{15}, צוה pi. *command* Jr $35_{8.14.18}$, ראה *see* 2 K 10_{15}, הלך *go* 2 K 10_{15}, בוא *come* 2 K 10_{23}, קרא *meet* 2 K 10_{15}, נתן *give* 2 K 10_{15}. <OBJ> ברך pi. *bless* 2 K 10_{15}, מצא *find* 2 K 10_{15}, עלה hi. *bring up* 2 K 10_{15}, רכב hi. *cause to ride* 2 K 10_{15}. <CSTR> בְּנֵי יְהוֹנָדָב *sons of Jehonadab* Jr 35_{16}, קוֹל *voice of* Jr 35_{8}, דִּבְרֵי *words of* Jr 35_{14}, מִצְוַת *command of* Jr 35_{18}. <APP> אָב *father* Jr $35_{8.18}$, בֵּן *son* 2 K $10_{15.23}$ Jr $35_{8.14.16}$.

3. appar. father of Jehokim, Seal 336 (6th cent.)

⇒ ״ *Y.* + נדב *impel.*

יְהוֹנָתָן 82.0.16.7 pr.n.m. **J(eh)onathan, 1.** son of Saul, ident. with יוֹנָתָן *Jonathan* at 1 S $13_{2.3.16.22.22}$ 14_{1+22t} 19_{1} 1 C 10_{2}, <SUBJ> היה *be* 1 S 23_{16}, אמר *say* 1 S $14_{6.8}$ $19_{2.4}$ 20_{1+11t} 23_{16}, דבר pi. *speak* 1 S $19_{2.4}$ 20_{18}, נגד hi. *tell* 1 S $19_{2.7}$ 20_{9}, קרא *call* 1 S 19_{7} $20_{37.38}$, ענה *answer* 1 S $20_{28.32}$, שׁבע ni. *swear* 1 S 20_{42}, hi. *cause to swear* 1 S 20_{17}, ידע *know* 1 S $20_{3.5.9.33.39}$, גלה *uncover* ear 1 S $20_{12.13}$, ni. *reveal oneself* 1 S 14_{8}, פשׁט htp. *strip oneself* 1 S 18_{4}, כרת *cut,* i.e. make, covenant 1 S 18_{3} 20_{16} 23_{18}, הלך *go* 1 S $23_{16.18}$, בוא *come* 1 S 21_{1}, hi. *bring* 1 S 19_{7} 20_{5}, יצא *go out* 1 S 19_{2} $20_{11.35}$, עלה *go up* 1 S 14_{8}, עבר *pass* 1 S $14_{6.8}$, שׁלח *send* 1 S $20_{12.13.18}$, pi. 1 S $20_{18.28}$, נטה *incline* 1 S 14_{6}, קלל *be swift* 2 S 1_{23}, גבר *be strong* 2 S 1_{23}, ירה *shoot* 1 S 20_{37}, hi. *shoot* 1 S $20_{18.35}$, קום *rise* 1 S $20_{25.34}$ 23_{16}, עמד *stand* 1 S 14_{8} 19_{2}, דמם *be still* 1 S 14_{8}, נעם *be pleasant* 2 S 1_{26}, אהב *love* 1 S 18_{1} 20_{17}, ni. *be loved* 2 S 1_{22}, חפץ *delight in* 1 S 19_{1}, נשׁק *kiss* 1 S 20_{40}, עצב ni. *be grieved* 1 S $20_{3.34}$, בכה *weep* 1 S 20_{40}, אכל *eat* 1 S 20_{34}, נתן *give* 1 S 18_{4} 20_{40}, עשׂה *do* 1 S $20_{4.5}$, יסף hi. *repeat* 1 S 20_{17}, חקר *search* 1 S

20$_{12}$, חזק pi. *strengthen* 1 S 23$_{16}$, פרד ni. *be separated* 2 S 1$_{23}$, נפל *fall* 2 S 1$_{12}$, מות *die* 1 S 20$_{13}$ 2 S 1$_{4.5}$, hi. *kill* 1 S 20$_{5}$.

<NOM CL> יְהוֹנָתָן ... חָלָל *Jonathan is ... slain* 2 S 1$_{25}$.

<OBJ> ילד hi. *beget* 1 C 8$_{33}$ 9$_{39}$, ענה *answer* 1 S 20$_{10}$, נכה hi. *kill* 1 S 20$_{32}$ 31$_{2}$ (||1 C 10$_{2}$ יוֹנָתָן), כלם hi. *put to shame* 1 S 20$_{34}$.

<CSTR> נַעַר יְהוֹנָתָן *lad of Jonathan* 1 S 20$_{38}$, בֶּן־ *son of* 2 S 9$_{6}$ 21$_{7}$, עַצְמוֹת *bones of* 2 S 21$_{12.13.14}$, נֶפֶשׁ *soul of* 1 S 18$_{1}$, קוֹל *voice of* 1 S 19$_{6}$, קֶשֶׁת *bow of* 2 S 1$_{22}$, שְׁמֻעַת ... יְהוֹנָתָן *report of*, i.e. about, ... *Jonathan* 2 S 4$_{4}$.

<APP> בֵּן *son* 1 S 19$_{1}$ 20$_{27.30(mss)}$ 23$_{16}$ 2 S 1$_{4.5.12.17}$ 4$_{4}$ 9$_{6}$ 21$_{7.12.13.14}$ 1 C 8$_{34}$ 9$_{40}$, אָח *brother* 2 S 1$_{26}$, נָעִים *pleasant one* 2 S 1$_{23}$.

<PREP> לְ of benefit, *to, for*, + עשׂה *do* 1 S 14$_{6}$ 20$_{13}$; of direction, *to*, + אמר *say* 1 S 14$_{6}$ 20$_{30}$; of possession, *of, (belonging) to* 1 S 20$_{40}$ 2 S 4$_{4}$ 9$_{3}$.

בְּ *against*, + חרה *be kindled* 1 S 20$_{30}$.

מִן *from, of*, + שׁאל *ask* 1 S 20$_{6.28}$.

אֶל *to*, + אמר *say* 1 S 14$_{8}$ 20$_{5.10.27}$, נגע hi. *reach* 1 S 14$_{8}$.

עַל *upon* 1 S 18$_{4}$; *for, on account of*, + צום *fast* 2 S 1$_{12}$, קין po. *lament* 2 S 1$_{17}$; טול עַל hi. *throw at* 1 S 20$_{32}$.

עִם *with* 1 S 14$_{6}$ 20$_{35}$, + בוא hi. *bring* 1 S 20$_{5}$, עשׂה *do* 1 S 20$_{13}$.

לִפְנֵי *before*, + אמר *say* 1 S 20$_{1}$.

בֵּין *between* 1 S 20$_{18}$ (+ David), + היה *be* 1 S 20$_{42}$ (+ David).

תַּחַת *beneath*, i.e. in one's place, + עמד *stand* 1 S 14$_{8}$.

בַּעֲבוּר *for the sake of*, + עשׂה *do* 2 S 9$_{1.7}$.

2. priest, son of Abiathar, ident. with יוֹנָתָן *Jonathan* at 1 K 1$_{42.43}$, <SUBJ> אמר *say* 2 S 17$_{20}$, נגד hi. *tell* 2 S 17$_{17.20}$, ראה ni. *be seen* 2 S 17$_{17}$, הלך *go* 2 S 17$_{17.20}$, בוא *come* 2 S 17$_{17}$, עלה *go up* 2 S 17$_{20}$, ירד *go down* 2 S 17$_{17}$, שׁוב *go back* 2 S 15$_{27}$, עבר *pass* 2 S 17$_{20}$, עמד *stand* 2 S 17$_{17}$, יכל *be able* 2 S 17$_{17}$. <NOM CL> שָׁם ... יְהוֹנָתָן *Jonathan is ... there* 2 S 15$_{36}$, אַיֵּה ... יְהוֹנָתָן *where is ... Jonathan?* 2 S 17$_{20}$. <OBJ> ראה *see* 2 S 17$_{17}$. <APP> בֵּן *son* 2 S 15$_{27.36}$. <PREP> לְ of direction, + נגד hi. *tell* 2 S 17$_{17}$.

3. son of David's brother Shimeah/Shimei, <SUBJ> נכה hi. *kill* 2 S 21$_{21}$||1 C 20$_{7}$. <APP> בֵּן *son* 2 S 21$_{21}$||1 C 20$_{7}$.

4. son of David's brother Shimeah, friend of Amnon, prob. err. for יוֹנָדָב *Jonadab*, <NOM CL> שמו [י]הונתן *his name was Jehonathan* 2 S 13$_{3(4QSam^a)}$ (MT יוֹנָדָב *Jonadab*).

5. uncle of David, <NOM CL> יְהוֹנָתָן ... יוֹעֵץ *Jonathan was ... a counsellor* 1 C 27$_{32}$ (+ אִישׁ־מֵבִין וְסוֹפֵר הוּא *he was a man of understanding and a scribe*). <APP> דּוֹד *uncle* 1 C 27$_{32}$.

6. one of David's warriors, ident. with יוֹנָתָן *Jonathan* at ||1 C 11$_{34}$, <APP> בֵּן *son* 2 S 23$_{32}$ (if em. יְהוֹנָתָן : שַׁמָּה *Jonathan, Shammah* to יְהוֹנָתָן בֶּן־שַׁמָּה *Jonathan, son of Shammah*).

7. one of David's treasurers, son of Uzziah, <NOM CL> עַל הָאוֹצָרוֹת ... יְהוֹנָתָן *over the treasuries was ... Jonathan* 1 C 27$_{25}$. <APP> בֵּן *son* 1 C 27$_{25}$.

8. scribe at time of Jeremiah, <CSTR> בֵּית יְהוֹנָתָן *house of Jonathan* Jr 37$_{15.20}$ 38$_{26}$. <APP> סֹפֵר *scribe* Jr 37$_{15.20}$.

9. Levite, <SUBJ> למד pi. *teach* 2 C 17$_{8}$, סבב *turn* 2 C 17$_{8}$. <NOM CL> עִמָּהֶם ... יְהוֹנָתָן *with them was ... Jehonathan* 2 C 17$_{8}$. <APP> לֵוִי *Levite* 2 C 17$_{8}$.

10. head of postexilic priestly family, <NOM CL> לִשְׁמַעְיָה יְהוֹנָתָן *(belonging) to Shemaiah was Jehonathan* Ne 12$_{18}$.

11. priest to tribe of Dan, descendant of Gershom, <SUBJ> היה *be* Jg 18$_{30}$ (+ כֹּהֵן *priest*). <APP> בֵּן *son* Jg 18$_{30}$.

12. priest, son of Eliashib, ident. with יְהוֹחָנָן *Jehohanan*, <CSTR> לִשְׁכַּת יְהוֹנָתָן *chamber of Jehonathan* Ezr 10$_{6(mss)}$ (L יְהוֹחָנָן *Jehohanan*). <APP> בֵּן *son* Ezr 10$_{6(mss)}$ (L יְהוֹחָנָן *Jehohanan*).

13. father of Niklah, in tenancy agreement, <CSTR> בן יהונתן *son of Jehonathan* Mur 24 4$_{5}$ ([בן]) 4$_{20}$ (יהונת[ן]).

14. son of Joseph, in deed of sale, <APP> בַּר *son* Mur 29 2$_{9}$.

15. father of Hanin, in deed of sale, <CSTR> בר יהונתן *son of Jehonathan* Mur 30 1$_{4}$ 2$_{17}$.

16. father of Honia, <CSTR> בר יהונתן *son of Jehonathan* Mur 30 1$_{6}$ 2$_{26}$.

17. son of Joseph, signatory to deed of sale, <SUBJ> חתם *seal* Mur 30 2$_{9}$. <APP> בַּר *son* Mur 30 2$_{9}$, בֵּן *son* Mur 30 2$_{34}$ (יהוס[ף]).

18. son of Eleazar, signatory to deed of sale, <SUBJ> חתם *seal* Mur 30 2$_{9}$. <APP> בַּר *son* Mur 30 2$_{9}$ ([בר]).

19. son of Honia, signatory to deed of sale, <SUBJ>

חתם *seal* Mur 30 2_{10}. <APP> בַּר *son* Mur 30 2_{10}.

20. writer of letter, ident. with יונתן *Jonathan* at MurEpJonathan$_1$, <SUBJ> כתב *write* MurEpJonathan$_{10}$ ([כת]בה). <APP> בַּר *son* MurEpJonathan$_{10}$.

21. Jonathan (Alexander) Jannaeus, high priest, ident. with ינתן on Coins 15 17, <APP> כֹּהֵן *priest* Alexander Jannaeus Coins 12 13 14, מֶלֶךְ *king* Alexander Jannaeus Coin 5 5A 6 8 perh. 9.

⇒ ׳י *Y.* + נתן *give.*

יְהוֹסֵף 1.0.15.3 pr.n.m. **J(eh)oseph, 1.** tribe descended from son of Jacob, usu. יוֹסֵף *Joseph*, <CSTR> בני יהוסף *sons of Joseph* 11QT $24_{13(mg)}$ (יוסף corrected in mg to יהוסף).

2. nation of Israel, usu. יוֹסֵף *Joseph*, <PREP> בְּ of place, *in*, + שִׂים *place* testimony Ps 81_6.

3. Frey 1285_4 (יהוסף נזר *Joseph the Nazirite*; others [יוסי בן דרן *Jose son of ...*; others יהויעמד *Jehojaamod*), <CSTR> בן יהוסף *son of Joseph* Frey 1285_4. <APP> נָזִיר *Nazirite* Frey 1285_4.

4. Frey 1285_{14}, <APP> גְּלִילִי *Galilaean* Frey 1285_{14}.

5. Frey 1285_{16}.

6. Frey 1286_8 (יה[ו]סף; others יהסף).

7. son of Simeon, signatory of lease, <SUBJ> כתב *write* 5/6ḤevBA 44_{30}. <APP> בֵּן *son* 5/6ḤevBA 44_{30}.

8. father of Judah, <CSTR> בן יהוסף *son of Joseph* 5/6 ḤevBA 44_{31}.

9. father of Simeon, perh. ident. with §7, בן יהוסף *son of Joseph* 5/6ḤevBA 44_{33}.

10. son of Addai, in deed of sale, Mur 22 1$_4$ $2_{5.7.21}$, <APP> בַּר *son* Mur 22 1_4, בֵּן *son* Mur 22 2_{21} (יה[ו]סף).

11. father of Halipha, in tenancy agreement, <CSTR> בן יהוסף *son of Joseph* Mur 24 3_5 ([בן יהו]סף) 3_{19}.

12. in deed of sale, <APP> בַּר *son* Mur 29 verso$_5$ (יהו[ס]ף).

13. father of Jehonathan, in deed of sale, <CSTR> בר יהוסף *son of Joseph* Mur 30 $2_{9.34}$ (יה[וסף]).

14. son of Ariston, <SUBJ> לקח *take* MurEpBeth-Mashiko$_3$. <APP> בֵּן *son* MurEpBeth-Mashiko$_3$.

15. father of Eleazar, <CSTR> בן יהוסף *son of Joseph* MurEpBeth-Mashiko$_9$.

16. son of Joseph, <APP> בַּר *son* MurEpBeth-Mashiko$_{12}$, עֵד *witness* MurEpBeth-Mashiko$_{12}$.

17. father of Joseph, <CSTR> בר יהוסף *son of Joseph* MurEpBeth-Mashiko$_{12}$.

18. father of Jacob, CSTR> בן יהוסף *son of Joseph* MurEpBeth-Mashiko$_{13}$.*

⇒ ׳י *Y.* + יסף hi. *add.*

יְהוֹעַדָּה 2 pr.n.m. **Jehoaddah,** son of Ahaz, descendant of Saul, appar. ident. with יַעְרָה *Jarah* at 1 C 9_{42}, <SUBJ> ילד hi. *beget* 1 C 8_{36}. <OBJ> ילד hi. *beget* 1 C 8_{36}.

⇒ ׳י *Y.* + עדה *adorn.*

יְהוֹעַדָּן 2.0.0.1 pr.n.f. **Jehoaddan, 1.** mother of Amaziah, <NOM CL> שֵׁם אִמּוֹ יְהוֹעַדָּן *his mother's name as Jehoaddan* 2 K $14_{2(Qr)}$‖2 C 25_1 (2 K 14_2 Kt יהועדין *Jehoaddin*).

2. daughter of Uriah, <APP> בַּת *daughter* Seal 855 (7th cent.). <PREP> לְ of possession, *of, (belonging) to* Seal 855 (7th cent.).*

⇒ ׳י *Y.* + עדן *delight.*

יהועדין, see יְהוֹעַדָּן *Jehoaddan.*

[יְהוֹעַז] 0.0.0.3 pr.n.m. **Jehoaz, 1.** father of Nehemiah, <CSTR> בן יהועז *son of Jehoaz* Arad ost. 31_3.

2. Arad ost. 40_2 (יהו[עז]).

3. appar. son of Ahab, <PREP> לְ of possession, *of, (belonging) to* Seal 156 (T. eṣ-Ṣafi, 7th cent.).

4. son of Mattan, <APP> בֵּן *son* Seal 574 (T. Beit Mirsim?, 7th/6th cent.). <PREP> לְ of possession, *of, (belonging) to* Seal 156 (T. eṣ-Ṣafi, 7th cent.).

⇒ ׳י *Y.* + עזז *be strong,*

[יְהוֹעֶזֶר] 0.0.0.3 pr.n.m. **Jehoezer, 1.** son of Obadiah, <APP> בֵּן *son* Seal 26 (6th cent.). <PREP> לְ of possession, *of, (belonging) to* Seal 26 (6th cent.).

2. appar. son of Igdaliah, <PREP> לְ of possession, *of, (belonging) to* Seal 421 (7th cent.).

3. Stamp/Coin 3 (Ramat Raḥel, 5th/4th cent.), <PREP> לְ of possession, *of, (belonging) to* Stamp/Coin 3 (ליהעזר; others יהוד *Jehud;* Ramat Raḥel, 5th/4th cent.).

4. governor of Jehud, or perh. potter, <APP> פֶּחָא

governor (others פֶּחָרָא *potter*) Stamp/Coin 14 15 (יהעזר; others לזבדיו *[belonging] to Zebadiah;* others עזבק *Azbuk*; both 5th/4th cent.).
⇒ ׳י *Y.* + עזר *help.*

[יְהוֹעֵלִי] 0.0.0.1 pr.n.[m.] **Jehoale,** Seal 916.
⇒ ׳י *Y.* + עלה *go up.*

[יְהוֹעָנָה] 0.0.0.1 pr.n.[m.] **Jehoanah,** Samaria Coin 38.
⇒ ׳י *Y.* + ענה *answer.*

יְהוֹצָדָק 8 pr.n.m. **Jehozadak,** high priest at time of exile and father of high priest Joshua, ident. with יוֹצָדָק *Jozadak* at Ezr $3_{2.8}$ 10_{18} Ne 12_{26}, <SUBJ> הלך *go* 1 C 5_{41}. <OBJ> ילד hi. *beget* 1 C 5_{40}. <CSTR> בֶּן־יְהוֹצָדָק *son of Jehozadak* Hg $1_{1.12.14}$ $2_{2.4}$ Zc 6_{11} (or em. יְהוֹשֻׁעַ בֶּן־יְהוֹצָדָק הַכֹּהֵן הַגָּדוֹל *Joshua, the son of Jehozadak, the high priest* to זְרֻבָּבֶל בֶּן־שְׁאַלְתִּיאֵל *Zerubbabel, the son of Shealtiel*).
⇒ ׳י *Y.* + צדק *be righteous.*

[יְהוֹקִם] 0.0.0.3 pr.n.[m.] **Jehokim, 1.** Seal 335 (8th/6th cent.). **2.** appar. son of Jehonadab, Seal 336 (6th cent.). **3.** appar. father of Pedaiah, Seal 512 (T. Beit Mirsim?, 7th/6th cent.). **4.** Seal 671 (יהוק[ם]; T. Beit Mirsim?, 7th /6th cent.).
⇒ ׳י *Y.* + קום hi. *raise up.*

יְהוֹרָם 29.0.0.1 pr.n.m. **Jehoram, 1.** king of Judah, son of Jehoshaphat, ident. with יוֹרָם *Joram* at 2 K $8_{21.23.24}$ 11_2 1 C 3_{11}, <SUBJ> היה *be* 2 K 8_{16} (mss יוֹרָם *Joram*) 2 C 21_9 (‖2 K 8_{21} יוֹרָם), הלך *go* 2 K 8_{16}‖2 C 21_5 2 C 21_9, קום *rise* 2 C $21_{4.9}$, עבר *pass* 2 C 21_9, חזק htp. *strengthen oneself* 2 C 21_4, מלך *reign* 1 K 22_{51}‖2 C 21_1 2 K 8_{16}‖2 C 21_5, קדשׁ hi. *consecrate* 2 K 12_{19}, עשׂה *do* 2 K 8_{16}‖2 C 21_5 2 C 21_9, זנה hi. *prostitute* 2 C 21_9, נדח hi. *lead astray* 2 C 21_9, נכה hi. *strike* 2 C 21_9, הרג *kill* 2 C $21_{4.9}$.

<NOM CL> בֶּן־שְׁלֹשִׁים וּשְׁתַּיִם שָׁנָה יְהוֹרָם *Jehoram was a son of thirty-two years,* i.e. thirty-two years old 2 C 21_5.

<CSTR> בֶּן־יְהוֹרָם *son of Jehoram* 2 K $8_{25.29}$‖2 C $22_{1.6}$, בַּת ... יְהוֹרָם *daughter of ... Jehoram* 2 C 22_{11}.

<APP> אָב *father* 2 K 12_{19}, בֵּן *son* 1 K 22_{51}‖2 C 21_1 2 K 1_{17} 8_{16} (mss יוֹרָם *Joram*), מֶלֶךְ *king* 2 K $8_{25.29}$‖2 C $22_{1.6}$ 2 K 1_{17} 12_{19} 2 C 22_{11}.

<PREP> לְ of direction, *to,* + נתן *give* 2 C 21_3; of possession, *of, (belonging) to* 2 K 1_{17}, + היה *be* 2 K 8_{16}‖2 C 21_5 (2 K mss יוֹרָם *Joram*); אֶל *to,* + בוא *come* 2 C 21_9; introducing object, + סבב *surround* 2 C 21_9 (‖2 K 8_{21} יוֹרָם); עַל *against,* + עור hi. *stir up* 2 C 21_{16}.

2. king of Israel, son of Ahab, ident. with יוֹרָם *Joram* at 2 K $8_{16.25.28.29}$ $9_{14.24.29}$ 2 C $22_{5.7}$, <SUBJ> אמר *say* 2 K 3_6 $9_{17.21.22.23}$, ראה *see* 2 K 9_{22}, הלך *go* 2 K 3_6, יצא *go out* 2 K 3_6 9_{21}, עלה *go up* 2 K 3_6, שׁוב *go back* 2 K 9_{15}, סור *turn aside* 2 K 3_1, hi. *remove* 2 K 3_1, הפך *turn* 2 K 9_{23}, נוס *flee* 2 K 9_{23}, שׁלח *send* 2 K 3_6, קרא *meet* 2 K 9_{21}, מצא *find* 2 K 9_{21}, מלך *reign* 2 K 1_{17} 3_1, עשׂה *do* 2 K 3_1, דבק *cling* 2 K 3_1, פקד *muster* 2 K 3_6, לחם ni. *fight* 2 K 9_{15}, חלה *be sick* 2 C 22_6, רפא htp. *be healed* 2 K 9_{15}, כרע *bow down* 2 K 9_{24}. <OBJ> ראה *see* 2 C 22_6, נכה hi. *strike* 2 K $9_{15.24}$, נשׂא *lift* 2 K 9_{24}, שׁלך hi. *cast* 2 K 9_{24}. <APP> אִישׁ *man,* i.e. each one 2 K 9_{21}, בֵּן *son* 2 K 3_1 2 C $22_{5.6}$, מֶלֶךְ *king* 2 K 3_6 $9_{15.21}$ 2 C 22_5. <PREP> בְּ *against,* + פשׁע *rebel* 2 K 3_6; כְּ *as* 2 K 3_6; עִם *with,* + יצא *go out* 2 C 22_7; אֵת *with,* + הלך *go* 2 K 3_6 2 C 22_5.

3. priest at time of Jehoshaphat, <NOM CL> עִמָּהֶם אֱלִישָׁמָע וִיהוֹרָם *with them were Elishama and Jehoram* 2 C 17_8. <APP> כֹּהֵן *priest* 2 C 17_8.

4. Seal 779 (Lachish), <PREP> לְ of possession, *of, (belonging) to* Seal 779 ([ל]יהורם; Lachish).
⇒ ׳י *Y.* + רום *be high.*

יְהוֹשַׁבְעַת 3 pr.n.f. **Jehoshabeath, Jehosheba**—יְהוֹשֶׁבַע (2 K 11_2)—daughter of Joram, king of Judah, and wife of Jehoiada the priest, <SUBJ> היה *be* 2 C 22_{11}, לקח *take* 2 K 11_2‖2 C 22_{11}, גנב *steal* 2 K 11_2‖2 C 22_{11}, נתן *give,* i.e. place 2 K 11_2‖2 C 22_{11} (if ins. וַתִּתֵּן *and she placed*), סתר hi. *hide* 2 C 22_{11}. <APP> אִשָּׁה *wife* 2 C 22_{11}, בַּת *daughter* 2 C 2 K 11_2‖22_{11} 2 C 22_{11}, אָחוֹת *sister* 2 K 11_2.
⇒ ׳י *Y* + (?) שֶׁבַע *abundance.*

יְהוֹשֻׁעַ 218.1.1.4 pr.n.m. **J(eh)oshua**—יְהוֹשׁוּעַ—**1.** son of Nun, descendant of Ephraim, ident. with הוֹשֵׁעַ *Hoshea* at Nm $13_{8.16}$ and יֵשׁוּעַ *Jeshua* at Ne 8_{17}, <SUBJ> היה *be* Jos 5_{13}, חיה *live* Nm 14_{38}, pi. *let live* Jos 9_{15}, hi. *let live*

Jos 6$_{25}$, זקן *be old* Jos 13$_{1}$ 23$_{1.2}$, אמר *say* Ex 32$_{17}$ Nm 11$_{28}$ 14$_{6}$ Jos 1$_{10.11}$ 2$_{1}$ 3$_{5.6.7.9.10}$ 4$_{5.17.20}$ 5$_{13.14}$ 6$_{6.8.10.16.22}$ 7$_{2.7.10.19.25}$ 8$_{3}$ 9$_{8.22}$ 10$_{12.18.22.24.25}$ 17$_{15.17}$ 18$_{3.8}$ 20$_{1}$ 22$_{1.7}$ 24$_{2.19.22.27}$, דבר pi. *speak* Jos 4$_{10}$ 9$_{22}$ 10$_{12}$ 20$_{1}$, קרא *call* Jos 4$_{4}$ 6$_{6}$ 9$_{22}$ 10$_{24}$ 22$_{1}$ 23$_{2}$ 24$_{1}$, *read* Jos 8$_{30.35}$, ענה *answer* Nm 11$_{28}$, צוה pi. *command* Jos 1$_{10.16}$ 3$_{7}$ 4$_{1.8.15.17}$ 6$_{10}$ 8$_{3.29}$ 10$_{27}$ 18$_{8}$, שׁאל *ask* Jos 19$_{49}$, הגה *meditate* Jos 1$_{1}$, שׁבע hi. *cause to swear* Jos 6$_{26}$, ברך pi. *bless* Jos 14$_{13}$ 22$_{6.7}$, שׁמע *hear* Ex 32$_{17}$ Jos 6$_{2}$ 14$_{6}$, ראה *see* Jos 5$_{13}$ 6$_{2}$ 8$_{1.21}$, ידע *know* Jos 14$_{6}$, ירא *fear* Dt 3$_{21}$ 31$_{7}$ Jos 8$_{1}$ 10$_{8}$ 11$_{6}$, ערץ *be terrified* Jos 1$_{1}$, חתת *be dismayed* Dt 31$_{7}$ Jos 1$_{1}$ 8$_{1}$, כתב *write* Jos 8$_{30}$ 24$_{26}$.

הלך *go* Dt 31$_{14}$ Jos 1$_{1}$ 5$_{13}$ 8$_{13}$ 23$_{2}$, בוא *come* Nm 14$_{30}$ 27$_{18}$ Dt 1$_{38}$ 31$_{7}$ Jos 3$_{1}$ 10$_{9}$ 11$_{7.21}$ 13$_{1}$ 23$_{1.2}$, hi. *bring* Dt 31$_{7}$ (mss)$_{.23}$, יצא *go out* Ex 17$_{9}$ Nm 27$_{18}$, עלה *go up* Jos 8$_{1.3.10}$ 10$_{6.7.9.36}$, hi. *bring up* Jos 7$_{6.24}$, סור *turn aside* Jos 1$_{1}$, hi. *remove* Jos 11$_{15}$, מושׁ hi. *depart* Ex 33$_{11}$ (Sam qal), נסע *set out* Jos 3$_{1}$, עבר *pass* Nm 14$_{6}$ Dt 3$_{21.28}$ 31$_{3}$ Jos 1$_{1}$ 3$_{1}$ 10$_{29.31.34}$, שׁוב *go back* Jos 5$_{2}$ 8$_{21}$ 10$_{15.38.43}$ 11$_{10}$, hi. *bring back* Jos 8$_{26}$, סבב *go round* Jos 6$_{2}$, hi. *cause to go round* Jos 6$_{10}$, קרב *draw near* Jos 8$_{3}$, hi. *bring near* Jos 7$_{16}$, נוס *flee* Jos 8$_{3.15}$, קום *rise* Ex 24$_{13}$ Jos 1$_{1}$ 7$_{10}$ 8$_{1.3}$, hi. *raise* Jos 4$_{9.20}$ 24$_{26}$, שׁכם hi. *rise early* Jos 3$_{1}$ 6$_{12}$ 7$_{16}$ Jos 8$_{10}$, נשׂא *lift* Jos 5$_{13}$, נשׁל *remove* Jos 5$_{15}$, שׁלח *send* Jos 1$_{16}$ 2$_{1}$ 6$_{25}$ 7$_{2.22}$ 8$_{3.9}$ 18$_{3}$, pi. Jos 22$_{6.7}$ 24$_{28}$ Jg 2$_{6}$, אסף *gather* Jos 24$_{1}$, נטה *stretch out* Jos 8$_{18.18.26}$, תור *spy* Nm 14$_{6}$, יתר ni. *remain* Nm 26$_{65}$, שׁאר hi. *let remain* Jos 10$_{28.29.33.36.38.40}$, עזב *leave* Jg 2$_{21}$, עמד *stand* Nm 27$_{18}$ Dt 1$_{38}$ Jos 5$_{15}$, יצב htp. *stand* Dt 31$_{14}$, ישׁב *dwell* Jos 19$_{49}$, לין *lodge* Jos 3$_{1}$ 8$_{9}$, חנה *encamp* Jos 10$_{31}$, נפל *fall* Jos 5$_{14}$ 7$_{6.10}$ 11$_{7}$, hi. *cause to fall*, i.e. allot Jos 23$_{2}$, שׁחה htpal. *bow* Jos 5$_{14}$, ירה *cast* lot Jos 18$_{3}$, שׁלך hi. *cast* lot Jos 18$_{8.10}$.

חזק *be strong* Dt 31$_{7.23}$ Jos 1$_{1.16}$, אמץ *be courageous* Dt 31$_{7.23}$ Jos 1$_{1.16}$, שׂכל hi. *succeed* Jos 1$_{1}$, צלח hi. *prosper* (trans.) Jos 1$_{1}$, עשׂה *do* Ex 17$_{10}$ Jos 1$_{1}$ 5$_{2.3.15}$ 6$_{2}$ 8$_{1}$ 9$_{3.15.24}$ 10$_{1.28.29.34.36.38}$ 11$_{9.15.18}$, מלא *be full* Dt 34$_{9}$, pi. *wholly follow* Nm 32$_{12}$, כלה pi. *finish* Jos 10$_{20}$ 19$_{51}$, בנה *build* Jos 8$_{30}$ 19$_{49}$, שׁמר *keep* Jos 1$_{1}$, שׂים *place* Jos 8$_{10.28}$ 24$_{25}$, נתן *give* Nm 32$_{28}$ Jos 9$_{27}$ 11$_{23}$ 12$_{7}$ 14$_{6.13}$ 15$_{13}$ 17$_{14}$ 22$_{7}$, נחל pi. *divide for inheritance* Jos 14$_{1}$ 19$_{51}$, hi. *cause to inherit* Dt 1$_{38}$ 3$_{28}$ 31$_{7}$ Jos 1$_{1}$, חלק pi. *divide* Jos 18$_{10}$ 19$_{51}$, לקח *take* Jos 4$_{1}$ 7$_{24}$ 8$_{1.10}$ 11$_{16.23}$ 24$_{26}$, לכד *capture* Jos 10$_{1.28.31.34.36.38.42}$ 11$_{10.12.16}$, *take by lot* Jos 7$_{16}$ (or em. וַיִּלְכֹּד *and he took* to וַיִּלָּכֵד *and it was taken*, i.e. ni.), בזז *plunder* Jos 8$_{1}$, נתק hi. *draw out* Jos 8$_{3}$, בחר *choose* Ex 17$_{9}$ Jos 8$_{3}$, פקד *muster* Jos 8$_{10}$, נצל hi. *deliver* Jos 9$_{24}$, ישׁע hi. *save* Jos 10$_{6}$, עזר *help* Jos 10$_{6}$, קדשׁ pi. *sanctify* Jos 7$_{10}$.

קרע *tear* Nm 14$_{6}$ Jos 7$_{6}$, מול *circumcise* Jos 5$_{2.3.4.7}$, כרת *cut off* Jos 11$_{21}$, *cut*, i.e. make, covenant Jos 9$_{6.15}$ 24$_{25}$, hi. *cut off* Jos 23$_{2}$, עקר pi. *hamstring* Jos 11$_{6.9}$, לחם ni. *fight* Ex 17$_{9.10}$ Jos 10$_{29.31.36.38}$, חלשׁ *defeat* Ex 17$_{13}$, נכה hi. *strike* Jos 8$_{21}$ 10$_{20+10t}$ 11$_{10.12.16}$ 12$_{7}$, נגע ni. *be struck* Jos 8$_{15}$, חרם hi. *destroy* Jos 8$_{26}$ 10$_{1.28.34.36.38.40}$ 11$_{10.12.21}$, שׂרף *burn* Jos 8$_{28}$ 11$_{6.9.10.13}$, תלה *hang* Jos 8$_{28}$ 10$_{26}$, מות *die* Jos 24$_{29}$ Jg 2$_{8.21}$, hi. *kill* Jos 10$_{26}$ 11$_{16}$.

<NOM CL> אֵלֶּה שְׁמוֹת הָאֲנָשִׁים ... יְהוֹשֻׁעַ *these are the names of the men ... Joshua* Nm 34$_{17}$, יְהוֹשֻׁעַ בְּנוֹ *Joshua was his son* 1 C 7$_{27}$, גבור בן חיל יהושע *Joshua was a mighty one, a son of valour* Si 46$_{1}$.

<OBJ> ענה *answer* Jos 1$_{16}$ 7$_{20}$ 9$_{24}$, צוה pi. *command* Nm 27$_{18.22}$ 32$_{28}$ Dt 3$_{21.28}$ 31$_{23}$ Jos 1$_{1}$ 4$_{10.10}$ 8$_{27}$ 11$_{15}$, קרא *call*, i.e. name Nm 13$_{16}$, summon Dt 31$_{14}$, meet Jos 8$_{3.21}$, ירא *fear* Jos 4$_{14}$, בוא hi. *bring* Nm 14$_{6}$, עמד hi. *cause to stand* Nm 27$_{18.22}$, עזב *leave* Dt 31$_{7}$ Jos 1$_{1}$, רפה hi. *abandon* Dt 31$_{7}$ Jos 1$_{1}$, לקח *take* Nm 27$_{18.22}$, חזק pi. *encourage* Dt 1$_{38}$, hi. Dt 3$_{28}$, אמץ pi. *strengthen* Dt 3$_{28}$, גדל pi. *make great* Jos 3$_{7}$ 4$_{14}$, רגם *stone* Nm 14$_{6}$, עכר *trouble* Jos 7$_{25}$, רמה pi. *deceive* Jos 9$_{22}$, קבר *bury* Jos 24$_{29}$ Jg 2$_{8}$.

<CSTR> אָזְנֵי יְהוֹשֻׁעַ *ears of Joshua* Ex 17$_{14}$, יַד *hand*, i.e. power, *of* Jg 2$_{23}$, יְמֵי *days of* Jos 24$_{31}$ Jg 2$_{7}$, מוֹת *death of* Jg 1$_{1}$ (or em. יְהוֹשֻׁעַ *Joshua* to מֹשֶׁה *Moses*) CD 5$_{4}$ (... מות ויהושוע ויושוע *death ... and Joshua and Joshua* [appar. dittography]).

<APP> אִישׁ *man* Nm 27$_{18}$, בֵּן *son* Ex 33$_{11}$ Nm 11$_{28}$ 14$_{6.30.38}$ 26$_{65}$ 27$_{18}$ 32$_{12.28}$ 34$_{17}$ Dt 1$_{38}$ 31$_{23}$ 34$_{9}$ Jos 1$_{1}$ 2$_{1.23}$ 6$_{6}$ 14$_{1}$ 17$_{4}$ 19$_{49.51}$ 21$_{1}$ 24$_{29}$ Jg 2$_{8}$ 1 K 16$_{34}$ Si 46$_{1}$, נַעַר *lad* Ex 33$_{11}$, מְשָׁרֵת *minister* Ex 24$_{13}$ 33$_{11}$ Nm 11$_{28}$ Jos 1$_{1}$ Si 46$_{1}$, עֶבֶד *servant* Jos 24$_{29}$ Jg 2$_{8}$.

<PREP> לְ of direction, *to* Jos 15$_{13}$, + אמר *say* Ex 17$_{10}$ Jos 11$_{9}$, ספר pi. *tell* Jos 2$_{23}$, נגד pu. *be told* Jos 10$_{17}$, קרא *call*, i.e. summon Dt 31$_{7}$, נתן *give* Nm 14$_{6}$ Jos 1$_{1}$ 19$_{49}$; of benefit, *for* Jos 5$_{13}$, + שׁאל *inquire* Nm 27$_{18}$, לחם ni. *fight* Dt 3$_{21}$.

בְּ *against*, + היה *be* Jos 24$_{27}$; חפץ בְּ *delight in* Nm 14$_{6}$.

אֶל *to* + אמר *say* Ex 17$_{9}$ Dt 31$_{7}$ Jos 1$_{1}$ 22$_{4}$ 3$_{7}$ 4$_{1.14}$ 5$_{2.9.15}$

6$_{2}$ 7$_{3.7}$ 8$_{1.18}$ 9$_{6.8.8}$ 10$_{8}$ 11$_{6}$ 13$_{1}$ 14$_{6}$ 24$_{21.24}$, דבר pi. *speak* Jos 4$_{8}$ 17$_{14(mss)}$ 20$_{1}$ 21$_{1}$, שׁמע *listen* Dt 34$_{9}$, הלך *go* Jos 9$_{6}$, בוא *come* Jos 2$_{23}$ 18$_{3.9}$, hi. *bring* Jos 7$_{23}$ 18$_{3}$, יצא hi. *bring out* Jos 10$_{24}$, נגשׁ *draw near* Jos 14$_{6}$ 21$_{1}$, קרב hi. *bring near* Jos 8$_{23}$, שׁוב *go back* Jos 7$_{3}$ 10$_{21}$ 18$_{8}$, שׁלח *send* Jos 10$_{6}$.

עַל *upon*, + סמך *lay* hand Nm 27$_{18.22}$ Dt 34$_{9}$, נתן *give*, i.e. place Nm 27$_{18}$.

עִם *with* Jos 10$_{7}$, + היה *be* Dt 31$_{7.23}$ Jos 1$_{1.16}$ 3$_{7}$, דבר pi. *speak* Jos 24$_{27}$, לחם ni. *fight* Jos 9$_{2}$.

אֵת *with* Nm 14$_{6}$ 27$_{18}$ Jos 8$_{10}$, + היה *be* Jos 6$_{27}$, דבר pi. *speak* Jos 17$_{14}$, עבר *pass over* Nm 32$_{28}$, שׁלם hi. *make peace* Jos 10$_{4}$.

בְּתוֹךְ *among*, + אחז ni. *take possession* Nm 32$_{28}$.

בְּיַד *by means of*, + דבר pi. *speak* 1 K 16$_{34}$.

לִפְנֵי *before*, + הלך *go* Dt 31$_{7}$, קרב *draw near* Jos 17$_{4}$, יצב htp. *stand* Jos 1$_{1}$, כבשׁ ni. *be subdued* Nm 32$_{28}$.

בִּפְנֵי *before, against*, + עמד *stand* Jos 10$_{8}$.

אַחֲרֵי *after*, + יצא *go out* Jos 8$_{3}$, רדף *chase* Jos 8$_{16}$, ארך hi. *prolong* days Jos 24$_{31}$ Jg 2$_{7}$.

<COLL> + מִבְּחֻרָיו *(one) of his chosen* Nm 11$_{28}$ (Sam^{mss} מִבְּחִירָיו *[one] of his chosen*)

2. Beth-shemeshite, <CSTR> שְׂדֵה יְהוֹשֻׁעַ *field of Joshua* 1 S 6$_{14.18}$. <APP> בֵּית־הַשִּׁמְשִׁי *Beth-shemeshite* 1 S 6$_{14.18}$.

3. governor of Jerusalem at time of Josiah, <CSTR> שַׁעַר יְהוֹשֻׁעַ *gate of Joshua* 2 K 23$_{8}$. <APP> שַׂר *prince*, i.e. governor 2 K 23$_{8}$.

4. high priest, son of Jehozadak, <SUBJ> היה *be* Zc 3$_{3}$, אמר *say* Hg 1$_{1}$, שׁמע *hear* Hg 1$_{12}$ Zc 3$_{8}$, הלך *go* Zc 3$_{6}$, עמד *stand* Zc 3$_{1.3}$, שׁמר *keep* Zc 3$_{6}$, עשׂה *do* Hg 2$_{4}$, דין *judge* Zc 3$_{6}$, חזק *be courageous* Hg 2$_{2}$, לבשׁ pass. *be clothed* Zc 3$_{3}$. <OBJ> ראה hi. *show* Zc 3$_{1}$, לבשׁ hi. *clothe* Zc 3$_{3}$. <CSTR> רֹאשׁ יְהוֹשֻׁעַ *head of Joshua* Zc 6$_{11}$ (or em.; see App.), רוּחַ *spirit of* Hg 1$_{14}$. <APP> בֵּן *son* Hg 1$_{1.12.14}$ 2$_{2.4}$ 6$_{11}$ (or em. יְהוֹשֻׁעַ בֶּן־יְהוֹצָדָק הַכֹּהֵן הַגָּדוֹל *Joshua, the son of Jehozadak, the high priest* to זְרֻבָּבֶל בֶּן־שְׁאַלְתִּיאֵל *Zerubbabel, the son of Shealtiel*), כֹּהֵן *priest* Hg 1$_{1.12.14}$ 2$_{2.4}$ Zc 3$_{1.8}$ 6$_{11}$ (or em.; see above). <PREP> לְ of direction, *to*, + נתן *give* Zc 3$_{6}$; בְּ of place, *among* Hg 2$_{2}$; introducing object, + עוד hi. *admonish* Zc 3$_{6}$; אֶל *to*, + היה *be* Hg 1$_{1}$, אמר *say* Hg 2$_{2}$ Zc 3$_{3}$ 6$_{11}$ (or em.; see App.); מֵעַל *from*, + עבר hi. *remove* Zc 3$_{3}$; אֵת *with* Hg 2$_{4}$; לִפְנֵי *before*, + עמד *stand* Zc 3$_{3}$, ישׁב *sit* 3$_{8}$, נתן *give*, i.e. place 3$_{9}$.

5. son of Asaiah, <APP> בֵּן *son* Seal 27 (Palestine, 7th cent.). <PREP> לְ of possession, *of, (belonging) to* Seal 27 (Palestine, 7th cent.).

6. son of Mathaniah and father of Ephroah, <CSTR> בן יהושע *son of Joshua* Seals 520 521 (both T. Beit Mirsim?, 7th/6th cent.). <APP> בֵּן *son* Seal 521 (T. Beit Mirsim?, 7th/6th cent.).

7. appar. father of Maliah, Seal 875 (8th/7th cent.).

⇒ ׳י *Y.* + ישׁע hi. *save*.

יְהוֹשָׁפָט 84 pr.n.m. **Jehoshaphat, 1.** king of Judah, son of Asa and Azubah, <SUBJ> היה *be* 2 C 17$_{12}$, אמר *say* 1 K 22$_{4.5.7.8}$||2 C 18$_{3.4.6.7}$ 2 K 3$_{7.11.12}$ 2 C 19$_{4.8}$ 20$_{5.20}$, צוה pi. *command* 2 C 19$_{8}$, קרא *call* 2 C 20$_{3}$, זעק *cry out* 1 K 22$_{32}$||2 C 18$_{31}$, קשׁב hi. *pay attention* 2 C 20$_{15}$, יעץ ni. *take counsel* 2 C 20$_{20}$, ברך pi. *bless* 2 C 20$_{25}$, ירא *fear* 2 C 20$_{3.15}$, חתת *be dismayed* 2 C 20$_{15}$, הלך *go* 1 K 22$_{4}$||2 C 18$_{3}$ 1 K 22$_{42}$||2 C 20$_{31}$ 2 K 3$_{7}$ 2 C 17$_{3.12}$, בוא *come* appar. 1 K 22$_{30}$||2 C 18$_{29}$ (or em. הִתְחַפֵּשׂ וָבֹא *disguise yourself and come* to אֶתְחַפֵּשׂ וְאָבֹא *I will disguise myself and come*) 2 C 20$_{25.27}$, יצא *go out* 2 C 19$_{4}$, ירד *go down* 1 K 22$_{2}$||2 C 18$_{1}$ 2 K 3$_{12}$ 2 C 20$_{15}$, עלה *go up* 1 K 22$_{29}$||2 C 18$_{28}$ 2 K 3$_{7}$ 2 C 18$_{1}$, שׁוב *go back* 2 C 19$_{1.4}$ 20$_{27}$, hi. *bring back* 2 C 19$_{4}$, סור *turn aside* (intrans.) 1 K 22$_{42}$||2 C 20$_{31}$, hi. *remove* 2 C 17$_{5}$, בער pi. *remove* 1 K 22$_{46}$ 2 C 19$_{2}$, שׁלח *send* 2 C 17$_{5}$, מצא *find* 2 C 20$_{15.25}$, קדד *bow* 2 C 20$_{18}$, קהל ni. *be gathered* 2 C 20$_{25}$, עמד *stand* 2 C 20$_{5.20}$, hi. *appoint* 2 C 19$_{4.8}$ 20$_{20}$, ישׁב *sit* 1 K 22$_{10}$||2 C 18$_{9}$, *dwell* 2 C 19$_{4}$, מלך *reign* 1 K 15$_{24}$||2 C 17$_{1}$ 1 K 22$_{41.41}$||2 C 20$_{31.31}$, גדל *be great* 2 C 17$_{12}$.

דרשׁ *inquire* 1 K 22$_{7}$||2 C 18$_{6}$ 2 K 3$_{11}$ 2 C 17$_{3}$ 19$_{2}$ 20$_{3}$ 22$_{9}$, חזק htp. *strengthen oneself* 2 C 17$_{1}$, נתן *give*, i.e. place 2 C 17$_{1}$ 20$_{3}$, חתן htp. *become related by marriage* 2 C 18$_{1}$, חבר pi. *make an ally of* 2 C 20$_{35}$, htp. *make an alliance with* 2 C 20$_{35.37}$, חפשׂ htp. *disguise oneself* 1 K 22$_{30}$ ||2 C 18$_{29}$ (or em.; see above), לבשׁ *wear* 1 K 22$_{30}$||2 C 18$_{29}$, בזז *plunder* 2 C 20$_{25}$, נצל pi. *strip off* 2 C 20$_{25}$, קדשׁ hi. *consecrate* 2 K 12$_{19}$, עשׂה *do* 1 K 22$_{42}$||2 C 20$_{31}$ 1 K 22$_{46}$, *make* 1 K 22$_{49(Qr)}$||2 C 20$_{35}$ (1 K 22$_{49}$ Kt עשׁר appar. *be rich with*), בנה *build* 2 C 17$_{12}$, כון hi. *establish* 2 C 19$_{2}$, לחם ni. *fight* 1 K 22$_{46}$, שׁלם hi. *make peace* 1 K 22$_{45}$, עזר *help* 2 C 19$_{2}$, אהב *love* 2 C 19$_{2}$, אבה *be willing* 1 K 22$_{50}$,

שׁכב *lie down* 1 K 22_{51}||2 C 21_1, קבר ni. *be buried* 1 K 22_{51}||2 C 21_1.

<NOM CL> יְהוֹשָׁפָט בֶּן־שְׁלֹשִׁים וְחָמֵשׁ שָׁנָה *Jehoshaphat was a son of thirty-five years,* i.e. thirty-five years old 1 K 22_{42}, יְהוֹשָׁפָט בְּנוֹ *Jehoshaphat was his son* 1 C 3_{10}.

<OBJ> ראה *see* 1 K 22_{32}||2 C 18_{31}, שׁמע *hear* 2 C 20_{20}, סות hi. *allure* 2 C 18_1, עזר *help* 2 C 18_{31}, שׂמח pi. *cause to rejoice* 2 C 20_{27}.

<CSTR> בֶּן־יְהוֹשָׁפָט *son of Jehoshaphat* 2 K 1_{17} 8_{16} 2 C 22_9, בְּנֵי *sons of* 2 C $21_{2.2}$, פְּנֵי *presence of* 2 K 3_{14}, מַלְכוּת *kingdom of* 2 C 20_{30}, דַּרְכֵי *ways of* 2 C 21_{12}, דִּבְרֵי *deeds of* 1 K 22_{46}||2 C 20_{34}.

<APP> אִישׁ *man,* i.e. each one 1 K 22_{10}||2 C 18_9, אָב *father* 2 K 12_{19} 2 C 21_{12}, בֵּן *son* 1 K 15_{24}||2 C 17_1 1 K 22_{41} 2 C 20_{31}, מֶלֶךְ *king* 1 K $22_{2.10.29}$||2 C $18_{9.28}$ 1 K 22_{52} 2 K $3_{1.7.12(mss)}$ 8_{16} (or del. וִיהוֹשָׁפָט מֶלֶךְ יְהוּדָה *and Jehoshaphat, king of Judah*) 8_{16} 12_{19} 2 C 18_3 $19_{1.2}$ $20_{15.35}$ 21_2.

<PREP> לְ of direction, *to,* + אמר *say* 2 C 20_{15}, נגד hi. *tell* 2 C 20_2, בוא hi. *bring* 2 C 17_{11}, נתן *give* 2 C 17_5, נוח hi. *give rest* 2 C 20_{30}; of possession, *of, (belonging) to* 1 K 22_{52} 2 K 3_1 2 C 20_{15}, + היה *be* 2 C $17_{5.12}$ 18_1; of benefit, *to, for,* + זבח *slaughter* 2 C 18_1.

כְּ *as* 1 K 22_4||2 C 18_3 2 K 3_7.

מִן of direction, *from,* + סות hi. *allure* 2 C 18_{31}.

אֶל *to,* + אמר *say* 1 K $22_{4.8.18.30}$||2 C $18_{3.7.17.29}$ 1 K 22_{50} 2 C 19_2, שׁלח *send* 2 K 3_7.

עַל *to, against* 2 C 19_2, + נבא htp. *prophesy* 2 C 20_{37}, בוא *come* 2 C $20_{1.2}$, סור *turn* 1 K 22_{32}, סבב *turn* 2 C 18_{31}.

עִם *with,* + היה *be* 2 C 17_3, מצא ni. *be found* 2 C 19_2, לחם ni. *fight* 2 C 17_{10}.

לִפְנֵי *before,* + נבא htp. *prophesy* 1 K 22_{10}||2 C 18_9.

מֵאַחֲרֵי *from (following) after,* + שׁוב *turn* (intrans.) 1 K 22_{32}||2 C 18_{31}.

תַּחַת *instead of,* + מלך *reign* 1 K 22_{51}||2 C 21_1.

2. recorder at time of David and Solomon, son of Ahilud, <NOM CL> יְהוֹשָׁפָט ... מַזְכִּיר *Jehoshaphat was ... recorder* 2 S 8_{16}||1 C 18_{15}=2 S 20_{24} 1 K 4_3. <APP> בֵּן *son* 2 S 8_{16}||1 C 18_{15}=2 S 20_{24} 1 K 4_3.

3. official of Solomon, son of Paruah, <NOM CL> יְהוֹשָׁפָט ... בְּיִשָּׂשכָר *Jehoshaphat was ... in Issachar* 1 K $4_{17(mss)}$ (L בְּיִשָּׂשכָר). <APP> בֵּן *son* 1 K 4_{17}.

4. father of Jehu, king of Israel (or grandfather of Jehu, if בֶּן־יְהוֹשָׁפָט *son of Jehoshaphat* follows נִמְשִׁי *Nimshi*), <CSTR> בֶּן־יְהוֹשָׁפָט *son of Jehoshaphat* 2 K $9_{2.14}$.

5. in pl.n. עֵמֶק יְהוֹשָׁפָט **valley of Jehoshaphat,** as place of judgment, appar. near Jerusalem, Jl $4_{2.12}$ Ophel ost.$_{2.3}$ (both [יהו]שפט; others ירת *Jereth;* others [ ]ידתן).

⇒ י׳ *Y.* + שׁפט *judge.*

יָהִיר 2 adj. **proud,** used attributively of גֶּבֶר *man* Hb 2_5, זֵד *presumptuous one* Ps 21_{24} (זֵד יָהִיר לֵץ שְׁמוֹ *a proud presumptuous one—scoffer is his name*).*

יָהֵל, see אהל I *pitch tent.*

יְהַלֶּלְאֵל 2 pr.n.m. **Jehallelel, 1.** descendant of Judah, <CSTR> בְּנֵי יְהַלֶּלְאֵל *sons of Jehallelel* 1 C 4_{16}.

2. Levite, father of Azariah, <CSTR> בֶּן־יְהַלֶּלְאֵל *son of Jehallelel* 2 C 29_{12}.

3. Kuntillet ʿAjrud inscr. E1_1, <OBJ> ברך pi. *bless* Kuntillet ʿAjrud inscr. E1_1 ([יהל[לאל). <PREP> לְ of direction, *to,* + אמר *say* Kuntillet ʿAjrud inscr. E1_1 ([ליהל[לאל).

⇒ הלל *praise* + אֵל *God.*

יַהֲלֹם 3 n.[m.] perh. **onyx**—mss יַהֲלֹם—semi-precious stone in Aaron's breastplate (Ex 28_{18}||39_{11}), <NOM CL> הַטּוּר הַשֵּׁנִי נֹפֶךְ סַפִּיר וְיָהֲלֹם *the second row is emerald, sapphire and onyx* Ex 28_{18}||39_{11}, כָּל־אֶבֶן יְקָרָה מְסֻכָתֶךָ אֹדֶם פִּטְדָה וְיָהֲלֹם *every precious stone was your covering—ruby, topaz and onyx* Ezk 28_{13}.*

יַהַץ 9 pl.n. **Jahaz**—+ ה- of direction, יַהְצָה (יָהְצָה), Sam יָחְצָה Nm 21_{23})—Levitical city in territory of Reuben, perh. Kh. Iskander, 46 km SSW of Amman, <SUBJ> היה *be* Jos 13_{18} (+ גְּבוּל *border*). <OBJ> נתן *give* Josh 21_{36} 1 C 6_{63} (both + מִגְרָשׁ *pasture*). <PREP> בְּ of place, *in, at,* + חנה *encamp* Jg 11_{20}; אֶל *to,* + בוא *come* Jr 48_{21}; עַד *as far as,* + שׁמע ni. *be heard* Is 15_4, נתן *give* voice Jr 48_{34}; ה- of direction, *to(wards), at,* + בוא *come* Nm 21_{23}, יצא *go out* Dt 2_{32}.

יָהְצָה, יַהְצָה, see יַהַץ *Jahaz.*

יוֹאָב 145 pr.n.m. **Joab**—יֹאָב—**1.** son of David's sister Zeruiah and commander of David's army, **<SUBJ>** היה *be* 2 S 2$_{18}$ 1 C 11$_{6}$, אמר *say* 2 S 2$_{14.26.27}$ 10$_{9}$||1 C 19$_{10}$ 2 S 11$_{18}$ 12$_{27}$ 14$_{2.22.31.32}$ 2 S 18$_{11.14.20.21.22}$ 19$_{6}$ 20$_{9.17.20}$ 24$_{3}$ ||1 C 21$_{3}$ 1 K 1$_{41}$, דבר pi. *speak* 2 S 3$_{27}$ 1 K 1$_{41}$ 2$_{30}$, ענה *answer* 2 S 20$_{20}$ 1 K 2$_{30}$, נגד hi. *tell* 2 S 11$_{18}$ 14$_{33}$, צוה pi. *command* 2 S 11$_{18}$ 14$_{19}$, ברך pi. *bless* 2 S 14$_{22}$, שׁבע ni. *swear* 2 S 19$_{6}$ 1 K 1$_{41}$, קדשׁ hi. *consecrate* 1 C 26$_{28}$, ראה *see* 2 S 10$_{9}$||1 C 19$_{10}$, שׁמע *hear* 2 S 20$_{17}$, ידע *know* 2 S 2$_{26}$ 11$_{16}$ 14$_{1}$ 19$_{6}$, אבה *be willing* 2 S 14$_{29}$, פקד *number* 2 S 24$_{2.4}$, ספר *count* 1 C 21$_{2}$, מנה *count* 1 C 27$_{24}$.

הלך *go* 2 S 2$_{32}$ 10$_{9}$ 14$_{21.23}$ 20$_{20}$ 1 C 21$_{2}$, htp. *go about* 1 C 21$_{4}$, בוא *come* 2 S 2$_{24}$ 3$_{22.23.24}$ 10$_{14}$||1 C 19$_{15}$ 2 S 14$_{29.31.32.33}$ 19$_{6}$ 24$_{4}$ 1 C 20$_{1}$ 21$_{4}$, hi. *bring* 2 S 14$_{23}$ 1 C 21$_{2}$, יצא *go out* 2 S 2$_{13}$ 3$_{26}$ 20$_{8}$ 24$_{4}$||1 C 21$_{4}$ 1 K 2$_{30}$, עלה *go up* 1 K 11$_{15}$, שׁוט *go about* 2 S 24$_{2.4}$, עבר *pass* 2 S 24$_{4}$, רדף *pursue* 2 S 2$_{24}$ 20$_{10}$, שׁוב *go back* 2 S 2$_{30}$ 10$_{14}$||1 C 19$_{15}$ (1 C if em. וַיָּבֹא *and he came* to וַיָּשָׁב *and he went back*) 2 S 11$_{14}$ 20$_{22}$ Ps 60$_{2}$, hi. *bring back* 2 S 14$_{21}$, נגשׁ *draw near* 2 S 10$_{13}$ ||1 C 19$_{14}$, קרב *draw near* 2 S 20$_{16}$, פגשׁ pi. *meet* 2 S 2$_{13}$, מצא *find* 2 S 14$_{22}$, קבץ *gather* 2 S 2$_{30}$, שׁלח *send* 2 S 3$_{26}$ 11$_{6.6.18.22}$ 12$_{27}$ 14$_{2}$ 18$_{29}$, בחר *choose* 2 S 10$_{9}$||1 C 19$_{10}$, ערך *arrange* 2 S 10$_{9}$||1 C 19$_{10}$, נטה *incline* 1 K 2$_{28}$, hi. *turn aside* trans. 2 S 3$_{27}$, סבב pi. *turn* trans. 2 S 14$_{20}$, נהג *lead* 1 C 20$_{1}$, נוס *flee* 1 K 2$_{28.29}$, פגע *fall upon* 1 K 2$_{31}$, נפל *fall* 2 S 14$_{22}$, שׁחה htpal. *bow down* 2 S 14$_{22}$, ישׁב *sit* 2 S 2$_{13}$, *remain* 1 K 11$_{16}$, חנה *encamp* 2 S 11$_{11}$ 24$_{4}$, קום *rise* 2 S 14$_{23.31}$, יצב htp. *stand* 2 S 18$_{12}$, יחל hi. *wait* 2 S 18$_{14}$, חזק hi. *hold* 1 K 2$_{28}$, *make strong* 2 S 11$_{25}$, htp. *take courage* 2 S 10$_{9}$||1 C 19$_{10}$, חשׂך *restrain* 2 S 18$_{16}$, נשׁק *kiss* 2 S 20$_{9}$, בקשׁ pi. *seek* 2 S 20$_{17}$.

נתן *give* 2 S 18$_{11}$ 24$_{9}$||1 C 21$_{5}$, i.e. place 2 S 10$_{9}$||1 C 19$_{10}$ 2 S 11$_{16}$ 1 K 2$_{5}$, יהב *give*, i.e. place 2 S 11$_{14}$, שׂים *place* 2 S 14$_{3.19}$ 1 K 2$_{5}$, לקח *take* 2 S 14$_{2}$ 18$_{14}$, שׁמר *keep* 2 S 11$_{16}$ 18$_{12}$, חלל hi. *begin* 1 C 27$_{24}$, כלה pi. *finish* 1 C 27$_{24}$, עשׂה *do* 2 S 14$_{20.21(mss)}$ 1 K 2$_{5}$, ישׁע hi. *save* 2 S 10$_{9}$ ||1 C 19$_{10}$, עזר *help* 1 K 1$_{7}$, חיה pi. *repair* 1 C 11$_{8}$, תקע *blow* trumpet 2 S 2$_{28}$ 18$_{16}$ 20$_{22}$, *thrust* dart 2 S 18$_{14}$, שׁפך *shed* blood 1 K 2$_{31}$, קרע *tear* 2 S 3$_{31}$, חגר *gird oneself* 2 S 3$_{31}$, pass. *be girded* 2 S 20$_{8}$, ספד *mourn* 2 S 3$_{31}$, לחם ni. *fight* 2 S 12$_{26.27}$, צור *besiege* 2 S 11$_{1}$||1 C 20$_{1}$, לכד *capture* 2 S 12$_{26.27}$, הרס *tear down* 2 S 11$_{25}$ 1 C 20$_{1}$, שׁחת hi. *destroy* 2 S 11$_{1}$||1 C 20$_{1}$ 2 S 20$_{20}$, בלע pi. *destroy* 2 S 20$_{17.20}$, כרת hi. *cut off* 1 K 11$_{16}$, נכה hi. *strike* 2 S 3$_{27}$ 20$_{10}$ 1 K 11$_{15}$ Ps 60$_{2}$ 1 C 20$_{1}$, הרג *kill* 2 S 3$_{30}$ 1 K 2$_{5.31}$, מות *die* 1 K 2$_{30}$ 11$_{21}$, hi. *kill* 2 S 20$_{17}$, קבר pi. *bury* 1 K 11$_{15}$, ni. *be buried* 1 K 2$_{33}$.

<NOM CL> בְּנֵי צְרוּיָה אַבְשַׁי וְיוֹאָב וַעֲשָׂה־אֵל *the sons of Zeruiah were Abishai, Joab and Asahel* 1 C 2$_{16}$, ... יוֹאָב עַל־הַצָּבָא *Joab was ... over the army* 2 S 8$_{16}$||1 C 18$_{15}$, var. 2 S 20$_{23}$ (אֶל *to*, i.e. over; ms[corr] עַל), שַׂר־צָבָא לַמֶּלֶךְ יוֹאָב *the commander of the king's army was Joab* 1 C 27$_{34}$, הַאַתָּה יוֹאָב *are you Joab?* 2 S 20$_{17}$.

<OBJ> צוה pi. *command* 2 S 18$_{5.12}$, שׁלח *send* 2 S 10$_{7}$ ||1 C 19$_{8}$ 2 S 11$_{1}$ 14$_{29.32}$, חזק pi. *encourage* 2 S 11$_{25}$, מות hi. *kill* 1 K 2$_{33}$, קבר *bury* 1 K 2$_{30}$.

<CSTR> אֵם יוֹאָב *mother of Joab* 2 S 17$_{25}$, אֲחִי *brother of* 1 S 26$_{6}$ 2 S 18$_{2}$ 23$_{18.24}$||1 C 11$_{20.26}$ 1 C 27$_{7}$, אַנְשֵׁי *men of* 2 S 20$_{7}$, נַעֲרֵי *lads of* 2 S 20$_{11}$, רֹאשׁ *head of* 2 S 3$_{29}$ 1 K 2$_{33}$, יַד *hand of* 2 S 14$_{19}$ 18$_{2}$ 20$_{10}$, יַד־יְמִין *right hand of* 2 S 20$_{9}$, בֵּית *house of* 2 S 3$_{29}$, חֶלְקַת *field of* 2 S 14$_{30}$, כְּלֵי *weapons of* 2 S 18$_{15}$ 23$_{37}$||1 C 11$_{39}$, שְׁלוֹם *peace of* 2 S 11$_{7}$.

<APP> בֵּן *son* 2 S 2$_{13.18}$ 8$_{16}$||1 C 18$_{15}$ 2 S 14$_{1}$ 1 K 1$_{7}$ 2$_{5.22}$ 1 C 11$_{6}$ 26$_{28}$ 27$_{24}$, אָח *brother* 2 S 2$_{22}$, אָדוֹן *lord* 2 S 11$_{11}$, שַׂר *commander* 2 S 24$_{2}$ 1 K 1$_{19}$ 11$_{15.21}$, עֶבֶד *servant* 2 S 14$_{19.20}$.

<PREP> לְ of benefit, *to, for*, + היה *be* 2 S 10$_{9}$||1 C 19$_{10}$, שׁאל *ask* 1 K 2$_{22}$, אור ni. *be light* 2 S 2$_{32}$; of direction, *to* 2 S 20$_{20}$, + אמר *say* 2 S 20$_{17}$, נגד hi. *tell* 2 S 3$_{23}$ 18$_{10.11}$, ho. *be told* 2 S 19$_{2}$, קרא *call*, i.e. invite 1 K 1$_{19}$, שׁחה htpal. *bow down* 2 S 18$_{21}$; of possession, *of, (belonging) to* 2 S 14$_{30.31}$.

חפץ בְּ *delight in* 2 S 20$_{11}$; פגע בְּ *fall upon* 1 K 2$_{29.30.33}$.

מִן of comparison, *(more) than*, + חזק *be strong* 2 S 10$_{9}$||1 C 19$_{10}$.

אֶל *to*, + היה *be* 2 S 10$_{9}$||1 C 19$_{10}$, אמר *say* 2 S 2$_{14}$ 3$_{31}$ 11$_{25}$ 14$_{21.32}$ 18$_{12.22}$ 20$_{16.21}$ 24$_{2}$||1 C 21$_{2}$, דבר pi. *speak* 2 S 20$_{16}$, קרא *call* 2 S 2$_{26}$, שׁלח *send* 2 S 11$_{6}$ 14$_{29.32}$, נשׂא *lift* 2 S 2$_{22}$, שׁלך hi. *cast* 2 S 20$_{22}$, ho. *be cast* 2 S 20$_{21}$, כתב *write* 2 S 11$_{14}$, תעב ni. *be abominable* 1 C 21$_{6(mss)}$; *over, against*, + חזק *be strong* 2 S 24$_{4}$.

עַל *upon* 2 S 18$_{11}$; *over, against*, + חזק *be strong* 2 S 24$_{4(mss)}$||1 C 21$_{4}$.

עִם *with* 2 S 10$_{13}$||1 C 19$_{14}$, + היה *be* 1 K 1$_{7}$, בוא hi.

bring 2 S 3_{22}, שׁלח *send* 2 S 11_{1}.

אֵת *with* 2 S $3_{23.31}$ 20_{15}, לחם ni. *fight* 2 S 11_{17}, תעב ni. *be abominable* 1 C 21_{6}.

עַד *unto*, + בוא *come* 1 K 2_{28}.

מִפְּנֵי *from before*, + נוס *flee* 2 S 10_{13}||1 C 19_{14}.

תַּחַת *instead of*, + היה *be* 2 S 19_{14}, שׂים *place* 2 S 17_{25}, נתן *give*, i.e. place 1 K 2_{33}.

אַחֲרֵי *after* 2 S 20_{11}, + עבר *pass* 2 S 20_{13}.

2. Judahite, son of Seraiah, <OBJ> ילד hi. *beget* 1 C 4_{14}. <APP> אָב *father* 1 C 4_{14}.

3. name of postexilic family, <CSTR> בְּנֵי יֵשׁוּעַ וְיוֹאָב *sons of Jeshua and Joab* Ezr 2_{6}||Ne 7_{11} (Ezr 2_{6} lacks וְ) Ezr 8_{9}.

4. Seal 9 (Carthage), <PREP> לְ of possession, *of, (belonging) to* Seal 9 (ליואב; others לאביהו *[belonging] to Abijah*; Carthage).

⇒ '' *Y*. + אָב *father*.

יוֹאָח 11 pr.n.m. **Joah, 1.** recorder at time of Hezekiah, son of Asaph, <SUBJ> אמר *say* 2 K $18_{18.26}$||Is $36_{3.11}$, נגד hi. *tell* 2 K 18_{37}||Is 36_{22}, בוא *come* 2 K 18_{37}||Is 36_{22}, יצא *go out* 2 K 18_{18}||Is 36_{3}. <APP> בֵּן *son* 2 K $18_{18.37}$||Is $36_{3.22}$, מַזְכִּיר *recorder* 2 K $18_{18.37}$||Is $36_{3.22}$, קרע pass. ptc. *one torn*, i.e. wearing torn garments 2 K 18_{37}||Is 36_{22}. <PREP> אֶל *to*, + אמר *say* 2 K 18_{18}||Is 36_{3}.

2. recorder at time of Josiah, son of Joahaz, <SUBJ> בוא *come* 2 C 34_{8}, חזק pi. *repair* 2 C 34_{8}, נתן *give* 2 C 34_{8}. <OBJ> שׁלח *send* 2 C 34_{8}. <APP> בֵּן *son* 2 C 34_{8}, מַזְכִּיר *recorder* 2 C 34_{8}.

3. Levite, son of Zimmah, descendant of Gershom, <NOM CL> יוֹאָח בְּנוֹ *Joah was his son* 1 C 6_{6}.

4. son of Obed-edom, <NOM CL> יוֹאָח הַשְּׁלִישִׁי *Joah was the third (son)* 1 C 26_{4}.

5. Levite, son of Zimmah, associated with reforms of Hezekiah, <SUBJ> בוא *come* 2 C 29_{12}, קום *rise* 2 C 29_{12}, אסף *gather* 2 C 29_{12}, קדשׁ htp. *sanctify oneself* 2 C 29_{12}, טהר pi. *cleanse* 2 C 29_{12}. <NOM CL> מִן־הַגֵּרְשֻׁנִּי יוֹאָח *from (among) the Gershonites was Joah* 2 C 29_{12}. <CSTR> בֶּן־יוֹאָח *son of Joah* 1 C 29_{12}. <APP> בֵּן *son* 2 C 29_{12}.

⇒ '' *Y*. + אָח *brother*.

יוֹאָחָז 4 pr.n.m. **Joahaz, 1.** king of Israel, son of Jehu, ident. with יְהוֹאָחָז *Jehoahaz* at 2 K 10_{35} $13_{1.4.7.8.9.10.22.25.25}$ $14_{8.17}$ 2 C $25_{17.25}$, <CSTR> בֶּן־יוֹאָחָז *son of Joahaz* 2 K 14_{1}.

2. king of Judah, son of Josiah, ident with יְהוֹאָחָז *Jehoahaz* at 2 K $23_{30.31.34}$ 2 C 36_{1}, and appar. with יוֹחָנָן *Johanan* at 1 C 3_{15}, <SUBJ> מלך *reign* 2 C 36_{2} (||2 K 23_{31} יְהוֹאָחָז *Jehoahaz*). <NOM CL> בֶּן־שָׁלוֹשׁ וְעֶשְׂרִים שָׁנָה יוֹאָחָז *Joahaz was a son of twenty-three years*, i.e. twenty-three years old 2 C 36_{2} (||2 K 23_{31} יְהוֹאָחָז *Jehoahaz*). <OBJ> סור hi. *remove* 2 C 36_{2}, לקח *take* 2 C 36_{4} (||2 K 23_{34} יְהוֹאָחָז *Jehoahaz*), בוא hi. *bring* 2 C 36_{4}. <APP> אָח *brother* 2 C 36_{4}.

3. father of Joah, <CSTR> בֶּן־יוֹאָחָז *son of Jehoahaz* 2 C 34_{8}. ⇒ '' *Y*. + אחז *hold*.

יוֹאֵל 19.0.0.3 pr.n.m. **Joel**—I יאל—**1.** firstborn son of Samuel, and father of Kohathite singer Heman, <SUBJ> היה *be* 1 S 8_{2} (וַיְהִי שֶׁם־בְּנוֹ הַבְּכוֹר יוֹאֵל *and the name of his firstborn son was Joel*). <NOM CL> יוֹאֵל הַבְּכֹר *Joel was the firstborn* 1 C 6_{13} (if ins. יוֹאֵל). <CSTR> בֶּן־יוֹאֵל *son of Joel* 1 C 6_{18} 15_{17}. <APP> בֵּן *son* 1 C 6_{18}.

2. descendant of Simeon, perh. son of Joshibiah (if em. וְיֵהוּא *and Jehu* to וְהוּא *and he* [Joel] was the son of Joshibiah), 1 C 4_{35}.

3. Reubenite, <CSTR> בֶּן־יוֹאֵל *son of Joel* 1 C 5_{8}, בְּנֵי *sons of* 1 C 5_{4} (or em. יוֹאֵל בְּנוֹ *Joel was his son*).

4. chief of Gad, <NOM CL> יוֹאֵל הָרֹאשׁ *Joel was the chief* 1 C 5_{12}.

5. chief of Issachar, son of Izrahiah, <NOM CL> בְּנֵי יִזְרַחְיָה ... יוֹאֵל *the sons of Izrahiah were ... Joel* 1 C 7_{3}.

6. one of David's warriors, appar. ident. with יִגְאָל *Igal* at 2 S 23_{36}, <NOM CL> גִּבּוֹרֵי הַחֲיָלִים ... יוֹאֵל *the mighty ones of the armies were ... Joel* 1 C 11_{38}. <APP> אָח *brother* 1 C 11_{38} (or em. אֲחִי *brother of* to בֶּן־ *son of* Nathan).

7. chief of Manasseh, son of Pedaiah, <NOM CL> לַחֲצִי שֵׁבֶט מְנַשֶּׁה יוֹאֵל *(belonging) to the half-tribe of Manasseh was Joel* 1 C 27_{20}. <APP> בֵּן *son* 1 C 27_{20}.

8. member of Nebo family, husband of non-Jewish wife, <NOM CL> מִבְּנֵי נְבוֹ ... יוֹאֵל *of the sons of Nebo were ... Joel* Ezr 10_{43}.

9. Benjaminite, overseer of Jerusalem, son of Zichri, <NOM CL> יוֹאֵל ... פָּקִיד *Joel was ... overseer* Ne 11_{9}.

<APP> בֵּן *son* Ne 11$_{9}$.

10. Levite, son of Azariah, <CSTR> בֶּן־יוֹאֵל *son of Joel* 1 C 6$_{21}$. <APP> בֵּן *son* 1 C 6$_{21}$.

11. Kohathite Levite associated with reforms of Hezekiah, son of Azariah, <SUBJ> בוא *come* 2 C 29$_{12}$, קום *rise* 2 C 29$_{12}$, אסף *gather* 2 C 29$_{12}$, קדשׁ htp. *sanctify oneself* 2 C 29$_{12}$, טהר pi. *cleanse* 2 C 29$_{12}$. <APP> בֵּן *son* 1 C 29$_{12}$, לֵוִי *Levite* 1 C 29$_{12}$.

12. Gershonite Levite, <SUBJ> עלה hi. *bring up* 1 C 15$_{11}$, קדשׁ htp. *sanctify oneself* 1 C 15$_{11}$. <NOM CL> לִבְנֵי גֵרְשׁוֹם יוֹאֵל *(belonging) to the sons of Gershom was Joel* 1 C 15$_{7}$, בְּנֵי לַעְדָּן ... יוֹאֵל *the sons of Ladan were ... Joel* 1 C 23$_{8}$, יוֹאֵל ... עַל־אוֹצְרוֹת בֵּית י׳ *Joel was ... over the treasuries of the house of Y.* 1 C 26$_{22}$. <APP> בֵּן *son* 1 C 26$_{22}$, אָח *brother* 1 C 26$_{22}$, שַׂר *chief* 1 C 15$_{7}$, לֵוִי *Levite* 1 C 15$_{11}$. <PREP> לְ of direction, *to*, + אמר *say* 1 C 15$_{11}$, קרא *call*, i.e. summon 1 C 15$_{11}$.

13. prophet, son of Pethuel, <APP> בֵּן *son* Jl 1$_{1}$. <PREP> אֶל *to*, + היה *be* Jl 1$_{1}$.

14. Seal 681 (T. Beit Mirsim?, 7th/6th cent.).

15. son of Jehucal, <APP> בֵּן *son* Seal 869 (8th cent.). <PREP> לְ of possession, *of, (belonging) to* Seal 869 (8th cent.).

16. son of Jeshua, <APP> בַּר *son* Stamp/Coin 11 (5th cent.).

⇒ י *Y.* + אֵל *God.*

[יוֹאָמָן] 0.0.0.1 pr.n.[m.] **Joaman,** appar. son of Abdi, Seal 172 (7th cent.).

⇒ ״ *Y.* + אמן *be trustworthy.*

[יוֹאֹר] 0.0.0.1 pr.n.[m.] **Joor,** <PREP> לְ of possession, *of, (belonging) to* Seal 249 (8th cent.).

⇒ ״ *Y.* + אוֹר *light.*

יוֹאָשׁ 47 pr.n.m. **Joash**—יֹאָשׁ—**1.** father of Gideon (Jerubbaal), <SUBJ> אמר *say* Jg 6$_{31}$, יצא hi. *bring out* Jg 6$_{30}$. <CSTR> בֶּן־יוֹאָשׁ *son of Joash* Jg 6$_{29}$ 7$_{14}$ 8$_{13.29.32}$, קֶבֶר *tomb of* Jg 8$_{32}$. <APP> אָב *father* Jg 8$_{32}$, אֲבִיעֶזְרִי *Abiezrite* Jg 6$_{11}$. <PREP> לְ of possession, *of, (belonging) to* Jg 6$_{11}$; אֶל *to*, + אמר *say* Jg 6$_{30}$; *against*, + עמד *stand* Jg 6$_{31(Gnz)}$; עַל *against*, + עמד *stand* Jg 6$_{31}$.

2. son of Ahab, <APP> בֵּן *son* 1 K 22$_{26}$||2 C 18$_{25}$ (בֶּן־הַמֶּלֶךְ *son of the king*). <PREP> אֶל *to*, + שׁוב hi. *bring back* 1 K 22$_{26}$||2 C 18$_{25}$.

3. king of Judah, son of Ahaziah and Zibiah, ident. with יְהוֹאָשׁ *Jehoash* at 2 K 12$_{1.2.3.5.7.8.19}$ 14$_{13}$, <SUBJ> היה *be* 2 K 11$_{2}$||2 C 22$_{11}$, אמר *say* 2 C 24$_{4}$, זכר *remember* 2 C 24$_{22}$, עשׂה *do* 2 K 12$_{20}$ 14$_{3}$ 2 C 24$_{2}$ (||2 K 12$_{3}$ יְהוֹאָשׁ *Jehoash*), חדשׁ pi. *repair* 2 C 24$_{4}$, קבץ *gather* 2 C 24$_{4}$, הרג *kill* 2 C 24$_{22}$, מות *die* 2 K 12$_{21}$. <NOM CL> בֶּן־שֶׁבַע שָׁנִים יֹאָשׁ *Joash was a son of seven years*, i.e. seven years old 2 C 24$_{1}$ (||2 K 12$_{1}$ יְהוֹאָשׁ *Jehoash*). <OBJ> לקח *take* 2 K 11$_{2}$||2 C 22$_{11}$, גנב *steal* 2 K 11$_{2}$||2 C 22$_{11}$, נתן *give*, i.e. place 2 K 11$_{2}$||2 C 22$_{11}$ (2 K if ins. וַתִּתֵּן *and she placed*), סתר hi. *hide* 2 K 11$_{2}$||2 C 22$_{11}$, נכה hi. *strike* 2 K 12$_{21}$, קבר *bury* 2 K 12$_{21}$. <CSTR> בֶּן־יוֹאָשׁ *son of Joash* 2 K 14$_{1.17}$||2 C 25$_{25}$ 2 K 14$_{23}$ 25$_{23}$ (||2 K 14$_{13}$ יְהוֹאָשׁ *Jehoash*), לֵב יוֹאָשׁ *heart of Joash* 2 C 24$_{4}$, דִּבְרֵי *deeds of* 2 K 12$_{20}$. <APP> אָב *father* 2 K 14$_{3}$, בֵּן *son* 2 K 11$_{2}$||2 C 22$_{11}$ 2 K 13$_{1}$ 1 C 3$_{11}$ 2 C 25$_{23}$ (or del.), מֶלֶךְ *king* 2 K 13$_{1.10}$ 14$_{1}$ 2 C 24$_{22}$. <PREP> לְ of possession, *of, (belonging) to* 2 K 13$_{1.10}$; of benefit, *for*, + נשׂא *take* wife 2 C 24$_{2}$; עִם *with*, + עשׂה *do* kindness 2 C 24$_{22}$; אֵת *with*, + עשׂה *do* judgment 2 C 24$_{24}$; תַּחַת *instead of*, + מלך *reign* 2 K 12$_{21}$.

4. king of Israel, son of Jehoahaz, ident. with יְהוֹאָשׁ *Jehoash* at 2 K 13$_{10.25}$ 14$_{8.9.11.13.15.16.17}$, <SUBJ> אמר *say* 2 C 25$_{18}$ (||2 K 14$_{9}$ יְהוֹאָשׁ *Jehoash*), הלך *go* 2 C 25$_{17}$, עלה *go up* 2 C 25$_{21}$ (||2 K 14$_{11}$ (יְהוֹאָשׁ), ירד *go down* 2 K 13$_{14}$, שׁלח *send* 2 C 25$_{18}$, שׁוב hi. *bring back* 2 K 13$_{25}$, מלך *reign* 2 K 13$_{9}$, עשׂה *do* 2 K 13$_{12}$, ראה htp. *look at one another* 2 C 25$_{17.21}$, לחם ni. *fight* 2 K 13$_{12}$, נכה hi. *strike* 2 K 13$_{25}$, תפשׂ *seize* 2 C 25$_{23}$ (||2 K 14$_{13}$ (יְהוֹאָשׁ), לקח *take* 2 K 13$_{14}$, בכה *weep* 2 K 13$_{14}$, שׁכב *lie down* 2 K 13$_{13}$, קבר ni. *be buried* 2 K 13$_{13}$. <CSTR> בֶּן־יוֹאָשׁ *son of Joash* 2 K 14$_{23.27}$ Ho 1$_{1}$ Am 1$_{1}$, דִּבְרֵי יוֹאָשׁ *deeds of Joash* 2 K 13$_{12}$, מוֹת *death of* 2 C 25$_{25}$ (||2 K 14$_{17}$ יְהוֹאָשׁ *Jehoash*). <APP> בֵּן *son* 2 K 13$_{9}$ 14$_{1}$ 2 C 25$_{25}$, מֶלֶךְ *king* 2 K 13$_{14}$ 14$_{1.23}$ 2 C 25$_{18.23.25}$. <PREP> לְ of direction, *to*, + אמר *say* 2 K 13$_{14}$; of possession, *of, (belonging) to* 2 K 14$_{1}$; אֶל *to*, + שׁלח *send* 2 C 25$_{17}$ (||2 K 14$_{8}$ (יְהוֹאָשׁ).

4. one of David's warriors, son of Shemaah, <APP> בֵּן *son* 1 C 12$_{3}$.

5. son of Shelah, descendant of Judah, <SUBJ> בעל

be lord 1 C 4_{22}, שׁוב *return* 1 C 4_{22} (if em. וְיָשֻׁבִי לָחֶם *and Jashubi-lahem* to וַיָּשֻׁבוּ בֵית לָחֶם *and they returned to Bethlehem*). <NOM CL> בְּנֵי שֵׁלָה ... וְיוֹאָשׁ *the sons of Shelah were ... and Joash* 1 C 4_{22}.*
⇒ ׳י *Y.*

יוֹב 1 pr.n.m. **Job,** son of Issachar, appar. ident. with יָשׁוּב *Jashub* at Nm 26_{24} 1 C 7_1, <NOM CL> בְּנֵי יִשָּׂשכָר ... יוֹב *the sons of Issachar were ... Job* Gn 46_{13} (or em. יָשׁוּב *Jashub*).
⇒ cf. also אִיּוֹב *Job*.

יוֹבָב 9 pr.n.m. **Jobab, 1.** son of Joktan, grandson of Eber and descendant of Shem, <OBJ> ילד *beget* Gn 10_{29}||1 C 1_{23}.

2. king of Edom, son of Zerah, <SUBJ> מלך *reign* Gn 36_{33}||1 C 1_{44}, מות *die* Gn 36_{34}||1 C 1_{45}. <APP> בֵּן *son* Gn 36_{33}||1 C 1_{44}. <PREP> תַּחַת *instead of*, + מלך *reign* Gn 36_{34}||1 C 1_{45}.

3. king of Madon, <APP> מֶלֶךְ *king* Jos 11_1. <PREP> אֶל *to*, + שׁלח *send* Jos 11_1.

4. Benjaminite, son of Shaharaim and Hodesh, <OBJ> ילד hi. *beget* 1 C 8_9.

5. Benjaminite, son of Elpaal, grandson of Shaharaim, <NOM CL> זְבַדְיָה ... וְיוֹבָב בְּנֵי אֶלְפָּעַל *Zebadiah ... and Jobab were sons of Elpaal* I C 8_{18}.

יוֹבֵל I $_{27.0.25}$ n.m. **ram**—יֹבֵל; pl. יוֹבְלִים (יֹבְלִים), Q יובלות; cstr. Q יבלי; sf. Q יובליהם—**1. ram, ram's horn,** <SUBJ> משׁך *draw out*, i.e. be sounded Ex 19_{13}. <CSTR> קֶרֶן הַיּוֹבֵל *horn of the ram* Jos 6_5, שופרות היובל *trumpets of the ram's horn* 1QM 7_{14}, שׁוֹפְרוֹת הַיּוֹבְלִים *trumpets of the rams' horns* Jos $6_{4.6}$ (יוֹבְלִים) $6_{8.13}$ (הַיֹּבְלִים).

2. Jubilee, i.e. **(year of) remission,** the fiftieth year, inaugurated by blowing of ram's horn; in the Book of Jubilees a period of seven weeks of years, <SUBJ> היה *be* Lv $25_{10.11}$ (both + שָׁנָה *year*) Nm 36_4 (+ לְ *to* Israelites). <NOM CL> יוֹבֵל הִיא *it is a jubilee* Lv 25_{12}(Qr). <OBJ> חיה *live* 2QJub[a] 23_8, שׁלם hi. *complete* 4QJub[f] 23_{11} ([ישלימו]). <CSTR> יובל גמול *jubilee of Gamul* 4QOtot 1.7_{10}, [יובלי עולם] *jubilees of everlastingness*, i.e. everlasting jubilees 4QBer[a] 1.2_{12}, יובלי שנים *jubilees of years* 4QpsJub[c] 2_2 4QpsEzek[c] 3.2_4 (יבלי); שבוע היובל *week of the jubilee* 11QMelch 2_7, שְׁנַת הַיֹּבֵל *year of the jubilee* Lv $25_{13.28.40.50.52.54}$ $27_{17.18.23}$ (all seven הַיֹּבֵל) 27_{24} 4QMishA 2.1_6 ([ש]נת) 11QMelch 2_2, שנת היובלים *year of the jubilees* 4QOtot 1.7_{18}, אות הי[ו]בלים *sign of the jubilees* 4QOtot 1.7_{18}, אתות היובל *signs of the jubilee* 4QOtot 1.5_{16} (אתות הי]ובל) $1.6_{5.12}$ ([אתות היוב]ל) 1.7_8 ([אתות]), סוף היובל *end of the jubilee* 4QOtot 1.6_5 ([סוף]) 1.7_7 ([ה]יו[בל]) 1.7_{16} (היובל]) 11QMelch 2_7 (ס[וף היו]בל) 3_{13} ([סוף ה]יובל), קץ היו[בל] *end of the jubilee* 11QJub 4_{14}, שלמות עשרה יבלי *completion of ten jubilees of* 4QpsEzek[c] 3.2_4. <ADJ> שֵׁנִי *second* 4QOtot 1.5_{16} ([הי]ובל [השני]) 4QMishA 2.1_6, שְׁלִישִׁי *third* 4QOtot 1.6_5 (השל[י]שי) 1.6_5 ([השלישי]), רְבִיעִי *fourth* 4QOtot 1.6_{12} ([היוב]ל), שִׁשִּׁי *sixth* 4QOtot 1.7_7 ([ה]יו[בל הששי]) 1.7_8 ([הששי]), שְׁבִיעִי *seventh* 4QOtot 1.7_{16} (היובל ה]שביעי) 4QpsMos[e] 1_6, שְׁמִינִי *eighth* 11QJub 4_{14} (היו]בל השמיני]), עֲשִׂירִי *tenth* 11QMelch 2_7 ([היו]בל), הוּא *that* 4QpsMos[e] 2.1_3, זֶה *this* 4QpsJub[b] 1_6. <PREP> לְ of time, *on, at* 4QOtot 1.7_{10} ([ליובל]) 4QMishA 4.2_{13}; *according to* CD 16_4 (ספר מחלקות העתים ליוביליהם ובשבועותיהם *book of the division of the times according to their jubilees and weeks*); of possession, *of, (belonging) to* 4QapJoshua[b] 12_5; of benefit, *to, for*, + נתן *give* 4QJub[a] 2_9 ([ויתן] ... [ליובלים]); בְּ of place, time, *in*, + היה *be* 4QpsMos[e] 2.1_3 ([ב]יובל), יצא *go out*, i.e. be released Lv $25_{28.30.31.33}$ 27_{21}, שׁכח *forget* 4QpsMos[e] 1_6, פרר hi. *break* 4QpsMos[e] 2.1_3 ([ב]יובל); מִן *from* 4QJub[b] 3_5; אַחַר *after* Lv 25_{15} 6QapProph 1_3, + קדשׁ hi. *dedicate* Lv 27_{18}. <COLL> + דְּרוֹר *liberty* Lv 25_{10}; [שני]ם יובלים *two jubilees* 4QJub[f] 23_{11}, שלושה יובלים *three jubilees* 2QJub[a] 23_8, ששה יובלי *six jubilees of* 4QpsJub[c] 2_3, תשע[ת ה]יובלים *the nine jubilees* 11QMelch 2_7, עשרה יבלי *ten jubilees of* 4QapJoseph[b] 3.2_4.

Also 4QM[g] 8_3 ([יו]בל) 4QpsJub[b] 2_3 4QapJoseph[b] 9_2 ([י]ובלים) 10_2 11QMelch 3_8 ([הי]ובל).*
⇒ יוֹבֵל II *Jobel*.

[יוֹבֵל] II pr.n.m. **Jobel,** father of Gaal, <CSTR> בֶּן־יוֹבֵל *son of Jobel* Jg 9_{26} (if em. עֶבֶד *Ebed*).
⇒ יוֹבֵל I *ram*.

יוּבַל I $_{1.0.4}$ n.[m.] **stream**—pl. cstr. Q יולבי—(unless

יוֹבֵל *channel,* i.e. ptc. of יבל *bring*), <SUBJ> היה *be* 1QIsa[a] 30$_{25}$. <CSTR> יובלי מים *streams of water* 1QIsa[a] 30$_{25}$ 44$_{4}$ (MT יִבְלֵי *streams of* in both). <PREP> לְ of direction, *to,* + שׁלח *send* 1QH 8$_{7}$ (ליובל[ו]); אֶל *to,* + שׁלח *send* 1QH 8$_{10}$; עַל *beside,* + שׁלח pi. *send* roots Jr 17$_{8}$ (or em. יוּבַל *channel* + מַיִם *water*), צמח *grow* 1QIsa[a] 44$_{4}$.

⇒ יבל *bring.*

[יוּבָל] II 1 pr.n.m. **Jubal**—יוּבָל—son of Lamech and Adah, <SUBJ> היה *be* Gn 4$_{21}$ (+ אָב *father* of those who play lyre and pipe). <NOM CL> שֵׁם אָחִיו יוּבָל *his brother's name was Jubal* Gn 4$_{21}$.

⇒ (?) יבל *bring.*

[יוֹבָנָה] 0.0.0.3 pr.n.[m.] **Jobanah,** appar. father of Menahem, perh. ident. with יהבנה *Jehobanah* on Seals 488 and 771, Seals 197 (Ramat Raḥel) 457 (י[ו]בנה; T. el-Judeideh) 788 (Jerusalem; all three 8th cent.).

⇒ ׳י *Y.* + בנה *build.*

[יוֹד] 0.0.1 n.[m.] **yodh,** the Hebrew letter, appar. in ref. to Y., <CSTR> משפטי יוד *judgments of Yod,* i.e. Y. 4QShir[b] 10$_{12}$ (or em. ידו *of his hand*).*

[יוּדָן] 0.0.0.1 pr.n.m. **Judan, 1.** rabbi, <APP> בֵּן *son* Beth-Shearim tomb inscr. 22, רַבִּי *rabbi* Beth-Shearim tomb inscr. 22. <PREP> לְ of possession, *of, (belonging) to* Beth-Shearim tomb inscr. 22 (שלושת בניו שלרבי יודן *the three sons of Rabbi Judan*).

2. Al-Minya inscr. (HN 118; others חדן *Haddan*).

יוֹזָבָד 11 pr.n.m. **Jozabad, 1.** conspirator against Joash, son of Shimeath, appar. ident. with זָבָד *Zabad* in ||2 C 24$_{26}$, <SUBJ> נכה hi. *strike* 2 K 12$_{22}$ (mss יוֹזָכָר *Jozacar*). <APP> בֵּן *son* 2 K 12$_{22}$.

2. one of David's warriors, <APP> גְּדֵרָתִי *Gederathite* 1 C 12$_{5}$.

3. Manassite chief, supporter of David, <SUBJ> נפל *fall,* i.e. desert 1 C 12$_{21}$ (or em. יוֹזָכָר *Jozacar*).

4. overseer at time of Hezekiah, <NOM CL> יוֹזָבָד ... פְּקִידִים *Jozabad, ... were overseers* 2 C 31$_{13}$.

5. Levite chief in time of Josiah, <SUBJ> רום hi. *present* 2 C 35$_{9}$. <APP> שַׂר *chief* 2 C 35$_{9}$.

6. priest, son of Pashhur, husband of non-Jewish wife, <NOM CL> מִבְּנֵי פַּשְׁחוּר ... יוֹזָבָד *of the sons of Pashhur was ... Jozabad* Ezr 10$_{22}$.

7. Levite, husband of non-Jewish wife, <NOM CL> מִן־הַלְוִיִּם יוֹזָבָד *of the Levites was Jozabad* Ezr 10$_{23}$.

8. Levite, son of Jeshua, <NOM CL> עִמָּהֶם יוֹזָבָד *with them was Jozabad* Ezr 8$_{33}$ (ms יוֹנָדָב *Jonadab*). <APP> בֵּן *son* Ezr 8$_{33}$, לֵוִי *Levite* Ezr 8$_{33}$.

9. Levite, law-interpreter, <SUBJ> בין hi. *explain* Ne 8$_{7}$.

10. Levite, director of temple works, <NOM CL> יוֹזָבָד עַל־הַמְּלָאכָה הַחִיצֹנָה *Jozabad was over the outside work* Ne 11$_{16}$. ⇒ ׳י *Y.* + זבד *endow.*

יוֹזָכָר 1 pr.n.m. **Jozacar, 1.** conspirator against Joash, son of Shimeath, appar. ident. with זָבָד *Zabad* in ||2 C 24$_{26}$, <SUBJ> נכה hi. *strike* 2 K 12$_{22(mss)}$ (L יוֹזָבָד *Jozabad*). <APP> בֵּן *son* 2 K 12$_{22}$.

2. Manassite chief, supporter of David, <SUBJ> נפל *fall,* i.e. desert 1 C 12$_{21}$ (if em. יוֹזָבָד *Jozabad*).

⇒ ׳י *Y.* + זכר *remember.*

[יוֹזָן] 0.0.0.1 pr.n.m. **Jozan,** Seal 371 (8th cent.), <APP> בֵּן *son* Seal 371 (ב[ן]; 8th cent.). <PREP> לְ of possession, *of, (belonging) to* Seal 371 (8th cent.).

⇒ ׳י *Y.* + אזן *hear.*

יוֹחָא 2 pr.n.m. **Joha, 1.** Benjaminite, son of Beriah, <NOM CL> זְבַדְיָה ... וְיוֹחָא בְּנֵי בְרִיעָה *Zebadiah ... and Joha were sons of Beriah* 1 C 8$_{16}$.

2. one of David's warriors, son of Shimri, <NOM CL> גִּבּוֹרֵי הַחֲיָלִים ... יוֹחָא *the mighty men of the armies were ... Joha* 1 C 11$_{45}$. <APP> אָח *brother* 1 C 11$_{45}$, תִּיצִי *Tizite* 1 C 11$_{45}$.

יוֹחָנָן 24.1.3.2 pr.n.m. **Johanan, 1.** son of Kareah, army captain loyal to Gedaliah, <SUBJ> אמר *say* Jr 40$_{13.15}$ 42$_{1}$ 43$_{2}$, דבר *speak* Jr 40$_{16}$, שׁמע *hear* Jr 41$_{11}$ 42$_{1}$ 43$_{4.5}$, הלך *go* Jr 40$_{15}$ 41$_{11.16}$, בוא *come* 2 K 25$_{23}$||Jr 40$_{8}$ Jr 40$_{13}$ 41$_{16}$ 43$_{5}$, שׁוב hi. *bring back* Jr 41$_{16}$ (or em. הֵשִׁיב מֵאֵת *he brought back from* to שָׁבָה אֹתָם *he captured them*), נגשׁ *draw near* Jr

42_1, שׁלח *send* Jr $42_{1.8}$, ישׁב *dwell* 2 K 25_{23}||Jr 40_8 Jr 41_{16} 43_4, שׁאר ni. *remain* Jr 42_1, ירא *fear* 2 K 25_{23}||Jr 40_8 41_{16}, עבד *serve* 2 K 25_{23}||Jr 40_8, מצא *find* Jr 41_{11}, לחם ni. *fight* Jr 41_{11}, נכה hi. *strike* Jr 40_{15}, לקח *take* Jr $41_{11.16}$ 43_5, עשׂה *do* Jr 40_{16} 42_1. <OBJ> ראה *see* Jr 41_{13} 42_1, ענה *answer* Jr 42_1, גלה hi. *exile* Jr 43_2, מות hi. *kill* Jr 43_2. <APP> בֵּן *son* 2 K 25_{23}||Jr 40_8 Jr $40_{13.15.16}$ $41_{11.13.14.15.16}$ $42_{1.8}$ $43_{2.4.5}$. <PREP> לְ of direction, *to*, + אמר *say* 2 K 25_{23}||Jr 40_8, נגד hi. *tell* Jr 42_1, שׁבע ni. *swear* 2 K 25_{23}||Jr 40_8; of benefit, *to, for*, + יטב *be good* 2 K 25_{23}||Jr 40_8 Jr 42_1; introducing object, + אמן hi. *believe* Jr 40_{13}; בְּ *against*, + היה *be* Jr 42_1, סות hi. *incite* Jr 43_2; אֶל *to*, + אמר *say* Jr 40_{16} $42_{1.8}$, קרא *call* Jr 42_8, הלך *go* Jr 41_{14}; אֵת *with* Jr 41_{13}, מִפְּנֵי *from*, + מלט ni. *escape* Jr 41_{15}, בַּעַד *for*, + פלל htp. *pray* Jr 42_1.

2. postexilic high priest, <SUBJ> ילד hi. *beget* Ne 12_{11} (if em. יוֹנָתָן *Jonathan*). <OBJ> ילד hi. *beget* Ne 12_{11} (if em. יוֹנָתָן *Jonathan*). <CSTR> יְמֵי יוֹחָנָן *days of … Johanan* Ne $12_{22.23}$. <APP> בֵּן *son* Ne 12_{23}.

3. son of king Josiah, <NOM CL> הַבְּכוֹר יוֹחָנָן *the first-born was Johanan* 1 C 3_{15}.

4. son of Elioenai, descendant of David, <NOM CL> בְּנֵי אֶלְיוֹעֵינַי … יוֹחָנָן *the sons of Elioenai were … Johanan* 1 C 3_{24}.

5. priest, son of Azariah, <SUBJ> ילד hi. *beget* 1 C 3_{36}. <OBJ> ילד hi. *beget* 1 C 3_{35}.

6. one of David's warriors, 1 C 12_5.

7. one of David's Gadite warriors, <NOM CL> יוֹחָנָן הַשְּׁמִינִי *Johanan was the eighth* 1 C 12_{13}.

8. member of Azgad family, returning exile with Ezra, <NOM CL> מִבְּנֵי עַזְגָּד יוֹחָנָן *of the sons of Azgad was Johanan* Ezr 8_{12}. <APP> בֵּן *son* Ezr 8_{12}.

9. high priest, father of Simeon, <CSTR> בן יוחנן *son of Johanan* Si 50_1.

10. appar. father of Abishai, in deed of sale, <COLL> ירשי אבשי יוחנן *the heirs of Abishai (son of) Johanan* Mur 22 1.1_3.

11. high priest, <APP> כֹּהֵן *priest* Stamp/Coin 49 (4th cent.).

12. son of Josek (others Joseph), <APP> בֵּן *son* Bene Ḥezir tomb inscr. <PREP> לְ of possession, *of, (belonging) to* Bene Ḥezir tomb inscr.

13. prob. Johanan Hyrcanus II, 4QMishC[e] 2_5.

14. perh. Johanan Maccabaeus, <OBJ> יכח hi. *rebuke* 4QRebukes 1.2_3 ([הוכיחו]). <APP> בֵּן *son* 4QRebukes 1.2_3 ([בן מת]תיה *son of Mattathiah*).

⇒ ״ *Y.* + חנן *be gracious*.

יוּטָּה, see יֻטָּה *Juttah*.

יוֹיָדָע 5 pr.n.m. **Joiada, 1.** son of Paseah, repairer of the walls of Jerusalem, <SUBJ> חזק hi. *strengthen*, i.e. repair Ne 3_6, קרה pi. *lay beams* Ne 3_6, עמד hi. *cause to stand*, i.e. place Ne 3_6. <APP> בֵּן *son* Ne 3_6. <PREP> עַל־יַד *beside*, + חזק hi. *strengthen*, i.e. repair Ne 3_6.

2. high priest, son of Eliashib, <SUBJ> ילד hi. *beget* Ne 12_{11}. <OBJ> ילד hi. *beget* Ne 12_{10}. <CSTR> בְּנֵי יוֹיָדָע *sons of Joiada* Ne 13_{28}, … יְמֵי *days of* … Ne 12_{22}. <APP> בֵּן *son* Ne 13_{28}, כֹּהֵן *priest* Ne 13_{28}.

⇒ ״ *Y.* + ידע *know*.

יוֹיָכִין 1 pr.n.m. **Joiachin,** king of Judah, ident. with יְהוֹיָכִין *Jehoiachin* at 2 K $24_{6.8}$||2 C $36_{8.10}$ 2 K $24_{12.15}$ $25_{27.27}$||Jr $52_{31.23}$, יְכָנְיָהוּ *Jeconiah* at Jr 24_1 27_{20} 28_4 29_2 Est 2_6 1 C $3_{16.17}$, and כָּנְיָהוּ *Coniah* at Jr $22_{24.28}$ 37_1, <CSTR> גָּלוּת … יוֹיָכִין *exile of Joiachin* Ezk 1_2. <APP> מֶלֶךְ *king* Ezk 1_2.

⇒ ״ *Y.* + כון *be established*.

יוֹיָקִים 4 pr.n.m. **Joiakim,** high priest, son of Jeshua, ident. with יְהוֹיָקִים *Jehoiakim* at 1 C 9_{10} (if em.), <SUBJ> ילד hi. *beget* Ne 12_{10}. <OBJ> ילד hi. *beget* Ne 12_{10}. <CSTR> בֶּן־יוֹיָקִים *son of Joiakim* Ne 11_{10} (if em. יוֹיָרִיב יָכִין *Joiarib, Jachin* to יוֹיָקִים בֶּן־ *Joiakim son of*), יְמֵי יוֹיָקִים *days of Joiakim* Ne $12_{12.26}$. <APP> בֵּן *son* Ne 11_{10} (if em.; see Cstr.) 12_{26}.

⇒ ״ *Y.* + קום *rise*.

יוֹיָרִיב 5.0.11 pr.n.m. **Joiarib**—Q יירִיב—**1.** head of priestly family, son of Jedaiah, ident. with יְהוֹיָרִיב *Jehoiarib* at 1 C 9_{10}, <CSTR> בֶּן־יוֹיָרִיב *son of Joiarib* Ne 11_{10} (or em. יוֹיָקִים *Joiakim*).

2. head of priestly family, <SUBJ> עלה *go up* Ne 12_6. <PREP> לְ of possession, *of, (belonging) to* Ne 12_{19}.

3. Judahite, son of Zechariah, <CSTR> בֶּן־יוֹיָרִיב *son* *of Joiarib* Ne 11$_5$. <APP> בֵּן *son* Ne 11$_5$.

4. member of Ezra's company, <SUBJ> בין hi. *understand* Ezr 8$_{16}$ (or del.). <PREP> שׁלח לְ *send for* Ezr 8$_{16}$ (or del.).

5. name of priestly course (derived from Jehoiarib at 2 C 24$_7$) and its period of office, <NOM CL> [התשיעי 31] [יירי]ב *the ninth (month), 31 (days), is,* i.e. begins with, *Joiarib* 4QMishA 4.1$_{11}$, [ברביעית] ... יוי[רי]ב *in the fourth (year) is ... Joiarib* 4QMishF^a 1$_5$, השלישית ... יויריב *(in) the third year is ... Joiarib* 4QMishF^b 1$_2$, ... בחו[דש] יויריב *in the (first) month is ... Joiarib* 4QMishF^b 1$_4$. <PREP> בְּ of time, *in, at, during* 4QOtot 7$_2$ (ב[יויריב]) 4QMishA 1.2$_3$ 4.3$_7$ 4.5$_{13}$ (ב[יורי]ב) 4QMishB^a 1.1$_5$ 2.1$_3$ 2.2$_2$ 2.3$_{2.6}$ (ב[יויריב]) 2.3$_9$ ((ב[יויר]יב) 4QMishB^b [ב]יוי[רי]ב). <COLL> בששה יוי[ר]יב *on the sixth of Joiarib* 4QMishB^a 1.2$_7$.

⇒ יְ Y. + ריב *strive.*

[יוֹיָשָׁע] pr.n.[m.] 0.0.0.1 **Joiasha,** Samaria ost. 36 ([יויש]ע) Samaria-Sebaste ost. 1142, <PREP> לְ of possession, *of, (belonging) to* Samaria-Sebaste ost. 1142.

⇒ יְ Y. + ישׁע *save.*

יוֹכֶבֶד 2 pr.n.f. **Jochebed,** Levite, wife of Amran and mother of Aaron, Moses and Miriam, <SUBJ> ילד *bear* Ex 6$_{20}$ Nm 26$_{59}$. <NOM CL> שֵׁם אֵשֶׁת עַמְרָם יוֹכֶבֶד *the name of Amran's wife was Jochebed* Nm 26$_{59}$. <OBJ> לקח *take* as wife Ex 6$_{20}$, ילד *bear* Nm 26$_{59}$. <APP> בַּת *daughter* Nm 26$_{59}$, דּוֹדָה *aunt* Ex 6$_{20}$.

יְ *Y.* + כבד *be heavy.*

יוּכַל 1 pr.n.m. **Jucal,** court official of Zedekiah, son of Shelemiah, ident. with יְהוּכַל *Jehucal* at Jr 37$_3$, <SUBJ> שׁמע *hear* Jr 38$_1$. <APP> בֵּן *son* Jr 38$_1$.

⇒ יְ Y. + יכל *be able.*

[יוֹכִן] 0.0.0.3 pr.n.[m.] **Jochin,** servant of Eliakim, <CSTR> נער יוכן *servant of Jochin* Seals 108 (נ[ע]ר; Beth-Shemesh) 277 (נע]ר]; Ramat Raḥel) 486 (T. Beit Mirsim; all three 8th cent.).

⇒ יְ *Y.* כון *be established.*

יוֹם I 2268.53.525.15 n.m. **day**—I יֹם; cstr. יוֹם (Q, I יֹם); sf. יוֹמָם ,יוֹמוֹ ,יוֹמְךָ; du. יוֹמַיִם (יוֹמָיִם); pl. יָמִים (יָמִם, Q יימים, יָמִין, Q יומים); + ה- of direction יָמִימָה; cstr. יְמֵי (Q יומי), יְמוֹת; sf. יָמַי (יָמָי), יָמֶיךָ (Q ימיכה); יָמַיִךְ ,יָמָיו (Q יומיו, Q ימו), יָמֶיהָ ,יָמֵינוּ ,יְמֵיכֶם ,יְמֵיהֶם (Q ימיהמה).

1. day, as opposed to night, **daytime** (e.g. Gn 1$_5$ 7$_4$ 8$_{22}$ 31$_{39}$ Ex 10$_{13}$ 24$_{18}$ 34$_{28}$ 2 S 3$_{35}$ Is 27$_3$ 62$_6$ Jr 36$_{30}$ Ho 4$_5$ Am 5$_8$ Jon 2$_1$ Jb 17$_{12}$ Est 4$_{16}$).

2. day, of 24 hours (e.g. Gn 1$_{5+5t}$ Lv 15$_{13}$ 1 K 5$_2$ Jon 3$_4$).

3. particular **day,** e.g. sabbath (Ex 16$_{25}$ 20$_8$ 31$_{15}$ 35$_3$ Lv 24$_8$ Nm 15$_{32}$ 28$_9$ Dt 5$_{12}$ Jr 17$_{21}$ Ezk 46$_1$ Ps 92$_1$ Ne 10$_{32}$ 13$_{15.17.19.22}$ 4QOrd^b 3$_2$), day of atonement (Lv 23$_{27}$ 25$_9$ 1QLitPr 1$_6$ 4QOtot 7$_2$ 11QPs^a 27$_8$ 11QT 25$_{11}$), day of first fruits (Nm 28$_{26}$), of trumpet blast (Nm 29$_1$), of new moon (Ezk 46$_1$), of Purim (Est 9$_{28}$); birthday Gn 40$_{20}$ perh. Jb 1$_4$.

4. day of Y., of judgment, etc. (e.g. Is 2$_{12}$ 3$_{14}$ [if em.] 10$_3$ 13$_6$ 22$_5$ Ezk 7$_{19}$ 13$_5$ 30$_3$ Jl 1$_{15}$ Am 5$_{18}$ Ob$_{15}$ Zp 1$_7$ Zc 14$_1$ Ml 3$_{23}$).

5. day, as a particular point in time (e.g. Gn 3$_5$ 4$_{14}$ 5$_1$ 7$_{13}$ 15$_{18}$ 17$_{23}$ 19$_{37}$ 22$_4$ 26$_{32}$ 30$_{35}$ 33$_{16}$ Ex 2$_{18}$ 5$_6$ 14$_{13}$ 32$_{28}$ Lv 9$_4$ 12$_3$ 13$_5$ 16$_{30}$ Nm 7$_1$ Jos 4$_9$ 1 S 1$_4$ 2 S 1$_2$ 1 K 1$_{25}$ 2 K 3$_6$ Is 2$_{11}$ Jr 1$_{10}$ Ps 2$_7$ Jb 1$_6$ Est 1$_{10}$ Siloam tunnel inscr.$_3$).

6. day, as part of a date (e.g. Gn 7$_{11}$ 8$_3$ Ex 12$_{18}$ 16$_1$ Lv 23$_6$ Nm 9$_3$ 28$_{16}$ 29$_{12}$ 33$_3$ Jos 5$_{10}$ 1 K 12$_{32}$ Ezk 45$_{21}$ Hg 1$_1$ Zc 1$_7$ Est 3$_{12}$ Dn 10$_4$ Ezr 10$_{16}$ 2 C 7$_{10}$).

7. pl. **days** of life, **lifespan** (e.g. Gn 3$_{14.17}$ 5$_{4+9t}$ 6$_3$ 9$_{29}$ 10$_{25}$ 11$_{32}$ 14$_1$ 25$_7$ 26$_1$ 35$_{28}$ 47$_{28}$ Ex 20$_{12}$ 1 S 7$_{13}$ 17$_{12}$ 25$_{28}$ 1 K 1$_6$ 3$_{11}$ 5$_1$ 2 K 8$_{20}$ Is 1$_1$ 7$_1$ Jr 1$_2$ 35$_1$ Ho 1$_1$ Am 1$_1$ Mc 1$_1$ Zp 1$_1$ Zc 14$_5$ Ps 103$_{15}$ 116$_2$ Jb 7$_1$ 14$_1$ 32$_7$ Ne 8$_{17}$ 1 C 1$_{19}$ 2 C 1$_{11}$ 13$_{20}$ Si 46$_{1.7}$ 48$_{18}$ 1QSa 1$_7$).

8a. sg. **day, time** (e.g. Gn 6$_{5}$).

8b. pl. **days, time** (e.g. Gn 6$_{4}$ 27$_{41}$ 29$_{21}$ Ex 2$_{11}$ Nm 13$_{20}$ Dt 4$_{32}$ Jos 3$_{15}$ 1 S 2$_{31}$ 7$_{2}$ Is 7$_{17}$ Ec 7$_{10}$); specified period of time (e.g. Gn 41$_{1}$ Dt 2$_{14}$ Jg 19$_{2}$ 2 S 13$_{23}$ 1 K 2$_{11}$ 14$_{20}$ Jr 28$_{3.11}$); unspecified period of time (e.g. Gn 4$_{3}$ 24$_{55}$ 26$_{8}$ 38$_{12}$ 40$_{4}$ Nm 9$_{22}$ Dt 1$_{19}$ Jg 11$_{4}$ 14$_{8}$ 15$_{1}$ 1 K 17$_{7}$ Is 32$_{10}$ Dn 11$_{33}$ Ne 1$_{4}$).

9. pl. יָמִים **year** (e.g. Lv 25$_{29}$ Jg 17$_{10}$ 1 S 1$_{21}$ 2$_{19}$ 20$_{6}$ 27$_{7}$ 29$_{3}$ [זֶה־יָמִים אוֹ־זֶה שְׁנָתַיִם *a year or two years*; if em. שָׁנִים days or *years* to שְׁנָתַיִם] 2 S 14$_{26}$ 2 C 21$_{19}$ [or em.; see Cstr.]); מִיָּמִים יָמִימָה *from year to year* (Ex 13$_{10}$ Jg 11$_{40}$ 21$_{19}$ 1 S 1$_{3}$ 2$_{19}$ 4QCommGenD 3$_{2}$).

<SUBJ> היה *be* Gn 1$_{5+5t}$ 5$_{4+9t}$ 6$_{3}$ 9$_{29}$ 11$_{32}$ 35$_{28}$ 47$_{9.28}$ Ex 12$_{14}$ Lv 25$_{8}$ Nm 29$_{1}$ 1 S 1$_{4}$ 14$_{1}$ 27$_{7}$ 2 S 24$_{13}$ 2 K 4$_{8.11.18}$ Is 56$_{12}$ Jr 20$_{14}$ 33$_{20}$ (if em.; see Coll.) Zc 14$_{7}$ Ps 109$_{8}$ Jb 1$_{6.13}$ 2$_{1}$ 3$_{4}$ Ec 7$_{10}$ 4QpsJub^{a} 2.2$_{12}$ ([ויהי]ו) 11QT 17$_{3}$ (והי[ה]) 19$_{7}$ (היו[ם]) 25$_{10}$ 27$_{5.8}$, רבה *be many* Gn 38$_{12}$ Dt 11$_{21.21}$ 1 S 7$_{2}$ Pr 9$_{11}$, בוא *come* 1 S 2$_{31}$ 26$_{10}$ 2 K 20$_{17}$||Is 39$_{6}$ Is 3$_{14}$ (if em. עַמִּים: *peoples* to יוֹם : עַמּוֹ *his people. The day of* Y. *comes*) 13$_{9}$ Jr 7$_{32}$ 9$_{24}$ 16$_{14}$ 19$_{6}$ 23$_{5.7}$ 30$_{3}$ 31$_{27.31.38(Qr)}$ 33$_{14}$ 46$_{21}$ 47$_{4}$ 48$_{12}$ 49$_{2}$ 51$_{47.52}$ 50$_{31}$ Ezk 7$_{10}$ 21$_{30.34}$ Ho 9$_{7.7}$ Jl 1$_{15}$ 2$_{1.2.2}$ 3$_{4}$ Am 4$_{2}$ 8$_{11}$ 9$_{13}$ Mc 7$_{4}$ (if em. בָּאָה *it* [f.] *has come* to בָּא *it* [m.] *has come*) Zp 2$_{2}$ (perh. יוֹם II *wind*) 14$_{1}$ Ml 3$_{19.19.23}$ Ps 37$_{13}$ Ec 2$_{16}$ 12$_{1}$ 4QpsEzek^{a} 1$_{2}$ CD 7$_{11}$, קרב *draw near* Gn 27$_{41}$ 47$_{29}$ Dt 31$_{14}$ 1 K 2$_{1}$ Ezk 12$_{23}$, נגע hi. *draw near* Ezk 7$_{12}$, קדם pi. *come before* Jb 20$_{27}$, נשׂג hi. *attain to* Gn 47$_{9}$, אחז *take hold of* Jb 30$_{16}$, עבר *pass* Gn 50$_{4}$ Zp 2$_{2}$ (or em. עָבַר יוֹם *a day has passed* to עֹבֵר chaff *passes*; or perh. יוֹם II *wind*) Ps 144$_{4}$ Jb 17$_{11}$, קלל *be swift* Jb 7$_{6}$ 9$_{25}$, מהר pi. *hasten* 4QpsEzek^{a} 3$_{3}$, בהל htp. *hasten* 4QpsEzek^{a} 3$_{2}$, נקף hi. *go round* Jb 1$_{5}$, שׁבת *cease* Gn 8$_{22}$, פנה *turn*, i.e. decline Jr 6$_{4}$ Ps 90$_{9}$, ערב *be evening* Pr 7$_{9}$ (if em.; see Cstr.), חמם *be hot* Gn 18$_{1}$ 1 S 11$_{11}$ 2 S 4$_{5}$, נפל *fall*, i.e. be void Nm 6$_{12}$, ירד *go down* Jg 19$_{11}$ Arad ost. 40$_{11}$ ([י]רד), נטה *decline* Jg 19$_{8}$, חנה *decline* Jg 19$_{9}$, רפה *be weak*, i.e. wane Jg 19$_{9}$, חשׁך *be dark* Ezk 30$_{18}$, קדר *be dark* Mc 3$_{6}$.

עשׂה ni. *be done*, i.e. kept Est 9$_{28}$, יצר pu. *be formed* Ps 139$_{16}$ (or em. יָמִים יֻצָּרוּ *days were formed* to יוֹם יוֹם יֻצָּרוּ *day by day they were formed*), כון ni. *be established* Jb 15$_{32}$, חרץ pass. *be decided* Jb 14$_{5}$, חתך ni. *be determined* 4QCommGenA 1$_{2}$, צפן pass. *be treasured*, i.e. fixed 4QapPs^{b} 31$_{6}$, מלא *be fulfilled* Gn 25$_{24}$ 29$_{21}$ 50$_{3.3}$ Lv 8$_{33}$ 12$_{4.6}$ Nm 6$_{5.13}$ 1 S 18$_{26}$ 2 S 7$_{12}$||1 C 17$_{11}$ Jr 25$_{34}$ Ezk 5$_{2}$ Lm 4$_{18}$ Est 1$_{5}$ 2$_{12}$ Dn 10$_{3}$ 1QS 7$_{21}$ 8$_{27}$ 4QD^{f} 2$_{13}$ 4QRitMar 102$_{1}$ 4QRitPur 11.10$_{2}$ (במילא[ת) CD 10$_{1}$, ni. *be fulfilled* Ex 7$_{25}$, כלה *be finished* Jr 20$_{18}$ Ps 102$_{4}$ (or em. מֵעַי *my innards*, or מִימַי *my [bodily] tumours*) Jb 7$_{6}$, תמם *be finished* Dt 34$_{8}$, שׁלם *be complete* Is 60$_{20}$ 4QTobit^{e} 4$_{1}$ 4QpsEzek^{a} 13.2$_{2}$ 4QMMT A$_{21}$, ארך *be long* Gn 26$_{8}$ Ezk 12$_{22}$, hi. *be long* Ex 20$_{12}$ Dt 5$_{16}$ 25$_{15}$, משׁך ni. *be prolonged* Is 13$_{22}$, מעט *be few* CD 10$_{9}$, ילד *bear* Pr 27$_{1}$, אנשׁ pass. *be incurable*, i.e. disastrous Jr 17$_{16}$, ברך pass. *be blessed* Jr 20$_{14}$, ארר pass. *be cursed* Jr 20$_{14.14}$, אבד *perish* Jb 3$_{3}$, זעך ni. *be extinguished* Jb 17$_{1}$ (or em. זעך to עזב ni. *be abandoned*; mss דעך ni. *be extinguished*), ירא ni. *be feared* Jl 3$_{4}$ Ml 3$_{23}$, בעת pi. *terrify* Jb 3$_{5}$, בער *burn* Ml 3$_{19}$, להט pi. *blaze* Ml 3$_{19}$, פוח *breathe* Ca 2$_{17}$ 4$_{6}$ (both perh. יוֹם II *wind*), אמר *speak* Jb 32$_{7}$, נבע hi. *pour out* Ps 19$_{3}$, זכר ni. *be remembered* Est 9$_{28}$, כתב pass. *be written* Ps 139$_{16}$, יעד pass. *be appointed* 1QM 1$_{10}$.

<NOM CL> הֶבֶל יָמָי *my days are a breath* Jb 7$_{16}$, צֵל יָמֵינוּ *our days are a shadow* Jb 8$_{9}$, הַיָּמִים יְמֵי בִּכּוּרֵי עֲנָבִים *the time was the time of the firstfruits of grapes* Nm 13$_{20}$, י[ו]ם [הכפו]רים ה[וא]ה ס[וף היו]בל העשירי *the day of atonement is the end of the tenth jubilee* 11QMelch 2$_{7}$, שַׁבָּת הַיּוֹם *today is a sabbath* Ex 16$_{25}$, sim. Ex 20$_{10}$ Dt 5$_{14}$, היום מועדו *today is his appointed time* 1QM 17$_{5}$, הַיּוֹם הַזֶּה יוֹם בְּשֹׂרָה הוּא *this day is a day of good news* 2 K 7$_{9}$, יוֹם עֶבְרָה הַיּוֹם הַהוּא *that day is a day of wrath* Zp 1$_{15}$, יום מלחמה היום הזה *this day is a day of war* 1QM 15$_{12}$ (יום corrected to מועד *appointed time of*), יוֹם־צָרָה וְתוֹכֵחָה וּנְאָצָה הַיּוֹם הַזֶּה *this day is a day of distress and rebuke and contempt* 2 K 19$_{3}$||Is 37$_{3}$, הֲלֹא־חֹשֶׁךְ יוֹם י׳ *is not the day of* Y. *darkness?* Am 5$_{20}$, גוית שם ימי אין מספר *the body of the name is days (of) without number*, i.e. eternal Si 37$_{25(Dmg)}$, טובת חי ימי מספר *the goodness of a life is (measured in) days of (great) number*, or *the good things of life last only for days that can be numbered* Si 41$_{13(B)}$, sim. 41$_{13(B)}$.

הַיָּמִים ... שְׁלֹשִׁים וּשְׁמֹנֶה שָׁנָה *the time was ... thirty-eight years* Dt 2$_{14}$, sim. 1 K 2$_{11}$ 11$_{42}$ 14$_{20}$ 2 K 10$_{36}$ Ps 90$_{10}$ 1 C 29$_{27}$, יְמֵי שְׁנֵי מְגוּרַי שְׁלֹשִׁים וּמְאַת שָׁנָה *the days of the years of my sojourning are a hundred and thirty years* Gn 47$_{9}$, שְׁלֹשֶׁת יָמִים הֵם *they are three days* Gn 40$_{12.18}$, עוֹד הַיּוֹם

גָּדוֹל *the day is still great*, i.e. it is still daylight Gn 297, גָּדוֹל הַיּוֹם הַהוּא *that day is great* Jr 307, sim. Ho 22 Jl 211, קָרוֹב הַיּוֹם *the day is near* Ezk 77, sim. Dt 3235 Ezk 303, קָרוֹב יוֹם י׳ *the day of Y. is near* Is 136 Jl 115 414 Ob15 Zp 17.14, sim. Ezk 303, טוֹב יוֹם בַּחֲצֵרֶיךָ מֵאָלֶף *a day in your courts is better than a thousand (elsewhere)* Ps 8411, הלוא טוב יום אחד ... מעשר[ה] *is not one day better ... than ten?* 4Q185 1.25, sim. 4QsapHymn 1,23, טוֹב ... יוֹם הַמָּוֶת מִיּוֹם הִוָּלְדוֹ *better is ... the day of death than the day of his birth* Ec 71, למה מיו[ם יום] *why is one day (better) than another?* Si 367(Segal), כָּל־יְמֵי עָנִי רָעִים *all the days of the afflicted one are evil* Pr 1515, הַיּוֹם קָדוֹשׁ הוּא לי׳ *today is holy to Y.* Ne 89, vars. Ne 810.11.

יוֹם לי׳ *there is a day to Y.*, i.e. Y. has a day Is 212, sim. Is 225 348 Jr 4610 Ps 7416, יָמִים רַבִּים לְיִשְׂרָאֵל לְלֹא אֱלֹהֵי אֱמֶת *Israel had many days without the true God* 2 C 153, יוֹם נָקָם בְּלִבִּי *a day of vengeance was in my heart* Is 634, בא במעוזיה יום הזכרון *on the 4th of Maaziah is a day of memorial* 4QMishA 4.36, sim. 4.37 4.42.3 4.55.6 4.61 4Q MishBa 2.22 2.31 ([י]ום), בו יום הריב *on it is the day of dispute* 4QMystb 92, בְּכָל־מְדִינָה וּמְדִינָה ... יוֹם טוֹב *in every province ... it was a good day*, i.e. a day of feasting Est 817, כִּימֵי הָעֵץ יְמֵי עַמִּי *the days of my people are as the days of a tree* Is 6522, כִּימֵי שָׂכִיר יָמָיו *his days are as the days of a hired servant* Jb 71, sim. Jb 105.5, יָמַי כְּצֵל *my days are like a shadow* Ps 10212, var. 1 C 2915 4QAdmon 1.25, כֶּחָצִיר יָמָיו *his days are as grass* Ps 10315, מֵעֵת הוּסַר הַתָּמִיד ... יָמִים *from the time when the continual burnt offering is removed ... there will be* one thousand two hundred and ninety *days* Dn 1211.

כַּמָּה יְמֵי שְׁנֵי חַיַּי *how many are the days of the years of my life?* 2 S 1935, כַּמָּה יְמֵי *how many are the days of?* Gn 478 Ps 11984, הֲלֹא־מְעַט יָמַי *are not my days few?* Jb 1020 (or em.; see Cstr.), מה מצער ימיך *your days are few* Si 3032, מה יומו *what is his day?*, i.e how will it be? Si 911, הִנֵּה הַיּוֹם *here is the day* 1 S 245 Ezk 710, לָמָּה־זֶּה לָכֶם יוֹם י׳ *why would you have the day of Y.?* Am 518, יום גדול *it is a great day* 1QS 104, הוּא הַיּוֹם *it is the day* Ezk 398 CD 82 1915, sim. 1QM 110 11QMelch 215, יוֹם הַכִּפֻּרִים הוּא *it is the day of atonement* Lv 2327 11QT 2511, var. 2328, הואה יום הזכרון *it is the day of memorial* 4QMishBa 2.22 2.26 ([הואה יו]ם) 2.31 ([הואה י]ום [הזכרון]) 2.35 (הואה יו[ם] [הזכרון]) 2.39 ([הזכר]ון) 11QMelch 27 (י]ום [הכפ]ורים), ה[וא יו]ם שבעה עשר *it is a day*, i.e. in that day Mc 712, יוֹם הוּא *it is the fourteenth day* 4QCommGenA 110, sim. 4Q CommGenA 113.19, זֶה הַיּוֹם *this is the day* Jg 414 Ps 11824 Lm 216, יום רביעי [ב]מלכיה זה אחד בחודש העשירי *the fourth day of Malchijah is the first (day) of the tenth month* 4QMishCd 1.23, אֵלֶּה יְמֵי *these are the days of* Gn 257, יֵשׁ־יוֹם *there is a day* Jr 316, לֹא יוֹם *it is not a day* Zc 147, עוֹד אַרְבָּעִים יוֹם *there are yet forty days* Jon 34.

<OBJ> רבה hi. *increase* Jb 2918, בוא hi. *bring* Is 717 Jr 1718 Lm 121, קרב hi. *bring near* Ezk 224, קום pi. *confirm* Est 931, קרא *call* Is 612 Lm 121, i.e. name Gn 15 Is 585, ברך pi. *bless* Gn 23 Ex 2011, קדשׁ pi. *sanctify* Gn 23 Ex 2011 Dt 512 Jr 1722.24.27 Ne 1322 11QT 278 CD 1017, חדשׁ pi. *renew* Lm 521, יעד *appoint* 1QM 1314, נגד *tell (concerning)* 4QJuba 220 ([אגיד]), ראה *see* Lm 216, חזה *see* Jb 241, ידע *know* Gn 272 Ps 3718, חשׁב pi. *consider* Ps 776, זכר *remember* Ex 133 208 Dt 163 327 Is 6311 Ezk 1622.43 2319 Ps 1377 1435 Ec 519 Ec 118, בחר *choose* Is 585, רצה *accept* Jb 146, קבל pi. *take* 1 C 2112, אהב *love* Ps 3413, אוה htp. *desire* Jr 1716 Am 518, אוץ *desire* or hasten Jr 1716 (if em. אַצְתִּי מֵרֹעֶה *I have* not *run from being a shepherd* to אַצְתִּי יוֹם רָעָה *I have* not *hastened the day of evil*), קוה pi. *wait for* Lm 216, נשׂג hi. *attain to* Gn 479, מצא *find* Lm 216, גאל *reclaim* Jb 34, דרשׁ *seek* Jb 34, נתן *give* Ezk 45 Ps 396 Ec 815.

עשׂה *do*, i.e. keep Dt 515 Est 917+7t 2 C 3023.23, spend Ec 612,* שׁמר *keep* Ex 1217 Dt 512 4QJubc 227 ([ישמר]ו) CD 618 1017, מלא pi. *fill* Ex 2326 Is 6520 4QBéat 14.213, כלה pi. *complete* Ezk 48 4327 Ps 789 Jb 2113(Qr) 3611, שׁלם hi. *complete* CD 1010 11QT 458, בלה pi. *consume* Jb 2113(Kt), ברא *create* Jr 3325 (if em. אִם־לֹא בְרִיתִי יוֹמָם וָלָיְלָה *if my covenant is not*, i.e. does not persist, *by day and [by] night* to אִם־לֹא בָרָאתִי יוֹם וָלָיְלָה *if I had not*, or, *surely I have, created day and night*), נזר hi. *spend* day *as a Nazirite* Nm 612, שׁאל *ask* 1 K 311‖2 C 111, ספר *count* Lv 1513.28 2316 Ezk 4426 11QT 1813 1913 2113.14 4515, מנה *count* Ps 9012, יסף hi. *add* Ps 617 Pr 1027, חצה *divide* Ps 5224, כול pilp. *endure* Ml 32, ארך hi. *prolong* Dt 426.40 533 119 1720 227=11QT 655 Dt 3018 3247 Jos 2431 Jg 27 1 K 314 Is 5310 Pr 2816 Ec 813 11QT 5921, קצר pi. *shorten* Ps 10315 Si 3024, hi. *shorten* Ps 8946, פקד *visit*, i.e. punish Ho 2$_{15}$, חשך hi. *darken* Am 5$_{8}$, ארר *curse* Jb 3$_{8}$ (or em. יָם *sea*),* קלל pi. *curse* Jb 3$_{1}$, חלל pi. *defile* Ne 13$_{17}$, בעת pi. *terrify* Jb 3$_{4}$.

<CSTR> יוֹם י׳ *day of Y.* Is 3$_{14}$ (if em. עַמִּים: *peoples* to עַמּוֹ: יוֹם *his people. The day of* Y. comes)* 13$_{6.9}$ Ezk 13$_{5}$ Jl 1$_{15}$ 2$_{1.11}$ 3$_{4}$ 4$_{14}$ Am 5$_{18.18.20}$ Ob$_{15}$ Zp 1$_{7.14.14}$ Ml 3$_{23}$, מַלְכֵּנוּ *of our king* Ho 7$_{5}$, אָחִיךָ *of your brother* Ob$_{12}$ (or em. בְּיוֹם־אָחִיךָ *at the day of your brother* to בְּמוֹ אָחִיךָ/ בְּאָחִיךָ *at your brother*), מְצַפֶּיךָ *of your watchers* Mc 7$_{4}$.

יְמֵי אֱנוֹשׁ *days of a mortal* Jb 10$_{5}$, גָּבֶר *of a man* Jb 10$_{5}$, פְּלִשְׁתִּים *of the Philistines* Jg 15$_{20}$, אָבִיו ... *of his father* Gn 26$_{15.18}$, אֲבֹתֵינוּ *of our fathers* Ezr 9$_{7}$, אֲבֹתֵיכֶם *of your fathers* Jl 1$_{2}$ Ml 3$_{7}$, בֶּן־ ... *of the son of* Ne 8$_{17}$ (בִּן־) 12$_{23.26}$ 2 C 30$_{26}$ 4QMMT C$_{18}$, בְּנוֹ *of his son* 1 K 21$_{29}$, בְּנֵיכֶם *of your sons* Dt 11$_{21}$, עֶבֶד *of a servant* Ps 119$_{84}$, שָׂכִיר *of a hired servant* Lv 25$_{50}$ Jb 7$_{1}$, עַמִּי *of my people* Is 65$_{22}$, מֶלֶךְ *of a king* Is 23$_{15}$ Ps 61$_{7}$, מֶלֶךְ ... *of the king of* Ezr 4$_{5}$ 1 C 4$_{41}$ 5$_{17.17}$ 2 C 30$_{26}$, מַלְכֵי *of the kings of* 2 K 23$_{22}$ Ne 9$_{32}$, הַזְּקֵנִים *of the elders* Jos 24$_{31}$ Jg 2$_{7}$, הַפֶּחָה ... *of the governor* Ne 12$_{26}$, הַשּׁוֹפֵט *of the judge* Jg 2$_{18}$, הַשֹּׁפְטִים *of the judges* 2 K 23$_{22}$, הַכֹּהֵן ... *of the priest* Ne 12$_{26}$, הַסּוֹפֵר ... *of the scribe* Ne 12$_{26}$, תְּמִימִם *of the blameless ones* Ps 37$_{18}$, רָשָׁע *of the wicked one* Jb 15$_{20}$, עָנִי *of the afflicted one* Pr 15$_{15}$, יוֹם רָעָה *day of evil* Jr 17$_{16}$ (if em. מֵרֹעֶה *from being a shepherd*).*

יְמֵי *days of*, + pr.n. Abijah 2 C 13$_{20}$, Abraham Gn 26$_{1.15.18}$ 4QpsJub^{a} 2.2$_{12}$, Adam Gn 5$_{4.5}$, Ahaz Is 1$_{1}$, Amraphel Gn 14$_{1}$, Ahasuerus Est 1$_{1}$, Ahaz Is 7$_{1}$, Artaxerxes Ezr 4$_{7}$, Asa 1 K 22$_{47}$, Asaph Ne 12$_{46}$, Cyrus Ezr 4$_{5}$, David 2 S 21$_{1}$ 1 K 2$_{1}$ Ne 12$_{46}$ 1 C 7$_{2}$, Eliashib Ne 12$_{22}$, Enoch Gn 5$_{23}$, Enosh Gn 5$_{11}$, Esarhaddon Ezr 4$_{2}$, Ezra Ne 12$_{26}$, Gideon Jg 8$_{28}$, Hezekiah Is 1$_{1}$ Jr 26$_{18}$ 1 C 4$_{41}$ 2 C 32$_{26}$, Isaac Gn 35$_{28}$ 4QpsJub^{a} 2.2$_{12}$, Israel Gn 47$_{29}$, Jaddua Ne 12$_{22}$, Jael Jg 5$_{6}$, Jacob Gn 47$_{28}$ 4QpsJub^{a} 2.2$_{12}$, Jared Gn 5$_{20}$, Jehoahaz 2 K 13$_{22}$, Jehoiada 2 C 24$_{14}$, Jehoiakim Jr 1$_{3}$ 35$_{1}$ Ne 12$_{12.26}$, Jeroboam Ho 1$_{1}$ Am 1$_{1}$ 1 C 5$_{17}$ 4QMMT C$_{19}$ (י]מי יר[ובעם), Johanan Ne 12$_{22.23}$, Joiada Ne 12$_{22}$, Joshua Jos 24$_{31}$ Jg 2$_{7}$ Ne 8$_{17}$ 12$_{7}$, Josiah Jr 1$_{2}$ 3$_{6}$ Jr 36$_{2}$ Zp 1$_{1}$, Jotham Is 1$_{1}$ Mc 1$_{1}$ 1 C 5$_{17}$, Kenan Gn 5$_{14}$, Lamech Gn 5$_{31}$, Levi 4QpsJub^{a} 2.2$_{12}$ (לו[י]), Mahalalel Gn 5$_{17}$, Methuselah Gn 5$_{27}$, Moses Si 46$_{7}$, Nehemiah Ne 12$_{26.47}$, Noah Gn 9$_{29}$ Is 54$_{9}$ (if em. כִּי מֵי *for the water of* to כִּימֵי *as the days of*), Pekah 2 K 15$_{29}$, Samuel 1 S 7$_{13}$ 2 C 35$_{18}$, Saul 1 S 17$_{12}$ 1 C 5$_{10}$ 13$_{3}$, Seth Gn 8$_{8}$, Shamgar Jg 5$_{6}$, Solomon 1 K 5$_{5}$ 10$_{21}$||2 C 9$_{20}$ 1 K 11$_{25}$ 2 C 30$_{26}$ 4QpsEzek^{b} 1.2$_{8}$ ([שלמה]) 4QMMT C$_{18}$, Terah Gn 11$_{32}$, Uzziah Is 1$_{1}$ Ho 1$_{1}$ Am 1$_{1}$ Zc 14$_{5}$, Zechariah 2 C 26$_{5}$, Zerubbabel Ne 12$_{47}$.

יְמֵי חַיֵּי *days of the life of* Ec 6$_{12}$ 9$_{9}$ 2QJub^{b} 46$_{1}$ ([ימי חיי]), חַיַּי *of my life* Ps 23$_{6}$ (חַיָּי) 27$_{4}$ 4QJub^{g} 25$_{9}$ (חיא corrected to חי׳), חַיֶּיךָ *of your life* Gn 3$_{14.17}$ Dt 4$_{9}$ 6$_{2}$ 16$_{3}$ Jos 1$_{5}$ Ps 128$_{5}$ Si 3$_{12}$ 4QTobit^{e} 2$_{4}$ (חן[ייכה]), חַיָּיו *of his life* Dt 17$_{19}$ Jos 4$_{14}$ 1 S 1$_{11}$ 7$_{15}$ 1 K 5$_{1}$ 11$_{34}$ 15$_{5.6}$ 2 K 25$_{29.30}$||Jr 52$_{33.34}$ (2 K 25$_{30}$ חַיָּו) Ec 5$_{17}$ (חַיָּו; Gnz חַיָּיו) 5$_{19}$ 8$_{15}$ Si 3$_{13}$, חַיֶּיהָ *of her life* Pr 31$_{12}$ (mss חַיֶּיהָ) 4QJub^{h} 36$_{23}$ (י[מ]י) 11QT 57$_{18}$, חַיֵּינוּ *of our life* Is 38$_{20}$, חַיֵּיהֶם *of their life* Ec 2$_{3}$ 4QpsEzek^{a} 34$_{2}$, יְמֵי חֶלְדִּי *days of my lifespan* Jb 10$_{20}$ (if em. יָמַי יֶחְדָּל appar. *my days, let it cease*), יְמֵי שָׁנָה *days of the year* Jb 3$_{6}$ 1QM 2$_{4}$ (השנה) 11QPs^{a} 27$_{6}$ (השנה), שְׁנֵי *of the years of* Gn 25$_{7}$ 47$_{8.9.9.9}$ 2 S 19$_{35}$, שָׁנָיו *of his years* Ec 6$_{3}$ 2 C 21$_{19}$ (if em. לְיָמִים שְׁנַיִם *of two years* to יְמֵי שָׁנָיו), שְׁנוֹתֵינוּ *of our years* Ps 90$_{10}$, יְמֵי מְגוּרֵיהֶם *days of their sojourning* Gn 47$_{9}$, נְעוּרַיִךְ *of your youth* Ezk 16$_{22}$ (נְעוּרָיִךְ) 16$_{43.60}$ (נְעוּרָיִךְ), נְעוּרֶיהָ *of her youth* Ezk 23$_{19}$ Ho 2$_{17}$, עֲלוּמָיו *of his youth* Ps 89$_{46}$ Jb 33$_{25}$, בְּחוּרוֹתֶךָ *of your youth* Ec 11$_{9}$ 12$_{1}$ (בְּחוּרֹתֶיךָ), יום הבריאה *day of creation* 4QpsJub^{a} 1$_{7}$ 11QT 29$_{9}$ (הבריה), ימי מלכתו *days of its kingdom* 4QpsMose^{e} 1$_{4}$, ממשלת *of the dominion of* 1QS 2$_{19}$ (יומי), ממשלתו *of his dominion* 4QpsHod^{b} 1$_{4}$.

יוֹם צָרָה *day of distress* Jr 16$_{19}$ Ob$_{12.14}$ Na 1$_{7}$ Hb 3$_{16}$ Ps 20$_{2}$ 50$_{15}$ Pr 24$_{10}$ (or em.; see Prep.) 25$_{19}$ Si 3$_{15(A)}$ 6$_{8}$ 51$_{10.12}$ 4QapPs^{a} 7.1$_{3}$, צָרָתִי *of my distress* Gn 35$_{3}$ Ps 77$_{3}$ 86$_{7}$, צָרָה וּמְצוּקָה *of distress and anguish* Zp 1$_{15}$, צָרָה וְתוֹכֵחָה וּנְאָצָה *of distress and rebuke and contempt* 2 K 19$_{3}$||Is 37$_{3}$, תּוֹכֵחָה *of rebuke* Ho 5$_{9}$, מְהוּמָה וּמְבוּסָה וּמְבוּכָה *of discomfiture and trampling and confusion* Is 22$_{5}$, אֵיד *of calamity* Jb 21$_{30}$, אֵידִי *of my calamity* 2 S 22$_{19}$||Ps 18$_{19}$ 4QapPs^{b} 24$_{7}$ (א[ידי]), אֵידֶךָ *of your calamity* Pr 27$_{10}$, אֵידוֹ *of his calamity* Ob$_{13.13}$, אֵידָם *of their calamity* Dt 32$_{35}$ Jr 18$_{17}$ 46$_{21}$ Ob$_{13}$, נָכְרוֹ *of his misfortune* Ob$_{12}$, מַפַּלְתֶּךָ *of your fall* Ezk 32$_{10}$, מַפַּלְתֵּךְ *of your* (f.) *fall* Ezk 26$_{18}$ 27$_{27}$, שֹׁאָה וּמְשׁוֹאָה *of ruin and devastation* Zp 1$_{15}$ Si 51$_{10}$ (שואה), יום הווה *day of destruction* 1QM 1$_{11}$, יום אבדן *day of destruction of* the nations 4QpsEzek^{a} 1$_{2}$, יוֹם הֶרֶג *day of slaugh-*

ter Is 30$_{25}$, הֲרֵגָה *of slaughter* Jr 12$_{3}$ 1QH 15$_{17}$, הַמַּגֵּפָה *of the plague* Nm 25$_{18}$, הַמָּוֶת *of death* Ec 7$_{1}$ 8$_{8}$ Si 30$_{32}$, מות *of the death of* CD 5$_{3}$, מוֹתִי *of my death* Gn 27$_{2}$, מוֹתוֹ *of his death* Jg 13$_{7}$ 1 S 15$_{35}$ 2 K 15$_{5}$||2 C 26$_{21}$ (2 K מֹתוֹ) Jr 52$_{11.34}$, מוֹתָהּ *of her death* 2 S 6$_{23}$, מֻתָן *of their death* 2 S 20$_{3}$.

יְמֵי הַמָּצוֹר *days of the siege* Ezk 5$_{2}$, מְצוּרֵךְ *of your siege* Ezk 4$_{8}$, חָרְפִּי *of my reproach* Jb 29$_{4}$, עֹנִי *of affliction* Jb 30$_{16.27}$, עָנְיָהּ וּמְרוּדֶיהָ *of her affliction and wandering* Lm 1$_{7}$, ימי מצרפותיו *days of its trials* CD 20$_{27}$.

יוֹם עֶבְרָה *day of wrath* Zp 1$_{15}$ Pr 11$_{4}$ Si 5$_{8}$ 34$_{6(Bmg).6(B)}$ 4QapPs^{b} 31$_{7}$, עֶבְרַת *of the wrath of* Y. Ezk 7$_{19}$ Zp 1$_{18}$, עֲבָרוֹת *of wrath* Jb 21$_{30}$, חֲרוֹן *of the wrath of* Is 13$_{13}$ Lm 1$_{12}$, אַף *of the anger of* Y. Zp 2$_{3}$ Lm 2$_{22}$, אַפֶּךָ *of your anger* Lm 2$_{21}$, אַפּוֹ *of his anger* Ps 110$_{5}$ Jb 20$_{28}$ Lm 2$_{1}$, זַעַם *of indignation* Ezk 22$_{24}$, זַעְמִי *of my indignation* Is 10$_{5}$ (if em. בְּיָדָם *in their hand* to בְּיוֹם *in the day of*), המשפט *of the judgment* 1QpHab 12$_{14}$ 13$_{2}$ 1QpMic 8$_{8}$ ([משפט]) 3QpIsa 1$_{6}$ ([י]ום), משפטו *of its ordinance* 1QS 10$_{7}$, יוֹם פְּקֻדָּה *day of visitation* Is 10$_{3}$, יְמֵי הַפְּקֻדָּה *days of the visitation* Ho 9$_{7}$, יוֹם נָקָם *day of vengeance* Is 34$_{8}$ 61$_{2}$ 63$_{4}$ Pr 6$_{34}$ Si 5$_{7(A)}$ 1QM 7$_{5}$ 1QS 9$_{23}$ 10$_{19(mg)}$, נָקָם וְשִׁלֵּם *of vengeance and recompense* Dt 32$_{35(Sam)}$ (MT לִי נָקָם וְשִׁלֵּם *mine is vengeance and recompense*; or em. וְשִׁלֵּם to וְשִׁלֵּם *and recompense*), נְקָמָה *of vengeance* Jr 46$_{10}$, יְמֵי הַשִּׁלֻּם *days of recompense* Ho 9$_{7}$, יום הריב *day of the dispute* 4QMyst^{b} 9$_{2}$, יוֹם מִלְחָמָה *day of battle* Ho 10$_{14}$ Am 1$_{14}$ Pr 21$_{31}$ 1QM 7$_{6}$ (המלחמה) 15$_{12}$ (יום corrected to מועד *appointed time of*) Kuntillet ʻAjrud add. inscr. 3$_{2.3}$ (both ים מלח[מה]), מִלְחֶמֶת appar. *of the battle of* 1 S 13$_{22}$, מלחמתם *of their battle* 1QM 1$_{12}$, קְרָב *of battle* Zc 14$_{3}$ Ps 78$_{9}$ 1QM 13$_{14}$, קְרָב וּמִלְחָמָה *of battle and war* Jb 38$_{33}$, נֶשֶׁק *of weapons*, i.e. battle Ps 140$_{8}$, חֵילֶךָ *of your power* Ps 110$_{3}$, הַמַּעֲשֶׂה *of the deed* 1 S 20$_{19}$, יְשׁוּעָה *of salvation* Is 49$_{8}$, ישעך *of your salvation* 11QPs^{a} 22$_{4}$, רָצוֹן *acceptance* Is 58$_{5}$, רָע *of evil* Am 6$_{3}$, יְמֵי רָע *days of evil* Ps 49$_{6}$ Ps 94$_{13}$ (or em. מִימֵי *from days of* to מֵימֵי *waters of*), יוֹם רָעָה *day of evil* Jr 17$_{17.18}$ 51$_{2}$ Ps 27$_{5}$ 41$_{2}$ Pr 16$_{4}$ Ec 7$_{14}$ Si 6$_{10}$ 34$_{6(Bmg)}$, יְמֵי רָעָה *days of evil* Ec 12$_{1}$, יוֹם פִּשְׁעוֹ *day of his transgression* Ezk 33$_{12}$, ימי חמס *days of violence* Si 49$_{3}$, יוֹם גְּאוֹנָיִךְ *day of your pride* Ezk 16$_{56}$, נִטְעֵךְ *of your planting* Is 17$_{11}$, ימי גורלה *days of her lot* 4Q418 86$_{2}$, [י]מי כבודכה *days of your glory* 4QRitPur 1.12$_{11}$.

יוֹם מָחָר *day of the morrow*, i.e. in the future Gn 30$_{33}$ Is 56$_{12}$ Pr 27$_{1}$, מָחֳרָת *of the morrow*, i.e. the next day Nm 11$_{32}$, אֶתְמוֹל *of previous time*, i.e. yesterday Ps 90$_{4}$, הַחֹדֶשׁ *of the month/new moon* Ex 40$_{2}$ 1 S 20$_{34}$ Ezk 46$_{1.6}$, ימי חודש *days of the new moon* 1QS 10$_{3}$ 11QT 43$_{2}$ ([החודש]), יוֹם הַכֵּסֶא *day of the full moon* Pr 7$_{20}$, הַשַּׁבָּת *of the sabbath* Ex 20$_{8.11}$ 31$_{15}$ 35$_{3}$ Lv 24$_{8.8}$ Nm 15$_{32}$ 28$_{9}$ Dt 5$_{12.15}$ Jr 17$_{21}$ $_{+6t}$ Ezk 46$_{1.4.12}$ Ps 92$_{1}$ Ne 10$_{32}$ 13$_{15.17.19.22}$ 4QHalakhah^{a} 1$_{6}$ 4QSD 7.1$_{3.5.6.7}$ 7.2$_{1}$ (ה[שבת]) 7.2$_{4}$ ([השבת]) 4QD^{e} 2.1$_{18}$ ([השבת]) 6.4$_{17}$ (השב[ת]) 4QTohA 1.2$_{2.3}$ (יו[ם]) 4QDibHam^{a} 1.7$_{4}$ 4QOrd^{b} 3$_{2}$ (שבת) CD 6$_{18}$ 10$_{17.17.22}$ 11$_{2.13}$, ימי השבתות *days of the sabbaths* 11QT 13$_{17}$ (השו[בתות]) 43$_{2}$, יוֹם הַבִּכּוּרִים *day of the firstfruits* Nm 28$_{26}$ 4QHalakhah^{a} 5$_{4}$ ([י]ום ה[בכורים]) 4Q365a 2.1$_{2}$, ימי הבכורים *days of the firstfruits* 11QT 43$_{3}$, יוֹם כִּפֻּרִים *day of atonement* Lv 23$_{27}$ (הַכִּפֻּרִים) 23$_{28}$ 25$_{9}$ (הַכִּפֻּרִים) 1QpHab 11$_{7}$ (הכפורים) 1QLitPr 1$_{6}$ (כפורים) 4QOtot 7$_{2}$ ([הכפורים]) 4QMishA 4.3$_{7}$ 4.4$_{3}$ (הכפ[ורים]) 4.5$_{6}$ 4.6$_{1}$ 4QMishB^{a} 2.2$_{2}$ (all three הכפורים) 2.3$_{1}$ (י[ום הכפורים]) 4QMishC^{c} 1$_{6}$ ([הכפורים]) 11QPs^{a} 27$_{8}$ (ים הכפורים) 11QT 25$_{11}$ (כפורים), תְּרוּעָה *of trumpet blast* Nm 29$_{1}$, שׁוֹפָר וּתְרוּעָה *of ram's horn and trumpet blast* Zp 1$_{16}$, זֶבַח *of sacrifice* Zp 1$_{8}$, זִבְחֲכֶם *of your sacrifice* Lv 19$_{6}$, קָרְבָּנוֹ *of his offering* Lv 7$_{15}$, ימי [קורבן] *days of the offering of* 11QT 11$_{12}$, יום הניפת *day of the waving of* the sheaf 11QT 18$_{10}$, הנף *of the waving of* the sheaf 11QT 11$_{10}$, יום הזכרון *the day of memorial* 4QOtot 8$_{4}$ (יום הזכר[ון]) 4QMishA 4.3$_{6}$ 4.4$_{2}$ (הזכ[רון]) 4.5$_{5}$ 4QMishB^{a} 2.2$_{2.6}$ ([יו]ם) 2.3$_{1}$ ([י]ום [הזכרון]) 2.3$_{5}$ ([יו]ם [הזכרון]) 2.3$_{9}$ (הזכר[ון]) 4QLiturgy 1.1$_{5}$ (זכרון), יוֹם אַשְׁמָתוֹ *day of his guilt offering* Lv 5$_{24}$, צוֹם *of fast* Jr 36$_{6}$ 1QpHab 11$_{8}$, צֹמְכֶם *of your fast* Is 58$_{3}$, התענית *of fasting* CD 6$_{19}$, חֲתֻנָּתוֹ *of his wedding* Ca 3$_{11}$.

ימי קיץ *days of summer* Si 50$_{8}$, יוֹם קָצִיר *day of harvest* Is 18$_{4(mss)}$ (L *in the heat of* בְּחֹם) Pr 25$_{13}$ (or em. בְּחֹם), יְמֵי קָצִיר *days of harvest* Jos 3$_{15}$ 2 S 21$_{9}$, קְצִיר *of the harvest of* Gn 30$_{14}$ Jg 15$_{1}$, בִּכּוּרֵי *of firstfruits of* Nm 13$_{20}$, הַפּוּרִים *of Purim* Est 9$_{28.31}$ (הַפֻּרִים), הַמִּשְׁתֶּה *of the feast* Jg 14$_{12}$ Jb 1$_{5}$, יוֹם מִשְׁתֶּה וְשִׂמְחָה *day of feasting and joy* Est 9$_{17.18}$, יְמֵי מִשְׁתֶּה וְשִׂמְחָה *days of feasting and joy* Est 9$_{22}$, הֶחָג *of the festival* Ezk 45$_{23}$, יום חג *day of the feast of* 11QT 43$_{7}$, יְמֵי חַג *days of the festival of* Ho 9$_{5}$, חַגֵּנוּ *of our feast* Ps 81$_{4}$, יוֹם מוֹעֵד *day of the appointed feast* Lm 2$_{7.22}$ Ho 9$_{5}$

12_{10} Si $50_{6.8}$, יום מועד *day of the appointed feast of* 11QT $43_{7.8}$, מועדו *of its appointed feast* 11QT 43_9, ימי המועדים *days of the appointed feasts* 11QT 43_{15}, המועדות *of the appointed feasts* 11QPs^a 27_8, תעודה *of appointment*, i.e. appointed days 4QCryptA 3.2_8 (י[מ]י), ימי [החתנה] *days of the wedding* 4QTobit^e 4_1.

יוֹם אוֹר *day of light*, i.e. daylight Am 8_9 (or em. בְּיוֹמוֹ *in its day*, i.e. at once), קָדִים *of the east wind* Is 27_8, קָרָה *of cold* Na 3_{17} Pr 25_{30}, הַשֶּׁלֶג *of snow* 2 S 23_{20}||1 C 11_{22}, הַגֶּשֶׁם *of rain* Ezk 1_{28}, סַגְרִיר *of persistent rain* Pr 27_{15}, סוּפָה *of the whirlwind* Am 1_{14}, עָנָן *of cloud* Ezk 30_3 Jl 2_2, עָנָן וַעֲרָפֶל *of cloud and darkness* Ezk 34_{12} Zp 1_{15}, חֹשֶׁךְ *of darkness* Jb 15_{23}, יְמֵי הַחֹשֶׁךְ *days of darkness* Ec 11_8, יוֹם חֹשֶׁךְ וַאֲפֵלָה *day of darkness and gloom* Jl 2_2 Zp 1_{15}, הַקָּהָל *of the assembly* Dt 9_{10} 10_4 18_{16}, יִזְרְעֶאל *of Jezreel* Ho 2_2, יְרוּשָׁלָםִ *of Jerusalem* Ps 137_7, מִדְיָן *of Midian* Is 9_3, מִצְרַיִם *of Egypt* Ezk 30_9, מַסָּה *Massah* Ps 95_8, יְמֵי הַגִּבְעָה *days of Gibeah* Ho 9_9 10_9.

יְמֵי אֵבֶל *days of mourning of*, i.e. for Gn 27_{41}, אֶבְלֵךְ *of your mourning* Is 60_{20}, בְּכִי *of weeping* Dt 34_8, בְּכִיתוֹ *of his weeping*, i.e. of weeping for him Gn 50_4, רְעָבוֹן *of famine* Ps 37_{19}, הֶבְלִי *of my vanity*, i.e. my vain days Ec 7_{15}, הֶבְלֶךָ *of your vanity*, i.e. your vain days Ec 9_9, הַחֲנֻטִים *of the embalming* Gn 50_3, מְרוּקֵיהֶן *of their rubbings*, i.e. beautification Est 2_{12}, נַחֲלָה *of sickness* Is 17_{11}, הַבְּעָלִים *of the Baals* Ho 2_{15}, מִלֻּאֵיכֶם *of your ordination* Lv 8_{33}, נִזְרוֹ *of his Naziriteship* Nm $6_{4.8.12.13}$, נֶדֶר *of the vow of* Nm 6_5, הַמַּעֲשֶׂה *of the work* Ezk 46_1 11QT $43_{16.17}$, צְבָאִי *of my service* Jb 14_{14}.

יוֹם הַטָּמֵא *day of the impure thing*, i.e. when a thing is impure Lv 14_{57}, יְמֵי נִדַּת *days of the impurity of* Lv 12_2 4QSD 7.2_{15} 4QD^a 6.2_6 ([י]מי), נִדָּתָהּ *of her impurity* Lv 15_{25}, ימי [נדתו] *days of his impurity* 4QNidd 2.1_2, יְמֵי זוֹב *days of the discharge* Lv 15_{25} 4QTohA 1.1_4 (הזוב), זוֹבָהּ *of her discharge* Lv 15_{26}, יוֹם הַטָּהֹר *day of the pure thing* Lv 14_{57}, יוֹם טָהֳרָתוֹ *day of his purification* Lv 14_2 Nm 6_9 4QOrd^c 1.1_3 ([י]ו[ם טהרת[ו]), יום טהרתם *day of their purification* 4QOrd^c 1.1_5 (ט]הרתם) 1.1_8 (ט]הרת[ם]), ימי טה[רתו] *days of his purification* 4QTohA 1.1_9 4QRitPur 11.10_2 (טה[רתו]), יְמֵי טָהֳרָהּ *days of her purification* Lv $12_{4.6}$, יוֹם קֹדֶשׁ *day of holiness*, i.e. holy day Ne 10_{32}, ימי קודש *days of holiness* 1QS 10_5 11QT 43_{17} (הקודש), יוֹם קָדְשִׁי *day of my holiness*, i.e. my holy day Is 58_{13}, יוֹם טוֹבָה *day of prosperity* Ec 7_{14}, יום ה[שלום] *the day of peace* 11QMelch 2_{15}, ימי שלוה *days of peace* Si 47_{13}, יוֹם שִׂמְחַתְכֶם *day of your joy* Nm 10_{10}, יוֹם שִׂמְחַת *day of the joy of* Ca 3_{11}, יוֹם בְּשֹׂרָה *day of good news* 2 K 7_9, יום [ה]ליכת *day of the going of* 4QJub^h 35_{10}.

ים הנקבה *day of the breach* Siloam tunnel inscr.$_3$, יוֹם מוּסַד *day of the founding of* the temple of Y. 2 C 8_{16} (if em. הַיּוֹם מוּסַד appar. *the day [when there was] the founding of*), יוֹם קְטַנּוֹת *day of small things* Zc 4_{10}, ימי מספר *days of a number*, i.e. numerous days or days that can be numbered Si 36_9 $41_{13(B)}$, ימי אין מספר *days (of) without number*, i.e. eternal Si 37_{25} 41_{13}.

יְמֵי הָעֵץ *days of a tree* Is 65_{22}, הָאָרֶץ *of the earth* Gn 8_{22}, שָׁמַיִם *of the heavens* Dt 11_{21} Ps 89_{30} (שָׁמַיִם) Si 45_{15} 50_{24}, שֶׁבַע *of seven* sabbaths of years Lv 25_8, קֶדֶם *of old* 2 K 19_{25}||Is 37_{26} Is 23_7 51_9 Jr 46_{26} Mc 7_{20} Ps 44_2 Lm 1_7 2_{17} Si 36_{16}, עוֹלָם *of old* Dt 32_7 (יְמוֹת) Is $63_{4.11}$ Am 9_{11} Mc 5_1 (+ מִקֶּדֶם *from of old*) 7_{14} Ml 3_4 Si 44_2 (ימות) 1QH 1_{15}, עד *of eternity* 4Q410 1_7.

יְמֵי אֲשֶׁר *the days when* Lv 13_{46} Nm 9_{18}, מִימֵי הִיא *from days (of) she is*, perh. she has been like this from long ago Na 2_9 (or em. מֵימֶיהָ *her waters*).

יוֹם *day of*, i.e. day when, followed by (1) inf. cstr. of verb היה *be* Ex 10_6 Ezk 34_{12}, הלך *go* 1 K 2_8 1QJub^b 35_{10} ([ל]כת), בוא *come* Ezk 38_{18} 44_{27} Ml 3_2 4QHalakhah^a 5_6, hi. *bring* Lv 23_{15} 1 S 29_6 11QT 18_{11} 19_{11}, יצא *go out* Dt 16_3 Jos 9_{12} 2 K $23_{7.42}$ Si 40_1 1QDM 2_6 (צ[את]נו), hi. *bring out* Jr 7_{22} 11_4 34_{13}, עלה *go up* Jg 19_{30} Is 11_{16} Ho 2_{17}, ni. *be taken up* Ex 40_{37}, hi. *bring up* 1 S 8_8 2 S 7_6 Jr 11_7, ירד *go down* Ezk 31_{15} 4QJub^h 38_{13} (י[ום]), שׁוב *go back* Ezk 33_{12} Si 40_1, עבר *cross* 4QpsJub^b 6_4, שׁלח *send* Jos 14_{11}, קרב hi. *bring near*, i.e. offer 11QT 43_{10}, זבח *sacrifice* 4QMMT B_{11} ([זב]חם), גלה *be exiled* Jg 18_{30}, אסף ni. *be gathered* CD 19_{35} 20_{13}, ישׁב *dwell* 1 S 7_2, עמד *stand* Ob$_{11}$, עזב *leave* 4QpsEzek^c 3.3_5, סור *turn aside* CD 7_{12} 14_1, אמר *say* Jos 6_{10}, דבר pi. *speak* CD 15_7, צוה pi. *command* Lv 7_{38}, קרא *call* Ps 20_{10}, ראה *see* Ex 10_{28} CD 9_{22}, ni. *appear* Lv 13_{14}, שׁמע *hear* Nm $30_{6.8.9.13.15}$ 11QT 53_{20} 54_3, ידע *know* Dt 9_{25} CD 16_6, אכל *eat* Gn 2_{17} 3_5, עשׂה *make* Gn 2_4, ni. *be made* Ezk 43_{18}, ברא *create* Gn 5_1 5QRègle 24_3 ([י]ום [ב]ראם), ni. *be created* Gn 5_2 Ezk $28_{13.15}$, ילד ni.

be born Ho 2$_5$ Ec 7$_1$, ho. *be born* Gn 40$_{20}$ Ezk 16$_{4.5}$, גמל ni. *be weaned* Gn 21$_8$, יסד ni. *be founded* Ex 9$_{18(Sam)}$ (MT הַיּוֹם *the day [when]*), בחר *choose* Ezk 20$_5$, קנה *buy* Ru 4$_5$, מכר *sell* Ne 13$_{15}$, כבד ni. *be glorified* Ezk 39$_{13}$, נתן *give* Jos 10$_{12}$ 1 K 17$_{14(Qr)}$, לקח *take* Ezk 24$_{25}$, ni. *be taken* 1 S 21$_7$, שׁבה *take captive* Ob$_{11}$, קום *rise* Zp 3$_8$, hi. *erect* Nm 9$_{15}$, נוח hi. *give rest* Is 14$_3$, נפל *fall* 1 S 29$_3$, פקד *visit* Ex 32$_{34}$ Jr 27$_{22}$ Am 3$_{14}$, נחל hi. *cause to inherit* Dt 21$_{16}$, משׁח *anoint* Lv 7$_{36}$, ni. *be anointed* Lv 6$_{13}$ Nm 7$_{10.84}$, טהר pi. *cleanse* Ezk 36$_{33}$, קרב hi. *bring near*, i.e. offer Lv 7$_{16}$, נוף hi. *wave* Lv 23$_{12}$, כון hi. *arrange* Na 2$_4$, מלא *be fulfilled* Lv 8$_{33}$, חבשׁ *bind* Is 30$_{26}$, חזק hi. *hold* Jr 31$_{22}$, נכה hi. *strike* Nm 3$_{13}$ 8$_{17}$ 2 S 21$_{12}$, ענה pi. *afflict* 2 S 13$_{32}$ Is 58$_5$, לחם ni. *fight* Zc 14$_3$, כלה pi. *finish* Nm 7$_1$, אבד *perish* Ob$_{12}$, חטא *sin* Ezk 33$_{13}$, פרר hi. *violate* 4QpsMos^e 2.1$_5$.

(2) pf. of verb, דבר pi. *speak* Ex 6$_{28}$ Nm 3$_1$ Dt 4$_{15}$ Jr 36$_2$, קרא *call* Ps 138$_3$, קרב hi. *bring near*, i.e. offer Lv 7$_{35}$, נצל hi. *deliver* 2 S 22$_1$||Ps 18$_1$, עזב *leave* 2 K 8$_6$.

(3) impf. of verb, קרא *call* Ps 56$_{10}$ 102$_3$ Lm 3$_{57}$, ירא *fear* Ps 56$_4$.

(4) nom. cl., בְּיוֹם צַר לִי *in the day of*, i.e. when there was, *distress to me* Ps 59$_{17}$ 102$_3$.

יְמֵי *days of*, i.e. days when, followed by (1) inf. cstr. of verb, היה *be* Jg 18$_{31}$ 1 S 22$_4$ 25$_{7.16}$, הלך htp. *go about* 1 S 25$_{15}$, יצא *go out* Mc 7$_{15}$, נזר hi. *be a Nazirite* Nm 6$_6$, שׁפט *judge* Ru 1$_1$, דרשׁ *seek* 2 C 26$_5$, ילד ho. *be born* 4Q Jub^h 36 $_{20}$ ([הולדתו]), ספר *count* 4QD^h 5$_5$, סגר ni. *be confined* 4QRitPur 67$_2$ ([הסגרו]).

(2) inf. abs. שׁמם ho. *be desolate* Lv 26$_{34.35}$ 2 C 36$_{21}$.

(3) pf. of verb, סגר hi. *shut up* Lv 14$_{46}$.

(4) impf. of verb, יְמֵי אֱלוֹהַּ יִשְׁמְרֵנִי *the days when God watched over me* Jb 29$_2$.

יְמוֹת *days of*, i.e. days when, followed by pf. of verb, ענה pi. *afflict* Ps 90$_{15}$.

יומי *days of*, followed by inf. cstr. of מאס *reject* 1QS 3$_5$, עמד *stand* 4QapPs^b 31$_6$ (unless noun עֹמֶד *standing*, i.e. existence).

בֶּן ... יָמִים *son of ... days*, i.e. so many days old Gn 17$_{12}$ 21$_4$, מְלֵא *(one) full of*, i.e. aged Jr 6$_{11}$, שְׂבַע *(one) satisfied of*, i.e. aged Gn 35$_{29}$ Jb 42$_{17}$ 1 C 29$_{28}$ 2QJub^a 23$_8$, ימי *of my days* 4QJub^d 21$_1$ ([שבע]), עול *child of*, i.e. a few days old Is 65$_{20}$, קְצַר *short (one) of*, i.e. of few days Jb 14$_1$, [ט]מאי הימם *impure ones of days* 4QOrd^c 1.1$_9$.

גְּנֻבְתִי יוֹם *one stolen of*, i.e. by, *day* Gn 31$_{39}$, קְשֵׁה־יוֹם *hard one of day*, i.e. whose day is hard Jb 30$_{25}$, אֹרְרֵי־יוֹם *ones who curse the day* Jb 3$_8$.

רוּחַ הַיּוֹם *wind of the day* Gn 3$_8$ (unless יוֹם II *storm*), עֶצֶם *bone of*, i.e. selfsame, day Gn 7$_{13}$ 17$_{23.26}$ Ex 12$_{17.41.51}$ Lv 23$_{14.21.23.29.30}$ Dt 32$_{48}$ Jos 5$_{11}$ 10$_{27}$ Ezk 2$_3$ 24$_{2.2}$, שֵׁם *name of* Ezk 24$_2$ Arad ost. 2$_4$ (הים), קוֹל יוֹם *sound of the day of* Y. Zp 1$_{14}$, נְכוֹן הַיּוֹם *established one*, i.e. fullness, *of the day* Pr 4$_{18}$, עֶרֶב יוֹם *evening of the day* Pr 7$_9$ (or em. בַּעֲרֹב יוֹם *when the day becomes evening*).

כִּמְרִירֵי יוֹם *blackness of the day*, i.e. eclipses Jb 3$_5$, מרירי יום *bitter things of the day* Si 11$_{4.4(B)}$, מרורי *bitter things of* 1QH 5$_{34}$, טוב[ת] *bounty of* Si 11$_{25}$ 14$_{14}$, רעת *evil of* Si 11$_{25}$ ([יו]ם).

מֶמְשֶׁלֶת הַיּוֹם *dominion of the day* Gn 1$_{16}$, מָחֳרַת *morrow of*, i.e. the next day 1 C 29$_{21}$, דָּת *edict of* Est 9$_{13}$, דְּבַר יוֹם *thing of a day* Ex 5$_{13.19}$ 16$_4$ Lv 23$_{37}$ 1 K 8$_{59}$ 2 K 25$_{30}$||Jr 52$_{34}$ Dn 1$_5$ Ezr 3$_4$ Ne 11$_{23}$ 12$_{47}$ 1 C 16$_{37}$ 2 C 8$_1$ 8$_{14}$ 31$_{16}$ 4QPentPar^b 23$_7$ 4QRP^c 23$_7$ 4QM^a 1$_8$ 11QT 29$_4$ ([דבר]), [ד]עת [י]מי (יום) *knowledge of days of* 4QCryptA 3.2$_8$, [מ]חזה ימינו *vision of our days* 4QMyst^b 8$_1$.

חֹדֶשׁ יָמִים *month of days*, i.e. a whole month Gn 24$_{55}$ (if ins. חֹדֶשׁ) 29$_{14}$ Nm 11$_{20.21}$ 11QT 63$_{14}$ (חודש), יֶרַח *month of* Dt 21$_{13}$ 2 K 15$_{13}$, דֶּרֶךְ יוֹם *journey of a day* Nm 11$_{31.31}$ 1 K 19$_4$, דֶּרֶךְ ... יָמִים *journey of* (a specified number of) *days* Gn 30$_{36}$ 31$_{23}$ Ex 3$_{18}$ 5$_3$ 8$_{23}$ Nm 10$_{33.33}$ 33$_8$ 2 K 3$_9$ 4QAges^a 5$_3$ 11QT 43$_{13}$ 52$_{14}$, מַהֲלַךְ ... יָמִים *a journey of* (a specified number of) *days* Jon 3$_{3.4}$, אוֹר שִׁבְעַת הַיָּמִים *the light of seven days* Is 30$_{26}$, לֶחֶם יוֹמָיִם *bread of*, i.e. sufficient for, *two days* Ex 16$_{29}$, זֶבַח הַיָּמִים *sacrifice of the year*, i.e. yearly sacrifice 1 S 1$_{21}$ 2$_{19}$ 20$_6$, עוֹלַת יוֹם בְּיוֹם *burnt offering of a day in a day*, i.e. daily burnt offering Ezr 3$_4$ 11QT 29$_4$ ([יום] ביומו), מנוחת יום *resting of the day of* 1QpHab 11$_7$, שכר שני ימים *earnings of two days* CD 14$_{13}$.

מִסְפַּר הַיָּמִים *number of the days* Nm 14$_{34}$ 1 S 27$_7$ 2 S 2$_{11}$ Ezk 4$_{4.5.9}$ Si 37$_{25}$ 41$_{13(Bmg, M)}$ (ימים) 4QD^a 1$_7$ ([מספר]), מִסְפַּר יְמֵי ([י]מים) *number of the days of* Ec 2$_3$ 5$_{17}$ 6$_{12}$, מִסְפַּר יָמֶיךָ *number of your days* Ex 23$_{26}$ Jb 38$_{21}$, מספר ימיו *number of his days* Si 26$_1$, אֹרֶךְ יָמִים *length of days* Ps 21$_5$ 23$_6$ 91$_{16}$ 93$_5$ Jb 12$_{12}$ Pr 3$_{2.16}$ Lm 5$_{20}$ 1QH 13$_{18}$ 1QM

1$_{9}$ 1QS 4$_{7}$ 4QsapHymnA 1.1$_{1}$ (all four אורך) 4QRitMar 20$_{2}$ ([אור]ך) Kuntillet ʿAjrud inscr. D2 (ארך ימם; others ברך ימם), אֹרֶךְ יָמֶיךָ *length of your days* Dt 30$_{20}$ 1QDM 2$_{5}$ (אורך ימ[יכה]) 4Q416 2.3$_{19}$ (ארוך ימיכה) 4Q418 137$_{4}$ (אורך ימיכה), תכון ימיהם *measure of their days* 1QM 6$_{12.14}$, מִדַּת יָמַי *measure of my days* Ps 39$_{5}$, שני היום *years of the day* 11QJub 4$_{30}$, דְּמִי יָמַי *the middle of my days* Is 38$_{10}$ (or em.; see Coll., §3a), חֲצִי יָמָיו *half*, i.e. middle, *of his days* Jr 17$_{11(Qr)}$, יָמָי *of my days* Ps 102$_{25}$, רֹב יָמִים *multitude of days* Is 24$_{22}$ Zc 8$_{4}$ Ec 11$_{1}$ (הַיָּמִים *of the days*) 1QH 17$_{15}$ (רוב), רוב ימו *multitude of his days* 4QJub^{f} 23$_{12}$, תקופות יום *the circuits of the day* 1QH 12$_{5}$, תְּקֻפוֹת הַיָּמִים *the circuits of days*, i.e. the course of time 1 S 1$_{20}$ 1QH 12$_{5}$, מבוא יום *coming of the day* 1QS 10$_{10}$, מַחֲצִית הַיּוֹם *half of the day*, i.e. midday Ne 8$_{3}$, שלישית *third of* 11QT 35$_{8}$, רְבִעִית *a quarter of* Ne 9$_{3}$.

דִּבְרֵי הַיָּמִים *events of the days*, i.e. chronicles 1 K 14$_{19.29}$ 15$_{7.23.31}$ 16$_{5.14.20.27}$ 22$_{39.46}$ 2 K 1$_{18}$ 8$_{23}$ 10$_{34}$ 12$_{20}$ 13$_{8.12}$ =14$_{15}$ 14$_{18.28}$ 15$_{6+6t}$ 16$_{19}$ 20$_{20}$ 21$_{17.25}$ 23$_{38}$ 24$_{5}$ Est 2$_{23}$ 6$_{1}$ 10$_{2}$ Ne 12$_{23}$ 1 C 27$_{24}$.

קֵץ (...) יָמִים *end of (...) days*, i.e. course of time Gn 4$_{3}$ 41$_{1}$ 2 S 14$_{26}$ 1 K 17$_{17}$ Jr 13$_{6}$ 42$_{7}$ Ne 13$_{6}$ 4QCommGenA 1$_{18}$, קֵץ הַיָּמִין *end of the days* Dn 12$_{13}$, קֵץ ... יוֹם *end of ... day(s)* Gn 8$_{6}$ Nm 13$_{25}$ Dt 9$_{11}$ 4QCommGenA 1$_{12}$, קְצֵה ... יוֹם *end of ... day(s)* Gn 8$_{3}$ Jos 3$_{2}$ 9$_{16}$ (both יָמִים) 2 S 24$_{8}$, קְצָת יָמִים *end of days* Dn 1$_{15.18}$ (הַיָּמִים), סוף ... יום *end of ... days* 4QCommGenA 1$_{9}$, מועד יום *appointed feast of the day of* 11QT 43$_{10}$, [מו]עדי יום *appointed times of the day* 4QParGenEx 2$_{12}$, מוֹעֵד הַיָּמִים *appointed time of the days*, i.e. the time appointed 1 S 13$_{11}$, שְׁבֻעוֹת יָמִים appar. *weeks of days* Ezk 45$_{21}$ (or em. שִׁבְעַת *seven* days), [חלו]קות ימי *divisions of the days of* 4QJub^{h} 36$_{20}$.

אַחֲרִית הַיָּמִים *end of the days*, i.e. the end of time* Gn 49$_{1}$ Nm 24$_{14}$ Dt 4$_{30}$ 31$_{29}$ Is 2$_{2}$||Mc 4$_{1}$ Jr 23$_{20}$ 30$_{24}$ 48$_{47}$ 49$_{39}$ Ezk 38$_{16}$ Ho 3$_{5}$ Dn 10$_{14}$ 1QpHab 2$_{6}$ 9$_{6}$ 1QSa 1$_{1}$ 4QMidrEschat^{a} 1$_{2.12.15.19}$ 4QMidrEschat^{b} 10$_{5.7}$ ([הימים]) 9$_{14}$ ([אחרית]) 9$_{10}$ 11$_{2}$ (ה[י]מים) 4QCat 1$_{1}$ 2$_{1}$ (ה[ימי]ם) 4QpIsa^{a} 5$_{10}$ 8$_{17}$ ([אח]רית הימים) 4QpIsa^{b} 2$_{1}$ 4QpIsa^{c} 4.2$_{14}$ (ה[ימים]) 13$_{3}$ ([אחר]ית) 14$_{2}$ ([אח]רית הימ[ים]) 23.2$_{10}$ 4QpIsa^{d} 1$_{7}$ ([א]חרית הימים) 4QpNah 3.2$_{2}$ 4Q178 3$_{4}$ ([אחר]ית הימ[ים]) 4QCommGenA 4$_{2}$ 4QMMT C$_{14}$ ([אחרי]ת) C$_{21}$ 4QDibHam^{a} 1.3$_{14}$ 4QPrFêtes^{c} 7$_{5}$ 11QMelch 2$_{4}$ CD 4$_{4}$ 6$_{11}$.

שְׁנֵי הַיָּמִים *the two days* Est 9$_{27}$ 4QCommGenA 1$_{9}$ (ימים) CD 14$_{13}$ (ימים), שְׁלֹשֶׁת יָמִים *three days* Gn 30$_{36}$ 40$_{12.13.18.19}$ 42$_{17}$ Ex 3$_{18}$ 5$_{3}$ 8$_{23}$ 10$_{22.23}$ 15$_{22}$ 19$_{15}$ Lv 12$_{4}$ Nm 10$_{33.33}$ 33$_{8}$ Jos 1$_{11}$ 2$_{16.22}$ 3$_{2}$ 9$_{16}$ Jg 14$_{14}$ 19$_{4}$ 1 S 9$_{20}$ 2 S 20$_{4}$ 24$_{13}$||1 C 21$_{12}$ Am 4$_{4}$ Jon 3$_{3}$ Est 4$_{16}$ 10$_{8.9}$ (both הַיָּמִים) 2 C 10$_{5}$ 1QSa 1$_{26}$ 11QT 43$_{13}$ 45$_{12}$ 52$_{14}$ (all four שלושת), אַרְבַּעַת *four* Jg 11$_{40}$ Arad ost. 2$_{3}$ (הימם), שֵׁשֶׁת *six* Ex 16$_{26}$ 20$_{9.11}$ 23$_{12}$ 24$_{16}$ 31$_{15.17}$ 34$_{21}$ 35$_{2}$ Lv 12$_{5}$ 23$_{3}$ Dt 5$_{13}$ 16$_{8}$ Jos 6$_{3.14}$ Ezk 46$_{1}$ (יְמֵי *days of*) 4QJub^{a} 2$_{17}$ 11QT 11$_{12}$ (ימי), שִׁבְעַת *seven* Gn 7$_{10}$ (הַיָּמִים) 8$_{10.12}$ 31$_{23}$ 50$_{10}$ Ex 7$_{25}$ 12$_{15.19}$ 13$_{6}$ 22$_{29}$ 23$_{15}$ 29$_{30.35.37}$ 34$_{18}$ Lv 8$_{33.33.35}$ 12$_{2}$ 13$_{4+7t}$ 14$_{8.38}$ 15$_{13.19.24.28}$ 22$_{27}$ 23$_{6+7t}$ Nm 12$_{14.14.15}$ 19$_{11.14.16}$ 28$_{17.24}$ 29$_{12}$ 31$_{19}$ Dt 16$_{3.4.13.15}$ Jg 14$_{12}$ (יְמֵי) 14$_{17}$ (הַיָּמִים) 1 S 10$_{8}$ 11$_{3}$ 13$_{8}$ 31$_{13}$||1 C 10$_{12}$ 1 K 8$_{65}$||2 C 7$_{8}$ 1 K 8$_{65}$ 16$_{15}$ 20$_{29}$ 2 K 3$_{9}$ Is 30$_{26}$ (הַיָּמִים) Ezk 3$_{15.16}$ 43$_{25.26}$ 44$_{26}$ 45$_{21}$ (if em.; see above) 45$_{23}$ (יְמֵי) 45$_{23}$ (הַיָּמִים) Jb 2$_{13}$ Est 1$_{5}$ Ezr 6$_{22}$ Ne 8$_{18}$ 1 C 9$_{25}$ 2 C 7$_{9.9}$ 30$_{21.22}$ (הַיָּמִים) 30$_{23.23}$ 35$_{17}$ 4QCommGenA 1$_{15.18}$ 4QD^{a} 6.1$_{11}$ 6.2$_{3}$ 4QD^{g} 1.2$_{9}$ 4QMMT B$_{67}$ ([שבעת י]מים) 4QRitMar 97$_{2}$ (ימ[ים]) 4QRitPur 11.10$_{2}$ (ימי) 11QT 15$_{4}$ ([הימים]) 15$_{14}$ ([ימ]ים) 17$_{11.12}$ (הימים) 45$_{15}$ 49$_{6.7}$ 50$_{12.13}$, שְׁמֹנַת *eight* Gn 17$_{12}$ 21$_{4}$, עֲשֶׂרֶת *ten* 1 S 25$_{38}$ (הַיָּמִים) Jr 42$_{7}$ Ne 5$_{18}$ 4QD^{a} 10.2$_{6}$ 4QD^{e} 7.1$_{14}$ ([עשר]ת), ארבע[ת] עשר *fourteen* 4QTobit^{e} 4$_{1}$.

עֶת־יוֹם בְּיוֹם *time of a day in a day*, i.e. from day to day 1 C 12$_{23}$.

כָּל־יוֹם *every day, all the day* Ps 7$_{12}$ (or em.; see Prep.) 88$_{10}$ 140$_{3}$ 145$_{2}$ Est 2$_{11}$ (יוֹם וָיוֹם) 11QPs^{a} 27$_{6}$ (כול יום ויום) 11QT 15$_{1}$ ([כו]ל יום ויום) 15$_{3}$ ([כ]ול יום ויום) 15$_{5}$ ([כול י]ום) 17$_{12}$ (כול יום ויום) Mur 47$_{4}$ GnzPs 1$_{22}$ ([כל יום]) 3$_{3}$ (ויום) 4$_{25}$.

כֹּל יוֹם *all the day of* Nm 11$_{32}$.

כָּל־הַיּוֹם *all the day/time* Gn 6$_{5}$ Ex 10$_{13}$ Nm 11$_{32}$ Dt 28$_{32}$ 33$_{12}$ Jg 9$_{45}$ (כֹּל) 1 S 19$_{24}$ 28$_{20}$ Is 28$_{24}$ 51$_{13}$ 52$_{5}$ 62$_{6}$ 65$_{2.5}$ Jr 20$_{7.8}$ Ho 12$_{2}$ Ps 25$_{5}$ 32$_{3}$ 35$_{28}$ 37$_{26}$ 38$_{7.13}$ 41$_{2}$ 42$_{4}$ 44$_{9.16.23}$ 52$_{3}$ 56$_{2.3.6}$ 71$_{8.15.24}$ 72$_{15}$ 73$_{14}$ 74$_{22}$ 86$_{3}$ 88$_{18}$ 89$_{17}$ 102$_{9}$ 119$_{97}$ Pr 21$_{26}$ 23$_{17}$ Lm 1$_{13}$ 3$_{3.14.62}$ 1QH 5$_{17}$ 11$_{6}$ (both כול) 1QS 10$_{16}$ (כול) 4Q415 2.2$_{3}$ 4Q418 126.2$_{10}$ 127$_{2}$ (all three כול) 11QPs^{a} 19$_{17}$ (כול).

כָּל־הַיָּמִים *all the days* Gn 43$_{9}$ 44$_{32}$ Dt 4$_{10.40}$ 5$_{29}$=4QTestim$_{4}$ (כול היומים) Dt 6$_{24}$ 11$_{1}$ 12$_{1}$ 14$_{23}$ 18$_{5}$ 19$_{9}$ 28$_{29.33}$ 31$_{13}$ Jos 4$_{24}$ Jg 16$_{16}$ 1 S 1$_{28}$ 2$_{32.35}$ 18$_{29}$ 20$_{31}$ 23$_{14}$ 27$_{11}$ 28$_{2}$ 2 S 13$_{37}$ 2 S 19$_{14}$ 1 K 5$_{15}$ 8$_{40}$||2 C 6$_{31}$ 1 K 8$_{40}$||2 C 7$_{16}$ 1 K

11$_{36.39}$ 12$_7$||2 C 10$_7$ 1 K 14$_{30}$||2 C 12$_{15}$ 2 K 8$_{19}$||2 C 21$_7$ 2 K 13$_3$ 17$_{37}$ Jr 31$_{36}$ 32$_{39}$ 33$_{18}$ 35$_{19}$ Jb 1$_5$ 1QH 15$_9$ 17$_{14}$ (both כול) 1QDM 1$_6$ ([כול]) 4QJub[a] 2$_{22}$ 4QJub[c] 2$_{26}$ 4QJub[d] 21$_{24}$ (כול היימים) 4QJub[f] 39$_6$ ([כו]ל הימ[ים]) 4QpsJub[b] ([כו]ל [ה]ימים) 4QDibHam[a] 1.4$_8$ (כול) 4QBéat 3.3$_1$ (כול [הימ]ים) 11QT 29$_{10}$ 46$_4$ 50$_{10}$ 51$_{16}$ 59$_{15}$ 60$_{11}$ (all six כול).

כל יומים *all the days* 4QMishA 8$_3$.

כָּל־יְמֵי *all the days of* Gn 3$_{14}$ (כֹּל) 5$_{5+8t}$ 8$_{22}$ 9$_{29}$ Lv 13$_{46}$ 14$_{46}$ 15$_{25.26}$ 26$_{34}$ (כֹּל) 26$_{35}$ Nm 6$_4$ (כֹּל) 6$_{5.6.8}$ (כֹּל) 9$_{18}$ Dt 4$_9$ 6$_2$ 16$_3$ (all three כֹּל) 17$_{19}$ Jos 1$_5$ 3$_{15}$ (both כֹּל) 4$_{14}$ 24$_{25.25}$ Jg 2$_{7.7.18}$ (all five כֹּל) 18$_{31}$ 1 S 1$_{11}$ 7$_{13.15}$ 14$_{52}$ (all three כֹּל) 22$_4$ 25$_{7.15.16}$ 1 K 5$_{1.5}$ (כֹּל) 11$_{25.34}$ 15$_{5.6}$ 2 K 13$_{22}$ 23$_{22}$ (both כֹּל) 2 K 25$_{29}$||Jr 52$_{33}$ 2 K 25$_{30}$||Jr 52$_{34}$ (כֹּל) Is 38$_{20}$ 63$_9$ Ps 23$_6$ 27$_4$ 128$_5$ Jb 14$_{14}$ 15$_{20}$ Pr 15$_{15}$ 31$_{12}$ (כֹּל) Ec 9$_{9.9}$ Ezr 4$_5$ 2 C 24$_{2.14}$ 36$_{21}$ Si 3$_{12.13}$ 1QH 1$_{15}$ 1QM 2$_4$ (כול) 1QS 2$_{19}$ 3$_5$ (both כול יומי) 2QJub[b] 46$_1$ ([כו]ל ימי) 4Q Tobit[e] 2$_4$ ([כ]ו[ל]) 4QJub[g] 25$_9$ ([כו]ל) 4QJub[h] 36$_{23}$ (כול [י]מי) 4QpsJub[a] 2.2$_{12}$ ([כו]ל) 4QpsJub[c] 1$_3$ (כול) 4QTohA 1.1$_4$ (כול) 4QapJoseph[b] 15$_3$ (כל ימ[י]) 4QLiturgy 1$_7$ ([כ]ול) 4QpsHod[b] 1$_4$ 4QRitPur 67$_1$ (כול [ימי]) 11QPs[a] 27$_6$ (כול) 11QT 57$_{18}$ (כול).

כל ימי *all my days* 4QpsEzek[a] 9.2$_2$, כָּל־יָמֶיךָ *all your days* Dt 12$_{19}$ 23$_7$ 1 K 3$_{13}$ 4QTobit[e] 2$_3$ (כול ימיכה), כָּל־יָמָיו *all his days* Dt 22$_{19.29}$=11QT 66$_{11}$ 1 K 15$_{14}$||2 C 15$_{17}$ 2 K 12$_3$ 15$_{18}$ Ec 2$_{23}$ 5$_{16}$ 2 C 18$_7$ 34$_{33}$ 4QOrd[a] 1.2$_7$ 2$_{10}$ (both כול) 11QT 16$_4$ (כול), כָּל־יָמֵינוּ *all our days* Jr 35$_8$ Ps 90$_{9.14}$, כָּל־יְמֵיכֶם *all your days* Jr 35$_7$, כָּל־יְמֵיהֶם *all their days* 1 K 15$_{16.32}$ =11QT 45$_{13}$ (כול ימיהמה).

<APP> עֶרֶב *evening* Gn 1$_{5+5t}$, בֹּקֶר *morning* Gn 1$_{5+5t}$, שָׁבוּעַ *week* Dn 10$_{2.3}$ (both שְׁלֹשֶׁת/שְׁלֹשָׁה שָׁבֻעִים יָמִים *three weeks, days*, i.e. a period of three weeks), חֹדֶשׁ *month* Jg 19$_2$ (יָמִים אַרְבָּעָה חֳדָשִׁים *days, four months*, i.e. a period of four months), שָׁנָה *year* Gn 41$_1$ (שְׁנָתַיִם יָמִים *two years, days*, i.e. a period of two years) 47$_{28}$ 2 S 13$_{23}$ 14$_{28}$ Jr 28$_{3.11}$ (all four שְׁנָתַיִם יָמִים) 1QS 7$_{21}$ 8$_{10.25.27}$ 9$_2$ (all five שנתים ימים) 4QS[d] 3.2$_3$ (שנתים [י]מים) 4QpsEzek[a] 6$_1$ ([שנת]ים ימים) 7$_5$ (שנתים י[מים]) 4QMMT A$_{21}$, מִסְפָּר *number* Nm 9$_{20}$ (יָמִים מִסְפָּר *days, a number*, i.e. a few days; or em. יְמֵי מִסְפָּר *days of a number*; Sam יָמִים בְּמִסְפָּר perh. *days according to number*), צוֹם *fast* Is 58$_4$, בְּרִית *covenant* Jr 33$_{20.25}$ (if em. יוֹמָם *by day*), שִׂמְחָה *joy* 2 C 30$_{23}$ (שִׁבְעַת־יָמִים שִׂמְחָה *seven days, joy*, i.e. seven days of joy).

<ADJ> טוֹב *good*, i.e. day of feasting 1 S 25$_8$ Est 8$_{17}$ 9$_{19.22}$, גָּדוֹל *great* Jl 3$_4$ Ml 3$_{23}$ 1QS 10$_4$ 4QSD 7.2$_4$ (י[ום]), תָּמִים *whole* Jos 10$_{13}$, אַחֵר *another* 2 S 18$_{20}$ 2 K 6$_{29}$ 2 C 30$_{23}$, מַר *bitter* Am 8$_{10}$, אֶחָד *one* Gn 1$_5$ 27$_{45}$ 33$_{13}$ Lv 22$_{28}$ Nm 11$_{19}$ 1 S 23$_4$ 9$_{15}$ 1 K 5$_2$ 20$_{29}$ Is 9$_{13}$ 10$_{17}$ 47$_9$ 66$_8$ Jon 3$_4$ Hg 1$_1$ Zc 3$_9$ 14$_7$ Est 3$_{13}$ 8$_{12}$ Ezr 3$_6$ 10$_{13.16.17}$ Ne 5$_{18}$ 8$_2$ 2 C 28$_6$ Si 46$_4$ 4QpIsa[c] 4.1$_5$ 4Q185 1.2$_5$ 4QJub[f] 33$_{14}$ ([אחד]) 4QCommGenA 1$_{13.19}$ (אח[ד]) 4QD[e] 3.2$_{18}$ 4QpsEzek[e] 65$_9$ 4QMMT B$_{36}$ 4QsapHymn 1.2$_3$ 4Q423 7$_6$ 11QT 52$_6$, pl. *a few* Gn 27$_{44}$ 29$_{20}$ Dn 11$_{20}$, אַחֲרוֹן *last* Is 30$_8$ Pr 31$_{25}$, רִאשׁוֹן *first, former* Ex 12$_{15.15.16}$ Lv 23$_{7.35.39.40}$ Nm 6$_{12}$ 7$_{12}$ 28$_{18}$ Dt 4$_{32}$ 10$_{10}$ 16$_4$ Jg 20$_{22}$ Zc 8$_{11}$ Ec 7$_{10}$ Dn 10$_{12}$ Ne 8$_{18}$ 4QRP[c] 23$_{10}$ (הרישו[ן]) 4QpsMos[e] 1$_4$ 11QT 45$_9$ 49$_{17}$ 50$_{14}$ (במים *with water* corrected to בים), קַדְמֹנִי *former* Ezk 38$_{17}$, שֵׁנִי *second* Gn 1$_8$ Ex 2$_{13}$ Nm 7$_{18}$ 29$_{17}$ Jos 6$_{14}$ 10$_{32}$ 20$_{24.25}$ 1 S 20$_{34}$ 41$_4$ Ezk 43$_{22}$ Est 7$_2$ Ne 8$_{13}$ 4QJub[a] 1$_4$ (ביו[ם השני]) 4QMishC[b] 1$_4$ (י[ום]) 11QT 24$_{12}$ 28$_2$ ([וביום] השני), שְׁלִישִׁי *third* Gn 1$_{13}$ 22$_4$ 31$_{22}$ 34$_{25}$ 40$_{20}$ 42$_{18}$ Ex 19$_{11.16}$ Lv 7$_{17.18}$ 19$_{6.7}$ Nm 7$_{24}$ 19$_{12.12.19}$ 29$_{20}$ 31$_{19}$ Jos 9$_{17}$ Jg 20$_{30}$ 1 S 30$_1$ 2 S 1$_2$ 1 K 3$_{18}$ 12$_{12.12}$||2 C 10$_{12.12}$ 2 K 20$_{5.8}$ Ho 6$_2$ Est 5$_1$ 4QJub[a] 2$_7$ (השל[ישי]) 11QT 24$_{13}$ 28$_6$ 45$_9$ (השל[ישי]) 49$_{18}$ 50$_{14}$, רְבִיעִי *fourth* Gn 1$_{19}$ Nm 7$_{30}$ 29$_{23}$ Jg 19$_5$ Ezr 8$_{33}$ 2 C 20$_{26}$ 4QCommGenA 1$_{9.11}$ 4QMishC[b] 1$_3$ (ר[ביעי]) 4QMishC[d] 1.2$_3$ 3$_2$ (רביע[י]) 4QMishE[a] 1$_3$ (רב[יעי]) 4QRP[c] 23$_{11}$ (הרב[יעי]) 4QDibHam[a] 3.2$_5$ (י[ום]) 11QT 24$_{14}$ 28$_9$ 50$_{15}$, חֲמִישִׁי *fifth* Gn 1$_{23}$ Nm 7$_{36}$ 29$_{26}$ Jg 19$_8$ 4QCommGenA 1$_9$ 11QT 24$_{15}$, שִׁשִּׁי *sixth* Gn 1$_{31}$ Ex 16$_{5.22.29}$ Nm 7$_{42}$ 29$_{29}$ 4QJub[a] 2$_{13}$ (ב[יום]) 4QHalakhah[a] 1$_7$ (י[ום]) 4QCommGenA 1$_9$ 4QPrQuot 11$_{20}$ (י[ום]) 4Q RitPur 1.12$_1$ 11QT 24$_{16}$ CD 10$_{14}$, שְׁבִיעִי *seventh* Gn 2$_{2.2.3}$ Ex 12$_{15.16}$ 13$_6$ 16$_{27.29.30}$ 20$_{10.11}$ 23$_{12}$ 24$_{16}$ 31$_{15.17}$ 34$_{21}$ 35$_2$ Lv 13$_{5.6.27.32.34.51}$ 14$_{9.39}$ 23$_{3.8}$ Nm 6$_9$ 7$_{42}$ 19$_{12.12.19.19}$ Nm 28$_{25}$ 29$_{32}$ 31$_{19.24}$ Dt 5$_{14}$ 16$_8$ Jos 6$_{4.15}$ Jg 14$_{15.17.18}$ 2 S 12$_{18}$ 1 K 20$_{29}$ Est 1$_{10}$ 4QJub[a] 2$_1$ ([השביעי]) 2$_{17}$ (השב[יעי]) 2$_{20}$ (ה[שביבי]) 4QD[a] 6.1$_4$ 4QNidd 2.2$_4$ 3$_2$ (ה[שביעי]) 11QT 17$_{15}$ 45$_{15}$ 49$_{19}$ 50$_4$, שְׁמִינִי *eighth* Ex 22$_{29}$ Lv 9$_1$ 12$_3$ 14$_{10.23}$ 15$_{14.29}$ 22$_{27}$ 23$_{36.39}$ Nm 6$_{10}$ 7$_{54}$ 29$_{35}$ 1 K 8$_{66}$ Ezk 43$_{27}$ Ne 8$_{18}$ 2 C 7$_9$ 4QD[a] 6.2$_4$ 4QMMT B$_{72}$ 11QT 45$_5$, תְּשִׁיעִי *ninth* Nm 7$_{60}$, עֲשִׂירִי *tenth* Nm 7$_{66}$, רַב pl. *many* Gn 21$_{26}$ 37$_{34}$ Ex 2$_{23}$ Lv 15$_{25}$ Nm 9$_{19.20(ms)}$ 20$_{15}$ Dt 1$_{46}$ 2$_1$ 20$_{19}$ Jos 11$_{18}$ 22$_3$ 23$_1$ 24$_7$ 2 S 14$_2$ 1 K 2$_{38}$ 3$_{11}$||2 C 1$_{11}$ 1 K 18$_1$ Jr 13$_6$

32$_{14}$ 35$_{7}$ 37$_{16}$ Ezk 12$_{27}$ 38$_{8}$ Ho 3$_{3.4}$ Est 1$_{4}$ Dn 8$_{26}$ 1 C 7$_{22}$ 2 C 15$_{3}$ 4QTohA 1.1$_{6}$ ([רבי[ם) 11QT 59$_{21}$.

הוּא *that* Gn 15$_{18}$ 26$_{32}$ 30$_{35}$ 33$_{16}$ 48$_{20}$ Ex 5$_{6}$ 8$_{18}$ 10$_{13}$ 13$_{8}$ 14$_{30}$ 32$_{28}$ Lv 22$_{30}$ 27$_{33}$ Nm 6$_{11}$ 9$_{6.6}$ 11$_{32}$ 32$_{10}$ Dt 21$_{23}$ =11QT 64$_{11}$ Dt 27$_{11}$ 31$_{17.17.18.22}$ Jos 4$_{14}$ 6$_{15}$ 8$_{25}$ 9$_{27}$ 10$_{14.28.35}$ 14$_{9.12.12}$ 24$_{25}$ Jg 3$_{30}$ 4$_{23}$ 5$_{1}$ 6$_{32}$ 9$_{45}$ 20$_{15.21.26.35.46}$ 1 S 3$_{2.12}$ 4$_{12}$ 6$_{15.16}$ 7$_{6.10}$ 8$_{18.18}$ 9$_{24}$ 10$_{9}$ 12$_{18}$ 14$_{18.23.24.31.37}$ 16$_{13}$ 18$_{2.9}$ 19$_{24}$ 20$_{26}$ 21$_{8.11}$ 22$_{18.22}$ 27$_{6}$ 30$_{25}$ 31$_{6}$ 2 S 2$_{17}$ 3$_{37}$ 5$_{8}$ 6$_{9}$ ||1 C 13$_{12}$ 2 S 11$_{12}$ 18$_{7.8}$ 19$_{3.3.4}$ 23$_{10}$ 24$_{18}$ 1 K 8$_{64}$ 13$_{3}$ 16$_{16}$ 22$_{25.35}$||2 C 18$_{24.34}$ 2 K 3$_{6}$ Is 2$_{11.17.20}$ 3$_{7.18}$ 4$_{1.2}$ 5$_{30}$ 7$_{18.20.21.23}$ 10$_{20.27}$ 11$_{10.11}$ 12$_{1.4}$ 17$_{4.7.9}$ 19$_{16+5t}$ 20$_{6}$ 22$_{8.12.20.25}$ 23$_{15}$ 24$_{21}$ 25$_{9}$ 26$_{1}$ 27$_{1.2.12.13}$ 28$_{5}$ 29$_{18}$ 30$_{23}$ 31$_{7}$ 52$_{6}$ Jr 4$_{9}$ 25$_{33}$ 30$_{7.8}$ 39$_{10.16}$ 39$_{17}$ 46$_{10}$ 48$_{41}$ 49$_{22.26}$ 50$_{30}$ Ezk 20$_{6}$ 23$_{38.39}$ 24$_{26.27}$ 29$_{21}$ 30$_{9}$ 38$_{10.14.18.19}$ 39$_{11.22}$ 45$_{22}$ Ho 1$_{5}$ 2$_{18.20.23}$ Jl 4$_{18}$ Am 2$_{16}$ 8$_{3.9.13}$ 9$_{11}$ Ob$_{8}$ Mc 2$_{4}$ 4$_{6}$ 5$_{9}$ 7$_{11}$ Zp 1$_{9.10.15}$ 3$_{11.16}$ Hg 2$_{23}$ Zc 2$_{15}$ 3$_{10}$ 6$_{10}$ 9$_{16}$ 11$_{11}$ 12$_{3.4.6.8.9}$ 13$_{1.2.4}$ 14$_{4+6t}$ Ps 146$_{4}$ Jb 3$_{4}$ Est 5$_{9}$ 8$_{1}$ 9$_{11}$ Ne 4$_{10}$ 8$_{17}$ 12$_{43.44}$ 13$_{1}$ 1 C 16$_{7}$ 29$_{21.22}$ 2 C 15$_{11}$ 35$_{16}$ 1QM 18$_{5}$ 4QBibPar 1$_{12}$ 4QpIsa^{c} 13$_{4}$ (ה[הו]אה) 4QJub^{h} 36$_{17}$ ([ביו]ם [ההוא]) 4QCommGenA 1$_{4}$ 2$_{2}$ perh. 4QparaKings 55$_{3}$ (ליום הואה) 4QZedek 1$_{3}$ ([הה]וא) 4QM^{a} 1$_{9.11}$ 4QPrQuot 1.3$_{14}$ (ה[יו]ם) 11QT 20$_{12}$.

הֵם *those* Gn 6$_{4}$ Ex 2$_{11.23}$ Dt 17$_{9}$ 19$_{17}$ 26$_{3}$ Jos 20$_{6}$ Jg 17$_{6}$ 18$_{1.1}$ 19$_{1}$ 20$_{27.28}$ 21$_{25}$ 1 S 3$_{1}$ 28$_{1}$ 2 S 16$_{23}$ 1 K 3$_{2}$ 2 K 10$_{32}$ 15$_{37}$ 20$_{1}$||Is 38$_{1}$ Jr 31$_{29.33}$ 33$_{15.16}$ 50$_{20}$ Ezk 38$_{17}$ Zc 8$_{6.10}$ Est 1$_{2}$ 2$_{21}$ 10$_{2}$ Ne 6$_{17}$ 13$_{15.23}$ 2 C 32$_{24}$, הֵמָּה *those* 2 K 18$_{4}$ Jr 3$_{16.18}$ 5$_{18}$ 50$_{4}$ Jl 3$_{2}$ 4$_{1}$ Zc 8$_{23}$ 4QpsJub^{b} 5$_{2}$ ([ה]ימים ההמ[ה]) 4QapJoshua^{a} 23$_{3}$ ([ההמ]ה) 4QpsEzek^{c} 3.2$_{7}$ 6QPriestProph 1$_{8}$ ([בימ]ים ההם) 11QT 56$_{1}$ ([בימים הה]מה) 61$_{9}$.

זֶה *this* Gn 7$_{11.13}$ 17$_{23.26}$ 26$_{33}$ 33$_{13}$ 39$_{11}$ 47$_{26}$ 48$_{15}$ 50$_{20}$ Ex 10$_{6}$ 12$_{14.17.17.41.51}$ 13$_{13}$ 19$_{1}$ Lv 8$_{34}$ 16$_{30}$ 23$_{14.21.28.29.30}$ Nm 22$_{30}$ Dt 2$_{22.25.30}$ 3$_{14}$ 4$_{20.38}$ 5$_{24}$ 6$_{24}$ 8$_{18}$ 10$_{8.15}$ 11$_{4}$ 26$_{16}$ 27$_{9}$ 29$_{3.27}$ 32$_{48}$ 34$_{6}$ Jos 3$_{7}$ 4$_{9}$ 5$_{9.11}$ 6$_{25}$ 7$_{25.26.26}$ 8$_{28.29}$ 9$_{27}$ 10$_{27}$ 13$_{13}$ 14$_{14}$ 15$_{63}$ 16$_{10}$ 22$_{3.3.17.22}$ 23$_{8.9}$ Jg 1$_{21.26}$ 6$_{24}$ 9$_{19}$ 10$_{4.15}$ 12$_{3}$ 15$_{19}$ 18$_{12}$ 19$_{30}$ 1 S 5$_{5}$ 6$_{18}$ 8$_{8}$ 11$_{13}$ 12$_{2.5}$ 14$_{45}$ 17$_{10.46.46}$ 22$_{8.13}$ 24$_{11.20}$ 25$_{32.33}$ 26$_{21.24}$ 27$_{6}$ 28$_{18}$ 29$_{3.6.8}$ 30$_{25}$ 2 S 3$_{38}$ 4$_{3.8}$ 6$_{8}$||1 C 13$_{11}$ 2 S 7$_{6}$||1 C 17$_{5}$ 2 S 14$_{2}$ 16$_{12}$ 18$_{18.20.20}$ 1 K 1$_{30}$ 2$_{26}$ 3$_{6}$ 8$_{8}$||2 C 5$_{9}$ 1 K 8$_{24}$||2 C 6$_{15}$ 1 K 8$_{61}$ 9$_{13.21}$||2 C 8$_{8}$ 1 K 10$_{12}$ 12$_{19}$||2 C 10$_{19}$ 1 K 14$_{14}$ 2 K 2$_{22}$ 7$_{9}$ 8$_{22}$||2 C 21$_{10}$ 2 K 14$_{7}$ 16$_{6}$ 17$_{23.34.41}$ 2 K 20$_{17}$||Is 39$_{6}$ 2 K 21$_{15}$ Jr 1$_{10}$ 3$_{25}$ 7$_{25}$ 11$_{5.7}$ 25$_{3.18}$ 32$_{20.31}$ 35$_{14}$ 36$_{2}$ 44$_{2.6.10.22.23}$ Ezk 2$_{3}$ 20$_{29}$ 24$_{2.2}$ 40$_{1}$ Hg 2$_{15.18.19}$ Est 1$_{18}$ 3$_{14}$ 4$_{11}$ 8$_{13}$ Dn 9$_{27}$ Ezr 9$_{7.7.15}$ Ne 9$_{10.32}$ 1 C 4$_{41.43}$ 5$_{26}$ 1 C 28$_{7}$ 1QM 15$_{12}$ 1QDM 2$_{1}$ (ה[יו]ם) 2$_{6}$ ([היום]) 3$_{9}$ 4QBibPar 1$_{9}$ 4QJub^{c} 2$_{27}$ ([הז]ה) 4QJub^{h} 35$_{12}$ 36$_{18}$ ([ביו]ם הזה) 4Q392 2$_{3}$ 4QPrayer^{e} 1$_{2}$ 4QM^{a} 11.2$_{16}$ 4QRitMar 2$_{7}$ 4QPrQuot 1.3$_{2}$ (הי[ו]ם) 70$_{4}$ 4QDibHam^{a} 1.6$_{4}$ 11QT 17$_{3}$ 18$_{3}$ 19$_{7}$ ([היו]ם הזה) 19$_{15}$ 21$_{8}$ ([ביו]ם הזה) 21$_{9}$ (בי[ום] הזה) 21$_{12}$ 22$_{13.15}$ 25$_{9.10.12}$ 27$_{5.8}$ 5/6ḤevBA 44$_{3}$ Meṣad Ḥashavyahu ost. 1$_{9}$, אֵלֶּה *these* Zc 8$_{9.15}$ Est 1$_{5}$ 9$_{26.27.28.31}$ 4QLiturgy 1.1$_{9}$ 11QT 17$_{12}$ ([הא]לה) 43$_{4}$ (באלה הימים).

<PREP> לְ *as*, or simply introducing predicate, + היה *be* Gn 1$_{14}$.

לְ *within (a period of), after*, + היה *be* Gn 7$_{10}$ 2 S 13$_{23}$, בוא *come* Ezr 10$_{8}$, קבץ ni. *be gathered together* Ezr 10$_{9}$, מטר hi. *rain* Gn 7$_{4}$, שׁלם *be finished* Ne 6$_{15}$.

לְ *in, during, at* 1QS 10$_{5}$ perh. 11QJub fr. 7$_{1}$ (ל[יום]) perh. 11QT 43$_{17}$ (לימי erased), + בוא *come* Pr 7$_{20}$, יצא *go out* 11QT 45$_{5}$, יבל ho. *be led* Jb 21$_{30}$, יצב htp. *stand* 1QM 2$_{4}$, חזק *be strong* Ezk 22$_{14}$, לחם ni. *fight* 1QM 1$_{11}$, חשׂך *spare* Jb 21$_{30}$, נגע *touch* 4QTohA 1.1$_{4.6}$.

לְ *on, at, by*, + היה *be* Ml 3$_{17}$, כון ni. *be prepared* Ex 19$_{11.15}$, עשׂה *do* Ho 9$_{5.5}$.

לְ *for (a period of)* Ezk 12$_{27}$ Ezr 10$_{13}$ Si 37$_{25(Dmg)}$, + היה *be* 1 K 5$_{2}$ 4QHod^{b} 5$_{5}$, קדשׁ pi. *sanctify* 2 C 29$_{17}$, נתן *give* 1QH 1$_{15}$ ([ותתנם]), קרב hi. *bring near*, i.e. offer 11QT 17$_{12}$, חצה *divide* 11QT 15$_{4}$ (לשבעת [הימים]).

לְ *for*, i.e. lasting until, + היה *be* Is 30$_{8}$.

לְ *concerning* Dn 8$_{26}$ 10$_{14}$, + שׁאל *ask* Dt 4$_{32}$.

לְ *consisting of* 4QCommGenA 2$_{3}$.

לְ *according to* 4QOtot 1.7$_{18}$ ([לימ]י).

לְ *with respect to* Jb 30$_{1}$ 32$_{4.6}$.

לְ of benefit, *to, for* Dt 32$_{35(Sam)}$ (MT לִי *to me*) Ps 92$_{1}$ 1QM 7$_{5}$ (+ עָתוּד *prepared*) perh. 15$_{15}$ 1QLitPr 1$_{6}$ perh. 4QparaKings 26$_{2}$ perh. 55$_{3}$ 11QPs^{a} 27$_{6.8.8}$, + היה *be* 1QS 9$_{23}$, קדשׁ hi. *sanctify* Jr 12$_{3}$ 1QH 15$_{17}$, חשׂך *withhold* Jb 38$_{23}$, נתן *give* 4QJub^{a} 2$_{9}$ ([ויתן] ... לימ[ים]), פעל *make* Pr 16$_{4}$, כון ho. *be prepared* Pr 21$_{31}$, יעד ni. *be gathered* 1QM 15$_{3}$.

לְ of direction, *(in)to*, + בוא *come* 4QAstrCrypt 1.2$_{2.3}$ (both [תבוא ליום]) 1.2$_{6}$, שׁוב *go back* Jb 33$_{25}$, נבע hi. *pour out* Ps 19$_{3}$, נגע hi. *reach* Dn 12$_{12}$, משׁל *have dominion* 4QAstrCrypt 1$_{7}$ ([ת]משול ... ליום).

לְ of possession, *(belonging) to, of* Am 5$_{20}$ 2 C 21$_{19}$

1QS 10$_{3}$.

לְ introducing object, + נדה pi. *thrust aside* Am 6$_{3}$, בוז *despise* Zc 4$_{10}$, קרא *call*, i.e. name Est 9$_{26}$, אוה htp. *desire* 11QPs^{a} 22$_{4}$.

חכה לְ pi. *wait for* Zp 3$_{8}$, נוח לְ *rest*, i.e. wait, *for* Hb 3$_{16}$, עשׂה לְ ni. *be made*, i.e. prepared, *for* Ne 5$_{18}$, עָתִיד לְ *ready for* Est 3$_{14}$ 8$_{14(Qr)}$, שׂים לְ *place as*, i.e. make into Jb 17$_{12}$ Si 36$_{9}$, הפך לְ ni. *be turned into* Est 9$_{22}$, שׂחק לְ *laugh at* Pr 31$_{25}$.

הָהּ לַיּוֹם *alas for the day!* Ezk 30$_{2}$ Jl 1$_{15}$ (אֲהָהּ).

מִיּוֹם־לְיוֹם *from day to day, day after day*, + בשׂר pi. *give news* Ps 96‖1 C 16$_{23}$ (אֶל־יוֹם *to day*; or em. מִיָּם אֶל־/לְיָם *from sea to sea*), נוח hi. *leave over* 4QMMT B$_{10}$, נפל hi. *cast* lot Est 3$_{7}$, עבר htp. *pass over*, i.e. procrastinate Si 5$_{7(C)}$ 4QErr 1$_{2}$ ([מיום]), חרשׁ hi. *be silent* CD 9$_{6}$, נטר *keep* CD 7$_{3}$.

לַיּוֹם *for the day*, i.e. each day 1 C 26$_{17.17}$ 11QT 13$_{11}$ ([ליום]), + עשׂה *make*, i.e. offer Ex 29$_{36.38}$ Nm 28$_{24}$ Ezk 43$_{25}$ 45$_{23.23}$ 46$_{13}$, קרב hi. *bring near*, i.e. offer Nm 7$_{11.11}$ 28$_{3}$, נתן *give* Jr 37$_{21}$, אכל *eat* Ezk 4$_{10}$; לִשְׁלֹשֶׁת יָמִים *every three days*, + בוא hi. *bring* Am 4$_{4}$; לְיוֹם בְּיוֹם *for a day in a day*, i.e. day after day, + עשׂה *do* 2 C 24$_{11}$, משׁל *rule* 4QapPs^{b} 1$_{8}$; לכול יום ויום *every day* 11QT 15$_{1.3}$ (כ[ול יום ויום]) 15$_{5}$ ([לכול י]ום ויום), + שׁיר pol. *sing* 11QPs^{a} 27$_{6}$.

לְ *every* seven days, + בוא *come* 1 C 9$_{25}$.

לַיָּמִים *for the year, per year*, + נתן *give* Jg 17$_{10}$; מִיָּמִים לַיָּמִים *every year* 2 S 14$_{26}$; לְיָמִים מִיָּמִים *in the course of time*, + היה *be* 2 C 21$_{19}$.

בְּ of time, *in, on, within, among* Gn 47$_{9}$ Ex 13$_{6}$ 31$_{15}$ Lv 7$_{35}$ 23$_{3.6.8.34.35}$ Nm 3$_{1}$ 7$_{84}$ 28$_{9.16.17.18}$ Dt 16$_{8}$ Jos 14$_{11}$ Jg 17$_{6}$ 18$_{1}$ 20$_{27}$ 21$_{25}$ 1 S 21$_{8}$ Is 10$_{5}$ (if em.; see Cstr.) 18$_{4(mss)}$ Jr 16$_{19}$ 17$_{17}$ Ezk 22$_{24}$ (or em.; see below) 24$_{25}$ 23$_{12}$ Ob$_{11.11}$ Na 1$_{7}$ 2$_{4}$ Pr 25$_{13}$ (or em.; see Cstr.) 25$_{19}$ 27$_{15}$ Ec 8$_{8}$ Ne 8$_{18}$ 12$_{7.22.26.46}$ 1 C 7$_{2}$ 12$_{23}$ Si 44$_{7(Bmg)}$ 50$_{8.9}$ 1QM 1$_{12}$ 1QDM 3$_{9}$ 4$_{4}$ 1Q69 15$_{1}$ 4QpIsa^{c} 4.1$_{5}$ perh. 4QpHos^{b} 4$_{1}$ 4QJub^{a} 2$_{13}$ (ב[יו]ם) 4QJub^{h} 36$_{23}$ ([בכול י]מי) 4QpsJub^{a} 1$_{9}$ 4QCitJub 1.1$_{13}$ (בימ[ים]) 4QCommGenA 2$_{1}$ 4QHalakhah^{a} 1$_{7}$ (ב[יו]ם) 4QSD 7.1$_{5}$ 7.2$_{4}$ ([בי]ום) 7.2$_{1.4}$ 4QD^{a} 3.4$_{1}$ ([ב]יום) 4QNidd 1.1$_{4}$ 2.1$_{3}$ perh. 4QMyst^{a} 18$_{2}$ 4QMishA 1.3$_{14}$ 4QOrdo 2$_{3}$ ([בי]ום) 3$_{1}$ (בי[ום]) 4$_{2}$ 5$_{3}$ ([בי]ום) 4QRP^{c} 23$_{11}$ ([ב]יום) 4Q365a 2.1$_{2}$ 4QapJoseph^{b} 15$_{3}$ (בכל ימ[י]) 4QapJoshua^{a} 23$_{3}$ 4QapPs^{a} 7.1$_{3}$ 4QpsEzek^{c} 2$_{6}$ ([ב]ימיהם) 3.3$_{5}$ 4QpsEzek^{e} 65$_{2.9}$ 4QLiturgy 1.1$_{5.9}$ 4QBapt 8$_{3}$ (ביו[ם]) 32$_{2}$ (בי[ום]) 4Q418 184$_{2}$ 4Q423 7$_{6}$ 4QpsHod^{b} 1$_{4}$ 4QJonathan 3$_{2}$ 4QMMT C$_{18}$ 4QRitMar 2$_{7}$ perh. 202$_{1}$ perh. 4QPrQuot 140$_{2}$ (בי[ום]) perh. 174$_{1}$ (בי[ום]) 4QDibHam^{a} 1.7$_{4}$ 3.2$_{5}$ (ב[יו]ם) 4QPrFêtes^{c} 131.2$_{9}$ 4QRitPur 1.12$_{1}$ 4QOrd^{b} 3$_{2}$ 6QPriestProph 1$_{6.9}$ 6QHymn 8$_{2}$ 11QJub 4$_{30}$ (ב[יום]) 11QT 24$_{16}$ 27$_{10}$ 28$_{2}$ ([וביום]) 28$_{6.9}$ 43$_{2.2.3}$ Mur 47$_{4}$.

+ היה *be* Gn 6$_{4}$ 14$_{1}$ 26$_{1.32}$ 34$_{25}$ 40$_{20.20}$ Ex 2$_{11.23}$ 6$_{28}$ 12$_{16.16}$ 16$_{5.26.27}$ 19$_{16}$ 35$_{2}$ Lv 9$_{1}$ 14$_{2.9}$ 23$_{7.36.39.39}$ Nm 7$_{1}$ 28$_{25.26}$ 29$_{12.35}$ Dt 17$_{9}$ 19$_{17}$=11QT 61$_{9}$ Dt 21$_{16}$ 26$_{3}$ 27$_{2}$ Jos 6$_{15}$ 20$_{6}$ Jg 14$_{15.17}$ 15$_{1}$ 18$_{31}$ 19$_{5}$ 1 S 3$_{1.2}$ 13$_{22}$ 14$_{18}$ 28$_{1}$ 30$_{1}$ 2 S 1$_{2}$ 2$_{17}$ 12$_{18}$ 18$_{7}$ 19$_{3}$ 21$_{1}$ 1 K 2$_{37}$ 3$_{18}$ 20$_{29}$ 2 K 20$_{19}$‖Is 39$_{8}$ Is 4$_{2}$ 7$_{1.18.20.23}$ 10$_{20.27}$ 11$_{10.11.16}$ 14$_{3}$ 17$_{4.9}$ 19$_{16.18.19.23.24}$ 22$_{20}$ 23$_{15}$ 24$_{21}$ 27$_{12.13}$ 28$_{5}$ 30$_{25.26}$ Jr 1$_{2.3}$ 4$_{9}$ 25$_{33}$ 26$_{18}$ 30$_{8}$ 35$_{1}$ 39$_{16}$ 41$_{4}$ 48$_{41}$ 49$_{22}$ 51$_{2}$ Ezk 1$_{28}$ 16$_{56}$ 30$_{9}$ 38$_{18.18.19}$ 39$_{11}$ 43$_{27}$ 45$_{21}$ Ho 1$_{1.1.5}$ 2$_{18.23}$ 5$_{9}$ Jl 1$_{2.2}$ Am 8$_{9}$ (or em.; see Cstr.) Mc 1$_{1}$ 5$_{9}$ Zp 1$_{1.8.10}$ Hg 1$_{1}$ Zc 1$_{7}$ 12$_{3.8.9}$ 13$_{1.2.4}$ 14$_{6+5t}$ Ps 110$_{3}$ Jb 29$_{4}$ Ru 1$_{1}$ Ec 6$_{3}$ 7$_{14}$ Ec 12$_{3}$ Lm 2$_{22}$ Est 1$_{1.2}$ 5$_{1}$ Dn 10$_{2.4}$ 12$_{12}$ Si 46$_{1}$ 1QM 7$_{6}$ 4QBibPar 1$_{12}$ 4QpsEzek^{b} 1.2$_{8}$ 4QBapt 10$_{10}$ 6QPriestProph 1$_{8}$ (בימ[ים]) 11QT 56$_{1}$ ([יהיה בימים]).

חיה *live* Ezk 33$_{12}$, שׁאר ni. *remain* 1 K 22$_{47}$, ישׁב *remain* 2 S 11$_{12}$ Ezr 10$_{16}$, hi. *cause to be inhabited* Ezk 36$_{33}$, חנה *encamp* Na 3$_{17}$, הלך *go* Gn 30$_{14}$ Jr 3$_{18}$, htp. *go about* Est 2$_{11.11}$, בוא *come* Ex 16$_{1}$ 19$_{1}$ Jos 9$_{17}$ Jg 13$_{10}$ 1 S 4$_{12}$ 10$_{9}$ 2 S 24$_{18}$ 1 K 12$_{12}$‖2 C 10$_{12}$ 2 K 15$_{29}$ Is 47$_{9}$ Jr 17$_{27}$ 50$_{4}$ Ezk 23$_{39}$ 24$_{26}$ Ob$_{13}$ Zc 6$_{10}$ Pr 27$_{10}$ Est 9$_{11}$ Ne 13$_{19}$ 2 C 29$_{17}$ 32$_{26}$ 1QM 18$_{5}$ 4QMMT B$_{72}$ C$_{19}$ (בי[מי]), hi. *bring* Lv 14$_{23}$ Nm 6$_{10.13}$ 1 K 21$_{29.29}$ Jr 17$_{24}$ Ne 10$_{32}$ 13$_{15}$ 4QHalakhah^{a} 5$_{4}$ ([בי]ום) 4QZedek 1$_{3}$ ([יב]וא), יצא *go out* Ex 2$_{13}$ 16$_{29}$ Jg 20$_{25}$ 2 K 3$_{6}$ Ezk 30$_{9}$ Est 5$_{9}$ 4QCommGenA 2$_{2}$ 4QD^{a} 6.2$_{4}$, hi. *bring out* Jr 17$_{22}$ 4QSD 7.1$_{6}$ ([יו]ציא), ירד *go down* Ex 19$_{11}$, עלה *go up* Jg 20$_{30}$ 1 K 12$_{33}$ 22$_{35}$ ‖2 C 18$_{34}$ 2 K 20$_{5.8}$ 23$_{29}$ 24$_{1}$ Ezk 38$_{10}$ Si 48$_{18}$ 4QJub^{f} 39$_{6}$ ([יעלה ... בכו]ל הימ[ים]), *cause to go up*, i.e. offer 11QT 18$_{10}$, שׁוב *go back* Gn 33$_{16}$ Lv 14$_{39}$ 1 S 6$_{16}$ 1 K 12$_{12}$‖2 C 10$_{12}$ Ps 56$_{10}$, hi. *restore* Jl 4$_{1(Qr)}$, סבב *go round* Jos 6$_{4.14.15}$, עבר *pass* Is 28$_{19}$, hi. *cause to pass* Lv 25$_{9}$, נסע *set out* Nm 33$_{3}$, הפך *turn* Ps 78$_{9}$, ברח *flee* 1 S 21$_{11}$, נוס *flee* Am 2$_{16}$ Zc 14$_{5}$, נדד *flee* Is 17$_{11}$ (if em. נֵד *heap of* to נָד *it has fled*), מושׁ *move* Is 22$_{25}$, *remove* Zc 3$_{9}$, עדה hi. *remove* Pr

25$_{20}$, מהר pi. *be quick* Ps 102$_{3}$, גנב htp. *go stealthily* 2 S 19$_{4}$, נוח *rest* Gn 8$_{4}$ Ex 20$_{11}$, ישן *sleep* 4QJub^{h} 36$_{17}$ ([וישנו] ב[יו]ם) 36$_{18}$ ([וישן ... ב[יו]ם]), נפל *fall* Ex 32$_{28}$ Jos 8$_{25}$ Jg 20$_{46}$ Ezk 27$_{27}$ 1QM 1$_{9}$ 4QpNah 3.2$_{6}$ 4QSD 7.1$_{7}$, כשל *stumble* Ho 4$_{5}$ (if em.; see Coll.), ni. Ezk 33$_{12}$, hi. *make stumble* 1QpHab 11$_{8}$, פוץ ni. *be scattered* Ezk 34$_{12}$, קדם pi. *confront* 2 S 22$_{19}$||Ps 18$_{19}$, עמד *stand* Jg 20$_{28}$ Ezk 13$_{5}$ Zc 14$_{4}$ Si 6$_{8}$, קום hi. *raise up* Ex 40$_{2}$ Ho 6$_{2}$ Am 9$_{11}$, *fulfil* 1 S 3$_{12}$, דלג *leap* Zp 1$_{9}$, שׁכם hi. *rise early* Jg 19$_{8}$, שׁלח pi. *send* 1 K 8$_{66}$ Ob$_{13}$ 2 C 7$_{10}$, ערב htp. *be mingled* 4QTohA 1.1$_{6}$.

מלך *rule* Si 47$_{13}$, hi. *make king* 1 K 16$_{16}$, עשׂה *do, make* Gn 5$_{1}$ 21$_{8}$ 42$_{18}$ Ex 31$_{15}$ Lv 8$_{34}$ 23$_{12}$ Nm 9$_{3.5.6.11}$ Jos 5$_{10}$ 2 S 23$_{10}$ 1 K 11$_{12}$ 12$_{32}$ Is 58$_{13}$ Jr 5$_{18}$ Ezk 45$_{22.25}$ 46$_{12}$ Hg 1$_{15}$ Ca 8$_{8}$ 1 C 5$_{10}$ 2 C 7$_{9}$ Si 46$_{7}$ 49$_{3}$ 4QJub^{a} 2$_{4}$ (... ב[יו]ם [עשה]) 2$_{6}$ perh. 4QapPs^{b} 1$_{3}$ (בימי corrected to ביומי or בימו; but perh. = *by means of an oath*) 4QpsMos^{e} 1$_{4}$ 11QT 17$_{15}$ 24$_{12.13.14.15}$ 27$_{5}$ CD 10$_{14}$ 11$_{2}$, פעל *do* Hb 1$_{5}$ Ps 44$_{2.2}$, יצר *form* Gn 2$_{4}$, בנה *build* 1 K 16$_{34}$ Am 9$_{11}$, ni. *be built* Si 50$_{2}$, שׂוג pilp. *fence about* Is 17$_{11}$, נשׂא *lift* Gn 22$_{4}$ Is 3$_{7}$ Jr 17$_{21.27}$ Ezk 20$_{5.6}$ Mc 2$_{4}$, סור *depart* Ne 9$_{19}$ (בְּיוֹמָם appar. *during their day*; mss יוֹמָם *by day*) CD 16$_{4}$, hi. *remove* Gn 30$_{35}$ Is 3$_{18}$, הגה *remove* Is 27$_{8}$, מאס *reject* Is 31$_{7}$, ערך *arrange* Lv 24$_{8.8}$ Jg 20$_{22}$, קרב *draw near* Nm 9$_{6}$ Jg 20$_{24}$ Lm 3$_{57}$ 4QD^{e} 2.1$_{18}$, hi. *bring near*, i.e. offer Lv 6$_{13}$ Nm 7$_{10+15t}$ 29$_{17+5t}$ Ezk 43$_{22}$ 44$_{27}$ 46$_{4.6}$ 4QRP^{c} 23$_{10}$ 11QT 13$_{17}$ 17$_{12}$ (בכול יום ויום) 19$_{15}$ 25$_{12}$, זבח *sacrifice* Dt 16$_{4}$ 1 S 6$_{15}$ Ne 12$_{43}$ 2 C 15$_{11}$ 4QMMT B$_{36}$ 11QT 52$_{6}$, חגג *celebrate festival* Lv 23$_{39}$, פקד *visit* Ex 32$_{34}$ Is 27$_{1}$ Am 3$_{14}$, *enrol* CD 15$_{7}$ 11QT 57$_{2}$ ([יפ]קו[דו]), ni. *be appointed* Ne 12$_{44}$, פלה hi. *set apart* Ex 8$_{18}$, קדשׁ pi. *sanctify* Nm 6$_{11}$ 1 K 8$_{64}$, hi. Nm 3$_{13}$ 8$_{17}$, גדל *be great* Zc 12$_{11}$, pi. *make great* Jos 4$_{14}$, שׂגב ni. *be exalted* Is 2$_{11.17}$, פלא ni. *be wonderful* Zc 8$_{6}$, שׁפט *judge* Jg 15$_{20}$ 4QsapDidB 6$_{3}$, עטר pi. *crown* Ca 3$_{11.11}$, עזר *help* Is 49$_{8}$, אבל hi. *cause to mourn* Ezk 31$_{15}$, htp. *mourn* Dn 10$_{2}$, חלל hi. *begin* 2 K 10$_{32}$ 15$_{37}$, מרה *rebel*, i.e. contend with 4QD^{e} 6.5$_{17}$ ([ימר]).

אמר *say* Dt 31$_{17}$ Jg 14$_{18}$ 2 S 5$_{8}$ 2 K 6$_{29}$ Is 12$_{1.4}$ 20$_{6}$ 25$_{9}$ Jr 3$_{6}$ 31$_{29}$ Est 1$_{10}$ 7$_{2}$, ni. *be said* Zp 3$_{16}$, דבר pi. *speak* Dt 9$_{10}$ 10$_{4}$ Jos 10$_{12}$ 14$_{12}$ 1 S 20$_{26}$ 2 S 22$_{1}$||Ps 18$_{1}$ Ezk 12$_{25}$ 38$_{17}$ CD 10$_{17}$, נגד hi. *tell* Ex 13$_{8}$, ho. *be told* Gn 31$_{22}$, ספר pi. *tell* GnzPs 4$_{25}$, בשׂר pi. *give news* 2 S 18$_{20}$, קרא *call* Ex 24$_{16}$ Is 22$_{12}$ Zc 3$_{10}$ Ps 50$_{15}$ 88$_{10}$ 116$_{2}$ 4QapPs^{b} 24$_{7}$, i.e. name Gn 5$_{2}$ Jg 6$_{32}$, *read* Jr 36$_{6}$, ni. *be called* Est 3$_{12}$, *be read* Ne 13$_{1}$, ענה *answer* Gn 30$_{33}$ 35$_{3}$ 1 S 8$_{18}$ 14$_{37}$ Ps 20$_{2.10}$ 102$_{3}$ 138$_{3}$, ברך pi. *bless* Gn 48$_{20}$ Ps 145$_{2}$ 4QLiturgy 1.1$_{3}$ 4QPrQuot 37.12$_{13.23}$ (both [יברכו]) Kuntillet 'Ajrud add. inscr. 3$_{2.3}$, הלל pi. *praise* Ps 119$_{164}$, נבא ni. *prophesy* Jr 26$_{18}$ Ezk 38$_{17}$, צוה pi. *command* Ex 5$_{6}$ Lv 7$_{36.38}$ Dt 27$_{11}$ Jr 7$_{22}$ 11$_{4}$, שׁאל *ask* Dt 18$_{16}$, עוד hi. *warn* Jr 11$_{7}$ Ne 13$_{15}$, שׁבע ni. *swear* Jos 14$_{9}$, קלל pi. *curse* 1 K 2$_{8}$, יכח hi. *rebuke* 1QS 5$_{26}$, שׁיר *sing* Jg 5$_{1}$, ho. *be sung* Is 26$_{1}$, ענה pi. *sing* Is 27$_{2}$, זעק *cry out* 1 S 8$_{18}$, נהם *growl* Is 5$_{30}$, ילל *howl* 4QpsEzek^{c} 5$_{4}$, hi. Am 8$_{3}$, תקע *sound trumpet* Nm 10$_{10}$.

ראה *see* Lv 13$_{5.6.27.32.34.51}$ Dt 4$_{15}$ 1 K 22$_{25}$||2 C 18$_{24}$ Jr 18$_{17}$ (or em. hi. *show*) Ob$_{12.13}$ Ec 7$_{14.15}$ Ec 8$_{16}$ Ne 13$_{15.23}$ 4QD^{a} 6.1$_{4}$, חזה *see* Am 1$_{1.1}$, נבט hi. *look* Is 22$_{8}$, שׁעה *gaze at* Is 17$_{7}$, שׁמע *hear* Nm 30$_{8}$ (unless transfer בְּיוֹם שָׁמְעוֹ *on the day when he hears* to follow לָהּ *to her*) Jos 14$_{12}$ 2 S 19$_{3}$ Is 29$_{19}$ Zc 8$_{9}$ Ne 8$_{2}$, חרשׁ hi. *be silent* Nm 30$_{8}$ (if transfer; see above) 30$_{15}$, ידע *know* 1 S 22$_{22}$ 3$_{37}$ 2 K 24$_{2}$ Is 19$_{21}$ 52$_{6}$ Ezk 38$_{14}$, ni. *be known* Pr 12$_{16}$, hi. *make known* CD 9$_{22}$, בין hi. *understand* Ne 8$_{2}$, יעץ *give counsel* 2 S 16$_{23}$, זמם *purpose* Zc 8$_{15}$, זכר *remember* Ezk 16$_{60}$ Ec 12$_{1}$ Lm 2$_{1}$, ni. *be remembered* Si 3$_{15}$, ירא *fear* 2 S 6$_{9}$||1 C 13$_{12}$ Ps 49$_{6}$, כתב *write* Dt 31$_{22}$ Ezr 4$_{7}$, ni. *be written* Ne 12$_{22}$ 1 C 4$_{41}$, חרץ ni. *be decided* 4QBéat 22$_{2}$, ישׁע hi. *save* Ex 14$_{30}$ 1 S 14$_{23}$ Zc 9$_{16}$, ni. *be saved* Jr 23$_{6}$ 33$_{16}$ Si 34$_{6}$, נצל hi. *deliver* Jr 39$_{17}$ Ezk 7$_{19}$ 33$_{12}$ Zp 1$_{18}$ 1QpHab 12$_{14}$, ni. *be delivered* Si 34$_{6(Bmg)}$, מלט pi. *deliver* Ps 41$_{2}$ Si 51$_{12}$, גנן *protect* Zc 12$_{8}$, חמל *spare* Pr 6$_{34}$, יעל hi. *profit* Pr 11$_{4}$ Si 5$_{8}$, חשׁב ni. *be reckoned* 1 K 10$_{21}$||2 C 9$_{20}$, צלח *succeed* Jr 22$_{30}$, hi. *cause to succeed* 2 C 26$_{5}$, כון ni. *be prepared* 2 C 35$_{16}$, pol. *be established* Ezk 28$_{13}$.

ילד ni. *be born* Jb 3$_{3}$, pi. *assist to give birth* CD 11$_{13}$, pu. *be born* Jr 20$_{14}$, חיל ho. *be brought to birth* Is 66$_{8}$, פרה *be fruitful*, i.e. multiply Jr 3$_{16}$, רבה *increase* Jr 3$_{16}$, hi. *make many* Ne 6$_{17}$, פרח *flourish* Ps 72$_{7}$, צמח hi. *cause to grow* Jr 33$_{15}$ Ezk 29$_{21}$, יחשׂ htp. *be enrolled by genealogy* 1 C 5$_{17,17}$, מלא ni. *be paid in full* Jb 15$_{32}$ (בְּלֹא יוֹמוֹ *when it is not his day*, i.e. before his time; or em. תִּמָּלֵא to תְּמַל *it will wither*, from מלל), שׂבע *be satisfied* Ps 37$_{19}$, נחל hi. *cause to inherit* Si 30$_{32}$ ([הנח]ל), פתח ni. *be opened* Gn 3$_{5}$ Ezk 24$_{27}$ 46$_{1.1}$, בקע ni. *break out* Gn 7$_{11.11}$ 4QComm

GenA 1$_{4}$, פלג ni. *be divided* Gn 10$_{25}$ 1 C 1$_{19}$, שקל ni. *be weighed* Ezr 8$_{33}$, שמח *rejoice* Ob$_{12}$ Ps 90$_{14}$ 11QT 21$_{9}$ (בי[ום]) 25$_{9}$, חדה *rejoice* Jb 3$_{6}$, יטב hi. *make glad* Ec 11$_{9}$, גדל hi. *act boastfully* Ob$_{12}$, נוא hi. *restrain* Nm 30$_{6.9}$ 11QT 53$_{20}$, קצף *be angry* Est 2$_{21}$, חזק hi. *seize* Is 4$_{1}$ Zc 8$_{23}$, pu. *be repaired* Si 50$_{1}$.

פרר hi. *annul* Nm 30$_{13}$ 11QT 54$_{3}$, ho. *be annulled* Zc 11$_{11}$, סתר hi. *hide* Dt 31$_{18}$ Ps 102$_{3}$, ni. *hide oneself* 1 S 20$_{19}$, צפן *hide* Ps 27$_{5}$, כסה pi. *cover* Nm 9$_{15}$, סכך *cover* Ps 140$_{8}$, חלה *be sick* 2 K 20$_{1}$||Is 38$_{1}$ 2 C 32$_{24}$, יבש *be dry* Gn 8$_{14}$, רשע hi. *do wickedly* CD 20$_{27}$, טמא *be unclean* Lv 13$_{14}$, ni. *defile oneself* 4QHalakhah[a] 1$_{6}$ ([הטמ]יא), pi. *defile* Ezk 23$_{38}$, חטא pi. *purify* Nm 19$_{19}$, htp. *purify oneself* Nm 19$_{12.12.12.12}$ 31$_{19.19}$, נזה hi. *sprinkle* Nm 19$_{19.19}$ 11QT 49$_{18.19}$ 50$_{4.14.15}$, שפך *pour* Jl 3$_{2}$, נגר ni. *be poured* Jb 20$_{28}$, hi. *pour*, i.e. deliver up perh. 4QapPs[b] 31$_{7}$ ([תגיר]), רחץ *wash* 4QOrd[c] 1.1$_{3}$ (בי[ו]ם) 1.1$_{5.8}$ 11QT 45$_{9}$ 49$_{17}$ 50$_{14}$ (במים *with water* corrected to בים), כבס pi. *wash* Nm 31$_{24}$ 4QOrd[c] 1.1$_{3}$ (בי[ו]ם) 1.1$_{5.8}$ 11QT 45$_{9.15}$, טבל *immerse* 4QTohA 1.2$_{2}$ (ט[בו]ל), נטף *drip* Jl 4$_{18}$, טהר pi. *cleanse* 11QT 49$_{13}$, כבד pi. *cleanse* 11QT 49$_{11}$, כפר pi. *make atonement* Lv 16$_{30}$ 11QT 21$_{8}$ ([בי[ו]ם]) 22$_{15}$, pu. *be atoned* 1QDM 3$_{11}$, כרת *cut* Ezk 16$_{4}$, i.e. make, covenant Gn 15$_{18}$ Jos 24$_{25}$ Jr 31$_{32}$ 34$_{13}$ Ho 2$_{20}$, מול ni. *be circumcised* Lv 12$_{3}$ CD 16$_{6}$, גלח pi. *shave* Nm 6$_{9.9}$ Is 7$_{20}$, חפר *dig* Gn 26$_{15.18}$, קבר *bury* Dt 21$_{23}$=11QT 64$_{11}$, בער pi. *kindle* fire Ex 35$_{3}$, שרף ni. *be burned* Lv 7$_{17}$, חרה *burn* Nm 32$_{10}$ Dt 31$_{17}$, זעם *be indignant* Ps 7$_{12}$ (or em. בְּכָל־יוֹם *every day* to בִּכְלַיִּים *with the knaves*).

נתן *give, place* Gn 16$_{29}$ Ex 22$_{29}$ Lv 5$_{24}$ 27$_{33}$ Dt 24$_{15}$ Jos 9$_{27}$ 1 S 12$_{18}$ 27$_{6}$ 1 K 13$_{3}$ Jr 39$_{10}$ Ezk 43$_{18}$ Est 8$_{1}$ Ne 12$_{47.47}$ 1 C 16$_{7}$ 22$_{9}$, שים *place* 1 S 21$_{7}$ Zc 12$_{6}$, יסף ho. *be added* 4QD[a] 6.1$_{11}$, סגר hi. *deliver up* Ob$_{14}$, לקח *take* Lv 14$_{10}$ 15$_{14.29}$ 23$_{40}$ 1 S 18$_{2}$ Hg 2$_{23}$ Ne 10$_{32}$ 4QSD 7.1$_{3}$ ([יקח]), לכד *capture* Jos 10$_{28.32.35}$, אסף *gather* Mc 4$_{6}$, ni. *gather together* Ne 8$_{13}$ 9$_{1}$, לקט *gather* Ex 16$_{22}$ 4QD[e] 3.2$_{18}$, קשש po. *gather* Nm 15$_{32}$, קהל ni. *be gathered together* Est 8$_{12}$ 9$_{1.1.15}$ 2 C 20$_{26}$, פקד htp. *be mustered* Jg 20$_{15}$, קנה *buy* Ru 4$_{5}$, לוה ni. *be joined* Zc 2$_{15}$, מצא *find* Is 58$_{3}$, ni. *be found* Si 6$_{10}$, שלך hi. *cast* Is 2$_{20}$, ho. *be cast* Jr 36$_{30}$ Ezk 16$_{5}$, בקש pi. *seek* Jg 18$_{1}$ 4QpIsa[c] 13$_{4}$ ([יבק]שו), pu. *be sought* Jr 50$_{20}$, דרש *seek* Ps 77$_{3}$ 1 C 13$_{3}$ 2 C 26$_{5}$, ציד htp. *take as one's provision* Jos 9$_{12}$, אכל *eat, consume* Gn 31$_{40}$ Ex 12$_{18}$ 1 S 9$_{24}$ 20$_{34}$ 2 S 18$_{8}$ Am 1$_{14}$ 1 C 29$_{22}$ 11QT 22$_{13}$ 43$_{15.16}$ CD 10$_{22}$, ni. *be eaten* Lv 7$_{15.16.18}$ 19$_{6.7}$ 22$_{30}$ 11QT 20$_{12}$ 43$_{4.17.17}$ 4QMMT B$_{11}$ ([נאכלת]), רעה *graze* Is 30$_{23}$, שתה *drink* 1 C 29$_{22}$, צום *fast* Jg 20$_{26}$ 1 S 7$_{6}$.

רפה hi. *forsake* Si 51$_{10.10}$, htp. *show oneself weak* Pr 24$_{10}$ (or em. בַּיָּם *in the sea*), עלף htp. *be faint* Am 8$_{13}$, עצר *retain* 2 C 13$_{20}$, נגש ni. *be hard pressed* 1 S 14$_{24}$, עוה hi. *commit iniquity* 2 S 19$_{20}$, עכר *trouble* Jos 7$_{25}$, פשע *rebel* 2 K 8$_{20}$||2 C 21$_{8}$, רעם hi. *thunder* 1 S 7$_{10}$, רעש *shake* Is 13$_{13}$, חרד *tremble* Ezk 32$_{10}$, גשם pu. *be rained upon* Ezk 22$_{24}$ (if em. גֻּשְׁמָהּ *her rain* to גֻּשְׁמָה *she will be rained upon*), חשך hi. *darken* Am 8$_{9}$, בוש *be ashamed* Zp 3$_{11}$, חדל *cease* Jg 5$_{6.6}$, שקט *be quiet* Jg 8$_{28}$ 2 C 13$_{23}$, שבת *rest* Gn 2$_{2.3}$ Ex 16$_{30}$ 23$_{12}$ 31$_{17}$ 34$_{21}$ 4QJub[a] 2$_{1.17.20}$ (לשבותם[בו]), hi. *cause to cease* Ex 12$_{15}$ Jr 16$_{9}$ 4QJub[d] 21$_{24}$, שחט *slaughter* Lv 22$_{28}$, הרג *kill* Lm 2$_{21}$ Est 8$_{12}$ 2 C 28$_{6}$, אבד *perish* Ps 146$_{4}$ 4QpsEzek[c] 3.2$_{7}$, pi. *destroy* Est 3$_{13}$ 8$_{12}$, hi. *destroy* Ob$_{8}$, כלה pi. *destroy* 1QpHab 13$_{2}$, *finish* Gn 2$_{2}$ Ne 3$_{34}$ (or em. בַּיּוֹם *in a day* to בִּנְיָנָם *their structure*) 2 C 29$_{17}$, שחת hi. *destroy* Jg 20$_{21.35}$, שמד hi. *destroy* Est 8$_{12}$, חרם hi. *destroy* Jos 10$_{35}$, דמם ni. *be destroyed* Jr 49$_{26}$ 50$_{30}$, שדד *destroy* Ho 10$_{14}$, בזז *plunder* Est 8$_{12}$, ספה ni. *be swept away* Si 5$_{7}$, נכה hi. *strike* 1 S 14$_{31}$ 2 S 23$_{20}$||1 C 11$_{22}$ 1 K 20$_{29}$ Zc 12$_{4}$ Siloam tunnel inscr.$_{3}$, ho. *be struck* Nm 25$_{18}$, מחץ *shatter* Ps 110$_{5}$, כנע *subdue* Jg 4$_{23}$, ni. *be subdued* Jg 3$_{30}$, לחם ni. *fight* Zc 14$_{3}$, שבר *break* 4QpsEzek[d] 1.2$_{4}$, ni. *be broken* Dn 11$_{20}$, עסס *crush* Ml 3$_{21}$, יגה hi. *cause grief* Lm 1$_{12}$, תלה *hang* 2 S 21$_{12}$, זקן *be old* 1 S 17$_{12}$, מות *die* Gn 2$_{17}$ Ex 10$_{28}$ 1 S 2$_{34}$ 31$_{6}$, hi. *put to death* 1 S 22$_{18}$ 2 K 2$_{26}$ (or em. בַּיּוֹם הַזֶּה *in this day* to בָּזֶה or עִם זֶה *in spite of this*), ho. *be put to death* 1 S 11$_{13}$ 2 S 21$_{9}$.

בְּעֶצֶם הַיּוֹם הַזֶּה *on this selfsame day*, + היה *be* Ex 12$_{41.51}$ Ezk 40$_{1}$, בוא *come* Gn 7$_{13}$, יצא hi. *bring out* Ex 12$_{17}$, דבר pi. *speak* Dt 32$_{48}$, קרא *proclaim* Lv 23$_{21}$, עשה *do* Lv 23$_{28.30}$, מול *circumcise* Gn 17$_{23}$, ni. *be circumcised* Gn 17$_{26}$, ענה pu. *be afflicted* Lv 23$_{29}$, htp. *afflict oneself* 11QT 25$_{12}$, סמך *lean*, i.e. besiege Ezk 24$_{2}$, אכל *eat* Jos 5$_{11}$.

דְּבַר יוֹם בְּיוֹמוֹ *the thing of a day for its day*, i.e. what is appropriate or due each day Ex 5$_{13.19}$ 16$_{4}$ Lv 23$_{37}$ 1 K 8$_{59}$ 2 K 25$_{30}$||Jr 52$_{34}$ Dn 1$_{5}$ Ezr 3$_{4}$ Ne 11$_{23}$ 12$_{47}$ 1 C 16$_{37}$ 2 C 8$_{13}$ (בְּיוֹם *for a day*) 8$_{14}$ 31$_{16}$ 4QPentPar[b] 23$_{7}$ (דבר

(יום[ ]) 4QM^{a} 1$_{8}$ ([ביומו]).

עולת [יום] ביומו *burnt offering of a day in a day*, i.e. daily burnt offering 11QT 29$_{4}$.

לְיוֹם בְּיוֹם *for a day in a day*, i.e. day after day 2 C 24$_{11}$ 4QapPs^{b} 1$_{8}$.

יוֹם בְּיוֹם *day after day* Ne 8$_{18}$ 2 C 30$_{21}$; בוא בַּיָּמִים *come into days*, i.e. become old Gn 18$_{11}$ 24$_{1}$ Jos 13$_{1.1}$ 23$_{1.2}$ 1 K 1$_{1}$.

בְּ *concerning*, + ירה hi. *teach* Lv 14$_{57.57}$, הלל htp. *boast* Pr 27$_{1}$.

בְּ *over* Ps 136$_{8}$ (מֶמְשֶׁלֶת בַּיּוֹם *dominion over the day*), + משל *rule* Gn 1$_{18}$ 4QJub^{a} 2$_{8}$; ראה בְּ *look at*, i.e. gloat over Ob$_{12}$ (or em.; see Cstr.).

מִבֵּין בְּ *during* Si 50$_{6}$.

כְּ *as* Dt 33$_{25}$ (or em. כְּיַמֶּיךָ *as your seas*) Is 54$_{9}$ (if em.; see Cstr.) 65$_{22}$ Am 8$_{10}$ Ps 90$_{4}$ Jb 7$_{1}$ 10$_{5.5}$ Si 50$_{24}$ perh. 4QpsEzek^{e} 70$_{1}$ ([כימ]י) perh. 4QSap^{b} 1.1$_{5}$ perh. 4QPrQuot 33.11$_{3}$, + היה *be* Gn 29$_{20}$ Lv 25$_{50}$ Jos 10$_{14}$ Si 45$_{15}$, רבה *be many* Dt 11$_{21}$, נתן *give*, i.e. make Jb 29$_{2}$, שׂים *place*, i.e. make Ps 89$_{30}$, אור hi. *give light* Ps 139$_{12}$.

כְּ *as in* Zc 8$_{11}$, + היה *be* Lv 15$_{25}$, עמד *stand* Dt 10$_{10}$, שׁכן *dwell* Jr 46$_{26}$, ישׁב hi. *cause to dwell* Ho 12$_{10}$, יצג hi. *place* Ho 2$_{5}$, נתן *give* Lm 2$_{7}$, נחל htp. *inherit* Si 36$_{16}$, עשׂה *do*, i.e. keep Est 9$_{22}$, ראה hi. *show* Mc 7$_{15}$, עור *awake* Is 51$_{9}$, קרא *call* Lm 2$_{22}$, ענה *answer* Ho 2$_{17.17}$, טמא *be unclean* Lv 12$_{2}$ 4QSD 7.2$_{15}$ 4QD^{a} 6.2$_{6}$ ([וטמאה] ... [כ]י[מי]), חתת hi. *shatter* Is 9$_{3}$, שׁחת pi. *act corruptly* Ho 9$_{9}$, לחם ni. *fight* Zc 14$_{3}$, עמק hi. *deepen* Ho 9$_{9}$, קשׁה hi. *harden* Ps 95$_{8}$, רעה *graze* Mc 7$_{14}$, ערב *be sweet* Ml 3$_{4}$.

כְּ *about* Is 23$_{15}$, *(in) about*, + היה *be* 1 S 25$_{38}$; *(for) about*, + אוץ *hasten* Jos 10$_{13}$.

כְּ *according to*, + ישׁב *remain* Dt 14$_{6}$, שׂמח pi. *make glad* Ps 90$_{15}$; כימם *according to the days*, i.e. a few days ago, + אסם *store* Meṣad Ḥashavyahu ost. 1$_{5.7}$.

כַּיּוֹם (1) *at about this day*, i.e. now, + עמד *stand* 1 S 9$_{27}$, צום *fast* Is 58$_{4}$.

(2) *first of all*, + מכר *sell* Gn 25$_{31}$, שׁבע ni. *swear* Gn 25$_{33}$ 1 K 1$_{51}$ (mss הַיּוֹם *today*), קטר hi. *burn* 1 S 2$_{16}$, דרשׁ *seek* 1 K 22$_{5}$||2 C 18$_{4}$.

כַּיּוֹם הַזֶּה *as at this day* Dn 9$_{7}$, + היה *be* Dt 4$_{20}$ 1 K 8$_{61}$ Jr 44$_{6}$, קרא *befall* Jr 44$_{23}$, עשׂה *do* Gn 50$_{20}$, נתן *give* Dt 2$_{30}$ 4$_{38}$ Jr 11$_{5}$ 15$_{18}$, צוה pi. *command* Dt 8$_{18}$, בחר *choose* Dt 10$_{15}$, שׁלח *cast* Dt 29$_{27}$, מלא pi. *fulfil* 1 K 8$_{24}$||2 C 6$_{15}$, עשׂה *make, do* Jr 32$_{20}$ Dn 9$_{15}$ 1 C 28$_{7}$, שׁאר ni. *remain* Ezr 9$_{15}$.

כְּהַיּוֹם *at about this day*, i.e. now, + מצא *find* 1 S 9$_{13}$, שׁוב hi. *bring back* Ne 5$_{11}$.

כְּהַיּוֹם הַזֶּה (1) *as at this day* Dn 9$_{7(Or)}$, + היה *be* Jr 44$_{22}$, חיה pi. *keep alive* Dt 6$_{24}$, ישׁב *sit* 1 K 3$_{6}$, קום *rise* 1 S 22$_{13}$, hi. *raise up* 1 S 22$_{8}$, נתן ni. *be given* Ezr 9$_{7}$, עשׂה *make* Ne 9$_{10}$, רצה *expiate* 4QDibHam^{a} 1.6$_{4}$.

(2) *on this particular day*, + היה *be* Gn 39$_{11}$.

עת כיום *a time at about this day*, i.e. now, at this time Lachish ost. 2$_{3.3}$ 4$_{1}$ 5$_{3}$ ([עת כים]) 5$_{3}$ 8$_{2}$ (both [עת כ]ים) 8$_{2}$ ([עת]).

כְּיוֹם בְּיוֹם *as (he did) day by day*, + נגן pi. *play stringed instrument* 1 S 18$_{10}$.

כְּפִי *according to*, + שׂכל hi. *enlighten* 1QSa 1$_{7}$.

מִן *from, since, after* 2 K 8$_{6}$ Is 23$_{7}$ Ezk 28$_{15}$ 39$_{22}$ Mc 5$_{1}$ Na 2$_{9}$ (or em.; see Cstr.) Ezr 9$_{7}$ Ne 5$_{14}$ Si 40$_{1}$ 44$_{2.7(B)}$ 2 C 30$_{26}$ 1QDM 2$_{6}$ ([מ]יום) 4QpsJub^{b} 6$_{4}$ 4QD^{h} 5$_{5}$ 4QMMT C$_{19(ms\ d)}$, 5QRègle 24$_{3}$ ([מי]ום) 11QT 43$_{7.9}$ CD 19$_{35}$ 20$_{13}$, + היה *be* Dt 9$_{24}$ Jos 23$_{1}$ Jg 11$_{4}$ 15$_{1}$ 1 S 7$_{2}$ 30$_{25}$ 2 K 21$_{15}$ Lm 1$_{7}$ Ne 4$_{10}$, חיה hi. *revive* Ho 6$_{2}$, ישׁב *dwell* 1 C 17$_{5}$, דבר pi. *speak* Jr 36$_{2.2}$, קרא *read* Ne 8$_{18}$, צוה pi. *command* Nm 15$_{23}$ Jb 38$_{12}$ Lm 2$_{17}$, ברך pi. *bless* Hg 2$_{19}$, שׁבע ni. *swear* Mc 7$_{20}$, חרשׁ hi. *be silent* Nm 30$_{15}$, שׁמע ni. *be heard* Dn 10$_{12}$, ראה *see* Ex 10$_{6}$, זוע *tremble* Si 48$_{12}$, בוא *come* CD 7$_{12}$ 14$_{1}$, שׁוב *go back* Jg 14$_{8}$, צלח *rush* 1 S 16$_{13}$, מצא *find* 1 S 29$_{3.6.8}$ Ne 9$_{32}$, ni. *be found* 1 S 25$_{28}$, חלל hi. *begin* Ezr 3$_{6}$ 4QpsMos^{e} 2.1$_{5}$ ([ו]ח[ל]ו), פתח ni. *be opened* CD 5$_{3}$, פקד ni. *be mustered* Ezk 38$_{8}$, נצל ni. *be saved* 1QpMic 8$_{8}$, עשׂה *do* 1 S 8$_{8}$ Is 37$_{3}$ Ne 8$_{17}$ 1QJub^{b} 35$_{10}$ (=4QJub^{h} 35$_{10}$ [ועשׂ]ה), ni. *be done, kept* 2 K 23$_{22}$ 2 C 35$_{18}$, שׂים *place* Hg 2$_{15.18.18}$, pass. *be placed*, i.e. determined 2 S 13$_{32}$, כון ni. *be established* 2 C 8$_{16}$ (if em.; see below), אכל *eat* Ex 12$_{15}$, זבח *sacrifice* Ezr 4$_{2}$, בחר *choose* 1 K 8$_{16}$||2 C 6$_{5}$, רצה ni. *be accepted* Lv 22$_{27}$, חכר *rent* Mur 24 2$_{13}$ 3$_{11}$ 5$_{8}$, ספר *count* Lv 23$_{15}$ 11QT 18$_{11}$ 19$_{11}$ 21$_{12}$ ([ספר]תמה), עין *eye* 1 S 18$_{9(Qr)}$, מרה hi. *be rebellious* Dt 9$_{24}$, עצב *grieve* 1 K 1$_{6}$ (מִיָּמָיו *since his days*, i.e. throughout his life), כעס hi. *anger* 2 K 21$_{15}$, חטא *sin* Ho 10$_{9}$, שׁלם hi. *bring to an end* Is 38$_{12.13}$.

מִיּוֹם *from today*, i.e. henceforth Is 43$_{13}$ Ezk 48$_{35}$;

לְיָמִים מִיָּמִים *in the course of time* 2 C 21$_{19}$.

מִן causative, *on account of*, + חרף *reproach* Jb 27$_{6}$.

מִן privative, *away from, without*, + שׁקט hi. *make quiet* Ps 94$_{13}$ (or em.; see Cstr.).

מִן of comparison, *(more) than* Ec 7$_{1}$ Si 36$_{7(Segal)}$ (מ[יו]ם) 4QJub^{c} 2$_{26}$ (מ[כל הימים]).

מִיּוֹם־לְיוֹם *from day to day, day after day, from one day to the next*, + בשׂר pi. *give news* Ps 96$_{2}$||1 C 16$_{23}$ (אֶל־יוֹם *to day*; or em.; see above), נפל hi. *cast* lot Est 3$_{7}$, נוח hi. *leave over* 4QMMT B$_{10}$, עבר htp. *pass over*, i.e. procrastinate Si 5$_{7(C)}$ (A אֶל) 4QErr 1$_{2}$ ([מיום]), חרשׁ hi. *be silent* Nm 30$_{15}$ (אֶל) CD 9$_{6}$, נטר *keep* CD 7$_{3}$.

מִיָּמִים יָמִימָה *from year to year*, lit. from days to days Jg 21$_{19}$ 4QCommGenD 3$_{2}$, + שׁמר *keep* Ex 13$_{10}$, הלך *go* Jg 11$_{40}$, עלה *go up* 1 S 1$_{3}$, hi. *bring up* 1 S 2$_{19}$.

לְמִן *from*, + היה *be* Ex 9$_{18}$ Dt 4$_{32}$ 9$_{7}$ Jr 32$_{31}$, ישׁב *dwell* 2 S 7$_{6}$, בוא *come* Is 7$_{17}$, שׁלח *send* Jr 7$_{25}$, סור *turn aside* Ml 3$_{7}$, ראה ni. *be seen* Jg 19$_{30}$, מרה hi. *be rebellious* Dt 9$_{7}$, ענה pi. *afflict* 2 S 7$_{11}$, בלה pi. *wear out*, i.e. trouble 1 C 17$_{10}$, כבס pi. *wash* 2 S 19$_{25}$, עשׂה *do* 2 S 19$_{25}$ 2 K 19$_{25}$, שׂים *place* Hg 2$_{18}$.

עַל *on*, + בוא *come* 1 S 25$_{8}$, שׁכן *dwell* Jb 3$_{4}$, יפע hi. *shine* Jb 3$_{4}$.

עַל *upon*, i.e. in addition to 2 C 21$_{15}$ (יָמִים עַל־יָמִים *day upon day*), + יסף hi. *add* 2 K 20$_{6}$||Is 38$_{5}$ Ps 61$_{7}$.

עַל *on account of*, + פנה hi. *turn* Jr 47$_{4}$.

שׁמם עַל ni. *be appalled at* Jb 18$_{20}$.

עַד *until, unto, by (the time of)* Gn 19$_{37.38}$ 26$_{33}$ 35$_{20}$ Jg 12$_{6}$ 6$_{24}$ 15$_{19}$ Ezr 9$_{7}$ Si 40$_{1}$ 4QBibPar 1$_{9}$ 4QpsJub^{a} 1$_{7}$ 4Q392 2$_{3}$ 4QPrayer^{e} 1$_{2}$ 11QT 43$_{8}$, + היה *be* Ex 12$_{6}$ Jos 4$_{9}$ 14$_{14}$ Jg 13$_{7}$ 18$_{30}$ 1 S 27$_{6}$ 2 S 4$_{3}$ 6$_{23}$ 20$_{3}$ 1 K 8$_{8}$||2 C 5$_{9}$ 2 K 15$_{5}$||2 C 26$_{21}$ 2 K 18$_{4}$ 2 K 21$_{15}$ Jr 25$_{3}$ 27$_{22}$ 32$_{31}$ 4QHalakhah^{a} 5$_{6}$ 4QCommGenA 1$_{6}$ 11QT 46$_{4}$, יתר ni. *remain* Lv 19$_{6}$, ישׁב *dwell* Dt 2$_{22}$ Jos 6$_{25}$ 13$_{13}$ 15$_{63}$ 16$_{10}$ Jg 1$_{21}$ 2 S 7$_{6}$||1 C 17$_{5}$ 2 K 16$_{6}$ Jr 38$_{28}$ 1 C 4$_{43}$, שׁכן hi. *cause to dwell* 11QT 29$_{9}$, עמד *stand* Jos 23$_{14}$, קום hi. *raise* Jos 7$_{26}$ 8$_{29}$, הלך htp. *go about* 1 S 12$_{2}$, בוא *come* 11QT 39$_{7}$, hi. *bring* 1 C 5$_{26}$, יצא *go out* Lv 8$_{33}$ Jos 6$_{10}$, עלה hi. *bring up* 1 K 9$_{21}$||2 C 8$_{8}$ 4QJub^{h} 38$_{13}$ ([מעלים ... עד יו]ם), נסע *journey* Ex 40$_{37}$, שׁוט *wander* 1QDM 3$_{10}$, רכב *ride* Nm 22$_{30}$, דרך *tread* 1 S 5$_{5}$, גלה *be exiled* 2 K 17$_{23}$, עזב *forsake* Jos 22$_{3}$, שׁלח *send* Jr 7$_{25}$, מצא *find* 1 S 29$_{3.6.8}$ Ne 9$_{32}$, אמר *say* 2 C 35$_{25}$, דבר pi. *speak* Jr 36$_{2}$, קרא *read* Ne 8$_{18}$, יכח hi. *rebuke* CD 20$_{5}$, כתב pass. *be written* Ne 12$_{23}$, אכל *eat* Gn 32$_{33}$ Ex 12$_{15.18}$ 11QT 43$_{7}$, *devour* 1QH 8$_{30}$ (עד ימימה), שׁתה *drink* Jr 35$_{14}$, נתן *give, place* Dt 29$_{3}$ Jos 9$_{27}$ Jr 52$_{11}$, ni. *be given* Jr 52$_{34}$, שׂים *place* Gn 47$_{26}$ Jos 8$_{28}$ 1 S 30$_{25}$ 2 K 10$_{27}$, נוח hi. *place* 1 S 6$_{18}$, עשׂה *do* Jos 23$_{8}$ 1 S 8$_{8}$ 2 S 19$_{25}$ 2 K 17$_{34.41}$ Ne 8$_{17}$, ni. *be done* 2 K 23$_{22}$, ברא ni. *be created* 4QJub^{b} 2$_{3}$ ([הנ]ברא), בנה ni. *be built* 1 K 3$_{2}$, כון ni. *be established* 2 C 8$_{16}$ (or em. עַד־הַיּוֹם *until the day* to מִיּוֹם *from the day*), גבר *prevail* 4QCommGenA 1$_{8}$, רעה *pasture*, i.e. lead Gn 48$_{15}$, אצר *store up* 2 K 20$_{17}$||Is 39$_{6}$, פתח *open* 1QH 9$_{32}$ (פתח[ה]), ראה *see* Ex 10$_{6}$ 1 S 15$_{35}$, ni. *be seen* Jg 19$_{30}$ 1 K 10$_{12}$, קרא *call*, i.e. name Dt 3$_{14}$ Jos 5$_{9}$ 7$_{26}$ Jg 10$_{4}$ 18$_{12}$ 2 S 6$_{8}$||1 C 13$_{11}$ 1 K 9$_{13}$ 2 K 14$_{7}$ 2 C 20$_{26}$, ni. *be called*, i.e. named 2 S 18$_{18}$ Ezk 20$_{29}$, עוד hi. *warn* Jr 11$_{7}$, ידע *know* Dt 34$_{6}$, טמא ni. *defile oneself* Ezk 20$_{31}$, בדל hi. *separate* Dt 10$_{8}$, כעס hi. *anger* 2 K 21$_{15}$, חטא *sin* Jr 3$_{25}$, פשׁע *rebel* 1 K 12$_{19}$||2 C 10$_{19}$ 2 K 8$_{22}$||2 C 21$_{10}$, אבד pi. *destroy* Dt 11$_{4}$, חרם hi. *destroy* 1 C 4$_{41}$, שׁבר *break* Si 47$_{7}$, דכא pu. *be humbled* Jr 44$_{10}$, טהר htp. *cleanse oneself* Jos 22$_{17}$, כבס pi. *wash* 2 S 19$_{25}$, רפה ni. *be healed* 2 K 2$_{22}$, כלה pi. *finish* Ezr 10$_{17}$, קטר pi. *burn* 2 K 18$_{4}$, תפשׂ *seize* 1QS 10$_{19(mg)}$, גרע *withhold* 4QJub^{h} 35$_{12}$ ([עד] היום ... [גרע]).

עַד־עֶצֶם הַיּוֹם הַזֶּה *until this selfsame day*, + אכל *eat* Lv 23$_{14}$ 11QT 18$_{3}$ ([תואכלו עד עצם]), שׂים *place* Jos 10$_{27}$, פשׁע *transgress* Ezk 2$_{3}$.

לִפְנֵי *before* today, + היה ni. *occur* Zc 8$_{10}$, שׁמע *hear* Is 48$_{7}$, קלל *be swift*, i.e. pass away swiftly Jb 24$_{18}$ (if em. עַל־פְּנֵי־מַיִם *upon the face of the waters* to לִפְנֵי יוֹמָם *before their day*).

אַחֲרֵי *after*, + כרת *cut*, i.e. make, covenant Jr 31$_{33}$.

תַּחַת *in return for*, + שׁלם pi. *repay* 1 S 24$_{20}$.

מִלְּבַד *apart from* 4QNarrD 2$_{4}$.

בֵּין *between*, + בדל hi. *divide* Gn 1$_{14}$; *at an interval of, every* ten days, + היה *be* Ne 5$_{18}$, עשׂה ni. *be made*, i.e. prepared Ne 5$_{18}$.

<COLL> 1. יוֹם :: לַיְלָה *night* Gn 1$_{5.14.16.18}$ 7$_{4.12}$ 31$_{39.40}$ Ex 10$_{13}$ 24$_{18}$ 34$_{28}$ Nm 11$_{32}$ Dt 9$_{9.11.18.25}$ 10$_{10}$ 1 S 19$_{24}$ 30$_{12}$ 1 K 8$_{29}$ 19$_{8}$ Is 27$_{3}$ 28$_{19}$ 62$_{6}$ Jr 33$_{20}$ 36$_{30}$ Jon 2$_{1}$ Zc 14$_{7}$ Ps 19$_{3.3}$ 74$_{16}$ 136$_{9}$ Jb 2$_{13}$ 3$_{3}$ Ec 8$_{16}$ Ne 4$_{16}$ 1QS 10$_{10}$ 4QJub^{a} 2$_{8}$ 4QCommGenA 1$_{6}$ 4QParGenEx 2$_{7.12}$; + לַיְלָה Is

38$_{12.13}$ Ho 4$_{5}$ Ps 77$_{3}$ 88$_{2}$ 90$_{4}$ Jb 7$_{12}$; יוֹם וָלַיְלָה *day and night* Gn 8$_{22}$ Jr 33$_{20}$ (if em. יוֹמָם וָלַיְלָה *by day and by night*); לַיְלָה וָיוֹם *by night and by day* 1 K 8$_{29}$ Is 27$_{3}$ Est 4$_{16}$ 4QPrQuot 218$_{4}$ GnzPs 4$_{10}$; יוֹם וָיוֹם *every day, day after day* Est 2$_{11}$ 3$_{4}$ 11QPs^{a} 27$_{6}$ 11QT 15$_{1.3}$ ([יום ויום]) 15$_{5}$ ([י]ום ויום) 17$_{12}$.

+ בֹּקֶר *morning* Ps 73$_{14}$, עֶרֶב *evening* Jr 6$_{4}$ 4QJonathan 3$_{2}$, חֹדֶשׁ *new moon, month* Ps 81$_{4}$ Jb 14$_{5}$ 1QM 2$_{4}$, כֵּסֶה *full moon* Ps 81$_{4}$, יֶרַח *month* Jb 3$_{6}$ 29$_{2}$, שַׁבָּת *sabbath* 1QM 2$_{4}$ 11QT 19$_{13}$ 21$_{13}$, שָׁבוּעַ *week* 11QT 19$_{13}$ 21$_{13}$.

|| שָׁנָה *year* Gn 1$_{14}$ 1 S 29$_{3}$ Is 61$_{2}$ Ps 78$_{33}$ Jb 36$_{11}$ Pr 3$_{2}$; + שָׁנָה *year* Gn 29$_{20}$ 35$_{28}$ 47$_{8.9.28}$ Is 63$_{4}$ Ezk 4$_{6.6}$ Ps 61$_{7}$ 77$_{6}$ Jb 10$_{5}$ 15$_{20}$ Pr 10$_{27}$; || עֵת *time* Is 49$_{9}$ Jr 33$_{15}$ 46$_{21}$ 50$_{4.20}$ Ezk 7$_{7.10}$ Jl 4$_{1}$ Ps 37$_{19}$ Jb 38$_{23}$; + עֵת *time* Jr 50$_{31}$ Ezk 21$_{30}$ Pr 8$_{30}$ Si 30$_{24.32}$ Lachish ost. 2$_{3.3}$ 4$_{1}$, מוֹעֵד *season* Gn 1$_{14}$ 1QM 2$_{4}$, תְּמוֹל *yesterday* Ex 5$_{14}$ 1 S 20$_{27}$ 2 S 15$_{20}$; || אֶתְמוֹל *yesterday* Si 38$_{22}$; + שִׁלְשֹׁם *the day before yesterday* Ex 5$_{14}$, מָחָר *tomorrow* Ex 19$_{10}$ Jos 22$_{18}$ 2 S 11$_{12}$ 2 K 6$_{28}$ Si 10$_{10}$, קֵץ *end* Lm 4$_{18}$, מֵאָז *from of old* Is 48$_{7}$, תָּמִיד *continually* Is 51$_{13}$ 52$_{5}$ 62$_{6}$ 11QPs^{a} 27$_{6}$.

|| חַיִּים *life* Ps 34$_{13}$, רוּחַ *spirit* Jb 17$_{1}$; + כֹּחַ *strength* Ps 102$_{24}$, שָׁלוֹם *peace* Jb 3$_{2}$, עֹשֶׁר *riches* Pr 3$_{16}$, כָּבוֹד *honour* Pr 3$_{16}$.

2. יוֹם + numeral, one Gn 1$_{5}$ 27$_{45}$ 33$_{13}$ 1 S 2$_{34}$ 9$_{15}$ 1 K 5$_{2}$ Is 9$_{13}$ 10$_{17}$ Is 47$_{9}$ Jon 3$_{4}$ Hg 1$_{1}$ Zc 3$_{9}$ 14$_{7}$ Est 3$_{13}$ 8$_{12}$ Ezr 3$_{6}$ 10$_{13.16.17}$ Ne 5$_{18}$ 8$_{2}$ 2 C 28$_{6}$ Si 46$_{4}$ 11QT 52$_{6}$, two 2 S 1$_{1}$ Est 9$_{27}$ Ezr 10$_{13}$ 2 C 21$_{19}$ (or em.; see Cstr.) Si 38$_{17}$ 4QAges^{a} 5$_{3}$ 4QCommGenA 1$_{9.13.19}$ 4QMishA 1.3$_{14}$ (יום שנים *the second day*) CD 14$_{13}$, three Gn 30$_{36}$ 40$_{12.13.18.19}$ 42$_{17}$ Ex 3$_{18}$ 5$_{3}$ 8$_{23}$ 10$_{22.23}$ 15$_{22}$ 19$_{15}$ Lv 12$_{4}$ Nm 10$_{33.33}$ 33$_{8}$ Jos 1$_{11}$ 2$_{16.22}$ 3$_{2}$ 9$_{16}$ Jg 14$_{14}$ 19$_{4}$ 1 S 9$_{20}$ 30$_{12}$ 2 S 20$_{4}$ 24$_{13}$ ||1 C 21$_{12}$ 1 K 12$_{5}$||2 C 10$_{5}$ 2 K 2$_{17}$ Am 4$_{4}$ Jon 2$_{1}$ 3$_{3}$ Est 4$_{16}$ Ezr 8$_{15.32}$ 10$_{8.9}$ Ne 2$_{11}$ 1 C 12$_{40}$ 2 C 20$_{25}$ 1QSa 1$_{26}$ 11QT 43$_{13}$ 45$_{8.12}$ 52$_{14}$, four Jg 11$_{40}$ Arad ost 2$_{3}$, five Nm 11$_{19}$ 1 S 6$_{19}$ (if em. חֲמִשִּׁים *fifty* to חָמֵשׁ יוֹם *five days*) 4QCommGenA 1$_{7}$,* six Ex 16$_{26}$ 20$_{9.11}$ 23$_{12}$ 24$_{16}$ 31$_{15.17}$ 34$_{21}$ 35$_{2}$ Lv 12$_{5}$ 23$_{3}$ Dt 5$_{13}$ 16$_{8}$ Jos 6$_{3.14}$ Ezk 46$_{1}$ 4QJub^{a} 2$_{17}$ 11QT 11$_{12}$ CD 14$_{21}$, seven Gn 7$_{4}$ 8$_{10.12}$ 31$_{23}$ Ex 7$_{25}$ 12$_{15.19}$ 13$_{6}$ 22$_{29}$ 23$_{15}$ 29$_{30.35.37}$ 34$_{18}$ Lv 8$_{33.33.35}$ 12$_{2}$ 13$_{4+7t}$ 14$_{8.38}$ 15$_{13.19.24.28}$ 22$_{27}$ 23$_{6+7t}$ Nm 12$_{14.14.15}$ 19$_{11.14.16}$ 28$_{17.24}$ 29$_{12}$ 31$_{19}$ Dt 16$_{3.4.13.15}$ Jg 14$_{12.17}$ 1 S 6$_{19}$ (if em. שִׁבְעִים *seventy* to שֶׁבַע יוֹם *seven days*)* 10$_{8}$ 11$_{3}$ 13$_{8}$ 31$_{13}$||1 C 10$_{12}$ 1 K 8$_{65}$||2 C 7$_{8}$ 1 K 8$_{65}$ 16$_{15}$ 20$_{29}$ 2 K 3$_{9}$ Is 30$_{26}$ Ezk 3$_{15.16}$ 43$_{25.26}$ 44$_{26}$ 45$_{21}$ (if em.; see Cstr.) 45$_{23.23}$ Jb 2$_{13}$ Est 1$_{5}$ Ezr 6$_{22}$ Ne 8$_{18}$ 1 C 9$_{25}$ 2 C 7$_{9.9}$ 30$_{21.22.23.23}$ 35$_{17}$ 4QCommGenA 1$_{15.18}$ 4QSD 7.2$_{15}$ 4QD^{a} 6.1$_{11}$ 6.2$_{3}$ 4QD^{e} 7.1$_{14}$ 4QD^{g} 1.2$_{9}$ 4QTohA 1.1$_{4.6.9}$ 4QapPent 2$_{9}$ 4QMMT B$_{67}$ ([שבעת י]מים) 4QRitMar 97$_{2}$ (ימי[ם]) 4QRitPur 11.10$_{2}$ 11QT 15$_{4}$ ([הימים]) 15$_{14}$ (ימי[ם]) 17$_{11.12}$ 45$_{15}$ 49$_{6.7}$ 50$_{12.13}$, eight(h) Gn 17$_{12}$ 21$_{4}$ 2 C 29$_{17.17}$, ten Gn 24$_{55}$ (יָמִים אוֹ עָשׂוֹר *days or ten*, i.e. ten days or so) Nm 11$_{19}$ Jr 42$_{7}$ Dn 1$_{12.14.15}$ Ne 5$_{18}$ 2 C 36$_{9}$ 1QS 7$_{10.11.15}$ 4QD^{a} 10.2$_{6}$ 4QCommGenA 1$_{13}$ 1QDM 3$_{10}$ ([עש]ור) 3$_{11}$ (ע[שר]) 4QSD 1.1$_{3}$ ([ע]שרת י[מ]ים) 4QNarrA 4$_{3}$ (יו[ם]), eleven(th) Nm 7$_{72}$ Dt 1$_{2}$, twelf(th) Nm 7$_{78}$, thirteen(th) Est 3$_{12}$ 9$_{1}$, fourteen(th) Ex 12$_{6.18}$ Nm 9$_{3.5.11}$ 28$_{16}$ Jos 5$_{10}$ 1 K 8$_{65}$ Ezk 45$_{21}$ Est 9$_{15.19.21}$ 4QTobit^{e} 4$_{1}$ (ארבע[ת] עשר) 4QCommGenA 1$_{8.10}$ ([יו]ם), fifteen(th) Ex 16$_{1}$ Lv 23$_{6.34.39}$ Nm 28$_{17}$ 29$_{12}$ 33$_{3}$ 1 K 12$_{32.33}$ Ezk 45$_{25}$ Est 9$_{21}$ 4QD^{a} 10.2$_{13}$ (חמשת [עשר]) 11QT 27$_{10}$, sixteen(th) 2 C 29$_{17}$, seventeen(th) Gn 7$_{11}$ 8$_{4}$ 4QCommGenA 2$_{1}$, twenty Nm 11$_{19}$ 2 S 24$_{8}$ 4QD^{d} 11.1$_{6}$ ([יו]ם), twenty-one (twenty-first) Ex 12$_{18}$ Dn 10$_{13}$, twenty-three (twenty-third) 2 C 7$_{10}$, twenty-four(th) Hg 1$_{15}$ 2$_{18}$ Zc 1$_{7}$ Dn 10$_{4}$ Ne 9$_{1}$, twenty-fifth 4QPrQuot 37.12$_{1\ 3}$ (חמשה ו[עשרים]), twenty-sixth 4QCommGen A1$_{6}$ 4QPrQuot 37.12$_{23}$ (ששה ו[עשרים]), twenty-seven Gn 8$_{14}$, thirty Lv 12$_{4}$ Nm 20$_{29}$ Dt 34$_{8}$ Est 4$_{11}$ 1QS 7$_{10.12.13.14}$ (=4QS^{e} 1.1$_{13}$ ש[ש]ים *sixty*) 7$_{15}$ 4QSD 1.1$_{4.9.11}$ 4QD^{a} 10.2$_{6}$, forty Gn 7$_{4.12.17}$ 8$_{6}$ 50$_{3}$ Ex 24$_{18}$ 34$_{28}$ Nm 13$_{25}$ 14$_{34}$ Dt 9$_{9.11.18.25}$ 10$_{10}$ 1 S 17$_{16}$ 1 K 19$_{8}$ Ezk 4$_{6}$ Jon 3$_{4}$ 2QJub^{a} 23$_{7}$ 4QCommGenA 1$_{6}$ 4QParGen Ex 2$_{7}$ ([ארבעים]), forty-nine 11QT 21$_{13}$, fifty Lv 23$_{16}$ 11QT 18$_{13}$ ([חמשים]) 19$_{13}$ 21$_{14}$, fifty-two Ne 6$_{15}$, sixty Lv 12$_{5}$ 1QS 7$_{8(mg)}$ 4QS^{e} 1.1$_{13}$ (ש[ש]ים=1QS 7$_{14}$ שלושים *thirty*), a hundred 4QD^{a} 10.2$_{1}$, a hundred and fifty Gn 7$_{24}$ 8$_{3}$ 4QCommGenA 1$_{7.9}$, a hundred and eighty Est 1$_{4}$, two hundred 4QD^{a} 10.2$_{1}$ ([מאת]ים), three hundred and sixty-four 4QCommGenA 2$_{3}$ 4QMMT A$_{21}$ (שלוש [מאות וש]שים וארבעה), three hundred and ninety Ezk 4$_{5.9}$, one thousand two hundred and ninety Dn 12$_{11}$, one thousand three hundred and thirty-five Dn 12$_{12}$.

3. Adverbial usages, **a.** יוֹם (1) *for* (a specified number of) *days*, + היה *be* Gn 7$_{12.17}$ Ex 24$_{18}$ 34$_{28}$ 4QCommGenA 1$_{6}$, חיה *live* 4QJub^{f} 33$_{14}$, הלך *go* 1 K 19$_{8}$ Is 38$_{10}$ (if em. בִּדְמִי יָמַי אֵלֵכָה *in the middle of my days I [must] go* to בְּדָמִי יָמַי אֵלֵכָה I said *in my sorrow, I have marched my days*),* עמד *stand* Dn 10$_{13}$, חיל *wait* Gn 8$_{10}$, יחל ni. *wait* Gn 8$_{12}$, מטר hi. *rain* Gn 7$_{4}$, גבר *prevail* Gn 7$_{24}$ 4QComm GenA 1$_{7}$, עמד *stand* Ex 21$_{21}$ Dt 10$_{10}$, יצב htp. *stand* 1 S 17$_{46}$, ישׁב *remain* Lv 12$_{4.5}$ Dt 9$_{9}$, נפל htp. *prostrate oneself* Dt 9$_{18}$, דפק *drive* Gn 33$_{13}$, עשׂה *make* 1 K 8$_{65}$, אכל *eat* Nm 11$_{19.19}$ Ezk 4$_{9}$ Est 4$_{16}$, שׁתה *drink* Est 4$_{16}$, קרא ni. *be called* Est 4$_{11}$, ראה hi. *show* Est 1$_{4}$, תור *spy* Nm 14$_{34}$, נשׂא *bear* Nm 14$_{34.34}$ Ezk 4$_{6.6.6}$, שׁית *place* Si 38$_{17}$, בכה *weep* Nm 20$_{29}$ Dt 34$_{8}$ 2QJub^{a} 23$_{7}$, ענשׁ ni. *be punished* 1QS 7$_{8(mg)}$ 7$_{12.13.14.15}$ 4QSD 1.1$_{4.9}$ (both [ונענש]) 1.1$_{11}$ 4QD^{a} 10.2$_{1}$ 4QD^{d} 11.1$_{6}$ ([ונענ]ש ... [יו]ם), בדל hi. *be separated* 4QD^{a} 10.2$_{6}$ ([הובדל]) 10.2$_{11}$ ([והובדל] ... [יו]ם).

(2) *in* (a specified number of) *days*, + שׁכל *bereave* Gn 27$_{45}$, עשׂה *make* Ex 20$_{11}$, גלה *uncover* ear 1 S 9$_{15}$, ספה ni. *be swept away* 1 S 27$_{1}$, כרת hi. *cut off* Is 9$_{13}$, אכל *devour* Is 10$_{17}$.

(3) *on the day of, in the day (when)* Ps 78$_{42}$, + היה *be* Ezk 39$_{13}$, רחק *be distant* Mc 7$_{11}$, חרד *tremble* Ezk 26$_{18}$, חלה hi. *be sick* Ho 7$_{5}$.

(4) *by day*, + היה *be* 1 K 8$_{29}$ Jr 33$_{20}$ (if em. יוֹמָם *by day*), נצר *guard* Is 27$_{3}$, עמד *stand* GnzPs 4$_{10}$, צעק *cry out* Ps 88$_{2}$ (or em. יוֹמָם *by day*), פתח pass. *be open* 1 K 8$_{29}$.

(5) *day after day*, + שׁכם hi. *rise early* Jr 7$_{25}$ (or del. יוֹם; ms יוֹם יוֹם *day after day*), שׁלח *send* Jr 7$_{25}$ (or del. יוֹם; ms יוֹם יוֹם).

b. הַיּוֹם (1) *this day, that day, today* Gn 31$_{48}$ 40$_{7}$ 42$_{13.32}$ Dt 1$_{10}$ 4$_{4}$ 5$_{3}$ 29$_{14}$ 31$_{2.27}$ Jos 14$_{10.11}$ 1 S 9$_{12}$ 12$_{17}$ 2 S 3$_{39}$ 19$_{23.36}$ Jb 23$_{2}$ Ru 4$_{9.10}$ Ne 9$_{36}$ 35$_{21}$ 1QM 17$_{5}$ Si 10$_{10}$ 38$_{22}$, + היה *be* 1 S 14$_{38}$ 2 S 19$_{23}$ 1 K 12$_{7}$, רבב *be many* 1 S 25$_{10}$, ישׁב *remain* 2 S 11$_{12}$, הלך *go* Jos 23$_{14}$ 1 S 10$_{2}$ 2 K 4$_{23}$, בוא *come* Gn 24$_{42}$ Ex 2$_{18}$ 1 S 9$_{12}$ 20$_{27}$ 2 S 19$_{21}$ Est 5$_{4}$, יצא *go out* Ex 13$_{4}$ 4QM^{a} 1$_{9}$ ([י]צאו), עלה *go up* 4QM^{a} 1$_{11}$ ([ע]לות), ירד *go down* 1 K 1$_{25}$, גרשׁ pi. *expel* Gn 4$_{14}$, נוס flee 1 S 4$_{16}$, נוע hi. *cause to wander* 2 S 15$_{20(Qr)}$, עבר *pass* Gn 30$_{32}$ Dt 2$_{18}$ 9$_{1}$, קרב *draw near* Dt 20$_{3}$ 1QM 10$_{3}$, hi. *bring near*, i.e. offer Lv 10$_{19}$, שׁלח *send* Lachish ost. 4$_{8}$ ([הים]), גלל *roll* Jos 5$_{9}$ 1 S 14$_{33}$ (or em. הַיּוֹם to הֲלֹם *hither*), פנה *turn* Dt 29$_{17}$, שׁוב *go back* Jos 22$_{16.18.29}$ Jr 34$_{15}$, יפע hi. *shine out* 1QM 18$_{10}$, אוץ *hasten* 1QM 18$_{12}$, סגר pi. *deliver up* 1 S 17$_{46}$ 26$_{8}$, גרשׁ pi. *expel* 1 S 26$_{19}$, עמד *stand* Dt 29$_{14}$ 2 K 6$_{31}$ Ps 119$_{91}$, נצב ni. *stand* Dt 29$_{9}$, קום *rise* Jg 9$_{18}$, hi. *raise*, i.e. establish Dt 29$_{12}$, שׁוב hi. *restore* 2 S 16$_{3}$, ילד *beget* Ps 2$_{7}$, חדשׁ pi. *renew* 4QPrQuot 1.3$_{2}$ (הי[ו]ם).

אמר *say* Est 1$_{18}$, ni. *be said* Gn 22$_{14}$, hi. *proclaim* Dt 26$_{17.18}$, דבר *speak* Dt 5$_{1}$, נגד hi. *declare* Dt 26$_{3}$ 30$_{18}$ 1 S 24$_{19}$ 2 S 19$_{7}$ Jr 42$_{21}$ Zc 9$_{12}$, צוה pi. *command* Ex 34$_{11}$ Dt 6$_{6}$ 7$_{11}$ 8$_{1.11}$ 10$_{13}$ 11$_{8.13.27.28}$ 13$_{19}$=11QT 55$_{14}$ Dt 15$_{5.15}$ 19$_{9}$ 26$_{16}$ 27$_{1.4.10}$ 28$_{1.13.14.15}$ 30$_{2.8.11.16}$ 1QDM 1$_{9}$ 2$_{2}$ ([הי]ום) 2$_{4}$ ([מצו]ך) 11QT 54$_{6}$, שׁבע ni. *swear* 1 K 1$_{51(mss)}$ (L כַּיּוֹם *first of all*), ברך pass. *be blessed* 1 K 5$_{21}$, פלל htp. *pray* 1 K 8$_{28}$ Ne 1$_{6}$, ידה hi. *give thanks* Is 38$_{19}$, שׁמע *hear* Gn 21$_{26}$ (לֹא שָׁמַעְתִּי בִּלְתִּי הַיּוֹם *I have not heard apart from*, i.e. until, *this day*) Ps 95$_{7}$, קרא ni. *be called*, i.e. named 1 S 9$_{9}$, ראה *see* Ex 14$_{13}$ Dt 5$_{24}$, ni. *appear* Lv 9$_{4}$ 1 K 18$_{15}$, hi. *show* Lachish ost. 5$_{9}$ (others ה מה ... *what?*), זכר hi. *cause to be remembered* Gn 41$_{9}$, ידע *know* Dt 1$_{39}$ 4$_{39}$ 9$_{3}$ 11$_{2}$ Jos 22$_{31}$ 2 S 14$_{22}$ 19$_{7}$, ni. *be known* 1 K 18$_{36}$, hi. *make known* Pr 22$_{19}$, גלה ni. *uncover oneself* 2 S 6$_{20}$, לקח *take* 2 K 2$_{3.5}$, לקט pi. *gather* Ru 2$_{19}$, בחר *choose* Jos 24$_{15}$.

כבד ni. *honour oneself* 2 S 6$_{20}$, בושׁ hi. *shame* 2 S 19$_{6}$, עוד hi. *testify, warn* Dt 32$_{46}$ Jr 42$_{19}$ Arad ost. 24$_{19}$, *cause to testify* Dt 4$_{26}$ 8$_{19}$ 30$_{19}$, שׁפט *judge* Jg 11$_{27}$ 2 S 18$_{31}$, מלט pi. *deliver* 2 S 19$_{6}$, פתח pi. *loosen*, i.e. set free Jr 40$_{4}$, צלח hi. *cause to succeed* Ne 1$_{11}$, אכל *eat* Ex 16$_{25}$ Lv 10$_{19}$ 1 S 9$_{19}$ 14$_{28.30}$ 2 K 6$_{28}$, קרה hi. *cause to occur* Gn 24$_{12}$, עשׂה *do* Gn 31$_{43}$ Ex 14$_{13}$ Dt 12$_{8}$ 31$_{21}$ 1 S 11$_{13}$ 14$_{45}$ 2 S 3$_{8}$ 1 K 13$_{11}$ Ru 2$_{19}$, נתן *give, place* Ex 32$_{29}$ Dt 4$_{9}$ 11$_{26.32}$ 30$_{15}$ 1 S 24$_{11}$ 26$_{33}$ 1 K 1$_{48}$ 20$_{13}$ Jr 1$_{18}$, מצא *find* Ex 16$_{25}$, קנה *buy* Gn 47$_{23}$, חכר *rent* Mur 24 1$_{6}$ ([חכרתי ... היו]ם) 3$_{6}$ 5$_{5}$ ([ח]כרת) 8$_{4}$ ([חכרתי ... היו]ם), שׁלם pi. *pay* vows Pr 7$_{14}$, כלה pi. *complete* Ru 3$_{18}$, לבן *make bricks* Ex 5$_{14}$, חלל hi. *begin* 1 S 22$_{15}$, קדשׁ *be holy* 1 S 21$_{6}$, pi. *sanctify* Ex 19$_{10}$, חתן htp. *become son-in-law* 1 S 18$_{21}$, מלא *fill* Ex 32$_{29}$, pi. *fill* hand, i.e. consecrate 1 C 29$_{5}$, כרת *cut*, i.e. make, covenant Dt 29$_{11}$ 4QJub^{a} 1$_{5}$, גדע ni. *be cut off* Jg 21$_{6}$, פקד *lay a charge* 2 S 3$_{8}$, ni. *be lacking* Jg 21$_{3}$, מרד *rebel* Jos 22$_{16.18}$, מאס *reject* 1 S 10$_{19}$, שׁבת hi. *cause to cease* Ru 4$_{14}$, נגף *strike* 1 S 4$_{3}$, קרע *tear* 1 S 15$_{28}$, פשׁט *make a raid* 1 S 27$_{10}$, מות *die* 2 S 19$_{7}$, ho. *be put to death* 2 S 19$_{23}$ 2 K 2$_{24}$.

(2) *today*, i.e. a specified number of days *ago*, e.g.

חָלִ֫יתִי הַיּוֹם שְׁלֹשָׁה *I became sick today three*, i.e. three days ago 1 S 30$_{13}$; + אבד *be lost* 1 S 9$_{20}$.

(3) *for* (a specified number of) *days*, + נפל htp. *prostrate oneself* Dt 9$_{25}$.

(4) *by day*, + היה *be* Ne 4$_{16}$, כשׁל *stumble* Ho 4$_{5}$ (or em. יוֹמָם *by day*, or בַּיּוֹם *in the day*).

(5) עוֹד הַיּוֹם *still today*, i.e. this same day, + עמד *stand* Is 10$_{32}$.

(6) בְּעוֹד הַיּוֹם *while it was still day*, + ברה hi. *feed* 2 S 3$_{35}$.

c. הַיּוֹם הַזֶּה *this day* 1 S 12$_{5}$ 26$_{21}$ 2 S 18$_{20}$ Jr 44$_{2}$, + היה *be* 1QDM 2$_{1}$ ([היו]ם הזה [תהיה]), ni. *become* Dt 27$_{9}$, ראה *see* 1 S 24$_{11}$, גדל *be great* 1 S 26$_{24}$, חלל hi. *begin* Dt 2$_{25}$ Jos 3$_{7}$, עלה *go up* Jg 12$_{3}$, יצא hi. *bring out* 1QDM 2$_{6}$ ([היום] הזה ... [הוציא]), שׁלח *send* 1 S 25$_{32}$, בשׂר pi. *give news* 2 S 18$_{20}$, נתן *give* 2 S 4$_{8}$, שׁוב hi. *repay* 2 S 16$_{12}$, חלק *divide* 5/6ḤevBA 44$_{3}$, פקד hi. *appoint* Jr 1$_{10}$, נפל *fall* 2 S 3$_{38}$, ישׁע hi. *save* Jos 22$_{22}$, נצל hi. *deliver* Jg 10$_{15}$, כלא *withhold* 1 S 25$_{33}$, עשׂה *do* Jg 9$_{19}$ 1 S 28$_{18}$ 1 K 1$_{30}$, חרף pi. *reproach* 1 S 17$_{10}$.

d. זֶה הַיּוֹם *this day*, + כרת hi. *cut off* 1 K 14$_{14}$.

e. זה ימם *these days*, i.e. a few days ago, + לקח *take* Meṣad Ḥashavyahu ost. 1$_{9}$.

f. הַיָּמִים/יָמִים (1) *for* (a specified number of) *days, for (some) time*, + היה *be* Gn 40$_{4}$ Ex 10$_{22}$ 22$_{29}$ Lv 15$_{19}$ 22$_{27}$ 25$_{29}$ Nm 9$_{20}$ Jg 19$_{2}$ 1 S 29$_{3}$ Jon 2$_{1}$ Dn 10$_{2}$ Ne 2$_{11}$ 1 C 12$_{40}$ 2 C 20$_{25}$, חיה *live* Jr 35$_{7}$, גור *sojourn* Gn 21$_{34}$, ישׁב *dwell, remain* Gn 24$_{55}$ 27$_{44}$ 29$_{14}$ (חֹדֶשׁ יָמִים *month of days*) Lv 8$_{35}$ 12$_{4.5}$ 14$_{8}$ 23$_{42}$ Nm 20$_{15}$ Dt 1$_{46}$ Jos 2$_{22}$ 24$_{7}$ Jg 19$_{4}$ 2 S 1$_{1}$ 14$_{28}$ 2 K 23$_{8}$ Jr 37$_{16}$ Ezk 3$_{15}$ Ho 3$_{3.4}$ Jb 2$_{13}$ Ezr 8$_{32}$ 4Q Dg 1.2$_{9}$ 4QMMT B$_{67}$ ([י]שב ... [י]מים), חנה *encamp* Nm 9$_{22}$ 31$_{19}$ 1 K 20$_{29}$ Ezr 8$_{15}$, עמד *stand* Jr 32$_{14}$, קום *rise* Ex 10$_{23}$, הלך *go* Ex 15$_{22}$ 1 K 12$_{5}$||2 C 10$_{5}$, בוא *come* 11QT 45$_{12}$, יצא *go out* Lv 8$_{33}$, עלה hi. *bring up* 4QParGenEx 2$_{7}$, שׁוב *go back* 4QS^{d} 3.2$_{3}$ ([י]מים), סבב *go round* Dt 2$_{1}$, כשׁל ni. *stumble* Dn 11$_{33}$, חבה ni. *hide oneself* Jos 2$_{16}$, מצא *be found* Ex 12$_{19}$, כון ni. *be established* 1QS 8$_{10}$, עזב *forsake* Jos 22$_{3}$, מלך *reign* 1 K 16$_{15}$ 2 C 36$_{9}$, אבל htp. *mourn* Gn 37$_{34}$ 2 S 14$_{2}$ Dn 10$_{2}$ Ne 1$_{4}$ 1 C 7$_{22}$, אסף *gather* Gn 42$_{17}$, לקט *gather* Ex 16$_{26}$, צור *besiege* Dt 20$_{19}$, בזז *plunder* 2 C 20$_{25}$, עשׂה *do, make, offer* Gn 50$_{10}$ Ex 23$_{12}$ 31$_{17}$ Nm 28$_{24}$ Dt 16$_{13}$ Jos 6$_{3.14}$ 11$_{18}$ 1 K 8$_{65}$||2 C 7$_{8}$ 1 K 8$_{65}$ Ezk 43$_{25}$ 45$_{23}$ Est 1$_{5}$ Ezr 6$_{22}$ Ne 8$_{18}$ 2 C 7$_{9.9}$ 30$_{21}$ 35$_{17}$ 11QT 17$_{11}$, ni. *be done* Ex 31$_{15}$ 35$_{2}$ Lv 23$_{3}$, עבד *work* Ex 20$_{9}$ 34$_{21}$ Dt 5$_{13}$, כפר pi. *atone* Ex 29$_{37}$ Ezk 43$_{26}$, קדשׁ pi. *sanctify* 1QSa 1$_{26}$, נתן *give* Arad ost. 2$_{3}$, ראה ni. *be seen* Dt 16$_{4}$, hi. *show* Est 1$_{4}$, שׁכח *forget* Jr 2$_{32}$, ni. *be forgotten* Ec 2$_{16}$, שׁאל ni. *be asked* 1QS 8$_{25}$, בחן ni. *be tested* 1QS 9$_{2}$, אכל *eat* Ex 12$_{15}$ 13$_{6}$ 23$_{15}$ 34$_{18}$ Lv 23$_{6}$ Nm 11$_{19.19}$ Dt 16$_{3.8}$ 1 S 20$_{12}$ 1 K 17$_{15}$ Est 4$_{16}$ 2 C 30$_{22}$ 4QapPent 2$_{9}$, ni. *be eaten* Ex 13$_{7}$ Nm 28$_{17}$ Ezk 45$_{21}$, שׁתה *drink* 1 S 30$_{12}$ Est 4$_{16}$, צום *fast* 1 S 31$_{13}$||1 C 10$_{12}$, קרב hi. *bring near*, i.e. offer Lv 23$_{8.36}$, חגג *celebrate festival* Lv 23$_{39.41}$ Nm 29$_{12}$ Dt 16$_{15}$, שׂמח *rejoice* Lv 23$_{40}$, סגר ni. *be shut up* Nm 12$_{14.15}$, hi. *shut up* Lv 13$_{4+7t}$ 14$_{38}$, כסה pi. *cover* Ex 24$_{16}$, לבשׁ *wear* Ex 29$_{30}$, מלא pi. *fill* Ex 29$_{35}$ Lv 8$_{33}$ 11QT 15$_{14}$ ([ימי]ם), ארך hi. *be long* Nm 9$_{19}$, חסר *decrease* 4QComm GenA 1$_{9}$, טמא *be unclean* Lv 12$_{2}$ 15$_{24}$ Nm 19$_{11.14.16}$ 4Q SD 7.2$_{15}$ 11QT 49$_{6.7}$ 50$_{12.13}$, כלם ni. *be ashamed* Nm 12$_{14}$, זוב *flow* Lv 15$_{25}$, חלה ni. *be sick* Dn 8$_{27}$, תנה pi. *mourn* Jg 11$_{40}$, בכה *weep* Jg 14$_{17}$, ענשׁ ni. *be punished* 1QS 7$_{10.10.11}$ 4QSD 1.1$_{3}$ ([ונענש] ... י[מ]ים) 4QD^{a} 10.2$_{6.13}$ 4QD^{e} 7.1$_{14}$ CD 14$_{21}$ ([נ]ענש), יחל hi. *wait* 1 S 10$_{8}$ 13$_{8(Qr)}$ (Kt ni.) 4QCommGenA 1$_{15}$, רפה hi. *let alone* 1 S 11$_{3}$, נסה pi. *test* Dn 1$_{12.14}$.

(2) *within, during* (a specified number of) *days*, + נגד hi. *tell* Jg 14$_{14}$, זעק hi. *call together* 2 S 20$_{4}$.

(3) *after* (many) *days, in* (a specified number of) *days' time*, + היה *be* 1 K 18$_{1}$, רגז *tremble* Is 32$_{10}$.

(4) (a specified number of) *days ago*, + אבד *be lost* 1 S 9$_{20}$.

(5) with בְּעוֹד *within* (a specified number of) *days, in* (a specified number of) *days' time*, + נשׂא *lift* Gn 40$_{13.19}$, עבר *cross* Jos 1$_{11}$, שׁוב hi. *bring back* Jr 28$_{3}$, שׁבר *break* Jr 28$_{11}$.

g. יְמֵי *(during the) days of, (throughout the) days of*, + היה *be* Ezk 46$_{1}$, אכל *eat* Gn 3$_{14.17}$ 4QTohA 1.1$_{9}$, נגד hi. *tell* Jg 14$_{12}$, זכר *remember* Lm 1$_{7}$, עשׂה *do*, i.e. offer Ezk 45$_{23}$, לוה *be joined to* Ec 8$_{15}$, סגר pass. *be closed* Ezk 46$_{1}$.

h. יוֹמוֹ *on his day*, + עשׂה *make*, i.e. hold, a feast Jb 1$_{4}$.

i. יוֹמַיִם *for two days*, + עמד *stand* Ex 21$_{21}$, חנה *encamp* Nm 9$_{22}$, אכל *eat* Nm 11$_{19}$.

j. יוֹם וָיוֹם/יום יום *day after day* Nm 10$_{34}$ (if em. יוֹמָם *by day*) 4QpsEzek^{a} 16.2$_{8}$, + היה *be* Pr 8$_{30}$, אמר *say* Est 3$_{4}$,

דבר pi. *speak* Gn 39$_{10}$, דרשׁ *seek* Is 58$_{2}$, לקט *gather* Ex 16$_{5}$, שׁקד *watch* Pr 8$_{34}$, שׁלם pi. *pay* vows Ps 61$_{9}$, עמס *carry* Ps 68$_{20}$, שׁית *place* Ps 13$_{3}$ (if em. יוֹמָם *by day* to יום (יוֹם)), יצר pu. *be formed* Ps 139$_{16}$ (if em.; see Subj.).

k. יוֹם בְּיוֹם *day after day*, + קרא *read* Ne 8$_{18}$, הלל pi. *praise* 2 C 30$_{21}$.

l. יָמִים עַל־יָמִים *day upon day*, i.e. day after day, + יצא *go out* 2 C 21$_{15}$.

m. כל יום (1) *all the day*, i.e. continually, + גור *attack* Ps 140$_{3}$, רדף *pursue* GnzPs 3$_{3}$ (אדריף appar. error for ארדוף *I will pursue*), ספר pi. *tell* GnzPs 1$_{22}$ (יספר כל] [יספר); (2) *all the day of*, + קום *rise* Nm 11$_{32}$.

n. כָּל־הַיּוֹם *all the day/time* Gn 6$_{5}$ Ps 44$_{16}$ 74$_{22}$ 119$_{97}$ Lm 3$_{62}$, + היה *be* Jr 20$_{7.8}$ Ps 72$_{14}$ Lm 3$_{14}$, הלך pi. *go about* Ps 38$_{7}$, קום *rise* Nm 11$_{32}$, נפל *fall* 1 S 19$_{24}$, נהג pi. *drive* Ex 10$_{13}$, רדף *pursue* Ho 12$_{2}$, סבב *surround* Ps 88$_{18}$, הפך *turn* Lm 3$_{3}$, חפף *shelter* Dt 33$_{12}$, פרשׂ pi. *spread* hands Is 65$_{2}$, כלה *fail* Dt 28$_{32}$, לחם ni. *fight* Jg 9$_{45}$, אכל *eat* 1 S 28$_{20}$, יקד *burn* Is 65$_{5}$, חרשׁ *plough* Is 28$_{24}$, פחד pi. *fear* Is 51$_{13}$, אמר *say* Ps 42$_{4.11}$, ספר pi. *recount* Ps 71$_{15}$, הגה *utter* Ps 35$_{28}$ 38$_{13}$ 71$_{24}$, קרא *cry* Ps 86$_{3}$, הלל pi. *boast* Ps 44$_{9}$, htp. *boast* Ps 52$_{3}$, ברך pi. *bless* Ps 72$_{15}$, חרף pi. *reproach* Ps 102$_{9}$, גיל *rejoice* Ps 89$_{17}$, שׂיח *meditate* 4Q418 126.2$_{10}$, pol. *meditate* 1QH 11$_{6}$, חשׁה *be silent* Is 62$_{6}$, קוה pi. *wait* Ps 25$_{5}$ 11QPs^{a} 19$_{17}$, אוה htp. *desire* Pr 21$_{26}$, קנא pi. *be jealous* Pr 23$_{17}$, מלא ni. *be filled* Ps 71$_{8}$, נאץ htpo. *be spurned* Is 52$_{5}$, בלה *be worn out* Ps 32$_{3}$, נתן *give*, i.e. place Lm 1$_{13}$, שׁען ni. *lean* 1QS 10$_{16}$, חנן *be gracious* Ps 37$_{26}$, לוה hi. *lend* Ps 37$_{26}$, עצב pi. *hurt* Ps 56$_{6}$, שׁאף *trample upon* Ps 56$_{3}$, לחץ *oppress* Ps 56$_{2}$, דכא pi. *crush* 1QH 5$_{17}$, נגע pass. *be struck* Ps 72$_{14}$, הרג pu. *be killed* Ps 44$_{23}$.

o. כָּל־הַיָּמִים *all the days*, i.e. for ever, continually Dt 31$_{13}$ 1 S 27$_{11}$ 2 C 12$_{15}$, + היה *be* Dt 28$_{29.33}$ 1 S 2$_{32}$ 18$_{29}$ 2 S 19$_{14}$ 1 K 5$_{15}$ 8$_{40}$||2 C 7$_{16}$ 1 K 11$_{36}$ 12$_{7}$||2 C 10$_{7}$ 1 K 14$_{30}$ Jr 31$_{36}$ 1QH 17$_{14}$, עמד *stand* Jr 35$_{19}$, ישׁב *sit* 4QDibHam^{a} 1.4$_{8}$, מצא ni. *be found* 11QT 59$_{15}$, רצה ni. *be accepted* 4Q Jub^{a} 2$_{22}$ ([ירצה]), איב *be an enemy* 1 S 18$_{29}$, צוק hi. *press* Jg 16$_{16}$, עשׁק pass. *be oppressed* Dt 28$_{29.33}$, גזל pas. *be robbed* Dt 28$_{29}$, רצץ pass. *be crushed* Dt 28$_{33}$, חטא *sin* Gn 43$_{9}$ 44$_{32}$, ירא *fear* Dt 4$_{10}$ 14$_{23}$ Jr 32$_{39}$, נתן *give* Dt 4$_{40}$ 2 K 8$_{19}$||2 C 21$_{7}$ 2 K 13$_{3}$, שׂים *place* 1 S 28$_{2}$, שׁמר *keep* Dt 5$_{29}$ 11$_{1}$, עשׂה *do* 2 K 17$_{37}$ Jb 1$_{5}$, שׁרת pi. *minister* Dt 18$_{5}$, ברך pi. *bless* 11QT 60$_{11}$, ירשׁ *possess* Dt 12$_{1}$ 11QT 51$_{16}$, שׁאל hi. *lend* 1 S 1$_{28}$, הלך *go* Dt 19$_{9}$, htp. *go about* 1 S 2$_{35}$, ירא *fear* Jos 4$_{24}$ 1 K 8$_{40}$||2 C 6$_{31}$, כון ni. *be established* 1 S 20$_{31}$, hi. *prepare* 11QT 29$_{10}$, בקשׁ pi. *seek* 1 S 23$_{14}$ 2 K 2$_{17}$, אבל htp. *mourn* 2 S 13$_{37}$, ענה pi. *afflict* 1 K 11$_{39}$, כרת ni. *be cut off* Jr 33$_{18}$, אהב *love* 1 K 5$_{15}$ 1QH 15$_{9}$ ([יא]הבו), שׂכה *cover* 4QBéat 3.3$_{1}$ (כול הימ[ים]).

p. כֹּל/כָּל־יְמֵי *all the days of* Nm 6$_{8}$ Dt 6$_{24}$, + היה *be* Lv 15$_{25}$ 1 S 7$_{13}$ 14$_{52}$ 26$_{16}$ 1 K 11$_{25}$ 15$_{6}$ 2 C 24$_{14}$ 1QS 3$_{5}$ (כול יומי) 11QT 57$_{18}$, בוא *come* Lv 14$_{46}$ Nm 6$_{6}$, עבר *pass* Nm 6$_{5}$, סור *turn aside* Dt 4$_{9}$ 1 K 15$_{5}$, רדף *pursue* Ps 23$_{6}$, קום hi. *erect* Jg 18$_{31}$, עמד htp. *stand* Jos 1$_{5}$, שׁכב *lie* Lv 15$_{26}$, ישׁב *dwell* 1 S 22$_{4}$ 1 K 5$_{5}$ Ps 27$_{4}$, חנה *encamp* Nm 9$_{18}$, עזב *forsake* Si 3$_{12}$, שׁבת *cease* Gn 8$_{22}$, *rest* Lv 26$_{35}$, יחל pi. *wait* Jb 14$_{14}$, טמא *be unclean* Lv 13$_{46}$, רצה *enjoy* Lv 26$_{34}$ 2 C 36$_{21}$, אכל *eat* Nm 6$_{4}$ 2 K 25$_{29}$||Jr 52$_{33}$, ראה *see* Ps 128$_{5}$ Ec 9$_{9.9}$, זכר *remember* Dt 16$_{3}$, שׁמר *keep* Dt 6$_{2}$, עשׂה *do* 2 C 24$_{2}$ 1QS 2$_{19}$ (כול יומי), נתן *give* 1 S 1$_{11}$, ni. *be given* 2 K 25$_{30}$||Jr 52$_{34}$, לקח *take* 4QJub^{g} 25$_{9}$ ([כול] ימי ... [אקח]), שׁית *place* 1 K 11$_{34}$, עלה hi. *cause to go up*, i.e. offer 2 C 24$_{14}$, גמל *repay* Pr 31$_{12}$, נשׂא pi. *carry* Is 63$_{9}$, ירא *fear* Jos 4$_{14}$, עבד *serve* Jos 24$_{31.31}$ Jg 2$_{7.7}$ 1 K 5$_{1}$, קרא *read* Dt 17$_{19}$, *call* 4QTohA 1.1$_{4}$, נגן pi. *play stringed instrument* Is 38$_{20}$, מלא *be full*, i.e. overflow Jos 3$_{15}$, פקד *miss* 1 S 25$_{15}$, ni. *be missing* 1 S 25$_{7}$, ישׁע hi. *save* Jg 2$_{18}$, שׁפט *judge* 1 S 7$_{15}$, לחץ *oppress* 2 K 13$_{22}$, חיל htpol. *writhe in fear* Jb 15$_{20}$, פרר hi. *frustrate* Ezr 4$_{5}$, כלם hi. *put to shame* Si 3$_{13}$.

q. כָּל־יָמֶיךָ *all your days*, + היה *be* 1 K 3$_{13}$ 4QTobit^{e} 2$_{3}$ (הי[ה]), עזב *forsake* Dt 12$_{19}$, דרשׁ *seek* Dt 23$_{7}$, זכר *remember* 4QTobit^{e} 2$_{3}$ ([ז]כר).

r. כָּל־יָמָיו *all his days* Ec 2$_{23}$, + היה *be* 1 K 15$_{14}$||2 C 15$_{17}$ 11QT 16$_{4}$ ([יהיה]), עשׂה *do* 2 K 12$_{3}$, נתן *give* 4QOrd^{b} 1.2$_{7}$, שׁלח pi. *send away*, i.e. divorce Dt 22$_{19.29}$=11QT 66$_{11}$ 4QOrd^{a} 2$_{10}$, סור *turn aside* 2 C 34$_{33}$, נבא htp. *prophesy* 2 C 18$_{7}$, חטא hi. *cause to sin* 2 K 15$_{18}$, אכל *eat* Ec 5$_{16}$.

s. כָּל־יָמֵינוּ used adverbially, *all our days*, + שׁתה *drink* Jr 35$_{8}$

t. כָּל־יְמֵיכֶם *all your days*, + ישׁב *dwell* Jr 35$_{7}$.

u. כָּל־יְמֵיהֶם *all their days*, + היה *be* 1 K 15$_{16.32}$, בוא *come* 11QT 45$_{13}$ (כול ימיהמה).

4. Other collocations, הַיּוֹם אֲשֶׁר (and vars.) *the day when, the day of which* Dt 4$_{10}$ 12$_{1}$ 31$_{13}$ 1 S 20$_{31}$ 1 K 8$_{40}$

||2 C 6$_{31}$ 1QDM 1$_6$ 11QT 50$_{10}$, + היה *be* Dt 4$_{32}$ Jg 14$_{17}$ 1 S 29$_8$ 2 S 2$_{11}$, ישב *remain* Dt 1$_{46}$ 1 S 27$_{11}$, עמד *stand* Dt 4$_{10}$, שכב *lie* Ezk 4$_9$, נפל htp. *prostrate oneself* Dt 9$_{25}$, הלך *go* Dt 2$_{14}$, בוא *come* Is 7$_{17}$, יצא *go out* Dt 9$_7$ 2 S 19$_{20}$ 2 K 21$_{15}$ Jr 7$_{25}$ 11QT 49$_{13}$, hi. *bring out* 1 K 8$_{16}$||2 C 6$_5$ 11QT 49$_{11}$, עלה hi. *bring up* 1 C 17$_5$, עבר *cross* Dt 27$_2$, נוח *rest* Est 9$_{22}$, שכן *dwell* 11QT 46$_4$ (ש[ו]כן), קום appar. *impose obligation* CD 16$_4$ (or em. pi.), שלם pi. *fulfil* 11QT 39$_7$, פקד *visit*, i.e. punish CD 8$_2$ 19$_{15}$, שפך *pour* 4QD^a 3.4$_1$ ([תשפוך]), אמר *say* 1 S 24$_5$, דבר pi. *speak* Ezk 39$_8$, צוה pi. *command* 2 S 7$_{11}$||1 C 17$_{10}$ Ne 5$_{14}$, ברא *create* Dt 4$_{32}$, ילד *bear* Jr 20$_{14}$, pu. *be born* Jr 20$_{14}$, בנה *build* Jr 32$_{31}$, יסד pu. *be founded* Hg 2$_{18}$, נתן *give, place* Jg 4$_{14}$ Dn 10$_{12}$, פדה *ransom* Ps 78$_{42}$, עשה *do* Ezk 22$_{14}$ Ml 3$_{17.21}$, ברא *create* 11QT 29$_9$, נזר hi. *be a Nazirite* Nm 6$_5$, מלך *reign* 1 K 2$_{11}$ 11$_{42}$ 14$_{20}$ 10$_{36}$ 1 C 29$_{27}$, hi. *cause to reign* 11QT 57$_2$, לכד ni. *be captured* Jr 38$_{28}$, שבר pi. *hope* Est 9$_1$.

בְּיוֹם שֶׁיְּדֻבַּר־בָּהּ *on the day when she is spoken for* Ca 8$_8$, בַּיּוֹם שֶׁיָּזֻעוּ *on the day when they tremble* Ec 12$_3$.

יוֹם קָרְאוּ נֹצְרִים *a day (when) the sentries call* Jr 31$_6$, יוֹם אִוָּלֶד בּוֹ *the day in which I was born* Jb 3$_3$, יָמֶיהָ לָלֶדֶת *her days to give birth* Gn 25$_{24}$, הַיּוֹם לֶכֶת הַמֶּלֶךְ *the day (when) the king went* 2 S 19$_{25}$, יום ישוב *the day (when) he returns* CD 20$_5$.

הַיּוֹם *today, this day, that day* Gn 4$_{14}$ 19$_{37.38}$ 21$_{26}$ 22$_{14}$ 24$_{12.42}$ 30$_{32}$ 31$_{43.48}$ 35$_{20}$ 40$_7$ 41$_9$ 42$_{13.32}$ 47$_{23}$ Ex 2$_{18}$ 5$_{14}$ 13$_4$ 14$_{13.13}$ 16$_{25.25.25}$ 19$_{10}$ 32$_{29.29}$ 34$_{11}$ Lv 9$_4$ 10$_{19.19}$ Dt 1$_{10.39}$ 2$_{18}$ 4$_{4.8.26.39}$ 5$_{1.3}$ 6$_6$ 7$_{11}$ 8$_{1.11.19}$ 9$_{1.3}$ 10$_{13}$ 11$_{2+6t}$ 12$_8$ 13$_{19}$ 15$_{5.15}$ 19$_9$ 20$_3$ 26$_{3.17.18}$ 27$_{1.4.10}$ 28$_{1.13.14.15}$ 29$_{9+5t}$ 30$_{2+6t}$ 31$_{2.21.27}$ 32$_{46}$ Jos 5$_9$ 14$_{10.11}$ 22$_{16.16.17.17.29.31}$ 23$_{14}$ 24$_{15}$ Jg 9$_{18}$ 11$_{27}$ 21$_{3.6}$ 1 S 4$_{3.12}$ 9$_{9.12.12.19.20}$ 10$_{2.19}$ 11$_{13}$ 12$_{17}$ 14$_{28.30.33.38}$ 15$_{28}$ 18$_{21}$ 20$_{27}$ 21$_6$ 22$_{15}$ 24$_{11.19}$ 25$_{10}$ 26$_{8.19.23}$ 27$_{10}$ 30$_{13}$ 2 S 3$_{8.8.39}$ 6$_{20}$ 11$_{12}$ 14$_{22}$ 15$_{20}$ 16$_3$ 18$_{31}$ 19$_{6+9t}$ 1 K 1$_{25.48}$ 2$_{24}$ 5$_{21}$ 8$_{28}$ 12$_7$ 13$_{11}$ 18$_{15.36}$ 20$_{13}$ 2 K 2$_{3.5}$ 4$_{23}$ 6$_{31}$ 10$_{27}$ Is 38$_{19}$ Jr 1$_{18}$ 34$_{15}$ 40$_4$ 42$_{19}$ 42$_{21}$ Ezk 20$_{31}$ Zc 9$_{12}$ Ps 2$_7$ 95$_7$ 119$_{91}$ Jb 23$_2$ Pr 7$_{14}$ 22$_{19}$ Ru 2$_{19.19}$ 3$_{18}$ 4$_{9.10.14}$ Est 1$_{18}$ 5$_4$ Ne 1$_{6.11}$ 8$_{9.10.11}$ 9$_{32}$ 1 C 29$_5$ 2 C 20$_{26}$ 35$_{21.25}$ Si 10$_{10}$ 38$_{22}$ 47$_7$ 1QM 10$_3$ 17$_5$ 18$_{10.12}$ 1QDM 1$_9$ 2$_2$ (ה[י]ום) 2$_4$ perh. 4QTobit^e 8$_1$ 4QJub^a 1$_5$ perh. 4QMyst^b 13$_1$ 4QapJoshua^a 3.2$_4$ 4Qpara Kings 9$_5$ 4QRitMar 10$_2$ ([ה]יום) 4QPrQuot 1.3$_2$ (הי[ו]ם) perh. 1.3$_4$ (if חום is error for היום) 1.3$_9$ 29.8$_{20}$ ([היו]ם) 66$_1$ (ה[י]ום) 70$_4$ 4QRitPur 1.12$_9$ 42.2$_5$ ([ה]י[ו]ם) 11QPs^a 19$_{17}$ Mur 24 1$_6$ ([היו]ם) 2$_{13}$ 3$_{6.11}$ 5$_{5.8}$ Lachish ost. 4$_8$ ([הים]) 5$_9$ (others ה מה ... *what?*) Arad 24$_{19}$.

יוֹם *today* Is 43$_{13}$ 48$_7$.

וַיְהִי הַיּוֹם *and it happened one day, on a certain day* 1 S 14$_1$ 2 K 4$_{8.11.18}$ Jb 1$_{6.13}$ 2$_1$.

הִנֵּה הַיּוֹם בָּא *behold the day is coming* Ml 3$_{19}$, sim. Zc 14$_1$, הִנֵּה יָמִים בָּאִים *behold the days are coming* 1 S 2$_{31}$ 2 K 20$_{17}$||Is 39$_6$ Jr 7$_{32}$ 9$_{24}$ 16$_{14}$ 19$_6$ 23$_{5.7}$ 30$_3$ 31$_{27.31.38(Qr)}$ 33$_{14}$ 48$_{12}$ 49$_2$ 51$_{47.52}$ Am 4$_2$ 8$_{11}$ 9$_{13}$.

שְׁלֹשֶׁת יָמִים דֶּבֶר *three days of pestilence* 2 S 24$_{13}$, sim. 1 C 21$_{12}$, כַּבִּיר מֵאָבִיךָ יָמִים *greater than your father with respect to days*, i.e. older than your father Jb 15$_{10}$, יָמֵינוּ עֲלֵי־אָרֶץ *our days upon the earth* Jb 8$_9$, יָמִים עַל־שָׁנָה perh. *days over a year*, i.e. just over a year Is32 $_{10}$, יָמִים אֵין מִסְפָּר *days without number* Jr 2$_{32}$, יוֹם לַשָּׁנָה *a day for a year* Ezk 4$_{6.6}$, יום ושנים *a day or two* Si 38$_{17}$, יוֹם לִבְנוֹת *a day to build* Mc 7$_{11}$, דָּוִיד זָקֵן וְשָׂבַע יָמִים *David was old and satisfied (with respect to) days* 1 C 23$_1$, sim. 2 C 24$_{15}$, וישבע ימו *and he became satisfied (with respect to) his days* 4QJub^f 23$_{10}$.

Also 1Q29 12$_1$ 4QpHos^b 25$_2$ 4Q178 2$_3$ 9$_2$ perh. 4QCit Jub 1.2$_1$ 4QD^e 3.1$_{20}$ perh. 4QMyst^a 82$_4$ perh. 89$_2$ perh. 4QMyst^b 2.2$_1$ 4QMishA 2.2$_3$ 4.2$_{10}$ 6$_2$ (ימ[י]ם) 4QMishC^d 1.2$_1$ 4QparaKings 114$_3$ ([י]מים) 4QpsEzek^a 3$_5$ 4QBapt 10$_5$ 12$_{10}$ 4Q418 137$_5$ 238$_5$ 4QsapHymnA 1.1$_{12}$ 4QRit Mar 11$_3$ ([היו]ם) 24$_5$ 156$_1$ 4QPrQuot 10.5$_2$ 48$_5$ 61$_1$ 64$_8$ ([ה]יום]) 72$_4$ 82$_3$ 133$_1$ 217$_1$ 4QPrFêtes^c 255$_1$ 4QShir^b 143$_1$ 4QSela 8.2$_9$ 4QBéat 37$_2$ 6QCal 1$_2$.

<SYN> שָׁנָה *year*, עֵת *time*, אֶתְמוֹל *yesterday*, חַיִּים *life*, רוּחַ *spirit*.

<ANT> לַיְלָה *night*.*

⇒ יוֹמָם *by day*.

*יוֹם II 3 n.m. **wind, 1. storm,** <SUBJ> בוא *come* Is 21$_1$ (if em. יָם *sea* to יוֹם *storm*, and move athnach), עבר *pass* Zp 2$_2$, ירד *go down* Jg 19$_{11}$ Arad ost. 40$_{11}$ (ירד[י]), פוח *blow* Ca 2$_{17}$ 4$_6$. <OBJ> ארר *curse* Jb 3$_8$ (or em. יָם *sea*). <CSTR> רוּחַ הַיּוֹם *wind of the storm* Gn 3$_8$ (unless יוֹם I *day*).*

2. breath, <CSTR> קְשֵׁה־יוֹם *one hard of*, i.e. with failing, *breath* Jb 30$_{25}$.

יוֹמָם $_{52.0.21}$ adv. **by day**—appar. noun, **day(time)** at Jr 15$_{9}$ 33$_{20.25}$ Ezk 30$_{16}$ (see Coll.) Ne 9$_{19}$ 1QH 12$_{7}$ 1QM 14$_{13}$ 4QPrQuot 1.3$_{10}$ 7.4$_{1}$ 14.6$_{1}$ 15,6$_{6}$ 33.10$_{1}$ 51$_{5(mg)}$.

+ היה *be* 1 S 25$_{16}$ 1 K 8$_{59}$ Is 4$_{6}$ (or del. יוֹמָם) 60$_{19}$ Jr 33$_{20}$ (or em. יוֹם *day*) Ps 42$_{4}$ 11QT 57$_{10}$ (+ תָּמִיד *continually*), חיה *live* 4QPrFêtes[b] 39$_{1}$ ([יו]מם), כבה *be extinguished* Is 34$_{10}$ (+ לְעוֹלָם *for ever*), כבד *be heavy* Ps 32$_{4}$, הלך *go* Ex 13$_{21.21}$ Nm 14$_{14}$ Dt 1$_{33}$, בוא *come* Jr 50$_{27}$, מושׁ *depart* Ex 13$_{22}$, סור *depart* Ne 9$_{19(mss)}$ (L בְּיוֹמָם appar. *during their day*), גלה *go into exile* Ezk 12$_{3}$, יצא hi. *take out* Ezk 12$_{4.7}$, ירד *run down* with tears, i.e. weep Jr 14$_{17}$ Lm 2$_{18}$ (hi.), ישׁב *sit* Lv 8$_{35}$, נוח *rest* 2 S 21$_{10}$, עטף htp. *be faint* 1QH 8$_{29}$, כשׁל *stumble* Ho 4$_{5}$ (if em. הַיּוֹם *by day*), עלה ni. *raise oneself* Nm 9$_{21}$ (or em.; see Coll.), עוף *fly* Ps 91$_{5}$, עמד *stand* Is 21$_{8}$ (+ תָּמִיד), hi. *set up* Ne 4$_{3}$, נחה hi. *lead* Ps 78$_{14}$ Ne 9$_{12}$, סבב po. *surround* Ps 55$_{11}$, נתן *give* Jr 31$_{35}$, שׁית *place* Ps 13$_{3}$ (or em. יוֹם יוֹם *every day*), פגשׁ pi. *encounter* Jb 5$_{14}$, פחד *fear* Dt 28$_{66}$, הסס *be silent* 1QH 10$_{15}$, הגה *meditate* Jos 1$_{8}$ Ps 1$_{2}$, קרא *call* Ps 22$_{3}$, צוה pi. *command* Ps 42$_{9}$, פלל htp. *pray* Ne 1$_{6}$, שׁוע pi. *cry for help* Ps 88$_{2}$ (if em. אֱלֹהֵי יְשׁוּעָתִי יוֹם־צָעַקְתִּי *the God of my salvation, by day I cry* to אֱלֹהֵי יְשׁוּעָתִי יוֹמָם צָעַקְתִּי *O my God, I cry for help by day; my cry*), דרשׁ *seek*, i.e. study 1QS 6$_{6}$ (+ תָּמִיד), בכה *weep* Jr 8$_{23}$, עשׂה *do* Jg 6$_{27}$, perh. ברא *create* Is 4$_{5}$, פתח pass. *be open* 2 C 6$_{20}$, pi. *open* Is 60$_{11}$ (or em. ni. or pu. *be opened*; + תָּמִיד), חתם pi. *keep sealed* Jb 24$_{16}$, נכה hi. *strike* Ps 121$_{6}$, עבד *serve* Jr 16$_{13}$, בדל hi. *separate* 4Q392 1$_{6}$.

In nom. cl., Ex 40$_{38}$ Nm 10$_{34}$ (or em. יוֹם יוֹם *day after day*) Jr 15$_{9}$ 33$_{25}$ (or em. אִם־לֹא בְרִיתִי יוֹמָם וָלָיְלָה *if my covenant is not*, i.e. does not persist, *by day and [by] night* to אִם־לֹא בָרָאתִי יוֹם וָלָיְלָה *if I had not*, or, *surely I have, created day and night*) 1 C 9$_{33}$ 4QPrQuot 11.5$_{4}$.

<COLL> גַּם־לַיְלָה גַּם־יוֹמָם *both by night and by day* 1 S 25$_{16}$, כִּי־יוֹמָם וָלַיְלָה עֲלֵיהֶם בַּמְּלָאכָה *for by day and (by) night it was upon them in the work*, i.e. they were on duty day and night 1 C 9$_{33}$.

מבוא יומם *entrance of*, i.e. the coming of, *daytime* 1QH 12$_{7}$ 1QM 14$_{13}$ (מ[בו]א), אור היומם *light of the day* 4QPr Quot 1.3$_{10}$ 7.4$_{1}$ 14.6$_{1}$ ([או]ר) 15,6$_{6}$ 33.10$_{1}$ (או[ר]) 51$_{5(mg)}$, וְנֹף צָרֵי יוֹמָם *and as for Noph, (there) are enemies of*, i.e. who attack during, *daytime* Ezk 30$_{16}$ (or em. וְנָפוֹצוּ מַיִם *and the waters will be dispersed* or וְנִפְרְצוּ חוֹמֹתֶיהָ *and its walls will be broken down*), ממשלת אור לגבול יומם *dominion of light as a boundary by day* 4Q408 1$_{8}$.

יוֹמָם וָלַיְלָה *by day and by night* Ex 13$_{21}$ Lv 8$_{35}$ Nm 9$_{21}$ (or em. יוֹם וָלַיְלָה *a day and a night*) Jos 1$_{8}$ 1 K 8$_{59}$ Is 60$_{11}$ Jr 8$_{23}$ 16$_{13}$ 33$_{20.25}$ (or em. both יוֹם וָלַיְלָה *day and night*) Ps 1$_{2}$ 32$_{4}$ 42$_{4}$ 55$_{11}$ Lm 2$_{18}$ Ne 1$_{6}$ 4$_{3}$ 1 C 9$_{33}$ 2 C 6$_{20}$ 1QH 8$_{29}$ 10$_{15}$ (ולי[לה]) 1QM 14$_{13}$ 1QS 6$_{6}$ 4QsapDidA $_{10}$ (ולי[ל]ה) 4Q417 1.1$_{22}$ 4QPrFêtes[b] 41$_{2}$ 11QT 57$_{10}$, לַיְלָה וְיוֹמָם *by night and by day* Dt 28$_{66}$ Is 34$_{10}$ Jr 14$_{17}$.

יוֹמָם *by day* :: לַיְלָה *(by) night* Ex 13$_{21.22}$ 40$_{38}$ Nm 14$_{14}$ Dt 1$_{33}$ Jg 6$_{27}$ 1 S 25$_{16}$ 2 S 21$_{10}$ Is 4$_{5}$ 21$_{8}$ Jr 31$_{35}$ Ps 22$_{3}$ 78$_{14}$ 91$_{5}$ Ne 9$_{12}$ 1QH 12$_{7}$ 4Q392 1$_{6}$.

יוֹמָם + בַּלַּיְלָה *during the night* Ps 42$_{9}$ 121$_{6}$, בְּלַיְלָה *at night* Ne 9$_{19}$, כַּלַּיְלָה *as the night* Jb 5$_{14}$, בָּעֶרֶב *in the evening* Ezk 12$_{4.7}$.

Also 4QMyst[a] 10$_{10}$ 4QPrQuot 10.5$_{3}$ 4QRitPur 51.2$_{14}$.

<ANT> לַיְלָה *by night*.

⇒ יוֹם *day*.

יָוָן $_{12.0.3}$ pr.n.m. **Javan, 1.** son of Japheth and grandson of Noah, <NOM CL> בְּנֵי יֶפֶת ... יָוָן *the sons of Japheth were ... Javan* Gn 10$_{2}$ 1 C 1$_{5}$. <CSTR> בְּנֵי יָוָן *sons of Javan* Gn 10$_{4}$ 1 C 1$_{7}$.

2. a people in Asia Minor, §1 being its eponymous ancestor, <SUBJ> ראה *see* Is 66$_{19}$, שׁמע *hear* Is 66$_{19}$, נתן *give* Ezk 27$_{13.19}$ (or del.). <NOM CL> יָוָן ... רֹכְלַיִךְ *Javan ... were your merchants* Ezk 27$_{13}$. <APP> אִי *coastland* Is 66$_{19}$. <PREP> אֶל *send* Is 66$_{19}$. <COLL> + תֻּבַל *Tubal* Is 66$_{19}$ Ezk 27$_{13}$, מֶשֶׁךְ *Meshech* Ezk 27$_{13}$, וְדָן *Vedan* Ezk 27$_{19}$ (or del.); יָוָן מְאוּזָּל *Javan from Uzal* Ezk 27$_{19(mss)}$ (L מְאוּזָּל; or del. יָוָן).

3. Greece, <CSTR> מֶלֶךְ יָוָן *king of Greece* Dn 8$_{21}$ 4Qp Nah 3.1$_{2}$, מלכי *kings of* CD 8$_{11}$=20$_{24}$ 4QpNah 3.2$_{3}$, שַׂר *prince of* Dn 10$_{20}$, מַלְכוּת *kingdom of* Dn 11$_{2}$. <COLL> יָוָן as vocative, *O Greece* Zc 9$_{13}$ (or del. עַל־בָּנַיִךְ יָוָן *against your sons, O Greece*).

⇒ יְוָנִי *Greek*.

יָוֵן 2 n.[m.] **mire**—cstr. יְוֵן—<CSTR> יְוֵן מְצוּלָה *mire of the deep* Ps 69$_{3}$; טִיט הַיָּוֵן *mud of the mire* Ps 40$_{3}$. <PREP> בְּ of place, *in*, + טבע *sink* Ps 69$_{3}$.

יוֹנָדָב 8 pr.n.m. **Jonadab, 1.** son of David's brother Shimeah, friend of Amnon, ident. with יְהוֹנָדָב *Jehonadab* at 2 S 13$_{5}$, and perh. ident. with יְהוֹנָתָן *Jonathan* at 2 S 21$_{21}$||1 C 20$_{7}$, <SUBJ> אמר *say* 2 S 13$_{3.35}$, דבר pi. *speak* 2 S 13$_{35}$, ענה *answer* 2 S 13$_{32}$, כלה pi. *finish* 2 S 13$_{35}$. <NOM CL> שְׁמוֹ יוֹנָדָב *his name was Jonadab* 2 S 13$_{3}$ (4QSam^{a} [י]הונתן *Jehonathan*), יוֹנָדָב אִישׁ חָכָם מְאֹד *Jonadad was a very astute man* 2 S 13$_{3}$. <APP> בֵּן *son* 2 S 13$_{3.32}$, אָח *brother* 2 S 13$_{3.32}$. <PREP> לְ of direction, *to*, + אמר *say* 2 S 13$_{3}$, נגד hi. *tell* 2 S 13$_{3}$.

2. son of Rechab and founder of the Rechabite community, ident. with יְהוֹנָדָב *Jehonadab* at 2 K 10$_{15.15.23}$ Jr 35$_{8.14.16.18}$, <SUBJ> צוה pi. *command* Jr 35$_{6.10}$. <APP> אָב *father* Jr 35$_{6.10}$, בֵּן *son* Jr 35$_{6.19}$. <PREP> לְ of possession, *of, (belonging) to* Jr 35$_{19}$.

3. Levite, son of Jeshua, <NOM CL> עִמָּהֶם יוֹזָבָד *with them was Jozabad* Ezr 8$_{33(ms)}$ (L יוֹזָבָד *Jozabad*). <APP> בֵּן *son* Ezr 8$_{33(ms)}$, לֵוִי *Levite* Ezr 8$_{33(ms)}$.

⇒ ״ *Y.* + נדב *impel.*

יוֹנָה I 33.0.6 n.f. **dove**—cstr. יוֹנַת; sf. יוֹנָתִי; pl. יוֹנִים; cstr. יוֹנֵי—**1. dove, pigeon,** <SUBJ> בוא *come* Gn 8$_{11}$, שׁוב *go back* Gn 8$_{9.12}$, מצא *find* Gn 8$_{9}$, יסף *add*, i.e. do again Gn 8$_{12}$, קנן pi. *nest* Jr 48$_{28}$, פתה *be simple*, i.e. silly Ho 7$_{11}$ (+ אֵין לֵב *without sense*). <NOM CL> עֵינַיִךְ יוֹנִים *your eyes are doves* Ca 1$_{15}$ 4$_{1}$. <OBJ> בוא hi. *bring* Gn 8$_{9}$, שׁלח pi. *send* Gn 8$_{8.10.12}$ 4QCommGenA 1$_{14.18}$ ([שלח א[ת ה]יונה]) 1$_{20}$ ([משלח את היונ[ה]), לקח *take* Gn 8$_{9}$. <CSTR> כַּנְפֵי יוֹנָה *wings of a dove* Ps 68$_{14}$; יוֹנֵי הַגֵּאָיוֹת *doves of the valleys* Ezk 7$_{16}$, יוֹנַת אֵלֶם *dove of silence* Ps 56$_{1}$ (or em. יְוָנַת אִיִּים in the *Greek of the coastlands*, or em. אֵלֶם to אֵלִים *of terebinths*); בֶּן־יוֹנָה *son of a dove* Lv 12$_{6}$ (|| תֹּר *turtledove*, + כֶּבֶשׂ *lamb*) 4Q424 2$_{2}$, בְּנֵי יוֹנָה *sons of a dove* Lv 1$_{14}$ (הַיּוֹנָה *of the dove*) 5$_{7.11}$ 12$_{8}$ 14$_{22.30}$ (הַיּוֹנָה) 15$_{14.29}$ Nm 6$_{10}$ 11QT 38$_{10}$ (היונה; all ten || תֹּר) 60$_{9.10}$ (both היונה), קוֹל יוֹנִים *sound of doves* Na 2$_{8}$, דִּבְיוֹנִים *dung of doves* 1 K 6$_{25(Qr)}$ (Kt חרייונים *dung of doves*). <PREP> כְּ *as* Ps 55$_{7}$ Ca 5$_{12}$, + היה *be* Jr 48$_{28}$ Ezk 7$_{16}$ Ho 7$_{11}$, הגה *moan* Is 38$_{14}$ (|| סוּס *swallow*, עָגוּר *crane*) 59$_{11}$ (|| דֹּב *bear*), עוף *fly* Is 60$_{8}$ (+ עָב *cloud*), חרד *tremble* Ho 11$_{11}$ (|| צִפּוֹר *bird*).

2. יוֹנָתִי **my dove,** term of affection for female lover, <SUBJ> ראה hi. *show* Ca 2$_{14}$, שׁמע hi. *cause to hear* Ca 2$_{14}$, פתח *open* Ca 5$_{2}$. <NOM CL> יוֹנָתִי ... אַחַת הִיא ... בָּרָה הִיא *my dove ... is one, ... she is pure* Ca 6$_{9}$. <APP> אָחוֹת *sister* Ca 5$_{2}$, רַעְיָה *companion* Ca 5$_{2}$, תָּם *perfect one* Ca 5$_{2}$ 6$_{9}$. <COLL> יוֹנָתִי *O my dove* Ca 2$_{14}$ 5$_{2}$.

Also perh. 4QTanḥ 34$_{2}$ 4QCommGenD 1$_{1}$.

<SYN> §1 תֹּר *turtledove*, סוּס *swallow*, עָגוּר *crane*, צִפּוֹר *bird*, דֹּב *bear*.*

⇒ יוֹנָה II *Jonah*.

יוֹנָה II 19 pr.n.m. **Jonah,** prophet, son of Amittai, <SUBJ> היה *be* Jon 2$_{1}$ 4$_{1}$, אמר *say* Jon 2$_{2}$ 3$_{4}$ 4$_{1.8}$, נגד hi. *tell* Jon 1$_{7}$, קרא *call* Jon 1$_{1.5}$ 2$_{2}$ 3$_{1.4}$, שׁוע *call for help* Jon 2$_{2}$, פלל htp. *pray* Jon 2$_{2}$ 4$_{1}$, שׁאל *ask* Jon 4$_{8}$, נדר *vow* Jon 2$_{2}$, ראה *see* Jon 4$_{5}$, נבט hi. *look* Jon 2$_{2}$, ידע *know* Jon 1$_{7}$ 4$_{1}$, זכר *remember* Jon 2$_{2}$, חוס *pity* Jon 4$_{9}$, ירא *fear* Jon 1$_{7}$, שׂמח *rejoice* Jon 4$_{6}$, הלך *go* Jon 1$_{1}$ 3$_{1.3}$, בוא *come* Jon 1$_{3}$ 3$_{4}$, יצא *go out* Jon 4$_{5}$, ירד *go down* Jon 1$_{3.5}$ 2$_{2}$, ישׁב *sit* Jon 4$_{5}$, קום *rise* Jon 1$_{1.3.5}$ 3$_{1.3}$, ברח *flee* Jon 1$_{3.7}$ 4$_{1}$, גרשׁ ni. *be expelled* Jon 2$_{2}$, שׁכב *lie down* Jon 1$_{5}$, רדם ni. *be in a deep sleep* Jon 1$_{5}$, נתן *give* Jon 1$_{3}$, שׁלם pi. *pay* Jon 2$_{2}$, זבח *sacrifice* Jon 2$_{2}$, חלל hi. *begin* Jon 3$_{4}$, יסף hi. *add*, i.e. *do again* Jon 2$_{2}$, קדם pi. *do beforehand* Jon 4$_{1}$, עשׂה *make* Jon 4$_{5}$, גדל pi. *make great* Jon 4$_{9}$, עמל *toil* Jon 4$_{9}$, עלף htp. *be faint* Jon 4$_{8}$, אבד *perish* Jon 1$_{5}$, מות *die* Jon 4$_{8}$.

<NOM CL> יוֹנָה ... אֲשֶׁר מִגַּת הַחֵפֶר *Jonah ... who was from Gath-hepher* 2 K 14$_{25}$.

<OBJ> ענה *answer* Jon 2$_{2}$, נשׂא *lift* Jon 1$_{7.15}$, טול hi. *throw* Jon 1$_{7.15}$, שׁלך *throw* Jon 2$_{2}$, סבב po. *surround* Jon 2$_{2}$, אפף *surround* Jon 2$_{2}$, בלע *swallow* Jon 2$_{1}$, קיא *vomit* Jon 2$_{11}$.

<CSTR> רֹאשׁ יוֹנָה *head of Jonah* Jon 4$_{8}$.

<APP> בֵּן *son* 2 K 14$_{25}$ Jon 1$_{1}$, עֶבֶד *prophet* 2 K 14$_{25}$, נָבִיא *prophet* 2 K 14$_{25}$.

<PREP> לְ of direction, *to*, + אמר *say* Jon 1$_{5}$, עשׁת htp. *give thought* Jon 1$_{5}$; of benefit, *to, for*, + עשׂה *do, make* Jon 1$_{7}$ 4$_{5}$; of possession, *of, (belonging) to* Jon 1$_{7}$ 2$_{2}$; *on the part of*, + חרה *be angry* Jon 4$_{1.9}$; introducing object, + נצל hi. *deliver* Jon 4$_{6}$; מִן of direction, *from*, + לקח *take* Jon 4$_{1}$; אֶל *to*, + היה *be* Jon 1$_{1}$ 3$_{1}$, אמר *say* Jon 1$_{7}$ 4$_{9}$, דבר *speak* Jon 3$_{2}$, קרב *draw near* Jon 1$_{5}$, רעע *be bad* Jon 4$_{1}$; עַל *upon, over*, + נפל *fall* Jon 1$_{7}$, עבר *pass* Jon 2$_{2}$, עטף על htp. *faint within* Jon 2$_{2}$; מֵעַל לְ *over*, + עלה *go up* Jon 4$_{6}$;

בְּיַד *by means of, through*, + דבר pi. *speak* 2 K 14$_{25}$; בַּעַד *behind* Jon 2$_{2}$.

→ יוֹנָה I *dove*.

יוֹנָה III *oppressor*, see ינה *oppress*.

[יְוָנִי] 1 gent. **Greek**—pl. יְוָנִים—**1.** as plural noun, **Greeks**, <CSTR> בְּנֵי הַיְּוָנִים *sons of the Greeks* Jl 4$_{6}$.

2. as sing. noun, a particular **Greek**, in ref. to Alexander, <SUBJ> בגד *betray* Hb 2$_{5}$ (if em. יַיִן *wine*).*

3. as adj., **Greek**, הַחֶרֶב הַיְּוָנִיָּה *the Greek sword* Jr 46$_{16}$ 50$_{16}$ (if em. in both חֶרֶב הַיּוֹנָה *a sword that oppresses*).

→ יָוָן *Javan*.

יוֹנֵק, see ינק, Qal, §2, *(male) infant, shoot*.

יוֹנֶקֶת, see ינק, Qal, §3, *female infant, shoot*.

*__[יְוָנִית]__ n.f. **Greek (language)**, <CSTR> יְוָנִת אִיִּים *Greek of the distant coastlands* Ps 56$_{1}$ (if em. יוֹנַת אֵלֶם *dove of silence*). <PREP> עַל *according to* Ps 56$_{1}$ (if em.; see Cstr.).

→ יָוָן *Javan*.

יוֹנָתָן 42.0.3.3 pr.n.m. **Jonathan**—I יִנתן—**1.** son of Saul, ident. with יְהוֹנָתָן *J(eh)onathan* at 1 S 14$_{6}$ and freq., <SUBJ> היה *be* 1 S 14$_{40.49}$, אמר *say* 1 S 14$_{1.12.29}$, נגד hi. *tell* 1 S 14$_{1.43.43}$, שׁמע *hear* 1 S 14$_{27}$, הלך *go* 1 S 14$_{3}$, עלה *go up* 1 S 14$_{12.13}$, עבר *pass* 1 S 14$_{1.4}$, שׁלח *send* 1 S 14$_{27}$, שׁוב hi. *bring back* 1 S 14$_{27}$, ישׁב *dwell* 1 S 13$_{16}$, בקשׁ pi. *seek* 1 S 14$_{4}$, טבל *dip* 1 S 14$_{27}$, טעם *taste* 1 S 14$_{29.43}$, לכד ni. *be taken by lot* 1 S 14$_{41.42}$, עשׂה *do* 1 S 14$_{43.45}$, נכה hi. *strike* 1 S 13$_{3}$ 14$_{14}$, מות *die* 1 S 14$_{39.43.44.45.45}$, hi. *kill* 1 S 19$_{1}$.

<NOM CL> אֵין יוֹנָתָן *Jonathan was not (there)* 1 S 14$_{17}$.

<OBJ> ענה *answer* 1 S 14$_{12}$, פדה *ransom* 1 S 14$_{45}$, נכה hi. *kill* 1 C 10$_{2}$ (||1 S 31$_{2}$ יְהוֹנָתָן).

<APP> בֵּן *son* 1 S 13$_{16.22}$ 14$_{1.39.40.42}$ 19$_{1}$.

<PREP> לְ of possession, *of, (belonging) to*, + מצא ni. *be found* 1 S 13$_{22}$; בְּ of place, *in* 1 S 14$_{39}$; אֶל *to*, + אמר *say* 1 S 14$_{43}$, דבר pi. *speak* 1 S 19$_{1}$; עִם *with* 1 S 14$_{21}$, + היה *be* 1 S 13$_{2}$,; אֵת *with* 1 S 13$_{22}$; בֵּין *between*, + נפל hi. *cause* lot *to fall* 1 S 14$_{42}$ (+ Saul); לִפְנֵי *before*, + נפל *fall* 1 S 14$_{13}$; אַחֲרֵי *after*, + עלה *go up* 1 S 14$_{12}$.

2. priest, son of Abiathar, ident. with יְהוֹנָתָן *J(eh)onathan* at 2 S 15$_{27.36}$ 17$_{17.20}$, <SUBJ> אמר *say* 1 K 1$_{43}$, ענה *answer* 1 K 1$_{43}$, בוא *come* 1 K 1$_{42}$, בשׂר pi. *give news* 1 K 1$_{42}$. <APP> בֵּן *son* 1 K 1$_{42}$.

3. son of Kareah, army captain loyal to Gedaliah, Jr 40$_{8}$ (lacking in mss and ||2 K 25$_{23}$), <SUBJ> בוא *come* Jr 40$_{8}$, ישׁב *dwell* Jr 40$_{8}$, ירא *fear* Jr 40$_{8}$, עבד *serve* Jr 40$_{8}$. <APP> בֵּן *son* Jr 40$_{8}$. <PREP> לְ of direction, *to*, + אמר *say* Jr 40$_{8}$, שׁבע ni. *swear* Jr 40$_{8}$; of benefit, *to, for*, + יטב *be good* Jr 40$_{8}$.

4. member of Adin family, father of Ebed, exile returning with Ezra, <CSTR> בֶּן־יוֹנָתָן *son of Jonathan* Ezr 8$_{6}$.

5. opponent of Ezra, son of Asahel, <SUBJ> עמד *stand* against Ezr 10$_{15}$. <APP> בֵּן *son* Ezr 10$_{15}$.

6. head of priestly Malluchi family, <NOM CL> לִמְלִיכוּ יוֹנָתָן *(belonging) to Melichu was Jonathan* Ne 12$_{14(Qr)}$ (Kt למליכי *to Malluchi*).

7. father of Asaphite temple musician Zechariah, <CSTR> בֶּן־יוֹנָתָן *son of Jonathan* Ne 12$_{35}$.

8. Judahite, son of Jada, <NOM CL> בְּנֵי יָדָע ... יוֹנָתָן *the sons of Jada were ... Judah* 1 C 2$_{32}$. <CSTR> בְּנֵי יוֹנָתָן *sons of Jonathan* 1 C 2$_{33}$.

9. one of David's warriors, son of Shagee, ident. with יְהוֹנָתָן *Jehonathan* at ||2 S 23$_{32}$, <NOM CL> גִּבּוֹרֵי הַחֲיָלִים ... יוֹנָתָן *the mighty ones of valour were ... Jonathan* 1 C 11$_{34}$. <APP> הֲרָרִי *Hararite* 1 C 11$_{34}$ (unless Hararite refers to Shagee).

10. postexilic high priest, <SUBJ> ילד hi. *beget* Ne 12$_{11}$ (or em. יוֹחָנָן *Johanan*). <OBJ> ילד hi. *beget* Ne 12$_{11}$ (or em. יוֹחָנָן *Johanan*).

11. leader in Ezra's caravan, Ezr 8$_{16(mss)}$ (L אֶלְנָתָן *Elnathan*), <SUBJ> בוא hi. *bring* Ezr 8$_{16(mss)}$, דבר pi. *speak* Ezr 8$_{16(mss)}$. <OBJ> צוה pi. *command* Ezr 8$_{16(mss)}$. <APP> ראשׁ *head* Ezr 8$_{16(mss)}$ (or em. אִישׁ *man*). <PREP> שׁלח לְ appar. *send for* Ezr 8$_{16(mss)}$.

12. Samaria ost. 45, <COLL> יונתן מיצ[ת] *Jonathan from Jazith* Samaria ost. 45 (others יו נתן[ ] *Nathan*).

13. writer of letter, ident. with יהונתן *Jehonathan* at MurEpJonathan$_{1\ 0}$, <APP> בֵּן *son* MurEpJonathan$_{1}$. <PREP> מִן of direction, *from* MurEpJonathan$_{1}$.

14. Jonathan (Alexander) Jannaeus, high priest, ident. with יהונתן *Jehonathan* on Coins 5 5A 6 8 9 12 13 14, <APP> כֹּהֵן *priest* Alexander Jannaeus Coins 15 17, מֶלֶךְ *king* 4QJonathan 2$_{2}$ 3$_{8}$ ([המלן]ך). <PREP> לְ perh. of benefit, *to, for* 4QJonathan 3$_{8}$; עַל perh. *for, on behalf of* 4QJonathan 2$_{2}$.

15. high priest, prob. ident. with §14, <APP> כֹּהֵן *priest* Alexander Jannaeus Seal.

⇒ י' Y. + נתן *give*.

יוסה, see יוֹסֵי *Jose*.

[יוֹסֵי] 0.0.1.1 pr.n.m. **Jose**—Q, I יוסה—short form of יוֹסֵף *Joseph*, **1.** Frey 1285$_{4}$ (יוסי'; others יהוסף *Joseph*; others יהויעמד *Jehojaamod*), <CSTR> בן יוסי *son of Jose* Frey 1285$_{4}$. <APP> בֵּן *son* Frey 1285$_{4}$.

2. Kfar Baram inscr., <SUBJ> עשׂה *make* Kfar Baram inscr. (יוסה), <APP> בֵּן *son* Kfar Baram inscr., לֵוִי *Levite* Kfar Baram inscr.

3. recipient of letter, <APP> בֵּן *son* MurEpJonathan$_{1}$ ([בן]). <PREP> לְ of direction, *to* MurEpJonathan$_{1}$.

יוֹסֵף 210.1.6.3 pr.n.m. **Joseph**—I יסף—**1.** son of Jacob and Rachel, <SUBJ> היה *be* Gn 37$_{2}$ 39$_{2.6.10.20.22}$ 41$_{39}$ Ex 1$_{5}$, חיה *live* Gn 50$_{22}$, hi. *keep alive* Gn 47$_{23}$, אמר *say* Gn 37$_{5.13}$ 39$_{7}$ 40$_{6.8.12.18}$ 41$_{16.25.54.55}$ 42$_{7.9.14.18}$ 43$_{16.17.26.30}$ 44$_{4.15}$ 45$_{3.4.9.17.21}$ 46$_{31}$ 47$_{1.16.23}$ 48$_{9.18}$ 50$_{19.24}$, דבר pi. *speak* Gn 41$_{25}$ 42$_{7.14.23}$ 44$_{2}$ 45$_{27}$ 50$_{4.21}$, קרא *cry* Gn 45$_{1}$, *call*, i.e. name Gn 41$_{51}$, ענה *answer* Gn 40$_{18}$ 41$_{16}$, נגד hi. *tell* Gn 37$_{5}$ 46$_{31}$ 47$_{1}$, ספר *count* Gn 41$_{49}$, pi. *tell* Gn 37$_{5}$, צוה pi. *command* Gn 42$_{25}$ 45$_{17}$ 50$_{2}$, שׁבע ni. *swear* Gn 47$_{29}$, hi. *cause to swear* Gn 50$_{25}$ Ex 13$_{19}$, שׁאל *ask* Gn 40$_{6}$ 43$_{26}$, מאן pi. *refuse* Gn 39$_{7}$, פתר *interpret* Gn 40$_{22}$ 41$_{15}$, ראה *see* Gn 37$_{13}$ 40$_{6}$ 41$_{41}$ 42$_{7}$ 43$_{16.26}$ 48$_{17}$ 50$_{23}$, ni. *present oneself* Gn 46$_{29}$, ידע *know* Gn 47$_{5}$ Ex 1$_{8}$ 4QapJoseph^{b} 1$_{10}$ ([י]דע), htp. *make oneself known* Gn 45$_{1}$, נכר hi. *recognize* Gn 42$_{7.8}$, שׁמע *hear* Gn 39$_{10}$ 42$_{23}$, חלם *dream* Gn 37$_{5}$ 42$_{9}$, זכר *remember* Gn 42$_{9}$, ירא *fear* Gn 42$_{18}$, ירה hi. *show* Gn 46$_{28}$, בכה *weep* Gn 42$_{23}$ 43$_{30}$ 45$_{9}$ 46$_{29}$ 50$_{1.17}$, ספד *lament* Gn 50$_{8}$, אפק htp. *restrain oneself* Gn 43$_{30}$ 45$_{1}$, נשׁק *kiss* Gn 45$_{9}$ 50$_{1}$, נחם pi. *comfort* Gn 50$_{19}$.

הלך *go* Gn 37$_{13.17}$, בוא *come* Gn 37$_{13.23}$ 39$_{10}$ 40$_{6}$ 41$_{14}$ 43$_{25.26.30}$ 47$_{1.15}$ 48$_{2}$ 50$_{8}$, hi. *bring* Gn 37$_{2}$ 47$_{7.14}$, יצא *go out* Gn 39$_{10}$ 41$_{45.46}$ 43$_{30}$, hi. *bring out* Gn 48$_{12}$, עלה *go up* Gn 46$_{29}$ 46$_{31}$ 50$_{4.7}$, ירד ho. *be brought down* Gn 39$_{1}$, נגשׁ ni. *draw near* Gn 33$_{7}$, hi. *bring near* Gn 48$_{9.13}$, קרב *draw near* Gn 37$_{17}$, שׁוב *go back* Gn 42$_{23}$ 50$_{4.14}$, hi. *bring back* Gn 37$_{13}$ 50$_{15}$, שׁלח *send* Gn 45$_{21.27}$, pi. *send* Gn 45$_{21}$, קרא *meet* Gn 46$_{29}$, תעה *wander* Gn 37$_{13}$, עבר *pass* Gn 41$_{46}$, hi. *cause to pass* Gn 47$_{20}$ (Sam עבד *enslave*), סור hi. *remove* Gn 48$_{17}$, טול ho. *be thrown* 4QapJoseph^{b} 1$_{10}$, נפל *fall* Gn 45$_{9}$ 46$_{29}$ 50$_{1}$, עמד *stand* Gn 41$_{46}$, hi. *place* Gn 47$_{7}$, ישׁב *dwell* Gn 50$_{22}$, hi. *cause to dwell* Gn 47$_{5.11}$, סבב *turn* Gn 42$_{23}$, עזב *leave* Gn 39$_{10}$, נוס *flee* Gn 39$_{10}$, מהר pi. *hasten* Gn 43$_{30}$, מצא *find* Gn 37$_{17}$ 39$_{4}$ 50$_{4}$, נשׂא *lift* Gn 43$_{26}$ 47$_{29}$, *forgive* Gn 50$_{17}$, אסף *gather* Gn 42$_{14}$, קבץ *gather* Gn 41$_{46}$, לקט pi. *gather* Gn 47$_{14}$, צבר *heap up* Gn 41$_{49}$, בקשׁ pi. *seek* Gn 37$_{13}$ 43$_{30}$.

עשׂה *do* Gn 39$_{2.7.10.22}$ 40$_{12}$ 47$_{29}$ 50$_{8}$ 4QapJoseph^{a} 9$_{2}$ ([לעשׂ]ות יוס[ף]), שׁרת pi. *serve* Gn 39$_{4}$ 40$_{4}$, יכל *be able* Gn 45$_{1}$, מלך *reign* Gn 37$_{5}$, משׁל *rule* Gn 37$_{5}$ 45$_{26}$, שׁחה htpal. *bow down* Gn 33$_{7}$, ילד hi. *beget* Gn 48$_{3}$, פתח *open* Gn 41$_{56}$, יהב *give* Gn 47$_{15}$, נתן *give, place* Gn 41$_{46}$ 45$_{3.17.21}$ 47$_{11.16.17}$, שׂים *place* Gn 47$_{5.26.29}$, ho. *be placed* Gn 50$_{26(Sam)}$, שׁית *place* Gn 46$_{4}$, יצג htp. *place* Gn 47$_{1}$, לקח *take* Gn 42$_{23}$ 48$_{1.9.13}$, קנה *purchase* Gn 47$_{20.23}$, שׁבר hi. *sell grain* Gn 41$_{56}$ (if em. וַיִּשְׁבֹּר qal to וַיַּשְׁבֵּר hi. *and he sold grain*) 42$_{6}$, מכר ni. *be sold* Ps 105$_{17}$, טרף pu. *be torn* Gn 37$_{33}$, רעה *pasture* Gn 37$_{2}$, כול pilp. *provide for* Gn 45$_{9}$ 47$_{12}$ 50$_{19}$, נהל pi. *refresh* Gn 47$_{17}$.

חטא *sin* Gn 39$_{7}$, שׁכב *lie down* Gn 39$_{7.10}$, תמך *take hold of* Gn 48$_{17}$, אלם pi. *bind* sheaves Gn 37$_{5}$, אסר *bind* Gn 42$_{23}$ 46$_{29}$, pass. *be imprisoned* Gn 40$_{3}$, גנב pu. *be stolen* Gn 40$_{12}$, שׂטם *bear a grudge* Gn 50$_{15}$, קבר *bury* Gn 47$_{29}$ 50$_{4.7.14}$, רחץ *wash* Gn 43$_{30}$, גלח pi. appar. *shave oneself* Gn 41$_{14}$ (or em. וַיְגַלַּח to וַיִּגָּלַח ni. *and he shaved himself*), חלף pi. *change* clothes Gn 41$_{14}$, חדל *cease* Gn 41$_{49}$, נכר htp. *act as a stranger* Gn 42$_{7}$, מות *die* Gn 50$_{26}$ Ex 1$_{6}$.

<NOM CL> יוֹסֵף הוּא הַשַּׁלִּיט *Joseph was the ruler* Gn 42$_{6}$, בְּנֵי רָחֵל יוֹסֵף וּבִנְיָמִן *the sons of Rachel were Joseph and Benjamin* Gn 35$_{24}$, var. Gn 46$_{19}$, אֵלֶּה בְּנֵי יִשְׂרָאֵל ... יוֹסֵף *these are the sons of Israel ... Joseph* 1 C 2$_{2}$, אֵין־יוֹסֵף *Joseph was not (there)* Gn 37$_{29}$, var. Gn 42$_{36}$, יוֹסֵף בֶּן־שְׁלֹשִׁים שָׁנָה *Joseph was a son of thirty years*, i.e. thirty

years old Gn 41$_{46}$, אֲנִי יוֹסֵף *I am Joseph* Gn 45$_{3.4}$, יוֹסֵף חַי *Joseph is alive* Gn 45$_{26.28}$.

<OBJ> שׁאל *ask* Gn 37$_{13}$, קרא *call*, i.e. summon Gn 41$_{14}$, ענה *answer* Gn 45$_{3}$, שׁבע hi. *cause to swear* Gn 50$_{4}$, ברך pi. *bless* Gn 48$_{15}$, ראה *see* Gn 37$_{17}$ 45$_{28}$, נכר hi. *recognize* Gn 42$_{8}$, ידע *cause to know* Gn 41$_{39}$, זכר *remember* Gn 40$_{12.23}$, שׁכח *forget* Gn 40$_{23}$, נשׁה pi. *cause to forget* Gn 41$_{51}$, בוא hi. *bring* Gn 37$_{28}$ 48$_{21}$, יצא *bring out* Gn 40$_{12}$, עלה hi. *bring up* Gn 37$_{28}$, רוץ hi. *bring quickly* Gn 41$_{14}$, שׁלח *send* Gn 37$_{13}$ 45$_{4}$, מצא *find* Gn 37$_{13}$, אהב *love* Gn 37$_{3}$, שׂנא *hate* Gn 37$_{3.5}$, ילד *bear* Gn 30$_{25}$, שׂים *place* Gn 33$_{2}$ 40$_{12}$ 45$_{4.9}$, ישׂם *place* Gn 50$_{26}$, נתן *give*, i.e. place Gn 39$_{20}$ 41$_{41.42}$, פקד *place in charge of* Gn 40$_{4}$, hi. Gn 39$_{4}$, רכב hi. *cause to ride* Gn 41$_{42}$, לקח *take* Gn 37$_{23}$ 39$_{20}$, קנה *purchase* Gn 39$_{1}$, מכר *sell* Gn 37$_{28}$ 45$_{4}$, פרה hi. *make fruitful* Gn 41$_{51}$, שׁלך hi. *cast* Gn 37$_{23}$, לבשׁ hi. *dress* Gn 41$_{42}$, פשׁט hi. *strip* Gn 37$_{23}$, תפשׂ *take hold of* Gn 39$_{10}$, נכל htp. *deal craftily with* Gn 37$_{17}$, גמל *repay* Gn 50$_{15.17}$, מות hi. *kill* Gn 37$_{17}$, חנט *embalm* Gn 50$_{26}$.

<CSTR> בֶּן־יוֹסֵף *son of Joseph* Nm 27$_{1}$ 32$_{33}$ 36$_{12}$ 17$_{2}$ 36$_{1(mss)}$, בְּנֵי *sons of* Gn 46$_{27}$ 48$_{8}$, אֲחִי *brother of* Gn 42$_{4}$, אֲחֵי־ *brothers of* Gn 42$_{3.6}$ 45$_{16}$ 50$_{15}$, בְּכוֹר *firstborn of* Nm Jos 17$_{1}$, אֲדֹנֵי *master of* Gn 39$_{20}$, יַד־ *hand of* Gn 39$_{6.20}$ 41$_{42}$, בִּרְכֵּי *knees of* Gn 50$_{23}$, עַצְמוֹת *bones of* Ex 13$_{19}$ Jos 24$_{32}$, שֵׁם *name of* Gn 41$_{45}$, כְּתֹנֶת *robe of* Gn 37$_{31}$, בֵּית *house of* Gn 43$_{17}$ (בֵּיתָה *to the house of*) 43$_{18.19.24}$ 44$_{14}$ (both בֵּיתָה) 50$_{8}$, דְּבַר *word of* Gn 44$_{2}$, דִּבְרֵי *words of* Gn 45$_{27}$, יְמֵי *days of* Gn 50$_{23(Sam)}$.

<APP> בֵּן *son* Gn 37$_{2}$ 45$_{9.25}$ 47$_{29}$ 48$_{2}$ 50$_{26}$.

<PREP> לְ of benefit, *to, for*, + עשׂה *make* Gn 37$_{3}$, שׂים *place* Gn 43$_{30}$, ילד *bear* Gn 41$_{50}$ 46$_{20}$, ni. *be born* Gn 46$_{20}$ 48$_{3}$, pu. *be born* Gn 41$_{50}$ 46$_{27}$.

לְ of direction, *to*, + אמר *say* Gn 37$_{5.13}$ 40$_{9}$ 47$_{17.29}$ 48$_{1}$ (or em. וַיֹּאמֶר *and he said* to וַיֵּאָמֶר ni. *and it was said*) 50$_{17}$, דבר pi. *speak* Gn 37$_{3}$ (if em. דַּבְּרוֹ *to speak [to] him* to דַּבֵּר לוֹ *to speak to him*), נגד hi. *tell* Gn 37$_{13}$, ספר pi. *tell* Gn 40$_{8.9}$, קרא *call* Gn 47$_{29}$, שׁחה htpal. *bow down* Gn 37$_{5}$ 42$_{6}$ 43$_{26}$, בוא hi. *bring* Gn 43$_{26}$, נתן *give* Gn 41$_{45}$ 48$_{9.21}$.

לְ of possession, *of, (belonging) to* Gn 50$_{17}$.

בְּ introducing object, + גער *rebuke* Gn 37$_{5}$, קנא pi. *be jealous of* Gn 37$_{5}$.

כְּ *as* Gn 41$_{39}$ 44$_{15}$, + ילד ni. *be born* Si 49$_{15}$.

מִן of direction, *from*, + חשׂך *withhold* Gn 39$_{7}$; of comparison, *(greater) than* Gn 39$_{7}$, + גדל *be great* Gn 41$_{39}$.

מֵעַל *from*, + יצא hi. *cause to go out* Gn 45$_{1}$.

אֶל *to*, + היה *be* Gn 45$_{9}$ (+ קָרוֹב *near*), אמר *say* Gn 37$_{13}$ 40$_{6.16}$ 41$_{15.39.41.44}$ 42$_{9}$ 43$_{26}$ 45$_{17}$ 46$_{30}$ 47$_{5}$ 48$_{3.11.21}$, דבר pi. *speak* Gn 39$_{10}$ 41$_{17}$ 50$_{17}$, צוה pi. *command* Gn 50$_{16}$ (or em. וַיְצַוּוּ *and they commanded* to וַיִּגְּשׁוּ *and they drew near*), הלך *go* Gn 41$_{55}$, בוא *come* Gn 41$_{57}$ 45$_{17}$ 46$_{31}$ 47$_{5}$ 48$_{3}$, hi. *bring* Gn 42$_{18}$ 47$_{17}$, ירד *go down* Gn 45$_{9}$, נגשׁ *draw near* Gn 45$_{4}$ 50$_{16}$ (if em.; see above), שׁלח *send* Gn 46$_{28}$, נשׂא *lift* eyes Gn 39$_{7}$, נטה *extend* kindness Gn 39$_{21}$.

עַל *upon* Gn 37$_{23}$; *beside*, + נצב ni. *stand* Gn 45$_{1}$; *concerning*, + שׁמע *hear* Gn 41$_{15}$; *against*, + חשׁב *devise* Gn 50$_{19}$.

עִם *with*, + היה *be* Gn 48$_{21}$, עלה *go up* Gn 50$_{8}$, עשׂה *do* Gn 40$_{12}$, לקח *take* Gn 47$_{1(Sam)}$ 48$_{1}$.

אֵת *with*, + היה *be* Gn 39$_{2.21}$, עלה *go up* Gn 50$_{14}$, ידע *know*, i.e. be concerned about Gn 39$_{7}$, דבר pi. *speak* Gn 45$_{9}$.

בִּגְלַל *on account of*, + ברך pi. *bless* Gn 39$_{5}$.

לִפְנֵי *before*, + קרא *call* Gn 41$_{42}$, עמד *stand* Gn 43$_{15}$, ישׁב *sit* Gn 43$_{30}$, נפל *fall* Gn 44$_{14}$ 50$_{17}$.

נֶגֶד *before*, + מות *die* Gn 47$_{15}$.

מִפְּנֵי *in the presence of*, + בהל ni. *be dismayed* Gn 45$_{3}$.

<COLL> וַתִּקְרָא אֶת־שְׁמוֹ יוֹסֵף *and she called his name Joseph* Gn 30$_{24}$.

2. tribe claiming §1 as eponymous ancestor, <SUBJ> עמד *stand* Dt 27$_{12}$, ברך pi. *bless* Dt 27$_{12}$. <NOM CL> בֵּן פֹּרָת יוֹסֵף *Joseph is the son of a fruit-bearer* (tree), i.e. a fruitful bough Gn 49$_{22}$, יוסף ... לנגב *Joseph is ... in the south* 11QT 39$_{12}$. <CSTR> בְּנֵי יוֹסֵף *sons of Joseph* Nm 1$_{10.32}$ 13$_{7}$ (if em.; see §4) 13$_{11}$ (if em.; see below) 26$_{28.37}$ 34$_{23}$ 36$_{1.5}$ Jos 14$_{4}$ 16$_{1.4}$ 17$_{14.16}$ 18$_{11}$ 24$_{32}$ Jg 1$_{22(mss)}$ 1 C 5$_{1}$ 7$_{29}$ 11QT 24$_{13}$ (corrected in mg to יהוסף) 44$_{13}$, בְּנֵי יַעֲקֹב וְיוֹסֵף *sons of Jacob and Joseph* Ps 77$_{16}$, רֹאשׁ יוֹסֵף *head of Joseph* Gn 49$_{26}$ Dt 33$_{16}$, מַטֵּה *tribe of* Nm 13$_{11}$ (or em. מַטֵּה *tribe of* to בְּנֵי *sons of*), בֵּית *house of* Jos 17$_{17}$ 18$_{5}$ Jg 1$_{22.23.35}$, אֹהֶל *tent of* Ps 78$_{67}$ (+ Ephraim), שַׁעַר *gate of* Ezk 48$_{32}$ 11QT 44$_{13.14}$. <APP> בֵּן *son* 1 C 5$_{1}$ 7$_{29}$. <PREP> לְ *concerning*, + אמר *say* Dt 33$_{13}$; of possession, *of, (belonging) to* Ezk 47$_{13}$ (if em.; see Coll.) 1 C 5$_{1(mss)}$ (L לִבְנֵי

יוֹסֵף *to the sons of Joseph*) 5_{2}. <COLL> יוֹסֵף חֲבָלִים perh. *Joseph (shall have) portions* Ezk 47_{13} (or em. לְיוֹסֵף חֲבָלִים *to Joseph shall be two portions*).

3. tribes and kingdom of northern kingdom of Israel (distinction from §2 not alw. clear), <OBJ> נהג *lead* Ps 80_{2} (+ Israel). <CSTR> בֵּית יוֹסֵף *house of Joseph* 2 S 19_{21} 1 K 11_{28} Am 5_{6} Ob$_{18}$ (+ Jacob, Esau) Zc 10_{6} (+ Judah), עֵץ *stick of* Ezk 37_{19}, שְׁאֵרִית *remnant of* Am 5_{15}, שֵׁבֶר *ruin of* Am 6_{6}. <PREP> לְ of benefit, *to, for* Ezk 37_{16}.

4. Issacharite, father of Igal, <CSTR> בֶּן־יוֹסֵף *son of Joseph* Nm 13_{7} (or em. לִבְנֵי יוֹסֵף *of the sons of Joseph*, i.e. §2).

5. member of Binnui family, husband of non-Jewish wife, <NOM CL> יוֹסֵף ... בְּנֵי בִנּוּי *the sons of Binnui were ... Joseph* Ezr 10_{42}.

6. priest, head of the Shebaniah family, <NOM CL> לִשְׁבַנְיָה יוֹסֵף *(belonging) to Shebaniah was Joseph* Ne 12_{14}.

7. Asaphite temple musician, <NOM CL> לִבְנֵי אָסָף זַכּוּר וְיוֹסֵף *of the sons of Asaph were Zaccur and Joseph* 1 C 25_{2}. <PREP> לְ of direction, *to*, + יצא (of lot) *go out*, i.e. fall 1 C 25_{9}.

8. father of Saal, <CSTR> בן יסף *son of Joseph* Seal 631 (T. Beit Mirsim?, 7th/6th cent.).

9. father of Eleazar, Honia, Joazar, Judah, Simeon, Johanan, <CSTR> בני יוסף *sons of Joseph* Bene Ḥezir tomb inscr.

10. son of Honia, <APP> בֵּן *son* Bene Ḥezir tomb inscr. <PREP> לְ of possession, *of, (belonging) to* Bene Ḥezir tomb inscr. (ל[יו]סף).

11. perh. father of Tobijah, <CSTR> [בן יו]סף *son of Joseph* 4QRebukes 1.2$_{7}$.

Also 4QapJoseph[b] 1$_{14.20}$ (יו]סף]).

⇒ יְ *Y.* + יסף *add.**

יוֹסִפְיָה 1 pr.n.m. **Josiphiah,** member of Bani family, father of Shelomith in Ezra's caravan, <CSTR> בֶּן־יוֹסִפְיָה *son of Josiphiah* Ezr 8_{10}.

⇒ יסף *add* + יְ *Y.*

[יוֹסְתֵּר] 0.0.0.1 pr.n.m. **Joster,** father of Shimea, <CSTR> בן יוסתר *son of Joster* Seal 346 (7th/6th cent.).

⇒ יְ *Y.* + סתר *hide.*

יוֹעֵאלָה 1 pr.n.m. **Joelah,** Benjaminite, one of David's warriors, son of Jeroham, <APP> בֵּן *son* 1 C 12_{8} (mss יַעְלָה *Jaalah*).

יוֹעֵד 1 pr.n.m. **Joed,** Benjaminite, son of Pedaiah, <CSTR> בֶּן־יוֹעֵד *son of Joed* Ne 11_{7}. <APP> בֵּן *son* Ne 11_{7}.

⇒ יְ *Y.* + עוד *bear witness.*

יוֹעֶזֶר 1.0.0.2 pr.n.m. **Joezer, 1.** one of David's warriors, <APP> קָרְחִי *Korahite* 1 C 12_{7}. **2.** papMurPalimp[b]4. **3.** son of Joseph, <APP> בֵּן *son* Bene Ḥezir tomb inscr.

⇒ יְ *Y.* + עזר *help.*

[יוֹעֵלְיָהוּ] 0.0.0.2 pr.n.m. **Joiliah, 1.** appar. son of Ishmael, <PREP> לְ of possession, *of, (belonging) to* Seal 724 (7th cent.).

2. father of Malchiah, <CSTR> בן יועליהו *son of Joiliah* Bulla 930 (7th cent.). ⇒ יעל *profit* + יְ *Y.*

יוֹעֵץ, see יעץ *counsel.*

יוֹעָשׁ 2 pr.n.m. **Joash, 1.** Benjaminite, son of Becher, <NOM CL> יוֹעָשׁ ... בְּנֵי בֶכֶר *the sons of Becher were ... Joash* 1 C 7_{8}.

2. one of David's officials, <NOM CL> עַל־אוֹצְרוֹת הַשֶּׁמֶן יוֹעָשׁ *over the storehouses of oil was Joash* 1 C 27_{28}.

⇒ יְ *Y.*

[יוֹעָשָׂה] 0.0.0.2 pr.n.m. **Joasah, 1.** Kuntillet 'Ajrud inscr. E1, <OBJ> ברך pi. *bless* Kuntillet 'Ajrud inscr. E1. <PREP> לְ of direction, *to*, + אמר *say* Kuntillet 'Ajrud inscr. E1.

2. appar. son of Zaccur, Seal 171 (7th cent.).

⇒ יְ *Y.* + עשׂה *do.*

יוֹצֵאת, see יצא *go out.*

יוֹצָדָק 4 pr.n.m. **Jozadak,** father of high priest Jeshua, ident. with יְהוֹצָדָק *Jehozadak* at Hg $1_{1.12.14}$ $2_{2.4}$ Zc 6_{11} 1 C $5_{40.41}$, <CSTR> בֶּן־יוֹצָדָק *son of Jozadak* Ezr $3_{2.8}$ 10_{18} Ne 12_{26}.

⇒ יְ *Y.* + צדק *be righteous.*

יוֹצֵר, see יצר *form.*

יוֹקִים 1.0.0.1 pr.n.m. **Jokim**—I יוקם—**1.** Judahite, son of Shelah, <NOM CL> בְּנֵי שֵׁלָה ... יוֹקִים *the sons of Shelah were ... Jokim* 1 C 4_{22} (or em. יוֹקִים to אֶת־בֵּית צֹבֵעַ וְרֹקֵם *with the house of the dyer and embroiderer*).

2. father of Asaiah, <CSTR> בן יוקם *son of Jokim* Seal 38 (8th cent.).

⇒ ׳י *Y.* + קום hi. *raise up.*

יוֹרֶא I, see ירה II, ho. *be given drink.*

יוֹרֶא II, see יוֹרֶה I *early rain.*

יוֹרָה 1 pr.n.m. **Jorah,** head of family of returning exiles, appar. ident. with חָרִיף *Hariph* at Ne 7_{24} 10_{19}, <CSTR> בְּנֵי יוֹרָה *sons of Jorah* Ezr 2_{18} (or em. חָרִיף *Hariph*).

יוֹרֶה I $_{3.0.2}$ n.[m.] **early rain**—Sam יוֹרֶא—from end of October to beginning of December, <OBJ> ירד hi. *send down* Jl $2_{23(mss)}$ (L מוֹרֶה *early rain;* ‖ מַלְקוֹשׁ *latter rain*) 11QBer 1_8 (‖ מַלְקוֹשׁ, + מָטָר *rain,* טַל *dew,* גֶּשֶׁם *rain*), נתן *give* Dt 11_{14} Jr 5_{24} (both ‖ מַלְקוֹשׁ). <APP> גֶּשֶׁם *rain* Jr $5_{24(Qr)}$ Jl $2_{23(mss)}$ 1QH 8_{16}, מָטָר *rain* Dt 11_{14}. <PREP> כְּ *as* 1QH 8_{16}. <SYN> מַלְקוֹשׁ *latter rain.**

⇒ ירה II *water.*

יוֹרֶה II, see ירה II *water.*

יוֹרַי 1 pr.n.m. **Jorai,** Gadite, son of Abihail, <NOM CL> אֲחֵיהֶם ... יוֹרַי *their brothers were ... Jorai* 1 C 5_{13}.

⇒ ׳י *Y.*

יוֹרָם 20 pr.n.m. **Joram**—יֹרָם—**1.** king of Judah, son of Jehoshaphat, ident. with יְהוֹרָם *Jehoram* at 1 K 22_{51} 2 K 1_{17} $8_{16.25.20}$ 12_{19} 2 C $21_{1.3.5.9.16}$ $22_{1.6.11}$, <SUBJ> היה *be* 2 K $8_{16(mss)}$ (L יְהוֹרָם *Jehoram*), הלך *go* 2 K $8_{16(mss)}$, עבר *pass* 2 K 8_{21} (‖2 C 21_9 יְהוֹרָם), קום *rise* 2 K 8_{21}, מלך *reign* 2 K $8_{16(mss)}$, עשׂה *do* 2 K $8_{16(mss).23}$, נכה hi. *strike* 2 K 8_{21}, שׁכב *lie down* 2 K 8_{24}, קבר ni. *be buried* 2 K 8_{24}. <NOM CL> יוֹרָם בְּנוֹ *Joram was his son* 1 C 3_{11}. <CSTR> בַּת ... יוֹרָם *daughter of ... Joram* 2 K 11_2, דִּבְרֵי יוֹרָם *deeds of Joram* 2 K 8_{23}. <APP> בֵּן *son* 2 K $8_{16(mss)}$ (L יְהוֹרָם *Jehoram*), מֶלֶךְ *king* 2 K 11_2. <PREP> אֶל introducing object, + סבב *surround* 2 K 8_{21} (‖2 C 21_9 יְהוֹרָם); תַּחַת *instead of,* + מלך *reign* 2 K 8_{24}.

2. king of Israel, son of Ahab, ident. with יְהוֹרָם *Jehoram* at 2 K 1_{17} $3_{1.6}$ $9_{15.17.21.24}$ 2 C $22_{5.6.6.7}$, <SUBJ> היה *be* 2 K 9_{14}, שׁמר *watch* 2 K 9_{14}, שׁוב *go back* 2 K 8_{29}‖2 C 22_5, לחם ni. *fight* 2 K 8_{29}, חלה *be sick* 2 K 8_{29}, רפא htp. *be healed* 2 K 8_{29}‖2 C 22_5, שׁכב *lie down* 2 K 9_{16}. <OBJ> ראה *see* 2 K 8_{29}‖2 C 22_5 2 K 9_{16}, נכה hi. *strike* 2 K 8_{28}‖2 C 22_5 2 K 8_{29}. <APP> בֵּן *son* 2 K $8_{16.25.28.29}$ 9_{29}, מֶלֶךְ *king* 2 K $8_{16.25.29}$. <PREP> לְ of possession, *of, (belonging) to* 2 K $8_{16.25}$ 9_{29}; אֶל *to,* + בוא *come* 2 C 22_7; *against,* + קשׁר htp. *conspire* 2 K 9_{14} (or em. אֶל to עַל *against*); אֶת *with,* + הלך *go* 2 K 8_{28}.

3. Levite, treasury official at time of David, <NOM CL> יֹרָם בְּנוֹ *Joram was his son* 1 C 26_{25}.

4. son of Toi the king of Hamath, ident. with הֲדוֹרָם *Hadoram* in ‖1 C 18_{10}, <SUBJ> שׁאל *ask* 2 S 8_{10}, ברך pi. *bless* 2 S 8_{10}. <OBJ> שׁלח *send* 2 S 8_{10}. <APP> בֵּן *son* 2 S 8_{10}.

5. brother of Tibni, <SUBJ> 1 K 16_{22} (if ins. וְיוֹרָם אָחִיו *and Joram his brother*). <APP> אָח *brother* 1 K 16_{22} (if em.; see Subj.).

⇒ ׳י *Y.* + רום *be high.*

יוּשַׁב חֶסֶד 1 pr.n.m. **Jushab-hesed,** son of Zerubbabel, <NOM CL> בְּנֵי זְרֻבָּבֶל ... יוּשַׁב חֶסֶד *the sons of Zerubbabel were ... Jushab-hesed* 1 C $3_{20(mss)}$ (L בֶּן־ *the son of* Zerubbabel was; or em. יוּשַׁב to יָשׁוּב *Jashub* or יָשׁוֹב *Jashob;* perh. del. חֶסֶד).

⇒ ישׁב *sit* + חסד *be loyal.*

יוֹשַׁבְיָה, see יוֹשַׁוְיָה *Joshaviah.*

יוֹשִׁבְיָה 1 pr.n.m. **Joshibiah,** Simeonite, son of Seraiah, <CSTR> בֶּן־יוֹשִׁבְיָה *son of Joshibiah* 1 C 4_{35}. <APP> בֵּן *son* 1 C 4_{35}.

⇒ ׳י *Y.* + ישׁב *sit.*

יוֹשָׁה 1 pr.n.m. **Joshah,** Simeonite, son of Amaziah, <APP> בֵּן *son* 1 C 4_{34}.

יוֹשַׁוְיָה 1 pr.n.m. **Joshaviah,** one of David's warriors, son of Elnaam, <NOM CL> גִּבּוֹרֵי הַחֲיָלִים ... יוֹשַׁוְיָה *the mighty men of the armies were ... Joshaviah* 1 C 11$_{46}$ (ms יוֹשַׁבְיָה *Joshabiah*). <APP> בֵּן *son* 1 C 11$_{46}$.

יוֹשָׁפָט 2 pr.n.m. **Joshaphat, 1.** one of David's warriors, <NOM CL> גִּבּוֹרֵי הַחֲיָלִים ... יְהוֹשָׁפָט *the mighty men of the armies were ... Joshaphat* 1 C 11$_{43}$. <APP> מִתְנִי *Mithnite* 1 C 11$_{43}$.

2. priest and trumpeter in procession of ark to Jerusalem, <SUBJ> חצצר *sound trumpet* 1 C 15$_{24}$. <APP> כֹּהֵן *priest* 1 C 15$_{24}$.

⇒ '' *Y.* + שׁפט *judge.*

יוֹתָם 24 pr.n.m. **Jotham, 1.** youngest son of Jerubbaal (Gideon), <SUBJ> יתר ni. *remain* Jg 9$_{5}$, אמר *say* Jg 9$_{7}$, קרא *call* Jg 9$_{7}$, הלך *go* Jg 9$_{7.21}$, ברח *flee* Jg 9$_{21}$, נוס *flee* Jg 9$_{21}$, עמד *stand* Jg 9$_{7}$, ישׁב *dwell* Jg 9$_{21}$, נשׂא *lift* voice Jg 9$_{7}$, חבא ni. *hide oneself* Jg 9$_{5}$. <CSTR> קִלְלַת יוֹתָם *curse of Jotham* Jg 9$_{57}$. <APP> בֵּן *son* Jg 9$_{5.57}$. <PREP> לְ of direction, *to,* + נגד hi. *tell* Jg 9$_{7}$; אֶל *to,* + שׁמע *listen* Jg 9$_{7}$.

2. king of Judah, son of Uzziah (Azariah) and Jerusha(h), <SUBJ> היה *be* 2 K 15$_{32}$ 2 C 27$_{7}$, בוא *come* 2 C 27$_{1}$, מלך *reign* 2 K 15$_{7}$||2 C 26$_{23}$ 2 K 15$_{32}$ 15$_{32}$||2 C 27$_{1}$ 2 C 27$_{7}$, שׁפט *judge* 2 K 15$_{5}$||2 C 26$_{21}$, עשׂה *do* 2 K 15$_{32}$ ||2 C 27$_{1}$ 2 K 15$_{36}$, כון hi. *establish* 2 C 27$_{6}$, בנה *build* 2 C 27$_{1}$, לחם ni. *fight* 2 C 27$_{1}$, חזק *be strong,* i.e. prevail 2 C 27$_{1}$, htp. *show oneself strong* 2 C 27$_{6}$, שׁכב *lie down* 2 K 15$_{38}$||2 C 27$_{9}$, קבר ni. *be buried* 2 K 15$_{38}$ (וַיִּקָּבֵר lacking in mss). <NOM CL> יוֹתָם בְּנוֹ *Jotham was his son* 1 C 3$_{12}$, בֶּן־עֶשְׂרִים וְחָמֵשׁ שָׁנָה יוֹתָם *Jotham was a son of twenty-five years,* i.e. twenty-five years old 2 C 27$_{1}$, יוֹתָם עַל־הַבַּיִת *Jotham was over,* i.e. in charge of, *the house* 2 K 15$_{5}$||2 C 26$_{21}$. <OBJ> קבר *bury* 2 C 27$_{9}$. <CSTR> בֶּן־יוֹתָם *son of Jotham* 2 K 15$_{30}$ (if em.; see Cstr.) 16$_{1}$ Is 7$_{1}$, דִּבְרֵי *deeds of* 2 K 15$_{36}$||2 C 27$_{7}$, (...) יְמֵי *days of (...)* Is 1$_{1}$ Ho 1$_{1}$ Mc 1$_{1}$ 1 C 5$_{17}$. <APP> בֵּן *son* 2 K 15$_{5.7}$||2 C 26$_{21.23}$ 2 K 15$_{30}$ (lacking in ms) 15$_{32}$ Is 7$_{1}$, מֶלֶךְ *king* 2 K 15$_{32}$ Is 1$_{1}$ Ho 1$_{1}$ Mc 1$_{1}$ 1 C 5$_{17}$. <PREP> לְ of direction, *to,* + שׁוב hi. *bring back,* i.e. render 2 C 27$_{1}$, נתן *give* 2 C 27$_{1}$; of possession, *of, (belonging) to* 2 K 15$_{30}$ (lacking in ms; or em. לְיוֹתָם בֶּן־עֻזִּיָּה *of Jotham the son of Uzziah* to אָחָז בֶּן־יוֹתָם *of Ahaz the son of Jotham*); תַּחַת *instead of,* + מלך *reign* 2 K 15$_{38}$||2 C 27$_{9}$.

3. Calebite, son of Jahdai, <NOM CL> בְּנֵי יָהְדַּי רֶגֶם וְיוֹתָם *the sons of Jahdai were Regem and Jotham* 1 C 2$_{47}$.

⇒ '' *Y.* + תמם *be perfect.*

יוֹשֶׁר, see יֹשֶׁר *uprightness.*

יוֹתֵר 9.5.2.1 n.m. **surplus**—יֹתֵר—**1. remainder, surplus,** <OBJ> חרם hi. *destroy* 1 S 15$_{15}$. <PREP> מִן *from* Arad ost. 5$_{13}$. <COLL> יותר על ארבעת perh. *the remainder over four* 1Q30 1$_{5}$.

2. excess, abundance, <NOM CL> טוב עובד ויותר *better is a worker and,* i.e. with, *excess* of wealth Si 10$_{27}$ (unless יתר ptc. *one who abounds in* wealth). <CSTR> יותר הון *excess of wealth* Si 10$_{27}$; חיי יותר *life of abundance* Si 40$_{18(Bmg, M)}$ (M יתר; + שָׂכָר *remuneration;* B חיי יין *life of wine* and strong drink).

3. advantage, superiority, <NOM CL> כִּי מַה־יּוֹתֵר לֶחָכָם *for what advantage does the wise one have?* Ec 6$_{8}$ (4QQoh[a] כמה יותר *how much advantage?*), מַה־יֹּתֵר לָאָדָם *what advantage does the human being have?* Ec 6$_{11}$ (or em. יִתְרוֹן *advantage*), טוֹבָה חָכְמָה ... וְיֹתֵר *wisdom is good ... and (is) an advantage* Ec 7$_{11}$, אֵין יוֹתֵר *there is no advantage* Ec 2$_{15}$ (if em. אָז *then* to אַיִן), הוא יותר *it is the advantage* 1QMyst 1.2$_{3}$.

4. as adv., **a. excessively, too (much),** + חכם *be wise* Ec 2$_{15}$ (or §2, if em. אָז *then* to אַיִן *there is not*), htp. *make oneself wise* Ec 7$_{16}$ (+ הַרְבֵּה *greatly*).

b. more, + קלה ni. *be despised* Si 10$_{31(A)}$ (B יָתֵר *more*).

c. יוֹתֵר מִן (1) **more than,** + עשׂה *do* honour Est 6$_{6}$, זהר ni. *be warned* Ec 12$_{12}$; followed by suffix in ref. to Haman Est 6$_{6}$, pronoun הֵמָּה *they* Ec 12$_{12}$.

(2) **too much for, beyond,** ביותר ממך אל תמר perh. *do not rebel against what is beyond you* Si 3$_{23}$, אל תערב יתר ממך *do not stand surety too much for you,* i.e. beyond your means Si 8$_{13}$.

d. יוֹתֵר שֶׁ- **besides,** יֹתֵר שֶׁהָיָה קֹהֶלֶת חָכָם עוֹד לִמַּד־דַּעַת *besides being wise, Koheleth also taught knowledge* Ec 12$_{9}$.

⇒ יתר *exceed.*

[יְזֶבֶל] 0.0.0.1 pr.n.[f.] **Jezebel,** Seal 215 (8th/7th cent.).

יזואל, see יְזִיאֵל *Jeziel.*

[יְזִיאֵל] 1 pr.n.m. **Jeziel,** one of David's warriors, 1 C 12$_{3(Qr)}$ (Kt יזואל *Jezuel*). ⇒ אֵל + (?) נזה *sprinkle.*

יִזִּיָּה 1 pr.n.m. **Izziah,** member of Parosh family, husband of non-Jewish wife, <NOM CL> מִבְּנֵי פַרְעֹשׁ ... יִזִּיָּה *of the sons of Parosh was ... Izziah* Ezr 10$_{25}$.
⇒ נזה *sprinkle,* + ׳י *Y.*

יָזִיז 1 pr.n.m. **Jaziz,** one of David's officers, <NOM CL> עַל־הַצֹּאן יָזִיז *over the flocks was Jaziz* 1 C 27$_{31}$. <APP> הַגְרִי *Hagrite* 1 C 27$_{31}$.

יִזְלִיאָה 1 pr.n.m. **Izliah,** Benjaminite, son of Elpaal, <NOM CL> בְּנֵי אֶלְפָּעַל ... יִזְלִיאָה *the sons of Elpaal were ... Izliah* 1 C 8$_{18}$.

יזן 1 vb. **be on heat**—Pu. 1 Ptc. מְיֻזָּנִים—appar. **be aroused sexually, be on heat,** <SUBJ> סוּס *horse* Jr 5$_{8}$ (mss מוזנים *well fed,* i.e. זון ho.; + שׁכה hi. *have [large] testicles;* ms שׁמם hi. *ravage;* or em. אשׁך hi. *have [large] testicles* or משׁך *drag*) Si 36$_{6(Segal)}$ ([כסוס מיזן]).

[יְזַנְיָה], see יְזַנְיָהוּ *Jezaniah.*

יְזַנְיָהוּ 2 pr.n.m. **Jezaniah**—יְזַנְיָה—son of Hoshaiah, appar. ident. with עֲזַרְיָה *Azariah* at Jr 43$_{2}$ (or em. עֲזַרְיָה *Azariah* to יְזַנְיָה *Jezaniah*), <SUBJ> אמר *say* Jr 42$_{1}$, ענה *answer* Jr 42$_{1}$, שׁמע *hear* Jr 42$_{1}$, הלך *go* Jr 42$_{1}$, שׁלח *send* Jr 42$_{1}$, שׁאר ni. *remain* Jr 42$_{1}$, עשׂה *do* Jr 42$_{1}$. <OBJ> ראה *see* Jr 42$_{1}$. <APP> בֵּן *son* Jr 42$_{1}$. <PREP> לְ of direction, *to,* + נגד hi. *tell* Jr 42$_{1}$; of benefit, *to, for,* + יטב *be good* Jr 42$_{1}$; בְּ *against,* + היה *be* Jr 42$_{1}$; מִן of direction, *from,* + מנע *withhold* Jr 42$_{1}$; אֶל *to,* + שׁלח *send* Jr 42$_{1}$; בַּעַד *for,* + פלל htp. *pray* Jr 42$_{1}$.

2. Maacathite, army captain loyal to Gedaliah, perh. ident. with §1, Jr 40$_{8}$ (mss and ||2 K 25$_{23}$ יַאֲזַנְיָהוּ *Jaazaniah*), <SUBJ> בוא *come* Jr 40$_{8}$, ישׁב *dwell* Jr 40$_{8}$, ירא *fear* Jr 40$_{8}$, עבד *serve* Jr 40$_{8}$, אסף *gather* Jr 40$_{8}$, שׂים *place* Jr 40$_{8}$, תפשׂ *hold* Jr 40$_{8}$. <APP> בֵּן *son* Jr 40$_{8}$. <PREP> לְ of direction, *to,* + שׁבע ni. *swear* Jr 40$_{8}$; of benefit, *to, for,* + יטב *be good* Jr 40$_{8}$. ⇒ אזן *hear* + ׳י *Y.*

[יֶזַע] 1 n.[m.] **sweat**—יָזַע—i.e. clothes that cause sweat, <PREP> בְּ *with,* + חגר *gird oneself* Ezk 44$_{18}$.
⇒ see also ידע V *sweat.*

יִזְרָח 1 gent. **Izrahite,** <NOM CL> הַחֲמִישִׁי שַׁמְהוּת הַיִּזְרָח *the fifth (commander) was Shamhuth the Izrahite* 1 C 27$_{8}$ (or em. הַזַּרְחִי *the Zerahite*). <APP> Shamhuth 1 C 27$_{8}$.
⇒ זרח *shine.*

יִזְרַחְיָה 3 pr.n.m. **Izrahiah, 1.** Issacharite, son of Uzzi, <NOM CL> בְּנֵי עֻזִּי יִזְרַחְיָה *the sons of Uzzi were Izrahiah* 1 C 7$_{3}$ (Seb בֶּן *the son of* Uzzi *was*). <CSTR> בְּנֵי יִזְרַחְיָה *sons of Izrahiah* 1 C 7$_{3}$. **2.** Levite, singer at dedication of wall of Jerusalem, <NOM CL> הַפָּקִיד יִזְרַחְיָה *the overseer was Izrahiah* Ne 12$_{42}$.
⇒ זרח *shine* + ׳י *Y.*

יִזְרְעֶאל I 2 pr.n.m. **Jezreel, 1.** son of Hosea, <OBJ> קרא *call* name Ho 1$_{4}$.

2. Judahite, son of Etam, <NOM CL> אֵלֶּה בְּנֵי עֵיטָם יִזְרְעֶאל *these were the sons of Etam, Jezreel* 1 C 4$_{3}$ (if em. אֲבִי *father of* Etam).
⇒ זרע *sow* + אֵל *God.*

יִזְרְעֶאל II 34 pl.n. **Jezreel**—L יִזְרְעֶאל (2 K 9$_{15}$); + ה- of direction יִזְרְעֶאלָה—**1.** town in Issachar, prob. Zer'în, 32 km SW of Tiberias; as representing Israel (Ho 2$_{24}$), <OBJ> ענה *answer* Ho 2$_{24}$. <CSTR> עֵמֶק יִזְרְעֶאל *valley of Jezreel* Jos 17$_{16}$ Jg 6$_{33}$ Ho 1$_{5}$, חֵלֶק *territory of* 1 K 21$_{23}$ (if em.; see below) 2 K 9$_{10.36.37}$, חֵל *rampart of* 1 K 21$_{23}$ (or em. חֵל to חֵלֶק *territory of*), שָׂרֵי *rulers of* 2 K 10$_{1}$ (or em. הָעִיר *of the city;* ms שֹׁמְרוֹן *of Samaria*), דְּמֵי *blood of* Ho 1$_{4}$, יוֹם *day of* Ho 2$_{2}$. <PREP> בְּ of place, *in, at* 1 S 29$_{1}$ 1 K 21$_{1}$ 2 K 9$_{17}$, + שׁאר ni. *remain* 2 K 10$_{11}$, נגד hi. *tell* 2 K 9$_{15}$, ראה *see* 2 K 8$_{29}$||2 C 22$_{6}$, רפא htp. *be healed* 2 K 8$_{29}$ ||2 C 22$_{6}$ 2 K 9$_{15}$; מִן *from* 2 S 4$_{4}$; אֶל *over,* + מלך hi. *make king* 2 S 2$_{9}$; מִתַּחַת לְ *below* 1 K 4$_{12}$; ה- of direction, *to(wards), at,* + היה *be* Jos 19$_{18}$, הלך *go* 1 K 18$_{45}$ 2 K 9$_{16}$,

בוא *come* 1 K 18$_{46}$ 2 K 9$_{30}$ 10$_{6}$, שׁלח *send* 2 K 10$_{7}$. <COLL> יִזְרְעֶאל used adverbially, *to Jezreel*, + עלה *go up* 1 S 29$_{11}$.

2. town in Judah, perh. T. Ṭarrāme, 9 km SW of Hebron, <NOM CL> בָּהָר שָׁמִיר ... וְיִזְרְעֶאל *in the hill country were Shamir ... and Jezreel* Jos 15$_{56}$. <PREP> מִן *from* 1 S 25$_{43}$.

⇒ זרע *sow* + אֵל *God*; יִזְרְעֵאלִי *Jezreelite*.

יִזְרְעֵאלִי 13 gent. **Jezreelite**—fem. sing. יִזְרְעֵאלִית (יִזְרְעֵלִית)—inhabitant of Jezreel, **1.** in Issachar, <SUBJ> אמר *say* 1 K 21$_{4}$, דבר pi. *speak* 1 K 21$_{4}$, מאן pi. *refuse* 1 K 21$_{15}$, נתן *give* 1 K 21$_{6.15}$. <APP> Naboth 1 K 21$_{1.4.6.7.15.16}$ 2 K 9$_{21.25}$. <CSTR> כֶּרֶם נָבוֹת הַיִּזְרְעֵאלִי *vineyard of Naboth the Jezreelite* 1 K 21$_{7.15.16}$, חֶלְקַת *field of* 2 K 9$_{21.25(mss)}$, שְׂדֵה *field of* 2 K 9$_{25}$ (שְׂדֵה lacking in mss). <PREP> לְ of direction, *to*, + אמר *say* 1 K 21$_{6}$; of possession, *of, (belonging) to*, + היה *be* 1 K 21$_{1}$; אֶל *to*, + דבר pi. *speak* 1 K 21$_{6}$.

2. in Judah, <SUBJ> עלה *go up* 2 S 2$_{2}$, ישׁב *dwell* 1 S 27$_{3}$, שׁבה ni. *be taken captive* 1 S 30$_{5}$. <APP> Ahinoam 1 S 27$_{3}$ 30$_{5}$ 2 S 2$_{2}$ 3$_{2}$‖1 C 3$_{1}$, אִשָּׁה *wife* 1 S 27$_{3}$ 30$_{5}$ 2 S 2$_{2}$. <PREP> לְ of agent, *by, through* 2 S 3$_{2}$‖1 C 3$_{1}$.

⇒ יִזְרְעֶאל *Jezreel*.

[יַחְבָּה], see יְחֻבָּה *Jehubbah*.

[יְחֻבָּה] 1 pr.n.m. **Jehubbah,** Asherite, son of Shemer (ms שׁוֹמֵר *Shomer*), <NOM CL> בְּנֵי שָׁמֶר ... יחבה *the sons of Shemer were ... Jehubbah* 1 C 7$_{34(Kt)}$ (unless Kt יַחְבָּה *Jahbah* mss, Qr וְחֻבָּה *and Hubbah*).

יחד 3.1.8 vb. **be united—Qal** 2.1 Impf. 3fs תֵּחַד, 2ms תֵּחַד—**be united,** intrans. **join (with), come together,** <SUBJ> בֵּן *son* Si 34$_{14(Bmg)}$, מֶלֶךְ *king* of Babylon Is 14$_{20}$, לֵב *heart* Ps 86$_{3}$ (if em. יַחְדּוּ *together* to יָחֵד *[with a] united* heart), כָּבוֹד *glory* Gn 49$_{6}$ (Sam יחר *let it* not *be angry*; or em. כָּבֵד my *liver*, i.e. I, and/or יחד *let it* not *rejoice* or *see*; + בוא *come*),* חֶבֶר *company* Ps 122$_{3}$ (if em. שֶׁחֻבְּרָה־לָּהּ יַחְדָּו *that is joined together* to שֶׁחֶבְרָתָהּ לָהּ יַחַד *whose company is united with her*), שֵׁבֶט *tribe* Dt 33$_{5}$ (if em. יַחַד *together* to יְחַד *coming together of*), לַיְלָה *night* Jb 3$_{6}$ (if em. יִחַד *let it* not *rejoice* to יֵחַד *let it* not *be united*, or em. יֵחַד *let it not be seen*).* <PREP> לְ *with*, + עִיר *city* Ps 122$_{3}$ (if em.; see Subj.); בְּ of place, *in*, + קְבוּרָה *burial* Is 14$_{20}$, טֶנֶא *basket* Si 34$_{14(Bmg)}$; *with*, + קָהָל *company* Gn 49$_{6}$ (or em. חדה *rejoice* with, or *look* at), יוֹם *day* Jb 3$_{6}$ (if em.; see Subj.); עִם *with*, + רֵעַ *neighbour* perh. Si 34$_{14(Bmg)}$; אֵת *with*, + מֶלֶךְ *king* Is 14$_{20}$.

Pi. 1 Impv. יַחֵד—**unite,** יַחֵד לְבָבִי לְיִרְאָה שְׁמֶךָ *unite my heart*, i.e. give me an undivided heart, *to fear your name* Ps 86$_{11}$ (mss אֶת־שְׁמֶךָ *your name*; or em. יַחֵד to יִחַדְ *let* my heart *rejoice* to fear your name).

Htp. 0.0.10 Impf. Q ייחד; 2ms תתיחד; inf. Q להיחד, ליחד, להחיד—**1.** usu. intrans. **be united, join** (Qumran) community; appar. intrans. **be united with** (1QS 9$_{6}$), <SUBJ> אִישׁ *man* 1QS 3$_{7}$ (וברוח קדושה ליחד באמתו *and by a holy spirit to be united with his truth* unless *and by the community's holy spirit in his truth*, i.e. יַחַד *community*) 5$_{20}$ (להיחד לעדה *to be united with the congregation* unless *for the community, that is, for the congregation*, i.e. יַחַד) 9$_{6}$ (להיחד קודש קודשים *to be united with the holy of holies* unless *for the community, the holy of holies*, i.e. יַחַד), אֱנוֹשׁ *human being* 1QH 11$_{11}$, אֶזְרָח *native* Israelite 1QSa 1$_{9}$; subj. not specified, 1QS 1$_{8}$ 5$_{14}$ 1QH fr. 2$_{10}$ 4Q416 2.4$_{5}$.

<PREP> בְּ be united *with*, + עֵצָה *council* 1QS 1$_{8}$, עֵדָה *congregation* 1QSa 1$_{9}$, אֱמֶת *truth* 1QS 3$_{7}$ (unless ליחד = *of the community*); *in respect of*, + עֲבוֹדָה *work* 1QS 5$_{14}$, + הוֹן *wealth* 1QS 5$_{14}$; לְ be united *with*, + עֵדָה *congregation* 1QS 5$_{20}$ (unless להיחד = *for the community*); עִם *with*, + אִישׁ evil *man* 1QS 5$_{14}$, בֵּן *son* 1QH 11$_{11}$ fr. 2$_{10}$, אִשָּׁה *wife* 4Q416 2.4$_{5}$.

2. perh. **be declared as one,** תתיחד מלכי מפי כל משרתך *may your unity be declared, O my king, from the mouth of each of your servants* GnzPs 4$_{12}$.*

⇒ יַחַד *unity*, יַחְדָּו *together*, יָחִיד *only*.

יַ֫חַד 45.1.168 n.[m.] **unity**—יַ֫חַד—**1. unity** (but distinction from §2 oft. uncertain; in §§1-2, לְיַחַד and בְּיַחַד may sometimes be adverb, *together*), <CSTR> יחד כול אנשי *unity of all the men* of my counsel 1QH 14$_{18}$, רנ[נ]ה *of song* 1QH 3$_{23}$ 11$_{14}$; [מ]משלת יחד *dominion of unity* 4Q Shir[b] 2.1$_{9}$. <PREP> לְ *as, for*, + היה *be* 1 C 12$_{18}$ (יִהְיֶה־לִּי

עֲלֵיכֶם לֵבָב לְיַחַד *I will have a heart towards you for unity*, i.e. we will be one, or *for a community*, i.e. in order to form an alliance, as §2); בְּ of place/time, *in*, + בוא *come* 1QH 3$_{22}$, נגש ho. *be brought* 1QH 14$_{18}$, יעד ni. *be assembled* 1QH fr. 10$_{6}$, הלל pi. *praise* 1QH 3$_{23}$, חדש htp. *be renewed* 1QH 11$_{14}$. <COLL> יַחַד || מַעֲמָד *service* 1QH 3$_{22}$; + עדה *congregation* 1QH 3$_{22}$.

2. community,* esp. Qumran community, <SUBJ> היה *be* 4QS^d 1.1$_2$ (1QS 5$_2$ ליחד *as a community*). <OBJ> חבר hi. *unite* 11QPs^a 18$_1$. <CSTR> יחד אל *community of God* 1QS 1$_{12}$ 2$_{22}$, קודש *of holiness* 1QS 9$_2$, עולמים *of eternity* 1QS 3$_{12}$, אמת *of truth* 1QS 2$_{24}$, אמתו *of his truth* 1QS 2$_{26}$ ([י]חד) 4QS^c 1.3$_1$ (יח[ד]), ברית עולם *of a covenant of eternity* 1QS 5$_5$, עצתו *of his counsel* 1QS 3$_6$, שמחה *of joy* 1QM 14$_4$, רשעה *of wickedness* 4QAges^b 1$_2$.

אנשי היחד *men of the community* 1QS 5$_1$ (4QS^d 1.1$_1$ התורה *of the Law*) 5$_3$ (4QS^d 1.1$_2$ 4QS^b 5$_3$ הרבים *the many*) 5$_{16}$ 6$_{21}$ 7$_{20.24}$ (היחו[ד]) 8$_{11.16}$ 9$_{6.7.10.19}$ 1Q31 1$_1$ 4QpIsa^e 9$_3$ (היח[ד]) 4QMidrEschat^b 5$_1$ (הי[חד]) 4QCommGenA 5$_5$ 4QCommGenC 4$_4$ (הי[ח]ד) 4QS^b 5$_8$ 4QRebukes 1.1$_1$ CD 20$_{32}$ (היחיד), יורה *teacher of* CD 20$_{14}$ (if em. היחיד *of the unique one*), מורה *teacher of* CD 20$_1$ (if em. היחיד), עצת *council of* 1QpHab 12$_4$ 1QS 3$_2$ (יחד) 5$_7$ 6$_3$ (החיד) 6$_{10.13.14.16}$ 7$_{2.22.24}$ 8$_{1.5}$ (erased העצת) 8$_{22}$ 11$_8$ 1QpMic 10$_8$ 1QSa 1$_{26}$ (יחד; + תעודת מלחמה *convocation of war*) 1$_{27}$ 2$_{2.11}$ 1QSb 4$_{26}$ (יחד) 4QpIsa^d 1$_2$ (+ [ה]כוהנם והע[ם] *the priests and the people*) 4QpPs^a 1.2$_{14}$ 4QMidrEschat^a 3$_{17}$ 4QMidrEschat^b 14$_5$ 4QS^d 1.1$_6$ 4QS^c 1.3$_3$ 4QSD 1.2$_3$ (ה[יח]ד) 7.2$_{7.8}$ (היח[ד]) 4QBer^a 7.2$_1$, עדת *congregation of* 1QSa 2$_{21}$ 4QpPs^a 3.4$_{19}$ 4QHod^a 7.2$_7$, סוד *council of* 1QS 6$_{19}$, גורל *lot of* 1QH 6$_{13}$ (unless §3f), אמת *truth of* 1QS 5$_3$ (unless §3a), רוח *spirit of* 4QRebukes 1.2$_6$ (היח[ד]), מדרש *investigation of* 1QS 6$_{24}$ (יחד; unless §3a), משפטי *judgements of* 1QS 6$_{15}$ 4QD^e 3.3$_{19}$, סרך *rule of* 1QS 1$_1$ (ס[רך]) 1$_{16}$ 4QS^a 1$_1$ 4QS^b 1.2$_4$ (both סרך), יסוד *foundation of* 1QS 7$_{17.18}$ 8$_{10}$, בית *house of* 1QS 9$_6$, שולחן *table of* 1QSa 2$_{17}$ (שול[חן יחד]; unless §3a) appar. 2$_{18}$ (השולחן; unless §3a), ברית *covenant of* 1QS 3$_{12}$ 8$_{16}$ (|| אנשי היחד) 1QSb 5$_{21}$, הון *property of* 1QS 7$_6$.

<APP> קודש קודשים *holy of holies* 1QS 9$_6$ (unless יחד htp. *be united*).

<PREP> לְ of direction, *to(wards)*, + קרב *approach* 1QS 6$_{22}$, יסף ni. *be added* 1QS 8$_{19}$, אסף ni. *be gathered* 1QS 5$_7$, לוה ni. *be joined* 1QS 5$_6$=4QS^b 5$_6$=4QS^d 1.1$_5$, סור hi. *cause to depart* 4QAges^b 1$_2$; of benefit, *for*, + עשׂה *do*, i.e. fulfil, statutes 1QS 5$_{20}$ (להיחד לעדה *for the community, that is, for the congregation* unless *to be united with the congregation*, i.e. יחד htp. *be united*), בדל hi. *separate* holy house 1QS 9$_6$ (להיחד קודש קודשים *for the community, the holy of holies* unless *to be united with the holy of holies*, i.e. יחד htp.); of possession, *of, (belonging) to* 1QS 3$_7$ (וברוח קדושה ליחד *and by the community's holy spirit* in his truth, unless *and by a holy spirit to be united* with his truth, i.e. יחד htp.), + היה *be* 1QS 6$_{23}$; *as*, + היה *be* 1QS 5$_2$ (4QS^d 1.1$_2$ יחד to be *a community*) 8$_{12}$, perh. ברא *create* Israel 4Q408 1$_3$, יסד pi. *establish* foundation of truth 1QS 5$_5$=4QS^b 5$_5$=4QS^d 1.1$_4$.

בְּ of place, *in, among* 4Q415 11$_3$ 4Q418 167$_5$, + היה *be* 1QS 2$_{24}$, דרש *investigate* 1QS 5$_{21}$ 6$_8$, תכן *examine* 4Q418 167$_6$, קרא *read* 1QS 6$_8$, שקד *watch* 1QS 6$_7$, ידע *know* place 1QS 2$_{22}$, חשב htp. *be reckoned* 4QS^c 1.3$_1$, perh. קום hi. *establish* covenant 1QS 5$_{21}$ (unless relevant verb is נדב htp. *volunteer*), יסר htp. *be disciplined* 1QS 3$_6$, בוא *come* perh. 4Q418 199$_1$ (הבא ביחד *the one who enters the community*), hi. *bring* 1QS 1$_{12}$, שוב *go back* 1QS 5$_{22}$, מול *circumcise* 1QS 5$_5$, רום pol. *exalt* name 1QM 14$_4$, אכל *eat* 4QS^b 5$_9$ ([ב]יחד), ברך pi. *bless* 1QS 6$_8$ 4QBer^b 5$_{11}$ ([ולברך]), אמר *say* 4QBer^a 7.2$_1$; *against* perh. 4QAges^b 1.2$_1$ (אשמה ביחד *a sin against the community*), + בגד *betray* 1QS 7$_{23}$.

עַל *concerning*, + בקר pi. *inspect* 4QSD 1.2$_6$.

בְּתוֹךְ *among*, + מלא *fill* 1QS 6$_{18}$ (במולאת לו שנה *when he has completed a year* among the community).

<COLL> יַחַד + ישראל *Israel* 1QS 5$_5$, עֵדָה *congregation* 1QS 5$_{20}$ (unless יחד ni. *be at one with*), קֹדֶשׁ *holiness* 1QS 5$_6$ 4QS^d 1.1$_5$ (קדש), בַּיִת *house* 1QS 5$_6$ 9$_6$ (unless יחד htp. *be united*), + סוֹד *council* 1QS 2$_{24}$, עֵצָה *council* 1QS 2$_{22.24}$, עָוֶל *injustice* 1QS 5$_1$ 4QS^b 5$_8$.

3. (distinctions among the following oft. unclear) as adv., **together, all together** (with the same senses as יַחְדָּו *together*), in ref. to, **a.** proximity or unity, with verb היה *be* 4QJub^a 2$_{21}$ 4QapJoseph^b 1$_{10}$, שׁאנן palel *be at ease* Jb 3$_{18}$, תמם *be used up* 4Q418 103.2$_9$, יקשׁ ni. *be ensnared* 4QBéat 14.2$_{27}$, עשׂה *do* 1QS 5$_3$ (unless §2), *do*, i.e. offer 11QT 24$_{13}$, ni. *be made* 4QJub^{a} 2$_{23}$, פעל *do* Gnz Ps 4$_{23}$, שׂים *place* Mc 2$_{12}$, ערך *prepare* 1QM 2$_{9}$ (unless §3e) 1QSa 2$_{18}$ (unless §2), נשׂא *lift* Jb 6$_{2}$, pi. *exalt* 4QShir Shabb^{d} 1.1$_{42}$, אשׁם *incur guilt* 4QapPs^{b} 79$_{3}$, אבד *perish* 4QBéat 14.2$_{16}$, אסף ni. *gather* intrans. 2 S 10$_{15}$ (mss יַחְדָּו *together*), יעד ni. *gather* 1QH 4$_{24}$ 1QSa 2$_{17}$ (unless §2), ni. *argue* Is 43$_{26}$, מלא htp. *gather oneself* Jb 16$_{10}$, הלך htp. *walk* 1QS 4$_{18}$ 4Q416 2.3$_{21}$ 4QBéat 14.2$_{15}$, שׁוב *go back* 4QpPs^{a} 1$_{11}$, נחת *go down* Jb 17$_{16}$, עלה hi. *bring up* 1QH 5$_{22}$, שׁפל ho. *be brought low* Si 11$_{6}$, נפל *fall* 2 S 21$_{9}$, עמד *stand* Is 50$_{8}$, ישׁב *dwell* Ps 133$_{1}$, *sit* 11QT 57$_{13}$, שׁאר ni. *remain* 1 S 11$_{11}$, יסד ni. appar. *sit in conclave* Ps 2$_{2}$ 31$_{14}$ (or em. סוד ni. *take counsel*), לין htpol. *stay night together* 4QMidrEschat^{b} 19$_{3}$, נדב htp. *volunteer* 1QS 5$_{10}$, אכל *eat* 1QS 6$_{2}$, לחם ni. *wage war* 1 S 17$_{10}$ 1QM 1$_{11}$, יעץ ni. *consult* 1QS 6$_{3}$, שׁמע hi. *proclaim* 1QH 11$_{26}$, ספר ni. *recount* 1QH fr. 10$_{7}$ 4QHod^{a} 3.1$_{5}$, לחשׁ htp. *whisper* Ps 41$_{8}$, ברך pi. *bless* 1QS 6$_{3}$, רנן *shout for joy* Jb 38$_{7}$, pi. *shout for joy* Ps 98$_{8}$, הלל pi. *praise* 4QShirShabb^{d} 1.2$_{15}$, רום pol. *exalt* 4QHod^{a} 7.1$_{13}$, יעץ *give counsel* 4QS^{d} 1.2$_{7}$, שׁפט *decide* 1QS 6$_{24}$ (unless §2), ברך pi. *bless* 4QS^{d} 1.2$_{7}$, בכה *weep* Jb 31$_{38}$, ליץ hi. *mock* 4QWiles 1$_{2}$; in nom. cl., יַחַד שִׁבְטֵי יִשְׂרָאֵל *the tribes of Israel were together* Dt 33$_{5}$ (unless *the community of the tribes of Israel*, as §2; or em. יֵחַד *coming together of*).*

b. inclusiveness or entirety, i.e. **both ... and, (both /all) alike, both/all (of them, etc.),** e.g. לְהַשְׁמִיד אֹתִי וְאֶת־בְּנִי יַחַד *to destroy me and my son together*, i.e. both me and my son 2 S 14$_{16}$, יַחַד עָשִׁיר וְאֶבְיוֹן *rich and poor together*, i.e. both rich and poor Ps 49$_{3}$ (+ גַּם ... גַּם *both ... and*), הַיֹּצֵר יַחַד לִבָּם *the one who fashions the hearts of them all* Ps 33$_{15}$ (unless יַחַד *he sees*, i.e. חדה II), יַחַד חֻבְּאוּ עֲנִיֵּי־אָרֶץ *the poor of the land all alike are hidden* Jb 24$_{4}$ Ps 49$_{11}$ (unless יַחַד *he sees*, i.e. חדה II) 62$_{10}$ 74$_{6}$ (or em. פִּתּוּחֶיהָ יָחַד *its carvings all together* to פִּתּוּחֵי הַיָּחִד *carvings of the only one*) 141$_{10}$ (if em.; see §3d) Jb 21$_{26}$ 34$_{29}$ (unless יַחַד *he looks at*, i.e. חדה II) 40$_{13}$ Si 25$_{24}$, במבוא מועדים לימי חודש יחד תקופתם *at the beginning of the appointed times on the days of the new moon, with their turning point* 1QS 10$_{3}$, לאלפיהם ולרבואותם יחד עם קדושיכה *for their thousands and for their tens of thousands together, with your holy ones* 1QM 12$_{4}$ (unless §3f).

c. exclusivity, i.e. **alone,** אֲנַחְנוּ יַחַד נִבְנֶה *we alone will build* Ezr 4$_{3}$, יַחַד אָנֹכִי עַד־אֶעֱבוֹר perh. *I alone pass on* Ps 141$_{10}$ (or §3c *all alike*, if יַחַד belongs with preceding clause), אליו [תש]וקתמה יחד *their only desire is towards it* 1QM 13$_{12}$.

d. degree, i.e. **altogether, utterly,** with נדד *flee* Is 22$_{3}$, כמר ni. (of compassion) *be warm* Ho 11$_{8}$, בושׁ *be ashamed* Is 44$_{11}$, חפר *be ashamed* Ps 40$_{15}$ (mss יַחְדָּו *altogether*) 70$_{3}$ (if ins. יַחַד), יצת hi. *burn* Is 27$_{4}$, חזק *strengthen* 1QM 10$_{6}$ (unless §3e), חפשׂ pi. *search out* 1QH 10$_{34}$, ינה *suppress* Ps 74$_{8}$, נקף hi. *surround* Ps 88$_{18}$, עשׂה *make* appar. Jb 10$_{8}$ (or em. יַחַד סָבִיב *altogether round about* to אַחַר סַבּוֹתָ *afterwards you turned*), רנן *cry out* 1QS 10$_{17}$; with negative, **at all,** יַחַד לֹא יְרוֹמֵם *he does not raise (them) up at all* Ho 11$_{7}$ (or em. הַאֶחְדַּל אֲרַחֵם *shall I cease to have compassion?*).

e. time, **(1) at the same time,** e.g. אֶשֹּׁם וְאֶשְׁאַף יָחַד *I will gasp and pant at the same time* Is 42$_{14}$ 45$_{8}$, לחזיק יחד בכול גבורי חיל *to strengthen all the mighty warriors at the same time* 1QM 10$_{6}$ (unless §3d); **(2) at once,** יִגְוַע כָּל־בָּשָׂר יָחַד *all flesh would expire at once* Jb 34$_{15}$, ועורכיה כול העדה יחד *the whole congregation preparing it together* 1QM 2$_{9}$ (unless §3a).

f. association, יַחַד **together,** כֹּהֲנָיו וְשָׂרָיו יחד *his priests and princes together* Jr 48$_{7(Kt)}$ (Qr יַחְדָּו *together*), מלאכי קודש עם צבאותם יחד *angels of holiness together with their armies* 1QM 7$_{6}$, לאלפיהם ולרבואותם יחד עם קדושיכה *for their thousands and for their tens of thousands together, with your holy ones* 1QM 12$_{4}$ (unless §3b), ... ויהמו ובנגינות יחד תלונתם עם שאה ומשווה *and they will murmur* my contention on the harp, *and with music their murmuring, together with storm and uprising* 1QH 5$_{30}$, הביאותה ... ובגורל יחד עם מלאכי פנים *you will bring* your glory to all the men of your council, *and into the lot together with the angels of the presence* 1QH 6$_{13}$ (unless §2), [נטעת]ה מטע ברוש ותדהר עם תאשור יחד *you have planted a plantation of juniper and plane, together with pine(s)* 1QH 8$_{5}$, יַחַד יָבֹאוּ גְדוּדָיו *his troops come on together* Jb 19$_{12}$.*

Also 1QH fr. 46$_{5}$, 1QSb 5$_{6}$ (unless רוחו) 4QMidr Eschat^{b} 22$_{2}$ 4QBer^{a} 20$_{4}$ 4QBer^{c} 1$_{1}$ 4QMyst^{a} 20$_{3}$ 4Qap Joseph^{b} 1$_{9}$ 4QParaKings 20$_{2}$ 4QShirShabb^{c} 1$_{3}$ 4$_{5}$ 4Q

ShirShabb[f] 36_1 4QBapt 10_7 4Q415 9_8 4Q476 3.1_6 4QM[a] $1\text{-}3_{10}$ $8\text{-}10_1$ $14\text{-}15_{11}$ 24_4 4QM[b] 1_{12} 4QRitMar 5_3 7_3 19_4 21_3 260_2 4QRitPur 84_2 4QBéat 3.2_8 14.2_9.

⇒ יחד *be united.*

יַחְדָּו 98.4.6 adv. **together**—יַחְדָּיו—**together** (with the same senses as יַחַד, §3 *together*), in ref. to, **1.** proximity or unity, **(all) together, as one,** with ענה *answer* Ex 19_8, רנן pi. *shout for joy* Is $52_{8.9}$, ראה *see* Is 40_5, יעץ ni. *take counsel* Is 45_{21} Ps 71_{10} 83_6 (or em. יַחְדָּו to יַחְדּוּ *they rejoice* [from חדה], or אֶחָד with *one* mind, or יַחַד *[with a] united* heart) Ne 6_7, מרק hi. *make sweet* counsel Ps 55_{15}, קשׁר *conspire* Ne 4_2, חבר pu. *be joined* Ps 122_3 (or em. שֶׁחֻבְּרָה־לָּהּ *that is joined together for itself* to שֶׁחֶבְרָהּ *whose company*, or em. שֶׁחֻבְּרָה to שֶׁחֶבְרָה *whose community* is together), שׁאג *roar* Jr 51_{38}, הלך *go* Gn $22_{6.8.19}$ Is 45_{16} (or em. יַחְדָּו to נֶחֱרָיו *those who are incensed against him*, i.e. חרה ni.; or del.) Am 3_3, בוא *come* Jr 3_{18} Jb 9_{32}, יצא *go out* Zc 10_4 (unless join יַחְדָּו with following verse), hi. *bring out* Is 43_{17} (unless שׁכב *lie down*), עבר *pass* Ps 48_5, נגשׁ htp. *draw near* Is 45_{20} (1QIsa[a] ואתיו *and come*), קרב *draw near* Is 41_1, יעד ni. *meet by appointment* Jb 2_{11} Ne 6_2, אסף ni. *gather* (intrans.) 2 S 10_{15} (mss) (L יַחַד *together*) Jg 6_{33}, קבץ ni. *gather* (intrans.) Is 43_9 Ps 102_{23}, htp. *gather* (intrans.) Jos 9_2 Ho 2_2, נוס *flee* Jr 46_{21}, רום pol. *exalt* Ps 34_4, עמד *stand* Is 48_{13}, ישׁב *dwell* Gn $13_{6.6}$ 36_7 Dt 25_5, חנה *encamp* Jos 11_5, שׁכב *lie down* Is 43_{17} (or יצא hi. *bring out*), רבץ *lie down* Is 11_7, נפל *fall* 2 S 2_{16} Jr 46_{12}, נצה ni. *strive* Dt 25_{11}, בזז *plunder* Is 11_{14}, אכל *eat* Jg 19_6, שׁתה *drink* 11QPs[a] 18_{12}, אסר pu. *be captured* Is 22_3, מות *die* 1 S 31_6‖1 C 10_6; with nom cl., יַחְדָּו הֵמָּה עַל־יְהוּדָה *together they are against Judah* Is 9_{20}, עֵגֶל וּכְפִיר וּמְרִיא יַחְדָּו *the calf and the lion and the fatling shall be together* Is 11_6 (or em. מְרִיא to יִמְרְאוּ *they shall become fat*), Ps 122_3 (if em.; see above).

2. inclusiveness or entirety, i.e. **both … and, (both /all) alike, both/all (of them, etc.),** e.g. הַטָּמֵא וְהַטָּהוֹר יַחְדָּו יֹאכְלֶנּוּ *the unclean and the clean alike shall eat of it* Dt 12_{22}, הטמא והטהור בכה יחדיו *the unclean and the clean among you alike* may eat of it 11QT 52_{11}, sim. 11QT 53_4, יַחְדָּו יַחֲלֹקוּ *they shall share alike* 1 S 30_{24}, וּבָעֲרוּ שְׁנֵיהֶם יַחְדָּו *and both of them shall burn together* Is 1_{31}, בָּהֶם עַמִּים יְנַגַּח יַחְדָּו *with them he will gore the peoples, all of them* Dt 33_{17} (or em. יַחְדָּו to יֶדְחֶה *he will push* them to the ends of the earth), הֲלֹא שָׂרַי יַחְדָּו מְלָכִים *are not my commanders all kings?* Is 10_8, Ex 26_{24}‖36_{29} Dt 15_{22} 2 S 2_{13} Is 1_{28} 18_6 31_3 $41_{20.23}$ 66_{17} Jr 5_5 6_{11} 31_{24} Zc 10_4 (if em. יַחְדָּו: וְהָיוּ *together; and they shall be* to יַחְדָּו יִהְיוּ *together they shall be*, i.e. they shall all be) Ps 14_3 ‖53_4 Jb 24_{17} Pr 22_{18} (or em. יַחְדָּו to כְּיָתֵד *as a tent-peg*) Lm 2_8 Si 35_8 50_{17}.

3. exclusivity, i.e. **alone,** אֲנַחְנוּ יַחְדָּו *we were alone* 1 K 3_{18}.

4. degree, i.e. **altogether, utterly,** מִשְׁפְּטֵי־יי׳ אֱמֶת צָדְקוּ יַחְדָּו *the ordinances of Y. are truth, they are righteous altogether* Ps 19_{10}, פֹּשְׁעִים נִשְׁמְדוּ יַחְדָּו *transgressors shall be utterly destroyed* Ps 37_{38} 40_{15}(mss) (L יַחַד *altogether*).

5. association, יַחְדָּו **together,** לֹא־תַחֲרֹשׁ בְּשׁוֹר־וּבַחֲמֹר יַחְדָּו *you shall not plough with an ox and an ass together* Dt 22_{10}=11QT 52_{13}, בְּרוֹשׁ תִּדְהָר וּתְאַשּׁוּר יַחְדָּו *the juniper, the plane and the pine together* Is 41_{19} 60_{13}, וְהָלַךְ מַלְכָּם בַּגּוֹלָה הוּא וְשָׂרָיו יַחְדָּו *and their king shall go into exile, he and his princes together* Am 1_{15}, לבוש צמר ופשתים יחדיו *wearing wool and linen together* 4QD[f] 3_{10}, Dt 22_{11} 2 S 12_3 Is 43_{17} (if transfer athnach) 65_7 Jr $6_{12.21}$ 13_{14} $31_{8.13}$ (or em. יַחְדּוּ *they shall rejoice*, from חדה)* 48_7(Qr) (Kt יחד *together*) 49_3 $50_{4.33}$ Si 7_{12} 34_{12}.

6. activity, יַחְדָּו modifying two verbs, **both,** יַחְדָּו אֶשְׁכְּבָה וְאִישָׁן *I both lie down and sleep* Ps 4_9, Is 46_2 Ps 35_{26}.*

Also 4QDiscourse 2.2_1.

⇒ יחד *be united.*

יַחְדּוֹ 1 pr.n.m. **Jahdo,** Gadite, son of Buz, <CSTR> בֶּן־יַחְדּוֹ *son of Jahdo* 1 C 5_{14}.

⇒ חדה *rejoice* + יו׳ *Y.*

יַחְדִּיאֵל 1 pr.n.m. **Jahdiel,** Manassite, head of family, <NOM CL> אֵלֶּה רָאשֵׁי בֵית־אֲבוֹתָם … יַחְדִּיאֵל *these were the heads of their fathers' houses … Jahdiel* 1 C 5_{24}.

⇒ חדה *rejoice* + אֵל *God.*

יֶחְדְּיָהוּ 2 pr.n.m. **Jehdeiah, 1.** Levite, son of Shubael, <NOM CL> לִבְנֵי שׁוּבָאֵל יֶחְדְּיָהוּ *of the sons of Shubael was*

Jehdeiah 1 C 24_{20}.

2. Meronothite, one of David's officers, <NOM CL> עַל־הָאֲתֹנוֹת יֶחְדְּיָהוּ *over the she-asses was Jehdeiah* 1 C 27_{30}. <APP> מֵרֹנֹתִי *Meronothite* 1 C 27_{30}.

⇒ חדה *rejoice* + י׳ *Y.*

יחואל, see יְחִיאֵל *Jehiel.*

[יְחוֹעֶלִי] 0.0.0.1 pr.n.[m.] **Jehoeli,** <CSTR> כרם יחועלי *vineyard of Jehoeli* Samaria ost. 55_2 60 (יחועל[י]).

[יַחֲזָא] 0.0.0.1 pr.n.[m.] **Jahaza,** T. Gat jar inscr., <PREP> לְ of possession, *of, (belonging) to* T. Gat jar inscr.

יַחֲזִיאֵל 6 pr.n.m. **Jahaziel, 1.** Benjaminite, one of David's warriors, 1 C 12_5.

2. priest at time of David, <NOM CL> בְּנָיָהוּ וְיַחֲזִיאֵל ... בַּחֲצֹצְרוֹת *Benaiah and Jahaziel were ... with the trumpets* 1 C 16_6. <APP> כֹּהֵן *priest* 1 C 16_6.

3. Levite, son of Hebron, <NOM CL> יַחֲזִיאֵל הַשְּׁלִישִׁי *Jahaziel was the third (son)* 1 C 23_{19} 24_{23}.

4. Asaphite Levite, son of Zechariah, <SUBJ> אמר *say* 2 C 20_{14}. <APP> בֵּן *son* 2 C 20_{14}. <PREP> עַל *upon,* + היה *be* 2 C 20_{14}.

5. member of Zattu family, father of Shecaniah, <CSTR> בֶּן־יַחֲזִיאֵל *son of Jahaziel* Ezr 8_5.

⇒ חזה *see* + אֵל *God.*

יַחְזְיָה 1.0.0.1 pr.n.m. **Jahzeiah**—I יחזיהו—**1.** son of Tikvah, opponent of Ezra's measures against foreign wives, <SUBJ> עמד *stand* against Ezr 10_{15}. <APP> בֵּן *son* Ezr 10_{15}.

2. Arad ost 63, <PREP> אֶל *to,* + שׁלח *send* Arad ost. 63 (יחזי[הו]).

3. Hebron jar inscr. 1, <PREP> לְ of possession, *of, (belonging) to* Hebron jar inscr. 1.

⇒ חזה *see* + י׳ *Y.*

יחזיהו, see יַחְזְיָה *Jahzeiah.*

[יְחָזָק] 0.0.0.1 pr.n.[m.] **Johazak,** Seal 83 (Nablus, 8th cent.).

⇒ י׳ *Y.* + חזק *be strong.*

יְחֶזְקֵאל 3.1.14 pr.n.m. **Ezekiel, 1.** priest and prophet, son of Buzi, <SUBJ> היה *be* Ezk 24_{24} (+ לְמוֹפֵת *as a sign*), ראה *see* Si 49_8 4QpsEzek[a] 4_5 (יחזק[אל]), עשׂה *do* Ezk 24_{24}, אמר *say* CD 19_{11} (יחזקאל erased), נגד hi. *tell* Si 49_8, זכר hi. *mention* Si 49_8. <OBJ> שׁוב hi. *bring back,* i.e. turn away 4QpsEzek[a] 3_4. <CSTR> ספר יחזקאל *the book of Ezekiel* 4QMidrEschat[a] 3_{16} 4QMidrEschat[b] 9_{13}, ד[בר]י *words of* 4QpsEzek[a] 1_1, יד *hand of* CD 3_{21} 19_{12}. <APP> בֵּן *son* Ezk 1_3, כֹּהֵן *priest* Ezk 1_3, נָבִיא *prophet* 4QMidrEschat[b] 9_{13}, פָּנִים *face* 4QpsEzek[a] 3_4. <PREP> אֶל *to,* + היה *be* Ezk 1_3.

2. head of priestly family at time of David, <PREP> לְ of direction, *to,* + יצא (of lot) *go out* 1 C 24_{15}.

3. priestly course, claiming §2 as its eponymous ancestor, and the period of its office, <PREP> בְּ of time, *in, at, during* 4QMishA 1.2_2 4.5_{12} $4.6_{5.9}$ 4Q MishB[a] 1.1_4 2.3_7 4QMishC[b] 2_3.

⇒ חזק *be strong* + אֵל *God.*

יְחִזְקִיָּה, see חִזְקִיָּהוּ *Hezekiah.*

יְחִזְקִיָּהוּ, see חִזְקִיָּהוּ *Hezekiah.*

יַחְזֵרָה 1 pr.n.m. **Jahzerah,** member of Immer family, ancestor of priest, son of Meshullam, appar. ident. with אַחְזַי *Ahzai* at Ne 11_{13}, <CSTR> בֶּן־יַחְזֵרָה *son of Jahzerah* 1 C 9_{12}.

[יְחִי] 0.0.0.1 pr.n.[m.] **Jehi,** Seal 885 (7th cent.).

⇒ היה *live.*

יְחִיאֵל 14 pr.n.m. **Jehiel, 1.** Levite, musician at time of David, <NOM CL> עִמָּהֶם ... יְחִיאֵל *with them were ... Jehiel* 1 C 15_{18}, שְׁמִירָמוֹת וִיחִיאֵל ... בִּנְבָלִים *Shemiramoth and Jehiel ... were on harps* 1 C 15_{20}, sim. 16_5. <APP> אָח *brother* 1 C 15_{18}.

2. Gershonite Levite at time of David, <NOM CL> הָרֹאשׁ יְחִיאֵל *the chief was Jehiel* 1 C 23_8. <CSTR> יַד יְחִיאֵל *hand,* i.e. charge, *of Jehiel* 1 C 29_8. <APP> גֵּרְשֻׁנִּי *Gershonite* 1 C 29_8.

3. son of Hachmoni, attendant to David's sons, <NOM CL> וִיחִיאֵל ... עִם־בְּנֵי הַמֶּלֶךְ *and Jehiel was ... with the sons of the king* 1 C 27$_{32}$.

4. son of Jehoshaphat, <APP> בֵּן *son* 2 C 21$_{2}$, אָח *brother* 2 C 21$_{2}$.

5. Levite, temple official at time of Hezekiah, <NOM CL> מִן־בְּנֵי הֵימָן יְחִיאֵל *of the sons of Heman were Jehiel* 2 C 29$_{14(Qr)}$ (Kt יחואל *Jehuel*), וִיחִיאֵל וַעֲזַרְיָהוּ ... פְּקִידִים *and Jehiel and Azariah ... were overseers* 2 C 31$_{13}$.

6. leading official of temple at time of Josiah, <NOM CL> חִלְקִיָּה וּזְכַרְיָהוּ וִיחִיאֵל נְגִידֵי בֵּית הָאֱלֹהִים *Hilkiah and Zechariah and Jehiel were leaders of the house of God* 2 C 35$_{8}$.

7. member of Joab family, father of Obadiah, <CSTR> בֶּן־יְחִיאֵל *son of Jehiel* Ezr 8$_{9}$.

8. member of Elam family, father of Shecaniah, <CSTR> בֶּן־יְחִיאֵל *son of Jehiel* Ezr 10$_{2}$.

9. member of Harim family, husband of non-Jewish wife, <NOM CL> מִבְּנֵי חָרִם ... וִיחִיאֵל *of the sons of Harim were ... and Jehiel* Ezr 10$_{21}$.

10. member of Elam family, husband of non-Jewish wife, appar. not ident. with §9, <NOM CL> מִבְּנֵי עֵילָם ... וִיחִיאֵל *of the sons of Elam were ... and Jehiel* Ezr 10$_{26}$.

⇒ חיה *live* + אֵל *God.*

יְחִיאֵלִי 2 pr.n.m. **Jehieli,** Gershonite Levite, son of Ladan, perh. ident. with יְחִיאֵל §2 *Jehiel* at 1 C 23$_{8}$ 29$_{8}$, <NOM CL> לְלַעְדָּן ... יְחִיאֵלִי *(belonging) to Ladan was ... Jehieli* 1 C 26$_{21}$. <CSTR> בְּנֵי יְחִיאֵלִי *sons of Jehieli* 1 C 26$_{22}$.

⇒ חיה *live* + אֵל *God.*

יָחִיד 12.0.7 adj. **only**—sf. יְחִידְךָ (יְחִידֶךָ, Q יחידכה); fem. יְחִידָה; sf. יְחִידָתִי; masc. pl. יְחִידִים; sf. Q יחידיהן—**1. only,** used as noun, **only one,** (1) masc., <SUBJ> היה *be* Pr 4$_{3}$ (‖ רַךְ *tender;* + לִפְנֵי אִמִּי *before my mother* [mss לִבְנֵי אִמִּי *of the sons of my mother*]). <OBJ> לקח *take* Gn 22$_{2}$, חשׂך *withhold* Gn 22$_{12.16}$, אהב *love* Gn 22$_{2}$ 4QpsJub^{a} 2.1$_{11}$, עלה hi. *offer as burnt offering* Gn 22$_{2}$. <CSTR> אֵבֶל יָחִיד *mourning of,* i.e. for, *an only one* Jr 6$_{26}$ Am 8$_{10}$, פִּתּוּחֵי הַיָּחִד *carvings of the only one* Ps 74$_{6}$ (if em. פִּתּוּחֶיהָ יַחַד *its carvings all together*). <APP> בֵּן *son* Gn 22$_{2.12.16}$. <PREP> לְ *of,* + שׁכל pi. *be bereft of children* 4QapLam^{a} 2$_{9}$, עַל *upon,* + חמל *show compassion* 4Q416 2.2$_{13}$; *for* Zc 12$_{10}$ (מִסְפֵּד עַל־הַיָּחִיד *mourning for an only one*).

(2) fem., <NOM CL> הִיא יְחִידָה *she was (his) only one* Jg 11$_{34}$. <OBJ> נצל hi. *deliver* Ps 22$_{21}$ (‖ נֶפֶשׁ *soul*), שׁוב hi. *bring back* Ps 35$_{17}$ (‖ נֶפֶשׁ).

2. lonely, solitary, a. in nom. cl. used predicatively of worshipper Ps 25$_{16}$ (יָחִיד וְעָנִי אָנִי *I am lonely and afflicted*).

b. as noun, **solitary one,** <OBJ> ישׁב hi. *cause to dwell* Ps 68$_{7}$ (or em. מוֹשִׁיב *causes to dwell* to מֵשִׁיב *brings back,* i.e. שׁוב hi.; + אָסִיר *prisoner*).

3. unique, 1. used attributively of יוֹרֶה *one who teaches, teacher* CD 20$_{14}$ (יורה היחיד; unless יַחַד *unity*), מוֹרֶה *teacher* CD 20$_{1}$ (מורה היחיד; unless יַחַד *unity*).

2. used as predicative adj. or noun, **unique one,** <NOM CL> מה הואה יחיד *how unique he is* 4Q417 1.1$_{6}$.*

Also 4QCommGenA 3$_{9}$ 4QPrFêtes 7$_{4}$.

⇒ יחד *be united.*

[יְחִיָּה] 1 pr.n.m. **Jehiah**—וִיחִיָּה—**1.** Levite, gatekeeper for the ark, <NOM CL> עֹבֵד אֱדֹם וִיחִיָּה שֹׁעֲרִים לָאָרוֹן *Obed-edom and Jehiah were gatekeepers for the ark* 1 C 15$_{24}$.

2. appar. father of Shebaniah, Seal 476 (others עזריהו *Azariah;* Lachish, 8th cent.).

⇒ חיה *live* + ״ *Y.*

יחיהו, see יְחִיָּה *Jehiah.*

יָחִיל 1 n.[m.] **waiting,** <COLL> טוֹב וְיָחִיל וְדוּמָם appar. *good and waiting and silence* Lm 3$_{26}$ (or em. טוֹב וְיָחִיל דּוּמָם *(he) is good, and one should wait in silence,* or וְיָחִיל וְדָמַם חַסְדּוֹ *and he waits but his loyalty has ceased,* i.e. יחל hi.).*

⇒ יחל *wait.*

יחל I 41.0.7 vb. **wait**—Ni. 2 Pf. נוֹחֲלָה; + waw וַיִּיָּחֶל—**wait,** <SUBJ> Noah Gn 8$_{12}$ (or em. וַיִּיָּחֶל to וַיְיַחֵל, i.e. pi.), perh. 1 S 13$_{8(Kt)}$ (but prob. וייחל is pi.), לָבִיא *lion* (fem.) Ezk 19$_{5}$ (unless יחל II *be desperate;* or em. נוֹחֲלָה *she waited* to נוֹאֲלָה *she was foolish,* i.e. יאל ni.). <PREP> לְ

according to, + מוֹעֵד *appointed time* perh. 1 S 13$_{8(Kt)}$ (but prob. וייחל is pi.). <COLL> וַיִּיָּחֶל עוֹד שִׁבְעַת יָמִים אֲחֵרִים *and he waited another seven days* Gn 8$_{12}$ (or em.; see Subj.), var. perh. 1 S 13$_{8(Kt)}$ (but prob. וייחל is pi.).

Pi. 24.0.5 Pf. יִחַלְנוּ ,(יִחֵלוּ) יִחֲלוּ ,יִחַלְתִּי ,יִחַלְתָּנִי; impf. יְיַחֵל (יְיַחֵלוּ) ,(יְיַחֵלוּן) ,אֲיַחֵל (אֲיַחֲלָה); + waw Q ויחל; impv. יַחֵל; ptc. מְיַחֵל ,מְיַחֲלִים—**1. wait, hope,** <SUBJ> Israel Ps 130$_{7}$ (or em. יַחֵל *hope,* O Israel to יֹחֵל *let* Israel *hope,* i.e. hi.) 131$_{3}$, לְאֹם *nation* Is 41$_{1}$ (if em. יַחֲלִיפוּ כֹחַ *let them renew [their] strength* to (נִחְכִי) יַחֲלוּ לְתוֹכַחְתִּי *wait for my reproof [before me]*), Job Jb 6$_{11}$ 13$_{15}$ 14$_{14}$ 30$_{26}$, Noah Gn 8$_{10.12}$ (both if em.; see Coll.) 4QCommGenA 1$_{15}$, Saul 1 S 13$_{8(Kt)}$ (unless וייחל is ni.), נָבִיא *prophet* Ezk 13$_{6}$ (or em. וְיִחֲלוּ *and they hope* to וַיָּחֵלּוּ *and they began,* i.e. חלל hi.), worshipper Ps 33$_{22}$ 69$_{4}$ 71$_{14}$ (or em. אֲיַחֵל *I will hope* to אָחוּל *I will exult,* from חול *dance*) 119$_{43.49}$ (if em.; see §2 Subj.) 119$_{74.81.114.147}$ 1QH 9$_{10}$ 11$_{31}$, עֶבֶד *servant* Jg 3$_{25}$ (if em.; see Coll.), יֹשֶׁבֶת *inhabitants* Mc 1$_{12}$ (if em. כִּי חָלָה *for she has waited,* from חיל, to אֵיךְ/מִי יִחֲלָה *how has she waited!*), אִי *coastland* Is 42$_{4}$ 51$_{5}$, טַל *dew* Mc 5$_{6}$, רְבִיב *rain* Mc 5$_{6}$; subj. not specified, Ps 31$_{25}$ 33$_{18}$ 147$_{11}$ Jb 29$_{21.23}$ Si 40$_{13}$ (if em. מחול אל חול *from sand to sand* [B; Bmg חיל מחיל *wealth from weath*] to מיחל אל חיל *one who hopes for wealth*) 4QVisSam 7$_{3}$ 4QWays^{b} 11$_{4}$ CD 8$_{4}$.

<PREP> לְ (wait) *for,* (hope) *in,* + Y. Ps 31$_{25}$ 33$_{22}$ 69$_{4}$ Jb 13$_{15(Qr)}$, Job Jb 29$_{23}$, אִישׁ *man* Mc 5$_{6}$, תּוֹרָה *law* Is 42$_{4}$, מִשְׁפָּט *ordinance* Ps 119$_{43}$, דָּבָר *word* Ps 119$_{74.81.114.147}$, חֶסֶד *loyalty* Ps 33$_{18}$ 147$_{11}$ 1QH 9$_{10}$, טוֹב *good* Mc 1$_{12}$ (if em.; see Subj.) 1QH 11$_{31}$, מַרְפֵּא *healing* CD 8$_{4}$, תּוֹכַחַת *reproof* Is 41$_{1}$ (if em.; see Subj.), אוֹר *light* Jb 30$_{26}$.

לְ *according to,* + מוֹעֵד *appointed time* 1 S 13$_{8(Kt)}$ (unless וייחל is ni.).

כְּ *as (for),* + מָטָר *rain* Jb 29$_{23}$.

אֶל (hope) *in, for,* + Y. Ps 130$_{7}$ (or em.; see Subj.) 131$_{3}$, חַיִל *wealth* Si 40$_{13}$ (if em.; see Subj.).

עַל (wait) *for,* (hope) *in,* + זְרוֹעַ *arm* Is 51$_{5}$, דָּבָר *word* Ps 119$_{49}$ (if em.; see §2 Subj.).

<COLL> יחל pi. || קוה pi. *wait* Mc 5$_{6}$ Jb 30$_{26}$; + קוה pi. Is 51$_{5}$, כלה *be exhausted,* i.e. *languish* Ps 119$_{81}$, ארך hi. *hold back* soul Jb 6$_{11}$, דמם *be silent* Jb 29$_{21}$, ירא *fear* Ps 33$_{18}$ 147$_{11}$; followed by infinitive of קום pi. *fulfil* Ezk 13$_{6}$ (or em.; see Subj.).

+ adverb or noun used adverbially, תָּמִיד *continually* Ps 71$_{14}$, אֵיךְ *how!* Mc 1$_{12}$ (if em.; see Subj.), מִי *how!* Mc 1$_{12}$ (if em.; see Subj.), כָּל־יְמֵי צְבָאִי אֲיַחֵל *all the days of my service I would wait* Jb 14$_{14}$, וַיְיַחֶל עוֹד שִׁבְעַת יָמִים אֲחֵרִים *and he waited another seven days* Gn 8$_{10}$ (if em. וַיָּחֶל *and he waited,* from חיל) 8$_{12}$ (if em. וַיִּיָּחֶל *and he waited,* i.e. יחל ni.) 4QCommGenA 1$_{15}$, var. 2 S 13$_{8(Kt)}$ (unless וייחל is ni.); וַיְיַחֲלוּ עַד־בּוֹשׁ *and they waited unto shaming,* i.e. until they were ashamed Jg 3$_{25}$ (if em. וַיָּחִילוּ *and they waited,* from חיל).

2. cause to hope, <SUBJ> Y. Ps 119$_{49}$ (or §1, if em. יִחַלְתָּנִי *you have caused me to hope* to יִחַלְתִּי *I have hoped*). <OBJ> worshipper Ps 119$_{49}$ (or em.; see Subj.). <PREP> עַל *in,* + דָּבָר *word* Ps 119$_{49}$ (or em.; see Subj.).

<SYN> §1 קוה pi. *wait.*

Hi. 15.0.2 Pf. הוֹחַלְתִּי (הוֹחָלְתִּי); impf. 2ms תּוֹחֵל ,אוֹחִיל (אוֹחִילָה ,אֹחִילָה); + waw וָאוֹחִל ;וְהוֹחַלְתִּי; impv. הוֹחִילִי—**wait, hope,** <SUBJ> Israel Ps 130$_{7}$ (if em.; see Pi. Subj.), Elihu Jb 32$_{11.16}$, Jeremiah Jr 4$_{19(Qr}$ (unless יחל II hi. *despair;* Kt אחולה *I writhe,* from חיל), Joab 2 S 18$_{14}$ (or em. אֹחִילָה *I will wait* to אָחֵלָּה *I will begin,* i.e. חלל hi.; mss אחולה appar. *I will be in pain*), Job Jb 35$_{14}$ (if em. וּתְחוֹלֵל *and you wait,* i.e. חיל pol., to וְהוֹחֵל *and wait*), Micah Mc 7$_{7}$, Saul 1 S 10$_{8}$ 13$_{8(Qr)}$, עֶבֶד *servant* Jg 3$_{25}$ (if em.; see Coll.), מַלְאָךְ *messenger* 2 K 6$_{33}$ (or em. הַמַּלְאָךְ *the messenger* to הַמֶּלֶךְ *the king*), worshipper Ps 37$_{7}$ (if em. הִתְחוֹלֵל *wait longingly,* i.e. חיל htpol. to הוֹחֵל *wait*) 38$_{16}$ 130$_{5}$ Lm 3$_{21}$ (unless יחל II hi. *despair*) 3$_{24}$ 1QH 7$_{18}$ fr. 4$_{17}$, נֶפֶשׁ *soul* Ps 42$_{6.12}$ 43$_{5}$, impersonal Lm 3$_{26}$ (if em. יָחִיל *waiting* to יָחִיל *one should wait*).

<PREP> לְ (wait) *for,* (hope) *in,* + Y. 2 K 6$_{33}$ Mc 7$_{7}$ Ps 37$_{7}$ (if em.; see Subj.) 38$_{16}$ 42$_{6.12}$ 43$_{5}$ Jb 35$_{14}$ (if em.; see Subj.) Lm 3$_{25}$, תְּשׁוּעָה *salvation* Lm 3$_{26}$ (if em.; see Subj.), דָּבָר *word* Ps 130$_{5}$ Jb 32$_{11}$.

לְ *according to,* + מוֹעֵד *appointed time* 1 S 13$_{8(Qr)}$.

בְּ *with,* + כֹּל *all* of my being 1QH fr. 4$_{17}$.

אֶל (hope) *in,* + Y. Ps 130$_{7}$ (if em.; see Pi. Subj.).

לִפְנֵי *before,* + אִישׁ *man* 2 S 18$_{14}$ (or em.; see Subj.).

<COLL> יחל hi. + קוה pi. *wait* Ps 130$_{5}$, צפה בְּ *look to* Mc 7$_{7}$, אזן hi. *listen (for)* Jb 32$_{11}$.

+ adverb or noun used adverbially, מָה *how?* 2 K 6$_{33}$,

דּוּמָם *(in) silence* Lm 3$_{26}$ (if em. יָחִיל וְדוּמָם *waiting and silence* to יָחִיל דּוּמָם *one should wait in silence*), תּוֹחֵל שִׁבְעַת יָמִים *you shall wait seven days* 1 S 10$_{8}$, var. 13$_{8(Qr)}$; וַיּוֹחִילוּ עַד־בּוֹשׁ *and they waited unto shaming*, i.e. until they were ashamed Jg 3$_{25}$ (if em. וַיָּחִילוּ *and they waited*, from חיל).*

⇒ יָחִיל *waiting*, תּוֹחֶלֶת *hope*, יַחְלְאֵל *Jahleel*, יַחְלְאֵלִי *Jahleelite*.

*יחל II $_{4.1.1}$ vb. **be desperate—Ni.** $_{1.1}$ Pf. נוֹחָלָה; ptc. Si נוחל—**1. be desperate, be uncertain,** <SUBJ> תִּקְוָה *hope* Ezk 19$_{5}$ (unless יחל I *wait*; || אבד *perish*).

2. wrestle, <SUBJ> אֹהֵב *friend* Si 37$_{5(Bmg)}$ (unless נוחל is from נחל *inherit*; D לחם ni. *fight*). <PREP> עִם *with*, + זָר *stranger* Si 37$_{5(Bmg)}$.

Hi. $_{3}$ Pf. הוֹחַלְתִּי; impf. אוֹחִיל (Qr אוֹחִילָה)—**despair,** <SUBJ> Elihu Jb 32$_{11}$ (unless יחל I hi. *wait*), Jeremiah Jr 4$_{19(Qr)}$ (unless יחל I hi. *wait*; Kt אחולה *I writhe*, from חיל), worshipper Lm 3$_{21}$ (unless יחל I *wait*). <PREP> לְ *on account of*, + דָּבָר *word* Jb 32$_{11}$ (unless יחל I hi. *wait*).

Ho. $_{0.0.1}$ Ptc. Q מוחלה—**be sick,** <SUBJ> subj. not specified, 11QBer 1.2$_{12}$.

יַחְלְאֵל $_{2}$ pr.n.m. **Jahleel,** son of Zebulun, <NOM CL> בְּנֵי זְבוּלֻן ... יַחְלְאֵל *the sons of Zebulun were ... Jahleel* Gn 46$_{14}$. <PREP> לְ of possession, *of, (belonging) to* Nm 26$_{26}$.

⇒ יחל *wait* + אֵל *God*; יַחְלְאֵלִי *Jahleelite*.

יַחְלְאֵלִי $_{1}$ gent. **Jahleelite,** collective for descendants of Jahleel, <CSTR> מִשְׁפַּחַת הַיַּחְלְאֵלִי *family of the Jahleelites* Nm 26$_{26}$.

⇒ יחל *wait* + אֵל *God*; יַחְלְאֵל *Jahleel*.

יחם $_{6}$ vb. **be hot—Qal** $_{2}$ + waw וַיֶּחֱמוּ, 3fpl וַיֵּחַמְנָה (unless both forms from חמם *be warm*)—**conceive,** <SUBJ> צֹאן *flock* Gn 30$_{38.39}$. <PREP> אֶל *at, by*, + מַקֵּל *rod* Gn 30$_{39}$.

Pi. $_{6}$ Impf. יֶחֱמַתְנִי; inf. cstr. יַחֵם (יַחְמֵנָה)—**conceive,** <SUBJ> אֵם *mother* Ps 51$_{7}$ (+ חיל polal *be brought to birth*), צֹאן *flock* Gn 30$_{41.41}$ 31$_{10}$. <OBJ> worshipper Ps 51$_{7}$. <PREP> בְּ of place, *among*, + מַקֵּל *rod* Gn 30$_{41}$; of accompaniment, *in, with*, + חֵטְא *sin* Ps 51$_{7}$. <COLL> בְּכָל־יַחֵם הַצֹּאן *whenever the flock were on heat* Gn 30$_{41}$ (or em. בְּכָל־עֵת *at every time when*), בְּעֵת יַחֵם הַצֹּאן *at the time when the flock were on heat* Gn 31$_{10}$.

⇒ see also חמם *be warm*, חמה II *be hot*.

יַחְמוּר $_{2}$ n.[m.] **roebuck,** permitted for food (Dt 14$_{5}$), on Solomon's menu (1 K 5$_{3}$), <OBJ> אכל *eat* Dt 14$_{5}$ (|| אַיָּל *deer*, צְבִי *gazelle*). <PREP> לְבַד מִן *apart from* 1 K 5$_{3}$ (|| אַיָּל *deer*, צְבִי *gazelle*, + בַּרְבּוּר *goose*).

<SYN> אַיָּל *deer*, צְבִי *gazelle*.

יַחְמַי $_{1}$ pr.n.m. **Jahmai,** Issacharite, son of Tola, <NOM CL> בְּנֵי תוֹלָע ... יַחְמַי *the sons of Tola were ... Jahmai* 1 C 7$_{2}$.

⇒ חֵמָה III *protection*.

[יְחָמֵל] $_{0.0.0.1}$ pr.n.[m.] **Johamal,** Kh. el-Qom decanter inscr.

⇒ ״י + חמל *spare*.

[יַחְמַלְיָהוּ] $_{0.0.0.2}$ pr.n.[m.] **Jahmaliah, 1.** appar. son of Maaseiah, Seal 51 (Palestine, 7th cent.). **2.** appar. father of Sheba, Seal 337 (8th–6th cent.).

⇒ חמל *spare* + ״י.

יחן $_{0.1}$ vb. **dwell—Qal** $_{0.1}$ Impf. ייחן (unless from חנה *encamp*)—<SUBJ> אזן ptc. *one who listens* Si 4$_{15}$. <PREP> בְּ of place, *in*, + חֶדֶר *chamber* Si 4$_{15}$ (בחדרי מבית *in the chambers of my house*).

[יְחָן] $_{0.0.0.1}$ pr.n.[m.] **Johan,** Seal 914, <PREP> לְ of possession, *of, (belonging) to* Seal 914.

⇒ ״י *Y.* + חנן *be gracious*.

[יְחָנֶה] $_{0.0.1}$ pr.n.m. **Jannes,** opponent of Moses, <OBJ> קום hi. *raise up* CD 5$_{18}$.

⇒ ״י *Y.* + חנן *be gracious*.

[יְחָנְנִי] $_{0.0.0.1}$ pr.n.[m.] **Jehonneni,** appar. father of Pan, <CSTR> בן יחנני *son of Jehonneni* Seal 392 (Lachish, c. 700).

⇒ חנן *be gracious*.

יָחֵף 5 adj. **barefoot,** used predicatively with הלך *go* 2 S 15$_{30}$ Is 20$_{2.3}$ (both || עָרוֹם *naked*), נהג *lead* Is 20$_{4}$ (|| עָרוֹם); without verb, מִנְעִי רַגְלֵךְ מִיָּחֵף *withhold your foot from (being) barefoot* Jr 2$_{25}$.

<SYN> עָרוֹם *naked.*

יַחְצְאֵל 3 pr.n.m. **Jahzeel**—יַחֲצִיאֵל—son of Naphtali, <NOM CL> בְּנֵי נַפְתָּלִי יַחְצְאֵל וְגוּנִי ... *the sons of Naphtali were Jahzeel and Guni ...* Gn 46$_{24}$ 1 C 7$_{13(mss)}$ (L יַחֲצִיאֵל *Jahziel*). <PREP> לְ of possession, *of, (belonging) to* Nm 26$_{48}$.

⇒ חצה *divide* + אֵל *God;* יַחְצְאֵלִי *Jahzeelite.*

יַחְצְאֵלִי 1 gent. **Jahzeelite,** collective for descendants of Jahzeel, <CSTR> מִשְׁפַּחַת הַיַּחְצְאֵלִי *family of the Jahzeelites* Nm 26$_{48}$.

⇒ יַחְצְאֵל *Jahzeel.*

יָ֫חְצָה, see יַ֫הַץ *Jahaz.*

[יְחַצִי] pr.n.[m.] **Johazi,** Arad inscr. 101, <PREP> לְ of possession, *of, (belonging) to* Arad inscr. 101 (ל[י]חצי; others חצי *half*).

יַחֲצִיאֵל, see יַחְצְאֵל *Jahzeel.*

יחר, see אחר *delay.*

יחשׂ 20 vb. **register—Htp.** Pf. הִתְיַחֲשׂוּ; ptc. מִתְיַחְשִׂים; inf. הִתְיַחֵשׂ (הִתְיַחְשָׂם)—**1. be genealogically registered, register oneself, be enrolled, declare ancestry.**

<SUBJ> Reuben (but perh. Joseph) 1 C 5$_{1}$, Israel 1 C 9$_{1}$ (+ כתב pass. *be written*), בֵּן *son* of Gad 1 C 5$_{17}$, appar. כֹּהֵן *priest* 2 C 31$_{18}$, חֹר *noble* Ne 7$_{5}$ (+ יַחַשׂ *genealogy*), עַם *people* Ne 7$_{5}$, סָגָן *prefect* Ne 7$_{5}$, appar. דָּבָר *word* 2 C 12$_{15}$ (or em. לְהִתְיַחֵשׂ *in order to declare ancestry* to זֶה לְהִתְיַחֵשׂ *this was for registration*, as §2).

<PREP> לְ *in accordance with,* + בְּכֹרָה *firstborn's privilege* 1 C 5$_{1}$; introducing object, + קָהָל *assembly* 2 C 31$_{18}$; בְּ of place/time, *in, during,* + יוֹם *day* 1 C 5$_{17.17}$; of accompaniment, *with,* + טַף *children* 2 C 31$_{18}$, בֵּן *son* 2 C 31$_{18}$ (or del.), בַּת *daughter* 2 C 31$_{18}$ (or del.), אִשָּׁה *woman* 2 C 31$_{18}$ (or del.).

2. inf. as noun, **a. (genealogical) registration,** <NOM CL> וְאֵלֶּה רָאשֵׁי אֲבֹתֵיהֶם וְהִתְיַחְשָׂם *and these are the heads of their fathers' (houses) with their registration* Ezr 8$_{1}$, וְעִמּוֹ הִתְיַחֵשׂ לִזְכָרִים *and with him was the registration of* 150 *males* Ezr 8$_{3}$, זֹאת מוֹשְׁבֹתָם וְהִתְיַחְשָׂם לָהֶם *this was (the manner of) their settlement, and registration was to them,* i.e. their populations were accounted for, or, *this was their settlement and their registration* 1 C 4$_{33}$, שְׁמוֹנִים וְשִׁבְעָה אֶלֶף הִתְיַחְשָׂם לַכֹּל *eighty-seven thousand was the registration of all of them* 1 C 7$_{5}$, וְהִתְיַחְשָׂם עֶשְׂרִים וּשְׁנַיִם אֶלֶף וּשְׁלֹשִׁים וְאַרְבָּעָה *and their registration was 22,034* 1 C 7$_{7}$, sim. 7$_{9.40}$, הֵמָּה בְחַצְרֵיהֶם הִתְיַחְשָׂם *and as for them, their registration was by their villages* 1 C 9$_{22}$, וְאֵת הִתְיַחֵשׂ הַכֹּהֲנִים לְבֵית אֲבוֹתֵיהֶם *and the registration of the priests was according to their ancestral houses* 2 C 31$_{17}$ (or em. וזאת *this was* the registration).

<CSTR> הִתְיַחֵשׂ הַכֹּהֲנִים *registration of the priests* 2 C 31$_{17}$, סֵפֶר הִתְיַחֵשׂ הָעוֹלִים *the document of registration of those who went up* to Jerusalem Ne 7$_{5}$ (if em. סֵפֶר הַיַּחַשׂ הָעוֹלִים *the document of registration, namely [of] those who went up*).

<PREP> בְּ of instrument, *by (means of), through,* בְּהִתְיַחֵשׂ לְתֹלְדוֹתָם *through registration according to their generations* 1 C 5$_{7}$; מִלְּבַד *apart from,* מִלְּבַד הִתְיַחְשָׂם לִזְכָרִים ... לְכָל־הַבָּא לְבֵית־יי *apart from their registration of males ... of all who came to the house of Y.,* i.e. excluding all (male) visitors to the temple 2 C 31$_{16}$ (or em. מִלְּבַד to כֹּל כְּדֵי *all in accordance with*).

2b. registered person, <CSTR> כָּל־הִתְיַחֵשׂ בַּלְוִיִּם *every registered person among the Levites* 2 C 31$_{19}$. <PREP> לְ of direction, *to,* + נתן *give* 2 C 31$_{19}$.

3. ptc. as noun, perh. as title of document, **those who are registered,** <OBJ> בקשׁ pi. *seek* Ezr 2$_{62}$||Ne 7$_{64}$. <APP> כְּתָבָם הַמִּתְיַחְשִׂים *their document, 'those who are registered'* Ezr 2$_{62}$||Ne 7$_{64}$. <PREP> בְּ בקשׁ pi. *investigate* Ezr 2$_{62}$||Ne 7$_{64}$ (if ins. בְּ).*

⇒ יַחַשׂ *genealogy.*

יַ֫חַשׂ 1.0.3 n.[m.] **genealogy, (genealogical) registration**—Q יחוש (Q יחוס); pl. Q יחשים—<CSTR> סֵפֶר הַיַּחַשׂ *document of registration* Ne 7$_{5}$ (or em. סֵפֶר הִתְיַחֵשׂ *docu* *ment of registration of*, i.e. יחשׂ htp.). <PREP> בְּ *in, with* 4QDa 5.2$_{14}$, + עלה *go up*, i.e. enter into registration 4Q TohBa 1$_{2}$.

Also 4QTohD 1$_{3}$.*

⇒ יחשׂ *register*.

יַחַת 8 pr.n.m. **Jahath**—יָחַת—**1.** Judahite, son of Reaiah, <SUBJ> ילד hi. *beget* 1 C 4$_{2}$. <OBJ> ילד hi. *beget* 1 C 4$_{2}$.

2. Gershonite Levite, <NOM CL> יַחַת בְּנוֹ *Jahath was his son* 1 C 6$_{5}$. <CSTR> בֶּן־יַחַת *son of Jahath* 1 C 6$_{28}$. <APP> בֵּן *son* 1 C 6$_{28}$.

3. Gershonite Levite, son of Shimei, perh. ident. with §2, <SUBJ> היה *be* 1 C 23$_{11}$ (+ רֹאשׁ *head*). <NOM CL> … בְּנֵי שִׁמְעִי יַחַת *the sons of Shimei were Jahath* … 1 C 23$_{10}$.

4. Levite, son of Shelomoth, <NOM CL> לִבְנֵי שְׁלֹמוֹת יַחַת *of the sons of Shelomoth was Jahath* 1 C 24$_{22}$.

5. Merarite Levite, overseer of repairs to temple at time of Josiah, <SUBJ> פקד ho. *be appointed* 2 C 34$_{12}$, נצח pi. *appoint* 2 C 34$_{12}$.

יטב 114.8.2.1 vb. **be good—Qal** 44.0.1 Impf. יִיטַב (יֵטַב), 3fs תִּיטַב, תִּיטְבִי; + waw וַיִּיטַב, 3fs וַתִּיטַב, וַיִּיטְבוּ—**be good,** i.e. **go well** (Gn 12$_{13}$ 40$_{14}$ Dt 4$_{14}$ 5$_{16.29}$ 6$_{3.18}$ 12$_{25.28}$ 22$_{7}$ 2 K 25$_{24}$||Jr 40$_{9}$ Jr 7$_{23}$ 38$_{20}$ 42$_{6}$ Ps 49$_{19}$ [if em.; see Subj.] Ru 3$_{1}$), **be pleasing** (Gn 34$_{18}$ 41$_{37}$ 45$_{16}$ Lv 10$_{19.20}$ Dt 1$_{23}$ Jos 22$_{30.33}$ 1 S 18$_{5}$ 20$_{13}$ [if em.; see Prep.] 24$_{5}$ 2 S 3$_{36}$ 18$_{4}$ 1 K 3$_{10}$ Ps 69$_{32}$ Ne 2$_{6}$ Est 1$_{21}$ 2$_{4}$ 5$_{14}$), **find favour** (Ne 2$_{5}$ Est 2$_{4.9}$), **be glad** (Jg 18$_{20}$ 19$_{6.9}$ 1 K 21$_{7}$ Ru 3$_{7}$ Ec 7$_{3}$ 11$_{9}$ [if em.; see Subj.]); יטב מִן **be (in a) better (position) than** (Na 3$_{8}$).

<SUBJ> impersonal Gn 12$_{13}$ 40$_{14}$ 45$_{16}$ Lv 10$_{19.20}$ Dt 4$_{14}$ 5$_{15.29}$ 6$_{18}$ 12$_{25.28}$ 22$_{7}$ Jos 22$_{30}$ 1 S 18$_{5}$ 20$_{13}$ (if em.; see Prep.) 24$_{5}$ 2 S 3$_{36}$ 2 K 25$_{24}$||Jr 40$_{9}$ Jr 7$_{23}$ 38$_{20}$ 42$_{6}$ Ps 49$_{19}$ (if em. תֵּיטִיב לָךְ appar. *it prospers because of you*, i.e. hi., to יִיטַב לוֹ *it goes well for him*; or em. תִּיטַב לָהּ *it* [the life] *does well*, i.e. prospers) Ru 3$_{1}$ Ne 2$_{6}$, אֲשֶׁר *that which* 2 S 18$_{4}$, עֶבֶד *servant* Ne 2$_{5}$, נַעֲרָה *young woman* Est 2$_{4.9}$, לֵב *heart* Jg 18$_{20}$ 19$_{6}$ 1 K 21$_{7}$ Ru 3$_{7}$ Ec 7$_{3}$ 11$_{9}$ (if em. וִיטִיבְךָ *and let it make you glad*, i.e. hi., to וְיִטַב *and let it be glad* or וְיִיטַבְךָ *and let it be glad for you*),* לֵבָב *heart* Jg 19$_{9}$, דָּבָר *word* Gn 34$_{18}$ 41$_{37}$ Dt 1$_{23}$ Jos 22$_{33}$ 1 K 3$_{10}$ Est 1$_{21}$ 2$_{4}$ 5$_{14}$, עִיר *city* Na 3$_{8}$; subj. not specified, 4QapMes 2.1$_{7}$.

<PREP> לְ in ref. to subj. of יטב, + נֶפֶשׁ *soul* Ps 49$_{19}$ (if em.; see Subj.).

לְ of benefit, *to, for*, + Y. Ps 69$_{32}$, Israel(ites) Dt 4$_{40}$ 5$_{16}$ 6$_{3.18}$ 12$_{25.28}$ 22$_{7}$ Jr 7$_{23}$, עַם *people* Dt 5$_{29}$ Jr 42$_{6}$, נְטֹפָתִי *Netophathite*, Abram Gn 12$_{13}$, Ishmael 2 K 25$_{24}$||Jr 40$_{9}$, Jaazaniah/Jezaniah 2 K 25$_{24}$||Jr 40$_{9}$ Jr 42$_{6}$, Johanan 2 K 25$_{24}$||Jr 40$_{9}$ Jr 42$_{6}$, Jonathan Jr 40$_{9}$, Seraiah 2 K 25$_{24}$||Jr 40$_{9}$, Zedekiah Jr 38$_{20}$, אִישׁ *man* 2 K 25$_{24}$||Jr 40$_{9}$ Ps 49$_{19}$ (if em.; see Subj.), בֵּן *son* Dt 4$_{40}$ 5$_{29}$ 12$_{25.28}$ 2 K 25$_{24}$||Jr 40$_{9}$ Jr 42$_{6}$, בַּת *daughter* Ru 3$_{1}$, מֶלֶךְ *king* Jr 38$_{20}$, שַׂר *chief* Gn 40$_{14}$ 2 K 25$_{24}$||Jr 40$_{9}$ Jr 42$_{6}$.

לְ of time, *for*, + עוֹלָם *eternity* Dt 5$_{29}$.

בְּ of place, *in*, + עַיִן *eye*, i.e. sight Gn 34$_{18}$ 41$_{37}$ 45$_{16}$ Lv 10$_{19.20}$ Dt 1$_{23}$ Jos 22$_{30.33}$ 1 S 18$_{5}$ 24$_{5}$ 2 S 3$_{36}$ 18$_{4}$ 1 K 3$_{10}$ Est 1$_{21}$ 2$_{4.4.9}$; of time, *in*, + יוֹם *day* Ec 11$_{9}$ (if em.; see Subj.).

מִן of comparison, *(more) than*, + שׁוֹר *ox* Ps 69$_{32}$, פַּר *bull* Ps 69$_{32}$, No-amon, i.e. Thebes Na 3$_{8}$.

אֶל *to*, + אָב *father* 1 S 20$_{13}$ (יִיטַב אֶל־אָבִי אֶת־הָרָעָה עָלֶיךָ *it is pleasing to my father to do you harm*, or em. יֵיטִב appar. *it is pleasing*, i.e. hi.); עַל *upon*, + אֲדָמָה *land* Dt 5$_{16}$; לִפְנֵי *before*, + Haman Est 5$_{14}$, מֶלֶךְ *king* Ne 2$_{5.6}$; עַד *until*, + עוֹלָם *eternity* Dt 12$_{25}$; בַּעֲבוּר *on account of, for the sake of*, + Sarai Gn 12$_{13}$, אִשָּׁה *wife* Gn 12$_{13}$.

<COLL> יטב + אָרַךְ יָמִים hi. *prolong days* Dt 4$_{40}$ 5$_{16}$ 22$_{7}$, חיה *live* Jr 38$_{20}$, נשׂא חֶסֶד *find favour* Est 2$_{9}$.

Hi. 70.8.1.1 Pf. הֵיטִיב, הֵיטַבְתָּ, הֵיטַבְתְּ, הֵיטִיבוּ; impf. יֵיטִיב (יֵיטִב, יֵיטִיב, יֵיטֵב), 3fs תֵּיטִיב, 2ms תֵּיטִיב (Si תטיב), תֵּיטִיבוּ, יֵיטִיבוּ, (אֵיטִיבָה) אֵיטִיב, תֵּיטִבִי; + waw וְהֵיטִב, וַתֵּיטֵב; (ויטיבך) וַיֵּיטֶב וְהֵיטִבֹתִי, 3fs וַתֵּיטַב; impv. Si היטב (Si הֵיטִיבוּ, הֵיטִיבִי, (הֵיטִיבָה, היטיב); ptc. מֵיטִיב (מֵטִב), מֵיטִיבִים, מֵיטִבֵי (מֵיטִבֵי); inf. abs. הֵיטֵיב (הֵיטֵב), cstr. הֵיטִיב (הֵיטִיבוֹ, הֵיטִבְךָ, הֵיטִיבִי)—**1. a. do good, deal well, act benevolently** (Gn 12$_{16}$ 32$_{10.13.13}$ Ex 1$_{20}$ Lv 5$_{4}$ Nm 10$_{32}$ Jos 24$_{20}$ Jg 17$_{13}$ 1 S 25$_{31}$ Is 41$_{23}$ Jr 10$_{5}$ Ezk 36$_{11}$ Mc 2$_{7}$ [or em.; see Subj.] Zp 1$_{12}$ Ps 49$_{19}$ [if em.; see Subj.] 119$_{68}$ 125$_{4}$ Si 12$_{1.2}$ 14$_{5.13}$ 39$_{27}$ 51$_{18[B]}$ Kuntillet ‘Ajrud inscr. D2); to one's self, i.e. **find enjoyment** (Si 14$_{11}$).

b. do good to, benefit (Dt 8$_{16}$ 28$_{63}$ 1 S 2$_{32}$ Jr 18$_{10}$ 32$_{40.41}$ Zc 8$_{15}$ Ps 51$_{20}$ Jb 24$_{21}$).

2. do good ethically (Gn 4$_{7.7}$ Is 1$_{17}$ Jr 4$_{22}$ 13$_{23}$ Jon 4$_{4.9.9}$ Ps 36$_{4}$ [or §5, if em.; see Obj.]).

3. intrans. **prosper** (Ps 49$_{19}$ [or em.; see Subj.]).

4. be good, pleasing (1 S 20$_{13}$ [or em.; see Prep.]).

5. make good, improve (Ho 10$_{1}$ Mc 2$_{7}$ [if em.; see Subj.] Pr 15$_{2}$ [or em.; see Subj.] 17$_{22}$ Si 13$_{5}$), i.e. **amend** one's ways, deeds (Jr 7$_{3.5.5}$ 18$_{11}$ 26$_{13}$ 35$_{15}$), **direct** one's way (Jr 2$_{33}$),* **make ready** (Ps 36$_{4}$ [if em.; see Obj.]), **beautify** head (2 K 9$_{30}$), **dress** lamp (Ex 30$_{7}$); with מִן of comparison, **make better, make greater (than)** (1 K 1$_{47}$ Ru 3$_{10}$).

6. make glad, make merry (Jg 19$_{22}$ Pr 15$_{12}$ Ec 11$_{9}$ [or em.; see Subj.]).

7a. do well, do thoroughly, be skilful (Dt 5$_{28}$ 18$_{17}$ 1 S 16$_{17}$ Is 23$_{16}$ Jr 1$_{12}$ Ezk 33$_{32}$ Mc 7$_{3}$ Ps 33$_{3}$ Pr 30$_{29.29}$).

b. inf. abs. הֵיטֵב **well, thoroughly, utterly,** with טחן *grind* Dt 9$_{21}$, שׁאל *ask* Dt 13$_{15}$, דרשׁ *inquire* Dt 17$_{4}$ 19$_{18}$, באר pi. *explain* Dt 27$_{8}$, צוה pi. *command* 1QDM 1$_{5}$, שׁבר pi. *break* 2 K 11$_{18}$.

<SUBJ> Y. Gn 32$_{10.13.13}$ Ex 1$_{20}$ Nm 10$_{32}$ Dt 8$_{16}$ 28$_{63}$ Jos 24$_{20}$ Jg 17$_{13}$ 1 S 2$_{32}$ 25$_{31}$ Jr 18$_{10}$ 32$_{41}$ 1 K 1$_{47}$ Ezk 36$_{11}$ Mc 2$_{7}$ (if em.; see below) Zp 1$_{12}$ Zc 8$_{15}$ Ps 51$_{20}$ 119$_{68}$ 125$_{4}$ Kuntillet 'Ajrud inscr. D2, gods Is 41$_{23}$, images Jr 10$_{5}$, Israel(ites) Dt 18$_{17}$ Is 1$_{17}$ Jr 2$_{33}$ 7$_{3.5.5}$ Ho 10$_{1}$ Mc 7$_{3}$, Tyre Is 23$_{16}$, עַם *people* Dt 5$_{28}$ Jr 4$_{22}$ 26$_{13}$, Aaron Ex 30$_{7}$, Ben Sira Si 51$_{18(B)}$, Cain Gn 4$_{7}$, Jeremiah Jr 1$_{12}$, Jezebel 2 K 9$_{30}$, Ruth Ru 3$_{10}$, אִישׁ *man* Jg 19$_{22}$ 1 S 16$_{17}$ Jr 18$_{11}$ 35$_{15}$, בֵּן *son* Si 12$_{1.2}$ 14$_{11.13}$, *son* of man Ezk 33$_{32}$, שַׂר *prince* Jr 26$_{13}$, פַּרְעֹה *Pharaoh* Gn 12$_{16}$, יֹשֵׁב *inhabitant* Jr 28$_{11}$ 35$_{15}$, עָשִׁיר *rich one* Si 13$_{5}$, רַע *bad*, i.e. mean, *one* Si 14$_{5}$, wicked one Ps 36$_{4}$ Jb 24$_{21}$, worshipper Ps 33$_{3}$, לִמֻּד *one accustomed to* Jr 13$_{23}$, נֶפֶשׁ *soul*, i.e. person Lv 5$_{4}$, לֵב *heart* Pr 15$_{13}$ 17$_{22}$ Ec 11$_{9}$ (or em.; see Qal, Subj.), לָשׁוֹן *tongue* Pr 15$_{2}$ (or em. תֵּיטִיב *it makes good* to תַּטִּיף *it drips*, or תֵּבַת *[is] an ark of* knowledge), דָּבָר *word* Mc 2$_{7}$ (or em. דְּבָרַי יֵיטִיבוּ *my words do good* to דְּבָרָיו יֵיטִיב *he makes his words good*), שָׁלוֹשׁ *three* Pr 30$_{29}$, אַרְבַּע *four* Pr 30$_{29}$, אֵלֶּה *these* Si 39$_{27(Segal)}$ ([א]לה), impersonal 1 S 20$_{13}$ Jon 4$_{4.9.9}$ Ps 49$_{19}$ (or em. תֵּיטִיב לָךְ appar. *it prospers because of you* to תֵּיטִיב לוֹ *you do good to him*, or יִיטַב לוֹ *it goes well for him*, i.e. qal).

<OBJ> Israel(ites) Dt 8$_{16}$ 28$_{63}$ 1 S 2$_{32}$, גּוֹי *nation* Jr 18$_{10}$, מַמְלָכָה *kingdom* Jr 18$_{10}$, עִיר *city* Jr 32$_{40.41}$, Jerusalem Zc 8$_{15}$, Zion Ps 51$_{20}$, בַּיִת *house* of Judah Zc 8$_{15}$, בָּחוּר *youth* Ec 11$_{9}$ (or em.; see Qal, Subj.), אַלְמָנָה *widow* Jb 24$_{21}$, לֵב *heart* Jg 19$_{22}$, פָּנִים *countenance* Pr 15$_{13}$, רֹאשׁ *head* 2 K 9$_{30}$, שֵׁם *name* 1 K 1$_{47}$, דַּעַת *knowledge* Pr 15$_{2}$ (or em.; see Subj.), דָּבָר *word* Mc 2$_{7}$ (if em.; see Subj.) Si 13$_{5}$, טוֹב *good* Nm 10$_{32}$, טוֹבָה *good* Jr 18$_{10}$ (הַטּוֹבָה אֲשֶׁר אָמַרְתִּי לְהֵיטִיב אוֹתוֹ *the good that I had said I would do to it*), חֶסֶד *kindness* Ru 3$_{10}$, גֵּהָה *healing* Pr 17$_{22}$ (or em. גֵּהָה to גְּוִיָּה *body*), דֶּרֶךְ *way* Jr 2$_{33}$ 7$_{3.5}$ 18$_{11}$ 26$_{13}$, מַעֲלָל *deed* Jr 7$_{3.5}$ 18$_{11}$ 26$_{13}$ 35$_{15}$, מַצֵּבָה *pillar* Ho 10$_{1}$, נֵר *lamp* Ex 30$_{7}$, אָוֶן *trouble* Ps 36$_{4}$ (if join לְהֵיטִיב with following verse), כָּל־אֲשֶׁר *all that which* Dt 5$_{28}$ 18$_{17(mss)}$ (L lacks כָּל־).

<PREP> לְ of direction, benefit, (do good) *to, for,* or introducing object, + עַם *people* Jos 24$_{20}$, Abram Gn 12$_{16}$, Micah Jg 17$_{13}$, אִישׁ *man* Ps 49$_{19}$ (if em.; see Subj.), בֵּן *son* Si 14$_{11}$, אָדוֹן *lord* 1 S 25$_{31}$, מְיַלֶּדֶת *midwife* Ex 1$_{20}$, טוֹב *good one* Ps 125$_{4}$ Si 39$_{27}$ (ל[ט]ובים), יָשָׁר *upright one* Ps 125$_{4}$, צַדִּיק *righteous one* Si 12$_{2}$, אֹהֵב *friend* Si 14$_{13}$, מִי *whom?* Si 12$_{1}$ 14$_{5}$.

לְ *with respect to,* + כֹּל אֲשֶׁר *everything that* Lv 5$_{4}$; *because of,* + Y. Ps 49$_{19}$ (or em.; see Subj.).

בְּ of time, *in, at,* + אַחֲרִית *end* Dt 8$_{16}$, יוֹם *day* Ec 11$_{9}$ (or em.; see Subj.); of accompaniment, *with, in,* + רָצוֹן *pleasure* Ps 51$_{20}$.

מִן of comparison, *(more) than,* + שֵׁם *name* 1 K 1$_{47}$, רֵאשָׁה *beginning* Ezk 36$_{11}$, רִאשׁוֹן *first (kindness)* Ru 3$_{10}$.

אֶל *to,* + אָב *father* 1 S 20$_{13}$ (יֵיטִב אֶל־אָבִי אֶת־הָרָעָה עָלֶיךָ *it is pleasing to my father to do you harm*, or em. יִיטָב *it is pleasing*, i.e. qal).

עִם *with, to,* + Jacob Gn 32$_{10.13}$, בֵּן *son* Si 13$_{5}$, Israel(ites) Nm 10$_{32}$, הלך ptc. *one who walks* Mc 2$_{7}$ (עִם הַיָּשָׁר הוֹלֵךְ *with the one who walks uprightly* to עִם עַמּוֹ יִשְׂרָאֵל *with his people Israel*).

בַּעֲבוּר *on account of, for the sake of,* + אִשָּׁה *woman* Gn 12$_{16}$.

<COLL> יטב hi. ‖ רבה hi. *multiply* Dt 28$_{63}$ Is 23$_{16}$, גדל pi. *make great* 1 K 1$_{47}$; :: רעע hi. *do evil* Lv 5$_{4}$ Is 1$_{18}$ 41$_{23}$ Jr 4$_{22}$ 10$_{5}$ 13$_{23}$ Zp 1$_{12}$; + טוב *be good* Nm 10$_{32}$ Ho 10$_{1}$, עשׂה מִשְׁפָּט *do justice* Jr 7$_{5}$, שׁוב מִן *turn away from* evil way Jr 18$_{11}$.

inf. abs. + finite form of יטב hi. Gn 32$_{13}$ Jr 7$_{5}$.

inf. cstr. of יטב hi. *do well, do thoroughly* + ראה *see* Jr 1_{12}, נגן pi. *play musical instrument* 1 S 16_{17} Is 23_{16} Ezk 33_{32} Ps 33_{3}, רעע hi. *do evil* Mc 7_{3} (if em. עַל־הָרַע כַּפַּיִם לְהֵיטִיב *their hands are upon the evil to do it well* to לְהָרַע כפיהם היטיבו *their hands are skilful at doing evil*).

מֵיטִבֵי צָעַד *skilful of*, i.e. in their, *step* Pr 30_{29}, מֵיטִבֵי לָכֶת *skilful of*, i.e. at, *walking* Pr 30_{29}, הַהֵיטֵב חָרָה־לָךְ *does it do good (in that) it is angry to you?*, i.e. do you do well to be angry? Jon 4_{9}, vars. $4_{4.9}$.

<SYN> רבה hi. *multiply*, גדל pi. *make great*.

<ANT> רעע hi. *do evil*.*

→ מֵיטָב *best*, מְהֵיטַבְאֵל *Mehetabel*, יָטְבָה *Jotbah*, יָטְבָתָה *Jotbathah*; see also טוֹב *be good*.

יָטְבָה 1 pl.n. **Jotbah,** town of Haruz, maternal grandfather of Amon, king of Judah, perh. Kh. Čefāt, 14 km N of Nazareth, <PREP> מִן *from, of* 2 K 21_{19}.

→ יטב *be good*.

יָטְבָתָה 3 pl.n. **Jotbathah,** station of the exodus, perh. ʿĒn Ṭāba, 8 km SW of Elath, <PREP> בְּ of place, *in*, + חנה *encamp* Nm 33_{33} Dt $10_{7(Sam)}$; מִן of direction, *from*, + נסע *journey* Nm 33_{34}. <COLL> יָטְבָתָה *to Jotbathah*, with נסע *journey* Dt 10_{7}.

→ יטב *be good*.

יֻטָּה 2 pl.n. **Juttah**—יוּטָּה—town in Judah allocated to priests, perh. Yaṭṭa, 9 km S of Hebron, <OBJ> נתן *give* Jos 21_{16} (+ מִגְרָשׁ *pasture land*). <NOM CL> וּבָהָר ... יוּטָּה *and in the hill country was ... Juttah* Jos 15_{55}.

יְטוּר 3 pr.n.m. **Jetur, 1.** tenth son of Ishmael, <SUBJ> שׁכן *dwell* Gn 25_{12}. <NOM CL> אֵלֶּה שְׁמוֹת בְּנֵי יִשְׁמָעֵאל ... יְטוּר *these are the names of the sons of Ishmael ... Jetur* Gn 25_{12}, sim. 1 C 1_{31}.

2. tribe descended from §1, <PREP> עִם *with*, + עשׂה *make* war 1 C 5_{19}.

***יטשׁ** 2 vb. **clash, dash—Qal** 2 + waw 3fs וַתִּטֹּשׁ, וַיִּטְּשֵׁהוּ (unless both from נטשׁ I *leave*, or II = יטשׁ)—**1. clash,** i.e. be joined with a clash, <SUBJ> מִלְחָמָה *battle* 1 S 4_{2}.

2. dash, <SUBJ> זָר *foreigner* Ezk 31_{12}. <OBJ> אֶרֶז *cedar* Ezk 31_{12}. <PREP> אֶל *on*, + הַר *mountain*.

יַיִן 141.17.17.31 n.m. **wine**—יַיִן (Pr 20_{1}), יַיִן, ין (Samaria ost.); cstr. יֵין—**wine;** also wine-induced **stupor** (Gn 9_{24}).

<SUBJ> היה *be* Nm 28_{14} (or del. יַיִן) Is 5_{12} 11QT 47_{6}, ישׁן *grow old* Si 9_{10}, פתח ni. *be opened* Jb 32_{19}, יצר ni. *be formed* Si 34_{27}, קדשׁ *be consecrated* Hg 2_{12}, אדם htp. *be red* Pr 23_{31}, perh. עשׁן pass. *be smoked* Lachish ost. 25 (יין עשן *smoked wine*, or perh. *wine of Ashan*), שׁתה ni. *be drunk* Si $34_{28.29}$, בוא *come* Dn 10_{3}, הלך *go* Pr 23_{31} (htp.) Ca 7_{10}, יצא *go out* 1 S 25_{37} (+ מִן *from*), עבר *pass*, i.e. overcome Jr 23_{9}, דבב *glide over* Ca 7_{10}, נתן *give* Pr 23_{31}, לקח *take* Ho 4_{11}.

שׂמח pi. *make joyful* Ps 104_{15} Ec 10_{19}, עלץ hi. *cause to rejoice* Si 40_{18}, בחן *test* Si $34_{26(Segal)}$ (if em.; see Nom. Cl.), דלק hi. *inflame* Is 5_{11}=4QpIsa[b] 2_{3} (יין ידלקם), בגד *betray* Hb 2_{5} (or ins. אִישׁ *man of* wine, i.e. drunkard, or em. הוֹי *woe*, or יָהִין *make light*, or יְוָנִי *Greek* [Alexander], or יֹנֶה *oppressor* [Nebuchadrezzar], or הַיּוֹן *Hiyon* [Canaanite deity]; 1QpHab 8_{3} הוֹן *wealth*),* פחז hi. *make reckless* Si $19_{2(Segal)}$ (יו[פח]יזו), חמר *foam* Ps 75_{9} (unless חמר III *be red* and unless כּוֹס *cup* is subj.; see Coll.; or em. יֵין חֶמֶר *wine of fermentation*).

<NOM CL> לֵץ הַיַּיִן *wine is a scoffer* Pr 20_{1} (mss הַיַּיִן), כן היין חדשׁ אוהב חדשׁ *a new friend is new wine* Si 9_{10}, כן היין למצות לצים *so is wine to the strife of scoffers* Si $34_{26(B)}$ (Bmg כי היית מצות *for it is the strife* of scoffers; or em. כן היין לבות לצים *so does wine test the hearts of scoffers* or כן שׁכר *so is strong drink* to the strife of scoffers), היין חיים לאנושׁ *wine is life to a person* Si 34_{27}, שׂמחת לב ושׂשׂון ועדוי יין appar. *wine is (conducive to) joy of heart, rejoicing, and conception* Si 34_{28} (or em. עֵדֶן/עִדּוּן *luxury*), יַיִן לְפָנָיו *wine was (set) before him* Ne 2_{1} (or em. לְפָנַי *before me*), כאב ראשׁ לענה וקלון יין *wine is headache, wormwood and dishonour* Si 34_{29}, יֵין מַלְכוּת רָב *the royal wine was abundant* Est 1_{7}, נִסְכּוֹ יַיִן *its drink offering will be wine* Lv $23_{13(Qr)}$, ונסכו יין רבןיעית ההין *and its drink offering shall be wine, a fourth of a hin* 11QT 13_{13a}, [בשׁמן רביעית ההין ו]יין לנסך *with oil, a quarter of a hin, and wine for a drink offering* 11QT 18_{6}, והיין מיום מועד התירושׁ עד השׁנה השׁנית *and (they shall drink) the wine from the day of the festival of the new wine until the next year* 11QT 43_{7}, חֲמַת

תַּנִּינִם יֵינָם *their wine is serpents' venom* Dt 32_{33}=CD $8_{9(A)}$ =CD $19_{22(B)}$, ויינם הוא דרכיהם *and their wine is their ways* CD $8_{10(A)}$=CD $19_{23(B)}$, לֶחֶם וָיַיִן יֶשׁ־לִי *I have bread and wine* Jg 19_{19}, למתניהו יין *the wine is Mattaniah's* Decanter inscr. (7th cent.), אַיֵּה דָּגָן וָיָיִן *where is grain and wine?* Lm 2_{12}, למי היין חיים *to whom is wine life?* Si 34_{27}, [לחל]ץ היין מח[צרת] perh. *to*, i.e. received from, *Helez is the wine from Hazeroth* Samaria ost. 26_2.

<OBJ> אהב *love* Pr 21_{17}, ראה *see* Pr 23_{31}, אמר *say*, i.e. mention 2 C 2_{14}, אסף *gather* Jr $40_{10.12}$, בוא hi. *bring* Gn 27_{25} Ne 13_{15} 1 C 12_{41}, יצא hi. *take out* Gn 14_{18} Ps 104_{15}, נתן *give* Pr 31_6 Ne 2_1 2 C 2_9 Lachish ost. 9_4 ([יין]) Arad ost. 2_2 4_2 8_5 10_2 ([נתן]) 11_3, *place* 2 C 11_{11}, לקח *take* Is 56_{12} 11QT 43_{15}, נשׂא *take* Dn 1_{16} Ne 2_1, שׁלח *send* 2 C 2_{14} perh. Arad ost. 61_2, שׁבר *buy (food)* Is 55_1, עשׂה *prepare* Nm 15_5, מסך *mix*, i.e. prepare Ho 7_5 (if em. מָשַׁךְ יָדוֹ *he drew his hand* to מָסַךְ יֵינוֹ *he mixed his wine*) Pr $9_{2.5}$, קרב hi. *bring* Nm $15_{7.10}$, סבב hi. *bring* Arad ost. 2_5, סור hi. *remove* 1 S 1_{14}, שׁבת hi. *remove* Jr 48_{33}, דרך *trample* Is 16_{10}, נסך *pour out* Ho 9_4 11QT 21_{10}, שׁתה *drink* Lv 10_9 Nm 6_{20} Dt 28_{39} 29_5 32_{38} Jg $13_{4.7.14}$ 1 S 1_{15} 2 S 16_2 Is 5_{22} 22_{13} 24_9 Jr $35_{5.6.6.8.14}$ Ezk 44_{21} Jl 1_5 4_3 (or del. שׁתה) Am 2_8 5_{11} 9_{14} Mc 6_{15}=1QpMic 17-18_3 Zp 1_{13} (or del.) Jb $1_{13.18}$ Pr 4_{17} 31_4 Ca 5_1 Ec 9_7 Si 9_{10} 34_{27} 4Q416 2.2_{19}=4Q 417 1.2_{24} 11QT 21_7 ([לשתות יין חדש]), שׁקה hi. *cause to drink* Gn $19_{32.33.34.35}$ Jr 35_2 Am 2_{12} Ps 60_5, סבא *drink* Pr 23_{20}, appar. אכל *eat* 11QT 43_{15}, קטר hi. *burn* 11QT 34_{13}, perh. אגר *gather* Dt 28_{39}.

<CSTR> יֵין חֶלְבּוֹן *wine of Helbon* Ezk 27_{18} Ho 14_8 (if em. לְבָנוֹן *of Lebanon*), יין כחל *wine of Kohel* Hebron jar inscr. 1 (unless כָּחֹל *blue* wine), [ין שמידע] *wine of Shemiada* Samaria ost. 62_1, [י]ן כרם התל[*wine of the vineyard of the tell* Samaria ost. 20_2 (others מכרם *from the vineyard* for [י]ן) 53_1 54_1 72_1 73_2 ([כרם]), יֵין מַלְכוּת *wine of (the) kingdom*, i.e. royal wine Est 1_7, עֲנוּשִׁים *of those fined* Am 2_8, יין נסכו *wine of its drink offering* 11QT 34_{13}, יֵין נְסִיכָם *wine of their drink offering* Dt 32_{38} (Sam נִסְכָּם *of their drink offering*), יין האגנת *wine of the bowls* Arad ost. 1_9, יֵין הָרֶקַח *wine of spice*, i.e. spiced wine Ca $8_{2(Gnz)}$, חֶמֶר *of fermentation* Ps 75_9 (if em. יַיִן חָמַר perh. *wine foams*; see Coll.), הַטּוֹב appar. *of goodness*, i.e. good wine Ca 7_{10} (but perh. טוֹב V *perfume*), מִשְׁתָּיו *of his drinking(s)* Dn $1_{5.8.16}$ (מִשְׁתֵּיהֶם *of their drinking*), חֲמָסִים *of violence* Pr 4_{17}.

שֹׁתֵי יַיִן *drinkers of wine* Jl 1_5, סֹבְאֵי *drinkers of* Pr 23_{20}, הֲלוּמֵי *those struck of*, i.e. overcome with Is 28_1, גֶּפֶן *vine of* Nm 6_4 Jg 13_{14}, חֹמֶץ *vinegar of*, i.e. made from Nm 6_3, כּוֹס *cup of* Jr 25_{15}, גְּבִיעַ *cup of* Jr 35_5 (if em. גְּבִעִים מְלֵאִים יַיִן *cups filled (with) wine* to גְּבִיעַ יַיִן *cup of wine*), מִזְרְקֵי *bowls of* Am 6_6, נֹאד *skin of* 1 S 16_{20}, נֹאדוֹת *skins of* Jos $9_{4.13}$ (הַיַּיִן), נֵבֶל *jar of* 1 S 1_{24} 10_3 (יַיִן) 25_{18} (נִבְלֵי־) 2 S 16_1 Ne 5_{18} (if em. כָּל־ *all* wine) Samaria ost. 1_2 ([י]ן) 3_2 ([יין]) 5_3 6_3 7_3 ([נבל ין]) 8_3 ([יין]) 9_3 ([נ]בל ין]) 10_3 11_1 ([נ]בל ין]) 12_3 13_3 14_3 15_2 ([נ]בל ין]) 89_1 ([נ]בל ין]), בֵּית *house of* Ca 2_4 (הַיָּיִן; Gnz הַיַּיִן), (...) אֹצְרוֹת *storehouses of* ... 1 C 27_{27} (הַיַּיִן) 2 C 11_{11} (יַיִן), מִשְׁתֵּה *the banquet of* Est 5_6 $7_{2.7.8}$ Si 34_{31} $35_{5.5.5}$ 49_1, מקום היין *the place of wine* Si 35_4, בְּלוֹ ... יַיִן *gift of ... wine* Ne 5_{15} (if em. בְּלֶחֶם וָיַיִן *for [the price of] bread and wine* to בְּלוֹ לֶחֶם וָיַיִן *gift of bread wine* or del. יַיִן), חיי *life of* Si $40_{18(B)}$ (Bmg חיי יותר, M חיי יתר *life of abundance*), חסר *lacking of*, i.e. in Si 34_{27}, מוסר לחם ויין *discipline of bread and wine* Si 34_{12}, תגאולת שמן ויין *pollution (consisting) of oil and wine* 11QT 49_{12}, כָּל־ *all wine* Ne 5_{18} (or em. נֵבֶל יַיִן *jar of wine*).

<APP> נֶסֶךְ *drink offering* Ex 29_{40} Nm 28_{14} (or del. יַיִן) Decanter inscr. (7th cent.), תִּירוֹשׁ *new wine* 11QT 21_7 ([יין]), רֶקַח *spice*, i.e. spiced wine Ca 8_2 (Gnz יֵין הָרֶקַח *wine of spice*, i.e. spiced wine), בַּת *bath* 2 C 2_9 Arad ost. 1_3 2_2 3_2 4_2 8_5 9_3 ([יין]) 10_2 11_3 61_2 ([י]ין) 4QOrd[b] 1.1_4, הִין *hin* Lv 23_{13} Nm $15_{5.7.10}$ 28_{14} (or del. יַיִן) 11QT 13_{13a} 19_{14}, חֹמֶר *homer* Arad ost. 2_5, מַאֲכָל *food* 1 C 12_{41}, חֵמָה *anger* Jr 25_{15} (or del. חֵמָה; or em. כּוֹס הַיַּיִן הַחֵמָה *cup of wine, of anger* to כּוֹס יֵין הַחֶמֶר appar. *cup of fermented wine*), תַּרְעֵלָה *reeling* Ps 60_5, כֹּל *all* Dt 14_{26}.

<ADJ> חָדָשׁ *new* Si 9_{10} 11QT 19_{14} $21_{7.10}$, יָשָׁן *old* Samaria ost. 4_3 ([ין ישן]) 5_3 7_3 ([ין י]שן) 8_3 ([ין ישן]) 9_3 ([י]ן) 10_3 12_3 13_3 14_3 15_2 ([ין ישן]) 101_1 perh. 6_3, perh. כָּחֹל *blue* Hebron jar inscr. 1 (unless כֹּחֵל wine of *Kohel*).

<PREP> לְ *concerning*, + נטף hi. *drop*, i.e. preach Mc 2_{11}.

בְּ of place, *in*, + כבס pi. *wash* Gn 49_{11}; of instrument, *by (means of), with*, + סחר *trade* Ezk 27_{18} (or del. בְּ), גאל htp. *defile oneself* Dn 1_8; of cause, *on account of* 2 S 13_{28} Est 1_{10}, + שׁגה *reel* Is 28_7; partitive, *(some) of, from* (among) Ne 5_{18}, + שׁתה *drink* Pr 9_5; *in exchange for*, + נתן *give* Dt 14_{26}, מכר *sell* Jl 4_3; *for (the price of)*, + לקח *take* Ne 5_{15} (or em. בְּ to בְּלוֹ *gift of* bread and wine, and/or del. יַיִן); introducing object, + משׁך *draw* Ec 2_3.

כְּ *as* Ho 14_8 Jb 32_{19} Ca 7_{10}, appar. + המה *be boisterous* (or em. וְשָׁתוּ הָמוּ *and they will drink, they were boisterous* to וְשָׁתוּ דָם/דָמָם *and they will drink [their] blood* as though it were wine); *as though it were*, + שׁתה *drink* Zc 9_{15} (כְּמוֹ), שׂמח *rejoice* Zc 10_7 (כְּמוֹ *as though* their heart *were full of* wine).

מִן of direction, *from*, + יקץ *awake* from stupor Gn 9_{24}=4QCommGenA 1.2_5, נזר hi. *abstain* Nm 6_3; of possession, *of, (belonging) to* Ho 7_5 (חֲמַת מִיַּיִן *heat of wine*; or em. חֲמָתָם יַיִן *their poison is wine*), of instrument, *by (means of)*, + רון htpo. *be overcome* Ps 78_{65} (unless רנן htpol. *cry out* on account of); partitive, *(some) of* 11QT 34_{13}, + שׁתה *drink* Gn 9_{21} Jr 51_7, שׁקה hi. *cause to drink* Ca 8_2, נתן *give* Arad ost. 1_9 3_2, מנה pi. *appoint* Dn 1_5; of cause, *on account of* Is 51_{21}, + בלע ni. *be confused* Is 28_7; comparative, *(more) than* Gn 49_{12} (unless מִן of cause) Ca 1_2 4_{10}, + זכר hi. *mention*, i.e. extol Ca 1_4, ערב *be sweet* 4QapJoseph[b] 3_5.

נגע אֶל *touch* Hg 2_{12}.

עַל *over* Is 24_{11}, + אחר pi. *delay* Pr 23_{30}, מנה pu. *be appointed* 1 C 9_{29}, גבר htp. *display arrogance* Si 34_{25} (perh. עַל = *on account of* or *concerning*); *in addition to*, + קרב hi. *present* 11QT 19_{15}.

<COLL> יַיִן (...) לַנֶּסֶךְ *wine for a drink offering* Nm $15_{5.7.10}$ 11QT 18_6 19_{14}; לְהַרְבֵּה + יַיִן *as an abundance* Ne 5_{18}, לָרֹב *in abundance* 1 C 12_{41}.

שָׁכְרוּ וְלֹא־יַיִן *become drunk but not (with) wine* Is 29_9, כָּל־נֵבֶל יִמָּלֵא יָיִן *every jar will be filled (with) wine* Jr 13_{12}. 12, גְּבִעִים מְלֵאִים יַיִן *cups filled (with) wine* Jr 35_5 (or em. גְּבִיעַ יַיִן *cup of wine*), יֵין חֶלְבּוֹן וְצֶמֶר צָחַר *wine of Helbon and tawny wool* Ezk 27_{18} (if em. דַּמֶּשֶׂק סֹחַרְתֵּךְ ... בְּיֵין חֶלְבּוֹן *Damascus trades (with) you ... in wine of Helbon* and tawny wool), הֶחֱלוּ שָׂרִים חֲמַת מִיָּיִן *the princes became ill (with) the heat that is from the wine* Ho 7_5 (or em. חֲמָתָם יַיִן with *their heat [which was caused by] wine* or em. יַיִן to יָדוֹ *his hand*), כּוֹס בְּיַד־י׳ יַיִן חָמַר מָלֵא מֶסֶךְ *a cup is in Y.'s hand, it foams with wine, it is full of mixed wine* Ps 75_9.

יַיִן || אִשָּׁה *woman* Si 19_2, שֵׁכָר *strong drink* Lv 10_9 Nm $6_{3.3}$ Dt 14_{26} 29_5 Jg $13_{4.7.14}$ 1 S 1_{15} Is 5_{22} 28_7 29_9 56_{12} Mc 2_{11} Pr 20_1 $31_{4.6}$ Si $40_{18(B).20}$, תִּירוֹשׁ *new wine* Ho 4_{11}, נֶסֶךְ *drink-offering* 11QT 21_{10}, מִנְחָה *offering* 11QT 34_{13}, חָלָב *milk* Is 55_1, חֵלֶב *fat* Dt 32_{38}, מַאֲכָל *food* 2 C 11_{11}, אֹכֶל *food* 11QT 47_6, מַשְׁקֶה *liquid* 11QT 47_6, לֶחֶם *bread* Gn 14_{18} Jg 19_{19} 1 S 25_{18} Hg 2_{12} Ps 104_{15} Pr 4_{17} Ec 9_7 Ne 5_{15} Si 34_{12} Lachish ost. 9_4 ([יין]), בָּשָׂר *flesh* Pr 23_{20} Dn 10_3, נָזִיד *stew* Hg 2_{12}, פַּתְבַּג *delicacies* Dn 1_5 (פַּת־בַּג) $1_{8.16}$, תַּעֲנוּג *delicacy* 4Q416 2.2_{19}, פְּרִי *fruit* Am 9_{14}, קַיִץ *summer fruit* Jr $40_{10.12}$, צִמּוּק *bunch of raisins* 1 C 12_{41}, עֵנָב *grape* Ne 13_{15}, תְּאֵנָה *fig* Ne 13_{15}, דְּבֵלָה *fig-cake* 1 C 12_{41}, גֶּפֶן *vine* Ho 14_8, שֶׁמֶן *oil* Jr 40_{10} Hg 2_{12} Pr 21_{17} (יַיִן־וְשֶׁמֶן) 1 C 9_{29} 12_{41} (יַיִן־וְשֶׁמֶן) 2 C $2_{9.14}$ 11_{11} 11QT 18_6 ([שמן]) 43_{15} 47_6 49_{12}, סֹלֶת *flour* 1 C 9_{29}, קֶמַח *flour* 1 C 12_{41} Arad ost. 8_5 (קם), בֹּשֶׂם *spice* 1 C 9_{29}, דָּגָן *corn* 4QOrd[b] 1.1_4 11QT 43_{15}, חִטָּה *wheat* 2 C $2_{9.14}$, שְׂעֹרָה *barley* 2 C $2_{9.14}$, בָּקָר *cattle* Dt 14_{26} 1 C 12_{41} 11QT 43_{15}, פַּר *young bull* 11QT 34_{13}, נֵתַח *piece* 11QT 34_{13}, צֹאן *flock* Dt 14_{26} 1 C 12_{41} 11QT 43_{15}, צֶמֶר *wool* Ezk 27_{18}, כִּנּוֹר *lyre* Is 5_{12}, נֵבֶל *lute* Is 5_{12}, תֹּף *timbrel* Is 5_{12}, חָלִיל *flute* Is 5_{12}, לְבוֹנָה *incense* 1 C 9_{29}, כְּלִי *vessel* 1 C 9_{29}, לֵחָה *liquid* 11QT 49_{12}.

יַיִן + שֵׁכָר *strong drink* Is 5_{11} 24_9 28_7 11QT 21_{10}, תִּירוֹשׁ *new wine* Mc 6_{15}=1QpMic 17-18_3 Si $34_{25.27}$ 11QT 43_7, מֵישָׁר appar. *new wine* Ca 1_4 7_{10}, מִמְסָךְ *mixed drink* Pr 23_{30}, דָּם *blood* of grapes Gn 49_{11}, עֵנָב *grape* 11QT 21_7, חָלָב *milk* Gn 49_{12} Ca 5_1, יַעַר *honeycomb* Ca 5_1, דְּבַשׁ *honey* Ca 5_1, דָּגָן *corn* 11QT 43_7, אֹכֶל *food* 4Q416 2.2_{19} =4Q417 1.2_{24}, לֶחֶם *bread* Ec 10_{19}, זֵרֹעַ *vegetable* Dn 1_{16}, שֶׁמֶן *oil* Ps 104_{15} Ca 4_{10} 11QT 43_7, יִצְהָר *fresh oil* 11QT 43_7, אוֹב *wineskin* Jb 32_{19}, כּוֹס *cup* Pr 23_{31} 4Q416 2.2_{19} =4Q417 1.2_{24}, גֶּפֶן *vine* 11QT 21_7, כֶּרֶם *vineyard* Dt 28_{39} Is 16_{10} Jr 48_{33} Am 5_{11} 9_{14} Zp 1_{13} (unless del.) 1 C 27_{27}, עַיִן *eye* Gn 49_{21}, דּוֹד *love* Ca $1_{2.4}$ 4_{10}, עוֹלָה *burnt offering* 11QT 19_{15}.

Also perh. Ps 141_5 (יָנִי perh. *my wine*, unless *let it* not *frustrate*, as mss יָנִיא; or em. יָנְאָ *let it not befit*, from נאה)* Samaria ost. 44_3.

<SYN> אִשָּׁה *woman*, שֵׁכָר *intoxicating drink*, חָלָב *milk*, חֵלֶב *fat*, לֶחֶם *bread*, מַאֲכָל *food*, בָּשָׂר *flesh*, נָזִיד *stew*, פַּתְבַּג *delicacies*, קַיִץ *summer fruit*, עֵנָב *grape*, צִמּוּק *bunch of raisins*, תְּאֵנָה *fig*, דְּבֵלָה *fig-cake*, שֶׁמֶן *oil*, סֹלֶת *flour*,

קֶמַח *flour,* בֹּשֶׂם *spice,* דָּגָן *corn,* חִטָּה *wheat,* שְׂעֹרָה *barley,* גֶּפֶן *vine,* בָּקָר *cattle,* צֹאן *flock,* כִּנּוֹר *lyre,* נֶבֶל *lute,* צֶמֶר *wool,* לְבוֹנָה *incense,* כְּלִי *vessel,* לֵחָה *liquid.**

[יִישׁוֹר] $_{0.0.1}$ n.[m.] **uprightness—**cstr Q יישור—<CSTR> יישור אמתכה *the uprightness of your truth* 1QH 6$_{10}$ (others יושיר or יושור, i.e. יֹשֶׁר *uprightness*). <PREP> כְּ *in accordance with,* + שפט *judge* 1QH 6$_{10}$.

יַד (1 S 4$_{13}$), see יָד *hand.*

*יכה $_1$ vb. **crouch—Ho.** $_1$ Impf. 3mpl תֻּכּוּ (unless תכה pu. *be led, be assembled*)—**crouch,** <SUBJ> קָדוֹשׁ *holy one* Dt 33$_3$. <PREP> לְ *at,* + רֶגֶל *foot* Dt 33$_3$.

יְכָנְיָה, see יְכָנְיָה *Jeconiah.*

יכח $_{59.1.37}$ vb. **contend—Ni.** $_{3.1}$ Impf. נִוָּכְחָה; ptc. נוֹכָח, נֹכַחַת (Si נכוחה)—**be justified** (Gn 20$_{16}$), **be adjudged, be understood** (Si 6$_{22[B]}$), **reason together** (Is 1$_{18}$), appar. **be acquitted** (Jb 23$_7$), <SUBJ> Y. Is 1$_{18}$, Israel(ites) Is 1$_{18}$, Sarah Gn 20$_{16}$, יָשָׁר *just one* Jb 23$_7$, מוּסָר *discipline* Si 6$_{22}$ (2Q18 [המוסר ... היא נ]כח). <PREP> לְ of agent, *by (means of),* + רַבִּים *many* Si 6$_{22(A)}$ (נְכוֹחָה, i.e. נוֹכְחָה she is *adjudged;* Segal נְכוֹחָה she is *straightforward;* 2Q18 [נ]כח *he is straightforward*); עִם *by,* + אֱלוֹהַּ *God* Jb 23$_7$; perh. אֵת *in the presence of,* + כֹּל *all* Gn 20$_{16}$.

Hi. $_{54.0.36}$ Pf. הוֹכִיחַ (הוֹכַח, הֹכִיחַ, Q הוכיחו), הֹכַחְתָּ (Q הוכחתה), הֹכַחְתִּיו; impf. יוֹכִיחַ (יוֹכַח, יוֹכִיחֶךָ, יוֹכִחֵנִי), יוֹכִחֵנוּ, Q יוכיחנו), 2ms תּוֹכִיחַ (תּוֹכַח, תּוֹכִיחֵנִי), אוֹכִיחַ (אוֹכִיחֲךָ, אוֹכִיחֶךָ), יוֹכִיחוּ, תּוֹכִיחוּ (תּוֹכִחֶךָ); + waw וְהוֹכִיחַ; Sam ויוכיח (וַיּוֹכַח); impv. הוֹכַח; ptc. מוֹכִיחַ (1QpHab מוכיחו), מוֹכִיחִים, Q מוכיחי; inf. הוֹכֵחַ, הוֹכִיחַ, הוֹכַח—**1. give reproof, reprove** (Gn 21$_{25}$ Lv 19$_{17.17}$ 2 S 7$_{14}$ Jr 2$_{19}$ Ezk 3$_{26}$ Ho 4$_4$ Ps 6$_2$ 38$_2$ 50$_{8.21}$ 94$_{10}$ 105$_{14}$||1 C 16$_{21}$ 141$_5$ Jb 5$_{17}$ 6$_{25.25}$ 13$_{10.10}$ 19$_5$ 22$_4$ 40$_2$ Pr 3$_{12}$ 9$_{7.8.8}$ 15$_{12}$ 19$_{25}$ 25$_{12}$ 28$_{23}$ 30$_6$ 1QH 6$_4$ 9$_{23}$ 12$_{28}$ 18$_{12}$ fr. 2$_6$ 1QS 5$_{24.26}$ 1QSb 5$_{22}$ 4QCommGenA 4$_5$ 4QapJoseph[b] 1$_{28}$ 4Q418 222$_3$ 4QHod[f] 3$_2$ 4QPseud[b] 5.1$_6$ 4QRebukes 1.2$_{5.7}$ 4QShir[b] 18.2$_8$ CD 7$_2$ 20$_{4.17}$), **correct** (Jb 6$_{26}$), **appoint** (Gn 24$_{14.44}$),* **decide** (Gn 31$_{37}$ Is 11$_3$ Jb 9$_{33}$ 16$_{21}$), **give justice** (Gn 31$_{42}$ Is 2$_4$||Mc 4$_3$ 11$_4$ Pr 10$_{10}$ [if em.; see Subj.]), **administer justice** (2 K 19$_4$||Is 37$_4$ Is 29$_{21}$ Am 5$_{10}$ Hb 1$_{12}$=1QpHab 5$_1$ Pr 24$_{25}$ 1 C 12$_{18}$), **argue** (Jb 13$_{3.15}$ 15$_3$ 32$_{12}$ 1QS 9$_{16.17}$ 4QAdmonPar 3.2$_7$), **plead, defend oneself** (1QH 1$_{25}$), **declare, acknowledge (as just)** (1QS 10$_{11}$).

<SUBJ> Y. Gn 24$_{14.44}$ 2 S 7$_{14}$ 2 K 19$_4$||Is 37$_4$ Is 2$_4$||Mc 4$_3$ Ps 6$_2$ 38$_2$ 105$_{14}$||1 C 16$_{21}$ Pr 3$_{12}$ 30$_6$ (if em.; see below), שַׁדַּי *Shaddai* Jb 22$_4$, אֵל *God* Jb 13$_{10.10}$ 1QH 9$_{23}$ perh. 18$_{12}$ 1QSb 5$_{22}$ (ל[א]ל ... [ל]הוכיח), אֱלֹהִים *God* Gn 24$_{14}$ 31$_{42}$ 2 K 19$_4$||Is 37$_4$ Is 2$_4$||Mc 4$_3$ Ps 50$_{8.21}$ 1 C 12$_{18}$, אֱלוֹהַּ *God* Jb 5$_{17}$ Pr 30$_6$ (or em. אֱלוֹהַּ *God* to ׳י *Y.*) perh. 4QAdmonPar 3.2$_7$, צוּר *rock,* i.e. God Hb 1$_{12}$=1QpHab 5$_1$, Abraham Gn 21$_{25}$, Eliphaz Jb 6$_{26}$, Job Jb 13$_3$, Jacob 4QCommGenA 4$_5$, Job's comforters Jb 19$_5$, אֱנוֹשׁ *human being* 1QH 1$_{25}$, אִישׁ *man* Ezk 3$_{26}$ Ho 4$_4$ 1QS 5$_{24.26}$ 4QS[d] 3.3$_{1.2}$ CD 7$_2$ 10$_4$, בֵּן *son* of Israel Lv 19$_{17(mss).17(mss)}$=CD 9$_{7.7}$, אָח *brother* Gn 31$_{37}$, יסר ptc. *one who disciplines* Ps 94$_{10}$, צַדִּיק *righteous one* Ps 141$_5$, חָכָם *wise one* Jb 15$_3$, recipient of wisdom Pr 9$_{8.8}$ 15$_{12}$ 19$_{25}$, מַשְׂכִּיל *instructor* 1QS 10$_{11}$, עֵדָה *congregation* Lv 19$_{17.17}$ (mss lack עֵדָה in both), חֹטֶר *shoot* Is 11$_{3.4}$, נֵצֶר *shoot* Is 11$_{3.4}$, מְשׁוּבָה *apostasy* Jr 2$_{19}$, עֵדוּת *testimony* 4QapJoseph[b] 1$_{28}$, הוֹכֵחַ *reproof* Jb 6$_{25}$ (see §2); subj. not specified, (1) ptc. מוֹכִיחַ *one who reproves* Is 29$_{21}$ Am 5$_{10}$ Jb 9$_{33}$ 32$_{12}$ 40$_2$ Pr 10$_{10}$ (if em. וֶאֱוִיל שְׂפָתַיִם יִלָּבֵט *and one who is foolish of lips will be thrust down* to וּמוֹכִיחַ יַעֲשֶׂה שָׁלוֹם *but one who adjudges rightly will make peace*) 24$_{25}$ 25$_{12}$ 28$_{23}$ 1QH 6$_4$ 12$_{28}$ fr. 2$_6$ 4QHod[f] 3$_2$ 4QShir[b] 18.2$_8$ CD 20$_{17}$; (2) other, 1QS 9$_{16.17}$.

<OBJ> אֱלוֹהַּ *God* Jb 40$_2$, Abimelech Gn 21$_{25}$, Hananiah Notos 4QRebukes 1.2$_5$, Joseph 4QapJoseph[b] 1$_{28}$, Reuben 4QCommGenA 4$_5$, Tobijah 4QRebukes 1.2$_7$ ([טוביה] ... יוכ[י]חו), Zophar Jb 13$_{10}$, Israel(ites) Ps 50$_{8.21}$, appar. Jr 2$_{19}$ Hb 1$_{12}$=1QpHab 5$_1$, psalmist Ps 6$_2$ 38$_2$ 141$_5$, אָדָם *human being* Pr 28$_{23}$, אִישׁ *man* CD 20$_4$, אֱנוֹשׁ *person* Jb 5$_{17}$, בֵּן *son* 4QRebukes 1.2$_7$ ([בן] ... יוכ[י]חו), נַעֲרָה *girl* Gn 24$_{14}$, אִשָּׁה *woman, wife* Gn 24$_{44}$, אָח *brother* CD 7$_2$ 9$_7$, עָמִית *companion* Lv 19$_{17}$, רֵעַ *neighbour* 1QS 5$_{24.26}$, זֶרַע *offspring* 2 S 7$_{14}$, מֶלֶךְ *king* Ps 105$_{14}$||1 C 16$_{21}$, לֵץ *scoffer* Pr 9$_8$, פֹּשֵׁעַ *transgressor* 4Q418 222$_3$, מִלָּה *word* Jb 6$_{26}$, מִשְׁפָּט *judgment* 1QS 10$_{11}$, דֶּרֶךְ *way* Jb 13$_{15}$, מוּם *blemish* Pr 9$_7$, חֶרְפָּה *reproach* Jb 19$_5$, אֲשֶׁר *one whom* Y.

loves Pr 3$_{12}$; obj. not specified, Ps 94$_{10}$.

<PREP> לְ of benefit, *for*, + Isaac Gn 24$_{14}$, בֵּן *son* Gn 24$_{44}$, עֶבֶד *servant* Gn 24$_{14}$; administer justice *to, for*, + עָנָו *poor one* Is 11$_{4}$, עַם *people* Is 2$_{4}$ (|| Mc 4$_{3}$, + גּוֹי *nation*); *on behalf of*, + גֶּבֶר *man*; Jb 16$_{21}$; *before, in the presence of*, + רֵעַ *companion* Jb 16$_{21}$; *in accordance with*, + מִשְׁמָע *report* Is 11$_{3}$; argue *against*, + Job Jb 32$_{12}$; introducing indirect object, + רָשָׁע *wicked one* Pr 9$_{7}$, חָכָם *wise one* Pr 9$_{8}$, לֵץ *scoffer* Pr 15$_{12}$, בין ni. ptc. *intelligent one* Pr 19$_{25}$, יֵצֶר *form* 1QH 18$_{12}$.

בְּ of place/time, *in, at, during*, + שַׁעַר *gate* Is 29$_{21}$ Am 5$_{10}$, יוֹם *day* 1QS 5$_{26}$; of instrument, *with, by (means of)*, + דָּבָר *word* Jb 15$_{3}$, מִלָּה *word* Jb 15$_{3}$, שֵׁבֶט *rod* 2 S 7$_{14}$, נֶגַע *blow* 2 S 7$_{14}$; of accompaniment, *with, in (a state of)*, + אַף *anger* Ps 6$_{2}$, קֶצֶף *anger* Ps 38$_{2}$, מִישׁוֹר *uprightness* Is 11$_{4}$ 1QSb 5$_{22}$ ([ל]הוכיח במי[שור]), אֱמֶת *truth* 1QS 5$_{24}$ (א[מ]ת), צֶדֶק *righteousness* CD 20$_{17}$, עֲנָוָה *humility* 1QS 5$_{24}$, אַהֲבָה *love* 1QS 5$_{24}$, אֱמוּנָה *faithfulness* 2QapMoses 1$_{2}$ (באמ[ו]נה), רָז *mystery* 1QH 9$_{23}$; *on account of*, + דָּבָר *word, matter*, 2 K 19$_{4}$||Is 37$_{4}$; introducing object, + Ithiel Pr 30$_{6}$ (or em. אִיתִיאֵל *Ithiel* to לָאִיתִי אֵל *I am weary, O God*, or לְאֵה אֶת־[הָ]אֵל *one who has wearied himself with God* or לֹא אָנֹכִי/אֲנִי אֵל *I am not God* or לֹא אִתִּי אֵל *God is not with me* or לוּ אִתִּי אֵל *if only God were with me*), Ucal Pr 30$_{6}$ (or em. וְאֻכָל *and Ucal* to וָאֵכֶל *and I am exhausted* or וָאֻכָל *and I have endured* or וְאֻכָל *that I should prevail* or וַיּוּכָל *and he has prevailed*), recipient of wisdom Pr 30$_{1}$ (if em.; see above), worshipper 1QH 9$_{23}$, perh. בֵּן *son* 4Q474 1$_{3}$ ([י]כח), עָפָר *dust* 1QH 12$_{28}$.

כְּ *in accordance with*, + מִצְוָה *commandment* CD 7$_{2}$, נַעֲוָה *iniquity* 1QS 10$_{11}$, מַעַל *unfaithfulness* CD 20$_{4}$ (כְּפִי *in accordance with*).

מִן *on account of*, + יִרְאָה *fear* Jb 22$_{4}$; אֶל *in the presence of, before*, + פָּנִים pl. *faces* Jb 13$_{15}$; *against*, i.e. with, + אֵל *God* Jb 13$_{3}$; עַל *on account of*, + appar. Israel(ites) Ps 105$_{14}$||1 C 16$_{21}$, זֶבַח *sacrifice* Ps 50$_{2}$, זנח hi. inf. *stench* (or perh. *rejection*) 4QPseud^{b} 5.1$_{6}$; *against*, + Job Jb 19$_{5}$; *concerning*, + עָוֹן *iniquity* 1QH 1$_{25}$; עִם *with* 4QAdmonPar 3.2$_{7}$, + אֱלוֹהַּ *God* Jb 16$_{21}$, בֶּן *son* Jb 16$_{21}$ (or em. וּבֶן־אָדָם *and with a son of a person* on behalf of his companion to וּבֵין־אָדָם *and between a person* and their companion); בֵּין *between*, + Bildad Jb 9$_{33}$, Job Jb 9$_{33}$, בֵּן *son* Jb 16$_{21}$ (if em.; see עִם *with*), שְׁנַיִם *two*, i.e. the two of us Gn 31$_{37}$; עַל־אוֹדוֹת *concerning*, + בְּאֵר *well* Gn 21$_{25}$.

<COLL> אֲשֶׁר בְּהַעֲוֹתוֹ וְהוֹכַחְתִּיו *whom, when he sins, I shall reprove* 2 S 7$_{14}$; יכח hi. with noun used adverbially, אֶמֶשׁ *evening*, i.e. last night Gn 31$_{42}$, דַּעַת *(with) knowledge* 1QS 9$_{17}$, מִשְׁפָּט *(with) judgment* 1QS 9$_{17}$; יכח hi. || שׁפט *judge* Is 11$_{3.4}$ CD 20$_{17}$, יסר pi. *discipline* Jr 2$_{19}$ Ho 4$_{4}$ Ps 6$_{2}$ 38$_{2}$, ריב htpol. *dispute* 1QS 9$_{16}$; + שׁפט *judge* Is 2$_{4}$||Mc 4$_{3}$.

<SYN> שׁפט *judge*, יסר pi. *discipline*, ריב *contend*.

2. inf. appar. as noun, **reproof, rebuke,** <SUBJ> יכח hi. *reprove* Jb 6$_{25}$ (וּמַה־יּוֹכִיחַ הוֹכֵחַ מִכֶּם *but how does reproof from you reprove?*). <CSTR> הוכח הכשר *rebuke of propriety* 4Q417 1.1$_{2}$. <PREP> בְּ of accompaniment, *with* 4QS^{d} 1.2$_{6}$ (=1QS 6$_{1}$ בתוכחת *with rebuke*) 4QD^{a} 7.1$_{4}$ CD 9$_{3}$, + ידע hi. *make known* CD 9$_{18}$; בְּלֹא *without* 4Q417 1.1$_{2}$. <COLL> הוכח לפני עדים *rebuke before witnesses* 4QS^{d} 1.2$_{6}$ (ע[דים]; =1QS 6$_{1}$ בתוכחת *with rebuke*) CD 9$_{3}$, הוכיח למבקר *rebuke before the overseer* CD 9$_{18}$.

Also 4QBer^{a} 20$_{2}$ 4QapPent 10.1$_{9}$ 4QapJoseph^{b} 18$_{2}$ 4QRebukes 1.1$_{3}$ 2$_{1}$.

Ho. 1 Pf. הוּכַח—**be reproved,** <SUBJ> אִישׁ *man* 4QWays^{b} 1a.2$_{11}$ ([איש י]וכח), גֶּבֶר *man* Jb 33$_{19}$, psalmist Ps 73$_{14}$ (if em. תּוֹכַחְתִּי *my reproof* to הוּכַחְתִּי *I have been reproved*). <PREP> לְ of place/time, *in, at, during*, + בֹּקֶר *morning* Ps 73$_{14}$ (if em.); בְּ of instrument, *by (means of)*, + מַכְאוֹב *pain* Jb 33$_{19}$; עַל *upon*, + מִשְׁכָּב *bed* Jb 33$_{19}$. <COLL> [י]וכח תוכחת משכיל *he shall be reproved (with) the reproof of the instructor* 4QWays^{b} 1a.2$_{11}$.

Htp. 1.0.1 Impf. יִתְוַכָּח; inf. Q התוכח—**1. argue,** <SUBJ> Y. Mc 6$_{2}$. <PREP> עִם *with*, i.e. against, + Israel Mc 6$_{2}$.

2. inf. cstr. as noun, **argument, controversy,** <PREP> בְּ of accompaniment, *with, in*, + עמד *stand* 4QapPs^{b} 76$_{10}$. <COLL> התוכח עמ[ו] *controversy with him* (Y.) 4QapPs^{b} 76$_{10}$.*

→ תּוֹכֵחָה *reproof*, תּוֹכַחַת *reproof*.

יכיליה, see יְכָלְיָהוּ *Jecoliah*.

יָכִין 8.0.6 pr.n.m. **Jachin, 1.** son of Simeon, appar. ident. with יָרִיב *Jarib* at 1 C 4$_{24}$, <NOM CL> בְּנֵי שִׁמְעוֹן ... יָכִין

the sons of Simeon were … Jachin Gn 46$_{10}$ Ex 6$_{15}$. <PREP> לְ of possession, *of, (belonging) to* Nm 26$_{12}$.

2. priest of David's time, eponymous ancestor of priestly family, מִן־הַכֹּהֲנִים ... יָכִין *of the priests was … Jachin* 1 C 9$_{10}$ (or em. וִיהוֹיָרִיב וְיָכִין: וַעֲזַרְיָה *and Jehoiarib, and Jachin, and Azariah* to יְהוֹיָרִיב בֶּן־עֲזַרְיָה בֶּן־יְהוֹיָקִים *Jehoiarib, the son of Azariah, the son of Jehoiakim*). <PREP> לְ of direction, *to*, + יצא (of lot) *go out* 1 C 24$_{17}$.

3. priestly course (derived from §2) and its period of office, <PREP> בְּ of time, *in, at, during* 4QOtot 1.8$_3$ 4QMishA 1.3$_{12}$ 4.6$_{10}$ 4QMishB^a 2.1$_2$ 2.2$_7$ 2.3$_2$.

4. head of postexilic priestly family, <NOM CL> מִן־הַכֹּהֲנִים ... יָכִין *of the priests was … Jachin* Ne 11$_{10}$ (or em. יוֹיָרִיב יָכִין *Joiarib, Jachin* to יוֹיָקִים בֶּן־ *Joiakim, the son of*). <APP> בֶּן *son* Ne 11$_{10}$ (or em.; see Nom. Cl.).

5. right-hand pillar before temple, perh. first word of prayer at the pillar, or inscription on the pillar.* <OBJ> קרא *call* name 1 K 7$_{21}$||2 C 3$_{17}$.

⇒ י׳ *Y.* + כון *be established*; יָכִינִי *Jachinite*.

יָכִינִי 1 gent. **Jachinite,** collective for descendants of Jachin, <CSTR> מִשְׁפַּחַת הַיָּכִינִי *family of the Jachinites* Nm 26$_{12}$.

⇒ יָכִין *Jachin*.

יכל 207.4.19.1 vb. **be able—Qal** 207.4.19.1 Pf. יָכֹל (יָכוֹל), יָכְלָה, יָכֹלְתִּי (יָכָלְתִּיו), יָכְלוּ (יָכְלוּ); impf. יוּכַל (יוּכָל), 3fs תּוּכַל, 2ms תּוּכַל (תּוּכָל), תּוּכְלִי, אוּכַל (אוּכָל), יוּכְלוּ (יוּכָלוּ, יָכְלוּ, יָכָלוּ, יוּכְלוּן), תּוּכְלוּ, נוּכַל (נוּכְלָה); + waw וַיֻּכַל, וְיָכָלְתָּ, 2ms וַתּוּכַל; ptc. I יכלם; inf. abs. יָכֹל (יָכוֹל), inf. cstr. יְכֹלֶת—**1. be able,** usu. in negative or conditional clause and in ref. to physical ability, but also to what is permitted by custom (e.g. Gn 34$_{14}$ 43$_{32}$ Jg 21$_{18}$ Ru 4$_6$), law (e.g. Dt 12$_{17}$ 16$_5$ 17$_{15}$ 21$_{16}$ 22$_{3.19.29}$), ritual purity (Nm 9$_6$), reverence, awe (e.g. Ex 19$_{23}$ 33$_{20}$ 40$_{35}$ 1 K 8$_{11}$||2 C 5$_{14}$ 2 C 7$_2$), and will (e.g. Gn 19$_{22}$ Nm 22$_{18}$ 24$_{13}$).

<SUBJ> Y. Gn 19$_{22}$ Nm 14$_{16}$ Dt 9$_{28}$ Jr 18$_6$ 44$_{22}$ Hb 1$_{13}$ Ps 78$_{19.20}$, 2 C 32$_{14}$, אֱלֹהִים *god* 2 C 32$_{13.13.14.15}$, Bel Is 46$_2$, Nebo Is 46$_2$, Israel(ites) Ex 15$_{23}$ Dt 7$_{17.22}$ 12$_{17}$ 14$_{24}$ 16$_5$ 17$_{15}$ 22$_3$ 28$_{27.35}$ Jg 2$_{14}$, Egypt(ians) Gn 43$_{32}$ Ex 7$_{21.24}$, Judah Jg 1$_{19}$ (if ins. יָכְלוּ *they were* not *able*) Ne 4$_4$, בֵּית *house* of Israel and Judah Jr 11$_{11}$, עַם *people* Ex 19$_{23}$ Jos 7$_{13}$ 24$_{19}$, קָהָל *assembly* 2 C 30$_3$, Abram Gn 13$_6$ 15$_5$, Ahijah 1 K 14$_4$, Ahimaaz 2 S 17$_{17}$, Balak Nm 22$_{6.11.37}$, Balaam Nm 22$_{18.38}$ 24$_{13}$, Boaz Ru 4$_6$, David 1 S 17$_{33.39}$ 2 S 12$_{23}$ 1 K 5$_{17}$ 1 C 21$_{30}$, Eli 1 S 3$_2$ 4$_{15}$, Esau Jr 49$_{10}$, Ezekiel Ezk 47$_5$, Gemariah Arad ost. 40$_{14}$, Gideon Jg 8$_3$, Hezekiah 2 K 18$_{23.29}$||Is 36$_{8.14}$, Ish-bosheth 2 S 3$_{11}$, Israel (Jacob) Gn 48$_{10}$, Jephthah Jg 11$_{35}$, Jeremiah Jr 20$_9$ 36$_5$, Jeroboam 1 K 13$_4$, Job Jb 33$_5$, Jonathan 2 S 17$_{17}$, Joseph Gn 45$_1$, Laban Gn 24$_{50}$, Lot Gn 13$_6$ 19$_{19}$, Moses Ex 18$_{18.23}$ 33$_{20}$ 40$_{35}$ Nm 11$_{14}$ Dt 1$_9$ 31$_2$, Nehemiah Ne 6$_3$ Arad ost. 40$_{14}$, Pekah 2 K 16$_5$=Is 7$_1$, Rachel Gn 31$_{35}$, Rezin 2 K 16$_5$=Is 7$_1$.

אָדָם *human being* Ec 6$_{10}$ 8$_{17}$, אֱנוֹשׁ *human being* 1QH 15$_{13}$, אִישׁ *man* Gn 13$_{16}$ 44$_1$ Nm 9$_6$ 13$_{31}$ Dt 21$_{16}$ 22$_{19.29}$ 1 S 17$_9$ 1 K 13$_{16}$ 2 K 3$_{26}$ Jon 1$_{13}$ Ec 1$_8$ 4QShir^b 30$_6$ 11QT 66$_{11}$, בַּעַל *husband* Dt 24$_4$, אִשָּׁה *woman* Ex 2$_3$, אָב *father* 1 K 5$_{17}$, בֵּן *son* Gn 34$_{14}$ Nm 22$_{6.11}$ Jos 15$_{63}$ 17$_{12}$ 2 K 4$_{40}$ 16$_5$=Is 7$_1$ Ezr 2$_{59}$||Ne 7$_{61}$ Arad ost. 40$_{14}$, of Israel Ex 12$_{39}$ Jos 7$_{12}$ Jg 21$_{18}$ 1 K 9$_{21}$, בַּת *daughter* Is 47$_{11.12}$, אָח *brother* Gn 29$_8$ 37$_4$ 44$_{26.26}$ 45$_3$, נַעַר *lad* Gn 44$_{22}$, מֶלֶךְ *king* Nm 22$_{6.11}$ 1 K 20$_9$ 2 K 16$_5$=Is 7$_1$ Ho 5$_{13}$ 2 C 30$_3$, שַׂר *prince* 2 C 30$_3$, נָשִׂיא *prince* Jos 9$_{19}$, גִּבּוֹר *mighty one* Jr 14$_9$ (or em. כְּגִבּוֹר *as a mighty one* to כְּגֶבֶר *as a man*), עֶבֶד *servant* Dn 10$_{17}$, חַרְטֹם *magician* Ex 8$_{14}$ 9$_{11}$, כֹּהֵן *priest* 1 K 8$_{11}$||2 C 5$_{14}$ Lm 4$_{14}$ 2 C 7$_2$ 29$_{34}$, נָבִיא *prophet* Lm 4$_{14}$, worshipper Ps 40$_{13}$ Lm 1$_{14}$ GnzPs 4$_{26}$, חָכָם *wise one* Ec 8$_{17}$, ידע ptc. *one who knows* Is 29$_{11}$, צֹפֶה *sentry* Is 56$_{10}$, צַדִּיק *righteous one* Ezk 33$_{12}$, שׂנא ptc. *one who hates* 4QMyst^a 6$_{24}$, אוֹיֵב *enemy* Ps 18$_{39}$, פעל ptc. *one who does* evil Ps 36$_{13}$, פתה ptc. *simple one* Si 8$_{17}$, לָמֵד *one accustomed to* Jr 13$_{23}$, אֹזֶן *ear* Jr 6$_{10}$.

אֶרֶץ *land* Gn 36$_7$ Am 7$_{10}$ Pr 30$_{21}$ 4QJub^d 21$_{19}$, יָם *sea* Is 57$_{20}$ Jr 49$_{23}$, מַיִם *water* Ca 8$_7$, כְּלִי *vessel* Jr 19$_{11}$, מִזְבֵּחַ *altar* 2 C 7$_7$, זָהָב *gold* Ezk 7$_{19}$ Zp 1$_{18}$, כֶּסֶף *silver* Ezk 7$_{19}$ Zp 1$_{18}$, נְכֹחָה *uprightness* Is 59$_{14}$, עות pu. ptc. *crooked thing* Ec 1$_{15}$, חֶסְרוֹן *deficiency* Ec 1$_{15}$, כֹּל *everyone* 1QH 7$_{29}$ 15$_{14}$, מִי *who?* 1 S 6$_{20}$ 1 K 3$_9$ Jb 4$_2$ Ec 7$_{13}$ Si 31$_{10}$ 1QS 11$_{20}$ 1QH 11$_{24}$ 4QM^h 6$_5$, אֵלֶּה *these* Ezr 2$_{59}$||Ne 7$_{61}$; subject not specified, Ex 10$_5$ Jg 14$_{13.14}$ 1QH 15$_{21}$ 16$_2$ ([יוכ]ל) fr. 1$_2$ 4QpIsa^c 57$_1$ 4QpZeph 1$_2$ 4QJub^f 12$_2$ 11QT 43$_{13.13}$.

<PREP> מִפְּנֵי *on account of*, + מִקְנֶה *cattle* Gn 36$_7$, שְׁחִין *boil* Ex 9$_{11}$, מִלְחָמָה *war* 1 K 5$_{17}$.

<COLL> **a.** (1) followed by inf. cstr. + לְ of חיה *live* Ezk 33$_{12}$, דבר pi. *speak* Ec 1$_8$ Dn 10$_{17}$, ענה *answer* Gn 45$_3$, נגד hi. *tell* Jg 14$_{13.14}$ Ezr 2$_{59}$||Nc 7$_{61}$, ספר pi. *relate* 1QH 11$_{24}$, נבח *bark* Is 56$_{10}$, ראה *see* Gn 44$_{26}$ 48$_{10}$ Ex 10$_5$ 33$_{20}$ 1 S 3$_2$ 4$_{15}$ 1 K 14$_4$ Ps 40$_{13}$, ni. *be seen* 2 S 17$_{17}$, אפק htp. *restrain oneself* Gn 45$_1$, קשב hi. *pay attention* Jr 6$_{10}$, שפט *judge* 1 K 3$_9$, דין *contend* Ec 6$_{10}$, מנה ni. *be counted* Ec 1$_{15}$, מהה htpalp. *wait* Ex 12$_{39}$, יצב htp. *position oneself* 1QH 7$_{29}$, ישב *dwell* Gn 13$_6$, הלך *go* 1 S 17$_{33.39}$ 1 C 21$_{30}$, בוא *come* Ex 40$_{35}$ Dt 31$_2$ Is 59$_{14}$ Jr 36$_5$ 2 C 7$_2$, hi. *bring* Nm 14$_{16}$ Dt 9$_{28}$ 11QT 43$_{13}$, יצא *go out* Dt 31$_2$ Jr 11$_{11}$, עלה *go up* Ex 19$_{23}$ Nm 13$_{31}$, ירד *go down* Gn 44$_{26}$ Ne 6$_3$, קום *rise* Gn 31$_{35}$ Jos 7$_{12.13}$, עמד *stand* Ex 9$_{11}$ Jg 2$_{14}$ 1 S 6$_{20}$ 1 K 8$_{11}$||2 C 5$_{14}$ GnzPs 4$_{26}$, סור *turn aside* (intrans.) Si 34$_{10}$, שוב *go back* Dt 24$_4$ Jg 11$_{35}$ 1 K 13$_{16}$, hi. *bring back* 2 S 3$_{11}$ 12$_{23}$ 1 K 13$_4$, עבר *pass* Ezk 47$_5$, i.e. transgress Nm 22$_{18}$ 24$_{13}$, שלח *send* 11QT 66$_{11}$ Arad ost. 40$_{14}$, pi. *send away*, i.e. divorce Dt 22$_{19.29}$, עזב *leave* Gn 44$_{22}$, מלט ni. *escape* Gn 19$_{19}$, מצא *find* Ec 8$_{17.17}$, לחם ni. *fight* Nm 22$_{11}$ 1 S 17$_9$ 2 K 16$_5$=Is 7$_1$, ירש hi. *dispossess* Dt 7$_{17}$ Jos 15$_{63}$ 17$_{12}$ Jg 1$_{19}$ (in em.; see Subj.), חרם hi. *destroy* 1 K 9$_{21}$, כלה pi. *destroy* Dt 7$_{22}$, כבה pi. *extinguish* Ca 8$_7$, בכר pi. *regard as firstborn* Dt 21$_{16}$, נגע *touch* Jos 9$_{19}$, מנה *count* Gn 13$_{16}$, צפן hi. *hide* Ex 2$_3$, עלם htp. *hide oneself* Dt 22$_3$, כסה pi. *cover* Si 8$_{17}$, ספר *count* Gn 15$_5$, תכן pi. *measure* 4QShir[b] 30$_6$, רפא *heal* Ho 5$_{13}$, ni. *be healed* Dt 28$_{27.35}$, *be mended* Jr 19$_{11}$, תקן *be straight* Ec 1$_{15}$, pi. *make straight* Ec 7$_{13}$, אכל *eat* Gn 43$_{32}$ Dt 12$_{17}$ 2 K 4$_{40}$, שתה *drink* Ex 7$_{21.24}$ 15$_{23}$, זבח *sacrifice* Dt 16$_5$, נתן *give, place* Gn 34$_{14}$ Dt 17$_{15}$ Jg 21$_{18}$ 2 K 18$_{23}$||Is 36$_{14}$, נשא *bear* Gn 36$_7$ Nm 11$_{14}$ Jr 44$_{22}$ 11QT 43$_{13}$, כול hi. *contain* Am 7$_{10}$ 2 C 7$_7$, *direct* 1QS 11$_{20}$ 15$_{13.21}$, לקח *take* Dt 24$_4$, עשׂה *do* Gn 19$_{22}$ 34$_{14}$ Nm 9$_6$ Jg 8$_3$ 1 K 20$_9$ Jr 18$_6$ 2 C 30$_3$, רעע hi. *do evil* Si 34$_{10}$, עבד *serve* Jos 24$_{19}$, בנה *build* 1 K 5$_{17}$ Ne 4$_4$, ערך *arrange* Ps 78$_{19}$, שנה ni. *be repeated* 1QH 15$_{14}$, פשט hi. *flay* 2 C 29$_{34}$, נצל hi. *deliver* 2 K 18$_{29}$||Is 36$_{14}$ Ezk 7$_{19}$ Zp 1$_{18}$ 2 C 32$_{13.14.14.15}$, ישע hi. *save* Jr 14$_9$, גאל *redeem* Ru 4$_6$, יטב hi. *do good* Jr 13$_{23}$.

(2) followed by inf. cstr. without לְ of דבר pi. *speak* Gn 24$_{50}$ 37$_4$ Nm 22$_{38}$, קום *rise* Ps 18$_{39}$ 36$_{13}$ Lm 1$_{14}$, עמד *stand* Ex 18$_{23}$, נשא *bear* Gn 44$_1$ Dt 1$_9$ 14$_{24}$ Pr 30$_{21}$, יעל hi. *profit* Is 47$_{12}$, כבד pi. *honour* Nm 22$_{37}$, מלט pi. *deliver* Is 46$_2$, כפר pi. *expiate* Is 47$_{11}$, עשׂה *do* Ex 18$_{18}$, נתן *give* Ps 78$_{20}$.

(3) preceded by inf. cstr. without לְ of שׁקט hi. *be quiet* Is 57$_{20}$ Jr 49$_{23}$, עצר *restrain* Jb 4$_2$, נבט hi. *look* Hb 1$_{13}$.

(4) without inf. cstr., but with implied reference to preceding verb, e.g. נִלְאֵיתִי כַּלְכֵל וְלֹא אוּכָל *I am weary of holding it in, and I cannot* Jr 20$_9$, Gn 29$_8$ Ex 8$_{14}$ 2 K 3$_{26}$ Is 29$_{11}$ Jon 1$_{13}$ Si 43$_{30}$; with implied reference to following verb, אִם־תּוּכַל הֲשִׁיבֵנִי *if you are able, answer me* Jb 33$_5$.

(5) with preceding subordinated verb, וְנֶחְבָּה לֹא יוּכָל *and he is not able to hide himself* Jr 49$_{10}$ (or em. וְנַחְבֹּה, i.e. inf. abs.).

(6) with following subordinated verb, אוּלַי אוּכַל נַכֶּה־בּוֹ *perhaps I shall be able (so that) we shall defeat him* Nm 22$_6$ (or em. נוּכַל *we shall be able*), נְגֹאֲלוּ בַּדָּם בְּלֹא יוּכְלוּ יִגְּעוּ בִּלְבֻשֵׁיהֶם *they were so defiled with blood that none could touch their garments* Lm 4$_{14}$.

b. יכל + adverb, עוֹד *again* Ex 2$_3$ Dt 31$_2$ Jg 2$_{14}$ 2 S 3$_{11}$ Jr 44$_{22}$.

c. other collocations, מִבִּלְתִּי יְכֹלֶת *for lack of being able*, i.e. because he was unable Nm 14$_{16}$ Dt 9$_{28}$; inf. abs. + finite form of יכל, Nm 22$_{38}$ 2 C 32$_{13}$.

2. be capable of, attain, <SUBJ> Y. Jb 42$_2$, Israel(ites) Ho 8$_5$, מֶלֶךְ *king* Jr 38$_5$, worshipper Ps 139$_6$. <OBJ> נִקָּיוֹן *innocence* Ho 8$_5$, דָּבָר *thing* Jr 38$_5$, כֹּל *everything* Jb 42$_2$. <PREP> לְ introducing object, + דַּעַת *knowledge* Ps 139$_6$; אֵת *with*, i.e. against, + Gedaliah Jr 38$_5$, Pashhur Jr 38$_5$, Shephatiah Jr 38$_5$, בֵּן *son* Jr 38$_5$.

3. endure, a. trans., <SUBJ> Y. Is 1$_{13}$, worshipper Ps 101$_5$. <OBJ> גְּבַהּ *exalted one* Ps 101$_5$, רְחַב לֵבָב *one broad of heart*, i.e. arrogant Ps 101$_5$, אָוֶן *iniquity* Is 1$_{13}$, עֲצָרָה *solemn assembly* Is 1$_{13}$, קרא pi. inf. *proclaiming* of assemblies Is 1$_{13}$, חֹדֶשׁ *new moon* Is 1$_{13}$, שַׁבָּת *sabbath* Is 1$_{13}$.

b. intrans., <SUBJ> Esther Est 8$_{6.6}$, Job Jb 31$_{23}$. <PREP> מִן of cause, *on account of*, + שְׂאֵת *exaltation* Jb 31$_{23}$. <COLL> אֵיכָכָה אוּכַל וְרָאִיתִי *how can I endure and*, i.e. when, *I see?* Est 8$_{6.6}$.

4a. prevail, succeed, <SUBJ> Y. Jr 20$_7$, Israel(ites) Jr

3_{5}, Moab Is 16_{12}, Agur Pr 30_{1} (if em.; וְאֻכָל *and Ucal* to וָאֻכָל *and I prevailed*, or וַיּוּכָל *and he prevailed*), David 1 S $26_{25.25}$ (|| עשׂה *do*), Jacob Gn 32_{29} Ho 12_{5}, Rachel Gn 30_{8}, בֵּן *son* Zc 9_{15} (if em. אָכְלוּ *and they shall devour* to וְיָכְלוּ *and they shall prevail*) Pr 30_{1} (if em.; see above), רֹדֵף *persecutor* Jr 20_{11}, אוֹיֵב *enemy* Ps 13_{5} (if em.; see §4b Obj.) 21_{12}, שׂנא ptc. *one who hates* Ps 21_{12}, רוּחַ *spirit* 1 K 22_{22}||2 C 18_{21}, גַּל *wave* Jr 5_{22}. <COLL> inf. abs. + finite form of יכל, 1 S 26_{25}.

b. prevail (against), overcome, <SUBJ> Israel(ites) Nm $13_{30.30}$, עַם *people* Jr 1_{19} 15_{20}, Goliath 1 S 17_{9}, Jeremiah Jr 15_{16} (if em. וָאֹכְלֵם *and I ate them* to וָאוּכְלֵם *and I prevailed against them*), Haman Est 6_{13} (:: נפל *fall*), אִישׁ *man* Gn 32_{26} Jr 38_{22} Ob_{7}, אֱנוֹשׁ *person* Jr 20_{10}, מֶלֶךְ *king* Jr 1_{19}, שַׂר *prince* Jr 1_{19}, סֶרֶן *lord* of Philistines Jg 16_{5}, כֹּהֵן *priest* Jr 1_{19}, אוֹיֵב *enemy* Ps 13_{5}, מִי *who?* Si 5_{3}; subj. not specified, Ps 129_{2}. <OBJ> worshipper Ps 13_{5} (or em. יְכָלְתִּיו *I have prevailed against him* to יָכֹלְתִּי לוֹ *I have prevailed against him*, or יָכֹלְתִּי *I have prevailed*), דָּבָר *word* Jr 15_{16} (if em.; see Subj.), כֹּחַ *strength* Si 5_{3}. <PREP> לְ *against*, or introducing object, + Esau (Edom) Ob_{7}, Jacob Gn 32_{26}, Jeremiah Jr 1_{19} 15_{20} 20_{10}, Mordecai Est 6_{13}, Samson Jg 16_{5}, Zedekiah Jr 38_{22}, אִישׁ *man* 1 S 17_{9}, worshipper Ps 13_{5} (if em.; see Obj.) 129_{2}, אֶרֶץ *land* Nm 13_{30}. <COLL> inf. abs. + finite form of יכל , Nm 13_{30}.

c. overrun, of ledges of temple building overrunning upper chambers, <SUBJ> אַתִּיק *ledge* Ezk 42_{5} (if em. יֹאכְלוּ *they ate*, i.e. used up space, from אכל, to יָכְלוּ *they overran*). <PREP> מִן of direction, *from*, + לִשְׁכָּה *chamber* Ezk 42_{5} (if em.; see Subj.).*

⇒ יְכָלְיָהוּ *Jecoliah*, יְהוּכַל *Jehucal*, יוּכַל *Jucal*.

יְכָלְיָה, see יְכָלְיָהוּ *Jecoliah.*

יְכָלְיָהוּ 2 pr.n.f. **Jecoliah**—יְכָלְיָה (mss יְכוֹלְיָה)—mother of Azariah (Uzziah), king of Judah, <NOM CL> שֵׁם אִמּוֹ יְכָלְיָהוּ מִירוּשָׁלָםִ *his mother's name was Jecoliah of Jerusalem* 2 K 15_{2}||2 C $26_{3(Qr)}$ (יְכָלְיָה מִן־יְרוּשָׁלָםִ; mss יְכוֹלְיָה; Kt יכיליה perh. *Jeciliah*).*

⇒ יכל *be able* + ״ *Y.*

יְכָנְיָה 7.0.0.1 pr.n.m. **Jeconiah**—יְכָנְיָהוּ, יְכוֹנְיָה—**1.** king of Judah, son of Jehoiakim, ident. with יְהוֹיָכִין *Jehoiachin* at 2 K $24_{6.8}$||2 C $36_{8.9}$ 2 K $24_{12.15}$ $25_{27.27}$ Jr 52_{31}, and כָּנְיָהוּ *Coniah* at Jr $22_{24.28}$ 37_{1}, <SUBJ> יצא *go out* Jr 29_{2}. <NOM CL> יְכָנְיָה בְנוֹ *Jeconiah was his son* 1 C 3_{16}. <OBJ> גלה *exile* Jr 27_{20}, hi. *exile* Jr 24_{1} Est 2_{6}, בוא hi. *bring* Jr 24_{1}, שׁוב hi. *bring back* Jr 28_{4}. <CSTR> בְּנֵי יְכָנְיָה *sons of Jeconiah* 1 C 3_{17} (Seb בֵּן *son of*). <APP> בֵּן *son* Jr 24_{1} 27_{20} 28_{4}, מֶלֶךְ *king* Jr 24_{1} 27_{20} 28_{4} 29_{2} Est 2_{6}. <PREP> עִם *with*, + גלה ho. *be exiled* Est 2_{6}.

2. army commander, son of Elnathan, Lachish ost. 3_{15} (כניהו[י]; others כניהו *Coniah*), <SUBJ> בוא *come* Lachish ost. 3_{15}, ירד *go down* Lachish ost. 3_{15}, שׁלח *send* Lachish ost. 3_{15}. <APP> בֵּן *son* Lachish ost. 3_{15}, שַׂר *commander* Lachish ost. 3_{15}.

3. son of Hechel, <APP> בֵּן *son* Seal 746 (c. 700). <PREP> לְ of possession, *of, (belonging) to* Seal 746 (c. 700).

⇒ כון hi. *establish* + ״ *Y.*

יְכָנְיָהוּ, see יְכָנְיָה *Jeconiah.*

ילד 499.7.39 vb. **give birth—Qal** 214.3.23 Pf. יָלַד (יָלֶד, יָלְדָתוּ, יְלָדַתְךָ, יְלָדַתְנִי, יָלֶדָה) יָלְדָה, (יָלְדוֹ, יְלָדֵךְ, יְלָדֵךְ, יְלִדְתִּיךָ, יְלָדֶתְךָ) יָלַדְתִּי, (יְלִדְתֶּנוּ, יְלִדְתִּנִי, יְלִדְתָּ) יָלַדְתְּ, (יְלִדְתִּיהוּ, יְלִדְנוּ, יָלְדוּ, יָלַדְנוּ); impf. יֵלֵד, 3fs תֵּלֵד, תֵּלְדִי, אֵלֵד, וְיָלְדוּ, וְיָלַדְתְּ, וְיָלְדָה + waw; תֵּלְדוּ, תֵּלַדְנָה, (יֵלֵדוּן) יֵלְדוּ (וְיָלֶדוּ); 3fs וַתֵּלֶד, וָאֵלֵד, וַיֵּלְדוּ, וַתֵּלַדְנָה, (וַתֵּלַדְןָ); ptc. יֹלֵד (יוֹלֵד, sf. יֹלַדְתְּ), (יֹלַדְתְּ) יֹלֶדֶת, (יֹלְדָיו, יֹלַדְתָּהּ), יֹלְדוֹת; ptc. pass. יָלוּד, יְלוּדִים; inf. יָלֹד, לֶדֶת (לַת) [1 S 4_{19}], לֵדָה [Ho 9_{11}], לִדְתִּי, לִדְתָּהּ, Q לדתמה, לִדְתָּנָה).

1. bear, give birth (to), usu. of mother, including animals (e.g. Gn 30_{39} $31_{8.8}$ Jb 39_{1}) and birds (Jr 17_{11}); also of Moses as mother (Nm 11_{12}), of both mother and father (Zc $13_{3.3}$), of stone as mother (Jr 2_{27}); of God (as rock) as mother (Dt 32_{18}), of Y. as father begetting (Ps 2_{7}), of Y. as giving birth to hoar frost (Jb 38_{29}); of one giving birth to deception (Ps 7_{15} Jb 15_{35}); appar. of countries (Is 26_{18}) and cities (Is 51_{18} 66_{7} Ezk 16_{20} perh. Is 54_{1}); in denying that a male bears young (Jr 30_{6}); of the day producing events (Pr 27_{1}); **issue** statute (Zp 2_{2}), perh. **be born** (Ec 3_{2} [:: מות *die*]).

<SUBJ> Y. Ps 2_{7}, Abigail 1 C 2_{17}, Abihail, wife of

Abishur 1 C 2_{29}, Abihail, wife of Rehoboam 2 C 11_{19}, Abijah 1 C 2_{24} (or em. Abihu), Adah, wife of Lamech Gn 4_{20}, Adah, wife of Esau Gn 36_{4}, Asenath Gn 41_{50} 46_{20}, Basemath Gn 36_{4} (Sam Mahalath), Bathsheba 2 S 12_{24}, Bilhah Gn $30_{3.5.7}$ 46_{25} 4QTNaph 1_{10}, Elisheba Ex 6_{23}, Ephah (secondary wife of Caleb) 1 C 2_{46}, Ephraim Ho $9_{11.16}$, Ephrath 1 C 2_{19}, Eve Gn $4_{1.2}$, Gomer Ho $1_{3.6.8}$, Hagar Gn $16_{11.15.15.16}$ 21_{9} 25_{12}, Hammolecheth 1 C 7_{18}, Hannah 1 S 1_{20} 2_{21}, Hannah, grandmother of Naphtali 4QTNaph 1_{4}, appar. Jerusalem Is 51_{18} Ezk 16_{20}, perh. Is 54_{1}, Jochebed Ex 6_{20} Nm 26_{59}, appar. people of Judah Is 26_{18}, Judahite 1 C 4_{18}, Keturah Gn 25_{2}‖1 C 1_{32}, Leah Gn 29_{32+5t} $30_{9.17.19.20.21}$ 34_{1} 46_{15}, Maacah, secondary wife of Caleb 1 C $2_{48.49}$ (or em. hi. *beget*, with Shaaph as subj.), Maacah, wife of Machir 1 C 7_{16}, Maacah, wife of Rehoboam 2 C 11_{20}, Michal 2 S 21_{8} (or em. Merab), Milcah Gn $22_{20.23}$ $24_{24.47}$, Moses Nm 11_{12}, Naarah 1 C 4_{6}, Naomi Ru 1_{12}, Oholah Ezk $23_{4.37}$, Oholibah Ezk $23_{4.37}$, Oholibamah Gn $36_{5.14}$, Rachel Gn $30_{1.23.25}$ $35_{16.16.17}$ $46_{22(Sam)}$ 4QTNaph 1_{9}, Rebekah Gn $25_{24.26}$, Reumah Gn 22_{24}, Rizpah 2 S 21_{8}, Ruth Ru 4_{13}, Sarai/Sarah Gn $16_{1.2}$ 17_{17} (or del. Sarah) $17_{19.21}$ 18_{13} $21_{2.3.7}$ 24_{36} 4QRP^{b} 1_{3} ([י]לדה), Shua Gn $38_{3.4.5.5}$, Tamar Gn $38_{27.28}$ 1 C 2_{4} Ru 4_{12}, Timna Gn 36_{12} 4QCommGenA 4_{1}, Zillah Gn 4_{22}, Zilpah Gn $30_{10.12}$, Zion Is 66_{7} (or ins. יֹלֵדָה *one who gives birth* as subj.) 66_{8}, Zipporah Ex 2_{22}.

Aramaean woman 1 C $7_{14.14}$, Egyptian woman Gn 21_{9} 25_{12}, Hebrew women Ex 1_{19}, אִשָּׁה *woman, wife* Gn 3_{16} $4_{1.2.17.25}$ 16_{1} 17_{19} 24_{36} 25_{2} 36_{14} 44_{27} Ex 2_{2} 21_{4} Lv $12_{2.5}$ Nm 26_{59} Dt 21_{15} 25_{6} Jg 11_{2} $13_{2.3.5.7.24}$ 1 S $4_{19.19.20}$ 2 S 11_{27} $12_{15.24}$ 1 K $3_{17.18.18.21}$ 2 K 4_{17} Jr 29_{6} 1 C $2_{24.29}$ 4_{18} $7_{16.23}$ 4QD^{a} 6.2_{5} 4QRP^{b} 1_{3} ([י]לדה) 11QT 48_{16}, appar. Gn 20_{17}, אֵם *mother* Nm 26_{59} (if em. אֹתָהּ *her* to אִמָּהּ *her mother*) Jr 15_{10} 16_{3} 20_{14} 22_{26} Zc $13_{3.3}$ 1 C 4_{9} 4QTNaph 1_{10}, appar. Pr 23_{25} Ca 6_{9}, אָב *father* Zc $13_{3.3}$.

בַּת *daughter* Gn 6_{4} 17_{17} 31_{43} 36_{14} 41_{50} 46_{20} Ex $6_{23.25}$ Nm 26_{59} 2 S $21_{8.8}$ Jr 29_{6} Ho 1_{3} 1 C $2_{21.35}$ 2 C $11_{19.20}$ 4QAges^{a} 1_{8} ([בנות ... וי]לדו) 4QAges^{b} 2_{2} (וילד[ו]), בְּכִירָה *firstborn daughter* Gn 19_{37}, אָחוֹת *sister* Ex 6_{23} 1 K 11_{20} 1 C 7_{18}, דּוֹדָה *(paternal) aunt* Ex 6_{20}, כַּלָּה *daughter-in-law* 1 S $4_{19.19.20}$ Ru 4_{15} 1 C 2_{4}, אָמָה *female servant* Gn 20_{17}, שִׁפְחָה *female servant* Gn 25_{12} $30_{7.10.12}$, פִּילֶגֶשׁ *secondary wife* Gn 22_{24} Jg 8_{31} 1 C 1_{32} $2_{46.48.49}$ (or em. hi. *beget*, with Shaaph as subj.) $7_{14.14}$, נְבִיאָה *prophet* (fem.) Is 8_{3}, עַלְמָה *young woman* Is 7_{14}, צְעִירָה *young(er) daughter* Gn 19_{38}, רַכָּה *tender one* Dt 28_{57}, עֲקָרָה *barren one* 1 S 2_{5} Jb 24_{21}, הָרָה *one who is pregnant* Is 26_{17}, יֹלֵדָה *one who bears* Is 66_{7} (if ins. יֹלֵדָה) Mc 5_{2}.

זָכָר *male* Jr 30_{6}, עַם *people* Is 65_{23} (or em. hi. *beget*), עֵדָה *assembly* of the impious Jb 15_{35}, יָעֵל pl. *mountain goat* Jb 39_{1}, perh. 39_{2}, אַיֶּלֶת *hind* Jr 14_{5} Jb 39_{2}, קֹרֵא *partridge* Jr 17_{11}, חַיָּה *beast* Ezk 31_{6}, צֹאן *flock* Gn 30_{39} $31_{8.8}$, צוּר *rock*, i.e. God Dt 32_{18}, אֶבֶן *stone* Jr 2_{27}, יָם *sea* Is 23_{4}, יוֹם *day* Pr 27_{1}, appar. רָז *secret* Si 8_{18}, מִי *who?* Is 49_{21} Jb 38_{29}; subj. not specified, Nm 26_{59} (or em. אֹתָהּ bore *her* to אִמָּהּ *her mother* bore) 2 S 3_{2} 1 K 1_{6} Jr 15_{9} 50_{12} Zp 2_{2} (or em. לֶדֶת חֹק before *a decree is issued* to לֹא תִדַּחֲקוּ before *you are crushed*) Ps 7_{15} Pr 17_{25} Ca 8_{5} Ec 3_{2}.

<OBJ> Aaron Ex 6_{20} Nm 26_{59}, Abel Gn 4_{2}, Abiezer 1 C 7_{18}, Abihu Ex 6_{23}, Abijah 2 C 11_{20}, perh. Achsah 1 C 2_{49} (or em. hi. *beget*), Adonijah 1 K 1_{6}, Ahban 1 C 2_{29}, Ahuzzam 1 C 4_{6}, Amalek Gn 36_{12} 4QCommGenA 4_{1}, Amasa 1 C 2_{17}, Ashhur 1 C 2_{24}, Asriel 1 C 7_{14}, Attai, son of Jarha 1 C 2_{35}, Attai, son of Rehoboam 2 C 11_{20}, Babylon Jr 50_{12}, Bethuel Gn 22_{20} $24_{24.47}$, Bilhah 4QTNaph 1_{4}, Buz Gn 22_{20}, Cain Gn 4_{1}, Chesed Gn 22_{20}, Coniah Jr 22_{26}, Dan 4QTNaph 1_{10}, Dinah Gn 34_{1} 46_{15}, Eleazar Ex 6_{23}, Eliphaz Gn 36_{4}, Enoch Gn 4_{17}, Ephraim Gn 46_{20}, Esau Gn 25_{26}, Gaham Gn 22_{24}, Gazez 1 C 2_{46} (or em. Gazen), Genubath 1 K 11_{20}, Haahashtari 1 C 4_{6}, Haran 1 C 2_{46}, Hazo Gn 22_{20}, Heber 1 C 4_{18}, Hepher 1 C 4_{6}, Hur 1 C 2_{19}.

Isaac Gn 17_{21} 4QRP^{b} 1_{3} ([ישחק] אשר י[לדה]), Ishbak Gn 25_{2}‖1 C 1_{32}, Ishhod 1 C 7_{18}, Ishmael Gn 16_{16} 25_{12}, Ithamar Ex 6_{23}, Jabal Gn 4_{20}, Jacob Gn 25_{26}, Jalam Gn $36_{5.14}$, Jekuthiel 1 C 4_{18}, Jered 1 C 4_{18}, appar. Jeremiah Jr 20_{14}, Jeush, son of Esau Gn $36_{5.14}$, Jeush, son of Rehoboam 2 C 11_{19}, Jidlaph Gn 22_{20}, Jochebed Nm 26_{59} (if em. אֹתָהּ bore *her* to אִמָּהּ *her mother* bore), Jokshan Gn 25_{2}‖1 C 1_{32}, Joseph Gn 30_{25}, Kemuel Gn 22_{20}, Korah Gn $36_{5.14}$, Maacah Gn 22_{24}, Machir 1 C 7_{14}, Mahlah 1 C 7_{18} (or del. Mahlah), Manasseh Gn 46_{20}, Medan Gn 25_{2}‖1 C 1_{32}, Midian Gn 25_{2}‖1 C 1_{32}, Miriam Ex $6_{20(mss)}$

Nm 26$_{59}$, Molid 1 C 2$_{29}$, Moses Ex 6$_{20}$ Nm 26$_{59}$, Moza 1 C 2$_{46}$.

Nadab Ex 6$_{23}$, Perez Ru 4$_{12}$ 1 C 2$_{4}$, Phinehas Ex 6$_{25}$, Pildash Gn 22$_{20}$, Reuel Gn 36$_{4}$, Segub 1 C 2$_{21}$, Shaaph 1 C 2$_{49}$ (or em. hi. *beget*, with Shaaph as subj.), Sheber 1 C 2$_{48}$, Shelah Gn 38$_{5}$, Shelomith 2 C 11$_{20}$ (or em. שְׁלֹמוֹת *Shelomoth*), Shemariah 2 C 11$_{19}$, Sheva 1 C 2$_{49}$ (or em. hi.), Shuah Gn 25$_{2}$||1 C 1$_{32}$, Tahash Gn 22$_{24}$, Tebah Gn 22$_{24}$, Temeni 1 C 4$_{6}$, Tirhanah 1 C 2$_{48}$, Uz Gn 22$_{20}$, Zaham 2 C 11$_{19}$, Zerah 1 C 2$_{4}$, Zimran Gn 25$_{2}$||1 C 1$_{32}$, Ziza 2 C 11$_{20}$.

בֵּן *son* Gn 3$_{16}$ 4$_{25}$ 16$_{11.15.15}$ 17$_{19}$ 19$_{37.38}$ 21$_{2.3.7.9}$ 22$_{20}$ 24$_{36}$ 29$_{32.33.34.34.35}$ 30$_{5+7t}$ 31$_{43}$ 38$_{3.4.5}$ 46$_{15}$ Ex 2$_{2.22}$ 21$_{4}$ Dt 21$_{15}$ 25$_{6(Sam)}$ 28$_{57}$ Jg 8$_{31}$ 11$_{2}$ 13$_{3.5.7.24}$ 1 S 1$_{20}$ 2$_{21}$ 4$_{20}$ 2 S 11$_{27}$ 12$_{24}$ 21$_{8.8}$ 1 K 3$_{21}$ 11$_{20}$ 2 K 4$_{17}$ Is 7$_{14}$ 8$_{3}$ 51$_{18}$ 66$_{8}$ Jr 16$_{3}$ 29$_{6}$ Ezk 16$_{20}$ 23$_{4.37}$ Ho 1$_{3.6.8}$, Ps 2$_{7}$ Pr 17$_{25}$ 23$_{25}$ Ru 1$_{12}$ 4$_{13.15}$ 1 C 7$_{16.23}$ 2 C 11$_{19}$ 4QTNaph 1$_{9}$ 11QJub 4$_{7}$, בַּת *daughter* Gn 30$_{21}$ 34$_{1}$ 46$_{15}$ Ex 21$_{4}$ Nm 26$_{59}$ (if em. אֹתָהּ bore *her* to אִמָּהּ *her mother* bore) 1 S 2$_{21}$ Jr 16$_{3}$ 29$_{6}$ Ezk 16$_{20}$ 23$_{4.37}$ 1 C 2$_{49}$ (or em. hi. *beget*), בְּכוֹר *firstborn* Gn 22$_{20}$ Dt 25$_{6}$ (Sam בֵּן *son*), יֶלֶד *child* 2 S 12$_{15}$, זָכָר *male (child)* Lv 12$_{2}$ 4QSD 7.2$_{14}$ ([וילדה זכר]) 4QD^{a} 6.2$_{5}$, נְקֵבָה *female (child)* Lv 12$_{5}$ 4QSD 7.2$_{16}$, אָח *brother* Gn 4$_{2}$ 22$_{20}$ 4QTNaph 1$_{10}$, אָחוֹת *sister* Nm 26$_{59}$, אָב *father* Gn 22$_{20}$ (or del. אָב) 1 C 2$_{24.49}$ (or em. hi. *beget* father) 4$_{18.18.18}$ 7$_{14}$, אֵם *mother* 4QTNaph 1$_{4}$, אִישׁ *man* Jr 15$_{10}$ Zc 13$_{3.3}$, נֶפֶשׁ *person* Gn 46$_{18.22(Sam)}$ 46$_{25}$, עַם *people* Nm 11$_{12}$, בֵּית *house* of Israel Jr 2$_{27}$, יוֹנָה *dove* Ca 6$_{9}$, תַּמָּה *perfect one* Ca 6$_{9}$, שְׁנַיִם *two (sons)* Gn 44$_{27}$, שִׁבְעָה *seven (children)* 1 S 2$_{5}$ Jr 15$_{9}$.

גִּבּוֹר *mighty one* 4QAges^{a} 1$_{8}$ (וי[ל]דו) 4QAges^{b} 2$_{2}$ (וילד[ו] ... [בנות]), עָקֹד *striped one* Gn 30$_{39}$ 31$_{8}$, נָקֹד *speckled one* Gn 30$_{39}$ 31$_{8}$, טָלוּא *spotted one* Gn 30$_{39}$, רוּחַ *wind* Is 26$_{18}$, כְּפוֹר *frost* Jb 38$_{29}$, קַשׁ *chaff* Is 33$_{11}$, חֹק *statute* Zp 2$_{2}$ (or em. לֶדֶת חֹק before *a decree is issued* to לֹא תִדַּחֲקוּ before *you are crushed*), שֶׁקֶר *deception* Ps 7$_{15}$, מָה *what?* Pr 27$_{1}$.

אֵלֶּה *these* Gn 22$_{23}$ 46$_{18.25}$ Is 49$_{21}$; obj. not specified, Gn 16$_{1.2}$ 18$_{13}$ 30$_{1.9}$ 35$_{16}$ Jg 13$_{2.3.3}$ 1 S 4$_{19}$ 1 K 3$_{17.18.18}$ Is 26$_{17}$ 54$_{1}$ 65$_{23}$ 66$_{7}$ (unless ins. בֵּן after יָלָדָה) Jr 17$_{11}$ Ezk 31$_{6}$ Ho 9$_{11.16}$ Mc 5$_{2}$ Jb 24$_{21}$ Ca 8$_{5}$ Ec 3$_{2}$ 1 C 4$_{9}$ Si 8$_{18}$.

<PREP> לְ of benefit, *for*, or *during* 4QAges^{b} 2$_{2}$ 11QJub 4$_{7}$, + Y. Ezk 16$_{20}$ 23$_{37}$, Aaron Ex 6$_{23.25}$, Abishur 1 C 2$_{29}$, Abra(ha)m Gn 16$_{1.15.16}$ 17$_{19.21}$ 21$_{2.3.7(Sam).9}$ 25$_{2.12}$ 4QRP^{b} 1$_{3}$ ([י]לדה), Adriel 2 S 21$_{8}$, Amram Ex 6$_{20}$ Nm 1$_{27}$ 12$_{15}$, Eliphaz Gn 36$_{12}$ 4QCommGenA 4$_{1}$, Esau Gn 36$_{4.14}$, Gideon Jg 26$_{59}$, Ashhur 1 C 4$_{6}$, Caleb 1 C 2$_{19}$, David 2 S 1 8$_{31}$, Gilead Jg 11$_{2}$, Hadad 1 K 11$_{20}$, Hezron, son of Perez 1 C 2$_{24}$, Hosea Ho 1$_{3}$, Jacob Gn 30$_{1+6t}$ 34$_{1}$ 46$_{15.18}$ 46$_{22(Sam)}$ 46$_{25}$, Jarha 1 C 2$_{35}$, Joseph Gn 41$_{50}$ 46$_{20}$, Judah Ru 4$_{12}$ 1 C 2$_{4}$, Levi Nm 26$_{59}$, Nahor Gn 22$_{20.23}$ 24$_{24.47}$, Rehoboam 2 C 11$_{19}$, Zion Is 49$_{21}$, אִישׁ *husband, man*, Gn 29$_{34}$ 30$_{20}$ Dt 21$_{15}$, בֵּן *son* 2 S 21$_{8}$ 4QCommGenA 4$_{1}$, אָח *brother* Gn 22$_{20.23}$, אָב *father* Gn 44$_{27}$, אָדוֹן *master* Gn 24$_{36}$, עֶבֶד *servant* Gn 44$_{27}$ Ex 21$_{4}$, זְקֻנִים *old age* Gn 21$_{2.7}$.

לְ *at*, + מוֹעֵד *season* Gn 17$_{21}$ 21$_{2}$ 2 K 4$_{17}$; (destined) for, + בֶּהָלָה *dismay* Is 65$_{23}$.

בְּ of place/time, *in, at*, + Chezib Gn 38$_{5}$ (Sam Cozeba), Egypt Nm 26$_{59}$, Paddan-Aram Gn 46$_{15}$, בַּיִת *house* 1 K 3$_{17}$, אֶרֶץ *land* Jr 16$_{3}$, שָׁנָה *year* Gn 17$_{21}$; of accompaniment, *with, in*, + עֶצֶב *pain* Gn 3$_{16}$ (Sam עִצָּבוֹן *pain*) 1 C 4$_{9}$; כְּ *at*, + עֵת *time* 2 K 4$_{17}$; עַל *upon*, + בֶּרֶךְ *knee* Gn 30$_{3}$; עִם *with*, + אִשָּׁה *woman* 1 K 3$_{17}$; תַּחַת *beneath*, + פֹּארָה *bough* Ezk 31$_{6}$; אַחֲרֵי *after*, + Absalom 1 K 1$_{6}$, זִקְנָה after reaching *old age* Gn 24$_{36}$.

<COLL> with noun used adverbially, הַיּוֹם *today* Ps 2$_{7}$, ספו appar. *(at) its end* Si 8$_{18}$; וַתֹּסֶף לָלֶדֶת *and she added*, i.e. she once more, *gave birth* Gn 4$_{2}$, עֵת לָלֶדֶת *a time to give birth* Ec 3$_{2}$, יָמֶיהָ לָלֶדֶת *her days to give birth* Gn 25$_{24}$, עֵת לִדְתָּנָה *time of their giving birth* Jb 39$_{2}$, עֵת לֶדֶת יַעֲלֵי־סָלַע *the time when mountain goats give birth* Jb 39$_{1}$, כֹּחַ אַיִן לְלֵדָה *there is no strength to give birth* 2 K 19$_{3}$ ||Is 37$_{3}$, חָפְרָה יוֹלַדְתְּכֶם *the one who has borne you is disgraced* Jr 50$_{12}$, עמד מִלֶּדֶת *stand from*, i.e. cease, *giving birth* Gn 29$_{35}$ 30$_{9}$.

לֵדָה *(giving) birth* + בֶּטֶן *womb* Ho 9$_{11}$, הֵרָיוֹן *conception* Ho 9$_{11}$.

ילד + הרה *conceive* Gn 4$_{1.17}$ 19$_{37}$ 21$_{2}$ 25$_{24}$ 29$_{32.33.34.35}$ 30$_{5.7.17.19.23}$ 38$_{3.4}$ Ex 2$_{2.22(mss)}$ Nm 11$_{12}$ Jg 13$_{3.5.7}$ 1 S 1$_{20}$ 2$_{21}$ (Q ותלד עוד *and she gave birth again*) 4$_{19}$ 2 K 4$_{17}$ Is 7$_{14}$ 8$_{3}$ 26$_{18}$ 33$_{11}$ Ho 1$_{3.6.8}$ Ps 7$_{15}$ Jb 15$_{35}$ 1 C 7$_{23}$, זרע hi. *conceive* Lv 12$_{2}$ (or em. זרע hi. to ni. *be sown*), דגר *incubate* Jr 17$_{11}$, חבל pi. *be pregnant* Ca 8$_{5}$, כרע *crouch down*

1 S 4$_{19}$ Jb 39$_{2}$, קשׁה pi. *be hard in bearing*, i.e. have hard labour Gn 35$_{16}$ קרב hi. *approach childbirth* Is 26$_{17}$, חול *writhe* in labour Is 23$_{4}$ 26$_{17.18}$ 54$_{1}$ 66$_{7.8}$, pol. *bring to birth* Jb 39$_{1}$, פלח pi. *bring forth* Jb 39$_{2}$, שׁלח *send forth*, i.e. deliver young Jb 39$_{2}$, זעק *cry out* Is 26$_{17}$, pol. *bear* Dt 32$_{18}$, מלט hi. *give birth (to)* Is 66$_{7}$, יצא *go out* Gn 25$_{26}$, בנה ni. *become mother of sons* Gn 16$_{2}$ 30$_{3}$.

ילד + לקח *take* wife Gn 25$_{2}$ Ex 6$_{20.23.25}$ Jr 29$_{6}$ Ru 4$_{13}$ 1 C 2$_{19.21}$ 2 C 11$_{19.20}$, קנה *acquire* Gn 4$_{1}$, ידע *know* sexually Gn 4$_{1.17.25}$, יהב *give* children Gn 30$_{1}$, נתן *give* a son Gn 17$_{17}$ 30$_{5}$, *give* a daughter in marriage Jr 29$_{6}$ 1 C 2$_{35}$, זקן *be old* Gn 18$_{13}$, רפא *heal* Gn 20$_{17}$.

ילד + ינק hi. *nurse* Gn 21$_{7}$ 1 K 3$_{21}$, גמל *wean* 1 K 11$_{20}$ Ho 1$_{8}$, מול *circumcise* Gn 21$_{3}$, גדל *grow up* Gn 25$_{26}$ Jg 11$_{2}$ 1 S 2$_{21}$ Ru 1$_{12}$, pi. *bring up* Is 23$_{4}$ 49$_{21}$ 51$_{18}$ Ho 9$_{11}$, רום pol. *raise* young women Is 23$_{4}$, יסף hi. *add*, i.e. bear again Gn 38$_{5}$, רבה *become many* Jr 29$_{6}$, מעט *become few* Jr 29$_{6}$, חמם *be warm*, i.e. breed Gn 30$_{39}$, עצר *close* womb Gn 20$_{17}$, שׁכל pi. *bereave* Ho 9$_{11}$, דקר *pierce*, i.e. put to death Zc 13$_{3}$.

<ANT> מות *die*.

2. beget, of father or eponymous ancestor (or at Gn 4$_{18.18.18}$ 10$_{8.13.15.24.24.26}$ 22$_{23}$ 25$_{3}$ em. יָלַד *he begat* to יִלַּד pi. in same sense),* <SUBJ> Arpachshad Gn 10$_{24}$‖1 C 1$_{18}$, Bethuel Gn 22$_{23}$ (Sam hi.), Canaan Gn 10$_{15}$‖1 C 1$_{13}$, Cush Gn 10$_{8}$ (Sam hi.)‖1 C 1$_{10}$, Egypt Gn 10$_{13}$‖1 C 1$_{11}$, Ephraim Ho 5$_{7}$, Irad Gn 4$_{18}$, Israel Ho 5$_{7}$, Jokshan Gn 25$_{3}$, Joktan Gn 10$_{26}$‖1 C 1$_{20}$, perh. Judah Ho 5$_{7}$ (unless del. Judah), Mehijael Gn 4$_{18}$ (or em. Mehujael), Methushael Gn 4$_{18}$, Shelah Gn 10$_{24}$‖1 C 1$_{18}$.

בֵּן *son* perh. Gn 6$_{4}$ (unless subj. is בַּת *daughter*, as §1; Sam hi. *beget*), אָב *father* Pr 23$_{22}$, appar. מֶלֶךְ *king* Dn 11$_{6}$ (unless em. הַיֹּלְדָהּ *he who begat her* to הַיַּלְדָּה *girl*), זֶה *(this) one* Pr 23$_{22}$; subj. not specified, Pr 17$_{21}$ 23$_{24}$.

<OBJ> Abimael Gn 10$_{26}$‖1 C 1$_{20}$, Almodad Gn 10$_{26}$ ‖1 C 1$_{20}$, Amorite Gn 10$_{15}$‖1 C 1$_{13}$, Anamim Gn 10$_{13}$ ‖1 C 1$_{11}$, Arkite Gn 10$_{15}$‖1 C 1$_{13}$, Arvadite Gn 10$_{15}$‖1 C 1$_{13}$, Caphtorite Gn 10$_{13}$‖1 C 1$_{11}$, Casluhim Gn 10$_{13}$‖1 C 1$_{11}$, Dedan Gn 25$_{3}$, Diklah Gn 10$_{26}$‖1 C 1$_{20}$, Ebal 1 C 1$_{22}$ (or em. Obal), Eber Gn 10$_{24}$‖1 C 1$_{18}$, Girgashite Gn 10$_{15}$‖1 C 1$_{13}$, Hadoram Gn 10$_{26}$‖1 C 1$_{20}$, Hamathite Gn 10$_{15}$‖1 C 1$_{13}$, Havilah Gn 10$_{26}$‖1 C 1$_{20}$, Hazarmaveth Gn 10$_{26}$‖1 C 1$_{20}$, Heth Gn 10$_{15}$‖1 C 1$_{13}$, Hivite Gn 10$_{15}$ ‖1 C 1$_{13}$, Jebusite Gn 10$_{15}$‖1 C 1$_{13}$, Jerah Gn 10$_{26}$‖1 C 1$_{20}$, Jobab Gn 10$_{26}$‖1 C 1$_{20}$, Lamech Gn 4$_{18}$, Lehabim Gn 10$_{13}$‖1 C 1$_{11}$, Ludim Gn 10$_{13}$‖1 C 1$_{11}$.

Mehujael Gn 4$_{18}$, Methushael Gn 4$_{18}$, Naphtuhim Gn 10$_{13}$ (or em. Pethumhim)‖1 C 1$_{11}$, Nimrod Gn 10$_{8}$ (Sam hi.)‖1 C 1$_{10}$, Obal Gn 10$_{26}$ (Sam עיבל), Ophir Gn 10$_{26}$‖1 C 1$_{20}$, Pathrusim Gn 10$_{13}$‖1 C 1$_{11}$, Rebekah Gn 22$_{23}$, Sheba, son of Joktan Gn 10$_{26}$‖1 C 1$_{20}$, Sheba, son of Jokshan Gn 25$_{3}$, Shelah Gn 10$_{24}$‖1 C 1$_{18}$, Sheleph Gn 10$_{26}$‖1 C 1$_{20}$, Sidon Gn 10$_{15}$‖1 C 1$_{13}$, Sinite Gn 10$_{15}$‖1 C 1$_{13}$, Uzal Gn 10$_{26}$ (Sam איזל)‖1 C 1$_{20}$, Zemarite Gn 10$_{15}$ ‖1 C 1$_{13}$.

בֵּן *son* Ho 5$_{7}$ Pr 23$_{22}$, בְּכוֹר *firstborn* Gn 10$_{15}$, בַּת *daughter* Dn 11$_{6}$ (unless em. הַיֹּלְדָהּ *he who begat her* to הַיַּלְדָּה *girl*), חָכָם *wise (one)* Pr 23$_{24}$, כְּסִיל *dullard* Pr 17$_{21}$.

<PREP> לְ of benefit, *to, for*, + בֵּן *son* Gn 6$_{4}$.

3. ptc. as noun, **one who bears,** <SUBJ> חול *writhe* in labour Is 66$_{7}$ (if ins. יֹלֵדָה after תָּחִיל), ילד *give birth* Is 66$_{7}$ (if ins. יֹלֵדָה after תָּחִיל) Mc 5$_{2}$. <OBJ> קבץ pi. *gather* Jr 31$_{8}$. <CSTR> צִירֵי יוֹלֵדָה *pangs of one who bears* a child Is 21$_{3}$ 1QH 5$_{31}$, חֶבְלֵי *labour pains of* Ho 13$_{13}$, תּוֹרַת *law of (for)* Lv 12$_{7}$ (יֹלֶדֶת). <PREP> כְּ *like* Jr 6$_{24}$ 22$_{23}$ 30$_{6}$ (or del. כַּיּוֹלֵדָה *like a woman in labour*) 50$_{43}$ Mc 4$_{9.10}$ Ps 48$_{7}$, + חול *writhe* Is 13$_{8}$ Si 48$_{19}$, פעה *groan* Is 42$_{14}$, נשׁם *pant* Is 42$_{14}$, שׁאף *gasp* Is 42$_{14}$, אחז *hold* Jr 49$_{24}$ (or del. כַּיּוֹלֵדָה *like a woman in labour*). <COLL> ילד ptc. + יַחְדָּו *together* Jr 31$_{8}$; + Zion Mc 4$_{10}$, הָרָה *one who is pregnant* Jr 31$_{8}$.

4a. pass., **be born,** הואה המולד אשר הוא ילוד עליו *this is the birthday on which he was born* 4QCrypt 1.2$_{8}$, sim. 2.1$_{8}$.

4b. pass. ptc. as noun, **one who is born, child,** <SUBJ> היה *be* 1 C 14$_{4}$, צדק *be righteous* Jb 15$_{14}$ (+ אֱנוֹשׁ *human being*), זכה *be pure* Jb 25$_{4}$, ישׁב *dwell* 1QS 11$_{21}$. <NOM CL> אָדָם יְלוּד אִשָּׁה קְצַר יָמִים וּשְׂבַע־רֹגֶז *a human being, one born of a woman, is short of days and surfeited with turmoil* Jb 14$_{1}$, מה ילוד אשה *what is one born of woman?* 1QH 13$_{14}$. <OBJ> נתן *give* 1 K 3$_{26.27}$ (mss יֶלֶד *child* in both). <CSTR> יְלוּד אִשָּׁה *one born of a woman* Jb 14$_{1}$ 15$_{14}$ 25$_{4}$ Si 10$_{18}$ 1QH 13$_{14}$ 18$_{12.16}$ (א[שה]) 18$_{23}$ ([אשה]) 1QS 11$_{21}$ 4Q482 1$_{4}$ (אש[ה]) 4QapLam[b] 1$_{5}$; שְׁמוֹת הַיִּלּוּדִים *the names of those who were born* 1 C 14$_{4}$, אשמות

ילוד *guilt of one born of* 1QH 18$_{12}$, [פ]שע *transgression of* 1QH 18$_{16}$. <APP> אָדָם *human being* Jb 14$_1$. <ADJ> חַי *living* 1 K 3$_{26.27}$. <PREP> לְ of direction, *to* perh. 4QapLam^b 1$_5$, + בשׂר pi. *announce* 1QH 18$_{23}$; נָאוֶה לְ *appropriate to* Si 10$_{18}$ (or em. נֶחֱלַק לְ *was apportioned to*; + אֱנוֹשׁ). <COLL> + יֵצֶר *form*, i.e. vessel, *of* clay 1QH 18$_{12}$.

Also perh. 4QMyst^a 28$_{1.2}$ (unless in both יִלּוֹד *born*) 4Q423 2$_5$.

Ni. 37.2.8 Pf. נוֹלַד, mss נוֹלְדוּ; impf. יִוָּלֵד (יִוָּלֶד), 2ms תִּוָּלֵד, אִוָּלֵד, יִוָּלְדוּ; + waw וַיִּוָּלֵד, וַיִּוָּלְדוּ; ptc. נוֹלָד (נוֹלַד־), נוֹלָדִים; inf. הִוָּלֵד (הִוָּלְדוֹ), הִוָּלְדָהּ, הִוָּלְדָהּ—**1. be born,** perh. **become** (Jb 11$_{12}$), <SUBJ> Abihu Nm 26$_{60}$, Bilhah 4QTNaph 1$_4$, Eleazar Nm 26$_{60}$, Ephraim Gn 46$_{20}$, Er 1 C 2$_3$, Ibhar 1 C 3$_{5(mss)}$, Irad Gn 4$_{18}$, Isaac Gn 21$_5$, Ithamar Nm 26$_{60}$, Jerahmeel 1 C 2$_9$, Job Jb 3$_3$ 38$_{21}$, Josiah 1 K 13$_2$, Manasseh Gn 46$_{20}$, Nadab Nm 26$_{60}$, Onan 1 C 2$_3$, Ram 1 C 2$_9$, Shelah 1 C 2$_3$.

בֵּן *son* Gn 10$_1$ 21$_{3.5}$ 48$_5$ Dt 23$_9$ 2 S 5$_{13}$ 14$_{27}$ 1 K 13$_2$ Ps 78$_6$ Jb 1$_2$ 1 C 2$_9$ 3$_1$ 22$_9$ 26$_6$ 4QpsJub^a 2.1$_8$ 4QSela 8.2$_3$, בְּכוֹר *firstborn* Dt 15$_{19}$ 2 S 3$_{2(Qr)}$ (Kt appar. qal) 11QT 52$_7$, זָכָר *male* Dt 15$_{19}$, בַּת *daughter* 2 S 5$_{13}$ 14$_{27}$ Jb 1$_2$, אָח *brother* Pr 17$_{17}$, אֵם *mother* Ho 2$_5$, מֶלֶךְ *king* Ec 4$_{14}$, אִישׁ *man* 1 C 7$_{21}$ 20$_6$, גֶּבֶר *man* Si 49$_{15}$, אָדָם *human being* Jb 15$_7$ 4QDibHam^c 131$_6$ ([א]דם), עַם *people* Ps 22$_{32}$, גֵּר *sojourner* 11QT 40$_6$ ([נולד]ו), גּוֹי *nation* Is 66$_8$, שׁוֹר *ox* Lv 22$_{27}$, כֶּשֶׂב *sheep* Lv 22$_{27}$, עֵז *goat* Lv 22$_{27}$, עַיִר *ass* Jb 11$_{12}$ (or em.; see Coll.), שְׁלוֹשָׁה *three (children)* 1 C 2$_3$, שִׁשָּׁה *six (children)* 1 C 3$_4$, אֵלֶּה *these (children)* 1 C 3$_{5(mss)}$; subj. not specified, Gn 17$_{17}$ (Sam hi.) Ec 7$_1$.

<PREP> לְ *(destined) to*, + מַלְכוּת *kingship* Ec 4$_{14}$ (if em. בְּ of accompaniment), צָרָה *distress* Pr 17$_{17}$; ילד לְ ni. *be born to* (father; perh. לְ of benefit), + Aaron Nm 26$_{60}$, Abraham Gn 21$_{3.5}$ 4QpsJub^a 2.1$_8$ ([לאברה]ם), Absalom 2 S 14$_{27}$, David 2 S 3$_2$ 1 C 3$_{1.4.5(mss)}$ 22$_9$, Edomite Dt 23$_9$, Egyptian Dt 23$_9$, Enoch Gn 4$_{18}$, Ham Gn 10$_1$, Japheth Gn 10$_1$, Job Jb 1$_2$, Jesse 4QSela 8.2$_3$, Joseph Gn 46$_{20}$ 48$_4$, Judah 1 C 2$_3$, Shem Gn 10$_1$, Shemaiah 1 C 26$_6$, בֵּן *son* Gn 10$_1$ 17$_{17}$ 4QSela 8.2$_3$, רָפָא appar. *Rephaim* 1 C 20$_6$, בַּיִת *house* of David 1 K 13$_2$.

בְּ of place/time, *in, among, on* 4QPrayer^m 2$_5$, + Israel 11QT 40$_6$, Hebron 2 S 3$_2$ 1 C 3$_{1.4}$, Jerusalem 1 C 3$_{5(mss)}$, אֶרֶץ *land* 1 C 7$_{21}$, specif. land of Egypt Gn 46$_{20}$ 48$_5$, בָּקָר *cattle* Dt 15$_{19}$ 11QT 52$_7$, צֹאן *flock* Dt 15$_{19}$ 11QT 52$_7$, יוֹם *day* Jb 3$_3$; of accompaniment, *with, in (a state of)*, + מַלְכוּת *kingship* Ec 4$_{14}$ (or em. בְּ to לְ).

כְּ *as*, + Joseph Si 49$_{15}$.

מִן of agent/instrument, *by (means of), through, of*, + אִשָּׁה *woman* Ezr 10$_3$, בַּת *daughter* 1 C 2$_3$.

<COLL> with adverb or noun used adverbially, פַּעַם אֶחָד *all at once* Is 66$_8$, רִאשׁוֹן *first* Jb 15$_7$, אָז *then* Jb 38$_{21}$, אַחֲרֵי כֵן *afterwards* 4QpsJub^a 2.1$_8$ ([אח]רי כן), דּוֹר *(in) generation* Dt 23$_9$, וְעַיִר פֶּרֶא אָדָם יִוָּלֵד *or can a domesticated ass [or] a wild ass be born human?* Jb 11$_{12}$ (or em. וְעַיִר פֶּרֶד יִוָּלֵד *or can a domesticated ass be born a stallion?* or וְעַיִר פֶּרֶא אָדָם יוֹלִד *or can a domesticated ass [or] a wild ass beget a human being?* or וְעַיִר פֶּרֶא אֲדָמָה יִוָּלֵד *can a domesticated ass be born a wild ass of the steppe?*), יוֹם הִוָּלְדָהּ *day of her birth* Ho 2$_5$, יוֹם הִוָּלְדוֹ *day of his birth* Ec 7$_1$ (+ יוֹם הַמָּוֶת *day of death*); ילד ni. + הרה pu. *be conceived* Jb 3$_3$, חיל pol. *be born* Jb 15$_7$.

2. ptc. as noun, **one who is born,** <NOM CL> ונולד ממנו מפח נפש *and one born of him is a trap to the soul* Si 30$_{12(B)}$ (Bmg וילוד ממך perh. error for וילוד ממך *and there is born of you* a trap to the soul). <OBJ> יצא hi. *expel* Ezr 10$_3$ (+ אִשָּׁה *woman*).

Also 4Q418 119$_3$ 4QBéat 19$_1$.

Nu. 2 Pf. נוּלְּדוּ—**be born,** <SUBJ> אֵלֶּה 1 C 3$_5$ (mss ni.) 20$_{8(Seb)}$. <PREP> ילד לְ nu. *be born to*, + David 1 C 3$_5$, *be descended from*, + רָפָא appar. *Rephaim* 1 C 20$_8$; בְּ of place, *in*, + Jerusalem 1 C 3$_5$, Gath 1 C 20$_8$.

Pi. 9.0.1 Impf. Q יילד; ptc. מְיַלֶּדֶת, מְיַלְּדֹת (מְיַלְּדוֹת); inf. יַלֶּדְכֶן—**1. act as midwife** (to), **deliver,** <SUBJ> אִישׁ *man* CD 11$_{13}$, מְיַלֶּדֶת *midwife* Ex 1$_{16}$. <OBJ> Hebrew women Ex 1$_{16}$, בְּהֵמָה *beast* CD 11$_{13}$. <PREP> בְּ of time, *on*, + יוֹם sabbath *day* CD 11$_{13}$ (=4QD^f בשבת *on the sabbath*).

2. ptc. as noun, **midwife,** <SUBJ> אמר *say* Gn 35$_{17}$ 38$_{28}$ Ex 1$_{19}$, ראה *see* Ex 1$_{16}$, ירא *fear* Ex 1$_{17.21}$, חיה pi. *let live* Ex 1$_{17.18}$, בוא *come* Ex 1$_{19}$, לקח *take* Gn 38$_{28}$, עשׂה *do* Ex 1$_{17.18}$, קשׁר *bind* Gn 38$_{28}$, ילד pi. *act as midwife (to)* Ex 1$_{16}$, מות hi. *kill* Ex 1$_{16}$. <ADJ> עִבְרִי *Hebrew* Ex 1$_{15}$. <PREP> לְ *to*, + אמר *say* Ex 1$_{15.18}$, קרא *call* Ex 1$_{18}$, עשׂה *do, give*, Ex 1$_{21}$, יטב hi. *deal well (with)* Ex 1$_{20}$; אֶל *to*, + דבר pi. *say* Ex 1$_{17}$. <COLL> [ש]תי המיל[דות] *the two mid-*

wives 4QParGenEx 3$_{2}$.

3. beget (if em.; see Qal, §2, and Pu.).

Pu. $_{27}$ Pf. יֻלַּד (יֻלָּד), יֻלְּדָה, יֻלַּדְתִּי, יֻלְּדוּ (יֻלָּדוּ), יֻלַּדְתֶּם; ptc. יוּלָּד—**be born,** sometimes **be descended from** (e.g. 2 S 21$_{20.22}$), <SUBJ> Coniah Jr 22$_{26}$, Dan Jg 18$_{29}$, appar. Jeremiah Jr 20$_{14}$, Rebekah Gn 24$_{15}$, בֵּן *son* Gn 4$_{26}$ ||1 C 1$_{19}$ 10$_{25}$ 35$_{26}$ 36$_{5}$ 41$_{50}$ 46$_{22}$ (Sam qal) 46$_{27}$ 50$_{23}$ Jr 20$_{15}$ Ru 4$_{17}$, בַּת *daughter* Gn 6$_{1}$, נַעַר *lad* Jg 13$_{8}$, יֶלֶד *child* Is 9$_{5}$, אָב *father* Jg 18$_{29}$, אֵם *mother* Jr 22$_{26}$, אִישׁ *man* 2 S 21$_{20.22}$ Ps 87$_{5}$, אָדָם *humanity* Jb 5$_{7}$ (or em. pi. or hi. *beget*), הַר *mountain* Ps 90$_{2}$, אַרְבַּע *four* 2 S 21$_{22}$, זֶה *this (one)* Ps 87$_{4}$, *each (one)* Ps 87$_{6}$, אֵלֶּה *these* 2 S 3$_{5}$; subj. not specified, Gn 10$_{21}$ 17$_{17(Sam)}$.

<PREP> לְ *to*, + Bethuel Gn 24$_{15}$, David 2 S 3$_{5}$, Eber Gn 10$_{25}$||1 C 1$_{19}$, Esau Gn 36$_{5}$, Israel, i.e. Jacob Jg 18$_{29}$, Jacob Gn 35$_{26}$ 46$_{22}$ (Sam qal), Joseph Gn 41$_{50}$ 46$_{27}$, Naomi Ru 4$_{17}$, Rapha 2 S 21$_{20.22}$, Seth Gn 4$_{26}$, Shem Gn 10$_{21}$, בֵּן *son* Gn 17$_{17(Sam)}$ (MT ni.) 24$_{15}$, אָח *brother* Gn 24$_{15}$, אָב *father* Jr 20$_{15}$, אָדָם *humanity* Gn 6$_{1}$, עַם *people*, i.e. Israel Is 9$_{5}$, עָמָל *mischief* Jb 5$_{7}$ (or em.; see Subj.); בְּ *in*, + Gath 2 S 21$_{22}$, Hebron 2 S 3$_{5}$, Paddan-Aram Gn 35$_{26}$, Zion Ps 87$_{5}$, אֶרֶץ *land* of Canaan Gn 36$_{5}$, יוֹם *day* Gn 50$_{23(Sam)}$ (MT עַל *upon* the knees of Joseph) Jr 20$_{14}$; עַל *upon*, + בֶּרֶךְ *knee* Gn 50$_{23}$ (Sam בִּימֵי *in the days of* Joseph).

<COLL> ילד pu. + שָׁם *there* Jr 22$_{26}$ Ps 87$_{4.6}$; + חול pol. *bring to birth* Ps 90$_{2}$.

Hi. $_{176.2.7}$ Pf. הוֹלִיד (הֹלִיד), הוֹלַדְתָּ, הוֹלִידוּ (הוֹלְדוּ); impf. יוֹלִיד, 2ms תּוֹלִיד, אוֹלִיד, Si תולידו; + waw וְהוֹלִיד (וְהוֹלִידָה), וְהוֹלִידוּ, וַיּוֹלֶד; ptc. מוֹלִיד (Si מולידו), מוֹלִדִים; inf. הוֹלִיד, הוֹלִידוֹ—**beget,** <SUBJ> Y. Is 66$_{9.9}$ 1QSa 2$_{11}$ (יולי; unless הלך hi. *lead*), Abijah 2 C 13$_{21}$, Abishua 1 C 5$_{31}$, Abraham Gn 25$_{19}$ 1 C 1$_{34}$ perh. 4QAges^{a} 1$_{5}$, Adam Gn 5$_{3.4.4}$, Ahaz 1 C 8$_{36}$||9$_{42}$, Ahimaaz 1 C 5$_{35}$, Ahitub, grandson of Meraioth 1 C 5$_{34}$, Ahitub, grandson of Azariah 1 C 5$_{38}$, Amariah, son of Meraioth 1 C 5$_{33}$, Amariah, son of Azariah 1 C 5$_{37}$, Amminadab Ru 4$_{20}$ ||1 C 2$_{10}$, Arpachshad Gn 11$_{12.13.13}$, Attai, son of Jarha 1 C 2$_{36}$, Azariah, son of Jehu 1 C 2$_{39}$, Azariah, son of Ahimaaz 1 C 5$_{35}$, Azariah, son of Johanan 1 C 5$_{37}$, Azariah, son of Hilkiah 1 C 5$_{40}$, Benjamin 1 C 8$_{1}$, Bethuel Gn 22$_{23(Sam)}$, Boaz Ru 4$_{21}$||1 C 2$_{12}$, Bukki 1 C 5$_{31}$, Caleb 1 C 2$_{18}$, Chelub 1 C 4$_{11}$ (or em. Caleb), Cush Gn 10$_{8(Sam)}$, David 1 C 14$_{3}$, Eber Gn 11$_{16.17}$, Eleasah 1 C 2$_{40}$, Eleazar 1 C 5$_{30}$, Eliashib Ne 12$_{10}$, Enoch Gn 5$_{21.22}$, Enosh Gn 5$_{9.10.10}$, Ephlal 1 C 2$_{37}$, Eshton 1 C 4$_{12}$.

Gilead Jg 11$_{1}$, Haran, son of Terah Gn 11$_{27}$, Haran, son of Ephah 1 C 2$_{46}$, Heber 1 C 7$_{32}$, Heglam 1 C 8$_{7}$, Helez 1 C 2$_{39}$, Hezekiah 2 K 20$_{18}$||Is 39$_{7}$, Hezron, son of Perez Ru 4$_{19}$, Hilkiah 1 C 5$_{39}$, Hur 1 C 2$_{20}$, Isaac 4QpsJub^{b} 7$_{3}$ ([ישחק]), Ishmael Gn 17$_{20}$, Israel(ites) Dt 4$_{25}$ 28$_{41}$ perh. Is 59$_{4}$, Jacob 4QpsJub^{a} 2.2$_{11}$ 4QpsJub^{b} 7$_{3}$ ([יעקב הוליד]), Jahath 1 C 4$_{2}$, Jared Gn 5$_{18.19}$, Jehoaddah 1 C 8$_{36}$ (||9$_{42}$ Jarah; or em. Jadah, mss Jehoaddah), Jehu 1 C 2$_{38}$, Jekamiah 1 C 2$_{41}$, Jeshua Ne 12$_{10}$, Jesse Ru 4$_{22}$ 1 C 2$_{13}$, Joash 2 C 24$_{3}$, Johanan 1 C 5$_{36}$, Joiada Ne 12$_{11}$, Joiakim Ne 12$_{10}$, Jonathan Ne 12$_{11}$ (or em. Jonathan to Johanan), Joseph Gn 48$_{6}$, Kenan Gn 5$_{12.13.13}$, Kish 1 C 8$_{33}$||9$_{39}$, Kohath Nm 26$_{58}$, Koz 1 C 4$_{8}$, Lamech Gn 5$_{28.30}$.

Machir Nm 26$_{29}$, Mahalalel Gn 5$_{15.16}$, Meonothai 1 C 4$_{14}$, Meraioth 1 C 5$_{32}$, Merib-baal 1 C 8$_{34}$||9$_{40}$ (Meribaal), Methuselah Gn 5$_{25.26}$, Mikloth 1 C 8$_{32}$||9$_{38}$, Moza 1 C 8$_{37}$||9$_{43}$, Nahor Gn 11$_{24.25.25}$, Nahshon Ru 4$_{20}$||1 C 2$_{11}$, Nathan 1 C 2$_{36}$, Ner 1 C 8$_{33}$||9$_{39}$, Noah Gn 5$_{32}$ 6$_{10}$, Obed, son of Boaz Ru 4$_{22}$||1 C 2$_{12}$, Obed, son of Ephlal 1 C 2$_{38}$ (or em. Jobab), Peleg Gn 11$_{18.19.19}$, Perez Ru 4$_{18}$, Phinehas 1 C 5$_{30}$, Ram Ru 4$_{19}$||1 C 2$_{10}$ (or em. Aram or Arran), Reaiah 1 C 4$_{2}$, Rehoboam 2 C 11$_{21}$, Rekem 1 C 2$_{44}$, Reu Gn 11$_{20.21.21}$.

Salmon Ru 4$_{21}$ (or em. Salmah or Salman) 1 C 2$_{11}$ (Salma), Saul 1 C 8$_{33}$||9$_{39}$, Segub 1 C 2$_{22}$, Seraiah, son of Kenaz 1 C 4$_{14}$, Seraiah, son of Azariah 1 C 5$_{40}$, Serug Gn 11$_{22.23.23}$, Seth Gn 5$_{6.7.7}$, Shaaph 1 C 2$_{49}$ (if em. qal *give birth*, with Maacah as subj.), Shaharaim 1 C 8$_{8}$ (or em. Ahiram) 8$_{9.11}$, Shallum, son of Sismai 1 C 2$_{41}$, Shallum, son of Zadok 1 C 5$_{39}$, Shelah Gn 11$_{14.15.15}$, Shem Gn 11$_{10.11}$, Shema 1 C 2$_{44}$, Sismai 1 C 2$_{40}$, Terah Gn 11$_{26.27}$, appar. Tirhanah 1 C 2$_{49}$ (if em. qal), Uri 1 C 2$_{20}$, Uzzi 1 C 5$_{32}$, Zabad 1 C 2$_{37}$, Zadok, father of Ahimaaz 1 C 5$_{34}$, Zadok, father of Shallum 1 C 5$_{38}$, Zerahiah 1 C 5$_{32}$, Zimri 1 C 8$_{36}$||9$_{42}$.

בֵּן *son* Gn 6$_{4(Sam)}$ 11$_{11}$ Dt 28$_{41}$ Ezk 18$_{14}$ 1 C 2$_{18}$ 4$_{2}$, בַּת *daughter* Gn 11$_{11}$ Dt 28$_{41}$, אָח *brother* 1 C 4$_{11}$ (unless em.

to אָב *father*), אָב *father* Is 45$_{10}$ Jr 16$_{3}$ 1 C 4$_{11(mss)}$, אִישׁ *man* Ezk 18$_{10}$ Ec 6$_{3}$ perh. Si 41$_{9(M)}$, אָדָם *humanity* Jb 5$_{7}$ (if em. pu. or pi.),* גֵּר *sojourner* Ezk 47$_{22}$, רַע *evil person* Si 11$_{33}$, עַם *people* Is 65$_{23}$ (if em.; MT qal), גּוֹלָה *exile* Jr 29$_{6}$, עַיִר *(domesticated) ass* Jb 11$_{12}$ (if em. ni.; see Ni., Coll.), גֶּשֶׁם *rain* Is 55$_{10}$, שֶׁלֶג *snow* Is 55$_{10}$; subj. not specified Lv 25$_{45}$ Jb 38$_{28}$ Ec 5$_{13}$ Si 41$_{9(Bmg)}$ CD 7$_{7}$ 19$_{3}$.

<OBJ> Abinadab, son of Saul 1 C 8$_{33}$||9$_{39}$ (or em. Amminadab in both), Abishua 1 C 5$_{30}$, Abram Gn 11$_{26.27}$, Ahihud 1 C 8$_{7}$, Ahimaaz 1 C 5$_{34}$, Ahitub, grandson of Meraioth 1 C 5$_{33}$, Ahitub, grandson of Azariah 1 C 5$_{37}$, Ahumai 1 C 4$_{2}$, Alemeth 1 C 8$_{36}$||9$_{42}$, Amariah, son of Meraioth 1 C 5$_{33}$, Amariah, son of Azariah 1 C 5$_{37}$, Amminadab Ru 4$_{19}$||1 C 2$_{10}$, Amram Nm 26$_{58}$, Anub 1 C 4$_{8}$, Arpachshad Gn 11$_{10.11}$, Azariah, son of Jehu 1 C 2$_{38}$, Azariah, son of Ahimaaz 1 C 5$_{35}$, Azariah, son of Johanan 1 C 5$_{36}$, Azariah, son of Hilkiah 1 C 5$_{39}$, Azmaveth 1 C 8$_{36}$||9$_{42}$ (or em. Azmoth in both).

Bela 1 C 8$_{1}$, Beth-rapha 1 C 4$_{12}$, Bezalel 1 C 2$_{20}$, Binea 1 C 8$_{37}$||9$_{43}$ (1 C mss Chinea; or em. Binea in both to Baana), Boaz Ru 4$_{21}$||1 C 2$_{11}$, Bukki 1 C 5$_{31}$, David Ru 4$_{22}$, Eber Gn 11$_{14.15}$, Eleasah 1 C 2$_{39}$, Eliab 1 C 2$_{13}$, Eliashib Ne 12$_{10}$, Elishama 1 C 2$_{41}$, Enoch Gn 5$_{18.19}$, Enosh Gn 5$_{6.7}$, Ephlal 1 C 2$_{37}$, Esh-baal 1 C 8$_{33}$||9$_{39}$, Gazez 1 C 2$_{46}$ (or em. Jahdai), Gilead Nm 26$_{29}$, Ham Gn 5$_{32}$ 6$_{10}$, Haran, son of Terah Gn 11$_{26.27}$, Helez 1 C 2$_{39}$, Hezron Ru 4$_{18}$, Hilkiah 1 C 5$_{39}$, Hotham 1 C 7$_{32}$, Isaac Gn 25$_{19}$ 1 C 1$_{34}$ 4QAges^{a} 1$_{5}$.

Jacob 4QpsJub^{b} 7$_{3}$ ([י]עקב), Jaddua Ne 12$_{11}$, Jahath 1 C 4$_{2}$, Jair 1 C 2$_{22}$, Japheth Gn 5$_{32}$ 6$_{10}$, Japhlet 1 C 7$_{32}$, Jared Gn 5$_{15.16}$, Jehoaddah 1 C 8$_{36}$ (or em. Jarah or Jehoiada)||9$_{42}$ (Jarah; or em. Jarah to Jadah, mss Jehoaddah), Jehozadak 1 C 5$_{40}$, Jehu 1 C 2$_{38}$, Jekamiah 1 C 2$_{41}$, Jephthah Jg 11$_{1}$, Jesse Ru 4$_{22}$||1 C 2$_{12}$, Jeuz 1 C 8$_{9}$, Joab 1 C 4$_{14}$, Jobab 1 C 8$_{9}$, Johanan 1 C 5$_{35}$, Joiada Ne 12$_{10}$, Joiakim Ne 12$_{10}$, Jonathan, son of Joiada Ne 12$_{11}$ (or em. Johanan), Jonathan, son of Saul 1 C 8$_{33}$||9$_{39}$, Kenan Gn 5$_{9.10}$, Kish 1 C 8$_{33}$ (or em. to Abner)||9$_{39}$, Lahad 1 C 4$_{2}$, Lamech Gn 5$_{25.26}$, Levi 4QpsJub^{a} 2.2$_{11}$ 4QpsJub^{b} 7$_{3}$ ([הוליד]), Lot Gn 11$_{27}$, Mahalalel Gn 5$_{12.13}$, Malcam 1 C 8$_{9}$, Malchishua 1 C 8$_{33}$||9$_{39}$, Mehir 1 C 4$_{11}$, Meraioth 1 C 5$_{32}$, Mesha 1 C 8$_{9}$, Methuselah Gn 5$_{21.22}$, Micah 1 C 8$_{34}$||9$_{40}$, Mirmah 1 C 8$_{9}$, Moza 1 C 8$_{36}$||9$_{42}$ (or em. Massa).

Nahor, son of Serug Gn 11$_{22.23}$, Nahor, son of Terah Gn 11$_{26.27}$, Nahshon Ru 4$_{20}$||1 C 2$_{10}$, Nathan 1 C 2$_{36}$, Nimrod Gn 10$_{8(Sam)}$, Noah Gn 5$_{30}$, Obed, son of Boaz Ru 4$_{21}$||1 C 2$_{12}$, Obed, son of Ephlal 1 C 2$_{37}$, Ophrah 1 C 4$_{14}$, Paseah 1 C 4$_{12}$, Peleg Gn 11$_{16.17}$, Phinehas 1 C 5$_{30}$, Raham 1 C 2$_{44}$, Ram Ru 4$_{19}$ (or em. Aram or Arran), Rebekah Gn 22$_{23(Sam)}$, Reu Gn 11$_{18.19}$.

Saaph 1 C 2$_{49}$ (if em. qal), Sachia 1 C 8$_{9}$, Salmah Ru 4$_{20}$ (or em. Salman or Salmon)||1 C 2$_{11}$, Saul 1 C 8$_{33}$ ||9$_{39}$, Seraiah 1 C 5$_{40}$, Serug Gn 11$_{20.21}$, Seth Gn 5$_{4}$, Shallum, son of Sismai 1 C 2$_{40}$, Shallum, son of Zadok 1 C 5$_{38}$, Shammai 1 C 2$_{44}$, Shelah Gn 11$_{12.13}$ (or em. Kenan in both), Shem Gn 5$_{32}$ 6$_{10}$, Sheva 1 C 2$_{49}$ (if em. qal), Shimeah 1 C 8$_{32}$ (or em. Shimeam as || 9$_{38}$), Shomer 1 C 7$_{32}$ (or em. Shemer), Shua 1 C 7$_{32}$, Sismai 1 C 2$_{40}$, Tehinnah 1 C 4$_{12}$, Terah Gn 11$_{24.25}$, Uri 1 C 2$_{20}$, Uzza 1 C 8$_{7}$, Uzzi 1 C 5$_{31}$, Zabad 1 C 2$_{36}$, Zadok, father of Ahimaaz 1 C 5$_{34}$, Zadok, father of Shallum 1 C 5$_{38}$, Zerahiah 1 C 5$_{32}$, Zibia 1 C 8$_{9}$, Zimri 1 C 8$_{36}$||9$_{42}$, Zobebah 1 C 4$_{8}$.

בֵּן *son* Gn 5$_{4+9t}$ 6$_{10}$ 11$_{13+6t}$ Dt 4$_{25}$ 2 K 20$_{18}$||Is 39$_{7}$ Jr 16$_{3}$ 29$_{6}$ Ezk 18$_{10.14}$ 47$_{22}$ Ec 5$_{13}$ 1 C 14$_{3}$ 2 C 11$_{21}$ 13$_{21}$ 24$_{3}$ CD 7$_{7}$ 19$_{3}$, בַּת *daughter* Gn 5$_{4+8t}$ 11$_{13+6t}$ Jr 16$_{3}$ 29$_{6}$ 1 C 14$_{3}$ 2 C 11$_{21}$ 13$_{21}$ 24$_{3}$ CD 7$_{7}$, בְּכוֹר *firstborn* 1 C 2$_{13}$ 8$_{1}$ 1QNoah 3$_{3}$ ([ב]כור), מוֹלֶדֶת *offspring* Gn 48$_{6}$, אָחוֹת *sister* 1 C 7$_{32}$, אָב *father* 1 C 2$_{44}$ 4$_{12.14}$, מִשְׁפָּחָה *family* Lv 25$_{45}$ 1 C 4$_{8}$, מָשִׁיחַ *Messiah* 1QSa 2$_{11}$ (יולי; unless הלך hi. *lead*), נָשִׂיא *prince* Gn 17$_{20}$, מֵאָה *a hundred (children)* Ec 6$_{3}$, אֶרֶץ *land* Is 55$_{10}$, אָוֶן *iniquity* Is 59$_{4}$, רַע *evil* Si 11$_{33}$, אֵגֶל *drop (of dew)* pl. Jb 38$_{28}$, מָה *what* Is 45$_{10}$; obj. not specified Is 65$_{23}$ (if em. qal) 1 C 8$_{8.9.11}$ Si 41$_{9(Bmg)}$.

<PREP> לְ introducing object, + עָמָל *mischief* Jb 5$_{7}$ (if em. pu. or pi.); appar. of benefit, *for*, + בֵּן *son* Gn 6$_{4}$ (Sam) (MT qal *give birth* to, of women); בְּ *in*, + דְּמוּת *likeness* Gn 5$_{3}$, אֶרֶץ *land* Lv 25$_{45}$ Jr 16$_{3}$, שָׂדֶה *field* of Moab 1 C 8$_{8}$; כְּ *according to*, + צֶלֶם *image* Gn 5$_{3}$; מִן of instrument, *by means of, with*, + Hodesh 1 C 8$_{9}$, Hushim 1 C 8$_{11}$ (or em. to Mehusham), אִשָּׁה *wife* 1 C 8$_{9}$; אֵת *with*, + Azuba 1 C 2$_{18}$, Jerioth 1 C 2$_{18}$, אִשָּׁה *wife* 1 C 2$_{18}$;

אַחֲרֵי *after*, + Ephraim Gn 48$_{6}$, Manasseh Gn 48$_{6}$; בְּתוֹךְ *among*, + appar. Israel Ezk 47$_{22}$.

<COLL> ילד hi. + לקח *take* wife Jr 29$_{6}$ 1 C 14$_{3}$, נשׂא *take* wife 2 C 13$_{21}$ 24$_{3}$, הרה *conceive* Is 59$_{4}$, חול *writhe, be in labour* Is 45$_{10}$, שׁבר hi. *bring to birth* Is 66$_{9}$, צמח hi. *cause to grow* Is 55$_{10}$; :: עצר *close* womb Is 66$_{9}$.

<ANT> עצר *close* womb.

Ho. 3 Inf. הֻלֶּדֶת ,הוּלֶּדֶת—**be born,** <SUBJ> Jerusalem Ezk 16$_{4}$, פַּרְעֹה *Pharaoh* Gn 40$_{20}$. <COLL> יוֹם הֻלֶּדֶת אֶת־פַּרְעֹה *Pharaoh's birthday* Gn 40$_{20}$, יוֹם הוּלֶּדֶת אֹתָךְ *day of your birth* Ezk 16$_{4.5}$ (הֻלֶּדֶת); ילד ho. + כרת שׁר *cut umbilical cord* Ezk 16$_{4}$, בְּמַיִם רחץ *bathe in water* after birth Ezk 16$_{4}$, מלח ho. *be rubbed* with salt, after birth Ezk 16$_{4}$, חתל ho. *be wrapped* Ezk 16$_{4}$.

Htp. 1 + waw וַיִּתְיַלְדוּ—**register genealogy,** <SUBJ> עֵדָה the whole *assembly* Nm 1$_{18}$.

<PREP> לְ *by*, + בַּיִת *house* of their fathers Nm 1$_{18}$; בְּ *according to*, + מִסְפָּר *number* of names Nm 1$_{18}$; עַל *according to*, + מִשְׁפָּחָה *clan* Nm 1$_{18}$.

→ יֶלֶד *child*, וָלָד *child*, יַלְדָּה *girl*, יִלּוֹד *born*, יָלִיד *born*, יַלְדוּת *youth*, מוֹלֶד *birth (sign)*, מוֹלֶדֶת *offspring*, תּוֹלֵדָה *generation*, אֶלְתּוֹלַד *Eltolad*, מוֹלִיד *Molid*, מוֹלָדָה *Moladah*, תּוֹלָד *Tolad*.*

יֶלֶד 89.2.4 n.m. **male child**—יָלֶד; cstr. יֶלֶד; pl. יְלָדִים; cstr. יַלְדֵי; sf. יַלְדֵי, יְלָדָיו, יְלָדֶיהָ, יַלְדֵיהֶם, יַלְדֵיהֶן—**male child** (e.g. Ex 1$_{17.18}$ Jl 4$_{3}$ Zc 8$_{5}$), as distinct from יַלְדָּה *girl*; plural is male children (e.g. Zc 8$_{5}$), though it may include females (e.g. Ex 21$_{4}$ Ezr 10$_{1}$); **youth** (e.g. 1 K 12$_{8.10.14}$‖2 C 10$_{8.10.14}$ Dn 1$_{4.10.13.15.17}$), **young** of birds and wild animals (Jb 38$_{41}$ 39$_{3}$), **unborn child, foetus** (Ex 21$_{22}$ [Sam וָלָד *foetus*]).

<SUBJ> היה *be* Ex 2$_{10}$ 21$_{4}$ 1 S 1$_{2}$ 2 S 6$_{23}$ (or em. וָלָד *child*) 12$_{18}$, גמל ni. *be weaned* Gn 21$_{8}$, אנשׁ ni. *be incurable* 2 S 12$_{15}$ (or del. יֵאָנַשׁ).

חיה *live* 1 S 12$_{22}$ 1 K 17$_{22}$, גדל *grow up* Gn 21$_{8}$ Ex 2$_{10}$ 1 K 12$_{8.10}$‖2 C 10$_{8.10}$ 2 K 4$_{18}$, מות *die* 2 S 12$_{18+8t}$ 1 K 14$_{12}$ 2 K 4$_{18}$, ראה *see* Is 29$_{23}$ (or del.), ידע *know* Dn 1$_{4}$, שׂכל hi. *have insight* Dn 1$_{4}$, בין hi. *understand* Dn 1$_{4}$, יעץ ni. *consider* 1 K 12$_{8}$, דבר pi. *speak* 1 K 12$_{10}$‖2 C 10$_{10}$, אמר *say* 1 K 12$_{10}$ 2 K 4$_{18}$, שׁוע pi. *cry out* Jb 38$_{41}$, קדשׁ hi. *sanctify* Is 29$_{23}$, קבב *curse* Si 41$_{7}$, שׂמח *rejoice* Ne 12$_{43}$, שׂחק pi. *play* Zc 8$_{5}$, רקד pi. *leap* Jb 21$_{11}$, אכל *eat* Dn 1$_{13.15}$.

בוא *come* 11QT 39$_{7}$, יצא *go out* 2 K 4$_{18}$ Ec 4$_{13}$, *abort* Ex 21$_{22}$, נגשׁ *approach* Gn 33$_{6.7}$, תעה *wander* Jb 38$_{41}$, שׁוב *return* 2 S 12$_{23}$, עמד *stand* Ec 4$_{15}$, *stand* before, i.e. serve, 1 K 12$_{8}$‖2 C 10$_{8}$ Dn 1$_{4.4}$, hi. *remain* Si 40$_{19}$, שׁחה htpal. *bow down* Gn 33$_{6.7}$, רבץ *lie down* Is 11$_{7}$, ישׁב *sit* 2 K 4$_{18}$ (or em. שׁכב *lie*), מלך *rule* Ec 4$_{13}$, פלח pi. *cleave open* Jb 39$_{3}$, חבל pi. *destroy* 6QAllegory 1$_{5}$.

<NOM CL> לְחַנָּה אֵין יְלָדִים *Hannah had no children* 1 S 1$_{2}$, הֲלוֹא־אַתֶּם יִלְדֵי־פֶשַׁע *are you not children of sin?* Is 57$_{4}$, הֲבֵן יַקִּיר לִי אֶפְרַיִם אִם יֶלֶד שַׁעֲשֻׁעִים *is Ephraim my precious son, is he a child of delight(s)?* Jr 31$_{20}$ (or del. הֲ and אִם), יְלָדִים אֲשֶׁר אֵין־בָּהֶם כָּל־מוּם *youths in whom there is no defect* Dn 1$_{4(Qr)}$, יְלָדִים ... אֲשֶׁר כֹּחַ בָּהֶם *youths ... in whom there is strength* to teach, Dn 1$_{4}$, הַיְלָדִים אֲשֶׁר כְּגִילְכֶם *the youths who are of your generation* Dn 1$_{10}$, הַיְלָדִים רַכִּים *the children are delicate* Gn 33$_{13}$, הַיֶּלֶד חַי *the child was alive* 2 S 12$_{21.22}$, טוֹב יֶלֶד מִסְכֵּן וְחָכָם *better a poor and wise youth* than an old and foolish king Ec 4$_{13}$.

כולם ילדים *all of them are children* 4QMidrEschat[b] 8$_{4}$, הִנֵּה ... הַיְלָדִים *here are ... the children* Is 8$_{18}$, יֶשׁ־לָנוּ ... יֶלֶד *we have ... a (male) child* Gn 44$_{20}$, אֵין לָהּ יֶלֶד *she* (Sarah) *had no child* Gn 11$_{30(Sam)}$ (MT וָלָד *child, foetus*), הַיֶּלֶד אֵינֶנּוּ *the boy is not here* Gn 37$_{30}$.

<OBJ> אהב *love* Gn 44$_{20}$, חיה pi. *let live* Ex 1$_{17.18}$, ראה *see* Gn 33$_{5}$ Ex 2$_{6}$, למד pi. *teach* Dn 1$_{4}$, גדל pi. *educate* Dn 1$_{4}$.

בוא hi. *bring* Ex 2$_{10}$ 2 K 4$_{18}$ Dn 1$_{4.17}$, שׁוב hi. *bring back* 2 S 12$_{23}$, ירד hi. *bring down* 1 K 17$_{23}$, נתן *give, place* Gn 21$_{14}$ 30$_{26}$ 1 K 3$_{25.26(mss).27(mss)}$ (L יִלּוֹד *child*) 17$_{23}$ Is 8$_{18}$ Jl 4$_{3}$ 4QD[a] 6.2$_{11}$ ([תתן את הי]לד), לקח *take* Gn 32$_{23.23}$ Ex 2$_{9}$ 1 K 17$_{23}$ 2 K 4$_{1}$ Ru 4$_{16}$, הלך hi. *take* Ex 2$_{9}$, משׁה *draw* Ex 2$_{10}$, נשׂא *carry* 2 K 4$_{18.18}$, שׂים *put* Gn 33$_{2.2}$ Ex 2$_{3}$, שׁית *put* Ru 4$_{16}$ (or del.), שׁכב hi. *lay down* 2 K 4$_{18}$, ילד *bear* 2 S 12$_{15}$, ינק hi. *nurse* Ex 2$_{7.9.9}$, חנן *be gracious (to)* Gn 33$_{5}$.

שׁלך hi. *throw* Gn 21$_{15}$, חצה *divide* Gn 33$_{1}$, גזר *cut* 1 K 3$_{25}$, נגף *strike* 2 S 12$_{15}$, הרג *kill* Gn 4$_{23}$, שׁחט *slaughter* Is 57$_{5}$ (שֹׁחֲטֵי הַיְלָדִים *those who slaughter children*), בשׁל pi. *cook* Lm 4$_{10}$.

<CSTR> יֶלֶד זְקֻנִים *child of (his) old age* Gn 44$_{20}$, שַׁעֲשֻׁעִים *of delight* Jr 31$_{20}$, יַלְדֵי הָעִבְרִים *children of the*

Hebrews Ex 2$_{6}$, נָכְרִים *of foreigners* Is 2$_{6}$, פֶּשַׁע *of sin* Is 57$_{4}$ (יַלְדֵי), זְנוּנִים *of prostitution* Ho 1$_{2}$, ילדי צדק *children of righteousness* 4QBark[d] 2.1$_{12}$.

אֵם הַיֶּלֶד *mother of the boy* Ex 2$_{8}$, נֶפֶשׁ *soul*, i.e. life, *of* 1 K 17$_{21.22}$ (both יֶלֶד), מוֹת *death of (the) boy* Gn 21$_{16}$ (יֶלֶד), בְּשַׂר *flesh of* 2 K 4$_{34}$, מַרְאֶה *appearance of* Dn 1$_{13}$, עֲצַת *advice of* 1 K 12$_{14}$‖2 C 10$_{14}$, רֶגֶל הַיְלָדִים *foot*, i.e. pace, *of the children* Gn 33$_{14}$, שֹׁחֲטֵי *those who slaughter* Is 57$_{5}$.

שְׁנֵי יְלָדַי *my two children* 2 K 4$_{1}$, שְׁנֵי יְלָדֶיהָ *her two sons* Ru 1$_{5}$, אַרְבָּעִים וּשְׁנַיִם יְלָדִים *forty-two boys* 2 K 2$_{24}$, אַחַד עָשָׂר יְלָדָיו *his eleven sons* Gn 32$_{23}$, כָּל־הַיְלָדִים *all the youths* Dn 1$_{15}$ (or del. כָּל).

<APP> קָהָל *assembly* Ezr 10$_{1}$, טוֹב *good (one)* Dn 1$_{4}$.

<ADJ> קָטָן *small*, i.e. young, Gn 44$_{20}$, חַי *living* 1 K 3$_{25.26(mss).27(mss)}$, מִסְכֵּן *poor* Ec 4$_{13}$, חָכָם *wise* Ec 4$_{13}$, שֵׁנִי *second* Ec 4$_{15}$, זֶה *this* Ex 2$_{9}$ 1 K 17$_{21}$, אֵלֶּה *these* Dn 1$_{10.17}$ (הַיְלָדִים הָאֵלֶּה אַרְבַּעְתָּם *all four of these young men*).

<PREP> לְ of direction, *to* + נתן *give* knowledge Dn 1$_{17}$, שׂים *place*, i.e. give, name Dn 1$_{4}$, קרא *call*, i.e. give name Ru 4$_{16}$; of benefit, *to, for*, + מנה pi. *appoint* Dn 1$_{4}$, עשׂה ni. *be done* Ex 2$_{3}$; of possession, *of, (belonging) to*, 2 K 4$_{26}$ (הֲשָׁלוֹם לַיָּלֶד *is the child well?*).

בְּ of place, *in, among* Dn 1$_{4}$; of instrument, *by (means of), with*, + נחם pi. *comfort* 4QBark[d] 2.1$_{12}$; *in exchange (for)*, + עבד *serve* Gn 30$_{26}$; *against*, + חטא *sin* Gn 42$_{22}$, שׂפק hi. perh. *strike (hands)* with Is 2$_{6}$ (unless שׂפק hi. *find satisfaction* with [בְּ of instrument]).

מִן partitive, *(one) of, (some) of* Ex 2$_{6}$, + מצא ni. *be found* Dn 1$_{17}$, בקע pi. *tear apart* 2 K 2$_{24}$; of comparison, *(more) than* Si 40$_{19}$, + זעף perh. *be thin* Dn 1$_{10}$.

אֶל *to*, + הלך *go* 2 S 12$_{23}$.

עַל *over*, + שׁכב *lie* 2 K 4$_{34}$, גהר *bend* 2 K 4$_{34.35}$ (or del.), מדד htpo. *measure*, i.e. stretch *oneself* 1 K 17$_{21}$ (or em. נפח *breathe*), חמל עַל *have pity on* Ex 2$_{6}$; עִם *with*, + הלך pi. *go* Ec 4$_{15}$; אֵת *with*, + דבר pi. *speak* Dn 1$_{17}$, יעץ ni. *consult together* 1 K 12$_{8}$‖2 C 10$_{8}$.

<COLL> יֶלֶד ‖ אִישׁ *man* Gn 4$_{23}$ Ezr 10$_{1}$, אִשָּׁה *wife* Gn 30$_{26}$ 33$_{5}$ Ex 21$_{4}$ Ho 1$_{2}$ Ezr 10$_{1}$ 11QT 39$_{7}$, עִיר *city* Si 40$_{19(B)}$; :: יַלְדָּה *girl* Zc 8$_{5}$ 6QAllegory 1$_{5}$.

יֶלֶד + בֵּן *son* Gn 21$_{8}$ Ex 1$_{17}$ 2$_{3.10}$ 21$_{4}$ 1 K 3$_{25}$ 17$_{23}$ 2 K 4$_{26.34}$ Is 57$_{4}$ Jr 31$_{20}$ Jb 39$_{3}$ Ru 4$_{16}$, בַּת *daughter* Ex 21$_{4}$, אָח *brother* Gn 42$_{22}$ 44$_{20}$, אָחוֹת *sister* Ex 2$_{3.7}$, אָב *father* Gn 44$_{20}$ 2 K 4$_{18}$ Si 41$_{7}$, אֵם *mother* Gn 44$_{20}$ 1 K 17$_{23}$ 2 K 4$_{18}$, אמן ptc. *foster mother* Ru 4$_{16}$, אִישׁ *man* 2 K 4$_{26}$ Ru 1$_{5}$, אִשָּׁה *woman* Gn 32$_{23}$ Ex 21$_{4}$ 1 S 1$_{2}$ 2 S 12$_{15}$ 2 K 4$_{1}$ Ru 1$_{5}$ Lm 4$_{10}$, נַעַר *lad* Gn 44$_{20}$ Ex 2$_{6}$ 2 S 12$_{15}$ 2 K 2$_{24}$ 4$_{26.34}$ Is 11$_{7}$, עֲוִיל *child* Jb 21$_{11}$, יִלּוֹד *child* 1 K 3$_{25}$ (mss יֶלֶד), יַלְדָּה *girl* Jl 4$_{3}$.

יֶלֶד + אָדוֹן *master* Ex 21$_{4}$, עֶבֶד *servant* Gn 33$_{5}$ Dn 1$_{10.13}$, שִׁפְחָה *female servant* Gn 32$_{23}$ 33$_{2.6}$, זָקֵן *elder, old man* 1 K 12$_{8}$‖2 C 10$_{8}$ 12$_{14}$ Zc 8$_{5}$, זְקֵנָה *old woman* Zc 8$_{5}$, מְיַלֶּדֶת *midwife* Ex 1$_{17.18}$, מֵינֶקֶת *nurse* Ex 2$_{7}$, אַלְמָנָה *widow* 1 K 17$_{21}$, עַם *people* Ezr 10$_{1}$, מצא ptc. *one who finds* wisdom Si 40$_{19}$, זֶרַע *offspring* Is 57$_{4}$, עֹרֵב *raven* Jb 38$_{41}$.

<SYN> אִישׁ *man*, אִשָּׁה *wife*, עִיר *city*.

<ANT> יַלְדָּה *girl*.*

⇒ ילד *give birth*.

יַלְדָּה 3.0.1 n.f. **girl**—pl. יְלָדוֹת—<SUBJ> שׂחק pi. *play* Zc 8$_{5}$, נתן ni. *be given (up)* Dn 11$_{6(ms)}$ (וְהַיַּלְדָּה *and the girl*; L וְהַיֹּלְדָהּ *the one who begot her*; or em. to וְיַלְדָּהּ *and her girl* or וִילָדֶיהָ *and her children*), חבל pi. *destroy* 6Q Allegory 1$_{5}$ (חב[לה]). <OBJ> לקח *take* Gn 34$_{4}$, מכר *sell* Jl 4$_{3}$. <ADJ> זֹאת *this* Gn 34$_{4}$. <COLL> + אִשָּׁה *wife* Gn 34$_{4}$; :: יֶלֶד *male child* Zc 8$_{5}$ 6QAllegory 1$_{5}$. <ANT> יֶלֶד *male child*.*

⇒ ילד *give birth*.

יַלְדוּת 3 n.f. **youth**—sf. יַלְדוּתֶךָ (יַלְדֻתֶיךָ)—as period of life, **youth** (Ec 11$_{9.10}$); **young men** (Ps 110$_{3}$), <NOM CL> הַיַּלְדוּת ... הָבֶל *youth is ... vanity* Ec 11$_{10}$. <CSTR> טַל יַלְדֻתֶיךָ *the dew of your young men* Ps 110$_{3}$ (or em. לְךָ טַל יַלְדֻתֶיךָ *to you [come] the dew of your young men* to כְּטַל יְלִדְתִּיךָ *like dew I have given birth to you*, i.e. ילד qal, §2). <PREP> בְּ of time, *in, during*, + שׂמח *rejoice* Ec 11$_{9}$. <COLL> יַלְדוּת *youth* + בְּחוּרִים *youth* Ec 11$_{9}$, שַׁחֲרוּת *blackness* of hair Ec 11$_{10}$.*

⇒ ילד *give birth*.

ילה 1 vb. **be anxious—Qal** 1 + waw 3fs וַתֵּלַהּ (unless from להה *languish*)—**be anxious, be distressed**, <SUBJ> אֶרֶץ *land* Gn 47$_{13}$ (Sam ותלא *it was weary*). <PREP> מִפְּנֵי *on account of*, + רָעָב *famine* Gn 47$_{13}$.

יָלוּד, see ילד *give birth*, Qal, §4.

יִלּוֹד $_{6}$ adj. **born**—pl. יִלֹּדִים, יִלּוֹדִים—with same meaning as יָלוּד pass. ptc. *one who is born*, from ילד, Qal, §4b; used attributively of בֵּן *son* Ex 1$_{22}$ (Sam + לָעִבְרִים *to the Hebrews*) 2 S 12$_{14}$ (+ לְךָ *to you*, i.e. David) Jr 16$_{3}$, בַּת *daughter* Jr 16$_{3}$, עַם *people* Jos 5$_{5}$. <COLL> עַל־הַבָּנִים וְעַל־הַבָּנוֹת הַיִּלּוֹדִים בַּמָּקוֹם הַזֶּה *concerning the sons and daughters who are born in this place* Jr 16$_{3}$; אֵלֶּה שְׁמוֹת הַיִּלֹּדִים לוֹ בִּירוּשָׁלָםִ *these are the names of those born to him* (David) *in Jerusalem* 2 S 5$_{14}$.

Also perh. 4QMyst^{a} 28$_{1.2}$ (unless both ילד pass. ptc.).*

⇒ ילד *give birth.*

יָלוֹן $_{1}$ pr.n.m. **Jalon,** Judahite, son of Ezrah, <NOM CL> בְּנֵי עֶזְרָה ... וְיָלוֹן *the sons of Ezrah were ... and Jalon* 1 C 4$_{17(Seb, mss)}$ (L בֶּן־ *son of*; or em. וְיָלוֹן וַתַּהַר *and Jalon; and she conceived* to וַיּוֹלֶד יֶתֶר *and Jether begat*).

[יָלִיד] $_{13}$ adj. **born**—cstr. יְלִיד; pl. יְלִידֵי—used as noun, **one (who is) born, descendant,** <SUBJ> אכל *eat* Lv 22$_{11}$, מול ni. *be circumcised* Gn 17$_{12.13.27}$. <NOM CL> אִם־ יְלִיד בַּיִת הוּא *is he*, i.e. Israel, *a home-born slave?* Jr 2$_{14}$. <OBJ> ראה *see* Nm 13$_{28}$, לקח *take* Gn 17$_{23}$, ירשׁ hi. *dispossess* Jos 15$_{14}$. <CSTR> יְלִיד בַּיִת *one born of*, i.e. to, *a household*, i.e. home-born slave Gn 17$_{12}$ (בָּיִת) 17$_{13}$ (בֵּיתְךָ) 17$_{27}$ (בָּיִת) Lv 22$_{11}$ (בֵּיתוֹ; Sam יְלִידֵי) Jr 2$_{14}$, יְלִידֵי בֵיתוֹ *ones born of*, i.e. to, *his household*, i.e. home-born slaves Gn 14$_{14}$ 17$_{23}$ Lv 22$_{11(Sam)}$, יְלִידֵי הָעֲנָק *descendants of Anak* Nm 13$_{22}$ (Sam יְלִידֵי עֲנָק) 13$_{28}$ (יְלִדֵי) Jos 15$_{14}$ (or del.), הָרָפָה *of Rapha* 2 S 21$_{16.18}$||1 C 20$_{4}$ (2 S יְלִדֵי; 1 C מִילִדֵי הָרְפָאִים *of the descendants of the Rephaim*); כָּל־ יְלִידֵי *all those born of*, i.e. to, his household Gn 17$_{23}$. <APP> Ahiman, Sheshai, and Talmai Nm 13$_{22}$ Jos 15$_{14}$, חָנִיךְ *retainer* Gn 14$_{14}$. <PREP> בְּ partitive, *(one) of* 2 S 21$_{16.18}$; מִן partitive, *(one) of* 1 C 20$_{4}$. <COLL> יְלִיד + מִקְנַת־כֶּסֶף *purchase of silver*, i.e. bought slave Gn 17$_{12.13.23.27}$, עֶבֶד *servant* Jr 2$_{14}$, קִנְיַן כַּסְפּוֹ *acquisition of his silver*, i.e. his property Lv 22$_{11}$.*

⇒ ילד *give birth.*

ילל $_{27.0.2}$ vb. **howl—Hi.** $_{27.0.2}$ Impf. יְיֵלִיל, אֵילִיל, יְיֵלִילוּ, תְּיֵלִילוּ, (Q ילילו) יְהֵילִילוּ; + waw וָאֵילִילָה, וְהֵילַל; impv. הֵילֵל, הֵילִילִי, הֵילִילוּ—**howl, wail, lament,** <SUBJ> appar. Y. Jr 48$_{31}$, Heshbon Jr 49$_{3}$, Moab Is 15$_{2}$ 16$_{7}$, appar. Micah Mc 1$_{8}$, perh. Israel Is 13$_{6}$ Jr 51$_{8}$ Ezk 30$_{2}$, בֶּן *son*, i.e. Ezekiel Ezk 21$_{17}$, מֹשֵׁל *ruler* Is 52$_{5}$ (or em. ילל hi. to הלל pi. *praise* ruler; 1QIsa^{a}, mss הלל poel *mock* ruler), יֹשֵׁב *inhabitant* Is 23$_{6}$ Jr 47$_{2}$ 48$_{20(Kt)}$ Zp 1$_{11}$, רֹעֶה *shepherd* Jr 25$_{34}$, מְשָׁרֵת *minister* Jl 1$_{13}$, כֹּרֵם *vinedresser* Jl 1$_{11}$, עזב ptc. *one who abandons* Y. Is 65$_{14}$, appar. sinner 4QPs Ezek^{c} 5$_{4}$, בְּרוֹשׁ *juniper* Zc 11$_{2}$, אַלּוֹן *oak* Zc 11$_{2}$, שַׁעַר *gate* Is 14$_{31}$, אֳנִיָּה *ship* Is 23$_{1.14}$, כֹּל *everyone* Is 15$_{3}$ 16$_{7}$; subj. not specified Jr 48$_{39}$.

<PREP> לְ of benefit, *for*, + Moab Is 16$_{7}$ (or del. לְמוֹאָב); בְּ of place/time, *in, on*, + יוֹם *day* 4QpsEzek^{c} 5$_{4}$, רְחוֹב *square* Is 15$_{3}$; מִן *from*, + שֶׁבֶר *crushing* of spirit Is 65$_{14}$; עַל *on account of, over, upon*, + Babylon Jr 51$_{8}$, Medeba Is 1$_{2}$, Moab Jr 48$_{31}$, Nebo Is 15$_{2}$, חִטָּה *wheat* Jl 1$_{11}$, שְׂעֹרָה *barley* Jl 1$_{11}$, גַּג *roof* Is 15$_{3}$, זֹאת *this* Mc 1$_{8}$.

<COLL> ילל hi. || זעק *cry out* Is 14$_{31}$ 15$_{3}$ (+) 65$_{14}$ Jr 25$_{34}$ 47$_{2}$ 48$_{20.31}$ (+) 49$_{3}$ Ezk 21$_{17}$ (+) Ho 7$_{14}$, ספד *lament* Jl 1$_{13}$ Mc 1$_{8}$, בושׁ hi. *be ashamed* Jl 1$_{11}$; + הגה *moan* Is 16$_{7}$ Jr 48$_{31}$, בכה *weep* Is 15$_{2}$, מוג ni. *be melted* Is 14$_{31}$, הלך *go* barefoot and naked Mc 1$_{8}$, ירד *go down* weeping Is 15$_{3}$, עשׂה *make* lamentation Mc 1$_{8}$; :: רנן *exult* Is 65$_{14}$.

Also 4QparaGenEx G$_{1}$.

<SYN> זעק *cry out*, ספד *lament*, בושׁ hi. *be ashamed.*

<ANT> רנן *exult.**

⇒ יְלֵל *howling*, יְלָלָה *howling*

יְלֵל $_{1}$ n.[m.] **howling,** <CSTR> יְלֵל יְשִׁמֹן *howling of*, i.e. heard in, *the wilderness* Dt 32$_{10}$ (or em. וְלֵיל יְשִׁמֹן *and a night of wilderness*; Sam ובתהללות ישן[ ]מנהו perh. *and he placed him in shining places*). <APP> תֹּהוּ *waste* Dt 32$_{10}$.*

⇒ ילל *howl.*

יְלָלָה $_{5}$ n.f. **howling**—cstr. יִלְלַת (L יְלָלַת); sf. יִלְלָתָהּ—<SUBJ> היה *be* Zp 1$_{10}$, נקף hi. *go around* appar. Is 15$_{8}$ perh. Is 15$_{8}$ (but prob. nom. cl.). <NOM CL> בְּאֵר אֵילִים יִלְלָתָהּ *her howling is (even at) Beer Elim* Is 15$_{8}$ (unless del. יִלְלָתָהּ). <CSTR> יִלְלַת הָרֹעִים *the howling of the*

shepherds Zc 11$_{3}$, אַדִּירֵי *of the nobles* of the flock Jr 25$_{36}$. <COLL> יְלָלָה || זְעָקָה *cry* Is 15$_{8}$, צְעָקָה *outcry* Jr 25$_{36}$ Zp 1$_{10}$ (+), שְׁאָגָה *roaring* Zc 11$_{3}$. <SYN> זְעָקָה *cry*, צְעָקָה *outcry*, שְׁאָגָה *roaring*.*
→ ילל *howl*.

יָלַע, see לעע *be rash*.

יַלֶּפֶת 2 n.f. **scab,** disqualifying priests from serving (Lv 21$_{20}$), and animals from being sacrificed (Lv 22$_{22}$), <SUBJ> היה *be* Lv 21$_{20}$ (unless יַלֶּפֶת = *man with scab*; + מְרוֹחַ אָשֶׁךְ *one crushed of testicle*, גָּרָב *eczema*, תְּבַלֻּל *confusion* of sight, דַּק *thin one*, גִּבֵּן *hunchbacked*, שֶׁבֶר *fracture* of hand or foot), קרב *draw near* Lv 21$_{20}$ (if יַלֶּפֶת = *man with scab*). <OBJ> קרב hi. *bring near*, i.e. offer Lv 22$_{22}$ (+ עַוֶּרֶת *blindness*, שָׁבוּר *broken one*, חָרוּץ *mutilated one*, יַבֶּלֶת *running sore*, גָּרָב *eczema*). <APP> אֵלֶּה *these* Lv 22$_{22}$. <PREP> מִן partitive, *(some) of*, + נתן *give*, i.e. place Lv 22$_{22}$.

יֶלֶק 9 n.m. **locust**—יֶלֶק—collective, <SUBJ> בוא *come* Ps 105$_{34}$ (|| אַרְבֶּה *locust*), עוף *fly* Na 3$_{16}$, אכל *eat* Jl 1$_{4}$ (+ גָּזָם *locust*) 2$_{25}$ (|| גָּזָם; both || אַרְבֶּה, חָסִיל *locust*), פשׁט *strip, shed (sheaths of wings)* Na 3$_{16}$. <CSTR> יֶתֶר הַיֶּלֶק *remainder of*, i.e. what is left by, *the locust* Jl 1$_{4}$. <APP> חַיִל *army* Jl 2$_{25}$. <ADJ> סָמָר *bristling* Jr 51$_{27}$. <PREP> כְּ *as* Jr 51$_{14.27}$, + אכל *eat* Na 3$_{15}$ (or del.), כבד htp. *make oneself heavy*, i.e. numerous Na 3$_{15}$ (|| אַרְבֶּה *locust*). <COLL> יֶלֶק אֵין מִסְפָּר *locusts without number* Ps 105$_{34(mss)}$ (L וְאֵין).
<SYN> אַרְבֶּה *locust*, גָּזָם *locust*, חָסִיל *locust*.

יַלְקוּט 1 n.[m.] **pouch,** carried by shepherd, <PREP> בְּ of place, *in*, + שׂים *place* 1 S 17$_{40}$ (+ כְּלִי הָרֹעִים *shepherds' pouch*).
→ לקט *gather*.

יָם 392.2.35 n.m. **sea**—cstr. יַם (יָם); + ה- of direction יָמָּה; cstr. יָמָּה; sf. יַמָּהּ; pl. יַמִּים—**1. sea,** in general (e.g. Gn 1$_{10}$ Jos 19$_{29}$ 1 K 5$_{23}$ Is 5$_{30}$ Jr 5$_{22}$ Ezk 25$_{16}$ Ho 2$_{1}$ Am 5$_{8}$ Jon 1$_{9}$ Mc 7$_{19}$ Na 1$_{4}$ Hb 1$_{14}$ Zc 9$_{4}$ Ps 8$_{9}$ Jb 7$_{12}$ Pr 8$_{29}$ Ec 1$_{7}$ Lm 2$_{13}$ Est 10$_{1}$ Ne 9$_{6}$ 1 C 16$_{32}$ 2 C 8$_{18}$ Si 43$_{23}$ 1QH 11$_{4}$ 2$_{12}$ 3$_{14.15}$ 6$_{23}$ 8$_{17}$ 13$_{9}$ 1QM 10$_{13}$ 1QpHab 3$_{11}$ 6$_{2}$ 11$_{2}$ 1QS 3$_{4}$ 4QpNah 1$_{3}$ 5$_{3}$ 4QVisSam 4.2$_{4}$ 4QpsJub[a] 2.1$_{6}$ 4Q AdmonPar 3.2$_{10}$ 4Q418 119$_{4}$ 4QJonathan A$_{7}$ 4QM[a] 11.1$_{15}$ 4QShir[b] 14 4QapMes 5.2$_{2}$ 5Q14 1$_{1}$); perh. personified, **Yam** (e.g. Hb 3$_{8}$ Ps 74$_{13}$ Jb 3$_{8}$ [if em.] 7$_{12}$ 26$_{12}$).

2. particular sea, **a.** יָם הַמֶּלַח *Dead Sea* (Gn 14$_{3}$ Nm 34$_{3.12}$ Dt 3$_{17}$ 4$_{49}$ Jos 3$_{16}$ 12$_{3}$ 15$_{2.5}$ 18$_{19}$ 2 K 14$_{25}$ Ezk 47$_{8.18}$ Jl 2$_{20}$ Zc 14$_{8}$ 2 C 20$_{2}$). **b.** יַם־סוּף *Red Sea*, lit. *Sea of Reeds* (Ex 10$_{19}$ [or em. יָמָּה סוּף *to the sea of reeds* to יָמִין *southward*]* 13$_{18}$ 15$_{4.22}$ 23$_{31}$ Nm 14$_{25}$ 21$_{4}$ 33$_{10.11}$ Dt 1$_{40}$ 2$_{1}$ 11$_{4}$ Jos 2$_{10}$ 4$_{23}$ 24$_{6}$ Jg 11$_{16}$ 1 K 9$_{26}$, Is 11$_{15}$ Jr 49$_{21}$ Zc 10$_{11}$ [if em.; see App.] Ps 106$_{7.7}$ [or em.; see under Prep., בְּ] 106$_{9.22}$ 136$_{13.15}$ [or del.] Ne 9$_{9.11.11}$ 2 C 8$_{17}$ 1QM 11$_{10}$ 4QM[a] 18$_{5}$ [[י]ם]). **c.** הַיָּם הַגָּדוֹל *the Great Sea*, i.e. Mediterranean (Nm 34$_{6.7}$ Jos 1$_{4}$ 9$_{1}$ 15$_{12.47}$ 23$_{4}$ Ezk 47$_{10.15.19.20}$), also called הַיָּם הָאַחֲרוֹן *the Western Sea* (Dt 11$_{24}$ 34$_{2}$ Jl 2$_{20}$), and יָם פְּלִשְׁתִּים *the Sea of the Philistines* (Ex 23$_{31}$) 48$_{28}$ Jon 1$_{4+9t}$ 2$_{4}$ Zc 14$_{8}$ (Ezr 3$_{7}$); as the direction, **west** (Gn 12$_{8}$ 13$_{14}$ 28$_{14}$ Ex 26$_{22.27}$ 27$_{12}$ 36$_{27.32}$ 38$_{12}$ Nm 2$_{18}$ 3$_{23}$ 35$_{5}$ Dt 3$_{27}$ 33$_{23}$ Jos 15$_{4.8.10.11.12}$ 16$_{3.8}$ 18$_{12.14. 14.15}$ 19$_{11.26. 34.34}$ 22$_{7}$ 24$_{6}$ 1 K 7$_{25}$ Is 11$_{14}$ 49$_{12}$ Ezk 41$_{12}$ 42$_{19}$ 45$_{7.7.7}$ 46$_{19}$ 47$_{20.20}$ perh. 48$_{1+20t}$ Ho 11$_{10}$ Zc 14$_{4}$ [or del.] perh. Ps 139$_{9}$ Dn 8$_{4}$ 1 C 9$_{24}$ 4Q365a 3$_{4}$ 3QTr 9$_{7}$ 11QT 38$_{14}$ 39$_{13}$ 40$_{9.12}$). **d.** יָם־כִּנֶּרֶת *Sea of Chinnereth*, i.e. Sea of Galilee (Nm 34$_{11}$ Jos 12$_{3}$ 13$_{27}$).

3. sea of bronze (in temple) (1 K 7$_{23+5t}$||2 C 4$_{2+5t}$ 2 K 16$_{17.17.17}$ 25$_{13.16}$ Jr 27$_{19}$ 1 C 18$_{8}$).

4. perh. **pool, basin, tank, vat** (3QTr 10$_{8.15}$).*

<SUBJ> היה *be* Nm 34$_{6.12}$ Jos 17$_{10}$ (+ גְּבוּל *border*), מלא *be full* Ec 1$_{7}$, המה *be in tumult* Is 17$_{12}$ Jr 6$_{23}$ 50$_{42}$ 1QH 3$_{15}$, חיל *be in labour* Is 23$_{4}$, גרשׁ ni. *be churned up* Is 57$_{20}$,* שׁתק *be quiet* Jon 1$_{11.12}$, חרב *be dried up* Ps 106$_{9}$.

אמר *say* Is 23$_{4}$ Jb 28$_{14}$, הלל pi. *praise* Ps 69$_{35}$, ברך pi. *bless* 4QShir[b] 14 (יב[רכו]הו), ראה *see* Ps 114$_{3}$, בוא *come* Jb 38$_{8}$, הלך *go* Jon 1$_{11.13}$, שׁוב *return* Ex 14$_{27}$, עלה *go up* Jr 51$_{42}$, hi. *bring up* Ezk 26$_{3}$, נוס *flee* Ps 114$_{3.5}$, עמד *stand* Jon 1$_{15}$ (+ זַעְפּוֹ *its*, i.e. the sea's, *raging*), כסה pi. *cover* Ex 15$_{10}$ Ps 78$_{53}$, יסף *increase* Jb 38$_{8}$, סער *rage* Jon 1$_{11.13}$, רעם *thunder* Ps 96$_{11}$ 98$_{7}$ 1 C 16$_{32}$, גיח *burst out* Jb 38$_{8}$, ילד *give birth* Is 23$_{4}$, גדל pi. *bring up* youths Is 23$_{4}$, רום pol. *raise* young girls Is 23$_{4}$.

<NOM CL> חֵיל יָם *(its) rampart is a sea* Na 3$_{8}$ (or em.

חֵילָהּ *its rampart* is a sea, or del. יָם), אֲשֶׁר־לוֹ הַיָּם *the sea is his* Ps 95$_{5}$ (perh. del. אֲשֶׁר), זֶה הַיָּם *there is the sea* Ps 104$_{25}$ (perh. del. זֶה), הֲיָם־אָנִי *Am I the sea?* Jb 7$_{12}$, הוּא יָם הַמֶּלַח *that is, the Salt Sea*, i.e. Dead Sea Gn 14$_{3}$, יָם הָעֲרָבָה יָם הַמֶּלַח *the sea of the Arabah, that is, the Salt Sea* Dt 3$_{17}$ Jos 3$_{16}$ 12$_{3}$ (יָם־הַמֶּלַח), הים הם כל הכ[תיים] *'the sea' is all the Kittim* 1QpNah 1$_{3}$, הַיָּם עֲלֵיהֶם מִלְמָעְלָה *the sea was upon them from above*, i.e. resting upon them, 1 K 7$_{25}$.

<OBJ> קרא *call* Gn 1$_{10}$ (+ מִקְוֵה הַמַּיִם *gathering of the waters*), ידע *know* 1 K 9$_{27}$||2 C 8$_{18}$, הלך hi. *drive back* Ex 14$_{21}$, בוא *come* 4QM^{a} 11.1$_{15}$ (באי ים *those who come of*, i.e. on, *the sea*), hi. *bring* Jos 24$_{7}$, ירד *go down* Is 42$_{10}$ Ps 107$_{23}$ 1QH 3$_{14}$, hi. *bring down* 2 K 16$_{17}$, נקף hi. *go around* 1 K 7$_{24}$ (or del.)||1 C 4$_{3}$, עבר *cross, reach*, Is 16$_{8}$ 23$_{2}$ Jr 48$_{32}$, הפך *transform* Ps 66$_{6}$, צפה *watch*, i.e. face (towards) 3QTr 9$_{7}$, סוך *shut in* Jb 38$_{8}$, ירשׁ *take possession of* Dt 33$_{23}$.

ברא *create* 1QH 1$_{14}$, נתן *place* 1 K 7$_{39}$ 2 K 16$_{17}$ 2 C 4$_{10}$, שׂים *place*, i.e. make, Ex 14$_{21}$ Jb 41$_{23}$ (+ מֶרְקָחָה *ointment pot*), עשׂה *make* Ex 20$_{11}$ 1 K 7$_{23}$||1 C 4$_{2}$ 1 K 7$_{44}$ Jon 1$_{9}$ Ps 95$_{5}$ 146$_{6}$ Ne 9$_{6}$ 1 C 18$_{8}$ 4QapMes 5.2$_{2}$ ([עשה]), יבשׁ pi. *dry up* Na 1$_{4}$ (or em. hi. *dry up*), hi. *dry up* Jos 4$_{23}$ Na 1$_{4}$ (if em. from pi. *dry up*), חרב hi. *dry up* Is 50$_{2}$ 51$_{10}$ Jr 51$_{36}$.

שׁבר pi. *shatter* 2 K 25$_{13}$ Jr 52$_{17}$, רגע *disturb* Is 51$_{15}$ (or em. רגע to גער *rebuke*) Jr 31$_{35}$ Jb 26$_{12}$, רעשׁ hi. *cause to quake* Hg 2$_{6}$, פרר po. *divide* Ps 74$_{13}$, בקע *split* Ps 78$_{13}$ Ne 9$_{11}$, גזר *separate* Ps 136$_{13}$, גער *rebuke* Is 51$_{15}$ (if em. רגע *disturb*), ארר *curse* Jb 3$_{8}$ (if em. יוֹם *day* to יָם).*

<CSTR> יָם־הַמֶּלַח *Sea of Salt*, i.e. Dead Sea, Gn 14$_{3}$ (+ עֵמֶק הַשִּׂדִּים *Valley of Siddim*) Nm 34$_{3}$ (יָם־הַמֶּלַח) 34$_{12}$ Dt 3$_{17}$ Jos 3$_{16}$ (both יָם־הַמֶּלַח) 12$_{3}$ 15$_{2.5}$ 18$_{19}$ (יָם־הַמֶּלַח), הָעֲרָבָה *of the Arabah*, i.e. Dead Sea, Dt 3$_{17}$ 4$_{49}$ 2 K 14$_{25}$, סוּף *of reeds*, i.e. Red Sea, Ex 10$_{19}$ (or em. יָמָּה סוּף *to the Sea of Reeds* to יָמִין *southward*) 13$_{18}$ 15$_{4.22}$ 23$_{31}$ Nm 14$_{25}$ 21$_{4}$ Dt 1$_{40}$ 2$_{1}$ 11$_{4}$ Jos 2$_{10}$ 4$_{23}$ 24$_{6}$ Jg 11$_{16}$ 1 K 9$_{26}$ Jr 49$_{21}$ Ps 106$_{7}$ (or em.; see under Prep., בְּ) 106$_{9.22}$ (יָם) 136$_{13.15}$ (or del.) Ne 9$_{9}$ (יָם) 1QM 11$_{10}$ ([סו]ף) 4QM^{a} 18$_{5}$ ([י]ם), מִצְרַיִם *of Egypt*, i.e. Red Sea, Is 11$_{15}$ Zc 10$_{11}$ (if em.; see App.), פְּלִשְׁתִּים *of the Philistines*, i.e. Mediterranean Sea, Ex 23$_{31}$, כִּנְרוֹת *of Chinneroth, Galilee* Nm 34$_{11}$ (כִּנֶּרֶת), Jos 12$_{3}$ (or em. כִּנֶּרֶת) Jos 13$_{27}$, ים בית חמים perh. *pool of the house of hot waters* 3QTr 10$_{15}$ (others המים *of waters*), יָם הַנְּחֹשֶׁת *sea of bronze* 2 K 25$_{13}$ Jr 52$_{17}$ 1 C 18$_{8}$ (mss יָם).

יֹדְעֵי הַיָּם *those who know the sea* 1 K 9$_{27}$||2 C 8$_{18}$ (יוֹדְעֵי יָם), באי ים *those who come of*, i.e. to, *the sea* 4QM^{a} 11.1$_{15}$, יוֹרְדֵי הַיָּם *those who go down of*, i.e. to, *the sea* Is 42$_{10}$ (or em. יַאְדִּרֵהוּ יָם *he will make the sea glorious*) Ps 107$_{23}$ Si 43$_{23}$ 1QH 3$_{14}$ (ימים), חֹבְלֵי *sailors of* Ezk 27$_{29}$, נְשִׂיאֵי *princes of* Ezk 26$_{16}$.

דג [י]מים *fish of the seas* 4QBer^{b} 3$_{3}$, דְּגַת הַיָּם *fish of the sea* Gn 1$_{26.28}$ Ezk 47$_{10}$ 1QpHab 6$_{2}$, דְּגֵי *fishes of* Gn 9$_{2}$ Nm 11$_{22}$ Ezk 38$_{20}$ Ho 4$_{3}$ Hb 1$_{14}$ Zp 1$_{3}$ Ps 8$_{9}$ Jb 12$_{8}$.

גְּבוּל הַיָּם *border of the sea* Nm 34$_{6.6}$ Jos 15$_{12}$ (גְּבוּל יָם הַיָּמָּה appar. *the border of the sea*, i.e. the western border, *was towards the* great *sea*; or em. גְּבוּל יָמָּה הַיָּם *[the] border to the south was the* great *sea*), *of the west* Ezk 45$_{7}$ (or em. יָם to יָמָּה *to the* border *of the west*) 48$_{21}$ (יָמָּה), חֶבֶל *territory of* Zp 2$_{5.6}$, חול *sand of* Gn 32$_{13}$ 41$_{49}$ Is 10$_{22}$ Jr 15$_{8}$ (יַמִּים) 33$_{22}$ Ho 2$_{1}$ Ps 78$_{27}$ Jb 6$_{3}$ (יַמִּים), חוֹף *shore of* Gn 49$_{13}$ Dt 1$_{7}$ Jos 9$_{1}$ Jg 5$_{17}$ Jr 47$_{7}$ Ezk 25$_{16}$, שְׂפַת *shore of* Gn 22$_{17}$ Ex 14$_{30}$ Jos 11$_{4}$ Jg 7$_{12}$ 1 S 13$_{5}$ 2 S 17$_{11(mss)}$ 1 K 5$_{9}$ (or del.) 9$_{26}$ 2 C 8$_{17}$ 4QpsJub^{a} 2.1$_{6}$, כֶּתֶף *slope of* Nm 34$_{11}$, קְצֵה *end of* Nm 34$_{3}$ Jos 13$_{27}$ 15$_{2}$, חוג ימים *circle of the seas* 1QM 10$_{13}$, לְשׁוֹן הַיָּם *tongue*, i.e. inlet, *of the sea* Jos 15$_{5}$ 18$_{19}$ Is 11$_{15}$, מְבוֹאֹת *entrances of* Ezk 27$_{3}$ (or em. מְבוֹאֹת יָם to מְבוֹא הַיָּם *entrance of the sea*), אִיֵּי *islands of* Is 11$_{11}$ 24$_{15}$ Est 10$_{1}$ 1QpHab 3$_{11}$, אֲפִיקֵי *channels of* 2 S 22$_{16}$ (or em. יָם to מַיִם *water*),

גַּלֵּי *waves of* Is 48$_{18}$, מִשְׁבְּרֵי *breakers of* Ps 93$_{4}$, נחשולי ימים *gales of the seas* 1QH 2$_{12}$, מַעֲמַקֵּי־יָם *depths of the sea* Is 51$_{10}$ 4Q418 119$_{4}$ (הים), מְצֻלוֹת *depths of* Mc 7$_{19}$ Ps 68$_{23}$, תהום *depth of* 4QJonathan 1$_{7}$, קַרְקַע הַיָּם *bottom of the sea* Am 9$_{3}$, שָׁרְשֵׁי *roots*, i.e. bottom, *of* Jb 36$_{30}$, נִבְכֵי *springs of* Jb 38$_{16}$ (יָם), עֵבֶר *other side of* Dt 30$_{13}$, תּוֹךְ *midst of* Ex 14$_{23}$, לֵב־ *heart of* Ex 15$_{8}$ Ezk 27$_{4.25.26.27}$ 28$_{2.8}$ Ps 46$_{3}$ (all seven לֵב יַמִּים) Pr 23$_{34}$ 30$_{19}$ (both יָם), לְבַב *heart of* Jon 2$_{4}$ (יַמִּים) 4QBibPar 14.1$_{7}$ (ים), בָּמֳתֵי *back of* Jb 9$_{8}$ (mss עָב back of *a cloud*), מֵי *waters of* Ex 15$_{19}$ Am 5$_{8}$ 9$_{6}$ Ps 33$_{7}$ 1QpHab 11$_{2}$, מָעוֹז *refuge of* Is 23$_{4}$ (or del.).

דֶּרֶךְ יָם *way of the sea* Nm 14$_{25}$ 21$_{4}$ Dt 1$_{40}$ 2$_{1}$ 1 K 18$_{43}$ Is 8$_{23}$ (הַיָּם), *of the western side* Ezk 41$_{12}$ (הַיָּם), אָרְחוֹת יַמִּים *ways of (the) seas* Ps 8$_{9}$, מִדְבַּר־יָם oracle of *the steppe* *of (the) sea* Is 21$_{1}$ (or em. מִדְבָּר oracle of *[the] steppe*, or מִדְבָּר יֶהֱמֶה *the steppe will be in tumult*, or מְדַבְּרִים oracle of *ones who speak*; or מִדְבַּר דֶּרֶךְ הַיָּם oracle of *the steppe along the sea route*; 1QIsa^{a} דבר ים oracle concerning *the matter of the sea*).*

נַהֲמַת־יָם *groaning of the sea* Is 5$_{30}$, שְׁאוֹן *roar of* Ps 65$_{8}$ (יַמִּים), גֵּאוּת *swelling* Ps 89$_{10}$ 4QapPs^{b} 14$_{4}$ (גא[ות הים]), זעף ימים *anger of the seas* 1QH 6$_{23}$, שֶׁפַע יַמִּים *abundance of the seas* Dt 33$_{19}$, מִבְטָח ... יָם *confidence of the sea* Ps 65$_{6}$, הֲמוֹן *wealth of* Is 60$_{5}$ (יָם), אֳנִיּוֹת *ships of* Ezk 27$_{9}$ (הַיָּם).

קִדְמַת הַיָּם *east of the sea* Ezk 39$_{11}$, פְּאַת־יָם *western side* Ex 27$_{12}$ 38$_{12}$ Nm 35$_{5}$ Jos 18$_{14.14}$ Ezk 45$_{7.20.20}$ 48$_{1}$ (־פְּאַת קָדִים הַיָּם appar. *the side of the east [and the side of] the west*; or em. מִפְּאַת קָדִימָ[ה] [וְ]עַד פְּאַת יָמָּה *from the eastern side to the western side*) 48$_{2+14t}$ (all fifteen יָמָּה), אַחֲרִית יָם *end of (the) west*, Ps 139$_{9}$, רוּחַ־יָם *west wind* or *sea wind*, i.e. north wind Ex 10$_{19}$,* *western side*, Ezk 42$_{19}$ (הַיָּם).

<APP> צָרָה *distress* Zc 10$_{11}$ (or em. וְעָבַר בַּיָּם צָרָה *and he shall pass in the sea, distress* to וְעָבְרוּ בְיַם מִצְרַיִם *and they will pass through the sea of Egypt*), גְּבוּל *border* Jos 15$_{47(Kt)}$, appar. יצא ho. ptc. *that which is taken out*, i.e. water Ezk 47$_{8}$ (or em. אֶל־הַיָּמָּה הַמּוּצָאִים *to the sea, those that are taken out* to אֶל־הַיָּם הֵם מוּצָאִים *to the sea they are taken out* or אֶל־הַמַּיִם הַמּוּצָאִים *to the waters that are taken out* or אֶל־הַמַּיִם הַחֲמוּצִים *to the bitter waters*).

<ADJ> גָּדוֹל *great* Nm 34$_{6.7}$ Jos 1$_{4}$ 9$_{1}$ 15$_{12}$ 15$_{47(Qr)}$ 23$_{4}$ Ezk 47$_{10.15.19.20}$ 48$_{28}$ Ps 104$_{25}$ 4QM^{g} 4$_{2}$ (הו[גדול]), אֶחָד *one* 1 K 7$_{44}$‖2 C 4$_{15}$ 2 K 25$_{16}$ Jr 52$_{20}$, אַחֲרוֹן *last*, i.e. western Dt 11$_{24}$ 34$_{2}$ Jl 2$_{20}$ Zc 14$_{8}$, רָחָב *wide* Ps 104$_{25}$, רָחוֹק *distant* Ps 65$_{6}$ (or em. עַמִּים distant *peoples*), קַדְמוֹנִי *eastern* sea, i.e. Dead Sea, Ezk 47$_{18}$ Jl 2$_{20}$ Zc 14$_{8}$.

<PREP> לְ of direction, *to* 4QpNah 5$_{3}$ 4Q365a 3$_{4}$ (לימה) 11QT 38$_{14}$ 39$_{13}$ 40$_{9.12}$, + עלה *go up* Jos 19$_{11}$; of benefit, *to, for*, Jr 5$_{22}$, + עשׂה *do* Jos 4$_{23}$, שׂים *assign* Pr 8$_{29}$; of possession, *(belonging) to* Ps 114$_{5}$; *as*, or introducing predicate, + היה *be* 1QH 8$_{17}$; indicating object, + כסה pi. *cover* Is 11$_{9}$.

בְּ of place, *in(to), at, upon, by, through* Gn 1$_{22}$ Ex 20$_{11}$ Lv 11$_{9.10}$ 1 K 10$_{22}$ Is 27$_{1}$ Jr 46$_{18}$ Ezk 26$_{18}$ 32$_{2}$ Jon 1$_{4}$ Ps 77$_{20}$ 106$_{7}$ (or em. עַל־יָם בְּיַם־סוּף they rebelled *at the sea, at the sea of reeds* to עֹלִים בְּיַם־סוּף *those who went into the sea of reeds* rebelled; בְּךָ עַל־יַם־סוּף they rebelled *against you*, or עֶלְיוֹן (against) *the Most High*)* 1QH 13$_{9}$ 3QTr 10$_{8.15}$ 4QVisSam 4.2$_{4}$ 4QAdmonPar 3.2$_{10}$ 4QapMes 5.2$_{2}$ ([בם]), + היה *be* Ezk 26$_{17}$, שׁמע ni. *be heard* Jr 49$_{21}$, בוא *come* Ex 14$_{28}$ 15$_{19}$, דרך *tread* Hb 3$_{15}$, רמשׂ *creep* Ps 69$_{35}$, עבר *pass* Zc 10$_{11}$, שׁלח *send* Is 18$_{2}$, נתן *give*, i.e. make Is 43$_{16}$, עשׂה *do* Ps 135$_{6}$ 1QM 11$_{10}$, *make* 146$_{6}$ Ne 9$_{6}$, שׂים *place* Ps 89$_{26}$, *cause to be* 1 K 5$_{23}$ (or del. בַּיָּם), רָמָה *throw* Ex 15$_{1.21}$, יָרָה *throw* Ex 15$_{4}$, נער pi. *shake off*, i.e. hurl Ps 136$_{15}$, נכה hi. *strike* Zc 9$_{4}$, קדשׁ htp. *sanctify oneself* 1QS 3$_{4}$.

מוג ni. *be melted* Jr 49$_{23}$ (or em. נָמֹגוּ בַּיָּם דְּאָגָה *they are melted, there is anxiety in the sea* to נָמוֹג לִבָּם מִדְּאָגָה *their hearts melt away with anxiety*), שׁבר ni. *be broken* Ezk 27$_{34}$ (if em. מִיַּמִּים *from the seas* to בַּיַּמִּים *on the seas*), רחץ *wash* 2 C 4$_{6}$.

בְּ *against* Hb 3$_{8}$, + גער *rebuke* Na 1$_{4}$ Ps 106$_{9}$.

כְּ *as* Is 57$_{20}$ Lm 2$_{13}$ (or em. כַּיָּם *as the sea* to כּוֹס *cup*, + שֶׁבֶר *breaking*), + המה *roar* Jr 6$_{23}$ 50$_{42}$.

אֶל *(in)to*, Ezk 47$_{19}$, + היה Ezk 48$_{28}$ (if em. עַל *to*), בוא *come* Ezk 47$_{8}$ (or em. אֶל־הַיָּמָּה *to the sea* to אֶל־הַמַּיִם *to the waters*), hi. *bring* Ezr 3$_{7}$, הלך *go* Ec 1$_{7}$, יצא *go out* Zc 14$_{8.8}$, נדח hi. *banish* Jl 2$_{20.20}$, טול hi. *hurl* Jon 1$_{4.5.12.15}$.

מִן of direction, *from* the sea Ezk 47$_{15}$ Na 3$_{8}$ (or em. מִיָּם *from a sea* to מַיִם *waters*) Zc 9$_{10}$, + היה *be* Ezk 47$_{17}$, נשׁת ni. *be dry* Is 19$_{5}$, צהל *cry out* Is 24$_{14}$, שׁבת ni. *be destroyed* Ezk 26$_{17}$ (if em. ישׁב ni. *be inhabited*), שׁבר ni. *be broken* Ezk 27$_{34}$ (or em. מִיַּמִּים to בַּיַּמִּים *in the seas*), בוא *come* Mc 7$_{12}$, יצא *go out* Ezk 27$_{33}$, אזל *go away* Jb 14$_{11}$, עלה hi. *bring up* Is 63$_{11}$, גוז *pass* Nm 11$_{31}$ (or em. hi. *bring*), נסע *set out* Nm 33$_{11}$, hi. *lead out* Ex 15$_{22}$, נוע *totter* Am 8$_{12}$, ישׁב ni. *be inhabited* Ezk 26$_{17}$ (or em. שׁבת ni. *be destroyed*), קבץ *gather* Ps 107$_{3}$ (or em. מִיָּם *from the sea* to מִיָּמִין *from the south*), נחל hi. *give as inheritance* Si 44$_{21}$, שׁית *place* border Ex 23$_{31}$, תאה pi. *mark out* border Nm 34$_{7}$, רדה *rule* Ps 72$_{8}$.

מִן *from* the west Is 49$_{12}$, + עלה *go up* 1 K 18$_{44}$ (or em. עֹלָה מִיָּם *going up from the west* to מַעֲלֶה מַיִם *taking up waters*), חרד *come trembling* Ho 11$_{10}$; *on* the west Gn 12$_{8}$ Jos 8$_{9.12.13}$ 11$_{2.3}$, + פגע *reach* Jos 19$_{34}$.

מִן of comparison, *(more) than* Jb 11$_{9}$ (+ רָחָב *wide*).

עַל *by, at, on* Jos 5_{1} 2 S 17_{11} 1 K 4_{20} (mss עַל־שְׂפַת־הַיָּם *by the seashore* in both) Is 10_{26} (or em. עַל *by* the sea, to עֲלֵיהֶם *upon them,* or em. עָלָיו *upon him*) perh. 4Q NarrA 9_{1} 5Q14 1_{1}, + מרה *rebel* Ps 106_{7} (or em. עַל־יָם עֹלִים בְּיַם־סוּף *at the sea, at the sea of reeds* to בְּיַם־סוּף *those who went into the sea of reeds,* or עֶלְיוֹן בְּיַם־סוּף *(against) the Most High at the sea of reeds*), שׁמע *hear* Ne 9_{9}, בוא hi. *bring* 2 C 2_{15}, ישׁב *dwell* Nm 13_{29}, חנה *encamp* Ex $14_{2.9}$ Nm 33_{10}, עשׂה *do* Ps 106_{22}, יסד *establish* Ps 24_{2}.

עַל *over,* + נטה *extend* hand Ex $14_{16.21.26.27}$ Is 23_{11}, כסה pi. *cover* Hb 2_{14} (or em. עַל־יָם *over the sea* to עֲלֵיהֶם *over them*); עַל *to(wards),* + היה *be* Ezk 48_{28} (mss אֶל *to;* mss עַד *unto*), ירד *go down* Jos 3_{16}; עַל *concerning,* + אמר *say* Jr 27_{19} (or del.).

עַד *unto,* Dt 3_{17} 4_{49} 11_{24} 34_{2} Jos 1_{4} $12_{3.3}$ Jr 48_{32} (or del.) Zc 9_{10} 4QMg 4_{2} 4QSela 8.2_{4} ([ועד הים]), + היה Ezk 48_{28} (if em. עַל *to*), בוא *come* Mc 7_{12} (if em.; see Coll.), הלך *go* Jg 11_{16}, שׁלח pi. *send out* , Ps 80_{12}, נוע *totter* Am 8_{12}, מדד *measure* Ezk 47_{18} (if em. עַל *to*), נחל hi. *give as inheritance* Si 44_{21}, שׁית *set* border Ex 23_{31}, שׁוב hi. *restore* 2 K 14_{25}, רדה *have dominion* Ps 72_{8}, נפל hi. *cause to drop,* i.e. allocate, territory Jos 23_{4} (if ins. עַד).

בֵּין *between* Ex 14_{2} (+ מִגְדֹּל *Migdol*), + נטע *pitch* tent, Dn 11_{45} (+ הר *mountain*); בְּתוֹךְ *in(to) the middle of, through* Ezk 27_{32}, + בוא *come* Ex $14_{16.22}$, + היה *be* Ezk 26_{5}, הלך *go* Ex 14_{29} 15_{19}, עבר *pass* Nm 33_{8} Ne 9_{11}, נער pi. *shake off,* i.e. hurl Ex 14_{27}; תַּחַת *beneath* 1 K 7_{44}||2 C 4_{15}; בְּעֵבֶר *beyond* Jr 25_{22}; מֵעֵבֶר לְ *beyond* Dt 30_{13}, בוא *come* 2 C 20_{2}.

ה- of direction, *to(wards) the west, sea* Gn 13_{14} Ex $26_{22.27}$ $36_{27.32}$ Nm 2_{18} Jos 5_{1} (or del. יָמָּה) 12_{7} $15_{12.46}$ Jos 19_{11} 22_{7} Is 11_{14} Ezk 45_{7} 46_{19} (or del. יָמָּה) 48_{1} (if em.; see Cstr.) 48_{2+19t} 4Q365a 3_{4} (לימה), + היה *be* Nm 34_{5} (Sam הַיָּם) Jos $15_{4.11}$ 16_{3} 16_{8} 17_{9} 19_{29} 1 C 9_{24}, בקע ni. *be split* Zc 14_{4} (or del. יָמָּה), בוא *come* Jos 24_{6} Ezk 47_{8} (or em. אֶל־הַיָּמָּה *to the sea* to אֶל־הַמַּיִם *to the waters* or אֶל־הַיָּם הֵם *to the sea they*), הלך *go* Jos 16_{8}, יצא *go out* Jos 16_{6} 18_{15}, עלה *go up* Jos 18_{12}, שׁוב *go back* Jos 19_{34}, סבב ni. *go around* Jos 15_{10}, ירד *go down* Jos 16_{3} 1 K 5_{23}, פגע *reach* Jos 19_{26}, פנה *turn* 1 K 7_{25}||1 C 4_{4}, נשׂא *raise* eyes Dt 3_{27}, נגח pi. *thrust* Dn 8_{4}, תקע *drive* Ex 10_{19} (or em. יָמָּה סוּף *to the sea of reeds* to יָמִין *southward*), חנה *encamp* Nm 3_{23}, פרץ *spread* Gn 28_{14}.

<COLL> יָם *O sea* Ps 114_{5} (הַיָּם); הַיָּם הַגָּדוֹל מְבוֹא הַשֶּׁמֶשׁ *the great sea (in) the setting of the sun,* i.e. west Jos 23_{4}, יָבוֹא ... יָם מִיָּם *one will come ... to sea from sea* Mc 7_{12} (or em. מִיָּם עַד יָם *from sea to sea*).

יָם *west* + קֶדֶם *east* Gn 12_{8} 13_{14} 28_{14} Nm 35_{5} Dt 3_{27} Is 11_{14} Ezk 45_{7}, קָדִים *east* Ezk 42_{19} $45_{7.7}$ 47_{20} 48_{1+19t}, מִזְרָח *east* Jos 11_{3} $19_{26.34}$ 1 K 7_{25}||2 C 4_{4} Am 8_{12} Zc 14_{4} Ps 107_{3} 1 C 9_{24}, נֶגֶב *south* Gn 13_{14} 28_{14} Nm 35_{5} Dt 3_{27} Jos 11_{2} 15_{8} $18_{14.14.15}$ 19_{34} 1 K 7_{25} Ezk 47_{20} $48_{10.16.17.34}$ Zc 14_{4} (or del.) Dn 8_{4} 1 C 9_{24}, דָּרוֹם *south* Dt 33_{23} Ezk 42_{19}, צָפוֹן *north* Gn 13_{14} 28_{14} Nm 35_{5} Dt 3_{27} Jos 8_{13} 11_{2} $15_{8.10.11}$ $18_{12.12}$ 19_{26} 1 K 7_{25}||2 C 4_{4} Is 49_{12} Ezk 42_{19} 46_{19} 47_{20} $48_{10.16.17.34}$ Am 8_{12} Zc 14_{4} (or del.) Ps 107_{3} Dn 8_{4} 1 C 9_{24}, מַעֲרָב *west* Ps 107_{3} Dn 8_{4}.

יָם *sea* + אֶרֶץ *earth* Gn $1_{10.22.26.28}$ 9_{2} Ex 20_{11} Nm 11_{31} Dt 34_{2} Jos 1_{4} Is 5_{30} 11_{9} Ezk 27_{29} Ho 4_{3} Jl 2_{20} Am 5_{8} Hb 2_{14} Hg 2_{6} Ps 46_{3} 65_{6} 69_{35} 96_{11} 135_{6} 146_{6} Jb 11_{9} 12_{8} Pr 8_{29} Ne 9_{6} 1 C 16_{32} 4QAdmonPar 3.2_{10}, אֲדָמָה *earth* Gn 9_{2} Ezk 38_{20} Zp 1_{3}, חָרָבָה *dry land* Ex 14_{21}, יַבָּשָׁה *dry land* Ex $14_{16.22.29}$ 15_{19} Jon $1_{9.13}$ Ps 66_{6} Ne 9_{11}, יַבֶּשֶׁת *dry land* Ps 95_{5}, שָׁמַיִם *heavens* Gn $1_{26.28}$ 9_{2} 22_{17} Ex 20_{11} Jr 33_{22} Ezk 38_{20} Ho 4_{3} Am 9_{6} Jon 1_{9} Zp 1_{3} Hg 2_{6} Ps 8_{9} 69_{35} 96_{11} 135_{6} 146_{6} Jb 9_{8} Pr 30_{19} Ne 9_{6} 1 C 16_{32}, הַר *mountain* Nm 13_{12} Dt 1_{7} 33_{19} Jos 9_{21} 11_{3} 12_{7} 18_{12} Jr 46_{18} Ezk 38_{20} Mc 7_{12} Ps 46_{3}.

יָם *sea* + מַיִם *waters* Ex $14_{21.22.26.28.29}$ $15_{8.10.22}$ Jos 3_{16} Is 11_{9} 18_{2} 19_{5} 43_{16} 50_{2} Ezk 47_{8} Na 3_{8} Hb 2_{14} 3_{15} Zc 14_{8} Ps 74_{13} 77_{20} 78_{13} 93_{4} 107_{23} Jb 14_{11} Pr 8_{29} Ne 9_{11} 1QS 3_{4}, נָהָר *river* Ex 23_{31} Dt 1_{7} 11_{24} Jos 1_{4} Is 11_{15} 19_{5} 48_{18} Mc 7_{12} Zc 9_{10} Ps 66_{6} 72_{8} 80_{12} Jb 14_{11} 1QS 3_{4}, נַחַל *stream* Jos $15_{4.47}$ 16_{8} 17_{9} 19_{11} Ec 1_{7}, תְּהוֹם *deep* Is 51_{10} Jb 28_{14} 38_{16} 1QH 1_{14} 3_{15}, מְצוּלָה *deep* Jb 41_{23} Ne 9_{11}.

ימים מעיני תהום appar. *seas from the springs of the deep* 4QBer[a] 5_{9}, ים של גי perh. *pool of the valley of* 3QTr 10_{8} (unless גי = גַּת *press of;* others גיא *valley of*).

Also 4QCommGenB 3_{1}, perh. 4QSD 3_{3} 4QMg 4_{1} 6_{5} 4QNarrA 7_{2} 4QShir[b] 143_{1}.*

יְמוּאֵל 2 pr.n.m. **Jemuel,** son of Simeon, <NOM CL> בְּנֵי שִׁמְעוֹן יְמוּאֵל *the sons of Simeon were Jemuel ...* Gn 46_{10} Ex 6_{15}. ⇒ אֵל *God.*

[יְמוֹנִי], see יְמָנִי *right.*

יְמִימָה 1 pr.n.f. **Jemimah,** Job's firstborn daughter after his restoration, וַיִּקְרָא שֵׁם־הָאַחַת יְמִימָה *and he called the first one's name Jemimah* Jb 42$_{14}$.*

יָמִין I 139.3.26.1 n.f. **right (side)**—Si ימים; I ימן; + ־ה of direction Sam הימינה; cstr. יְמִין; sf. יְמִינִי, יְמִינְךָ (יְמִינֶךָ), יְמִינֶךָ, יְמִינוֹ, יְמִינָהּ (יְמִינָהּ), יְמִינָם—**1.** oft. **right, right-hand side.**

2. perh. specif. **south,** Gn 13$_9$ Ex 10$_{19}$ (if em. יָמָּה סוּף *to the Sea of Reeds*) Jos 17$_7$ 1 S 23$_{19.24}$ 2 S 24$_5$ (if em. וּמִן *and from*) Is 9$_{19}$ Ezk 16$_{46}$ Zc 12$_6$ Ps 89$_{13}$ (or em. יַמִּים *seas* or אֲמָנָה *Amanah*) Jb 23$_9$.

3. right hand, Gn 48$_{13}$ 48$_{14.18}$ Jg 5$_{26}$ 16$_{29}$ Is 41$_{13}$ 44$_{20}$ 45$_1$ Ezk 21$_{27}$ Ps 26$_{10}$ 45$_5$ 89$_{26.43}$ 109$_6$ 137$_5$ 144$_{8.11}$ Jb 40$_{14}$ Pr 3$_{16}$ 27$_{16}$ Ca 2$_6$=8$_3$ Dn 12$_7$ Si 47$_5$ GnzPs 1$_{25}$ 1QS 11$_{4.5}$, perh. Is 63$_{12}$ 2 K 12$_{10(Kt)}$ Jon 4$_{11}$ Ps 16$_8$; specif. right hand of Y., Ex 15$_{6.6.12}$ Is 41$_{10}$ 48$_{13}$ 62$_8$ Hb 2$_{16}$ Ps 16$_{11}$ 17$_7$ 18$_{36}$ 20$_7$ 21$_9$ 44$_4$ 48$_{11}$ 60$_7$||108$_7$ 63$_9$ 74$_{11}$ 77$_{11}$ 78$_{54}$ 80$_{16}$ 89$_{14}$ 98$_1$ 118$_{15.16.16}$ (or del.) 138$_7$ 139$_{10}$ Lm 2$_{3.4}$ GnzPs 2$_{13}$ 1QM 4$_7$ 1QH 17$_{18}$ 18$_7$ 1QLitPr 3.2$_7$ 4Q451 1$_3$, perh. Dt 33$_2$ Ps 80$_{18}$ Si 33$_7$ 4QMyst^b 8$_1$.

<SUBJ> מלא *be full* Ps 26$_{10}$ 48$_{11}$, רום *be high* Ps 89$_{14}$, pol. *exalt* Ps 118$_{16}$, אדר ni. *be majestic* Ex 15$_6$, כלא *be restrained* Ps 74$_{11}$ (if em. כַּלֵּה impv. *destroy* to כְּלֻאָה *restrained* and change verse division), perh. שׁנה *be changed* Ps 77$_{11}$ (unless שְׁנוֹת = *years of* the right hand of Elyon).

אחז *hold* Ps 139$_{10}$, תמך *hold* Ps 63$_9$, חבק pi. *embrace* Ca 2$_6$=8$_3$, טפח pi. *extend* heavens Is 48$_{13}$, מצא *find* Ps 21$_9$, קנה *acquire* Ps 78$_{54}$, ישׁע hi. *save* Ps 44$_4$ 98$_1$ Jb 40$_{14}$, סעד *sustain* Ps 18$_{36}$, נטע *plant* Ps 80$_{16}$, עשׂה *do* Ps 118$_{15.16}$ (or del.), רעץ *shatter* Ex 15$_6$, כתב *write* 1QLitPr 3.2$_7$, ירה hi. *show* Ps 45$_5$, שׁכח *forget*, perh. lose ability, or *wither* Ps 137$_5$ (unless יָמִין is obj. of שׁכח *forget*, or em. ni. *be forgotten* or כחשׁ *fail* or כחשׁ pi. *cause* right hand *to fail*).

<NOM CL> יְמִינָם יְמִין שָׁקֶר *their right hand is a right hand of deceit* Ps 144$_{8.11}$ (unless יָמִין IV *oath*).

<OBJ> זרז pi. *strengthen* Si 33$_{7(Bmg)}$ (ימים), רום hi. *raise* Dn 12$_7$ Ps 89$_{43}$, שׁוב hi. *take back*, i.e. withdraw Ps 74$_{11}$ (or em.; see Subj.) Lm 2$_3$, שׁלח *send*, i.e. extend Gn 48$_{14}$ (Sam יַד־יְמִינוֹ *his right hand*) Jg 5$_{26}$, נטה *extend* Ex 15$_{12}$, שׂים *place* Gn 48$_{18}$ Ps 89$_{26}$, שׁית *place* Gn 48$_{14}$, אמץ pi. *strengthen* Si 33$_{7(B)}$, חזק hi. *strengthen* or *hold* Is 41$_{13}$, תמך *hold* GnzPs 1$_{25}$, ברא *create* Ps 89$_{13}$ (or em. יַמִּים *seas* or אֲמָנָה *Amanah*), perh. קרא *meet* Pr 27$_{16}$ (or em. וְשֶׁמֶן יָמִין יִקְרָא *and oil encounters his right hand* to וּשְׁמָהּ יָמִין יִקְרָא *but her name is called propitious*, i.e. יָמִין III, or שְׁמוֹ נֶאֱמָן יִקְרָא *his name is called reliable*).

<CSTR> יְמִין י״ *right hand of Y.* Hb 2$_{16}$ Ps 118$_{15.16.16}$ (or del. יְמִין), עֶלְיוֹן *of Elyon* Ps 77$_{11}$, צָרָיו *of his adversaries* Ps 89$_{43}$, ימין אל *right hand of God* (as slogan on banner) 1QM 4$_7$, עוזך *of your strength* 1QH 17$_{18}$ 18$_7$ (עוזכה), עוזו *of his strength* 1QIsa^b 42$_8$ (י[מ]ין), יְמִין צִדְקִי *right hand of my righteousness, salvation*, i.e. my saving right hand Is 41$_{10}$, שָׁקֶר *of deceit* Ps 144$_{8.11}$.

יְמִין יוֹאָב *right-hand side of Joab* 2 S 20$_9$, מֹשֶׁה *of Moses* Is 63$_{12}$ (unless יָמִין §3 *right hand*), אֶבְיוֹן *of a poor person* Ps 109$_{31}$, הַגֻּלָּה *of the bowl* Zc 4$_3$ (or em. מִימִינָהּ *on its right side*), הַמְּנוֹרָה *of the lampstand* Zc 4$_{11}$, הַיְשִׁימוֹן south *of Jeshimon* 1 S 23$_{19}$ (מִימִין) 23$_{24}$, הָעִיר *of the city* 2 S 24$_5$ (or em. וּמִן *and from* the city), לימ[ין ה]שער הזה *to the right of this gate* 4Q365a 2.1$_5$=11QT 38$_9$ (לימ[ין ה]שער), כו[ו]ל ימין שער לוי *everything to the right of the gate of Levi* 11QT 44$_5$, ימין המערכה *right of the battle line* 1QM 6$_7$.

מעשי ימין *deeds of the right hand of* 1QH 17$_{18}$, עוזו [ימינכ]ה *might of your right hand* 4Q451 1$_3$, גבורות ימינך *mighty deeds of your right hand* GnzPs 2$_{13}$, גְּבוּרוֹת יֵשַׁע יְמִינוֹ *mighty deeds of salvation of his right hand* Ps 20$_7$ (mss גְּבוּרַת *might of* salvation), שְׁנוֹת appar. *years of*, i.e. dealt out by, the right hand of the Most High Ps 77$_{11}$ (unless שְׁנוֹת יְמִין עֶלְיוֹן *the right hand of the Most High has changed*), כּוֹס יְמִין *cup of*, i.e. in, *the right hand of* Hb 2$_{16}$, אִישׁ יְמִינֶךָ *man of your right (hand)* Ps 80$_{18}$, משען ימיני eternal existence is the *support of my right hand* 1QS 11$_4$ (unless *a support is at my right hand*), משענת ימיני his strength is the *support of my right hand* 1QS 11$_5$.

שׁוֹק הַיָּמִין *thigh of the right-hand side*, i.e. right thigh Ex 29$_{22}$||Lv 8$_{25}$ Lv 7$_{32.33}$ 8$_{25}$ 9$_{21}$ Nm 18$_{18}$ 11QT 20$_{15}$ 22$_9$, יֶרֶךְ יְמִינוֹ *hip of his right-hand side* Jg 3$_{16.21}$, עֵין יָמִין *eye of (the) right side*, i.e. right eye 1 S 11$_{2}$, יְמִינוֹ *of his right-hand side* Zc 11$_{17.17}$ (or em. עֵין יְמִינוֹ to עֵינוֹ *his eye*).

יַד־יְמִינוֹ *the hand of his right-hand side*, i.e. his right hand Gn 48$_{14(Sam).17}$ Jg 3$_{15}$ 20$_{16}$, יְמִינְךָ *of your right-hand side* Ezk 39$_{3}$ (יד יְמִינְךָ) Ps 121$_{5}$ (יַד יְמִינֶךָ), יְמִינִי *of my right-hand side* Jr 22$_{24}$ (יַד יְמִינִי) Ps 73$_{23}$, יְמִינָם *of their right-hand side* Jg 7$_{20}$, יְמִין יוֹאָב *of Joab's right-hand side* 2 S 20$_{9}$.

<PREP> לְ *at, by, on, to(wards)* Ec 10$_{2}$ Ne 12$_{31}$ 1QM 9$_{14}$ ([ל]ימין) perh. 4QD^{a} 6.4a$_{2}$ 4Q365a 2.1$_{5}$=11QT 38$_{9}$ ([לימ]ין) 11QT 13$_{5}$ 15$_{11}$, + הלך *go* Ne 12$_{31}$ (if em. וְתַהֲלֻכֹת *and processions* were on the right to וְהָאַחַת הֹלֶכֶת *and the first went* to the right) 4QDibHam^{a} 1.2$_{14}$ ([ללכת]), hi. *cause to go* Is 63$_{12}$, ישב *sit* 1 K 2$_{19}$ Ps 110$_{1}$, hi. *seat* Si 12$_{12}$ (+ אֵצֶל *beside*), עמד *stand* Ps 109$_{31}$ 1QM 6$_{7}$, נצב ni. *stand* Ps 45$_{10}$ (or change verse division, leaving לִימִינְךָ in nom. cl.).

בְּ of place, *in* right hand Is 44$_{20}$ Ps 16$_{11}$ Pr 3$_{16}$ Lm 2$_{4}$ (if em.; see Coll.), + היה *be* Ezk 21$_{27}$, נתן *give*, i.e. place Si 47$_{5}$; of instrument, *by (means) of, with*, + שׁבע ni. *swear* Is 62$_{8}$, לקח *take* Gn 48$_{13}$, נתן *give*, i.e. place 2 K 12$_{10(Kt)}$, תמך *hold* Is 41$_{10}$, לפת *hold* Jg 16$_{29}$, חזק hi. *hold* Is 45$_{1}$, עזר *help* Is 41$_{10}$, אמץ pi. *strengthen* Is 41$_{10}$, עשׂה *do* 1QH 18$_{7(Licht)}$ ([לעשות]), perh. ירשׁ *possess* Ps 44$_{4}$ (with ellipsis of prep.), perh. נהל pi. *lead* 1QH 18$_{7}$, perh. ישׁע hi. *save* Ps 17$_{7}$; perh. *at, by*, + חסה *seek refuge* Ps 17$_{7}$; perh. *against*, + קום htpol. *arise* Ps 17$_{7}$.

מִן of direction, *from*, + היה *be* Siloam tunnel inscr.$_{3}$ (כי הית זדה בצר מימן ו[עד שמא]ל *for there was a fissure in the rock from right to left*), יצא *go out* 11QT 45$_{4}$ (מימ[י]ן); *at, by, on, to(wards)* Ex 14$_{22.29}$ Dt 33$_{2}$ 1 S 23$_{19}$ 2 S 16$_{6}$ 2 K 23$_{13}$ Zc 4$_{3}$ Ps 16$_{8}$ 1QM 8$_{5}$ 4QM^{a} 1$_{14}$, + ישב *dwell* Ezk 16$_{46}$, לקח *take* Gn 48$_{13}$, נתן *give*, i.e. place 1 K 7$_{39}$||2 C 4$_{6}$ 2 K 12$_{10(Qr)}$ 2 C 4$_{7}$, נוח hi. *place* 1 K 7$_{49}$ 2 C 4$_{8}$, קום hi. *raise* column 2 C 3$_{17}$, עמד *stand* 1 K 22$_{19}$ Ezk 10$_{3}$, נפל *fall* Ps 91$_{7}$.

עַל *at, by, on, to(wards)* Zc 4$_{11}$ Ps 110$_{5}$ Ne 8$_{4}$, + היה *be* Zc 6$_{13}$ (if em. עַל־כִּסְאוֹ *by his throne* to עַל־יְמִינוֹ *at his right-hand side*), עמד *stand* Zc 3$_{1}$ Ps 109$_{6}$ 1 C 6$_{24}$ 2 C 18$_{18}$, קום *arise* Jb 30$_{12}$, פנה *turn* (intrans.) Gn 24$_{49}$ (or em. אֶל *to*), נטה *turn* (intrans.) 2 S 2$_{19.21}$, גזר *snatch* Is 9$_{19}$, אכל *eat*, i.e. destroy Zc 12$_{6}$.

אֶל *at, by, on, to(wards)* Ezk 1$_{10}$, + הלך *go* Jos 17$_{7}$ 1 S 23$_{24}$, פנה *turn* (intrans.) Gn 24$_{49}$ (if em. עַל).

בֵּין *between*, אֲשֶׁר לֹא־יָדַע בֵּין־יְמִינוֹ לִשְׂמֹאלוֹ *who did not know between their right (hand) and their left (hand)* Jon 4$_{11}$.

<COLL> מִימִין לְ *to the right of* 2 K 23$_{13}$ Ezk 10$_{3}$, אֶל־הַיָּמִין לְ *to the right of* Ezk 1$_{10}$.

[וי]מינכה פקדת *and with your right hand you deposit* a purse with a creditor 4Q418 81$_{(Strugnell)}$ (others [צ]פוניכה the purse of *your treasures*, as ||4Q416 2.2$_{5}$).

יָמִין used adverbially, *(to the) right, south* 11QT 44$_{5}$, + חנה *encamp* 2 S 24$_{5}$ (or em. וַיַּחֲנוּ בַעֲרוֹעֵר יְמִין *and they encamped at Aroer to the south of* to וַיָּחֵלּוּ מֵעֲרוֹעֵר וּמִן *and they started out from Aroer and from* the city), הלך *go* 1QS 1$_{15}$, סור *depart* Nm 20$_{17(Sam)}$ Dt 2$_{27}$ 5$_{32}$ 17$_{11}$=11QT 56$_{7}$ Dt 17$_{20}$ 28$_{14}$ Jos 1$_{7}$ 23$_{6}$ 1 S 6$_{12}$ 2 K 22$_{2}$||2 C 34$_{2}$ 1QS 3$_{10}$, נטה *turn* (intrans.) Nm 20$_{17}$ 22$_{26}$ Pr 4$_{27}$ 4QD^{a} 11$_{17}$, עטף *turn* (intrans.) Jb 23$_{9}$, פרץ *break out* Is 54$_{3}$, פרד ni. *separate oneself* Gn 13$_{9}$ (Sam הימינה *to the right*, with -ה of direction), נבט hi. *look* Ps 142$_{5}$, תקע *drive* locusts Ex 10$_{19}$ (if em. יָמָּה סוּף *to the sea of reeds* to יָמִין *southward*).*

הוֹשִׁיעָה יְמִינְךָ *save (me with) your right hand* Ps 60$_{7}$ ||108$_{7}$, תּוֹשִׁיעֵנִי יְמִינֶךָ perh. *you save me with your right hand* Ps 138$_{7}$ (unless *your right hand saves me*), נִצָּב יְמִינוֹ כְּצָר *his right hand set like an enemy* Lm 2$_{4}$ (or em. חֵץ בִּימִינוֹ appar. *an arrow is in his right hand*).

יָמִין || יַד *(left) hand* Jg 5$_{26}$ Is 48$_{13}$ Ps 21$_{9}$ 26$_{10}$ 74$_{11}$ 80$_{18}$ (+) 89$_{14.26}$ 138$_{7}$ 139$_{10}$ Si 33$_{7(Bmg)}$ 1QLitPr 3.2$_{7}$ (+), זְרוֹעַ *arm* Is 62$_{8}$ 63$_{12}$ Zc 11$_{17.17}$ (all three +) Ps 44$_{4}$ 89$_{14}$ (+) 89$_{26}$ 98$_{1}$ Si 33$_{7(B)}$ GnzPs 1$_{25}$, צַד *side* Ps 91$_{7}$, אוֹר *light* of face Ps 44$_{4}$, עֲנָוָה *humility* Ps 18$_{36}$ (or em. עֶזְרָה *help*).

יָמִין :: שְׂמֹאל *left-hand side, left hand, north* Gn 13$_{9}$ 24$_{49}$ 48$_{13.13.14}$ Ex 14$_{22.29}$ Nm 20$_{17}$ 22$_{26}$ Dt 2$_{27}$ 5$_{32}$ 17$_{11}$=11QT 56$_{7}$ Dt 17$_{20}$ 28$_{14}$ Jos 1$_{7}$ 23$_{6}$ Jg 7$_{20}$ 16$_{29}$ 1 S 6$_{12}$ 2 S 2$_{19.21}$ 16$_{6}$ 1 K 7$_{39}$||2 C 4$_{6}$ 1 K 7$_{49}$ 22$_{19}$||2 C 18$_{18}$ 2 K 22$_{2}$||2 C 34$_{2}$ Is 9$_{19}$ 54$_{3}$ Ezk 1$_{10}$ 16$_{46}$ 39$_{3}$ Jon 4$_{11}$ Zc 4$_{3.11}$ 12$_{6}$ Jb 23$_{9}$ Pr 3$_{16}$ 4$_{27}$ Ca 2$_{6}$=8$_{3}$ Ec 10$_{2}$ Dn 12$_{7}$ Ne 12$_{31}$ 1 C 6$_{24}$ 2 C 3$_{17}$ 4$_{7.8}$ 1QS 1$_{15}$ 3$_{10}$ 1QM 6$_{7}$ 8$_{5}$ 9$_{14}$ ([ל]ימין) 4QD^{a} 11$_{17}$ ([ושמאול]) 4QM^{a} 1$_{14}$ 4QDibHam^{a} 1.2$_{14}$ 11QT 13$_{5}$ ([לשמאל]) 44$_{5}$ 45$_{4}$ (מימ[י]ן) Siloam tunnel inscr.$_{3}$ ([שמא]ל), צָפוֹן *north* Ps 89$_{13}$ (or em. יַמִּים *seas* or אֲמָנָה *Amanah*, with צָפוֹן *Zaphon*, both names of mountains).

<SYN> יָד *(left) hand,* זְרוֹעַ *arm,* צַד *side,* אוֹר *light* of face, עֲנָוָה *humility.*

<ANT> שְׂמֹאל *left (side),* perh. צָפוֹן *north* Ps 89_{13}.*

→ ימן *go right,* יְמָנִי *right,* בִּנְיָמִין *Benjamin,* יָמִין II *Jamin.*

יָמִין II 6 pr.n.m. **Jamin, 1.** son of Simeon, <NOM CL> בְּנֵי שִׁמְעוֹן יְמוּאֵל וְיָמִין *the sons of Simeon were Jemuel and Jamin* Gn 46_{10}‖Ex 6_{15}‖1 C 4_{24} (1 C נְמוּאֵל *Nemuel*). <PREP> לְ of possession, *of, (belonging) to* Nm 26_{12} (+ Nemuel). **2.** Judahite, son of Ram and grandson of Jerahmeel, <SUBJ> היה *be* 1 C 2_{27} (or em. יָבִין *Jabin*). **3.** Levite, interpreter of the law under Ezra (or del. Jamin). <SUBJ> בין hi. *explain* Ne 8_7. <APP> לֵוִי *Levite* Ne 8_7 (if del. וְ *and* the Levites).

→ יָמִינִי *Jaminite;* יָמִין I *right (side).*

[יָמִין] III 1 adj. **propitious,** וּשְׁמָהּ יָמִין יִקְרָא the north is a harsh wind *but its name is called propitious* Pr 27_{16} (if em. וְשֶׁמֶן יְמִינוֹ יִקְרָא whoever encloses a contentious woman encloses the wind *and his right hand encounters oil*).

* **[יָמִין]** IV 2 n.[m.] **oath**—<NOM CL> יְמִינָם יְמִין שָׁקֶר *their oath is an oath of deceit* Ps $144_{8.11}$ (unless יָמִין I *right hand*).

יָמִינִי 1 gent. **Jaminite,** Simeonite, of the family of Jamin, used collectively, <CSTR> מִשְׁפַּחַת הַיָּמִינִי *family of the Jaminite(s)* Nm 26_{12}.

→ יָמִין *Jamin.*

יְמִינִי I 4 gent. **Benjaminite,** ident. with בֶּן־יְמִינִי *Benjaminite* at Jg 3_5 19_{16} 1 S 9_{21} 22_7 2 S 16_{11} 19_{17} 1 K 2_8 Ps 7_1 1 C 27_{12}, as collective noun, **Benjaminites** (perh. adj. at 1 S 9_1 2 S 20_1 Est 2_5 *Benjaminite* man), <CSTR> אִישׁ יְמִינִי *man of (the) Benjaminites* 1 S 9_1 (or em. בֶּן־אִישׁ יְמִינִי *son of a man of the Benjaminites* to מִבִּנְיָמִן *of Benjamin*) 2 S 20_1 Est 2_5, אֶרֶץ־יְמִינִי *land of (the) Benjaminites* 1 S 9_4.

→ בִּנְיָמִן *Benjamin.*

[יְמִינִי] II, see יְמָנִי *right.*

יַמְלֵךְ 1 pr.n.m. **Jamlech,** Simeonite, 1 C 4_{34}, <APP> אֵלֶּה *these* 1 C 4_{34}.

→ מלך *rule.*

יֵמִם 1 n.[m.] perh. **hot spring(s)** or **mule(s)** or **marsh fish(es)*** or **snake(s),** <OBJ> מצא *find* in the steppe Gn 36_{24} (or em. מַיִם *water* or חַמִּים *hot waters*).

ימן 5 vb. **go right—Hi.** 5 Impf. תְּאֲמִינוּ, אֵימִינָה; impv. הֵימִינוּ; ptc. מַיְמִינִים; inf. הֵמִין—**be right-handed, go to right (side), stay on right (side),** <SUBJ> עַם *people* Is 30_{21} (:: שׂמאל hi. *go to left*), Abram Gn 13_9 (:: שׂמאל hi.), נשׁק ptc. *one who arms himself* with bow 1 C 12_2 (:: שׂמאל hi.); subj. not specified, 2 S 14_{19} Ezk 21_{21} (both :: שׂמאל hi.).

<ANT> שׂמאל hi. *go to left.**

Also 4QApJoshua[b] $1_{6(WA)}$ (Newsom וּמִן *and from*).

→ יָמִין I *righ (side),* יִמְנָה *Imnah,* יְמָנִי *right side,* תֵּימָן *south.*

יִמְנָה 5 pr.n.m. **Imnah, 1.** son of Asher, <NOM CL> בְּנֵי אָשֵׁר יִמְנָה *the sons of Asher were Imnah ...* Gn 46_{17}‖1 C 7_{30}. <CSTR> מִשְׁפַּחַת הַיִּמְנָה *family of the Imnites* Nm 26_{44}. <PREP> לְ of possession, *(belonging) to, of* Nm 26_{44}.*

2. Levite, father of Kore, <CSTR> בֶּן־יִמְנָה *son of Imnah* 2 C 31_{14}. <ADJ> לֵוִי *Levite* 2 C 31_{14};

→ ימן *go right.*

יְמָנִי 33.0.2 adj. **right**—Kt ימוני (Ezk 4_6), ימיני (2 C 3_{17}); fem. יְמָנִית—**1. right, southern,** used attributively of אֹזֶן *ear* Ex 29_{20}‖Lv $8_{23.24}$=11QT 16_3 ([ידו הימנית]) Lv $14_{14.17.25.28}$, רֶגֶל *foot* Ex 29_{20}‖Lv $8_{23.24}$=11QT 16_2 (אוזנו] [הימנית) Lv $14_{14.17.25.28}$, יָד *hand* Ex 29_{20}‖Lv $8_{23.24}$=11QT 16_3 ([ידו הימנית]) Lv $14_{14.17.25.28}$, אֶצְבַּע *finger* Lv $14_{16.27}$, כָּתֵף *shoulder,* i.e. side, of temple 1 K 6_8 7_{39} 2 K 11_{11}‖2 C 23_{10} Ezk 47_1 (or em. הַכָּתֵף *the side* and del. הַבַּיִת *of the house*) 2 C 4_{10} (if em.; see §2), of gateway Ezk 47_2, צַד *side* of Ezekiel Ezk 4_6, עַמּוּד *column* 1 K 7_{21}, אֶבֶן *stone* 1Q29 2_2 (הא]בן הימנית]).

2. used as noun, **right-hand one, southern one,** <CSTR> שֵׁם־יְמִינִי *the name of the right-hand one* 1 C $3_{17(Qr)}$, מִכֶּתֶף הַיְמָנִית *on the side of the southern one* 2 C

4_{10} (or em. to מִכְּתֶף הַבַּיִת הַיְמָנִית *on the southern side of the temple*). <COLL> יְמָנִי :: שְׂמָאלִי *left* Lv $14_{16.27}$ 1 K 7_{21}||2 C 3_{17} (§2) 2 K 11_{11}||2 C 23_{10} Ezk 4_6.

<ANT> שְׂמָאלִי *left*.*

⇒ יָמִין *right (side)*, ימן *go right*.

יִמְנָע 1 pr.n.m. **Imna,** Asherite, son of Hemel, <NOM CL> בְּנֵי חֵלֶם אָחִיו ... יִמְנָע *the sons of his brother Helem were ... Imna* 1 C $7_{35(mss)}$.

⇒ מנע *withhold*.

ימר, see אמר htp. *boast*, מור hi. *exchange*.*

יִמְרָה 1 pr.n.m. **Imrah,** Asherite, son of Zophah, <NOM CL> בְּנֵי צוֹפַח ... יִמְרָה *the sons of Zophah were ... Imrah* 1 C 7_{36}.

⇒ מרה *be obstinate*.

ימשׁ 1 vb. **touch—Hi.** 1 Impv. הֵימִשֵׁנִי (Qr הֲמִשֵּׁנִי *remove me*)—**feel,** <SUBJ> נַעַר *lad* Jg $16_{26(Kt; mss)}$. <OBJ> עַמּוּד *pillar* Jg 16_{26}.

⇒ משׁשׁ *feel*.

ינה 19.0.3 vb. **oppress—Qal** 5 Impf. נִינָם; ptc. fs יוֹנָה—**1. oppress, treat violently,** <SUBJ> צֹרֵר *foe* Ps 74_8, עִיר *city* Zp 3_1, חֶרֶב *sword* Jr $25_{38(mss)}$ (L חֲרוֹן *anger of* the oppressive one; or em. חַרְבּוֹ הַגְּדוֹלָה *his great sword*) 46_{16} 50_{16} (or em. in both חֶרֶב הַיּוֹנָה *a sword that oppresses* to הַיּוֹנָה sword of *the oppressor*, as §2, or הַחֶרֶב הַיְוָנִיָּה *the Greek sword*). <OBJ> Israelite(s) Ps 74_8.

2. ptc. as noun, **oppressor,** <SUBJ> בגד *betray* Hb 2_5 (if em. הַיַּיִן *the wine* to הַיּוֹנָה *the oppressor*, i.e. Nebuchadrezzar; 1QpHab 8_3 הוֹן *wealth*), <CSTR> חֲרוֹן הַיּוֹנָה *burning of the oppressor* Jr 25_{38} (mss חֶרֶב *sword*), חֶרֶב הַיּוֹנָה *sword of the oppressor* Jr 46_{16} 50_{16} (if em.).

Hi. 14.0.3 Pf. הוֹנָה, Q הוניתה (Q הונות), הוֹנוּ; impf. יוֹנֶה, 2ms תּוֹנֶה (תּוֹנֻּוּ), יוֹנוּ ,תּוֹנוּ (תֹּנוּ); ptc. מוֹנַיִךְ; inf. הוֹנָתָם—**oppress,** <SUBJ> Israelite(s) Ex 22_{20} (|| לחץ *oppress*) Dt 23_{17}, עַם *people* Jr 22_3 (|| חמס *treat violently*) Ezk 22_{29}, אִישׁ *man* Lv $25_{14.17}$ Ezk 18_7, בֵּן Israelite *son* Lv 19_{33}, *son* Ezk $18_{12.16}$, מֶלֶךְ *king* Jr 22_3 (|| חמס *treat violently*), נָשִׂיא *prince* Ezk 22_7 45_8 46_{18}, שַׂר *prince* 4QpPsa 3_7, עֶבֶד *servant* Jr 22_3 (|| חמס *treat violently*); subj. not specified, Is 49_{26} 4Q418 97_1 127_4. <OBJ> עַם *people* Ezk 45_8 46_{18} 4QpPsa 3_7, אִישׁ *man* Ezk $18_{7.16}$, אָח *brother* Lv 25_{14}, עָמִית *fellow* Lv 25_{17}, אַלְמָנָה *widow* Jr 22_3 Ezk 22_7, יָתוֹם *orphan* Jr 22_3 Ezk 22_7, אֶבְיוֹן *poor one* Ezk 18_{12} 22_{29}, עָנִי *poor one* Ezk 18_{12} 22_{29}, עֶבֶד *slave* Dt 23_{17}, גֵּר *sojourner* Ex 22_{20} Lv 19_{33} Jr 22_3. <PREP> בְּ *in, with*, + הֲלִיכָה *way of life* 4Q418 127_4; מִן of direction, oppress (so as to drive out) *from*, + אֲחֻזָּה *inheritance* Ezk 46_{18} (or del. אֲחֻזָּה).

<SYN> לחץ *oppress*, חמס *treat violently*.*

יָנוֹחַ 3 pl.n. **Janoah**— + ה- of direction יָנוֹחָה—**1.** appar. in Ephraim, <PREP> מִן of direction, *from*, + ירד *go down* Jos 16_7; יָנוֹחָה (with ה- of direction), *at, in, to, into*, + עבר *pass by* Jos 16_6.

2. in northern Galilee, perh. ident. with Yānūḥ, 10 km N of Tyre, <OBJ> לקח *take*, i.e. capture 2 K 15_{29}.

⇒ נוח *settle*.

יָנוּם 1 pl.n. **Janum**—Kt ינים—in Judah appar. near Hebron Jos 15_{53}, <NOM CL> וּבָהָר ... וְיָנוּם *and in the hill country were ... and Janum* Jos $15_{53(Qr)}$.

⇒ (?) נום *fall asleep*.

[יְנִיקָה] 1 n.f. **shoot**—pl. sf. יְנִיקוֹתָיו—<CSTR> רֹאשׁ יְנִיקוֹתָיו *head of its shoots*, i.e. topmost twigs Ezk 17_4 (or em. יֹנְקוֹתָיו in same sense, i.e. ינק, Qal, §3b).

⇒ ינק *suck*.

ינק 31.0.4 vb. **suck—Qal** 16.0.3 Impf. אִינַק, תִּינַק, יִינָק, תִּינְקוּ, יִינָקוּ; + waw Q וינקו, וַתִּינָקְתְּ, וִינַקְתֶּם; ptc. יוֹנֵק (יֹנֵק), יוֹנְקוֹתֶיהָ ,(יֹנְקוֹתָיו) יוֹנְקוֹתָיו ,יוֹנַקְתּוֹ ,(יונ[קים]) Q יונק ,יוֹנְקֵי ,יֹנְקִים—**1. suck, be suckled (at), feed (on),** <SUBJ> Jacob Dt 32_{13} (if em. hi.), Zebulun and Issachar Dt 33_{19}, Zion Is $60_{16.16}$, עַם *people* 1QIsaa 65_3 (if וינקו is not נקה ni. *be emptied*), Job Jb 3_{12} (+ שַׁד *breast*), אָח *brother* Ca 8_1, אהב ptc. *one who loves* Is 66_{11} (|| מצץ *suck*, שׂבע *be satisfied*) 66_{12} (or em.; see §3), אבל htp. ptc. *one who mourns* Is $66_{11.12}$ (or em.), רָשָׁע *wicked one* Jb 20_{16}, חָנֵף *impious one* Jb 20_{16}. <OBJ> שַׁד *breast* or *wealth* Is 60_{16}, שַׁד *breast* 1QIsaa 65_3 (if em. ידים *hands* to שדים *breasts* and if וינקו is not נקה ni. *be emptied*)* Ca 8_1, חָלָב

milk Is 60$_{16}$, דְּבַשׁ *honey* Dt 32$_{13}$ (if em.), שֶׁמֶן *oil* Dt 32$_{13}$ (if em.), שֶׁפַע *abundance* of the sea Dt 33$_{19}$, שָׂפוּן *hidden thing* Dt 33$_{19}$, רֹאשׁ *poison* Jb 20$_{16}$. <PREP> מִן of direction, *from*, + סֶלַע *rock* Dt 32$_{13}$ (if em.), חַלָּמִישׁ *flint* Dt 32$_{13}$ (if em.); partitive, *(some) of*, + שַׁד *breast* or *wealth* Is 66$_{11}$; עַל *upon*, + אֶבֶן *stone* 1QIsa^a 65$_3$ (if וינקו is not נקה ni. *be emptied* into vaginas [אָבְנַיִם]).

2. masc. ptc., יוֹנֵק, as noun, **a. (male) infant, suckling child,** <SUBJ> עטף ni. *faint* Lm 2$_{11}$, שׁעע pilp. *play* Is 11$_8$. <OBJ> נשׂא *raise*, i.e. carry Nm 11$_{12}$ CD 11$_{11}$ (=4QD^e 6.2$_{16}$ [היונק]), כרת hi. *cut off* Jr 44$_7$, אסף *gather* Jl 2$_{16}$. <CSTR> יֹנְקֵי שָׁדָיִם *infants of*, i.e. at, *breasts* Jl 2$_{16}$, לְשׁוֹן יוֹנֵק *tongue of infant* Lm 4$_4$, פִּי עוֹלְלִים וְיֹנְקִים *mouth of children and infants* Ps 8$_3$. <PREP> כְּ *like, as*, + פצה *open* 1QH 7$_{21}$ ([יונ]קים), עַד *unto*, i.e. including + מות hi. *kill* 1 S 15$_3$, + נכה hi. *strike* 1 S 22$_{19}$. <COLL> עוֹלֵל || יֹנֵק *child* 1 S 15$_3$ 22$_{19}$ Jr 44$_7$ Jl 2$_{16}$ Ps 8$_3$ Lm 2$_{11}$ 4$_4$ (+) 1QH 7$_{21}$ (עולול), גמל pass. ptc. *weaned child* Is 11$_8$, אֹמֵן *nurse* Nm 11$_{12}$ 1QH 7$_{21}$ CD 11$_{11}$ (=4QD^f 5.1$_7$ [האומן]), בָּחוּר *youth* Dt 32$_{25}$, אִישׁ *man* Dt 32$_{25}$ 1 S 15$_3$ 22$_{19}$ Jr 44$_7$, אִשָּׁה *woman* 1 S 15$_3$ 22$_{19}$ Jr 44$_7$, בְּתוּלָה *young woman* Dt 32$_{25}$, שׁוֹר *ox* 1 S 15$_3$ 22$_{19}$, שֶׂה *sheep* 1 S 15$_3$ 22$_{19}$, גָּמָל *camel* 1 S 15$_3$, חֲמוֹר *donkey* 1 S 15$_3$ 22$_{19}$.

2b. shoot, <PREP> כְּ *as*, + עלה *go up*, i.e. grow Is 53$_2$ (or em. יֹנֶקֶת, as §3b; || שֹׁרֶשׁ *root*).

2c. nurse, <PREP> לְ *to, towards*, + בהל htp. *hasten* 4QTNaph 1$_5$.

3. fem. ptc., יֹנֶקֶת, **a. female (suckling) infant,** <SUBJ> נשׂא ni. *be carried* Is 66$_{12}$ (if em. וִינַקְתֶּם עַל־צַד תִּנָּשֵׂאוּ *and you will nurse; you will be carried at the side* to וְיֹנַקְתָּהּ/וְיֹנְקֹתָם עַל־צַד תִּנָּשֵׂא *and her female infant/and their female infants will be carried at the side*; or em. (וְיֹנְקֹתָם), שׁעע polp. *be played with* Is 11$_8$ (if em. תְּשָׁעֳשָׁעוּ *you will be played with* to תְּשָׁעֳשָׁע *she* [infant] *will be played with*).

3b. shoot (singular used collectively at Jb 8$_{16}$ 14$_7$ 15$_{30}$), <SUBJ> הלך *go* Ho 14$_7$ (+ שֹׁרֶשׁ *root*), יצא *go out*, i.e. grow Jb 8$_{16}$ (|| שֹׁרֶשׁ), חדל *cease* Jb 14$_7$. <OBJ> שׁלח pi. *send (away)* Ps 80$_{12}$ (|| קָצִיר *branch*), יבשׁ pi. *dry up* Jb 15$_{30}$. <CSTR> רֹאשׁ יְנִיקוֹתָיו *head of its shoots*, i.e. topmost twigs Ezk 17$_4$ (if em. יְנִיקוֹתָיו in same sense) 17$_{22}$. <PREP> כְּ *as*, + עלה *go up*, i.e. grow Is 53$_2$ (if em. יוֹנֵק [§2b]; || שֹׁרֶשׁ).

<SYN> §1 מצץ *suck*, שׂבע *be satisfied*; §2a עוֹלֵל *child*, גמל pass. ptc. *weaned child*; §2b שֹׁרֶשׁ *root*; §3b שֹׁרֶשׁ *root*, קָצִיר *branch*.

Hi. 15.0.1 Pf. הֵינִקָה (Q הניקה), הֵינִקוּ; impf. 3fs תֵּינִק; + waw וַיֵּינִקֵהוּ, 3fs וַתֵּינֶק (וַתְּנִיקֵהוּ); ptc. מֵינֶקֶת (מֵינִקְתּוֹ), מֵינִיקוֹת (מֵינִיקֹתַיִךְ), מֵנִקְתָּהּ, Q מנקת), מֵנִקְתּוֹ; impv. הֵינִקֵהוּ; inf. הֵינִיק—**1. suckle (with), feed (with),** <SUBJ> Y. Dt 32$_{13}$ (or em. qal, with Jacob as subj.), Deborah 4QTNaph 1$_1$, Sarah Gn 21$_7$, אִשָּׁה *woman* Ex 2$_{7.9}$ 1 S 1$_{23}$ 1 K 3$_{21}$, אֵם *mother* Ex 2$_9$, גָּמָל *camel* Gn 32$_{16}$, תַּן *jackal* Lm 4$_3$. <OBJ> (1) recipient of feeding, Rebekah 4QTNaph 1$_1$, Jacob Dt 32$_{13}$ (or em.), בֵּן *son* Gn 21$_7$ 1 S 1$_{23}$ 1 K 3$_{21}$, יֶלֶד *child* Ex 2$_{7.9.9}$, גּוּר *cub* Lm 4$_3$; (2) food, דְּבַשׁ *honey* Dt 32$_{13}$ (or em.), שֶׁמֶן *oil* Dt 32$_{13}$ (or em.). <PREP> לְ of benefit, *for*, + בַּת *daughter* of Pharaoh Ex 2$_9$, מִן of direction, *from*, + סֶלַע *rock* Dt 32$_{13}$ (or em.), חַלָּמִישׁ *flint* Dt 32$_{13}$ (or em.); בְּ of accompaniment, *in (a state of), with*, + טָהֳרָה *purity* 4QD^a 6.2$_{11}$; עַד *until*, + גמל inf. *weaning* 1 S 1$_{23}$. <COLL> ינק hi. חלץ שַׁד *expose breast* Lm 4$_3$, + ילד *give birth* Gn 21$_7$.

2. fem. ptc., מֵינֶקֶת, as noun, **(wet)nurse,** <SUBJ> היה *be* Is 49$_{23}$ (+ שָׂרָה *prince* [fem.]), מות *die* Gn 35$_8$, קבר ni. *be buried* Gn 35$_8$. <OBJ> שׁלח pi. *send away* Gn 24$_{59}$, גנב *steal* 2 K 11$_2$, נתן *give*, i.e. place 2 K 11$_2$||2 C 22$_{11}$ (if ins. נתן at 2 K). <CSTR> מֵינֶקֶת רִבְקָה *Rebekah's nurse* Gn 35$_8$. <APP> Deborah Gn 35$_8$. <COLL> || אֹמֵן *nurse* Is 49$_{23}$, + Joash 2 K 11$_2$||2 C 22$_{11}$, Rebekah Gn 24$_{59}$, אִישׁ *man* Gn 24$_{59}$, עֶבֶד *servant* Gn 24$_{59}$.

<SYN> §2 אֹמֵן *nurse*.*

→ יְנִיקָה *shoot*.

יַנְשׁוּף 3 n.m. perh. **screech owl**—יַנְשׁוּף—unclean bird, <SUBJ> אכל ni. *be eaten* Lv 11$_{17}$, שׁכן *dwell* Is 34$_{11}$. <OBJ> אכל *eat* Dt 14$_{16}$, שׁקץ pi. *despise* Lv 11$_{17}$.*

יסד I 41.2.16 vb. **establish—Qal** 19.1.11 Pf. יָסַד (יְסָדָהּ, Q יסדם), יָסַדְתָּ, יְסָדָהּ (Q יסדתה, יסדתני, יְסַדְתּוֹ, יְסַדְתָּם), יְסַדְתִּיךָ, Q יסדו; ptc. יֹסֵד, Q יסודים ([יוסד]י, perh. יסודי); inf. יְסוֹד (יְסֹד, יְסֹדִי, יָסְדוֹ)—**1. establish, found, lay foundations, accumulate** (2 C 31$_7$), **educate** (Si 10$_1$), **decree** (Ezr 7$_9$ [if em.]).

<SUBJ> Y. 1QIsa[b] 28_{16} (MT; 1QIsa[a] pi.) 51_{13} 54_{11} =4QpIsa[d] 1_{1} (or em. וְיִסַּדְתִּיךְ *and I have established you* to יְסֹדֹתַיִךְ *your foundations* are) Am 9_{6} Hb 1_{12}=1QpHab 5_{1} Zc 12_{1} Ps 24_{2} 78_{69} (אֲדֹנָי *my Lord*) 89_{12} $104_{5.8}$ 119_{152} Jb 38_{4} Pr 3_{19} 1QH 5_{9} (אדוני *my Lord*) 9_{17} 4QD[a] 11_{9} 4QShirShabb[a] 1.1_{10} ([י]סדם) 1.1_{19} 4QShirShabb[b] 17_{5} appar. 5Q Règle 1_{3}, צוּר *rock*, i.e. Y. Hb 1_{12}=1QpHab 5_{1}, אֵל *God* Ps 102_{26} (11QPs[a] נוסדה the earth *was established*; + לְפָנִים *of old*) 1QSb 3_{21}, Ezra Ezr 7_{9} (if em. יְסֻד *establishment*), Assyria Is 23_{13}, שֹׁפֵט *judge* Si 10_{1}, יָד *hand* Is 48_{13}, עֲרֵמָה *heap* 2 C 31_{7}; subj. not specified, Ezr 3_{12}.

<OBJ> appar. Jerusalem Is 54_{11}, worshipper 1QH 5_{9}, כֹּהֵן *priest* 4QShirShabb[a] 1.1_{19}, עֲנִיָּה *afflicted one* (fem.) Is 54_{11}, סֹעֲרָה *storm-tossed one* (fem.) Is 54_{11}, לֹא נֻחָמָה *uncomforted one* (fem.) Is 54_{11}, עַם *people* Si 10_{1} 4QD[a] 11_{9}, perh. גּוֹי *nation* Hb 1_{12}=1QpHab 5_{1}, רוּחַ *spirit* 1QH 9_{12}, שָׁמַיִם *heavens* Ps 89_{12}, אֶרֶץ *land, earth* Is 23_{13} 48_{13} 51_{13} Zc 12_{1} Ps 24_{2} 78_{69} 89_{12} 102_{26} 104_{5} Jb 38_{4} Pr 3_{19}, תֵּבֵל *world* Ps 89_{12}, מְלֹא *fullness* Ps 89_{12}, בַּיִת *house* Ezr 3_{12}, אֲגֻדָּה *vault* Am 9_{6}, מָקוֹם *place* Ps 104_{8}, אֶבֶן *stone* 1QIsa[b] 28_{16}.

מִצְוָה *commandment* Ps 119_{152}, עֵדָה *testimony* Ps 119_{152} (or em. עֵדוּת *testimony* or פִּקּוּד *precept*), עֵצָה *council* 4QpIsa[d] 1_{2}, סוֹד *council* appar. 4QShirShabb[a] 1.1_{10}, שָׁלוֹם *peace* 1QSb 3_{21}, הוֹד *majesty* (ה[ו]ד) =4QShirShabb[d] 1.1_{17} (ויברך ליוסד[י הוד]) *and he will bless those who establish majesty*; =4QShirShabb[f] 3.2_{7} ויברך ליסודי ה[ו]ד perh. *and he will bless the foundations of majesty*), מַעֲשֶׂה *deed* 1QS 3_{25}, מַעֲלָה *ascent* to Jerusalem Ezr 7_{9} (if em. יְסֻד *establishment*).

<PREP> לְ of benefit, *for*, + 4QShirShabb[a] 1.1_{10} [י]סדם (ל[ו] *he established them for himself*) 1.1_{19} 4QShirShabb[b] 17_{5}, צִי *ship* Is 23_{13}, הַר *mountain* Ps 104_{8}, בִּקְעָה *valley* Ps 104_{8}; *as*, + קָדוֹשׁ *holy one* 4QShirShabb[a] 1.1_{10} [י]סדם (ל[ו] לקד[ושי]), יכח hi. ptc. *one who reproves* 1QpHab 5_{1}; *in accordance with*, + מִשְׁפָּחָה *family* 4QD[a] 11_{9}, אֻמָּה *people* 4QD[a] 11_{9}, לָשׁוֹן *tongue* 4QD[a] 11_{9}.

בְּ of place, *in*, + Zion 1QIsa[b] 28_{16}; of instrument, *with*, + חָכְמָה *wisdom* Pr 3_{19}, סַפִּיר *sapphire* Is 54_{11} (or em. וְיִסַּדְתִּיךְ *and I have established you* with sapphire to יְסֹדֹתַיִךְ *your foundations* are sapphire).

עַל *upon*, + אֶרֶץ *earth* Am 9_{6}, יָם *sea* Ps 24_{2}, מְכוֹנָה *foundation* Ps 104_{5}.

<COLL> יסד with יכח hi. *reprove* Hb 1_{12}, קרב *approach* 4QShirShabb[b] 17_{5} (ל[קרוב]); with adverb of time, לְעוֹלָם *forever* Ps 78_{69} 1QSb 3_{21} (עד לעולמי *for eternity* 1QSb 3_{21}), לְפָנִים *of old* Ps 102_{26}; יסד ‖ כון pol. *establish* Ps 24_{2} Pr 3_{19}, נטה *extend* heavens Is $51_{13.16}$ (if em. נטע *plant*) Zc 12_{1}, טפח pi. *extend* heavens Is 48_{13}, נטע *plant* heavens Is 51_{16} (or em.); + בנה *build* Am 9_{6} Ps 78_{69}, קום hi. *establish* Is 23_{13}, ערר po. *destroy* Is 23_{13} (or em. ערר pol. *agitate*), ידע *know* 1QH 9_{12}.

Also 4QTime 2_{1} (קודשו יסדם *[of] his holiness has established them* unless *his holiness is their foundation*, i.e. יְסוֹד).

<SYN> כון pol. *establish*, נטע *plant*, נטה *extend*, טפח pi. *extend*, ידע *know*.

Ni. 2.1.2 Pf. Q נוסדה ,נוֹסְדוּ; impf. תִּוָּסֵד; inf. הִוָּסְדָה, הִוָּסְדָם—**be established**, **<SUBJ>** Egypt Ex 9_{18}, רַבִּים *many* Ps 31_{14}, סרר ptc. *those who rebel* against the way CD 2_{7}, תעב ptc. pi. *those who abhor* the statute CD 2_{7}, אֶרֶץ *earth* 11QPs[a] 102_{26} (MT יָסַדְתָּ *you established* the earth), הֵיכָל *temple* Is 44_{28}, מִשְׁפָּט *judgment* 4Q418 69.2_{5} (=4Q417 18_{2} [משפט]). **<COLL>** סיד ni. ‖ היה *be* 4Q418 69.2_{5} (=4Q417 18_{2} [היה]), בנה ni. *be rebuilt* Is 44_{28}. **<SYN>** היה *be*, בנה ni. *be rebuilt*.

Pi. 7.1.3 Pf. יִסַּד (יִסְּדָה), יִסַּדְתָּ, יִסְּדוּ, יִסְּדֶנָּה; impf. Si. תיסד; + waw וַיְיַסְּדוּ; ptc. Q מיסדי; inf. יַסֵּד—**establish**; also **decree** (Est 1_{8} Ezr 7_{9} [if em.]), perh. **re-establish, repair*** (Zc 4_{9} Ezr 3_{10}).

<SUBJ> Y. Is 14_{32} 28_{16} (1QIsa[b] qal) Ps 8_{3}, אֵל *God* 1QS 3_{25}, Bethelite 1 K 16_{34}, David 1 C 9_{22}, Hiel 1 K 16_{34}, Samuel 1 C 9_{22}, Solomon 2 C 3_{3} (if em. ho.), Ezra Ezr 7_{9} (if em. יְסֻד *establishment*), אִישׁ *man* Jos 6_{26} 1QS 5_{5}= 4QS[b] 5_{5}=4QS[d] 1.1_{4}, מֶלֶךְ *king* Est 1_{8}, רֹאֶה *seer* 1 C 9_{22}, בֹּנֶה *builder* Ezr 3_{10}, יָד *hand* Zc 4_{9}, בְּרָכָה *blessing* Si 3_{9}, אֶבֶן *stone* 1 K 5_{31}.

<OBJ> Jericho Jos 6_{26} 1 K 16_{34}, Zion Is 14_{32}, דַּעַת *knowledge* 4QShirShabb[d] 1.1_{24} (מיסדי ד[עת]; others מוסדי ד[עת] *foundations of knowledge*), אֶבֶן *stone* Is 28_{16}, בַּיִת *house* 1 K 5_{31} (+ אַבְנֵי גָזִית *with hewn stones*) Zc 4_{9}, הֵיכָל *temple* Ezr 3_{10}, מוּסָד *foundation* 1QS 5_{5} (=4QS[b] 5_{5} מסד=4QS[d] 1.1_{4} [מוסד]), עִיר *city* Jos 6_{26}, שֹׁעֵר *gatekeeper* 1 C 9_{22}, מַעֲלָה *ascent* to Jerusalem Ezr 7_{9} (if em. יְסֻד

establishment), מִדָּה *measurement* 2 C 3$_3$ (if em. ho.), עֹז *strength* Ps 8$_3$, שֹׁרֶשׁ *root* Si 3$_9$.

<PREP> לְ of benefit, *for*, + Israel =1QS 5$_5$=4QS^b 5$_5$ =4QS^d 1.1$_4$, יַחַד *community* 1QS 5$_5$=4QS^b 5$_5$=4QS^d 1.1$_4$; of purpose, *in order to*, + עשׂה *do* Est 1$_8$, בנה *build* 2 C 3$_3$ (if em. ho.), שׁבת hi. *put an end to* Ps 8$_3$; בְּ of place, *in*, + Zion Is 28$_{16}$; *at the cost of*, + Abiram 1 K 16$_{34}$, בְּכוֹר *first-born* Jos 6$_{26}$ 1 K 16$_{34}$, בֶּאֱמוּנָתָם ... יִסַּד *he established (them) ... in their (office of) trust* or *on account of their reliability* 1 C 9$_{22}$ (or em. בַּאֲבֹתָם *on account of their ancestors*); עַל *upon*, + רוּחַ *spirit* 1QS 3$_{25}$, i.e. give orders to, + רַב *great one* Est 1$_8$; לְמַעַן *on account of*, + צֹרֵר *adversary* Ps 8$_3$; מִפִּי *from the mouth of*, + עוֹלֵל *child* Ps 8$_3$, יֹנֵק *male infant* Ps 8$_3$.

<COLL> יסד pi. ‖ בצע pi. *complete* Zc 4$_9$; + בנה *build* Jos 6$_{26}$, 1 K 16$_{34}$, נצב hi. *erect* Jos 6$_{26}$; :: נתשׁ *uproot* Si 3$_9$.

<SYN> בצע pi. *complete*. <ANT> נתשׁ *uproot*.

Pu. 6 Pf. יֻסַּד (יָסַּד); ptc. מְיֻסָּד, מְיֻסָּדִים; Kt מיסדות—**1. be established, be set;** perh. **be re-established, be repaired*** (Hg 2$_{18}$ Zc 8$_9$), <SUBJ> עַמּוּד *pillar* Ca 5$_{15}$, בַּיִת *house* 1 K 6$_{37}$ Zc 8$_9$, הֵיכָל *temple* Hg 2$_{18}$ Zc 8$_9$ Ezr 3$_6$, שׁוֹק *leg* Ca 5$_{15}$. <PREP> לְ of purpose, *for*, + בנה ni. inf. *rebuilding* Zc 8$_9$; בְּ of place/time, *in*, + Zion Is 28$_{16(mss)}$, יֶרַח *month* 1 K 6$_{37}$, שָׁנָה *year* 1 K 6$_{37}$; עַל *upon*, + אֶדֶן *base* Ca 5$_{15}$. <COLL> with adverb of time, יוֹם *day* in which Zc 8$_9$, הַיּוֹם *today* Hg 2$_{18}$; יסד pu. + בנה *build* 1 K 6$_{37}$, כלה *be finished* 1 K 6$_{37}$.

2. ptc. as noun, **foundation,** <NOM CL> מְיֻסָּד אֲבָנִים יְקָרוֹת אֲבָנִים גְּדֹלוֹת *(the) foundation was of splendid stones, huge stones* 1 K 7$_{10}$. <CSTR> מיסדות הַצְּלָעוֹת *foundations of the side chambers* Ezk 41$_{8(Kt)}$ (Qr מוּסְדוֹת *foundations*; or em. מַסָּדוֹת *foundations*).

Ho. 3 Ptc. מוּסָּד; inf. הוּסַד—**be established,** <COLL> מוּסָד מוּסָּד *a (well-)established foundation* Is 28$_{16}$ (mss lack מוּסָּד), עַל הוּסַד בֵּית־י׳ *on account of the establishing of the house of Y.* Ezr 3$_{11}$, וְאֵלֶּה הוּסַד שְׁלֹמֹה לִבְנוֹת appar. *and these are what Solomon established for building* 2 C 3$_3$ (or em. הַמִּדּוֹת אֲשֶׁר יִסַּד and these are *the measurements that* Solomon *established* for building).*

⇒ יְסַד *establishment*, יְסוֹד *foundation*, יְסוּדָה *foundation*, מוֹסָד *foundation*, מוּסָּד *foundation*, מוֹסָדָה *foundation*, מוּסָדָה *foundation*, מַסָּד *foundation*.

יסד II 2 vb. **plot—Ni.** 2 Pf. נוֹסְדוּ; inf. הִוָּסְדָם—**conspire,** <SUBJ> רֹזֵן *ruler* Ps 2$_2$, רַב pl. *many* Ps 31$_{14}$. <PREP> עַל *against*, + Y. Ps 2$_2$, מָשִׁיחַ *anointed one* Ps 2$_2$ (or del. עַל־י׳ וְעַל־מְשִׁיחוֹ *against Y. and his anointed*), worshipper Ps 31$_{14}$ (or em. סוד ni. *hold counsel*). <COLL> יסד ni. + יַחַד *together* Ps 2$_2$ 31$_{14}$.

[יְסַד] 1 n.m. **establishment**—cstr. יְסַד—<NOM CL> הוּא יְסַד הַמַּעֲלָה *it was the establishment of the return from exile*, lit. ascent Ezr 7$_9$ (or em. הוּא נִסָּן יָסַד/יִסַּד *it was Nisan; he* [Ezra] *decreed* the return).*

⇒ יסד *establish*.

יְסוֹד 20.1.22 n.m. **foundation**—Q ישוד; cstr. יְסוֹד; sf. יְסֹדוֹ (Q יסודו), יְסוֹדָם; pl. Q יסודים, יסודות; cstr. Si יסודי; sf. יְסוֹדֶיהָ (וִיסֹדֶיהָ), Q יסודותיהו; יְסוֹדֹתֶיהָ—**foundation, base,** esp. of altar* (Ex 29$_{12}$ Lv 4$_{7.18.25.30.34}$ 5$_9$ 8$_{15}$ 9$_9$); **re-establishment, repair** (2 C 24$_{27}$);* perh. **thigh*** (Hb 3$_{13}$ [+ צַוָּאר *neck*]); **founding principle** (CD 19$_{4[B]}$); **authority** (1QS 7$_{17}$); perh. **pillar** of community (1QSa 1$_{12}$).

<SUBJ> גלה ni. *be exposed* Ezk 13$_{14}$, זוע htpalp. *be shaken* 1QS 8$_8$, חושׁ hi. *fall apart* 1QS 8$_8$, הרס ni. *be destroyed* Ezk 30$_4$, יצק ho. *be emptied out*, i.e. be destroyed Jb 22$_{16}$, כתב pass. *be written* 2 C 24$_{27}$, רעשׁ *quake* Si 16$_{19}$, מוט ni. *be moved* Pr 12$_3$ (if em. שֹׁרֶשׁ צַדִּיקִים *the root of the righteous* will not be moved, to יְסוֹד עוֹלָם *a foundation of eternity*).*

<NOM CL> יְסוֹד עוֹלָם *the foundation is for ever* Pr 10$_{25}$, יסוד בשרי *my flesh is the foundation* 4QShir^b 48.2$_4$, בֶּעָפָר יְסוֹדָם *their foundation is in the dust* Jb 4$_{19}$, יסודי הרים לשרפה *the foundations of the mountains shall be as a burning* 1QH 3$_{31}$, אתה ... יסוד הא[מת] *you are ... the foundation of truth* 4QShir^b 52.3$_1$, [א]לא יסדות *these are the foundations* of the walls of the community 4QD^a 10.1$_{11}$.

<OBJ> נבט hi. *look at* Si 16$_{19}$, גלה pi. *uncover* Mc 1$_6$, ערה pi. *expose* Hb 3$_{13}$ (עָרוֹת יְסוֹד עַד־צַוָּאר perh. *exposing [from] the thigh up to the neck* to צוּר exposing the foundation down to the *rock* and/or em. עֵרִיתָ/עֵרִית *you have exposed*), אכל *eat*, i.e. destroy Lm 4$_{11}$.

<CSTR> יסודי תבל *foundations of the world* Si 16$_{19}$, יסוד הבריאה *the foundation of creation* CD 4$_{21}$, יְסוֹד עוֹלָם

a foundation of eternity Pr 12$_3$ (if em.; see Subj.), יסודי הרים *foundations of the mountains* 1QH 3$_{31}$, ישוד עם *foundation of the nation* 4QDᵃ 5.2$_9$, יסוד היחד *authority of the community* 1QS 7$_{17.18}$, יסוד היחד *founding principles of the community* 1QS 8$_{10}$, יְסוֹד בֵּית *foundation of the house of* 2 C 24$_{27}$, יסדות אוש[י] *the foundations of the walls of* 4QDᵃ 10.1$_{11}$, יסוד [הרק]יע *base of the vault* 4QMishA 1.1$_2$, הַמִּזְבֵּחַ *of the altar* Ex 29$_{12}$ Lv 4$_{30.34}$ 5$_9$ 8$_{15}$ 9$_9$, מִזְבֵּחַ *of the altar of* Lv 4$_{7.18.25}$ 11QT 34$_8$ 52$_{21}$, יסוד רוח *foundation of the spirit of* 1QS 9$_3$, יסודי הברית *foundations of the covenant* CD 10$_6$, יסוד הא[מת] *the foundation of truth* 4QShirᵇ 52.3$_1$, יסודי פשע *foundations of sin* 4QShir Shabbᶜ 1$_5$, יסודי קץ *foundations of time*, i.e. the established time 1QH 12$_8$; שַׁעַר הַיְסוֹד *gate of the foundation* 2 C 23$_5$, כול יסודי *all foundations of* 4QShirShabbᶜ 1$_5$.

<PREP> לְ *as*, + היה *be* 1QS 9$_3$; בְּ of place, *in, at*, + אור hi. *shine* 4QMishA 1.1$_2$; of accompaniment, *in, with*, + יצב htp. *take one's position* 1QSa 1$_{12}$; *in*, + כון ni. *be established* 1QS 8$_{10}$, בין pol. *instruct* CD 10$_6$; introducing object, + ירה hi. *teach* 4QDᵃ 5.2$_9$; מִן of direction, *from*, + זוע *tremble* 1QS 7$_{18}$.

מִן of direction, *from* 4QShirᵇ 73$_3$.

אֶל *to, at*, + מצה ni. *be pressed out* Lv 5$_9$, שׁפך *pour out* Ex 29$_{12}$ Lv 4$_{7.18.25.30.34}$, יצק *pour out* Lv 8$_{15}$ 9$_9$; עַד *until, as far as*, + ערה pi. *make bare*, i.e. tear down Ps 137$_7$; כְּמִשְׁפַּט *according to the rule of*, i.e. in accordance with, + הלך htp. *go about* CD 19$_{4(B)}$ (כמשפט היסודים כסרך התורה *according to the founding principles, according to the rule of the law* (=7$_{8(A)}$ היסורים *the precepts*; or em. האסרים *the vows*, i.e. אִסָּר, and/or כדרך *according to the way of* the law).*

Also 4QMishCᵃ 2$_4$ 4Q365a 3$_2$ 4QShirᵇ 44.1$_5$.

⇒ יסד *establish.*

יְסוּדָה 1 n.f. **foundation**—sf. יְסוּדָתוֹ—**foundation,** <NOM CL> יְסוּדָתוֹ בְּהַרְרֵי קֹדֶשׁ *his foundation is in the holy mountains* Ps 87$_1$.*

⇒ יסד *establish.*

[יָסוּר] n.[m.] 1 **one who departs**—cstr./sf. Kt יסורי—יסורי בָּאָרֶץ יִכָּתֵבוּ perh. *those who depart from me/him will be inscribed in the (under)world* or *those who depart of the land*, i.e. those in the land who depart, *will be inscribed* Jr 17$_{13}$ (Qr וְסוּרַי *and those who depart from me*).*

⇒ סור *depart.*

יִסּוֹר 1.1.10 n.[m.] **reprover; punishment, instruction**—cstr. Si יסור; pl. Q יסורים; cstr. Q יסורי; sf. Q יסוריך, יסוריה, יסורו—**1. reprover** or **one who is to be disciplined,** <SUBJ> ריב *contend* Job 40$_3$ (or em. יָסוּר *he will depart*; + מוֹכִיחַ *reprover*). **2.** appar. **punishment, pain, torture,** <CSTR> מטעמי זבד לא[י]ש יודע יסור מעים *delicacies given as a gift are a punishment of (the) bowels to a knowing person* Si 40$_{29(M[Yadin])}$ (B מטעמו ... סוד מעים *his delicacy ... is a secret of the bowels*; Bmg יסור מזעים *torture that makes indignant*, i.e. זעם hi.). <PREP> בְּ of instrument, *by means of*, + שׁוב hi. *bring back* 1QH 17$_{22}$, אפק htp. *restrain oneself* 4QBéat 3.2$_4$; indicating object, + מאס *reject* 4QBéat 5$_{10}$. <COLL> יִסּוֹר ‖ נֶגַע *plague* 4Q Béat 3.2$_4$, תּוֹכֵחָה *rebuke* 4QBéat 5$_{10}$.

<SYN> נֶגַע *plague*, תּוֹכֵחָה *rebuke.*

3. instruction, precept,* <OBJ> ידע hi. *make known* 1QLitPr 3.2$_7$. <CSTR> יסורי צדק *the precepts of righteousness* 1QS 3$_1$ 4QDᵃ 11$_7$=4QDᵉ 7.1$_{21}$ (both הצדק), הברית *of the covenant* 6.4$_{17}$ (ובי[סו]רי); ‖ ספר ההג[י] *the book of meditation*; 4QDᵃ 8.3$_6$ ישו[די] הברית *the founding principles of the covenant*=CD 10$_6$ יסודי *the founding principles of* the covenant), כל יסורו *all his precepts* CD 7$_5$ (or em. יסורי *precepts of* the covenant), כבוד *of glory* 1Q LitPr 3.2$_7$. <PREP> בְּ of place/time, *in*, + בין pol. *be expert (in)* 4QDᵉ 6.4$_{17}$ (4QDᵃ 8.3$_6$ בישו[די הברית] *in the founding principles of the covenant*=CD 10$_6$ ביסודי *in the founding principles of* the covenant); *against*, + געל *loathe* 1QS 3$_1$ 4QDᵃ 11$_7$, עַל־פִּי *in accordance with*, + הלך htp. *go about*, i.e. conduct life CD 7$_5$; כְּמִשְׁפַּט *according to the rule of*, i.e. in accordance with, + הלך htp. CD 7$_{8(A)}$ (כמשפט היסורים כסרך התורה *according to the precepts, according to the rule of the law* (=19$_{4[B]}$ היסודים *the founding principles*; or em. האסרים *the vows*, i.e. אִסָּר, and/or כדרך *according to the way of* the law).

<COLL> מַעֲלָה *step* 1QLitPr 3.2$_7$.

Also 4QDᵃ 6.1c$_1$ (יסורו erased).

<SYN> מַעֲלָה *step.*

⇒ יסר *discipline.*

יִסְכָּה 1 pr.n.f. **Iscah,** daughter of Haran and sister of Milcah Gn 11$_{29}$, <CSTR> אֲבִי יִסְכָּה *father of Iscah* Gn 11$_{29}$.
⇒ (?) סוך *anoint.*

יִסְמַכְיָהוּ 1 pr.n.m. **Ismachiah,** Levite, official under Hezekiah, <NOM CL> יִסְמַכְיָהוּ וּמַחַת וּבְנָיָהוּ פְּקִידִים *Ismachiah and Mahath and Benaiah were overseers* 2 C 31$_{13}$.
⇒ סמך *support* + יִ Y.

יסף 215.5.40 vb. **add—Qal** 34.0.3 Pf. יָסַף (יָסֵף), יָסְפָה, יָסַפְתָּ, יָסְפוּ (יָסֵפוּ); + waw וְיָסַף, וְיָסְפָה, וְיָסַפְתָּ, וְיָסַפְתִּי; impv. סְפוּ, Q ספי; ptc. יוֹסֵף, יֹסְפִים—**1. add, increase, regenerate** roots (2 K 19$_{30}$||Is 37$_{31}$).

<SUBJ> Y. Gn 30$_{24}$ Lv 26$_{21}$ 2 K 20$_{6}$||Is 38$_{5}$ (if em. hi. to qal in both) Is 26$_{15.15}$ (mss lack יסף) Jr 45$_{3}$, אֱלֹהִים *God* 2 K 20$_{6}$||Is 38$_{5}$ (if em. hi. in both), Ariel Is 29$_{1}$, Israel appar. Dt 19$_{9}$, Judah Jr 7$_{21}$, Solomon 1 C 19$_{6}$, אִישׁ *man* Lv 22$_{14}$, עָנָו *humble one* Is 29$_{19}$, קדשׁ hi. ptc. *one who consecrates* house Lv 27$_{15.19}$, עַם *people* 1 S 12$_{19}$, נִשְׁאָרָה *remnant* 2 K 19$_{30}$||Is 37$_{31}$, פְּלֵיטָה *remnant* 2 K 19$_{30}$||Is 37$_{31}$, קִרְיָה *city* 1QIsa^{a} 29$_{1}$; subj. not specified, Lv 27$_{13.27}$.

<OBJ> בֵּן *son* Gn 30$_{24}$, שִׂמְחָה *joy* Is 29$_{19}$, יָגוֹן *grief* Jr 45$_{3}$, מַכְאֹב *pain* Jr 45$_{3}$, מַכָּה *wound* Lv 26$_{21}$, חֲמִישִׁית *fifth part* Lv 22$_{14}$ 27$_{13.15.19.27}$, עֹלָה *burnt offering* Jr 7$_{21}$, שֹׁרֶשׁ *root* 2 K 19$_{30}$||Is 37$_{31}$, עִיר *city* Dt 19$_{9}$, שָׁנָה *year* 2 K 20$_{6}$||Is 38$_{5}$ (if em. hi. in both) Is 29$_{1}$.

<PREP> לְ of direction, *to,* + Rachel Gn 30$_{24}$, גּוֹי *nation* Is 26$_{15.15}$ (lacking in ms); לְמַטָּה *below* 2 K 19$_{30}$||Is 37$_{31}$; בְּ of cause, *on account of* Y. Is 29$_{19}$; כְּ *in accordance with,* + חַטָּאת *sin* Lv 26$_{21}$; עַל *(in addition) to,* + Israelites Lv 26$_{21}$, עֵרֶךְ *valuation* Lv 27$_{13.15.19.27}$, חַטָּאת *sin* 1 S 12$_{19}$, זֶבַח *sacrifice* Jr 7$_{21}$, קֹדֶשׁ *sacred thing* Lv 22$_{14}$, שְׁמוּעָה *report* 1 C 19$_{6}$, עִיר *town* Dt 19$_{9}$, יוֹם *day* 2 K 20$_{6}$||Is 38$_{5}$ (if em. hi.), שָׁנָה *year* Is 29$_{1}$.

2. as auxiliary verb expressing repetition, continuation, etc., **do again** (Gn 8$_{12}$ 38$_{26}$ Nm 32$_{15}$ Jg 13$_{21}$ 1 S 7$_{13}$ 4QCommGenA 1$_{19.20}$), **do more** (Dt 5$_{22}$ Is 29$_{14}$ [if em. hi. to qal]), **go on to do** (Lv 26$_{18}$), **continue to do** (Nm 11$_{25}$ Dt 5$_{25}$ 20$_{8}$=11QT 62$_{2}$ 1 S 27$_{4[Qr]}$ 2 S 2$_{28}$ 2 K 6$_{23}$).

<SUBJ> Y. Lv 26$_{18}$ Nm 32$_{15}$ Dt 5$_{22}$ Is 29$_{14}$ (if em. hi.; אֲדֹנָי), Israel Dt 5$_{25}$, Judah Gn 38$_{26}$, Midian Jg 8$_{28}$, Samuel 1 S 15$_{35}$, Saul 1 S 27$_{4(Qr)}$, זָקֵן *elder* Nm 11$_{25}$, שֹׁטֵר *officer* Dt 20$_{8}$=11QT 62$_{2}$ (Sam hi.), מַלְאָךְ *angel* Jg 13$_{21}$, עַם *people* 2 S 2$_{28}$, גְּדוּד *troop* 2 K 6$_{23}$, יוֹנָה *dove* Gn 8$_{12}$ 4QCommGenA 1$_{19}$ ([ה]יונה) 1$_{20}$ ([היונ]ה ... יספ[ה]).

<COLL> יסף with inf. cstr. (oft. introduced by לְ [e.g. Gn 38$_{26}$ Lv 26$_{18}$ Nm 32$_{15}$ Dt 5$_{25}$ Jg 8$_{28}$]) of ראה *see* 1 S 15$_{35}$, ni. *appear* Jg 13$_{21}$, שׁמע *hear* Dt 5$_{25}$, דבר pi. *speak* Dt 20$_{8}$ (Sam hi.)=11QT 62$_{2}$, appar. 5$_{22}$, ידע *know* Gn 38$_{26}$, פלא hi. *amaze* Is 29$_{14}$ (if em. hi.), בקשׁ pi. *seek* 1 S 27$_{4(Qr)}$, בוא *come* 1 S 7$_{13}$ 2 K 6$_{23}$, נוח hi. *leave* Nm 32$_{15}$, שׁוב *go back* Gn 8$_{12}$ 4QCommGenA 1$_{19.20}$, נשׂא *raise* head Jg 8$_{28}$, לחם ni. *fight* 2 S 2$_{28}$, יסר pi. *discipline* Lv 26$_{18}$.

יסף + עוֹד *again, more* Gn 8$_{12}$ 38$_{26}$ Nm 32$_{15}$ Dt 5$_{25}$ Jg 13$_{21}$ 1 S 7$_{13}$ 27$_{4(Qr)}$ 2 S 2$_{28}$ 2 K 6$_{23}$ 4QCommGenA 1$_{19.20}$, שֶׁבַע *seven times, sevenfold* Lv 26$_{18.21}$ (וְיָסַפְתִּי עֲלֵיכֶם מַכָּה שֶׁבַע *and I will add a wound to you seven times,* as §1).

וַיִּתְנַבְּאוּ וְלֹא יָסָפוּ *and they prophesied but did not continue* Nm 11$_{25}$ (Sam אסף ni. *be gathered;* or em. סוף *cease*).

Ni. 6.1.7 Pf. נוֹסַף; + waw וְנוֹסַף, וְנוֹסְפָה; ptc. נוֹסָף, נוֹסָפוֹת; inf. Q הוסיף (Q לוסף, Q ליוסף)—**1. be added,** <SUBJ> חַי *living one* 4QD^{a} 6.1$_{4.10}$ (both מן החי *some of the living*) 6.1$_{11}$ ([מן הח]יות), דָּבָר *word* Jr 36$_{32}$, נַחֲלָה *inheritance* Nm 36$_{3.4}$, יוֹם *day* 4QMMT A$_{20}$ ([יום ... נו]סף), שָׁנָה *year* Pr 9$_{11}$ (if em. hi. *add* to ni. *be added*); subj. not specified Pr 11$_{24}$ perh. Si 43$_{27}$. <PREP> בְּ of time, *on,* יוֹם *day* 4QD^{a} 6.1$_{10}$; of instrument, *by (means of),* + חָכְמָה *wisdom* Pr 9$_{11}$ (if em. hi.); אֶל *to,* + מֵת *dead one* 4QD^{a} 6.1$_{4}$ ([אל] המת) 6.1$_{10}$; עַל *to,* + מֵת *dead one* 4QD^{a} 6.1$_{11}$, דָּבָר *word* Jr 36$_{32}$, נַחֲלָה *inheritance* Nm 36$_{3.4}$. <COLL> יסף ni. + גרע ni. *be diminished* Nm 36$_{3.4}$; יסף ni. + עוֹד *again* Jr 36$_{32}$ Pr 11$_{24}$ perh. Si 43$_{27}$.

2. join (oneself to), <SUBJ> עַם *people* Ex 1$_{10}$, מִתְנַדֵּב *volunteer* 1QS 6$_{14}$ 1QpMic 10$_{7}$, כֹּל *everyone* 1QS 8$_{19}$ CD 13$_{11}$. <PREP> לְ of direction, *to,* + יַחַד *community* 1QS 8$_{19}$, עֵדָה *congregation* CD 13$_{11}$; עַל *to,* + שׂנא ptc. *one who hates* Ex 1$_{10}$, בָּחִיר *elect* 1QpMic 10$_{7}$, עֵצָה *council* 1QS 6$_{14}$. <COLL> יסף ni. + finite verb, עלה *go up* Ex 1$_{10}$, לחם ni. *wage war* Ex 1$_{10}$.

3. ptc. as noun, **something additional,** of a punishment, <SUBJ> שִׁית *place* Is 15$_{9}$.

Hi. 174.4.30 Pf. הֹסִיף, הוֹסַפְתִּי; impf. יוֹסִיף (יֹסִיף, יֹסֵף, יוֹסֵף, יוֹסֶף, יוֹסִף), 3fs תּוֹסִיף (תֹּסִף, תֹּסִיף, תּוֹסִף, תֹּסֵף), 2ms תּוֹסִיף (תֹּסִיף, תּוֹסִף, תֹּסֵף, תֹּסֶף, תּוֹסֶף, תּוֹסְף, תּוֹסַף), תּוֹסִפִי (תּוֹסִפִי), אוֹסִיף (אֹסִיף, אֹסִף, אֹסֵף, אוֹסֵף, אֹסִפָה), יוֹסִיפוּ (יוֹסִפוּ, יֹסִפוּ, יֹסִיפוּ, יוֹסִפוּן), תֹּסִפוּן (תּוֹסִיפוּ, תֹּסִפוּ, תֹּאסִפוּן, Sam תוסיפון), perh. Si נוסף (unless ni.); + waw וְהוֹסַפְתִּי (וְהֹסַפְתִּי), Q והוסיפו; וַיֹּסֶף (וַיּוֹסֶף, וַיֹּאסֶף), וַתּוֹסֶף (וַתֹּסֶף), וַיֹּסִפוּ (וַיֹּסִיפוּ, וַיּוֹסִפוּ, וַיּוֹסִיפוּ); ptc. Si מוֹסִיף, מוֹסִפִים; inf. הוֹסִיף (Q לוסיף)—**1. add, increase, gain** (e.g. Pr 1$_{5}$ 9$_{9}$ 16$_{24}$ 19$_{4}$ Ec 1$_{16}$), **multiply** (e.g. Is 1$_{5}$ Pr 23$_{28}$), **restore** (Jb 42$_{10}$), **surpass** (1 K 10$_{7}$), **use** hand **again** (Is 11$_{11}$), **give further cause for** (Ne 13$_{18}$).

<SUBJ> Y. Nm 22$_{19}$ Dt 1$_{11}$ 2 S 12$_{8}$ 24$_{3}$||1 C 21$_{3}$ 2 K 20$_{6}$||Is 38$_{5}$ (or em. qal in both) Is 11$_{11}$ Ezk 5$_{16}$ Ps 115$_{14}$ Jb 42$_{10}$, אֲדֹנָי *Lord* Ezk 5$_{16}$, אֱלֹהִים *God* Dt 1$_{11}$ 2 S 12$_{8}$ 24$_{3}$ 2 K 20$_{6}$||Is 38$_{5}$ (or em. qal in both) Ps 61$_{7}$ 71$_{14}$, David 1 C 17$_{18}$, Israel Dt 4$_{2}$ 13$_{1}$=11QT 54$_{6}$ Is 1$_{5}$ Job Jb 34$_{37}$ appar. 2 C 28$_{13}$, Kittim 1QpHab 6$_{1}$, Koheleth Ec 1$_{16}$, Oholibah Ezk 23$_{14}$, Rehoboam 1 K 12$_{11.14}$||1 C 10$_{11.14}$, Solomon 1 K 10$_{7}$ 1 C 22$_{14}$.

אִישׁ *man* Lv 27$_{31}$ Nm 5$_{7}$ 4QCryptA 3.2$_{5}$ (ה]וסיפו]) 3.2$_{6.8}$ (הו]סיפו]); or em. preceding אהבו *love*, with אִישׁ as subj., to אהבי *those who love* loyalty, as new subj. in 3.2$_{6.8}$) 4Q416 2.3$_{6}$, אִשָּׁה *woman* Nm 5$_{7}$, אָחוֹת *sister* Ezk 23$_{14}$, בֵּן *son* Si 5$_{5}$, חָכָם *wise man* Pr 1$_{5}$, חר *noble* Ne 13$_{18}$, נָכְרִיָּה *foreign woman* Pr 23$_{28}$, זוֹנָה *prostitute* Pr 23$_{28}$ (or em. זָרָה *strange woman*), כֹּהֵן *priest* 1QpHab 8$_{12}$, נֶפֶשׁ *person* Lv 5$_{16.24}$, טְהוֹר *one who is pure* of hands Jb 17$_{9}$, שמר ni. ptc. *one who is cautious* Si 37$_{31(B, D)}$, אהב ptc. *one who loves* 4QCryptA 3.2$_{6.8}$ (if em.), צַדִּיק *righteous one* Pr 9$_{9}$, יָשָׁר *upright one* 4QBark^{c} 1.1$_{2}$, פֶּתִי *simple one* 1QH 1$_{35}$ ([פתיים]), ידע ptc. *one who knows* 4QCryptA 3.2$_{6}$ ([יו]דעי]), חול htpol. ptc. appar. *wicked one* Si 3$_{27}$ (or em. הול htpol. ptc. *madman*), recipient of wisdom Pr 30$_{6}$, עַם *people* Ezr 10$_{10}$, רֵעַ *neighbour* perh. 1QH 5$_{33}$ (ויוספיה; =4QHod^{c} 1.4$_{6}$ ויוספוהו; unless from אסף *gather*), רַבִּים *many* Si 37$_{31(Bmg)}$.

לֵב *mind* Pr 16$_{23}$, מֶתֶק *sweetness* of lips Pr 16$_{21}$ (or em. מֶתֶק *sweetness* to מֶתֶג *bridle*, i.e. control of lips), כּוֹס *cup* of God's wrath 1QpHab 11$_{15}$, יִרְאָה *fear* Pr 10$_{27}$, מִצְוָה *commandment* Pr 3$_{2}$, תּוֹרָה *teaching* perh. Pr 3$_{2}$, עֶצֶב *toil* Pr 10$_{22}$, תְּבוּאָה *produce* Lv 19$_{25}$, הוֹן *wealth* Pr 19$_{4}$, שָׁנָה *year* Pr 9$_{11}$ (or em. hi. to ni. *be added*); subj. not specified, Ps 120$_{3}$ Ec 1$_{18.18}$ 3$_{14}$ perh. Si 43$_{27}$ 4Q416 2.4$_{7}$ 4Q418 81$_{17}$.

<OBJ> רֵעַ *friend* Pr 19$_{4}$, בֹּגֵד *traitor* Pr 23$_{28}$, חֲמִישִׁית *fifth part* Lv 5$_{16.24.31}$ Nm 5$_{7}$, חַיִּים *life* Si 37$_{31}$, שָׁלוֹם *peace* Pr 3$_{2}$, חָכְמָה *wisdom* Ec 1$_{16}$ perh. 4Q418 137$_{2}$ ([חכ]מת]), עָרְמָה *prudence* 1QH 1$_{35}$, דַּעַת *knowledge* Ec 1$_{18}$ 4QCryptA 3.2$_{8}$ (הו]סיפו ד]עת]), מִצְוָה *commandment* Dt 13$_{1}$, לֶקַח *learning* Pr 1$_{5}$ 9$_{9}$ 16$_{21.23}$ 4QCryptA 3.2$_{5}$ (ה]וסיפו לק[ח]) 4Q418 81$_{17}$ perh. 221$_{3}$ (]סיף[ ]) 4QBark^{c} 1.1$_{2}$, נֶדֶר *vow* 4Q416 2.4$_{7}$, נְדָבָה *freewill offering* 4Q416 2.4$_{7}$ ([נדבנ[ה]), עֲנָוָה *humility* 4QCryptA 3.2$_{7}$, פֶּשַׁע *rebellion* Jb 34$_{37}$, סָרָה *apostasy* Is 1$_{5}$, עָוֹן *iniquity* Si 3$_{27}$ 5$_{5}$ 1QpHab 8$_{12}$, אֹמֶץ *might* Jb 17$_{9}$ 4QCryptA 3.2$_{6}$, חָרוֹן *anger* Ne 13$_{18}$, מַכְאוֹב *pain* Ec 1$_{18}$, צוּקָה *distress* perh. 1QH 5$_{33}$ (ויוספיה; =4QHod^{c} 1.4$_{6}$ ויוספוהו; unless from אסף *gather*), רָעָב *famine* Ezk 5$_{16}$, הוֹן *wealth* 1QpHab 6$_{1}$, תְּבוּאָה *produce* 4QD^{a} 6.4$_{8}$ ([להו]סיף לו ת[בואתו]), אֹרֶךְ *length* Pr 3$_{2}$, מִדָּה *measurement* or *tribute* 4QWays^{a} 2$_{3}$ ([להו]סיף]), יוֹם *day* Ps 61$_{7}$ Pr 10$_{27}$, שָׁנָה *year* 2 K 20$_{6}$||Is 38$_{5}$ (or em. qal in both) Pr 3$_{2}$, יָד *hand* Is 11$_{11}$ (or em.; see Coll.), כֹּל *everything* Jb 42$_{10}$, מָה *what?* Nm 22$_{19}$ 1 C 17$_{18}$.

<PREP> לְ of direction, *to* 4QD^{a} 6.4$_{8}$ ([להו]סיף]) 4Q418 137$_{2}$ perh. 4QPrQuot 15.5$_{10}$, + David 2 S 12$_{8}$, בֵּן *son* Pr 3$_{2}$, recipient of wisdom Pr 9$_{11}$, בין hi. ptc. *one who understands* perh. 4Q418 221$_{3}$ (]סיף[ ]), of benefit, *for*, + Israel(ites) Lv 19$_{25}$, לָשׁוֹן *tongue* Ps 120$_{3}$; *concerning*, + כָּבוֹד *honour* 1 C 17$_{18}$ (or em. לְכָבוֹד *concerning honour* to your servant to לְכַבֵּד *to honour* your servant); לְמִשְׁנֶה *increase twofold* Jb 42$_{10}$; introducing object, + צוּקָה *distress* perh. 1QH 5$_{33}$.

בְּ of instrument, *by (means of)*, + חָכְמָה *wisdom* Pr 9$_{11}$ (or em. ni. *be added*).

כְּ *as (though it were)*, + דָּג *fish* 1QpHab 6$_{1}$.

מִן of comparison, *(more) than*, + כֹּל *everyone* Ec 2$_{9}$.

אֶל *to*, + Y. 1 C 17$_{18}$, עַם *people* 2 S 24$_{3}$ (mss אֶת־הָעָם *the people*), שְׁמוּעָה *report* 1 K 10$_{7}$ (mss עַל *to, upon*), תַּזְנוּת *fornication* Ezk 23$_{14}$, כֹּל *everything* Ec 3$_{14}$.

עַל *to*, + Israel Dt 1$_{11}$ Ezk 5$_{16}$ Ne 13$_{18}$ Ps 115$_{14}$, בֵּן *son* Ps 115$_{14}$, עַם *people* 1 C 21$_{3}$, כֹּהֵן *priest* 1QpHab 8$_{12}$, כֹּל *everyone* Ec 1$_{16}$, שָׂפָה *lip* Pr 16$_{23}$, דָּבָר *word, matter* Dt 4$_{2}$ 13$_{1}$=11QT 54$_{6}$ Pr 30$_{6}$, תְּהִלָּה *praise* Ps 71$_{14}$, עֹל *yoke* 1 K

12$_{11.14}$||1 C 10$_{11.14}$, אַשְׁמָה *guilt* Ezr 10$_{10}$ 2 C 28$_{13}$, חַטָּאת *sin* Jb 34$_{37}$ 2 C 28$_{13}$, עָוֹן *iniquity* Si 3$_{27}$ 5$_{5}$, קָלוֹן *dishonour* 1QpHab 11$_{15}$ ([ע]ל [כול ק]ל[ו]נו), רוֹשׁ *poverty* 4Q416 2.3$_{6}$, רֹאשׁ *head, principal part* Nm 5$_{7}$, מַעֲשֵׂר *tithe* Lv 27$_{31}$, אֶבֶן *stone* 1 C 22$_{14}$, עֵץ *wood* 1 C 22$_{14}$, נַחֲלָה *inheritance* 4Q418 162$_{3}$ ([או]סיף), יוֹם *day* 2 K 20$_{6}$||Is 38$_{5}$ (unless em. both hi. to qal) Ps 61$_{7}$, אֲשֶׁר *that which* Lv 5$_{16.24}$.

עִם *to*, + בְּרָכָה *blessing* Pr 10$_{22}$ (or em. עַל *to*), שָׁלָל *spoil* 1QpHab 6$_{1}$.

<COLL> יסף hi. with inf. cstr. of חלל pi. *profane* Ne 13$_{18}$, בין htpol. *understand* 4QBark^{c} 1.1$_{2}$; with noun used adverbially, חָכְמָה *wisdom* 1 K 10$_{7}$, טוֹב *prosperity* 1 K 10$_{7}$; כָּהֵנָּה וְכָהֵנָּה *according to those things and according to those things*, i.e. twice as much more 2 S 12$_{8}$, כָּהֵם וְכָהֵם *according to those (people) and according to those (people)* a hundred times 2 S 24$_{3}$, י׳ ... יֹסֵף עֲלֵיכֶם כָּכֶם אֶלֶף פְּעָמִים *may Y. ... add to you as (many) as you are a thousand times* Dt 1$_{11}$, sim. 2 S 24$_{3}$||1 C 21$_{3}$; יסף + עוֹד *again* 1 C 17$_{18}$ Si 43$_{27}$; יוֹסִיף י׳ שֵׁנִית *Y. will (again) use* his hand *a second time* Is 11$_{11}$ (or em. שַׁנּוֹת will again *raise* his hand, as §2).

יסף hi. || נתן *give* Ps 120$_{3}$ (or em. נתן pu. *be given*; ms יסף ho. *be added*), גדל hi. *increase* Ec 1$_{16}$ (or em. qal *become great*); + גדל *become great* Ec 1$_{16}$ (if em. hi.) 2$_{9}$, שׁלם pi. *restore* Lv 5$_{24}$, גאל *redeem* Lv 27$_{31}$, ברך ptc. pass. *be blessed* Ps 115$_{14}$; :: גרע *diminish* Dt 4$_{2}$ 13$_{1}$=11QT 54$_{6}$ Ec 3$_{14}$, קצר *be short* Pr 10$_{27}$.

<SYN> נתן *give*, גדל hi. *increase*. **<ANT>** גרע *diminish*, קצר *be short*.

2. do again (e.g. Gn 4$_{2}$ Ex 8$_{25}$ Nm 22$_{15}$ Dt 3$_{26}$ Jg 2$_{21}$), **continue to do** (e.g. Gn 4$_{12}$ Ex 5$_{7}$ Dt 18$_{16}$ Jos 7$_{12}$ 1 S 3$_{21}$ 1QS 2$_{11}$ 4QBer^{a} 7.1$_{8}$), **do more** (e.g. Gn 37$_{5}$ Dt 25$_{3}$ 1 S 3$_{17}$ 2 S 3$_{9}$ 11QPs^{a} 24$_{15}$), **cause to do again** (Gn 44$_{23}$), **happen again** (in the future) (Ex 11$_{6}$ Jl 2$_{2}$ [both :: היה ni. *happen* in the past]).

<SUBJ> Y. Gn 8$_{21.21}$ Jos 7$_{12}$ 23$_{13}$ Jg 2$_{21}$ 10$_{13}$ 1 S 3$_{6.8.21}$ 11$_{11}$ (אֲדֹנָי) 14$_{44}$ 20$_{13}$ 29$_{14}$ (אֲדֹנָי) 2 K 21$_{8}$||2 C 33$_{8}$ Is 7$_{10}$ (or em. Y. to Isaiah) 8$_{5}$ Ho 1$_{6}$ 9$_{15}$ Am 7$_{8}$ 8$_{2}$ Ps 77$_{8}$ (אֲדֹנָי) Ru 1$_{17}$ Lm 4$_{22}$, אֱלֹהִים *God* Jos 23$_{13}$ 1 S 3$_{17}$ 25$_{22}$ 2 S 3$_{9.35}$ 19$_{14}$ 1 K 2$_{23}$ 2 K 6$_{31}$, *gods* 1 K 19$_{2}$ 20$_{10}$.

Aaron Ex 9$_{28}$, Abner 2 S 2$_{22}$, Abraham Gn 18$_{29}$ 25$_{1}$, Ahab 1 K 16$_{33}$, Ahaz 2 C 28$_{22}$, Ahimaaz 2 S 18$_{22}$, Amos Am 7$_{13}$, Balaam Nm 22$_{25}$, Balak Nm 22$_{15}$, David 1 S 23$_{4}$ 2 S 7$_{20}$, Edom Ezk 36$_{12}$, Elihu Jb 36$_{1}$, Ephraim Ho 13$_{2}$, Esther Est 8$_{3}$, Eve Gn 4$_{2}$, Gaal Jg 9$_{37}$ (or em. Gaal to Goal), Isaiah Is 7$_{10}$ (if em. Y. to Isaiah), Israel(ites) Dt 13$_{12}$ Jg 3$_{12}$ 4$_{1}$ 10$_{6}$ 13$_{1}$ 20$_{23.28}$ Jr 31$_{12}$, appar. Dt 17$_{16}$ =11QT 56$_{18}$ Dt 18$_{16}$ 28$_{68}$ Ho 13$_{2}$ Ps 78$_{17}$, Jacob perh. Jr 31$_{12}$, Jephthah Jg 11$_{14}$, Job Jb 27$_{1}$ 29$_{1}$ 40$_{5.32}$, Jonah Jon 2$_{5}$, Jonathan 1 S 20$_{17}$, Moses Ex 9$_{28}$ 10$_{28.29}$ Dt 3$_{26}$, Noah Gn 8$_{10}$ 4QCommGenA 1$_{16}$, Pharaoh Ex 8$_{25}$ 9$_{34}$, Philistines 2 S 5$_{22}$ 1 C 14$_{13}$, Saul 1 S 18$_{29}$ 19$_{21}$ 27$_{4(Kt)}$ (Qr qal), Shua Gn 38$_{6}$.

אִישׁ *man* Jg 20$_{22}$, אֱנוֹשׁ *person* Ps 10$_{18}$, אִשָּׁה *wife* Gn 4$_{2}$, בֵּן *son* 2 S 7$_{10}$ 18$_{22}$ 1 C 14$_{9}$, אָח *brother* Gn 37$_{5}$ (or del. יסף hi.), נַעַר *lad* 1 S 9$_{8}$, בְּתוּלָה *young woman* Is 23$_{12}$ Am 5$_{2}$, עֶבֶד *servant* Gn 44$_{23}$ Ex 9$_{34}$, מֶלֶךְ *king* 2 K 24$_{7}$, קָצִין *ruler* Is 1$_{13}$, שֹׁטֵר *officer* Dt 20$_{8(Sam)}$ (MT qal), שֹׁפֵט *judge* Dt 25$_{3.3}$, כֹּהֵן *priest* Lm 4$_{15}$ 1QS 2$_{11}$, לֵוִי *Levite* 1QS 2$_{11}$, נָבִיא *prophet* Lm 4$_{15}$, מַלְאָךְ *angel* Nm 22$_{26}$, דבר pi. ptc. *one who speaks* 2 S 14$_{10}$, עָרֵל *uncircumcised one* Is 52$_{1}$, טָמֵא *impure one* Is 52$_{1}$, מְעֻשָּׁקָה *one who is crushed* Is 23$_{12}$, דרשׁ ptc. *one who seeks* 4QpNah 3.3$_{7}$, כְּמַרְאֵה אָדָם *(one who is) like (the appearance of) a human* Dn 10$_{18}$, בְּלִיַּעַל *worthlessness* Na 2$_{1}$ (or em. בָּךְ *against you* to בֶּן *son of* worthlessness).

עַם *people* Ex 14$_{13}$ Jg 20$_{22}$ (or del. עָם) 2 S 3$_{34}$ (Q del. עָם) Is 1$_{13}$ 51$_{22}$, שְׁאָר *remnant* Is 10$_{20}$, נִשְׁאָר *remaining (Israelite)* Dt 19$_{20}$=11QT 61$_{11}$, פְּלֵיטָה *remnant* Is 10$_{20}$, עַיִן *eye* Jb 20$_{9}$, פָּנִים *face* of Y. Lm 4$_{16}$, אֲדָמָה *earth* Gn 4$_{12}$, אֶרֶץ *earth* Is 24$_{20}$, הַר *mountain* of Israel Ezk 36$_{12}$, יָם *sea* Jb 38$_{11}$, צְעָקָה *cry* Ex 11$_{6}$, אַף *anger* 2 S 24$_{1}$, נֶגַע *plague* 11QPs^{a} 24$_{12}$, אֹמֶץ *might* 11QPs^{a} 24$_{15}$ (מה אוסיף אומ[צם] *what more can their might do?*), מִלְחָמָה *war* 1 S 19$_{8}$, יוֹם *day* appar. Jl 2$_{2}$; subj. not specified, Is 47$_{1.5}$ Ps 41$_{9}$ Jb 34$_{32}$ Pr 19$_{19}$ 23$_{35}$ 4Q417 1.1$_{18.20}$.

<PREP> לְ of direction, *to*, + Abner 2 S 3$_{9}$; בְּ of place/time, *in, at*, + יוֹם *day* Is 10$_{20}$ 11$_{11}$, עֵת *time* 2 C 28$_{22}$, רִאשֹׁנָה *beginning* 2 S 7$_{10}$ 1 C 17$_{9}$; עַד *until*, + שָׁנָה *year* Jl 2$_{2}$, עוֹלָם *eternity* Ex 14$_{13}$; אַחֲרֵי *after*, + יוֹם *day* of Y. Jl 2$_{2}$.

<COLL> יסף hi. + עוֹד *(yet) again* Gn 8$_{12.21.21}$ 18$_{29}$ 37$_{5}$ (or del. יסף hi.) 37$_{8}$ Ex 10$_{29}$ 14$_{13}$ Nm 22$_{15}$ Dt 3$_{26}$ 13$_{12}$ (Sam, mss) 17$_{16}$=11QT 56$_{18}$ Dt 19$_{20}$ =11QT 61$_{11}$ Dt 28$_{68}$ Jg 9$_{37}$ 1 S 3$_{6}$ 18$_{29}$ 23$_{4}$ 27$_{4(Kt)}$ (Qr qal) 2 S 5$_{22}$ 7$_{20}$ 14$_{10}$ 18$_{22}$ Is

8$_{5}$ 10$_{20}$ 23$_{12}$ 51$_{22}$ 52$_{1}$ Jr 31$_{12}$ Ezk 36$_{12}$ Ho 1$_{6}$ Am 7$_{8.13}$ 8$_{2}$ Na 2$_{1}$ Zp 3$_{11}$ Ps 10$_{18}$ 77$_{8}$ 78$_{17}$ Pr 19$_{19}$ 23$_{35}$ 4QpNah 3.3$_{7}$ 4Q417 1.1$_{18}$ ([עו]ד) 1.1$_{20}$ perh. 4Q418 199$_{2}$; וַיֹּסֶף י׳ ... בַּשְּׁלִישִׁית *and Y.* called *again a third time* 1 S 3$_{8}$, אִם־תַּצִּיל עוֹד תּוֹסִף *if you rescue* an angry person *once, you must do it again* Pr 19$_{19}$; כֹּה יַעֲשֶׂה ... וְכֹה יוֹסִיף *thus may* God *do ... and thus may he do again* 1 S 3$_{17}$, sim. 1 S 14$_{44}$ 20$_{13}$ 25$_{22}$ 2 S 3$_{9.35}$ 19$_{14}$ 1 K 2$_{23}$ 19$_{2}$ 20$_{10}$ 2 K 6$_{31}$ Ru 1$_{17}$.

יסף hi. + inf. cstr. of היה *be* Jos 7$_{12}$ 1 S 19$_{8}$, בוא hi. *bring* Is 1$_{13}$ (unless יסף hi. + רמס *trample*), עבר *pass* Nm 22$_{26}$ Na 2$_{1}$, נגשׁ *approach* Jg 20$_{23}$, עלה *go up* 2 S 5$_{22}$, קום *arise* Is 24$_{20}$ Am 5$_{2}$ Ps 41$_{9}$, עמד *stand* Ex 9$_{28}$, יצא *go out* Jg 20$_{28}$ 2 K 24$_{7}$, שׁוב *go back* Dt 17$_{16}$=11QT 56$_{18}$ 11QPs^{a} 24$_{12}$, שׁלח *send* Nm 22$_{15}$, pi. *send away* Gn 8$_{10}$ 4QComm GenA 1$_{16}$, סור hi. *remove* 2 C 33$_{8}$, תעה hi. *lead astray* 4QpNah 3.3$_{7}$, נוד hi. *cause to wander* 2 K 21$_{8}$, גלה hi. *(take into) exile* Lm 4$_{22}$, שׁען ni. *lean* Is 10$_{20}$, נשׂא *raise* Jb 27$_{1}$ 29$_{1}$, שׁנה pi. *raise* Is 11$_{11}$ (if em. שֵׁנִית *a second time*), נתן *give* Gn 4$_{12}$ Ex 5$_{7}$, קנה *acquire* Is 11$_{11}$.

ראה *see* Gn 44$_{23}$ Ex 10$_{28.29}$ 14$_{13}$ Dt 28$_{68}$, ni. *appear* 1 S 3$_{21}$, נבט hi. *look* Jon 2$_{5}$ Lm 4$_{16}$, שׁמע *hear* Dt 18$_{16}$, אמר *say* 2 S 2$_{22}$, דבר pi. *speak* Gn 18$_{29}$ Nm 22$_{19}$ (§1) Dt 3$_{26}$ 20$_{8}$ (Sam) (MT qal) Jg 9$_{37}$ 2 S 7$_{20}$ Is 7$_{10}$ 8$_{5}$, קרא *call* 1 S 3$_{6.8}$, שׁאל *ask* 1 S 23$_{4}$, ענה *answer* 1 S 9$_{8}$, שׁבע hi. *adjure* 1 S 20$_{17}$, זכר *remember* Jb 40$_{32}$, ברך pi. *bless* 4QBer^{a} 7.1$_{8}$, נבא ni. *prophesy* Am 7$_{13}$, עלז *exult* Is 23$_{12}$, גבה *be proud* Zp 3$_{11}$, רצה *desire* Ps 77$_{8}$, בקשׁ pi. *seek* 1 S 27$_{4(Kt)}$ (Qr qal), פלא hi. *amaze* Is 29$_{14}$ (or em. qal), ירא *fear* 1 S 18$_{29}$, בכה *weep* 2 S 3$_{34}$.

שׁתה *drink* Is 51$_{22}$, גור *sojourn* Lm 4$_{15}$, עשׂה *do* Dt 13$_{12}$ 19$_{20}$=11QT 61$_{11}$ Jg 3$_{12}$ 4$_{1}$ 10$_{6}$ 13$_{1}$ 1 K 16$_{33}$, פעל *do* Jb 34$_{32}$, ילד *give birth* Gn 4$_{2}$, שׁכל pi. *make childless* Ezk 36$_{12}$, חטא *sin* Ex 9$_{34}$ Ho 13$_{2}$ Ps 78$_{17}$, שׂנא *hate* Gn 37$_{5}$ (unless del. יסף hi.) 37$_{8}$, תלל hi. *deceive* Ex 8$_{25}$, מעל *sin* 2 C 28$_{22}$, קלל pi. *curse* Gn 8$_{21}$, ערך *array* battle line Jg 20$_{22}$, ענה pi. *afflict* 2 S 7$_{10}$, בלה pi. *wear out*, i.e. trouble 1 C 17$_{9}$, ערץ *cause to tremble* Ps 10$_{18}$, נגע *touch* 2 S 14$_{10}$, נכה hi. *strike* Nm 22$_{25}$ Dt 25$_{3}$, *destroy* Gn 8$_{21}$, חרה *burn* 2 S 24$_{1}$, רמס *trample* Is 1$_{13}$ (unless יסף hi. + בוא hi. *bring*), ירשׁ hi. *dispossess* Jos 23$_{13}$ Jg 2$_{21}$, דאב *languish* Jr 31$_{12}$, ישׁע hi. *rescue* Jg 10$_{13}$.

יסף hi. + finite verb, אהב *love* Ho 9$_{15}$, ראה *see* Dt 18$_{16}$, שׁזף *glimpse* Jb 20$_{9}$, אמר *say* 2 S 18$_{22}$ Jb 36$_{1}$ 1QS 2$_{11}$, דבר pi. *speak* Jb 40$_{5}$ Est 8$_{3}$, קרא *call* Is 47$_{1.5}$, בוא *come* Is 52$_{1}$ Jb 38$_{11}$, עבר *pass*, i.e. pardon Am 7$_{8}$ 8$_{2}$, שׁלח *send* Jg 11$_{14}$ 1 S 19$_{21}$, בקשׁ pi. *seek* Pr 23$_{35}$, עמד *stand* Nm 22$_{26}$, נטשׁ ni. *spread out* 2 S 5$_{22}$, נגע *touch* Dn 10$_{18}$, לקח *take* wife Gn 25$_{1}$, ילד *give birth* Gn 38$_{5}$, רחם pi. *pity* Ho 1$_{6}$, כבד hi. *harden* Ex 9$_{34}$, נכה hi. *strike* Dt 25$_{3}$, פשׁט *raid* 1 C 14$_{13}$, שׁמד hi. *exterminate* Jos 7$_{12}$.

Also 4QMyst^{a} 6.2$_{18}$ 30$_{5}$ 4Q416 2.2$_{10}$ 4QNarrA 14$_{5}$ 4QRitMar 3$_{1}$ (כהוסיפ[כם]) 4QBéat 2$_{3}$.

<SYN> היה ni. *happen*.

Ho. 1.0.2 Impf. ms יוּסַף (Q [erased] יושף)—**be added,** וּמַה־יּוֹסִיף לָךְ *and what will be added to you?* Ps 120$_{3(ms)}$ (L מַה־יֹּסִיף *what will he add?*), אם יוסף מן החי ... ואם לו [ליוסף מן החי]יות *if there must be added from the living (hair) ... or if is not to be added from the living (hairs)* 4QD^{a} 6.1$_{10}$ (ליוסף appar. error for inf. לְהוּסַף or impf. יוּסַף).*

⇒ יוֹסֵף *Joseph*, יוֹסֵי *Jose*, יָסָף *Jasoph*, יוֹסִפְיָה *Josiphiah*, אֶבְיָסָף *Ebiasaph*, אֶלְיָסָף *Eliasaph*.

[יָסָף] 0.0.0.1 pr.n.m. **Jasoph,** Seal 632 (T. Beit Mirsim?, 7th/6th cent.), <CSTR> בן יסף *son of Jasoph* Seal 632 (T. Beit Mirsim?, 7th/6th cent.).

⇒ יסף *add*.

יסר I 44.4.19 vb. **discipline—Qal** 5 Impf. יְסַּרְנִי, אֶסֳּרֵם; ptc. יֹסֵר; inf. יָסֹר—**discipline, warn, instruct, train,** <SUBJ> Y. Is 8$_{11}$ (or em. pi.; 1QIsa^{a} סור hi. *cause to depart*) Ho 10$_{10}$ (or em. pi.) Ps 94$_{10}$ (+ יכח hi. *reprove*, למד pi. *instruct*), Chenaniah 1 C 15$_{22}$ (see Prep.; or em. Conaniah; mss Benaiah); subj. not specified Pr 9$_{7}$ (+ יכח hi.). <OBJ> Isaiah Is 8$_{11}$, Israel Ho 10$_{10}$, לֵץ *scoffer* Pr 9$_{7}$, גּוֹי *nation* Ps 94$_{10}$. <PREP> בְּ *in, concerning*, + מַשָּׂא perh. *music* or *transport* 1 C 15$_{22}$ (יָסֹר בַּמַּשָּׂא *he gave instruction in music/transport*, i.e. inf. abs., unless יָסֹר is noun, an *instructor* in music/transport; or em. יָשַׂר *he ruled*, from שׂרר); מִן *(away) from, so as not to*, + הלך inf. *walk(ing)* Is 8$_{11}$.

Ni. 5.1.1 Impf. יִוָּסֵר, 2ms Si תוסר, אִוָּסֵר, תִּוָּסְרוּ, Q נוסרה; + waw וְנִוַּסְּרוּ; impv. הִוָּסְרוּ—**accept discipline** (Jr 6$_{8}$ Ps 2$_{10}$ [|| שׂכל hi. *be prudent*]), **be disciplined** (Lv 26$_{23}$ Jr 31$_{18}$ Pr 29$_{19}$ [+ בין *understand* Pr 29$_{19}$], perh. 4QHod^{a} 3.1$_{4}$), **become wise** (Si 6$_{33}$ [|| ערם hi. *become pru* *dent,* חכם htp. *become wise*]), <SUBJ> Ephraim Jr $31_{18.19}$ (or em. הֻוְדְעִי perh. *my being made to know* to הִוָּסְרִי *my being disciplined*), Israel(ites) Lv 26_{23}, Jerusalem Jr 6_{8}, אִשָּׁה *woman* Ezk 23_{48} (if em. ntp.), בֵּן *son* Si 6_{33}, שֹׁפֵט *judge* Ps 2_{10} (or em. הִוָּסְרוּ *be disciplined* to הִוָּסְדוּ *be established*), עֶבֶד *servant* Pr 29_{19}, appar. נדר ptc. *one who vows* 4QD^{a} 8.2$_{5}$, worshipper(s) 4QHod^{a} 3.1$_{4}$. <PREP> לְ of benefit, *for*, + Y. Lv 26_{23}; of agent, *by*, + Y. appar. 4Q Hod^{a} 3.1$_{4}$; בְּ of instrument, *by (means of)*, + דָּבָר *word* Pr 29_{19}, אֵלֶּה *these (things)* Lv 26_{23}. <SYN> שׂכל hi. *be prudent.*

Pi. $_{32.3.8}$ Pf. יִסַּר (יִסְּרוּנִי ,יִסְּרַנִי), mss יסרני ,יסרו (יִסְּרוֹ), יִסְּרָתּוּ, יִסַּרְתָּ (Q יסר]תה) ,(יִסַּרְתִּי ,יִסַּרְתַּנִי ,יִסַּרְתִּיךָ) ,יִסְּרוּ; impf. יְיַסֵּר ,תְּיַסְּרֵנִי ,תְּיַסְּרֶךָּ ,תְּיַסְּרֵנוּ ,אֲיַסֵּר; impv. יַסֵּר (Si יסיר, יַסְּרֵנִי); ptc. מְיַסֶּרְךָ; inf. יַסֹּר ,יַסְּרָה, יַסֶּרְךָ (יַסְּרְךָ)—**discipline, punish, warn;** also **instruct, train** (Is 28_{26} perh. Ho 7_{15} Ps 94_{12} Jb 4_{3}, unless at Ho 7_{15} Jb 4_{3} יסר II pi. *strengthen*), perh. **educate, make wise** concerning ways of the world (Si 7_{23} [+ נשׂא *raise*, i.e. cause to marry wife] 30_{2} [Segal] [‖ למד pi. *teach*] 30_{13} [+ כבד hi. *make* yoke *heavy*, פן באולתו *lest in his folly*]) 4QD^{a} 9.3$_{6}$.

<SUBJ> Y. Lv $26_{18.28}$ Dt 4_{36} 8_{5} Is 8_{11} (if em. qal) 28_{26} Jr 10_{24} 30_{11}‖46_{28} 31_{18} Ho 7_{12} (if em. hi.) 7_{15} 10_{10} (if em. qal) 10_{10} (if em. אֶאֱסֳרֵם *I shall bind them* to אֲיַסְּרֵם *I shall punish them*) Ps 6_{2} $16_{7(mss)}$ 38_{2} 94_{12} $118_{18.18}$ 1QH 7_{22} (יסר]תה]), אֲדֹנָי *Lord* Ps 39_{12} appar. 4QDibHam^{a} 1.3$_{6}$, אֱלֹהִים *God* Dt 8_{5}, חָכְמוֹת *Wisdom* Si 4_{17} (or em. אסר *bind*), Job Jb 4_{3}, Rehoboam 1 K $12_{11.14}$, אִישׁ *man* Dt 8_{5} 4QDib Ham^{a} 1.3$_{6}$ 6_{15}, אָב *father* Dt 21_{18} 1 K $12_{11.14}$‖2 C $10_{11.14}$ 11QT 64_{3}, אֵם *mother* Dt 21_{18} Pr 31_{1} 11QT 64_{3}, בֵּן *son* Si 7_{23} 30_{13}, זָקֵן *elder* Dt 22_{18} 11QT 65_{14}, appar. בקר pi. ptc. *overseer* 4QD^{a} 9.3$_{6}$, כִּלְיָה *kidney*, i.e. conscience Ps 16_{7}, רָעָה *evil* Jr 2_{19}; subj. not specified Pr 19_{18} 29_{17} Si 30_{2} (Segal).

<OBJ> Isaiah Is 8_{11} (if em. qal), Jeremiah Jr 10_{24} (or em. יַסְּרֵנִי *punish me* to יַסְּרֵנוּ *punish us [Israel]*), Lemuel Pr 31_{1}, appar. David Ps 6_{2} 16_{7} 38_{2}, psalmist Ps 118_{18}, Ephraim Jr 31_{18} Ho 7_{12} (if em. hi.) perh. Ho 7_{15} (or del. יסר pi.), Israel(ites) Lv $26_{18.28}$ Dt 4_{36} Jr 2_{19} 10_{24} (if em.) 30_{11}‖46_{28} Ho 10_{10} (if em.) 10_{10} (if em.) appar. 4QDib Ham^{a} 1.3$_{6}$, אִישׁ *man* Dt 22_{18} Ps 39_{12} 11QT 65_{14}, גֶּבֶר *man* Ps 94_{12}, בֵּן *son* Dt 8_{5} 21_{18} Pr 19_{18} 29_{17} Si 7_{23} $30_{2(Segal).13}$ 4QD^{a} 9.3$_{6}$ 4QDibHam^{a} 1.3$_{6}$ appar. 6_{15} ([את בנו]) 11QT 64_{3}, בַּת 4QD^{a} 9.3$_{6}$ ([בנותם]), טַף *child* 4QD^{a} 9.3$_{6}$, מֶלֶךְ *king* Pr 31_{1}, חרשׁ ptc. *one who ploughs* Is 28_{26}, עַם *people* 1 K $12_{11.11.14.14}$‖2 C $10_{11.11.14.14}$, שׁמע ptc. *one who hears* Wisdom Si 4_{17} (or em. אסר *bind*), רַבִּים *many* or *aged* Jb 4_{3},* לֵב *heart* 1QH 17_{22} (יסר]תה]), perh. זְרוֹעַ *arm* Ho 7_{15}, דָּבָר *word* Pr 31_{1}.

<PREP> לְ *in accordance with*, + מִשְׁפָּט *judgment* Is 28_{26} Jr 30_{11}‖46_{28}, רָעָה *wickedness* Ho 7_{12} (if em. hi.); בְּ of instrument, *by (means of)*, + רוּחַ *spirit* 4QD^{a} 9.3$_{6}$, אַהֲבָה *love* 4QD^{a} 9.3$_{6}$, עַקְרָב *scorpion* 1 K $12_{11.14}$, שׁוֹט *whip* 1 K $12_{11.14}$‖2 C $10_{11.14}$, אֵסוּר *bond* Si 4_{17} (or em. אֵסוּר *punishment*, or יסר pi. to אסר *bind* with bonds), נִסְתָּר *secret* 1QH 17_{22} ([בנס]תרותיך]); *in accordance with*, + מִשְׁפָּט *judgment* Jr 10_{24}, חֵמָה *anger* Ps 6_{2} 38_{2}; *in respect of*, + תּוֹכַחַת *reproof* Ps 39_{12}; מִן *(away) from, so as not to*, + הלך inf. *walk(ing)* Is 8_{11} (if em.); עַל *on account of*, + חַטָּאת *sin* Lv $26_{18.28}$, עָוֹן *iniquity* Ps 39_{12}.

<COLL> יסר pi. with noun used adverbially, לַיְלָה *night* Ps 16_{7}, שֶׁבַע *seven times, sevenfold* Lv $26_{18.28}$, כִּלְיוֹתָי *in my kidneys* Ps $16_{7(mss)}$.

יסר pi. ‖ יכח hi. *reprove* Jr 2_{19} Ps 6_{2} 38_{2}, חזק pi. *strengthen* Ho 7_{15} Jb 4_{3}, לקח *take* 11QT 65_{14}, ענשׁ *fine* 11QT 65_{14}, ירה hi. *teach* Is 28_{26}, למד pi. *teach* Ps 94_{12}; + נקה pi. *leave unpunished* Jr 30_{11}‖46_{28}, תפשׂ *seize* 11QT 64_{3}, יצא hi. *bring out* 11QT 64_{3}.

Also 4QWays^{b} 1a.1$_{6}$ ([א]ותו ליסרו]).

<SYN> יכח hi. *reprove*, חזק pi. *strengthen*, לקח *take*, ירה hi. *teach*, למד pi. *teach.*

Hi. $_{1}$ Impf. אַיְסִרֵם (mss אַיְסִירֵם)—perh. **punish,** אַיְסִרֵם כְּשֵׁמַע לַעֲדָתָם *I shall punish them* (Ephraim) *as their congregation have heard* Ho 7_{12} (or em. אֶאֱסְרֵם כְּשֵׁמַע לַעֲדָתָם *I shall seize them as soon as their swarm is heard* or אֲיַסְּרֵם כְּשֵׁמַע לְרָעָתָם *I shall punish them in accordance with the notice of their wickedness* or אֲסִירֵם לְצָרָתָם *I shall transfer them to their oppression*).

Htp. $_{0.0.5}$ Q התיסר ,התוסרו; + waw Q והתיסרו; ptc. Q מתיסרים; inf. Q לתיסר—**be taught, be instructed,*** <SUBJ> אִישׁ *man*, i.e. early member, of community 1QS 9_{10} 4QD^{e} 7.1$_{16}$, רִאשׁוֹן *first one*, perh. founding member CD 4_{8} (התוסרו)=4QD^{e} 1.2b$_{3}$ ([התי]סרו]), חזק hi. ptc. *one who holds firm* to judgments CD 20_{31}, appar. כֹּל *all* 1QS

3$_{6}$, subj. not specified 4QD^{e} 7.1$_{15}$ (כל המתיסרים *all those who have been disciplined*). <PREP> בְּ of place/time, *in*, + יַחַד *community* 1QS 3$_{6}$; be instructed *in*, be taught *about*, + פֵּרוּשׁ *interpretation* of law CD 4$_{8}$, מִשְׁפָּט *judgment* CD 20$_{31}$ (+ אזן hi. *listen* to voice of teacher of righteousness) 1QS 9$_{10}$ (+ שׁפט ni. *be judged*); עַד *until*, + שָׁבוּעַ *week* 4QTohB^{a} 2$_{1}$. <COLL> החלו ... לתיסר *they began ... to be instructed* 1QS 9$_{10}$.

Ntp. 1 + waw וְנִוַּסְּרוּ—**accept discipline,** <SUBJ> אִשָּׁה *woman* Ezk 23$_{48}$ (or em. וְנוֹסְרוּ, ni., in same sense).*

→ יִסּוֹר *reprover, punishment,* מוּסָר *discipline,* אִסּוּר *punishment.*

יסר II 2 vb. **be strong—Pi.** Pf. יִסַּרְתִּי, יִסַּרְתָּ—**strengthen** (unless both יסר I pi. *train*), <SUBJ> Y. Ho 7$_{15}$, Job Jb 4$_{3}$ (both ‖ חזק pi. *strengthen*). <OBJ> רַבִּים *many* Jb 4$_{3}$, זְרוֹעַ *arm* perh. Ho 7$_{15}$. <SYN> חזק pi. *strengthen.**

יָסַר, see יסר I, Qal, *instruct.*

יָע 9 n.m. **fire-shovel**—pl. יָעִים; sf. יָעָיו—for cleaning altar (Ex 27$_{3}$‖38$_{3}$ Nm 4$_{14}$ 1 K 7$_{40.45}$‖2 C 4$_{11.16}$ 2 K 25$_{14}$‖Jr 52$_{18}$). <OBJ> עשׂה *make* Ex 27$_{3}$‖38$_{3}$ (both ‖ סִיר *pot,* מִזְרָק *basin,* מִזְלָג *meat-fork,* מַחְתָּה *bucket*) 1 K 7$_{40(mss).45}$‖2 C 4$_{11.16}$, נתן *give*, i.e. place Nm 4$_{14}$ (‖ מַחְתָּה, מִזְלָג, מִזְרָק), לקח *take* 2 K 25$_{14}$‖Jr 52$_{18}$ (both ‖ סִיר, מְזַמֶּרֶת *snuffer,* כַּף *basin*). <APP> כְּלִי *utensil* Nm 4$_{14}$.

<SYN> סִיר *pot,* מִזְרָק *basin,* מִזְלָג *meat-fork,* מַחְתָּה *bucket,* מְזַמֶּרֶת *snuffer,* כַּף *basin.*

→ יעה *sweep together.*

יַעְבֵּץ I 1 pl.n. **Jabez,** town in Judah, appar. near Bethlehem 1 C 2$_{55}$, <CSTR> יֹשְׁבֵי יַעְבֵּץ *dwellers of Jabez* 1 C 2$_{55(Qr)}$.

יַעְבֵּץ II 3 pr.n.m. **Jabez,** Judahite, <SUBJ> היה *be* 1 C 4$_{9}$, כבד ni. *be honourable* 1 C 4$_{9}$, קרא *call* 1 C 4$_{10}$.

יעד 29.0.17 vb. **appoint—Qal** 5.0.3 Pf. יָעֲדוֹ (יְעָדָהּ, Q יעדם), Q יעדתה (Q יעדתנו); impf. Q יעוד, יְיעָדֶנָּה—**appoint, designate,** <SUBJ> ’’ *Y.* Jr 47$_{7}$, אֵל *God* Jb 25$_{5}$ (if em. עַד *unto*, i.e. even, the moon) 1QM 1$_{10}$ 13$_{14}$, אֱלֹהִים *God* 4QShir^{b} 2.2$_{7}$, מֶלֶךְ *king* 2 S 20$_{5}$, אָדוֹן *master* Ex 21$_{8.9}$, מִי *who?* Mc 6$_{9}$; subj. not specified, 1QM 13$_{18}$.

<OBJ> Judah 2 S 20$_{5}$, בַּת *daughter* Ex 21$_{8.9}$, worshipper 1QM 13$_{18}$, חֶרֶב *sword* Jr 47$_{7}$, יָרֵחַ *moon* Jb 25$_{5}$ (if em. עַד *unto*, i.e. even, *the moon* to יָעַד God *has appointed* the moon; unless עַד is short form of יָעַד)*, יוֹם *day* 1QM 1$_{10}$ 13$_{14}$; obj. not specified, Mc 6$_{9}$ 4QShir^{b} 2.2$_{7}$.

<PREP> לְ of benefit, *to, for* 1QM 13$_{18}$, + אֵל *God* 1QM 1$_{10}$ 13$_{14}$, אָדוֹן *master* Ex 21$_{8(Qr)}$, בֵּן *son* Ex 21$_{9}$; *as,* + מִלְחָמָה *war* 1QM 1$_{10}$.

מִן of direction, *from,* + אָז *then*, i.e. ancient times 1QM 1$_{10}$.

אֶל *to,* + Ashkelon Jr 47$_{7}$, חוֹף *shore* of the sea Jr 47$_{7}$.

Ni. 19.0.11 Pf. נוֹעֲדוּ (נוֹעָדוּ), נוֹעַדְתִּי (נֹעַדְתִּי), Q נועדנו; impf. אִוָּעֵד, Q יועדו, נִוָּעֵד (נִוָּעֲדָה); + waw וַיִּוָּעֲדוּ; ptc. נוֹעָדִים (Q נועדי)—**appear, reveal oneself, gather oneself, agree, have appointment with, be companion to** (1QH 5$_{23}$), <SUBJ> ’’ *Y.* Ex 25$_{22}$ 29$_{42.43}$ 30$_{6.36}$ Nm 17$_{19}$, עֵדָה *congregation* Nm 10$_{3}$ 14$_{35}$ 16$_{11}$ 27$_{3}$ 1 K 8$_{5}$‖2 C 5$_{6}$, חַיִל *army* 1QM 15$_{3}$, Bildad Jb 2$_{11}$, Eliphaz Jb 2$_{11}$, Geshem Ne 6$_{2}$, Korah Nm 16$_{11}$, Nehemiah Ne 6$_{2.10}$, Sanballat Ne 6$_{2}$, Shemaiah Ne 6$_{2}$, Solomon 1 K 8$_{5}$‖2 C 5$_{6}$, Zophar Jb 2$_{11}$, אֱנוֹשׁ *human being* 1QSa 2$_{2}$, אִישׁ *man* 1QSa 2$_{22}$, מֶלֶךְ *king* Jos 11$_{5}$ 1 K 8$_{5}$‖2 C 5$_{6}$ Ps 48$_{5}$, נָשִׂיא *prince* Nm 10$_{4}$, חָכָם *wise one* 1QSa 2$_{17}$, גֵּאֶה *proud one* 4QHod^{a} 7.1$_{18}$, worshipper 1QH fr 10$_{6}$, דרשׁ ni. ptc. *one who inquires of* 1QH 4$_{24}$, ידע ptc. *one who has insight* 1QSa 2$_{17}$, רֹאשׁ *head*, i.e. leader Nm 10$_{4}$ 1QSa 2$_{17}$, שְׁנַיִם *two* Am 3$_{3}$, כֹּל *all* 1QH 5$_{23}$ 4QShirShabb^{d} 1.1$_{25}$; subj. not specified, 4QShirShabb^{a} 7$_{1}$ 4QShirShabb^{d} 1.1$_{27}$ 4QPrayer^{e} 3$_{2}$.

<PREP> לְ of direction, *to,* + Moses Ex 29$_{42}$ 30$_{6.36}$ Nm 17$_{19}$, בֵּן Israelite *son* Ex 25$_{22}$ 29$_{42.43}$ Nm 17$_{19}$, עֵצָה *council* 1QSa 2$_{2}$; of benefit, *to, for,* + יוֹם *day* 1QM 15$_{3}$, בְּרִית *covenant* 1QH 4$_{24}$; *at,* + שֻׁלְחָן *table* 1QSa 2$_{17}$; בְּ of place, *in, at,* + כְּפִיר *village* Ne 6$_{2}$, בִּקְעָה *plain* Ne 6$_{2}$, יַחַד *community* 1QH fr. 10$_{6}$; אֶל *to, at,* + Moses Nm 10$_{3.4}$, בַּיִת *house* of God Ne 6$_{10}$, פֶּתַח *entrance* of tent of meeting Nm 10$_{3}$; עַל *upon*, i.e. with, + Solomon 1 K 8$_{5}$‖2 C 5$_{6}$; *against,* + ’’ *Y.* Nm 14$_{35}$ 16$_{11}$ 27$_{3}$; אֶל־תּוֹךְ *among,* + הֵיכָל *temple* Ne 6$_{10}$; עִם *with,* + Belial 1QM 15$_{3}$, ידע ptc. *one who has insight* 1QH fr 10$_{6}$.

<COLL> ברכו לנועדי צדק *bless those appointed for*

righteousness 4QShirShabb[d] 1.1$_{27}$.

Hi. $_{3.0.1}$ Impf. יוֹעִידֵנִי (יְעִדֵנִי)—**summon,** <SUBJ> מִי *who?* Jr 49$_{19}$ 50$_{44}$ Jb 9$_{19}$ 4QM[a] 11.1$_{17}$. <OBJ> ׳י Y. Jr 49$_{19}$ 50$_{44}$, Job Jb 9$_{19}$, worshipper 4QM[a] 11.1$_{17}$.

Ho. $_{2.0.1}$ Ptc. מוּעָדִים, מֻעָדוֹת—**be ordered, be directed, be placed, be destined** (1QH 5$_{7}$), <SUBJ> לָבִיא *lion* 1QH 5$_{7}$, דוּד *basket* of fruit Jr 24$_{1}$, פָּנִים *face,* i.e. edge of glittering sword Ezk 21$_{21}$. <PREP> לְ of benefit, *to, for,* + בֵּן *son* of guilt 1QH 5$_{7}$; לִפְנֵי *before,* + הֵיכָל *temple* of Y. Jr 24$_{1}$.*

⇒ עֵדָה *congregation,* מוֹעֵד *appointed time,* (?) עֵת *time,* מוֹעָד *rank,* מוּעָדָה *appointment,* נוֹעַדְיָה *Noadiah.*

יַעְדָּה $_{2}$ pr.n.m. **Jadah**—L. יַעְרָה—Benjaminite, son of Ahaz, <SUBJ> ילד hi. *be father of* 1 C 9$_{42(mss)}$. <OBJ> ילד hi. *be father of* 1 C 9$_{42(mss)}$.

עדה *adorn.*

[יֶעְדּוֹ] $_{1}$ pr.n.m. **Iddo**—יעדי *Iddi*—prophet in time of Jeroboam, <CSTR> חֲזוֹת יֶעְדּוֹ *visions of Iddo* 2 C 9$_{29(mss; Qr)}$ (Kt יעדי *Iddi*). <APP> חֹזֶה *seer* 2 C 9$_{29(mss; Qr)}$ (Kt יעדי *Iddi*).

עדה *adorn.*

יעדי, see יֶעְדּוֹ *Iddo.*

יעה $_{1}$ vb. **sweep together—Qal** $_{1}$ + waw וְיָעָה—<SUBJ> בָּרָד *hail* Is 28$_{17}$. <OBJ> מַחְסֶה *refuge* of lies Is 28$_{17}$.

⇒ יָע *fire-shovel.*

יְעוּאֵל $_{1}$ pr.n.m. **Jeuel,** Judahite, member of the Zerah family, <NOM CL> יְעוּאֵל וַאֲחֵיהֶם שֵׁשׁ־מֵאוֹת וְתִשְׁעִים *Jeuel and their brothers were six hundred and ninety (persons)* 1 C 9$_{6}$. <APP> בֵּן *son* 1 C 9$_{6}$.

⇒ (?) יעה *sweep together.*

יְעוּץ $_{1}$ pr.n.m. **Jeuz,** Benjaminite, son of Shaharaim, <OBJ> ילד hi. *be father of* 1 C 8$_{10}$.

⇒ עוץ *conceal.*

יָעוּר, see יָעִיר *Jair.*

יְעוֹרִים, see יַעַר *wood.*

יְעוּשׁ $_{9}$ pr.n.m. **Jeush**—Kt יעיש—**1.** son of Esau and Edomite chief, <NOM CL> בְּנֵי עֵשָׂו אֱלִיפַז ... וִיעוּשׁ *the sons of Esau were Eliphaz ... and Jeush* 1 C 1$_{35}$, <OBJ> ילד *bear child* Gn 36$_{5(Qr).14(Qr)}$. <APP> אַלּוּף *chief* Gn 36$_{18}$, בֵּן *son* Gn 36$_{18}$.

2. Benjaminite, son of Bilhah, <NOM CL> בְּנֵי בִלְהָן יְעוּשׁ *the sons of Bilhan were Jeush ...* 1 C 7$_{10(Qr)}$,

3. Levite, son of Shimei, <SUBJ> רבה hi. *make many,* i.e. have many sons 1 C 23$_{11}$. <NOM CL> בְּנֵי שִׁמְעִי יַחַת ... וִיעוּשׁ *the sons of Shimei were Jahath ... and Jeush* 1 C 23$_{10}$.

4. son of Rehoboam, king of Judah, <OBJ> ילד *bear child* 2 C 11$_{19}$. <APP> בֵּן *son* 2 C 11$_{19}$

5. Benjaminite, son of Eshek 1 C 8$_{39}$. <NOM CL> בְּנֵי עֵשֶׁק ... יְעוּשׁ *the sons of Eshek were ... Jeush ...* 1 C 8$_{39}$. <COLL> יְעוּשׁ הַשֵּׁנִי *Jeush the second (son)* 1 C 8$_{39}$.

⇒ עושׁ *aid.*

יעז $_{1}$ vb. **insult—Ni.** $_{1}$ ptc. נוֹעָז—**be insolent,** <SUBJ> עַם *people* Is 33$_{19}$ (or em. לעז *speak foreign language*).

יַעֲזִיאֵל $_{1}$ pr.n.m. **Jaaziel,** Levite musician in time of David, <APP> אָח *brother* 1 C 15$_{18}$.

⇒ עזז *be strong* + אֵל *God.*

יַעֲזִיָּהוּ $_{2}$ pr.n.m. **Jaaziah,** Merarite Levite <CSTR> בְּנֵי יַעֲזִיָּהוּ *the sons of Jaaziah* 1 C 24$_{26}$. <PREP> לְ of possession, *(belonging) to, of* 1 C 24$_{27}$.

⇒ עזז *be strong* + ׳י *Y.*

יַעְזֵיר $_{13}$ pl.n. **Jazer**—יַעְזֵר—in Transjordan, former Amorite city allocated to Gad, but later part of Moab Nm 21$_{32}$ 32$_{1.3.35}$ Jos 13$_{25}$ 21$_{39}$ 2 S 24$_{5}$ Is 16$_{8.9}$ Jr 48$_{32.32}$ 1 C 6$_{66}$ 26$_{31}$.

<SUBJ> היה *be* Jos 13$_{25}$. <OBJ> רגל pi. *spy out* Nm 21$_{32}$, נכה hi. *conquer* Nm 32$_{3}$, בנה *build* Nm 32$_{35}$, נתן *give* Jos 21$_{39}$ 1 C 6$_{66}$. <CSTR> יָם יַעְזֵר *sea of Jazer* Jr 48$_{32}$, אֶרֶץ יַעְזֵר *land of Jazer* Nm 32$_{1}$, בְּכִי יַעְזֵר *weeping of Jazer* Is 16$_{9}$ Jr 48$_{32}$. <APP> אֶרֶץ *land* Nm 32$_{3}$. <PREP> בְּ of place, *in, at,* + מצא ni. *be found* 1 C 26$_{31}$; אֶל *to, at,* + חנה

encamp 2 S 245; עַד *until*, + נגע *reach* Is 168. <COLL> יַעְזֵיר גִּלְעָד *Jazer in Gilead* 1 C 2631.

⇒ עזר *help* + ״ *Y.*

יעט 1 vb. **cover—Qal** 1 Pf. יְעָטָנִי—<SUBJ> ״ *Y.* Is 6110 (‖ לבשׁ hi. *clothe*; or em. עטה hi. *wrap one in*), אֱלֹהִים *God* Is 6110 (‖ לבשׁ hi. *clothe*; or em. עטה hi. *wrap one in*). <OBJ> worshipper Is 6110. <COLL> מְעִיל צְדָקָה יְעָטָנִי *he has covered me with a robe of righteousness* Is 6110.

<SYN> לבשׁ hi. *clothe*.

⇒ see also עטה *wrap*.

יְעִיאֵל 13 pr.n.m. **Jeiel**—Kt יעואל—**1.** Reubenite 1 C 57. **2.** Benjaminite, ancestor of Saul 1 C 935. **3.** son of Hotham, one of David's warriors 1 C 1144. **4.** Levite musician in time of David 1 C 1518.21 165.5. **5.** Asaphite Levite 2 C 2014. **6.** secretary to Uzziah 2 C 2611. **7.** Levite in reign of Hezekiah 2 C 2913. **8.** Levite in reign of Josiah 2 C 359. **9.** companion of Ezra Ezr 813. **10.** member of Nebo family Ezr 1043.

<SUBJ> ישׁב *dwell* 1 C 935(Qr), נצח pi. *supervise* 1 C 1521, רום hi. *raise*, i.e. provide 2 C 359. <NOM CL> הָרֹאשׁ יְעִיאֵל *the head*, i.e. the chief, *was Jeiel* 1 C 57, שָׁמָע וִיעִיאֵל בְּנֵי חוֹתָם *Shama and Jeiel were the sons of Hotham* 1 C 1144(Qr), עִמָּהֶם ... יְעִיאֵל *with them were ... Jeiel* 1 C 1518. <CSTR> בֶּן־יְעִיאֵל *son of Jeiel* 2 C 2014, יַד יְעִיאֵל *hand of Jeiel*, i.e. by means of Jeiel 2 C 2611(Qr). <APP> אָב *father* 1 C 935(Qr), אָח *brother* 1 C 1518, בֵּן *son* Ezr 1043 2 C 2913(Qr), גִּבּוֹר *warrior* 1 C 1144(Qr), לֵוִי *Levite* 1 C 165.5, סוֹפֵר *secretary* 2 C 2611(Qr), שֵׁם *name* Ezr 813. <PREP> מִן partitive, *some of, (any)one of* Ezr 1043.

⇒ יעה *sweep together* + אֵל *God*.

יָעִיר 1 pr.n.m. **Jair**—Kt יעור—father of Elhanan who slew the brother of Goliath 1 C 205, <CSTR> בֶּן־יָעִיר *son of Jair* 1 C 205.

⇒ עור *rouse oneself*.

יְעִישׁ, see יְעוּשׁ *Jeush*.

יַעְכָּן 1 pr.n.m. **Jachan,** Gadite chief 1 C 513, <APP> אָח *brother* 1 C 513. ⇒ see also עָכָן *Achan*.

יעל 23.3.3 vb. **profit—Hi.** 23.3.3 Pf. הוֹעִיל; impf. יוֹעִיל (Q יועל), Si 2ms תוֹעִיל, אוֹעִיל, יוֹעִילוּ (יועלו) יועילוך, יעילו, יועלו), ptc. נוֹעִיל; inf. מוֹעִיל; הוֹעֵל, הוֹעִיל—**be of use, get profit, get advantage,** <SUBJ> אֵל *god* Is 4410, פֶּסֶל *image* Is 4410 Hb 218, עַם *people* Is 305.6, Job Jb 2115 353, בֵּן *son* Si 3821, נבא ni. ptc. *one who prophesies* Jr 2332, רֹעֶה *shepherd* Jr 1213, friends of Job Jb 2115, worshipper 4QShirb 485 (אוע[ל]), פִּרְחָח *rabble* Jb 3013.

צְדָקָה *righteousness* Is 5712, מַעֲשֶׂה *deed* Is 5712, חָמוּד *desirable object* Is 449, אוֹצָר *treasure* Pr 102, הוֹן *wealth* Pr 114, נְכָסִים *wealth* Si 58, תֹּהוּ *useless object*, perh. image 1 S 1221 (‖ נצל hi. *deliver*), דָּבָר *word* Jr 78, מִלָּה *word* Jb 153; subj. not specified, Is 4712 4817 Jr 28.11 1619 Si 137 1QH 620 4QapJoshuaa 231 4QDibHama 1.520.

<OBJ> Israelite(s) Is 5712.

<PREP> לְ of benefit, *to, for*, + עַם *people* Jr 2332, כֹּל *everyone* Is 305; introducing object, + הַוָּה *ruin* Jb 3013; בְּ of time, *in, during*, + יוֹם *day* Pr 114 Si 58; מִן of instrument, *by (means of)*, + דֶּרֶךְ *way* 1QH 620.*

<SYN> נצל hi. *deliver*.

⇒ יָעֵל *Jael*.

יָעֵל I 2 n.m. **wild goat**—pl. יְעֵלִים; cstr. יַעֲלֵי—<SUBJ> ילד *give birth* Jb 391. <CSTR> יַעֲלֵי־סָלַע *wild goats of the rocks*, i.e. living among the rocks Jb 391. <PREP> לְ of benefit, *to, for* Ps 10418.

⇒ יַעֲלָה *wild she-goat*, (?) יָעֵל II *Jael*.

יָעֵל II 6 pr.n.f. **Jael,** assassin of Sisera, wife of Heber the Kenite, <SUBJ> ברך pu. *be blessed* Jg 524.24, בוא *come* Jg 421, יצא *go out* Jg 418.22, ראה hi. *show* Jg 422, לקח *take* Jg 421, שׂים *place* Jg 421, כסה pi. *cover* Jg 418, תקע *thrust* Jg 421, קרא *call* Jg 418.22, אמר *say* Jg 418.22.

<NOM CL> יָעֵל אֵשֶׁת חֶבֶר הַקֵּינִי *Jael was the wife of Heber the Kenite* Jg 417 524. <CSTR> אֹהֶל יָעֵל *tent of Jael* Jg 417, יְמֵי יָעֵל *days of Jael* Jg 56.*

⇒ (?) יָעֵל I *wild goat*, יעל *profit*.

יַעֲלָה 1 n.f. **wild she-goat,** <CSTR> יַעֲלַת־חֵן *she-goat of grace*, i.e. pleasing woman Pr 519; יְצוּעֵי יַעֲלָה *couch(es) of (his) she-goat*, i.e. concubine Gn 494 (if em. יְצוּעִי עָלָה *he went up to my couch*).* ⇒ יָעֵל *wild goat*.

יַעְלָה 2 pr.n.m. **Jaalah**—יַעֲלָא—member of class of 'Solomon's servants', <CSTR> בְּנֵי יַעְלָה *sons of Jaalah* Ezr 2₅₆ Ne 7₅₈ (יַעֲלָא).*

→ יעל *profit,* (?) יָעֵל I *wild goat.*

יַעְלָם 4 pr.n.m. **Jalam,** son of Esau and Oholibamah, eponymous ancestor of Edomite tribe, <SUBJ> ישׁב *dwell* Ps 55₂₀ (if em.; see יָעֵן *ostrich*). <NOM CL> בְּנֵי עֵשָׂו אֱלִיפַז ... וְיַעְלָם *the sons of Esau were Eliphaz ... and Jalam* 1 C 1₃₅. <OBJ> ילד *give birth (to)* Gn 36₅.₁₄. <APP> אַלּוּף יַעְלָם *a chief, Jalam* Gn 36₁₈.

→ (?) עלם I n. *be concealled,* or עלם II hi. *be dark.*

[יָעֵן] I 1 n.[m.] **ostrich***—pl. Qr יְעֵנִים [Kt ענים]—בַּת־עַמִּי לְאַכְזָר כַּיְעֵנִים בַּמִּדְבָּר *the daughter of my people has become cruel, like ostriches in the steppe* Lm 4₃(Qr) (unless יָעֵן II *bedouin;* or em. בְּנוֹת *daughters of*), כְּנַף־יְעֵנִים *wing(s) of ostriches* Jb 39₁₃ (if em. רְנָנִים *ostriches*).

[יָעֵן] II 1 n.[m.] **bedouin***—pl. Qr יְעֵנִים [Kt ענים]—בַּת־עַמִּי לְאַכְזָר כַּיְעֵנִים בַּמִּדְבָּר *the daughter of my people has become cruel, like bedouin, in the steppe* Lm 4₃(Qr) (unless יָעֵן I *ostrich;* or em. בְּנוֹת *daughters of*), יִשְׁמָעֵאל וִיעֵנִים וְיֹשְׁבֵי קֶדֶם *Ishmael and the bedouin and those who dwell in the east* Ps 55₂₀ (if em. יִשְׁמַע אֵל וְיַעֲנֵם וְיֹשֵׁב קֶדֶם *God hears and humbles them, even he who is enthroned of old;* or em. יִשְׁמָעֵאל וְיַעְלָם יֹשֵׁב קֶדֶם *Ishmael and Jalam dwell in the east*).

יַעַן I 96.0.3 conj. **because, 1.** יַעַן conj. of cause, **because, since, a.** followed by pf. and waw consecutive with impf. of היה *be* Ezk 20₂₄ 34₈, גבה *be high* Ezk 28₂, מצא ni. *be found* 1 K 14₁₃, גלה ni. *be revealed* Ezk 16₃₆, רכך *be soft* 2 K 22₁₉‖2 C 34₂₇, נקם ni. *be avenged* Ezk 25₁₂.₁₅ (in both inf., not pf.), הלך *go* Ezk 20₁₆, עלה *go up* 2 K 19₂₈‖Is 37₂₉, נשׂא *raise,* i.e. bear, reproach Ezk 36₆, שׁלח pi. *send away* 1 K 20₄₂, שׁלך hi. *throw* Ezk 23₃₅ (inf., not pf.), נתן *give,* i.e. place, heart Ezk 28₂, נטה *extend* hand Pr 1₂₄, נגר hi. *hand over* Ezk 35₅, טעה hi. *mislead* Ezk 13₁₀, שׁכח *forget* Ezk 23₃₅, מאס *despise* Lv 26₄₃ 1 S 15₂₃ Ezk 20₁₆.₂₄ 4QpsMos[d] 1.24, געל *abhor* Lv 26₄₃ 4QpsMos[d] 1.24, טהר pi. *purify* Ezk 24₁₃, טמא pi. *defile* Ezk 5₁₁, חלל pi. *defile* Ezk 20₁₆.₂₄, מעל *sin* Ezk 15₈, אשׁם *sin* Ezk 25₁₂ (inf., not pf.), פשׁע *sin* Ho 8₁, עבר *transgress* covenant Ho 8₁, שׂמח *rejoice* Ezk 25₆ (inf., not pf.), אמן hi. *trust* Nm 20₁₂, בטח *trust* Is 30₁₂ (inf., not pf.), שׁען ni. *rely* Is 30₁₂ (inf., not pf.), דרשׁ *seek* Ezk 34₈ (inf., not pf.), משׁח *anoint* Is 61₁, אמר *say* Ezk 28₂ 29₉ (or em. inf.) 36₂, דבר pi. *speak* Is 65₁₂ 66₄ Jr 35₁₇, קרא *call* Is 65₁₂ 66₄ Jr 35₁₇ Pr 1₂₄, חזה *see* Ezk 13₈ (inf., not pf.), כנע ni. *humble oneself* 2 K 22₁₉‖2 C 34₂₇, בכה *weep* 2 K 22₁₉‖2 C 34₂₇, קרע *tear* clothes 2 K 22₁₉‖2 C 34₂₇, רעה *tend* sheep Ezk 34₈.₈ (inf., not pf.).

b. followed by impf. of הדף *push* Ezk 34₂₁, נגח *gore* Ezk 34₂₁, לקח *take* Am 5₁₁ (inf., not impf.).

c. followed by inf. cstr. of היה *be* Ezk 22₁₉ 29₆ 34₈ 35₅, שׁפך ni. *be poured* Ezk 16₃₆, זכר ni. *be remembered* Ezk 21₂₉, hi. *cause to be remembered* Ezk 21₂₉, מאס *despise* Is 30₁₂, המן *be tumultuous* Ezk 5₇ (or em. מרה *rebel*), רגז htp. *become angry* 2 K 19₂₈‖Is 37₂₉, נתן *give,* i.e. place, heart Ezk 28₆, בטח *trust* Jr 48₇, מכר htp. *sell oneself* 1 K 21₂₀, אמר *say* Jr 23₃₈ Ezk 25₃.₈ 29₉ (if em. pf.) 35₁₀ 36₁₃ (if em. ptc.), דבר pi. *speak* Jr 5₁₄ Ezk 13₈, עשׂה *do* Jr 7₁₃ Ezk 20₂₄ 25₁₂.₁₅, מחא *strike* hand Ezk 25₆, רקע *stamp* foot Ezk 25₆, בשׁס po. *trample* Am 5₁₁ (or em. בוס *trample* or שׁבס *impose [corn] tax*), כאב hi. *hurt* Ezk 13₂₂ (if em. כאה hi. *dishearten*).

d. followed by לְ + inf. of חזק pi. *strengthen* Ezk 13₂₂.

e. followed by inf. abs. of שׁמם *make desolate* Ezk 36₃ (or em. שַׁמּוֹת וְשָׁאֹף *making desolate and crushing* to שָׂמֹחַ וְשָׁאֹט *rejoicing and despising*).

f. followed by ptc. of אמר *say* Ezk 36₁₃ (or em. inf.).

<COLL> יַעַן וּבְיַעַן *for indeed* or *just because* Lv 26₄₃ (Sam יַעַן בְּיַעַן in same sense) Ezk 13₁₀ 36₃(mss) (L יַעַן בְּיַעַן) 4QpsMos[d] 1.24 (יען ביען), אִם־לֹא יַעַן *I swear that because* Ezk 34₈; with following verb negated Nm 20₁₂ Ezk 20₁₆.₂₄ 34₈.₈; result clause beginning with waw consecutive with pf. 1 K 20₄₂ 2 K 19₂₈‖Is 37₂₉ Is 65₁₂ (יַעַן follows) Jr 7₁₃ Ezk 15₈ (יַעַן follows) 34₂₁, with impf. 1 S 15₂₃; beginning with imperative Ezk 13₁₀, לָכֵן *therefore* Nm 20₁₂ Is 30₁₂ Ezk 5₇ 13₂₂ 25₁₂ 28₂ 34₈ 35₅.₁₀ 36₂.₃.₆.₁₃, עַל כֵּן *therefore* 4QpsMos[d] 1.24, הִנֵּה *behold* perh. 1 K 21₂₀ Jr 5₁₄ Ezk 13₈, לָכֵן הִנְנִי *therefore, behold, I* Jr 23₃₈ 35₁₇ (יַעַן follows לָכֵן ... הִנְנִי) Ezk 16₃₆ 22₁₉ 25₃.₆ (or del. הִנְנִי) 25₈

25_{15} 28_6 29_6 (לָכֵן ... הִנְנִי) 29_9, וְגַם אָנֹכִי *I too* 2 K 22_{19}||2 C 34_{27} (וְגַם־אֲנִי) Is 66_4 (יַעַן follows גַּם־אֲנִי) Ezk 5_{11} (וְגַם־אֲנִי) 20_{15} (יַעַן follows וְגַם־אֲנִי) 20_{24} (יַעַן follows גַּם־אֲנִי) Pr 1_{24} (גַּם־אֲנִי), גַּם־אַתְּ *you too* Jr 48_7 Ezk 23_{35} (וְגַם־).

2. יַעַן as prep., **on account of,** + תּוֹעֵבָה *abomination* Ezk 5_9, בַּיִת *house* Hg 1_9, מָה *what?* Hg 1_9.

3. יַעַן אֲשֶׁר as conj. of cause, **because, since,** also **inasmuch as** (1 K 8_{18}||2 C 6_8), followed by pf. and waw consecutive with impf. of היה *be* 1 K 8_{18}||2 C 6_8 1 K 11_{11} 14_7 2 K 21_{15} Ezk 44_{12} (if em. waw consecutive with pf.) 2 C 1_{11}, רום *be high* Ezk 31_{10}, גבה *be high* Ezk 31_{10}, הלך *go* 1 S 30_{22} 1 K 11_{33} $14_{7.7}$ 16_2, עזב *abandon* 1 K 11_{33} Jr 19_4, שׁחה htpal. *bow down* 1 K 11_{33}, רום hi. *raise* 1 K 14_7 16_2, קום hi. *establish* CD 9_7, רדף *pursue* Ps 109_{16}, שׁלח *send* 2 K 1_{16} Jr 29_{25} (or em.; see Coll.) 29_{31}, שׁלך hi. *throw* 1 K 14_7, מלא *fill* Jr 19_4, pi. *do wholeheartedly* Dt 1_{36} Jos 14_{14}, עשׂה *do* Gn 22_{16} 1 K $14_{7.15}$ 2 K 10_{30} $21_{11.15}$ Jr 29_{23} 35_{18}, רעע hi. *do evil* 1 K 14_7 2 K 21_{11}, חטא hi. *tempt* 1 K 16_2 2 K 21_{11}, רגז *anger* Ezk 16_{43}, בטח hi. *cause to trust* Jr 29_{31}, נאף pi. *commit adultery* Jr 29_{23}, נכר pi. *alienate* Jr 19_4, כרת hi. *cut off* Ezk 21_9 (pf. with impf. value, unless יַעַן אֲשֶׁר final, as §4), שׁמר *keep* 1 K 11_{11} Jr 35_{18}, נתן *give* 1 K 14_7, *extend* branches Ezk 31_{10}, *cause to be* 1 K 14_7 16_2, חשׂך *withhold* Gn 22_{16}, קרע *tear* 1 K 14_7, עבר *transgress* Jg 2_{20}, אמר *say* 1 K 20_{36} Ezk 26_2, דבר pi. *speak* Jr 29_{23}, שׁאל *ask* 1 K $3_{11.11.11.11.11}$ 2 K 21_{15}, שׁרת pi. *serve* Ezk 44_{12} (if em. waw consecutive with pf.) 2 C $1_{11.11.11}$, נבא ni. *prophesy* Jr 29_{31}, שׁמע *hear* 1 K 20_{28} Jr 25_8 35_{18}, זכר *remember* Ezk 16_{43} Ps 109_{16}, שׁרת pi. *serve* Ezk 44_{12} (if em. impf.), קטר pi. *burn incense* Jr 19_4, בנה *build* Jr 19_4; followed by impf. and waw consecutive with pf. of שׁרת pi. *serve* Ezk 44_{12} (or em. pf.), היה *be* Ezk 44_{12} (or em. waw consecutive with impf.).

<COLL> יַעַן אֲשֶׁר followed by negative verb Gn 22_{16} 1 S 30_{22} 1 K $3_{11.11.11}$ 11_{33} 14_7 20_{36} 2 K 21_{15} Jr 25_8 Ezk 16_{43} 44_{12} (if em. waw consecutive with pf.) Ps 109_{16} 2 C $1_{11.11}$ CD 9_7; result clause beginning with waw consecutive with pf. 1 K 14_{15} 20_{28} 2 K 21_{15} (in both יַעַן אֲשֶׁר follows) Jr 19_4, with impf. Ezk 31_{10} (if em. simple waw), לָכֵן *therefore* 1 K 14_7 2 K 21_{11} Jr 29_{31} 35_{18} Ezk 21_9 (unless יַעַן אֲשֶׁר final, as §2b) 26_2, עַל־כֵּן *therefore* Jos 14_{14} Ezk 44_{12}, כִּי *therefore* Gn 22_{16}, הִנֵּה *behold* 1 K 3_{10} 11_{33} (precedes יַעַן אֲשֶׁר) 16_2 20_{36} Jr 25_8, גַּם־אֲנִי *I too* Jg 2_{20} Ezk 16_{43} (וְגַם־), הוּא יִרְאֶנָּה *he will see it* Dt 1_{36} (precedes יַעַן אֲשֶׁר), הַחָכְמָה וְהַמַּדָּע נָתוּן לָךְ *wisdom and knowledge shall be given to you* 2 C 1_{11} (or em. אֶתֵּן *I shall give*); appar. without result clause, Jr 29_{25} (or em. יַעַן אֲשֶׁר אַתָּה שָׁלַחְתָּ בִשְׁמְכָה *because you sent in your own name* to שָׁלַח בִּשְׁמוֹ *he sent in his name*) Ps 109_{16}.

4. יַעַן אֲשֶׁר as final conj., **so that,** followed by impf. of ראה *see* Ezk 12_{12} (or em. יַעַן אֲשֶׁר לֹא־יִרְאֶה he will cover his face *so that he does not see* to לְמַעַן אֲשֶׁר לֹא־יֵרָאֶה *so that he will not be seen*).

5. יַעַן כִּי as conj. of cause, **because, since,** followed by pf. and waw consecutive with impf. of היה *be* Is 29_{13}, גבה *be high* Is 3_{16}, הלך *go* Is 3_{16}, נגשׁ ni. *approach* Is 29_{13}, רחק pi. *distance* Is 29_{13}, יעץ *advise* Is 7_5, מאס *despise* Nm 11_{20} Is 8_6, מרה *rebel* 1 K 13_{21}, בכה *weep* Nm 11_{20}, כנע ni. *humble oneself* 1 K 21_{29}. <COLL> result clause beginning with waw consecutive with pf. Is 3_{16}, כֹּה *thus* Is 7_5, (וְ)לָכֵן הִנֵּה *(and) therefore, behold* Is 8_6 29_{13} (הִנְנִי).*

יַעַן II 1 pl.n. **Jaan,** וַיָּבֹאוּ דָּנָה יַעַן perh. *and they came to Dan, (to) Jaan* or *to Dan-jaan* 2 S 24_6 (or em. יַעַר to Dan *of the wood* or וְעִיּוֹן to Dan *and Ijon*; or דָּן וּמִדָּן *to Dan, and from Dan* they turned).
⇒ (?) ענה *answer.*

יַעֲנָה I 8 n.f. **desert**—alw. with בַּת־ *daughter of,* in ref. to unclean, desert-dwelling, bird, **ostrich** or **eagle owl,** <CSTR> בַּת הַיַּעֲנָה *daughter of the desert,* i.e. *ostrich* or *eagle owl* Lv 11_{16}||Dt 14_{15} Is 13_{21} 34_{13} 43_{20} Jr 50_{39} Mc 1_8 Jb 30_{29} (all six בְּנוֹת יַעֲנָה).*

יַעֲנָה II 8 n.f. **greed**—alw. with בַּת־ *daughter of,* i.e. unclean, desert-dwelling, bird, **ostrich** or **eagle owl,** <CSTR> בַּת הַיַּעֲנָה *daughter of greed,* i.e. *ostrich* or *eagle owl* Lv 11_{16}||Dt 14_{15} Is 13_{21} 34_{13} 43_{20} Jr 50_{39} Mc 1_8 Jb 30_{29} (all six בְּנוֹת יַעֲנָה).*

יַעְנַי 1 pr.n.m. **Janai,** Gadite chief in Bashan, <SUBJ> ישׁב *dwell* 1 C 5_{12}. <NOM CL> יַעְנַי וְשָׁפָט בַּבָּשָׁן *Janai and Shaphat were in Bashan* 1 C 5_{12}. <APP> בֵּן *son* 1 C 5_{12}.
⇒ ענה *answer.*

יעף I $_{8}$ vb. **be weary—Qal** $_{8}$ Pf. יָעֲפוּ; impf. יִיעַף, יִיעֲפוּ (יִעָפוּ); + waw וַיִּיעַף—<SUBJ> ״ Y. Is 40$_{28}$ (|| יגע *be tired*), אֱלֹהִים *God* Is 40$_{28}$ (|| יגע *be tired*), Babylon Jr 51$_{64}$, לְאֹם *people* Jr 51$_{58}$ Hb 2$_{13}$, Daniel Dn 9$_{21}$ (unless יעף II *be swift*), נַעַר *youth* Is 40$_{31}$ (|| יגע *be tired*), חָרָשׁ *artificer* Is 44$_{12}$, קוה ptc. *one who waits* Is 40$_{31}$ (|| יגע *be tired*; :: הלך *go*), בקשׁ pi. ptc. *one who seeks* Jr 2$_{24}$; subj. not specified, 4Q418 69.2$_{13}$.

<PREP> בְּ *in, with,* + קֵץ *time* 4Q418 69.2$_{13}$; בְּדֵי *in exchange for,* + אֵשׁ *fire* Jr 51$_{58}$, רִיק *nothingness* Hb 2$_{13}$.

<SYN> יגע *be tired.* <ANT> הלך *go.**

⇒ יָעֵף *weary;* see also עיף *be weary.*

יעף II $_{1}$ vb. **be swift—Ho.** $_{1}$ Ptc. מֻעָף (mss מוּעָף)—**be swift,** <SUBJ> Gabriel Dn 9$_{21}$ (unless יעף I *be weary,* of Daniel), אִישׁ *man* Dn 9$_{21}$. <PREP> בְּ *in, with,* + יְעָף *flying* Dn 9$_{21}$.

⇒ יְעָף *flying.*

יָעֵף $_{4}$ adj. **weary**—pl. יְעֵפִים—**1.** used atrributively of, + אִישׁ *man* Jg 8$_{15}$. **2.** as predicative adj. or noun **weary one,** <SUBJ> שׁתה *drink* 2 S 16$_{2}$. <PREP> לְ of direction, *to,* + נתן *give* Is 40$_{29}$; אֵת *with,* + עות *sustain* Is 50$_{4}$.*

⇒ יעף *be weary.*

יְעָף I $_{1}$ n.m. **weariness**—<PREP> בְּ perh. of cause, *on account of,* + יעף ho. *be weary* Dn 9$_{21}$.

⇒ יעף I *be weary.*

יְעָף II $_{1}$ n.m. **flying**—<PREP> בְּ perh. of cause, *on account of,* + יעף ho. *be swift* Dn 9$_{21}$.

⇒ יעף II *be swift.*

[יַעְפּוּר] $_{0.0.1}$ pl.n. **Jaapur,** town, location unknown, 4Q Sela 1.1$_{4}$.

יעץ $_{80.4.7}$ vb. **advise—Qal** $_{57.3.2}$ Pf. יָעַץ (יָעָץ, יְעָצַנִי, יְעָצָה), יָעַצְתָּ, יָעַצְתִּי, יָעֲצוּ (יְעָצֻהוּ); impf. אִיעָצָה (אִיעָצְךָ, אִיעָצֵךְ); ptc. יוֹעֵץ (יֹעֵץ, יֹעֲצֵךְ), fs sf. יֹעַצְתּוֹ, pl. יוֹעֲצִים (יֹעֲצִים), cstr. יֹעֲצֵי, sf. יֹעֲצַיִךְ, יוֹעֲצָיו (יֹעֲצָיו), pass. יְעוּצָה—**advise, counsel.**

1a. <SUBJ> ״ *Y.* Is 14$_{24.27}$ 19$_{12.17}$ 23$_{9}$ Jr 49$_{20}$ 50$_{45}$ (both || חשׁב *determine*) Ps 16$_{7}$ 32$_{8}$, Syria Is 7$_{5}$, Ephraim Is 7$_{5}$, Ahithophel 2 S 16$_{23}$ 17$_{7.15.21}$, Balaam Nm 24$_{14}$, Balak Mc 6$_{5}$, Bildad Jb 26$_{3}$, Hushai 2 S 17$_{11}$, Jeremiah Jr 38$_{15}$ (|| נגד hi. *declare*), Nathan 1 K 1$_{12}$, Nebuchadrezzar Jr 49$_{30}$ (|| חשׁב), אִישׁ *man* Ezk 11$_{2}$ (|| חשׁב), בֵּן *son* of Remaliah Is 7$_{5}$, חֹתֵן *father-in-law* Ex 18$_{19}$, מֶלֶךְ *king* Jr 49$_{30}$ Mc 6$_{5}$, נָדִיב *noble* Is 32$_{8}$, זָקֵן *elder* 1 K 12$_{8}$||2 C 10$_{8}$ 1 K 12$_{13}$, כִּילַי *scoundrel* Is 32$_{7}$; subj. of pass. עֵצָה *counsel* Is 14$_{24}$, מִי *who?* Is 23$_{8}$; subj. not specified, Na 1$_{11}$ (|| חשׁב) Hb 2$_{10}$ Ps 62$_{5}$.

<OBJ> Absalom 2 S 17$_{15}$, Balak Nm 24$_{14}$, Bathsheba 1 K 1$_{12}$, Moses Ex 18$_{19}$, Rehoboam 1 K 12$_{8}$||2 C 10$_{8}$, Zedekiah Jr 38$_{15}$, מֶלֶךְ *king* 1 K 12$_{8}$||2 C 10$_{8}$ 1 K 12$_{13}$, זָקֵן *elder* 2 S 17$_{15}$, worshipper Ps 16$_{7}$, דֶּרֶךְ *way* Si 37$_{7(B)}$, עֵצָה *counsel* 2 S 16$_{23}$ 17$_{7}$ Is 19$_{17}$ Jr 49$_{20.30}$ 50$_{45}$ Ezk 11$_{2}$, זִמָּה *plan* Is 32$_{7}$, נְדִיבָה *noble action* Is 32$_{8}$, רָעָה *evil* Is 7$_{5}$, בְּלִיַּעַל *worthlessness* Na 1$_{11}$, בֹּשֶׁת *shame* Hb 2$_{10}$, זֹאת *this (action)* Is 23$_{8.9}$.

<PREP> לְ of benefit, *to, for,* + בַּיִת *house* Hb 2$_{10}$; introducing object, + לֹא *one devoid* of wisdom Jb 26$_{3}$; בְּ of place/time, *in, at, during,* + עִיר *city* Ezk 11$_{2}$, יוֹם *day* 2 S 16$_{23}$, פַּעַם *time* 2 S 17$_{7}$; אֶל *against,* + Babylon Jr 50$_{45}$, Edom Jr 49$_{20}$; עַל *upon,* + אֶרֶץ *earth* Is 14$_{26}$; *against,* + Egypt Is 19$_{12.17}$, Tyre Is 23$_{8}$, עַם *people* 2 S 17$_{21}$, Ahaz Is 7$_{5}$, David 2 S 17$_{21}$, יֹשֵׁב *inhabitant* Jr 49$_{30}$.

<COLL> אִיעָצֵךְ נָא עֵצָה *let me counsel you with counsel* 1 K 1$_{12}$.

<SYN> נגד hi. *declare,* חשׁב *determine.*

1b. ptc. as noun, **counsellor,** <SUBJ> היה *be* 2 C 22$_{3.4}$, גיח *burst out* 1QH 3$_{10}$, נוף hi. *wave* hand Si 37$_{7(B)}$, רום hi. *present* offering Ezr 8$_{25}$, אבד perish Mc 4$_{9}$, אמר *say* Si 37$_{7(D)}$.

<NOM CL> זְכַרְיָהוּ בְנוֹ יוֹעֵץ *Zechariah his son was a counsellor* 1 C 26$_{14}$, יְהוֹנָתָן ... יוֹעֵץ *Jonathan ... was a counsellor* 1 C 27$_{32}$, אֲחִיתֹפֶל יוֹעֵץ *Ahithophel was a counsellor* 1 C 27$_{33}$, יועץ בליעל עם לבבם *a counsellor of Belial is with their hearts* 1QH 6$_{21}$, אך יש יועץ *surely there is a counsellor* Si 37$_{7(B)}$, אֵין יוֹעֵץ *there is no counsellor* Is 41$_{28}$.

<OBJ> סור hi. *remove* Is 3$_{2}$ (|| שַׂר *prince,* שֹׁפֵט *judge,* נָבִיא *prophet,* קֹסֵם *diviner,* זָקֵן *elder,* חָכָם *wise one*), הלך hi. *lead away* Jb 12$_{17}$, שׁוב hi. *bring back* Is 1$_{26}$ (|| שֹׁפֵט *judge*), שׁלח *send* 2 S 15$_{12}$, סכר *bribe* Ezr 4$_{5}$, הלל pi. *praise* Si 44$_{3}$, קרא *call* Is 9$_{5}$.

<CSTR> יֹעֲצֵי אָרֶץ *counsellors of the earth* Jb 3$_{14}$, פַּרְעֹה *of Pharaoh* Is 19$_{11}$, יוֹעֵץ דָּוִד *counsellor of David* 2 S 15$_{12}$, יועץ בליעל *a counsellor of Belial* 1QH 6$_{21}$, יֹעֲצֵי שָׁלוֹם *counsellors of peace* Pr 12$_{20}$; חַכְמֵי יֹעֲצֵי *wise ones of the counsellors of* Is 19$_{11}$, רֹב יוֹעֵץ *greatness*, i.e. abundant number, *of counsellor(s)* Pr 11$_{14}$ 24$_{6}$, רֹב יוֹעֲצִים *greatness*, i.e. abundant number, *of counsellors* Pr 15$_{22}$, כל יועץ *every counsellor* Si 37$_{7(B)}$.

<APP> Ahithophel 2 S 15$_{12}$, מֶלֶךְ *king* Ezr 7$_{28}$, אִישׁ *man* Si 44$_{3}$, פֶּלֶא *marvellous one* 1QH 3$_{10}$, שֵׁם *name* Is 9$_{5}$.

<PREP> לְ of benefit, *to, for* Pr 12$_{20}$; *as*, + נתן *give*, i.e. make 2 C 25$_{16}$; מִן of direction, *from*, + שמר *keep* Si 37$_{8}$; לִפְנֵי *before*, + נטה hi. *extend* Ezr 7$_{28}$; עִם *with*, + שכב *lie down* Jb 3$_{14}$.

<SYN> שַׂר *prince*, שֹׁפֵט *judge*, נָבִיא *prophet*, קֹסֵם *diviner*, זָקֵן *elder*, חָכָם *wise one*.

Ni. 22.1.2 Pf. נוֹעָץ, נוֹעֲצוּ; impf. Q יועץ, Si 2ms תועץ, נִוָּעֲצָה, יִוָּעֲצוּ; + waw וַיִּוָּעַץ, וַיִּוָּעֲצוּ; ptc. נוֹעָץ, נוֹעָצִים; inf. Q להיעץ—**take counsel together, deliberate, decide, give counsel, allow oneself to be advised** (Pr 13$_{10}$), **advise (after consultation)** (1 K 12$_{6}$).

<SUBJ> Amaziah 2 C 25$_{17}$, David 1 C 13$_{1}$, Hezekiah 2 C 32$_{3}$, Jehoshaphat 2 C 20$_{21}$, Nehemiah Ne 6$_{7}$, Sanballat Ne 6$_{7}$, Rehoboam 1 K 12$_{6.8}$‖2 C 10$_{6.8}$, בֵּן *son* CD 3$_{5}$, יֶלֶד *youth* 1 K 12$_{9}$‖2 C 10$_{9}$, מֶלֶךְ *king* 1 K 12$_{6.8}$‖2 C 10$_{6.8}$ 1 K 12$_{28}$ 2 K 6$_{8}$ 2 C 25$_{17}$ 30$_{2}$, שַׂר *prince* 2 C 30$_{2}$, זָקֵן *elder* 1 K 12$_{6}$‖2 C 10$_{6}$, worshipper Si 37$_{10}$, שֹׁמֵר *watcher* Ps 71$_{10}$, אוֹיֵב *enemy* Ps 83$_{6}$, קָהָל *assembly* 2 C 30$_{2.23}$, מִי *who?* Is 40$_{14}$; subj. not specified, Is 45$_{21}$ Pr 13$_{10}$ 1QS 6$_{3}$ 4QapPs^{b} 69$_{3}$.

<PREP> בְּ of place, *in, at*, + Jerusalem 2 C 30$_{2}$; אֶל *to, with*, + עַם *people* 2 C 20$_{21}$, עֶבֶד *servant* 2 K 6$_{8}$, לֵב *heart* 4QapPs^{b} 69$_{3}$; עַל *against*, + מִצְוָה *commandment* CD 3$_{5}$; אֵת *with*, + זָקֵן *elder* 1 K 12$_{6}$‖2 C 10$_{6}$, יֶלֶד *youth* 1 K 12$_{8}$ ‖2 C 10$_{8}$; עִם *with*, + חָם *father-in-law* Si 37$_{10}$, שַׂר *commander* 1 C 13$_{1}$ 2 C 32$_{3}$, גִּבּוֹר *warrior* 2 C 32$_{3}$.

<COLL> נוֹעֲצוּ יַחְדּוֹ *they have taken counsel together* Ps 71$_{10}$, נוֹעֲצוּ לֵב יַחְדּוֹ *they have taken counsel with one heart together*, i.e. with one purpose in mind Ps 83$_{6}$, נִוָּעֲצָה יַחְדּוֹ *let us take counsel together* Ne 6$_{7}$, יחד יועצו *they shall give counsel in unity* 1QS 6$_{3}$.

Hi. 0.0.1 Impf. תועצני—as Qal, **advise, counsel,** תועצני *you advise me* 4Q417 1.2$_{17}$.

Htp. 1.0.1 Impf. יִתְיָעֲצוּ; ptc. Q מתיעצים—**take counsel,** <SUBJ> אוֹיֵב *enemy* Ps 83$_{4}$; subj. not specified, 4QapPs^{b} 45$_{5}$. <PREP> עַל *against*, + צָפוּן *protected one* Ps 83$_{4}$, worshipper 4QapPs^{b} 45$_{5}$."

⇒ עֵצָה *counsel*, מוֹעֵצָה *plan*.

יעק, see עוק *be hindered.*

יַעֲקֹב 350.6.39 pr.n.m. **Jacob**—יַעֲקוֹב—**1.** 215.1.29 patriarch, son of Isaac and father of tribes of Israel, Gn 25$_{26.27.28.29.30.31.33.33.34}$ 27$_{6.11.15.17.19.21.22.22.30.30.36.41.41.42.46}$ 28$_{1.5.6.7.10.16.18.20}$ 29$_{1.4.10.10.11.11.12.13.15.18.20.21.28}$ 30$_{1.1.2.4.5.7.9.10.12.16.17.19.25.31.36.36.37.40.41.42}$ 31$_{1.2.3.4.11.17.20.22.24.25.25.26.29.31.32.33.36.36.43.45.46.47.51.53.54}$ 32$_{1.3.4.5.7.8.10.19.21.25.26.27.28.30.31.33}$ 33$_{1.10.17.18}$ 34$_{1.3.5.5.6.7.7.13.19.25.27.30}$ 35$_{1.2.4.4.5.6.9.10.10.14.15.20.22.23.26.27.29}$ 36$_{6}$ 37$_{1.2.34}$ 42$_{1.1.4.29.36}$ 45$_{25.27}$ 46$_{2.5.5.6.8.8.15.18.19.22.25.26.26.27}$ 47$_{7.7.8.9.10.10.28.28}$ 48$_{2.3}$ 49$_{1.2.24.33}$ 50$_{24}$ Ex 1$_{1.5}$ 2$_{24}$ 3$_{6.15.16}$ 4$_{5}$ 6$_{3.8}$ 33$_{1}$ Lv 26$_{42}$ Nm 32$_{11}$ Dt 1$_{8}$ 6$_{10}$ 9$_{5.27}$ 29$_{12}$ 30$_{20}$ 34$_{4}$ Jos 24$_{4.4.42}$ 1 S 12$_{8}$ 1 K 18$_{31}$ 2 K 13$_{23}$ 17$_{34}$ Jr 33$_{26}$ Ho 12$_{13}$ Ob$_{10}$ Ml 1$_{2.2}$ 3$_{6}$ Ps 77$_{16}$ 105$_{6.23}$ 1 C 16$_{13}$ 1QJub^{b} 35$_{9.10}$ 4QBibPar 3$_{3}$ 4QTNaph 1$_{7.10}$ 4QJub^{a} 1$_{7.28}$ 2$_{20}$ 4QJub^{f} 37$_{13}$ 14$_{1}$ 4QJub^{g} 25$_{12}$ 4QJub^{h} 35$_{9.13.15.16.17.17.17.20}$ 38$_{1.4}$ 4QpsJub^{a} 2.2$_{11.11.12}$ 4QpsJub^{b} 7$_{3.5}$ 4QCommGenA 4$_{3}$ 4QRP^{b} 3.2$_{6}$ 4QapJoshua^{b} 17$_{4}$ 19$_{2}$ 22.2$_{13}$ 4QNarrC 1$_{3.6}$ 4QPatr 8$_{1}$ 4QapMes 4$_{7}$ 5QRègle 2$_{6}$ 6QD 5$_{4}$ CD 3$_{3.4}$ 4$_{15}$.

<SUBJ> חיה *live* Gn 47$_{28}$, ידע *know* Gn 28$_{16}$ 31$_{32}$, ראה *see* Gn 29$_{10}$ 31$_{2}$ 32$_{3.21.31}$ 33$_{1.10}$ 42$_{1}$, שמע *hear* Gn 28$_{7}$ 31$_{1}$ 34$_{5}$, אהב *love* Gn 29$_{18}$ 4QJub^{h} 35$_{20}$, יכל *be able*, i.e. have ability over Gn 32$_{29}$, ילד hi. *become father of* 4QpsJub^{a} 2.2$_{11}$, צרר *be anxious* Gn 32$_{8}$, ירא *fear* Gn 31$_{31}$ 32$_{8}$, שכב *lie down* Gn 30$_{16}$, יקץ *wake up* Gn 28$_{16}$, גור *sojourn* Gn 32$_{5}$ Ps 105$_{23}$, ישב *dwell* Gn 25$_{27}$ 35$_{1}$ 37$_{1}$, תקע *pitch tent* Gn 31$_{25}$, חנה *encamp* Gn 33$_{18}$, חרשׁ hi. *keep silent* Gn 34$_{5}$, אסף ni. *be gathered* Gn 49$_{33}$, יתר ni. *be left* Gn 32$_{25}$, שמד ni. *be exterminated* Gn 34$_{30}$.

בוא *come* Gn 29$_{21}$ 30$_{4.16.16}$ 33$_{18}$ 35$_{6.9.27}$ 46$_{6.8}$ 1 S 12$_{8}$ 4QTNaph 1$_{7}$, נגשׁ *draw near* Gn 27$_{22}$ 29$_{10}$, הלך *go* Gn 28$_{5.7.10.20}$ 29$_{1}$ 30$_{25}$ 32$_{2}$ 1QJub^{b} 35$_{10}$, יצא *go out* Gn 27$_{30}$ 28$_{10}$ 47$_{10}$, שוב *go back* Gn 30$_{31}$ 31$_{3}$, ירד *go down* Jos 24$_{4}$, עלה *go up* Gn 35$_{1}$, קום *arise* Gn 31$_{17}$ 35$_{1}$ 46$_{5}$, שכם hi. *rise early*

Gn 28$_{18}$, נסע *march on* Gn 33$_{17}$, ברח *flee* Gn 31$_{20.22}$ 35$_{1}$ Ho 12$_{13}$, נהג pi. *lead away* Gn 31$_{26}$, אסף *draw back* feet Gn 49$_{33}$, חצה *divide* Gn 32$_{8}$ 33$_{1}$, פרד hi. *separate* Gn 30$_{40}$, שׂים *place* Gn 28$_{18}$ 30$_{41.42}$ 37$_{34}$, שׁית *place* Gn 30$_{40.40}$, לקח *take* Gn 27$_{46}$ 28$_{6.6.18}$ 30$_{37}$ 31$_{1.45}$, נתן *give* Gn 25$_{34}$ 30$_{40}$.

עשׂה *do* Gn 29$_{28}$ 31$_{1.26}$ 33$_{17}$ 35$_{1}$, עבד *serve* Gn 29$_{15.18.20}$ Ho 12$_{13}$, רעה *pasture flock* Gn 30$_{31.36}$, שׁמר *keep* Gn 30$_{31}$, כלה pi. *finish* Gn 49$_{33}$, מלא pi. *fulfil* Gn 29$_{28}$, שׁקה hi. *give drink* Gn 29$_{10.11}$, יצק *pour out* Gn 28$_{18}$ 35$_{14}$, זיד hi. *boil* Gn 25$_{29}$, קנה *buy* Jos 24$_{32}$, נשׂא *raise* Gn 29$_{1.11}$ 31$_{17}$ 33$_{1}$, רקם hi. *erect stone* Gn 31$_{45}$, נצב hi. *set up* Gn 35$_{14.20}$, בנה *build* Gn 33$_{17}$, מצא *find* Gn 33$_{10}$, טמן *hide* Gn 35$_{4}$, שׁלח *send* Gn 31$_{4}$ 32$_{4}$ 42$_{4}$, גלל *roll away* Gn 29$_{10}$, פצל pi. *peel* bark Gn 30$_{37}$, קרע *tear* Gn 37$_{34}$, גנב *steal*, i.e. deceive Gn 31$_{20.26}$, אבק ni. *wrestle* Gn 32$_{25}$, שׂרה *strive* Gn 32$_{29}$, גוע *expire* Gn 49$_{33}$, קבר *bury* Gn 35$_{29}$.

זבח *sacrifice* Gn 31$_{54}$, נסך hi. *make drink offering* Gn 35$_{14}$, כפר pi. *make atonement* Gn 32$_{21}$, נדר *make vow* Gn 28$_{20}$, שׁבע ni. *swear oath* Gn 31$_{53}$, שׁאל *ask* Gn 32$_{30}$, קרא *call* Gn 31$_{4.47.54}$ 32$_{3.31}$ 33$_{17}$ 35$_{15}$ 49$_{1}$ 4QBibPar 3$_{3}$, ni. *be called* Gn 35$_{10}$, אמר *say* Gn 25$_{31.33}$ 27$_{11.19}$ 28$_{16}$ 29$_{4.18.21}$ 30$_{25.31}$ 31$_{11.31.31.36.46}$ 32$_{3.5.10.21.28.30}$ 33$_{10}$ 34$_{30}$ 35$_{2}$ 42$_{1.4.36}$ 46$_{2}$ 47$_{9}$ 48$_{3}$, ni. *be said*, i.e. be called Gn 32$_{29}$, ענה *answer* Gn 31$_{31.36}$, נגד hi. *declare* Gn 29$_{12.15}$ 31$_{20}$ 49$_{1}$, ספר pi. *relate* Gn 29$_{13}$, צוה pi. *command* Gn 32$_{5}$ 49$_{33}$, ריב *reproach* Gn 31$_{36}$, אבל htp. *observe mourning rites* Gn 37$_{34}$, בכה *weep* Gn 29$_{11}$, ברך pi. *bless* Gn 47$_{7.10}$.

<NOM CL> יַעֲקֹב אִישׁ תָּם *Jacob was a perfect man* Gn 25$_{27}$, שִׁמְךָ יַעֲקֹב *your name is Jacob* Gn 35$_{10}$, עַבְדְּךָ יַעֲקֹב אַחֲרֵינוּ *your servant Jacob is behind us* Gn 32$_{21}$.

<OBJ> ידע *know* 4QJub^{h} 35$_{9}$, ילד hi. *become father of* 4QpsJub^{a} 2.2$_{11}$ 4QpsJub^{b} 7$_{3}$, בוא hi. *bring* Gn 29$_{13}$ 47$_{7}$, נשׂג hi. *overtake* Gn 31$_{25}$, אהב *love* Gn 25$_{28}$ Ml 1$_{2}$ 4QJub^{h} 35$_{13}$, רצה *be favourable to* Gn 33$_{10}$, עמד hi. *position* Gn 47$_{7}$, נתן *give* Jos 24$_{4}$ 4QJub^{g} 25$_{12}$, נשׂא *raise*, i.e. carry Gn 46$_{5.5}$, חלם hi. *make strong* Si 49$_{10}$, שׁמר *keep* Gn 28$_{20}$ 4QJub^{h} 35$_{17}$, לבשׁ hi. *clothe* Gn 27$_{15}$, שׂכר *hire* Gn 30$_{16}$, שׂטם *bear grudge* Gn 27$_{41}$, עכר *bring taboo on* Gn 34$_{30}$.

באשׁ hi. *make odious* Gn 34$_{30}$, שׁכל pi. *make childless* Gn 42$_{36}$, ענה pi. *oppress* 1QJub^{b} 35$_{9}$, נכה hi. *strike* Gn 34$_{30}$, הרג *kill* Gn 27$_{41}$ 4QJub^{h} 35$_{15}$ ([יע[קו]ב]), קרא *meet* Gn 29$_{13}$ 30$_{16}$ 32$_{7}$, שׁלח *send* Gn 28$_{5}$, pi. *send away* Gn 28$_{6}$ 30$_{25}$, קרא *call* Gn 25$_{26}$ 27$_{36}$, אמר *say* Gn 31$_{11}$ 46$_{2}$, צוה pi. *command* Gn 28$_{1}$, ברך pi. *bless* Gn 27$_{30.41}$ 28$_{1.6.6}$ 32$_{30}$ 35$_{9}$ 48$_{3}$.

<CSTR> אֲבִיר יַעֲקֹב *mighty one of Jacob* Gn 49$_{24}$ Si 51$_{12}$, אֹהֶל־יַעֲקֹב *tent of Jacob* Gn 31$_{33}$, אָהֳלֵי *tents of* Jr 30$_{18}$ Ml 2$_{12}$, אֱלֹהֵי *God of* Ex 3$_{6.15.16}$ 4$_{5}$ 4QJub^{h} 35$_{17}$ ([י]עקוב), אֵם *mother of* Gn 28$_{5}$, אַף *anger of* Gn 30$_{2}$, אֵשֶׁת *wife of* Gn 46$_{19}$, בֵּית *house of* Gn 46$_{27}$ 3QJub 3$_{3}$, בְּכוֹר *firstborn of* Gn 35$_{23}$ 46$_{8}$, בן יעקב *son of Jacob* CD 4$_{15}$, בְּנֵי יַעֲקֹב *sons of Jacob* Gn 34$_{7.13.25.27}$ 35$_{5.22.26}$ 46$_{26}$ 49$_{2}$ 1 K 18$_{31}$ 2 K 17$_{34}$ Ml 3$_{6}$ Ps 77$_{16}$ 105$_{6}$||1 C 16$_{13}$ 4Q Jub^{a} 1$_{28}$ ([בני י]עקב) 4QJub^{h} 38$_{4}$ 4QapJoseph^{b} 1$_{13}$ 4QapJoshua^{b} 22.2$_{13}$ CD 3$_{4}$.

בַּת יַעֲקֹב *daughter of Jacob* Gn 34$_{3.7.19}$, זֶרַע *seed of* Jr 33$_{26}$ 4QJub^{a} 2$_{20}$, יַד *hand of* Gn 27$_{17}$, יְמֵי *days of* Gn 47$_{28}$, ימי ... יעקוב *days of ... Jacob* 4QpsJub^{a} 2.2$_{12}$, יֶרֶךְ יַעֲקֹב *thigh of*, i.e. loins of, *Jacob* Ex 1$_{5}$, כַּף־יֶרֶךְ *socket of hip-joint of* Gn 32$_{26.33}$, פְּנֵי *face of* Gn 36$_{6}$, קוֹל *voice of* Gn 27$_{22}$, רוּחַ *spirit of* Gn 45$_{27}$, שבטי יעקב *tribes of Jacob* Si 33$_{13}$, שֵׁמַע יַעֲקֹב *report of*, i.e. about, *Jacob* Gn 29$_{13}$, ברכות יעקוב *blessings of Jacob* 4QCommGenA 4$_{3}$, תּוֹלְדוֹת יַעֲקֹב *generations of Jacob* Gn 37$_{2}$.

<APP> Abraham 2 K 13$_{23}$, אָב *father* Dt 1$_{8}$ 6$_{10}$ 9$_{5}$ 29$_{12}$ 30$_{20}$ 4QTNaph 1$_{7.10}$ 4QJub^{h} 38$_{1}$ 4QRP^{b} 4b.1$_{8}$, בֵּן *son* Gn 27$_{17.42}$ 4QRP^{b} 3.2$_{6}$, אָח *brother* Gn 27$_{41}$ Ob$_{10}$ 1QJub^{b} 35$_{9.10}$, עֶבֶד *servant* Gn 32$_{21}$ Dt 9$_{27}$ 4QapJoshua^{b} 19$_{2}$ ([י]עקב), אהביך יעקב *your friend, Jacob* 4QapJoseph^{b} 1$_{21}$, שֵׁם *name* Gn 25$_{26}$ 27$_{36}$ 32$_{29}$ 35$_{10}$.

<PREP> לְ of direction, *to*, + ידע ni. *be known* Ex 6$_{3}$, נתן *give* Gn 28$_{20}$ 29$_{28}$ 30$_{9.31}$ Ex 6$_{8}$, קרא *call* Gn 27$_{42}$, אמר *say* Gn 28$_{1}$ 29$_{15}$ 31$_{26.51}$ 35$_{10}$ 4QpsEzek^{a} 45$_{4}$ 4QpsEzek^{d} 2$_{3}$, נגד hi. *declare* Gn 42$_{29}$ 48$_{2}$, שׁבע ni. *swear oath* Gn 50$_{24}$ Ex 33$_{1}$ Nm 32$_{11}$ Dt 1$_{8}$ 6$_{10}$ 9$_{5}$ 29$_{12}$ 30$_{20}$ 34$_{4}$ 4QJub^{a} 1$_{7}$ ([יע[קו]ב]).

לְ of benefit, *to, for* Ml 1$_{2}$ 4QJub^{f} 14$_{1}$ ([יעקו]ב) 4QNarr C 1$_{3.6}$, + עשׂה *do* Gn 30$_{31}$, לקח *take* Gn 28$_{6}$, בקשׁ pi. *seek* 4QJub^{f} 37$_{13}$, מכר *sell* Gn 25$_{33}$, מסר *hand down* CD 3$_{3}$, ילד *bear child* Gn 30$_{1.5.7.10.12.17.19}$ 34$_{1}$ 46$_{15.18.25}$, pu. *be born* Gn 46$_{22}$.

לְ of possession, *(belonging) to, of* Gn 32$_{19}$ 46$_{26}$, + היה *be* Gn 30$_{42}$; *on the part of*, + חרה *be angry* Gn 31$_{36}$; introducing object, + חבק pi. *embrace* Gn 29$_{13}$, נשׁק pi. *kiss fervently* Gn 29$_{13}$, זכר *remember* Dt 9$_{27}$.

בְּ introducing object, + פגע *meet* Gn 32$_{2}$.

אֶל *to*, + ראה ni. *appear* Gn 35$_{1.9}$ 48$_{3}$ Ex 6$_{3}$, בוא *come* Gn 42$_{29}$ 45$_{25}$ 48$_{2}$, יצא *go out* Gn 34$_{6}$, שׁוב *go back* Gn 32$_{7}$, נתן *give* Gn 35$_{4}$, קרא *call* Gn 28$_{1}$, אמר *say* Gn 25$_{30}$ 27$_{6.21.42}$ 30$_{1}$ 31$_{3.11.43}$ 32$_{10}$ 35$_{1}$ 47$_{8}$, דבר pi. *speak* 4QJub^{h} 38$_{1}$ ([יעק]וב), ידע hi. *make known* 5QRègle 2$_{6}$.

עַל *upon*, + היה *be* Gn 42$_{36}$; *concerning*, + צוה pi. *command* Gn 28$_{6}$, דאג hi. *worry about* 4QJub^{h} 35$_{17}$ ([יעקו]ב); אַחַר *after*, + הלך *go* 4QRP^{b} 4b.1$_{8}$, דלק *hotly pursue* Gn 31$_{36}$; אַחֲרֵי *after* 4QRP^{b} 3.2$_{6}$; אֵת *with* 2 K 13$_{23}$, + בוא *come* Ex 1$_{1}$, זכר *remember* Ex 2$_{24}$, דבר pi. *speak* Gn 34$_{6}$ 35$_{14.15}$; בֵּין *between*, + שׂים *place* Gn 30$_{36}$ (+ Laban), ירה *erect* pillar Gn 31$_{51}$ (+ Laban); עִם *with*, + היה *be* Gn 28$_{20}$ 31$_{3}$, יטב hi. *make good* Gn 32$_{10}$, דבר pi. *speak* Gn 31$_{24.29}$, כרת *make covenant* 4Qap Joseph^{b} 3$_{9}$ 11QT 29$_{10}$; מֵעִם *(from) with*, + גזל *take by force* Gn 31$_{31}$.

<COLL> זָכַרְתִּי אֶת־בְּרִיתִי יַעֲקוֹב *I have remembered my covenant with Jacob* Lv 26$_{42}$.

Also 4QJub^{h} 35$_{16}$ 4QpsJub^{b} 7$_{5}$ 4QapJoshua^{b} 17$_{4}$ 4Q Patr 8$_{1}$ 4QapMes 4$_{7}$ 6QD 5$_{4}$ ([י]עקב).

2. 135.5.7 name of people claiming Jacob (§1) as their ancestor, sometimes ‖ Israel, e.g. Nm 23$_{7}$ Dt 33$_{10}$ Is 14$_{1}$ Ps 14$_{7}$, often difficult to distinguish from §1, Gn 49$_{7}$ Ex 19$_{3}$ Nm 23$_{7.10.21.23.23}$ 24$_{5.17.19}$ Dt 32$_{9}$ 33$_{4.10.28}$ 2 S 23$_{1}$ Is 2$_{3.5.6.7}$ 3$_{9}$ 8$_{17}$ 9$_{7}$ 10$_{20.21}$ 14$_{1.1}$ 17$_{4}$ 27$_{6.9}$ 29$_{22.22.23}$ 40$_{27}$ 41$_{8.14.21}$ 42$_{24}$ 43$_{1.22.28}$ 44$_{1.2.5.21.23}$ 45$_{4.4.19}$ 46$_{3}$ 48$_{1.12.20}$ 49$_{5.6.26}$ 58$_{1.14}$ 59$_{20}$ 60$_{16}$ 65$_{9}$ Jr 2$_{4}$ 5$_{20}$ 10$_{16.25}$ 30$_{7.10.10.18}$ 31$_{7.11}$ 33$_{26}$ 46$_{27.27.28}$ 51$_{19}$ Ezk 20$_{5}$ 28$_{25}$ 37$_{25}$ 39$_{25}$ Ho 10$_{11}$ 12$_{3}$ Am 3$_{13}$ 6$_{8}$ 7$_{2.5}$ 8$_{7}$ 9$_{8}$ Ob$_{17.18}$ Mc 1$_{5.5}$ 2$_{7.12}$ 3$_{1.8.9}$ 4$_{2}$ 5$_{6.7}$ 7$_{20}$ Na 2$_{3}$ Ml 2$_{12}$ Ps 14$_{7}$ 20$_{2}$ 22$_{24}$ 24$_{6}$ 44$_{5}$ 46$_{8.12}$ 47$_{5}$ 53$_{7}$ 59$_{14}$ 75$_{10}$ 76$_{7}$ 78$_{5.21.71}$ 79$_{7}$ 81$_{2.5}$ 84$_{9}$ 85$_{2}$ 87$_{2}$ 94$_{7}$ 99$_{4}$ 105$_{10}$ 114$_{1.7}$ 132$_{2.5}$ 135$_{4}$ 146$_{5}$ 147$_{19}$ Lm 1$_{17}$ 2$_{2.3}$ 1 C 16$_{17}$ 4QPs^{b} 5$_{6}$ 4QpsEzek^{a} 5$_{5}$ 4Q S1* 1$_{2}$ 5Q25.3$_{2}$ 11QPs^{a} 18$_{7}$ CD 20$_{17}$.

<SUBJ> שׁמע *hear* Is 44$_{1}$ 48$_{12}$, עין *dwell* Dt 33$_{28}$ (if em. עֵין *fountain of* to עָן *dwells*), עמד *stand* 4QMidrEschat^{b} 10$_{15}$, שׁקט *be at peace* Jr 30$_{10}$ 46$_{27}$, שׁאן palal *be undisturbed* Jr 30$_{10}$ 46$_{27}$, בושׁ *be ashamed* Is 29$_{22}$, ירא *fear* Is 43$_{1}$ 44$_{2}$ Jr 30$_{10}$ 46$_{27.28}$, קום *arise* Am 7$_{2.5}$, שׁוב *go back* Jr 30$_{10}$ 46$_{27}$, שׂדד pi. *harrow* Ho 10$_{11}$, שׁרשׁ hi. *put out roots* Is 27$_{6}$, זכר *remember* Is 44$_{21}$, קרא *call* Is 43$_{22}$, אמר *say* Is 40$_{27}$, גיל *rejoice* Ps 14$_{7}$ 53$_{7}$.

<NOM CL> אַתָּה ... יַעֲקֹב *you are ... Jacob* Is 41$_{8}$, יַעֲקֹב חֶבֶל נַחֲלָתוֹ *Jacob is the allotted portion of his heritage* Dt 32$_{9}$ (or em. יַעֲקֹב חֶבֶל נַחֲלָתוֹ יִשְׂרָאֵל Y. is the portion *of Jacob, Israel is the allotted portion of his heritage*).

<OBJ> ברא *create* Is 43$_{1}$, בחר *choose* Is 41$_{8}$ Ps 135$_{4}$, רחם pi. *have compassion on* Is 14$_{1}$, אסף *gather* Mc 2$_{12}$, שׁוב pol. *bring back* Is 49$_{5}$, גאל *redeem* Is 43$_{1}$ 44$_{23}$ 48$_{20}$, פדה *redeem* Jr 31$_{11}$, נתן *give* Is 42$_{24}$ 43$_{28}$, אכל *eat*, i.e. devour Jr 10$_{25}$ Ps 79$_{7}$, ארר *curse* Nm 23$_{7}$.

<CSTR> אֲבִיר יַעֲקֹב *mighty one of Jacob* Is 49$_{26}$ 60$_{16}$ Ps 132$_{2.5}$, אָהֳלֵי *tents of* Jr 30$_{18}$ (יַעֲקוֹב) Ml 2$_{12}$, אֵל *God of* Ps 146$_{5}$, אֱלוֹהַּ *God of* Ps 114$_{7}$ (mss אֱלֹהֵי *God of*), אֱלֹהֵי *God of* 2 S 23$_{1}$ Is 2$_{3}$‖Mc 4$_{2}$ Ps 20$_{2}$ 46$_{8.12}$ 75$_{10}$ 76$_{7}$ 81$_{2.5}$ 84$_{9}$ 94$_{7}$ 132$_{2.5}$ Si 46$_{14}$, אדון יעקוב *Lord of Jacob* 11QPs^{a} 18$_{7}$.

בֵּית יַעֲקֹב *house of Jacob* Ex 19$_{3}$ Is 2$_{5.6}$ 8$_{17}$ 10$_{20}$=4QIsa^{c} 4.2$_{11}$ (יעקוב) Is 14$_{1}$ 29$_{22}$=4QpIsa^{c} 18$_{4}$ ([בית יעקוב]) Is 46$_{3}$ 48$_{1}$ 58$_{1}$ Jr 2$_{4}$ 5$_{20}$ Ezk 20$_{5}$ Am 3$_{13}$ 9$_{8}$ Ob$_{17.18}$ Mc 2$_{7}$ 3$_{9}$ Ps 114$_{1}$, בני יעקב *sons of* CD 3$_{4}$ 4$_{15}$ 4QTestim$_{28}$ (בני [יעקוב]) 5Q25 3$_{2}$ 11QT 23$_{7}$ (בני יעקו[ב]), גְּאוֹן יַעֲקֹב *pride of Jacob* Am 6$_{8}$ 8$_{7}$ Na 2$_{3}$ (or em. גֶּפֶן) Ps 47$_{5}$, זֶרַע *seed of* Is 45$_{19}$ Jr 33$_{26}$ Ps 22$_{24}$ Si 46$_{10}$ 4QDibHam^{a} 1.5$_{7}$ (both יעקוב).

חֵלֶק יַעֲקֹב *portion of Jacob* Jr 10$_{16}$ 51$_{19}$ (יַעֲקוֹב), יְשׁוּעוֹת *saving acts of*, i.e. for Ps 44$_{5}$, כְּבוֹד *glory of* Is 17$_{4}$, מֶלֶךְ *king of* Is 41$_{21}$, מִשְׁכְּנוֹת *dwelling places of* Ps 87$_{2}$, נְאוֹת *habitations of* Lm 2$_{2}$, נַחֲלַת *inheritance of* Is 58$_{14}$, עוֹן *iniquity of* Is 27$_{9}$, עֵין *fountain of* Dt 33$_{28}$ (or em. עָן Jacob *dwells*), עֲפַר *dust of* Nm 23$_{10}$.

פֶּשַׁע יַעֲקֹב *transgression of Jacob* Mc 1$_{5.5}$, קְדוֹשׁ *holy one of* Is 29$_{23}$, קְהִלַּת *assembly of* Dt 33$_{4}$, רָאשֵׁי *heads of*, i.e. rulers of Mc 3$_{1}$, שְׁאָר *remnant of* Is 10$_{21}$, שְׁאֵרִית *remnant of* Mc 5$_{6.7}$, שְׁבוּת *fortunes of* Ezk 39$_{25(Qr)}$, שִׁבְטֵי *tribes of* Is 49$_{6}$, שְׁבִית *captivity of* Ps 85$_{2(Qr)}$, שֵׁם *name of* Is 44$_{5}$, תּוֹלַעַת *worm of* Is 41$_{14}$.

<APP> עֶבֶד *servant* Is 44$_{1.2}$ 45$_{4}$ 48$_{20}$ Jr 30$_{10}$ 46$_{27.28}$; יַעֲקֹב־אֵל *Jacob-el* Dt 33$_{28}$ (if em. יַעֲקֹב אֶל־ *Jacob; to*).

<PREP> לְ of direction, *to* 4QPs^{b} 5$_{6}$, + נתן *give* Ezk 28$_{25}$ 37$_{25}$ Mc 7$_{20}$, אמר ni. *be said* Nm 23$_{23}$, נגד hi. *declare* Mc 3$_{8}$ Ps 147$_{19}$, צוה pi. *command* Lm 1$_{17}$; of benefit, *to, for* Jr 30$_{7}$ 4QS1* 1$_{2}$, + עמד hi. *establish* Ps 105$_{10}$‖1 C 16$_{17}$, ירה hi. *teach* Dt 33$_{10}$, רנן *shout joyfully* Jr 31$_{7}$.

בְּ *in, with*, + נבט hi. *look at* Nm 23$_{21}$, שׁוב *go back* Is 59$_{20}$, עשׂה *execute* Ps 99$_{4}$, קום hi. *establish* Ps 78$_{5}$, רעה *pasture flock* Ps 78$_{71}$, משׁל *rule* Ps 59$_{14}$, חלק pi. *divide* Gn

49_{7}, בער *burn* Lm 2_{3}, למד pi. *teach* Si 45_{5}; *against* Nm 23_{23}, + נשׂק ni. *be kindled* Ps 78_{21}, שׁלח *send* Is 9_{7}.

מִן of direction, *from*, + דרך *go out* Nm 24_{17}, יצא hi. *bring out* Is 65_{9}; of agent, *by (means of)*, + רדה *rule* Nm 24_{19}; עַל *upon*, + פקד *inflict punishment* Ho 12_{3}; לְמַעַן *for the sake of* Is 45_{4}.

<COLL> מַה־טֹּבוּ אֹהָלֶיךָ יַעֲקֹב *how excellent are your tents, O Jacob* Nm 24_{5}, זֶה דּוֹר מְבַקְשֵׁי פָנֶיךָ יַעֲקֹב *this is the generation of those who seek your face, O Jacob* Ps 24_{6} (unless em. פָּנֶיךָ *your face* to אֱלֹהֵי *the God of*), ושבי פשע יעקב שמרו ברית *but the penitents from sin (among) Jacob kept the covenant* of God CD 20_{17}.

יִשְׂרָאֵל *Israel* || יַעֲקֹב *Jacob* Gn 49_{7} Ex 19_{3} Nm $23_{7.10.21.23}$ $24_{5.17}$ Dt 33_{10} 2 S 23_{1} Is 9_{7} 27_{6} 40_{27} 41_{14} 42_{24} $43_{1.22.28}$ $44_{1.5.21.23}$ 45_{4} 46_{3} $48_{1.12}$ $49_{5.6}$ Jr 2_{4} 30_{10} 46_{27} Ezk 39_{25} Mc $3_{1.8.9}$ Na 2_{3} Ps 22_{24} $78_{5.21.71}$ 105_{10} 135_{4} 147_{19} 1 C 16_{17}.

יַעֲקֹב *Jacob* || יִשְׂרָאֵל *Israel* Is 10_{20} 41_{8} Mc 1_{5} Ps 105_{23} 114_{1} 1 C 16_{13}.

3. 0.0.2 principal party in correspondence, <APP> בֵּן *son* MurEpBeth-Mashiko$_{3.10}$. <PREP> מִן of direction, *from*, + לקח *take* MurEpBeth-Mashiko$_{3}$.

4. 0.0.1 notary acting on behalf of Jacob the son of Judah, <APP> בֵּן *son* MurEpBeth-Mashiko$_{13}$.*

Also 4QpsEzek^{a} 5_{5}.

⇒ (?) עקב *grasp by heel*; יַעֲקֹבָה *Jaakobah.*

יַעֲקֹבָה $_{1}$ pr.n.m. **Jaakobah,** Simeonite chief, <APP> אֵלֶּה *these* 1 C 4_{36}.

⇒ יַעֲקֹב *Jacob.*

יַעֲקָן $_{1}$ pr.n.m. **Jaakan,** Horite chief in Edom, perh. ident. with עֲקָן *Akan* (Gn 36_{27}), <NOM CL> בְּנֵי־אֵצֶר ... זַעֲוָן יַעֲקָן *the sons of Ezer were ... Zaavan and Jaakan* 1 C 1_{42}.

⇒ בְּנֵי־יַעֲקָן *Bene-jaakan.*

יַעַר I $_{57.0.5}$ n.m. **forest**—יָעַר; + ־ה of direction יַעְרָה; cstr. יַעַר; sf. יַעְרוֹ (יַעְרוֹ), יַעְרָהּ; pl. יְעָרִים—**wood, forest, thicket,** <SUBJ> רבה hi. *increase* 2 S 18_{8} (וַיֶּרֶב הַיַּעַר לֶאֱכֹל *and the forest consumed more* victims), ירד *go down* Is 32_{19} (or em. בְּרֶדֶת הַיַּעַר *when the forest goes down* to בְּרֶדֶת הָעִיר *at the descent of the city*)* Zc 11_{2}, רנן pi. *shout for joy* Is 44_{23}.

<NOM CL> יַעַר הוּא *it is a forest* Jos 17_{18}.

<OBJ> עשׂה *produce* 4QJub^{a} 2_{7}, חשׂף *strip bark* Ps 29_{9} (if em. יְעָרִים; unless יַעֲרָה II), בער *burn* Ps 83_{15}, כרת *cut down* Jr 46_{23}, שׁקה hi. *water* Ec 2_{6}.

<CSTR> יַעַר אֶפְרַיִם *forest of Ephraim* 2 S 18_{6}, חֶרֶת *of Hereth* 1 S 22_{5}, הַלְּבָנוֹן *of Lebanon* 1 K 7_{2} $10_{17.21}$||2 C $9_{16.20}$, הַנֶּגֶב *of the Negeb* Ezk 21_{3}, הַשָּׂדֶה *of the field* Ezk 21_{2}, כַּרְמִלּוֹ *of its plantation*, i.e. dense forest 2 K 19_{23}||Is 37_{24}.

עֵץ הַיַּעַר *tree(s) of the forest* Ezk 15_{6}, יַעְרוֹ *of his forest* Is 10_{19}, עֲצֵי יַעַר *trees of the forest* Is 7_{2} 44_{14} (יָעַר) Ezk 15_{2} (הַיָּעַר) Ps 96_{12} (יָעַר) Ca 2_{3} (הַיַּעַר) 1 C 16_{33} (הַיָּעַר), סִבְכֵי הַיַּעַר *thickets of the forest* Is 9_{17} 10_{34}, שְׂדֵי־יָעַר *fields of (the) forest* Ps 132_{6} (unless יַעַר III *Jaar*, or *Kiriath-jearim*; or del. יַעַר or em. יָעִיר *Jair*, i.e. Bethlehem, or יָעַד the field *he appointed*; mss שְׂדֵה *field of*),* [חי]ת יער *beast of the forest* 1QH 8_{8}, חַיְתוֹ־יָעַר *beast(s) of the forest* Ps 50_{10} 104_{20}, בֵּית יַעַר *house of the forest of* 1 K 7_{2} $10_{17.21}$||2 C $9_{16.20}$ Is 22_{8} (הַיַּעַר), בָּמוֹת יָעַר *high places of (the) forest* Jr 26_{18}||Mc 3_{12}, מצולו[ת] יערים *depths of the forests* 4QBer^{a} 5_{3}, כְּבוֹד יַעְרוֹ *glory of his forest* Is 10_{18}.

<ADJ> בָּצוּר *inaccessible* Zc 11_{2}.

<PREP> לְ of direction, *to*, + אמר *say* Ezk 21_{3}; *as*, + חשׁב ni. *be considered* Is 29_{17} 32_{15}, שׂים *place*, i.e. make Ho 2_{14}.

בְּ of place, *in, at* Is 56_{9} Jr 12_{8}, + היה *be* 2 S 18_{6}, ישׁב *dwell* 4QJub^{h} 34_{4}, לין *spend night* Is 21_{13}, ישׁן *sleep* Ezk 34_{25}, בוא *come* Dt 19_{5} 1 S 14_{25}, שׁלך hi. *throw* 2 S 18_{17}, יצת hi. *kindle fire* Jr 21_{14}, שׁאג *roar* Am 3_{14}.

מִן of direction, *from* Jr 5_{6} 10_{3} Ps 80_{14}, + יצא *go out* 2 K 2_{24}, חטב *gather firewood* Ezk 39_{10}.

אֶל *to*, + בוא *come* 1 S 14_{26}, נבא ni. *prophesy* Ezk 21_{2}.

יַעְרָה (with ־ה- of direction), *at, in, to, into*, etc. *(the wood of)*, + עלה *go up* Jos 17_{15}.

יַעַר (without ־ה- of direction), *at, in, to, into*, etc. *(the wood of)*, + בוא *come* 1 S 22_{5}.

<COLL> שֹׁכְנִי לְבָדָד יַעַר *I dwell alone (in) a forest* Mc 7_{14}.*

Also 4QapJoseph^{a} 12_{1}.

⇒ יַעַר III *Jaar.*

יַעַר II $_{1}$ n.m. **honeycomb**—sf. יַעְרִי—<OBJ> אכל *eat* Ca 5_{1}.

⇒ יַעְרָה I *honeycomb.*

יַעַר III 1 pl.n. **Jaar**—יָעַר—prob. ident. with קִרְיַת יְעָרִים *Kiriath-jearim*, mod. Dēr el Azhar, 14 km N of Jerusalem, <CSTR> שְׂדֵי־יָעַר *fields of Jaar* Ps 132$_{6}$. <APP> אֶפְרָתָה *Ephrathah* Ps 132$_{6}$.
→ יַעַר *forest*.

יַעֲרָה I 1 n.f. **honeycomb**—cstr. יַעֲרַת—<CSTR> יַעֲרַת הַדְּבָשׁ *comb of the honey*, i.e. the honeycomb 1 S 14$_{27}$. <PREP> בְּ *in*, + טבל *dip* 1 S 14$_{27}$.
→ יַעַר II *honeycomb*.

[יַעֲרָה] 1 II n.f. **kid**—pl. יְעָרוֹת—חשׂף pi. *bring to premature birth* Ps 29$_{9}$ (unless יַעַר I *forest*).

יַעְרָה 2 pr.n.m. **Jarah**, descendant of Saul, perh. ident. with יְהוֹעַדָּה *Jehoaddah* at 1 C 8$_{36}$, <SUBJ> ילד hi. *be father of* 1 C 9$_{42}$ (mss יַעְדָּה *Jadah*). <OBJ> ילד hi. *be father of* 1 C 9$_{42}$ (mss יַעְדָּה *Jadah*).

יַעֲרֵי אֹרְגִים 1 pr.n.m. **Jaare-oregim**, father of Elhanan who slew Goliath, <CSTR> בֶּן־יַעֲרֵי אֹרְגִים *son of Jaare-oregim* 2 S 21$_{19}$.
→ יַעַר *forest* + ארג *weave*.

יַעֲרֶשְׁיָה 1 pr.n.m. **Jareshiah**, Benjaminite, son of Jeroham (or em. Jeremoth), <NOM CL> יַעֲרֶשְׁיָה וְאֵלִיָּה וְזִכְרִי בְּנֵי יְרֹחָם *Jareshiah and Elijah and Zichri were the sons of Jeroham* 1 C 8$_{27}$.
→ ? + יה *Y*.

[יַעַשׂ] 0.0.0.1 pr.n.m. **Jaas**, Samaria ost. 48$_{3}$, <APP> Ahimelech Samaria ost. 48$_{3}$. <PREP> לְ of benefit, *to*, *for* Samaria ost. 48$_{3}$.
→ עשׂה *do*.

יַעֲשׂוֹ 1 pr.n.m. **Jaasu**—Qr יַעֲשָׂי—member of Bani family, husband of a non-Jewish wife Ezr 10$_{37}$, <NOM CL> מִבְּנֵי בָנִי ... יַעֲשָׂי *of the sons of Bani were ... Jaasu* Ezr 10$_{37(Qr)}$.
→ עשׂה *do*.

יַעֲשִׂיאֵל 2 pr.n.m. **Jaasiel**, **1.** one of David's warriors, <NOM CL> גִּבּוֹרֵי הַחֲיָלִים ... יַעֲשִׂיאֵל הַמְּצֹבָיָה *the warriors of the armies were ... Jaasiel the Mezobaite* 1 C 11$_{47}$. <ADJ> מְּצֹבָיָה *Mezobaite* 1 C 11$_{47}$
2. Benjaminite chief, <NOM CL> לְבִנְיָמִן יַעֲשִׂיאֵל בֶּן־אַבְנֵר *(belonging) to Benjamin was Jaasiel the son of Abner* 1 C 21$_{27}$. → עשׂה *do* + אֵל *God*.

יִפְדְיָה 1 pr.n.m. **Iphdeiah**, Benjaminite, son of Shashak, <NOM CL> יִפְדְיָה וּפְנִיאֵל בְּנֵי שָׁשָׁק *Iphdeiah and Penuel were the sons of Shashak* 1 C 8$_{25}$. → פדה *redeem* + יה *Y*.

יפה 7.5.1 vb. **be beautiful—Qal** 5.4.1 Pf. Q יפה, יָפִית, יָפוּ; + waw וַתִּיפִי, וַיִּיף; ptc. Si יפה, pl. Si יפים—**be beautiful, be befitting,** <SUBJ> Jerusalem Ezk 16$_{13}$, אִשָּׁה *woman* Si 26$_{16}$ ([אִ]שה) 36$_{26(mg)}$, מֶלֶךְ *king* Ps 45$_{2}$ (if em. יָפְיָפִיתָ to יָפִיתָ), אַהֲבָה *love*, i.e. lovely one Ca 7$_{7}$ (|| נעם *be pleasant*), דּוֹד *love* Ca 4$_{10}$, אֶרֶז *cedar* Ezk 31$_{7}$, פַּעַם *foot* Ca 7$_{2}$, דָּבָר *word* Si 35$_{5}$; subj. not specified, Si 14$_{16}$ 4QAges^{a} 2.2$_{2}$.
<PREP> בְּ *in, with*, + גֹּדֶל *greatness* Ezk 31$_{7}$, מְאֹד *excessiveness* Ezk 16$_{13}$, נַעַל *sandal* Ca 7$_{2}$; מִן of comparison, *(more) than*, + בֵּן *son* Ps 45$_{2}$ (if em.; see Subj.).
<COLL> וַתִּיפִי בִּמְאֹד מְאֹד *and you became exceedingly beautiful* Ezk 16$_{13}$.
<SYN> נעם *be pleasant*.
Pi. 1 + waw וַיְיַפֵּהוּ—**decorate, make beautiful,** <SUBJ> subj. not specified, Jr 10$_{4}$ (or em. צפה pi. *overlay*). <OBJ> עֵץ *tree* Jr 10$_{4}$. <PREP> בְּ of instrument, *by (means of), with*, + זָהָב *gold* Jr 10$_{4}$, כֶּסֶף *silver* Jr 10$_{4}$.
Ho. 0.1 Ptc. Si מ[ה]ופין—**be regarded as beautiful,** <SUBJ> דָּבָר *word* Si 13$_{22}$.
Htp. 1 Impf. תִּתְיַפִּי—**make oneself beautiful,** <SUBJ> שָׁדוּד *devastated one* Jr 4$_{30}$. <PREP> לְ of benefit, *to, for*, + שָׁוְא *vanity* Jr 4$_{30}$.
Pealal 1 Pf. יָפְיָפִיתָ—**be fair,** <SUBJ> מֶלֶךְ *king* Ps 45$_{2}$ (or em. יָפִיתָ, i.e. qal). <PREP> מִן of comparison, *(more) than*, + בֵּן *son* Ps 45$_{2}$ (or em. יָפִיתָ, i.e. qal).*
→ יָפֶה *beautiful*, יְפֵה־פִיָּה *handsome*, יָפוֹ *Joppa*, יְפָיָהוּ *Jephaiah*, יְפִי *beauty*, (?) יְפוֹת *harmony*.

[יָפָה], see יְפוֹת *harmony*.

יָפֶה 42.0.4 adj. **fair**—cstr. יְפֵה; fs יָפָה; cstr. יְפַת; sf. יָפָתִי; f.pl. יָפוֹת; cstr. יְפוֹת—**fair,* attractive, beautiful, pleas**

ing, 1. used attributively of אִשָּׁה *woman* Jb 42_{15} Pr 11_{22} 11QT 63_{11}, אָחוֹת *sister* 2 S 13_{1}, נַעֲרָה *girl* 1 K $1_{3.4}$, בְּתוּלָה *young woman* Am 8_{13}, חִטָּה *wheat* Mur 24 2_{16} 3_{15} 4_{15} 5_{11} ([יפות]).

2. used as noun or predicative adj., **fair (one),** <SUBJ> היה *be* Gn 29_{17} $39_{6.6}$ 2 S 14_{27}, ידע *know* Ca 1_{8}, הלך *go* Ca $2_{10.13}$ (both ‖ רַעְיָה *beloved one*), קום *arise* Ca $2_{10.13}$ (both ‖ רַעְיָה), עלה *go up* Gn $41_{2.18}$, שׁקף ni. *look down* Ca 6_{10}.

<NOM CL> הָאִשָּׁה ... יְפַת־תֹּאַר *the woman was ... beautiful in form* 1 S 25_{3}, כֻּלָּךְ יָפָה *all of you is beautiful,* i.e. you are entirely beautiful Ca 4_{7}, יָפָה אַתְּ *you are the* (fem.) *beautiful one* Ca 6_{4}, הִנְּךָ יָפֶה *behold, you are the* (masc.) *beautiful one* Ca 1_{16}, הִנָּךְ יָפָה *behold, you are the* (fem.) *beautiful one* Ca 1_{15} $4_{1.1}$, יָפָה הִיא *she is beautiful* Gn $12_{14(Qr)}$, הַיָּפָה בַּנָּשִׁים *O (most) beautiful among women* Ca 5_{9} 6_{1}. <OBJ> עשׂה *make* Ezk 31_{9}, אכל *eat* Gn 41_{4}.

<CSTR> יְפֵה מַרְאֶה *beautiful of,* i.e. in, *appearance* 1 S 17_{42}, יְפַת־מַרְאֶה *beautiful of,* i.e. in, *appearance* Gn 12_{11} 29_{17} 39_{6} 2 S 14_{27}, יְפוֹת מַרְאֶה *fair ones of appearance* Gn 41_{2}, יְפֹת הַמַּרְאֶה *the fair ones of appearance* Gn 41_{4}, יְפַת־תֹּאַר *beautiful one of form* Gn 29_{17} 39_{6} Dt 21_{11} 1 S 25_{3} Est 2_{7}, יְפֹת תֹּאַר *fair ones of form* Gn 41_{18}, יְפֵה עֵינַיִם *beautiful of eyes*, i.e. with beautiful eyes 1 S 16_{12}, יְפֵה פְרִי־תֹאַר an olive tree, *fair with fine fruit* Jr 11_{16}, יְפֵה עָנָף *fair of branches*, i.e. with fair branches Ezk 31_{3}, יְפֵה נוֹף *fair of height*, i.e. beautiful in height Ps 48_{3}, יְפֵה קוֹל *beautiful of voice*, i.e. with a beautiful voice Ezk 33_{32}.

אִישׁ־יָפֶה *a beautiful man* 2 S 14_{25}, אֵשֶׁת יְפַת־תֹּאַר *a beautiful woman*, lit. a woman beautiful of form Dt 21_{11}.

<APP> אִשָּׁה *woman* Gn 12_{11}, נַעֲרָה *girl* Est 2_{7}, פַּר *young bull* Gn $41_{2.4.18}$, זֹאת *this (one)* Ca 6_{10}.

<PREP> עִם *with* 1 S 16_{12}, + היה *be* 1 S 17_{42}.

<COLL> אֶת־הַכֹּל עָשָׂה יָפֶה בְעִתּוֹ *he has made everything beautiful in its time* Ec 3_{11}, אֲשֶׁר־רָאִיתִי אָנִי טוֹב אֲשֶׁר־יָפֶה לֶאֱכוֹל *that which I have seen is good is that (it is) pleasant to eat* Ec 5_{17}.*

<SYN> רַעְיָה *beloved one.*

⇒ יפה *be beautiful.*

יְפֵה־פִיָּה 1 adj. **handsome**—(mss יְפֵיפִיָּה)—used as attributive adj. of עֶגְלָה *heifer* Jr 46_{20}.

⇒ יפה *be beautiful.*

יָפוֹ 4 pl.n. **Joppa**—יָפוֹא—seaport town of Israel, <APP> יָם *sea* Ezr 3_{7} 2 C 2_{15}. <PREP> אֶל *to*, + בוא hi. *bring* Jon 1_{3}; עַל *to*, + בוא hi. *bring* 2 C 2_{15}; מוּל *opposite* Jos 19_{46}; יָפוֹ (without ה- of direction, *to, towards, etc.*), + ירד *go down* Jon 1_{3}.

⇒ יפה *be beautiful.*

*[**יְפוֹת**] 0.1 **harmony**—pl. Q יפות—perh. דורש בתורה ... על יפות איש לרעהו *explaining the Torah ... in harmony, each to their companion* 1QS 6_{7} (unless על יפות = עֲלִיפוֹת, i.e. חֲלִיפוֹת *in turns*).

⇒ (?) יפה *be beautiful.*

יפח 1 vb. **breathe—Htp.** 1 Impf. תִּתְיַפֵּחַ—**gasp for breath,** <SUBJ> בַּת *daughter* of Zion Jr 4_{31}.

⇒ יָפֵחַ I *breathing out.*

[**יָפֵחַ**] I 1 adj. **breathing out**—cstr. יְפֵחַ—as noun, **one breathing out, puffing out,** <SUBJ> קום *rise* Ps 27_{12} (+ עֵד *witness*). <CSTR> יְפֵחַ חָמָס *one breathing out violence* Ps 27_{12}.

⇒ יפח *breathe.*

*__יָפֵחַ__ II 8 n.m. **witness**—יָפֵחַ; cstr. יְפִיחַ (יָפֵחַ, יְפֵחַ)—(unless יָפִיחַ I *breathing out*, or פוח hi. *blow*) usu. false witness, <SUBJ> מלט ni. *escape* Pr 19_{5}, אבד *die* Pr 19_{9}, קום *arise* against worshipper Ps 27_{12}, נגד hi. *tell*, i.e. speak with, righteousness Pr 12_{17}, כזב pi. *lie* Hb 2_{3}, נצל hi. *rescue* deceit Pr 14_{25}. <NOM CL> יָפִיחַ כְּזָבִים עֵד שָׁקֶר *a false witness is a lying witness* Pr 14_{5}, כִּי עוֹד חָזוֹן לַמּוֹעֵד וְיָפֵחַ לַקֵּץ *for there is still a vision for the appointed time and a witness for the end* Hb 2_{3} (or em. עֵד the vision is *a witness*). <OBJ> שׂנא *hate* Pr 6_{19}. <CSTR> יָפִיחַ כְּזָבִים *witness of lies*, i.e. false witness Pr 6_{19} $14_{5.25}$ $19_{5.9}$ (all five ‖ עֵד *witness*), אֱמוּנָה *of truth* Pr 12_{17} (‖ עֵד), חָמָס *of violence* Ps 27_{12} (יָפֵחַ; or em. וְיָפִיחוּ *and they blow* violence, or וִיפֵחֵי *and witnesses of*; ‖ עֵד).

<SYN> עֵד *witness.*

[**יִפְטָר**] 0.0.0.1 pr.n.m. **Jophtar,** Seal 459_{1} (Gezer).

⇒ פטר *separate.*

יְפִי 19.2.5 n.m. **beauty**—יוֹפִי (יֹפִי)—cstr. יְפִי; sf. יָפְיֵךְ (Q יפך), יָפְיָהּ, יָפְיוֹ, יָפְיֵךְ; pl. Q יפים—<NOM CL> הֶבֶל הַיֹּפִי *beauty is vanity* Pr 31$_{30}$, היפים בשערם *(they) were the handsome ones by their hair* 11QPs^{a} 28$_{10}$, מַה־יָּפְיוֹ *what,* i.e. how great, *is his beauty* Zc 9$_{17}$ (|| טוּב *goodness*)

<OBJ> ראה hi. *show* Est 1$_{11}$, כלל *make complete* Ezk 27$_{4.11}$, תעב pi. *make abomination of* Ezk 16$_{25}$, אוה htp. *desire* Ps 45$_{12}$, חמד *desire* Pr 6$_{25}$.

<CSTR> יְפִי חָכְמָתֶךָ *beauty of your wisdom* Ezk 28$_{7}$, יפי התור *the handsome one of form* 11QPs^{a} 28$_{9}$, יפי המראה *the handsome one of appearance* 11QPs^{a} 28$_{9}$, יפי מראיה *beauty of his appearance* 4Q418 167$_{5}$; כְּלִיל יֹפִי *perfect of,* i.e. in, *beauty* Ezk 28$_{12}$, כְּלִילַת יֹפִי *perfect of beauty* Ezk 27$_{3}$ Lm 2$_{15}$, מִכְלַל־יֹפִי *perfect of beauty* Ps 50$_{2}$.

<PREP> בְּ of instrument, *by (means of), with,* + דמה *be like* Ezk 31$_{8}$, גבה *be exalted* Ezk 28$_{17}$, יצא *go out* Ezk 16$_{14}$; *in, with,* + חזה *see* Is 33$_{17}$, בטח *trust* Ezk 16$_{15}$; אֶל *to,* + נבט hi. *look on* Si 9$_{8}$; עַל *against,* + ריק hi. *draw sword* Ezk 28$_{7}$; תַּחַת *instead of* Is 3$_{24}$.

<SYN> טוּב *goodness.*

Also Si 45$_{12}$ 1QNoah 12$_{1}$.*

⇒ יפה *be beautiful.*

[יְפִיָּהוּ] 0.0.0.1 pr.n.m. **Jephaiah,** Seal 477 (Lachish 8th/7th cent.).*

⇒ יפה *be beautiful* + ״ *Y.*

יָפִיחַ, see יָפֵחַ II *witness.*

יָפִיעַ I 4 pr.n.m. **Japhia, 1.** king of Lachish in time of Joshua Jos 10$_{3}$. **2.** son of David, <SUBJ> ילד ni. *be born* 1 C 3$_{7}$. <APP> שֵׁם *name* 2 S 5$_{15}$||1 C 14$_{6}$, אֵלֶּה *these* 1 C 3$_{7}$. <PREP> אֶל *to,* + שׁלח *send* Jos 10$_{3}$.

⇒ יפע *shine forth.*

יָפִיעַ II 1 pl.n. **Japhia,** on border of Zebulun Jos 19$_{12}$, <PREP> יָפִיעַ (without ה- of direction, *to, towards, etc.*), + עלה *go up* Jos 19$_{12}$.

⇒ יפע *shine forth.*

יְפֵיפִיָּה, see יְפֵה־פִיָּה *handsome.*

יַפְלֵט 3 pr.n.m. **Japhlet,** Asherite, son of Heber, <OBJ> ילד hi. *be father of* 1 C 7$_{32}$. <CSTR> בְּנֵי יַפְלֵט *sons of Japhlet* 1 C 7$_{33.33}$.

⇒ פלט *escape;* יַפְלֵטִי *Japhletite.*

יַפְלֵטִי 1 gent. **Japhletite**—הַיַּפְלֵטִי—as collective, **Japhletites,** <CSTR> גְּבוּל הַיַּפְלֵטִי *boundary of the Japhletites* Jos 16$_{3}$.

⇒ יַפְלֵט *Japhlet.*

יְפֻנֶּה 16.1 pr.n.m. **Jephunneh, 1.** Judahite, father of Caleb, <CSTR> בֶּן־יְפֻנֶּה *son of Jephunneh* Nm 13$_{6}$ 14$_{6.30.38}$ 26$_{65}$ 32$_{12}$ 34$_{19}$ Dt 1$_{36}$ Jos 14$_{6.13.14}$ 15$_{13}$ 21$_{12}$ 1 C 4$_{15}$ 6$_{41}$ Si 46$_{7}$.

2. Asherite, son of Jether, <NOM CL> בְּנֵי יֶתֶר יְפֻנֶּה *the sons of Jether were Jephunneh* 1 C 7$_{38}$.

⇒ פנה *turn.*

יפע 8.2.32 vb. **shine forth—Hi.** 8.2.32 Pf. הוֹפִיעַ (Q הופע), הוֹפַעְתָּ (Q הופעתה), Q הופיעו; impf. Si יופיע (Q יפיע), 3fs תּוֹפַע (Q תופיע), Q יפיעו; + waw Q והופעתי; וַתּוֹפַע, Q ותופע; impv. הוֹפִיעָה, Q הופיעי; ptc. Si מופיע; inf. Q הופע (Q הופיע, אופיע)—**shine forth, rise, appear in radiance, appear, reveal oneself** (Si 12$_{15}$), **announce** (1QH 18$_{6}$), <SUBJ> ״ *Y.* Dt 33$_{2}$ (|| זרח *shine*) Ps 94$_{1}$, אֱלֹהִים *God* Ps 50$_{2}$, אֱלוֹהַּ *God* Jb 10$_{3}$ 37$_{15}$, אֵל *God* Ps 94$_{1}$ 1QH 4$_{23}$ 9$_{31}$, אֲדֹנָי *Lord* 1QH 4$_{6}$, כָּבוֹד *glory* of God 4QShir^{b} 1$_{7}$ CD 20$_{25}$, Belial 1QH 7$_{3}$, אִישׁ *man* of arrogance Si 12$_{15}$, כֹּהֵן *priest* 1QpHab 11$_{7}$, worshipper 1QH 7$_{24}$, ישׁב ptc. *one who sits* Ps 80$_{2}$.

Jerusalem 1QM 12$_{13}$, שֶׁמֶשׁ *sun* Si 43$_{2(M)}$, אוֹר *light* 1QH 9$_{26}$, נְהָרָה *bright light* Jb 3$_{4}$, מָאוֹר *luminary* 1QS 10$_{2}$, יוֹם *day* 1QM 18$_{10}$, יֵצֶר *inclination* 1QH 5$_{32}$, מַעֲשֶׂה *deed* CD 20$_{3.6}$, אֱמֶת *truth* 1QH 11$_{26}$; subj. not specified, Jb 10$_{22}$ 1QM 1$_{16}$ 1QH 18$_{6}$ 1Q36.14$_{4}$ ([הופי]ע) 4QParaKings 49$_{6}$ 4QConfess 1.2$_{6}$ 4Q408 1$_{5.8.10}$ 4QsapHymn 1.2$_{14}$ 4Q418 130$_{1}$ 200$_{2}$ 4QHod^{a} 7.2$_{2.3.10}$ 4QHod^{b} 8.1$_{3}$ 4QapMes 4$_{5}$.

<OBJ> אוֹר *light* Jb 37$_{15}$ 4QHod^{a} 7.2$_{2}$, פְּאֵר *crown* 4Q 408 1$_{5}$, מֶמְשָׁלָה, *dominion* 4Q408 1$_{8.10}$, גְּבוּרָה *might* 4QHod^{a} 7.2$_{10}$, יֵצֶר *inclination* 1QH 7$_{3}$, אֱמֶת *truth* 4QHod^{b} 8.1$_{3}$, שָׁלוֹם *peace* 4QHod^{a} 7.2$_{3}$, שְׁמוּעָה *report* 1QH 18$_{6}$ ([ש]מועות).

<PREP> לְ of direction, *to,* + Israel CD 20$_{25}$; of benefit,

to, for, + worshipper 1QM 18_{10} 1QH $4_{6.23}$ 5_{32}; *as*, + אוֹרָה *light* 1QH $4_{6.23}$, מָרֹר *bitterness* 1QH 5_{32}; *in*, + כָּבוֹד *glory* 1QH 11_{26} 4QHod^{b} 8.1_{3}; introducing object, + worshipper 1QH 9_{31}.

בְּ of instrument, *by (means of)*, + כֹּחַ *strength* 1QH 4_{23}; of accompaniment, *with, in*, + עֶזְרָה *help* 1QM 1_{16}, רִנָּה *joy* 1QM 12_{13}; *in*, + אוֹר *light* 1QH 7_{24}, כָּבוֹד *glory* 1QH 9_{26}, שֶׂכֶל *insight* 1QH 9_{31}, אֹמֶר *word* 4QShir^{b} 1_{7}.

מִן of direction, *from*, + Zion Ps 50_{2}, הַר *mountain* Dt 33_{2}, זְבֻל *dwelling place* 1QS 10_{2}, נְעוּרִים *youth* 1QH 9_{31}; אֶל *to* 1QpHab 11_{7}; עַל *upon*, + יוֹם *day* Jb 3_{4}, עֵצָה *counsel* Jb 10_{3}; בְּקֶרֶב *among*, + worshipper 4QConfess 1.2_{6}.

<COLL> תופיע תבל *you will shine out on the world* 4Q 418 130_{1}.

<SYN> זרח *shine*.

Also 1Q36.14_{4}.*

⇒ יִפְעָה *brightness*, יָפִיעַ *Japhia*, מֵיפַעַת *Mephaath*.

[יִפְעָה] I 2 n.f. **splendour**—sf. יִפְעָתֶךָ—<OBJ> חלל pi. *profane* Ezk 28_{7} (unless יִפְעָה II *arrogance*). <PREP> עַל perh. *for the sake of*, + שחת pi. *ruin* wisdom Ezk 28_{17}.*

⇒ יפע *shine forth*.

[יִפְעָה] II 2 n.f. **arrogance***—sf. יִפְעָתֶךָ—<OBJ> חלל pi. *profane* Ezk 28_{7} (unless יִפְעָה I *splendour*). <PREP> עַל perh. *for the sake of*, + שחת pi. *ruin* wisdom Ezk 28_{17}.

[יָפְקַד] 0.0.0.1 pr.n.m. **Jophkad**—Seal 459_{1} (Gezer).

⇒ פקד *appoint*.

יפר* 1 vb. **be many—Hi.** 1 **esteem,** אוֹקִיר אֱנוֹשׁ מִפָּז וְאָדָם מִכֶּתֶם אוֹפִיר *I shall value a mortal more than gold and a human being I shall esteem more than fine gold* Is 13_{12} (unless אוֹפִיר = *Ophir*).

[יִפְרַעְיוֹ] 0.0.0.1 pr.n.[m.] **Iphraio,** <PREP> לְ of possession, *of, (belonging) to* Seal 177 (Samaria, 8th cent.).

⇒ פרע *let loose* + יו *Y*.

יֶפֶת 11.0.2 pr.n.m. **Japheth**—יָפֶת—third son of Noah, <SUBJ> ראה *see* Gn 9_{23}, שׁכן *dwell* Gn 9_{27}, בוא *come* Gn 7_{13}, הלך *go* Gn 9_{23}, יצא *go out* Gn 9_{18}, לקח *take* Gn 9_{23}, שׂים *place* Gn 9_{23}, כסה pi. *cover* Gn 9_{23}.

<NOM CL> בְּנֵי נֹחַ שֵׁם חָם וָיָפֶת *the sons of Noah were Shem, Ham and Japheth* 1 C 1_{4} (if ins. בְּנֵי), וְאֵלֶּה תּוֹלְדֹת בְּנֵי־נֹחַ שֵׁם חָם וָיָפֶת *and these are the generations of the sons of Noah: Shem, Ham and Japheth* Gn 10_{1}. <OBJ> ילד hi. *be father of* Gn 5_{32} 6_{10}. <CSTR> בְּנֵי יֶפֶת *sons of Japhet* Gn 10_{2}‖1 C 1_{5} 4QM^{f} 14_{4}, אֲחִי יֶפֶת *brother of Japhet* Gn 10_{21}. <APP> בֵּן *son* Gn 7_{13} 9_{18}. <PREP> לְ of benefit, *to, for*, + היה *be* Gn 9_{27}, ילד ni. *be born* Gn 10_{1}, פתה hi. *provide ample room* Gn 9_{27}.

Also 4QNarrC 1_{2}.

⇒ (?) פתה *be simple*.

יִפְתָּח I 29 pr.n.m. **Jephthah,** Gileadite, judge in Israel, <SUBJ> היה *be* Jg $11_{1.6.8.9}$ 12_{2}, ישׁב *dwell* Jg 11_{3}, קבר ni. *be buried* Jg 12_{7}, בוא *come* Jg 11_{34}, הלך *go* Jg $11_{6.8.11}$, עבר *pass by* Jg $11_{29.29.29.32}$ 12_{1}, ברח *flee* Jg 11_{3}, קבץ *gather* Jg 12_{4}, שׁוב hi. *bring back*, i.e. restore Jg 11_{13}, נחל *receive inheritance* Jg 11_{2}.

יסף hi. *do again* Jg 11_{14}, שׁלח *send* Jg $11_{12.14.28}$, לחם ni. *fight* Jg $11_{8.9.32}$ $12_{1.4}$, נכה hi. *strike* Jg 12_{4}, מות *die* Jg 12_{7}, זעק *cry* Jg 12_{2}, קרא *call* Jg 12_{1}, אמר *say* Jg $11_{7.9.15.30}$ 12_{2}, דבר pi. *speak* Jg 11_{11}, נדר *make vow* Jg 11_{30}, שׁפט *judge* Jg 12_{7}.

<OBJ> ילד hi. *become father of* Jg 11_{1}, קרא *meet* Jg 11_{34}, שׁוב hi. *bring back* Jg 11_{9}, לקח *take* Jg 11_{5}, שׂים *place* Jg 11_{11}, שׁלח *send* 1 S 12_{11}, ישׁע hi. *save* Jg 12_{2}, גרשׁ pi. *drive out* Jg $11_{2.7}$, שׂנא *hate* Jg 11_{7}.

<CSTR> בַּת יִפְתָּח *daughter of Jephthah* Jg 11_{40}, מַלְאֲכֵי יִפְתָּח *messengers of Jephthah* Jg 11_{13}, דִּבְרֵי יִפְתָּח *words of Jephthah* Jg 11_{28}. <ADJ> גִּלְעָדִי *Gileadite* Jg $11_{1.40}$ 12_{7}. <PREP> לְ of direction, *to*, + אמר *say* Jg $11_{2.6}$ 12_{1}; אֶל *to*, + בוא *come* Jg $11_{7.12}$, שׁוב *go back* Jg 11_{8}, לקט htp. *gather around* Jg 11_{3}, אמר *say* Jg $11_{8.10}$; עַל *upon*, + היה *be* Jg 11_{29}, שׂרף *burn* Jg 12_{1}; לִפְנֵי *before*, + נתן *give* Jg 11_{9}; עִם *with*, + הלך *go* Jg 12_{1}, יצא *go out* Jg 11_{3}.

⇒ פתח *open*.

יִפְתָּח II 1 pl.n. **Iphtah,** in lowland of Judah Jos 15_{43}, <NOM CL> בַּשְּׁפֵלָה ... יִפְתָּח *in the lowland was ... Iphtah* Jos 15_{43}. <APP> עִיר *city* Jos 15_{43}.

⇒ פתח *open*.

יִפְתַּח־אֵל, see גֵּי יִפְתַּח־אֵל *Ge-Iphtahel.*

יצא 1067.20.156.1 vb. **go out.**

Qal 785.14.120 Pf. יָצָא, יָצְאָה (יָצָאָה), יָצָאתָ, יָצָאתִי (Kt יצתי [Job 1_{21}]), יָצְאוּ (יָצָאוּ, יָצָאנִי), יְצָאתֶם, יָצָאנוּ; impf. יֵצֵא (Si יצאך), 3fs תֵּצֵא, 2ms תֵּצֵא, תֵּצְאִי, אֵצֵא (אֵצְאָה), יֵצְאוּ (יֵצֵאוּ), 3fpl תֵּצֶאנָה, תֵּצְאוּ (תֵּצֵאוּ), נֵצֵא; + waw וַיָּצָא, וַיֵּצְאָה, וַיָּצָאתָ, וַיָּצָאת, וַיֵּצְאוּ, וִיצָאתֶם, וִיצָאנוּ; וַיֵּצֵא, 3fs וַתֵּצֵא, וָאֵצֵא (וָאֵצְאָה), וַיֵּצְאוּ (וַיֵּצֵאוּ), 3fpl וַתֵּצֶאנָה (וַתֵּצֶאןָ); impv. צֵא (צְאָה), צְאִי, צְאוּ (צֵאוּ), צֶאנָה; ptc. יֹצֵא (יוֹצֵא), יֹצֵאת (יוֹצֵאת, יֹצָא), יֹצְאִים (יוֹצְאִים), יֹצְאֵי (יוֹצְאֵי), יֹצְאוֹת (יוֹצְאוֹת, יֹצְאֹת); inf. abs. יָצֹא (יָצוֹא); cstr. צֵאת (צֵאתִי, צֵאתְךָ, צֵאתֵךְ, צֵאתֵךְ, צֵאתוֹ, צֵאתֵנוּ, צֵאתְכֶם, צֵאתָם, Q צאתמה).

1. intransitive, go out, come out, set out, leave, depart, march (into battle); of river, **flow** (Gn 2_{10}), of sun, **rise** (Gn 19_{23} Jg 5_{31}), of peoples, **be descended** (e.g. 1 C 2_{53}), of land sold, **be returned** (e.g. Lv 25_{28}), of money, **be spent** (e.g. 2 K 12_{13}), of prisoner, **surrender** (e.g. 2 K 24_{12}), of lot, **fall** (e.g. Nm 33_{54} Jos 16_1), of foetus, **come out early, abort** (Ex 21_{22} Ps 144_{14}), of intestines, **drop, prolapse** (2 C $21_{15.19}$), **protrude** (e.g. Ne 3_{25} 11QT 41_{12}); perh. **fulfil duty** (Ec 7_{18}), perh. **depart** life, **die*** (Si 30_{40}), of metal, **flow** from crucible (Ex 32_{24} Jb 23_{10} Pr 25_4 [unless יצא II *shine*]).*

2. transitive, **go out from, leave** (Gn 44_4 Ex $9_{29.33}$ Nm 35_{26} Dt 14_{22} 2 K 20_4 Si 6_{35}).

<SUBJ> Y. Ex 11_4 Jg 4_{14} 5_4 2 S 5_{24} Is 26_{21} 42_{13} Mc 1_3 Hb 3_{13} Zc 14_3 Ps 44_{10} 60_{12} 68_8 108_{12} 1 C 14_{15}, Belial 1QM 1_4, כְּרוּב *cherub* Ezk 10_{19}, מַלְאָךְ *angel* Nm 22_{32} 2 K 19_{35} ||Is 37_{36} Zc $2_{7.7}$ 5_5 4QShirShabb[f] 20.2_9, *messenger* Ezk 30_9, שָׂטָן *adversary* Jb 1_{12} 2_7.

Aaron Ex 4_{14} 8_8 12_{31} 28_{35} Lv 8_{33} 9_{23} 10_7 $16_{17.18.24}$ Nm $12_{4.4.5}$ (or em. בוא *come*) 4QapMos[a] 1.2_8 (… ואה[רון] [וי]צא), Abimelech Jg 9_{29}, Abiram Nm 16_{27}, Abner 2 S 2_{12}, Abra(ha)m Gn 11_{31} (or em. וַיֵּצְאוּ *and they went out* to וַיֵּצֵא *and* Terah *went out*, or hi.) $12_{4.5}$ 24_5 4QCommGenA $2_{10.13}$ ([אב]רם), Ahaziah 2 K $9_{21.21}$ 2 C 22_7, Araunah 2 S 24_{20}, Asa 2 C 14_9, Asshur Gn 10_{11}, Asher 4QJub[h] 38_6 ([יצאו]), Azariah 2 C 15_2, Balak Nm 22_{36}, Benaiah 1 K 2_{46}, Ben-hadad 1 K $20_{31.33}$, Benjamin 4QJub[h] 38_8 ([ויצא … בנימי]ן), Cain Gn 4_{16}, Dan 4QJub[h] 38_6 ([יצאו]), Dathan Nm 16_{27}, David 1 S $17_{35.55}$ $18_{5.13}$ 19_8 $20_{11.11}$ 21_6 23_{13} 24_9 28_1 29_6 2 S 13_{39} (or ins. נֶפֶשׁ *soul* of David) 18_3 $19_{8.8}$ 2 S 21_{17} 1 C 12_{18} $14_{8.15}$ 4QDescDavid 1_5, Dinah Gn 34_1, Ebed-melech Jr 38_8, Ehud Jg $3_{23.24}$, Eldad Nm 11_{26}, Eleazar Lv 10_7 Nm 31_{13}, Eliakim 2 K 18_{18}||Is 36_3, Elijah 1 K $19_{11.13}$, Elisha 2 K 2_{21} 5_{11}, Enoch 4QJub[h] 38_8 (… ויצא] [חנוך]), Ezekiel Ezk $3_{22.23.25}$, Gaal Jg $9_{27.33.35.38.39}$, Gad 4QJub[h] 38_5 ([ויצאו]), Gehazi 2 K 5_{27}, Haman Est 5_9, Hamor Gn 34_6, Hananiah Arad ost. 16_3, Hathach Est 4_6, Hezekiah 2 K 18_7, Hiram 1 K 9_{12}.

Isaac Gn 24_{63} 4QJub[d] 21_{26}, Isaiah 2 K 20_4 (or del. יָצָא) Is 7_3, Ishmael Jr 41_6, Issachar 4QJub[h] 38_7 ([יששכר]), Ithamar Lv 10_7, Jacob Gn 27_{30} 28_{10} 31_{13} 47_{10} Mc 2_{13} (people), Jael Jg $4_{18.22}$, Jehu 2 K 9_{11} 10_9, Jeconiah Jr 29_2, Jehoiachin 2 K 24_{12}, Jehoshaphat 2 C 19_4 $20_{20.20}$, Jehu 2 C 19_2, Jeremiah Jr 1_5 14_{18} 19_2 20_{18} $37_{4.12}$, Jeroboam 1 K 11_{29} 12_{25}, Joab 2 S 2_{13} 3_{26} 20_8 $24_{4.7}$ 1 K 2_{30} 1 C 21_4, Joah 2 K 18_{18}||Is 36_3, Job Jb 1_{21} 3_{11} 23_{10} 29_7 31_{34}, Jonah Jon 4_5, Jonathan 1 S 19_3 $20_{11.11.35}$, Joram 2 K $9_{21.21}$, Joseph Gn $39_{12.15}$ (mss lack וַיֵּצֵא) $41_{45.46}$ 43_{31} Ps 81_6, Joshua Ex 17_9 Nm 27_{21} Jos 14_{11}, Josiah 2 C 35_{20}, Judah 4QJub[h] 38_5 ([ויצאו יהודה]), Laban Gn 31_{33}, Leah Gn 30_{16}, Levi Gn 34_{26} 4QJub[h] 38_6 ([לוי … [יצאו]), Lot Gn 11_{31} (or em.; see Abraham) 12_5 $19_{6.14}$, Medad Nm 11_{26}, Michal 2 S 6_{20}, Miriam Nm $12_{4.4.5}$ (or em. בוא *come*), Mordecai Est 4_1 8_{15}, Moses Ex $2_{11.13}$ $8_{8.25.26}$ $9_{29.33}$ $10_{6.18}$ $11_{8.8.8}$ 12_{31} 18_7 33_8 $34_{18.34.34}$ Lv 9_{23} Nm 11_{24} $12_{4.4}$ 31_{13} Dt 4_{46} 31_2.

Naphtali 4QJub[h] 38_5 ([ויצאו]), Nebuchadrezzar Jr 43_{12}, Nehemiah Ne 2_{13}, Noah Gn $8_{16.18}$ 4QCommGenA 2_2 4QCommGenD 3_2, Oded 2 C 28_9, Og Nm 21_{33} Dt 3_1

29$_{6}$, Ornan 1 C 21$_{21}$, Othniel Jg 3$_{10}$, Rebekah Gn 24$_{15.45}$, Reuben 4QJub^{h} 38$_{7}$, Ruth Ru 2$_{22}$, Samson Jg 16$_{20}$, Samuel 1 S 9$_{14.26}$, Sarai Gn 11$_{31}$ (or em.; see under Abraham) 12$_{5}$, Saul 1 S 9$_{26}$ 13$_{10}$ 23$_{13.15}$, Sennacherib 2 K 19$_{27}$ ||Is 37$_{28}$, Shallum Jr 22$_{11}$, Shebna 2 K 18$_{18}$||Is 36$_{3}$, Shimei 1 K 2$_{36.37.42}$, Sihon Nm 21$_{23}$ Dt 2$_{32}$ 29$_{6}$, Simeon, son of Jacob Gn 34$_{26}$ 4QJub^{h} 38$_{8}$ ([ויצא שמעון]), Simeon, son of Johanan Si 50$_{5}$, Solomon 1 K 3$_{7}$ 2 C 1$_{10}$, Terah Gn 11$_{31}$ 4QCommGenA 2$_{8}$, Tirhakah 2 K 19$_{9}$||Is 37$_{9}$, Uriah 2 S 11$_{8.13}$, Uzziah 2 C 26$_{6.18.20}$, Zebulun Dt 33$_{18}$ 4QJub^{h} 38$_{7}$ ([זבולון]), Zedekiah Jr 38$_{17.18.21}$ 39$_{4.4}$, Zerah 2 C 14$_{8}$.

Amorite Dt 1$_{44}$, Aramaean 2 K 5$_{2}$ 7$_{12}$, Benjaminite Jg 20$_{25}$, Caphtorite Dt 2$_{23}$, Cherethite 2 S 20$_{7.7}$, Edom Nm 20$_{18.20}$, Eshtaolite 1 C 2$_{53}$, Hebrew Dt 15$_{16}$ 1 S 14$_{11}$, Hivite Jos 9$_{12}$, Jerusalem 2 C 20$_{17}$, Judah 2 C 20$_{17.20.20}$, Moab Jr 48$_{9}$ (or em. נָצֹא תֵצֵא *it will go flying away* to נָצֹה תִצֶּה *it will indeed be ruined*), Pelethite 2 S 20$_{7.7}$, Philistine Gn 10$_{14}$ 1 C 1$_{12}$, Shunamite 2 K 4$_{37}$, Zorathite 1 C 2$_{53}$, Chemosh Jr 48$_{7}$, Israel(ites) Ex 15$_{22}$ (Sam hi.) 23$_{15}$ Dt 9$_{7}$ 11$_{10}$ 16$_{3.3.6}$ 20$_{1}$=11QT 61$_{13}$ Dt 21$_{10}$=11QT 63$_{10}$ Dt 23$_{5.10}$ 24$_{9}$ 25$_{17}$ Jos 2$_{10}$ Jg 2$_{15}$ 1 S 4$_{1}$ 2 K 7$_{12}$ 13$_{5}$ Is 48$_{20}$ 55$_{12}$ Mc 7$_{15}$ Ps 105$_{38}$ 114$_{1}$ 121$_{8}$ 2 C 31$_{1}$ 4QapPent 2$_{10}$ 11QT 46$_{13}$, worshipper Ps 88$_{9}$.

אָדָם *human being* Ps 104$_{23}$ Jb 14$_{2}$ perh. Si 16$_{14}$, אֱנוֹשׁ *person* Si 14$_{22}$, אִישׁ *man* Gn 44$_{4}$ Ex 12$_{22}$ 16$_{29}$ Nm 27$_{17}$ 30$_{3}$ 31$_{28}$ Dt 13$_{14}$=11QT 55$_{3}$ Dt 23$_{11.13}$ 24$_{5}$ Jos 2$_{5}$ 5$_{4.6}$ 8$_{14.17}$ Jg 1$_{24}$ 11$_{3}$ 19$_{23.27}$ 20$_{20}$ 1 S 7$_{11}$ 11$_{10}$ 17$_{4}$ 23$_{13}$ 28$_{1}$ 30$_{21}$ 2 S 11$_{17.23}$ 13$_{9}$ 16$_{5.5.7.7}$ 20$_{7.7}$ 1 K 20$_{17.18.18}$ 2 K 10$_{25}$ 18$_{31}$||Is 36$_{16}$ 39$_{4}$ 52$_{7}$ Ezk 9$_{7.7}$ 47$_{3}$ Dn 9$_{22}$ 1QM 2$_{8.8}$ 3$_{1.7}$ 7$_{3.16}$ perh. 7$_{17}$ 9$_{3}$ 16$_{4}$ ([י]צאו]) 1QS 7$_{23}$ 9$_{9}$ 4QD^{e} 7.1$_{11}$ ([האיש]) 4QM^{c} 1$_{6}$ ([אנ]שי]) 11QT 58$_{16}$ CD 11$_{10.11}$, זָכָר *male* Jos 5$_{4}$, גֶּבֶר *man* Lm 3$_{7}$, אִשָּׁה *woman* Gn 8$_{16.18}$ 12$_{5}$ Ex 15$_{20}$ 21$_{3}$ Dt 24$_{2}$ 1 S 18$_{6}$ 2 K 8$_{3}$ Am 4$_{3}$ Zc 5$_{9}$ Pr 7$_{15}$ Ru 1$_{7}$, אָב *father* 1 S 22$_{3}$ 2 K 21$_{15}$ Jr 7$_{25}$, אֵם *mother* 1 S 22$_{3}$ 2 K 4$_{21}$ 24$_{12}$.

בֵּן *son* Gn 8$_{16.18}$ 9$_{18}$ 11$_{31}$ 12$_{5}$ 27$_{3}$ 42$_{15}$ Lv 8$_{33}$ 24$_{10}$ 25$_{41.54}$ Dt 13$_{14}$=11QT 55$_{3}$ Jg 8$_{30}$ 9$_{26}$ 2 S 10$_{8}$||1 C 19$_{9}$ (of Ammon) 2 S 16$_{11}$ 1 K 2$_{46}$ 1 K 8$_{19}$||2 C 6$_{9}$ 2 K 2$_{3}$ 18$_{18.18}$||Is 36$_{3.3}$ 2 K 20$_{18}$||Is 39$_{7}$ Jr 22$_{11}$ 41$_{6}$ Ezk 44$_{19}$ 5QRègle 2$_{8}$ ([בני]), specif. son of Israel Ex 12$_{31}$ 14$_{8}$ 19$_{1}$ Nm 1$_{1}$ 9$_{1}$ 26$_{4}$ 27$_{21}$ 33$_{1.3.38}$ Dt 4$_{45.46}$ 20$_{1.28}$ 21$_{24}$ 1 K 6$_{1}$ 8$_{9}$||2 C 5$_{10}$ 20$_{16}$ Jr 10$_{20}$ Ne 8$_{15}$ 1QDM 1$_{1}$ ([צ]את בני י]שר[אל]) 2$_{6}$ ([צ]את[נו]) 4QJub^{a} 1.1$_{1}$ ([בנ]י ישראל]), of Benjamin Jg 20$_{14.21.31}$ 21$_{21}$, of human being Si 40$_{1}$, of animal Jb 39$_{4}$, of worthlessness Dt 13$_{14}$, בַּת *daughter* Gn 24$_{13}$ Ex 21$_{7.11}$ Jg 11$_{34}$ 21$_{21}$ Mc 4$_{10}$ Ca 3$_{11}$, אָח *brother* Gn 25$_{26}$ 38$_{29.30}$ 42$_{15}$ Lv 25$_{41.54}$ Dt 15$_{16}$ Jg 9$_{27}$ Jr 29$_{16}$ 11QPs^{a} 28$_{9}$, חָתָן *son-in-law* Gn 19$_{14}$ Jl 2$_{16}$ Ps 19$_{6}$, כַּלָּה *daughter-in-law* Gn 11$_{31}$ Jl 2$_{16}$, עַלְמָה *young woman* Gn 24$_{43}$, בְּתוּלָה *young woman* Jr 31$_{4}$, נַעֲרָה *girl* 1 S 9$_{11}$, נַעַר *boy* 1 K 20$_{17}$ 2 K 2$_{23}$, יֶלֶד *male child* Ex 21$_{22}$ 2 K 4$_{18}$ Ec 4$_{14}$, וָלָד *foetus* Ex 21$_{22(Sam)}$, דּוֹד *beloved* Ca 7$_{12}$, אַהֲבָה *beloved one* Ca 7$_{12}$ (if em. אַהֲבָה *love*), יָפֶה *beautiful one* Ca 1$_{8}$, צַדִּיק *righteous one* Pr 12$_{13}$, perh. עָנִי *poor one* Jb 24$_{5}$, ירא ptc. *one who fears* Ml 3$_{20}$ Ec 7$_{18}$, בקשׁ pi. ptc. *one who seeks* Ex 33$_{7}$, יֹשֵׁב *inhabitant* Ezk 15$_{7}$ 39$_{9}$ Mc 1$_{11}$ 2 C 20$_{20.20}$, לבשׁ pass. ptc. *one who is clothed* Ezk 10$_{7}$, perh. רָשָׁע *wicked one* Ps 109$_{7}$, אהב ptc. *one who loves* money Ec 5$_{14}$, מֵת *dead one* Nm 12$_{12}$ 11QT 49$_{14}$.

מֶלֶךְ *king* Gn 14$_{8.17}$ 17$_{6}$ 35$_{11}$ Jos 8$_{14}$ 11$_{4}$ 1 S 8$_{20}$ 24$_{15}$ 26$_{20}$ 2 S 11$_{1(Qr)}$ 15$_{16.17}$ 18$_{2}$ 19$_{20}$ 1 K 20$_{21}$ 2 K 3$_{6}$ 9$_{21.21}$ 11$_{8}$ 19$_{9.27}$||Is 37$_{9.28}$ 2 K 24$_{7.12}$ Jr 17$_{19}$ 22$_{11}$ 29$_{2}$ 39$_{4}$ Dn 11$_{11.44}$ 1 C 20$_{1}$ 2 C 23$_{7}$ 11QT 58$_{15.18.19.20.21}$, שַׂר *prince* 1 S 18$_{30.30}$ 2 S 24$_{4.7}$ 2 K 24$_{12}$ Jr 29$_{2}$ 1QSa 1$_{17(erased)}$ (שרי ... [לצאת]) 4QM^{a} 1$_{9}$ ([י]צאו]), נָשִׂיא *prince* Nm 31$_{13}$ Ezk 44$_{3}$ 46$_{2.8.10.12.12}$, פַּרְעֹה *Pharaoh* Ex 7$_{15}$ 8$_{16}$, גְּבִירָה *queen mother* Jr 29$_{2}$, מֹשֵׁל *ruler* Jr 30$_{21}$, נֹגֵשׂ *ruler* Zc 10$_{4}$ (or del.), אָדוֹן *lord* Jg 19$_{27}$ 2 S 19$_{20}$ Dn 10$_{20}$, בַּעַל *lord* Jg 9$_{27}$ 19$_{23}$, ראשׁ *head* 1QM 9$_{11}$ 1QSa 1$_{17(mg)}$ (רשי ... [לצאת]).

כֹּהֵן *priest* Lv 14$_{3.38}$ 21$_{12}$ Nm 31$_{13}$ 1 K 8$_{10}$ Ezk 42$_{14}$ 44$_{19}$ 2 C 5$_{11}$ 24$_{5}$ 1QM 7$_{9.13}$ 1Q29 2$_{4}$ ([הכו]הן]) 4QM^{a} 1$_{9}$ ([י]צאו ... ה[כוהנ]ים]) 4QM^{c} 1$_{4}$, לֵוִי *Levite* Ezk 44$_{19}$ 2 C 24$_{5}$ 1QM 7$_{14}$ 4QM^{a} 1$_{9}$ ([י]צאו]), מְשֹׁרֵר *singer* 2 C 20$_{21}$, הלל pi. ptc. *one who praises* 2 C 20$_{21}$, שֹׁטֵר *overseer* Ex 5$_{10}$ (or em. יצא to אוץ *urge*) 5$_{20}$, נֹגֵשׂ *taskmaster* Ex 5$_{10}$, מַשְׂכִּיל *instructor* 1QS 10$_{13}$, סֹפֵר *scribe* 2 K 18$_{18}$||Is 36$_{3}$, מַזְכִּיר *recorder* 2 K 18$_{18}$||Is 36$_{3}$, זָקֵן *elder* Dt 21$_{2}$ 1 S 11$_{3}$, שֹׁפֵט *judge* Dt 21$_{2}$, מְשָׁרֵת *servant* 2 K 6$_{15}$, שׁאב ptc. *one who draws (water)* Gn 24$_{11}$, רָץ *runner* Est 3$_{15}$ 8$_{14}$, עמד ptc. *one who stands* Jg 3$_{19}$, סָרִיס *eunuch* 2 K 24$_{12}$ Jr 29$_{2}$, חָרָשׁ *artisan* Jr 29$_{2}$, מַסְגֵּר *smith* Jr 29$_{2}$, עֶבֶד *servant* Gn 42$_{15}$ Ex 21$_{2.3.4.5.7}$ 2 S 2$_{12.13}$ 1 K 20$_{31.39}$ 2 K 24$_{12}$ Si 30$_{40}$, נשׂא *one who raises*, i.e. carries, Y.'s vessels Is 52$_{11.11.12}$.

אָסוּר *prisoner* Is 49$_{9}$, רֹדֵף *pursuer* Jos 2$_{7}$, פָּלִיט *survivor* 2 K 9$_{15}$, פְּלֵיטָה *survivor* 2 K 19$_{31}$||Is 37$_{32}$, חשׁב *planner* Na 1$_{11}$, חרב hi. ptc. *one who lays waste* Is 49$_{17}$, רֹצֵחַ *killer*

Nm 35$_{26}$, מַשְׁחִית *destroyer* 1 S 13$_{17}$ Jr 4$_{7}$, אוֹיֵב *enemy* Dt 28$_{7}$ Ps 41$_{7}$ (ms lacks יצא), גִּבּוֹר *warrior* 2 S 20$_{7.7}$ Jr 46$_{9}$ 11QT 58$_{16}$, פָּרָשׁ *rider* 1QM 6$_{9.11}$, בוא ptc. *one who comes*, i.e. member of camp CD 13$_{4}$, בחר pass. ptc. *chosen one* 2 C 25$_{5}$, perh. שׁוב *one who turns*, i.e. convert CD 4$_{3}$ 6$_{5}$, שׁלח htp. ptc. *one who is expelled* 4QD^{a} 11$_{14}$, חזק hi. ptc. *one who holds* CD 20$_{27}$ (ל[צ]את), תפשׂ ptc. *one who seizes*, i.e. joins, battle Nm 31$_{27}$, הרס pi. ptc. *one who overthrows* Is 49$_{17}$.

זֶרַע *seed* Gn 15$_{14}$ 2 S 7$_{12}$, בָּשָׂר all *flesh* Is 66$_{24}$, עַם *people* Ex 11$_{8}$ 13$_{3.4.8}$ 16$_{4}$ 34$_{18}$ Nm 11$_{20}$ 21$_{33}$ 22$_{5.11}$ Dt 23$_{2}$ 3$_{1}$ 28$_{6.19.25}$ Jos 5$_{4.4.5.5}$ 8$_{5.6}$ 11$_{4}$ Jg 9$_{33.42.43}$ 1 S 11$_{7}$ 14$_{41}$ 2 S 15$_{17}$ 18$_{4.6}$ 1 K 8$_{44}$ 20$_{16}$ 2 K 7$_{16}$ Jr 2$_{37}$ 15$_{1.2}$ 50$_{8}$ 51$_{45}$ Ezk 36$_{20}$ 46$_{9.9.9.10}$ Hg 2$_{5}$ Ne 8$_{16}$, גּוֹי *nation* Jos 5$_{6}$ Jr 9$_{2}$, שְׁאֵרִית *remnant* 2 K 19$_{31}$||Is 37$_{32}$ Mc 2$_{13}$, עֵדָה *congregation* Ex 16$_{1}$ 35$_{20}$ Nm 27$_{21}$, בַּיִת *house* Lv 25$_{30.31}$ 2 S 15$_{16}$ Jr 11$_{11.11}$ Ps 114$_{1}$ perh. CD 20$_{22}$, צָבָא *army* Ex 12$_{41}$, חַיִל *army* 1 S 17$_{20}$ Jr 37$_{5.7}$ 2 C 26$_{11}$, מַחֲנֶה *camp* Jos 11$_{4}$, מַעֲרָכָה *battle-line* 1 S 17$_{8}$ 1QM 16$_{12}$ 4QM^{a} 1$_{15}$ ([תצא]) 4QM^{c} 1$_{9.10}$, מַצָּב *garrison* 1 S 13$_{23}$, מַחֲלֹקֶת *division* 1 C 27$_{1}$, דֶּגֶל *battalion* 1QM 6$_{1.4}$ 8$_{3}$.

נֶפֶשׁ *soul* Gn 12$_{5}$ 35$_{18}$ Ca 5$_{6}$ Si 38$_{23}$, נְשָׁמָה *breath* Jb 26$_{4}$, רוּחַ *spirit* 1 K 22$_{21.22.22}$||2 C 18$_{20.21.21}$ Ps 146$_{4}$ 4QShirShabb^{f} 23.1$_{10}$, *wind* Zc 6$_{5}$, לֵב *heart* Gn 42$_{28}$, עַיִן *eye* Ps 73$_{7}$ (or em. עָוֹן *iniquity*), יָד *hand* Ru 1$_{13}$, קוֹל *sound* Jr 30$_{19}$ 1QM 16$_{8}$, דָּם *blood* 4QD^{e} 4$_{4}$, שְׁכָבָה *lying down*, i.e. emission, of seed Lv 15$_{16.32}$ 22$_{4}$ 4QTohA 1.1$_{8}$ ([תצ]א), שִׁלְיָה *afterbirth* Dt 28$_{57}$, perh. פַּרְשְׁדֹנָה *bowel* Jg 3$_{22}$ (unless פַּרְשְׁדֹן *anus* or *vestibule* with ה- of direction; or em. פֶּרֶשׁ *faeces*; or del. with יצא; or subj. Ehud or לַהַב *blade*), מֵעִים *intestines* 2 C 21$_{15.19}$.

תּוֹרָה *law* Is 2$_{3}$=Mc 4$_{2}$ 51$_{4}$, דָּבָר *matter* Gn 24$_{50}$ Est 1$_{17}$, *word* Jos 6$_{10}$ Is 2$_{3}$||Mc 4$_{2}$ 55$_{11}$ Jr 44$_{17}$ Ezk 33$_{30}$ Est 1$_{19}$ 7$_{8}$ Dn 9$_{23}$, מָשָׁל *proverb* Si 6$_{35}$, מִשְׁפָּט *judgment* Ho 6$_{5}$ Hb 1$_{4.7}$ Ps 17$_{2}$ GnzPs 4$_{20}$, אֱמֶת *truth* 1QS 4$_{19}$, כָּבוֹד *glory* Ezk 10$_{18}$, חָכְמָה *wisdom* 4QapPs^{b} 76$_{8}$, תֹּכֶן *measurement*, i.e. decision 1QS 5$_{3}$, צְדָקָה *righteousness* Is 45$_{23}$ 62$_{1}$, יֵשַׁע *salvation* Is 51$_{5}$, יְשׁוּעָה *salvation* 4QSela 8.2$_{13}$ (... [תצא] [ישוע]ת), שְׂאֵת *dignity* Hb 1$_{7}$, הָדָר *majesty* Lm 1$_{6}$, טוֹב *good* Lm 3$_{38}$, perh. שָׂכָר *reward* Si 16$_{14}$ (unless subj. is אָדָם *human being*), תּוֹדָה *thanksgiving* Jr 30$_{19}$, שֵׁם *name* Ezk 16$_{14}$ 1 C 14$_{17}$ 2 C 26$_{15}$, שְׁגָגָה *error* Ec 10$_{5}$.

עָתָק *arrogance* 1 S 2$_{3}$ (or em. עֹשֶׁק *oppression*), קֶצֶף *anger* Nm 17$_{11}$, חֵמָה *anger* Jr 4$_{4}$=21$_{12}$ (unless יצא II *shine*), זַעַם *indignation* Si 5$_{7}$, רֶשַׁע *wickedness* 1 S 24$_{14}$, רָעָה *evil* Jr 25$_{32}$ Lm 3$_{38}$ 4Q185 1.2$_{8}$, חֲנֻפָּה *profaneness* Jr 23$_{15}$, אָלָה *curse* Zc 5$_{3}$, צְפִירָה perh. *doom* Ezk 7$_{10}$, עָוֹן *iniquity* Ps 73$_{7}$ (if em. עַיִן *eye*), אָוֶן *iniquity* Jb 5$_{6}$, מָדוֹן *strife* Pr 22$_{10}$, עֵסֶק *concern* Si 7$_{25}$, אָסוֹן *harm* Si 38$_{18}$.

חַיָּה *beast* Gn 8$_{19}$, סוּס *horse* Zc 6$_{6.8}$ Jb 39$_{21}$, בָּרֹד *mottled horse* Zc 6$_{6}$, לָבָן *white horse* Zc 6$_{6}$, אָמֹץ *dappled horse* Zc 6$_{7}$, פָּרָה *cow* Am 4$_{3}$, דֹּב *bear* 2 K 2$_{24}$, עֵגֶל *calf* Ex 32$_{24}$, רֶמֶשׂ *creeping things* Gn 8$_{19}$, צֶפַע *snake* Is 14$_{29}$, אַרְבֶּה *locust* Pr 30$_{27}$, עָשׁ *moth* Si 42$_{13(B)}$, סָס *moth* Si 42$_{13(M)}$, עוֹף *bird* Gn 8$_{19}$, עֹרֵב *raven* Gn 8$_{7.7}$ 4QCommGenD 3$_{4.4}$ ([העו]רב) 3$_{5.5}$ ([העו]רב), שֹׁרֶשׁ *root* 4QCryptA 2.2$_{1}$ ([יצ]או), חֹטֶר *shoot* Is 11$_{1}$ 4QM^{g} 5$_{2}$, יוֹנֶקֶת *shoot* Jb 8$_{16}$, חוֹחַ *thorn* Jb 31$_{40}$.

מֶרְכָּבָה *chariot* 1 K 10$_{29}$ Zc 6$_{1}$, קֶשֶׁת *bow*, i.e. arrow Jb 20$_{25}$, חֵץ *arrow* Zc 9$_{14}$, חֵצִי *arrow* 2 K 9$_{24}$, חֲנִית *spear* 2 S 2$_{23}$, זֶרֶק *javelin* 1QM 8$_{10}$, חֶרֶב *sword* Ezk 21$_{9}$, לַהַב *blade* Jg 3$_{22}$ (unless subj. Ehud or פַּרְשְׁדֹנָה *bowel*), *flame* Jb 41$_{13}$, לֶהָבָה *flame* Nm 21$_{28}$ Jr 48$_{45}$, אֵשׁ *fire* Ex 22$_{5}$ Lv 9$_{24}$ 10$_{2}$ Nm 16$_{35}$ 21$_{28}$ Jg 9$_{15.20.20}$ Jr 48$_{45}$ Ezk 5$_{4}$ 19$_{14}$, סְעָרָה *whirlwind* Jr 23$_{19}$ 30$_{23}$, רֶשֶׁף *plague* Hb 3$_{5}$, הֶגֶה *rumbling* Jb 37$_{2}$, בָּרָק *(lightning) flash* Ezk 1$_{13}$ Jb 20$_{25}$, עָשָׁן *smoke* Jb 41$_{12}$.

שֶׁמֶשׁ *sun* Gn 19$_{23}$ Jg 5$_{31}$ Is 13$_{10}$ Si 43$_{2(Bmg; M)}$ (B צרה *distress*) 4QPrQuot 40.2$_{4}$ ([ ]השמש]) 56.2$_{3}$ ([בצ]את השמש]) 1.3$_{1}$ ([השמש]) 1.3$_{12}$ ([ב]צא[ת השמש]) 1.3$_{23}$ ([בצ]את השמש]) 29.8$_{11}$ ([בצא]ת השמש]) 33.11$_{1}$ (בצ[א]ת) 92$_{1}$ ([בצ]את השמש]) 137$_{2}$ ([השמש]) perh. 4QUnidD 1$_{4}$ ([שמ]ש), כּוֹכָב *star* Ne 4$_{15}$, מָאוֹר *luminary* 4QPrQuot 215$_{6}$ ([בצא]ת).

יָם *sea* Jb 38$_{8}$, מַיִם *water* Ex 17$_{6}$ Nm 20$_{11}$ Jg 15$_{19}$ Ezk 47$_{1.8.12}$ Zc 14$_{8}$, נָהָר *river* Gn 2$_{10}$, נַחַל *wadi* Dt 8$_{7}$, עַיִן *spring* Dt 8$_{7}$, מַעְיָן *spring* Jl 4$_{18}$, תְּהוֹם *deep* Dt 8$_{7}$, קֶרַח *frost* Jb 38$_{29}$, שָׂדֶה *field* Lv 27$_{21}$, מִדְבָּר *steppe* Nm 21$_{13}$, גּוֹרָל *lot* Nm 33$_{54}$ Jos 16$_{1.2}$ 19$_{1.17.24.32.40}$ 21$_{4}$ 1 C 24$_{7}$ 25$_{9}$ 26$_{14}$ 1QS 6$_{16.18.21}$ 9$_{7}$ 1QSa 1$_{16}$ 4QTohD 1$_{4}$ (הגור[ל]) 4QWays^{b} 1a.1$_{4}$ ([יצ]א) CD 13$_{4}$, גְּבוּל *border* Nm 34$_{4.9}$ (גְּבֻל) Jos 15$_{3.4.9.11.11}$ 16$_{6.7}$ 18$_{11.15.15.17.17}$ 19$_{12.13.27.34.47}$, דֶּרֶךְ *way* Ezk 21$_{24}$, עִיר *city* Ezk 26$_{18}$ Am 5$_{3.3}$, שַׁעַר *gate* 11QT 41$_{12}$, מִגְדָּל *tower* 1QM 9$_{13}$ (מג[ד]לות), עִזָּבוֹן *merchandise* Ezk 27$_{33}$, רַב *great(ness)* of rust Ezk 24$_{12}$.

צִפּוּי *covering* Is 30$_{22}$, אֲפֻדָּה *ephod* Is 30$_{22}$, קָנֶה *branch* of candlestick Ex 25$_{32.33.35}$ 37$_{18.19.21}$, קֶרֶן *horn* Dn 8$_{9}$,

מִגְדָּל *tower* Ne $3_{25.26.27}$, מִמְכָּר *sale* Lv 25_{28}, מַשְׂאֵת *gift* 2 S 11_{8}, כְּלִי *vessel* Pr 25_{4} (unless יצא II *shine*; or em. כֻּלּוֹ *all of it* [dross]), בָּשָׂר *meat* Nm 11_{20}, יַיִן *wine* 1 S 25_{37}, תְּבוּאָה *produce* Dt 14_{22}, לֶחֶם *food* Jb 28_{5}, אֵיפָה *ephah* Zc 5_{6}, אֵזוֹב *hyssop* 1 K 5_{13}, מָתוֹק *sweet thing* Jg 14_{14}, מַאֲכָל *food* Jg 14_{14}, מַשְׁקֶה *drink* 4QTohA 2.1_{7}, קַו *line* Jr $31_{39(Qr)}$ Ps 19_{5} (or em. קַוָּם *their line* to קוֹלָם *their sound*), קֵץ *end* 2 C 21_{19}, שָׁנָה *year* Ex 23_{16}.

רִאשׁוֹן *first (one)* Gn 25_{25} 11QT 45_{4}, רִאשֹׁנָה *former (thing)* Is 48_{3} 11QT 45_{6}, זֶה *this (one)* Gn 38_{28} 11QT 45_{5}, זֹאת *this (thing)* Is 28_{29}, אֵלֶּה *these* Jos 8_{22} 1 K 20_{19}, חֲצִי *half* Zc $14_{2.8.8}$, חֲמִישִׁית *fifth* 11QT 58_{16}, מַעֲשֵׂר *tenth* 11QT $58_{5.6}$, אֶחָד *one* Gn 44_{28} 2 K 4_{39} 4QpIsaa 8_{24}, חֲמִשִּׁים *fifty* 4QJubh 38_{5} ([חמשים] ... [יצאו]) 38_{6} ([חמשים] ... [ויצא]) 38_{7} (חמ[שים]) 38_{8} ([חמשים] ... [ויצא]).

Subj. not specified, Gn 9_{10} 15_{4} $34_{24.24}$ 46_{26} Ex 1_{5} 16_{27} Nm 13_{+13t} 26_{2} 31_{36} Jos 2_{19} 6_{1} Jg $11_{31.36}$ 13_{14} 1 S 11_{7} 1 K 15_{17}‖2 C 16_{1} 2 K 11_{7} 11_{9}‖2 C 23_{8} 2 K 12_{13} Is 48_{1} Jr 6_{25} Jr 5_{6} 21_{9} 38_{2} Mc 5_{1} Zc 5_{5} 8_{10} Ps 109_{7} (unless רָשָׁע *wicked one* is subj.) 144_{14} Pr 25_{8} (or em. hi. *take out*) 1 C 5_{18} 7_{11} $12_{34.37}$ 2 C 15_{5} 25_{5} 26_{11} Si 10_{28} 38_{17} 1QM 4_{9} 4QpPsa 1.3_{4} 4QDe 7.1_{13} 4QMa $1_{8.9}$ ([י]אצאו) 11QT 33_{6} 36_{8} 53_{15} 54_{5}.

<OBJ> בֵּן *son* Si 6_{35}, עִיר *city* Gn 44_{4} Ex $9_{29.33}$ 2 K $20_{4(Kt)}$ (Qr חָצֵר *court*; or del. יצא), גְּבוּל *border* Nm 35_{26}, שָׂדֶה *field* Dt 14_{22}.

<PREP> לְ of direction, *to, towards, into, onto*, + Abijah 1 C 24_{7}, Asa 1 K 15_{17}, Asaph 1 C 25_{9}, Bilgah 1 C 24_{7}, Delaiah 1 C 24_{7}, Eliashib 1 C 24_{7}, Gamul 1 C 24_{7}, Hakkoz 1 C 24_{7}, Happizzez 1 C 24_{7}, Harim 1 C 24_{7}, Hezir 1 C 24_{7}, Huppah 1 C 24_{7}, Immer 1 C 24_{7}, Issachar Jos 19_{17}, Jachin 1 C 24_{7}, Jakim 1 C 24_{7}, Jedaiah 1 C 24_{7}, Jehezkel 1 C 24_{7}, Jehoiarib 1 C 24_{7}, Jeshebeab 1 C 24_{7}, Jeshua 1 C 24_{7}, Joseph 1 C 25_{9}, Maaziah 1 C 24_{7}, Malchijah 1 C 24_{7}, Mijamin 1 C 24_{7}, Pethahiah 1 C 24_{7}, Seorim 1 C 24_{7}, Shechaniah 1 C 24_{7}, Simeon Jos 19_{1}, מֶלֶךְ *king* Jr 37_{7}, עַם *people* 4Q185 1.2_{8}, מַטֶּה *tribe* Jos $19_{1.24.40}$, מִשְׁפָּחָה *family* Jos 21_{4}, בֵּן *son* (of tribe of) Jos $19_{17.32.32}$, נדב htp. ptc. *one who offers oneself* 1QS $6_{18.21}$, אֶרֶץ *land* Jr 23_{15}, מִדְבָּר *steppe* 2 C 20_{20}, עִיר *city* 2 C 24_{5}, צָפוֹן *north* 4QJubh 38_{7} ([לצפון]) 11QT 46_{13}, דָּרוֹם *south* 4QJubh 38_{5} ([ויצא]), מִזְרָח *east* 4QJubh 38_{6} ([יצאו למזרח]), מַעֲרָב *west* 4QJubh 38_{5} (ל[מערב] ... [ויצא]), נֵצַח *eternity* Hb 1_{4} 1QS 4_{19}, מִלְחָמָה *battle* Nm 21_{33} Dt 2_{32} 3_{1} 20_{1}=11QT 61_{13} Dt 21_{10} =11QT 63_{10} Jg 3_{10} $20_{14.20.28}$ 2 S 21_{17} 1 K 8_{44} 1 C 7_{11} 1QM 4_{9} 6_{11} 16_{12} 4QMa 1_{15} ([ת]צא מלחמה) 11QT $58_{5.15}$, perh. Nm 29_{6} Jos 8_{14} 1 S 4_{1}, צָבָא *military service* Nm $31_{27.28}$ 1QM $2_{8.8}$, מַעֲרָכָה *battle line* 1QM 3_{7}, מוֹעֵד *(appointed) meeting* 1 S 20_{35}.

יצא לַחוּץ *go outside* Ps 41_{7} (ms lacks יצא) 11QT 41_{12} 46_{13}; יצא מִחוּצָה לְ *go out from*, + מַחֲנֶה *camp* 4QMa 1_{9} ([י]אצאו); יצא אֶל־מִחוּץ לְ *go out from*, + מַחֲנֶה *camp* Lv 14_{3} perh. Nm 31_{13} Dt 23_{11}.

לְ of benefit, *for*, + Israel Ezk 16_{14}, צֹרֵף *smith* Pr 25_{4} (unless יצא II *shine*; or em. לַצֹּרֵף כֶּלִי *a vessel* comes out *for the smith* to נִצְרַף כֻּלּוֹ *all of it purified*); of purpose, *for (the purpose of)*, + מִלְחָמָה *war* 1 K 20_{18}, יֵשַׁע *salvation* Hb 3_{13}, שָׁלוֹם *peace* 1 K 20_{18}, פֹּעַל *work* Ps 104_{23}, עֲבֹדָה *work* Ps 104_{23}, רִיב *dispute* Pr 25_{8} (or em. לָרִב *for dispute* to לָרֹב *to many*); *at, by*, + רֶגֶל *foot* Hb 3_{5}, מוֹעֵד *appointed time* 4QCommGenD 3_{2}, קֵץ *end* 4QCommGenA 2_{2}, יוֹם *day* 11QT 45_{5}; *as*, + חָפְשִׁי *freed one* Ex 21_{2}, שָׂטָן *adversary* Nm 22_{32}, עֶזְרָה *help* Jr 37_{7}, גְּדוּד *troop* 2 C 26_{11}; *in accordance with*, + צָבָא *army* Nm 33_{1}, מֵאָה *hundred* 2 S 18_{4}, אֶלֶף *thousand* 2 S 18_{4}; *concerning*, + דָּבָר *matter* 1QS 5_{3}.

בְּ of place, *in(to), on, along, through(out), among* perh. 11QT 33_{6}, + עַם *people* 2 C 19_{4}, גּוֹי *nation* Ezk 16_{14}, הַר *mountain* Dt 8_{7}, בִּקְעָה *valley* Dt 8_{7}, perh. מִדְבָּר *steppe* Jb 24_{5}, אֶרֶץ *land* Ps 19_{5} 1 C 14_{17}, קִיר *wall* 1 K 5_{13} (perh. בְּ *from* wall), שַׁעַר *gate* Jr 17_{19} 39_{4} Mc 2_{13} Ne 2_{13} 11QT 36_{8}, מִלְחָמָה *war* 1 C 14_{15}, מַחֲנֶה *army* 1 S 28_{1} 29_{6}, דֶּרֶךְ *way* Dt $28_{7.25}$ Ezk 46_{8}, גּוֹלָה *exile* Jr 29_{16} 48_{7} Zc 14_{2}, עָקֵב *footprint* Ca 1_{8}.

בְּ of time, *on, at, during*, + יֹבֵל *jubilee* (year) Lv $25_{28.30.31}$ 27_{21}, שָׁנָה *year* Lv 25_{54}, שְׁבִיעִי *seventh* (year) Ex 21_{2}, חֹדֶשׁ *month* Ex 13_{4} 23_{15} 34_{18}, יוֹם *day* Ex 2_{13} $13_{3(Sam)}$ 16_{29} Jg 20_{25} 2 K 3_{6} Ezk 30_{9} Jl 4_{18} Zc 14_{8} Est 5_{9} 4QCommGenA 2_{2}, עֶרֶב *evening* 2 S 11_{13}, צָהֳרַיִם *noon* 1 K 20_{16}, שַׁבָּת *sabbath* CD $11_{10.11}$, תְּחִלָּה *beginning* Dn 9_{23}, רִאשֹׁנָה *first (time)*, i.e. beginning 1 K 20_{17}.

בְּ of accompaniment, *with* perh. 4QBéat 14.2_{22}, + עַם *people* Nm 20_{20}, רְכוּשׁ *property* Gn 15_{14}, תֹּף *timbrel* Ex 15_{20} Jg 11_{34} 1 S 18_{6}, שָׁלִישׁ perh. *triangle* 1 S 18_{6}, מָחוֹל *dance* Jr 31_{4}, מְחוֹלָה *dance* Ex 15_{20} Jg 11_{34}, לְבוּשׁ *clothing* Est 8_{15}, חֶרֶב *sword* Nm 20_{18}, יָד strong *hand* Nm 20_{20},

לָשׁוֹן *tongue* of fire 4QapMos^b 1.2_1, צָבָא *army* Nm 31_{36} Dt 24_5 Ps 44_{10} 60_{12} 108_{12}, חַיִל *army* 2 C 14_8; *in (a state of)*, + שִׂמְחָה *joy* 1 S 18_6 Is 55_{12}, חֵמָה *anger* Dn 11_{44} (חֵמָא) 1QM 1_4, שָׁלוֹם *peace* Jr 43_{12}, גְּבוּרָה *might* Jg 5_{31}, יָד high *hand*, i.e. defiantly Ex 14_8 Nm 33_3, גַּף *body*, i.e. on his own Ex $21_{3.4}$, חִפָּזוֹן *haste* Dt 16_3 Is 52_{12}, חֵקֶר *searching* Si 14_{22}.

בְּ of instrument, *by (means of), on*, + רֶגֶל *foot* 2 S $15_{16.17}$; partitive, (whoever goes out to battle) *from among* Israel Nm 1_3 26_2; of cause, *on account of*, + יֳפִי *beauty* Ezk 16_{14}, פֹּעַל *work* Jb 24_5, דָּבָר king's *word* Est 3_{15} 8_{14}; *against*, + Naomi Ru 1_{13}; בְּיַד *under the leadership of* Moses Nm 33_1.

כְּ *as*, + גִּבּוֹר *warrior* Is 42_{13}, זָהָב *gold* Jb 23_{10}, נֹגַהּ *brightness* Is 62_1, אֵשׁ *fire* Jr 4_4=21_{12} (unless יצא II *shine*), בָּרָק *lightning* Zc 9_{14}, צִיץ *blossom* Jb 14_2; כְּפַעַם בְּפַעַם *as occasion with occasion*, i.e. as usual Jg 16_{20}; *in accordance with*, + מַעֲשֶׂה *deed* Si 16_{14}, סֶרֶךְ *rule* 1QM 7_{17} (ס[רך]).

מִן of direction, *from* 4QTohA 1.1_8 (תצ[א ממנו]) 11QJub 12_{28} (מ[ן]) 11QT 51_1 ([היו]צא מהמ[ה]), + Y. Gn 24_{50} Is 51_4, Abimelech Jg 9_{20}, Abram Gn 17_6, Bildad Jb 26_4, Nabal 1 S 25_{37}, Hezekiah 2 K 20_{18}=Is 39_7, Babylon Is 48_{20}, Beer-sheba Gn 28_{10}, Bethel Jos 16_2, Bethlehem Mc 5_1, Caphtor Dt 2_{23}, Eden Gn 2_{10}, Egypt Ex 13_3 (Sam ins. אֶרֶץ *land of* Egypt) 13_8 23_{15} 34_{18} Nm 11_{20} $22_{5.11}$ Dt $4_{45.46}$ 16_6 23_5 24_9 25_{17} Jos 2_{10} $5_{4.4.5.6}$ 1 K 10_{29} 2 K 21_{15} Jr 37_5 Hg 2_5 Ps 114_1 2 C 5_{10} 4QapPent 2_{10}, Gibeah Jg $20_{21.25}$, Haran Gn 12_4 11QJub fr. 8_3 (מ[ן חרן]), Heshbon Nm 21_{28} Jr 48_{45}, Jerusalem 2 S 19_{20} 20_7 1 K 11_{29} 2 K 19_{31}||Is 37_{32} Is 2_3=Mc 4_2 Jr 29_2 37_{12} Zc 14_8 1QM 7_3, Jordan Jos 16_1, Keilah 1 S 23_{13}, Mahanaim 2 S 2_{12}, Mizpah 1 S 7_{11} Jr 41_6, Nineveh Na 1_{11}, Samaria 1 K 20_{17} 2 K 3_6, Seir Jg 5_4, Tyre 1 K 9_{12}, Ur Gn 11_{31} 4QCommGenA 2_8, Zion Is 2_3 =Mc 4_2 Is 49_{17} 4QSela 8.2_{13} (תצא מצי[ון]), Danites Jos 19_{47}, Jacob, i.e. people of Israel Jr 30_{19}, Chaldaeans Hb 1_7, אִישׁ *man* Lv 15_{16} 22_4, בַּת *daughter* Lm 1_6, עַם *people* Ex 16_{27} Ps 114_1, גּוֹי *nation* Jr 25_{32}, אֵלֶּה *these (families)* 1 C 2_{53}, בַּעַל *lord* Jg 9_{20}, רָשָׁע *evil one* 1 S 24_{14}, אֹכֵל *eater* Jg 14_{14}, עַז *strong one* Jg 14_{14}.

רָעָה *evil* Jr 9_2 11_{11}, צָרָה *distress* Pr 12_{13}, דִּין *judgment* Si 38_{18} (or em. דְּוֹן from *grief*), עֵצָה *counsel* 1QS 9_9 perh. 11QT 58_{20}.

אֶרֶץ *land* Gn 10_{11} 31_{13} Ex 16_1 19_1 Nm 1_1 9_1 26_4 $33_{1.38}$ Dt 9_7 $16_{3.3}$ 1 K 6_1 8_9 2 K 24_7 Jr 7_{25} 50_8 Ezk 21_{24} 36_{20} Mc 7_{15} Jb 28_5 1QDM 1_1 ([צא]ת ... [מאר]ץ) 2_6 (צ[את]נו) 4QapJoshua^b 12_4 (מאר[ץ]) CD 4_3 6_5, גְּבוּל *border* Nm 21_{13}, קִרְיָה *city* Nm 21_{28} Mc 4_{10}, עִיר *city* Jos 8_{22} Jg 1_{24} 9_{43} 1 S 18_6 1 K 20_{19} 2 K 2_{23} 7_{12} 9_{15} Jr 5_6 39_4 52_7 Ezk 24_{12} Jon 4_5 11QT 45_4 CD 20_{22}, מַכְתֵּשׁ *hollow* Jg 15_{19}, הַר *mountain* 2 K 19_{31}||Is 37_{32}, צוּר *rock* Ex 17_6, יַעַר *forest* 2 K 2_{24}, כֶּרֶם *vineyard* Jg 21_{21}, גֶּפֶן *vine* Jg 13_{14}, גֵּזַע *stump* Is 11_1 4QM^g 5_2, שֹׁרֶשׁ *root* Is 14_{29}, מַטֶּה *branch* Ezk 19_{14}, אָטָד *bramble* Jg 9_{15}, חֹר *hole* 1 S 14_{11}, מְעָרָה *cave* 1 S 24_9, דֶּרֶךְ *way* Ezk 44_3, עָפָר *dust* Jb 5_6, אֵשׁ *fire* Ezk 1_{13} 15_7, יָם *sea* Ezk 27_{33}, מַיִם *water* Is 48_1 (or em. מֵעִים pl. *insides*).

מִקְדָּשׁ *sanctuary* Lv 21_{12} Ezk 47_{12} 2 C 26_{18}, קֹדֶשׁ *sanctuary* 1 K 8_{10} Ezk 42_{14} 2 C 5_{11}, אֹהֶל *tent* Gn 31_{33}, בַּיִת *house* Ex 13_3 Lv 14_{38} Dt 24_2 Jg 9_{20} 2 S 11_8 Jr 38_8 Jl 4_{18} Zc 10_4 Ec 4_{14} Ne 3_{25} Si 50_5 11QT 49_{14} Arad ost. 16_3, חֶדֶר *chamber* Jl 2_{16}, חֻפָּה *bridal chamber* Jl 2_{16} Ps 19_6, מַחֲנֶה *camp* 1 S 13_{17} 17_4 2 K 7_{12}, מַעֲרָכָה *battle-line* 1QM 9_{13}, גֹּרֶן *threshing-floor* 1 C 21_{21}, תֵּבָה *ark* Gn $8_{16.19}$ 9_{18} 4QCommGenA 2_2 4QCommGenD 3_2, דֶּלֶת *door* Jos 2_{19} Jg 11_{31}, קִיר *wall* 11QT 41_{12}, שַׁעַר *gate* 1QM $7_{9.16}$ 8_3, מְנוֹרָה *lampstand* Ex $25_{33.35}$ $37_{19.21}$, תַּעַר *sheath* Ezk 21_9, בֶּגֶד *garment* Si 42_{13}, מָקוֹם *place* Gn 19_{14} Ex 16_{29} Is 26_{21} Jr 4_7 22_{11} Mc 1_3 Ru 1_7, זֶה *this (place)* Gn 42_{15}, שָׁם *there* Gn 10_{14} 24_5 Dt 11_{10} Jos 19_{34} Jg 21_{24} 2 S 16_5 1 K 2_{36} 12_{25} Is 52_{11} Jr 43_{12} 1 C 1_{12}.

לֵב *heart* 2 K 9_{24}, רֶחֶם *womb* Nm 12_{12} Jr 1_5 20_{18} Jb 38_8 Si 40_1, בֶּטֶן *womb* Jb 1_{21} 3_{11} 38_{29} Ec 5_{14}, מֵעֶה pl. *loins* Gn 15_4 2 S 7_{12} 16_{11} Is 48_1 (if em. מַיִם *water*), חֲלָצַיִם *loins* Gn 35_{11} 1 K 8_{19}||2 C 6_9, גֵּוָה *back* Jb 20_{25} (or em. גַּו *back*), אֲחֹרַיִם *back* 2 S 2_{23}, מְרֹרָה *gall bladder* Jb 20_{25}, צַד *side* Ex 25_{32} 37_{18}, אַף *nose* Nm 11_{20}, נָחִיר *nostril* Jb 41_{12}, פֶּה *mouth* Nm 30_3 Jos 6_{10} Jg 11_{36} 1 S 2_3 Is 45_{23} 48_3 55_{11} Jr 44_{17} Jb 37_2 41_{13} Lm 3_{38} Est 7_8 4QapPs^b 76_8 11QT 53_{15} 54_5, perh. hair Ezk 5_4, חֵלֶב *fat* Ps 73_7, צְעִיר *little (horn)* Dn 8_9 (or del. מִן), אֶחָד *one (horn)* Dn 8_9.

מִן of cause, *on account of*, + חֳלִי *sickness* 2 C 21_{15}; אֶל־מִן *to(wards)*, + נֶגֶב *south* Jos 15_3; עַד־לְמִן *to*, + רָחוֹק *(great) distance* 2 C 26_{15}.

אֶל *to(wards), into*, + Abimelech Jg 9_{33}, Elisha 2 K 2_3, Jehu 2 C 22_7, Mordecai Est 4_6, Nahash 1 S 11_3, Rabsaris

2 K 18₁₈, Rabshakeh 2 K 18₁₈||Is 36₃, Tartan 2 K 18₁₈, Cabul Jos 19₂₇, Daberath Jos 19₁₂, Geliloth Jos 18₁₇, Ammonites 1 S 11₁₀, Chaldaeans Jr 38₂, אִישׁ *man* Gn 19₆.₆ Jg 19₂₃.₂₃, אָב *father* 2 K 4₁₈, בֵּן *son* 2 C 22₇, אָח *brother* Ex 2₁₁, עַם *people* Dt 28₇ 2 S 18₂ Ezk 44₁₉, גּוֹי *nation* Jr 25₃₂, בַּיִת *house* of Israel Ezk 5₄, מֶלֶךְ *king* 1 K 20₃₁.₃₃ 2 K 8₃ 18₃₁||Is 36₁₆ 2 K 24₁₂(mss), שַׂר *chief* Jr 38₁₇.₁₈, קֹצֵר *reaper* 2 K 4₁₈, עֶבֶד *servant* 2 K 9₁₁, מַעֲרָכָה *rank* 1 S 17₂₀, עִיר *city* Nm 22₃₆ Jos 15₉ (or del. עִיר), מַעֲבָר *pass* 1 S 13₂₃, כָּתֵף *slope* Jos 15₁₁, מַעְיָן *spring* Jos 18₁₅, מוֹצָא *spring* 2 K 2₂₁, מִדְבָּר *steppe* Ex 15₂₂ (Sam hi.), נֶגֶב *south* 2 S 24₇, גְּלִילָה *district* Ezk 47₈, שָׂדֶה *field* 2 K 4₃₉, בִּקְעָה *valley* Ezk 3₂₂.₂₃, גַּיְא *valley* Jr 19₂, אֶרֶץ *land* Zc 6₆.₈, רְחוֹב *square* Est 4₆, אֹהֶל *tent* Ex 33₇.₈ Nm 12₄, פֶּתַח *entrance* Lv 14₃₈, מִזְבֵּחַ *altar* Lv 16₁₈, חָצֵר *court* Ezk 42₁₄ 44₁₉.₁₉ (or del. אֶל־הֶחָצֵר), רָעָה from one *evil* to another Jr 9₂, אֲשֶׁר *(the place) that* Nm 33₅₄.

אֶל *against*, + Israel(ites) 2 S 11₂₃, בָּשָׂר *flesh* Ezk 21₉, גִּבּוֹר *warrior* 2 C 14₈, אוֹיֵב *enemy* Dt 28₂₅ 1QM 9₃ perh. 4QM[a] 1₉ ([י]צאו); אֶל *concerning*, + Absalom 2 S 13₃₉ (mss עַל *on account of*).

עַל *on, over*, + אֶרֶץ *land* Gn 19₂₃ Ps 81₆ (or em. מִן *from*), פָּנִים *(sur)face* of land Zc 5₃, גַּנָּה *garden* Jb 8₁₆; *against*, + אוֹיֵב *enemy* Dt 20₁=11QT 61₁₃ Dt 21₁₀=11QT 63₁₀ Dt 23₁₀ 1 K 8₄₄ 11QT 58₁₅.

עַל *to*, + מֶלֶךְ *king* 2 K 24₁₂ (mss אֶל *to*), גִּבְעָה *hill* Jr 31₃₉ (mss עַד *unto*), אִשָּׁה *woman* Est 1₁₇ (or em. אֶל *to*); *in accordance with, by*, + פֶּה *mouth*, i.e. command Nm 27₂₁ 1QS 9₇ 11QT 58₁₉.₂₁ CD 13₄ 20₂₇ (לְ[צ]את), עֵצָה *council* 1QS 6₁₆; *on account of*, + Absalom 2 S 13₃₉(mss); be spent *on*, + בַּיִת *house* 2 K 12₁₃.

מֵעַל *from (upon)*, + Amnon 2 S 13₉, Eglon Jg 3₁₉, מִפְתָּן *threshold* Ezk 10₁₈.

כְּפִי *in accordance with*, + תְּעוּדָה *summons* 1QM 2₈.

אֵת *with*, + Abram, Lot, and Sarai Gn 11₃₁ (or em. hi., Terah *took* them out, with אֵת as object-marker), Achish 1 S 28₁ 29₆, אִישׁ *man* 2 S 21₁₇, עַם *people* Jr 29₁₆, מֶלֶךְ *king* 1 S 22₃ 2 K 11₈; perh. fulfil duty *in respect of* everything Ec 7₁₈.

מֵאֵת *from (with)*, + Y. Nm 16₃₅ Ezk 33₃₀, Abraham 4QJub[d] 21₂₆, Jacob Gn 44₂₈, נָבִיא *prophet* Jr 23₁₅, פַּרְעֹה *Pharaoh* Ex 5₂₀, זֶה *this (path)* Jr 2₃₇.

עִם *with* 4QapMos[b] 1.2₁, + Asher 4QJub[h] 38₆ ([יצאו]), Benjamin 4QJub[h] 38₈ ([ויצאו]), Dan 4QJub[h] 38₆ ([יצאו]), Enoch 4QJub[h] 38₈ ([ויצאו]), Gad 4QJub[h] 38₅ ([ויצאו]), Issachar 4QJub[h] 38₇, Jehoram 2 C 22₇, Jephthah Jg 11₃, Judah 4QJub[h] 38₅ ([ויצאו]), Naphtali 4QJub[h] 38₅ ([ויצאו]), Reuben 4QJub[h] 38₇, Simeon 4QJub[h] 38₈ ([ויצאו]), Zebulun 4QJub[h] 38₇, בֵּן *son* 4QJub[h] 38₈ ([ויצאו]), אָח *brother*, i.e. fellow Israelite, Lv 25₄₁.₅₄, עַם *people* 2 S 18₂, אִישׁ *man* 1QM 6₁₁, נַעֲרָה *girl* Ru 2₂₂, מֶלֶךְ *king* 11QT 58₅.₆.₁₆, עֶבֶד *servant* Ex 21₃, כֹּהֵן *priest* 1QM 7₁₄, מַעֲרָכָה *battle-line* 1QM 7₁₇; *against*, + Benjamin Jg 20₂₀, בֵּן *son* of Benjamin, Jg 20₂₈, of Israel Jg 20₁₄; *on account of*, + חֳלִי *illness* 2 C 21₁₉.

מֵעִם *from (being with)*, + Y. Is 28₂₉, David 2 S 3₂₆, פַּרְעֹה *Pharaoh* Ex 8₈.₂₅.₂₆ 9₃₃ 10₆.₁₈ 11₈, Israelite Lv 25₄₁ Dt 15₁₆, בֵּן *son* Lv 25₄₁, פָּנִים *face* Jb 1₁₂.

עַד *until*, + יוֹם *day* Jos 6₁₀.

בְּקֶרֶב *among, into*, + Jacob Jr 30₂₁, מִלְחָמָה *war* 1 K 20₃₉; מִקֶּרֶב *from among*, + Israel Dt 13₁₄=11QT 55₃; בֵּין *between* sons of Judah and sons of Joseph Jos 18₁₁; אֶל־בֵּין *(to) between*, + מַעֲרָכָה *battle-line* 1QM 7₉.₁₄; מִבֵּין *from between*, + Sihon Jr 48₄₅ (mss מִבֵּית *from the house of* Sihon), חָלָל *slain one* 4QM[c] 1₄, רֶגֶל *leg* Dt 28₅₇, הַר *mountain* Zc 6₁, גַּלְגַּל *wheel* 4QShirShabb[f] 20.2₉ ([ג]לגלי); מִתּוֹךְ *from among*, + Babylon Is 52₁₁ Jr 51₄₅, עַם *people* Ex 12₃₁; בְּתוֹךְ *among, through*, + Egypt Ex 11₄, בֵּן *son* of Israel Lv 24₁₀, עַם *people* Jr 37₄, בַּיִת *house* of Israel Ezk 3₂₅, עִיר *city* Est 4₁.

אַחֲרֵי *after* 1QM 6₁, + perh. Abishai 2 S 20₇, Miriam Ex 15₂₀, Saul 1 S 11₇, Uriah 2 S 11₈, Israel Jos 8₁₇, עַם *people* Jos 8₆, אִישׁ *man* Jos 2₇, דֶּגֶל *battalion* 1QM 6₄, חָכְמָה *wisdom* Si 14₂₂, תְּבוּנָה *understanding* Si 14₂₂, דּוֹב *bear* 1 S 17₃₅, אֲרִי *lion* 1 S 17₃₅, מִי *whom?* 1 S 24₁₅; אֶל־אַחֲרֵי *after*, + סוּס black *horse* Zc 6₆ (or em. אֶל־אֶרֶץ הַיָּם *to the west*); אַחַר *after*, + Samuel 1 S 11₇.

לִפְנֵי *in front of, in the presence of*, + Asa 2 C 15₂, Barak Jg 4₁₄, David 2 S 5₂₄||1 C 14₁₅, Zerah 2 C 14₉, Israel 1 S 18₁₆, Judah 1 S 18₁₆, Philistine 1 C 14₈, הָמוֹן *multitude* 2 C 20₁₇, עֵדָה *congregation* Nm 27₁₇ 1QSa 1₁₇ ([לצאת]), עַם *people* 1 S 8₂₀ 18₁₃ Ps 68₈ 2 C 1₁₀, perh. אָדָם *human being* Si 16₁₄, בֵּן *son* 1 C 12₁₈, מֶלֶךְ *king* 2 S 24₄, בַּעַל *lord* Jg 9₃₉, חָלוּץ *armed man* 2 C 20₂₁, צָבָא *army* 2 C 28₉, רֹאשׁ

head 4QapMos^{a} 1.2$_{8}$ ([ו[י]צא לפני כ[ול ראשי] *and he shall go out before all the heads of*); אֶל־פְּנֵי *in the presence of* Jehoshaphat 2 C 19$_{2}$; מִלִּפְנֵי *from before, from the presence of*, + Y. Gn 4$_{16}$ Lv 9$_{24}$ 10$_{2}$ Nm 17$_{11}$ Ezk 30$_{9}$ Ps 17$_{2}$ GnzPs 4$_{20}$, Moses Ex 35$_{20}$, Elisha 2 K 5$_{27}$, מֶלֶךְ *king* Est 1$_{19}$ 8$_{15}$, פַּרְעֹה *Pharaoh* Gn 47$_{10}$, שַׁלִּיט *ruler* Ec 10$_{5}$, רַב pl. *many* 1QS 7$_{23}$; מֵאֵת פְּנֵי *from the presence of* Y. Jb 2$_{7}$; לְעֵינֵי *in the sight of* all Egypt Nm 33$_{3}$.

תַּחַת *instead of*, + חִטָּה *wheat* Jb 31$_{40}$; מִתַּחַת *from under*, + יָד *hand*, i.e. control (of) 2 K 13$_{5}$, מִפְתָּן *threshold* Ezk 47$_{1}$; נֶגֶד *in front of*, + קַו *line* Jr 31$_{39(Qr)}$ (or em. נֶגְדּוֹ *in front of it* to נֶגְבָּה *southwards*), אִשָּׁה *each one* (fem.) Am 4$_{3}$ (or em. ho. *be taken out*).

+ ה of direction, *to(wards), into*, + Gibeon 2 S 2$_{12}$, Hukkok Jos 19$_{34}$, Jahaz Dt 2$_{32}$, Luz Jos 16$_{2}$, Ziphron Nm 34$_{9}$, צָפוֹן *north* 1 C 26$_{14}$, מִזְרָח *east* Jos 16$_{1}$, קָדִים *east* Ezk 47$_{1}$, פֶּתַח *entrance* Gn 19$_{6}$, אֹהֶל *tent* Nm 11$_{26}$, מִסְדְּרוֹן perh. *vestibule* Jg 3$_{23}$, perh. פַּרְשְׁדֹן *anus* or *vestibule* Jg 3$_{22}$ (unless פַּרְשְׁדֹנָה *bowel*), מַיִם *water* Ex 7$_{15}$ 8$_{16}$, יָם *sea* Jos 16$_{6}$ 18$_{15}$, מִדְבָּר *steppe* Nm 21$_{23}$, שָׁם *there* Dt 23$_{13}$ 4QOrd^{a} 5$_{5}$ 11QT 46$_{13}$, חוּץ *outside* Gn 39$_{12.15}$ (mss lack יצא in both) Jos 2$_{19}$ 1 S 9$_{26}$; without ה- of direction, + Assyria Gn 10$_{11}$ (unless אַשּׁוּר *Asshur* is subj. of יצא), En-shemesh Jos 18$_{17}$, Jabneel Jos 15$_{11}$, Jordan Jos 16$_{7}$, Rimmon Jos 19$_{13}$, הַר *mountain* Ne 8$_{15}$, שָׂדֶה *field* Gn 27$_{3}$ Jg 9$_{27.42}$ 1 S 20$_{11.11.35}$ 2 S 11$_{23}$ 18$_{6}$ Jr 6$_{25}$ 14$_{18}$ Ca 7$_{12}$, נַחַל *wadi* Jos 15$_{4}$, קָדִים *east* Ezk 47$_{3}$.

<COLL> יֹצְאֵי הַתֵּבָה *those who go out of the ark* Gn 9$_{10}$, יֹצְאֵי שַׁעַר עִירוֹ *those who go out of the gate of his city* Gn 34$_{24.24}$, יֹצְאֵי יְרֵכוֹ *those who go out of his thigh* (and var.) Gn 46$_{26}$ Ex 1$_{5}$ Jg 8$_{30}$, יֹצֵא צָבָא *one who goes to war* Nm 1$_{3+13t}$ 26$_{2}$ 2 C 25$_{5}$, יֹצְאֵי צָבָא *those who go to war* 1 C 5$_{18}$ 7$_{11}$ 12$_{34.37}$ 2 C 26$_{11}$ (יוֹצְאֵי in all three), חֵלֶק הַיֹּצְאִים בַּצָּבָא *portion of those who go out with the army* Nm 31$_{36}$, יֹצְאֵי הַשַּׁבָּת *those who go out*, i.e. off duty, *on the sabbath* 2 K 11$_{7}$ 11$_{9}$||2 C 23$_{8}$ (יוֹצְאֵי).

הַיּוֹם אֲשֶׁר־יָצָאתָ *the day on which you left* Dt 9$_{7}$, בְּיוֹם צֵאתְךָ *on the day you left* 1 K 2$_{37.42}$, יוֹם צֵאתְךָ *the day you left* Dt 16$_{3}$, יְמֵי צֵאתְךָ *the days when you left* Mc 7$_{15}$, ביום אשר יצא המת *on the day when the dead one leaves*, i.e. is taken out 11QT 49$_{14}$, הַיּוֹם אֲשֶׁר יָצְאוּ *the day on which they left* Jr 7$_{25}$, מוֹעֵד צֵאתְךָ *the appointed time of your departure* Dt 16$_{6}$, בְּיוֹם צֵאתֵנוּ *on the day we left* Jos 9$_{12}$, בראשית צאת *at the beginning of going out*, i.e. when one goes out 1QS 10$_{13}$, בְּכֹל אֲשֶׁר יָצְאוּ *whenever they went out* Jg 2$_{15}$, עֵת צֵאת הַמְּלָכִים *the time when kings go out* 2 S 11$_{1(Qr, mss)}$ (Kt המלאכים *messengers*) 1 C 20$_{1}$, מיום צאתו *from the day he goes out* Si 40$_{1}$, עת תצא הראישונה *the time when the first one goes out* 11QT 45$_{6}$.

אשר יצא הגורל *for whom the lot falls* 1QSa 1$_{16(mg)}$; מֵעֲלוֹת הַשַּׁחַר עַד צֵאת הַכּוֹכָבִים *from the rising of the dawn to the coming out of the stars* Ne 4$_{15}$, צֵאת הַשֶּׁמֶשׁ *rising of the sun* Jg 5$_{31}$; ויתן לך ... כיוצא בהם *that he might give you ... like that which goes out for them*, i.e. like them/theirs Si 10$_{28(A)}$, ושית אבלו כיוצא בו *and perform mourning for him like that which goes out for him*, i.e. to the extent he deserves it Si 38$_{17}$.

יצא + noun used adverbially, חוּץ *outside* Dt 23$_{13}$, פֶּרֶץ *(through) breach* Am 4$_{3}$ (or em. וּפְרָצִים תֵּצֶאנָה *and through breaches you will pass* to וַעֲרֻמּוֹת תּוּצֶאנָה *and naked you will be taken out* or פְּצוּרוֹת תּוּצֶאנָה *pushed along, you will be taken out* or פְּרוּצוֹת תּוּצֶאנָה *broken, you will be taken out*), דֶּרֶךְ *by way (of)* Jr 39$_{4}$ 52$_{7}$ Ezk 46$_{9.9}$, *in the direction (of)* Jr 39$_{4}$, פֶּתַח *(out of) entrance* Jb 31$_{34}$ (unless יצא transitive, *go out from* the entrance), שַׁעַר *(through) gate* Jb 29$_{7}$ (unless יצא transitive), לַיְלָה *(by) night* Jr 39$_{4}$ 52$_{7}$ Ne 2$_{13}$, חֵמָה *(in) anger* Jr 23$_{19}$ 30$_{23}$, אַמָּה *(for a number of) cubit(s)* 11QT 41$_{12}$, שָׁנָה שָׁנָה *year by year* Dt 14$_{22}$, חֹדֶשׁ בְּחֹדֶשׁ לְכֹל חָדְשֵׁי הַשָּׁנָה *month by month, every month of the year* 1 C 27$_{1}$.

יצא + other adverb, אָז *then* 1QS 4$_{19}$, אַחַר *afterwards* 4QCommGenA 2$_{10}$, אַחֲרֵי־כֵן *afterwards* Gn 15$_{14}$ 25$_{26}$ Ex 11$_{8}$, אָנָה *where?* Jr 15$_{2}$, אָנֶה וָאָנָה *(to) anywhere at all* 1 K 2$_{36}$, חִנָּם *at no cost* Ex 21$_{2.11}$, פתאם *suddenly* Si 5$_{7}$, כֵּן *thus* 4QWays^{b} 1a.1$_{4}$.

יצא + noun used predicatively, מַחֲנֶה *(as) army* Dt 23$_{10}$, אֶלֶף *(as) thousand* Am 5$_{3}$, מֵאָה *(as) hundred* Am 5$_{3}$, רָשָׁע *(as) guilty one* Ps 109$_{7}$, ראשון *first* 4QJub^{h} 38$_{5}$ ([ויצאו]), חָפְשִׁי *freely* Ex 21$_{5}$; וַיֵּצֵא ... שָׂמֵחַ וְטוֹב לֵב *he left happy and contented* Est 5$_{9}$, sim. 4QJub^{d} 21$_{26}$, יָצְאוּ מְבֹהָלִים וּדְחוּפִים *they left with great haste and urgency* Est 8$_{14}$, var. Est 3$_{15}$.

יצא infinitive + יצא finite, Gn 8$_{7}$ 27$_{30}$ Nm 35$_{26}$ 2 S 16$_{5}$ 18$_{2}$ 2 K 5$_{11}$ Jr 38$_{17}$ 48$_{9}$ (if em. נצא *fly*) 4QCommGenD 3$_{4.5}$; יצא followed by inf. of הלך *go* Gn 11$_{31}$ 12$_{5}$ Jos 9$_{12}$ Jg

19$_{27}$ 2 K 9$_{15}$ Jr 37$_{12}$ 1QM 7$_{3}$ 1QS 7$_{23}$ 9$_{9}$, קרא *meet* Gn 14$_{17}$ 30$_{16}$ Ex 4$_{14}$ 18$_{7}$ Nm 20$_{18.20}$ 21$_{23.33}$ 22$_{36}$ 31$_{13}$ Dt 1$_{44}$ 2$_{32}$ 3$_{1}$ 29$_{6}$ Jos 8$_{5.14.22}$ Jg 4$_{18.22}$ 11$_{31.34}$ 20$_{25.31}$ 1 S 4$_{1}$ 9$_{14}$ 13$_{10}$ 17$_{55}$ 18$_{6}$ 30$_{21}$ 2 S 6$_{20}$ 18$_{6}$ 2 K 9$_{21}$ Is 7$_{3}$ Jr 41$_{6}$ Zc 2$_{7}$ Jb 39$_{21}$ Pr 7$_{15}$ 2 C 35$_{20}$ 4QDibHam^{a} 1.4$_{7}$ 28$_{9}$, רדף *pursue* 2 S 20$_{7}$, חבה ni. *hide oneself* 2 K 7$_{12}$, ראה *see* Gn 34$_{1}$ 1 K 9$_{12}$ Jr 20$_{18}$, דבר pi. *speak* Gn 34$_{6}$, נגד hi. *tell* 2 K 9$_{15(Qr)}$, צעק *cry* 2 K 8$_{3}$, בקשׁ pi. *seek* 1 S 23$_{15}$ 26$_{20}$, שׁחר pi. *seek* Pr 7$_{15}$, פקד *muster* 2 S 24$_{4}$, *punish* Is 26$_{21}$, שׁאב *draw* water Gn 24$_{13.43}$ 1 S 9$_{11}$, שׂוח perh. *meditate* Gn 24$_{63}$, שׂכל hi. *instruct* Dn 9$_{22}$, חול *dance* Jg 21$_{21}$, שׁיר *sing* 1 S 18$_{6(Qr)}$, שׁכב *lie down* 2 S 11$_{13}$, שׂים *cause to be* Jr 4$_{7}$, נפל hi. *bring down* 1QM 8$_{10}$, נכה hi. *strike* 2 S 5$_{24}$||1 C 14$_{15}$, לחם ni. *fight* 2 K 19$_{9}$||Is 37$_{9}$ 1QM 1$_{4}$, ערך *array* 1 S 17$_{8}$ 1 C 12$_{37}$ 4QM^{a} 1$_{8}$, שׁמד hi. *destroy* Dn 11$_{44}$, חרם hi. *destroy* Dn 11$_{44}$, חזק pi. *strengthen* 2 K 12$_{13}$, מלך *rule* Ec 4$_{14}$.

יצא :: בוא *come* Gn 31$_{33}$ Ex 21$_{3}$ 28$_{35}$ Lv 9$_{23}$ 16$_{17}$ Nm 22$_{36}$ (+) 27$_{17.21}$ Dt 9$_{7}$ 23$_{11}$ 28$_{6.19}$ 29$_{6}$ (+) 31$_{2}$ Jos 6$_{1}$ 14$_{11}$ Jg 3$_{24}$ 9$_{15}$ (+) 1 S 9$_{14}$ 13$_{10}$ (+) 17$_{20}$ 18$_{6}$ (both +) 18$_{13.16}$ 29$_{6}$ 30$_{21}$ 2 S 16$_{5}$ 24$_{7}$ (all three +) 1 K 3$_{7}$ 15$_{17}$||2 C 16$_{1}$ 2 K 4$_{37}$ 11$_{9}$ 19$_{27}$||Is 37$_{28}$ Jr 17$_{19}$ 37$_{4}$ Ezk 7$_{10}$ (+) 42$_{14}$ 44$_{3}$ 46$_{8.9.9.10.10}$ Mc 4$_{10}$ (+) Zc 8$_{10}$ 1 C 21$_{4}$ 27$_{1}$ 2 C 1$_{10}$ 15$_{5}$ 22$_{7}$ (+) 23$_{7.8}$ 1QS 10$_{13}$ 11QT 36$_{8}$ 45$_{5}$ 58$_{19}$ CD 11$_{10.11}$ 13$_{4}$ 20$_{27}$, ישׁב *sit* 2 K 19$_{27}$ 2 C 19$_{4}$ 1QS 10$_{13}$ (+), שׁוב *go back* Gn 8$_{7}$ Jb 1$_{21}$ 4QD^{e} 7.1$_{13}$.

יצא + יבל ho. *be brought* Isa 55$_{12}$ (1QIsa^{a} הלך *go* for יבל), קום *arise* Gn 31$_{13}$ Ex 12$_{31}$ 2 S 19$_{8}$ Ezk 3$_{22.23}$ 1QS 10$_{13}$, נוס *flee* Gn 39$_{12.15}$ (mss lack יצא) Dt 28$_{7.25}$, ברח *flee* Is 48$_{20}$||Jr 39$_{4}$=52$_{7}$, פנה *turn* Ex 10$_{6}$, סור *depart* Is 52$_{11.11}$, עמד *stand* 1 K 19$_{11.13}$ 22$_{21}$ 2 K 10$_{9}$, שׁכם hi. *arise early* Jos 8$_{14}$, הלך htp. *go around* 1 C 21$_{4}$, אבד *die* Si 30$_{40}$.

Also 1QpMic 12$_{3}$ 4Q365a 2.2$_{4}$ 4QapJoshua^{a} 3.2$_{3}$ 4Q paraKings 21$_{3}$ (יו[צ]א) 4Q418 211$_{2}$ 11QJub fr. 7$_{1}$ ([יו]צא) 11QT 4$_{2}$.

<ANT> בוא *come*, ישׁב *sit*, שׁוב *go back*.

Hi. 277.6.36 Pf. הוֹצִיא (הוֹצִיאַ֫נִי, הוֹצִיאֲךָ, הוֹצֵאֲךָ, Q הוציאכה, הוֹצִיאָ֫נוּ, הוֹצִיאָם), הוֹצֵאתָ (הֵצֵאתָ֫נִי, הוֹצֵאתָ֫נוּ), הוֹצֵאתִי (הוֹצֵאתִ֫יךָ, הוֹצֵאתִ֫יהָ, הוֹצֵאתִים), הוֹצִיאוּ, הוֹצֵאתֶם; impf. יוֹצִיא (יֹצֵא, Q יוצי, יוֹצִיאֵ֫נִי, יוֹצִיאֵם, Q יוציאנו, Q יוציאה), 3fs תּוֹצִיא (תּוֹצֵא), 2ms תּוֹצִיא (תֹּצִיא, תּוֹצִיאֵ֫נִי), אוֹצִיא (אוֹצִיאָה), יוֹצִיאוּ (יֹצִאוּ, Kt יציאו [Jr 8$_{1}$], יֹצִאוּ, יוֹצִיאוּם), תּוֹצִיאוּ, נוֹצִיא; + waw וְהוֹצִיא, וְהוֹצֵאתָ (Q וְהוֹצֵאתִי, וְהוֹצֵאתְ), וְהוֹצֵאתַ֫נִי, וְהוֹצֵאתוֹ, וְהֹצֵאתָ, והוצאתה, וְהוֹצֵאתֶם (Q והוציאוהו), וְהוֹצִיאוּ (וְהוֹצֵאתִים, וְהֹצֵאתִי); וַיֹּצֵא (וַיֹּצֵא, וַיּוֹצִיא, וַיּוֹצֵא, וַיּוֹצִאֵ֫נִי, וַיּוֹצִאֲךָ, וַיֹּצִאֲךָ, וַיּוֹצִאָהּ, וַיּוֹצִאֵ֫נוּ, וַיֹּצִיאֵ֫נוּ, וַיֹּצִאֵ֫נוּ, וַיּוֹצִיאֵם, Sam וַיּוֹצִאֵ֫הוּ [Ex 15$_{22}$]), וַיּוֹצִיאוּ (וַיֹּצִיאוּ, וַיֹּצִאוּ, וַיּוֹצִאֻ֫הוּ, וַיּוֹצִאֻ֫הוּ), 3fs וַתּוֹצֵא, 2ms וַתֹּצֵא (וַתּוֹצִיאֵ֫נוּ), וָאוֹצִיא (וָאֹצִיא, Kt ואוצאה [Ezr 8$_{17}$] וָאוֹצִיאֵם); impv. הוֹצֵא (Qr הַיְצֵא, הוֹצִיא, הוֹצִיאָה, הוֹצִיאֵ֫נִי, הוֹצִיאוּהָ, הוֹצִיאֻ֫הוּ), הוֹצִיאוּ, הוֹצִיאִי (הוֹצִיאֵם, הוֹצִיאָהּ); ptc. מוֹצִיא (מוֹצֵא, מוֹצִא, מוֹצִיאִי, מוֹצִיאֲךָ, מוֹצִיאוֹ, מוֹצִיאָם), מוֹצִיאִים (מוֹצְאֵי; inf. cstr. הוֹצִיא (Q הוצי, הוֹצִיאִי, הוֹצִאִי, הוֹצִיאֲךָ, Q הוציאכה, הוֹצִיאוֹ, הוֹצִיאֵ֫הוּ, הוֹצִיאָם, הוֹצִיאָ֫נוּ)—**take out, bring out, produce** (e.g. Jr 15$_{19}$), **lead out** (e.g. Ex 6$_{26}$),* **cause to appear** (e.g. Jr 51$_{10}$), **exact** money (e.g. 2 K 15$_{20}$), **expel** (e.g. Ezr 10$_{3}$), **give in marriage** (Si 7$_{25}$), perh. **cast into** weapon (Is 54$_{16}$).*

<SUBJ> Y. Gn 15$_{5.7}$ Ex 6$_{6.7}$ 7$_{4.5}$ 12$_{17}$ 12$_{42.51}$ 13$_{3.9.14.16}$ 16$_{6.32}$ 18$_{1}$ 20$_{2}$ 29$_{46}$ 32$_{11.12}$ Lv 19$_{36}$ 22$_{33}$ 23$_{43}$ 25$_{38.42}$ 26$_{13.45}$ Nm 15$_{41}$ Nm 20$_{16}$ 23$_{22}$ 24$_{8}$ Dt 1$_{27}$ 4$_{20.37}$ 5$_{6.15}$ 6$_{12.21.23}$ 7$_{8.19}$ 8$_{14.15}$ 9$_{26.28.28.29}$ 13$_{6.11}$ 16$_{1}$ 26$_{8}$ 29$_{24}$ Jos 24$_{5.6}$ Jg 2$_{12}$ 6$_{8}$ 2 S 22$_{20.49}$ 1 K 8$_{16.21.51.53}$ 9$_{9}$ Is 43$_{8.17}$ 65$_{9}$ Jr 7$_{22}$ 10$_{13}$ 11$_{4}$ 31$_{32}$ 32$_{21}$ 34$_{13}$ 50$_{25}$ 51$_{10.16.44}$ Ezk 11$_{7(mss).9}$ 20$_{6.9.10.14.22.34.38.41}$ 21$_{8.10}$ 28$_{18}$ 34$_{13}$ 37$_{1}$ 38$_{4}$ 42$_{1.15}$ 46$_{21}$ 47$_{2}$ Mc 7$_{9}$ Zc 5$_{4}$ Ps 18$_{20}$ 25$_{15.17}$ 31$_{5}$ 37$_{6}$ 66$_{12}$ 68$_{7}$ 78$_{16}$ 105$_{37.43}$ 107$_{14.28}$ 135$_{7}$ 136$_{11}$ 142$_{8}$ 143$_{11}$ Jb 10$_{18}$ 12$_{22}$ Dn 9$_{15}$ Ne 9$_{7.15}$ 2 C 6$_{5}$ 7$_{22}$ Si 38$_{4}$ 44$_{23}$ ([ויו]צ[י]א) 1QH 1$_{29}$ 4$_{25}$ 4QpsEzek^{b} 1.2$_{6}$ 4QDibHam^{a} 1.5$_{10}$ 11QPs^{a} 26$_{14}$ 11QT 54$_{16}$, perh. 4QBibPar 1$_{16}$ 4QpsEzek^{c} 3.2$_{5}$ (א[וציא]) 4QpsMos^{d} 2$_{2}$.

Aaron Ex 6$_{13.26}$ 16$_{3}$ Nm 20$_{10}$ 1 S 12$_{8}$, Asa 2 C 16$_{2}$, Cyrus Ezr 1$_{7.8}$, David 2 S 5$_{2}$ 12$_{30.31}$||1 C 20$_{2.3}$ 1 C 11$_{2}$, Eleazar Nm 19$_{3}$, Eliezer Ezr 10$_{19}$, Elnathan Jr 26$_{23}$, Evilmerodach Jr 52$_{31}$, Ezekiel Ezk 12$_{7.7}$, Ezra Ezr 8$_{17(Kt)}$, Gedaliah Jr 39$_{14}$ Ezr 10$_{19}$, Gideon Jg 6$_{18.19}$, Hadadezer 2 S 10$_{16}$, Hilkiah 2 K 23$_{4}$, Jarib Ezr 10$_{19}$, Jehoiada 2 K 11$_{12}$, Jeremiah Jr 15$_{19}$, Jeshua Ezr 10$_{19}$, Joash Jg 6$_{30}$, Job Jb 15$_{13}$ 38$_{32}$, Joseph Gn 48$_{12}$, Josiah 2 K 23$_{6}$, Lot Gn 19$_{5.8.12}$, Maaseiah Ezr 10$_{19}$, Melchizedek Gn 14$_{18}$, Menahem 2 K 15$_{20}$, Moses Ex 3$_{10.11.12}$ 4$_{6.7}$ 6$_{13.26}$ 14$_{11}$ 15$_{22(Sam)}$ (MT qal) 16$_{3}$ 19$_{17}$ Lv 24$_{14}$ Nm 17$_{24}$ 20$_{8.10}$ Dt 9$_{12}$ 1 S 12$_{8}$, Nebuchadnezzar Ezr 1$_{7}$, Noah Gn 8$_{17}$, Pashhur Jr 20$_{3}$, Pharaoh Ex 6$_{27}$, Rahab Jos 2$_{3}$, Ruth 2$_{18}$, Zerubbabel Zc 4$_{7}$.

Ephraim Ho 9$_{13}$, Judah Jr 17$_{22}$, Israel(ites) Ex 12$_{46}$ Dt 14$_{28}$ 17$_{5}$=11QT 55$_{20}$ Dt 22$_{24}$=11QT 66$_{1}$ ([והו]ציאו) Is 48$_{20}$

Ezr 10$_{3}$ 11QT 49$_{11}$, perh. אָדָם *human being* Ps 104$_{14}$ (unless subj. is Y.), אִישׁ *man* Gn 19$_{16.17}$ 43$_{23}$ Nm 13$_{32}$ 14$_{36}$ 27$_{17}$ Dt 22$_{14.19}$=11QT 65$_{8.15}$ Dt 24$_{11}$ Jos 6$_{22}$ Jg 19$_{22.24.25}$ 1 K 21$_{13}$ Jr 26$_{23}$ 38$_{23}$ 2 C 23$_{11}$ 4QOrd^{a} 2$_{8}$ 4QHalakhah^{a} 1$_{4}$ 4QSD 7.1$_{5}$ (יו[צ׳א א׳]ש) CD 11$_{7.7.8}$, אִשָּׁה *woman* 1 K 17$_{13}$.

אָב *father* Dt 21$_{19}$=11QT 64$_{3}$ Dt 22$_{15}$=11QT 65$_{9}$ Jb 8$_{10}$, אֵם *mother* Dt 21$_{19}$=11QT 64$_{3}$ Dt 22$_{15}$=11QT 65$_{9}$, אַלְמָנָה *widow* 1 K 17$_{13}$, בֵּן *son* Si 7$_{25}$ 1QSa 1$_{23}$, of Israel Ex 12$_{39}$ Lv 24$_{23}$ Jos 10$_{22.23.24}$, of humankind, i.e. Ezekiel Ezk 12$_{4.5.6}$, דּוֹד *uncle* Am 6$_{10}$ (or em. וּנְשָׂאוֹ דּוֹדוֹ וּמְסָרְפוֹ *and [if] his uncle, the one who must burn him, lift him up* to take out bones, to וְנִשְׁאֲרוּ מְתֵי מִסְפָּר *and [if] there remain a few people* to take out bones), נַעַר *lad* Jos 6$_{23.23}$, זָקֵן *old man* Jg 19$_{22}$, *elder* Dt 22$_{21}$ 1 K 21$_{10.13}$.

מֶלֶךְ *king* Gn 14$_{18}$ Ex 6$_{27}$ Jr 17$_{22}$ Ezr 1$_{7.8}$, נָשִׂיא *prince* Ezk 12$_{12}$, בַּעַל *lord* Jg 19$_{22.24}$, חֹר *noble* 1 K 21$_{10.13}$ Ne 6$_{19}$, שַׂר *prince* Gn 40$_{14}$ 2 K 11$_{15}$||2 C 23$_{14}$, פָּקוּד *officer* 2 K 11$_{15}$||2 C 23$_{14}$, שָׁלִישׁ *officer* 2 K 10$_{26}$, מַלְאָךְ *messenger* 1 C 19$_{16}$, כֹּהֵן *priest* Lv 4$_{12.21}$ 6$_{4}$ 14$_{45}$ 2 K 23$_{4.4}$ 24$_{13}$ Ezk 46$_{20}$ 2 C 29$_{16}$ perh. 11QT 22$_{11}$, Levite 1 C 9$_{28}$ 2 C 29$_{5.16}$, גִּבּוֹר *mighty one* of the gatekeepers 1 C 9$_{28}$, חַרְטֹם *magician* Ex 8$_{14}$, סֹחֵר *trader* 1 K 10$_{29}$ 2 C 1$_{17.17}$, רַכָּב *rider* 1 K 22$_{34}$ ||2 C 18$_{33}$, מְרַגֵּל *spy* Jos 6$_{23}$, רָץ *guard* 2 K 10$_{26}$, עשׂה ptc. *one who does* work 2 K 12$_{12}$, חָרָשׁ *artisan* Is 54$_{16}$, שֹׁמֵר *keeper* 2 K 23$_{4}$, מְשָׁרֵת *servant* 2 S 13$_{18}$, עֶבֶד *servant* Gn 24$_{53}$ Is 42$_{1.3}$ perh. 42$_{7}$, זֹנָה *prostitute* 4QWiles 1$_{1}$ (הזונ[ה]), ירא ptc. *one who fears* Si 35$_{16}$, מִתְנַדֵּב *volunteer* 1QS 6$_{20}$, דֹּרֵשׁ *interpreter* of law CD 6$_{8}$, כְּסִיל *fool* Pr 29$_{11}$, יֹשֵׁב *inhabitant* Is 42$_{7}$ Jr 17$_{22}$, פְּלֵטָה *remnant* Ezk 14$_{22}$ (if em. פְּלֵטָה הַמּוּצָאִים בָּנִים וּבָנוֹת *a remnant, those who are taken out, sons and daughters* to מוֹצִאִים a remnant *bringing out* sons and daughters).

עַם *people* Dt 28$_{38}$, 2 C 23$_{11}$, בַּיִת *house* of rebellion Ezk 24$_{6}$, עֵדָה *congregation* Nm 15$_{36}$, לֵב *heart* Ec 5$_{1}$, אֶרֶץ *earth* Gn 1$_{12.24}$ Is 61$_{11}$, אֲדָמָה *land* Hg 1$_{11}$, מַטֶּה *staff* Nm 17$_{23}$, שַׁעַר *gate* 1QH 6$_{31}$, מִיץ *pressing* Pr 30$_{33.33.33}$, מִי *who?* Is 40$_{26}$; subj. not specified, Gn 38$_{24}$ 45$_{1}$ Lv 16$_{27}$ 2 S 13$_{9}$ 2 K 10$_{22}$ Jr 8$_{1}$ Jb 28$_{11}$ Pr 10$_{18}$ 2 C 9$_{28}$ 34$_{14}$ Si 37$_{11}$ 1QS 7$_{13.15}$ 4QMMT B$_{31}$ 4Q418 81$_{18}$ 4QBéat 14.2$_{20.25}$.

<OBJ> Abra(ha)m Gn 15$_{5.7}$ Ne 9$_{7}$, Ariel Ezr 8$_{17(Kt)}$, Athaliah 2 K 11$_{15}$||2 C 23$_{14}$, David 2 S 22$_{20.49}$, Eliezer Ezr 8$_{17(Kt)}$, Elnathan Ezr 8$_{17(Kt).17(Kt)}$, Ezekiel Ezk 37$_{1}$ 42$_{1.15}$ 46$_{21}$ 47$_{2}$, Gog Ezk 38$_{4}$, Jarib Ezr 8$_{17(Kt)}$, Jehoiachin Jr 52$_{31}$, Jeremiah Jr 20$_{3}$, 39$_{14}$, Job Jb 10$_{18}$, Joiarib Ezr 8$_{17(Kt)}$, Joseph Gn 40$_{14}$, Lot Gn 19$_{16.17}$, Meshullam Ezr 8$_{17(Kt)}$, Naboth 1 K 21$_{10.13}$, Nathan Ezr 8$_{17(Kt)}$, Rahab Jos 6$_{23}$, Shemaiah Ezr 8$_{17(Kt)}$, Simeon Gn 43$_{23}$, Tamar Gn 38$_{24}$ 2 S 13$_{18}$, Uriah Jr 26$_{23}$, Zechariah Ezr 8$_{17(Kt)}$.

Aramaean 2 S 10$_{16}$||1 C 19$_{16}$, Israel(ites) Ex 15$_{22(Sam)}$ 18$_{1}$ Nm 20$_{16}$ 23$_{22}$ 24$_{8}$ Dt 1$_{27}$ 4$_{20.37}$ 5$_{6.15}$ 6$_{12.21.23}$ 13$_{6.11}$ 2 S 5$_{2}$ 1 K 8$_{16}$ Jr 32$_{21}$ Ezk 20$_{6.9.10.14}$ 136$_{11}$ 1 C 11$_{2}$ 2 C 7$_{22}$ perh. 4QpsMos^{d} 2$_{2}$ ([אתכם]) 4QDibHam^{a} 1.5$_{10}$ 11QT 54$_{16}$, Jacob, i.e. Israelites Nm 23$_{22}$ 24$_{8}$.

אִישׁ *man* Gn 19$_{5}$ 45$_{1}$ Nm 15$_{36}$ Dt 17$_{5}$=11QT 55$_{20}$ Jos 2$_{3}$ Jg 19$_{22}$ 2 S 13$_{9}$ Si 44$_{23}$, אִשָּׁה *woman* Gn 19$_{17}$ Dt 17$_{5}$=11QT 55$_{20}$ Dt 22$_{14}$ Jos 6$_{22}$ Jr 38$_{23}$ Ezr 10$_{3.19}$, אָב *father* Jos 6$_{23}$ 24$_{6}$ 1 S 12$_{8}$ 1 K 8$_{21.53}$ 9$_{9}$ Jr 7$_{22}$ 11$_{4}$ 31$_{32}$ 34$_{13}$, אֵם *mother* Jos 6$_{23}$, אָח *brother* Nm 20$_{16}$ Jos 6$_{23}$, בֵּן *son* Gn 19$_{12}$ 48$_{12}$ Dt 21$_{19}$=11QT 64$_{3}$ Jg 6$_{30}$ 2 K 11$_{12}$||2 C 23$_{11}$ Jr 38$_{23}$ Ezk 14$_{22}$ (if em. פְּלֵטָה הַמּוּצָאִים בָּנִים וּבָנוֹת *a remnant, those who are taken out, sons and daughters* to מוֹצִאִים a remnant *bringing out* sons and daughters) Ho 9$_{13}$ 4QpsEzek^{b} 1.2$_{6}$, of Israel Ex 3$_{10.11}$ 6$_{6.7.13.26.27}$ 7$_{4.5}$ 12$_{51}$ 14$_{11}$ 16$_{3.6}$ 29$_{46}$ Lv 22$_{33}$ 23$_{43}$ 25$_{38}$ 26$_{13}$ Nm 15$_{41}$ Jg 2$_{12}$ 6$_{8}$ Ezk 20$_{22}$, בַּת *daughter* Gn 19$_{8.12.17}$ Jg 19$_{24}$ Ezk 14$_{22}$ (if em.) Si 7$_{25(A)}$, חָתָן *son-in-law* Gn 19$_{12}$, כַּלָּה *daughter-in-law* Gn 38$_{24}$, נַעֲרָה *girl* Dt 22$_{21(Qr).24(Qr)}$, בְּתוּלָה *young woman* Jg 19$_{24}$, פִּילֶגֶשׁ *secondary wife* Jg 19$_{24.25}$, רִאשׁוֹן *ancestor* Lv 26$_{45}$, ילד ni. ptc. *one born* Ezr 10$_{3}$.

מֶלֶךְ *king* Jos 10$_{22.23.24}$ 1 K 22$_{34}$||2 C 18$_{33}$ Jr 52$_{31}$, נָשִׂיא *prince* Ezk 37$_{1}$, רֹאשׁ *head* Ezr 8$_{17(Kt)}$, מֵבִין *instructor* Ezr 8$_{17(Kt)}$, קלל pi. ptc. *one who curses* Lv 24$_{14.23}$, אַסִּיר *prisoner* Is 42$_{7}$, אָסִיר *prisoner* Ps 68$_{7}$ 107$_{14}$, עֶבֶד *servant* Lv 25$_{42}$, עשׂה ptc. *one who does* work Ps 107$_{28}$, יֹשֵׁב *inhabitant* Ps 107$_{14}$, ירד ptc. *one who goes down* Ps 107$_{28}$, מֹרֵד *rebel* Ezk 20$_{38}$, פֹּשֵׁעַ *sinner* Ezk 20$_{38}$, מֵת *dead one* 11QT 49$_{11}$, שְׁנַיִם *two (fornicators)* Dt 22$_{24}$=11QT 66$_{1}$ (והוציאו את] [שניהמה]), ירשׁ ptc. *one who inherits* Is 65$_{9}$, עִזּוּז *mighty one* Is 43$_{17}$, פָּרָשׁ *rider* Ezk 38$_{4}$, worshipper Ps 18$_{20}$ 25$_{17}$ 31$_{5}$ 66$_{12}$.

עַם *people* Ex 3$_{10.12}$ 7$_{4}$ 13$_{3.9.14.16}$ 19$_{17}$ 20$_{2}$ 32$_{11.12}$ Dt 7$_{8.19}$ 8$_{14.15}$ 9$_{12.26.28.28.29}$ 16$_{1}$ 26$_{8}$ Jos 24$_{5}$ 2 S 12$_{31}$||1 C 20$_{3}$ 1 K 8$_{16.51}$ Is 43$_{8}$ Jr 32$_{21}$ Ps 105$_{37.43}$ Dn 9$_{15}$ 2 C 6$_{5}$, בַּיִת *house*

Lv 14$_{45}$, of Israel Ex 16$_{32}$ Ezk 11$_{7.9}$ 20$_{34.41}$, מִשְׁפָּחָה *family* Jos 6$_{23}$, שֵׁבֶט *tribe* Dt 29$_{24}$, עֵדָה *congregation* Ex 16$_{3}$ Lv 19$_{36}$ Nm 20$_{8}$ 27$_{17}$ 1QSa 1$_{23}$, מַמְלָכָה *kingdom* 4QpsEzek[c] 3.2$_{5}$ ([א]וצ׳א), צָבָא *host* Ex 7$_{4}$ 12$_{17.42}$ Is 40$_{26}$, חַיִל *army* Is 43$_{17}$ Ezk 38$_{4}$.

מֶרְכָּבָה *chariot* 1 K 10$_{29}$ 2 C 1$_{17.17}$, עִיר *city* Mc 7$_{9}$, אוֹצָר *treasure* 2 K 24$_{13.13}$, כֶּסֶף *silver* 2 K 12$_{12}$ 15$_{20}$ 2 C 16$_{2}$ 34$_{14}$, זָהָב *gold* 2 C 16$_{2}$, נַחֲלָה *inheritance* Dt 9$_{26.29}$ 1 K 8$_{51}$, יְקָר *preciousness* Jr 15$_{19}$, תְּרוּפָה *healing* Si 38$_{4}$, שָׁלָל *booty* 2 S 12$_{30}$‖1 C 20$_{2}$, עֲבוֹט *pledge* Dt 24$_{11}$, מְלָאכָה *work*, i.e. earnings 1QS 6$_{20}$, הוֹן *wealth* 1QS 6$_{20}$, מַשָּׂא *load* Jr 17$_{22}$.

מִשְׁפָּט *judgment* Is 42$_{1.3}$ 1QH 4$_{24}$, רִיב *dispute* Pr 30$_{33}$, אֹמֶר *word* 4QBéat 14.2$_{20}$ ([אמר־]כה), מִלָּה *word* Jb 8$_{10}$ 15$_{13}$ 4QsapDidA 1$_{4}$, דָּבָר *word* Ec 5$_{1}$ Ne 6$_{19}$ 4QWays[b] 3$_{3}$ ([יוצ־]א דברו), מַבָּע *utterance* 1QH 1$_{29}$, זֹאת *this (message)* Is 48$_{20}$, תַּעֲלֻמָה *secret* Jb 28$_{11}$, תַּחְבֻּלוֹת *prudence* Si 35$_{16}$, חָכְמָה *wisdom* Si 35$_{16(Bmg, E)}$ (E [יוצ־]או), אֱמֶת *truth* 1QH 4$_{25}$, צְדָקָה *righteousness* Jr 51$_{10}$ Ps 37$_{6}$, הֶבֶל *vanity* 4QWiles 1$_{1}$, רַע *evil* Si 37$_{11(B)}$, דִּבָּה *evil report* Nm 13$_{32}$ 14$_{36}$ Pr 10$_{18}$, אָלָה *curse* Zc 5$_{4}$, שֵׁם bad *name* Dt 22$_{14.19}$=11QT 65$_{8.15}$ 4QOrd[a] 2$_{8}$, נִדָּה *impurity* 2 C 29$_{5}$, טֻמְאָה *impurity* 2 C 29$_{16.16}$, מַחְסוֹר *need* 4Q418 81$_{18}$,

יָד *hand* Ex 4$_{6.7}$ 1QS 7$_{13.15}$, רֶגֶל *foot* Ps 25$_{15}$, עֶצֶם *bone* Jr 8$_{1.1.1.1.1}$ Am 6$_{10}$, דָּם *blood* Pr 30$_{33}$, נֶפֶשׁ *soul* Gn 1$_{24}$ Ps 142$_{8}$ 143$_{11}$, בְּתוּל *(token of) virginity* Dt 22$_{15}$=11QT 65$_{9}$.

מַיִם *water* Nm 20$_{8.10}$ Dt 8$_{15}$ Ne 9$_{15}$, נוֹזֵל *stream* Ps 78$_{16}$, מַזָּרוֹת *Mazzaroth* (constellation) Jb 38$_{32}$, דֶּשֶׁא *grass* Gn 1$_{12}$, עֵשֶׂב *plants* Gn 1$_{12}$, פֶּרַח *bud* Nm 17$_{23}$, צֶמַח *sprout* Is 61$_{11}$, עֵץ *tree* Gn 1$_{12}$, *wood* Lv 14$_{45}$, זֶרַע *seed* Gn 1$_{12}$ Dt 28$_{38}$, *offspring* Is 65$_{9}$ Ezk 20$_{6.9.10.14}$, אֶבֶן *stone* Lv 14$_{45}$ Zc 4$_{7}$, עָפָר *dust* Lv 14$_{45}$, דֶּשֶׁן *ashes* Lv 6$_{4}$ 4QMMT B$_{31}$ (דשא), אֵשׁ *fire* Ezk 28$_{18}$, רוּחַ *wind* Jr 10$_{13}$ 51$_{16}$ Ps 135$_{7}$ 11QPs[a] 26$_{14}$ ([רוח]), *spirit* Pr 29$_{11}$, צַלְמָוֶת *deep shadow* Jb 12$_{22}$.

בְּהֵמָה *beast* Gn 1$_{24}$ CD 11$_{7}$, חַיָּה *beast* Gn 1$_{24}$ 8$_{17}$, סוּס *horse* 1 K 10$_{29}$ Is 43$_{17}$ Ezk 38$_{4}$ 2 C 1$_{17.17}$ 9$_{28}$, פַּר *bull* Lv 4$_{12.21}$ 16$_{27}$, פָּרָה *heifer* Nm 19$_{3}$, שָׂעִיר *goat* Lv 16$_{27}$, רֶמֶשׂ *creeping thing* Gn 1$_{24}$, כֵּן *gnat* Ex 8$_{14}$, צֹאן *flock* Ezk 34$_{13}$.

בָּשָׂר *flesh* Jg 6$_{19}$, לֶחֶם *bread* Gn 14$_{18}$ Ps 104$_{14}$, עֻגָה *cake* 1 K 17$_{13}$, בָּצֵק *dough* Ex 12$_{39}$, חֶמְאָה *curd* Pr 30$_{33}$, מָרָק *broth* Jg 6$_{19}$, יַיִן *wine* Gn 14$_{18}$, מַאֲכָל *food* 4QSD 7.1$_{5}$ ([יו]צ׳א ... מאכ[ל]), מַשְׁקֶה *drink* 4QLeqeṭ 1$_{5}$ ([מש]קיהם), בֶּלַע *food* Jr 51$_{44}$, מִנְחָה *cereal offering* Jg 6$_{18}$ Ezk 46$_{20}$, אָשָׁם *guilt offering* Ezk 46$_{20}$, חַטָּאת *sin offering* Ezk 46$_{20}$, מַעֲשֵׂר *tithe* Dt 14$_{28}$.

בֶּגֶד *garment* Gn 24$_{53}$, לְבוּשׁ *garment* 2 K 10$_{22}$, כְּלִי *vessel* Gn 24$_{53.53}$ 2 K 23$_{4}$ Is 54$_{16}$ Jr 50$_{25}$ 1QH 6$_{31}$ 4QSD 7.1$_{5}$ (יו[צ׳א) CD 6$_{8}$, Ezk 12$_{4.5.6.7.7.12}$ Ezr 1$_{7.7.8}$ 1 C 9$_{28}$, מַצֵּבָה *pillar* 2 K 10$_{26}$, אֲשֵׁרָה *Asherah* 2 K 23$_{6}$, מַטֶּה *staff* Nm 17$_{24}$, חֶרֶב *sword* Ezk 21$_{8.10}$, רֶכֶב *chariot* Is 43$_{17}$, קַו *line* 1QH 1$_{29}$, חֶלְאָה *rust* Ezk 24$_{6}$.

<PREP> לְ of direction, *to, to a state of*, + Elijah 1 K 17$_{13}$, Solomon 2 C 9$_{28}$, Tobiah Ne 6$_{19}$, בֹּנֶה *builder* 2 K 12$_{12}$, חָרָשׁ *artisan* 2 K 12$_{12}$, דרשׁ ptc. *one who seeks* 4Q418 81$_{18}$, גּוֹי *nation* Is 42$_{1}$, אוֹר *light* Mc 7$_{9}$ Jb 12$_{22}$, מֶרְחָב *broad place*, i.e. freedom 2 S 22$_{20}$ Ps 18$_{20}$, מֵישָׁר *evenness* 1QH 4$_{25}$, רְוָיָה *saturation* Ps 66$_{12}$ (or em. רְוָחָה *relief*), נַחַל *wadi* 2 C 29$_{16}$, מֶלֶךְ *king* 1 K 10$_{29}$ 2 C 1$_{17}$, נֵצַח perh. *victory* 1QH 4$_{25}$; of benefit, *for*, + Israelites Dt 8$_{15}$, עֵדָה *congregation* Nm 20$_{8}$, קָהָל *assembly* Nm 20$_{10}$, עֹבֵד *worshipper* 2 K 10$_{22}$, רָז *mystery* 1QH 1$_{29}$, חֶשְׁבּוֹן *thought* 1QH 1$_{29}$; *in accordance with*, + אֱמֶת *truth* Is 42$_{3}$ (unless לֶאֱמֶת = *indeed*),* נֵתַח *piece* Ezk 24$_{6}$; *for (the purpose of)*, + מַעֲשֶׂה *work* Is 54$_{16}$.

אֶל־מִחוּץ לְ *(to) outside*, + מַחֲנֶה *camp* Lv 4$_{12.21}$ 6$_{4}$ 24$_{14.23}$ Nm 15$_{36}$ 19$_{3}$, עִיר *city* Lv 14$_{45}$; מִחוּץ לְ *outside*, + עִיר *city* 1 K 21$_{13}$, Jerusalem 2 K 23$_{6}$; אֶל־מִבֵּית לְ *to within, behind*, + שְׂדֵרָה *rank* of soldiers 2 K 11$_{15}$ (‖2 C 23$_{14}$ lacks לְ).

בְּ of place/time, *in(to), on, through*, + קִיר *wall* Ezk 12$_{5.12}$, יוֹם *day* Ex 12$_{17.51}$ (both בְּעֶצֶם הַיּוֹם הַזֶּה *on this very day*) 4QSD 7.1$_{5}$ ([יו]צ׳א); of instrument, *by (means of), with*, + חֹזֶק *strength* of hand Ex 13$_{3.14.16}$, כֹּחַ *strength* Ex 32$_{11}$ Dt 4$_{37}$ 9$_{29}$, יָד strong *hand* Ex 13$_{9}$ 32$_{11}$ Dt 5$_{15}$ 6$_{21}$ 7$_{8}$ 9$_{26}$ 26$_{8}$ Jr 32$_{21}$ Dn 9$_{15}$, זְרוֹעַ *arm* Dt 5$_{15}$ 9$_{29}$ 26$_{8}$ Jr 32$_{21}$ (אֶזְרוֹעַ), רוּחַ *spirit* Ezk 37$_{1}$; of accompaniment, *in (a state of), with* (but distinction from foregoing not alw. certain), + כֶּסֶף *silver* Ps 105$_{37}$, זָהָב *gold* Ps 105$_{37}$, שָׂשׂוֹן *rejoicing* Ps 105$_{43}$, רִנָּה *rejoicing* Ps 105$_{43}$, כּוֹשָׁרָה perh. *prosperity* Ps 68$_{7}$, שֶׁפֶט *judgment* Ex 7$_{4}$, מוֹרָא *fear* Dt 26$_{8}$ Jr 32$_{21}$, אוֹת *sign* Dt 26$_{8}$ Jr 32$_{21}$, מוֹפֵת *sign* Dt 26$_{8}$ Jr 32$_{21}$, עֲלָטָה *darkness* Ezk 12$_{6.7}$, דַּעַת *knowledge* 4QBéat 7.2$_{5}$ (מיצאת בלוא [דעת]); *for the sake of*, + רָעָה *evil* Ex 32$_{12}$; *in accordance with*, + מִסְפָּר *number* Is 40$_{26}$ 1 C 9$_{28}$, עֵצָה *advice* Ezr 10$_{3}$.

מִן of direction, *from*, + Israel Si 44$_{23}$, Jacob Is 65$_{9}$, Judah Is 65$_{9}$, Egypt Ex 3$_{10.11.12}$ 6$_{27}$ 12$_{39}$ 13$_{9.14.16}$ 14$_{11}$ 18$_{1}$ Nm 20$_{16}$ 23$_{22}$ 24$_{8}$, Dt 4$_{20.37}$ 6$_{21}$ 9$_{12.26}$ 16$_{1}$ 26$_{8}$ Jos 24$_{6}$ 1 S 12$_{8}$ 1 K 8$_{16.51.53}$ Jr 26$_{23}$ 2 C 1$_{17}$ 9$_{28}$, Jerusalem Ezr 1$_{7}$, Memphis 4QpsEzek[b] 1.2$_{6}$, Ur Gn 15$_{7}$ Ne 9$_{7}$.

עַם *people* Ezk 20$_{34.41}$ 34$_{13}$, אוֹיֵב *enemy* 2 S 22$_{49}$, אֶרֶץ *land* Ex 6$_{13.26.27(mss, Sam)}$ 7$_{4}$ 12$_{17.42.51}$ 16$_{6.32}$ 20$_{2}$ 29$_{46}$ 32$_{11}$ Lv 19$_{36}$ 22$_{33}$ 23$_{43}$ 25$_{38.42}$ 26$_{13.45}$ Nm 15$_{41}$ Dt 1$_{27}$ 5$_{6}$ 6$_{12}$ 8$_{14}$ 13$_{6.11}$ 29$_{24}$ Jg 2$_{12}$ 1 K 8$_{21}$ 9$_{9}$ Jr 7$_{22}$ 11$_{4}$ 31$_{32}$ 32$_{21}$ 34$_{13}$ Ezk 20$_{6.9.10.38}$ Ps 104$_{14}$ Dn 9$_{15}$ 2 C 6$_{5}$ 7$_{22}$ 9$_{28}$ Si 38$_{4}$ 11QT 54$_{16}$, בַּיִת *house* Gn 40$_{14}$ Ex 12$_{46}$ 13$_{14}$ 20$_{2}$ Dt 5$_{6}$ 6$_{12}$ 8$_{14}$ 13$_{11}$ Jg 6$_{8}$ 2 K 23$_{6}$ Jr 17$_{22}$ 34$_{13}$ 52$_{31}$ Is 42$_{7}$ Am 6$_{10}$ 4QHalakhah[a] 1$_{4}$ 11QT 49$_{11}$ CD 11$_{7.7}$, סֻכָּה *booth* CD 11$_{8}$ (:: בוא hi. *bring*), אֹהֶל *tent* 4QSD 7.1$_{5}$ ([יו]צ֯יא), הֵיכָל *temple* 2 K 23$_{4}$, קֹדֶשׁ *sanctuary* 2 C 29$_{5}$, אוֹצָר *storehouse* Jr 10$_{13}$ 51$_{16}$ Ps 135$_{7}$ 2 C 16$_{2}$ 11QPs[a] 26$_{14}$ (מאו[צרותיו]), מַחֲנֶה *camp* Ex 19$_{17}$, *battle-front* 1 K 22$_{34}$‖2 C 18$_{33}$, חָצֵר *court* 4QErr 1$_{6}$, מַסְגֵּר *prison* Is 42$_{7}$ Ps 142$_{8}$, מַהְפֶּכֶת *stocks* Jr 20$_{3}$, תַּעַר *sheath* Ezk 21$_{8.10}$, רֶשֶׁת *net* Ps 25$_{15}$ 31$_{5}$, צוּר *rock* Dt 8$_{15}$, סֶלַע *rock* Nm 20$_{8.10}$ Ps 78$_{16}$ Ne 9$_{15}$, מְעָרָה *cave* Jos 10$_{22.23}$, קֶבֶר *grave* Jr 8$_{1}$, כּוּר *furnace* Dt 4$_{20}$ Jr 11$_{4}$, מָקוֹם *place* Gn 19$_{12}$ 4QHalakhah[a] 1$_{4}$, זֶה *this (place)* Ex 13$_{3}$, שָׁם *there* Dt 5$_{15}$ 6$_{23}$ 9$_{28}$ Jos 6$_{22}$ 2 K 24$_{13}$.

יָד *hand* 4QpsEzek[c] 3.2$_{5}$ ([א]וציא) 4QpsMos[d] 2$_{2}$ ([מארץ]), לֵב *heart* Jb 8$_{10}$ Si 35$_{16}$, פֶּה *mouth* Jr 51$_{44}$ Jb 15$_{13}$, חֵיק *bosom* Ex 4$_{6(Sam, mss).7}$, רֶחֶם *womb* Jb 10$_{18}$, זוֹלֵל *worthlessness* Jr 15$_{19}$, מְצוּקָה *distress* Ps 25$_{17}$ 107$_{28}$, צָרָה *distress* Ps 143$_{11}$, חֹשֶׁךְ *darkness* Ps 107$_{14}$, נֶשֶׁף *twilight* Si 35$_{16}$, צַלְמָוֶת *deep shadow* Ps 107$_{14}$.

מִן partitive, *(any) of*, + בָּשָׂר *flesh* Ex 12$_{46}$; of cause, *on account of* Dt 9$_{28}$ (מִבְּלִי יְכֹלֶת י׳ *on account of Y.'s inability*), + שִׂנְאָה *hatred* Dt 9$_{28}$; at, after, + קָצֶה *end* Dt 14$_{28}$.

אֶל *to*, + Joshua 10$_{22.23.24}$, Chaldaean Jr 38$_{23}$, Israelite Dt 24$_{11}$, אִישׁ *man* Gn 19$_{5}$ 43$_{23}$ Jg 19$_{25}$, בֵּן *son* of Israel Nm 13$_{32}$ 17$_{24}$ 11QT 22$_{11}$, אָח *brother* Gn 19$_{8}$, זָקֵן *elder* Dt 21$_{19}$ =11QT 64$_{3}$ Dt 22$_{15}$=11QT 65$_{9}$, הֹרֵג *killer* Ho 9$_{13}$, בַּיִת *house* Jr 39$_{14}$, אֶרֶץ *land* Ezk 20$_{6}$, מִדְבָּר *steppe* Ex 15$_{22(Sam)}$ (MT qal) 16$_{3}$, נַחַל *stream* 2 K 23$_{6}$, מָקוֹם *place* Lv 4$_{12}$ 6$_{4}$ 14$_{45}$, שֶׁפֶךְ *(place of) pouring* Lv 4$_{12}$, פֶּתַח *entrance* Dt 22$_{21}$, חָצֵר *court* Ezk 42$_{1}$ 46$_{20.21}$, שַׁעַר *gate* Dt 17$_{5}$ 21$_{19}$=11QT 64$_{3}$ Dt 22$_{24}$=11QT 66$_{1}$ ([והוציאו ... אל שער]).

עַל *upon*, + כָּתֵף *shoulder* Ezk 12$_{7}$; *to*, + Iddo Ezr 8$_{17(Kt)}$; *for (the benefit of)*, + רַבִּים *many* 1QS 6$_{20}$; עַל *against*, + אִשָּׁה *woman* Dt 22$_{14}$=11QT 65$_{8}$, בְּתוּלָה *young woman* Dt 22$_{19}$=11QT 65$_{15}$ 4QOrd[a] 2$_{8}$; exact money *from*, + Israel 2 K 15$_{20}$, גִּבּוֹר *warrior* 2 K 15$_{20}$; *in accordance with, by*, + צָבָא *army* Ex 6$_{26}$ 12$_{51}$; *concerning*, + אֶרֶץ *land* Nm 14$_{36}$; מֵעַל *from (upon)*, + Amnon 2 S 13$_{9}$, Joseph Gn 45$_{1}$.

עַד *unto*, + קָצֶה *end* Is 48$_{20}$.

אֵת *with*, + Noah Gn 8$_{17}$.

בְּיַד *through, by the agency of*, + סֹחֵר *trader* 1 K 10$_{29}$ 2 C 1$_{17}$; עַל־יַד *under (the charge of)*, + Mithredath Ezr 1$_{8}$; מֵעִם *from (with)*, + בֶּרֶךְ *knee* Gn 48$_{12}$; מִתַּחַת *from under*, + סְבָלָה *burden* Ex 6$_{6.7}$, בֶּגֶד *garment* 1QS 7$_{13}$; מִתּוֹךְ *from (among)*, + Egypt Ex 7$_{5}$ Ps 136$_{11}$, עִיר *city* Ezk 11$_{7.9}$, כְּרוּב *cherub* Ezk 28$_{18}$, כּוּר *furnace* 1 K 8$_{51}$; לִפְנֵי *in the presence of*, + אֱלֹהִים *God* Ec 5$_{1}$; לְעֵינֵי *in the sight of*, + גּוֹי *nation* Ezk 20$_{14.22}$ 4QDibHam[a] 1.5$_{10}$; בִּפְנֵי *in the sight of* Y. Dt 4$_{37}$; מִלִּפְנֵי *from the presence of* Y. Nm 17$_{24}$.

+ ה- of direction, *to(wards)*, + חוּץ *outside* Gn 15$_{5}$ 19$_{17}$ Ex 12$_{46}$ Dt 24$_{11}$ 2 C 29$_{16}$, שַׁעַר *gate* Dt 22$_{15}$.

<COLL> יצא hi. + noun used adverbially, take out *(in)to*, + שָׂדֶה *field* Dt 28$_{38}$, אוֹר *light* Jb 28$_{11}$, חוּץ *outside* Jg 19$_{25}$ 2 S 13$_{18}$; *by (means of), with*, + אוֹת *sign* Dt 7$_{19}$, מוֹפֵת *sign* Dt 7$_{19}$, יָד *hand* Dt 7$_{19}$, זְרוֹעַ *arm* Dt 7$_{19}$, דֶּרֶךְ by *way* of Ezk 42$_{15}$ 47$_{2}$; *during, by*, + לַיְלָה *night* Dt 16$_{1}$, שַׁבָּת *sabbath* 4QHalakhah[a] 1$_{4}$; ביום אשר הוציאו *on the day that they bring* 11QT 49$_{11}$; יצא hi. + inf. of הרג *kill* Ex 32$_{12}$, כלה pi. *destroy* Ex 32$_{12}$, שחח *recline* 1QS 7$_{15}$; יצא hi. :: בוא hi. *bring* e.g. Nm 27$_{17}$ 2 S 5$_{2}$ 1 C 9$_{28}$ CD 11$_{8}$.

Also 4QpsJub[b] 1$_{3}$ (להוצ[יא]) 4QConfess 1.1$_{8}$ 4Q408 1$_{7}$ 4Q415 1.1$_{4}$.

<ANT> בוא hi. *bring*.*

Ho. $_{5}$Pf. הוּצָאָה; ptc. מוּצֵאת, מוּצָאִים, מוּצָאוֹת—**be taken out, be brought out,** <SUBJ> Tamar Gn 38$_{25}$, אִשָּׁה *woman* Jr 38$_{22}$ Am 4$_{3}$ (if em. qal *go out*), בֵּן *son* Ezk 14$_{22}$ (or em. פְּלֵטָה הַמּוּצָאִים בָּנִים וּבָנוֹת *a remnant, those who are taken out, sons and daughters* to מוֹצִאִים a remnant *bringing out* sons and daughters), בַּת *daughter* Ezk 14$_{22}$ (or em.), כַּלָּה *daughter-in-law* Gn 38$_{25}$, אֶרֶץ *land* appar. Ezk 38$_{8}$, פָּרָה *cow* Am 4$_{3}$ (if em.); subj. not expressed, Ezk 47$_{8}$ (or em. אֶל־הַיָּמָּה הַמּוּצָאִים *to the sea, namely those [waters] that are taken out* to אֶל־הַמַּיִם הַחֲמוּצִים *to the bitter waters*). <PREP> אֶל *to*, + שַׂר *commander* Jr 38$_{22}$; מִן of direction, *from*, + עַם *people* Ezk 38$_{8}$.*

→ יָצִיא *coming out*, יְצִיאָה *outlet*, מוֹצָא *going out*, מוֹצָאָה *origin*, תּוֹצָאָה *extremity*, צֶאֱצָא *offspring*, מוֹצָא *Moza*.

***יצא** II 3 vb. **be pure—Qal** 1 + waw וַיֵּצֵא—**shine, flash,** <SUBJ> כְּלִי *vessel* Pr 25$_{4}$ (unless יצא I *go out* of crucible), חֵמָה *anger* Jr 4$_{4}$=21$_{12}$ (unless יצא I *go out*). <PREP> לְ of benefit, *for*, + צֹרֵף *smith* Pr 25$_{4}$; כְּ *as*, + אֵשׁ *fire* Jr 4$_{4}$=21$_{12}$.

יצב 48.7.27 vb. **stand—Htp.** 48.7.27 Pf. Si התיצבתי, הִתְיַצְּבוּ; impf. Q יתיצבו, אֶתְיַצְּבָה, תִּתְיַצֵּב, (יִתְיַצָּב, יִתְיַצֵּב) יִתְיַצֵּב; + waw וַיִּתְיַצְּבוּ, וַתֵּתַצַּב, וַיִּתְיַצֵּב; impv. הִתְיַצֵּב, וְהִתְיַצְּבוּ, (הִתְיַצָּבָה), הִתְיַצְּבוּ; inf. הִתְיַצֵּב—**stand, position oneself, stand firm** (1 S 3$_{10}$ 10$_{19}$), **appear, arrive, resist** (Jos 1$_{5}$).

<SUBJ> י׳ *Y.* Ex 34$_{5}$ 1 S 3$_{10}$, מַלְאָךְ *angel* of Y Nm 22$_{22}$, שָׂטָן *Satan* Jb 2$_{1}$, עַם *people* Ex 14$_{13}$ 19$_{17}$ 1 S 12$_{7.16}$, Judah 2 C 20$_{17}$, פְּלִשְׁתִּי *Philistine* 1 S 17$_{16}$, Ahimaaz 2 S 18$_{30}$, Balak Nm 23$_{3.15}$, Caleb Si 46$_{7}$, Habakkuk Hb 2$_{1}$, Jehoshaphat 2 C 20$_{17}$, Joab 2 S 18$_{13}$, Job Jb 33$_{5}$, Joshua Dt 31$_{14}$ Jos 24$_{1}$ Si 46$_{7}$, Moses Ex 8$_{16}$ 9$_{13}$ Dt 31$_{14}$, Nathan Si 47$_{1}$, Saul 1 S 10$_{23}$, Shammah 2 S 23$_{12}$||1 C 11$_{14}$, Ben Sira Si 39$_{32}$.

אִישׁ *man* Nm 11$_{16}$ Dt 7$_{24}$ 11$_{25}$ Jos 1$_{5}$ Pr 22$_{29.29}$ 1QM 16$_{5}$ 17$_{11}$ ([התיצ]בם) 1QSa 1$_{20.21}$, אָב *father* of congregation 1QM 2$_{3}$, בֵּן *son* 1 S 10$_{19}$ Jb 1$_{6}$ 2$_{1}$ Si 8$_{8}$, אָחוֹת *sister* Ex 2$_{4}$, מֶלֶךְ *king* Ps 2$_{2}$ 2 C 20$_{17}$, כֹּהֵן *priest* 2 C 11$_{13}$ 1QM 8$_{3}$, רֹאשׁ *head*, i.e. leading official Jos 24$_{1}$ 1QM 2$_{3.4}$ 1QSa 1$_{16}$, שֹׁפֵט *judge* Jos 24$_{1}$, לֵוִי *Levite* 2 C 11$_{13}$, זָקֵן *elder* Nm 11$_{16}$ Jos 24$_{1}$, פִּנָּה *corner*, i.e. chief Jg 20$_{2}$.

שֹׁטֵר *officer* Nm 11$_{16}$ Jos 24$_{1}$, רֹפֵא *physician* Si 38$_{3}$, רָשָׁע *wicked one* Ps 36$_{5}$, גִּבּוֹר *warrior* 1QH 12$_{30}$, פָּרָשׁ *rider* Jr 46$_{4}$, יֹשֵׁב *inhabitant* 2 C 20$_{17}$, זוֹנָה *prostitute* 4QWiles 1$_{12}$, חֵלֶק *creature* Si 36$_{13}$, פָּקוּד *one who is enlisted* 1QM 2$_{4}$, בָּחִיר *chosen one* 1QS 11$_{16}$, הלל ptc. *one who is deluded* Ps 5$_{6}$ GnzPs 1$_{3}$, worshipper 1QH 3$_{24}$ 1QSa 1$_{11.12.14}$, רוּחַ *spirit* 1QH 3$_{21}$ 11$_{13}$, מַעֲשֶׂה *work, creature* 1QH 10$_{11}$, מִי *who?* Dt 9$_{2}$ Ps 94$_{16}$ Jb 41$_{2}$ Si 46$_{3}$, אֵלֶּה *these* Zc 6$_{5}$ 1QM 2$_{5}$ 1QSa 2$_{8}$, כֹּל *everyone* 1QH 7$_{29}$; subj. not specified, 2 S 21$_{5}$ Jr 46$_{14}$ Jb 38$_{14}$ 2 C 20$_{6}$ 1QM 8$_{17}$ (התיצ[בו]) 1QH 12$_{28}$ 1QH fr. 7$_{11}$ 4QD^{b} 4$_{9}$ 4QShirShabb^{a} 1.1$_{13}$ ([מתיצ]בים) 4QPrFêtes^{c} 22$_{3}$ ([י]תיצבו) 4QBéat 15$_{4}$ CD 10$_{7}$.

<PREP> לְ of benefit, *to, for*, + worshipper Ps 94$_{16}$; *at*, + מוֹעֵד *appointed time*, i.e. festival 1QM 2$_{4}$, חֹדֶשׁ *new moon* 1QM 2$_{4}$, שַׁבָּת *sabbath* 1QM 2$_{4}$, יוֹם *day* 1QM 2$_{4}$; *according to*, + שֵׁבֶט *tribe* 1 S 10$_{19}$, אֶלֶף *thousand(s)* 1 S 10$_{19}$.

בְּ of place, *in, at*, + תַּחְתִּית *lowest part*, i.e. foot, *of* mountain Ex 19$_{17}$, גְּבוּל *border*, i.e. realm, of wickedness 1QH 3$_{24}$, דֶּרֶךְ *way* Nm 22$_{22}$, הֵיכָל *temple* 4QShirShabb^{a} 1.1$_{13}$, אֹהֶל *tent* Dt 31$_{14}$, קָהָל *assembly* Jg 20$_{2}$, שַׁעַר *gate* 1QM 2$_{3}$ 4QWiles 1$_{12}$, מַעֲמָד *position* 1QH 3$_{21}$ 11$_{13}$.

בְּ of accompaniment, + כּוֹבַע *helmet* Jr 46$_{4}$.

בְּ *against*, + פָּנִים *face* Dt 7$_{24}$ 11$_{25}$; *at*, + מִשְׁמָע *hearing* 1QSa 1$_{11}$; *among*, + רֹאשׁ *head*, i.e. leading official 1QSa 1$_{14}$, יְסוֹד *founding member* 1QSa 1$_{12}$; *in*, + עֲבוֹדָה *service* 1QSa 1$_{16}$, מִלְחָמָה *battle* 1QSa 1$_{21}$.

מִן of direction, *from*, + גְּבוּל *border* 2 C 11$_{13}$; *at*, + רָחוֹק *distance* Ex 2$_{4}$, רֹאשׁ *head*, i.e. beginning Si 39$_{32}$.

עַל *upon, beside, before*, + י׳ *Y.* Jb 1$_{6}$ 2$_{1.1}$, אָדוֹן *Lord* Zc 6$_{5}$, עֵדָה *congregation* 1QSa 1$_{20}$, Rehoboam 2 C 11$_{13}$, מָצוֹר *tower* Hb 2$_{1}$, דֶּרֶךְ *way* Ps 36$_{5}$, מַעֲמָד *position* 1QM 8$_{3.17}$ 16$_{5}$ 17$_{11}$, עֹלָה *burnt offering* Nm 23$_{3.15}$ 1QM 2$_{5}$, זֶבַח *sacrifice* 1QM 2$_{5}$.

בְּתוֹךְ *among*, + עַם *people* 1 S 10$_{23}$, עֵדָה *congregation* 1QSa 2$_{8}$, חֶלְקָה *allotted portion of ground* 2 S 23$_{12}$||1 C 11$_{14}$.

לְנֶגֶד *before*, + עַיִן *eye* Ps 5$_{6}$ GnzPs 1$_{3}$.

לִפְנֵי *before*, + י׳ *Y.* 1 S 10$_{19}$ Jb 41$_{2}$, אֱלֹהִים *God* Jos 24$_{1}$, אֵל *God* 1QS 11$_{16}$ 1QH 11$_{13}$, פַּרְעֹה *Pharaoh* Ex 8$_{16}$ 9$_{13}$, מֶלֶךְ *king* Pr 22$_{29}$, שַׂר *prince* Si 8$_{8}$, נָדִיב *noble* Si 38$_{3}$, David Si 47$_{1}$, Joshua Jos 1$_{5}$ Si 46$_{3}$, בֵּן *son* Dt 9$_{2}$, חָשׁוּךְ *darkened one* Pr 22$_{29}$, יכח hi. ptc. *one who reproves* 1QH 12$_{28}$, כָּבוֹד *glory* 1QH 10$_{11}$, אַף *anger* 1QH 12$_{30}$, חֵמָה *wrath* 1QH 7$_{29}$.

מִפְּנֵי *before* Si 36$_{13}$.

עִם *with*, + י׳ *Y.* 2 C 20$_{6}$, אֱלֹהִים *God* 2 C 20$_{6}$, Moses Ex 34$_{5}$ Nm 11$_{16}$, צָבָא *host* of the holy ones 1QH 3$_{21}$.

<COLL> הִתְיַצֵּב כֹּה *position yourself here* Nm 23$_{15}$, וַיִּתְיַצֵּב אַרְבָּעִים יוֹם *and he positioned himself for forty days* 1 S 17$_{16}$, תִּתְיַצֵּב מִנֶּגֶד *you would have stood aloof* 2 S 18$_{13}$, להתיצב תמיד *to take up one's position continually* 1QM 2$_{3}$.

יצג 16.1 vb. **place—Hi.** 15 Pf. הִצִּיגַנִי (Qr), הִצַּגְתִּיו; impf. 2ms

וַיַּצִּיגוּ, (וַיַּצִּגֵם, וַיַּצִּג) וַיַּצֵּג; וְהִצַּגְתִּיהָ + waw ;אַצִּיגָה, תַּצִּיג (וַיַּצִּגוּ); impv. הַצִּיגוּ; ptc. מַצִּיג; inf. הַצֵּג—**set down, place, bring one forward, produce.**

<SUBJ> י״ Y. Ho 2_5, אֱלוֹהַּ God Jb 17_6, בַּיִת house of Israel Am 5_{15}, פְּלִשְׁתִּי Philistine 1 S 5_2, Esau Gn 33_{15}, Gideon Jg 6_{37} 7_5 8_{27}, Jacob Gn 30_{38}, Joseph Gn 47_2, Judah Gn 43_9, Nebuchadrezzar Jr $51_{34(Qr)}$, מֶלֶךְ *king* Jr $51_{34(Qr)}$, רַךְ *tender one* Dt 28_{56}, עָנֹג *dainty one* Dt 28_{56}; subj. not specified, 2 S 6_{17}||1 C 16_1.

<OBJ> Jerusalem Jr 51_{34}, Benjamin Gn 43_9, Job Jb 17_6, אִישׁ *man* Gn 47_2, אֵם *mother* Ho 2_5, מִשְׁפָּט *justice* Am 5_{15}, אֲרוֹן *ark* of God 1 S 5_2, אֵפוֹד *ephod* Jg 8_{27}, מַקֵּל *shoot* Gn 30_{38}, גִּזָּה *fleece* Jg 6_{37}, כַּף *sole* of foot Dt 28_{56}, כֹּל *everyone* Jg 7_5.

<PREP> לְ *as*, + מְשֹׁל *by-word* of peoples Jb 17_6; בְּ of place, *in, at*, + Ophrah Jg 8_{27}, עִיר *city* Jg 8_{27}, גֹּרֶן *threshing floor* Jg 6_{37}, שַׁעַר *gate* Am 5_{15}, מָקוֹם *place* 2 S 6_{17}; מִן partitive, *some of, (any) one of*, + עַם *people* Gn 33_{15}; עַל *upon*, + אֶרֶץ *earth* Dt 28_{56}; אֵצֶל *beside*, + Dagon 1 S 5_2; בְּתוֹךְ *among*, + אֹהֶל *tent* 2 S 6_{17}||1 C 16_1; לִפְנֵי *before*, + Israel Gn 43_9, פַּרְעֹה *Pharaoh* Gn 47_2; עִם *with*, + Jacob Gn 33_{15}.

<COLL> הִצִּיגַנִי כְּלִי רִיק *he has made me (as) an empty vessel* Jr $51_{34(Qr)}$.

Ho. $_{1.1}$ Impf. יֻצַּג; ptc. Si מצגת—**be placed, be left behind,** <SUBJ> צֹאן *sheep* Ex 10_{24}, בָּקָר *cattle* Ex 10_{24}, תְּנוּפָה *wave-offering* Si 30_{18}.

<PREP> לִפְנֵי *before*, + גִּלּוּל *idol* Si $30_{18(B)}$ (Bmg lacks prep.).*

***יצד be firm—Pi. fasten,** וּבַמַּקָּבוֹת יְיַצְּדֵהוּ *and with hammers he fastens it* (image) Is 44_{12} (if em. יְצָרֵהוּ *he shapes it*).

***יצה** 2 vb. **order—Pi.** + waw וַיְצַו; impv. צַו—**give last injunctions** (unless צוה pi. *command*)—<SUBJ> David 1 K 2_1, Hezekiah 2 K 20_1. <OBJ> (indirect) Solomon 1 K 2_1. <PREP> לְ of direction, *to*, + בַּיִת *house(hold)* 2 K 20_1.

⇒ see also צוה pi. *command*.

יִצְהָר I $_{23.1.12}$ n.m. **fresh oil**—sf. יִצְהָרֶךָ—as product of land (e.g. Dt 7_{13} 11_{14} Jr 31_{12} Hg 1_{11} 2 C 32_{28}), and used for anointing (Zc 4_{14}).

<SUBJ> אמל pulal *languish* Jl 1_{10}.

<OBJ> אסף *gather* Dt 11_{14} (|| תִּירוֹשׁ *new wine*, דָּגָן *grain*), בוא hi. *bring* Ne 10_{38}, נתן *give* Ho 2_{10} 11QBer 1_9 (both || תִּירוֹשׁ ,דָּגָן), קדשׁ hi. *sanctify* 11QT 60_6 (|| תִּירוֹשׁ ,דָּגָן), שׁלח *send* Jl 2_{19} (|| תִּירוֹשׁ ,דָּגָן), שׁוק hi. *overflow with* Jl 2_{24}, שׁאר hi. *leave* Dt 28_{51} (|| תִּירוֹשׁ ,דָּגָן, + שֶׁגֶר *offspring*, עַשְׁתָּרוֹת *flocks*), ענה *answer* Ho 2_{24} (|| תִּירוֹשׁ ,דָּגָן), ברך pi. *bless* Dt 7_{13} (|| תִּירוֹשׁ ,דָּגָן, + פְּרִי *fruit*, שֶׁגֶר, עַשְׁתָּרוֹת).

<CSTR> חֵלֶב יִצְהָר *fat*, i.e. best, *of olive oil* Nm 18_{12}, רוב ... יצהר *plenty of ... fresh oil* 1QH 10_{24}, מַעְשַׂר ... יִצְהָרְךָ *tithe of ... your fresh oil* Dt 12_{17} 14_{23} Ne $13_{5.12}$ (both הַיִּצְהָר), [ראשית ה]יצהר *the beginning of the fresh oil* 11QT 21_{16}, רֵאשִׁית ... יִצְהָרְךָ *beginning*, i.e. firstfruits, *of ... your fresh oil* Dt 18_4 2 C 31_5, תְּבוּאַת יִצְהָר *produce of fresh oil* 2 C 32_{28}, מועד היצהר *the festival of the fresh oil* 4QRPc 23_9 11QT 11_{12}, sim. 11QT 43_9, תְּרוּמַת ... הַיִּצְהָר *offering of the fresh oil* Ne 10_{40}, זֵית יִצְהָר *olive(s) of fresh oil* 2 K 18_{32}, בְּנֵי־הַיִּצְהָר *sons of the new oil*, i.e. anointed ones Zc 4_{14} 4QCommGenC 4_2, מעשר הדגן והתירוש והיצהר *one tenth of the grain and the new wine and the fresh oil* 11QT 60_6, מְאַת הַכֶּסֶף וְהַדָּגָן הַתִּירוֹשׁ וְהַיִּצְהָר *hundredth part of the money and the grain, the new wine and the fresh oil* Ne 5_{11}.

<PREP> עַל *because of, over*, + נהר *be radiant* Jr 31_{12} (|| תִּירוֹשׁ *new wine*, דָּגָן *grain*, + בֵּן *young* of flock and herd); *upon*, + קרא *call for* drought Hg 1_{11} (|| תִּירוֹשׁ ,דָּגָן, אֶרֶץ *land*, הַר *mountain*, אָדָם *humankind*, בְּהֵמָה *beast*, + יְגִיעַ *labour*, אֲשֶׁר תּוֹצִיא הָאֲדָמָה *what the ground brings forth*).

<SYN> תִּירוֹשׁ *wine*, דָּגָן *grain*, אֶרֶץ *land*, הַר *mountain*, אָדָם *humankind*, בְּהֵמָה *beast*.

<COLL> [ח]לב ודבש דם ענב יצהר ובגד *milk and honey, the blood of the grape, fresh oil and clothing* Si 39_{26}.

Also 4QHalakhaha 5_1 4Mg 1_6 4QBera 5_6 4Q365a 2.1_1 4QPrFêtesb 13_3.*

⇒ צהר *press out oil;* יִצְהָר IIIzhar.

יִצְהָר II $_9$ pr.n.m. **Izhar,** Kohathite Levite, <NOM CL> בְּנֵי קְהָת ... יִצְהָר וְחֶבְרוֹן *the sons of Kohath were ... Izhar and Hebron* Ex 6_{18} Nm 3_{19} 1 C 5_{28} 6_3 23_{12}. <CSTR> בֶּן־יִצְהָר *son of Izhar* Nm 16_1 1 C 6_{23}, בְּנֵי יִצְהָר *the sons of Izhar* Ex 6_{21} 1 C 23_{18}.

⇒ יִצְהָרִי *Izharite;* יִצְהָר I *fresh oil.*

יִצְהָרִי 4 gent. **Izharite**—הַיִּצְהָרִי—collective, **Izharites**, <CSTR> מִשְׁפַּחַת הַיִּצְהָרִי *family of the Izrahites* Nm 3$_{27}$.

<PREP> לְ of possession, *(belonging) to, of* 1 C 24$_{22}$ 26$_{23}$. $_{29}$.

→ יִצְהָר *Izhar.*

יָצוּעַ I 5.3.3 n.m. **couch**—sf. יְצוּעִי; pl. cstr. יְצוּעֵי; sf. יְצוּעַי, Si יצועיך, יצועיו, יצעיה (Q יצועיה)—**couch, bed,** <NOM CL> יצועיה יצועי שחת *her couches are couches of corruption* 4QWiles 1$_{5}$.

<OBJ> רפד pi. *spread out* Jb 17$_{13}$, חלל pi. *profane* Gn 49$_{4}$ 1 C 5$_{1}$ Si 47$_{20}$.

<CSTR> יְצוּעֵי אָבִיו *beds of his father* 1 C 5$_{1}$, יצועי שחת *couches of corruption* 4QWiles 1$_{5}$; עֶרֶשׂ יְצוּעָי *couch of my bed* Ps 132$_{3}$.

<PREP> עַל *upon* 1QH 9$_{4}$, + זכר *remember* Ps 63$_{7}$, קום htpol. *rise up* Si 41$_{22}$, נשׂק hi. *kindle (sexual desire)* Si 34$_{19(B)}$ (Bmg יְצוּר *creature*); לִפְנֵי *before*, + שׁכב *lie down* 4QVis Sam 7$_{4}$.

<COLL> יְצוּעִי עָלָה *he went up (to) my couch* Gn 49$_{4}$ (or em. יְצוּעַ עָלָה you defiled *the couch of a she-goat*, i.e. secondary wife or יְצוּעֵי יַעֲלָה *couch[es] of [his] she-goat*, i.e. secondary wife),* משכב יצועי *when I laid down (upon) my couch* 1QS 10$_{14}$.

→ יצע *spread.*

יָצוּעַ II, see יָצִיעַ *terrace.*

[יְצוּר] 0.1 n.m. **creature**—sf. Si יצוריו—<PREP> עַל *upon*, + נשׂק hi. *kindle fire* Si 34$_{19(Bmg)}$ (B יָצוּעַ *couch*).

→ יצר *form.*

יִצְחָק 112.2.13 pr.n.m. **Isaac**—יִשְׂחָק (Jr 33$_{26}$ Am 7$_{9.16}$ Ps 105$_{9}$ [mss, ||1 C 16$_{16}$ יִצְחָק]), Q יסחק—Hebrew patriarch, son of Abraham and Sarah.

<SUBJ> היה *be* Gn 25$_{20}$, זקן *be old* Gn 27$_{1}$, עצם *be mighty* Gn 26$_{16}$, ראה *see* Gn 24$_{63}$, אהב *love* Gn 24$_{67}$ 25$_{28}$, חנה *encamp* Gn 26$_{17}$, גור *sojourn* Gn 35$_{27}$, ישׁב *dwell* Gn 24$_{62}$ 25$_{11}$ 26$_{6.17}$, ילד ni. *be born* Gn 21$_{5}$, hi. *become father of* 4QAges^{a} 1$_{5}$, גמל ni. *be weaned* Gn 21$_{8}$, נחם ni. *be comforted* Gn 24$_{67}$, אסף ni. *be gathered* Gn 35$_{29}$, בוא *come* Gn 24$_{62}$, hi. *bring* Gn 24$_{67}$, הלך *go* Gn 26$_{1.16.17}$, htp. *walk* Gn 48$_{15}$, יצא *go out* Gn 24$_{63}$, שׁוב *go back*, i.e. do again Gn 26$_{18}$.

עשׂה *do* Gn 27$_{37}$, כלה pi. *finish* Gn 27$_{30}$, חפר *dig* Gn 26$_{18}$, נטה *pitch* tent Gn 26$_{25}$, בנה *build* Gn 26$_{25}$, שׂים *place*, i.e. make Gn 27$_{37}$, נתן *give* Gn 27$_{37}$, סמך *sustain* Gn 27$_{37}$, שׁמר *keep* CD 3$_{3}$, לקח *take* Gn 24$_{67}$ 25$_{20}$, נשׂא *raise* Gn 24$_{63}$, שׁלח *send* Gn 28$_{5}$, pi. *send away* Gn 26$_{31}$ 28$_{6}$.

זרע *sow* Gn 26$_{12}$, מצא *obtain* harvest Gn 26$_{12}$, מושׁ *feel* Gn 27$_{21.22}$, צחק pi. *fondle* Gn 26$_{8}$, חרד *tremble* Gn 27$_{33}$, גוע *expire* Gn 35$_{29}$, מות *die* Gn 35$_{29}$, קבר *bury* Gn 25$_{9}$, קרא *call* Gn 26$_{18.20.25}$ 27$_{1}$ 28$_{1}$, אמר *say* Gn 22$_{7}$ 26$_{9.27}$ 27$_{1}$ $_{+8t}$ 28$_{1}$ 4QpsJub^{a} 2.2$_{2.4}$, דבר pi. *speak* Gn 27$_{5}$, ענה *answer* Gn 27$_{37.39}$, ברך pi. *bless* Gn 25$_{11}$ 27$_{33}$ 28$_{1.6.6}$, צוה pi. *command* Gn 27$_{46}$ 28$_{6}$, עתר *plead* Gn 25$_{21}$.

<NOM CL> יִצְחָק בֶּן־שִׁשִּׁים שָׁנָה *Isaac was the son of sixty years*, i.e. sixty years old Gn 25$_{26}$, בְּנֵי אַבְרָהָם יִצְחָק *the sons of Abraham were Isaac* 1 C 1$_{28}$.

<OBJ> ראה *see* Gn 24$_{64}$, ילד *bear child* Gn 17$_{21}$ 21$_{3}$, hi. *become father of* Gn 25$_{19}$ 1 C 1$_{34}$, מול *circumcise* Gn 21$_{4}$, נתן *give* Jos 24$_{3}$, לקח *take* Gn 22$_{2.3}$ 4QpsJub^{a} 2.1$_{11}$, עקד *tie up* Gn 22$_{9}$, עלה hi. *bring up*, i.e. offer up Gn 22$_{2}$, שׁלח pi. *send away* Gn 26$_{27}$, שׂנא *hate* Gn 26$_{27}$, קבר *bury* Gn 35$_{29}$ 49$_{31}$, קרא *call* Gn 17$_{19}$ 4QpsJub^{a} 2.1$_{9}$, ברך pi. *bless* Gn 26$_{12}$ 4QpsJub^{a} 2.2$_{10}$.

<CSTR> אֱלֹהֵי (...) יִצְחָק *God of (...) Isaac* Gn 28$_{13}$ 32$_{10}$ 46$_{1}$ Ex 3$_{6.15.16}$ 4$_{5}$ 1 K 18$_{36}$ 1 C 29$_{18}$ 2 C 30$_{6}$ 4QConfess 3$_{5}$, פַּחַד *fear*, or *thigh/posterity, of* Gn 31$_{42.53}$ (פַּחַד ... יִצְחָק),* צור יצחק *rock of Isaac* Si 51$_{12}$,, תּוֹלְדֹת *descendants of* Gn 25$_{19}$, בְּנֵי *sons of* 1 C 1$_{34}$, זֶרַע ... יִשְׂחָק *offspring of Isaac* Jr 33$_{26}$, בֵּית *house of* Am 7$_{16}$.

עַבְדֵי יִצְחָק *servants of Isaac* Gn 26$_{19.25.32}$, רֹעֵי *shepherds of* Gn 26$_{20}$, פְּנֵי *face*, i.e. presence, *of* Gn 27$_{30}$, עֵינֵי *eyes of* Gn 28$_{8}$, יְמֵי *days of* Gn 35$_{28}$, ימי ... ישחק *days of ... Isaac* 4QpsJub^{a} 2.2$_{12}$, שֵׁם ... יִצְחָק *name of ... Isaac* Gn 48$_{16}$, בָּמוֹת יִשְׂחָק *high places of Isaac* Am 7$_{9}$.

<APP> אָב *father* Gn 31$_{53}$ 32$_{10}$ 46$_{1}$ 48$_{15.16}$, בֵּן *son* Gn 22$_{2}$ 4QpsJub^{a} 2.1$_{11}$, שֵׁם *name* Gn 17$_{19}$ 4QpsJub^{a} 2.1$_{9}$.

<PREP> לְ of direction, *to* Ps 105$_{9}$ (שְׁבוּעָתוֹ לְיִשְׂחָק *his oath [given] to Isaac*]), + בוא hi. *bring* Gn 27$_{33}$, נתן *give* Gn 25$_{5}$ 35$_{12}$ Ex 6$_{8}$ Jos 24$_{4}$, קרא *call* Gn 26$_{9}$, אמר *say* Gn 26$_{32}$, ספר pi. *relate* Gn 24$_{66}$, נגד hi. *declare* Gn 26$_{32}$, שׁבע ni. *swear oath* Gn 50$_{24}$ Ex 33$_{1}$ Nm 32$_{11}$ Dt 1$_{8}$ 6$_{10}$ 9$_{5}$ 29$_{12}$ 30$_{20}$ 34$_{4}$.

לְ of benefit, *to, for* 1 C 16$_{16}$, + היה *be* Gn 24$_{67}$ 26$_{35}$, עתר ni. *be moved by entreaty* Gn 25$_{21}$, יכח hi. *determine* Gn 24$_{14}$, קום hi. *raise up* Si 44$_{22}$, לקח *take* Gn 24$_{4}$, מסר *hand down* CD 3$_{3}$, חקק *inscribe* 4Q185 1.2$_{4}$.

לְ introducing object, + נשק *kiss* Gn 27$_{26}$, זכר *remember* Ex 32$_{13}$ Dt 9$_{27}$.

בְּ of instrument, *by (means of), with*, + קרא ni. *be called* Gn 21$_{12}$; *with regard to*, + שׂטם hi. *accuse* 4QpsJub^{a} 2.1$_{10}$.

אֶל *to*, + ראה ni. *appear* Ex 6$_{3}$, בוא *come* Gn 26$_{27}$ 31$_{18}$ 35$_{27}$ 4QJub^{h} 35$_{9}$, נגשׁ *draw near* Gn 27$_{22}$, אמר *say* Gn 26$_{16}$ 27$_{1.46}$.

עַל *upon*, + שׂים *place* Gn 22$_{6}$; אֵת *with* 2 K 13$_{23}$, + קום hi. *establish* Gn 17$_{19.21}$, זכר *remember* Ex 2$_{24}$; מֵעַל *from (upon)*, + שׁלח pi. *send away* Gn 25$_{6}$; עִם *with*, + ירשׁ *take possession* Gn 21$_{10}$.

<COLL> וְזָכַרְתִּי ... אֶת־בְּרִיתִי יִצְחָק *and I will remember ... my covenant (with) Isaac* Lv 26$_{42}$.*

Also 4QAges^{b} 2$_{1}$ 4QpsJub^{b} 7$_{5}$ 4QD^{h} 4.1$_{9}$ 4QapJoshua^{b} 17$_{4}$.

⇒ צחק *laugh*.

[יִצְחָר] 1 pr.n.m. **Izhar**—Kt יצחר—Judahite, son of Asshur and Helah, <NOM CL> וּבְנֵי חֶלְאָה צֶרֶת יצחר *and the sons of Helah were Zereth (and) Izhar* 1 C 4$_{7(Kt)}$ (Qr וְצֹחַר *and Zohar*).

⇒ צַחַר *tawny*.

יָצִיא 1 adj. **coming out**—pl. cstr. יְצִיאֵי (Qr)—as noun, **one coming out**, <CSTR> מִיצִיאֵי מֵעָיו *from among the ones coming forth of his bowels*, i.e. his very own sons 2 C 32$_{21(Qr)}$.

⇒ יצא *go out*.

[יְצִיאָה] 0.0.1 n.f. **outlet**—cstr. Q יציאת—על פי יציאת המים *by the mouth of the water outlet* 3QTr 7$_{14}$; בציאת גי פלא *at the outlet of the valley of Pella* 9$_{15}$* (others בצחיאת גר *in the stony ground near to the cairn of* the thorn).

⇒ יצא *go out*.

[יָצִיעַ] 3 n.m. & f. **terrace**—only Qr יָצוּעַ, Kt יציע, lower projecting **storey** or **terrace** of temple, <NOM CL> הַיָּצִיעַ הַתַּחְתֹּנָה חָמֵשׁ בָּאַמָּה רָחְבָּהּ *the lowest terrace was five cubits broad* 1 K 6$_{6(Qr)}$. <OBJ> בנה *build* 1 K 6$_{5(Qr).10(Qr)}$. <ADJ> תַּחְתּוֹן *lowest one* 1 K 6$_{6(Qr)}$.

⇒ יצע *spread out*.

יָצַל, see אָצַל *take away*.

יצע 4.1.2 vb. **extend—Hi.** 2.1.2 Pf. Q הוצעת; impf. יַצִּיעַ, Si 2ms תצע, אַצִּיעָה, Q יציעו—**extend, spread out as couch,** <SUBJ> אָדָם *person* Is 58$_{5}$, בֵּן *son* Si 4$_{27}$, worshipper Ps 139$_{8}$; subj. not specified, 4QRitMar 20$_{4}$ 4QBéat 15$_{9}$.

<OBJ> נֶפֶשׁ *soul* Si 4$_{27}$, שַׂק *sackcloth* Is 58$_{5}$, אֵפֶר *ashes* Is 58$_{5}$.

<PREP> לְ of direction, *to*, + נָבָל *foolish one* Si 4$_{27}$.

<COLL> וְאַצִּיעָה שְׁאוֹל *and (if) I should spread a couch in Sheol* Ps 139$_{8}$.

Ho. 2 Impf. יֻצַּע—**be spread out as a couch,** <SUBJ> רִמָּה *maggot* Is 14$_{11}$, שַׂק *sackcloth* Est 4$_{3}$, אֵפֶר *ashes* Est 4$_{3}$.

<PREP> לְ of benefit, *to, for*, + רַב pl. *many* Est 4$_{3}$; תַּחַת *under*, + מֶלֶךְ *king* of Babylon Is 14$_{11}$.*

⇒ יָצוּעַ *couch*, יָצִיעַ *terrace*, מַצָּע *couch*.

יצק 55.3.6 vb. **pour out—Qal** 42.1.1 Pf. יָצַק (יְקָצָם), Q יצקתה; impf. אֶצֹּק (Si אצוק); + waw וַיִּצֹק, וְיָצַקְתָּ, וְיָצַק; 3fs וַתִּצֹּק, וַיִּצְקוּ (וַיִּצֶק); impv. יְצֹק (צַק); ptc. pass. יָצוּק, יְצֻקוֹת (יְצֻקִים) יְצוּקִים; inf. צֶקֶת—**pour out, cast, spread, dish up** food, **issue** statute (Si 16$_{22}$), <SUBJ> '' Y. Is 44$_{3.3}$, אֵל *God* 4QDibHam^{a} 1.5$_{15}$, עַם *people* 1 K 18$_{34}$, Israelite(s) Lv 2$_{6}$, Aaron Lv 9$_{9}$, Bezalel Ex 36$_{36}$ 37$_{3.13}$ 38$_{5}$, Elisha 2 K 3$_{11}$, Jacob Gn 28$_{18}$ 35$_{14}$, Moses Ex 25$_{12}$ 26$_{37}$ 29$_{7}$ Lv 8$_{12.15}$, Samuel 1 S 10$_{1}$, Tamar 2 S 13$_{9}$, אִישׁ *man* Nm 5$_{15}$, אִשָּׁה *woman* 2 K 4$_{4}$, נַעַר *lad* 2 K 9$_{6}$, מֶלֶךְ *king* 1 K 7$_{46}$||2 C 4$_{17}$, כֹּהֵן *priest* Lv 14$_{15.26}$, worshipper Si 16$_{22}$, נֶפֶשׁ *soul*, i.e. anyone Lv 2$_{1}$, אֶחָד *one* 2 K 4$_{40.41}$ 9$_{3}$.

בָּקָר *cattle* 2 C 4$_{3}$, בַּיִת *house* of rebellion Ezk 24$_{3}$, מַפָּל *fleshy belly* of crocodile Jb 41$_{15}$, דָּם *blood* 1 K 22$_{35}$, עָפָר *dust* Jb 38$_{38}$; subj. of pass., פְּקָעִים *gourds* 1 K 7$_{24}$, כָּתֵף *support* for laver 1 K 7$_{30}$, צוּר *rock* Jb 29$_{6}$, לֵב *heart* Jb 41$_{16.16}$, דָּבָר *thing* Ps 41$_{9}$; subj. not specified, Ex 38$_{27}$.

<OBJ> רוּחַ *spirit* Is 44$_{3}$ 4QDibHam^{a} 1.5$_{15}$, בְּרָכָה *blessing* Is 44$_{3}$, חֹק *statute* Si 16$_{22}$ (or em. נצר *keep* statute or רחק *be distant*, with חֹק as subj.), שֶׁמֶן *oil* Gn 28$_{18}$ 35$_{14}$ Lv 2$_{1.6}$ Nm 5$_{15}$ 2 K 9$_{6}$, מַיִם *water* 2 K 3$_{11}$ Is 44$_{3}$ Ezk 24$_{3}$, נֵזֶל

stream Is 44$_{3}$, דָּם *blood* Lv 8$_{15}$ 9$_{9}$, טַבַּעַת *ring* Ex 25$_{12}$||37$_{3}$ 37$_{13}$ 38$_{5}$, אֶדֶן *socket* Ex 26$_{37}$||36$_{36}$ 38$_{27.27}$, כְּלִי *utensil* 1 K 7$_{46}$||2 C 4$_{17}$, סִיר *pot* 1 K 7$_{46}$||2 C 4$_{17}$, יָעַ *fire-shovel* 1 K 7$_{46}$ ||2 C 4$_{17}$, מִזְרָק *basin* 1 K 7$_{46}$||2 C 4$_{17}$.

<PREP> לְ of direction, *to,* + מוּצָק *clod of dust* Jb 38$_{38}$.

לְ of benefit, *to, for,* + עַם *people* 2 K 4$_{41}$, אִישׁ *man* 2 K 4$_{40}$, אֲרוֹן *ark* Ex 25$_{12}$||37$_{3}$, שֻׁלְחָן *table* Ex 37$_{13}$, עַמּוּד *pillar* Ex 26$_{37}$||36$_{36}$.

בְּ of place, *in, at,* + כִּכָּר *district* of Jordan 1 K 7$_{46}$||2 C 4$_{17}$; *in, on,* + worshipper Ps 41$_{9}$, קָצָה *corner* of grating Ex 38$_{5}$, סִיר *pot* Ezk 24$_{3}$.

כְּ *as,* + אֶבֶן *stone* Jb 41$_{16}$, פֶּלַח *mill-stone* Jb 41$_{16}$.

מִן partitive, *some of, (any) one of,* + שֶׁמֶן *oil* Lv 8$_{12}$ 14$_{26}$.

אֶל *to, at,* + יְסוֹד *base* Lv 8$_{15}$ 9$_{9}$, חֵיק *hollow* of chariot 1 K 22$_{35}$, רֹאשׁ *head* 2 K 9$_{6}$.

עַל *upon,* + מַצֵּבָה *pillar* Gn 35$_{14}$, קָרְבָּן *offering* Nm 5$_{15}$, עֹלָה *burnt offering* 1 K 18$_{34}$, מִנְחָה *grain offering* Lv 2$_{1.6}$, כְּלִי *utensil* 2 K 4$_{4}$, עֵץ *wood* 1 K 18$_{34}$, צָמֵא *thirsty ground* Is 44$_{3}$, יַבָּשָׁה *dry ground* Is 44$_{3}$, זֶרַע *seed,* i.e. offspring Is 44$_{3}$, צֶאֱצָאִים *offspring* Is 44$_{3}$, worshipper 4QDibHam^{a} 1.5$_{15}$, רֹאשׁ *head* Gn 28$_{18}$ Ex 29$_{7}$ Lv 8$_{12}$ 1 S 10$_{1}$ 2 K 9$_{3.6(mss)}$, יָד *hand* of Elijah 2 K 3$_{11}$, כַּף *palm* of hand Lv 14$_{15.26}$, Leviathan Jb 41$_{15}$.

לִפְנֵי *before,* + Ammon 2 S 13$_{9}$.

עִמָּד *with,* + Job Jb 29$_{6}$.

Hi. 4 + waw וַיַּצִּקוּ (וַיַּצִּקֻם); ptc. מוּצֶקֶת (Kt מיצות)—**set down, pour out,** <SUBJ> לֵוִי *Levite* 2 S 15$_{24}$, מַלְאָךְ *messenger* Jos 7$_{23}$, הִיא *she* 2 K 4$_{5(Qr, mss)}$.

<OBJ> אֲרוֹן *ark* of God 2 Sam 15$_{24}$, אַדֶּרֶת *cloak* from Shinar Jos 7$_{23}$, כֶּסֶף *silver* Jos 7$_{23}$, לָשׁוֹן *tongue-shaped bar* of gold Jos 7$_{23}$.

<PREP> לִפְנֵי *before,* + '' *Y.* Jos 7$_{23}$.

Ho. 9.2.5 Pf. הוּצַק; impf. יוּצַק; ptc. מוּצָק (מֻצָק); cstr. מוּצַק; pl. Q מוצקות—**be emptied out, be poured out, be washed away, be cast, be firmly founded** (Jb 11$_{15}$), **1a.** <SUBJ> יָם *sea* 1 K 7$_{23}$||2 C 4$_{2}$, יְסוֹד *foundation* Jb 22$_{16}$, מַיִם *water* Si 15$_{16}$ 11QT 49$_{7}$, שֶׁמֶן *oil* Lv 21$_{10}$ 4QapMoses^{a} 1.1$_{9}$, אֵשׁ *fire* Si 15$_{16}$, כּוּר *furnace* Si 43$_{4(Bmg)}$ (B מצוק), כֹּתֶרֶת *capital* on column 1 K 7$_{16}$, רְאִי *mirror* Jb 37$_{18}$, חֵן *favour* Ps 45$_{3}$, כֹּל *everything* 1 K 7$_{33}$; subj. not specified, Jb 11$_{15}$.

<PREP> בְּ *in, on,* + שָׂפָה *lip* Ps 45$_{3}$.

עַל *upon,* + רֹאשׁ *head* Lv 21$_{10}$ 4QapMoses^{a} 1.1$_{9}$, אֹכֶל *food* 11QT 49$_{7}$.

לִפְנֵי *before,* + worshipper Si 15$_{16}$.

<COLL> מוּצַק נְחֹשֶׁת *being cast of,* i.e. in, *bronze* 1 K 7$_{16}$, נָהָר יוּצַק יְסוֹדָם *their foundation was washed away by a river* Jb 22$_{16}$.

1b. ptc. as noun, **cast (object), casting, liquid streams** (4QMMT B$_{55.56.57}$), <SUBJ> בדל hi. *separate* 4QMMT B$_{56}$.

<NOM CL> [כ]ור [נ]פוח מעשי מוצק *the furnace that is blown upon,* i.e. glowing, *is a wrought casting* Si 43$_{4(M)}$.

<CSTR> לחת מוצקות *moisture of the streams* 4QMMT B$_{57}$.

<PREP> עַל *concerning* 4QMMT B$_{55}$.*

→ יְצֻקָה *casting,* מוּצָק *casting,* מוּצֶקֶת *cast pipe.*

יְצֻקָה 1 n.f. **casting**—<PREP> בְּ of accompaniment, *with, in,* + יצק pass. *be cast* 1 K 7$_{24}$ (שְׁנֵי טוּרִים הַפְּקָעִים יְצֻקִים בִּיצֻקָתוֹ *two rows of panels, cast when it was cast*).*

→ יצק *pour out.*

יצר 63.11.19 vb. **form**—**Qal** 60.3.14 Pf. יָצַר (יָצָר, יְצָרָהּ), יָצַרְתָּ, יְצַרְתִּי (יְצַרְתָּם, יְצַרְתִּיךָ, יְצַרְתִּיו, יְצַרְתִּיהָ), יָצְרוּ (Q יצרתה, יצרום); impf. יִצְּרֵהוּ, אֶצָּרְךָ (Kt אצורך); + waw וַיִּצֶר (וַיִּיצֶר); ptc. יוֹצֵר (יֹצֵר, יֹצְרִי, יֹצֶרְךָ, יוֹצְרוֹ, יֹצְרוֹ, יֹצְרָהּ, יֹצְרֵנוּ), pl. יוֹצְרִים (יֹצְרִים), cstr. יֹצְרֵי; inf. Q ליצור—**form, fashion, create, shape, 1a.** <SUBJ> '' *Y.* Gn 2$_{7.8.19}$ 2 K 19$_{25}$||Is 37$_{26}$ Is 43$_{1.7}$ (both || ברא *create*) 43$_{21}$ 44$_{2}$ (|| עשה *make*) 44$_{21.24}$ 45$_{7}$ (|| ברא) 45$_{11.18}$ (|| ברא, עשה) 45$_{18}$ 46$_{11}$ (|| עשה) 49$_{5}$ Jr 1$_{5(Qr)}$ 10$_{16}$ 18$_{11}$ 33$_{2}$ (|| עשה) 51$_{19}$ Am 4$_{13}$ (|| ברא) 7$_{1}$ Zc 12$_{1}$ Ps 33$_{15}$ 94$_{9}$ 104$_{26}$, אֱלֹהִים *God* Gn 2$_{7.8.19}$ 2 K 19$_{25}$||Is 37$_{26}$ Am 4$_{13}$ Ps 74$_{17}$, אֵל *God* 1QH 1$_{8.15}$ 4$_{31}$, אֲדֹנָי *Lord* 1QH 3$_{21}$ 10$_{6.22}$ 15$_{22}$ perh. 4QDibHam^{a} 8$_{4}$, גּוֹי *nation* 1QpHab 12$_{13}$, אָב *father* 4Q416 2.3$_{17}$, אֵם *mother* 4Q416 2.3$_{17}$, חָרָשׁ *artisan* Is 44$_{12}$ (or em. יצר pi. *fasten*), כִּסֵּא הַוּוֹת *throne of destruction* Ps 94$_{20}$, יָד *hand* Ps 95$_{5}$, כֹּל *all* Is 44$_{9}$, מִי *who?* Is 44$_{10}$; subj. not specified, Is 22$_{11}$ 27$_{11}$ Si 51$_{12}$ 4QMyst^{a} 10$_{4}$ 4QAdmonPar 1.1$_{13}$ 4Q417 2.1$_{17}$ 4Q 423 5$_{4}$ 4QHymnSap 2$_{3}$.

<OBJ> אֵל *god* Is 44$_{10}$, אֶרֶץ *earth* Is 45$_{18.18}$, הַר *mountain* Am 4$_{13}$, יַבֶּשֶׁת *dry ground* Ps 95$_{5}$, עַם *people* Is 27$_{11}$ 43$_{21}$, Israel Is 43$_{1}$ 44$_{2.21.24}$ 45$_{11}$, Jeremiah Jr 1$_{5}$, אָדָם *human being* Gn 2$_{7.8}$, אָב *father* 4QDibHam^{a} 8$_{4}$, קָדוֹשׁ *holy*

one 4Q417 2.1$_{17}$, worshipper Is 49$_5$, מַעֲשֶׂה *creature* 4Q 423 5$_4$, Leviathan Ps 104$_{26}$, חַיָּה *beast* Gn 2$_{19}$, עוֹף *bird* Gn 2$_{19}$, גֹּבַי *swarm of locusts* Am 7$_1$, פֶּסֶל *image* Is 44$_{9.10.12}$ (or em. יצר pi. *fasten* and/or ins. פָּעֳלוֹ *his construction* as obj.) 1QpHab 12$_{13}$, אוֹר *light* Is 45$_7$, רוּחַ *spirit* Zc 12$_1$ 1QH 1$_{8.15}$ 4$_{31}$ 15$_{22}$, לֵב *heart* Ps 33$_{15}$, עַיִן *eye* Ps 94$_9$, עָמָל *distress* Ps 94$_{20}$, רָעָה *evil* Jr 18$_{11}$, קַיִץ *summer* Ps 74$_{17}$, חֹרֶף *winter* Ps 74$_{17}$, כֹּל *everyone, everything* Is 43$_7$ Jr 10$_{16}$ 51$_{19}$ Si 51$_{12}$ 4QAdmonPar 1.1$_{13}$; obj. not specified, 2 K 19$_{25}$||Is 37$_{26}$ Is 22$_{11}$.

<PREP> לְ of benefit, *to, for,* + "י Y. Is 43$_{21}$, אֵל *God* 1QH 4$_{31}$, סוֹד *council* 1QH 3$_{21}$, worshipper 1QH 10$_6$.

בְּ of time/place, *in, at, during,* + תְּחִלָּה *beginning* Am 7$_1$, תֵּבֵל *world* 1QH 1$_{15}$; of instrument, *by (means of), with,* + מַקֶּבֶת *hammer* Is 44$_{12}$ (or em. יצר pi. *fasten*), יָד *hand* 4Q423 5$_4$; *in, with,* + בֶּטֶן *womb* Jr 1$_5$, דְּמוּת *image* 4QDibHam^a 8$_4$.

מִן of direction, *from,* + עָפָר *dust* 1QH 3$_{21}$, אֲדָמָה *ground* Gn 2$_{7.19}$, יוֹם *day* 2 K 19$_{25}$||Is 37$_{26}$, רָחוֹק *distant time* Is 22$_{11}$, בֶּטֶן *womb* Is 44$_{2.24}$ 49$_5$.

עַל *against,* + אִישׁ *man* of Judah Jr 18$_{11}$, יֹשֵׁב *inhabitant* of Jerusalem Jr 18$_{11}$; of agent, *by (means of),* + חֹק *statute* Ps 94$_{20}$, רוּחַ *spirit* 4Q416 2.3$_{17}$.

בְּקֶרֶב *among,* + אָדָם *human being* Zc 12$_1$.

<SYN> ברא *create,* עשׂה *make.*

<COLL> הַיֹּצֵר יַחַד לִבָּם *who forms the hearts of all* Ps 33$_{15}$.

1b. ptc. as noun, **one who forms, creator, potter,** <SUBJ> חשׁב ni. *be considered* Is 29$_{16}$, פסל *hew out* Hb 2$_{18}$, רמס *tread* Is 41$_{25}$, בטח *trust* Hb 2$_{18}$.

<NOM CL> אַתָּה יֹצְרֵנוּ *you are our potter* Is 64$_7$, הֵמָּה הַיּוֹצְרִים *they are the potters* 1 C 4$_{23}$.

<CSTR> כְּלִי יוֹצֵר *vessel of the potter* 2 S 17$_{28}$ Jr 19$_{11}$ (הַיּוֹצֵר) Ps 2$_9$ Si 27$_8$, נֵבֶל יוֹצְרִים *jar of the potters* Is 30$_{14}$, בַּקְבֻּק יוֹצֵר *flask of the potter* Jr 19$_1$, בֵּית הַיּוֹצֵר *house of the potter* Jr 18$_{2.3}$, יַד *hand of* Jr 18$_{4.6}$, עֵינֵי *eyes of* Jr 18$_4$, יְדֵי יוֹצֵר *hands of the potter* Lm 4$_2$.

<PREP> לְ of direction, *to,* + אמר *say* Is 29$_{16}$ 45$_9$; כְּ *as* Jr 18$_6$; אֶל *to,* + שׁלך hi. *throw out* Zc 11$_{13.13}$ (or em. הָאוֹצָר *the treasury*); אֵת *with,* + ריב *contend* Is 45$_9$.

Also Si 36$_{13}$.

Ni. $_{1.8.1}$ Pf. נוֹצַר, Si נוצרה, Si נוצרתי, Si נוצרו, Q נוצרתם—**be formed,** <SUBJ> אֵל *god* Is 43$_{10}$, Jeremiah Si 49$_7$, Joshua Si 46$_1$, אָדָם *human being* Si 36$_{10}$, נָבִיא *prophet* Si 49$_7$, רַע *evil one* Si 37$_{3(D)}$, חֹשֶׁךְ *darkness* Si 11$_{16}$, שִׂכְלוּת *foolishness* Si 11$_{16}$, יַיִן *wine* Si 34$_{27}$, מְעַט *few* Si 49$_{14}$; subj. not specified, Si 40$_{15}$ 4Q418 69.2$_6$.

<PREP> לְ of benefit, *to, for,* + פֹּשֵׁעַ *transgressor* Si 11$_{16}$, שִׂמְחָה *joy* Si 34$_{27}$; כְּ *as,* + Enoch Si 49$_{14}$; מִן of direction, *from,* + עָפָר *dust* Si 36$_{10}$, חָמָס *violence* Si 40$_{15}$, רֶחֶם *womb* Si 49$_7$; *at,* + רֵאשִׁית *beginning* Si 34$_{27}$; עַל *upon,* + אֶרֶץ *earth* Si 49$_{14}$; לִפְנֵי *before,* + "י *Y.* Is 43$_{10}$.

Pu. $_{1.1}$ Pf. Q יוצר, יֻצָּרוּ—**be formed,** <SUBJ> יוֹם *day* Ps 139$_{16}$. <COLL> ויוצר יד מה יבין *and that which is formed by the hand or penis, what does it understand?* 1QS 11$_{22}$.

Ho. $_{1.0.1}$ Impf. יוּצַר; ptc. Q מוצרת—**be formed,** <SUBJ> כְּלִי *weapon* Is 54$_{17}$; subj. not specified, 4QBéat 10$_1$.

<PREP> עַל *against,* + Israelite(s) Is 54$_{17}$.*

⇒ יֵצֶר *formation,* יֵצֶר *inclination,* יָצוּר *creature,* יְצֻרִים *bodily members;* יֵצֶר *Jezer,* יִצְרִי I *Jezerite,* יִצְרִי II *Izri.*

יֵצֶר I $_{9.2.65}$ n.m. **formation, imagination**—cstr. יֵצֶר; sf. Q יצרי, יִצְרוֹ, יִצְרֵנוּ, Q יצרם—**formation,** i.e. nature and material of human person (Ps 103$_{14}$), perh. **creature, human being*** (Is 29$_{16}$ [|| מַעֲשֶׂה *product*] 1QH 18$_{13}$), **image** (Hb 2$_{18}$), **thinking, imagination, devising** (Gn 6$_5$ 8$_{21}$ Dt 31$_{21}$ Is 26$_3$ 1 C 28$_9$ 29$_{18}$ Si 27$_6$ 1QH 5$_6$ 4QAdmon 1.1$_3$ 4QD^e 1.1$_1$ 4QBer^a 7.2$_7$), **character** (e.g. 1QH 7$_{16}$ 1QJub^b 35$_9$), rarely, perh. **inclination, instinct** (e.g. Si 15$_{14}$ 4Q417 2.2$_{12}$ 11QPs^a 19.16).*

<SUBJ> היה *be* 1QH 2$_9$, תמם *be complete* 1QH fr. 3$_9$, סמך pass. *be unshakable* Is 26$_3$ 1QS 4$_5$ 8$_3$ 1QH 1$_{35}$ 2$_{9.36}$ 4QBark^e 12$_3$, יפע hi. *appear* 1QH 5$_{31}$, אבד *perish* 1QH fr. 3$_{10}$, אמר *say* Is 29$_{16}$, ירשׁ *possess* 11QPs^a 19$_{16}$.

<NOM CL> אני יצר *I am a creature* 1QH 18$_{25}$ fr. 3$_{11}$ 52$_3$ 4QHod^b 15$_2$, אני יצר החמר *I am the creature of clay* 1QH 1$_{21}$ 3$_{23}$ 12$_{32}$ (חמר) fr. 1$_8$, אני יצר העפר *I am the creature of dust* 1QH 18$_{31}$, אתה יצר *you are the creature* 11QHymn$^{b}_{1}$, יצר בשר הואה *it is the inclination of the flesh* 4Q418 2$_8$, בידך יצר כול רוח *the intent of every spirit is in your hand* 1QH 15$_{13}$, מה יצר חמר *what is a creature of clay?* 1QH 4$_{29}$.

<OBJ> ידע *know* Dt 31$_{21}$ Ps 103$_{14}$ 1QH 7$_{13.16}$ 1QJub^b 35$_9$ (י[וד]ע) 4QPrFêtes 2$_5$, שׂים *place* 1QH 10$_{23}$, סמך *sus*

tain 1QH 18_{13}, עשׂה *do* Dt 31_{21}, יצר *form*, i.e. make Is 29_{16} Hb 2_{18} (or em. יֹצֵר יִצְרוֹ *one who makes their image* [1QpHab יצריו *their images*] to יֹצְרוֹ *the one who makes it*), יפע hi. *manifest* 1QH 7_3.

<CSTR> יצר היותם *inclination of their existence* 1QH 7_3, יֵצֶר מַחֲשָׁבוֹת *devising of thoughts*, i.e. thinking 1 C 28_9, יֵצֶר מַחְשְׁבֹת לִבּוֹ *the devising of the thoughts of their heart*, i.e. their thinking Gn 6_5, יצר מחשבו[ות לבם] *the inclination of the thoughts of their heart* 4QapPs^{b} 76-77$_2$, יֵצֶר מַחְשְׁבוֹת לְבַב עַמֶּךָ *the devising of the thoughts of the heart of your people*, i.e. your people's thinking 1 C 29_{18}, יֵצֶר לֵב הָאָדָם *the thinking of the human heart* Gn 8_{21}, יצר לבנ[ו] *inclination of our hearts* 4QMyst^{a} 8_6, יצר בינה *the inclination of understanding* 4QMyst^{a} 8_7, יצר מבינתו *inclination of his understanding* 4Q417 2.1$_{11}$ ([י]צר) 4Q418 43_8, יצר אמינית *inclination of faithfulness* 4QConfess 1.2$_6$.

יצר לבם *the imagination of their heart* 4QAdmon 1.1$_3$, יצר בשר *intent of the flesh* 1QH 10_{23} 4Q416 1_{16} ([י]צר) 4Q418 2_8, יצר כול רוח *the intent of every spirit* 1QH 15_{13}, יצר מעשה *thinking of a creature* 1QH 7_{13}, יצר אשמה *the devising of sin* 1QH 6_{32} 4QD^{e} 1.1$_1$ 4QBer^{a} 7.2$_7$ (א[שמתכה]) CD 2_{16}, יצר עשו *Esau's character* 1QJub^{b} 35_9, יצר אחד *the character of each person* Si 27_6, יצר עבדכה *your servant's character* 1QH 7_{16}.

יצר החמר *the creature of clay* 1QH 1_{21} 3_{23} 4_{29} 11_3 $12_{26.32}$ 18_{12} (all five חמר) fr. 1_8 11_7 4QHod^{b} 15_2 (חמר) 4QShir^{b} 28_3 ([חמר]), העפר *of dust* 1QH 18_{31} fr. 3_5 (עפר) 3_{14} ([י]צר) 4QHod^{b} 11_8 (עפר), בשר *of flesh* 1QH fr. 50_2, רמיה *of deceit* 1QH fr. 3_9, עולה *of iniquity* 1QH fr. 3_{10}.

מחשבות יצר לבם *thoughts of the imagination of their heart* 4QAdmon 1.1$_3$, מחשבות יצר אשמה *thoughts of the devising of sin* 4QD^{e} 1.1$_1$ ([מ]חשבות) CD 2_{16}, כו[ל] מחשבות יצר א[שמתכה] *all the thoughts of the devising of your sin* 4QBer^{a} 7.2$_7$, מחשבת יצר רע perh. *thought(s) of (the) evil inclination* 4Q417 2.2$_{12}$, מחשבת יצרו *thoughts of his inclination* 1QS 5_5.

זמות יצרי perh. *the plans of my devising* 1QH 5_6, עול יצר *iniquity of the creature* 1QH fr. 2_{17}, יד יצרו *power of his inclination* Si 15_{14} (וישיתהו ביד חותפו ויתנהו ביד יצרו *and God placed them under the power of that which snatches them away*, i.e. their instincts or cravings, *and placed them under the power of their inclination*), עורלת יצר *foreskin of the inclination* 1QS 5_5, כָּל־יֵצֶר *every devising of* Gn 6_5 1 C 28_9, כול יצר *every creature of* 1QH fr. 3_9.

<ADJ> רַע *evil* 4Q417 2.2$_{12}$ 4QBark^{c} 1.1$_{10}$ 11QPs^{a} 19_{16}. <PREP> לְ of direction, *to*, + שׁמע hi. *announce* 1QH 18_{11}; of benefit, *to, for* 1QH 6_{32} 12_{26}, + פתח *open* 1QH 18_{13}; *as*, + היה *be* 1QH 13_5; *concerning*, + שׁמר *keep (in mind)* 1 C 29_{18}; introducing object, + יכח hi. *reprove* 1QH 18_{12}.

בְּ *in, with* 4QHod^{b} 11_8, + גבר hi. *be mighty to* 1QH 11_3, הלך htp. *walk* 4Q417 2.1$_{11}$ 4Q418 43_8; introducing object, + שׁמר *keep* 1QH fr 3_5; כְּ *as* 4QapPs^{b} 76-77$_2$; מִן of comparison, *more (than)* 1QH 9_{16}.

עַל *concerning, as evidence of*, + היה *be* Si 27_6 (על עבדת עץ יהי פרי כן חשבון על יצר אחד *as evidence of the service*, i.e. cultivation, *of a tree there is [its] fruit, so there is thought as evidence of the character of an individual*).

Also 1QH fr. 1_{13} 3_{18} 4QBéat 11_4 (מיצר מחשב[) 4QMyst^{a} 33_2 4Q417 2.1$_9$ 4Q418 43_7 ([י]צרה) 4Q418 217_1 ([י]צר) 4QHod^{b} 36_1 4QBark^{d} 4_2 4QBéat 11_4.*

⇒ יצר *form*.

יֵצֶר II 3 pr.n.m. **Jezer**—son of Naphtali, <NOM CL> בְּנֵי נַפְתָּלִי ... יֵצֶר *the sons of Naphtali were ... Jezer* Gn 46_{24} ||1 C 7_{13}. <PREP> לְ of possession, *(belonging) to, of* Nm 26_{49}. ⇒ יצר *form*.

[יֹצֶר] 0.0.1 n.m. **inclination**—Q יוצר—<ADJ> רַע *evil* 4QParGenEx 1_{12}. <PREP> בְּ of accompaniment, *with, in* 4QParGenEx 1_{12}.

⇒ יצר *form*.

יִצְרִי I 1 gent. **Jezerite,** collective **Jezerites,** <CSTR> מִשְׁפַּחַת הַיִּצְרִי *family of the Jezerites* Nm 26_{49}.

⇒ יצר *form*.

יִצְרִי II 1 pr.n.m. **Izri,** Levite musician, son of Jeduthan, prob. ident. with צְרִי *Zeri* (1 C 25_3), son of Jeduthun, <PREP> לְ of benefit, *to, for*, + יצא *go out* 1 C 25_{11}.

⇒ יצר *form*.

יְצֻרִים 1.0.1 n.m. **bodily members, inclinations**—cstr. Q יצרי; sf. יְצֻרַי—**limbs** or **inner organs, intents** or **incli**

nations, <NOM CL> וִיצֻרַי כַּצֵּל כֻּלָּם *and my members are all as the shadow* Jb 17$_{7}$. <OBJ> ידע *know* 1QH 11$_{20}$. <CSTR> יצרי גבר *inclinations of a man* 1QH 11$_{20}$.

⇒ יצר *form.*

יצת 30.2 vb. **kindle—Qal** 4 Impf. תִּצַּתְנָה, יִצַּתוּ; + waw וַתִּצַּת—**be kindled with fire, kindle, burn up,** <SUBJ> רִשְׁעָה *guilt* Is 9$_{17}$, קוֹץ *thorn-bush* Is 33$_{12}$, שַׁעַר *gate* of Babylon Jr 51$_{58}$, בַּת *daughter*, i.e. village Jr 49$_{2}$.

<PREP> בְּ *in, with,* + אֵשׁ *fire* Is 33$_{12}$ Jr 49$_{2}$ 51$_{58}$; introducing object, + סְבַךְ *thicket* Is 9$_{17}$.

Ni. 8.1 Pf. נִצְּתוּ, נִצְּתָה; + waw וְנִצְּתָה—**become inflamed, be burned up, break out,** <SUBJ> חֵמָה *anger* of Y. 2 K 22$_{13.17}$ Si 16$_{6}$, אֶרֶץ *land* Jr 9$_{11}$, הַר *mountain* Jr 9$_{9}$, Memphis Jr 46$_{19}$, עִיר *city* Jr 2$_{15(Qr)}$ (Kt נצה ni. *be destroyed*), שַׁעַר *gate* Ne 1$_{3}$ 2$_{17}$, נָוֶה *pasturage* Jr 9$_{9}$.

<PREP> בְּ of instrument, *by (means of), with,* + אֵשׁ *fire* Ne 1$_{3}$ 2$_{17}$; בְּ *against,* + עַם *people* 2 K 22$_{13}$, Judah 2 K 22$_{13}$, Josiah 2 K 22$_{13}$, גּוֹי *nation* Si 16$_{6}$, מָקוֹם *place* 2 K 22$_{17}$; כְּ *as,* + מִדְבָּר *steppe* Jr 9$_{11}$; מֵאֵין *without,* + יֹשֵׁב *inhabitant* Jr 46$_{19}$; מִבְּלִי *without,* + יֹשֵׁב *inhabitant* Jr 2$_{15}$, אִישׁ *man* Jr 9$_{9}$, עבר ptc. *one who passes by* Jr 9$_{11}$.

Hi. 18.1 Pf. הִצִּיתוּ, הִצַּתִּי, הִצִּית; impf. תַּצִּיתוּ; + waw וַיַּצֵּת־, וַיַּצִּיתוּ (וַיַּצִּתוּ); impf. הַצִּיתוּהָ (Kt הוציתיה); ptc. מַצִּית—**set on fire, set fire to,** <SUBJ> ′′ Y. Is 27$_{4}$ Jr 11$_{16}$ 17$_{27}$ 21$_{14}$ 43$_{12}$ 49$_{27}$ 50$_{32}$ Ezk 21$_{3}$ Am 1$_{14}$ Lm 4$_{11}$, עַם *people* Jg 9$_{49}$, Chaldaean Jr 32$_{29}$, גִּבּוֹר *warrior* Jos 8$_{8.19}$ Jr 51$_{30}$, עֶבֶד *servant* 2 S 14$_{30.30.31}$; subj. not specified, Si 49$_{6}$.

<OBJ> עִיר *city* Jos 8$_{8.19}$ Jr 32$_{29}$, קִרְיָה *city* Si 49$_{6}$, מִשְׁכָּן *dwelling place* Jr 51$_{30}$, צְרִיחַ *vault* Jg 9$_{49}$, חֶלְקָה *common field* 2 S 14$_{30.30.31}$, שָׁמִיר *thorn-bush* Is 27$_{4}$, שַׁיִת *weeds* Is 27$_{4}$, אֵשׁ *fire* Jr 11$_{16}$ 17$_{27}$ 21$_{14}$ 43$_{12}$ 49$_{27}$ 50$_{32}$ Ezk 21$_{3}$ Am 1$_{14}$ Lm 4$_{11}$.

<PREP> לְ of agent, *by (means of),* + קוֹל *voice* Jr 11$_{16}$; בְּ of place, *in, at,* + Zion Lm 4$_{11}$, עִיר *city* Jr 50$_{32}$, בַּיִת *house*, i.e. temple Jr 43$_{12}$, חוֹמָה *wall* Jr 49$_{27}$ Am 1$_{14}$, שַׁעַר *gate* Jr 11$_{16}$, יַעַר *forest* Jr 21$_{14}$ Ezk 21$_{3}$; of instrument, *by (means of),* + אֵשׁ *fire* Jos 8$_{8.19}$ 2 S 14$_{30.30.31}$ Jr 32$_{29}$; עַל *upon,* + עַם *people* Jg 9$_{49}$; *against,* + זַיִת *olive tree* Jr 11$_{16}$.

<COLL> אֲצִיתֶנָּה יָּחַד *I would burn them up together* Is 27$_{4}$.*

⇒ (?) יָצַת *Jazith.*

[יָצַת] 0.0.0.7 pl.n. **Jazith,** appar. location in NE Samaria in district of Hoglah Samaria ost. 9$_{1}$ 10$_{1}$ 19$_{2}$ 45$_{3}$ 47$_{2}$ 67$_{1}$ 80$_{1}$.

<PREP> מִן of direction, *from* Samaria ost. 9$_{1}$ 10$_{1}$ 19$_{2}$ 45$_{3}$ ([יצ]ת) 47$_{2}$ 67$_{1}$ ([יצ]ת).

Also Samaria ost. 80$_{1}$.

⇒ (?) יצת *kindle.*

יֶקֶב 16.0.1 n.m. **wine-vat**—יֶקֶב; sf. יִקְבֶךָ; pl. יְקָבִים; cstr. יִקְבֵי—**trough** or **channel** dug in rock, receptacle of juice trodden out in the wine-press (e.g. Nm 18$_{27.30}$ Dt 15$_{14}$ 16$_{13}$ Is 5$_{2}$ Ho 9$_{2}$); **wine-press** (Is 16$_{10}$ Jr 48$_{33}$ Jb 24$_{11}$).

<SUBJ> רעה *sustain* Ho 9$_{2}$, שוק hi. *overflow* Jl 2$_{24}$ 3$_{13}$, פרץ *break out* Pr 3$_{10}$.

<OBJ> חצב *hew out* Is 5$_{2}$, דרך *tread* Jb 24$_{11}$.

<CSTR> יֶקֶב־זְאֵב *wine-vat of Zeeb* Jg 7$_{25}$, יִקְבֵי הַמֶּלֶךְ *wine-vats of the king* Zc 14$_{10}$, יקב תירושכה *the press of your fresh wine* 4QBen 1$_{3}$; תְּבוּאַת יֶקֶב *produce of the wine-vat* Nm 18$_{30}$.

<PREP> בְּ of place, *in, at,* + הרג *slay* Jg 7$_{25}$, דרך *tread* Is 16$_{10}$; מִן of direction, *from* Nm 18$_{27}$, + ענק hi. *provide with* Dt 15$_{14}$, אסף *gather in* Dt 16$_{13}$, ישע hi. *save* 2 K 6$_{27}$, שבת hi. *cause to cease* Jr 48$_{33}$; אֶל *to,* + בוא *come* Hg 2$_{16}$; עַד *unto* Zc 14$_{10}$.

<COLL> יֶקֶב ‖ גֹּרֶן Nm 18$_{27.30}$ Dt 15$_{14}$ 16$_{13}$ 2 K 6$_{27}$ Ho 9$_{2}$ Jl 2$_{24}$.*

יְקַבְצְאֵל 1 pl.n. **Jekabzeel,** ident. with קַבְצְאֵל *Kabzeel* (Jos 15$_{21}$ 2 S 23$_{20}$‖1 C 11$_{22}$), in south of Judah, <PREP> בְּ of place, *in, at,* + ישב *dwell* Ne 11$_{25}$ (mss בְּקַבְצְאֵל) *in Kabzeel.*

⇒ קבץ *gather* + אֵל *God.*

יקד 8.1.1 vb. **be kindled—Qal** 3.1 Impf. יֵקַד; + waw וַתִּיקַד; ptc. יֹקֶדֶת (Si יוקדת)—**be kindled, burn,** <SUBJ> אֵשׁ *fire* Dt 32$_{22}$ Is 65$_{5}$ Si 16$_{6}$, יְקֹד *conflagration* Is 10$_{16}$.

<PREP> בְּ of place, *in, at,* + עֵדָה *congregation* Si 16$_{6}$; עַד *unto,* + שְׁאוֹל *Sheol* Dt 32$_{22}$.

<COLL> אֵשׁ יֹקֶדֶת כָּל־הַיּוֹם *a fire that burns all the day* Is 65$_{5}$.

Ho. 5.0.1 Impf. תּוּקַד (תּוּקָד)—**be kindled, be kept burning,** <SUBJ> אֵשׁ *fire* Lv 6$_{2.5.6}$ Jr 15$_{14}$ 17$_{4}$, שְׁאוֹל *Sheol*

1QM 14_{18}.

<PREP> לְ *as*, + שְׂרֵפָה *burning* 1QM 14_{18}; בְּ *in, on*, + מִזְבֵּחַ *altar* Lv $6_{2.5}$; עַל *upon*, + מִזְבֵּחַ *altar* Lv 6_6; *against*, + Jerusalem Jr 15_{14}; עַד *until*, + עוֹלָם *eternity* Jr $15_{14(mss)}$ 17_4.*

→ יְקֹד *conflagration*, יָקוּד *hearth*, מוֹקֵד *burning mass*, מוֹקְדָה *hearth*, יָקְדְעָם *Jokdeam*.

יְקֹד 2 n.m. **conflagration**—cstr. יְקוֹד—<SUBJ> יקד *be kindled* Is 10_{16}. <CSTR> יְקוֹד אֵשׁ *conflagration of a fire* Is 10_{16}.*

→ יקד *be kindled*.

יָקְדְעָם 1 pl.n. **Jokdeam,** in the Negeb of Judah, perh. Kh. Raq'a, near Ziph, <NOM CL> וּבָהָר שָׁמִיר ... וְיָקְדְעָם *and in the hill-country were Shamir ... and Jokdeam* Jos 15_{56}. <APP> עִיר *city* Jos 15_{56}.

→ יקד *be kindled* + (?) עַם *people*.

יָקֶה 1 pr.n.m. **Jakeh,** father or ancestor of Agur, author of proverbs, <CSTR> בֶּן־יָקֶה *son of Jakeh* Pr 30_1.

יְקָהָה 2 n.f. **obedience**—cstr. יִקְּהַת (יְקָהַת)—<NOM CL> לוֹ יִקְּהַת עַמִּים *to him (shall be) the obedience of the peoples* Gn 49_{10}. <CSTR> יִקְּהַת עַמִּים *obedience of the peoples* Gn 49_{10}, אֵם *of a mother* Pr 30_{17}. <PREP> לְ introducing object, + בוז *despise* Pr 30_{17}.

יָקוּד 1 n.m. **hearth**—<PREP> מִן of direction, *from*, + חתה *take away* Is 30_{14}.

→ יקד *be kindled*.

יָקוֹט 1 n.m. perh. **gossamer**—אֲשֶׁר יָקוֹט כִּסְלוֹ *whose confidence is gossamer* Jb 8_{14} (unless יָקוֹט *is cut off*, from קוט or קטט; or em. אֲשֶׁר יָקוֹט to קָרֵי קַיִט his confidence is [as] *threads of summer* or קִשְׁרֵי קַיִט *bands of summer* or חוּט קַיִץ *thread of summer*, i.e. gossamer, or קוִּים *threads* or קוּרִים *threads*, i.e. tenuous).*

יְקוּם 3.1.3 n.m. **living form**—<OBJ> זנח *reject* Si $43_{13(Bmg)}$, מחה *wipe out* Gn $7_{4.23}$, בלע *swallow* Dt 11_6.

<CSTR> יקום הבלי[הם] *their living forms of (their) vanity* 1QM 14_{12}, יקום הוותם *living forms of (their) destruction* 1QM 15_{11}; כָּל־יְקוּם *every living form* Gn $7_{4.23}$ Dt 11_6 1QM 14_{12} 15_{11} 4QMa 8_9 (יקו[ם]).

→ קום *arise, become*.

יָקוֹשׁ 1 n.[m.] **(game) hunter,** פַּח יָקוֹשׁ *a hunter's trap* Ho 9_8 Ps 91_3 (if em. יָקוּשׁ in same sense) Pr 6_5 (if em. יַד יָקוּשׁ from the *hand of a hunter*). <PREP> כְּ *as* Jr 5_{26} (if em. שַׁךְ יְקוּשִׁים *crouching of hunters* to יָשְׁרְכוּ שְׂבָכָה כִּיוֹקְשִׁים *they weave a net like hunters*).*

→ יקשׁ *trap*.

יָקוּשׁ 3.0.1 n.[m.] **(game) hunter**—pl. יְקוּשִׁים—<CSTR> שַׁךְ יְקוּשִׁים *crouching of hunters* Jr 5_{26} (or em. יָקוֹשׁ *hunter*), פַּח יָקוּשׁ *hunter's trap* Ps 91_3 (or em.) 4QapJoshuab 22.2_{10}, יַד יָקוּשׁ from the *hand of a hunter* Pr 6_5 (or em. פַּח *trap* or פַּח יָקוֹשׁ *a hunter's trap*).

Also 4QSapb 14_2 ([י]קוש).

→ יקשׁ *trap*.

יְקוּתִיאֵל 1 pr.n.m. **Jekuthiel,** Judahite, descendant of Mered, <NOM CL> יְקוּתִיאֵל אֲבִי זָנוֹחַ *Jekuthiel was the father*, or *founder, of Zanoah* 1 C 4_{18}. <OBJ> ילד *bear child* 1 C 4_{18}.

→ אֵל *God*.

* **יקח** 2 vb. **be shameless—Pi.** 2 Impf. יְקַחֲךָ, 2ms תְּקַחֲךָ—**embolden,** מַה־יִּקָּחֲךָ לִבֶּךָ *why has your heart emboldened you?* Jb 15_{12} (unless יִקָּחֲךָ = what *has taken from you* your mind?), וְאַל־תִּקָּחֲךָ בְּעַפְעַפֶּיהָ *and do not embolden yourself because of her eyes* (unless תִּקָּחֲךָ = *may she* not *captivate you* with her eyes).

Hi. be impudent, <SUBJ> Korah, Dathan, Abiram, and On Nm 16_1 (if em. וַיִּקַּח *and he took* to וַיַּקַּח *and he was impudent*).*

יָקְטָן 6 pr.n.m. **Joktan,** younger son of Eber and great grand-son of Shem Gn $10_{25.26.29}$||1 C $1_{19.20.23}$, <SUBJ> ילד *bear child* Gn 10_{26}||1 C 1_{20}. <NOM CL> שֵׁם אָחִיו יָקְטָן *the name of his brother was Joktan* Gn 10_{25}||1 C 1_{19}.

<CSTR> בְּנֵי יָקְטָן *sons of Joktan* Gn 10_{29}||1 C 1_{23}.

→ קטן *be small*.

יָקִים 2.0.9 pr.n.m. **Jakim, 1.** Benjaminite, son of Shimei 1 C 8_{19}, <NOM CL> בְּנֵי שִׁמְעִי ... וְזַבְדִּי : ... יָקִים ... *Jakim ... and Zabdi ... were the sons of Shimei* 1 C 8_{19}.

2. priest in time of David 1 C 24_{12}, <PREP> לְ of benefit, *to, for,* + יצא *go out* 1 C 24_8.

3. name of priestly course and its period of office 4QMishA 4.4_9 $4.5_{1.5}$ 4QMishB[a] 1.1_2 2.1_5 2.2_9 2.3_5 2.3_8 4QMishC[b] $1_{3.3}$ 4QMishF[a] 1_5 4QMishF[b] 1_2 2_2., <PREP> בְּ of time, *on, at, during* 4QMishA 4.4_9 $4.5_{1.5}$ 4QMish B[a] 1.1_2 2.1_5 2.2_9 2.3_5 2.3_8 4QMishC[b] $1_{3.3}$ 4QMishF[a] 1_5 4QMishF[b] 1_2 2_2.

⇒ קום *arise.*

[יְקִימְיָהוּ] 0.0.0.1 pr.n.m. **Jakimiah,** Seal 366_2 (7th cent.), <CSTR> בן יקימיהו *son of Jakimiah* Seal 366_2 (7th cent.).

⇒ קום *arise* + יה *Y.*

יַקִּיר 1 adj. **precious,** used attributively of בֵּן *son* Jr 31_{20}.*

⇒ יקר *be precious.*

יְקַמְיָה 3.0.0.13 pr.n.m. **Jekamiah**—I יקמיהו—**1.** Judahite and Jerahmeelite, son of Shallum, <SUBJ> ילד hi. *become father of* 1 C 2_{41}. <OBJ> ילד hi. *become father of* 1 C 2_{41}.

2. son of Jehoiachin, king of Judah 1 C 3_{18}. <NOM CL> בְּנֵי יְכָנְיָה אַסִּר ... יְקַמְיָה *the sons of Jeconiah the captive were ... Jekamiah* 1 C 3_{18}.

3. Arad ost. 24_{16}, <CSTR> בן יקמיהו *son of Jekamiah* Arad ost. 24_{16} (others ירמיהו *Jeremiah*). **4.** father of Adam, בן יקמיהו *son of Jekamiah* Arad ost. 39_1. **5.** Arad ost. 59_2, <APP> בֵּן *son* Arad ost. 59_2. **6.** Arad ost. 74_3 (יקמ[יהו]).

7. Seal 53_1 (Jerusalem), <PREP> לְ of possession, *(belonging) to, of* Seal 53_1 (Jerusalem). **8.** Seal 122_1 (8th cent.), <PREP> לְ of possession, *(belonging) to, of* Seal 122_1 (8th cent.). **9.** appar. father of Machi, Seal 153_2 (others שקניה *Shekaniah,* Judaea? 6th cent.). **10.** Seal 344_2 (7th cent.), <APP> Elijah Seal 344_2 (7th cent.). <PREP> לְ of possession, *(belonging) to, of* Seal 344_2 (7th cent.). **11.** Seal 511_2 (T. Beit Mirsim?, 7th/6th cent.), בן יקמיהו *son of Jekamiah* Seal 511_2 (T. Beit Mirsim?, 7th/6th cent.). **12.** Seal 575_1 (T. Beit Mirsim?, 7th/6th cent.), <PREP> לְ of possession, *(belonging) to, of* Seal 575_1 (T. Beit Mirsim?, 7th/6th cent.). **13.** Seal 576_1 (T. Beit Mirsim?, 7th/6th cent.), <PREP> לְ of possession, *(belonging) to, of* Seal 576_1 (T. Beit Mirsim?, 7th/6th cent.). **14.** Seal 577_1 (T. Beit Mirsim?, 7th/6th cent.), <PREP> לְ of possession, *(belonging) to, of* Seal 577_1 (T. Beil Mirsim?, 7th/6th cent.)

Also Seal 672_2 (T. Beit Mirsim?, 7th/6th cent.).

⇒ קום *arise* + יה *Y.*

יְקַמְעָם 2 pr.n.m. **Jekameam,** Levite, son of Hebron, <NOM CL> בְּנֵי חֶבְרוֹן ... וִיקַמְעָם הָרְבִיעִי *the sons of Hebron were ... and Jekameam the fourth* 1 C 23_{19} $24_{23(\text{mss})}$, וּבְנָי ... יְקַמְעָם הרביעי *and (?) my sons were ... Jekameam the fourth* 1 C 24_{23} (or rd. וּבְנֵי חֶבְרוֹן *and the sons of Hebron*). <ADJ> רְבִיעִי *fourth* 1 C 23_{19} 24_{23}.

⇒ קום *arise* + עַם *people.*

יָקְמְעָם 2 pl.n. **Jokmeam**—יָקְמֳעָם—**1.** Levitical town, ident. with יָקְנְעָם *Jokneam* (see below). **2.** Levitical city of refuge in Ephraim 1 C 6_{53}. <OBJ> נתן *give* 1 C 6_{53}. <PREP> מֵעֵבֶר לְ *on the other side of* 1 K 4_{12}.

⇒ קום *arise* + עַם *people.*

יָקְנְעָם 3 pl.n. **Jokneam**—יָקְמְעָם, יָקְנֳעָם (1 K 4_{12})—Levitical city in Zebulun, perh. T. Qaimūn 28 km S of Haifa, <OBJ> נתן *give* Jos 21_{34}. <CSTR> מֶלֶךְ־יָקְנְעָם *king of Jokneam* Jos 12_{22}, פְּנֵי יָקְנְעָם *face of,* i.e. east of, *Jokneam* Jos 19_{11}. <PREP> לְ of direction, *to* 1 K 4_{12}.

יקע 8 vb. **be dislocated—Qal** 4 Impf. 3fs תֵּקַע; + waw 3fs וַתֵּקַע—**be dislocated, be alienated, turn away with jerk,** <SUBJ> כַּף *hollow,* i.e. socket of thigh joint Gn 32_{26}, נֶפֶשׁ *soul* Jr 6_8 Ezk $23_{17.18}$.

<PREP> מִן of direction, *from,* + Jerusalem Jr 6_8, בֵּן *son* of Babylon Ezk 23_{17}.

מֵעַל *from (upon),* + Oholibah Ezk 23_{18}, אָחוֹת *sister* Ezk 23_{18}.

Hi. 3 Pf. הוֹקַעֲנוּם; + waw וְהוֹקִיעוּם; impv. הוֹקַע—**expose with broken limbs,** <SUBJ> Gibeonite 2 S $21_{6.9}$, Moses Nm 25_4.

<OBJ> רֹאשׁ *head,* i.e. leader of the people Nm 25_4, בֵּן *son* 2 S $21_{6.9}$.

<PREP> לְ of benefit, *to, for,* + יה *Y.* Nm 25_4 2 S 21_6; בְּ

of place, *in, at,* + הַר *mountain* 2 S 21$_{9}$, Gibeon 2 S 21$_{6}$; לִפְנֵי *before,* + ′י *Y.* 2 S 21$_{9}$; נֶגֶד *opposite,* + שֶׁמֶשׁ *sun* Nm 25$_{4}$.

Ho. $_{1}$ Ptc. מוּקָעִים—**be exposed with broken limbs,** <SUBJ> subj. not specified, 2 S 21$_{13}$.

יִקְפָּאוֹן, see קִפָּאוֹן *frost.*

יקץ $_{11}$ vb. **awake—Qal** $_{11}$ Impf. יִקְצוּ ,יִקַץ; + waw וַיִּיקַץ (וַיִּקֶץ ,וַיִּקַץ) ,וָאִיקָץ—**awake, be active,** <SUBJ> אֲדֹנָי *Lord* Ps 78$_{65}$, אֱלֹהִים *god* 1 K 18$_{27}$, Jacob Gn 28$_{16}$, Noah Gn 9$_{24}$, Samson Jg 16$_{14.20}$, Solomon 1 K 3$_{15}$, פַּרְעֹה *Pharaoh* Gn 41$_{4.7.21}$; subj. not specified, Hb 2$_{7}$.

<PREP> כְּ *as,* + יָשֵׁן *sleeping one* Ps 78$_{65}$.

מִן of direction, *from,* + יַיִן *wine* Gn 9$_{24}$, שֵׁנָה *sleep* Gn 28$_{16}$ Jg 16$_{14.20}$.*

→ see also קיץ *awake.*

יקר $_{11.1}$ vb. **be precious—Qal** $_{9}$ Pf. יָקְרָה ,יָקְרָתְ ,יָקַרְתִּי, יָקְרוּ; impf. יֵיקַר (יֵקַר), 3fs תֵּיקַר; + waw וַיֵּיקַר—**be precious, be valued** (Zc 11$_{13}$), **be honoured** (1 S 18$_{30}$), <SUBJ> Israel Is 43$_{4}$, רֹעֶה *shepherd* Zc 11$_{13}$, נֶפֶשׁ *soul* 1 S 26$_{21}$ 2 K 1$_{13.13.14}$, פִּדְיוֹן *ransom* of life Ps 49$_{9}$, דָּם *blood* Ps 72$_{14}$, שֵׁם *name* 1 S 18$_{30}$, רֵעַ *thought* Ps 139$_{17}$.

<PREP> בְּ *in, with,* + עַיִן *eye* 1 S 26$_{21}$ 2 K 1$_{13.14}$ Is 43$_{4}$ Ps 72$_{14}$; מֵעַל *from (upon),* + עָנִי *poor one* Zc 11$_{13}$.

Hi. $_{2.1}$ Impf. אוֹקִיר; impv. הֹקַר (Si הוקיר)—**1. make rare,** <SUBJ> ′י *Y.* Is 13$_{12}$ (אוֹקִיר *I shall make rare* + אוֹפִיר *Ophir*); subj. not specified, Pr 25$_{27}$ (if em. וְחֵקֶר כְּבֹדָם כָּבוֹד *and the searching of their glory is [itself] glory* to וְהֹקַר דִּבְרֵי כָבוֹד *and make rare words of honour;* or em. וּדְחֹק כָּבוֹד מִכָּבוֹד *and press,* i.e. extract, *glory from glory*). <OBJ> אֱנוֹשׁ *human being* Is 13$_{12}$, דָּבָר *word* Pr 25$_{27}$ (if em.). <PREP> מִן of comparison, *(more) than,* + פַּז *(fine) gold* Is 13$_{12}$.

2. perh. **make heavy, stay,*** <OBJ> רֶגֶל *foot,* i.e. keep away Pr 25$_{17}$. <PREP> מִן of direction, *from,* + בַּיִת neighbour's *house* Pr 25$_{17}$.

3. honour, הקיר מך ואל תתן לזד *honour the downtrodden but give nothing to the impudent* (i.e. הֹקִיר; or הָקֵיר *cool,* i.e. refresh, the downtrodden, from קרר *be cool*).*

→ יָקָר *precious,* יְקָר *preciousness,* יַקִּיר *precious.*

יָקָר I $_{36.1.7}$ adj. **precious**—cstr. יְקַר; יְקָרָה; cstr. יִקְרַת; pl. יְקָרִים ,יְקָרוֹת (יְקָרֹת)—**precious, rare, costly, valuable, weighty, noble, 1.** used attributively of אֶבֶן *stone* 2 S 12$_{30}$||1 C 20$_{2}$ 1 K 5$_{31}$ (unless יָקָר II *split*) 7$_{9.10.11}$ 10$_{2.10.11}$ ||2 C 9$_{1.9.10}$ Ezk 27$_{22}$ 28$_{13}$ Dn 11$_{38}$ 1 C 29$_{2}$ 2 C 3$_{6}$ 32$_{27}$ Si 45$_{11}$ 4QDibHam^{a} 1.4$_{10}$, שֹׁהַם *onyx stone* Jb 28$_{16}$, חָרוּץ *diligence* Pr 12$_{27}$ (or em. יָקָר הוֹן אָדָם חָרוּץ *precious is the wealth of a diligent person,* or הוֹן יָקָר לְאָדָם חָרוּץ *a diligent person has precious wealth*), נֶפֶשׁ *soul* Pr 6$_{26}$, בֵּן *son* 4QJub^{h} 35$_{17}$, בַּת *daughter* 4QapLam^{a} 1.2$_{13}$.

2. used predicatively, **precious one, rare one,** <SUBJ> היה *be* 1 S 3$_{1}$ Zc 14$_{6}$ (if em. קוֹר *cold*), קפא ni. *congeal* Zc 14$_{6(Qr)}$, הוֹן *wealth* Pr 1$_{13}$ 24$_{4}$.

<NOM CL> יָקָר בְּעֵינֵי ′י הַמָּוְתָה לַחֲסִידָיו, *precious in the eyes of Y. is the death of his loyal ones* Ps 116$_{15}$, בְּנֵי צִיּוֹן הַיְקָרִים *the precious sons of Zion* Lm 4$_{2}$, יָקָר מֵחָכְמָה מִכָּבוֹד סִכְלוּת מְעָט *a little folly is more weighty than wisdom (and) honour* Ec 10$_{1}$, כול יקר לי *every precious thing belongs to me* 4QM^{a} 11$_{14}$, יְקָרָה הִ״א wisdom *is precious* Pr 3$_{15}$, מַה־יָּקָר חַסְדְּךָ *how precious is your loyalty* Ps 36$_{8}$.

<OBJ> יצא hi. *bring out* Jr 15$_{19}$, נתן *give* 4QMishC^{a} 2$_{1}$.

<CSTR> יִקְרַת מוּסָד *precious* stone *of the foundation* Is 28$_{16}$, יְקַר כָּרִים *precious,* i.e. beauty, *of pastures* Ps 37$_{20}$, יקר קרן *precious one of the horn* 4QPrayers^{c} 1$_{1}$, יְקַר־רוּחַ *noble one of spirit* Pr 17$_{27(Qr)}$ (Kt וְקַר *and one who is cool* of spirit);* פִּנַּת יִקְרַת מוּסָד *corner stone of the precious (stone) of the foundation,* i.e. a precious corner stone as a foundation Is 28$_{16}$ 1QS 8$_{7}$, כול יקר *every precious thing* 4QM^{a} 11$_{14}$.

<PREP> בְּ of accompaniment, *with, in* Ps 45$_{10}$ perh. 4QPrayers^{c} 1$_{1}$ 11QShirShabb 1$_{2}$.

<COLL> וְיָרֵחַ יָקָר הֹלֵךְ *and the moon moving about in splendour* Jb 31$_{26}$.*

→ יקר *be precious.*

* **[יָקָר] II** $_{1}$ adj. **split**—pl. יְקָרוֹת—אֲבָנִים יְקָרוֹת *split stones* 1 K 5$_{31}$ (unless יָקָר I *precious*).

יְקָר $_{17}$ n.m. **preciousness**—cstr. יְקַר; sf. יְקָרָהּ ,יְקָרוֹ—**preciousness, precious articles, excellent price** (Zc 11$_{13}$), **honouring, esteeming,** <SUBJ> היה *be* Est 8$_{16}$.

<OBJ> ראה *see* Jb 28_{10}, hi. *show* Est 1_4, עשׂה *do*, i.e. bestow Est 6_3 (‖ גְּדוּלָּה *greatness*) 6_6, לקח *take* Ezk 22_{25} (‖ חֹסֶן *wealth*), נתן *give* Jr 20_5 Est 1_{20}.

<CSTR> אֶדֶר הַיְקָר *splendour of the price* Zc 11_{13}, כְּלִי יְקָר *jewel of preciousness* Pr 20_{15}, כָּל־יְקָר *every precious object* Jb 28_{10}, כָּל־יְקָרָהּ *all of its precious objects* Jr 20_5.

<PREP> בְּ *in, with*, + חפץ *delight in* Est $6_{7.9.9.11}$, לין *spend night* Ps $49_{13.21(mss)}$; introducing object, + בין *understand* Ps 49_{21}.

<SYN> חֹסֶן *wealth*, גְּדוּלָּה *greatness*.*

⇒ יקר *be precious*.

יקשׁ 8.6 vb. **trap—Qal** 3 Pf. יָקְשׁוּ, יָקַשְׁתִּי; ptc. יֹקְשִׁים—<SUBJ> י׳ *Y.* Jr 50_{24}, פעל ptc. *one who practises* iniquity Ps 141_9; subj. not specified, Ps 124_7.

<OBJ> פַּח *bird-trap* Ps 141_9.

<PREP> לְ of benefit, *to, for*, + Babylon Jr 50_{24}, worshipper Ps 141_9.

Ni. 4.6 Pf. נוֹקְשׁוּ, נוֹקַשְׁתָּ; impf. Si יוקשׁ, 2ms תִּוָּקֵשׁ; ptc. Si נוקשׁ—<SUBJ> עַם *people* Is 28_{13} (‖ לכד ni. *be taken*), Israelite(s) Dt 7_{25}, אִישׁ *man* Si $41_{2(M, Bmg)}$ (B נקשׁ ni. *be ensnared*), בֵּן *son* Pr 6_2 Si 9_5, worshipper 4QBéat 14.2_{27} ([נו]קשתה), רַב pl. *many* Is 8_{15} (‖ לכד ni.), פֶּתֶה *naive one* Si 34_7, כְּסִיל *foolish one* Si $34_{30(Bmg)}$ (B מוֹקֵשׁ *snare*), מִתְלַהְלֵהַּ *insane one* Si $35_{14.16}$.

<PREP> בְּ of instrument, *by (means of), with* + פָּסִיל *image* Dt 7_{25}, פְּנִינִים *corals* Si 34_7, רָצוֹן *favour* Si 35_{14}, אֵמֶר *word* Pr 6_2, תּוֹרָה *law* Si 35_{16}, כֹּל *everything* Si 41_2; *in*, עֹנֶשׁ *fine* Si 9_5.

<SYN> לכד ni. *be taken*.

Pu. 1 Ptc. יוּקָשִׁים—**be caught,** <SUBJ> בֵּן *son* of human being Ec 9_{12}.

<PREP> לְ *at*, + עֵת *time* Ec 9_{12}.*

⇒ יָקוֹשׁ *(game) hunter*, יָקוּשׁ *(game) hunter*, מוֹקֵשׁ *snare*; יָקְשָׁן *Jokshan*.

יָקְשָׁן 4 pr.n.m. **Jokshan,** son of Abraham and Keturah, <SUBJ> ילד *bear child* Gn 25_3. <OBJ> ילד *bear child* Gn 25_2 1 C 1_{32}. <CSTR> בְּנֵי יָקְשָׁן *sons of Jokshan* 1 C 1_{32}.

יקשׁ *trap*.

יָקְתְאֵל 2 pl.n. **Joktheel, 1.** in Judah near Lachish Jos 15_{38}. **2.** name given by Amaziah to Petra 2 K 14_7.

<NOM CL> בַּשְּׁפֵלָה ... יָקְתְאֵל *in the lowland was ... Joktheel* Jos 15_{38}. <OBJ> קרא *call* 2 K 14_7. <APP> שֵׁם *name* 2 K 14_7.

ירא I 378.13.62 vb. **fear—Qal** 328.9.36 Pf. יָרֵא, יָרְאָה (יָרֵאָה), יָרֵאתָ, יָרֵאתִי, יָרְאוּ (יְרֵאוּנִי, יְרֵאוּךָ, יְרֵאוּהוּ), יְרֵאתֶם (יְרָאתֶם Jos 4_{24}), יָרֵאנוּ; impf. יִירָא (יִרָאֲךָ), 3fs תִּירָא, 2ms תִּירָא, יִרְאוּ, יְרָאוּ, יִירְאוּ (יִירָאוּ), אִירָא (אִירָאֶנּוּ), תִּירְאִי (תִּירָאִי), תִּירָאֻם, תִּירְאוּן, תִּירְאוּ (תִּירָאוּ), (יִרָאוּךָ, יִירָאוּךָ, יִירָאוּן), נִירָא (Kt נרא); + waw וַיִּירָא (וַיִּרָא, וַיִּירָאֵנִי), וַיִּרְאוּ, וַיִּרָאוּ, וַיִּרֵאתָ, וַתִּירְאִי, וָאִירָא, וַיִּירְאוּ (וַיִּרְאוּ, וַיִּירָאוּ), 3fpl וַתִּירֶאןָ, וַתִּירָאוּ, וַנִּירָא; impv. יְרָא, יְראוּ; ptc. יָרֵא, cstr. יְרֵא, pl. יְרֵאִים, cstr. יִרְאֵי, sf. יְרֵאֶיךָ (Q יראיכה, לִירֵאֶיךָ), יְרֵאָיו (לִירֵאָיו), fem. cstr. יִרְאַת; inf. cstr. יִרְאָה (יְרֹא, לֵרֹא, יִרְאָתוֹ, יִרְאָתָם).

1. be afraid, fear, be fearful,* a. used absolutely, <SUBJ> Israel(ites) Dt 1_{21} 13_{12} 20_3=1QM 10_3 Dt 21_{21} =11QT 64_6 Dt 31_6 1 S 17_{11} Is $41_{10.13.23(Kt)}$ (Qr, 1QIsa[a] ראה *see*) $43_{1.5}$ 1QM 15_8, Jacob, i.e. Israel Is $41_{10.13}$ $43_{1.5}$ 44_2 Jr 30_{10} $46_{27.28}$, Jeshurun Is 44_2, Judah Jr 3_8 2 C $20_{15.17}$, Philistines 1 S 4_7, עַם *people* Ex 14_{13} 20_{20} Dt 17_{13} =11QT 56_{11} 1 S 12_{20} Hg 2_5 perh. 4QM[a] 11.2_{13} (ת[ירא]ו), בֵּית *house* of Israel/Judah Zc $8_{13.15}$, אִי *coastland* Is 41_{15}, Ashkelon Zc 9_5, Jerusalem Zp 3_{16} 2 C 20_{17}, Abiathar 1 S 22_{23}, Abra(ha)m Gn 15_1 $20_{11(Sam)}$, Adoni-zedek Jos 10_2, Ahaz Is 7_4, Daniel Dn 10_{12}, David 1 S 23_{17}, Elijah 1 K $19_{3(mss)}$, Gideon Jg 6_{23}, Hagar Gn 21_{17}, Job Jb 11_{15}, Jehoshaphat 2 C $20_{3.15}$, Joshua Dt 31_8 Jos 8_1, Isaac Gn 26_{24}, Jacob Gn 28_{17} 31_{31} 32_8, Mephibosheth 2 S 9_7, Moses Ex 2_{14}, Nehemiah Ne 2_2 6_{13}, Rachel Gn 35_{17}, Sarah Gn 18_{15}, Saul 1 S 28_5, Solomon 1 C 28_{20}, Uriah Jr 26_{19}.

אָדָם *human being* Gn 3_{10} (or em. וָאִירָא *and I feared* to וָאֵרֶא *and I saw*) Ps 64_{10}, אִישׁ *man* Gn 20_8 Dt $43_{18.23}$ Dt 20_8=11QT 62_3 1 S 17_{24} 23_3 Jon $1_{10.16}$ Ps 112_8 Dn 10_{19}, גֶּבֶר *man* Jr $17_{8(Kt)}$ (Qr ראה *see*), מַת *man* Is 41_{14}, אִשָּׁה *woman, wife* 1 S 4_{20} 28_{13} 1 K 17_{13}, אָב *father* 4QTobit[e] 5_3, אֵם *mother* 4QJub[g] 25_{10}, בֵּן *son* 1 C 22_{13} 28_{20}, of Israel Ex 14_{10}, בַּת *daughter* Ru 3_{11}, אָח *brother* Gn 42_{35} $50_{19.21}$, אָחוֹת *sister* Jr 3_8, כַּלָּה *daughter-in-law* 1 S 4_{20}, אַלְמָנָה *widow* 1 K 17_{13}, מֶלֶךְ *king* Jos 10_2 2 C 20_{15}, שַׂר *commander* 2 K 10_4 2 C 32_7, אָדוֹן *lord* Jg 4_{18}, קָצִין *chief* Jos 10_{25}, עֶבֶד *servant* Is $41_{10.13}$ 44_2 Jr 30_{10} $46_{27.28}$, נַעַר *lad* Jg 8_{20} 2 S 13_{28}

2 K 6_{16}, זָקֵן *elder* 2 K 10_4, אֹמֵן *guardian* 2 K 10_4, חָכָם *wise one* Pr 14_{16}, יֹשֵׁב *inhabitant* 2 C 20_{15}, worshipper Ps 46_3 49_6 (or em. אִירָא *I fear* to תִּרְאֶה *you look*) 56_4 (or em. אִירָא *I fear* to אֶקְרָא *I call*, or del.) $56_{5.12}$ 118_6 Lm 3_{57}.

מַלָּח *sailor* Jon 1_5, נשׂא ptc. *one who bears* armour 1 S 31_4||1 C 10_4, מהר ni. ptc. *hurried*, i.e. anxious, *one* Is 35_4, סער ptc. *storm-tossed one* Is 54_{14}, עָקָר *barren one* Is 54_4, עָנִי *afflicted one* Is 54_{14}, מְבַשֶּׂרֶת *messenger* Is 40_9, אוֹיֵב *enemy* Ps 64_5 (or em. יִירָאוּ *they* do not *fear* to יֵרָאוּ *they are* not *seen*), שׂנא pi. ptc. *one who hates* 4QJonathan 1_5 (מסנ[איך]), רעע hi. ptc. *evil one* Ps 64_5 (or em.; see above), פעל ptc. *one who does* evil Ps 64_5 (or em.; see above), friends of Job Jb 6_{21}, שׁאר ni. ptc. *one who remains* Dt 19_{20}=11QT 61_{11}, לֵב *heart* Ps 27_3, זֶרַע *seed* Is $41_{10.13}$, בְּהֵמָה *beast* Jl 2_{22}, צֹאן *flock* Jr 23_4, תּוֹלַעַת *worm* Is 41_{14}, אֲדָמָה *land* Jl 2_{21}, מִי *who?* Jg 7_3 Am 3_8; subj. not specified, Ps 49_{17} (or em. אַל־תִּירָא *do not fear* to אַל־תֵּרֶא *do not look*).

<PREP> בְּ of time, *in*, + יוֹם *day* Ps 49_6 (or em.; see Subj.).

<COLL> ירא || שׁתע *fear* Is $41_{23(Kt)}$ (1QIsa[a] ראה *see* || שׁמע *hear*), חתת *be dismayed* Dt 1_{21} Dt 31_8 Jos 8_1 10_{25} 1 S 17_{11} Jr 23_4 30_{10} 46_{27} 1 C 22_{13} 28_{20} 2 C 20_{17}, חפז *be alarmed* Dt 20_3, חרד *tremble* Is 41_5, ערץ *tremble* Dt 20_3, חיל *writhe* Zc 9_5, שׁמע *hear* Dt 13_{12} 17_{12} 19_{20}=11QT 61_{11} Dt 21_{21}=11QT 64_6, נבא ni. *prophesy* Am 3_8.

+ חתת *be dismayed* 2 C 20_{15} 32_7, ערץ *tremble* Dt 31_6, צרר *be narrow*, i.e. distressed Gn 32_8, רכך (of heart) *be weak* Dt 20_3=1QM 10_3 Is 7_4, רפה (of hands) *be weak* Zp 3_{16}, חרד (of heart) *tremble* 1 S 28_5, חזק (of hands) *be strong* Zc 8_{13}, סור *turn aside* from evil Pr 14_{16}, ראה *see* Gn 42_{35} Ex $14_{13.31}$ 34_{30} Dt 28_{10} 1 S 12_{24} 17_{24} $28_{5.13}$ 2 S 10_{19} 1 K 3_{28} Is 41_5 Zc 9_5 Ps 40_4 52_8 Jb 6_{21} 37_{24}.

:: חזק *be strong* Dt 31_6 Jos 10_{25} Is 35_4 1 C 22_{13} 28_{20} 32_7, אמץ *be courageous* Dt 31_6 Jos 10_{25} 1 C 22_{13} 28_{20} 32_7, זיד *be presumptuous* Dt 17_{13}=11QT 56_{11}, שׁקט hi. *be quiet* Is 7_4, עבר htp. *be arrogant* Pr 14_{16}.

ירא + adverb or noun used adverbially, מְאֹד *much* Gn 20_8 32_8 Ex 14_{10} Jos 10_2 1 S $17_{11.24}$ 31_4||1 C 10_4 2 K 10_4 (מְאֹד מְאֹד) Ne 2_2 (הַרְבֵּה מְאֹד *very much*) Arad ost. 111_2 ([י]רא), עוֹד *again* Jr 23_4, יוֹם *(in the) day (when)* Ps 56_4.

ירא with adj., חָרֵד *trembling* Jg 7_3, רַךְ *weak* of heart Dt 20_8=11QT 62_3.

אַל־תִּירָא *do not fear* (masc. sing.) Gn 15_1 26_{24} Dt 1_{21} Jos 8_1 Jg 4_{18} 6_{23} 1 S 22_{23} 23_{17} 2 S 9_7 2 K 1_{15} 2 K 6_{16} Is 7_4 Is $41_{10.13}$ $43_{1.5}$ 44_2 Jr 30_{10} $46_{27.28}$ Ps 49_{17} (or em.; see Subj.) Lm 3_{57} Dn $10_{12.19}$ 1 C 22_{13} 28_{20} 4QPseud[b] 1_9, אַל־תִּירְאִי/תִּירָאִי *do not fear* (fem. sing.) Gn 21_{17} 35_{17} 1 S 4_{20} 28_{13} 1 K 17_{13} Is 40_9 41_{14} 54_4 Jl 2_{21} Zp 3_{16} Ru 3_{11}, אַל־תִּירְאוּ/תִּירָאוּ *do not fear* (masc. pl.) Gn 43_{23} $50_{19.21}$ Ex 14_{13} 20_{20} Dt 20_3=1QM 10_3 Dt 31_6 Jos 10_{25} 1 S 12_{20} 2 S 13_{28} Is 35_4 Jl 2_{22} Hg 2_5 Zc $8_{13.15}$ 2 C $20_{15.17}$ 32_7 1QM 15_8 4QM[a] 11.2_{13} (ת[ירא]ו), לֹא תִירָא (as command) *you shall not fear* Dt 31_8.

1b. be afraid of (doing), fear (to do), <SUBJ> Aram(aeans) 2 S 10_{19}, Aaron Ex 34_{30} Nm 12_8, Elihu Jb 32_6, Gidon Jg 7_{10}, Isaac Gn 26_7, Lot Gn 19_{30}, Miriam Nm 12_8, Moses Ex 3_6, Samuel 1 S 3_{15}, אִישׁ *man* 2 S 1_{14}, בֵּן *son* of Israel Ex 34_{30}, עֶבֶד *servant* 2 S 12_{18}.

<COLL> ירא followed by inf. cstr. + לְ be afraid *to*, + אמר *say* Gn 26_7, דבר pi. *speak* Nm 12_8, נגד hi. *tell* 2 S 12_{18}, ירד *go down* Jg 7_{10}, שׁלח *send*, i.e. stretch, hand 2 S 1_{14}, ישׁב *dwell* Gn 19_{30}, ישׁע hi. *save* 2 S 10_{19}; followed by inf. cstr. + מִן be afraid *of*, + נגד hi. *tell* 1 S 3_{15}, חוה pi. *declare* Jb 32_6, נבט hi. *look* Ex 3_6, ירד *go down* Gn 46_3, נגשׁ *draw near* Ex 34_{30}; ירא + זחל *fear* Jb 32_6; אַל־תִּירָא *do not fear* Gn 46_3.

1c. be afraid of, fear someone or something, <SUBJ> Israel(ites) Dt 1_{29} 3_{33} 5_5 $7_{18.19}$ 20_1=11QT 61_{13} 1 K 3_{28} Is 8_{12} Zp 3_{13} (mss ראה *see*) 1QM 17_4, עַם *people* Dt 28_{10} 2 K 25_{26} Is 10_{24} 51_7 Jr 51_{46}, עֵדָה *congregation* Nm $14_{9.9}$, בַּיִת *house* of Israel Ezk 11_8, Jerusalem/Zion Is 51_{12} perh. 57_{11}, Abraham Gn 20_{10} (if em.; see Obj.), Adonijah 1 K $1_{50.51}$, David 1 S 21_{13}, Elijah 2 K 1_{15}, Gideon Jg 6_{27}, Ishbosheth 2 S 3_{11}, Ishmael 2 K 25_{24}||Jr 40_9, Jaazaniah 2 K 25_{24}||Jr 40_9, Jacob Gn 32_{12}, Jeremiah Jr 1_8, Job Jb $5_{21.22}$, Johanan 2 K 25_{24}||Jr 40_9 Jr $42_{11.11.11}$, Seraiah 2 K 25_{24}||Jr 40_9, Joshua Jos 10_8 11_6, Moses Nm 21_{34} Dt 3_2, Saul 1 S 15_{24} $18_{12.29}$ 28_{20}, אִישׁ *man* 2 K 25_{24}||Jr 40_9 Jr 41_{18} 51_{46} Ps 112_7, אִשָּׁה *woman, wife* Jr 41_{18} Pr 31_{21}, בֵּן *son* Dt 2_4 2 K 25_{24}||Jr 40_9 Pr 3_{25} 11QPsAp[A] 2_{11} ([בני]), of Israel 1 S 7_7, of man Ezk $2_{6.6}$ 3_9, בַּת *daughter* of Zion Zp 3_{13} (mss ראה *see*), טַף *children* Jr 41_{18}, אָדוֹן *lord* 2 K 19_6||Is 37_6, שַׂר *commander* 2 K 25_{24}||Jr 40_9 Dn 1_{10}, חֹר *noble* Ne 4_8, סָרִיס *eunuch* Jr 41_{18}, סָגָן *official* Ne 4_8, יֹשֵׁב *inhabitant* Jos 9_{24} Ps

6$_{5_9}$ Ps 91$_5$, ידע ptc. *one who knows* Is 51$_7$, worshipper Ps 3$_7$ 23$_4$ 27$_1$ 56$_5$ 119$_{120}$, גָּבֹהַּ *high one* Jb 41$_{26}$, שְׁאֵרִית *remnant* Jr 41$_{18}$ 42$_{16}$, יֶתֶר *remainder* Ne 4$_8$, מִי *who?* Ps 90$_{11}$ (if em. כְּיִרְאָתְךָ *according to your fear* to מִי יָרֵא תֹּךְ *who fears injury?*), subj. not specified, Ec 9$_2$ 12$_5$.

<OBJ> עַם *people* Nm 14$_{9.9}$ 1 S 15$_{24}$, בַּיִת *house* Jg 6$_{27}$ Ezk 3$_9$, Abner 2 S 3$_{11}$, Esau Gn 32$_{12}$, Og Nm 21$_{34}$ Dt 3$_2$, Solomon 1 K 1$_{51}$, אִישׁ *man* Jg 6$_{27}$, מֶלֶךְ *king* Nm 21$_{34}$ Dt 3$_{2.22}$ 1 K 1$_{51}$ Dn 1$_{10}$, אָדוֹן *lord* Dn 1$_{10}$, לִוְיָתָן *Leviathan* Jb 41$_{26}$, דָּבָר *word* 1 S 28$_{20}$, שְׁבוּעָה *oath* Ec 9$_2$, יִרְאָה *(object of) fear* Jon 1$_{10.16}$, מוֹרָא *(object of) fear* Is 8$_{12}$, חַתְחַת *terror* Ec 12$_5$, חֶרְפָּה *reproach* Is 51$_7$, חֶרֶב *sword* Ezk 11$_8$, רַע *evil* Zp 3$_{13}$ (mss ראה *see*) Ps 23$_4$, תֹּךְ *injury* Ps 90$_{11}$ (if em.; see Subj.), מַכָּה *blow* 11QPsAp^a 2$_{11}$ ([ויירא]ו את המכה]), מִי *whom?* Is 57$_{11}$, מָה *what?* Gn 20$_{10}$ (if em. מָה רָאִיתָ *what did you see?* to מָה יָרֵאתָ *what did you fear?*); obj. not specified, 1QM 17$_4$.

<PREP> לְ *for (the sake of)*, + נֶפֶשׁ *soul*, i.e. life Jos 9$_{24}$, בַּיִת *house(hold)* Pr 31$_{21}$.

בְּ introducing object or *on account of*, + שְׁמוּעָה *report* Jr 51$_{46}$.

מִן introducing object or *on account of*, + Assyria(ns) Is 10$_{24}$, Israel(ites) Dt 28$_{10}$, עַם *people* Dt 2$_4$ 20$_1$=11QT 61$_{13}$, גּוֹי *nation* Dt 7$_{18}$, Ahab 4QparaKings 1$_2$, Jezebel 4Qpara Kings 1$_2$, אֱנוֹשׁ *human being* Is 51$_{12}$, בֵּן *son* Dt 1$_{29}$ Ezk 2$_6$, of man Is 51$_{12}$, מֶלֶךְ *king* Jos 10$_8$ Jr 42$_{11}$, עֶבֶד *servant* 2 K 25$_{24}$||Jr 40$_9$, גָּבֹהַּ *high one* Ec 12$_5$, חַיָּה *beast* Jb 5$_{22}$, חֶרֶב *sword* Jr 42$_{16}$, חֵץ *arrow* Ps 91$_5$, דָּבָר *word* Ezk 2$_6$, שְׁמוּעָה *report* Ps 112$_7$, מִשְׁפָּט *judgment* Ps 119$_{120}$, אוֹת *sign* Ps 65$_9$, פַּחַד *dread* Ps 91$_5$ Pr 3$_{25}$, שֹׁד *destruction* Jb 5$_{21}$, שׁוֹאָה *devastation* Pr 3$_{25}$, שֶׁלֶג *snow* Pr 31$_{21}$, רְבָבָה *ten thousand* Ps 3$_7$, מִי *whom?* Ps 27$_1$.

מִפְּנֵי introducing object or *on account of* Jr 1$_8$, + Chaldaeans 2 K 25$_{26}$||Jr 41$_{18}$, Israel(ites) Jos 9$_{24}$, Philistines 1 S 7$_7$, עַם *people* Dt 7$_{19}$, Achish 1 S 21$_{13}$, David 1 S 18$_{29}$, Solomon 1 K 1$_{50}$, מֶלֶךְ *king* Jos 11$_6$ 1 K 3$_{28}$ Jr 42$_{11.11}$, שַׂר *commander* 2 K 1$_{15}$, צַר *adversary* Ne 4$_8$, אֵשׁ *fire* Dt 5$_5$, דָּבָר *word* 2 K 19$_6$||Is 37$_6$.

מִלִּפְנֵי introducing object, + David 1 S 18$_{12}$.

<COLL> ירא || דאג *fear* Is 57$_{11}$; + ערץ *dread* Dt 1$_{29}$ Is 8$_{12}$, חתת *be dismayed* Is 51$_7$ Ezk 2$_6$ 3$_9$, שׁמע *hear* voice 1 S 15$_{24}$; :: שׂחק *laugh* Jb 5$_{22}$; ירא ... מֵעֲשׂוֹת *be too afraid of* someone ... *to do* Jg 6$_{27}$.

ירא + adverb, מְאֹד *much* Jos 9$_{24}$ 1 S 21$_{13}$; + פֶּן *lest* Gn 32$_{12}$, אֲשֶׁר לָמָּה *lest* Dn 1$_{10}$.

אַל־תִּירָא *do not fear* (masc. sing.) Nm 21$_{34}$ Dt 3$_2$ Jos 10$_8$ 11$_6$ 2 K 19$_6$||Is 37$_6$ Is 10$_{24}$ Jr 1$_8$ Ezk 2$_{6.6}$ 3$_9$ Jb 5$_{22}$ Pr 3$_{25}$, אַל־תִּירְאוּ *do not fear* (masc. pl.) Nm 14$_9$ 2 K 25$_{24}$||Jr 40$_9$ Is 51$_7$ Jr 10$_5$ 42$_{11.11}$ Ne 4$_8$, var. Nm 14$_9$ 1QM 17$_4$, לֹא תִירָא (as command) *you shall not fear* (masc. sing.) Dt 7$_{18}$ 20$_1$, לֹא־תִירְאוּ (as command) *you shall not fear* (masc. pl.) Is 8$_{12}$, vars. Dt 1$_{29}$ 3$_{22}$.

2a. fear Y.,* (other) gods, word of Y., etc.; sometimes **be afraid of** (e.g. Jr 5$_{22}$ Mc 7$_{17}$ Jb 9$_{35}$), but usu. **revere, be in awe of, <SUBJ>** Israel(ites) Lv 19$_{14.32}$ 25$_{17.36.43}$ Dt 5$_{29}$=4QTestim$_3$ Dt 6$_{2.13}$ 6$_{24}$ 8$_6$ 10$_{12.20}$ 13$_5$=11QT 54$_{14}$ Dt 14$_{23}$ Dt 28$_{58}$ 1 K 8$_{40}$||2 C 6$_{31}$, Amalek(ites) Dt 25$_{18}$, Babylonians, etc. 2 K 17$_{25}$, עַם *people* Ex 14$_{31}$ Dt 4$_{10}$ 31$_{12}$ Jos 4$_{24}$ (if em. יְרָאתֶם appar. *that you* [sons of Israel] *may fear* to יִרְאָתָם *that they* [the peoples] *may fear*, i.e. inf.) 24$_{14}$ 1 S 12$_{14.18.24}$ 1 K 8$_{43}$||2 C 6$_{33}$ Is 29$_{13}$ Jr 5$_{22.24}$ Hg 1$_{12}$, גּוֹי *nation* 2 K 17$_{28.41}$ Mc 7$_{16}$ Ps 102$_{16}$, בַּיִת *house* of Israel Jr 10$_5$, Jerusalem/Zion perh. Is 57$_{11}$, עִיר *city* Is 25$_3$ Jr 32$_{39}$ Zp 3$_7$, David 2 S 6$_9$||1 C 13$_{12}$, Habakkuk Hb 3$_2$ (or em. יָרֵאתִי *I have feared* to וְרָאִיתִי *and I have seen*), Hezekiah Jr 26$_{19}$, Job Jb 1$_9$ 9$_{35}$, Jonah Jon 1$_9$, Joseph Gn 42$_{18}$, Obadiah 1 K 18$_3$.

אֱנוֹשׁ *person* Ps 55$_{20}$, אִישׁ Dt 31$_{12}$ 2 K 17$_{32.33.34}$ Ps 112$_1$ Jb 37$_{24}$ Ne 7$_2$, אִשָּׁה *woman* Dt 31$_{12}$, בֵּן *son* Dt 31$_{13}$ Jos 22$_{25}$ Ps 72$_5$ (or em. יִירָאוּךָ *may they fear you* to וְיַאֲרִיךְ *and may he endure*, i.e. ארך hi.) Pr 3$_7$ 24$_{21}$, of Israel Jos 4$_{24}$ (unless em.; see above) Jg 6$_{10}$ 2 K 17$_{7.35.36.37.38.39}$ 4QMMT B$_{49}$ ([בני ישראל]) 11QT 46$_{11}$, טַף *children* Dt 31$_{12}$, מֶלֶךְ *king* Dt 17$_{19}$ Ps 102$_{16}$, Pharaoh Ex 9$_{30}$, עֶבֶד *servant* Ex 9$_{30}$ 1 K 18$_{12}$ 2 K 4$_1$ Ne 1$_{11}$, גֵּר *sojourner* Dt 31$_{12}$, לֵוִי *Levite* Ml 2$_5$, worshipper Ps 86$_{11}$, קָדוֹשׁ *holy one* Ps 34$_{10}$, מְיַלֶּדֶת *midwife* Ex 1$_{17.21}$, אַלּוּף *companion* Ps 55$_{20}$, מְיֻדָּע *familiar friend* Ps 55$_{20}$, עֵד *witness* CD 10$_2$ (עוד appar. error for עֵד), ירא ptc. *one who fears* Ec 8$_{12}$, עָנִי *afflicted one* Ps 72$_5$, רָשָׁע *wicked one* Ec 8$_{13}$, נטה hi. ptc. *one who turns* sojourner *aside* Ml 3$_5$, אֶרֶץ *earth* Ps 33$_8$, אֶפֶס *end* of earth Ps 67$_8$, מִי *who?* Is 50$_{10}$ Jr 10$_7$, מִי שֶׁ- *whoever* 4QMMT C$_{24}$, כָּל־אֲשֶׁר *all who* Ps 119$_{63}$; subj. not specified, Ex 9$_{20}$ Is 59$_{19}$ Pr 19$_{23}$ (if em. יִרְאַת י׳ לְחַיִּים *the fear of Y.*

[leads] to life Pr 19$_{23}$ to לֶחֶם יְרֵא אֶת־י׳ *he who fears Y.* shall be satisfied *with bread*) Ec 3$_{14}$ 5$_{6}$ 12$_{13}$.

<OBJ> Y. Gn 42$_{18}$ Ex 1$_{17.21}$ 14$_{31}$ Dt 4$_{10}$ 5$_{29}$=4QTestim$_{3}$ Dt 6$_{2.13.24}$ 8$_{6}$ 10$_{12}$ 13$_{5}$=11QT 54$_{14}$ Dt 14$_{23}$ 17$_{19}$ 25$_{18.58}$ 31$_{12.13}$ Jos 22$_{25}$ 24$_{14}$ 1 S 12$_{14.18.24}$ 2 S 6$_{9}$||1 C 13$_{12}$ 1 K 8$_{40.43}$||2 C 6$_{31.33}$ 1 K 18$_{3.12}$ 2 K 4$_{1}$ 17$_{25.28.32.33.34.36.39.41}$ Is 25$_{3}$ 29$_{13}$ 50$_{10}$ 57$_{11}$ Jr 5$_{22.24}$ 26$_{19}$ 32$_{39}$ Jon 1$_{9}$ Zp 3$_{7}$ Ml 2$_{5}$ 3$_{5}$ Ps 34$_{10}$ 55$_{20}$ 67$_{8}$ 72$_{5}$ 112$_{1}$ 119$_{63}$ Jb 1$_{9}$ 9$_{35}$ 37$_{24}$ Pr 3$_{7}$ 19$_{23}$ (if em.; see Subj.) 24$_{21}$ Ec 5$_{6}$ 12$_{13}$ Ne 7$_{2}$ CD 10$_{2}$, אֱלֹהִים *god* Jg 6$_{10}$ 2 K 17$_{7.35.37.38}$, מֶלֶךְ *king* Jr 10$_{7}$, שֵׁם *name* Dt 28$_{58}$ Is 59$_{19}$ Ps 86$_{11}$ 102$_{16}$ Ne 1$_{11}$, כָּבוֹד *glory* Is 59$_{19}$ Ps 102$_{16}$, דָּבָר *word* of God Ex 9$_{20}$, תּוֹרָה *law* 4QMMT C$_{24}$ (ה[ת]תור), פֹּעַל *work* Hb 3$_{2}$ (or em.; see Subj.).

<PREP> בְּ of time, *on*, + יוֹם *day* 2 S 6$_{9}$||1 C 13$_{12}$; כְּ *as*, + עַם *people* 1 K 8$_{43}$||2 C 6$_{33}$; מִן of direction, *from (the time of)*, + מַעֲרָב *west* Is 59$_{19}$, מִזְרָח *rising* of sun Is 59$_{19}$, נְעוּרִים *youth* 1 K 18$_{12}$; introducing object or of cause, *on account of*, + Y. Lv 19$_{14.32}$ 25$_{17.36.43}$ Mc 7$_{17}$ Ps 33$_{8}$, images Jr 10$_{5}$, מִקְדָּשׁ *sanctuary* 4QMMT B$_{49}$ 11QT 46$_{11}$; of comparison, *(more) than*, + רַב pl. *many* Ne 7$_{2}$; מִפְּנֵי introducing object or *on account of*, + Y. Ex 9$_{30}$ Hg 1$_{12}$; עִם *with*, + שֶׁמֶשׁ *sun* Ps 72$_{5}$; לִפְנֵי *before*, + יָרֵחַ *moon* Ps 72$_{5}$; מִלִּפְנֵי *(from) before*, + Y. Ec 3$_{14}$ 8$_{12.13}$.

<COLL> ירא || עבד *serve* Dt 6$_{13}$ 10$_{20}$ Jos 24$_{14}$ 1 S 12$_{14.24}$, כבד pi. *glorify* Is 25$_{3}$, גור *fear* Ps 33$_{8}$.

+ עבד *serve* Dt 10$_{12}$ 2 K 17$_{33.35.41}$, שחה htpal. *bow down* to 2 K 17$_{35.36}$, שמר *keep* commandments, etc. Dt 5$_{29}$=4QTestim$_{3}$ Dt 6$_{2}$ 8$_{6}$ 13$_{5}$ 17$_{19}$ 31$_{12}$ 2 K 17$_{37}$ Ps 119$_{63}$ Ec 12$_{13}$, עשׂה *do* according to commandments, etc. 2 K 17$_{34}$, הלך *walk* in ways Dt 8$_{6}$ 10$_{12}$ 2 C 6$_{31}$; *walk* after Dt 13$_{5}$=11QT 54$_{14}$, חפץ *delight* in commandments Ps 112$_{1}$, אהב *love* Dt 10$_{12}$, דבק *cling* to Dt 10$_{20}$ 13$_{5}$=11QT 54$_{14}$, שמע *hear* voice Dt 13$_{5}$=11QT 54$_{14}$ 1 S 12$_{14}$ Is 50$_{10}$, לקח *accept* discipline Zp 3$_{7}$, שׁבע ni. *swear* by name Dt 6$_{13}$ 10$_{20}$, חלה pi. *entreat* Jr 26$_{19}$, זבח *sacrifice* to 2 K 17$_{35.36}$, אמן hi. *believe* Ex 14$_{31}$, חיל *writhe* Jr 5$_{22}$, פחד *be afraid* Mc 7$_{17}$, חתת ni. *be in awe* Ml 2$_{5}$, סור *turn aside* from evil Pr 3$_{7}$, סור hi. *remove* gods Jos 24$_{14}$.

:: מרה hi. *rebel* 1 S 12$_{14}$.

ירא + adverb or noun used adverbially, מְאֹד *much* 1 S 12$_{18}$ 1 K 18$_{3}$, אֵיךְ *how?* 2 K 17$_{28}$, יוֹם *day* Dt 14$_{23}$ 1 K 8$_{40}$ ||2 C 6$_{31}$ Jr 32$_{39}$.

יִרְאָתָם אֹתִי מִצְוַת אֲנָשִׁים מְלֻמָּדָה *their fear of me is a commandment taught by men* Is 29$_{13}$.

לֹא תִירְאוּ (as command) *you shall not fear* (masc. pl.) Jg 6$_{10}$ 2 K 17$_{35.37.38}$.

2b. revere, be in awe of, respect a human or a thing, <SUBJ> Israel(ites) Lv 19$_{3.30}$ 26$_{2}$ Jos 4$_{14.14}$, עַם *people* 1 S 12$_{18}$ 14$_{26}$, אִישׁ *man* Lv 19$_{3}$, בֵּן *son* Pr 24$_{21}$. <OBJ> Joshua Jos 4$_{14}$, Moses Jos 4$_{14}$, Samuel 1 S 12$_{14}$, אָב *father* Lv 19$_{3}$, אֵם *mother* Lv 19$_{3}$, מֶלֶךְ *king* Pr 24$_{21}$, מִקְדָּשׁ *sanctuary* Lv 19$_{30}$ 26$_{2}$, שְׁבוּעָה *oath* 1 S 14$_{26}$. <COLL> ירא + שמר *keep* sabbaths Lv 19$_{3.30}$ 26$_{2}$.

2c. used absolutely, **fear, show reverence to, be in awe of,** God, or God's activity, <SUBJ> אָב *father* Jr 44$_{10}$, מֶלֶךְ *king* Jr 44$_{10}$, אִשָּׁה *wife* Jr 44$_{10}$, צַדִּיק *righteous one* Ps 52$_{8}$ (or em. וְיִרְווּ *and they shall be sated*; mss וְיִשְׂמָחוּ *and they shall rejoice*), רַב pl. *many* Ps 40$_{4}$, אֶרֶץ *earth* Ps 76$_{9}$. <COLL> ירא || שקט *be quiet* Ps 76$_{9}$; + דכא pu. *be humbled* Jr 44$_{10}$, הלך *walk* in law Jr 44$_{10}$, בטח *trust* in Y. Ps 40$_{4}$.

3. ptc. used as noun, **fearer, one who fears, one who reveres** Y., Y.'s name, etc. (alw. cstr. or with suffix in ref. to Y.; for other forms of ptc., see §§1-2), **a.** masc. <SUBJ> היה *be* Ml 3$_{16}$ Jb 1$_{1}$ 11QT 57$_{8}$, אמר *say* Ps 118$_{4}$, דבר ni. *speak* Ml 3$_{16}$, הלל pi. *praise* Ps 22$_{24}$, שׂמח *rejoice* Ps 119$_{74}$, ברך pi. *bless* Ps 135$_{20}$, pu. *be blessed* Ps 128$_{4}$, כבד ni. *be honoured* Si 10$_{20(B)}$, ראה *see* Ps 119$_{74}$, שמע *hear* Ps 66$_{16}$, ידע *know* Ps 119$_{79(Kt)}$, בין *understand* Si 35$_{16.16(B)}$, בחר *choose* Ps 25$_{12}$, בטח *trust* Ps 115$_{11}$, נצר *keep* 4QBéat 5$_{8}$, הלך *go* Ps 66$_{16}$ 128$_{1}$ Pr 14$_{2}$, htp. perh. 4QBéat 5$_{8}$, יצא *go out* Ml 3$_{20}$ Ec 7$_{18}$, hi. *bring out* Si 35$_{16.16(B)}$, שוב *go back* Ps 119$_{79}$, פושׁ *spring about* Ml 3$_{20}$, נוס htpol. *flee* Ps 60$_{6}$, פגע *meet* Si 36$_{1}$, עסס *tread* Ml 3$_{20}$, נשׂג hi. *reach* Si 6$_{16}$, שלם pu. *be repaid* Pr 13$_{13}$, עשׂה *do* Si 15$_{1}$. <NOM CL> מִי זֶה ... יְרֵא י׳ *who is ... the one who fears Y.?* Ps 25$_{12}$, יראיך לפניך תמיד *those who fear you are before you continually* 4QapPs^{b} 46$_{6}$. <OBJ> ישׁע hi. *save* Ps 145$_{19}$, חמל *spare* Ml 3$_{16}$, חלץ pi. *deliver* Ps 34$_{8}$, כבד pi. *honour* Ps 15$_{4}$, ברך pi. *bless* Ps 115$_{13}$, ירה hi. *teach* Ps 25$_{12}$, ידע hi. *cause to know* Ps 25$_{14}$, רצה *be pleased with* Ps 147$_{11}$.

<CSTR> יְרֵא י׳ *one who fears Y.* Ps 25$_{12}$ 128$_{1.4}$ Pr 14$_{2}$ Si 15$_{1}$ 14$_{4}$ 26$_{3}$ 35$_{16}$ 36$_{1}$, יִרְאֵי י׳ *those who fear Y.* Ml 3$_{16.16}$ Ps 15$_{4}$ 22$_{24}$ 115$_{11.13}$ 118$_{4}$ 135$_{20}$ Si 35$_{16(B)}$, יְרֵא אֱלֹהִים *one who fears God* Jb 1$_{1.8}$ 2$_{3}$ Ec 7$_{18}$ Si 10$_{20.24}$ (([י]רא), יִרְאֵי אֱלֹהִים

those who fear God Ps 66$_{16}$ Ec 8$_{12}$ (הָאֱלֹהִים) 4QBéat 5$_{8}$ ([י]ראי אלוהים) 11QT 57$_{8}$ (אלוהים), ירא אל *one who fears God* Si 6$_{16}$, יראי אל *those who fear God* 1QSb 1$_{1}$ (יראו[י אל]) 4QPrayer^{d} 1.1$_{1}$ CD 20$_{19.20}$, יִרְאֵי שְׁמִי *those who fear my name* Ml 3$_{20}$, שְׁמֶךָ *your name* Ps 61$_{6}$, מִצְוָה *(the) commandment* Pr 13$_{13}$; חלק ירא *portion of one who fears* Si 26$_{3}$, יְרֻשַּׁת יִרְאֵי *heritage of those who fear* Ps 61$_{6}$, אַשְׁרֵי כָּל־יְרֵא *happiness of everyone who fears* Ps 128$_{1}$, רְצוֹן־יְרֵאָיו *desire of those who fear him* Ps 145$_{19}$, כָּל־יְרֵא *all who fear* Ps 128$_{1}$, כָּל־יִרְאֵי *all those who fear* Ps 66$_{16}$, כול יראריכה *all those who fear you* 4QShir^{b} 52.3$_{5}$.

<APP> אִישׁ *man* Ml 3$_{16}$ Ps 25$_{12}$ Jb 1$_{8}$ 2$_{3}$, גֶּבֶר *man* Ps 128$_{4}$, קָטָן *small one* Ps 115$_{13}$, גָּדוֹל *great one* Ps 115$_{13}$, עֲרִירִי *childless one* Si 16$_{4}$.

<PREP> לְ of benefit, *to, for* Ps 25$_{14}$ 85$_{10}$ 119$_{38}$ (if em. לְיִרְאָתֶךָ *concerning your fear* to לִירֵאֶיךָ *to those who fear you*) 4QShir^{b} 52.3$_{5}$, + היה *be* Ec 8$_{12}$, צפן *treasure up* Ps 31$_{20}$, אנה pi. *allow to happen* Si 15$_{13}$; לְ of direction, *to*, + נתן *give* Ps 60$_{6}$ 111$_{5}$, גלה ni. *be revealed* CD 20$_{20}$; לְ of possession, *of, (belonging) to* Ps 34$_{10}$; לְ *concerning* Ml 3$_{16}$, + כתב ni. *be written* CD 20$_{19}$; זרח לְ *rise over* Ml 3$_{20}$; מִן of comparison, *(greater) than* Si 10$_{24}$ (מ[ן י]רא); מִן partitive, *(from) among* 4QPrayer^{d} 1.1$_{1}$; אֶל *to(wards)* Ps 33$_{18}$; עַל *upon, for, towards* Ps 103$_{17}$, + גבר *be mighty* Ps 103$_{11}$, רחם *have compassion* Ps 103$_{13}$; נֶגֶד *before*, + שׁלם pi. *pay* vows Ps 22$_{26}$, ספר pi. *tell* 4Q apPs^{b} 31$_{4}$, גיל *rejoice* 4QapPs^{b} 33$_{5}$ ([יראו]יך); בְּתוֹךְ *among*, + הלל pi. *fear* 1QH 12$_{3}$; סָבִיב לְ *around*, + חנה *encamp* Ps 34$_{8}$.

<COLL> ירא ptc. *one who fears* || זֶרַע *seed* Ps 22$_{24}$, בַּיִת *house* Ps 135$_{20}$; + אִישׁ *man* 11QT 57$_{8}$, תָּם *blameless (one)* Jb 1$_{1}$, גִּבּוֹר *mighty one* 11QT 57$_{8}$; + ptc. of חשׁב *think* Ml 3$_{16}$, ידע *know* Ps 119$_{79(Qr)}$, חסה *seek refuge* Ps 31$_{20}$, יחל pi. *wait* Ps 33$_{18}$ 147$_{11}$, תפשׂ *seize* law Si 15$_{1}$, סור *depart* from evil Jb 1$_{1.8}$ 2$_{3}$, שׂנא *hate* gain 11QT 57$_{8}$.

b. fem. <SUBJ> הלל htp. *be praised* Pr 31$_{30}$. <CSTR> יִרְאַת־י׳ *one who fears Y.* Pr 31$_{30}$. <APP> אִשָּׁה *woman* Pr 31$_{30}$.

Also 4QapPs^{b} 48$_{4}$ perh. 50$_{4}$ (וירה) 4QapMes 1.1$_{5}$ 4Q Béat 32$_{2}$ 4QSap^{b} 5$_{5}$ perh. 4QShir^{b} 20.2$_{2}$ perh. Ḥorvat ʿUza bowl inscr.$_{4}$ (unless ירא is from ראה *see*).

<SYN> §1a חתת *be dismayed*, חפז *be alarmed*, חרד *tremble*, ערץ *tremble*, חיל *writhe*, שׁמע *hear*, נבא ni. *prophesy*; §1c דאג *fear*; §2a עבד *serve*, כבד pi. *glorify*, גור *fear*; §2c שׁקט *be quiet*; §3a זֶרַע *seed*, בַּיִת *house*.

<ANT> §1a חזק *be strong*, אמץ *be courageous*, זיד *be presumptuous*, שׁקט hi. *be quiet*, עבר htp. *be arrogant*; §1c שׂחק *laugh*; §2a מרה hi. *rebel*.

Ni. 45.4.17 Pf. נוֹרָא; impf. תִּוָּרֵא; ptc. נוֹרָא, נוֹרָאָה, Q נוראים, נוראות, נוֹרָאוֹת (נוֹרָאֹת, נֹרָאוֹת, נוֹרְאֹתֶיךָ)—**1. be feared, be revered, be terrible; make oneself feared.***

<SUBJ> Y. Ps 66 76$_{13}$ 130$_{4}$ 139$_{14}$ (if em. נוֹרָאוֹת *fearfully* to נוֹרֵאתָ *you are feared*), אִישׁ *man* Si 9$_{18}$ (if em. ביטה נורא בעד איש לשון perh. *a fearful chatterer is behind a talkative man* to ביטה : נורא בעיר *voluble* sage. *Feared in the city* is a talkative man), אֵל *god* 4QShirShabb^{a} 2$_{2}$ (+ כבד ni. *be honoured*). <PREP> לְ of benefit, *to, for*, + מֶלֶךְ *king* Ps 76$_{13}$; of agent, *by*, + מוֹסָד *council* 4QShirShabb^{a} 2$_{2}$. <COLL> + noun used adverbially, עֲלִילָה *(with respect to) deeds* Ps 66$_{5}$.

2. ptc. as adj. (some cases may be §1), **a. feared, dreaded, dreadful,*** (1) attributively of אֶרֶץ *land* Is 21$_{1}$, מִדְבָּר *steppe* Dt 1$_{19}$ 8$_{15}$ (both || גָּדוֹל *great*), קֶרַח *ice* Ezk 1$_{22}$, עַם *people* Is 18$_{2.7}$ (both עַם נוֹרָא מִן־הוּא וָהָלְאָה *a people dreaded far and near*), בטה ptc. *chatterer* perh. Si 9$_{18}$ (ביטה; or em.; see §1).

(2) predicatively of גּוֹי *nation* Hb 1$_{7}$ (|| אָיֹם *terrible*).

b. terrible, fear-inspiring, inspiring reverence, (1) attributively of אֵל *God* Dt 7$_{21}$ 10$_{17}$ (|| גִּבּוֹר *mighty*) Dn 9$_{4}$ Ne 1$_{5}$ 9$_{32}$ (|| גִּבּוֹר; all five || גָּדוֹל *great*) 1QM 10$_{1}$ (|| גָּדוֹל), אֲדֹנָי *Lord* Ne 4$_{8}$ (|| גָּדוֹל), שֵׁם *name* Dt 28$_{58}$ (|| כבד ni. ptc. *glorious*) Ps 89$_{9}$ (+ רַב *great*, ערץ ni. ptc. *terrible*) 99$_{3}$ (|| גָּדוֹל), מַרְאֶה *appearance* Jg 13$_{6}$, כְּלִי *vessel* Si 43$_{2(M)}$, קֶרַח *frost* 4QpsEzek^{a} 4$_{14}$ ([הקרח] [הנור]א), יוֹם *day* of Y. Jl 3$_{4}$ Ml 3$_{23}$ (both || גָּדוֹל), רָז *mystery* 1QH 13$_{14}$ ([רזי]) 4QpsHod^{b} 3.1$_{23}$, מַחֲשָׁבָה *device* 4QD^{a} 1$_{6}$ (מח[שבות אל] [הנורא]ות).

(2) in nom. cl., predicatively of, or in ref. to, Y. Ex 15$_{11}$ (מִי כָּמֹכָה ... נוֹרָא תְהִלֹּת *who is like you ... [who is] inspiring [with respect to] praises?*; + אדר ni. ptc. *majestic*) Zp 2$_{11}$ (or em. נוֹרָא to נִרְאָה *he will show himself*) Ps 47$_{3}$ 68$_{36}$ 76$_{5}$ (if em. נָאוֹר you *shine*, i.e. אור ni. ptc., to נוֹרָא you are *terrible*) 76$_{8}$ 89$_{8(mss)}$ 96$_{4}$||1 C 16$_{25}$ (+ גָּדוֹל *great*, הלל pu. ptc. *praiseworthy*) 4QMyst^{c} 3a$_{5}$ 4QapPs^{b} 50$_{3}$ 4Q apJoseph^{b} 1$_{29}$ (+ קָדוֹשׁ, גָּדוֹל *holy*, גִּבּוֹר *mighty*, אַדִּיר *majestic*, פלא ni. ptc. *wonderful*), עֶלְיוֹן *the Most High* Ps 47$_{3}$,

Elijah Si 48$_4$, שֵׁם *name* Ml 1$_{14}$ Ps 111$_9$ (|| קָדוֹשׁ *holy*), מָקוֹם *place* Gn 28$_{17}$, הוֹד *splendour* Jb 37$_{22}$, יוֹם *day* Jl 2$_{11}$ (|| גָּדוֹל), חֹדֶשׁ *new moon* Si 43$_8$, מַעֲשֶׂה *deed* Ps 66$_3$ Si 43$_{2(B)}$, מוֹרָא *fear* 4QShirShabb^{e} 23.1$_{13}$, אֲשֶׁר *that which* Ex 34$_{10}$.

<COLL> נוֹרָא *terrible, fear-inspiring;* + בַּגּוֹיִם *among the nations* Ml 1$_{14}$, במזמת אפו *in the plan of his anger* 4QMyst^{c} 3a$_5$, עַל־כָּל־אֱלֹהִים *above all gods* Ps 96$_4$||1 C 16$_{25}$ 4QShirShabb^{e} 23.1$_{13}$, עַל־כָּל־סְבִיבָיו *above all around him* Ps 89$_8$, מִמִּקְדָּשֶׁיךָ *from your sanctuary* (or em. מִמִּקְדָּשׁוֹ *from his sanctuary*) Ps 68$_{36}$; + adverb, מְאֹד *very* Jg 13$_6$, מַה־נּוֹרָא *how terrible!* Gn 28$_{17}$ Ps 66$_3$ Si 43$_{2(B).8}$ 48$_4$.

3. ptc. as noun, **a.** masc. **awesome one, awesome thing,** <OBJ> זמר pi. *sing praise to* 4QShirShabb^{d} 1.1$_{42}$ ([זמ]רו ... [נ]ורא), עשׂה *do* 11QT 2$_1$ ([נורא הוא אשר אנ]י [עוש]ה) *it is an awesome thing that I am doing*). <CSTR> [נ]ורא כוח *awesome one of strength,* i.e. whose strength is awsome 4QShirShabb^{d} 1.1$_{42}$, נוראי כוח *awsome ones of strength* 11QShirShabb 5$_3$. <APP> אֱלֹהִים *god* 4QShirShabb^{d} 1.1$_{42}$ (אלו[הים נ]ורא) 11QShirShabb 5$_3$. <PREP> אֶל *concerning* 4Q418 43$_1$ (אל הנוראים תשכיל ראש perh. *you will teach the poor concerning awesome things*).

b. fem. pl. ptc. נוֹרָאוֹת, (1) as noun, **terrible deeds, terrible things,** <OBJ> ראה *see* Dt 10$_{21}$, עשׂה *do* Dt 10$_{21}$ 2 S 7$_{23}$ (both || גְּדוּלָּה *great deed*) Is 64$_2$ Ps 106$_{22}$ (|| גְּדוֹלָה, פלא ni. ptc. *wonderful deed*), פלא hi. *make wonderful* 4QShir^{b} 35$_5$ (יהללוהו בהפלא נוראות *they will praise him for making wonderful his terrible deeds*), ירה hi. *teach* Ps 45$_5$. <CSTR> עֱזוּז נוֹרְאֹתֶיךָ *the might of your terrible deeds* Ps 145$_6$ (+ גְּדוּלָּה *great deed*), שֵׁם ... נֹרָאוֹת *name of,* i.e. for, *terrible deeds* 1 C 17$_{21}$ (|| גְּדוּלָּה). <APP> אֵלֶּה *these* Dt 10$_{21}$. <COLL> נוראות [משנות עולמים] *terrible deeds from years of long ago* 4QDibHam^{a} 8$_3$ (|| פלא ni. *wonderful deed*).

(2) used adverbially, **fearfully, terribly,** of פלא ni. *be wonderful* Ps 139$_{14}$ (or em.; see §1), ענה *answer* Ps 65$_6$.

Also 4QShirShabb^{e} 58$_2$ 4QBark^{e} 7$_2$ (ונור[א]) 4QM^{a} 11.1$_8$ 4QShir^{b} 192$_1$.

<SYN> §2a גָּדוֹל *great,* אָיֹם *terrible;* §2b גִּבּוֹר *mighty,* גָּדוֹל *great,* כבד ni. ptc. *glorious,* קָדוֹשׁ *holy;* §3 גְּדוּלָּה *great deed.*

Pi. $_{5.0.9}$ Pf. יֵרְאֻנִי; ptc. Q מירא, מְיָרְאִים, Q מיראיו; inf. יָרְאָם, יָרְאֵנִי—**1. cause fear,** <SUBJ> worshipper 8QHymn 1$_1$. <PREP> בְּ of accompaniment, *with, in,* + שֵׁם *name* 8QHymn 1$_1$.

2. make afraid, <SUBJ> Geshem Ne 6$_9$, Sanballat Ne 6$_9$, Tobiah Ne 6$_{9.19}$, עַם *people* 2 S 14$_{15}$, עַרְבִי *Arab* Ne 6$_9$, עֶבֶד *servant* 2 C 32$_{18}$, נָבִיא *prophet* Ne 6$_{14}$, יֶתֶר *remainder* Ne 6$_9$. <OBJ> Nehemiah Ne 6$_{9.14.19}$, עַם *people* 2 C 32$_{18}$, אִשָּׁה *woman* 2 S 14$_{15}$. <COLL> || בהל pi. *terrify* 2 C 32$_{18}$.

3. cause to be feared, <SUBJ> worshipper 4QShir^{b} 35$_6$. <OBJ> אֵל *God* 4QShir^{b} 35$_6$. <PREP> בְּ of place, time, *in,* + קֵץ *end* of generations 4QShir^{b} 35$_6$.

Also perh. 4QCrypt 1.3$_5$ (מיראות) 4QShir^{b} 8$_4$ 11$_5$ 111$_{6.7}$ (both [מ]יראיו) 121$_3$ 191$_2$.

<SYN> בהל pi. *terrify.**

⇒ יִרְאָה *fear,* מוֹרָא *fear.*

***ירא II** $_2$ vb. **drink deeply (of)—Qal** $_2$ Impf. 2ms תֵּרֶא; impv. רְאוּ, אַל־תֵּרֶא יַיִן *do not drink deeply of wine* Pr 23$_{31}$ (unless ראה *see*), טַעֲמוּ וּרְאוּ כִּי־טוֹב י' *taste and drink deeply, for Y. is sweet* Ps 34$_9$ (unless ראה), מָתַי אָבוֹא וְאֵרֶא פְּנֵי אֱלֹהִים *when can I come and drink deeply of the presence of God?* Ps 42$_3$ (if em. וְאֵרָאֶה *that I might appear* before God; mss וְאֶרְאֶה *that I might see*).

Hi. force to drink deeply, הִרְאִיתָה עַמְּךָ קָשָׁה הִשְׁקִיתָנוּ יַיִן תַּרְעֵלָה *you made your people drink deeply of the cup, you have given us wine of reeling to drink* Ps 60$_5$ (if em. הִרְאִיתָה *you made us see*).

Ho. be allowed to drink deeply, וּמַרְוֶה גַּם־הוּא יוֹרָא *and one who gives to drink will be allowed to drink deeply* Pr 11$_{25}$ (if em. יוֹרֶא *be given drink,* i.e. רוה II *water,* ho.).

יִרְאָה $_{44.8.5}$ n.f. **fear**—cstr. יִרְאַת; sf. יִרְאָתִי, יִרְאָתְךָ, (יִרְאָתֶךָ), Q (יראתכה), יִרְאָתוֹ—**1. fear** of someone or something, **dread, terror,** <SUBJ> בוא *come* Ps 55$_6$. <NOM CL> יִרְאָה לָהֶם *terror was to them,* i.e. they inspired terror Ezk 1$_{18}$ (or em. וָאֵרֶאֶה *and I saw* them). <OBJ> נתן *give,* i.e. place Dt 2$_{25}$ Ezk 30$_{13}$. <CSTR> יִרְאַת שָׁמִיר וָשַׁיִת *fear of briers and thorns* Is 7$_{25}$, יראת רוח *fear of a* backsliding *spirit* 1QS 8$_{12}$. <ADJ> גָּדוֹל *great* Jon 1$_{10.16}$. <PREP> מִן of cause, *on account of,* + סתר pi. *hide* 1QS 8$_{12}$. <COLL> || רַעַד *trembling* Ps 55$_6$ (יִרְאָה וָרַעַד *fear and trembling*), פַּחַד *dread* Dt 2$_{25}$, גֹּבַהּ *height* Ezk 1$_{18}$; + פַּלָּצוּת *shuddering* Ps 55$_6$; יִרְאָה used adverbially, (1) *(for) fear of,* + בוא *come* Is 7$_{25}$; (2) *(with) fear,* + ירא *fear* Jon 1$_{10.16}$ (both ... וַיִּירְאוּ

יִרְאָה גְדוֹלָה *and they feared … [with] a great fear*, i.e. they feared greatly).

2. fear of Y., **reverence, devotion;** sf. usu. objective (i.e. referring to Y.), but subjective (i.e. referring to the one who fears Y.) at Jb 4$_{6}$ 22$_{4}$, <SUBJ> היה *be* Ex 20$_{20}$, עמד *stand*, i.e. remain Ps 19$_{10}$ (or em.; see Nom. Cl.), יסף hi. *increase* days Pr 10$_{27}$, שׂנא *hate* Pr 8$_{13}$ (or del. יִרְאַת י׳ שְׂנֹאת רָע *the fear of Y. is to hate evil*).

<NOM CL> רֵאשִׁית חָכְמָה יִרְאַת י׳ *the fear of Y. is the beginning of wisdom* Ps 111$_{10}$, sim. Jb 28$_{28}$ Pr 1$_{7}$ 9$_{10}$ 15$_{33}$, יִרְאַת י׳ מְקוֹר חַיִּים *the fear of Y. is a fountain of life* Pr 14$_{27}$, תוּשִׁיָּה יִרְאַת שְׁמֶךָ *the fear of your name is sound wisdom* Mc 6$_{9}$ (if em. יִרְאֶה appar. *he sees* to יִרְאַת *fear of*), יראת י׳ חיים *the fear of Y. is life* Si 50$_{29}$, יִרְאַת י׳ הִיא אוֹצָרוֹ *the fear of Y. is his treasure* Is 33$_{6}$, תפארתם יראת י׳ *their glory is the fear of Y.* Si 10$_{22(B)}$ (A י[רא]ת אֱלֹהִים *the fear of God;* Bmg ביראת י׳ *in the fear of Y.*), הֲלֹא יִרְאָתְךָ כִּסְלָתֶךָ *is not your fear your confidence?* Jb 4$_{6}$, אֵין־יִרְאַת אֱלֹהִים *there is no fear of God* Gn 20$_{11}$ Si 16$_{2}$, יִרְאַת י׳ טְהוֹרָה *the fear of Y. is pure* Ps 19$_{10}$ (or em. יִרְאַת to אִמְרַת *word of*), יראת אלהים כעדן ברכה *the fear of God is like an Eden of blessing* Si 40$_{27}$, יִרְאַת י׳ לְחַיִּים *the fear of Y. (leads) to life* Pr 19$_{23}$ (or em. יְרֵא אֶת־י׳ לֶחֶם *the one who fears Y.* shall be satisfied *with bread*), משניהם [יר]את אֱלֹהִים *better than both of them is the fear of God* Si 40$_{26}$.

<OBJ> נתן *give*, i.e. place Jr 32$_{40}$, בחר *choose* Pr 1$_{29}$, בין *understand* Pr 2$_{5}$, למד pi. *teach* Ps 34$_{12}$, עשׂה *do* Ps 111$_{10}$, עזב *forsake* Jb 6$_{14}$, פרר hi. *frustrate* Jb 15$_{4}$.

<CSTR> יִרְאַת י׳ *fear of Y.* Is 11$_{2.3}$ 33$_{6}$ Ps 19$_{10}$ (or em.; see Nom Cl.) 34$_{12}$ 111$_{10}$ Jb 28$_{28(mss)}$ Pr 1$_{7.29}$ 2$_{5}$ 8$_{13}$ (or del.) 9$_{10}$ 10$_{27}$ 14$_{26.27}$ 15$_{16.33}$ 16$_{6}$ 19$_{23}$ (or em.; see Nom. Cl.) 22$_{4}$ 2 C 19$_{9}$ Si 10$_{22(B)}$ 16$_{2}$ 40$_{26}$ 50$_{29}$, אֲדֹנָי *of my Lord* Jb 28$_{28}$, אֱלֹהִים *of God* Gn 20$_{11}$ Ne 5$_{15}$ 2 C 26$_{5}$ (if em.; see Prep.) Si 9$_{16}$ 10$_{22(A)}$ (י[רא]ת) 40$_{26}$ ([יר]את) 40$_{27}$, אֱלֹהֵינוּ *of our God* Ne 5$_{9}$, אל *of God* Si 35$_{12}$ 1QSb 5$_{25}$, שַׁדַּי *of Shaddai* Jb 6$_{14}$, עליון *of the Most High* Si 6$_{17}$; רוּחַ … יִרְאַת *spirit of … the fear of* Y. Is 11$_{2}$, עֵקֶב … יִרְאַת *consequence of … the fear of* Y. Pr 22$_{4}$.

<APP> עֲנָוָה *humility* Pr 22$_{4}$ (unless em. עֲנָוָה יִרְאַת *humility, fear of* to עֲנָוָה וְיִרְאַת *humility and fear of*).

<PREP> בְּ of accompaniment, *with, in* Pr 14$_{26}$ 15$_{16}$ Si 9$_{16}$ 10$_{22(Bmg)}$ 35$_{12}$ 40$_{26}$, + עבד *serve* Ps 2$_{11}$ (ms בְּשִׂמְחָה *with joy*), הלך *walk* Ne 5$_{9}$, עשׂה *do* 2 C 19$_{9}$, בין hi. *cause to understand* 2 C 26$_{5}$ (if em. בִּרְאֹת *when* God *saw* to בְּיִרְאַת *in the fear of* God); of instrument, *by (means of), through,* + סור *turn aside* Pr 16$_{6}$ (unless em. סוּר מֵרָע *turning aside from evil* to מוּסַר רָע *the discipline of evil*); introducing object, + בין htpol. *consider* Si 6$_{17}$; רוח בְּ hi. *smell*, i.e. delight, *in* Is 11$_{3}$.

כְּ *according to* Ps 90$_{11}$ (or em. וּכְיִרְאָתְךָ appar. *and in accordance with the fear of you* is your anger, to וּמִיִּרְאַת *or* who knows *any of*, i.e. has any idea of, *the fear of* your anger? or וּמִי רֹאֶה/יָרֵא תֹּקֶף *and who sees/fears the harshness of* your anger? or וּבְיִרְאָתְךָ *or that against those who fear you* is your anger?, as §3).

מִן of comparison, *(more) than*, + קשׁח hi. *make hard* Is 63$_{17}$ (תַּקְשִׁיחַ לִבֵּנוּ מִיִּרְאָתֶךָ *you have made our heart harder than your fear*, i.e. so hard that we cannot fear you); of cause, *on account of*, + יכח hi. *reprove* Jb 22$_{4}$; of instrument, *by (means) of*, + כנע hi. *subdue* 4QShir[b] 35$_{7}$ (מיראו[תו]); מִפְּנֵי *on account of* Ne 5$_{15}$.

<COLL> יִרְאָה ‖ דַּעַת *knowledge* Is 11$_{2}$ Pr 9$_{10}$ 1QSb 5$_{25}$; + דַּעַת *knowledge* Is 33$_{6}$ Pr 1$_{29}$ 2$_{5}$, דֶּרֶךְ *way* Is 63$_{17}$, יְשׁוּעָה *salvation* Is 33$_{6}$, חָכְמָה *wisdom* Is 33$_{6}$, שִׂיחָה *meditation* Jb 15$_{4}$, מִצְוָה *commandment* Si 6$_{17}$, רְעָדָה *trembling* Ps 2$_{11}$, תֹּם *integrity* Jb 4$_{6}$, חֶסֶד *loyalty* Pr 16$_{6}$, אֱמֶת *faithfulness* Pr 16$_{6}$, אֱמוּנָה *faithfulness* 2 C 19$_{9}$, לֵבָב שָׁלֵם *a whole heart* 2 C 19$_{9}$.

3. perh. **one who fears, reveres*** (unless §2 in each case), also used collectively, <NOM CL> מוֹשֵׁל יִרְאַת אֱלֹהִים *a ruler is one who fears God* 2 S 23$_{3}$ (mss בְּיִרְאַת ruling *in the fear of* God, as §2). <CSTR> יִרְאַת י׳ *those who fear (of) Y.* Pr 23$_{17}$, אֱלֹהִים *(of) God* 2 S 23$_{3}$. <PREP> לְ of possession, *of, (belonging) to* Ps 119$_{38}$ (אִמְרָתֶךָ אֲשֶׁר לְיִרְאָתֶךָ *your promise, which is to those who fear you*; or em. לִירֵאֶיךָ in same sense); בְּ of place, *among*, + שׁחה htpal. *worship* Ps 5$_{8}$; *against* Ps 90$_{11}$ (if em. וּכְיִרְאָתְךָ appar. *and in acccordance with the fear of you*, as §2); קנא בְּ pi. *be jealous of* Pr 23$_{17}$.

Also 4QVisSam 5$_{3}$ 4Q185 2$_{5}$ 4QapJosh[a] 14$_{5}$.

<SYN> §1 גֹּבַהּ *height*, רַעַד *trembling*, פַּחַד *dread*; §2 דַּעַת *knowledge*.*

⇒ ירא *fear.*

יִרְאוֹן 1 pl.n. **Iron,** or **Yiron,** city in Naphtali, prob. mod. Yarun, in N Galilee Jos 19$_{38}$, <NOM CL> ... עָרֵי הַמִּבְצָר יִרְאוֹן *the fortified cities are ... Iron* Jos 19$_{38}$.

[יִרְאִוִּיָּהוּ] 0.0.0.1 pr.n.m. **Irivvijah,** Seal 328 (7th/6th cent.).

⇒ ראה *see* + ״ *Y*.

יִרְאִיָּיה 2 pr.n.m. **Irijah,** son of Shemeliah, Benjaminite sentry who arrested Jeremiah Jr 37$_{13.14}$, <SUBJ> שׁמע *hear* Jr 37$_{14}$, תפשׂ *take hold of* Jr 37$_{13.14}$, בוא hi. *bring* Jr 37$_{14}$.

<NOM CL> וּשְׁמוֹ יִרְאִיָּיה בֶּן־שֶׁלֶמְיָה *and his name was Irijah who was the son of Shemeliah* Jr 37$_{13}$.

⇒ ראה *see* + ״ *Y*.

יָרֵב 2 adj. **great,** used attributively of מֶלֶךְ Assyrian *king* Ho 5$_{13}$ 10$_{6}$ (unless מֶלֶךְ יָרֵב = *a king, may he contend,* i.e. from ריב *contend;* or em. מֶלֶךְ/מַלְכִּי רָב *great king*).*

⇒ see also רבב *be great.*

יְרֻבַּעַל 14.0.0.1 pr.n.m. **Jerubbaal**—יְרֻבָּעַל—**1.** name given to Gideon* (Jg 6$_{32}$ 7$_{1}$ 8$_{29.35}$ 9$_{1.2.5.16.19.24.28.57}$ 1 S 12$_{11}$), ident. with יְרֻבֶּשֶׁת *Jerubbesheth* (2 S 11$_{21}$), <SUBJ> ישׁב *dwell* Jg 8$_{29}$, חנה *encamp* Jg 7$_{1}$, שׁכם hi. *rise up early* Jg 7$_{1}$, הלך *go* Jg 8$_{29}$.

<NOM CL> יְרֻבַּעַל הוּא גִדְעוֹן *Jerubbaal is Gideon* Jg 7$_{1}$.

<OBJ> קרא *call* Jg 6$_{32}$, שׁלח *send* 1 S 12$_{11}$.

<CSTR> בֵּית יְרֻבַּעַל *house of Jerubbaal* Jg 8$_{35}$, בֶּן־יְרֻבַּעַל *son of Jerubbaal* Jg 9$_{1.5.28.57}$, בְּנֵי יְרֻבַּעַל *sons of Jerubbaal* Jg 9$_{2.5.24}$.

<PREP> עִם *with,* + עשׂה *do* Jg 9$_{16.19}$.

2. Stamp/Coin 47$_{1}$ (Samaria?, 4th cent.).

⇒ ריב *contend* + בַּעַל *Baal.*

יָרָבְעָם 104.1.0.3 pr.n.m. **Jeroboam, 1.** first king of the northern kingdom of Israel 1 K 11$_{26.28.29.31.40.40}$ 12$_{2.2.3.12.15.20.25.26.32}$ 13$_{1.4.33.34}$ 14$_{1.2.2.4.5.6.7.10.10.10.11.13.13.14.16.17.19.20.30}$ 15$_{1.6.7.9.25.29.29.30.34}$ 16$_{2.3.7.19.26.31}$ 21$_{22}$ 22$_{53}$ 2 K 3$_{3}$ 9$_{9}$ 10$_{29.31}$ 13$_{2.6.11}$ 14$_{24}$ 15$_{9.18.24.28}$ 17$_{21.21.22}$ 23$_{15}$ 2 C 9$_{29}$ 10$_{2.2.3.12.15}$ 11$_{4.14}$ 13$_{1.2.3.4.6.8.13.15.19.20}$.

1. <SUBJ> היה *be* 1 K 11$_{40}$, שׁכב *lie down* 1 K 14$_{20}$, ישׁב *dwell* 1 K 12$_{2.25}$, עמד *stand* 1 K 13$_{1}$, hi. *position* 1 K 12$_{32}$, שׁמע *hear* 1 K 12$_{2}$‖2 C 10$_{2}$ 2 C 13$_{4}$, בוא *come* 1 K 12$_{3.12}$ ‖2 C 10$_{3.12}$, שׁוב *go back* 1 K 12$_{20}$ 13$_{33}$ 2 C 10$_{2}$, *do again* 1 K 13$_{33}$, יצא *go out* 1 K 11$_{29}$ 12$_{25}$, קום *arise* 1 K 11$_{40}$ 2 C 13$_{6}$, סבב hi. *bring around* 2 C 13$_{13}$, רום hi. *raise* 1 K 11$_{26}$, ברח *flee* 1 K 11$_{40}$ 12$_{2}$, לקח *take* 1 K 11$_{31}$, עשׂה *do* 1 K 12$_{32.32.32.32.33}$ 2 K 23$_{15}$ 2 C 13$_{8}$.

שׁלח *stretch* hand 1 K 13$_{4.4}$, ערך *arrange battle order* 2 C 13$_{3}$, בנה *build* 1 K 12$_{25.25}$, מלך *rule* 1 K 14$_{20}$, עלה hi. *bring up,* i.e. enact, offering 1 K 12$_{32}$, זבח pi. *offer sacrifice* 1 K 12$_{32}$, נדא hi. *seduce from allegiance to* 2 K 17$_{21(Kt)}$, מרד *rebel* 2 C 13$_{6}$, נדח hi. *lead astray* 2 K 17$_{21(Qr)}$, זנה hi. *exclude* 2 C 11$_{14}$, חטא *sin* 1 K 14$_{16}$ 15$_{30}$ Si 47$_{23}$ (חׄ[ט]א), hi. *cause to sin* 1 K 14$_{16}$ 15$_{30.34}$ 16$_{26}$ 22$_{53}$ 2 K 3$_{3}$ 10$_{29.31}$ 13$_{2.6.11}$ 14$_{24}$ 15$_{9.18.24.28}$ 17$_{21}$ 23$_{15}$ Si 47$_{23}$ (ו[יח]טיא), נגף *strike blow* 2 C 13$_{15}$, מות *die* 2 C 13$_{20}$, אמר *say* 1 K 12$_{26}$ 14$_{2}$, דבר pi. *speak* 1 K 12$_{3}$‖2 C 10$_{3}$.

<NOM CL> הָאִישׁ יָרָבְעָם גִּבּוֹר חָיִל *the man Jeroboam was a mighty warrior* 1 K 11$_{28}$.

<OBJ> נתן *give,* i.e. place 1 K 14$_{7}$, מצא *find* 1 K 11$_{29}$, רום hi. *raise,* i.e. exalt 1 K 14$_{7}$, מלך hi. *make king* 1 K 12$_{20}$ 2 K 17$_{21}$, נגף *strike blow* 2 C 13$_{20}$, מות hi. *kill* 1 K 11$_{40}$, קרא *call* 1 K 12$_{20}$‖2 C 10$_{3}$.

<CSTR> בֵּית יָרָבְעָם *house,* i.e. dynasty, *of* 1 K 13$_{34}$ 14$_{10.10.13.14}$ 15$_{29}$ 16$_{3.7}$ 21$_{22}$ 2 K 9$_{9}$ 13$_{6}$, אֵשֶׁת *wife of* 1 K 14$_{2.4.5.6.17}$, בֶּן *son of* 1 K 14$_{1}$ 15$_{25}$, דֶּרֶךְ *way of* 1 K 15$_{34}$ 16$_{2.19.26}$ 22$_{53}$, חַטֹּאֵי *sins of* 2 K 10$_{29}$, חַטֹּאות *sin of* 1 K 14$_{16}$ 15$_{30}$ 16$_{31}$ 2 K 3$_{3}$ 10$_{31}$ 13$_{2.11}$ 14$_{24}$ 15$_{9.18.24.28}$ 17$_{22}$, כֹּחַ *strength of* 2 C 13$_{20}$, ... מִלְחֲמוֹת *wars of* 2 C 12$_{15}$, [ימי] *days of* 4QMMT C$_{19}$ ([יר]ובעם), דִּבְרֵי *acts of* 1 K 14$_{19}$.

<APP> אִישׁ *man* 1 K 11$_{26}$, בֵּן *son* 1 K 11$_{26}$ 12$_{2.15}$‖2 C 10$_{2.15}$ 1 K 15$_{1}$ 2 K 17$_{21}$ 23$_{15}$ 2 C 9$_{29}$ 13$_{6}$ Si 47$_{23}$, מֶלֶךְ *king* 1 K 15$_{1.9}$ 2 C 13$_{1}$.

<PREP> לְ of direction, *to,* + נתן *give* 1 K 11$_{31}$, אמר *say* 1 K 11$_{31}$ 14$_{7}$; of benefit, *to, for,* + שׁאר hi. *leave over* 1 K 15$_{29}$; of possession, *(belonging) to, of* 1 K 14$_{11.13}$ 15$_{9}$ 2 C 13$_{1}$; *with respect to,* + כרת hi. *cut off* 1 K 14$_{10}$; מִן of direction, *from,* + לכד *capture* 2 C 13$_{19}$; אֶל *to,* + הלך *go* 2 C 11$_{4}$, דבר pi. *speak* 1 K 12$_{15}$‖2 C 10$_{15}$; עַל *concerning* 2 C 9$_{29}$, + דבר pi. *speak* 1 K 14$_{2}$; אַחֲרֵי *after,* + רדף *pursue* 2 C 13$_{19}$; בֵּין *between,* + היה *be* 1 K 14$_{30}$ 15$_{6}$ (both + Rehoboam) 15$_{7}$ (+ Abijam) 2 C 13$_{2}$ (+ Abijah); תַּחַת

instead of, + מלך *rule* 1 K 14_{20}.

2. king of Israel, son of Jehoash, <SUBJ> שׁכב *lie down* 2 K 14_{29}, ישׁב *sit* 2 K 13_{13}, מלך *rule* 2 K $14_{16.23}$, מות *die* Am 7_{11}. <CSTR> בֵּית *house of*, i.e. dynasty of Am 7_9, בֶּן *son of* 2 K 15_8, דִּבְרֵי *acts of* 2 K 14_{28}, יַד *hand of* 2 K 14_{27}, יְמֵי *days of* Ho 1_1 Am 1_1 1 C 5_{17}. <APP> מֶלֶךְ *king* 2 K 15_1 Am 7_{10}, בֵּן *son* 2 K $14_{16.23}$. <PREP> לְ *(belonging) to, of* 2 K 15_1; אֶל *to*, + שׁלח *send* Am 7_{10}.

3. Hazor inscr. 6_1, <PREP> לְ of possession, *(belonging) to, of* Hazor inscr. 6_1 (ירבע[ם]).

4. Seal 68_2 (Megiddo, 8th cent.). <CSTR> עבד ירבעם *servant of Jeroboam* Seal 68_2.

5. Stamp/Coin 47_1 (Samaria?, 4th cent.).

⇒ רבה *be great* + עָם *people*.

יְרֻבֶּשֶׁת 1 pr.n.m. **Jerubbesheth,** ident. with יְרֻבַּעַל *Jerubbaal* (Jg 6_{32} 7_1 $8_{29.35}$ $9_{1.2.5.16.19.24.28.57}$ 1 S 12_{11}) and גִּדְעוֹן *Gideon*, <CSTR> בֶּן־יְרֻבֶּשֶׁת *son of Jerubbesheth* 2 S 11_{21}.

⇒ ריב *contend* + בֹּשֶׁת *shame*.

ירד I $_{379.8.31.2}$ vb. **go down—Qal** $_{306.7.26.2}$ Pf. יָרַד (רַד Jg 19_{11}, יָרֵד), יָרְדָה (יָרֵדָה), יָרַדְתָּ (יָרַדְתְּ), יָרַדְתִּי, יָרְדוּ, יָרַדְנוּ; impf. יֵרֵד (יֵרַד), 3fs תֵּרֵד (תֵּרַד, תֵּרֶד 1 K $1_{10.12}$), 2ms תֵּרֵד, אֵרֵד (אֵרְדָה־, Sam אֵרְדָה Ex 3_8), יֵרְדוּ, 3fpl תֵּרַדְנָה, נֵרֵד (נֵרְדָה); + waw וְיָרַד, וְיָרַדְתָּ, Qr וְיָרַדְתְּ (Ru 3_3), וְיָרַדְתִּי, וְיָרְדוּ, וְיָרַדְנוּ; וַיֵּרֶד (וַיֵּרַד, Gnz וַיֵּרֵד 1 S 15_{12}), 3fs וַתֵּרֶד, וָאֵרֵד, וַיֵּרְדוּ, וַנֵּרֶד; impv. רֵד (רְדָה, רֵדָה, יְרַד Jg 5_{13}), רְדִי, רְדוּ; ptc. יוֹרֵד (יֹרֵד), יֹרֶדֶת (Q יורדת, יֹרְדָה), יוֹרְדִים (יֹרְדִים), יוֹרְדֵי (יֹרְדֵי), יוֹרְדוֹת (יֹרְדוֹת); inf. abs. יָרֹד; cstr. רֶדֶת (ירד Si 30_{17}, רִדְתִּי, Qr יָרְדִי־ Ps 30_4, רִדְתָּהּ, רְדָה Gn 46_3, רִדְתּוֹ, Q רדתנו, Q יורדם).

go down, come down, march down, descend, swoop down, of birds of prey (Gn 15_{11}), **dismount** (Jg 4_{15} 1 S 25_{23}), **step down** (Lv 9_{22}), **lead down,** of way (Pr 7_{27}), of steps (Ne 3_{15}), **sink** (Dt 28_{43} Lm 1_9 Ps 104_8), in water (Ex 15_5 Jon 2_7), of waves (Ps 107_{26}), **fall,*** of rain, etc. (Ex 9_{19} Nm 11_9 Is 52_4), of city (Dt 20_{20}), of horse and rider (Hg 2_{22}), **fall down,** of wall (Dt 28_{52}), **be felled,** of forest (Zc 11_2), **flow down,*** of water (Jos $3_{13.16.16}$ 4QapJoshua[b] $12_{1.2}$), of oil (Ps $133_{2.3}$), of tears (Si 32_{18}), **(over)flow with** tears, of eyes (Jr 9_{17} 13_{17} 14_{17} Ps 119_{136} Lm 1_{16} 3_{48}), **decline,** of shadow (2 K 20_{11} Is 38_8), **be over,** of day(light) (Jg 19_{11} Arad ost. 40_{10}).

appar. **go up** into mountainous country (Jg 1_9 15_8 1 S $23_{4.6.8.11}$ 2 S 5_{17} 2 K 2_2 6_{18} 10_{13} 1 C 11_{15}),* but perh. sometimes **go south, go down country*** (Nm $34_{11.12}$ Jos 15_{10} 18_{13} 1 S 23_{25} 25_1), **roam** upon mountains (Jg 11_{37}),* **be present*** (1 S 29_4 Is 34_7 Jr 48_{15}).

<SUBJ> Y. Gn $11_{5.7}$ 18_{21} 46_4 Ex 3_8 (Sam וְאֵרְדָה *and I will come down* for וָאֵרֵד *and I came down*) Ex $19_{11.18.20}$ 34_5 Nm $11_{17.25}$ 12_5 Jg 5_{13} 2 S 22_{10}||Ps 18_{10} Is 31_4 63_{14} 64_2 Mc 1_3 (or del. ירד) Ps 18_{10} 144_5 Ne 9_{13} Si 16_{18}, Aaron Lv 9_{22}, Abigail 1 S $25_{20.23}$, Abishai 1 S 26_6, Abra(ha)m Gn 12_{10}, Adonijah 1 K 1_{25}, Ahab 1 K 18_{44} $21_{16.18}$, Ahaziah 2 K $1_{4.6.16}$ 8_{29}||2 C $22_{6(mss)}$ 9_{16}, Ahimaaz 2 S 17_{18}, Azariah 2 C 22_6, Barak Jg 4_{14}, Barzillai 2 S 19_{32}, Benaiah 2 S $23_{20.21}$||1 C $11_{22.23}$ 1 K 1_{38}, Coniah Lachish ost. 3_{14}, David 1 S $17_{28.28}$ 20_{19} (or em. תֵּרֵד *you will go down* to תִּפָּקֵד *you will be … missed*) 23_4 (mss lack ירד) 23_{25} $25_{1.20}$ (mss הלך *go* instead of ירד) 29_4 2 S 5_{17} 21_{15}, Elead 1 C 7_{21}, Eleazar Nm 20_{28}, Elijah 1 K 21_{18} 2 K $1_{9.11.15.15}$ 2_2, Elisha 2 K 2_2, Ezer 1 C 7_{21}, Gideon Jg $7_{9.10.10.11.11}$, Isaac Gn 26_2, Jacob Gn 37_{35} (+ אָבֵל *as a mourner*) 45_9 46_3 Jos 24_4, Jehoshaphat 1 K 22_2 2 K 2_2 2 C 18_2 20_{16}, Jeremiah Jr $18_{2.3}$ 22_1 36_{12}, Joash 2 K 13_{14}, Jonah Jon $1_{3.3.5}$ 2_7, Jonathan 2 S 17_{18}, Judah Gn 38_1 $43_{4.5}$ $44_{26.26}$, Mephibosheth 2 S 19_{25}, Moses Ex $19_{14.21.24.25}$ $32_{1.7.15}$ $34_{29.29}$ Nm 20_{28} Dt $9_{12.15}$ 10_5, Naaman 2 K 5_{14}, Naomi Ru $3_{3(Kt)}$, Nathan 1 K 1_{38}, Nehemiah Ne $6_{3.3}$, Pelethite 1 K 1_{38}, Purah Jg $7_{10.11}$, Rebekah Gn $24_{16.45}$, Ruth Ru $3_{3(Qr).6}$, Samson Jg $14_{1.5.7.19}$ 15_8 (mss הלך *go*), Samuel 1 S $9_{25.27}$ 10_8, Saul 1 S $9_{25.27}$ 10_8 $14_{36.37}$ 15_{12} $23_{11.11}$ 26_2 (mss הלך *go* instead of ירד) 1 S 26_{10}, Shimei 2 S $19_{17.21}$ 1 K 2_8, Shuthelah 1 C 7_{21}, Simeon Si 50_{20}, Sisera Jg 4_{15}, Uriah 2 S $11_{8.9.10.10.13}$, Zadok 1 K 1_{38}.

Amalekite Nm 14_{45}, Benjaminite 2 S 19_{17} 1 K 2_8, Canaanite Nm 14_{45}, Cherethite 1 K 1_{38}, Gileadite 2 S 19_{32}, Israel(ite) Jg 5_1 (if em. יְרַד שָׂרִיד לְאַדִּירִים *come down, O remnant of noble ones* to יָרַד יִשְׂרָאֵל בָּאַדִּירִים *Israel came down with noble ones*) 1 S 13_{20}, Judah 2 C 20_{16}, Kenite 1 S 15_6, Philistine 1 S 13_{12}, Sidonian Ezk 32_{30}, Tishbite 1 K 21_{18}, psalmist Ps $30_{4(Qr).10}$.

Assyria Ezk 31_{15} (or em. תְּאַשּׁוּר *box tree*), Beth-Millo 2 K 12_{21}, Egypt Ezk 32_{19}, Elam Ezk 32_{24}, Jerusalem Lm

1$_{9}$ (or em. ho.), Meshech Ezk 32$_{27}$, Tubal Ezk 32$_{27}$.

אָב *father* Gn 45$_{9}$ Nm 20$_{15}$ Dt 10$_{22}$ 26$_{5}$ Jg 14$_{5}$ (or del. אָב) 14$_{10}$ 2 K 5$_{14}$, אֵם *mother* Jg 14$_{5}$ (or del. אֵם), בֵּן *son* Gn 42$_{2.38}$ Jos 24$_{4}$ Jg 1$_{9.34}$ 2 S 19$_{17.25}$ 23$_{20.21}$||1 C 11$_{22.23}$ 1 K 1$_{38}$ 2$_{8}$ 2 K 8$_{29}$=2 C 22$_{6}$ Is 30$_{2}$ 1 C 7$_{21}$ Si 50$_{20}$ 4QJub^{h} 38$_{13}$, Lachish 3$_{14}$, of Israel Jg 3$_{27.28}$ (if em. רדף *follow* to ירד) 3$_{28}$, בַּת *daughter* Ex 2$_{5}$ Jg 11$_{37}$ Is 47$_{1}$ perh. Jr 48$_{18(Qr)}$ perh. Ezk 32$_{19}$, אָח *brother* Gn 42$_{3}$ 43$_{4.5}$ 44$_{23.26.26}$ Jg 16$_{31}$ 1 S 22$_{1}$ 2 K 10$_{13}$ 4QapJoshua^{a} 6.1$_{5}$ ([י]ורדי), עַם *people* Dt 28$_{43}$ Jg 5$_{11.13(mss)}$ 9$_{36.37}$ 1 S 14$_{36}$ 23$_{8}$ Is 32$_{19(ms)}$ 52$_{4}$ Ezk 31$_{12}$ (or em. ירד to נדד *flee*), אָדָם *human being* Nm 16$_{30.33}$ Jb 33$_{24}$, אִישׁ *man* Gn 43$_{15.20}$ Jos 2$_{23}$ Jg 4$_{14}$ 15$_{11.12}$ 1 S 17$_{8}$ 25$_{20}$ 29$_{4}$ 2 K 1$_{6(ms).9.11}$ 1QM 7$_{6}$ CD 11$_{1}$, *each (one)* Hg 2$_{22}$ (or del. אִישׁ), נַעַר *lad, servant* Jg 7$_{10.11}$, נַעֲרָה *girl* Gn 24$_{16}$, בְּתוּלָה *young woman* Is 47$_{1}$, מַלְאָךְ *angel* Gn 28$_{12}$, *messenger* 2 K 6$_{33}$ (or em. מֶלֶךְ *king*), מָשִׁיחַ *anointed one* 1 S 26$_{10}$, מִבְחָר *chosen one* Ex 15$_{5}$ Jr 48$_{15}$, כֹּהֵן *priest* 1 K 1$_{38}$ Si 50$_{20}$, נָבִיא *prophet* 1 K 1$_{38}$.

מֶלֶךְ *king* 1 S 23$_{20.20}$ 1 K 21$_{18}$ 22$_{2}$ 2 K 1$_{4.6.16}$ 2$_{2.2(mss).2}$ 7$_{17}$ (or em. מַלְאָךְ *messenger*) 8$_{29}$ (ms lacks מֶלֶךְ; ||2 C 22$_{6}$) 9$_{16}$ 13$_{14}$ Ps 72$_{6}$ 2 C 20$_{16}$, נָשִׂיא *chief* Ezk 26$_{16}$, שְׁלֹשָׁה *three* chiefs 2 S 23$_{13(Qr)}$||1 C 11$_{15}$, שְׁלֹשִׁים *thirty* chiefs 2 S 23$_{13(Kt)}$, נָסִיךְ *chief* Ezk 32$_{30}$, שַׂר *commander* Lachish ost. 3$_{14}$, מְחֹקֵק *commander* Jg 5$_{14}$, עֶבֶד *servant* Ex 11$_{8}$ 2 S 19$_{21}$ 21$_{15}$.

רֹכֵב *rider* Hg 2$_{22}$, חֹבֵל *sailor* Ezk 27$_{29}$, מַלָּח *sailor* Ezk 27$_{29}$, תֹּפֵשׂ ptc. *one who handles* oar Ezk 27$_{29}$, עֹזֵר *helper* Ezk 31$_{17}$ (if em. זְרוֹעַ *arm*), נחל ptc. *one who possesses* 4QWiles 1$_{11}$, דּוֹד *(male) beloved* Ca 6$_{2.11}$ (unless רַעְיָה *[female] companion*), יוֹשֵׁב *inhabitant* 1 S 6$_{21}$ Jr 48$_{18}$ 2 C 20$_{16}$, בַּיִת *house(hold)* Jg 16$_{31}$ 1 S 22$_{1}$, חַיִל *army* Ex 15$_{5}$ 2 K 6$_{18}$, חֶבֶל *band* of prophets 1 S 10$_{5}$, הָמוֹן *multitude* Is 5$_{14}$ perh. Ezk 32$_{18}$ 32$_{21.24.27}$, שָׂרִיד *remnant* Jg 5$_{1}$ (or em.; see above), רִאשׁוֹן *(the) first* 2 S 19$_{21}$, הֶרֶג *slain one* Is 14$_{19}$, מְטֹעָן *pierced one* Is 14$_{19}$, עָרֵל *uncircumcised one* perh. Ezk 32$_{21.24}$, אוֹיֵב *enemy* Ps 55$_{16}$, שַׁאֲנָן *one at ease* Amos 6$_{2}$, הָדָר *honour*, i.e. honoured one Is 5$_{14}$, גְּאוֹן *pride* of her strength Ezk 30$_{6}$, עָלֵז *exulting (one)* Is 5$_{14}$, רוּחַ *spirit* Ec 3$_{21}$ 4QD^{a} 6.1$_{12}$ 4QD^{g} 1.1$_{7}$.

פְּרִי *fruit*, i.e. offspring Jr 50$_{27}$ (if em. פַּר *bull*), עַיִן *eye* Jr 9$_{17}$ 13$_{17}$ 14$_{17}$ Ps 119$_{136}$ Lm 1$_{16.16}$ (or del. עַיִן) 3$_{48}$, דִּמְעָה *tears* Si 32$_{18}$, זְרוֹעַ *arm* Ezk 31$_{17}$ (or em. זֶרַע *seed*, עֹזֵר *helper*, or גוע *expire*), רֶגֶל *foot* Pr 5$_{5}$ 4QWiles 1$_{3}$, בְּהֵמָה *beast* Is 63$_{14}$, רְאֵם *wild ox* Is 34$_{7}$, פַּר *bull* Is 34$_{7}$ Jr 50$_{27}$ (or em. פְּרִי *fruit*, i.e. offspring), סוּס *horse* Hg 2$_{22}$, עַיִט *bird of prey* Gn 15$_{11}$, מָן *manna* Nm 11$_{9}$, שֶׁמֶן *oil* Ps 133$_{2.2}$ (unless זָקָן *beard* is subj.; or del.), צֹאָה *excrement* 11QT 46$_{15}$, עַמּוּד *column* of cloud Ex 33$_{9}$ Nm 12$_{5}$, צֵל *shadow* 2 K 20$_{11}$ Is 38$_{8}$ (or ins. שֶׁמֶשׁ *sun*), שֶׁמֶשׁ *sun* Is 38$_{8}$ (if ins. שֶׁמֶשׁ) 38$_{8}$, אֵשׁ *fire* 2 K 1$_{10.10.12.12.14}$ 2 C 7$_{1.3}$, עָפָר *dust* Dt 28$_{24}$, בָּרָד *hail* Ex 9$_{19}$, שֶׁלֶג *snow* Is 52$_{4}$ Si 43$_{17(Bmg, M)}$, גֶּשֶׁם *rain* Is 52$_{4}$, טַל *dew* Nm 11$_{9}$ Ps 133$_{3}$, מַיִם *water* Jos 3$_{13.16.16}$ Ezk 47$_{1.8}$ 4QapJoshua^{b} 12$_{1.2}$ (both [המים]), גַּל *wave* Ps 107$_{26}$, נַחַל *wadi* Dt 9$_{21}$, בִּקְעָה *valley* Ps 104$_{8}$, יַעַר *forest* Is 32$_{19}$ Zc 11$_{2}$, עֵץ *tree* Ezk 31$_{17}$, תְּאַשּׁוּר *box tree* Ezk 31$_{15}$ (if em. אַשּׁוּר *Assyria*), זֶרַע *seed* Ezk 31$_{17}$ (if em. זְרוֹעַ *arm*), גְּבוּל *border* Nm 34$_{11.11.12}$ Jos 15$_{10}$ 16$_{7}$ 17$_{9}$ 18$_{13.16.16.16.17.18}$, גּוֹרָל *lot* Jos 16$_{3}$, דֶּרֶךְ *way* of Sheol Pr 7$_{27}$.

עִיר *city* Dt 20$_{20}$, חוֹמָה *wall* Dt 28$_{52}$, מַעֲלָה *step* Ne 3$_{15}$, מַצֵּבָה *memorial stone* Ezk 26$_{11}$ (or em. תֵּרֵד *it will fall* to יוֹרִד Y. *will cause* memorial stones *to fall*), מְחִלָּה *shaft* 11QT 32$_{13}$, מֶרְכָּבָה *chariot* Ex 15$_{5}$, חֶרֶב *sword* Is 34$_{5}$, אֵפוֹד *ephod* 1 S 23$_{6}$, עֲטָרָה *crown* Jr 13$_{18}$, מַרְאָשׁוֹת perh. *head-dress* Jr 13$_{18}$ (or em. מֵרָאשֵׁיכֶם *from your heads* or מֵרַאשׁוֹתֵיכֶם in same sense), שַׁלְשֶׁלֶת *chain* 11QT 34$_{15}$, יוֹם *day* Jg 19$_{11}$ Arad ost. 40$_{10}$ ([י]רדים), כָּבוֹד *glory* Ps 49$_{18}$ 2 C 7$_{3}$, תִּקְוָה *hope* Jb 17$_{16}$, טוֹבָה *good* Jb 17$_{16}$ (if em. וְתִקְוָתִי *and my hope* to וְטוֹבָתִי *and my good*), רַע *evil* Mc 1$_{12}$, חָמָס *violence* Ps 7$_{17}$, שָׁאוֹן *uproar* of revellers Is 5$_{14}$, דָּבָר *word* Pr 18$_{8}$ 26$_{22}$, כּוֹכָב *star* 1QM 11$_{7}$.

כֹּל *everyone* Is 15$_{3}$, כָּל־אֲשֶׁר *everything that* belonged to them Nm 16$_{30.33}$, מִי *who?* 1 S 26$_{6}$ Pr 30$_{4}$; subj. not specified, Jg 7$_{24}$ 1 S 30$_{24}$ Is 31$_{1}$ 38$_{8}$ 42$_{10}$ Ezk 26$_{20.20}$ 31$_{14.16}$ 32$_{18.24.25.29.30}$ Jl 4$_{13}$ Ps 22$_{30}$ 28$_{1}$ 30$_{4(Kt)}$ 88$_{5}$ 107$_{23}$ 115$_{17}$ 143$_{7}$ Jb 7$_{9}$ Pr 1$_{12}$ Si 30$_{17}$ 43$_{24}$ 1QH 3$_{14}$ 8$_{28}$.

<OBJ> דִּמְעָה *tear* Jr 9$_{17}$ 13$_{17}$ 14$_{17}$, פֶּלֶג *stream* of water, i.e. tears Ps 119$_{136}$ Lm 3$_{48}$, מַיִם water, i.e. tears Lm 1$_{16}$.

<PREP> לְ of direction, *to(wards)*, + poet Jg 5$_{13}$ (or Y., if em. לִי *to me* to לוֹ *to him*), Egypt 4QJub^{h} 38$_{13}$ (למצרים), Samaria 2 C 18$_{2}$, שְׁאוֹל *Sheol* Si 30$_{17(mg)}$, שַׁעַר *gate* Jg 5$_{11}$ Mc 1$_{12}$, בַּיִת *house* 2 S 11$_{8}$, גַּן *garden* Ca 6$_{2}$, עֲרוּגָה *bed* of spice Ca 6$_{2}$, אֶרֶץ *ground* Ezk 26$_{11}$ Ec 3$_{21}$, עֵמֶק *valley* Jg 13$_{4}$, קָצֶב *extremity* of mountain Jon 2$_{7}$, טֶבַח *slaughter* Jr 48$_{15}$ 50$_{27}$.

נֵרֶד לִשְׁלוֹם perh. *we have come down to (ask after) the welfare of* 2 K 10$_{13}$.

לְ of motive, *for, in order to find*, + עֶזְרָה *help* Is 31$_1$.

לְ *before*, + עַיִן *eye*, i.e. in sight Ex 19$_{11}$.

בְּ of place/time, *in, into, among, on, at*, + גִּבּוֹר *warrior* Jg 5$_{13}$, מַחֲנֶה *camp* Jg 7$_{9.11}$, סֻלָּם *flight of steps* Gn 28$_{12}$, מַעֲלָה *step*, of sundial 2 K 20$_{11}$ Is 38$_8$, אֳנִיָּה *ship* Jon 1$_3$ Ps 107$_{23}$, יָד *hand* 1 S 23$_6$, אֵשׁ *fire* Ex 19$_{18}$, עָנָן *cloud* Ex 34$_5$ Nm 11$_{25}$, תְּחִלָּה *beginning* Gn 43$_{20}$, קָצֶה *end* of city 1 S 9$_{27}$, סֵתֶר *shelter* of mountain 1 S 25$_{20}$, מִלְחָמָה *battle* 1 S 26$_{10}$ 29$_4$ 30$_{24}$, בִּקְעָה *valley* Is 63$_{14}$, מְצוֹלָה *depths* Ex 15$_5$, שְׁאוֹל *Sheol* Is 5$_{14}$ (if em. הֲדָרָהּ וַהֲמוֹנָהּ וּשְׁאוֹנָהּ *her honour, her multitude and her uproar* to הֲדָרוֹ וַהֲמוֹנוֹ וּשְׁאוֹנוֹ *his honour, his multitude and his uproar*), נֶפֶשׁ *throat* of Sheol Is 5$_{14}$ (or em.), רֶדֶת *descent* Is 32$_{19(ms)}$.

בְּ of essence, *as, (consisting) of*, + נֶפֶשׁ seventy *persons* Dt 10$_{22}$.

בְּ of instrument, *by (means of), with*, + חֶרֶב *sword* Hg 2$_{22}$ (or del. בְּחֶרֶב).

בְּ of accompaniment, *with, in (a state of)*, + אַדִּיר *noble one* Jg 5$_{13}$ (if em.; see Subj.), כְּלִי *weapon(s)* Ezk 32$_{27}$, שֵׁבֶט *club* 2 S 23$_{21}$||1 C 11$_{23}$, בְּכִי *weeping* Is 15$_3$.

בְּ *according to*, + שֶׁמֶשׁ *sun* Is 38$_8$.

בְּ *despite*, + חִתִּית *terror* Ezk 32$_{30}$.

כְּ *as*, + אֶבֶן *stone* Ex 15$_5$, מָטָר *rain* Ps 55$_{16}$.

מִן of direction, *from*, + Egypt Gn 12$_{10}$, Jacob 1QM 11$_7$, Janoah Jos 16$_7$, Machir Jg 5$_{14}$, Migdol Ezk 30$_6$, Rogelim 2 S 19$_{32}$, Shepham Nm 34$_{11}$, שָׁמַיִם *heaven* 2 K 1$_{10.10.12.12.14}$ Is 52$_4$ 2 C 7$_1$, כָּבוֹד *glory* Jr 48$_{18}$, רֹאשׁ *head* Jg 9$_{36}$ Jr 13$_{18}$ (if em. מַרְאֲשֹׁתֵיכֶם *your head-dress* to מֵרָאשֵׁיכֶם *from your heads* or מֵרָאשׁוֹתֵיכֶם in same sense), מְקָרֶה *ceiling* 11QT 34$_{15}$, הַר *mountain* Ex 19$_{14}$ 32$_{1.15}$ 34$_{29.29}$ Nm 20$_{28}$ Dt 9$_{15.21}$ 10$_5$ Jos 2$_{23}$ Jg 3$_{27}$ 4$_{14}$, בָּמָה *high place* Jg 9$_{25}$ 1 S 10$_5$, שָׁמַיִם *heaven* 4QapPs^b 69$_{5a}$, זֶה *this (place)* Dt 9$_{12}$, עִיר *city* Ne 3$_{15}$, צֵל *shadow* Ezk 31$_{12}$ (or em. ירד to נדד *flee*), מִטָּה *bed* 2 K 1$_{4.6.16}$, אֳנִיָּה *ship* Ezk 27$_{29}$, כָּתֵף *side* Ezk 47$_1$.

מֵעַל *from (upon)*, + כִּסֵּא *throne* Ezk 26$_{16}$, מֶרְכָּבָה *chariot* Jg 4$_{15}$, חֲמוֹר *ass* 1 S 25$_{23}$.

מֵאֵת *from (with)*, + Y. Mc 1$_{12}$, אָח *brother* Gn 38$_1$.

מֵעִם *from (with)*, + טַבּוּר *centre of* land Jg 9$_{37}$.

מִתּוֹךְ *from among*, + Amalekite 1 S 15$_6$.

אֶל *to(wards)*, + Ahab 2 C 18$_2$, David 1 S 22$_1$, Elisha 2 K 3$_{12}$ 6$_{18.33}$ 7$_{17}$ 13$_{14}$, Geshem Ne 6$_3$, Goliath 1 S 17$_8$, Joseph Gn 45$_9$, Moses Ex 11$_8$, Saul 1 S 10$_8$ 13$_2$ 26$_6$, Sanballat Ne 6$_3$, Philistine 1 S 13$_{20(ms)}$ 17$_8$, בֵּן *son* Gn 37$_{35}$ 45$_9$ 2 K 3$_{12}$, אִישׁ *man* 2 S 23$_{21}$||1 C 11$_{23}$ 2 K 7$_{17}$, אִשָּׁה *woman* Jg 14$_{10}$, עַם *people* Ex 19$_{14.25}$, מֶלֶךְ *king* 1 K 22$_2$ 2 K 1$_{15}$, חָלָל *slain one* Ezk 31$_{17}$, רֹאשׁ *head*, i.e. top, of mountain Ex 19$_{20}$, כָּתֵף *shoulder*, i.e. mountain slope Jos 18$_{16}$, קָצֶה *end* Jos 18$_{16}$ Jg 7$_{11}$ (or em. אֶל־קְצֵה *to the end of* to לְצַפּוֹת *to spy on*), גְּבוּל *border* Jos 16$_3$, מִדְבָּר *steppe* 1 S 25$_1$ 26$_2$, מְצוּדָה *stronghold* 2 S 5$_{17}$, סְעִיף *cleft* of rock Jg 15$_{11}$, שַׁחַת *pit* Ps 30$_{10}$, אֶבֶן *stone* of grave Is 14$_{19}$ (or em. אֶדֶן *base*), אֶרֶץ *ground* Ezk 32$_{24}$, כֶּרֶם *vineyard* 1 K 21$_{16}$, גַּן *garden* of nuts Ca 6$_{11}$, בַּיִת *house* 2 S 11$_{9.10.10.13}$, חֶדֶר *chamber* of death Pr 7$_{27}$, מַחֲנֶה *camp* Jg 7$_{10}$ 1 S 26$_6$, יַרְכָּה *innermost part* of ship Jon 1$_5$, מָקוֹם *place* Ps 104$_8$ (2QPs ולכו[ל] perh. *even to every* place for אֶל־ *to* the place).

אֶל־תּוֹךְ *into*, + בּוֹר *pit* 11QT 46$_{15}$.

עַל *upon*, + Edom Is 34$_5$, עַם *people* Dt 28$_{24}$ Is 34$_5$, אָדָם *human being* Ex 9$_{19}$, פֶּגֶר *corpse* Gn 15$_{11}$, קָדְקֹד *skull* Ps 7$_{17}$, זָקָן *beard* Ps 133$_{2.2}$, לְחִי *cheek* Si 32$_{18}$, בְּהֵמָה *beast* Ex 9$_{19}$, שָׁמַיִם *heaven* Si 16$_{18.18}$, אֶרֶץ *earth* Si 16$_{18}$, תְּהוֹם *deep* Si 16$_{18}$, הַר *mountain* Ex 19$_{11.18.20}$ Jg 11$_{37}$ Ps 133$_3$ Ne 9$_{13}$, מַחֲנֶה *camp* Nm 11$_9$, בַּיִת *house* 2 C 7$_3$, פֶּה *mouth, opening* of garment Ps 133$_2$, יַרְכָּה *recess* of pit 4QBéat 22$_3$, טַל *dew* Nm 11$_9$, שֶׁבֶר *breakdown* of people Lm 3$_{48}$.

עַל of direction, *to(wards)*, + יָם *sea* Jos 3$_{16}$, הַר *mountain* Jos 18$_{13}$, עֲרָבָה *steppe* Ezk 47$_8$, לִשְׁכָּה *room* Jr 36$_{12}$.

עַל *against*, + הָמוֹן *multitude* 2 C 20$_{16}$.

לִפְנֵי *ahead of*, + Samuel 1 S 10$_8$.

אַחֲרֵי *after*, + Barak Jg 4$_{14}$, Ehud Jg 3$_{28}$ (if em.; see Subj.) 3$_{28}$, Philistines 1 S 14$_{36.37}$, אִישׁ *man* Ps 49$_{18}$.

אֵת *with*, + David 1 S 26$_6$, Judah Gn 44$_{23}$, Assyria Ezk 31$_{17}$ (or em.; see Subj.), אָח *brother* Gn 44$_{23}$, שַׂר *commander* 2 K 1$_{15.15}$, עֶבֶד *servant* Gn 44$_{23}$, חָלָל *slain one* Ezk 32$_{30}$, תְּאַשּׁוּר *box tree* Ezk 31$_{17}$ (if em.; see Subj.).

עִם *with*, + Ehud Jg 3$_{27}$, David 1 S 26$_6$ 2 S 21$_{15}$, Jacob Gn 46$_4$, Reuben Gn 42$_{38}$, בֵּן *son* Gn 42$_{38}$, אִישׁ *man* 2 S 19$_{17}$, שַׂר *commander* 1 S 29$_4$, הֵם *them*, not specified Is 34$_7$, אַבִּיר *mighty one*, i.e. bull Is 34$_7$.

עַד *unto*, + Gezer Jos 16$_3$, גְּבוּל *border* Jos 16$_3$.

+ ה- of direction, *into, to(wards)*, + Egypt Gn 26$_{2}$ 46$_{3.4}$ Nm 20$_{15}$ Dt 10$_{22}$ 26$_{5}$ Jos 24$_{4(mss)}$, Jordan Nm 34$_{12}$, Naarath Jos 16$_{7}$, Timnah Jg 14$_{1.5}$, שְׁאוֹל *Sheol* Gn 37$_{35}$ Nm 16$_{30.33}$ Ezk 31$_{15.17}$, עַיִן *spring* Gn 24$_{16.45}$, יָם *sea*, i.e. west Jos 16$_{3}$, שָׁם *there* Gn 42$_{2}$ 1 S 22$_{1}$.

without ה- of direction, *into, to(wards)*, + Philistine 1 S 13$_{20}$, Arabah Jos 18$_{18}$, Ashkelon Jg 14$_{19}$, Ataroth Jos 16$_{7}$, Ataroth-addar Jos 18$_{13}$, Bethel 2 K 2$_{2}$, Beth-shemesh Jos 15$_{10}$, Egypt Gn 43$_{15}$ Jos 24$_{4}$ Is 30$_{2}$ 31$_{1}$ 52$_{4}$ 4QpsJub^{b} 1$_{3}$, En-rogel Jos 18$_{16}$, Gath Amos 6$_{2}$, Gilgal 1 S 10$_{8}$ 13$_{2}$ 15$_{12}$, Joppa Jon 1$_{3}$, Keilah 1 S 23$_{4.8}$, Riblah Nm 34$_{11}$, Silla 2 K 12$_{21}$, Syene Ezk 30$_{6}$, שְׁאוֹל *Sheol* Ezk 32$_{27}$ Ps 55$_{16}$ Jb 7$_{9}$ Si 30$_{17}$, בַּד *bar* of Sheol Jb 17$_{16}$ (or em. בַּדֵּי *bars of* to הַעִמָּדִי will they go down *with me* to Sheol?), מָוֶת *death* Pr 5$_{5}$, בּוֹר *pit* Ps 30$_{4(Qr)}$, שַׁחַת *pit* Jb 33$_{24}$, חֶדֶר *chamber* of belly Pr 18$_{8}$ 26$_{22}$, עִיר *city* 1 S 9$_{25}$, בַּיִת *house* Jr 18$_{2.3}$ 22$_{1}$ 36$_{12}$, גֹּרֶן *threshing floor* Ru 3$_{3.6}$, נַחַל *wadi* Jos 17$_{9}$, גַּיְא *valley* Jos 18$_{16}$, תְּהוֹם *deep* Ps 107$_{26}$ 4Q418 115$_{2}$ ([תהמ[ת), מִדְבָּר *steppe* 1 S 25$_{1(mss)}$, סֶלַע *rock* 1 S 23$_{25}$, אֶבֶן *stone* of Bohan Jos 18$_{17}$, זֶה *this (place)* 1 S 17$_{28}$, שָׁם *there* 2 S 17$_{18}$ 1 K 21$_{18}$.

<COLL> יוֹרְדֵי בוֹר *descenders of*, i.e. those who go down to, *the pit* Is 38$_{18}$ (יוֹרְדֵי־) Ezk 26$_{20.20}$ 31$_{14.16}$ 32$_{18.24.25.29.30}$ Ps 28$_{1}$ 30$_{4(Kt)}$ (Qr יָרְדִי *my descending* into the pit) 88$_{5}$ 143$_{7}$ Pr 1$_{12}$, יורדי שאול *those who go down to Sheol* 1QH 8$_{29}$, יוֹרְדֵי עָפָר *those who go down to the dust* Ps 22$_{30}$, יוֹרְדֵי הַיָּם *those who go down to*, i.e. travel, *the sea* Is 42$_{10}$ (or em. יַאְדִּירֻהוּ יָם *let [the] sea glorify him*) Ps 107$_{23}$ Si 43$_{24}$ 1QH 3$_{14}$ (ימים), יֹרְדֵי דוּמָה *those who go down into silence* Ps 115$_{17}$.

טוב ... לירד שאול מכאב עומד *it is better ... to go down to Sheol than (to suffer) an enduring pain* Si 30$_{17}$, כול נוחליה ירדו שחת *all who possess her will go down to the pit* 4QWiles 1$_{11}$, כארבה ישכון רדתו *its* (snow's) *coming down is as (when) locusts settle* Si 43$_{17(Bmg, M)}$.

ירד + adverb, or noun used adverbially, מַהֵר *hastily* Dt 9$_{12}$, מְאֹד *greatly* Jg 19$_{11}$ 1 S 20$_{19}$, פְּלָאִים *in an extraordinary way* Lm 1$_{9}$ (or em.; see Subj.), מָטָּה מָטָּה *lower and lower* Dt 28$_{43}$, לְמַטָּה *downwards* Ec 3$_{21}$ 11QT 32$_{13}$, מִתַּחַת *from beneath* Ezk 47$_{1}$, מִלְמַעְלָה *from above* Jos 3$_{13.16}$, בָּרִאשֹׁנָה *of old* Is 52$_{4}$, הַיּוֹם *today* 1 K 1$_{25}$, מָחָר *tomorrow* 2 C 20$_{16}$, לַיְלָה *by night* 1 S 14$_{36}$, לְקֵץ שָׁנִים *after (some) years* 2 C 18$_{2}$, כֵּן *thus* 4QMyst^{a} 6.2$_{17}$; + adj. used predicatively, חַי *alive* Nm 16$_{30.33}$ Ps 55$_{16}$.

וַיֵּרֶד מֵעֲשֹׂת הַחַטָּאת *he stepped down from offering a sin offering* Lv 9$_{22}$.

inf. abs. of ירד + finite form of verb Gn 43$_{20}$.

ירד + לְ + inf. to express purpose, + בוא *go* Lachish 3$_{14}$, עלה hi. *take up* Ex 3$_{8}$, קרא *meet* Jg 7$_{24}$ 1 S 25$_{20}$ 2 S 19$_{17.21.25}$ 1 K 2$_{8}$ 21$_{18}$, לחם ni. *fight* Jg 1$_{9}$, צבא *fight* Is 31$_{4}$, צור *lay siege* 1 S 23$_{8}$ (mss צוד *hunt*), ירש *take possession* 1 K 21$_{16.18}$, רשע hi. *do evil* 4QWiles 1$_{3}$, נצל hi. *rescue* Ex 3$_{8}$, לקח *take* 1 C 7$_{21}$, לקט *gather* Ca 6$_{2}$, גור *sojourn* Gn 11$_{5}$ Is 52$_{4}$, נתן *give* Jg 15$_{12}$, רעה *tend* Ca 6$_{2}$, אסר *bind* Jg 15$_{12}$, לטש *sharpen* 1 S 13$_{20}$, רחץ *bathe* Ex 2$_{5}$ CD 11$_{1}$, שבר *buy* food Gn 43$_{20}$, צפה pi. *spy on* Jg 7$_{11}$ (if em.; see Prep.), ראה *see* Gn 11$_{5}$ 2 K 8$_{29}$||2 C 22$_{6}$ 9$_{16}$ Ca 6$_{11.11}$; יָרַדְתָּ ... לְמַעַן רְאוֹת *you came down in order to see* 1 S 17$_{28}$.

ירד || עלה *go up* Ps 104$_{8}$, שׁוב *go back* Ps 7$_{17}$, נפל *fall* Zc 11$_{2}$.

ירד + עלה *go up* Ex 19$_{20}$ 2 C 20$_{16}$, hi. *take up* Gn 46$_{4}$ Ex 3$_{8}$ Jg 16$_{31}$ 1 S 6$_{21}$ 10$_{8}$, נחת *go down* Jb 17$_{16}$, הלך *go* Ex 19$_{24}$ 32$_{1}$ Jg 11$_{37}$ 1 S 15$_{6}$ Is 30$_{2}$ Am 6$_{2}$, דרך *tread* Mc 1$_{3}$ (or del. דרך or ירד), יצא *go out* Ezk 47$_{1.8}$ Mc 1$_{3}$, בוא *come* Jg 14$_{5}$ 1 S 20$_{19}$ 2 S 23$_{13}$ Ezk 47$_{8}$ Jl 4$_{13}$ Jon 1$_{3}$, סור *withdraw* 1 S 15$_{6}$, עבר *pass over* 1 S 15$_{12}$ Am 6$_{2}$, נזל *flow* Jr 9$_{17}$, דמע *weep* Jr 13$_{17}$ (or del. דמע), בכה *weep* Jr 13$_{17}$, נפל *fall* Ezk 30$_{6}$, קום *rise* Dt 9$_{12}$ Jg 7$_{9}$ 1 S 23$_{4}$ (mss lack קום and ירד) 25$_{1}$ 26$_{2}$ 1 K 21$_{16.18}$ 2 K 1$_{15}$ Jr 18$_{2}$, נשׂא *raise* Si 50$_{20}$, עמד *stand* Ex 33$_{9}$ Nm 12$_{5}$, יצב htp. *stand* Ex 34$_{5}$.

ירד :: עלה *go up* Gn 28$_{12}$ 2 K 14$_{6.16}$ Jb 7$_{9}$ Pr 30$_{4}$ Ec 3$_{21}$ 4QD^{a} 6.1$_{12}$ QD^{g} 1.1$_{7}$.

Also 4QMidrEschat^{a} 4$_{5}$ 4QMidrEschat^{b} 10$_{15}$ 4QapPs^{b} 52$_{3}$ 4QPrFêtes^{b} 36$_{1}$ 4QPrFêtes^{c} 256$_{1}$.

Hi. 67.1.4 Pf. הוֹרִד, הוֹרַדְתָּנוּ (Jos 2$_{18}$), הוֹרִידוּ (הוֹרִדֻהוּ), הוֹרִדְנוּ; impf. Q יורד, תּוֹרֵד (תּוֹרִדֵנִי), (תּוֹרִדֵם, יוֹרִידוּ), אוֹרִיד (אוֹרִדְךָ, אוֹרִידְךָ, אוֹרִידֵם), (יֹרִדוּ, יוֹרִדֵנִי, יוֹרִדוּךְ); + waw וְהוֹרַד, וְהוֹרַדְתָּ, וְהוֹרַדְתִּי (וְהוֹרַדְתִּיךָ, וְהוֹרַדְתִּים), (וַיֹּרֶד, וַיּוֹרֶד (וַיֹּרִדֵהוּ, וַיֹּרִדֵם), וְהוֹרַדְתֶּם, (וְהוֹרִדוּ) וְהוֹרִידוּ, וַתּוֹרֶד (וַתֹּרֶד, וַתּוֹרִדֵם), וַיּוֹרִידוּ (וַיֹּרִדוּ, וַיֹּרִידוּ, וַיֹּרִדֵהוּ), 3fs (וַיֹּרִידוּם); impv. הוֹרֵד (הוֹרִדֵהוּ, הוֹרִידֵמוֹ), הוֹרִידִי, הוֹרִידוּ; ptc. מוֹרִיד; inf. cstr. הוֹרִיד (הוֹרִדִי, הוֹרִדֵהוּ).

take down, bring down, lead down, send down

rain (Ezk 34$_{26}$ 11QBer 1$_{7}$), to Sheol (Gn 42$_{38}$ 1 K 2$_{6}$), **cast down** into Sheol (1 S 2$_{6}$ Ezk 32$_{18}$), to ground (Is 63$_{6}$), **pull down** from height, (Jr 49$_{16}$||Ob$_{4}$), from heaven (Ob$_{3}$), **take off** jewellery (Ex 33$_{5}$), **lower** pitcher (Gn 24$_{18.46}$), sack (Gn 44$_{11}$), **let down** through window (Jos 2$_{15}$ 1 S 19$_{12}$), **bow** head (Lm 2$_{10}$), **cause to flow down**, saliva (1 S 21$_{14}$), streams (Ps 78$_{16}$), **let** tears **run down** (Lm 2$_{18}$), **subdue** peoples, inhabitants (2 S 22$_{48}$ Is 10$_{13}$ Ps 56$_{8}$), enemies (Ps 59$_{12}$), **deduct** (4QD^{f} 2$_{1}$), perh. **remove** (Mur 24 2$_{12}$).

<SUBJ> Y. Ezk 26$_{11}$ (if em. תֵּרֵד *it will fall* to יוֹרִד *he will cause to fall*) 1 S 2$_{6}$ 2 S 22$_{48}$ (4QSam^{a} רדד *subdue*) Is 43$_{14}$ (unless ירד II hi. *cause to appear*) 63$_{6}$ Jr 49$_{16}$||Ob$_{4}$ Jr 51$_{40}$ Ezk 26$_{20}$ 31$_{16}$ 34$_{26}$ Ho 7$_{12}$ Jl 2$_{23}$ 4$_{2}$ Am 9$_{2}$ Ps 55$_{24}$ 56$_{8}$ 59$_{12}$ 78$_{16}$ Jb 30$_{19}$ (if em. ירה hi. *cast* to ירד hi.) 4QTobit^{e} 6$_{6}$ 11QBer 1$_{7}$, Aaron Num 4$_{5}$, Ahaz 2 K 16$_{17}$, Benaiah 1 K 1$_{33}$, David 1 S 21$_{14}$, Elijah 1 K 17$_{23}$ 18$_{40}$, Ezekiel Ezk 32$_{18}$ (or em. וְהוֹרִדֵהוּ *and send it down* to וַהֲדָרָהּ *and her honour*) Si 48$_{6}$, Gideon Jg 7$_{4.5}$, Jehoiada 2 K 11$_{19}$||2 C 23$_{20}$, Joab 1 K 2$_{6}$, Joseph Gn 39$_{1}$, Judah Gn 44$_{21.31}$, Michal 1 S 19$_{12}$, Nathan 1 K 1$_{33}$, Rahab Jos 2$_{15.18}$, Rebekah Gn 24$_{18.46}$, Reuben Gn 42$_{38}$, Shimei 1 K 2$_{9}$, Zadok 1 K 1$_{33}$, Benjaminite 1 K 2$_{9}$, Carian 2 K 11$_{19}$ (||2 C 23$_{20}$, if em. וַיּוֹרֶד *and he brought down* to וַיֹּרִידוּ *and they brought down*), Levite Num 1$_{51}$ 1 S 6$_{15}$, Ishmaelite Gn 39$_{1}$, Philistine Jg 16$_{21}$, אָח *brother* Gn 42$_{38}$ 43$_{7.11}$ 44$_{29}$ 45$_{13}$, בֵּן *son* Nm 4$_{5}$ 1 K 1$_{33}$ 2$_{6.9}$, of Israel Ex 33$_{5}$, בַּת *daughter* Ezk 32$_{18}$, עַם *people* 2 K 11$_{19}$ (||2 C 23$_{20}$ if em.; see above), אִישׁ *man* Gn 43$_{22}$ (Sam לקח *take* for ירד hi.) 44$_{11}$ Dt 1$_{25}$, נַעַר *lad, servant* 1 S 30$_{15.15.16}$, בְּתוּלָה *young woman* Lm 2$_{10}$, נַעֲרָה *girl* Gn 24$_{18}$, כֹּהֵן *priest* 1 K 1$_{33}$ 2 K 11$_{19}$ (||2 C 23$_{20}$ if em.; see above), נָבִיא *prophet* 1 K 1$_{33}$, חָכָם *wise one* Pr 21$_{22}$, זָקֵן *elder* Dt 21$_{4}$=11QT 63$_{1}$ ([ו]הור[ידו]), מֶלֶךְ *king* 2 K 16$_{17}$ Is 10$_{13}$, שַׂר *commander* 2 K 11$_{19}$ (||2 C 23$_{20}$ if em.; see above), רָץ *runner, messenger* 2 K 11$_{19}$ (||2 C 23$_{20}$ if em.; see above), עֶבֶד *servant* Gn 44$_{21.31}$ 1 S 30$_{15.15.16}$ 1 K 5$_{23}$, זָר *stranger* Ezk 28$_{8}$, צַר *enemy* Am 3$_{11}$ (unless em. ho.), עָרִיץ *ruthless one* Ezk 28$_{8}$, אֹרְחָה *caravan* of Ishmaelites Gn 37$_{25}$, מִי *who?* Ob$_{3}$; subj. not specified, Jos 8$_{29}$ 1 K 1$_{53}$.

<OBJ> Adonijah 1 K 1$_{53}$, Benjamin Gn 44$_{21}$, David 1 S 19$_{12}$ 30$_{15.15.16}$, Job Jb 30$_{19}$ (if em.; see Subj.), Samson Jg 16$_{21}$, Solomon 1 K 1$_{33}$, Assyria Ezk 31$_{16}$ (or em. תְּאַשּׁוּר *box tree*), Babylon(ian) Jr 51$_{40}$, Edom(ite) Jr 49$_{16}$||Ob$_{4}$ Ob$_{3}$, Egypt perh. Ezk 32$_{18}$ (or em. אוֹתָהּ *her* to אַתָּה *you*), Ephraim(ite) Ho 7$_{12}$, Israel(ite) Am 9$_{2}$, Tyre Ezk 26$_{20}$.

אָב *father* Gn 45$_{13}$, אָח *brother* Gn 43$_{7}$, בַּת perh. Ezk 32$_{18}$ (or em. וְהוֹרִדֵהוּ אוֹתָהּ *and cast it* (multitude) *down, her* (Egypt) and the daughters, to וַהֲדָרָהּ אַתָּה *and her honour, you*), עַם *people* Jg 7$_{4.5}$ 2 S 22$_{48}$ Ps 56$_{8}$, גּוֹי *nation* Jl 4$_{2}$, אִישׁ *man* Jos 2$_{15.18}$ Ps 55$_{24}$, יֶלֶד *child* Gn 44$_{21}$ 1 K 17$_{23}$, מֶלֶךְ *king* 2 K 11$_{19}$||2 C 23$_{20}$ Si 48$_{6}$, נָגִיד *prince* Ezk 28$_{8}$, נִכְבָּד *honoured one* Si 48$_{6}$, נָבִיא *prophet* 1 K 18$_{40}$, יוֹשֵׁב *inhabitant* Is 10$_{13}$, שֹׁכֵן *one who dwells* Jr 49$_{16}$||Ob$_{4}$ Ob$_{3}$, בָּרִיחַ *fugitive* Is 43$_{14}$ (unless ירד II hi. *cause to appear*; or em. בְּרִיחַ *bar* or perh. *noble* or בָּחוּר *youth* or בַּר *cargo ship*), שׁוֹרֵר *enemy* Ps 59$_{12}$, הָמוֹן *multitude* Ezk 32$_{18}$, נְבֵלָה *corpse* Jos 8$_{29}$, רֹאשׁ *head* Lm 2$_{10}$, שֵׂיבָה *grey hair* Gn 42$_{38}$ 44$_{29.31}$ 1 K 2$_{6.9}$, דִּמְעָה *tears* Lm 2$_{18}$ Si 32$_{19}$ (if em. מרודיה *her homeless ones* to מורידה *the one who causes it to run down*), רִיר *saliva* 1 S 21$_{14}$, עֶגְלָה *heifer* Dt 21$_{4}$=11QT 63$_{1}$ ([ו]הור[ידו]).

מִשְׁכָּן *tabernacle* Num 1$_{51}$, פָּרֹכֶת *curtain* Num 4$_{5}$, אֲרוֹן *ark* of Y. 1 S 6$_{15}$, אַרְגַּז *box* 1 S 6$_{15}$, כִּיּוֹר *laver* 2 K 16$_{17(Kt)}$, יָם *sea*, i.e. laver 2 K 16$_{17}$, אַמְתַּחַת *sack* Gn 44$_{11}$, כַּד *pitcher* Gn 24$_{18.46}$, מִנְחָה *gift* Gn 43$_{11}$, עֲדִי *jewellery* Ex 33$_{5}$, כֶּסֶף *silver* Gn 43$_{22}$, מַצֵּבָה *memorial stone* Ezk 26$_{11}$ (if em.; see Subj.), חוֹמָה *wall* of daughter of Zion Lm 2$_{18}$, עֵץ *timber* 1 K 5$_{23}$, פְּרִי *fruit* Dt 1$_{25}$, בָּטְנִים *pistachio nuts* Gn 43$_{11}$, שָׁקֵד *almond* Gn 43$_{11}$, נְכֹאת *gum* Gen 37$_{25}$ 43$_{11}$, צֳרִי *balm* Gn 37$_{25}$ 43$_{11}$, לֹט *ladanum* Gn 37$_{25}$ 43$_{11}$, דְּבַשׁ *honey* Gn 43$_{11}$, נוֹזֵל *stream* Ps 78$_{16}$, גֶּשֶׁם *rain* Ezk 34$_{26}$ Jl 2$_{23}$ 11QBer 1$_{7}$, מָטָר *rain* 11QBer 1$_{7}$, יוֹרֶה *early rain* 11QBer 1$_{7}$, מַלְקוֹשׁ *latter rain* 11QBer 1$_{7}$, טַל *dew* 11QBer 1$_{7}$, נֵצַח *glory*, or perh. *juice*, i.e. blood Is 63$_{6}$, עֹז *strength* Am 3$_{11}$ (or em. ho.) Pr 21$_{22}$, עִשָּׂרוֹן *tenth* 4QD^{f} 2$_{1}$, כֹּל *everything* Mur 24 2$_{12}$.

<PREP> לְ of direction, *to(wards), into*, + בֵּן *son* of Zion Jl 2$_{23}$, אִישׁ *man* Gn 43$_{11}$, חֹמֶר *clay* Jb 30$_{19}$ (if em.; see Subj.), אֶרֶץ *ground* Ezk 26$_{11}$ (if em.; see Subj.) Is 63$_{6}$ Lm 2$_{10}$, שַׁחַת *pit* Ezk 28$_{8}$, בְּאֵר *pit* Ps 55$_{24}$ (or em. באר || בּוֹר *cistern*).

בְּ of place/time, *in, through*, + יָד *hand* Gn 43$_{22}$, חַלּוֹן

window Jos 2$_{18}$, עֵת *time* Ezk 34$_{26}$; בְּ of accompaniment, *with, in (a state of)*, + דָּם *blood* 1 K 2$_{9}$, אַף *anger* Ps 56$_{8}$, יָגוֹן *grief* Gn 42$_{38}$ 44$_{31}$, רָעָה *disaster* Gn 44$_{29}$, שָׁלוֹם *peace* 1 K 2$_{6}$; בְּ of instrument, *by (means of), with*, + חֶבֶל *rope* Jos 2$_{15}$.

בְּעַד *through*, + חַלּוֹן *window* Jos 2$_{15}$ 1 S 19$_{12}$.

כְּ *as*, + אַבִּיר *mighty one* Is 10$_{13}$ (or em. כְּאָבִיר *as the mighty one*, i.e. God, or בֶּעָפָר *into the dust* or בָּאֵפֶר *into the dust*), אַיִל *ram* Jr 51$_{40}$, כַּר *lamb* Jr 51$_{40}$, עוֹף *bird* Ho 7$_{12}$, נָהָר *river* Ps 78$_{16}$, נַחַל *wadi* Lm 2$_{18}$.

מִן of direction, *from*, + Lebanon 1 K 5$_{23}$, מִשְׁפָּחָה *family* Am 3$_{11}$ (or em. ho.), בַּיִת *house* of Y. 2 K 11$_{19}$||2 C 23$_{20}$, עֲלִיָּה *upper room* 1 K 17$_{23}$, מִטָּה *bed* Si 48$_{6}$, עֵץ *tree*, i.e. gibbet Jos 8$_{29}$, גֹּרֶן *threshing-floor* 4QD^{f} 2$_{1}$, שָׁם *there* Jr 49$_{16}$||Ob$_{4}$ Am 9$_{2}$.

מֵעַל *from upon*, + Rebekah Gn 24$_{46}$, בֵּן *son* of Israel Ex 33$_{5}$, עֵץ *tree*, i.e. gibbet Jos 10$_{27}$, מִזְבֵּחַ *altar* 1 K 1$_{53}$, בָּקָר bronze *oxen* 2 K 16$_{17}$.

אֶל *to(wards), into*, + Joseph Gn 44$_{21}$, Moses Dt 1$_{25}$, Israel(ites) Dt 1$_{25}$, עַם *people* Ezk 26$_{20}$, אָדוֹן *lord* Gn 44$_{21}$, גְּדוּד *troop* 1 S 30$_{15.15}$, זָקָן *beard* 1 S 21$_{14}$ (mss עַל *upon*), Gihon 1 K 1$_{33}$ (mss עַל *to*), מַיִם *water* Jg 7$_{4.5}$, נַחַל *wadi* Dt 21$_{4}$=11QT 63$_{4}$ ([ו]הורן[ידו]) 1 K 18$_{40}$, עֵמֶק *valley* Jl 4$_{2}$, אֶרֶץ *land* of lowest (places) Ezk 32$_{18}$.

עַל *upon*, + יָד *hand* Gn 24$_{18}$ 1 S 21$_{14(mss)}$, אֶרֶץ *land* 11QBer 1$_{7}$; עַל *to*, + Gihon 1 K 1$_{33(mss)}$, שַׁחַת *pit* Si 48$_{6}$; עַד *to*, + שְׁאוֹל *Sheol* 4QTobit^{e} 6$_{6}$ (שאולה); אֵת *with*, + אִישׁ *man* 1QM 7$_{6}$, ירד ptc. *those who go down* to the pit Ezk 26$_{20}$ (mss אֶל *to*) 31$_{16}$ 32$_{18}$; תַּחַת *under*, + David 2 S 22$_{48}$.

+ ה- of direction, *into, to(wards)*, + Egypt Gn 37$_{25}$, Gaza Jg 16$_{21}$, שְׁאוֹל *Sheol* Gn 42$_{38}$ 44$_{31}$ Ezk 31$_{16}$, אֶרֶץ *ground* Gn 44$_{11}$, יָם *sea* 1 K 5$_{23}$, בַּיִת *house* 1 K 17$_{23}$, שָׁם *there* Gn 39$_{1}$.

without preposition or ה- of direction, *into, to(wards)*, + אֶרֶץ *earth* Ob$_{3}$, שְׁאוֹל *Sheol* Gn 44$_{29}$ 1 S 2$_{6}$ 1 K 2$_{6.9}$.

<COLL> ירד hi. + adverb, יוֹמָם וָלַיְלָה *(by) day and night* Lm 2$_{18}$, הֵנָּה *here* Gn 45$_{13}$.

ירד hi. followed by inf. of purpose, + שׁבר *buy* food Gn 43$_{22}$.

ירד hi. || נוע hi. *cause to wander* Ps 59$_{12}$; ירד hi. :: קום hi. *erect* Num 1$_{51}$, עלה hi. *raise* 1 S 2$_{6}$; + עלה *go up* Am 9$_{2}$ Pr 21$_{22}$, יצא hi. *bring out* Ps 78$_{16}$.

Ho. 6.0.1 Pf. הוּרַד; impf. 2ms תּוּרָד (Is 14$_{15}$); + waw וְהוּרַדְתָּ, וְהוּרַד—**be taken down, be brought down, be stripped** (Am 3$_{11}$ [if em. hi.]).

<SUBJ> Joseph Gn 39$_{1}$, Pharaoh Ezk 31$_{18}$, מֶלֶךְ *king* Is 14$_{15}$ Ezk 31$_{18}$, הָמוֹן *multitude* Ezk 31$_{18}$, Jerusalem Lm 1$_{9}$ (if em. qal), מִשְׁכָּן *tabernacle* Nm 10$_{17}$, חֵלֶק *portion* 1 S 30$_{24(mss\ Kt)}$, גָּאוֹן *pride* Is 14$_{11}$ Zc 10$_{11}$ 4QpsEzek^{a} 41$_{3}$ ([גאון]), עֹז *strength* Am 3$_{11}$ (if em. hi.).

<PREP> בְּ of place, time, *in(to)*, + מִלְחָמָה *battle* 1 S 30$_{24(mss\ Kt)}$, יוֹם *day* 4QpsEzek^{a} 41$_{3}$ ([בימיהם]); מִן of direction, *from*, + מִשְׁפָּחָה *family* Am 3$_{11}$ (if em. hi.); אֶל *to(wards), into*, + אֶרֶץ lowest *land* Ezk 31$_{18}$, שְׁאוֹל *Sheol* Is 14$_{15}$, יַרְכָה *innermost part* of pit Is 14$_{15}$; אֵת *with*, + עֵץ *tree* Ezk 31$_{18}$.

+ ה- of direction, *into, to(wards)*, + Egypt Gn 39$_{1}$.

without ה- of direction, *into, to(wards)*, + שְׁאוֹל *Sheol* Is 14$_{11}$.

<COLL> ירד ho. + noun used adverbially, פְּלָאִים *in an extraordinary way* Lm 1$_{9}$ (if em.; see Subj.).*

⇒ מוֹרָד *slope*; (?) יֶרֶד *Jared*.

ירד II 1 vb. **appear—Hi.** Impf. + waw וְהוֹרַדְתִּי—**cause to appear**, unless ירד I hi. *bring down*, <SUBJ> Y. Is 43$_{14}$. <OBJ> בָּרִיחַ *fugitive* Is 43$_{14}$ (or em. בְּרִיחַ *bar* or perh. *noble* or בָּחוּר *youth* or בַּר *cargo ship*).*

יֶרֶד 7 pr.n.m. **Jared**—יֶרֶד—**1.** antediluvian Sethite, father of Enoch and grandfather of Methuselah Gn 5$_{15.16.18.19.20}$ 1 C 1$_{2}$, <SUBJ> חיה *live* Gn 5$_{18.19}$, ילד hi. *become father of* Gn 5$_{19}$. <OBJ> ילד hi. *become father of* Gn 5$_{15.16}$. <CSTR> יְמֵי־יֶרֶד *days of Jared* Gn 5$_{20}$.

2. Judahite, <OBJ> ילד *bear child* 1 C 4$_{18}$. <APP> אָב *father* 1 C 4$_{18}$. <COLL> קֵינָן מַהֲלַלְאֵל יֶרֶד *Kenan, Mahalalel, Jared* 1 C 1$_{2}$.

⇒ (?) ירד *go down*.

יַרְדֵּן I 181.0.3 pl.n. **Jordan**—הַיַּרְדֵּן; + ה- of direction הַיַּרְדֵּנָה; cstr. יַרְדֵּן—**1.** river flowing from Sea of Galilee to Dead Sea (Gn 32$_{11}$ Dt 3$_{27}$ 31$_{2}$ Jos 1$_{2.11}$ 4$_{22}$), with its fords (Jg 3$_{28}$ 12$_{5.6}$), its environs (Jos 22$_{11}$), its plain, around Jericho (Gn 13$_{10.11}$ 1 K 7$_{46}$||2 C 4$_{17}$), its region

(Ps 42$_{7}$).

<SUBJ> היה *be* Jos 13$_{23.27}$ 19$_{22.33}$, מלא *be full*, i.e. overflow Jos 3$_{15}$ 4QapJoshua[b] 12$_{6}$, גבל *form border* Jos 18$_{20}$ (or em. יִגְבֹּל־אֹתוֹ the Jordan *bordered it* to וּגְבֻל the Jordan *and [its] border* were to the east), סבב *turn around* Ps 114$_{3.5}$, גיח *burst out* Jb 40$_{23}$ (unless יַרְדֵּן II *river*).

<NOM CL> הַיַּרְדֵּן מִזְרַח הַשָּׁמֶשׁ *the Jordan is to the east of the sun*, i.e. to the east Jos 19$_{34}$.

<OBJ> עבר *cross over* Gn 32$_{11}$ Nm 32$_{21.29}$ 33$_{51}$ 35$_{10}$ Dt 2$_{29}$ 3$_{27}$ 4$_{21.22.26}$ 9$_{1}$ 11$_{31}$ 12$_{10}$ 27$_{2.4.12}$ 30$_{18}$ 31$_{2.13}$ 32$_{47}$ Jos 1$_{2.11}$ 3$_{14}$ 4$_{1.22}$ 24$_{11}$ Jg 10$_{9}$ 1 S 13$_{7}$ 2 S 2$_{29}$ 10$_{17}$ 17$_{22.22}$ 19$_{37.40.42}$ 24$_{5}$ 1 C 12$_{16}$ 19$_{17}$ 1QDM 1$_{10}$ 2$_{2}$, hi. *bring across* Nm 32$_{5}$ Jos 7$_{7}$ 2 S 19$_{16}$, שׁלח pi. *escort* 2 S 19$_{32(Qr)}$, נתן *give* Dt 3$_{17}$, *give*, i.e. make Jos 22$_{25}$, לכד *seize*, i.e. capture Jg 7$_{24.24}$.

<CSTR> יַרְדֵּן יְרֵחוֹ *Jordan of*, i.e. at, *Jericho* Nm 22$_{1}$ 26$_{3.63}$ 31$_{12}$ 33$_{48.50}$ 34$_{15}$ 35$_{1}$ 36$_{13}$ Jos 13$_{32}$ 16$_{1}$ 20$_{8}$ 1 C 6$_{63}$.

אֶרֶץ יַרְדֵּן *land of the Jordan* Ps 42$_{7}$, גְּלִילוֹת הַיַּרְדֵּן *territories of the Jordan* Jos 22$_{10.11}$ (unless pl.n. *Geliloth of the Jordan*), כִּכַּר *district of the Jordan* Gn 13$_{10}$ 1 K 7$_{46}$||2 C 4$_{17}$, קְצֵה *border of* Jos 15$_{5.5}$ 18$_{19}$, דֶּרֶךְ *way of* Jos 2$_{7}$, יַד *hand of*, i.e. beside Nm 13$_{29}$, מִזְרַח *east of* 1 C 6$_{63}$, מֵי *waters of* Jos 3$_{8.13.13}$ 4$_{7.18.23}$ 5$_{1}$, מֵימֵי *waters of* Jos 4$_{7}$, מַעְבְּרוֹת *fords of* Jg 3$_{28}$ 12$_{5.6}$, פְּנֵי *face of*, i.e. east of 1 K 17$_{3.5}$, שְׂפַת *lip*, i.e. bank, *of* 2 K 2$_{13}$, עֵבֶר *opposite side of* Dt 4$_{49}$ Jos 13$_{27}$ Is 8$_{23}$, גְּאוֹן *magnificence of*, i.e. thickets Jr 12$_{5}$ 49$_{19}$ 50$_{44}$ Zc 11$_{3}$.

<PREP> בְּ of place, *in, at*, + עמד *stand* Jos 3$_{8}$, עבר *cross over* Jos 3$_{11}$ 4$_{7}$ 2 S 19$_{19}$, טבל *dip* 2 K 5$_{14}$, רחץ *wash* 2 K 5$_{10}$.

מִן of direction, *from* Jos 23$_{4}$, + היה *be* Jos 18$_{12}$, יצא *go out* Jos 16$_{1}$, עלה *go up* Jos 4$_{16.17.19}$, דבק *follow closely* 2 S 20$_{2}$, לקח *take* Jos 4$_{20}$, נכה hi. *strike* 2 K 10$_{33}$.

עַל *upon, at, by* Nm 26$_{3.63}$ 31$_{12}$ 33$_{48.50}$ 35$_{1}$ 36$_{13}$, + עמד *stand* 2 K 2$_{7}$, חנה *encamp* Nm 33$_{49}$, בנה *build* Jos 22$_{10}$.

בְּתוֹךְ *among, in*, + עמד *stand* Jos 3$_{17}$ 4$_{10}$, קום hi. *raise up* Jos 4$_{9}$; מִתּוֹךְ *from (among)*, + עלה *go up* Jos 4$_{18}$, נשׂא *raise* Jos 4$_{3.8}$; אֶל־תּוֹךְ *to (among)*, + עבר *cross over* Jos 4$_{5}$.

בְּעֵבֶר *on the other side of, beyond* Gn 50$_{10.11}$ (unless §2) Dt 3$_{8.25}$ 4$_{46.47}$ 11$_{30}$ Jos 2$_{10}$ 5$_{1}$ 9$_{1.10}$ Jg 10$_{8}$ 1 S 31$_{7}$, + ישׁב *dwell* Jos 7$_{7}$ 24$_{8}$, שׁכן *settle* Jg 5$_{17}$, נתן *give* Dt 3$_{20}$ Jos 1$_{14.15}$ 13$_{8}$ 22$_{4.7(Qr)}$, בדל hi. *separate* Dt 4$_{41}$, נכה hi. *strike* Jos 12$_{7}$, ירשׁ *take possession of* Jos 12$_{1}$, דבר pi. *speak* Dt 1$_{1}$, באר pi. *explain* Dt 1$_{5}$.

מֵעֵבֶר לְ *on the other side of, beyond* Nm 22$_{1}$ 32$_{19.32}$ Jos 17$_{5}$ 20$_{8}$ Jg 7$_{25}$ 1 C 6$_{63}$ 12$_{38}$ 26$_{30}$, + נתן *give* Nm 35$_{14}$ Jos 14$_{3}$, לקח *take* Nm 34$_{15}$ Jos 18$_{7}$, נחל *take possession of* Nm 32$_{19}$.

עַד *unto*, + בוא *come* Jos 3$_{1.15}$ 2 S 19$_{16}$, הלך *go* 2 K 6$_{2}$ 7$_{15}$, לקח *take* Jg 11$_{13}$, ירשׁ *take possession of* Jg 11$_{22}$.

הַיַּרְדֵּנָה (with ה- of direction), *at, in, to, into*, etc. *the Jordan*, + בוא *come* Jg 8$_{4}$ 2 K 6$_{4}$, ירד *go down* Nm 34$_{12}$, שׁלח *send* 2 K 2$_{6}$.

הַיַּרְדֵּן (without ה- of direction), *at, in, to, into*, etc. *(the Jordan)* Ezk 47$_{18}$, + יצא *go out* Jos 16$_{7}$, עבר *pass by* 2 S 19$_{32}$, צלח *rush* 2 S 19$_{18}$, קרא *meet* 1 K 2$_{8}$.

2. perh. town in SW Canaan, perh. Kh. 'Irq,* <PREP> בְּעֵבֶר *on the other side of, beyond*, i.e. across from Jordan Gn 50$_{10.11}$.*

* יַרְדֵּן II $_{1}$ n.m. **river**, <SUBJ> גיח *burst out* Jb 40$_{23}$ (unless יַרְדֵּן I *Jordan*).

ירה I $_{31.0.6}$ vb. **throw—Qal** $_{13}$ Pf. יָרָה, יָרִיתִי, Q ירו; + waw וַיָּרִיתִי; וַנִּירָם; impv. יְרֵה; ptc. יֹרֶה, יוֹרִים (יֹרִים); inf. יָרֹה, יְרוֹת (יְרוֹא)—**1. throw, shoot; erect** pillar (Gn 31$_{51}$), **lay** cornerstone (Jb 38$_{6}$).

<SUBJ> ʼʼ *Y.* Ex 15$_{4}$, Joash 2 K 13$_{17}$, Jonathan 1 S 20$_{36.37}$, Joshua Jos 18$_{6}$, Laban Gn 31$_{51}$, Israel Nm 21$_{30}$ (unless וַנִּירָם appar. = *we became exalted*, from רום; or em. וְנִינָם *and their posterity*, or וְנִירָם *and their land* or *their yoke*, i.e. dominion, or וּבְיָדֵנוּ *and by our hand*), מֶלֶךְ *king* 2 K 13$_{17}$, רָשָׁע *wicked one* Ps 11$_{2}$, פעל ptc. *one who practises* iniquity Ps 64$_{5}$, מִתְלַהְלֵהַּ *insane one* Pr 26$_{18}$, חִשָּׁבוֹן *war engine* 2 C 26$_{15}$, מִי *who?* Jb 38$_{6}$; subj. not specified, 2Q32.2$_{1}$.

<OBJ> Moabites Nm 21$_{30}$, תָּם *blameless one* Ps 64$_{5}$, מֶרְכָּבָה *chariot* Ex 15$_{4}$, גַּל *cairn* Gn 31$_{51}$, מַצֵּבָה *pillar* Gn 31$_{51}$, אֶבֶן *stone* Jb 38$_{6}$, גּוֹרָל *lot* Jos 18$_{6}$, חֵצִי *arrow* 1 S 20$_{36.37}$ Pr 26$_{18}$, זִק *flaming arrow* Pr 26$_{18}$, מָוֶת *death* Pr 26$_{18}$.

<PREP> לְ of benefit, *to, for*, + בֵּן Israelite *son* Jos 18$_{6}$; introducing object, + יָשָׁר *upright one* Ps 11$_{2}$.

בְּ of place, *in, at,* + יָם *sea* Ex 15$_{4}$, מִסְתָּר *secret place* Ps 64$_{5}$; of instrument, *by (means of), with,* + חֵץ *arrow* 2 C 26$_{15}$.

בְּמוֹ *in,* + אֹפֶל *darkness* Ps 11$_{2}$; בֵּין *between,* + Laban Gn 31$_{51}$ (+ Jacob); לִפְנֵי *before,* + ״ *Y.* Jos 18$_{6}$, אֱלֹהִים *God* Jos 18$_{6}$.

2. ptc. as noun, **archer,** <SUBJ> ירה hi. *shoot* 2 C 35$_{23}$. <PREP> מִן of agent, *by (means of), with,* + חיל *be in pain* 1 C 10$_{3}$.

Ni. 1 Impf. יִיָּרֶה—**be shot,** <SUBJ> נגע ptc. *one who touches* Ex 19$_{13}$.

Hi. 15.0.5 Pf. הוֹרָנִי; impf. יוֹרֶה, אוֹרֶה, יֹרוּ (Q יורו, יִרְהוּ): + waw וַיֹּור (וַיֹּרֵם), וַיֹּורוּ (Kt ויראו); ptc. מוֹרֶה, מוֹרִים (Kt מוראים 2 S 11$_{24}$)—**shoot, throw, 1a.** <SUBJ> Y. Jb 30$_{19}$, אֱלֹהִים *God* Ps 64$_{8}$, Joash 2 K 13$_{17}$, Jonathan 1 S 20$_{20.36}$, Moses Ex 15$_{25}$, אִישׁ *man* 2 S 11$_{20}$, מֶלֶךְ *king* 2 K 13$_{17}$ 19$_{32}$||Is 37$_{33}$, גִּבּוֹר *warrior* 1QH 2$_{26}$ (unless פרר hi. *break*), יוֹרֶה *archer* 2 C 35$_{23}$, מוֹרֶה *archer* 2 S 11$_{24}$, פעל ptc. *one who practises* iniquity Ps 64$_{5}$, רָשָׁע *wicked one* 4QpNah 3.4$_{2}$; subj. not specified, 1QH 3$_{27}$ (unless פרר hi. *break*) 5$_{27}$ 4QHod[c] 1.3$_{10}$.

<OBJ> Job Jb 30$_{19}$, עֵץ *tree* Ex 15$_{25}$, חֵץ *arrow* 1 S 20$_{20.36}$ Ps 64$_{8}$ 1QH 2$_{26}$ 3$_{27}$, גּוֹרָל *lot* 4QpNah 3.4$_{2}$, עָפָר *dust* 4QHod[c] 1.3$_{10}$.

<PREP> לְ of direction, *to, (in)to,* + חֹמֶר *mud* Jb 30$_{19}$; introducing object, + מֶלֶךְ *king* 2 C 35$_{23}$, חֵץ *arrow* 1QH 5$_{27}$.

אֶל *to,* + עֶבֶד *servant* 2 S 11$_{24}$.

עַל *for,* + נִכְבָּד *honourable one* 4QpNah 3.4$_{2}$.

מֵעַל *from (upon),* + חוֹמָה *wall* 2 S 11$_{20.24}$.

<COLL> וַאֲנִי שְׁלֹשֶׁת הַחִצִּים צִדָּה אוֹרֶה *and I will shoot three arrows at its side* 1 S 20$_{20}$.

1b. ptc. as noun, **archer,** <SUBJ> מצא *find* 1 S 31$_{3}$||1 C 10$_{3}$, ירה hi. *shoot* 2 S 11$_{24}$.

<PREP> מִן of agent, *by (means of), with,* + חיל *be in pain* 1 S 31$_{3}$.*

→ יוֹרֶה *archer,* מוֹרֶה *archer;* יוֹרָה *Jorah,* יְרוּאֵל *Jeruel,* יְרִיאֵל *Jeriel,* יְרִיָּהוּ *Jeriah.*

ירה II 3 vb. **water—Hi.** 2 Impf. יוֹרֶה—**1. water, rain upon,** <SUBJ> מַלְקוֹשׁ *late rain* Ho 6$_{3}$ (or em. יַרְוֶה late rain that *soaks* the earth, from רוה hi.). <OBJ> אֶרֶץ *earth* Ho 6$_{3}$ (or em.). **2. cause to rain down,** <SUBJ> ״ *Y.* Ho 10$_{12}$. <OBJ> צֶדֶק *righteousness* Ho 10$_{12}$. <PREP> לְ perh. of benefit, *to, for,* + Israel Ho 10$_{12}$.

Ho. 1 Impf. יוֹרָא (mss יוֹרֶה)—**be given drink,** <SUBJ> רוה hi. ptc. *one who provides drink* Pr 11$_{25}$ (or em. יוֹרֶה or יִרְוֶה *be given drink* or יוֹרָא *be allowed to drink deeply* or יוּאָר one who curses *will be cursed*).*

→ יוֹרֶה *early rain,* מוֹרֶה *early rain;* see also רוה *water.*

ירה III 45.0.30 vb. **teach—Qal** 0.0.3 Ptc. Q יורה (יוריה)—ptc. as noun, **teacher, one who teaches,** מצות יוריהם *the commandment[s] of the one who teaches them* CD 3$_{8}$, עד עמד יורה הצדק *until the teacher of righteousness has arisen* 6$_{11}$, ומיום האסף יורה היחיד *and from the day of the ingathering,* i.e. death, *of the unique teacher* 20$_{14}$ (or em. היחד of *the community*).

Also CD 19$_{35(erased)}$.

Hi. 45.0.27 Pf. הוֹרָהוּ, Q הוריתה (הוֹרְתָנִי), Q הוריתי (הוֹרֵיתִיךָ); impf. יוֹרֶה (יוֹרֵנוּ, יוֹרֵנוּ, יוֹרֵם, יֹרֵם), 3fs תֹּרְךָ (תֹּרֶךָּ), תּוֹרֵם, אוֹרְךָ, יוֹרוּ (יוֹרוּךָ, Q יורוכה, Q יורוהו); + waw וַיּוֹרֵהוּ (וַיּוֹרֵנִי); וְהוֹרֵיתִי; impv. הוֹרֵנִי (הֹרֵנִי), הוֹרוּנִי; ptc. מוֹרֶה (Q מורי, מוֹרַי, מוֹרֶיךָ); inf. הורות (הוֹרוֹתָם)—**1. teach, instruct.**

<SUBJ> ״ *Y.* Ex 4$_{12.15}$ 15$_{25}$ 1 K 8$_{36}$ Is 2$_{3}$||Mc 4$_{2}$ Ps 25$_{8.12}$ 27$_{11}$ 32$_{8}$ 86$_{11}$ 119$_{33.102}$, אֱלֹהִים *God* Is 2$_{3}$||Mc 4$_{2}$ Is 28$_{26}$, אֵל *God* Jb 36$_{22}$ 1QS 10$_{13}$ 11$_{17}$ 1QSb 3$_{23}$, אֲדֹנָי *Lord* 1QH 6$_{9}$, Aaron Lv 10$_{11}$, Bezaleel Ex 35$_{34}$, Jehoiada 2 K 12$_{3}$, Job 27$_{11}$, Judah Gn 46$_{28}$, Moses Ex 24$_{12}$, Oholiab Ex 35$_{34}$, Samuel 1 S 12$_{23}$.

אִישׁ *man* of God Jg 13$_{8}$, *man* Pr 6$_{13}$, אָב *father* Jb 8$_{10}$ Pr 4$_{4.11}$, נָבִיא *prophet* Is 9$_{14}$, כֹּהֵן *priest* Dt 17$_{10.11}$ 24$_{8}$ 2 K 12$_{3}$ 17$_{27.28}$ Ezk 44$_{23}$ Mc 3$_{11}$ 2 C 15$_{3}$ (or del.), לֵוִי *Levite* Dt 17$_{10.11}$ 24$_{8}$ 33$_{10}$ Ezk 44$_{23}$, worshipper 4QHod[b] 7$_{3}$, friend of Job Jb 6$_{24}$, רַב pl. *many* perh. 1QpHab 10$_{11}$, בְּהֵמָה *beast* Jb 12$_{7}$, יָמִין *right hand* Ps 45$_{5}$, עֵץ *tree* Hb 2$_{19}$, שִׂיחַ *shrub* Jb 12$_{8}$, אֶבֶן *stone* Hb 2$_{19}$, מִי *who?* Is 28$_{9}$; subj. not specified, Lv 14$_{57}$ Hb 2$_{18}$ 1QH[b] 1$_{9}$ 4QpIsa[a] 8$_{23}$ 4QpIsa[c] 21$_{6}$ 4QpHos[a] 5$_{2}$ 4QUnid 7$_{1}$ 4QJub[a] 1$_{2}$ 4QD[a] 5.2$_{9}$ 4QHod[f] 1$_{2}$ 4QBark[a] 1.3$_{4}$ 11QT 56$_{6}$.

<OBJ> (1) person taught, עַם *people* 1 S 12$_{23}$ 1 K 8$_{36}$ Is 2$_{3}$||Mc 4$_{2}$ Ezk 44$_{23}$ 1QSb 3$_{23}$, גּוֹי *nation* 2 K 17$_{27.28}$, שְׁאֵרִית *remnant* 1QH 6$_{9}$, Israelite(s) Dt 17$_{10.11}$, Aaron

Ex 4_{15}, Jehoash 2 K 12_3, Job Jb 6_{24} 8_{10}, Manoah Jg 13_8, Moses Ex $4_{12.15}$ 15_{25}, אִישׁ *man* Ps 25_{12}, אִשָּׁה *woman* Jg 13_8, בֵּן Israelite *son* Ex 24_{12} Lv 10_{11}, *son* Pr $4_{4.11}$, מֶלֶךְ *king* Ps 45_5, worshipper Ps 27_{11} 32_8 86_{11} $119_{33.102}$ 1QS 10_{13} 11QT 56_6, טָהוֹר *clean one* Lv 14_{57}, טָמֵא *unclean one* Lv 14_{57}, חַטָּא *sinful one* Ps 25_8, friend of Job Jb $12_{7.8}$ 27_{11}; obj. not specified, Is 28_{26} Jb 34_{32} 4QpIsa^a 8_{23}.

(2) thing taught, שֶׁקֶר *falsehood* Is 9_{14} Hb 2_{18}, תּוֹרָה *law* Dt 17_{10} 33_{10}, חֹק *statute* Lv 10_{11}, מִשְׁפָּט *judgment* Dt 33_{10} 2 K 17_{27}, נוֹרָא *awesome deed* Ps 45_5, דֵּעָה *knowledge* Is 28_9 1QS 11_{17}, דֶּרֶךְ *way* 1 K 8_{36} Ps 27_{11} 86_{11} 119_{33} 4QBark^a 1.3_4, אֲשֶׁר *that which* 1QS 10_{13}, כֹּל *everything* Dt 24_8; obj. not specified, Is 28_{26} Jb 34_{32}.

<PREP> לְ of direction, *to*, + Israel Dt 33_{10}, Jacob Dt 33_{10}.

בְּ of place/time, *in, along, on*, + דֶּרֶךְ *way* 1 S 12_{23} Ps $25_{8.12}$ 32_8, יוֹם *day* Lv $14_{57.57}$; of instrument, *by (means of), with*, + יָד *hand* of God Jb 27_{11}, אֶצְבַּע *finger* Pr 6_{13}; of exchange, *for*, + מְחִיר *price* Mc 3_{11}; introducing object, + מַעֲשֶׂה *deed* 1QpHab 10_{11}, אַשְׁמָה *guilt* 4QHod^b 7_3, יְסוֹד *foundation* 4QD^a 5.2_9.

מִן of direction, *from*, + דֶּרֶךְ *way* Is 2_3||Mc 4_2; בֵּין *between*, + קֹדֶשׁ *holiness* Ezk 44_{23} (+ טָמֵא *uncleanness*); לִפְנֵי *before*, + Jacob Gn 46_{28}.

<COLL> לְהוֹרֹת לְפָנָיו גֹּשְׁנָה *to show (the way) before him to Goshen* Gn 46_{28}.

3. ptc. as noun, **teacher,** <SUBJ> אסף ni. *be gathered*, i.e. die CD 20_1, עמד *arise* 4QpPs^a 1.3_{15}, ירה hi. *teach* 1QpMic 8_6 (אשר הואה [יורה] *who teaches* the law), ידע hi. *teach* CD 1_{11}, בנה *build* 4QpPs^a 1.3_{15}. <NOM CL> [הצדיק] הוא מורה הצדק *the righteous one is the teacher of righteousness* 1QpHab 1_{13}. <OBJ> כון hi. *establish* 4QpPs^a 1.3_{15}, קום hi. *establish* CD 1_{11}, perh. ישר pi. *direct* 4QpPs^a 1.3_{15}, עזר *help* 1QpHab 5_{10}, ידע hi. *teach* 1QpHab 7_4, בלע pi. *swallow* 1QpHab 11_5.

<CSTR> מורה הצדק *the teacher of righteousness* 1QpHab 1_{13} 2_2 ([בדברי] מורה הצדקה trust in *the words of the teacher of righteousness*) 5_{10} (+ תוכחת *reproof of* the teacher) 7_4 8_3 9_9 (+ בעוון *because of sin of*, i.e. against, the teacher; others בעיין *in the sight of*) 11_5 1QpMic 8_6 (מורי) 4QpPs^a 1.3_{15} ([ה]צדק) 1.3_{19} (מור[ה הצדק]) 3.4_{27} ([הצדק]) 4QpPs^b 1_4 (+ [נס]תרות/[ע]תרות *prayers/secrets of the teacher*) 2_2 ([מ]ורה הצד[ק]) CD 1_{11} (מורה צדק), מורה היחיד *the teacher of the unique one*, i.e. unique teacher CD 20_1 (or em. היחד of *the community*) 20_{32} (מורה צדק); קול מורה *voice of the teacher* CD $20_{28.32}$ (+ צדק teacher of *righteousness*).

<APP> כֹּהֵן *priest* 4QpPs^a 1.3_{15}. <PREP> בְּ appar. *to*, + דבר pi. *speak* 4QpPs^a 1.3_{15} ([ד]בר בו *commanded him*; others [ב]חר בו *chose him*); אֱמוּנָה בְּ their *trust in* the teacher 1QpHab 8_3; עַל *concerning* 1QpHab 7_4 1QpMic 8_6 ([על]) 4QpPs^a $1.3_{15.19}$ (מור[ה]) 3.4_{27}; אַחַר *after*, + רדף *pursue* 1QpHab 11_5.

Ho. be taught,* נֶפֶשׁ תּוּרֶךָ *a soul taught by you* Ps 74_{19} (if em. נֶפֶשׁ תּוֹרֶךָ *the soul of your dove*).*

→ מוֹרֶה *teacher*, תּוֹרָה *law*.

***ירה IV** $_2$ vb. **be led—Hi. lead** Pf. הֹרֵתִיךָ, impf. 2ms + sf. תֹּרֵם—<SUBJ> יי *Y.* 2 C 6_{27}, אֱלֹהִים *God* 2 C 6_{27}, אָב *father* Pr 4_{11}. <OBJ> עַם *people* 2 C 6_{27}, בֵּן *son* Pr 4_{11}. <PREP> בְּ of place, *in, on, along*, + דֶּרֶךְ *way* Pr 4_{11}; אֶל *in(to)*, + דֶּרֶךְ *way* 2 C 6_{27}.

***ירה** $_1$ vb. **be terrified—Qal** $_1$ Impf. תִּרְהוּ—<SUBJ> Israel Is 44_8 (|| פחד *tremble*; 1QIs^a ירא *fear*), Jacob Is 44_8 (|| פחד).

<SYN> פחד *tremble*.

יְרוּאֵל $_1$ pl.n. **Jeruel,** region in steppe of Judah near Ziz 2 C 20_{16}, <CSTR> מִדְבַּר יְרוּאֵל *steppe of Jeruel* 2 C 20_{16}.

→ (?) ירה *throw* + אֵל *God*.

יָרוֹחַ $_1$ pr.n.m. **Jaroah,** Gadite, son of Gilead and leader of the tribe of Gad 1 C 5_{14}, <CSTR> בֶּן־יָרוֹחַ *son of Jaroah* 1 C 5_{14}. → (?) יָרֵחַ *moon*.

יָרוּם $_6$ adj. **exalted—1.** as predicative adj. or noun, **exalted one** (unless יָרוּם is impf. 3ms of רום *be high*), <NOM CL> יָרוּם אֱלֹהֵי צוּר *the God of the rock of* my salvation *is an exalted one* Ps 18_{47}||2 S 22_{47}, עַבְדִּי יָרוּם *my servant is the exalted one* Is 52_{13}, צוּר־יָרוּם *the rock is an exalted one* Ps 61_3, יָרוּם רֹאשִׁי *my head is an exalted one* Ps 27_6, יָרוּם לְבָבוֹ *his heart is an exalted one* Dn $11_{12(Kt)}$.

→ רום *be exalted*.

יָרוֹק 1.0.1 n.m. **green plants**—<OBJ> דרשׁ *search out* Jb 39$_{8}$, אכל *eat* 4QParGenEx 3$_{11}$. <CSTR> כָּל־יָרוֹק *every verdant plant* Jb 39$_{8}$ 4QParGenEx 3$_{11}$.

→ יָרָק *herbage*.

יְרוּשָׁא 2 pr.n.f. **Jerusha**—יְרוּשָׁה—daughter of Zadok, wife of Uzziah, mother of Jotham king of Judah 2 K 15$_{33}$ 2 C 27$_{1}$, <NOM CL> שֵׁם אִמּוֹ יְרוּשָׁא *the name of his mother was Jerusha* 2 K 15$_{33}$||2 C 27$_{1}$ (יְרוּשָׁה).*

→ ירשׁ *take possession of*.

יְרוּשָׁלַם 641.2.29.5 pl.n. **Jerusalem**—יְרוּשָׁלַיִם (יְרוּשָׁלֶם), Q ירושלים (ירושלם), I ירשלם; + ־ה of direction יְרוּשָׁלַיְמָה (יְרוּשָׁלְמָה, יְרוּשָׁלָיְמָה)—capital of all Israel and centre of temple worship, first a Canaanite city-state (Jos 10$_{1.3.5.23}$), conquered by David (2 S 5$_{6}$); captured by Nebuchadrezzar (2 K 25$_{1}$), and later centre of postexilic community (Ezr 1$_{11}$ 2$_{11}$ Ne 2$_{11.17}$).

<SUBJ> היה *be* Is 64$_{9}$ Jr 26$_{18}$||Mc 3$_{12}$ Jl 4$_{17}$ Lm 1$_{17}$ 4QJub^{a} 1$_{28}$, טהר *be clean* Jr 13$_{27}$, גלה *be exiled* 4QMMT C$_{19}$, שׁכן *dwell* Jr 33$_{16}$, בנה pass. *be built* Ps 122$_{3}$, ni. *be built* Is 44$_{28}$, ישׁב *be inhabited* Jl 4$_{20}$ Zc 2$_{8}$ 7$_{7}$ 12$_{6}$ 14$_{11}$, ni. Is 44$_{26}$, נתן ni. *be given* 2 K 19$_{10}$||Is 37$_{10}$, לכד ni. *be captured* Jr 38$_{28.28}$, ישׁע ni. *be saved* Jr 4$_{14}$, קרא ni. *be called* Zc 8$_{3}$, יסר ni. *be warned* Jr 6$_{8}$.

עלה *go up* Jr 51$_{50}$, שׁוב pol. *turn aside* Jr 8$_{5}$, עור htpol. *rouse oneself* Is 51$_{17}$, נער htp. *shake oneself* Is 52$_{2}$, קום *arise* Is 51$_{17}$ 52$_{2}$, לבשׁ *clothe oneself* Is 52$_{1}$, כבס pi. *wash* Jr 4$_{14}$, כשׁל *stumble* Is 3$_{8}$, חטא *sin* Lm 1$_{8}$, שׁתה *drink* Is 51$_{17}$, זכר *remember* Lm 1$_{7}$, אמר *say* Jr 51$_{35}$, שׁיר *sing* 4QTobit^{e} 7.2$_{1}$, שׁבח pi. *praise* Ps 147$_{12}$.

<NOM CL> וִירוּשָׁלַם אָהֳלִיבָה *and Oholibah is Jerusalem* Ezk 23$_{4}$, יְרוּשָׁלַם הָרִים סָבִיב לָהּ *as the mountains are round about Jerusalem* Ps 125$_{2}$, יְרוּשָׁלַם חֲרֵבָה *Jerusalem is desolate* Ne 2$_{17}$, ירושלם מכון שבתיך *Jerusalem is the place of your dwelling* Si 36$_{18}$.

הִיא יְרוּשָׁלָם *it is Jerusalem* Jos 15$_{8}$ 18$_{28}$ Jg 19$_{10}$ 1 C 11$_{4}$, sim. 1QpHab 12$_{7}$, ירושלים היא המקום *Jerusalem is the place* 4QMMT B$_{32}$||B$_{60}$, [ירו]שלם היא [העיר] *Jerusalem is the city* 4QapPs^{a} 1$_{2}$, ירושלים היאה מחנה *Jerusalem is a camp* of holiness 4QMMT B$_{60}$, ירושלים היא ראש *Jerusalem is head* of the camps of Israel 4QMMT B$_{61}$.

זֹאת יְרוּשָׁלַם *this is Jerusalem* Ezk 5$_{5}$, הֲלוֹא יְרוּשָׁלָם *is it not Jerusalem?* Mc 1$_{5}$, אוֹי לָךְ יְרוּשָׁלַם *woe to you, O Jerusalem* Jr 13$_{27}$.

<OBJ> ראה *see* Is 33$_{20}$, ברא *create* Is 65$_{18}$, בנה *build* Mc 3$_{10}$ Ps 147$_{2}$ Dn 9$_{25}$, בחר *choose* 1 K 11$_{13.36}$ 2 K 21$_{7}$||2 C 33$_{7}$ 2 K 23$_{27}$, שׂים *place*, i.e. make Is 62$_{7}$ Zc 12$_{2.3}$ Ps 79$_{1}$, נתן *give*, i.e. make Jr 9$_{10}$ 25$_{18}$, עמד hi. *maintain* 1 K 15$_{4}$, עלה hi. *bring up* Ps 137$_{6}$, חפשׂ *search out* Zp 1$_{12}$, מלא pi. *fill* 2 K 21$_{16}$ 24$_{4}$.

יטב hi. *do good to* Zc 8$_{15}$, רחם pi. *show compassion to* Zc 1$_{12}$ Si 36$_{18}$, נצל hi. *deliver* 2 K 18$_{35}$||Is 36$_{20}$, גאל *redeem* Is 52$_{9}$ Kh. Beit Lei graf. 5$_{2(Cross)}$, טהר pi. *cleanse* 2 C 34$_{3.5}$, עזב *forsake* Ne 3$_{8}$, שׁכח *forget* Ps 137$_{5}$, מאס *reject* 2 K 23$_{27}$, זרה pi. *scatter* Zc 2$_{2}$, מחה *wipe out* 2 K 21$_{13}$, גלה hi. *exile* 2 K 24$_{14}$ 1 C 5$_{41}$, שׁקה hi. *cause to drink* Jr 25$_{18}$, זכר *remember* 4QNarrC 1$_{19}$, חקק *mark out* Ezk 4$_{1}$, מדד *measure* Zc 2$_{6}$, ידע hi. *make known* Ezk 16$_{2}$.

<CSTR> אֱלָהּ יְרוּשְׁלֶם *God of* Jerusalem Ezr 7$_{19}$, אֱלֹהֵי *God of* 2 C 32$_{19}$ Kh. Beit Lei graf. 5$_{2(Naveh)}$ (ירשלם), ארץ *land of* 4QpsEzek^{a} 16.1$_{3}$, סְבִיבוֹת *environs of* Jr 17$_{26}$ Ps 79$_{3}$ Ne 12$_{28.29}$, סְבִיבֵי *environs of* Jr 32$_{44}$ 33$_{13}$, מְסִבֵּי *surroundings of* 2 K 23$_{5}$, פֶּלֶךְ *district of* Ne 3$_{9.12}$, גִּבְעַת *hill of* Is 10$_{32}$, מדבר *steppe of* 1QM 1$_{3}$, חוק ירושלם *boundary of Jerusalem* 4QTestim$_{29}$, גבול *boundary of* 4QpIsa^{a} 5$_{13}$, חָרְבוֹת יְרוּשָׁלַם *waste places of Jerusalem* Is 52$_{9}$ Dn 9$_{2}$, רְחֹבוֹת *streets of* Zc 8$_{4}$, חוֹמַת *wall of* 1 K 3$_{1}$ 9$_{15}$ 2 K 14$_{13}$ Ne 1$_{3}$ 2$_{17}$ 12$_{27}$ 2 C 25$_{23}$ 36$_{19}$, חוֹמֹת *walls of* 2 K 25$_{10}$||Jr 39$_{8}$||52$_{14}$ Ne 2$_{13}$ (mss חוֹמַת *wall of*) Ps 51$_{20}$ (חוֹמוֹת) Ne 4$_{1}$ (חֹמוֹת; mss חוֹמַת), אַרְמְנוֹת *palaces of* Jr 17$_{27}$ Am 2$_{5}$, בָּתֵּי *houses of* 2 K 25$_{9}$||Jr 52$_{13}$ Is 22$_{10}$ Jr 19$_{13}$, חוּצוֹת *streets of* Jr 5$_{1}$ 7$_{17}$ (יְרוּשָׁלָם) 7$_{34}$ 11$_{6.13}$ 14$_{16}$ 33$_{10}$ 44$_{6.9}$ (יְרוּשָׁלָם) 44$_{17}$ (יְרוּשָׁלָם) 44$_{21}$, שַׁעַר *gate of* Mc 1$_{12}$, שַׁעֲרֵי *gates of* Jr 1$_{15}$ 17$_{19.21.27}$ 22$_{19}$ Lm 4$_{12}$ Ne 7$_{3}$ 13$_{19}$.

עַם *people of* 2 C 32$_{18}$, קְהַל *assembly of* 2 C 20$_{5}$, שְׁאֵרִית *remnant of* Jr 24$_{8}$, אִישׁ *man of* 2 C 20$_{27}$, בְּנֵי *sons of* Jl 4$_{6}$ 2 C 28$_{10}$, בַּת *daughter of* 2 K 19$_{21}$||Is 37$_{22}$ Mc 4$_{8}$ Zp 3$_{14}$, Zc 9$_{9}$ Lm 2$_{13.15}$, בְּנוֹת *daughters of* Ca 1$_{5}$ 2$_{7}$ 3$_{5.10}$ 5$_{8.16}$ 8$_{4}$ GnzPs 3$_{16}$, בְּתוּלֹת *young women of* Lm 2$_{10}$, מֶלֶךְ *king of* Jos 10$_{1.3.5.23}$ 12$_{10}$, מְבַשֶּׂרֶת *herald of* Is 40$_{9}$ (unless app.), נְבִיאֵי *prophets of* Jr 23$_{14.15}$, כוהני *priests of* 1QpHab 9$_{4}$ 4QpNah 3.1$_{11}$ 4QpsEzek^{c} 3.3$_{6}$ (כהני), זִקְנֵי *elders of* 2 K 23$_{1}$ 2 C 34$_{29}$, שָׂרֵי *princes of* Jr 29$_{2}$ 34$_{19}$, חֹרֵי *nobles of* Jr

27$_{20}$, בּוֹנֵה *builder of* Ps 147$_2$, יוֹשֵׁב *inhabitant of* Is 5$_3$ 8$_{14}$ 22$_{21}$ Zc 12$_{7.8.10}$, יוֹשְׁבֵי *inhabitants of* Jos 15$_{63}$ 2 K 23$_2$ Jr 4$_4$ 8$_1$ 11$_{2.9.12}$ 13$_{13}$ 17$_{20.25}$ 18$_{11}$ 19$_3$ 25$_2$ 32$_{32}$ 35$_{13.17}$ 36$_{31}$ 42$_{18}$ Ezk 11$_{15}$ 12$_{19}$ 15$_6$ Zp 1$_4$ Zc 12$_5$ 13$_1$ Dn 9$_7$ Ezr 4$_6$ Ne 7$_3$ 2 C 20$_{15.18.20}$ 21$_{11.13}$ 22$_1$ 31$_4$ 32$_{22.26.33}$ 33$_9$ 34$_{30.32}$ 35$_{18}$ 4QD^a 5.1$_{12}$.

צֹאן *flocks of* Ezk 36$_{38}$, מִנְחַת *grain offering of* Ml 3$_4$, טוּב *prosperity of* Ps 128$_5$, שְׁבוּת *fortunes of* Jl 4$_1$, שְׁלוֹם *peace of* Ps 122$_6$, יוֹם *day of* Ps 137$_7$, מָצוֹר *siege of* Ezk 4$_7$, גָּלוּת *deportation of* Jr 1$_3$, גָּלוּת *exile of* Jr 40$_1$ Ob$_{20}$, גְּאוֹן *arrogance of* Jr 13$_9$, אָזְנֵי *ears*, i.e. hearing, *of* Jr 2$_2$, לֵב *heart of* Is 40$_2$, דְּמֵי *blood(stains) of* Is 4$_4$, פְּנֵי *face*, i.e. east, *of* 1 K 11$_7$ 2 K 23$_{13}$ Zc 14$_4$, נֶגֶב *south of* Zc 14$_{10}$, קֶרֶב *middle of* Jr 6$_1$, תּוֹךְ *middle of* Ezk 22$_{19}$, עֲצַת *plan of* Jr 19$_7$, צְוָחַת *wail of* Jr 14$_7$, שִׂמְחַת *joy of* Ne 12$_{43}$, כָּל־ *all of* 2 K 24$_{14}$.

<APP> הַר *mountain* Is 66$_{20}$, עַם *people* Jr 8$_5$, גּוֹי *nation* Jr 25$_{18}$, עִיר *city* 1 K 11$_{36}$ 2 K 23$_{27}$ Ezk 4$_1$ Dn 9$_{16}$ 4QapLam^a 1.1$_8$, קִרְיָה *city* Si 36$_{18}$, מְבַשֶּׂרֶת *herald of* Is 40$_9$ (unless cstr.), שְׁבִי *captive one* Is 52$_2$.

<PREP> לְ of direction, *to*, + קוה ni. *be gathered* Jr 3$_{17}$, אסף ni. *be assembled* 2 C 30$_3$, בוא *come* Ezr 3$_8$ Ne 13$_7$ 2 C 30$_{11}$, hi. *bring* Ezr 8$_{30}$ Ne 12$_{27}$ 2 C 32$_{23}$, הלך *go* 2 C 11$_{14}$, עלה *go up* Ezr 1$_3$, hi. *bring up* Ezr 1$_{11}$, שׁוב *go back* Zc 1$_{16}$ Ezr 2$_1$||Ne 7$_6$ 2 C 34$_7$, נתן *give* Is 41$_{27}$, שׁלח *send* 1 C 21$_{15}$ 2 C 19$_1$, אמר *say* 2 K 18$_{22}$||Is 36$_7$||2 C 32$_{12}$ Is 44$_{26.28}$ Jr 4$_3$ Ezk 16$_3$, ni. *be said* Jr 4$_{11}$ Zp 3$_{16}$.

לְ of benefit, *to, for*, + קנא pi. *be jealous* Zc 1$_{14}$, עשׂה *do* Is 10$_{11}$ Ne 2$_{12}$; introducing object, + נשׁא hi. *deceive* Jr 4$_{10}$, קרא *call* Jr 3$_{17}$.

בְּ of place, *in, at* 2 S 5$_{14}$ 15$_{14}$ 1 K 11$_{36}$ 12$_{27}$ 2 K 23$_9$ Is 28$_{14}$ 31$_9$ Jr 29$_{25}$ 34$_8$ 36$_9$ Ezk 12$_{10}$ Zc 12$_6$ Ec 1$_1$ 2$_{7.9}$ Ezr 1$_{3.4.5}$ 2$_{68}$ 7$_{27}$ 8$_{29}$ Ne 2$_{20}$ 11$_{22}$ 2 C 2$_6$ 30$_{1.2.14.26}$ 32$_9$ 1QpPs 9$_2$ 4QpIsa^b 2$_{7.10}$ 4QpIsa^c 23.2$_{11}$, + היה *be* 2 K 24$_{20}$||Jr 52$_3$ Jl 3$_5$ Zc 14$_{21}$ Ec 1$_{12}$ Ne 13$_6$ 1 C 14$_4$ 2 C 17$_{13}$ 30$_{26}$ 2 C 33$_4$, גדל *be great* Zc 12$_{11}$, ישׁב *dwell* Jos 15$_{63}$ Jg 1$_{21}$ 2 S 9$_{13}$ 11$_1$|| 1 C 20$_1$ 2 S 11$_{12}$ 14$_{28}$ 16$_3$ 1 K 2$_{38}$ 2 K 22$_{14}$||2 C 34$_{22}$ Is 30$_{19}$ Jr 35$_{11}$ Ne 11$_{1.1.2.3.4.6}$ 1 C 8$_{28.32}$ 9$_{3.34.38}$ 2 C 11$_{15}$ 19$_4$ 32$_{10}$, שׁכן *dwell* 1 C 23$_{25}$.

ראה ni. *be seen* 2 K 23$_{24}$, ילד ni. *be born* 1 C 3$_5$, מצא ni. *be found* 2 C 30$_{21}$ 34$_{32}$, יתר ni. *be left over* Is 4$_3$ Jr 27$_{18}$, קבר ni. *be buried* 2 K 14$_{20}$, נחם pu. *be comforted* Is 66$_{13}$, בוא *come* Is 52$_1$ Jr 36$_9$ Ezk 21$_{25}$, עבר hi. *cause to pass through*, i.e. make proclamation Ezr 10$_7$ Ne 8$_{15}$, סור hi. *remove* 2 C 36$_3$, נתן *give*, i.e. place 1 K 10$_{27}$||2 C 1$_{15}$||9$_{27}$ 1 K 15$_4$ Ezr 9$_9$, *give*, i.e. raise voice 2 C 24$_9$, שׂים *place* 2 K 21$_{1.4.7}$||2 C 33$_7$, חזק htp. *make oneself powerful* 2 C 12$_{13}$, עמד hi. *install* Ne 6$_7$ 2 C 19$_8$, נוח hi. *station* 1 K 10$_{26}$||2 C 1$_{14}$||9$_{25}$.

עשׂה *do* Jr 15$_4$ 2 C 26$_{15}$ 28$_{24}$ Lachish ost. 6$_{10}$ (וביר[שלם]), *do*, i.e. perform, passover 2 K 23$_{23}$||2 C 35$_1$ 2 C 30$_5$, ni. *be practised* Ml 2$_{11}$ Dn 9$_{12}$, בצע pi. *bring to completion* Is 10$_{12}$, לקח *take* 1 C 14$_3$, נטה *pitch tent* 2 C 1$_4$, בנה *build* 1 K 2$_{36}$ 9$_{19}$||2 C 8$_6$ Ezr 1$_2$||2 C 36$_{23}$ 1 C 5$_{36}$ 6$_{17}$ 2 C 3$_1$ 26$_9$ 33$_{15}$, מלך *rule* 2 S 5$_5$ 1 K 2$_{11}$ 11$_{42}$||2 C 9$_{30}$ 1 K 14$_{21}$||2 C 12$_{13}$ 1 K 15$_2$||2 C 13$_2$ 1 K 15$_{10}$ 22$_{42}$||2 C 20$_{31}$ 2 K 8$_{17.26}$||2 C 21$_5$ 22$_2$ 2 K 12$_2$ 14$_2$||2 C 25$_1$ 2 K 15$_{2.33}$||2 C 27$_1$ 2 K 16$_2$||2 C 28$_1$ 2 K 18$_2$||2 C 29$_1$ 2 K 21$_{1.19}$||2 C 33$_{1.21}$ 2 K 22$_1$||2 C 34$_1$ 2 K 23$_{31.33.36}$||2 C 36$_{2.5.9}$ 2 K 24$_{8.18}$||Jr 52$_1$||2 C 36$_{11}$ Is 24$_{23}$ 1 C 3$_4$ 29$_{27}$ 2 C 21$_{20}$ 24$_1$ 26$_3$ 27$_8$, hi. *make king* 2 C 36$_1$.

בקשׁ pi. *seek* Zc 8$_{22}$, כול pilp. *provide* 2 S 19$_{34}$, מכר *sell* Ne 13$_{16}$, נחם pi. *console* 4QBark^a 1.1$_6$, שׁחה htpal. *prostrate oneself* 2 K 18$_{22}$ Is 27$_{13}$, קדשׁ hi. *make holy* 2 C 36$_{14}$, נסה pi. *test* 2 C 9$_1$, שׁבר *break* Ezk 4$_{16}$, קשׁר *conspire* 2 K 14$_{19}$||2 C 25$_{27}$, קבר *bury* 2 C 28$_{27}$, כתב pass. *be written* Is 4$_3$, ספר pi. *relate* Ps 102$_{22}$, דבר pi. *speak* Jr 34$_6$, שׁמע hi. *proclaim* Jr 4$_5$, גיל *rejoice* Is 65$_{19}$ 66$_{10}$.

בְּ *against*, + נתך *be poured out* 2 C 12$_7$, לחם ni. *fight* Jg 1$_8$ Zc 14$_{14}$ Ne 4$_2$; introducing object, + בחר *choose* Zc 1$_{17}$ 2$_{16}$ 3$_2$ 2 C 6$_6$.

כְּ *as* Ca 6$_4$.

מִן of direction, *from* 2 K 14$_2$||2 C 25$_1$ 2 K 15$_2$ 24$_8$ 2 C 26$_3$, + בוא *come* Ezk 33$_{21}$, hi. *bring* 2 C 24$_6$, הלך *go* 2 S 15$_{11}$ 1 K 2$_{41}$, hi. *bring* 2 K 24$_{15}$, יצא *go out* 2 S 19$_{20}$ 20$_7$ 1 K 11$_{29}$ 2 K 19$_{31}$||Is 37$_{32}$ Is 2$_3$||Mc 4$_2$ Jr 29$_2$ 37$_{12}$ Zc 14$_8$ 1QM 7$_4$, hi. *bring out* Ezr 1$_7$, שׁוב *go back* Dn 9$_{16}$, סור hi. *remove* Is 3$_1$, נתן *give*, i.e. utter voice Jl 4$_{16}$ Am 1$_2$, לקח *take* 2 S 5$_{13}$, כרת hi. *cut off* Zc 9$_{10}$, גלה *be exiled* Jr 27$_{20}$, hi. *exile* Jr 24$_1$ 29$_{1.4}$ 52$_{29 (mss)}$, ho. *be exiled* Est 2$_6$, שׁלח *send* Jr 29$_1$, pi. *send away* Jr 29$_{20}$.

מִן of comparison, *(more) than* Is 10$_{10}$.

אֶל *to*, + בוא *come* Jr 39$_1$ Ezr 7$_9$ Ne 2$_{11}$ 2 C 23$_2$ 24$_{23}$, אסף *gather* Zc 14$_2$, ni. *be gathered* Ezr 3$_1$ 2 C 12$_5$, עלה *go up* Zc 14$_{17}$ Ezr 7$_7$, שׁוב *go back* 2 C 20$_{27}$, קהל hi. *assemble*

1 C 15$_{3}$ 28$_{1}$ 2 C 5$_{2}$, שׂים *place* Ezk 21$_{7}$, סמך *lean*, i.e. besiege Ezk 24$_{2}$, שׁלח pi. *send away* Ezk 14$_{21}$, נבא ni. *prophesy* Ezk 13$_{16}$.

עַל *upon, to, in* Ps 68$_{30}$ Ec 1$_{16}$, + ראה ni. *be seen* 4QapPs[a] 1$_{6}$, בוא *come* 2 K 25$_{1}$||Jr 52$_{4}$ Jr 52$_{12}$, hi. *bring* 2 K 21$_{12}$ Is 66$_{20}$ Jr 44$_{2}$ Ezk 14$_{22}$, עלה *go up* 1 K 14$_{25}$ 2 K 12$_{18}$, נטה *stretch out* 2 K 21$_{13}$, pass. *be stretched out* 1 C 21$_{16}$, ni. *be stretched out* Zc 1$_{16}$, ידד *throw*, i.e. cast, lot Ob$_{11}$, גנן *protect* Is 31$_{5}$, חמל *show compassion* Jr 15$_{5}$, כון hi. *establish* throne Si 47$_{11}$, מלך hi. *make king* 2 C 36$_{4.10}$, פקד *visit*, i.e. punish Jr 44$_{13}$, שׁפך *pour out* anger Ezk 9$_{8}$, צור *besiege* Jr 32$_{2}$ 37$_{5}$ Dn 1$_{1}$, לחם ni. *fight* Jr 34$_{1.7}$, שׁמע hi. *proclaim* Jr 4$_{16}$.

עַל *concerning*, + חזה *see* Is 1$_{1}$ 2$_{1}$ Mc 1$_{1}$, אמר *say* Ezk 26$_{2}$, שׁאל *ask* Ne 1$_{2}$, צוה pi. *command* Ne 7$_{2}$; *against* 2 C 32$_{2}$, + היה *be* Zc 12$_{2}$ 2 C 24$_{18}$ 29$_{8}$ 32$_{25}$, בוא *come* Zc 12$_{9}$ 14$_{16}$, עלה *go up* 2 C 12$_{2.9}$, שׁפך *heap up* siege-ramp Jr 6$_{6}$, צבא *conduct war* Zc 14$_{12}$.

מֵעַל *from (upon)*, + עלה *go up* 2 K 12$_{19}$ Jr 37$_{5.11}$.

אֵת *with*, + שׂמח *rejoice* Is 66$_{10}$.

בְּתוֹךְ *among*, + שׁכן *dwell* Zc 8$_{3.8}$, לין *spend night* Ne 4$_{16}$, עבר *pass through* Ezk 9$_{4}$, שׁלם pi. *pay* vow Ps 116$_{19}$.

לְמַעַן *for the sake of*, + היה *be* 1 K 11$_{32}$, שׁקט *be at peace* Is 62$_{1}$, נתן *give* 1 K 11$_{13}$.

מִחוּץ לְ *outside*, + לין *spend night* Ne 13$_{20}$, יצא hi. *bring out* 2 K 23$_{6}$, שׂרף *burn* 2 K 23$_{4}$.

מִקֶּרֶב *from (among)*, + עוז hi. *bring to shelter* Jr 6$_{1}$.

עַד *unto* 2 S 20$_{2}$, + בוא *come* 2 C 12$_{4}$, נגע *reach* Mc 1$_{9}$.

עִם *with* 2 C 20$_{17}$.

יְרוּשָׁלַםְ (with ה- of direction), *at, in, to, into*, etc. *Jerusalem*, + בוא *come* 1 K 10$_{2}$, hi. *bring* Ezk 8$_{3}$, רכב hi. *carry in chariot* 2 K 9$_{28}$, שׁלח *send* Is 36$_{2}$||2 C 32$_{9}$.

יְרוּשָׁלַםְ (without ה- of direction), *at, in, to, into*, etc. *(Jerusalem)*, + ישׁב *dwell* Jg 1$_{21}$, שׁכן *dwell* Ps 135$_{21}$, אסף ni. *be assembled* 2 C 30$_{13}$, קבץ ni. *be assembled* Ezr 10$_{7.9}$ 2 C 15$_{10}$, יתר ni. *be left over* Jr 27$_{21}$, בוא *come* 2 S 10$_{14}$||1 C 19$_{15}$ 2 S 15$_{37}$ 16$_{15}$ 19$_{26}$ 20$_{3}$ 24$_{8}$ 1 K 3$_{15}$ 12$_{21}$||2 C 11$_{1}$ 2 K 14$_{13}$ 18$_{17}$ 25$_{8}$ Jr 27$_{3}$ 35$_{11}$ Ezk 17$_{12}$ Dn 1$_{1}$ Ezr 3$_{8}$ 7$_{8}$ 8$_{32}$ 1 C 21$_{4}$ 2 C 11$_{16}$ 20$_{28}$ 4QpNah 3.1$_{2}$, hi. *bring* Jg 1$_{7}$ 1 S 17$_{54}$ 2 S 8$_{7}$||1 C 18$_{7}$ 2 S 14$_{23}$ 2 K 23$_{30}$ Ne 13$_{15}$ 2 C 1$_{13}$ 25$_{23}$ 33$_{13}$, הלך *go* 2 S 5$_{6}$||1 C 11$_{4}$ Ezr 8$_{31}$, hi. *bring* 2 C 35$_{24}$, עלה *go up* 2 S 19$_{35}$ 1 K 12$_{28}$ 2 K 16$_{5}$||Is 7$_{1}$ 2 K 24$_{10}$, hi. *bring up* 2 C 2$_{15}$, שׁוב *go back* 2 S 12$_{31}$||1 C 20$_{3}$ 2 S 17$_{20}$ 20$_{22}$ 2 K 23$_{20}$ 2 C 14$_{14}$ 19$_{8}$, hi. *bring back* 2 S 15$_{8.29}$, נוס *flee* 1 K 12$_{18}$||2 C 10$_{18}$, קהל *assemble* 1 K 8$_{1}$, שׁלח *send* 2 K 18$_{17}$, *stretch out* hand 2 S 24$_{16}$.

<COLL> עַל־חוֹמֹתַיִךְ יְרוּשָׁלַםִ הִפְקַדְתִּי שֹׁמְרִים *upon your walls, O Jerusalem, I have appointed watchers* Is 62$_{6}$, בִּימִינוֹ הָיָה הַקֶּסֶם יְרוּשָׁלַםִ *in his right hand is the decision for Jerusalem* Ezk 21$_{27}$, עֹמְדוֹת הָיוּ רַגְלֵינוּ בִּשְׁעָרַיִךְ יְרוּשָׁלָםִ *our feet have been standing within your gates, O Jerusalem* Ps 122$_{2}$, העדה ירושלים *the congregation that is in Jerusalem* 1QM 3$_{11}$, הופיעי ברנות ירושלים *shine forth in jubilation, O Jerusalem* 1QM 12$_{13}$.

יְרוּשָׁלַםִ *Jerusalem* || יְהוּדָה *Judah* 1 K 14$_{21}$ 2 K 18$_{22}$||Is 36$_{7}$ 2 K 23$_{1.2.24}$ Is 1$_{1}$ 2$_{1}$ Jr 4$_{3.4.5}$ 11$_{2.9}$ 13$_{9}$ 17$_{20.25}$ 18$_{11}$ 19$_{7}$ 25$_{2}$ 27$_{20.21}$ 29$_{2}$ 32$_{32}$ 34$_{19}$ 35$_{13}$ Jl 4$_{1.6}$ Zp 1$_{4}$ Zc 2$_{2}$ Ml 3$_{4}$ Dn 9$_{7}$ Ezr 1$_{3}$ 4$_{6}$ 9$_{9}$ 10$_{7}$ 1 C 5$_{41}$ 2$_{6}$ 11$_{14}$ 20$_{5.15.17.18.27}$ 24$_{6.9.18.23}$ 28$_{10}$ 29$_{8}$ 32$_{12.33}$ 34$_{3.5.29.30}$ 35$_{24}$ 36$_{4.10}$.

יְהוּדָה *Judah* || יְרוּשָׁלַםִ *Jerusalem* 2 K 21$_{12}$ 24$_{20}$ Is 3$_{1.8}$ 5$_{3}$ Jr 36$_{31}$ 40$_{1}$ 52$_{3}$ Zc 14$_{21}$ Ezr 2$_{1}$||Ne 7$_{6}$.

יְרוּשָׁלַםִ *Jerusalem* || צִיּוֹן *Zion* 2 K 19$_{31}$||Is 37$_{22}$ Zc 1$_{14}$.

צִיּוֹן *Zion* || יְרוּשָׁלַםִ *Jerusalem* 2 K 19$_{21}$||Is 37$_{22}$ Is 2$_{3}$||Mc 4$_{2}$ Is 4$_{3}$ 10$_{12}$ 24$_{23}$ 30$_{19}$ 31$_{9}$ 40$_{9}$ 41$_{27}$ 62$_{1}$ Jl 3$_{5}$ 4$_{16}$ Am 1$_{2}$ Mc 4$_{8}$ Zp 3$_{14}$ Zc 9$_{9}$ Ps 102$_{22}$.

Also 1QM 12$_{17}$ 4QTanḥ 1.1$_{3}$ 4QMidrEschat[b] 11$_{15}$ 4QAges[a] 5$_{4}$ 4QJub[b] 2$_{4}$ 4QapJoseph[b] 1$_{8}$ 4QpsEzek[a] 16.2$_{5}$ 4QpsEzek[e] 62.2$_{1}$ Seal 479$_{1}$ (Lachish, 8th/7th cent.) Stamp/Coin 21 (3rd cent.).*

⇒ (?) ירשׁ *take possession of*.

יָרֵחַ 27.2.1 n.m. **moon**—sf. יְרֵחֲךָ—<SUBJ> חשׁך *be darkened* Ec 12$_{2}$ (+ שֶׁמֶשׁ *sun*, כּוֹכָב *star*, אוֹר *light*), קדר *be darkened* Jl 2$_{10}$ 4$_{15}$ (both + שֶׁמֶשׁ), דמם *be motionless* Jos 10$_{12.13}$ (both + שֶׁמֶשׁ), עמד *stand still* Hb 3$_{11}$ (+ שֶׁמֶשׁ), אסף ni. *withdraw oneself* Is 60$_{20}$, הפך ni. *be turned into* Jl 3$_{4}$ (+ שֶׁמֶשׁ), שׁחה htpal. *prostrate oneself* Gn 37$_{9}$ (+ שֶׁמֶשׁ, כּוֹכָב).

הלך *go* Jb 31$_{26}$, ארח hi. *set on journey* Si 43$_{6(M)}$ (B ירח ירח appar. *the moon, as for the moon*), אור hi. *give light* Is 60$_{19}$ Ezk 32$_{7}$, נגה hi. *cause light to shine* Is 13$_{10}$, אהל hi. *shine* Jb 25$_{5}$ (יַאֲהִיל *it shines*; ms יָהֵל *it shines*, i.e. הלל hi.), נכה hi. *strike* Ps 121$_{6}$ (+ שֶׁמֶשׁ), הלל pi. *praise* Ps 148$_{3}$ (+ כּוֹכָב, שֶׁמֶשׁ).

<OBJ> ראה *see* Dt 4$_{19}$ (+ כּוֹכָב, שֶׁמֶשׁ) Ps 8$_4$ (+ כּוֹכָב), עשׂה *make* Ps 104$_{19}$ 136$_9$ (+ שֶׁמֶשׁ), כון pol. *establish* Ps 8$_4$ (+ כּוֹכָב).

<CSTR> חֻקֹּת יָרֵחַ *statutes*, i.e. fixed order, *of* Jr 31$_{35}$.

<ADJ> מָלֵא *full* Si 50$_6$.

<PREP> לְ of direction, *to*, + שׁטח *spread out* Jr 8$_2$, קטר pi. *burn incense* 2 K 23$_5$; introducing object, + שׁחה htpal. *prostrate oneself* Dt 17$_3$ 11QT 55$_{18}$.

כְּ *as* Si 50$_6$, + כון ni. *be established* Ps 89$_{38}$.

לִפְנֵי *before*, + ירא *fear* Ps 72$_5$.

עַד *unto*, i.e. even Jb 25$_5$ (or em. עַד *unto* to עִדֵּר the moon *was diminished*, or יָעַד *he has appointed*, or גָּעַר *he has rebuked*, or צִוָּה לְ *he has commanded* the moon, or עָד the moon *goes round*, or עָדָה *passes*).*

<COLL> יָרֵחַ *moon* + שֶׁמֶשׁ *sun*, e.g. Gn 37$_9$ Jos 10$_{12.13}$ Is 60$_{19}$ Ps 72$_5$ Jb 3$_{11}$, עַד־בְּלִי יָרֵחַ *until the moon is no more* Ps 72$_7$.*

⇒ יֶרַח *month*, יֶרַח *Jerah*, יָרוֹחַ *Jaroah*.

יֶרַח I $_{12.0.4.9}$ n.m. **month**—cstr. יֶרַח; pl. יְרָחִים; cstr. יַרְחֵי; sf. or du. I ירחו—perh. <NOM CL> ירחו אסף ירחו זרע *his two months are harvest, his two months are sowing* Gezer calendar$_1$, ירחו לקש *his two months are the time of late grass* Gezer calendar$_2$, ירחו זמר *his two months are pruning* Gezer calendar$_6$.

<OBJ> נחל ho. *be possessor of* Jb 7$_3$, עשׂה *make* 4QJub[a] 2$_8$, ספר *number* Jb 39$_2$.

<CSTR> יֶרַח יָמִים *month of days*, i.e. a full month Dt 21$_{13}$ 2 K 15$_{13}$, ירח צח *month of Zah* Arad ost. 20$_2$, perh. ירח קצר *month of harvest* Gezer Calendar$_{4.5}$, perh. ירח עצד פשת *month of flax-pulling* Gezer Calendar$_3$, perh. ירח קץ *month of summer fruit* Gezer Calendar$_7$, יַרְחֵי־שָׁוְא *months of emptiness* Jb 7$_3$, יַרְחֵי־קֶדֶם *months of antiquity* Jb 29$_2$; גֶּרֶשׁ יְרָחִים *produce of the months* Dt 33$_{14}$, מִסְפַּר *number of* Jb 3$_6$, רשית *beginning of* 1QS 10$_5$, [כ]ול ירחי *all the months of* 4QPrFêtes 131.1$_5$.

<APP> אֵתָנִים *Ethanim* 1 K 8$_2$, בּוּל *Bul* 1 K 6$_{38}$, זִו *Ziv* 1 K 6$_{37}$.

<PREP> בְּ of time, *in, during*, + יסד pu. *be founded* 1 K 6$_{37}$, כלה *be completed* 1 K 6$_{38}$, קהל ni. *assemble* 1 K 8$_2$, כחד hi. *destroy* Zc 11$_8$.

כְּ *as* Jb 29$_2$.

<COLL> וַתִּצְפְּנֵהוּ שְׁלֹשָׁה יְרָחִים *and she hid him for three months* Ex 2$_2$,

וּבָכְתָה אֶת־אָבִיהָ וְאֶת־אִמָּהּ יֶרַח יָמִים *and she shall weep for her father and her mother for a full month* Dt 21$_{13}$, וַיִּמְלֹךְ יֶרַח־יָמִים בְּשֹׁמְרוֹן *and he reigned for a full month in Samaria* 2 K 15$_{13}$.*

Also 2QapProph 3$_2$. ⇒ יָרֵחַ *moon*.

יֶרַח II $_2$ pr.n.m. **Jerah**—יָרַח—Shemite, son of Joktan Gn 10$_{26}$ 1 C 1$_{20}$, <OBJ> ילד *bear child* Gn 10$_{26}$‖1 C 1$_{20}$.

⇒ יָרֵחַ *moon*.

יְרֵחוֹ, see יְרִיחוֹ *Jericho*.

יְרֹחָם $_{10}$ pr.n.m. **Jeroham, 1.** Ephraimite (Levite in 1 C 6$_{27.34}$), son of Elihu, father of Elkanah and grandfather of Samuel, <CSTR> בֶּן־יְרֹחָם *son of Jeroham* 1 S 1$_1$ 1 C 6$_{19.27.34}$. <APP> בֵּן *son* 1 C 6$_{12}$. **2.** Benjaminite leader, <CSTR> בְּנֵי יְרֹחָם *sons of Jeroham* 1 C 8$_{27}$. **3.** Benjaminite, <CSTR> בְּנֵי יְרֹחָם *sons of Jeroham* 1 C 12$_8$. **4.** Danite, father of Azarel, <CSTR> בֶּן־יְרֹחָם *son of Jeroham* 1 C 27$_{22}$. **5.** military officer, father of Azariah, <CSTR> בֶּן־יְרֹחָם *son of Jeroham* 2 C 23$_1$. **6.** Benjaminite, ancestor of post-exilic family, <CSTR> בֶּן־יְרֹחָם *son of Jeroham* 1 C 9$_8$. **7.** priest, father of Adaiah, <CSTR> בֶּן־יְרֹחָם *son of Jeroham* Ne 9$_{12}$ 1 C 9$_{12}$. ⇒ רחם *be compassionate*.

יְרַחְמְאֵל $_{8.0.0.1}$ pr.n.m. **Jerahmeel, 1.** clan within Israel, <SUBJ> ילד ni. *be born* 1 C 2$_9$. <CSTR> בְּנֵי יְרַחְמְאֵל *sons of Jerahmeel* 1 C 2$_{25.33}$, בְּכוֹר *firstborn of* 1 C 2$_{27}$, אֲחִי *brother of* 1 C 2$_{42}$. <APP> בֵּן *son* 1 C 2$_9$. <PREP> לְ of possession, *(belonging) to, of*, + היה *be* 1 C 2$_{26}$.

2. Levite, son of Kish, <APP> בֵּן *son* 1 C 24$_{29}$.

3. officer and son of Jehoiakim who arrested Jeremiah, <OBJ> צוה pi. *command* Jr 36$_{26}$.

4. son of a king, perh. ident, with §3, <NOM CL> ירחמאל בן המלך *Jerahmeel was the son of the king* Seal 508$_1$ (T. Beit Mirsim?, 7th/6th cent.). <PREP> לְ of possession, *(belonging) to, of* Seal 508$_1$ (T. Beit Mirsim?, 7th/6th cent.).

⇒ רחם *be compassionate* + אֵל *God*; יְרַחְמְאֵלִי *Jerahmeelite*.

יְרַחְמְאֵלִי 2 gent. **Jerahmeelite**—plur. or collective sing. noun, **Jerahmeelites,** <CSTR> עָרֵי הַיְּרַחְמְאֵלִי *cities of the Jerahmeelites* 1 S 30$_{29}$, נֶגֶב הַיְּרַחְמְאֵלִי *Negeb of the Jerahmeelites* 1 S 27$_{10}$.
⇒ יְרַחְמְאֵל *Jerahmeel.*

יַרְחָע 2 pr.n.m. **Jarha,** Egyptian servantof Sheshan, a Jerahmeelite, <NOM CL> שְׁמוֹ יַרְחָע *his name was Jarha* 1 C 2$_{34}$. <APP> עֶבֶד *servant* 1 C 2$_{35}$. <PREP> לְ of direction, *to,* + נתן *give* 1 C 2$_{35}$.

ירט 2 vb. **be precipitate—Qal** 2 Pf. יָרַט; impf. יִרְטֵנִי—**be precipitate, be steep** (Nm 22$_{32}$), **push into another's hands** (Jb 16$_{11}$), <SUBJ> אֵל *God* Jb 16$_{11}$, דֶּרֶךְ *way* Nm 22$_{32}$. <OBJ> Job Jb 16$_{11}$. <PREP> עַל *upon, into,* + יָד *hand* of wicked one Jb 16$_{11}$; לְנֶגֶד *before,* + מַלְאָךְ *angel* of Y. Nm 22$_{32}$.

יְרִיאֵל 1 pr.n.m. **Jeriel,** Issacharite, son of Tola, <NOM CL>
וּבְנֵי תוֹלָע עֻזִּי וּרְפָיָה וִירִיאֵל *the sons of Tola were Uzzi and Rephaiah and Jeriel* 1 C 7$_{2}$.
⇒ ראה *see* + אֵל *God.*

[יָרִיב] I 3 n.[m.] **adversary**—sf. יְרִיבֶךָ; pl. sf. יְרִיבַי (יְרִיבָי), mss יְרִיבַיִךְ (Gnz יְרִיבַךְ)—<OBJ> ריב *contend (with)* Lm 3$_{58}$ (if em. רִיב *contention*). <CSTR> יְרִיבֵי נַפְשִׁי *adversaries of my soul* Lm 3$_{58}$ (if em.), קוֹל יְרִיבָי *voice of my adversaries* Jr 18$_{19}$ (or em. רִיב). <PREP> אֵת *with* (but perh. object-marker), + ריב *contend* Is 49$_{25}$ (1QIsa^{a} רִיב; :: בֵּן your *son*) Ps 35$_{1}$ (mss רִיב; || לחם ptc. *one who fights* with me). <SYN> לחם ptc. *one who fights.* <ANT> בֵּן *son.**
⇒ ריב *contend.*

יָרִיב II 3 pr.n.m. **Jarib, 1.** son of Simeon and grandson of Jacob and Leah, <NOM CL> בְּנֵי שִׁמְעוֹן ... יָרִיב *the sons of Simeon were ... Jarib* 1 C 4$_{24}$. **2.** companion of Ezra, <PREP> לְ of direction, *to,* + שׁלח *send* Ezr 8$_{16}$. **3.** priest, husband of non-Jewish wife, <SUBJ> מצא ni. *be found* Ezr 10$_{18}$.
⇒ ריב *contend.*

יְרִיבַי 1 pr.n.m. **Jeribai,** son of Elnaam and one of David's warriors 1 C 11$_{46}$, <NOM CL> גִּבּוֹרֵי הַחֲיָלִים ... יְרִיבַי *the warriors of the armies were ... Jeribai* 1 C 11$_{46}$.
⇒ ריב *contend.*

[יְרִידָה] 0.0.1 n.f. **descent**—sf. Q ירידתו—ירידתו מלמעלא *the descent into it is from high up* 3QTr 10$_{1}$, בירדא לסמל *in the descent to the left* 1$_{13}$ (others בירד אל סמל *while descending to the left;* בירכא לסמל *on the left-hand side*).*
⇒ ירד *go down.*

יְרִיָּה, see יְרִיָּהוּ *Jeriah.*

יְרִיָּהוּ 3 pr.n.m. **Jeriah**—יְרִיָּה—Kohathite Levite, eldest son of Hebron, <NOM CL> בְּנֵי חֶבְרוֹן יְרִיָּהוּ *the sons of Hebron were Jeriah* 1 C 23$_{19}$ 24$_{23(mss)}$, וּבְנֵי יְרִיָּהוּ *and my sons were Jeriah* 1 C 24$_{23(L)}$,
יְרִיָּה הָרֹאשׁ לַחֶבְרוֹנִי *Jeriah was the chief of the Hebronites* 1 C 26$_{31}$.
⇒ ראה *see* + אֵל *God.*

יְרִיחֹה, see יְרִיחוֹ *Jericho.*

יְרִיחוֹ 58.0.3 pl.n. **Jericho**—יְרֵחוֹ (יְרִיחֹה, יְרֵחוֹ)—city near the Jordan, mod. T. es-Sulṭān (e.g. Nm 22$_{1}$ Dt 32$_{49}$ Jos 2$_{2.3}$ 6$_{1}$ 2 K 25$_{5}$).
<SUBJ> היה *be* Jos 18$_{21}$, סגר *be closed* Jos 6$_{1}$.
<OBJ> ראה *see* Jos 2$_{1}$, רגל pi. *spy out* Jos 6$_{25}$, נתן *give* Jos 6$_{2}$, בנה *build* Jos 6$_{26}$ 1 K 16$_{34}$.
<CSTR> בִּקְעַת יְרֵחוֹ *valley of Jericho* Dt 34$_{3}$, עַרְבוֹת יְרִיחוֹ *plains of Jericho* Jos 3$_{16}$ 5$_{10}$ 2 K 25$_{5}$||Jr 39$_{5}$||52$_{8}$, מִזְרָח *east border of* Jos 4$_{19}$, כָּתֵף *shoulder of* Jos 18$_{12}$, מֵי *waters of* Jos 16$_{1}$, מֶלֶךְ *king of* Jos 2$_{2.3}$ 10$_{28.30}$ 12$_{9}$, בַּעֲלֵי־ *lords of* Jos 24$_{11}$, אַנְשֵׁי יְרֵחוֹ *men of Jericho* Ne 3$_{2}$, בְּנֵי *sons of Jericho* Ezr 2$_{34}$||Ne 7$_{36}$.
<APP> עִיר *city* Jos 6$_{26}$ 18$_{21}$.
<PREP> לְ of benefit, *to, for,* + עשׂה *do* Jos 8$_{2}$ 9$_{3}$ 10$_{1}$; בְּ of place, *in, at, by* 2 K 25$_{5.15}$ 4QParaKings 9$_{8}$, + היה *be* Jos 5$_{13}$, ישׁב *dwell* 2 S 10$_{5}$||1 C 19$_{5}$ 2 K 2$_{18}$; introducing object, + פגע *reach* Jos 16$_{7}$; מִן of direction, *from* 3QTr

5$_{13}$, + עלה *go up* Jos 16$_{1}$, שׁלח *send* Jos 7$_{2}$; אֶל *to*, + בוא *come* Jos 24$_{11}$; עַל־פְּנֵי *opposite* Dt 32$_{49}$ 34$_{1}$; נֶגֶד *opposite*, + עבר *pass over* Jos 3$_{16}$; יְרִיחוֹ (without ה- of direction), *at, in, to, into,* etc. *(Jericho)*, + בוא *come* 2 K 2$_{4}$, שׁלח *send* 2 K 2$_{4}$; יְרֵחוֹ (without ה- of direction), *at, in, to, into,* etc. *Jericho*, + בוא hi. *bring* 2 C 28$_{15}$.

<COLL> מֵעֵבֶר לְיַרְדֵּן יְרֵחוֹ *opposite the Jordan (at) Jericho*, + חנה *encamp* Nm 22$_{1}$ 33$_{48}$, לקח *take* Nm 34$_{15}$, נתן *give*, i.e. appoint Jos 20$_{8}$ (יְרִיחוֹ) 1 C 6$_{63}$, נחל pi. *distribute* Jos 13$_{32}$ (יְרִיחוֹ), פקד *muster* Nm 26$_{63}$ (יְרִיחוֹ), דבר pi. *speak* Nm 33$_{50}$ 35$_{1}$, בכה *weep* 4QapJoshua^{a} 14$_{2}$; וַיֵּצֵא ... מִיַּרְדֵּן יְרִיחוֹ *and it went out ... from the Jordan (at) Jericho* Jos 16$_{1}$, אֲשֶׁר עַל יַרְדֵּן יְרֵחוֹ *which is by the Jordan (at) Jericho* Nm 31$_{12}$.

יְרֵמוֹת, see יְרִימוֹת *Jerimoth*.

יְרִימוֹת 7.0.0.1 pr.n.m. **Jerimoth**—יְרִמוֹת—**1.** Benjaminite, son of Bela, <NOM CL> וּבְנֵי בֶלַע ... וִירִימוֹת *and the sons of Bela were ... Jerimoth* 1 C 7$_{7}$.

2. Merarite Levite, son of Mushi, <NOM CL> בְּנֵי מוּשִׁי ... וִירִימוֹת *the sons of Mushi were ... and Jerimoth* 1 C 24$_{30}$.

3. Benjaminite warrior 1 C 12$_{6}$.

4. Levite of the line of Heman, musician, ident. with יְרֵמוֹת *Jeremoth* (1 C 25$_{22}$), <NOM CL> בְּנֵי הֵימָן ... וִירִימוֹת *the sons of Heman were ... and Jerimoth* 1 C 25$_{4}$.

5. Naphtalite, son of Azriel, <NOM CL> לְנַפְתָּלִי יְרִימוֹת בֶּן־עַזְרִיאֵל *belonging to Naphtali was Jerimoth the son of Azriel* 1 C 27$_{19}$.

6. son of David and father of Mahalath the wife and cousin of Rehoboam, <CSTR> בַּת־יְרִימוֹת *daughter of Jerimoth* 2 C 11$_{18}$.

7. Levite, temple treasury official under Hezekiah, <NOM CL> וִיחִיאֵל ... וִירִימוֹת ... פְּקִידִים *and Jehiel ... and Jerimoth ... were overseers* 2 C 31$_{13}$.

8. Seal 361$_{1}$, <PREP> לְ of possession, *(belonging) to, of* Seal 361$_{1}$ (7th cent.).

→ (?) ירם *be high*.

יְרִיעָה 54.0.1 n.f. **curtain**—pl. יְרִיעוֹת (יְרִיעֹת); cstr. יְרִיעוֹת (יְרִיעֹת); sf. יְרִיעֹתַי, יְרִיעוֹתֵיהֶם—of tent (Is 54$_{2}$ Jr 4$_{20}$ 10$_{20}$ 49$_{29}$ Hb 3$_{7}$ Ca 1$_{5}$), specif. of tabernacle, (e.g. Ex 26$_{1.2.2.2.8.8}$ Nm 4$_{25}$ 2 S 7$_{2}$||1 C 17$_{1}$).

<SUBJ> נטה hi. *be stretched out* Is 54$_{2}$, חבר *be joined* Ex 26$_{3.3}$, לקח ni. *be taken* Jr 49$_{29}$ (|| אֹהֶל *tent*), שׁדד pu. *be devastated* Jr 4$_{20}$ (|| אֹהֶל *tent*), רגז *tremble* Hb 3$_{7}$.

<OBJ> עשׂה *make* Ex 26$_{7.7}$||36$_{14.14}$, חבר pi. *join* Ex 26$_{6.9}$||36$_{10.16}$ 36$_{13.10}$, כפל *double over* Ex 26$_{9}$, נשׂא *raise* Nm 4$_{25}$, קום hi. *raise up* Jr 10$_{20}$.

<CSTR> יְרִיעוֹת אֶרֶץ *curtains of the land of* Hb 3$_{7}$, יְרִיעֹת הָאֹהֶל *the curtains of the tent* Ex 26$_{12.13}$, הַמִּשְׁכָּן *of the tabernacle* Nm 4$_{25}$, יְרִיעוֹת מִשְׁכְּנוֹתַיִךְ *curtains of your dwelling place* Is 54$_{2}$, יְרִיעֹת עִזִּים *curtains of goats' hair* Ex 26$_{7}$||36$_{14}$ 4QpsEzek^{d} 17$_{2}$ (יריעות), יְרִיעוֹת שְׁלֹמֹה *curtains of Solomon* Ca 1$_{5}$.

שְׂפַת הַיְרִיעָה *lip*, i.e. edge, *of the curtain* Ex 26$_{4.4.10.10}$||36$_{11.11.17.17}$, קָצֶה *edge of* Ex 26$_{5}$||36$_{12}$, אֹרֶךְ *length of* Ex 26$_{2.8}$||36$_{9.15}$, אֹרֶךְ יְרִיעֹת *length of the curtains of* Ex 26$_{13}$, רֹחַב הַיְרִיעָה *breadth of the curtain* Ex 36$_{15}$, חֲמֵשׁ הַיְרִיעֹת *five curtains* Ex 26$_{3.9}$||36$_{10.16}$, חֲצִי הַיְרִיעָה *half of the curtain* Ex 26$_{12}$, כָּל־הַיְרִיעֹת *all of the curtains* Ex 26$_{2}$||36$_{9}$.

<PREP> לְ of benefit, *to, for* Ex 26$_{2.8}$||36$_{9.15}$.

בְּ *in, with, on* 4QpsEzek^{d} 17$_{2}$, + עדף *be left over* Ex 26$_{12}$, עשׂה *make* Ex 26$_{5}$||36$_{12}$.

כְּ *as* Ps 104$_{2}$.

בְּתוֹךְ *among*, + ישׁב *dwell* 2 S 7$_{2}$.

תַּחַת *underneath* 1 C 17$_{1}$.

<COLL> וְאֶת־הַמִּשְׁכָּן תַּעֲשֶׂה עֶשֶׂר יְרִיעֹת *you shall make the tabernacle with ten curtains* Ex 26$_{1}$||36$_{8}$.

הַיְרִיעָה הָאַחַת *one curtain* Ex 26$_{2.8}$||36$_{9.15}$, הַיְרִיעָה הָאֶחָת *one curtain* Ex 26$_{2.5.8}$||36$_{9.12.15}$, חָמֵשׁ יְרִיעֹת *five curtains* Ex 26$_{3}$||36$_{10}$, שֵׁשׁ הַיְרִיעֹת *six curtains* Ex 26$_{9}$||36$_{16}$, עֶשֶׂר יְרִיעֹת *ten curtains* Ex 26$_{1}$||36$_{8}$, עַשְׁתֵּי־עֶשְׂרֵה יְרִיעֹת *eleven curtains* Ex 26$_{7.8}$||36$_{14.15}$.

הַיְרִיעָה הַשִּׁשִּׁית *the sixth curtain* Ex 26$_{9}$.

<SYN> אֹהֶל *tent*.

→ ירע *quiver*.

יְרִיעוֹת 1 pr.n.f. **Jerioth**, one of the two wives of the Judahite Caleb 1 C 2$_{18}$, <OBJ> ילד hi. *become father of* 1 C 2$_{18}$.

→ ירע *tremble*.

יָרֵךְ 34.0.1 n.f. **thigh, side, base**—cstr. יֶרֶךְ; sf. יְרֵכִי, יְרֵכְךָ, יְרֵכָהּ, יְרֵכוֹ; du. יְרֵכַיִם; sf. יְרֵכַיִךְ; Sam יְרֵכֶיהָ—**1. thigh, hip, hip joint,** perh. **genitals;*** as food (Ezk 24$_4$), <SUBJ> נפל *fall* Nm 5$_{21.22}$ (if em. hi. *cause to fall*) 5$_{27}$ (all three || בֶּטֶן *womb, abdomen*). <OBJ> נתן *give*, i.e. cause (to fall) Nm 5$_{21}$, נפל hi. *cause to fall* Nm 5$_{22}$ (or em.), אסף *gather* Ezk 24$_4$ (|| כָּתֵף *shoulder*). <CSTR> יֶרֶךְ אַבְרָהָם *thigh of Abraham* Gn 24$_9$, יַעֲקֹב *of Jacob* Gn 32$_{26.33}$ Ex 1$_5$ (יֶרֶךְ־), יְמִינוֹ *of his right side*, i.e. his right thigh Jg 3$_{16.21}$; כַּף הַיָּרֵךְ *socket of the hip joint* Gn 32$_{33}$, כַּף־יֶרֶךְ *socket of hip joint of* Gn 32$_{26.33}$, יְרֵכוֹ *of his hip-joint* Gn 32$_{26}$, חַמּוּקֵי יְרֵכַיִךְ *the curves of your thighs* Ca 7$_2$ (Gnz חָמוּקֵי), יֹצְאֵי יֶרֶךְ־ *those going out of the thigh of* Jacob, i.e. Jacob's own children Ex 1$_5$, יֹצְאֵי יְרֵכוֹ *those going out of his thigh* Gn 46$_{26}$ Jg 8$_{30}$. <APP> נֵתַח *cut* of meat Ezk 24$_4$. <PREP> עַל *upon*, + צלע *limp* Gn 32$_{32}$; *against, next to* Ca 3$_8$, + נכה hi. *strike* Jg 15$_8$ (+ שׁוֹק *leg, thigh*), ספק *clap (hand)* Jr 31$_{19}$ (or em. יְמֵי I groaned for *the days of* shame) Ezk 21$_{17}$ (if em. אֶל in same sense), שׂים *place* sword Ex 32$_{27}$, חגר *gird* sword Jg 3$_{16}$ Ps 45$_4$; מֵעַל *from (against)*, + לקח *take* sword Jg 3$_{21}$ (+ בֶּטֶן *abdomen*); עַד *unto*, + היה *be*, i.e. extend Ex 28$_{42}$ (+ מֹתֶן from the *hip* to the thigh); תַּחַת *under*, + שׂים *place* hand (in oath ritual) Gn 24$_{2.9}$ 47$_{29}$.

2. north or south **side** of tabernacle, altar, <CSTR> יֶרֶךְ הַמִּשְׁכָּן *side of the tabernacle* Ex 40$_{22.24}$ Nm 3$_{29.35}$, הַמִּזְבֵּחַ *of the altar* Lv 1$_{11}$ 2 K 16$_{14}$. <PREP> עַל *at, on*, + שׂים *place* cult objects Ex 40$_{22.24}$, נתן *give*, i.e. place, altar 2 K 16$_{14}$, שׁחט *slaughter* sacrificial beast Lv 1$_{11}$, חנה *encamp* Nm 3$_{29.35}$.

3. base of lampstand, <SUBJ> היה *be* of one piece with the lampstand Ex 25$_{31}$||37$_{17}$ (|| קָנֶה *reed*, i.e. shaft). <PREP> עַד *unto* Nm 8$_4$ (|| פֶּרַח *flower*, i.e. petal).

4. deepest place, hollow, recess of cistern (בּוֹר) or vault (צְרִיחַ), <CSTR> ירך קרקעו *the deepest place of its base*, i.e. right at the bottom, or *a hollow of*, i.e. in, *its base* 3QTr 1$_7$ (others זֶרֶב appar. *lining, plaster* of base; בור בקרקעו). <APP> תָּוֶךְ *middle* 6$_2$, רוּחַ *side* 3QTr 9$_8$ (others ב[צ]ריח *in the vault*). <PREP> בְּ of place, *in* 3QTr 1$_7$ 6$_2$ (בירך כלין *in the recess are vessels*; others בור בן[ו] כלין *a cistern, in which are vessels*, or בת מטבלין *a bath of untithed goods*), + חפר *dig* (unless pass. *be dug*, i.e. buried) 9$_8$ (others זֶרֶב).

<SYN> §1 בֶּטֶן *womb, abdomen*, כָּתֵף *shoulder*; §3 קָנֶה *reed*, i.e. shaft, פֶּרַח *flower*, i.e. petal.

⇒ יַרְכָה *flank*.

יַרְכָה 28.0.1.1 n.f. **flank**—sf. יַרְכָתוֹ, יַרְכָתָם (Qr ירכתים); du. יַרְכָתַיִם (יַרְכָתָיִם); cstr. יַרְכְּתֵי־—**flank, side, rear, distant part, innermost part,** in ref. to **distant border,** of Zebulun (Gn 49$_{13}$), in dual to **distant part, innermost part** of any object (e.g. Jg 19$_{1.18}$ 2 K 19$_{23}$||Is 37$_{24}$ Is 14$_{15}$ Ps 128$_3$), <NOM CL> יַרְכָתוֹ עַל־צִידֹן *its distant border is at Sidon* Gn 49$_{13}$, הַר־צִיּוֹן יַרְכְּתֵי־צָפוֹן *Mount Zion is in the remotest parts of the north* Ps 48$_3$.

<CSTR> יַרְכְּתֵי־אָרֶץ *remotest parts of the earth* Jr 6$_{22}$ 25$_{32}$ 31$_8$ 50$_{41}$, צָפוֹן *of the north* Is 14$_{13}$ Ezk 38$_{6.15}$ 39$_2$ Ps 48$_3$, הַר־אֶפְרַיִם *of Mount Ephraim* Jg 19$_{1.18}$, לְבָנוֹן *of Lebanon* 2 K 19$_{23}$||Is 37$_{24}$, יַרְכְּתֵי הַמְּעָרָה *innermost parts of the cave* 1 S 24$_4$, יַרְכְּתֵי הַמִּשְׁכָּן *rear of the tabernacle* Ex 26$_{22}$||36$_{27}$, הַבַּיִת *of the house* 1 K 6$_{16(Qr;mss)}$ Am 6$_{10}$, יַרְכְּתֵי בֵיתֶךָ *recesses of your house* Ps 128$_3$, הַסְּפִינָה *of the ship* Jon 1$_5$, יַרְכְּתֵי־בוֹר *depths of the pit* Is 14$_{15}$ Ezk 32$_{23}$ 4QBéat 22$_3$.

<PREP> לְ of benefit, *to, for*, + עשׂה *make* Ex 26$_{22}$||36$_{27}$; *at* Ex 26$_{27}$||36$_{32}$; בְּ of place, *in, at* Ezk 46$_{19(Qr)}$ Am 6$_{10}$ Ps 128$_3$ Ophel monumental inscr.$_3$, + ישׁב *dwell* 1 S 24$_4$ Is 14$_{13}$, גור *sojourn* Jg 19$_1$, נתן ni. *be given*, i.e. be placed Ezk 32$_{23}$; *in, with*, + עשׂה *make* Ex 26$_{23}$||36$_{28}$; מִן of direction, *from*, + עור ni. *be stirred up* Jr 6$_{22}$ 25$_{32}$ 50$_{41}$, בוא *come* Ezk 38$_{15}$, עלה hi. *bring up* Ezk 39$_2$, קבץ pi. *gather together* Jr 31$_8$; *at*, + בנה *build* 1 K 6$_{16}$; אֶל *to*, + ירד *go down* Jon 1$_5$ 4QBéat 22$_3$, ho. *be brought down* Is 14$_{15}$; עַד *unto*, + עבר *pass by* Jg 19$_{18}$.

<COLL> עָלִיתִי ... יַרְכְּתֵי לְבָנוֹן *I have gone up ... (to) the remotest parts of Lebanon* 2 K 19$_{23}$||Is 37$_{24}$.

Also 4QParaKings 44$_2$ (ירכת[י]).

⇒ יָרֵךְ *thigh*.

*__ירם__ 6 vb. **be high—Qal** Impf. + waw וַנִּירָם; pass. ptc. יָרוּם—(unless יָרוּם = *it/he will be high*, i.e. from רום, and וַנִּירָם = *and we shot at them*, from ירה), **1.** active, **become high, exalted,** וַנִּירָם אָבַד חֶשְׁבּוֹן *and we became exalted but Heshbon passed away* Nm 21$_{30}$. **2.** pass., **be**

exalted, be high (Ps 61$_3$), <SUBJ> ״י *Y.* Ps 18$_{47}$ (+ ברך pass. *be blessed*), עֶבֶד *servant* Is 52$_{13}$ (|| נשׂא ni. *be raised,* גבה *be high*), ראשׁ *head* of worshipper Ps 27$_6$, לֵבָב *heart* of multitude Dn 11$_{12(Kt)}$ (Qr וְרָם *and is high;* || נשׂא ni.), צוּר *rock,* i.e. mountain Ps 61$_3$. <PREP> עַל *over,* + אוֹיֵב *enemy* Ps 27$_6$. <SYN> נשׂא ni. *be raised,* גבה *be high.*

→ (?) יְרִימוֹת *Jerimoth,* יְרֵמוֹת *Jeremoth,* יְרֵמַי *Jeremai,* (?) יַרְמוּת *Jarmuth,* (?) יִרְמְיָהוּ *Jeremiah;* see also רום *be high.*

יָרָם, see יוֹרָם *Joram.*

יַרְמוּת 7 pl.n. **Jarmuth, 1.** town in the lowland of Judah, mod. Kh. Yarmūk 30 km SW of Jerusalem, <NOM CL> בַּשְּׁפֵלָה אֶשְׁתָּאוֹל ... יַרְמוּת *in the lowland were Eshtaol ... Jarmuth* Jos 15$_{35}$. <CSTR> מֶלֶךְ יַרְמוּת *king of Jarmuth* Jos 10$_{3.5.23}$ 12$_{11}$. <PREP> בְּ of place, *in, at,* + ישׁב *dwell* Ne 11$_{29}$.

2. Levitical city in Isaachar, <OBJ> נתן *give* Jos 21$_{29}$.

→ (?) ירם *be high.*

יְרָמוֹת, see יְרֵמוֹת *Jeremoth.*

יְרֵמוֹת 6 pr.n.m. **Jeremoth, 1.** Benjaminite, son of Becher, <NOM CL> וּבְנֵי בֶכֶר זְמִירָה וְיוֹעָשׁ ... וִירֵמוֹת *and the sons of Becher were Zemirah and Joash ... and Jeremoth* 1 C 7$_8$.

2. Merarite Levite, son of Mushi, ident. with יְרִימוֹת *Jerimoth* (1 C 24$_{30}$), <NOM CL> בְּנֵי מוּשִׁי ... וִירֵימוֹת *the sons of Mushi were ... and Jeremoth* 1 C 23$_{23}$.

3. Benjaminite, descendant of Elpaal, perh. ident. with יְרֹחָם *Jeroham* (1 C 24$_{30}$), <NOM CL> וּבְנֵי אֶלְפַּעַל עֵבֶר ... וִירֵמוֹת *and the sons of Elpaal were Eber ... and Jeremoth* 1 C 8$_{14}$.

4. Levite, member of the Heman family of musicians, ident. with יְרִימוֹת *Jerimoth* (1 C 25$_4$) <PREP> לְ of possession, *(belonging) to, of* 1 C 25$_{22}$.

5. member of Elam family, husband of non-Jewish wife, <APP> בֵּן *son* Ezr 10$_{26}$.

6. member of Zattu family, husband of non-Jewish wife, <APP> בֵּן *son* Ezr 10$_{27}$.

→ ירם *be high.*

יְרֵמַי 1.0.0.1 pr.n.m. **Jeremai, 1.** member of Hashum, husband of non-Jewish wife Ezr 10$_{33}$, <APP> בֵּן *son* Ezr 10$_{33}$.

2. Seal 307$_1$, <PREP> לְ of possession, *(belonging) to, of* Seal 307$_1$ (6th/5th cent.).

יִרְמְיָה, see יִרְמְיָהוּ *Jeremiah.*

יִרְמְיָהוּ 144.1.7.12 pr.n.m. **Jeremiah**—יִרְמְיָה—**1.** Manassite chief, <APP> ראשׁ *head,* i.e. principal leader 1 C 5$_{24}$.

2. Benjaminite, one of David's warriors, 1 C 12$_5$. **3.** Gadite, another of David's warriors, <APP> אִישׁ *man* 1 C 12$_{11}$, גִּבּוֹר *warrior* 1 C 12$_{11}$. <COLL> יִרְמְיָה הַחֲמִשִׁי *Jeremiah the fifth* 1 C 12$_{11}$. **4.** Gadite, a third of David's warriors, <APP> אִישׁ *man* 1 C 12$_{14}$, גִּבּוֹר *warrior* 1 C 12$_{14}$. <COLL> יִרְמְיָהוּ הָעֲשִׂירִי *Jeremiah the tenth* 1 C 12$_{14}$.

5. father of Hamutal the wife of Josiah, <CSTR> בַּת־יִרְמְיָהוּ *daughter of Jeremiah* 2 K 23$_{31}$ 24$_{18}$||Jr 52$_1$.

6. prophet and priest, the son of Hilkiah, from Anathoth, <SUBJ> היה *be* 4QpsEzek^a 16.2$_4$, כלא *be imprisoned* Jr 32$_2$, סתר ni. *be hidden* Jr 36$_{19}$, שׁמע *hear* Jr 42$_4$, ישׁב *dwell* Jr 37$_{16.21}$ 38$_{13.28}$ 39$_{14}$ 40$_6$, בוא *come* Jr 19$_{14}$ 37$_{4.12.16}$ 40$_6$ 43$_7$, הלך *go* Jr 28$_{11}$ 4QpsEzek^a 16.1$_6$, יצא *go out* Jr 37$_{4.12}$, טבע *sink* Jr 38$_6$, נפל *fall,* i.e. desert Jr 37$_{13.14}$, עשׂה *do* Jr 38$_{12}$, לקח *take* Jr 36$_{32}$, נתן *give* Jr 36$_{32}$, שׂים *place* Jr 38$_{12}$, חלק hi. *participate in distribution* Jr 37$_{12}$.

שׁלח *send* Jr 29$_1$, מנע *hold back* Jr 42$_4$, כחד pi. *hide* Jr 38$_{14}$, מות *die* Jr 38$_{9.24}$, כתב *write* Jr 51$_{60}$, קרא *call* Jr 36$_4$, אמר *say* Jr 20$_3$ 21$_3$ 26$_{12}$ 28$_{5.6.15}$ 32$_6$ 35$_{18}$ 37$_{14.17.17.18}$ 38$_{15.17.20}$ 42$_4$ 44$_{20.24}$ 51$_{61}$ CD 8$_{20}$, דבר pi. *speak* Jr 25$_2$ 26$_{7.8.8}$ 34$_6$ 36$_4$ 38$_1$ 43$_{1.2}$ 45$_1$, נגד hi. *declare* Jr 38$_{15.27}$ 42$_4$, פלל htp. *pray* Jr 37$_3$ 42$_{2.4}$, צוה pi. *command* Jr 36$_{5.8}$ 51$_{59}$, יעץ *give counsel* Jr 38$_{15}$, נבא ni. *prophesy* Jr 20$_1$ 25$_{13}$ 26$_{12}$, htp. Jr 29$_{27}$, קין pol. *utter lament* 2 C 35$_{25}$.

<OBJ> שׁמע *hear* Jr 20$_1$ 26$_7$, עלה hi. *bring up* Jr 38$_{10.13}$, משׁך *draw up* Jr 38$_{13}$, יצא hi. *bring out* Jr 20$_3$, לקח *take* Jr 36$_{26}$ 38$_{6.14}$ 39$_{14}$ 40$_1$ 43$_6$, תפשׂ *take hold of* Jr 26$_8$ 37$_{13}$, שׁלך hi. *throw* Jr 38$_{6.9}$, נתן *give,* i.e. place Jr 20$_2$ 26$_{24}$ 37$_{4.15.17}$ 38$_{7.16}$ 39$_{14}$, פקד hi. *assign* Jr 37$_{21}$, שׁלח *send* Jr 26$_{12}$ 42$_5$ 43$_2$, pi. *send away* Jr 38$_6$ 40$_1$, סתר hi. *hide* Jr 36$_{26}$, נכה hi. *strike* Jr 20$_2$ 37$_{15}$, מות hi. *kill* Jr 38$_{15.16}$, שׁאל *ask* Jr 38$_{14.27}$,

ענה *answer* Jr 44_{15}.

<CSTR> צַוְּאר יִרְמְיָה *neck of Jeremiah* Jr $28_{10.12}$, אָזְנֵי יִרְמְיָהוּ *ears of Jeremiah* Jr 29_{29}, פִּי *mouth of* Jr $36_{4.27.32}$ 45_1 Ezr 1_1||2 C 36_{22} 2 C 36_{21}, קול ימריה *voice of Jeremiah* 4QpsEzek^a 16.1_8, יַד יִרְמְיָהוּ *hand of*, i.e. by means of, *Jeremiah* Jr 37_2 50_1 Si 49_7, דִּבְרֵי *words of* Jr 1_1 26_{20} 36_{10} 51_{64} 4QpsEzek^a 39_2 ((ירמי[ה]), ספר ירמ[יה] *book of Jeremiah* 4QCat 1_4.

<APP> נָבִיא *prophet* Jr 20_2 25_2 $28_{5.6.10.11.12.15}$ $29_{1.29}$ 32_2 34_6 $36_{8.26}$ $37_{2.3.13}$ $38_{9.10.14}$ $42_{2.4}$ 43_6 45_1 $46_{1.13}$ 47_1 49_{34} 50_1 51_{59} Dn 9_2 2 C 36_{12} 4QpsEzek^a $16.1_{2.6}$ 25_1 (יר[מיהו]) 4QpsEzek^e 3_5 (י[רמיה]).

<PREP> לְ of direction, *to*, + נתן *give* Jr 37_{21}; לְ of benefit, *to*, *for*, + עשׂה *do* Jr 38_9; introducing object, + לקח *take* Jr 40_2; בְּ introducing object, + גער *rebuke* Jr 29_{27}, תפשׂ *take hold of* Jr 37_{14}; מִן of direction, *from*, + חרשׁ hi. *become silent* Jr 38_{27}; אֶל *to*, + היה *be* Jr 7_1 11_1 14_1 18_1 21_1 27_1 28_{12} 29_{30} 30_1 $32_{1.6.26}$ $33_{1.19.23}$ $34_{1.8.12}$ $35_{1.12}$ $36_{1.27}$ 37_6 39_{15} 40_1 42_7 43_8 44_1 46_1 47_1 49_{34} Dn 9_2, שׁמע *hear* Jr 37_{14} 38_{15}, קהל ni. *be assembled* Jr 26_9, בוא *come* Jr 38_{27}, hi. *bring* Jr 37_{14}, שׁלח *send* Jr 37_3, pi. *send away* Jr 38_{11}, אמר *say* Jr $38_{12.14.19.24}$ 40_2 $42_{2.5}$ 43_2, דבר pi. *speak* Jr 46_{13}, שׁבע ni. *swear oath* Jr 38_{16}; עַל *upon*, *to*, + היה *be* Jr 25_1; *against*, + קצף *be angry* Jr 37_{15}, חשׁב *plan*, i.e. plot Jr 18_{18}; *concerning*, + צוה pi. *command* Jr 39_{11}; אֵת *with*, + היה *be* Jr 26_{24}; לִפְנֵי *before*, + נפל *fall*, i.e. come Jr 42_2; מִלִּפְנֵי *from (before)*, + כנע ni. *humble oneself* 2 C 36_{12}.

<COLL> מָה־אַתָּה רֹאֶה יִרְמְיָהוּ *what do you see, O Jeremiah?* Jr 1_{11} 24_3.

Also 4QpsEzek^a 16.2_3 ((ירמי[ה]) 16.2_6.

7. Rechabite, son of Haazziniah and father of Jaazaniah, <CSTR> בֶּן־יִרְמְיָהוּ *son of Jeremiah* Jr 35_3.

8. priest who returned from exile with Zerubbabel, <SUBJ> עלה *go up* Ne 12_1. <APP> כֹּהֵן *priest* Ne 12_1. <PREP> לְ of possession, *(belonging) to, of* Ne 12_{12}.

9. priest, signatory of covenant in time of Nehemiah, <NOM CL> עַל הַחֲתוּמִים נְחֶמְיָה ... יִרְמְיָה *upon (the documents) that were sealed are Nehemiah ... (and) Jeremiah* Ne 10_3 (or em. הַחוֹתְמִים *those who sealed*, i.e. signed, or אֵלֶּה הַחוֹתְמִים *these are the signatories*).

10. Judahite prince at dedication of walls of Jerusalem <COLL> יְהוּדָה וּבִנְיָמִן וּשְׁמַעְיָה וְיִרְמְיָה *Judah and Benjamin and Shemaiah and Jeremiah* Ne 12_{34}.

11. Lachish ost. 1_4, <CSTR> בן ירמיהו *son of Jeremiah* Lachish ost. 1_4. **12.** Arad ost 24_{15}, <CSTR> בן ירמיהו *son of Jeremiah* Arad ost 24_{15}. **13.** Arad ost. 80_2. **14.** Seal 58_2, <APP> Jeremiah, Seal 58_2 (Egypt). <PREP> לְ of possession, *(belonging) to, of* Seal 58_2 (Egypt). **15.** Seal 248_1, <PREP> לְ of possession, *(belonging) to, of* Seal 248_1 (8th cent.). **16.** Seal 258_1, <PREP> לְ of possession, *(belonging) to, of* Seal 258_1 (Lachish, 7th cent.). **17.** Seal 364_1, <PREP> לְ of possession, *(belonging) to, of* Seal 364_1 (8th/7th cent.). **18.** Seal 411_2, appar. son of Jeremiah, Seal 411 (Beth-Shemesh, 7th/6th cent.). **19.** Seal 578_1, <PREP> לְ of possession, *(belonging) to, of* Seal 578_1 (T. Beit Mirsim?, 7th/6th cent.). **20.** Seal 763_2, <CSTR> בן ירמיהו *son of Jeremiah* Seal 763_2 (c. 700). **21.** Seal 894_2, <CSTR> בן ירמיהו *son of Jeremiah* Seal 894_2 (7th cent.). **22.** Seal 899_1, <PREP> לְ of possession, *(belonging) to, of* Seal 899_1 (Babylon?, 8th/7th cent).

⇒ (?) ירם *be high* + Y.

ירע 1 vb. **tremble—Qal** 1 Pf. יָרְעָה—**tremble, be faint-hearted,** <SUBJ> נֶפֶשׁ *soul* Is 15_4 (1QIsa^a ירע, perh. יֵרַע *is troubled*, from רעע *be evil*). <PREP> לְ of benefit, *to, for*, + חָלוּץ *armed one* Is 15_4.*

⇒ תִּרְעַת *majesty*, יְרִיעֹת *Jerioth*; see also ירה *be terrified*.

יִרְפְּאֵל 1 pl.n. **Irpeel,** town in Benjamin, prob. mod. Rafat, 10 km NW of Jerusalem Jos 18_{27}, <SUBJ> היה *be* Jos 18_{27}. <APP> עִיר *city* Jos 18_{27}.

⇒ רפא *heal* + אֵל *God*.

ירק 3.0.1 vb. **spit—Qal** 3 Pf. יָרַק; + waw וַיָּרְקָה; Q וירקו; inf. יָרֹק—**spit** in another's face as curse Nm 12_{14} Dt 25_9, <SUBJ> אָב *father* Nm 12_{14}, יְבָמָה *brother's wife* Dt 25_9; subj. not specified, Nm 12_{14} 4QErr 1_4.

<PREP> בְּ introducing object, + פָּנִים *face* Nm 12_{14} Dt 25_9.*

יָרָק 5 n.m. **herbage**—cstr. יְרַק—collective, **herbage, vegetables** (Dt 11_{10} 1 K 21_2 2 K 19_{26}||Is 37_{27} Pr 15_{17}), <CSTR> יְרַק דֶּשֶׁא *green shoots of grass* 2 K 19_{26}||Is 37_{27};

גַּן הַיָּרָק *the garden of vegetables* Dt 11$_{10}$ 1 K 21$_{2}$ (יָרָק), אֲרֻחַת יָרָק *a ration of vegetable(s)* Pr 15$_{17}$.*

→ יֶרֶק *grass, plants,* יְרַקְרַק *greenish,* יָרוֹק *green plants,* יֵרָקוֹן *rust,* (?) יַרְקוֹן *Jarkon.*

יֶרֶק 6.0.4 n.m. **grass, plants**—cstr. יֶרֶק—**grass** (Gn 1$_{30}$ 9$_{3}$ Ex 10$_{15}$ Nm 22$_{4}$ Is 15$_{6}$ Ps 37$_{2}$), <SUBJ> היה *be* Is 15$_{6}$, יתר ni. *be left over* Ex 10$_{15}$ 4QTohA 2.2$_{4}$, נבל *wither* Ps 37$_{2}$.

<OBJ> טהר *cleanse* 4QTohA 2.2$_{4}$, לחך *lick up* Nm 22$_{4}$.

<CSTR> יֶרֶק הַשָּׂדֶה *green plants of the field* Nm 22$_{4}$, יֶרֶק עֵשֶׂב perh. *foliage of plants* Gn 9$_{3}$; כָּל־יֶרֶק *every plant* Gn 1$_{30}$ Ex 10$_{15}$, כול הירק *all the plants* 4QTohA 2.2$_{4}$.

<PREP> כְּ *as* Gn 9$_{3}$ Ps 37$_{2}$; מִן of direction, *from* 4QTohA 2.1$_{8}$; שֶׁל *of* 5/6 Hev BA fr2$_{3}$ 5/6 Hev BA 46$_{1}$.*

→ יָרָק *herbage.*

יַרְקוֹן 1 pl.n. **Jarkon,** Danite wadi, perh. mod. Nahr el-ʿAuğa 6 km N of Joppa Jos 19$_{46}$, <CSTR> מֵי הַיַּרְקוֹן *waters of the Jarkon* Jos 19$_{46}$.*

→ (?) יָרָק *herbage.*

יֵרָקוֹן 6.0.1 n.m. **rust**—disease of grain, **rust** or **mildew** (1 K 8$_{37}$), **paleness** of face (Jr 30$_{6}$), <SUBJ> היה *be* 1 K 8$_{37}$‖2 C 6$_{28}$ (both ‖ שִׁדָּפוֹן *blight*).

<PREP> לְ of direction, *(in)to,* + הפך ni. *be turned to* Jr 30$_{6}$ (‖ שִׁדָּפוֹן).

בְּ of instrument, *by (means of), with,* + נכה hi. *strike* Dt 28$_{22}$ (‖ שַׁחֶפֶת *consumption,* קַדַּחַת *fever,* חַרְחֻר *violent heat,* חֶרֶב *sword,* שִׁדָּפוֹן, דַּלֶּקֶת *inflammation*) Am 4$_{9}$ Hg 2$_{17}$ (both ‖ שִׁדָּפוֹן).

<SYN> שַׁחֶפֶת *consumption,* קַדַּחַת *fever,* חַרְחֻר *violent heat,* חֶרֶב *sword,* שִׁדָּפוֹן *blight,* דַּלֶּקֶת *inflammation.*

Also 4QTwoWays 2$_{6}$.*

→ יָרָק *herbage.*

יָרְקְעָם 1 pr.n.m. **Jorkeam,** Calebite, son of Raham 1 C 2$_{44}$, <CSTR> אֲבִי יָרְקְעָם *father of Jorkeam* 1 C 2$_{44}$, perh. also pl.n. ident. with יָקְדְעָם *Jokdeam* (Jos 15$_{56}$).*

יְרַקְרַק 3 adj. **greenish**—f.pl. יְרַקְרַקֹּת—**1.** attributively of שְׁקַעֲרוּרָה *depression* in wall Lv 14$_{37}$; predicatively (with היה *be*) of נֶגַע *wound* Lv 13$_{49}$ (יְרַקְרַק אוֹ אֲדַמְדָּם *greenish or reddish*). **2.** perh. as noun, **leaf,*** וְאֶבְרוֹתֶיהָ בִּירַקְרַק חָרוּץ *and her wings are (covered) with leaf of gold* Ps 68$_{14}$.*

→ יָרָק *herbage.*

ירשׁ I 230.5.32 vb. **take possession of—Qal** 160.1.18 Pf. יָרַשׁ (Q ירשנה, ירשני), יָרַשְׁתָּ, יָרְשׁוּ (Q רשו), יְרֵשְׁנוּ; impf. יִירַשׁ (יִירָשֶׁם, יִירָשֶׁךָ, יִירָשְׁךָ, יִירַשׁ, יָרַשׁ), תִּירַשׁ (תִּירָשֶׁנּוּ, תִּירָשׁ), תִּירְשׁוּ (יִירָשׁוּם, יִירָשׁוּהָ, יִירָשׁוּ, יְרֵשׁוּ) יִירְשׁוּ, אִירָשֶׁנָּה (נִירָשָׁה) נִירַשׁ, (תִּירָשׁוּן, תִּירָשׁוּ); + waw Q וירש, וִירַשְׁתָּ (Q וִירֵשׁוּהָ, וִירֵשׁוּךָ), Q וירשו (וִירִשְׁתֶּם, וִירִשְׁתָּהּ, וירשתה, וַיִּירָשׁוּהָ (וַיִּירָשֵׁם); וִירַשְׁנוּהָ, וִירִשְׁתֶּם; impv. רֵשׁ (רֵשׁ), יְרָשָׁה, רְשׁוּ; ptc. יוֹרֵשׁ (יֹרֵשׁ), יֹרֶשֶׁת, pl. יוֹרְשִׁים (יֹרְשָׁיו, יֹרְשִׁים), cstr. Q ירשי (Q יורשי); inf. רֶשֶׁת (רֶשֶׁת, רִשְׁתְּךָ, רִשְׁתּוֹ, רִשְׁתָּהּ, יָרְשֵׁנוּ, Q ירשתו, רשתם).

1. take possession of, inherit from, displace from property, dispossess, drive out, <SUBJ> Israel Nm 21$_{24.32.35}$ Dt 4$_{1}$ 9$_{1}$ Jos 21$_{43}$ 23$_{5}$ Jg 11$_{21.22}$ Jr 30$_{3}$ 32$_{23}$ 49$_{2}$ Ezk 36$_{12}$ Am 2$_{10}$, Judah Jr 30$_{3}$, בֵּית *house* of Jacob Ob$_{17}$, עֵדָה *congregation* of the poor ones 4QpPs[a] 1.3$_{11}$, Chaldaean(s) Hb 1$_{6}$, Mount Seir Ezk 35$_{10}$, נֶגֶב *Negeb* Ob$_{19}$, שְׁפֵלָה *Shephelah* Ob$_{19}$, עַם *people* Nm 13$_{30}$ Dt 10$_{11}$ Jos 1$_{11.11}$ 24$_{8}$ Jg 18$_{7}$ Is 60$_{21}$ 63$_{18}$ Jr 30$_{3}$ 32$_{23}$ Ezk 36$_{12}$ Ps 105$_{44}$ 1 C 28$_{8}$, גּוֹי *nation* Hb 1$_{6}$, Israelite(s) Dt 1$_{21}$ 2$_{24}$ 3$_{12.18}$ 4$_{5.14.22.26}$ 5$_{31.33}$ 6$_{1.18}$ 7$_{1}$ 8$_{1}$ 9$_{4.5.6.23}$ 11$_{8+7t}$ 12$_{1.2.29.29}$ 15$_{4}$ 16$_{20}$ 17$_{14}$ 18$_{14}$ 19$_{1.2.14}$ 21$_{1}$ 23$_{21}$ 25$_{19}$ 26$_{1}$ 28$_{21.63}$ 30$_{5.16.18}$ 31$_{3.13}$ 32$_{47}$ Jg 11$_{24}$ Is 61$_{7}$ Am 9$_{12}$ Ezr 9$_{11}$ Ne 9$_{22}$ 11QT 50$_{15}$ 56$_{12}$ CD 1$_{7}$ 8$_{14}$ 19$_{27}$, Danite(s) Jg 18$_{9}$, Amalek Jg 3$_{13}$, Milcom Jr 49$_{1}$, עַמּוֹנִי *Ammonite(s)* Dt 2$_{21}$, גָּדִי *Gadite(s)* Jos 1$_{15}$, נַפְתָּלִי *Naphtalite(s)* Dt 33$_{23}$, רְאוּבֵנִי *Reubenite(s)* Jos 1$_{15}$.

Abishai Mur 22 1$_{3}$ (אב[ש]י) 22 2$_{11.12(Milik)}$ ([אב[שי), Abra(ha)m Gn 15$_{8}$ Ezk 33$_{24}$, Ahab 1 K 21$_{15.16.18.19}$, Benjamin Ob$_{19}$, Caleb Nm 13$_{30}$, Eliezer 4QpsJub[a] 2.1$_{4}$, Esau Jos 24$_{4}$, Hanin Mur 22 1$_{3}$ 22 2$_{11}$, Jacob Gn 28$_{4}$, Jephthah Jg 11$_{24}$, Moses Nm 13$_{30}$ Dt 2$_{31.31}$ 3$_{12}$ 4$_{47}$, Oreb Ps 83$_{13}$, Zalmunna Ps 83$_{13}$, Zebah Ps 83$_{13}$, Zeeb Ps 83$_{13}$, אָדָם *human being* perh. 4Q185 1.2$_{14}$, אָב *father* Dt 30$_{5}$ Ps 44$_{4}$ Ne 9$_{15.22.23}$, אָח *brother* Dt 3$_{20}$ Jos 1$_{15}$ 1 C 28$_{8}$, בֵּן *son* Gn 15$_{3.4}$ 21$_{10}$ Lv 25$_{46}$ Dt 1$_{39}$ 2$_{12.22}$ Jos 19$_{47}$ Jg 3$_{13}$ Is 14$_{21}$ Ne 9$_{24.25}$, Israelite *son* Lv 20$_{24.24}$ Nm 33$_{53}$ 36$_{8}$ Dt 1$_{8}$ 4$_{47}$ Jos 12$_{1}$ 18$_{3}$ Jg 2$_{6}$ 4QpsEzek[a] 3$_{3}$, בַּת *daughter* Nm

36$_{8}$, טַף *child* Dt 1$_{39}$.

מֶלֶךְ *king* Jg 11$_{23.24}$, רֹאשׁ *head*, i.e. ancestral head of family Jos 23$_{5}$, שֹׁפֵט *judge* Jos 23$_{5}$, זָקֵן *elder* Jos 23$_{5}$, שֹׁטֵר *official* Jos 23$_{5}$, שִׁפְחָה *female servant* Pr 30$_{23}$, ברך pu. ptc. *one who is blessed* Ps 37$_{22}$, קוה ptc. *one who waits* Ps 37$_{9}$, חסה ptc. *one who takes refuge* Is 57$_{13}$, עבר ptc. *one who passes over* 1QDM 1$_{10}$ (לרש[תה]), יֹשֵׁב *inhabitant* Ezk 33$_{25.26}$, worshipper Ps 37$_{34}$.

בָּחִיר *chosen one* Is 65$_{9}$, צַדִּיק *righteous one* Ps 37$_{29}$, עָנִי *poor one* Ps 37$_{11}$, רַע *evil (one)* Ezk 7$_{24}$, גָּלוּת *exile* Ob$_{20}$, זֶרַע *seed*, i.e. offspring Gn 22$_{17}$ 24$_{60}$ Is 54$_{3}$ Ps 25$_{13}$ Si 46$_{9}$, שְׁאֵר *blood relation* Nm 27$_{11}$, חֲצִי *half* tribe of Manasseh Jos 1$_{15}$, יֵצֶר *inclination* 11QPs^{a} 19$_{16}$, הוא *he* Gn 15$_{4}$, קָאַת *hawk* Is 34$_{11}$, קִפּוֹד *hedgehog* Is 34$_{11}$, קִמּוֹשׁ *nettles* Ho 9$_{6}$; subj. not specified, Gn 15$_{7}$ Jos 13$_{1}$ Jg 14$_{15}$ 2 S 14$_{7}$ 2 K 17$_{24}$ Is 34$_{17}$ 65$_{9}$ Ps 69$_{36}$ 1QH fr. 45$_{4}$ 4QTohB^{a} 2$_{2}$ 4QDiscourse 2.1$_{6}$ 4QapJoshua^{a} 11$_{8}$ 4QapJerB 22$_{1}$ 4QpsEzek^{a} 5$_{1}$ 4QBéat 14.2$_{13}$ 11QT 50$_{15}$ Mur 30 2$_{22}$.

<OBJ> (1) object possessed, אֶרֶץ *land* Gn 15$_{7.8}$ 28$_{4}$ Nm 13$_{30}$ 21$_{24.35}$ 33$_{53}$ Dt 1$_{8.39}$ 2$_{31}$ 3$_{12.18.20}$ 4$_{1.5.14.22.26.47}$ 5$_{31.33}$ 6$_{1.18}$ 7$_{1}$ 8$_{1}$ 9$_{4.5.6.23}$ 10$_{11}$ 11$_{8+6t}$ 12$_{1}$ 15$_{4}$ 16$_{20}$ 17$_{14}$ 19$_{1.2.14}$ 23$_{21}$ 25$_{19}$ 26$_{1}$ 28$_{21.63}$ 30$_{5.5.16}$ Jos 1$_{11.11.15.15}$ 12$_{1}$ 13$_{1}$ 18$_{3}$ 21$_{43}$ 23$_{5}$ 24$_{8}$ Jg 2$_{6}$ 11$_{21}$ 18$_{9}$ Is 14$_{21}$ 60$_{21}$ Jr 30$_{3}$ 32$_{23}$ Ezk 33$_{24.25.26}$ 35$_{10}$ Am 2$_{10}$ Ps 25$_{13}$ 37$_{9.11.22.29.34}$ 44$_{4}$ Ezr 9$_{11}$ Ne 9$_{15.22.22.22.23.24}$ 1 C 28$_{8}$ 1QDM 1$_{10}$ 4QpsEzek^{a} 5$_{1}$ 11QT 50$_{15.16}$ 56$_{12}$ CD 1$_{7}$, אֲדָמָה *land* Lv 20$_{24.24}$ Dt 21$_{1}$ 30$_{18}$ 31$_{13}$ 32$_{47}$.

Edom Is 34$_{11.17}$, Gilead Ob$_{19}$, Samaria 2 K 17$_{24}$, Zion Ps 69$_{36}$, גּוֹי *nation* CD 8$_{14}$ 19$_{27}$, יָם *sea* Dt 33$_{23}$, הַר *mountain* Jos 24$_{4}$ Is 57$_{13}$ 65$_{9.9}$ Ezk 36$_{12}$ Ob$_{19}$ 4QpPs^{a} 1.3$_{11}$, גְּבוּל *border* Jg 11$_{22}$, כֶּרֶם *vineyard* 1 K 21$_{15.16.18}$ Ne 9$_{25}$, זַיִת *olive orchard* Ne 9$_{25}$, שָׂדֶה *field* Ob$_{19.19}$, דָּרוֹם *south* Dt 33$_{23}$, עִיר *city* Dt 9$_{1}$ Jg 3$_{13}$ Ob$_{20}$, Leshem Jos 19$_{47}$, מִקְדָּשׁ *sanctuary* Is 63$_{18}$, בַּיִת *house* Ezk 7$_{24}$ Ne 9$_{25}$, מִשְׁכָּן *dwelling place* Hb 1$_{6}$, נָוֶה *pasturage* Ps 83$_{13}$, שַׁעַר *gate* Gn 22$_{17}$ 24$_{60}$, בּוֹר *cistern* Ne 9$_{25}$, עֵץ *tree* Ne 9$_{25}$, אֲחֻזָּה *possession* Lv 25$_{46}$, נַחֲלָה *inheritance* Nm 27$_{11}$ 36$_{8.8}$ Si 46$_{9}$, מוֹרָשׁ *possession* Ob$_{17}$, מַחְמָד *precious object* Ho 9$_{6}$, מִשְׁנֶה *double portion* Is 61$_{7}$, עָמָל *toil* Ps 105$_{44}$, עֶצֶר *restraint* Jg 18$_{7}$, אֲשֶׁר *that which* Jg 11$_{24}$, כָּל־אֲשֶׁר *all of that* Jg 11$_{24}$; obj. not specified, 4Q185 1.2$_{14}$.

(2) person dispossessed, עַם *people* Dt 9$_{1}$ Jg 11$_{23}$, גּוֹי *nation* Dt 9$_{1}$ 11$_{23}$ 12$_{2.29.29}$ 18$_{14}$ 31$_{3}$ Is 54$_{3}$ Am 9$_{12}$, Gad Jr 49$_{1}$, אֱמֹרִי *Amorite(s)* Nm 21$_{32}$, חֹרִי *Horite(s)* Dt 2$_{12.22}$, פְּלִשְׁתִּי *Philistine(s)* Jg 14$_{15}$ Ob$_{19}$, רְפָאִים *Rephaim* Dt 2$_{21}$, שְׁאֵרִית *remnant* of Edom Am 9$_{12}$, Abra(ha)m Gn 15$_{3.4.4}$ 4QpsJub^{a} 2.1$_{4}$, גְּבִרָה *mistress* Pr 30$_{23}$, worshipper 4QBéat 14.2$_{13}$.

<PREP> לְ of benefit, *to, for*, + Oreb Ps 83$_{13}$, Zalmunna Ps 83$_{13}$, Zebah Ps 83$_{13}$, Zeeb Ps 83$_{13}$.

בְּ of place/time, *on, in, at*, + עֵת *time* Dt 3$_{12}$, אֶרֶץ *land* Is 61$_{7}$; of instrument, *by (means of), with*, + חֶרֶב *sword* Ps 44$_{4}$; introducing object, + נַחֲלָה *inheritance* 4QTohB^{a} 2$_{2}$.

מִן of direction, *from*, + Arnon Nm 21$_{24}$.

עַד *unto*, + Jabbok Nm 21$_{24}$.

עִם *with*, + Isaac Gn 21$_{10}$, בֵּן *son* Gn 21$_{10}$.

2. ptc. as noun, **possessor, inheritor, conqueror,** <NOM CL> אִם־יוֹרֵשׁ אֵין *is there no heir?* Jr 49$_{1}$.

<OBJ> בוא hi. *bring* Mc 1$_{15}$, ירשׁ *take possession of* Jr 49$_{2}$.

<PREP> לְ of direction, *to*, + נתן *give* Jr 8$_{10}$.

Ni. 4 Impf. יִוָּרֵשׁ, 2ms תִּוָּרֵשׁ, אִוָּרֵשׁ—**be deprived of property, become poor,** <SUBJ> Agur Pr 30$_{9}$, Jacob Gn 45$_{11}$, בַּיִת *house(hold)* Gn 45$_{11}$, worshipper Pr 20$_{13}$, סֹבֵא *drunkard* Pr 23$_{21}$, זוֹלֵל *glutton* Pr 23$_{21}$, כָּל־אֲשֶׁר־לָךְ *all that is yours* Gn 45$_{11}$.

Pi. 1 Impf. יְיָרֵשׁ—**take possession of,** <SUBJ> צְלָצַל *crickets* Dt 28$_{42}$. <OBJ> עֵץ *tree* Dt 28$_{42}$, פְּרִי *fruit* of your land Dt 28$_{42}$.

Hi. 65.4.14 Pf. הוֹרִישׁ (הֹרִישׁ, הוֹרִישׁוּ), הוֹרַשְׁתָּ (הוֹרַשְׁתָּנוּ), הוֹרִישׁוּ (הוֹרַשְׁתִּים, הוֹרַשְׁתָּם); impf. יוֹרִישׁ (יוֹרִישְׁךָ, יוֹרְשֶׁנּוּ, יוֹרְשֶׁנָּה, Q יורשי, Q יורישם), Si 3fs תורישנו, 2ms תּוֹרִישׁ (תּוֹרִישֵׁנִי, תּוֹרִישֵׁמוֹ), תּוֹרִישׁוּ, אוֹרִישׁ (אוֹרִישֵׁם); + waw וְהוֹרַשְׁתֶּם, וַיּוֹרֶשׁ (וַיֹּרֶשׁ, וַיֹּרִשֵׁם), וְאוֹרִשֶׁנּוּ; ptc. מוֹרִישׁ (מוֹרִישָׁם); inf. הוֹרֵשׁ (הוֹרִישׁ, הוֹרִישׁוֹ, הוֹרֵישׁ, הוֹרִישָׁם)—**take possession of, cause to possess, drive out, dispossess, make suffer** (Jb 13$_{26}$), **make poor** (1 S 2$_{7}$), **cast out** (Jb 20$_{15}$).

<SUBJ> ״ Y. Ex 34$_{24}$ Nm 14$_{12}$ Dt 4$_{38}$ 9$_{4.5}$ 11$_{23}$ 18$_{12}$ Jos 13$_{6}$ 23$_{5.9.13}$ Jg 2$_{21.23}$ 11$_{23}$ 1 S 2$_{7}$ 1 K 14$_{24}$ 21$_{26}$ 2 K 16$_{3}$‖2 C 28$_{3}$ 2 K 17$_{8}$ 21$_{2}$‖2 C 33$_{2}$ GnzPs 3$_{12.21}$ 11QT 60$_{20}$, אֲדֹנָי *Lord* Zc 9$_{4}$, אֱלֹהִים *God* Dt 9$_{5}$ 18$_{12}$ Jos 23$_{5.13}$ Jg 11$_{23}$ Ps 44$_{3}$ 2 C 20$_{7}$, *god* Jg 11$_{24}$, אֵל *God* Jos 3$_{10}$ Jb 13$_{26}$ 20$_{15}$ Si

32_{23}, Chemosh Jg 11_{24}.

עַם *people* Dt 7_{17}, Israel Nm $21_{32(Qr)}$ Dt 9_3 (|| אבד hi. *exterminate*) Jg 1_{28}, Israelite(s) Ezr 9_{12}, בַּיִת *house* of Joseph Jos 17_{18}, Asher Jg $1_{31.32}$, Caleb Jos 14_{12} 15_{14} Jg 1_{20}, Ephraim Jg 1_{29}, Joshua 4QSela 1.2_3, Judah Jg $1_{19.19}$, Manasseh Jg 1_{27}, Moses Jos 13_{12}, Naphtali Jg 1_{33}, Zebulun Jg 1_{30}.

חָלוּץ *armed one* Nm 32_{21}, גִּבּוֹר *warrior* Jos 8_7, בֵּן *son* Nm 32_{39} 2 C 20_{11} Si 6_1, Israelite *son* Nm $33_{52.53.55}$ Jos 13_{13} 15_{63} 16_{10} $17_{12.13}$ Jg 1_{21}, זֶרַע *seed*, i.e. offspring Nm 14_{24}, גְּוִיָּה *body* 4Q416 2.2_{18}, יָד *hand* Ex 15_9, חָכְמָה *wisdom* Si 15_6, זַעַם *anger* Si 39_{23}; subj. not specified, Jos 3_{10} 17_{13} Jg 1_{28} Si 20_{22} 4QpIsa^c 31_4 4QpPs^b 1_7 4Q185 1.2_{15} 4QParaKings 104_3 4QConfess 2_7 4Q418 81_3.

<OBJ> (1) object possessed, אֶרֶץ *land* Nm 14_{24} 33_{53}, הַר *mountain* Jg 1_{19}, Beth-shean Jg 1_{27}, Tanach Jg 1_{27}, Tyre Zc 9_4, עִיר *city* Jos 8_7 17_{12}, נַחֲלָה *inheritance* 4QpPs^b 1_7 4Q418 81_3 GnzPs 3_{21}, חַיִל *riches* Jb 20_{15}, עָוֹן *iniquity* Jb 13_{26}, חֶרְפָּה *reproach* Si 6_1, קָלוֹן *shame* Si 6_1, שֵׁם *name* Si 6_1 15_6, שֵׁבֶט *sceptre* Si 32_{23}; obj. not specified, Si 15_6 4Q185 1.2_{15}.

(2) person dispossessed, עַם *people* Nm 14_{12}, גּוֹי *nation* Ex 34_{24} Dt 4_{38} 7_{17} $9_{3.4.5}$ 11_{23} 18_{12} Jos $23_{5.9.13}$ Jg 2_{23} 1 K 14_{24} 2 K 16_3||2 C 28_3 2 K 17_8 21_2||2 C 33_2 Ps 44_3 Si 39_{23} 11QT 60_{20}.

עֲנָקִים *Anakim* Jos 14_{12}, אֱמֹרִי *Amorite(s)* Nm 21_{32} 32_{39} Jos 3_{10} Jg 11_{23} 1 K 21_{26} 4QSela 1.2_3, כְּנַעֲנִי *Canaanite(s)* Jos 3_{10} 16_{10} $17_{13.18}$ Jg $1_{28.29.32}$, גְּשׁוּרִי *Geshurite(s)* Jos 13_{13}, גִּרְגָּשִׁי *Girgashite(s)* Jos 3_{10}, חִתִּי *Hittite(s)* Jos 3_{10}, חִוִּי *Hivite(s)* Jos 3_{10}, יְבוּסִי *Jebusite(s)* Jos 3_{10} 15_{63} Jg 1_{21}, מַעֲכָתִי *Maacathite(s)* Jos 13_{13}, פְּרִזִּי *Perizzite(s)* Jos 3_{10}, Israelite(s) Ex 15_9 2 C 20_{11}, רְפָאִים *Rephaim* appar. Jos 13_{12}, צִידֹנִי *Sidonian(s)* Jos 13_6.

Job Jb 13_{26}, אִישׁ *man* 4Q418 81_3, מֶלֶךְ *king* Jg 11_{24}, אוֹיֵב *enemy* Nm 32_{21}, יֹשֵׁב *inhabitant* Nm $33_{52.55}$ Jos 13_6 15_{63} Jg 1_{19+10t} 2 C 20_7, בֵּן *son* of Anak Jos 15_{14} Jg 1_{20}, נֶפֶשׁ *soul* Si 20_{22}.

<PREP> לְ of direction, *to*, + צֶאֱצָאִים *offspring* 4Q185 1.2_{15}; introducing object, + בֵּן *son* Ezr 9_{12} perh. 4QConfess 2_7, אֶבְיוֹן *poor one* GnzPs 3_{21}.

בְּ of instrument, *by (means of), with*, + אִוֶּלֶת *folly* Si 20_{22}.

מִן of direction, *from*, + יְרֵשָׁה *possession* 2 C 20_{11}, בֶּטֶן *belly* Jb 20_{15}, שָׁם *there* Jos 15_{14} Jg 1_{20} 4QSela 1.2_3; partitive, *some of, (any)one of*, + גּוֹי *nation* Jg 2_{21}.

מִפְּנֵי *(from) before*, + עַם *people* Ex 34_{24} Jg 11_{23}, Israel Dt 4_{38} $9_{4.5}$ 11_{23} Jos 23_9 Jg 2_{21} 11_{23}, Israelite(s) Dt 18_{12}, חָלוּץ *armed one* Nm 32_{21}, Israelite *son* Nm $33_{52.55}$ Jos 3_{10} 13_6 1 K 14_{24} 21_{26} 2 K 16_3||2 C 28_3 2 K 17_8 21_2||2 C 33_2, רֹאשׁ *head*, i.e. ancestral head of family Jos 23_9, שֹׁפֵט *judge* Jos 23_9, זָקֵן *elder* Jos 23_9, שֹׁטֵר *official* Jos 23_9.

מִלִּפְנֵי *(from) before*, + עַם *people* 2 C 20_7, Israel Jos $23_{5.13}$ 2 C 20_7, Israelite(s) 11QT 60_{20}, רֹאשׁ *head*, i.e. ancestral head of family Jos $23_{5.13}$, שֹׁפֵט *judge* Jos $23_{5.13}$, זָקֵן *elder* Jos $23_{5.13}$, שֹׁטֵר *official* Jos $23_{5.13}$.

עַד *until*, + עוֹלָם *eternity* Ezr 9_{12}.

<COLL> אַתָּה יָדְךָ גּוֹיִם הוֹרַשְׁתָּ *you (with) your hand have driven out the nations* Ps 44_3.

<SYN> אבד hi. *exterminate*.*

→ יְרֵשָׁה *possession*, יְרֻשָּׁה *possession*, רֶשֶׁת *net*, מוֹרָשׁ *possession*, מוֹרָשָׁה *possession*, יְרוּשָׁא *Jerusha*, מוֹרֶשֶׁת *Moresheth*, מוֹרַשְׁתִּי *Moreshethite*.

ירשׁ II 1 vb. **press—Qal** 1 Impf. 2ms תִּירוֹשׁ—<SUBJ> Israel Mc 6_{15}=1QpMic 17_2 (|| דרך *tread*). <SYN> דרך *tread*.

→ תִּירוֹשׁ *new wine*.

יְרֵשָׁה 2.0.1 n.f. **possession**—acquired by conquest Nm $24_{18.18}$, <SUBJ> היה *be* Nm 24_{18} (Sam ירושה *possession*) 24_{18} 1QM 11_7.*

→ ירשׁ *take possession of*.

יְרֻשָּׁה 14 n.f. **possession**—cstr. יְרֻשַּׁת; sf. יְרֻשָּׁתוֹ, יְרֻשָּׁתְךָ, יְרֻשַּׁתְכֶם—acquired by conquest Dt $2_{5.9.12.19}$ 3_{20} Jos $12_{6.7}$ Jg 21_{17} Jr 32_8 Ps 61_6 2 C 20_{11}, <OBJ> נתן *give* Dt 3_{20}, ירשׁ hi. *cause to possess* 2 C 20_{11}.

<CSTR> יְרֻשַּׁת פְּלֵיטָה *possession of the escaped one*, i.e. the survivors' possession Jg 21_{17}, יְרֻשַּׁת יִרְאֵי שְׁמֶךָ *the inheritance of the fear of your name* Ps 61_6; אֶרֶץ יְרֻשָּׁתוֹ *land of his possession* Dt 2_{12}, מִשְׁפַּט הַיְרֻשָּׁה *judgment*, i.e. right, *of the possession* Jr 32_8.

<PREP> לְ of direction, *to*, + שׁוּב *go back* Dt 3_{20}.

מִן of direction, *from*, + גרשׁ pi. *drive out* 2 C 20_{11}.

<COLL> כִּי־יְרֻשָּׁה לְעֵשָׂו נָתַתִּי אֶת־הַר שֵׂעִיר *for I have given Mount Seir to Esau as a possession* Dt 2$_{5}$, כִּי לֹא־אֶתֵּן לְךָ מֵאַרְצוֹ יְרֻשָּׁה *for I will not give to you from any of his land as a possession* Dt 2$_{9}$, var. 2$_{19}$, נָתַתִּי אֶת־עָר יְרֻשָּׁה *I have given Ar as a possession* Dt 2$_{9}$, וַיִּתְּנָהּ מֹשֶׁה עֶבֶד־יְהוָה יְרֻשָּׁה *and Moses the servant of Y. gave it as a possession* Jos 12$_{6}$, וַיִּתְּנָהּ יְהוֹשֻׁעַ לְשִׁבְטֵי יִשְׂרָאֵל יְרֻשָּׁה *and Joshua gave it to the tribes of Israel as a possession* Jos 12$_{7}$.*

→ ירשׁ *take possession of.*

[יָרֹת] 0.0.0.2 pl.n. **Jaroth,** appar. in vicinity of Jerusalem Ophel ost.3.3, <CSTR> עמק ירת *valley of Jaroth* Ophel ost.3.3.

יִשְׂחָק, see יִצְחָק *Isaac.*

יְשִׂימִאֵל 1 pr.n.m. **Jesimiel,** Simeonite chief 1 C 4$_{36}$.

→ אֵל *God* + שׂים *place.*

יִשְׂרָאֵל 2512.21.354.22 pr.n.m. **Israel, 1.** patriarch, originally named Jacob, son of Isaac and Rebekah, husband of Leah, Rachel, Bilhah and Zilpah, eponymous ancestor of tribes of Israel, <SUBJ> היה *be* Gn 35$_{10}$ (+ שֵׁם *name*), יכל *be able* Gn 48$_{10}$, נגשׁ hi. *bring near* Gn 48$_{10}$, נסע *set out* Gn 35$_{21}$ 46$_{1}$, שׁחה htpal. *bow down* Gn 47$_{31}$, נטה *extend*, i.e. pitch, tent Gn 35$_{21}$, שׂים *place* Gn 48$_{20}$, שׁית *place* Gn 48$_{14}$, שׂכל pi. *place* hands *crosswise* Gn 48$_{14}$, שׁלח *send*, i.e. stretch, hand Gn 48$_{14}$, ישׁב *dwell* Gn 47$_{27}$, *sit* 48$_{2}$, שׁכן *dwell* Gn 35$_{22}$, אמר *say* Gn 37$_{13}$ 43$_{6.11}$ 45$_{28}$ 46$_{30}$ 47$_{29.31}$ 48$_{8.11.21}$, קרא *call* Gn 47$_{29}$, ברך pi. *bless* Gn 48$_{20}$, ראה *see* Gn 48$_{8.10}$, שׁמע *hear* Gn 35$_{22}$, אהב *love* Gn 37$_{3}$, נשׁק *kiss* Gn 48$_{10}$, חבק pi. *embrace* Gn 48$_{10}$, חזק htp. *strengthen oneself* Gn 48$_{2}$, עשׂה *make* Gn 37$_{3}$.

<NOM CL> בְּנֵי יִצְחָק עֵשָׂו וְיִשְׂרָאֵל *the sons of Isaac were Esau and Israel* 1 C 1$_{34}$.

<OBJ> חנט *embalm* Gn 50$_{2.2}$, קרא *call* name 35$_{10}$, שׂים *place*, i.e. call, name 2 K 17$_{34}$, קרא *meet* Gn 46$_{29}$.

<CSTR> אֵל אֱלֹהֵי יִשְׂרָאֵל *God, the God of Israel* Gn 33$_{20}$, י׳ אֱלֹהֵי אַבְרָהָם יִצְחָק וְיִשְׂרָאֵל *Y., God of Abraham, Isaac and Israel* 1 K 18$_{36}$ 1 C 29$_{18}$ 2 C 30$_{6}$, בֶּן־ *son of* Ezr 8$_{18}$ 1 C 5$_{1}$ 6$_{23}$ 7$_{29}$, בְּנֵי *sons of* Gn 42$_{5}$ 45$_{21}$ 46$_{5.8}$ 50$_{25}$ Ex 1$_{1}$, יְמֵי־ *days of* Gn 47$_{29}$, יְמִין *right side of* Gn 48$_{13}$, שְׂמֹאל *left side of* Gn 48$_{13}$, עֵינֵי *eyes of* Gn 48$_{10}$.

<APP> אָב *father* Gn 43$_{8.11}$ 46$_{29}$ 49$_{2}$.

<PREP> לְ of direction, *to*, + אמר *say* Gn 37$_{13}$ 46$_{2}$; of possession, *of, (belonging) to* 37$_{3}$ 46$_{1}$; introducing object, + זכר *remember* Ex 32$_{13}$; בְּ *against*, + עשׂה *do* Gn 34$_{7}$ (unless בְּיִשְׂרָאֵל = *among the Israelites*, i.e. §2); אֶל *to*, + אמר *say* Gn 43$_{8}$, שׁמע *listen* Gn 49$_{2}$.

<COLL> לֹא יַעֲקֹב יֵאָמֵר עוֹד שִׁמְךָ כִּי אִם־יִשְׂרָאֵל *your name shall not longer be called Jacob, but Israel* Gn 32$_{29}$.

Israel + Jacob Gn 32$_{29}$ 35$_{10}$ 46$_{2}$ 47$_{27}$ 48$_{2}$ 49$_{2}$, Abraham Ex 32$_{13}$, Isaac Ex 32$_{13}$, Ephraim Gn 48$_{13.14.20}$.

2. nation regarding §1 as its eponymous ancestor, <SUBJ> היה *be* 1 S 14$_{40}$ 2 S 24$_{9}$ 1 K 9$_{7}$ 18$_{31}$ 2 K 9$_{14}$ Is 19$_{24}$ Jr 2$_{14}$ 46$_{27}$ Ho 8$_{8}$ Ps 114$_{2}$ 1 C 21$_{5}$, ni. *become* Dt 27$_{9}$, אבה *be willing* Is 42$_{24}$ Ps 81$_{12}$, אמן ni. *be trustworthy* Ps 78$_{37}$, hi. *trust* Ps 78$_{22.32}$, אשׁם *be guilty* Ho 10$_{2}$, בושׁ *be ashamed* Ho 10$_{6}$, באשׁ ni. *be odious* 1 S 13$_{4}$, זור *be strange* Ps 78$_{30}$, חפז *be alarmed* Dt 20$_{3}$ 1QM 10$_{3}$, חתת *be dismayed* 1 S 17$_{11}$, רבה *be many* Dt 6$_{3}$, hi. *make many* Ho 10$_{1}$, רכך *be weak* Dt 20$_{3}$, שׂבע *be satisfied* Ps 78$_{29}$, סרר *be stubborn* Ho 4$_{16}$ CD 4$_{14}$, יכל *be able* Ex 15$_{23}$ Jos 7$_{13}$ Jg 2$_{14}$, גבר *be mighty* Ex 17$_{11}$, חזק *be strong* Jg 1$_{28}$, ישׁע ni. *be saved* Is 45$_{17}$ CD 5$_{19}$ (= 4QD[b] 2$_{2}$ [בהרשע י[שראל *when he did evil to Israel*), בהל ni. *be dismayed* 2 S 4$_{1}$, נגף ni. *be struck* Jos 8$_{15}$ (if em. נגע ni. *[pretend to] be defeated*) 1 S 4$_{2.10}$ 1 K 8$_{33}$ ||2 C 6$_{24}$, בלע ni. *be confused* or *be swallowed* Ho 8$_{8}$, יגע *be weary* Is 43$_{22}$, יחשׂ htp. *be enrolled* 1 C 9$_{1}$, כחד ni. *be hidden* Ho 5$_{3}$, בדל ni. *be separate* Ezr 9$_{1}$, חלק ni. *be divided* 1 K 16$_{21}$, צמד ni. *attach oneself* Nm 25$_{3}$.

הלך *go* Ex 15$_{22}$ Dt 10$_{12}$ Jos 14$_{10}$ Jg 2$_{22}$ 11$_{16.18}$ 1 K 8$_{36}$ ||2 C 6$_{27}$ 12$_{16}$ 2 K 13$_{6.11}$ Is 43$_{2}$ Jr 3$_{6}$ 31$_{2}$ Ps 81$_{13}$ 1 C 11$_{4}$ 2 C 10$_{16}$, pi. Ps 81$_{14}$, בוא *come* Ex 15$_{23}$ Nm 21$_{1}$ Dt 9$_{1}$ 31$_{11}$ Jg 11$_{16.18.18}$ 1 S 2$_{14}$ 1 K 12$_{1}$ Ps 105$_{23}$ 2 C 10$_{1.3}$, hi. *bring* 2 S 5$_{2}$, קרב *draw near* Dt 20$_{3}$, יצא *go out* 2 C 31$_{1}$, ירד *go down* 1 S 13$_{20}$, עלה *go up* Jos 10$_{6}$ Jg 11$_{13.16}$ 1 K 16$_{17}$ Is 11$_{16}$ 1 C 13$_{6}$, hi. *take up* 1 C 13$_{6}$ 15$_{3.28}$, קום *rise* Jos 7$_{13}$ 2 K 3$_{24}$, עמד *stand* Jos 8$_{33}$ Jg 2$_{14}$ 1 S 17$_{3}$ Ho 10$_{9}$ 2 C 7$_{6}$, רום hi. *raise*, i.e. contribute Ezr 8$_{25}$, נשׂא hi. *bring* ropes 2 S 17$_{13}$, נפל *fall* Ps 78$_{28}$ (if em. hi. *cause* Israel *to fall*), כשׁל *stumble* Ho 14$_{2}$, ni. Ho 5$_{5}$, רגז *tremble* 1 C 17$_{9}$, ערץ *tremble* Dt 20$_{3}$ 1QM 10$_{3}$, דלל *be low* Jg 6$_{6}$, רכב *ride* horse Ho 14_{4}.

עבר *pass* Nm 20_{21} 21_{23} Dt 9_{1} Jos 3_{17} 4_{22} $11_{17.19.20}$ Is 43_{2}, *transgress* Jos 7_{11} Dn 9_{11}, סבב *go round* Jg 11_{18}, סור *depart* Dn 9_{11}, שׁוב *go back* Jos 8_{21} 8_{24} $10_{38.43}$ 1 K 8_{33}||2 C 6_{24} 2 K 17_{13} Is 44_{22} Jr $3_{7.7.12}$ $4_{1.1}$ Ho $14_{2.3}$ Ps $78_{34.41}$ 1 C 9_{2} (if em. ישׁב *dwell*) 2 C 15_{4}, hi. *take back* Jr 30_{3}, *remove* Jos 7_{13} Jr 4_{1}, הפך *turn* Jos 7_{8}, נטה *turn* Nm 20_{21}, נוד *wander* Jr 4_{1}, נוס *flee* Jos 8_{15} 1 S 4_{17} 2 S 19_{9}, שׁלח *send* Nm 21_{21} Jg $11_{17.17.19}$ 1 K 12_{20}, קבץ *gather* 1 S 7_{6} 25_{1}, ni. *assemble* 1 C 11_{1} 4QM^{a} 16_{4} (יקב[צו]), אסף ni. *be gathered* 2 S 17_{11} Is 49_{5}, רדף *pursue* Jos 8_{24} 10_{10} 11_{8} 1 K 20_{20}, קרא *meet* Am 4_{12}, גלה *be exiled* 2 K 17_{23} Am $7_{11.17}$, פוץ ni. *be scattered* 1 K 22_{17}||2 C 18_{16}, נתשׁ ni. *be uprooted* Am 9_{15}.

מצא *find* Ex 15_{22}, ni. *be found* Jr 46_{27} Ezr 8_{25} 2 C 31_{1} 35_{18}, שׂים *place* Jos 7_{11} Jg 1_{28} 20_{29} 1 K 2_{15}, נתן *give* Ezk 27_{17} Ne 12_{47}, ni. *be given* 4QpNah 3.1_{12}, מכר *sell* Am 2_{6}, לקח *take* Nm 21_{25} Jos 7_{11} Jg $11_{13.15}$ Ho $14_{3.3}$, נצל hi. *rescue* 1 S 7_{14}, עזב *leave* 2 C 12_{1} 4QPseud^{b} 5.1_{7}.

אהב *love* Dt 10_{12} 1 S 18_{16} Ho 9_{1}, אוה *desire* Ps $78_{29.30}$, בטח *trust* Ps 78_{22} 115_{9} (mss בֵּית יִשְׂרָאֵל *house of Israel*), זכר *remember* Is 44_{21} Ps $78_{35.42}$, נשׁה *forget* Is 44_{21}, שׁכח *forget* Ho 8_{14}, ידע *know* Jos 3_{7} 22_{22} Jg 3_{1} 1 S 3_{20} 2 S 3_{37} 17_{10} Is 1_{3} 45_{4} Ho 8_{2} 9_{7} (or em. רעע *do evil*), ירא *fear* Dt 10_{12} 13_{12} 20_{3} 21_{21} Jos 4_{14} 1 S 17_{11} Is 43_{1} Ho 10_{3} 1QM 10_{3}, נכר hi. *recognize* Is 63_{16}, ראה ni. *appear* Dt 31_{11}, שׁמע *hear* Dt 4_{1} 5_{1} $6_{3.4}$ 9_{1} 13_{12} 20_{3}=11QT 61_{15} Dt 21_{21} 27_{9} Jg 3_{4} 1 S 13_{4} 17_{11} 1 K 3_{28} 12_{20} 2 K 21_{9} Is 42_{24} 44_{1} 48_{12} Ps 81_{9} Dn 9_{11} 1 C 29_{23} 2 C 13_{4} 1QM 10_{3}, hi. *cause to be heard* 1 C 15_{28}.

בקשׁ pi. *seek* Ho 7_{10} 2 C 15_{4}, דרשׁ *seek* Ps 78_{34}, שׁחר pi. *seek eagerly* Ps 78_{34}, יחל pi. *await* Ps 130_{7} 131_{3}, זנח *reject* Ho 8_{3}, כבד pi. *glorify* Ps 50_{15}, פאר htp. *glorify oneself* Jg 7_{2}, צדק pi. *justify* Jr 3_{11}, שׂחק pi. *play*, i.e. dance 1 C 13_{8}, שׂמח *rejoice* 1 K 4_{20} Ho 9_{1} Ps 147_{7}||53_{7} 149_{2}.

אמר *say* Nm 20_{14} 21_{2} Jg 11_{19} 1 S 7_{6} 1 S 12_{1} Ho 10_{3} 13_{10} $14_{3.4}$ Ps 118_{2} 124_{1} 129_{1} 1 C 11_{1}, דבר pi. *speak* Is 40_{27} Ho 10_{4} 2 C 10_{3}, קרא *call* 1 K 12_{20} Ps 50_{15}, pu. *be called* Is 48_{12}, רוע hi. *raise a shout* 1 S 4_{5} Zp 3_{14}, זעק *cry out* Ho 8_{2}, סכת hi. *be silent* Dt 27_{9}, ברך pi. *bless* Gn 48_{20} (or em. pu. *be blessed* or htp. *bless oneself*), חנן htp. *make supplication* 1 K 8_{33}||2 C 6_{24}, ידה hi. *confess* 1 K 8_{33}||2 C 6_{24}, פלל htp. *pray* 1 K $8_{30.33}$||2 C $6_{21.24}$, ספד *lament* 1 S 25_{1} 28_{3} 1 K $14_{13.18}$, שׁיר *sing* Nm 21_{17} Ho 7_{10}, ראה *see* Ex $14_{30.31}$ Dt 29_{1} Jos 8_{21} 1 K 12_{16}||2 C $10_{16(mss)}$.

חנה *encamp* Ex 19_{2} Jg 11_{18} 1 S 4_{1} 28_{4} 29_{1} 2 S 17_{26}, ערך *arrange* battle line 1 S 17_{21}, צור *besiege* 1 K 15_{27}, לכד *capture* Jos 10_{37}, בזז *plunder* Jos 8_{27}, חרם hi. *destroy* Jos 10_{37}, שׁמד hi. *destroy* 4QapJoseph^{b} 3_{10} (שראל[י]), שׂרף *burn* Jos 7_{25} 11_{13}, שׁבר pi. *shatter* 2 C 31_{1}, שׁדד po. *destroy* Ho 10_{2}, גדע pi. *hew down* 2 C 31_{1}, נתץ pi. *tear down* 2 C 31_{1}, סחב *drag* 2 S 17_{13}, קרע *tear* 2 K 17_{21}, htp. *be torn* 4QpsEzek^{c} 2_{7}, ערף *break* altars Ho 10_{2}, לחם ni. *fight* Jos 10_{36}, שׁלף *draw* sword 1 C 21_{5}, נכה hi. *strike* Nm 21_{24} Jos 8_{21} $8_{22.24}$ $10_{10.10.37}$ $11_{8.8}$ Jg 11_{21} 2 K 3_{24} Ho 14_{6} (or em. נטה *stretch out* roots), סקל *stone* Jos 7_{25}, רגם *stone* Jos 7_{25} 1 K 12_{18}, עצב hi. *cause pain* Ps 78_{40}, עכר *trouble* 1 K 18_{18}, תוה hi. *wound* Ps 78_{41}, הרג *kill* Jos 8_{24} Ps 78_{34}.

עשׂה *do* Nm 22_{2} 24_{18}=1QM 11_{7} Dt 2_{12} 6_{3} Jg 3_{12} Jr $3_{6.7}$ Ezk 25_{14} Ezr 10_{5} 1 C 12_{33} 4QpsMos^{e} 1_{3}, *make* 1 K 14_{15} Am 9_{14}, *celebrate* festival 1 K 8_{65}||2 C 7_{8} 2 C 35_{18}, פעל *do* Ho 7_{1}, שׁמר *keep* Dt 6_{3} Jg 2_{22} 2 K 17_{13} 21_{8} Ho 12_{13}, ni. *be guarded* Ho 12_{14}, עבד *serve* Dt 10_{12} Jos $10_{29.31.34}$ 24_{31} Ho 12_{13}.

רעע hi. *do evil* Ho 9_{7} (if em. ידע *know*), חטא *sin* Jos 7_{11} 1 S 7_{6} 1 K 8_{33}||2 C 6_{24} Is 42_{24} Ho 10_{9} (or em. חַטַּאת *sin of* Israel) Ps 78_{32} Dn 9_{11} Jr 46_{27}, תעה *err* Ezk $44_{10.10}$ CD 3_{14}, פשׁע *rebel* 1 K 12_{19}||2 C 10_{19}, מרה hi. *be rebellious* Ps 78_{40}, נאץ pi. *commit adultery* Jr 3_{8}, זנה *prostitute oneself* Jg 8_{27} Jr 3_{6} Ho 4_{15} 9_{1}, טמא ni. *defile oneself* Ho 5_{3} 6_{10}, כזב pi. *lie* Ps 78_{36}, כחשׁ pi. *deceive* Jos 7_{11}, פתה pi. *deceive* Ps 78_{36}, נסה pi. *test* Ps 78_{41}, כעס hi. *anger* 1 K 14_{15}, גנב *steal* Jos 7_{11}, בזה *despise* CD 7_{18}.

זבח *sacrifice* 1 K 8_{62} Ps 50_{14}, נדר *vow* Nm 21_{2}, שׁלם pi. *pay* vows Ho 14_{3} Ps 50_{14}, שׁבע ni. *take an oath* Ezr 10_{25}, כרת *cut*, i.e. make, covenant 2 S 3_{21} Ho 10_{4}, מלך *reign* perh. 1QM 12_{16} (שראל[י]), hi. *make king* 1 K 12_{20} 16_{16} 2 K 17_{21} 2 C 10_{1}, ירשׁ *(dis)possess* Nm 21_{24} Dt 9_{1} Jos 21_{43} Jg 1_{28} (hi.) $11_{21.22}$ Jr 30_{3} 49_{2}, hi. Jg 1_{28}.

ישׁב *dwell* Gn 47_{27} Nm $21_{25.31}$ 25_{1} Jos 10_{15} 21_{43} Jg $11_{17.26}$ 2 S 11_{11} 1 K 5_{5} 11_{16} Ezk 38_{14} 9_{14} Ezr 2_{70}||Ne 7_{72} Ne 11_{3} 1 C 9_{2} (or em. שׁוב *return*), שׁכן *dwell* Nm 24_{2} Dt 33_{28} Jr 23_{6} (or em. יְרוּשָׁלַםִ *Jerusalem*) 1 C 17_{9}, בנה *build*

Ho 8_{14}, קבר *bury* 1 S 25_1 28_3 1 K $14_{13.18}$, זרע *sow* Jg 6_3, נטע *plant* Am 9_{14}, פרח *sprout* Is 27_6 Ho 14_6, צוץ *blossom* Is 27_6, אכל *eat* 1 K 4_{20} Am 9_{14} Ps 78_{29} 124_1, שׁתה *drink* 1 K 4_{20} Am 9_{14}, צום *fast* 1 S 7_6, רעה *graze* Jr 50_{19}, שׁאב *draw (water)* 1 S 7_6, שׁפך *pour out* 1 S 7_6, כון hi. *prepare* Am 4_{12}, כלה *complete* Jos 8_{24} 4QapJoseph[b] 3_{10} ([י]שראל).

<NOM CL> בְּנִי בְכֹרִי יִשְׂרָאֵל *Israel is my son, my first-born* Ex 4_{22}, גֶּפֶן ... יִשְׂרָאֵל *Israel was ... a vine* Ho 10_1, הַעֶבֶד יִשְׂרָאֵל *is Israel a servant?* Jr 2_{14}, יְהוּדָה וְיִשְׂרָאֵל רַבִּים *Judah and Israel were many* 1 K 4_{20}, לֹא־אַלְמָן יִשְׂרָאֵל וִיהוּדָה *Israel and Judah are not widowed* Jr 51_5, יִשְׂרָאֵל שֵׁבֶט נַחֲלָתוֹ *Israel is the tribe of his possession* Jr 10_{16}, נַעַר יִשְׂרָאֵל *Israel was a lad* Ho 11_1, קֹדֶשׁ יִשְׂרָאֵל *Israel was holy* Jr 2_3 4QMMT B_{76}, שֶׂה פְזוּרָה יִשְׂרָאֵל *Israel is a scattered flock* Jr 50_{17}, ישראל למלכות עולמים *Israel shall be an eternal dominion* 1QM 19_8.

<OBJ> ראה *see* Nm 24_2 1 K 22_{17}||2 C 18_{16}, קרא *call* Jr 23_6, זכר *remember* 4QNarrC 1_{19} (ישרא corrected to ירושלם *Jerusalem*), כנה pi. *surname* Is 45_4 Si 36_{17}, צוה pi. *command* Jos 7_{11} 2 K 21_8 Ne 8_1, שׁבע hi. *adjure* Ezr 10_5, נסה pi. *test* Jg 2_{22} $3_{1.4}$, שׁפט *judge* Jg 3_{10} 4_4 $10_{2.3}$ 12_{7+6t} 15_{20} 16_{31} 1 S 4_{18} $7_{15.16.17}$ 2 K 23_{22}, ירה hi. *teach* 1 K 8_{36} ||2 C 6_{27}, יכח hi. *reprove* Ps 50_8, חרף pi. *reproach* 1 S 17_{25} 2 S 21_{21}||1 C 20_7, זעם *curse* Nm 23_7, קלל pi. *curse* Jos 24_9, קנא hi. *make jealous* 4QapJoseph[b] 1_{12}, בחר *choose* Ps 135_4 1QM 10_9, אמן hi. *trust* Jg 11_{20}, אהב *love* 1 K 10_9 Ho 11_1 14_5 2 C 9_8 4QDibHam[a] 1.4_5, ברך pi. *bless* Nm 24_1 Dt 26_{15} Jos 8_{33} 24_{10} 2 C 31_8, יטב hi. *gladden* 1 S 2_{32}, קדשׁ pi. *sanctify* Ezk 37_{28}, חטא hi. *cause to sin* 1 K 14_{16} $15_{26.30.34}$ $16_{2.13.19.26}$ 21_{22} 22_{53} 2 K 3_3 $10_{29.31}$ $13_{2.11}$ 14_{24} $15_{9.18.24.28}$ 17_{21} 23_{15} Si 47_{23} (יח[טיא]), תעה hi. *mislead* 2 K 21_9 Jr 23_{13} CD 5_{20}.

הלך hi. *lead* Ezk 36_{12}, נחה hi. *lead* 2 K 18_{11} (or em. שֹׁמְרוֹן *Samaria*), בוא hi. *bring* 1 C 11_2, יצא hi. *take out* Ex 18_1 1 K 8_{16} Jr 32_{21} Ps 136_{11} 1 C 11_2, שׁלח pi. *send away* Ex $5_{2.2}$ 14_5 2 S 11_1 Jr 3_8 Ps 81_{13}, נסע hi. *cause to set out* Ex 15_{22}, קרב hi. *bring near* Jos 7_{16}, שׁוב hi. *take back* 1 K 8_{34}||2 C 6_{25} CD 6_1, pol. Jr 50_{19}, סור hi. *remove* 2 K 17_{23} 23_{27}, שׂוג hi. *remove* Ho 10_9, עבר *pass by*, i.e. forgive Am 8_2, hi. *make pass through* Ps 136_{14}, דרך *tread* Dt 33_{29}, עלה hi. *take up* Jos 7_{24} 1 S 10_{18} Ho 12_{14} Am 9_7 1 C 17_5, נפל hi. *cause to fall* Ps 78_{28} (or em. qal *fall*, with Israel as subj.).

אסף *gather* 2 S 10_{17}||1 C 19_{17}, קבץ *gather* 1 S 7_5 28_4 2 S 3_{21} 1 K 18_{19}, קהל hi. *gather* 1 C 13_5 15_3, מנה *count* 2 S 24_1 1 C 21_1, ספר *count* 1 C 21_2, פקד *muster* 2 S 24_4 2 K 3_6, קרא *meet* Nm 21_{23} Jos 11_{20} 1 S 4_2 2 S 18_6, מצא *find* Ho 9_{10}.

אבד pi. *destroy* Mc 1_{15} (if em. כְּבוֹד *glory of* Israel to מְאַבֵּד *destroyer of*), שׁחת pi. *destroy* Ho 13_9, hi. Ps 78_{45}, כלה pi. *destroy* 4QDibHam[a] 1.5_7, שׁבר *break* 4QpsEzek[d] 1.2_5, בלע pi. *swallow* Lm 2_5, אכל *eat*, i.e. destroy Is 9_{11} Ps 78_{45}, hi. *feed* Ps 81_{17}, שׁטף *overwhelm* Is 43_2, בלה pi. *wear out*, i.e. trouble 1 C 17_9, נגף *strike* 2 C 13_{15}, נכה hi. *strike*, i.e. defeat Jg 3_{13} 1 K 14_{15} 1 C 21_7, זרה *scatter* 1 K 14_{15} Zc 2_2, pi. Jr 31_{10} , נדח hi. *banish* 2 K $17_{21(Qr)}$ (Kt נדא hi. *expel*) 4QDibHam[a] 1.5_{11} 1.6_{12} (ישר[אל] ... [הדחתם]), גלה hi. *exile* 2 K 17_6 18_{11}, עזב *abandon* 1 K 6_{13}, כרת hi. *cut off* 1 K 9_7, נתשׁ *uproot* 1 K 14_{15} Jr 12_{14}, ירשׁ *(dis)possess* Jr 49_2, כוה *burn* Is 43_2, אסר *bind* Ho 7_{12} (if em. יסר pi. *punish*) $10_{10.10}$, שׁסה *plunder* Jg 2_{14}, רדף *pursue* Ho 8_3, לחץ *oppress* 1 S 10_{18} 2 K $13_{4.6.22}$, עכר *trouble* 1 K 18_{17} 1 C 2_7, געל *abhor* 4QDibHam[a] 1.5_7, ערב *mix* 4QRebukes 1.2_6 (ישר[אל]), רשׁע *do evil to* 4QD[b] 2_2 ([י]שראר).

מגן pi. *hand over* to enemy Ho 11_8, מכר *sell* Jg 2_{14} 3_8 10_7, נתן *give* Jg 2_{14} 1 S 28_{19} 1 K 11_{38} 14_{16} Is 42_{24} 43_{28}, i.e. allow (to pass), Nm 20_{21} 21_{23}, i.e. establish, 1 C 17_{22}, שׂים *place* 4QShir[b] 2.1_7 ([י]שראל), כון pol. *establish* 2 S 7_{24}, ברא *create* Is 43_{15} 4Q408 1_3, יצר *form* Is 43_1 44_{21}, רבה hi. *increase* 1 C 27_{23}, נטע *plant* 2 S 7_{10} Am 9_{15} 1 C 17_9, ישׁב hi. *settle* 2 K 17_6, נחל hi. *cause to inherit* Dt 13_8 Jr 12_{14} Si 46_1, רעה *tend* 2 S 5_2 7_7 Ho 4_{16} 1 C 11_2, שׁמר *keep* Ps 121_4 Si 51_{12} 11QPsAp[a] 1_{10} (שומר יש[ראל]), עבד *serve* 2 S 10_{19} 2 C 35_3, שׂבע hi. *satisfy* Ps 81_{17}.

ישׁע hi. *save* Ex 14_{30} Jg 3_{31} $6_{14.15.36.37}$ 10_1 13_5 1 S $14_{23.39}$ 2 S 3_{18} 2 K 14_{27} Jr 30_{10} 46_{27} Ho 13_{10} 14_4 1QM 10_3 4QMidrEschat[a] 3_{13}, נצל hi. *deliver* Jos 24_{10} 1 S 10_{18} 14_{48} 4QDibHam[a] 1.6_{12} (ישר[אל]), חלץ pi. *deliver* Ps 50_{15}, גאל *redeem* Is 43_1 44_{22} 49_7 Si 51_{12}, פדה *ransom* Dt 21_8 Ps 25_{22} 78_{42} 130_8 1 C 17_{21}, חנן *be gracious to* 4QDibHam[a] 1.5_{11}.

<CSTR> י׳ אֱלֹהֵי(־)יִשְׂרָאֵל *Y., God of Israel* Ex 5_1 32_{27} 34_{23} Jos $7_{13.19.20}$ 8_{30} $9_{18.19}$ $10_{40.42}$ $13_{14.33}$ 14_{14} 22_{24} $24_{2.23}$

יִשְׂרָאֵל

Jg 4$_6$ 5$_{3.5}$ 6$_8$ 11$_{21.23}$ 21$_3$ 1 S 2$_{30}$ 10$_{18}$ 14$_{41}$ 20$_{12}$ 23$_{10.11}$ 25$_{32.34}$ 2 S 12$_7$ 1 K 1$_{30.48}$ 8$_{15.17.20}$

8$_{23.25}$∥2 C 6$_{4.7.10.14.16}$ 1 K 11$_{9.31}$ 14$_{7.13}$ 15$_{30}$ 16$_{13.26.33}$ 17$_{1.14}$ 22$_{54}$ 2 K 9$_6$ 10$_{31}$ 14$_{25}$ 18$_5$ 19$_{15}$ 2 K 19$_{20}$∥Is 37$_{21}$ 2 K 21$_{12}$ 22$_{15.18}$∥2 C 34$_{23.26}$ Is 17$_6$ 21$_{17}$?24$_{15}$ Jr 11$_3$ 13$_{12}$ 21$_4$ (or del.) 23$_2$ 24$_5$ 25$_{15}$ 30$_2$ 32$_{36}$ 33$_4$ 34$_{2.13}$ 37$_7$ 42$_9$ 45$_2$ Ezk 44$_2$ Ml 2$_{16}$ Ps 41$_{14}$ 106$_{48}$∥1 C 16$_{36}$ Ru 2$_{12}$ Ezr 1$_3$ 4$_{1.3}$ 6$_{21}$ 7$_6$ 9$_{15}$ 1 C 15$_{12.14}$ 16$_4$ 22$_6$ 23$_{25}$ 24$_{19}$ 28$_4$ 29$_{10}$ 2 C 2$_{11}$ 6$_{17}$ 11$_{16}$ 13$_5$ 15$_{4.13}$ 20$_{19}$ 29$_{10}$ 30$_{1.5}$ 32$_{17}$ 33$_{16.18}$ 36$_{13}$ Si 50$_{22}$ 4QSel^a 8.2$_5$ (אלוהי) 4QapJoshua^b 22.2$_5$ ([י]שראל) GnzPs 2$_6$ 3$_{10}$ 4$_{16}$, י׳ צְבָאוֹת אֱלֹהֵי *Y. of hosts, God of* 2 S 7$_{27}$ Is 21$_{10}$ 37$_{16}$ Jr 7$_{3.21}$ 9$_{14}$ 16$_9$ 19$_{3.15}$ 25$_{27}$ 27$_{4.21}$ 28$_{2.14}$ 29$_{4.8.21.25}$ 31$_{23}$ 32$_{14}$ 32$_{15}$ 35$_{13.18}$ (or em. י׳) 35$_{19}$ (or del.) 39$_{16}$ 42$_{15.18}$ 43$_{10}$ 44$_{2.11.25}$ 46$_{25}$ 48$_1$ 50$_{18}$ 51$_{33}$ Zp 2$_9$ 1 C 17$_{24}$, אֱלֹהִים אֱלֹהֵי *God, God of* Ps 68$_9$ 72$_{18}$ (or del. אֱלֹהִים) Ezr 6$_{22}$, י׳־אֱלֹהִים צְבָאוֹת אֱלֹהֵי *Y. the God, Sebaoth, God of* Ps 59$_6$.*

אֱלֹהֵי יִשְׂרָאֵל *God of Israel* (without a preceding title) Ex 24$_{10}$ Nm 16$_9$ Jos 22$_{16}$ 1 S 1$_{17}$ 5$_{7.8.10.11}$ 6$_{3.5}$ 2 S 23$_3$ 1 K 8$_{26}$ Is 29$_{23}$ 41$_{17}$ 45$_3$ 45$_{15}$ 48$_1$ 48$_2$ 52$_{12}$ Jr 35$_{17}$ 38$_{17}$ 44$_7$ Ezk 8$_4$ 9$_3$ 10$_{19.20}$ 11$_{22}$ 43$_2$ Ho 8$_2$ (if em. אֱלֹהַי יְדַעֲנוּךָ *my God, we have known you* to יְדַעֲנוּךָ אֱלֹהֵי *we have known you, God of* Israel) Ps 69$_7$ 72$_{18}$ (if del. אֱלֹהִים) Ezr 3$_2$ 8$_{35}$ 9$_4$ 1 C 4$_{10}$ 5$_{26}$ 2 C 29$_7$ 4QJub^a 1$_{28}$ ([אלהי ישראל]) 4QpsEzek^c 2$_5$, אֵל *God of* Ps 68$_{36}$ 1QM 1$_{10}$ 6$_6$ 10$_8$ 13$_{1.2.13}$ 14$_{4.4}$ 15$_{13}$ 16$_1$ 18$_{3.6}$ 1QS 3$_{24}$ perh. 4QMidrEschat^a 2$_{18}$ (י[שר]אל) 4QMidrEschat^b 10$_9$ (ישרא[ל]) 4QNidd 2.2$_5$ 4QBapt 7.2$_3$ ([אל]) 4QM^a 11.2$_{16}$ (ישר[אל]) 4QM^b 1$_{12}$ 4QRitMar 8$_5$ 9$_{2.14}$ 14$_4$ 24$_2$ 30$_3$ ([אל יש]ראל) 101$_1$ ([אל ישר]אל) 104$_4$ ([אל י]שראל) 105$_1$ 4QPrQuot 1.3$_6$ (א[ל ישראל]) 1.3$_{18}$ ([אל]) 7.4$_6$ (יש[ראל]) 33.10$_6$ ([ישר]אל) 33.10$_{20}$ 14.6$_2$ 15.6$_{8.12}$ (ישרא[ל]) 40.2$_3$ ([ישראל]) 41.2$_4$ ([אל ישרא]ל) 48$_{3.7}$ 51$_6$ (both יש[ראל]) 51$_{12.15.17}$ (both [אל ישר]אל) 62$_1$ ([אל יש]ראל) 65$_4$ (יש[ראל]) 66$_2$ (ישרא[ל]) 67$_1$ ([אל יש]ראל) 68$_2$ (יש[ראל]) 69$_2$ (ישר[אל]) 74$_3$ ([י]שראל) 74$_5$ ([אל יש]ראל) 90$_2$ (יש[ראל]) 92$_2$ ([אל] יש[ראל]) 184$_1$ (יש[ראל]) 215$_4$ ([א]ל) 217$_2$ ([אל ישרא]ל) 218$_2$ ([אל י]שרא[ל]) 4QRitPur 29.7$_{21}$ (יש[ראל]) 11.10$_5$ (ישר[א]ל) 1.12$_{2.8}$ (א[ל ישאר]ל) 41$_3$ (ישר[אל]) 42$_3$ ([אל י]ש[ראל]) 64$_5$ (יש[ראל]) 11QBer 1$_2$ ([אל י]שראל).

as other titles of Y., צוּר יִשְׂרָאֵל *rock of Israel* 2 S 23$_3$ Is 30$_{29}$, אֶבֶן *stone of* Gn 49$_{24}$ 4QCommGenC 7$_3$, אֲבִיר *strong one of* Is 1$_{24}$, אוֹר־ *light of* Is 10$_{17}$, מִקְוֵה *hope of* Jr 14$_8$ 17$_{13}$, קְדוֹשׁ *holy one of* 2 K 19$_{22}$ Is 1$_4$ 5$_{19.24}$ 10$_{20}$ 12$_6$ 17$_7$ 29$_{19}$ 30$_{11.12.15}$ 31$_1$ 41$_{14.16.20}$ 43$_{3.14}$ 45$_{11}$ 47$_4$ 48$_{17}$ 49$_7$ 54$_5$ 55$_5$ 60$_{9.14}$ Jr 50$_{29}$ 51$_5$ Ps 71$_{22}$ 78$_{41}$ 89$_{19}$ Si 50$_{17}$ 4QpIsa^b 2$_8$ 4QparaKings 15$_8$, perh. תְּהִלּוֹת *praises of* Ps 22$_4$ (or em. תְּהִלַּת *praise of*).

בְּנֵי(־)יִשְׂרָאֵל *sons of Israel* Gn 32$_{33}$ 36$_{31}$ Ex 1$_{7.9.12.13}$ 2$_{23.25}$ 3$_{9.10.11.13.14.15}$ 4$_{29.31}$ 5$_{14.15.19}$ 6$_{5+8t}$ 7$_{2.4.5}$ 9$_{4.6.26.35}$ 10$_{20.23}$ 11$_{7.10}$ 12$_{27+8t}$ 13$_{2.18.19}$ 14$_{2+9t}$ 15$_{1.19}$ 16$_{1+9t}$ 17$_{1.7}$ 19$_{1.3.6}$ 20$_{22}$ 24$_{5.11.17}$ 25$_{2.22}$ 27$_{20.21}$ 28$_{1+7t}$ 29$_{28.28.43.45}$ 30$_{12.16.16.31}$ 31$_{13.16.17}$ 32$_{20}$ 33$_{5.6}$ 34$_{30.32.34.35}$ 35$_{1.4.20.29.30}$ 36$_3$ 39$_{6.7.14.32.42}$ 40$_{36}$ Lv 1$_2$ 4$_2$ 7$_{23+5t}$ 9$_3$ 10$_{11.14}$ 11$_2$ 12$_2$ 15$_{2.31}$ 16$_{5.16.19.21.34}$ 17$_{2.5.12.13.14}$ 18$_2$ 19$_2$ 20$_{2.2}$ 21$_{24}$ 22$_{2.3.15.18.32}$ 23$_{2+5t}$ 24$_{2+5t}$ 25$_{2.33.46.55}$ 26$_{46}$ 27$_{2.34}$ Nm 1$_{2+5t}$ 2$_{2.32.33.34}$ 3$_{8+11t}$ 5$_{2.4.6.9.12}$ 6$_{2.23.27}$ 8$_{6+13t}$ 9$_{2+9t}$ 10$_{12.28}$ 11$_4$ 13$_{2.3.24.26.32}$ 14$_{2+5t}$ 15$_{2+6t}$ 16$_2$ 17$_{3+7t}$ 18$_{5+12t}$ 19$_{2.9.10}$ 20$_{1+5t}$ 21$_{10}$ 22$_{1.3}$ 25$_{6+5t}$ 26$_{2+6t}$ 27$_{8.11.12.20.21}$ 28$_2$ 30$_{1.2}$ 31$_{2+7t}$ 32$_{7.9.17.18.28}$ 33$_{1+5t}$ 34$_{2.13.29}$ 35$_{2.8.10.15.34}$ 36$_{1+10t}$ Dt 1$_3$ 3$_{18}$ 4$_{44.45.46}$ 10$_6$ 23$_{18}$ 24$_7$ 28$_{69}$ 31$_{19.19.22.23}$ 32$_{8.49.51.51.52}$ 33$_1$ 34$_{8.9}$ Jos 1$_2$ 2$_2$ 3$_{1.9}$ 4$_{4+6t}$ 5$_{1+6t}$ 6$_1$ 7$_{1.1.12.23}$ 8$_{31.32}$ 9$_{17.18.26}$ 10$_{4.11.12.20.21}$ 11$_{14.19.22}$ 12$_{1.6.7}$ 13$_{6.13.22}$ 14$_{1.1.5}$ 17$_{13}$ 18$_{1.2.3.10}$ 19$_{49.51}$ 20$_{2.9}$ 21$_{1.3.8.41}$ 22$_{9+9t}$ 24$_{32}$ Jg 1$_1$ 2$_{4.6.11}$ 3$_{2+10t}$ 4$_{1+5t}$ 6$_{1.2.6.7.8}$ 8$_{28.33.34}$ 10$_{6+6t}$ 11$_{27.33}$ 13$_1$ 19$_{12.30}$ 20$_{1+15t}$ 21$_{5.6.18.24}$ 1 S 2$_{28}$ 7$_{4.6.7.7.8}$ 9$_2$ 10$_{18}$ 11$_8$ 14$_{18}$ 15$_6$ 17$_{53}$ 2 S 7$_{6.7}$ 21$_{2.2.2}$ 1 K 6$_{1.13}$ 8$_{1.9.63}$ 9$_{20.21.22}$ 11$_2$ 12$_{17.24.33}$ 14$_{24}$ 18$_{20}$ 19$_{10.14}$ 20$_{15.27.27.29}$ 21$_{26}$ 2 K 8$_{12}$ 13$_5$ 16$_3$ 17$_{7.8.9.22.24}$ 18$_4$ 21$_{2.9}$ Is 17$_{3.9}$ 27$_{12}$ 31$_6$ 66$_{20}$ Jr 3$_{21}$ 16$_{14.15}$ 23$_7$ (or em. בֵּית *house of* Israel) 23$_8$ (if em. בֵּית) 31$_{33}$ (if em. בֵּית) 32$_{30}$ 32$_{30.32}$ 50$_{4.33}$ Ezk 2$_3$ (or em. בֵּית) 3$_1$ (if em. בֵּית) 4$_3$ (if em. בֵּית) 4$_{13}$ 6$_5$ 12$_{24}$ (if em. בֵּית) 18$_2$ (if em. בֵּית) 20$_{44}$ (or del.) 28$_{25}$ (if em. בֵּית) 35$_5$ (or em. בֵּית) 37$_{16.16}$ (if em. בֵּית) 37$_{21}$ 43$_7$ 44$_{9.15}$ (or em. בֵּית in all three) 47$_{22}$ 48$_{11}$ Ho 2$_{1.2}$ 3$_{1.4.5}$ 4$_1$ 8$_6$ (if em. בֵּית) Jl 4$_{16}$ Am 2$_{11}$ 3$_1$ (or em. בֵּית *house of* Israel) 3$_{12}$ 4$_5$ 9$_7$ Ob$_{20}$ Mc 5$_2$ Ps 103$_7$ 148$_{14}$ Dn 1$_3$ Ezr 3$_1$ 6$_{16.21}$ 7$_7$ Ne 1$_{6.6}$ 2$_{10}$ 7$_{72}$ (or del.) 8$_{14.17}$ 9$_1$ 10$_{40}$ 13$_2$ 1 C 1$_{43}$ (or del.) 2$_1$ 6$_{49}$ 27$_1$ 2 C 5$_{2.10}$ 6$_{11}$ 7$_3$ 8$_{2.8.9}$ 10$_{17.18}$ 13$_{12.16.18}$ 28$_{3.8}$ 30$_{6.21}$ 31$_{1.5.6}$ 33$_{2.9}$ 34$_{33}$ 35$_{17}$ Si 45$_{16.17.23}$ 51$_{12}$ 1QS 1$_{23}$ 1QDM 1$_1$ ([בני] [י]שר[אל]) 1$_4$ (ישרא[ל]) 2$_5$ ([בני י]שראל) 2$_{11}$ (בנ[י ישרא]ל) 4$_1$ ([בני ישר]אל) 4$_5$ (ישר[אל]) 1Q29 5$_4$ ([בני י]ש[רא]ל) 2QJub^b 1$_4$ ([בני ישראל]) 4QJub^a 1.1$_1$ (בנ[י ישראל]) 4QpsJub^f fr. 8$_1$ (ישרא[ל]) fr. 8$_2$ (ישר[א]ל) 4QS^b 2$_2$ ([ישראל]) 4QTobit^e 6$_7$ (ישר[אל]) 4QD^e 6$_{11}$ 4QMyst^a 39$_1$ (ישר[אל]) 68$_2$ (ישר[אל]) 4QPentPar^b 6$_5$ ([בני ישראל]) 23$_{3.4}$ 4Q365a

2.1$_{2}$ 4QapJoshua^{a} 14$_{1}$ ([ישראל]) 14$_{3}$ (יש]ראל]) 4QapPs^{a} 1$_{3}$ (ב]נ[י]) 4QpsEzek^{a} 2$_{4}$ 3$_{3}$ 7$_{6}$ 4$_{2}$ ([ישרא]ל) 16.1$_{6}$ 16.2$_{7}$ 4QpsEzek^{c} 3.2$_{10}$ 4.1$_{3}$ 4QpsMos^{d} 1.2$_{2}$ 4QpsEzek^{e} 36$_{5}$ 4QApocJer^{c} 1.1$_{6}$ 1.2$_{7}$ 4QMMT^{a} 8.3$_{48}$ ([בני ישראל]) 4QBark^{a} 2.1$_{12}$ (בנ]י ישרא]ל) 4QRedInk 5$_{2}$ ([יש]ראל) 4QPrQuot 79$_{4}$ ([ב]ני יש]ראל) 4QOrd^{b} 10.2$_{2}$ 11$_{2}$ 11QT 21$_{8.15}$ (ב]ני יש]ראל) 22$_{11.11}$ 26$_{11}$ 27$_{2.4}$ 29$_{5}$ 37$_{5}$ 39$_{7.12}$ (בנ'[יש]ר[אל) 40$_{3}$ 42$_{14}$ 45$_{14}$ 46$_{7}$ 51$_{6.8}$ 57$_{2}$ 58$_{19}$ 64$_{6.10}$ CD 4$_{2}$ 14$_{4.5}$=4QD^{a} 23.5 (both [בני ישראל]).*

עַם יִשְׂרָאֵל *people of Israel* 2 S 18$_{7}$ 19$_{41}$ Ezr 2$_{2}$ Ne 7$_{7}$ Si 37$_{25(B)}$ (Bmg, D ישורון *Jeshurun*), עֲדַת *congregation of* Ex 12$_{3.6.19.47}$ Lv 4$_{13}$ Nm 16$_{9}$ 32$_{4}$ Jos 22$_{18.20}$ 1 K 8$_{5}$ 11QPs^{a} 122$_{4}$ 2 C 5$_{6}$ 1QSa 1$_{20}$ 2$_{12}$ 11QT 39$_{5}$ ([ישראל]), קְהַל *assembly of* Lv 16$_{17}$ Dt 31$_{30}$ Jos 8$_{35}$ 1 K 8$_{14.14.22.55}$ 12$_{3}$ 1 C 13$_{2}$ 2 C 6$_{3.3.12.13}$ Si 50$_{13.20}$ 1Q29 3$_{3}$ (ק[ה]ל or כו]ל] *all*) 4QapMos^{c} 2.2$_{6}$ 11QT 39$_{5}$ ([ישראל]), מִקְרָאֵי *convocations of* Ps 68$_{27}$ (if em. מְקוֹר *source of*), חבור *company of* CD 12$_{8}$ (= 4QD^{b} 9.3$_{3}$ חבר).

בֵּית יִשְׂרָאֵל *house of Israel* Ex 16$_{31}$ 40$_{38}$ Lv 10$_{6}$ 17$_{3.8.10}$ 22$_{18}$ Nm 20$_{29}$ Jos 21$_{45}$ 1 S 7$_{2.3}$ 2 S 1$_{12}$ 6$_{5.15}$ 12$_{8}$ 16$_{3}$ 1 K 12$_{21}$ 20$_{31}$ Is 5$_{7}$ 14$_{2}$ 46$_{3}$ 63$_{7}$ Jr 2$_{4.26}$ 3$_{18}$ 3$_{20}$ 5$_{11.15}$ 9$_{25}$ 10$_{1}$ 11$_{10.17}$ 13$_{11}$ 18$_{6.6}$ 23$_{7}$ (if em. בְּנֵי *sons of*) 23$_{8}$ (or del. בֵּית or em. בְּנֵי) 31$_{27.31}$ 31$_{33}$ (or em. בְּנֵי) 33$_{14.17}$ 48$_{13}$ Ezk 2$_{3}$ (if em. בְּנֵי) 3$_{1}$ (or em. בְּנֵי) 3$_{4.5.7.7.17}$ 4$_{3}$ (or em. בְּנֵי) 4$_{4.5}$ 5$_{4}$ 6$_{11}$ 8$_{6.10.11.12.14}$ 9$_{9}$ 11$_{5.15}$ 12$_{6.9}$ 12$_{10.24}$ (or em. בְּנֵי) 12$_{27}$ 13$_{5.9}$ 14$_{4.5.6.7.11}$ 17$_{2}$ 18$_{6+6t}$ 20$_{1.3}$ (if em. in both זִקְנֵי *elders of*) 20$_{13+6t}$ 22$_{18}$ 24$_{21}$ 28$_{24.25}$ (or em. בְּנֵי) 29$_{6.16.21}$ 33$_{7.10.11.20}$ 34$_{30}$ 35$_{5}$ (if em. בְּנֵי) 35$_{15}$ 36$_{10+6t}$ 37$_{11.16}$ (or em. בְּנֵי) 39$_{12.22.23.25.29}$ 40$_{4}$ 43$_{7}$ (if em. בְּנֵי) 43$_{7}$ 43$_{10}$ 44$_{6.6.12.15}$ (if em. בְּנֵי) 44$_{22}$ (or del. בֵּית) 45$_{6.8.17.17}$ Ho 1$_{4.6}$ 5$_{1}$ (or em. שָׂרֵי *princes of* Israel) 6$_{10}$ (or em. בֵּית־אֵל *Bethel*, or בֵּית שְׁאָן *Beth Shean*) 10$_{15}$ (if em. בֵּית־אֵל *Bethel*) 12$_{1}$ Am 3$_{1}$ (if em. בְּנֵי־ *sons of*) 5$_{1.3.4.25}$ 6$_{1.11}$ 7$_{10}$ 9$_{9}$ Mc 1$_{5}$ 3$_{4.9}$ Zc 8$_{13}$ Ps 98$_{3}$ 115$_{9(mss)}$ 115$_{12}$ 118$_{2(mss)}$ 135$_{19}$ Ru 4$_{11}$ 1QM 17$_{7}$ (ב]ית י]שראל) 4QpIsa^{a} 8$_{3}$ 4QparaKings 43$_{1}$ ([יש]ראל) 4QpsEzek^{e} 56$_{3}$ MurEpBeth Mashiko7 5/6ḤevEp 12$_{4}$.

בָּתֵּי יִשְׂרָאֵל *houses of Israel* Is 8$_{14}$=CD 7$_{12}$ 4QD^{e} 3.2$_{19}$, שִׁבְטֵי *tribes of* Gn 49$_{16.28}$ Ex 24$_{4}$ Dt 29$_{20}$ 33$_{5}$ Jos 3$_{12.17}$ 4$_{14}$ 12$_{7}$ 24$_{1}$ Jg 18$_{1}$ 20$_{2.10.12}$ 21$_{5.8.15}$ 1 S 2$_{28}$ 9$_{21}$ 10$_{20}$ 2 S 5$_{1}$ 7$_{7}$ 15$_{2.10.17}$ 19$_{10}$ 20$_{14}$ 24$_{2}$ 1 K 8$_{16}$ 11$_{32}$ 14$_{21}$ 2 K 21$_{7}$ Ezk 37$_{19}$ 47$_{13.21.22}$ 48$_{19.29.31}$ Ho 5$_{9}$ Zc 9$_{1}$ (or em. שָׁאטֵי *those who scorn* Israel or שֹׁפְטֵי צֶמֶר *judges of Zemer*) Ps 78$_{55}$ 1 C 17$_{6}$ (if em. שֹׁפְטֵי) 27$_{16.22}$ 29$_{6}$ 2 C 6$_{5}$ 11$_{16}$ 12$_{13}$ 33$_{7}$ Si 45$_{11}$ (ש]בטי יש]ראל) 1QM 2$_{7}$ 3$_{14}$ (ש]בטי ישרא]ל) 5$_{1}$ 4QpIsa^{d} 1$_{7}$ 4QMMT B$_{61}$ ([י]שראל) 11QT 18$_{16}$ 21$_{3}$, מַטּוֹת *tribes of* Nm 31$_{4}$ Jos 22$_{14}$ 11QT 19$_{14}$, מִשְׁפְּחוֹת *families of* Jr 31$_{1}$ (or em. מִשְׁפַּחַת *family of*), זרע *seed of* 4QDibHam^{a} 1.3$_{19}$ CD 12$_{22}$.

צְבָא יִשְׂרָאֵל *army of Israel* 1 K 2$_{32}$ 2 C 25$_{7}$, צִבְאוֹת *armies of* 1 K 2$_{5}$, אֹרֵב *ambush of*, i.e. by Jg 20$_{33}$, גְּדוּד *troop of* 2 C 25$_{9}$, מַחֲנֶה *camp of* Ex 14$_{19.20}$ Jos 6$_{18.23}$ Jg 7$_{15}$ 1 S 28$_{19}$ 2 S 1$_{3}$ 2 K 3$_{24}$, [מ]חנות *camps of* 4QMMT B$_{62}$, הֲמוֹן *multitude of* 2 S 6$_{19}$ 2 K 7$_{13(Qr).13}$, רב *multitude of* 1QS 5$_{22}$ (ריב before erasure), אַלְפֵי *thousands of* Nm 1$_{16}$ 10$_{4.36}$ 31$_{5}$ Jos 22$_{14.21.30}$ 1QSa 1$_{14}$ 4QCommGenA 5$_{3}$ (א]ל[פי) 11QT 19$_{16}$, רִבְבֹת *myriads of* Nm 23$_{10}$ (if em. רֹבַע *quarter*, or *dust*, *of*), בְּחוּרֵי *chosen ones of* 1 S 26$_{2}$ 2 S 10$_{9(Qr)}$ 1Q37 1$_{3}$ 4QpIsa^{e} 6$_{1}$ (ב]חיר[י) 4QpPs^{a} 11$_{2}$ ([בחירי]) 4QMidrEschat^{a} 3$_{19}$ 4QTohB^{a} 3$_{2}$ (בחירי] ישרא]ל) CD 4$_{4}$, גִּבֹּרֵי *warriors of* Ca 3$_{7}$, חַלְלֵי *slain ones of* Jr 51$_{49}$, מַעַרְכֹת *ranks of* 1 S 17$_{8.10.45}$ (both מַעַרְכוֹת), אוֹיְבֵי *enemies of* 2 C 20$_{29}$.

פְּלֵיטַת יִשְׂרָאֵל *remnant of Israel* Is 4$_{2}$, שְׁאָר *remnant of* Is 10$_{20}$ Ne 11$_{20}$ 4QpIsa^{a} 1$_{2}$ ([שאר י]שראל), שְׁאֵרִית *remnant of* Jr 6$_{9}$ 31$_{7}$ Ezk 9$_{8}$ 11$_{13}$ Mc 2$_{12}$ Zp 3$_{13}$ 1 C 12$_{39}$ (שֵׁרִית, or em. שְׁאֵרִית) 34$_{9}$, אֱמוּנֵי *faithful ones of* 2 S 20$_{19}$, נְצוּרֵי *preserved ones of* Is 49$_{6(Qr)}$ (or em. נִצְרֵי *shoots of*), נִדְחֵי *banished of* Is 11$_{12}$ 56$_{8}$ Ps 147$_{2}$ Si 51$_{12}$, גלות *exile of* 4QpsMos^{d} 3$_{6}$.

אִישׁ(־)יִשְׂרָאֵל *man of Israel* Nm 25$_{8.8.14}$ Dt 27$_{14}$ 29$_{9}$ Jos 9$_{6.7}$ 10$_{24}$ Jg 7$_{8.14.23}$ 8$_{22}$ 9$_{55}$ 20$_{11+12t}$ 21$_{1}$ 13$_{6.20}$ 14$_{22.24}$ 17$_{2.19.24.25}$ 2 S 15$_{13}$ 16$_{15.18}$ 17$_{14.24}$ 19$_{42.43.44.44}$ 20$_{2}$ 23$_{9}$ 1 K 8$_{2}$ 1 C 10$_{1.7}$ 16$_{3}$ 2 C 5$_{3}$ 1QS 2$_{22}$, אַנְשֵׁי *men of* 1 S 7$_{11}$ 8$_{22}$ 11$_{15}$ 17$_{52}$ 31$_{1.7.7}$ 2 S 2$_{17}$ 15$_{6}$ 4QParGenEx 3$_{7}$ (א]נשי ישר]אל), מְתֵי *men*, or *weevils*, *of* Is 41$_{14}$, בְּכֹר *firstborn of* Ex 6$_{14}$ Nm 1$_{20}$ 26$_{5}$ 1 C 5$_{1.3}$ (all three בְּכוֹר), זֶרַע *offspring of* 2 K 17$_{20}$ Is 45$_{25}$ Jr 31$_{36.37}$ Ps 22$_{24}$ Ne 9$_{2}$ Ezk 44$_{22}$ (if del. בֵּית *house of*) 1 C 16$_{13}$ (or em. זֶרַע אַבְרָהָם *offspring of Abraham*), בְּנוֹת *daughters of* Dt 23$_{18}$ Jg 11$_{40}$ 2 S 1$_{24}$, בְּתוּלַת *young woman of*, i.e. who is Dt 22$_{19}$=11QT 65$_{15}$ Jr 18$_{13}$ 31$_{4.21}$ Am 5$_{2}$ 4QOrd^{a} 2$_{8}$.

מֶלֶךְ יִשְׂרָאֵל *king of Israel* 1 S 24$_{15}$ 26$_{20}$ 29$_{3}$ 2 S 6$_{20}$ 1 K 15$_{9.16.17.19.32}$ 20$_{2+12t}$ 21$_{18}$ 22$_{2+16t}$||2 C 18$_{3+16t}$ 1 K 22$_{41.45}$ 2 K 3$_{4+7t}$ 5$_{5.6.7.8}$ 6$_{9+5t}$ 7$_{6}$ 8$_{16.25.26}$ 9$_{21}$ 13$_{14.16.18}$ 14$_{1+6t}$ 15$_{1}$.

$_{29.32}$ 16$_{5.7}$ 18$_{1.9.10}$ 21$_3$ 23$_{13}$ 24$_{13}$ Is 7$_1$ 41$_9$ Ho 1$_1$ 10$_{15}$ Am 1$_1$ 7$_{10}$ Mc 1$_{14}$ (if em. מַלְכֵי *kings of*) Pr 1$_1$ (mss עַל king *over* Israel) Ezr 3$_{10}$ Ne 13$_{26}$ 1 C 5$_{17}$ 2 C 8$_{11}$ 16$_{1.3}$ 20$_{35}$ 21$_2$ (or em. יְהוּדָה *Judah*) 22$_5$ 25$_{17.18.21.23.25}$ 28$_{5.19}$ (or em. יְהוּדָה) 29$_{27}$ 30$_{26}$ 35$_{3.4}$ 4QparaKings 3$_2$ ([מל]ך), specif. in ref. to Y. Is 44$_6$ Zp 3$_{15}$ (or em. יִמְלֹךְ Y. *will rule*), מַלְכֵי *kings of* 1 K 14$_{19}$ 15$_{31}$ 16$_{5.14.20.27.33}$ 22$_{39}$ 2 K 1$_{18}$ 8$_{18}$ 10$_{34}$ 13$_{8.12.13}$ 14$_{15}$ 14$_{16.28.29}$ 15$_{11.15.21.26.31}$ 16$_3$ 17$_{2.8}$ 23$_{19.22}$ Mc 1$_{14}$ (or em. מֶלֶךְ) 1 C 9$_1$ 2 C 20$_{34}$ 21$_{6.13}$ 25$_{26}$ 27$_7$ 28$_{2.26.27}$ 32$_{32}$ 33$_{18}$ (or del.) 35$_{18.27}$ 36$_8$ 4QMMT C$_{23}$ (ישרא[ל]).

נְשִׂיאֵי *princes of* Nm 1$_{44}$ 4$_{46}$ 7$_{2.84}$ Ezk 19$_1$ 21$_{17.30}$ 22$_6$ 45$_9$, נשיא ישראל *prince of* Mur 24 2$_3$ (נסיא [י]שרא[ל]) 2$_{10}$ ([נ]סיא [ישר]אל) 3$_2$ ([ישראל]) 3$_9$ ([נסיא ישר]אל) 4$_3$ (נש[י]א [י]שר[אל]) 4$_{18}$ (נסיא ישרא[ל]) 5$_3$ (נסיא [יש]ראל) 5$_7$ (נסיא) 6$_3$ ([ישרא]ל) 6$_8$ ([נשיא]) 7$_3$ ([נש]יא ישראל]) 9$_3$ (נסיא [יש]ראל) 10$_2$ ([נשיא יש]ראל) 5/6ḤevBA 44$_{2.7}$ 5/6 ḤevBA 45$_3$ fr. 2$_2$ Bar-Kochba Revolt Year 1 Coin 169 Bar-Kochba Revolt Year 2 Coin 193, שָׂרֵי *princes of* 1 C 22$_{17}$ 23$_2$ 28$_1$ 2 C 12$_6$ 21$_4$, משיח ישראל *anointed one of Israel* 1QSa 2$_{14}$ ([מש]יח) 2$_{20}$ CD 13$_1$ (משוח ...) 14$_{19}$ (משיח ...) 19$_{11}$ ([מש]יח ...) 4QparaKings 16$_2$ ([מ]שיח ... ישר[א]ל), משיחי ... *anointed ones of* ... 1QS 9$_{11}$, שֹׁפֵט יִשְׂרָאֵל *judge of Israel* Mc 4$_{14}$, שֹׁפְטֵי *judges of* Nm 25$_5$ 1 C 17$_6$ (or em. שִׁבְטֵי *tribes of*), חוֹקְקֵי *commanders of* Jg 5$_9$, זִקְנֵי *elders of* Ex 3$_{16.18}$ 12$_{21}$ 17$_{5.6}$ 18$_{12}$ 24$_{1.9}$ Lv 9$_1$ Nm 11$_{16.30}$ 16$_{25}$ Dt 27$_1$ 31$_9$ Jos 7$_6$ 8$_{10}$ 24$_1$ 1 S 4$_3$ 8$_4$ 2 S 3$_{17}$ 5$_3$ 17$_{4.15}$ 1 K 8$_{1.3}$ Ezk 14$_1$ 20$_{1.3}$ (em. both זִקְנֵי בֵית *elders of the house of*) 1 C 11$_3$ 15$_{25.28}$ 2 C 5$_2$ (or em. כָּל־ *all* Israel) 5$_4$, נְבִיאֵי *prophets of* Ezk 13$_{2.16}$ 38$_{17}$, רוֹעֵי *shepherds of* Ezk 34$_{2.2}$ (רֹעֵי־), קדו[שי] *holy ones of* 4QTohA 1.1$_6$, שבי ישראל *converts of Israel* (i.e. שׁוב ptc.; unless *captives of*, i.e. שְׁבִי) 4QD^a 5.1$_{15}$ CD 4$_2$ 6$_5$ 8$_{16}$ 19$_{29}$, [ר]שעי *wicked ones of* 4QpPs^a 1.3$_{12}$, קֶרֶן *horn of* Lm 2$_3$, קוֹל *voice of* Nm 21$_3$, יַד *hand of* Jos 10$_{30.32}$ 11$_8$ Jg 3$_{30}$ 1 S 14$_{12.37}$ Ezk 25$_{14}$, רֶגֶל *foot of* 2 K 21$_8$ 2 C 33$_8$, ראש *head of* Si 44$_{23}$.

אֶרֶץ יִשְׂרָאֵל *land of Israel* 1 S 13$_{19}$ 2 K 5$_{2.4}$ 6$_{23}$ Ezk 27$_{17}$ 38$_8$ (if em. הָרֵי *mountains of*) 40$_2$ 47$_{18}$ 1 C 22$_2$ 2 C 2$_{16}$ 30$_{25}$ 34$_7$ (if em. אַרְצוֹת *lands of*) 4QparaKings 1$_4$ (א[רץ]) 4QMMT B$_{63}$ 11QT 58$_6$, אַדְמַת *soil of* Ezk 7$_2$ 11$_{17}$ 12$_{19}$ 12$_{22}$ 13$_9$ 18$_2$ (or em. בְּנֵי *sons of*) 20$_{38.42}$ 21$_{7.8}$ 25$_{3.6}$ 33$_{24}$ 36$_6$ 37$_{12}$ 38$_{18.19}$ 4QpsEzek^b 1.2$_2$, גְּבוּל *border of* Jg 19$_{29}$ 1 S 7$_{13}$ 11$_7$ 27$_1$ 2 S 21$_5$ (גְּבֻל) 1 K 1$_3$ 2 K 10$_{32}$ 14$_{25}$ Ezk 11$_{10.11}$ Ml 1$_5$ 1 C 21$_{12}$ 4QpNah 5$_5$ (ישרא[ל]), נַחֲלַת *inheritance of* Jg 20$_6$, הַר *hill country of* Jos 11$_{16.21}$, הָרֵי *mountains of* Ezk 6$_{2.3}$ 19$_9$ 33$_{28}$ 34$_{13}$ 34$_{14}$ 35$_{12}$ 36$_{1.1.4.8}$ 37$_{22}$ 38$_8$ (or em. אֶרֶץ *land of*) 39$_{2.4.17}$, הַר מְרוֹם *mountain of the height of* Ezk 17$_{23}$ 20$_{40}$, הָרֵי מְרוֹם *mountains of the height of* Ezk 34$_{14}$, רום *height of* 4QpPs^a 1.3$_{11}$ (ישר[אל]), מֵימֵי *waters of* 2 K 5$_{12}$, עָרֵי *cities of* 1 S 18$_6$ 1 K 15$_{20}$ 2 K 13$_{25}$ Ezk 39$_9$ 2 C 16$_4$ 11QT 58$_5$ CD 12$_{19}$, מקומות *places of* Kfar Alma inscr. Kfar Baram inscr., מִקְדְּשֵׁי *sanctuaries of* Am 7$_9$, מְקוֹר *fountain of* Ps 68$_{27}$ (or em. מְקוֹרֵי *fountains of*, or em. מִקְרָאֵי *sacred assemblies of*), מקד[ש י]שראל *sanctuary of Israel* 4QMidrEschat^a 3$_6$.

מַמְלֶכֶת יִשְׂרָאֵל *kingship of*, i.e. over, Israel 1 S 24$_{21}$ 4QpsEzek^c 3.2$_7$, מַמְלְכוּת *kingship of* 1 S 15$_{28}$ 11QT 59$_{18}$, ממשלת *dominion of* 1QM 17$_8$, פְּקֻדַּת *overseeing of* 1 C 26$_{30}$, יְשׁוּעַת *salvation of* Ps 14$_7$||Ps 53$_{7(mss)}$ 4QSela 8.2$_{14}$ (ישוע[ת ישראל]), תְּשׁוּעַת *salvation of* Jr 3$_{23}$, ברית *covenant of* 1QM 17$_7$, גאלת *redemption of* Mur 22 1$_1$ (גאולת [י]שר]אל) 24 1$_1$ ([גאול]ת [ישראל]) 2$_2$ 3$_2$ ([גאלת י]שראל) 4$_2$ 5$_2$ ([י]שראל) 6$_2$ ([גאלת]) 7$_2$ ([גאל]ת ישרא[ל]) 9$_2$ (גאלת [י]שראל) Mur29 1$_1$ 2$_1$ ([גא]לת יש]רא[ל) Mur 30 1$_1$ (גאלת [ישראל) 30 2$_8$ (גאולת) Bar Kochba IOU$_2$ (ל[גאלת]; 2nd cent. CE) Bar-Kochba Revolt Year 1 Coins 165 166 169 171 173 176, חר *freedom of* Bar-Kochba Revolt Year 2 Coins 176 178 181 183 (ישאל) 185 186 187 (ישאל) 190A 193 (ישאל), כְּבוֹד *glory of* Mc 1$_{15}$ (or em. מְאַבֵּד *he will destroy* Israel), תִּפְאֶרֶת *glory of* Lm 2$_1$, נֵצַח *glory of* 1 S 15$_{29}$, חֶמְדַּת *desire of* 1 S 9$_{20}$, גְּאוֹן *pride of* Ho 5$_5$ 7$_{10}$ Na 2$_3$ (or em. גֶּפֶן *vine of*), טהרת *purity of* 4QBapt 10$_8$ 4QRitPur 7.11$_2$ ([ט]הרת ישר[אל]).

רָעַת ... יִשְׂרָאֵל *evil of ... Israel* Jr 7$_{12}$, אַשְׁמַת *guilt of* Ezr 10$_{10}$ perh. 4QPseud^b 5.1$_{10}$ (אשמות ...), חַטַּאת *sin of* 1 K 8$_{34}$ Ho 10$_{8.9}$ (if em. חָטָאתָ *you have sinned, Israel*) Dn 9$_{20}$, עֲוֹן *sin of* Jr 50$_{20}$, פִּשְׁעֵי *sins of* Am 2$_6$ 3$_{14}$ Mc 1$_{13}$, מעל ישראל *faithlessness of Israel* CD 20$_{23}$, עורון *blindness of* CD 16$_3$, שְׁבוּת יִשְׂרָאֵל *captivity of Israel* Jr 30$_3$ 33$_7$ (or em. יְרוּשָׁלַםִ of *Jerusalem*) Am 9$_{14}$, עֳנִי *affliction of* 2 K 14$_{26}$, לַחַץ *oppression of* 2 K 13$_4$.

שֵׁם יִשְׂרָאֵל *name of Israel* 2 K 14$_{27}$ Is 44$_5$ 48$_1$ Ps 83$_5$ 1QM 3$_{13}$ 5$_1$, חֻקּוֹת *laws of* 2 K 17$_{19}$, משפטי ישראל *ordinances of Israel* 4QMMT B$_{53}$, עֵדוּת יִשְׂרָאֵל *testimony of Is-*

rael Ps 122$_4$ (or em. עֲדַת *congregation of*), זְמִרוֹת *songs of* 2 S 23$_1$, מַעֲשֵׂה *deed of* 2 C 17$_4$.

מִקְנֵה יִשְׂרָאֵל *cattle of Israel* Ex 9$_{4.7}$ Ezk 45$_{15}$ (if em. מַשְׁקֵה *watered soil of* Ezk 45$_{15}$), גֶּפֶן *vine of* Na 2$_3$ (if em. גְּאוֹן *pride of*), שקל ישראל *shekel of Israel* Jewish War Year 1 Coin 148 Jewish War Year 2 Coin 151 Jewish War Year 4 Coin 158 Jewish War Year 5 Coin 164, מִנְחַת יִשְׂרָאֵל *offering of Israel* 1 S 2$_{29}$, כִּסֵּא *throne of* 1 K 2$_4$ 8$_{20.25}$ 9$_5$ 10$_9$ 2 K 10$_{30}$ 15$_{12}$ 2 C 6$_{10.16}$ 4QDibHam^a 1.4$_7$, נֵר *lamp of* 2 S 21$_{17}$, קֶשֶׁת *bow of* Ho 1$_5$, רֶכֶב *chariot of* 2 K 2$_{12}$ 13$_{14}$.

רֹבַע יִשְׂרָאֵל *quarter*, or *dust*, *of Israel* Nm 23$_{10}$ Nm 23$_{10}$ (or em. רִבְבֹת *myriads of*).

כָּל־יִשְׂרָאֵל *all Israel* Ex 18$_{25}$ Nm 16$_{34}$ Dt 1$_1$ 5$_1$ 11$_6$ (ms lacks כָּל־) 13$_{12}$ 18$_6$=11QT 60$_{14}$ Dt 21$_{21}$ 27$_9$ 29$_1$ 31$_{1.7.11.11}$ 32$_{45}$ 34$_{12}$ Jos 3$_7$ 7$_{24}$ (or em. הָעָם all *the people*) 7$_{25}$ 8$_{15.21.24.33}$ 10$_{15+6t}$ 23$_2$ Jg 8$_{27}$ 20$_{34}$ 1 S 2$_{14.22}$ 3$_{20}$ 4$_{1.5}$ 7$_5$ 11$_2$ 12$_1$ 13$_4$ 14$_{40}$ 17$_{11}$ 18$_{16}$ 19$_5$ 24$_3$ 25$_1$ 28$_{3.4}$ 2 S 3$_{12.21.37}$ 4$_1$ 5$_5$ 8$_{15}$ 10$_{17}$ 14$_{25}$ 15$_6$ 16$_{21.22}$ 17$_{10.11.13}$ 18$_{17}$ 19$_{12}$ 1 K 1$_{20}$ 2$_{15}$ 3$_{28}$ 4$_{1.7}$ 5$_{27}$ 8$_{38}$ (כֹּל...) 8$_{62.65}$ 11$_{16.42}$ 12$_{1.16.18.20}$ 14$_{13.18}$ 15$_{27.33}$ 16$_{16.17}$ 18$_{19}$ 22$_{17}$ 2 K 3$_6$ 9$_{14}$ 10$_{21}$ Ml 3$_{22}$ Dn 9$_{7.11}$ Ezr 2$_{70}$ 8$_{25.35}$ 10$_5$ Ne 7$_{72}$ 12$_{47}$ 13$_{26}$ 1 C 9$_1$ 11$_{1.4}$ (or em. כָּל־אֲנָשָׁיו *all his men*) 11$_{10}$ 12$_{39}$ 13$_{5.6.8}$ 14$_8$ 15$_3$ 17$_6$ 18$_{14}$ 19$_{17}$ 21$_{4.5}$ 28$_{4.8}$ 29$_{21.23.25.26}$ 2 C 1$_{2.2}$ 5$_2$ (if em. זִקְנֵי *elders of*) 6$_{29}$ (כָּל...) 7$_{6.8}$ 9$_{30}$ 10$_{1.3.16.16}$ 11$_{3.13}$ 12$_1$ 13$_{4.15}$ 18$_{16}$ 24$_5$ 28$_{23}$ 29$_{24.24}$ 30$_{1.5.6}$ 31$_1$ 35$_{3.18}$ (כָּל...) 1Q29 3$_3$ ([כו]ל or ק[ה]ל *assembly of*) 4QpNah 3.3$_3$ 4QD^a 5.1$_{18}$ (כול) 4QM^a 16$_4$ (כול) 4QM^g 6$_2$ (כול ישר[אל]) 4QapMos^c 1.1$_7$ (ישׂ[רא]ל) 4Q408 1$_{3.4}$ 6$_2$ 4QapMes 2.3$_5$ CD 3$_{14}$ 16$_1$.

<APP> בָּחִיר *elect* Is 45$_4$, הָמוֹן *multitude* 2 K 7$_{13(Kt)}$, כֹּל *all* 2 S 2$_9$, מְשֻׁבָה *apostate* Jr 3$_{6.8.11.12}$, נַחֲלָה *possession* Is 19$_{25}$ Jl 4$_2$ Ps 78$_{71}$, עֶבֶד *servant* 1 K 8$_{36}$ Ps 136$_{22}$, עַם *people* Dt 21$_{8.8}$=11QT 63$_{6.7}$ Jg 11$_{23}$ 1 S 9$_{16}$ 15$_1$ 2 S 3$_{18}$ 5$_{2.12}$ 6$_{21}$ 7$_7$ 7$_{8.10.11.23.24}$||1 C 17$_{7.9.10.21.22}$ 2 S 24$_4$ 1 K 6$_{13}$ 8$_{16}$ 8$_{16+7t}$||2 C 6$_{5+7t}$ 1 K 8$_{52.56.59.66}$||2 C 7$_{10}$ 1 K 14$_7$ 16$_{2.2.21}$ 2 K 9$_6$ Is 10$_{22}$ Jr 7$_{12}$ 12$_{14}$ 23$_{13}$ 30$_3$ 33$_{21}$ Ezk 14$_9$ 25$_{14}$ 36$_8$ 36$_{12}$ 38$_{14.16}$ 39$_7$ Jl 4$_2$ Am 7$_{8.15}$ 8$_2$ 9$_{14}$ Ps 135$_{12}$ Dn 9$_{20}$ Ezr 9$_1$ 1 C 11$_{2.2}$ 14$_2$ 2 C 6$_6$ 7$_{10}$ 20$_7$ 31$_8$ 35$_3$ Si 36$_{17}$ 1QM 10$_9$ 4QapPs^b 76$_5$ (ישרא[ל]) 4Q417 24$_1$ (ישר[אל]) 4QDibHam^a 1.2$_{11}$ 1.4$_9$ 1.5$_{11}$ 1.6$_{12}$ (ישר[אל]) Kfar Alma inscr., קָהָל *assembly* 1 C 28$_8$, יַחַד *community* 1QS 5$_5$, צָבָא *army* 2 S 20$_{23}$, קָדוֹשׁ *holy one* 4QAdmonPar 1.1$_{10}$ (ק[דשו ישרא[ל] perh. *his holy one, Israel*).

<PREP> לְ of direction, *to* perh. 4QD^a 5.1$_{11}$, + אמר *say* Ps 50$_{12}$ 2 C 1$_{2.2}$ CD 19$_{27}$, ni. *be said* Nm 23$_{23}$, דבר pi. *speak* Dt 6$_3$, נגד hi. *tell* Mc 3$_8$ Ps 147$_{19}$, קרא *call* Jos 23$_2$ Is 45$_4$, ירה hi. *teach* Dt 33$_{10}$, למד pi. *teach* Si 45$_5$, נטף hi. *drip*, i.e. teach CD 1$_{14}$, בין hi. *explain* 2 C 35$_{3(Qr)}$, גלה ni. *be revealed* 4QpNah 3.3$_3$, בוא hi. *bring* Ps 78$_{29}$, שׁוב hi. *bring back* 2 K 14$_{28}$ (if em. בְּ *in* Israel), נפל hi. *cause to fall*, i.e. *apportion* Jos 13$_6$, כחשׁ ni. *cringe* Dt 33$_{29}$, pi. perh. Ps 81$_{14}$, שׁוב *go back* 1 S 7$_{14}$, נתן *give* Dt 26$_{15}$ Jos 11$_{23}$ 21$_{43}$ 1 K 8$_{56}$ 2 K 13$_5$ Is 46$_{13}$ Am 9$_{14}$ Ps 78$_{21}$ 135$_{12}$ 136$_{22}$ 2 C 20$_{10}$, נוח hi. *give rest* Jos 23$_1$, יפע hi. *shine out* CD 19$_{26}$.

לְ of benefit, *to, for* Ps 73$_1$ (or em. לַיָּשָׁר אֵל *God is* good *to the upright one*) 1QM 2$_9$ 15$_1$ (לישר[אל]) 1QS 8$_5$ 9$_6$ 4QS^b 1.2$_4$ 4QD^a 5.1$_{18}$ 4QNidd 1.1$_5$ perh. 4QapMos^c 1.1$_7$ (לכול יש[רא]ל) 5$_2$ perh. 4QpsEzek^e 23$_2$ (לישרא[ל]) 4QMMT C$_{32}$ perh. 4QNarrC 1$_4$ (לישרא[ל]) perh. 1$_{11}$ (ל[י]שראל) 4QM^a 11.2$_{18}$ (ל[י]שראל) perh. 4QSl* 1$_3$ CD 15$_5$, + היה *be* Is 11$_{16}$ Jr 2$_{31}$ Ho 14$_6$ 1 C 17$_{22}$ 2 C 28$_{23}$, יטב *be good* Dt 6$_3$, עשׂה *do* Ex 18$_{1.9}$ Jos 24$_{31}$ Jg 2$_{7.10}$ 1 S 15$_2$ 2 S 7$_{23}$ 15$_6$ 1 K 8$_{66}$||2 C 7$_{10}$ Ho 10$_3$ Am 4$_{12}$, שׂים *place* 1 S 8$_1$ 30$_{25}$ 1 C 17$_9$, עמד hi. *establish* Ps 105$_{10}$||1 C 16$_{17}$, קום hi. *establish* CD 3$_{13}$, יסד *found* 1QS 5$_5$, שׁאר hi. *leave* CD 1$_5$, נשׂא *raise*, i.e. yield, *fruit* Ezk 36$_8$ (or del. Israel), כפר pi. *atone* Dt 21$_8$=11QT 63$_6$, אמר *say*, i.e. designate, burnt offering 2 C 29$_{24}$, זבח *sacrifice* 1 C 29$_{21}$, בזז *plunder* Jos 8$_{27}$, לחם ni. *fight* Jos 10$_{14.42}$ 1QM 10$_3$.

לְ of possession, *of, (belonging) to* 1 S 17$_{46}$ Jr 49$_1$ Ho 10$_1$ Ps 81$_5$ 122$_4$ Dn 9$_7$ Ezr 4$_3$ 8$_{29}$ 10$_2$ 1 C 17$_{24}$ 22$_1$ 2 C 15$_3$ 16$_{11}$ 23$_2$ 24$_6$ 4QConfess 2$_7$ 11QT 58$_4$, + היה *be* Jos 8$_{22}$ 1 K 11$_{25}$ Jr 31$_9$ 1 C 21$_3$ 2 C 6$_{29}$ 35$_3$ 4QCommGenA 5$_1$; ילד לְ pu. *be born to* Jg 18$_{29}$, צרר *be narrow*, i.e. distressing, *to* Jg 10$_9$.

לְ of agent, *by*, + מצא ni. *be found* 2 C 15$_4$, שׁלם ni. *be completed* 4QD^e 3.2$_{21}$.

לְ introducing object, + רפא *heal* Ho 7$_1$, צוק hi. *constrain* 1 K 11$_{25}$ (if em. קוץ בְּ *loathe*), עזר *help* 2 K 14$_{26}$, קהל hi. *assemble* 2 C 24$_6$ (if em. הַקָּהָל *the congregation* of Israel), קרא *call*, i.e. name 4QDibHam^a 1.3$_6$ (ל[י]שראל).

בְּ of place, *in, among, through* Nm 18$_{14}$ 23$_{23}$ Jg 17$_6$ 18$_1$

19$_{1}$ 21$_{25}$ 1 S 9$_{9}$ 18$_{18}$ 26$_{15}$ 1 K 18$_{36}$ 2 K 1$_{3.6.16}$ 5$_{8.15}$ 6$_{12}$ Ezk 39$_{7}$ Ps 76$_{2}$ Ru 4$_{7.7}$ 1 C 12$_{41}$ 2 C 11$_{13}$ 1QS 5$_{6}$ 8$_{9}$ 1QSa 1$_{6}$ 2$_{2}$ 4QD[a] 5.1c-d$_{2}$ (בי[ש]ראל) 4QparaKings 43$_{3}$ 4Q Pseud[b] 5.1$_{2}$ perh. 4QShir[b] 2.2$_{10}$, + היה *be* Nm 18$_{14}$ Jg 11$_{39}$ 18$_{19}$ 21$_{3}$ 2 S 13$_{13}$ Ezk 44$_{29}$ 45$_{8.16}$ 1QS 8$_{4.12}$ 9$_{3}$, ראה ni. *be seen* Jg 5$_{8}$, מצא ni. *be found* 2 C 34$_{33}$, קרא ni. *be called* Dt 25$_{10}$ Ru 4$_{14}$, תנה pi. *recount* Jg 5$_{11}$, משׁל *use a proverb* Ezk 12$_{23}$ 18$_{3}$, למד pi. *teach* Ezr 7$_{10}$, ישׁב *dwell* Lv 23$_{42}$, גור *sojourn* Lv 20$_{2}$ 22$_{18}$ Ezk 14$_{7}$, יסף hi. *assemble* 2 S 6$_{1}$.

הלך *go* 2 C 30$_{6}$, htp. *go* 1 C 17$_{6}$ 21$_{4}$, יצא *go out* Nm 1$_{3.45}$ 26$_{2}$, עלה *go up* Ps 78$_{21}$, קום *arise* Dt 34$_{10}$ Jg 5$_{7}$, hi. *establish* Dt 25$_{7}$, נשׂא *raise up* Ho 13$_{1}$ (or em. ni. *be exalted*), נפל *fall* 2 S 3$_{38}$ Is 9$_{7}$, עבר hi. *cause to pass* 2 C 30$_{5}$, שׁאר hi. *leave* Jg 6$_{4}$ 1 K 19$_{18}$, שׁוב *go back* 4QMMT C$_{21}$ (ישר[אל]), hi. *bring back* 2 K 14$_{28}$ (or em. לְ *for* Israel), נתן *give* Nm 18$_{21}$ 2 S 24$_{15}$ Is 8$_{18}$ Ezk 39$_{11}$ 44$_{28}$ 1 C 21$_{14}$, שׁלח *send* 2 K 10$_{21}$, שׂים *place* Ps 78$_{5}$, עשׂה *do* Dt 22$_{21}$ Jos 7$_{15}$ Jg 20$_{6.10}$ 1 S 3$_{11}$ 11$_{13}$ 14$_{45}$ 17$_{25}$ Jr 29$_{23}$ 32$_{20}$ 2 C 24$_{16}$ 4QJub[f] 33$_{14}$ 4QapJoshua[b] 22.2$_{13a}$, עשׂה ni. *be done* Dt 17$_{4}$=11QT 55$_{20}$ 2 S 13$_{12}$ Ml 2$_{11}$ 2 C 35$_{18}$ 11QT 55$_{6}$, בנה *build* CD 3$_{19}$, פתח ni. *be opened* CD 5$_{3}$, חמד pass. *be desired* 11QT 57$_{21}$.

קדשׁ hi. *consecrate* firstborn Nm 3$_{13}$, זיד hi. *be presumptuous* 11QT 56$_{11}$, שׁחת hi. *destroy* Jg 20$_{21}$, כרת hi. *cut off* survivor 1 K 14$_{10}$ 21$_{21}$ 2 K 9$_{8}$, קצה *cut off* 2 K 10$_{32}$ (or em. לְקְצוֹף בְּ *be angry with* Israel, or לָקוּץ בְּ *feel a loathing for* Israel), מות hi. *bring death* 2 S 20$_{19}$ 21$_{4}$, מות ho. *be put to death* 2 S 19$_{23}$, מאס *reject* Ps 78$_{59}$, חדל *cease* Jg 5$_{7}$, פוץ hi. *scatter* Gn 49$_{7}$, שׁאר ni. *remain* 2 C 34$_{21}$, פרע *let alone* Jg 5$_{2}$.

בְּ of instrument, *by (means of), with,* + באשׁ hi. *put to shame* 1 S 27$_{12}$, פאר htp. *glorify oneself* Is 44$_{23}$ 49$_{3}$.

בְּ *against,* + ראה *see* Nm 23$_{21}$, נגשׁ *approach* 1 S 7$_{10}$, שׁלח pi. *send* Ps 78$_{45.49}$, pu. *be sent* CD 4$_{13}$, נפל hi. *cause to fall* Jr 3$_{12}$, פשׁע *rebel* 2 K 1$_{1}$, אנף htp. *be angry*, חרה *burn* (anger) Nm 25$_{3}$ 32$_{13}$ Jg 2$_{14.20}$ 3$_{8}$ 10$_{7}$ 2 S 24$_{1}$ 2 K 13$_{3}$ CD 20$_{16}$, עלה *go up* (anger) Ps 78$_{31}$, לחם ni. *wage war* Nm 21$_{1.23}$ Jos 24$_{9}$ Jg 11$_{25}$ 1 S 28$_{1}$ 31$_{1}$ 2 K 6$_{8}$.

בְּ introducing object, + בחר *choose* 2 S 10$_{9(Kt)}$ (Qr בְּחוּרֵי יִשְׂרָאֵל appar. *chosen men of Israel*) Is 14$_{1}$ Is 44$_{1}$ Ezk 20$_{5}$ 1 C 19$_{10}$, רעה *tend* Ps 78$_{71}$, עוד hi. *warn* 2 K 17$_{13}$ Ps 50$_{7}$, קוץ *abhor* 1 K 11$_{25}$ (or em. צוק *constrain*), בער *burn* Is 43$_{2}$, נכה hi. *strike* Jg 20$_{31}$, תפשׂ *catch* CD 4$_{16}$.

בְּ *over,* + משׁל *rule* Jg 14$_{4}$ Mc 5$_{1}$ 2 C 7$_{18}$ perh. 1QpHab 8$_{10}$.

כְּ *as* Dt 33$_{29}$ 2 S 7$_{23}$ 1 C 17$_{21}$ 1QM 10$_{9}$, + היה *be* 2 S 14$_{25}$, ירא *fear* 1 K 8$_{43}$ 2 C 6$_{33}$.

אֶל *to* Nm 32$_{14}$ Ml 1$_{1}$, + אמר *say* Dt 20$_{3}$ 29$_{1}$, 1 S 12$_{1}$ 14$_{40}$ 2 C 11$_{3}$ (or del.), דבר pi. *speak* Dt 1$_{1}$ 27$_{9}$ 31$_{1}$ 32$_{45}$ Jr 30$_{4}$, קרא *call* Dt 5$_{1}$ 29$_{1}$, נבא ni. *prophesy* Am 7$_{15}$, שׁמע *listen* 1 K 12$_{16}$, בוא *come* Am 8$_{2}$, עלה *go up* 1 S 7$_{7}$, נתן *give* Jr 3$_{8}$, שׁלח *send* 2 K 17$_{6}$.

אֶל *over,* + כון hi. *establish* 1 S 13$_{13}$ (or em. עַל *over*), משׁח *anoint* 2 K 9$_{3.6.12}$ (or em. עַל in all three).

מִן of direction, *from,* Ho 8$_{6}$ (or em. נִקָּיֹן בְּנֵי *purity, sons of* Israel) Ezr 2$_{59}$ Ne 7$_{61}$ 2 C 8$_{7}$ Si 47$_{2}$, + בוא *come* 2 C 30$_{25}$, גלה *depart* 1 S 4$_{21.22}$, שׁוב *go back* Nm 25$_{4}$ Ho 14$_{5}$ 4QDibHam[a] 1.2$_{11}$, קבץ *gather* 2 C 24$_{5}$, בדל hi. *separate* Ne 13$_{3}$, כרת hi. *cut off* Is 9$_{13}$, בער pi. *destroy* Dt 17$_{12}$ =11QT 56$_{10}$ Dt 19$_{13}$ 22$_{22}$ Jg 20$_{13}$ 11QT 63$_{8}$, שׁמד hi. *exterminate* 2 K 10$_{28}$, מחה ni. *be wiped out* Dt 25$_{6}$ Jg 21$_{17}$, סתר ni. *be hidden* 1QS 8$_{11}$, pu. 4QpsEzek[c] 3.2$_{9}$, hi. *hide* 4QpsEzek[c] 3.3$_{5}$ ([מיש]ראל) CD 1$_{3}$, צמח pi. *cause to sprout* CD 1$_{7}$, גדע ni. *be hewn down* Jg 21$_{6}$, כרת ni. *be cut off* Ex 12$_{15}$ Nm 19$_{13}$; *(from) before,* + היה *be* free of obligation Nm 32$_{22}$.

מִן partitive, (1) *(some) of,* 1 K 8$_{41}$ Ezr 10$_{25}$, + פקד ni. *be missing* Jg 21$_{3}$, סור *be removed* 2 C 15$_{17}$, בוא *come* Jg 20$_{34}$, קבץ *gather* Ezr 7$_{28}$, קבץ ni. *gather* Ezr 10$_{1}$ (or em. מִירוּשָׁלַםִ *some from Jerusalem*), נפל *fall* 1 S 4$_{10}$ 1 C 21$_{14}$ 2 C 13$_{17}$ 15$_{9}$, בחר *choose* Ex 18$_{25}$ 1 S 13$_{2}$ 24$_{3}$, עלה hi. *impose* 1 K 5$_{27}$, שׂכר *hire* 2 C 25$_{6}$, שׁבה *take captive* Nm 21$_{1}$, מות *die* Nm 21$_{6}$.

(2) *from among* Dt 18$_{6}$=11QT 60$_{12}$ 1QS 6$_{13}$ perh. 4QD[a] 5.2$_{12}$ 4QCommMal 1.2$_{1}$ 4QpsEzek[a] 2$_{2}$ 11QT 49$_{9}$, + קום *arise* Nm 24$_{17}$ 1QM 11$_{6}$ CD 7$_{20}$, hi. *raise up* CD 6$_{2}$, עמד *stand,* i.e. arise CD 20$_{1}$, ברר pass. *be chosen* CD 10$_{5}$.

מִן of comparison, *(more) than* Dt 9$_{1}$.

מִקֶּרֶב *from (among),* + סור hi. *remove* Jos 7$_{13}$.

מִתּוֹךְ *from (among),* + שׁמד hi. *destroy* Ezk 14$_{9}$.

עַל *upon, over* Ps 68$_{35}$ 125$_{5}$ 128$_{6}$ 2 C 2$_{3}$ 24$_{9}$ 5/6ḤevEp 1$_{1}$ Tiberias inscr. (others ישׁרון *Jeshurun*), + קרא ni. *be called* Si 47$_{18}$, שׂים *place* 1 S 11$_{2}$, עבר *pass* 1 C 29$_{30}$, מטר

hi. *send rain* Ps 78$_{21}$, יצא hi. *bring out*, i.e. impose obligation 2 K 15$_{20}$, רחם pi. *have mercy* Si 36$_{17}$.

עַל *over, in charge of* 2 S 7$_{26}$ 19$_{23}$ 1 K 4$_{7}$ 16$_{16}$ Pr 1$_{1(mss)}$ (L מֶלֶךְ *king of* Israel) 1 C 26$_{29}$ 29$_{25}$, + היה *be* 1 S 15$_{26}$ 2 S 5$_{2}$ 7$_{8}$ 1 K 13$_{5}$ 4$_{1}$ 8$_{16}$ 11$_{37}$ Ec 1$_{12}$ 1 C 11$_{2}$ 17$_{7}$ 28$_{4}$ 2 C 6$_{5.6}$, עשׂה *do*, i.e. exercise, kingship 1 K 21$_{7}$, נתן *give*, i.e. place 1 K 13$_{4}$ 14$_{7}$ 16$_{2}$ Ne 13$_{26}$ 2 C 13$_{5}$ 4QSel[a] 8.2$_{11}$ (על [ישׂ]רא[ל]), כון hi. *establish* 1 S 13$_{13}$ (if em. אֶל *over* Israel) 2 S 5$_{12}$ 1 C 14$_{2}$ 22$_{10}$, קום hi. *establish* 2 S 3$_{10}$ 1 K 9$_{5}$ 14$_{14}$, צוה pi. *command*, i.e. appoint 1 S 25$_{30}$ 2 S 6$_{21}$ 7$_{11}$ 1 C 17$_{10}$ 22$_{12}$, מלך *rule* 1 S 13$_{1}$ 16$_{1}$ 23$_{17}$ 2 S 2$_{9.10}$ 5$_{5}$ 8$_{15}$ 1 K 2$_{11}$ 6$_{1}$ 11$_{42}$ 15$_{25.25.33}$ 16$_{8.23.29.29}$ 22$_{52.52}$ 2 K 3$_{1}$ 10$_{36}$ 13$_{1.10}$ 15$_{8.17.23.27}$ 17$_{1}$ 1 C 18$_{14}$ 29$_{26.27}$ 2 C 1$_{13}$ 9$_{30}$, hi. *make king* 1 S 12$_{1}$ 15$_{35}$ 1 K 12$_{20}$ 1 C 12$_{39}$ 23$_{1}$ 28$_{4}$, שׂרר *rule* Jg 9$_{22}$, משׁל *rule* 11QT 59$_{15}$, משׁח *anoint* as king, prince 1 S 9$_{16}$ 15$_{1.17}$ 2 S 5$_{3.17}$ 12$_{7}$ 1 K 19$_{16}$ 2 K 9$_{3.6.12}$ (if em. אֶל *over* Israel) 1 C 11$_{3}$, ni. *be anointed* as king 1 C 14$_{8}$, ישׁב *sit* on throne 1 C 28$_{5}$, לכד *capture* kingship 1 S 14$_{47}$.

עַל *against* 2 K 3$_{27}$ 1 C 27$_{24}$ 2 C 28$_{13}$, + עזז *be strong*, i.e. prevail Jg 6$_{2}$, חזק pi. *strengthen* Jg 3$_{12}$, חזק htp. *strengthen oneself* 2 C 17$_{1}$, עמד *stand* 1 C 21$_{1}$, עלה *go up* Ezk 38$_{16}$, נבא ni. *prophesy* Am 7$_{16}$, פקד *visit*, i.e. bring punishment Am 3$_{14}$, יסף hi. *increase* wrath Ne 13$_{18}$.

עַל *to* Ezr 7$_{11}$ 4QPrQuot 1.3$_{10}$ ([עלי]כה) 29.8$_{11}$ ([ע]ליכה) 29.8$_{21}$ ([עליכה יש]ראל) 33.10$_{17}$ ([עליכה ישר]אל) 33.11$_{5.13}$ ([י]שראל) 15.6$_{7}$ ([ישראל]) 41.2$_{1}$ ([י]שראל) 42$_{3}$ (עלי[כ]ה [ישרא]ל) 48$_{2}$ ([עליכה יש]ראל) 48$_{6}$ (ע[ליכה י]שראל) 65$_{5}$ ([ע]ליכה [ישרא]ל) 66$_{3}$ ([עלי]כה), + שׁלח *send* 2 C 30$_{1}$, נתן *give* 1 C 22$_{9}$ 2 C35$_{25}$, צוה pi. *command* 1 C 16$_{40}$ (or em. עַל־בְּנֵי *upon the sons of* Israel), לוה ni. *join oneself* 4QpNah 3.3$_{5}$.

עַל *for, on behalf of* Ezr 3$_{11}$ 1QS 1$_{22}$ 4QOrd[b] 2.2$_{4}$ ([י]שראל), + צוה pi. *command* Ml 3$_{22}$ 1 C 22$_{13}$, קרב hi. *bring near*, i.e. offer Ezr 8$_{35}$, כפר pi. *make atonement* Ne 10$_{34}$ 1 C 6$_{34}$ 2 C 29$_{24}$.

עַל *concerning* Zc 12$_{1}$ 1 C 11$_{10}$, + דבר pi. *speak* Nm 10$_{29}$ Jr 36$_{2}$ (or em. עַל־יְרוּשָׁלַםִ *concerning Jerusalem*), שׁפט ni. *plead* Jl 4$_{2}$, חזה *see* Am 1$_{1}$, כתב pass. *be written* 4QD[a] 11$_{3}$.

מֵעַל *from*, + סור hi. *remove* 1 S 17$_{26}$, עצר ni. *be restrained* 2 S 24$_{25}$, לוה ni. *be joined* Is 14$_{1}$.

עִם *with, for* 2 C 25$_{7}$ CD 16$_{1}$, + היה *be* Dt 18$_{1}$ 1 S 14$_{21}$, הלך *go* 1QM 10$_{3}$, עלה *go up* 1 K 20$_{26}$, כשׁל *stumble* Ho 5$_{5}$ (or del. יִשְׂרָאֵל), לקח *take* Ho 14$_{3}$, עשׂה *do* Dt 33$_{21}$ Jg 8$_{35}$, חזק pi. *strengthen* 1 C 11$_{10}$, ריב *quarrel* Jg 11$_{25}$, יכח htp. *contend* Mc 6$_{2}$, לחם ni. *wage war* Ex 17$_{8}$ Jos 9$_{2}$ 11$_{5}$ Jg 11$_{4.5.20}$ 1 S 13$_{5}$ 2 C 11$_{1}$, כרת *cut*, i.e. make, covenant CD 15$_{9}$.

אֵת *with*, + היה *be* 2 S 21$_{15}$, כרת *cut*, i.e. make, covenant Ex 34$_{27}$, שׁלם hi. *make peace* Jos 10$_{1}$ 2 S 10$_{19}$.

מֵעִם *from*, + שׁאל *ask* Dt 10$_{12}$.

מֵאֵת *from*, + לקח *take* 1 S 7$_{14}$ CD 16$_{14}$.

מֵעַל *from*, + סור hi. *remove* 1 S 17$_{26}$.

לִפְנֵי *before*, + נתן *place*, Jos 11$_{6}$, נגף *strike* Jg 20$_{35}$ 1 S 7$_{10}$, ni. *be struck* 2 S 10$_{15.19}$ 2 K 14$_{12}$ 1 C 19$_{16.19}$ 2 C 25$_{22}$, המם *confuse* Jos 10$_{10}$, ברך pi. *bless* 4QM[g] 1$_{0}$ ([וברכם] בשם לפני [י]שראל *and he blessed them by name before Israel*), עמד *stand* 4QPseud[b] 5.1$_{11}$ ([ע]מוד).

מִלִּפְנֵי *from before*, + נוס *flee* 1 C 19$_{18}$, ירשׁ hi. *dispossess* 2 C 20$_{7}$; מִפְּנֵי *from before*, + נוס *flee* Ex 14$_{25}$ Jos 10$_{11}$ 2 S 10$_{18}$ 2 K 3$_{24}$ 4QM[g] 4$_{3}$ ([וינוס]ו), ירשׁ hi. *dispossess* Jg 11$_{23}$.

נֶגֶד *before*, + עשׂה *do* 2 S 12$_{12}$, כבד pi. *give honour* 1 S 15$_{30}$.

לְעֵינֵי *in the sight of* 1 C 28$_{8}$ 4QOrd[a] 2$_{2}$ ([יש]ראל), + אמר *say* Jos 10$_{12}$, בוא *come* 2 S 16$_{21}$, עשׂה *do* Dt 34$_{12}$, גדל pi. *make powerful* 1 C 29$_{25}$; בְּעֵינֵי *in the sight of* 2 S 3$_{19}$, + גדל pi. *make powerful* Jos 3$_{7}$ 4$_{14}$.

אַחֲרֵי *after*, + יצא *go out* Jos 8$_{17}$, רדף *pursue* Jos 8$_{17}$ 2 S 2$_{28}$ 18$_{16}$.

בְּקֶרֶב *among* Jos 7$_{13}$ Jl 2$_{27}$, + היה *be* Jos 10$_{1}$, ישׁב *live* Jos 6$_{25}$ 13$_{13}$, נתן *set* Dt 21$_{8}$=11QT 63$_{7}$, שׂים *place* plumbline Am 7$_{8}$, ארך hi. *prolong* days Dt 17$_{20}$, בלע *swallow* Dt 11$_{6}$; בְּתוֹךְ *among*, + ידע hi. *make known* Ezk 39$_{7}$, קדשׁ htp. *sanctify oneself* 4QDibHam[a] 1.4$_{9}$.

בֵּין *between*, + היה *be* 1 S 7$_{14}$, ישׁב *remain* 1 K 22$_{1}$, פלה hi. *distinguish* Ex 11$_{7}$, פרר hi. *break* Zc 11$_{14}$.

בַּעֲבוּר *for the sake of*, + נשׂא ni. *be exalted* 1 C 14$_{2}$, נשׂא pi. *exalt* 2 S 5$_{12}$; לְמַעַן *for the sake of* Is 45$_{4}$; בְּעַד *on behalf of*, + זעק *cry out*, 1 S 7$_{9}$, פלל htp. *pray* 1 S 7$_{5}$; עַל אוֹדֹת *on account of*, + עשׂה *do* Ex 18$_{8}$.

<COLL> יִשְׂרָאֵל *O Israel* Ex 32$_{4.8}$ Dt 6$_{4}$ 9$_{1}$ 10$_{12}$ 20$_{3}$ =11QT 61$_{15}$ Dt 27$_{9}$ 33$_{29}$ Jos 7$_{13}$ 2 S 1$_{19}$ 20$_{1}$ 1 K 12$_{16.28}$ Is 10$_{22}$ 40$_{27}$ 41$_{8}$ 43$_{1.22}$ 44$_{1.21.21}$ 48$_{12}$ 49$_{3}$ Jr 3$_{12}$ 4$_{1}$ Jr 30$_{10}$ Ezk 13$_{4}$ Ho 4$_{15}$ 9$_{1}$ 10$_{9}$ 11$_{8}$ 13$_{9}$ Am 4$_{12.12}$ Zp 3$_{14}$ 3$_{15}$ (if em.

מֶלֶךְ *king of* Israel) Ps 50$_{7}$ 81$_{9}$ 115$_{9}$ (or em. בֵּית *house of* Israel, or em. יִשְׂרָאֵל בָּטַח בַּי׳ *Israel trusted in Y.*) 130$_{7}$ (or em. יַחֵל יִשְׂרָאֵל אֶל־י׳ *Israel will wait for Y.*) 131$_{3}$ 2 C 10$_{16}$ 13$_{4}$ 1QM 10$_{3}$ 4QPseud^{b} 5.1$_{7.11}$ 4QPrQuot 1.3$_{10.17}$ 29.8$_{11.21}$ 33.10$_{17}$ (both ישר[אל]) 33.11$_{5.13}$ ([י]שראל) 15.6$_{7}$ ([ישראל]) 41.2$_{1}$ ([י]שראל) 42$_{3}$ (ישרא[ל]) 48$_{2}$ (יש]ראל]) 48$_{6}$ ([י]שראל) 65$_{5}$ (ישרא[ל]) 66$_{3}$.

Israel + Jacob Gn 32$_{29.33}$ 34$_{7}$ 35$_{10.22}$ 46$_{2.5.8}$ 48$_{2}$ 49$_{2.7.24}$ Ex 1$_{1}$ 3$_{15.16}$ 19$_{3}$ Nm 23$_{7.10.21.23}$ 24$_{5.17}$=1QM 11$_{6}$ Dt 33$_{10.28}$ Jos 24$_{32}$ 2 S 23$_{1}$ 1 K 18$_{31}$ 2 K 17$_{34}$ Is 9$_{7}$ 10$_{20}$ 14$_{1}$ 27$_{6}$ 29$_{23}$ 40$_{27}$ 41$_{8}$ 41$_{14}$ 42$_{24}$ 43$_{1.22.28}$ 44$_{1.5.21.23}$ 45$_{4}$ 46$_{3}$ 48$_{1.12}$ 49$_{5.6}$ Jr 2$_{4}$ 10$_{16}$ 30$_{10}$ 31$_{7}$ 46$_{27}$ Ezk 20$_{5}$ 28$_{25}$ 39$_{25}$ Ho 12$_{13}$ Mc 1$_{5}$ 2$_{12}$ 3$_{1.8.9}$ Na 2$_{3}$ Ps 14$_{7}$ 22$_{24}$ 53$_{7}$ 78$_{5.21.71}$ 81$_{5}$ 105$_{10.23}$ 114$_{1}$ 135$_{4}$ 147$_{19}$ Lm 2$_{3}$ 1 C 16$_{13.17}$ Si 45$_{5}$.

+ Ephraim Jg 3$_{27}$ 4$_{5}$ 10$_{1.9}$ 19$_{1}$ 1 S 14$_{22}$ 2 S 2$_{9}$ 18$_{6}$ 2 K 14$_{13}$ Is 17$_{3}$ Jr 31$_{9}$ 50$_{19}$ Ezk 37$_{16.19}$ Ho 5$_{3.3.5}$ (or del. יִשְׂרָאֵל) 5$_{9}$ 6$_{10}$ 7$_{1}$ 10$_{6}$ 11$_{8}$ 12$_{1}$ 13$_{1}$ 2 C 13$_{4}$ 15$_{9}$ 25$_{7.23}$ 30$_{1}$ 31$_{1}$ 34$_{9}$ 4QPseud^{b} 5.1$_{10}$; Joseph Ezk 37$_{16.19}$; Samaria Ho 7$_{1}$ Am 3$_{12}$ 6$_{1}$.

+ Benjamin Jg 10$_{9}$ 20$_{10+8t}$ 21$_{1.6.15.17.18}$ 1 S 9$_{16.21}$ 10$_{20}$ 13$_{2}$ 2 S 2$_{9}$ 3$_{19}$ 1 K 12$_{21}$ Ezr 4$_{1}$ 2 C 11$_{1.3}$ 15$_{9}$ 31$_{1}$ 34$_{9}$.

+ Judah Ex 35$_{30}$ Jos 7$_{1.16}$ 11$_{21}$ Jg 10$_{9}$ 19$_{1}$ 20$_{18}$ 1 S 11$_{8}$ 17$_{52}$ 18$_{16}$ 2 S 2$_{10}$ 3$_{10}$ 5$_{5}$ 11$_{11}$ 12$_{8}$ 19$_{12.41.42.43.44}$ 20$_{2}$ 21$_{2}$ 24$_{1.9}$ 1 K 1$_{35}$ 2$_{32}$ 4$_{20}$ 5$_{5}$ 12$_{17.20.21}$ 14$_{21}$ 15$_{9.17.25.33}$ 16$_{8.23.29}$ 22$_{2.10.29.41.52}$ 2 K 3$_{1.9}$ 8$_{16.25}$ 9$_{21}$ 13$_{1.10.12}$ 14$_{1+8t}$ 15$_{1+5t}$ 17$_{1.13.18.19}$ 18$_{1.5}$ 21$_{12}$ 22$_{18}$ 23$_{22.27}$ Is 5$_{7}$ 7$_{1}$ 11$_{12}$ 48$_{1}$ Jr 3$_{8.11.18}$ 5$_{11}$ 9$_{25}$ 11$_{10.17}$ 12$_{14}$ 13$_{11}$ 19$_{3}$ 23$_{6}$ 24$_{5}$ 27$_{21}$ 30$_{3}$ 30$_{4}$ 31$_{23.27.31}$ 32$_{30.32}$ 33$_{4.7.14}$ 34$_{2}$ 35$_{13.17}$ 36$_{2}$ 37$_{7}$ 42$_{15}$ 44$_{2.7.11}$ 50$_{4.20.33}$ 51$_{5}$ Ezk 9$_{9}$ 25$_{3}$ 27$_{17}$ 37$_{16.19}$ 48$_{31}$ Ho 1$_{1}$ 2$_{2}$ 4$_{15}$ 5$_{5}$ 8$_{14}$ 12$_{1}$ Am 1$_{1}$ Mc 1$_{5}$ 5$_{1}$ Zc 2$_{2}$ 8$_{13}$ 11$_{14}$ Ml 2$_{11}$ Ps 76$_{2}$ 114$_{2}$ Lm 2$_{5}$ Dn 9$_{7}$ Ezr 1$_{3}$ 4$_{1}$ Ne 11$_{3.20}$ 1 C 2$_{1}$ 5$_{17}$ 9$_{1}$ 13$_{6}$ 21$_{5}$ 28$_{4}$ 2 C 10$_{17}$ 11$_{1.3}$ 13$_{15.16.18}$ 15$_{9}$ 16$_{1.11}$ 18$_{3.9.28}$ 20$_{35}$ 21$_{13}$ 23$_{2}$ 24$_{5.6.9}$ 25$_{17+5t}$ 25$_{26}$ 27$_{7}$ 28$_{19.26}$ 30$_{1.6.25}$ 31$_{1.6}$ 32$_{32}$ 33$_{9.16}$ 34$_{9.21.26}$ 35$_{18.27}$ 36$_{8}$.

+ Jerusalem Jos 10$_{1}$ 2 S 5$_{5}$ 11$_{1}$ 16$_{3.15}$ 20$_{2}$ 1 K 2$_{11}$ 8$_{1}$ 11$_{32.42}$ 12$_{18.21.28}$ 14$_{21}$ 2 K 8$_{26}$ 14$_{13}$ 16$_{5}$ 21$_{7.12}$ 23$_{13.27}$ Is 7$_{1}$ 8$_{14}$ 66$_{20}$ Jr 19$_{3}$ 27$_{21}$ 29$_{4.25}$ 32$_{32}$ 35$_{13.17}$ 42$_{18}$ 44$_{2}$ Ezk 9$_{8}$ 11$_{15}$ 12$_{10.19}$ 13$_{16}$ 21$_{7}$ Jl 4$_{16}$ Ob$_{20}$ Mc 1$_{5}$ Zp 3$_{14}$ Zc 2$_{2}$ Ml 2$_{11}$ Ps 147$_{2}$ Ec 1$_{12}$ Dn 9$_{7}$ Ezr 1$_{3}$ 3$_{1}$ 5$_{1}$ 7$_{7.13.15}$ 8$_{29}$ Ne 11$_{3}$ 1 C 11$_{4}$ 15$_{3}$ 21$_{4}$ 23$_{25}$ 28$_{1}$ 29$_{27}$ 2 C 1$_{13}$ 5$_{2}$ 6$_{6}$ 9$_{30}$ 10$_{18}$ 11$_{1.16}$ 12$_{13}$ 19$_{8}$ 21$_{13}$ 23$_{2}$ 24$_{6.9}$ 25$_{23}$ 28$_{27}$ 30$_{1.5.21.26}$ 33$_{7.9}$ 34$_{7.9}$ 35$_{18}$.

+ Amalek Ex 17$_{8.11}$ 1 S 15$_{2}$; Amorites Nm 21$_{21.25.31}$ 22$_{2}$ Dt 4$_{46}$ Jos 5$_{1}$ 10$_{12}$ Jg 3$_{5}$ 10$_{8.11}$ 11$_{19.21.23}$ 1 S 7$_{14}$ 2 S 21$_{2}$ 1 K 9$_{20}$ 21$_{26}$ Is 17$_{9}$ Ezr 9$_{1}$ 2 C 8$_{7}$; Aram Nm 23$_{7}$ Ho 12$_{12}$ Zc 9$_{1}$.

+ Egypt Gn 47$_{27}$ Ex 2$_{23}$ 3$_{10.11.16.18}$ 6$_{11.13.26.27}$ 7$_{4.5}$ 9$_{4}$ 12$_{27.40.42.51}$ 13$_{18}$ 14$_{5.8.20}$ 16$_{1.6}$ 18$_{1}$ 19$_{1}$ 32$_{4.8}$ Lv 23$_{43}$ 25$_{55}$ Nm 3$_{13}$ 8$_{17}$ 14$_{2}$ 26$_{4}$ 33$_{1.38}$ 44$_{5.46}$ 29$_{2}$ Jos 5$_{6}$ 24$_{32}$ Jg 6$_{8}$ 11$_{13.16}$ 19$_{30}$ 1 S 10$_{18}$ 15$_{2.6}$ 2 S 7$_{6}$ 1 K 6$_{1}$ 8$_{9.16.65}$ 12$_{28}$ 2 K 7$_{6}$ 17$_{7}$ Is 11$_{16}$ 19$_{24.25}$ 27$_{12}$ 31$_{1}$ 43$_{3}$ Jr 9$_{26}$ 16$_{14}$ 23$_{7}$ 32$_{20.21}$ 34$_{13}$ 37$_{7}$ 42$_{15.18}$ 46$_{25}$ Ezk 20$_{5}$ 29$_{6}$ Ho 11$_{1}$ 12$_{13}$ Am 3$_{1}$ 9$_{7}$ Ps 105$_{23}$ 114$_{1}$ 1 C 13$_{5}$ 17$_{21}$ 2 C 5$_{10}$ 6$_{5}$ 7$_{8}$ 20$_{10}$ 4QpsEzek^{d} 1.2$_{5}$.

+ Ethiopia(ns) Is 43$_{3}$ Am 9$_{7}$; Gilead Nm 36$_{1}$ Jos 22$_{9.13.32}$ Jg 10$_{8.17}$ 11$_{5}$ 12$_{7}$ 20$_{1}$ 2 S 2$_{9}$ 17$_{26}$ 1 K 17$_{1}$ 2 K 15$_{29}$ Jr 50$_{19}$ Ezk 47$_{18}$.

+ Philistines 1 S 13$_{4.5.19}$ 14$_{22.37.47}$ 17$_{2.3.19.21.46.52}$ 27$_{1}$ 28$_{1.4.19}$ 29$_{3}$ 31$_{1.7}$ 2 S 3$_{18}$ 5$_{17}$ 19$_{9}$ 21$_{15}$ 23$_{9}$ 1 K 15$_{27}$ Is 9$_{12}$ Am 9$_{7}$ 1 C 10$_{1}$ 14$_{8}$.

+ Aaron Ex 4$_{29}$ 5$_{1}$ 6$_{13.26.27}$ 7$_{2}$ 11$_{10}$ 12$_{28.31.50}$ 16$_{2.6.9.10}$ 18$_{12}$ 24$_{1.9}$ 27$_{21}$ 28$_{1.12.29.30.38}$ 29$_{28}$ 34$_{30}$ Lv 7$_{34}$ 9$_{1}$ 10$_{6}$ 16$_{21}$ 17$_{2}$ 21$_{24}$ 22$_{2.18}$ Nm 1$_{3.44}$ 3$_{9.38}$ 4$_{46}$ 6$_{23}$ 8$_{11.19.20}$ 13$_{26}$ 14$_{2.5}$ 17$_{5.6.21}$ 18$_{8.20.28}$ 20$_{12.24.29}$ 25$_{11}$ 26$_{64}$ 33$_{1.38}$ Dt 10$_{6}$ Ps 115$_{12}$ 135$_{19}$ Ne 12$_{47}$ 1 C 6$_{34}$ 24$_{19}$ 1QM 3$_{13}$ 5$_{1}$ 1QS 9$_{11}$ 4QMidr Eschat^{a} 4$_{7}$ ([י]שראל) CD 1$_{7}$ 6$_{2}$ 10$_{5}$ 13$_{1}$ 14$_{19}$ 19$_{11}$ 20$_{1}$.

+ Isaac Am 7$_{9.16}$; Levi Ne 10$_{10}$ 1QM 5$_{1}$ CD 10$_{5}$.

+ עַם *people* 2 S 16$_{18}$ Is 1$_{3}$ Jl 4$_{16}$ Mc 6$_{2}$ Ps 50$_{7}$ 81$_{9.12.14}$ 148$_{14}$, אָדָם *humanity* Jr 32$_{20}$, עֶבֶד *servant* 1 K 8$_{36}$‖2 C 6$_{27}$ Jr 46$_{27}$, בְּנֵי־צִיּוֹן *sons of Zion* Ps 149$_{2}$, בַּת *daughter* of Jerusalem/Zion Zp 3$_{14}$ Lm 2$_{1}$, זֶרַע אַבְרָהָם *seed of Abraham* Is 41$_{8}$.

Also Si 45$_{22}$ 1QM 17$_{5}$ 1QDM 2$_{1}$ 45$_{1}$(both [י]שראל) 1Q37 1$_{1}$ ([ישרא[ל]) 1Q58 1$_{3}$ ([יש]ראל) 4QOrd^{a} 1.2$_{17}$ 4Qp Isa^{c} 4.2$_{7}$ 4QMidrEschat^{b} 8$_{7}$ ([ישרא[ל]) 4QAges^{b} 2$_{3}$ 4Q CommGenB 1$_{2}$ ([י]שראל) 4QCommGenC 5$_{6}$ ([ישר[אל]) 17$_{1}$ ([י]שראל) 4QD^{b} 8$_{7}$ (יש]רא[ל) 13$_{1}$ ([י]שראל) 4QD^{d} 10.2$_{11}$ 4Q365a 1$_{4}$ ([ישר[אל) 4QMyst^{a} 10$_{3}$ ([ישרא[ל]) 13a$_{2}$ ([י]שראל) 66$_{3}$ ([ישרא[ל]) 68$_{1}$ 82$_{3}$ 4QapJoseph^{a} 4$_{2}$ 4Qap Joseph^{b} 1$_{6}$ 2$_{12}$ ([יש]ראל) 4QapMos^{c} 3$_{3}$ 4QapJoshua^{a} 18.2$_{4}$ ([י]שראל) 4QapJoshua^{b} 12$_{8}$ 4QparaKings 4$_{2}$ ([ישר[אל) 38$_{1}$ ([יש]ראל) 38$_{1}$ 48$_{5}$ ([ישרא[ל]) 112$_{4}$ ([י]שראל) 132$_{2}$ 4QpsEzek^{a} 7$_{5}$ ([י]שראל) 4QpsEzek^{d} 1.2$_{4}$ 4Qps Mos^{d} 3$_{7}$ ([י]שראל) 4QpsEzek^{e} 77$_{1}$ 4QConfess 4$_{4}$ ([יש]ראל) 4QJonathan 2$_{4}$ 4QNarrA 10$_{2}$ ([ישרא[ל])

4QMa 11.1$_{10}$ 20$_{2}$ (both [י]שראל) 25$_{1}$ (ישר[אל]) 4QMe 1$_{1}$ (ישר[אל]) 4QMf 3$_{4}$ (יש[ראל]) 4QRitMar 11$_{2}$ 14$_{8}$ (both [י]שראל) 21$_{4}$ 47$_{1}$ (יש[ראל]) 163$_{1}$ ([ישרא]ל) 242$_{1}$ ([י]שרא[ל]) 255$_{2}$ ([י]שראל) 289$_{1}$ (יש[ראל]) 4QPrQuot 36a 11$_{9}$ ([ישר]אל) 15$_{16}$ ([י]שראל) 15$_{17}$ 28$_{4}$ 131$_{2}$ ([ישר]אל) 135$_{2}$ ([י]שראל) 4QpsHistB 1$_{6}$ 4QDibHama 73a ([י]שראל) 4QPrFêtes 26$_{1}$ ([ישרא]ל) 44$_{2}$ ([י]שרא[ל]) 4QShirb 2.1$_{5}$ ([ישרא]ל) 76$_{2}$ ([י]שראל) 4QRitPur 29.7$_{20}$ ([י]שראל) 4Q apMes 15$_{3}$ ([י]שראל) 11QBer 2$_{2}$ ([י]שראל).*

→ יִשְׂרְאֵלִי *Israelite.*

יַשַׂרְאֵלָה 1 pr.n.m. **Jesharelah** (unless em. אֲשַׂרְאֵלָה *Asarelah*, as 1 C 25$_{2}$), Asaphite musician of David, <NOM CL> הַשְּׁבִעִי יַשַׂרְאֵלָה *the seventh (lot) was (for) Jesharelah* 1 C 25$_{14}$. <APP> בֵּן *son* 1 C 25$_{14}$.

יִשְׂרְאֵלִי 5 gent. **Israelite**—fs יִשְׂרְאֵלִית—**1.** as sing. noun, <CSTR> בֶּן הַיִּשְׂרְאֵלִית *son of the Israelite (woman)* Lv 24$_{10}$. <APP> יִתְרָא הַיִּשְׂרְאֵלִי *Ithra the Israelite* 2 S 17$_{25}$. **2.** as attributive adj. of אִישׁ *man* Lv 24$_{10}$, אִשָּׁה *woman* Lv 24$_{10.11}$.

→ יִשְׂרָאֵל *Israel.*

יִשָּׂשכָר 43.0.5 pr.n.m. **Issachar**—Q יש שכר—**1.** ninth son of Jacob, <NOM CL> בְּנֵי לֵאָה ... יִשָּׂשכָר וּזְבוּלֻן *the sons of Leah were ... Issachar and Zebulun* Gn 35$_{23}$. <OBJ> קרא *call* Gn 30$_{18}$. <CSTR> בְּנֵי יִשָּׂשכָר *sons of Issachar* Gn 46$_{13}$. <APP> בֵּן *son* 1 C 2$_{1}$, שֵׁם *name* Gn 30$_{18}$ Ex 1$_{3}$.

2. usu. tribe with §1 as eponymous ancestor, with its assoc. territory, <SUBJ> שמח *be glad* Dt 33$_{18}$, עמד *stand* Dt 27$_{12}$.

<NOM CL> יִשָּׂשכָר חֲמֹר גָּרֶם *Issachar is an ass of (strong) bone(s)* Gn 49$_{14}$, וְיִשָּׂשכָר כֵּן appar. *and thus was Issachar*, or em. וּכְיִשָּׂשכָר *and as Issachar* thus was Barak), וְעַל גְּבוּל שִׁמְעוֹן ... יִשָּׂשכָר *and upon the border of Simeon was ... Issachar* Ezk 48$_{25}$, יש שכר ... לים *Issachar is ... on the west* 11QT 39$_{13}$.

<CSTR> גְּבוּל יִשָּׂשכָר *border of Issachar* Ezk 48$_{26}$, שַׁעַר *gate of* Ezk 48$_{33}$ 11QT 41$_{4}$ 44$_{16}$, מַטֵּה *tribe of* Nm 1$_{29}$ 2$_{5}$ 13$_{7}$ Jos 21$_{6.28}$ 1 C 6$_{47.57}$, בֵּית *house of* 1 K 15$_{27}$, מִשְׁפְּחֹת *families of* Nm 26$_{25}$ 1 C 7$_{5}$, אִישׁ *man of* Jg 10$_{1}$, בְּנֵי *sons of* Nm 1$_{28}$ 2$_{5}$ 10$_{15}$ 26$_{23}$ 34$_{26}$ Jos 19$_{17.23}$ 1 C 7$_{1}$ 12$_{33}$ 11QT 44$_{16}$, נְשִׂיא *prince of* Nm 7$_{18}$, עולת יש שכר *burnt offering of Issachar* 11QT 24$_{15}$.

<APP> אֵלֶּה *these* Dt 27$_{12}$.

<PREP> לְ of benefit, *to, for*, + יצא *go out* Jos 19$_{17}$; of possession, *(belonging) to, of* Nm 1$_{8}$ 1 C 27$_{18}$; בְּ of place, *in, at* Jos 17$_{10}$ Jg 5$_{15}$ 1 K 4$_{17}$, + היה *be* Jos 17$_{11}$; כְּ *as* Jg 5$_{15}$ (if em.); מִן partitive, *some of, (any)one of* 2 C 30$_{18}$; עַד *unto* 1 C 12$_{41}$.

3. Levite, gatekeeper at time of David, son of Obed-edom, <APP> בֵּן *son* 1 C 26$_{5}$. <COLL> יִשָּׂשכָר הַשְּׁבִיעִי *Issachar the seventh* 1 C 26$_{5}$.

→ שׂכר *hire.*

יֵשׁ 138.43.22 part. **(there) is**—יֶשׁ־; sf. יֶשְׁכֶם, יֶשְׁךָ, יֶשְׁנוֹ (יֶשְׁכֶם)—**1.** as part., linking a subject to a complement (*X is*), or as the complement of an indefinite subject (*there is X*).

a. subjects (e.g. יֵשׁ י׳ בַּמָּקוֹם הַזֶּה *Y. is in this place* Gn 28$_{16}$), **(1)** nouns, י׳ *Y.* Gn 28$_{16}$ Ex 17$_{7}$ Jg 6$_{13}$ 2 C ?5$_{9}$, אֱלֹהִים *God* 1 S 17$_{46}$ Ps 58$_{12}$, אֱלוֹהַּ *God* Is 44$_{8}$, אָדָם *human being* Jon 4$_{11}$ Ec 2$_{21}$, אִישׁ *man* Gn 47$_{6}$ Dt 29$_{17}$ Jg 4$_{20}$ 2 K 2$_{16}$ Si 10$_{30(B)}$, אֶחָד *one (person)* Ec 4$_{8}$, רֵעַ *companion* Pr 18$_{24(Seb)}$, אִשָּׁה *woman* Dt 29$_{17}$ Ezr 10$_{44}$ Si 36$_{26(Bmg)}$, אָב *father* Gn 44$_{19.20}$ Jb 38$_{28}$, אָח *brother* Gn 43$_{7}$ 44$_{19.26}$, יֶלֶד *child* Gn 44$_{20}$, עֶבֶד *servant* 2 K 10$_{23}$ (מֵעֲבָדֶי *any of the servants of*), נִכְבָּשָׁה *female captive* Ne 5$_{5}$, מַלְאָךְ *messenger* Jb 33$_{23}$, רֹאֶה *seer* 1 S 9$_{11.12}$ (with ellipsis of subj.), נָבִיא *prophet* 2 K 5$_{8}$, צַדִּיק *righteous one* Gn 18$_{24}$ Ec 8$_{14}$, יָשָׁר *upright one* 2 K 10$_{15.15.15}$ (both with ellipsis of subj.; or em. יֹשֶׁר *uprightness*), חָכָם *wise one* Si 37$_{19.20.22.23}$, מַשְׂכִּיל *intelligent one* Ps 14$_{2}$=53$_{3}$, מוֹכִיחַ *one who reproves* Jb 9$_{33}$, גֹּאֵל *redeemer* Ru 3$_{12}$, דַּיָּן *judge* Jb 19$_{29}$ (if em. שַׁדִּין appar. know *how to judge* to שֶׁיֵּשׁ־דַּיָּן *that there is a judge*), אֹהֵב *friend* Si 6$_{8.9.10}$, דַּל *pauper* Si 10$_{30(A)}$, רָשָׁע *evildoer* Ec 8$_{14}$, מִשְׁפָּחָה *family* Dt 29$_{17}$, שֵׁבֶט *tribe* Dt 29$_{17}$, גּוֹי *nation* 1 K 18$_{10}$, מַמְלָכָה *kingdom* 1 K 18$_{10}$, זָכָר *male (animal)* or *ram* Ml 1$_{14}$ (or em. זָכֶה *unblemished [beast]*).

יָד *hand* Gn 31$_{29}$ Mc 2$_{1}$ Si 5$_{1}$, כֶּרַע *leg* 11QT 48$_{5}$, עַיִן *eye* Is 43$_{8}$, לָשׁוֹן *tongue* 1QMyst 1.1$_{10}$=4QMysta 1$_{2}$ (היש שפה ולשון מחזקת בה *is there a lip or a tongue that holds to it?*), שָׂפָה *lip* 1QMyst 1.1$_{10}$=4QMysta 1$_{2}$, רוּחַ *spirit* Ps 135$_{17}$, *wind* Si 39$_{28(Segal)}$ (יש [רוחות] *there are winds*), נֶפֶשׁ *soul*

2 K 9$_{15}$ (אִם־יֵשׁ נַפְשְׁכֶם appar. *if your soul is [so disposed]*; mss אִם־יֵשׁ אֶת־נַפְשְׁכֶם *if it is with*, i.e. agreeable to, *your soul*) Jb 16$_{4}$.

דֶּרֶךְ *way* Pr 14$_{12}$=16$_{25}$, מָקוֹם *place* Gn 24$_{23}$, עָפָר *dust*, i.e. land Mur 24 3$_{7}$, מוֹצָא *source* Jb 28$_{1}$, עֵץ *tree* Nm 13$_{20}$, שֶׁבֶר *grain* Gn 42$_{1.2}$, תֶּבֶן *straw* Jg 19$_{19}$, מִסְפּוֹא *fodder* Jg 19$_{19}$, אֹכֶל *food* Si 36$_{23(B)}$, מַאֲכָל *food* Si 36$_{23(Bmg)}$, לֶחֶם *bread* Jg 19$_{19}$ 1 S 21$_{5}$, מָעוֹג *cake* 1 K 17$_{12}$, יַיִן *wine* Jg 19$_{19}$, חוֹתָם *seal* 4QṬohA 2$_{3}$, כְּלִי *vessel* 4QṬohB^{b} 14$_{(PC)}$ (חרש אשר [הוא י]ש במזבח *a clay vessel that is on the altar*; WA: [לוא הוג]ש that *is not presented*), חֶרֶב *sword* Nm 22$_{29}$ 1 S 21$_{9}$, חֲנִית *spear* 1 S 21$_{9}$, אֵפוֹד *ephod* Jg 18$_{14}$, תְּרָפִים *teraphim* Jg 18$_{14}$, פֶּסֶל *image* Jg 18$_{14}$, מַסֵּכָה *image* Jg 18$_{14}$, עֹשֶׁר *wealth* Si 30$_{19}$, מַטְמוֹן *treasure* Jr 41$_{8}$, סְגֻלָּה *private treasure* 1 C 29$_{3}$ (or em. יֶשׁ־לִי *there is to me* to שֶׁלִּי *my* house), זָהָב *gold* Pr 20$_{15}$ 1 C 29$_{3}$, כֶּסֶף *silver* 1 C 29$_{3}$, יִתְרוֹן *profit* Ec 2$_{13}$, שָׂכָר *payment* Jr 31$_{16}$ Ec 4$_{9}$ 2 C 15$_{7}$ Si 16$_{14}$.

יוֹם *day* Jr 31$_{6}$, מוֹעֵד *appointed time* Si 36$_{8}$, עֵת *time* Ec 8$_{6}$ Si 38$_{13}$, אַחֲרִית *end* Pr 23$_{18}$=24$_{14}$, מִשְׁפָּט *judgment* Ec 8$_{6}$, דָּבָר *word* 2 K 3$_{12}$ Jr 27$_{18}$ 37$_{17.17}$ (with ellipsis of subj.) Ec 1$_{10}$ 6$_{11}$ 1QS 6$_{12.13}$ 1QSa 2$_{9}$ ([דבר]), מִלָּה *word* Jb 33$_{32}$, מִסְפָּר *number* Jb 25$_{3}$ Si 37$_{25}$ ([מספר יש לימים] *there is a number to days*), perh. עֵרֶךְ *array* 1QMyst 12$_{2}$, דֵּעָה *knowledge* Ps 73$_{11}$, בִּינָה *understanding* 4QMyst^{b} 8$_{6}$ 4QapPs^{b} 76$_{13}$, טַעַם *taste* Jb 6$_{6}$, תִּקְוָה *hope* Jr 31$_{17}$ Jb 11$_{18}$ 14$_{7}$ Pr 19$_{18}$ Ru 1$_{12}$ Lm 3$_{29}$, מִקְוֶה *hope* Ezr 10$_{2}$ 1QH 3$_{20}$ 6$_{6}$ 9$_{14}$ fr. 1$_{7}$, תּוֹחֶלֶת *hope* 1QH fr. 1$_{7}$, בִּטָּחוֹן *security* Ec 9$_{4}$, כֹּחַ *strength* Mc 6$_{14}$ (if em. וְיֶשְׁחֲךָ בְּקִרְבֶּךָ perh. *and your dysentery is within your bowels* to וְיֵשׁ־כֹּחַ בְּקִרְבֵּךְ/בְּקִרְבָּהּ *and there is strength in your/her womb*) 2 C 25$_{8}$ 4QapPs^{b} 76$_{9(mg)}$, מַרְפֵּא *healing* Si 36$_{28}$, טָהֳרָה *purification* 11QT 49$_{15}$.

עָוֹן *iniquity* 1 S 20$_{8}$ 2 S 14$_{32}$, עָוֶל *iniquity* Ps 7$_{4}$, עַוְלָה *iniquity* Jb 6$_{30}$, appar. שֶׁקֶר *falsehood* Jr 23$_{26}$, רָעָה *evil* Ec 5$_{12}$=6$_{1}$=10$_{5}$, הֶבֶל *vanity* Ec 8$_{14}$, בֹּשֶׁת *shame* Si 4$_{21.21}$, מאום *defect* 11QT 52$_{17}$, מַכְאוֹב *pain* Lm 1$_{12}$, מַכָּה *blow* Si 36$_{23}$, מִלְחָמָה *war* 2 C 16$_{9}$.

רַב *much* Gn 33$_{9}$, רֹב *abundance* Pr 20$_{15}$, כֹּל *everything* Gn 33$_{11}$ 39$_{4}$ (כָּל־יֶשׁ־לוֹ *everything [that] there belonged to him*; mss, Sam כָּל־אֲשֶׁר יֶשׁ־לוֹ, as 39$_{5.8}$, in same sense) 39$_{5.8}$ 11QT 58$_{3}$ Mur 30 2$_{23}$, אֲשֶׁר *who(ever)* Dt 29$_{14}$ 2 S 9$_{1}$, מָה *what?* 1 S 21$_{4}$ 2 S 19$_{29}$ 2 K 4$_{2}$ Ne 5$_{2.3.4}$ (all three וְיֵשׁ אֲשֶׁר אֹמְרִים *and there were those who were saying*).

(2) ptc. as substantivized relative clause (e.g. יש מרים ומשפיל *there is one who raises and lowers* Si 7$_{11}$, אך יש אהב שם אהב *but there is one who loves the name of friend*, i.e. who is a friend in name only Si 37$_{1[D]}$), Jr 5$_{1}$ 14$_{22}$ Jb 5$_{1}$ Pr 11$_{24}$ 12$_{18}$ 13$_{7}$ Si 7$_{11}$ 10$_{30(A)}$ 11$_{11.12}$ 12$_{18}$ ([י]ש) 20$_{5(Segal)}$ (יש [מחרי]ש *there is one who is silent*) 20$_{5}$ ([וי]ש) 20$_{6.6.22.23}$ 37$_{1(Bmg, D).7.12(B)}$ (Bmg, D אִישׁ *man*).

(3) לְ + inf. as subj. Gn 23$_{8}$ 2 K 4$_{13}$ 2 C 25$_{9}$ 4Q416 2.2$_{10}$=4Q418 8$_{10}$.

(4) finite verb as subj. of asyndetic relative clause Si 11$_{18}$ (ו[יש] יח[י]ב שכרו perh. *and there is one who deserves his reward*; Segal ו[הוא] *and he*); with subj. not expressed Pr 3$_{28}$ Si 14$_{11.11}$ 25$_{21(Segal)}$ (ועל יש לה [אל] תחמ]ד *and do not desire that which is hers*, i.e. the woman herself; unless יֵשׁ *property*, as §2; or em. על יש לה to אשה do not desire *a woman*) 43$_{30}$ Si 44$_{8.9}$ 48$_{16}$ (all three יש מהם *there are among them*, i.e. some of them).

b. complements (e.g. יֶשׁ־שֶׁבֶר בְּמִצְרָיִם *there is grain in Egypt* Gn 42$_{1}$), **(1)** prepositions, oft. לְ of possession, *of, (belonging) to*; also, בְּ *in, among, on* Gn 28$_{16}$ 42$_{1.2}$ 47$_{6}$ Nm 22$_{29}$ Dt 29$_{17}$ Jg 18$_{14}$ 1 S 9$_{11}$ 20$_{8}$ 2 S 14$_{32}$ 2 K 4$_{2}$ 5$_{8}$ Jr 14$_{22}$ 23$_{26}$ 41$_{8}$ Jon 4$_{11}$ Mc 6$_{14}$ (if em. וְיֶשְׁחֲךָ בְּקִרְבֶּךָ perh. *and your dysentery is within your bowels* to וְיֶשׁ־כֹּחַ בְּקִרְבֵּךְ/בְּקִרְבָּהּ *and there is strength in your/her womb*) Ml 1$_{14}$ Ps 7$_{4}$ 58$_{12}$ 73$_{11}$ 135$_{17}$ Jb 6$_{6.30}$ 2 C 25$_{8}$ 4QṬohB^{b} 14$_{(PC)}$ ([י]ש במזבח) 4QapPs^{b} 76$_{9(mg)}$ 11QT 52$_{17}$ Mur 24 3$_{7}$, *with* Si 36$_{28(Bmg, C)}$ perh. 4Q418 210$_{2}$, *on account of* Si 20$_{5}$ 1QH 9$_{14.14}$, בְּקֶרֶב *among* Ex 17$_{7}$, בְּתוֹךְ *inside* Gn 18$_{24}$, כְּ *as* Lm 1$_{12}$, כְּפִי *in accordance with* Si 6$_{8}$, מִן *among* Ezr 10$_{44}$ Si 36$_{8}$ 44$_{8.9}$ 48$_{16}$, *by way of* Si 11$_{18}$ ([י]ש), *on account of* Si 20$_{6.22.23(Segal)}$, מֵאֵת *from* Jr 37$_{17.17}$ (with ellipsis of prep.), מִבַּלְעֲדֵי *apart from* Is 44$_{8}$, אֵת *with* Gn 23$_{8}$ 44$_{26}$ 2 K 2$_{16}$ 3$_{12}$ 9$_{15(mss)}$ 10$_{15}$ (or em. הֲיֵשׁ אֶת־לְבָבְךָ *is there* an upright one *with your heart?* to הֲיֵשׁ לְבָבְךָ עִם־לְבָבִי *is your heart* upright *with my heart?*) 10$_{15.15}$ (both with ellipsis of prep.) Jr 27$_{18}$ Pr 3$_{28}$ Si 5$_{12}$ 1QS 6$_{12.13}$ 4QMyst^{b} 8$_{6}$, עִם *with* Jg 6$_{13}$ 2 K 10$_{23}$ 2 C 16$_{9}$, עַל perh. *at the command of* Jb 33$_{23}$, בֵּין *between* Jb 9$_{33}$, לִפְנֵי *in front of* 1 S 9$_{12}$ Pr 14$_{12}$=16$_{25}$, תַּחַת *under* 1 S 21$_{4.5}$ (with ellipsis of prep.) 21$_{9}$ Ec 10$_{5}$, *instead of* Jb 16$_{4}$, בִּגְלַל *on account of*

Si 10$_{30(A)}$.

(2) adverbs, פֹּה *here* Dt 29$_{14}$ Jg 4$_{20}$ 1 S 21$_{9}$ 2 K 10$_{23}$, עוֹד *still* 2 S 9$_{1}$ 2 S 19$_{29}$ Si 43$_{30}$, תָּמִיד *always* Si 37$_{12(B)}$; noun used adverbially, בֵּית *(in the) house of* Gn 24$_{23}$.

(3) adjectives, 2 K 10$_{15(mss)}$ (הֲיֵשׁ לְבָבְךָ יָשָׁר *is your heart upright?*) Pr 18$_{24}$ (יֵשׁ אֹהֵב דָּבֵק מֵאָח *there is a friend more clinging than a brother*) Ru 3$_{12}$ (יֵשׁ גֹּאֵל קָרוֹב מִמֶּנִּי *there is a redeemer more closely related than I am*) Si 36$_{23}$ (Segal) (אך יש אוכל [מאוכל נעים] *but there is food more pleasant than any other*) 36$_{26(Segal)}$ ([אך יש אשה מאשה] [יפה] *but there is a woman fairer than any other woman*).

(4) לְ + infinitive, Pr 18$_{24(Seb)}$ (יֵשׁ רֵעִים לְהִתְרֹעֵעַ *there are companions to keep company with*; MT אִישׁ *a man of*, i.e. with, companions).

(5) imperative, Si 5$_{12}$ 14$_{11.11}$.

(6) participle equivalent to relative clause, Ec 7$_{15.15}$ Ne 5$_{2.3.4}$ Si 6$_{9}$ 10$_{30(A)}$ 37$_{19.20(B)}$ 1QMyst 1.1$_{10}$=4QMyst^{a} 1$_{2}$.

(7) relative clause introduced by אֲשֶׁר or -שֶׁ, Ec 1$_{10}$ 2$_{21}$ 5$_{12}$=6$_{1}$ 8$_{14.14.14}$ Si 38$_{13}$.

(8) asyndetic relative clause, Si 36$_{23(Bmg)}$ (אך יש מאכל ממאכל תנעם *but there is food that is more pleasant than any other*) 36$_{26(B)}$ (אך יש מכה ממכה תנעם *but there is a blow that is more pleasant than any other*) 37$_{20(D)}$ (ויש חכם בדברו ימאס *and there is a wise person who is despised because of what he says*) 37$_{22}$ (יש חכם לנפשו יחכם *there is a wise person who [alone] considers himself wise*), 37$_{23(D)}$ (ויש חכם לעמו יחכם *and there is a wise person who is considered wise by his people*) 39$_{28(Segal)}$ (יש [רוחות למשפט נו]צרו *there are winds that are kept for judgment*).

(9) none of the above, 1 K 18$_{10}$ 2 K 4$_{13}$ Is 43$_{8}$ Jr 5$_{1}$ 31$_{6}$ Ps 14$_{2}$=53$_{3}$ Jb 5$_{1}$ 11$_{18}$ 33$_{32}$ Pr 11$_{24}$ 12$_{18}$ 13$_{7}$ 19$_{18}$ 20$_{15}$ 23$_{18}$ =24$_{14}$ Ec 4$_{8}$ 9$_{4}$ Lm 3$_{29}$ Si 4$_{21.21}$ 6$_{10}$ 7$_{11}$ 11$_{11.12.18}$ ([ו]יש) Si 20$_{5(Segal).6.23}$ 37$_{1(Bmg, D).7}$.

<COLL> יֵשׁ with pronom. sf. expressing subject, יֶשְׁךָ *you are*, יֶשְׁנוֹ *he is*, etc., complemented by ptc. Gn 24$_{42.49}$ 43$_{4}$ Dt 13$_{4}$=11QT 54$_{12}$ Jg 6$_{36}$, by prep. 1 S 14$_{39}$, by noun Est 3$_{8}$; with resumptive pronom. sf., Dt 29$_{14}$ (אֶת־אֲשֶׁר יֶשְׁנוֹ פֹּה *with whomever is here*).

הֲיֵשׁ *is there?* Gn 24$_{23}$ 43$_{7}$ 44$_{19}$ Ex 17$_{7}$ Nm 13$_{20}$ Dt 13$_{4}$ Jg 4$_{20}$ 1 S 9$_{11}$ 2 S 9$_{1}$ (הֲכִי יֵשׁ־) 2 K 4$_{13}$ 10$_{15}$ Is 44$_{8}$ Jr 14$_{22}$ 23$_{26}$ (or del. -הֲ or em. הַשְּׁמִי *is my name?*) 37$_{17}$ Ps 14$_{2}$ =53$_{3}$ Jb 5$_{1}$ 6$_{30}$ 25$_{3}$ 38$_{28}$ 1QMyst 1.1$_{10}$=4QMyst^{a} 1$_{2}$ 1Q Myst 12$_{2}$ 4QMyst^{b} 8$_{6}$ 4QapPs^{b} 76$_{13}$.

יֵשׁ וָיֵשׁ *there is and there is*, i.e. yes indeed 2 K 10$_{15}$.

יֵשׁ :: אַיִן *(there is) not* Gn 44$_{26}$ Ex 17$_{7}$ Nm 13$_{20}$ Dt 29$_{14}$ Jg 4$_{20}$ 19$_{19}$ (+) 1 K 18$_{10}$ Is 44$_{8}$ (+) Pr 13$_{7}$ (+) Ne 5$_{5}$ Si 5$_{12}$ 30$_{19}$ (+); אַיִן(־)יֵשׁ־ *(there) is not* 1 S 21$_{9(mss)}$ (L אַיִן; or em. אַיֵּן *where* is? or אִם *is* there? or הֵן *behold*, there is) Ps 135$_{17}$ (or del. יֵשׁ־), לֹא יֵשׁ־ *there is not* Jb 9$_{33}$ (mss לוּ as *if only* there were, as Nm 22$_{29}$; Jb 16$_{4}$).

2. as noun, **property,** <SUBJ> ספה ni. *be swept away* Pr 13$_{23}$ (or em. רָשׁ *pauper*). <OBJ> נחל hi. *bequeath* Pr 8$_{21}$ (+ וְאֹצְרֹתֵיהֶם אֲמַלֵּא *and that I might fill their treasuries*). <CSTR> מחלקת נחלה ויש *the distribution of inheritance and property* Si 43$_{3(M)}$ (B מחלוקת; Bmg יֹשֶׁר *and uprightness*).

3. יֵשׁ אֲשֶׁר appar. as conditional conj., **if, whenever,** Nm 9$_{20.21}$ (both + יִהְיֶה הֶעָנָן and if *the cloud stayed*).

Also 4QSD 5$_{1}$ 4QHod^{c} 3$_{3}$.

<ANT> §1 אַיִן *not*.

[יִשְׁאָל] 1.0.0.1 pr.n.m. **Ishal**—Kt Or ישאל (Qr [L] וּשְׁאָל *and Sheal*)—**1.** member of Bani family, husband of non-Jewish wife, <NOM CL> מִבְּנֵי בָנִי ... ישאל *of the sons of Bani were ... Ishal* Ezr 10$_{29(Kt Or)}$.

2. Seal 213$_{1}$ (Jerusalem, 7th cent.), <PREP> לְ of possession, *(belonging) to, of* Seal 213$_{1}$ (Jerusalem, 7th cent.).

⇒ שׁאל *ask*.

ישׁב 1085.20.82.1 vb. **sit—Qal** 1036.13.80.1 Pf. יָשַׁב (יָשָׁב), יָשְׁבָה, יָשַׁבְתָּ (Si ישבתה), יָשַׁבְתְּ, יָשַׁבְתִּי, יָשְׁבוּ (יָשָׁבוּ), יְשַׁבְתֶּם, יָשַׁבְנוּ; impf. יֵשֵׁב (יֵשֶׁב), 3fs תֵּשֵׁב, 2ms תֵּשֵׁב, תֵּשְׁבִי (תֵּשֵׁבִי), אֵשֵׁב (אֵשֵׁבָה, אֵשְׁבָה), יֵשְׁבוּ (יֵשֵׁבוּ), תֵּשְׁבוּ (תֵּשֵׁבוּ), נֵשֵׁב; + waw וְיָשַׁב, וְיָשְׁבָה, וְיָשַׁבְתָּ (וְיָשַׁבְתָּה), וְיָשַׁבְתְּ, וְיָשְׁבוּ (וְיָשָׁבוּ), וִישַׁבְתֶּם, וְיָשַׁבְנוּ; וַיֵּשֶׁב (וַיֵּשֵׁב), 3fs וַתֵּשֶׁב, וָאֵשֵׁב (וָאֵשְׁבָה), וַנֵּשֶׁב, וַתֵּשְׁבוּ, וַיֵּשְׁבוּ (וַיֵּשֵׁבוּ); impv. שֵׁב (שֵׁב־, שְׁבָה, Q שיבנה), שְׁבִי, שְׁבוּ (שֵׁבוּ); ptc. יֹשֵׁב (יוֹשֵׁב, יֹשְׁבִי), יֹשֶׁבֶת (יֹשָׁבֶת, יוֹשֶׁבֶת, יֹשְׁבָה, Kt ישבתי), יֹשְׁבִים (יוֹשְׁבִים), יֹשְׁבֵי (יֹשְׁבֵיהֶן, יוֹשְׁבֵיהֶם, יוֹשְׁבֶיהָ, יֹשְׁבֶיהָ, יוֹשְׁבָיו, יֹשְׁבָיו, יוֹשְׁבֵי), יֹשְׁבֹת (יֹשְׁבוֹת, Q יושבות); inf. abs. יָשֹׁב (שׁוֹב Jr 42$_{10}$); inf. cstr. שֶׁבֶת (שָׁבֶת, שִׁבְתִּי, שִׁבְתְּךָ (שִׁבְתֶּךָ, Si שבתיך), שִׁבְתּוֹ, שִׁבְתָּהּ, שִׁבְתֵּנוּ, שִׁבְתְּכֶם, שִׁבְתָּם).

1. sit (e.g. Gn 18$_{1}$ 19$_{1}$ 31$_{34}$ 38$_{14}$ Ex 2$_{15}$ 11$_{5}$ 17$_{12}$ Lv 15$_{4}$

Dt 6$_{7}$ 17$_{18}$ Jg 3$_{20}$ 1 S 1$_{9}$ 20$_{5}$ 2 S 18$_{24}$ 1 K 1$_{13}$ 13$_{20}$ 2 K 1$_{8}$ 4$_{20}$ Is 3$_{26}$ Jr 32$_{12}$ Ezk 2$_{6}$ Jl 4$_{12}$ Mc 4$_{4}$ Zc 3$_{8}$ Ps 1$_{1}$ Est 1$_{2}$ Si 34$_{12}$).

2. sit down* (e.g. Gn 21$_{16}$ Ex 32$_{6}$ Dt 23$_{14}$ 1 S 28$_{23}$ Jon 4$_{5}$ Ru 4$_{2}$).

3. sit on throne, be enthroned,* of king (e.g. Dt 17$_{18}$ Si 40$_{3(B)}$ 4QCommGenA 5$_{2}$ perh. Is 10$_{13}$), of Babylon as queen (Is 47$_{8}$), of Y. (e.g. 1 S 4$_{4}$ 2 S 6$_{2}$||1 C 13$_{6}$ 2 K 19$_{15}$ ||Is 37$_{16}$ 40$_{22}$ Ps 2$_{4}$ 9$_{11}$ 22$_{3}$ 29$_{10.10}$ 47$_{9}$ 55$_{20}$ [or em.; see Subj.] 80$_{2}$ 99$_{1}$ 102$_{13}$ 113$_{5}$ 123$_{1}$ Lm 5$_{19}$).

4. lie down, rest (e.g. Ps 127$_{2}$).

5. remain, stay, of persons (e.g. Gn 22$_{5}$ 27$_{44}$ 44$_{33}$ Ex 16$_{29}$ Lv 8$_{35}$ 12$_{4}$ Nm 22$_{8}$ Dt 1$_{6}$ 9$_{9}$ Jos 2$_{22}$ Jg 6$_{18}$ 2 S 1$_{1}$ 2 K 2$_{2}$ Jr 37$_{16}$), of objects (e.g. Gn 49$_{24}$ [or em.; see Subj.] 1 S 5$_{7}$ 2 S 6$_{11}$ Jr 30$_{18}$ Ps 125$_{1}$).

6. dwell, inhabit* (e.g. Gn 19$_{29.30}$ Ex 23$_{33}$ Lv 20$_{22}$ 25$_{18}$ Nm 13$_{18}$ Dt 2$_{4}$ 23$_{17}$ Jos 6$_{25}$ 7$_{7}$ 15$_{63}$ Jg 1$_{21}$ 6$_{10}$ 1 S 27$_{5}$ 2 S 7$_{5}$ 1 K 2$_{36}$ 3$_{17}$ 2 K 6$_{1}$ 25$_{24}$||Jr 40$_{9}$ Is 6$_{5}$ 10$_{24}$ Jr 2$_{6}$ 27$_{11}$ 35$_{9}$ Ezk 12$_{2}$ 28$_{25}$ 36$_{17}$ Ho 4$_{3}$ Am 3$_{12}$ Na 1$_{5}$ Hg 1$_{4}$ Ps 9$_{12}$ 101$_{7}$ Jb 15$_{28}$ Pr 21$_{19}$ Lm 1$_{3}$ Est 9$_{19}$ Ezr 2$_{70}$||Ne 7$_{72}$ Ne 3$_{26}$ 1 C 4$_{28}$ 2 C 19$_{4}$).

7. settle* (e.g. Gn 4$_{16}$ 11$_{2.31}$ 13$_{12.18}$ 19$_{30}$ 20$_{1.15}$ 26$_{6}$ 34$_{10.21.23}$ 35$_{1}$ 36$_{8}$ 37$_{1}$ 45$_{10}$ 47$_{4}$ Dt 12$_{29}$).

8. be inhabited, populated (e.g. Is 13$_{20}$ 45$_{18}$ 1QIsa^{a} 44$_{26}$ Jr 17$_{6}$ 50$_{13.39}$ Ezk 26$_{20}$ [or em.; see Subj.] 29$_{11}$ 35$_{9(Kt)}$ 36$_{35}$ Jl 4$_{20}$ Zc 2$_{8}$ 7$_{7.7}$ 9$_{5}$ 12$_{6}$ 14$_{10}$ Si 16$_{4.4(B)}$ [[תשנ]ב]).

9. be set, of eye, as jewel (Ca 5$_{12}$), of teeth, in order (4QCrypt 2.1$_{3}$).

10. be established, stand, endure, e.g. of throne (Ps 122$_{5}$).

11. perh. **sit in worship*** (Is 65$_{4}$ Ps 23$_{6}$ 27$_{4}$ 84$_{5}$ 133$_{1}$ 140$_{14}$).

12. with לְ, **wait for** (Ex 24$_{14}$ Jg 16$_{9}$ Jr 3$_{2}$).

13. ptc. as noun (distinction from §6 oft. unclear), **inhabitant.**

<SUBJ> Y. Ex 15$_{17}$ Nm 10$_{36}$ (if em. שׁוּבָה *return* to שְׁבָה *dwell*) 1 S 4$_{4}$ 2 S 6$_{2}$||1 C 13$_{6}$ 2 S 7$_{5.6}$||1 C 17$_{4.5}$ appar. 2 S 15$_{8(Qr)}$ (or em. יָשׁוֹב to הָשֵׁב, i.e. hi. inf. abs. שׁוב hi. *bring back*) 1 K 8$_{13.27.30.39.43.49}$||2 C 6$_{2.18.21.30.33.39}$ 1 K 22$_{19}$||2 C 18$_{18}$ 2 K 19$_{15}$||Is 37$_{16}$ Is 6$_{1}$ Jl 4$_{12}$ Ps 9$_{5.8.12}$ 22$_{4}$ 29$_{10.10}$ 33$_{14}$ 47$_{9}$ 68$_{17}$ 99$_{1}$ 102$_{13}$ 113$_{5}$ 132$_{14}$ Lm 5$_{19}$ Si 36$_{18}$ 4QapPs^{b} 76$_{12}$, אֵל *God* Ps 55$_{20}$ (or em. יִשְׁמַע אֵל וְיַעֲנֵם וְיֹשֵׁב קֶדֶם *God hears and humbles them, even the one who is enthroned of old* to יִשְׁמָעֵאל ויענים וְיֹשְׁבֵי קֶדֶם *Ishmael and the bedouin and those who dwell in the east* or יִשְׁמָעֵאל וְיַעְלָם יֹשֵׁב קֶדֶם *Ishmael and Jalam dwell in the east*) *god* Is 44$_{13}$, פֶּסֶל *image* Is 44$_{13}$.

Amalekite Nm 13$_{29}$ 14$_{25.45}$, Amorite Gn 14$_{7}$ Nm 13$_{29}$ Dt 1$_{44}$ Jos 24$_{8}$ Jg 1$_{35}$, Arab 2 C 26$_{7}$, Aram(aean) 1 K 22$_{1}$ 2 K 16$_{6(Kt)}$, Asher(ite) Jg 1$_{32}$ 5$_{17}$, Avvim Dt 2$_{23}$, Baasha 1 K 15$_{21}$, Cananite Gn 13$_{7}$ Nm 13$_{29}$ 14$_{25.45}$ 21$_{1}$ Dt 11$_{30}$ Jos 16$_{10.10}$ 17$_{12.16}$ Jg 1$_{10.27.29.29.30}$ 1 K 9$_{16}$, Caphtorim Dt 2$_{23}$, Carmelite 1 S 27$_{3}$, Edomite 2 K 16$_{6(Qr)}$, Emim Dt 2$_{10}$, Geshurite Jos 13$_{13}$, Gittite 2 S 15$_{19}$, Hittite Nm 13$_{29}$, Hivite Jos 9$_{7}$, Horite Dt 2$_{12}$, Israel(ite) Gn 47$_{27}$ Nm 20$_{15}$ 21$_{25.31}$ 25$_{1}$ Dt 1$_{6.45(Sam).46}$ 3$_{29}$ 6$_{7}$ 8$_{12}$ 11$_{19.30}$ 12$_{10.10.29}$ 13$_{13}$ =11QT 55$_{2}$ ([לש]בת) Dt 17$_{14}$=11QT 56$_{12}$ Dt 19$_{1}$ 23$_{14}$ 26$_{1}$ 28$_{30}$ 29$_{15}$ 30$_{20}$ Jos 21$_{43}$ Jg 11$_{17.26}$ 2 S 11$_{11}$ 1 K 5$_{5}$ 11$_{16}$ 22$_{1}$ Jr 8$_{14}$ 9$_{5}$ (or em. שׁוּב *repent*) Ezk 34$_{25.28}$ 38$_{14}$ 39$_{26}$ Ho 9$_{3}$ Am 9$_{14}$ Mc 5$_{3}$ 7$_{8}$ Zc 14$_{11}$ Ps 69$_{36}$ 137$_{1}$ Ezr 2$_{70}$||Ne 7$_{72}$ Ezr 8$_{32}$ Ne 11$_{3}$, Jebusite Nm 13$_{29}$ Jos 15$_{63}$ Jg 1$_{21}$, Jew Jr 32$_{12}$ 44$_{1.1}$ Est 5$_{13}$ 6$_{10}$ 9$_{19}$ Ne 4$_{6}$, Judah 2 S 11$_{11}$ 1 K 5$_{5}$ Jr 31$_{24}$ 44$_{26}$ Jl 4$_{20}$ Lm 1$_{3}$ 2 C 32$_{10}$, Maacathite Jos 13$_{13}$, Moab(ite) Dt 2$_{29}$ Jr 48$_{18}$ Ru 2$_{7}$, Naamathite Jb 2$_{13}$, Naphtali Jg 1$_{33}$, Perizzite Gn 13$_{7}$, Philistine 1 S 31$_{7}$||1 C 10$_{7}$ 2 C 28$_{18}$, Rephaim Dt 2$_{20}$ Jos 12$_{4}$, Shuhite Jb 2$_{13}$, Shumanite 2 K 4$_{13}$, Temanite Jb 2$_{13}$, Tishbite 1 K 17$_{5.9}$ 2 K 1$_{8}$, Tyrians Ne 13$_{16}$, people from various cities 2 K 17$_{24.25}$.

Ashkelon Zc 9$_{5}$, Babylon Is 13$_{20}$ Jr 50$_{13.39}$, Jerusalem/Zion Is 3$_{26}$ 5$_{2}$ (or em. שְׁבִיָּה *captive*) 44$_{26(1QIsa^{a})}$ (MT ho.) 65$_{21}$ Jr 3$_{2}$ Jl 4$_{20}$ Zc 2$_{8}$ 7$_{7}$ 12$_{6}$ 14$_{10.11}$, Kedar Is 42$_{11}$, No-amon, i.e. Thebes Na 3$_{8}$, Samaria Ezk 16$_{46}$, Tyre Ezk 26$_{20}$ (or em. לֹא תֵשֵׁבִי *you shall not be inhabited* to לֹא תָשֻׁבִי *you shall not return*) 27$_{3}$.

עַם *people* Ex 32$_{6}$ Nm 13$_{18.19.19.28}$ 20$_{1}$ 22$_{5}$ Jos 7$_{7}$ 24$_{7.13.15}$ Jg 18$_{7}$ 20$_{26}$ 21$_{2}$ 1 S 12$_{11}$ 13$_{16}$ Is 30$_{19}$ 32$_{18}$ 33$_{24}$ 65$_{4.21}$ Jr 25$_{5}$ 29$_{16}$ 42$_{10.10.13.14}$ 43$_{4}$ 44$_{15}$ 49$_{1}$ Ezk 38$_{8.12.14}$ Am 9$_{14}$ Hg 1$_{4}$ Ps 68$_{11}$ Ezr 2$_{70}$||Ne 7$_{72}$ Ezr 10$_{9}$ 4QapJoseph^{b} 1$_{20}$, גּוֹי *nation* Jos 5$_{8}$ 2 K 17$_{29}$ Jr 27$_{11}$ 49$_{31}$ Ezk 31$_{6}$, שֵׁבֶט *tribe* Jg 18$_{1}$ 1 C 5$_{22}$, עֵדָה *congregation* Ex 16$_{3}$, קָהָל *assembly* Ne 8$_{17}$, מִשְׁפָּחָה *family* 1 C 4$_{28}$, בַּיִת *house* Gn 46$_{34}$ 50$_{22}$ 1 S 27$_{3}$ 2 S 2$_{3}$ Jr 35$_{7.9.10.11}$ Ezk 28$_{25.26.26}$ 36$_{17.28}$ 39$_{26}$ Am 5$_{11}$, פְּלֻגָּה *section of tribe* Jg 5$_{16}$, גֹּלָה *exiles* Jr 29$_{5.28}$ Ezk 3$_{15.15}$, גְּדוּד *troop* 1 K 11$_{24}$, חַיָּה *flock* perh. Ps 68$_{11}$ (but prob.

חַיָּתֵךְ *your dwelling place*).

Aaron Lv 8$_{35}$, Abdon 1 C 8$_{32}$ 9$_{38}$, Abiathar 1 S 22$_{23}$ 2 S 15$_{29}$, Abigail 1 S 27$_{3}$, Abimelech Jg 9$_{41}$, Abner 1 S 20$_{25}$, Abra(ha)m Gn 11$_{31}$ 13$_{6.6.12.18}$ 16$_{3}$ 18$_{1}$ 20$_{1.15}$ 22$_{19}$ 24$_{3}$ 4QCommGenA 2$_{9}$, Absalom 2 S 14$_{28}$ 15$_{8}$, Admatha Est 1$_{14}$, Adonijah 1 K 1$_{24}$, Ahasuerus Est 1$_{2}$, Ahinoam 1 S 27$_{3}$, Ahio 1 C 8$_{32}$ 9$_{38}$, Alma 5/6ḤevBA 44$_{5}$, Amaziah 2 K 14$_{10}$||2 C 25$_{19}$, Athaiah Ne 11$_{4}$, Baal 1 C 8$_{32}$ 9$_{38}$, Baruch Jr 36$_{15}$, Bela 1 C 5$_{8.9}$, Bildad Jb 2$_{13}$, Boaz Ru 4$_{1}$, Cain Gn 4$_{16}$, Carshena Est 1$_{14}$, David 1 S 19$_{2.18}$ 20$_{5.5.19}$ 22$_{5}$ 23$_{14.14.18.25}$ 24$_{1.4}$ 26$_{3}$ 27$_{3.5.7.11}$ 2 S 1$_{1}$ 5$_{9}$||1 C 11$_{7}$ 2 S 7$_{18}$||1 C 17$_{16}$ 2 S 11$_{1}$||1 C 20$_{1}$ 2 S 18$_{24}$ 1 C 17$_{1}$ 4QDibHam^{a} 1.4$_{7}$, Deborah Jg 4$_{5}$, Delaiah Jr 36$_{12}$, Eglon Jg 3$_{20}$, Eli 1 S 1$_{9}$ 4$_{13}$, Elijah 1 K 17$_{5.9.19}$ 19$_{4}$ 2 K 1$_{9}$ 4QparaKings 9$_{6}$, Eliphaz Jb 2$_{13}$, Elisha 2 K 2$_{2.4.6.18}$ 6$_{1.2.32}$, Elishama Jr 36$_{12}$, Elkanah 1 C 9$_{16}$, Elnathan Jr 36$_{12}$, Ephron Gn 23$_{10}$, Esau Gn 36$_{7.8}$ 4QJub^{h} 36$_{19}$, Ezekiel Ezk 3$_{15(Qr)}$ (וָאֵשֵׁב; Kt ואשר *and who*; or em. אֲשֶׁר *who*) 3$_{15}$ 8$_{1}$, Ezra Ezr 9$_{3.4}$, Gaal Jg 9$_{41}$, Gedaliah Jr 40$_{10}$, Gedor 1 C 8$_{32}$ 9$_{38}$, Gemariah Jr 36$_{12}$.

Hagar Gn 21$_{16.16}$, Haman Est 3$_{15}$, Hannah 1 S 1$_{23}$, Hezekiah 2 C 32$_{10}$, Huldah 2 K 22$_{14}$||2 C 34$_{22}$, Hushai 2 S 16$_{18}$, Isaac Gn 24$_{62}$ 25$_{11}$ 26$_{6.17}$, Isaiah Is 6$_{5}$, Ittai 2 S 15$_{19}$, Jacob/Israel Gn 25$_{27}$ 27$_{44}$ 29$_{14.19}$ 35$_{1}$ 37$_{1}$ 48$_{2}$, Jacob (son of Judah) MurEpBeth-Mashiko$_{4}$, Jehonathan 5/6 ḤevEp 12$_{3}$ (יהו[נ]תן ... יושב[י]ן), Jehoshaphat 1 K 22$_{10}$ ||2 C 18$_{9}$ 2 C 18$_{9}$ 19$_{4}$, Jeiel/Jeuel 1 C 8$_{29}$ (if ins. יְעִיאֵל or יְעוּאֵל) 9$_{35}$, Jephthah Jg 11$_{3}$, Jeremiah Jr 15$_{17.17}$ 16$_{8}$ 37$_{16.21}$ 38$_{13.28}$ 39$_{14}$ 40$_{5.6}$, Jeroboam, son of Nebat 1 K 12$_{2}$ (or em.; see Prep.) 12$_{25}$, Jeroboam, son of Joash 2 K 13$_{13}$, Jerubbaal Jg 8$_{29}$, Joab 1 K 11$_{16}$, Job Jb 2$_{8}$ 29$_{25}$, Johanan Jr 41$_{17}$ 42$_{10.10.13.14}$ 43$_{4}$, Jonah Jon 4$_{5.5}$, Joseph Gn 50$_{22}$, Joshua Jos 19$_{50}$, Jothan Jg 9$_{21}$, Kish 1 C 8$_{32}$ 9$_{38}$, Lot Gn 11$_{31}$ 13$_{6.6.12}$ 14$_{12}$ 19$_{1.29.30.30.30}$, Maaseiah Ne 11$_{4}$, Machir Nm 32$_{40}$, Marsena Est 1$_{14}$, Masbala 5/6ḤevEp 12$_{3}$ (יושב[י]ן), Memucan Est 1$_{14}$, Mephibosheth 2 S 9$_{13}$, Meres Est 1$_{14}$, Mikloth 1 C 8$_{32}$ 9$_{38}$, Mordecai Est 2$_{19.21}$ 5$_{13}$ 6$_{10}$, Moses Ex 2$_{15.15.21}$ 17$_{12}$ 18$_{13.14}$ Dt 9$_{9}$.

Nadab 1 C 8$_{32}$ 9$_{38}$, Naomi Ru 1$_{4}$, Nehemiah Ne 1$_{4}$, Ner 1 C 9$_{38}$, Nergal-sharezer Jr 39$_{3}$, Og Dt 1$_{4}$, Oholibah Ezk 23$_{41}$, Orpah Ru 1$_{4}$, Rachel Gn 31$_{34}$, Rahab Jos 2$_{15}$ 6$_{25}$, Rahab (sea monster) Is 30$_{7}$ (רַהַב הֵם שָׁבֶת perh. *they are Rahab that sits still*; or em. to רָהְבָּהּ מָשְׁבָּת *her noise stilled*, or em. הֵם שָׁבֶת to הַמָּשְׁבָּת *the silenced one*, i.e. שׁבת ho. ptc.), Rehoboam 2 C 11$_{5}$, Ruth Ru 1$_{4}$ 2$_{14.23}$, Samgar-nebo Jr 39$_{3}$, Samson Jg 15$_{8}$, Samuel 1 S 19$_{18}$, Sarai Gn 11$_{31}$, Sarsechim Jr 39$_{3}$, Saul 1 S 14$_{2}$ 19$_{9}$ 22$_{6}$ 28$_{23}$, Sennacherib 2 K 19$_{27.36}$||Is 37$_{28.37}$, Shethar Est 1$_{14}$, Shimei 1 K 2$_{36.38}$, Sihon Dt 1$_{4}$ 3$_{2}$ 4$_{46}$ Jos 12$_{2}$, Simeon (son of Kosiba) Mur 24 2$_{4}$ 3$_{4}$ ([שמעון] ... ש[י]שב) 4$_{4}$ (שמע[ו]ן) 5$_{3}$, Sisera Jg 4$_{2}$, Solomon 1 K 1$_{13.17.30.35.46}$ 2$_{12}$ 7$_{8}$ 8$_{20}$||2 C 6$_{10}$ 1 C 28$_{5}$ 29$_{23}$ 2 C 2$_{2}$ 4QpsEzek^{a} 13.2$_{2}$, Tamar, daughter-in-law of Judah Gn 38$_{11.11.14}$, Tamar, daughter of David 2 S 13$_{20}$, Tarshish Est 1$_{14}$, Tehinnah 5/6ḤevBA 44$_{5}$, Terah Gn 11$_{31}$ Jos 24$_{2}$, Tola Jg 10$_{1}$, Uriah 2 S 11$_{12.12}$, Uzziah 2 C 26$_{21}$, Zadok 2 S 15$_{29}$, Zechariah 1 C 9$_{38}$, Zecher 1 C 8$_{32}$, Zedekiah Jr 36$_{12}$, Zimri 1 K 16$_{11}$, Zophar Jb 2$_{13}$, Zur 1 C 8$_{32}$.

אִישׁ *man* Gn 34$_{21.22.23}$ Ex 16$_{29}$ Jos 2$_{22}$ 8$_{9}$ Jg 10$_{1}$ 17$_{10}$ 19$_{4.15}$ 20$_{47}$ 1 S 24$_{4}$ 27$_{3}$ 2 S 2$_{3}$ 10$_{5}$||1 C 19$_{5}$ 1 K 5$_{5}$ 8$_{25}$||2 C 6$_{16}$ 1 K 13$_{14.20}$ 21$_{13}$ 22$_{10}$||2 C 18$_{9}$ 2 K 7$_{3.4}$ 18$_{27}$||Is 36$_{12}$ 2 K 25$_{24}$||Jr 40$_{9}$ Jr 22$_{30}$ 25$_{5}$ 29$_{32}$ 33$_{17}$ 35$_{15}$ 49$_{18.33}$ 50$_{40}$ 51$_{43}$ Ezk 14$_{1}$ 20$_{1}$ Mc 4$_{4}$ Zc 6$_{13}$ Ps 1$_{1}$ Ru 4$_{2.2}$ Ezr 10$_{16}$ Ne 11$_{2.3}$ 1 C 4$_{43}$ 2 C 18$_{9}$ 1QS 6$_{4.9}$ 7$_{20}$ 1QSa 2$_{13.16}$ 11QT 59$_{14.17}$ 5/6 ḤevEp 12$_{3}$ (יושב[י]ן), גֶּבֶר *man* Lm 3$_{28}$, בַּעַל *husband* Pr 31$_{23}$ Si 25$_{18}$, אִשָּׁה *woman, wife* Lv 12$_{4.5}$ 15$_{20.22.23.26}$ 31$_{9}$ Dt 21$_{13}$=11QT 63$_{13}$ Jos 1$_{14}$ Jg 4$_{5}$ 13$_{9}$ 1 S 1$_{23}$ 27$_{3}$ 1 K 3$_{17}$ 2 K 22$_{14}$||2 C 34$_{22}$ Jr 41$_{17}$ Ezk 8$_{14}$ Ho 3$_{3}$ Zc 5$_{7}$ Pr 9$_{14}$ Ru 1$_{4}$ 2 C 8$_{11}$ 4QDg 1.2$_{8}$ ([אשה] ... [ת]שב) perh. 4QTohC 1$_{4}$ ([אשה]), אָדָם *human being* Jr 2$_{6}$.

אָב *father* Gn 27$_{19}$ 45$_{10}$ 47$_{6}$ Jos 24$_{2}$ 1 S 22$_{4}$ Ezk 37$_{25}$ 1 C 8$_{29}$ 9$_{35}$, אֵם *mother* 1 S 22$_{4}$ 1 K 2$_{19}$, בֵּן *son* Gn 11$_{31}$ 27$_{44}$ 29$_{14}$ 34$_{10.10.16}$ Lv 8$_{35}$ Nm 32$_{6.40}$ Dt 2$_{4.8.12.21.22.22.29}$ Jos 19$_{50}$ 22$_{33}$ Jg 1$_{16}$ 8$_{29}$ 10$_{1}$ 18$_{28}$ 21$_{23}$ 2 S 16$_{3}$ 1 K 1$_{13.17.30.35}$ 3$_{6}$ 21$_{13}$ 2 K 4$_{38}$ 6$_{1.2}$ 10$_{30}$ 15$_{12}$ Is 49$_{20}$ Jr 36$_{12.15}$ 40$_{10}$ 41$_{17}$ 42$_{10.10.13.14}$ 43$_{4}$ Ezk 33$_{31}$ 37$_{25}$ Ps 132$_{12}$ Ru 1$_{4}$ Ne 11$_{3.4.6.25}$ 1 C 5$_{8.9.10.11.16.22.23}$ 7$_{29}$ 8$_{32}$ 9$_{3.38}$ 28$_{5}$ Si 8$_{14}$ 34$_{12.18}$ 1QSa 2$_{13}$ ([בני]) Mur 24 2$_{4}$ 3$_{4}$ 4$_{4}$ ([בן]) 5$_{3}$ MurEpBeth-Mashiko$_{4}$ 5/6ḤevBA 44$_{5}$, of Israel Ex 12$_{40}$ Lv 18$_{3}$ 20$_{22}$ 23$_{42}$ 25$_{18.19}$ 26$_{5.35}$ Nm 33$_{53.55}$ 35$_{34}$ Jos 19$_{47}$ Jg 3$_{5}$ 6$_{10}$ 20$_{26}$ 1 K 12$_{17}$ ||2 C 10$_{17}$ 2 K 13$_{5}$ Ezk 37$_{25.25}$ Ho 3$_{4}$ Am 3$_{12}$ Ne 8$_{14}$ 2 C 31$_{6}$ 4QRP^{c} 23$_{5}$, of man, i.e. mortal Ezk 2$_{6}$ 12$_{2}$ Si 40$_{3(B)}$ CD 14$_{6}$, בַּת *daughter* Jr 50$_{39}$ (בְּנוֹת יַעֲנָה *young of ostriches*) Ru 3$_{18}$ Lm 4$_{21}$ Si 42$_{11(Bmg)}$ ([ת]שב), כַּלָּה *daughter-in-law*

Gn 11$_{31}$ 38$_{11.11}$, אָח *brother* Gn 37$_{25}$ 46$_{34}$ 47$_{6}$ Dt 24$_{8}$ 25$_{5}$ Jg 9$_{41}$ Ps 133$_{1}$ 2 C 10$_{10}$ 1QSa 2$_{13}$ ([א]חיו), אָחוֹת *sister* Ezk 16$_{46}$.

נַעַר *lad* Gn 21$_{20.21}$ 22$_{5}$ 1 S 1$_{22}$ 2 K 4$_{20}$, נַעֲרָה *young woman* Gn 24$_{55}$ Ru 2$_{7}$, בְּתוּלָה *young woman* Is 47$_{1.1.5}$, טַף *children* Nm 32$_{17}$ Dt 3$_{19}$ Jos 1$_{14}$ Jr 41$_{17}$, מֶלֶךְ *king* Nm 21$_{1.34}$ Dt 1$_{4.4}$ 3$_{2}$ 4$_{46}$ 17$_{18}$=11QT 56$_{20}$ Jos 12$_{2}$ Jg 3$_{20}$ 1 S 20$_{24.25}$ 2 S 7$_{1.2.18}$||1 C 17$_{16}$ 2 S 19$_{9.9}$ 1 K 2$_{19}$ 15$_{18}$||2 C 16$_{2}$ 1 K 22$_{10}$||2 C 18$_{9}$ 2 K 11$_{19}$ 14$_{10}$||2 C 25$_{19}$ 2 K 15$_{5}$||2 C 26$_{21}$ 2 K 19$_{27.36}$||Is 37$_{28.37}$ Jr 13$_{13.18}$ 17$_{25}$ 22$_{2.4}$ 29$_{16}$ 36$_{22}$ 38$_{7}$ Jon 3$_{6}$ Ps 61$_{8}$ Pr 20$_{8}$ Est 1$_{2}$ 3$_{15}$ 5$_{1}$ 2 C 18$_{9}$ 32$_{10}$ 4QM^{a} 11.1$_{12}$, גְּבִירָה *queen mother* Jr 13$_{18}$, שֵׁגָל *queen* Ne 2$_{6}$, פַּרְעֹה *Pharaoh* Ex 11$_{5}$ 12$_{29}$, שַׂר *prince* Nm 22$_{8}$ 2 K 9$_{5}$ 25$_{24}$||Jr 40$_{9}$ Jr 17$_{25}$ 26$_{10}$ 36$_{12}$ 39$_{3}$ 41$_{17}$ 42$_{10.10.13.14}$ 43$_{4}$ Ps 119$_{23}$ Est 1$_{14}$ Ne 11$_{1}$ 11QT 42$_{16}$, נָשִׂיא *prince* Ezk 26$_{16}$ 44$_{3}$ Si 41$_{17(B)}$ 11QT 42$_{16}$ Mur 24 2$_{4}$ 3$_{4}$ ([יו]שב) 4$_{4}$ ([נ]ש[יא]) 5$_{3}$, נָגִיד *prince* Ezk 28$_{2}$, חֹר *noble* 1 K 21$_{8.11}$, אָדוֹן *lord* Gn 24$_{37}$ Ps 110$_{1}$, רַב־סָרִיס *Rabsaris* Jr 39$_{3}$, רַב־מָג *Rabmag* Jr 39$_{3}$, גִּבּוֹר *warrior* Jos 8$_{9}$ Jr 51$_{30}$, עֶבֶד *servant* Gn 44$_{33}$ 47$_{4}$ Nm 22$_{19}$ Dt 23$_{17}$ 1 S 27$_{5}$, סָרִיס *eunuch* Jr 41$_{17}$.

זָקֵן *elder* Ex 24$_{14}$ 1 K 21$_{8.11}$ 2 K 6$_{32}$ Zc 8$_{4}$ Lm 2$_{10}$ 1QS 6$_{8}$ 11QT 42$_{16}$, כֹּהֵן *priest* 1 S 1$_{9}$ 2 K 17$_{27.28}$ Ezr 2$_{70}$||Ne 7$_{72}$ Ne 11$_{3}$ 1QS 6$_{8}$ 1QSa 2$_{13}$ CD 14$_{6}$, לֵוִי *Levite* Nm 35$_{2.3}$ Jos 14$_{4}$ 21$_{2}$ Jg 17$_{11}$ 19$_{4}$ Ezr 2$_{70}$||Ne 7$_{72}$ Ne 11$_{3}$ 11QT 57$_{13}$ CD 14$_{6}$, נָבִיא *prophet* 1 K 13$_{11.20.25}$, נְבִיאָה *prophet* (fem.) Jg 4$_{5}$ 2 K 22$_{14}$||2 C 34$_{22}$, מְשֹׁרֵר *singer* Ezr 2$_{70}$||Ne 7$_{72}$, שֹׁעֵר *gatekeeper* Ezr 2$_{70}$||Ne 7$_{72}$, נָתִין *temple servant* Ezr 2$_{70}$||Ne 7$_{72}$ Ne 3$_{26}$ 11$_{3.21}$, worshipper Ps 26$_{4.5}$ 27$_{4}$ 139$_{2}$, שֹׁפֵט *judge* Is 16$_{5}$, חָכָם *wise one* 1QSa 2$_{16}$, ידע ptc. *knowledgeable one* 1QSa 2$_{16}$ ([ידעיהם]), סֹפֵר *secretary* Jr 36$_{12}$ 1 C 2$_{55(Kt)}$, מַשְׂכִּיל *instructor* 1QS 10$_{14}$, יֹצֵר *potter* 1 C 4$_{23}$, בְּכוֹר *firstborn* Gn 43$_{33}$, צָעִיר *young one* Gn 43$_{33}$, צָרוּעַ *leper* Lv 13$_{46}$ 4QMMT B$_{66}$ ([י]שב), זוב ptc. *one who has a discharge* Lv 15$_{4.6}$ 4QTohA 1.1$_{5}$, טהר htp. ptc. *one who undergoes purification* Lv 14$_{8}$, שקט ptc. *quiet one* Ezk 38$_{11}$, דכא ni. ptc. *oppressed one* Si 11$_{5}$, דרשׁ ptc. *one who seeks* Is 16$_{5}$, מָהִיר *quick one* Is 16$_{5}$, נוס ptc. *one who flees* Nm 35$_{32}$ (if em. לָנוּס *to flee* to לַנָּס *for the one who flees*), רֹצֵחַ *killer* Nm 35$_{25.28.32}$ (unless em.; see above) Jos 20$_{4.6}$, אוֹיֵב *enemy* Lv 26$_{32}$ 4QapJoseph^{b} 1$_{20}$, רָשָׁע *wicked one* Ps 10$_{8}$ 50$_{20}$ (or em. תֵּשֵׁב *you sit* to בֹּשֶׁת *shame*), זוֹנָה *prostitute* 4QWiles 1$_{7}$ ([הזונ]ה)).

יֹשֵׁב *inhabitant* Ex 23$_{33}$ Jos 9$_{16.22}$ Jr 25$_{5}$ 35$_{15}$ 49$_{8.30}$ Zp 1$_{13}$ 1 C 4$_{23}$, גֵּר *sojourner* 2 C 30$_{25}$ CD 14$_{6}$, אֶזְרָח *native* Lv 23$_{42}$, רֵעַ *friend* Zc 3$_{8}$ Jb 2$_{13}$ Pr 3$_{29}$, female lover Ca 2$_{3}$, אמן ni. ptc. *faithful one* Ps 101$_{6}$, יָשָׁר *upright one* Ps 140$_{14}$, עשׂה ptc. *one who does* Ps 101$_{7}$, נגע hi. ptc. *one who causes to touch*, i.e. joins together Is 5$_{8(1QIsa^{a})}$ (MT וְהוּשַׁבְתֶּם *and you are made to dwell*, i.e. ho.), מַלְאָךְ *angel* Jg 6$_{11.18}$, *messenger* Ml 3$_{3}$, גֹּאֵל *redeemer* Ru 4$_{1.1}$, הֵילֵל *shining one* Is 14$_{13}$, עָדִין *voluptuous one* Is 47$_{8.8}$, עָשִׁיר *rich one* Ec 10$_{6}$, דַּל *poor one* Ps 74$_{21}$ (if em. אַל־יָשֹׁב *let him not go back*, from שׁוב, to אַל־יֵשֵׁב *let him not live*), מַמְזֵר *bastard* Zc 9$_{6}$, קצץ pass. ptc. *one cut*, i.e. with corners of hair cut Jr 9$_{25}$, נשׂא pass. ptc. *one lifted of* face, i.e. shown favour Jb 22$_{8}$, ראה ptc. *one who sees* Est 1$_{14}$, זֶרַע *seed*, i.e. descendants Jr 23$_{8}$ 2 C 20$_{8}$, ראשׁ *head* Ezr 10$_{16}$ Ne 11$_{3}$ 1 C 9$_{34}$ 1QSa 2$_{14.16}$ 11QT 42$_{16}$, עַיִן *eye* Ca 5$_{12}$, שֵׁן *tooth* 4Q Crypt 2.1$_{3}$, שְׁאֵרִית *remnant* Jr 41$_{17}$ 44$_{14}$, שְׁאָר *remainder* 1QS 6$_{9}$, אֹרֵב *ambush* Jg 16$_{9.12}$.

מִקְנֶה *cattle* Dt 3$_{19}$ Jos 1$_{14}$, צִי *wild animal* Jr 50$_{39}$, כְּפִיר *young lion* Ps 17$_{12}$ Jb 38$_{40}$, לָבִיא *lion* Jb 38$_{40}$, עֵץ *tree* perh. Ezk 31$_{17}$, קֶשֶׁת *bow* Gn 49$_{24}$ (or em. וַתֵּשֶׁב *and it remained* to וַתִּשָּׁבֵר *and it was broken*, or וַתֵּשַׁב *and it was splintered*), אֲרוֹן *ark* 1 S 5$_{7}$ 7$_{2}$ 2 S 6$_{11}$||1 C 13$_{14}$ 2 S 7$_{2}$ 11$_{11}$, אַרְמוֹן *palace* Jr 30$_{18}$, אֶרֶץ *land* Jr 17$_{6}$ Ezk 29$_{11}$ Zc 1$_{11}$, עִיר *city* Jr 17$_{25}$ 31$_{24}$ Ezk 35$_{9(Kt)}$ 36$_{35}$ Zp 2$_{15}$ 7$_{7}$ Lm 1$_{1}$ Si 16$_{4.4(B)}$ ([תשב]), הַר *mountain* Ps 125$_{1}$, שְׁפֵלָה *lowland* Zc 7$_{7}$, נֶגֶב *Negeb* Zc 7$_{7}$, צְבִי *glory* Is 13$_{20}$, תִּפְאֶרֶת *beauty* Is 13$_{20}$, צְדָקָה *righteousness* Is 32$_{16}$, אַחֵר *another one* Is 65$_{22}$, אֶחָד *one* 2 K 17$_{28}$ Ne 11$_{1}$, שְׁנַיִם *two* Jg 19$_{6}$, מָאתַיִם *two hundred* 1 S 25$_{13}$, רַב pl. *many* Si 11$_{5}$, זֶה *this* 2 S 11$_{12}$, אֵלֶּה *these* 2 S 2$_{13}$ 1 C 4$_{41}$ 8$_{28}$, מִי *who?* 1 K 1$_{20.27}$, כֹּל *everyone* Ezk 38$_{11}$.

subj. not specified, Gn 11$_{2}$ Lv 15$_{6}$ Jg 5$_{10}$ 1 S 30$_{24}$ 1 K 14$_{8}$ Is 9$_{1}$ 10$_{13}$ 23$_{18}$ 24$_{6}$ 28$_{6}$ 40$_{22.22}$ 42$_{7}$ 45$_{18}$ 47$_{14}$ 58$_{12}$ (or em.; see Coll.) Jr 8$_{16}$ 10$_{17}$ 12$_{4}$ 21$_{9}$ 24$_{8}$ 36$_{30}$ 38$_{2}$ 44$_{13}$ 46$_{8}$ 47$_{2}$ Ezk 12$_{19}$ 32$_{15}$ 39$_{6}$ Ho 4$_{3}$ 14$_{8}$ Am 8$_{8}$ 9$_{5}$ Na 1$_{5}$ Hb 2$_{8.17}$ Ps 2$_{4}$ 24$_{1}$ 69$_{13.26}$ 80$_{2}$ 91$_{1}$ 98$_{7}$ 107$_{10.34}$ 123$_{1}$ 127$_{2}$ Jb 15$_{28}$ 24$_{13}$ (mss יָשׁוּבוּ *they go back*) Pr 21$_{9.19}$ 23$_{1}$ 25$_{24}$ Ru 4$_{4}$ Ca 8$_{13}$ 1 C 1$_{40}$ 1QpHab 4$_{8}$ 1QSb 3$_{1}$ 4QCommGenA 5$_{2}$ 4Q TohA 1.1$_{1.1.2}$ 4QBer^{a} 5$_{1}$ 11QT 43$_{12}$ CD 7$_{6}$ 19$_{2}$ GnzPs 4$_{3}$ Arad ost. 18$_{10}$.

<PREP> לְ in ref. to subj. of ישׁב, Hagar Gn 21$_{16}$, נַעַר

lad Gn 22$_{5}$, unspecified Jb 15$_{28}$; לְ of benefit, *for*, + David Jr 13$_{13}$ 22$_{4}$ Ps 132$_{12}$, Jehu 2 K 10$_{30}$ 15$_{12}$; לְ (wait) *for*, + Delilah Jg 16$_{9}$, Joshua Ex 24$_{14}$, Moses Ex 24$_{14}$, מְשָׁרֵת *minister* Ex 24$_{14}$, רֵעַ *friend*, i.e. lover Jr 3$_{2}$; לְ *for (the purpose of)*, + מִשְׁפָּט *judgment* Ps 122$_{5}$, אֶרֶב *lying in wait* Jb 38$_{40}$; לְ of place, *at, on, over*, + פֶּתַח *entrance* Pr 9$_{14}$, חוֹף *coast* Jg 5$_{17}$, יָד *side* 1 S 4$_{13(Qr)}$ (if em.; see Coll.), יָמִין *right hand* 1 K 2$_{19}$ Ps 110$_{1}$, מִזְרָח *east* 1 C 5$_{9}$, אֶרֶץ *ground* Is 3$_{26}$ 47$_{1}$ Jb 2$_{13}$ Lm 2$_{10}$, כִּסֵּא *throne* Ps 9$_{5}$, מַבּוּל *flood* Ps 29$_{10}$ (unless לְמַבּוּל = *since*, or *before, the [time of] the flood*);* לְ of direction, time, *to, for*, + נֶצַח *eternity* Is 13$_{20}$ Jr 50$_{39}$, עוֹלָם *eternity* Jr 17$_{25}$ Jl 4$_{20}$ Ps 9$_{8}$ 29$_{10}$ 102$_{13}$ 125$_{1}$ Lm 5$_{19}$, עַד *eternity* Ps 132$_{12}$, דֹּר *generation* Jl 4$_{20}$; לְ of accompaniment, *in, with*, + Hosea Ho 3$_{3}$, בֶּטַח *security* Lv 25$_{18.19}$ 26$_{5}$ Jg 18$_{7}$ 1 K 5$_{5}$ Is 47$_{8}$ Jr 49$_{31}$ Ezk 28$_{26.26}$ 34$_{25.28}$ 38$_{8.14}$ 39$_{6.26}$ Zp 2$_{15}$ Zc 14$_{11}$ Pr 3$_{29}$ 4QRP^{c} 23$_{5}$; לְ *as*, + מֶלֶךְ *king* 1 C 29$_{23}$.

בְּ of place, *in, on, at, among* perh. 4QM^{a} 11.1$_{13}$, + אֶרֶץ *land* Gn 4$_{16}$ 13$_{7.12}$ 16$_{3}$ 24$_{37.62}$ 34$_{21}$ 37$_{1}$ 45$_{10}$ 46$_{34}$ 47$_{4.6}$ 47$_{27}$ Ex 2$_{15}$ 23$_{33}$ Lv 18$_{3}$ 20$_{22}$ 26$_{5.32}$ Nm 13$_{19.28.29}$ 21$_{31}$ 33$_{53.55}$ 35$_{32.34}$ Dt 2$_{20}$ 11$_{31}$ 12$_{10.29}$ 17$_{14}$=11QT 56$_{12}$ Dt 26$_{1}$ 29$_{15}$ Jos 1$_{14}$ 17$_{12.16}$ 21$_{43}$ 22$_{33}$ 24$_{15}$ Jg 1$_{27}$ 6$_{10}$ 11$_{3}$ 2 K 25$_{24}$||Jr 40$_{9}$ Is 9$_{1}$ 24$_{6}$ Jr 12$_{4}$ 24$_{8}$ 31$_{24}$ 42$_{10.10.13}$ 43$_{4}$ 44$_{1.1.13.15.26}$ Ezk 12$_{19}$ 32$_{15}$ 36$_{28}$ 37$_{25}$ Ho 4$_{3}$ 9$_{3}$ Am 8$_{8}$ 9$_{5}$ Jb 22$_{8}$ Pr 21$_{19}$ Lm 4$_{21}$ 1 C 5$_{11.23}$ 2 C 20$_{8}$ 4QBer^{a} 5$_{1}$ CD 13$_{21}$, אֲדָמָה *land* Jr 27$_{11}$, תֵּבֵל *world* Na 1$_{5}$ Ps 24$_{1}$ 98$_{7}$ GnzPs 4$_{3}$, גּוֹי *nation* Lm 1$_{3}$, מַלְכוּת *kingdom* Est 1$_{14}$, עִיר *city* Gn 13$_{12}$ 19$_{29}$ Nm 13$_{19}$ 21$_{25}$ 32$_{17}$ 35$_{25.28}$ Dt 3$_{19}$ 19$_{1}$ Jos 10$_{50}$ 20$_{6}$ 24$_{13}$ Jg 11$_{26}$ 18$_{28}$ 21$_{23}$ 1 S 27$_{5}$ 31$_{7}$||1 C 10$_{7}$ 2 S 2$_{3}$ 1 K 9$_{16}$ 12$_{17}$||2 C 10$_{17}$ 1 K 13$_{25}$ 21$_{11}$ 17$_{24}$ Jr 8$_{16}$ 21$_{9}$ 29$_{16}$ 38$_{2}$ 46$_{8}$ 47$_{2}$ 49$_{1}$ Est 9$_{19}$ Ezr 2$_{70}$||Ne 7$_{72}$ Ne 11$_{3.3}$ 2 C 19$_{10}$ 31$_{6}$, קִרְיָה *city* Hb 2$_{8.17}$, חָצֵר *village* Dt 2$_{23}$ 1 C 9$_{16}$, *court* Jr 32$_{12}$ 37$_{21}$ 38$_{13.28}$, בַּת *daughter*, i.e. village Jg 11$_{26}$ Ne 11$_{25}$ 1 C 5$_{16}$.

Adullam Ne 11$_{25}$, Aijalon Jg 1$_{35}$, Ar Dt 2$_{10.29}$, Aram 2 S 15$_{8}$, Aroer Jg 11$_{26}$ 1 C 5$_{8}$, Arumah Jg 9$_{41}$, Ashdod Zc 9$_{6}$, Ashtaroth Dt 1$_{4}$ Jos 12$_{4}$, Azekah Ne 11$_{25}$, Babylon Jr 50$_{39}$, Bashan 1 C 5$_{16}$, Beer-sheba Gn 22$_{19}$ Ne 11$_{25}$ 1 C 4$_{28}$, Beth-biri 1 C 4$_{28}$, Bethel 1 K 13$_{11}$ 2 K 17$_{28}$, Beth-marcaboth 1 C 4$_{28}$, Beth-pelet Ne 11$_{25}$, Bethuel 1 C 4$_{28}$, Bilhah 1 C 4$_{28}$, Damascus 1 K 11$_{24}$ 15$_{18}$||2 C 16$_{2}$, Dibon Ne 11$_{25}$, Edrei Dt 1$_{4}$ Jos 12$_{4}$, Egypt Gn 50$_{22}$ Ex 12$_{40}$ Nm 20$_{15}$ 1 K 12$_{2}$ (or em. וַיֵּשֶׁב יָרָבְעָם בְּמִצְרָיִם *and Jeroboam dwelt in Egypt* to וַיָּשָׁב יָרָבְעָם מִמִּצְרָיִם *and Jeroboam returned from Egypt*), En-gedi 5/6ḤevBA 44$_{5}$, En-rimmon Ne 11$_{25}$, Ezem 1 C 4$_{28}$, Gath 1 S 27$_{3}$, Geba 1 S 13$_{16}$, Gerar Gn 26$_{6}$, Geruth Chimham Jr 41$_{17}$, Geshur 2 S 15$_{8}$, Gezer Jos 16$_{10}$ Jg 1$_{29}$, Gibeah 1 S 22$_{6}$, Gibeon 1 C 8$_{29}$ 9$_{34}$, Gilead Nm 32$_{40}$ 1 C 5$_{16}$, Gurbaal 2 C 26$_{7}$, Haran 4QpsJub^{a} 2.1$_{2}$ ([ישׁ]ב) 4QCommGenA 2$_{9}$, Har-heres Jg 1$_{35}$, Harosheth-hagoiim Jg 4$_{2}$, Hazazon-tamar Gn 14$_{7}$, Hazar-shual Ne 11$_{25}$ 1 C 4$_{28}$, Hazar-susim 1 C 4$_{28}$, Heshbon Nm 21$_{34}$ Dt 1$_{4}$ 3$_{2}$ 4$_{46}$ Jos 12$_{2}$ Jg 1$_{10}$ 11$_{26}$, Horesh 1 S 23$_{18}$, Hormah 1 C 4$_{28}$, Jarmuth Ne 11$_{25}$, Jekabzeel Ne 11$_{25}$, Jericho 2 S 10$_{5}$||1 C 19$_{5}$ 2 K 2$_{18}$, Jerusalem Jos 15$_{63}$ 2 S 9$_{13}$ 11$_{1}$||1 C 20$_{1}$ 2 S 11$_{12}$ 14$_{28}$ 16$_{3}$ 1 K 2$_{38}$ 2 K 22$_{14}$||2 C 34$_{22}$ Is 30$_{19}$ 33$_{24}$ Jr 35$_{10}$ Zc 12$_{6}$ 14$_{11}$ Ezr 2$_{70}$||Ne 7$_{72}$ (if ins. יְרוּשָׁלַםִ) Ne 11$_{1.1.2.3.4.6}$ 13$_{16}$ 1 C 8$_{28}$. 8$_{32}$ 9$_{3.34.38}$ 2 C 11$_{5}$ 19$_{4}$ 32$_{10}$, Jeshua Ne 11$_{25}$, Judah 2 C 30$_{25}$, Kadesh Nm 20$_{1}$ Dt 1$_{46}$ Jg 11$_{17}$, Kiriath-arba Ne 11$_{25}$, Kiriath-jearim 1 S 7$_{2}$, Lachish Ne 11$_{25}$, Leshem Jos 19$_{47}$, Meconah Ne 11$_{25}$, Memphis Jr 44$_{1}$, Migdol Jr 44$_{1}$, Mizpah Jr 40$_{10}$, Moladah Ne 11$_{25}$ 1 C 4$_{28}$, Naioth 1 S 19$_{18}$, Nineveh 2 K 19$_{36}$||Is 37$_{37}$, Pathros Jr 44$_{15}$, Samaria Am 3$_{12}$, Seir Dt 2$_{4.8.12.22.29}$, Shaalabim Jg 1$_{35}$, Shaaraim 1 C 4$_{28}$, Sharmir Jg 10$_{1}$, Shechem Jg 9$_{41}$ 1 K 12$_{25}$, Shittim Nm 25$_{1}$, Sodom Gn 14$_{12}$, Tahpanhes Jr 44$_{1}$, Tirzah 1 K 15$_{21}$, Tolad 1 C 4$_{28}$, Zanoah Ne 11$_{25}$, Ziklag 2 S 1$_{1}$ Ne 11$_{25}$ 1 C 4$_{28}$, Zoar Gn 19$_{30}$, Zorah Ne 11$_{25}$.

הַר *mountain, hill country* Gn 19$_{30}$ 36$_{8}$ Nm 13$_{29}$ 14$_{45}$ Dt 1$_{6.44}$ 9$_{9}$ Jg 10$_{1}$ 1 S 23$_{14}$ Is 14$_{13}$, עֹפֶל *mound* Ne 3$_{26}$ 11$_{21}$, גַּיְא *valley* Dt 3$_{29}$, עֵמֶק *valley* Nm 14$_{25}$, עֲרָבָה *Arabah* Dt 11$_{30}$, מִדְבָּר *steppe* Gn 21$_{20.21}$ Jos 24$_{7}$ 1 S 23$_{14.14.25}$ 26$_{3}$ Jr 9$_{25}$ Ezk 34$_{25}$, נַחַל *wadi* 1 K 17$_{5}$, מִגְרָשׁ *pasture* 1 C 5$_{16}$, שָׂדֶה *field* Jg 13$_{9}$ 1 S 27$_{7.11}$ Ne 11$_{25}$, כַּרְמֶל *plantation* Is 32$_{16}$, גַּן *garden* Ca 8$_{13}$, חַיָּה *flock* Ps 68$_{11}$.

שַׁעַר *gate* Gn 19$_{1}$ Jr 38$_{7}$ 39$_{3}$ Ezk 44$_{3}$ Est 2$_{19.21}$ 5$_{13}$ 6$_{10}$, פֶּתַח *entrance* Gn 38$_{14}$ Jr 26$_{10}$, רְחוֹב *square, street* of city Jg 19$_{15}$ Zc 8$_{4}$ Ezr 10$_{9}$, בַּיִת *house* Dt 6$_{7}$ 11$_{19}$ 19$_{1}$ 21$_{13}$=11QT 63$_{13}$ Dt 28$_{30}$ Jg 8$_{29}$ 1 S 19$_{9}$ 2 S 7$_{1.2.6}$||1 C 17$_{1.1.5}$ 1 K 3$_{17}$ 2 K 6$_{32}$ 14$_{10}$||2 C 25$_{19}$ 2 K 15$_{5}$ Ezk 8$_{1}$ Am 5$_{11}$ Hg 1$_{4}$ Ps 27$_{4}$ Est 5$_{1}$ 1 C 13$_{14}$ 2 C 2$_{2}$ 8$_{11}$, סֻכָּה *booth* Lv 23$_{42.42}$ 2 S 11$_{11}$ Ne 8$_{14.17}$, אֹהֶל *tent* 2 K 13$_{5}$ Is 16$_{5}$ Jr 35$_{7.10}$ Ps 69$_{26}$ 1 C 5$_{10}$ perh. 4QSapHymn 1.2$_{10}$ ([באהל לש]בת

in a tent to dwell in), נָוֶה *habitation* Is 32_{18}, מִשְׁכָּן *dwelling place* Is 32_{18}, מְנוּחָה *resting place* Is 32_{18}, מְצָד *stronghold* 1 S 23_{14} 24_{1} Jr 51_{30} 1 C 11_{7}, מְצוּדָה *stronghold* 1 S 22_{5} 2 S 5_{9}, הֵרוֹדִיס *Herodium* Mur 24 2_{4} ([בהרד]יס) 3_{4} ([יו]שב [בהרד]יס) 4_{4} ([בהרודיס]) 5_{3}, קֶבֶר *tomb* Is 65_{4}, מְעָרָה *cave* Gn 19_{30}, גֹּרֶן *threshing floor* 2 C 18_{9}, חֶדֶר *chamber* Jg $16_{9.12}$, עֲלִיָּה *upper chamber* Jg 3_{20}, חוֹמָה *wall* Jos 2_{15}, יַרְכָּה *side* 1 S 24_{4} Is 14_{13}, מוֹשָׁב *seat* Ps 1_{1}, כִּסֵּא *throne* 4QM^{a} 11.1_{12}.

נְתִיבָה *path* Jb 24_{13} (mss יָשׁוּבוּ *they go back*), סֶלַע *rock* Jg 20_{47}, סְעִיף *cleft* Jg 15_{8}, צָמָא perh. *dry ground* Jr 48_{18} (unless em. בַּצָּמָא to בַּצֹּאָה *in filth*), אֵלוֹן *terebinth* Gn 13_{18}, טוֹב *good (place)* Gn 20_{15}, שֵׁפֶל *low estate* Ec 10_{6}, דָּם *blood* Lv 12_{4} 4QSD 7.2_{17} (ת[שב]), צֵל *shade* Ezk $31_{6.17}$ Ho 14_{8} Jon 4_{5} Ca 2_{3}, לֵב *heart* of sea Ezk 28_{2}, מָצוֹר *seige* Jr 10_{17} 2 C 32_{10}, מַאֲרָב *ambush* Ps 10_{8}, מֶרְחָק *distance* 11QT 43_{12}, קָצֶה *end* 1 S 14_{2}, סוֹד *company* Jr 15_{17} 4QRitMar 19_{1} 23_{4} ([י]שבו בסו[ד]), שָׁמַיִם *heaven* Ps 2_{4} 123_{1}, סֵתֶר *secret place* 1 S 19_{2} Ps 91_{1}, מִסְתָּר *hiding place* Ps 17_{12}, מְעֹנָה *den* Jb 38_{40}, חֹשֶׁךְ *darkness* Mc 7_{8}, אֲחֻזָּה *possession* Ne 11_{3}, מָקוֹם *place* Dt 23_{17}, תֹּכֶן *measurement*, i.e. rank 1QS 6_{9}, זֶה *this (place)* Nm 22_{19}, אֵלֶּה *these (places)* 1 C 7_{29}.

בְּ *beside* Na 3_{8}; בְּ of time, *on*, + יוֹם *day* 2 S 11_{12} Ezr 10_{16}, חֹדֶשׁ *month* Jr 36_{22} Ne 8_{14}; בְּ of essence, *as*, + אֵיתָן *continuous one* Gn 49_{24} (or em.; see Subj.); בְּ of accompaniment, *with, in*, אֱמֶת *faithfulness* Is 16_{5}, מְלָאכָה *work* 1 C 4_{23}, מִשְׁפָּט *judgment* 4QapPs^{b} 76_{12}, בְּאֵין חוֹמָה *without walls* Ezk 38_{11}; כְּ *as*, + עֲרָבִי *Arab* Jr 3_{2}, כְּפַעַם בְּפַעַם *as a time in a time*, i.e. as at other times 1 S 20_{25}, כִּתְמוֹל שִׁלְשׁוֹם *as yesterday and the day before* 2 K 13_{5}, כְּהַיּוֹם הַזֶּה *as at this day* 1 K 3_{6}; כְּ *according to*, + בְּכֹרָה *firstborn's privilege* Gn 43_{33}, צְעִירָה *youth* Gn 43_{33}, יוֹם *day* Dt 1_{46}, מִשְׁפָּט *manner* Jg 18_{7}, סֶרֶךְ *rule* CD 7_{6} 19_{2}, תֹּכֶן *rank* 1QS 6_{4}, מִדָּה *measure* 4QTohA 1.1_{2}; כְּ *about*, + שָׁנָה *year* Ru 1_{4}; מִן of direction, *from, at*, + Dan 1 K 5_{5}, יָד *side* 1 S 20_{25}, צַד *side* Ru 2_{14}, יָמִין *right*, i.e. south Ezk 16_{46}, קֶדֶם *east* Jon 4_{5}, זֶה *this (side)* 2 S 2_{13}.

מִן of time, *since*, + עוֹלָם *ancient time* Jos 24_{2}; מִמָּחֳרָת *on the morrow* 2 S 11_{12}; מִן of cause, *on account of*, + עֲרִירִי *childless one* Si 16_{4}, קֶצֶף *anger* Jr 50_{13}, רֹב *multitude* Zc 2_{8}, אֶחָד *one* Si $16_{4.4(B)}$; מִן of comparison, *than (with)*, + אִשָּׁה *wife* Pr $21_{9.19}$ 25_{24}.; לְמִן *from*, + שַׁעַר *gate* Zc 14_{10}, מִגְדָּל *tower* Zc 14_{10}; *since*, + יוֹם *day* 2 S 7_{6}.

אֶל *to, at, upon*, + אֲדָמָה *land* Jr 35_{15}, נָהָר *river* Ezk 3_{15}, לֶחֶם *food* 1 S $20_{24(Qr)}$, שֻׁלְחָן *table* 1 K 13_{20}, כִּסֵּא *throne* Jr 29_{16}, מוֹשָׁב *seat* 1 S 20_{25}, מִטָּה *bed* 1 S 28_{23}, עַקְרָב *scorpion* Ezk 2_{6}.

עַל *upon, in, at* 4QapJoseph^{b} 1_{20}, + אֶרֶץ *land* Lv $25_{18.19}$ 25_{35} Nm 13_{18} 1 K 8_{27}||2 C 6_{18} Ezk 26_{19} $37_{25.25}$ 4QRP^{c} 23_{5} 4QapPs^{b} 69_{6}, אֲדָמָה *land* Dt 30_{20} Jr 23_{8} 25_{5} Ezk $28_{25.26}$ 36_{17} 39_{26}, חוּג *circle* Is 40_{22}, תּוֹצָאוֹת *extremities* 1 C 5_{16}, שְׂמֹאל *left*, i.e. north Ezk 16_{46}, תְּרָפִים *teraphim* Gn 31_{34}, מַד perh. *carpet* Jg 5_{10}, מִטָּה *bed* Gn 48_{2} 1 S $28_{23(mss)}$ Ezk 23_{41}, כִּסֵּא *throne* Ex 11_{5} 12_{29} Dt 17_{18} =11QT 56_{20} 1 S 1_{9} 4_{13} 1 K $1_{13.17.20.24.27.30.35.46.48}$ $2_{12.19}$ 3_{6} $8_{20.25}$||2 C $6_{10.16}$ 1 K 16_{11} $22_{10.19}$||2 C $18_{9.18}$ 2 K 10_{30} 11_{19} 13_{13} 15_{12} Is 6_{1} 16_{5} Jr 13_{13} 17_{25} $22_{2.4.30}$ 33_{17} 36_{30} Zc 6_{13} Ps 47_{9} Pr 9_{14} 20_{8} Est 1_{2} 5_{1} 1 C 28_{5} 29_{23} Si 11_{5} 4Qps Ezek^{a} 13.2_{2} ([על כסא]) 4QDibHam^{a} 1.4_{7} 11QT $59_{14.17}$, מוֹשָׁב *seat* 1 S 20_{25}, שֻׁלְחָן *table* Si 34_{12}, מָבוֹא *entrance* Ezk 27_{3}, פִּנָּה *corner* Pr 21_{9} 25_{24}, רֹאשׁ *top* of hill 2 K 1_{9}, טַבּוּר *centre* of earth Ezk 38_{12}, פָּנִים *face*, i.e. region 1 C 5_{10}, אֶבֶן *stone* Ex 17_{12}, חוֹמָה *wall* 2 K 18_{27}||Is 36_{12}, כְּלִי *vessel* Lv $15_{4.6.6.22.23.26}$ 4QTohA 1.1_{5} 4QTohC 1_{4} ([כלי ... עליו]), בֶּרֶךְ *knee* 2 K 4_{20}, דָּם *blood* Lv 12_{5} 4QSD 7.2_{15} ([תשב על דם]), עָפָר *dust* Is 47_{1}, אֵפֶר *ashes* Jon 3_{6}, מִלֵּאת *setting* Ca 5_{12}, סֶרֶךְ *order* 4QCrypt 2.$1_{3.6}$, כֹּל *anything* Lv 15_{20}.

עַל *beside*, + מְזוּזָה *doorpost* 1 S 1_{9}, בְּאֵר *well* Ex 2_{15}, בְּרֵכָה *pool* 2 S 2_{13}, סִיר *pot* Ex 16_{3}, כְּלִי *vessel* 1 S 25_{13} 30_{24}, נָהָר *river* Ps 137_{1}, יָם *sea* Nm 13_{29}; עַל *(with authority) over*, + Israel 1 C 28_{5}; עַל *for (the purpose of)*, + לֶחֶם *food* 1 S $20_{24(Kt)}$, מִשְׁפָּט *judgment* Is 28_{6}; עַל *according to*, + מִשְׁפָּט *custom*, i.e. as previously Jr 30_{18}; עַל יַד *beside*, + Jordan Nm 13_{29}.

עִם *with, at* 4QRitMar 19_{1}, + Israel(ite) Dt 23_{17}, Achish 1 S $27_{3.5}$, Balaam Nm 22_{8}, Laban Gn 27_{44} $29_{14.19}$, Micah Jg 17_{10}, אִישׁ *man* 1 S 5_{7}, מַת *man* Ps 26_{4}, אָח *brother* Gn 27_{44} 1 C 8_{32} 9_{38}, זָקֵן *elder* Jos 20_{4} Pr 31_{23}, מֶלֶךְ *king* 1 S 20_{5} 22_{4} 2 S 15_{19} 1 C 4_{23} 11QT 57_{13}, שֹׁפֵט *judge* Si 8_{14}, רָשָׁע *wicked one* Ps 26_{5}, worshipper Ps 101_{6}, Beer-lahai-roi Gn 25_{11}.

אֵת *with* Jr 16_{8}, + אָדָם *human beings* 2 C 6_{18}, עַם *people* Jg 1_{16}, David 1 S 22_{23}, Elisha 2 K 6_{32}, Gedaliah Jr $40_{5.6}$,

Hamor Gn $34_{10.16.22.23}$, Job Jb 2_{13}, Naboth 1 K 21_{8}, Shechem Gn $34_{10.16.22.23}$, אִישׁ *man* Gn $34_{22.23}$ Ex 2_{21} Jg 17_{11}, אָב *father* Jg 19_{4}, חֹתֵן *father-in-law* Jg 19_{4}, אֵם *mother* Gn 24_{55}, חָמוֹת *mother-in-law* Ru 2_{23}, בֵּן *son* Jos 15_{63} Jg 1_{21} Jr $40_{5.6}$ Pr 3_{29}, אָח *brother* Gn 24_{55}, פָּנִים *face*, i.e. presence Ps 140_{14}, אִי *jackal* Jr 50_{39}, אֲשֶׁר *(the one) who* 2 S 16_{18}.

עַד *unto*, + Baal-meon 1 C 5_{8}, Beer-sheba 1 K 5_{5}, Nebo 1 C 5_{8}, Salecah 1 C 5_{11}, שַׁעַר *gate* Zc 14_{10}, יֶקֶב *winepress* Zc 14_{10}, מִלֵּאת *setting* Ca $5_{12(Gnz)}$, מָקוֹם *place* Zc 14_{10}; עַד *until*, + יוֹם *day* Jos 6_{25} 15_{63} 16_{10} Jg 1_{21} 2 S 7_{6} 2 K 16_{6} Jr 38_{38} 1 C 4_{43}, עֶרֶב *evening* Jg 21_{2}, צָהֳרַיִם *noon* 2 K 4_{20}, גֹּלָה *exile* 1 C 5_{22}, עוֹלָם *eternity* 1 S 1_{22} Ezk 37_{25}; עַד לְ *until*, + מִנְחָה *offering* Ezr 9_{4}.

בֵּין *between, among*, + רֵעַ *friend* Si 25_{18}, רַב pl. *many* Si 34_{18}, Ai Jos 8_{9}, Bethel Jos 8_{9}, Kadesh Gn 20_{1}, Shur Gn 20_{1}, מִשְׁפָּת *sheepfold* Jg 5_{16}, שַׁעַר *gate* 2 S 18_{24} $19_{9.9}$.

בְּתוֹךְ *among, within*, + Hittite Gn 23_{10}, עַם *people* 2 K 4_{13} Is 6_{5} Jr 29_{32} 39_{14} $40_{5.6}$, גּוֹי *nation* Ezk 31_{17}, גֹּלָה *exile* Ezk 3_{15}, בַּיִת *house* Ezk 12_{2}, יְרִיעָה *curtain* 2 S 7_{2}, אֵיפָה *ephah* Zc 5_{7}, אֵפֶר *ashes* Ps 2_{8}, מִרְמָה *deceit* Jr 9_{5} (or em.; see Subj.).

בְּקֶרֶב *among, within*, + Canaanites Gn 24_{3} Jg $1_{32.33}$ 3_{5}, Ephraim Jos 16_{10} Jg 1_{29}, Israel(ites) Dt 23_{17} Jos 6_{25} $9_{16.22}$, Zebulun Jg 1_{30}, אֶרֶץ *land* 1QIsa[a] 5_{8}.

לְפִי *according to*, + כָּבוֹד *honour* 1QSa $2_{13.14}$ ([לפי] [כבודו]) 2_{16}.

מִפְּנֵי *on account of*, + Abimelech Jg 9_{21}, אָח *brother* Jg 9_{21}, יֹשֵׁב *inhabitant* Nm 32_{17}.

לִפְנֵי *before*, + ״י *Y.* Jg 20_{26} 2 S 7_{18}‖1 C 17_{16} Is 23_{18}, אֱלֹהִים *God* Jg 21_{2} Ps 61_{8}, Joshua Zc 3_{8}, Elisha 2 K 4_{38} 6_{1}, Ezekiel Ezk 14_{1} 20_{1}, Joseph Gn 43_{33}, אִישׁ *man* 1QS 5_{4}, בֵּן *son* Ezk 33_{31}, כֹּהֵן *priest* 1QS 6_{4} 1QSa 2_{16} ([הכוהן]), מָשִׁיחַ *messiah* 1QSa 2_{13} ([לפניו]) $2_{14.16}$ (both [מש]יח).

נֶגֶד *before, opposite*, + Naboth 1 K 21_{13}, בֵּן *son* 1 C 5_{11}, אָח *brother* 1 C 8_{32} 9_{38}, אוּר *fire* Is 47_{14}; נֹכַח *opposite*, + פֶּתַח *entrance* Est 5_{1}; מוּל *opposite*, + Beth-peor Dt 3_{29}, Gilgal Dt 11_{30}; מִמּוּל *opposite*, + Balak Nm 22_{5}, בֵּן *son* Nm 22_{5}, מֶלֶךְ *king* Nm 22_{5}; מִחוּץ לְ *outside*, + אֹהֶל *tent* Lv 14_{8} 4QMMT B_{66} ([י]שב חוץ [לאוהלו]); בְּעֵבֶר *beyond*, + Jordan Jos 7_{7} 24_{8}, נָהָר *river* Jos 24_{2}; אֵצֶל *beside*, + מֶלֶךְ *king* Ne 2_{6}, צַר *enemy* Ne 4_{6}, אֵלוֹן *terebinth* Dt 11_{30}, אֶבֶן *stone* 1 S 20_{19}; אַחַר *behind*, + אִישׁ *man* 1QS 7_{20}; אַחֲרֵי *after*, + מֶלֶךְ *king* 1 K 1_{27}, אָדוֹן *lord* 1 K 1_{27}; תַּחַת *in (its own) place*, + Jerusalem Zc 12_{6} 14_{10}; תַּחַת *in place of, instead of*, + Avvim Dt 2_{23}, David 1 C 29_{23}, Hagrites 1 C 5_{22}, Horite Dt $2_{12.22}$, Jetur 1 C 5_{22}, Meunim 1 C $4_{41(Qr)}$ (Kt Meinim), Naphish 1 C 5_{22}, Nodab 1 C 5_{22}, Rephaim Dt 2_{21}, עַם *people* Dt 2_{21}, גּוֹי *nation* Jos 5_{8}, David 1 K 1_{30}, אִישׁ *man*, i.e. each one Ex 16_{29}, נַעַר *lad* Gn 44_{33}, מֶלֶךְ *king* 1 K 1_{30}; תַּחַת *under*, + אֵלָה *terebinth* Jg 6_{11} 1 K 13_{14}, אֶשֶׁל *tamarisk* 1 S 22_{6}, גֶּפֶן *vine* 1 K 5_{5} Mc 4_{4}, רִמּוֹן *pomegranate tree* 1 S 14_{2}, רֹתֶם *broom tree* 1 K 19_{4}, תְּאֵנָה *fig tree* 1 K 5_{5} Mc 4_{4}, תֹּמֶר *palm* Jg 4_{5}, סֻכָּה *booth* Jon 4_{5}.

<COLL> ישב *dwell* ‖ שכן *dwell* Is 32_{16} Jr 50_{39}, לין *lodge* Is 65_{4}, htpol. Ps 91_{1}, גור *sojourn* Jr $49_{18.33}$ 50_{40}, עבר *pass through* Jr 51_{43}, סור *turn aside* Ru $4_{1.1}$, שקט *be quiet* Zc 1_{11}, משל *rule* Zc 6_{13}.

+ שכן *dwell* Jg 5_{17} Jb 29_{25} 4QWiles 1_{7}, גור *sojourn* Gn 20_{1}, חנה *encamp* Gn 26_{17}, שכב *lie* Lv 15_{20} Dt 6_{7} 11_{19} 4QTohA 1.1_{1}, קום *rise* Dt 6_{7} 11_{19} Is 52_{2} (unless em.; see Subj.), ראם *rise* Zc 14_{10}, דמם *be silent* Lm 2_{10} 3_{28}, שמם po. *be appalled* Ezr $9_{3.4}$, בכה *weep* Ne 1_{4}, אבל htp. *mourn* Ne 1_{4}, אכל *eat* 5/6ḤevEp 12_{3} (יושב[י]ן), שתה *drink* 5/6ḤevEp 12_{3} (יושב[י]ן).

ישב *dwell* :: הלך *go* Dt 6_{7} 11_{19}, בוא *come* 2 K 19_{27}‖Is 37_{28}, יצא *go out* 2 K 19_{27}‖Is 37_{28}, מוט ni. *be moved* Ps 125_{1}, קום *rise* Ps 127_{2} 139_{2} 1QS 10_{14}, חרב *be desolate* Si $16_{4.4(B)}$ ([תשב]).

ישב *dwell* followed by inf. of purpose, אכל *eat* Gn 37_{25} Ex 32_{6} 1 S $20_{5.24}$ Jr 16_{8} Ezk 44_{3}, לחם *eat* Pr 23_{1}, שתה *drink* Ex 32_{6} Jr 16_{8} Est 3_{15}, שפט *judge* Ex 18_{13} Jl 4_{12} 4QapPs[b] 76_{12}, בקר pi. *inquire* Ps 27_{4}, דרש *inquire* Ezr 10_{16}, חזה *see* Ps 27_{4}.

ישב *dwell* + adverb or noun used adverbially, פֹּה *here* Nm 32_{6} 2 K $2_{2.4.6}$ $7_{3.4}$ Ps 132_{14} Ru $4_{1.2}$ 4QparaKings 9_{6}, שָׁם *there* Gn $11_{2.31}$ 26_{17} 35_{1} Dt 13_{13}=11QT 55_{2} ([לש]בת שמה) Jos 22_{2} Jg 9_{21} 21_{2} 1 S 1_{22} 27_{5} 2 S 15_{29} 1 K 2_{36} 7_{8} 11_{16} $17_{9.19}$ 2 K $6_{1.2}$ 16_{6} $17_{25.27.29}$ Jr 2_{6} 37_{16} 42_{14} 44_{14} $49_{18.33}$ 50_{40} Ezk $3_{15.15}$ Ps 69_{36} 122_{5} (שָׁמָּה) 137_{1} Ru 1_{4} 4_{1} Ezr 8_{32} 1 C $4_{23.40.43}$ 2 C 28_{18} 4QJub[h] 36_{19} ([שמ]ה) 11QT 42_{16} ([שמה]), עוֹד *again* Jr 50_{39}, מְעַט *a little*, i.e. for a short time Ru 2_{7}, מִנֶּגֶד *opposite* Gn 21_{16}, חוּץ *outside* Dt 23_{14}, יַחְדָּו *together* Gn $13_{6.6}$ 36_{7} Dt 25_{5} Jr 31_{24}, יַחַד

together Ps 133$_{1}$ 11QT 57$_{13}$, בֶּטַח *securely* Dt 12$_{10}$ 1 S 12$_{11}$, אֵיכָה לָמָּה *why?* Jg 5$_{16}$ 1 S 27$_{5}$, עַל־מָה *why?* Jr 8$_{14}$, אֵיכָה *how!* Lm 1$_{1}$, כֵּן *thus* CD 14$_{6}$, לְפָנִים *formerly* Dt 2$_{10.12.20}$ 1 C 4$_{40}$, אֶרֶץ *(in) earth* Is 45$_{18}$, פֶּתַח *(at) entrance* Gn 18$_{1}$ Lv 8$_{35}$, בַּיִת *(in) house* Gn 38$_{11.11}$ 2 S 6$_{11}$ 7$_{5}$||1 C 17$_{4}$ 2 S 13$_{20}$ Is 44$_{13}$ Jr 36$_{22}$ Ru 2$_{7}$ 2 C 26$_{21}$ MurEpBeth-Mashiko$_{4}$ (אבית משכו *in Beth-Mashiko*) Arad ost. 18$_{10}$, אֹהֶל *(in) tent* Gn 25$_{27}$ Is 40$_{22}$, מַחֲנֶה *(in) camp* Mur 24 2$_{4}$ (במחנ[ה]) 5$_{3}$ CD 7$_{6}$ 19$_{2}$, מוֹשָׁב *(in) dwelling place* 4QTohA 1.1$_{1}$, עִיר *(in) city* Nm 35$_{2.3}$ Jos 14$_{14}$ 21$_{2}$, חָצֵר *(in) village* Is 42$_{11}$, נְתִיבָה *(in) path* Is 58$_{12}$ (unless em. נְתִיבוֹת *paths* to נְתִיצוֹת *ruins*), נֶגֶב *(in) Negeb* Nm 21$_{1}$, צִיּוֹן *(in) Zion* Ps 9$_{12}$, נַחֲלָה *(in) inheritance* Jg 18$_{1}$, יָד *(at) side* 1 S 4$_{13(Qr)}$ (unless em. לְיַד *at the side of*), כְּרוּב *(upon) cherub* 1 S 4$_{4}$ 6$_{2}$||1 C 13$_{6}$ 2 K 19$_{15}$||Is 37$_{16}$ Ps 80$_{2}$ (all י׳ צְבָאוֹת יֹשֵׁב הַכְּרֻבִים, or sim., *Y. [who] is enthroned upon the cherubim*) 99$_{1}$, תְּהִלָּה *(upon) praise* perh. Ps 22$_{4}$, כִּסֵּא *(on) throne* Si 40$_{3(B)}$ 4QCommGenA 5$_{2}$, רְבָבָה *(with) ten thousand* Nm 10$_{36}$ (if em.; see Subj.), דּוּמָם *(in) silence* Is 47$_{5}$, יוֹם *(for) day(s)* Gn 27$_{44}$ Lv 12$_{4.5}$ 14$_{8}$ 23$_{42}$ Nm 20$_{15}$ Dt 1$_{46}$ 9$_{9}$ Jos 2$_{22}$ 24$_{7}$ Jg 19$_{4}$ 1 S 27$_{7.11}$ 2 S 1$_{1}$ 14$_{28}$ 1 K 2$_{38}$ 5$_{5}$ Jr 35$_{7}$ 37$_{16}$ Ezk 3$_{15}$ Ho 3$_{3.4}$ Ps 27$_{4}$ Jb 2$_{13}$ Ezr 8$_{32}$ 4QSD 7.2$_{15}$ ([יום תשב]) 7.2$_{17}$ ([ימים תש]ב) 4QD^{g} 1.2$_{8}$ ([ת]שב) 4QMMT B$_{66}$ ([י]שב]), הַיּוֹם *today* 2 S 11$_{12}$, יוֹמָם *by day* Lv 8$_{35}$, לַיְלָה *(by) night* Lv 8$_{35}$, *(for) night(s)* Dt 9$_{9}$ Jb 2$_{13}$, הַלַּיְלָה *tonight* Nm 22$_{19}$, מָחָר *tomorrow* 2 S 11$_{12}$, חֹדֶשׁ *(for) month(s)* Jg 20$_{47}$ 2 S 6$_{11}$||1 C 13$_{14}$ 1 K 11$_{16}$, שָׁנָה *(for) year(s)* 2 S 14$_{28}$ 1 K 22$_{1}$ Ezk 29$_{11}$ 4QpsJub^{a} 2.1$_{2}$ (י[שב] ... שנ[ה]) 4QCommGenA 2$_{9}$, קֶדֶם *from of old* Ps 55$_{20}$ (or em., so that קֶדֶם = *in the east*; see אֵל *God*, under Subj.), עוֹלָם *(for) eternity* 1 K 8$_{13}$||2 C 6$_{2}$ Ps 61$_{8}$, מוֹשָׁב *time of dwelling* Ex 12$_{40}$, פְּרָזָה *(as) unwalled city* Zc 2$_{8}$, רֹאשׁ *(as) head* Jb 29$_{25}$, מְצָרֵף *(as) refiner* Ml 3$_{3}$, מְטַהֵר *(as) purifier* Ml 3$_{3}$, שֹׁפֵט *judge* Ps 9$_{5}$, מֶלֶךְ *(as) king* Ps 29$_{10}$, אַלְמָנָה *(as) widow* Gn 38$_{11}$ Is 47$_{8}$, וַתֵּשֶׁב תָּמָר וְשֹׁמֵמָה *and Tamar dwelt as a desolate woman* 2 S 13$_{20}$, כלם ni. ptc. *(as) a humiliated one* Ps 74$_{21}$ (if em.; see Subj.); pl.n. used adverbially, *in, at,* + Jabez 1 C 2$_{55(Kt)}$.

ישב *dwell* + noun used predicatively, רִאשֹׁנָה *first* Est 1$_{14}$ 1QS 6$_{8}$ (לרשונה), בָּדָד *alone* Lv 13$_{46}$ Jr 15$_{17}$ Lm 1$_{1}$ 3$_{28}$ 4QTohA 1.1$_{1}$ 1.2$_{8}$ ([בדד]), לְבַד *alone* Ex 18$_{14}$, בַּד *alone* Is 5$_{8(1QIsa^a)}$, רחוק *distant* 4QTohA 1.1$_{1.2}$.

ישב *dwell* + אַיִן *there is not*, i.e. without, followed by מֶלֶךְ *king* Ho 3$_{4}$, שַׂר *prince* Ho 3$_{4}$, כִּסֵּא *throne* Is 47$_{1}$, זֶבַח *sacrifice* Ho 3$_{4}$, מַצֵּבָה *pillar* Ho 3$_{4}$, אֵפוֹד *ephod* Ho 3$_{4}$, תְּרָפִים *teraphim* Ho 3$_{4}$.

מָכוֹן לְשִׁבְתְּךָ *a place for your dwelling* Ex 15$_{17}$ 1 K 8$_{13}$||2 C 6$_{2}$, מְכוֹן שִׁבְתְּךָ, and vars. *the place of your dwelling* 1 K 8$_{39.43.49}$||2 C 6$_{30.33.39}$ Ps 33$_{14}$ 2 C 6$_{21}$ Si 36$_{18}$, מְקוֹם שִׁבְתְּךָ *the place of your dwelling* 1 K 8$_{30}$, ונתן שבנ[תו] *and he shall give his sitting*, i.e. compensate him for time spent inactive 4QHalakhah^{a} 4$_{2}$, הָהָר חָמַד אֱלֹהִים לְשִׁבְתּוֹ *the mountain that God desired for his dwelling* Ps 68$_{17}$, בָּתִּים לְשִׁבְתֵּנוּ *houses for us to live in* Jr 35$_{9}$, כַּיָּמִים אֲשֶׁר יְשַׁבְתֶּם *according to the days when you remained* Dt 1$_{46}$, יְדַעְתֶּם אֵת אֲשֶׁר־יָשַׁבְנוּ *you know how we dwelt* Dt 29$_{15}$, בַּיִת לְשִׁבְתִּי *a house for me dwelling* 2 S 7$_{5}$, לָשֶׁבֶת יְצָרָהּ *he formed it to be inhabited* Is 45$_{18}$, הֶעְמִיקוּ לָשֶׁבֶת *they make deep to dwell*, i.e. dwell in the depths Jr 48$_{8.30}$, הַמַּגְבִּיהִי לָשָׁבֶת *the one who raises himself to sit*, i.e. sits on high Ps 113$_{5}$, מְאַחֲרֵי־שֶׁבֶת *(ones who are) late to rest* Ps 127$_{2}$, בראשית ... לשבת *at the beginning of sitting*, i.e. when one sits 1QS 10$_{14}$, תאהל שבת *she pitches her tent to dwell* 4QWiles 1$_{7}$.

ישב *dwell* pl. cstr. ptc. followed by prep., יֹשְׁבֵי לָבֶטַח *those who dwell in security* Ezk 38$_{11}$, יֹשְׁבֵי בְּאֶרֶץ *those who dwell in a land of* Is 9$_{1}$, יֹשְׁבֵי בְצִלּוֹ *those who dwell in his shadow* Ho 14$_{8}$, יֹשְׁבֵי בָהּ *those who dwell in it* Is 24$_{6}$ Jr 8$_{16}$ 12$_{4}$ 46$_{8}$ 47$_{2}$ Ezk 32$_{15}$ Am 9$_{5}$ (both יוֹשְׁבֵי) Na 1$_{5}$ Hb 2$_{8.17}$ Ps 24$_{1}$ 98$_{7}$ 107$_{34}$ 4QBer^{a} 5$_{1}$, יֹשְׁבֵי עַל־מִדִּין *those who sit upon carpets* Jg 5$_{10}$, יֹשְׁבֵי עַל־טַבּוּר הָאָרֶץ *those who dwell at the centre of the earth* Ezk 38$_{12}$.

ישב *dwell* pl. cstr. ptc., other verbal uses, יֹשְׁבֵי הָאִיִּים לָבֶטַח *those who dwell in the coastlands securely* Ezk 39$_{6}$, יֹשְׁבֵי חֹשֶׁךְ *those who sit in darkness* Is 42$_{7}$, יֹשְׁבֵי חֹשֶׁךְ וְצַלְמָוֶת *those who sit in darkness and gloom* Ps 107$_{10}$, יֹשְׁבֵי שַׁעַר *those who sit in the gate* Ps 69$_{13}$, יוֹשְׁבֵי בֵיתֶךָ *those who dwell in your house* Ps 84$_{5}$.

13. יוֹשֵׁב ptc. as noun (distinction from §6 oft. unclear), **inhabitant**, sg. oft. used collectively (e.g. Gn 4$_{20}$ 50$_{11}$ Nm 14$_{14}$ 2 S 5$_{6}$ Is 5$_{3}$ Jr 48$_{43}$ Ezk 7$_{7}$ Am 1$_{5}$ Zc 12$_{7}$); fem. sing. used collectively Is 12$_{6}$ Jr 21$_{13}$ 46$_{19}$ 48$_{18.19}$ 51$_{35}$ Mc 1$_{11.11.12.13.15}$ Zc 2$_{11}$; fem. pl. 1 S 27$_{8}$.

<SUBJ> היה *be* Jos 17$_{11.11.11.11}$ Jg 1$_{33}$ 2 K 19$_{26}$||Is 37$_{27}$ Jr

23_{14} 48_{28} 50_3 51_{62} Ezk 27_8, ירא *be afraid* Is 10_{24} Ps 65_9 2 C 20_{15}, גור *fear* Ps 33_8, מוג ni. *melt* Ex 15_{15} Jos $2_{9.24}$ Ps 75_4, חתת *be dismayed* 2 K 19_{26}||Is 37_{27} 2 C 20_{15}, בעת ni. *be terrified* 1QH 3_{13}, רגז *tremble* Jl 2_1, בוש *be ashamed* 2 K 19_{26}||Is 37_{27}, נפל *fall* Is 26_{18} 2 C 20_{18}, שחה htpal. *prostrate oneself* 2 C 20_{18}, כנע ni. *humble oneself* 2 C 32_{26}, אמר *say* Jos 9_{11} Is 20_6 Jr 48_{19} 51_{35} Ezk 11_{15} 33_{24} 1 C 11_5, דבר pi. *speak* Mc 6_{12}, רנן *shout for joy* Is 12_6 42_{11}, צהל *cry* Is 12_6, זעק *cry* Jr 11_{12}, שיר *sing* Is 42_{10} (unless em.; see below), הלל pi. *praise* MasShirShabb 1_9 ([הללו]), דמם *be silent*, perh. *weep* Is 23_2, ילל hi. *wail* Is 23_6 Jr 47_2 Zp 1_{11}, שאל *ask* Jr 48_{19}, בקש pi. *seek* Zc 8_{21}, חלה pi. *entreat* Zc 8_{21}, ראה *see* Gn 50_{11} Is 18_3, צפה *watch* Jr 48_{19}, שמע *hear* Jos 7_9 9_3 1 S 31_{11} Is 18_3 Jr 17_{20} 19_3 2 C 20_{20}, אזן hi. *hear* Jl 1_2 Ps 49_2, קשב hi. *pay attention* 2 C 20_{15}, ידע *know* Is 9_8 Ezk 29_6 GnzPs 2_{16}, למד *learn* Is 26_9 GnzPs 2_{16}, אמן hi. *believe* Lm 4_{12} 2 C 20_{20}, עבד *serve* GnzPs 2_{16}, אכל *eat* Ezk 12_{19}, שתה *drink* Ezk 12_{19}, זנה *prostitute oneself* Ex 34_{15}.

קדם pi. *go before* Is 21_{14} GnzPs 2_{16}, אתה hi. *bring* Is 21_{14}, הלך *go* Jr 11_{12} 20_6 Zc 8_{21}, בוא *come* Jr $17_{20.25}$ Zc 8_{20}, יצא *go out* Ezk 39_9 Mc 1_{11}, עלה *go up* 2 K 23_2||2 C 34_{30}, ירד *go down* 2 C 20_{15}, שוב *go back* GnzPs 2_{16}, עוז hi. *flee for safety* Is 10_{31}, עבר *pass* Is $23_{2.6}$ 24_5 Mc 1_{11}, חלף *pass* Is 24_5, עזב *leave* Jr 48_{28}, מלט ni. *escape* Zc 2_{11}, סור hi. *remove* Jr 4_4, נשא *lift* Ezk 39_9, עמד *stand* Jr 48_{19}, ישב *dwell* Jr $49_{8.30}$, שכן *dwell* Jr 48_{28}, חיל *writhe* Mc 1_{12}, מצא *find* 2 C 20_{15}, זבח *sacrifice* Ex 34_{15}, קטר pi. *burn incense* Jr 11_{12}, צלח hi. *succeed* 2 C 20_{20}, שלם hi. *make peace* Jos 10_1 11_{19}, שפט *judge* Is 5_3, מלך hi. *make king* 2 C 22_1, כעס hi. *anger* Jr 32_{32}.

עשה *do, make* Jr 32_{32} 46_{19} 51_{24} 2 C 32_{33} 33_9 34_{32} 35_{18}, מלא pi. *fill* Jr $13_{13.13}$, נתן *give, place* Ezk 26_{17} (or em. הַיַּבָּשָׁה *the dry land*; or del.) 2 C 31_4, חטא hi. *cause to sin* 4QSela 8.2_{10}, רתם *attach* Mc 1_{13}, חזק hi. *repair* Ne 3_{13}, בנה *build* Ne 3_{13}, שמם *be appalled* Ezk 27_{35}, אדר hi. *glorify* Is 42_{10} (if em. יֹרְדֵי הַיָּם *those who go down to the sea* to יַאְדִּירֻהוּ יָם *let the sea glorify him*), גדל pi. *magnify* GnzPs 2_{16}, עמק hi. *make deep* Jr $49_{8.30}$, בער pi. *burn* Ezk 39_9, שלק hi. *burn* Ezk 39_9, בזז *plunder* Ezk 39_9, שלל *despoil* Ezk 39_9, חטב *cut* Ezk 39_9, מול ni. *circumcise oneself* Jr 4_4, חרה *dwindle away* Is 24_6 (unless חָרוּ from חור *become pale* or חור *become feeble*), מות *die* Is 51_6.

<NOM CL> אֵין־יוֹשֵׁב *there is no inhabitant* Jr 4_{29} 44_2, אֵלֶּה ... יֹשְׁבֵי הָאָרֶץ *these are ... the inhabitants of the land* Gn 36_{20}, הֵנָּה יֹשְׁבוֹת הָאָרֶץ *they were the inhabitants of the land* 1 S 27_8, הֵמָּה הַיּוֹצְרִים וְיֹשְׁבֵי נְטָעִים וּגְדֵרָה *they were the potters and inhabitants of Netaim and Gederah* 1 C 4_{23}, הַיּוֹשְׁבִים הָרִאשֹׁנִים ... יִשְׂרָאֵל הַכֹּהֲנִים הַלְוִיִּם וְהַנְּתִינִים *the first dwellers were ... Israel, the priests, the Levites and the temple servants* 1 C 9_2 (or em. הַיּוֹשְׁבִים *those who dwelt* to הַשָּׁבִים *those who returned*, i.e. שוב ptc.), יֹשְׁבֵיהֶן קִצְרֵי־יָד *their inhabitants are short of strength* 2 K 19_{26}||Is 37_{27}, שָׁם ... יֹשְׁבֵי הָאָרֶץ *there ... there were the inhabitants of the land* 1 C 11_4, יֹשְׁבֶיהָ כַּחֲגָבִים *its inhabitants are like grasshoppers* Is 40_{22}, כְּרֹאשׁ עִיר כֵּן יֹשְׁבָיו *as the head of a city, so are its inhabitants* Si 10_2.

<OBJ> הפך *overthrow* Gn 19_{25}, ירש hi. *dispossess* Nm $33_{52.55}$ Jos 13_6 15_{63} Jg 1_{19+11t} 2 C 20_7, כנע hi. *subdue* Ne 9_{24}, קיא *vomit* Lv 18_{25}, ברח hi. *put to flight* 1 C 8_{13}, אכל *devour* Nm 13_{32}, אחז *seize* Ex 15_{14}, נדח hi. *turn away* Dt 13_{14}=11QT 55_3 ([י]ושבי), גרש pi. *expel* Jos 24_{18}, קלע *sling out* Jr 10_{18}, , פוץ hi. *scatter* Is 24_1, שחח hi. *bring low* Is 26_5, נכה hi. *strike* Dt 13_{16}=11QT 55_6 Jg 1_{17} 21_{10} Jr 21_6, הרג *kill* Jos 8_{24}, שמד hi. *destroy* Jos 9_{24}, חרם hi. *destroy* Jos 8_{26}, כרת hi. *cut off* Am $1_{5.8}$, ארר *curse* Jg 5_{23}, קוץ *loathe* Si 50_{26}, זנה hi. *lead into prostitution* 2 C $21_{11.13}$, תעה hi. *lead astray* 2 C 33_9, ישע hi. *save* 1 S 23_5 2 C 32_{22}, כון hi. *establish* 1QH 1_{14} (יוש[ביהם]), נתן *give, place* Ex 23_{31} Ezk 15_6 Mc 6_{12} Ne 9_{24} 1 C 22_{18}, מלא pi. *fill* Is 23_2 (unless em. מִלְאוּךְ : וּבְמַיִם *they filled you. And in the waters* to מַלְאָכָיו : בַּמַּיִם *his messengers in the waters*), אסף *gather* Jl 1_{14}.

<CSTR> יֹשֵׁב *inhabitant of*, + pl.n. Dor Jg $1_{27(Kt)}$, Jerusalem Jg 1_{21} Is 5_3 8_{14} 22_{21} Zc 12_7 (יֹשֵׁב) $12_{8.10}$, Moab Jr 48_{43}, Samaria Is 9_8, Zephath Jg 1_{17}, Zion Is 10_{24} (יֹשֵׁב).

יֹשְׁבֵי *inhabitants of*, + pl.n. Aijalon 1 C 8_{13} (יוֹשְׁבֵי), Acco Jg 1_{31}, Ai Jos $8_{24.26}$, Arvad Ezk 27_8, Babylon Jr $50_{34.35}$ 51_{12}, Beth-anath Jg $1_{33.33}$, Beth-shemesh Jg $1_{33.33}$, Canaan Ex 15_{15}, Chaldaea Jr 51_{24} (יוֹשְׁבֵי) 51_{35}, Debir Jos 15_{15} Jg 1_{11} (יוֹשְׁבֵי), Dedan Jr 49_8, Dor Jos 17_{11} Jg $1_{27(Qr)}$, En-dor Jos 17_{11}, En-tappuah Jos 17_7 (or em. יֹשְׁבֵי to יָשׁוּב *Jashub*), Egypt Ezk 29_6 4QNarrC 1_{14}

(יו[שב]), Gath 1 C 8_{13} (יוֹשְׁבֵי), Geba 1 C 8_6 (יוֹשְׁבֵי), Gebim Is 10_{31}, Gederah 1 C 4_{23}, Gibeah Jg 20_{15}, Gibeon Jos 9_3 10_1 11_{19}, Gilead Jg 10_{18} 11_8, Hazor Jr 49_{30}, Ibleam Jg 1_{27} (יוֹשְׁבֵי), Jabesh-gilead Jg $21_{9.10.12}$ 1 S 31_{11}, Jabez 1 C $2_{55(Qr)}$, Jebus 1 C 11_5.

Jerusalem Jos 15_{63} (יוֹשְׁבֵי) 2 K 23_2‖2 C 34_{30} Jr 4_4 8_1 (יוֹשְׁבֵי) $11_{2.9.12}$ 13_{13} 17_{20} 18_{11} (יוֹשְׁבֵי) 19_3 25_2 32_{32} $35_{13.17}$ (both יוֹשְׁבֵי) 36_{31} 42_{18} Ezk 11_{15} 12_{19} (יוֹשְׁבֵי) 15_6 Zp 1_4 (יוֹשְׁבֵי) Zc 12_5 13_1 Dn 9_7 (יוֹשְׁבֵי) Ezr 4_6 Ne 7_3 2 C $20_{15.18.20}$ $21_{11.13}$ 22_1 31_4 (יוֹשְׁבֵי) $32_{22.26.33}$ 33_9 $34_{9(Kt).32}$ 35_{18} (יוֹשְׁבֵי), Judah Ezr 4_6, Keilah 1 S 23_5, Kiriath-jearim 1 S 6_{21}, Kitron Jg 1_{30} (יוֹשְׁבֵי), Megiddo Jos 17_{11} Jg 1_{27} (יוֹשְׁבֵי), Moab Jr 48_{28}, Nahalol Jg 1_{30} (יוֹשְׁבֵי), Netaim 1 C 4_{23}, Pekod Jr 50_{21} (יוֹשְׁבֵי), Philistia Ex 15_{14} Si 50_{26} (יושבי) 4QNarrC 1_{14} (יו[שב]), Seir 2 C 20_{23} (יוֹשְׁבֵי) Si 50_{26} (יושבי), Sela Is 42_{11}, Sidon Jg 1_{31} (יוֹשְׁבֵי) Ezk 27_8, Taanach Jos 17_{11}, Teman Jr 49_{20}, Tyre Ps 83_8, Zanoah Ne 3_{13}.

יוֹשֶׁבֶת *inhabitant of* (fem. sing.), + pl.n. Aroer Jr 48_{19}, Lachish Mc 1_{13}, Mareshah Mc 1_{15}, Maroth Mc 1_{12}, Shaphir Mc 1_{11}, Zaanan Mc 1_{11}, Zion Is 12_6 Jr 51_{35}, יוֹשֶׁבֶת בַּת *inhabitant of the daughter of* Jr 46_{19} 48_{18} (יֹשֶׁבֶת) Zc 2_{11}, הָעֵמֶק *of the valley* Jr 21_{13} (יֹשֶׁבֶת).

יֹשֵׁב הָאָרֶץ *inhabitant of the land* Gn 34_{30} 50_{11} Ex $34_{12.15}$ Nm 14_{14} (all four יוֹשֵׁב) Jos 24_{18} Jg 11_{21} 2 S 5_6 Is 24_{17} (all three יוֹשֵׁב) Is 26_{21} Jr 47_2 Ezk 7_7 (both יוֹשֵׁב) 11QT $2_{4.12}$ (both [יושב הארץ]) CD 4_{14} (יושב), יֹשְׁבֵי הָאָרֶץ *inhabitants of the land* Gn 36_{20} Ex 23_{31} Nm 32_{17} $33_{52.55}$ Jos $2_{9.24}$ 7_9 9_{24} 13_{21} Jg $1_{32.33}$ 2_2 (יוֹשְׁבֵי) Is 24_6 (אֶרֶץ) Jr 1_{14} 6_{12} 10_{18} (יוֹשְׁבֵי) 13_{13} 17_{25} $25_{29.30}$ Ho 4_1 Jl 1_2 (both יוֹשְׁבֵי) 1_{14} 2_1 Zp 1_{18} Zc 11_6 Ps 33_{14} Ne 9_{24} 1 C 11_4 22_{18} 2 C 20_7 CD 10_9 (יושבי), יֹשְׁבֵי אֶרֶץ *inhabitants of the land of* Is 21_{14}, יֹשְׁבוֹת הָאָרֶץ *inhabitants of the land* 1 S 27_8, יֹשְׁבֵי אַרְצֵנוּ *inhabitants of our land* Jos 9_{11}, יוֹשְׁבֵי הָאֲרָצוֹת *inhabitants of the lands* 2 C 15_5, יושבי האדמה *inhabitants of the land* 1QH fr. 5_{12}, יֹשְׁבֵי תֵבֵל *inhabitants of the world* Is 18_3 $26_{9.18}$ Ps 33_8 Lm 4_{12} 4QpNah 1_9 (יושבי) GnzPs 2_{16} (יושבי), חֶלֶד *of the world* Is $38_{11(mss)}$ (יוֹשְׁבֵי) Ps 49_2, חֶדֶל *of the world* Is 38_{11} (יוֹשְׁבֵי), יושבי עפר *dwellers of*, i.e. in, the dust 1QH 3_{13}.

[י]שב ער[י]הם *inhabitant of their cities* 4QDᵉ 7.2_{14}, יֹשְׁבֵי הָעִיר *inhabitants of the city* Dt 13_{16}=11QT 55_6 (יושבי) Jr 21_6, עִירָם *of their city* Dt 13_{14}=11QT 55_3 (י[ו]שבי עירמה), הֶעָרִים *of the cities* Gn 19_{25}, עָרִים *of cities* Zc 8_{20}, עָרֵי *of the cities of* Ezk 39_9, יוֹשֵׁב הָהָר *inhabitant of the hill-country* Jg 1_9, יֹשֵׁב הַר *inhabitant of the hill-country of* Jg 3_3, יֹשְׁבֵי הַר *inhabitants of the mountain of* 2 C 20_{23}, יֹשְׁבֵי הָהָר *inhabitants of the hill-country* Jos 10_6 13_6, יֹשְׁבֵי הָעֵמֶק *inhabitants of the valley* Jg 1_{19}, יֹשֵׁב הָאִי *inhabitant of the coastland* Is 20_6, יֹשְׁבֵי אִי *inhabitants of the coastland* Is $23_{2.6}$, הָאִיִּים *of the coastlands* Ezk 27_{35}, חֶבֶל *of the territory of* Zp 2_5, קְצוֹת *of the ends* Ps 65_9, הַמַּכְתֵּשׁ *of the mortar* Zp 1_{11}, מָרוֹם *of the height* Is 26_5, יושבי מרומי *inhabitants of the heights of* MasShirShabb 1_9, הֶחֳרָבוֹת *of the desolations* Ezk 33_{24}, יֹשְׁבֵי אַחַת *inhabitants of one (town)* Zc 8_{21}.

יֹשֵׁב אֹהֶל *dweller of*, i.e. one who dwells in, *a tent* Gn 4_{20}, יֹשְׁבֵי בֵיתֶךָ *dwellers of*, i.e. those who dwell in, *your house* Jr 20_6, ישב [מ]חניהם *dweller of*, i.e. one who dwells in, *their camps* 4QDᵉ 7.2_{14}.

יֹשְׁבֵי לֵב קָמָי appar. *inhabitants of those who rise against me* (לֵב קָמָי cipher for כַּשְׂדִּים *Chaldaea*) Jr 51_1.

אֲבִי יֹשֵׁב *father of one who dwells* Gn 4_{20}, מִשְׁפְּחוֹת ... יֹשְׁבֵי *families of ... the inhabitants of* 1 C $2_{55(Qr)}$, אֶרֶץ ... יוֹשֵׁב *land of ... the inhabitant of* Jg 11_{21}.

עַצְמוֹת יוֹשְׁבֵי *bones of the inhabitants of* Jr 8_1, עֲוֹן יֹשֵׁב *iniquity of the inhabitant of* Is 26_{21}, תִּפְאֶרֶת *beauty of* Zc 12_7, מִשְׁמְרוֹת יֹשְׁבֵי *guards of the inhabitants of* Ne 7_3, אַשְׁרֵי יוֹשְׁבֵי *happiness of*, i.e. happy are, *the inhabitants of* Ps 84_5, מעשי ישבי *deeds of the inhabitants of* 4QapPsᵇ 69_{5a}.

כָּל יוֹשֵׁב *every inhabitant* Jr 47_2 4QSela 8.2_{10} ([כל]), כל ישב *every inhabitant of* 4QDᵉ $7.2_{14.14}$ ([י]שב), כול יושב[ים] *all the inhabitants* 4QparaKings 140_1, כָּל־יֹשְׁבֵי *all the inhabitants of* Gn 19_{25} Ex 15_{15} Nm 33_{52} Jos $2_{9.24}$ 7_9 (כֹּל) $8_{24.26}$ 9_{24} 13_6 Jg 10_{18} 11_8 (both כֹּל) 2 K 23_2 Is 18_3 Jr 1_{14} $13_{13.13}$ 17_{20} 20_6 (both כֹּל) $25_{5.29.30}$ 35_{17} (כֹּל יוֹשְׁבֵי) 51_{24} (כֹּל יוֹשְׁבֵי) Ezk 27_{35} (כֹּל) 29_6 Jl 1_2 (כֹּל יוֹשְׁבֵי) 1_{14} 2_1 (both כֹּל) Zp 1_4 (יוֹשְׁבֵי) 1_{18} Ps $33_{8.14}$ 49_2 Lm 4_{12} (כֹּל) 2 C 15_5 (יוֹשְׁבֵי) 4QpsEzekᵉ 8_2 ([יושב]) 11QT 55_3 (כול [י]ושבי), כָּל־יֹשְׁבֶיהָ *all its inhabitants* Lv 25_{10} Ezk 26_{17} (יוֹשְׁבֶיהָ) Ps 75_4 4QBerᵃ 5_1 (כול יוש[ביה]), כול יוש[ביהם] *all their inhabitants* 1QH 1_{14}.

<APP> Amorite Jos 10_{6} 24_{18} Jg 11_{21}, Canaanite Gn 34_{30} 50_{11} Jg $1_{9.17.32.33}$ Ne 9_{24}, Hivite Jos 11_{19} Jg 3_{3}, Jebusite Jos 15_{63} Jg 1_{21} 2 S 5_{6}||1 C 11_{4}, Perizzite Gn 34_{30}, עַם *people* Is 10_{24} 2 C 31_{4}, Evi Jos 13_{21}, Hur Jos 13_{21}, Reba Jos 13_{21}, Rekem Jos 13_{21}, Zur Jos 13_{21}, בֵּן *son* Gn 36_{20}, נָשִׂיא *prince* Jos 13_{21}, נָסִיךְ *prince* Jos 13_{21}, סֹחֵר *merchant* Is 23_{2}, צוּר *rock* Jr 21_{13}.

<ADJ> רִאשׁוֹן *first* 1 C 9_{2}.

<PREP> לְ of benefit, *for, to* Lv 25_{10} 4QD^{e} 7.2_{14}, + היה *be* Is 22_{21}, עשׂה *do, make* Jr 19_{12} 46_{19}, פתח ni. *be opened* Zc 13_{1}; לְ *for*, i.e. with, + כרת *cut*, i.e. make, covenant Ex $34_{12.15}$ Jg 2_{2} 11QT $2_{4.12}$ (both [ליושב]); לְ of direction, *to*, + אמר *say* Jr 35_{13} 2 C 20_{15} 31_{4}, שׁלם pi. *repay* Jr 51_{24}, נתן *give* Ezk 26_{17}, ni. *be given* Ezk 33_{24}; לְ *towards, against* Zc $12_{5(ms)}$, + היה *be* Is 8_{14}, בוא hi. *bring* Mc 1_{15}, רגז hi. *cause disquiet* Jr 50_{34}; לְ of possession, *(belonging) to, of* Dn 9_{7} 1 C $8_{6.13}$ 2 C 20_{15}, + היה *be* Jg 10_{18} 11_{8}; לְ *concerning*, + אמר *say* Ezk 12_{19}; לְ introducing object, + ישׁע hi. *save* Jr 11_{12}, כלה pi. *make an end of* 2 C 20_{23}.

בְּ *by, among* perh. 1QH fr. 5_{12}, + באשׁ hi. *cause to be despised* Gn 34_{30}, מצא ni. *be found* Jr 11_{9}; בְּ *against* CD 10_{9}, + לחם ni. *fight* Jg 1_{9}, עלה *go up* Jr 48_{18}, עשׂה *do* Ne 9_{24}.

מִן of direction, *from* perh. 4QparaKings 140_{1}, + אסף *gather* 2 C $34_{9(Kt)}$; מִן partitive, *(some) of* Jg 21_{9}, + יתר hi. *let remain* Nm 33_{55}, מצא ni. *be found* Jg 21_{12}; צרר מִן *be too narrow for* Is 49_{19}.

אֶל *to*, + אמר *say* Nm 14_{14}, דבר pi. *speak* Jr $11_{2(mss)}$ 25_{2}, ענה *sing* Jr 25_{30}, הלך *go* Jos 17_{7} (or em.; see Cstr.) Jg 1_{11} 2 S 5_{6}, בוא *come* Ezk 7_{7}, עלה *go up* Jos 15_{15}, שׁלח *send* 1 S 6_{21}; אֶל *against* Jr 21_{13} 50_{35}, + בוא hi. *bring* Jr 35_{17}, עלה *go up* Jr 50_{21}, נתן *give*, i.e. place Jr 26_{15}, חשׁב *devise* Jr 49_{20}, עור hi. *stir up* Jr 51_{1}; אֶל *upon* Jr 51_{35}; אֶל *concerning*, + דבר pi. *speak* Jr 51_{12}; שׁגח אֶל hi. *gaze at* Ps 33_{14}.

עַל *upon* Is 24_{17} Jr 48_{43} CD 4_{14}, + שׁפך *pour out* Zc 12_{10}, נתך ni. *be poured out* Jr 42_{18}, חמל *have compassion* Zc 11_{6}; עַל *against* 2 C 15_{5} 34_{27}, + בוא hi. *bring* 2 K 22_{16} ||2 C 34_{24} Jr 25_{9} 36_{31} 2 C 34_{28}, נטה *stretch out* hand Zp 1_{4}, hi. *stretch out* hand Jr 6_{12}, עמד *stand* 2 C 20_{23}, דבר pi. *speak* 2 K 22_{19}, קרא *call* Jr 25_{29}, כתב *write* Ezr 4_{6}, פתח ni. *be opened* Jr 1_{14} (unless em. תִּפָּתַח *it shall be opened* to תְּנֻפַּח/תֻּפַּח *it shall be fanned* or תִּפָּנֶה *it shall turn*); עַל *to*, + אמר *say* Jr 18_{11}, דבר pi. *speak* Jr 11_{2}; עַל *on account of*, + היה *be* Mc 7_{13}.

עִם *with* Is 38_{11} Ho 4_{1} Ps 83_{8}; אֵת *with*, + עשׂה *do* Zp 1_{18}; בְּקֶרֶב *among*, + ישׁב *dwell* Jg $1_{32.33}$; לְבַד מִן *besides* Jg 20_{15}; מִפְּנֵי *on account of*, + ישׁב *dwell* Nm 32_{17}; תַּחַת *on account of*, + חנף *be polluted*, or *be outraged* Is 24_{5}; אַחֲרֵי *after*, + חרם hi. *destroy* Jr 50_{21}; בַּעַד *behind*, i.e. around, + גנן *cover* Zc 12_{8}.

<COLL> יֹשֵׁב *inhabitant* || שֹׁכֵן *inhabitant* Is 18_{3}, אִישׁ *man* Is 5_{6} Jr 4_{4} $11_{2.9}$ 17_{25} 18_{11} 32_{32} 35_{13} 36_{31} Zp 3_{6} Dn 9_{7}, אָדָם *human being* Is 6_{11} Jr 33_{10}, מֶלֶךְ *king* Jr 8_{1} $17_{20.25}$ 19_{3} 32_{32} 2 C 20_{15}, שַׂר *prince* Jr 17_{25} 32_{32}, כֹּהֵן *priest* Jr 8_{1} 32_{32} 2 C 35_{18}, לֵוִי *Levite* 2 C 35_{18}, נָבִיא *prophet* Jr 8_{1} 13_{13} 32_{32}.

יֹשֵׁב *inhabitant* + מֶלֶךְ *king* Lm 4_{12}, שַׂר *prince* Jr 50_{35}, זָקֵן *elder* Jos 9_{11} Jl $1_{2.14}$, כֹּהֵן *priest* 2 K 23_{2}||2 C 34_{30}, לֵוִי *Levite* 2 C 34_{30}, נָבִיא *prophet* 2 K 23_{2}, חָכָם *sage* Jr 50_{35}, Babylon Jr 51_{1}, Benjamin 2 C $34_{9(Kt)}$, Chaldaean Jr 50_{35}, Ephraim 2 C $34_{9(Kt)}$, Manasseh 2 C $34_{9(Kt)}$, Israel Dn 9_{7} 2 C $34_{9(Kt)}$ 2 C 35_{18}, Judah Jr 17_{20} Zp 1_{4} 2 C $20_{15.18.20}$ $21_{11.13}$ 32_{33} 33_{9} $34_{9(Kt)}$ 2 C 35_{18}, עַם *people* 2 K 23_{2}||2 C 34_{30} Is 9_{8}, גּוֹי *nation* Jr 25_{9}, אֶרֶץ *land* Jr 25_{9} Ps 33_{8} Ps 75_{4}, עִיר *city* Jr 11_{12} 26_{15}, בַּיִת *house* Is 8_{14} 22_{21} Zc 12_{10} 13_{1}, אִי *coastland* Is 42_{10}, מָקוֹם *place* 2 K 22_{19}||2 C 34_{27} Jr 19_{2} 2 C 34_{28}, בְּהֵמָה *beast* Jr 33_{10}.

הוֹי יֹשְׁבֵי חֶבֶל הַיָּם *woe to the inhabitants of the territory of the sea* Zc 2_{5}.

מֵאֵין יֹשֵׁב *without inhabitant* Is 5_{9} 6_{11} Jr 4_{7} 26_{9} 33_{10} 34_{22} 44_{22} 48_{9} $51_{29.37}$ Zp 2_{5} 3_{6} 6QapProph 1_{3} ([מאין] יושב), מִבְּלִי יֹשֵׁב *without inhabitant* Jr 2_{15} 9_{10}, יוֹשֵׁב לְמֵאָדָם וְעַד־בְּהֵמָה *an inhabitant (consisting of) either human or beast* Jr 51_{62}, var. 50_{3}.

יֹשֵׁב ptc. *O inhabitant* Is 5_{3} 12_{6} 21_{14} $23_{2.6}$ 24_{17} Jr 21_{13} 22_{23} 46_{19} $48_{18.19.28.43}$ $49_{8.30}$ Ezk 7_{7} Zp 1_{11}.

Also perh. 1QpPs 16_{1} perh. 1Q29 1_{6} 2QapProph 1_{1} 4QBibPar 14.1_{8} 4QTanḥ 8_{16} 4QpsJub^{b} 1_{4} 4QMyst^{a} 98_{1} 4QpsEzek^{a} 5_{3} (וישב[תה]) 4QHod^{a} 12_{2} (ישבת[י]) 11QPs Ap^{a} A_{10} 11QShirShabb 3_{3} (ישב[ו]) 11QT 44_{1} MassShir Shabb 1_{9}.

<SYN> §§1-11 שׁכן *dwell*, לין *lodge*, גור *sojourn*, עבר *pass through*, סור *turn aside*, שׁקט *be quiet*, משׁל *rule*; §13

שֹׁכֵן *inhabitant*, אִישׁ *man*, אָדָם *human being*, מֶלֶךְ *king*,, שַׂר *prince*, כֹּהֵן *priest*, לֵוִי *Levite*, נָבִיא *prophet* Jr 8_{1} 13_{13} 32_{32}.

<ANT> §§1-11 הלך *go*, בוא *come*, יצא *go out*, מוט ni. *be moved*, קום *rise*, חרב *be desolate*.

Ni. 8.2 Pf. נוֹשָׁבָה, נוֹשָׁבוּ; + waw וְנֹשְׁבוּ; ptc. נוֹשֶׁבֶת (נוֹשָׁבֶת), נוֹשָׁבוֹת—**1. be inhabited,** perh. **be habitable** (Ex 16_{35}), <SUBJ> אֶרֶץ *land* Ex 16_{35} Jr 6_{8}, עִיר *city* Jr 22_{6} Ezk 12_{20} 26_{19} 36_{10} (|| בנה ni. *be built*) Si 10_{3}, חָרְבָּה *waste* Ezk 38_{12}. <PREP> בְּ of cause, *on account of*, + שֵׂכֶל *wisdom* Si 10_{3}.

2. יוֹשֶׁבֶת, fem. ptc. as noun, **inhabited one,** of city (Ezk 26_{17}), world (Si 43_{4}), <SUBJ> אבד *perish* Ezk 26_{17} (or em. נוֹשֶׁבֶת *inhabited one* to נִשְׁבַּתְּ *you have been made to cease*). <OBJ> גמר *destroy* Si 43_{4}. <APP> עִיר *city* Ezk 26_{17} (or em.; see Subj.). <COLL> as vocative, Ezk 26_{17} (or em.; see Subj.). <SYN> §1 בנה ni. *be built*.

Pi. 1 + waw וְיִשְּׁבוּ—**establish,** <SUBJ> בֵּן *son* of east Ezk 25_{4} (|| נתן *give*, i.e. place). <OBJ> טִירָה *settlement* Ezk 25_{4}. <PREP> בְּ of place, *in*, + בֵּן *son* of Ammon Ezk 25_{4}. <SYN> נתן *give*, i.e. place.

Hi. 38.5.2 Pf. הֹשִׁיב (הוֹשִׁיבַנִי, Q הושיבכה), Q הושבתה, הֹשַׁבְתִּי, הֹשִׁיבוּ; impf. 3fs Si תושיבנו (Si תשיבנו), 2ms תּוֹשִׁיבֵנִי (Si תושיבהו), אוֹשִׁיבְךָ, יוֹשִׁיבוּ; + waw Si והושבתך, וְהוֹשַׁבְתִּי (וְהוֹשַׁבְתִּיךָ, וְהֹשַׁבְתִּים, וְהוֹשְׁבוֹתִים Zc 10_{6}); וַיֹּשֶׁב (וַיּוֹשֶׁב, וַיּוֹשֵׁב, וַיּוֹשִׁבֵנִי, וַיֹּשִׁיבֵם), וַתּוֹשֵׁב, וַיּוֹשִׁיבוּ (וַיֹּשִׁבֵם, וַיֹּשְׁבוּם), וַתֹּשִׁיבוּ, וָאֹשֵׁב; impv. הוֹשֵׁב, הוֹשִׁיבוּ; ptc. מוֹשִׁיב (מוֹשִׁיבִי); inf. הוֹשִׁיב (הוֹשִׁיבִי, Si הושיבו).

1. cause to sit, allow to sit, place, <SUBJ> Y. 1 S 2_{8} 1 K 2_{24} Ps 113_{8} Si 10_{14} 4Q416 2.3_{11}, עַם *people* 2 C 23_{20}, בֵּן *son* Si 8_{11} 12_{12}, בַּת *daughter* Si $42_{11(B)}$ (והושבתך; Bmg והובישתך *and she will shame you*, i.e. בוש hi.), זָקֵן *elder* 1 K $21_{9.10.12}$, שַׂר *prince* 2 C 23_{20}, אַדִּיר *noble* 2 C 23_{20}, חֹר *noble* 1 K $21_{9.10.12}$, מֹשֵׁל *ruler* 2 C 23_{20}, אוֹיֵב *enemy* Ps 143_{3}, חָכְמָה *wisdom* Si 11_{1}.

<OBJ> Hannah 1 S $2_{8(mss)}$, Naboth 1 K $21_{9.12}$, Solomon 1 K 2_{24}, אִישׁ *man* 1 K 21_{10} perh. 4QBark[b] 4_{2} ([אנשי]), בֵּן *son* 1 K 21_{10}, מֶלֶךְ *king* 1 K 2_{24} 2 C 23_{20}, אֶבְיוֹן *needy one* 1 S 2_{8} Ps 113_{8} (if em. לְהוֹשִׁיבִי perh. *to cause me to sit* to לְהוֹשִׁיבוֹ *to cause him to sit*), דַּל *poor one* 1 S 2_{8} Ps 113_{8} (if em.; see above) Si 11_{1}, עָנִי *afflicted one* Si 10_{14}, worshipper Ps 113_{8} (unless em.; see above) 143_{3}, שֹׂנֵא ptc. *one who hates*, i.e. enemy Si 12_{12}, לֵץ *scorner* Si 8_{11}; obj. not specified, 4Q416 2.3_{11}. <PREP> לְ *at*, + יָמִין *right hand* Si 12_{12}; בְּ of place, *in, at*, + רֹאשׁ *head* 1 K $21_{9.12}$, מַחֲשָׁךְ *dark place* Ps 143_{3}, עֵדָה *assembly* Si $42_{11(Segal)}$ (ב[ע]דת]); כְּ *as*, + מֵת *dead one* Ps 143_{3}, אֹרֵב *ambush* Si 8_{12}; עַל *upon*, + כִּסֵּא *throne* 1 K 2_{24} 2 C 23_{20}; עִם *with*, + נָדִיב *noble* 1 S 2_{8} Ps 113_{8} 4Q416 2.3_{11}; בֵּין *among*, + נָדִיב *noble* Si 11_{1}; נֶגֶד *opposite*, + Naboth 1 K 21_{10}; לִפְנֵי *before*, + בֵּן *son* Si 8_{11}; תַּחַת *in place of, instead of*, + גֵּאֶה *proud one* Si 10_{14}. <COLL> ישׁב hi. || עמד hi. *cause to stand* Si 12_{12}.

2. accommodate, cause to dwell, (re)settle, <SUBJ> Y. 1 S 12_{8} (if em. וַיֹּשְׁבוּם *and they caused them to dwell* to וַיֹּשִׁיבֵם *and he caused then to dwell*) Jr 32_{37} Ezk 26_{20} 36_{11} Ho 11_{11} (or em. וְהוֹשַׁבְתִּים *and I will make them dwell* to וַהֲשִׁיבֹתִים *and I will bring them back*, i.e. שׁוב hi.) Zc 10_{6} (or em. וְהוֹשְׁבוֹתִים *and I will make them dwell* to וַהֲשִׁיבֹתִים) Ps 4_{9} 68_{7} (or em. מוֹשִׁיב *causes to dwell* to מֵשִׁיב *brings back*, i.e. שׁוב hi.) 107_{36} 113_{9} (or em. מוֹשִׁיבִי *causing to dwell* to מְשִׁיבִי *restoring*, i.e. שׁוב hi.)* Lm 3_{6}, Aaron 1 S 12_{8} (unless em.; see above), Joseph Gn $47_{6.11}$, Moses 1 S 12_{8} (unless em.; see above), Solomon 2 C 8_{2}, גֶּבֶר *man* Lm 3_{6}, בֵּן *son* of Israel Lv 23_{43}, מֶלֶךְ *king* 2 K $17_{6.24.26}$.

<OBJ> Israel 2 K 17_{6} Ezk 36_{11} Ho 11_{11} (or em.; see Subj.), Tyre Ezk 26_{20}, אָב *father* Gn $47_{6.11}$ 1 S 12_{8}, בֵּן *son* of Israel 2 C 8_{2}, אָח *brother* Gn $47_{6.11}$, עִיר *city* Jr 32_{37}, גּוֹי *nation* 2 K 17_{26}, people from various cities 2 K 17_{24}, בַּיִת *house* Zc 10_{6} (or em.; see Subj.), יָחִיד *solitary one* Ps 68_{7} (or em.; see Subj.), רָעֵב *hungry one* Ps 107_{36}, עָקָר *barren one* Ps 113_{9}, worshipper Ps 4_{9}. <PREP> לְ of accompaniment, *in, with*, + בֶּטַח *security* Jr 32_{37} Ps 4_{9}; בְּ of place, *in, at, on*, + Habor 2 K 17_{6}, Halath 2 K 17_{6}, אֶרֶץ *land* Ezk 26_{20}, עִיר *city* 2 K $17_{6.24.26}$, סֻכָּה *booth* Lv 23_{43}, נָהָר *river* 2 K 17_{6}, מֵיטָב *best (part)* Gn 47_{6}, מַחְשָׁךְ *dark place* Lm 3_{6}, מָקוֹם *place* 1 S 12_{8}; כְּ *as*, + מות ptc. *dead one* Lm 3_{6}, חָרְבָּה *waste* Ezk 26_{20}; *as in*, + קֶדֶם *former time* Ezk 36_{11}; עַל *in*, + בַּיִת *house* Ho 11_{11} (or em.; see Subj.); אֵת *with*, + ירד ptc. *one who goes down* Ezk 26_{20}; תַּחַת *instead of*, + בֵּן *son* of Israel 2 K 17_{24}; ה- of direction, *in*, + בַּיִת *house* Ps 68_{7} (or em.; see Subj.). <COLL> + adverb or noun used adverbially, לְבָדָד *alone* Ps 4_{9}, שָׁם *there*

Ps 107$_{36}$ 2 C 8$_2$, בַּיִת *(in) a house* Ps 113$_9$.

3. cause to be inhabited, populate, <SUBJ> Y. Ezk 36$_{33}$, זֶרַע *descendants* Is 54$_3$. <OBJ> עִיר *city* Is 54$_3$ Ezk 36$_{33}$.

4. cause to remain, leave, <SUBJ> David 1 S 30$_{21(mss)}$ (וַיֹּשִׁיבֵם *and he left them;* L וַיֹּשִׁיבֻם *and* David's men *left them*), אִישׁ *man* 1 S 30$_{21}$. <OBJ> אִישׁ *man* 1 S 30$_{21}$. <PREP> בְּ of place, *at,* + נַחַל *wadi* 1 S 30$_{21}$.

5. marry, <SUBJ> Israelites Ezr 10$_2$, יְהוּדִי *Jew* Ne 13$_{23.27}$, עָם *people* Ezr 10$_{10}$, אִישׁ *man* Ezr 10$_{17}$, בֵּן *son* Ezr 10$_{18}$, כֹּל *everyone* Ezr 10$_{14}$. <OBJ> אִשָּׁה *woman* Ezr 10$_{2.10.14.17.18}$ Ne 13$_{23.27}$. <COLL> + מעל *act unfaithfully* Ezr 10$_{2.10}$ Ne 13$_{27}$.

<SYN> §1 עמד hi. *cause to stand.*

Ho. 2 Pf. הוּשַׁבְתֶּם; impf. 3fs תּוּשָׁב—**1. be made to dwell,** <SUBJ> נגע hi. ptc. *one who causes to touch,* i.e. joins together Is 5$_8$ (1QIsa^a וישבתם *and you dwell,* i.e. qal). <PREP> בְּקֶרֶב *within,* + אֶרֶץ *land* Is 5$_8$. <COLL> + adverb לְבַד *alone* Is 5$_8$. **2. be inhabited,** <SUBJ> Jerusalem Is 44$_{26}$ (1QIsa^a תשב, i.e. Qal; + בנה ni. *be built*), עִיר *city* Ezk 35$_{9(mss)}$ (L [Kt] תישבנה *they will* not *be inhabited,* i.e. ישׁב qal; [Qr] תָּשֹׁבְנָה *they will* not *return,* i.e. שׁוּב qal).*

⇒ שֶׁבֶת *seat,* מוֹשָׁב *seat,* יְשִׁיבָה *sitting,* תּוֹשָׁב *sojourner,* שִׁיבָה *stay,* יֶשֶׁבְאָב *Jeshebeab,* יֹשֵׁב בַּשֶּׁבֶת *Josheb-basshebeth,* יָשְׁבְקָשָׁה *Joshbekashah,* יוֹשִׁבְיָה *Joshibiah.*

יֶשֶׁבְאָב 1.0.6 pr.n.m. **Jeshebeab, 1.** priest in time of David, 1 C 24$_{13}$. <PREP> לְ of benefit, *to, for,* + יצא *go out* 1 C 24$_{13}$.

2. priestly course and the period of its office, 4QOtot 1.6$_{19}$ 1.8$_5$ 4QMishA 4.1$_{14}$ 4.5$_{2.7}$ 4QMishB^a 1.1$_3$ 2.3$_4$ 4QMishF^a 1$_1$ 4QMishH 1.2$_3$. <NOM CL> בחמשית ישב]אב] *in the fifth is Jeshebeab* 4QMishF^a 1$_1$, בשנה הח]משית[ישבאב *in the fifth year is Jeshebeab* 4QMishH 1.2$_3$. <PREP> בְּ of time, *on, at, during* 4QOtot 1.6$_{19}$ 4QMishA 4.5$_{2.7}$ 4QMishB^a 1.1$_3$ 2.3$_4$.

Also 4QOtot 1.8$_5$ 4QMishA 4.1$_{14}$.

⇒ אָב *father* + ישׁב *dwell, endure.*

יֹשֵׁב בַּשֶּׁבֶת 1 pr.n.m. **Josheb-basshebeth,** one of David's warriors, <APP> שֵׁם *name* 2 S 23$_8$ (or em. יִשְׁבַּעַל *Ishbaal*), תַּחְכְּמֹנִי *Tahchemonite* 2 S 23$_8$.

⇒ ישׁב *dwell.*

יִשְׁבָּח 1 pr.n.m. **Ishbah,** Judahite, son of Mered, <OBJ> הרה *conceive* 1 C 4$_{17}$.

⇒ (?) שׁבח *praise.*

יִשְׁבִּי 1 pr.n.m. **Ishbi,** Philistine giant, <SUBJ> חגר *be belted with* 2 S 21$_{16(Qr)}$, נכה hi. *strike* 2 S 21$_{16(Qr)}$, אמר *say,* i.e. think 2 S 21$_{16(Qr)}$. <NOM CL> יִשְׁבִּי בְּנֹב *Ishbi was in Nob* 2 S 21$_{16(Qr)}$.

⇒ ישׁב *dwell.*

יָשֻׁבִי לֶחֶם 1 pr.n.m. **Jashubi-lehem,** Judahite, descendant of Shelah, <NOM CL> בְּנֵי שֵׁלָה ... יָשֻׁבִי לָחֶם *the sons of Shelah were ... Jashubi-lehem* 1 C 4$_{22}$.

⇒ לֶחֶם *bread* + שׁוּב *go back.*

[יִשְׁבַּעַל] pr.n.m. **Ishbaal,** perh. warrior and army commander of David, <SUBJ> עור pol. *brandish weapon* 1 C 11$_{11}$ (if em. יָשָׁבְעָם *Jashobeam*). <NOM CL> יִשְׁבַּעַם ... רֹאשׁ הַשְּׁלוֹשִׁים *Ishbaal ... was chief of the thirty* 1 C 11$_{11}$ (if em.), עַל הַמַּחֲלֹקֶת הָרִאשׁוֹנָה לַחֹדֶשׁ הָרִאשׁוֹן יִשְׁבַּעַם *over the first division of the first month was Ishbaal* 1 C 27$_2$ (if em. יָשָׁבְעָם *Jashobeam*).

<APP> בֶּן *son* 1 C 11$_{11}$ 27$_2$.

יָשָׁבְעָם 3 pr.n.m. **Jashobeam,** Korahite, warrior of David's 2 S 23$_8$ 1 C 11$_{11}$ 12$_7$ 27$_2$, <SUBJ> עור pol. *brandish weapon* 1 C 11$_{11}$ (unless em. to יִשְׁבַּעַל *Ishbaal*).

<NOM CL> יָשָׁבְעָם ... רֹאשׁ הַשְּׁלוֹשִׁים *Jashobeam ... was chief of the thirty* 1 C 11$_{11}$ (unless em.), עַל הַמַּחֲלֹקֶת הָרִאשׁוֹנָה לַחֹדֶשׁ הָרִאשׁוֹן יָשָׁבְעָם *over the first division of the first month was Jashobeam* 1 C 27$_2$ (unless em. to יִשְׁבַּעַל *Ishbaal*).

<APP> בֶּן *son* 1 C 11$_{11}$ 27$_2$, קָרְחִי *Korahite* 1 C 12$_7$.

⇒ (?) שׁוּב *go back* + עַם *people.*

יִשְׁבָּק 2 pr.n.m. **Ishbak,** son of Abraham and Keturah, <OBJ> ילד *bear child* Gn 25$_2$ 1 C 1$_{32}$.

יָשְׁבְּקָשָׁה 2 pr.n.m. **Joshbekashah,** Hemanite musician, <NOM CL> לְהֵימָן ... יָשְׁבְּקָשָׁה *to Heman ... was Joshbekashah* 1 C 25$_{4}$. <APP> בֵּן *son* 1 C 25$_{4.24}$, אָח *brother* 1 C 25$_{24}$. <PREP> לְ of possession, *(belonging) to, of* 1 C 25$_{24}$.

יָשׁוּב I $_{3.0.0.1}$ pr.n.m. **Jashub, 1.** son of Issachar, <NOM CL> לִבְנֵי יִשָּׂשכָר ... יָשׁוּב *of the sons of Issachar were ... Jashub* 1 C 7$_{1(Qr)}$. <PREP> לְ of possession, *(belonging) to, of* Nm 26$_{24}$.

2. member of Bani family, husband of non-Jewish wife, <NOM CL> מִבְּנֵי בָּנִי ... יָשׁוּב *of the sons of Bani were ... Jashub* Ezr 10$_{29}$.

3. father of Obadiah, <CSTR> בן ישב *son of Jashub* Seal 34$_{2}$ (Cyrene, 7th cent.).

⇒ שׁוּב *go back.*

[יָשׁוּב] II $_{0.0.0.1}$ pl.n. **Jashub, 1.** in Samaria, perh. Yāsūf 13 km S of Nāblus, <PREP> מִן of direction, *from* Samaria ost. 48$_{3}$; אֶל *to,* + הלך *go* Jos 17$_{7}$ (if em. יֹשְׁבֵי *inhabitants of* to יָשׁוּב *Jashub).*

⇒ שׁוּב *go back;* יָשֻׁבִי *Jashubite.*

יָשׁוּבִי $_{1}$ gent. **Jashubite,** collective, **Jashubites,** <CSTR> מִשְׁפַּחַת הַיָּשׁוּבִי *family of the Jashubites* Nm 26$_{24}$.

⇒ יָשׁוּב *Jashub.*

יִשְׁוָה $_{2}$ pr.n.m. **Ishvah,** son of Asher, <NOM CL> וּבְנֵי אָשֵׁר יִמְנָה וְיִשְׁוָה *and the sons of Asher were Imnah and Ishvah* Gn 46$_{17}$‖1 C 7$_{30}$.

⇒ שׁוה *be like.*

יְשׁוֹחָיָה $_{1}$ pr.n.m. **Jeshohaiah,** Simeonite chief, 1 C 4$_{36}$.

יִשְׁוִי I $_{4}$ pr.n.m. **Ishvi, 1.** son of Asher, as also יִשְׁוָה *Ishvah,* <NOM CL> וּבְנֵי אָשֵׁר יִמְנָה וְיִשְׁוָה וְיִשְׁוִי *and the sons of Asher were Imnah and Ishvah and Ishvi* Gn 46$_{17}$‖1 C 7$_{30}$. <PREP> לְ of possession, *(belonging) to, of* Nm 26$_{44}$.

2. son of Saul and brother of Jonathan, <SUBJ> היה *be* 1 S 14$_{49}$.

⇒ שׁוה *be like.*

יִשְׁוִי II $_{1}$ gent. **Ishvite,** collective, **Ishvites,** <CSTR> מִשְׁפַּחַת הַיִּשְׁוִי *family of the Ishvites* Nm 26$_{24}$.

⇒ יִשְׁוִי *Ishvi.*

יֵשׁוּעַ I $_{27.2.15}$ pr.n.m. **Jeshua, Joshua** (§1)—I ישע—**1.** son of Nun and servant of Moses, conqueror of land of Israel (usu. יְהוֹשֻׁעַ *Joshua*), <SUBJ> כלה pi. *complete* 4QTestim$_{21}$. <CSTR> יְמֵי יֵשׁוּעַ *days of Joshua* Ne 8$_{17}$. <APP> בֵּן *son* Ne 8$_{17}$ 1QDM 1$_{12}$. <PREP> לְ of direction, *to,* + קרא *call* 1QDM 1$_{12}$; אֶל *to,* + אמר *say* 1QDM 1$_{12}$.

2. priest in the time of David, <PREP> לְ of benefit, *to, for,* + יצא *go out* 1 C 24$_{11}$.

3. Levite in the time of Hezekiah, <NOM CL> וְעַל־יָדוֹ עֵדֶן וּמִנְיָמִן וְיֵשׁוּעַ *and at his hand were Eden and Miniamin and Jeshua,* i.e. assisting him 2 C 31$_{15}$.

4. postexilic head of family, <CSTR> בְּנֵי יֵשׁוּעַ *sons of Jeshua* Ezr 2$_{6}$‖Ne 7$_{11}$.

5. high priest contemporary with Zerubbabel, and son of Jozadak, <SUBJ> קום *arise* Ezr 3$_{2}$, חלל hi. *begin* Ezr 3$_{8}$, בנה *build* Ezr 3$_{2}$ 4$_{3}$, עמד hi. *cause to stand,* i.e. appoint Ezr 3$_{8}$, אמר *say* Ezr 4$_{3}$. <OBJ> צוה pi. *command* Ezr 4$_{3}$. <CSTR> בְּנֵי יֵשׁוּעַ *sons of Jeshua* Ezr 10$_{18}$, בֵּית יֵשׁוּעַ *house of Jeshua* Ezr 2$_{36}$‖Ne 7$_{39}$. <APP> Zerubbabel Ezr 2$_{2}$ Ne 12$_{1}$, בֵּן *son* Ezr 10$_{18}$. <PREP> עִם *with,* + בוא *come* Ezr 2$_{2}$, עלה *go up* Ne 12$_{1}$.

6. Levite family head, <SUBJ> קום *arise* Ne 9$_{4}$, עמד *stand* Ezr 3$_{9}$, אמר *say* Ne 9$_{5}$, בין hi. *grant understanding* Ne 8$_{7}$. <NOM CL> הַלְוִיִּם וְיֵשׁוּעַ ... בִּנּוּי *the Levites were (both) Jeshua ... (and) Binnui* Ne 10$_{10}$ (mss lack וְ), sim. Ne 12$_{8}$, וְרָאשֵׁי הַלְוִיִּם חֲשַׁבְיָה שֵׁרֵבְיָה וְיֵשׁוּעַ *and the heads of the Levites were Hashabiah and Sherebiah and Jeshua* Ne 12$_{24}$. <CSTR> בְּנֵי יֵשׁוּעַ *sons of Jeshua* Ezr 2$_{40}$‖Ne 7$_{43}$. <APP> בֵּן *son* Ne 12$_{24}$.

7. Levite, father or family of Jozabad, <CSTR> בֶּן־יֵשׁוּעַ *son of Jeshua* Ezr 8$_{33}$.

8. Levite, father or family of Ezer the ruler of Mizpah, <CSTR> בֶּן־יֵשׁוּעַ *son of Jeshua* Ne 3$_{19}$.

9. Levite, interpreter of the law, <SUBJ> קום *arise* Ne 9$_{4}$, זעק *cry out* Ne 9$_{4}$, בין hi. *grant understanding* Ne 8$_{7}$.

10. Levite, son of Azaniah, <NOM CL> הַלְוִיִּם וְיֵשׁוּעַ ... בִּנּוּי *the Levites were (both) Jeshua ... (and) Binnui* Ne 10$_{10}$ (mss lack וְ).

11. father of Simeon and grandson of Sira, <CSTR>

בן ישוע *son of Jeshua* Si 50$_{27}$ 51$_{30}$.

12. name of priestly course and its period of service, <CSTR> [ב׳את י]שוע *entrance of*, i.e. beginning of, *Jeshua* 4QMishC^{d} 3$_2$. <PREP> בְּ of time, *on, at, during* 4QOtot 7$_1$ 4QMishA 1.2$_6$ 1.3$_9$ 4.1$_{13}$ 4.3$_5$ 4QMishB^{a} 1.1$_7$ 2.1$_5$ 2.2$_{1.3}$ 4QMishB^{b} 1.1$_6$.

13. 5QTopon 1$_1$, <SUBJ> היה *be* 5QTopon 1$_1$.

14. Mur 29$_3$, <CSTR> בת ישוע *daughter of Jeshua* Mur 29$_3$.

15. MurEpBeth-Mashiko$_{1.8}$, <APP> בֵּן *son* MurEp Beth-Mashiko$_8$. <PREP> מִן of direction, *from* MurEp Beth-Mashiko$_1$.

16. MurEpBeth-Mashiko$_2$, <PREP> לְ of direction, *to* MurEpBeth-Mashiko$_2$.

17. MurEpBarC^{a}1, <APP> בֵּן *son* MurEpBarC^{a}1. <PREP> לְ of direction, *to* MurEpBarC^{a}1.

18. MurEpBarC^{b}1, <APP> בֵּן *son* MurEpBarC^{b}1. <PREP> לְ of direction, *to* MurEpBarC^{b}1.

19. Seal 63$_3$, <CSTR> אשת ישע *wife of Jeshua* Seal 63$_3$.

20. Seal 146$_1$ (Judaea?, c. 600). <PREP> לְ of possession, *(belonging)to, of* Seal 146$_1$ (Judea?, c. 600).

21. Stamp/Coin 11$_2$ (5th cent.), <CSTR> בר ישע *son of Jeshua* Stamp/Coin 11$_2$ (5th cent.).

Also 4QMishA 4.1$_{13}$.

⇒ ישע *save*.

יֵשׁוּעַ II 1 pl.n. **Jeshua,** town in southern Judah, perh. ident. with שְׁמַע *Shema* (Jos 15$_{26}$). <PREP> בְּ of place, *in, at*, + ישׁב *dwell* Ne 11$_{26}$.

⇒ ישע *save*.

יְשׁוּעָה 78.1.22 n.f. **salvation**—יְשׁוּעָתָה (יְשֻׁעָתָה); cstr. יְשׁוּעַת; sf. יְשׁוּעָתִי (יְשֻׁעָתִי) יְשׁוּעָתְךָ (יְשֻׁעָתֶךָ, Q ישועתכה), יְשׁוּעָתֵךְ, יְשׁוּעָתוֹ (יְשֻׁעָתוֹ), יְשׁוּעָתָהּ, יְשׁוּעָתֵנוּ; pl. יְשׁוּעוֹת (יְשֻׁעוֹת, יְשׁוּעֹת); cstr. יְשׁוּעוֹת—**1. salvation, deliverance, prosperity, help,** <SUBJ> היה *be* Is 33$_2$ 49$_6$ 51$_{6.8}$ (both ‖ צְדָקָה *righteousness*), ידע *know* Ps 67$_3$, רחק *be far away* Is 59$_{11}$, יצא *go out* Is 62$_1$ (‖ צְדָקָה), עבר *pass away* Jb 30$_{15}$, שׂגב pi. *make high* Ps 69$_{30}$.

<NOM CL> יְשׁוּעָתִי ... י׳ *Y. is ... my salvation* Ps 140$_8$, אֵל יְשׁוּעָתִי *God is my salvation* Is 12$_2$, חסדי אל ישועתי לעד *the loyalties of God are my salvation for ever* 1QS 11$_{12}$, הָאֵל יְשׁוּעָתֵנוּ *God is our salvation* Ps 68$_{20}$, קְרוֹבָה יְשׁוּעָתִי *my salvation is near* Is 56$_1$, רָחוֹק מֵרְשָׁעִים יְשׁוּעָה *salvation is far away from the wicked* Ps 119$_{155}$.

יְשֻׁעָתֵךְ אָנִי *I am your salvation* Ps 35$_3$, הוּא ... יְשׁוּעָתִי *he is ... my salvation* Ps 62$_{3.7}$, לַי׳ יְשׁוּעָתָה *salvation belongs to Y.* Jon 2$_{10}$, sim. Ps 3$_9$, מִמֶּנּוּ יְשׁוּעָתִי *from him is my salvation* Ps 62$_2$, אֵין יְשׁוּעָתָה *there is no salvation* Ps 3$_3$.

<OBJ> ראה *see* Ex 14$_{13}$ Is 52$_{10}$ Ps 98$_3$ 2 C 20$_{17}$, אהב *love* Ps 70$_5$, עשׂה *do*, i.e. enact Ex 14$_{13}$ 1 S 14$_{45}$ Is 26$_{18}$, פעל *do*, i.e. enact Ps 74$_{12}$, נתן *give*, i.e. place Ps 14$_7$ 53$_7$, שׁית *place* Is 26$_1$, גדל hi. *make great* Ps 18$_{51(Qr)}$, קרא *call* Is 60$_{18}$, ידע hi. *make known* Ps 98$_2$, בשׂר pi. *publish news of* Ps 96$_2$‖1 C 16$_{23}$, שׁמע hi. *proclaim* Is 52$_7$, צוה pi. *command* Ps 44$_5$.

<CSTR> יְשׁוּעַת י׳ *salvation of Y.* Ex 14$_{13}$ 2 C 20$_{17}$; אֱלֹהֵינוּ *of our God* Is 52$_{10}$ Ps 98$_3$, ישועות אל *salvations of God* 1QM 4$_{13}$, יְשׁוּעַת יִשְׂרָאֵל *salvation of Israel* Ps 14$_7$ 53$_7$ (יְשֻׁעוֹת perh. *salvations of*),* יַעֲקֹב *of Jacob* Ps 44$_5$, עולם *of eternity* 1QH 15$_{16}$.

אל ישועות *God of salvations* 1QS 1$_{19}$, אֱלֹהֵי יְשׁוּעָתִי *God of my salvation* Ps 88$_2$, צוּר *rock of* Ps 89$_{27}$, צוּר יְשֻׁעָתוֹ *rock of his salvation* Dt 32$_{15}$, מִגְדּוֹל יְשׁוּעוֹת *tower of deliverances* 2 S 22$_{51(Qr)}$, שערי *gates of* 1QM 18$_7$, אהל ישועה *tent of salvation* 4QHod^{a} 7.1$_{12}$, מַעַיְנֵי הַיְשׁוּעָה *springs of salvation* Is 12$_3$, חֹסֶן יְשׁוּעֹת *treasures of salvations* Is 33$_6$, כּוֹבַע יְשׁוּעָה *helmet of salvation* Is 59$_{17}$, כּוֹס־יְשׁוּעוֹת *cup of deliverances* Ps 116$_{13}$, יוֹם יְשׁוּעָה *day of salvation* Is 49$_8$, עת ישועה *time of salvation* 1QM 1$_5$, תוחלת ישועתך *expectation of your salvation* 11QPs^{a} 22$_3$, רוח ישועות *spirit of salvation* 4QBark^{e} 5$_3$, קוֹל *voice of*, i.e. sound of Ps 118$_{15}$, תעודות *testimonies of* 1QM 14$_5$, רנ[ות] *jubilations of* 4QShir^{b} 1$_5$, כנור *lyre of* 1QH 11$_{23}$ 4QHod^{a} 1$_5$ ([כנור]) 4QShir^{b} 10$_8$.

<ADJ> גָּדוֹל *great* 1 S 14$_{45}$, זֹאת *this* 1 S 14$_{45}$.

<PREP> לְ of direction, *to* Ps 119$_{123}$, + קוה pi. *wait* Gn 49$_{18}$ Is 59$_{11}$ (‖ מִשְׁפָּט *judgment*) 11QPs^{a} 22$_8$, שׂבר pi. *wait* Ps 119$_{166}$, תאב *long for* Ps 119$_{174}$; of benefit, *to, for*, + פתח *open*, i.e. enlarge 1QH 15$_{16}$; לְ *as* Jb 13$_{16}$, + היה *be* Ex 15$_2$ 2 S 10$_{11}$ Is 12$_2$ Ps 118$_{4.21}$, הלך *go* Ps 80$_3$.

בְּ of instrument, *by (means of), with* Ps 21$_6$, פקד *visit* Ps 106$_4$, פאר pi. *glorify* Ps 149$_4$, שׂמח pi. *make glad* Si 32$_{25}$; בְּ *in, with*, + שׂמח *be glad* 1 S 2$_1$ Is 25$_9$, גיל *rejoice* Ps

9$_{15}$ 13$_6$ 21$_2$, שׂישׂ *rejoice* Ps 35$_9$ 1QM 13$_{13}$, רנן pi. *shout joyfully* Ps 20$_6$ 1QS 10$_{17}$, בטח *trust* Ps 78$_{22}$; בְּ introducing object, + ראה *see* CD 20$_{34}$, hi. *show* Ps 91$_{16}$.

מִן of direction, *from* Ps 22$_2$; אֶל *to*, + קרא *call* 4QapPs^b 15$_9$.

<COLL> כִּי תִרְכַּב עַל ... מַרְכְּבֹתֶיךָ יְשׁוּעָה *for you have ridden upon ... your chariots victoriously* Hb 3$_8$.

2. perh. in pl. sometimes **saviour,*** י׳ ... יְשׁוּעוֹת מְשִׁיחוֹ *Y. is ... the saviour of his anointed one* Ps 28$_8$, אוֹדֶנּוּ יְשׁוּעֹת פָּנַי אֱלֹהָי *I shall praise him, my saviour, my presence, my God* Ps 42$_{12}$=43$_5$, sim. 42$_6$ (if em. פָּנָיו [of] *his face/presence*).

<SYN> §1 צְדָקָה *righteousness*, מִשְׁפָּט *judgment*.

Also 1QH 12$_3$ fr. 18$_5$ 4Q185 1.2$_{13}$ 4QM^a 15$_7$ 4QPrQuot 48$_6$ (ישו[ע]תכה) 4QShir^b 38$_3$ ([י]שועתו).*

⇒ ישׁע *save*.

[יְשׁוּר] 0.0.1 n.m. **uprightness**—cstr. Q ישור—<CSTR> ישור לבבי *uprightness of my heart* 1QS 11$_2$. <PREP> עם *with* 1QS 11$_2$.

⇒ ישׁר *be straight*.

[יֶשַׁח] 1 n.m. perh. **dysentery**—sf. יֶשְׁחֲךָ—**dysentery,* faeces,** or perh. **semen,*** <NOM CL> וְיֶשְׁחֲךָ בְּקִרְבֶּךָ *and your dysentery is within your bowels* Mc 6$_{14}$ (or em. וְיֵשׁ־כֹּחַ בְּקִרְבֵּךְ/בְּקִרְבָּהּ *and there is strength in your belly/her womb* or וַאֲשֶׁר בְּקִרְבֶּךָ *and whatever is in your belly*).

יָשַׁט 3.4 vb. **extend—Hi.** 3.4 Impf. יוֹשִׁיט, 2ms Si תושיט (תושט); + waw וַיּוֹשֶׁט; impv. Si הושיט—**extend, hold out,** <SUBJ> בֵּן *son* Si 7$_{32}$, מֶלֶךְ *king* Est 4$_{11}$ 5$_2$ 8$_4$; subj. not specified, Si 34$_{14.18}$.

<OBJ> שַׁרְבִיט *sceptre* Est 4$_{11}$ 5$_2$ 8$_4$, יָד *hand* Si 7$_{32}$ 34$_{14.18}$.

<PREP> לְ of direction, *to* Est 4$_{11}$, + Esther Est 5$_2$ 8$_4$, אֶבְיוֹן *poor one* Si 7$_{32}$; לִפְנֵי *before*, + רֵעַ *neighbour* Si 34$_{18}$.

Ho. 0.1 Ptc. Si מושטת—**be stretched out,** <SUBJ> יָד *hand* Si 43$_1$. <PREP> לְ of direction, *to*, + שְׂאֵת *exaltation* Si 43$_1$.

יִשַׁי 41.1.4 pr.n.m. **Jesse**—יִשַׁי—grandson of Ruth and Boaz and father of David (e.g. 1 S 16$_{1.3.5.8}$ Is 11$_{1.10}$ Ps 72$_{20}$ Ru 4$_{17.22}$), <SUBJ> עבר hi. *make pass by* 1 S 16$_{9.10}$, ילד hi. *become father of* Ru 4$_{22}$, לקח *take* 1 S 16$_{20}$, קרא *call* 1 S 16$_8$, אמר *say* 1 S 17$_{17}$, צוה pi. *command* 1 S 17$_{20}$.

<NOM CL> שְׁמוֹ יִשַׁי *his name was Jesse* 1 S 17$_{12}$.

<OBJ> ילד hi. *become father of* Ru 4$_{22}$ 1 C 2$_{12}$, קדשׁ pi. *sanctify* 1 S 16$_5$.

<CSTR> אֲבִי יִשַׁי *father of Jesse* Ru 4$_{17}$, בֶּן *son of* 1 S 20$_{27.30.31}$ 22$_{7.8.9.13}$ 25$_{10}$ 2 S 20$_1$ 23$_1$ 1 K 12$_{16}$‖2 C 10$_{16}$ Ps 72$_{20}$ 1 C 10$_{14}$ 12$_{19}$ 29$_{26}$ 2 C 11$_{18}$ Si 45$_{25}$, בן *son of* 11QPs^a 27$_2$ 28$_3$, בְּנֵי *sons of* 1 S 17$_{13}$, גֶּזַע *stump of* Is 11$_1$ 4QM^g 5$_2$, שֹׁרֶשׁ *root of* Is 11$_{10}$ GnzPs 1$_{15}$.

<APP> עֶבֶד *servant* 1 S 17$_{58}$.

<ADJ> בֵּית־הַלַּחְמִי *the Bethlehemite* 1 S 16$_{1.18}$ 17$_{58}$.

<PREP> לְ of direction, *to*, + קרא *call* 1 S 16$_3$; of possession, *(belonging) to, of* 1 S 16$_{18}$.

אֶל *to*, + שׁלח *send* 1 S 16$_{1.19.22}$, אמר *say* 1 S 16$_{10.11.11}$.

[יָשִׁיב] 1 pr.n.m. **Jashib**—Qr ישוב—son of Issachar, <NOM CL> לִבְנֵי יִשָּׂשכָר ... יָשִׁיב *of the sons of Issachar were ... Jashub* 1 C 7$_{1(Kt)}$.

⇒ שׁוב *go back*.

[יְשִׁיבָה] 0.1 n.f. **sitting**—sf. Si ישיבתי—**sitting** of teacher, i.e. **teaching,** perh. **academy,** <PREP> בְּ שׂמח *rejoice in* Si 51$_{29}$ (+ שִׁירָה *song*).

⇒ ישׁב *sit*.

יִשִּׁיָּה 6 pr.n.m. **Isshiah, 1.** Issacharite chief, <NOM CL> וּבְנֵי יִזְרַחְיָה ... יִשִּׁיָּה *and the sons of Izrahiah were ... Isshiah* 1 C 7$_3$,

2. member of Harim family, husband of non-Jewish wife, <NOM CL> וּבְנֵי חָרִם ... יִשִּׁיָּה *and the sons of Harim were ... Isshiah* Ezr 10$_{31}$.

3. Levite, son of Uzziel, <NOM CL> בְּנֵי עֻזִּיאֵל ... יִשִּׁיָּה הַשֵּׁנִי *the sons of Uzziel were ... Isshiah the second* 1 C 23$_{20}$, אֲחִי מִיכָה יִשִּׁיָּה *the brother of Micah was Isshiah* 1 C 24$_{25}$. <CSTR> בְּנֵי יִשִּׁיָּה *sons of Isshiah* 1 C 24$_{25}$. <ADJ> שֵׁנִי *second* 1 C 23$_{20}$.

4. Levite, head of Rehabiah family, <NOM CL> הָרֹאשׁ יִשִּׁיָּה *the chief was Isshiah* 1 C 24$_{21}$.

יִשִּׁיָּהוּ 1 pr.n.m. **Isshiah,** one of David's warriors, 1 C 12$_{7}$.

יְשִׁימוֹן 13 n.m. & pl.n. **desert, Jeshimon**—יְשִׁימֹן (יְשִׁמֹן, יְשִׁמֹן); cstr. יְשִׁימוֹן—**1.** as noun in ref. to **desert** or **steppe,** <CSTR> יְשִׁימוֹן דֶּרֶךְ *desert of a way,* i.e. a path through a wasteland Ps 107$_{4}$; יְלֵל יְשִׁמֹן *howling of the desert* Dt 32$_{10}$.

<PREP> בְּ of place, *in, at,* + צעד *step* Ps 68$_{8}$, תעה *wander* Ps 107$_{4}$, שׂים *place* Is 43$_{19}$ (|| מִדְבָּר *steppe*), נתן *give* Is 43$_{20}$ (|| מִדְבָּר), עצב hi. *grieve* Ps 78$_{40}$, נסה pi. *test* Ps 106$_{14}$.

2. wasteland in the Negev near Ziph and Maon, <CSTR> פְּנֵי הַיְשִׁימֹן *face,* i.e. east of, *of Jeshimon* 1 S 26$_{1.3}$, מִימִין הַיְשִׁימוֹן *the right hand of,* i.e. the south of, *Jeshimon* 1 S 23$_{19}$, יְמִין הַיְשִׁימוֹן *the right hand of,* i.e. the south of, *Jeshimon* 1 S 23$_{24}$.

<PREP> עַל *upon* 1 S 26$_{1.3}$.

3. wasteland in the Transjordan near Peor, <CSTR> פְּנֵי הַיְשִׁימֹן *face,* i.e. east of, *of Jeshimon* Nm 21$_{20}$ 23$_{28}$. <PREP> עַל *upon,* + שׁקף ni. *look down* Nm 21$_{20}$ 23$_{28}$.

<SYN> מִדְבָּר *steppe.*

⇒ ישׁם *be desolate.*

[יְשִׁימָה] 1 n.f. **desolation**—pl. Kt ישׁימות—<NOM CL> ישׁימות עָלֵימוֹ appar. *may desolations be upon them* Ps 55$_{16}$ (Qr יַשִּׁי מָוֶת *may death be deceitful against them*).

⇒ ישׁם *be desolate.*

יְשִׁימוֹת, see בֵּית יְשִׁימוֹת *Beth-jeshimoth.*

יָשִׁישׁ 4.2 adj. **aged (one)**—pl. יְשִׁישִׁים—**1.** attributive adj. with אֱנוֹשׁ *human being* Si 8$_{5}$.

2. as predicative adj. or noun, **aged (one),** <SUBJ> עמד *stand* Jb 29$_{8}$, קום *arise* Jb 29$_{8}$.

<NOM CL> אַתֶּם יְשִׁישִׁים *you are the aged ones* Jb 32$_{6}$, יָשִׁישׁ בָּנוּ *the aged one(s) are among us* Jb 15$_{10}$.

<CSTR> ישׁישׁ ... מוסר *discipline of ... an aged one* Si 42$_{8(B)}$.

<PREP> בְּ *in, with* Jb 12$_{12}$.

יְשִׁישַׁי 1 pr.n.m. **Jeshishai,** Gadite chief, son of Jahdo, <CSTR> בֶּן־יְשִׁישַׁי *son of Jeshishai* 1 C 5$_{14}$.

ישׁם 4 vb. **be desolate—Qal** 4 Impf. 3fs תֵּשַׁם (תֵּשָׁם), 3fpl תִּישַׁמְנָה; + waw וַתֵּשַׁם—<SUBJ> אֲדָמָה *land* Gn 47$_{19}$, אֶרֶץ *land* Ezk 12$_{19}$ 19$_{7}$, בָּמָה *high place* Ezk 6$_{6}$.

⇒ יְשִׁימוֹת *desolations,* יְשִׁימוֹן *Jeshimon.*

יִשְׁמָא 1 pr.n.m. **Ishma,** Judahite chief, <APP> אֵלֶּה *these* 1 C 4$_{3}$.

יִשְׁמָעֵאל 48.0.1.20 pr.n.m. **Ishmael, 1.** son of Abraham and Hagar, <SUBJ> חיה *live* Gn 16$_{16}$ 17$_{18}$, מול ni. *be circumcised* Gn 17$_{26}$, קבר *bury* Gn 25$_{9}$. <NOM CL> בְּנֵי אַבְרָהָם ... יִשְׁמָעֵאל *the sons of Abraham were ... Ishmael* 1 C 1$_{28}$, יִשְׁמָעֵאל בְּנוֹ בֶּן־שְׁלֹשׁ עֶשְׂרֵה שָׁנָה *Ishmael his son was the son of thirteen years,* i.e. thirteen years old Gn 17$_{25}$. <OBJ> ילד *bear child* Gn 16$_{16}$ 25$_{12}$, לקח *take* Gn 17$_{23}$, קרא *call* Gn 16$_{11.15}$. <CSTR> בְּנֵי יִשְׁמָעֵאל *sons of Ishmael* Gn 25$_{13.16}$ 1 C 1$_{31}$ 1QM 2$_{13}$, בַּת *daughter of* Gn 28$_{9}$ 36$_{3}$, בְּכוֹר *firstborn of* Gn 25$_{13}$||1 C 1$_{29}$, תֹּלְדֹת *descendants of* Gn 25$_{12}$, חַיֵּי *life of* Gn 25$_{17}$. <APP> בֵּן *son* Gn 17$_{23.25.26}$ 25$_{9.12}$, שֵׁם *name* Gn 16$_{11.15}$. <PREP> לְ of benefit, *to, for,* + שׁמע *hear* Gn 17$_{20}$; אֶל *to,* + הלך *go* Gn 28$_{9}$.

2. Benjaminite, son of Azel and descendant of Saul, <APP> שֵׁם *name* 1 C 8$_{38}$ 9$_{44}$.

3. military officer, father of Zebadiah, <CSTR> בֶּן־יִשְׁמָעֵאל *son of Ishmael* 2 C 19$_{11}$.

4. Judaean official, son of Jehohanan, <PREP> לְ *namely* 2 C 23$_{1}$.

5. son of Nethaniah and assassin of Gedaliah, the governor of Judah, <SUBJ> בוא *come* 2 K 25$_{23.25}$ Jr 40$_{8}$ 41$_{1}$, הלך *go* Jr 41$_{6.10.15}$, יצא *go out* Jr 41$_{6}$, עבר *pass by* Jr 41$_{10}$, קום *arise* Jr 41$_{2}$, פגשׁ *meet* Jr 41$_{6}$, קרא *meet* Jr 41$_{6}$, חדל *refrain* Jr 41$_{8}$, עשׂה *do* Jr 41$_{11}$, מלא pi. *fill* Jr 41$_{9}$, אכל *eat* Jr 41$_{1}$, שׁלך hi. *throw down* Jr 41$_{9}$, שׁבה *take captive* Jr 41$_{10.10.14}$, נכה hi. *strike* 2 K 25$_{25}$ Jr 40$_{14.15}$ 41$_{2.3.9.16.18}$, שׁחט *slay* Jr 41$_{7}$, מות hi. *kill* Jr 41$_{2.8}$, מלט ni. *escape* Jr 41$_{15}$, בכה *weep* Jr 41$_{6}$, אמר *say* Jr 41$_{6}$. <OBJ> מצא *find* Jr 41$_{12}$, שׁלח *send* Jr 40$_{14}$, נכה hi. *strike* Jr 40$_{15}$. <APP> בֵּן *son* 2 K 25$_{23.25}$ Jr 40$_{8.14.15}$ 41$_{1+10t}$. <PREP> אֶל *to, concerning,* + אמר *say* Jr 41$_{8}$, דבר *speak* Jr 40$_{16}$; אֵת *with* Jr 41$_{13}$; מֵאֵת *from (with),* + שׁוב hi. *bring back* Jr 41$_{16}$; עִם *with,* +

לחם ni. *fight* Jr 41_{12}.

6. member of Pashhur family and husband of non-Jewish wife, <NOM CL> מִבְּנֵי פַּשְׁחוּר ... יִשְׁמָעֵאל *of the sons of Pashhur were ... Ishmael* Ezr 10_{22}.

7. Kenyon inscr. 1796_1, <PREP> לְ of possession, *(belonging) to, of* Kenyon inscr. 1796_1.

8. Seal 45_1 (ישמעא[ל]; Jerusalem). **9.** Seal 53_2 (Jerusalem), <PREP> לְ of possession, *(belonging) to, of* Seal 53_2 (Jerusalem). **10.** Seal 418_1 (8th/7th cent.), <PREP> לְ of possession, *(belonging) to, of* Seal 418_1 (8th/7th cent.). **11.** Seal 427_2 (7th cent.), <PREP> לְ of possession, *(belonging) to, of* Seal 427_2 (7th cent.). **12.** Seal 578_2 (T. Beit Mirsim?, 7th/6th cent.), <PREP> לְ of possession, *(belonging) to, of* Seal 578_2 (ישמעא[ל]; T. Beit Mirsim?, 7th/6th cent.). **13.** Seal 579_1 (T. Beit Mirsim?, 7th/6th cent.), <PREP> לְ of possession, *(belonging) to, of* Seal 579_1 (T. Beit Mirsim?, 7th/6th cent.). **14.** Seal 580_1 (T. Beit Mirsim?, 7th/6th cent.), <PREP> לְ of possession, *(belonging) to, of* Seal 580_1 (ישמ]עאל]; T. Beit Mirsim?, 7th/6th cent.).

15. Seal 581_1 (T. Beit Mirsim?, 7th/6th cent.), <PREP> לְ of possession, *(belonging) to, of* Seal 581_1 (ישמ]עאל]; T. Beit Mirsim?, 7th/6th cent.). **16.** Seal 582_1 (T. Beit Mirsim?, 7th/6th cent.). <PREP> לְ of possession, *(belonging) to, of* Seal 582_1 (ישמ]עאל]; T. Beit Mirsim?, 7th/6th cent.). **17.** Seal 589_2 (T. Beit Mirsim?, 7th/6th cent.), <PREP> לְ of possession, *(belonging) to, of* Seal 589_2 (T. Beit Mirsim?, 7th/6th cent.). **18.** Seal 601_2 (T. Beit Mirsim?, 7th/6th cent.), <CSTR> בן ישמעאל *son of Ishmael* Seal 601_2 (T. Beit Mirsim?, 7th/6th cent.). **19.** Seal 602_2 (T. Beit Mirsim?, 7th/6th cent.), <CSTR> [בן] ישׁ]מעאל] *son of Ishmael* Seal 602_2 (T. Beit Mirsim?, 7th/6th cent.).

20. Seal 664_2 (T. Beit Mirsim?, 7th/6th cent.), <CSTR> בן ישמעאל *son of Ishmael* Seal 664_2 (T. Beit Mirsim?, 7th/6th cent.). **21.** Seal 673_2 (T. Beit Mirsim?, 7th/6th cent.), Seal 673_2 (T. Beit Mirsim?, 7th/6th cent.). **22.** Seal 714_2 (7th cent.), <CSTR> בן ישמעאל *son of Ishmael* Seal 714_2 (7th cent.). **23.** Seal 724_2 (7th cent.), <PREP> לְ of possession, *(belonging) to, of* Seal 724_2 (7th cent.). **24.** Seal 770_1 (Ophel, 7th cent.).

25. Seal 778_2 (T. el-Ḥesi, 7th/6th cent.), <PREP> לְ of possession, *(belonging) to, of* Seal 778_2 (T. el-Ḥesi, 7th/6th cent.). **26.** Seal 803_2 (City of David, 7th/6th cent.), <PREP> לְ of possession, *(belonging) to, of* Seal 803_2 (City of David, 7th/6th cent.).

⇒ אֵל *God* + שׁמע *hear*, יִשְׁמְעֵאלִי *Ishmaelite.*

יִשְׁמְעֵאלִי 8 gent. **Ishmaelite**—יִשְׁמְעֵלִי; pl. יִשְׁמְעֵאלִים—

1. collective, **Ishmaelites,** <SUBJ> ירד hi. *bring down* Gn 39_1. <NOM CL> יִשְׁמְעֵאלִים הֵם *they were Ishmaelites* Jg 8_{24}. <CSTR> אֹרְחַת יִשְׁמְעֵאלִים *caravan of the Ishmaelites* Gn 37_{25}, אָהֳלֵי *tents of* Ps 83_7, יַד הַיִּשְׁמְעֵאלִים *the hand of the Ishmaelites* Gn 39_1. <PREP> לְ of direction, *to,* + מכר *sell* Gn $37_{27.28}$.

2. as sing. noun, a particular **Ishmaelite,** יֶתֶר הַיִּשְׁמְעֵאלִי *Jether the Ishmaelite* 1 C 2_{17}, אוֹבִיל הַיִּשְׁמְעֵאלִי *Obil the Ishmaelite* 1 C 27_{30}.

⇒ יִשְׁמָעֵאל *Ishmael.*

יִשְׁמַעְיָה 1 pr.n.m. **Ishmaiah,** one of David's warriors (1 C 12_4).

⇒ Y. + שׁמע *hear.*

יִשְׁמַעְיָהוּ 1 pr.n.m. **Ishmaiah,** Zebulunite prince, son of Obadiah, <NOM CL> לִזְבוּלֻן יִשְׁמַעְיָהוּ בֶּן־עֹבַדְיָהוּ *for Zebulun was Ishmaiah the son of Obadiah* 1 C 27_{19}. <APP> בֵּן *son* 1 C 27_{19}.

⇒ Y. + שׁמע *hear.*

יִשְׁמְעֵלִי, see יִשְׁמְעֵאלִי *Ishmaelite.*

יִשְׁמְרַי 1 pr.n.m. **Ishmerai,** Benjaminite chief, <NOM CL> יִשְׁמְרַי וְיִזְלִיאָה וְיוֹבָב בְּנֵי אֶלְפָּעַל *Ishmerai and Izliah and Jobab were the sons of Elpaal* 1 C 8_{18}.

ישׁן I 16.1.2 vb. **sleep—Qal** 15.1 Pf. יָשֵׁנוּ ,יָשַׁנְתִּי; impf. יִישָׁן, תִּישַׁן ,אִישָׁן (אִישַׁן), יִשְׁנוּ; + waw וַיִּישַׁן (Q וישן), וָאִישָׁנָה; ptc. יָשֵׁן; inf. לִישׁוֹן—**be asleep, sleep, go to sleep,** <SUBJ> אֲדֹנָי *Lord* Ps 44_{24} (:: קיץ hi. *awake*), Elijah 1 K 19_5 (+ שׁכב *lie down*), Isaac 4QJubh 36_{18}, Job Jb 3_{13}, אָדָם *human being* Gn 2_{21}, פַּרְעֹה *Pharaoh* Gn 41_5 (+ חלם *dream*), שַׂר *prince* Jr 51_{57} (:: קיץ hi.), פֶּחָה *governor* Jr 51_{57} (:: קיץ hi.), סֶגֶן *prefect* Jr 51_{57} (:: קיץ hi.).

חָכָם *wise one* Jr 51$_{57}$ (:: קִיץ hi.), רָשָׁע *wicked one* Pr 4$_{16}$, עָשִׁיר *rich one* Ec 5$_{11}$, גִּבּוֹר *warrior* Jr 51$_{57}$ (:: קִיץ hi.), יֹשֵׁב *inhabitant* Jr 51$_{39}$ (:: קִיץ hi.), שֹׁמֵר *keeper* Ps 121$_{4}$ (|| נוּם *slumber*), worshipper Ps 3$_{6}$ (+ שׁכב; :: קִיץ hi.) 4$_{9}$ (+ שׁכב) 13$_{4}$, צֹאן *sheep* Ezk 34$_{25}$, כּוֹכָב *star* Si 43$_{10(Bmg)}$ (B שחח ni. *be bowed down*, i.e. relax guard), אֲשֶׁר *whoever* 1QS 7$_{10}$; subj. not specified, Is 5$_{27}$ (||נוּם).

<OBJ> שֵׁנָה *sleep* Jr 51$_{39.57}$.

<PREP> בְּ of place, *in, at*, + יַעַר *forest* Ezk 34$_{25}$; *in, with*, + אַשְׁמוּרָה *night watches* Si 43$_{10}$, מוֹשָׁב *sitting*, i.e. session 1QS 7$_{10}$.

<SYN> נוּם *slumber*. <ANT> קִיץ hi. *awake*.

Pi. 1 + waw וַתְּיַשְּׁנֵהוּ—**cause to fall asleep,** <SUBJ> Delilah Jg 16$_{19}$.

<OBJ> Samson Jg 16$_{19}$.

<PREP> עַל *upon*, + בֶּרֶךְ *knee* Jg 16$_{19}$.*

→ יָשֵׁן *sleeping*, יָשֵׁן *Jashen*, שֵׁנָה *sleep*, יְשֵׁנָה *sleep*.

ישן II 3.2.1 vb. **be old—Qal** 0.1 Pf. Si ישן—**become old,** <SUBJ> יַיִן *wine* Si 9$_{10}$.

Ni. 3.0.1 Pf. Q נושנת ,נוֹשַׁנְתֶּם; ptc. נוֹשֶׁנֶת ,נוֹשָׁן—**become old,** (of disease) **become advanced** (Lv 13$_{11}$), <SUBJ> Israelite(s) Dt 4$_{25}$, צָרַעַת *skin disease* Lv 13$_{11}$ 11QT 48$_{17}$, יָשָׁן *old grain* Lv 26$_{10}$.

<PREP> בְּ of place, *in, at*, + אֶרֶץ *land* Dt 4$_{25}$.

Htp. 0.1 Impv. Si התישן—**make oneself old,** <SUBJ> בֵּן *son* Si 11$_{20}$.

<PREP> בְּ of instrument, *by (means of), with*, + מְלָאכָה *work* Si 11$_{20}$.*

→ יָשָׁן *old thing*, יְשָׁנָה *Jeshannah*.

יָשָׁן 8.1.0.14 adj. **old**—fs יְשָׁנָה, pl. יְשָׁנִים—**1.** attributive adj. with אוֹהֵב *friend* Si 9$_{10}$, תְּבוּאָה *produce* Lv 25$_{22}$, מֶגֶד *choice fruit* Ca 7$_{14}$, יַיִן *wine* Samaria ost. 1$_{3}$ 3$_{2}$ ([י]שן) 4$_{3}$ ([ישן]) 5$_{3}$ 6$_{4}$ 7$_{2}$ (ישן[י]) 8$_{3}$ ([ישן]) 9$_{3}$ 10$_{4}$ 12$_{4}$ 13$_{3}$ 14$_{3}$ 15$_{2}$ ([ישן]) 101$_{1}$, בְּרֵכָה *pool* Is 22$_{11}$, שַׁעַר *gate* Ne 3$_{6}$ 12$_{39}$.

2. as predicative adj. or noun, **old (one), old (object),** <OBJ> יצא hi. *bring out* Lv 26$_{10}$, אכל *eat* Lv 25$_{22}$ 26$_{10}$.

→ ישן *become old*.

יָשֵׁן I 9 adj. **asleep**—fs. יְשֵׁנָה, pl. יְשֵׁנִים; cstr. יְשֵׁנֵי—**1.** as predicative adj. or noun, **asleep,** <NOM CL> ... שָׁאוּל יָשֵׁן *Saul was ... sleeping* 1 S 26$_{7}$, אֲמָתְךָ יְשֵׁנָה *your female servant is asleep* 1 K 3$_{20}$, יָשֵׁן אֹפֵהֶם *their anger is asleep* Ho 7$_{6}$, כֻּלָּם יְשֵׁנִים *all of them were asleep* 1 S 26$_{12}$, אֲנִי יְשֵׁנָה *I was asleep* Ca 5$_{2}$, יָשֵׁן הוּא *he is asleep* 1 K 18$_{27}$.

<CSTR> יְשֵׁנֵי אַדְמַת *sleeping ones of*, i.e. in, *the earth of* Dn 12$_{2}$, שִׂפְתֵי יְשֵׁנִים *lips of those asleep* Ca 7$_{10}$.

<PREP> כְּ *as*, + קִיץ hi. *awake* Ps 78$_{65}$.

מִן partitive, *some of, (any)one of* Dn 12$_{2}$.*

→ ישן *sleep*.

יָשֵׁן II 1 pr.n.m. **Jashen,** one of David's warriors, <CSTR> בְּנֵי יָשֵׁן *sons of Jashhen* 2 S 23$_{32}$.

→ ישן *sleep*.

יְשָׁנָה 1 pl.n. **Jeshanah,** town on southern border of northern Israel near Bethel, perh. Burj el-Isāneh 25 km N of Jerusalem 2 C 13$_{19}$, <OBJ> לכד *capture* 2 C 13$_{19}$.

<APP> עִיר *city* 2 C 13$_{19}$.

[יְשֵׁנָה] 0.1 n.f. **sleep**—Si ישינה—<COLL> מכאוב ונדד ישינה *pain and fleeting sleep* Si 34$_{20}$ (or em. נדדי שנ[י]ה *restlessness of sleep* [Smend]).

→ ישן *sleep*.

ישע 205.7.37.3 vb. **save—Ni.** 21.1.3 Pf. נוֹשַׁעְנוּ ,נוֹשַׁעְתֶּם ,נוֹשַׁע; impf. נִוָּשֵׁעַ ,תִּוָּשְׁעוּן ,(אִוָּשֵׁעָה) אִוָּשֵׁעַ ,תִּוָּשְׁעִי ,תִּוָּשַׁע ,יִוָּשַׁע (נִוָּשֵׁעָה); impv. הִוָּשְׁעוּ; ptc. נוֹשָׁע; inf. Si הושע—**be saved, be victorious, be helped, receive help,** <SUBJ> אֶפֶס *end* of earth Is 45$_{22}$, Israel Is 45$_{17}$ Ps 80$_{4.8.20}$ 1QM 10$_{8}$ 6QD 3$_{2}$ CD 5$_{19}$, Judah Jr 23$_{6}$ 33$_{16}$, Jacob Jr 30$_{7}$, Joseph Ps 80$_{4.8.20}$, עַם *people* Dt 33$_{29}$ Is 30$_{15}$, עֵדָה *congregation* Nm 10$_{9}$, David 2 S 22$_{4}$||Ps 18$_{4}$, Jeremiah Jr 17$_{14}$, Moses Nm 10$_{9}$, בַּת *daughter* of my people Jr 8$_{20}$, מֶלֶךְ *king* Zc 9$_{9}$ Ps 33$_{16}$, worshipper Ps 119$_{117}$, הלך ptc. *one who goes* Pr 28$_{18}$, רב pl. *many* Si 34$_{6}$ (|| נצל ni. *be delivered*), Jerusalem Jr 4$_{14}$; subj. not specified, Is 64$_{4}$.

<PREP> בְּ of time, *in, on*, + יוֹם *day* of wrath Si 34$_{6}$; of instrument, *by (means of)*, + ׳י *Y.* Dt 33$_{29}$ Is 45$_{17}$, רֹב *greatness* of the army Ps 33$_{16}$; *in, with*, + שׁוּבָה *returning* Is 30$_{15}$.

מִן of direction, *from*, + אֹיֵב *enemy* Nm 10$_{9}$ 2 S 22$_{4}$||Ps

18$_{4}$ 1QM 10$_{8}$, צָרָה *distress* Jr 30$_{7}$.

<SYN> נצל ni. *be delivered.*

Hi. $_{184.6.34.3}$ Pf. הוֹשִׁיעַ (הוֹשִׁעַ, Si השיע, הוֹשִׁיעוֹ, הוֹשַׁעְתָּנוּ, Si הושעתני), הוֹשַׁעְתָּ, הוֹשִׁיעָה, (הוֹשִׁיעָם, הוֹשַׁעְתֶּם, הוֹשַׁעְתִּים) הוֹשַׁעְתִּיךָ; impf. יוֹשִׁיעַ (יוֹשִׁעַ, יֹשַׁע, יֹשִׁעֵנוּ, יוֹשִׁיעֵנוּ, יוֹשִׁיעֶנּוּ, יוֹשִׁיעֵךְ, יוֹשִׁיעֲךָ, יוֹשִׁיעֵנִי, יְהוֹשִׁיעַ, תֹּשִׁעֵנִי, תּוֹשִׁיעֵנִי, תּוֹשִׁעַ) 2ms תּוֹשִׁיעַ (יוֹשִׁיעֵם, יֹשַׁעֲכֶם), יוֹשִׁיעוּ (Q יושעו, אוֹשִׁיעַ (אוֹשִׁיעֵם, אוֹשִׁיעֵךְ), תּוֹשִׁיעֵנוּ), וְהוֹשַׁעְתָּ + waw תּוֹשִׁיעוּן; (יוֹשִׁיעוּם, יוֹשִׁיעֻךְ, יוֹשִׁיעוּךָ), וַיּוֹשִׁעָן, וַיֹּשַׁע) וַיּוֹשַׁע; (Q והושעתים, Q והושעתיהו) וְהוֹשַׁעְתִּי, Si וישעוהו, וָאוֹשִׁיעָה, וַתּוֹשַׁע, (Si ויושיעם); impv. הוֹשַׁע (הוֹשִׁיעָה, הוֹשָׁעָה, הוֹשִׁעֵנִי, הוֹשִׁיעֵנוּ); ptc. מוֹשִׁיעַ (מוֹשִׁיעוֹ, מוֹשִׁיעֵךְ, מוֹשִׁיעֲךָ, מוֹשִׁעֵךְ, מֹשִׁעִי, מֹשִׁיעַ, מוֹשִׁיעָם), pl. מוֹשִׁיעִים (מוֹשִׁעִים); inf. הוֹשֵׁעַ (הֹשֵׁעַ, הוֹשִׁיעַ, הוֹשִׁיעֵךְ, הוֹשִׁיעָהּ, הוֹשִׁיעֵנִי, הוֹשִׁיעֲךָ)—**1a. help, rescue, spare, deliver, save, come to the aid of, defend cause of,** <SUBJ> ׳׳ *Y.* Ex 14$_{30}$ Dt 20$_{4}$ Jg 7$_{7}$ 10$_{12.13}$ 1 S 4$_{3}$ 7$_{8}$ 14$_{6.23.39}$ 17$_{47}$ 25$_{26}$ 2 S 3$_{18}$ 8$_{6.14}$||1 C 18$_{6.13}$ 2 S 22$_{28}$||Ps 18$_{28}$ 2 K 6$_{27}$ 14$_{27}$ 19$_{19.34}$||Is 37$_{20.35}$ Is 33$_{22}$ 38$_{20}$ 43$_{12}$ 49$_{25}$ 63$_{1}$ Jr 2$_{27}$ 14$_{8}$ 15$_{20}$ (|| נצל hi. *deliver*) 17$_{14}$ 30$_{10.11}$ 31$_{7}$ 42$_{11}$ (|| נצל hi.) 46$_{27}$ Ezk 34$_{22}$ 36$_{29}$ 37$_{23}$ Ho 1$_{7.7}$ Hb 1$_{2}$ Zp 3$_{17.19}$ Zc 8$_{7.13}$ 9$_{16}$ 10$_{6}$ 12$_{7}$ Ps 6$_{5}$ 7$_{2}$ (|| נצל hi.) 12$_{2}$ 20$_{7.10}$ 22$_{22}$ 28$_{9}$ 31$_{3.17}$ 34$_{7.19}$ 36$_{7}$ 37$_{40}$ 55$_{17}$ 71$_{2}$ (|| נצל hi., פלט pi. *rescue*) 71$_{3}$ 86$_{2}$ 106$_{8.10.47}$ 107$_{13.19}$ 109$_{26.31}$ 116$_{6}$ 118$_{25}$ 119$_{94.146}$ 145$_{19}$ Pr 20$_{22}$ 1 C 11$_{14}$ 2 C 32$_{22}$ 4QapPs[b] 31$_{2}$ 11QT 59$_{11.18}$ Lachish ost. 8$_{4}$ Kh. Beit Lei graf. 7$_{1}$.

אֱלֹהִים *God* Ex 14$_{30}$ Jg 6$_{36.37}$ 1 S 7$_{8}$ 10$_{19}$ 2 S 22$_{3}$ 2 K 19$_{19}$||Is 37$_{20}$ Is 25$_{9}$ 35$_{4}$ Zp 3$_{17}$ Zc 9$_{16}$ Ps 3$_{8}$ 7$_{2}$ (|| נצל hi.) 7$_{11}$ Ps 44$_{8}$ 54$_{3}$ 59$_{3}$ (|| נצל hi.) 60$_{7}$ 69$_{2.36}$ 76$_{10}$ 106$_{47}$||1 C 16$_{35}$ Ps 108$_{7}$ 109$_{26}$ Jb 5$_{15}$ 2 C 20$_{9}$ Si 33$_{1}$ 51$_{3}$ 1QM 10$_{4}$ 4QShir[b] 10$_{9}$, *gods* Jg 10$_{14}$ Jr 2$_{28}$ 11$_{12}$, אֱלוֹהַּ *God* Jb 22$_{29}$, אֵל *God* Is 45$_{20}$ Ps 57$_{4}$ 86$_{16}$ Si 48$_{20}$ 1QM 11$_{3}$ 4QpPs[a] 3.4$_{21}$ 4Q183 1.2$_{3}$ 4QD[a] 5.1$_{18}$ 4QBer[c] 1$_{5}$ 4QapJoseph[b] 1$_{16}$, *god* Is 46$_{7}$, אֲדֹנָי *Lord* 1QH 2$_{23}$ 3$_{6}$ ([הוש]עתה), עֶלְיוֹן *Most High* Si 48$_{20}$, אֲשֵׁרָה *Asherah* Kh. el-Qom tomb inscr. 3$_{3}$, מַלְאָךְ *angel* Is 63$_{9}$, אַשּׁוּר *Assyria* Ho 14$_{4}$, גּוֹי *nation* Lm 4$_{17}$ 4QpHos[a] 2$_{14}$, אֲרָם *Syrian(s)* 2 S 10$_{19}$||1 C 19$_{19}$, Abigail 1 S 25$_{33}$, David 1 S 23$_{2.5}$ 4QMidrEschat[a] 3$_{13}$, Gideon Jg 6$_{14.15}$ 8$_{22}$, Joab 2 S 10$_{11}$||1 C 19$_{12}$, Joshua Jos 10$_{6}$, Moses Ex 2$_{17}$, Shamgar Jg 3$_{31}$, Tiglath-pileser 2 K 16$_{7}$, Tola Jg 10$_{1}$.

אִישׁ *man* Jg 12$_{2.3}$ 1 S 9$_{16}$, בֵּן *son* Si 4$_{9}$, נַעַר *lad* Jg 13$_{5}$, רֹאשׁ *head* of Israel Jos 22$_{22}$, מֶלֶךְ *king* 2 S 14$_{4}$ 2 K 6$_{26.27}$ 2 K 16$_{7}$ Ho 13$_{10}$ Ps 72$_{4.13}$, אָדוֹן *lord* 1 S 25$_{31}$ 2 K 6$_{26}$, שֹׁפֵט *judge* Jg 2$_{16.18}$, נָבִיא *prophet* Si 49$_{10}$, מוֹשִׁיעַ *deliverer* Jg 3$_{9}$ Ne 9$_{27}$, גִּבּוֹר *warrior* Jr 14$_{9}$ Zp 3$_{17}$, עָשִׁיר *rich one* Si 13$_{6}$ (unless שׁעע hi. *flatter*), עֵצָה *counsel* Is 47$_{13}$, יָד *hand* Jg 7$_{2}$ Is 59$_{1}$ 1QS 6$_{27}$ 4QapPs[a] 1.2$_{4}$ CD 9$_{9.10}$, חֶרֶב *sword* Ps 44$_{7}$, זְרוֹעַ *arm* Is 59$_{16}$ 63$_{5}$ Ps 44$_{4}$ 98$_{1}$, יָמִין *right hand* Ps 98$_{1}$ 138$_{7}$ Jb 40$_{14}$, זֶה *this one* 1 S 10$_{27}$, מִי *who?* 4QPrayer[c] 3$_{2}$, כֹּל *everyone* Jg 6$_{31}$; subj. not specified, Dt 22$_{27}$ 28$_{29.31}$ 1 S 11$_{3}$ Is 47$_{15}$ Jb 26$_{2}$ 4QpsJub[b] 5$_{1}$ 4QRP[c] 6a.2$_{3}$ 4QapJoseph[b] 8$_{3}$ 4QDiscourse 2.2$_{10}$ 4QapPs[b] 15$_{2}$ 42$_{2}$ 4QapJerB 7$_{3}$ 4QpsEzek[a] 16.2$_{10}$ 4QpsEzek[c] 3.2$_{5}$ 4Q418 32$_{2}$ (משי[ע]) 11QT 59$_{8}$ 66$_{8}$.

<OBJ> בַּעַל *Baal* Jg 6$_{31}$, עַם *people* 1 S 9$_{16}$ 2 S 3$_{18}$ 2 K 19$_{19}$||Is 37$_{20}$ Is 63$_{9}$ Jr 31$_{7}$ 42$_{11}$ Zc 8$_{7}$ Ps 28$_{9}$ 106$_{47}$||1 C 16$_{35}$, Israel Ex 14$_{30}$ Jg 2$_{16.18}$ 3$_{31}$ 6$_{14.15.36.37}$ 7$_{7}$ 10$_{1}$ 13$_{5}$ 1 S 10$_{19}$ 14$_{23.39}$ 2 S 3$_{18}$ 2 K 14$_{27}$ Jr 14$_{8}$ 30$_{10.11}$ 46$_{27}$ Ho 13$_{10}$ 14$_{4}$ 1QM 10$_{4}$ 11$_{3}$ 4QMidrEschat[a] 3$_{13}$, Israelite(s) Ex 14$_{30}$ Is 25$_{9}$ 33$_{22}$ Ps 44$_{8}$, Jacob Si 49$_{10}$, מַמְלָכָה *kingdom* 4QpsEzek[c] 3.2$_{5}$, בַּיִת *house* of Israel Ezk 36$_{29}$ Zc 8$_{13}$, of Judah Ho 1$_{7.7}$ Zc 8$_{13}$, of Joseph Zc 10$_{6}$, חֲצִי *half* tribe of Manasseh Jos 22$_{22}$, שְׁאֵרִית *remnant* Jr 31$_{7}$, Abishai 2 S 10$_{11}$||1 C 19$_{12}$, Ahaz 2 K 16$_{7}$, David 2 S 8$_{6.14}$||1 C 18$_{13}$ 22$_{3}$, Gideon Jg 7$_{7}$, Hezekiah 2 K 19$_{19}$||Is 37$_{20}$ Is 38$_{20}$ 2 C 32$_{22}$, Jephthah Jg 12$_{2}$, Jeremiah Jr 15$_{20}$ 17$_{14}$, Johanan Jr 42$_{11}$, Joseph 4QapJoseph[b] 1$_{16}$.

אָדָם *human being* Ps 36$_{7}$, אִישׁ *man* Jg 8$_{22}$, אִשָּׁה *woman* 2 K 6$_{27.27}$, אָב Israelite *father* Ps 106$_{8.10}$ Ne 9$_{27}$, בֵּן Israelite *son* Jg 3$_{9}$ 10$_{12.13.14}$ 1 S 7$_{8}$ Ezk 37$_{23}$, *son* of Reuben Jos 22$_{22}$, of Gad Jos 22$_{22}$, *son* 1 S 10$_{27}$ 2 S 10$_{19}$||1 C 19$_{19}$ Is 49$_{25}$, בַּת *daughter* Ex 2$_{17}$ Is 47$_{13.15}$, מֶלֶךְ *king* Jr 2$_{27.28}$ Ps 20$_{10}$, שַׂר *prince* Jr 2$_{27.28}$ 42$_{11}$, כֹּהֵן *priest* Jr 2$_{27.28}$, נָבִיא *prophet* Jr 2$_{27.28}$, זָקֵן *elder* 1 S 4$_{3}$ 11$_{3}$, עֶבֶד *servant* Ps 86$_{2}$, יֹשֵׁב *inhabitant* 1 S 23$_{2}$ 2 C 32$_{22}$, מָשִׁיחַ *anointed one* Ps 20$_{7}$.

צַדִּיק *righteous one* Ps 37$_{40}$, יָשָׁר *upright one* Ps 7$_{11}$, אֶבְיוֹן *poor one* Jb 5$_{15}$, עָנָו *humble one* Ps 76$_{10}$, עָנִי *humble one* 2 S 22$_{28}$||Ps 18$_{28}$ Ps 34$_{7}$, שַׁח *one with downcast eyes* Jb 22$_{29}$, דַּכָּא *crushed one* of spirit Ps 34$_{19}$, צֹלֵעָה *lame one* Zp 3$_{19}$, זֶרַע *seed*, i.e. offspring Jr 30$_{10}$ 46$_{27}$, צוק ho. ptc. *one who is oppressed* Si 4$_{9}$, מהר ni. ptc. *fearful one* Is 35$_{4}$, קרא ptc. *one who calls* Ps 145$_{19}$, worshipper Ps 3$_{8}$ 6$_{5}$ 7$_{2}$

22$_{22}$ 31$_{3.17}$ 44$_7$ 54$_3$ 55$_{17}$ 57$_4$ 59$_3$ 69$_2$ 71$_{2.3}$ 119$_{94.146}$ 138$_7$ Si 51$_3$ 4QapPs^{a} 1.2$_4$ 4QapPs^{b} 31$_2$, Zion Ps 69$_{36}$, Keilah 1 S 23$_2$, עִיר *city* 2 K 19$_{34}$||Is 37$_{35}$, אֹהֶל *tent* of Judah Zc 12$_7$, צֹאן *flock* Ezk 34$_{22}$, בְּהֵמָה *beast* Ps 36$_7$, יָד *hand* 1 S 25$_{26}$, זְרוֹעַ *arm* Jb 26$_2$, נֶפֶשׁ *soul* Ps 72$_{13}$ 1QH 2$_{23}$ 3$_6$; obj. not specified, Is 46$_7$ Zc 9$_{16}$ Ps 107$_{13.19}$ Si 33$_1$ 48$_{20}$ 4QpHos^{a} 2$_{14}$ 4QpPs^{a} 3.4$_{21}$ 11QT 59$_{11.18}$.

<PREP> לְ of benefit, *to, for*, + י׳ *Y.* Is 59$_{16}$ 63$_5$ 98$_1$, אָדוֹן *lord* 1 S 25$_{31}$, אִישׁ *man*, i.e. community member 1QS 6$_{27}$ CD 9$_{10}$, David 1 C 18$_6$ Job Jb 40$_{14}$, אָב Israelite *father* Ps 44$_4$, בֵּן *son* Ps 72$_4$, worshipper Pr 20$_{22}$.

לְ introducing object Kh. el-Qom tomb inscr. 3$_3$, + Israel Jg 7$_2$, Israelite(s) Dt 28$_{31}$, David 1 S 25$_{33}$, אִישׁ *man* Jos 10$_6$, בֵּן *son* Ps 86$_{16}$ 4QapPs^{b} 15$_2$, נַעֲרָה *young woman* Dt 22$_{27}$ 11QT 66$_8$, יֹשֵׁב *inhabitant* Jr 11$_{12}$, worshipper Ps 116$_6$ Si 13$_6$ CD 9$_9$, עִיר *city* Jr 11$_{12}$.

בְּ of place, *in, at*, + עִיר *city* Ho 13$_{10}$, כֹּל *everywhere* 2 S 8$_{6.14}$||1 C 18$_{6.13}$.

בְּ of time, *in, on*, + יוֹם *day* Ex 14$_{30}$ 1 S 14$_{23}$ Zc 9$_{16}$, עֵת *time* Jg 10$_{14}$ Jr 2$_{28}$ 11$_{12}$ 14$_8$.

בְּ of instrument, *by (means of)*, + י׳ *Y.* Ho 1$_7$, אֱלֹהִים *God* Ho 1$_7$, אִישׁ *man* Jg 7$_7$, פָּרָשׁ *rider* Ho 1$_7$, חֶסֶד *loyalty* Ps 31$_{17}$ 1QH 2$_{23}$, קֶשֶׁת *bow* Ho 1$_7$, חֶרֶב *sword* 1 S 17$_{47}$ Ho 1$_7$, חֲנִית *spear* 1 S 17$_{47}$, מִלְחָמָה *battle* Ho 1$_7$, סוּס *horse* Ho 1$_7$, יָד *hand* Jg 6$_{36.37}$ 2 S 3$_{18}$ 2 K 14$_{27}$ 1QM 11$_3$, רֹב *greatness* 1 S 14$_6$, מְעַט *little* 1 S 14$_6$, שֵׁם *name* Ps 54$_3$.

מִן of direction, *from*, + אֶרֶץ *land* Jr 30$_{10}$ 46$_{27}$ Zc 8$_{7.7}$, רָחוֹק *far away* Jr 30$_{10}$ 46$_{27}$, מוֹשָׁב *dwelling place* Ezk 37$_{23}$, אִישׁ *man* Ps 59$_3$, שֹׁפֵט *judge* Ps 109$_{31}$, רֹדֵף *pursuer* Ps 7$_2$, צַר *adversary* Ps 44$_8$, צוק hi. ptc. *one who oppresses* Si 4$_9$, רָעָה *evil* 1 S 10$_{19}$, מְצוּקָה *affliction* Ps 107$_{13.19}$, צָרָה *distress* 1 S 10$_{19}$ Is 46$_7$ Ps 34$_7$ 4QpHos^{a} 2$_{14}$, חָמָס *violence* 2 S 22$_3$.

טֻמְאָה *uncleanness* Ezk 36$_{29}$, מְשׁוּבָה *faithlessness* Ezk 37$_{23(mss)}$, חֶרֶב *sword* Jb 5$_{15}$, יָד *hand*, i.e. power, *of* Ex 14$_{30}$ Jg 2$_{16.18}$ 8$_{22}$ 10$_{12}$ 12$_2$ 13$_5$ 1 S 7$_8$ 9$_{16}$ 2 S 3$_{18.18}$ 2 K 19$_{19}$||Is 37$_{20}$ Ps 106$_{10}$ Jb 5$_{15}$ Ne 9$_{27}$ 2 C 32$_{22}$ Si 48$_{20}$ 4QpPs^{a} 3.4$_{21}$ 4QapJoseph^{b} 1$_{16}$ 11QT 59$_{11.18.18}$, כַּף *hand*, i.e. power, *of* Jg 6$_{14}$ 1 S 4$_3$ 2 K 16$_{7.7}$, פֶּה *mouth* Ps 22$_{22}$ Jb 5$_{15}$.

לְמַעַן *for sake of*, + שֵׁם *name* Ps 106$_8$.

מִפְּנֵי *on account of*, + רָעָה *evil* 11QT 59$_8$.

<COLL> אַל־תּוֹשִׁיעֵנוּ הַיּוֹם הַזֶּה: *do not spare us today* Jos 22$_{22}$, וְהֹשֵׁעַ יָדִי לִי *and saving myself (with) my own hand* 1 S 25$_{33}$, וַיּוֹשַׁע י׳ תְּשׁוּעָה גְדוֹלָה: *and Y. saved (with) a great salvation* 1 C 11$_{14}$.

<SYN> נצל hi. *deliver*, פלט pi. *rescue*.

1b. ptc. as noun, **saviour, deliverer,** **<SUBJ>** עלה *go up* Ob$_{21}$, שׁפט *judge* Ob$_{21}$, פלה hi. *treat with distinction* Ps 17$_7$.

<NOM CL> אֲנִי ... מוֹשִׁיעֵךְ *I am ... your saviour* Is 43$_3$, אֲנִי י׳ מוֹשִׁיעֵךְ *I am Y. your saviour* Is 49$_{26}$, 60$_{16}$, ... אַתָּה מוֹשִׁיעַ *you are ... the saviour* Is 45$_{15}$, אֵין מוֹשִׁיעַ *there is no saviour* 2 S 22$_{42}$||Ps 18$_{42}$ 4QpsEzek^{c} 3.2$_{11}$ 4QpsEzek^{e} 1.2$_3$, sim. Is 43$_{11}$, מוֹשִׁיעַ אַיִן *there is no saviour* Ho 13$_4$.

<OBJ> קום hi. *raise up* Jg 3$_{9.15}$, נתן *give* 2 K 13$_5$ Ne 9$_{27}$, שׁלח *send* Is 19$_{20}$, שׁכח *forget* Ps 106$_{21}$.

<APP> אֵל *God* Is 45$_{21}$ Ps 106$_{21}$.

<PREP> לְ *as*, + היה *be* Is 63$_8$.

<COLL> אֱלֹהֵי צוּרִי אֶחֱסֶה־בּוֹ ... מֹשִׁעִי *O God of my rock, in whom I take refuge ... my saviour* 2 S 22$_3$, הוֹשִׁיעָה נָּא ... הַצְלִיחָה נָּא *save, pray ... cause (us) to prosper, pray* Ps 118$_{25}$.*

⇒ יֵשַׁע *salvation*, יֶשַׁע *salvation*, יְשׁוּעָה *salvation*, שׁוֹעַ *noble one*, שׁוּעַ *Shua*, שׁוּעַ *opulence*, שׁוּעָא *Shua*, יִשְׁעִי *Ishi*, יְשַׁעְיָהוּ *Isaiah, Jeshaiah*, הוֹשֵׁעַ *Hosea*, הוֹשַׁעְיָה *Hoshaiah*, יְהוֹשֻׁעַ *Joshua*, יֵשׁוּעַ *Jeshua*, יֵשְׁעָא *Jeshua*, יִשְׁעִי *Ishi*, מוֹשָׁעָה *saving acts*, מֵישַׁע *Mesha*, מֵישָׁע *Mesha*, תְּשׁוּעָה *salvation*.*

יֵשַׁע $_{36.2.11.3}$ n.m. **salvation**—יֶשַׁע; cstr. יֵשַׁע; sf. יִשְׁעִי, יִשְׁעֲךָ (Q ישעכה), יִשְׁעֵךְ, יִשְׁעוֹ, יִשְׁעֵנוּ—**help, liberation, salvation, favour, fortune,** **<SUBJ>** בוא *come* Is 62$_{11}$, יצא *go out* Is 51$_5$.

<NOM CL> יִשְׁעִי ... י׳ *Y. is ... my salvation* Ps 27$_1$, שמך ישעי *your name is my salvation* 4QapPs^{b} 24$_7$, קָרוֹב לִירֵאָיו יִשְׁעוֹ *his salvation is near to those who fear him* Ps 85$_{10}$, עַל־אֱלֹהִים יִשְׁעִי *upon God is my salvation* Ps 62$_8$, ישעי לנגד עיניך *my salvation is before your eyes* 4QapPs^{b} 33$_8$.

<OBJ> נתן *give* Ps 85$_8$, צלח hi. *make prosper* 2 S 23$_5$, שׂגב *have great prosperity* Jb 5$_{11}$, פרה *bear fruit* Is 45$_8$, ידע hi. *make known* 11QPs^{a} 18$_2$, גלה hi. *reveal* 1QH 5$_{12}$ CD 20$_{20}$.

<CSTR> יֵשַׁע אֱלֹהִים *salvation of God* Ps 50$_{23}$, יֵשַׁע עַמֶּךָ *salvation of your people* Hb 3$_{13}$.

[א]לוהי ישע *God of salvation* 4QShir^{a} 2$_{2}$, אֱלֹהֵי יִשְׁעִי *God of my salvation* Mc 7$_{7}$ Hb 3$_{18}$ Ps 18$_{47}$ 25$_{5}$ 27$_{9}$ Si 51$_{1}$ 4QapPs^{b} 31$_{6}$, יִשְׁעֵךְ *of your salvation* Is 17$_{10}$, יִשְׁעוֹ *of his salvation* Ps 24$_{5}$, יִשְׁעֵנוּ *of our salvation* Ps 65$_{6}$ 79$_{9}$ 85$_{5}$ 1 C 16$_{35}$, צוּר יִשְׁעִי *rock of my salvation* 2 S 22$_{47}$, צוּר יִשְׁעֵנוּ *rock of our salvation.*

גבור ישעי *warrior of my salvation* Si 51$_{10}$, מולדי ישע *offspring of salvation* 4Q417 1.1$_{11}$, גְּבֻרוֹת יֵשַׁע *mighty acts of salvation* Ps 20$_{7}$, קֶרֶן יִשְׁעִי *horn of my salvation* 2 S 22$_{3}$||Ps 18$_{3}$, בִּגְדֵי־יֶשַׁע *garments of salvation* Is 61$_{10}$, מָגֵן יִשְׁעֶךָ *shield of your salvation* 2 S 22$_{36}$||Ps 18$_{36}$, יום ישעך *day of your salvation* 11QPs^{a} 22$_{4}$, שְׂשׂוֹן יִשְׁעֶךָ *joy of your salvation* Ps 51$_{14}$, אֱמֶת *truth of* Ps 69$_{14}$, כָּל־יִשְׁעִי *all of my salvation* 2 S 23$_{5}$.

<PREP> לְ *to, for,* + יצא *go out* Hb 3$_{13.13}$, קוה pi. *wait* 4QapPs^{b} 33$_{9}$; בְּ *in, with,* + שׁית *place* Ps 12$_{6}$; introducing object, + ראה hi. *show* Ps 50$_{23}$; מִן of direction, *from,* + רחק *be far away* Jb 5$_{4}$.

<COLL> כֹּהֲנֶיהָ אַלְבִּישׁ יֶשַׁע *I will clothe its priests with salvation* Ps 132$_{16}$.

Also 4QapJoshua^{b} 19$_{1}$.*

→ ישע *save.*

יֵשַׁע 1 n.m. **salvation**—sf. יִשְׁעֲכֶם—<SUBJ> בוא *come* Is 35$_{4}$.

→ ישע *save.*

[יְשַׁעְאָ] 0.0.0.1 pr.n.m. **Jeshua,** Seal 425$_{2}$ (7th/6th cent.).

→ ישע *save.*

יִשְׁעִי 5 pr.n.m. **Ishi, 1.** Judahite, son of Appaim, <NOM CL> בְּנֵי אַפַּיִם יִשְׁעִי *the sons of Appaim were Ishi* 1 C 2$_{31}$. <CSTR> בְּנֵי יִשְׁעִי *the sons of Ishi* 1 C 2$_{31}$.

2. Calebite Judahite chief, <CSTR> בְּנֵי יִשְׁעִי *the sons of Ishi* 1 C 4$_{20}$.

3. Manassite chief, <APP> רֹאשׁ *head,* i.e. chief 1 C 5$_{24}$.

4. Simeonite chief, <CSTR> בְּנֵי יִשְׁעִי *the sons of Ishi* 1 C 4$_{42}$.

→ ישע *save.*

יְשַׁעְיָהוּ 39.1.5.12 pr.n.m. **Isaiah** (§1), **Jeshaiah** (§§2-19)—יְשַׁעְיָה; I. ישעהו—**1.** son of Amoz and Judaean prophet, <SUBJ> היה *be* 2 K 20$_{4}$, חזה *see* Is 1$_{1}$ 2$_{1}$ 13$_{1}$, בוא *come* 2 K 20$_{1}$||Is 38$_{1}$ 2 K 20$_{14}$||Is 39$_{3}$, הלך *go* Is 20$_{2.2.3}$, יצא *go out* 2 K 20$_{4}$ Is 7$_{3}$, קרא *meet* Is 7$_{3}$, עשׂה *do* Is 20$_{2}$, שׁלח *send* 2 K 19$_{20}$||Is 37$_{21}$, פתח pi. *loosen* Is 20$_{2}$, חלץ *remove sandal* Is 20$_{2}$, קרא *call* 2 K 20$_{11}$, אמר *say* 2 K 19$_{6}$||Is 37$_{6}$ 2 K 20$_{1.7}$||Is 38$_{1.21}$ 2 K 20$_{9.14.16}$||Is 39$_{5}$ CD 6$_{8}$, דבר pi. *speak* 2 K 20$_{19}$||Is 39$_{8}$.

<CSTR> חֲזוֹן יְשַׁעְיָהוּ *vision of Isaiah* Is 1$_{1}$, יַד *hand of,* i.e. (by) means of Is 20$_{2}$ Si 48$_{20}$ CD 4$_{13}$, דברי ישעיה *words of Isaiah* CD 7$_{10}$, ספר *book of* 4QMidrEschat^{a} 3$_{15}$ 4QTanḥ 1$_{4}$.

<APP> בֵּן *son* 2 K 19$_{2.20}$||Is 37$_{2.21}$ 2 K 20$_{1}$||Is 38$_{1}$ Is 1$_{1}$ 2$_{1}$ 13$_{1}$ 20$_{2}$ CD 4$_{13}$ 7$_{10}$, נָבִיא *prophet* 2 K 19$_{2}$||Is 37$_{2}$ 2 K 20$_{1.11.14}$||Is 39$_{3}$ 4QMg 5$_{1}$ CD 4$_{13}$ 7$_{10}$, עֶבֶד *servant* Is 20$_{3}$.

<PREP> אֶל *to,* + היה *be* 2 K 20$_{4}$||Is 38$_{4}$, בוא *come* 2 K 19$_{5}$||Is 37$_{5}$, שׁלח *send* 2 K 19$_{2}$||Is 37$_{2}$, אמר *say* 2 K 20$_{8.19}$ ||Is 39$_{8}$ Is 7$_{3}$.

2. Levite musician, son of Jeduthun, <NOM CL> בְּנֵי יְדוּתוּן ... יְשַׁעְיָהוּ *the sons of Jeduthun were ... Jeshaiah* 1 C 25$_{3}$. <APP> Asaph 1 C 25$_{15}$, בֵּן *son* 1 C 25$_{15}$. <PREP> לְ of benefit, *to, for,* + יצא *go out* 1 C 25$_{15}$.

3. Levite, temple treasurer, <NOM CL> לֶאֱלִיעֶזֶר ... יְשַׁעְיָהוּ *belonging to Eliezer was ... Jeshaiah* 1 C 26$_{25}$.

4. member of the Elam family, son of Athaliah, <NOM CL> מִבְּנֵי עֵילָם יְשַׁעְיָה *of the sons of Elam were Jeshaiah* Ezr 8$_{7}$. <APP> בֵּן *son* Ezr 8$_{7}$.

5. Merarite Levite, <NOM CL> אִתּוֹ יְשַׁעְיָה מִבְּנֵי מְרָרִי *with him was Jeshaiah of the sons of Merari* Ezr 8$_{19}$.

6. Benjaminite family head, <CSTR> בֶּן־יְשַׁעְיָה *son of Jeshaiah* Ne 11$_{7}$.

7. Judahite, son of Hananiah, <NOM CL> בֶּן־חֲנַנְיָה ... יְשַׁעְיָה *the son(s) of Hananiah were ... Jeshaiah* 1 C 3$_{21}$.

8. Jerusalem Jar inscr.$_{1}$, <PREP> לְ of possession, *(belonging) to, of* Jerusalem Jar inscr.$_{1}$.

9. Ketef Hinnom inscr. 2$_{19}$, <PREP> לְ of possession, *(belonging) to, of* Ketef Hinnom inscr. 2$_{19}$.

10. Seal 52$_{1}$ (Palestine), <PREP> לְ of possession, *(belonging) to, of* Seal 52$_{1}$ (Palestine). **11.** Seal 211$_{1}$ (Kiriath-jearim, 7th/6th cent.), <PREP> לְ of possession, *(belonging) to, of* Seal 211$_{1}$ (Kiriath-jearim, 7th/6th cent.). **12.** Seal 294$_{2}$ (Hebron, 8th cent.), <PREP> לְ of possession, *(belonging) to, of* Seal 294$_{2}$ (Hebron, 8th cent.) ([ישעיה]ו]). **13.** Seal 408$_{1}$ (Wadi ed-Daliyeh, seal 4th cent.), <APP> בֵּן *son* Seal 408$_{1}$ (Wadi ed-Daliyeh, seal 4th cent.) (ישע[יהו]). <PREP> לְ of possession, *(belonging) to, of* Seal 408$_{1}$ (Wadi ed-Daliyeh, seal 4th cent.). **14.** Seal 420$_{2}$ (8th/7th cent.), <PREP> לְ of possession, *(belonging) to, of* Seal 420$_{2}$ (8th/7th cent.).

15. Seal 426$_{2}$ (7th cent.), <PREP> לְ of possession, *(belonging) to, of* Seal 426$_{2}$ (7th cent.). **16.** Seal 583$_{1}$ (T. Beit-Mirsim?, 7th/6th cent.), <APP> בֵּן *son* Seal 583$_{1}$ (T. Beit-Mirsim?, 7th/6th cent.). <PREP> לְ of possession, *(belonging) to, of* Seal 583$_{1}$ (T. Beit-Mirsim?, 7th/6th cent.). **17.** Seal 584$_{1}$ (T. Beit-Mirsim?, 7th/6th cent.), <PREP> לְ of possession, *(belonging) to, of* Seal 584$_{1}$ (T. Beit-Mirsim?, 7th/6th cent.) ([י]שעיהו). **18.** Seal 591$_{2}$ (T. Beit-Mirsim?, 7th/6th cent.), Seal 591$_{2}$ (T. Beit-Mirsim?, 7th/6th cent.).Seal 591$_{2}$ (T. Beit-Mirsim?, 7th/6th cent.) ([ישעי]הו). **19.** Seal 862$_{1}$ (7th cent.), <PREP> לְ of possession, *(belonging) to, of* Seal 862$_{1}$ (7th cent.).

⇒ Y. + ישׁע *save.*

יְשֻׁעָתָה, see יְשׁוּעָה *salvation.*

יָשְׁפֵה 3 n.m. **jasper** or perh. a kind of **quartz,** <SUBJ> שׁבץ pu. *be set in gold* Ex 28$_{20}$, סבב ho. *be set,* i.e. be surrounded with Ex 39$_{13}$.

<NOM CL> הַטּוּר הָרְבִיעִי ... יָשְׁפֵה *the fourth row is ... jasper* Ex 28$_{20}$‖39$_{13}$, ... כָּל־אֶבֶן יְקָרָה מְסֻכָתֶךָ אֹדֶם פִּטְדָה וְיָשְׁפֵה *every precious stone was your covering—ruby, topaz ... and jasper* Ezk 28$_{13}$.

יִשְׁפָּה 1 pr.n.m. **Ispah,** Benjaminite, son of Beriah, <NOM CL> יִשְׁפָּה ... בְּנֵי בְרִיעָה *Ispah ... were sons of Beriah* 1 C 8$_{16}$.

יִשְׁפָּן 1 pr.n.m. **Ishpan,** Benjaminite, son of Shashak, <NOM CL> יִשְׁפָּן וָעֵבֶר וֶאֱלִיאֵל ... בְּנֵי שָׁשָׁק׃ *Ishpan and Eber and Eliel ... were the sons of Shashak* 1 C 8$_{22}$.

[יִשְׁפָּט] 0.0.0.1 pr.n.m. **Ishpat,** Arad ostr. 53$_{1}$.

⇒ שׁפט *judge.*

ישׁר 25.1.11 vb. **be straight—Qal** 13.1 Pf. יָשַׁר, יָשְׁרָה, יָשְׁרוּ; impf. יִישַׁר, יִישְׁרוּ; + waw וַיִּשַׁר, וַתִּישַׁר, וַיִּשַּׁרְנָה—**be straight, be upright, be level, be right, go straight ahead, please,** <SUBJ> אִשָּׁה *woman* Jg 14$_{7}$, בֵּן *son* 4QJub^{d} 21$_{15}$, פַּר *young bull* 1 S 6$_{12}$, עִיר *city* 1 K 9$_{12}$, אֹרַח *path* Si 39$_{24(Segal)}$ (ארחו[ת]), נֶפֶשׁ *soul* Hb 2$_{4}$, דָּבָר *matter* 1 S 18$_{20.26}$ 2 S 17$_{4}$ 1 C 13$_{4}$ 2 C 30$_{4}$, הִיא *she* Jg 14$_{3}$, אֲשֶׁר *who* Jr 27$_{5}$; subj. not specified, Nm 23$_{27}$ Jr 18$_{4}$ 11QShir Shabb 3$_{6}$ ([י]שרו).

<PREP> בְּ of place, *in, at,* + מֵישָׁר *level place* Si 39$_{24(Bmg)}$; *in, with* Hb 2$_{4}$, + מַעֲשֶׂה *deed* 4QJub^{d} 21$_{15}$, דֶּרֶךְ *way* 1 S 6$_{12}$, עַיִן *eye* Nm 23$_{27}$ Jg 14$_{3.7}$ 1 S 18$_{20.26}$ 2 S 17$_{4.4}$ 1 K 9$_{12}$ Jr 18$_{4}$ 27$_{5}$ 1 C 13$_{4.4}$ 2 C 30$_{4}$.

Pi. 9.0.8 Pf. Q יִשַּׁרְתִּי, ישרתה; impf. יְיַשֵּׁר (יְיַשֶּׁר־), תְּיַשֵּׁר, אֲיַשֵּׁר (אֲיַשֵּׁר, Kt אושר), Q תישרו; + waw וַיְּיַשְּׁרֵם (Kt ויישרם); impv. יַשְּׁרוּ; ptc. מְיַשְּׁרִים; inf. Q לישר—**level, direct, go straight ahead, keep precisely,** <SUBJ> יי *Y.* Is 45$_{2.13}$ Pr 3$_{6}$ GnzPs 1$_{10}$, אֵל *God* 1QH 7$_{14}$, Hezekiah 2 C 32$_{30}$, אִישׁ *man* Pr 15$_{21}$, worshipper Ps 119$_{128}$ 1QH 6$_{24}$ 12$_{34}$, צְדָקָה *righteousness* Pr 11$_{5}$; subj. not specified, Is 40$_{3}$ Pr 9$_{15}$ 1QS 4$_{2}$ 4QpPs^{a} 1.3$_{17}$ 4QTanḥ 38$_{1}$ 4QWays^{b} 1a.1$_{5}$ 4QHod^{f} 3$_{1}$.

<OBJ> הָדוּר *mountainous land* Is 45$_{2(Qr)}$ (1QIsa^{a} הררים *mountains,* 1QIsa^{b} הרורים appar. *mountains*), מְסִלָּה *highway* Is 40$_{3}$, דֶּרֶךְ *way* Is 45$_{13}$ Pr 11$_{5}$ 1QS 4$_{2}$ 1QH 6$_{24}$ 12$_{34}$ 4QpPs^{a} 1.3$_{17}$, אֹרַח *path* Pr 3$_{6}$ 9$_{15}$, פַּעַם *step* 1QH 7$_{14}$, כֹּחַ *strength* GnzPs 1$_{10}$, מַיִם *waters* 2 C 32$_{30}$, כֹּל *all* Ps 119$_{128}$.

<PREP> לְ of direction, *to,* + מַטָּה *downward* 2 C 32$_{30}$, נְתִיבָה *path* 1QH 7$_{14}$, אֱמֶת *truth* 4QpPs^{a} 1.3$_{17}$; of benefit, *to, for,* + אֱלֹהִים *God* Is 40$_{3}$; *according to,* + פִּקּוּד *precept* Ps 119$_{128}$ (if em.); בְּ *in, with,* + מַעֲשֶׂה *deed* GnzPs 1$_{10}$.

לִפְנֵי *before* 1QS 4$_{2}$; עַל פְּנֵי *upon,* + מַיִם *water* 1QH 6$_{24}$.

<COLL> אִישׁ ... יְיַשֶּׁר־לָכֶת *a man ... makes straight his going* Pr 15$_{21}$.

Pu. 1.0.1 Impf Q יושר; ptc. מְיֻשָּׁר—**be evenly hammered,** <SUBJ> זָהָב *gold* 1 K 6$_{35}$; subj. not specified, GnzPs 3$_{3}$.

<PREP> בְּ *in, with,* + עַיִן *eye* GnzPs 3$_{3}$.

Hi. 2.0.1 Impf. יַיְשִׁרוּ; impv. הַיְשַׁר (Kt הושר)—**level, look straight ahead,** <SUBJ> יי *Y.* Ps 5$_{9}$, בֵּן *son* 4QJub^{d} 21$_{25}$, עַפְעַפַּיִם *eyelids* Pr 4$_{25}$.

<OBJ> דֶּרֶךְ *way* Ps 5$_{9}$.

<PREP> לִפְנֵי *before*, + worshipper Ps 5$_{9}$; נֶגֶד *opposite*, + בֵּן *son* Pr 4$_{25}$; בְּ of place, *in, at*, + עֲרָבָה *desert* Is 40$_{3}$; *in, with*, + שָׁלוֹם *peace* 4QJub^{d} 21$_{25}$.*

⇒ יישׁור *uprightness*, יָשָׁר *upright one*, יֹשֶׁר *uprightness*, יֵשֶׁר *Jesher*, יְשָׁרָה *uprightness*, יְשֻׁרוּן *Jeshurun*, מֵישָׁר *uprightness*, מִישׁוֹר *level place*.

יָשָׁר $_{118.1.31}$ adj. **straight (one)**—cstr. יְשַׁר; fs יְשָׁרָה; pl. יְשָׁרִים; cstr. יִשְׁרֵי; fpl יְשָׁרוֹת—**1.** attributive adj. with אִישׁ *man* Jb 1$_{8}$ 2$_{3}$ Pr 21$_{2}$ 4QapJoshua^{a} 3.2$_{6}$ 4Q424 3$_{8}$, אָדָם *human being* Ec 7$_{29}$, דֶּרֶךְ *way* 1 S 12$_{23}$ Jr 31$_{9}$ Ps 107$_{7}$ Pr 14$_{12}$ 16$_{25}$ Ezr 8$_{21}$ Si 11$_{15}$, לֵבָב *heart* 2 K 10$_{15}$, רֶגֶל *foot* Ezk 1$_{7}$, מִשְׁפָּט *judgment* Ne 9$_{13}$.

2. predicative adj. or noun, **straight (one), upright (one), correct (one),** <SUBJ> היה *be* Jb 1$_{1}$, שׂמח *be glad* Ps 107$_{42}$, שׁמם *be horrified* Jb 17$_{8}$, חזה *see* Ps 11$_{7}$, ראה *see* Ps 107$_{42}$, ישׁב *dwell* Ps 140$_{14}$, שׁכן *dwell* Pr 2$_{21}$, כחד ni. *be destroyed* Jb 4$_{7}$, הלך *go* Mc 2$_{7}$, יסף hi. *increase* 4QBark^{c} 1.1$_{2}$, נחל hi. *cause to inherit* 4QSap^{b} 16$_{3}$, כון hi. *establish* Pr 21$_{29}$, פלס pi. *make smooth* Is 26$_{7}$, נטה hi. *divert* 4QWiles 1$_{14}$, בקשׁ pi. *seek* Pr 29$_{10}$, רדה *rule* Ps 49$_{15}$, הלל htp. *make one's boast* Ps 64$_{11}$, רנן hi. *make one shout joyfully* Ps 32$_{11}$, יכח ni. *argue together* Jb 23$_{7}$.

<NOM CL> יָשָׁר י׳ *Y. is upright* Ps 25$_{8}$ 92$_{16}$, יְשָׁרִים דַּרְכֵי י׳ *the ways of Y. are upright ones* Ho 14$_{10}$, פִּקּוּדֵי י׳ יְשָׁרִים *the precepts of Y. are upright ones* Ps 19$_{9}$, יָשָׁר דְּבַר־י׳ *the word of Y. is upright* Ps 33$_{4}$, יָשָׁר מִשְׁפָּטֶיךָ *upright are your judgments* Ps 119$_{137}$, הַלְוִיִּם יִשְׁרֵי לֵבָב *the Levites were upright ones of heart* 2 C 29$_{34}$, כַּנְפֵיהֶם יְשָׁרוֹת *their wings were straight* Ezk 1$_{23}$, כֻּלָּם ... יְשָׁרִים *all of them are ... upright* Pr 8$_{9}$.

יָשָׁר הוּא *he is upright* Dt 32$_{4}$, יָשָׁר אַתָּה *you are upright* 1 S 29$_{6}$ Jb 8$_{6}$, אָז יָשָׁר בְּעֵינֶיךָ *then it would be right in your eyes* 2 S 19$_{7}$, דֶּרֶךְ אֱוִיל יָשָׁר בְּעֵינָיו *the way of a fool is right in his eyes* Pr 12$_{15}$, יְשָׁרָם כִּמְסוּכָה *their upright one is as a thorn hedge* Mc 7$_{4}$ (if em.), ספות ישר אל הראוש *its lips (shall be) straight up to the head* 1QM 5$_{12}$, אַחֲרָיו כָּל־יִשְׁרֵי־לֵב *after it are all the upright ones of heart* Ps 94$_{15}$, יְשָׁרִים עִמּוֹ *upright ones are with him* Dn 11$_{17}$.

יָשָׁר בָּאָדָם אָיִן *there is no upright one among human beings* Mc 7$_{2}$, איש הבהב ל[וא] ישר *the greedy man is not upright* 4QsapHymnA 2$_{1}$.

<OBJ> ראה *see* 2 K 10$_{3}$ (‖ טוֹב *good*) Ps 37$_{37}$, עשׂה *do* Ex 15$_{26}$ Dt 6$_{18}$ (‖ טוֹב) 12$_{8.25.28}$ (‖ טוֹב) 13$_{19}$ 21$_{9}$ Jg 17$_{6}$ 21$_{25}$ 1 K 11$_{33.38}$ 14$_{8}$ 15$_{5.11}$‖2 C 14$_{1}$ 1 K 22$_{43}$‖2 C 20$_{32}$ 2 K 10$_{30}$ 12$_{3}$‖2 C 24$_{2}$ 2 K 14$_{3}$‖2 C 25$_{2}$ 2 K 15$_{3}$‖2 C 26$_{4}$ 2 K 15$_{34}$ ‖2 C 27$_{2}$ 2 K 16$_{2}$‖2 C 28$_{1}$ 18$_{3}$‖2 C 29$_{2}$ 2 K 22$_{2}$‖2 C 34$_{2}$ Jr 34$_{15}$ 2 C 31$_{20}$ 1QS 1$_{2}$ 4QMMT C$_{31}$ 11QT 53$_{7}$ 55$_{14}$ 59$_{17}$ 63$_{8}$ CD 3$_{6}$ 8$_{7}$ 19$_{20}$, פעל *do* Pr 20$_{11}$ 21$_{8}$, שׁגה hi. *mislead* Pr 28$_{10}$, עוה hi. *pervert* Jb 33$_{7}$, טבח *slay* Ps 37$_{14}$, ישׁע hi. *save* Ps 7$_{11}$, נצל hi. *deliver* Pr 11$_{6}$ 12$_{6}$, בין hi. *cause to understand* 1QS 4$_{22}$, דבר *speak* Pr 16$_{13}$.

<CSTR> יִשְׁרֵי־לֵב *upright ones of heart* Ps 7$_{11}$ 11$_{2}$ 32$_{11}$ 36$_{11}$ 64$_{11}$ 94$_{15}$ 97$_{11}$, יִשְׁרֵי לֵבָב *upright ones of heart* 2 C 29$_{34}$ 4QD^{a} 5.1$_{2}$, יְשַׁר־דָּרֶךְ *upright one of the way* Pr 29$_{27}$, יִשְׁרֵי־דָרֶךְ *upright ones of the way* Ps 37$_{14}$ 1QH 2$_{10}$.

סוֹד יְשָׁרִים *council of the upright* Ps 111$_{1}$, דּוֹר *generation of* Ps 112$_{2}$, בֵּין *interval of* Pr 14$_{9}$, אֹהֶל *tent of* Pr 14$_{11}$, מְסִלַּת *highway of* Pr 16$_{17}$, אֹרַח *path of* Pr 15$_{19}$, מוֹת *death of* Nm 23$_{10}$, תֻּמַּת *integrity of* Pr 11$_{3}$, בִּרְכַּת *blessing of* Pr 11$_{11}$, צִדְקַת *righteousness of* Pr 11$_{6}$, פִּי *mouth of* Pr 12$_{6}$, סֵפֶר הַיָּשָׁר *book of the upright one* Jos 10$_{13}$ 2 S 1$_{18}$, תְּפִלַּת יְשָׁרִים *prayer of upright ones* Pr 15$_{8}$, פקודי *directives of* CD 20$_{2}$, כָּל־הַיָּשָׁר *every right act* Dt 12$_{8}$ Jr 40$_{5}$, כָּל־הַיְשָׁרָה *every right act* Mc 3$_{9}$, כָּל־יִשְׁרֵי *all the upright ones of* Ps 32$_{11}$ 64$_{11}$ 94$_{15}$ 4QD^{a} 5.1$_{2}$ (כול).

<PREP> לְ of direction, *to*, + ירה *shoot* Ps 11$_{2}$; of benefit, *to, for* Ps 97$_{11}$ 1QH 2$_{10}$ 4QShir^{a} 1$_{9}$ 4QShir^{b} 10$_{7}$ 60$_{1}$, + אוה ni. *be fitting* Ps 33$_{1}$, צפן *store up* Pr 2$_{7}$, זרח *shine* Ps 112$_{4}$, משׁך *extend* Ps 36$_{11}$, יטב hi. *do good to* Ps 125$_{4}$; introducing object, + חזה *see* 4Q424 3$_{3}$; בְּ *in, with*, + עשׂה *do* Ps 111$_{8}$, חיה *live* 4QpPs^{a} 1.3$_{1}$; כְּ *as* Jos 9$_{25}$ Jr 26$_{14}$; אֶל *to*, + הלך *go* Jr 40$_{4.5}$; אֵת *with* Pr 3$_{32}$; עִם *with*, + חשׁב htp. *be accounted* 1QS 3$_{1}$, יטב hi. *do good to* Mc 2$_{7}$; תַּחַת *instead of* Pr 21$_{18}$. <COLL> הולכי ישר *those who walk uprightly* 4QWiles 1$_{15}$.

<SYN> טוֹב *good*.

Also 4QMyst^{a} 79$_{2}$ 4QParaKings 38$_{6}$ 4QsapHymnA 1.2$_{6}$ 4QDibHam^{a} 17.2$_{5}$ 4QRitMar 163$_{2}$.*

⇒ ישׁר *be straight*.

יֵשֶׁר $_{1}$ pr.n.m. **Jesher,** Calebite, Judahite, son of Hezron, <APP> בֵּן *son* 1 C 2$_{18}$.

⇒ ישׁר *be straight*.

יֹשֶׁר $_{14.4.7}$ n.m. **uprightness**—Si, Q יושר; cstr. יֹשֶׁר, Q יושר; sf. יָשְׁרוֹ—**uprightness, straightness, honesty, integrity,** <SUBJ> נצר *preserve* Ps 25_{21} (|| תֹּם *integrity*), חשׂך ni. *be witheld* Si 9_{17}.

<NOM CL> א[ין] עמו ישר *uprightness is not with him* 4QJub[h] 35_9.

<OBJ> ידע *know* 4QShir[b] 2.2_9, עשׂה *do* Si 48_{16} 4QCitJub 1.2_3, נגד hi. *declare* Jb 33_{23}.

<CSTR> יֹשֶׁר לְבָבְךָ *integrity of your heart* Dt 9_5 Ps 119_7, יֹשֶׁר לְבָבִי *uprightness of my heart* 1 C 29_{17}, יֹשֶׁר־לִבִּי *uprightness of my heart* Jb 33_3, יושר אמתכה *uprightness of your truth* 1QH 6_{10} (others יִישׁוֹר *uprightness*), ישר לבבך *the uprightness of your heart* CD $8_{14(A)}$ (=$19_{27[B]}$ יושר), יושר ישרים *the uprightness of the upright ones* 4QShir[b] 2.2_9.

אָרְחוֹת יֹשֶׁר *paths of uprightness* Pr 2_{13}, מַעְגְּלֵי־יֹשֶׁר *tracks of uprightness* Pr 4_{11} 4QWiles 1_{17}, מכוני יוש[ר] *residences of the upright ones* 4QBer[a] 1.2_7, מחלקות ... ישר *division of ... uprightness* Si $42_{3(Bmg)}$ (B יֵשׁ *property*), אִמְרֵי־יֹשֶׁר *words of honesty* Jb 6_{25}, רוח יושר וענוה *a spirit of uprightness and humility* 1QS 3_8.

<APP> מִשְׁפָּט *judgment* Si 4_9.

<PREP> בְּ of cause, *on account of*, + בוא *come* to inherit Dt 9_5 CD $8_{14(A)}$=$19_{27(B)}$; of accompaniment, *in (a state of), with*, + הלך *go* 1 K 9_4 Pr 14_2, נדב htp. *offer freely* 1 C 29_{17}; ידה hi. *praise* Ps 119_7.

כְּ *in accordance with*, + שׁפט *judge* 1QH 6_{10} (others יִישׁוֹר *uprightness*).

מִן of direction, *from*, + חשׂך *withold* Pr 11_{24}.

עַל *on account of*, + נכה hi. *strike* Pr 17_{26}.

<COLL> כָּתוּב יֹשֶׁר דִּבְרֵי אֱמֶת appar. *words of truth written in uprightness* Ec 12_{10} (mss וְכָתַב *and he wrote* words of truth in uprightness; or em. וְכָתוֹב *and to write* words of truth in uprightness), לכ[ול] הול[כי יו]שר bless *all who walk in righteousness* 4QShirShabb[d] 1.1_{17}.

<SYN> תֹּם *integrity*.

Also 4QBéat 8_4.*

⇒ ישׁר *be straight*.

יְשָׁרָה $_{2.0.1}$ n.f. **uprightness**—cstr. יִשְׁרַת—<OBJ> עקשׁ pi. *pervert* Mc 3_9. <CSTR> יִשְׁרַת לֵבָב *uprightness of heart* 1 K 3_6. <PREP> בְּ *in, with* 4QapJoshua[b] 10_3, + הלך *go* 1 K 3_6.*

⇒ ישׁר *be straight*.

יְשֻׁרוּן $_{4.1}$ pr.n.m. **Jeshurun**—Si ישורון—poetic name for Israel, <SUBJ> שׁמן *be fat* Dt 32_{15}, בעט *kick* Dt 32_{15}. <CSTR> חיי ישורון *life of Jeshurun* Si $37_{25(Bmg;D)}$. <PREP> בְּ of place, *in, at*, + היה *be* Dt 33_5; introducing object, + בחר *choose* Is 44_2. <COLL> אֵין כָּאֵל יְשֻׁרוּן *there is no one like God, O Jeshurun* Dt 33_{26}.*

⇒ ישׁר *be straight*.

יָשֵׁשׁ $_1$ adj. **aged (one),** predicative adj. or noun, **aged one,** <APP> בָּחוּר *youth* 2 C 36_{17}. <PREP> עַל *upon*, + חמל *show compassion* 2 C 36_{17}.

יָתֵד $_{24.0.1}$ n.f. **peg**—cstr. יְתַד (יְתֶד); pl. יְתֵדוֹת; cstr. יִתְדוֹת; sf. יִתְדֹתָם, יְתֵדֹתֶיהָ, יְתֵדוֹתָיו, יְתֵדֹתַיִךְ—**peg, pin, nail,** of wooden tent **peg** (Jg $4_{21.21.22}$ 5_{26} Is 33_{20} 54_2 Ezk 15_3), metal tent **pin** (Ex $27_{19.19}$ $35_{18.18}$ $38_{20.31.31}$ 39_{40} Nm 3_{37} 4_{32}), **peg** in plaster wall for hanging cloak, etc. (Is $22_{23.25}$ Ezr 9_8), digging **stick** (Dt 23_{14}), **peg** for beating weft on loom (Jg $16_{14.14}$), leader of the people (Zc 10_4).

<SUBJ> היה *be* Dt 23_{14}, תקע pass. *be secured* Is 22_{25}, יצא *go out* Zc 10_4, מושׁ *fall away* Is 22_{25}.

<NOM CL> כָּל־יְתֵדֹתָיו וְכָל־יִתְדֹת הֶחָצֵר נְחֹשֶׁת *all of its pegs and all the pegs of the court are of bronze* Ex 27_{19}, כָּל־הַיְתֵדֹת ... נְחֹשֶׁת *all the pegs ... are of bronze* Ex 38_{20}, פְּקֻדַּת מִשְׁמֶרֶת ... יְתֵדֹתָם *the office of the charge* of the sons of Merari was ... *their pegs* Nm 3_{37}, זֹאת מִשְׁמֶרֶת מַשָּׂאָם ... יְתֵדֹתָם *this is the charge of their burden ... their pegs* Nm 4_{32}, הַיָּתֵד בְּרַקָּתוֹ *the tent peg was in his temple* Jg 4_{22}.

<OBJ> בוא hi. *bring* Ex 39_{40}, עשׂה *make* Ex $35_{18.18}$ 38_{31}, חזק pi. *make strong* Is 54_2, נתן *give* Ezr 9_8, לקח *take* Jg 4_{21} Ezk 15_3, תקע *drive* Jg 4_{21}, נסע *remove* Jg 16_{14} Is 33_{20}.

<CSTR> יִתְדֹת הֶחָצֵר *pegs of the court* Ex 27_{19} 35_{18} 38_{31}, הַמִּשְׁכָּן *of the tabernacle* Ex 35_{18} 38_{31}, יְתַד הָאֹהֶל *peg of the tent* Jg 4_{21}; כל ... יתד *every peg* CD 12_{17}, כָּל־הַיְתֵדֹת *all the pegs* Ex 38_{20}, כָּל־יִתְדֹת *all pegs of* Ex 27_{19}, כָּל־יְתֵדֹתָיו *all of its pegs* Ex 27_{19}.

<APP> כֹּל *all* Ex 35_{18}.

<PREP> לְ of direction, *to*, + שׁלח *send*, i.e. extend, hand Jg 5₂₆ (+ הַלְמוּת *hammer*).*

בְּ of instrument, *by (means of), with*, + תקע *beat hair* Jg 16₁₄.

<COLL> תְּקַעְתִּיו יָתֵד *I will secure him as a peg* in a sure place Is 22₂₃.

יָתוֹם 42.2.4 n.m. **orphan**—pl. יְתוֹמִים (יְתֹמִים); sf. יְתֹמֶיךָ, יְתוֹמָיו (יְתֹמָיו)—<SUBJ> היה *be* Ex 22₂₃, שׂבע *be satisfied* Dt 14₂₉ 26₁₂, בוא *come* Dt 14₂₉, אכל *eat* Dt 14₂₉ 26₁₂, שׂמח *rejoice* Dt 16₁₁.₁₄, צעק *cry out* Ex 22₂₂ (+ אַלְמָנָה *widow*), רחם pu. *be shown compassion* Ho 14₄ (or del.).

<NOM CL> הַיָּתוֹם ... אֲשֶׁר בְּקִרְבֶּךָ *the orphan who is in your midst* Dt 16₁₁, הַיָּתוֹם ... אֲשֶׁר בִּשְׁעָרֶיךָ *the orphan who is in your gates* Dt 14₂₉ 16₁₄.

<OBJ> חיה pi. *rear* Jr 49₁₁, שׁפט *judge* Is 1₁₇.₂₃, רחם pi. *pity* Is 9₁₆, עזב *leave* Jr 49₁₁, ענה pi. *afflict* Ex 22₂₁ Zc 7₁₀, עשׁק *oppress* Jr 7₆, ינה hi. *oppress* Jr 22₃ Ezk 22₇, עזד *abandon* 1QH 5₂₀, בזז *plunder* Is 10₂, רצח *kill* CD 6₁₇.

<CSTR> מִשְׁפַּט יָתוֹם *judgment of an orphan* Dt 10₁₈ 24₁₇ (גֵּר יָתוֹם *of sojourner [and] orphan*; ms גֵּר וְיָתוֹם *of sojourner and orphan*; or del. יָתוֹם) 27₁₉ (גֵּר־יָתוֹם), דִּין *judgment of* Jr 5₂₈, צעקת יתום *cry of an orphan* Si 32₁₇, שועת *shout of* 4QBark[a] 1.2₂ (יתומים), כָּל־אַלְמָנָה וְיָתוֹם *every widow and orphan* Ex 22₂₁. <PREP> לְ of direction, *to*, + נתן *give* Dt 26₁₂.₁₃; of benefit, *for*, + היה *be* (of gleanings) Dt 24₁₉.₂₀.₂₁; of possession, *of, (belonging) to*, + היה *be* Si 4₁₀ (היה כאב ליתומים *be like a father to orphans*).

<COLL> יָתוֹם ‖ אַלְמָנָה *widow* Ex 22₂₁.₂₂.₂₃ (both +) Dt 10₁₈ 14₂₉.₂₉.₂₉ 16₁₁.₁₄ 24₁₇ (+; or del. יָתוֹם) 24₁₉.₂₀.₂₁ 26₁₂.₁₃ 27₁₉ Is 1₁₇.₂₃ (both +) 9₁₆ 10₂ (+) Jr 5₂₈ (if em. אֶבְיוֹן *poor one*) 7₆ 22₃ Ezk 22₇ Zc 7₁₀ Si 4₁₀ 32₁₇ (+) CD 6₁₇ (+), בֵּן *son* Ex 22₂₃ (+) Dt 16₁₁.₁₄, בַּת *daughter* Dt 16₁₁.₁₄, גֵּר *sojourner* Dt 10₁₈ (+) 14₂₉.₂₉.₂₉ 16₁₁.₁₄ 24₁₇ (or del. יָתוֹם) 24₁₉.₂₀.₂₁ 26₁₂.₁₃ 27₁₉ Jr 7₆ 22₃ Ezk 22₇ (+) Zc 7₁₀, לֵוִי *Levite* Dt 14₂₉.₂₉.₂₉ 16₁₁.₁₄ 26₁₂.₁₃, עֶבֶד *servant* Dt 16₁₁.₁₄, אָמָה *female servant* Dt 16₁₁.₁₄, עָנִי *poor one* Zc 7₁₀, רָשׁ *poor one* 1QH 5₂₀; + אָב *father* Ezk 22₇ Si 4₁₀, אֵם *mother* Ezk 22₇, אֶבְיוֹן *poor one* Jr 5₂₈ (or em. אַלְמָנָה *widow*), נָקִי *innocent one* Jr 7₆ 22₃.

Also 1Q69 7₁.

<SYN> אַלְמָנָה *widow*, בֵּן *son*, בַּת *daughter*, גֵּר *sojourner*, לֵוִי *Levite*, עֶבֶד *servant*, אָמָה *female servant*, עָנִי *poor one*, רָשׁ *poor one*.*

[יָתוּר] 1 n.[m.] **outcrop**—cstr. יְתוּר—(unless **searching**, from תור *search out*) יְתוּר הָרִים מִרְעֵהוּ *the outcrops of the mountains are his pasture* Jb 39₈ (or em יָתוּר *he searches out* mountains as his pasture).*

⇒ יתר *exceed*.

יַתִּיר 4 pl.n. **Jattir**—יַתִּר—Levitical city in Judah, perh. Kh. ʿAttir SW of Hebron, <NOM CL> בָּהָר שָׁמִיר וְיַתִּיר וְשׂוֹכֹה *in the hill country were Shamir and Jattir and Socoh* Jos 15₄₈. <OBJ> נתן *give* Jos 21₁₄‖1 C 6₄₂. <PREP> בְּ of place, *in, at* 1 S 30₂₇.

יִתְלָה 1 pl.n. **Ithlah,** village in southern Danite territory, <SUBJ> היה *be* Jos 19₄₂.

⇒ תלה *hang*.

[יָתֻם] 0.0.0.2 pr.n.m. **Jathum, 1.** Seal 158₁ (Gaza, 5th cent.). **2.** Seal 766₁ (7th cent.), <PREP> לְ of possession, *(belonging) to, of* Seal 158₁ (Gaza, 5th cent.) Seal 766₁ (7th cent.).

יִתְמָה 1 pr.n.m. **Ithmah,** Moabite, one of David's warriors, <NOM CL> גִּבּוֹרֵי הַחֲיָלִים ... יִתְמָה *the warriors of the armies were ... Ithmah* 1 C 11₄₆. <ADJ> מוֹאָבִי *Moabite* 1 C 11₄₆.

[יתן] I vb. **be constant—Qal, be constant,** <SUBJ> לֶחֶם *bread* Is 33₁₆ (if em. נִתָּן bread *will be given* to יִתַּן *will be constant*), שֶׁרֶשׁ *root* of righteous ones Pr 12₁₂ (if em. יִתֵּן *he will give* root to יָתַן; or em. יִכֹּן *will be established* or בְּאֵיתָן *is perpetual*).

⇒ (?) יֹתָן *Jothen*.

* **[יתן] II** vb. **give—Qal, give, cause to be,** וְאֹיְבַי יָתַתָּה לִּי עֹרֶף *and you gave me my enemies (as) a neck*, i.e. you made them flee from me 2 S 22₄₁ (if em. תַּתָּה, from נתן *give* [as ‖Ps 18₄₁ נָתַתָּה], in same sense), הָאֵל הַמְאַזְּרֵנִי חָיִל וַיִּתֵּן תָּמִים דַּרְכִּי *the God who girds me with strength*

and the donor whose dominion is complete Ps 18$_{33}$ (if em. וַיִּתֵּן *and who has made* my way sound).

⇒ see also נתן *give.*

[יֹתֵן] 0.0.0.1 pr.n.m. **Jothen,** Seal 158$_1$ (Gaza, 5th cent.), <PREP> לְ of possession, *(belonging) to, of* Seal 158$_1$ (Gaza, 5th cent.).

⇒ יתן I *be constant.*

יַתְנִיאֵל 1 pr.n.m. **Jathniel,** Kohathite gatekeeper, <APP> בֵּן *son* 1 C 26$_2$. <ADJ> רְבִיעִי *fourth* 1 C 26$_2$.

⇒ אֵל *God* + נתן *give.*

יִתְנָן 1 pl.n. **Ithnan,** town in the Negeb of Judah, <SUBJ> היה *be* Jos 15$_{23}$. <APP> עִיר *town* Jos 15$_{23}$.

יתר 105.1.18 vb. **exceed—Qal,*** ptc. as noun, **affluent one,** as title of Y., הָאֵל מָעוּזִי חָיִל וְיֹתֵר תָּמִים דַּרְכּוֹ *the God, my fortress, a strong one, and the affluent one whose dominion is complete* 2 S 22$_{33}$ (if em. וַיַּתֵּר תָּמִים דַּרְכִּי [Qr] perh. *and releases,* i.e. makes, *my way sound;* ||Ps 18$_{33}$ וַיִּתֵּן *and who gives,* i.e. makes [or em. וְיֹתֵן *and the donor*]).

Ni. 82.0.10 Pf. נוֹתַר (נֹתַר), נוֹתְרָה, נוֹתַרְתִּי, נוֹתְרוּ (נֹתְרוּ), נוֹתַרְתֶּם; impf. יִוָּתֵר (יִוָּתֵר), וַיִּוָּתְרוּ; + waw וַיִּוָּתֵר, וָאִוָּתֵר; ptc. נוֹתָר (נֹתָר), נוֹתֶרֶת, נוֹתָרִים, נוֹתָרוֹת (נֹתָרֹת)—**1a. remain, be left (over);** perh. **be enriched*** (Pr 2$_{21}$). <SUBJ> עַם *people* 1 K 9$_{20}$||2 C 8$_7$ Is 30$_{17}$, עֲנָק *Anak(im)* Jos 11$_{22}$, שֵׁבֶט *tribe* Jos 18$_2$, Eleazar Lv 10$_{16}$, Elijah 1 K 18$_{22}$ 19$_{10.14}$, Ithamar Lv 10$_{16}$, Jacob Gn 32$_{25}$, Jotham Jg 9$_5$, אִישׁ *man* Nm 26$_{65}$ Am 6$_9$ Dn 10$_{13}$, בֵּן *son* Lv 10$_{16}$ Jos 17$_{2.6}$ 21$_{5.20.26.34.40}$ 1 K 9$_{21}$||2 C 8$_8$ 1 C 6$_{46.55.62}$ 24$_{20}$, בַּת *daughter* Is 1$_8$, יֶלֶד *child* Gn 44$_{20}$, פְּלֵטָה *survivor* Ezk 14$_{22}$, תָּמִים *blameless one* Pr 2$_{21}$, חזק hi. ptc. *one who holds fast* CD 3$_{13}$, צֹאן *sheep* Gn 30$_{36}$, יֶרֶק *green plant* Ex 10$_{15}$, זָהָב *gold* 1 K 15$_{18}$, כֶּסֶף *silver* 1 K 15$_{18}$, הָמוֹן *riches* 2 C 31$_{10}$.

נְשָׁמָה *breath* Jos 11$_{11}$ 1 K 17$_{17}$, כְּלִי *vessel* Jr 27$_{18.19.21}$, עִיר *city* Jr 34$_7$, פֶּרֶץ *breach* Ne 6$_1$, יֶתֶר *remnant* 4QpIsa^c 12$_4$, יֶרֶק *verdant plant* 4QTohA 2.2$_4$, דָּבָר *thing* 2 K 20$_{17}$||Is 39$_6$, שָׁנָה *year* Lv 27$_{18}$ 1QM 2$_{6.10.14}$, שֵׁם *name* Ex 28$_{10}$, אֶחָד *one* 2 S 13$_{30}$ 17$_{12}$ Ps 106$_{11}$, שְׁלִשִׁית *third* Zc 13$_8$, כֹּל *all* Jg 8$_{10}$ 1 S 2$_{36}$ Is 7$_{22}$ Zc 14$_{16}$ 11QT 43$_{11}$, אֲשֶׁר *one that* 2 S 9$_1$ 1QDM 3$_2$ ([יו]תר); subj. not specified, Ex 12$_{10}$ 29$_{34}$ Lv 2$_{3.10}$ 6$_9$ 7$_{16.17}$ 8$_{32}$ 10$_{12.12}$ 14$_{18.29}$ 19$_6$ 1 S 25$_{34}$ 2 K 4$_7$ Is 4$_3$ (|| שׁאר ni. *be remaining*) Ezk 48$_{15.18.21}$ 1Q30.1$_5$.

<PREP> לְ of benefit, *to, for,* + Aaron Lv 2$_{3.10}$, Nabal 1 S 25$_{34}$, בֵּן *son* Lv 2$_{3.10}$, נָשִׂיא *prince* Ezk 48$_{21}$, בַּיִת *house* of Saul 2 S 9$_1$.

בְּ of place, *in, at,* + אֶרֶץ *land* Jos 11$_{22}$ 1 K 9$_{21}$ Ezk 14$_{22}$ Zc 13$_8$ Pr 2$_{21}$, עִיר *city* Jr 27$_{19}$, אוֹצָר *treasury* 1 K 15$_{18}$, בַּיִת *house* Jr 27$_{18}$ Am 6$_9$.

בְּ of accompaniment, *with, in,* + David 2 S 17$_{12}$.

בְּ partitive, *some of, (any)one of,* + אִישׁ *man* 2 S 17$_{12}$, בֵּן *son* Jos 18$_2$, עֵץ *tree* Ex 10$_{15}$, עֵשֶׂב *plant* Ex 10$_{15}$, בָּשָׂר *flesh* Lv 8$_{32}$, לֶחֶם *bread* Lv 8$_{32}$, שֶׁמֶן *oil* Lv 14$_{18}$.

בְּ *in, with,* + בֵּן *son* 1 K 17$_{17}$, אֹרֶךְ *length* Ezk 48$_{18}$, חוֹמָה *wall* Ne 6$_1$.

אֶל *to,* + Lachish Jr 34$_7$, Azekah Jr 34$_7$.

עַל *upon* 1Q30.1$_5$, + אֶבֶן *stone* Ex 28$_{10}$.

מִן partitive, *some of, (any)one of,* + גּוֹי *nation* Zc 14$_{16}$, Amorite 1 K 9$_{20}$||2 C 8$_7$, Hittite 1 K 9$_{20}$||2 C 8$_7$, Hivite 1 K 9$_{20}$||2 C 8$_7$, Jebusite 1 K 9$_{20}$||2 C 8$_7$, Perizzite 1 K 9$_{20}$||2 C 8$_7$, מַטֶּה *tribe* 1 C 6$_{62}$, מִשְׁפָּחָה *family* Jos 21$_{40}$ 1 C 6$_{46}$, מַחֲנֶה *army* Jg 8$_{10}$, אִישׁ *man* Nm 26$_{65}$, בֵּן *son* Jos 21$_{20}$ 2 S 13$_{30}$, צַר *adversary* Ps 106$_{11}$, חזק hi. ptc. *one who holds fast* CD 3$_{13}$, בָּשָׂר *flesh* Ex 12$_{10}$ 29$_{34}$ Lv 7$_{17}$, מוֹעֵד *appointed festival* 11QT 43$_{11}$, מִנְחָה *grain offering* Lv 2$_{3.10}$ 6$_9$, קָרְבָּן *offering* Lv 7$_{16}$, שֶׁמֶן *oil* Lv 14$_{29}$.

אַחֲרֵי *after,* + Amorite 1 K 9$_{21}$||2 C 8$_8$, Hittite 1 K 9$_{21}$||2 C 8$_8$, Hivite 1 K 9$_{21}$||2 C 8$_8$, Jebusite 1 K 9$_{21}$||2 C 8$_8$, Perizzite 1 K 9$_{21}$||2 C 8$_8$.

בְּקֶרֶב *within,* + אֶרֶץ *land* Is 7$_{22}$.

מֵאֵת (from) with, + מַטֶּה *tribe* Jos 21$_{34}$.

עַד *until,* + אוֹר *light* 1 S 25$_{34}$, בֹּקֶר *morning* Ex 12$_{10}$, יוֹם *day* Lv 19$_6$, שָׁנָה *year* Lv 27$_{18}$.

<COLL> וַיִּוָּתֵר יַעֲקֹב לְבַדּוֹ *and Jacob remained by himself* Gn 32$_{25}$, וַיִּוָּתֵר הוּא לְבַדּוֹ *and he remained by himself* Gn 44$_{20}$.

<SYN> שׁאר ni. *be remaining.*

1b. ptc. as noun, **that which is left over, remaining (one),** <SUBJ> עמד *stand* 1 S 30$_9$, נוס *flee* 1 K 20$_{30}$.

<OBJ> רפשׂ *trample* Ezk 34$_{18}$, שׂרף *burn* Ex 29$_{34}$, קבר pi. *bury* Ezk 39$_{14}$, אכל *eat* 11QT 20$_{11}$.

<PREP> לְ of benefit, *to, for*, + עשׂה *do* Jg 21$_{7.16}$.

Hi. 23.1.8 Pf. הוֹתִיר (הוֹתִרְךָ, הוֹתִירְךָ), הוֹתָרָה; impf. יוֹתִיר (יוֹתֵר, Q יתר), 2ms תּוֹתֵר, אוֹתִיר, תּוֹתִירוּ, נוֹתַר; + waw וְהוֹתַרְתִּי; וַיּוֹתֵר, וַתּוֹתַר, וַיּוֹתִרוּ; impv. הוֹתֵר; ptc. Q מותר; inf. הוֹתִיר, הוֹתֵר—**leave over, leave behind, have remaining; give abundantly, enrich** (Dt 28$_{11}$); **have precedence**(Gn 49$_4$), <SUBJ> ׳י *Y.* Dt 28$_{11}$ 30$_9$ Is 1$_9$ Ezk 6$_8$ 12$_{16}$ 39$_{28}$, אֱלֹהִים *God* Dt 30$_9$ Ps 79$_{11}$, אֵל *God* CD 2$_{11}$, עַם *people* 2 K 4$_{43.44}$, David 2 S 8$_4$‖1 C 18$_4$, Reuben Gn 49$_4$, Ruth Ru 2$_{14.18}$, אִישׁ *man* Ex 16$_{19.20}$ Dt 28$_{54}$, בֵּן Israelite *son* Nm 33$_{55}$, כֹּהֵן *priest* 2 C 31$_{10}$, לֵוִי *Levite* 2 C 31$_{10}$, בָּרָד *hail* Ex 10$_{15}$, קֵץ *age* 1QpHab 7$_7$; subj. not specified, Ex 36$_7$ Jr 44$_7$ Si 30$_{38}$ 4QpsEzek[a] 10.14 4Q416 2.2$_{10}$ 4Q417 1.1$_{18}$ 4Q418 126.2$_{15}$ 292$_1$ ([מו]תירכה) 4Q 424 1$_{11}$ ([מותירן]ים) 4QSap[b] 1.2$_3$ (unless יֶתֶר *remnant*).

<OBJ> Israelite(s) Dt 28$_{11}$ 30$_9$, אִישׁ *man* Ezk 12$_{16}$, בֵּן *son* Dt 28$_{54}$ Ps 79$_{11}$, רֶכֶב *chariot* 2 S 8$_4$‖1 C 18$_4$, עֵשֶׂב *plant* Ex 10$_{15}$, פְּרִי *fruit* Ex 10$_{15}$, שְׁאֵרִית *remnant* Jr 44$_7$, פְּלֵיטָה *remnant* CD 2$_{11}$, אֲשֶׁר *that which* Ru 2$_{18}$.

<PREP> לְ of benefit, *to, for* 4Q416 2.2$_{10}$, + Israelite(s) Jr 44$_7$, שָׂרִיד *survivor* Is 1$_9$, אֶרֶץ *land* CD 2$_{11}$.

בְּ *in, with*, + מַעֲשֶׂה *deed* Dt 30$_9$, פְּרִי *fruit* Dt 30$_{9.9.9}$, שְׁרִירוּת *stubbornness* of heart 4QSap[b] 1.2$_3$.

מִן of direction, *from*, + חֶרֶב *sword* Ezk 12$_{16}$, רָעָב *famine* Ezk 12$_{16}$, דֶּבֶר *pestilence* Ezk 12$_{16}$.

מִן partitive, *some of, (any)one of*, + בַּיִת *house* of Israel Ezk 12$_{16}$ 39$_{28}$, יֹשֵׁב *inhabitant* Nm 33$_{55}$, רֶכֶב *chariot* 2 S 8$_4$‖1 C 18$_4$, בָּשָׂר *flesh* Ex 12$_{10}$, לֶחֶם *bread* Ex 16$_{19.20}$, זֶבַח *sacrifice* Lv 22$_{30}$.

עַל *against*, + אָדָם *human being* Si 30$_{38}$.

עַד *until*, + בֹּקֶר *morning* Ex 12$_{10}$ 16$_{19.20}$ Lv 22$_{30}$.*

⇒ יֶתֶר *remnant*, יֶתֶר *more*, יֶתֶר *Jether*, יִתְרָא *Ithra*, יִתְרָה *abundance*, יִתְרוֹ *Jethro*, יִתְרִי *Ithrite*, יוֹתֵר *remainder*, יֹתֶרֶת *appendage*, יִתְרוֹן *profit*, יִתְרָן *Ithran*, הוֹתִיר *Hothir*, מוֹתָר *abundance*, מֵיתָר *cord*, יַתִּיר *Jattir*.

יַתִּר, see יַתִּיר *Jattir*.

[יָתֵר] 0.3.2 adv. **more**—Q יתיר—**1. (even) more,** המתכבד בדלתו בעשרו מתכבד יתר *whoever is honoured in their poverty will be even more honoured in their wealth* Si 10$_{31}$, והנקלה בעשרו בדלתו נקלה יתר *and whoever is despised in his wealth is even more despised in his poverty* Si 10$_{31(B)}$ (A יוֹתֵר *more*). **2.** substantivized, **more** or **one who has more,** אל תערב יתר ממך *do not pledge more than you have* or *do not stand surety for one who is greater than you* Si 8$_{13}$, יתיר או חסר *remaining or lacking*, i.e. more or less Mur 30 1$_3$ (ר[או חס]ר) 2$_{14}$ ([ח]סר).

⇒ יתר *exceed*.

יֶתֶר I 96.1.1.2 n.m. **remnant**—sf. יִתְרוֹ, יִתְרָם; pl. יְתָרִים; sf. Si יתריו—usu. **remnant, remainder, rest** (but perh. **totality, all, majority**);* **excess, abundance** (Is 56$_{12}$ Ps 17$_{14}$ 31$_{24}$ Jb 22$_{20}$ Pr 17$_7$ Dn 8$_9$); **pre-eminence** (Gn 49$_{3.3}$); perh. **wealth** (Hb 2$_8$).*

<SUBJ> היה *be* Nm 31$_{32}$, כתב pass. *be written* 1 K 11$_{41}$ 14$_{19.29}$ 15$_{7.23.31}$ 16$_{5.14.20.27}$ 22$_{39.46}$‖2 C 20$_{34}$ 2 K 1$_{18}$ 8$_{23}$ 10$_{34}$ 12$_{20}$ 13$_{8.12}$ 14$_{15.18}$‖2 C 25$_{26}$ 2 K 14$_{28}$ 15$_6$‖2 C 26$_{22}$ 2 K 15$_{11.15.21.26.31.36}$‖2 C 27$_7$ 2 K 16$_{19}$‖2 C 28$_{26}$ 2 K 20$_{20}$ ‖2 C 32$_{32}$ 2 K 21$_{17}$‖2 C 33$_{18}$ 2 K 21$_{25}$ 23$_{28}$‖2 C 35$_{26}$ 2 K 24$_5$‖2 C 36$_8$ 2 C 13$_{22}$, כרת ni. *be cut off* Zc 14$_2$, יתר ni. *remain* 4QpIsa[c] 12$_4$, שׁוב *go back* Mc 5$_2$, שׁלל *plunder* Hb 2$_8$, נחל *take possession of* Zp 2$_9$.

<NOM CL> אַתָּה ... יֶתֶר שְׂאֵת וְיֶתֶר עָז *you are the pre-eminent one of pride and the pre-eminent one of power* Gn 49$_3$.

<OBJ> אסף *gather* 2 S 12$_{28}$, גלה hi. *exile* 2 K 25$_{11.11}$‖Jr 52$_{15.15}$ Jr 39$_9$, עשׂה *make* Is 44$_{19}$, נתן *give* Dt 3$_{13}$ 2 S 10$_{10}$ ‖1 C 19$_{11}$, נוח hi. *leave* Ps 17$_{14}$, רמס *tread* Ezk 34$_{18}$, אכל *eat* Ex 10$_5$ 23$_{11}$ Jl 1$_{4.4.4}$ Jb 22$_{20}$.

<CSTR> יֶתֶר עָז *pre-eminent one of strength* Gn 49$_3$, שְׂאֵת *of pride* Gn 49$_3$.

יֶתֶר הַגִּלְעָד *remainder of Gilead* Dt 3$_{13}$, הַגּוֹיִם *of the nations* Jos 23$_{12}$, גּוֹי *of a nation* Zp 2$_9$, הָאֱמֹרִי *of the Amorites* 2 S 21$_2$, הָרְפָאִים *of the Rephaim* Dt 3$_{11}$ Jos 12$_4$ 13$_{12}$, הָעָם *of the people* Jg 7$_6$ 1 S 13$_2$ 2 S 10$_{10}$‖1 C 19$_{11}$ 2 S 12$_{28}$ 1 K 12$_{23}$ 2 K 25$_{11}$‖Jr 52$_{15}$ Jr 39$_{9.9}$ Zc 14$_2$ Ne 4$_{8.13}$, העמים *of the peoples* 1QpHab 9$_7$, מַמְלָכוּת *of the kingdom* Jos 13$_{27}$, הַשְּׁבָטִים *of the tribes* Ezk 48$_{23}$, הֶהָמוֹן *of the multitude* 2 K 25$_{11}$, כָּל־יֶתֶר עַמִּים perh. *all the wealth of peoples* Hb 2$_8$.

יֶתֶר בָּנָיו *remainder of his sons* Dt 28$_{54}$, אֶחָיו *of his brothers* Mc 5$_2$, הַקָּדֵשׁ *of the sacred male(s)* 1 K 22$_{47}$, נְבִיאִים *of the prophets* Ne 6$_{14}$, זִקְנֵי *of the elders of* Jr 29$_1$, הָאָמוֹן *of the artisan(s)* Jr 52$_{15}$, אֹיְבֵינוּ *of our enemies* Ne 6$_1$, הַפְּלֵטָה

of the survivor, i.e. that which has survived Ex 10_{5}, הַגָּזָם *of the locust*, i.e. what is left by the locust Jl 1_{4}, הָאַרְבֶּה *of the locust* Jl 1_{4}, הַיֶּלֶק *the locust* Jl 1_{4}, הַכֵּלִים *of the vessels* Jr 27_{19}, הַבָּז *of the spoil* Nm 31_{32}, הַשֶּׁמֶן *of the oil* Lv 14_{17}, מִרְעֵיכֶם *of your pasture* Ezk 34_{18}, שְׁנוֹתָי *of my years* Is 38_{10}.

יֶתֶר דִּבְרֵי *remainder of the acts of* 1 K 11_{41} $14_{19.29}$ $15_{7.31}$ $16_{5.14.20.27}$ $22_{39.46}$||2 C 20_{34} 2 K 1_{18} 8_{23} 10_{34} 12_{20} $13_{8.12}$ $14_{15.18}$||2 C 25_{26} 2 K 14_{28} 15_{6}||2 C 26_{22} 2 K $15_{11.15.21.26.31.36}$||2 C 27_{7} 2 K 16_{19}||2 C 28_{26} 2 K 20_{20}||2 C 32_{32} 2 K 21_{17}||2 C 33_{18} 2 K 21_{25} 23_{28}||2 C 35_{26} 2 K 24_{5}||2 C 36_{8} 2 C 13_{22}, יֶתֶר כָּל־דִּבְרֵי *remainder of all the acts of* 1 K 15_{23}.

חיי יתר [ש]כר *life of the wealth of understanding* Si 40_{18}, שְׂפַת־יֶתֶר *lips of excess*, i.e. arrogant speech Pr 17_{7}, כֹּל יֶתֶר *all the remainder of* Jg 7_{6}, perh. *all the wealth of* Hb 2_{8}.

<APP> גָּדוֹל *great* Is 56_{12}.

<PREP> לְ of direction, *to*, + שׁמע ni. *be heard*, i.e. be reported Ne 6_{1}, נגד hi. *declare* Ne 2_{16}; introducing object, + זכר *remember* Ne 6_{14}.

בְּ *against*, + רעע *be evil* Dt 28_{54}; introducing object, + דבק *join* Jos 23_{12}; אֶל *to*, + שׁלח *send* Jr 29_{1}, אמר *say* 1 K 12_{23} Ne $4_{8.13}$; עַל *concerning*, + אמר *say* Jr 27_{19}; *because of*, + שׁלם pi. *recompense* Ps 31_{24}.

מִן partitive, *some of, (any)one of* Jos 12_{4} 2 S 21_{2} Arad ost. 5_{13}, + שׁאר ni. *be remaining* Dt 3_{11} Jos 13_{12}, נתן *give*, i.e. place Lv 14_{17}.

<COLL> פֻּקַּדְתִּי יֶתֶר שְׁנוֹתָי in the gates of Sheol *I am appointed for the remainder of my years* Is 38_{10}, וַתִּגְדַּל־יֶתֶר *and it became great exceedingly* Dn 8_{9}.

Also 4QSap[b] 1.2_{3} (unless verb יתר *exceed*).*

⇒ יתר *exceed*.

יֶתֶר II 6.1 n.m. **cord**—sf. יִתְרָם; pl. יְתָרִים—**cord, bow-string, tent ropes, sinews**, <SUBJ> נסע ni. *be pulled up* Jb 4_{21}.

<OBJ> בוא hi. *bring* Si 14_{24}, עלה hi. *bring up* Jg 16_{8}, נתק pi. *tear up* Jg 16_{9}, פתח pi. *loosen* Jb 30_{11}.

<PREP> בְּ of instrument, *by (means of), with*, + אסר bind Jg 16_{7}; עַל *upon*, + כון pol. *prepare* Ps 11_{2}.

<COLL> שִׁבְעָה יְתָרִים *seven bow-strings* Jg $16_{7.8}$.

⇒ יתר *exceed*.

יֶתֶר III 9 pr.n.m. **Jether, 1.** ident. with יִתְרוֹ *Jethro*, father in law of Moses, Kenite priest and chief, Ex 4_{18} (ms, Sam יִתְרוֹ), <APP> חֹתֵן *father-in-law* Ex 4_{18}. <PREP> אֶל *to*, + שׁוב *go back* Ex 4_{18}.

2. eldest son of Gideon, <APP> בְּכוֹר *firstborn* Jg 8_{20}. <PREP> לְ of direction, *to*, + אמר *say* Jg 8_{20}.

3. Judahite chief, son of Jada, <SUBJ> מות *die* 1 C 2_{32}. <NOM CL> בְּנֵי יָדָע ... יֶתֶר *the sons of Jada ... were Jether* 1 C 2_{32}.

4. Judahite, son of Ezrah, <NOM CL> בֶּן־עֶזְרָה יֶתֶר *the son(s) of Ezrah were Jether* 1 C 4_{17}.

5. Asherite, warrior and chief, <CSTR> בְּנֵי יֶתֶר *the sons of Jether* 1 C 7_{38}.

6. father of Amasa and husband of David's sister Abigail, <NOM CL> אֲבִי עֲמָשָׂא יֶתֶר *the father of Amasa was Jether* 1 C 2_{17} (=1 S 17_{25} יִתְרָא *Ithra*). <CSTR> בֶּן־יֶתֶר *son of Jether* 1 K $2_{5.32}$.

⇒ יתר *exceed*.

יֹתֵר, see יוֹתֵר *remainder*.

יִתְרָא 1.0.1 pr.n.m. **Ithra, 1.** father of Amasa and husband of David's sister Abigail, ident. with יֶתֶר *Jether* at 1 K $2_{5.32}$ 1 C 2_{17}, <NOM CL> שְׁמוֹ יִתְרָא *his name was Ithra* 2 S 17_{25} (=1 C 2_{17} יֶתֶר *Jether*).

2. temple servant, 4QNetin 1_{3}.

⇒ יתר *exceed*.

יִתְרָה 2 n.f. **abundance**—cstr. יִתְרַת—<SUBJ> אבד *perish* Jr 48_{36}. <OBJ> עשׂה *do*, i.e. produce Is 15_{7} Jr 48_{36}.*

⇒ יתר *exceed*.

יִתְרוֹ 9 pr.n.m. **Jethro**, father in law of Moses, Kenite priest and chief Ex 3_{1} 4_{18} $18_{1.2.5.6.9.10.12}$, <SUBJ> שׁמע *hear* Ex 18_{1}, בוא *come* Ex $18_{5.6}$, לקח *take* Ex $18_{2.12}$, אמר *say* Ex 4_{18} 18_{10}, חדה *rejoice* Ex 18_{9}. <NOM CL> אֲנִי חֹתֶנְךָ *I am your father-in-law* Ex 18_{6}. <CSTR> צֹאן יִתְרוֹ *sheep of Jethro* Ex 3_{1}. <APP> חֹתֵן *father-in-law* Ex 3_{1} $4_{18(ms, Sam)}$ (L יֶתֶר *Jether*) $18_{1.2.5.6.12}$, כֹּהֵן *priest* Ex 3_{1} 18_{1}. <PREP> אֶל *to*, + שׁוב *go back* Ex $4_{18(ms, Sam)}$ (L יֶתֶר *Jether*).

⇒ יתר *exceed*.

יִתְרוֹן 10 n.m. **profit**—cstr. יִתְרוֹן—**profit, surplus, benefit, advantage,** <NOM CL> יִתְרוֹן אֶרֶץ בַּכֹּל *the profit of the land is in the whole* Ec 5₈, מַה־יִּתְרוֹן לָאָדָם *what profit is it to a human being?* Ec 1₃, מַה־יִּתְרוֹן הָעוֹשֶׂה *what profit does the worker have?* Ec 3₉, מַה־יִּתְרוֹן לוֹ *what profit is it to him?* Ec 5₁₅, אֵין יִתְרוֹן *there is no advantage* under the sun Ec 2₁₁ 10₁₁, יֵשׁ יִתְרוֹן לַחָכְמָה *there is benefit to wisdom* Ec 2₁₃. <CSTR> יִתְרוֹן הָאוֹר *advantage of the light* Ec 2₁₃, יִתְרוֹן אֶרֶץ *profit of the land* Ec 5₈, יִתְרוֹן דַּעַת *advantage of knowledge* Ec 7₁₂. <PREP> כְּ *as* Ec 2₁₃. <COLL> יִתְרוֹן הַכְשֵׁיר חָכְמָה *wisdom is an advantage for success* Ec 10₁₀.*
⇒ יתר *exceed.*

יִתְרִי 3 gent. **Ithrite, 1.** collective, **Ithrites,** <NOM CL> מִשְׁפְּחוֹת קִרְיַת יְעָרִים הַיִּתְרִי *the families of Kiriath-jearim were the Ithrites* 1 C 2₅₃.
2. as sing. noun, a particular **Ithrite,** עִירָא הַיִּתְרִי גָּרֵב הַיִּתְרִי *Ira the Ithrite, Gareb the Ithrite* 2 S 23₃₈‖1 C 11₄₀.
⇒ יתר *exceed.*

יִתְרָן 3 pr.n.m. **Ithran, 1.** ancestor of a Horite clan in Edom, <NOM CL> בְּנֵי דִישָׁן ... יִתְרָן *the sons of Dishon were ... Ithran* Gn 36₂₆‖1 C 1₄₁ (דִּישׁוֹן).
2. Asherite, son of Zophah, <NOM CL> בְּנֵי צוֹפַח ... יִתְרָן *the sons of Zophah were ... Ithran* 1 C 7₃₇.
⇒ יתר *exceed.*

יִתְרְעָם 2 pr.n.m. **Ithream,** son of David, <SUBJ> ילד ni. *be born* 2 S 3₅₍Qr;mss₎ 1 C 3₃. <APP> בֵּן *son* 2 S 3₅ 1 C 3₃. <ADJ> שִׁשִּׁי *sixth* 2 S 3₅ 1 C 3₃.
⇒ עַם *people* + יתר *exceed.*

יֹתֶרֶת 11.0.1 n.f. **appendage**—יוֹתֶרֶת—**appendage, lobe,** or **fatty mass** at opening of liver of sacricial animals, <OBJ> כסה pi. *cover* Ex 29₁₃.₂₂, לקח *take* Lv 8₁₆.₂₅, סור hi. *remove* Lv 3₄.₁₀.₁₅ 4₉ 7₄ 4QJub[e] 21₈, קטר hi. *burn as incense* Lv 9₁₀. <CSTR> יֹתֶרֶת הַכָּבֵד *lobe of the liver* Ex 29₂₂ Lv 8₁₆.₂₅ 9₁₉ 4QJub[e] 21₈.
⇒ יתר *exceed.*

יְתֵת 2 pr.n.m. **Jetheth,** Edomite chief, <APP> אַלּוּף *chief* Gn 36₄₀‖1 C 1₅₁.

כ

כְּ +2471.+c.153.+c.550.+17 prep. **as**—**1.** vocalized **a.** כְאֶ, כַאְ, כָאֱ, כָאֶ, before א, ה, ח, or ע; exceptions are כֵּאלֹהִים, כַּאבִיר; כַּאדֹנָי/כַּי׳; כֵּאלֹהָיו; **b.** כְּ usu. before any consonant other than א, ה, ח, or ע; c. כָּהֵמָּה, כָּאֵלֶּה, כָּזֶה; **c.** before a definite noun, כַּ, כָּ, or כֶּ (except כְּהַיּוֹם). **d.** with sf., כָּכֶם (כָּכֶם), כָּהֶם (כָּהֵם, כָּהֵמָּה), כָּהֵן (כָּהֵנָּה); other suffixes are attached to כְּמוֹ. **2.** Kt בְּ and Qr כְּ: Jos 4$_{18}$ 6$_{5}$ Jg 19$_{25}$ 1 S 11$_{6.9}$ 2 S 5$_{23}$ Est 3$_{4}$.

1. as, like, comparing **a.** divine and human actions, e.g. הֲכַיּוֹצֵר הַזֶּה לֹא אוּכַל לַעֲשׂוֹת *can I not act like this potter?* Jr 18$_{6}$; also Is 42$_{13}$ Zc 14$_{3}$. **b.** divine actions and actions of beasts or birds, e.g. כְּנֶשֶׁר יָעִיר קִנּוֹ ... י׳ בָּדָד יַנְחֶנּוּ *as an eagle stirs up its nest … Y. alone guides him* Dt 32$_{11}$. **c.** human actions and actions of beasts or birds, e.g. אֶהְגֶּה כַּיּוֹנָה *I moan like a dove* Is 38$_{14}$, also Hb 2$_{5}$ Ps 42$_{2}$. **d.** human actions, e.g. אַל־תִּשְׂמַח יִשְׂרָאֵל אַל־תָּגֵל כָּעַמִּים *do not rejoice, Israel, do not exult like (other) nations* Ho 9$_{1}$ (if em. אֶל־גִּיל perh. rejoice *for joy*). **e.** deities, e.g. וַיְדַבְּרוּ אֶל־אֱלֹהֵי יְרוּשָׁלִַם כְּעַל אֱלֹהֵי עַמֵּי הָאָרֶץ *and they spoke of the God of Jerusalem as of the gods of the peoples of the earth* 2 C 32$_{19}$. **f.** people and deities, e.g. וִהְיִיתֶם כֵּאלֹהִים *you will be like God* or *like gods* or *like angels* Gn 3$_{5}$. **g.** people, e.g. כִּי כָמוֹךָ כְּפַרְעֹה *for you* (Joseph) *are like Pharaoh* Gn 44$_{18}$, וַיְהִי כְּמַחֲרִישׁ *and he was like one deaf* 1 S 10$_{27}$; also Gn 42$_{30}$. **h.** persons and natural objects, e.g. וְשַׂמְתִּי אֶת־זַרְעֲךָ כַּעֲפַר הָאָרֶץ *and I shall make your descendants like the dust of the earth* Gn 13$_{16}$; also Gn 22$_{17}$ 25$_{25}$ Ps 1$_{3}$ 18$_{43}$ 44$_{23}$ 49$_{13}$ 68$_{3}$ 125$_{1}$ 127$_{4}$. **i.** of natural objects, e.g. כֻלָּהּ מַשְׁקֶה ... כְּגַן־י׳ כְּאֶרֶץ מִצְרַיִם the plain of Jordan *was well watered … like the garden of Y., like the land of Egypt* Gn 13$_{10}$; also Ex 16$_{40}$ Is 29$_{2.4.7}$ Jr 50$_{9}$ Ps 122$_{3}$ 139$_{12}$ Pr 10$_{26}$. **j.** human and divine attributes, e.g. וְאִם זְרוֹעַ כָּאֵל לָךְ *have you an arm like God?* Jb 40$_{9}$. **k.** human attributes and attributes of objects, beasts, or birds, e.g. מְשַׁוֶּה רַגְלַי כָּאַיָּלוֹת *he makes my feet like (the feet of) hinds* Ps 18$_{34}$; also Ps 58$_{5}$ Jb 9$_{26}$ 11$_{16}$ Pr 16$_{27}$ 20$_{2}$ Ca 6$_{10}$ 8$_{10}$. **l.** events or situations, e.g. וְכָשְׁלוּ ... כְּמִפְּנֵי חֶרֶב *they will stumble as (one stumbles) before the sword* Lv 26$_{37}$, וַיְשַׁסְּעֵהוּ כְּשַׁסַּע הַגְּדִי *he tore it* (a lion) *as one tears a kid* Jg 14$_{6}$; also 2 S 3$_{34}$ Is 1$_{7}$ 5$_{17.24}$ 9$_{3}$ 10$_{13.15}$ 13$_{6}$ 17$_{6}$ 23$_{5}$ 51$_{9}$ 61$_{10}$ 62$_{1}$ 63$_{2}$ Ezk 26$_{10}$ Ps 89$_{30.37}$ 95$_{8}$ Jb 29$_{2.23}$ 30$_{5}$ Ec 10$_{5}$ Lm 1$_{20}$ 2$_{7}$ Dn 11$_{29}$.

2. special cases of comparison, **a.** of approximation, e.g. וְתַחַת רַגְלָיו כְּמַעֲשֵׂה לִבְנַת הַסַּפִּיר *and beneath his feet (was) as it were a pavement of sapphire stone* Ex 24$_{10}$, כְּנֶגַע *something like a plague* Lv 14$_{35}$, כְּמַרְאֵה־אֵשׁ *like the appearance of fire* Nm 9$_{15}$; also Nm 23$_{22}$ Ezk 1$_{4.26.27}$ Dn 8$_{15}$ 10$_{16.18}$. **b.** of unattainables, e.g. הֲנִמְצָא כָזֶה אִישׁ *can a man like this be found?* Gn 41$_{38}$, אֵין קָדוֹשׁ כַּי׳ *there is no one holy like Y.* 1 S 2$_{2}$. **c.** of uniqueness, e.g. וְלֹא הָיָה כַּיּוֹם הַהוּא לְפָנָיו וְאַחֲרָיו *there was not a day like it before or since* Jos 10$_{14}$, הֲנִהְיָה כַּדָּבָר הַגָּדוֹל הַזֶּה *has anything as great as this happened?* Dt 4$_{32}$. **d.** of idealization, e.g. בִּקֵּשׁ י׳ לוֹ אִישׁ כִּלְבָבוֹ *Y. has sought a man after his own heart* 1 S 3$_{14}$; also Jr 3$_{15}$. **e.** of inequality, e.g. הַמַּסֵּכָה צָרָה כְּהִתְכַּנֵּס *the covering is too narrow to wrap oneself in* Is 28$_{20}$. **f.** כָּזֶה, כָּאֵלֶּה, כָּזֹאת, etc., e.g. וַתִּקְרֶאנָה אֹתִי כָּאֵלֶּה *things such as these have happened to me* Lv 10$_{19}$; also Jg 13$_{23}$ 15$_{7}$ 19$_{30}$ Is 66$_{8}$.

3. as … so, indicating equivalence (with one or more repetitions of כְּ), of **a.** ritual, e.g. כַּחַטָּאת כָּאָשָׁם תּוֹרָה אַחַת לָהֶם *as for the sin offering, so for the guilt offering, there (will be) one regulation for them* Lv 7$_{7}$. **b.** persons, e.g. כַּגֵּר כָּאֶזְרָח *as much the sojourner as the native* Lv 24$_{16}$; also Lv 24$_{22}$ Nm 15$_{15}$ Dt 1$_{17}$ Jos 8$_{33}$ Is 24$_{2}$ (with 12 instances of כְּ) Ezk 18$_{4}$ Ho 4$_{9}$. **c.** of possessions, e.g. כָּמוֹנִי כָמוֹךָ כְּעַמִּי כְעַמֶּךָ כְּסוּסַי כְּסוּסֶיךָ *I am as you are: my people are your people, my horses are your horses* 1 K 22$_{4}$. **d.** quantity, e.g. כִּי כְּחֵלֶק הַיֹּרֵד בַּמִּלְחָמָה וּכְחֵלֶק הַיֹּשֵׁב *for the share of whoever goes down to battle is to be the same as the share of whoever remains* 1 S 30$_{24}$. **e.** כְּ ... כֵּן, e.g. כִּשְׁמוֹ כֶּן־הוּא *as is his name, so is he* 1 S 25$_{25}$; also Ho 4$_{7}$ Ps 48$_{11}$. **f.** state or quality, e.g. כְּכֹחִי אָז וּכְכֹחִי עָתָּה *I am as strong now as then* Jos 14$_{11}$.

4. indicating approximate number, **about, around, approximately,** of **a.** persons, e.g. וַיִּסְעוּ ... כְּשֵׁשׁ־מֵאוֹת אֶלֶף רַגְלִי *and they journeyed ... about 600,000 on foot* Ex 12$_{37}$, כָּהֵם וְכָהֵם *however many these might be* 2 S 24$_{3}$; also Jos 4$_{13}$ 7$_{3}$ Jg 20$_{39}$ 1 S 9$_{22}$. **b.** measurement or quantity, e.g. וּכְאַמָּתַיִם עַל־פְּנֵי הָאָרֶץ *about two cubits above the ground* Nm 11$_{31}$; also Ru 2$_{17}$. **c.** time or space, e.g. רָחוֹק יִהְיֶה ... כְּאַלְפַּיִם אַמָּה בַּמִּדָּה *it will be ... about 2000 cubits away* Jos 3$_{4}$, כִּי כְפֶשַׂע בֵּינִי וּבֵין הַמָּוֶת *for there is (only) about a step between me and death* 1 S 20$_{3}$, לֹא־אָץ לָבוֹא כְּיוֹם תָּמִים the sun *did not hasten to set for about a whole day* Jos 10$_{13}$. **d.** of area, e.g. כְּבַחֲצִי מַעֲנָה צֶמֶד שָׂדֶה *about half a furrow in a yoke of land* 1 S 14$_{14}$.

5. in accordance with, after, וַיִּקְרָא שֵׁם הָעִיר כְּשֵׁם בְּנוֹ חֲנוֹךְ *he called the name of the city after the name of his son Enoch* Gn 4$_{17}$; also Jos 19$_{47}$.

6. indicating time, **at, when, as, a.** with verbs, כְּבוֹא אַבְרָם מִצְרָיְמָה *when Abram came into Egypt* Gn 12$_{14}$ (sim. Gn 19$_{17}$ 24$_{30}$ 29$_{13}$ 38$_{29}$ 39$_{13}$ 2 C 12$_{1}$), כִּשְׁמֹעַ עֵשָׂו אֶת־דִּבְרֵי אָבִיו *when Esau heard his father's words* Gn 23$_{34}$, וַיַּשְׁכִּמוּ כַּעֲלוֹת הַשַּׁחַר *and they rose at the dawning of the day* Jos 6$_{15}$, וְהִיא כְפֹרַחַת *and when it budded* Gn 40$_{10}$, וַיְהִי כְּדַבְּרָהּ אֶל־יוֹסֵף יוֹם יוֹם *and it happened, as she spoke to Joseph day after day* Gn 39$_{10}$ (sim. Dt 20$_{2.9}$), לָכֵן כֶּאֱכֹל קַשׁ לְשׁוֹן אֵשׁ *as the tongue of the fire devours the stubble* Is 5$_{24}$ (also Is 18$_{5}$ Ezk 22$_{22}$ Jb 2$_{10}$), וְהָיָה כִּרְאוֹתוֹ כִּי אֵין הַנַּעַר *and it shall be when he sees the lad is not (with us)* Gn 44$_{31}$, וְעַתָּה כְּבֹאִי אֶל־עַבְדְּךָ אָבִי *now when I come to your servant my father* Gn 44$_{30}$, כְּבֹאֲכֶם הָעִיר *when you enter the city* 1 S 9$_{13}$ (sim. Is 30$_{19}$ Dn 11$_{2}$), כְּטוֹב לֵב־אַמְנוֹן בַּיַּיִן *when Amnon is happy with wine* 2 S 13$_{28}$.

b. with nouns, adverbs, etc., e.g. שׁוֹב אָשׁוּב אֵלֶיךָ כָּעֵת חַיָּה *I shall certainly return to you at the time (spring) is reviving* Gn 18$_{10}$, הִנְנִי מַמְטִיר כָּעֵת מָחָר *tomorrow at (about) this time I shall cause it to rain* Ex 9$_{18}$ (sim. Ex 11$_{4}$ Nm 23$_{23}$ Jos 11$_{6}$ Is 8 $_{23}$), נִגָּפִים הֵם לְפָנֵינוּ כְּבָרִאשֹׁנָה *they are beaten before us as before* Jg 20$_{32}$ (sim. 1 K 13$_{6}$ Is 1$_{26}$ Jr 33$_{7.11}$), וַיְהִי כְּמִשְׁלֹשׁ חֳדָשִׁים *and it happened about three months later* Gn 38$_{24}$ 1 S 25$_{38}$ Ru 1$_{4}$.

7. perh. possessive, **of,*** אֹרַח כַּנָּשִׁים *the way of women* Gn 18$_{11}$ (or em. כְּאֹרַח נָשִׁים *as the way of women*).

→ כְּמוֹ *as.*

כאב $_{8.2}$ vb. **hurt—Qal** $_{4.1}$ Impf. יִכְאַב (יִכְאָב); ptc. כֹּאֵב (כּוֹאֵב), כֹּאֲבִים—**be in pain,** <SUBJ> worshipper Ps 69$_{30}$, בָּשָׂר *flesh* Jb 14$_{22}$ (‖ אבל *mourn*), לֵב *heart* Pr 14$_{13}$, Shechemites Gn 34$_{25}$; subj. not specified, Si 13$_{5}$. <PREP> לְ of benefit, *to, for,* + דַּל *poor one* Si 13$_{5}$; בְּ *in, with,* + שׂחק inf. as noun, *laughter* Pr 14$_{13}$; עַל *for, on behalf of,* + גֶּבֶר *man* Jb 14$_{22}$. <SYN> אבל *mourn.*

Hi. $_{4.1}$ Pf. הִכְאַבְתִּיו; impf. תַּכְאִיב, יַכְאִיב; ptc. מַכְאִיב—**hurt, ruin,*** <SUBJ> ״ *Y.* Ezk 13$_{22}$, אֱלוֹהַּ *God* Jb 5$_{18}$, Jehoram 2 K 3$_{19}$, Jehoshaphat 2 K 3$_{19}$, בֵּן *son* Si 4$_{3}$, מֶלֶךְ *king* 2 K 3$_{19}$, false prophets Ezk 13$_{22}$ (if em. כאה hi. *discourage*), קוֹץ *thorn* Ezk 28$_{24}$ (‖ מאר hi. *inflict sore*). <OBJ> צַדִּיק *righteous one* Ezk 13$_{22}$, חֶלְקָה *portion of land* 2 K 3$_{19}$, קֶרֶב *inward parts,* i.e. feelings Si 4$_{3}$, לֵב *heart* of righteous Ezk 13$_{22}$. <PREP> בְּ of instrument, *by (means of), with,* + אֶבֶן *stone* 2 K 3$_{19}$. <SYN> מאר hi. *inflict sore.**

→ כְּאֵב *pain,* מַכְאוֹב *pain.*

כְּאֵב $_{6.4.2}$ n.m. **pain**—Q כאיב; cstr. כְּאֵב; sf. כְּאֵבִי—**pain, anguish,** <SUBJ> היה *be* Jr 15$_{18}$, גדל be great Jb 2$_{13}$, אמן ni. *be continuous* Si 30$_{17}$, עכר ni. *be untouchable* Ps 39$_{3}$, חשך ni. *be restrained* Jb 16$_{6}$, אנשׁ pass. *be incurable* Is 17$_{11}$ 1QH 5$_{28}$ 8$_{28}$, עמד *stand,* i.e. continue Si 30$_{17}$. <NOM CL> כאב ראשׁ ... יין נשתה *pain of the head,* i.e. headache, *is ... as wine that is drunk* in strife and vexation Si 34$_{29}$. <CSTR> כְּאֵב לֵב *pain of the heart* Is 65$_{14}$, כאב נפשׁו *pain of his soul* Si 4$_{6}$, ראשׁ *of the head* Si 34$_{29}$. <PREP> לְ *as,* or introducing predicate, + היה *be* 1QH 5$_{28}$, פרח *break out* 1QH 8$_{28}$; בְּ *in, with,* + צעק *cry out* Si 4$_{6}$; מִן of comparison, *more (than)* Si 30$_{17.17}$; of cause, *because of,* + צעק *cry out* Is 65$_{14}$. <COLL> כאיב אנושׁ לאין עצור *an incurable pain that cannot be stopped* 1QH 8$_{28}$; כְּאֵב + נֶגַע *stroke* 1QH 5$_{28}$ 8$_{28}$ (נ[יג]ע׳).*

→ כאב *hurt.*

כאה $_{3.0.2}$ vb. **be discouraged—Ni.** $_{2.0.2}$ + waw וְנִכְאָה; ptc. נִכְאָה, Q נכאים, Q נכאי—**1. be discouraged,*** <SUBJ> מֶלֶךְ *king* of the north Dn 11$_{30}$. **2.** ptc. as noun, **discouraged one, downcast one,** <OBJ> בער hi. *kindle* 1QM 11$_{10}$, רדף *persecute* Ps 109$_{16}$ (+ אִישׁ עָנִי וְאֶבְיוֹן *poor and needy man*), מות pol. *kill* Ps 109$_{16}$. <CSTR> נִכְאֵה לֵבָב *discouraged one of heart* Ps 109$_{16}$, נכאי רוח *downcast ones* *of spirit* 1QM 11_{10}. <PREP> בְּ introducing object, + נחם pi. *comfort* 1QS 10_{21}.

Hi. 1 Inf. הַכְאוֹת—**discourage,** יַעַן הַכְאוֹת לֵב־צַדִּיק שֶׁקֶר *on account of discouraging the heart of the righteous one (with) falsehood* Ezk 13_{22} (or em. הַכְאִיב *hurting* and/or del. שֶׁקֶר).

[כָּאוֹר] 0.0.1 adj. **repulsive**—Q כאורה—ושמתיך כאורה *and I will make you repulsive* 4QpNah 3.3_1 (=Na 3_6 כְּרֹאִי *as a spectacle*).

→ כאר II *be repulsive.*

[כאף] 0.2 vb. **bend—Pi.** 0.1 Impv. Si כיף—**bend, bow,** <SUBJ> subj. not specified, Si 30_{12}. <OBJ> ראשׁ *head* Si 30_{12}. <PREP> בְּ *in, at,* + נְעֻרוֹת *youth* Si 30_{12}.

Hi. 0.1 Impv. Si הכאף—**bow, bend,** <SUBJ> בֵּן *son* Si 4_7. <OBJ> ראשׁ *head* Si 4_7. <PREP> לְ of direction, *to,* + שִׁלְטוֹן *powerful one* Si 4_7.

כאר I 1 vb. perh. **bind—Qal** 1 Pf. mss כָּאֲרוּ; ptc. mss כָּאֲרֵי (L כָּאֲרִי)—**bind,** <SUBJ> עֵדָה *congregation* of wicked Ps $22_{17(mss)}$ (or em. אָסְרוּ *they bound* or כָּאֲרוּ *as though to pluck [at]*). <OBJ> יָד *hand* Ps $22_{17(mss)}$, רֶגֶל *foot* Ps $22_{17(mss)}$.*

כאר II 1.0.1 vb. **be repulsive—Qal** 1 Pf. mss כָּאֲרוּ (L כָּאֲרִי)—**be repulsive,** <SUBJ> יָד *hand* Ps $22_{17(mss)}$, רֶגֶל *foot* Ps $22_{17(mss)}$ (or em. po. *mutilate* or אסר *bind* hands and feet).

Pi. 0.1 + waw Q וכארום—**consider repulsive,** <SUBJ> רַב pl. *many* 4QpNah 3.3_4 (+ שׂנא *hate*). <OBJ> דרשׁ ptc. *one who seeks* 4QpNah 3.3_4. <PREP> עַל *on account of,* + זָדוֹן *presumptuousness* 4QpNah 3.3_4.

Po. mutilate,* <SUBJ> עֵדָה *congregation* Ps $22_{17(mss)}$. <OBJ> יָד *hand* Ps $22_{17(mss)}$, רֶגֶל *foot* Ps $22_{17(mss)}$ (if em. כָּאֲרוּ *they are repulsive* to כֹּאֲרוּ *they mutilated*).

→ כָּאוֹר *repulsive.*

כָּאֲרִי, see כרה *excavate.*

כַּאֲשֶׁר, see אֲשֶׁר *which.*

כבד 113.22.56.1 vb. **be heavy—Qal** 23.0.1 Pf. כָּבֵד (כָּבֵד), כָּבְדָה (כָּבֵדָה), כָּבְדוּ; impf. יִכְבַּד (יִכְבָּד), 3fs תִּכְבַּד, יִכְבְּדוּ, נִכְבַּד, וַתִּכְבְּדִי; + waw וַיִּכְבַּד, 3fs וַתִּכְבַּד; impv. Q כבוד—**1. be heavy, be weighty, be numerous, be burdensome, be honoured, weigh heavily.**

<SUBJ> יי *Y.* Is 66_5, Tyre Ezk 27_{25}, מֶלֶךְ *king* 2 S 13_{25}, עֶבֶד *servant* 2 S 13_{25}, בֵּן *son* Jb 14_{21}, עֲבוֹדָה *labour* Ex 5_9 Ne 5_{18}, מִלְחָמָה *war* Jg 20_{34} 1 S 31_3||1 C 10_3, חַטָּאת *sin* Gn 18_{20}, פֶּשַׁע *transgression* Is 24_{20}, עָוֹן *iniquity* Ps 38_5, כַּעַשׂ *vexation* Jb 6_3, אֶכֶף *pressure* Jb 33_7, יָד *hand* Jb 23_2, specif. of Y. 1 S $5_{6.11}$ Ps 32_4, of house of Joseph Jg 1_{35}, לֵב *heart* of Pharaoh Ex 9_7, עַיִן *eye* of Israel Gn 48_{10}, אֹזֶן *ear* Is 59_1, שֵׂעָר *hair* 2 S 14_{26}.

<PREP> בְּ of place, *in, among,* + לֵב *heart* of seas Ezk 27_{25}; מִן of comparison, *more (than),* + חוֹל *sand* of sea Jb 6_3; of cause, *because of,* + זֹקֶן *old age* Gn 48_{10}; privative, *without,* + שׁמע inf. as noun *hearing* Is 59_1, *for,* + worshipper Ps 38_5; אֶל *to, on, upon,* + Ashdodite 1 S 5_6, Saul 1 S 31_3; עַל *upon,* + אֶרֶץ *earth* Is 24_{20}, Ashdodite 1 S $5_{6(mss)}$, עַם *people* Ne 5_{18}, Absalom 2 S 13_{25} 14_{26}, Job Jb 33_7, Saul 1 S $31_{3(mss)}$||1 C 10_3, אִישׁ *man* Ex 5_9, בֵּן *son* 2 S 13_{25}, worshipper Ps 32_4, אֲנָחָה *sigh* Jb 23_2.

<COLL> יוֹמָם וָלַיְלָה תִּכְבַּד *day and night* your hand *was heavy* upon me Ps 32_4.

2. honour, respect, 4Q416 2.3_{15} (כבוד; = 4Q418 9_{17} כבד, prob. pi.), <SUBJ> subj. not specified, 4Q416 2.3_{15}. <OBJ> אָב *father* 4Q416 2.3_{15}, אֵם *mother* 4Q416 2.3_{15}. <PREP> בְּ of accompaniment, *with, in,* + רוֹשׁ *poverty* 4Q 416 2.3_{15}, מִצְעָד *step* 4Q416 2.3_{15}.

Ni. 30.10.33 Pf. נִכְבַּד, נִכְבַּדְתָּ (נִכְבָּדְתָּ), Q נכבדתה), Q נכבדתי, Si נכבדו; impf. Q יכבד, אֶכָּבֵד (אֶכָּבְדָה), (אֶכָּבֵדָה); + waw וְנִכְבַּדְתִּי; impv. הִכָּבֵד; ptc. נִכְבָּד, נִכְבָּדִים, נִכְבַּדֵּי, Q נכבדיו, נִכְבַּדֶּיהָ, נִכְבַּדֵּיהֶם, נִכְבָּדוֹת; inf. Q הכבד (הִכָּבְדִי), Q הכבדכה—**1. be made heavy, be honoured, be glorious, enjoy respect, behave with dignity, reveal one's glory.***

<SUBJ> יי *Y.* Ex $14_{4.17.18}$ Lv 10_3 Is 26_{15} Ezk 28_{22} 39_{13} Hg 1_8, אֱלֹהִים *God* Si 33_4, אֵל *God* 1QM $11_{8(mg)}$ (with erasure of להלחם *to fight*) 4QMyst[c] $3_{4.5.6}$ ([נ]כבד; || הדר ni. *be honoured*) 4QShirShabb[d] 1.1_4 (=MasShirShabb 2_{13} אל כבוד *God of glory*), אֲדֹנָי *Adonai* 1QH 2_{24}, Israel Is 43_4 (|| יקר *be precious*), Abishai 2 S 23_{19}||1 C 11_{21}, Amaz–

iah 2 K 14_{10}, Benaiah 2 S 23_{23}||1 C 11_{25}, David 1 S 22_{14} 2 S 6_{22}, Jabez 1 C 4_9, אִישׁ *man* 1 S 9_6 Si $10_{30(B)}$ 1QH 10_{27}, נַעַר *youth* Gn 34_{19}, מֶלֶךְ *king* 2 S 6_{20} 4QMyst[a] 9_3 ([מ]לך]), שַׂר *prince* Nm 22_{15} Si $10_{24(B)}$, מֹשֵׁל *ruler* Si 10_{24}, שֹׁפֵט *judge* Si 10_{24}, עֶבֶד *servant* of Y. Is 49_5, עָשִׁיר *rich one* Si $10_{30(B)}$, דַּל *poor one* Si $10_{30(A)}$, ירא ptc. *one who fears* Si 10_{20}, קָדוֹשׁ *holy one* 4QShirShabb[a] 2_2 (|| ni. *be revered*), לֵבָב *heart* 4QMyst[c] 2a2, ראשׁ *head* Si 10_{20}, בָּשָׂר *flesh* 1QH 9_{16} (+ גבר *be mighty*), זֶרַע *seed*, i.e. offspring Si 10_{19}, שֵׁם *name* Dt 28_{58} (|| ירא ni. *be revered*) Si 47_{18} 1QS 6_{27} 4QPrayers[c] 1_2 ([שם]), קוֹל *voice* 1QM 10_{10} 1QH fr. 12_5 4QShirShabb[d] 1.2_{12}, אֵלֶּה *these* Si 44_7; subj. not specified, Si $10_{30(A)}$ 10_{31}.

<PREP> לְ *in*, + מִשְׁמָע *hearing* 4QShirShabb[d] 1.2_{12}; בְּ of place/time, *in, among, at, during* 4QShirShabb[b] 14.1_5, + עַם *people* Si $33_{4(Bmg)}$ 4QMyst[c] 3_6 ([נ]כבד]), דּוֹר *generation* Si 44_7, אוֹיֵב *enemy* 1QM $11_{8(mg)}$ (with erasure of להלחם *to fight*), עוֹלָם *eternity* 4QPrayers[c] 1_2, מַחֲנֶה *camp* 4QShirShabb[a] 2_2; of authority, *over*, + Pharaoh Ex $14_{4.17.18}$, חַיִל *army* Ex $14_{4.17}$, רֶכֶב *chariot* Ex $14_{17.18}$, פָּרָשׁ *horseman* Ex $14_{17.18}$; *in, with*, + בַּיִת *house* 1 S 22_{14}, עַיִן *eye* of Y. Is 49_5, *eye* Si $10_{31(B)}$, עֹשֶׁר *riches* Si 10_{31}, אֹרֶךְ *length* 4QMyst[c] 3_4 (באו[רך]), שְׁנַיִם *two* 1 C 11_{21}; of instrument, *by (means of), with*, + מִשְׁפָּט *judgment* 1QH 2_{24}.

מִן of direction, *from*, + שְׁלֹשָׁה *three* 2 S 23_{19}||1 C 11_{21}, שְׁלֹשִׁים *thirty* 2 S $23_{19(mss)}$ 23_{23}||1 C 11_{25}; of comparison, *more (than)* 1QH fr. 11_8, + אָח *brother* 1 C 4_9 Si 10_{20}, רֵעַ *neighbour* 1QH 10_{27}, בַּיִת *house* of his father Gn 34_{19}, יֵצֶר *form* 1QH 9_{16}, אֵלֶּה *these* Nm 22_{15}.

עַל־פְּנֵי *before*, + עַם *people* Lv 10_3; בִּגְלַל *on account of*, + שֵׂכֶל *understanding* Si $10_{30(A)}$, עֹשֶׁר *riches* Si $10_{30(A)}$; לְפִי *according to*, + דַּעַת *knowledge* 1QH 10_{27}; בְּתוֹךְ *among*, + Sidon Ezk 28_{22}, בֵּן *son* 1QNoah 13_3 ([בני]); לְעֵינֵי *before*, + worshipper Si 33_4; עִם *with*, + אָמָה *female servant* 2 S 6_{22}.

<COLL> מַה־נִּכְבַּד הַיּוֹם *how* the king of Israel *honoured himself today* 2 S 6_{20}, מה כבד לבב *how honoured is the heart* 4QMyst[c] 2a2, יוֹם הִכָּבְדִי *on the day when I shall be glorified* Ezk 39_{13}.

2. ptc. as noun, **honourable one, glorious one,*** <SUBJ> דבר pu. *be spoken* Ps 87_3, נתן ni. *be given* Si 11_6, נפל *fall* 4QpNah 3.2_9 ([נ[כ]בדים]). <NOM CL> כִּנְעָנֶיהָ נִכְבַּדֵּי־אָרֶץ *her traders were the honourable ones of the earth* Is 23_8. <OBJ> ירד hi. *bring down* Si 48_6, קלל hi. *treat with contempt* Is 23_9, אסר *bind* Ps 149_8.

<CSTR> נִכְבַּדֵּי־אָרֶץ *honourable ones of the earth* Is $23_{8.9}$, נִכְבַּדֵּי־מַיִם *heavy ones of water*, i.e. (springs) with an abundance of water Pr 8_{24}; אלוהי הנכבד[ים] *God of the glorious ones* 4QShirShabb[a] 3.2_9, מלך נכבדים *king of the glorious ones* 1QH 10_8 (|| אֵל *god*), יד נכבדי[ו] *hand of his glorious ones* 4Q419 6_1, כוח הנכבד[ים] *strength of the glorious ones* 1Q29 3_5, יגון ... נכבד[ינו] perh. *grief of ... our honoured ones* 4QPrFêtes[c] 16_4 (+ זָקֵן *elder*), ברכות נכבדים *blessings of honourable ones* 11QPs[a] 22_{13}, כָּל־נִכְבַּדֵּי *all the honourable ones of* Is 23_9.

<PREP> לְ of direction, *to*, + שׁוב hi. *bring back* 1QM 14_{11}; בְּ *against*, + רהב *assail* Is 3_5 (|| זָקֵן *elder*); עַל *on behalf of*, + ידד *cast* lots Na 3_{10}; introducing object, + בוז *despise* 1QpHab 4_2. <COLL> גבוריו ונכבדיו *his warriors and his honourable ones* 4QpNah 3.4_4, נ[כ]בדים [ומוש]לים *honourable ones and rulers* 4QpNah 3.2_9.

Also 1QNoah 3_3 1Q39 1_4 4QpNah 3.3_9 4QMyst[c] 5_4 ([נכבד]) 9_3 ([נכב]ד]) 4Q418 75_1 4QM[a] 12_2 4QRitPur 72_3 ([ונכבד]).

<SYN> §1, הדר ni. *be honoured*, ירא ni. *be revered*, יקר *be precious*; §2, זָקֵן *elder*, אֵל *god*.

Pi. 38.6.20.1 Pf. כִּבַּדְתָּנִי (כִּבַּדְתּוֹ), כִּבְּדוּ (כִּבְּדוּנִי), כִּבַּדְנוּךָ; impf. יְכַבֵּד (יְכַבְּדֻנְנִי), 3fs תְּכַבֵּדךָ (Q תכבדכה), 2ms Q תכבד, תְּכַבְּדוּ, יְכַבְּדוּ, אֲכַבְּדֵהוּ; + waw Q ויכבדום, וְתִכַּבֵּד; impv. כַּבֵּד (Q כבדהו), כַּבְּדוּהוּ; ptc. מְכַבֵּד (מְכַבְּדוֹ, מְכַבְּדַי, מְכַבְּדֶיךָ, Q מכבדיכה, I מכבדם, Q מכבדנו); inf. כַּבֵּד (כַּבְּדְךָ)—**1. honour, make honourable;*** perh. specif. **honour with banquet, fête*** (Ps 15_4 $50_{15.23}$ 91_{15}).

<SUBJ> ״ *Y.* 1 S 2_{30} Is 60_{13} Ps 91_{15} (+ חלץ pi. *deliver*), אֲדֹנָי *Adonai* perh. 4QHod[b] 7_8 ([כבד[תני]) 4QapMes 2.2_7, Israel Is 43_{23} Ps 50_{15}, Israelite(s) Ex 20_{12}||Dt 5_{16} Is 58_{13} 4QpHos[a] 2_5, עַם *people* Is 25_3 29_{13} Ps 50_{15} (+ חלץ pi. *deliver*), גּוֹי *nation* Ps 86_9 4QDibHam[a] 1.4_{11}, זֶרַע *seed*, i.e. offspring of Jacob Ps 22_{24}, Balak Nm $22_{17.37}$ 24_{11}, David 2 S 10_3||1 C 19_3, Eli 1 S 2_{29}, Jacob 4QJub[h] 35_{13} (+ עשה רָצוֹן *do will*), Manoah Jg 13_{17}, Samuel 1 S 15_{30}.

אִישׁ *man* 1QSa 1_{18}, אִשָּׁה *wife* Jg 13_{17}, בֵּן *son* Ml 1_6 Pr

3$_{9}$ Si 3$_{8}$ 7$_{31}$ 10$_{28}$, מֶלֶךְ *king* Dn 11$_{38.38}$ 4Q418 158$_{5}$, עֶבֶד *servant* Ml 1$_{6}$, worshipper Ps 86$_{12}$ 1QSb 4$_{28}$, זבח ptc. *one who sacrifices* Ps 50$_{23}$, חנן ptc. *one who is gracious* Pr 14$_{31}$, חַיָּה *beast* Is 43$_{20}$, תַּן *jackal* Is 43$_{20}$, יַעֲנָה *ostrich* Is 43$_{20}$, חָכְמָה *wisdom* Pr 4$_{8}$, מִי *who?* Si 10$_{29}$; subj. not specified, Jg 9$_{9}$ 1 S 2$_{30}$ (:: בזה *despise*) Is 24$_{15}$ Si 3$_{6}$ 10$_{23}$ Ps 15$_{4}$ 4Q416 2.3$_{10}$ 4Q416 2.3$_{18}$ 4Q418 9$_{17}$ (= 4Q416 2.3$_{15}$ qal) 55$_{10}$ (+ רבה הָדָר hi. *increase glory*) 81$_{4.11}$ Hazor inscr. 5.

<OBJ> יי *Y.* 1 S 2$_{30}$ Is 24$_{15}$ 25$_{3}$ 43$_{20.23}$ Ps 22$_{24}$ Pr 3$_{9}$ 4QapPent 9$_{2}$, אֲדֹנָי *Lord* Is 29$_{13}$, אֱלֹהִים *God* Ps 50$_{15}$ 4QapPent 9$_{2}$, *gods* Jg 9$_{9}$, אֱלוֹהַּ *God* Ps 50$_{23}$, אֵל *God* Si 7$_{31}$ perh. 4Q418 81$_{4}$, עֹשֶׂה *creator* Pr 14$_{31}$, מַלְאָךְ *angel* of Y. Jg 13$_{17}$, עַם *people* 4QDibHam[a] 1.4$_{11}$, עִיר *city* 4QDibHam[a] 1.4$_{11}$, Zion 4QDibHam[a] 1.4$_{11}$, Balaam Nm 22$_{17.37}$ 24$_{11}$, Isaac 4QJub[h] 35$_{13}$, Rebekah 4QJub[h] 35$_{13}$, Saul 1 S 15$_{30}$, אִישׁ *man* Jg 9$_{9}$ Si 10$_{23}$ 4Q418 55$_{10}$, אָב *father* Ex 20$_{12}$||Dt 5$_{16}$ 2 S 10$_{3}$||1 C 19$_{3}$ Ml 1$_{6}$ Si 3$_{8}$ 4Q416 2.3$_{18}$ 4Q418 9$_{17}$ ([אבן]יכה; = 4Q416 2.3$_{15}$ qal), אֵם *mother* Ex 20$_{12}$ ||Dt 5$_{16}$ Si 3$_{6}$ 4Q416 2.3$_{18}$ 4Q418 9$_{17}$ ([אמכ]ה; = 4Q416 2.3$_{15}$ qal), בֵּן *son* 1 S 2$_{29}$ Pr 4$_{8}$.

אָדוֹן *lord* Ml 1$_{6}$, מֵרֵעַ *companion* 1QSa 1$_{18}$, עֶבֶד *servant* 4QapJoseph[b] 1$_{3}$ (unless עֹבֵד *worshipper*), worshipper 4QHod[b] 7$_{8}$ ([כבד]תני), ירא ptc. *one who fears* Ps 15$_{4}$, חָסִיד *loyal one* 4QapMes 2.2$_{7}$, קָדוֹשׁ *holy one* 4Q418 81$_{11}$, קלל hi. ptc. *one who despises* Si 10$_{29}$, תעה pi. ptc. *one who leads astray* 4QpHos[a] 2$_{5}$, נֶפֶשׁ *soul*, i.e. self Si 10$_{28}$, שֵׁם *name* of Y. Is 24$_{15}$ Ps 86$_{12}$ 1QSb 4$_{28}$, שַׁבָּת *sabbath* Is 58$_{13}$, בַּיִת *house* 4QDibHam[a] 1.4$_{11}$, מָקוֹם *place* Is 60$_{13}$, קֹדֶשׁ *holiness* 1QSb 4$_{28}$; obj. not specified, Ps 91$_{15}$ 4Q416 2.3$_{10}$ Hazor inscr. 5.

<PREP> לְ of direction, *to*, + עוֹלָם *eternity* Ps 86$_{12}$; introducing object, + אֱלוֹהַּ *God* Dn 11$_{38.38}$, שֵׁם *name* Ps 86$_{9}$.

בְּ of place, *in, among*, + אוּר *east* Is 24$_{15}$, אִי *island* Is 24$_{15}$; of instrument, *by (means of), with*, + מַעֲשֶׂה *deed* Si 3$_{8}$, עֲנָוָה *humility* Si 10$_{28}$, זַיִת *olive tree* Jg 9$_{9}$, זָהָב *gold* Dn 11$_{38}$, כֶּסֶף *silver* Dn 11$_{38}$, אֶבֶן precious *stone* Dn 11$_{38}$, חֲמֻדוֹת *valuable gifts* Dn 11$_{38}$, מַאֲמָר *command* Si 3$_{8}$; *in, with*, + שָׂפָה *lip* Is 29$_{13}$, זֶבַח *sacrifice* 1QIsa[a] 43$_{23}$; of accompaniment, *with, in*, + רוּשׁ *poverty* 4Q418 9$_{17}$ ([ברוש]כה; = 4Q416 2.3$_{15}$ qal), מִצְעָד *step* 4Q418 9$_{17}$ (= 4Q416 2.3$_{15}$ qal), זֶה *this* 4Q418 81$_{4}$.

מִן of direction, *from*, + הוֹן *wealth* Pr 3$_{9}$; of comparison, *more (than)* 1Q26 1$_{5}$, + יי *Y.* 1 S 2$_{29}$, רֵעַ *neighbour* 4Q418 55$_{10}$; עַל *upon*, + כִּסֵּא *throne* 4QapMes 2.2$_{7}$; נֶגֶד *opposite*, + זָקֵן *elder* 1 S 15$_{30}$; לְמַעַן *for the sake of*, + כָּבוֹד *glory* 4Q416 2.3$_{18}$.

<COLL> זְבָחֶיךָ לֹא כִבַּדְתָּנִי *you have not honoured me with your sacrifices* Is 43$_{23}$.

2. make dull, insensitive, <SUBJ> Egyptian 1 S 6$_{6}$, Philistine 1 S 6$_{6}$, Pharaoh 1 S 6$_{6}$. <OBJ> לֵב *heart* 1 S 6$_{6}$, לֵבָב *heart* 1 S 6$_{6}$.

3. cleanse, <SUBJ> Israelites 11QT 49$_{11}$. <OBJ> בַּיִת *house* 11QT 49$_{11}$. <PREP> בְּ of time, *in, on*, + יוֹם *day* 11QT 49$_{11}$; מִן *from, of*, + תְּגְאֹלֶת *defilement* 11QT 49$_{11}$. Also perh. 4QShirShabb[f] 66$_{2}$ perh. 4Q415 2.2$_{1}$. <ANT> בזה *despise*.

Pu. 3 Impf. יְכֻבָּד; ptc. מְכֻבָּד—**be honoured,** perh. also **be enriched,*** <SUBJ> שמר ptc. *one who keeps* Pr 13$_{18}$ 27$_{18}$, קָדוֹשׁ *holy one*, i.e. day Is 58$_{13}$.

Hi. 17.2.1 Pf. הִכְבַּדְתִּים, הִכְבַּדְתָּ, הִכְבִּיד; impf. Si 2ms תכביד; + waw וַיַּכְבֵּד; impv. Si הכבד; ptc. מַכְבִּיד; inf. הַכְבֵּד—**make heavy, deal heavily with, make unresponsive,* harden, let something weigh heavily,** perh. **multiply** (Jr 30$_{19}$ [|| רבה hi. *multiply*] Jb 35$_{16[mss]}$ [L כבר hi. *multiply*]); **bring to honour, glorify** (e.g. GnzPs 4$_{6}$), <SUBJ> יי *Y.* Ex 10$_{1}$ GnzPs 4$_{6}$, perh. Is 8$_{23}$ (:: קלל hi. *lighten*) Jr 30$_{19}$ Lm 3$_{7}$, Israelite(s) Zc 7$_{11}$, גֶּבֶר *man* Hb 2$_{6}$, אָב *father* 1 K 12$_{10}$||2 C 10$_{10}$ (:: קלל hi. *lighten*) 1 K 12$_{14}$||2 C 10$_{14}$, בֵּן *son* Si 8$_{15}$ (or em. תכביד *you will make heavy* to יכביד *he will make heavy* [אַכְזָרִי]), בְּתוּלָה *virgin* daughter of Babylon Is 47$_{6}$, Pharaoh Ex 8$_{11.28}$ 9$_{34}$, Job Jb 35$_{16(mss)}$, פֶּחָה *governor* Ne 5$_{15}$, אַכְזָרִי *cruel one* Si 8$_{15}$ (if em.); subj. not specified, Is 6$_{10}$ 2 C 25$_{19}$ Si 30$_{13}$.

<OBJ> עֹל *yoke* 1 K 12$_{10.14}$||2 C 10$_{10.14}$ Is 47$_{6}$ Si 30$_{13}$, נְחֹשֶׁת *bronze fetter* Lm 3$_{7}$, עַבְטִיט *pledge* Hb 2$_{6}$, רָעָה *evil* Si 8$_{15}$, דֶּרֶךְ *way* of the sea Is 8$_{23}$, אֹהֶל *tent* of Jacob Jr 30$_{19}$, מִלָּה *word* Jb 35$_{16(mss)}$, תּוֹרָה *law* GnzPs 4$_{6}$, מִצְוָה *commandment* GnzPs 4$_{6}$, לֵב *heart* Ex 8$_{11.28}$ 9$_{34}$ 10$_{1}$, אֹזֶן *ear* Is 6$_{10}$ Zc 7$_{11}$.

<PREP> מִן privative, *without*, + שמע inf. as noun *hearing* Zc 7$_{11}$; עַל *upon*, + גֶּבֶר *man* Hb 2$_{6}$, עַם *people* Ne

515; עַל יְדֵי *through, by means of,* + אמן ni. ptc. *faithful one* GnzPs 46; עַל פִּי *through, by means of,* + עֶבֶד *servant* GnzPs 46. <ANT> קלל hi. *lighten.*

Htp. 2.5.1 Impf. Si, Q תתכבד; impv. הִתְכַּבְּדִי ,הִתְכַּבֵּד; ptc. L מִתְכַּבֵּד (mss מִתַכַּבֵּד)—**multiply, increase, put on airs, honour oneself, glorify oneself,** perh. **be fêted** (Pr 129),* <SUBJ> Nineveh Na 315.15, בֵּן *son* Si 310; subj. not specified, Pr 129 Si 1026 ((תתכבד[ד]) 1027(A) (מת]כבד[)) 1031.31 4Q416 2.220.

<PREP> בְּ of instrument, *by (means of), with,* + קָלוֹן *shame* of your father Si 310; *in, with,* + דַּלָּה *poverty* Si 1031, מַחְסוֹר *lack* 4Q416 2.220, עֹשֶׁר *riches* Si 1031; כְּ *as,* + יֶלֶק *locust* Na 315, אַרְבֶּה *locust* Na 315. *

→ כָּבֵד I *heavy,* כָּבֵד II *liver,* כֹּבֶד *heaviness,* כִּבּוּד *heaviness,* כְּבֵדֻת *difficulty,* כָּבוֹד *glory,* כְּבוּדָּה *glory, property.*

כָּבֵד I 41.5.4 adj. **heavy**—cstr. כְּבַד (כֶּבֶד); pl. כְּבֵדִים; cstr. כִּבְדֵי—**heavy** (Ex 918.24 1 S 418 1 K 124.11||2 C 104.11 Ps 385 11QT 592.6, specif. heavy of ear, i.e. hard of hearing 4Q424 32, heavy of mouth/tongue, i.e. slow of speech Ex 410.10, heavy of tongue, i.e. with difficult language Ezk 35.6, heavy, i.e. full, of iniquity Is 14), **burdensome** (Ex 1818 Nm 1114 Pr 273) **dense** (Ex 1916), **massive** (Is 322), **numerous** (Gn 509 Ex 820 1238 Nm 2020 1 K 39 102 ||2 C 91 2 K 614 4QParGenEx 310), **rich** (Gn 132), **deep, profound** (Gn 5010.11), **severe** (Gn 1210 4131 431 474.13 Ex 93), **obstinate** (Ex 714 Si 326.27), **unresponsive** (Ps 43), **weary** (Ex 1712).

1. used attributively of עַם *people* Nm 2020 1 K 39 Is 14 Ezk 35.6 Si 1617, אִישׁ *man* 4Q424 32 ([איש]), חַיִל *army* 1 K 102||2 C 91 2 K 614, מַחֲנֶה *company* Gn 509, מִקְנֶה *cattle* Ex 1238, עָרֹב *swarm of insects* Ex 820, חָסִיל *locust* 4Q ParGenEx 310, דֶּבֶר *plague* Ex 93, בָּרָד *hail* Ex 918.24, עָנָן *cloud* Ex 1916, עֹל *yoke* 1 K 124.11||2 C 104.11 Si 401 11QT 592.6, מַשָּׂא *burden* Ps 385, סֶלַע *rock* Is 322, לֵב *heart* Ex 714 Si 326.27, מִסְפֵּד *mourning* Gn 5010 (|| גָּדוֹל *great*), אֵבֶל *mourning* Gn 5011.

<COLL> כִּבְדֵי לָשׁוֹן *heavy of tongue* Ezk 35.6, כבד אזן *heavy of ear,* i.e. hard of hearing 4Q424 34, כֶּבֶד עָוֹן *heavy of,* i.e. full with, *iniquity* Is 14.

2. used predicatively of Abram Gn 132, Moses Ex 410.10, עַם *people* Nm 1114, אִישׁ *man* 1 S 418, בֶּן *son* of human being Ps 43, לֵב *heart* Ex 714, יָד *hand* Ex 1712, רָעָב *famine* Gn 1210 4131 431 474.13, דָּבָר *matter* Ex 1818, כַּעַס *vexation* Pr 273.

<COLL> כְּבַד־פֶּה *heavy of mouth* Ex 410, כְּבַד לָשׁוֹן *heavy of tongue* Ex 410, כבד אזן *heavy of ear* 4Q424 34, כִּבְדֵי לֵב *heavy of heart* Ps 43 (if em. כְּבוֹדִי לִכְלִמָּה *my glory [will be] as an insult*).

3. used adverbially, **in great numbers,** וַיָּנַח ... כָּבֵד מְאֹד *and* the locusts *rested* upon all Egypt *in very great numbers* Ex 1014.

4. used as noun, **that which is heavy** (Si 302), **that which is numerous** (2 K 1817||Is 362), כבד ממך [מה] תשא *how can you bear that which is heavier than you?* Si 302, חֵיל כָּבֵד *an army of that which is numerous,* i.e. a great army 2 K 1817||Is 362.*

<SYN> §1 גָּדוֹל *great.*

→ כבד *be heavy.*

כָּבֵד II 14.0.3 n.m. **liver**—sf. כְּבֵדִי ,כְּבֵדוֹ—**liver** of animal (Ex 2913.22 Lv 34.10.15 49 74 816.25 910.19 Pr 723), as seat of human emotion* (Lm 211; also Gn 496 Ps 76 169 3013 579 1082, if em. כָּבֹד *glory* in all six), consulted in divination (Ezk 2126).

<SUBJ> שׁפך ni. *be poured out* Lm 211. <OBJ> פלח pi. *split open* Pr 723. <CSTR> יֹתֶרֶת הַכָּבֵד *appendage of the liver* Ex 2922 Lv 816.25 919 perh. 4QJube 218 (היותרת הכבד) 11QT 158 167 206 (both [יותרת הכבד]) 2315. <PREP> בְּ *at, with,* + ראה *see,* i.e. consult for divination Ezk 2126; מִן of direction, *from,* + קטר hi. *burn* Lv 910; עַל *upon* 4QJubd 218 (ה]כבד[על), + לקח *take* Ex 2913, סור hi. *remove* Lv 49 74, קרב hi. *bring near,* i.e. offer Lv 34.10.15.*

→ כבד *be heavy.*

כֹּבֶד 4.0.2 n.m. **heaviness**—cstr. כֹּבֶד (Q כבוד, Q כובוד)—**weight** of battle (Is 2115), of clouds (Is 3027), **mass** of corpses (Na 33), stones (Pr 273), **dullness** of hearing (1QS 411), **hardness** of heart (1QS 411).

<NOM CL> כֹּבֶד־אֶבֶן *a stone is heavy* Pr 273, לרוח עולה ... כבוד אוזן ... וכובוד לב *(belonging) to the spirit of falsehood are ... heaviness of ear ... and heaviness of heart* 1QS 411. <CSTR> כֹּבֶד מִלְחָמָה *heaviness of,* i.e. oppress–

iveness of, *the war* Is 21$_{15}$, כֹּבֶד פֶּגֶר *heaviness of*, i.e. mass of, *corpse(s)* Na 3$_3$ (=4QpNah 3.2$_4$ כבוד), כבוד אוזן *heaviness of ear*, i.e. dullness of hearing 1QS 4$_{11}$ (+ עִוָּרוֹן *blindness*, קְשִׁי *stiffness* of neck), כובוד לב *heaviness*, i.e. hardness, *of heart* 1QS 4$_{11}$, כֹּבֶד מַשָּׂאָה perh. *heaviness of*, i.e. thickness of, *the uplifted*, i.e. clouds Is 30$_{27}$. <PREP> מִפְּנֵי *from (before)*, + נדד *flee* Is 21$_{15}$.*

⇒ כבד *be heavy*.

כְּבֵדֻת 1 n.f. **heaviness, awkwardness,** <PREP> בְּ *in, with*, + נהג pi. *drive* chariot Ex 14$_{25}$.*

⇒ כבד *be heavy*.

כבה 24.2.2 vb. **be extinguished—Qal** 14.0.1 Pf. כָּבוּ; impf. יִכְבֶּה, 3fs תִּכְבֶּה—**be extinguished, go out, die** (of wrath of Y.), sometimes perh. **fall down, subside,*** <SUBJ> רָשָׁע *wicked one* 4QapPsb 50$_2$ ([יכבו]), אֶרֶץ *land* Is 34$_{10}$, חַיִל *army* Is 43$_{17}$, עִזּוּז *powerful one* Is 43$_{17}$, סוּס *horse* Is 43$_{17}$, רֶכֶב *chariot* Is 43$_{17}$, אֵשׁ *fire* Lv 6$_{5.6}$ Is 66$_{24}$ Jr 17$_{27}$ Pr 26$_{20}$, נֵר *lamp* of God 1 S 3$_3$ Pr 31$_{18}$, לֶהָבָה *flame* Ezk 21$_{3.4}$, חֵמָה *wrath* 2 K 22$_{17}$ Jr 7$_{20}$ (:: בער *burn*) 2 C 34$_{25}$.

<PREP> בְּ of time, *in, at*, + לַיְלָה *night* Pr 31$_{18}$. <ANT> בער *burn*. <COLL> לַיְלָה וְיוֹמָם לֹא תִכְבֶּה *night and day it shall not be extinguished* Is 34$_{10}$.

Pi. 10.2.1 Pf. כִּבּוּ; impf. תְּכַבֶּה, יְכַבֶּנָּה, Si יכבו; + waw וַיְכַבּוּ; ptc. מְכַבֶּה; inf. כַּבּוֹת (כַּבּוֹתְךָ)—**extinguish, quench,** <SUBJ> ׳׳ *Y.* Ezk 32$_7$, מִשְׁפָּחָה *family* 2 S 14$_7$, David 2 S 21$_{17}$, אָב Israelite *father* 2 C 29$_7$, עֶבֶד *servant* of Y. Is 42$_3$, מַיִם *water* Ca 8$_7$ (|| שֶׁטֶף *flood*), אֵשׁ *fire* Si 3$_{30}$, מַתָּן *gift* Pr 21$_{14}$ (if em. כפה *subdue*); subj. not specified, Is 1$_{31}$ Jr 4$_4$ 21$_{12}$ (all three :: בער) Am 5$_6$ (:: אכל *devour*) Si 51$_4$ 4QapPsb 24$_2$.

<OBJ> Pharaoh Ezk 32$_7$, אֵשׁ *fire* Si 51$_4$ נֵר *lamp* 2 S 21$_{17}$ 2 C 29$_7$, פִּשְׁתָּה *wick* Is 42$_3$, גַּחֶל *coal* 2 S 14$_7$, מַיִם *water* Si 3$_{30}$, אַהֲבָה *love* Ca 8$_7$, אַף *anger* Pr 21$_{14}$ (if em.). <PREP> לְ of benefit, *to, for*, + Bethel Am 5$_6$; עַד *until* 4QapPsb 24$_2$. <SYN> שֶׁטֶף *flood*. <ANT> בער *burn*, אכל *devour*.*

⇒ כֵּבָה *dimness*.

[כֵּבָה] 0.1 n.f. **dimness**—pl. Si כבות—<CSTR> כבות אש *dimness of a fire* Si 51$_4$. <PREP> מִן partitive, *without* Si 51$_4$.

⇒ כבה *be extinguished*.

כָּבוֹד 199.32.315 n.m. (rarely f.) **glory**—כָּבוֹד (כָּבֹד); cstr. כְּבוֹד; sf. כְּבוֹדִי (כְּבֹדִי), כְּבוֹדְךָ (Q כבודכה), כְּבוֹדֵךְ, כְּבוֹדוֹ (כְּבֹדוֹ), כְּבוֹדָהּ, כְּבוֹדְכֶם, כְּבוֹדָם (כְּבֹדָם, Q כבודמה)—**1. glory, splendour, majesty,** as attributes of Y. (e.g. Is 42$_8$ 48$_{11}$ Ps 19$_2$ 24$_{7.8.9.10}$ 29$_3$ 1 C 16$_{29}$); as manifestation of Y. (e.g. Ex 33$_{13.18.22}$ Dt 5$_{24}$ Is 60$_2$ 66$_{18}$ Ps 97$_6$); as essence and power of Y. (e.g. Ex 24$_{16}$ Nm 14$_{21}$ Is 6$_3$ 24$_{23}$ Ps 72$_{19}$).

2. honour, reputation, wealth, of people and things (e.g. Gn 31$_1$ 45$_{13}$ Is 10$_{18}$ 22$_{24}$ Ezk 31$_{18}$ Hb 2$_{16}$ Dn 11$_{39}$).

3. appar. **soul,* inner being** of humans (Gn 49$_6$ Ps 7$_6$ 16$_9$ 30$_{13}$ 57$_9$ 108$_2$ [or em. כָּבֵד my *liver*, i.e. my*self*, in all six]).

<SUBJ> היה *be* Is 11$_{10}$ Hg 2$_9$ Ps 104$_{31}$ 2 C 17$_5$ 18$_1$ 32$_{27}$ (all three || עֹשֶׁר *riches*), רבה *be numerous* Ps 49$_{17}$, יחד *be joined* Gn 49$_6$, אסף *be rearguard* Is 58$_8$ (or em. pi. with same meaning), דלל *be unimportant* Is 17$_4$, דמם *be silent* Ps 30$_{13}$, כלה *be ended* Is 21$_{16}$, גלה ni. *be revealed* Is 40$_5$ 4QpNah 3.3$_4$ (בה[ג]לות), ראה ni. *appear* Ex 16$_{10}$ Lv 9$_{6.23}$ Nm 14$_{10}$ 16$_{19}$ 17$_7$ 20$_6$ Is 60$_2$ 4QPrEnosh 1.2$_3$, יפע hi. *shine out* 4QShirb 1$_7$, עלה ni. *be taken up* Ezk 9$_3$, נתן ni. *be given* Is 35$_2$, כתב pass. *be written* 4QTanḥ 8$_{13}$, קלה ni. *be of little account* Is 16$_{14}$, אוה ni. *be fitting* Pr 26$_1$, ni. *be erased* Si 44$_{13(M)}$ ([ימח]ה).

בוא *come* Is 60$_{13}$ Ezk 43$_{2.4}$ Mc 1$_{15}$, גלה *depart* 1 S 4$_{21.22}$ Ho 10$_5$, עבר *pass by* Ex 33$_{22}$, ירד *go down* Ps 49$_{18}$, עלה *go up* Ezk 11$_{23}$, יצא *go out* Ezk 10$_{18}$, עור *arouse oneself* Ps 57$_9$, רום *arise* Ezk 3$_{12}$ (if em.) 10$_4$, עוף htpol. *fly away* Ho 9$_{11}$, עמד *stand* Ezk 3$_{23}$ 10$_{18}$, שׁכן *dwell* Ps 85$_{10}$ 4QJuba 1$_2$ ([וישכן כ]בוד), שׁלח *send* Zc 2$_{12}$, זרח *shine* Is 60$_1$, מלא *fill* Ex 40$_{34.35}$ 1 K 8$_{11}$||2 C 5$_{14}$ Ezk 43$_5$ 44$_4$ 2 C 7$_{1.2}$ Si 42$_{16(M)}$ 4QNarrC 1$_8$ 4QBarka 1.1$_3$, גיל *rejoice* Ps 16$_9$, זמר pi. *sing praise* Ps 30$_{13}$, שׁלם *be complete* 4QPrQuot 1.3$_{16}$ ([כב]ודו).

<NOM CL> אַתָּה ׳׳ ... כְּבוֹדִי *you O Y. are ... my glory* Ps 3$_4$, sim. 11QPsa 24$_{13}$, אדר נציב כבודם perh. *the majesty of pillars is their glory* 4QapPsb 31$_7$, בָּרוּךְ כְּבוֹד־׳׳ *blessed be the glory of Y.* Ezk 3$_{12}$ (or em. רום *arise*), גָּדוֹל

כְּבוֹד־י׳ *great is the glory of Y.* Ps 138_{5}, גָּדוֹל כְּבוֹדוֹ *great is his glory* Ps 21_{6}, כבוד איש כבוד אביו *the glory of a man is the glory of his father* Si 3_{11}, חֵקֶר כְּבֹדָם כָּבוֹד *the searching of their glory is glory* Pr 25_{27} (or em. הֹקַר דִּבְרֵי כָבוֹד *and be sparing with,* or *value, honourable words*), כְּבוֹדוֹ מְתֵי רָעָב *its honoured one(s) are men of hunger* Is 5_{13} (mss מֵתֵי *dying of* hunger), כל כבוד חפתה *its canopy is all of (its) glory* Si 40_{27}.

כְּבוֹדִי חָדָשׁ עִמָּדִי *my glory is fresh with me* Jb 29_{20}, מְלֹא כָל־הָאָרֶץ כְּבוֹדוֹ *all of the earth is full of his glory* Is 6_{3}, עֵקֶב עֲנָוָה ... כָּבוֹד *the reward of humility is ... honour* Pr 22_{4}, שָׁם כְּבוֹד אֱלֹהֵי יִשְׂרָאֵל *the glory of the God of Israel was there* Ezk 8_{4}.

כָּבוֹד לָאִישׁ *there is honour for a man* Pr 20_{3}, לא כבוד הוא לך *it is not glory for you* Si 3_{10}, להם כול כבוד אדם *all the glory of Adam shall be theirs* 1QS 4_{23}, כבודכה לאין מדה *your glory is without measure* 1QH 5_{20} (+ גְּבוּרָה *might*), כבוד ... ביד בוטה *honour ... is within the grasp of one who speaks impetuously* Si $5_{13(A)}$, כבודו בסוד אל[ים] perh. *his glory is in the council of the gods* 4QShirShabb^{a} 1.2_{9}, [הכ]בוד באור אורתם *the glory is in the light of their light* 4QShirShabb^{d} 1.1_{45}, בהדר תשבחות כבוד מלכותו *in the splendour of praise is the glory of his kingdom* 4QShir Shabb^{d} 1.1_{32}, בִּשְׂמֹאולָהּ עֹשֶׁר וְכָבוֹד *in her left hand are riches and honour* Pr 3_{16}, כבוד ייי על כל מעשיו *the glory of Y. is over all his works* Si $42_{16(B)}$, עַל־אֱלֹהִים ... כְּבוֹדִי *upon God ... is my honour* Ps 62_{8}, עַל הַשָּׁמַיִם כְּבוֹדוֹ *his glory is over the heavens* Ps 113_{4}, עַל כָּל־הָאָרֶץ כְּבוֹדֶךָ *your glory is over all the earth* Ps $57_{6.12}$ 108_{6}, כְּבוֹד י׳ עַל־הַבָּיִת *the glory of Y. was over the temple* 2 C 7_{3}, כְּבוֹד אֱלֹהֵי יִשְׂרָאֵל עֲלֵיהֶם *the glory of the God of Israel was upon them* Ezk 10_{19} 11_{22}.

עֹשֶׁר־וְכָבוֹד אִתִּי *riches and honour are with me* Pr 8_{18}, כול כבוד אתכה הוא *all glory is with you* 1QH 11_{8} (+ דֵּעָה *knowledge,* כֹּחַ *strength*), [כ]בוד רוב הדר אתם *glory and an abundance of honour are with them* 4Q418 69.2_{14}, כבודי עם בני המלך *my glory is with the sons of the king* 4QM^{a} 11.1_{18}, כבודכה בתוכ[נו] perh. *your glory is among us* 4QDibHam^{a} 6_{11}, הַכָּבוֹד מִלְּפָנֶיךָ *the honour is from you* 1 C 29_{12}, נֶגֶד זְקֵנָיו כָּבוֹד *in the presence of his elders is glory* Is 24_{23}, אַיֵּה כְבוֹדִי *where is my glory?* Ml 1_{6}, עַד־מֶה כְבוֹדִי לִכְלִמָּה *how long will my glory be a shameful thing?* Ps 4_{3}, כָּבֹד מִכֹּל כְּלִי חֶמְדָּה *there is the glory of every precious object* Na 2_{10}, כבודו לע[ד] perh. *his glory is for ever* 4Q419 1_{10}.

<OBJ> ידע *know* Hb 2_{14} 1QH 6_{12} (‖ אֱמֶת *truth*) 15_{20} (‖ כֹּחַ *strength*) fr. 5_{9} fr. 10_{3} ([כבוד]כה) 4QParGenEx 2_{9}, hi. *proclaim* Ps 145_{12} 1QH 1_{30} (+ פלא ni. ptc. *wonder*) 13_{13} 11QPs^{a} 18_{3}, ראה *see* Ex 16_{7} Nm 14_{22} Is 35_{2} 62_{2} $66_{18.19}$ Ps 63_{3} (‖ עֹז *strength*) 97_{6} 4QDibHam^{a} 1.4_{8}, hi. *show* Ex 33_{18} Dt 5_{24}, שׁמע hi. *make known* 4QShirShabb^{f} 23.1_{9}, ירא *fear* Is 59_{19} Ps 102_{16}, פחד *dread* perh. 4QPoet^{b} 2_{4}, בוא hi. *bring* 1QH 6_{12} ([כ]בודכה), עלה hi. *bring up* Is 8_{7}, רום hi. *raise* 1QH 15_{17}, pol. *exalt* 4QShirShabb^{a} 1.2_{13} MasShirShabb 1_{10}, שׁכן hi. *settle* Ps 7_{6} 11QT 29_{9}, עשׂה *make* Gn 31_{1}, תמך *take hold of* Pr 11_{16} 29_{23}, מצא *find* Pr 21_{21} Si 4_{13} GnzPs 3_{1}, שׂים *place,* i.e. give Jos 7_{19} Is 42_{12} 11QPs^{a} 28_{5}, נתן *give* 1 S 6_{5} 1 K 3_{13} Is 42_{8} 48_{11} Jr 13_{16} Ezk 39_{21} Ml 2_{2} Ps 84_{12} 115_{1} Pr 26_{8} Ec 6_{2} 2 C 1_{12} 32_{33} Si 49_{5} 2QJub^{b} 46_{2} ([כב]ודם) 4QPrEnosh 1.2_{12} (כבודכ[ה]), יהב *give* 4QHod^{a} 7.1_{13} (‖ גֹּדֶל *greatness*), סמך *lean,* i.e. place 4QPrEnosh 1.2_{8} (שמת[ה]), יהב *give* Ps $29_{1.2}$ $96_{7.8}$‖1 C $16_{28.29}$, חלק *divide* Si 44_{2}, כול hi. *contain* 1QS 11_{20}, חרת *engrave* 4QShirShabb^{f} 23.2_{3}.

נחל *inherit* Pr 3_{35} Si $37_{26(D)}$ 4Q417 1.1_{11} 4QBéat 14.2_{14}, רבה hi. *increase* Dn 11_{39} 4Q418 81_{5}, ימר hi. *exchange* Jr 2_{11}, מור hi. *change* Ho 4_{7} Ps 106_{20}, מכר hi. *sell* 4Q416 2.2_{18}, תלה *hang* Is 22_{24}, נטה *extend* Is 66_{12}, עטר pi. *crown with* Si 45_{25}, עזב *forsake* Is 10_{3}, פשׁט hi. *strip* Jb 19_{9}, כלה pi. *destroy* Is 10_{18}, אמר *say* Ps 29_{9} 145_{11}, שׁאל *ask* 2 C 1_{11}, נגד hi. *declare* Gn 45_{13} Is 66_{19}, ספר pi. *relate* Ps 19_{2} 96_{3}‖1 C 16_{24} Est 5_{11} 1QH 11_{6} (+ גְּבוּרָה *might*) 12_{30} 13_{11} fr. 2_{4} 4QShirShabb^{a} 2_{5} GnzPs 2_{11} 4_{25}, הגה *utter* 4QShirShabb^{d} 1.1_{36}, זמר pi. *sing praise* Ps 66_{2}, הלל pi. *praise* 4QShirShabb^{a} 2_{1}, צוה pi. *command* GnzPs 4_{4} (+ הוד *splendour,* הָדָר *honour*), גדל pi. *magnify* GnzPs 2_{18}, הדר *honour* 11QPs^{a} 24_{9}.

<CSTR> כְּבוֹד י׳ *glory of Y.* Ex $16_{7.10}$ 24_{17} $40_{34.35}$ Lv $9_{6.23}$ Nm $14_{10.21}$ 16_{19} 17_{7} 20_{6} 1 K 8_{11}‖2 C 5_{14} Is 35_{2} 40_{5} 58_{8} 60_{1} Ezk 1_{28} $3_{12.23}$ $10_{4.4.18}$ 11_{23} $43_{4.5}$ 44_{4} Hb 2_{14} Ps 104_{31} 138_{5} 2 C $7_{1.2.3}$ Si 42_{16} 4QJub^{a} 1_{2} ([כ]בוד יהו[ה]) 11QPs^{a} 18_{3}, [כ]בוד אדני *the glory of the Lord* Si $42_{16(M)}$, כְּבֹד אֱלֹהִים *the glory of God* Pr 25_{2} 4QapMos^{c} 2.2_{9} (כבוד אלוהים) MasShirShabb 2_{24}, כְּבוֹד אֱלֹהֵי *the glory of the*

God of Ezk 8$_4$ 9$_3$ 10$_{19}$ 11$_{22}$ 43$_2$ 1QSb 4$_{25}$ 4QShir^b 1$_7$ (אלוהי׳), כבוד אלוהותכ[ה] *glory of your divinity* 4QBer^b 2$_8$, כְּבוֹד־אֵל *the glory of God* Ps 19$_2$ 1QM 4$_6$ (|| צֶדֶק *righteousness*, מִשְׁפָּט *judgment*) 4$_8$ (|| רוֹמָם *exaltation*, גֹּדֶל *greatness*, תִּשְׁבֹּחַת *praise*) 1QS 10$_9$ 1QNoah 13$_1$ Mur 6 1$_6$, כבוד על[יון] *glory of the Most High* 4QParGenEx 2$_9$.

כְּבוֹד־שְׁמֶךָ *glory of your name* Ps 79$_9$, שְׁמוֹ *of his name* Ps 66$_2$ 96$_8$||1 C 16$_{29}$, כְּבוֹד הוֹדֶךָ *the glory of your majesty* Ps 145$_5$, הָדָר *of the honour of* Ps 145$_{12}$, כבוד נפלאותו *glory of his wonder* 4QShirShabb^f 3.2$_3$, מראה *of the vision* GnzPs 3$_{26}$, מראי *of the appearance of* 4QShirShabb^f 23.2$_8$, עולם *of eternity* Si 49$_{12}$ 1QH 13$_6$ 1QSb 3$_4$ (ע[ו]לם) 4Q 417 2.1$_{13}$ ([עולם]) 4Q418 126.2$_8$, עד *of eternity* 1QH 11$_{27}$ (|| שָׁלוֹם *peace*), נצח *of eternity* 4QHod^a 7.2$_9$.

כבוד איש *the glory of a man* Si 3$_{11}$, אביך *of your father* Si 3$_{12}$, אביו *of his father* Si 3$_{11}$, כְּבוֹד בְּנֵי *glory of the sons* of Israel Is 17$_3$, כבוד המלך *glory of the king* 4QShir Shabb^a 1.2$_9$ 4QShirShabb^f 23.1$_9$, מלך *of the king of* 4Q ShirShabb^a 2$_5$ 4QShirShabb^f 24$_3$, כְּבֹד מְלָכִים *the glory of kings* Pr 25$_2$, כבוד השופט *glory of the judge* 4QHod^a 7.1$_{19}$, כְּבוֹד מַלְכוּתְךָ *glory of your kingdom* Ps 145$_{11}$ 1QM 12$_7$ (מלכותכה), מַלְכוּתוֹ *of his kingdom* Est 1$_4$ 4QShir Shabb^d 1.1$_{32}$ 1.2$_{10}$ 4QShirShabb^f 23.1$_3$ 4QShir^a 1$_5$ Gnz Ps 4$_4$, גּוֹיִם *of the nations* Is 66$_{12}$, כבוד אדם *glory of Adam* 1QH 17$_{15}$ 1QS 4$_{23}$, כְּבוֹד יִשְׂרָאֵל *glory of Israel* Mc 1$_{15}$, יַעֲקֹב *of Jacob* Is 17$_4$, כבוד יהודה *glory of Judah* 4QpNah 3.3$_4$, כְּבוֹד הַלְּבָנוֹן *the glory of Lebanon* Is 35$_2$ 60$_{13}$, מוֹאָב *of Moab* Is 16$_{14}$, קֵדָר *of Kedar* Is 21$_{16}$, הַבַּיִת *of the house* Hg 2$_9$, כְּבוֹד בֵּית *weight of the house of* Is 22$_{24}$, כְּבוֹד בֵּיתוֹ *splendour of his house* Ps 49$_{17}$, כְּבוֹד יַעְרוֹ *glory of his forest* Is 10$_{18}$, כְּבוֹד עָשְׁרוֹ *splendour of his riches* Est 5$_{11}$, [כב]וד מעשיו *glory of his deeds* 11QShirShabb 1$_3$, שחקים *of the clouds* 4QPrEnosh 1.2$_8$, מרכבות *of the chariots of* 4QShirShabb^f 20.2$_{11}$.

אֵל־הַכָּבוֹד *the God of glory* Ps 29$_3$ MasShirShabb 2$_{13}$, אלהות כבודו *divinity of his glory*, i.e. his glorious divinity 4QShirShabb^d 1.1$_{33}$, מלאך *angel of* 4QShir^b 20.1$_2$, מלאכי כבוד *angels of glory* 4QShirShabb^f 17$_4$, כבודו *of his glory* 4QShir^b 35$_4$, איש כבוד *man of glory* 1QM 12$_{10}$ 4QM^b 1$_3$ ([איש]), מֶלֶךְ הַכָּבוֹד *the king of glory* Ps 24$_{7.8.9.10.10}$, מלך הכבוד *the king of glory* 1QM 12$_8$=19$_1$ 4QShir Shabb^d 1.1$_3$ ([מ]ל[ך]) 1.1$_{31}$ 1.2$_{25}$ 4QShirShabb^f 15.2$_7$ ([הכבו]ד) 11QShirShabb 1$_5$ 5$_6$ 4QShir^a 1$_1$ ([מ]לך) 4Q Shir^b 52.3$_4$ (הכב[ו]ד), רוח כבוד *spirit of glory* 4QShir Shabb^f 14.1$_1$ ([ר]וח כב[וד]) 23.2$_9$, א[ור] *light of* 4QShir Shabb^f 1$_5$, אור כבודו *light of his glory* 4QPrQuot 21$_1$, מאורות *luminaries of* 4QShir^b 2.1$_8$, מַרְאֵה כְּבוֹד *appearance of glory of* Ex 24$_{17}$, דְּמוּת כְּבוֹד־ *likeness of the glory of* Ezk 1$_{28}$, דמות כבוד[כה] *likeness of your glory* 4QDib Ham^a 8$_4$, נֹגַהּ כְּבוֹד *shining of the glory of* Ezk 10$_4$, הֲדַר *honour of* Ps 145$_5$, הדר כבודכה *honour of your glory* 1QH 12$_{15}$ 16$_3$ ([הדר כ]בודך), [ת]שבחות הכבוד *praises of glory* 4QMidrEschat^b 10$_1$, תהלי כבודכה *praises of your glory* 4QPrQuot 51$_9$, כבודו *of his glory* 4QShir^b 10$_7$, הודות כבודכה *thanksgiving of your glory* 4QShir^b 63.2$_3$, רנות כבודכה *cries of your glory* 4QPrQuot 29.8$_{10}$, עֵינֵי כְבוֹדוֹ *eyes of*, i.e. presence of, *his glory* Is 3$_8$, פי כבודכה *mouth*, i.e. word, *of your glory* 1QH 6$_{14}$, רגלי *feet of* 4Q Ber^a 1.2$_1$ (+ יְקָר *honour*), קול הכבו[ד] *sound of glory* 4Q ShirShabb^f 18$_4$.

מלכות כבוד *kingdom of the glory of* 4Q ShirShabb^f 24$_3$, כב[וד]כה *of your glory*, i.e. your glorious kingdom 4Q ShirShabb^b 14.1$_6$, כבודו *of his glory*, i.e. his glorious kingdom 4QShirShabb^d 1.1$_{25}$ 4QShir Shabb^f 23.2$_{12}$, [ש]מי כבודמה *heaven of their glory*, i.e. their glorious heaven 4QBer^b 2$_3$ (+ פֶּלֶא *wonder*), רקיע כבודו *firmament of his glory* 4QShirShabb^f 23.1$_7$, מִשְׁכַּן כְּבוֹדֶךָ *dwelling place of your glory* Ps 26$_8$, זבול כבודכה *dwelling place of your glory* 1QM 12$_2$, מעון כבוד *habitation of glory* 1QS 10$_3$ 4QShir^a 1$_4$ ([מע]ון), מעון כבודכה *habitation of your glory* 1QH fr. 9$_7$, בתי כבודם *houses of their glory* 4QShir^a 8$_{11}$, היכלי כבודו *temples of his glory* 11QShirShabb 1$_7$, דביר *inner sanctuary of* 4QShirShabb^a 1.1$_4$, דבירי כבוד *inner sanctuaries of glory* 4QShirShabb^f 14.1$_6$ ([ד]בירי) 11QShirShabb 3$_3$, פתחי *entrances of* 4Q ShirShabb^f 23.1$_8$, שערי *gates of* 4QPrQuot 33.10$_7$ ([שערי כ]בוד) 51$_5$ ([כבו]ד), כִּסֵּא כָבוֹד *seat of honour* 1 S 2$_8$ Is 22$_{23}$ Jr 17$_{12}$ 4QpIsa^a 8$_{19}$ ([כ]סא), כִּסֵּא כְבוֹדֶךָ *throne of your glory* Jr 14$_{21}$, כסאי כבוד *thrones of the glory of* 4Q ShirShabb^f 23.1$_3$ (corrected from כסאיכה בוד), כסאי כבודו *thrones of his glory* 11QShirShabb 1$_6$, מושב כבוד *seat of honour* Si 7$_4$, כבודו *of his glory* 4QShirShabb^f 20.2$_9$, מושבי כבוד *seats of glory* 4QShirShabb^f 20.2$_4$, שולחן *table of* 1QM 2$_6$, מקוי *stores of* 1QH 12$_{29}$ (|| דַּעַת *knowledge*) 4QShir^b 52.3$_2$

(הכבוד), מעין *fount of* 1QS 11$_{7}$, פלגי כבודכה *channels of your glory* 4QBen 1$_{5}$, [יס]וד כבודך *foundation of your glory* 1QH 16$_{9}$, ארץ כבוד *land of glory* 4QDibHam^{a} 8$_{7}$.

מַרְכְּבוֹת כְּבוֹדֶךָ *chariots of your glory*, i.e. your glorious chariots Is 22$_{18}$ 4QBer^{a} 1.2$_{2}$ (כבודכה), מרכבות כבודו *chariots of his glory* 4QShirShabb^{f} 20.2$_{3.5}$, [ג]לגלי כבודו *wheels of his glory* 4QShirShabb^{f} 20.2$_{10}$, שבילי כבוד *paths of glory* 1QH 7$_{15}$ (+ שָׁלוֹם *peace*), זִיז כְּבוֹדָהּ *teat of her glory*, i.e. her glorious breast Is 66$_{11}$, כבודך *of your glory* 11QPs^{a} 22$_{5}$, פארת כבוד *branch of glory* 1QH 8$_{22}$, שֹׂבַע ... כָּבוֹד *satisfaction of ... honour* 1 C 29$_{28}$, שלמות כבוד *retribution of glory* 4QpsEzek^{e} 62.2$_{2}$, רחמי כבודו *compassion of his glory* 4QShirShabb^{f} 13$_{2}$, ברכות כבוד *blessings of the glory of* 11QShirShabb q$_{4}$, הפלא כבודו appar. *wonder of his glory* 4QAges^{b} 1.2$_{3}$, הוד *splendour of* 4QShirShabb^{f} 13$_{4}$, עֹשֶׁר כְּבוֹד *riches of the glory of* Est 1$_{4}$, רב כבוד *abundance of glory* Si 44$_{2}$, רוב כבודו *abundance of his glory* 4Q418 126.2$_{9}$ (+ כֹּחַ *strength*, טוב *goodness*), כבודך *of your glory* 4QBark^{a} 1.2$_{14}$ ([ר]וב) 11QPs^{a} 22$_{4}$, מדת כבודכה *measure of your glory* 4Q418 159.2$_{6}$, נחלת *inheritance of* 4Q416 2.3$_{12}$, כליל *crown of* 1QS 4$_{7}$ 1QH 9$_{25}$, פארי כבדו *crowns of his glory* 4Q408 1$_{5}$, בגדי כבוד *garments of glory* Si 6$_{31}$ 50$_{11}$, רוקמת *variegated stuff of* 4QShirShabb^{f} 20.2$_{11}$, עדי *ornaments of* 1QM 12$_{15}$=19$_{7}$, לבני כבודם *bricks of their glory*, i.e. their glorious bricks 4QShirShabb^{f} 19$_{6}$ ([כ]בודם) 11QShirShabb f$_{4}$ ([ל]בני), שם כבוד *name of glory*, i.e. glorious name 4Q Ber^{a} 16$_{1}$, *name of glory of* 4QBer^{b} 2$_{8}$ MasShirShabb 2$_{24}$ GnzPs 2$_{4}$ 3$_{8}$ 4$_{14}$, שֵׁם כְּבוֹדֶךָ *the name of your glory* Ne 9$_{5}$ 4QBer^{a} 7.1$_{7}$ (כבודכה) 4QBer^{b} 5$_{11}$ (שם כבו[דכה]), שֵׁם כְּבוֹדוֹ *name of his glory* Ps 72$_{19}$ 4QShir Shabb^{d} 1.1$_{29}$ Gnz Ps 2$_{5}$ 3$_{8}$ 4$_{15}$, צעד כבו[דו] *step of his glory* 4QMyst^{c} 6$_{2}$.

מועדי כבוד *festivals of glory*, i.e. glorious festivals 4QBer^{a} 1.2$_{10}$ 4QPrQuot 1.3$_{13}$ (כ[בוד]) 1.3$_{15}$ (כב[וד]) 4QPrFêtes^{b} 4QPrFêtes^{b} 13$_{2}$, חג כבוד *festival of glory* 4QPrQuot 33.11$_{23}$, [י]מי כבודכה *days of your glory* 4QRitPur 1.12$_{11}$, שבועות כבודו *weeks of his glory* 4QPrQuot 42$_{5}$, חֵקֶר כְּבֹדָם *searching of their glory* Pr 25$_{27}$, בשת כבוד *shame (worthy) of glory* Si 4$_{21(A)}$, בדני *figures of* 4QShirShabb^{f} 19$_{2}$ ([בדני]) 11QShirShabb j$_{2}$ ([ב]דני כב[וד]), צורות *images of* 4QShirShabb^{f} 19$_{6}$, תבנית *form of* 4QShirShabb^{d} 1.2$_{3}$, מראת כבו[ו]ד *vision of glory* 1QLitPr3.2$_{6}$, מראה כבודך *vision of your glory* GnzPs 2$_{24}$, דְּבַר כְּבוֹד־ *word of*, i.e. account of, *the glory of* Ps 79$_{9}$, דברי כבוד *words of the glory of* 4QShirShabb^{f} 3.2$_{3}$ 4QDibHam^{a} 2.7$_{3}$ ([דב]רי), דברי כבודו *words of his glory* 4QapPent 9$_{4}$, תעודות כבודכה *testimonies of your glory* 1QM 13$_{8}$, מעשי כבודו *works of his glory* 4QShir Shabb^{f} 23.2$_{12}$ 4QPoet^{b} 1$_{3}$ MasShirShabb 1$_{6}$, [מחשבת כבו]דכה *plan of your glory* 1QM 14$_{14}$, מחשבת כבודו *plan of his glory* 1QS 3$_{16}$, מזמת כבוד[ו] *plan of his glory* 4Q ShirShabb^{c} 3.2$_{13}$, יסורי כבוד *regulations of glory* 1QLitPr 3.2$_{7}$, [ב]רית כבודו *covenant of his glory* 1Q54 1$_{2}$ (others [גבו]רות *mighty acts of*), חכמת *wisdom of* 1QS 4$_{18}$, שכל *wisdom of* 4QShirShabb^{f} 23.2$_{13}$ ([כב]ודו), בינות *understanding of* 4QShirShabb^{a} 1.1$_{6}$, אמת *truth of* 1QH 3$_{35}$, טהרת כבוד *purity of glory* 1QS 4$_{5}$, רום *height of* 1QS 10$_{12}$ (|| קֹדֶשׁ *holiness*) 4QBer^{a} 1.2$_{4}$ (+ הָדָר *honour*, קֹדֶשׁ), מרומי כ[בודו] *heights of his glory* 11QShirShabb 1$_{1}$, אף כבודו *anger of his glory* 4QShirShabb^{f} 23.1$_{12}$, מפלג כבודו *section of his glory* 4QPrQuot 1.3$_{7}$, קץ כבודכה *time of your glory* 1QH 12$_{22}$, עדן כבוד *Eden of glory* 1QH 8$_{20}$, כָּל־כָּבוֹד *all the glory* Is 4$_{5}$ 21$_{16}$ 1QH 11$_{8}$ (כול), כֹּל כְּבוֹד *all glory of* Is 22$_{24}$ Si 40$_{27}$ 1QH 17$_{15}$ (כול) 1QS 4$_{23}$ (כול) Mur 6 1$_{6}$, כָּל־כְּבוֹדִי *all my glory* Gn 45$_{13}$, כול כבודכה *all your glory* 1QH 12$_{30}$ fr. 2$_{4}$ fr. 5$_{9}$, כָּל־כְּבוֹדוֹ *all his glory* Is 8$_{7}$ 4QMyst^{c} 4$_{3}$ (כול).

<ADJ> רִאשׁוֹן *former* Hg 2$_{3}$, רַב *great* 4QTanḥ 8$_{13}$, זֶה *this* Gn 31$_{1}$.

<PREP> לְ of direction, *to*, + יסף hi. *add* 1 C 17$_{18}$, שׁוב hi. *restore* 4Q416 2.3$_{9}$; of benefit, *to, for* 1QS 10$_{9}$ perh. 1QNoah 13$_{1}$ 1QSb 4$_{25}$ perh. 1Q38 2$_{2}$ perh. 4QparaKings 50$_{4}$ perh. 4QShirShabb^{e} 11$_{3}$ perh. 4QDibHam^{a} 7$_{5}$ GnzPs 3$_{16}$ (|| תִּפְאֶרֶת *beauty*), + עשׂה *make* Ex 28$_{2.40}$ (|| תִּפְאֶרֶת) 1QH 10$_{12}$ fr. 2$_{5}$ ([לכ]בודכה), ברא *create* Is 43$_{7}$ 4QDibHam^{a} 1.3$_{4}$, כון pol. *be prepared* Si 49$_{12}$, hi. *establish* 1QH 6$_{10}$ 7$_{24}$ ([הכי]נותה) 18$_{22}$, נטה *stretch* 1QH 1$_{10}$, נטע *plant* 1QH 8$_{5}$ ([נטעת]ה), פלא hi. *make wonderful* 1QH fr. 2$_{16}$, אור hi. *shine* 1QM 1$_{9}$ (+ שָׁלוֹם *peace*, בְּרָכָה *blessing*, שִׂמְחָה *joy*, אֹרֶךְ *length* of days), יפע hi. *shine out* 1QH 11$_{27}$; of possession, *of, (belonging) to* 1QH 9$_{17}$ (|| חָכְמָה *wisdom*, + גְּבוּרָה *might*); *as*, + היה *be* Is 4$_{2}$ (|| צְבִי *beauty*) Si 51$_{17}$; *any* 2 C 26$_{18}$; introducing object, + ידה hi. *confess* 4QShirShabb^{d} 1.1$_{38}$.

בְּ of instrument, *by (means of), with*, + קדשׁ ni. *be*

sanctified Ex 29$_{43}$, pi. *sanctify* 11QT 29$_8$, שׁרת pi. *minister* Si 45$_7$, שׂמח *rejoice* Si 35$_2$; of accompaniment, *in, with,* or of cause, *on account of* Si 43$_{12(M)}$ 50$_{13}$ 1QM 12$_7$ 4QM[a] 11.1$_{14}$, perh. 1QSb 3$_4$ ([בכבו]ד) 4QMyst[c] 4$_3$ 4QBapt 12$_9$ ([בכבודכ]ה) 4Q418 126.2$_8$ 4QHod[a] 3.1$_2$ 4QShir[b] 81$_5$ 95$_2$, + אדר ni. *be majestic* Si 43$_{11}$ (בכ[בוד]), הדר ni. *be glorious* Si 43$_{11(Bmg)}$ (בכ[בוד]), נשׂא ni. *be exalted* 1Q Noah 13$_2$ ([י]נשׂא; || הָדָר *honour,* תִּפְאֶרֶת *beauty*), דמה *be like* Ezk 31$_{18}$ 4QM[a] 11.1$_{15}$, רום *be raised* Ps 112$_9$, גבר htp. *display might* 1QH 18$_8$ ([בכבו]דכה), חזק htp. *show oneself strong* Si 3$_{12}$, שׁכב *lie down* Is 14$_{18}$, ראה *see* Hg 2$_3$, ni. *appear* Ps 102$_{17}$, יפע hi. *shine out* 1QH 9$_{26}$, נתן *give,* i.e. place Si 44$_{19}$ 47$_{20}$, פאר pi. *endow* Si 45$_8$, קדשׁ *sanctify* 1QSb 3$_4$, htp. *sanctify oneself* 4QDibHam[a] 3.2$_6$, נקף hi. *surround* boundary Si 43$_{12(B)}$, אמר htp. *boast* Is 61$_6$, עלז *exult* Ps 149$_5$, גיל *rejoice* 4QShirShabb[f] 23.1$_7$, שׂמח *rejoice* 11QPs[a] 22$_{15}$; introducing object, + נחל hi. *cause to inherit* 1QH 17$_{15}$, ידע *know* 4Q417 2.1$_{13}$; בטח בְּ *trust in* GnzPs 3$_{26}$ (+ שֵׁם *name,* דָּבָר *word,* דֶּרֶךְ *way*); נבט בְּ hi. *look at* 1QH 10$_{20}$.

כְּ *as* Ezk 3$_{23}$, + היה *be* Is 17$_3$ Zc 2$_9$.

מִן of direction, *from,* + ירד *go down* Jr 48$_{18}$, מלא pi. *fill* Si 36$_{19}$, מנע *withhold* Nm 24$_{11}$; of comparison, *more (than)* Ec 10$_1$, + גבר *be mighty* 1QpHab 11$_{12}$ (:: קָלוֹן *contempt*); of agent, *by (means of), with,* + אור hi. *shine* Ezk 43$_2$; privative, *without,* + שׂבע *be sated* Hb 2$_{16}$ (:: קָלוֹן *contempt*).

עַל *over, upon* Is 4$_5$ Hb 2$_{16}$, + גיל *rejoice* Ho 10$_5$ (or em. ילל hi. *wail*); *concerning* 4QpsHod[c] 2$_2$; עִם *with,* + הלך htp. *go* 4QShirShabb[f] 20.2$_{11}$; בְּתוֹךְ *within,* + חזק hi. *hold* 4QShirShabb[f] 23.2$_8$; לִפְנֵי *before* Pr 15$_{33}$ 18$_{12}$ Si 45$_{25}$, + חזק htp. *show oneself strong* Si 42$_{17}$, יצב htp. *stand* 1QH 10$_{11}$; מִלִּפְנֵי *from before* 4QapMos[c] 2.2$_9$ GnzPs 4$_{26}$; לְנֶגֶד *in the presence of* 1QH 10$_{10}$ (+ גְּבוּרָה *might*), + יצב htp. *stand* GnzPs 1$_3$; בַּעֲבוּר *for the sake of* 1QpHab 10$_{11}$, + פלא hi. *do wonders* 1QH 4$_{28}$; לְמַעַן *for the sake of,* + טהר pi. *purify* 1QH 11$_{10}$, כבד pi. *honour* 4Q416 2.3$_{18}$, שׂים *place* 4QShir[b] 28$_2$ ([ש]מתה); לְפִי *according to,* + ישׁב *sit* 1QSa 2$_{14.15.17}$, ברך pi. *bless* 1QSa 2$_{21}$ (... יבר[כו] [לפי]), הלך htp. *walk* 4QShir[b] 2.1$_{10}$; תַּחַת *under,* + יקד *burn* Is 10$_{16}$; מִתַּחַת *from under* 4QShirShabb[f] 46$_3$.

<COLL> וְיִמָּלֵא כְבוֹד־י׳ *and* all the earth *shall be filled with the glory of Y.* Nm 14$_{21}$, וְיִמָּלֵא כְבוֹדוֹ אֶת־כֹּל הָאָרֶץ *and may the whole earth be filled with his glory* Ps 72$_{19}$, מלא ארצכה כבוד *fill your land with glory* 1QM 12$_{12}$=19$_4$ (|| בְּרָכָה *blessing*), וּמִלֵּאתִי אֶת־הַבַּיִת הַזֶּה כָּבוֹד *and I will fill this house with splendour* Hg 2$_7$, וְכָבוֹד וְהָדָר תְּעַטְּרֵהוּ *and you have crowned him with glory and honour* Ps 8$_6$ (|| הָדָר *honour*), שִׂימוּ כָבוֹד תְּהִלָּתוֹ *make his praise glorious* Ps 66$_2$, כָּבוֹד תִּקָּחֵנִי *you will receive me with glory* Ps 73$_{24}$, אֲזַמְּרָה אַף־כְּבוֹדִי *I will sing even with my soul* Ps 108$_2$, הוד כבוד ותהלת עז *majesty, glory and mighty praise* Si 45$_{12}$, כבודו משׂעיר *his glory from Seir* 1QpMic 12$_2$.

Also Si 37$_{26(C)}$ 45$_{20}$ 47$_8$ (כ[בוד]) 1QH fr. 4$_{19}$ fr. 17$_5$ fr. 56$_2$ 1QpMic 6$_2$ 1QSb 5$_{18}$ 4QCommGenC 9$_3$ 4QMyst[a] 63$_4$ 75$_2$ 4QapPent 9$_{3.4}$ 4QapPs[b] 18$_4$ 4QShirShabb[a] 1.1$_9$ 21$_2$ ([כבו]ד) 4QShirShabb[b] 63$_{.6}$ 16$_4$ ([כבו]דו) 31$_2$ ([כבו]דו) 34$_2$ ([כב]וד) 4QShirShabb[c] 3.1$_3$ 8$_5$ (הנבוד perh. error for הכבוד) 4QShirShabb[d] 1.2$_4$ 4QShir Shabb[f] 15.2$_5$ 17$_8$ 20.1$_3$ 20.2$_7$ 35$_2$ 46$_1$ 50$_2$ 73$_2$ 4Q416 2.4$_{11}$ 4Q417 20$_5$ 4Q418 84$_3$ ([כב]ודה) 255$_1$ 4Q423 8$_4$ 4Qsap HymnA 1.1$_1$ ([כב]וד) 4QHod[a] 7.2$_{13}$ 4QBark[a] 1.1$_7$ 4Q Bark[e] 54$_a$ 4QpsHod[b] 2$_1$ ([כבו]ד) 3.1$_{19}$ ([כ]בודכה) 3.1$_{24}$ 4QPrayer[m] 1.2$_6$ 4Q476 1$_6$ 3.2$_5$ ([כבו]ד) 4QM[a] 11.1$_{13}$ perh. 4QRitMar 9$_{15}$ ([כבו]דו) 14$_5$ 18$_1$ 22$_2$ 57$_1$ 95$_2$ 99$_5$ 108$_1$ ([כב]ודכה) 155$_5$ 156$_3$ ([כ]בודו) 195$_1$ ([כבו]ד) 287$_2$ ([כ]בוד) 4QPrQuot 15.6$_4$ 20.6$_1$ ([כבו]דם) 24$_2$ ([כב]ודו) 37.12$_{22}$ 40.2$_{5.8}$ 45$_4$ 51$_{18}$ ([כ]בודו) 89$_2$ ([כ]בודו) 153$_1$ ([כ]בודו) 4QDibHam[a] 1.7$_{12}$ 3.2$_{18}$ ([כבו]ד) 47$_1$ 4QPr Fêtes[c] 108$_2$ ([כבו]ד) 131.2$_2$ ([כ]בודכה) 278$_1$ 4QShir[b] 90$_1$ ([הכבו]ד) 111$_5$ 124$_2$ 208$_1$ 4QRitPur 51.2$_5$ 6QapSamKgs 24.2$_2$ ([כבו]ד) 66$_2$ ([כ]בוד) 6QHymn 2$_2$ ([כבו]ד) 12$_1$ ([כבו]ד) 11QHymn[a] 1$_4$ 11QShirShabb 1$_1$ ([כב]ודו) k$_6$ ([כבו]ד) l$_4$ s$_1$.

<SYN> תִּפְאֶרֶת *beauty,* צְבִי *beauty,* הָדָר *honour,* רוֹמָם *exaltation,* גֹּדֶל *greatness,* תִּשְׁבַּחַת *praise,* בְּרָכָה *blessing,* עֹשֶׁר *riches,* עֹז *strength,* כֹּחַ *strength,* קֹדֶשׁ *holiness,* צֶדֶק *righteousness,* אֱמֶת *truth,* חָכְמָה *wisdom,* דַּעַת *knowledge,* מִשְׁפָּט *judgment.* <ANT> קָלוֹן *contempt.**

⇒ כבד *be heavy.*

[כִּבּוּד] n.[m.] **heaviness,** <CSTR> [כי]בוד לב *heaviness of heart* 4QSap[b] 24$_2$.

⇒ כבד *be heavy.*

כְּבוּדָּה 3 n.f. **wealth** (Ps 45$_{14}$), **property** (Jg 18$_{21}$), <NOM CL> כָּל־כְּבוּדָּה בַת־מֶלֶךְ פְּנִימָה perh. they will seek your favour with *all kinds of wealth; the daughter of the king is within* Ps 45$_{14}$ (or em. כָּל־כְּבוּדָּה פְּנִינִים with *all glory, corals*). <OBJ> שִׂים *place* Jg 18$_{21}$ (+ מִקְנֶה *livestock*, טַף *infants*). <CSTR> כָּל־כְּבוּדָּה *all wealth* Ps 45$_{14}$. <APP> מִטָּה כְּבוּדָּה *couch, wealth,* i.e. a sumptuous couch Ezk 23$_{41}$ (or em. רְבוּדָה *extended* couch). <PREP> עַל *upon,* + ישׁב *sit* Ezk 23$_{41}$.*

⇒ כבד *be heavy.*

כָּבוּל 2 pl.n. **Cabul—1.** city on border of Asher, perh. ident. with Kābûl 4 km SE of Akko, Jos 19$_{27}$. **2.** area of 20 cities given by Solomon to Hiram, 1 K 9$_{13}$, <CSTR> אֶרֶץ כָּבוּל *land of,* i.e. area of, *Cabul* 1 K 9$_{13}$. <PREP> אֶל *to,* + יצא *go out* Jos 19$_{27}$.

כַּבּוֹן 1 pl.n. **Cabbon**—in Judah near Lachish, <SUBJ> היה *be* Jos 15$_{40}$. <APP> עִיר *city* Jos 15$_{40}$.

[כִּבּוּס] 0.0.1 n.[m.] **washing** of garments, <CSTR> טמא כבוס *unclean one of washing,* i.e. unclean person with washed garments CD 11$_{22}$.

⇒ כבס *wash.*

כְּבִיר 2 n.m. **braided article**—cstr. כְּבִיר—perh. **cushion** or **quilt**, made from goats' hair 1 S 19$_{13.16}$, <NOM CL> כְּבִיר הָעִזִּים מְרַאֲשֹׁתָיו *the cushion of goats' hair was at its head* 1 S 19$_{16}$. <OBJ> שִׂים *place* 1 S 19$_{13}$. <CSTR> כְּבִיר הָעִזִּים *the cushion of goats' hair* 1 S 19$_{13.16}$.

כַּבִּיר 10.0.1 adj. **strong**—pl. כַּבִּירִים, Q כבירות—**strong, powerful, mighty, 1.** used attributively of מַיִם *water* Is 17$_{12}$ 28$_{2}$, רוּחַ *wind* Jb 8$_{2}$.

2. used as predicative adj. or noun, **strong (one), powerful (deed),** <NOM CL> אֵל כַּבִּיר *God is a mighty one* Jb 36$_{5}$ (unless §3), שְׁאָר ... לוֹא כַבִּיר *the remnant will ... not be powerful* Is 16$_{14}$, כַּבִּיר מֵאָבִיךָ יָמִים *whose days are greater than your father,* i.e. who is older than your father Jb 15$_{10}$, כַּבִּיר כֹּחַ לֵב *the strength of (his) heart,* i.e. (his) understanding, *is mighty* Jb 36$_{5}$ (unless §3). <OBJ> מצא *find* Jb 31$_{25}$, רעע *break* Jb 34$_{24}$, רשׁע hi. *pronounce guilty* Jb 34$_{17}$ (unless §3).

3. perh. as divine title, **the aged one,*** הֶן־אֵל כַּבִּיר וְלֹא יִמְאָס כַּבִּיר כֹּחַ לֵב *behold, God, the aged one, the omnipotent one who is contemptuous, the aged one, mighty of heart* Jb 36$_{5}$ (if em. לֹא *not* contemptuous), וְאִם צַדִּיק כַּבִּיר תַּרְשִׁיעַ *and if you were righteous, would you condemn the aged one?* Jb 34$_{17}$. Also 4QTohD 1$_{3}$.

⇒ כבר *be great.*

כֶּבֶל 2.0.2 n.m. **fetter**—pl. Q כבלים; cstr. כַּבְלֵי—<OBJ> נתן *give,* i.e. place MurEpBarC^{a}$_{5}$. <CSTR> כַּבְלֵי בַרְזֶל *fetters of iron* Ps 149$_{8}$. <PREP> בְּ of place, instrument, *in, by (means of), with,* + אסר *bind* Ps 149$_{8}$, לכד ni. *be caught* 1QH 8$_{34}$, ענה pi. *force* Ps 105$_{18}$.

[כַּבְלוּלָה] 0.0.2 pr.n.[f.] **Cablulah,** in deed of sale as occupant of neighbouring land, <NOM CL> צפון כבלולה *in the north is Cablulah* Mur 30 1$_{4}$ 2$_{17}$.

כבס 48.0.30 vb. **wash—Qal** 3 Ptc. כּוֹבֵס—ptc. as noun, **fuller,*** <CSTR> שְׂדֵה כוֹבֵס *field of the fuller* 2 K 18$_{17}$||Is 36$_{2}$ Is 7$_{3}$.

Pi. 41.0.29 Pf. כִּבֵּס (כִּבֶּס), כִּבְּסוּ (Q כיבסו), כִּבַּסְתֶּם; impf. יְכַבֵּס, תְּכַבְּסֵנִי, תְּכַבְּסִי, Q יכבסו; + waw וְכִבֶּס; וַיְכַבְּסוּ; impv. כַּבְּסִי (כַּבְּסֵנִי); ptc. מְכַבְּסִים—**wash, launder, clean.**

<SUBJ> אֱלֹהִים *God* Ps 51$_{4.9}$, עַם *people* Ex 19$_{10.14}$, Israelite(s) Lv 13$_{58}$ Jr 2$_{22}$ 1QM 14$_{2}$ 11QT 49$_{13}$, Judah Gn 49$_{11}$, Jerusalem Jr 4$_{14}$, Aaron Lv 6$_{20}$, Mephibosheth 2 S 19$_{25}$, אָדָם *human being* Lv 13$_{6}$ 11QT 50$_{8}$, אִישׁ *man* Lv 13$_{34}$ 15$_{5}$ Nm 31$_{24}$ 4QTohA 1.1$_{3}$ 1.2$_{9}$ ([אי]שׁ) 11QT 45$_{8.9}$ (both [אי]שׁ) 45$_{15}$ appar. CD 11$_{4}$ (or em. כיבסו *they washed* to כובסו *they were washed,* i.e. pu.), נֶפֶשׁ *self* Lv 17$_{15.16}$, בֵּן *son* Lv 6$_{20}$, כֹּהֵן *priest* Nm 19$_{7}$, לֵוִי Levite Nm 8$_{7.21}$, טָהוֹר *purified one* Lv 15$_{8}$, טָמֵא *unclean one* Nm 19$_{19}$ 4Q zOrd^{c} 1.1$_{6.9}$ (טמא[ט]).

ישׁב ptc. *one who sits* Lv 15$_{6}$, שׁכב ptc. *one who lies down* Lv 14$_{47}$, אסף ptc. *one who gathers* Nm 19$_{10}$, נגע ptc. *one who touches* Lv 15$_{7.21.22.27}$ 4QTohA 1.1$_{9}$ 11QT 51$_{3}$, נזה hi. ptc. *one who sprinkles* Nm 19$_{21}$, נשׂא ptc. *one who raises* Lv 11$_{25.28.40}$ 15$_{10}$ 11QT 51$_{4}$, שׁלח pi. ptc. *one who releases* Lv 16$_{26}$, זוב ptc. *one who has a discharge* Lv

15_{13} 4QDg 1.2_6 ([הזב]) 4QTohA 1.1_5, שׂרף ptc. *one who burns* Lv 16_{28} Nm 19_8, אכל ptc. *one who eats* Lv 11_{40} 14_{47}, טהר pi. ptc. *one who is pronounced clean* Lv $14_{8.9}$, כֹּל *anyone* Lv 15_{11} 11QT $49_{17.18.20}$, אֲשֶׁר *one who* perh. 4QTohA 1.2_1 (ר[אש]); subj. not specified, Lv 13_{54} Ml 3_2 4QMMT B_{66} 11QT $50_{13.14.15}$.

<OBJ> worshipper Ps $51_{4.9}$, לְבוּשׁ *garment* Gn 49_{11}, בֶּגֶד *garment* Lv $11_{25.28.40.40}$ $13_{6.34.58}$ $14_{8.9.47.47}$ 15_{5+8t} $16_{26.28}$ 17_{15} Nm $8_{7.21}$ $19_{7.8.10.19.21}$ 31_{24} 2 S 19_{25} 1QH 14_2 4QDa 6.1c3 4QDg 1.2_6 (בנ[ד]יו) 4QTohA 1.$1_{3.5}$ 1.2_8 (כ[בס] [בגדיו]) 4QRitPur 11.10_3 51.2_7 (יכס *let him cover* corrected to יכבס) 11QT $45_{8.9.15}$ $49_{17.20}$ $50_{8.13.14.15}$ $51_{3.4}$, שִׂמְלָה *mantle* Ex $19_{10.14}$, שַׂלְמָה *garment* 11QT 49_{18}, כְּלִי *vessel* Lv 13_{58} 11QT 49_{20}, שְׁתִי *woven garment* Lv 13_{58}, עֵרֶב *woven garment* Lv 13_{58}, לֵב *heart* Jr 4_{14}, מַנְעוּל *lock* 11QT 49_{13}, מְזוּזָה *doorpost* 11QT 49_{13}, מַשְׁקוֹף *lintel* 11QT 49_{13}, אָסַף *threshold* 11QT 49_{13}, אֲשֶׁר *that which* Lv 13_{54}.

<PREP> בְּ of place, time, *in, at,* + מָקוֹם *place* Lv 6_{20}, יוֹם *day* 4QOrdc 1.1_3 (ב[יו]ם) 11QT $45_{8.9.15}$ $49_{17.20}$ $50_{13.14.15}$; of instrument, *by (means of), with,* + יַיִן *wine* Gn 49_{11}, מַיִם *water* Nm 19_8 4QTohA 1.2_8 ([כ]בס) 1.2_9 4QOrdc 1.$1_{6.9}$ 4QRitPur 11.10_3 ([במ]ים) 51.2_7 (יכס *let him cover* corrected to יכבס) 11QT 49_{13} appar. CD 11_4 (or em.; see Subj.), נֶתֶר *natron* Jr 2_{22}.

מִן of direction, *from,* + עָוֹן *iniquity* Ps 51_4, רָעָה *evil* Jr 4_{14}.

<COLL> כבס ‖ טהר *be clean* Lv $13_{6.34}$ 14_8 15_{13}, + טהר 4QOrdc 1.$1_{6.9}$ 11QT 49_{20} $50_{8.15}$ $51_{3.4}$, טהר htp. *cleanse oneself* Nm 8_7, ‖ רחץ *wash* Lv $14_{8.9}$ $15_{5.6.7.8.10.11.13.21.22.27}$ $16_{26.28}$ $17_{15.15.16}$ Nm $19_{7.8.19}$ 1QH 14_2 4QTohA 1.$1_{3.5}$ 1.2_1 4QOrdc 1.$1_{3.6.9}$ 11QT $45_{8.9.15}$ $49_{17.18.20}$ $50_{8.13.14.15}$ $51_{3.4}$, כבס + שׁוף pass. *be rubbed* 1QH 11_4, כבס :: טמא *be unclean* Lv $11_{25.28.40}$ $15_{5.6.7.8.10.11.21.22.27}$ $17_{15.15}$ Nm $19_{7.8.10}$.

<SYN> טהר *be clean,* רחץ *wash.* **<ANT>** טמא *be unclean.* Also 4QTohA 1.2_9.

Pu. 2 Pf. כֻּבַּס—**be washed, <SUBJ>** בֶּגֶד *garment* Lv 13_{58} 15_{17} CD 11_4 (if em. כיבסו *they washed* to כובסו *they were washed*), כְּלִי *clothing* Lv 13_{58}, שְׁתִי *woven garment* Lv 13_{58}, עֵרֶב *woven garment* Lv 13_{58}, עוֹר *skin* Lv 15_{17}. **<PREP>** בְּ of instrument, *by (means of), with,* + מַיִם *water* Lv 15_{17} CD 11_4 (if em.; see Subj.). **<COLL>** וְכֻבַּס שֵׁנִית *then it shall be washed a second time* Lv 13_{58}.

Htp. 0.0.1 Impf. Q יתכבסו—**be washed, <SUBJ>** בֶּגֶד *garment* 11QT 49_{16}, שַׂק *sack* 11QT 49_{16}, עוֹר *skin* 11QT 49_{16}.

Hotp. 2 Pf. הֻכַּבֵּס—**be washed, <SUBJ>** בֶּגֶד *garment* Lv $13_{55.56}$, כְּלִי *clothing* Lv $13_{55.56}$, שְׁתִי *woven garment* Lv $13_{55.56}$, עֵרֶב *woven garment* Lv $13_{55.56}$.*

⇒ כִּבּוּס *washing.*

כבר 2.0.1 vb. **be great—Hi.** 2.0.1 Pf. Q הכביר; impf. יַכְבִּר; ptc. מַכְבִּיר—**1. multiply,** בִּבְלִי־דַעַת מִלִּין יַכְבִּר *without knowledge, he multiplies words* Jb 35_{16} (mss כבד hi. *make heavy*). **2.** perh. ptc. as noun, **abundance,** יִתֶּן־אֹכֶל לְמַכְבִּיר *he gives food in abundance* (unless *he gives food as one who multiplies,* i.e. generously) Jb 36_{31}. Also 1Q36 1_4.

Pi. 1 Inf. כַּבֵּר—inf. as adverb, **thoroughly,*** וְאֶצְרֹף כַּבֹּר סִיגָיִךְ *I shall thoroughly refine your dross* Is 1_{25} (unless כַּבֹּר = so that it becomes *like soap*).

⇒ כַּבִּיר *strong.*

כְּבָר I 9.0.2 adv. **already, now—1. already, long ago,** before pf. of היה *be* Ec 1_{10} 3_{15}, מות *die* 4_2, אבד *die* 9_6, קרא ni. *be called* 6_{10}, ספר pi. *relate* 4QTobe 4_5, רצה *desire* Ec 9_7, עשׂה *do* 2_{12}, perh. שׁכח ni. *be forgotten* 2_{16} (but see §3); ptc. of ידע *know* 4QTobe 4_3 (כבר אני יודע *I already know*). **2. now,** in nom. cl., כְּבָר הוּא *it is (happening) now* Ec 3_{15}. **3.** perh. as prep., **during,** בְּשֶׁכְּבָר הַיָּמִים הַבָּאִים הַכֹּל נִשְׁכָּח *for during the days to come, everything will have been forgotten* (or, as §1, *everything has already been forgotten [in] the days to come*) Ec 2_{16}.

כְּבָר II 8.0.2 pl.n. **Chebar**—river or canal near Babylon, linked to Euphrates, **<CSTR>** נְהַר־כְּבָר *river of Chebar* Ezk $1_{1.3}$ $3_{15.23}$ $10_{15.20.22}$ 43_3 4QpsEzeke 6_{5_4} (ר[נה]). **<PREP>** עַל *beside,* + זעק *cry out* 4QpsMosd 1.2_3 ([זועקים]).

כְּבָרָה I 1 n.f. **sieve—<PREP>** בְּ of instrument, *by (means of), with,* + נוע ni. *be shaken,* i.e. sifted Am 9_9.*

[כִּבְרָה] II 3 n.f. **stretch (of land)**—cstr. כִּבְרַת—(unless

כְּ *about* + בָּרָה *mile*, in much the same sense),* <NOM CL> בְּעוֹד כִּבְרַת־אֶרֶץ לָבֹא אֶפְרָתָה *while there was still a stretch of land*, i.e. some distance, *to come to Ephrath* Gn 48_{7}, וַיְהִי־עוֹד כִּבְרַת־הָאָרֶץ לָבוֹא אֶפְרָתָה *and there was still a stretch of the land*, i.e. some distance, *to come to Ephrath* Gn 35_{16}, וַיֵּלֶךְ מֵאִתּוֹ כִּבְרַת־אָרֶץ *and he went from him a region of the land*, i.e. some distance 2 K 5_{19}.

כִּבְרָה, see כִּבְרָה II *stretch*.

כֶּבֶשׂ $_{107.1.23}$ n.m. **ram**—pl. כְּבָשִׂים; sf. כְּבָשַׂי—male sheep, perh. young **lamb,** as distinct from אַיִל *ram* (e.g. Ezk 46_{6}) and from כִּבְשָׂה *ewe*, perh. *ewe lamb*, usu. sacrificial animal (e.g. Ex $29_{38.39.40.41}$ Lv 4_{32} Is 1_{11} Ezk 46_{4} 2 C $29_{21.22.32}$)as wool for clothing (Jb 31_{20} Pr 27_{26}).*

<SUBJ> היה *be* Ezk 46_{6}, יבל ho. *be brought* Jr 11_{19}, רעה *graze* Is 5_{17}, שׁלם pi. *complete* 4QHalakhah[a] 7_{1} (‖ שׁוֹר *ox*, עֵז *goat*).

<NOM CL> קָרְבָּנוֹ ... כֶּבֶשׂ־אֶחָד *his offering was ... one ram* Nm 7_{15+10t}, כְּבָשִׂים לִלְבוּשֶׁךָ *rams are for your clothing* Pr 27_{26}, כְּבָשִׂים ... לְזֶבַח הַשְּׁלָמִים five *rams were ... for the sacrifice of the peace offerings* Nm 7_{17+11t}, הכבשים אשר לעולה *the rams that are for the burnt offering* 4Q 365a 1_{6}, כְּבָשִׂים בְּנֵי־שָׁנָה *rams, sons of one year*, i.e. one year old Ex 29_{38} Lv 23_{19} Nm 7_{17+13t} $28_{3.9.11.19.27}$ 29_{2+9t}, sim. Lv 23_{18}, כֶּבֶשׂ בֶּן־שְׁנָתוֹ *the ram is a son of one year*, i.e. one year old Nm $6_{12.14}$ Ezk 46_{13}, sim. Lv 23_{12} Nm 7_{15+10t}, כבש אחד לאהרון ול]בנו] *one ram shall be for Aaron and his son* 11QT 21_{1}, sim. $21_{1.2}$, ביום שלישי ... כבשים ארבעה עשר *on the third day there shall be ... fourteen rams* 11QT 28_{7}, sim. 28_{3} ([כבשים]) 28_{10}.

<OBJ> לקח *take* Lv 9_{3} (‖ עֵגֶל *ox*), $14_{10.12.21.24}$, נתן *give* 11QT 21_{1} ([ונתנו] ... [כבש]) $22_{12.12.13}$ (all three ‖ אַיִל *ram*), רום hi. *contribute* 2 C 35_{7}, בוא hi. *bring* Lv 4_{32} 12_{6} Nm 6_{12} 2 C 29_{21}, עלה hi. *bring up*, i.e. offer up 1 C 29_{21}, קרב hi. *bring near*, i.e. offer Lv 23_{18} Nm 6_{14} $28_{3.11.19.27}$ 29_{8+8t} Ezk 46_{4} Ezr 8_{35} 11QT 13_{17} ([כבשים]) 17_{13} (+ פַּר *bull*, אַיִל *ram*, שָׂעִיר *he-goat*) $20_{2.7}$ (11QT[b] ויקריבו] ... כבש]ים) 25_{5} ([כבשי]ם ... [והק]רבתמה]) 25_{13} (‖ פַּר *bull*, אַיִל *ram*, + שָׂעִיר *he-goat*), עשׂה *do*, i.e. offer Ex $29_{39.39.41}$ Lv $23_{12.19}$ Nm $28_{4.4.8}$ 29_{2} Ezk $46_{13.15}$ 11QT 13_{11} (הכבש... [תעשה]) 14_{12} ([ועשיתמה]) 23_{6} ([ויעשו] ... כב[ש]) 27_{3} ([ה]כבשים), שׁחט *slaughter* Lv $14_{13.25}$ 2 C 29_{22}, אכל *eat* 4QHalakhah[a] 7_{1} ([יאכל]) 11QT $22_{12.12.13}$.

<CSTR> כֶּבֶשׂ הָאָשָׁם *ram of the guilt offering* Lv $14_{24.25}$, שְׁנֵי כְבָשִׂים *two rams* Lv 23_{20} Nm 28_{9} 11QT 13_{17} ([כבשים]); גֵּז כְּבָשַׂי *fleece of my rams* Jb 31_{20}, דַּם ... כְּבָשִׂים *blood of ... rams* Is 1_{11}, שְׁנֵי־כְבָשִׂים *two rams* Lv 14_{10} 23_{19}, שֵׁשֶׁת כְּבָשִׂים *six rams* Ezk 46_{6}, שִׁבְעַת כְּבָשִׂים *seven rams* Lv 23_{18} Nm $28_{21.29}$ $29_{4.10}$ (all four הַכְּבָשִׂים) 11QT 14_{18} ([שב]עת הכבשים).

<APP> קָרְבָּן *gift* Nm 6_{14} 7_{21} 28_{3}, עֹלָה *burnt offering* Nm $28_{11.19.27}$ 29_{2+9t} Ezk 46_{4} Ezr 8_{35} 1 C 29_{21} 2 C 29_{32} 11QT 14_{12} ([עולה]) 17_{13} 20_{7} (11QT[b] [עולה ... כבש]ים) 23_{6} ([עולה] ... כב[ש]) 25_{5} (עול[ה] ... [כבשי]ם) 25_{13}, שֶׁלֶם *peace offering* 11QT 20_{2} ([של]מים), צֹאן *small cattle* 2 C 35_{7}, בֵּן *son* 11QT $13_{10.17}$ 14_{1} (all three [כבשים בני]) 14_{12} 17_{13} 20_{2} ([בני]) 20_{7} (11QT[b] [כבש]ים) 23_{6} (כב[ש ... בן]) 25_{5} ([כבש]ים ב[ני]) 25_{13} 28_{10}.

<ADJ> אַלּוּף *obedient* Jr 11_{19} (or ins. וְ a ram *and* a cow), תָּמִים *free of blemish* Lv $23_{12.18}$ Ezk 46_{13} 11QT 13_{10} ([כבשים]) 13_{17} 14_{1} both ([כבשים ... תמימים]) 14_{12} ([תמימים]) 17_{13} 25_{13} (תמימים erased), אֶחָד *one* Nm 7_{15} Lv 14_{21} 11QT 13_{11} ([הכבש האחד]) $14_{6.18}$ 21_{1} (כבש] [אחד) $21_{1.2}$ $22_{12.12.13}$ 23_{6} ([כב]ש אחד]) 28_{02} (לכבש] [האחד) 29_{1} ([לכבשים]).

<PREP> לְ of direction, *to, for* Ex 29_{40}; of benefit, *to, for* Nm $28_{7.13.29}$ 29_{4+9t} Ezk 46_{5} perh. 4Q418 185_{3} 11QT $14_{6.6}$ ([ל]שבעה הכבשים]) 14_{18} 28_{02} ([לכבש]), + היה *be* Nm 28_{14} Ezk 46_{11}, עשׂה *do* 11QT $24_{7.7}$ ([ל]כבש וכבש]) 28_{1} (לא[רבעה עשר] הכבשים), i.e. prepare Nm 15_{5} Ezk 46_{7}, *do*, i.e. offer Nm 28_{21}; *concerning* 11QT 17_{15} (ל[כב]שים) 20_{10} (11QT[b] [לכבשים]) 22_{4} (לכ[בש]ים) 25_{15} $28_{5.9}$ (all three ‖ פַּר *bull*, אַיִל *ram*, שָׂעִיר *goat*).

בְּ *among* Nm 15_{11}; כְּ *as* Jr 11_{19} Ho 4_{16}; מִן of direction, *from*, + לקח *take* Ex 12_{5}, רום hi. *raise*, i.e. offer 11QT 20_{15}; partitive, *from (among)*, + נתן *give* 11QT 21_{01} ([ונתנו] ... מן [הכבשים]); אֶל *to*, + חבר pu. *be joined to* Si 13_{17}; עַל *upon, over*, + נוף hi. *wave* Lv 23_{20}; עִם *with*, + גור *sojourn* Is 11_{6} (‖ גְּדִי *kid*).

<COLL> דַּם ... כְּבָשִׂים ... לֹא חָפָצְתִּי *I have no delight in ... the blood of ... rams* Is 1_{11}, הַכֶּבֶשׂ הָאֶחָד *the one ram* Ex 29_{39}, לַכֶּבֶשׂ הָאֶחָד *for the one ram* Ex 29_{40} Nm 15_{5} $28_{7.13.21.29}$ $29_{4.10.15}$ 11QT $14_{6.18}$ ([לכבש]) 28_{02} ([לכבש האחד]),

הַכֶּבֶשׂ אֶחָד *the one ram* Nm 28_{4} 11QT 13_{11} ([הכבש] [האחד]), כֶּבֶשׂ אֶחָד *one ram* Lv 14_{21} Nm 7_{15} 11QT 21_{1} ([כבש אחד]) $21_{1.2}$ $22_{12.12.13}$ 23_{6} ([כב]ש אחד]), כְּבָשִׂים ... שְׁנַיִם *two ... rams* Ex 12_{38} 11QT 13_{10} ([כבשים] ... [שנים]), כְּבָשִׂים ... הַכֶּבֶשׂ הַשֵּׁנִי *the second ram* Ex $29_{39.41}$ Nm $28_{4.8}$, ... כְּבָשִׂים ... חֲמִשָּׁה *five ... rams* Nm 7_{17+11t}, שִׁשָּׁה כְבָשִׂים *six rams* Ezk 46_{4}, כְּבָשִׂים שִׁבְעָה *seven rams* 2 C 29_{21} 11QT 17_{13} 29_{012} ([כב]שים שב[עה]), כְּבָשִׂים ... שִׁבְעָה *seven ... rams* Nm 28_{11} $29_{2.8.36}$ 11QT 14_{1} ([כבשים ... שבעה]) 14_{12} 20_{7} (11QT^{b} [כבש]ים) 25_{5} ([כבשי]ם ... שבע[ה]) 25_{13}, sim. Nm $28_{19.27}$ 11QT 14_{6} ([לשבעה הכבשים]), ... כְּבָשִׂים ... אַרְבָּעָה עָשָׂר *fourteen ... rams* Nm 29_{13+6t} 11QT 20_{2} 22_{3} ([כב]שים) 28_{3} ([כבשים ארבעה] עשר) $28_{7.10}$, sim. Nm 29_{15} 11QT 28_{1} ([ארבעה עשר] הכבשים), כְּבָשִׂים שִׁבְעִים וְשִׁבְעָה *seventy-seven rams* Ezr 8_{35}, כְּבָשִׂים מָאתָיִם *two hundred rams* 2 C 29_{32}, כְּבָשִׂים אֶלֶף *a thousand rams* 1 C 29_{21}.

Also 4QLiturgy 1.2_{3} 4QRitMar 8_{2} (כ[בשים]). <SYN> אַיִל *ram*, פַּר *bull*, גְּדִי *kid*, שָׂעִיר *goat*, עֵז *goat*, עֵגֶל *ox*, שׁוֹר *ox*.

⇒ כִּבְשָׂה *ewe*.

כַּבְשָׂה, see כִּבְשָׂה *ewe*.

כִּבְשָׂה 8 n.f. **ewe**—כִּבְשָׂה; cstr. כִּבְשַׂת; pl. כְּבָשֹׂת; cstr. כִּבְשֹׂת—female sheep, perh. young **ewe lamb** (Gn $21_{28.29.30}$ Lv 14_{10} Nm 6_{14} 2 S $12_{3.4.6}$), <NOM CL> ... כַּבְשָׂה בַּת־שְׁנָתָהּ *the ewe lamb ... was a daughter of its year*, i.e. one year old Lv 14_{10} Nm 6_{14}, לָרָשׁ ... כִּבְשָׂה אַחַת *the poor man had ... one ewe* 2 S 12_{3}, מָה הֵנָּה שֶׁבַע כְּבָשֹׂת הָאֵלֶּה *what are these seven ewes?* Gn 21_{29}.

<OBJ> נצב hi. *set aside* Gn $21_{28.29}$, קרב hi. *bring near*, i.e. offer Nm 6_{14}, לקח *take* Gn 21_{30} Lv 14_{10} 2 S 12_{4}, עשׂה *do*, i.e. prepare 2 S 12_{4}, שׁלם pi. *restore* 2 S 12_{6}.

<CSTR> כִּבְשַׂת הָאִישׁ *ewe of the man* 2 S 12_{4}, כִּבְשׂת הַצֹּאן *ewes of the flock* Gn 21_{28}. <APP> קָרְבָּן *gift* Nm 6_{14}. <ADJ> תְּמִים *free of blemish* Lv 14_{10} Nm 6_{14}, אֵלֶּה *these* Gn 21_{29}. <COLL> כִּבְשָׂה אַחַת *one ewe* Lv 14_{10} (כַּבְשָׂה) 2 S 12_{3}, שֶׁבַע כְּבָשֹׂת *seven ewe lambs* Gn $21_{28.29.30}$.*

⇒ כֶּבֶשׂ *ram*.

כבשׁ 14.0.2 vb. **subdue—Qal** 8.0.1 Impf. יִכְבֹּשׁ; + waw וְכָבְשׁוּ, וַתִּכְבְּשׁוּ, וַיִּכְבְּשׁוּם; impv. כִּבְשֻׁהָ; ptc. כֹּבְשִׁים; inf. כִּבּוֹשׁ—**subdue, make subservient, rape** woman (Est 7_{8}), <SUBJ> אֵל *God* Mc 7_{19}, עַם *people* Jr $34_{11(Qr)}$, Israelite(s) Ne 5_{5}, Ephraim Zc 9_{15}, Judah Zc 9_{15}, Haman Est 7_{8}, אָדָם *human being* Gn 1_{28}, אִישׁ *man* Jr 34_{16}, בֵּן *son* of Israel 2 C 28_{10}, שַׂר *prince* Jr $34_{11(Qr)}$.

<OBJ> אֶרֶץ *earth* Gn 1_{28}, מַלְכָּה *queen* Est 7_{8}, בֵּן *son* Ne 5_{5} 2 C 28_{10}, בַּת *daughter* Ne 5_{5}, עֶבֶד *servant* Jr $34_{11.16}$, שִׁפְחָה *female servant* Jr $34_{11.16}$, עָוֹן *iniquity* Mc 7_{19}, אֶבֶן sling *stone* Zc 9_{15}.

<PREP> לְ of benefit, *to, for*, + בֵּן *son* of Israel 2 C 28_{10}; *as*, + עֶבֶד *servant* Ne 5_{5} 2 C 28_{10}, שִׁפְחָה *female servant* 2 C 28_{10}; בְּ of place, *in, at*, + בַּיִת *house* Est 7_{8}; עִם *with*, + מֶלֶךְ *king* Est 7_{8}.

Also perh. 4QMishC^{b} 5_{1} 4Q483 1_{1} ([וכיבשו]ה), or [וכובשי]ם).

Ni. 5.0.1 Pf. נִכְבְּשָׁה; ptc. נִכְבָּשׁוֹת—**be subdued, be degraded,** <SUBJ> אֶרֶץ *land* Nm $32_{22.29}$ Jos 18_{1} 1 C 22_{18}, בַּת *daughter* Ne 5_{5}. <PREP> לִפְנֵי *before*, + י׳ *Y.* Nm 32_{22} 1 C 22_{18}, עַם *people* 1 C 22_{18}, עֵדָה *congregation* Jos 18_{1}, בֵּן *son* of Gad Nm 32_{29}, *son* of Reuben Nm 32_{29}.

Also 4QpsEzek^{a} 9.1_{4}.

Pi. 1 Pf. כִּבֵּשׁ—**subdue, subjugate,** <SUBJ> David 2 S 8_{11}. <OBJ> גּוֹי *nation* 2 S 8_{11}.

Hi. 1 + waw וַיַּכְבִּישׁוּם—**subdue, subjugate,** <SUBJ> עַם *people* Jr $34_{11(Kt)}$, שַׂר *prince* Jr $34_{11(Kt)}$. <OBJ> עֶבֶד *servant* Jr 34_{11}, שִׁפְחָה *female servant* Jr 34_{11}.*

⇒ כֶּבֶשׁ *footstool*, כִּבְשָׁן *furnace*.

כֶּבֶשׁ 1 n.m. **footstool,** <SUBJ> אחז ho. *be attached* 2 C 9_{18}. <NOM CL> כֶּבֶשׁ בַּזָּהָב *the footstool was of gold* 2 C 9_{18}.*

⇒ כבשׁ *subdue*.

כִּבְשָׁן 4.1.1 n.m. **kiln, furnace** (Gn 19_{28} Ex $9_{8.10}$ 19_{18}), <SUBJ> בער pi. *burn* Si 27_{5}. <CSTR> קִיטֹר הַכִּבְשָׁן *smoke of the furnace* Gn 19_{28}, עֶשֶׁן *smoke of* Ex 19_{18}, פִּיחַ כִּבְשָׁן *soot of the furnace* Ex $9_{8.10}$ (הַכִּבְשָׁן). <PREP> בְּ of place, *in* 1QH 9_{5}.*

⇒ כבשׁ *subdue*.

* **[כבת] be humble—Ni. be humbled,** וְסוּרַי בָּאָרֶץ יִכָּבֵתוּ *those who depart from me will be humbled in the*

(under)world Jr 17$_{13(Qr)}$ (if em. יִכָּתֵבוּ *will be inscribed;* || בּוֹשׁ *be ashamed*). <SYN> בושׁ *be ashamed.*

כַּד 18.0.0.1 n.f. **jar**—cstr. כַּד; sf. כַּדָּהּ, כַּדֵּךְ; pl. כַּדִּים—as container for water, flour, etc. (Gn 24$_{14.15.16.17.18.20.43.45.46}$ Jg 7$_{16.16.19.20}$ 1 K 17$_{12.14.16}$ 18$_{34}$ Ec 12$_6$), perh. **cup** of fate (Jb 21$_{20}$ [if em. כִּיד *misfortune*), perh. silver **goblet** (3QTr 2$_{11}$ 7$_{10}$ [others בַּד silver *bar*]).

<SUBJ> כלה *be consumed* 1 K 17$_{14.16}$, שׁבר ni. *be broken* Ec 12$_6$. <NOM CL> כַּדָּהּ עַל־שִׁכְמָהּ *her jar was upon her shoulder* Gn 24$_{15.45}$, הַכַּדִּים אֲשֶׁר בְּיָדָם *the jars that were in their hands* Jg 7$_{19}$. <OBJ> נטה hi. *incline* Gn 24$_{14}$, ירד hi. *bring down* Gn 24$_{18.46}$, נתן *give* Jg 7$_{16}$, מלא *fill* 1 K 18$_{34}$, pi. Gn 24$_{16}$, ערה pi. *empty* Gn 24$_{20}$, שׁבר *break* Jg 7$_{20}$, נפץ *smash* Jg 7$_{19}$, ראה *see* Jb 21$_{20}$ (if em.).

<CSTR> כַּד הַקֶּמַח *jar of meal* 1 K 17$_{14.16}$, כד הצער *jar of the shepherd boy* T. el-'Oreme ost. <ADJ> רֵיק *empty* Jg 7$_{16}$. <PREP> מִן of direction, *from,* + גמא hi. *cause to sip* Gn 24$_{17}$, שׁקה hi. *give drink to* Gn 24$_{43}$; בְּתוֹךְ *inside* Jg 7$_{16}$. <COLL> אַרְבָּעָה כַדִּים *four jars* 1 K 18$_{34}$, כדים של כסף שש *six jars* (or *goblets*) *of silver* 3QTr 2$_{11}$ 7$_{10}$.

כַּדּוּר 2 n.m. **ball, skein** of yarn (Is 22$_{18}$), **circular** encampment (Is 29$_3$), <OBJ> צנף *wind up* Is 22$_{18}$ (if em.). <COLL> צָנוֹף יִצְנָפְךָ צְנֵפָה כַּדּוּר *he will certainly roll you up (like) that which is rolled up (into) a ball* Is 22$_{18}$ (or em. כִּצְנֹף הַכַּדּוּר *as when he rolled up the ball*), חָנִיתִי כַדּוּר עָלָיִךְ *I have encamped in a circle about you* Is 29$_3$ (mss כְּדָוִד *as David*).

כַּדְכֹּד 2 n.m. **agate**—article of beauty or commerce (Is 54$_{12}$ Ezk 27$_{16}$), <OBJ> נתן *give,* i.e. exchange Ezk 27$_{16}$ (+ נֹפֶךְ *emerald,* אַרְגָּמָן *purple cloth,* רִקְמָה *embroidery,* בּוּץ *fine linen,* רָאמוֹת *corals*). <COLL> וְשַׂמְתִּי כַּדְכֹד שִׁמְשֹׁתַיִךְ *and I will make your battlements of agate* Is 54$_{12}$.*

***כדם** 1 n.f. **bind—Qal** 1 Ptc. כְּדֻמָה—pass. **be bound, be held captive,** or **be anchored,** מִי כְצוֹר כְּדֻמָה בְּתוֹךְ הַיָּם *who is like Tyre, captive in the middle of the sea?* or *anchored far out to sea?* Ezk 27$_{32}$ (unless כְּ *as* + דֻּמָה *silent one* or *fortress*; or em. נִדְמָה *is silent* or *is destroyed* like, or *be likened* to, Tyre).

כְּדָרְלָעֹמֶר 5 pr.n.m. **Chedorlaomer**—כְּדָר־לָעֹמֶר—king of Elam at time of Abraham (Gn 14$_{1.4.5.9.17}$), <SUBJ> בוא *come* Gn 14$_5$. <NOM CL> כְּדָרְלָעֹמֶר מֶלֶךְ עֵילָם *Chedorlaomer was king of Elam* Gn 14$_1$. <OBJ> עבד *serve* Gn 14$_4$, נכה hi. *strike* Gn 14$_{17}$.

<CSTR> יְמֵי ... כְּדָרְלָעֹמֶר *days of ... Chedorlaomer* Gn 14$_1$.

<PREP> אֵת *with,* + ערך *enter into battle* Gn 14$_9$.

כֹּה 582 adv. **thus—1.** usu. adverb of manner, **so, thus, in this way,** oft. as demonstrative, **this (is what)** (Y. has said, showed me, you are to do, etc.).

a. כֹּה (sometimes כֹה־) before pf. or impf. of verb, היה *be* (impf.) Gn 15$_5$ Is 24$_{13}$, ראה hi. *show* (pf.) Am 7$_{1.4.7}$ 8$_1$, עשׂה *do* (pf.) Nm 32$_8$ Jos 6$_{14}$ 1 S 27$_{11}$ Ezk 23$_{39}$ Ne 13$_{18}$ 2 C 24$_{11}$, (impf.) Nm 8$_7$ Dt 7$_5$ Jos 6$_3$ 1 S 3$_{17}$ 14$_{44}$ 20$_{13}$ 25$_{22}$ 2 S 3$_{9.35}$ 19$_{14}$ 1 K 2$_{23}$ 19$_2$ 20$_{10}$ 2 K 6$_{31}$ Am 4$_{12}$ Ru 1$_{17}$ 2 C 19$_{9.10}$, ni. *be done* (impf.) 1 S 11$_7$ 17$_{27}$ Jr 5$_{13}$ (or del.), יסף hi. *add* (impf.) 1 S 3$_{17}$ 14$_{44}$ 20$_{13}$ 25$_{22}$ 2 S 3$_{9.35}$ 19$_{14}$ 1 K 2$_{23}$ 19$_2$ 20$_{10}$ 2 K 6$_{31}$ Ru 1$_{17}$, נתן *give* (impf.) 1 K 5$_{25}$, דבר pi. *speak* (pf.) Gn 24$_{30}$ 1 K 2$_{30}$, (impf.) Nm 23$_{5.16}$ 1 K 12$_{10}$, ענה *answer* (pf.) 1 K 2$_{30}$, ברך pi. *bless* (pf.) Jos 17$_{14(mss)}$ (see §5), (impf.) Nm 6$_{23}$, קלל pi. *curse* (impf.) 2 S 16$_{10(Qr)}$.

b. כֹּה (sometimes כֹה־) before אמר *say,* כֹּה אָמַר י׳ *thus has said Y.* (293 times in MT) Ex 4$_{22}$ 5$_1$ 7$_{17.26}$ 8$_{16}$ 9$_{1.13}$ 10$_3$ 11$_4$ 32$_{27}$ Jos 7$_{13}$ 24$_2$ Jg 6$_8$ 1 S 2$_{27}$ 10$_{18}$ 15$_2$ 2 S 7$_{5.8}$||1 C 17$_{4.7}$ 2 S 12$_{7.11}$ 24$_{12}$||1 C 21$_{10}$ 1 K 11$_{31}$ 12$_{24}$||2 C 11$_4$ 1 K 13$_{2.21}$ 14$_7$ 17$_{14}$ 20$_{13.14.28.42}$ 21$_{19.19}$ (or del.) 22$_{11}$||2 C 18$_{10}$ 2 K 1$_{4.6.16}$ 2$_{21}$ 3$_{16.17}$ 4$_{43}$ 7$_1$ 9$_{3.6.12}$ 19$_{6.20.32}$||Is 37$_{6.21.33}$ 2 K 20$_{1.5}$||Is 38$_{1.5}$ 2 K 21$_{12}$ 22$_{15.16.18}$||2 C 34$_{23.24.26}$ Is 8$_{11}$ 18$_4$ 29$_{22}$ 31$_4$ 43$_{1.14.16}$ 44$_{2.6.24}$ 45$_{1.11.14.18}$ 48$_{17}$ 49$_{7.8.25}$ 50$_1$ 52$_3$ 56$_{1.4}$ 65$_8$ 66$_{1.12}$ Jr 2$_{2.5}$ 4$_{3.27}$ 5$_{14}$ 6$_{6.9.16.21.22}$ 7$_{3.20}$ (if del. אֲדֹנָי *Adonai*) 7$_{21}$ 8$_4$ 9$_{6.14.16.22}$ 10$_{2.18}$ 11$_{3.11.21.22}$ 12$_{14}$ 13$_{1.9.12.13}$ 14$_{10.15}$ 15$_{2.19}$ 16$_{3.5.9}$ 17$_{5.19.21}$ 18$_{11.13}$ 19$_{1.3.11.15}$ 20$_4$ 21$_{4.8.12}$ 22$_{1.3.6.11.18.30}$ 23$_{2.15.16.38}$ 24$_{5.8}$ 25$_{8.15.27.28.32}$ 26$_{2.4.18}$ 27$_{2.4.16.19.21}$ 28$_{2.11.13.14.16}$ 29$_{4.8.10.16.17.21.25.31.32}$ 30$_{2.5.12.18}$ 31$_{2.7.15.16.23.35.37}$ 32$_{3.14.15.28.36.42}$ 33$_{2.4.10.12.17.20.25}$ 34$_{2.2.4.13.17.18.19}$ 36$_{29.30}$ 37$_{7.9}$ 38$_{2.3.17}$ 39$_{16}$ 42$_{9.15.18}$ 43$_{10}$ 44$_{2.7.11.25.30}$ 45$_{2.4}$ 47$_2$ 48$_{1.40}$ 49$_{1.7.12.28.35}$ 50$_{18.33}$ 51$_{1.33.36.58}$ Ezk 11$_5$ 21$_8$ 30$_6$ Am 1$_{3.6.9.11.13}$ 2$_{1.4.6}$ 3$_{11}$ (if del. אֲדֹנָי) 3$_{12}$ 5$_3$ (if del. אֲדֹנָי) 5$_{4.16}$ 7$_{17}$ Mc 2$_3$ 3$_5$ Na 1$_{12}$ Hg 1$_{2.5.7}$ 2$_{6.11}$ Zc 1$_{3.4.14.16.17}$ 2$_{12}$

3$_{7}$ 6$_{12}$ 7$_{9}$ 8$_{2.3.4.6.7.9.14.19.20.23}$ 11$_{4}$ Ml 1$_{4}$ 1 C 21$_{11}$ 2 C 12$_{5}$ 20$_{15}$ 21$_{12}$.

כֹּה־אָמַר הָאֵל י׳ *thus has the God, Y., said* Is 42$_{5}$, כֹּה אָמַר הָאֱלֹהִים *thus has God said* 2 C 24$_{20}$, כֹּה אָמַר אֲדֹנָי *thus has said Adonai* Is 21$_{16}$ Ezk 21$_{14}$ (mss add י׳), כֹּה אָמַר אֲדֹנַיִךְ י׳ *thus has said your Lord, Y.* Is 51$_{22}$, כֹּה אָמַר אֲדֹנָי י׳ *thus has said Adonai, Y.* (134 times in MT) Is 7$_{7}$ 10$_{24}$ 22$_{15}$ 28$_{16}$ 30$_{15}$ 49$_{22}$ 52$_{4}$ 65$_{13}$ Jr 7$_{20}$ (or del. אֲדֹנָי) Ezk 2$_{4}$ 3$_{11.27}$ 5$_{5.7.8}$ 6$_{3.11}$ 7$_{2.5}$ 11$_{7.16.17}$ 12$_{10.19.23.28}$ 13$_{3.8.13.18.20}$ 14$_{4.6.21}$ 15$_{6}$ 16$_{3.36.59}$ 17$_{3.9.19.22}$ 20$_{5.27.30.39}$ 21$_{3.14(mss).29.31.33}$ 22$_{3.19.28}$ 23$_{22.28.32.35.46}$ 24$_{3.6.9.21}$ 25$_{3.6.8.12.13.15.16}$ 26$_{3.7.15.19}$ 27$_{3}$ 28$_{2.6.12}$ 28$_{22.25}$ 29$_{3.8.13.19}$ 30$_{2.10.13.22}$ 31$_{10.15}$ 32$_{3.11.25.27}$ 34$_{2.10.11.17.20}$ 35$_{3.14}$ 36$_{2.3.4.5.6.7.13.22.33.37}$ 37$_{5.9.12.19.21}$ 38$_{3.10.14.17}$ 39$_{1.17.25}$ 43$_{18}$ 44$_{6.9}$ 45$_{9.18}$ 46$_{1.16.13}$ Am 3$_{11}$ 5$_{3}$ (or del. אֲדֹנָי in both) Ob$_{1}$, כֹּה אָמַר קְדוֹשׁ יִשְׂרָאֵל *thus has the holy one of Israel said* Is 30$_{12}$ (or del.), כֹּה אָמַר רָם וְנִשָּׂא *thus has the exalted and elevated one said* Is 57$_{15}$.

כֹּה אָמַר פַּרְעֹה *thus has Pharaoh said* Ex 5$_{10}$, כֹּה אָמַר הַמֶּלֶךְ *thus has the king said* 1 K 2$_{30}$ (־כֹּה) 22$_{27}$||2 C 18$_{26}$ 2 K 1$_{11}$ 2 K 9$_{18.19}$ 18$_{19}$ (all four ־כֹּה) 18$_{29}$||Is 36$_{4}$ (־כֹּה) 2 K 18$_{29.31}$||Is 36$_{14.16}$ (2 K מֶלֶךְ אַשּׁוּר *the king of Assyria said*; Is הַמֶּלֶךְ אַשּׁוּר).

כֹּה אָמַר עַבְדְּךָ *thus has your servant said* Gn 32$_{5}$, כֹּה אָמַר בִּנְךָ *thus has your son said* Gn 45$_{9}$, כֹּה אָמַר אָחִיךָ *thus has your brother said* Nm 20$_{14}$, כֹּה אָמַר בָּלָק *thus has Balak said* Nm 22$_{16}$, sim. Jg 11$_{15}$ (Jephthah) 2 S 16$_{7}$ (Shimei) 1 K 20$_{3.5}$ (Ben-hadad in both) 2 K 19$_{3}$||Is 37$_{3}$ (Hezekiah) Am 7$_{11}$ (Amos) Ezr 1$_{2}$||2 C 36$_{23}$ (Cyrus) 2 C 32$_{10}$ (Sennacherib).

כֹּה אָמַר *thus he said* (not followed by subject) 2 S 19$_{1}$, כֹּה אָמְרוּ *thus they said* Jos 22$_{16}$, כֹּה יֹאמַר *thus he is to say* Gn 31$_{8}$ 1 S 20$_{7}$ 2 S 15$_{26}$, כֹּה יֹאמְרוּ *thus they are to say* 1 S 14$_{9.10}$, כֹּה תֹאמַר *thus you* (sg.) *are to say* Ex 3$_{14.15}$ 19$_{3}$ 20$_{22}$ 2 S 7$_{8}$||1 C 17$_{7}$ 2 S 11$_{25}$ 1 K 12$_{10}$||2 C 10$_{10}$ Jr 23$_{27}$ 45$_{4}$ Ezk 33$_{27}$, כֹּה תֹאמְרוּ *thus you* (pl.) *are to say* Gn 50$_{17}$ 1 S 18$_{25}$ 2 K 22$_{18}$ Jr 23$_{35}$ 27$_{4}$ 37$_{7}$ 2 C 34$_{26}$, כֹּה תֹאמְרוּן *thus you* (pl.) *are to say* Gn 32$_{5}$ 1 S 11$_{9}$ 2 K 19$_{6.10}$||Is 37$_{6.10}$ Jr 21$_{3}$ (תֹּאמְרֻן), אִם־כֹּה אֹמַר *if thus I say* 1 S 20$_{22}$.

c. כֹּה forms subject or predicate of nom. cl., כֹּה נְאֻם־י׳ *thus is the declaration of Y.* Jr 9$_{21}$ (or del.), כֹּה מִשְׁפָּטוֹ *thus was his custom* 1 S 27$_{11}$, כֹּה מַבָּטֵנוּ *thus is our hope* Is 20$_{6}$, הֲלוֹא כֹה דְבָרִי *is not my word thus?* Jr 23$_{29}$ (or del. כֹּה or em. כָּל *every* word of mine, or כֹּוֶה does not my word *scorch?*).

d. **<COLL>** כֹּה before verb, עשׂה *do* (impf.) Ex 5$_{15}$, (inf.) Nm 22$_{30}$, עלל po. *act harshly* (pf.) Lm 2$_{20}$, אמר *say* (pf.) 1 S 25$_{6}$; כֹּה יַעֲשֶׂה־לְּךָ אֱלֹהִים וְכֹה יוֹסִיף אִם *thus may God do to you and thus may he continue (to do), if* 1 S 3$_{17}$, sim. (all with עשׂה ... יסף impf. in imprecation) 1 S 14$_{44}$ 20$_{13}$ 25$_{22}$ 2 S 3$_{9.35}$ 19$_{14}$ 1 K 2$_{23}$ 19$_{2}$ 20$_{10}$ 2 K 6$_{31}$ Ru 1$_{17}$.

2. adverb of place or direction, **(over) here, (over) there, hither, thither, on this side, on that side,** after שׂים *place* Gn 31$_{37}$, קרה ni. *meet* Nm 23$_{3}$ (if ins. כֹּה) 23$_{15}$ (or em. קרא *call*), יצב htp. *position oneself* Nm 23$_{15}$ 2 S 18$_{30}$, פנה *turn* Ex 2$_{12.12}$, נטשׁ *let* quail *lie* Nm 11$_{31.31}$, דבק *cling*, i.e. stay, with Ru 2$_{8}$ (כֹּה before verb). **<COLL>** כְּדֶרֶךְ יוֹם כֹּה *about a day's journey on this side* Nm 11$_{31.31}$, כֹּה ... כֹּה *here ... there* Ex 2$_{12}$ Nm 11$_{31}$ 23$_{15}$.

3. as compound adverb בְּכֹה **in this way,** עַד־כֹּה, **here, this place, now, this time,** with verb היה *be* 1 K 18$_{45.45}$, שׁמע *hear*, i.e. obey Ex 7$_{16}$, הלך *go* Gn 22$_{5}$ (+ פֹּה *here*), אמר *say* 1 K 22$_{20.20}$ (וַיֹּאמֶר זֶה בְּכֹה וְזֶה אֹמֵר בְּכֹה) *and this one spoke in this way and the other one spoke in this way*; ||2 C 18$_{19}$ כָּכָה *thus* both times), ברך pi. *bless* Jos 17$_{14}$ (or del. עַד־כֹּה or ־עַד; mss lack ־עַד, with כֹּה *thus* has Y. *blessed* me). **<COLL>** וַיְהִי עַד־כֹּה וְעַד־כֹּה וְהַשָּׁמַיִם הִתְקַדְּרוּ *and meanwhile the skies grew dark* 1 K 18$_{45}$.

Also perh. 4QOrd[b] 28$_{2}$.

כהה I 8 vb. **be dim—Qal** 5 Pf. כָּהֲתָה; impf. יִכְהֶה; + waw וַתִּכְהֶ֫יןָ, וַתֵּכַהּ; inf. כָּהֹה—of eyes, **be dim, be weak,** **<SUBJ>** עֶבֶד *servant* of Y. Is 42$_{4}$, עַיִן *eye* Gn 27$_{1}$ Dt 34$_{7}$ Zc 11$_{17}$ Jb 17$_{7}$.

<PREP> מִן privative, *without*, + ראה inf. as noun, *seeing* Gn 27$_{1}$; of cause, *because of*, + כַּעַשׂ *vexation* Jb 17$_{7}$, רוּחַ *spirit* Ezk 21$_{12}$ (if em. Qal).

Pi. 3 Pf. כֵּהֲתָה, כִּהָה—**be disheartened, be colourless,** of spots on skin (Lv 13$_{6.56}$), **<SUBJ>** נֶגַע *mark* (of skin disease) Lv 13$_{6.56}$, רוּחַ *spirit* Ezk 21$_{12}$ (or em. Qal).*

→ כֵּהֶה *dim*, כֵּהָה *lessening*.

כהה II 1 vb. **rebuke—Pi.** 1 Pf. כִּהָה—**rebuke, restrain,**

<SUBJ> Eli 1 S 3$_{13}$. <PREP> בְּ introducing object, + בֵּן *son* 1 S 3$_{13}$.*

כהה III 0.0.1 vb. **be blunt—Qal** 0.0.1 Impf. Q יכהו—<SUBJ> כְּלִי *weapon* 1QM 17$_1$ (+ שׁנן *sharpen*). <PREP> עד *until* 1QM 17$_1$.

כֵּהָה 1 n.f. **lessening,** assuaging of wound, <NOM CL> אֵין־כֵּהָה *there is no lessening to your wound* Na 3$_{19}$.*
→ כהה I *be dim.*

כֵּהֶה 7.0.1 adj. **dim**—cstr. Q כהה (Q כ ה), fs כֵּהָה; pl. כֵּהוֹת—**dim, colourless, dull, fearful, glowing, smoky, 1.** used attributively of רוּחַ *spirit* Is 61$_3$, בַּהֶרֶת *spot* Lv 13$_{39}$, פִּשְׁתָּה *wick* Is 42$_3$.

2. used as predicative adj. or noun, **dim (one), colourless (one),** <SUBJ> בוא *come* CD 15$_{16}$, קרא *read* 4QD^b 5.3$_2$. <NOM CL> הִיא כֵּהָה *it is dim* Lv 13$_{21.26.28}$. <CSTR> כהה עינים *one dim of eyes,* i.e. with poor eyesight CD 15$_{16}$ (=4QD^a 8.1$_7$ כה) 4QD^b 5.3$_2$ ([עינ[י]ם); כול כהה *every dim one* 4QD^b 5.3$_2$. <COLL> הֵחֵלּוּ כֵהוֹת his eyes *began (to be) dim* 1 S 3$_2$ (or em. כהה *be dim*).*
→ כהה I *be dim.*

[כְּהוּנָּה], see כְּהֻנָּה *priesthood.*

כהן 23.3.1 vb. **be priest, serve as priest—Pi.** Pf. כִּהֵן; impf. יְכַהֵן; + waw וַיְכַהֵן, וַיְכַהֲנוּ; וְכִהֵן, וְכִהֲנוּ; inf. כַּהֵן (כַּהֲנוֹ)—**1. be priest, serve as priest,*** <SUBJ> Aaron Ex 28$_{1.3}$ (+ קדשׁ pi. *sanctify*) 28$_{4.41}$ 29$_1$ 29$_{44}$ 30$_{30}$ (all three + קדשׁ pi.) 31$_{10}$||35$_{19}$||39$_{41}$ 40$_{13}$ (+ קדשׁ pi.) Lv 7$_{35}$ Si 45$_{15}$ (+ שׁרת pi. *minister,* ברך pi. *bless*), Nadab and Abihu Ex 28$_1$, Ithamar Ex 28$_1$ 1 C 24$_2$, Eleazar Ex 28$_1$ Nm 3$_4$ Dt 10$_6$ 1 C 24$_2$, Azariah 1 C 5$_{36}$, אָח *brother* Ex 28$_{1.4.41}$ 29$_1$, בֵּן *son* Ex 28$_{1.4.41}$ 29$_{1.44}$ 30$_{30}$ 31$_{10}$||35$_{19}$||39$_{41}$ 40$_{15}$ Lv 7$_{35}$ Nm 3$_3$ Si 51$_{12}$ (sons of Zadok), כֹּהֵן *priest* Ex 31$_{10}$ ||35$_{19}$||39$_{41}$ Lv 16$_{32}$ Nm 3$_3$ (both + מלא יָד pi. *fill the hand,* i.e. ordain) perh. Ho 4$_6$, לֵוִי *Levite* Ezk 44$_{13}$ 2 C 11$_{14}$, עַם *people* perh. Ho 4$_6$.

<PREP> לְ of benefit, *to, for,* + Y. Ex 28$_{1.3.4.41}$ 29$_1$ 29$_{44}$ 30$_{30}$ 40$_{13.15}$ Lv 7$_{35}$ Ezk 44$_{13}$ Ho 4$_6$ 2 C 11$_{14}$ appar. Si 45$_{15}$; בְּ of place, *in,* + בַּיִת *house,* i.e. temple 1 C 5$_{36}$; תַּחַת *instead of,* + Aaron Dt 10$_6$, אָב *father* Lv 16$_{32}$; עַל־פְּנֵי *before the face of,* i.e. during the lifetime of, + Aaron Nm 3$_4$, אָב *father* Nm 3$_4$.

2. act as a priest (without being one), <SUBJ> David 4QSela 8.2$_7$ ([דויד]), Samuel Si 46$_{13}$. <COLL> יכהן שם [ראישון מ]זבח על[הס]לע הזה] *he was first to act as priest there at the altar upon this rock* 4QSela 8.2$_7$.

3. perh. **consecrate,** or **parade like a priest, flaunt,*** כְּחָתָן יְכַהֵן פְּאֵר *like a bridegroom, who consecrates,* or *flaunts, a turban* Is 61$_{10}$ (or em. כון hi. or pol. *place;* 1QIsa^a ככוהן כחתן פאר *like a priest, like a bridegroom* he wraps me in *a turban*).
→ כֹּהֵן *priest,* כְּהֻנָּה *priesthood.*

כֹּהֵן 752.4.181.21 n.m. **priest**—כֹּהֵן (Q, I כוהן, I כה, כוה); cstr. כֹּהֵן; pl. כֹּהֲנִים (Q כוהנים, I כהנם); cstr. כֹּהֲנֵי (Q כוהני); sf. Q כוהניכה, כֹּהֲנָיו, כֹּהֲנֶיהָ, כֹּהֲנַי, כֹּהֲנֵינוּ—sg. used collectively at Is 24$_8$ 28$_7$ Jr 6$_{13}$ 8$_{10}$ 14$_{18}$ 18$_{18}$ 23$_{11.33.34}$ Ezk 7$_{26}$ Ho 4$_9$ Lm 2$_6$, perh. Ho 4$_4$ Lm 2$_{20}$)*—usu. Israelite cultic officials of Y. offering sacrifice (e.g. Lv 6$_{15.19}$ 14$_{19}$ 15$_{15.30}$ Ezk 43$_{27}$ 46$_2$), sounding trumpets or rams' horns in battle, in royal ceremonies, etc. (e.g. Nm 10$_8$ Jos 6$_4$ 1 C 15$_{24}$ 2 C 13$_{14}$ Si 50$_{16}$ 1QM 7$_{15}$), making judicial decisions (e.g. 2 K 17$_{27}$ Ezk 44$_{23}$ Mc 3$_{11}$ Ml 2$_8$ 2 C 15$_3$), etc.; sometimes priests of other gods (e.g. Gn 41$_{45.50}$ Ex 3$_1$ 1 S 5$_5$ 6$_2$ 2 K 10$_{19}$ 11$_{18}$ Jr 48$_7$ 49$_3$ 2 C 13$_9$) and non-Levitical priests (e.g. Jg 17$_5$ 2 S 8$_{18}$).

<SUBJ> היה *be* Jg 18$_{19.19.30}$ 2 S 8$_{18}$ 20$_{26}$ 1 K 1$_8$ 2$_{27}$ 13$_{33}$ Zc 6$_{13}$ Ne 10$_{39}$ 12$_{12}$ 2 C 13$_9$ 29$_{34}$ 1QM 7$_{12}$ 8$_{12}$ 9$_{1.7}$ (הכו[הנ]ים) 16$_9$ ([ה]כוהני[ם]) 17$_{14}$ 1QS 1$_{18}$ 4QPseud^b 1$_5$ (כוהנ[ן]) 4QShir^b 35$_4$ 11QT 15$_{15}$, יכל *be able* 1 K 8$_{11}$||2 C 5$_{14}$ 2 C 7$_2$, חזק *be strong* Hg 2$_4$, pi. *strengthen* 1QM 7$_{12}$ 15$_6$ 16$_{13}$, אמן ni. *be reliable* 1 S 2$_{35}$, בדל ni. *be separated* Ezr 9$_1$ 10$_{16}$ (or em. hi. *separate*) Ne 10$_{29}$, אסף ni. *be gathered* Ne 8$_{13}$, קבץ *gather* 1QpHab 9$_4$, ni. *be gathered* 1 C 13$_2$, יחשׂ *be genealogically registered* 2 C 31$_{17}$, קדשׁ pu. *be consecrated* Ezk 48$_{11}$ (if em. לַכֹּהֲנִים הַמִּקְדָּשׁ מִבְּנֵי צָדוֹק *to the priests of the sons of Zadok was the consecrated area* to לַכֹּהֲנִים הַמְקֻדָּשִׁים בְּנֵי צָדוֹק *to the consecrated priests, the sons of Zadok*), htp. *consecrate oneself* Ex 19$_{22}$ 1 C 15$_{14}$ 2 C 5$_{11}$ 29$_{34}$ 30$_{3.24}$, חרץ pass. *be destined* 1QM 15$_4$, שׁמם ni. *be horrified* Jr 4$_9$, כלם ni. *be ashamed* 2 C 30$_{15}$, בושׁ hi.

be ashamed Jr 2_{26}, גוע *expire* Lm 1_{19}, הרג ni. *be killed* Lm 2_{20}.

הלך *go* Jos 6_{13} 2 K 17_{27} 22_{14} Jr 49_{3} 1QpHab 11_{4}, pi. *go* 1QM 7_{12}, htp. *go about* 1QM 15_{6} 4QpsEzek^{c} 2_{4}, בוא *come* Lv $14_{36.36.44.48}$ 1 K 1_{32} Ezk 42_{14} 2 C 7_{2} $23_{4.6}$ $26_{16.17.17}$ 1QM 8_{2} 9_{7} (הכו[הנ]ים) 1QSa 2_{12} ([הכוה]ן) CD 13_{5}, hi. *bring* Lv 4_{16} 1 K 8_{6}||2 C 5_{7} Ezr 8_{30} Ne 8_{2} 1QM 7_{10}, קרב *approach* Ezk 44_{15} 4QShirShabb^{a} 1.1_{20} (ה[קר]בים), hi. *bring near* Nm 5_{16}, specif. *offer* as sacrifice Lv $1_{5.13.15}$ 5_{8} $7_{8.8.9}$ 6_{16} 11QT 23_{9} 15_{16}, נגשׁ ni. *approach* Dt 20_{2}=11QT 61_{15} Dt 21_{5}=11QT 63_{3} 1QM 16_{13} 19_{11}, hi. *bring near* CD 3_{21}, דרך *tread* 1 S 5_{5}, יצא *go out* Lv $14_{3.38}$ Nm 31_{13} 1 K 8_{10}||2 C 5_{11} Jr 48_{7} 1QM $7_{10.13}$ 1Q29 2_{2} ([הכו]הן) 4QM^{a} 1_{9} ([י]צאו ... ה[כוהנ]ים) 4QM^{c} 1_{4}, hi. *take*, i.e. order, warriors *out* 2 C 23_{14}, עבר *pass* Jos 4_{11} 6_{8} Jr 34_{19} 1QS 2_{19}, *transgress* 1QpHab 8_{16} ([עב]ר), שׁוב *go back* Lv 14_{39}, פנה *turn* to Uzziah 2 C $26_{20.20}$, רדף *pursue* 1QpHab 11_{4}, שׁגה *stray*, i.e. stagger, because of wine Is 28_{7}, מושׁ *depart* 1QS 6_{4} CD 13_{2}.

ירד *go down* 1 K 1_{38}, עלה *go up* Nm 33_{38} Jos 4_{18} 2 K 12_{11} 23_{2}||2 C 34_{30} 2 K 23_{9} Ne 12_{1}, hi. *take up* ark, etc. 1 K 8_{4}||2 C 5_{5}, specif. *offer* as sacrifice Lv 14_{20} Ezk 43_{24} 2 C 29_{21} 35_{14}, קום *arise* Ezr 1_{5} 3_{2} 10_{10} Ne $3_{1.1}$ 2 C 30_{27}, עמד *stand* Dt 17_{12}=11QT 56_{9} Jos 3_{17} 4_{10} 1 K 8_{11}||2 C 5_{14} Ezk 44_{15} Zc 3_{1} Ezr 2_{63}||Ne 7_{65} Ne 12_{41} 2 C 7_{6} 29_{26} 35_{10} 1QM 10_{2} 15_{4} 16_{13} $18_{5.5}$ 4QpPs^{a} 1.3_{15} 4QM^{c} $1_{1.4}$ ([ועמ]דו) 11QT 15_{15} CD 13_{5}, hi. *cause to stand* before Y. Lv 14_{11} Nm 5_{18}, נצב ni. *stand* Jg 18_{17}, יצב htp. *stand* 2 C 11_{13} 1QM 8_{2}, שׁלח *send*, i.e. stretch, hand 1QS $6_{5.5}$ 1QSa 2_{19} ([וישל]ח) 4QD^{f} 2_{4} ([הכוה]נים) 4QpHos^{b} 2_{3}, נשׂא *raise*, i.e. carry, ark Jos $3_{3.14}$ 4_{10} $6_{4.6.6.12.13}$ 8_{33} 1 K 8_{3}, *count* Nm 31_{26}, רום hi. *raise*, i.e. remove Lv 2_{9}, נפל *fall* Ps 78_{64}, hi. *cast* lot Ne 10_{35}, ישׁב *sit* 1 S 1_{9} 1QS 6_{8}, *dwell* 2 K 17_{27} Ezr 2_{70}||Ne 7_{72} Ne 11_{3} 1 C 9_{2}, ערב htp. *intermingle* 4QMMT B_{80} ([מקצת הכהנים ו]העם מתרבים *some of the priests and the [lay-]people intermingle*).

נתן *give* 1 S 21_{7} 2 K 11_{10}||2 C 23_{9} 2 K 22_{10}||2 C 34_{18}, specif. *place* Lv 1_{7} 4_{7} $14_{14.17.28.29}$ 2 K 12_{10} 11QT 26_{3} ([ונתן הכו]הן), pass. *be appointed* Ne 13_{4}, ni. *be given (over)* Ezr 9_{7}, שׂים *place* 2 K 11_{18}, סדר *order* 1QM 15_{4} $17_{10(mg)}$, גמל *repay* 1QpHab 12_{2}, נחל pi. *apportion* Jos 14_{1} 19_{51}, ערך *arrange* Lv $1_{8.12}$ 11QT 9_{13}, hi. *value* Lv $27_{8.12.14.14}$, מצא *find* book 2 K 23_{24} 2 C 34_{14}, קבל pi. *receive* money, blood Ezr 8_{30} 2 C 29_{22}, קנה *acquire* Lv 22_{11}, תפשׂ *seize* Jr 26_{8}, לקח *take* Lv $4_{5.25.30.34}$ $14_{12.14.15.24.25}$ Nm $5_{17.17.25}$ 6_{19} 17_{4} $19_{4.6}$ $31_{51.54}$ Dt 26_{4} 1 S 2_{14} 1 K 1_{39} 2 K $12_{6.10}$ Ezk 45_{19} CD 16_{14}, קמץ *take handful* Lv 5_{12} Nm 5_{26}.

לבשׁ *be clothed* Ex 29_{30} Lv 6_{3} Ps 132_{9}||2 C 6_{41} 1QM 7_{10} 4QTohB^{b} 1_{9} 11QT 15_{15} (ל[בו]שׁ), pu. Ezr 3_{10}, חגר *be girded* Jl 1_{13}, אכל *eat* Lv 6_{19} Ezk 42_{13} 44_{31} 11QT 19_{5} ([ואכלום]) 20_{12} (יוא[כ]לום), שׁתה *drink* Ezk 44_{21} 11QT 21_{4} ([הכוהנים י]שׁתו), סחר *trade* Jr 14_{18}, תמם hi. *add up* money 2 K 22_{4} (or em. נתך hi. *melt* or חתם *seal*), חשׁב pi. *calculate* value Lv $27_{18.23}$ 2 K 12_{11}, בנה *build* 2 K 16_{11} Ne $3_{1.1}$ 4QpPs^{a} 1.3_{15}, חזק hi. *strengthen*, i.e. repair Ne $3_{22.28}$, pi. 2 K 12_{7}, הרס *breach* cordon around Mt Sinai Ex 19_{24}, רדה *rule* Jr 5_{31}, פקד *muster* Nm $26_{63.64}$, ho. *be appointed* 4QD^{a} 11_{8} CD 14_{6} 4QD^{e} 7.1_{16} ([המ]ופקד), פטר *dismiss* 2 C 23_{8}.

נוף hi. *wave* Lv 14_{24} $23_{10.11.20}$ Nm 6_{20}, טבל *dip* finger Lv $4_{6.17}$ $14_{5.16.48}$, זרק *scatter* Lv $1_{5.11}$ $3_{2.8}$ (if ins. כֹּהֵן) $3_{13(Sam)}$ 6_{19} 7_{14} 17_{6} 2 K 16_{15} 2 C $29_{22.22}$ 30_{16} 35_{11} 4QTohB^{c} 1_{9} ([הכו]הן) 11QT 22_{5} ([וזרק]ו), נזה hi. *sprinkle* Lv 14_{27}, שׁלך hi. *throw* salt Ezk 43_{24}, יצק *pour* Lv 14_{26}, סגר hi. *enclose*, i.e. isolate, diseased person Lv $13_{4.5.21.26.31.33}$ CD 13_{5}.

שׁרת pi. *minister* Dt 17_{12}=11QT 56_{9} Dt 21_{5}=11QT 63_{3} 1 K 8_{11}||2 C 5_{14} Jr 33_{21} Ezk 44_{15} 45_{4} Jl 1_{9} 2_{17} Ne $10_{37.40}$ 2 C 13_{10} 4QShirShabb^{a} 1.1_{8} ([כוה]ני) 11QT 15_{15} ([לשׁר]ת), שׁמר *keep* Ezk 44_{15}=CD 3_{21} Ezk 48_{11} 1QS $5_{2.9}$, עשׂה *do* Nm 5_{30} 31_{31} 2 K $16_{11.16}$ Jr 32_{32} Ne 9_{34} 2 C 35_{18} 4QpsEzek^{a} 16.1_{10}, specif. *prepare* sacrifice Lv 6_{15} 14_{19} $15_{15.30}$ Ezk 43_{27} 46_{2}, פעל *do* 1QpHab 12_{8}, יסף hi. *do again* 1QS 2_{11}, שׁחט *slaughter* 2 C 29_{24}, משׁח *anoint* 1 K $1_{34.45}$, pass. *be anointed* Nm 3_{3} (see also Adj.), כבס pi. *wash* Nm 19_{7}, בער pi. *burn* wood Lv 6_{5}, בשׁל pi. *boil* Ezk 46_{20} 2 C 35_{10}, קטר hi. *burn in sacrifice* Lv $1_{9.17}$ $2_{2.9.16}$ $3_{11.16}$ $4_{10.31.35}$ $7_{5.31}$ 2 K 23_{8} (pi.) 11QT 22_{5} 34_{13}, כפר pi. *atone* Lv $4_{20.26.31.35}$ 5_{6+5t} 7_{7} 12_{8} $14_{18.20.29.31}$ $15_{15.30}$ 16_{32} 19_{22} Nm $15_{25.28.28}$, טהר pi. *purify, declare purified* Lv $12_{6(Sam, ms)}$ (if em. qal *be pure* at 12_{7}) 13_{6+6t} 14_{5} (or em. qal) $14_{11.48}$ Ezk 43_{24} Ne 12_{30} 2 C $29_{16.18}$ 4QTohB^{c} 1_{9} ([הכו]הן), htp. *purify oneself* Ezr 6_{20} Ne 12_{30}, מול *circumcise* 1QpHab 11_{12}.

טמא *be impure* Nm 19$_{7}$ Ezk 44$_{25}$, pi. *make impure* 2 K 23$_{8(ms)}$ 1QpHab 12$_{8}$, *declare impure* Lv 13$_{3+10t}$ 11QT 48$_{17}$, גאל htp. *be defiled* 1QM 9$_{7}$ (הכו[הנ]ים), חנף *be impious* Jr 23$_{11}$, חלל pi. *profane* Zp 3$_{4}$, hi. *profane* 1QM 9$_{7}$ (הכו[הנ]ים), בזה *despise* Y.'s name Ml 1$_{6}$, חמס *be violent* Ezk 22$_{26}$ Zp 3$_{4}$ 4QpsMos^{e} 2.1$_{9}$, חטא *sin* Lv 4$_{3}$, pi. *offer as sin offering* or *sprinkle* 2 C 29$_{24}$, רשע hi. *act wickedly* 1QpHab 9$_{9}$, מרד *rebel* 1QpHab 8$_{16}$, שׁגג *err* 11QT 34$_{14}$, שׁלל *despoil* 1QpHab 8$_{16}$ ([לשלול]), בלע pi. *destroy* 1QpHab 11$_{4}$, ספה *sweep away* 1QpHab 11$_{12}$, כלה pi. *finish* 4QapMos^{b} 1.2$_{2}$.

ברך pi. *bless* Dt 21$_{5}$=11QT 63$_{3}$ Jos 8$_{33}$ 2 C 30$_{27}$ 1QM 13$_{1}$ (הכוה[נים]) 1QS 1$_{18}$ 2$_{1}$ 1QSa 2$_{19}$ 4QD^{f} 2$_{4}$ (ה[כו]הנים] [...]לבר[ך), hi. *bless* 1QS 6$_{5.5}$, זעם *curse* 1QM 13$_{1}$ (ה[כו]הנים), כתב *write* curses Nm 5$_{23}$, pass. *be written*, i.e. registered Ne 12$_{22}$ 1QS 7$_{2}$, קרא *read (aloud)* Jr 29$_{29}$ 1QM 13$_{4}$, ni. *be called*, i.e. designated Is 61$_{6}$ 1Qp Hab 8$_{8}$, ראה *see*, i.e. examine, disease Lv 13$_{3+25t}$ 14$_{3.44}$ 4QD^{a} 6.1$_{2.4.10}$ 4QD^{d} 7$_{7(mg)}$ 4QD^{g} 1.1$_{8.14}$, ho. *be shown* Lv 13$_{49}$, שׁמע *hear* Ex 18$_{1}$ Jos 22$_{30}$ Jr 20$_{1}$ 26$_{7}$ Ho 5$_{1}$ Hg 1$_{12}$ Zc 3$_{8}$, hi. *cause to be heard* Si 50$_{16}$ 1QS 1$_{21}$, אמר *say* Dt 20$_{2}$ =11QT 61$_{15}$ Nm 5$_{21}$ 31$_{21}$ Jg 18$_{6.18}$ 1 S 14$_{36}$ 21$_{10}$ 2 K 11$_{15}$ ||2 C 23$_{14}$ 2 K 22$_{8}$ Jr 2$_{8}$ 21$_{1}$ 23$_{34}$ 26$_{11}$ Hg 2$_{12.13}$ Ne 8$_{9}$ 2 C 31$_{10}$ 1QM 10$_{2}$ 13$_{1}$ (ה[כו]הנים) 1QS 2$_{1.11}$, דבר pi. *speak* Nm 26$_{3}$ Dt 20$_{2}$=11QT 61$_{15}$ Dt 27$_{9}$ 2 K 22$_{14}$ 1QM 10$_{2}$ 4QapMos^{b} 1.2$_{2}$ CD 14$_{6}$, ספר *count* 4QD^{a} 6.1$_{10}$, pi. *tell* 1QS 1$_{21}$, שׁאל *ask* Jr 23$_{33}$, בקר pi. *inquire* Lv 13$_{36}$, דרשׁ *interpret* 1QS 5$_{9}$ 1Q29 5$_{2}$ 4QBer^{d} 1$_{4}$ ([י]דר[וש]), בין pol. *understand* CD 13$_{2}$ 14$_{6}$, אות ni. *agree* 2 K 12$_{9}$, ענה *answer* 1 S 21$_{5}$ Hg 2$_{12.13}$ 1QM 13$_{1}$ (ה[כו]הנים) 4QD^{a} 11$_{8}$, צוה pi. *command* Lv 13$_{54}$ 14$_{4.5.36.40}$ 2 K 11$_{9.15}$ 2 C 23$_{8}$ 4QD^{a} 6.1$_{9}$ 4QM^{g} 5$_{5}$, נצח pi. *direct* 1QM 8$_{8.12}$ 9$_{1.2}$, ירה hi. *teach* Dt 24$_{8}$ 2 K 12$_{3}$ 17$_{27}$ Mc 3$_{11}$ 2 C 15$_{3}$, שׁבע hi. *adjure* Nm 5$_{19.21}$.

רוע hi. *sound* trumpet 2 C 13$_{12}$ Si 50$_{16.16}$ 1QM 8$_{8.12}$ 9$_{1.2.7}$ (הכו[הנ]ים) 16$_{9}$ (הכוהני[ם]) 17$_{12.14}$ 18$_{3}$ 4QM^{a} 1$_{17}$ 4QM^{c} 1$_{3}$, תקע *sound* trumpet Nm 10$_{8}$ 1QM 7$_{15}$ 8$_{2.3.5.7.13.14}$ (ה[כו]הנים) 8$_{16}$ ([יתקעו]) 9$_{3.6}$ 16$_{3.4.6.12}$ (הכו[ה]נים) 17$_{10(mg).11}$, ram's horn Jos 6$_{4.16}$, חצצר hi. *sound* trumpet 1 C 15$_{24}$ 2 C 5$_{12}$ 7$_{6}$ 13$_{14}$, ספד *mourn* Jl 1$_{13}$, אבל *mourn* Jl 1$_{9}$, אנח ni. *groan* Lm 1$_{4}$, בכה *weep* Jl 2$_{17}$ Ezr 3$_{12}$, שׂמח *rejoice* 2 C 30$_{25}$, הלל pi. *praise* 2 C 30$_{21}$.

<NOM CL> אַתָּה־כֹהֵן לְעוֹלָם *you are a priest for ever* Ps 110$_{4}$, הוּא כֹהֵן *he was a priest* Gn 14$_{18}$, אין הוא כוהן *he is not a priest* 11QT 35$_{5}$, אֵלֶּה הַכֹּהֲנִים *these are the priests* Ne 10$_{9}$ 12$_{1}$, זָבוּד בֶּן־נָתָן כֹּהֵן רֵעֶה הַמֶּלֶךְ *Zabud, son of Nathan, a priest, was king's companion* 1 K 4$_{5}$ (or del. כֹּהֵן; mss Zaccur for Zabud), עֲזַרְיָהוּ ... הַכֹּהֵן *Azariah ... was the priest* 1 K 4$_{2}$, צָדוֹק וְאֶבְיָתָר כֹּהֲנִים *Zadok and Abiathar were priests* 2 S 20$_{25}$ 1 K 4$_{4}$, צָדוֹק ... וַאֲחִימֶלֶךְ ... כֹּהֲנִים *Zadok ... and Ahimelech ... were priests* 2 S 8$_{17}$||1 C 18$_{16}$ (mss), שָׁם שְׁנֵי בְנֵי־עֵלִי ... כֹּהֲנִים *there the two sons of Eli ... were priests* 1 S 1$_{3}$, הכוהנים הם שבי ישראל *the priests are the converts* (or *captives*) *of Israel* CD 4$_{2}$.

הַכֹּהֲנִים ... בְּכָל־עָרֵי יְהוּדָה *the priests ... were in all the cities of Judah* Ne 11$_{20}$, הַכֹּהֲנִים בַּחֲצֹצְרוֹת תָּמִיד *the priests were with trumpets continually* 1 C 16$_{6}$, בעצת היחד ... כוהנים שלושה *in the council of the community there shall be ... three priests* 1QS 8$_{1}$, הַכֹּהֲנִים ... הַקְּרֹבִים אֵלַי *the priests ..., who are near to me* Ezk 43$_{19}$, עַל הֶחָתוּם ... כֹּהֲנֵינוּ *upon the sealed document are ... (the names of) our priests* Ne 10$_{1}$, כֹּהֵן הָרֹאשׁ עֲלֵיכֶם *the chief priest is over you* 2 C 19$_{11}$, לוֹ אֶבְיָתָר הַכֹּהֵן *Abiathar the priest is his* 1 K 2$_{22}$ (if em. וּלְאֶבְיָתָר *and for Abiathar*), עִמּוֹ כֹּהֲנִים *priests were with him* 2 C 26$_{17}$, sim. 5$_{12}$ 17$_{8}$, הַכֹּהֲנִים אֲשֶׁר לְבֵית־י״ *the priests who belong to the house of Y.* Zc 7$_{3}$, הַכֹּהֲנִים אֲשֶׁר בַּעֲנָתוֹת *the priests who are in Anathoth* Jr 1$_{1}$, הַכֹּהֲנִים אֲשֶׁר בְּנֹב *the priests who were in Nob* 1 S 22$_{11}$, הכוהנים לראשונה *the priests shall be first* CD 14$_{3.5}$, כוהניו טהורי[ם] perh. *his priests are pure* 4QPseud^{b} 3$_{3}$.

<OBJ> הלך hi. *lead* naked Jb 12$_{19}$, בוא hi. *bring* 2 K 23$_{8}$ 2 C 29$_{4}$ 4QpsEzek^{a} 16.1$_{5}$, עזב *leave* 1 C 16$_{39.39}$, שׁלח *send* 1 K 14$_{4}$ Jr 37$_{3}$, אסף *gather* 1 C 23$_{2}$, קבץ *gather* 2 C 24$_{5}$, נדח hi. *expel* 2 C 13$_{9}$, גלה hi. *exile* 2 K 17$_{27.28}$, עמד hi. *cause to stand*, i.e. place, establish 1 K 12$_{32}$ Ezr 3$_{10}$ 2 C 11$_{15}$ 35$_{2}$, קום hi. *raise*, i.e. establish, appoint 1 S 2$_{35}$, יסד *establish* 4QShirShabb^{a} 1.1$_{19}$, מלא pi. *fill* with drunkenness Jr 13$_{13}$, נתן *give* 1 K 2$_{35}$ Jr 29$_{26}$ 1QpHab 9$_{9}$, לקח *take* Jg 18$_{24.27}$ 2 K 25$_{18.18}$||Jr 52$_{24.24}$ 4QpsEzek^{a} 16.1$_{5}$.

עשׂה *make*, i.e. appoint 1 K 12$_{31}$ 13$_{33}$ 2 K 17$_{32}$ 2 C 13$_{9}$, לבשׁ hi. *clothe* in victory Ps 132$_{16}$, הדר *honour* Si 7$_{31}$, קדשׁ hi. *treat as holy* Si 7$_{29}$, נאץ *reject* Lm 2$_{6}$, ענה *humiliate* 1QpHab 9$_{9}$, נכה hi. *strike* 2 K 10$_{11}$, הרג *slay* 1 S 22$_{21}$ 2 K 11$_{18}$, מות hi. *kill* 1 S 22$_{17}$, זבח *kill* 1 K 13$_{2}$ 2 K 23$_{20}$,

בלע pi. *destroy* 1QpHab 11_{12}.

ראה hi. *show* Zc 3_{1}, שׁאל *ask* Hg 2_{11}, קרא *call* 1 S $22_{11.11}$ 2 K 10_{19} Ne 5_{12}, עוד hi. *call as witness* Is 8_{2}, ענה *answer* 1 S 21_{6}, צוה pi. *command* Nm 32_{28} Jos 3_{8} $4_{16.17}$ 2 K 16_{15} 22_{12} $23_{4.4}$, בחר *choose* 1QSb 3_{22}, ברך pi. *bless* 1QSb 3_{22} ([לברך]), בין hi. *teach* CD 13_{5}.

<CSTR> כֹּהֵן י׳ *priest of Y.* 1 S 14_{3}, כֹּהֲנֵי י׳ *priests of Y.* 1 S $22_{17.21}$ Is 61_{6} 2 C 13_{9}, כֹּהֵן הַבַּעַל *priest of Baal* 2 K 11_{18}||2 C 23_{17}, כֹּהֲנֵי דָגוֹן *priests of Dagon* 1 S 5_{5}, כֹּהֵן אֹן *priest of On* Gn $41_{45.50}$ (אוֹן) 46_{20}, בֵּית־אֵל *of Bethel* Am 7_{10}, מִדְיָן *of Midian* Ex 2_{16} 3_{1} 18_{1}, כהן דאר *priest of Dor* Seal 323, כוהני ירושלם *priests of Jerusalem* 1QpHab 9_{4} 4QpsEzek^{c} 3.3_{6} (כהני ירושלים), כֹּהֲנֵי בָמוֹת *priests of the high places* 1 K 12_{32} 13_{2} (both הַבָּמוֹת) $13_{33.33}$ 2 K 17_{32} $23_{9.20}$ (both הַבָּמוֹת), כוהן קורב *priest of the inner sanctum* 4QShirShabb^{d} 1.2_{24}, כוהני *priests of* 4QShirShabb^{a} 1.1_{3} ([קורב]) 1.1_{8} ([כוה]ני]) $1.1_{17.19}$ 4QShirShabb^{d} 1.2_{19} 4QShirShabb^{f} 20.2_{1}, כוהני מרומי רום *priests of highest heaven* 4QShirShabb^{a} 1.1_{20}, השם *of repute* 4QpIsa^{a} 8_{24}, רוש *of the head*, i.e. the chief priests 4QShirShabb^{b} 13_{3}, כֹּהֵן מִשְׁנֶה *priest of second (order)*, i.e. deputy high priest 2 K 23_{4} (if em. כֹּהֲנֵי *priest of*) 25_{18}||Jr 52_{24} (הַמִּשְׁנֶה).

אַדְמַת הַכֹּהֲנִים *land of the priests* Gn $47_{22.26}$, גְּבוּל *boundary of* Ezk 48_{13}, מַמְלֶכֶת כֹּהֲנִים *kingdom of priests* Ex 19_{6} 4QDibHam^{a} 4_{10} ([ממלכת כו]הנים), ממלכות כוהנים *kingdom of priests* 4QM^{a} 16_{3}, עִיר־הַכֹּהֲנִים *city of the priests* 1 S 22_{19}, עָרֵי *cities of* 2 C 31_{15}, חֲצַר *court of* 2 C 4_{9}, מגזת הכוהן *ford of the priest* 3QTr 6_{14}, [מו]עדי הכוהנים *assembly places of the priests* 4QpIsa^{a} 1_{4}, מַחְלְקוֹת הַכֹּהֲנִים *divisions of the priests* 1 C $28_{13.21}$ 2 C 8_{14} 31_{2}, מְנָת *portion of* 2 C 31_{4}, תְּרוּמַת *contribution of* Ne 13_{5}, חטאת הכוהנים *sin offering of the priests* 11QT 35_{11}, זבחי *sacrifices of* 11QT 37_{12}, מִנְחַת כֹּהֵן *cereal offering of a priest* Lv 6_{16}, קדש כהנם *holy thing of priests* Ivory pomegranate inscr., תּוֹשַׁב כֹּהֵן *sojourner*, perh. bound labourer, *of a priest* Lv 22_{10}, נַעַר הַכֹּהֵן *servant of the priest* 1 S $2_{13.15}$, חֶבֶר כֹּהֲנִים *company of priests* Ho 6_{9} (or em. חִבְּרוּ priests *have joined together* or חֻבְּאוּ priests *are hidden*), ... עצת [ה]כוהנים *council of ... the priests* 4QpIsa^{d} 1_{2}, שָׂרֵי הַכֹּהֲנִים *princes of the priests* Ezr $8_{24.29}$ 10_{5} 2 C 36_{14}, רָאשֵׁי *heads of* Ne 12_{7} 1QM 2_{1} (הכוהנים), פְּקִיד כֹּהֵן *officer of the priest* 2 C 24_{11}, זִקְנֵי הַכֹּהֲנִים *elders of the priests* 2 K 19_{2}||Is 37_{2} Jr 19_{1}, בְּנֵי הַכֹּהֲנִים *sons of the priests* Ezr 2_{61} (or del. בְּנֵי) 10_{18} Ne 12_{35} 1 C 9_{30} 4QMMT B_{12} ([בני] הכוה[נים]) B_{26} ([בני] הכו[הנ]ים), בַּת־כֹּהֵן *daughter of a priest* Lv $22_{12.13}$.

פְּנֵי כֹהֲנִים *face of priests* Lm 4_{16}, עֵינֵי הַכֹּהֵן *eyes of the priest* Lv 13_{12}, יַד *hand of* Nm 5_{18}, יד כוהניו *hand of his priests* 4Q419 1_{3}, יַד הַכֹּהֲנִים under the *charge of the priests* 2 C 23_{18}, כַּף הַכֹּהֵן *hand of the priest* Lv $14_{15.18.26.29}$, לֵב *heart of* Jg 18_{20}, פי הכוהן *mouth*, i.e. word, *of the priest* 1QpHab 2_{8}, פי הכוהנים *mouth*, i.e. word, *of the priests* (unless עַל פִּי compound prep. *according to*) 1QS 5_{2} 6_{19} 11QT 57_{1} ([פי]), שִׂפְתֵי כֹהֵן *lips of a priest* Ml 2_{7}, עַצְמוֹת כֹּהֲנִים *bones of priests* Jr 8_{1} (הַכֹּהֲנִים) 2 C 34_{5}, רַגְלֵי הַכֹּהֲנִים *the feet of the priests* Jos $3_{13.15}$ $4_{3.9.18}$, נֶפֶשׁ *soul*, i.e. appetite, *of* Jr 31_{14}, נבלת כוהניכה *bodies of your priests* 4QTanḥ 1.1_{3}, כָּתְנֹת כֹּהֲנִים *tunics of priests* Ezr 2_{69}||Ne 7_{71} Ne 7_{69} (כָּתְנוֹת).

מְרִיבֵי כֹהֵן *contenders of*, i.e. with, *a priest* Ho 4_{4} (or em. רִיבִי הַכֹּהֵן with you is *my contention, O priest* or אֲנִי רָב הַכֹּהֵן with you *I contend, O priest*), [דב]ירי כול כוהני *inner sanctuaries of all the priests of* 4QShirShabb^{f} 20.2_{1}, עֲוֹנוֹת כֹּהֲנֶיהָ *iniquities of its priests* Lm 4_{13}, מוֹת הַכֹּהֵן הַגָּדוֹל *the death of the high priest* Nm $35_{25.28.28.32(ms,\ Sam)}$ Jos 20_{6}, בְּרִית הַכֹּהֲנִים *covenant of the priests* Ne $13_{29(ms)}$, מִשְׁפַּט *entitlement of* Dt 18_{3}, *practice of* 1 S 2_{13}, *judgment of* 1QSa 1_{2}, הִתְיַחֵשׂ־הַכֹּהֲנִים *genealogical registration of the priests* 2 C 31_{17}, כְּעֶרְכְּךָ הַכֹּהֵן appar. *according to the valuation of the priest* Lv 27_{12}.

כָּל־כֹּהֵן *every priest* Ezk 4_{21}, כָּל־הַכֹּהֲנִים *all the priests* 2 K 23_{8} Jr 29_{25} 2 C 5_{11} 26_{20}, כָּל־כֹּהֲנֵי *all the priests of* 2 K 23_{20} 4QShirShabb^{f} 20.2_{1} (כול כוהני), כָּל־כֹּהֲנָיו *all his priests* 2 K 10_{19}.

<APP> Aaron Ex 31_{10}||35_{19}||39_{41} 38_{21} Lv 1_{7} 7_{34} 13_{2} 21_{21} Nm $3_{6.32}$ $4_{16.28.33}$ 7_{8} 17_{2} 18_{28} $25_{7.11}$ $26_{1.64}$ 33_{38} Jos $21_{4.13}$ Ezr 7_{5}, Abiathar 1 S 23_{9} 30_{7} 2 S $15_{35.35}$ 17_{15} 19_{12} 1 K $1_{7.19.25.42}$ $2_{22.26}$ 1 C 15_{11}, Ahimelech 1 S $21_{2.3}$ 22_{11}, Amariah 2 C 19_{11}, Amasai 1 C 15_{24}, Amaziah Am 7_{10}, Azariah 2 C $26_{17.20}$ 31_{10}, Benaiah 1 C 15_{24} 16_{6}, Elam Ne 12_{41}, Eleazar Nm 17_{4} $19_{3.4}$ $26_{3.63}$ $27_{2.19.21.22}$ 31_{6+9t} $32_{2.28}$ 34_{17} Jos 14_{1} 17_{4} 19_{51} 21_{1} $22_{13.31.32}$ Ne 12_{41} Bar-Kochba Revolt Year 1 Coin 166 167 173 Year 3 Coin 213 (both אלעזר) Bene Ḥezir tomb inscr. (Frey 1394), Eli 1 S 1_{9}

2$_{11}$ 14$_{3}$, Eliakim Ne 12$_{41}$, Eliashib Ne 3$_{1.20}$ 13$_{4.28}$, Eliezer 1 C 15$_{24}$, Elioenai Ne 12$_{41}$, Elishama 2 C 17$_{8}$, Ezekiel Ezk 1$_{3}$, Ezer Ne 12$_{41}$, Ezra Ezr 7$_{11}$ 10$_{10.16}$ Ne 8$_{2.9}$ 12$_{26}$, Hananiah Ne 12$_{41}$, Hilkiah 2 K 22$_{4.8.10}$||2 C 34$_{9.14.18}$ 2 K 22$_{12.14}$ 23$_{4.24}$ Seal 734 (8th/7th cent.), Honiah Bene Ḥezir tomb inscr.

Jahaziel 1 C 16$_{6}$, Jehohanan Ne 12$_{41}$, Jehoiada 2 K 11$_{9.9.15}$||2 C 23$_{8.8.14}$ 2 K 12$_{3.8.10}$ Jr 29$_{26}$ 1 C 27$_{5}$ 2 C 22$_{11}$ 23$_{9}$ 24$_{2.20.25}$, Jehoram 2 C 17$_{8}$, Jethro Ex 3$_{1}$ 18$_{1}$, Joezer Bene Ḥezir tomb inscr. (Frey 1394), Johanan Stamp /Coin 49 (4th cent.; יוחנ[ן]) Si 50$_{1}$ Hyrcanus I Coin 26 27 Bene Ḥezir tomb inscr. Hyrcanus II Coin 18 18A 19 20 22 23, Jonathan Alexander Jannaeus Coin 12 13 14 17 Alexander Jannaeus Seal, Joshaphat 1 C 15$_{24}$, Joshua Hg 1$_{1.12.14}$ 2$_{2.4}$ Zc 3$_{1.8}$ 6$_{11}$, Judah Aristobulus Coin 28 29 Bene Ḥezir tomb inscr., Maaseiah Ne 12$_{41.41}$, Malchijah Ne 12$_{41}$, Mattan 2 K 11$_{18}$||2 C 23$_{17}$, Mattathias Antigonus Coin 30 (מתתי]ה הכ[הנ) 31 34 (כה[נ]), Melchizedek 4QShirShabb^{b} 11$_{3}$ (מלכי]צדק[), Meremoth Ezr 8$_{33}$, Micaiah Ne 12$_{41}$, Miniamin Ne 12$_{41}$, Nethanel 1 C 15$_{24}$, Pashhur Jr 20$_{1}$, Phinehas Jos 22$_{30}$, Potiphera Gn 41$_{45.50}$ 46$_{20}$, Seraiah 2 K 25$_{18}$||Jr 52$_{24}$, Shebaniah 1 C 15$_{24}$, Shelemiah Ne 13$_{13}$, Shemaiah Ne 12$_{41}$, Simeon Bene Ḥezir tomb inscr., Uriah 2 K 16$_{10.11.}$ $_{11.15.16}$ Is 8$_{2}$, Uzzi Ne 12$_{41}$, Zadok 2 S 15$_{27.35}$ 17$_{15}$ 19$_{12}$ 1 K 1$_{8+7t}$ 2$_{35}$ 1 C 15$_{11}$ 16$_{39}$ 24$_{6}$, Zechariah Ne 12$_{41}$ 1 C 15$_{24}$ Seal 323$_{2}$, Zephaniah 2 K 25$_{18}$||Jr 52$_{24}$ Jr 21$_{1}$ 29$_{25.29}$ 37$_{3}$.

לֵוִי *Levite* Dt 17$_{9.18}$ 18$_{1}$ 24$_{8}$ 27$_{9}$ Jos 3$_{3}$ 8$_{33}$ Is 66$_{21}$ (mss add וְ *and* Levites in all three) Jr 33$_{18.21}$ Ezk 43$_{19}$ 44$_{15}$ 2 C 5$_{5}$ 23$_{18}$ 30$_{27}$ (mss add וְ in all three), perh. Ezr 10$_{5}$ Ne 10$_{29.35}$ 11$_{20}$, אִישׁ *man* Lv 21$_{9}$ Ne 11$_{3}$ 1QS 6$_{4}$ 1QSa 2$_{13}$ 4QTohB^{c} 1$_{6}$ CD 13$_{2}$, אָח *brother* Ezr 3$_{2.8}$ 6$_{20}$ Ne 3$_{1}$ 1 C 16$_{39}$ 1QM 13$_{1}$ (ה[כו]הנים) 15$_{4}$ (הכ[והנים]) 4QD^{a} 5.2$_{4}$, בֵּן *son* Lv 1$_{5.7.11}$ 2$_{2}$ 3$_{2}$ 13$_{2}$ 21$_{1}$ Nm 3$_{3}$ 10$_{8}$ Dt 21$_{5}$=11QT 63$_{3}$ Dt 31$_{9}$ Jos 21$_{19}$ 1 S 1$_{1}$ 14$_{3}$ 22$_{11}$ 30$_{7}$ 1 K 4$_{5}$ Jr 20$_{1}$ 21$_{1}$ 29$_{25}$ 37$_{3}$ Ezk 1$_{3}$ 44$_{15}$ Hg 1$_{1.12.14}$ 2$_{2.4}$ Ezr 8$_{33}$ Zc 6$_{11}$ Ne 10$_{39}$ 13$_{28}$ 1 C 27$_{5}$ 2 C 13$_{8}$ 26$_{17}$ 29$_{21}$ 30$_{26}$ 31$_{19}$ 35$_{14.14}$ Si 50$_{1.16}$ 1QS 5$_{2.9}$ 1QSa 1$_{2.16.24}$ 2$_{3.13}$ ([בני]) 1QSb 3$_{22}$ 4QD^{a} 5.1$_{16}$ ([ב]ני) 4QTohD 1$_{4}$ (לכוה[נים]) 4QM^{c} 1$_{1}$ 11QT 9$_{13}$ 22$_{5}$ 34$_{13}$ 35$_{5}$ (ה[כוהנים בני]) 44$_{4}$ Seal 734 (8th/7th cent.) Bene Ḥezir tomb inscr. (Frey 1394), מוֹרֶה *teacher* 4QpPs^{a} 1.3$_{15}$, קָרִיא *one invited* 1QSa 2$_{13}$ ([קוראי]), רַב pl. *many* 4QpNah 3.2$_{9}$, פָּקִיד *overseer* 4QBer^{d} 1$_{4}$ (הפ[קיד]), רֹאשׁ *head*, i.e. chief (usu. כֹּהֵן הָרֹאשׁ) 2 K 25$_{18}$||Jr 52$_{24}$ Ezr 7$_{5}$ (הַכֹּהֵן) 1 C 27$_{5}$ (הַכֹּהֵן רֹאשׁ) 2 C 19$_{11}$ 24$_{11}$ 26$_{20}$ 31$_{10}$ (הַכֹּהֵן) 1QM 2$_{1}$ 15$_{4}$ 16$_{13}$ (=4QM^{a} 10.2$_{13}$ הכוהן הרוש) 18$_{5}$ 19$_{11}$ (הרו[אש]) 4QM^{g} 5$_{5}$ (כוהן [הרואש]), מִשְׁנֶה *second one* 11QT 31$_{4}$.

<ADJ> גָּדוֹל *great*, i.e. chief, high Lv 21$_{10}$ Nm 35$_{25.28.28.32.(ms, Sam)}$ Jos 20$_{6}$ 2 K 12$_{11}$ 22$_{4}$||2 C 34$_{9}$ 2 K 22$_{8}$ 23$_{4}$ Hg 1$_{1.12.14}$ 2$_{2.4}$ Zc 3$_{1.8}$ 6$_{11}$ Ne 3$_{1.20}$ 13$_{28}$ 2 C 34$_{9}$ 3QTr 6$_{14}$ 4QMishC^{e} 2$_{4}$ (ג[דול]) 11QT 15$_{15}$ 23$_{9}$ 25$_{16}$ 26$_{3}$ (הכו[הן] [ה]גדול) 31$_{5}$ (הכוהן הג[דול]) 58$_{18}$ Hyrcanus I Coin 26 Aristobulus Coin 28 29 Alexander Jannaeus Coin 12 13 14 Alexander Jannaeus Seal (גדל) Hyrcanus II Coin 18 18A 19 20 22 23 Antigonus Coin 30 31 (both [גדול]), אַחֲרוֹן *last* 1QpHab 9$_{4}$ 4QpHos^{b} 2$_{3}$, מָשִׁיחַ *anointed* Lv 4$_{3.5.16}$ 6$_{15}$ 4QapMos^{a} 1.1$_{9}$ 4QapMos^{b} 1.1$_{1}$, טָהוֹר *pure* 4QTohB^{c} 1$_{6}$, תָּמִים *blameless* 1QS 8$_{1}$, רָשָׁע *wicked* 1QpHab 8$_{8}$ 9$_{9}$ (ה[ר]שע) 11$_{4}$ 12$_{2.8}$, אֶחָד *one* 1QM 7$_{12}$.

<PREP> לְ of direction, *to* Temple area inscr. (להכ[הן]), + יצא *go out* 4QTohD 1$_{4}$ (לכוה[נים]), נתן *give* Lv 7$_{32.34}$ 22$_{14}$ Nm 5$_{10}$ 18$_{28}$ 31$_{29.41}$ Dt 18$_{3}$ 1 S 2$_{15}$ Ezk 44$_{30}$ Ezr 7$_{11}$ 2 C 35$_{8}$ 31$_{19}$, נתן *give* 11QT 22$_{11}$, שׁלם pi. *repay* 1QpHab 12$_{2}$, רום hi. *raise*, i.e. contribute 2 C 35$_{8}$, קרא *call* 1 S 6$_{2}$ 1 K 1$_{19.25.26.32}$ 2 K 12$_{8.8}$||1 C 15$_{11.11}$, אמר *say* 1 S 21$_{3}$ 1 K 2$_{26}$ 2 C 29$_{21}$, נגד hi. *tell* Lv 14$_{35}$ 2 S 15$_{35}$ Ne 2$_{16}$, ידע hi. *make known* 4QD^{e} 7.1$_{16}$, פשׁר *interpret* 1QDM 1$_{3}$ (פש[ור] ... ללו[י]ים וכול ה[כוהנים] *interpret ... to the Levites and all the priests*), גלה ni. *be revealed* 1QS 5$_{9}$, ידע htp. *confess* CD 9$_{13}$; שׁאל לְ *inquire of* 11QT 58$_{18}$.

לְ of benefit, *to, for* Ne 12$_{44}$ 4QHalakah^{a} 6$_{9}$ perh. 4QShirShabb^{b} 4$_{2}$, + היה *be* Lv 23$_{20}$, בוא hi. *bring* Ex 39$_{41}$ Ne 10$_{37.38}$, עשׂה *make* Ex 31$_{10}$||35$_{19}$ 11QT 37$_{8}$ (וע[ש]יתמה), pass. *be made* 11QT 37$_{10}$, כון hi. *prepare* 2 C 35$_{14.14}$, עמד hi. *establish* divisions 2 C 31$_{2}$, שׁחט *slaughter* Ezr 6$_{20}$, חרם hi. *devote* 4QHalakah^{a} 10$_{2}$ (וה[חרימו]), שׁאל *ask*, i.e. request 1 K 2$_{22}$ (or em.; see Nom. Cl.).

לְ of possession, *of, (belonging) to* Gn 47$_{22}$ Ex 2$_{16}$ Lv 7$_{8.9.14}$ 14$_{13}$ Dt 18$_{1}$ Nm 5$_{8}$ 6$_{20}$ Jr 33$_{18}$ Ezk 40$_{45.46}$ 46$_{19}$ (if em. אֶל־הַכֹּהֲנִים *to the priests* to אֲשֶׁר לַכֹּהֲנִים *that belong to the priests*) 48$_{10.11}$ Ne 13$_{30}$ 1 C 24$_{6.31}$ 2 C 4$_{6}$ 26$_{18}$ 4QMMT B$_{63.64}$ 11QT 15$_{18}$ (לכוהני[ם]) 58$_{13}$ 60$_{9}$, + היה *be* Lv 5$_{13}$ 27$_{21}$ Nm 5$_{9.10}$ 2 K 12$_{17}$ Ezk 44$_{30}$ 45$_{4}$ 11QT 8$_{1}$ (11QT^{b}

([לכוהנים י]היה) 19$_{5}$ ([יה]יו) 22$_{10}$ 44$_{4}$ CD 9$_{13.15}$.

לְ (to serve) as, + היה be Jg 17$_{5.10.12.13}$ 18$_{4.19}$ 4QHalakaha^{a} 10$_{3}$ ([והיתה]) 4QShirShabb^{a} 1.1$_{3}$, בחר choose 1 S 2$_{28}$, לקח take Is 66$_{21}$, משׁח anoint 1 C 29$_{22}$; against, + נתן give, i.e. make, into fortress Jr 1$_{18}$; namely Ne 9$_{32}$ 2 C 23$_{4}$.

בְּ of place, among 4QShirShabb^{a} 1.1$_{17}$, partitive, among, some of, (any) of Lv 6$_{22}$ 7$_{6}$ Ps 99$_{6}$ 2 C 31$_{19}$ 4QShirShabb^{b} 13$_{3}$ 4QShirShabb^{d} 1.2$_{19}$; against, + שׁלח send, i.e. stretch, hand 4QpPs^{a} 1.2$_{18}$; introducing object, + דבר pi. command 4QpPs^{a} 1.3$_{15}$ (ד[בר]; others בחר choose), בחר choose Dt 21$_{5}$=11QT 63$_{3}$, פגע strike 1 S 22$_{17.18.18}$, שׁלל despoil 1QpHab 8$_{16}$ (ויש[ללו]), בין consider Ezr 8$_{15}$.

כְּ as, + היה be Is 24$_{2}$ Ho 4$_{9}$ (or del.).

מִן of direction, from perh. 4QMyst^{a} 67$_{3}$ perh. 4QShirShabb^{d} 1.2$_{24}$, + אבד disappear Jr 18$_{18}$ Ezk 7$_{26}$; of possession, of Ezk 44$_{22}$; of comparison, more (than), + קדשׁ htp. consecrate oneself 2 C 29$_{34}$; partitive, (some) of, (any) of, (from) among Lv 13$_{2}$ Jr 1$_{1}$ Ezr 2$_{61}$||Ne 7$_{63}$ (if em. in Ezr מִבְּנֵי of the sons of the priests to מִן of the priests) Ezr 3$_{12}$ Ne 11$_{10}$||1 C 9$_{10}$ 1QS 7$_{2}$ (אחד מן הכוהנים one of the priests) 4QpIsa^{a} 8$_{24}$ (אחד מכוהני one of the priests of) 4QD^{e} 4$_{5}$ (א[י]ש [מן] הכהנים a man, i.e. one, of the priests) 11QT 35$_{5}$ (איש מה[כוהנים] a man from among the priests) 57$_{12}$ (מן הכוהנים שנים עשר twelve of the priests), + בוא come 2 K 17$_{28}$, הלך hi. take 2 K 17$_{27}$, עלה go up Ezr 7$_{7}$, עמד hi. establish 2 C 19$_{8}$.

אֶל to Ezk 46$_{19}$ (or em. לְ of possession), + היה be, i.e. come Ezk 1$_{3}$ Hg 1$_{1}$, שׁמע listen Dt 17$_{12}$=11QT 56$_{9}$, ראה ni. appear Lv 13$_{7.19}$, hi. show Lv 13$_{7}$, בוא come Lv 13$_{16}$ Dt 17$_{9}$ 26$_{3}$ 1 S 21$_{2}$ 2 K 11$_{9}$ 2 C 34$_{9}$, hi. bring Lv 2$_{2}$ 5$_{8.12.18.25}$ 12$_{6}$ 14$_{23}$ 15$_{29}$ 17$_{5}$ 23$_{10}$ Nm 5$_{15}$ 6$_{10}$ 31$_{12}$, ho. be brought Lv 13$_{2.9}$ 14$_{2}$, נגשׁ come near Jos 21$_{1}$, קרב hi. bring near Lv 2$_{8}$, יצא go out 1QM 9$_{3}$, עלה go up 2 K 22$_{4}$, נתן give Lv 15$_{14}$ Nm 19$_{3}$ Dt 31$_{9}$ Ezk 43$_{19}$, שׁלח send 2 S 19$_{12}$ 2 K 16$_{10}$ Jr 29$_{1.25.25}$, קרא call Jos 6$_{6}$, אמר say Lv 21$_{1}$ Nm 32$_{2}$ Jos 3$_{6}$ 1 S 14$_{19}$ 23$_{9}$ 30$_{7}$ 2 S 15$_{27}$ 17$_{15}$ 2 K 12$_{5.8}$ Jr 26$_{16}$ Hg 2$_{2}$ Zc 7$_{3.5}$, דבר pi. speak 1 S 14$_{19}$ Jr 27$_{16}$.

עַל to(wards) Ne 12$_{44}$, + שׁלח send 1 C 13$_{2}$; for, on behalf of, + כפר pi. atone Lv 16$_{33}$, קרב hi. bring near, i.e. offer 11QT 25$_{16}$; concerning 2 C 8$_{15}$ 1QpHab 8$_{8.16}$ 9$_{4.9}$ 11$_{4.12}$ 12$_{2}$ 4QpHos^{b} 2$_{3}$ (ע[ל]) 4QpPs^{a} 1.3$_{15}$; + דרשׁ עַל question 2 C 31$_{9}$.

לִפְנֵי before, in the presence of 1QM 7$_{15}$, + עמד stand Nm 27$_{2.21}$ Dt 19$_{17}$=11QT 61$_{8}$, hi. cause to stand, i.e. present Lv 27$_{8.11}$ Nm 3$_{6}$ 27$_{19.22}$, קרב approach Jos 17$_{4}$, הלך go Jos 6$_{9}$, בוא come 4QapMos^{a} 1.1$_{9}$ 11QT 58$_{18}$, זרח appear 2 C 26$_{19}$, יעד ni. be assembled 1QSa 2$_{3}$, שׁלח send, i.e. stretch, hand 1QSa 2$_{19}$ ([ישלח]), כתב write 1 C 24$_{6}$; לְעֵינֵי before, in the presence of, + אמר say Jr 28$_{1.5}$, צוה pi. command Nm 27$_{22}$.

עַל פִּי according to 1QSa 1$_{16}$ ([על פ]י) 1$_{24}$; אֵת with Jr 33$_{21}$; עִם with, + היה be 1 K 1$_{7}$, יצא go out 1QM 7$_{13}$, זעף be angry 2 C 26$_{19}$, כרת hi. destroy name Zp 1$_{4}$; מִקְצָת some of 4QMMT B$_{80}$; מִלִּפְנֵי perh. at the dictation of, + כתב write Dt 17$_{18}$=11QT 56$_{21}$; נֶגֶד facing, + עמד stand Jos 8$_{33}$; alongside, + שׁרת pi. minister 2 C 8$_{14}$; אַחַר after, + סרך rank 1QM 2$_{1}$; עַד unto, מִנָּבִיא וְעַד־כֹּהֵן from prophet unto priest, i.e. both of them Jr 6$_{13}$ 8$_{10}$; תַּחַת in place of, + נתן give, i.e. install as Jr 29$_{26}$.

<COLL> לְלֹא כֹהֵן without a priest 2 C 15$_{3}$, וְעַתָּה אֲלֵיכֶם הַמִּצְוָה הַזֹּאת הַכֹּהֲנִים and now this commandment is for you, O priests Ml 2$_{1}$, חֲזַק ... כֹּהֵן be strong ..., O priest Hg 2$_{4}$, רִיבִי הַכֹּהֵן my contention is with you, O priest Ho 4$_{4}$ (if em. מְרִיבֵי כֹהֵן contenders of a priest).

כֹּהֵן לַי״ priest of Y. 1 K 2$_{27}$, sim. 1 S 1$_{3}$ 2 C 26$_{17}$ (both כֹּהֲנִים priests), כֹּהֵן לְאֵל עֶלְיוֹן priest of El-elyon Gn 14$_{18}$, כֹּהֵן לְלֹא אֱלֹהִים priest of non-gods 2 C 13$_{9}$, כֹּהֲנִים לַבָּמוֹת וְלַשְּׂעִירִים וְלָעֲגָלִים priests of the high places, satyrs, and calves 2 C 11$_{15}$, הַכֹּהֵן לַצָּבָא the priest for the army Nm 31$_{6}$, כֹּהֵן לְשֵׁבֶט priest of a tribe Jg 18$_{19}$, sim. 18$_{30}$ (כֹּהֲנִים), כֹּהֵן לְבֵית אִישׁ אֶחָד priest to the house of just one man Jg 18$_{19}$, כֹּהֵן לְדָוִד priest of David 2 S 20$_{26}$, כֹּהֵן לְאוּרִים וְתֻמִּים a priest of, i.e. with, urim and thummim Ezr 2$_{63}$, var. ||Ne 7$_{65}$, כוהן בעד[ת אל] priest in the assembly of God 4QShirShabb^{b} 11$_{3}$, עצת היחד [ה]כוהנים והע[ם] council of the community, the priests and the people 4QpIsa^{d} 1$_{2}$.

כוהנים שנים two priests 4QOrd^{a} 2$_{4}$, כוהנים שלושה three priests 1QS 8$_{1}$ 4QpsEzek^{c} 2$_{4}$, שבעה כוהנים seven priests 1QM 7$_{10}$.

לֵוִי || כֹּהֵן Levite (see also App.) 1 K 8$_{4}$ Ezr 1$_{5}$ 2$_{70}$||Ne 7$_{72}$ Ezr 3$_{8.10.12}$ 6$_{20}$ (or del. (כֹּהֵן)) 7$_{7}$ 8$_{29.30}$ 9$_{1}$ Ne 8$_{13}$ 10$_{1}$ 11$_{3}$||1 C 9$_{2}$ 12$_{1.30.44.44}$ 13$_{29(ms).30}$ 1 C 13$_{2}$ 15$_{11.14}$ 23$_{2}$ 24$_{6.31}$ 28$_{13.21}$ 2 C 7$_{6}$ 8$_{14.15}$ 11$_{13}$ 13$_{9.10}$ 19$_{8}$ 23$_{4}$ 24$_{5}$ 29$_{4.26}$ 30$_{15.21.25}$ 31$_{2.2.4.9.17.19}$ 34$_{30}$ 35$_{8.10.11.18}$ 1QM 7$_{15}$ 1QS 1$_{18}$ 2$_{11}$ 4Q

Md 1$_{2}$ 11QT 57$_{12}$ 58$_{13}$ 61$_{8}$ CD 14$_{3.5}$, + לֵוִי Ne 8$_{9}$ 10$_{39}$ 13$_{5.13}$ 2 C 23$_{6}$ 29$_{34.34}$ 30$_{16}$ 35$_{14}$ 1QM 7$_{13}$ 8$_{8}$ 13$_{1}$ (ה[כו]הנים) 1QS 1$_{21}$ 2$_{19}$ 4QMa 1$_{9}$ (ה[כוהנ]ים והלויי[ן]ם) 4QMd 1$_{3}$ 11QT 21$_{4}$ ([הכוהנ]ים) 22$_{10.11}$ CD 3$_{21}$.

כֹּהֵן || נָבִיא *prophet* 1 K 18$_{32.34.38.44.45}$ 2 K 10$_{19}$ 2 K 23$_{2}$ Is 28$_{7}$ Jr 2$_{8.26}$ 4$_{9}$ 5$_{31}$ 6$_{13}$ 8$_{1.10}$ 13$_{13}$ 14$_{18}$ 18$_{18}$ 23$_{11.33.34}$ 26$_{7.8.11.16}$ 29$_{1}$ 32$_{32}$ Ezk 7$_{26}$ Mc 3$_{11}$ Zp 3$_{4}$ Zc 7$_{3}$ Lm 2$_{20}$ 4$_{13}$ Ne 9$_{32}$, + נָבִיא 2 K 19$_{2}$||Is 37$_{2}$ Jr 27$_{16}$ 28$_{1.5}$ 29$_{29}$ 37$_{3}$ Hg 1$_{1.12}$ 2 C 35$_{18}$; || זָקֵן *elder* Dt 31$_{9}$ 1 K 8$_{3}$ Jr 29$_{1}$ Ezk 7$_{26}$ Lm 1$_{19}$ 4$_{16}$ Ezr 3$_{12}$ 1QS 6$_{8}$, + זָקֵן Jos 8$_{33}$ 2 S 17$_{15}$ 19$_{12}$ 2 K 19$_{2}$||Is 37$_{2}$ Jr 19$_{1}$ 1QM 13$_{1}$; || מֶלֶךְ *king* 4QpNah 3.2$_{9}$ 4QpsEzeka 16.1$_{10}$, שַׂר *prince* 4QpNah 3.2$_{9}$, שֹׁפֵט *judge* 11QT 61$_{8}$.

כֹּהֵן || אָב *father* Jg 17$_{10}$ 18$_{19}$, כֹּהֵן + בֵּן *son* of Zadok CD 3$_{21}$, of Israel 4QpsEzeka 16.1$_{5}$ CD 14$_{3.5}$, אִישׁ *man* 1QSa 1$_{2}$ 4QpPsa 1.2$_{18}$, עַם *people* 4QShirb 35$_{4}$, גֵּר *sojourner* CD 14$_{3.5}$, כֹּמֶר *priest (of foreign god)* Zp 1$_{4}$, מְשָׁרֵת *minister* 4QShirb 35$_{4}$, מַלְאָךְ *angel* 4QShirb 35$_{4}$, צָבָא *army* 4QShirb 35$_{4}$.

כֹּהֵן || תּוֹרָה *law* 2 C 15$_{3}$, + תּוֹרָה Lv 7$_{7}$ 14$_{2}$ Nm 5$_{30}$ 31$_{21}$ Dt 17$_{18}$ 31$_{9}$ 2 K 22$_{8}$ 23$_{24}$ Jr 2$_{8}$ 18$_{18}$ Ezk 7$_{26}$ 22$_{26}$ Zp 3$_{4}$ Hg 2$_{11}$ Ml 2$_{7}$ Ezr 3$_{2}$ Ne 8$_{2.9.13}$ 9$_{34}$ 10$_{29.35.37}$ 12$_{44}$ 2 C 23$_{18}$ 30$_{16}$ 31$_{4}$ 34$_{14}$.

Also 4QpIsac 12$_{6}$ (הכ[והנים]) 4QDa 6.1$_{2}$ (הכוה[ן]) 4QDb 10$_{2}$ 4QBerd 2$_{3}$ (הכוה[נים]) 4QpsEzeka 43$_{2}$ 4QShirShabba 1.1$_{12}$ (כו[הני]) 4QShirShabbb 11$_{1}$ (כוהנ[י]) 4QMa 21$_{2}$ (הכ[והנים]) 4QRitPur 116$_{1}$ 4QBéat 6$_{3}$ 11QT 17$_{1}$ Mount Gerizim stone inscr. 1.

<SYN> לֵוִי *Levite*, נָבִיא *prophet*, זָקֵן *elder*, אָב *father*, תּוֹרָה *law*.

→ כהן *act as priest*, כְּהֻנָּה *priesthood*.

כְּהֻנָּה 14.1.12 n.f. **priesthood**—Si, Q כהונה; cstr. כְּהֻנַּת (Q כהונת); sf. Q כְּהֻנָּתָם, כְּהֻנַּתְכֶם, כוהנתנו (Q כהונתם); pl. כְּהֻנּוֹת—**priesthood, priestly office; priestly duty** (1 S 2$_{36}$).*

<SUBJ> היה *be* Ex 29$_{9}$ Si 45$_{24}$ 4QapMes 11$_{3}$ (כהונה ת[היה]). <NOM CL> כְּהֻנַּת י׳ נַחֲלָתוֹ *the priesthood of Y. is his inheritance* Jos 18$_{7}$ (mss נַחֲלָתָם *their inheritance*), וכוהנתנו מה במעוניהם *and what (value) is our priesthood in their dwelling places?* 4QShirShabba 2$_{6}$. <OBJ> נתן *give* Nm 18$_{7}$ (+ עֲבֹדַת מַתָּנָה *as a service of gift*, i.e. given as a favour), שׁמר *keep* Nm 3$_{10}$ 18$_{7}$, בקשׁ pi. *seek*, i.e. aspire to Nm 16$_{10}$.

<CSTR> כְּהֻנַּת י׳ *priesthood of Y.* Jos 18$_{7}$, עוֹלָם *of eternity* Ex 40$_{15}$ Nm 25$_{13}$=1QSb 3$_{26}$ (כהונת [עולם]); AHL ([כהו]נת קורבו, כהונ[תו]) *priesthood(s) of his sanctuary* 4QShirShabbf 8$_{5}$, [כוה]נות פלא *priesthood of wonder* 4QShirShabbd 1.2$_{21}$; עֲוֹן כְּהֻנַּתְכֶם *iniquity of your priesthood* Nm 18$_{1}$, גָּאֳלֵי הַכְּהֻנָּה *defilement(s) of the priesthood* Ne 13$_{29}$, בְּרִית *covenant of* Ne 13$_{29}$ (ms הַכֹּהֲנִים *of the priests*) 1QSb 3$_{26}$, שמן משחית כהונתם *anointing oil of their priesthood* 1QM 9$_{8}$, שמן כהונתם *oil of their priesthood* 4QMc$_{5}$, בְּרִית כְּהֻנַּת עוֹלָם perh. *a covenant of eternal priesthood* Nm 25$_{13}$ =1QSb 3$_{26}$, ראשי נשיאי כוה[נות פלא] *chiefs of the princes of the wonderful priesthood* 4QShirShabbd 1.2$_{21}$=4QShirShabbf 8$_{6}$, [שב]עת דבירי כהונו[ת] *seven sanctuaries of priesthood* 4QShirShabbf 7$_{7}$, אַחַת הַכְּהֻנּוֹת *a single priestly duty* 1 S 2$_{36}$, שבע [כהו]נת קורבו *seven priesthoods of his sanctuary* 4QShirShabbf 8$_{5}$.

<ADJ> כהונה גדולה *high priesthood* Si 45$_{24}$. <PREP> לְ *as*, + היה *be* Ex 40$_{15}$; מִן *from, so as not to share in*, + גאל pu. *be defiled* Ezr 2$_{62}$||Ne 7$_{64}$. <COLL> שבע [כוה]נות perh. *seven priesthoods* 4QShirShabbd 1.2$_{22}$.

Also 1QDM 4$_{8}$ 4QShirShabba 1.2$_{19}$ (כוהנו[ת]) 4QShirShabbf 7$_{8}$ ([כ]הונתו) 8$_{7}$ (כוה[נות]) 4QPrQuot 64$_{3}$ 72$_{6}$ 81$_{2}$ 4QapMes 8$_{9}$ (כ[הונה]).

→ כֹּהֵן *priest*.

כּוּב 1 pl.n. **Cub**, country in Africa or Arabia, <SUBJ> נפל *fall* Ezk 30$_{5}$ (|| Ethiopia, Put, Lud, Arabia; or em. לוּב *Libya*).

כּוֹבַע 6 n.m. **helmet**—כּוֹבַע; cstr. כּוֹבַע; pl. כּוֹבָעִים—<NOM CL> כּוֹבַע נְחֹשֶׁת עַל־רֹאשׁוֹ *a helmet of bronze was upon his head* 1 S 17$_{5}$, כֻּלָּם מָגֵן וְכוֹבַע *all of them have shield and helmet* Ezk 38$_{5}$. <OBJ> לבשׁ *clothe oneself with* Is 59$_{17}$, כון hi. *prepare* 2 C 26$_{14}$ (+ מָגֵן *shield*, רֹמַח *lance*, שִׁרְיוֹן *coat of mail*, קֶשֶׁת *bow*), תלא *hang* Ezk 27$_{10}$ (+ מָגֵן *shield*). <CSTR> כּוֹבַע נְחֹשֶׁת *a helmet of bronze* 1 S 17$_{5}$, כּוֹבַע יְשׁוּעָה *a helmet of salvation* Is 59$_{17}$. <PREP> בְּ of accompaniment, + יצב htp. *position oneself* Jr 46$_{4}$.

→ קוֹבַע *helmet*.

כוה 2.1 vb. **burn—Qal burn,** הֲלוֹא כֹה דְבָרִי כָּאֵשׁ *does not my word burn like fire?* Jr 23$_{29}$ (if em. כֹּה is not, *thus* my word, like fire?).

Also perh. 4QShir^{b} 73$_{1}$ (הכווה).

Ni. 2.1 Impf. Si 3fs תכוה, 2ms תִּכָּוֶה, 3fpl תִּכָּוֶינָה—**be burned, be scorched,** <SUBJ> Israel Is 43$_{2}$, Jacob Is 43$_{2}$, רֶגֶל *foot* Pr 6$_{28}$, עַיִן *eye* Si 43$_{4}$.

⇒ כְּוִיָּה *burn,* כִּי III *burn,* מִכְוָה *burn.*

[כּוֹזֵבָא], see כֹּזֵבָא *Cozeba.*

כּוֹחַ, see כֹּחַ *strength.*

כְּוִיָּה 2 n.f. **burn,** <OBJ> נתן *give* Ex 21$_{25.25}$. <PREP> תַּחַת *instead of, for,* + נתן *give* Ex 21$_{25}$.

⇒ כוה *burn.*

[כּוּךְ] n.[m.] **crypt,** בביבא הגדולא של הכוך כל[י]ן בית הכוך *in the large drain of the crypt are vessels of the crypt* 3QTr 12$_{8}$ (others של הברך כלבית הברך *of Habbaruch, going towards Beth-habbaruch,* or בזך ... בזך *basin ... basin,* or של הבזך כלבית הבזך *of Habbazach on the way to Beth-habbazach,* or של הבור [ב]בית הבור *of the cistern in the place of the cistern*), תחת סף הכוך ככרין *under the threshold of the crypt are 42 talents* 12$_{2}$ (others הבור *the cistern*).*

כּוֹכָב 37.2.12 n.m. **star**—cstr. כּוֹכַב; pl. כּוֹכָבִים; cstr. כּוֹכְבֵי; sf. כּוֹכְבֵיהֶם—usu. **star;** perh. at Am 5$_{26}$ **royal ensign,*** <SUBJ> היה *be* 1QH 1$_{12}$ ([והיו]; || מָאוֹר *luminary,* + רוּחַ *spirit*), זכך *be pure* Jb 25$_{5}$ (+ יָרֵחַ *moon*), חשך *be darkened* Jb 3$_{9}$ Ec 12$_{2}$ (|| שֶׁמֶשׁ *sun,* יָרֵחַ, אוֹר *light*), דרך *advance* Nm 24$_{17}$=1QM 11$_{6}$=CD 7$_{19}$ (|| שֵׁבֶט *sceptre*), יצא *go out* Ne 4$_{15}$, אסף *remove,* i.e. withhold Jl 2$_{10}$ 4$_{15}$, לחם ni. *fight* Jg 5$_{20}$, הלל hi. *let shine* Is 13$_{10}$ (|| כְּסִיל *star*), שׁחה htpal. *bow down* Gn 37$_{9}$, רנן *sing* Jb 38$_{7}$, הלל pi. *praise* Ps 148$_{3}$.

<NOM CL> הכוכב הוא דורש התורה *the star is the interpreter of the law* CD 7$_{18}$, לילה ירח וכוכבים *by night are the moon and the stars* 4Q392 1$_{6}$.

<OBJ> ראה *see* Dt 4$_{19}$ (|| שֶׁמֶשׁ *sun,* יָרֵחַ *moon*) Ps 8$_{4}$ (|| יָרֵחַ *moon*), צפה *watch* 3QpsJub^{a} 2.1$_{5}$, כון pol. *establish* Ps 8$_{4}$ (|| יָרֵחַ *moon*), עשׂה *make* Gn 1$_{16}$ (|| מָאוֹר *luminary*) Ps 136$_{9}$ (|| יָרֵחַ *moon*) 4QJub^{a} 2$_{8}$ ([עשה]; || יָרֵחַ), אור hi. *cause to shine* perh. 4QapPs^{b} 1$_{5}$ (ויהיר), קדר hi. *darken* Ezk 32$_{7}$, ספר *count* Gn 15$_{5}$, רמס *trample* Dn 8$_{10}$.

<CSTR> כּוֹכְבֵי הַשָּׁמַיִם *stars of the heavens* Gn 22$_{17}$ 26$_{4}$ Ex 32$_{13}$ (הַשָּׁמָיִם) Dt 1$_{10}$ 10$_{22}$ 28$_{62}$ Is 13$_{10}$ Na 3$_{16}$ Ne 9$_{23}$ (הַשָּׁמָיִם) 1 C 27$_{23}$ 4QRitMar 27$_{4}$ ([כוכב]י השמים), כּוֹכְבֵי־אֵל *stars of God* (unless *mighty stars*) Is 14$_{13}$,* כּוֹכַב אֱלֹהֵיכֶם *star of your god* Am 5$_{26}$, כוכב אור *star of light,* i.e. shining star Si 50$_{6}$, כּוֹכְבֵי אוֹר *stars of light* Ps 148$_{3}$, כּוֹכְבֵי בֹקֶר *stars of the morning* Jb 38$_{7}$, כּוֹכְבֵי נִשְׁפּוֹ *stars of its twilight* Jb 3$_{9}$.

רֹאשׁ כּוֹכָבִים *head of,* i.e. height of, *the stars* Jb 22$_{12}$, הדר כוכב *splendour of the stars* Si 43$_{9(B)}$, חֻקֹּת ... כּוֹכָבִים *statutes,* i.e. fixed times, *of ... the stars* Jr 31$_{35}$, [מאור]ות כוכבים *luminaries of the stars* 4QMyst^{a} 5$_{1}$, כָּל־כּוֹכְבֵי *all stars of* Ps 148$_{3}$.

<PREP> לְ of possession, *of, (belonging) to* Ps 147$_{4}$; בְּ introducing object, + חזה *see* Is 47$_{13}$; כְּ *as* Gn 22$_{17}$ 26$_{4}$ Ex 32$_{13}$ Dt 1$_{10}$ 10$_{22}$ 28$_{62}$ Ne 9$_{23}$ 1 C 27$_{23}$, + זהר hi. *shine* Dn 12$_{3}$; מִן of comparison, *more (than),* + רבה hi. *increase* Na 3$_{16}$; partitive, *some of, (any)one of,* + נפל hi. *bring down* Dn 8$_{10}$; עִם *with* 4QRitMar 27$_{4}$; בֵּין *among,* + שׂים *place* Ob$_{4}$; בַּעַד introducing object, + חתם *seal* Jb 9$_{7}$; מִמַּעַל לְ *above,* + רום hi. *elevate* Is 14$_{13}$.

Also 4QJub^{h} 56$_{2}$ 4QNarrA 2.1$_{2}$ 11QJub 12$_{16}$ ([הכוכ]בים) 12$_{17}$ ([הכוכב]ים).

<SYN> אוֹר *light,* מָאוֹר *luminary,* שֶׁמֶשׁ *sun,* יָרֵחַ *moon,* שֵׁבֶט *sceptre.**

[כּוֹכָבָה] 0.0.1 pl.n. **Cochaba,** perh. Kōkab, 15 km NNW of Nazareth, 5QTopon 5$_{1}$.

כול 37.7.8.4 vb. **contain—Qal** 1.0.1.4 Pf. כָּל, I 1cs כלת; impf. Q יכול; + waw I ויכל; ptc. I כל—**lay hold of, seize, measure,** <SUBJ> עֶבֶד *servant* Meṣad Ḥashavyahu ost. 1$_{5.6}$ (both + אסם *store*), מִי *who?* Is 40$_{12}$ 4QShir^{b} 30$_{5}$ ([מי]); subj. not specified, Gezer calendar$_{5}$ Meṣad Ḥashavyahu ost. 1$_{8}$. <OBJ> קָצִיר *grain* Meṣad Ḥashavyahu ost. 1$_{6.8}$, עָפָר *dust* of the earth Is 40$_{12}$ 4QShir^{b} 30$_{5}$. <PREP> בְּ of place, *in(to),* or instrument, *by (means of), with,* + שָׁלִישׁ *third (measure)* Is 40$_{12}$ 4QShir^{b}

30$_{5}$ ([בשליש]).

Pilp. 23.4.3 Pf. כִּלְכֵּל (כִּלְכְּלָם), כִּלְכַּלְתֶּם, כִּלְכְּלוּ, Q כלכלנו; impf. יְכַלְכֵּל (יְכַלְכֶּלְךָ, Si יכלכלנה), Q תכלכל, אֲכַלְכֵּל, יְכַלְכְּלוּךָ (יְכַלְכְּלֵהוּ); + waw וְכִלְכַּלְתִּי; וַיְכַלְכֵּל (וַיְכַלְכְּלֵם), וָאֲכַלְכְּלֵם; ptc. מְכַלְכֵּל, Si מכלכלת; inf. כַּלְכֵּל—**contain, hold in, restrain, provide for, sustain, support, endure, manage** or **measure*** (Ps 112$_{5}$), <SUBJ> שָׁמַיִם *heavens* 1 K 8$_{27}$||2 C 6$_{18}$ 2 C 2$_{5}$, 'י *Y.* Ps 55$_{23}$, אֱלוֹהַּ *God* Ne 9$_{21}$ (+ חסר *be lacking*), Barzillai 2 S 19$_{33}$, Jeremiah Jr 20$_{9}$ (+ יכל *be able*), Job Si 49$_{9}$, Joseph Gn 45$_{11}$ 47$_{12}$ 50$_{21}$, Obadiah 1 K 18$_{4.13}$, אִישׁ *man* Ps 112$_{5}$, אִשָּׁה *woman* 1 K 17$_{9}$ Si 25$_{22}$, בֵּן *son* Ru 4$_{15}$, מֶלֶךְ *king* 2 S 19$_{34}$ 20$_{3}$, נִצָּב *overseer* 1 K 4$_{7}$ 5$_{7}$ (+ עדר pi. *omit*), רֹעֶה *shepherd* Zc 11$_{16}$, אַלְמָנָה *widow* 1 K 17$_{9}$, חסר ptc. *one who lacks* Si 6$_{20}$, עֹרֵב *raven* 1 K 17$_{4}$, רוּחַ *spirit* of a man Pr 18$_{14}$, אֶחָד *one* governor 1 K 4$_{7}$, מִי *who?* Ml 3$_{2}$ 4Q185 1.1$_{8}$ (both + עמד *stand*); subj. not specified, Si 45$_{24}$.

<OBJ> אֱלֹהִים *God* 1 K 8$_{27}$||2 C 6$_{18}$ 2 C 2$_{5}$, Barzillai 2 S 19$_{34}$, Elijah 1 K 17$_{4.9}$, אִשָּׁה *woman* 2 S 20$_{3}$, אָב *father* Gn 47$_{12}$, אָב Israelite *ancestor* Ne 9$_{21}$, אָח *brother* of Joseph Gn 45$_{11}$ 47$_{12}$ 50$_{21}$, טַף *child* Gn 50$_{21}$, מֶלֶךְ *king* 2 S 19$_{33}$ 1 K 4$_{7}$ 5$_{7}$, נָבִיא *prophet* 1 K 18$_{4.13}$, פִּלֶגֶשׁ *secondary wife* 2 S 20$_{3}$, נִצָּבָה *wretched one* Zc 11$_{16}$, worshipper Ps 55$_{23}$, קָרֵב *one who approaches* 1 K 5$_{7}$, בַּיִת *house(hold)* Gn 47$_{12}$ 1 K 4$_{7}$, מִקְדָּשׁ *sanctuary* Si 45$_{24}$, מַחֲלֶה *sickness* Pr 18$_{14}$, שֵׂיבָה *old age* Ru 4$_{15}$, יוֹם *day* Ml 3$_{2}$, כֹּל *all* Si 49$_{9}$, חָכְמָה *wisdom* Si 6$_{20}$, דָּבָר measure *word* or *manage* affair Ps 112$_{5}$.

<PREP> בְּ of place, *in, at*, + Jerusalem 2 S 19$_{34}$, שִׁיבָה *stay* 2 S 19$_{33}$ (or em. שֶׁבֶת *dwelling*); מִדְבָּר *steppe* Ne 9$_{21}$; of instrument, *by (means of), with*, + מִשְׁפָּט *justice* Ps 112$_{5}$; לְפִי *according to*, + טַף *child* Gn 47$_{12}$ (unless לְפִי הַטָּף provide food *for the mouth[s] of the children*); עִם *with*, + מֶלֶךְ *king* 2 S 19$_{34}$.

<COLL> וַיְכַלְכֵּל יוֹסֵף אֶת־אָבִיו ... לֶחֶם *and Joseph provided his father ... with bread* Gn 47$_{12}$, וְכִלְכְּלָם לֶחֶם וָמָיִם *and he provided them with bread and water* 1 K 18$_{4}$, sim. 1 K 18$_{13}$.

Also 4QConfess 1.1$_{10}$ 4Q418 46$_{2}$.

Polp. 1 Pf. כָּלְכְּלוּ—**be provided with,** <SUBJ> בֵּן Israelite *son* 1 K 20$_{27}$.

Hi. 12.0.3 Pf. Q הכיל; impf. יָכִיל (יְכִילֶנּוּ, Q יכילה), יָכִילוּ (יָכִלוּ); inf. הָכִיל—**hold, contain, endure, restrain** (1QS 6$_{12}$), <SUBJ> אֶרֶץ *land* Am 7$_{10}$, גּוֹי *nation* Jr 10$_{10}$, אִישׁ *man*, i.e. overseer 1QS 6$_{12}$ (יכיל *he will restrain*; others וכול *and any*), Jeremiah Jr 6$_{11}$, מִזְבֵּחַ *altar* of bronze 1 K 8$_{64}$||2 C 7$_{7}$, יָם *sea* 1 K 7$_{26}$||2 C 4$_{5}$, מָקוֹר *spring* 4Q418 103.2$_{6}$, בּוֹר *cistern* Jr 2$_{13}$ (or em. כלא *retain*), כִּיּוֹר *wash-basin* 1 K 7$_{38}$, כּוֹס *cup* Ezk 23$_{32}$, חֶרֶב *sword* Ezk 21$_{33}$ (or em. לְכָלָה *for destruction*), מִי *who?* Jl 2$_{11}$ 4QM^{a} 11.1$_{7}$.

<OBJ> אִישׁ *man*, i.e. community member 1QS 6$_{12}$ (יכיל; others וכול *and any* man), עֹלָה *burnt offering* 1 K 8$_{64}$||2 C 7$_{7}$, מִנְחָה *cereal offering* 1 K 8$_{64}$||2 C 7$_{7}$, חֵלֶב *fat* of peace offering 1 K 8$_{64}$||2 C 7$_{7}$, מַיִם *water* Jr 2$_{13}$, בַּת *bath* (liquid measure) 1 K 7$_{26.38}$ 2 C 4$_{5}$, מַרְבָּה *abundance* Ezk 23$_{32}$ (if em.), זַעַם *indignation* Jr 10$_{10}$, יוֹם *day* of Y. Jl 2$_{11}$, דָּבָר *word* Am 7$_{10}$, appar. wisdom 4Q185 2.2$_{12}$.

Htpalp. 0.2.1 Impf. Si יתכלכל, Q יתכלכלו—**withstand, restrain oneself,** <SUBJ> בֵּן *son* of unrighteousness 4QShir^{b} 1$_{8}$, חבר ptc. *one who is joined* to impudent women Si 12$_{15}$, מִי *who?* Si 43$_{3(B)}$. <PREP> לִפְנֵי *before*, + חֹרֶב *heat* Si 43$_{3(B)}$.

Htpol. 0.1 Impf. Si יתכולל—**withstand,** <SUBJ> מִי *who?* Si 43$_{3(M)}$. <PREP> לִפְנֵי *before*, + חֹרֶב *heat* Si 43$_{3(M)}$.*

⇒ כל III *measure*.

כּוּמָז 2.1 n.m. **ornament,** for woman's neck and breast (Ex 35$_{22}$ Nm 31$_{50}$ Si 35$_{5}$), <NOM CL> כומז אודם על ניב זהב *an ornament of ruby is upon a necklace of gold* Si 35$_{5(B)}$. <OBJ> מצא *find* Nm 31$_{50}$ (|| אֶצְעָדָה *bracelet*, צָמִיד *bracelet*, טַבַּעַת *ring*, עָגִיל *anklet*), בוא hi. *bring* Ex 35$_{22}$ (|| נֶזֶם *earring*, טַבַּעַת *ring*, חָח *brooch*). <CSTR> כומז אודם *ornament of ruby* Si 35$_{5(B)}$.

Also perh. 4QRitMar 20$_{4}$ (כו[מז]).

כון 217.15.101 vb. **be upright—Ni.** 65.6.29 Pf. נָכוֹנָה, נָכֹנוּ (נָכוֹנוּ); impf. יִכּוֹן, 3fs תִּכּוֹן; יִכֹּנוּ (Q יכונו); + waw וַתִּכּוֹן; impv. הִכּוֹן, הִכּוֹנוּ; ptc. נָכוֹן (נְכוֹן), נְכוֹנָה, נְכֹנִים, נְכוֹנִים, Q נכונות; inf. Q הכון (Q הנכון)—**1. be firm, be secure, be sure, be ready, be lasting, be established, stand firm,** <SUBJ> תֵּבֵל *world* Ps 93$_{1}$ 96$_{10}$||1 C 16$_{30}$, הַר *mountain* of house of Y. Is 2$_{2}$||Mc 4$_{1}$, דֶּרֶךְ *way* Ps 119$_{5}$ Pr 4$_{26}$ 1QH 4$_{31}$ 7$_{31}$, Gog Ezk 38$_{7}$, Israel Am 4$_{12}$, עַם *people* Ex 19$_{11.15}$

1QH 4_{14}, מַמְלָכָה *kingdom* 1 K 2_{46}, מַלְכוּת *kingdom* 1 S 20_{31} 1 K 2_{12}, עֵדָה *congregation* Jr 30_{20}, עֵצָה *council* 1QS 8_5, בַּיִת *house* Jg $16_{26.29}$ 2 S 7_{26}||1 C 17_{24}, כִּסֵּא *throne* 2 S 7_{16}||1 C 17_{14} 1 K 2_{45} Ps 89_{38} 93_2 Pr 16_{12}, אֱמוּנָה *faithfulness* Ps 89_3 (if em.; see Hi.), אֱמֶת *truth* appar. 1QH 9_{32}, צְדָקָה *righteousness* Si 40_{17} 1QH 8_2 (צדק[תכה]).

Elijah Si 48_{10}, Jonathan 1 S 20_{31}, Moses Ex 34_2, worshipper Ps 38_{18}, אִישׁ *man* Ps 140_{12}, אָדָם *human being* Pr 12_3, אֱנוֹשׁ *human being* Si 34_{19}, בֵּן *son* Si 5_{11}, זֶרַע *seed*, i.e. offspring Ps 102_{29} Jb 21_8, דבר ptc. *speaker* Ps 101_7, הלך ptc. *one who goes* 1QH 4_{22}, רָשָׁע *wicked one* 1QLitPr 3.2_5, שָׂפָה *lip* Pr 12_{19}, שַׁד *breast* Ezk 16_7, לֵב *heart* Ps $57_{8.8}$ 78_{37} 108_2 112_7 4QUnidC 1_4, יָד *hand* Ps 89_{22}, קַו *line* 1QH 8_{21}, מוֹצָא *going out* Ho 6_3, יוֹם *day* Jb 15_{23} Pr 4_{18}, שַׁחַר *dawn* 1QH 4_6.

מִשְׁפָּט *judgment* 1QS 10_{20}, שֶׁפֶט *act of judgment* Pr 19_{29}, אֵיד *disaster* Jb 18_{12}, רוּחַ *spirit* Ps 51_{12}, תְּפִלָּה *prayer* Ps 141_2, מְלָאכָה *work* 2 C 8_{16}, עֲבוֹדָה *service* 2 C 29_{35} $35_{10.16}$, מַחֲשָׁבָה *plan* Pr 16_3 20_{18} 1QH 4_{13}, דָּבָר *word* Pr 22_{18} 1QMyst 1.1_8 perh. 4QapMes 2.3_2 ([דבר]), *thing* Gn 41_{32}, *act* Dt 13_{15}=11QT 55_5 Dt 17_4=11QT 55_{20}, חָזוֹן *vision* 1QH 4_{18}, חֹק *statute* CD 5_{12}, אֵלֶּה *these* 1QS 8_{10}, כֹּל *all* Jos 8_4; subj. not specified, Ex 8_{22} (+ עשׂה *do*) Ne 8_{10} Si $36_{24(\mathrm{Bmg})}$ 4QShir[b] 63.2_4.

<PREP> לְ of direction, *to*, + עַד *eternity* Pr 12_{19} Si 40_{17} 1QH 8_2, נֵצַח *eternity* 1QH $4_{13.22}$ 7_{31}; of benefit, *to, for*, + לֵץ *scoffer* Pr 19_{29}, יַחַד *community* 4Q418 172_3 (ליחן[ד]), צֶלַע *stumbling* Jb 18_{12}, עֲבוֹדָה *service* 4QShir[b] 63.2_4, עֵת *time* Si 48_{10}; *on, in*, + יוֹם *day* Ex $19_{11.15}$, בֹּקֶר *morning* Ex 34_2.

בְּ of instrument, *by (means of)*, + יָד *hand* 1 K 2_{46} Jb 15_{23}, צְדָקָה *righteousness* Pr 16_{12}, רֶשַׁע *injustice* Pr 12_3, עֵצָה *counsel* Pr 20_{18}; of accompaniment, *with, in*, + אֱמֶת *truth* 1QH 4_{14} fr. 2_{15} 1QS 8_5, יְסוֹד *foundation*, i.e. institution, of community 1QS 8_{10}, בְּרִית *covenant* 4QUnidC 1_4 (ברן[ית]); of place/time, *in, at*, + שָׁמַיִם *heavens* Ps 89_3 (if em.), אֶרֶץ *land* Ps 140_{12}, יוֹם *day* 2 C 35_{16}.

כְּ *as*, + שַׁחַר *dawn* Ho 6_3, יָרֵחַ *moon* Ps 89_{38}; מִן of direction, *from*, + אָז *then*, i.e. long time ago Ps 93_2.

עַל *upon*, + עַמּוּד *pillar* Jg $16_{26.29}$, שָׂפָה *lip* Pr 22_{18}; לְנֶגֶד *before*, + עַיִן *eye* Ps 101_7; לִפְנֵי *before*, + ״ *Y.* 2 S 7_{26}||1 C 17_{24} 1 K 2_{45} Jr 30_{20} Ps 141_2, אֲדֹנָי *Adonai* perh. 1QLitPr 3.2_5, אֱלֹהִים *God* 2 S 7_{26}, אֵל *God* Ps 102_{29}, רָשָׁע *wicked one* Jb 21_8; עַד *until*, + עוֹלָם *eternity* 2 S 7_{16}||1 C 17_{14} 1 K 2_{45}; עִם *with*, + אֵל *God* Ps 78_{37}, David Ps 89_{22}, עֶבֶד *servant* Ps 89_{22}; מֵעִם *from (with)*, + אֱלֹהִים *God* Gn 41_{32}.

<COLL> יִכּוֹן עוֹלָם *it shall be established eternally* Ps 89_{38}, תִּכּוֹן תְּפִלָּתִי קְטֹרֶת *let my prayer be established as incense* Ps 141_2, יִכֹּנוּ יַחְדָּו *they will be ready together* upon your lips Pr 22_{18}, נכון הדבר לבוא *the word is sure to come about* 1QMyst 1.1_8; כון ni. + adverb, אֵיכָה *how* 4Q418 172_3.

2. ptc. as noun, **certainty, correctness, established thing, a.** masc., <PREP> אֶל־נָכוֹן *of a certainty*, + בוא *come* 1 S 26_4, שׁוב *go back* 1 S 23_{23}. <COLL> נָכוֹן used adverbially, *correctly*, + ענה *answer* 4QBéat 14.2_{25}, נבע *utter* perh. 4QBéat 23.2_1 (ונ[כון]).

b. fem., <NOM CL> אֵין בְּפִיהוּ נְכוֹנָה *there is no certainty in its mouth* Ps 5_{10}. <CSTR> חוקי נכונות *statutes of established things*, i.e. established statutes 1QH 18_{23}. <COLL> נְכוֹנָה used adverbially, *correctly, certainly*, + דבר pi. *speak* Jb $42_{7.8}$, ענה *answer* Si 5_{11}.

Also Si 34_{20} (נבון corrected to נכון) 4QMyst[a] 34_1 4Q415 9_7 4Q418 122.1_1 4QBéat 7.2_5 11_2 perh. 21_9 ([ ]נכין; others נכון).

Polel $_{30.1.5}$ Pf. כּוֹנֵן (כּוֹנְנָה) כּוֹנַנְתָּ, (Q כוננתה, כּוֹנַנְתָּה, כּוֹנְנוּ (כּוֹנָנוּ), (Q כוננתי) כּוֹנַנְתִּי, (כּוֹנַנְתָּה); impf. יְכוֹנֵן; + waw וַיְכֹנְנֶךָ, וַיְכוֹנְנֶהָ (Si ויכוננהו, וַיְכֹנְנֶךָ [Dt 32_6]), וְכֹנַנְתִּי, וְכוֹנֵן, וַיְכוֹנְנוּנִי, וַתְּכוֹנֵן, וַיְכוֹנְנוּ (כּוֹנְנֵהוּ, כּוֹנְנָה); impv. כּוֹנֵן, ptc. Si מכונן—**prepare, establish, appoint, fashion, grant permanence to, take aim, direct;** perh. **ascertain** (Jb 8_8).*

<SUBJ> ״ *Y.* Dt 32_6 (|| עשׂה *make*) 2 S 7_{13}||1 C 17_{12} Is 45_{18} (|| עשׂה *make*) 62_7 Ps 7_{10} 8_4 9_8 21_{13} 24_2 40_3 (|| קום hi. *raise up*) 99_4 119_{90} Pr 3_{19} GnzPs 1_{10} (|| ישׁר pi. *make straight*), אֲדֹנָי *Adonai* Ps $90_{17.17}$, אֱלֹהִים *God* 2 S 7_{24} Is 45_{18} (|| עשׂה *make*) Ps 48_9 68_{10} Ps $90_{17.17}$, אֵל *God* 1QNoah 15_2 4QHod[b] 7_7, עֶלְיוֹן *Most High* Ps 87_5, יָד *hand* of Y. Ex 15_{17} Ps 119_{73} (|| עשׂה *make*), Abraham Si $44_{23(B)}$, Job Jb 8_8 (or em. בין pol. *understand*), רָעֵב *hungry one* Ps 107_{36}, רָשָׁע *wicked one* Ps 11_2, מֵצִיק *oppressor* Is 51_{13}, אֶחָד *one* Jb 31_{15}; subj. not specified, Hb 2_{12} Ps 7_{13}.

<OBJ> תֵּבֵל *world* Ps 24_2, שָׁמַיִם *heavens* Pr 3_{19}, יָרֵחַ *moon* Ps 8_4, כּוֹכָב *star* Ps 8_4, אֶרֶץ *land* Is 45_{18} Ps 119_{90},

Zion Ps 87$_5$, עַם *people* Dt 32$_6$ 2 S 7$_{24}$, Israel 2 S 7$_{24}$, Jerusalem Is 62$_7$, עִיר *city* Ps 48$_9$ 107$_{36}$, קִרְיָה *city* Hb 2$_{12}$, מִקְדָּשׁ *sanctuary* Ex 15$_{17}$, כִּסֵּא *throne* 2 S 7$_{13}$||1 C 17$_{12}$ Ps 9$_8$, אָשֻׁר *step* Ps 40$_3$, מַעֲשֶׂה *work* Ps 90$_{17.17}$, דֶּרֶךְ *way* Gnz Ps 1$_{10}$, נַחֲלָה *inheritance* Ps 68$_{10}$, מֵישָׁר *uprightness* Ps 99$_4$, Isaac Si 44$_{23}$, צַדִּיק *righteous one* Ps 7$_{10}$, worshipper Ps 119$_{73}$ Jb 31$_{15}$, רֶגֶל *foot* 4QHod^b 7$_5$, קֶשֶׁת *bow* Ps 7$_{13}$, חֵץ *arrow* Ps 11$_2$.

<PREP> לְ of benefit, *to, for,* + אֱלֹהִים *God* 2 S 7$_{24}$, מִשְׁפָּט *judgment* Ps 9$_8$; *as,* + עַם *people* 2 S 7$_{24}$; of instrument, *by (means of)* or introducing object, + חֵקֶר *searching* of their fathers Jb 8$_8$.

בְּ of place, *in,* + רֶחֶם *womb* Jb 31$_{15}$, דֶּרֶךְ *way* 4QHod^b 7$_5$; of instrument, *by (means of), with,* + עַוְלָה *injustice* Hb 2$_{12}$, מֵיתָר *bow-string* Ps 21$_{13}$, בְּרָכָה *blessing* Si 44$_{23}$, תְּבוּנָה *understanding* Pr 3$_{19}$.

אֶל *to,* + מִצְוָה *commandment* GnzPs 1$_{10}$; עַל *upon,* + פָּנִים *face* Ps 21$_{13}$, worshipper Ps 90$_{17}$, נָהָר *river* Ps 24$_2$, יֶתֶר *bow-string* Ps 11$_2$; עַד *until,* + עוֹלָם *eternity* 2 S 7$_{13}$ ||1 C 17$_{12}$ 2 S 7$_{24}$ Ps 48$_9$.

Also 1QH fr. 47$_3$ 11QHymn^a 1$_1$.

<SYN> עשׂה *make,* קום hi. *raise up,* ישׁר pi. *make straight.*

Polal 2.1 Pf. כּוֹנָנוּ—**be prepared,** <SUBJ> הֵיכָל *temple* Si 49$_{12}$, מִצְעָד *step* Ps 37$_{23}$, אֶבֶן precious *stone* Ezk 28$_{13}$. <PREP> לְ of benefit, *to, for,* + כָּבוֹד *glory* Si 49$_{12}$; מִן of agent, *by (means of),* + ׳׳ *Y.* Ps 37$_{23}$.

Hi. 110.7.62 Pf. הֵכִין (Q היכין, הֱכִינַנִי, הֱכִינוֹ, הֱכִינָהּ), הֲכִינֹתִי (הכינותמה Q, הכינותם Q, הֱכִינֹתָ) הֲכִינוֹתָה (הֲכִנֹתִי, הֲכִינוֹתִי), הֵכִינוּ (הֵכַנּוּ 2 C 29$_{19}$); impf. יָכִין (Q יהכין), 3fs תָּכִין, 2ms תָּכִין (תְּכִינֶה, תָּכֵן), אָכִין (אָכִינָה); + waw וַיָּכֶן (וַהֲכִינֹתִי) וַהֲכִינוֹתִי (וַהֲכִינֹתָה) וַהֲכִינוֹתָ, 2ms Q ותכן, וַיָּכִינוּ; impv. הָכֵן (Si הכין), הָכִינוּ; ptc. מֵכִין; inf. הָכִין (Q הכינו)—**1. prepare, determine, establish, appoint, create, accomplish, make firm, consider.**

<SUBJ> ׳׳ *Y.* Ex 23$_{20}$ 1 S 13$_{13}$ 2 S 5$_{12}$||1 C 14$_2$ 2 S 7$_{12}$ ||1 C 17$_{11}$ 1 K 2$_{24}$ (|| ישׁב hi. *place*) Jr 10$_{12}$ 33$_2$ 51$_{15}$ Zp 1$_7$ Ps 10$_{17}$ 89$_3$ (or em. תִּכֹּן your faithfulness *will stand firm,* i.e. ni.) 89$_5$ 103$_{19}$ 119$_{133}$ 147$_8$ Pr 8$_{27}$ 16$_9$ 1 C 22$_{10}$ 28$_7$ 29$_{18}$ 2 C 17$_5$ Si 47$_{11}$ 11QPs^a 26$_{11}$, אֲדֹנָי *Adonai* 1QH 7$_{9.13}$ 10$_{22}$ (+ יצר *form*) 11$_{34}$ perh. 13$_7$ ([הכי]נותה) perh. 13$_{10}$ 15$_{14.15.19.22}$ ([ה]הכינותה; + יצר *form*) fr. 15$_6$ ([ה]כינותה) 4QBark^a 1.2$_4$, appar. Y. 4QD^c 1$_6$ 11QT 29$_{10}$, אֱלֹהִים *God* Ex 23$_{20}$ Jr 10$_{12}$ Ps 65$_{7.10.10}$ 68$_{11}$ 74$_{16}$ 78$_{20}$ Jb 28$_{27}$ 1 C 29$_{18}$ 2 C 29$_{36}$, אֵל *God* Si 37$_{15}$ 47$_{13}$ 1QH 1$_{14.19.28}$ 2$_{17}$ 6$_{10}$ 7$_{24}$ ([הכי]נותה) 7$_{25}$ (both [א]לי) 10$_{22}$ 12$_{11.34}$ ([הכינ]ותני) 18$_{22}$ (+ גבר hi. *strengthen*) fr. 4$_{15}$ ([הכינו]תה) 1QS 3$_{15}$ 10$_{20}$ 11$_{11.13.16}$ 1QSb 3$_{20}$ 4QpPs^a 1.3$_{16}$ 4QAges^a 1$_2$ 4QHod^b 7$_8$ (הכינ[ו]תה) 4QpsHod^b 3.1$_{22}$.

Egypt Jr 46$_{14}$, Gog Ezk 38$_7$, Israelite(s) Dt 19$_3$, Ephraimite(s) Jg 12$_6$, Gebalite(s) 1 K 5$_{32}$, Ziphite(s) 1 S 23$_{22}$, עַם *people* Ex 16$_5$ Jos 1$_{11}$ 2 C 20$_{33}$, בַּיִת *house* of Israel 1 S 7$_3$, קָהָל *assembly* 1 C 29$_{16}$, דּוֹר *generation* Ps 78$_8$.

Balak Nm 23$_{1.29}$, David 1 C 15$_{1.3.12}$ 22$_{3.5.5.14.14}$ 28$_2$ 29$_{2.3.16.19}$ 2 C 1$_4$ 2$_6$ 3$_1$ Si 47$_9$ GnzPs 1$_{16}$, Elijah Si 48$_{10}$, Ezekiel Ezk 4$_{3.7}$, Ezra Ezr 7$_{10}$, Haman Est 6$_4$ 7$_{10}$, Jehoshaphat 2 C 19$_3$, Jeshua Ezr 3$_3$, Job Jb 11$_{13}$ 29$_7$, Joshua Jos 4$_4$, Josiah 2 C 35$_{20}$, Jotham 2 C 27$_6$, Manasseh 2 C 33$_{16(Kt)}$, Rehoboam 2 C 12$_{14}$, Samuel Si 46$_{13}$, z1 K 6$_{19}$, Uzziah 2 C 26$_{14}$.

אִישׁ *man* Gn 43$_{25}$ Jr 10$_{23}$ 1QS 3$_9$, גֶּבֶר *man* 1QH 2$_{17}$, אָדָם *human being* 4QBéat 3.2$_4$, אֱנוֹשׁ *human being* 1QH 15$_{11}$ 1QS 11$_{10}$, אָב *father* 2 C 2$_6$, בֵּן *son* Pr 24$_{27}$ 1 C 9$_{32}$ 4QSela 8.2$_5$ ([י]כין]), אָח *brother* Ezr 3$_{3.3}$ 1 C 12$_{40}$ 2 C 35$_{15}$, חָרָשׁ *artisan* Is 40$_{20}$, עֶבֶד *servant* 2 C 2$_8$ GnzPs 1$_{16}$, יָשָׁר *upright one* Pr 21$_{29(Kt)}$, רָשָׁע *wicked one* Ps 7$_{14}$ Jb 27$_{16.17}$, יֹשֵׁב *inhabitant* Ezk 7$_{14}$, בֹּנֶה *builder* 1 K 5$_{32.32}$, כֹּהֵן *priest* Ezr 3$_3$ 2 C 29$_{19}$ 31$_{11.11}$, לֵוִי *Levite* 2 C 31$_{11.11}$ 35$_{4(Qr)}$ 35$_{6.14.14.15}$, בָּשָׂר *flesh* 1QH 15$_{21}$, לֵב *heart* 4QWiles 1$_2$, בֶּטֶן *inner self* Jb 15$_{35}$, רוּחַ *spirit* perh. 4Q415 11$_8$, שֹׁרֶשׁ *root* of Jesse GnzPs 1$_{16}$.

אֲשֶׁר עַל־בֵּיתוֹ *one who was over his house,* i.e. his steward Gn 43$_{16}$, נְמָלָה *ant* Pr 6$_8$ 30$_{25}$, סֶרֶךְ *rule* CD 14$_{12}$, כֹּל *everyone* 2 C 30$_{19}$; subj. not specified, Jos 3$_{17}$ 4$_3$ Is 9$_6$ (|| סעד *support*) 14$_{21}$ Jr 51$_{12}$ Na 2$_4$ Ps 57$_7$ Jb 38$_{41}$ 2 C 12$_1$ Si 35$_2$ 4Q418 81$_{18}$ 11QPs^a 26$_{14}$ (|| עשׂה *make*) perh. 4QPrFêtes^c 12.1$_3$ (unless מבין *one who understands*).

<OBJ> תֵּבֵל *world* Jr 10$_{12}$ 51$_{15}$ 4Q418 159.2$_7$ 11QPs^a 26$_{14}$, שָׁמַיִם *heavens* Pr 8$_{27}$, שֶׁמֶשׁ *sun* Ps 74$_{16}$, מָאוֹר *luminary* Ps 74$_{16}$, אוֹר *light* 1QH 7$_{24}$ ([אור אשר הכי]נותה]), שַׁחַר *dawn* 11QPs^a 26$_{11}$, תְּקוּפָה *circuit* 1QH 12$_{11}$, צָבָא *host* of heaven 4Q416 1$_7$, אֶרֶץ *earth* Jr 33$_2$, הַר *mountain* Ps 65$_7$, מָקוֹם *place* Ex 23$_{20}$ 1 C 15$_{1.3.12(mss)}$, בַּיִת *house* 2 C 35$_{20}$ Si 47$_{13}$, מִקְדָּשׁ *sanctuary* 11QT 29$_{10}$, דְּבִיר *inner*

sanctuary 1 K 6$_{19}$, לִשְׁכָּה *hall* 2 C 31$_{11}$, מַבְנִית *building* 1QH 7$_{8}$, אשׁ *foundation* 1QH 7$_{8}$ 1QSb 3$_{20}$, דֶּרֶךְ *way* Dt 19$_{3}$ Pr 21$_{29}$ 2 C 27$_{6}$, מוֹשָׁב *seat* Jb 29$_{7}$, צַעַד *step* Jr 10$_{23}$ Pr 16$_{9}$ Si 37$_{15}$ 1QH 15$_{11.21}$ 1QS 11$_{10}$, פַּעַם *step* Ps 119$_{133}$ 1QS 3$_{9}$ 11$_{13}$.

David 2 S 5$_{12}$||1 C 14$_{2}$, Solomon 1 K 2$_{24}$, אִישׁ *man* Jos 4$_{4}$, זֶרַע *seed*, i.e. offspring Ps 89$_{5}$, יֹשֵׁב *inhabitant* 1QH 1$_{14}$ ([יוש]ביהם), חָכָם *skilled one* 2 C 2$_{6}$, צַדִּיק *righteous one* 1QH 15$_{15}$, מוֹרֶה *teacher* 4QpPs^a 1.3$_{16}$, רָשָׁע *wicked one* 1QH 15$_{19}$, worshipper 1QH 10$_{22}$ 12$_{34}$ (הכינ[ו]תני), שְׁאֵרִית *remnant* 1QH 6$_{10}$, מִחְיָה *preservation of life*, i.e. survivor 1QH 6$_{10}$, כִּסֵּא *throne* Ps 103$_{19}$ 1 C 22$_{10}$ Si 47$_{11}$, מַמְלָכָה *kingdom* 1 S 13$_{13}$ 2 S 7$_{12}$ 2 C 17$_{5}$ Si 46$_{13}$, מַלְכוּת *kingdom* 1 C 17$_{11}$ 28$_{7}$ 2 C 12$_{1}$, מִשְׂרָה *dominion* Is 9$_{6}$, שֶׁבַח *praise* GnzPs 1$_{16}$, אֱמוּנָה *faithfulness* Ps 89$_{3}$, אֱמֶת *truth* 4QM^a 11.1$_{10}$, חָכְמָה *wisdom* Jb 28$_{27}$, דַּעַת *knowledge* 4QHod^b 7$_{8}$ (הכינ[ו]תה), מַחֲשָׁבָה *plan* 1QS 3$_{15}$, תְּעוּדָה *destiny* 1QH 1$_{19}$, מוֹעֵד *appointed time* 4QD^c 1$_{6}$ ([מועדי]), רָז *mystery* 4QM^a 11.1$_{10}$, perh. מַעֲנֶה *reply* 1QH 11$_{34}$, טוֹב *good* 4QpsHod^b 3.1$_{22}$ (בטובכה with prep. erased).

פַּר *bull* Nm 23$_{1.29}$, מַטְבֵּחַ *slaughter-yard* Is 14$_{21}$, מִנְחָה *present* Gn 43$_{16}$, זֶבַח *sacrifice* Zp 1$_{7}$, מִזְבֵּחַ *altar* Ezr 3$_{3}$ 2 C 33$_{16}$, צֹרֶךְ *need* Si 35$_{2}$, צֵידָה *provisions* Jos 1$_{11}$, צַיִד *provisions* Jb 38$_{41}$, הָמוֹן *abundance* 1 C 29$_{16}$, מָטָר *rain* Ps 147$_{8}$, שְׁאֵר *flesh* Ps 78$_{20}$, לֶחֶם *food* Pr 6$_{8}$ 30$_{25}$, דָּגָן *grain* Ps 65$_{10.10}$, פְּרִי *fruit* 1QH 1$_{28}$, עֵץ *wood* 1 K 5$_{32}$ 1 C 22$_{10}$ 29$_{2}$ 2 C 2$_{8}$, *gallows* Est 6$_{4}$ 7$_{10}$, אֶבֶן *stone* 1 K 5$_{32}$ 1 C 22$_{10}$ 29$_{2}$, נְחֹשֶׁת *bronze* 1 C 29$_{2}$ 4QSela 8.2$_{5}$ ([נחושת ... יכין]), בַּרְזֶל *iron* 1 C 22$_{3}$ 29$_{2}$ 4QSela 8.2$_{5}$ ([יכין]), כֶּסֶף *silver* 1 C 22$_{14}$ 29$_{2}$ 4QSela 8.2$_{5}$ ([ברזל יכין]), זָהָב *gold* 1 C 22$_{14}$ 29$_{2}$ 4QSela 8.2$_{5}$ ([יכין]).

מַלְבּוּשׁ *clothing* Jb 27$_{16}$, מַעֲשֶׂה *work* 1QS 11$_{16}$, מְלָאכָה *work* Pr 24$_{27}$, פְּעֻלָּה *work* 1QH 15$_{14}$ (פעולת[ו]) 15$_{22}$ 4QAges^a 1$_{2}$, חֵפֶץ *requirement* CD 14$_{12}$, צֶדֶק *righteousness* 4Q416 1$_{15}$ (=4Q418 2$_{7}$ הבין *to understand*), מִרְמָה *deceit* Jb 15$_{35}$, פַּחוּז *wantonness* 4QWiles 1$_{2}$, פֶּסֶל *image* Is 40$_{20}$, רֶשֶׁת *net* Ps 57$_{7}$, אֶרֶב *ambush* Jr 51$_{12}$, כְּלִי *weapon* Ps 7$_{14}$, *utensil* 2 C 29$_{19}$, רֶכֶב *chariot* Na 2$_{4}$, פָּנִים *face* Ezk 43$_{7}$, לֵב *heart* Ps 10$_{17}$ 78$_{8}$ Jb 11$_{13}$ 2 C 12$_{14}$ 1QH 7$_{13}$ 4QBéat 3.2$_{4}$, לֵבָב *heart* 1 S 7$_{3}$ 1 C 29$_{18}$ 2 C 19$_{3}$ 20$_{33}$ 30$_{19}$, רֶגֶל *foot* 1QH 7$_{25}$ 4QBark^a 1.2$_{4}$, נְגִינָה *string music* Si 47$_{9}$, אֵלֶּה *these* 1QH 13$_{7}$ ([הכינותה]) 13$_{10}$, כֹּל *everything* Ezk 7$_{14}$ 1 C 29$_{3}$ 1QH 18$_{22}$, אֲשֶׁר *that which* Ex 16$_{5}$.

<PREP> לְ of benefit, *to, for*, + Y. 11QT 29$_{10}$, אֶרֶץ *earth* Ps 147$_{8}$, Egypt Jr 46$_{14}$, Gog Ezk 38$_{7}$, Israelite(s) Dt 19$_{3}$, עַם *people* Jos 1$_{11}$ Ps 78$_{20}$ 2 C 29$_{36}$, צָבָא *army* 2 C 26$_{14}$, Balaam Nm 23$_{1.29}$, Mordecai Est 6$_{4}$ 7$_{10}$, Solomon 2 C 2$_{8}$, אִישׁ *man* 1 C 12$_{40}$, בֵּן *son* Is 14$_{21}$, אָח *brother* 2 C 35$_{6}$, כֹּהֵן *priest* 2 C 35$_{14.14}$, לֵוִי *Levite* 2 C 35$_{14.14}$, שֹׁעֵר *gatekeeper* 2 C 35$_{15}$, דֹּרֵשׁ *seeker* 4QD^c 1$_{6}$, עָנִי *poor one* Ps 68$_{11}$, אֲרוֹן *ark* of God 1 C 15$_{1.3.12}$ 2 C 1$_{4}$, עֹרֵב *raven* Jb 38$_{41}$, בַּיִת *house* 1 C 22$_{5.14}$ 29$_{2.3}$, דֶּלֶת *door* 1 C 22$_{3}$, פַּעַם *step* Ps 57$_{7}$, מַסְמֵר *nail* 1 C 22$_{3}$, מְחַבְּרוֹת *clamps* 1 C 22$_{3}$, שֵׁם *name* Si 47$_{13}$, פֹּעַל *work* 1QH 11$_{34}$ (לפועו[ל]כה), תּוֹרָה *law* 4QBark^a 1.1$_{12}$, כָּבוֹד *glory* 1QH 6$_{10}$ 7$_{24}$ (הכ[י]נותה) 18$_{22}$, מוֹעֵד *appointed time* 1QH 15$_{15}$.

לְ of direction, *to, on*, + אֱלֹהִים *God* 2 C 20$_{33}$, דֶּרֶךְ *way* 1QS 11$_{13}$ 4QBark^a 1.2$_{4}$ 4QBéat 3.2$_{4}$.

לְ *as*, + מֶלֶךְ *king* 2 S 5$_{12}$||1 C 14$_{2}$, סוֹד *foundation* 1QH 7$_{9}$; *in*, + רֹב *abundance* 1 C 22$_{5}$ 2 C 2$_{8}$; *according to*, + בַּיִת *house* 2 C 35$_{4}$; introducing object, + חֵפֶץ *desire* 4Q418 88$_{1}$ (לכו[ל] חפציכה).

בְּ of instrument, *by (means of)*, + יָד *hand* 2 C 17$_{5}$, פֶּה *mouth*, i.e. word 1QH 2$_{17}$, רָצוֹן *will* 1QH 10$_{22}$ (ברצו[נכה]), כֹּחַ *strength* Ps 65$_{7}$, טוֹבָה *goodness* Ps 68$_{11}$, עֳנִי *misery* 1 C 22$_{14}$, חָכְמָה *wisdom* Jr 10$_{12}$ 51$_{15}$ 1QH 1$_{14.19}$ (הכ[י]נותה) 11QPs^a 26$_{14}$, דַּעַת *knowledge* 11QPs^a 26$_{11}$, אֱמֶת *truth* Si 37$_{15}$, אִמְרָה *word* Ps 119$_{133}$, עֵצָה *counsel* 1QH 6$_{10}$; of place/time, *in, at*, + שָׁמַיִם *heavens* Ps 89$_{3}$ 103$_{19}$, מָקוֹם *place* 2 C 3$_{1}$, מִישׁוֹר *level place* 1QH 7$_{25}$ (במ[ישור]), רְחוֹב *square* Jb 29$_{7}$, חוּץ *outside* Pr 24$_{27}$, בַּיִת *house* 2 C 31$_{11}$, קַיִץ *summer* Pr 6$_{8}$ 30$_{25}$, יוֹם *day* Na 2$_{4}$, סוֹד *council* 1QH fr. 9$_{10}$; of accompaniment, *with, in*, + צֶדֶק *righteousness* 1QS 11$_{16}$; *according to*, + מַחֲשָׁבָה *plan* 1QS 11$_{11}$ 4Q418 46$_{1}$ (במחשב[ות]), לִמּוּד *teaching* 1QH 7$_{13}$ (בל[מודיכה]), אֱמֶת *truth* 1QH 7$_{13}$, טוֹב *good* 4QpsHod^b 3.1$_{22}$ (ב erased).

כְּ *according to*, + בְּרִית *covenant* 11QT 29$_{10}$.

מִן of time, place, *from, since*, + רֶחֶם *womb* 1QH 15$_{15}$, תֹּכֶם *innards* 4QHod^b 7$_{8}$ (הכינ[ו]תה), קֶדֶם *ancient time* 1QH 13$_{7}$ ([הכינותה מקדם]) 13$_{10}$ 15$_{22}$ (הכ[ינותה מקדם]); partitive, *some of, (any)one of*, + בֵּן *son* of Israel Jos 4$_{4}$.

אֶל *to*, + '' *Y.* 1 S 7$_{3}$ 1 C 29$_{16}$, אֱלֹהִים *God* 1 C 29$_{18}$, Israel 1 S 13$_{13}$, מָצוֹר *siege* Ezk 4$_{7}$, מַחֲבַת *plate* Ezk 4$_{3}$; עַל

over, upon, + Israel 1 S 13$_{13(mss)}$ 2 S 5$_{12}$‖1 C 14$_{2}$ 1 C 22$_{10}$, Jerusalem Si 47$_{11}$, מְכוֹנָה *place* Ezr 3$_{3}$, סֶלַע *rock* 1QH 7$_{9}$.

בְּתוֹךְ *among,* + בַּיִת *house* 1 K 6$_{19}$; בֵּין *between,* טוֹב *good* 4Q416 1$_{15}$ (בין טוב לר[ע] *between good and evil;* =4Q418 2$_{7}$ להבין *to understand*); לִפְנֵי *before,* + ״י Y. 2 C 27$_{6}$, אֱלֹהִים *God* 2 C 27$_{6}$, מָוֶת *death* 1 C 22$_{5}$; לְפִי *according to,* + רָז *mystery* 1QH 15$_{19}$ ([לפי רזי]); עַד *until,* + עוֹלָם *eternity* 1 S 13$_{13}$ Ps 89$_{5}$ 1 C 22$_{10}$; עַד־לְ *until (to),* + עוֹלָם *eternity* 1 C 28$_{7}$.

<COLL> לְהָכִין שַׁבַּת שַׁבָּת *to prepare (it) every Sabbath* 1 C 9$_{32}$; כון hi. + adverb, אָז *then* 4Q418 81$_{18}$, מאז *from of old* 4QM^{a} 11.1$_{10}$; + noun used adverbially, יוֹם *day* 11QT 29$_{10}$.

2. ptc. as noun, **preparer,** <CSTR> מכין טובי *preparer of my goodness* 1QS 10$_{12}$ (or em. מכון *base of;* ‖ מָקוֹר *source,* מָעוֹן *spring,* + רוּם *height,* גְּבוּרָה *might,* צֶדֶק *righteousness*). <COLL> אומר ... לעליון מכין טובי *I will say ... to the Most High, 'preparer of my goodness'* 1QS 10$_{22}$.

Also 4QMyst^{a} 8$_{1}$ 4Q415 9$_{7}$ 4Q418 55$_{6}$ 114$_{2}$ 4QHod^{a} 6$_{4}$ 4QRitMar 3$_{3}$ 4Q518 1$_{3}$ perh. 4QHymnPr 29$_{2}$ 4QBéat 23.2$_{3}$.

<SYN> §1, ישׁב hi. *place,* סעד *support;* §2, מָקוֹר *source,* מָעוֹן *spring.*

Ho. 6.0.4 Pf. הוּכַן (הֻכַן, הוּכָן); impf. Q תוכן; ptc. מוּכָן, מוּכָנִים—**be established, be set up, be made ready; be fit** for marriage (4QD^{f} 3$_{9}$).

<SUBJ> Topheth Is 30$_{33}$, בַּיִת *house* Zc 5$_{11}$, כִּסֵּא *throne* Is 16$_{5}$, סֹכֵךְ *mantelet* Na 2$_{6}$, שְׁפַתַּיִם *pegs* or *ledges* Ezk 40$_{43}$, סוּס *horse* Pr 21$_{31}$, חֵלֶק *portion* 4QpsEzek^{a} 9.2$_{3}$, אֲשֶׁר *one who* 4QD^{f} 3$_{9}$; subj. not specified, CD 10$_{22}$. <PREP> לְ of benefit, *to, for,* + בַּת *daughter* 4QD^{f} 3$_{9}$, מֶלֶךְ *king* Is 30$_{33}$, יוֹם *day* Pr 21$_{31}$; בְּ of instrument, *by (means of), with,* + חֶסֶד *loyalty* Is 16$_{5}$; of place, *in,* + בַּיִת *house* Ezk 40$_{43}$; כְּ *as,* + בֶּגֶד *garment* 4QpUnid 2$_{2}$.

Htpol. 4.0.1 Impf. יִתְכּוֹנֵן, תִּכּוֹנֵן (תִּכּוֹנָנִי), יִכּוֹנָנוּ (Q יתכונו)—**be firmly founded; form oneself in battle array,** <SUBJ> אֵל *god* 4QShirShabb^{f} 23.1$_{11}$, אוֹיֵב *enemy* Ps 59$_{5}$, פֹּעַל *worker* of iniquity Ps 59$_{5}$, עִיר *city* of Sihon Nm 21$_{27}$ (‖ בנה ni. *be built*), בַּיִת *house* Pr 24$_{3}$ (‖ בנה ni. *be built*); subj. not specified, Is 54$_{14}$. <PREP> בְּ of instrument, *by (means of), with,* + צְדָקָה *righteousness* Is 54$_{14}$, תְּבוּנָה *understanding* Pr 24$_{3}$; עַל *against,* + אֹמֶר *word* 4QShirShabb^{f} 23.1$_{2}$. <SYN> בנה ni. *be built.**

→ כֵּן *correct,* מָכוֹן *place,* מְכוֹנָה *base,* תְּכוּנָה *place.*

[כַּוָּן] 2 n.m. **cake**—pl. כַּוָּנִים—as offering (Jr 7$_{18}$ 44$_{19}$), <OBJ> עשׂה *make* Jr 7$_{18}$ 44$_{19}$.

כּוּן 1 pl.n. **Cun,** appar. in Syria, a city of Hadadezer, perh. ident. with Kūna S of Beretān, <NOM CL> מִטִּבְחַת וּמִכּוּן עָרֵי הֲדַדְעֶזֶר *from Tibhath and from Cun, cities of Hadadezer* 1 C 18$_{8}$. <PREP> מִן of direction, *from,* + לקח *take* 1 C 18$_{8}$.

[כּוֹנָנָה] 0.0.1 n.f. **bowl**—cstr. pl. Q כוננות—in list of altar vessels, <CSTR> כוננות הכסף *bowls of silver* 11QT 33$_{14}$ (+ מִזְרָק *dish,* קַשְׂוָה *cup,* מַחְתָּה *fire-pan*). <PREP> לְ *to, for* 11QT 33$_{14}$.

כּוֹנַנְיָהוּ, see כָּנַנְיָהוּ *Conaniah.*

כּוֹס I 31.0.7 n.f. **cup, purse**—cstr. כּוֹס; sf. כּוֹסִי, Q כוסכה, Q כוסם; pl. כּוֹסוֹת (Q כסות)—**1. cup, drinking cup,** for wine, etc. (e.g. Gn 40$_{11.11.11.13.21}$ 1 K 7$_{26}$ Jr 35$_{5}$), container of judgment (e.g. Is 51$_{17.22}$ Jr 25$_{15}$ 49$_{12}$ Ps 75$_{9}$ 1Qp Hab 11$_{14}$), of blessing (Ps 23$_{6}$), **lot,** i.e. fortune, destiny, <SUBJ> בוא *come* 4QpNah 3.4$_{6}$, סבב *go around* Hb 2$_{16}$, עבר *pass* Lm 4$_{21}$, בלע *swallow* 1QpHab 11$_{14}$.

<NOM CL> כּוֹסִי ... ״י *Y. is ... my lot* Ps 16$_{5}$, כּוֹסִי רְוָיָה *my cup is satiation,* i.e. full Ps 23$_{5}$, כּוֹס שַׁמָּה וּשְׁמָמָה כּוֹס אֲחוֹתֵךְ שֹׁמְרוֹן *a cup of horror and desolation is the cup of your sister Samaria* Ezk 23$_{33}$, כּוֹס־זָהָב בָּבֶל בְּיַד־״י *Babylon was a cup of gold in the hand of Y.* Jr 51$_{7}$, אין כוסות *there are no cups* 4Q416 2.2$_{19}$ (=4Q417 1.2$_{24}$ כסית), כּוֹס בְּיַד־״י *the cup is in the hand of Y.* Ps 75$_{9}$, כּוֹס פַּרְעֹה בְּיָדִי *the cup of Pharaoh was in my hand* Gn 40$_{11}$, תחת הפנא הדרומית אמות תשע ... כוסות *underneath the south corner at nine cubits are ... cups* 3QTr 3$_{3}$ (‖ מִזְרָק *dish,* מְנַקִּית *bowl,* קְסָוָה *vase,* + כְּלִי *vessel*).

<OBJ> נתן *give,* i.e. place Gn 40$_{11.13.21}$ Jr 35$_{5}$ Ezk 23$_{31}$, לקח *take* Is 51$_{22}$ Jr 25$_{15.17.28}$, נשׂא *raise* Ps 116$_{13}$, שׁתה *drink* Is 51$_{17}$ Jr 49$_{12}$ Ezk 23$_{32}$, שׁקה hi. *cause to drink* Jr 16$_{7}$.

<CSTR> כּוֹס יְמִין יי׳ *cup of the right hand of Y.* Hb 2$_{16}$, פַּרְעֹה *of Pharaoh* Gn 40$_{11.11.13}$, אֲחוֹתֵךְ *of your sister* Ezk 23$_{32.33}$, כּוֹס־זָהָב *cup of gold* Jr 51$_{7}$, כּוֹס הַיַּיִן *the cup of wine* Jr 25$_{15}$, כּוֹס־יְשׁוּעוֹת *cup of salvation* Ps 116$_{13}$, כּוֹס תַּנְחוּמִים *cup of consolations* Jr 16$_{7}$, הַתַּרְעֵלָה *of staggering* Is 51$_{17.22}$, שַׁמָּה וּשְׁמָמָה *of horror and desolation* Ezk 23$_{33}$, כוס חמת *cup of the wrath of* 1QpHab 11$_{14}$, כּוֹס חֲמָתִי *cup of my wrath* Is 51$_{22}$, חֲמָתוֹ *of his wrath* Is 51$_{17}$.

קֻבַּעַת כּוֹס *the bowl of the cup of* Is 51$_{17.22}$, שְׂפַת־כּוֹס *lip*, i.e. brim, *of cup* 1 K 7$_{26}$‖2 C 4$_{5}$, מְנָת כּוֹסָם *portion of their cup* Ps 11$_{6}$.

<PREP> בְּ *in, with,* + נתן *give* Pr 23$_{31(Qr)}$; כְּ *as* 4Qps Ezek^{b} 1.3$_{1}$; מִן of direction, *from,* + שׁתה *drink* 2 S 12$_{3}$; אֶל *to, into,* + שׂחט *squeeze out* Gn 40$_{11}$. <SYN> מִזְרָק *dish*, מְנַקִּית *bowl*, קְשָׂוָה *vase*.*

2. purse, <OBJ> פקד *deposit* 4Q416 2.2$_{4}$ ([פק]דת), לקח *take* 4Q417 1.2$_{8}$ ([יקח]). <CSTR> כוס צפוניכה *purse of your treasures* 4Q416 2.2$_{4}$.

כּוֹס II 3 n.m. perh. **tawny owl**—cstr. כּוֹס—unclean bird.

<OBJ> שׁקץ pi. *abominate* Lv 11$_{17}$, אכל *eat* Dt 14$_{16}$. <CSTR> כּוֹס חֳרָבוֹת *owl of waste places* Ps 102$_{7}$. <PREP> כְּ *as,* + היה *be* Ps 102$_{7}$.*

[כּוֹסְבָא] 0.0.10 pr.n.m. **Cosiba**—Q כוסבה—father of Simeon Bar Cochba/Cosiba, leader of second Jewish revolt, <CSTR> בן כוסבא *son of Cosiba* Mur 24 2$_{3}$ 3$_{3.20}$ ([בן כוס[ב]א]) 5$_{2}$ (כ[וס]בא) 7$_{3}$ ([בן כוס[בא]) MurEpBarC^{a} 1$_{1}$ (כוכבה) 5/6ḤevBA 44$_{1.7}$ 5/6ḤevBA 45$_{2}$ fr. 2$_{2}$, בר *son of* 5/6ḤevEp 1$_{1}$ (כוסבה) 5/6ḤevEp 12$_{1}$.

כור 1 vb. perh. **bind**—**Qal** 1 Pf. mss כָּרוּ (i.e. כָּרוּ, unless כָּרוּ, from כרה I or IV; L כָּאֲרִי)—**bind,** <SUBJ> עֲדָה *congregation* of wicked Ps 22$_{17(mss)}$ (or em. אָסְרוּ *they bound*). <OBJ> יָד *hand* Ps 22$_{17(mss)}$, רֶגֶל *foot* Ps 22$_{17(mss)}$.

כּוּר 9.2.11 n.m. **smelting-pot**—cstr. כּוּר—**1.** small **furnace,** <SUBJ> נפח pass. *be blown* Si 43$_{4(B)}$, ni. *be blown* 4Q416 4$_{2}$, בחן *test* Si 34$_{26}$. <NOM CL> [כ]ור [נ]פוח מעשי מוצק *the furnace that is blown upon*, i.e. glowing, *is a wrought casting* Si 43$_{4(M)}$, כּוּר לַזָּהָב *the furnace is for gold* Pr 17$_{3}$ 27$_{21}$. <OBJ> ידע *know* 1QH 1$_{22}$ (+ סוֹד *foundation*, מָקוֹר *source*, מִבְנֶה *structure*).

<CSTR> כור נופחים *furnace of the smiths* 1QH 5$_{16}$, כּוּר הַבַּרְזֶל *the furnace of iron* Dt 4$_{20}$ 1 K 8$_{51}$ Jr 11$_{4}$, עֳנִי *of affliction* Is 48$_{10}$, כור העוון *furnace of iniquity* 1QH 1$_{22}$, חרון *of wrath* 4QBéat 22$_{4}$; יְקֹד כֻּרִים *kindling of furnaces* Ps 37$_{20}$ (if em.).

<PREP> בְּ of place, *in(to)* 1QM 5$_{11}$ 4QBéat 22$_{4}$, + בוא *come* 4Q424 1$_{5}$, בחר *test* Is 48$_{10}$, זקק pu. *be purified* 1QH 5$_{16}$; מִן of direction, *from,* + יצא hi. *bring out* Dt 4$_{20}$ Jr 11$_{4}$.

אֶל־תּוֹךְ *into,* + קבץ *gather* Ezk 22$_{20}$; בְּתוֹךְ *within* Ezk 22$_{18}$, נתך ni. *be poured out*, i.e. melted Ezk 22$_{22}$ CD 20$_{3}$; מִתּוֹךְ *from (within),* + יצא hi. *bring out* 1 K 8$_{51}$.

2. crucible of conception, **womb,** <NOM CL> המה כור הוריכה *they* (parents) *are the crucible of your conception* 4Q416 1.3$_{17}$. <CSTR> כור הריה *womb of pregnant woman* 1QH 3$_{8.10.12}$, הוריכה *of your conception* 4Q416 1.3$_{17}$. <PREP> בְּ of place, *in,* + חיל hi. *cause writhing* 1QH 3$_{8}$, הפך ni. *come* 1QH 3$_{12}$; מִן of direction, *from,* + גיח *burst out* 1QH 3$_{10}$.

⇒ כִּיר *cooking-furnace.*

[כּוֹר] 0.0.0.1 pl.n. **Chor,** perh. ident. with Kur SW of Samaria, <PREP> מִן of direction, *from* Samaria ost. 49$_{4}$ (others כסר *Kaser*).

כּוֹר עָשָׁן 1 pl.n. **Chor-ashan,** appar. ident. with Ashan at Jos 15$_{42}$ 19$_{7}$ 1 C 4$_{32}$ 6$_{44}$, <PREP> בְּ of place, *in, at* 1 S 30$_{30(mss)}$ (L בּוֹר־עָשָׁן *Borashan*).

כּוֹרֶשׁ 16 pr.n.m. **Cyrus**—כֹּרֶשׁ—king of Medes and Persians, conqueror of the Babylonian empire, <SUBJ> יצא hi. *bring out* Ezr 1$_{7.8}$, שׁלם hi. *bring to completion* Is 44$_{28}$, אמר *say* Ezr 1$_{2}$‖2 C 36$_{23}$, צוה pi. *command* Ezr 4$_{3}$. <CSTR> רוּחַ כּוֹרֶשׁ *spirit of Cyrus* Ezr 1$_{1}$ (כֹּרֶשׁ) 2 C 36$_{22}$, כָּל יְמֵי *all the days of* Ezr 4$_{5}$, רִשְׁיוֹן *authorisation of* Ezr 3$_{7}$. <APP> מֶלֶךְ *king* Dn 1$_{21}$ 10$_{1}$ Ezr 1$_{1.1.2}$‖2 C 36$_{22.22.23}$ Ezr 1$_{7.8}$ 4$_{3.5}$, רֹעֶה *shepherd* Is 44$_{28}$, מָשִׁיחַ *anointed one* Is 45$_{1}$. <PREP> לְ of direction, *to,* + אמר *say* Is 44$_{28}$ 45$_{1}$; of possession, *of, (belonging) to* Dn 10$_{1}$ Ezr 1$_{1}$‖2 C 36$_{22}$ Dn 1$_{21}$.

כּוּשׁ $_{30.0.2}$ pr.n.m. **Cush, 1.** son of Ham and father of Nimrod, <SUBJ> ילד *bear child* Gn 10$_{8}$||1 C 1$_{10}$, <NOM CL> ... בְּנֵי חָם כּוּשׁ *the sons of Ham were Cush* ... Gn 10$_{6}$||1 C 1$_{8}$, <CSTR> בְּנֵי כּוּשׁ *sons of Cush* Gn 10$_{7}$||1 C 1$_{9}$.

2. descendants of foregoing (Ezk 30$_{9}$ 38$_{5}$) with their territory (e.g. 2 K 19$_{9}$||Is 37$_{9}$ Is 11$_{11}$ 18$_{1}$ Jb 28$_{19}$). <SUBJ> עצם *be mighty* Na 3$_{9}$, רוץ hi. *cause to run*, i.e. hasten Ps 68$_{32}$ (or em. רום hi. *raise*), תפשׂ *take hold of* Jr 46$_{9}$, נפל *fall* Ezk 30$_{5}$ 4QpsEzek[a] 1$_{4}$ (ל[פו]י). <NOM CL> כּוּשׁ עָצְמָה *Cush is its might* Na 3$_{9(mss)}$, כּוּשׁ ... אִתָּם *Cush is ... with them* Ezk 38$_{5}$, [כוש מעבו]ר לים *Cush is beyond the sea* 4QpsEzek[a] 9.2$_{5}$. <OBJ> נתן *give* Is 43$_{3}$, חרד hi. *terrify* Ezk 30$_{9}$. <CSTR> אֶרֶץ כּוּשׁ *land of Cush* Gn 2$_{13}$, גְּבוּל *border of* Ezk 29$_{10}$, נַהֲרֵי־כוּשׁ *rivers of Cush* Is 18$_{1}$ Zp 3$_{10}$ 4QpsEzek[a] 9.1$_{4}$ ([כוש]), מֶלֶךְ־ *king of* 2 K 19$_{9}$||Is 37$_{9}$, גָּלוּת כּוּשׁ *exiles of Cush* Is 20$_{4}$, אָהֳלֵי *tents of* Hb 3$_{7}$ (if em. כּוּשָׁן *Cushan*), סְחַר־כּוּשׁ *profit of Cush* Is 45$_{14}$, פִּטְדַת־ *chrysolith of* Jb 28$_{19}$. <PREP> בְּ of place, *in, at*, + היה *be* Ezk 30$_{4}$; מִן of direction, *from*, + קנה *buy* Is 11$_{11}$; of cause, *on account of*, + בושׁ *be ashamed* Is 20$_{5}$, חתת *be shattered* Is 20$_{5}$; עַל *against* Is 20$_{3}$; עַד *until, as far as*, + מלך *rule* Est 1$_{1}$ 8$_{9}$; עִם *with* Ps 87$_{4}$.

3. Benjaminite, <NOM CL> כּוּשׁ בֶּן־יְמִינִי *Cush was a Benjaminite* Ps 7$_{1}$. <CSTR> דִּבְרֵי־כוּשׁ *deeds of Cush* Ps 7$_{1}$.

⇒ כּוּשִׁי *Cushite.*

כּוּשִׁי I $_{24}$ gent. **Cushite**—כֻּשִׁי; fs כֻּשִׁית; pl. כּוּשִׁים (כֻּשִׁים, כֻּשִׁיִּים)—**1.** as plur. or collective sing. noun, **Cushites,** <SUBJ> היה *be* 2 C 16$_{8}$, בוא *come* 2 C 12$_{3}$, נוס *flee* 2 C 14$_{11}$. <NOM CL> גַּם־אַתֶּם כּוּשִׁים חַלְלֵי חַרְבִּי הֵמָּה *you too, O Cushites, are the victims of my sword* Zp 2$_{12}$, כֻּשִׁים בְּמִצְעָדָיו *the Cushites (follow) in his steps* Dn 11$_{43}$. <OBJ> נגף *strike* 2 C 14$_{11}$.

<CSTR> בְּנֵי כֻּשִׁיִּים *sons of the Cushites* Am 9$_{7}$, יַד כּוּשִׁים *hand of the Cushites* 2 C 21$_{16}$. <APP> עַם *people* 2 C 12$_{3}$. <PREP> מִן partitive, *some of, (any)one of*, + נפל *fall* 2 C 14$_{12}$.

2. as sing. noun, a particular **Cushite,** <SUBJ> שׁמע *hear* Jr 38$_{7}$, בוא *come* 2 S 18$_{31}$, יצא *go out* 2 C 14$_{8}$, רוץ *run* 2 S 18$_{21}$, הפך *change* Jr 13$_{23}$, שׁחה htpal. *bow down* 2 S 18$_{21}$, אמר *say* 2 S 18$_{31.32}$ Jr 38$_{12}$. <OBJ> עבר *pass by* 2 S 18$_{23}$, צוה pi. *command* Jr 38$_{10}$. <APP> Ebed-melech Jr 38$_{7.10.12}$ 39$_{16}$, Zerah 2 C 14$_{8}$. <PREP> לְ of direction, *to*, + אמר *say* Jr 39$_{16}$; אֶל *to*, + אמר *say* 2 S 18$_{32}$; אַחֲרֵי *after*, + רוץ *run* 2 S 18$_{22}$.

3. as attributive adj., **Cushite,** + אִשָּׁה *woman* Nm 12$_{1.1}$.

⇒ כּוּשׁ *Cush.*

כּוּשִׁי II $_{2}$ pr.n.m. **Cushi, 1.** great-grandfather of Jehudi, <CSTR> בֶּן־כּוּשִׁי *son of Cushi* Jr 36$_{14}$. **2.** son of Gedaliah and father of prophet Zephaniah, <CSTR> בֶּן־כּוּשִׁי *son of Cushi* Zp 1$_{1}$.

כּוּשָׁן $_{1}$ gent. **Cushan,** appar. Arabian nomadic tribe, <CSTR> אָהֳלֵי כוּשָׁן *tents of Cushan* Hb 3$_{7}$ (or em. כּוּשׁ *of Cush*).

⇒ (?) כּוּשׁ *Cush.*

כּוּשַׁן רִשְׁעָתַיִם $_{4}$ pr.n.m. **Cushan-rishathaim**—כּוּשַׁן רִשְׁעָתָיִם—perh. play on רִשְׁעָתַיִם *double wickedness*—king of Mesopotamia Jg 3$_{8.8.10.10}$, <OBJ> נתן *give* Jg 3$_{10}$, עבד *serve* Jg 3$_{8}$. <CSTR> יַד כּוּשַׁן רִשְׁעָתַיִם *hand of Cushan-rishathaim* Jg 3$_{8}$. <APP> מֶלֶךְ *king* Jg 3$_{8.10}$. <PREP> עַל *over*, + עזז *be strong* Jg 3$_{10}$.

⇒ כּוּשׁ (?) *Cush*, רָשָׁע *wicked one.*

כּוֹשָׁרוֹת $_{1}$ n.f. **prosperity, success; perh. skill, music;** or perh. **Cosharoth,** Canaanite goddesses of conception and childbirth, מוֹצִיא אֲסִירִים בַּכּוֹשָׁרוֹת *leading out captives into prosperity*, or *with music*, or *among the Cosharoth* Ps 68$_{7}$.*

כּוּת $_{2}$ pl.n. **Cuth**—כּוּתָה—city in Mesopotamia, from which inhabitants were resettled in northern Israel (2 K 17$_{24.30}$), perh. ident. with Kûtû, mod. T. Ibrāhīm 30 km NE of Babylon, <CSTR> אַנְשֵׁי־כוּת *people of Cuth* 2 K 17$_{30}$. <PREP> מִן of direction, *from*, + בוא hi. *bring* 2 K 17$_{24}$.

כּוֹתֶרֶת, see כֹּתֶרֶת *capital.*

כזב $_{16.1.4}$ vb. **lie—Qal** $_{1}$ Ptc. כֹּזֵב—**lie,** <SUBJ> אָדָם *human being* Ps 116$_{11}$.

Ni. $_{2}$ Pf. נִכְזַבְתָּ, נִכְזָבָה—**be declared false,** <SUBJ> worshipper Pr 30$_{6}$, תּוֹחֶלֶת *hope* Jb 41$_{1}$.

Pi. $_{12.1.4}$ Pf. כִּזֵּב; impf. אֲכַזֵּב, תְּכַזְּבִי, יְכַזֵּב; ptc. Q מכזבים; inf. כַּזֶּבְכֶם—**lie, deceive, cheat, fail;** perh. **declare false** (Jb 34$_{6}$ [or em.]), <SUBJ> יי *Y.* Ps 89$_{36}$, אֵל *God* Nm 23$_{19}$ (|| נחם htp. *change one's mind*) Jb 34$_{6}$ (if em. אֲכַזֵּב *I lie/declare false* to יְכַזֵּב *he lies*), Job Jb 6$_{28}$ 34$_{6}$ (or em. יְכַזֵּב *he lies;* or אִכָּזֵב ni. or אֲכֻזַּב pu. *I am proved a liar*), אִישׁ *man* 2 K 4$_{16}$ Mc 2$_{11}$, בַּת *daughter* of people Ezk 13$_{19}$, אָדוֹן *lord* 2 K 4$_{16}$, בָּחוּר *choice one* Ps 78$_{36}$, עֵד *witness* Pr 14$_{5}$, worshipper Si 16$_{21}$, מַיִם *water* Is 58$_{11}$, מָקוֹר *source* 1QSb 1$_{4}$ ([יכז]ב), perh. אֶשֶׁד *watercourse* 1QH 5$_{16}$ (השדים; + מוש *depart*), חָזוֹן *vision* Hb 2$_{3}$; subj. not specified, Is 57$_{11}$ 4Q417 1.1$_{22}$.

<OBJ> רוּחַ *wind* Mc 2$_{11}$, שֶׁקֶר *falsehood* Mc 2$_{11}$.

<PREP> לְ of direction, *to* 4Q417 1.1$_{22}$, + עֶלְיוֹן *Most High* Ps 78$_{36}$, עַם *people* Ezk 13$_{19}$, David Ps 89$_{36}$; בְּ of instrument, *by (means of), with,* + לָשׁוֹן *tongue* Ps 78$_{36}$; *in, with,* + סֵתֶר *secrecy* Si 16$_{21}$; introducing object, + שִׁפְחָה *female servant* 2 K 4$_{16}$; עַל *concerning* or *despite* (if em. ni./pu.) or introducing object, + מִשְׁפָּט *judgment* Jb 34$_{6}$; עַל־פְּנֵיכֶם *before you* or *to your face* Jb 6$_{28}$.

<COLL> כזב pi. *fail,* + inf. פתח *open* 1QH 5$_{16}$. Also 4Q apJoseph[b] 18$_{4}$ 4Q410 1$_{8}$. <SYN> נחם htp. *change one's mind.*

Pu. be declared a liar, <SUBJ> Job Jb 34$_{6}$ (if em.).*

Hi. $_{1}$ Impf. יַכְזִיבֵנִי—**make one a liar,** <SUBJ> מִי *who?* Jb 24$_{25}$. <OBJ> Job Jb 24$_{25}$.

→ אַכְזָב *deceitful,* כָּזָב *lie.*

כָּזָב $_{31.5.18}$ n.m. **lie**—pl. כְּזָבִים; sf. כִּזְבֵיהֶם—**lie(s), falsehood,** of false prophecies (e.g. Ezk 13$_{6.7.9}$ 21$_{34}$ 22$_{38}$), images as false gods (Am 2$_{4}$).

<SUBJ> מצא ni. *be found* 1QS 10$_{22}$ (|| מִרְמָה *deceit,* + כַּחַשׁ *lie,* נְבָלָה *lewdness*), תעה hi. *lead astray* Am 2$_{4}$. <NOM CL> כָּזָב בְּנֵי אִישׁ *the sons of mankind are a lie* Ps 62$_{10}$ (|| הֶבֶל *vanity*), אין כזב בכל דברך *there is no lie in all your word* GnzPs 4$_{22}$. <OBJ> חזה *see* Ezk 13$_{6.8}$, שמע *hear* Ezk 13$_{19}$, שִׂים *place,* i.e. make Is 28$_{15}$ (|| שֶׁקֶר *falsehood*), רבה hi. *make many* Ho 12$_{2}$, רצה *take pleasure* Ps 62$_{5}$, בקשׁ pi. *seek* Ps 4$_{3}$, פוח *utter* Pr 6$_{19}$ 14$_{5.25}$ 19$_{5.9}$, דבר *speak* Ps 5$_{7}$ 58$_{4}$, pi. *speak* Jg 16$_{10.13}$ Ho 7$_{13}$ Zp 3$_{13}$ Dn 11$_{27}$, קסם *divine* Ezk 13$_{9}$ 21$_{34}$ 22$_{28}$.

<CSTR> אִישׁ כָּזָב *man of a lie,* i.e. liar Pr 19$_{22}$ 1QpHab 2$_{2}$ 5$_{11}$ (both הכזב) 4QpPs[a] 1.1$_{18}$ (הכזב) 3.4$_{14}$ (א[י]ש הכזב) CD 50$_{15}$ (הכזב), אנשי כזב *men of lies,* i.e. liars Si 15$_{8.20}$, עֵד־כְּזָבִים *witness of lies,* i.e. false witness Pr 21$_{28}$, נביאי כזב *prophets of lies* 1QH 4$_{16}$ (+ תְּעוּת *error*), מטיף הכזב *spreader of lies* 1QpHab 10$_{9}$ 11$_{1}$ ([מטי]ף) 1QpMic 10$_{4}$ CD 8$_{13}$ (כזב), מליצי כזב *mediators of lies* 1QH 2$_{31}$ (+ חֵלֶק *smooth thing*) 4$_{10}$ (|| רְמִיָּה *deceit*), לשון כזביהם *tongue of their lies,* i.e. their lying tongue 4QpNah 3.2$_{8}$ (|| שֶׁקֶר *falsehood,* מִרְמָה *deceit*), מַחְסֵה כָזָב *refuge of lies* Is 28$_{17}$, מִקְסַם כָּזָב *divination of a lie* Ezk 13$_{7}$, לֶחֶם כְּזָבִים *bread of lies,* i.e. deceptive bread Pr 23$_{3}$, מטעמי כזב *delicacies of a lie* Si 36$_{24}$, מימי כזב *waters of falsehood* CD 1$_{15}$, תוחלת כזב *expectation of a lie,* i.e. a false expectation Si 31$_{1}$, דְּבַר־כָּזָב *word of a lie* Pr 30$_{8}$, אמרי כזב *words of a lie* 4QapJoseph[a] 1$_{13}$ (|| שֶׁקֶר *falsehood*).

<APP> קֶסֶם *divination* Ezk 13$_{6}$. <PREP> לְ *concerning,* + נטף hi. *drip,* i.e. teach CD 19$_{26}$. <COLL> שָׂטֵי כָזָב *those who go astray (after) false ones,* i.e. false gods Ps 40$_{5}$=Si 51$_{2}$. <SYN> שֶׁקֶר *falsehood,* רְמִיָּה *deceit,* מִרְמָה *deceit,* הֶבֶל *vanity.*

→ כזב *lie.*

כֹּזֵבָא $_{1.0.1}$ pl.n. **Cozeba**—Q כוזבא—**1.** appar. location in lowland of Judah 1 C 4$_{22}$, <CSTR> אַנְשֵׁי כֹזֵבָא *men of Cozeba* 1 C 4$_{22}$. **2.** perh. Dēr el-Qelṭ, 1 km NNW of Jericho, <COLL> יציאת של המים של הכוזבא *the water-outlet of Cozeba* 3QTr 7$_{14}$.

כָּזְבִּי $_{2}$ pr.n.f. **Cozbi,** daughter of Zur, chief of Midian Nm 25$_{15.18}$, <SUBJ> נכה ho. *be struck down* Nm 25$_{18}$. <NOM CL> שֵׁם הָאִשָּׁה ... כָּזְבִּי *the name of the woman was ... Cozbi* Nm 25$_{15}$. <CSTR> דְּבַר כָּזְבִּי *the matter of Cozbi* Nm 25$_{18}$. <APP> בַּת *daughter* Nm 25$_{15.18}$, אָחוֹת *sister* Nm 25$_{18}$.*

כְּזִיב I $_{1}$ pl.n. **Chezib,** town in Judah, perh. ident. with Achzib at Jos 15$_{44}$ Mc 1$_{14}$, וְהָיָה בִכְזִיב בְּלִדְתָּהּ אֹתוֹ *and he (Judah) was at Chezib when she gave birth to him* (Shelah) Gn 38$_{5}$ (Sam בכזבה *in Cozeba*).

כְּזִיב II $_{1}$ n.[m.] **menopause,*** <PREP> בְּ *in, with,* וְהִיא בִכְזִיב בְּלִדְתָּהּ אֹתוֹ *and she* [daughter of Shua] *was in menopause when she gave birth to him* Gn 38$_{5}$ (if em. וְהָיָה *and he was* to וְהִיא *and she*).

כֹּחַ I $_{125.11.94}$ n.m. **strength**—כּוֹחַ; sf. כֹּחִי, כֹּחֲךָ (כֹּחֶךָ), Si כוחך, Q כוחכה), כֹּחוֹ (Si, Q כוחו), כֹּחָהּ (Q כוחה), Q כוחנו, כֹּחֲכֶם, כֹּחָם (Q כוחם)—**strength, power, violence, ability, wealth,** only used in sing., of **strength, power** of humans (e.g. Dt 8$_{17}$ Jos 17$_{17}$ Jg 16$_{5}$ Ho 7$_{9}$ Mc 3$_{8}$), physical and intellectual **ability, efficiency** of humans (e.g. Gn 31$_{6}$ Ec 9$_{10}$ Dn 1$_{4}$ 1 C 26$_{8}$ 29$_{2.14}$ 2 C 2$_{5}$ 1Q Sa 1$_{19}$), acts of **violence** Ec 4$_{1}$, **wealth** of humans (e.g. Pr 5$_{10}$ 24$_{10}$ Ezr 26$_{9}$ Si 44$_{6}$), **power** of Y. (e.g. Ex 9$_{16}$ 15$_{6}$ Dt 4$_{37}$ 2 K 17$_{36}$ Jr 27$_{5}$), **produce** of soil (Gn 4$_{12}$ Jb 31$_{39}$).

<SUBJ> היה *be* 1 S 28$_{20.22}$ Dn 8$_{7}$, יכל *be able* Si 5$_{3}$, גדל *be great* Nm 14$_{17}$, עצם *be mighty* Dn 8$_{24}$, תמם *be used up* Lv 26$_{20}$ 4Q423 3$_{1}$ ([ת]ם ... כו]חה]), כלה *be exhausted* Ps 71$_{9}$, יבשׁ *be dry* Ps 22$_{16}$, ידע ni. *be known* Jg 16$_{9}$, בוא *come* 1QS 3$_{2}$ (|| דַּעַת *knowledge,* הוֹן *wealth*), שׁאר ni. *be left* Dn 10$_{8}$, סור *depart* Jg 16$_{17.19}$, עשׂה *do, make* Dt 8$_{17}$ 1QM 11$_{5}$ (+ עֹצֶם *might*), עמד *stand,* i.e. remain Dn 10$_{17}$, כשׁל *stumble,* i.e. fail Ps 31$_{11}$ Ne 4$_{4}$ GnzPs 1$_{26}$, עזב *forsake* Ps 38$_{11}$.

<NOM CL> אֵל ... כַּבִּיר כֹּחַ לֵב *God is ... a mighty one who has strength of understanding,* i.e. great understanding Jb 36$_{5}$, תִּפְאֶרֶת בַּחוּרִים כֹּחָם *the glory of youths is their strength* Pr 20$_{29}$, מִיַּד עֹשְׁקֵיהֶם כֹּחַ *from the hand of their oppressors (comes) violence* Ec 4$_{1}$, צַר כֹּחֶכָה *your strength is scarce* Pr 24$_{10}$, רַב כֹּחוֹ *great is his strength* Jb 39$_{11}$.

כֹּחַ גָּדוֹל לָךְ *you have great power* Jos 17$_{17}$, כֹחוֹ לֵאלֹהוֹ *his strength is as his god* Hb 1$_{11}$, כֹחוֹ בְמָתְנָיו *his strength is in his loins* Jb 40$_{16}$, בְּיָדְךָ כֹּחַ *in your hand is power* 1 C 29$_{12}$ 2 C 20$_{6}$, עוד בו כח *strength is still in him,* i.e. he still has strength Si 41$_{1}$, כֹּחַ בָּהֶם *ability is in them* Dn 1$_{4}$, כוח ... בלהבי אש *strength is ... with flames of fire* CD 2$_{5}$ (|| גְּבוּרָה *might,* חֵמָה *anger*), בַּמֶּה כֹּחוֹ גָדוֹל *in what (lies) his great strength* Jg 16$_{5.15}$ (כֹּחֲךָ *your strength*), איו כח *where is strength?* 4QConfess 2$_{5}$, אַתָּה כֹּחִי *you are my strength* Gn 49$_{3}$.

מַה־כֹּחִי *what is my strength?* Jb 6$_{11}$, sim. 1QH 3$_{24}$, גַּם־כֹּחַ יְדֵיהֶם לָמָּה לִּי *why should I profit from the strength of their hands?* Jb 30$_{2}$, אִם־כֹּחַ אֲבָנִים כֹּחִי *is my strength the strength of stones?* Jb 6$_{12}$, לֹא־כֹחַ *there is no strength* Jb 26$_{2}$ Lm 1$_{6}$, אַיִן כֹּחַ *there is no strength* 2 K 19$_{3}$||Is 37$_{3}$, אֵין כֹּחַ *there is no strength* Is 44$_{12}$ Dn 11$_{15}$ Ezr 10$_{13}$ 2 C 14$_{10}$ 4Q 185 1.1$_{7}$ (+ מִקְוֶה *hope*) 4QapPs[b] 53.1$_{4}$ ([א]ין), var. 4Q416 2.2$_{16}$, אִם־אֵין־בִּי כֹחַ *is there no power in me?*, i.e. do I not have power? Is 50$_{2}$, יש בכם כח *there is strength in you* 4Q apPs[b] 76$_{9}$, יֶשׁ־כֹּחַ בֵּאלֹהִים *there is power in God* 2 C 25$_{8}$, אֵין בָּנוּ כֹּחַ *there is no power in us* 2 C 20$_{12}$, אֵין־בָּהֶם כֹּחַ *there was no strength in them* 1 S 30$_{4}$.

<OBJ> שׂבע *be satiated with* Pr 5$_{10}$, מלא *be filled with* Mc 3$_{8}$, ראה hi. *show* Ex 9$_{16}$, ידע *know* 1QH 15$_{20}$ (+ כָּבוֹד *glory*) 4QDibHam[a] 1.2$_{10}$ (+ חֶסֶד *loyalty*), hi. *make known* Si 38$_{5}$, נגד hi. *declare* Ps 111$_{6}$, גבר pi. *make great* GnzPs 3$_{14}$ (+ כִּסֵּא *throne*), נתן *give* Dt 8$_{18}$ Is 40$_{29}$ 4Q423 2$_{3}$, *give,* i.e. yield Gn 4$_{12}$, זכר *remember* 1QH 4$_{35}$, בוא hi. *bring* 1QS 1$_{11}$ (|| דַּעַת *knowledge,* הוֹן *wealth*) 4QS[c] 1.3$_{3}$ (= 1QS 3$_{2}$ qal with כֹּחַ as subj.), עצר *retain* Dn 10$_{8.16}$ 11$_{6}$ 1 C 29$_{14}$ 2 C 2$_{5}$ 13$_{20}$ 22$_{9}$ 1QH 10$_{11.12}$ ([כוח]) fr. 10$_{3}$ 4QVisSam 3.2$_{1}$, סמך *support* Si 44$_{6}$, עור hi. *stir up* Dn 11$_{25}$ (|| לֵב *heart*), תכן pi. *regulate* 1QS 1$_{12}$ (+ דַּעַת, הוֹן), ישׁר pi. *make straight* GnzPs 1$_{10}$, חלף hi. *renew* Is 40$_{31}$ 41$_{1}$ Si 43$_{30}$, אמץ pi. *strengthen* Am 2$_{14}$ Na 2$_{2}$ Pr 24$_{5}$, כלה pi. *use up* Is 49$_{4}$, כשׁל hi. *make unsteady* Lm 1$_{14}$, חסר pi. *cause deficiency* Si 34$_{30}$, ענה pi. *subdue* Ps 102$_{24(Qr)}$, אכל *eat* Ho 7$_{9}$ Jb 31$_{39}$ 4QapJoseph[b] 1$_{15}$ (+ עֶצֶם *bone*), תמם hi. *make an end of* 1QH 5$_{29}$ (|| בָּשָׂר *flesh*), כלה pi. *make an end of* 1QH 5$_{36}$.

<CSTR> כוח אל *strength of God* 1QM 4$_{12}$ (|| מִלְחָמָה *battle,* נְקָמָה *vengeance,* רִיב *strife,* גְּמוּל *recompense,* שִׁלּוּם *requital,* גְּבוּרָה *might,* + כָּלָה *destruction*) 4Q418 126.2$_{9}$ (+ רֹב *abundance,* טוּב *goodness*), כוח אלוהי *strength of the God of* 11QShirShabb 5$_{3}$, כח אלוה[יך] *strength of your God* 4QapPs[a] 1.2$_{4}$, כֹּחַ אֲדֹנָי *strength of the Lord* Nm 14$_{17}$, כוח הנכבד[ים] *strength of the glorious ones* 1Q29 3$_{5}$, כֹּחַ הַסַּבָּל *strength of the porter* Ne 4$_{4}$, כֹּחַ שׁוֹר *strength of an ox* Pr 14$_{4}$, כֹּחַ חַיִל *strength of might* 2 C 26$_{13}$, כוח גבורה *strength of might* 1QH fr. 7$_{9}$ (=4QHod[a] גבורתכה *of your might*), כוח גבורתכה *strength of your might* 1QH 18$_{8}$ fr. 15$_{4}$ (גבורתך) 1QS 11$_{19}$ (=4QS[j] 1$_{7}$ גבורתך), כוח גבורתו *strength of his might* 1QH 4$_{32}$ 4Q418 159.2$_{3}$ ([גב]ורתו; + צֶדֶק *righteousness*) 4QShir[a] 1$_{3}$ (גבו[ת]ו) 4QShir[b] 81$_{2}$ ([גב]ורתו), כֹּחַ מַעֲשָׂיו *strength of his deeds* Ps 111$_{6}$, [כו]ח יד *strength of the hand of* 4QPrQuot 1.3$_{5}$, כוח ידכה *strength of your*

hand 1QH 4$_{35}$ 1QM 11$_{1}$, ידיכה *of your hands* 4Q418 88$_{4}$, כּוֹחַ הַזְּרוֹעַ *strength of the arm* Dn 11$_{6}$, כֹּחַ הָאֲכִילָה *strength of*, derived from, *the food* 1 K 19$_{8}$, כֹּחַ יָדִי *strength of my hand* Is 10$_{13}$, כֹּחַ יְדֵיהֶם *strength of their hands* Jb 30$_{2}$, כֹּחַ לֵב *strength of heart*, i.e. understanding Jb 36$_{5}$, כֹּחַ אֲבָנִים *strength of stones* Jb 6$_{12}$.

אַמִּיץ כֹּחַ *mighty of strength* Is 40$_{26}$ Jb 9$_{4}$, אמיצי כוח *mighty ones of strength* 4QD^{a} 5.1$_{8}$, גִּבֹּרֵי כֹחַ *mighty ones of strength* Ps 103$_{20}$ 1QH 8$_{11}$ 10$_{35}$ (both גבורי כוח) 4QShir^{a} 1$_{3}$ (גבורי כוח), גְּדָל־כֹּחַ *great of strength* Na 1$_{3}$, רַב־כֹּחַ *great of strength* Ps 147$_{5}$, שַׂגִּיא־כֹחַ *great of strength* Jb 37$_{23}$, עצומי כח *mighty ones of strength* 4QConfess 2$_{8}$ (+ חַיִל *power*), [נ]ורא כוח *dreadful one of power* 4QShirShabb^{d} 1.1$_{42}$, נוראי *dreadful ones of* 11QShirShabb 5$_{3}$, מַאֲמַצֵּי־כֹחַ *exertions of strength* Jb 36$_{19}$, רָב־כֹּחַ *abundance of strength* Jb 23$_{6}$ 30$_{18}$ (unless כֹּחַ III *suppuration*), רוב כוח *greatness of the strength of* 1Q29 3$_{5}$, רֹב כֹּחוֹ *abundance of his strength* Is 63$_{1}$, רוב כוחכה *abundance of your strength* 1QH 9$_{14}$, המון כוחו *tumult of his strength* 1QH 3$_{34}$, כוחכה *of your strength* 4QLam^{b} 1$_{8}$, אמוץ כוח *might of strength* 1QH 2$_{8}$ (+ חֹזֶק *strength*) perh. 4QapMes 5.1$_{6}$ (אמץ), עוז כחו *might of his strength* 4Q185 2.2$_{15}$, גדול כוחך *greatness of your strength* 1QH 14$_{23}$ (+ פלא ni. ptc. *wonderful deed*) 4QDibHam^{a} 1.2$_{7}$ (כוחכה).

זְרוֹעַ כֹּחוֹ *arm of his strength*, i.e. his strong arm Is 44$_{12}$, יְגִיעֵי כֹחַ *exhausted ones of strength*, i.e. those devoid of strength Jb 3$_{17}$, חֲמַת כֹּחוֹ *anger of his strength* Dn 8$_{6}$, חסר כחו *lack of his strength* Si 34$_{4}$, כול כוח *all strength* 4QMyst^{a} 2$_{13}$, כָּל־כֹּחִי *all my ability* Gn 31$_{6}$ 1 C 29$_{2}$, כול כוחו *all his strength* 4QMidrEschat^{a} 2$_{16}$.

<APP> חַיִל *might* Si 40$_{26}$. <ADJ> גָּדוֹל *great* Ex 32$_{11}$ Dt 4$_{37}$ 9$_{29}$ Jos 17$_{17}$ Jg 16$_{5.6.15}$ 2 K 17$_{36}$ Jr 27$_{5}$ 32$_{17}$ Ne 1$_{10}$ 1QH 15$_{20}$ 1QPrLit 3.2$_{4}$ 4QDibHam^{a} 1.2$_{10}$ 4QPrFêtes^{c} 97.1$_{4}$ ([הגדול]), זֶה *this* Jg 6$_{14}$.

<PREP> לְ of benefit, *to, for* Jb 9$_{19}$; *concerning*, + פקד *examine* CD 13$_{11}$ (|| גְּבוּרָה *might*, הוֹן *wealth*, שֵׂכֶל *understanding*, מַעֲשֶׂה *deed*).

בְּ of instrument, *by (means of), with* Zc 4$_{6}$ (|| חַיִל *might*) Pr 14$_{4}$ 1 C 26$_{8}$ 4QHod^{a} 7.2$_{21}$ 4QPrQuot 1.3$_{5}$ (בכו[ח]) 4QPrFêtes^{c} 55$_{3}$ 4QShir^{b} 2.2$_{5}$ 81$_{2}$, + גבר *be mighty* 1 S 2$_{9}$, עצם *be mighty* Dn 8$_{24}$, חפשׂ htp. *be disguised*, perh. disfigured, Jb 30$_{18}$, נצל ni. *be delivered* Ps 33$_{16}$ (|| חַיִל), עלה hi. *bring up* Nm 14$_{13}$ 2 K 17$_{36}$ (|| זְרוֹעַ *arm*), יצא hi. *bring out* Ex 32$_{11}$ (|| יָד *hand*) Dt 4$_{37}$ (|| פָּנִים *face*) 9$_{29}$ (|| זְרוֹעַ), נהל pi. *lead* 1QH 18$_{8}$, רום hi. *raise* Is 40$_{9}$, עמד *stand* Dn 8$_{22}$.

עשׂה *do, make* Is 10$_{13}$ Jr 10$_{12}$ (|| חָכְמָה *wisdom*) 27$_{5}$ 32$_{17}$ (both || זְרוֹעַ) 51$_{15}$ (|| חָכְמָה) Ec 9$_{10}$ 2 C 26$_{13}$ 1QM 11$_{5}$ (|| עֹז *strength*, + חַיִל *might*) 11QPs^{a} 26$_{14}$ (|| חָכְמָה), ברא *create* 1QH 1$_{13}$, כון hi. *establish* Ps 65$_{7}$, משׁך *prolong* Jb 24$_{22}$, חלף hi. *renew* 4QapMes 2.2$_{6}$, ידע hi. *make known* 4QM^{a} 11.1$_{23}$, שׂגב hi. *prove oneself great* Jb 36$_{22}$, רגע *stir up* Jb 26$_{12}$, עבד *serve* Gn 31$_{6}$, נטה *bend down*, i.e. push Jg 16$_{30}$, נוף hi. *wave* Si 43$_{16(M)}$, פדה *redeem* Ne 1$_{10}$, זעם hi. *cause to curse* Si 43$_{16(B)}$, רטשׁ pu. *be dashed in pieces* 1QM 11$_{1}$.

בְּ of accompaniment, *in, with* Ps 29$_{4}$ (|| הָדָר *majesty*) 1QH 9$_{17}$ 10$_{10}$ 11$_{8}$ (both + כָּבוֹד *glory*, גְּבוּרָה *might*) 1QM 13$_{13}$ 4QBer^{a} 2$_{2}$ perh. 4Q418 88$_{4}$ 126.2$_{9}$ perh. 159.2$_{3}$ perh. 210$_{2}$ 4QHod^{a} 7.2$_{13}$ perh. 4QHod^{b} 25$_{1}$ 4QPseud^{b} 8$_{3}$ (+ חַיִל *power*) 11QShirShabb 5$_{3}$, + הלך *go* Jg 6$_{14}$ 1 K 19$_{8}$, יפע hi. *shine out* 1QH 4$_{23}$, בקשׁ pi. *seek* 4QMidrEschat^{a} 2$_{16}$, עוז hi. *seek refuge* 1QH 7$_{17.19}$, אדר ni. *be glorious* Ex 15$_{6}$, שׂושׂ *rejoice* Jb 39$_{21}$, חזק htp. *strengthen oneself* 1QH 12$_{35}$ ([את]חזק), רעם hi. *thunder* 4QAdmon 1.1$_{3}$ (בכח[ו]).

בְּ introducing object, + ידע *know* 1QH 4$_{32}$, בין hi. *understand* 1QLitPr 3.2$_{4}$ 4QPrFêtes^{c} 97.1$_{4}$ (הב[ינו]), *cause to understand* 1QH fr. 15$_{4}$.

כְּ *as* Jos 14$_{11.11}$ Ezr 2$_{69}$ 1 C 29$_{2}$ Si 9$_{14}$; מִן of direction, *from*, + שׁחד *grant gift* Jb 6$_{22}$; of cause, *on account of*, + בהל ni. *be dismayed* 4QShir^{a} 1$_{3}$; privative, *without*, + עמד *stand* Jr 48$_{45}$.

כַּאֲשֶׁר *according to*, + ספר pi. *relate* GnzPs 2$_{23}$ (+ רוּחַ *spirit*); עַל *upon*, + שׁען ni. *lean*, i.e. depend upon Si 5$_{1}$; עִם *with* 1QS 11$_{19}$; לְפִי *according to*, + נתן *give* 1QSa 1$_{19}$ (יתנ[ו]).

<COLL> לאשר אין כוחכה אל תגע *do not touch anything for which your strength is not (sufficient)* 4Q416 2.2$_{16}$.

Also 1QH fr. 9$_{9}$ 4QBer^{a} 13$_{3}$ perh. 4QparaKings 90$_{2}$ 115$_{1}$ 4QpsEzek^{e} 4$_{3}$ perh. 24$_{2}$ perh. 4Q417 1.1$_{24}$ (but prob. כחכה = *like a hook*) 4Q423 1.2$_{9}$ 4QHod^{a} 7.2$_{18}$ 4QHod^{b} 13$_{1}$ 4QPseud^{b} 5.1$_{7}$ 4QM^{a} 25$_{3}$.

<SYN> חַיִל *might*, גְּבוּרָה *might*, עֹז *strength*, הָדָר *majesty*, יָד *hand*, פָּנִים *face*, זְרוֹעַ *arm*, לֵב *heart*, בָּשָׂר *flesh*, חָכְמָה *wisdom*, שֵׂכֶל *understanding*, דַּעַת *knowledge*, הוֹן

wealth, מַעֲשֶׂה *deed,* חֵמָה *anger,* מִלְחָמָה *battle,* נְקָמָה *vengeance,* רִיב *strife,* גְּמוּל *recompense,* שִׁלּוּם *requital.*

כֹּחַ II 1.0.1 n.[m.] **lizard,** an unclean beast, <NOM CL> זֶה לָכֶם הַטָּמֵא בַּשֶּׁרֶץ ... הַכֹּחַ *this is what is unclean for you among the swarming things ... the lizard* Lv 11$_{29}$. <OBJ> טמא pi. *declare unclean* 11QT 50$_{21}$.

* **כֹּחַ III** 1 n.m. **suppuration**—בְּרָב־כֹּחַ יִתְחַפֵּשׂ לְבוּשִׁי *my clothing is saturated with much suppuration* Jb 30$_{18}$ (unless כֹּחַ I *effort*).

כחד 32.0.5 vb. **hide—Ni.** 10.0.2 Pf. נִכְחָדוּ ,(נִכְחָד) נִכְחַד; impf. יִכָּחֵד; + waw וַתִּכָּחֵד; ptc. נִכְחָדוֹת ,נִכְחֶדֶת—**be hidden, effaced, destroyed,** <SUBJ> Israel Ho 5$_{3}$, אָדָם *human being* 4QBéat 3.2$_{5}$ ([י]כחד; others פחד *dread*), פַּרְעֹה *Pharaoh* Ex 9$_{15}$, יָשָׁר *upright one* Jb 4$_{7}$, קִים *adversary* Jb 22$_{20}$, כחד ni. ptc. *what is to be destroyed* Zc 11$_{9}$, אַשְׁמָה *act of guilt* Ps 69$_{6}$, עִיר *city* Jb 15$_{28}$, עֹצֶם *bone* Ps 139$_{15}$, חָכְמָה *wisdom* 4QMyst[b] 1$_{5}$ 5$_{5}$, דָּבָר *matter* 2 S 18$_{13}$; subj. not specified, Zc 11$_{9.16}$.

<PREP> מִן of direction, *from,* + י׳ *Y.* Ho 5$_{3}$ Ps 139$_{15}$, אֱלֹהִים *God* Ps 69$_{6}$, מֶלֶךְ *king* 2 S 18$_{13}$, אֶרֶץ *earth* Ex 9$_{15}$. <COLL> [בעת י]כחד *in the day when he is destroyed* 4Q Béat 3.2$_{5}$ (others [ביום] פחד *in a day of dread*).

Pi. 16.0.2 Pf. כִּחֵד, כִּחַדְתִּי, כִּחֲדוּ (כִּחֲדוּ); impf. 2ms תְּכַחֵד, תְּכַחֲדִי, אֲכַחֵד, תְּכַחֲדוּ, תְּכַחֵד—נְכַחֵד—**keep hidden, cover up,** <SUBJ> אֱלֹהִים *God* 4QapPs[b] 31$_{6}$, Jerusalem Is 3$_{9}$ (:: נגד hi. *declare*), Egyptian Gn 47$_{18}$, Judah Is 3$_{9}$ (:: נגד hi. *declare*), Achan Jos 7$_{19}$, Jeremiah Jr 38$_{14.25}$, Job Jb 6$_{10}$ 27$_{11}$, Samuel 1 S 3$_{17.17.18}$, אִשָּׁה *woman* 2 S 14$_{18}$, חָכָם *wise one* Jb 15$_{28}$ (:: נגד hi. *declare*), worshipper Ps 40$_{11}$ 78$_{4}$ (:: ספר pi. *declare*); subj. not specified, Jr 50$_{2}$, <OBJ> חֶסֶד *loyalty* Ps 40$_{11}$, אֱמֶת *truth* Ps 40$_{11}$, דָּבָר *word* 1 S 3$_{17}$ 2 S 14$_{18}$ Jr 38$_{14}$, אֵמֶר *word* Jb 6$_{10}$, עָוֹן *iniquity* 4QapPs[b] 31$_{6}$.

<PREP> לְ of direction, *to,* + קָהָל *assembly* Ps 40$_{11}$; בְּ of place, *in, at,* + קָהָל *assembly* Ps 40$_{11(mss)}$; מִן of direction, *from,* + Eli 1 S 3$_{17.17.18}$, Joshua Jos 7$_{19}$, אָב *father* Jb 15$_{28}$, בֵּן *son* Ps 78$_{4}$, מֶלֶךְ *king* 2 S 14$_{18}$ Jr 38$_{14}$, אָדוֹן *lord* Gn 47$_{18}$, שַׂר *prince* Jr 38$_{25}$.

Also perh. 1QH fr. 6$_{9}$ (unless יכחד is ni.). <ANT> נגד hi. *declare,* ספר pi. *declare.*

Hi. 6.0.1 Pf. Q הִכְחַדְתִּיו ,הכחדתם; impf. יַכְחִידֶנָּה, נַכְחִידֵם; + waw וָאַכְחִיד ,וַיַּכְחֵד; inf. הַכְחִיד—**hide, destroy, efface,** <SUBJ> י׳ *Y.* Ex 23$_{23}$, אֱלֹהִים *God* 4QapJoshua[a] 22.1$_{1}$, מַלְאָךְ *angel* 2 C 32$_{21}$, appar. Zechariah Zc 11$_{8}$, רָשָׁע *wicked one* Jb 20$_{12}$, אֹיֵב *enemy* Ps 83$_{5}$; subj. not specified, 1 K 13$_{34}$.

<OBJ> עַם *people* Ps 83$_{5}$, Amorite Ex 23$_{23}$, Canaanite Ex 23$_{23}$, Hittite Ex 23$_{23}$, Hivite Ex 23$_{23}$, Jebusite Ex 23$_{23}$, Perizzite Ex 23$_{23}$, שַׂר *prince* 2 C 32$_{21}$, נָגִיד *leader* 2 C 32$_{21}$, גִּבּוֹר *warrior* 2 C 32$_{21}$, רֹעֶה *shepherd* Zc 11$_{8}$, רָעָה *evil* Jb 20$_{12}$.

<PREP> בְּ of place, *in, at,* + מַחֲנֶה *camp* 2 C 32$_{21}$; of cause, *on account of,* + אַשְׁמָה *guilt* 4QapJoshua[a] 22.1$_{1}$; מִן privative, *without,* i.e. from being, + גּוֹי *nation* Ps 83$_{5}$; תַּחַת *under,* + לָשׁוֹן *tongue* Jb 20$_{12}$.

כחל 1 vb. **paint (eyes)—Qal** 1 Pf. כָּחַלְתְּ—<SUBJ> Oholah Ezk 23$_{40}$, Oholibah Ezk 23$_{40}$. <OBJ> עַיִן *eye* Ezk 23$_{40}$ ⇒ כָּחֹל *blue.*

* **[כָּחֹל]** 0.0.0.1 adj. **blue**—יין כחל *blue,* i.e. dark, *wine* Hebron jar inscr. 1 (unless כֹּחֵל wine of *Cohel*).
⇒ כחל *paint (eyes).*

* **[כֹּחֵל]** 0.0.0.1 pl.n. **Cohel,** perh. Bēt Kāḥil 6 km NW of Hebron, <CSTR> יין כחל *wine of Cohel* Hebron jar inscr. 1 (unless כָּחֹל *blue* wine).

[כֹּחְלִת] 0.0.4 pl.n. **Cohlith,** perh. Bēt Kāḥil 6 km NW of Hebron, or Kh. Kuḥlah 27 km ENE of Beer-sheba, <CSTR> מזרח כחלת *east of Cohlith* 3QTr 2$_{13}$, צפון *north of* 3QTr 4$_{11}$ 12$_{10}$. <COLL> תל של כחלת *hill of Cohlith* 3QTr 1$_{9}$.

כחס 0.0.1 vb. **lie—Pi.** 0.0.1 Impf. יכחס—**lie,** <SUBJ> אֲשֶׁר *one who* 1QS 7$_{3}$. <PREP> בְּ of accompaniment, *with, in,* + מַדָּע *knowledge,* i.e. knowingly 1QS 7$_{3}$.

כחשׁ 22.2.2 vb. **deny; submit—Qal** 1 Pf. כָּחַשׁ—perh. **be lean** or **be worn out, be exhausted,** וּבְשָׂרִי כָּחַשׁ מִשָּׁמֶן *and my flesh is exhausted of fat* or *is lean, without fat* Ps 109$_{24}$.

Ni. $_1$ Impf. יִכָּחֲשׁוּ; Q אכחש—**cringe, submit,** perh. **feign obedience,** <SUBJ> בֵּן *son* of foreigner 2 S 22$_{45}$ $_{(mss)}$||Ps 18$_{45}$ (if em. pi.; or del.), אֹיֵב *enemy* Dt 33$_{29}$ Ps 66$_3$ (if em. pi.). <PREP> לְ *before,* + Israel Dt 33$_{29}$, David 2 S 22$_{45(mss)}$||Ps 18$_{45}$ (if em. pi.; or del.), אֱלֹהִים *God* Ps 66$_3$ (or em. ni.); לִפְנֵי *before* Y. 4QNonCanPs^b 33$_9$ (unless pi.).*

Pi. $_{19.2.2}$ Pf. כִּחֵשׁ כִּחֵשׁ (כִּחֶשׁ), כִּחֲשׁוּ; impf. יְכַחֵשׁ יְכַחֵשׁ (יְכַחֶשׁ), Si 2ms תכחש, תְּכַחֲשׁוּן, יְכַחֲשׁוּ; + waw וְכִחַשְׁתִּי; 3fs וַתְּכַחֵשׁ; inf. כַּחֵשׁ—**be unfaithful** to God (24$_{27}$ Jb 31$_{28}$ Is 59$_{13}$ Jr 5$_{12}$), **be deceitful** to person (Lv 5$_{21}$ 19$_{11}$), appar. **betray** companion (Si 37$_{6[Bmg]}$), **tell lies** (Gn 18$_{15}$ Lv 5$_{22}$ 1 K 13$_{18}$ Zc 13$_4$ perh. Jb 8$_{18}$ Pr 30$_9$ Si 7$_{13}$), perh. **conceal** (Jos 7$_{11}$). **2.** of oil, wine, **fail, be exhausted** (Ho 9$_2$ Hb 3$_{17}$). **3.** as Ni., **cringe, submit,** perh. **feign obedience** (Ps 18$_{45}$ 66$_3$ 4QapPs^b 33$_9$).

<SUBJ> עַם *people* Jos 24$_{27}$, Israel(ites) Lv 19$_{11}$ (|| שׁקר pi. *lie*) Jos 7$_{11}$ Is 59$_{13}$, בַּיִת *house* of Israel and Judah Jr 5$_{12}$, Agur Pr 30$_9$, Job Jb 31$_{28}$, Sarah Gn 18$_{15}$, אִישׁ *man* 4QOrd^a 2$_9$ 4QSD 1.1$_9$, נֶפֶשׁ *person* Lv 5$_{21}$ (|| מעל *be unfaithful*) 5$_{22}$, בֵּן *son* Si 7$_{13}$, specif. son of foreigner Ps 18$_{45}$ (or em. ni.), נָבִיא *prophet* 1 K 13$_{18}$ Zc 13$_4$, worshipper 4QapPs^b 33$_9$, אֹיֵב *enemy* Ps 66$_3$ (or em. ni.), מְשַׂנֵּא *enemy* Ps 81$_{16}$, מַעֲשֶׂה *produce* of olive Hb 3$_{17}$, תִּירוֹשׁ *new wine* Ho 9$_2$, מָקוֹם *place* Jb 8$_{18}$; subj. not specified, Si 37$_{6(Bmg)}$ (B, D שׁכח *forget*).

<OBJ> חָבֵר *companion* Si 37$_{6(Bmg)}$.

<PREP> לְ cringe *before,* + ׳י *Y.* Ps 81$_{16}$ (or em. מְשַׂנְאֵי ׳י *those who hate Y.* to מְשַׂנְאֵיהֶם *those who hate them* [Israel] cringe before him), אֱלֹהִים *God* Ps 66$_3$ (or em. ni.), David Ps 18$_{45}$ (or del. or em. ni.); *be false* to, + אֵל *God* Jb 31$_{28}$, אִישׁ *man* of God 1 K 13$_{18}$.

בְּ of place, fail *among* Israel Ho 9$_2$, betray *in,* + קְרָב *war* Si 37$_6$; of accompaniment, *with, in,* + מַדָּע *knowledge* 4QSD 1.1$_9$ ([במ]דעו); of cause, *on account of,* + רֹב *abundance* of might Ps 66$_3$ (or em. ni.); *concerning,* + impious person Jb 8$_{18}$, פִּקָּדוֹן *deposit* Lv 5$_{21}$, תְּשׂוּמֶת *security* Lv 5$_{21}$, גָּזֵל *robbery* Lv 5$_{21}$, אֲבֵדָה *lost object* Lv 5$_{22}$; be unfaithful *to,* + ׳י *Y.* Is 59$_{13}$ Jr 5$_{12}$, אֱלֹהִים *God* Jos 24$_{27}$; be deceitful *to,* + עָמִית *companion* Lv 5$_{21}$ 19$_{11}$.

עַל *concerning,* + בְּתוּלָה *young woman* 4QOrd^a 2$_9$; *on account of,* + חֵטְא *sin* 4QapPs^b 33$_9$ (ח[טא]י); appar. tell lies *by means of,* + כַּחַשׁ *lie* Si 7$_{13}$.

לִפְנֵי *before,* + אֱלֹהִים *God* 4QapPs^b 33$_9$ ([א]לה[י]ן).

4. inf. as noun, **lying,** אָלֹה וְכַחֵשׁ וְרָצֹחַ וְגָנֹב וְנָאֹף פָּרָצוּ *cursing and lying and murder and theft and adultery have broken out* Ho 4$_2$.

<SYN> §1 מעל *be unfaithful,* שׁקר pi. *lie.*

Htp. $_1$ Impf. יִתְכַּחֲשׁוּ—**cringe, submit,** <SUBJ> בֵּן *son* of foreigner 2 S 22$_{45}$ (mss ni.). <PREP> לְ *before* David 2 S 22$_{45}$.*

→ כַּחַשׁ *lie,* כֶּחָשׁ *untruthful.*

כַּחַשׁ $_{6.2.4}$ n.m. **lie**—כַּחַשׁ; sf. כַּחֲשִׁי; pl. sf. כַּחֲשֵׁיהֶם—**1. lie, deceit,** <SUBJ> שׁמע ni. *be heard* 1QS 10$_{22}$ (|| נְבָלָה *lewdness,* + מִרְמָה *deceit,* כָּזָב *lie*). <NOM CL> כֻּלָּהּ כַּחַשׁ *all of it,* i.e. the city, *is a lie* Na 3$_1$, א]ין כחש ב[כל מעשיך *there is no deceit in any of your works* GnzPs 4$_{22}$, ... לרוח עולה כחש *belonging to the spirit of falsehood are ... deceit* 1QS 4$_9$ (|| רְמִיָּה *deceit*). <CSTR> כחש עוון *deceit of iniquity* 1QS 10$_{22}$; פְּרִי־כָחַשׁ *fruit of lies* Ho 10$_{13}$. <ADJ> אַכְזָרִי *cruel* 1QS 4$_9$.

<PREP> בְּ of instrument, *by (means of), with,* + שׂמח pi. *make one glad* Ho 7$_3$; of accompaniment, *in, with,* + סבב *encompass* Ho 12$_1$, הלך htp. *walk* 4QpNah 3.2$_2$ (ו[י]תהלכו; || שֶׁקֶר *falsehood*); מִן of cause, *on account of,* + ספר pi. *declare* Ps 59$_{13}$ (|| אָלָה *curse*).

אֶל בוֹשׁ *be ashamed of* Si 41$_{17(B)}$; עַל appar. *by means of,* + כחשׁ pi. *tell lies* Si 7$_{13}$; בוֹשׁ עַל *be ashamed of* Si 41$_{17(Bmg, M)}$.

2. emaciation, sickliness, <SUBJ> קום *arise* Jb 16$_8$, ענה *answer* Jb 16$_8$.

<SYN> §1, אָלָה *curse,* רְמִיָּה *deceit,* שֶׁקֶר *falsehood.* נְבָלָה *lewdness.*

→ כחשׁ *deny.*

[כֶּחָשׁ] $_{1.0.1}$ adj. **untruthful**—pl. כֶּחָשִׁים—**1. untruthful,** used as attributive adj., + בֵּן *son* Is 30$_9$. **2. weak,** used predicatively with מצא ni. *be found* 4QpsJub^a 2.2$_8$ (:: אמן ni. ptc. *faithful*).

<ANT> §2 אמן ni. ptc. *faithful.*

→ כחשׁ *deny.*

כִּי I $_{+4488.+151.+898.10}$ conj. **for**—Q כיא, Q כאם (= כי אם).

כִּי

1. with causal clause, **for, because,** p. 384a
2. with 'object' clause, **that,** p. 384b
3. with relative clause, **that, which,** p. 386a
4. with purpose clause, **so that,** p. 386a
5. with conditional/temporal clause, **if, when,** p. 386b
6. with concessive clause, **although,** p. 387a
7. כִּי עַתָּה or כִּי אָז **then (by) now,** p. 387a
8. with adversative clause, **rather, yet, nonetheless, except,** p. 387b
9. as emphatic or phatic particle, **surely, indeed; now, then, in fact, namely; how!,** p. 388a
10. as adverb of consequence, **so, therefore,** p. 388b
11a. כַּאֲשֶׁר ... כִּי כֵן **just as ... so too,** p. 388b
11b. כִּי ... כֵּן perh. **as ... so,** p. 388b
12a. as interrogative particle, p. 389a
12b. as interrogative pronoun, **who?,** p. 389a
13. appar. as prep., **despite; on account of,** p. 389a
14. כִּי אִם in various senses, p. 389a
15. כִּי in other compound conjunctions, p. 390b

1. usu. introducing causal or explanatory clause, **for, because, since, inasmuch as, in that.**

a. oft. with causal clause following main clause, e.g. וַיְקַדֵּשׁ אֹתוֹ כִּי בוֹ שָׁבַת מִכָּל־מְלַאכְתּוֹ *and he sanctified it because on it he rested from all his work* Gn 2$_{3}$, לְזֹאת יִקָּרֵא אִשָּׁה כִּי מֵאִישׁ לֻקֳחָה־זֹּאת *this one shall be called Woman because she was taken from a man* Gn 2$_{23}$, וָאִירָא כִּי־עֵירֹם אָנֹכִי *and I was afraid, because I was naked* Gn 3$_{10}$, וַתָּשָׁב אֵלָיו אֶל־הַתֵּבָה כִּי־מַיִם עַל־פְּנֵי כָל־הָאָרֶץ *and* the dove *returned to him to the ark, for the waters were upon the face of all the earth* Gn 8$_{9}$, הֱטִיבֹתָ כִּי הָיָה עִם־לְבָבֶךָ *you did well insasmuch as this was in your mind* 1 K 8$_{18}$||2 C 6$_{8}$ (הֱטִיבוֹתָ), חָטָאנוּ כִּי־דִבַּרְנוּ בַי׳ *we have sinned in that we spoke against Y.* Nm 21$_{7}$, לספר אשר שלחתה אל עבדך אמש כי לב [ע]בדך דוה *to tell your servant what you sent him yesterday, for the heart of your servant is sick* Lachish ost. 3$_{6}$ (others שלח אד[נ׳] לעבדך what *my lord sent to your servant*), לוא אשיב לאיש גמול רע בטוב ... כיא את אל משפט כול חי *shall not give anyone a recompense of evil for good ..., for with God (alone) is the judgment of every living being* 1QS 10$_{18}$, לוא יומת כיא צדיק הואה *he is not to die, for he is righteous* 4QapMos^{a} 1.1$_{6}$, [וישמ]ע קל אש קו[ר]א אל רעו כי הית זדה בצר *and the voice of a man was heard, calling to his companion, because there was a fissure in the rock* Siloam tunnel inscr.$_{3}$ (others נשמ]ע] a voice *was heard*), perh. כאנוש הם כי יעצל ובן אדם כי ידמה *are they like a human being, inasmuch as he is idle, or a mortal, inasmuch as he is destroyed?* 4Q418 55$_{11}$, זַעֲקַת סְדֹם וַעֲמֹרָה כִּי־רָבָּה וְחַטָּאתָם כִּי כָבְדָה מְאֹד׃ אֵרְדָה־נָּא *because the outcry from Sodom and Gomorrah is great and because their sin is very serious, I shall go down* Gn 18$_{20}$ (§1b; unless §9).

b. with causal clause preceding main clause, כִּי עָשִׂיתָ זֹּאת אָרוּר אַתָּה *because you have done this, cursed are you* Gn 3$_{14}$, e.g. Gn 3$_{17}$ 18$_{20.20}$ Ex 1$_{21}$ 2 S 7$_{27}$||1 C 17$_{25}$ Is 28$_{15}$ Jr 29$_{15}$ Ho 8$_{11}$ Hb 2$_{8}$ perh. Ps 63$_{4}$ 91$_{9}$ perh. Jb 35$_{15}$ 1 C 15$_{13}$.

c. it is because, e.g. וְעַל הִשָּׁנוֹת הַחֲלוֹם ... כִּי־נָכוֹן הַדָּבָר *and concerning the difference in the dreams ..., it is because the word* of God *is determined* Gn 41$_{32}$.

2. introducing substantival clause, either object or subject clause, and either verbal or nominal,* **that;** also **how** (e.g. 'remember how'), e.g. וְיָדְעוּ כִּי אֲנִי י׳ *and they will know that I (am) Y.* Ex 29$_{46}$ Ezk 5$_{13}$ 6$_{10.14}$ 7$_{27}$ 12$_{15.16}$ 24$_{27}$ 25$_{11.17}$ 26$_{6}$ 28$_{22.23.26}$ 29$_{9.21}$ 30$_{8.19.25.26}$ 32$_{15}$ 33$_{29}$ 34$_{27.30}$ 35$_{15}$ 36$_{38}$ 38$_{23}$ 39$_{6.28}$ 4QpsEzek^{a} 2$_{4}$ 4QpsEzek^{b} 1.2$_{1}$ 4QpsEzek^{d} 8$_{6}$, ואדעה כיא בידו משפט כול חי *and I know that in his hand is the judgment of every living being* 1QS 10$_{16}$, וַיַּרְא אֱלֹהִים אֶת־הָאוֹר כִּי טוֹב *and God saw that the light was good* Gn 1$_{4}$ (unless §9), וַיַּגֵּד לָהֶם ... פִּשְׁעֵיהֶם כִּי יִתְגַּבָּרוּ *and he told them ... that their sins were outrageous* Jb 36$_{9}$ (§2a), וְאֵת בְּקִיעֵי עִיר־דָּוִד רְאִיתֶם כִּי־רָבּוּ *and you saw that the breaches in the city of David were great* Is 22$_{9}$ (§2a; unless §9).

a. preceded by verb in main clause, ראה *see* Gn 1$_{4+5t}$ 3$_{6.6}$ 6$_{2.5}$ 12$_{14}$ 13$_{10}$ 16$_{4.5}$ 26$_{28}$ 28$_{6}$=4QRP^{b} 3.2$_{7}$ Gn 28$_{8}$ 29$_{31}$ 30$_{1.9}$ 31$_{5}$ 32$_{26}$ 37$_{4}$ 38$_{14}$ 39$_{3.13}$ 40$_{16}$ 42$_{1}$ 44$_{31}$ 45$_{12}$ 46$_{30}$ 48$_{17}$ 49$_{15.15}$ 50$_{15}$ Ex 2$_{2.12}$ 3$_{4}$ 8$_{11}$ 9$_{34}$ 16$_{29}$ 20$_{22}$ 32$_{1.25}$ 33$_{13}$ 34$_{35}$ Nm 20$_{29}$ 24$_{1}$ Dt 4$_{3}$ (unless §1a) 5$_{24}$ 28$_{10}$ 32$_{36.39}$ Jos 8$_{21.21}$ Jg 6$_{22}$ 9$_{55}$ 12$_{3}$ 16$_{18}$ 18$_{26}$ 20$_{36.41}$ 1 S 5$_{7}$ 10$_{14.24}$ 12$_{12.17}$ 13$_{6.11}$ 14$_{29}$ 17$_{51}$ 23$_{15}$ 24$_{12}$ 26$_{3}$ 28$_{21}$ 31$_{5.7.7}$||1 C 10$_{5.7.7}$ 2 S 10$_{6.9.14.15.19}$||1 C 19$_{6.10.15.16.19}$ 2 S 12$_{19}$ 17$_{23}$ 20$_{12}$ 1 K 11$_{28}$ 12$_{16}$ ||2 C 10$_{16\text{(mss)}}$ 1 K 16$_{18}$ 20$_{7}$ 21$_{29}$ 22$_{33}$||2 C 18$_{32}$ 2 K 3$_{26}$ 5$_{7}$

6$_{32}$ 11$_{1}$||2 C 22$_{10}$ 2 K 12$_{11}$||2 C 24$_{11}$ 2 K 13$_{4}$ Is 41$_{20}$ 59$_{16}$ Jr 2$_{19}$ 3$_{8}$ perh. Ezk 12$_{3}$ (unless §6) 19$_{5}$ 21$_{4}$ 23$_{13}$ Jon 3$_{10}$ Ps 25$_{19}$ 34$_{9}$ 37$_{13}$ 119$_{159}$ Jb 2$_{13}$ 22$_{12}$ 32$_{5}$ Ru 1$_{18}$ Ec 2$_{24}$ 3$_{22}$ 4$_{4}$ 8$_{17}$ 9$_{11}$ Lm 1$_{11.20}$ Est 3$_{5}$ 7$_{7}$ 1 C 21$_{28}$ 28$_{10}$ 2 C 12$_{7}$ 15$_{9}$ 32$_{2}$ Si 30$_{26}$ 51$_{27}$ 4QAges^{a} 2.2$_{9}$ 4QapPs^{b} 69$_{1}$ 4Q416 2.2$_{11}$=4Q 417 1.2$_{15}$ ([ור]אה), ni. *be seen* Is 16$_{12}$, hi. *show* 2 K 8$_{10}$, נבט hi. *see* Lm 1$_{11}$ 4QPrFêtes^{c} 16$_{6}$.

שׁמע *hear* Gn 14$_{14}$ 29$_{33}$ 34$_{5}$ 39$_{15}$ 42$_{2}$ 43$_{25}$ Ex 4$_{31.31}$ 18$_{1}$ Nm 14$_{14}$ 21$_{1}$ 22$_{36}$ Jos 9$_{16}$ 10$_{1.1}$ 14$_{12}$ Jg 20$_{3}$ 1 S 7$_{7}$ 14$_{22}$ 22$_{6}$ 23$_{10}$ 25$_{4.7.39}$ 2 S 4$_{1}$ 5$_{17}$||1 C 14$_{8}$ 2 S 8$_{9}$||1 C 18$_{9}$ 2 S 11$_{26}$ 2 S 16$_{21}$ 1 K 1$_{11}$ 5$_{15}$ 11$_{21}$ 12$_{20}$ 20$_{31.31}$ 21$_{15.16}$ 2 K 3$_{21}$ 5$_{8}$ 19$_{8}$||Is 37$_{8}$ 2 K 20$_{12}$||Is 39$_{1}$ 2 K 25$_{23}$ Jr 38$_{7.25}$ 40$_{7.7.11.11}$ Ps 62$_{12}$ 141$_{6}$ (unless §1a) Ru 1$_{6}$ Lm 1$_{21}$ Ezr 4$_{1}$ Ne 3$_{33}$ 4$_{1.1.9}$ 2 C 20$_{29}$ 4Q418 55$_{8}$ perh. 4QMyst^{a} 3c$_{3}$, ni. *be heard* Ne 6$_{1}$.

ידע *know* Gn 3$_{5.7}$ 8$_{11}$ 12$_{11}$ 15$_{8.13}$ 20$_{6.7}$ 22$_{12}$ 24$_{14}$ 31$_{6.32}$ 33$_{13}$ 38$_{9.16}$ 42$_{23.33.34}$ 43$_{7}$ 44$_{15.27}$ Ex 3$_{19}$ 4$_{14}$ 6$_{7}$ 7$_{5.17}$ 8$_{6.18}$ 9$_{14.29.30}$ 10$_{2.7}$ 14$_{4.18}$ 16$_{6.12}$ 18$_{11}$ 31$_{13}$ 32$_{22}$ 34$_{29}$ Lv 23$_{43}$=4Q RP^{c} 23$_{2}$ (ידע[ו]) Nm 11$_{16}$ 16$_{28.28.30}$ 22$_{34}$ Dt 3$_{19}$ 4$_{35.39}$ 7$_{9}$ 8$_{5}$ 9$_{3.6}$ 11$_{2}$ 20$_{20}$ 29$_{5}$ 31$_{29}$ Jos 2$_{9.9.9}$ 3$_{7.10}$ 4$_{24}$ 8$_{14}$ 22$_{31}$ 23$_{13.14}$ Jg 6$_{37}$ 13$_{16.21}$ 14$_{4}$ 15$_{11}$ 16$_{20}$ 17$_{13}$ 18$_{14}$ 20$_{34}$ 1 S 3$_{20}$ 4$_{6}$ 6$_{9}$ 12$_{17}$ 14$_{3}$ 17$_{28.46.47}$ 18$_{28}$ 20$_{3.7.9.30.33}$ 22$_{17.22}$ 23$_{9}$ 24$_{12.21}$ 26$_{4}$ 28$_{1.14}$ 29$_{9}$ 2 S 1$_{5.10}$ 2$_{26}$ 3$_{25.37.38}$ 5$_{12.12}$||1 C 14$_{2.2}$ 2 S 11$_{16}$ 14$_{1.22}$ 17$_{8.10}$ 19$_{7.21.23}$ 1 K 2$_{15.37.42}$ 5$_{17.20}$ 8$_{43}$||2 C 6$_{33}$ 1 K 8$_{60}$ 14$_{2}$ 17$_{24}$ 18$_{37}$ 20$_{7.13.28}$ 22$_{3}$ 2 K 2$_{3.5}$ 4$_{1.9}$ 5$_{7.8.15}$ 7$_{12}$ 10$_{10}$ 19$_{19}$||Is 37$_{20}$ Is 41$_{20.23}$ 45$_{3.6}$ 48$_{4}$ 49$_{23.26}$ 50$_{7}$ 60$_{16}$ Jr 2$_{19}$ 3$_{13}$ (unless §1a) 10$_{23}$ 11$_{19}$ 13$_{12}$ 16$_{21}$ 24$_{7}$ (unless §1a) 26$_{15}$ 32$_{8}$ 40$_{14}$ 42$_{19.22}$ 44$_{15.29}$ Ezk 2$_{5}$ 6$_{7.13}$ 7$_{4.9}$ 10$_{20}$ 11$_{10.12}$ 12$_{20}$ 13$_{9.14.21.23}$ 14$_{8.23}$ 15$_{7}$ 16$_{62}$ 17$_{21.24}$ 20$_{12.20.38.42.44}$ 21$_{10}$ 22$_{16.22}$ 23$_{49}$ 24$_{24}$ 25$_{5.7}$ 28$_{24}$ 29$_{6.16}$ 33$_{33}$ 35$_{4.9.12}$ 36$_{11.23.36}$ 37$_{6.13.14.28}$ 39$_{7.22.23}$ Ho 2$_{10}$ 11$_{3}$ Jl 2$_{27}$ 4$_{17}$ Jon 1$_{10.12}$ 4$_{2}$ Zc 2$_{13.15}$ 4$_{9}$ 6$_{15}$ 11$_{11}$ Ml 2$_{4}$ Ps 4$_{4}$ 20$_{7}$ 41$_{12}$ 46$_{11}$ 56$_{10}$ 59$_{14}$ 83$_{19}$ 94$_{11}$ 100$_{3}$ 109$_{27}$ 119$_{75.152}$ 135$_{5}$ 140$_{13}$ Jb 5$_{24.25}$ 9$_{2.28}$ 10$_{7.13}$ 11$_{6}$ 12$_{9}$ 13$_{18}$ 15$_{23}$ 19$_{6}$ 20$_{5}$ 42$_{2}$ Pr 7$_{23}$ 9$_{18}$ 28$_{22}$ Ru 3$_{11}$ Ec 3$_{12.14}$ 11$_{9}$ Ne 6$_{16}$ 9$_{10}$ 13$_{10}$ 1 C 29$_{17}$ 2 C 13$_{5}$ 25$_{16}$ 33$_{13}$ Si 9$_{13}$ 33$_{5}$ 36$_{22}$ 46$_{6}$ ([דע]ת) 46$_{10}$ 1QH 2$_{22.33}$ ([יד]עו) 3$_{20}$ 4$_{30}$ 6$_{6}$ 7$_{16}$ 9$_{14}$ ([כ]י) 11$_{7}$ 13$_{19}$ ([כי]א) 14$_{11.13}$ 15$_{12.13.22.23.26}$ 16$_{4.10.11.16}$ (אד[עה כי]) 18$_{21}$ fr. 1$_{9}$ 1QS 10$_{16}$ 4QJub^{i} 21$_{3}$ ([וידעו כי]א) 4QJub^{a} 1$_{5}$ ([יד]עו) 4QJub^{h} 37$_{23}$ 4QMyst^{a} 72$_{3}$ ([י]דעו כיא) 4QMidrEschat^{a} 4$_{8}$ ([י]דע) CD 1$_{8}$ Lachish ost. 4$_{10}$ Arad ost. 40$_{13}$ ([כי]) 4QparaKings 9$_{5}$ ([היד]עתה) 4QpsMos^{d} 1.2$_{7}$ ([כ]י) 4QM^{h} 1$_{4}$ CD 1$_{8}$ GnzPs 2$_{14.18}$, ni. *be known* Gn 41$_{21}$ Ex 21$_{36}$ 33$_{16}$ 1 K 18$_{36}$ Ru 3$_{14}$ 1QMyst^{a} 1.1$_{8}$, hi. *cause to know* Dt 8$_{3}$ perh. 4QapMos^{c} 2.2$_{8}$, בין *understand* 1 S 3$_{8}$ 2 S 12$_{19}$, hi. *understand* Is 43$_{10}$ perh. 57$_{1}$ (unless §9) Mc 4$_{12}$ (unless §1a) Dn 8$_{17}$ 1QH 17$_{21}$ 4QVisSam 3$_{6}$ ([בי]נו) 4QpsMos^{e} 2.1$_{6}$ CD 1$_{10}$, שׂכל hi. *understand* Is 41$_{20}$, אמן hi. *believe* Ex 4$_{5}$ Jb 9$_{16}$ 39$_{12.24}$ (כִּי־קוֹל שׁוֹפָר appar. he does not believe *that a sound is the trumpet*) Lm 4$_{12}$, perh. בטח *trust* Jb 40$_{23}$ (unless §6), טעם *taste*, i.e. discern Ps 34$_{9}$ Pr 31$_{18}$.

אמר *say* Jg 15$_{2}$ Is 3$_{10}$ Jb 36$_{10}$ Ec 5$_{5}$ 1 C 21$_{18}$, קרא *cry* Is 40$_{2.2.2}$, ענה *answer* Is 14$_{32}$, נגד hi. *tell* Gn 3$_{11}$ 12$_{18}$ 29$_{12.12}$ 31$_{20}$ 45$_{26}$ (unless §9) Dt 26$_{3}$ 30$_{18}$ Jg 4$_{12}$ 14$_{9}$ 1 S 3$_{13}$ 10$_{16}$ 22$_{21}$ 2 S 7$_{11}$ 12$_{18}$ 19$_{7}$ Jr 48$_{20}$ 51$_{31}$ Ps 22$_{32}$ (unless §1a) 92$_{16}$ Jb 36$_{9}$ 1QM 10$_{1}$, ho. *be told* Gn 31$_{22}$ Ex 14$_{5}$ Jg 9$_{47}$ 1 S 23$_{7.13}$ 27$_{4}$ 1 K 2$_{29.41}$, ספר pi. *tell* Ps 48$_{15}$ (unless §1a or §9), בשׂר pi. *give news* 2 S 18$_{19}$, htp. *receive news* 2 S 18$_{31}$, גלה *uncover* ear, i.e. tell 1 S 22$_{8}$, שׁבע ni. *swear* Gn 22$_{16}$ Jos 2$_{12}$ 2 S 19$_{8}$ Jr 22$_{5}$ 49$_{13}$ Am 4$_{2}$ Dn 12$_{7}$ (unless §1a, §2c, or §9), hi. *adjure* 1 K 18$_{10}$, נחם ni. *repent* Gn 6$_{6.7}$ 1 S 15$_{11.35}$, שׂים *place* in hearing Ex 17$_{14}$, *consider* Is 41$_{20}$ Jb 1$_{8}$ 2$_{3}$, שׁוב hi. *take back* to heart, i.e. consider Dt 4$_{39}$, זכר *remember* Dt 5$_{15}$ 15$_{15}$ 16$_{12}$ 24$_{18.22}$ Jg 9$_{2}$ Ps 42$_{5}$ 78$_{35.39}$ Jb 7$_{7}$ 10$_{9}$ 36$_{24}$ Ec 11$_{8}$ Si 8$_{5}$ 9$_{12}$ 14$_{12}$ 34$_{13}$ 41$_{3(B)}$ (ז[כו]ר) 4Q416 2.3$_{2}$ 4QapLam^{b} 1$_{1}$ 4QDibHam^{a} 5.2$_{3}$ 6$_{6}$ ([ז]כור) 8$_{1}$ ([זכו]ר), hi. *cause to be mentioned* Is 12$_{4}$, עוד hi. *call to witness* Dt 4$_{26}$, *warn* Dt 8$_{19}$ Jr 42$_{20}$ Am 3$_{14}$, נכר hi. *recognize* 1 K 20$_{41}$ Is 61$_{9}$, שׁכח *forget* Jb 39$_{15}$, כתב ni. *be written* Ps 102$_{20}$ (unless §1a or §2c), טוב *be good* 2 S 18$_{3}$ Ps 119$_{71}$ Jb 10$_{3.3}$ 13$_{9}$ Ru 2$_{22}$ Lm 3$_{27}$, יטב *be good* 1 K 3$_{10}$, רעע *be evil*, i.e. displease Is 59$_{15}$, שׁמם htpo. *be astounded* Is 59$_{16}$, אוה pi. *desire* 4Q418 127$_{2}$, perh. חפץ *desire* 4Q418 94$_{3}$ ([ח]פץ).

b. preceded in main clause by nom. cl. or by noun and היה *be*, תִּהְיֶה־לִּי לְעֵדָה כִּי חָפַרְתִּי אֶת־הַבְּאֵר הַזֹּאת *you*, or *it*, *will be to me as a witness that I dug this well* Gn 21$_{30}$, זֶה־לְּךָ הָאוֹת כִּי אָנֹכִי שְׁלַחְתִּיךָ *this is your sign that is I who have sent you* Ex 3$_{12}$, מַה־זֹּאת עָשִׂינוּ כִּי־שִׁלַּחְנוּ אֶת־יִשְׂרָאֵל *what is this that we have done, that we have let Israel go?* Ex 14$_{5}$, מַה־בֶּצַע כִּי נַהֲרֹג אֶת־אָחִינוּ *what advantage is it that we kill our brother?* Gn 37$_{26}$, הַמְעַט מִכֶּם כִּי־הִבְדִּיל אֱלֹהֵי יִשְׂרָאֵל אֶתְכֶם *is it too small a thing for you that the God of Israel has separated you?* Nm 16$_{9}$, זה חפצי ... כי אחיה לפניך תמיד *... this is my desire ... that I should* *live in your presence continually* GnzPs 3$_{2}$, [מ]ה בשר כיא *what is flesh that?* 4QMyst[c] 5$_{3}$, Ex 13$_{9.16}$ 31$_{17}$ (unless §1a in all three) Nm 16$_{13}$ Jos 22$_{34}$ 24$_{22}$ 1 S 12$_{5}$ 2 K 20$_{8}$||Is 38$_{22}$ 2 K 20$_{9}$ Jr 22$_{21}$ (unless §1a) 44$_{29}$ Ezk 24$_{19}$ Ps 119$_{50.71}$ Jb 6$_{10}$ (unless §1a) 13$_{16}$ 39$_{27}$ (unless כִּי II *vulture*) Ru 1$_{13}$ (unless §1a) 4$_{9}$ Ec 9$_{3}$.

c. introducing direct speech (distinction from §§1a, 2a, 9 not alw. clear), וַיֹּאמֶר כִּי־עַתָּה הִרְחִיב י׳ לָנוּ *and he said, Now Y. has made room for us* Gn 26$_{22}$, וַיֹּאמֶר אֵלָיו י׳ כִּי אֶהְיֶה עִמָּךְ *and Y. said to him, I am with you* Jg 6$_{16}$, perh. אֵת שֵׁם הַשֵּׁנִי קָרָא אֶפְרָיִם כִּי־הִפְרַנִי אֱלֹהִים *the name of the second he called Ephraim, saying, God has made me fruitful* Gn 41$_{52}$, Gn 4$_{23.25}$ 21$_{30}$ 29$_{32.33}$ 32$_{31}$ 41$_{51}$ Ex 2$_{10}$ 17$_{16}$ 18$_{4}$ 22$_{8}$ Jos 2$_{24}$ 22$_{34}$ Jg 10$_{10}$ (וְכִי עָזַבְנוּ *and, We have forsaken*; mss כִּי *for* we have forsaken, as §1a) 1 S 1$_{20}$ 13$_{11}$ 2 S 11$_{23}$ 1 K 1$_{13.17.30}$ 11$_{22}$ 20$_{5}$ 2 K 8$_{13}$ Is 39$_{8}$ 45$_{23}$ Jr 2$_{35}$ 29$_{10}$ Ezk 33$_{10}$ Ps 59$_{8}$ 118$_{2.3.4}$ 1 C 4$_{9}$ 2 C 28$_{23}$ perh. CD 3$_{18}$ perh. GnzPs 1$_{14}$.

3. perh. as relative particle, **that, which, (one) who,*** perh. אז תצא לנצח אמת תבל כיא להתגוללה בדרכי רשע *then truth will appear for ever (in) the world, which has polluted itself by ways of ungodliness* 1QS 4$_{19}$, בל י[בוא זר] ... כי ראה בלא הכיר perh. *no stranger shall come ..., (one) who sees but does not recognize* 1QH 8$_{13}$.

4. introducing clause of consequence or purpose, **(with the result) that, (in order) that, (so) that, (such) that.**

מֶה־חָטָאתִי לָךְ כִּי־הֵבֵאתָ עָלַי ... חֲטָאָה גְדֹלָה *how have I sinned against you, that you have brought about for me ... a great sin?* Gn 20$_{9}$, מָה רָאִיתָ כִּי עָשִׂיתָ אֶת־הַדָּבָר הַזֶּה *what did you see*, i.e. what was your purpose, *that you did this thing?* Gn 20$_{10}$, מַה־תִּתֶּן־לִי כִּי תָבוֹא אֵלָי *what will you give me, that you may come to me?* Gn 38$_{16}$, לֹא־עָשִׂיתִי מְאוּמָה כִּי־שָׂמוּ אֹתִי בַּבּוֹר *I have done nothing that they should have put me in the dungeon* Gn 40$_{15}$, מִי אָנֹכִי כִּי אֵלֵךְ אֶל־פַּרְעֹה *who am I that I should go to Pharaoh?* Ex 3$_{11}$, מה אפהו אדם ... כי תשכילנו *what then is a human being ... that you make him understand?* 1QH 10$_{4}$, perh. השמר מאד כי[ן] *be very careful to* 4Q418 123.2$_{7}$, מי עבדך כלב כי שלח אדני *who is your servant, a dog, such that my lord has sent* the king's document? Lachish ost. 6$_{3}$ (sim. 2$_{4}$ 5$_{4}$), Gn 31$_{36}$ Ex 3$_{11}$ 16$_{7}$ 32$_{21}$ Nm 11$_{12.29}$ 16$_{11.13}$ 22$_{28}$ Jg 8$_{6.15}$ 9$_{28.38}$ 11$_{12}$ 13$_{17}$ 14$_{3}$ 18$_{23}$ 1 S 11$_{5}$ 17$_{26.43}$ 18$_{18}$ 20$_{1}$ 21$_{16}$ 22$_{8}$ 28$_{22}$ 29$_{8}$ 2 S 7$_{18}$||1 C 17$_{16}$ 2 S 9$_{8}$ 10$_{3}$||1 C 19$_{3}$ 2 S 19$_{23.35}$ 1 K 18$_{9}$ 2 K 5$_{7}$ 8$_{13}$ 18$_{20.35}$||Is 36$_{5.20}$ Is 7$_{13}$ 22$_{1.16}$ 29$_{16}$ 43$_{22}$ 57$_{11}$ Jr 2$_{5}$ 4$_{30.30.30}$ 37$_{18}$ 48$_{9.27}$ perh. 51$_{62}$ (unless §1a) Ezk 8$_{17}$ Ho 1$_{6}$ Mc 4$_{9}$ Hb 2$_{18.18}$ 3$_{8}$ Ml 3$_{14.14}$ (unless all four §5) Ps 8$_{5.5}$ 114$_{5}$ Jb 3$_{12}$ 6$_{11.11}$ 7$_{12.17.17}$ 10$_{6}$ 15$_{13.14.14}$ 16$_{3}$ 21$_{15}$ 38$_{20.20}$ 41$_{2}$ 1 C 29$_{14}$ 2 C 4$_{18}$ 32$_{14}$ perh. Si 46$_{11}$ (למען ... וגם כי *in order to ... and also so that*) 1QH 10$_{12}$ 15$_{21}$.

5. introducing conditional clause (sometimes with temporal aspect), **if, supposing that, in the case that, when,*** כִּי תַעֲבֹד אֶת־הָאֲדָמָה לֹא־תֹסֵף תֵּת־כֹּחָהּ *when you till the ground, it shall no more yield its strength* Gn 4$_{12}$, אָז תִּנָּקֶה מֵאָלָתִי כִּי תָבוֹא אֶל־מִשְׁפַּחְתִּי *then you will be free from my oath, when you come to my family* Gn 24$_{41}$, כִּי תִקְנֶה עֶבֶד עִבְרִי שֵׁשׁ שָׁנִים יַעֲבֹד *when you buy a Hebrew slave, he shall serve six years* Ex 21$_{2}$, כִּי שִׁבְעָתַיִם יֻקַּם־קָיִן וְלֶמֶךְ שִׁבְעִים וְשִׁבְעָה *if Cain is avenged sevenfold, then Lamech (will be avenged) seventy-sevenfold* Gn 4$_{24}$, כיא תבוא מלחמה ... והריעות[מה] בחצוצרות *when a war comes ..., you shall blow on the trumpets* 1QM 10$_{6}$, והיה כיא יערוכו השולחן ... הכוהן ישלח ידו *and (it will be) that when they set the table ..., the priest will extend his hand* 1QS 6$_{4}$, perh. [ולוא ימלט מידו כי בידו ירד] *and he will not escape from his control if he comes under his control* 4QJub[h] 35$_{16}$, perh. [ו]כי יריבון אנ[שים] *and when men struggle* 4QHalakhah[a] 3.1$_{2}$, וכיא יקום השבט ... ובאתה *but if the tribe arises ..., then you are to come* 4QapMos[a] 1.1$_{5}$, או כי ילכו לעיר *or if they go to a city* 4QapMos[b] 1.3$_{2}$, רָעָב כִּי־יִהְיֶה בָאָרֶץ *if there be famine in the land* 1 K 8$_{37}$ (§5), Gn 6$_{1}$ 12$_{12}$ 26$_{8}$ 27$_{1}$ 30$_{33}$ perh. 31$_{37}$ 31$_{49}$ 32$_{18}$ 43$_{21}$ 44$_{24}$ 46$_{33}$ Ex 1$_{10}$ 3$_{21}$ 7$_{9}$ 9$_{15}$ 12$_{25.26.48}$ 13$_{5.11.14.15}$ 18$_{16}$ 20$_{25}$ 21$_{7.14.18.20.22.26.28.33.35.36.37}$ 22$_{4.5.6.9.13.15.26}$ 23$_{4.5.23}$ 30$_{12}$ Lv 1$_{2}$ 2$_{1.4}$ 4$_{2}$ 5$_{1.3.4.5.15.17.21.23}$ 7$_{21.25}$ 11$_{37.38.39}$ 12$_{2}$ 13$_{2.9.16.18.24.29.31.38.40.42.47.51}$ 14$_{34}$ 15$_{2.8.13.16.19.25.25}$ 19$_{5.20.23.33}$ 20$_{27}$ 21$_{9}$ 22$_{9.11.12.13.14.21.27.29}$ 23$_{10}$ 24$_{15.17.19}$ 25$_{2.14}$=4QD[f] 3$_{4}$ (כי [תמכור] *if you sell*) Lv 25$_{20.25.26.29.35.39.47}$ 27$_{2.14}$ Nm 5$_{6.12.20.20}$ 6$_{2.9}$ 9$_{10.14}$ 10$_{9.32}$ 11$_{13}$ 15$_{2.8.14.22}$ 18$_{26}$ 19$_{14}$ 27$_{8}$ 30$_{3.4}$ 32$_{15}$ 33$_{51}$ 34$_{2}$ 35$_{10}$ Dt 4$_{25.29}$ 6$_{10.20.25}$ 7$_{1.17}$ 11$_{29}$ 12$_{20.21.29}$ 13$_{2.7.13.19}$ 14$_{24.24}$ 15$_{7.12.13.16.21}$ 17$_{2.8.14}$=11QT 56$_{12}$ Dt 18$_{6.9}$ =11QT 60$_{16}$ Dt 18$_{21}$ 19$_{1.9.11.16}$ 20$_{1}$=11QT 61$_{12}$ Dt 20$_{10}$ =11QT 62$_{5}$ Dt 20$_{19}$ 21$_{1.9.10}$=11QT 63$_{10}$ Dt 21$_{15.18.22}$

=11QT 64$_{2.9}$ Dt 22$_{6.8.8.13}$=11QT 65$_{2.5.6.7}$ Dt 22$_{22.23.28}$ =11QT 66$_{8}$ Dt 23$_{10.11.22.23.25.26}$ 24$_{1.3.5.7.10.19.20.21}$ 25$_{1.5.11}$ 26$_{1.12}$ 28$_{2.9.13}$ 30$_{1}$=4QMMT C$_{13}$ Dt 30$_{10.10}$ 31$_{20.21}$ 32$_{36}$ Jos 4$_{6}$ 8$_{5}$ 17$_{13}$ 20$_{5}$ 22$_{7.28}$ 24$_{20}$ Jg 1$_{28}$ 2$_{18}$ 6$_{7}$ 8$_{1}$ 12$_{5}$ 15$_{3}$ 16$_{16.25}$ 21$_{22}$ 1 S 1$_{12}$ 10$_{7}$ 17$_{48}$ 20$_{13.18}$ 22$_{22}$ 24$_{20}$ 25$_{30}$ 2 S 3$_{9}$ 6$_{13}$ 7$_{1}$ 7$_{12}$||1 C 17$_{11}$ 2 S 16$_{10(Kt)}$ (Qr כֹּה *thus*) 19$_{26}$ 1 K 5$_{15}$ 8$_{35.36.37.37.37.37.44.46}$||2 C 6$_{26.27.28.28.28.28.34.36}$ 1 K 19$_{2}$ 2 K 2$_{23}$ 4$_{29.29}$ 7$_{12}$ 18$_{22}$||Is 36$_{7}$ Is 1$_{12}$ 3$_{6}$ 8$_{19.21}$ 10$_{12}$ perh. 16$_{4}$ (unless §1a) 16$_{12}$ 19$_{20}$ 28$_{15.18}$ 30$_{21.21}$ 40$_{7}$ 43$_{2.2}$ 54$_{6}$ 58$_{7}$ Jr 2$_{26}$ 3$_{16}$ 5$_{19}$ 12$_{1.5.6}$ 13$_{21.22}$ 14$_{12.12}$ 15$_{2}$ 16$_{10}$ 17$_{6.8}$ 18$_{22}$ 23$_{33}$ 25$_{28}$ 29$_{13}$ 32$_{5}$ 38$_{15.15.25}$ 42$_{6.20}$ 44$_{19}$ 46$_{22}$ Ezk 3$_{19.21}$ 14$_{9.13.23}$ 18$_{5.21}$ 21$_{12.12}$ 25$_{3.3.3}$ 33$_{2.6.9}$ 46$_{12.16.17}$ Ho 4$_{14.14}$ 11$_{1}$ Am 5$_{17}$ Mc 5$_{4.4.5.5}$ Hb 1$_{5}$ 2$_{18}$ 3$_{8}$ Zc 7$_{5.6.6}$ 13$_{3}$ Ml 1$_{4.8.8}$ Ps 8$_{4}$ 11$_{3}$ 13$_{5}$ perh. 21$_{12}$ (unless §1a) 32$_{3}$ 41$_{12}$ 49$_{17.17}$ 58$_{11}$ 62$_{11}$ 63$_{12}$ 71$_{23}$ 75$_{3}$ 90$_{4}$ 102$_{1}$ 120$_{7}$ 127$_{5}$ Jb 1$_{5}$ 3$_{22}$ 5$_{21}$ 7$_{13}$ 19$_{28}$ 21$_{15}$ 22$_{3.3}$ 22$_{29}$ 27$_{8.8.9}$ 29$_{11}$ 31$_{14.14.21.26.29}$ 35$_{3}$ 36$_{13}$ 37$_{4.20.20}$ 38$_{5.40.41}$ Pr 3$_{25}$ 4$_{3}$ (unless §1a or §9) 4$_{8}$ 6$_{30.30}$ 19$_{18}$ 22$_{18}$ 23$_{1.13.22.31.31}$ 24$_{12}$ 26$_{25}$ 30$_{4.22.22.23.23}$ Ru 1$_{12.17}$ Ec 6$_{11}$ Lm 1$_{19}$ 3$_{28}$ Si 32$_{17}$ 46$_{3}$ 51$_{18(B)}$ 1QS 5$_{20}$ 6$_{4.11}$ 10$_{2}$ 4QOrd^{a} 2$_{8}$ 11QPs Ap^{a} 4$_{12}$ ([כי]) 11QT 45$_{7}$ 49$_{5}$ 50$_{10}$ 53$_{1}$ ([כי]) 53$_{14.16}$ 58$_{3}$ 64$_{6}$ GnzPs 2$_{15}$.

6. introducing concessive clause, **although,** לֹא־נָחָם אֱלֹהִים דֶּרֶךְ אֶרֶץ פְּלִשְׁתִּים כִּי קָרוֹב הוּא *God did not lead them by way of the land of the Philistines, although it was near* Ex 13$_{17}$, perh. וכי שלח אדני על דבר בית הרפד אין שם אדם *and although my lord has sent (instructions) concerning the matter of Beth-haraphid, no one is there* Lachish ost. 4$_{4}$, perh. צו ... כי משפט מות הואה *command* the Israelites to observe this matter *even though it is a judgment of death* 4QJub^{f} 33$_{13}$, Ex 34$_{9}$ Dt 29$_{18}$ Jos 14$_{12}$ 17$_{18.18.18}$ perh. 1 S 1$_{5}$ 15$_{35}$ 2 S 1$_{9}$ Is 12$_{1}$ 30$_{4}$ 63$_{16}$ Jr 46$_{23}$ 49$_{16}$ 50$_{11.11.11}$ 51$_{5.53.53}$ Ezk 2$_{6}$ Ho 7$_{14}$ 13$_{15}$ perh. Mc 1$_{12}$ (unless §1a) 7$_{8.8}$ Na 2$_{3}$ Hb 3$_{17}$ Zc 8$_{6}$ 9$_{2}$ perh. Ps 27$_{10}$ (unless §9) 37$_{24}$ 44$_{20}$ 49$_{19}$ 71$_{15}$ appar. 116$_{10}$ (or em. לָכֵן *therefore*) 119$_{83}$ 138$_{6}$ perh. Jb 6$_{20}$ Pr 6$_{35}$ 29$_{19}$ Ec 4$_{14}$ (כִּי גַּם appar. *even though*) perh. 8$_{6}$ (unless §1a) Est 1$_{20}$ Ezr 9$_{13}$.

7. כִּי עַתָּה or כִּי אָז introducing apodosis of conditional sentence, **then (by) now,** כִּי לוּלֵא הִתְמַהְמָהְנוּ כִּי־עַתָּה שַׁבְנוּ זֶה פַעֲמָיִם *for if we had not delayed, then by now we would have returned twice* Gn 43$_{10}$, Gn 31$_{42}$ Nm 22$_{29.33}$ 1 S 13$_{13}$ (if em. לֹא *not* to לֻא *if*) 14$_{30}$ 2 S 2$_{27}$ 19$_{7(Qr)}$ Jr 26$_{15}$ Jb 8$_{6}$ 11$_{15}$ 13$_{19}$ 22$_{26}$.

8. with adversative clause, **a. (but) rather,** לֹא־תִקְרָא אֶת־שְׁמָהּ שָׂרָי כִּי שָׂרָה שְׁמָהּ *you shall not call her name Sarai, but rather Sarah is her name* Gn 17$_{15}$ (unless §1a, *for Sarah is her name*), לֹא מְרַגְּלִים אַתֶּם כִּי כֵנִים אַתֶּם *you are not spies; rather, you are honest men* Gn 42$_{34}$, ולוא האזינו לדברכה כי אמרו לחזון דעת לא נכון *and they did not listen to your word; instead, they said of the vision of knowledge, It is not true* 1QH 4$_{17}$, Gn 24$_{4}$ 45$_{8}$ Ex 4$_{1.10}$ 16$_{8}$ 19$_{13}$ 23$_{24}$ 34$_{13}$ Nm 27$_{3}$ 35$_{31}$ 36$_{7.9}$ Dt 4$_{26}$ 5$_{3}$ 7$_{8}$ 8$_{3}$ 9$_{5}$ perh. 11$_{7}$ 13$_{10}$ 15$_{8}$ 20$_{17}$ 21$_{17.23}$=11QT 64$_{11}$ Dt 29$_{14.19}$ 30$_{14}$ 32$_{47}$ Jos 11$_{20}$ 17$_{18}$ perh. 18$_{7}$ (unless §1a) 22$_{27.28}$ Jg 2$_{17}$ 11$_{16}$ 1 S 6$_{3}$ 30$_{24}$ 2 S 20$_{21}$ 1 K 9$_{22}$||2 C 8$_{9}$ 1 K 11$_{34}$ 21$_{15}$ 2 K 14$_{6.16}$ 6$_{12}$ 12$_{8}$ Is 10$_{7}$ 23$_{18}$ 28$_{27}$ 30$_{5}$ 62$_{4.9}$ 65$_{20.23}$ Jr 1$_{7}$ 14$_{12.13}$ 22$_{12}$ 31$_{33}$ 32$_{4}$ 34$_{3}$ 35$_{7}$ 38$_{23}$ 39$_{12(Qr)}$ 43$_{3}$ 44$_{17}$ 49$_{12}$ 51$_{26}$ Ezk 7$_{4}$ 10$_{11}$ 12$_{25.25}$ 14$_{18}$ perh. 18$_{11}$ (unless §1a or §9) 46$_{9}$ Am 7$_{14}$ Zc 8$_{12}$ Ps 44$_{4}$ 75$_{8}$ 115$_{1}$ 118$_{17}$ Jb 5$_{7}$ 9$_{18}$ Ec 6$_{2}$ Est 1$_{16}$ 6$_{13}$ Dn 9$_{18}$ Ezr 4$_{3}$ Ne 6$_{8.12}$ 1 C 29$_{1}$ 2 C 6$_{9}$ 16$_{12}$ 17$_{4}$ 18$_{7}$ 19$_{6}$ 20$_{15}$ 25$_{4}$ 26$_{18}$ 33$_{23}$ 35$_{21.22}$ Si 30$_{26}$ 1QH 4$_{17}$ 1QS 5$_{15}$ 3QJub 1$_{2}$ CD 8$_{15}$ 19$_{28}$, perh. 4QapJoseph^{c} 1$_{6}$=4QapJoseph^{b} 19$_{4}$ 4Q392 1$_{6}$ 4QMMT B$_{65}$ 4QBéat 3.2$_{6}$.

b. yet, nonetheless, כִּי־יָלַדְתִּי בֵן לִזְקֻנָיו *yet I have borne him a son in his old age* Gn 21$_{7}$, Ex 5$_{11}$ 33$_{3}$ Jg 1$_{19}$ 1 S 17$_{39}$ 28$_{13}$ 29$_{8}$ 2 S 18$_{3}$ 1 K 8$_{27}$||2 C 6$_{18}$ 1 K 15$_{4}$ Is 7$_{16}$ perh. 8$_{23}$ (unless §1a) 14$_{1}$ 49$_{25}$ 57$_{20}$ 66$_{8}$ Jr 2$_{34}$ 12$_{11}$ 18$_{15.20}$ 22$_{17}$ 23$_{18}$ 30$_{17}$ 49$_{10}$ 51$_{5}$ Ezk 29$_{13}$ perh. Ho 5$_{1}$ (unless §1a) Am 6$_{12.14}$ 9$_{8}$ perh. Mc 1$_{12}$ (unless §1a) Ml 3$_{8}$ Ps 14$_{6}$ 37$_{20}$ 38$_{16}$ 130$_{4}$ 141$_{8}$ (or em. וְאָנֹכִי *and I*) Jb 4$_{5}$ 23$_{10}$ perh. 23$_{17}$ perh. 36$_{18}$ Ec 5$_{6}$ 8$_{12}$ 9$_{4}$ 2 C 12$_{8}$ 20$_{12}$ 28$_{27}$ 30$_{18}$ Si 40$_{14}$ 1QH 4$_{12.18}$ 1QS 11$_{2}$ 11QT 48$_{6}$ CD 14$_{2}$ perh. Lachish ost. 4$_{12}$ (unless §1a or §9).

c. except, לוא כוחנו ... עשה חיל כיא בכוחכה *our strength ... has not done valiantly, except by your power* 1QM 11$_{5}$, אֵין־חֵפֶץ לַמֶּלֶךְ בְּמֹהַר כִּי בְּמֵאָה עָרְלוֹת פְּלִשְׁתִּים *the king has no pleasure in any bride-price except one consisting of a hundred foreskins of Philistines* 1 S 18$_{25}$ (mss כִּי אִם *except*).

d. לֹא כִּי **(1) rather, instead,** לֹא כִּי צָחָקְתְּ *instead you did laugh* Gn 18$_{15}$, 19$_{2}$ 42$_{12}$ Jos 5$_{14}$ 24$_{21}$ Jg 15$_{13}$ 1 S 2$_{16(Qr)}$ 10$_{19(mss)}$ (L לוֹ כִּי *to him, but*) 12$_{12}$ 2 S 16$_{18}$ 24$_{24}$ 1 K 2$_{30}$ 3$_{22.22.23}$ 2 K 20$_{10}$ Is 30$_{16}$ perh. Jr 2$_{25}$ (but לוֹא כִּי perh. *no, rather*, as §8a) 42$_{14}$ 1 C 21$_{24}$; **(2) nonetheless,** לֹא כִּי שָׁלֵחַ

תְּשַׁלְּחֵנִי *nonetheless, you are to dispatch me* 1 K 11$_{22}$ (mss לֹא כִּי), כיא פ[ת]א[י]ם עבר[ו] ויענשו *nonetheless, the guileless sin and are punished* 4QD^{b} 9.5$_{5}$ (=CD 14$_{2}$ כי פתאום ונענשו appar. *but suddenly they are indeed punished*).

9. as emphatic particle, **surely, indeed;*** or merely phatic, **now, then, in fact, namely;** also with the interrogative particle הֲ (Gn 27$_{36}$ 29$_{15}$ 1 S 10$_{1}$ 2 S 9$_{1}$ 13$_{28}$ 23$_{19}$ [unless §12b] Jb 6$_{22}$); as exclamatory adverb, **how!***

כִּי שִׂיחַ וְכִי־שִׂיג לוֹ וְכִי־דֶרֶךְ לוֹ *surely he is in meditating or busy or on a journey* 1 K 18$_{27}$, כי לוא רמה תודה לכה *surely a maggot cannot give thanks to you* 11QPs^{a} 19$_{1}$, כִּי־זֶה לְבַדּוֹ יָבֹא לְיָרָבְעָם אֶל־קֶבֶר יַעַן נִמְצָא־בוֹ דָּבָר טוֹב *indeed he alone of Jeroboam's family will go to the grave, because something good is found in him* 1 K 14$_{13}$, כִּי לְכוּ־נָא אֶל־מְקוֹמִי *now go to my place* Jr 7$_{12}$, כִּי מַדּוּעַ לֹא עָלְתָה אֲרֻכַת בַּת־עַמִּי *then why has the healing of the daughter of my people not been effected?* Jr 8$_{22}$ (mss lack כִּי), וכי אמר אדני perh. *and in fact my lord said* Lachish ost. 3$_{8}$, הֲכִי קָרָא שְׁמוֹ יַעֲקֹב *does he (not) call himself Jacob?* Gn 27$_{36}$, הֲכִי־אָחִי אַתָּה *are you (not) my brother* Gn 29$_{15}$, הֲכִי יֶשׁ־עוֹד *is there still anyone?* 2 S 9$_{1}$, הֲלוֹא כִּי־מְשָׁחֲךָ י׳ *has not Y. anointed you?* 1 S 10$_{1}$, perh. [והזה] האיש ... כיא איש כוהן טהור *and the man is to sprinkle ... namely (a man who is) a pure priest* 4QTohB^{c} 1$_{6}$, אָמְנָם כִּי *truly indeed* Jb 12$_{2}$ Ru 3$_{12(Qr)}$.

זַעֲקַת סְדֹם וַעֲמֹרָה כִּי־רָבָּה וְחַטָּאתָם כִּי כָבְדָה מְאֹד *how great is the outcry from Sodom and Gomorrah, how very grave is their sin!* Gn 18$_{20}$ (if em. כָּבְדָה qal for [§1b] the outcry is great, to כְּבֵדָה, adj.), וַיַּרְא אֱלֹהִים אֶת־הָאוֹר כִּי טוֹב *and God saw the light—how good!* Gn 1$_{4}$ (unless §2a), וְאֵת בְּקִיעֵי עִיר־דָּוִד רְאִיתֶם כִּי־רָבּוּ *and you saw the breaches in the city of David—how great they had become!* Is 22$_{9}$ (unless §2a), מִן־הַשְּׁלֹשָׁה הֲכִי נִכְבָּד *of the thirty, how honoured was he!* 2 S 23$_{19}$, Gn 28$_{15}$ 31$_{16}$ 37$_{35}$ 42$_{16}$ 44$_{32}$ Ex 3$_{7.12}$ 4$_{25}$ 6$_{1}$ 10$_{10}$ Lv 18$_{29}$ 20$_{9}$ 23$_{29}$ Nm 11$_{18}$ 14$_{22}$ 20$_{24}$ 21$_{5.26}$ 22$_{17}$ 23$_{9.23}$ 26$_{62}$ 35$_{33}$ Dt 2$_{7}$ 3$_{11}$ 4$_{32}$ 5$_{25}$ 7$_{7}$ 11$_{31}$ 12$_{31}$ 15$_{11}$ 18$_{14}$ 22$_{26}$ 28$_{57}$ 29$_{15}$ 30$_{11}$ 32$_{4.28.32.35.40}$ Jos 11$_{10}$ Jg 1$_{34}$ 18$_{10}$ 20$_{39}$ 21$_{22.22}$ 1 S 2$_{2.21.24}$ 3$_{5.6.8.21}$ 9$_{13.24}$ 12$_{22.24}$ 14$_{39.44}$ 17$_{25}$ 20$_{3.12.26}$ 22$_{23}$ 25$_{34}$ 26$_{16.18}$ 27$_{8}$ 29$_{6}$ 2 S 2$_{27}$ 5$_{19}$ 7$_{6}$‖1 C 17$_{5}$ 2 S 7$_{22}$ 12$_{5.12}$ 13$_{12.15}$ 14$_{14.19}$ 19$_{23.27}$ 22$_{23.29.30.32}$‖Ps 18$_{23.29.30.32}$ 1 K 1$_{42}$ 2$_{24}$ 11$_{16}$ 14$_{13}$ 18$_{15}$ 19$_{20}$ 22$_{14}$‖2 C 18$_{13}$ 2 K 3$_{10.13.14}$ 5$_{7}$ 9$_{25}$ 13$_{7}$ 17$_{21}$ 23$_{22}$ 24$_{20}$‖Jr 52$_{3}$ Is 1$_{29.30}$ 26.12 32$_{4}$(5$_{7.10}$ 9$_{17}$ 10$_{13}$ 13$_{10}$ 15$_{1.1.6.6.9}$ 24$_{18}$ 26$_{5}$ 27$_{10}$ 28$_{8.10.11.19.20.27.28}$ 30$_{19.31}$ 32$_{13}$ 38$_{18}$ 48$_{8}$ 49$_{18.19.19}$ 51$_{3}$ 53$_{8}$ (unless §1a) 54$_{6.14.14}$ 55$_{12}$ 57$_{1.8}$ 60$_{2.9}$ 63$_{16}$ Jr 2$_{10.20.20}$ 4$_{15.18.18.20.31}$ 6$_{11}$ 7$_{22}$ 8$_{17}$ 9$_{2.19}$ 10$_{2.3.3}$ 14$_{5.18}$ 15$_{5}$ 18$_{12}$ 20$_{10}$ 22$_{22.24}$ 24$_{8}$ 25$_{38}$ 27$_{15}$ 29$_{16}$ 30$_{5.11}$ 31$_{20}$ 32$_{31}$ 35$_{16}$ 37$_{16}$ (or em. כִּי בָא *so he came* to וַיָּבֹא *and he came*) 38$_{4}$ 39$_{18}$ 46$_{18.21}$ 48$_{7.37}$ 49$_{19}$ =50$_{44}$ (or em. כֵּן *thus*) 50$_{15.31}$ 51$_{2.11.62}$ Ezk 7$_{13}$ 11$_{16.16}$ 14$_{21}$ 16$_{59}$ 18$_{32}$ 20$_{16}$ 23$_{8.46}$ 30$_{9}$ 35$_{6}$ 41$_{7}$ Ho 4$_{16}$ 5$_{3}$ 6$_{1.9}$ 8$_{6.7}$ 9$_{6.15}$ 10$_{3.5}$ 11$_{10}$ Jl 1$_{12}$ 2$_{11.11.11}$ Am 3$_{7}$ Ob$_{16}$ Jon 1$_{12}$ Mc 1$_{13}$ 4$_{5}$ 6$_{4}$ Zp 2$_{9.11}$ 3$_{13.20}$ 4$_{10}$ 9$_{17}$ 13$_{5}$ Ps 3$_{8}$ 9$_{19}$ 10$_{3.14}$ 16$_{8}$ 18$_{28}$ 21$_{4.7}$ 22$_{10.17}$ 25$_{6}$ 27$_{10}$ 31$_{4.11.14}$ 33$_{21}$ 37$_{22}$ 38$_{19}$ 42$_{6.12}$ 43$_{5}$ 44$_{4.7.23.26}$ 49$_{16}$ 51$_{18}$ 55$_{13}$ 56$_{3}$ 66$_{10}$ 73$_{4.21.27}$ 75$_{9}$ 76$_{11}$* 77$_{12}$ 83$_{6}$ 84$_{11}$ 85$_{9}$ perh. 89$_{3}$* 89$_{7.19}$ 90$_{7.9.10}$ 92$_{5.10.10}$ 94$_{14.15}$ 96$_{5}$‖1 C 16$_{26}$ Ps 102$_{10.15}$ 103$_{16}$ 112$_{6}$ 116$_{8.16}$ 118$_{10.11.12}$ 119$_{111}$ 122$_{5}$ 125$_{3}$ 128$_{2.4}$ 133$_{3}$ 139$_{4.13}$ 143$_{3}$ Jb 5$_{2}$ 6$_{3.21}$ (or em. כִּי to כֵּן *thus*) 8$_{8}$ 9$_{32}$ 11$_{16}$ 13$_{26}$ 14$_{7.16}$ 15$_{5.27}$ 17$_{4}$ 20$_{20}$ 21$_{28.30}$ 24$_{17}$ 27$_{3}$ 28$_{1}$ 30$_{23.26}$ 31$_{18}$ 33$_{14}$ 34$_{23.31.33.37}$ 36$_{27.31}$ 37$_{6}$ 39$_{14}$ 40$_{20}$ Pr 1$_{17}$ 2$_{18}$ 6$_{26}$ 7$_{6}$ 30$_{2}$ Ru 1$_{10.13}$ 2$_{21}$ 3$_{12}$ Ec 2$_{10}$ 5$_{2.6}$* 6$_{8.12}$ 7$_{7.13.20}$ 8$_{7.7.16}$ 9$_{1.5.12}$ Lm 1$_{10}$ 4$_{18}$ 9$_{4}$ Ezr 10$_{1}$ Ne 8$_{17}$ 1 C 4$_{40}$ 5$_{1.2.22}$ 9$_{26}$ 12$_{23}$ 21$_{24}$ 23$_{27}$ 26$_{10}$ 29$_{14.15}$ 2 C 6$_{13}$ 11$_{21}$ 12$_{13}$ 16$_{9}$ 20$_{10.26}$ 24$_{24.25}$ 28$_{21}$ 30$_{18.24}$ Lachish ost. 6$_{13}$ ([כ]י), perh. Gn 29$_{32}$ Lm 3$_{22.22}$* 4$_{3(Kt)}$ Si 3$_{16(A)}$* 1QIsa^{a} 3$_{24}$ 4QapJoseph^{b} 1$_{18.29}$ 2$_{7}$ 3$_{8}$ 4Qap Mos^{c} 2.2$_{11}$ perh. 4QSirShabb^{f} 23.1$_{12}$ (כ[י]א) perh. Gnz Ps 1$_{6}$ 4$_{9}$.

10. perh. as adv. introducing a consequence, **so, therefore,** e.g. כִּי יַעַן אֲשֶׁר עָשִׂיתָ אֶת־הַדָּבָר הַזֶּה ... : כִּי־בָרֵךְ אֲבָרֶכְךָ *for because you have done this thing ..., therefore I shall indeed bless you* Gn 22$_{17}$, וַיִּשָּׁבַע לְבִלְתִּי עָבְרִי אֶת־הַיַּרְדֵּן ... : כִּי אָנֹכִי מֵת בָּאָרֶץ הַזֹּאת *so he swore that I should not cross the Jordan ...; therefore, I shall die in this land* Dt 4$_{22}$, סוּרוּ טָמֵא קָרְאוּ ... כִּי נָצוּ גַּם־נָעוּ *keep away, unclean, they cried ..., so they fled and wandered* Lm 4$_{15}$, כִּי־יֹדֵעַ כָּל־יִשְׂרָאֵל כִּי־גִבּוֹר אָבִיךָ ... : כִּי יָעַצְתִּי *for all Israel knows that your father is a warrior ... Therefore, I advise* 2 S 17$_{11}$.

11a. כַּאֲשֶׁר ... כִּי כֵן **just as ... so too,** in fulfilment of oath, 2 S 3$_{9}$ 1 K 1$_{30}$; without כַּאֲשֶׁר, perh. כור ביתן מעשה לוטש כי היית מצות לצים *(just as) a palace furnace is something that cuts, so too is the commandment of scoffers* Si 36$_{26(Bmg)}$ (B כֵּן *thus*).

b. כִּי ... כֵּן perh. *as ... so*, כִּי־גָבְהוּ שָׁמַיִם מֵאָרֶץ כֵּן גָּבְהוּ דְרָכַי מִדַּרְכֵיכֶם perh. *as the heavens are higher than the* *earth so are my ways higher than your ways* Is 55$_{9}$ (or em. כְּגֹבַהּ lit. *as the being high* of the heavens; or כִּי כְגֹבַהּ *for/but as the being high*; 1QIsa[a] כגובה *like the height of*).*

12. appar. as interrogative, **a.** adverb, כִּי הָאָדָם עֵץ הַשָּׂדֶה *are the trees of the field human beings?* Dt 20$_{19}$ (or em. כִּי הֶאָדָם *are (they) indeed human beings?*, as §9), אַיֵּה אֱלֹהֵי חֲמָת ... כִּי־הִצִּילוּ אֶת־שֹׁמְרוֹן מִיָּדִי *where are the gods of Hamath ...? Did they save Samaria from my hand?* 2 K 18$_{34}$||Is 36$_{19}$ (or em. הַהִצִּילוּ in same sense).

b. pronoun, **who?,*** e.g. מִי יוֹדֵעַ עֹז אַפֶּךָ וּכִי רֹאֶה תוֹךְ עֶבְרָתֶךָ *who can know the force of your anger and who can look at the harshness of your anger?* Ps 90$_{11}$ (if em. וּכְיִרְאָתְךָ appar. *and in accordance with the fear of you is your anger*), אַיֵּה אֱלֹהֵי חֲמָת וְאַרְפָּד ... כִּי הִצִּילוּ אֶת־שֹׁמְרוֹן מִיָּדִי *where are the gods of Hamath and Arpad ... who delivered Samaria from my hand?* 2 K 18$_{34}$||Is 36$_{19}$ (unless §12a), שִׁחֶתְךָ יִשְׂרָאֵל כִּי־בִי בְעֶזְרֶךָ *should I destroy you, O Israel, who, pray, would be your helper?* Ho 13$_{9}$ (if em. שִׁחֶתְךָ *it has destroyed you*).

13. appar. as prep., **a. despite,** יַעַבְרוּ מֵעָלָיִךְ כִּי רָעָתֵכִי אָז תַּעֲלֹזִי *they pass from upon you; despite your evil you then rejoice* Jr 11$_{15}$ (or em. יַעֲבִרוּ מֵעָלַיִכִי רָעָתֵכִי *they cause your evil to pass from you*); **b. on account of,** וַיָּשָׁב לְהִתְרַפֵּא בְיִזְרְעֶאל כִּי הַמַּכִּים אֲשֶׁר הִכֻּהוּ בָרָמָה *and he returned to be healed in Jezreel on account of the wounds that they had inflicted on him at Ramah* 2 C 22$_{6}$ (mss and ||2 K 8$_{29}$ מִן be healed *from*; or ins. רַבִּים for *many* were the wounds).

14. כִּי אִם. **a. (but) rather,** לֹא יִירָשְׁךָ זֶה כִּי־אִם אֲשֶׁר יֵצֵא מִמֵּעֶיךָ הוּא יִירָשֶׁךָ *this one will not be your heir; rather, he who comes from within you will be your heir* Gn 15$_{4}$, לֹא יַעֲקֹב יֵאָמֵר עוֹד שִׁמְךָ כִּי אִם־יִשְׂרָאֵל *your name shall no more be called Jacob, but rather Israel* Gn 32$_{29}$, perh. וגם עצת לבבך כך כי אם אמון ממנו *thus also is the counsel of your heart; rather, (it is) even more trustworthy than him* (a God-fearing man) Si 37$_{13(D)}$ (or em. כי אין *for there is none* more trustworthy), [ואין כפורים לכ]פר על האיש כי א[ם להמיתו ...] *and there is no ransom to redeem the man* who does this great evil, for ever; *rather, he is to be killed* 4QJub[f] 33$_{13}$, ולוא קלל את חם כי אם בנו *and he did not curse Ham, but rather his son* 4QCommGenA 2$_{7}$, [אשר] לא ילך איש בשרירות לבו לתעות כי אם ליסד [מסד] אמת *a man is not to go in the stubbornness of his heart so as to err; rather, a foundation of truth is to be established* 4QS[d] 1$_{4}$, Gn 24$_{4(Seb)}$ 35$_{10}$ Ex 12$_{9}$ Lv 21$_{14}$ Nm 10$_{30}$ 26$_{33}$ Dt 7$_{5}$ 12$_{5.14.18}$ 16$_{6}$ Jos 17$_{3}$ 23$_{8}$ 1 S 2$_{15}$ 8$_{19}$ perh. 2 S 5$_{6}$ 13$_{33}$ 21$_{2}$ 1 K 8$_{19}$ 18$_{18}$ 22$_{8.18.31}$||2 C 18$_{17.30}$ 2 K 7$_{10}$ 10$_{23}$ 14$_{6}$ 17$_{36.39.40}$ 19$_{18}$||Is 37$_{19}$ 2 K 23$_{9}$ Is 33$_{21}$ (unless §1a) 55$_{10.11}$ 59$_{2}$ 65$_{6.18}$ Jr 3$_{10}$ 7$_{23.32}$ 9$_{23}$ 16$_{15}$ 19$_{6}$ 20$_{3}$ 23$_{8}$ 31$_{30}$ 38$_{4.6}$ 39$_{12(Kt)}$ Ezk 12$_{23}$ 33$_{11}$ 36$_{22}$ appar. 44$_{10}$ 44$_{22}$ Am 8$_{11}$ Zc 4$_{6}$ Ps 1$_{2.4}$ Pr 18$_{2}$ 23$_{17}$ 1 C 2$_{34}$ 23$_{22}$ Si 36$_{1}$ 1QH 14$_{20}$ perh. 4QTohB[c] 1$_{10}$ perh. 4QWays[b] 13$_{1}$ 4QDibHam[a] 1.4$_{13}$ 4QShir[b] 10$_{5}$ 11QT 3$_{6}$ 48$_{12}$ 52$_{14}$ 57$_{16}$ CD 4$_{11}$ 15$_{1}$ GnzPs 4$_{20}$ Silwan royal steward tomb inscr. 1$_{2}$ ([כי] אם).

b. followed by noun or noun-like structure (Gen 39$_{9}$ Est 5$_{12}$), as prep., **apart from, other than** (specif. **more than,** CD 11$_{5}$); or by inf. or prep., as conj., **except;** or by finite verb (Gn 32$_{27}$ Lv 22$_{6}$ 2 K 4$_{24}$ Am 3$_{7}$ Ru 3$_{18}$ Lm 5$_{22}$ Est 2$_{14}$), as conj., **unless.**

לֹא־נָתְנוּ חֵלֶק לַלְוִיִּם בָּאָרֶץ כִּי אִם־עָרִים לָשֶׁבֶת *they gave no share in the land to the Levites apart from cities to dwell in* Jos 14$_{4}$, מָה י׳ אֱלֹהֶיךָ שֹׁאֵל מֵעִמָּךְ כִּי אִם־לְיִרְאָה אֶת־י׳ *what does Y. your God ask from you except to fear Y.?* Dt 10$_{12}$, לְנֶפֶשׁ לֹא־יִטַּמָּא בְּעַמָּיו׃ כִּי אִם־לִשְׁאֵרוֹ הַקָּרֹב אֵלָיו *he is not to defile himself for one of his people's corpses except for (the corpse of) a close relative of his* Lv 21$_{2}$, לָאָרֶץ לֹא־יְכֻפַּר לַדָּם אֲשֶׁר שֻׁפַּךְ־בָּהּ כִּי־אִם בְּדַם שֹׁפְכוֹ *the land can not receive atonement for the blood shed in it except by the blood of the person who shed it* Nm 35$_{33}$, אל יקחה איש כי אם [בראות נשים] נאמנות *no man is to marry her except after examination by trustworthy women* 4QD[f] 3$_{13}$, אל ילך איש ... כי אם אלפים באמה *let no one go ... more than two thousand cubits* CD 11$_{5}$, לֹא אֲשַׁלֵּחֲךָ כִּי אִם־בֵּרַכְתָּנִי *I will not let you go unless you bless me* Gn 32$_{27}$, לֹא יֹאכַל מִן־הַקֳּדָשִׁים כִּי אִם־רָחַץ בְּשָׂרוֹ *he shall not eat of the holy things unless he has washed his flesh* Lv 22$_{6}$, [ל]וא אלך כי אם י[שלחני] *I shall not go unless he sends me* 4QJub[g] 27$_{6}$, ואל ידבר כי אם ל[ ] *and let him not speak unless it is to* 4QS[z] 1$_{7}$, ואל יעש איש דבר ... כי אם הודיע למבקר *and let no one do anything ... unless they have informed the overseer* CD 13$_{15}$, [לא יב]יאה כי אם דמה יצוא [לא יצא] *he is not to bring her unless her blood has indeed not issued* 4QD[e] 4$_{4}$, ביתו יאשם כי אם נלחץ *his house will be held guilty unless he was forced (to sin)* CD 5$_{15}$, מה אדבר כי אם פרחתה פי

how shall I speak unless you open my mouth? 1QH 12_{33}, Gn 28_{17} $39_{6.9}$ 42_{15} Nm 14_{30} 26_{65} 1 S $18_{25(mss)}$ $21_{5.7}$ $30_{17.22}$ 2 S 3_{13} (כִּי אִם־לִפְנֵי הֲבִיאֲךָ appar. *except on account of your bringing*, i.e. until you have brought) 12_{3} 19_{29} 1 K $17_{1.12}$ 2 K $4_{2.24}$ $5_{15.17}$ 9_{35} 13_{7} 23_{23} Is 42_{19} Jr 22_{17} 44_{14} Ezk 44_{25} Am 3_{7} Mc 6_{8} Ru 3_{18} Ec 3_{12} 5_{10} 8_{15} Lm 5_{22} Est $2_{14.15}$ 5_{12} Dn 10_{21} Ne $2_{2.12}$ 1 C 15_{2} 2 C 2_{5} 21_{17} 23_{6} Si $32_{13(Bmg)}$ 1QH 4_{31} $12_{33.34}$ 1QS 5_{14} 4QHalakhah^{a} 5_{1} 4QD^{a} 7.1_{3} (כי [א]ם) 4QD^{d} 8.2_{4} 4QTohA 1.1_{7} 4QMyst^{a} 3a.2_{6} CD 9_{5} $10_{22.23}$ $11_{3.18}$ $12_{8.13}$ 13_{14} GnzPs 2_{24}.

Perh. 4QJub^{h} 40_{7} ([כי] [אם]) 4QpsJub^{b} 6_{7} ([כי א]ם) 4QTohA 2.2_{6} 4QLeqeṭ 2_{7} 4QMyst^{a} 6.$2_{6.7}$ 20_{1} 42_{2} 4QMyst^{b} 5_{5} ([כ]י] אם) 4QM^{a} 10.2_{16} (כאם).

c. if not, otherwise, כַּסְפְּךָ ... לִי תִתֵּן : כִּי אִם־כָּעֵת מָחָר אֶשְׁלַח אֶת־עֲבָדַי *you are to give me ... your silver; otherwise, at this time tomorrow I shall send my servants* 1 K 20_{6}.

d. in oath or asseveration, **(1) I swear that, it is certainly the case that,** אִם־תַּעֲשׂוּן כָּזֹאת כִּי אִם־נִקַּמְתִּי בָכֶם *if you act like this, I will surely take revenge on you* Jg 15_{7}, כיא אם לכה המלחמה *surely the battle is yours!* 1QM 11_{1}, 1 S 21_{6} 26_{10} 2 S 15_{21} (mss כִּי *indeed*, as §9, for כִּי אִם) 2 K 5_{20} Jr 51_{14} Jb 42_{8} (or em. אִם־ to אֶת־, with כִּי *so that*, as §4, or *indeed*, as §9) Pr 23_{18} (or ins. תִּשְׁמְרֶנָּה for if *you observe these*, as §14e); **(2) if, surely not,** חַי־י׳ ... כִּי אִם־ נוֹתַר לְנָבָל *as Y. lives, ... if there remains to Nabal* 1 S 25_{34} (or em. כִּי אִם to כִּי *if* or אִם *if*), וְכֹה יֹסִיף כִּי אִם ... אֶטְעַם־ לֶחֶם *and thus may he continue (to do) if ... I taste food* 2 S 3_{35} (or em. לִי to do *to me*; or em. אִם/כִּי).

e. for if, that if, but if, even if, etc. (i.e. כִּי and אִם each have their own meaning), כי אם [יהיו נמ]נים אלה ואו[ף] אם לוא *for if these can be counted, and even if not* 4QpsJub^{a} 2.1_{6}, לֹא נְכַחֵד מֵאֲדֹנִי כִּי אִם־תַּם הַכֶּסֶף *we cannot hide from my lord that if the money has run out* Gn 47_{18}, כִּי אִם־אֵינְךָ מְשַׁלֵּחַ אֶת־עַמִּי הִנְנִי מַשְׁלִיחַ ... אֶת־הֶעָרֹב *but if you will not let my people go, behold I will send ... a swarm* Ex 8_{17}, כִּי אִם־זְכַרְתַּנִי אִתְּךָ כַּאֲשֶׁר יִיטַב לָךְ וְעָשִׂיתָ־נָּא עִמָּדִי חָסֶד *but if you remember me when things go well for you, please do me the favour* Gn 40_{14} (or em. אַךְ *but* if), appar. כי אם למילפנים פקד אל את מעשיהם ויחר אפו *for when in former times God punished their deeds, he would become angry* CD 5_{15} (or em. גַּם for *also*; =4QD^{a} 3.2_{3} כי *for*, without אִם), Ex 9_{2} 10_{4} 22_{22} 23_{22} appar. Nm 24_{22} Dt 11_{22} 1 S 14_{39} 20_{9} Is 10_{22} Jr 2_{22} 7_{5} 22_{24} 37_{10} Ho 9_{12} Am 5_{22}* Pr 2_{3} 19_{19} Ru $3_{12(Kt)}$ Ec 4_{10} 11_{8} Lm 3_{32} Est 4_{14} 2 C 25_{8} Si 30_{40} perh. 4QPatr 2_{1} 11QT 53_{11} Lachish ost. 4_{9} (unless §14a, §14b, or §14d[2]).

15. כִּי in other compound conjunctions. **a.** אַף כִּי **(1) indeed, really,** אַף כִּי־אָמַר אֱלֹהִים *God really said?* Gn 3_{1} (or em. הַאַף *did* God *really* say?); **(2) even, moreover,** וְאַף כִּי תִשְׁלַחְנָה *and you even sent* Ezk 23_{40}; **(3) even though,** אַף כִּי־עָשׂוּ לָהֶם עֵגֶל מַסֵּכָה ... לֹא עֲזַבְתָּם *even though they made themselves a molten calf, ... you did not forsake them* Ne 9_{18}; **(4) how much more (if),** הַיּוֹם מַמְרִים הֱיִתֶם עִם־י׳ וְאַף כִּי־אַחֲרֵי מוֹתִי *today you are rebellious against Y.; how much more after my death!* Dt 31_{27}, 1 S 14_{30} 21_{6} 23_{3} 2 S 4_{11} 2 K 5_{13} Pr 11_{31} 15_{11} 19_{7} 21_{27}; **(5) how much less (if),** בִּהְיוֹתוֹ תָמִים לֹא יֵעָשֶׂה לִמְלָאכָה אַף כִּי־אֵשׁ אֲכָלַתְהוּ *when it was whole, it was not used for anything; how much less if fire has consumed it!* Ezk 15_{5}, 1 K 18_{27}‖2 C 6_{18} perh. Hb 2_{5} Jb 9_{14} 15_{16} 25_{6} 35_{14} Pr 17_{7} 19_{10} 2 C 32_{15} Si 16_{11}.

b. גַּם כִּי **even though,** גַּם כִּי־תַרְבּוּ תְפִלָּה אֵינֶנִּי שֹׁמֵעַ *even though you increase your prayers, I shall not listen* Is 1_{15}, Ho 8_{10} 9_{16} Ps 23_{4} Pr 22_{6} Lm 3_{8}.

c. כִּי־עַל־כֵּן **because, since,** וְאֶקְחָה פַת־לֶחֶם ... כִּי־עַל־כֵּן עֲבַרְתֶּם עַל־עַבְדְּכֶם *and let me fetch a piece of bread ... since you have come to your servant* Gn 18_{5}, 19_{8} 33_{10} 38_{26} Nm 14_{43} Jg 6_{22} Jr 29_{28} 38_{4}.

d. עַל כִּי **because,** הֲלֹא עַל כִּי־אֵין אֱלֹהַי בְּקִרְבִּי מְצָאוּנִי הָרָעוֹת הָאֵלֶּה *have these evils not befallen me because my God is not among us,* lit. *me?* Dt 31_{17}, Jr 4_{28} Ml 2_{14} Ps 139_{14}.

e. תַּחַת כִּי **because,** וְתַחַת כִּי אָהַב אֶת־אֲבֹתֶיךָ ... וַיּוֹצִאֲךָ *and because he loved your ancestors ... he brought you out* Dt 4_{37} (or em. וַתֶּחִי *and you lived*; for he loved), Pr 1_{29}.

f. עֵקֶב כִּי **because,** לֹא־תָסוּר חֶרֶב מִבֵּיתְךָ ... עֵקֶב כִּי בְזִתָנִי *the sword will not depart from your house ... because you have despised me* 2 S 12_{10}, Am 4_{12}.

g. יַעַן כִּי **because, since,** יַעַן כִּי מָרִיתָ פִּי י׳ ... לֹא־תָבוֹא נִבְלָתְךָ אֶל־קֶבֶר אֲבֹתֶיךָ *because you have rebelled against the command of Y. ... your corpse shall not come to the tomb of your fathers* 1 K 13_{21}, Nm 11_{20} 1 K 21_{29} Is 3_{16} 7_{5} 8_{6} 29_{13}.

h. עַד כִּי **until,** וַיֵּלֶךְ הָלוֹךְ וְגָדֵל עַד כִּי־גָדַל מְאֹד *and he became greater and greater until he had become very great* Gn 26$_{13}$, 41$_{49}$ 49$_{10}$ 2 S 23$_{10}$ 2 C 26$_{15}$ Si 32$_{21(Bmg)}$.

i. אֶפֶס כִּי **(1) except that,** אֶפֶס כִּי־עַז הָעָם *except that the people is strong* Nm 13$_{28}$, Dt 15$_{4}$ 2 S 12$_{14}$ Am 9$_{8}$ (or del.); **(2) however,** הָלֹךְ אֵלֵךְ עִמָּךְ אֶפֶס כִּי לֹא תִהְיֶה תִּפְאַרְתְּךָ עַל־הַדֶּרֶךְ *I shall indeed go with you; however, your glory will not be upon the way* Jg 4$_{9}$ (or em. אֶפֶס to דֵּעַ *know* that); perh. **(3) because,** אפס כי [לא יד]עו *because they did not know* 1QH 2$_{33}$.

j. אַךְ כִּי **but,** שְׁמַע בְּקוֹלָם אַךְ כִּי־הָעֵד תָּעִיד בָּהֶם *listen to their voice, but solemnly warn them* 1 S 8$_{9}$.

k. אִם־לֹא כִּי **unless,** אֵיכָה יִרְדֹּף אֶחָד אֶלֶף ... אִם־לֹא כִּי־צוּרָם מְכָרָם *how could one pursue a thousand ... unless their rock had sold them?* Dt 32$_{30}$.

Also Si 41$_{7}$.

***כִּי II** 1 n.m. perh. **vulture,** יַגְבִּיהַּ נָשֶׁר וְכִי יָרִים קִנּוֹ *the eagle flies up and the vulture makes high her nest* Jb 39$_{27}$ (unless כִּי is it at your command *that* the eagle makes high?, as כִּי I, §2b, or interrogative, as כִּי I, §12).

כִּי III 1 n.m. **burn,** <NOM CL> וְהָיָה ... כִּי־תַחַת יֹפִי *and there will be ... a burn instead of beauty* Is 3$_{24}$ (1QIsa^{a} כי תחת יפי בשת *indeed* [i.e. כִּי I, §9], *instead of beauty, shame*).*

⇒ כוה *burn.*

כִּיד I 1 n.[m.] **misfortune**—sf. כִּידוֹ—<OBJ> ראה *see* Jb 21$_{20}$ (or em. פִּידוֹ *his ruin* or כַּדּוֹ *his cup*).

***כִּיד II** 1 **cup**—sf. כִּידוֹ—<OBJ> ראה *see* Jb 21$_{20}$ (or em. כַּדּוֹ *his cup*).

[כִּידוֹד] I 1 n.m. **spark**—pl. cstr. כִּידוֹדֵי—<SUBJ> מלט htp. *fly out* Jb 41$_{11}$. <CSTR> כִּידוֹדֵי אֵשׁ *sparks of a fire* Jb 41$_{11}$.*

***[כִּידוֹד] II** 1 n.m. **son**—pl. cstr. כִּידוֹדֵי—<SUBJ> מלט htp. *fly out* Jb 41$_{11}$. <CSTR> כִּידוֹדֵי אֵשׁ *sons of fire* Jb 41$_{11}$.

כִּידוֹן 9.1 n.m. **javelin**—כִּידֹן; cstr. כִּידוֹן—**javelin** or short curved **sword** (as כִּידָן),* <SUBJ> רנה *rattle* Jb 39$_{23}$ (|| חֲנִית *spear*). <NOM CL> כִּידוֹן נְחֹשֶׁת בֵּין כְּתֵפָיו *a javelin of bronze was between his shoulder blades* 1 S 17$_{6}$. <OBJ> חזק hi. *take hold of* Jr 6$_{23}$ 50$_{42}$, נוף hi. *wield* Si 46$_{2}$. <CSTR> כִּידוֹן נְחֹשֶׁת *javelin of bronze* 1 S 17$_{6}$; רַעַשׁ כִּידוֹן *clatter of the javelin* Jb 41$_{21}$. <PREP> בְּ of accompaniment, *with, in,* + בוא *come* 1 S 17$_{45}$; introducing object, + נטה *stretch out* Jos 8$_{18.18.26}$. <SYN> חֲנִית *spear.*

כִּידוֹר 1 n.[m.] perh. **attack,** תִּתְקְפֵהוּ כְּמֶלֶךְ עָתִיד לַכִּידוֹר *it overwhelms him, like a king ready for the attack* Jb 15$_{24}$.

[כִּידָן] 0.0.5 n.m. **(Spanish) sword, *gladius***—Q כידן; pl. Q כידנים—<NOM CL> ובידם רמח וכידן *and in their hand is spear and sword* 1QM 5$_{7}$, והכידנים ברזל ברור טהור בכור ומלובן *and the swords are to be of select iron purified in the furnace and whitened* like a mirror 5$_{11}$. <CSTR> אורך הכידן *the length of the sword* is one and a half cubits and its width four fingers 5$_{12}$, יד *hand,* i.e. hilt, *of* 5$_{14}$, מחזיקי מגן וכידן *wielders of shield and sword* 6$_{5}$.*

כִּידֹן 1 pr.n.m. **Chidon,** appar. ident. with Nacon (2 S 6$_{6}$), owner of threshing floor where the oxen stumbled when carrying the ark 1 C 13$_{9}$, <CSTR> גֹּרֶן כִּידֹן *threshing floor of Chidon* 1 C 13$_{9}$.

כִּיּוּן I 1.0.2 pr.n.m. **Kivvun,** appar. Saturn (Kevan/Kaiwan/Kayyamānu); vocalization may suggest כִּיּוּן 'reliable one' or, שִׁקּוּץ *abomination,* unless כִּיּוּן common noun, *pedestal* or *palanquin*; or em. כֵּן in same sense or כַּיִן *vagina,* i.e. fertility symbol, <NOM CL> כיון הצלמים הם ספרי הנביאים *Kivvun of the images are the books of the prophets* CD 7$_{17}$. <OBJ> נשׂא *raise* Am 5$_{26}$, גלה hi. *exile* CD 7$_{15}$. <CSTR> כיון הצלמים appar. *Kivvun of the images* CD 7$_{17}$. <APP> צֶלֶם *image* Am 5$_{26}$=CD 7$_{15}$.*

***כִּיּוּן II** 1.0.2 n.[m.] **pedestal** or **palanquin,** <NOM CL> כיון הצלמים הם ספרי הנביאים *the pedestal of the images are the books of the prophets* CD 7$_{17}$. <OBJ> נשׂא *raise* Am 5$_{26}$, גלה hi. *exile* CD 7$_{15}$. <CSTR> כיון הצלמים *pedestal of the images* CD 7$_{17}$, כִּיּוּן צַלְמֵיכֶם *the pedestal of your images* Am 5$_{26}$=CD 7$_{15}$.

כִּיּוֹר 23.0.10 n.m. **bowl**—כִּיֹּר; pl. כִּיֹּרוֹת (כִּיֹּרִים); sf. Q כיוריהמה—**1.** bronze **bowl, basin** for washing, i.e. **laver*** (Ex 30$_{18.28}$ 31$_9$ 35$_{16}$ 38$_8$ 39$_{39}$ 40$_{7.11.30}$ Lv 8$_{11}$ 1 K 7$_{30.38.38.38.38.40.43}$ 2 K 16$_{17}$ 2 C 4$_{6.14}$ 11QT 32$_{13}$). **2. pot** for cooking (1 S 2$_{14}$). **3.** movable **hearth** or **brazier** (Zc 12$_6$). **4. platform** for king in court of temple (2 C 6$_{13}$).

<SUBJ> כול hi. *contain* 1 K 7$_{38}$. <NOM CL> אַרְבַּע בָּאַמָּה הַכִּיּוֹר הָאֶחָד *the one basin*, i.e. each basin, *(measured) four by the cubit*, i.e. four cubits 1 K 7$_{38}$, כִּיּוֹר אֶחָד עַל־הַמְּכוֹנָה הָאַחַת *one basin was for each stand* 1 K 7$_{38}$. <OBJ> בוא hi. *bring* Ex 39$_{39}$, עשׂה *make* Ex 30$_{18}$||38$_8$ 31$_9$ 35$_{16}$ 1 K 7$_{38}$||2 C 4$_6$ 1 K 7$_{40.43}$||2 C 4$_{14}$ 2 C 6$_{13}$, נתן *give*, i.e. place Ex 40$_7$, שׂים *place* Ex 40$_{30}$, קדשׁ pi. *sanctify* Ex 40$_{11}$ ||Lv 8$_{11}$, משׁח *anoint* Ex 30$_{28}$ 40$_{11}$||Lv 8$_{11}$, סור hi. *remove* 2 K 16$_{17}$.

<CSTR> כִּיּוֹר אֵשׁ *brazier of fire* Zc 12$_6$, כִּיּוֹר נְחֹשֶׁת *basin of bronze* Ex 30$_{18}$||38$_8$, *platform of bronze* 2 C 6$_{13}$, כִּיֹּרוֹת נְחֹשֶׁת *basins of bronze* 1 K 7$_{38}$; בית הכיור *house of the laver* 11QT 33$_5$ ([בי]ת) 33$_{8.8}$ (ב[י]ת]) 33$_{9.11}$.

<PREP> לְ of benefit, *to, for* perh. 11QT 33$_5$ (לכיו[ר]), + עשׂה *make* 11QT 31$_{10}$; of possession, *of, (belonging) to* 11QT 35$_8$; בְּ *in, into*, + נכה hi. *strike*, i.e. thrust (into) 1 S 2$_{14}$; כְּ *as* Zc 12$_6$; מִתַּחַת לְ *from (underneath), with respect to* 1 K 7$_{30}$; לְתַחַת *below*, + הלך *go* 11QT 32$_{13}$ (ל[ת]חת); סָבִיב לְ *around*, + עשׂה *make* 11QT 32$_{12}$.

<COLL> הַכִּיּוֹר הָאֶחָד *one basin* 1 K 7$_{38.38.38}$ (אֶחָד), עֲשָׂרָה כִּיֹּרוֹת *ten basins* 1 K 7$_{38}$, הַכִּיֹּרֹת עֲשָׂרָה *the ten basins* 1 K 7$_{43}$, כִּיּוֹרִים עֲשָׂרָה *ten basins* 2 C 4$_6$.

Also 4QBer[b] 2$_1$.

[כִּיּוֹר] 0.0.2 n.[m.] **panelling**—cstr. Q כיור—**panelling, eaves** of gate to temple court, <CSTR> כיור ארז *panelling of cedar* 11QT 36$_{10}$; גובה הכיור *height of the eaves* 11QT 6$_5$. <COLL> מוקרה כיור ארז *it* (gate) *shall be beamed with panelling of cedar* 11QT 36$_{10}$.

כִּילַי 1 n.m. **villain**—<PREP> לְ of direction, *to*, + אמר ni. *be said* Is 32$_5$.

⇒ נכל *be crafty*.

כֵּילָף 1 n.f. **crowbar**—pl. כֵּילַפֹּת—<APP> כַּשִּׁיל *axe* Ps 74$_6$. <PREP> בְּ of instrument, *by (means of), with*, + הלם *break in pieces* Ps 74$_6$.

כִּימָה 3 n.f. **Pleiades**—<OBJ> עשׂה *make* Am 5$_8$ Jb 9$_9$ (both || כְּסִיל *Orion*). <CSTR> מַעֲדַנּוֹת כִּימָה *bands of the Pleiades* Jb 38$_{31}$.

*[כִּיּוּן] n.[m.] **vagina,** <OBJ> נשׂא *raise* Am 5$_{26}$ (if em. כִּיּוּן *Kivvun* or *pedestal*). <APP> צֶלֶם *image* Am 5$_{26}$ (if em.).*

כִּיס 5.2.1 n.m. **bag**—of **bag** or **purse** (Dt 25$_{13}$ Is 46$_6$ Mc 6$_{11}$ Pr 16$_{11}$ Si 18$_{33}$ 35$_5$), **bag** as the **lot** or **destiny** (Pr 1$_{14}$). <SUBJ> היה *be* Pr 1$_{14}$. <CSTR> כִּיס אַבְנֵי *bag of stones of* Mc 6$_{11}$, כיס זהב *purse of gold* Si 35$_5$; אַבְנֵי־כִיס *stones of*, i.e. weights in, *the bag* Pr 16$_{11}$. <PREP> בְּ of accompaniment, *with, in (the presence of)*, + זכה *be pure* Mc 6$_{11}$; *in, with* Si 18$_{33}$, + היה *be* Dt 25$_{13}$; מִן of direction, *from*, + זול *weigh out* Is 46$_6$; עַל *upon* Si 35$_5$. Also2 QapProph 4$_3$. <COLL> כִּיס אֶחָד *one bag*, i.e. destiny Pr 1$_{14}$.

כִּיר 1.0.1 n.m. **cooking-furnace**—du. כִּירַיִם—<SUBJ> נתץ ho. *be broken in pieces* Lv 11$_{35}$ (|| תַּנּוּר *oven*). <PREP> לְ of benefit, *to, for*, + עשׂה *make* 11QT 37$_{13}$. <SYN> תַּנּוּר *oven*.

⇒ כור *smelting pot*

כִּיֹּר, see כִּיּוֹר *pot*.

[כִּירְגָר] 0.0.1 n.[m.] perh. **cistern,** <PREP> בְּ of place, *in* 3QTr 10$_3$ (בכירגר מזקות שרו מהנחל הגדול) perh. *in the cistern next to the canals fed by the great wadi)*.

כִּישׁוֹר 1 n.[m.] **spindle** or perh. **spinning whorl** or **distaff,** <PREP> בְּ of place, *(on)to*, + שׁלח pi. *send* hands *away*, i.e. grasp Pr 31$_{19}$ (|| פֶּלֶךְ *spindle*).

<SYN> פֶּלֶךְ *spindle*.*

כָּכָה 37.3.11 adv. **thus**—Si כך—adverb, usu. of manner, **so, thus, in this way, 1.** verb usu. follows כָּכָה (but see Coll.), + היה *be* Ne 5$_{13}$ 4QJub[a] 2.1$_7$ 11QT 36$_{13}$ 43$_5$, ידע *know* Ec 11$_5$, עשׂה *do* Ex 29$_{35}$ Nm 8$_{26}$ 11$_{15}$ 15$_{12}$ Jos 10$_{25}$ 1 S 2$_{14}$ 1 K 1$_6$ Ho 10$_{15}$ Jb 1$_5$ 1QS 2$_{19}$ 4QM[a] 17$_5$ 11QT 24$_7$ 28$_{02}$ (both כ[כ]ה), ni. *be done* Nm 15$_{11}$ Dt 25$_9$ Est 6$_{9.11}$, רמה pi. *deceive* 1 S 19$_{17}$, שׁחת hi. *spoil* Jr 13$_9$, שׁבר *break* Jr

19_{11} 28_{11}, שׁקע *sink down* Jr 51_{64}, אכל *eat* Ezk 4_{13} 11QT 43_{5}, אמר *say* 1 K 14_{8}, יעץ *counsel* 2 S 17_{21}, גער *rebuke* Ne 5_{13}, שׁבע hi. *adjure* Ca 5_{9}.

<NOM CL> כך רשע לצדיק *so is the wicked one in relation to the righteous* Si 13_{17}, כך נאים דברים *so are fitting words* ... at a feast of wine Si 35_{5}, גם עצת לבבך כך *such is also the counsel of your heart* Si $37_{13(D)}$, מַדּוּעַ אַתָּה כָּכָה דַּל *why are you so dejected?* 2 S 13_{4}, אַשְׁרֵי הָעָם שֶׁכָּכָה לּוֹ *blessed is the people for whom it is so* Ps 144_{15}, [ככה מן] [הפנה] הזואת עד ש[ער] *thus shall be from this corner to the gate* of Issachar 11QT 41_{2}, ככה משער דן עד שער נפתלי *thus shall be from the gate of Dan to the gate of Naphtali* 11QT 41_{8}, ככה רוחב ואורך לכול רוחותיה *thus shall be the width and length of all its sides* 11QT 38_{13}.

<COLL> כָּכָה preceded by verb, + דמה *be like* Ezk 31_{18}, עשׂה *do* Nm 15_{13} Dt 29_{23} 1 K 9_{8}||2 C 7_{21} Jr 22_{8}, אכל *eat* Ex 12_{11}, אמר *say* 2 C $18_{19.19}$.

2. עַל־כָּכָה **concerning such a matter,** + ראה *see* Est 9_{26}, פצה hi. perh. *inform* (unless *declare free of obligation* on account of this) MurEpBeth-Mashiko$_{6}$.

3. לְעֻמַּת כָּכָה **in accordance with this, accordingly,** + קום pi. *oblige* Mur 24 3_{19} 4_{19} ([וקו]ים ... לע[מת]), מרק *complete (transaction)* Mur 30 1_{6} 2_{25}.

כִּכָּר I 13 n.f. **district**—cstr. כִּכַּר—sometimes perh. specif. **valley,*** <OBJ> ראה *see* Gn 13_{10}, hi. *show* Dt 34_{3}, בחר *choose* Gn 13_{11}, הפך *overthrow* Gn 19_{25}. <CSTR> כִּכַּר הַיַּרְדֵּן *district of the Jordan* Gn 13_{10} 1 K 7_{46}||2 C 4_{17}; אֶרֶץ הַכִּכָּר *land of the district* Gn 19_{28}, עָרֵי הַכִּכָּר *cities of the district* Gn 13_{12} 19_{29}, דֶּרֶךְ הַכִּכָּר *way of the district* 2 S 18_{23}, אַנְשֵׁי הַכִּכָּר *men of the district* Ne 3_{22}, כָּל־הַכִּכָּר *all of the district* Gn $19_{17.25}$. <PREP> בְּ of place, *in, at,* + עמד *stand* Gn 19_{17}, יצק *cast metal* 1 K 7_{46}||2 C 4_{17}; מִן of direction, *from,* + אסף ni. *be gathered* Ne 12_{28}.

⇒ כרר *go around.*

כִּכָּר II 55.0.47 n.f. **talent**—cstr. כִּכַּר; pl. כִּכָּרִים (Q ככרין, Q ככ); cstr. כִּכְּרֵי (כִּכְּרוֹת); du. כִּכָּרַיִם (כִּכְּרַיִם)—of any disk shaped objects, **1. loaf of bread,** (Ex 29_{23} Jg 8_{5} 1 S 2_{36} 10_{3} Jr 37_{21} Pr 6_{26} 1 C 16_{3}). **2. lead disk** or **cover** (Zc 5_{7}). **3. talent,** i.e. **disk** of gold or silver as unit of weight or value (e.g. Ex 25_{39} 2 S 12_{30} 2 K 23_{33} Est 3_{9} 2 C 27_{5}).

<SUBJ> היה *be* Ex $38_{24.27}$ 1 K 10_{14}||2 C 9_{13}, נשׂא ni. *be raised* Zc 5_{7}.

<NOM CL> מִשְׁקָלָהּ כִּכַּר זָהָב *its weight was a talent of gold* 2 S 12_{30}, נְחֹשֶׁת ... שִׁבְעִים כִּכָּר *the bronze was ... seventy talents* Ex 38_{29}, כולה ככרים *all of it was two talents* 11QT 9_{11}, כֶּסֶף ... מְאַת כִּכַּר *the silver was ... a hundred talents* Ex 38_{25}, הכל ככרין שש מאות *the total was six hundred talents* 3QTr 12_{7}, sim. 12_{9}, לשש מא[ו]ת האלף מאת ככר *for the six hundred thousand it shall be a hundred talents* 4QOrd[a] 1.2_{8}, כִּכָּר לָאָדֶן *a talent was for the pedestal* Ex 38_{27}.

<OBJ> שׂים *place,* i.e. impose 2 K 18_{14}, לקח *take* Ex 29_{23} 1 K 9_{28} 2 K 5_{23} 2 C 8_{18}, כון hi. *provide* 1 C $22_{14.14}$, נתן *give* Jg 8_{5} 1 K 10_{10}||2 C 9_{9} 2 K 15_{19} 23_{33} Jr 37_{21} 1 C $29_{7.7.7.7}$ 2 C 25_{9} 27_{5}, צור *tie up* 2 K 5_{23}, נשׂא *raise* 1 S 10_{3}, שׁלח *send* 1 K 9_{14} 1 C 19_{6}, חלק pi. *distribute* 1 C 16_{3}, שׁקל *weigh out,* i.e. pay 1 K 20_{39} Est 3_{9} Ezr $8_{26.26}$.

<CSTR> כִּכַּר לֶחֶם *loaf of bread* Ex 29_{23} 1 S 2_{36} (לֶחֶם) Jr 37_{21} Pr 6_{26} (לָחֶם) 1 C 16_{3}, כִּכְּרוֹת לֶחֶם *loaves of bread* Jg 8_{5} 1 S 10_{3}, כִּכַּר עֹפֶרֶת *cover of lead* Zc 5_{7}.

כִּכַּר־כֶּסֶף *a talent of silver* 1 K 20_{39} 2 K 15_{19} (כָּסֶף) 18_{14} 23_{33}||2 C 36_{3} Est 3_{9} 1 C 19_{6} 29_{4} 2 C 25_{6} (כָּסֶף) 27_{5}, כִּכַּר הַכֶּסֶף *the talent of silver* Ex 38_{27}, כִּכְּרֵי־כֶסֶף *talents of silver* 2 K 5_{5}, כִּכַּר זָהָב *a talent of gold* 2 S 12_{30}||1 C 20_{2} 1 K 9_{14} $10_{10.14}$ 2 K 18_{14} 23_{33}||2 C 36_{3}, כִּכְּרֵי זָהָב *talents of gold* 1 C 29_{4} GnzPs 2_{27}.

מִשְׁקַל כִּכָּר *weight of talent of* 1 C 20_{2}, משקל ככרין *weight of* specified number of *talents* 3QTr 1_{4} 12_{9} (+ מָנֶה *mina*), מחצית הככר *half a talent* 4QOrd[a] 1.2_{8}, מְאַת כִּכָּר *a hundred talents* Ex 38_{27} 2 C 25_{9} (הַכִּכָּר) 4QOrd[a] 1.2_{8}, מְאַת כִּכַּר *a hundred talents of* Ex $38_{25.27}$.

<APP> מִשְׁקָל *weight* 1 K 10_{14}||2 C 9_{13}, אֲגוֹרָה *payment* 1 S 2_{36}, עֹנֶשׁ *fine* 2 K 23_{33}, נְחֹשֶׁת *bronze* 1 C 29_{7}, בַּרְזֶל *iron* 1 C 29_{7}, כֶּסֶף *silver* 1 K 16_{24} 2 K 5_{23} Ezr 8_{26} 1 C 22_{14} 1 C 29_{7} 3QTr 1_{15} ([כ]כר ... [כ]סף) 2_{6} 3_{7} $4_{5.10.13.14}$ $5_{4.11}$ $8_{7.16}$ 10_{7} 12_{5}, זָהָב *gold* Ex 25_{39}||37_{24} 1 K 9_{28} 1 C 22_{14} 29_{7} 3QTr 7_{16} 8_{7} 10_{10} 12_{1} 11QT 9_{11} ([זהב]).

<PREP> לְ of benefit, *to, for,* + שׁחה htpal. *beseech* 1 S 2_{36}; *consisting of* Ezr 8_{26} (if em. כִּכָּרַיִם *two talents*) 2 C 3_{8}; בְּ of exchange, *for, with,* + קנה *buy* 1 K 16_{24}; מִן of comparison, *(more) than* GnzPs 2_{27}; עַד *until* Pr 6_{26}.

<COLL> ככרין שים *two talents* 3QTr 7_{16}, עֶשֶׂר כִּכְּרֵי־

כֶּסֶף *ten talents of silver* 2 K 5$_5$, ככרין עסר *ten talents* 3QTr 2$_9$, ככרין שבעשרה *seventeen talents* 3QTr 1$_4$, תֵּשַׁע וְעֶשְׂרִים כִּכָּר *twenty nine talents* Ex 38$_{24}$, שְׁלֹשִׁים כִּכַּר זָהָב *thirty talents of gold* 2 K 18$_{14}$, ארבעין [כ]כר *forty talents* 3QTr 1$_{15}$, ככרין ששין *sixty talents* 3QTr 12$_1$, ככרין ששין ושנין *sixty-two talents* 3QTr 10$_7$, שִׁבְעִים כִּכָּר *seventy talents* Ex 38$_{29}$ 3QTr 2$_6$ (ככרין שבעין) 4$_{12}$ (ככ שבעין), מֵאָה כִכָּר *a hundred talents* Ezr 8$_{26}$, מֵאָה כִּכַּר־כֶּסֶף *a hundred talents of silver* 2 K 23$_{33}$||2 C 36$_3$ 2 C 27$_5$, מֵאָה וְעֶשְׂרִים כִּכַּר זָהָב *a hundred and twenty talents of gold* 1 K 9$_{14}$ 10$_{10}$||2 C 9$_9$, ככ מאתין *two hundred talents* 3QTr 4$_{10}$, שְׁלֹשׁ מֵאוֹת כִּכַּר־כֶּסֶף *three hundred talents of silver* 2 K 18$_{14}$, ככרין שלש מאות *three hundred talents* 3QTr 10$_{10}$.

ככרין ארבע מאות *four hundred talents* 3QTr 7$_7$, אַרְבַּע־מֵאוֹת וְעֶשְׂרִים כִּכָּר *four hundred and twenty talents* 1 K 9$_{28}$, אַרְבַּע־מֵאוֹת וַחֲמִשִּׁים כִּכַּר זָהָב *four hundred and fifty talents of gold* 2 C 8$_{18}$, שֵׁשׁ מֵאוֹת כִּכָּרִים *six hundred talents* 2 C 3$_8$ 3QTr 12$_7$ (ככרין), שֵׁשׁ־מֵאוֹת וַחֲמִשִּׁים כִּכָּרִים *six hundred and fifty talents* Ezr 8$_{26}$, שֵׁשׁ מֵאוֹת שִׁשִּׁים וָשֵׁשׁ כִּכַּר זָהָב *six hundred and sixty six talents of gold* 1 K 10$_{14}$||2 C 9$_{13}$ (כִּכְּרֵי), ככרין תשע מאת *nine hundred talents* 3QTr 1$_8$.

אֶלֶף כִּכַּר־כֶּסֶף *a thousand talents of silver* 2 K 15$_{19}$ 1 C 19$_6$ (כֶּסֶף), כִּכָּרִים חֲמֵשֶׁת־אֲלָפִים *five thousand talents* 1 C 29$_7$, שִׁבְעַת אֲלָפִים כִּכַּר־כֶּסֶף *seven thousand talents of silver* 1 C 29$_4$, עֲשֶׂרֶת אֲלָפִים כִּכַּר־כֶּסֶף *ten thousand talents of silver* Est 3$_9$, כִּכָּרִים עֲשֶׂרֶת אֲלָפִים *ten thousand talents* 1 C 29$_7$, רִבּוֹ וּשְׁמוֹנַת אֲלָפִים כִּכָּרִים *eighteen thousand talents* 1 C 29$_7$, כִּכָּרִים מֵאָה־אֶלֶף *one hundred thousand talents* 1 C 22$_{14}$, sim. 1 C 29$_7$, אֶלֶף אֲלָפִים כִּכָּרִים *one million talents* 1 C 22$_{14}$, אלף אלפים ככרי זהב *one million talents of gold* GnzPs 2$_{27}$.

22 ככרין *twenty-two talents* 3QTr 2$_{15}$, 42 ככרין *forty-two talents* 3QTr 2$_2$ 12$_3$, 71 ככרין *seventy-one talents* 3QTr 12$_9$, 14 [ ]ככ *fourteen talents* 3QTr 4$_2$, 22 [ ]ככ *twenty-two talents* 3QTr 7$_2$, 4 ככ *four talents* 3QTr 8$_9$, 5 ככ *five talents* 3QTr 12$_1$, 7 ככ *seven talents* 3QTr 5$_4$, 9 ככ *nine talents* 3QTr 9$_{13}$ 10$_2$, 12 ככ *twelve talents* 3QTr 4$_{14}$ 10$_4$, 13 ככ *thirteen talents* 3QTr 3$_{13}$, 17 ככ *seventeen talents* 3QTr 8$_7$ 10$_{16}$, 21 ככ *twenty-one talents* 3QTr 6$_{10}$, 22 ככ *twenty-two talents* 3QTr 7$_{13}$, 23 1/2 ככ *twenty-three and a half talents* 3QTr 9$_6$, 23 ככ *twenty-three talents* 3QTr 5$_{11}$, 27 ככ *twenty-seven talents* 3QTr 6$_{13}$, 32 ככ *thirty-two talents* 3QTr 5$_{14}$, 40 ככ *forty talents* 3QTr 3$_7$ 11$_8$, 42 ככ *forty-two talents* 3QTr 6$_6$, 55 ככ *fifty-five talents* 3QTr 4$_5$, 60 ככ *sixty talents* 3QTr 7$_{17}$ 12$_5$, 66 ככ *sixty-six talents* 3QTr 8$_{13}$, 70 ככ *seventy talents* 3QTr 8$_{16}$, 80 ככ *eighty talents* 3QTr 10$_{14}$.

⇒ כרר *turn*.

כֹּל I $_{5408.143.2540.15}$ n.m. **all**—כּוֹל (Jr 33$_8$), כוול; cstr. כֹּל (כָּל, כָּל־ Ps 35$_{10}$); sf. 2ms כֻּלְּךָ, 2fs כֻּלֵּךְ (כֻּלָּךְ), כֻּלּוֹ (Q כולו, כֻּלֹּה, Q כולהו), 3fs כֻּלָּהּ (כֻּלָּא), כֻּלָּנוּ (Q כולנו), כֻּלְּכֶם (Q כולכם), כֻּלָּם (כּוּלָּם, כֻּלָּהֶם, כֻּלְהֶם, Q כולמה, כולמו), 3fpl כֻּלָּנָה (כֻּלְהֶנָה).

1. in absolute or with pronominal suffix or followed by אֲשֶׁר or a participle

2. In construct, as first element (*nomen regens*)

1. in absolute or with pronominal suffix or followed by אֲשֶׁר or a participle (sometimes with -הַ article/relative), **all, everyone, everything, everywhere, wherever, whenever, the total, the whole.**

<SUBJ> היה *be* Gn 42$_{36}$ 45$_{10}$ Lv 15$_{10}$ Dt 20$_{14}$ Jos 2$_{19}$ 6$_{17}$ 8$_4$ 2 S 9$_9$ 1 K 10$_2$||2 C 9$_1$ 2 K 24$_7$ Is 64$_5$ Jr 23$_{14}$ 50$_{13}$ Ezk 22$_{19}$ 35$_{15}$ Ec 3$_{14}$ 4$_{16}$ 1QH 1$_{20}$ 11$_{13}$ 1QH fr. 4$_{17}$ 1QM 7$_{3.5}$ 17$_5$ 4QJub[a] 2$_{15}$ 4QD[a] 8.1$_6$ 4QPrEnosh 3$_2$ 4QShirShabb[d] 1.1$_{22}$ 4QShirShabb[f] 13$_6$ 4Q417 1.1$_{20}$ 4QpsHod[b] 3.1$_{19}$ 4QJonathan 1.1$_{17}$ 4Q476 2$_4$ 4QPrFêtes[c] 198$_2$ 4QBéat 3.2$_5$ 11QPs[a] 27$_{10}$ CD 2$_9$, ni. *occur* 1QM 17$_5$ 1QS 2$_{24}$ 10$_8$ 11$_{11.11.18}$ 4QD[a] 2.1$_6$ 4QD[c] 1$_8$ 4QShirShabb[c] 4$_{12}$ 4Q417 18$_4$ 4Q418 69.2$_7$ 123.2$_3$, קרה *occur* Gn 42$_{29}$ Est 4$_7$ 6$_{13}$ 4QapLam[a] 1$_3$, הוה *become* 1QS 3$_{15}$, ברא ni. *be created* 4QJub[b] 2$_3$, בנה pass. *be built* 11QT 12$_{10}$, חיה *live* Jos 6$_{17}$ 2 K 10$_{19}$, יתר ni. *remain* Jg 8$_{10}$ 1 S 2$_{36}$ Is 7$_{22}$ Zc 14$_{16}$, שאר ni.

remain 2 K $10_{11.17}$ Ezr 1_4 4QD[a] 5.1_{12} 4QpsEzek[e] 3_4, עדף *remain* Ex 16_{23}, ילד *become father of* 4QMidrEschat[b] 8_4.

יכל *be able (to do)* 1QH 15_{14}, שׁנה *be different* Si 42_{24}, רבה *be numerous* Dt 8_{13}, עזז *be strong* 4QapJoshua[b] 6_3, גבר *be mighty* Si $39_{21.34(Bmg)}$ (B hi.), כבד ni. *be honoured* Is 23_9, pi. *honour* Ps 45_{14} (if em. כְּבוּדָּה all *wealth* to יְכַבְּדוּךְ all *will honour you*), צדק *be righteous* 1QH 9_{15}, פרה *be fruitful* 4QpsMos[e] 1_7, בושׁ *be ashamed* Is $30_{5(Qr)}$ (hi.; Kt באשׁ hi. *stink*; or em. כָּל־הַבָּא הֵבִישׁ *any who comes is put to shame*) 45_{16}, כלם ni. *be humbled* Is 45_{16}, פתה *be naïve* Si 34_7 11QPs[a] 18_3, פסד ni. *be damaged*, i.e. suffer loss Mur $24B_{13}$ D_{12}.

חמם *be hot* Ho 7_7, עשׁן *be wrapped in smoke* Ex 19_{18}, מוג ni. *be melted* Is 14_{31}, יצק ho. *be poured*, i.e. cast 1 K 7_{33}, צפה pu. *be overlaid* 11QT 5_{11} 6_8, חרה ni. *be angry* Is 41_{11} 45_{24}, צרר *be hostile* Ps 6_8 10_5 31_{12} 69_{20} 143_{12} 4QDibHam[a] 1.6_{16}, זור *be strange* Lv $22_{10.13}$ 4QapJoseph[b] 3_8 4QsapHymn A 1.1_{10}, ni. *be estranged* Ezk 14_5, טמא *be unclean* Lv $11_{32.33.35}$ 14_{36} $15_{20.20}$ Nm $19_{14.22}$ 4QTohA $1.1_{1.3.9}$, נגע pu. *be afflicted* in one's flesh 1QSa 2_5, צרע pass. *be leprous* Nm 5_2 11QT 45_{17}, זוב *have discharge* Nm 5_2.

דשׁן ni. *be fat* 1QH 10_{26}, כהה *be dim* 4QD[b] 5.3_2, כפף pass. *be bowed down* Ps 145_{14}, עשׁק pass. *be oppressed* Ps 103_6 Ec 4_1, ירשׁ ni. *be poor* Gn 45_{11}, חלה ni. *be ill* Ezk 34_{21}, חשׁל ni. *be feeble* Dt 25_{18}, בלה *be worn out* Is 50_9 Ps 102_{27}, עוה ni. *be perverted* 4QShirShabb[a] $1.1_{14.16}$ 4QShirShabb[d] $1.1_{16.25}$, תמם *be consumed* Jr 44_{12}, כלה *be destroyed* Is 31_3, הרג pass. *be killed* Pr 7_{26}, עזב ni. *be forsaken* 1QH 9_{18}, נדד ho. *be banished* 2 S 23_6, גלה ho. *be exiled* Jr 13_{19}, ספה ni. *be swept away* Is 13_{15}, כרת ni. *be cut off* Na 2_1, פחח ho. *be trapped* Is 42_{22}, שׂרף ni. *be burned* Jos 7_{15}, בקע ni. *be split open* 2 C 25_{12}, שׁפט ni. *be judged* CD 20_{24}, יסר htp. *be disciplined* 4QD[e] 7.1_{15}.

חמד pass. *be desired* 11QT 57_{21}, ברר pass. *be selected* 1 C 9_{22} 11QT 57_7, בחר ni. *be chosen* Si $39_{21.30(Bmg)}$, נקב ni. *be designated* Ezr 8_{20}, פקד pass. *be mustered* Nm $1_{45.46}$ $2_{9.16.24.31.32}$ 3_{39} 4_{46} 14_{29} 4QShirShabb[f] 20.2_{14}, ni. *be enrolled* CD 14_3, *be missing* 2 K 10_{19}, ho. *be due for punishment* Jr 6_6 (if em. כֻּלָּה *all of it* [fem.] to כֻּלּוֹ [masc.]), חרץ pass. *be designated* 1QM 16_{11}, ברך pass. *be blessed* 4QShirShabb[d] $1.1_{27.29}$, נגשׂ *be overseer* Zc 10_4, חלץ pass. *be armed* Nm $32_{21.27.29}$, קצץ pass. *be cut* Jr 9_{25} 25_{23}, נשׁך pass. *be bitten* Nm 21_8, מול pass. *be circumcised* Jr 9_{24}, פרס hi. *have divided hoof* Lv 11_3.

סכת ni. *be silent* Si 13_{23}, סתם pass. *be secret* Ezk 28_3, עלם ni. *be secret* Ec 12_{14}, שׁכח ni. *be forgotten* Ec 2_{16}, גלה ni. *be revealed* 1QS 1_8 5_9 $8_{1.15}$ $9_{13.19}$, חקה pu. *be engraved* 4QShirShabb[f] 15.2_4, חקק pass. *be engraved* 1QH 1_{23}, כתב pass. *be written* Jos 1_8 8_{34} 23_6 2 K 22_{13}‖2 C 34_{21} Is 4_3 Jr 25_{13} 1 C 16_{40} 4QMidrEschat[b] 10_{12} 4QDibHam[a] 1.6_{14}, ni. *be written* Ps 139_{16}, יחשׂ htp. *be genealogically registered* 1 C 5_{17} 2 C 31_{19}, דקק polpal *be exactly defined* CD 16_2, דרשׁ ni. *be sought* 1QH 4_{24}, רחק pu. *be distant* 4Q476 1_4, אסף ni. *be gathered* Si 8_7, קבץ ni. *be assembled* Is 48_{14} 49_{18} 60_4, htp. Is 44_{11}, יסף ni. *be added* CD 13_{11}, לוה ni. *be joined* Est 9_{27}, צמד ni. *be attached to* 1QH 5_{24}, ערב pi. *be intermixed* 11QT 35_{12}, בדל ni. *be separated* Ezr 6_{21} Ne 10_{29}.

מצא ni. *be found* Ex 35_{24} Dt 21_{17} Jg 20_{48} 2 K 20_{13}‖Is 39_2 Is 13_{15} 22_3 Dn 12_1 2 C 29_{29} $34_{32.33}$ 35_7 1QS 6_2 9_{20}, נתן ni. *be given* Ezk 31_{14} Est 2_{13}, שׁמר ni. *be kept* Si $42_{23(M)}$, נשׂא ni. *be raised* 2 K 20_{17}‖Is 39_6 Is 2_{12}, אוץ *be hasty* Pr 21_5, מהר ni. *be hasty* 4QShirShabb[d] 1.1_{20} 4QShirShabb[f] 13_3.

בוא *come* Gn $23_{10.18}$ 47_1 Nm 4_{3+6t} 19_{14} 31_{23} Jos 21_{45} 23_{14} 1 S 5_5 9_6 22_{11} 2 S 2_{23} 20_{12} Is 7_{19} 30_5 (if em. בושׁ hi. *be ashamed*) 60_6 Hb 1_9 Ps 71_{18} Jb 17_{10} Pr 2_{19} Ec 11_8 Ezr 3_8 9_{13} 10_8 Ne 9_{33} 2 C 7_{11} 13_9 31_{16} 1QpHab $2_{7.10}$ 1QS 1_{16} 2_{18} 5_7 8_{21} 1QSa $1_{4.26}$ 1QH 6_{27} 4QWays[b] 12_4 4Q474 1_9 11QT 49_6 CD 2_2 8_1 $13_{4.14}$ 19_{13} 20_2, hi. *bring* Ex $35_{5.21.22}$, ho. *be brought* Ezk 44_5 (if em. לִמְבוֹא *to the entrance of* to לְכָל־מְבוֹאֵי *to all who may be brought into*), הלך *go* Gn 32_{20} Lv $11_{27.42.42}$ 2 S 13_{25} Jr 23_{17} 30_{16} Ec 3_{20} 6_6 1QM 7_5 1QS $4_{6.12}$ 4QapJoseph[b] 9_4 4QShirShabb[d] 1.1_{17} 4Q418 81_{16} CD 1_{20} 4_7 11_{21} 19_{31}, htp. *walk* CD 7_4 14_1, ירד *go down* Nm 16_{33} Ps 22_{30} 115_{17} 4QparaKings 9_{10}, עלה *go up* Gn 13_1 50_{14} Is 22_1 Am 8_8 9_5 Pr 24_{31}, יצא *go out* Gn 9_{10} $34_{24.24}$ Nm 1_{3+13t} 26_2 30_3 Jos 2_{19} 2 K 11_7 Jr 5_6 Pr 30_{27} 11QT 53_{15}, ho. *be excluded* Ezk 44_5 (if em. מוֹצָאֵי all *exits of* to מוּצָאֵי all *who are excluded from*), שׁוב *go back* Jr 8_6 Jb 17_{10} Ne 4_9 Si 40_{11} 41_{10} 1QH 2_8 4QpPs[a] 2_2 4QD[a] 2.2_5 5.1_{15} 4QShirShabb[a] 1.1_{16} CD 15_7, עבר *pass* Lv 27_{32} 1 K 9_8‖2 C 7_{21} Jr 18_{16} 19_8 49_{17} 50_{13} Ezk 5_{14} 36_{34} Zp 2_{15} Ps 80_{13} 89_{42} Pr 26_{10} (if rd. עֹבְרִים כֹּל *all who pass by*) Lm 1_{12}

2$_{15}$ 1QH 8$_{8}$, *enter covenant* 1QS 1$_{19.24}$ ([כול]) 2$_{10}$, *transgress* Ex 30$_{13.14}$ 38$_{26}$ 1QH 4$_{26}$ 1QS 5$_{7.14}$ 4QMyst^{a} 59$_{3}$.

נסע *set out* Gn 46$_{1}$, קרב *approach* Dt 1$_{22}$, פנה *turn* Is 56$_{11}$, הפך *turn* Lv 13$_{13}$, סור *depart* Ps 14$_{3}$, סוג *depart* Ps 53$_{4}$, שׁגה *stray* Ps 119$_{118}$ Pr 20$_{1}$, תעה *stray* Is 53$_{6}$, עזב *forsake* Jr 17$_{13}$ Ezr 8$_{22}$ 4QapJoseph^{b} 1$_{27}$, רדף *pursue* Ps 7$_{2}$ Lm 1$_{3}$ 1QM 9$_{5}$ 4QMyst^{a} 8$_{7}$, ברח *flee* Gn 31$_{21}$, דלג *jump* Zp 1$_{9}$, רמשׂ *swarm* Gn 1$_{30}$ 8$_{19}$ Dt 4$_{18}$ Ps 69$_{35}$ 4QJub^{a} 2$_{13.14}$, שׁרץ *swarm* 4QJub^{a} 2$_{11}$, רכב *ride* Ezk 23$_{23}$ 38$_{15}$ Si 36$_{6(Segal)}$ ([רוכב]).

שׁכב *lie down* Ex 22$_{18}$ Is 14$_{18}$, נוח *rest* Is 7$_{19}$, קום *arise* Nm 30$_{10}$ 2 S 18$_{31.32}$, עמד *stand* Jg 3$_{19}$ 4Q417 1.1$_{16}$, נצב ni. *stand* Gn 45$_{1}$, יצב htp. *position oneself* 1QH 7$_{29}$, כרע *kneel* Is 65$_{12}$, כשׁל *stumble* 2 C 28$_{15}$, מטט *stumble* 11QPs^{a} 19$_{2}$, נפל *fall* Jos 8$_{24.25}$ Jg 20$_{46}$ Ezk 39$_{23}$ Ps 145$_{14}$, סוג hi. *displace* 4Q424 3$_{9}$, עמס *carry* Zc 12$_{3}$, גרר *carry off* 4QWays^{a} 2$_{7}$, נשׂא *raise* Lv 11$_{25}$ Ho 14$_{3}$ Hb 2$_{6}$, רום hi. *raise* Ex 35$_{24}$ 4QShirShabb^{d} 1.1$_{24}$, עור hi. *rouse* Ezr 1$_{5}$, עטה *cover* Mc 3$_{7}$, שׁלך hi. *throw* Is 19$_{8}$, מצא *find* Gn 4$_{14.15}$ Jos 2$_{23}$ Jr 50$_{7}$, נגע *reach* Ex 19$_{12}$ 29$_{37}$ 30$_{29}$ Lv 6$_{11.20}$ 11$_{24.27}$ 15$_{10.11.19.21.22.27}$ Nm 19$_{13}$ 31$_{19}$ Pr 6$_{29}$, *touch* 4QTohA 1.1$_{8}$ 4QTohB^{c} 1$_{3}$ 4QapJoseph^{b} 3$_{10}$ 11QT 50$_{12}$, תפשׂ *hold* Gn 4$_{21}$ Ezk 27$_{29}$, חזק hi. *take hold of* 1QM 5$_{4}$ 4Q418 69.2$_{8}$ CD 20$_{27}$, תמך *grasp firmly* 1QMyst 1.1$_{7}$ 4QBéat 12$_{2}$, נחל *take possession of* 4QWiles 1$_{8.11}$ 4Q418 81$_{14}$ 4QBéat 13$_{5}$, שׁמר *keep* Is 56$_{6}$ 4QJub^{h} 35$_{17}$ 4Q418 81$_{8}$, משׁל *rule* 4Q423 5$_{4}$.

שׁמע *hear* Gn 21$_{6}$ Lv 24$_{14}$ 1 S 3$_{11}$ 1 K 22$_{28}$||2 C 18$_{27}$ 2 K 21$_{12}$ Jr 19$_{3}$ Mc 1$_{2}$ Na 3$_{19}$ 1 C 28$_{12}$ 1QH 18$_{7}$ 11QPs^{a} 27$_{8}$, ni. *be heard* Si 42$_{23(Bmg)}$, hi. *obey* 4QS^{d} 1.2$_{3}$, ראה *see* Jg 19$_{30}$ Is 61$_{9}$ Ezk 28$_{18}$ Na 3$_{7}$ Ps 22$_{8}$ 64$_{9}$ Est 2$_{15}$ Si 37$_{24(D)}$ 4Q418 74$_{2}$ 11QPs^{a} 28$_{7}$, חזה *see* Jb 27$_{12}$ 1QH 2$_{15}$ 4QMidrEschat^{a} 4$_{9}$, נבט hi. *look* 1QH 10$_{3}$ 1QH fr. 6$_{8}$, שׁקד *watch* Is 29$_{20}$, ידע *know* 1 S 10$_{11}$ Is 9$_{8}$ 56$_{10}$ Jr 31$_{34}$ 48$_{17}$ Ezk 28$_{19}$ Jb 42$_{11}$ Est 1$_{13}$ Ne 10$_{29}$ 1QH 13$_{1}$ 14$_{15}$ 4QJub^{a} 1$_{28}$ ([כל]) 4QAges^{b} 2$_{5}$ 4QD^{e} 2.2$_{19}$ 4QBer^{a} 7.1$_{6}$ 4QDiscourse 2.2$_{9}$ 4QShirShabb^{a} 2$_{9}$ 4QShirShabb^{d} 1.1$_{19}$ 4QShirShabb^{f} 8$_{3}$ 3$_{19}$ 4QShir^{b} 2.1$_{2}$ 4QBéat 14.2$_{15}$ CD 1$_{1}$ GnzPs 2$_{14}$, בין hi. *understand* 1QH 2$_{18}$, htpol. *consider carefully* 1QH 10$_{2}$, שׁכח *forget* Jb 8$_{13}$.

שׂבר pi. *hope* Ps 104$_{27}$, קוה *wait* Ps 25$_{3}$, יחל pi. *wait* Ps 31$_{25}$ 4QapMes 1.2$_{4}$, חכה *wait* Is 30$_{18}$ 4QShirShabb^{d} 1.1$_{23}$ 4QShirShabb^{e} 2$_{4}$, בקשׁ pi. *seek* Ex 33$_{7}$ Jr 2$_{24}$ Ps 40$_{17}$||70$_{5}$ Ezr 8$_{22}$ Si 30$_{26}$ 4QJub^{h} 36$_{9}$ 4Q418 102$_{4}$, דרשׁ *seek* 2 C 15$_{13}$ 1QH 2$_{15.34}$ 4QD^{a} 3.2$_{13}$ 4QapJoseph^{b} 1$_{19}$ 4Q418 81$_{18}$ 103.2$_{5}$ 107$_{5}$ 126.2$_{11}$, חסה *seek refuge* 2 S 22$_{31}$||Ps 18$_{31}$ Ps 2$_{12}$ 5$_{12}$ 34$_{23}$, אוה htp. *desire* Ec 6$_{2}$, אהב *love* Is 1$_{23}$ 66$_{10}$ Jr 20$_{4.6}$ Ps 145$_{20}$ Lm 1$_{2}$ Est 5$_{14}$ 6$_{13}$ Si 37$_{1}$ 4QJub^{h} 35$_{20}$, pi. *love* Jr 22$_{20}$ 30$_{14}$ Ezk 16$_{33.37}$, כבד pi. *honour* Lm 1$_{8}$, בטח *trust* 2 K 18$_{21}$||Is 36$_{6}$ Ps 115$_{8}$||135$_{18}$, ירא *fear* Ps 66$_{16}$ 128$_{1}$ 4QShir^{b} 52.3$_{5}$, pi. *frighten* Ne 6$_{9}$, מאס *refuse* 1QS 2$_{25}$ 4QD^{a} 11$_{5}$ 4QBer^{f} 1$_{7}$ 4Q418 148.2$_{3}$ CD 7$_{9}$ 8$_{19}$ 19$_{5.32}$ 20$_{8}$, יסד *conspire* 4QShirShabb^{c} 1$_{5}$, שׂנא *hate* Ps 41$_{8}$ 129$_{5}$ Gnz Ps 1$_{24}$, pi. *hate* Pr 8$_{36}$ 1QH 15$_{19}$ 1QM 3$_{5}$ 11QPs^{a} 22$_{11}$, נאץ pi. *despise* Nm 14$_{23}$ Is 60$_{14}$ 1QH 7$_{22}$ 1QS 5$_{19}$ CD 1$_{2}$, שׁוט *despise* Ezk 28$_{26}$, לעג *mock* Jr 20$_{7}$, קלל pi. *curse* Jr 15$_{10}$.

אמר *say* Dt 1$_{22}$ Is 14$_{10}$ Ps 29$_{9}$ Si 37$_{1.7}$ 4QBer^{b} 7.2$_{1}$, קרא *call* Jl 3$_{5}$ Zp 3$_{9}$ Ps 86$_{5}$ 145$_{18.18}$, pass. *be called* 1 K 14$_{1.49}$, ni. *be called* Is 43$_{7}$ 4Q418 81$_{12}$, נגד ho. *be declared* Ru 2$_{11}$, ענה *answer* Is 14$_{10}$, שׁבע ni. *swear* Zc 5$_{3}$ Ps 63$_{12}$, יעץ *advise* Si 37$_{7}$, שׁפט *judge* Ps 148$_{11}$ Pr 8$_{16}$ 1QSa 1$_{29}$ perh. 1QMyst 9$_{4}$ 4QapPent 5$_{2}$ 4QBark^{f} 1.1$_{6}$, חתם *set one's seal* 1QH fr. 11$_{3}$ (unless noun חוֹתָם *seal*, or pu. pf. חתם), ידה hi. *praise* Ps 67$_{4=6}$, *confess* 4QShirShabb^{d} 1.1$_{20}$, שׁיר *sing* 2 C 35$_{25}$, עלז *exult* Ps 96$_{12}$||1 C 16$_{32}$ (עלץ), רנן pi. *exult* Jr 51$_{48}$ 1QM 14$_{2}$ 4QShirShabb^{d} 1.1$_{37}$, ילל hi. *wail* Is 15$_{3}$ 16$_{7}$, שׂמח *rejoice* Is 14$_{29}$ 24$_{7}$, המה *make a noise* Is 59$_{11}$ Ezk 7$_{16}$, ברך pi. *bless* 1QM 14$_{4}$.

ישׁב *dwell* Gn 19$_{25}$ Ex 15$_{15}$ Lv 25$_{10}$ Nm 33$_{52}$ Jos 2$_{9.24}$ 7$_{9}$ 8$_{24.26}$ 9$_{11.24}$ 13$_{6}$ Jg 10$_{18}$ 11$_{8}$ 2 K 23$_{2}$ Is 18$_{3}$ Jr 1$_{14}$ 13$_{13.13}$ 17$_{20}$ 25$_{2.29.30}$ 35$_{17}$ 47$_{2}$ 51$_{24}$ Ezk 12$_{19}$ 26$_{17}$ 27$_{35}$ 29$_{6}$ 32$_{15}$ 38$_{8.11}$ Ho 4$_{3}$ Jl 1$_{2.14}$ 2$_{1}$ Am 8$_{8}$ 9$_{5}$ Na 1$_{5}$ Hb 2$_{8.17}$ Zp 1$_{4.18}$ Ps 33$_{8.14}$ 75$_{4}$ Lm 4$_{12}$ 2 C 15$_{5}$ 1QSb 3$_{1}$ 4QpsEzek^{e} 8$_{2}$.

סרר *be stubborn* 1QS 10$_{21}$, מרה hi. *be obstinate* 4QpPs^{a} 2$_{3}$, פשׁע *sin* Jr 2$_{29}$, נאף pi. *commit adultery* Jr 9$_{1}$ Ho 7$_{4}$, זנה *prostitute oneself* Lv 20$_{5}$ Ps 73$_{27}$, בזה *depise* 1QH 4$_{22}$, ארב *wait in ambush* Mc 7$_{2}$, קבע *rob* Ml 3$_{9}$, גנב *steal* Zc 5$_{3}$, בצע *extort* Jr 6$_{13}$ 8$_{10}$ Pr 1$_{19}$, בגד *betray* Jr 12$_{1}$ Ps 59$_{6}$, קשׁר *plot* 1 S 22$_{8}$ 2 K 21$_{24}$||2 C 33$_{25}$ Ne 4$_{2}$, רשׁע hi. *condemn* CD 20$_{26}$, גור *attack* 1QH 7$_{12}$, הות pol. *attack* Ps 62$_{4}$, הרג *kill* Nm 31$_{19}$, רצח *kill* Dt 19$_{3}$, נכה hi. *strike* Nm 35$_{15.30}$ Jos 20$_{9}$ 2 S 5$_{8}$||1 C 11$_{6}$, טול hi. *throw spear* 1QM 6$_{4}$, פשׁט hi. *strip* the slain 1QM 7$_{2}$, בזז *plunder* Jr 30$_{16}$, שׁלל *plunder* Jr 50$_{10}$, שׁבה *take captive* Jr 50$_{33}$ Ps 106$_{46}$, לחץ *oppress*

Jg 6$_{9}$ Jr 30$_{20}$, ענה pi. *humiliate* Zp 3$_{19}$ 1QM 12$_{14}$, רעע hi. *do evil* GnzPs 3$_{25}$, שחת hi. *do evil* Si 49$_{4}$, נקם *exact vengeance* 1QS 2$_{6}$, שלם pi. *requite* 1QS 2$_{6}$, חלל pi. *profane* 4QJub^{c} 2$_{27}$.

עשׂה *do* Ex 31$_{14}$ 31$_{15}$||35$_{2}$ Lv 18$_{29}$ Dt 18$_{12}$ 22$_{5}$ 25$_{16.16}$ Is 19$_{10}$ Ml 2$_{17}$ 3$_{19}$ Ps 111$_{10}$ Si 16$_{14}$ 35$_{23}$ 1Q36.7$_{1}$ 11QT 60$_{19}$, ni. *be done* Lv 7$_{9}$ 13$_{51}$ Nm 4$_{26}$ Ezk 44$_{14}$ Ec 9$_{3.6}$ 2 C 34$_{13}$ 1QH 1$_{8}$ 10$_{9}$ 1QpHab 8$_{1}$ 1QS 9$_{24}$ 11$_{17}$ 4QJub^{c} 2$_{27}$ Mas ShirShabb 1$_{5}$, פעל *do* Ps 5$_{6}$ 6$_{9}$ 14$_{4}$ 94$_{4}$ 101$_{8}$ GnzPs 4$_{23}$ 1QH 14$_{14}$, יטב hi. *do good to* 1QDM 1$_{4}$, יסד *found* 4QapPs^{a} 2$_{3}$, צמח *sprout* 4QJub^{a} 2$_{7.10.12}$, ימר hi. *change* 4QJub^{a} 1$_{12}$, נדב ni. *be dedicated* 1QS 1$_{7.11}$, htp. *volunteer* Ezr 1$_{6}$ 3$_{5}$ 1QS 5$_{6.8}$ 6$_{13}$ 1QpMic 10$_{7}$, עזר *help* Ezk 30$_{8}$, עבד *serve*, i.e. worship Nm 4$_{37.41}$ 2 K 10$_{19.21.22}$ Ezk 20$_{40}$ Ps 97$_{7}$ 1QpHab 13$_{3}$ 4QJub^{f} 22$_{22}$ 4QapJoseph^{b} 8$_{8}$ 4QsapHymnA 10$_{3}$ GnzPs 1$_{8}$ 2$_{19}$, שׁרת pi. *minister* Pr 29$_{12}$, דרך *tread* Is 59$_{8}$, *draw* bow Jr 50$_{14.29}$, תאם hi. *have twins* Ca 4$_{2}$ =6$_{6}$, לבשׁ *be dressed* Zp 1$_{8}$, אחז *lay hold of* 1QS 2$_{9}$ 4QBer^{f} 1$_{4}$, pass. *be strapped* Ca 3$_{8}$, אזר pi. *gird oneself* 4QWiles 1$_{7}$, חגר *gird oneself* 2 K 3$_{21}$, סרך *set in order* 1QM 2$_{6}$, קדח *light fire* Is 50$_{11}$ CD 5$_{13}$, צרף *refine* Jr 10$_{14}$ =51$_{17}$, טעם *taste* 4QpsHod^{c} 2$_{7}$, אכל *eat* Ex 12$_{15.19}$ Lv 7$_{25}$ 17$_{14}$ Jr 2$_{3}$ 30$_{16}$ Ho 9$_{4}$ 4QRitPur 67$_{3}$, לקק *lick* Jg 7$_{5}$, שׁתה *drink* Ezk 31$_{14.16}$ Jl 1$_{5}$ 1QH 3$_{30}$ 4QHod^{b} 3$_{6}$ 4QHod^{f} 4.2$_{6}$, זבח *sacrifice* Zc 14$_{21}$, תקע *sound* trumpet Jg 7$_{18}$, אבל htp. *mourn* Is 66$_{10}$, מות *die* Gn 7$_{22}$ 20$_{7}$, גוע *die* Gn 6$_{17}$, אבד *die* Nm 17$_{27}$, *perish* CD 9$_{10}$.

<NOM CL> הכל ... שבע *the total is ... seven (talents)* 3QTr 1$_{10}$, כל שְׁלֹשִׁים וְשִׁבְעָה *(the) total was thirty-seven* 2 S 23$_{39}$, הַכֹּל מֵאָה שְׁלֹשִׁים וְתִשְׁעָה *the total was one hundred and thirty-nine* Ezr 2$_{42}$, הכול שש מאות וארבעת אלפים *the total was four thousand and six hundred (persons)* 1QM 6$_{10}$, הכל ככרין שש מאות *the total is six hundred talents* 3QTr 12$_{7}$, כל שש מאות ותשעה *the total is six hundred and nine* 3QTr 3$_{4}$, הַכֹּל עֲבָדֶיךָ *all are your servants* Ps 119$_{91}$, הַכֹּל בְּנֵי־חָיִל *all were sons of might*, i.e. valiant warriors 2 C 28$_{6}$, הַכֹּל עוֹלָה *all (of this) was a burnt offering* Ezr 8$_{35}$, הַכֹּל אֶרֶז *everything was cedar* 1 K 6$_{18}$, הַכֹּל נְחֹשֶׁת *everything was bronze* 2 K 25$_{17}$||Jr 52$_{22}$, הכול מעשיך *your deeds are everything* 1QH 16$_{8}$, הכל טובים *all are good* Si 39$_{16(Bmg).33(Bmg)}$, הַכֹּל הֶבֶל *all is vanity* Ec 1$_{2}$ (הָבֶל) 1$_{14}$ 2$_{11.17}$ 3$_{19}$ 12$_{8}$ (both הָבֶל).

לא הכל לכל טוב *not everything is good for everyone* Si 37$_{28(B)}$, כל אֲשֶׁר־אֵינֶנּוּ נָקֹד *every one that was not spotted* Gn 30$_{33}$, הַכֹּל לִפְנֵיהֶם *all is before them* Ec 9$_{1}$, הַכֹּל עַד לִכְלוֹת הָעֹלָה *everything lasted until the completion of the burnt offering* 2 C 29$_{28}$ (or del. הַכֹּל), הַכֹּל לַפְּסָחִים *everything was for the passover sacrifices* 2 C 35$_{7}$, הכל בכתב *all should be (recorded) in a document* Si 42$_{7}$, כול בידכם *everything is in your hands* 4QMyst^{a} 77$_{2}$, בידיך הכול *everything is in your hands* 4QD^{a} 11$_{9}$, כל שיש לי *everything that I have* Mur 30 2$_{23}$, הַכֹּל כַּאֲשֶׁר לַכֹּל *all is as that which is to all*, i.e. there is the same lot for all Ec 9$_{2}$, כֹּל אֲשֶׁר־לוֹ סְנַפִּיר *everything that has fins* Dt 14$_{9}$, כֹּל אֲשֶׁר אֵין־לוֹ סְנַפִּיר *everything that does not have fins* Lv 11$_{10}$ 11$_{12}$||Dt 14$_{10}$, כָּל־אֲשֶׁר־לוֹ בְּיָדֶךָ *all that is his is in your hand* Jb 1$_{12}$, כֹּל אֲשֶׁר בַּמָּיִם *everything that is in the waters* Dt 14$_{9}$, כל שבה חרם *everything that is in it is devoted* 3QTr 9$_{16}$, כל שבו *everything that is in it* Mur 30 1$_{4}$ 2$_{19}$, כֹּל שֶׁעִמָּהֶם *everyone who was with them* 1 C 5$_{20}$.

הוא הכל *he is all* Si 43$_{27}$, מִמְּךָ הַכֹּל *everything is from you* 1 C 29$_{14}$, כול עולם *everything is from eternity* 4QparaKings 15$_{4}$, [הכו]ל [ע]ל [מ]דר[ש] התורה *the whole is in accordance with the interpretation of the law* 4QD^{a} 11$_{20}$, לְךָ הַכֹּל *to you belongs everything* 1 C 29$_{16}$, לַי׳ ... כָּל־אֲשֶׁר־בָּהּ *to Y. (belongs) ... everything that is in it* Dt 10$_{14}$, לְךָ ... כֹּל בַּשָּׁמַיִם *to you (belongs) ... everything in heaven* 1 C 29$_{11}$, לְךָ כֹּל אֲשֶׁר לִמְפִי־בֹשֶׁת *all that belonged to Mephibosheth is yours* 2 S 16$_{4}$, יֶשׁ־לִי־כֹל *I have everything* Gn 33$_{11}$, אֵין כֹּל *there is nothing at all* Nm 11$_{6}$ Pr 13$_{7}$, וְלָרָשׁ אֵין־כֹּל *and the poor man had nothing at all* 2 S 12$_{3}$, אֵין לְשִׁפְחָתְךָ כֹל בַּבַּיִת *your servant has nothing at all in the house* 2 K 4$_{2}$.

כֻּלָּךְ יָפָה *all of you is beautiful* Ca 4$_{7}$, כֻּלּוֹ כְּאַדֶּרֶת שֵׂעָר *all of him was as a cloak of hair* Gn 25$_{25}$, כֻּלּוֹ חָנֵף *all of them are* (lit. *all of him is*) *irreligious* Is 9$_{16}$, כֻּלּוֹ מַחֲמַדִּים *all of him is desirable* Ca 5$_{16}$, כֻּלּוֹ שַׁלְאֲנַן *he is completely peaceful* (lit. *all of him is undisturbed*) Jb 21$_{23}$, מַעֲשֵׂה חָרָשִׁים כֻּלֹּה *all of it is the work of artisans* Ho 13$_{2}$, כֻּלֹּה זֶרַע אֱמֶת *all of it was (from) reliable seed* Jr 2$_{21}$, כולה ככרים *all of it is of two talents* 11QT 9$_{11}$.

כֻּלָּהּ מַשְׁקֶה *all of it was watered* (lit. *drink*) Gn 13$_{10}$, כֻּלָּהּ מִקְשָׁה אַחַת *all of it is a single hammered piece* Ex 25$_{36}$ ||37$_{22}$, כֻּלָּהּ עֹשֶׁק בְּקִרְבָּהּ *all of it is oppression in her midst*, i.e. it is full of oppression Jr 6$_6$ (Qr Or כֻּלּוֹ; or em. כֻּלּוֹ *all of it* as subj. of פקד ho. *be visited*), כֻּלָּהּ כַּחַשׁ פֶּרֶק מְלֵאָה *all of it is full of deceit (and) violence* Na 3$_1$.

כֻּלָּנוּ בְּנֵי אִישׁ־אֶחָד נָחְנוּ *all of us are sons of one man* Gn 42$_{11}$, עַמְּךָ כֻלָּנוּ *all of us are your people* Is 64$_8$, עמכה כולנו *all of us are your people* 4QDibHam[a] 6$_6$, כֻּלָּנוּ חַיִּים *all of us are alive* Dt 5$_3$, כֻּלָּנוּ מֵתִים *all of us (will be) dead* Ex 12$_{33}$, כֻּלָּנוּ הַיּוֹם מֵתִים *if all of us (were) dead today* 2 S 19$_7$, כלנו חייבים *all of us are guilty* Si 8$_5$, מַעֲשֵׂה יָדְךָ כֻּלָּנוּ *all of us are the work of your hands* Is 64$_7$, כולנו יחד *all of us are united* 4QRitMar 19$_4$.

חַיִּים כֻּלְּכֶם הַיּוֹם *all of you are alive today* Dt 4$_4$, בְּנֵי עֶלְיוֹן כֻּלְּכֶם *all of you are sons of the Most High* Ps 82$_6$, כֻּלְּכֶם בְּנֵי יִשְׂרָאֵל *all of you are sons of Israel* Jg 20$_7$, רֹפְאֵי אֱלִל כֻּלְּכֶם *all of you are worthless physicians* Jb 13$_4$, מְנַחֲמֵי עָמָל כֻּלְּכֶם *all of you are comforters of misery* Jb 16$_2$.

כֻּלָּם אֲנָשִׁים ... הֵמָּה *all of them are men* Nm 13$_3$, כֻּלָּם גִּבּוֹרִים *all of them are warriors* Jr 5$_{16}$, כֻּלָּם פְּגָרִים מֵתִים *all of them are dead corpses* 2 K 19$_{35}$||Is 37$_{36}$, כֻּלָּם חֲלָלִים *all of them are slain* Ezk 32$_{22.23.24}$, כֻּלָּם עֲרֵלִים *all of them are uncircumcised* Ezk 32$_{25.26}$, כֻּלָּם סָרֵי סוֹרְרִים *all of them are the most rebellious of the rebels* Jr 6$_{28}$.

כֻּלָּם כְּלָבִים אִלְּמִים *all of them are dumb dogs* Is 56$_{10}$, כולם שנים שנים *all of them are two, two*, i.e. they all come in pairs Si 36$_{15}$, כולם שבע מערכות *all of them are seven formations* 1QM 9$_4$, כֻּלָּם יְשֵׁנִים *all of them were sleeping* 1 S 26$_{12}$, כֻּלָּם קְדֹשִׁים *all of them are holy* Nm 16$_3$, כֻּלָּם צַדִּיקִים *all of them are righteous* Is 60$_{21}$, כֻּלָּם טְהוֹרִים *all of them are pure* Ezr 6$_{20}$, כֻּלָּם נְכֹחִים *all of them are straightforward* Pr 8$_9$, כלם טובים *all of them are good* Si 39$_{16(B).33(B)}$.

כֻּלָּם מָגֵן וְכוֹבָע *all of them are (with) shield and helmet* Ezk 38$_5$, כֻּלָּם נְחֹשֶׁת *all of them are bronze* Ezk 22$_{18}$, כֻּלָּם אָוֶן *all of them are falsity*, i.e. false Is 41$_{29}$, כֻּלָּם תֹּהוּ *all of them are null* Is 44$_9$, כֻּלָּם חֲמִשָּׁה *their total was five* 1 C 2$_6$.

כֻּלָּם לַאדֹנִי *all of them (belong to) my lord* 1 C 21$_3$, כֻּלָּם בְּשֵׁמוֹת *all of them were (designated) by name(s)* Ezr 10$_{16}$.

רָאשִׁים כֻּלָּם *all of them were heads* 1 C 7$_3$, גִּבּוֹרֵי חַיִל כֻּלָּם *all of them were mighty warriors* 1 C 12$_{22}$, מַרְאֵה שָׁלִשִׁים כֻּלָּם *all of them had* (lit. *were*) *the appearance of adjutants* Ezk 23$_{15}$, עָרִיצֵי גוֹיִם כֻּלָּם *all of them are the most ruthless of the nations* Ezk 32$_{12}$, בַּחוּרֵי חֶמֶד כֻּלָּם *all of them are desirable youths* Ezk 23$_{6.12.23}$ (חֶמֶד ... כֻּלָּם), לְבֻשֵׁי מִכְלוֹל כֻּלָּם *all of them had* (lit. *were*) *perfect clothes* Ezk 38$_4$, מְרִיאֵי בָשָׁן כֻּלָּם *all of them are fatlings of Bashan* Ezk 39$_{18}$, מַעֲשֵׂה יָדָיו כֻּלָּם *all of them are the work of his hands* Jb 34$_{19}$, מַעֲשֵׂה חֲכָמִים כֻּלָּם *all of them are the work of wise ones* Jr 10$_9$, שָׁמָּה ... כֻּלָּם *there ... are all of them* Ezk 32$_{30}$, כולם עתודים *all of them are prepared* 1QM 6$_{16}$.

וִיצֻרַי כַּצֵּל כֻּלָּם *and all my forms* (perh. limbs or thoughts) *are as a shadow* Jb 17$_7$ (or em. כָּלִים *are wasting away* or כָּלָם *have wasted away* [with enclitic ם-]).

<OBJ> ראה *see* Gn 1$_{31}$ 31$_{12.43}$ 45$_{13}$ Ex 18$_{14}$ Nm 22$_2$ 23$_{13}$ Dt 29$_1$ Jos 23$_3$ 2 K 20$_{15}$||Is 39$_4$ Ezk 40$_4$ Jb 13$_1$ Ec 7$_{15}$, hi. *show* Ex 25$_9$ Ezk 40$_4$, חזה *see* Is 48$_6$ Si 15$_{18}$ 44$_3$, שׁמע *hear* Ex 18$_1$ Dt 5$_{27}$ Jos 9$_9$ 1 S 2$_{22}$ 1 K 11$_{38}$ Ezk 44$_5$ 1 C 10$_{11}$, ידע *know* 2 S 3$_{25}$ 14$_{20}$ Ps 139$_4$ Jb 38$_{18}$ Est 4$_1$ 1QH fr. 5$_9$ 4QPrFêtes[c] 5.2$_4$, hi. *make known* Gn 41$_{39}$, בין hi. *understand* Pr 28$_5$ (unless כֹּל III *measure*) Ne 8$_2$ 1 C 25$_7$ 2 C 34$_{12}$ Si 4$_{11}$ 42$_{21}$ 4QPrayer[c] 2$_8$, אוה htp. *desire* Dt 5$_{21}$, חפץ *desire* Si 15$_{17}$ Mur 30 2$_{23}$, חמד *desire* Ex 20$_{17}$, שׂנא *hate* Si 15$_{11}$, זמם *plan* Gn 11$_6$.

אמר *say* Gn 21$_{12}$ 31$_{16}$ Ex 18$_{24}$ Dt 5$_{27}$ Jg 7$_4$ 1 S 8$_7$ 12$_1$ 2 K 10$_5$ Ru 3$_5$ Si 15$_{11}$, דבר *speak* Ex 6$_{29}$, pi. *speak* Ex 23$_{22}$ Dt 5$_{27.28}$ 18$_{18}$ 1 S 9$_6$ 2 S 3$_{19}$ 1 K 10$_2$||2 C 9$_1$ Jr 1$_{7.17}$ 26$_8$ Est 6$_{10}$, הגה *speak* 4QShirShabb[d] 1.1$_{36.37}$, ענה *answer* Ec 10$_{19}$, קרא *call* Gn 2$_{19}$ CD 6$_6$, צוה pi. *command* Gn 6$_{22}$ 7$_5$ Ex 7$_2$ 25$_{22}$ 29$_{35}$ 31$_{11}$ 35$_{10}$ 36$_1$ 38$_{22}$ 39$_{32.42}$ 40$_{16}$ Nm 1$_{54}$ 2$_{34}$ 8$_{20}$ 9$_5$ 15$_{23}$ Dt 18$_{18}$ 26$_{14}$ Jos 1$_{16}$ 2 K 18$_{12}$ Jr 1$_{7.17}$ 26$_8$ Jb 37$_{12}$ Ru 3$_6$ Est 4$_{17}$, נגד hi. *declare* Gn 45$_{13}$ 1 S 9$_{19}$ 19$_{18}$ 2 S 11$_{22}$ 1 K 19$_1$ Ezk 40$_4$ Ru 3$_{16}$ Est 4$_7$, ספר pi. *relate* Ex 18$_8$ Est 5$_{11}$ 6$_{13}$, כתב *write* 4QpsJub[c] 2$_4$, שׁאל *ask* Dt 18$_{16}$ Ec 2$_{10}$, ni. *be consulted* 1QS 6$_{16}$, בין hi. *understand* CD 8$_{12}$, ירה hi. *teach* Dt 17$_{10}$ 24$_8$, למד pi. *teach* Ps 119$_{99}$, מנה *count* 5QapMal 1$_5$, בחן *test* 4QapPs[b] 46$_5$, נסה pi. *test* Jg 3$_1$, שׁפט *judge* 4Q423 5$_5$, פקד *appoint (punishment)* Zp 3$_7$, אסר *bind*, i.e. vow Nm 30$_{10}$ 11QT 53$_{19}$, ברך pi. *bless* 2 S 6$_{12}$||1 C 13$_{14}$.

בוא hi. *bring* Gn 46$_{32}$ Dt 12$_{11}$ Ezk 14$_{22}$ 2 C 36$_{18}$, קרב hi. *bring near*, i.e. offer Lv 1$_{13}$ 22$_{20}$, ירד hi. *take down* Is 43$_{14}$, סור hi. *remove* Gn 30$_{35}$, יצא hi. *take out* Jos 6$_{22.23}$, עלה hi. *raise* 1 S 2$_{14}$ Hb 1$_{15}$ Ezr 1$_{11}$, שׁוב hi. *bring back* 1 S 30$_{19}$ 2 K 8$_6$, נשׂא *raise* Is 57$_{13}$ CD 12$_7$, קום hi. *raise*, i.e. establish 1 S 3$_{12}$, מצא *find* Ec 9$_{10}$, שׁלח *send* Ex 9$_{19}$ 2 S

11$_{22}$ 1 K 20$_{9}$, pi. *send away* Gn 12$_{20}$, אסף *gather* Mc 2$_{12}$ Zp 1$_{2}$, לקח *take* Gn 31$_{1}$ Jos 7$_{24}$ 11$_{19}$ 1 S 30$_{19}$ 2 S 19$_{31}$ Ps 49$_{18}$ 2 C 12$_{9}$ 4QD^{a} 9.3$_{4}$ 4QD^{e} 4$_{7}$, נתן *give* Gn 9$_{3}$ 24$_{36}$ 25$_{5}$ 28$_{22}$ 39$_{4.8}$ Lv 8$_{27}$ 27$_{9}$ Dt 2$_{36}$ Jos 11$_{6}$ 2 S 24$_{23}$||1 C 21$_{23}$ Jb 2$_{4}$ 2 C 36$_{17}$ Si 15$_{17}$ 4QpsJub^{b} 4$_{3}$ 4QParGenEx 2$_{13}$ 4Q Pseud^{b} 2$_{2}$, חזק pi. *take hold of* 4QMyst^{a} 6.1$_{17}$, יסף ni. *be added* 1QS 8$_{19}$, hi. *add* Jb 42$_{10}$, שׂים *place* Ex 29$_{24}$ Jb 34$_{13}$, שׁית *place* Ps 8$_{7.8}$, ho. *be placed* Ex 21$_{30}$, סרך *set in order* 4QWays^{b} 1.1$_{3}$, עזב *leave* Gn 39$_{6}$ 4QJub^{h} 39$_{13}$, שׁאר hi. *leave* Dt 28$_{55}$, כון hi. *establish* Ezk 7$_{14}$ 1QH 18$_{22}$ 4Q418 55$_{6}$, פתח *open* Gn 41$_{56}$, שׁמר *keep* Jos 22$_{2}$ 1 S 25$_{21}$.

עשׂה *do* Gn 11$_{6}$ 39$_{3.22}$ Ex 18$_{8.24}$ 19$_{8}$ 23$_{22}$ 24$_{7}$ 31$_{6}$ 35$_{10}$ 38$_{22}$ Nm 22$_{17}$ 23$_{26}$ Dt 1$_{30}$ 3$_{21}$ 4$_{34}$ 12$_{8.14}$ 29$_{8}$ Jos 9$_{10}$ 1 S 14$_{7}$ 19$_{18}$ 2 S 3$_{25}$ 7$_{3}$||1 C 17$_{2}$ 2 S 19$_{39}$ 21$_{14}$ 1 K 2$_{3}$ 11$_{41}$ 14$_{29}$ 15$_{7}$ (all three + יֶתֶר דִּבְרֵי *the rest of the words of*) 15$_{23}$ (+ יֶתֶר כָּל־דִּבְרֵי *the rest of all the words of*) 15$_{31}$ 16$_{14}$ (both + יֶתֶר דִּבְרֵי) 19$_{1}$ 20$_{9}$ 22$_{39}$ 2 K 8$_{23}$ 10$_{34}$ 12$_{20}$ 13$_{8.12}$ 14$_{28}$ 15$_{6.21.26.31}$ 21$_{17}$ 23$_{28}$ 24$_{5}$ (all fourteen + יֶתֶר דִּבְרֵי) Jr 32$_{23}$ 38$_{9}$ Ps 104$_{24}$ 115$_{3}$ 135$_{6}$ Pr 13$_{16}$ (if em. כָּל־עָרוּם *every astute person* does to כֹּל עָרוּם *an astute person* does *everything* [unless כֹּל III makes *measure*, i.e. measures]) Ru 2$_{11}$ 3$_{5.11.16}$ Ec 3$_{11}$ 8$_{3}$ 11$_{5}$ Ne 5$_{19}$ 1 C 29$_{19}$ 2 C 33$_{8}$ 34$_{16}$ 1QH 10$_{12}$ 16$_{9}$ 1QH fr. 2$_{5}$ 11$_{5}$ 13$_{6}$ 1Q29.7$_{2}$ 2QapProph 1$_{4}$ 4QJub^{h} 35$_{21}$ 36$_{7}$ 39$_{13}$ 4QD^{a} 11$_{9}$ 4QMyst^{a} 3a.2$_{11}$ 4QShirShabb^{c} 4$_{11}$ 4Q418 81$_{2}$ 4QShir^{b} 42$_{2}$ GnzPs 2$_{14}$, *make* Ex 20$_{11}$ Is 44$_{24}$ Ps 146$_{6}$ Pr 22$_{2}$ Ec 3$_{11}$ Ne 9$_{6.6}$ 11QT 12$_{11}$, perh. *cause* Ec 11$_{5}$, פעל *do* GnzPs 3$_{6}$, יכל *be able (to do)* Jb 42$_{2}$ Si 43$_{30}$, ברא *create* 4QBer^{b} 3$_{2.4}$, יצר *form* Jr 10$_{16}$=51$_{19}$ Si 51$_{12}$ 4QAdmon Par 1.1$_{13}$, קרה *befall* Ec 2$_{14}$ 9$_{11}$, צמח hi. *make grow* 4Q423 2$_{6}$, קטר hi. *burn incense* 4QJub^{d} 21$_{7.9}$ 4QJub^{e} 21$_{7.9}$, מכר *sell* 4QJub^{h} 36$_{14}$.

קנה *acquire* Ru 4$_{9.9}$, קטר pi. *burn incense* 11QT 23$_{17}$, hi. *burn incense* 11QT 34$_{13}$, טהר pi. *cleanse* 4QRitPur 12$_{6}$ 42$_{4}$, קדשׁ hi. *consecrate* 1 C 26$_{28.28}$, משׁח *anoint* Ex 40$_{9}$ ||Lv 8$_{10}$, נצל hi. *rescue* 1 S 30$_{18}$, חיה hi. *keep alive* Jos 2$_{13}$ 6$_{25}$, pi. *preserve alive* Ne 9$_{6}$, רפא hi. *heal* Si 43$_{22}$, צלח hi. *cause to prosper* Gn 39$_{3}$ Ps 1$_{3}$ (unless כֹּל is subj.), שׂכל hi. *cause to prosper* Dt 29$_{8}$ 1 K 2$_{3.3}$, *cause to understand* 1 C 28$_{19}$, נשׁק *kiss* 1Q31.1$_{2}$ CD 13$_{3}$, חסר *lack* Dt 8$_{9}$ Jr 44$_{18}$, נשׁא *make loan* CD 10$_{18}$, אכל *eat* Ex 10$_{12}$ 1QS 5$_{16}$, בלע *swallow* Nm 16$_{30}$, חלל poel *pierce* Pr 26$_{10}$ (or em. כָּל־עֹבְרִים *all who pass*), פלג pi. *split open* 1QH 13$_{13}$, בזז *plunder* Gn 34$_{29}$, גזל *rob* Jg 9$_{25}$, שׂרף *burn* Jos 6$_{24}$ 11QT 16$_{13}$, נכה hi. *strike* Ex 9$_{25}$ 2 K 15$_{16}$, רעע hi. *damage* Ps 74$_{3}$, חרם hi. *put to ban* Dt 13$_{16}$ Jos 6$_{21}$ 1 S 15$_{3}$, כלה pi. *destroy* 4QJub^{g} 48$_{5}$, שׁחת hi. *destroy* Is 65$_{8}$, שׁבת hi. *cause to cease* CD 11$_{23}$, ירשׁ hi. *possess* Jg 11$_{24}$, בלל *confuse* 4Q 417 2.1$_{10}$, סתר pi. *hide* 4Q418 126.2$_{5}$.

<CSTR> כֹּל in absolute, or with pronominal suffix, as second element of construct or construct chain (*nomen rectum*), אלהי הכל *God of all* Si 32$_{1}$ 45$_{23}$ (אלוה[י] כל) 5Q Règle 1$_{2}$ ([א]לוהי הכול) 11QShirShabb m$_{2}$ ([א]לוהי כול), אדון הכול *lord of all* 4QLiturgy 1.1$_{6.8}$ perh. 4QD^{a} 11$_{9}$ (אונ הו הכול), מל[ך ה]כול *king of all* 4QShirShabb^{a} 1.1$_{28}$, רוב כול *great one of all* 4QparaKings 104$_{9}$, גבורת כול *strong one of all* 1QS 10$_{12}$.

יַד־כֹּל *hand of everyone* Gn 16$_{12}$ 2 C 32$_{22}$, sim. 4Qpara Kings 31$_{2}$ 4Q418 81$_{7.17}$, יַד־כֻּלָּם *hand of all of them* Jg 7$_{16}$, יד כולמ[ה] *hand of all of them* 1QMyst 1.1$_{9}$, פְּנֵי כֻלָּם *faces of all of them* Na 2$_{11}$, רֹאשׁ כֻּלָּם *head of all of them* Am 9$_{1}$, עֵינֵי־כֹל *eyes of all* Ps 145$_{15}$, sim. 4QapMoses^{c} 1.1$_{3}$, פי כול *mouth of all* 4QMyst^{a} 3a.2$_{8}$, פי כולם *mouth of all of them* 1QH 11$_{24}$, [פ]י כולמה *mouth of all of them* 4QHod^{a} 1$_{6}$, רוח כול *spirit of all* 4Q416 2.2$_{3}$ (כו[ל]) 4Q 419 8.2$_{7}$.

בְּכוֹר כֹּל *firstborn of everyone* Nm 8$_{16}$ (or em. כָּל־בְּכוֹר *every firstborn of*) 4Q423 3$_{4}$, מַשְׂאֹת כֻּלָּם *portions of all of them* Gn 43$_{34}$, משאי כול *tasks of all* 4QShirShabb^{f} 23.1$_{5}$, מַעְשַׂר הַכֹּל *tithe of everything* 2 C 31$_{5}$, עֹלוֹת מִסְפַּר כֻּלָּם *burnt offerings of*, i.e. corresponding to, *the number of all of them* Jb 1$_{5}$, רֹב כֹּל *abundance of everything* Dt 28$_{47}$, חלבי כל *choice (one) of all* 4QapPs^{b} 1$_{9}$.

בִּכּוּרֵי כָּל־אֲשֶׁר *firstfruits of everything that* Nm 18$_{13}$, מעשי כול *deeds of all* 4QShir^{b} 52.3$_{3}$, תְּמוּנַת כֹּל *image of anything* Dt 4$_{23.25}$, תפארת כולם *beauty of all of them* 4Q Shir^{b} 1$_{5}$, חָזוּת הַכֹּל *vision of the totality* Is 29$_{11}$, אמונת כול *faithfulness of all* 4QShir^{b} 17$_{1}$, [פקו]דת כול *visitation of all* 4QRitMar 16$_{4}$, משפט כול *judgment of all* 4Qpara Kings 23$_{2}$, משפטי כול *judgments of all* 1QS 3$_{17}$, משפט כולם *judgment of all of them* 1QH 5$_{4}$ 1QH fr. 13$_{4}$ 4Q Myst^{b} 11$_{2}$ (כלם) 4Q418 1$_{3}$, חֹסֶר כֹּל *lack of all* Dt 28$_{48.57}$ (חֹסֶר־) Si 35$_{12}$ 11QT 59$_{3}$ (חסור כול), ערמת כול *understanding of all things* 1QS 4$_{6}$, דעת כולם *knowledge of all of them* 1QS 8$_{9}$, פטיש כול *sledgehammer of all* 4QNarrG 1$_{5}$.

<APP> (e.g.) Edom Ezk 36$_5$, Egypt Ezk 29$_2$, בַּיִת *house* of Israel Ezk 11$_{15}$, עַם *people* Mc 1$_2$ Ps 67$_{4=6}$, גּוֹי *nation* Ml 3$_9$, Jacob Mc 2$_{12}$, נָסִיךְ *prince* Ezk 32$_{30}$, עֲבוֹדָה *service* CD 11$_{23}$, אָשָׁם *guilt offering* CD 9$_{14}$, שׁוּם *evaluation* Mur 22 1$_2$, קִיר *wall* 11QT 33$_{11}$, שַׁעַר *gate* 11QT 46$_6$, בְּרִיחַ *bar* Is 43$_{14}$, מְנוֹרָה *lampstand* Zc 4$_2$, תֵּבֵל *world* Jb 34$_{13}$.

<PREP> לְ of direction, *to* Ps 145$_{18.18}$ (+ קָרוֹב *near*) 4QapPs^b 50$_2$ perh. 4QparaKings 35$_1$, + נבט hi. *look* Si 15$_{18(B)}$, נתן *give* Gn 45$_{22}$ 1 S 22$_7$ 4Q417 1.2$_3$, רוה hi. *water* 4QMyst^a 6.1$_{12}$, שׁמע *listen* Jos 22$_2$ 1 S 12$_1$ Jr 42$_{21}$ (all three + קוֹל *voice*), קרא *call* Is 40$_{26}$ Ps 147$_4$, אמר *say* Jg 6$_{31}$ Ezk 11$_{15}$ Ec 10$_3$, ידע hi. *make known* 4QRitPur^b 15$_3$; of benefit, *to, for* Lv 13$_{51}$ 2 C 30$_{17}$ perh. 1QH 1$_{19}$ 13$_5$ perh. 1QMyst 12$_3$ 4QMyst^a 1$_5$ 4QCreatA 1$_7$ perh. 4Q417 2.1$_9$ perh. 4Q417 2.1$_{10}$ 4Q418 43$_7$ perh. 4Q418 118$_3$ 4Qps Hod^b 3.1$_{18}$, + היה *be* 4QMMT B$_{15}$, כסה ni. *be covered* 4QS^h 2$_1$, נתן *give*, i.e. appoint Ezk 44$_{14}$, צלח *be useful* Jr 13$_{7.10}$ 1QMyst 1.2$_5$, קנה *acquire* 2 K 12$_{13}$; of possession, *of, (belonging) to* Gn 11$_6$ 20$_{16}$ 1 S 6$_4$ 1 K 7$_{37}$ Ho 5$_2$ Ml 2$_{10}$ Ps 119$_{63}$ Ec 3$_{1.19}$ 4$_{16}$ 9$_{2.3}$ 2 C 5$_{12}$ perh. 4QConfess 2$_6$, + היה *be* Ezk 37$_{22.24}$ Pr 1$_{14}$; of cause, *for, on account of*, + זעק *cry* Jr 48$_{31}$; introducing object, + חזק pi. *strengthen* 1 C 29$_{12}$, נקשׁ pi. *strike* Ps 109$_{11}$, עבר *transgress* 4Q410 1$_2$, אמר *say* Is 8$_{12}$, ברך pi. *bless* 4QShirShabb^e 2$_{1.2.6}$.

לְ *as*, + שׂים *place*, i.e. appoint 1 S 22$_7$; *according to* perh. Lv 5$_4$, + עשׂה *do* Ex 36$_1$, שׁפט *judge* perh. 4Q423 6$_3$; *concerning*, + שׁאל ni. *be asked* CD 14$_6$; *over, above* 1 C 29$_{11}$ (הַמִּתְנַשֵּׂא לְכֹל *raising oneself above all*), *in respect of* 2 K 12$_6$ Is 38$_{16}$ (לְכָל־בָּהֶן חַיֵּי perh. *in every respect, the life of* my spirit *is on account of them*; or em. לְךָ לִבִּי וְהָנַח י׳ *my heart is yours and let my spirit rest, O Y.*) Ezr 8$_{34}$ 1 C 7$_5$, + שׁמע *hear* 1 S 8$_7$ Jr 35$_8$, צוה pi. *command* Jos 1$_{18}$.

בְּ of place/time, *in, during* (i.e. בְּכֹל = *wherever/whenever*) Dt 4$_7$, + היה *be* 2 S 7$_9$||1 C 17$_8$, שׂכל hi. *be successful* Jos 1$_7$, צלח *be prosperous* 4QJub^d 21$_{23}$ 4QJub^f 21$_{23.23}$, הלך *go* 4QMyst^b 8$_4$, htp. *walk* 1QH 15$_{15}$ perh. 1Q51$_3$, יצא *go out* Jg 2$_{15}$ 2 K 18$_7$, קום hi. *raise up* CD 2$_{11}$, עשׂה *do* 4QJub^a 2$_2$, כלה pi. *complete* 4QJub^a 2$_{16}$, שׁלח *send* 1 S 18$_5$, פנה *turn* 1 S 14$_{47}$, ישׁע hi. *save* 2 S 8$_{6.14}$||1 C 18$_{6.13}$, שׁמר *keep* Gn 28$_{15}$, דבר pi. *speak* 2 S 7$_7$||1 C 17$_6$, שׂמח *rejoice* Ec 11$_8$; of accompaniment, *in, with* Gn 21$_{22}$ Jos 1$_9$ 1QH 2$_4$ perh. 1Q29.4$_1$ perh. 4Q415 13$_4$, + היה *be* Gn 39$_5$, חיה *live* 4QapPs^b 103$_2$; of instrument, *by (means of), with*, + ענה htp. *be afflicted* 1 K 2$_{26}$, גאל htp. *defile oneself* 4QapJoshua^b 3$_5$, טמא ni. *become impure* Ezk 23$_7$, נקשׁ ni. *be struck* by, i.e. stumble against Si 41$_{2(B)}$, רום hi. *raise* voice Si 43$_{30}$, שׁקץ pi. *make abominable* Lv 20$_{25}$; partitive, *(some) of* Ec 9$_6$, + נתן *give* Dt 21$_{17}$.

בְּ *over, in charge of*, + היה *be* Gn 39$_5$, מלך *rule* 2 S 3$_{21}$ 1 K 11$_{37}$ Arad ost. 88$_1$ ([בכ]ל), משׁל *rule* Gn 24$_2$ Ps 103$_{19}$ 1 C 29$_{12}$ 2QapProph 6$_3$ 4QJub^h 32$_{18}$ 4QapPs^b 1$_{7.7}$ 77$_{15}$ 4QNarrC 1$_7$, hi. *cause to rule* 4QJub^a 2$_{14}$; *in respect of* Ec 5$_8$, + ערך pass. *be arranged* 2 S 23$_5$, צלח hi. *be successful* Si 41$_1$, בין hi. *understand* GnzPs 1$_6$ CD 19$_{24}$ 4QparaKings 15$_2$ 4QMMT C$_{28}$, ברך pi. *bless* Gn 24$_1$, שׁמר *keep*, i.e. be on guard Ex 23$_{13}$, עשׂה *do* Dt 15$_{18}$; *(in exchange) for*, + נתן *give* silver Dt 14$_{26.26}$; *against* Gn 16$_{12}$, + נקשׁ *strike*, i.e. stumble Si 41$_{2(Bmg)}$; *according to* 2 S 7$_{22}$||1 C 17$_{20}$; ידע בְּ *know* 1QH 16$_6$; נבט בְּ hi. *look at* 1 S 23$_2$, בין בְּ hi. *understand* 1QH 13$_{14}$, htpol. *examine* Si 34$_{15(B)}$, שׂכל בְּ hi. *understand* 4Q418 197$_1$, נגע בְּ *touch* Nm 16$_{26}$ Jb 1$_1$.

כְּ *(just) as, in accordance with* (כְּכָל־אֲשֶׁר everywhere except Jb 24$_{24}$, unless כֹּל II *mallow* or em. כְּמַלּוּחַ *as a mallow*) 2 S 3$_{36}$ 15$_{15}$ 4QZedek 3$_6$, + עשׂה *do* Gn 6$_{22}$ 7$_5$ Ex 25$_9$ 29$_{35}$ 31$_{11}$ 39$_{32.42}$ 40$_{16}$ Nm 1$_{54}$ 2$_{34}$ 8$_{20}$ 9$_5$ Dt 12$_8$ 17$_{10}$ 24$_8$ 26$_{14}$ 1 S 25$_{30}$ 2 S 9$_{11}$ 1 K 8$_{43}$||2 C 6$_{33}$ 1 K 9$_4$||2 C 7$_{17}$ 2 K 10$_{30}$ 11$_9$||2 C 23$_8$ 2 K 14$_3$ 15$_3$||2 C 26$_4$ 2 K 15$_{34}$||2 C 27$_2$ 2 K 16$_{16}$ 18$_3$||2 C 29$_2$ 2 K 21$_8$ 23$_{32.37}$ 24$_9$ 24$_{19}$||Jr 52$_2$ Jr 11$_4$ 35$_{10.18}$ 36$_8$ 42$_{20}$ 50$_{21.29}$ Ezk 9$_{11(Qr)}$ (Kt כַּאֲשֶׁר) 24$_{24}$ Ru 3$_6$ Est 4$_{17}$ Lachish ost. 4$_{2.3.11}$ Arad ost. 60$_1$, אמר *say* Nm 30$_1$, דבר pi. *speak* Dt 1$_3$ Jos 4$_{10}$, שׁמע *hear* Jos 1$_{17}$, כתב ni. *be written* Est 3$_{12}$ 8$_9$ Lachish ost. 4$_3$, קום hi. *raise* Dt 18$_{16}$, נתן *give* Ex 21$_{30}$ 1 K 5$_{20}$ 8$_{56}$, לקח *take* Jos 11$_{23}$, סור hi. *remove* 2 K 24$_3$, לחם ni. *fight* Dt 1$_{30.41}$, שׁמר *keep (watch)* Lachish ost. 4$_{11}$, בנה *build* 2 K 16$_{11}$, כפר pi. *atone* 1 C 6$_{34}$; + קפץ ni. *be contracted* Jb 24$_{24}$ (or em. כְּמַלּוּחַ *as a mallow* and/or קטף ni. *be cut off* or קבץ ni. *be gathered*), נסה pi. *try* Dt 4$_{34}$, נכה hi. *strike* Jos 10$_{32.35.37}$, נוח hi. *give rest* Jos 21$_{44}$, תעב hi. *act abominably* 1 K 21$_{26}$, כעס hi. *anger* 1 K 22$_{54}$.

מִן of direction, *(away) from* CD 16$_3$ perh. 1QMyst 3$_1$ 4QparaKings 111$_3$ 4QpsEzek^d 18$_1$ 4QBapt 7.2$_4$ 11QT

58$_{14}$, + סתר ni. *be hidden* 4QMyst^{a} 6.2$_{4}$ 4QRitPur 5$_{15}$, סור *depart* 1 K 15$_{5}$, hi. *remove* Jos 11$_{15}$, שׂמאל hi. *go to left* 2 S 14$_{19}$, חסה *seek refuge* 1QH 9$_{29}$, נצל hi. *rescue* Ps 34$_{20}$, פלט pi. *rescue* 1QSb 1$_{7}$, שׁמר ni. *keep away* Jg 13$_{13}$, רשׁע hi. *make guilty* 1QlitPr 3.2$_{4}$, שׁבת *stop working* 4QJub^{a} 2$_{20}$; of comparison, *(more) than* Jr 17$_{9}$ (+ עָקֹב more *treacherous* than) Dn 11$_{2}$ (+ גָּדוֹל *greater*), + היה *be* Ec 2$_{7}$, כבד ni. *be glorified* 1QH fr. 11$_{8}$, יסף hi. *increase* Ec 2$_{9}$, צדק hi. *justify* 1QSb 4$_{22}$, נתן *give* 1 C 29$_{3}$ (perh. מִן = *in addition to*), רעע hi. *do evil* 1 K 14$_{9}$ 16$_{25.30}$ 2 K 21$_{11}$, קנא pi. *anger* 1 K 14$_{22}$; of cause, *on account of*, + כלם ni. *be ashamed* Ezk 16$_{54}$ 43$_{11}$, זוע *tremble* Si 48$_{12}$.

מִן partitive, *(some) of, (any) of, from among* Gn 7$_{22}$ Lv 5$_{22.26}$ 2 K 9$_{5}$ Ec 6$_{2}$ 4QMyst^{a} 60$_{3}$ perh. Ketef Hinnom inscr. 1$_{9}$, + היה *be* Jos 8$_{35}$, מצא ni. *be found* Dn 1$_{19}$, פקד ni. *be missing* 1 S 25$_{21}$, בוא *come* Gn 6$_{20}$ 7$_{8}$ (with ellipsis of מִן), hi. *bring* Gn 6$_{19}$, נפל hi. *cause to fall*, i.e. omit Est 6$_{10}$, נתן *give* tithe Gn 14$_{20}$, קדשׁ pi. *sanctify* CD 16$_{16}$, בחר *choose* 1QH 15$_{23}$, לקח *take* Gn 6$_{2}$ 14$_{23}$, שׁוב hi. *bring back* Lv 5$_{24}$, שׁאר hi. *leave* 1 S 25$_{22}$, אצל *withhold* Ec 2$_{10}$, חרם hi. *devote* Lv 27$_{28}$, מות *die* Ex 9$_{4}$, אכל *eat* Gn 27$_{33}$ Lv 11$_{9}$ Nm 6$_{4}$ Dt 14$_{9}$ Jg 13$_{14}$.

אֶל *to* perh. Si 39$_{16}$, + הלך *go* Jos 1$_{16}$, אמר *say* Gn 35$_{2}$, קרא *call* Ex 36$_{2}$ (with ellipsis of אֶל); *at*, + חיה *live* Ezk 47$_{9}$, שׂכל hi. *be successful* Pr 17$_{8}$.

עַל *above, upon, more than* 4QAdmon Par 1.1$_{5}$ 4Qap Joshua^{b} 32$_{4}$, + גלה ni. *be revealed* Si 42$_{16}$, גדל htp. *make oneself great* Dn 11$_{37}$, עלה *go up* Pr 31$_{29}$, appar. חלק *create* Si Si 34$_{13(Bmg)}$ (B עַל־כֵּן *therefore*); *over, in charge of*, + פקד hi. *appoint* Gn 39$_{5}$ Nm 1$_{50}$, מלך hi. *make king* 2 S 2$_{9}$; *against*, + פשׁט *rush out* Jg 9$_{44}$, דבר pi. *speak* Ezk 36$_{5}$, נבא ni. *prophesy* Ezk 29$_{2}$, עוד hi. *testify* 4QpsJub^{c} 2$_{3}$; *to*, + הלך *go* Jr 1$_{7}$, נטה hi. *turn* heart Pr 21$_{1}$; *(in addition) to*, + יסף hi. *add* Ec 1$_{16}$; *because of* 1QS 6$_{27}$, + מאס *reject* Jr 31$_{37}$; *concerning*, + דרשׁ *seek* Ec 1$_{13}$, תור *spy out* Ec 1$_{13}$.

כְּעַל *in accordance with*, + זכר hi. *recall* Is 63$_{7}$.

אַחֲרֵי *after* 4QJub^{a} 2$_{14}$.

אֵת perh. *in the presence of*, + יכח ni. *be vindicated* Gn 20$_{16}$.

בַּעַד *around*, + שׂוך *enclose* Jb 1$_{10}$, חתם *fix seal* 4QShir^{b} 30$_{3}$.

עִם *with* 1QH 3$_{4}$ 4QapJoseph^{b} 3$_{2}$, + הלך htp. *walk* 1QS 8$_{4}$, תפשׂ *take hold of* 4Q248$_{7}$.

מִפְּנֵי *before*, + שׁוב *go back* Pr 30$_{30}$, נוס *flee* Si 34$_{13}$, זוע htpal. *tremble* 1QS 11$_{4}$.

<COLL> כֹּל אֲשֶׁר *all that/who* Gn 1$_{31}$ 2$_{19}$ 6$_{2.17.22}$ 7$_{5.8.22.22}$ 9$_{2}$ 11$_{6}$ 12$_{20}$ 14$_{23}$ 19$_{12}$ 20$_{7.16}$ 21$_{12.22}$ 24$_{2.36}$ 25$_{5}$ 28$_{15.22}$ 30$_{33.35}$ 31$_{1.12.16.21.43}$ 34$_{29}$ 35$_{2}$ 39$_{3+5t}$ 41$_{56}$ 45$_{10.11}$ 46$_{1.32}$ 47$_{1}$ Ex 6$_{29}$ 7$_{2}$ 9$_{19.25}$ 10$_{12}$ 18$_{1.8.14.24}$ 19$_{8}$ 20$_{11.17}$ 21$_{30}$ 23$_{13.22}$ 24$_{7}$ 25$_{9.22}$ 29$_{35}$ 31$_{6.11}$ 35$_{10.21.24.24}$ 36$_{1.2}$ 38$_{22}$ 39$_{32.42}$ 40$_{9.16}$ Lv 5$_{4.22.24.26}$ 6$_{11.20}$ 8$_{10}$ 11$_{9+5t}$ 13$_{51}$ 14$_{36}$ 15$_{10.11.20.20}$ 16$_{26}$ 18$_{29}$ 20$_{25}$ 22$_{20}$ 27$_{9.28.32}$ Nm 1$_{50.54}$ 2$_{34}$ 4$_{16.26}$ 6$_{4}$ 8$_{20}$ 9$_{5}$ 15$_{23}$ 16$_{30.33}$ 18$_{13}$ 19$_{14.16.22}$ 22$_{2.17}$ 23$_{26}$ 30$_{1.10}$ 31$_{23}$ Dt 1$_{3.30.41}$ 3$_{21}$ 4$_{23.34}$ 5$_{21.27.27.28}$=4QTestim$_{2}$ Dt 8$_{13}$ 10$_{14}$ 12$_{8.11.14}$ 13$_{16}$ 14$_{9.9.26.26}$ 15$_{18}$ 17$_{10}$ 18$_{16.18}$=4QTestim$_{6}$ Dt 20$_{14}$ 21$_{17}$ 24$_{8}$ 26$_{14}$ 29$_{1.8}$ Jos 1$_{7+5t}$ 2$_{13.19.19}$ 4$_{10}$ 6$_{17+6t}$ 7$_{15.24}$ 8$_{35}$ 9$_{9.10}$ 10$_{32.35.37}$ 11$_{15.23}$ 15$_{46}$ 21$_{44}$ 22$_{2.2}$ 23$_{3}$ Jg 2$_{15}$ 3$_{1}$ 6$_{31}$ 7$_{4.5.18}$ 9$_{25.44}$ 1$_{24}$ 13$_{13.14}$ 1 S 2$_{14.22.32}$ 8$_{7}$ 9$_{6.19}$ 12$_{1}$ 14$_{7.47}$ 15$_{3}$ 18$_{5}$ 19$_{18}$ 25$_{6.21.21.22.30}$ 30$_{18.19}$ 2 S 3$_{19.21.25.36}$ 6$_{12}$ 7$_{3.7.9.22}$||1 C 17$_{2.6.8.20}$ 2 S 8$_{6}$||1 C 18$_{6}$ 2 S 8$_{14}$||1 C 18$_{13}$ 2 S 9$_{9.11}$ 11$_{22}$ 14$_{19.20}$ 15$_{15}$ 16$_{4.21}$ 18$_{32}$ 19$_{39}$ 21$_{14}$ 1 K 2$_{3.3.26}$ 5$_{20}$ 8$_{43}$||2 C 6$_{33}$ 1 K 8$_{56}$ 9$_{4}$||2 C 7$_{17}$ 1 K 10$_{2}$||2 C 9$_{1}$ 1 K 11$_{37.38.41}$ 14$_{9.22.29}$ 15$_{5.7.23.31}$ 16$_{14.25}$ 19$_{1}$ 20$_{4.9}$ 21$_{26}$ 22$_{39.54}$ 2 K 8$_{6.23}$ 10$_{5.30.34}$ 11$_{9}$||2 C 23$_{8}$ 2 K 12$_{6.13.20}$ 13$_{8.12}$ 14$_{3.28}$ 15$_{3+6t}$ 16$_{11.16.30}$ 18$_{3}$||2 C 29$_{2}$ 2 K 18$_{7.12}$ 20$_{13.15.17}$||Is 39$_{2.4.6}$ 2 K 21$_{8}$||2 C 33$_{8}$ 2 K 21$_{11.17}$ 23$_{28.32.37}$ 24$_{3.5.7.9.19}$||Jr 52$_{2}$ Is 8$_{12}$ 19$_{17}$ 63$_{7}$ Jr 1$_{7.7.17}$ 11$_{4}$ Jr 26$_{8}$ 31$_{37}$ 32$_{23}$ 35$_{8.10.18}$ 36$_{8}$ 38$_{9}$ 42$_{20.21}$ 50$_{21.29}$ 51$_{48}$ Ezk 9$_{11(Qr)}$ 12$_{14}$ 14$_{22}$ 16$_{54}$ 23$_{7}$ 24$_{24}$ 40$_{4.4}$ 43$_{11}$ 44$_{5.14}$ 47$_{9}$ Zp 3$_{7}$ Ps 1$_{3}$ 96$_{12}$ ||1 C 16$_{32}$ Ps 109$_{11}$ 115$_{3.8}$ 119$_{63}$ 135$_{6.18}$ 145$_{18}$ 146$_{6}$ Jb 1$_{10.11.12}$ 2$_{4}$ 37$_{12}$ 42$_{10}$ Pr 17$_{8}$ 21$_{1}$ Ru 2$_{11}$ 3$_{5.6.11.16}$ 4$_{9.9}$ Ec 1$_{13.16}$ 2$_{10}$ 3$_{14}$ 4$_{16}$ 6$_{2}$ 8$_{3}$ 9$_{3.6.10}$ Est 2$_{13}$ 3$_{12}$ 4$_{1.7.17}$ 5$_{11}$ 6$_{10.13}$ 8$_{9}$ Ezr 10$_{8}$ Ne 5$_{19}$ 9$_{6.6}$ 1 C 6$_{34}$ 10$_{11}$ 13$_{14}$ 28$_{12}$ 2 C 15$_{13}$ 34$_{16}$ Si 15$_{11}$ 34$_{15(Bmg)}$ 46$_{11}$ 1QH 1$_{14}$ 3$_{33}$ 14$_{10}$ 15$_{11.18}$ 17$_{24.24}$ 1QpHab 7$_{7}$ 1QS 1$_{3.4.17}$ 5$_{1.8.18.18.19}$ 9$_{25.26}$ 1QDM 4$_{6}$ 4QpPs^{a} 3$_{4}$ 4Q MidrEschat^{a} 2$_{6}$ 4QJub^{a} 1$_{9}$ 2$_{1.12.14.14.16}$ 4QJub^{f} 39$_{4}$ 4Q Jub^{h} 35$_{10}$ 36$_{10.12}$ 38$_{5}$ 39$_{12}$ 4QHalakah^{a} 13$_{5.6}$ 4QD^{a} 5.2$_{1}$ 4QD^{b} 5.3$_{1}$ 4QD^{e} 2.2$_{7}$ 5$_{20}$ 4QD^{f} 3$_{6.12}$ 4QTohA 2.2$_{3}$ 4QToh B^{c} 1$_{10}$ 4QNidd 2.1$_{2}$ 4QErr 1$_{3}$ 4QAdmon 1.1$_{1.6}$ 4Qap Joseph^{b} 1$_{18}$ 4QDiscourse 9$_{5}$ 4Qap Moses^{b} 1.2$_{3}$ 4QapPs^{b} 1$_{9}$ 4QpsEzek^{a} 12$_{7}$ 4QpsMos^{e} 1$_{3.5}$ 4QpsEzek^{e} 4$_{1}$ 4Q416 1$_{11}$ 3$_{6}$ 4Q418 2$_{3}$ 81$_{2}$ 208$_{1}$ 4QM^{h} 4$_{1}$ 4Q474 1$_{6}$ 4QRitMar 126$_{2}$ 4QDibHam^{a} 1.5$_{14}$ 1.7$_{8}$ 4QPrFêtes^{c} 31$_{5}$ 4QShir^{b} 37$_{4}$ 4QapMes 1.2$_{2}$ 11QPs Ap^{a} 1$_{12}$ 11QMelch 2$_{17.25}$ 11QT 29$_{5}$ 31$_{9}$ 43$_{10.13}$ 47$_{5.6}$ 49$_{6.8.16.17}$ 51$_{9}$ 54$_{4.5}$ 55$_{7}$ 56$_{6}$ 58$_{3}$ 60$_{5}$

62$_{10}$ CD 6$_{11}$ 12$_{3}$ 15$_{13}$ 16$_{8}$ 20$_{25}$ Lachish ost. 4$_{2.3}$ Arad ost. 21$_{7}$ (וכל אש[ר]) 40$_{6}$ ([כל אשר]) Kuntillet 'Ajrud add. inscr. 2$_{1}$.

הֵיבוּ, כָּל־אֲשֶׁר תִּפְנֶה שָׁם *everywhere you turn* 1 K 2$_{3}$, כָּל־אֲשֶׁר דִּבֵּרוּ *everything they spoke they did well (to speak)* Dt 5$_{28}$, כל מאשר ראיתי *all from those I have seen* 4QJub^{a} 2$_{20}$, כָּל־שֶׁ־ *all that* Ec 2$_{7.9}$ 11$_{8}$ 1 C 5$_{20}$ Si 15$_{17(B)}$ 34$_{15(B)}$, הכל של הדמע *the total of the offering* 3QTr 1$_{10}$, חסר כל *lacking in everything* Si 11$_{12}$, וְלָרָשׁ אֵין־כֹּל *and the poor man had nothing at all* 2 S 12$_{3}$, אֵין לְשִׁפְחָתְךָ כֹל בַּבַּיִת *your servant has nothing at all in the house* 2 K 4$_{2}$.

2. in construct, as first element (*nomen regens*) (usu. כָּל־), **all (of), every, each (of), the whole of,** immediately preceding a noun (absolute, construct, singular, plural) or adjective used as noun (the list is arranged alphabetically), אָב *father* Ps 39$_{13}$ 1 C 29$_{15}$ 4QMyst^{a} 76$_{3}$ 4Qap Mes 3.2$_{9}$, אֵב *greenness* 4QSD 7.2$_{14}$, אֲבֵדָה *lost object* Ex 22$_{8}$ Dt 22$_{3}$ CD 9$_{14}$, אֶבְיוֹן *poor one* 1QH 5$_{22}$, אַבִּיר *mighty one* Lm 1$_{15}$, אָבֵל *mourner* Is 61$_{2}$, אֵבֶל *mourning* 1QH 11$_{22}$ 4QHod^{a} 1$_{4}$, אֶבֶן *stone* Nm 35$_{23}$ Is 27$_{9}$ Ezk 27$_{22}$ 28$_{13}$ Pr 16$_{11}$ 1 C 29$_{2}$ Si 45$_{11}$ 4QBéat 3.3$_{3}$ GnzPs 2$_{29}$, אֲבָקָה *(aromatic) powder* Ca 3$_{6}$, אֲגַף *troop* Ezk 12$_{14}$ 17$_{21}$ 38$_{6.6.9}$ 39$_{4}$ 4QHod^{f} 4.2$_{4}$, *bank* 1QH 3$_{29}$, אֱדוֹם *Edom* 2 S 8$_{14}$||1 C 18$_{13}$ 2 S 8$_{14}$ Ezk 35$_{15}$, אָדָם *human being* Gn 7$_{21}$ Ex 9$_{19}$ Lv 16$_{17}$ Nm 12$_{3}$ 16$_{29.29.32}$ Jos 11$_{14}$ Jg 16$_{17}$ 1 K 5$_{11}$ 8$_{38}$||2 C 6$_{29}$ Jr 10$_{14}$ 31$_{30}$ 51$_{17}$ Ezk 38$_{20}$ Zc 8$_{10}$ Ps 39$_{6.12}$ 64$_{10}$ 116$_{11}$ Jb 21$_{33}$ 36$_{25}$ 37$_{7}$ Ec 3$_{13}$ 5$_{18}$ 7$_{2}$ 12$_{13}$ Si 13$_{15}$ 16$_{14}$ 30$_{38}$ 46$_{19}$ 4QMyst^{a} 69$_{3}$ 11QPsAp^{a} 2$_{8}$ 11QT 32$_{15}$ 49$_{9}$ 50$_{8}$ MurEpBarC^{a} 1$_{5}$ CD 9$_{1.2}$ 14$_{11}$, אֲדָמָה *land* Gn 47$_{20}$, אֹהֶל *tent* Gn 31$_{34}$ Nm 18$_{3}$, אַוָּה *desire* Dt 12$_{15.20.21}$ 18$_{6}$ 1 S 23$_{20}$ 11QT 60$_{13}$, אֱוִיל *fool* Pr 20$_{3}$ 4Q417 18$_{5}$ 4Q418 69.2$_{8}$, אָוֶן *iniquity* Ps 119$_{133}$, *trouble* Pr 12$_{21}$, אוֹן *strength* Ps 105$_{36}$ 4QParGenEx 3$_{12}$, אוֹצָר *treasury* 2 K 24$_{13}$ Jr 17$_{3}$ 20$_{5}$ 1 C 26$_{26}$, אוֹר *light* 4QpIsa^{d} 1$_{6}$ 4Q415 5$_{2}$, אוֹת *sign* Ex 4$_{28}$ Nm 14$_{11}$ Dt 34$_{11}$ 1 S 10$_{9}$ 4QBibPar 1$_{15}$ Lachish ost. 4$_{11}$, אוּט *storehouse* 4Q418 126.2$_{2}$ 4Q423 1.1$_{5}$, אֹזֶן *ear* 4Q474 1$_{10}$, אֶזְרָח *citizen* Lv 23$_{42}$ Nm 15$_{13}$ 1QSa 1$_{6}$ 4Q423 5$_{5}$, אָח *brother* Gn 16$_{12}$ 25$_{18}$ 27$_{37}$ 37$_{4}$ 45$_{15}$ Ex 1$_{6}$ Nm 16$_{10}$ Dt 18$_{7}$ 1 K 1$_{9}$ Is 66$_{20}$ Jr 7$_{15}$ 9$_{3.3}$ Jb 42$_{11}$ Pr 19$_{7}$ 1 C 12$_{33}$ 2 C 21$_{4}$ 1QM 15$_{7}$ 1QSa 2$_{12}$ 4QRP^{b} 1$_{1}$ 4QapJoseph^{b} 1$_{19}$ 11QT 60$_{14}$ Meṣad Ḥashavyahu ost. 1$_{10}$, אֶחָד *one* 1QS 1$_{13}$ (כול אחד מכול דברי אל *any one of all the words of God*), אָחוֹר *back* of oxen 1 K 7$_{25}$||2 C 4$_{4}$, אָחוֹת *sister* Jb 42$_{11}$, אִי *island* Zp 2$_{11}$, אֹיֵב *enemy* Ex 23$_{27}$ Dt 6$_{19}$ 12$_{10}$ 25$_{19}$ Jos 10$_{25}$ 21$_{44.44}$ 23$_{1}$ Jg 5$_{31}$ 8$_{34}$ 1 S 14$_{47}$ 2 S 3$_{18}$ 7$_{1.9.11}$||1 C 17$_{8.10}$ 2 S 19$_{10(ms)}$ 22$_{1}$ ||Ps 18$_{1}$ 2 K 17$_{39}$ 21$_{14}$ Mc 5$_{8}$ Ps 3$_{8}$ 6$_{11}$ 21$_{9}$ 89$_{43}$ Lm 1$_{21}$ 2$_{16}$ 3$_{46}$ Est 9$_{5}$ Ne 6$_{16}$ 1 C 22$_{9}$ 1QM 9$_{6}$ 10$_{1}$ 4QMidrEschat^{a} 3$_{7}$ 4QapLam^{a} 1$_{14}$ 4QPrayer^{e} 1$_{5}$ 11QT 59$_{19}$, אַיִל *ram* Ex 29$_{18}$ Lv 8$_{21}$ 11QT 15$_{3a}$ 35$_{14}$.

אִישׁ *man* Gn 17$_{27}$ 29$_{22}$ 45$_{1}$ Ex 4$_{19}$ 25$_{2}$ 35$_{21.22.23.29}$ 36$_{1.2}$ Lv 21$_{18.21}$ 22$_{3}$ Nm 14$_{22}$ Dt 2$_{16}$ 4$_{3}$ 21$_{21}$ 27$_{14}$ 29$_{9}$ Jos 1$_{18}$ 5$_{4}$ 6$_{3}$ 8$_{25}$ 10$_{2.24}$ Jg 3$_{29}$ 7$_{8.24}$ 9$_{49.51}$ 12$_{4}$ 20$_{11.33}$ 1 S 2$_{13}$ 11$_{1.15}$ 14$_{22.52}$ 17$_{19.24}$ 22$_{2.2.2}$ 30$_{22}$ 31$_{6.12}$||1 C 10$_{7.12}$ 2 S 1$_{11}$ 13$_{9.9}$ 15$_{2.4.22}$ 16$_{18}$ 17$_{12.14.24}$ 19$_{15.42.42.43}$ 20$_{2.13}$ 1 K 1$_{9}$ 8$_{2}$||2 C 5$_{3}$ 2 K 23$_{2}$||2 C 34$_{30}$ 2 K 24$_{16}$ 25$_{4}$||Jr 52$_{7}$ Jr 29$_{26}$ 39$_{4}$ 41$_{12}$ 42$_{17}$ 43$_{2}$ 44$_{15.26.27}$ 49$_{26}$ 50$_{30}$ 51$_{43}$ Ezk 9$_{6}$ 27$_{27}$ 39$_{20}$ Jl 4$_{9}$ Ob 7 Ps 76$_{6}$ Jb 37$_{7}$ Est 1$_{22}$ 4$_{11}$ Ezr 10$_{9.17}$ Ne 5$_{13}$ 11$_{2}$ 1 C 16$_{3}$ 2 C 2$_{16}$ 20$_{27}$ Si 10$_{23}$ 11$_{29}$ 1QH 4$_{20}$ 6$_{13.18}$ 1QM 1$_{5.15}$ 4$_{2}$ 7$_{5.12}$ 9$_{3}$ 15$_{4}$ 14$_{18}$ 1QS 2$_{1.4.22}$ 5$_{10.23}$ 6$_{12}$ (others יכיל איש *he will restrain a man*) 7$_{20.22}$ 8$_{16.21}$ 9$_{20}$ 1QSa 1$_{19}$ 2$_{3.4}$ 1Q31.1$_{1}$ 1Q36.7$_{2}$ 2QJub^{a}$_{2}$ 4QpPs^{a} 2$_{7}$ 4QTanḥ 17$_{3}$ 4QMidr Eschat^{b} 9$_{4}$ 10$_{14}$ 4QJub^{f} 33$_{14}$ 39$_{6}$ 4QD^{a} 6.1$_{14}$ 4QapPs^{b} 48$_{9}$ 4Q415 2.2$_{8}$ 4Q416 2.3$_{5}$ 4Q418 94$_{2}$ 4QWays^{b} 2$_{3}$ 4QM^{h} 4$_{2}$ 4QM^{a} 1$_{6}$ 4QShir^{b} 63.2$_{4}$ 63.3$_{5}$ 4QOrd^{c} 1.1$_{10}$ 5QRègle 1$_{13}$ 6QBen 1$_{2}$ 11QT 27$_{6}$ 35$_{2.3}$ 45$_{12.15}$ 49$_{8}$ 50$_{4.21}$ 64$_{5}$ CD 8$_{21}$ 9$_{2}$ 12$_{2}$ 19$_{33}$ 20$_{14}$, אֹכֶל *food* Gn 14$_{11}$ 41$_{35.48}$ Lv 11$_{34}$ Ps 107$_{18}$ 11QT 35$_{4}$ 47$_{6.12}$ 49$_{7}$, אֵל *god* Dn 11$_{36}$ 4QShirShabb^{a} 1.1$_{4}$ 4QShirShabb^{d} 1.1$_{14.18.30.35.38.38}$ 1.2$_{33.35}$ 4QShirShabb^{f} 13$_{2}$ 4QM^{a} 24$_{3}$ 11QMelch 2$_{14}$, אָלָה *curse* Dt 29$_{19.20}$ 30$_{7}$ 2 C 34$_{24}$ 1QS 2$_{15}$ 4QD 10$_{5}$, אֵלָה *terebinth* Ezk 6$_{13}$.

אֵלֶּה *these (things)* Gn 10$_{29}$||1 C 1$_{23}$ Gn 14$_{3}$ 15$_{10}$ 25$_{4}$ ||1 C 1$_{33}$ Gn 49$_{28}$ Lv 18$_{24.24}$ 20$_{23}$ 22$_{25}$ Dt 3$_{5}$ Jg 13$_{23}$ 20$_{25.35.44.46}$ 1 K 7$_{9}$ 2 K 10$_{9}$ Is 45$_{7}$ 66$_{2.2}$ Jr 2$_{34}$ 3$_{7}$ 5$_{19}$ 14$_{22}$ Ezk 16$_{30.43}$ 17$_{18}$ 18$_{11}$ Hg 2$_{13}$ Zc 8$_{12.17}$ Jb 12$_{9}$ 33$_{29}$ Ec 7$_{28}$ 11$_{9}$ Dn 12$_{7}$ Ezr 10$_{44}$ 1 C 2$_{23}$ 7$_{8.11.40}$ 8$_{38.40}$ 9$_{9}$ 12$_{39}$ 25$_{5.6}$ 26$_{8}$ 27$_{31}$ 29$_{17}$ 2 C 14$_{7}$ 21$_{2}$ 29$_{32}$ Si 35$_{13}$ ([כ]ל [א]לה) 37$_{15}$ 39$_{27}$ (Segal) (כל א[לה]) 39$_{30}$ 44$_{7}$ 4QpsMos^{e} 2.1$_{2}$ 4Q418 96$_{2}$ 123.2$_{5}$ 4QBark^{d} 3$_{4}$ 4QBark^{e} 5$_{3}$ 4QPrayer^{d} 1.1$_{2}$ 4QDibHam^{a} 1.6$_{4}$ 11QPs^{a} 27$_{11}$ 11QPsAp^{a} 3$_{7}$, אֱלֹהִים *gods* Gn 35$_{4}$ Ex 12$_{12}$ 18$_{11}$ 2 K 18$_{35}$||Is 36$_{20}$||2 C 32$_{14}$ Zp 2$_{11}$ Ps 95$_{3}$ 96$_{4.5}$||1 C 16$_{25.26}$ Ps 97$_{7.9}$ 135$_{5}$ 2 C 2$_{4}$ 4QShirShabb^{d} 1.1$_{2.32.32}$ 4QShirShabb^{f} 23.1$_{13}$ 24$_{3}$ MasShirShabb 2$_{5}$, אֱלוֹהַּ *god* Dn 11$_{37}$ 2 C 32$_{15}$, אַלּוֹן *oak* Is 2$_{13}$, אַלְמָנָה *widow*

Ex 22$_{21}$, אֶלֶף *thousand* 1 S 23$_{23}$, אֻמָּה *people* GnzPs 1$_{18.23}$ 2$_{11}$, אֱמֹרִי *Amorite* 4QSela 1.2$_{3}$, אֹמֶר *word* 1QS 9$_{25}$ 4QapJoseph^{a} 1$_{13}$ 4QapJoseph^{b} 3$_{6}$, אֵמֶר *word* Jos 24$_{27}$ Pr 8$_{8}$, אִמְרָה *word* Pr 30$_{5}$, אֱמֶת *faithfulness* Gn 32$_{11}$, אֱנוֹשׁ *human being* Jr 20$_{10}$ Si 38$_{5}$, אֲנָחָה *sighing* Is 21$_{2}$, אֳנִיָּה *ship* Is 2$_{16}$ Ezk 27$_{9}$, אָסוֹן *harm* Si 34$_{22}$, אָסִיר *prisoner* Gn 39$_{22}$ Lm 3$_{34}$, אֲסַפְסֻף *rabble* 4QMidrEschat^{b} 9$_{4}$, אִסָּר *vow* Nm 30$_{5.12.15}$, אָפִיק *channel* Is 8$_{7}$ Ezk 31$_{12}$ 35$_{8}$ Jl 4$_{18}$ 4QBer^{a} 5$_{2}$, אֲפֵלָה *darkness* 4Q392 1$_{5}$, אֶפֶס *end* Is 45$_{22}$ 52$_{10}$ Ps 22$_{28}$ 67$_{8}$ 98$_{3}$ Pr 30$_{4}$ Si 36$_{22}$, אַצִּיל *joint* Ezk 13$_{18}$, אֲרֻבָּה *window* 4QAdmon 1.1$_{4}$, אֶרֶז *cedar* Is 2$_{13}$ Ps 148$_{9}$ 4QBer^{a} 5$_{5}$, אֹרַח *way* Ps 25$_{10}$ 119$_{101.104.128}$ Jb 13$_{27}$ 33$_{11}$ 4QapLam^{a} 2$_{7}$ 4Q424 1$_{7}$, אֹרֶךְ *length* Ezk 48$_{13}$, אַרְמוֹן *fortress* Lm 2$_{5}$ 2 C 36$_{19}$ 4QapLam^{a} 1$_{10}$ 2$_{6}$.

אֶרֶץ *earth, land, ground* Gn 1$_{26.29}$ 2$_{11.13}$ 7$_{3}$ 8$_{9}$ 9$_{19}$ 11$_{1.4.8.9.9}$ 13$_{9.15}$ 17$_{8}$ 18$_{25}$ 19$_{31}$ 26$_{3.4}$ 41$_{19+9t}$ 45$_{8.20.26}$ 47$_{13}$ Ex 5$_{12}$ 7$_{19.21}$ 8$_{12.13.20}$ 9$_{9.9.14.16.22.24.25}$ 10$_{14.15.15.22}$ 11$_{6}$ 19$_{5}$ 32$_{13}$ 34$_{10}$ Lv 25$_{9.24}$ Nm 14$_{21}$ 21$_{26}$ Dt 11$_{3.25}$ 19$_{8}$ 28$_{52.52}$ 29$_{1.22}$ 34$_{1.2.11}$ Jos 1$_{4}$ 2$_{3.24}$ 3$_{11.13}$ 6$_{27}$ 9$_{24}$ 10$_{40.41}$ 11$_{16.16.23}$ 13$_{4}$ 21$_{43}$ 23$_{14}$ 24$_{3}$ Jg 6$_{37.39.40}$ 11$_{21}$ 1 S 13$_{3.19}$ 14$_{25}$ 17$_{46}$ 30$_{16}$ 2 S 15$_{23}$ 18$_{8}$ 24$_{8}$ 1 K 2$_{2}$ 4$_{10}$ 9$_{19}$||2 C 8$_{6}$ 1 K 10$_{24}$ 15$_{20}$ 2 K 5$_{15}$ 10$_{33}$ 15$_{29}$ 17$_{5}$ 19$_{11}$||Is 37$_{11}$ Is 6$_{3}$ 7$_{24}$ 10$_{14.23}$ 12$_{5}$ 13$_{5}$ 14$_{7.26}$ 25$_{8}$ 28$_{22}$ 37$_{18}$ 54$_{5}$=4QTanḥ 8$_{7}$ Jr 1$_{18}$ 4$_{20.27}$ 8$_{16}$ 12$_{11}$ 15$_{10}$ 16$_{15}$ 23$_{3.8.15}$ 25$_{11}$ 27$_{6}$ 32$_{37}$ 40$_{4.11}$ 44$_{26}$ 45$_{4}$ 50$_{23}$ 51$_{7+6t}$ Ezk 20$_{6.15}$ 22$_{4}$ 32$_{4}$ 35$_{14}$ 36$_{24}$ Mc 4$_{13}$ Hb 2$_{20}$ Zp 1$_{18}$ 3$_{8.19}$ Zc 1$_{11}$ 4$_{10.14}$ 5$_{3.6}$ 6$_{5}$ 13$_{8}$ 14$_{9.10}$ Ps 8$_{2.10}$ 19$_{5}$ 33$_{8}$ 45$_{17}$ 47$_{3.8}$ 48$_{3}$ 57$_{6.12}$ 66$_{1.4}$ 72$_{19}$ 83$_{19}$ 96$_{1.9}$||1 C 16$_{23.30}$ 97$_{5.9}$ 98$_{4}$ 100$_{1}$ 105$_{7}$||1 C 16$_{14}$ Ps 108$_{6}$ Jb 42$_{15}$ Lm 2$_{15}$ Dn 8$_{5}$ 9$_{7}$ 1 C 13$_{2}$ 14$_{17}$ 22$_{5}$ 2 C 9$_{28}$ 11$_{23}$ 15$_{8}$ 16$_{9}$ 34$_{7.33}$ Si 48$_{15}$ 1QM 2$_{7}$ 11$_{13}$ 4QJub^{a} 2$_{4.8.14}$ 4QJub^{d} 21$_{22.25}$ 4QJub^{f} 21$_{22}$ 4QJub^{h} 32$_{19.19}$ 40$_{1.3.3.4.6}$ 4QPrEnosh 2$_{2}$ 4QapJoseph^{b} 1$_{5.5}$ 4QDiscourse 2.1$_{4}$ 2.2$_{5}$ 4QapPs^{b} 69$_{2}$ 4QparaKings 105$_{5}$ 4QpsEzek^{c} 3.2$_{7}$ 4QParGenEx 3$_{8}$ 4QDibHam^{a} 1.4$_{3}$ 11QPsAp^{a} 3$_{3}$ 11QT 52$_{3}$ GnzPs 1$_{9}$ Kh. Beit Lei graf. 5$_{1}$, אשׁ *foundation* 1QH 7$_{4}$ 1QSb 3$_{20}$ 11QShirShabb 5$_{7}$, אִשָּׁה *woman* Ex 15$_{20}$ 35$_{25.26}$ Nm 31$_{17}$ Jg 21$_{11}$ 1 K 11$_{8}$ Jr 38$_{22.23}$ 44$_{15.24}$ Ezk 23$_{48}$ Est 1$_{17.20}$ 2$_{17}$ Ezr 10$_{3}$ 2 C 11$_{21}$ 4QTohA 1.1$_{6}$, אִשֶּׁה *fire offering* 1 S 2$_{28}$, אָשָׁם *guilt offering* Nm 18$_{9}$ CD 9$_{13}$, אַשְׁמָה *guilt* 11QT 18$_{7}$ 26$_{12}$ 59$_{9}$, אֶתְנָה *fee* Mc 1$_{7}$.

בְּאֵר *well* Gn 26$_{15}$, בֶּגֶד *garment* Lv 15$_{17}$ Nm 31$_{20}$ Ps 45$_{9}$ 4QBéat 3.3$_{6}$, בְּדִיל *tin* Is 1$_{25}$, בְּהֵמָה *beast* Gn 2$_{20}$ 3$_{14}$ 7$_{2.14}$ 8$_{1.20}$ 34$_{23}$ 36$_{6}$ Ex 22$_{9}$ Lv 11$_{2.26}$ 18$_{23}$ 20$_{16}$ 27$_{11}$ Nm 31$_{9.30}$ 32$_{26}$ Dt 3$_{7}$ 4$_{17}$ 5$_{14}$ 14$_{6}$ 27$_{21}$ Is 18$_{6}$ Ezk 32$_{13}$ Zc 14$_{15}$ Ps 148$_{10}$ 2 C 32$_{28}$ 4QBibPar 10$_{13}$ 4QJub^{a} 2$_{13}$ 11QT 52$_{16}$ 55$_{8}$, בָּחוּר *youth* 2 S 6$_{1}$ 10$_{9(mss)}$||1 C 19$_{10}$, בָּחִיר *chosen one* GnzPs 1$_{21}$ 1QH 14$_{15}$, בִּינָה *insight* 1QH fr. 15$_{8}$ 1Q29.13$_{2}$ 4QShirShabb^{a} 2$_{4}$, בַּיִת *house* Gn 7$_{1}$ 34$_{19}$ 41$_{51}$ 45$_{8}$ 47$_{12}$ 50$_{8}$ Ex 40$_{38}$ Lv 10$_{6}$ Nm 12$_{7}$ 20$_{29}$ Dt 6$_{22}$ Jos 2$_{18}$ Jg 16$_{31}$ 1 S 1$_{21}$ 7$_{2.3}$ 9$_{20}$ 22$_{1.11.15.16}$ 25$_{17}$ 2 S 3$_{19.29}$ 6$_{5.11.15.21}$ 9$_{9}$ 15$_{16}$ 19$_{21.29}$ 6$_{10.22.22}$ 7$_{1}$ 12$_{21.23}$ 13$_{32}$ 15$_{29}$ 16$_{11.12}$ 2 K 9$_{8}$ 20$_{13}$ 2 K 23$_{19}$ 25$_{9.9}$||Jr 52$_{13.13}$ Is 24$_{10}$ 32$_{13}$ 39$_{2}$ Jr 9$_{25}$ 13$_{11.11}$ 19$_{13}$ 35$_{3}$ Ezk 3$_{7}$ 5$_{4}$ 11$_{15}$ 12$_{10}$ 20$_{40}$ 36$_{10}$ 37$_{11.16}$ 39$_{25}$ 41$_{19}$ 45$_{6}$ Pr 31$_{21}$ Ne 4$_{10}$ 1 C 10$_{6}$ 28$_{4}$ 2 C 29$_{18}$ Si 11$_{30}$ 4QJub^{h} 40$_{7}$ 4QD^{e} 3.2$_{19}$ 4QTohA 1.1$_{2}$ 4QapPent 5$_{3}$ 11QT 33$_{11}$ 49$_{5}$ 50$_{11}$ MurEp Beth-Mashiko 1$_{7}$, בֵּית שְׁאָן *Beth-shean* 1 K 4$_{12}$ (or del.), בְּכוֹר *firstborn* Ex 11$_{5.5}$ 12$_{12.29.29}$ 13$_{2.13}$ (if em. פֶּטֶר *firstborn*) 13$_{13.15.15}$ 34$_{20}$ Nm 3$_{12+9t}$ 8$_{17.17.18}$ 33$_{4}$ Dt 15$_{19}$ Ezk 44$_{30}$ Ps 78$_{51}$ 105$_{36}$ 11QT 52$_{7}$ 60$_{2}$, בְּלִיַּעַל *Belial, wicked one* 1QH 3$_{28}$ 4QHod^{f} 4.2$_{3}$, בָּמָה *high place* Nm 33$_{52}$ 2 K 17$_{11}$.

בֵּן *son* Gn 10$_{21}$ 17$_{12}$ 37$_{3.35}$ Ex 1$_{22}$ 10$_{23}$ 11$_{7}$ 12$_{42.43.50}$ 16$_{6}$ 32$_{26}$ 34$_{30.32}$ Lv 7$_{10}$ 17$_{2}$ 21$_{24}$ 22$_{18}$ Nm 14$_{2.10.39}$ 17$_{24}$ 24$_{17}$ =4QTestim$_{13}$ Nm 27$_{21}$ Dt 3$_{18}$ Jos 3$_{1}$ 7$_{23}$ 20$_{9}$ Jg 2$_{4}$ 7$_{12}$ 9$_{2}$ 10$_{8}$ 20$_{1.26}$ 1 S 1$_{4}$ 14$_{52}$ 15$_{6}$ 2 S 7$_{7}$ 13$_{23.27.29.30.33}$ 1 K 1$_{19.25}$ 5$_{10}$ 8$_{39.63}$ 18$_{20}$ 20$_{15}$ 2 K 17$_{11}$ Is 51$_{18.18}$ 54$_{13}$ Jr 35$_{3}$ Ezk 23$_{23}$ 44$_{9.9}$ Ps 33$_{13}$ 89$_{48}$ Jb 1$_{3}$ 38$_{7}$ 41$_{26}$ Pr 31$_{5.8}$ Ezr 6$_{20}$ 10$_{7}$ Ne 9$_{2}$ 11$_{6}$ 1 C 2$_{4}$ 3$_{9}$ 26$_{11}$ 28$_{5}$ 29$_{24}$ 2 C 7$_{3}$ 11$_{23}$ 25$_{7}$ 31$_{1}$ 35$_{13}$ Si 16$_{17}$ 50$_{13}$ 1QH 4$_{32}$ 6$_{29.30}$ 7$_{11.29}$ 9$_{35}$ 11$_{9}$ 1QM 1$_{7}$ ([כול]) 1$_{9}$ 2$_{12.13.14}$ 3$_{6.9}$ 11$_{6.14}$ 13$_{10.16.16}$ 14$_{17}$ 17$_{8}$ 1QS 1$_{9.10}$ 2$_{16}$ 3$_{13.13.20.22.24}$ 4$_{5.15}$ 2QJub^{a} 2$_{2}$ 4QMidrEschat^{a} 4$_{1}$ 4QMidrEschat^{b} 11$_{12.16}$ 4QJub^{a} 1$_{28}$ 4QJub^{h} 36$_{22}$ 4QD^{a} 11$_{7}$ 4QBer^{a} 7.2$_{6}$ 4QCrypt A 1$_{1}$ 4QapJoseph^{a} 7$_{2}$ 4QapJoseph^{b} 1$_{21}$ 5$_{4}$ 17$_{2}$ 4QapPs^{a} 1.2$_{3}$ 4Q416 1$_{10}$ 4Q418 2$_{2}$ 126.2$_{9}$ 201$_{2}$ 4QHod^{a} 7.2$_{12}$ 4QRitMar 48$_{2}$ 4QShir^{b} 1$_{8}$ 4QBéat 8$_{3}$ 4QUnidD 1$_{2}$ 11QMelch 2$_{8.14}$ 11QT 23$_{01}$ 27$_{2}$ 33$_{9}$ 58$_{19}$ 60$_{11}$ 64$_{6}$ CD 20$_{34}$ GnzPs 1$_{5}$, בַּעַל *lord* Dt 15$_{2}$ Jg 9$_{2.3.6.46.47.51}$ Pr 1$_{17}$ 11QMelch 2$_{3}$, בִּקְעָה *valley-plain* 4QSela 1.1$_{3}$, בָּקָר *cattle* Nm 7$_{87.88}$ 4Q408 7$_{2}$, בַּקָּשָׁה *request* Ezr 7$_{6}$ GnzPs 3$_{2}$, בֵּרִי *Berite* 2 S 20$_{14}$, בְּרִיאָה *creation* Si 16$_{16}$ 4QBer^{b} 3$_{2}$ 4QDibHam^{a} 1.7$_{9}$, בְּרִית *covenant* 1QH 17$_{27}$, בֶּרֶךְ *knee* 1 K 19$_{18}$ Is 45$_{23}$ Ezk 7$_{17}$ 21$_{12}$, בְּרָכָה *blessing* Dt 28$_{2}$ Ne 9$_{5}$ Si 3$_{8}$ 1QS 4$_{7}$ 1QSb 1$_{5}$ 4QJub^{d} 21$_{25}$ 4QapJoshua^{b} 15$_{1}$ 4QShirShabb^{d} 1.1$_{28}$ 4QBéat 12$_{1}$ 11QShirShabb 1$_{3}$, בֹּשֶׂם *perfume* Ezk 27$_{22}$ Ca 4$_{10}$, בָּשָׂר *flesh* Gn 6$_{12.13.17.19}$ 7$_{15.16.21}$ 8$_{17}$ 9$_{11.15.15.16.17}$ Lv 4$_{11}$ 13$_{13}$ 15$_{16}$ 17$_{14.14.14}$ Nm 8$_{7}$ 16$_{22}$

18$_{15}$ 27$_{16}$ Dt 5$_{26}$ Is 40$_{5.6}$ 49$_{26}$ 66$_{16.23.24}$ Jr 12$_{12}$ 25$_{31}$ 32$_{27}$ 45$_{5}$ Ezk 10$_{12}$ 21$_{4.9.10}$ Jl 3$_{1}$ Zc 2$_{17}$ Ps 65$_{3}$ 136$_{25}$ 145$_{21}$ Jb 34$_{15}$ Pr 4$_{22}$ Si 8$_{19}$ 13$_{15.16}$ 14$_{17}$ 30$_{29 (Segal)}$ ([בשר]) 39$_{19}$ 41$_{4}$ 44$_{18}$ 45$_{4}$ 48$_{12}$ 50$_{17}$ 1QM 4$_{3}$ 15$_{13}$ 17$_{8}$ 1QSb 3$_{28}$ 1QlitPr 3.1$_{3}$ 4QJub^{a} 2$_{12}$ 4QJub^{e} 21$_{7}$ 4QD^{b} 1$_{8}$ 4QapPs^{b} 29$_{3}$ 4QShir^{b} 7$_{3}$ 35$_{1}$ 4QBéat 8$_{5}$ 11QPs^{a} 19$_{4}$ 11QT 45$_{16}$ CD 1$_{2}$ 2$_{20}$ GnzPs 3$_{22}$, בָּשָׁן *Bashan* Dt 3$_{10.13.13}$ Jos 12$_{5}$ 13$_{11.30}$, בֹּשֶׁת *shame* Si 41$_{16}$, בַּת *daughter* Gn 37$_{35}$ Ex 1$_{22}$ Nm 21$_{25}$ 36$_{8}$ Ec 12$_{4}$ Lm 3$_{51}$ 4QapLam^{a} 2$_{5.8}$ 4QJub^{g} 25$_{9}$ 11QT 57$_{15}$, בְּתוּלָה *virgin* Est 2$_{17}$, בִּתְרוֹן *morning* 2 S 2$_{29}$.

גֵּאֶה *proud one* Is 2$_{12}$ Jb 40$_{11.12}$, גֶּבֶא *cistern* CD 10$_{12}$, גָּבֹהַּ *exalted one* Jb 41$_{26}$ Pr 16$_{5}$, גֹּבַהּ *height* 11QT 5$_{7}$ 6$_{5}$, גְּבוּל *border* Gn 23$_{17}$ Ex 7$_{27}$ 10$_{14.19}$ 13$_{7}$ Dt 16$_{4}$ 28$_{40}$ Jg 11$_{22}$ 19$_{29}$ 1 S 11$_{3.7}$ 27$_{1}$ 2 S 21$_{5}$ 1 K 1$_{3}$ 2 K 10$_{32}$ Is 54$_{12}$ Jr 15$_{13}$ 17$_{3}$ Ezk 43$_{12}$ 45$_{1}$ 105$_{31}$ 1 C 21$_{12}$ 4QpNah 5$_{2}$ 4QParGen Ex 3$_{8.10}$, גְּבוּלָה *border* Ps 74$_{17}$, גִּבּוֹר *warrior* Jos 1$_{14}$ 10$_{7}$ 2 S 16$_{6}$ 20$_{7}$ 2 K 15$_{20}$ 24$_{14.16}$ Jr 26$_{21}$ 2 C 32$_{21}$ 1QH 6$_{33}$ 1QM 14$_{8.11}$ 4QShir^{a} 1$_{3}$ 11QT 58$_{16}$ GnzPs 1$_{25}$, גְּבוּרָה *strength* 2 K 10$_{34}$ 20$_{20}$ Mc 7$_{16}$ 1QH 11$_{8}$ 4QMyst^{a} 6.1$_{16}$ 4QShirShabb^{d} 1.1$_{21}$, גִּבְעָה *hill* 1 K 14$_{23}$ 2 K 17$_{10}$ Is 2$_{14}$ 30$_{25}$ Jr 2$_{20}$ 4$_{24}$ 16$_{16}$ Ezk 6$_{13}$ 20$_{28}$ 34$_{6}$ Am 9$_{13}$ Ps 148$_{9}$ 4QBer^{a} 5$_{2}$, גֶּבֶר *man* Jr 30$_{6}$ Si 10$_{5}$ 4QOrd^{b} 14$_{4}$, גַּג *roof* Jr 48$_{38}$, גְּדוּד *troops* 1QM 1$_{3}$, גָּדוֹל *great one* 2 K 8$_{4}$ Na 3$_{10}$ 4QPrayers^{a} 3$_{5}$, גְּדוּלָּה *greatness* 2 S 7$_{21}$||1 C 17$_{19}$ 1 C 17$_{19}$ Si 3$_{18}$, גָּדָה *riverbank* Jos 3$_{15}$ 4$_{18}$ Is 8$_{7}$ 1 C 12$_{6}$ 4QapJoshua^{b} 12$_{6}$, גְּדֵרָה *wall* Ps 89$_{41}$, גּוֹי *nation* Gn 18$_{18}$ 22$_{18}$ 26$_{4}$ Ex 34$_{10}$ Dt 11$_{23}$ 17$_{14}$ 26$_{19}$ 28$_{1}$ 29$_{23}$ 30$_{1}$ Jos 3$_{17}$ 4$_{1}$ 5$_{6.8}$ 23$_{3.4}$ 1 S 8$_{5.20}$ 2 S 8$_{11}$||1 C 18$_{11}$ 1 K 5$_{11}$ Is 2$_{2}$ 14$_{26}$ 25$_{7}$ 29$_{7.8}$ 34$_{2}$ Is 40$_{17}$ 43$_{9}$ 52$_{10}$ 61$_{11}$ 66$_{18.20}$ Jr 3$_{17}$ 9$_{25}$ 25$_{9.13.15.17}$ 26$_{6}$ 27$_{7}$ 28$_{11.14}$ 29$_{14.18}$ 30$_{11}$ 33$_{9}$ 36$_{2}$ 43$_{5}$ 44$_{8}$ 46$_{28}$ Ezk 25$_{8}$ 31$_{6}$ 39$_{21}$ Jl 4$_{2.11.12}$ Am 9$_{9.12}$ Ob$_{15.16}$ Hb 2$_{5}$ Hg 2$_{7.7}$ Zc 7$_{14}$ 12$_{3.9}$ 14$_{2.14.16.19}$ Ml 3$_{12}$ Ps 9$_{18}$ 59$_{6.9}$ 67$_{3}$ 72$_{11.17}$ 82$_{8}$ 86$_{9}$ 113$_{4}$ 117$_{1}$ 118$_{10}$ 147$_{20}$ Ne 6$_{16}$ 1 C 14$_{17}$ 2 C 32$_{15.23}$ Si 33$_{2}$ 46$_{6}$ 1QH 6$_{12}$ 1QM 4$_{12}$ 6$_{6}$ 14$_{7}$ 15$_{1.2}$ 16$_{1}$ 19$_{10}$ 1QpHab 3$_{4}$ 5$_{4}$ 13$_{1}$ 4QpIsa^{a} 8$_{4.20}$ 4QJub^{a} 1$_{13}$ 2$_{21}$ 4QJub^{h} 32$_{19}$ 4QMyst^{a} 10$_{3}$ 4QapJoseph^{b} 1$_{17}$ 9$_{3}$ 4QapJoshua^{a} 3.1$_{9}$ 4QapPs^{b} 77$_{16}$ 4QBark^{a} 1.1$_{7}$ 4QM^{a} 15$_{6}$ 4QM^{b} 2$_{1}$ 4QPrQuot 24$_{4}$ 4QDibHam^{a} 1.3$_{3.5}$ 1.4$_{8}$ 4QDibHam^{b} 125$_{4}$ 11QT 56$_{13}$ 58$_{3}$ GnzPs 1$_{19}$, גּוֹלָה *diaspora* Jr 28$_{6}$ 29$_{4.20.31}$, גּוֹרָל *party* 1QM 1$_{5}$ 4QBer^{a} 7.2$_{2.9}$ 4QShirShabb^{f} 46$_{2}$, גַּיְא *valley* Is 40$_{4}$=4QTanḥ 1$_{7}$ Ezk 31$_{12}$, גִּיל *rejoicing* 4Q418 69.2$_{4}$, גִּלּוּל *idol* 1 K 15$_{12}$ Ezk 6$_{13}$ 8$_{10}$ 20$_{31}$ 23$_{7}$ 36$_{25}$ 1QS 4$_{5}$ 4QMidrEschat^{a} 3$_{16}$, גָּלוּת *diaspora* Jr 28$_{4}$ 29$_{22}$ 40$_{1}$, גְּלִילָה *district* Jos 13$_{2}$ Jl 4$_{4}$, גִּלְעָד *Gilead* Dt 3$_{10}$, גְּמוּל *reward* Ps 103$_{2}$, גָּמָל *camel* Gn 24$_{20}$, גֶּרֶם *bone* 1QH 4$_{33}$, גֹּרֶן *threshing floor* Ho 9$_{1}$, גִּתִּי *Gittite* 2 S 15$_{18}$.

דְּבִיר *inner sanctuary* 4QShirShabb^{f} 23.1$_{13}$, דָּבָר *word, thing, matter* Gn 20$_{8}$ 24$_{66}$ 29$_{13}$ 45$_{27}$ Ex 4$_{28.30}$ 18$_{22.22.26}$ 19$_{7}$ 20$_{1}$ 22$_{8}$ 24$_{3.3.4.8}$ Lv 5$_{2}$ 8$_{36}$ Nm 16$_{31}$ 18$_{7}$ 31$_{23}$ Dt 1$_{18}$ 4$_{30}$ 9$_{10}$ 12$_{28}$ 13$_{1}$ 17$_{1.19}$ 23$_{10.20}$ 24$_{5}$ 27$_{3.8}$ 28$_{14.58}$ 29$_{28}$ 30$_{1}$ 31$_{12}$ 32$_{44.45.46.46}$ Jos 4$_{10}$ 8$_{34}$ 21$_{45}$ 23$_{14.15.15}$ Jg 9$_{3}$ 11$_{11}$ 18$_{10}$ 19$_{19}$ 1 S 3$_{17.18.19}$ 8$_{10.21}$ 19$_{7}$ 25$_{9.12}$ 2 S 7$_{17}$||1 C 17$_{15}$ 2 S 11$_{18.19}$ 13$_{21}$ 14$_{19}$ 15$_{11.35.36}$ 18$_{13}$ 1 K 6$_{38}$ 8$_{56}$ 10$_{3}$||2 C 9$_{2}$ 1 K 15$_{23}$ 18$_{36}$ 2 K 19$_{4}$ 22$_{16}$ 23$_{2}$||2 C 34$_{30}$ Is 37$_{17}$ Jr 7$_{27}$ 11$_{6.8}$ 16$_{10}$ 18$_{18}$ 25$_{13.30}$ 26$_{2.12.15.20}$ 27$_{12}$ 30$_{2}$ 32$_{17.27}$ 34$_{6}$ 36$_{2+11t}$ 38$_{27}$ 42$_{4.5}$ 43$_{1.1}$ 44$_{17}$ 51$_{60.61}$ Ezk 3$_{10}$ 11$_{25}$ 12$_{28}$ Am 7$_{10}$ Ps 52$_{6}$ Jb 33$_{1.13}$ Pr 14$_{15}$ Ru 4$_{7}$ Ec 1$_{8}$ 7$_{21}$ Est 9$_{26}$ Dn 1$_{20}$ Ne 11$_{24}$ 1 C 26$_{32}$ 27$_{1}$ 28$_{21}$ 2 C 8$_{15}$ 19$_{11.11}$ 23$_{19}$ Si 14$_{16}$ 34$_{13}$ 42$_{1.20}$ 48$_{13}$ Si 49$_{9 (Segal)}$ ([ד]בר) 1QH 17$_{23}$ 1QM 15$_{5}$ 1QpHab 2$_{8}$ 1QS 1$_{14}$ 3$_{11}$ 5$_{3.15.15}$ 6$_{4.11}$ 7$_{1.9}$ 8$_{11.23}$ 1QDM 2$_{9}$ 3$_{3}$ 1QlitPr 3.2$_{4}$ 4QMidrEschat^{b} 10$_{1}$ 4QJub^{a} 1$_{5.6.7}$ 2$_{1}$ 4QSD 1.1$_{11}$ 4QBer^{c} 1$_{4}$ 4QRP^{b} 3.2$_{5}$ 4Qap Moses^{b} 1.3$_{2}$ 4QapMoses^{c} 2.2$_{4}$ 4QapJoshua^{b} 18$_{7}$ 4QMMT B$_{26}$ C$_{14}$ 4Q408 5$_{3}$ 4QBapt 2.1$_{5}$ 4QWays^{a} 6$_{1}$ 4QRedInk 2$_{4}$ 4QRitPur 11$_{1}$ 11QT 49$_{5}$ 54$_{5}$ 57$_{10.14}$ 58$_{17}$ 59$_{10}$ MasShirShabb 1$_{2}$ MurEpJonathan 1$_{7.8}$ papMurPalimp^{b} 1$_{2}$ ([לכ]ל) 5/6ḤevEp 12$_{4}$ CD 9$_{16}$ 14$_{11}$ GnzPs 2$_{24}$ 4$_{22}$, דְּבַשׁ *honey* Lv 2$_{11}$, דָּג *fish* Gn 9$_{2}$ Nm 11$_{22}$, דָּגָה *fish* Dt 4$_{18}$ Ezk 29$_{4.5}$, דֶּגֶל *division* 4QShirShabb^{f} 20.2$_{14}$ 4QRitMar 27$_{3}$ 4QPrQuot 7.4$_{4}$, דּוֹר *generation* Ex 1$_{6}$ Nm 32$_{13}$ Dt 2$_{14}$ Jg 2$_{10}$ Ps 45$_{18}$ 71$_{18}$ (if em. לְדוֹר לְכָל־ *to a generation; to everyone* to לְכָל־דּוֹר *to every generation*) 145$_{13}$ Est 9$_{28}$ 1QH 1$_{16}$ 1QM 14$_{9}$ 4QJub^{d} 21$_{24.25}$ 4QJub^{f} 21$_{24}$ 23$_{11}$ 4QBéat 29$_{4}$ GnzPs 4$_{11}$, דָּם *blood* Ex 29$_{12}$ Lv 3$_{17}$ 4$_{7.18.30.34}$ 7$_{26.27}$ 17$_{10}$ 2 S 16$_{8}$ 2 K 16$_{15.15}$ 4QJub^{d} 21$_{18.19}$ 4QJub^{e} 21$_{6}$, דֵּעָה *knowledge* 1QH 11$_{8}$ 1QS 11$_{18}$ 4Q418 69.2$_{11}$, דַּעַת *knowledge* 1QS 1$_{11}$ 4QJub^{f} 23$_{11}$ 4Q418 117$_{1}$, דֶּרֶךְ *way* Dt 1$_{31}$ 5$_{33}$ 8$_{2}$ 10$_{12}$ 11$_{22}$ 32$_{4}$ Jos 2$_{22}$ 22$_{5}$ 24$_{17}$ 1 S 18$_{14}$ 1 K 8$_{39}$||2 C 6$_{30}$ 1 K 8$_{58}$ 16$_{26}$ 22$_{43}$ 2 K 7$_{15}$ 21$_{21}$ 22$_{2}$ Is 45$_{13}$ Jr 7$_{23}$ 16$_{17}$ 32$_{19}$ Ezk 16$_{31.47}$ Ho 9$_{8}$ Ps 91$_{11}$ 119$_{168}$ 139$_{3}$ 145$_{17}$ Jb 34$_{27}$ Pr 3$_{6}$ 3$_{31}$ 4$_{26}$ 16$_{2}$ 21$_{2}$ 2 C 28$_{26}$ Si 35$_{23}$ 1QH 7$_{31}$ 14$_{26}$ 1QS 2$_{2}$ 3$_{10}$ 4$_{1.2.11.18}$ 5$_{4}$ 1QSb 5$_{22}$ 2QapDavid 2$_{3}$ 4QWiles 1$_{8}$ 4QJub^{h} 35$_{13}$ 36$_{23}$ 4QMyst^{b} 7$_{3}$ 4QAdmon 1.1$_{3}$ 4QapPs^{b} 31$_{3}$ 4Q408 1$_{6}$ 4Q416 2.3$_{10.14}$ 4Q417 2.1$_{7}$ 2.2$_{11}$ 4Q418 9$_{9.10.15}$ 43$_{5}$ 55$_{4}$ 87$_{10}$ 4Q419 1$_{12}$ 4Q

Ways[b] 10$_{1}$ 4QBéat 12$_{3}$ 11QPs[a] 27$_{3}$ 11QT 58$_{21}$ CD 2$_{16}$ GnzPs 3$_{26}$, דֶּשֶׁן *fat* Ps 22$_{30}$.

הֶבֶל *vanity* Ps 39$_{6}$ (mss lack כָּל־), הָדָר *majesty* Lm 1$_{6}$ 4QBéat 14.2$_{5}$, הַוָּה *destruction* 1QH 2$_{6}$ 7$_{7}$, הוֹן *wealth* Ezk 27$_{12.18}$ Ps 119$_{14}$ Pr 1$_{13}$ 6$_{31}$ 24$_{4}$ Ca 8$_{7}$ 1QH 15$_{23}$ 1QS 1$_{13}$ 5$_{20}$ 1QSb 3$_{19}$ 4Q183.2$_{5}$ 4Q416 2.2$_{6}$ 4Q418 123.1$_{2}$ 4Q424 3$_{11}$ 11QT 57$_{21}$, הֵיכָל *temple* GnzPs 2$_{26}$, הָמוֹן *army, multitude* 2 S 6$_{19}$ 1 K 20$_{13.28}$ 2 K 7$_{13.13}$ Is 16$_{14}$ Ezk 7$_{12.13.14}$ 31$_{18}$ 32$_{12+7t}$ 39$_{11}$ 1 C 29$_{16}$ 2 C 32$_{7}$ 1QM 18$_{3}$ CD 2$_{1}$, הַר *mountain* Gn 7$_{19}$ Ex 34$_{3}$ Jos 11$_{21.21}$ 13$_{11}$ Jg 7$_{24}$ Is 2$_{14}$ 7$_{25}$ 11$_{9}$ 30$_{25}$ 40$_{4}$=4QTanḥ 1$_{8}$ Is 49$_{11}$ 65$_{25}$ Jr 3$_{6}$ 16$_{16}$ Ezk 34$_{6}$ 38$_{21}$ 4QapJoseph[b] 1$_{11}$.

זֹאת *this* Gn 41$_{39}$ Dt 32$_{27.29}$ (if ins. כָּל־) Jg 6$_{13}$ 1 S 22$_{15}$ 2 S 14$_{19}$ Is 5$_{25}$ =4QpIsa[b] 2$_{9}$=4QpIsa[c] 4.1$_{18}$ ([כול זאת]) Is 9$_{11.16.20}$ 10$_{4}$ Jr 3$_{10}$ Ho 7$_{10}$ Mc 1$_{5}$=1QpMic 1$_{5}$=8$_{2}$ (1$_{5}$ כול זא[ת], 8$_{2}$ [כול זאת]) Ps 44$_{18}$ 78$_{32}$ Jb 1$_{22}$ 2$_{10}$ Ne 10$_{1}$ 2 C 21$_{18}$ 31$_{1}$ 35$_{20}$ Si 48$_{15}$ 4QDibHam[a] 1.5$_{6}$ 4QPrayer[b] 1$_{2}$, זֵד *presumptuous one* Ml 3$_{19}$ 11QPs[a] 18$_{13}$, זֶה *this* Jg 20$_{16.17}$ Ec 8$_{9}$ 9$_{1.1}$ Est 5$_{13}$ Ne 13$_{6}$ 4QJub[f] 37$_{14}$ 4QpsJub[a] 2.2$_{7}$ 4QapJoseph[b] 1$_{10.14}$ 11QT 59$_{4}$, זֹה *this* Ec 7$_{23}$, זָהָב *gold* Ex 38$_{24}$ Nm 7$_{86}$ 31$_{52}$ 2 K 14$_{14}$||2 C 25$_{24}$ 4QD[d] 8.2$_{2}$ 4QD[e] 3.3$_{20}$, זְכוּר *male* Ex 23$_{17}$||34$_{23}$||Dt 16$_{16}$ Dt 20$_{13}$, זָכָר *male* Gn 17$_{10.12.23}$ 34$_{15.22.24.25}$ Ex 12$_{48}$ Lv 6$_{11.22}$ 7$_{6}$ Nm 1$_{2.20.22}$ 3$_{15.22.28.34.39}$ 18$_{10}$ 26$_{62}$ 31$_{7.17}$ Jg 21$_{11}$ 1 K 11$_{15.16}$ 2 C 31$_{19}$ Si 36$_{26}$ (כ[ל]) 42$_{12}$, זֵכֶר *remembrance* Is 26$_{14}$, זִמָּה *plan* 4QPseud[b] 5.1$_{9}$, זְמָן *set time* 5/6 ḤevBA 44$_{25}$, זַן *kind* Si 37$_{28}$, זְנוּת *prostitution* 4QOrd[b] 2.2$_{2}$, זָקָן *beard* Is 15$_{2}$ Jr 48$_{37}$, זָקֵן *elder* Gn 50$_{7}$ Ex 4$_{29}$ 12$_{21}$ 18$_{12}$ Dt 21$_{6}$ 31$_{9.28}$ 1 S 8$_{4}$ 2 S 5$_{3}$ ||1 C 11$_{3}$ 2 S 17$_{4}$ 1 K 8$_{3}$ 20$_{7.8}$ 2 K 23$_{1}$||2 C 34$_{29}$ 2 C 5$_{4}$ 1QM 13$_{1}$ 11QT 63$_{4}$, זֵרוּעַ *plant* 4QSD 6$_{1}$, זֶרַע *seed*, i.e. offspring Gn 46$_{6.7}$ Lv 11$_{37}$ 22$_{3}$ 2 K 11$_{1}$||2 C 22$_{10}$ 2 K 17$_{20}$ Is 45$_{25}$ Jr 7$_{15}$ 31$_{37}$ Ps 22$_{24.24}$ Est 10$_{3}$ Si 45$_{25}$ 46$_{10}$ 1QSb 3$_{2}$ 11QPsAp[a] 2$_{6}$, חֶבֶל *territory* Dt 3$_{4.13.14}$, *cord* Is 33$_{20}$, חֹבֵל *sailor* Ezk 27$_{29}$, חָבֵר *companion* Is 44$_{11}$ 4QJub[h] 37$_{25}$, חָגָב *locust* CD 12$_{14}$, חֶדֶר *chamber* Pr 20$_{27}$ 4Q185.1.3$_{12}$, חָדָשׁ *novelty* Ec 1$_{9}$, חֹדֶשׁ *month* 1 C 27$_{1}$ CD 14$_{13}$, חַוָּה *tent village* Jos 13$_{30}$, חוּם *brown* sheep Gn 30$_{35.40}$, חוֹמָה *wall* Is 2$_{15}$ Jr 1$_{15}$ Ezk 38$_{20}$ Ne 3$_{38}$ 2 C 32$_{5}$, חוּץ *street* Is 51$_{20}$ Ezk 26$_{11}$ Am 5$_{16}$ Na 3$_{10}$ Lm 2$_{19}$ (or del.) 4$_{1}$, חֹזֶה *seer* 2 K 17$_{13}$, חָזוֹן *vision* Ezk 12$_{22.23.24}$ Dn 1$_{17}$ 1 C 17$_{15}$ 4Q417 2.1$_{22}$, חִזָּיוֹן *vision* 2 S 7$_{17}$, חַטָּא *sinner* Am 9$_{10}$, חֵטְא *sin* Dt 19$_{15}$ Is 38$_{17}$ 11QT 61$_{6}$, חַטָּאת *sin, sin offering* Lv 6$_{23}$ 16$_{16.21.30.34}$ Nm 5$_{6}$ 16$_{26}$ 18$_{9}$ Dt 9$_{18}$ 19$_{15}$ 1 S 12$_{19}$ 1 K 15$_{3}$ 16$_{13}$ 2 K 13$_{11}$ 14$_{24}$ 17$_{22}$ Is 40$_{2}$=4QTanḥ 1$_{6}$ Jr 15$_{13}$ Ezk 18$_{14}$ 33$_{16}$ Mc 7$_{19}$ Ps 25$_{18}$ 85$_{3}$ 2 C 33$_{19}$ 1QS 3$_{22}$ 4QparaKings 7$_{4}$ 4QPrFêtes[b] 41$_{1}$ 11QT 26$_{12}$ 35$_{14}$ GnzPs 1$_{13}$, חַי *living being* Gn 3$_{20}$ 6$_{19}$ 8$_{21}$ Ps 143$_{2}$ 145$_{16}$ Jb 12$_{10}$ 28$_{21}$ 30$_{23}$ Ec 4$_{15}$ 9$_{4}$ Si 7$_{33}$ 40$_{1}$ 42$_{1.8.23(M)}$ 43$_{25}$ 44$_{23}$ 45$_{16}$ 46$_{20}$ 49$_{16}$ 1QH 15$_{22}$ 1QS 4$_{26}$ 9$_{12}$ 10$_{17.18}$ 4QTobit[e] 6$_{9}$ 4QMyst[a] 29$_{3}$ 4Q416 2.2$_{2}$ 3$_{2}$ 4Q417 2.1$_{19}$ 7$_{2}$ 4Q418 81$_{20}$ 180$_{2}$ 4QRitMar 39$_{2}$ 4QDib Ham[a] 6$_{22}$ 11QPs[a] 19$_{3}$ 24$_{7}$ 26$_{13}$ CD 12$_{21}$ GnzPs 1$_{2}$ 3$_{22}$, חַיָּה *beast* Gn 1$_{28.30}$ 2$_{19.20}$ 3$_{1.14}$ 7$_{14}$ 8$_{1.17.19}$ 9$_{2.5.10.10}$ Lv 11$_{27}$ Nm 35$_{3}$ Is 56$_{9.9}$ Jr 12$_{9}$ Ezk 31$_{6.13}$ 34$_{5.8}$ 39$_{17}$ Zp 2$_{14}$ Ps 50$_{10}$ 104$_{11.20}$ Jb 40$_{20}$ Dn 8$_{4}$ 1QH 8$_{8.19}$ 4QJub[a] 2$_{13}$ 4QShir[b] 1$_{4}$ CD 12$_{12}$, חַיִּים *life* 1QH 4$_{29}$ 4Q416 2.2$_{5}$ 4Q417 1.2$_{7}$ 4Q418 8$_{5}$, חַיִל *wealth* Gn 34$_{29}$ Nm 31$_{9}$, *army* Ex 14$_{4.17.28}$ 2 S 8$_{9}$||1 C 18$_{9}$ 1 K 20$_{1}$ 2 K 25$_{1.5.10}$||Jr 52$_{4.8.14}$ Jr 34$_{1}$ 37$_{10}$ 39$_{1}$ Ezk 32$_{31}$ 38$_{4}$ Est 8$_{11}$ 1QM 15$_{2}$ 18$_{1}$, חָכָם *wise one* Gn 41$_{8}$ Ex 28$_{3}$ 31$_{6}$ 35$_{10}$ 36$_{4.8}$ Jr 10$_{7}$ Jb 37$_{24}$ 1 C 22$_{15}$ 1QSa 1$_{27}$ 4Q418 81$_{20}$ 4QUnidA 2$_{2}$, חָכְמָה *wisdom* 1 K 5$_{10}$ 10$_{4}$ Ps 107$_{27}$ Dn 1$_{4}$ 1QH 3$_{15}$ 4QMyst[a] 3c$_{3}$ 4QMyst[b] 1b$_{4}$ 3$_{3}$ 4Q418 102$_{3}$ 115$_{3}$ 4QHod[f] 4.1$_{2}$, חֵלֶב *fat* Ex 29$_{13}$ Lv 3$_{3.9.14.16.17}$ 4$_{8.8.19.26.31.35}$ 7$_{3.23}$ 8$_{16.25}$ Nm 18$_{12.12.29}$ 4QJub[d] 21$_{8.8}$ 11QT 20$_{5}$, חֳלִי *sickness* Dt 7$_{15}$ 28$_{61}$ 4QMidrEschat[b] 10$_{2}$, חָלָל *slain one* 1QM 3$_{8}$, חֶלְקָה *plot of land* 2 K 3$_{19.25}$, חֶמְדָּה *desire* Dn 11$_{43}$, חֶמְדָּה *desire* 1 S 9$_{20}$ 4QDibHam[a] 1.4$_{11}$ GnzPs 3$_{15}$, חֵמָה *anger* Ps 78$_{38}$, חַמָּן *incense altar* 2 C 34$_{7}$, חָמָס *violence* 4QBibPar 1$_{8}$ 4Qap Joseph[b] 1$_{19}$, חָמֵץ *leavened bread* 4QSD 4$_{3}$, חֶסֶד *loyalty* Gn 32$_{11}$ Is 40$_{6}$ 1QS 1$_{22}$, חָסִיד *loyal one* Ps 31$_{24}$ 32$_{6}$ 148$_{14}$ 149$_{9}$ Si 51$_{12}$, חֹסֶן *treasure* Jr 20$_{5}$, חֶסֶר *lack* 4Q418 71$_{6}$ 4Q424 3$_{10}$, חֵפֶץ *pleasure* 2 S 23$_{5}$ 1 K 5$_{22.24}$ 9$_{11}$ 10$_{13}$||2 C 9$_{12}$ Is 44$_{28}$ 46$_{10}$ Ps 16$_{3}$ 111$_{2}$ Pr 3$_{15}$ 8$_{11}$ Ec 3$_{1.17}$ 8$_{6}$ 1QS 3$_{17}$ 4QMidrEschat[b] 10$_{2}$ 4Q418 88$_{1}$ 127$_{5}$ 128$_{3}$ 138$_{3}$ 158$_{3}$ 4Q423 2$_{6}$ CD 14$_{12}$, חֵץ *arrow* 1QH 3$_{16.27}$, חָצִיר *reed* Jb 8$_{12}$, חָצֵר *settlement* Jos 19$_{8}$ 1 C 4$_{33}$, חֹק *statute* Ex 15$_{26}$ Lv 10$_{11}$ 20$_{22}$ Nm 9$_{12}$ Dt 4$_{6}$ 6$_{24}$ 11$_{32}$ 1QH 15$_{12}$ 1QS 3$_{8}$ 5$_{7.20.22}$ 1QSa 1$_{5}$ 1QSb 3$_{24}$ 4QJub[a] 1$_{14}$ 4QD[a] 11$_{6}$ 4QTohA 2.1$_{2}$ 4QpsMos[e] 2.14$_{4}$ 4QM[h] 3$_{4}$ 4QSap[b] 1.1$_{4}$ 4QDibHam[a] 3.2$_{14}$ 6$_{3}$, חֻקָּה *statute* Lv 19$_{37}$ Nm 9$_{3}$ Dt 6$_{2}$ Ezk 18$_{19.21}$ 43$_{11.11}$ 44$_{5}$, חֹר *noble* Jr 27$_{20}$ 39$_{6}$, חֶרֶב *sword* 1QH 6$_{28}$, חָרְבָּה *waste* Is 51$_{3}$, חָרֵד *one who trembles* Ezr 9$_{4}$, חֲרָדָה *trembling* 2 K 4$_{13}$, חָרוֹן *burning* Zp 3$_{8}$ 4QBark[a] 1.2$_{6}$ 4QDibHam[a] 1.3$_{11}$, חַרְטֹם *magician* Gn 41$_{8}$ Dn 1$_{20}$ 4QJub[h] 40$_{1}$, חֵרֶם *devoted object* Lv

27$_{28.28.29}$ Nm 18$_{14}$ Ezk 44$_{29}$ 4QHalakah[a] 6$_9$ 4QD[e] 6.3$_{16}$, חֶרְפָּה *reproach* Si 42$_{14}$, חַרְצֹב *fetter* CD 13$_{10}$, חָרָר *dispute* Mur 30 2$_{25}$, חָרֵשׁ *artisan* Gn 4$_{22}$, חָרָשׁ *artisan* 2 K 24$_{14}$, חֹשֶׁךְ *darkness* Jb 20$_{26}$, חֵשֶׁק *desire* 1 K 9$_1$ 2 C 8$_6$.

טָהוֹר *pure one* Lv 7$_{19}$ Nm 18$_{11.13}$ 4QShirShabb[f] 3.2$_3$, טָהֳרָה *purity* 4QNidd 6$_1$ 11QT 47$_{17}$ 49$_{21}$, טוֹב *good thing* Jg 10$_{15}$ 1 S 11$_{10}$ 14$_{36}$ 15$_9$ Ps 34$_{11}$ Si 37$_{28(D)}$ 1QS 2$_2$ 1QDM 2$_3$ 1QMyst 1.2$_5$ 4QapJoshua[b] 15$_{3.3}$ 4Q418 127$_1$ 4QM[h] 2$_9$, טוּב *good thing* Gn 24$_{10}$ Ex 33$_{19}$ Dt 6$_{11}$ 26$_{11}$ 2 K 8$_9$ Ne 9$_{25}$, טוֹבָה *good thing* Ex 18$_9$ Jg 8$_{35}$ 1 K 8$_{66}$||2 C 7$_{10(mss)}$ Jr 32$_{42}$ 33$_{9.9}$ Si 11$_{30}$ 12$_5$, טִירָה *encampment* Nm 31$_{10}$, טַל *dew* 4QJub[a] 2$_7$, טָמֵא *impure one* Lv 7$_{19.21}$ 22$_4$ Nm 5$_2$ Jg 13$_4$ 4QOrd[c] 1.1$_5$ 11QT 45$_{17}$, טֻמְאָה *impurity* Lv 5$_3$ 22$_5$ Jg 13$_{7.14}$ Ezk 36$_{25.29}$ 2 C 29$_{16}$ 1QSa 2$_3$ 4QD[d] 8.2$_5$ 4QTohB[b] 1$_8$ 4QNidd 3$_5$ 4QRitPur 152$_2$ 11QT 47$_5$ 51$_6$ CD 7$_3$, טַף *children* Gn 34$_{29}$ Nm 31$_{18}$ 2 S 15$_{22}$ 2 C 31$_{18}$.

יְאֹר *river* 2 K 19$_{24}$||Is 37$_{25}$, יְבוּל *produce* 4QRitMar 9$_6$, יָבֵישׁ גִּלְעָד *Jabesh-Gilead* 1 C 10$_{11}$, יָגוֹן *torment* 4QBark[d] 2.1$_7$, יְגִיעַ *labour* Dt 28$_{33}$ Jr 20$_5$ Ezk 23$_{29}$ Ho 12$_9$ Hg 1$_{11}$, יָד *hand* Dt 2$_{37}$ 34$_{12}$ Is 13$_7$ Jr 48$_{37}$ Ezk 7$_{17}$ 21$_{12}$ Jb 20$_{22}$ Ne 10$_{32}$.

יְהוּדָה *Judah* 1 K 15$_{22}$||2 C 16$_6$ 2 K 22$_{13}$ Jr 7$_2$ 17$_{20}$ 20$_4$ 26$_{19}$ 36$_6$ 40$_{15}$ 44$_{11.24.26}$ Ne 13$_{12}$ 2 C 15$_{2.9.15}$ 17$_{5.19}$ 20$_{3.13.15.18}$ 23$_8$ 25$_5$ 31$_{1.20}$ 32$_{9.33}$ 34$_9$ 35$_{18.24}$, יְהוּדִי *Judaean, Jew* Jr 32$_{12}$ 40$_{11.12}$ 41$_3$ 44$_1$ Est 3$_{6.13}$ 4$_{13.16}$ 9$_{20.24.30}$.

יוֹם *day* Gn 3$_{14.17}$ 5$_{5+8t}$ 6$_5$ 8$_{22}$ 9$_{29}$ 43$_9$ 44$_{32}$ Ex 10$_{13}$ Lv 13$_{46}$ 14$_{46}$ 15$_{25.26}$ 26$_{34.35}$ Nm 6$_{4.5.6.8}$ 9$_{18}$ 11$_{32.32}$ Dt 4$_{9.10.40}$ 5$_{29}$=4QTestim$_4$ Dt 6$_{2.24}$ 11$_1$ 12$_{1.19}$ 14$_{23}$ 16$_3$ 17$_{19}$ 18$_5$ 19$_9$ 22$_{19.29}$ 23$_7$ 28$_{29.32.33}$ 31$_{13}$ 33$_{12}$ Jos 1$_5$ 3$_{15}$ 4$_{14}$ 24$_{31.31}$ Jg 2$_{7.7.18}$ 9$_{45}$ 16$_{16}$ 18$_{31}$ 1 S 1$_{11.28}$ 2$_{32.35}$ 7$_{13.15}$ 14$_{52}$ 18$_{29}$ 19$_{24}$ 20$_{31}$ 22$_4$ 23$_{14}$ 25$_{7.15.16}$ 27$_{11}$ 28$_{2.20}$ 2 S 13$_{37}$ 19$_{14}$ 1 K 3$_{13}$ 5$_{1.5.15}$ 8$_{40}$||2 C 6$_{31}$ 1 K 9$_3$||2 C 7$_{16}$ 1 K 11$_{25.34.36.39}$ 12$_7$||2 C 10$_7$ 1 K 14$_{30}$||2 C 12$_{15}$ 1 K 15$_{5.6}$ 1 K 15$_{14}$||2 C 15$_{17}$ 1 K 15$_{16.32}$ 2 K 8$_{19}$||2 C 21$_7$ 2 K 12$_3$ 13$_{3.22}$ 15$_{18}$ 17$_{37}$ 23$_{22}$ 25$_{29.30}$||Jr 52$_{33.34}$ Is 28$_{24}$ 38$_{20}$ 51$_{13}$ 52$_5$ 62$_6$ 63$_9$ 65$_{2.5}$ Jr 20$_{7.8}$ 31$_{36}$ 32$_{39}$ 33$_{18}$ 35$_{7.8.19}$ Ho 12$_2$ Ps 7$_{12}$ 23$_6$ 25$_5$ 27$_4$ 32$_3$ 35$_{28}$ 37$_{26}$ 38$_{7.13}$ 42$_{4.11}$ 44$_{9.16.23}$ 52$_3$ 56$_{2.3.6}$ 71$_{8.15.24}$ 72$_{15}$ 73$_{14}$ 74$_{22}$ 86$_3$ 88$_{10.18}$ 89$_{17}$ 90$_{9.14}$ 102$_9$ 119$_{97}$ 128$_5$ 140$_3$ 145$_2$ Jb 1$_5$ 14$_{14}$ 15$_{20}$ Pr 15$_{15}$ 21$_{26}$ 23$_{17}$ 31$_{12}$ Ec 2$_{23}$ 5$_{16}$ 9$_{9.9}$ Lm 1$_{13}$ 3$_{3.14.62}$ Est 2$_{11}$ Ezr 4$_5$ 2 C 18$_7$ 24$_{2.14}$ 34$_{33}$ 36$_{21}$ Si 3$_{12.13}$ 45$_{14}$ 1QH 1$_{15}$ 5$_{17}$ 11$_5$ 15$_9$ 17$_{14}$ 1QM 2$_4$ 1QS 2$_{19}$ 3$_5$ 10$_{16}$ 1Q39.1$_3$ 2QJub[b] 46$_{1.2.2}$ 4QOrd[a] 1.2$_7$ 2$_{10}$ 4QMidrEschat[a] 1$_{17}$ 4QTobit[e] 2$_{3.4}$ 4QJub[a] 2$_{22.24}$ 4QJub[c] 2$_{26}$ 4QJub[d] 21$_{2.24}$ 4QJub[f] 21$_{24}$ 23$_{10}$ 37$_{13}$ 39$_6$ 4QJub[g] 25$_9$ 4QJub[h] 35$_{7.12}$ 36$_{8.10.23}$ 37$_{18}$ 38$_{12}$ 4QpsJub[a] 2.2$_{10.11}$ 4QpsJub[b] 5$_2$ 7$_4$ 4QpsJub[c] 1$_3$ 4QTohA 1.1$_4$ 4QNidd 1$_2$ 4QMishA 8$_3$ 4Qap Joseph[b] 15$_3$ 4QpsEzek[a] 9.2$_2$ 4Q410 1$_7$ 4Q415 2.2$_3$ 4Q418 126.2$_{10}$ 127$_2$ 4QpsHod[b] 1$_4$ 4QDibHam[a] 1.4$_8$ 4QRitPur 67$_1$ 4QBéat 3.3$_1$ 11QPs[a] 27$_{6.6.8}$ 11QT 15$_3$ 16$_4$ 17$_{12}$ 29$_{10}$ 45$_{13}$ 46$_4$ 50$_{10}$ 51$_{16}$ 57$_{18}$ 59$_{15}$ 60$_{11}$ 66$_{11}$ Mur 47 1$_4$ GnzPs 3$_3$ 4$_{25}$, יחם inf. *mating (season)* Gn 30$_{41}$, יַיִן *wine* Ne 5$_{18}$, יֶלֶד *child* Dn 1$_{15}$, יָלִיד *child* Gn 17$_{23}$, יְסוֹד *foundation* 4QShirShabb[d] 1.1$_{41}$, יסור *teaching* CD 7$_5$, יֵצֶר *impulse* Gn 6$_5$ 1 C 28$_9$ 1QH 7$_{13}$ 1QH fr. 3$_9$, יְקוּם *living thing* Gn 7$_{4.23}$ Dt 11$_6$ 1QM 14$_{12}$ 15$_{11}$ 4QBer[a] 5$_2$, יְקָר *precious object* Jr 20$_5$ Jb 28$_{10}$ 4QM[a] 1.1$_{14}$, יָרוֹק *plant* Jb 39$_8$ 4QParGenEx 3$_{11}$, יְרוּשָׁלַםִ *Jerusalem* 2 K 24$_{14}$, יְרִיעָה *curtain* Ex 26$_2$ 36$_9$, יֶרֶק *green plant* Gn 1$_{30}$ Ex 10$_{15}$ 4QTohA 2.2$_4$.

יִשְׂרָאֵל *Israel* Ex 18$_{25}$ Nm 16$_{34}$ Dt 1$_1$ 5$_1$ 11$_6$ 13$_{12}$ 18$_6$ 21$_{21}$ 27$_9$ 29$_1$ 31$_{1.7.11.11}$ 32$_{45}$ 34$_{12}$ Jos 3$_{7.17}$ 4$_{14}$ 7$_{24.25}$ 8$_{15.21.24.33}$ 10$_{15+6t}$ 23$_2$ Jg 8$_{27}$ 20$_{34}$ 1 S 2$_{14.22}$ 3$_{20}$ 4$_{1.5}$ 7$_5$ 11$_2$ 12$_1$ 13$_{4.20}$ 14$_{40}$ 17$_{11}$ 18$_{16}$ 19$_5$ 24$_3$ 25$_1$ 28$_{3.4}$ 2 S 3$_{12.21.37}$ 4$_1$ 5$_5$ 8$_{15}$||1 C 18$_{14}$ 2 S 10$_{17}$||1 C 19$_{17}$ 2 S 11$_1$ 12$_{12}$ 14$_{25}$ 15$_6$ 16$_{21.22}$ 17$_{10.11.13}$ 18$_{17}$ 19$_{12}$ 1 K 1$_{20}$ 2$_{15}$ 3$_{28}$ 4$_{1.7}$ 5$_{27}$ 8$_{62.65}$||2 C 7$_8$ 1 K 11$_{16.42}$||2 C 9$_{30}$ 1 K 12$_{1.16}$||2 C 10$_{1.16}$ 1 K 12$_{18.20.20}$ 14$_{13.18}$ 15$_{27.33}$ 16$_{16.17}$ 18$_{19}$ 22$_{17}$||2 C 18$_{16}$ 2 K 3$_6$ 9$_{14}$ 10$_{21}$ Ml 3$_{22}$ Dn 9$_{7.11}$ Ezr 2$_{70}$||Ne 7$_{72}$ Ezr 8$_{25.35}$ 10$_5$ Ne 12$_{47}$ 13$_{26}$ 1 C 9$_1$ 11$_{1.4.10}$ 12$_{39}$ 13$_{5.6.8}$ 14$_8$ 15$_{3.28}$ 17$_6$ 21$_{4.5}$ 28$_{4.8}$ 29$_{21.23.25.26}$ 2 C 1$_{2.2}$ 7$_6$ 10$_{3.16}$ 11$_{3.13}$ 12$_1$ 13$_{4.15}$ 24$_5$ 28$_{23}$ 29$_{24.24}$ 30$_{1.5.6}$ 31$_1$ 35$_3$ 1Q29.3$_3$ 4QpNah 3$_3$ 4QD[a] 5.1$_{18}$ 4QM[g] 6$_2$ 4QapMoses[c] 1.1$_7$ 4Q408 1$_{3.4}$ 6$_2$ 4QM[a] 16$_4$ 11QT 60$_{12}$ CD 3$_{14}$ 15$_5$ 16$_1$, יֹשֵׁב *inhabitant* 4QD[a] 11$_{16.19.20}$ 4QBer[a] 5$_{1.1}$ 4QparaKings 140$_1$ 11QT 55$_{3.6}$ GnzPs 2$_{16}$ 4$_3$, יֵשַׁע *salvation* 2 S 23$_5$, יָשָׁר *right* Dt 12$_8$ Jr 40$_5$, *upright one* Ps 32$_{11}$ 64$_{11}$ 94$_{15}$ 4QD[a] 5.1$_2$, יְשָׁרָה *right* Mc 3$_9$, יָתֵד *peg* Ex 27$_{19.19}$ 38$_{20.31}$, יֶתֶר *remnant* Jg 7$_6$ Hb 2$_8$.

כָּבוֹד *glory* Gn 45$_{13}$ Is 4$_5$ Si 40$_{27}$ 1QH 11$_8$ 17$_{15}$ 1QH fr. 2$_4$ 1QS 4$_{23}$ 4QMyst[c] 4$_3$ Mur 6$_6$ CD 3$_{20}$, *wealth* Gn 31$_1$ Is 22$_{24}$, *multitude* Is 8$_7$ 21$_{16}$, כְּבוּדָּה *wealth* Ps 45$_{14}$ (or em. יְכַבְּדוּךָ all *will honour you*, as §1), כֹּהֵן *priest* 2 K 10$_{19}$ 23$_{8.20}$ Jr 29$_{25}$ Ezk 44$_{21}$ 2 C 5$_{11}$ 26$_{20}$ 1QDM 1$_3$ 4QShirShabb[f] 20.2$_1$ 11QT 16$_{01}$, כּוֹכָב *star* Ps 148$_3$, כֹּחַ *strength* Gn 31$_6$ 1 C 29$_2$ 4QMidrEschat[a] 2$_{16}$ 4QMyst[a] 21$_3$, כִּיּוֹר *entablature* 11QT 5$_{10}$ 6$_8$, כִּכָּר *environs* Gn 13$_{10.11}$ 19$_{17.25}$,

כְּלִי *vessel* Gn 31$_{37.37}$ Ex 25$_{9.39}$ 27$_{3.19}$ 30$_{27.28}$ 31$_{7.8.9}$ 35$_{13.16.22}$ 37$_{24}$ 38$_{3.3.30}$ 39$_{33.36.37.39.40}$ 40$_{9.10}$ Lv 8$_{11}$ 11$_{32.32.33.34}$ 13$_{49.52.53.57.58.59}$ 15$_{4.12.22.26}$ Nm 1$_{50.50}$ 3$_{8.36}$ 4$_{9+7t}$ 7$_{1.1}$ 19$_{15.18}$ 31$_{20.20.51}$ 35$_{22}$ 1 K 6$_{7}$ 7$_{45.47.48}$||2 C 4$_{16.18.19}$ 1 K 8$_{4}$ ||2 C 5$_{5}$ 1 K 10$_{21.21}$||2 C 9$_{20.20}$ 2 K 4$_{4}$ 12$_{14}$ 14$_{14}$||2 C 25$_{24}$ 2 K 23$_{4}$ 24$_{13}$ 25$_{14.16}$||Jr 52$_{18.20}$ Is 22$_{24}$ 54$_{17}$ Jr 28$_{3}$ 49$_{29}$ Ezk 15$_{3}$ Ho 13$_{15}$ Na 2$_{10}$ Ezr 1$_{11}$ Ne 13$_{8}$ 1 C 9$_{29}$ 12$_{34.38}$ 18$_{10}$ 23$_{26}$ 28$_{13.14.14.14}$ 2 C 5$_{1}$ 29$_{18.18.19}$ 32$_{27}$ 36$_{18.19}$ 1QH 2$_{25}$ 4QSD 6$_{3}$ 4QD[d] 8.2$_{4}$ 4QTohA 1.1$_{4}$ 1.2$_{4}$ 2.2$_{10.12}$ 4QapMes 4$_{8}$ 11QT 3$_{8}$ 49$_{14.15.15}$ 50$_{12.16.17}$ CD 11$_{2}$ 12$_{17}$ Gnz Ps 2$_{28}$, כלם ni. inf. *humiliation* Si 41$_{16}$, כְּנַעֲנִי *Canaanite* Jos 17$_{16}$ Jg 3$_{3}$, כָּנָף *wing* Gn 7$_{14}$ Ezk 17$_{23}$ 39$_{4.17}$ 4QAdmon 1.1$_{6}$, כִּנְרוֹת *Chinneroth* 1 K 15$_{20}$, כֶּסֶף *silver* Gn 47$_{14}$ Nm 7$_{85}$ Jos 6$_{19}$ 1 K 15$_{18}$ 2 K 12$_{5.5.10}$ 18$_{15}$, כַּעַס *provocation* 2 K 23$_{26}$ 4QpsEzek[e] 6-7$_{3}$, כָּפָר *village* Ezk 38$_{13}$, כֹּפֶר *bribe* Pr 6$_{35}$, כֶּרֶם *vineyard* Am 5$_{17}$, כְּרֵתִי *Cherethite* 2 S 15$_{18}$, כַּשְׂדִּי *Chaldaean* Ezk 23$_{23}$, כִּשְׁרוֹן *success* Ec 4$_{4}$, כִּתִּיִּים *Kittim* 4QpNah 1$_{3}$, כָּתֵף *shoulder* Ezk 29$_{7.18}$.

לְאֹם *people* Ps 148$_{11}$ 1QH 6$_{12}$ 1QMyst 1.1$_{9}$, לֵב *heart* Jg 16$_{17.18.18}$ 1 K 8$_{23}$||2 C 6$_{14}$ 1 K 8$_{48}$||2 C 6$_{38}$ 2 K 23$_{3}$ Jr 3$_{10}$ 24$_{7}$ 32$_{41}$ Ezk 21$_{12}$ Zp 3$_{14}$ Ps 9$_{2}$ 119$_{2.10.34.58.69.145}$ 138$_{1}$ Pr 3$_{5}$ Si 7$_{29}$ 39$_{35}$ 47$_{8}$ 1QH 14$_{26}$ 15$_{10}$ 1QS 5$_{8}$ 4QJub[a] 1$_{15}$ 4QJub[d] 21$_{2}$ 4QJub[h] 35$_{10.12.13}$ 36$_{20}$ 4QS[a] 1$_{2}$ 4QMyst[a] 10$_{5}$ 4QapMoses[a] 1.1$_{2.3}$ 4QDibHam[a] 1.2$_{13}$ CD 15$_{9.12}$ GnzPs 4$_{19}$, לֵבָב *heart* Dt 4$_{29}$ 6$_{5}$ 10$_{12}$ 11$_{13}$ 13$_{4}$ 26$_{16}$ 30$_{2.6.10}$ Jos 22$_{5}$ 23$_{14}$ 1 S 7$_{3}$ 12$_{20.24}$ 1 K 2$_{4}$ 8$_{48}$ 14$_{8}$ 2 K 10$_{31}$ 23$_{25}$ Is 1$_{5}$ 13$_{7}$ Jr 29$_{13}$ Ezk 36$_{5}$ Jl 2$_{12}$ Ps 86$_{12}$ 111$_{1}$ 1 C 28$_{9}$ 2 C 15$_{12.15}$ 22$_{9}$ 30$_{19}$ 31$_{21}$ 32$_{31}$ 34$_{31}$ 4QpsEzek[c] 3.2$_{1.2}$ 4QMMT C$_{15.16}$ 4QHymnSap 6$_{1}$ 4QShir[b] 22$_{4}$ 11QPs[a] 22$_{12}$ 11QT 54$_{13}$ 59$_{10}$, לְבָנוֹן *Lebanon* Jos 13$_{5}$, לְבֹנָה *frankincense* Lv 2$_{2.16}$ 6$_{8}$, לוּחַ *plank* Ezk 27$_{5}$, לֶחֶם *bread* Jos 9$_{5}$ Jr 37$_{21}$, לֵוִי *Levite* 2 S 15$_{24}$ Ne 11$_{18}$ 1 C 15$_{27}$ 2 C 30$_{22}$, לַיְלָה *night* Ex 10$_{13}$ 14$_{20.21}$ Lv 6$_{2}$ Nm 11$_{32}$ Jos 10$_{9}$ Jg 16$_{2.2}$ 19$_{25}$ 1 S 15$_{11}$ 19$_{24}$ 28$_{20}$ 31$_{12}$ 2 S 2$_{29.32}$ 4$_{7}$ Is 21$_{8}$ 62$_{6}$ Ho 7$_{6}$ Ps 6$_{7}$ 78$_{14}$ 1QS 6$_{7}$ 4QD[a] 6.4$_{1}$, לֶקֶט *gleanings* 4QD[a] 6.3$_{5}$, לָשׁוֹן *tongue* Is 45$_{23}$ 54$_{17}$ Zc 8$_{23}$ 4QapJoshua[b] 15$_{3.3}$ 4QPrQuot 42$_{3}$ 4QRitPur 3$_{12}$ CD 14$_{10}$, לִשְׁכָּה *hall* 1 C 28$_{12}$.

מְאֹד *might* Dt 6$_{5}$ 2 K 23$_{25}$ Si 7$_{30}$ 11QPs[a] 22$_{1}$ CD 12$_{10}$, מָאוֹר *light* Ezk 32$_{8}$, מְאוּמָה *(any)thing* Gn 39$_{23}$ 2 S 3$_{35}$ 1QS 5$_{16}$ Lachish ost. 3$_{12}$ (כל [מאומ]ה; others אל *to*), מַאֲכָל *food* Gn 6$_{21}$ 40$_{17}$ Hg 2$_{12}$ Si 36$_{23}$ 37$_{20}$, מַאֲמָץ *exertion* Jb 36$_{19}$, מְאַסֵּף *rear-guard* 4QapMoses[c] 2.1$_{6}$ מָבוֹא *entrance* Si 14$_{22}$, מִבְחָר *choice one* Dt 12$_{11}$, מַבְנִית *structure* 4QShirShabb[d] 1.1$_{43}$, מִבְצָר *fortress* Ho 10$_{14}$ Mc 5$_{10}$ Na 3$_{12}$ Hb 1$_{10}$, מִבְרָח *refugee* Ezk 17$_{21}$, מֶגֶד *choice gift* Ca 7$_{14}$, מָגוֹר *place of residence* 1QS 6$_{2}$, מְגִלָּה *scroll* Jr 36$_{23}$, מָגֵן *shield* 1 K 14$_{26}$ 1QM 9$_{14}$, מַגֵּפָה *plague* Ex 9$_{14}$, מִגְדָּל *tower* Is 2$_{15}$, מְגוֹרָה *horror* Ps 34$_{5}$, מִגְרָשׁ *pasture-land* 1 C 5$_{16}$, מִדְבָּר *steppe* Dt 1$_{19}$ 4QBer[a] 5$_{3}$, מִדָּה *measurement* 4QTohA 1.1$_{5}$ 2.2$_{9}$, מַדְהֵבָה *oppression* CD 13$_{9}$, מְדִינָה *province* Est 1$_{16.22}$ 2$_{3}$ 3$_{8.13.14}$ 4$_{3}$ 8$_{5.12.13.17}$ 9$_{2.4.20}$, מַדְוֶה *disease* Dt 7$_{15}$ 28$_{60}$, מִדְיָן *Midian* Jg 6$_{33}$, מְהוּמָה *confusion* 4QPseud[b] 1$_{6}$, מַהְפָּךְ *overturning* 4QShirShabb[d] 1.2$_{4}$, מוֹאָב *Moab* 2 K 3$_{21}$, מוֹטָה *yoke* Is 58$_{6}$, מוֹלֶדֶת *birth* 1QH 12$_{7}$, מוֹסָד *foundation* Ps 82$_{5}$ 4QAdmon 1.1$_{3}$ 4QShir[b] 10$_{12}$, מוֹעֵד *appointed time* Ezk 44$_{24}$ 45$_{17}$ Ho 2$_{13}$ Ps 74$_{8}$ Ezr 3$_{5}$ 1QH 1$_{24}$ 1QM 1$_{8}$ 12$_{3}$ 1QS 1$_{15}$ 3$_{26}$ ([מו]עדי) 4QBer[b] 1$_{3}$ 2$_{7}$ 4QPrEnosh 1.1$_{4}$ 4QM[a] 8$_{16}$ 4QRitMar 24$_{1}$ 4QPr Quot 29.8$_{21}$ 33.10$_{21}$ 41$_{3}$, מוֹפֵת *sign* Ex 4$_{21}$ 11$_{10}$ 4QShir[b] 49.2$_{5}$, מוֹצָא *exit* Ezk 42$_{11}$ (or em. כָּל־ to כְּ *as*) 44$_{5}$ (or em. בְּכֹל *in all* to וּלְ *and to*; or em. מוּצָאֵי all *who are excluded*, as §1) 4QShirShabb[f] 23.1$_{8}$ 11QShirShabb 1$_{7}$, *expression* Nm 30$_{13}$ Dt 8$_{3}$ Si 48$_{12}$, מוֹקֵשׁ *snare* 1QH 2$_{21}$ CD 14$_{2}$, מוֹרָא *terror* Dt 34$_{12}$, מוֹרֵד *rebel* CD 8$_{4}$, מוֹשָׁב *settlement* Ex 12$_{20}$ 35$_{3}$ Lv 3$_{17}$ 7$_{26}$ 23$_{3.14.21.31}$ Nm 35$_{29}$ 2 S 9$_{12}$ Ezk 6$_{6.14}$ 34$_{13}$ 37$_{23}$ 11QT 17$_{4}$ 21$_{9}$ 27$_{9}$, מוּם *blemish* Lv 22$_{21}$ Dt 15$_{21}$ Dn 1$_{4}$ 4QD[e] 5$_{14}$ 11QT 52$_{4.10}$, מוּסָר *correction* 4Q416 2.3$_{13}$ 4Q418 9$_{13}$, מוֹשְׁקֶה *drink* 11QT 49$_{7.9}$, מִזְבֵּחַ *altar* Lv 1$_{9}$ 1 K 6$_{22}$ Am 2$_{8}$ 2 C 33$_{15}$ 11QT 3$_{14}$, מְזִמָּה *plan* Ps 10$_{4}$ 1QH 5$_{10}$, מִזְרָע *sown land* Is 19$_{7}$.

מַחֲבָא *hiding place* 1 S 23$_{23}$, מְחִיר *price* 1QMyst 1.2$_{8}$, מַחֲלָה *illness* Ex 15$_{26}$ 1 K 8$_{37}$||2 C 6$_{28}$, מַחֲלֹקֶת *division* 4QJub[a] 1$_{26}$, מַחְמָד *precious thing* 1 K 20$_{6}$ Is 64$_{10}$ Lm 1$_{10}$ 2$_{4}$ Si 36$_{27}$, מַחְמֹד *desire* Lm 1$_{7(Qr)}$, מחמד *desire* Lm 1$_{7.11(Kt)}$, מַחְמֶצֶת *leavened food* Ex 12$_{20}$, מַחֲנֶה *camp* Gn 33$_{8}$ Nm 10$_{25}$ Jos 8$_{13}$ 10$_{5}$ 11$_{4}$ Jg 4$_{15.16}$ 7$_{14.18.21.22}$ 8$_{10.12}$ 1 S 29$_{1}$ 2 K 5$_{15}$ 6$_{24}$ CD 14$_{3.9}$ 1QM 7$_{7.7}$ 18$_{4}$ 4QD[a] 7.2$_{6}$ 4QShirShabb[a] 2$_{2}$ 4QShirShabb[f] 20.2$_{13}$, מַחְסוֹר *lack* Jg 19$_{20}$ 4Q416 2.2$_{1}$ 4Q417 1.2$_{3}$, מַחֲשָׁבָה *thought* Ps 56$_{6}$ Lm 3$_{60.61}$ 2 C 2$_{13}$ (מַחֲשֶׁבֶת) 1QH 3$_{33}$ 4$_{12}$ 13$_{9}$ 1QH fr. 20$_{4}$ 1QM 13$_{2}$ 1QpHab 3$_{5}$ 1QS 3$_{15}$ 4$_{4}$ 11$_{19}$ 4QBer[f] 1$_{2}$ 4QBer[a] 5$_{1}$ 7.2$_{7}$ 4QMyst[a] 3a.2$_{11}$ 4QShirShabb[d] 1.2$_{13.14}$ 4QShirShabb[f] 23.2$_{10}$ 4QsapDidB 4.2$_{3}$ 4QHod[a] 7.2$_{21}$ 4QHod[b] 13$_{4}$ 4QDibHam[a] 1.7$_{7}$ 4$_{4}$ 4QDibHam[c] 131$_{9}$ 4QShir[b] 23$_{4}$ 26$_{2}$ 37$_{4}$ 63.2$_{3}$, מַטֶּה

staff, tribe Nm 17$_{24}$ 31$_{4}$ Jos 22$_{14}$ Ps 105$_{16}$ 11QT 19$_{14}$ 21$_{1.2.12}$, מַטְעָם *delicacy* Si 37$_{29}$, מָטָר *rain* Si 40$_{16}$, מַיִם *water* Ex 7$_{20}$ 2 K 5$_{12}$ Is 32$_{20}$ 1QS 3$_{5}$ 4Q415 11$_{5}$, מִין *kind* 1QS 3$_{14}$ 4QJub^{a} 2$_{11}$, מִישׁוֹר *plain* Jos 13$_{9.16}$, מֵיתָר *cord* Jr 10$_{20}$, מַכָּה *blow* Dt 28$_{61}$ 1 S 4$_{8}$ Jr 19$_{8}$ 49$_{17}$ 50$_{13}$ Si 25$_{13}$ 4QD^{g} 1.1$_{2}$, מָכוֹן *place* Is 4$_{5}$, מֶכֶר *merchandise* Ne 13$_{16}$.

מַלְאָךְ *angel* Ps 148$_{2}$ 1QM 1$_{15}$ ([כו]ל) 1QS 4$_{12}$ 4QM^{g} 1$_{3}$ 4QDibHam^{a} 1.7$_{6}$ 11QPs^{a} 26$_{12}$ 11QPsAp^{a} 2$_{5}$ 11QBer 1$_{4}$ CD 2$_{6}$ GnzPs 1$_{23}$, מְלָאכָה *work* Gn 2$_{2.3}$ Ex 12$_{16}$ 20$_{9.10}$ 31$_{3.5}$ 35$_{24+5t}$ 36$_{1.4.7}$ 38$_{24}$ 39$_{43}$ Lv 7$_{24}$ 13$_{48}$ 16$_{29}$ 23$_{3+9t}$ Nm 28$_{18.25.26}$ 29$_{1.7.12.35}$ Dt 5$_{13.14}$ 1 S 15$_{9}$ 1 K 7$_{14.40}$ 1 K 7$_{51}$ ||2 C 5$_{1}$ Jr 17$_{22.24}$ Ps 73$_{28}$ Ne 10$_{34}$ 1 C 6$_{34}$ 22$_{15}$ 26$_{30}$ 28$_{13.19.20.21}$ 29$_{5}$ 2 C 8$_{16}$ Si 3$_{17}$ 1Q43$_{2}$ 4QJub^{a} 2$_{17.18.18}$ 4QJub^{c} 2$_{26}$ 4QRP^{c} 23$_{5.8}$ 11QT 14$_{10}$ 17$_{11.16}$ 19$_{8}$ 25$_{9}$ 27$_{6.9}$, מַלְבּוּשׁ *garment* Is 63$_{3}$, מָלוֹשׁ *kneading dough* 4QBark^{f} 1.1$_{2}$, מִלְחָמָה *war* Jg 3$_{1}$ 2 C 27$_{7}$, מֶלֶךְ *king* Jos 5$_{1.1}$ 9$_{1}$ 10$_{6.40.42}$ 11$_{5.12.17.18}$ 12$_{24}$ 2 S 10$_{19}$ 1 K 5$_{4.14}$ 10$_{15.23}$||2 C 9$_{14.22}$ 1 K 10$_{29}$||2 C 1$_{17}$ 1 K 16$_{33}$ 2 K 18$_{5}$ Is 14$_{9.18}$ 62$_{2}$ Jr 25$_{20+9t}$ Ho 7$_{7}$ Ps 72$_{11}$ 102$_{16}$ 138$_{4}$ 1 C 29$_{25}$ 2 C 9$_{23.26}$ 35$_{18}$ 1QpPs 10$_{1}$ 4QMyst^{a} 60$_{4}$ 4QsapHymnA 10$_{4}$ 4QM^{a} 11.1$_{12}$ GnzPs 1$_{24}$ 2$_{12}$, מַלְכוּת *kingdom* Jr 10$_{7}$ Est 1$_{20}$ 3$_{6}$ Dn 1$_{20}$ 11$_{17}$ Ezr 1$_{1}$ ||2 C 36$_{22}$ 1 C 29$_{30}$ 4QJub^{h} 40$_{6}$ 4QShirShabb^{d} 1.1$_{33}$, מַלְקוֹחַ *booty* Nm 31$_{11}$, מִמְכָּר *merchandise* Ne 13$_{20}$, מַמְלָכָה *kingdom* Dt 3$_{21}$ 28$_{35}$ Jos 11$_{10}$ 13$_{12.21.30}$ 1 S 10$_{18}$ 1 K 5$_{1}$ 10$_{20}$||2 C 9$_{19}$ 1 K 11$_{13.34}$ 2 K 19$_{15.19}$||Is 37$_{16.20}$ Is 23$_{17}$ Jr 15$_{4}$ 24$_{9}$ 25$_{26}$ 29$_{18}$ 34$_{1.17}$ Ps 135$_{11}$ Ezr 1$_{2}$||2 C 36$_{23}$ 1 C 29$_{30}$ 2 C 17$_{10}$ 20$_{6.29}$ 4QShirShabb^{b} 5$_{5}$, מֶמְשָׁלָה *rule* 2 K 20$_{13}$||Is 39$_{2}$ 2 C 32$_{9}$ 1QH 12$_{8}$ 13$_{11}$ 1QS 3$_{21}$ 9$_{24}$ 4QMyst^{a} 10$_{9}$ 4QPrEnosh 3$_{3.4}$, מִנְחָה *cereal offering* Lv 2$_{11}$ 6$_{16}$ 7$_{9.10}$ Nm 18$_{9}$ 1 S 2$_{29}$ Ps 20$_{4}$ 11QT 20$_{9}$, מְנַשֶּׁה *Manasseh* Jg 6$_{35}$ 7$_{23}$, מַס *melted one* 1QM 10$_{5}$, מִסְכְּנוֹת *storehouse* 2 C 16$_{4}$, מְסִלָּה *highway* perh. 2QapProph 6$_{2}$, מַסַּע *departure* Ex 40$_{36.38}$, מִסְפָּר *number* Nm 14$_{29}$ 2 C 26$_{12}$ 4QMyst^{a} 10$_{6}$.

מַעֲבָר *blow* Is 30$_{32}$, מַעְגָּל *track* Pr 2$_{9}$ 5$_{21}$, מַעְיָן *spring* Gn 7$_{11}$ 1 K 18$_{5}$ 2 K 3$_{19.25}$ Ps 87$_{7}$ 2 C 32$_{4}$ 4QCommGenA 1$_{5}$, מַעַל *unfaithfulness* Ezk 39$_{26}$ 4QHalakah^{a} 11$_{3}$, מַעֲמָד *position* Si 43$_{20}$ 4QShirShabb^{d} 1.1$_{12}$, מַעֲנֶה *answer* 1QH 7$_{13}$, מַעֲרָכָה *formation* 1QM 7$_{17}$ 15$_{6}$ 18$_{4}$ 1QSa 2$_{22}$ 4QM^{a} 1$_{14}$ 4QM^{c} 1$_{6}$, מַעֲרֹם *naked one* 2 C 28$_{15}$, *secret* Si 42$_{18}$, מַעֲשֶׂה *deed* Nm 16$_{28}$ 31$_{20}$ Dt 2$_{7}$ 11$_{7}$ 14$_{29}$ 15$_{10}$ 16$_{15}$ 24$_{19}$ 28$_{12}$ 30$_{9}$ Jos 24$_{31}$ Jg 2$_{7}$ 1 S 8$_{8}$ 1 K 13$_{11}$ 2 K 16$_{10}$ 22$_{17}$||2 C 34$_{25}$ 2 K 23$_{19}$ Is 10$_{12}$ 19$_{14}$ 26$_{12}$ Jr 7$_{13}$ Am 8$_{7}$ Mc 6$_{16}$ Hg 2$_{14.17}$ Ps 33$_{4.15}$ 103$_{22}$ 145$_{9.10.17}$ Ec 1$_{14}$ 2$_{11}$ 3$_{17}$ 8$_{9.17}$ 12$_{14}$ Est 10$_{2}$ Dn 9$_{14}$ 2 C 31$_{21}$ 32$_{30}$ Si 7$_{36}$ 14$_{19}$ 30$_{31}$ 32$_{11}$ 34$_{22}$ 35$_{23}$ 36$_{15}$ 37$_{16}$ 42$_{16.22}$ 43$_{28}$ 47$_{8}$ 1QH 1$_{6.7.9.26.30.33}$ 2$_{3}$ 3$_{12.23}$ 4$_{17.20.31.32.40}$ 6$_{8}$ 9$_{36}$ 10$_{8.11.36}$ 11$_{24.30}$ 13$_{8.14.19}$ 14$_{16}$ 15$_{20}$ 16$_{10.14}$ 1QH fr. 5$_{8}$ 12$_{3}$ 1QM 13$_{1}$ 15$_{9}$ 1QS 1$_{5.19}$ 2$_{5}$ 3$_{25}$ 4$_{3.20.23}$ 5$_{18.19}$ 10$_{17}$ 11$_{16}$ 1QSb 2$_{27}$ 1Q26.1$_{6}$ 4QTobit^{e} 6$_{1}$ 4QJub^{a} 1$_{11.11}$ 2$_{1.1.3.16}$ 4QJub^{d} 21$_{15.21.21.23.24}$ 4QJub^{f} 21$_{23.24}$ 4QJub^{h} 36$_{8}$ 4QD^{a} 1$_{3}$ 4QMyst^{a} 3a.2$_{3.10.15}$ 37$_{2}$ 4QCreatA 1$_{6}$ 4QPrEnosh 2$_{5}$ 4Q392 1$_{7}$ 4QShirShabb^{a} 1.1$_{5}$ 4QShirShabb^{d} 1.1$_{35}$ 4QShirShabb^{f} 19$_{5.6}$ 23.2$_{12}$ 33$_{2}$ 4Q417 1.1$_{6}$ 2.1$_{10}$ 4Q418 102$_{2}$ 148.1$_{3}$ 4Q423 4$_{2}$ 5$_{4}$ 7$_{4}$ 4QHod^{a} 7.2$_{11}$ 4QHod^{b} 2$_{2}$ 4QHod^{d} 1$_{5}$ 4QHod^{f} 3$_{1}$ 4QPrayer^{m} 1.2$_{8}$ 4QM^{h} 2$_{4}$ 4QShir^{b} 10$_{10}$ 18.2$_{7}$ 63.3$_{2}$ 63.4$_{1}$ 4QRitPur 5$_{16}$ 11QPs^{a} 18$_{7}$ 11QShirShabb 1$_{5}$ 7$_{1}$ 11QT 50$_{17}$ GnzPs 1$_{10.12}$ 2$_{22}$ 4$_{10.11.22}$, מַעֲשֵׂר *tithe* Lv 27$_{30.32}$ Nm 18$_{21.28}$ Dt 14$_{28}$ 26$_{12}$ Ml 3$_{10}$.

מִפְלָג *division* 4QShirShabb^{f} 23.1$_{7}$ 4QPrQuot 1.3$_{7}$ 15.6$_{11}$, מִפְעָל *deed* Si 15$_{19}$, מִצְוָה *commandment* Lv 4$_{2.13.22}$ 5$_{17}$ 26$_{14.15}$ Nm 15$_{22.39.40}$ Dt 5$_{29}$=4QTestim$_{3}$ Dt 5$_{31}$ 6$_{25}$ 8$_{1}$ 11$_{8.22}$ 13$_{19}$ 15$_{5}$ 19$_{9}$ 26$_{13.18}$ 27$_{1}$ 28$_{1.15}$ 30$_{8}$ 31$_{5}$ 1 K 6$_{12}$ 2 K 17$_{16}$ Jr 35$_{18}$ Ps 119$_{6.86.151.172}$ Ne 10$_{30}$ 1 C 28$_{8}$ 1QS 8$_{17}$ 4QJub^{a} 1$_{9.14}$ 4Q365^{a} 1$_{5}$ 4QapMoses^{a} 2.2$_{8}$ 4QapMoses^{c} 2.2$_{5}$ 4QpsMose^{e} 2.1$_{4}$ 4QsapHymnA 1.1$_{2}$ 11QT 55$_{13}$, מְצוּדָה *enticement* 1QH 3$_{26}$, מְצוּלָה *depth* Zc 10$_{11}$, מָצוֹק *hardship* 4QJub^{a} 1$_{8}$ 4QPseud^{b} 1$_{7}$, מִצְרַיִם *Egypt* Gn 41$_{55}$ 45$_{9}$ 47$_{15}$ Ex 7$_{24}$ 9$_{11}$ 10$_{6}$ 12$_{30}$ Nm 33$_{3}$ Dt 7$_{18}$ 2QJub^{b} 46$_{2}$, מִקְדָּשׁ *temple* 1QM 16$_{1}$ (מקוד[ש]) 11QT 45$_{8}$, מִקְוֶה *hope* 4QMyst^{a} 6.1$_{14}$, מִקְוֶה *pool* Ex 7$_{19}$ 4QapMes 5$_{3}$, מָקוֹם *place* Gn 18$_{26}$ 20$_{13}$ Ex 20$_{24}$ Nm 18$_{31}$ Dt 11$_{24}$ 12$_{2.13}$ Jos 1$_{3}$ 1 S 7$_{16}$ 30$_{31}$ Is 7$_{23}$ Jr 8$_{3}$ 24$_{9}$ 29$_{14}$ 40$_{12}$ 45$_{5}$ Ezk 34$_{12}$ Am 4$_{6}$ 8$_{3}$ Ml 1$_{11}$ Ps 103$_{22}$ Pr 15$_{3}$ Ezr 1$_{4}$ Ne 4$_{6}$ 12$_{27}$ 1QS 6$_{3}$ 4QapMes 1.3$_{4}$ 11QT 48$_{11}$ 51$_{19}$, מִקְטֶרֶת *incense altar* 2 C 30$_{14}$, מִקְנָה *purchase* Gn 17$_{23}$, מִקְנֶה *livestock, possession* Gn 31$_{18}$ 47$_{17}$ Ex 9$_{6}$ 34$_{19}$ Nm 31$_{9}$ 4QJub^{h} 35$_{10}$ 36$_{12}$, מַר *bitter thing* Pr 27$_{7}$, מַרְאֶה *appearance* Lv 13$_{12}$ 1QM 6$_{13}$, מַרְבִּית *increase* 1 S 2$_{33}$, מָרוֹם *height* 4QShirShabb^{a} 2$_{4}$ 4QShirShabb^{d} 1.1$_{34}$ 4QShirShabb^{f} 23.2$_{11}$, מֶרְחָק *distance* Is 8$_{9}$, מֶרְכָּב *seat* Lv 15$_{9}$, מַרְעִית *grazing land* Jr 10$_{21}$.

מַשָּׂא *burden* Nm 4$_{27.27}$ Ne 13$_{15}$, מְשׂוּרָה *volume* 1 C 23$_{29}$, מָשׂוֹשׂ *joy* Ho 2$_{13}$, מַשְׂכִּיל *teacher* 4Q418 81$_{17}$, מַשְׂכִּית *image* Nm 33$_{52}$, מִשְׁאָלָה *request* Ps 20$_{6}$ GnzPs 3$_{7}$, מִשְׁבָּר

breaker Jon 2$_{4}$ Ps 42$_{8}$ 88$_{8}$ 1QH 6$_{23}$ 4QHod^{c} 2.2$_{2}$, *birth channel* 1QH 3$_{10}$, מַשְׁחִית *destroyer* 1QH 3$_{38}$, מָשִׁיחַ *anointed one* 4QapMes 4$_{9}$, מִשְׁכָּב *bed* Lv 15$_{4.24.26}$ Ps 41$_{4}$, מִשְׁכָּן *tabernacle* Nm 4$_{16}$ Ps 87$_{2}$, מֹשֵׁל *ruler* GnzPs 3$_{14}$, מִשְׁלַח *undertaking* Dt 12$_{7.18}$ 15$_{10}$ 23$_{21}$ 28$_{8.20}$ 1QS 9$_{23}$ 4Q418 91$_{2}$ 4QShir^{b} 16$_{2}$, מִשְׁלַחַה *mission* 4QShirShabb^{f} 23.1$_{13}$, מִשְׁמָר *vigilance* Pr 4$_{23}$, מִשְׁעָן *support* Is 3$_{1.1}$, מִשְׁפָּחָה *family* Gn 12$_{3}$ 28$_{14}$ Nm 26$_{43}$ Jos 6$_{23}$ Jg 1$_{25}$ 9$_{1}$ 1 S 9$_{21}$ 20$_{6}$ 2 S 14$_{7}$ Jr 1$_{15}$ 2$_{4}$ 25$_{9}$ 31$_{1}$ Am 3$_{1.2}$ Zc 12$_{14}$ Ps 22$_{28}$ 1 C 4$_{27}$ 7$_{5}$ 1QSa 1$_{15}$ 4QMyst^{a} 67$_{2}$ 4QRitPur 51.2$_{11}$, מִשְׁפָּט *judgment* Ex 24$_{3}$ Lv 19$_{37}$ 20$_{22}$ Nm 9$_{3}$ 2 S 22$_{23}$||Ps 18$_{23}$ 1 K 6$_{38}$ Ps 119$_{13.160}$ Pr 16$_{33}$ 1QH 1$_{37}$ 7$_{35}$ 11$_{8}$ 14$_{20}$ 1QS 6$_{15}$ 1QSa 1$_{5}$ 1QSb 3$_{23}$ 1QDM 2$_{7.7}$ 4QJub^{a} 1$_{6}$ 4QapMoses^{b} 1.3$_{1}$ 4Q419 1$_{1}$ 4QHod^{b} 7$_{2}$ 4QM^{a} 4$_{3}$ CD 14$_{8}$, מַשְׁקֶה *drink* Lv 11$_{34}$, מִשְׁקָל *weight* Ezr 8$_{34}$ 4Q418 87$_{12}$, מִשְׁרָה *extract* Nm 6$_{3}$, מְשָׁרֵת *minister* GnzPs 4$_{12}$ 1QM 13$_{3}$ 4QBer^{b} 2$_{9.12}$, מֹת *human being* Jb 19$_{19}$, מַתָּנָה *gift* Ex 28$_{38}$ Nm 18$_{29}$ 11QT 29$_{6}$, מָתְנַיִם *loins* Ezk 29$_{7}$ Am 8$_{10}$ Na 2$_{11}$ 4QMidrEschat^{b} 10$_{3}$.

נְאָצָה *disparagement* Ezk 35$_{12}$ (or em. כָּל־ to קוֹל *sound of*), נְבוּאָה *prophecy* GnzPs 2$_{7}$ 3$_{11}$ 4$_{17}$, נָבִיא *prophet* 1 K 19$_{1}$ 22$_{10.12.22}$||2 C 18$_{9.11.21}$ 1 K 22$_{23}$ 2 K 10$_{19}$ 17$_{13}$, נֵבֶל *jar* Jr 13$_{12.12}$, נְבָלָה *folly* Jg 20$_{10}$, נְבֵלָה *corpse* Dt 14$_{21}$ Ezk 44$_{31}$ 11QT 48$_{5}$, נֶגֶב *Negeb* Jos 11$_{16}$, נָגוּעַ *affliction* 1QS 3$_{23}$, נָגִיד *leader* 1 C 13$_{1}$, נְגִינָה *music* 1QS 10$_{9}$, נֶגַע *blow* Dt 21$_{5}$ 1QH 1$_{18}$ 16$_{15}$ 4QM^{g} 1$_{8}$ 4Q417 2.2$_{9}$ 4QBark^{a} 1.2$_{11}$ 11QPs Ap^{a} 1$_{4}$ 11QT 63$_{4}$, *disease* Lv 14$_{54}$ 1 K 8$_{37}$||2 C 6$_{28}$, נְדָבָה *freewill offering* Lv 22$_{18}$ 23$_{38}$, נִדָּה *defilement* 1QpHab 8$_{13}$ 4QOrd^{b} 30$_{1}$, נָדִיב *one who is generous* Ex 35$_{5.22}$ 1 C 28$_{21}$ 2 C 29$_{31}$ 1QSb 3$_{27}$, נֶדֶר *vow* Nm 30$_{5.6.12.14.15}$ Dt 23$_{19}$ 11QT 53$_{19.20}$ 54$_{4}$, *votive offering* Lv 22$_{18}$ 23$_{38}$ Dt 12$_{17}$ 11QT 53$_{9}$, נָהָר *river* Na 1$_{4}$ 1QH 6, נָוֶה *dwelling place* Lm 2$_{2}$, נוֹעָד *companion* 1QH 5$_{23}$, נַחַל *river* 1 K 18$_{5}$ Ec 1$_{7}$ 4QBer^{a} 5$_{10}$, נַחֲלָה *inheritance* 4QpPs^{a} 3$_{1}$, נְחֹשֶׁת *bronze* Jr 52$_{17}$ (||2 K 25$_{13}$ lacks כָּל־), נֵכָר *foreignness* Ne 13$_{30}$, נִמְהָר *terrified one* 1QH 2$_{9}$, נָסוֹג *apostate one* CD 7$_{13}$, נָסִיךְ *prince* Ps 83$_{12}$, נֶסֶךְ *drink offering* 11QT 29$_{6}$, נַעֲוֶה *perverse one* 4Q416 2.1$_{7}$ 4Q417 1.1$_{13}$, נַעַר *lad* 2 S 13$_{32}$ Ne 5$_{16}$ 1QM 7$_{3}$ 4QD^{d} 8.2$_{6}$, נַעֲרָה *young woman* Est 2$_{3}$, נִפְלָאָה *wonder* Ex 3$_{20}$ Jg 6$_{13}$ Jr 21$_{2}$ Ps 9$_{2}$ 26$_{7}$ 105$_{2}$||1 C 16$_{9}$ Si 42$_{17}$ 1QH 1$_{34}$ 4QS^{j} 1$_{7}$ 4QBark^{a} 1.2$_{1}$ 4QBark^{d} 1$_{1}$ 4QNarrF 2$_{1}$ GnzPs 3$_{23}$, נֶפֶשׁ *soul* Gn 1$_{21}$ 9$_{10.12.15.16}$ 36$_{6}$ 46$_{15.22.25.26.26.27}$ Ex 1$_{5}$ 12$_{16}$ Lv 7$_{27}$ 11$_{10.46.46}$ 17$_{12.15}$ 21$_{11}$ 23$_{29.30}$ 24$_{17}$ Nm 19$_{11}$ 31$_{35}$ Dt 4$_{29}$ 6$_{5}$ 10$_{12}$ 11$_{13}$ 13$_{4}$ 26$_{16}$ 30$_{2.6.10}$ Jos 10$_{28+6t}$ 11$_{11}$ 22$_{5}$ 23$_{14}$ 1 S 22$_{22}$ 2 S 1$_{9(ms)}$ 1 K 2$_{4}$ 8$_{48}$||2 C 6$_{38}$ 2 K 23$_{3}$||2 C 34$_{31}$ 2 K 23$_{25}$ Jr 31$_{25}$ 32$_{41}$ 43$_{6}$ 52$_{30}$ Ezk 18$_{4}$ 47$_{9}$ 2 C 15$_{12}$ Si 37$_{28}$ 1QH 15$_{10}$ 1QS 5$_{9}$ 11$_{19}$ 4QJub^{h} 37$_{24}$ 4QS^{a} 1$_{2}$ 4QErr 1$_{12}$ 4QAdmon 1.1$_{1}$ 4QapMoses^{a} 1.1$_{2.3}$ 4QpsEzek^{c} 3.2$_{2}$ 4QMMT C$_{15.16}$ 4QBark^{d} 2.1$_{13}$ 4QDibHam^{a} 1.2$_{13}$ 11QT 25$_{11}$ 54$_{13}$ 59$_{10}$ CD 11$_{16}$ 12$_{12}$ 15$_{10.12}$, נָפַת דֹּאר *Naphath-dor* 1 K 4$_{11}$, נַפְתָּלִי *Naphtali* Dt 34$_{2}$, נְקֵבָה *female* Nm 31$_{15}$, נְקָמָה *vengeance* Lm 3$_{60}$, נֵר *lamp* 11QT 9$_{12}$, נָשִׂיא *prince* Ex 16$_{22}$ 34$_{31}$ Nm 13$_{2}$ 17$_{17.21}$ 31$_{13}$ Jos 9$_{19}$ Ezk 21$_{17}$ 26$_{16}$ 27$_{21}$ 32$_{29}$ 2 C 1$_{2}$ 4QShirShabb^{d} 1.1$_{26}$ 4QM^{a} 1$_{4.5}$, נִשְׁכָּה *chamber* 11QT 42$_{3}$, נְשָׁמָה *soul* Dt 20$_{16}$ Jos 10$_{40}$ 11$_{11.14}$ 1 K 15$_{29}$ Ps 150$_{6}$ 11QT 62$_{14}$, נֵתַח *piece (of meat)* Ezk 24$_{4}$, נְתִיבָה *path* Pr 3$_{17}$ GnzPs 3$_{5}$, נָתִין *temple servant* Ezr 2$_{58}$||Ne 7$_{60}$.

סְאוֹן *boot* Is 9$_{4}$, סָבִיב *surrounding area* (oft. as prep., *all around it*, etc.) Nm 22$_{4}$ Jr 21$_{14}$ 48$_{17.39}$ 49$_{5}$ 50$_{32}$ Ezk 28$_{24}$ Ps 76$_{12}$ 89$_{8}$ Dn 9$_{16}$ Ezr 1$_{6}$ 4QJub^{h} 36$_{12}$, סֵבֶל *forced labour* 1 K 11$_{28}$, סֶגֶן *governor* Jr 51$_{28}$, סוֹד *secret, counsel, council* Si 9$_{15}$ 42$_{1}$ 4QBer^{a} 1.2$_{3}$ 4QapPs^{b} 15$_{6}$ 4QShir Shabb^{d} 1.1$_{34}$ 4QShir^{b} 47.1$_{2}$ MasShirShabb 2$_{25}$ CD 14$_{9}$, סוּס *horse* Ex 14$_{9.23}$ Zc 12$_{4.4}$, סִיר *pot* Zc 14$_{21}$, סֶמֶל *image* Dt 4$_{16}$, סֵפֶר *document* Dn 1$_{17}$ 4Q418 148.2$_{7}$ Lachish ost. 3$_{11}$, סֶרֶךְ *order* 1QM 4$_{6.11}$ 7$_{17}$ 16$_{3}$ 4QM^{a} 1$_{19}$ 4QM^{c} 1$_{9}$, סֶרֶן *prince* Jg 16$_{27}$ 1 S 5$_{8.11}$ Si 46$_{18}$, סֵתֶר *secrecy* Si 16$_{21}$ (בכל סתר appar. *in complete secrecy*), עֶבֶד *servant* Gn 20$_{8}$ 40$_{20}$ 41$_{37}$ 50$_{7}$ Ex 7$_{29}$ 10$_{6}$ 11$_{8}$ 12$_{30.44}$ Dt 29$_{1}$ 34$_{11}$ 1 S 18$_{22.30}$ 19$_{1}$ 22$_{6.14}$ 2 S 11$_{9}$ 13$_{31.36}$ 15$_{14.18}$ 16$_{6.11}$ 19$_{6.15}$ 1 K 3$_{15}$ 2 K 9$_{7}$ 17$_{23}$ Jr 7$_{25}$ 25$_{4}$ 35$_{15}$ 36$_{24}$ 44$_{4}$ Ps 134$_{1}$ 135$_{9}$ Est 3$_{2}$ 4$_{11}$ Ne 9$_{10}$ 1QS 1$_{3}$ 4QPrayers^{b} 2$_{4}$ 4QapJoseph^{c} 1$_{2}$ 4QWays^{b} 9$_{3}$ 12$_{2}$, עֲבֹדָה *service* Ex 1$_{14.14}$ 27$_{19}$ 35$_{21}$ 39$_{32.42}$ Nm 3$_{26.31.36}$ 4$_{27.27.31.32.33}$ 18$_{4}$ Ezk 44$_{14}$ 1 C 6$_{33}$ 28$_{21.21}$ 2 C 35$_{16}$ 1QM 2$_{15}$ 13$_{5}$ 1QS 3$_{26.26}$ 4QMyst^{a} 10$_{8}$ 4QMyst^{c} 1$_{3}$ 4Q410 2$_{1}$ 4Q418 137$_{3}$ 4QShir^{b} 63.2$_{4}$ 63.3$_{5}$ CD 14$_{16}$, עֵבֶר *side* 1 K 5$_{4.4}$ Jr 49$_{32}$ 1QM 6$_{10}$ ([ע]ברי), עֶבְרָה *anger* Ps 85$_{4}$ 4Q418 211$_{3}$.

עֵדָה *congregation* Ex 12$_{3.47}$ 16$_{1.2.9.10}$ 17$_{1}$ 35$_{1.4.20}$ Lv 4$_{13}$ 8$_{3}$ 9$_{5}$ 10$_{6}$ 19$_{2}$ 24$_{14.16}$ Nm 1$_{2.18}$ 3$_{7}$ 8$_{9.20}$ 10$_{3}$ 13$_{26.26}$ 14$_{1.2.7.10.35.36}$ 15$_{24.25.26.33.35.36}$ 16$_{3}$ +7t 17$_{6}$ 20$_{1.22.27.29}$ 25$_{6}$ 26$_{2}$ 27$_{2.19.20.21.22}$ 31$_{27}$ Jos 9$_{18.19.21}$ 18$_{1}$ 22$_{12.16.18.20}$ Jg 21$_{13}$ 1 K 8$_{5}$ ||2 C 5$_{6}$ Jb 16$_{7}$ 1QM 2$_{5.9}$ 3$_{13}$ 4$_{15}$ 5$_{1}$ 1QpHab 5$_{12}$ 1QSa 1$_{1}$ 1QSa 1$_{23}$ 1QSa 2$_{12.21}$ 1QSb 3$_{3}$ 1QDM 1$_{2}$ 4QapMoses^{a} 2.2$_{6}$ 4QapMoses^{b} 1.3$_{1}$ 4QShirShabb^{f} 23.1$_{3}$ 4QM^{a} 16$_{2}$ 5Q

17 1$_2$ 11QT 22$_{02}$ 39$_6$ CD 7$_{20}$ 8$_{13}$ 19$_{26}$, עֵדֶר *herd* Gn 29$_{3.8}$, עוֹד *continuity*, i.e. all the while 2 S 1$_9$ (ms lacks עוֹד; or del. כָּל־) Jb 27$_3$, עָוֶל *iniquity* 1QS 6$_{15}$ 8$_{18}$ 9$_{21}$ 4Q418 161$_5$, עַוְלָה *iniquity* Ps 107$_{42}$ 1QH 14$_{15}$ 15$_{25}$ 4Q416 1$_{13}$ 4Q418 2$_5$, עוֹלָם *eternity, age* Ps 145$_{13}$ 4QTobit^{e} 6$_{5.10}$ 4QJub^{a} 1$_{26}$ 2$_1$ 4QBer^{a} 7.1$_7$ 4QapJoshua^{b} 14$_3$ GnzPs 3$_{17.20}$, עָוֹן *iniquity* Lv 16$_{21.22}$ Dt 19$_{15}$ Jr 33$_{8.8}$ Ezk 36$_{33}$ Am 3$_2$ Ps 51$_{11}$ 103$_3$ 130$_8$ Si 5$_6$ 1QH 17$_{15}$ 1QS 3$_{6.7}$ 11$_{14}$ 4QapLam^{a} 1$_2$ 4QSD 7.2$_9$ 4QD^{f} 3$_3$ 4QBer^{a} 7.2$_6$ 4QConfess 1.2$_5$ 11QMelch 2$_6$ 11QT 26$_{11.13}$ 58$_{17}$ 61$_6$, עוֹף *bird* Gn 1$_{21.30}$ 2$_{19}$ 7$_{14}$ 8$_{19.20}$ 9$_2$ Dt 14$_{20}$ 28$_{26}$ Jr 4$_{25}$ Ezk 31$_{6.13}$ 32$_4$ Ps 50$_{11}$ 1QH 8$_9$ 4QJub^{a} 2$_{11}$ 4QJub^{c} 21$_6$ 11QT 46$_3$, עוֹר *skin* Lv 13$_{12}$ 15$_{17}$ 4QD^{d} 8.2$_3$ 11QT 47$_7$, עֵז *goat* Gn 30$_{35}$, עֹז *strength* 2 S 6$_{14}$ 1 C 13$_8$ 4Q185.1.2$_{15}$ 4QapJoseph^{b} 1$_{18}$, עַיִן *eye* 1 S 11$_2$.

עִיר *city* Gn 18$_{28}$ Nm 21$_{25.25}$ 31$_{10}$ 35$_7$ Dt 2$_{34.34}$ 3$_{4.6.10}$ 20$_{15}$ Jos 10$_{37.39}$ 11$_{12.13}$ 13$_{10.17.21.25}$ 15$_{32}$ 16$_9$ 21$_{19+6t}$ Jg 11$_{26}$ 20$_{37.48}$ 1 S 4$_{13}$ 5$_{11}$ 6$_{18}$ 18$_6$ 2 S 12$_{31}$||1 C 20$_3$ 2 S 24$_7$ 1 K 22$_{39}$ 2 K 3$_{19.19}$ 17$_9$ 18$_{13}$||Is 36$_1$ Jr 1$_{15}$ 4$_{26.29.29}$ 19$_{15}$ 26$_2$ 31$_{24}$ 33$_{12}$ 34$_{1.7}$ 44$_2$ 48$_{8.24}$ 49$_{13}$ Ho 13$_{10}$ Am 4$_6$ Ru 1$_{19}$ Est 8$_{11.17}$ Ne 8$_{15}$ 10$_{38}$ 11$_{20}$ 1 C 6$_{45}$ 2 C 8$_{4.6.6}$ 11$_{12.23}$ 2 C 14$_{4.13.13}$ 17$_{2.9}$ 19$_5$ 20$_4$ 23$_2$ 28$_{25}$ 31$_{19}$ 33$_{14}$ 1QM 12$_{13}$ 19$_5$ 4QpIsa^{a} 5$_{12}$ 4QapLam^{a} 1$_{11}$ 4QapJoseph^{b} 2$_9$ 4QBark^{f} 1.1$_5$ 11QT 45$_{11}$ 48$_{14}$ 57$_5$, עלה hi. inf. *offering* 1 C 23$_{31}$, עֹלָה *burnt offering* 2 C 29$_{34}$ 4QWays^{b} 13$_2$, עֲלִילָה *(mis)deed* Ezk 20$_{43}$ 21$_{29}$ Zp 3$_{7.11}$ 1QS 4$_{1.21}$.

עַם *people* Gn 19$_4$ 26$_{11}$ 35$_6$ 41$_{40}$ 42$_6$ Ex 1$_{22}$ 11$_8$ 18$_{14.21.23}$ 19$_{5.8.11.16}$ 20$_{18}$ 23$_{27}$ 24$_3$ 32$_3$ 33$_{8.10.10.16}$ 34$_{10.10}$ Lv 9$_{23.24}$ 10$_3$ 16$_{33}$ Nm 11$_{11.12.13.14.29}$ 13$_{32}$ 15$_{26}$ 21$_{23.33.34.35}$ 32$_{15}$ Dt 2$_{32.33}$ 3$_{1.2.3}$ 4$_{19}$ 7$_{6.7.14.16.19}$ 10$_{15}$ 13$_{10}$ 14$_2$ 17$_{7.13}$ 20$_{11}$ 27$_{15+11t}$ 28$_{10.37.64}$ 30$_3$ Jos 1$_2$ 4$_{11.24}$ 5$_{4.5.5}$ 6$_5$ 7$_{3.3}$ 8$_{1.3.5.11.14.16}$ 10$_{7.21}$ 11$_7$ 24$_{2.17.18.27}$ Jg 4$_{13}$ 7$_{1.7}$ 9$_{34.48.49}$ 11$_{20.21}$ 14$_3$ 16$_{30}$ 20$_{2.8.16.26}$ 1 S 2$_{23}$ 9$_2$ 10$_{23.24.24.24.25}$ 11$_{4.15}$ 12$_{18.19}$ 13$_{7.22}$ 14$_{15.20.24.34.39}$ 15$_8$ 18$_5$ 23$_8$ 30$_6$ 2 S 2$_{28.30}$ 3$_{31+6t}$ 6$_{2.19.19}$ 8$_{15}$ 12$_{29.31}$||1 C 20$_3$ 2 S 15$_{17.23.23.24.30}$ 16$_{6.14.15}$ 17$_{2.3.3.16.22}$ 18$_{4.5}$ 19$_{3.9.9.10.40.41}$ 20$_{12.15.22}$ 1 K 1$_{39.40}$ 5$_{14}$ 8$_{38}$||2 C 6$_{29}$ 1 K 8$_{43}$||2 C 6$_{33}$ 1 K 8$_{53.60}$ 9$_7$||2 C 7$_{20}$ 1 K 9$_{20}$||2 C 8$_7$ 1 K 12$_{12}$||2 C 10$_{12}$ 1 K 18$_{21.24.30.30.39}$ 20$_{8.10.15}$ 2 K 10$_{9.18}$ 11$_{14.18.19.20}$||2 C 23$_{13.16.17.21}$ 2 K 14$_{21}$||2 C 26$_1$ 2 K 16$_{15}$ 23$_2$||2 C 34$_{30}$ 2 K 23$_{2.3.21}$ 25$_{26}$ Is 25$_{6.7}$ 56$_7$ Jr 19$_{14}$ 25$_{1.2.19}$ 26$_{7+7t}$ 27$_{16}$ 28$_{1.5.7.11}$ 29$_{1.16.25}$ 34$_{1.8.10.19}$ 36$_{9.9.10}$ 38$_{1.4}$ 41$_{10.13.14}$ 42$_{1.8}$ 43$_{1.4}$ 44$_{15.20.20.24}$ Ezk 31$_{12}$ 39$_{13}$ 45$_{16.22}$ Mc 4$_5$ Hb 2$_5$ Zp 1$_{11}$ 3$_{20}$ Hg 2$_4$ Zc 7$_5$ 11$_{10}$ 12$_{2.3.6}$ 14$_{12}$ Ml 2$_9$ Ps 47$_2$ 49$_2$ 96$_3$||1 C 16$_{24}$ Ps 97$_6$ 99$_2$ 106$_{48}$||1 C 16$_{36}$ Ps 116$_{14.18}$ Ru 4$_{9.11}$ Ec 4$_{16}$ Lm 1$_{11.18}$ 3$_{14}$ Est 1$_{5.16}$ 3$_{8.14}$ 8$_{13}$ 9$_2$ Dn 9$_6$ Ezr 1$_3$||2 C 36$_{23}$ Ezr 3$_{11}$ 10$_9$ Ne 8$_{1+10t}$ 9$_{10.32}$ 1 C 13$_4$ 16$_{43}$ 18$_{14}$ 28$_{21}$ 2 C 7$_{4.5}$ 23$_{5.6.10.20}$ 24$_{10}$ 29$_{36}$ 32$_{13}$ Si 50$_{19}$ 1QH 4$_{26}$ 1QM 1$_{12}$ ([כו]ל) 3$_{13}$ 8$_9$ 9$_1$ 10$_9$ 16$_{7.8}$ 17$_{13.14}$ 1QpHab 3$_{6.11}$ ([כ]ול) 3$_{13}$ ([כול]) 4$_{14}$ ([כו]ל) 6$_7$ 1QS 2$_{21}$ 6$_9$ 1QMyst 1.1$_8$ 1.2$_{10}$ 1QlitPr 3.2$_6$ 4QVisSam 3.2$_5$ 4QpIsa^{a} 8$_{21}$ 4QMidrEschat^{b} 9$_{14}$ 4Q185.1.2$_{8.10}$ 4QMyst^{a} 79$_8$ 4QapJerB 10$_6$ 4QpsEzek^{a} 12$_2$ 4QpsEzek^{e} 6-7$_2$ 4Q419 1$_7$ 4QM^{a} 13$_8$ 4QDibHam^{a} 1.4$_5$ 11QT 15$_7$ 21$_6$ 26$_{7.9}$ 56$_{10}$ 62$_7$ GnzPs 2$_6$ 3$_{10}$ 4$_{16}$, עַמּוּד *column* Ex 27$_{17}$ 38$_{17}$, עָמָל *trouble* Gn 41$_{51}$ Ec 1$_3$ 2$_{10.10.18.19.20.22}$ 3$_{13}$ 4$_{4.8}$ 5$_{17}$ 6$_7$, עֵמֶק *valley* Jr 31$_{40}$ 1 C 12$_{16}$.

עֵנָב *grape* 11QT 21$_7$, ענה pu. inf. *pain* Ps 132$_1$ (or em. עֲנָוָה), עָנָו *humble one* Zp 2$_3$ Ps 76$_{10}$ 4QTobit^{e} 2$_6$, עָפָר *dust* Ex 8$_{13}$ Lv 14$_{45}$, עֵץ *tree* Gn 1$_{29}$ 2$_{9.16}$ 3$_1$ 23$_{17}$ Ex 9$_{25}$ 10$_5$ Lv 19$_{23}$ Dt 12$_2$ 16$_{21}$ 22$_6$ 28$_{42}$ Jg 9$_{14}$ 2 S 6$_5$ 1 K 14$_{23}$ 2 K 3$_{19.25}$ 16$_4$||2 C 28$_4$ 2 K 17$_{10}$ Is 44$_{23}$ 55$_{12}$ 57$_5$ Jr 2$_{20}$ 3$_{6.13}$ Ezk 6$_{13}$ 15$_2$ 17$_{24}$ 20$_{28}$ 21$_{3.3.15}$ 31$_{4+6t}$ 47$_{12}$ Jl 1$_{12.19}$ Ps 96$_{12}$ Ca 4$_{14}$ Ne 10$_{36.38}$ 1QH 3$_{29}$ 8$_{6.9}$ 4QJub^{a} 2$_{12}$ 4QJub^{d} 21$_{13}$ 4QHalakah^{a} 6$_8$ 4QD^{a} 6.4$_2$ 4Q423 2$_1$ 11QT 38$_7$ 65$_2$ CD 12$_{15}$, עָצָב *image* Mc 1$_7$, עַצָּב *worker* Is 58$_3$, עֶצֶב *pain* Pr 14$_{23}$ 4QPrFêtes^{c} 16$_2$, עַצֶּבֶת *pain* Jb 9$_{28}$, עֵצָה *counsel* 2 S 16$_{23}$ Jr 18$_{23}$ Ps 20$_5$ Pr 1$_{25}$ 1QS 6$_9$ 8$_{18.25}$ 9$_9$ 11QT 57$_{15}$, עֶצֶם *bone* Is 38$_{13}$ Jr 23$_9$ Ps 22$_{15.18}$ 34$_{21}$ 35$_{10}$ 4QapJoseph^{b} 1$_{15}$ 4QMMT B$_{73}$, עֵרֶב *mixed people* Jr 50$_{37}$ Ezk 30$_5$ Ne 13$_3$, עֹרֵב *raven* Lv 11$_{15}$||Dt 14$_{14}$, עֲרָבָה *desert* Dt 4$_{49}$ Jos 12$_1$, עֶרְוָה *nakedness* 1QM 7$_7$ 10$_1$ 4QRitPur 3$_{17}$ 11QT 58$_{17}$, עָרוּם *astute person* Pr 13$_{16}$ (or em. כָּל־ to כֹּל an astute person does *everything*, as §1, or *makes measure*, i.e. measures, as כֹּל III), עֵרֶךְ *valuation* Lv 27$_{25}$, עָרֵל *uncircumcised one* Ex 12$_{48}$ 4QNarrA 2.2$_4$, עֵשֶׂב *plant* Gn 1$_{29}$ 2$_5$ Ex 9$_{22.25}$ 10$_{12.15}$ Dt 29$_{22}$ Is 42$_{15}$ Ps 105$_{35}$, עֹשֶׂה *worker* 2 C 34$_{13}$, עֹשֶׁר *wealth* Gn 31$_{16}$, עֵת *time* Ex 18$_{22.26}$ Lv 16$_2$ Ps 10$_5$ 34$_2$ 62$_9$ 106$_3$ 119$_{20}$ Jb 27$_{10}$ Pr 5$_{19}$ 6$_{14}$ 8$_{30}$ 17$_{17}$ Ec 9$_8$ Est 5$_{13}$ 4QJub^{d} 21$_{16}$ 4Q417 1.1$_1$ 4QM^{a} 1$_{17}$ GnzPs 2$_2$ 3$_{24}$, עַתּוּד *leader* Is 14$_9$, עָתוּד *prepared one* 1QM 9$_5$ 15$_2$.

פֶּגֶר *corpse* Jr 41$_9$ 4QM^{a} 15$_9$, פֶּה *mouth* 1 K 19$_{18}$ Is 9$_{11.16}$ 4QapDidA 1$_7$ 4QPrMercy 1$_5$, פַּח *trap* 1QH 3$_{26}$ 4QpPs^{a} 2$_9$, פַּחַד *trembling* 1QS 1$_{17}$, פֶּטֶר *firstborn* Ex 13$_{12.12.13}$ (or em. בְּכוֹר *firstborn*) 13$_{15}$ 34$_{19}$ Nm 18$_{15}$ Ezk 20$_{26}$, פְּלִשְׁתִּי *Philistine* 2 S 5$_{17}$||1 C 14$_8$ Jr 47$_4$, פְּלֵתִי *Pelethite* 2 S

15$_{18}$, פִּנָּה *corner* Pr 7$_{12}$ 2 C 28$_{24}$ 4QShirShabb^{d} 1.14$_{1}$, *leader* 1 S 14$_{38}$, פָּנִים *face* Is 25$_{8}$ Jr 30$_{6}$ Ezk 7$_{18}$ 21$_{3}$ Jl 2$_{6}$ Si 36$_{27(C)}$, *surface* Gn 2$_{6}$ 19$_{28}$ 41$_{56}$ Ezk 34$_{6}$ 1 C 5$_{10}$, פִּסֵּחַ *lame one* 1QM 7$_{4}$, פֶּסֶל *image* Is 21$_{9}$ Mc 1$_{7}$ 2 C 33$_{22}$ 1QpHab 12$_{12}$, פְּעוּלָּה *deed* 1QS 4$_{15}$, פֹּעַל *deed* Ps 77$_{13}$ 92$_{8.10}$ 143$_{5}$ Pr 16$_{4}$ Si 37$_{16}$, פִּקּוּד *precept* Ps 111$_{7}$, פְּקֻדָּה *visitation* 4Q416 1$_{9}$ 4Q417 2.1$_{14}$, פַּר *(young) bull* Lv 4$_{12}$ Jr 50$_{27}$, פֵּרוּשׁ *list* 1QM 4$_{7.8.12}$, פְּרִי *fruit* Ex 10$_{15}$ Lv 19$_{24}$ Dt 26$_{2}$ Is 27$_{9}$ Ec 2$_{5}$ Ne 10$_{36}$ 4QapPs^{b} 1$_{6}$ 4QParGenEx 3$_{10}$ 4Q423 2$_{1}$, פֶּשַׁע *sin* Lv 16$_{21}$ 1 K 8$_{50}$ Ezk 14$_{11}$ 18$_{22.28.30.31}$ 37$_{23}$ Ps 39$_{9}$ Pr 10$_{12}$ Lm 1$_{22}$ Si 10$_{6}$ 38$_{10}$ 1QH 17$_{11}$ 1QS 1$_{23}$ 4QOrd^{a} 1.2$_{2}$ 4QDibHam^{a} 1.6$_{2}$ 4QShir^{b} 18.2$_{9}$ 4QRitPur 7$_{9}$ GnzPs 1$_{13}$, פִּתּוּחַ *engraving* 2 C 2$_{13}$, פֶּתַח *entrance* 1 K 7$_{5}$ appar. Si 34$_{7(Bmg)}$, פֶּתִי *simple-minded one* 4Q418 221$_{2}$ CD 15$_{15}$.

צֹאן *flock* Gn 30$_{32}$ 31$_{8.8}$ 33$_{13}$ 1 S 30$_{20}$ Is 60$_{7}$, צֶאֱצָא *offspring* Is 34$_{1}$ 1QH 1$_{18}$ 2$_{38}$ 13$_{9}$ 1QM 10$_{13}$ 12$_{10}$ 19$_{2}$ 1QSb 2$_{28}$ 4QMyst^{a} 6.1$_{9}$ 4Q418 47$_{4}$ 264$_{1}$ 4QHod^{b} 20$_{8}$, צָבָא *army* Gn 2$_{1}$ Ex 12$_{41}$ Dt 4$_{19}$ 17$_{3}$ 2 S 3$_{23}$ 10$_{7}$||1 C 19$_{8}$ 2 S 20$_{23}$ 1 K 22$_{19}$||2 C 18$_{18}$ 2 K 17$_{16}$ 21$_{3.5}$||2 C 33$_{3.5}$ 2 K 23$_{4.5}$ Is 34$_{2.4.4}$ 45$_{12}$ Jr 8$_{2}$ 19$_{13}$ 51$_{3}$ Ps 33$_{6}$ 103$_{21}$ 148$_{2}$ Ne 9$_{6}$ 2 C 26$_{14}$, *host* 1QH 1$_{10}$ 1QM 12$_{2}$ 1QS 4$_{15}$ 1QSa 1$_{6.24}$ 4QapJoseph^{b} 6$_{3}$ 4QapPs^{b} 1$_{10}$ 4Q418 126.2$_{1}$ 4QM^{h} 2$_{3}$ 4QM^{a} 17$_{2}$ 11QT 55$_{18}$, צְבִי *beauty* Is 23$_{9}$, צַדִּיק *righteous one* 4QpsJub^{c} 1$_{1}$, צְדָקָה *righteousness* 1 S 12$_{7}$ Ezk 18$_{24}$ 33$_{13}$ Dn 9$_{16}$, צוּרָה *form* Ezk 43$_{11.11.11}$, צִידֹנִי *Sidonian* Jos 13$_{6}$ Ezk 32$_{30}$, צִיר *pang* 1QH 3$_{11}$, צֶלֶם *image* Nm 33$_{52}$, צָמֵא *thirsty one* Is 55$_{1}$ 1QH 8$_{16}$, צֶמַח *growth* 4Q418 58$_{3}$ 107$_{5}$, צַעַד *step* Jb 31$_{4}$ 34$_{21}$ 1QH fr. 2$_{6}$, צִפּוֹר *bird* Gn 7$_{14}$ Dt 4$_{17}$ 14$_{11}$ Ezk 17$_{23}$, צַר *oppressor* Jr 30$_{16}$, צַר *distress* 4QapPs^{b} 24$_{5}$, צָרָה *distress* 1 S 26$_{24}$ 2 S 4$_{9}$ 1 K 1$_{29}$ Is 63$_{9}$ Ps 25$_{22}$ 34$_{7.18}$ 54$_{9}$ 2 C 15$_{6}$ 1QH 15$_{16}$ 4QBark^{a} 1.3$_{1}$ 4QDibHam^{a} 1.6$_{8}$ 1.7$_{2}$, צָרִיךְ *needy person* Si 39$_{16(Bmg)}$, צֹרֶךְ *need* 2 C 2$_{15}$ Si 39$_{16(B).33}$ 42$_{23(M)}$ 11QT 47$_{9}$.

קָדוֹשׁ *holy one* Dt 33$_{3}$ Zc 14$_{5}$ 4QJub^{f} 33$_{12}$ 4QShirShabb^{a} 1.1$_{2.15.17}$ 4QShirShabb^{d} 1.1$_{24.31.40.45}$ 4QShirShabb^{f} 8$_{2}$ 4Q418 81$_{12}$ 4QPrayer^{m} 1.2$_{5}$ 4QPrQuot 40.2$_{7}$ 4QShir^{a} 1$_{2}$ 11QShirShabb q$_{3}$ CD 20$_{8}$, קֹדֶשׁ *sacred thing* Lv 12$_{4}$ Nm 5$_{9}$ 18$_{8}$ 2 K 12$_{19}$ Ezk 29$_{40}$ 44$_{13}$ 1 C 23$_{28}$ 2 C 24$_{7}$ 1QSb 3$_{2}$ 4QSD 7.2$_{17}$ 4QTohA 1.2$_{9}$ MasShirShabb 1$_{13}$ 11QT 60$_{3.3}$, קָהָל *assembly* Ex 12$_{6}$ 16$_{3}$ Lv 16$_{17}$ Nm 14$_{5}$ Dt 5$_{22}$ 31$_{30}$ Jos 8$_{35}$ 1 S 17$_{47}$ 1 K 8$_{14.14.22}$||2 C 6$_{3.3.12}$ 1 K 8$_{55}$ 12$_{3}$ Jr 26$_{17}$ Ezk 27$_{27.34}$ 32$_{22}$ 38$_{7}$ Ezr 2$_{64}$||Ne 7$_{66}$ Ezr 10$_{12.14}$ Ne 5$_{13}$ 8$_{17}$ 1 C 13$_{2.4}$ 29$_{1.10.20}$ 2 C 1$_{3}$ 6$_{13}$ 23$_{3}$ 28$_{14}$ 29$_{28}$ 30$_{2.4.23.25.25}$ 31$_{18}$ Si 50$_{13.20}$ 1QM 11$_{16}$ 15$_{10}$ 4QapMoses^{b} 1.2$_{2}$ 4QapMoses^{c} 2.2$_{3}$ 4QJonathan 1.1$_{13}$ 4QM^{a} 1$_{2}$, קוֹמָה *height* Ezk 13$_{18}$ 4Q474 1$_{13}$, קוֹרָה *beam* 4QShirShabb^{d} 1.14$_{3}$, קִיר *wall* 1 K 6$_{29}$ Ezk 41$_{17}$ 1QH 7$_{9}$ 4QShirShabb^{e} 5$_{6}$, קְלָלָה *curse* Dt 28$_{15.45}$ 29$_{26}$ 1QDM 1$_{10}$ 4QJub^{a} 1$_{6}$ 4QJub^{i} 21$_{2}$, קֶלַע *curtain* Ex 38$_{16}$, קָנֶה *stalk* 11QT 9$_{9}$, קִנְיָן *possession* Gn 36$_{6}$ Ps 105$_{21}$ Pr 4$_{7}$, קֵץ *age* 1QH 1$_{24}$ 13$_{9}$ 1QH fr. 20$_{4}$ 1QM 1$_{8}$ 1QpHab 7$_{13}$ 1QS 4$_{13.16.25}$ 10$_{5}$ 11$_{8}$ 1QSb 4$_{26}$ 5$_{18}$ 4QD^{a} 11$_{18.19}$ 4Q416 1$_{14}$ 4Q417 2.1$_{7}$ 4Q418 2$_{6}$ 69.2$_{14}$ 81$_{13}$ 4Q419 8.2$_{6}$ 4QHod^{a} 7.1$_{15}$ 7.2$_{4}$ 4QHod^{e} 1$_{5}$ 4QShir^{b} 63.1$_{4}$ 11QMelch 2$_{20}$ CD 6$_{10}$ 13$_{20}$ 15$_{7.10}$, קְצו *end* Is 26$_{15}$ Ps 65$_{6}$ 1QM 1$_{8}$, קָצִין *leader* Is 22$_{3}$, קָצִיר *harvest* Ru 2$_{21}$, קרא inf. *calling* 1 K 8$_{52}$, קָרֵב *one who approaches* Nm 17$_{28}$ 1 K 5$_{7}$ Si 12$_{13}$, קֶרֶב *innard* Ps 103$_{1}$ 11QT 16$_{13}$, קָרְבָּן *offering* Lv 2$_{13.13}$ 7$_{14}$ Nm 18$_{9}$ 4QWays^{b} 13$_{6}$ 11QT 20$_{13}$, קָרוֹב *near one* 1QH 14$_{14}$, קֶרֶן *horn* Ps 75$_{11}$ Lm 2$_{3}$, קֶרֶשׁ *plank* Ex 26$_{17}$ 36$_{22}$, קֶשֶׁת *bow* Is 5$_{28}$.

רֹאשׁ *head* Is 1$_{5}$ 15$_{2}$ Jr 48$_{37}$ Ezk 6$_{13}$ 7$_{18}$ 16$_{25}$ 29$_{18}$ Am 8$_{10}$ Ca 4$_{14}$ 1QM 2$_{7}$ 19$_{12}$ 1QSa 1$_{16.25}$ 2$_{15}$ 4QapMoses^{a} 2.2$_{8}$ 4QShirShabb^{b} 2$_{4}$ 4QShirShabb^{d} 1.13$_{4}$ 11QT 19$_{16}$, *chief* Nm 25$_{4}$ Dt 5$_{23}$ 1 K 8$_{1}$||2 C 5$_{2}$, רִאשׁוֹן *former one* 2 C 22$_{1}$ Si 44$_{22}$ 4QapJoseph^{b} 9$_{1}$, רַב *great one* Jr 39$_{13}$ Ps 89$_{51}$ (or em. רַבִּים *many* or *great ones* to דִּבַּת *rumour of* or כְּלִמַּת *insult of*) Est 1$_{8}$, רֶוַח *space, side* 11QT 30$_{10}$ 38$_{13}$, רוּחַ *spirit* Ezk 21$_{12}$ Hb 2$_{19}$ Pr 29$_{11}$ 1QH 1$_{9}$ 3$_{18}$ 7$_{29}$ 10$_{8}$ 15$_{13}$ 1QH fr. 45$_{6}$ 1QM 13$_{2.4.10.11}$ 15$_{14}$ 1QS 3$_{24}$ 4$_{20}$ 1Q36.15$_{5}$ 4QBibPar 14.1$_{2}$ 4QMidrEschat^{b} 11$_{14}$ 4QJub^{a} 2$_{2.2}$ 4QBer^{a} 2$_{1}$ 3$_{5}$ 7.2$_{3}$ 4QMyst^{c} 4$_{2}$ 4Q365^{a} 2.1$_{9}$ 4QparaKings 31$_{4}$ 4QShirShabb^{d} 1.1$_{35.37.38}$ 4QShirShabb^{f} 23.1$_{6.9}$ 4Q416 1$_{12}$ 4Q418 58$_{2}$ 73$_{1}$ 76$_{1}$ 81$_{1}$ 286$_{1}$ 4QpsHod^{b} 3.1$_{18}$ 4QM^{a} 15$_{10}$ 4Q Shir^{a} 1$_{5}$ 2$_{3}$ 4QShir^{b} 1$_{2}$ 35$_{7}$ 4QBéat 12$_{4}$ 8QHymn 2$_{6}$ 11Q Melch 2$_{13}$ 11QHymn^{a} 1$_{5}$, *wind* Jr 49$_{32.36}$ Ezk 5$_{10.12}$ 12$_{14}$ 17$_{21}$ Si 5$_{9}$, רוּם *lofty one* 4QShirShabb^{f} 3.2$_{4}$, רָז *mystery* 1QH 12$_{20}$ 1QH fr. 1$_{3}$ 1QM 14$_{9}$ 1QpHab 7$_{5}$ 4QMyst^{a} 3a.2$_{11}$, רָחוֹק *distance* 11QT 46$_{15}$, רַחֲמִים *compassion* Ps 145$_{9}$ 4Q423 2$_{5}$, רֶחֶם *womb* Gn 20$_{18}$ Ex 13$_{2}$ Nm 8$_{16}$, רְחוֹב *street* Ezk 16$_{24.31}$ Am 5$_{16}$, רִיב *dispute* Dt 21$_{5}$ 2 C 19$_{10}$ 11QT 63$_{4}$ CD 14$_{12}$, רֶכֶב *chariot* Ex 14$_{7}$ Jg 4$_{13.15}$ 2 S 8$_{4}$ ||1 C 18$_{4}$ 2 K 8$_{21}$||2 C 21$_{9}$ 1QM 6$_{11}$, רְכוּשׁ *property* Gn 12$_{5}$ 14$_{11.16}$ 31$_{18}$ Nm 16$_{32}$ Ezr 8$_{21}$ 10$_{8}$ 1 C 28$_{1}$ 2 C 21$_{14.17}$, רִמּוֹן *pomegranate* Jr 52$_{23}$,

רֶמֶשׂ *creeping thing* Gn $1_{25.26}$ 6_{20} 7_{14} $8_{17.19}$ 9_3 Ezk 38_{20}, רַע *evil* Gn 48_{16} Is 56_2 Ps 121_7 Pr 5_{14} 20_8 Si $51_{8.12}$ 1QH 14_{18} 1QS $1_{4.7}$ 2_3 5_1 4QJub^a 1_5 4QJub^d 21_{20} 4QPrFêtes^c 276_1 4QRitPur 65_2 4QBéat 14.2_{12}, *evil one* 4QdivProv 1_3, רֵעַ *companion* Jr 9_3 Pr 19_6 Lm 1_2 1QH 4_9 4QBer^a 7.1_3, רָעָה *evil* Gn 50_{15} Dt 31_{18} Jg 9_{57} 1 S 10_{19} 12_{20} 2 S 19_8 1 K 2_{44} 9_9||2 C 7_{22} 1 K 16_7 2 K 22_{20}||2 C 34_{28} Jr 1_{16} 16_{10} 19_{15} 22_{22} $32_{23.32.42}$ 33_5 35_{17} $36_{3.31}$ 41_{11} 44_2 $51_{24.60}$ Ezk 16_{23} 20_{43} Ho 7_2 9_{15} Jb 2_{11} 42_{11} Lm 1_{22} Dn 9_{13} Ne $13_{18.27}$ Si 25_{13} 47_{25} 2QJub^b 46_2 4QJub^f 37_{13}, רֹעֶה *shepherd* Gn 46_{34} Jr 22_{22}, רָצוֹן *desire* 2 C 15_{15} 1Q 29.5_2, רָקִיעַ *firmament* 11QShirShabb 1_4, רָשָׁע *wicked one* Ps 75_9 101_8 119_{119} 145_{20} Dn 12_{10} 1QpHab 5_5, רִשְׁעָה *wickedness* 4QpPs^a 2_6, רֶשֶׁף *pestilence* 4QJub^d 21_{20}.

שְׂאֹר *leaven* Lv 2_{11}, שָׂבָע *plenty* Gn 41_{30}, שָׂדֶה *field* Gn 14_7 Jg 20_6 2 S 9_7 Jr 12_4 4QBibPar 10_7, שֶׂה *lamb* Gn $30_{32.32}$, שָׂטָן *adversary* 1QH fr. 4_6 45_3, שִׂיחַ *shrub* Gn 2_5, שִׂיחָה *speech* Si 6_{35}, שְׂכִיָּה *ship* Is 2_{16}, שֶׂכֶל *intelligence* Si 42_{20} 1QS 9_{13} 4QMyst^a 8_8, שֹׁכֵן *inhabitant* 4QTestim$_{24}$ 4QapJoshua^b 22.2_{10} 4QsapHymnA 12_4, שִׂמְחָה *joy* Is 24_{11} Ec 2_{10}, שֵׂעָר *hair* Lv $14_{8.9.9}$, שָׂפָה *lip* Ps 12_4 1QH 8_{36} 4QShir^b 22_4, שַׂר *prince* Nm 23_6 2 S 18_5 2 K 24_{14} 25_{23} Is 34_{12} Jr $26_{12.21}$ 34_{10} $36_{12.12.14.21}$ 38_{27} 39_3 $40_{7.13}$ $41_{11.13.16}$ $42_{1.8}$ $43_{4.5}$ 52_{10} Ho 9_{15} Am 2_3 Est $1_{3.16.18}$ 2_{18} 3_1 9_3 Ezr 7_{28} 1 C 22_{17} 23_2 27_3 28_1 29_{24} 2 C $24_{10.23}$ 36_{14} 1QSb 3_{27} 4QapJoshua^a 19.2_7 GnzPs 3_{14}.

שְׁאָט *scorn* Ezk 25_6, שְׁאֵר *flesh* Lv 18_6, שְׁאֵרִית *remnant* Is 46_3 Jr 8_3 39_3 $41_{10.16}$ 42_2 43_5 44_{28} Ezk 5_{10} 9_8 Hg $1_{12.14}$ 1 C 12_{39} 2 C 34_9, שָׁבוּעַ *week* 4QNidd 1_2, *seven* 4QShirShabb^d 1.1_{26} 4QShirShabb^e 2_1 4QRitPur 4_1, שְׁבוּעָה *oath* Nm 30_{14} 4Q416 2.4_8 4Q418 10_9 11QT 54_2 CD 16_7, שֵׁבֶט *tribe* Dt 12_5 $18_{1.5}$ 29_{20} Jos 24_1 Jg $20_{2.10.12}$ 21_5 1 S 2_{28} 10_{20} 2 S 5_1 15_{10} 19_{10} 20_{14} 24_2 1 K 8_{16}||2 C 6_5 1 K 11_{32} 14_{21}||2 C 12_{13} 2 K 21_7||2 C 33_7 Ezk 48_{19} Zc 9_1 2 C 11_{16} Si 33_{13} 1QM 2_7 4QMMT B$_{33.61}$ 4QM^h 4_4 4QM^a 1_9 11QT 60_{10}, שְׁבִיל *way* Si 5_9 4QD^a 2.2_3, שֶׁבֶר *grain* Ne 10_{32}, שַׁבָּת *sabbath* 4QHalakah^a 1_4 4QparaKings 142_3, שְׁדֵמָה *field* Jr $31_{40(Qr)}$, שִׁיר *song* Am 8_{10} 11QPs^a 27_9, שָׁכֵן *neighbour* Dt 1_7 2 K $4_{3(Qr)}$ Jr 12_{14}, שָׁלוֹם *peace* Jr 33_9, שֻׁלְחָן *table* Is 28_8, שֶׁלֶט *shield* Ca 4_4, שָׁלָל *booty* Nm 31_{11} Dt $13_{17.17}$ 20_{14} Jos 11_{14} 1 S 30_{16} 2 C 24_{23} 1QpHab 6_1 11QT $55_{8.9}$ 62_{10}, שֵׁם *name* Ps 138_2, שָׁמַיִם *heaven* Gn 7_{19} Dt 2_{25} Jb 28_{24} 37_3 41_3 Dn 9_{12} 4QParGenEx 2_7, שָׁמֵן *fat one* Jg 3_{29}, שִׁנְאָב perh. *stream* 1QH 3_{29}, שָׁנָה *year* Is 38_{15} Est $9_{21.27}$ 1QDM 42_3 4QJub^b 2_2 4QMishA 2.1_5 4Q418 69.2_{12} 11QT 42_{13} Mur 24C$_{18}$ CD 2_{10} 4_{12}, שַׁעַר *gate* Dt 12_{15} 16_{18} $28_{52.52.55}$ Jr 17_{19} Ezk 21_{20} Ru 3_{11} Lm 1_4 11QT 36_{13} 51_{11} 52_{14}, שְׁפִי *bare height* Is 49_9 Jr 12_{12}, שִׁקּוּץ *abomination* 2 K 23_{24} Ezk 5_{11} 11_{18}, שֶׁקֶץ *abomination* Lv 7_{21}, שֶׁרֶץ *swarming creature* Gn 7_{21} Lv 11_{10+8t} 22_5 Dt 14_{19} 11QT 50_{21}, שְׁרִירוּת *stubbornness* 1QS 9_{10}, שֹׁרֶשׁ *root* 4Q416 2.3_{14} 4Q418 9_{15} 55_9.

תַּאֲוָה *desire* Ps 38_{10}, תֹּאַר *form* 4QsapHymnA 1.1_9, תְּבוּאָה *produce* Lv 25_7 Dt 14_{22} 16_{15} 2 K 8_6 Jb 31_{12} Pr 3_9 2 C 31_5 1Q26.1_6 2_2 4QBer^a 5_6 4QapPs^b 1_6 4Q423 3_2 4_2 5_7, תֵּבֵל *world* 1QH 6_{15} 4QCryptA 3.1_5 4QPr Enosh 1.2_7 4QapJoseph^b 1_{11} 4QapJoseph^b 1_{22} 4QapJoshua^a 12_2 4QapJoshua^b 30_2 4QPrayer^c 6_2 4QHymnPr 48_2 11QPs^a 22_{12}, תַּבְנִית *pattern* Ezk 8_{10} 11QShirShabb 5_2, תְּגֹאֶלֶת *defilement* 11QT 49_{11}, תַּגְמוּל *recompense* Ps 116_{12}, תְּהוֹם *abyss* Ps 135_6 148_7 4QAdmon 1.1_4, תְּהִלָּה *praise* Ps 9_{15} 71_{14} 106_2 4QapPs^a 1.1_8, תּוֹכַחַת *reproof* Pr 1_{30}, תּוֹעֵבָה *abomination* Lv $18_{26.27.29}$ Dt 12_{31} 14_3 20_{18} 1 K 14_{24} Jr 7_{10} Ezk $5_{9.11}$ $6_{9.11}$ $7_{3.8}$ 9_4 11_{18} 12_{16} 14_6 $16_{22.43.51}$ $18_{13.24}$ 22_2 33_{29} $44_{6.7}$ 2 C 34_{33} 36_{14} 1QH 11_{11} 1QS 4_{21} 4QJub^d 21_{23} 4QJub^f $21_{23.23}$ 4Q418 81_2 11QT 48_6 62_{16}, תּוֹצָאָה *departure* 4Q417 2.1_{12}, תּוֹרָה *law* Nm 5_{30} Dt 4_8 Jos 1_7 2 K 17_{13} 21_8 23_{25} Ezk 43_{11} 44_5 2 C 33_8 1QS 5_{16} 8_1 4QMidrEschat^a 4_2 4QJub^a 1_{14} 4QZedek 1_4, תּוּשִׁיָּה *prudence* Pr 18_1, תַּחֲלוּא *disease* Ps 103_3, תְּחִנָּה *supplication* 1 K 8_{38}||2 C 6_{29}, תִּכּוּן *rule* 1QS $9_{3.7}$ 4Q418 127_6, תִּכְלָה *extremity* Ps 119_{96}, תַּכְלִית *extremity* Jb 28_3, תְּלָאָה *hardship* Ex 18_8 Nm 20_{14} Ne 9_{32}, תְּמוּנָה *image* Ex 20_4 Dt 4_{15} 5_8, תָּמִים *perfect one* 1QH 1_{36} 4QShirShabb^d 1.1_{22} 4QShirShabb^e 2_3 4QShirShabb^f 13_6 4QShir^b 10_8, תְּנוּפָה *wave offering* Nm 18_{11} 4QBer^a 5_7 11QT 60_2, תְּעוּדָה *testimony* 1QM 13_8 4QPr Enosh 1.1_7 4QShirShabb^c 1_3 MasShirShabb 1_3, תַּעֲנוּג *delicacy* Si $37_{29(B)}$ 4QpPs^a 2_{10}, תַּעֲרֹבֶת *marital union* 4QMMT B$_{48.50}$, תְּפִלָּה *prayer* 1 K 8_{38}||2 C 6_{29} 1 K 8_{54} 5Q14 1_3, תְּקוּם *power* GnzPs 3_{17}, תְּקוּפָה *cycle* 4QJub^a 2_9, תֹּקֶף *power* Est 9_{29}, תְּרוּמָה *contribution* Ex 36_3 Nm 5_9 $18_{19.29}$ Ezk $44_{30.30}$ 48_{20} 4QOrd^b 2.2_3.

<COLL> עַל־כָּל־אֹדוֹת אֲשֶׁר *on account of all that* Jr 3_8, כָּל־עֻמַּת שֶׁבָּא appar. *just as he came* Ec 5_{15} (or em. כִּלְעֻמַּת שֶׁבָּא *as in accordance with [the way] that he came*);

־כָּל as part of pr.n.m. כָּל־חֹזֶה *Colhozeh* Ne 3$_{15}$ 11$_{5}$.

Also Si 36$_{7}$ 39$_{26}$ (כ[ל]) 40$_{5(Bmg)}$ 40$_{12}$ 43$_{33}$ 1QH 3$_{38}$ 6$_{18}$ 12$_{36}$ 14$_{6}$ 16$_{4.5}$ 1QH fr. 9$_{5.11}$ 11$_{2}$ 13$_{1}$ 15$_{5}$ 22$_{2}$ 56$_{2}$ 1QM 15$_{13}$ 1QSb 2$_{27}$ 5$_{19}$ 1QDM 4$_{6.9}$ 12$_{3}$ 1Q26.1$_{8.8}$ 1QMyst 1.1$_{1}$ 1.2$_{7.11}$ 2$_{2}$ 3$_{3}$ 1Q29.5$_{1}$ 1Q30.1$_{3}$ 1QlitPr 3.2$_{2}$ 1Q46.6$_{1}$ 2Q Juridicial 3$_{2}$ 2Q33.5$_{1}$ 4QOrd^{a} 1.2$_{9}$ 26$_{10}$ 5$_{8}$ 4QpIsa^{c} 23.2$_{1}$ 4QpIsa^{d} 2$_{1}$ 4QpHos^{b} 26$_{1}$ 4QpPs^{a} 2$_{10}$ 4QUnid 1$_{1}$ 5$_{3}$ 7$_{2}$ 12$_{1}$ 4QTanḥ 18$_{2}$ 21$_{2}$ 54$_{1}$ 4QMidrEschat^{a} 4$_{7}$ 4QAges^{a} 2.2$_{9}$ 4QWiles 1$_{11.12}$ 4Q185.1.2$_{15}$ 4QTobit^{e} 7.1$_{3}$ 4QJub^{a} 2$_{11}$ 4QpsJub^{b} 12$_{2}$ 4QCitJub 1.1$_{4.10}$ 4Q248$_{10}$ 4QHalakah^{a} 1$_{2}$ 4QSD 10$_{6}$ 4QD^{a} 5.1$_{14}$ 5.2$_{15}$ 6.1$_{2}$ 7.1$_{5}$ 16b$_{1}$ 52$_{3}$ 4QD^{b} 6$_{5}$ 4QD^{e} 2.1$_{21}$ 4QD^{g} 1.2$_{9}$ 4QTohA 1.3$_{7}$ 2.1$_{6}$ 4QTohB^{c} 1$_{3}$ 4Q Ber^{a} 4$_{4}$ 7.1$_{8}$ 8$_{2}$ 4QBer^{b} 3$_{3}$ 4$_{4}$ 5$_{11}$ 4Q Ber^{c} 1$_{3}$ 4QBer^{d} 1$_{5.7}$ 2$_{2}$ 4QPrayers^{a} 1$_{7}$ 3$_{3}$ 4QCryptA 2.1$_{2}$ 4QMyst^{a} 6.1$_{8}$ 12$_{2}$ 31$_{2}$ 36$_{1}$ 48$_{2}$ 54$_{4}$ 67$_{4}$ 99$_{1}$ 4QMishC^{e} 2$_{4}$ 4Q365^{a} 1$_{1}$ 4QPr Enosh 1.1$_{1}$ 1.2$_{4}$ 4QAdmon 1.1$_{5}$ 4Qap Joseph^{a} 1$_{8}$ 4Qap Joseph^{b} 2$_{3}$ 3$_{6}$ 11$_{2}$ 13$_{1}$ 4QDiscourse 10$_{3}$ 4QapMoses^{c} 6$_{1}$ 4Qap Joshua^{a} 3.1$_{3}$ 4Qap Joshua^{b} 15$_{2}$ 22.1$_{8}$ 4QapPs^{a} 6$_{1}$ 4Qap Ps^{b} 7$_{2}$ 14$_{2}$ 31$_{2}$ 37$_{2}$ 97$_{2}$ 4Qpara Kings 34$_{1}$ 83$_{1}$ 147$_{1}$ 4Qps Ezek^{a} 14$_{2}$ 22$_{2}$ 42$_{3}$ 4QpsEzek^{d} 6$_{3}$ 4QpsEzek^{e} 3$_{1}$ 17$_{2}$ 25$_{1}$ 4QMMT B$_{2}$ 4QShirShabb^{a} 1.2$_{5}$ 7$_{3}$ 4QShirShabb^{b} 24$_{3}$ 34$_{3}$ 38$_{2}$ 4QShirShabb^{e} 6$_{2}$ 15$_{1}$ 17$_{2}$ 4QShirShabb^{f} 2$_{2}$ 15.2$_{8}$ 19$_{3}$ 23.2$_{4}$ 84$_{1}$ 4Q408 1$_{5.9}$ 4$_{1}$ 6$_{3}$ 4QBapt 13$_{1}$ 22$_{2}$ 4Q 415 2.1$_{1}$ 4Q416 1$_{15}$ 2.3$_{13}$ 3$_{3}$ 14$_{2}$ 4Q417 2.1$_{5.15.22}$ 3$_{3}$ 5$_{3}$ 13$_{6}$ 15$_{2}$ 20$_{8}$ 4Q418 9$_{14}$ 28$_{1}$ 65$_{2}$ 69.2$_{9.11.15}$ 73$_{2}$ 81$_{4}$ 84$_{1}$ 89$_{2}$ 103.2$_{2.3}$ 126.2$_{3}$ 132$_{1}$ 139$_{3}$ 165$_{1}$ 167$_{1}$ 170$_{4}$ 177$_{6}$ 196$_{2}$ 198$_{1}$ 224$_{2}$ 227$_{1}$ 261$_{1}$ 282$_{1}$ 287$_{1}$ 4Q419 8.1$_{5}$ 4Q Ways^{a} 1$_{7}$ 4Q Ways^{b} 1.2$_{17}$ 11$_{2.6}$ 4QParGenEx 3$_{8}$ 4Q423 5$_{9.10}$ 8$_{3}$ 15$_{2}$ 24$_{3}$ 4Q424 4$_{2}$ 4Q sapDidB 4.2$_{4}$ 4QHod^{b} 3$_{4}$ 4QHod^{c} 2.2$_{12}$ 4Q Bark^{a} 5$_{2}$ 4Q Bark^{b} 4$_{1}$ 4QpsHod^{b} 3.1$_{15. 20.21}$ 4QPrayer^{c} 6$_{1}$ 4QPrayer^{e} 1$_{5}$ 4QPrayer^{i} 1$_{4}$ 4Q Prayer^{m} 2$_{7}$ 4QNarrB 3$_{1}$ 4QNarrC 4$_{1}$ 4Q469 1$_{3}$ 3$_{4}$ 4Q TwoWays 1$_{7}$ 2$_{3}$ 4Q476 1$_{1}$ 4Q476 3.2$_{3}$ 4Q PrMercy 1$_{9}$ 4Q 482 5$_{2}$ 4QSap^{b} 7$_{6}$ 8$_{4}$ 35$_{2}$ 37$_{1}$ 40$_{2}$ 4QM^{a} 1$_{20}$ 4QM^{g} 8.1$_{2}$ 4Q HymnSap 2$_{3}$ 3.1$_{2}$ 9$_{2}$ 4QHymnPr 10$_{3}$ 4QRitMar 9$_{7}$ 13$_{1}$ 21$_{1}$ 32$_{3}$ 48$_{3}$ 60$_{2}$ 84$_{1}$ 87$_{2}$ 98$_{2}$ 149$_{1}$ 200$_{1}$ 250$_{1}$ 280$_{1}$ 4QPrQuot 48$_{8}$ 56.2$_{4}$ 153$_{2}$ 216$_{4}$ 4QDibHam^{a} 2.7$_{4}$ 3.2$_{17}$ 4$_{3.9}$ 7$_{7}$ 17.2$_{2}$ 32$_{2}$ 34$_{2}$ 4QDibHam^{c} 124$_{1}$ 125$_{3}$ 4Q PrFêtes^{a} 2$_{1}$ 4QPrFêtes^{b} 18$_{2}$ 21$_{3}$ 30$_{1}$ 40$_{3}$ 4Q PrFêtes^{c} 4$_{2}$ 5.2$_{3}$ 7$_{2}$ 10.4$_{11}$ 24$_{3}$ 37$_{2}$ 58$_{8}$ 100$_{2}$ 131.1$_{11}$ 131.2$_{17}$ 177$_{2}$ 184.1$_{5}$ 204$_{1}$ 218$_{1}$ 4QShir^{a} 2$_{1}$ 4QShir^{b} 1$_{2}$ 2.2$_{3}$ 3$_{6.8}$ 7$_{2}$ 11$_{3}$ 12$_{2}$ 22$_{2}$ 49.2$_{7}$ 60$_{2}$ 63.2$_{2.5}$ 83$_{3}$ 88$_{2}$ 99$_{4}$ 108$_{2}$ 121$_{3}$ 122$_{2}$ 125$_{2}$ 127$_{3}$ 128$_{2}$ 134$_{2}$ 203$_{1}$ 4QRitPur 12$_{13}$ 15.1$_{6}$ 45.1$_{4}$ 45.2$_{5}$ 76$_{2}$ 81$_{2}$ 139$_{1}$ 4QOrd^{b} 11$_{4}$ 13$_{8}$ 24$_{4}$ 4Q517 30$_{1}$ 36$_{1}$ 4Q520 1$_{2}$ 4Qap Mes 1.2$_{14}$ 4QBéat 8$_{7}$ 13$_{6}$ 23.2$_{8}$ 29$_{1}$ 4QpsHod^{c} 3$_{5}$ 4QUnid E 1$_{10}$ 5QTopon 6$_{3}$ 5QapMal 3$_{1}$ 5QRègle 11$_{1}$ 5Q 16 2$_{1}$ 5Q22 1$_{4}$ 6QapSamKgs 22$_{2}$ 23$_{2}$ 36$_{2}$ 40$_{2}$ 6QProph 13$_{2}$ 22$_{1}$ 8QHymn 2$_{4}$ 11QMelch 3$_{5}$ 11QShirShabb 1$_{5.7.8}$ 3$_{6}$ 5$_{3}$ m$_{1}$ n$_{3}$ 11QT 3$_{5.13}$ 5$_{14}$ 7$_{6.8}$ 35$_{4}$ 37$_{2}$ 60$_{2}$ Mur 24A$_{14}$ Gezer calendar$_{5}$.

⇒ כלל *be complete.*

***כֹּל II** $_{1}$ n.[m.] **mallow** or another plant, כַּכֹּל יִקָּפְצוּן *like mallow they are contracted*, i.e. wilt Jb 24$_{24}$.

*** כֹּל III** $_{1}$ n.[m.] **measure,** אַנְשֵׁי־רָע לֹא־יָבִינוּ מִשְׁפָּט וּמְבַקְשֵׁי י׳ יָבִינוּ כֹל *evil men do not understand justice but those who seek Y. understand measure* Pr 28$_{5}$, כֹּל עָרוּם יַעֲשֶׂה בְדָעַת *an astute person makes measure intelligently* Pr 13$_{16}$ (if em. ־כָּל *every* astute person acts intelligently).

כלא $_{17.0.1}$ vb. **restrain—Qal** $_{14.0.1}$ Pf. כָּלְאָה, כְּלִתַנִי, אֶכְלָא, תִּכְלָא, תִּכְלָאִי, יִכְלֶה; impf. (כָּלוּ) כָּלְאוּ, כָּלָאתִי; impv. כְּלָאֵם; ptc. pass. כָּלֻא; inf. כְּלוֹא (Q כלו)—**hold back, withold, imprison,** pass. **be kept imprisoned,** <SUBJ> י׳ *Y.* Ps 40$_{12}$ 56$_{14}$ (if em. הֲלֹא *have* you *not* delivered my foot from stumbling? to כָּלִאתָ *you have held back*) 1 C 21$_{17}$ (if em. וּבְעַמְּךָ לֹא לְמַגֵּפָה appar. *and against your people, let not [your hand be] for striking* to וּבָעָם כְּלָא לַמַּגֵּפָה *but against the people restrain the striking*), שָׁמַיִם *heavens* Hg 1$_{10}$, אֶרֶץ *earth* Hg 1$_{10}$, תֵּימָן *south* Is 43$_{6}$, Abigail 1 S 25$_{33}$, Moses Nm 11$_{28}$, Zedekiah Jr 32$_{3}$, אִישׁ *man* Gn 23$_{6}$ 1 S 6$_{10}$, מֶלֶךְ *king* Jr 32$_{3}$ 4QapPs^{b} 33$_{8}$, אָדוֹן *lord* Nm 11$_{28}$, worshipper Ps 40$_{10}$ (:: בשׂר pi. *announce*) 119$_{101}$; subj. of pass. Jeremiah Jr 32$_{2}$, worshipper Ps 88$_{9}$; subj. not specified, Jr 29$_{26}$ (if em. לִכְלֹא *to restrain*) Ec 8$_{8}$.

<OBJ> David 1 S 25$_{33}$, Eldad Nm 11$_{28}$, Jeremiah Jr 32$_{3}$, Manasseh 4QapPs^{b} 33$_{8}$, Medad Nm 11$_{28}$, Jr 29$_{26}$, בֵּן *son*, i.e. calf 1 S 6$_{10}$, מֶלֶךְ *king* 4QapPs^{b} 33$_{8}$, יְבוּל *produce* Hg 1$_{10}$, רַחַם *compassion* Ps 40$_{12}$, קֶבֶר *grave* Gn 23$_{6}$, שָׂפָה *lip* Ps 40$_{10}$, רוּחַ *spirit* Ec 8$_{8}$, רֶגֶל *foot* Ps 56$_{14}$ (if em.) 119$_{101}$, מַגֵּפָה *striking* 1 C 21$_{17}$ (if em.).

<PREP> בְּ of place, *in, at,* + בַּיִת *house* 1 S 6$_{10}$, חָצֵר *court* of the guard Jr 32$_{2}$; מִן of direction, *from,* + Abra–

ham Gn 23$_{6}$, worshipper Ps 40$_{12}$, אֹרַח *path* Ps 119$_{101}$, דְּחִי *stumbling* Ps 56$_{14}$ (if em.), בוא inf. as noun, *entering* into blood, i.e. blood guilt 1 S 25$_{33}$; partitive, *some of, (any) one of*, + טַל *dew* Hg 1$_{10}$.

<COLL> כְּלִתַנִי הַיּוֹם הַזֶּה *you have restrained me this day* 1 S 25$_{33}$. Also perh. 4QShir[b] 60$_{3}$. <ANT> בשׂר pi. *announce*.

Ni. $_{3}$ + waw וַיִּכָּלְאוּ, וַיִּכָּלֵא—**be kept back, be restrained,** <SUBJ> עַם *people* Ex 36$_{6}$, גֶּשֶׁם *rain* Gn 8$_{2}$, מַיִם *waters* Ezk 31$_{15}$. <PREP> מִן of direction, *from*, + שָׁמַיִם *heavens* Gn 8$_{2}$, בוא hi. inf. as noun, *bringing* Ex 36$_{6}$.*

→ כֶּלֶא *confinement*, כְּלִיא *confinement*, מִכְלָה *fold*, כְּלָאָה *fold*.

כֶּלֶא I $_{10}$ n.m. **confinement**—sf. כִּלְאוֹ; pl. כְּלָאִים—**confinement, imprisonment, prison,** <SUBJ> חשׁב ni. *be reckoned* 1QH 5$_{38}$ (כל[א']). <CSTR> בֵּית הַכֶּלֶא *the house of imprisonment*, i.e. the prison 1 K 22$_{27}$||2 C 18$_{26}$ 2 K 17$_{4}$ 25$_{27}$ Is 42$_{7}$ (all three כֶּלֶא) Jr 37$_{15.18}$, בָּתֵּי כְלָאִים *houses of imprisonment*, i.e. prisons Is 42$_{22}$, בִּגְדֵי כִלְאוֹ *garments of his imprisonment* 2 K 25$_{29}$||Jr 52$_{33}$.

Also perh. 4Q415 16$_{2}$ perh. 32$_{2}$.*

→ כלא *restrain*.

* [כֶּלֶא] II n.[m.] **both,** הֲרִימוֹתָ יְמִין צָרָיו הִשְׂמַחְתָּ כֶּלֶא אוֹיְבָיו *you raised the right hand of his enemies, you lifted both (hands) of his adversaries* Ps 89$_{43}$ (if em. כָּל־ you gladdened *all* his adversaries).

כֶּלָא $_{1}$ n.m. **all**—<APP> Edom Ezk 36$_{5}$ (or em. כֻּלָּהּ *all of it*). <PREP> עַל *against*, + דבר pi. *speak* Ezk 36$_{5}$.

→ כלל *be complete*.

כִּלְאָב $_{1}$ pr.n.m. **Chileab,** a son of David, <SUBJ> ילד ni. *be born* 2 S 3$_{3}$. <NOM CL> מִשְׁנֵהוּ כִלְאָב *his second-born was Chileab* 2 S 3$_{3}$. <APP> בֵּן *son* 2 S 3$_{3}$.

[כְּלָאָה] $_{0.0.1}$ n.f. **fold**—pl. Q כלאת—**fold, enclosure,** <NOM CL> ללוקח ... וכלאת שעליו *(it belongs) to the purchaser ... and (also) the folds which are upon it* Mur 30 1$_{3}$ 2$_{15}$.

→ כלא *restrain*.

כִּלְאַיִם $_{4.0.5}$ n.m.du. **two kinds**—כִּלְאָיִם—of **two kinds** of cloth (Lv 19$_{19}$), forbidden intermixing of **two kinds** of cattle, seeds and vines (Lv 19$_{19.19}$ Dt 22$_{9}$); appar. **mixed kinds** of judges (4QMixedKinds 1$_{2}$); of unsuitable marriage partner (4QD[d] 9$_{2}$).

<SUBJ> היה *be* 4Q418 103.2$_{7}$. <NOM CL> הוא כלאים *it is two kinds* 4QD[d] 9$_{2}$. <OBJ> זרע *sow* 4Q418 103.2$_{8}$. <CSTR> בֶּגֶד כִּלְאַיִם *garment of two kinds* of material Lv 19$_{19}$, דייני כליים perh. *judges of mixed kinds* 4QMixed Kinds 1$_{2}$. <APP> [שור וחמור ולבוש צמר ופשתים] *ox and ass and garment of wool and linen together* 4QD[d] 9$_{2}$.

<COLL> בְּהֶמְתְּךָ לֹא־תַרְבִּיעַ כִּלְאַיִם *you shall not crossbreed your beasts with those of a different kind* Lv 19$_{19}$, שָׂדְךָ לֹא־תִזְרַע כִּלְאָיִם *you shall not sow your field with two kinds of seed* Lv 19$_{19}$, לוא לרבעה כלאים *it is not to lie down with a different kind* 4QMMT B$_{77}$, לֹא־תִזְרַע כַּרְמְךָ כִּלְאָיִם *you shall not sow your vineyard with two kinds of seed* Dt 22$_{19}$.

Also perh. 4Q418 29$_{1}$ ([ ]כלאי) perh. 4Q423 16$_{1}$ ([ ]כ[ל]א).

כָּלֵב I $_{34.2.0.1}$ pr.n.m. **Caleb, 1.** son of Jephunneh, one of the twelve spies, <SUBJ> חיה *live* Nm 14$_{38}$, ראה *see* Dt 1$_{36}$, יתר ni. *be left* Nm 26$_{65}$, בוא *come* Nm 14$_{24.30}$, דרך *tread* Dt 1$_{36}$, יצב htp. *stand firm* Si 46$_{7}$, מלא pi. *remain loyal* Nm 14$_{24}$ Dt 1$_{36}$ Jos 14$_{14}$, ירשׁ hi. *dispossess* Jos 15$_{14}$|| Jg 1$_{20}$, יהב *give* Jg 1$_{15}$, נתן *give* Jos 15$_{16.17}$||Jg 1$_{12.13.15.15}$, *give*, i.e. place Jg 1$_{15}$, הסה hi. *hush* Nm 13$_{30}$, קרע *tear* Nm 14$_{6}$, אמר *say* Jos 14$_{6}$ 15$_{16.18}$||Jg 1$_{12.14}$. <NOM CL> לְמַטֵּה יְהוּדָה כָּלֵב *to the tribe of Judah was Caleb* Nm 13$_{6}$ 34$_{19}$, כָּלֵב ... מִן־הַתָּרִים *Caleb ... was among the ones who had spied out* the land Nm 14$_{6}$. <OBJ> בוא hi. *bring* Nm 14$_{24}$, ברך pi. *bless* Jos 14$_{13}$.

<CSTR> אֲחִי כָלֵב *brother of Caleb* Jos 15$_{17}$||Jg 1$_{13}$ Jg 3$_{9}$, בְּנֵי כָלֵב *sons of Caleb* 1 C 4$_{15}$. <APP> אִישׁ *man* Nm 26$_{65}$, בֵּן *son* Nm 13$_{6}$ 14$_{6.30.38}$ 26$_{65}$ 34$_{19}$ Dt 1$_{36}$ Jos 14$_{6.13.14}$ 15$_{13}$ 21$_{12}$ 1 C 4$_{15}$ 6$_{41}$ Si 46$_{7}$, עֶבֶד *servant* Nm 14$_{24}$. <ADJ> קְנִזִּי *Kenizzite* Jos 14$_{6.14}$. <PREP> לְ of direction, *to*, + נתן *give* Dt 1$_{36}$ Jos 14$_{13}$ 15$_{13}$ 21$_{12}$ Jg 1$_{20}$ 1 C 6$_{41}$ Si 46$_{9}$, אמר *say* Jg 1$_{15}$; of possession, *(belonging) to, of*, + היה *be* Jos 14$_{14}$.

2. brother of Jerahmeel and son of Hezron, <SUBJ> לקח *take* 1 C 2$_{19}$, ילד hi. *become father* 1 C 2$_{18}$. <CSTR>

פִּילֶגֶשׁ כָּלֵב *secondary wife of Caleb* 1 C 2$_{46.48}$, בְּנֵי *sons of* 1 C 2$_{42.50}$, בַּת־כָּלֵב *daughter of Caleb* 1 C 2$_{49}$. <APP> אָח *brother* 1 C 2$_{42}$, בֵּן *son* 1 C 2$_{18}$. <PREP> לְ of benefit, *to, for,* + לקח *take* 1 C 2$_{19}$, ילד *bear child* 1 C 2$_{19}$.

3. Arad ost. 58$_{2}$, <APP> בֵּן *son* Arad ost. 58$_{2}$.

⇒ כָּלֵבִי *Calebite.*

כָּלֵב II $_{2}$ pl.n. **Caleb,** appar. place in desert of Judaea, <CSTR> נֶגֶב כָּלֵב *Negeb of Caleb* 1 S 30$_{14}$. <APP> אֶפְרָתָה *Ephrathah* 1 C 2$_{24}$. <PREP> בְּ of place, *in, at* 1 C 2$_{24}$ (or em. בְּכָלֵב אֶפְרָתָה וְאֵשֶׁת *in Caleb, Ephrathah; and the wife of* to בָּא כָלֵב אֶפְרָתָה אֵשֶׁת *Caleb came to Ephrathah wife of*).

*[**כַּלָּב**] n.m. **hunter,** <SUBJ> סבב *surround* worshipper Ps 22$_{17}$ (if em. כֶּלֶב *dog*). <PREP> מִיַּד *from (the hand of),* + נצל hi. *save* worshipper's soul Ps 22$_{21}$ (if em. כֶּלֶב from paw of *dog*).

כֶּלֶב I $_{32.3.2.3}$ n.m. **dog**—כֶּלֶב; pl. כְּלָבִים; cstr. כַּלְבֵי; sf. כְּלָבֶיךָ—**1. dog,** esp. as consuming corpses (1 K 14$_{11}$ 16$_{4}$ 21$_{19.19.23.24}$ perh. 22$_{38}$ 2 K 9$_{10.36}$ 4QMMT B$_{58}$) or carrion (Ex 22$_{30}$), as predatory (Is 56$_{11}$ [or em.] Ho 13$_{8}$ [if em.] Ps 57$_{5}$ [if em.] 59$_{7.15.16}$ 68$_{24}$ Si 11$_{30}$ [+ זְאֵב *bear*]), as attacking psalmist Ps 22$_{17.21}$* (or em. in both כַּלָּב *hunter*), offered in non-Yahwist sacrifice (Is 66$_{3}$), eaten (4QErr 1$_{5}$), as term of opprobrium (1 S 17$_{43}$ 2 S 16$_{9}$) or self-abasement (1 S 24$_{15}$ 2 S 9$_{8}$ 2 K 8$_{13}$ Ps 31$_{13}$ [if em.] 1 C 17$_{19}$ [if em.] Lachish ost. 2$_{4}$ 5$_{4}$ 6$_{3}$). **2.** perh. **devotee** of god* (Dt 23$_{19}$ [|| זֹנָה female *prostitute*] Jg 7$_{5}$ 1 K 21$_{19}$ 22$_{38}$ [|| זֹנָה, or em. זֵיָנוֹת *armour*]).

<SUBJ> ידע *know* Is 56$_{11}$, בוא *come* Si 11$_{30}$, סבב *surround* Ps 22$_{17}$, שׁוב *go back* Pr 26$_{11}$, סחב *drag off* Jr 15$_{3}$, להט *devour* or *bewitch* Ps 57$_{5}$ (if em. לָבִא *lion*; and/or em. לעט *devour*), אכל *eat* Ho 13$_{8}$ (if em. וְאֹכְלֵם שָׁם כְּלָבִיא *and I shall eat them there like a lion* to וַאֲכָלוּם שָׁם כְּלָבִים *and there dogs will eat them*) 4QMMT B$_{58}$, לקק *lap* water Jg 7$_{5}$, *lick up* blood 1 K 21$_{19.19}$ 22$_{38}$, אכל *eat* 1 K 14$_{11}$ 16$_{4}$ 21$_{23.24}$ 2 K 9$_{10.36}$, חרץ *sharpen* tongue, i.e. growl Ex 11$_{7}$, נבח *bark* Is 56$_{10}$, קלל pi. *curse* 2 S 16$_{9}$. <NOM CL> כֻּלָּם כְּלָבִים *all of them are dogs* Is 56$_{10}$, הֲכֶלֶב אָנֹכִי *am I a dog?* 1 S 17$_{43}$, מָה עַבְדְּךָ הַכֶּלֶב *what is your servant, a dog?* 2 K 8$_{13}$, מי עבדך כלב *who is your servant, a dog?* Lachish ost. 2$_{4}$ 5$_{4}$ 6$_{3}$. <OBJ> בוא hi. *bring* 4QMMT B$_{58}$, פקד *appoint* Jr 15$_{3}$ (|| עוֹף *bird,* בְּהֵמָה *beast;* + חֶרֶב *sword*), ערף *break neck of* Is 66$_{3}$, אכל *eat* 4QErr 1$_{5}$.

<CSTR> כַּלְבֵי צֹאנִי *dogs of my flock* Jb 30$_{1}$; רֹאשׁ כֶּלֶב *head of a dog,* perh. dog-faced baboon (*cynocephalus*)* 2 S 3$_{8}$, לְשׁוֹן כְּלָבֶיךָ *tongue of your dogs* Ps 68$_{24}$, אָזְנֵי־כָלֶב *ears of a dog* Pr 26$_{17}$, יַד כֶּלֶב *paw of the dog* Ps 22$_{21}$, מְחִיר כֶּלֶב *hire of a devotee* Dt 23$_{19}$. <APP> הַכְּלָבִים עַזֵּי־נֶפֶשׁ *dogs, mighty of appetite* Is 56$_{11}$ (or em. לִבְאִים/לְבָאִים *lions*). <ADJ> מֵת *dead* 1 S 24$_{15}$ 2 S 9$_{8}$ 16$_{9}$ 2 K 8$_{13}$ (if ins. מֵת) Ps 31$_{13}$ (if em. כְּמֵת מִלֵּב I am forgotten by the heart *like one who is dead* to כְּכֶלֶב מֵת I am forgotten *like a dead dog*), אִלֵּם *dumb* Is 56$_{10}$.

<PREP> לְ of direction, *to,* + שׁלך hi. *throw* Ex 22$_{30}$; of benefit, *to, for* Ec 9$_{4}$; כְּ *as* Pr 26$_{11}$ Si 11$_{30}$, + היה *be* Si 4$_{30}$, המה *growl* Ps 59$_{7.15}$, *as though I were,* + שׁכח *be forgotten* Ps 31$_{13}$ (if em.); אֶל *to,* + פנה *turn* 2 S 9$_{8}$; *with* Si 13$_{18}$ (מאיש שלום צבוע אל כלב) perh. *on account of a man, is there peace of jackal with dog?*; or em. מֵאַיִן *whence is there* peace?).

אַחֲרֵי *after,* + רדף *pursue* 1 S 24$_{15}$; עִם *with,* + שׁית *place* Jb 30$_{1}$; בְּתוֹךְ *among,* + שׁכב *lie down* Ps 57$_{5}$ (if em. לָבִא *lion;* or em. נַפְשִׁי בְּתוֹךְ *my soul is among* lions/dogs to וְיוֹשַׁע נַפְשִׁי מִתּוֹךְ *may he save my soul from among* lions/dogs); בַּעֲבוּר *on account of,* + עשׂה *do* 1 C 17$_{19}$ (if em. וּכְלִבְּךָ *and in accordance with your heart* to וְכַלְבְּךָ your servant *and your dog*).

Also Lachish ost. 12$_{1}$ (but perh. כְּלֵב *as the heart of* 21$_{3}$ (others כלא or כלע). <SYN> §1 עוֹף *bird,* בְּהֵמָה *beast;* §2 זֹנָה *prostitute.**

*__כֶּלֶב__ II $_{8.0.0.3}$ n.m. **servant**—sometimes **temple servant, hierodule,** <SUBJ> לקק *lap* water Jg 7$_{5}$ (+ בְּיָדָם *with their hands*), *lick up* blood 1 K 21$_{19.19}$ 22$_{38}$. <CSTR> רֹאשׁ כֶּלֶב *head of a servant,* i.e. chief slave 2 S 3$_{8}$; מְחִיר כֶּלֶב *hire of a (temple) servant* Dt 23$_{19}$. <NOM CL> הֲכֶלֶב אָנֹכִי *am I a servant?* 1 S 17$_{43}$, מָה עַבְדְּךָ הַכֶּלֶב *what is your slave, a temple servant?* 2 K 8$_{13}$, מי עבדך כלב *who is your slave, a temple servant?* Lachish ost. 2$_{4}$ 5$_{4}$ 6$_{3}$. <PREP> אֶל *to,* + פנה *turn* 2 S 9$_{8}$ (if em. מֵת *dead* dog, i.e. כֶּלֶב I).

כָּלֵבִי $_{1}$ gent. **Calebite**—as sing. noun, an individual

Calebite, <NOM CL> הוּא כָלִבִּי *he was a Calebite* 1 S 25$_{3(Qr)}$.
→ כָּלֵב *Caleb.*

כלה 206.6.37 vb. **be complete—Qal** 63.0.8 Pf. כָּלָה, כָּלְתָה, כָּלִיתִי, (כָּלָתָה), כָּלוּ (כָּלוֹ Ps 37$_{20}$, Q כלון), כְּלִיתֶם, כָּלִינוּ; impf. יִכְלֶה (יִכֶל), תִּכְלֶה, יִכְלוּ (יִכְלָיוּן); + waw וְכָלָה, וַתִּכְלֶינָה, וַתֵּכֶל; ptc. כָּלוֹת; inf. כְּלוֹת (כַּלֹּתוֹ), וּכְלִיתֶם (כְּלוֹתָם)—**be complete, be finished, be destroyed, be consumed, be weak, be dim** (Ps 69$_{4}$), **be determined, desire, disappear, perish.**

<SUBJ> 4QpsMos^{e} 1$_{9}$ ([יכ]לו]; others [יוכ]לו]), אִישׁ *man* Jr 44$_{27}$, בֵּן *son* Jr 16$_{4}$ Ml 3$_{6}$ 1QM 3$_{9}$, בַּת *daughter* Jr 16$_{4}$, נָבִיא *prophet* Ezk 13$_{14}$, worshipper Ps 39$_{11}$ 90$_{7}$, לֵץ *scoffer* Is 29$_{20}$, רָשָׁע *wicked one* Ps 37$_{20}$, זֹרֵעַ *sower* Jb 4$_{9}$, חֹרֵשׁ *plougher* Jb 4$_{9}$, עזב ptc. *one who forsakes* Is 1$_{28}$, שׂטן ptc. *one who accuses* Ps 71$_{13}$ (|| בושׁ *be ashamed*), צֹרֵר *adversary* 4QapPs^{b} 31$_{8}$, הלך ptc. *one who walks* 1QS 4$_{14}$, כָּבוֹד *glory* of Kedar Is 21$_{16}$, בַּיִת *house*, i.e. temple 1 K 6$_{38}$ 2 C 8$_{16}$, עֲבֹדָה *service* of tabernacle Ex 39$_{32}$, מְלָאכָה *work*, i.e. service of house of Y. 1 C 28$_{20}$ 2 C 29$_{34}$, עֹלָה *burnt offering* 2 C 29$_{28}$, רַחַם *compassion* Lm 3$_{22}$, רָעָה *evil* 1 S 20$_{7.9}$ 25$_{17}$ Est 7$_{7}$, עַוְלָה *injustice* 1QH 11$_{22}$, עָוֹן *iniquity* 4QHod^{a} 7.2$_{4}$ (|| שׁבת *cease*), זַעַם *indignation* Is 10$_{25}$ Dn 11$_{36}$, אַף *anger* Ezk 5$_{13}$, שֹׁד *destruction* Is 16$_{4}$, שֵׁבֶט *rod* of anger Pr 22$_{8}$.

עָנָן *cloud* Jb 7$_{9}$ (|| הלך *go away*), מַיִם *water* Gn 21$_{15}$ 4QPatr 5.2$_{3}$, דֶּשֶׁא *grass* Is 15$_{6}$, בָּצִיר *vintage* Is 24$_{13}$ 32$_{10}$, כַּד *jar* of meal 1 K 17$_{14.16}$, קָצִיר *harvest* Ru 2$_{23}$, יוֹם *day* Jr 20$_{18}$ Ps 102$_{4}$ Jb 7$_{6}$, קַיִץ *summer* Jr 8$_{20}$, שָׁנָה *year* Gn 41$_{53}$, כֹּחַ *strength* Ps 71$_{9}$, חַיִּים *life* Ps 31$_{11}$, רוּחַ *spirit* Ps 143$_{7}$, עַיִן *eye* Jr 14$_{6}$ Ps 69$_{4}$ 119$_{82.123}$ Jb 11$_{20}$ 17$_{2}$ (if em. תָּלֶן עֵינִי *my eye dwells* to תִּכְלֶן עֵינַי *my eyes fail*) 17$_{5}$ Lm 2$_{11}$ 4$_{17}$ 1QH 9$_{5}$, לֵבָב *heart* Ps 73$_{26}$, כִּלְיָה *kidney* Jb 19$_{27}$, בָּשָׂר *flesh* Jb 33$_{21}$ Pr 5$_{11}$, שְׁאֵר *flesh* Ps 73$_{26}$ Pr 5$_{11}$, נֶפֶשׁ *soul* Ps 84$_{3}$ (|| כסף ni. *long for*) 119$_{81}$, דָּבָר *word* of Y. Ezr 1$_{1}$||2 C 36$_{22}$, קֵץ *period* 4QMyst^{c} 3$_{8}$ ([כלו[ת]), שְׁלִישִׁי *third portion* Ezk 5$_{12}$, אֵלֶּה *these* Dn 12$_{7}$, כֹּל *everyone* Is 31$_{3}$.

<PREP> לְ of direction, *to,* + חָצֵר *court* Ps 84$_{3}$, תְּשׁוּעָה *salvation* Ps 119$_{81.123}$, אִמְרָה *word* Ps 119$_{82}$; *for (need of),* + מָנוֹחַ *rest* 1QH 9$_{5}$; *according to,* + מִשְׁפָּט *specification* 1 K 6$_{38}$; *concerning, in,* + דָּבָר *part* 1 K 6$_{38}$; לְאֵין *without (there being),* + שְׁאֵרִית *remnant* 1QS 4$_{14}$, פְּלֵטָה *escape* 1QS 4$_{14}$.

בְּ of instrument, *by (means of), with,* + חֶרֶב *sword* Jr 16$_{4}$, + רָעָב *famine* Jr 16$_{4}$ Ezk 5$_{12}$, יָגוֹן *trouble* Ps 31$_{11}$, אַף *anger* Ps 90$_{7}$, חֵמָה *wrath* 4QpsMos^{e} 1$_{9}$ ([יכ]לו]; others [יוכ]לו]); *in, with,* + בֹּשֶׁת *shame* Jr 20$_{18}$, אֶפֶס *nothingness* Jb 7$_{6}$, עָשָׁן *smoke* Ps 37$_{20}$ 102$_{4}$, חֵיק *bosom* Jb 19$_{27}$, דִּמְעָה *tears* Lm 2$_{11}$.

כְּ *as,* + עָשָׁן *smoke* Ps 37$_{20(mss)}$ 102$_{4(mss)}$; מִן of direction, *from,* + חֵמֶת *goat skin* Gn 21$_{15}$; of agent, *by (means of),* + תִּגְרָה *agitation* Ps 39$_{11}$, רוּחַ *spirit* Jb 4$_{9}$, פֶּה *mouth* of Jeremiah Ezr 1$_{1}$||2 C 36$_{22}$.

כלה אֶל *reach right up to, overtake,* + Haman Est 7$_{7}$ (or em. עַל), אָדוֹן *lord*, i.e. Nabal 1 S 25$_{17}$ (mss עַל); כלה עַל in same sense + בַּיִת Nabal's *house(hold)* 1 S 25$_{17}$.*

מֵאֵת *from (with),* + מֶלֶךְ *king* Est 7$_{7}$; מֵעִם *from (with),* + Saul 1 S 20$_{7}$, אָב *father* 1 S 20$_{9}$.

Also perh. 4QBer^{a} 8$_{1}$ 4QRitMar 133$_{1}$. <SYN> בושׁ *be ashamed,* כסף ni. *long for,* שׁבת *cease,* הלך *go away.*

Pi. 141.6.29 Pf. כִּלָּה (כִּלָּם) כִּלְּתָה, (כִּלַּתּוּ) כִּלִּיתָ, (כִּלִּיתָם) כִּלִּיתִי (כִּלִּיתִים) כִּלּוּ, (כִּלּוּנִי) כִּלִּיתֶם; impf. תְּכַלֶּה, יְכַלֶּה, אֲכַלֶּה (אֲכַלְךָ) אֲכַלֵּם, יְכַלּוּ, תְּכַלֶּינָה; + waw וְכִלָּה, וְכִלִּיתִי, וַיְכַל (וַיְכַלֵּהוּ), Si (ויכלם), וָאֲכַל, וַיְכַלּוּ; impv. Si כל, Q כַּלּוּ; ptc. מְכַלֶּה, מְכַלּוֹת; inf. כַּלֵּא (כַּלֵּה), כַּלּוֹת (כַּלּוֹתוֹ), Q (כלותמה), כלותם—**complete, finish, end,* use up, exhaust, destroy, exterminate;*** appar. **exhaust oneself, pine** (Ps 6$_{1}$ [if em.]).*

<SUBJ> ״ *Y.* Gn 18$_{33}$ Ex 31$_{18}$ 32$_{10.12}$ 33$_{3.5}$ Lv 26$_{44}$ Nm 16$_{21}$ 17$_{10}$ 25$_{11}$ Dt 28$_{21}$ 32$_{23}$ Is 10$_{18}$ Jr 5$_{3}$ 9$_{15}$ 14$_{12}$ 49$_{37}$ Ezk 5$_{13}$ 6$_{12}$ 7$_{8}$ 13$_{15}$ 20$_{8.21}$ 22$_{31}$ 43$_{8}$ Lm 4$_{11}$ Si 45$_{19}$ 4QapJoseph^{b} 3$_{10}$, אֲדֹנָי *Lord* Ps 59$_{14.14}$ 4QBark^{a} 1.2$_{5}$, אֱלֹהִים *God* Gn 2$_{2}$ 17$_{22}$ Jr 9$_{15}$ Ps 74$_{11}$ 78$_{33}$ Ezr 9$_{14}$ 4QShir^{b} 35$_{1}$ (לכלת; א[לו]הים) *for the destruction of* corrected to לכלות *to destroy),* אֱלוֹהַּ *God* Jb 9$_{22}$, אֵל *God* 1QH 5$_{36}$ (|| כשׁל hi. *cause to stumble)* 8$_{31}$ (|| תמם hi. *bring to an end)* 1QpHab 5$_{3}$ 13$_{3}$ 4QNarrD 1$_{3}$ (לכלות[ם]) 4QDibHam^{a} 1.5$_{8}$, Israel Jos 8$_{24}$ 2 C 31$_{1}$, Israelite(s) Lv 19$_{9}$ 23$_{22}$ Dt 7$_{22}$ 26$_{12}$, Jew Ne 3$_{34}$, Amalekite(s) 1 S 15$_{18}$, עַם *people* Ex 5$_{13}$ 2 C 24$_{10}$, גּוֹי *nation* Jr 10$_{25}$.

Aaron Lv 16$_{20}$ Nm 4$_{15}$, Adonijah 1 K 1$_{41}$, David 1 S 18$_{1}$ 24$_{17}$ 2 S 6$_{18}$ 13$_{39}$ (if em. וַיְכַל) 22$_{39}$ 1 C 16$_{2}$, Ehud Jg 3$_{18}$, Eleazar Jos 19$_{51}$ 1QDM 1$_{12}$, Ezekiel Ezk 4$_{6.8}$, Ezra Ezr 10$_{17}$, Hiram 1 K 7$_{40}$, Huram 2 C 4$_{11(Qr)}$, Isaac Gn

27$_{30}$, Jacob Gn 43$_{2}$ 49$_{33}$, Jehu 2 K 10$_{25}$, Jeremiah Jr 26$_{8}$ 43$_{1}$, Joab 1 C 27$_{24}$, Job Jb 31$_{16}$, Jonadab 2 S 13$_{36}$, Joshua Jos 10$_{20}$ 19$_{51}$ 24$_{20}$ 1QDM 1$_{12}$ 4QTestim$_{21}$, Moses Ex 34$_{33}$ 40$_{33}$ Nm 7$_{1}$ 16$_{31}$ 17$_{25}$ Dt 31$_{24}$ 32$_{45}$, Noah Gn 6$_{16}$, Rebekah Gn 24$_{19}$, Samson Jg 15$_{17}$, Saul 1 S 10$_{13}$ 13$_{10}$, Seraiah Jr 51$_{63}$, Simeon Si 50$_{14.19}$, Solomon 1 K 3$_{1}$ 6$_{9.14}$ 7$_{1}$ 8$_{54}$ ||2 C 7$_{1}$ 1 K 9$_{1}$ 2 C 7$_{11}$.

אִישׁ *man* 1 S 2$_{33}$ 2 S 21$_{5}$ Ezk 42$_{15}$ Ru 3$_{3.18}$ Ezr 10$_{17}$ 1QM 8$_{1}$, בֵּן *son* Nm 4$_{15}$ 1QDM 1$_{12}$ 4QMidrEschat^{a} 3$_{8}$, *son* of human being Ezk 43$_{23}$, *son* of Israel Jos 10$_{20}$ 19$_{49}$ 2 C 8$_{8}$ 31$_{7}$, of Ammon 2 C 20$_{23}$, of Moab 2 C 20$_{23}$, אָח *brother* Gn 43$_{2}$ 1QS 6$_{10}$, נַעַר *youth* Ru 2$_{21}$ Si 35$_{8}$, עֶבֶד *servant* Gn 24$_{15.45}$ Is 49$_{4}$, עֹשֶׂה *worker* 2 C 24$_{14}$, מַלְאָךְ *messenger* 2 S 11$_{19}$, שֹׁטֵר *officer* Ex 5$_{14}$ Dt 20$_{9}$, שֹׁפֵט *judge* 11QT 62$_{4}$, שַׂר *prince* 2 C 24$_{10}$, ראשׁ family *head* Jos 19$_{51}$, כֹּהֵן *priest* Ezk 43$_{27}$ 2 C 29$_{17}$ 1Q29 1$_{4}$ ([ל]כלות) 4QapMos^{b} 1.2$_{2}$, צַדִּיק *righteous one* Jb 36$_{11}$, אוֹיֵב *enemy* 2 S 22$_{38}$||Ps 18$_{38}$ Lm 2$_{22}$, זֵד *arrogant one* Ps 119$_{87}$, רָשָׁע *wicked one* Jb 21$_{13(Qr)}$, עָרִיץ *terrible one* 4QpPs^{a} 1.2$_{14}$, קרץ ptc. *one who purses lips* Pr 16$_{30}$, קרא ptc. pass. *one who is invited* 1 K 1$_{41}$, worshipper Ps 90$_{9}$ appar. 101$_{5}$ (if em.; see Obj.), אֲשֶׁר עַל־הַבַּיִת *one who was over the house*, i.e. steward Gn 44$_{12}$.

גָּמָל *camel* Gn 24$_{19.22}$, עֵגֶל *calf* Is 27$_{10}$, גֹּבַי *swarm of locusts* Am 7$_{2}$, רָעָב *famine* Gn 41$_{30}$, בֶּהָלָה *terror* Lv 26$_{16}$, שַׁחֶפֶת *consumption* Lv 26$_{16}$, קַדַּחַת *fever* Lv 26$_{16}$, חֶרֶב *sword* Ho 11$_{6}$ (|| אכל *devour*), אֵשׁ *fire* 1QM 11$_{11}$, רוּחַ *spirit* 2 S 13$_{39}$ (if ins.), צְרָרִים *innards* Ps 6$_{1}$ (if em. בְּכָל־צוֹרְרָי it has aged *on account of all my enemies* to בְּכָלֵה צוֹרְרָי *my innards* have aged *from pining*), אָלָה *curse* Zc 5$_{4}$, אֲשֶׁר *one who* 1QpHab 12$_{6}$; subj. not specified, 1 S 3$_{12}$ 1 K 22$_{11}$||2 C 18$_{10}$ 2 K 13$_{17.19}$ Ezk 20$_{13}$ Dn 9$_{24}$ 12$_{7}$ Ezr 9$_{1}$ 2 C 29$_{29}$ 31$_{1}$ Si 10$_{13}$ 38$_{26}$ 4QpNah 1$_{4}$ 4QpsEzek^{c} 3.2$_{9}$ (or em. למכל[י]ם *for those who destroy* to למלכ[י]ם *for the kings*) 11QT 33$_{15}$.

<OBJ> אֶרֶץ *land* Gn 41$_{30}$, כַּרְמֶל *orchard* Is 10$_{18}$, כָּבוֹד *glory* of forest Is 10$_{18}$, Israel(ites) Dt 28$_{21}$ Jr 5$_{3}$ 4QDibHam^{a} 1.5$_{8}$, Gibeonite(s) 2 S 21$_{5}$, Elam Jr 49$_{37}$, Kittim 4QpNah 1$_{4}$ (הכ[תיים]) Syrian 1 K 22$_{11}$||2 C 18$_{10}$ 2 K 13$_{17.19}$, עַם *people* Ex 32$_{10.12}$ 33$_{3.5}$ Jos 24$_{20}$ Jr 9$_{15}$ 14$_{12}$ Ezk 22$_{31}$ 1QpHab 5$_{3}$, גּוֹי *nation* Dt 7$_{22}$, עֵדָה *congregation* Nm 16$_{21}$ 17$_{10}$ Si 45$_{19}$, בַּיִת *house* of Israel Ezk 20$_{13}$ 43$_{8}$, Jacob Jr 10$_{25}$.

בֵּן *son* 2 C 8$_{8}$ 1QM 13$_{16}$ 4QMidrEschat^{a} 3$_{8}$, of Israel Lv 26$_{44}$ Nm 25$_{11}$, עֶבֶד *servant* 4QWays^{b} 9$_{3}$ (ל[כ]לות), worshipper Ps 119$_{87}$, תָּם *blameless one* Jb 9$_{22}$, אֶבְיוֹן *poor one* 1QpHab 12$_{6}$, עָנָו *humble one* 4QBark^{a} 1.2$_{5}$, אוֹיֵב *enemy* 2 S 22$_{39}$, רָשָׁע *wicked one* Jb 9$_{22}$ 1QpHab 13$_{3}$, גְּבַהּ *one who is proud* Ps 101$_{5}$ (if em. אֹתוֹ לֹא אוּכָל *him I cannot endure* to אֹתוֹ לַאֲכַלֶּא *him I shall indeed destroy*; or em. אִתּוֹ לֹא אוֹכֵל *with him I shall not eat*; || צמת hi. *destroy*),* עבד ptc. *one who serves* foreign gods 1QpHab 13$_{3}$, עשׂה ptc. *one who does* 4QpPs^{a} 1.2$_{14}$, בָּשָׂר *flesh*, i.e. strength 1QH 8$_{31}$, כֹּחַ *strength* Is 49$_{4}$ 1QH 5$_{36}$, מְלָאכָה *work* Gn 2$_{2}$ Ex 40$_{33}$, מַעֲשֶׂה *work* Ex 5$_{13}$, חֹק *allotted task* Ex 5$_{14}$, קָצִיר *harvest* Ru 2$_{21}$, מַרְבֵּק *fattening* Si 38$_{26}$, סָעִיף *branch* Is 27$_{10}$, חֵץ *arrow* Dt 32$_{23}$, צֹהַר *roof* Gn 6$_{16}$, בַּיִת *house* 1 K 6$_{9.14}$ 7$_{1}$ Zc 5$_{4}$ 2 C 7$_{11}$.

עַיִן *eye* Lv 26$_{16}$ 1 S 2$_{33}$ Jb 31$_{16}$, יָמִין *right hand* Ps 74$_{11}$, תְּלֻנּוֹת *grumblings* Nm 17$_{25}$, רִשְׁעָה *wickedness* 4QShir^{b} 35$_{1}$ (לכלת *for the destruction of* corrected to לכלות *to destroy*), רָעָה *evil* Pr 16$_{30}$, פֶּשַׁע *transgression* Dn 9$_{24}$, אַשְׁמָה *guilt* 1QM 11$_{11}$, אַף *anger* Ezk 7$_{8}$ 20$_{8.21}$, חֵמָה *anger* Ezk 5$_{13}$ 6$_{12}$ 13$_{15}$ Lm 4$_{11}$, מִדָּה *measurement* Ezk 42$_{15}$, בַּד *pole* Ho 11$_{6}$, יוֹם *day* Ezk 43$_{27}$ Ps 78$_{33}$ Jb 21$_{13}$ 36$_{11}$, שָׁנָה *year* Ps 90$_{9}$, דָּבָר *word* 1QDM 1$_{12}$ ([דברי]), *matter* Ru 3$_{18}$, זֹאת *this* 2 C 31$_{1}$, אֵלֶּה *these* Ezk 4$_{6}$ Ezr 9$_{1}$; obj. not specified, Lm 2$_{22}$.

<PREP> לְ of benefit, *to, for*, + תֹּהוּ *nothingness* Is 49$_{4}$; of direction, + עוֹלָם *eternity* 6QHymn 5$_{4}$ (לעו[למים]).

בְּ of place/time, *in, at, among, on*, + דֶּרֶךְ *way* Ex 33$_{3}$, מִדְבָּר *steppe* Ezk 20$_{21}$, אֶרֶץ *earth* Ps 119$_{87}$, יוֹם *day* Gn 2$_{2}$ Nm 7$_{1}$ Ne 3$_{34}$ 2 C 29$_{17}$, חֹדֶשׁ *month* 2 C 31$_{7}$; of instrument, *by (means of), with*, + יָד *hand* 1QpHab 5$_{3}$, חֶרֶב *sword* Jr 14$_{12}$, קִנְאָה *jealousy* Nm 25$_{11}$, אֵשׁ *fire* Ezk 22$_{31}$, חָרוֹן *heat* of anger Si 45$_{19}$ 4QBark^{a} 1.2$_{5}$, אַף *anger* Ezk 43$_{8}$, חֵמָה *anger* Ps 59$_{14}$, אַשְׁמָה *wickedness* 4QMidrEschat^{a} 3$_{8}$ (לכלותמ[ה באש]מה).

בְּ *in, with*, + אִישׁ *man* Ezr 10$_{17}$, קָטֹן *small one*, i.e. youngest Gn 44$_{12}$, טוֹב *goodness* Jb 21$_{13}$ 36$_{11}$, הֶבֶל *vanity* Ps 78$_{33}$; *against*, + Israelite(s) Dt 32$_{23}$, Israel Ezk 20$_{8}$, בַּיִת *house* of Israel Ezk 6$_{12}$, Jerusalem Ezk 5$_{13}$, קִיר *wall* Ezk 13$_{15}$, בֵּן *son* Ezk 20$_{21}$, יֹשֵׁב *inhabitant* Ezk 7$_{8}$, טוח ptc. *one who plasters* Ezk 13$_{15}$; introducing object, + יֹשֵׁב *inhabitant* 2 C 20$_{23}$.

כְּ *as*, + רֶגַע *moment* Nm 16_{21} 17_{10}; מִן of direction, *from*, + נֶפֶשׁ *soul* Is 10_{18} (+ עַד־בָּשָׂר *until flesh*, i.e. both of them); אֶל *to*, + אַמָּה *cubit* Gn 6_{16}.

מֵעַל *from (upon)*, + פָּנִים *face* of ground Ex 32_{12} 4QpNah 1_4, אֲדָמָה *ground* Dt 28_{21}; *against*, + 'י *Y.* Nm 17_{25}; מִקֶּרֶב *from (among)*, + חֵיק *bosom* Ps $74_{11(Qr)}$; עַד *until*, + בָּשָׂר *flesh* Is 10_{18} (+ מִנֶּפֶשׁ *from soul*, i.e. both of them), מוֹעֵד *set time* 1QH 8_{31}.

<COLL> לֹא תוּכַל כַּלֹּתָם מַהֵר *you shall not be able to destroy them quickly* Dt 7_{22}, עד לכלה *as far as destroying* 4QapJoshua[a] 3.1_7 (+ מעל *act unfaithfully*).

כלה followed by יצא *go out* 2 S 13_{39}, קום hi. *erect* Nm 7_1, קצר *reap harvest* Lv 19_9 23_{22}, אכל *eat* Gn 43_2 1 K 14_1 Am 7_2 Ru 3_3, שתה *drink* Gn $24_{19.22}$ Ru 3_3, שקת hi. *give drink to* Gn 24_{19}, עשׂה *do* 1 K 7_{40}||2 C 4_{11} 2 K 10_{25}, בנה *build* 1 K 3_1 9_1, שרת pi. *serve* Si $50_{14.19}$, כסה pi. *cover* Nm 4_{15}, קרב hi. *offer* Jg 3_{18}, עלה hi. *present burnt offering* 1 S 13_{10} 2 S 6_{18} 1 C 16_2 2 C 29_{29}, קטר hi. *burn*, i.e. sacrifice 11QT 33_{15}, חטא pi. *cleanse* Ezk 43_{23}, כפר pi. *make atonement* Lv 16_{20}, עשׂר hi. *tithe* Dt 26_{12}.

נכה hi. *strike* Jos 10_{20}, שמד hi. *destroy* 4QapJoseph[b] 3_{10}, נפץ pi. *smash* Dn 12_7, הרג *kill* Jos 8_{24}, אמר *say* Si 35_8, דבר pi. *speak* Gn 2_2 17_{22} 18_{33} $24_{15.45}$ Ex 31_{18} 34_{33} Nm 16_{31} Dt 20_9=11QT 62_4 Dt 32_{45} Jg 15_{17} 1 S 18_1 24_{17} 2 S 11_{19} 13_{36} Jr 26_8 43_1 1QS 6_{10} 1Q29 1_4 ([ל]כלות) 4QapMos[b] 1.2_2, צוה pi. *command* Gn 49_{33}, הלל pi. *praise* 4QTestim$_{21}$, ברך pi. *bless* Gn 27_{30}, פלל htp. *pray* 1 K 8_{54} ||2 C 7_1, נבא htp. *prophesy* 1 S 10_{13}, ידה hi. *give thanks* 4QTestim$_{21}$, קרא *read* Jr 51_{63}, נחל *distribute* Jos 19_{49}, חלק pi. *divide* Jos 19_{51}, כתב *write* Dt 31_{24}, שלך hi. *throw* 1QM 8_1.

Also 4QTanḥ 23_3 4Q185 1.3_{12} perh. 4QapPs[b] 33_1 5Q Règle 6_2.

<SYN> אכל *devour*, כשל hi. *cause to stumble*, תמם hi. *bring to an end*.

Pu. 2 Pf. כֻּלּוּ; + waw וַיְכֻלּוּ—**be completed, be finished,** <SUBJ> שָׁמַיִם *heavens* Gn 2_1, אֶרֶץ *earth* Gn 2_1, צָבָא *host* of stars Gn 2_1, תְּפִלָּה *prayer* Ps 72_{20}.*

→ כָּלֶה *longing*, כָּלָה *end*, כִּלָּיוֹן *annihilation*, מִכְלוֹת *perfection*, תִּכְלָה *perfection*, תַּכְלִית *completeness*.

כָּלֶה 1 adj. **longing**—f. pl. כָּלוֹת—<NOM CL> עֵינֶיךָ רֹאוֹת וְכָלוֹת אֲלֵיהֶם *your eyes are looking and longing for them* Dt 28_{32}.

→ כלה *be complete*.

כָּלָה 22.2.46 n.f. **end**—cstr. Q כלת—**end, destruction, annihilation, completion,** <SUBJ> נתך *be poured out* Dn 9_{27}, מוש *withdraw* Si 40_{10}.

<NOM CL> אין כלה *there is no end*, i.e. without end 1QH 5_{34}, כלת עולמים לכול גורל בליעל *eternal destruction shall be for all the lot of Belial* 1QM 1_5, כלה לכול גוי רשעה *destruction shall be for all the nations of wickedness* 1QM 15_2, כלה בלוא רחמיך *without your mercy there is destruction* 1QH 11_{18}, כָּלָה בְּיָדוֹ *destruction is in his hand*, i.e. power Dn 11_{16} (or em. כֻּלֹּה *all of it*), כָּלָה הִיא מֵעִם אָבִיו *destruction was (from) with his father*, i.e. his father's intention 1 S 20_{33}.

<OBJ> שמע *hear* Is 28_{22}, עשׂה *do*, i.e. carry out Is 10_{23} Jr 4_{27} $5_{10.18}$ $30_{11.11}$ $46_{28.28}$ Ezk 11_{13} 20_{17} Na $1_{8.9}$ Zp 1_{18} Ne 9_{31} 4QD[a] 1_4.

<CSTR> כלת אל *destruction of*, i.e. by, *God* 1QM 4_{12}, כלת בני *destruction of the sons of* darkness 1QM 1_{16}, [חרו]נו *of his wrath* 4QShirShabb[f] 23.1_{12} ([כל]ת), רשעה *of wickedness* 4QShir[b] 35_1 (לכלה corrected to לכלות *to destroy*), עולמים *of eternity*, i.e. eternal destruction 1QM 1_5 9_5 1QS 2_{15} 5_{13} (עולם) 4QHod[a] 7.2_8 (עולם) 4QM[a] 1_4 4QShir[a] 1_7 (עולם) 4QShir[b] 8_5([כל]ת עולם]); באר כלה *pit of destruction* 4QHod[a] 7.1_{19}, עת *season of* Si 44_{17}, כלמת *disgrace of* 1QS 4_{13} 4QBer[d] 1_2 ([כלמ]ת), מלחמת *war of*, i.e. destructive war 1QM 1_{10}, מלחמות *wars of* 4QM[a] 1_{14}, מגפח *slaughter of* 1QM 18_{12} (appar. error for מגפת), שרפת *burning of*, i.e. destructive burning 4QM[a] 17_6 ([כלה]), רדף *pursuit of*, i.e. destructive pursuit 1QM 9_6, קנאת *zeal of*, i.e. destructive zeal 1QH 12_{14}, עברת כל[ת] *fury of the destruction of* 4QShirShabb[f] 23.1_{12}, משפטי נגע וכלה perh. *judgments (consisting) of plague and destruction* 1QH fr. 3_{16}.

<ADJ> נִבְהָלָה *terrifying* Zp 1_{18}.

<PREP> לְ of direction, benefit, purpose, *to (the point of), for (the purpose of)* Ezk 13_{13} 1QH 9_3 fr. 5_8 1QM 1_{16} 9_5 1QpHab 9_{11} 1QS 5_{13} 4QHod[a] 7.2_8 4QPrayer[g] 1_2 ([לכל]ת) 4QShir[a] 1_7 4QShir[b] 8_5 ([לכל]ת) 35_1 (לכלה corrected to לכלות *to destroy*) 4QUnidC 1_3, + שחת hi. *destroy* 2 C 12_{12}, בער *burn* 1QS 2_{15}, רמס *trample* 1QH 6_{32}, שפט *judge*

1QpHab 12₅, נגף *strike* perh. 4QMᵃ 1₄, נתן *give* CD 1₅, פקד *visit*, i.e. punish CD 8₂ 19₁₄, אסף *gather* 1QM 14₅, המה *moan* 1QH 7₅, שׁחח htpol. *be bowed down* 1QH 8₃₂.

עַל *concerning* 4QpIsaᶜ 8₁ (others מלך *king of*); *until*, + בער *burn* 1QH 6₁₉, שׁוב *return* 1QH 3₃₆; עַד לְ *until* 4QapPsᵇ 24₃.

<COLL> עָשׂוּ כָּלָה *they have carried out completely* Gn 18₂₁, כְּשַׁלְּחוֹ כָּלָה *when he sends* you *away completely* Ex 11₁ (or em. כַּלָּה *bride*), כָּלָה יַעֲשֶׂה מְקוֹמָהּ *an end he will make of her place* Na 1₈ (or em. מְקוֹמָה *of opposition* or מְקָמֶיהָ *of her enemies* or בְּקָמָיו *against his enemies*), יפקוד אחריכה כלה *may he visit you with destruction* 1QS 2₆.

כלה באש מחשכים *destruction in the fire of darkness* 1QS 4₁₃, כלת אל בכול גוי הבל *destruction by God of every nation of vanity* 1QM 4₁₂, כלה בכל מענינו perh. *destruction among all our oppressors* 1QLitPr 3.1₆, כָּלָה וְנֶחֱרָצָה *destruction and what is determined*, i.e. determined destruction Is 10₂₃=4QpIsaᶜ 4.2₁₈ ([כלה ונחרצה]) Is 28₂₂ Dn 9₂₇ 1QH 3₃₆, כלה בבל appar. *destruction of Babylon* 4QpIsaᶜ 8₁ (others מלך *king of* Babylon); (לְאֵין + כָּלָה) שארית *without a remnant* 1QH 6₃₂ ([שא]רית) 1QM 14₅ 1QS 5₁₃, לאין [מספר] *without number* 1QH 6₃ (|| הַוָּה *destruction*).*

Also 1QH fr. 3₈ perh. 4QapPsᵇ 76₄.

<SYN> הַוָּה *destruction*.

⇒ כלה *be complete*.

כַּלָּה 34.0.1 n.f. **bride**—sf. כַּלָּתָהּ, כַּלָּתוֹ, (כַּלָּתֶךָ) כַּלָּתֵךְ; pl. sf. כַּלֹּתֶיהָ, כַּלֹּתַיִךְ—**daughter-in-law, bride, young wife,** <SUBJ> הרה *be pregnant* 1 S 4₁₉, בוא *come* Ca 4₈, קום *arise* Mc 7₆ Ru 1₆, יצא *go out* Jl 2₁₆, שׁוב *go back* 2 S 17₃ (if em. הַכֹּל *the whole* to כַּלָּה *bride*), עדה *adorn oneself* Is 61₁₀, ילד *bear child* 1 S 4₁₉ Ru 4₁₅ 1 C 2₄, זנה *prostitute oneself* Gn 38₂₄, נאף *commit adultery* Ho 4₁₃.₁₄ (both || בַּת *daughter*), לבב pi. *bewitch heart* Ca 4₉, שׁכח *forget* Jr 2₃₂.

<NOM CL> גַּן נָעוּל ... כַּלָּה *the bride ... is (as) a locked garden* Ca 4₁₂, כַּלָּתוֹ הִיא *she was his daughter-in-law* Gn 38₁₆, שְׁתֵּי כַלֹּתֶיהָ עִמָּהּ *two of her daughters-in-law were with her* Ru 1₇, רוּת ... כַּלָּתָהּ עִמָּהּ *Ruth ... her daughter-in-law was with her* Ru 1₂₂. <OBJ> לקח *take* Gn 11₃₁, שׁלח pi. *send away* Ex 11₁ (if em.), טמא pi. *defile* Ezk 22₁₁.

<CSTR> עֶרְוַת כַּלָּתְךָ *nakedness of your daughter-in-law* Lv 18₁₅, קוֹל כַּלָּה *voice of the bride* Jr 7₃₄ 16₉ 25₁₀ 35₁₁, שְׁתֵּי כַלֹּתֶיהָ *two of her daughters-in-law* Ru 1₇.₈. <APP> Ruth Ru 1₂₂ 2₂₂, Sarai Gn 11₃₁, Tamar Gn 38₁₁.₂₄ 1 C 2₄, אָחוֹת *sister* Ca 4₉, גַּן *garden* Ca 5₁.

<PREP> לְ of direction, *to*, + בוא *come* Ca 5₁, אמר *say* Gn 38₁₁ Ru 1₈ 2₂₀; כְּ *as* Is 49₁₈ 61₁₀; אֶל *to*, + אמר *say* Ru 2₂₂; עַל *upon, over* Is 62₅, + פקד *visit*, i.e. punish Ho 4₁₄ (|| בַּת); *beside, with*, + שׁכן *dwell* 4QBarkᵃ 1.1₆ ([ישכ]ן); אֵת *with*, + שׁכב *lie*, i.e. have sex with Lv 20₁₂. <SYN> בַּת *daughter*. <COLL> תִּטֹּפְנָה שִׂפְתוֹתַיִךְ כַּלָּה *your lips drip with honey, (my) bride* Ca 4₁₁, מַה־יָּפוּ דֹדַיִךְ אֲחֹתִי כַלָּה *how beautiful is your love, my sister, (my) bride* Ca 4₁₀.*

⇒ כְּלוּלֹת *betrothal*.

[כְּלֻהַי] 1 pr.n.m. **Cheluhi**—Kt כלהי (Qr כְּלוּהוּ)—of Bani family, married to non-Israelite, <APP> בֵּן *son* Ezr 10₃₅(Kt).

כְּלוּא 2 n.m. **confinement,** <CSTR> בֵּית הַכְּלוּא *the house of confinement*, i.e. prison Jr 37₄(Qr) 52₃₁(Qr).

⇒ כלא *restrain*.

כְּלוּב I 3.2 n.m. **basket**—**basket** for fruit (Am 8₁), **birdcage** (Jr 5₂₇=Si 11₃₀), <NOM CL> כְּלוּב מָלֵא עוֹף *the cage is full of birds* Jr 5₂₇ Si 11₃₀. <OBJ> אמר *say* Am 8₂. <CSTR> כְּלוּב קָיִץ *basket of summer fruit* Am 8₁.₂. <PREP> בְּ of place, *in, at*, + אחז pass. *be held fast* Si 11₃₀; כְּ *as* Jr 5₂₇ Si 11₃₀.

כְּלוּב II 2 pr.n.m. **Chelub, 1.** brother of Shuhah and father of Mehir 1 C 4₁₁. **2.** father of Ezri 1 C 27₂₆. <SUBJ> ילד hi. *become father* 1 C 4₁₁. <NOM CL> כְּלוּב אֲחִי־שׁוּחָה *Chelub was the brother of Shuhah* 1 C 4₁₁. <CSTR> בֶּן־כְּלוּב *son of Chelub* 1 C 27₂₆.

כְּלוּבַי 1 pr.n.m. **Chelubai**—כְּלוּבָי—appar. ident. with Caleb son of Hezron (כָּלֵב I, §2), <SUBJ> ילד ni. *be born* 1 C 2₉.

כְּלוּהוּ 1 pr.n.m. **Cheluhi**—Kt כְּלֻהַי—of Bani family, married to non-Jewish woman Ezr 10₃₅, <APP> בֵּן *son* Ezr 10₃₅(Qr).

כְּלוּלֹת 1 n.f.pl. **betrothal**—sf. כְּלוּלֹתָיִךְ—of time of **betrothal** (Jr 2$_2$), <CSTR> אַהֲבַת כְּלוּלֹתָיִךְ *love of your betrothal*, i.e. your love to me when you were betrothed Jr 2$_2$.

→ כַּלָּה *bride*.

כֶּלַח I 2 n.m. **old age**—כֶּלַח—<SUBJ> אבד *perish* Jb 30$_2$. <PREP> בְּ of accompaniment, *in (a state of), with*, + בוא *come* Jb 5$_{26}$ (or em. בְּלֵחֲךָ *in your moisture*, i.e. vigour, or בְּחֵילְךָ *in your strength*).*

כֶּלַח II 2 n.m. **vigour**—כֶּלַח—<SUBJ> אבד *perish* Jb 30$_2$. <PREP> בְּ of accompaniment, *in (a state of), with*, + בוא *come* Jb 5$_{26}$ (or em. בְּלֵחֲךָ *in your moisture*, i.e. vigour, or בְּחֵילְךָ *in your strength*).

כֶּלַח III 2 pl.n. **Calah**—כֶּלַח—city in Assyria, perh. ident. with modern T. Nimrûd, at NE junction of Tigris and upper Zab, <OBJ> בנה *build* Gn 10$_{11}$. <PREP> בֵּין *between*, + בנה *build* Gn 10$_{12}$ (+ Nineveh).

כָּל־חֹזֶה 2 pr.n.m. **Col-hozeh,** Judahite, son of Hazziah, <CSTR> בֶּן־כָּל־חֹזֶה *son of Col-hozeh* Ne 3$_{15}$ 11$_5$.

כְּלִי 324.7.65 n.m. **vessel**—כֶּלִי, Q כל; cstr. כְּלִי; sf. כֶּלְיְךָ; pl. כֵּלִים, Q כלין, Q כאלין; cstr. כְּלֵי; sf. כֵּלַי, כֵּלֶיךָ, כֵּלֵינוּ, כְּלֵיהֶם, כְּלֵיכֶם (כליהמה).

1. usu. household or cultic object, etc., **vessel, container, utensil, tool, implement, object, furniture, furnishings, goods, equipment, baggage,*** etc. (distinction from §§2 and 4 not alw. certain).

<SUBJ> היה *be* 2 S 8$_{10.10.10}$ CD 12$_{17}$ (+ יָתֵד *nail*, מַסְמֵר *peg*), יתר ni. *remain* Jr 27$_{18.21}$, מצא ni. *be found* 2 K 14$_{14}$ ||2 C 25$_{24}$, שׁנה *be different* Est 1$_7$ 8$_{27}$ (if em. שְׁנַיִם *two* vessels to שֹׁנִים *different*, i.e. exceptional, vessels), מלא *be full* 2 K 4$_6$, שׁבר ni. *be broken* Lv 6$_{21}$ 15$_{12}$ 11QT 50$_{17}$, שׁחת ni. *be spoiled* Jr 18$_4$, אבד *be destroyed* Ps 31$_{13}$ 1QH 4$_9$, טמא *be impure* Lv 15$_{4.26}$ 11QT 49$_8$ 50$_{12}$ (+ בַּיִת *house*) CD 12$_{17}$, טהר *be pure* Lv 13$_{58}$, חמד pass. *be desirable* Ezr 8$_{27}$, שׁמע ni. *be heard* 1 K 6$_7$, עשׂה pass. *be made* 2 K 23$_4$, ni. *be made* 2 K 12$_{14.14}$, *be used* Lv 11$_{32}$, כבס pu. *be washed* Lv 13$_{58}$, שׁטף ni. *be washed* Lv 15$_{12}$, שׁקל ni. *be weighed* Ezr 8$_{33}$, פתח pass. *be opened* Nm 19$_{15}$, טוח *be sealed with pitch* CD 11$_9$, בוא *come* Jr 27$_{18}$, יצא *go out* Pr 25$_4$, שׁוב ho. *be taken back* Jr 27$_{16}$, נשׂא *carry* 4QTohA 1.2$_5$.

<NOM CL> מִשְׁמַרְתָּם ... כְּלֵי הַקֹּדֶשׁ *their charge was ... the holy vessels* Nm 3$_{31}$, מִשְׁמֶרֶת ... כָּל־כֵּלָיו *the charge of* the Merarites ... *was all its utensils* Nm 3$_{36}$, ... כֹּל כְּלֵי זָהָב *all the vessels of ... were of gold* 1 K 10$_{21.21}$||2 C 9$_{20.20}$, הַכֵּלִים קֹדֶשׁ *the vessels are holy* Ezr 8$_{28}$, כְּלֵי נְחֹשֶׁת וּבַרְזֶל קֹדֶשׁ הוּא *the vessels of bronze and iron are holy* Jos 6$_{19}$, כֹּל כְּלִי פָתוּחַ ... טָמֵא הוּא *every open vessel ... is unclean* Nm 19$_{15}$, שָׁבוּ כְלֵיהֶם רֵיקָם *they returned (and) their vessels were empty* Jr 14$_3$, כֵּלִים אֲחֵרִים אָלֶף *other vessels (numbered) one thousand* Ezr 1$_{10}$, כָּל־הַכֵּלִים ... חֲמֵשֶׁת אֲלָפִים וְאַרְבַּע מֵאוֹת *all the vessels ... (totalled) five thousand four hundred* Ezr 1$_{11}$, הַאִישׁ הַזֶּה כָּנְיָהוּ אִם־כְּלִי *is this man Coniah* a despised broken pot *or a vessel?* Jr 22$_{28}$, [וגם] איש כ]לי חמר *and a man too is a vessel of clay* Si 36$_{10}$ (Segal), הכלים אשר בבית *the vessels that are in the house* 11QT 49$_{19}$, בתל של כחלת כלי דמע *in the hill of Kochlit are vessels of tithe* 3Q Tr1$_9$, sim. 3QTr 2$_{6.8}$ 3$_9$ 5$_6$ 8$_3$ 11$_{1.10.14}$ 12$_6$, תחת הפנא הדרומית ... כלי כסף וזהב *underneath the south corner ... are vessels of silver and gold* 3QTr 3$_2$, sim. 3QTr 11$_4$, כְּלִי הָרֹעִים אֲשֶׁר־לוֹ *a shepherds' bag that was his* 1 S 17$_{40}$, שָׁם כְּלֵי הַמִּקְדָּשׁ *there are the vessels of the sanctuary* Ne 10$_{40}$, אֵין עוֹד כֶּלִי *there is not another vessel* 2 K 4$_6$, מְרַק פִּגֻּלִים כְּלֵיהֶם *broth of unclean things is (in) their vessels* Is 65$_{4(Qr)}$ (1QIsa[a] בכליהמה *in their vessels*; or em. מִכְּלֵיהֶם *from their vessels*).

<OBJ> בוא hi. *bring* Ex 39$_{33.36.37.39.40}$ 1 K 10$_{25.25}$||2 C 9$_{24.24}$ (or del. second כְּלִי in 1 K) 1 K 15$_{15}$||2 C 15$_{18}$ Dn 1$_2$ 1 C 22$_{19}$ 2 C 36$_{18}$, עלה hi. *take up* 1 K 8$_4$||2 C 5$_5$, נגשׁ hi. *bring near* 2 K 4$_6$, שׁוב hi. *take back* Jr 28$_{3.6}$ Ne 13$_9$, יצא hi. *take out* 2 K 23$_4$ Is 54$_{16}$=CD 6$_8$ Ezk 12$_{4.7}$ Ezr 1$_7$ 4QSD 7.1$_5$ ([יוןציא]), אסף *gather* 2 C 28$_{24}$, נשׂא *raise*, i.e. carry, Nm 1$_{50}$ 4$_{26}$ Is 52$_{11}$ 1 C 23$_{26}$ 4QSD 7.1$_8$, take Jr 49$_{29}$.

שׁלח *send* Nm 31$_6$ 1 C 18$_{10}$ (or em. וְ *and* to בְּ send *with* vessels), נתן *give* Ex 22$_6$ (:: כֶּסֶף *silver*, i.e. money) Ezk 27$_{13}$, *place* Nm 4$_{10.14.14}$ Jos 6$_{24}$ 1 K 7$_{51}$||2 C 5$_1$ Ne 13$_5$, נוח hi. *place* Ezk 40$_{42}$, יצג hi. *place* Jr 51$_{34}$, נטשׁ *leave* 1 S 17$_{22}$, נוח hi. *leave* 1 K 7$_{47}$, פקד hi. *deposit* Is 10$_{28}$ (unless כְּלִי = *weapon*), זנח hi. *exclude* 2 C 29$_{19}$, טול hi. *throw* Jon 1$_5$, שׁלך hi. *throw* Nm 35$_{22}$ 2 K 7$_{15}$ (unless כְּלִי =

weapon) Ne 13$_{8}$, מצא *find* 2 C 20$_{25}$, לקח *take* Nm 4$_{12}$ 2 K 14$_{14}$ 25$_{14}$||Jr 52$_{18}$ Jr 49$_{29}$ Zc 11$_{15}$ 4QpsEzek^{a} 16.1$_{5}$, קבל pi. *receive* Ezr 8$_{30}$, שׁמר *keep* Nm 3$_{8}$ 1 S 17$_{22}$.

שׁאל *ask (for)* 2 K 4$_{3.3}$, כון hi. *prepare* 2 C 29$_{19}$, כבס pi. *wash* Lv 13$_{58}$ 11QT 49$_{19}$ (+ שַׂלְמָה *garment)* 49$_{20}$ (|| בֶּגֶד *garment)*, טהר pi. *purify* Lv 13$_{59}$ 2 C 29$_{18.18}$ 11QT 49$_{14}$ (+ בַּיִת *house*, רֵחַיִם *mill*, מְדוֹכָה *mortar)* 49$_{15.15}$ CD 10$_{12}$, חטא pi. *purify* Nm 31$_{20.20}$ (if em. htp. *be purified)*, קדשׁ pi. *consecrate* Ex 40$_{9}$ Nm 7$_{1.1}$, hi. *consecrate* 2 C 29$_{19}$, משׁח *anoint* Ex 30$_{27.27.28}$ 40$_{10}$ Lv 8$_{11}$, טבל *dip* 4QTohA 1.2$_{4.5}$, טמא pi. *declare impure* Lv 13$_{59}$, פקד *list* Nm 4$_{32}$.

עשׂה *make* Ex 25$_{39}$||37$_{24}$ (if em. אֵת make *with* at 25$_{39}$ to וְאֵת *and* the vessels) 31$_{7.8.8.9}$ 35$_{13.14.16}$ 37$_{16}$ 38$_{3.3.30}$ 1 S 8$_{12}$ 1 K 7$_{45.48}$||2 C 4$_{16.19}$ Jr 18$_{4}$ 46$_{19}$ Ezk 12$_{3}$ 1 C 18$_{8}$ 2 C 4$_{18}$ 24$_{14.14.14}$ 4QBark^{c} 1.1$_{2}$, מעט hi. *provide few* 2 K 4$_{3}$, כסה pi. *cover* Nm 4$_{9.15}$, תלה *hang* Ezk 15$_{3}$, שׁקל *weigh* Ezr 8$_{25.26}$, משׁשׁ pi. *feel* Gn 31$_{37}$, מלא pi. *fill* Gn 42$_{25}$ (+ שַׂק *sack)*, ריק hi. *empty* Jr 48$_{12}$ (|| נֵבֶל *jar)*, פתח *open* CD 11$_{9}$.

שׁסה *plunder* Ho 13$_{15}$ (or em. שׁאה hi. *ruin)*, שׂרף *burn* Lv 13$_{52}$, בער pi. *burn* Si 27$_{5}$, שׁבר *break* Jr 19$_{11}$, קצץ pi. *cut in pieces* 2 K 24$_{13}$ 2 C 28$_{24}$, שׁחת hi. *destroy* 2 C 36$_{19}$.

<CSTR> כְּלֵי י׳ *vessels of Y.* Is 52$_{11}$, כְּלֵי הַקֹּדֶשׁ *the vessels of holiness* Nm 3$_{31}$ 4$_{15}$ 18$_{3}$ 31$_{6}$ 1 K 8$_{4}$||2 C 5$_{5}$ 1 C 9$_{29}$ 22$_{19}$ (קֹדֶשׁ הָאֱלֹהִים *of the holiness of God)*, כלי קודשו *vessels of his holiness*, i.e. his holy vessels 4QapMes 8$_{8}$, כְּלֵי הָעֲבוֹדָה *vessels of the (temple) service* 1 C 9$_{28}$ 28$_{14.14}$ (both עֲבוֹדָה וַעֲבוֹדָה *of every kind of service)*, עֲבוֹדַת *of the service of* Ex 39$_{40}$ (עֲבֹדַת) 1 C 28$_{13}$, עֲבֹדָתָם *of their service* Nm 4$_{26}$, שָׁרֵת *of service* Nm 4$_{12}$ (הַשָּׁרֵת) 2 C 24$_{14}$, כלי מעשׂה *tools of work* CD 12$_{17}$.

כְּלֵי הַמִּקְדָּשׁ וְהַכֹּהֲנִים *vessels of the sanctuary and of the priests* Ne 10$_{40}$, הַמִּזְבֵּחַ *of the altar* Ex 38$_{3.30}$ Nm 4$_{14}$ 11QT 33$_{13}$, הַמִּשְׁכָּן *of the tabernacle* Ex 27$_{19}$, הָאֹהֶל *of the tent* Ex 31$_{7}$ Nm 3$_{8}$ (אֹהֶל מוֹעֵד *of the tent of meeting)*.

כְּלֵי בֵית י׳ *vessels of the house of Y.* Jr 27$_{16}$ (בֵּית־) 28$_{3.6}$ Ezr 1$_{7}$ (both בֵּית־) 2 C 36$_{7}$, Ne 13$_{8}$, בֵּית הָאֱלֹהִים *of the house of God* Dn 1$_{2}$ (בֵּית־) Ne 13$_{9}$ 2 C 28$_{24.24}$ (both בֵּית־) 36$_{18}$ 4QpsEzek^{a} 16.1$_{5}$, בֵּית־יַעַר הַלְּבָנוֹן *of the house of the forest of Lebanon* 1 K 10$_{21}$||2 C 9$_{20}$, בֵּית־טוֹבִיָּה *of the house of Tobiah* Ne 13$_{8}$, בֵּיתֶךָ *of your household* Gn 31$_{37}$.

כְּלִי זָהָב *vessel of gold* 2 K 12$_{14}$ Si 50$_{9}$, כְּלֵי זָהָב *vessels of gold* 2 S 8$_{10}$||1 C 18$_{10}$ (2 S כְּלֵי־) 1 K 10$_{25}$||2 C 9$_{24}$ 24$_{13}$ (הַזָּהָב) Est 1$_{7}$ 1 C 28$_{14}$ (if ins. כְּלֵי) 2 C 24$_{14}$ 3QTr 3$_{2}$ (כלי כסף וזהב) 12$_{6}$, כְּלֵי־כֶסֶף *vessel of silver* 2 K 12$_{14}$, כְּלֵי־כֶסֶף *vessels of silver* 2 S 8$_{10}$ 1 K 10$_{25}$||2 C 9$_{24}$ (כְּלֵי כֶסֶף) Ezr 1$_{6}$ 8$_{26}$ 1 C 18$_{10}$ (כְּלֵי זָהָב וָכֶסֶף) 28$_{14}$ (כְּלֵי הַכֶּסֶף) 2 C 24$_{14}$ (כְּלֵי זָהָב וָכֶסֶף) 3QTr 3$_{2}$ (כלי כסף וזהב) 12$_{6}$ (כל[י]).

כְּלִי נְחֹשֶׁת *vessel of bronze* Lv 6$_{21}$ 4QMMT B$_{6}$ ([נחושת]), כְּלֵי נְחֹשֶׁת *vessels of bronze* Jos 6$_{19.24}$ (הַנְּחֹשֶׁת) 2 S 8$_{10}$ 2 K 25$_{14}$||Jr 52$_{18}$ (both הַנְּחֹשֶׁת) Ezk 27$_{13}$ Ezr 8$_{27}$ 1 C 18$_{8}$ (הַנְּחֹשֶׁת) 11QT 49$_{15}$, כְּלִי בַרְזֶל *implement of iron* Nm 35$_{16}$ 1 K 6$_{7}$, כלי ... ברזל *vessels of ... iron* 11QT 49$_{15}$, כְּלִי־עֵץ *object of wood* Lv 11$_{32}$ Nm 31$_{20}$, *utensil of wood* Lv 15$_{12}$, כלי עץ *utensils of wood* 11QT 49$_{15}$, כְּלִי עֵץ־יָד *implement of wood in hand* Nm 35$_{18}$, כְּלִי־חֶרֶשׂ *vessel of clay* Lv 6$_{21}$ 11$_{33}$ 14$_{5.50}$ 15$_{12}$ Nm 5$_{17}$ Jr 32$_{14}$ (both כְּלִי־חָרֶשׂ) 4QTohA 2.2$_{10}$, כלי חרש *vessels of clay* 11QT 49$_{8}$ 50$_{17}$, [כ]לי חמר *vessel of clay* Si 36$_{10}$.

כְּלֵי הָאַגָּנוֹת *the vessels (consisting) of bowls* Is 22$_{24}$, הַנְּבָלִים *of jars* Is 22$_{24}$, שַׁמְנָהּ *of*, i.e. for, *its oil* Nm 4$_{9}$, מַשְׁקֶה *of drinking* 1 K 10$_{21}$||2 C 9$_{20}$, כְּלִי־עוֹר *article of skin* Lv 13$_{49.52}$ (כְּלִי הָעוֹר) 13$_{53.57.58}$ (כְּלִי הָעוֹר) 13$_{59}$ Nm 31$_{20}$ (unless in all seven כְּלִי = leather *clothing*, as §4), כלי אור *vessels of light* 4QPrQuot 1.3$_{9}$.

כְּלִי רֹעֶה *shepherd's equipment* Zc 11$_{15}$, כְּלִי הָרֹעִים *shepherds' bag* 1 S 17$_{40}$, כְּלִי יוֹצֵר *potter's vessel* 2 S 17$_{28}$ Jr 19$_{11}$ (הַיּוֹצֵר) Ps 2$_{9}$ Si 27$_{5}$, כְּלֵי רִכְבּוֹ *equipment of his chariot* 1 S 8$_{12}$, כְּלֵי הַבָּקָר *equipment of*, i.e. for, *the oxen* 2 S 24$_{22}$ (כְּלִי) 1 K 19$_{21}$, כְּלֵי גוֹלָה *baggage of*, i.e. for, *exile* Jr 46$_{19}$ Ezk 12$_{3.4.7}$, כְּלֵי מִשְׁמֶרֶת מַשָּׂאָם *objects of observance of their burden*, i.e. things they must carry Nm 4$_{32}$, כְּלֵי הַקָּטָן *the vessels of a small one*, i.e. the small vessels Is 22$_{24}$, כְּלִי רִיק *vessel of emptiness* Jr 51$_{34}$, כלי דמע *vessels of*, i.e. for, *tithe* 3QTr 1$_{9}$ 3$_{9}$ 8$_{3}$ 11$_{1.4.10.14}$ ([דמ]ע).

כְּלִי חֶמְדָּה *precious vessel* Jr 25$_{34}$ (or em. בְּלִי חֶמְלָה *without compassion)* Ho 13$_{15}$ Na 2$_{10}$ GnzPs 2$_{28}$, כְּלֵי חֶמְדָּה *precious vessels* 2 C 32$_{27}$, כְּלֵי חֲמֻדוֹת *precious vessels* 2 C 20$_{25}$, כְּלֵי חֶמְדַּת בֵּית־י׳ *precious vessels of the temple of Y.* 2 C 36$_{10}$ (חֶמְדַּת), כְּלֵי חֶמְדָּתָם *their precious vessels* Dn 11$_{8}$, כְּלֵי מַחֲמַדֶּיהָ *its precious vessels* 2 C 36$_{19}$, כלי דעת *vessels of knowledge* 4QBark^{c} 1.1$_{2}$.

מימי הכלי *water of the vessel* CD 10$_{13}$, כֶּסֶף הַכֵּלִים *silver of the vessels* Nm 7$_{85}$, תסובות כלי *rotations of vessels of* light 4QPrQuot 1.3$_{9}$, אחד כלי *one of the tools of* CD 12$_{18}$,

יֶתֶר הַכֵּלִים *remainder of the vessels* Jr 27₁₉, כָּל־הַכְּלִי *all the furniture* Lv 15₄.₂₆, כל הכלי *any (of the) vessel* Lv 13₂₂ (Sam) 4QDf 2₁₁ ([כל]ן), כָּל־כְּלִי *any vessel* Lv 11₃₂.₃₄ 15₂₂ Nm 19₁₅ (כֹּל) 35₂₂ Ezk 15₃ (כֶּלִי) 4QDe 6.4₂₁ 4QTohA 1.1₄ 1.2₄ (both כול) 2.2₁₀ GnzPs 2₂₈, [־כְּלִי־ן] כָּל־ *any vessel of* Lv 11₃₂.₃₃ 13₄₉.₅₂.₅₃.₅₇.₅₈.₅₉ 15₁₂ Nm 31₂₀.₂₀ 1 K 6₇ 12₁₄ Ho 13₁₅ Na 2₁₀ (כֹּל) CD 11₂ (כל כל), 12₁₇, כָּל־כֵּלִים *all vessels* Ezr 1₁₁ 11QT 49₁₅ (כול), כָּל־הַכֵּלִים *all the vessels* Ex 25₃₉ Nm 19₁₈ (כָּל־ lacking in mss, Sam) 1 K 7₄₅.₄₇.₄₈ 2 K 4₄ (or del. ־כָּל) 25₁₆||Jr 52₂₀ 2 C 25₂₄ 29₁₉ 11QT 50₁₆ (כול), [־כְּלֵי־ן] כָּל־ *all vessels of* Gn 31₃₇ (כֹּל) Ex 27₁₉ (כֹּל) 31₇ 38₃.₃₀ 39₄₀ Nm 3₈ 4₉.₁₂.₁₄ (כֹּל) 4₁₅.₂₆.₃₄(ms, Sam) Jos 6₁₉ (כֹּל ...) 1 K 8₄||2 C 5₅ 1 K 10₂₁.₂₁||2 C 9₂₀.₂₀ (both כֹּל) 2 K 24₁₃ 25₁₄||Jr 52₁₈ Is 22₂₄ (כֹּל) 22₂₄ Jr 28₃ Ne 13₈ 1 C 9₂₉ 18₁₀ (כֹּל) 28₁₃.₁₄ 2 C 32₂₇ 36₁₈ (both כֹּל) 36₁₉ 4QSD 6₃ ([כול כל]ן) 4QapMes 8₈ 11QT 49₁₅ 50₁₇ (both כול), כָּל־ כֵּלַי *all my goods* Gn 31₃₇, כָּל־כֵּלָיו *all its vessels* Ex 25₉ 27₃ 30₂₇.₂₈ 31₉ 35₁₃.₁₆ 38₃ 39₃₃.₃₆.₃₉ 40₉.₁₀ Lv 8₁₁ Nm 1₅₀.₅₀ 3₃₆ 4₁₄ 7₁.₁ 1 C 23₂₆ 2 C 29₁₈.₁₈ 11QT 49₁₄ 50₁₂ (both כול), כָּל־כֵּלֶיהָ *all its vessels* Ex 35₁₄(Gnz, Sam) 37₂₄ 39₃₇ Nm 4₁₀, כָּל־כְּלֵיהֶם *all their vessels* Nm 4₃₂ Jr 49₂₉ 2 C 4₁₆.

<APP> מִנְחָה *offering* 1 K 10₂₅, קֹדֶשׁ *holiness*, i.e. consecrated gift 1 K 15₁₅||2 C 15₁₈, appar. אֹהֶל *tent* 1 K 7₄₅ (Kt), כֹּל *everything* 2 C 36₁₈, אוֹצָר *treasury* Ho 13₁₅ (or ins. וְ *and* vessel), כֶּסֶף וְזָהָב *silver and gold* Dn 11₈.

<ADJ> טָהוֹר *pure* Is 66₂₀, רֵיק *empty* 2 K 4₃, חָדָשׁ *new* 4QTohBb 1₃, אֵלֶּה *these* 1 K 7₄₅(Qr) 2 K 25₁₆||Jr 52₂₀ (or del), אַחֵר *other* Jr 18₄ Ezr 1₁₀, אֶחָד *one* Ezk 4₉.

<PREP> לְ *for (the purpose of)* 11QT 33₁₃, + עשׂה *make* treasuries 2 C 32₂₇; of possession, *of, (belonging) to* 11QT 49₁₅, *as*, + חשׁב *reckon* 1QH 4₉; *plan (in respect) of* 1 C 28₁₃.₁₄.₁₄.₁₄; *namely* Nm 4₃₂; עשׂה לְ *do to* 11QT 50₁₆ (|| בֶּגֶד *garment*, עוֹר *skin*).

בְּ of place, *in, on, among, through* Lv 11₃₄ 1QIsaa 65₄ 4QSD 6₃ ([בכול כל]ן) 11QT 49₈, + היה *be* Lv 13₄₉, ראה ni. *appear* Lv 13₅₇, בוא hi. *bring* offering Is 66₂₀, פשׂה *spread* Lv 13₅₃, שׂים *place* Jos 7₁₁ 1 S 17₄₀ Jr 40₁₀, נתן *give*, i.e. place Jr 32₁₄ Ezk 4₉, לקח *take* Gn 43₁₁ Nm 5₁₇ 1 K 17₁₀, נשׂא *carry* 4QTohBb 1₃ ([נ]שא), נפל *fall* 4QTohA 2.2₁₀ ([י]פול [בו]), בשׁל pi. *boil* 4QMMT B₆, pu. *be boiled* Lv 6₂₁, עשׂה ni. *be done* 4QDf 2₁₁ ([כל]ן ... יעשה); of instrument, *by (means of), with*, + שׁרת pi. *minister* Nm 4₉, עלה hi. *bring up* CD 11₁₇ (+ סֻלָּם *ladder*, חֶבֶל *rope*), בשׁל pi. *boil* perh. 1 K 19₂₁, חזק pi. *strengthen*, i.e. encourage Ezr 1₆, נכה hi. *strike* Nm 35₁₆.₁₈; of accompaniment, *with* Nm 4₁₆, + שׁלח *send* 1 C 18₁₀ (if em. וְ *and* to בְּ *with*), ערב htp. *be mixed* 11QT 45₄ ([בכליה]מה]); *from*, + שׁקה hi. *cause to drink* Est 1₇; כְּלִי אֵין חֵפֶץ בּוֹ *a vessel in which there is no delight* Jr 22₂₈ 48₃₈ Ho 8₈ (both ־אֵין); נגע בְּ *touch* Lv 15₂₂ (or del. בְּכָל־כְּלִי) 4QTohA 1.1₄.

כְּ *as*, + היה *be* Ho 8₈ Ps 31₁₃, נפל *fall* Jr 25₃₄ (or em. כִּכְלִי חֶמְדָּה *like a precious vessel* to בִּכְלִי חֶמְלָה *without compassion*); *as (though it were)* Si 50₉, + שׁבר *break* Jr 48₃₈, יצא hi. *take out* Ezk 12₄.₇, נפץ pi. *shatter* Ps 2₉.

מִן of direction, *from* Is 65₄ (if ins. מִן), + ריק ho. *be emptied* Jr 48₁₁, אזל *go* 1 S 9₇; partitive, *(some) of* Est 1₇, + בוא hi. *bring* 2 C 36 4QDf 2₁₁ ([יב]א] ... כל]ן); of comparison, *(better) than* GnzPs 2₂₈; *(consisting) of*, כָּבֹד מִכֹּל כְּלִי־חֶמְדָּה *the wealth (consisting) of every precious vessel* (or em. כָּבֵד *heavy* on account of).

מִקְצָת *some of*, + נתן *give* Dn 1₂.

אֶל *to*, + הלך *go* Ru 2₉, קרב *approach* Nm 18₃; *into*, + ריק ho. *be emptied out* Jr 48₁₁, נתן *give*, i.e. place Nm 19₁₇ Dt 23₂₅, שׁלח *send*, i.e. extend, hand 1 S 17₄₉, שׁאב *draw (water)* CD 11₂; *among*, + חבא ni. *be hidden* 1 S 10₂₂; *over* or *in*, + שׁחט *slaughter* Lv 14₅.₅₀.

עַל *(up)on*, + ישׁב *sit* Lv 15₆.₂₂ (or del.) 15₂₃ 1 S 25₁₃ 30₂₄ (but perh. in both ישׁב עַל = *stay with*), נזה hi. *sprinkle* Nm 19₁₈; *into*, + יצק *pour* 2 K 4₄ (or em. אֶל *into*); *in charge of, over* 1 C 9₂₈, + מנה pu. *be appointed* 1 C 9₂₉.₂₉, פקד hi. *appoint* Nm 1₅₀; *about, concerning*, + אמר *say* Jr 27₂₁, חוס *pity*, i.e. concern oneself Gn 45₂₀.

אֵת *with*, + עשׂה *make* Ex 25₃₉ (||37₂₄ אֵת object-marker); עִם *with*, + בוא hi. *bring* Dn 11₈ (Gnz qal *come*) 2 C 36₁₀.

<COLL> כאלין של דמע *vessels of*, i.e. for, *tithe* 3QTr 5₆, כלי כסף וזהב של דמע *vessels of silver and gold of*, i.e. for, *tithe* 3QTr 3₂, כלי כסף וכלי זהב של דמע *vessels of silver and vessels of gold of*, i.e. for, *tithe* 3QTr 12₆.

מְלֵאָה בְגָדִים וְכֵלִים *full of clothes and vessels* 2 K 7₁₅ (unless כְּלִי = *weapon*), כָּל־הַכֵּלִים לַזָּהָב וְלַכֶּסֶף *all the vessels of gold and of silver* Ezr 1₁₁, כְּלֵי נְחֹשֶׁת ... שְׁנַיִם *two vessels of bronze* Ezr 8₂₇ (or em. שֹׁנִים *different*), כלין

כופרין עסרין perh. *twenty pitched vessels* 3QTr 10_{11}, כְּלֵי־ כֶּסֶף מֵאָה *one hundred silver vessels* Ezr 8_{26}.

2. weapon,* Gn 27_{3} 49_{5} Dt 1_{41} Jg 9_{54} $18_{11.16.17}$ 1 S 8_{12} 14_{1+8t} 16_{21} 17_{54} 20_{40} 21_{9} (|| חֶרֶב *sword*) $31_{4.4.5}$||1 C $10_{4.4.5}$ 1 S $31_{6.9.10}$||1 C 10_{10} 2 S 1_{27} 18_{15} 23_{37}||1 C 11_{39} 2 K 11_{8} ||2 C 23_{7} 2 K 11_{11} 20_{13}||Is 39_{2} Is 13_{5} 54_{17} Jr 21_{4} 22_{7} (perh. כְּלִי = *tool*, as §1) 50_{25} 51_{20} Ezk $9_{1.2}$ 32_{27} Ps 7_{14} (+ חֶרֶב, חֵץ *arrow*, קֶשֶׁת *bow*) Ec 9_{18} 1 C 10_{9} $12_{34.38}$ Si 12_{5} 1QH 2_{26} $6_{28.31}$ 1QM 7_{2} $8_{8.12}$ 16_{6} 17_{1} 1QpHab 6_{4} 4QapJoshua[b] 22.2_{11} 4QPseud[b] 8_{4}.

<SUBJ> היה *be* 4QapJoshua[b] 22.2_{11}=4QTestim$_{25}$ (ל[ה]יות), אבד *be destroyed* 2 S 1_{27}, יצר ho. *be formed* Is 54_{17}, בוא *come* Is 13_{5}, חבל pi. *destroy* Is 13_{5}, כרת *cut* Jr 22_{7}, נפל hi. *cause to fall* Jr 22_{7}.

<NOM CL> מַפֵּץ־אַתָּה לִי כְּלֵי מִלְחָמָה *you are my mace, weapons of war* Jr 51_{20} (or em. כְּלִי *weapon of*), כלי מלחמותם המה מוראם *their weapons of war are their objects of reverence* 1QpHab 6_{4}, כֵּלָיו בְּיָדוֹ *his weapons were in his hand* 2 K 11_{8}||2 C 23_{7} 2 K 11_{11}, כְּלִי מַשְׁחֵתוֹ בְּיָדוֹ *his weapon of destruction was in his hand* Ezk 9_{1}, כְּלִי מַפָּצוֹ בְּיָדוֹ *his weapon of destruction was in his hand* Ezk 9_{2} (or del.), כְּלֵי חָמָס מְכֵרֹתֵיהֶם perh. *weapons of violence are their counsels* Gn 49_{5} (unless כְּלֵי = *plans of*, as §6; or em. מַכְרֵתֵיהֶם *their knives* or מִכְמְרֹתֵיהֶם *their nets*; Sam כִּלּוּ perh. *they have completed* the violence of their plans).

<OBJ> יצא hi. *take out* Jr 50_{25} 1QH 6_{31}, סבב hi. *remove* Jr 21_{4}, כון hi. *prepare* Ps 7_{14}, עשׂה *make* 1 S 8_{12}, שׂים *place* 1 S 17_{54} 31_{10}||1 C 10_{10}, לקח *take* 1 S 21_{9}, נתן *give* 1 S 20_{40} Si 12_{5}, נשׂא *raise*, i.e. take Gn 27_{3} 1 C 10_{9}, *carry* for someone (i.e. נֹשֵׂא כֵלִים *armour bearer*) Jg 9_{54} 1 S 14_{1+8t} 16_{21} $31_{4.4.5}$||1 C $10_{4.4.5}$ 1 S 31_{6} 2 S 18_{15} 23_{37}||1 C 11_{39}, שׁמר *keep* 1QM 7_{2} (שומרי הכלים *keepers of the arms*), חגר *gird (on)* Dt 1_{41}, פשׁט hi. *strip (off)* 1 S 31_{9}, קדשׁ pi. *dedicate* Jr 22_{7}, שׁנן *sharpen* 1QM 17_{1}.

<CSTR> כְּלִי מַפָּצוֹ *his weapon of destruction* Ezk 9_{2}, כְּלִי מַשְׁחֵתוֹ *his weapon of destruction* Ezk 9_{1}, כלי לחם *weapons of war* Si 12_{5}, כְּלֵי מִלְחָמָה *weapons of war* Jg $18_{11.17}$ (הַמִּלְחָמָה) 2 S 1_{27} Jr 21_{4} (הַמִּלְחָמָה) 51_{20} (or em. כְּלִי *weapon of*) 1 C $12_{34.38}$ (if em. כְּלֵי צְבָא מִלְחָמָה *weapons of the army of war*) 1QM 8_{8} (המלמחה) 4QpIsa[c] 25_{3}, כְּלֵי מִלְחַמְתּוֹ *his weapons of war* Dt 1_{41} 1 S 8_{12} (כְּלֵי־) 1QH 6_{28} 1QM 16_{6} perh. 17_{1} (מלחמתה) 17_{12}, כְּלֵי מִלְחַמְתָּם *their weapons of war* Jg 18_{16} Ezk 32_{27} (כְּלֵי־) 4QPseud[b] 8_{4}, כלי מלחמות *weapons of war* 1QH 6_{31}, כלי מלחמותם *their weapons of war* 1QH 2_{26} 1QpHab 6_{4}, כְּלֵי קְרָב *weapons of war* Ec 9_{18}, כְּלֵי יוֹאָב *weapons of Joab* 2 S 18_{15} 23_{37} 1 C 11_{39}, חָמָס *of violence* Gn 49_{5} (Sam כִּלּוּ *they completed* violence) 4QTestim$_{25}$ 4QapJoshua[b] 22.2_{11}=4QTestim$_{25}$, זַעְמוֹ *of his indignation* Is 13_{5} Jr 50_{25}, מָוֶת *of death* Ps 7_{14} (כְּלֵי־).

שומרי הכלים *keepers of the arms* 1QM 7_{2}, בֵּית כֵּלָיו *house of his weapons*, i.e. his armoury 2 K 20_{13}||Is 39_{2}; כָּל־כְּלִי *every weapon* Is 54_{17}, כָּל־כְּלֵי *all weapons of* 1 C $12_{34.38}$ (כֹּל כְּלֵי) 1QH 2_{26}.

<APP> מַשְׁחִית *destroyer* Jr 22_{7}, מַעֲשֶׂה *deed* Si $43_{2(M)}$, מַפֵּץ *mace* Jr 51_{20}. <PREP> בְּ of instrument, *by (means of), with*, + קבל hi. *be arrayed* against Si 12_{5}; of accompaniment, *with* perh. 4QPseud[b] 8_{4}, + בוא *come* 1QH 6_{28}, ירד *go down* Ezk 32_{27}, רום hi. *raise* hand 1QM 16_{6} 17_{12}, סבב *surround* 1QH 2_{26}; נטה בְּ *stretch* hand *to*, i.e. seize 1QM 8_{8}. <COLL> אִישׁ וְכֵלָיו *each with their weapons* Jr 22_{7}, אִישׁ חָגוּר כְּלֵי מִלְחָמָה *men girded with weapons of war* Jg 18_{11}, sim. Jg $18_{16.17}$.

3. (musical) instrument,* in cultic context except Am 6_{5} (or em.), Ps 71_{22} Ne 12_{36} 1 C 15_{16} $16_{5.42}$ 23_{5} 2 C 5_{13} 7_{6} 23_{13} $29_{26.27}$ 30_{21} 34_{12} Si 39_{15}.

<OBJ> עשׂה *make* 1 C 23_{5}, חשׁב appar. *invent* or *reckon* Am 6_{5} (or em. כְּלֵי־שִׁיר *instruments of song* to כָּל־שִׁיר *every song* or כְּשִׁיר *as a song*).

<CSTR> כְּלִי־נֶבֶל *instrument (consisting) of a harp* Ps 71_{22}, כְּלֵי נְבָלִים *instruments (consisting) of harps* 1 C 16_{5}, כְּלֵי־שִׁיר *instruments of song* Am 6_{5} (or em.) Ne 12_{36} 1 C 15_{16} 16_{42} (כְּלֵי שִׁיר) 2 C 5_{13} (כְּלֵי הַשִּׁיר) 7_{6} 23_{13} (כְּלֵי הַשִּׁיר) 34_{12}, כְּלֵי דָוִיד *instruments of David* 2 C $29_{26.27}$ (דָּוִיד), כְּלֵי־עֹז *instruments of might* 2 C 30_{21} (or em. כָּל־ *all* might), כלי מינים *instruments of strings* Si 39_{15}. <PREP> בְּ of instrument, *by (means of), with*, + רום hi. *raise* sound 2 C 5_{13}, ידה hi. *praise* Ps 71_{22}, הלל pi. *praise* 1 C 23_{5} 2 C 30_{21}, שׁיר pol. *continually sing* 1 C 15_{16}; of accompaniment, *with* Ne 12_{36} 1 C 16_{5} 2 C 23_{13}, + עמד *stand* 2 C 7_{6} 29_{26}; בין בְּ hi. *be expert in* 2 C 34_{12}; עַל־יְדֵי appar. *alongside, accompanied by*, + חלל hi. *begin* 2 C 29_{27}.

4. clothing, jewel(lery),* ornament, Gn $24_{53.53}$ Ex $3_{22.22}$ $11_{2.2}$ $12_{35.35}$ 35_{22} Nm $31_{50.51}$ Dt 22_{5} (|| שִׂמְלָה *garment*)

1 S 6$_{8.15}$ Is 61$_{10}$ (‖ פְּאֵר *turban*) Ezk 16$_{17.39}$ 23$_{26}$ Jb 28$_{17}$ Pr 20$_{15}$.

<SUBJ> היה *be* Dt 22$_{5}$ 4QOrd[a] 2$_{6}$. <NOM CL> כְּלִי יְקָר שִׂפְתֵי־דָעַת *lips of knowledge are (as) a jewel of preciousness* Pr 20$_{15}$, אֲשֶׁר־בּוֹ כְּלֵי־זָהָב *in which were (the) ornaments of gold* 1 S 6$_{15}$, לֹא ... תְּמוּרָתָהּ כְּלִי־פָז *its exchange is not*, i.e. wisdom cannot be exchanged for, *jewellery of gold* Jb 28$_{17}$. <OBJ> בוא hi. *bring* Ex 35$_{22}$, יצא hi. *take out* Gn 24$_{53.53}$, שׂים *place* Ex 3$_{22.22}$ 1 S 6$_{8}$, לקח *take* Ezk 16$_{17.39}$ 23$_{26}$, קרב hi. *bring forward* in offering Nm 31$_{50}$, עדה *adorn oneself (with)* Is 61$_{10}$, שׁאל *ask (for)* Ex 3$_{22.22}$ 11$_{2.2}$ 12$_{35.35}$.

<CSTR> כְּלִי־גֶבֶר *clothing of a man* Dt 22$_{5}$ 4QOrd[a] 2$_{6}$, כְּלִי־זָהָב *ornament of gold* Nm 31$_{50}$, כְּלֵי זָהָב *ornaments of gold* Gn 24$_{53}$ Ex 3$_{22}$ 11$_{2}$ 12$_{35}$ 35$_{22}$ Nm 31$_{50(Seb)}$ (כְּלֵי־) 1 S 6$_{8}$ (כְּלֵי הַזָּהָב; mss כֹּל *all* the gold, טְחוֹרֵי *haemorrhoids of* gold) 6$_{15}$ (כְּלֵי־), כְּלֵי־כֶסֶף *ornaments of silver* Gn 24$_{53}$ Ex 3$_{22}$ 11$_{2}$ 12$_{35}$, כְּלִי מַעֲשֶׂה *ornament of making*, i.e. ornament wrought in metal Nm 31$_{51}$, כְּלִי יְקָר *jewel of preciousness* Pr 20$_{15}$, כְּלֵי תִפְאַרְתֵּךְ *your jewellery of beauty* Ezk 16$_{17.39}$ 23$_{26}$, כְּלִי־פָז *jewellery of gold* Jb 28$_{17}$; כָּל־כְּלִי *every ornament of* Ex 35$_{22}$ Nm 31$_{51}$ (כֹּל), כָּל־כְּלֵי *all ornaments of* Ex 35$_{22(mss)}$. <APP> קָרְבָּן *offering* Nm 31$_{50}$, אֶצְעָדָה *bracelet* 31$_{50}$, צָמִיד *bracelet* 31$_{50}$, טַבַּעַת *ring* Ex 35$_{22}$ (lacking in Sam, mss; mss וְ *and* every vessel) Nm 31$_{50}$, עָגִיל *anklet* Ex 35$_{22(Sam, mss)}$ 31$_{50}$, כּוּמָז *bead* Ex 35$_{22}$ Nm 31$_{50}$, חָח *brooch* Ex 35$_{22}$, נֶזֶם *earring* Ex 35$_{22}$.

5. boat, ship, <SUBJ> קוה ni. *be gathered* Is 60$_{9}$ (if em. כִּי־לִי אִיִּים יְקַוּוּ *because for me the islands wait*, to כְּלֵי אִיִּים יִקָּווּ *the ships of the islands are gathered*; + אֳנִיָּה *ship*). <CSTR> כְּלֵי־גֹמֶא *boats of papyrus* Is 18$_{2}$, כְּלֵי אִיִּים *the ships of the islands* Is 60$_{9}$ (if em.). <PREP> בְּ *in*, + שׁלח *send* ambassadors Is 18$_{2}$.

6. idea, tactic, plan, <NOM CL> כֵּלַי כֵּלָיו רָעִים *as for a villain, his plans are evil* Is 32$_{7}$ (+ זִמָּה *plan*),* perh. כְּלֵי חָמָס מְכֵרֹתֵיהֶם *tactics of violence are their counsels* Gn 49$_{5}$ (but see §2).

7. perh. **device, mechanism,** as description of sun and moon, Si 43$_{2(M).8}$, but sense in both perh. *weapon*, as §2; at 42$_{8}$, perh. **(military) signal,** <SUBJ> ירא ni. *be feared* Si 43$_{2(M)}$, רצף pi. *pave* Si 43$_{8(B)}$. <NOM CL> ... שמש כלי נורא *the sun ... is an awe-inspiring mechanism* Si 43$_{2(M)}$ (B מה נורא *how fearful*). <CSTR> כלי צבא נבלי שמים *a mechanism of*, i.e. for, *the host of clouds in the sky* Si 43$_{8}$.

8. perh. **body,** וַיִּהְיוּ כְלֵי־הַנְּעָרִים קֹדֶשׁ וְהוּא דֶּרֶךְ חֹל וְאַף כִּי הַיּוֹם יִקְדַּשׁ בַּכֶּלִי *and if the bodies of the young men are kept undefiled even on an ordinary journey, how much more today will they be undefiled in respect of their body* 1 S 21$_{6}$ (unless כְּלִי = *weapon* or *vessel*), תבוז לחייכה וגם תקל כלי חוקכה do not *despise your life nor belittle the body of your statute*, i.e. the body that belongs to you by law, i.e. your wife 4Q416 2.2$_{21}$* (or em. חיקכה *of your bosom*).

Also 4QMMT B$_{19}$ (כלי[ם]) perh. 4QDibHam[a] 15.2$_{2}$. <SYN> §1 נֵבֶל *jar*, בֶּגֶד *garment*, עוֹר *skin*; §2 חֶרֶב *sword*; §4 שִׂמְלָה *garment*, פְּאֵר *turban*. <ANT> §1 כֶּסֶף *silver*, i.e. money.

כֵּלַי 1 n.m. **villain,** <SUBJ> יעץ *plan* Is 32$_{7}$. <COLL> כֵּלַי כֵּלָיו רָעִים *as for the villain his devices are evil* Is 32$_{7}$.

⇒ כִּילַי *villain*.

כְּלִיא 1 n.m. **confinement,** <CSTR> בֵּית הַכְּלִיא *the house of confinement*, i.e. prison Jr 37$_{4(Kt)}$ 52$_{31(Kt)}$.*

⇒ כלא *restrain*.

[כִּלְיָה] 31.0.10 n.f. **kidney**—pl. כְּלָיוֹת (כְּלָית); cstr. כִּלְיוֹת; sf. כִּלְיוֹתַי, Q כליתו, כליותיה, כִּלְיוֹתֵיהֶם—alw. pl., **a.** as part of animal sacrificed to Y. (Ex 29$_{13.22}$‖Lv 8$_{16.25}$ Lv 3$_{4.4.10.10.15.15}$ 4$_{9.9}$ 7$_{4.4}$ 9$_{10.19}$ 4QJub[d/e] 21$_{8.8}$ 11QT 15$_{7}$ 16$_{8}$ 20$_{6}$ 23$_{15}$). **b.** as part of animal killed or sacrificed by Y. (Dt 32$_{14}$ [if em.] Is 34$_{6}$). **c.** as part of human body liable to suffer injury or to fail (Jb 16$_{13}$ 19$_{27}$ Lm 3$_{13}$). **d.** as seat of human conscience, joy, grief. etc. (Jr 11$_{20}$ [‖ לֵב *heart*] 12$_{2}$ [:: פֶּה *mouth*] 17$_{10}$ 20$_{12}$ Ps 7$_{10}$ [all three ‖ לֵב] 16$_{7}$ 26$_{2}$ [‖ לֵב] 73$_{21}$ [‖ לֵבָב *heart*] Pr 23$_{16}$ [‖ לֵב] 4QWiles 1$_{2}$ [+ לֵב] 4Q185 1.3$_{12[AHL]}$ [כליתו; Allegro כלותו *his destruction*; + חדרי בטן *innermost parts of the body*] 4QBark[c] 1.1$_{5.6}$, perh. Ps 139$_{13}$). **e.** consisting of highest quality fat, in ref. to choicest part of wheat (Dt 32$_{14}$ [or em.]).

<SUBJ> כלה *be ended*, i.e. fail Jb 19$_{27}$, עלז *exult* Pr 23$_{16}$, יסר pi. *discipline* Ps 16$_{7}$ (mss appar. יִסְּרַנִי כִלְיוֹתָי *he disciplines me (in) my kidneys*).

<OBJ> לקח *take* Ex 29$_{13.22.22}$‖Lv 8$_{16.25.25}$, שׂים *place* Ex

29$_{22}$, קרב hi. *bring near* in sacrifice Lv 3$_{4.10.15}$ 7$_{4}$ 11QT 15$_{7}$ 16$_{8}$ ([[והקריב ... הכל]יות), מצא hi. *bring* Lv 9$_{19}$, קטר hi. *burn* Ex 29$_{13.22}$||Lv 8$_{16.25}$ Lv 3$_{4.10.15}$ 4$_{9}$ 9$_{10}$ 4QJub^{d} 21$_{8}$ ([[תק]טיר] ... הכליות]) 4QJub^{e} 21$_{8}$, נוף hi. *offer as wave offering* Ex 29$_{22}$||Lv 8$_{25}$, רום hi. *raise*, i.e. remove Lv 4$_{9}$.

ראה *see* Jr 20$_{12}$, בחן *test* Jr 11$_{20}$ 17$_{10}$ Ps 7$_{10}$, צרף *test* Ps 26$_{2}$, שׁנן *sharpen* 4QBark^{c} 1.1$_{5}$, חפשׂ pi. *seek* 4Q185 1.3$_{12(AHL)}$, קנה *create* Ps 139$_{13}$, נתן *give*, i.e. place Lv 8$_{25}$, פלח pi. *split open* Jb 16$_{13}$, פתח *open* 4QBark^{c} 1.1$_{6}$.

<CSTR> חֵלֶב כִּלְיוֹת אֵילִים *fat of the kidneys of rams* Is 34$_{6}$, חֵלֶב כִּלְיוֹת כָּרִים *fat of the kidneys of lambs* Dt 32$_{14}$ (if em. חֵלֶב כִּלְיוֹת חִטָּה *fat of kidneys of wheat*, i.e. the choicest of wheat), שְׁתֵּי הַכְּלָיֹת *the two kidneys* Ex *29$_{13.22}$||Lv 8$_{16.25}$ Lv 3$_{4.10.15}$ 4$_{9}$ 7$_{4}$ 11QT 15$_{7}$ 16$_{8}$ ([[שתי הכל]יות).

<APP> אִשֶּׁה *fire offering* Lv 3$_{4.4.10.10.15.15}$, לֶחֶם *food* Lv 3$_{10.15}$, חֵלֶב *fat* Lv 4$_{9}$.

<PREP> בְּ *in(to)*, + בוא hi. *bring* arrows Lm 3$_{13}$; מִן of direction, *from* Jr 12$_{2}$; עַל *(up)on, attached to*, וְאֵת שְׁתֵּי הַכְּלָיֹת וְאֶת־הַחֵלֶב אֲשֶׁר עֲלֵיהֶן *and the two kidneys and the fat that is on them* Ex 29$_{13.22}$ Lv 3$_{4.10.15}$ (all three עֲלֵהֶן) 4$_{9}$ (Gnz lacks עֲלֵיהֶן) 7$_{4}$ 9$_{19}$ (if em. וְהַכְּלָיֹת *and the kidneys*) 11QT 15$_{7}$ (... [ואת] [שתי הכל]יות ... עליה[נה]) 16$_{8}$ ([ה]חלב ... עלי[הנה]), [ואת הכליות [ו]את ה]חלב אשר עליהן] *and the kidneys and the fat that is on them*4QJub^{e} 21$_{8}$, [ואת הכליות ו]כול החלב אשר עליהן *and the kidneys and all the fat that is on them* 4QJub^{d} 21$_{8}$; *as well as, with*, + סור hi. *remove* Lv 3$_{4.10.15}$ 4$_{9}$ 7$_{4}$ 11QT 20$_{6}$ ([על]); עִם *with*, + סור hi. *remove* caudal lobe 4QJub^{d} 21$_{8}$ 4Q Jub^{e} 21$_{8}$ ([תסיר[נה]) 11QT 23$_{15}$.

<COLL> וְאֶת־הַיֹּתֶרֶת עַל־הַכָּבֵד עַל־הַכְּלָיֹת *and* you are to remove *the lobe of the liver as well as the kidneys* Lv 3$_{4.10.15}$ 4$_{9}$ 7$_{4}$, sim. 4QJub^{d} 21$_{8}$ ([ואת היותרת על ה]כבד) 4QJub^{e} 21$_{8}$ (ואת היותרת הכבד עם הכליות) (עם הכליות) 11QT 20$_{6}$ (ואת [יותרת הכבד על]הכליות) 23$_{15}$ (ואת יותרת הכבד עם הכליות), וְאֶת־שְׁתֵּי הַכְּלָיֹת וְאֶת־חֶלְבְּהֶן *and the two kidneys and their fat* Lv 8$_{16.25}$ (Sam חֶלְבֵּיהֶן *their fat[s]* in both).

וְכִלְיוֹתַי אֶשְׁתּוֹנָן *and I was pricked (in) my kidneys* Ps 73$_{21}$, יִסְּרוּנִי כִלְיוֹתָי *he disciplines me (in) my kidneys* Ps 16$_{7(mss)}$.

Also 4QWiles 1$_{2}$.

<SYN> לֵב *heart*, לֵבָב *heart*. <ANT> פֶּה *mouth*.*

כִּלָּיוֹן 2.0.1 n.m. **destruction**—cstr. כִּלְיוֹן—**destruction, annihilation, failure** of eyes (Dt 28$_{65}$), <SUBJ> חרץ pass. *be determined* Is 10$_{22}$. <OBJ> נתן *give* Dt 28$_{65}$. <CSTR> כִּלְיוֹן עֵינַיִם *failure of eyes* Dt 28$_{65}$. <PREP> בְּ perh. of accompaniment, *with, in* 4QPrFêtes^{c} 242$_{1}$.

⇒ כלה *be complete*.

כִּלְיוֹן 3 pr.n.m. **Chilion,** Judahite, son of Elimelech, husband of Ruth (Ru 1$_{2.5}$ 4$_{9}$), <SUBJ> מות *die* Ru 1$_{5}$. <NOM CL> וְשֵׁם שְׁנֵי־בָנָיו מַחְלוֹן וְכִלְיוֹן *and the names of his two sons were Mahlon and Chilion* Ru 1$_{2}$. <PREP> לְ of possession, *(belonging) to, of* Ru 4$_{9}$.*

כָּלִיל I 15.3.4 adj. **whole**—cstr. כְּלִיל, f.s. cstr. כְּלִילַת—**1.** attributive adj., + עוֹלָה *burnt offering* 1 S 7$_{9}$.

2. predicative adj. or noun, **whole (one), complete (one), whole offering** (Lv 6$_{16.16}$ Dt 33$_{10}$ 1 S 7$_{9}$ Ps 51$_{21}$ 4QShirShabb^{f} 23.1$_{5}$, perh. Dt 13$_{17}$=11QT 55$_{9}$), **perfection** (Si 45$_{8}$, unless כָּלִיל II *crown*).*

<SUBJ> היה *be* Lv 6$_{16}$. <NOM CL> אֲנִי כְּלִילַת יֹפִי *I am a perfect one of beauty*, i.e. perfect in beauty, ... אַתָּה כְּלִיל יֹפִי *you are ... a perfect one of beauty*, i.e. perfect in beauty Ezk 28$_{12}$, כָּלִיל הוּא *it is complete* Ezk 16$_{14}$. <OBJ> שׂים *place* Dt 33$_{10}$, קטר *burn* Lv 6$_{15}$, אמר *say* Lm 2$_{15}$.

<CSTR> כְּלִיל יֹפִי *perfect one of beauty*, i.e. perfect in beauty Ezk 28$_{12}$, כְּלִילַת יֹפִי *perfect one of beauty*, i.e. perfect in beauty Ezk 27$_{3}$ Lm 2$_{15}$ (unless from כְּלִילָה *crown*), כליל תפארת *perfect one of beauty*, i.e. perfect in beauty Si 45$_{8(B)}$ (Bmg תפארתו *of his beauty*; unless כָּלִיל II *crown*), כְּלִיל תְּכֵלֶת *complete one of purple wool*, i.e. completely of purple wool Ex 28$_{31}$ 39$_{22}$ Nm 4$_{6}$, כְּלִיל הָעִיר *totality of the city* Jg 20$_{40}$; אלוהי כלילו *gods (in charge) of his whole offering* 4QShirShabb^{f} 23.1$_{5}$.

<COLL> וְשָׂרַפְתָּ ... כָּלִיל לַי׳ *and you shall burn ... as a whole offering to Y.* Dt 13$_{17}$=11QT 55$_{9}$, תַּחְפֹּץ ... עוֹלָה וְכָלִיל *you will have pleasure in ... burnt offerings and whole offerings* Ps 51$_{21}$, וילבישהו כליל תפארת *and he clothed him in perfection of beauty* Si 45$_{8}$ (unless כָּלִיל II *crown*).

3. adverbially, **completely, utterly,** with חלף *pass* *away* Is 2_{18} GnzPs 2_{21}, מֹשֵׁל *rule* Si $37_{18(B)}$, שׁלח pi. *send* Si $37_{18(Bmg, D)}$, קטר pi. *burn* Si 45_{14}.

Also 4QShirShabb^f 23.1$_6$.

→ כלל *be perfect*.

*[כָּלִיל] II $_{0.1.2}$ n.[m.] **crown**—cstr. Si, Q כליל—<NOM CL> פקודת כול הולכי בה ... כליל כבוד *the visitation of all those who walk in it will be ... a crown of glory* 1QS 4_7. <OBJ> לבשׁ hi. *clothe with* Si 45_8 (unless כָּלִיל I *perfection*). <CSTR> כליל כבוד *crown of glory* 1QH 9_{25} 1QS 4_7, כליל תפארת *crown of beauty* Si $45_{8(B)}$ (Bmg תפארתו *of his beauty*; unless כָּלִיל I *perfection*). <PREP> לְ *as*, or introducing predicate 1QH 9_{25}.

Also 1QSb 4_2 ([כלי]ל).

*[כְּלִילָה] $_1$ n.f. **crown**—cstr. כְּלִילַת—<CSTR> כְּלִילַת יֹפִי *crown of beauty* Lm 2_{15} (unless from כָּלִיל I *perfect one*).

כַּלְכֹּל $_{2.0.0.1}$ pr.n.m. **Calcol, 1.** son of Mahol, famous for wisdom, <APP> Ethan 1 K 5_{11}. <PREP> מִן of comparison, *(more) than*, + חכם *be wise* 1 K 5_{11}.

2. son of Zerah and grandson of Judah, <APP> בֵּן *son* 1 C 2_6.

3. Seal 868 (8th cent.), <PREP> לְ of possession, *(belonging) to, of* Seal 868 (8th cent.).

[כַּלְכֹּלְיָהוּ] $_{0.0.0.1}$ pr.n.m. **Calcoliah,** Seal 329 (7th–6th cent.), <PREP> לְ of possession, *(belonging) to, of* Seal 329 (7th–6th cent.).

כלל $_2$ vb. **perfect—Qal** $_2$ Pf. כָּלְלוּ—<SUBJ> בֵּן *son* of Arvad Ezk 27_{11}, בֹּנֶה *builder* Ezk 27_4. <OBJ> יֳפִי *beauty* Ezk $27_{4.11}$.

→ כֹּל *all*, כָּלִיל I *whole*, כְּלָל *total*, מִכְלוֹל *perfection*, מִכְלָל *perfection*, מַכְלֻלִים *choice garments*.

[כְּלָל] I $_{0.0.1}$ n.[m.] **total**—cstr. Q כלל—<CSTR> כלל חלליהם *total of their slain ones* 4QpNah 3.2$_6$. <PREP> לְ of possession, *of, (belonging) to* 4QpNah 3.2$_6$.*

כְּלָל II $_1$ pr.n.m. **Chelal,** of Pahath-moab family, husband of a non-Jewish wife, <APP> בֵּן *son* Ezr 10_{30}.

כלם I $_{38.5.1}$ vb. **humiliate—Ni.** $_{26.3.1}$ Pf. נִכְלַמְתְּ, נִכְלַמְתְּ, נִכְלַמְתִּי, נִכְלַמוּ, נִכְלָמְנוּ impf. 3fs תִּכָּלֵם, תִּכָּלְמִי, יִכָּלְמוּ, תִּכָּלְמוּ; impv. הִכָּלְמוּ; ptc. נִכְלָם, נִכְלָמִים, נִכְלָמוֹת; inf. הִכָּלֵם—**be humiliated, be ashamed, be put to shame, be confounded,** <SUBJ> Israel Is 45_{17} 54_4 Jr 22_{22}, Israelite(s) Jr 3_3, בַּיִת *house* of Israel Ezk 36_{32} $43_{10.11}$, עַם *people* 2 S 19_4, Ephraim Jr 31_{19}, Jerusalem Ezk $16_{54.61}$, Ezra Ezr 9_6, Miriam Nm 12_{14}, אִישׁ *man* 2 S 10_5||1 C 19_5, בַּת *daughter* Ezk 16_{27}, סור ptc. *one who departs* from Y. Jr $17_{13(Qr)}$ (if em. כתב ni. *be inscribed*).

כֹּהֵן *priest* 2 C 30_{15}, לֵוִי *Levite* 2 C 30_{15}, עֶבֶד *servant* of Y. Is 50_7, חָכָם *wise one* Jr 8_{12}, דַּךְ *oppressed one* Ps 74_{21}, יֹשֵׁב *inhabitant* Jr 6_{15} (if em.), בקשׁ pi. ptc. *one who seeks* Ps 35_4 69_7, חפץ ptc. *one who delights* Ps 40_{15}=70_3, פָּנִים *face* GnzPs 1_{27}, כֹּל *everyone* Is 41_{11} 45_{16} Si 41_{16}; subj. not specified, Si 20_{23} 41_{16}.

<PREP> לְ of direction, *to*, + עוֹלָם *eternity* GnzPs 1_{27}; בְּ of instrument, *by (means of), with*, + worshipper Ps 69_7; מִן of cause, *because of*, + רָעָה *wicked act* Jr 22_{22}, עָוֹן *iniquity* Ezk 43_{10}, כֹּל אֲשֶׁר *all that* Ezk 16_{54} 43_{11}; עַל *according to*, + מִשְׁפָּט *judgment* Si 41_{16}.

<COLL> כלם || בושׁ Is 41_{11} $45_{16.17}$ 54_4 Jr 8_{12} 22_{22} 31_{19} Ezk 36_{32} Ps 35_4 40_{15}=70_3 69_7 Ezr 9_6, בושׁ || כלם Is 50_7, תִּכָּלֵם שִׁבְעַת יָמִים *she shall be put to shame for seven days* Nm 12_{14}. <SYN> בושׁ *be ashamed*.

Hi. $_{10.2}$ Pf. הִכְלַמְנוּם, הִכְלִימוּ, הִכְלִמוּ; impf. יַכְלִים, Si תכלים, תַּכְלִימוּנִי (תַּכְלִימוּהָ); + waw וַתַּכְלִימֵנוּ; ptc. מַכְלִים; inf. הַכְלִים—**humiliate, shame, abuse,** <SUBJ> אֱלֹהִים *God* Ps 44_{10}, David 1 S 25_7, אָב *father* 1 S 20_{34}, בֵּן *son* Si 3_{13} 8_5, נַעַר *youth* 1 S 25_7 Ru 2_{15}, יֹשֵׁב *inhabitant* Jr 6_{15} (or em. ni. *be ashamed*), רֹעֶה *companion* Pr 28_7, רֵעַ *neighbour* Pr 25_8, Job's comforters Jb 19_3; subj. not specified, Jg 18_7 (or em. וְאֵין־מַכְלִים דָּבָר *and there was no one causing any humiliation* to וְאֵין־מַכֹּל דָּבָר *and there was nothing* in the land, or וְאֵין־מַחְסוֹר כָּל־דָּבָר *and there was no lack of anything* or וְאֵין מַכְלֵא מִדָּבָר *and there is no one restraining (us) from anything* or וְאֵין מֶלֶךְ מַדְבֵּר *and there was not a subjugating king*, unless כלם II hi. *speak*, דבר pi. *speak*; or מַחְסוֹר *lack*) Jb 11_3.

<OBJ> עַם *people* Ps 44_{10}, David 1 S 20_{34}, Job Jb 19_3,

Ruth Ru 2_{15}, אִישׁ *man* Si 8_5, אָב *father* Pr 28_7 Si 3_{13}, רֹעֶה *shepherd* 1 S 25_7, worshipper Pr 25_8. <COLL> אל תכלים אותו כל ימי חייו *you shall not put him to shame all the days of his life* Si 3_{13}.

Ho. 2 Pf. הָכְלָמְנוּ—**be ashamed, suffer harm,** <SUBJ> נַעַר *youth* 1 S 25_{15}, צָעִיר *young servant* Jr 14_3 (|| בושׁ *be ashamed*). <SYN> בושׁ *be ashamed*.*

⇒ כְּלִמָּה *insult*, כְּלִמּוּת *disgrace*.

***כלם** II 1 vb. **speak—Hi.** 1 Ptc. מַכְלִים—**speak,** perh. specif. **speak with authority, govern** וְאֵין־מַכְלִים דָּבָר *and no one spoke a word (with authority)* Jg 18_7 (unless כלם I hi. *humiliate*).

⇒ כְּלִמָּה II *speech*.

[כָּלֵם] 0.0.0.1 pr.n.m. **Chalem,** appar. place in Samaria Seal 185 (Samaria).

כִּלְמַד 1 pl.n. **Chilmad,** appar. trading centre in Assyria Ezk 27_{23}, <SUBJ> רכל *trade* Ezk 27_{23} (+ Haran, Canneh, Esen, Asshur; or em. כָּל־מָדַי *all the Medes*).

כְּלִמָּה I 30.0.4 n.f. **insult**—cstr. כְּלִמַּת; sf. כְּלִמָּתִי, כְּלִמָּתֶךָ, כְּלִמָּתוֹ, כְּלִמָּתָם; pl. כְּלִמּוֹת—**insult, reproach, disgrace,** <SUBJ> היה *be* 1QH 9_{22} ([הייתי]), שׁכח ni. *be forgotten* Jr 20_{11}, סוג ni. *depart* Mc 2_6 (or em. יַסִּג *they depart* to יַשִּׂגֵנוּ reproaches *overtake us*, or em. כְּלִמּוֹת to כְּלִמּוּת *disgrace*; unless כְּלִמָּה II *speech*),* כסה pi. *cover* Jr 3_{25} 51_{51} Ps 69_8. <NOM CL> כָּל־הַיּוֹם כְּלִמָּתִי נֶגְדִּי *my disgrace is before me all the day* Ps 44_{16}, אִוֶּלֶת הִיא־לוֹ וּכְלִמָּה *it is foolishness to him and a disgrace* Pr 18_{13}. <OBJ> שׁמע hi. *cause to hear* Ezk 36_{15}, ידע *know* Ps 69_{20} (|| בֹּשֶׁת *shame*, חֶרְפָּה *reproach*), נשׂא *raise*, i.e. bear Ezk $16_{52.52.54}$ $32_{24.25.29.30}$ $36_{6.7}$ 39_{26} 44_{13}.

<CSTR> כְּלִמַּת עוֹלָם *disgrace of eternity* Jr 20_{11}, כְּלִמַּת הַגּוֹיִם *disgrace of the nations* Ezk 34_{29} 36_{15}, sim. 36_6, כלמת כלה *disgrace of destruction* 1QS 4_{13} 4QBer[d] 1_2 (כלמ[ת]), כלמות חרפה *reproaches of shame* 4QBéat 15_7; מוּסַר כְּלִמָּתִי *rebuke of my disgrace*, i.e. that dishonours me Jb 20_3. <APP> בֹּשֶׁת *shame* Is 61_7.

<PREP> לְ of benefit, *to, for* Ps 4_3 (or em. כִּבְדֵי לֵב לָמָּה *why are the weights of [my] heart?*, i.e. why is my heart weighed down?), + היה *be* Is 30_3.

בְּ of accompaniment, *in, with* 4QBer[d] 1_2 (ב[כלמ]ת) 4QparaKings 49_8, + הלך *go* Is 45_{16}; מִן of direction, *from*, + סתר hi. *hide* Is 50_6; עִם *with* 1QS 4_{13}; מִפְּנֵי *because of*, + היה *be* Ezk 16_{63}; תַּחַת *instead of* Is 61_7; אַחַר *after*, + הלך *go* 4QJub[a] 1_9 ([אחר כ]ל[מתם]).

<COLL> יִלְבְּשׁוּ־בֹשֶׁת וּכְלִמָּה *may they be clothed with shame and disgrace* Ps 35_{26}, יִלְבְּשׁוּ ... כְּלִמָּה *may they be clothed ... with disgrace* Ps 109_{29}, יַעֲטוּ חֶרְפָּה וּכְלִמָּה *may they be covered with reproach and disgrace* Ps 71_{13}.

Also perh. 4QRitPur 51.2_{12} ([הכלמ]).

***[כְּלִמָּה]** II 1 n.f. **speech**—pl. כְּלִמּוֹת—<OBJ> נסג *forge* Mc 2_6 (לֹא יַסִּג כְּלִמּוֹת *he will not forge speeches*, if em. יַסִּג *speeches* depart; unless כְּלִמָּה I *reproach*).

כְּלִמּוּת 1 n.f. **disgrace**—<SUBJ> סוג *depart* Mc 2_6 (if em. כְּלִמּוֹת *reproaches*). <OBJ> נתן *give*, i.e. place Jr 23_{40} (|| חֶרְפָּה *reproach*). <CSTR> כְּלִמּוּת עוֹלָם *disgrace of eternity* Jr 23_{40}. <SYN> חֶרְפָּה *reproach*.

⇒ כלם *humiliate*.

כַּלְנֵה 3 pl.n. **Calneh**—כַּלְנוֹ—**1.** city in Babylonia, **1.** <NOM CL> רֵאשִׁית מַמְלַכְתּוֹ בָּבֶל וְאֶרֶךְ וְאַכַּד וְכַלְנֵה *the beginning of his kingdom was Babel and Erech and Accad and Calneh* Gn 10_{10} (or em. כֻּלָּנָה *all of them*).

2. appar. city in Syria, <NOM CL> הֲלֹא כְּכַרְכְּמִישׁ כַּלְנוֹ *is not Calneh like Carchemish* Is 10_9. <COLL> עִבְרוּ כַּלְנֵה *pass over to Calneh* Am 6_2.

כַּלְנוֹ, see כַּלְנֵה *Calneh*.

כמה 1 vb. **long for—Qal** 1 Pf. כָּמַהּ—**long for, yearn for, faint,** <SUBJ> בָּשָׂר *flesh* Ps 63_2. <PREP> לְ of direction, *to*, + אֱלֹהִים *God* Ps 63_2.

⇒ כִּמְהָם *Chimham* I, II.

כַּמָּה, see מָה *what*.

כַּמֶּה, see מָה *what*.

כִּמְהָם I 3 pr.n.m. **Chimham**—כִּמְהָן—son of Barzillai

and attendant of David, <SUBJ> עבר *pass by* 2 S 19$_{38.39.41}$ (mss כִּמְהָם). <APP> עֶבֶד *servant* 2 S 19$_{38}$.
⇒ כמה *long for.*

כִּמְהָם II $_1$ pl.n. **Chimham**—(Kt כמוהם Jr 41$_{17}$)—near Bethlehem, perh. compound גֵּרוּת כִּמְהָם *Geruth-Chimham* Jr 41$_{17(Qr)}$ (unless *lodging place of Chimham* .
⇒ כמה *long for.*

כִּמְהָן, see כִּמְהָם *Chimham.*

כְּמוֹ $_{+140.+7.+17}$ prep. **as**—sf. כָּמֹנִי (כָּמֹנִי), כָּמוֹךָ (כָּמֹכָה), Q כְּמוֹכֶם, (כָּמֹנוּ) כָּמֹנוּ, (כמוהה Q) כָּמֹהָ, כָּמֹהוּ, (כמוכה), כְּמוֹהֶם—alternative form of כְּ *like.*

1. כְּמוֹ without suffix, **as, like,** comparing **a.** divine action and action of natural object, e.g. הָיוֹ תִהְיֶה לִי כְּמוֹ אַכְזָב מַיִם לֹא נֶאֱמָנוּ *will you be to me like a deceitful (brook), waters that fail?* Jr 15$_{18}$. **b.** natural objects with natural objects, e.g. נִצְּבוּ כְמוֹ־נֵד נֹזְלִים *the floods stood up like a heap* Ex 15$_{8}$. **c.** persons with persons, e.g. כְּמוֹ חֲלָלִים *(I am) like the slain* Ps 88$_{6}$. **d.** persons with things, e.g. כֻּלָּם ... כְּמוֹ תַנּוּר *they are all ... like a heated oven* Ho 7$_{4}$. **e.** physical sensations with persons, e.g. הֲלוֹא חֲבָלִים יֹאחֱזוּךְ כְּמוֹ אֵשֶׁת לֵדָה *will not pangs seize you like a woman in labour?* Jr 13$_{21}$.

2. other uses, **a. when,** e.g. וּכְמוֹ הַשַּׁחַר עָלָה *when morning dawned* Gn 19$_{15}$. **b. now,** e.g. כְּמוֹ עַתָּה *as it is now* Ezk 16$_{57}$. **c.** comparing a future state with a previous one, e.g. וְרָבוּ כְּמוֹ רָבוּ *they will be as numerous as they were (once) numerous* Zc 10$_{8}$. **d. whether,** e.g. כְּמוֹ־חַי כְּמוֹ־חָרוֹן יִשְׂעָרֶנּוּ *whether green,* i.e. alive, *or ablaze, he will sweep them away* Ps 58$_{10}$. **e.** perh. **thus,** אִם־אָמַרְתִּי אֲסַפְּרָה כְמוֹ *if I said, I shall talk thus* Ps 73$_{15}$ (or em. כְּמוֹהָ *like it,* i.e. thus). **f. as in** (of time), e.g. כְּמוֹ־רָגַע *in a moment* Lm 4$_{6}$. **g.** כְּמוֹ ... כֵּן **in like manner, like ... so,** e.g. וְיֹשְׁבֶיהָ כְּמוֹ־כֵן יְמוּתוּן *its inhabitants will die in like manner* Is 51$_{6}$ (or em. כִּנִּים *[as] gnats*), כְּמוֹ הָרָה ... כֵּן הָיִינוּ *like a pregnant woman ... so were we* Is 26$_{17}$.

3. כָּמוֹ with suffix and a negative particle, expressing **a.** incomparability of God, e.g. מִי־כָמֹכָה בָּאֵלִם *who is like you among the gods?* Ex 15$_{11}$, כִּי־אֵין כָּמוֹךָ *for there is none like you* 2 S 7$_{22}$. **b.** incomparability of humans, e.g. אֵין־נָבוֹן וְחָכָם כָּמוֹךָ *there is no one as discerning and wise as you* Gn 41$_{39}$. **c.** incomparability of an event or a thing, e.g. הֲנִשְׁמַע כָּמֹהוּ *has its like been heard of?* Dt 4$_{32}$, לֹא הָיָה כֵן אַרְבֶּה כָּמֹהוּ *there never was such a swarm of locusts* Ex 10$_{14}$, לֹא תַעֲשׂוּ כָּמֹהוּ *you will make no other (oil) like it* Ex 30$_{32}$.

4a. כָּמוֹ with suffix, expressing equivalence among humans, e.g. אִם תִּהְיוּ כָמֹנוּ *you must become as we are* Gn 34$_{15}$, כִּי כָמוֹךָ כְּפַרְעֹה *for you are like Pharaoh himself* Gn 44$_{18}$, נָבִיא ... כָּמֹנִי יָקִים לְךָ י׳ *Y. will raise up for you a prophet ... like me* Dt 18$_{15}$, כָּמוֹךָ כְמוֹהֶם *as you are so were they* Jg 8$_{18}$, כָּמוֹנִי כָמוֹךָ *I am as you are* 1 K 22$_{4}$. **b.** equivalence of situations, attitudes, or actions, e.g. וּתְהִי אַחֲרִיתִי כָּמֹהוּ *may my latter end be like his* Nm 23$_{10}$, וְאָהַבְתָּ לְרֵעֲךָ כָּמוֹךָ *you must love your neighbour as (you love) yourself* Lv 19$_{18}$, לְמַעַן יָנוּחַ עַבְדְּךָ וַאֲמָתְךָ כָּמוֹךָ *that your manservant and your maidservant may rest as you (rest)* Dt 5$_{14}$, מַהֲרוּ עֲשׂוּ כָמוֹנִי *do quickly as I (have done)* Jg 9$_{48}$. **c.** value, כִּי־אַתָּה כָמֹנוּ עֲשָׂרָה אֲלָפִים *you are worth ten thousand of us* 2 S 18$_{3(mss)}$. **d. in accordance with,** כִּי כָל־הַגֹּנֵב מִזֶּה כָּמוֹהָ נִקָּה וְכָל־הַנִּשְׁבָּע מִזֶּה כָּמוֹהָ נִקָּה *every one who steals will be cut off in accordance with it* (the writing) *on one side and everyone who swears (falsely) will be cut off in accordance with it on the other side* Zc 5$_{3}$.
⇒ כְּ *as.*

כְּמוֹהָם, see כִּמְהָם II *Chimham.*

כְּמוֹשׁ $_{8.0.0.2}$ pr.n.m. **Chemosh**—(Kt כמיש Jr 48$_{7}$)—**1.** national god of Moab (Nm 21$_{29}$ Jg 11$_{24}$ Jr 48$_{7.13.46}$), with high place in Jerusalem (1 K 11$_{7.33}$ 2 K 23$_{13}$). **2.** Lachish ost. 8$_{3}$. **3.** Seal 185 (Samaria).

<SUBJ> יצא *go out* Jr 48$_{7(Qr)}$, ירשׁ hi. *grant possession* Jg 11$_{24}$. <NOM CL> כְּמוֹשׁ שִׁקֻּץ מוֹאָב *Chemosh is an abomination of Moab* 1 K 11$_{7}$ 2 K 23$_{13}$. <CSTR> עַם־כְּמוֹשׁ *people of Chemosh* Nm 21$_{29}$ Jr 48$_{46}$. <APP> אֱלֹהִים *God* Jg 11$_{24}$ 1 K 11$_{33}$. <PREP> לְ of benefit, *to, for,* + בנה *build* 1 K 11$_{7}$ 2 K 23$_{13}$; introducing object, + שׁחה htpalp. *worship* 1 K 11$_{33}$; מִן of cause, *because of, through,* + בושׁ *be ashamed* Jr 48$_{13}$.

Also Lachish ost. 8$_{3}$ Seal 185 (Samaria).

כְּמִישׁ, see כְּמוֹשׁ *Chemosh.*

כַּמֹּן 3 n.m. **cumin,** plant grown as condiment, <SUBJ> חבט ni. *be beaten out* Is 28$_{27}$. <OBJ> זרק *sprinkle,* i.e. sow Is 28$_{25}$. <PREP> עַל *upon, over,* + סבב ho. *be turned* Is 28$_{27}$.

כמס 1 vb. **store up—Qal** 1 Ptc. pass. כָּמֻס—<SUBJ> הוּא *it* Dt 32$_{34}$ (Sam כָּנוּס *be gathered up*).

כמר 4 vb. **be agitated—Ni.** 4 Pf. נִכְמְרוּ (נִכְמָרוּ)—**be agitated, be hot, burn,** <SUBJ> רֶחֶם *belly,* i.e. tender care Gn 43$_{30}$ 1 K 3$_{26}$ Ho 11$_{8}$ (if em.), נִחֻמִים *consolation* Ho 11$_{8}$ (or em. רֶחֶם), עוֹר *skin* Lm 5$_{10}$. <PREP> כְּ *as,* + תַּנּוּר *oven* Lm 5$_{10}$; אֶל *to, for,* + אָח *brother* Gn 43$_{30}$; עַל *for, on behalf of,* + בֵּן *son* 1 K 3$_{26}$; מִפְּנֵי *because of,* + זַלְעֲפוֹת רָעָב *ragings of famine* Lm 5$_{10}$.

כֹּמֶר 3 n.m. **priest**—pl. כְּמָרִים; sf. כְּמָרָיו—only of **priests** of foreign deities, <SUBJ> גיל *rejoice* Ho 10$_{5}$ (or em. ילל hi. *wail*). <OBJ> נתן *give,* i.e. install 2 K 23$_{5}$, שׁבת hi. *remove* 2 K 23$_{5}$. <CSTR> שֵׁם הַכְּמָרִים *the name of the priests* Zp 1$_{4}$. Also 4QapJoseph^{b} 1$_{3}$.

[כַּמְרִיר] 0.1 n.[m.] **darkness, eclipse,** <SUBJ> בעת pi. *terrify* Jb 3$_{5}$ (if em. כִּמְרִירֵי *as the bitter things of* the day). <OBJ> קלט pi. *disdain* perh. Si 11$_{4(B, D)}$ (A במרירי *in the bitter things of* the day, as 1QH 5$_{34}$) <CSTR> כַּמְרִירֵי יוֹם *darkness(es) of the day* Jb 3$_{5}$ Si 11$_{4(B, D)}$.*

[כָּן] 0.0.1 adv. **here,** <NOM CL> [הוא כן אצלי בעין גדן'] *he is here with me in En-gedi* MurEpJonathan$_{4}$.

כֵּן I 566.56.97.1 adv. **thus**—כֶּן־—**1.** adv. of manner, **so, thus, such, in this way, in the same way, accordingly, that is what ... is like;** oft. almost as noun, **this (thing), that (thing),** etc. (e.g. אֵת אֲשֶׁר דִּבֶּר י׳ אֶל־עֲבָדֶיךָ כֵּן נַעֲשֶׂה *that which Y. spoke to your servants, that thing we shall do* Nm 32$_{31}$, וְאַתָּה לֹא כֵן נָתַן לְךָ י׳ אֱלֹהֶיךָ *but for you, Y. your God has not permitted such things* Dt 18$_{14}$).

a. immediately followed by היה *be* Gn 41$_{13}$ Ex 26$_{24}$ (or em. עשׂה *do*) Lv 27$_{12}$ Nm 9$_{16}$ 13$_{33}$ 2 S 13$_{35}$ 16$_{19}$ 1 K 13$_{7}$ Is 14$_{24}$ 26$_{17}$ 29$_{8}$ 47$_{15}$ 55$_{11}$ Ezk 36$_{38}$ Zc 14$_{15}$ 4QMyst^{a} 6.2$_{11}$, שׁמע *hear* Jos 1$_{17}$ (or del. כֵּן), ראה *see* Ps 48$_{9}$, חזה *see* Ps 63$_{3}$ (בַּקֹּדֶשׁ *in holiness* intervenes), ידע *know* Pr 24$_{14}$, hi. *make known* Ps 90$_{12}$, כתב pass. *be written* 1QS 5$_{15}$ 2QJuridicial 1$_{3}$ 4QCitJub 1.1$_{8}$ CD 11$_{18}$, גדל *be great* 1 S 26$_{24}$, גבה *be high* Is 55$_{9}$, רבה *be numerous* Ex 1$_{12}$, hi. *make numerous* Jr 33$_{22}$, לבשׁ *be clothed* 2 S 13$_{18}$, שׁכל *be bereaved* 1 S 15$_{33}$, יצר ni. *be formed* Si 37$_{3(B)}$ (Bmg, D lack כֵּן), אוה ni. *be fitting* Pr 26$_{1}$ (לֹא *not* interrupts), שׁלח pu. *be sent out* Jg 5$_{15}$, אחר htp. *be late* Si 11$_{11}$ (הוּא *he* intervenes; but see §7e), מאס ni. *be rejected* Si 41$_{5(Bmg)}$ (B, M נין *offspring*), בושׁ hi. *be ashamed* Jr 2$_{26}$, כבד ni. *be honoured* Si 33$_{4}$ (לעיניהם *in their eyes* intervenes in mg.), אמן ni. *be trusted* Si 20$_{4}$, ברך pu. *be blessed* Ps 128$_{4}$, טהר *be pure* 11QT 47$_{15}$, סלל htpo. *be blocked* Si 39$_{24}$, נתך ni. *be poured out* Jr 42$_{18}$ 4Q424 1$_{5}$, ho. *be melted* Ezk 22$_{22}$, נצל ni. *be rescued* Am 3$_{12}$,אבד *die* Dt 8$_{20}$ Jg 5$_{31}$, שׁמד ni. *be destroyed* 4QJub^{f} 22$_{22}$, כרת ni. *be cut off* 4QapPs^{b} 33$_{9}$ ([א]כרת), מות *die* Is 51$_{6}$ (but כְּמוֹ־כֵן perh. *as lice* 1QIsa^{b} כמוכן perh. *as locusts*).

בוא *come* Ezk 23$_{44}$ Pr 26$_{2}$ (כֵּן קִלְלַת חִנָּם לוֹ תָבֹא *so a curse needlessly made comes back to him* [Qr]) Si 30$_{11}$ (כן בוצע בא *thus an extortioner comes*) 4QD^{c} 1$_{1}$ 4QAstr-Crypt 1$_{2}$ ([תבוא]) 1$_{3}$ ([כן תבוא]) 1$_{5}$ ([כן]) 1$_{11.12}$ (both [כן תבוא]) 1$_{14}$, hi. *bring* Jos 23$_{15}$ Jr 32$_{42}$ (כֵּן אָנֹכִי מֵבִיא *so I bring*), יצא *go out* 4QWays^{b} 1a.1$_{4}$, הלך *go* Ec 5$_{15}$, htp. *go* 4Q423 3$_{2}$, ירד *go down* Is 31$_{4}$ Jb 7$_{9}$ 4QMyst^{a} 6.2$_{17}$, עלה *go up* Ezk 41$_{7}$ (וְכֵן הַתַּחְתּוֹנָה יַעֲלֶה *and thus would the lower one ascend;* or em. וּמִן *and from* the lower one, it would ascend, or וְכֵן מִן *and so, from* the lower one, it would ascend), שׁוב *go back* Zc 8$_{15}$, hi. *bring back* 4Q416 2.3$_{4}$, הפך ni. *turn out* evil Si 39$_{27}$ (כן ... נהפכו *accordingly ..., they turn out*), קרב *approach* 1 K 2$_{7}$, נגשׁ hi. *bring near* 1QH 14$_{13}$, ho. *be brought near* 1QH 14$_{14}$, עזב *leave* 2 C 32$_{31}$ (כֵּן ... עֲזָבוֹ הָאֱלֹהִים *accordingly ..., God left him*), יצא hi. *take out* 1 K 10$_{29}$‖2 C 1$_{17}$ (כֵּן ... יֹצִאוּ *in the same way ... they would bring out*).

ישׁב *sit* CD 14$_{6}$, קום *arise* Lv 27$_{14}$, עמד *stand* Is 66$_{22}$ 1QM 6$_{9}$, רום hi. *raise,* i.e. present Nm 15$_{20}$ 18$_{2}$, נדד *wander* Pr 27$_{8}$ (כֵּן אִישׁ נוֹדֵד *so a person wanders*), רוץ *run* Jl 2$_{4}$, נהג *lead* Is 20$_{4}$, pi. *lead away* Is 63$_{14}$, נסע *set out* Nm 2$_{17.34}$, רדף *pursue* Ps 83$_{16}$, קבץ *gather* Ezk 22$_{20}$, ריק hi.

empty Hb 1$_{17}$, דבק hi. *cause to cling* Jr 13$_{11}$, ארך hi. *endure* Pr 28$_{2}$ (unless כֵּן III *right* or *stability*; or em. יֹדֵעַ כֵּן יַאֲרִיךְ through understanding *knowledgeable* people, the land *endures* to יִדְעָכוּן *many will be extinguished*), פרץ *extend* Ex 1$_{12}$, יחל hi. *wait* 2 S 18$_{14}$ (or em. לֹא־כֵן *not so* to לָכֵן *therefore* and/or יחל to חול *dance* or חלל hi. *begin*).

חלל hi. *begin* 4QAstrCrypt 1$_{9}$ ([כן יחל]), כון *be finished* 1QMyst 1.1$_{6}$, hi. *prepare* Ps 65$_{10}$, תמם hi. *complete* 2 S 20$_{18}$, נתן *give* Ps 127$_{2}$ (mss כִּי *for*) Pr 26$_{8}$, i.e. cause to be Jr 24$_{8}$ Ezk 15$_{6}$, permit Dt 18$_{14}$, ni. *be given*, i.e. inflicted Lv 24$_{20}$, רצה *accept* 4Q416 6$_{1}$, נזה hi. *cause to jump* Is 52$_{15}$ (or em. qal *sprinkle* or רגז *quake* or בזה *despise*).

חנה *encamp* Nm 2$_{34}$, צוץ *produce blossom* Ps 103$_{15}$, צמח hi. *cause to sprout* Is 61$_{11}$ (אֲדֹנָי י' *my Lord Y.* intervenes), שׁבר pi. *shatter* Is 38$_{13}$, שׂרף *burn* Jr 34$_{5}$, להט pi. *set alight* Si 9$_{8}$ (כן אהביה באש טלהט *thus she sets her lovers alight with fire*), שׂנא *hate* 1QS 4$_{24}$, תעב pi. *loathe* 1QH 14$_{21}$ 1QS 4$_{24}$, אכל *eat* Dt 12$_{22}$, עבד *serve* Jr 5$_{19}$ 4Q416 2.3$_{17}$, קרר hi. *keep cool* Jr 6$_{7}$, גנן *protect* Is 31$_{5}$, שׁלם pi. *repay* Jg 1$_{7}$, נצל hi. *rescue* 2 C 32$_{17}$ (לֹא *not* intervenes), ישׁע hi. *save* Zc 8$_{13}$, כפר pi. *atone* Si 3$_{30}$ (צְדָקָה *righteousness* intervenes) CD 4$_{10}$, נחל ho. *inherit* Jb 7$_{3}$, ירשׁ hi. *dispossess* Si 39$_{23}$.

עשׂה *do* Gn 6$_{22}$ 18$_{5}$ Ex 7$_{6}$ 12$_{28.50}$ 22$_{29}$ 23$_{11}$ 25$_{9}$ 26$_{4.17}$ 27$_{8}$ 36$_{11.22.29}$ 39$_{32.42.43}$ 40$_{16}$ Lv 4$_{20}$ 16$_{16}$ Nm 1$_{54}$ 5$_{4}$ 6$_{21}$ 8$_{4.20.22}$ 9$_{5.14}$ 14$_{28}$ 15$_{14}$ 17$_{26}$ 32$_{31}$ 36$_{10}$ Dt 3$_{21}$ 7$_{19}$ 20$_{15}$=11QT 62$_{11}$ Dt 22$_{3.3.3}$ Jos 10$_{1.39}$ 11$_{15}$ 14$_{5}$ Jg 7$_{17.17}$ 11$_{10}$ 14$_{10}$ 15$_{11}$ 1 S 1$_{7}$ 8$_{8}$ (הֵמָּה *they* intervenes) 2 S 3$_{9}$ 9$_{11}$ 12$_{31}$||1 C 20$_{3}$ 1 K 1$_{30}$ 2$_{38}$ 6$_{33}$ 7$_{18}$ 11$_{8}$ 12$_{32}$ 2 K 16$_{11}$ Is 10$_{11}$ 65$_{8}$ Jr 19$_{12}$ 28$_{6}$ 39$_{12}$ 42$_{5.20}$ (נגד hi. *tell* intervenes) 48$_{30}$ (if em.; see כֵּן II, III) Ezk 35$_{15}$ 45$_{20}$ Zc 1$_{6}$ Pr 24$_{29}$ Ne 5$_{12}$ Si 20$_{4}$ 38$_{8}$ (רֹקֵחַ *perfumer* intervenes) 1QS 9$_{15}$ 4Q417 13$_{3}$ 11QT 16$_{15}$ ([כן יעשה]) 24$_{11}$ Mur 7 3$_{2}$ ([אעש]ה) Lachish ost. 4$_{3}$, ni. *be done* Gn 34$_{7}$ (וְכֵן לֹא יֵעָשֶׂה perh. *and right was not done*, i.e. כֵּן III) Lv 24$_{19}$ Ezk 12$_{11}$.

ערג *long for* Ps 42$_{2}$ (נַפְשִׁי *soul* intervenes), אהב *love* Jr 14$_{10}$ Am 4$_{5}$, כעס hi. *anger* 1 S 1$_{7}$, זמם *plan* Zc 8$_{15}$ (שׁוּב *go back* intervenes), יסד pi. *determine* Est 1$_{8}$, נכר hi. *recognise* Jr 24$_{5}$, בגד *betray* Jr 3$_{20}$, סרר *rebel* CD 1$_{14}$, בקר pi. *investigate* Ezk 34$_{12}$, שׁקד *keep watch* Jr 31$_{28}$, צפף pilp. *whisper* Is 38$_{14}$, אמר *say* 1 K 1$_{36}$ Ezk 11$_{5}$ 33$_{10}$ Si 39$_{15}$, דבר *speak* 4Q424 3$_{5}$, pi. *speak* Ex 10$_{29}$ 2 S 7$_{17}$||1 C 17$_{15}$, קרא *call* Zc 7$_{13}$, נגד hi. *tell* Jr 42$_{20}$, צוה pi. *command* Jos 11$_{15}$ 1 K 13$_{9}$ Est 3$_{2}$, pu. *be commanded* Lv 8$_{35}$ 10$_{13}$, שׁאל *ask* CD 14$_{6}$ GnzPs 3$_{1}$, ni. *be asked* 1QS 6$_{4.9}$, שׁפט *judge* 4QpIsa[a] 8$_{23}$, ni. *plead* Ezk 20$_{36}$, שׁבע ni. *swear* Is 54$_{9}$, ברך pi. *bless* Ps 63$_{5}$, שׂחק *laugh* Ec 7$_{6}$, שׂישׂ *rejoice* Dt 28$_{63}$, נחם pi. *comfort* Is 66$_{13}$ (אָנֹכִי *I* intervenes) 4QBark[a] 1.1$_{6}$, שׂכל hi. *instruct* 1QS 9$_{18}$, בין hi. *instruct* 4QD[a] 9.3$_{5}$.

b. preceded by verb (or with ellipsis of verb from preceding clause, e.g. Si 7$_{4.12.20}$), היה *be* Gn 1$_{7.9.11.15.24.30}$ Ex 10$_{10.14.14}$ Jg 6$_{38}$ 2 K 2$_{10}$ 7$_{20}$ 15$_{12}$ Am 5$_{14}$ perh. Si 27$_{6}$ 4QpsEzek[a] 2$_{6}$ ([ויה]י כן]), רום ho. *be exalted* Si 47$_{2}$, קום hi. *establish* Si 44$_{22(Bmg)}$ (B בֵּן *son*), חלק *apportion* or create Si 39$_{25}$, עשׂה *do* Gn 29$_{28}$ 42$_{20.25}$ 45$_{21}$ 50$_{12}$ Ex 7$_{10.11.20.22}$ 8$_{3.13.14.20.22}$ 14$_{4}$ 16$_{17}$ 17$_{6}$ Nm 5$_{4}$ 8$_{3}$ 32$_{23}$ Dt 4$_{5}$ 12$_{4.30.31}$ 15$_{17}$ Jos 4$_{8}$ 5$_{15}$ 9$_{26}$ 10$_{23}$ Jg 2$_{17}$ 6$_{20.40}$ 21$_{23}$ 1 S 6$_{10}$ 30$_{23}$ 2 S 5$_{25}$ 16$_{10}$ 1 K 10$_{20}$||2 C 9$_{19}$ 1 K 14$_{4}$ 20$_{25}$ 22$_{22}$||2 C 18$_{21}$ Is 20$_{2}$ Jr 38$_{12}$ Ezk 12$_{7}$ Ps 147$_{20}$ Est 2$_{4}$ 6$_{10}$ 7$_{5}$ Ezr 10$_{16}$ Ne 5$_{15}$ 6$_{13}$ 8$_{17}$ 1 C 13$_{4}$ 2 C 1$_{12.12}$, ni. *be done* Gn 29$_{26}$ 2 S 13$_{12}$ Est 9$_{14}$, רעע hi. *do evil* Si 7$_{20(C)}$ (A ידע perh. *humble*), צום *fast* Est 4$_{16}$.

ידע *know* 1 S 23$_{17}$ Zc 11$_{11}$ Jb 9$_{2}$, חרשׁ *devise* Si 7$_{12}$, בקשׁ pi. *seek* Si 7$_{4}$, בחן *test* Si 34$_{26.26}$, אהב *love* Jr 5$_{31}$, perh. אמן hi. *believe* Si 45$_{13}$, אמר *say* 1 K 22$_{8}$||2 C 18$_{7}$ Ezr 10$_{12}$, דבר pi. *speak* Ex 6$_{9}$, נבא ni. *prophesy* 1 K 22$_{12}$||2 C 18$_{11}$, בקשׁ pi. *seek* Si 7$_{4}$.

c. in nom. cl., כֵּן הַכְּרוּב הַשֵּׁנִי *thus was the second cherub* 1 K 6$_{26}$, כֵּן הָעָם־הַזֶּה *that is what this people is like* Hg 2$_{14}$, כֵּן־הַגּוֹי הַזֶּה *that is what this nation is like* Hg 2$_{14}$, כֵּן הֶעָצֵל *so is the idler* Pr 10$_{26}$.

כֵּן אֲדֹנִי הַמֶּלֶךְ *thus is my lord the king* 2 S 14$_{17}$, כֵּן פַּרְעֹה *that is what Pharaoh is like* 2 K 18$_{21}$||Is 36$_{6}$, לֹא־כֵן עַבְדִּי מֹשֶׁה *my servant Moses is not so* Nm 12$_{7}$, כֵּן־אִישׁ *thus is a man* Pr 26$_{19}$ Si 6$_{1}$ 36$_{31}$ 4Q423 5$_{8}$, כן כל אנשים *so are all the men* CD 19$_{33}$, כן אבוהי *so is his father* 4Q416 2.3$_{16}$, כן אמו *so is his mother* 4Q416 2.3$_{16}$, כֵּן בְּנֵי הַנְּעוּרִים *thus are the sons of one's youth* Ps 127$_{4}$, כן ילוד perh. *so is one born* 4QMyst[a] 28$_{2}$, כן חנף *so is the irreligious one* Si 41$_{10(M)}$ (Bmg בן *son of* an irreligious one), כן עשיר *that is what a wealthy person is like* Si 13$_{17}$ (|| כָּךְ *thus*), כן רעהו *thus is his companion* Si 6$_{17}$, כֵּן רַעְיָתִי *that is what my companion is like* Ca 2$_{2}$, כֵּן דּוֹדִי *that is what my be-*

loved is like Ca 2_{3}, כן רוחם *so is their spirit* 1QH fr. 6_{4}, כן חובר אל אשת זדון *thus is a man who allies himself with an impudent woman* Si 12_{14}, [כ]ן כל שומרי עישאו *so are all the guardians of Esau* 4QJub^{h} 35_{17}, כן פשר דבר [על הבו]גדים *likewise the interpretation of the passage concerns the traitors* 1QpHab 2_{5}.

כֵּן דֶּרֶךְ אִשָּׁה *such is the way of a woman* Pr 30_{20}, כֵּן לֵב־הָאָדָם *such is the heart of a person* Pr 27_{19}, כֵּן מַרְאֵה הַנֹּגַהּ *that is what was the appearance of the brightness was like* Ezk 1_{28}, כֵּן רָחְבָּן *thus was their width* Ezk 42_{11}, כְּמוֹת זֶה כֵּן מוֹת זֶה *as one dies, so dies the other* Ec 3_{19}, כן מרעית עשיר דלים *in the same way, the poor are the grazing ground of the rich* Si 13_{19}, כֵּן כָּל־מַעֲשֵׂה יְדֵיהֶם *thus is every deed of their hands* Hg 2_{14}, כן כל כבוד חפתה *in this way, all that is glorious is its canopy* Si $40_{27(B)}$ (M עַל its canopy is *over* all that is glorious), לֹא־כֵן בֵּיתִי *is not my house thus?* 2 S 23_{5} (but perh. כֵּן V *secure*), כן כל אבדה *likewise is any lost object* CD 9_{14}.

כן חקך *thus is your decree* Si $38_{22(Bmg)}$ (B הוּא *it*), כן תוכחתו *thus is his reproof* Si 16_{12}, כֵּן כָּל־עֲצַת אֲחִיתֹפֶל *thus was all the counsel of Ahithophel* 2 S 16_{23}, כן המשפט *likewise is the ordinance* CD 15_{6} 16_{12}, כֵּן מִשְׁפָּטֶךָ *such is your judgment* 1 K 20_{40}, כן משפט כל באי בריתו *such is the judgment of all who entered his covenant* CD 8_{1}, sim. CD 8_{16} $19_{13.28}$ 20_{1}, כֵּן תְּהִלָּתְךָ *such is your praise* Ps 48_{11}, כֵּן הַדָּבָר הַזֶּה *that is what this word,* i.e. legal case, *is like* Dt 22_{26}=11QT 66_{7}, לֹא־כֵן הַדָּבָר *the matter is not so* 2 S 20_{21}, כֵּן דְּבַר הַמֶּלֶךְ *such was the word of the king* Est 1_{13}, כֵּן מִצְוַת דָּוִיד *such was the command of David* 2 C 8_{14}, כן אהבתו עם שנאתו *thus shall his love be, together with his hatred* 1QS 9_{16}.

כֵּן עֵינֵינוּ אֶל־י׳ *so our eyes are to Y.* Ps 123_{2}, כן מליציו *thus are his intermediaries* Si 10_{2}, כן יושביו *thus are its residents* Si 10_{2}, כן דורות בשר ודם *such are the generations of flesh and blood* Si 14_{18}, לֹא־כֵן הָרְשָׁעִים *the wicked are not so* Ps 1_{4}, כן שש מאות אלף רגלי *that is what the six hundred thousand on foot were like* Si 16_{10}, כֵּן בָּתֵּיהֶם *thus are their houses* Jr 5_{27} Si 11_{30}, כן מעשיו *thus are his deeds* Si 2_{18}, כן כול טוב *so is all good* 1QMyst 1.2_{5}, כֵּן אָרְחוֹת כָּל־שֹׁכְחֵי אֵל *such is the fate of all who forget God* Jb 8_{13}, כֵּן אָרְחוֹת כָּל־בֹּצֵעַ בָּצַע *such is the fate of every extortioner* Pr 1_{19} (or em. in both אַחֲרִית *end*), כן טמאת perh. *so is the impurity of* 4QNarrC 1_{17}.

כן לנוקם *so it is for an avenger* 1QS 7_{9}, כן לאיש הנפטר המושב הרבים *so it is for the man who leaves the session of the many* 1QS 7_{10}, [כן לבן א]דם *so it is for the son of man* 1QH 10_{28}, כן ללויים *so it is for the Levites* 4QM^{d} 1_{3}, כן למגרש *so it is for one divorcing* CD 13_{17}, כֵּן לַבָּקָר *so it was for the bulls* 2 C 35_{12}, כֵּן לְכָל־הֶעָרִים *so it is for all the cities* Jos 21_{42}, כֵּן לְשֵׁשֶׁת הַקָּנִים *so it is for the six branches* of the lampstand Ex 25_{33}||37_{19}, כֵּן לִפְאַת צָפוֹן בָּאֹרֶךְ *so it is for the north side in respect of length* Ex 27_{11}, כֵּן לָאֵלַמּוֹת *so it was for the vestibules* Ezk 40_{16}, כֵּן לָעֶרֶב *it was the same in the evening* 1 C 23_{30}, כֵּן מִמַּעַל perh. *so it was from above* 1 K 7_{29} (unless כֵּן IV *stand*).

כֵּן־אַתֶּם *that is what you are like* Jr 18_{6}, כֵּן־הוּא *that is what he is like* 1 S 25_{25} Pr 23_{7} perh. 4QapJoshua^{a} 20.2_{3}, *let it be so* Jos 2_{21}, כֵּן־הִיא *it is so* Jb 5_{27}, wisdom *is so* Si 6_{22} (if em. הוא *he*), [הו]א כן *it is so* 4QMMT B_{38}, כן מי שיש לו עושר *thus is one who has wealth* Si 30_{19}.

אִם־כֵּן *if it is so* Gn 25_{22} 43_{11}, לֹא־כֵן אָנֹכִי *I am not so* Jb 9_{35}, וַיִּרְאוּ כִּי־כֵן *and they saw … that it was so* 1 S 5_{7}, לֹא־כֵן *it is not so/let it not be so* Gn 48_{18} Ex 10_{11}.

<COLL> כְּ … כֵּן *as … thus* Gn 6_{22} Ex $39_{32.42}$ 40_{16} Lv 27_{12} Nm 1_{54} 2_{34} 6_{21} (כְּפִי *in accordance with*) $8_{4.20}$ $9_{5.14}$ 13_{33} 15_{20} Dt 8_{20} Jos 1_{17} 2_{21} Jg 11_{10} 1 S 8_{8} 25_{25} 2 S 7_{17} 9_{11} 13_{35} 14_{17} 1 K 12_{32} 2 K 16_{11} Is 26_{17} (כְּמוֹ) 31_{5} perh. 38_{13} 38_{14} 55_{9} (if em. כִּי *for* to כְּ) 61_{11} 63_{14} 66_{13} Jr 2_{26} 3_{20} (if em. אָכֵן בָּגְדָה *indeed, she has betrayed* to אַךְ כִּבְגֹד *but as the betrayal of*) 5_{27} 6_{7} 18_{6} $24_{5.8}$ 34_{5} $42_{5.20}$ Ezk 1_{28} 22_{20} (if ins. כְּ) 20_{22} 34_{12} 35_{15} 36_{38} 42_{11} Jl 2_{4} Zc 1_{6} Ps 42_{2} 48_{11} 83_{16} 103_{15} 123_{2} 127_{4} Pr 10_{26} 23_{7} (כְּמוֹ) $26_{1.2.8.19}$ $27_{8.19}$ Ca $2_{2.3}$ Ec 3_{19} 5_{15} (if em. כָּל־עֻמַּת שֶׁ *just as* to כְּלְעֻמַּת שֶׁ *as in accordance with [the way] that*) 2 C 32_{17} 7_{6} Si 2_{18} $6_{17.22}$ $10_{2.2}$ 16_{12} 30_{11} 47_{2} 1QH 14_{21} 1QS 9_{15} 1QMyst 1.1_{6} 4QJub^{h} 35_{17} ([כ]ן) 4Q416 $2.3_{16.16}$ 4Q424 1_{5} 3_{5} 4QBark^{a} 1.1_{6} 11QT 47_{15} CD 1_{14} Lachish ost. 4_{3}.

כְּמוֹ־כֵן *as thus,* i.e. likewise Is 51_{6} (unless כֵּן V *louse*).

כֵּן … כַּאֲשֶׁר *thus … (just) as* Gn 18_{5} 50_{12} Ex $7_{10.20}$ 10_{10} Nm 8_{3} Jos 4_{8} 2 S 5_{25} Ezk 12_{7} Am 5_{14} Ne 5_{12}.

כַּאֲשֶׁר … כֵּן *as … thus* Gn 41_{13} Ex 1_{12} 7_{6} $12_{28.50}$ 27_{8} 39_{43} Lv 4_{20} $24_{19.20}$ 27_{14} Nm 2_{17} 5_{4} 8_{22} 14_{28} 15_{14} 17_{26} 36_{10} Dt 12_{22} 22_{26}=11QT 66_{7} Dt 28_{63} Jos $10_{1.39}$ 11_{15} 14_{5} 23_{15} Jg 1_{7} 7_{17} 15_{11} 1 S 15_{33} 26_{24} 2 S 3_{9} $16_{19.23}$ 1 K $1_{30.37}$ 2_{38} Is

10$_{11}$ 14$_{24}$ 20$_{4}$ 29$_{8}$ 31$_{4}$ 52$_{15}$ 54$_{9}$ (if em. אֲשֶׁר *which*) 65$_{8}$ 66$_{22}$ Jr 5$_{19}$ (perh. כַּאֲשֶׁר = *because*) 13$_{11}$ 31$_{28}$ 32$_{42}$ 39$_{12}$ 42$_{18}$ Ezk 12$_{11}$ 15$_{6}$ 20$_{36}$ Am 3$_{12}$ Zc 1$_{6}$ 7$_{13}$ 8$_{13}$ Ps 48$_{9}$ Pr 24$_{29}$ Si 33$_{4}$ 4QJub^{f} 22$_{22}$ ([כאשר]), כֵּן ... כֵּן *thus ... thus*, i.e. as ... so Si 20$_{4}$, אֵיכָה ... כֵּן *how? ... thus* Dt 12$_{30}$, מדוע כן *why am I thus* formed Si 37$_{3}$.

2. perh. adv. of quantity, **in such quantity, so much, so many** (Ex 10$_{14}$ 1 K 10$_{12}$ Est 2$_{12}$); **in sufficient quantity** (Jg 21$_{14}$); **(the more ...) the more** (Ho 11$_{2}$ Ps 48$_{6}$), though כֹּה *thus* is also possible, לְפָנָיו לֹא־הָיָה כֵן אַרְבֶּה כָּמֹהוּ *before there had never been in such quantity (a swarm of) locusts like it* Ex 10$_{14}$, לֹא בָא־כֵן עֲצֵי אַלְמֻגִּים *timbers of almug had not come in such quantity* 1 K 10$_{12}$, שְׁנֵים עָשָׂר חֹדֶשׁ כִּי כֵּן יִמְלְאוּ יְמֵי מְרוּקֵיהֶן *twelve months, for so many were the days of their beautification* Est 2$_{12}$, sim. Gn 50$_{3}$, לֹא־מָצְאוּ לָהֶם כֵּן *they did not find* (women) *for themselves in sufficient quantity* Jg 21$_{14}$, קָרְאוּ לָהֶם כֵּן הָלְכוּ מִפְּנֵיהֶם *(the more) they called to them, the more they went (away) from them* Ho 11$_{2}$ (or em. כְּדֵי קָרְאִי/כְּקָרְאִי ... מִפָּנַי: הֵם *the more I called* to them, the more they went *from me; they* sacrifice to the baalim), כְּרֻבָּם כֵּן חָטְאוּ־לִי *as they increased, the more they sinned against me* Ho 4$_{7}$, הֵמָּה רָאוּ כֵּן תָּמָהוּ *(the more) they saw, the more they were amazed* Ps 48$_{6}$, גדול אתה כן תשפיל נפשך *the greater you are the more you should humble your soul* Si 3$_{18}$, כֵּן־מִשְׁחַת מֵאִישׁ מַרְאֵהוּ perh. *his appearance was so great a disfigurement from (that of) a man* Is 52$_{14}$ (or em. מָשְׁחָת his appearance *being* so much *disfigured*; 1QIsa^{a} משחתי thus *have I anointed* or *have I marred* his face more than [that of] any other man).

3. adv. of time, **then,** כְּבֹאֲכֶם הָעִיר כֵּן תִּמְצְאוּן אֹתוֹ בְּטֶרֶם יַעֲלֶה *as (soon as) you enter the city, then you will find him, before he goes up* 1 S 9$_{13}$ (mss כְּבֹאֲכֶם *when you enter*), כְּשַׁחֲרֵנוּ כֵּן נִמְצָאֶנוּ/נִמְצָאֵהוּ *as (soon as) we seek him, then we shall find him* Ho 6$_{3}$ (if em. כְּשַׁחַר נָכוֹן מוֹצָאוֹ *his going out is as established as the dawn*), יֵשֵׁב עוֹלָם ... כֵּן אֲזַמְּרָה שִׁמְךָ לָעַד *may he dwell forever* before God ..., *then/during that time, I shall praise your name forever* Ps 61$_{9}$, נוצר נביא: לנתוש... להרס וכן לבנת לנטע ולהשיב and he was from the womb *fashioned as a prophet, to uproot ..., to tear up and then to (re)build, to (re)plant, and to restore* Si 49$_{7}$.

4. appar. **also, too,** אִם־שְׁלֵמִים וְכֵן רַבִּים וְכֵן נָגֹזּוּ וְעָבָר *(even) if complete and (also) numerous, they too have been cut off and passed away* Na 1$_{12}$ (or em. אִם־שַׁלְמֵי מַיִם רַבִּים *though deluges be many* or אִם־מֹשְׁלִים הֵם וְרַבִּים *if they are rulers and mighty ones* or אִם־מֹשְׁלִים וְאִם רַבִּים *though they be rulers, though they be mighty ones*, and/or rd. וְעָבְרוּ *and they passed away*), מדין יוצא אסון כן רע לבב יבנה עצבה *from judgment comes harm and evil of heart produces pain* Si 38$_{18}$.

5. כֵּן ... כֵּן **as ... so,** כן תתן לאבתיו כן ירשנה *as she was given to his fathers, so shall he inherit her* 4Q185 1.2$_{14}$.

6. appar. preposition, **as, like,** וְיִשָּׂשכָר כֵּן בָּרָק בָּעֵמֶק שֻׁלַּח בְּרַגְלָיו *and Issachar, like Barak, was sent out, behind him into the valley* Jg 5$_{15}$ (or del. וְיִשָּׂשכָר כֵּן בָּרָק or em. וּכְיִשָּׂשכָר *and like Issachar*, so too was Barak, as §4).

7. compounded with preceding preposition, as adv. or conj.

a. אַחַר כֵּן **afterwards,** with verb, בוא *come* Lv 14$_{36}$ Dt 21$_{13}$ 1 S 10$_{5}$.

b. אַחֲרֵי־כֵן **afterwards,** with verb, בוא *come* Lv 16$_{26.28}$ Nm 4$_{15}$ 8$_{15.22}$, נסע *set out* 9$_{17}$, שׁוב *go back* Jr 34$_{11}$ 4QJub^{a} 2$_{17}$ ([ואחרי כן ישובו]), hi. *bring back* 49$_{6}$, יצא *go out* Gn 15$_{14}$ 25$_{26}$ Ex 11$_{8}$, נגשׁ *approach* 34$_{32}$, קום *arise* 1 S 24$_{9}$, עמד *arise* 4QMidrEschat^{a} 8$_{3}$, עשׂה *offer* sacrifice Ezr 3$_{5}$ (אַחֲרֵיכֵן), שׁלח *send* Jr 16$_{16}$, pi. *dispatch* Israelites Ex 3$_{20}$ 11$_{1}$, נתן *give* Jr 21$_{7}$, ni. *be given* 4QpPs^{a} 1.2$_{19}$ (ואחר[י] כן), פתח *open* Jb 3$_{1}$ 4QM^{c}$_{2}$, נכה hi. *strike* Jos 10$_{26}$, קבר *bury* Gn 23$_{19}$, עתר ni. *be appeased* 2 S 21$_{14}$, ראה *see* Gn 32$_{21}$, דבר pi. *speak* 45$_{15}$ (אַחֲרֵי כֵן), שׁמע *hear* 2 S 3$_{28}$ (מֵאַחֲרֵי כֵן), קרא *read* Jos 8$_{34}$, pass. *be called* Is 1$_{26}$, ילד ni. *be born* 4QpsJub^{a} 2.1$_{8}$ ([אחר[י), חבר htp. *make alliance* 2 C 20$_{35}$ (אַחֲרֵיכֵן), בנה *build* 33$_{14}$, שׁכן *dwell* Jr 46$_{26}$, אכל *eat* 1 S 9$_{13}$.

וַיְהִי אַחֲרֵי־כֵן *and it came to pass afterwards* Jg 16$_{4}$ 1 S 24$_{6}$ 2 S 2$_{1}$ 8$_{1}$||1 C 18$_{1}$ 2 S 10$_{1}$||1 C 19$_{1}$ 2 S 13$_{1}$ 15$_{1}$ (מֵאַחֲרֵי כֵן) 21$_{18}$||1 C 20$_{4}$ (אַחֲרֵיכֵן) 2 K 6$_{24}$ Jl 3$_{1}$ (וְהָיָה) 2 C 20$_{1}$ 24$_{4}$ (both אַחֲרֵיכֵן), הָרָעָב הַהוּא אַחֲרֵי־כֵן *that famine thereafter* Gn 41$_{31}$, בַּיָּמִים הָהֵם וְגַם אַחֲרֵי־כֵן *in those days, and afterwards too* 6$_{4}$, וַיִּנַּשֵּׂא ... מֵאַחֲרֵי־כֵן *and he was exalted ... from then on* 2 C 32$_{23}$; אַחֲרֵי־זֹאת *after this* Jb 42$_{16}$ Ezr 9$_{10}$, אַחֲרֵי כָל־זֹאת *after all this* 2 C 21$_{18}$ 35$_{20}$ (כָּל־).

c. בְּכֵן **then, afterwards,** perh. **thereupon*** (Ec 8$_{10}$), with verb, בוא *come* Est 4_{16}, ראה *see* Ec 8_{10} Si 13_7, אמר ni. *be said* 4QNarrC 1_4, שִׁיר *sing* 4QpsEzek^b 1.2_8, קבל pu. *be received* 1QSa 1_{11}, אכל *eat* 4QActs 1_3.

d. בַּעֲבוּר כֵּן **because of this, therefore,** with verb, קנה *acquire* Si 51_{21}; also Si 51_{20}.

e. כְּדֵי כֵן **in like measure, proportionately,** with verb, אחר htp. *be late* Si 11_{11} (if em. כְּדַי *as sufficiency*), נגשׁ hi. *bring near* Si 13_9.

e. לָכֵן **therefore,** see לָכֵן.

f. עַד־כֵּן **unto this, still,** with verb, נגד hi. *declare* Ne 2_{16} (mss עַל־כֵּן *therefore*).

g. עַל־כֵּן **therefore, because of this, that is why,** sometimes, perh. **indeed,*** with verb (only the first verb to follow is noted), היה *be* Dt 10_9 Jos 14_{14} 1 S 10_{12} Ec 5_1 Lm 1_8, משׁך *continue* Jr 31_3, חיל *endure* Jb 20_{21}, גדל *be great* 2 S 7_{22} Jr 5_{27}, גבה *be high* Ezk 31_5, חזק *be strong* 1 K 20_{23} Si 34_{11}, חרה *be hot*, i.e. angry Is 5_{25}, מלא *be full* Is 21_3 Ec 8_{11} Si 10_{13}, שׁלם *be fulfilled* 11QPs^a 24_{14}, רחק *be far* Is 59_9, חרה *dwindle away* Is 24_6, פוג *be feeble* Hb 1_4, רפה *be weak* Is 13_7, אבד *die* Jr 48_{36}, קלל ni. *be swift* Is 30_{16}, מלט ni. *be rescued* 2 C 16_7, יצב htp. *position oneself* Si 39_{32}, אצל ni. *be recessed* Ezk 42_6.

בוא *come* Gn 42_{21} 1 S 20_{29} Pr 6_{15}, hi. *bring* 1 K 9_9‖2 C 7_{22} (+ עַל אֲשֶׁר *because*), דרך *tread* 1 S 5_5, נסע *set out* Zc 10_2, נוס *flee* Is 30_{16} Si 34_{13} (mg על כל *above all*), יצא *go out* Pr 7_{15}, קום *arise* Ps 1_5, pi. *impose obligation* CD 16_1 (יקום appar. error for יקים), hi. *establish* Si 44_{21}, עמד *stand* Jr 48_{11}, כשׁל ni. *stumble* Jr 20_{11}, רגז hi. *cause to tremble* Is 13_{13}, ריק hi. *empty* Hb 1_{17}, שׁפך *pour* 4QDibHam^a 1.3_{10} (עלכן), נתן *give* Ex 16_{29}, *allow* Gn 20_6, *cause to be* Ezk 7_{20} 22_4, שׂים *place* Is 50_7, כלא *withhold* Hg 1_{10}, עזב *forsake* Gn 2_{24}, נשׂא *raise* Is 15_7 Ezk 44_{12} (+ יַעַן אֲשֶׁר *because*), רום hi. *raise* Ps 110_7, pol. *exalt* Jb 17_4, מצא *find* 2 S 7_{27}‖1 C 17_{25}, סתר hi. *hide* 4QpsMos^d 1.2_4.

קרא *happen* Jr 44_{23} (+ מִפְּנֵי אֲשֶׁר *because*), עשׂה *do* 1 S 28_{18} (+ כַּאֲשֶׁר *because*) Est 9_{19}, קדם pi. *do first* Jon 4_2, הלל htpo. *act madly* Jr 51_7, זנה *prostitute oneself* Ho 4_{13}, שׂכל hi. *prosper* Jr 10_{21}, נצר *keep* Ps 119_{129} (here and at Ps $45_{3.8}$ $119_{127.128}$ perh. עַל־כֵּן = *according to right, rightly*, i.e. כֵּן III), ישׁר pi. *keep precisely* or *declare just* Ps 119_{128}, משׁח *anoint* Ps 45_8, זבח *sacrifice* Ex 13_{15} Hb 1_{16}, מול ni. *be circumcised* CD 16_6, בנה *build* Ne 6_6, חצב *hew* Ho 6_5, זרע *sow* Is 17_{10}, hi. *conceive* 4QSD 7.2_{14} (כן כ[י תזריע]), נטע *plant* Is 17_{10}, מכר *sell* Gn 47_{22}, אכל *eat* Gn 32_{33}, *destroy* Is 24_6, נכה hi. *strike* Jr 5_6, פקד *visit*, i.e. punish Am 3_2.

ידה hi. *give thanks* 2 S 22_{50}‖Ps 18_{50} Ps 45_{18} Si 51_{12}, שׂמח *rejoice* Is 9_{16} Hb 1_{15}, ברך pi. *bless* Ex 20_{11} Ps 45_3, רחם pi. *pity* Is 27_{11}, כבד pi. *glorify* Is 24_{15} 25_3, יחל hi. *hope* Lm $3_{21.24}$, זכר *remember* Ps 42_7 (or em. עַל־כֹּל *above all*), שׁכח *forget* Ho 13_6, אהב *love* Ps 119_{127} Ca 1_3, מאס *reject* Jb 42_6, שׂנא *hate* Jr 12_8 Ps 119_{104}, ירא *fear* Ps 46_3, חלה *be anxious* Is 57_{10}, כלם ni. *be ashamed* Is 50_7, זחל *fear* Jb 32_6, בהל ni. *be dismayed* Jb 23_{15}.

קרא *call* Gn 11_9 16_{14} 19_{22} 21_{31} 25_{30} $29_{34.35}$ 30_6 31_{48} 33_{17} 50_{11} Ex 15_{23} Jos 7_{26} Jg 15_{19} 18_{12} 1 S 23_{28} 2 S 5_{20}‖1 C 14_{11} Est 9_{26} 1 C 11_7 2 C 20_{26}, אמר *say* Ex 5_{17} Lv 17_{12} Nm 18_{24} 21_{27} 1 S 19_{24} 2 S 5_8 Is 22_4 Jb 9_{22} 4QNarrC 1_{10}, ni. *be said* Gn 10_9 Nm 21_{14}, ענה *answer* Si 47_6, ירה hi. *teach* Ps 25_8, צוה pi. *command* Dt 5_{15} $15_{11.15}$ 19_7 $24_{18.22}$, לעע *be rash* Jb 6_3, צעק *cry out* Ex 5_8, המה *make a noise* Is 16_{11} Jr 31_{20} 48_{36}, אבל *mourn* Ho 4_3, בכה *weep* Is 16_9, ילל hi. *wail* Jr 48_{31} 4QpsEzek^c 5_4, רוע hi. *shout* Is 15_4 (or em. רעע *break*).

In nom. cl., עַל־כֵּן שֵׁם־הָעִיר בְּאֵר שֶׁבַע *therefore the name of the town was Beer-sheba* Gn 26_{33}, עַל־כֵּן רֹחַב־לַבַּיִת לְמָעְלָה *therefore, the breadth of the temple was upwards*, i.e. it became broader towards its top Ezk 41_7, עַל־כֵּן סְבִיבוֹתֶיךָ פַּחִים *therefore snares are around you* Jb 22_{10}, על כן לא מספר לתשועתו *therefore, there is no limit to his salvation* Si 39_{20}, על כן מקור מים *therefore my eye is a spring of water* 4QBark^f 1.1_3.

g. כִּי עַל־כֵּן (כִּי־עַל־כֵּן Gn 33_{10} Nm 10_{31} Jr 29_{28}) **because, seeing that, inasmuch as,** with verb, ראה *see* Gn 33_{10} Jg 6_{22}, מות *die* 2 S $18_{20(Qr)}$, ידע *know* Nm 10_{31}, רפה pi. *weaken* Jr 38_4, בוא *come* Gn 19_8, עבר *pass* Gn 18_5, שׁוב *go back* Nm 14_{43}, שׁלח *send* Jr 29_{28}, נתן *give* Gn 38_{26}.

h. אֲשֶׁר עַל־כֵּן **because**, with verb סור *depart* Jb 34_{27} (or em. עַל אֲשֶׁר *because*).*

Also 1Q36 14_3 4QD^c 6.3_{20} 4QTohA 1.3_1 4QAdmonPar 3.3_1 4QCreatB 1_2 (על כן) 4QpsEzek^a 5_2 (בכן) 36.2_5 (לכן) 4QapJoshua^a 3.2_5 ([כ]ן) 4QpsMos^d 3_3 (על כ[ן]; others על בנ[יהם] *for their sons*) 4QpsMos^e 2.1_2 4Q418

33$_4$ 122.17 4QNarrC 2$_1$ 4QpsHod^c 3$_5$ 5QfrProph 1$_5$.

כֵּן II 3.0.1 adj. **right, correct,** used predicatively, ... יָדַעְתִּי עֶבְרָתוֹ וְלֹא־כֵן בַּדָּיו לֹא־כֵן עָשׂוּ *I know ... his anger, and it is not just, boasts (that are) not true they have made* Jr 48$_{30}$ (or em. עֲבֹדָתוֹ וְלֹא־כֵן *his worship, and* his boasts *are not right* [כֵּן III]), מקצת דברינו כן *some of our practices are correct* 4QMMT C$_{30}$, כֵּן־הוּא *it is right* Gn 44$_{10}$.
⇒ כון *be upright*.

כֵּן III 10 n.m. **right** or **stability,** <SUBJ> עשׂה ni. *be done* Gn 34$_7$. <OBJ> עשׂה *do* Ec 8$_{10}$, בְּאָדָם מֵבִין יֹדֵעַ כֵּן יַאֲרִיךְ *with an intelligent (and) knowledgeable person its security will endure* Pr 28$_2$ (unless כֵּן I *thus,* or em. יִדְעָכוּן *they will be extinguished*), לֹא־כֵן בַּדָּיו לֹא־כֵן עָשׂוּ *his boasts are not right, (that which is) not right they have done* Jr 48$_{30}$ (if כֵּן without athnach), הוּא לֹא־כֵן יְדַמֶּה *he plans (that which is) not right* Is 10$_7$. <PREP> perh. עַל־כֵּן *according to right* as adverb, *rightly* Ps 45$_{3.8}$ 119$_{127.128.129}$ (unless all five עַל־כֵּן *therefore*).*

כֵּן IV 13 n.m. **stand**—כֶּן־; sf. כַּנּוֹ—usu. **stand, base** for basin (כִּיּוֹר) of tabernacle, and other objects (e.g.1 K 7$_{29.31}$); **platform, pedestal** (Am 5$_{26}$ [if em.]) or **(in) place (of)** (Dn 11$_{7.38}$, if not כֵּן VI *position*); **socket** of mast (תֹּרֶן, Is 33$_{23}$); **stock** of vine (גֶּפֶן, Ps 80$_{16}$ [if em.]), of king of south (Dn 11$_7$ [if em.]).

<NOM CL> כַּנּוֹ נְחֹשֶׁת *its base was bronze* Ex 30$_{18}$, וְעַל־הַשְּׁלַבִּים כֵּן מִמָּעַל perh. *and above the frame was a stand, above* 1 K 7$_{29}$ (or em. כֵּן מִמַּעַל *a stand; above;* but perh. כֵּן I *thus*). <OBJ> בוא hi. *bring* Ex 39$_{39}$, עשׂה *make* Ex 31$_9$ 35$_{16}$ 38$_8$ (+ נְחֹשֶׁת *in bronze*), חזק pi. *strengthen,* i.e. hold steady Is 33$_{23}$, משׁח *anoint* Ex 30$_{28}$ 40$_{11}$ Lv 8$_{11}$, נטע *plant* Ps 80$_{16}$ (if em. כַּנָּה *a stock* to כַּנָּהּ *its stock*), נשׂא *raise* Am 5$_{26}$ (if em. כִּיּוּן *Kivvun* to כֵּן *pedestal of* your images).

<CSTR> כֶּן־תָּרְנָם *socket of their mast* Is 33$_{23}$, מַעֲשֵׂה־כֵן *work of a stand,* i.e. *after the fashion of a stand* 1 K 7$_{31}$, כֵּן צַלְמֵיכֶם *the pedestal of your images* Am 5$_{26}$ (if em.). <PREP> עַל *upon,* + כבד pi. *honour* god Dn 11$_{38}$ (unless כֵּן VI *place*). <COLL> וְעָמַד מִנֵּצֶר שָׁרָשֶׁיהָ כַּנּוֹ *and an offshoot of her roots will stand on his* (king of south's) *platform* or *in his place* Dn 11$_7$ (or em. וְעָמַד to יַעֲמֹד *he will arise/stand* and/or מִנֵּצֶר שָׁרָשֶׁיהָ to נֵצֶר מִשָּׁרָשֶׁיהָ in same sense).

Also CD 7$_{17}$ (כיניי הצלמים appar. error for immediately following כיון הצלמים *Kivvun of the images*).*

כֵּן V 7.1.1 n.[m.] perh. **louse**—כֵּן; pl. כִּנִּים (כִּנָּם), perh. כִּנָּם, Si כִּנִּיוּם—**louse, maggot, gnat, mosquito,** perh. collective at Is 51$_6$, <SUBJ> היה *be* Ex 8$_{13}$ (כִּנָּם perh. *vermin*) 8$_{13.14}$ (כִּנָּם), בוא *come* Ps 105$_{31}$ (or em. hi. *bring* lice; + עָרֹב *swarm*). <NOM CL> כנים בכול גבול[ם] *lice were throughout all their borders* 4QParGenEx 3$_8$ (+ צְפַרְדֵּעַ *frog,* עָרֹב *swarm*). <OBJ> יצא hi. *take out* Ex 8$_{14}$, נחל *inherit* Si 10$_{11}$ (|| רֶמֶשׂ *insects,* תּוֹלֵעָה *worm*). <PREP> לְ *as,* + היה *be* Ex 8$_{12}$; כְּ *as,* + מות *die* Is 51$_6$ (unless כְּמוֹ־כֵן = *like thus,* i.e. likewise; 1QIsa^b כמוכן perh. *as locusts*). <SYN> רֶמֶשׂ *insects,* תּוֹלֵעָה *worm.*

[כֵּן] VI 5 n.[m.] **position**—sf. כַּנּוֹ, כַּנֶּךָ, כַּנִּי—**position, place, status, office,** <PREP> עַל *on, (on)to, in,* + שׁוב hi. *bring back,* i.e. restore Gn 40$_{13}$ 41$_{13}$, עמד *stand* Dn 11$_{20.21}$, כבד pi. *honour* god Dn 11$_{38}$ (but perh. כֵּן IV, god placed on a *stand*).*

[כַּנָּא] 0.0.1 n.[f.] **base**—Q כנא—במערא של הכנא של הרגם perh. *in the rock of the base of the stoning ground* 3QTr 6$_7$ (others הפנא של הרגב *the corner of the watchtower*).

* **[כֶּנֶד]** **jug,** כֹּנֵס כֶּנֶד מֵי הַיָּם נֹתֵן בְּאוֹצָרוֹת תְּהוֹמוֹת *gathering (into) a jug the waters of the sea, placing the deeps into storehouses* Ps 33$_7$ (if em. כַּנֵּד *like a heap;* or em. כְּנֹאד *like a flask*).

כנה 4.3.1 vb. **name—Pi.** 4.3 Pf. Si כיניתה; impf. יְכַנֶּה, אֲכַנֶּה (אֲכַנְּךָ); + waw Si ויכנוהו, ויכנהו—**grant title, give honorary name,** <SUBJ> '' *Y.* Is 45$_4$ Si 36$_{17}$ 44$_{23(Bmg)}$ (B כון pol. *establish*), Elihu Jb 32$_{21.22}$, בַּת *daughter* Si 47$_6$, זֶה *this one* Is 44$_5$ (or em. pu.). <OBJ> Israel Si 36$_{17}$ 44$_{23(Bmg)}$, Cyrus Is 45$_4$, David Si 47$_6$. <PREP> בְּ of instrument, *by (means of), with,* + שֵׁם *name* Is 44$_5$, בְּרָכָה *blessing* Si 44$_{23(B)}$ 47$_6$, בְּכוֹר *firstborn* Si 44$_{23(Bmg)}$; אֶל *to,* + אָדָם *human being* Jb 32$_{21}$. <COLL> ישראל בכור כיניתה *you have titled Israel the firstborn* Si 36$_{17}$.

Pu. 1.0.1 Pf. Q כונו; impf. יְכֻנֶּה—**be named,** <SUBJ> זֶה *this one* Is 44$_5$. <PREP> בְּ of instrument, *by (means of), with,* + שֵׁם *name* Is 44$_5$ 4QNetin 1$_2$ ([בש]מותיהם).*

כַּנָּה 1 n.f. **stock** of vine, <OBJ> נטע *plant* Ps 80$_{16}$ (or em. וְכַנָּה *and a stock* to וְכַנָּהּ *and its stock,* i.e. כֵּן IV, or וְגַנָּה *and a garden* or וְכוֹנְנָהּ *and restore it*).*

כַּנֵּה 1 pl.n. **Canneh,** appar. in Northern Mesopotamia, <SUBJ> רכל *conduct business,* i.e. trade Ezk 27$_{23}$.

כִּנּוֹר 42 n.m. **lyre**—cstr. Q כנור; sf. כִּנֹּרִי; pl. כִּנֹּרוֹת (כִּנּוֹרוֹת); sf. כִּנֹּרֹתֵינוּ, כִּנּוֹרַיִךְ—**lyre, harp.**

<SUBJ> היה *be* Is 5$_{12}$ (|| נֵבֶל *harp,* תֹּף *tambourine,* חָלִיל *flute*) Jb 30$_{31}$, עור *be aroused* Ps 57$_9$ 108$_3$ (both || נֵבֶל). <NOM CL> לִפְנֵיהֶם נֵבֶל וְתֹף וְחָלִיל וְכִנּוֹר *before them were harp and tambourine and flute and lyre* 1 S 10$_5$, כנור נבלי לתכון קודשו *my lyre (and) my harp are to the pattern of his holiness* 1QS 10$_9$. <OBJ> עשׂה *make* 1 K 10$_{12}$||2 C 9$_{11}$ (both || נֵבֶל) 11QPs[a] 28$_4$ (|| עוּגָב *pipe*), תלה *hang* Ps 137$_2$, לקח *take* 1 S 16$_{23}$ Is 23$_{16}$, תפשׂ *take hold of,* i.e. play Gn 4$_{21}$, נתן *give,* i.e. play Ps 81$_3$ (|| תֹּף).

<CSTR> כנור ישועות *lyre of salvation* 1QH 11$_{23}$ (|| נֵבֶל *harp*) 4QShir[b] 10$_8$; מְשׂוֹשׂ כִּנּוֹר *joy,* i.e. joyful sound, *of the lyre* Is 24$_8$, קוֹל כִּנּוֹרַיִךְ *voice,* i.e. sound, *of your lyres* Ezk 26$_{13}$. <APP> כְּלִי *musical instrument* 1 C 15$_{16}$, תֹּף *tambourine* Ps 149$_3$ Jb 21$_{12}$, נֵבֶל *harp* Ps 150$_3$ 1 C 15$_{28}$, מְצִלְתַּיִם *cymbal* 1 C 25$_6$ 2 C 5$_{12}$. <ADJ> נָעִים *pleasant* Ps 81$_3$.

<PREP> בְּ of instrument, accompaniment, *by (means of), with* 4QpIsa[c] 25$_3$ ([בכנו]רות; + תֹּף *tambourine*), + נשׂא *raise* song Jb 21$_{12(mss)}$, שׂחק pi. *make merry* 2 S 6$_5$ (|| תֹּף, נֵבֶל, מְנַעַנְעִים *sistrum,* צֶלְצְלִים *cymbals*), ידה hi. *praise* Ps 33$_2$ 43$_4$, הלל pi. *praise* Ps 150$_3$, זמר pi. *sing (praise)* Ps 71$_{22}$ 98$_5$ 147$_7$ 149$_3$ 1QH 11$_{23}$, שׁיר pol. *continually sing* 1 C 15$_{16}$, המה *make noisy* 1QH 5$_{30}$, הגה *groan* 1QH 11$_{22}$.

בְּ of accompaniment, *with, in* Ps 98$_5$ Ne 12$_{27}$ 1 C 15$_{21}$ 16$_5$ 25$_6$ 2 C 5$_{12}$, + היה *be* Is 30$_{32}$, בוא *come* 2 C 20$_{28}$ (|| נֵבֶל, חֲצוֹצְרָה *trumpet*), עלה hi. *bring up* 1 C 15$_{28}$, עמד hi. *position* 2 C 29$_{25}$ (|| נֵבֶל, מְצִלְתַּיִם *cymbal*), שׂחק pi. *make merry* 1 C 13$_8$, נגד hi. *declare* Ps 92$_4$, נבא ni. *prophesy* 1 C 25$_{1.3}$, שׁלח pi. *send away* Gn 31$_{27}$ (|| תֹּף), פתח *open* Ps 49$_5$ 4QShir[b] 10$_8$ ([יפת]חו); introducing object, + נגן pi. *play stringed instrument* 1 S 16$_{16}$.

כְּ *as* Jb 21$_{12}$, + המה *murmur* Is 16$_{11}$.

<SYN> תֹּף *tambourine,* נֵבֶל *harp,* חָלִיל *flute,* עוּגָב *pipe,* מְנַעַנְעִים *sistrum,* צֶלְצְלִים *cymbals,* מְצִלְתַּיִם *cymbals,* חֲצוֹצְרָה *trumpet.**

כָּנְיָהוּ 3.0.0.2 pr.n.m. **Coniah, 1.** appar. ident. with Jehoiachin, king of Judah in Jeremiah's time, taken captive to Babylon Jr 22$_{24.28}$ 37$_1$. **2.** Lachish ost. 3$_{15}$. **3.** Arad ost. 49$_1$.

1. <SUBJ> היה *be* Jr 22$_{24}$. <APP> אִישׁ *man* Jr 22$_{28}$, בֵּן *son* Jr 22$_{24}$ 37$_1$, מֶלֶךְ *king* Jr 22$_{24}$. <PREP> תַּחַת *instead of,* + מלך *rule* Jr 37$_1$.

2. <SUBJ> ירד *go down* Lachish ost. 3$_{15}$. <APP> בֵּן *son* Lachish ost. 3$_{15}$.

3. <CSTR> בני כניהו *sons of Coniah* Arad ost. 49$_1$.

[כִּנִּיּוֹם], see כֵּן V *louse.*

כַּנְלֹתְךָ, see נלה *obtain.*

כִּנָּם 2 n.[m.] **vermin** (unless simply pl. of כֵּן IV *louse*), <SUBJ> היה *be* Ex 8$_{13.14}$.

כְּנָנִי 1 pr.n.m. **Chenani,** Levite, <SUBJ> קום *arise* Ne 9$_4$, זעק *cry out* 9$_4$. <APP> לֵוִי *Levite* Ne 9$_4$.

כְּנַנְיָה 2 pr.n.m. **Chenaniah**—כְּנַנְיָהוּ 1 C 15$_{22}$—leader of Levite musicians, <SUBJ> כרבל pu. *be wrapped* 1 C 15$_{27}$, בין hi. *understand* 1 C 15$_{22}$, יסר *direct* 1 C 15$_{22}$. <APP> שַׂר *officer* 1 C 15$_{22.27}$.

כְּנַנְיָהוּ 1 pr.n.m. **Chenaniah, 1.** = כְּנַנְיָה. **2.** Levite administrator 1 C 26$_{29}$. <NOM CL> כְּנַנְיָהוּ וּבָנָיו לַמְּלָאכָה *Chenaniah and his sons were appointed for the work* 1 C 26$_{29}$.

כָּנַנְיָהוּ 3 pr.n.m. **Conaniah**—כּוֹנַנְיָהוּ—**1.** Levite collector of tithes in Hezekiah's time 2 C 31$_{12.13}$. **2.** Levite family head in Josiah's time 2 C 35$_9$. <SUBJ> רום hi. *raise,* i.e. provide 2 C 35$_9$. <NOM CL> נָגִיד כָּנַנְיָהוּ הַלֵּוִי *the leader* *was Conaniah the Levite* 2 C 31₁₂. <CSTR> יַד כּוֹנַנְיָהוּ *hand of Conaniah*, i.e. one who assisted Conaniah 2 C 31₁₃. <ADJ> לֵוִי *Levite* 2 C 31₁₂.

כנס 11.0.4 vb. **gather—Qal** 7.0.4 Pf. כָּנַסְתִּי; impv. Q כנס; ptc. כֹּנֵס, Q כונסים; inf. כְּנוֹס—**gather, collect,** <SUBJ> ״ Y. Ps 33₇, Eliezer, son of Samuel 5/6Ḥev 45 fr. 2₂, Koheleth Ec 2₈, Mordecai Est 4₁₆, אִישׁ *man* Ne 12₄₄, perh. אֲשֶׁר *one who* 4QOrd^a 1.2₄.₄ ([יכנס]); subj. not specified, Ec 2₂₆ (|| אסף *gather*) 3₅ 1 C 22₂ 11QT 34₇ (+ היה *be*). <OBJ> Jew Est 4₁₆, גֵּר *sojourner* 1 C 22₂, כֶּסֶף *silver* Ec 2₈, זָהָב *gold* Ec 2₈, מְנָת *portion* Ne 12₄₄, דָּם *blood* 11QT 34₇ ([הדם]), מַיִם *waters* Ps 33₇, כֹּל *all* 5/6 Ḥev 45 fr. 2₂ (כל מהפירות *all of the fruit*).

<PREP> לְ of benefit, *to, for,* + Koheleth Ec 2₈, כֹּהֵן *priest* Ne 12₄₄, לֵוִי *Levite* Ne 12₄₄, נֶפֶשׁ *soul*, i.e. self 5/6 Ḥev 45 fr. 2₂, בַּיִת *household* 4QOrd^a 1.2₄ (לבןיתו לוא [יכנס]), אֲשֶׁר *one who* 4QOrd^a 1.2₄; בְּ of place, *in(to),* + נִשְׁכָּה *chamber* Ne 12₄₄, מִזְרָק *dish* 11QT 34₇.

Also 4QpIsa^c 55₁. <SYN> אסף *gather*.

Pi. 3 Pf. כִּנַּסְתִּי (כִּנַּסְתִּים); impf. יְכַנֵּס—**gather, assemble,** <SUBJ> ״ Y. Ezk 22₂₁ 39₂₈ Ps 147₂. <OBJ> בַּיִת *house* of Israel Ezk 22₂₁ 39₂₈, נדח ni. ptc. as noun, *outcast* Ps 147₂. <PREP> עַל *to,* + אֲדָמָה *land* Ezk 39₂₈.

Htp. 1 Inf. הִתְכַּנֵּס—**wrap oneself,** <SUBJ> subj. not specified, Is 28₂₀.

→ מִכְנָס *trousers*, כְּנֶסֶת *congregation*.

[כְּנֶסֶת] 0.0.2 n.f. **congregation**—cstr. Q כנסת; sf. Q כנסתם—**congregation, assembly,** <SUBJ> פרד ni. *be dispersed* 4QpNah 3.3₇ (+ עֵצָה *council*). <NOM CL> היא כנסת *it is the assembly of* 4QCommGenA 5₆. <CSTR> כנסת אנשי *assembly of the men of* 4QCommGenA 5₆.

→ כנס *gather*.

כנע 36.4.15 vb. **be humble—Ni.** 25.1.5 Pf. נִכְנַע, נִכְנְעוּ; impf. יִכָּנַע, Q יכנעו; + waw וַיִּכָּנַע, 3fs וַתִּכָּנַע, 2ms וַתִּכָּנַע, וַיִּכָּנְעוּ; impv. Si היכנע, ptc. Q נוכנעים; inf. Q הכנע (Q הכנעו, הִכָּנְעוֹ)—**1. be humble(d), be subdued, humble oneself,** <SUBJ> עַם *people* Ps 106₄₂ 2 C 7₁₄, Midian Jg 8₂₈, Moab Jg 3₃₀, Philistines 1 S 7₁₃ 1 C 20₄, Ahab 1 K 21₂₉.₂₉, Amon 2 C 33₂₃, Hezekiah 2 C 32₂₆.₂₆, Josiah 2 K 22₁₉||2 C 34₂₇ 2 C 34₂₇, Manasseh 2 C 33₁₂.₁₉.₂₃, Rehoboam 2 C 12₁₂, Zedekiah 2 C 36₁₂, אִישׁ *man* 2 C 30₁₁, בֵּן *son* Si 4₂₅, בְּנֵי עַמּוֹן *Ammonites* Jg 11₃₃, בְּנֵי־יִשְׂרָאֵל *Israelites* 2 C 13₁₈, מֶלֶךְ *king* 2 C 12₆.₇.₇, שַׂר *prince* 2 C 12₆.₇.₇, יֹשֵׁב *inhabitant* 2 C 32₂₆, לֵבָב *heart* Lv 26₄₁, לֵב *heart* 4QDibHam^a 1.6₅, נֶפֶשׁ *soul* 4QapPs^b 45₂, רִשְׁעָה *wickedness* 1QM 1₆.

<PREP> בְּ of accompaniment, *in, with,* + גֹּבַהּ *pride* 2 C 32₂₆; of time, *in, on,* + יוֹם *day* Jg 3₃₀, עֵת *time* 2 C 13₁₈; לְאֵין *without (there being),* + שְׁאֵרִית *remnant* 1QM 1₆; אֶל *to,* + אֱלֹהִים *God* Si 4₂₅; לִפְנֵי *before,* + בְּנֵי־יִשְׂרָאֵל *Israelites* Jg 8₂₈; מִלִּפְנֵי *before,* + ״ *Y.* 1 K 21₂₉ 2 C 33₂₃ 34₂₇, אֱלֹהִים *God* 2 C 34₂₇, Jeremiah 2 C 36₁₂; מִפְּנֵי *before,* + ״ Y. 1 K 21₂₉ 2 K 22₁₉, אֱלֹהִים *God* 4QapPs^b 45₂ ([מלפנ]יך), בְּנֵי יִשְׂרָאֵל *Israelites* Jg 11₃₃; תַּחַת *under,* + יַד *hand* Jg 3₃₀ Ps 106₄₂.

2. ptc. as noun, **subdued one, oppressed one,** <PREP> לְ of benefit, *to, for* 1QS 10₂₆. Also 4QapPs^b 39₁ 75₃.

Hi. 11.3.10 Pf. הִכְנַעְתִּי, הִכְנִיעַ; impf. יַכְנִיעֵם (Q יכניענו), אַכְנִיעַ, תַּכְנִיעַ; + waw וַיַּכְנַע (וַיַּכְנִיעֵם), 2ms וַתַּכְנַע; impv. Si הכניע (הַכְנִיעֵהוּ); ptc. Q מכנעת; inf. Q הכניע (Q הכניעם)—**make humble, subdue,** <SUBJ> ״ *Y.* Dt 9₃ Jg 4₂₃(ms) Is 25₅ Ps 81₁₅ Ne 9₂₄ 1 C 17₁₀ 2 C 28₁₉ Si 46₁₈, אֱלֹהִים *God* Dt 9₃ Jg 4₂₃ Is 25₅ Ps 81₁₅ Si 33₉, אֵל *God* 1QM 17₅ (|| שפל hi. *abase*) 4QM^a 11.2₁₆, עֶלְיוֹן *Most High* Ps 107₁₂, David 2 S 8₁||1 C 18₁ Si 47₇ 1QM 11₃ (הכנ[י]ע), אִישׁ *man* 1QSa 1₂₁, Job Jb 40₁₂, יָד *hand* 1QM 1₁₄, worshipper 4QShir^b 35₇, דֶּגֶל *battalion* 1QM 6₅.

<OBJ> גּוֹי *nation* Dt 9₃ 1QSa 1₂₁, Philistines 2 S 8₁||1 C 18₁ 1QM 11₃ (הכנ[י]ע), Judah 2 C 28₁₉, Jabin Jg 4₂₃, יֹשֵׁב *inhabitant* Ne 9₂₄, אוֹיֵב *enemy* Ps 81₁₅ 1 C 17₁₀ 4QM^a 1₈ ([להכ]ניע [אויב]), צַר *adversary* Si 33₉ 47₇, גֵּאֶה *proud one* Jb 40₁₂, לֵב *heart* Ps 107₁₂, רוּחַ *spirit* 4QShir^b 35₇, נְצִיב *garrison* Si 46₁₈, מַעֲרָכָה *battle line* 1QM 6₅, שָׁאוֹן *uproar* of strangers Is 25₅.

<PREP> בְּ of time, *in, on,* + יוֹם *day* Jg 4₂₃; of instrument, *by (means of),* + שֵׁם *name* 1QM 11₃ (הכנ[י]ע), עָמָל *hardship* Ps 107₁₂; מִן of direction, *from,* + סָבִיב *all around* Si 47₇; *by (means of),* + יִרְאָה *fear* 4QShir^b 35₇ ([מירא]תו); לִפְנֵי *before,* + Israel Dt 9₃, אָב *father* of Israel Ne 9₂₄, בְּנֵי יִשְׂרָאֵל *Israelites* Jg 4₂₃.

<COLL> כנע hi. + noun used adverbially, פַּעַם *time* 1QM 11_{3} (הכנ[י]ע), perh. יוֹם *day* 4QM^{a} 11.2_{16}. Also 1QH fr. 9_{6} 4QShir^{b} 48.2_{3} 145_{3} ([להכנ]יע) 6QHymn 1_{6} ([להכני]ע). <SYN> שׁפל hi. *abase.**

[כִּנְעָה] $_{1}$ n.f. **bundle**—sf. כִּנְעָתֵךְ—<OBJ> אסף *gather,* i.e. pick up Jr 10_{17}.

כְּנַעַן I $_{9.0.1}$ pr.n.m. **Canaan**—כְּנָעַן—son of Ham, Gn $9_{18.22.25.26.27}$ $10_{6.15}$ 1 C $1_{8.13}$. <SUBJ> היה *be* Gn $9_{26.27}$, ילד *be father* Gn 10_{15}||1 C 1_{13}, ארר pass. *be cursed* Gn 9_{25}=4Q CommGenA 2_{6}. <NOM CL> בְּנֵי חָם כּוּשׁ וּמִצְרַיִם וּפוּט וּכְנָעַן *the sons of Ham were Cush and Egypt and Put and Canaan* Gn 10_{6}||1 C 1_{8}. <CSTR> אֲבִי כְנָעַן *father of Canaan* Gn $9_{18.22}$.*

כְּנַעַן II $_{84.0.5}$ pl.n. **Canaan,** land of Palestine, inhabited by Canaanites and others including Israelites, <OBJ> אבד hi. *destroy* Zp 2_{5}.

<CSTR> עֲצַבֵּי כְנָעַן *idols of Canaan* Ps 106_{38}, אֶרֶץ־כְּנַעַן *land of Canaan* Gn 11_{31} $12_{5.5}$ (all אַרְצָה *to the land of*) Gn 13_{12} 16_{3} 17_{8} $23_{2.19}$ 31_{18} (אַרְצָה) 33_{18} 35_{6} $36_{5.6}$ 37_{1} $42_{5.7.13.29}$ (אַרְצָה) 42_{32} 44_{8} 45_{17} (אַרְצָה) 45_{25} $46_{6.12.31}$ $47_{1.4.13.14.15}$ $48_{3.7}$ 49_{30} $50_{5.13}$ (אַרְצָה) Ex 6_{4} 16_{35} Lv 14_{34} 18_{3} 25_{38} Nm $13_{2.17}$ 26_{19} $32_{30.32}$ (Seb אַרְצָה) $33_{40.51}$ 34_{2} (הָאָרֶץ כְּנַעַן) 34_{2} (+ לִגְבֻלֹתֶיהָ *to the full extent of its boundaries*) 34_{29} 35_{10} (אַרְצָה) 35_{14} Dt 32_{49} Jos 5_{12} 14_{1} 21_{2} $22_{9.10.11.32}$ 24_{3} Jg 21_{12} Ezk 16_{29} 17_{4} Ps 105_{11}||1 C 16_{18} 4QJub^{h} 36_{20} 4QpsJub^{b} 3_{5} ([כנע]ן) 4QCommGenA 2_{10} 4QapJoshua^{b} 12_{6}, מַמְלְכוֹת כְּנָעַן *kingdoms of Canaan* Ps 135_{11}, עַם כְּנַעַן *people of Canaan,* i.e. merchants Zp 1_{11}, בְּנוֹת כְּנָעַן *daughters of Canaan* Gn $28_{1.6.8}$ 36_{2}, מֶלֶךְ־כְּנַעַן *king of Canaan* Jg $4_{2.23.24.24}$, מַלְכֵי כְנַעַן *kings of Canaan* Jg 5_{19}, יֹשְׁבֵי כְּנָעַן *inhabitants of Canaan* Ex 15_{15}, מִלְחֲמוֹת כְּנָעַן *wars of Canaan* Jg 3_{1}, שְׂפַת כְּנַעַן *lip of,* i.e. language of, *Canaan* Is 19_{18}.

<APP> אֶרֶץ *land* Zp 2_{5}. <PREP> אֶל *to,* i.e. concerning, + צוה pi. *command* Is 23_{11}; עַל *against* Zp 2_{5}.

Also 4QCommGenA 2_{13}.*

⇒ כְּנַעֲנִי *Canaanite.*

כְּנַעַן III $_{1}$ n.m. **merchant,** only in Ho 12_{8} (cf. עַם כְּנַעַן *people of Canaan,* i.e. merchants Zp 1_{11}), <COLL> כְּנַעַן בְּיָדוֹ מֹאזְנֵי מִרְמָה *a trader, in whose hands are false balances* Ho 12_{8}.

[כִּנְעָן] $_{1}$ n.m. **merchant**—pl. sf. כִּנְעָנֶיהָ—<NOM CL> כִּנְעָנֶיהָ נִכְבַּדֵּי־אָרֶץ *her traders were the honourable ones of the earth* Is 23_{8}.

⇒ כְּנַעַן *Canaan.*

כְּנַעֲנָה $_{5}$ pr.n.m. **Chenanah, 1.** Benjaminite warrior, son of Bilhan, <NOM CL> בְּנֵי בִלְהָן יְעוּשׁ וּבִנְיָמִן וְאֵהוּד וּכְנַעֲנָה *the sons of Bilhan were Jeush and Benjamin and Ehud and Chenaanah* 1 C $7_{10(Qr)}$.

2. father of the prophet Zedekiah, <CSTR> בֶּן־כְּנַעֲנָה *son of Chenaanah* 1 K $22_{11.24}$||2 C $18_{10.23}$.

כְּנַעֲנִי I $_{73.0.3}$ gent. **Canaanite**—f.s. כְּנַעֲנִית; m.pl. כְּנַעֲנִים—**1.** collective sing. (rarely plur.) noun, **Canaanites,** <SUBJ> היה *be* Jg 1_{30} 3_{3}, ראה *see* Gn 50_{11}, שׁמע *hear* Jos 7_{9} 9_{1}, ישׁב *dwell* Gn 13_{7} Nm 13_{29} $14_{25.45}$ Jos $16_{10.10}$||Jg $1_{29.29}$ Jos 17_{12}||Jg 1_{27} Jos 17_{16} Jg $1_{9.10.17.30}$ 3_{3} 1 K 9_{16}, ירד *go down* Nm 14_{45}, לחם ni. *fight* Jos 24_{11}, יאל hi. *resolve* Jos 17_{12}||Jg 1_{27}, חטא hi. *cause to sin* 4QSel^{a} 8.2_{9} ([הכנענ]י).

<NOM CL> הַכְּנַעֲנִי שָׁם *the Canaanites were there* Nm 14_{43}, הַכְּנַעֲנִי אָז בָּאָרֶץ *the Canaanites were then in the land* Gn 12_{6}, האמורי שם והכנענ[י] *the Amorites are there and the Cananites* 4QSel^{a} 8.2_{9}.

<OBJ> נתן *give* Gn 15_{21} Nm 21_{3} Jos 17_{13} 24_{11} Jg 1_{4} Ne 9_{24}, שׂים *place* Jg 1_{28}, גרשׁ *banish* Ex 34_{11} 11QT 2_{2} ([גורש] הכנעני ...), pi. *drive out* Ex 23_{28} 33_{2}, נשׁל *clear away* Dt 7_{1}, ירשׁ *possess* Ob$_{20}$ (if em. אֲשֶׁר *who* to יִרְשׁוּ *they shall possess*), hi. *drive out* Jos 3_{10} 16_{10}||Jg 1_{29} Jos 17_{18}, כנע hi. *subdue* Ne 9_{24}, נכה hi. *strike* Jg $1_{4.5.17}$, הרג *slay* 1 K 9_{16}, חרם hi. *destroy* Nm 21_{3} Dt 20_{17}=11QT 62_{14}.

<CSTR> אֶרֶץ הַכְּנַעֲנִי *land of the Canaanites* Ex 3_{17} $13_{5.11}$ Dt 1_{7} 11_{30} Jos 13_{4} Ezk 16_{3} Ne 9_{8}, גְּבוּל *border of* Gn 10_{19}, עָרֵי *cities of* 2 S 24_{7}, מְקוֹם *place of* Ex 3_{8}, מַלְכֵי *kings of* Jos 5_{1}, בְּנוֹת *daughters of* Gn $24_{3.37}$, מִשְׁפְּחוֹת *families of* Gn 10_{18}, כָּל־הַכְּנַעֲנִי *all the Canaanites* Jos 17_{16} Jg 3_{3}.

<APP> אֶרֶץ *land* Gn 15_{21}, גּוֹי *nation* Dt 7_{1}, Amorite Ex 23_{23}, מֶלֶךְ *king* Jos 9_{1} 11_{3}, בַּעַל *lord* Jos 24_{11}, יֹשֵׁב *inhabitant* Gn 50_{11} Ne 9_{24}, בָּהָר וּבַשְּׁפֵלָה וּבָעֲרָבָה וּבָאֲשֵׁדוֹת

הַכְּנַעֲנִי ... וּבַמִּדְבָּר וּבַנֶּגֶב *in the hill country, and in the lowland, and in the Arabah, and on the slopes, and in the steppe country and in the Negeb ... the (land of) the Canaanites* Jos 12$_{8}$.

<PREP> לְ of possession, *of, (belonging) to* Ezr 9$_{1}$; *as*, + חשׁב ni. *be reckoned* Jos 13$_{3}$; בְּ of instrument, *by (means of)*, + נסה pi. *test* Jg 3$_{3}$; of accompaniment, *with, in* Jos 17$_{16}$; *against*, + לחם ni. *fight* Jg 1$_{3.9}$; *to*, + באשׁ hi. *make odious* Gn 34$_{30}$; אֶל *to*, + בוא hi. *bring* Ex 23$_{23}$, הלך *go* Jg 1$_{10}$, עלה *go up* Jg 1$_{1}$, שׁלח *send* Jos 11$_{3}$; בְּקֶרֶב *among*, + ישׁב *dwell* Jg 1$_{32.33}$ 3$_{5}$.

2. sing. noun, an individual **Canaanite, <SUBJ>** שׁמע *hear* Nm 21$_{1}$ 33$_{40}$, ישׁב *dwell* Nm 21$_{1}$ 33$_{40}$. **<CSTR>** בֶּן־הַכְּנַעֲנִית *the son of a Canaanite (woman)* Gn 46$_{10}$ Ex 6$_{15}$. **<APP>** Bath-shua 1 C 2$_{3}$. **<PREP>** מִן of agent, *by (means of)*, + ילד ni. *be born* 1 C 2$_{3}$.

3. attributive adj., **Canaanite,** + אִישׁ *man* Gn 38$_{2}$.

Also 4QapMos[c] 1.1$_{8}$.*

→ כְּנַעַן II *Canaan.*

כְּנַעֲנִי II 3 n.m. **merchant**—pl. כְּנַעֲנִים—**<SUBJ>** היה *be* Zc 14$_{21}$. **<PREP>** לְ of direction, *to*, + נתן *give* Pr 31$_{24}$, בֵּין *between*, + חצה *divide* Jb 40$_{30}$.

→ כְּנַעַן III *merchant.*

כנף 1 vb. **hide—Ni.** 1 Impf. יִכָּנֵף—**hide oneself, <SUBJ>** מוֹרֶה *teacher* Is 30$_{20}$.

→ כָּנָף *wing.*

כָּנָף 109.1.19 n.f. **wing**—cstr. כְּנַף; sf. כְּנָפִי, כְּנָפֶךָ; du. כְּנָפַיִם (כְּנָפָיִם); pl. cstr. כַּנְפֵי, כַּנְפוֹת; sf. כְּנָפֶיךָ, כְּנָפַיִךְ, כְּנָפָיו, כַּנְפֵיהֶם, כְּנָפֶיהָ—**wing** of bird (e.g. Gn 1$_{21}$ Ex 19$_{4}$ Dt 32$_{11}$ Is 10$_{14}$ Ps 148$_{10}$ 4QShir[b] 97$_{1}$), insect (e.g. Lv 11$_{20}$ Dt 14$_{19}$ 11QT 48$_{5}$), cherubim (e.g. 1 K 6$_{24}$ Ezk 1$_{6}$ 2 C 3$_{11}$), seraphim (Is 6$_{2.2}$), wind (e.g. 2 S 22$_{11}$||Ps 18$_{11}$), dawn (Ps 139$_{9}$), etc., **skirt, hem, edge** of garment* (e.g. 1 S 15$_{27}$ Dt 22$_{12}$ Jr 2$_{34}$ Ezk 5$_{3}$ Ru 3$_{9}$ 4QWiles 1$_{4}$ 4QJub[f] 33$_{12}$), **flank** of army (1QM 9$_{11}$), **corner, end** of world (Is 11$_{12}$ 24$_{16}$ Ezk 7$_{2}$ Jb 37$_{3}$ 38$_{13}$ Dn 9$_{27}$), **winged creature** (Gn 7$_{14}$), **<SUBJ>** דבק *be joined* 2 C 3$_{12}$, פרד pass. *be outspread* Ezk 1$_{11}$, חפה ni. *be covered* Ps 68$_{14}$, עלס ni. *appear glad* Jb 39$_{13}$, שׁכן *dwell*, i.e. nest Ezk 17$_{23}$, בוא *come* Gn 7$_{14}$, יצא *go out* perh. 1QM 9$_{11}$, נגע *touch* 1 K 6$_{27.27.27}$, hi. *touch* 2 C 3$_{11.11.12}$, חבר *join* Ezk 1$_{9}$, פרשׂ *spread out* 2 C 3$_{13}$, רום *be raised* 4QShirShabb[f] 20.2$_{8}$, מות *die* 4QAdmon 1.1$_{6}$ (וי]מ[ת).

<NOM CL> חָמֵשׁ אַמּוֹת כְּנַף הַכְּרוּב *five cubits was (the length of) the wing of the cherub* 1 K 6$_{24.24}$, כַּנְפֵיהֶם יְשָׁרוֹת *their wings were straight*, i.e. stretched out Ezk 1$_{23}$, כַּנְפֵיהֶם ... מְלֵאִים עֵינַיִם *their wings were ... full of eyes* Ezk 10$_{12}$.

אַרְבַּע כְּנָפַיִם לְאֶחָד *four wings were to one of them*, i.e. each had four wings Ezk 10$_{21}$, שֵׁשׁ כְּנָפַיִם לְאֶחָד *each had six wings* Is 6$_{2}$, אַרְבַּע כְּנָפַיִם לְאַחַת לָהֶם *each had four wings* Ezk 1$_{6}$, כַּנְפֵיהֶם לְאַרְבַּעְתָּם *their wings were to the four of them*, i.e. all four of them had wings Ezk 1$_{8}$, לָהֵנָּה כְנָפַיִם *to them were wings*, i.e. they had wings Zc 5$_{9}$, כְּנָפַיִם כְּכַנְפֵי הַחֲסִידָה *the wings were as the wings of the stork* Zc 5$_{9}$.

<OBJ> ראה *see* 1 S 24$_{12}$, עשׂה *make* Pr 23$_{5}$, נדד *flutter* Is 10$_{14}$, נשׂא *raise* Ezk 10$_{16.19}$ 11$_{22}$ Ps 139$_{9}$, רום pol. *raise* 11QShirShabb 5$_{8}$ ([כ]נפיהם מרןוממים]), פרשׂ *extend* Ex 25$_{20}$||37$_{9}$ Dt 32$_{11}$ 1 K 6$_{27}$ 8$_{7}$ Jr 48$_{40}$ 49$_{22}$ Jb 39$_{26}$ 2 C 5$_{8}$ 4QDibHam[a] 6$_{8}$ 11QT 7$_{11}$, perh. specif. cover with garment in marriage ritual Ezk 16$_{8}$ Ru 3$_{9}$,* רפה pi. *let drop* Ezk 1$_{24.25}$, גלה pi. *uncover* Dt 23$_{1}$=11QT 66$_{12}$ Dt 27$_{20}$ 4QJub[f] 33$_{12}$ (גל[ה]) 11QT 66$_{13}$, כרת *cut off* 1 S 24$_{5.6.12}$.

<CSTR> כְּנַף הַכְּרוּב *wing of the cherub* 1 K 6$_{24.24.27}$ 2 C 3$_{11.12}$, כַּנְפֵי הַכְּרֻבִים *the wings of the cherubim* 1 K 6$_{27}$ 8$_{6}$||2 C 5$_{7}$ Ezk 10$_{5}$, sim. 2 C 3$_{11.13}$, כַּנְפֵי נְשָׁרִים *wings of eagles* Ex 19$_{4}$, כַּנְפֵי יוֹנָה *wings of a dove* Ps 68$_{14}$, כַּנְפֵי הַחֲסִידָה *the wings of the stork* Zc 5$_{9}$, כְּנַף־רְנָנִים *wing(s) of ostriches* Jb 39$_{13}$, כַּנְפֵי־רוּחַ *wings of the wind* 2 S 22$_{11}$||Ps 18$_{11}$ Ps 104$_{3}$ 1QH fr. 19$_{3}$, כַּנְפֵי־שָׁחַר *wings of the dawn* Ps 139$_{9}$, כְּנַף שִׁקּוּצִים *wing of desolations* Dn 9$_{27}$, כנפי דעת *wings of knowledge* 11QShirShabb 3$_{5}$.

כְּנַף אִישׁ *skirt*, i.e. robe, *of a man of* Zc 8$_{23}$, כְּנַף אָבִיו *skirt*, i.e. robe, *of his father* Dt 23$_{1}$=11QT 66$_{12}$ (אביהו) Dt 27$_{20}$ 4QJub[f] 33$_{12}$ (אביהו), אחיהו *of his brother* 11QT 66$_{13}$, כְּנַף בִּגְדוֹ *skirt of his garment* Hg 2$_{12}$, כְּנַף־הַמְּעִיל *skirt of the robe* 1 S 24$_{5}$, כְּנַף מְעִילְךָ *skirt of your robe* 1 S 24$_{12.12}$, כְּנַף־מְעִילוֹ *skirt of his robe* 1 S 15$_{27}$.

כַּנְפוֹת כַּנְפֵי בִגְדֵיהֶם *edges of their garments* Nm 15$_{38}$, כַּנְפוֹת כְּסוּתְךָ *corners of your clothing* Dt 22$_{12}$, כְּנַף הָאָרֶץ *corner* of the earth Is 24₁₆, כַּנְפוֹת הָאָרֶץ corners of the earth Is 11₁₂ Ezk 7₂ Jb 37₃ 38₁₃, כנפי הוניך corners of, i.e. extent of, your substance Si 38₁₁, כְּנַף־הָאֶחָד the wing of the one cherub 1 K 6₂₇||2 C 3₁₁.

בני כנף sons of wing, i.e. birds 1QM 10₁₄ (+ חַיָּה beast), בַּעַל כָּנָף lord of wing, i.e. bird Pr 1₁₇, בַּעַל כְּנָפַיִם lord of wings, i.e. bird Ec 10₂₀, עוֹף כָּנָף bird of wing, i.e. winged bird Gn 1₂₁ Ps 78₂₇ 1QH 8₉, צִפּוֹר bird of Dt 4₁₇ Ps 148₁₀ 4QShir^b 97₁, צִיצִת הַכָּנָף tassel of the edge of the garment Nm 15₃₈, קוֹל כַּנְפֵי voice, i.e. sound, of wings of Ezk 3₁₃ 10₅, קוֹל כַּנְפֵיהֶם voice, i.e. sound, of their wings Ezk 1₂₄, צְלָצַל כְּנָפָיִם buzzing of (insects') wings Is 18₁.

גְּדוֹל הַכְּנָפַיִם greatness of the wings Ezk 17₃, sim. Ezk 17₇, מֻטּוֹת כְּנָפָיו stretching of its wings Is 8₈, צֵל כְּנָפֶיךָ shadow of your wings Ps 17₈ 36₈ 57₂ 63₈, סֵתֶר hiding-place of Ps 61₅, קְצוֹת כְּנָפָיו ends of its wings 1 K 6₂₄.₂₄, כָּל־כָּנָף every wing, i.e. winged creature Gn 7₁₄ Ezk 17₂₃ 39₄.₁₇ 4QAdmon 1.1₆ (all five || צִפּוֹר bird).

<ADJ> אַחֵר other 2 C 3₁₁.₁₂.

<PREP> לְ of direction, to, + דבק be joined 2 C 3₁₂, נגע hi. touch 2 C 3₁₁.

בְּ of place, in 4QWiles 1₄; of instrument, by (means of), with perh. 4Q418 19₃, + ערך prepare Si 38₁₁, נגע touch Hg 2₁₂, סכך cover Ex 25₂₀||37₉, שׁסע pi. tear Lv 1₁₇, עוף fly 11QT 48₅; in, on Zc 5₉ Ml 3₂₀, + מצא ni. be found Jr 2₃₄, חזק hi. take hold of Zc 8₂₃, צור tie up Ezk 5₃, צרר wrap Ho 4₁₉, נשׂא raise, i.e. carry Hg 2₁₂; introducing object, + חזק hi. take hold of 1 S 15₂₇, אחז take hold of Jb 38₁₃.

כְּ as Zc 5₉.

מִן of direction, from, + שׁמע hear Is 24₁₆; מִתַּחַת from (underneath) Ezk 1₈.

אֶל to, + נגע touch 1 K 6₂₇; אֶל־תַּחַת beneath, + בוא hi. bring 1 K 8₆||2 C 5₇.

עַל upon Dn 9₂₇ 1QH fr. 19₃, + ראה ni. appear 2 S 22₁₁||Ps 18₁₁, הלך pi. go Ps 104₃, נשׂא raise Ex 19₁₄, עשׂה make Nm 15₃₈, שׁרה let loose Jb 37₃.

תַּחַת underneath Ezk 10₂₁, + ראה ni. appear Ezk 10₈, חסה seek refuge Ps 91₄ Ru 2₁₂.

<COLL> שתי הכ[נפים] the two wings 4QpsEzek^a 4₇, אַרְבַּע כַּנְפוֹת four corners of Dt 22₁₂ Is 11₁₂ Ezk 7₂, אַרְבַּע כְּנָפַיִם four wings Ezk 1₆, שֵׁשׁ כְּנָפַיִם six wings Is 6₂.₂.

Also 4QShirShabb^f 40₃ 4Q418 16₂ 4QShir^b 18.3₁₀.

<SYN> צִפּוֹר bird.*

⇒ כנף hide.

כִּנְּרוֹת, see כִּנֶּרֶת Chinnereth.

כִּנֶּרֶת ₇ pl.n. **Chinnereth, Chinneroth**—כִּנֶּרֶת (כִּנֲרוֹת, כִּנְּרוֹת, כִּנְרוֹת)—town in Naphtali, 40 km SW of Caesarea Philippi, Dt 3₁₇ Jos 11₂ 19₃₅ 1 K 15₂₀, with an adjacent sea of Chinneroth or Galilee (Nm 34₁₁ Jos 12₃ 13₂₇).

<NOM CL> עָרֵי מִבְצָר ... רַקַּת וְכִנֶּרֶת the fortified cities are ... Rakkath and Chinnereth Jos 19₃₅. <OBJ> נכה hi. strike 1 K 15₂₀. <CSTR> יָם־כִּנֶּרֶת sea of Chinnereth Nm 34₁₁ Jos 13₂₇, יָם כִּנְרוֹת sea of Chinneroth Jos 12₃*, נֶגֶב כִּנֲרוֹת south of Chinneroth Jos 11₂, כָּל־כִּנְרוֹת all Chinneroth 1 K 15₂₀. <PREP> מִן of direction, from, + נתן give Dt 3₁₇.

[כְּנָת] ₁ n.m. **associate**—pl. sf. כְּנָוֺתָיו—<CSTR> שְׁאָר כְּנָוֺתָיו remainder of his associates Ezr 4₇(Qr).

כֵּס, see כִּסֵּא throne.

כֶּסֶא ₂ n.m. **full moon**—כֶּסֶה—<CSTR> יוֹם הַכֶּסֶא day of the full moon Pr 7₂₀. <PREP> בְּ of time, on, at, + תקע blow trumpet Ps 81₄.*

כִּסֵּא ₁₃₅.₄.₂₁ n.m. **throne**—כִּסֵּה (1 K 10₁₉.₁₉ Jb 26₉); cstr. כִּסֵּא (כֵּס Ex 17₁₆); sf. כִּסְאִי, כִּסְאֲךָ (כִּסְאֶךָ, Q כסאכה), כִּסְאוֹ; pl. כִּסְאוֹת; sf. כִּסְאוֹתָם—**throne, seat of honour,** of Y. (Ex 17₁₆ 1 K 22₁₉ Is 6₁ Jr 3₁₇ 49₃₈ Ezk 1₂₆.₂₆ 10₁ 43₇ Ps 9₈ 11₄ 45₇ 47₉ 89₁₅.₃₇ 93₂ 97₂ 103₁₉ Jb 26₉ Lm 5₁₉ 1 C 28₅ 29₂₃), of kings, specif. kings of Israel (Dt 17₁₈= 11QT 56₂₀ 2 S 3₁₀ 7₁₃.₁₆||1 C 17₁₂.₁₄ 14₉ 1 K 1₁₃₊₉ₜ 2₄.₁₂.₁₉.₂₄.₃₃.₄₅ 3₆ 7₇ 8₂₀.₂₅||2 C 6₁₀.₁₆ 1 K 9₅||2 C 7₁₈ 10₉||2 C 9₈ 1 K 10₁₈.₁₉.₁₉||2 C 9₁₇.₁₈.₁₈ 1 K 16₁₁ 22₁₀.₁₉||2 C 18₉.₁₈ 2 K 10₃.₃₀ 11₁₉ 13₁₃ 15₁₂ Is 9₆ 16₅ 22₂₃ Jr 13₁₃ 14₂₁ 17₂₅ 22₂.₄.₃₀ 29₁₆ 33₁₇.₂₁ 36₃₀ Zc 6₁₃.₁₃ Ps 9₅ 89₅.₃₀.₄₅ 122₅.₅ 132₁₁.₁₂ 1 C 22₁₀ 2 C 23₂₀ Si 47₁₁), other kings (Gn 41₄₀ Ex 11₅ 12₂₉ Is 14₉.₁₃ 47₁ Jr 1₁₅ 43₁₀ Ezk 26₁₆ Jon 3₆ Hg 2₂₂ Ps 94₂₀ Jb 36₇ Pr 16₁₂ 20₈.₂₈ 25₅ 29₁₄ Est 1₂ 3₁ 5₁ Ne 3₇ Si

10_{14} 11_{5} 40_{3}); **seat, chair** (Jg 3_{20} 1 S 1_{9} 2_{8} $4_{13.18}$ 1 K 2_{19} 2 K 4_{10} 25_{28}||Jr 52_{32} Pr 9_{14}).

<SUBJ> היה *be* 2 S 7_{16}||1 C 17_{14} 1 K 2_{45} Ps 89_{37}, רום *be high* Is 6_{1} 4Q419 1_{9}, ישׁב *dwell*, i.e. be established Ps $122_{5.5}$, בוא *come* 4QBark^{a} 1.1_{7} (ויבו[א]), חבר *be allied with* Ps 94_{20}, כון ni. *be established* Ps 93_{2} Pr 16_{12} 25_{5} 29_{14}, ho. *be established* Is 16_{5}, נשׂא ni. *be raised* Is 6_{1}.

<NOM CL> כִּסְאֲךָ לְדֹר וָדוֹר *your throne is for generation to generation* Lm 5_{19}, כִּסְאֲךָ אֱלֹהִים עוֹלָם וָעֶד *your throne O God is for ever and ever* Ps 45_{7}, כִּסֵּא כָבוֹד ... מְקוֹם מִקְדָּשֵׁנוּ *a throne of glory ... is the place of our sanctuary* Jr 17_{12}, הַמֶּלֶךְ וְכִסְאוֹ נָקִי *the king and his throne are innocent* 2 S 14_{9}, הַשָּׁמַיִם כִּסְאִי *the heavens are my throne* Is 66_{1}, בַּשָּׁמַיִם כִּסְאוֹ *his throne is in the heavens* Ps 11_{4}, אֵין־כִּסֵּא *there is no throne* Is 47_{1}.

<OBJ> עשׂה *make* 1 K 10_{18}||2 C 9_{17}, נתן *give* 2 K 25_{28}||Jr 52_{32}, *give*, i.e. place Jr 1_{15}, נחל hi. *cause to inherit* 1 S 2_{8}, שׂים *place* 1 K 2_{19} 2 K 4_{10} (+ מִטָּה *bed*, שֻׁלְחָן *table*, מְנוֹרָה *lampstand*) Jr 43_{10} 49_{38} Ps 89_{30} Est 3_{1}, סעד *hold upright* Pr 20_{28}, רום hi. *raise* Is 14_{13}, קום hi. *raise up*, i.e. establish 2 S 3_{10} 1 K 9_{5}||2 C 7_{18}, כון pol. *establish* 2 S 7_{13}||1 C 17_{12} Ps 9_{8}, hi. *establish* Ps 103_{19} 1 C 22_{10} Si 47_{11} 4QMidr Eschat^{a} 3_{10}, בנה *build* Ps 89_{5}, גדל pi. *make great* 1 K $1_{37.47}$ GnzPs 3_{14} (+ כֹּחַ *strength*), ישׁב *sit on* Si $40_{3(B)}$ 4QComm GenA 5_{2}, שׁכן *settle on* Si $40_{3(B\ mg)}$, הפך *overturn* Hg 2_{22} Si 10_{14}, מגר pi. *throw down* Ps 89_{45}, קרא *call* Jr 3_{17}.

<CSTR> כֵּס יָהּ *throne of Y.* Ex 17_{16} (Sam כִּסֵּא; or em. נֵס *banner*), כִּסֵּא י״ *throne of Y.* Jr 3_{17} 1 C 29_{23}, כִּסֵּא אֲדֹנִי־הַמֶּלֶךְ *throne of my lord the king* 1 K $1_{27.37}$ (אֲדֹנִי הַמֶּלֶךְ דָּוִד *my lord king David*), כִּסֵּא הַמְּלוּכָה *the throne of kingship* 1 K 1_{46}, כִּסֵּא הַמַּמְלָכָה *throne of the kingdom* 2 C 23_{20}, כִּסֵּא מַמְלַכְתְּךָ *throne of your kingdom* 1 K 9_{5}, כִּסֵּא מַמְלַכְתּוֹ *throne of his kingdom* Dt 17_{18}=11QT 56_{20} 2 S 7_{13} 4QMidrEschat^{a} 3_{10}, כִּסֵּא מַמְלָכוֹת *throne of kingdoms* Hg 2_{22}, כִּסֵּא מַלְכוּת *throne of the kingdom of* 1 C 28_{5} 4Qap Mes 2.2_{7} 11QT 59_{17}, כִּסֵּא מַלְכוּתֶךָ *throne of your kingdom* 2 C 7_{18}, כִּסֵּא מַלְכוּתוֹ *throne of his kingdom* Est 1_{2} 5_{1} 1 C 22_{10} 4QShirShabb^{f} 20.2_{2}.

כִּסֵּא יִשְׂרָאֵל *throne of Israel* 1 K 2_{4} $8_{20.25}$||2 C $6_{10.16}$ 1 K 9_{5} 10_{9} 2 K 10_{30} 15_{12} 4QDibHam^{a} 1.4_{7}, כִּסֵּא בֵית־ *throne of the house of* Jr 33_{17}, כִּסֵּא דָוִד *throne of David* 2 S 3_{10} 1 K $2_{12.24.45}$ Is 9_{6} Jr 17_{25} $22_{2.30}$ 29_{16} 36_{30}, כסא אבותיו *throne of his fathers* 11QT 59_{14}, כִּסֵּא הַמְּלָכִים *throne of the kings* 2 K 11_{19} 25_{28}||Jr 52_{32}, כסא גאים *throne of proud ones* Si 10_{14}, כִּסֵּא פַּחַת *throne*, i.e. jurisdiction, *of the governor of* Ne 3_{7}, כסא מרכבה *throne of a chariot* 4QShirShabb^{f} 20.2_{8}, כִּסֵּא כָבוֹד *throne, seat of glory* 1 S 2_{8} Is 22_{23} Jr 17_{12} 4QpIsa^{a} 8_{19} (כ[ס]א; + נֵזֶר *crown*), כִּסֵּא כְבוֹדֶךָ *throne of your glory* Jr 14_{21}, כסאי כבוד *thrones of the glory of* 4Q ShirShabb^{f} 23.1_{3} (corrected from כסאיכה בוד), כסאי כבודו *thrones of his glory* 11QShirShabb 1_{6}, [כס]אי פלא *thrones of wonder*, i.e. wonderful thrones 11QShirShabb f$_{5}$, כִּסֵּא קָדְשׁוֹ *throne of his holiness*, i.e. his holy throne Ps 47_{9}, כסא עון *throne of iniquity* 4QBéat 14.2_{2}, כִּסֵּא־דִין *throne of judgment* Pr 20_{8}, כִּסֵּא הַוּוֹת *throne of destruction* Ps 94_{20}, כִּסֵּא־שֵׁן *throne of ivory* 1 K 10_{18}||2 C 9_{17}, כסא עוז *throne of strength* 4QM^{a} 11.1_{12}, כסאי עולמים *thrones of eternity* 11QShirShabb k$_{5}$.

עם כסאו *people of his throne* 4QShir^{b} 2.1_{10}, אוּלָם הַכִּסֵּא *the hall of the throne* 1 K 7_{7}, מְקוֹם כִּסְאִי *place of my throne* Ezk 43_{7}, מְכוֹן כִּסְאֶךָ *foundation of your throne* Ps 89_{15}, מְכוֹן כִּסְאוֹ *foundation of his throne* Ps 97_{2} 11QPs^{a} 26_{11}, מרום כסא *height of a throne* 11QShirShabb 3_{1}, דְּמוּת כִּסֵּא *likeness of a throne* Ezk $1_{26.26}$ 10_{1}, תבנית כסא *figure of a throne of* 4QShirShabb^{f} 20.2_{8}, פְּנֵי־כִסֵּה *face*, i.e. surface, *of the throne* Jb 26_{9} (or em. כֶּסֶה *moon*).

<ADJ> מָרוֹם *elevated* Jr 17_{12}, גָּדוֹל *great* 1 K 10_{18}||2 C 9_{17}.

<PREP> לְ of possession, *of, (belonging) to* 1 K $10_{19.19}$ ||2 C $9_{18.18}$ (unless at 9_{18} בַּזָּהָב לַכִּסֵּא מָאֳחָזִים = *in gold, attached to the throne*, or em. לַכִּסֵּא מְאֻחָזִים בַּזָּהָב *belonging to the throne, [all] covered in gold*) Ne 3_{7};* of benefit, *to, for* 11QShirShabb 1_{6}, + היה *be* 1 K 2_{33}, ישׁב hi. *cause to sit*, i.e. place Jb 36_{7}; *as*, + היה *be* Is 22_{23}, *with respect to*, + נתן *give* Jr 52_{32}; of direction, *to, on*, + ישׁב *sit* Ps 9_{5} 132_{12}, שׁית *place* Ps 132_{11}.

בְּ of place, *on*, + ישׁב *sit* 4QM^{a} 11.1_{12}; כְּ *as* 4QShir Shabb^{f} 20.2_{2}; מִן of direction, *from*, + קום *arise* Jon 3_{6}, hi. *raise* Is 14_{9}; of comparison, *greater (than)*, + גדל pi. *make great* 1 K $1_{37.47}$.

אֶל *to*, on, + ישׁב *sit* Jr 29_{16}.

עַל *upon* Is 9_{6} 4QBéat 14.2_{2}, + היה *be* Zc 6_{13}, נתן *give*, i.e. place 1 K 5_{19} 10_{9}||2 C 9_{8}, שׂים *place* 2 K 10_{3}, ישׁב *sit* Ex 11_{5} 12_{29} Dt 17_{18}=11QT 56_{20} 1 S 1_{9} 4_{13} 1 K 1_{13+8t} $2_{12.19}$

36 820.25||2 C 610.16 1 K 1611 2210.19||2 C 189.18 2 K 1030 1119 1313 1512 Is 61 Jr 1313 1725 222.4.30 3317 3630 Ps 479 Pr 914 208 Est 12 51 1 C 285 2923 Si 115 4QDibHama 1.47 11QT 5914.17, hi. *cause to sit*, i.e. place 1 K 224 2 C 2320, מלך *rule* Jr 3321, משׁל *rule* Zc 613, כבד pi. *honour* 4QapMes 2.27; *against* Ex 1716.

מֵעַל *from (upon)*, + כרת ni. *be cut off* 1 K 24 95, נתן *give* 2 K 2528, קום *arise* Jg 320, נפל *fall* 1 S 418, ירד *go down* Ezk 2616.

<COLL> רַק הַכִּסֵּא אֶגְדַּל מִמֶּךָּ *only with regard to the throne I will be greater than you* Gn 4140.*

Also 4Q418 864.

[כֹּסֶא] 0.0.0.1 pr.n.m. **Choseh**—Seal 107 (Beth-Shemesh, 8th cent.), <PREP> לְ of possession, *(belonging) to, of* Seal 107.

כסה 156.6.19 vb. **cover—Qal** 3 Ptc. כֹּסֶה, pass. כְּסוּי—**cover, conceal, forgive** (Ps 321), <SUBJ> אָדָם *human being* Pr 1223, עָרוּם *clever one* Pr 1216.23 (:: ידע ni. *be known*, קרא *proclaim*); subj. of pass. חֲטָאָה *sin* Ps 321 (|| נשׂא pass. *be raised*, i.e. be forgiven). <OBJ> דַּעַת *knowledge* Pr 1223, קָלוֹן *dishonour* Pr 1216. <SYN> נשׂא pass. *be raised*, i.e. be forgiven. <ANT> ידע ni. *be known*, קרא *proclaim*.

Ni. 2.1.3 Pf. Si נִכְסָתָה, נכסה, Q נכסו; Impf. 3fs Q תכסה; inf. הִכָּסוֹת—**be covered, be hidden,** <SUBJ> Babylon Jr 5142, דָּם *blood* Ezk 248, שֶׁמֶשׁ *sun* Si 432, אוֹר *light* 4QAstrCrypt 19, שְׁתֵּים עֶשְׂרֵה *twelve (parts of surface of moon)* 4QAstrCrypt 11 ([תכסה שתים ע]שרא), שְׁלֹשׁ עֶשְׂרֵה *thirteen (parts of surface of moon)* 4QAstrCrypt 13 ([שלוש [עשרא), אַרְבַּע עֶשְׂרֵה *fourteen (parts of surface of moon)* 4QAstrCrypt 15 ([ארבע עשרא תכס[ה).

<PREP> בְּ of instrument, *by (means of)*, + הָמוֹן *noise* of its waves Jr 5142.

Also 4QSh 21.

Pi. 136.3.16 Pf. כִּסִּיתָ, (כִּסַּתְנִי) כִּסְּתָה, (כִּסָּמוֹ, כִּסָּהוּ) כִּסָּה
(כִּסִּיתוֹ, כִּסִּיתִי) כִּסֵּתִי, כִּסִּיתִיךָ), כִּסּוּ, (כִּסּוּךְ) כִּסִּינוּ;
impf. יְכַסֶּה (Q יכס, יְכַסֶּנּוּ, יְכַסִּימוֹ, יְכַסֶּךָּ, יְכַסֵּךְ, יְכַסְיֻמוּ),
+ ;יְכַסֶּנָּה, אֲכַסֶּה, תְּכַסִּי, (תְּכַסֵּנוּ, תְּכַסֶּךָּ, תְּכַסֵּךְ, תְּכַס) תְּכַסֶּה
waw וְכִסָּה, 2ms Q וכסיתו, וְכִסּוּ; וַיְכַס (וַיְכַסֵּהוּ), 3fs וַתְּכַס,
מְכַסִּים, מְכַסֶּה, ptc. ;כַּסֵּנוּ .impv ;(וַיְכַסֻּהוּ) וַיְכַסּוּ, וַתְּכַסִּים מְכַסּוֹת; inf. כַּסּוֹת (כַּסֹּתוֹ)—**cover;** specif. **conceal** (Ps 325 4011 Pr 2813), with עַל, sometimes perh. **condone, forgive** (Dt 139 Pr 1012 Ne 337),* **clothe oneself;** perh. **uncover, reveal** (Ho 211 Ps 1439 Jb 3630 Pr 1011.18 2626).*

<SUBJ> ״ *Y.* Gn 1817 Is 2910 5116 Ezk 168.10 3115 327.7 Ps 853 (+ נשׂא *raise*, i.e. forgive) 1046 1478, אֱלֹהִים *God* Ps 4420 1046 1478 Ne 337, אֱלוֹהַּ *God* Jb 924, אֵל *God* Jb 3317 3630.32, כְּרוּב *cherub* 2 C 58, שָׂרָף *seraph* Is 62.2, Israelite(s) Dt 139 2212 2314 Is 587 11QT 5212 535, Egypt Jr 468, עַם *people* Nm 225.11, Jerusalem Ezk 1618, Aaron Nm 45.8.9.11.12.15, Ezekiel Ezk 126, Jael Jg 418.19, Japheth Gn 923, Job Jb 3133, Judah Gn 3726, Michal 1 S 1913, Shem Gn 923, Solomon Si 4715, Tamar Gn 3814 (Sam htp.) 3815.

אִישׁ *man* Ex 2133 Lv 1713 Ezk 187.16 Si 3518, גֶּבֶר *man* 4QOrda 27 (+ לבשׁ *wear*), בֵּן *son* Nm 45.8.9.11.12.15, אָח *brother* Gn 3726, מֶלֶךְ *king* Jon 36, נָשִׂיא *prince* Ezk 1212, כֹּהֵן *priest* Ml 213.16, חָכָם *wise one* Si 3518, worshipper Ps 325 4011 (|| כחד pi. *keep hidden*; :: אמר *say*) 1439, נֶאֱמָן *reliable one* Pr 1113, פֹּתֶה *naive one* Si 817, רָשָׁע *wicked one* Jb 1527, שְׂלָו *quail* Ex 1613, גָּמָל *camel* Is 606, צְפַרְדֵּעַ *frogs* Ex 82, אַרְבֶּה *locusts* Ex 105.15 4QParGenEx 310, רִמָּה *maggot* Jb 2126.

הוֹד *majesty* Hb 33, עָנָן *cloud* Ex 2415.16 4034 Lv 1613 Nm 915.16 177 Ezk 389.16 4QapMosc 2.210, יָם *sea* Ex 1510 Jos 247 Ps 7853, תְּהוֹם *deeps* of sea Ex 155, מַיִם *waters* Ex 1428 Is 119 Ezk 2619 Hb 214 Ps 1049 10611 Jb 2211 3834, אֶרֶץ *earth* Nm 1633 Is 2621 Ps 10617 Jb 1618, הַר *mountain* Ho 108, אָבָק *dust* Ezk 2610, טַל *dew* 1QM 129=192, חֹשֶׁךְ *darkness* Is 602, אֹפֶל *darkness* Jb 2317, כָּנָף *wing* Ezk 111.23.23.

חֵלֶב *fat* Ex 2913.22 Lv 33.9.14 48 73 11QT 156 205 (both [החלב המכסה]) 2314, פֶּה *mouth* of wicked one Pr 106.11, אַהֲבָה *love* Pr 1012, צָרַעַת *skin-disease* Lv 1312.13, כְּלִמָּה *disgrace* Jr 325 5151 Ps 698, בּוּשָׁה *shame* Ob10 Mc 710, בֹּשֶׁת *shame* Ps 4416, פַּלָּצוּת *shuddering* Ezk 718 Ps 556, חָמָס *violence* Hb 217, עָמָל *trouble* Ps 14010(Qr); subj. not specified, Ex 2613 2842 1 K 11 718.41.42||2 C 412.13 Ezk 247 3018 Ho 211 Pr 1018 179 2813 4Q416 2.23.

<OBJ> Edom Ob10, Egypt Ezk 3018, אֶרֶץ *land* Ex 82 Is 602 Jr 468 Ezk 389.16 Ps 1046.9 Si 4715 1QM 129=192, עַיִן *eye*, i.e. surface, of land Ex 105.15 Nm 225.11 4QParGenEx

3$_{10}$, שָׁמַיִם *heavens* Ezk 32$_7$ Hb 3$_3$ Ps 147$_8$, שֶׁמֶשׁ *sun* Ezk 32$_7$, תְּהוֹם *deep* Ezk 31$_{15}$, שֹׁרֶשׁ *root* of the sea Jb 36$_{30}$, הַר *mountain* Ex 24$_{15.16}$, Jerusalem Ezk 26$_{10}$, Tyre Ezk 26$_{19}$.

Israelite(s) Is 60$_6$ Jr 3$_{25}$, Egyptians Jos 24$_7$, David 1 K 1$_1$, Job Jb 22$_{11}$ 38$_{34}$, Sisera Jg 4$_{18.19}$, worshipper Is 51$_{16}$ Ps 44$_{16}$ 55$_6$, חַיִל *army* of Pharaoh Ex 14$_{28}$ 15$_5$, פָּרָשׁ *rider* Ex 14$_{28}$, שָׁלִישׁ *adjutant* Ex 15$_5$, אוֹיֵב *enemy* Ex 15$_{10}$ Ps 78$_{53}$, צַר *adversary* Ps 106$_{11}$, רָשָׁע *wicked one* Ps 140$_{10}$, עָרוֹם *naked one* Is 58$_7$, עֵירֹם *naked one* Ezk 18$_{7.16}$, פָּלִיט *fugitive* Ezk 7$_{18}$, אמר ptc. *one who says* Mc 7$_{10}$.

מַחֲנֶה *camp* Ex 16$_{13}$, מִשְׁכָּן *tabernacle* Ex 26$_{13}$ Nm 9$_{15.16}$, קֹדֶשׁ *sanctuary* Nm 4$_{15}$, אֹהֶל *tent* of meeting Ex 40$_{34}$ Nm 17$_7$, מִזְבֵּחַ *altar* Ml 2$_{13}$, כַּפֹּרֶת *mercy-seat* Lv 16$_{13}$, אֲרוֹן *ark* of the testimony Nm 4$_5$, כֹּתֶרֶת *capital* of column 1 K 7$_{18}$, גֻּלָּה *bowl*, i.e. projection of pillar 1 K 7$_{41.42}$||2 C 4$_{12.13}$, מְנוֹרָה *lampstand* Nm 4$_9$, כְּלִי *vessel* Nm 4$_{12.15}$.

צְדָקָה *righteousness*, i.e. saving act Ps 40$_{11}$, חָכְמָה *wisdom* Si 35$_{18(Bmg)}$, עָוֺן *iniquity* Ps 32$_5$, חַטָּאת *sin* Ps 85$_3$, פֶּשַׁע *transgression* Jb 31$_{33}$ Pr 10$_{12}$ (if em. עַל cover *over*, i.e. condone, sin, to עָוֺל cover *iniquity* [and] sin) 17$_9$ 28$_{13}$, שִׂנְאָה *hatred* Pr 10$_{18}$, גֵּוָה *pride* Jb 33$_{17}$ (or em. גֵּוֹה *his body*), חֶרְפָּה *reproach* 4Q418 177$_3$, חָמָס *violence* Ml 2$_{16}$ Pr 10$_{6.11}$, דָּם *blood* Gn 37$_{26}$ Lv 17$_{13}$ Jb 16$_{18}$ 11QT 52$_{12}$ 53$_5$, בָּשָׂר *flesh* Ex 28$_{42}$ Lv 13$_{13}$, עוֹר *skin* Lv 13$_{12}$, גְּוִיָּה *body* Ezk 1$_{11.23}$, ראשׁ *head* Is 29$_{10}$, פָּנִים *face* Gn 38$_{15}$ Is 6$_2$ Jr 51$_{51}$ Ezk 12$_{6.12}$ Ps 44$_{16}$ 69$_8$ Jb 9$_{24}$ 15$_{27}$ 4Q416 2.2$_3$, רֶגֶל *foot* Is 6$_2$, עֶרְוָה *nakedness* Gn 9$_{23}$ Ezk 16$_8$ Ho 2$_{11}$, בֶּגֶד *cloth* Nm 4$_{8.11}$, *garment* Ezk 16$_{18}$ 4QRitPur 11$_4$ appar. 51.2$_7$ (יכס corrected to יכבס), רֶכֶב *chariot* Ex 14$_{28}$, מֶרְכָּבָה *chariot* Ex 15$_5$, בּוֹר *pit* Ex 21$_{33}$, קֶרֶב *inner parts* of animal Ex 29$_{13.22}$ Lv 3$_{3.9.14}$ 7$_3$ 11QT 15$_6$ 20$_5$ (both [המכסה את הקרב]) 23$_{14}$, צֵאָה *excrement* Dt 23$_{14}$, סוֹד *secret* Si 8$_{17}$, דָּבָר *matter* Pr 11$_{13}$, אֲשֶׁר *that which* Gn 18$_{17}$; obj. not specified, Ho 10$_8$ Hb 2$_{17}$.

<PREP> לְ of possession, *of, (belonging) to*, + הֵנָּה *those* Ezk 1$_{23.23}$; introducing object, + יָם *sea* Is 11$_9$.

בְּ of instrument, *by (means of), with*, + מִכְסֶה *covering* Nm 4$_{8.11.12}$, פָּרֹכֶת *veil* Nm 4$_5$, כְּסוּת *clothing* Dt 22$_{12}$, בֶּגֶד *clothing* 1 S 19$_{13}$ 1 K 1$_1$, שַׂלְמָה *garment* 4QOrd^a 2$_7$, שְׂמִיכָה *rug* Jg 4$_{18}$, כָּנָף *wing* Is 6$_{2.2}$, חֵלֶב *fat* Jb 15$_{27}$, עָפָר *dust* Lv 17$_{13}$ 11QT 52$_{12}$ 53$_5$, עָב *cloud* Ps 147$_8$, עָנָן *cloud* Ezk 32$_7$, צַלְמָוֶת *deep darkness* Ps 44$_{20}$, מַיִם *water* appar. 4QRitPur 51.2$_7$ (יכס corrected to יכבס).

בְּ of place, time, + חֶרְפָּה *reproach* 4Q416 2.2$_3$ (בחרפת[נו]); of accompaniment, *in, with*, + נֶפֶשׁ *soul* Si 47$_{15}$, צָעִיף *shawl* Gn 38$_{14}$, צֵל *shadow* Is 51$_{16}$.

מִן of direction, *from*, + Abraham Gn 18$_{17}$, ראשׁ *head* Lv 13$_{12}$ (+ עַד־רַגְלָיו *unto its foot*), פָּנִים *face* Jb 23$_{17}$, גֶּבֶר *man* Jb 33$_{17}$.*

אֶל *to*, + י׳ Y. Ps 143$_9$.

כסה עַל pi. *cover (over)*,* + worshipper Ps 44$_{20}$, dead Jb 21$_{26}$, Korah and his associates Nm 16$_{33}$, Moses 4QapMos^c 2.2$_{10}$, עֵדָה *congregation* of Abiram Ps 106$_{17}$, הרג pass. ptc. *slain one* Is 26$_{21}$, קֶרֶב *entrails* Lv 4$_8$, דָּם *blood* Ezk 24$_7$, כַּף *hand* Jb 36$_{32}$, לְבוּשׁ *clothing* Ml 2$_{16}$, אֶרֶז *cedar* Ezk 31$_{15}$, יָם *sea* Hb 2$_{14}$, אֲרוֹן *ark* 2 C 5$_8$; perh. *condone*, + עָוֺן *iniquity* Ne 3$_{37}$, פֶּשַׁע *sin* Pr 10$_{12}$ (or em. עָוֺל cover *iniquity*), אִישׁ *man* 4QapMos^c 2.2$_{10}$, אִשָּׁה *wife* Dt 13$_9$, בֵּן *son* Dt 13$_9$, בַּת *daughter* Dt 13$_9$, אָח *brother* Dt 13$_9$, רֵעַ *friend* Dt 13$_9$.

אֵת *with*, + כְּלִי *vessel* Nm 4$_9$, נֵר *lamp* Nm 4$_9$, מֶלְקָחַיִם *snuffers* Nm 4$_9$, מַחְתָּה *pan* Nm 4$_9$.

בְּתוֹךְ *within*, + לֵב *heart* Ps 40$_{11}$.

<COLL> וַיְכַסֵּהוּ הֶעָנָן שֵׁשֶׁת יָמִים *and the cloud covered it (the mountain) for six days* Ex 24$_{16}$, וָאֲכַסֵּךְ מֶשִׁי *and I covered you with silk* Ezk 16$_{10}$, יְכַסֶּה־בֶּגֶד *he will cover* the naked one *with a garment* Ezk 18$_7$, sim. Ezk 18$_{16}$, לְכַסּוֹת ... עָפָר *to cover ... with dust* Ezk 24$_7$, עָנָן יְכַסֶּנָּה *he shall cover it with a cloud* Ezk 30$_{18}$, וַיְכַס שַׂק *and he covered (himself) with sackcloth* Jon 3$_6$, כַּסּוֹת דִּמְעָה *to cover* the altar *with tears* Ml 2$_{13}$, וְכִסָּה חָמָס *and he covered* his garment *with violence* Ml 2$_{16}$, תְּהוֹם ... כִּסִּיתוֹ *you have covered it ... with the deep* Ps 104$_6$, כִּסָּה־אוֹר *he covers it with lightning* Jb 36$_{30}$.

Also 4QD^h 5$_2$ 4QMyst^a 6.2$_3$ 4Q418 127$_2$ ([יכסן) 4QBark^e 7$_3$. <SYN> כחד pi. *keep hidden*. <ANT> אמר *say*.

Pu. 7.2 Pf. כֻּסּוּ; impf. יְכֻסֶּה (Si יכוסה); + waw וַיְכֻסּוּ; ptc. Si. מכוסה, מְכֻסִּים, מְכֻסּוֹת—**be covered,** <SUBJ> David 1 C 21$_{16}$, זָקֵן *elder* 1 C 21$_{16}$, שׂנא ptc. *one who hates* Si 12$_8$, הַר *mountain* Gn 7$_{19.20}$ Ps 80$_{11}$, חַלּוֹן *window* Ezk 41$_{16}$, פָּנִים *face* of ground Pr 24$_{31}$, שֵׁם *name* Ec 6$_4$; subj. not specified, Si 3$_{21}$.

<PREP> בְּ of instrument, *by (means of), with*, + חֹשֶׁךְ *darkness* Ec 6$_4$, שַׂק *sackcloth* 1 C 21$_{16}$, רָעָה *evil* Si 12$_8$; מִן

of direction, *from,* + בֵּן *son* Si 3$_{21}$. <COLL> כָּסּוּ הָרִים צִלָּהּ *the mountains were covered with its shade* Ps 80$_{11}$, כָּסּוּ פָנָיו חֲרֻלִּים *its face was covered with weeds* Pr 24$_{31}$.

Htp. 9 Impf. יִתְכַּסּוּ; + waw וַתִּתְכַּס, וַיִּתְכַּס; ptc. מִתְכַּסֶּה, מִתְכַּסִּים—**cover oneself, hide oneself,** <SUBJ> Ahijah 1 K 11$_{29}$, Eliakim 2 K 19$_{2}$||Is 37$_{2}$, Hezekiah 2 K 19$_{1}$||Is 37$_{1}$, Rebekah Gn 24$_{65}$, Shebna 2 K 19$_{2}$||Is 37$_{2}$, כֹּהֵן *priest* 2 K 19$_{2}$||Is 37$_{2}$, אָדָם *human being* Jon 3$_{8}$, בְּהֵמָה *beast* Jon 3$_{8}$, שִׂנְאָה *hatred* Pr 26$_{26}$; subj. not specified, Is 59$_{6}$.

<PREP> בְּ of instrument, *by (means of), with,* + שַׂק *sackcloth* 2 K 19$_{1.2}$||Is 37$_{1.2}$, מַעֲשֶׂה *deed* Is 59$_{6}$, מַשָּׁאוֹן *deception* Pr 26$_{26}$; *in, with,* + שַׂלְמָה *mantle* 1 K 11$_{29}$. <COLL> יִתְכַּסּוּ שַׂקִּים *let them be covered with sackcloth* Jon 3$_{8}$.*

⇒ כְּסוּי *covering,* כְּסוּת *covering,* מִכְסֶה *covering,* מְכַסֶּה *covering.*

כֶּ֫סֶה, see כֶּסֶא *full moon.*

כִּסֵּה, see כִּסֵּא *throne.*

כָּסוּי 2 n.m. **covering**—cstr. כְּסוּי—<OBJ> נתן *give,* i.e. place Nm 4$_{6}$, פרשׂ *spread* Nm 4$_{14}$. <CSTR> כְּסוּי עוֹר *covering of skin* Nm 4$_{6.14}$.*

⇒ כסה *cover.*

כְּסוּת 8.0.1 n.f. **covering**—cstr. כְּסוּת; sf. כְּסוּתוֹ, כְּסוּתְךָ, כְּסוּתָהּ, כְּסוּתָם—**clothing** (Ex 21$_{10}$ 22$_{26}$ Dt 22$_{12}$ Is 50$_{3}$ Jb 24$_{7}$ 31$_{19}$); **covering** of eyes (Gn 20$_{16}$), Abaddon (Jb 26$_{6}$). <NOM CL> הוּא כְסוּתוֹ לְבַדָּהּ *it is his only covering* Ex 22$_{26(Qr)}$, הוּא־לָךְ כְּסוּת עֵינַיִם *it is for you (as) a covering of the eyes,* i.e. exoneration Gn 20$_{16}$, אֵין כְּסוּת בַּקָּרָה *there is no covering in the cold* Jb 24$_{7}$, אֵין כְּסוּת לָאֲבַדּוֹן before God, *there is no covering for Abaddon* Jb 26$_{6}$, אֵין כְּסוּת לָאֶבְיוֹן *there is no covering for the poor* Jb 31$_{19}$. <OBJ> שׂים *place,* i.e. make Is 50$_{3}$, גרע *diminish* Ex 21$_{10}$. <CSTR> כְּסוּת עֵינַיִם *covering of the eyes* Gn 20$_{16}$; כַּנְפוֹת כְּסוּתְךָ *corners of your clothing* Dt 22$_{12}$. Also 4QD^{e} 3.3$_{20}$ ([ו]כסות[ו]) 4QapPs^{b} 15$_{10}$.*

⇒ כסה *cover.*

כסח 2 vb. **cut off—Qal** 2 Ptc. pass. fs כְּסוּחָה, pl. כְּסוּחִים—**be cut off, cut down,** <SUBJ> קוֹץ *thorn-bush* Is 33$_{12}$, גֶּפֶן *vine* Ps 80$_{17}$ (or em. כְּסָחוּהָ *they have cut it down*); subj. not specified, Ps 80$_{17}$ (if em.). <OBJ> גֶּפֶן *vine* Ps 80$_{17}$ (if em.).

[כֵּסְיָה] 1 n.f. **great throne, rump***—<PREP> עַל *upon* Ex 17$_{16}$ (L כֵּס יָהּ *throne of Y.*; or em. נֵס *banner* of Y.).

כְּסִיל I 70.5.1 n.m. **fool**—pl. כְּסִילִים—as foolish in practical matters, shameless in religious matters, sluggish in repayment of debts, etc.*

<SUBJ> בטח *be careless* Pr 14$_{16}$, עבר htp. *be angry* Pr 14$_{16}$, הלך *go* Ec 2$_{14}$, רום hi. *raise,* i.e. receive, shame Pr 3$_{35}$ (unless כְּסִיל is obj. of מֵרִים *receives,* or em. מָרוֹם fools inherit *the height of* shame, or מֹרָשִׁים fools *inherit* shame or מְמִירִים fools *exchange* glory for shame, or מַרְבִּים fools *increase* shame, or מְרִיַם כְּסִילִים *the desire of fools* is shame), יצא hi. *bring out* Pr 10$_{18}$ 29$_{11}$, עשׂה *do* Pr 10$_{23}$, שׁנה *do again* Pr 26$_{11}$, נתן *give,* i.e. offer sacrifice Ec 4$_{17}$, שׁמר *keep* Si 20$_{7}$, חפץ *take pleasure* Pr 18$_{2}$, חבק *fold hands* Ec 4$_{5}$, פרשׂ *flaunt* folly Pr 13$_{16}$, בוזה *despise* Pr 15$_{20}$, שׂנא *hate* Pr 1$_{22}$, בלע pi. *devour* Pr 21$_{20}$, אבד *perish* Ps 49$_{11}$ (|| בַּעַר *fool*), שׂחק *laugh* Ec 7$_{6}$, בין *understand* Ps 92$_{7}$, hi. *have discernment* Pr 8$_{5}$, שׂכל hi. *have insight* Ps 94$_{8}$.

<NOM CL> הוּא כְסִיל *he is a fool* Pr 10$_{18}$ 19$_{1}$ 28$_{26}$. <OBJ> ילד *bear child* Pr 17$_{21}$, פגשׁ *meet* Pr 17$_{12}$, שׂכר *hire* Pr 26$_{10}$, נכה hi. *strike* Pr 17$_{10}$, ענה *answer* Pr 26$_{4.5}$.

<CSTR> רֹעֶה כְסִילִים *companion of fools* Pr 13$_{20}$, טובת כסילים *good actions of fools* Si 20$_{13}$, שַׁלְוַת כְּסִילִים *ease of fools* Pr 1$_{32}$, אִוֶּלֶת *folly of* Pr 14$_{8.24}$, תּוֹעֲבַת *abomination of,* i.e. to Pr 13$_{19}$, עֲמַל הַכְּסִילִים *the toil of fools* Ec 10$_{15}$, מוסר כסיל ... *discipline of ... a fool* Si 42$_{8(B)}$, מִקְרֵה הַכְּסִיל *the fate of the fool* Ec 2$_{15}$, משפטי כסיל *judgments of a fool* 4QMyst^{c} 2a$_{1}$.

יַד־כְּסִיל *hand of a fool* Pr 17$_{16}$ 26$_{6}$, לֵב כְּסִיל *heart of a fool* Ec 10$_{2}$, לֵב כְּסִילִים *heart of fools* Pr 12$_{23}$ 16$_{7}$ Ec 7$_{4}$, קוֹל כְּסִיל *voice of a fool* Ec 5$_{2}$, שִׂפְתֵי *lips of* Pr 18$_{6}$, שִׂפְתוֹת *lips of* Ec 10$_{12}$, פִּי־כְסִיל *mouth of a fool* Pr 18$_{7}$, פִּי כְסִילִים *mouth of fools* Pr 15$_{2.14(Qr)}$ 26$_{7.9}$, עֵינֵי כְסִיל *eyes of a fool* Pr 17$_{24}$, אָזְנֵי *ears of* Pr 23$_{9}$, גֵּו כְּסִילִים *back of fools* Pr 19$_{29}$ 26$_{3}$, חֵיק *bosom of* Ec 7$_{9}$, שִׁיר *song of* Ec 7$_{5}$, מְרִיַם *desire of* Pr 3$_{35}$ (if em.).*

<APP> אָדָם *human being* Pr 15$_{20}$ 21$_{20}$, אִישׁ *man* Pr 14$_{7}$

Si 34_{20}, בֵּן *son* Pr 10_1 17_{25} 19_{13}, מֶלֶךְ *king* Ec 4_{13}. <PREP> לְ of benefit, *to, for* Pr 10_{23} 26_{12} 29_{20} Si 34_{30}, + אוה ni. *be fitting* Pr 19_{10} 26_1, נתן *give* Pr 26_8; בְּ *in, with* Ec 5_3 9_{17}; מִן of comparison, *(more) than*, + יתר *have advantage* Ec 6_8; עִם *with* Ec 2_{16} Si 34_{20}; בְּקֶרֶב *among*, + ידע ni. *be known* Pr 14_{33}; מִנֶּגֶד לְ *(from) opposite*, + הלך *go* Pr 14_7. Also 4QapPs[b] 46_3 (כ[ס]ילים). <SYN> בַּעַר *fool.**
→ כסל *be foolish.*

כְּסִיל II 4.0.1 pr.n.m. **Orion**—pl. Qכסילים; sf. כְּסִילֵיהֶם—**Orion; (in pl.) star** (of Orion) (Is 13_{10} 4QapPs[b] 1_5), <SUBJ> הלל hi. *let shine* Is 13_{10} (|| כּוֹכָב *star*). <OBJ> עשׂה *make* Am 5_8 Jb 9_9 (both + כִּימָה *Pleiades*), אור hi. *cause to shine* 4QapPs[b] 1_5 (ויהיר). <CSTR> מֹשְׁכוֹת כְּסִיל *cords of Orion* Jb 38_{31}. <SYN> כּוֹכָב *star.**

כְּסִיל III 1 pl.n. **Chesil,** town in S of Judah, <SUBJ> היה *be* Jos 15_{30}. <APP> עִיר *city* Jos 15_{30}.

כְּסִילוּת 1 n.f. **stupidity**—<CSTR> אֵשֶׁת כְּסִילוּת *woman of stupidity* or *Lady Folly* Pr 9_{13}.*
→ כסל *be foolish.*

כסל 1 vb. **be foolish—Qal** 1 Impf. יִכְסְלוּ—**be foolish, be stupid,** <SUBJ> חָכָם *wise (one)* Jr 10_8 (|| בער *be foolish*). <SYN> בער *be foolish.**
→ כְּסִיל I *fool*, כְּסִילוּת *stupidity*, כֶּסֶל I *stupidity*, כִּסְלָה *stupidity.*

כֶּסֶל I 6.0.1 n.m. **stupidity**—sf. כִּסְלוֹ, כִּסְלֵךְ, כִּסְלִי, Q כסלכמה, כִּסְלָם—**stupidity; confidence,** <SUBJ> קוט *break in pieces* Jb 8_{14} (or em. קִרֵי קַיִט *threads of summer*). <NOM CL> קִרֵי קַיִט כִּסְלוֹ *his confidence is (as) threads of summer* Jb 8_{14} (if em.), כֶּסֶל לָמוֹ *they have confidence* Ps 49_{14}. <OBJ> שׂים *place* Ps 78_7 Jb 31_{24}. <CSTR> רֶשַׁע כֶּסֶל *wrong of stupidity* Ec 7_{25}. <PREP> בְּ of essence, *as*, + היה *be* Pr 3_{26} (unless כֶּסֶל II at your *thigh*, i.e. side; + רֶגֶל *foot*). Also 4QMyst[b] 1_2.*
→ כסל *be foolish.*

כֶּסֶל II 7.1.3 n.m. **thigh**—כֶּסֶל; pl. כְּסָלִים; sf. כְּסָלַי—<SUBJ> מלא *be full* Ps 38_8. <PREP> בְּ of place, *at* your *thigh*, i.e. side, + היה *be* Pr 3_{26} (unless כֶּסֶל I *confidence*; + רֶגֶל *foot*); עַל *upon* Lv $3_{4.10.15}$ 4_9 7_4 11QT 15_8 16_9 (both [על]) 20_7 ([על הכסלים]) 23_{16}, + עשׂה *make*, i.e. accumulate, fat Jb 15_{27}.*

[כְּסֶלָא] 0.0.0.2 pr.n.m. **Choselah, 1.** <CSTR> בן כסלא *son of Choselah* Seal 632 (T. Beit Mirsim? 7th/6th cent.). **2.** Seal 887 (7th cent.).

כִּסְלָה 2 n.f. **stupidity; confidence**—sf. כִּסְלָתֶךָ—<NOM CL> הֲלֹא יִרְאָתְךָ כִּסְלָתֶךָ *is not your fear your confidence* Jb 4_6. <PREP> לְ of direction, *to*, + שׁוב *go back* Ps 85_9.*
→ כסל *be foolish.*

כִּסְלֵו 2.0.1 pr.n.[m.] **Chislev,** ninth month of Babylonian-based calendar, corresponding to November/ December, <CSTR> חֹדֶשׁ־כִּסְלֵו *month of Chislev* Ne 1_1. <PREP> לְ of possession, *of, (belonging) to* 5/6ḤevBA 45_1; בְּ of time, *in, at* Zc 7_1.

כְּסָלוֹן 1 pl.n. **Chesalon,** location on border of tribe of Judah, perh. ident. with Keslā 16 km W of Jerusalem, <NOM CL> הִיא כְסָלוֹן *it is Chesalon* Jos 15_{10}.

כִּסְלוֹן 1 pr.n.m. **Chislon,** Benjaminite, father of Elidad, appointed to divide portion of land, <CSTR> בֶּן־כִּסְלוֹן *son of Chislon* Nm 34_{21}.

[כַּסְלֻחִי] 2 gent. **Casluhite**—pl. כַּסְלֻחִים—perh. of territory or inhabitants of Lower Egypt, <OBJ> ילד *give birth (to)* (of Egypt) Gn 10_{14}||1 C 1_{12}. <PREP> מִן of direction, *from*, + יצא *go out* (of Philistines) Gn 10_{14}||1 C 1_{12} (or del. אֲשֶׁר יָצְאוּ מִשָּׁם פְּלִשְׁתִּים *whence the Philistines went out* or move to after כַּפְתֹּרִים *Caphtorites*).*

כִּסְלֹת תָּבוֹר 1 pl.n. **Chisloth-tabor,** location in Zebulun, <CSTR> גְּבוּל כִּסְלֹת תָּבֹר *border of Chisloth-tabor* Jos 19_{12}.

כסם 2.0.1 vb. **clip—Qal** 2 Impf. יִכְסְמוּ; inf. כָּסוֹם—<SUBJ> כֹּהֵן *priest* Ezk 44_{20}; subj. not specified, Ezk 44_{20}. <OBJ> רֹאשׁ *head*, i.e. hair Ezk 44_{20}.

Pi. 0.0.1 + waw Q ויכסמוהו—**tear off, ravage,** <SUBJ> חֲזִיר *wild boar* 4QAdmonPar 2.3$_6$ ([חזו]ירים).
⇒ כֻּסֶּמֶת *spelt.*

כְּסָמִים, see כֻּסֶּמֶת *spelt.*

כֻּסֶּמֶת 3 n.f. **spelt**—pl. כֻּסְּמִים—a wheat grain with split awn, <SUBJ> נכה pu. *be ruined* Ex 9$_{32}$ (|| חִטָּה *wheat*). <OBJ> נתן *give*, i.e. place Ezk 4$_9$ (|| חִטָּה), שׂים *place*, i.e. plant Is 28$_{25}$, לקח *take* Ezk 4$_9$ (||חִטָּה). <SYN> חִטָּה *wheat*.
⇒ כסם *clip*.

כסס 1 vb. **reckon—Qal** 1 Impf. תָּכֹסּוּ—<SUBJ> עֵדָה *congregation* of Israel Ex 12$_4$. <PREP> עַל *on behalf of*, + שֶׂה *lamb* Ex 12$_4$.

כסף I 6 vb. **long for—Qal** 3 Impf. יִכְסוֹף, 2ms תִּכְסֹף—<SUBJ> אֵל *God* Jb 14$_{15}$, אַרְיֵה *lion* Ps 17$_{12}$ (+ טרף *tear*). <PREP> לְ of direction, *to*, + מַעֲשֶׂה *work* of your hands Jb 14$_{15}$.

Ni. 3 Pf. נִכְסְפָה ,נִכְסַפְתָּה; ptc. נִכְסָף; inf. נִכְסוֹף—**long for, be ashamed,** Zp 2$_1$ (unless כסף II in same sense), <SUBJ> גּוֹי *nation* Zp 2$_1$, Jacob Gn 31$_{30}$, נֶפֶשׁ *soul* Ps 84$_3$ (+ כלה *be faint*); subj. not specified, Gn 31$_{30}$. <PREP> לְ of direction, *to*, + בַּיִת *house* of your father Gn 31$_{30}$.

* **כסף** II 1 vb. **be ashamed—Ni.** Ptc. נִכְסָף—הַגּוֹי לֹא נִכְסָף *O nation that is not ashamed* Zp 2$_1$.
⇒ כֶּסֶף II *disappointment*, כֹּסֵף *disappointment*.

כֶּסֶף I 403.4.49.6 n.m. **silver**—כָּסֶף; cstr. כֶּסֶף; sf. כַּסְפִּי, כַּסְפְּךָ (כַּסְפֶּךָ), כַּסְפְּכֶם, כַּסְפֵּנוּ, כַּסְפֵּךְ, כַּסְפָּם; pl. sf. כַּסְפֵּיהֶם—**silver,** as found in earth (Job 28$_1$ perh. Pr 2$_4$), melted in crucible (Ezk 22$_{18.20.22}$ Zc 13$_9$), material of valuable objects (e.g. Gn 24$_{53}$ 44$_2$), especially images (e.g. Ex 20$_{23}$ Dt 29$_{16}$), or, oft., for purchase or payment, **money,*** **price; silver object(s)** (1 C 29$_{2.5}$).

<SUBJ> היה *be* Lv 25$_{50}$ 2 K 12$_{17}$ Is 1$_{22}$ Ezk 22$_{18}$ Jb 22$_{25}$, מצא ni. *be found* 2 K 18$_{15}$ 22$_9$, אסף pu. *be gathered* Zc 14$_{14}$, לקח pu. *be taken* Jg 17$_2$, שׁוב ho. *be taken back* Gn 42$_{28}$, perh. נוח ho. *be deposited* 3QTr 9$_{10}$ (כסף מנח הרב *much gold is deposited*; others כסף מן החרם *silver from the consecrated offerings*; כסף מנה חרם *a mina of silver, a consecrated offering*),* נתן pass. *be given* Est 3$_{11}$, רבה *be increased* Dt 8$_{13}$, יכל *be able* Ezk 7$_{19}$ Zp 1$_{18}$, רקע pu. *be beaten* Jr 10$_9$, צרף pass. *be refined* Ps 12$_7$, טהר *be pure* Nm 31$_{22}$, זקק pu. *be refined* 1 C 29$_4$ 1QH 5$_{16}$, שׁקל ni. *be weighed* Jb 28$_{15}$ Ezr 8$_{33}$, תכן pu. *be weighed* 2 K 12$_{12}$, חשׁב ni. *be considered* 1 K 10$_{21}$||2 C 9$_{20}$ 2 K 22$_7$, בחר ni. *be chosen* Pr 10$_{20}$, מאס ni. *be rejected* Jr 6$_{30}$, תמם *be finished* Gn 47$_{15.18}$, אפס *cease* Gn 47$_{15.16}$.

בוא *come* Gn 43$_{23}$ Nm 31$_{22}$, ho. *be brought* 2 K 12$_{10.14.17.17}$ 22$_4$||2 C 34$_9$ Jr 10$_9$, עבר *pass* among merchants, i.e. be valid currency Gn 23$_{16}$ perh. 2 K 12$_5$ (unless עֹבֵר = *pass* into the number of mustered men; or em. עֵרֶךְ silver of *valuation*),* עמד hi. *establish* progress Si 40$_{25}$ (Segal) (כס[ף יעמידו רג]ל), נצל hi. *deliver* Ezk 7$_{19}$ Zp 1$_{18}$, ענה *answer*, i.e. satisfy Ec 10$_{19}$.

<NOM CL> עֲצַבֵּי הַגּוֹיִם כֶּסֶף *the images of the nations are silver* Ps 135$_{15}$, עֲצַבֵּיהֶם כֶּסֶף *their images are silver* Ps 115$_4$, הַכֶּסֶף ... נְדָבָה *the silver is ... a freewill offering* Ezr 8$_{28}$, כֶּסֶף־אִישׁ בְּפִי אַמְתַּחְתּוֹ *everyone's money was in the mouth of his sack* Gn 43$_{21}$, כַּסְפֵּנוּ בְּמִשְׁקָלוֹ *our money was with its (total) weight* Gn 43$_{21}$, אֶלֶף־וּמֵאָה הַכֶּסֶף *one thousand, one hundred (shekels) was the silver* Jg 17$_2$, וְכֶסֶף ... מְאַת כִּכַּר *and the silver ... was one hundred talents* Ex 38$_{25}$,

אַדְנֵיהֶם כֶּסֶף *their sockets are of silver* Ex 26$_{21}$||36$_{26}$ 26$_{25}$||36$_{30}$ (both כָּסֶף), וָוֵי הָעַמֻּדִים ... כֶּסֶף *the nails of the pillars ... shall be of silver* Ex 27$_{10.11}$||38$_{10.11}$ 38$_{12.17}$ (כָּסֶף), וָוֵיהֶם כֶּסֶף *their nails are of silver* Ex 27$_{17}$||38$_{19}$ (כָּסֶף) 38$_{17(Sam)}$ (כָּסֶף), רַב הַכֶּסֶף *great was the silver* 2 K 12$_{11}$|| 2 C 24$_{11}$, כֻּלָּם כֶּסֶף *all of them have become (as) silver* Ezk 22$_{18}$ (if כֶּסֶף moved), צִפּוּי רָאשֵׁיהֶם כֶּסֶף *the plating of their capitals was silver* Ex 38$_{17}$, sim. 38$_{19}$, מְלֹא בֵיתוֹ כֶּסֶף וְזָהָב *the fullness of his house was silver and gold* Nm 22$_{18}$ 24$_{13}$.

בשוא המעבא של מנס ... [כ]סף *in the plastered cistern of Manos is ... silver* 3QTr 1$_{14}$, sim. 3QTr 2$_6$ 9$_{10}$ 12$_{5.7}$, כסף ... בהיכל[ו]תיכה *... let there be silver ... in your fields* 1QM 12$_{12(mg)}$, כַּסְפּוֹ הוּא *it is his money* Ex 21$_{21}$, כַּסְפְּךָ ... לִי־הוּא *your silver ... is mine* 1 K 20$_3$, לִי הַכֶּסֶף *the silver is mine* Hg 2$_8$, הַכֶּסֶף אִתִּי *the silver is with me* Jg 17$_2$, כַּסְפָּם ... אִתָּם *their silver ... is with them* Is 60$_9$, הַכֶּסֶף

תַּחְתֶּיהָ *the silver is underneath it* Jos 7$_{21.22}$.

אֵין כֶּסֶף *there is no money*, i.e. without payment Ex 21$_{11}$, i.e. without considering the cost 1 K 10$_{21}$ (אֵין כֶּסֶף לֹא נֶחְשָׁב *there was no price; it was not considered*; ||2 C 9$_{20}$ lacks לֹא), אין [פ]ה כסף וזהב *there is no silver or gold here* Silwan royal steward tomb inscr. 1$_{1}$, אֲשֶׁר אֵין־לוֹ כָּסֶף *whoever has no money* Is 55$_{1}$ (unless כֶּסֶף III *food*), אֵין־לָנוּ כֶּסֶף וְזָהָב *we have no (claim for) silver or gold* 2 S 21$_{4(Qr)}$ (Kt אֵין־לִי *I have no*).

<OBJ> בוא hi. *bring* Gn 47$_{14}$ Ex 35$_{5}$ 1 K 7$_{51}$||2 C 5$_{1}$ (if del. וְ *and* the silver) 1 K 15$_{15}$||2 C 15$_{18}$ 2 K 12$_{5}$ Is 60$_{17}$ Ca 8$_{11}$ Dn 11$_{8}$ 2 C 9$_{14}$ 17$_{11}$ 4QDibHam^{a} 1.4$_{10}$ 11QT 43$_{14}$, שׁוב hi. *take back* Gn 42$_{25}$ 43$_{12.21}$ Ex 21$_{34}$ Jg 17$_{3.4}$ Ne 5$_{11}$, עבר hi. *cause to pass* Nm 31$_{22}$, יצא hi. *take out* 2 K 12$_{12}$ 15$_{20}$ 2 C 16$_{2}$ 34$_{14}$, ירד hi. *take down* Gn 43$_{22}$, עלה hi. *take up* Jg 16$_{18}$, נשׂא *raise*, i.e. carry off 1 K 10$_{22}$||2 C 9$_{21}$ 2 K 7$_{8}$ Ezk 38$_{13}$, שׁלח *send* 2 C 16$_{3}$ Arad ost. 16$_{5}$ ([ה]כ[סף]), שׁלך hi. *throw* Ezk 7$_{19}$, שׂים *place* Gn 43$_{22}$ 44$_{1.2}$, אסף *gather* 2 C 24$_{11}$, קבץ *gather* 2 C 24$_{5}$, כנס *gather* Ec 2$_{9}$, לקט pi. *gather* Gn 47$_{14}$, צבר *amass* Zc 9$_{3}$ Jb 27$_{16}$, עשׂה *make*, i.e. amass Ezk 28$_{4}$, *make* silver *into* Ho 8$_{4}$, צור *tie up* Dt 14$_{25}$ 2 K 12$_{11}$ (unless צור III *melt down*; or em. יצר *form*, i.e. reshape, or ערה *empty*).

נתן *give* Gn 20$_{16}$ 23$_{13}$ 24$_{35}$ 45$_{22}$ Ex 21$_{32}$ 22$_{6}$ Lv 25$_{37}$ Nm 3$_{48}$ Dt 14$_{26}$ 22$_{19}$=11QT 65$_{14}$ Dt 22$_{29}$=11QT 66$_{10}$ Jg 9$_{4}$ 16$_{5}$ 17$_{10}$ 2 S 18$_{11}$ 1 K 7$_{51}$||2 C 5$_{1}$ 1 K 20$_{5}$ 21$_{2}$ 2 K 12$_{10.12.16}$ 18$_{15}$ 22$_{9}$ 23$_{35.35}$ Ezk 27$_{12}$ (if del. בְּ *in exchange for* silver) Ps 15$_{5}$ Ezr 2$_{69}$||Ne 2$_{70}$ Ezr 3$_{7}$ Ne 7$_{69.71}$ 1 C 29$_{3.7}$ 2 C 34$_{9}$ (or em. נתך hi. *pour*) perh. 4QD^{b} 4$_{10}$ ([יתן]), *place* Jos 6$_{24}$ 2 K 12$_{10}$, *cause* silver *to be* 1 K 10$_{27}$||2 C 1$_{15}$||9$_{27}$.

מצא *find* Gn 44$_{8}$, לקח *take* Gn 43$_{12}$ Ex 25$_{3}$ 30$_{16}$ Nm 3$_{49.50}$ Jos 7$_{24}$ Jg 17$_{4}$ 2 K 5$_{26}$ 12$_{8.9}$ 14$_{14}$ 16$_{8}$ perh. 25$_{15}$||Jr 52$_{19}$ (see Coll.) Jl 4$_{5}$ Zc 6$_{11}$ 11$_{13}$ Pr 8$_{10}$, קנה *acquire* Si 51$_{28}$, לוה *borrow* Ne 5$_{4}$, hi. *lend* Ex 22$_{24}$, נשׁא *lend* Ne 5$_{10}$, כון hi. *provide* 1 C 22$_{14}$ 29$_{2}$ 4QSela 8.2$_{5}$ ([יכין]), ענשׁ *fine* Dt 22$_{19}$=11QT 65$_{14}$, שׁקל *weigh* Gn 23$_{16}$ Ex 22$_{16}$ 2 S 18$_{12}$ Is 46$_{6}$ 55$_{2}$ Jr 32$_{9.10}$ Ezr 8$_{25}$, רבה hi. *multiply* Dt 17$_{17}$=11QT 56$_{19}$ Ho 2$_{10}$ Si 47$_{18}$ 11QT 56$_{17}$, חצה *divide* Ex 21$_{35}$, חלק *divide* Jb 27$_{17}$, טהר pi. *cleanse* Ml 3$_{3}$, צרף *refine* Zc 13$_{9}$ Ps 66$_{1}$, קדשׁ hi. *consecrate* Jg 17$_{30}$ 2 S 8$_{11}$||1 C 18$_{11}$, עבד *worship* 11QT 59$_{3}$, נתך hi. *pour*, i.e. empty out 2 K 22$_{4}$||2 C 34$_{9}$ (if em. in both) 2 K 22$_{9}$||2 C 34$_{17}$, גנב *steal* Gn 44$_{8}$, אכל *eat*, i.e. use up Gn 31$_{15}$, בזז *plunder* Na 2$_{10}$, נגשׂ *exact* 2 K 23$_{35}$.

ראה *see* Gn 42$_{27}$, hi. *show* 2 K 20$_{13}$||Is 39$_{2}$, אהב *love* Ec 5$_{9}$, שׂבע *be satisfied (with)* Ec 5$_{9}$, חמד *desire* Dt 7$_{25}$=11QT 2$_{8}$, חשׁב *esteem* Is 13$_{17}$, pi. *calculate* Lv 27$_{18}$, מנה *count* 2 K 12$_{11}$, תמם hi. *sum up* 2 K 22$_{4}$ (or em. נתך hi. *pour* or חתם *stamp*).

<CSTR> כֶּסֶף פְּקוּדֵי *silver of the mustered ones of* the congregation Ex 38$_{25}$, הַכֵּלִים *of the vessels* Nm 7$_{85}$, תּוֹעָפוֹת *of eminence* Jb 22$_{25}$, סִיגִים *of dross* Pr 26$_{23}$.

כֶּסֶף־אִישׁ *money of each one* Gn 43$_{21}$ 44$_{1}$, כֶּסֶף נַפְשׁוֹת *money (in payment) of persons* 2 K 12$_{5}$, מִקְנָתוֹ *of his purchase* Lv 25$_{51}$, מִמְכָּרוֹ *of his sale* Lv 25$_{50}$, עֶרְךְ *valuation* 2 K 12$_{5}$ (if em. עֹבֵר money that *passes* to merchants, i.e. valid currency), עֶרְכְּךָ *of your valuation* Lv 27$_{15.19}$, כסף ערכו *money of its valuation* CD 16$_{18}$ (=4QD^{a} 8.2$_{3}$), כֶּסֶף הערכים *of the valuation* 4QOrd^{a} 1.2$_{6}$ 4QD^{e} 2.2$_{9}$, כֶּסֶף הַשָּׂדֶה *money of the field* Gn 23$_{13}$, מְחִיר *of*, i.e. for, its *price* 1 K 21$_{2}$, שִׁבְרוֹ *of*, i.e. for, *his grain* Gn 44$_{2}$, הַכִּפֻּרִים *of atonement* Ex 30$_{16}$, הַפִּדְיוֹם *of redemption* Nm 3$_{49.51}$ (הַפְּדֻיִים), הַקֳּדָשִׁים *of the sacred objects* 2 K 12$_{5}$, אָשָׁם *of*, i.e. from, *guilt offering(s)* 2 K 12$_{17}$, חַטָּאוֹת *of sin offerings* 2 K 12$_{17}$.

צְרוֹר הַכֶּסֶף *the pouch of*, i.e. for, *money* Pr 7$_{20}$, צְרוֹר־כַּסְפּוֹ *pouch of his money* Gn 42$_{35}$, צְרוֹרוֹת כַּסְפֵּיהֶם *pouch of their money* Gn 42$_{35}$, שדת כסף *chest of money* 3QTr 1$_{3}$, אֲגוֹרַת כֶּסֶף *payment of money* 1 S 2$_{36}$, מִקְנַת־כֶּסֶף *purchase of*, i.e. bought for, *money* Gn 17$_{12.27}$ Ex 12$_{44}$ (כָּסֶף), מִקְנַת כַּסְפֶּךָ *purchase of your money* Gn 17$_{13}$, מִקְנַת כַּסְפּוֹ *purchase of his money* Gn 17$_{23}$, קִנְיַן כַּסְפּוֹ *an acquisition of*, i.e. through, *his money* Lv 22$_{11}$, נֶשֶׁךְ כֶּסֶף *interest of*, i.e. from, *money* Dt 23$_{20}$, צֵל הַכָּסֶף *the shelter of money* Ec 7$_{12}$, שְׁאָר הַכֶּסֶף *remainder of the money* 2 C 24$_{14}$, פָּרָשַׁת perh. *exact amount of* Est 4$_{7}$, דְּבַר *matter of* Gn 43$_{18}$, מִשְׁנֶה־כֶסֶף *double of*, i.e. twice as much *money* Gn 43$_{15(mss)}$.

אֱלֹהֵי כֶסֶף *gods of silver* Ex 20$_{23}$, אֱלִילֵי כַסְפּוֹ *his images of silver* Is 2$_{20}$ 31$_{7}$, פְּסִילֵי כַסְפֶּךָ *your images of silver* Is 30$_{22}$, מַשְׂכִּיּוֹת כָּסֶף *images of silver* Pr 25$_{11}$, רַצֵּי־כָסֶף *pieces of silver* Ps 68$_{31}$ (mss רָצֵי־ *ones who run of*, i.e. after, silver; or em. רֹצֵי *those desirous of* silver), תְּרוּמַת כֶּסֶף *contribution of silver* Ex 35$_{24}$, שֹׁחַד כֶּסֶף *bribe of silver* 1 K

15$_{19}$, בֶּצַע כֶּסֶף *profit of silver* Jg 5$_{19}$, סְחַר־כֶּסֶף *profit of silver* Pr 3$_{14}$, מִכְמַנֵּי ... הַכֶּסֶף *the hidden treasures of ... silver* Dn 11$_{43}$.

שֶׁקֶל כֶּסֶף *shekel of silver* Gn 23$_{15}$ (שֶׁקֶל־) 23$_{16}$ Lv 27$_{3.16}$ (כֶּסֶף) 1 S 9$_{8}$ (כֶּסֶף), כִּכַּר־ *talent of* Ex 38$_{27}$ (כִּכַּר הַכֶּסֶף) 1 K 20$_{39}$ 2 K 5$_{5}$ (כִּכְּרֵי־) 5$_{22}$ 15$_{19}$ (כֶּסֶף) 18$_{14}$ 23$_{33}$‖2 C 36$_{3}$ Est 3$_{9}$ 1 C 19$_{6}$ 29$_{4}$ 2 C 25$_{6}$ (כֶּסֶף) 27$_{5}$ Arad ost. 16$_{5}$ (הו[כ]סף 8 ש), נְטִילֵי כֶסֶף *ones laden of*, i.e. with, *silver* Zp 1$_{11}$, טִירַת כָּסֶף *battlement of silver* Ca 8$_{9}$, מִטּוֹת ... כֶּסֶף *couches of ... silver* Est 1$_{6}$, מְנֹרוֹת הַכֶּסֶף *the lampstands of silver* 1 C 28$_{15}$, שֻׁלְחָנוֹת *the tables of* 1 C 28$_{16}$ (הַכָּסֶף), חֲצוֹצְרֹת *trumpets of* Nm 10$_{2}$, רְתֻקוֹת *chains of* Is 40$_{19}$, חֶבֶל הַכֶּסֶף *the cord of silver* Ec 12$_{6}$, נְקֻדּוֹת הַכָּסֶף perh. *the beads of silver* Ca 1$_{11}$, אַדְנֵי־כֶסֶף *sockets of silver* Ex 26$_{19}$‖36$_{24}$ 26$_{32}$‖36$_{36}$ (both כָּסֶף), גְּלִילֵי *rods of* Est 1$_{6}$.

כְּלֵי־כֶסֶף *vessels of silver* Gn 24$_{53}$ Ex 3$_{22}$ 11$_{2}$ 12$_{35}$ 2 S 8$_{10}$ 1 K 10$_{25}$‖2 C 9$_{24}$ (כְּלֵי כֶסֶף) 2 K 12$_{14}$ (כְּלִי־כָסֶף *vessel of silver*) Ezr 1$_{6}$ 8$_{26}$ 1 C 18$_{10}$ (כְּלֵי זָהָב וָכֶסֶף) 28$_{14}$ (כְּלֵי הַכֶּסֶף) 2 C 24$_{14}$ (כְּלֵי זָהָב וָכֶסֶף) 3QTr 3$_{2}$ 12$_{6}$ (כל[י]), מִזְרְקֵי־ *basins of*, Nm 7$_{84}$, אֲגַרְטְלֵי־ *baskets of* Ezr 1$_{9}$, כְּפוֹרֵי *bowls of silver* Ezr 1$_{10}$ 1 C 28$_{17}$ (הַכֶּסֶף), כוננות הכסף perh. *the bowls of silver* 11QT 33$_{14}$, קַעֲרַת־כֶּסֶף *dish of silver* Nm 7$_{13+11t}$, קַעֲרֹת *dishes of* Nm 7$_{84}$, סִפּוֹת *bowls of* 2 K 12$_{14}$, גְּבִיעַ הַכֶּסֶף *the cup of silver* Gn 44$_{2}$.

קְבֻצַת כֶּסֶף *gathering of silver* Ezk 22$_{20}$, הִתּוּךְ *melting of* Ezk 22$_{22}$, [חמ]שית כסף *a fifth of the money of* its valuation 4QD^{a} 8.2$_{3}$, עֲשֶׂרֶת כֶּסֶף *ten (pieces) of silver* Jg 17$_{10}$, אֶלֶף *a thousand (pieces) of* Gn 20$_{16}$, אַלְפֵי זָהָב וָכָסֶף *thousands (of pieces of) gold and silver* Ps 119$_{72}$, כָּל־הַכֶּסֶף *all the silver* 1 K 15$_{18}$ 2 K 14$_{14}$‖2 C 25$_{24}$ (כָּל־הַזָּהָב־וְהַכֶּסֶף) 4QD^{f} 2$_{9}$ (כו[ל] הזהב והכסף), *all the money* Gn 47$_{14}$ 2 K 12$_{10}$, כָּל־כֶּסֶף *all (the) money* 2 K 12$_{5}$, כֹּל כֶּסֶף *all the silver* Jos 6$_{19}$, *all the silver of* Nm 7$_{85}$, *all the money of* 2 K 12$_{5}$.

<APP> אֱלֹהִים *god* 11QT 59$_{3}$, דָּבָר any *thing* Nm 31$_{22}$, תְּרוּמָה *contribution* Ex 35$_{5}$, מִנְחָה *offering* 4QDibHam^{a} 1.4$_{10}$, קֹדֶשׁ *holy thing* 1 K 7$_{51}$‖2 C 5$_{1}$ (if del. וְ *and* the silver) 15$_{15}$‖2 C 15$_{18}$, שֶׁקֶל *shekel* Ex 21$_{32}$ Lv 5$_{15}$ (perh. cstr.) 27$_{6.6}$ Nm 18$_{16}$ Jos 7$_{21}$ 2 S 24$_{24}$ 2 K 15$_{20}$ Jr 32$_{9}$ Ne 5$_{15}$ (perh. cstr.) Meṣad Ḥashavyahu ost. 6$_{2}$, כִּכָּר *talent* 1 K 16$_{24}$ 2 K 5$_{23}$ 1 C 22$_{14}$ 29$_{7}$ 3QTr 1$_{14}$ ([כ]סף ... כ[כר]) 2$_{6}$ 3$_{6}$ 4$_{4.10.12.14}$ 5$_{4.11}$ 8$_{6.16}$ (all nine ככ) 10$_{6}$ 12$_{5}$ (ככ), מָנֶה *mina* 3QTr 9$_{10}$ (others מנח *deposited*), מִשְׁנֶה *double (amount)* Gn 43$_{12.15}$, חַיִל *wealth* Zc 14$_{14}$, סְגֻלָּה *treasure* 1 C 29$_{3}$, כְּלִי *vessel* Dn 11$_{8}$, קְעָרָה *dish* Nm 7$_{85}$, מִזְרָק *basin* Nm 7$_{13+11t}$, גִּלּוּל *image* Dt 29$_{16}$, שִׁקּוּץ *abomination* Dt 29$_{16}$, מַעֲשֶׂה *work* 1QM 5$_{5}$ 11QT 59$_{3}$.

<ADJ> מָלֵא *full* Gn 23$_{9}$ 1 C 21$_{22.24}$, אַחֵר *other* Gn 43$_{22}$, רַב *much* 3QTr 9$_{10}$ (הרב; others חרם *consecrated offering*).

<PREP> לְ of benefit, *to, for* Pr 17$_{3}$ 27$_{21}$, כון hi. *provide* 1 C 29$_{2}$, נתן *give* 1 C 29$_{5}$, עשׂה *make* treasuries 2 C 32$_{27}$; of possession, *of, (belonging) to* Jb 28$_{1}$ 1 C 22$_{16}$ 29$_{5}$; *(consisting) of* Ho 9$_{6}$ (or em. מַחְמַדֵּי כַסְפָּם *their desirable things of silver*, unless כֶּסֶף II *disappointment*) Ezr 1$_{11}$ 2 C 21$_{3}$; *for (the purpose of)*, + שׁלח *send* 1 K 20$_{7}$.

בְּ of instrument, *by (means of), with, through*, + חפה ni. *be covered* Ps 68$_{14}$, כבד pi. *honour* Dn 11$_{38}$, יפה pi. *decorate* Jr 10$_{4}$, נשׂא pi. *assist* Ezr 1$_{4}$; *as (though you were)*, + צרף *refine* Is 48$_{10}$; of accompaniment, *with* perh. 4QD^{b} 7$_{4}$ ([בכס]ף) perh. 4QD^{f} 3$_{1}$, + שׁוב *go back* Jos 22$_{8}$, יצא hi. *take* Israel *out* Ps 105$_{37}$; of essence, *in, (consisting) of* 1QM 5$_{8.14}$; *in respect of*, + כבד *be heavy*, i.e. rich Gn 13$_{2}$; עשׂה בְּ *work in/with* Ex 31$_{4}$‖35$_{32}$ 2 C 2$_{6.13}$.

בְּ *with, (in exchange) for* Mur 22 1$_{4}$, + גאל ni. *be redeemed* Is 52$_{3}$, נתן *give* Gn 23$_{9}$ 14$_{25}$ Dt 2$_{28}$ 1 K 21$_{6.15}$ Ezk 27$_{12}$ (or del. בְּ, with כֶּסֶף as obj. of נתן) 1 C 21$_{22}$, כרה *buy* Dt 2$_{6}$, קנה *buy* 2 S 24$_{24}$‖1 C 21$_{24}$ Is 43$_{24}$ Jr 32$_{25.44}$ Am 8$_{6}$, *acquire* wisdom Si 51$_{25}$ (בְּלֹא *not in exchange for*), שׁבר *buy (food)* Dt 2$_{6}$ Is 55$_{1}$, hi. *sell (food)* Dt 2$_{28}$, מכר *sell* Dt 21$_{14}$ Am 2$_{6}$ 11QT 43$_{14}$ Mur 30 2$_{20}$, שׁתה *drink* water Lm 5$_{4}$, קסם *practise divination* Mc 3$_{11}$.

כְּ *as (though they/it were)* 1QH 5$_{16}$, + זקק pi. *refine* Ml 3$_{3}$, בקשׁ pi. *seek* Pr 2$_{4}$.

מִן of direction, *from*, + הגה *remove* dross Pr 25$_{4}$; of comparison, *(more) than* Si 40$_{25}$ (ומשׁ[ניהם]), + בחר ni. *be chosen* Pr 8$_{19}$ 16$_{16}$ 22$_{1}$; *from, (out) of*, עשׂה ni. *be made* 2 K 12$_{14}$, לקח *take* Ezk 16$_{17}$, עשׂה *make* Ho 13$_{2}$; *in proportion to*, + שׁוב hi. *take back*, i.e. repay Lv 25$_{51}$; partitive, *(any) of*, + בוא hi. *bring* 4QD^{f} 2$_{9}$ (מכו[ל] ... הכסף).

עִם *with*, + קדשׁ hi. *consecrate* 2 S 8$_{11}$‖1 C 18$_{11}$.

בְּלִי *without*, + אכל *eat* Jb 31$_{39}$.

<COLL> כֶּסֶף *silver* after (and oft. ‖ to) זָהָב *gold* Ex 25$_{3}$ 26$_{32}$ 31$_{4}$ 35$_{5.32}$ 36$_{36}$ Nm 31$_{22}$ Jos 7$_{21}$ 1 K 10$_{21.22}$‖2 C

$9_{20.21}$ 2 K 12_{14} 14_{14}||2 C 25_{24} 2 K 23_{35} 25_{15} Is 40_{19} 46_6 60_{17} Jr 52_{19} Ezk 7_{19} $16_{13.17}$ 28_4 Hb 2_{19} Zc 14_{14} Ml 3_3 Ps 119_{72} Jb 3_{15} Pr 25_{11} Ca 1_{11} Est 1_6 Dn $11_{38.43}$ Ezr $1_{9.10.11}$ 2_{69}||Ne 7_{70} Ne 7_{71} 1 C 18_{10} $22_{14.16}$ $28_{14.15.16.17}$ $29_{2.3.4.5.7}$ 2 C $2_{6.13}$ 9_{14} 24_{14} Si 40_{25} 47_{18} 1QH 5_{16} ([כז]הב) 1QM $5_{5.8.14}$ 4QD[f] 2_9 4QSela 8.2_5.

כֶּסֶף *silver* before (and oft. || to) זָהָב *gold* Gn 13_2 $24_{35.53}$ 44_8 Ex 3_{22} 11_2 12_{35} 20_{23} Nm 7_{84} 22_{18} 24_{13} Dt 7_{25}=11QT 2_8 Dt 8_{13} 17_{17}=11QT 56_{19} Dt 29_{16} Jos $6_{19.24}$ $7_{21.24}$ 22_8 2 S $8_{10.11}$||1 C 18_{11} 21_4 1 K 7_{51}||2 C 5_1 1 K 10_{25} ||2 C 9_{24} 1 K $15_{15.18.19}$||2 C $16_{2.3}$ 1 K $20_{3.5.7}$ 2 K 5_5 7_8 12_{14} 16_8 18_{14} 20_{13} $23_{33.35}$||2 C 36_3 Is $2_{7.20}$ 13_{17} 30_{22} 31_7 39_2 60_9 Jr $10_{4.9}$ Ezk 7_{19} 38_{13} Ho 2_{10} 8_4 Jl 4_5 Na 2_{10} Zp 1_{18} Hg 2_8 Zc 6_{11} 13_9 Ml 3_3 Ps 105_{37} 115_4 135_{15} Jb 28_1 Pr 17_3 22_1 27_{21} Ca 3_{10} Ec 2_8 12_6 Est 1_6 Dn 11_8 Ezr $1_{4.6}$ $8_{25.26.28.30.33}$ 2 C 1_{15} 15_8 21_3 24_{14} 32_{27} Si 51_{28} 1QM $12_{12(mg)}$=19_5 ([כסף וזהב]) 3QTr 3_2 8_6 12_6 4QapJoseph[b] 8_7 ([כ]סף) 4QDibHam[a] 1.4_{10} 11QT 3_5 56_{17} 59_3.

כֶּסֶף אוֹ־כֵלִים *money or goods* Ex 22_6.

הוּא תָּפוּשׂ זָהָב וָכֶסֶף *it is seized (of)*, i.e. overlaid with, *gold and silver* Hb 2_{19}=1QpHab 12_{16} (הוא תפוש זהב] [וכסף), מְחֻשָּׁקִים כֶּסֶף all the pillars of the court will *be bound with silver* Ex 27_{17}||Ex 38_{17}, עַמּוּדָיו עָשָׂה כֶסֶף *its columns he made of silver* Ca 3_{10}, וַתַּעְדִּי זָהָב וָכֶסֶף *and you adorned yourself with gold and silver* Ezk 16_{13}, וַתִּמָּלֵא אַרְצוֹ כֶּסֶף וְזָהָב *and his land was filled with silver and gold* Is 2_7, הַמְמַלְאִים בָּתֵּיהֶם כָּסֶף *who fill their houses with silver* Jb 3_{15}, שני דודין מלאין כסף *two pots full of silver* 3QTr 4_8, אֲשֶׁר־כֶּסֶף כָּסֶף perh. *what was of silver, silver* he took, or, *whatever was of silver* 2 K 25_{15}||Jr 52_{19}.

כֶּסֶף after numeral (not cstr.) for number of silver coins, חֲמִשָּׁה *five* 2 K 6_{25} 4QOrd[a] 1.2_{11} ([חמ[שה)), עֲשָׂרָה *ten* 2 S 18_{11}, חֲמִשָּׁה עָשָׂר *fifteen* Ho 3_2, עֶשְׂרִים *twenty* Gn 37_{28}, שְׁלֹשִׁים *thirty* Zc $11_{12.13}$, חֲמִשִּׁים *fifty* Dt 22_{29}=11QT 66_{10}, שִׁבְעִים *seventy* Jg 9_4, שְׁמֹנִים *eighty* 2 K 6_{25}, מֵאָה *one hundred* Dt 22_{19}=11QT 65_{14}, מָאתַיִם *two hundred* Jg 17_4, שֵׁשׁ מֵאוֹת *six hundred* 1 K 10_{29}||2 C 1_{17}, אֶלֶף *one thousand* 2 S 18_{12} Is 7_{23} Ca 8_{11}, אֶלֶף[־]וּמֵאָה *eleven hundred* Jg 16_5 17_3.

כֶּסֶף before numeral (not cstr.) for quantity (in talents) of silver, ארבעין *forty* 3QTr 1_{14} ([כ]סף... [כ]כר), ששין ושנין *sixty-two* 3QTr 10_6, שבעין *seventy* 3QTr 2_6 4_{12}, מאתין *two hundred* 3QTr 4_{10}; 40 כסף ככ *forty talents of silver* 3QTr 3_6, sim. (quantity in brackets) 3QTr 4_4 (45) 4_{10} (12) 5_4 (7) 5_{11} (23) 8_6 (17; כסף וזהב *silver and gold*) 8_{16} 12_5 (60).

כסף 40 זוז *forty zuzim of silver* Mur 22 1_4, כסף ש[מו]נים שמונה זוז *eighty-eight zuzim of silver* Mur 30 2_{20}, כסף זוזין מאה ששין *a hundred and sixty zuzim of silver* 5/6ḤevBA 46, כֶּסֶף ... חֲמִשִּׁים וּמֵאָה *one hundred and fifty pieces of silver* 1 K 10_{29}||2 C 1_{17}, בדין של כסף שש *six bars of silver* 3QTr 2_{11} 7_{10}.

ש 8 ה[כ]סף *8 sh(ekels) of silver* Arad ost. 16_5, [כ]ס[ף] 6 *6 (pieces) of silver* Arad ost. 48_2, כסף 10 *10 (pieces) of silver* Arad ost. 29_6.

Also Arad ost. 16_8 24_5 (כס[ף]).

<SYN> זָהָב *gold.*

<ANT> כְּלִי *vessel.**

כֶּסֶף II $_1$ n.[m.] **disappointment**—מַחְמַד לְכַסְפָּם *(that which they) desire is for*, i.e. results in, *their disappointment* Ho 9_6 (or em. מַחְמַדָּם *their desire*).

⇒ כסף II *be ashamed.*

* **[כֶּסֶף]** III $_1$ n.[m.] **food**—כֶּסֶף—כָּסֶף—אֲשֶׁר אֵין־לוֹ כָּסֶף *whoever has no food* Is 55_1 (unless כֶּסֶף I *silver*).

* **[כֹּסֶף]** n.[m.] **disappointment**—מַחְמַד לְכָסְפָּם *that which they desire results in disappointment* Ho 9_6 (if em. מַחְמַד לְכַסְפָּם *their treasures of silver*, or see כֶּסֶף II).

⇒ כסף II *be ashamed.*

כָּסִפְיָא $_2$ pl.n. **Casiphia,** in Babylonia, <APP> מָקוֹם *place* Ezr $8_{17.17}$. <PREP> בְּ of place, *in, at* Ezr $8_{17.17}$.

[כָּסֵר] $_{0.0.0.1}$ pl.n. **Caser,** appar. in Samaria, <PREP> מִן of direction, *from* Samaria ostr. 49_3.

כֶּסֶת $_2$ n.f. **band**—pl. כְּסָתוֹת; sf. כִּסְּתוֹתֵיכֶנָה—of **bands** used for magical purposes, <OBJ> תפר pi. *sow together* Ezk 13_{18}. <PREP> אֶל *against* Ezk 13_{20}.

כעס $_{54.1.3}$ vb. **be angry—Qal** $_6$ Pf. כָּעַס (כָּעָס); impf. אֶכְעַס; + waw וַיִּכְעַס; inf. כָּעוֹס—**be angry, vexed,**

<SUBJ> '' *Y.* Ezk 16$_{42}$, Asa 2 C 16$_{10}$, Sanballat Ne 3$_{33}$ (|| חרה *be angry*), רָשָׁע *wicked one* Ps 112$_{10}$, בַּעַל *master*, i.e. possessor of riches Ec 5$_{16}$; subj. not specified, Ec 7$_{9}$. <PREP> אֶל *to, with*, + רֹאֶה *seer* 2 C 16$_{10}$. <SYN> חרה *be angry*.

Pi. $_{2}$ Pf. כִּעֲסוּנִי, כִּעֲסַתָּה—**provoke (to anger),** <SUBJ> Israelite(s) Dt 32$_{21}$, צָרָה *rival-wife* 1 S 1$_{6}$. <OBJ> '' *Y.* Dt 32$_{21}$, Hannah 1 S 1$_{6}$. <PREP> בְּ of instrument, *by (means of)*, + הֶבֶל *image* Dt 32$_{21}$. <COLL> וְכִעֲסַתָּה צָרָתָהּ גַּם־כַּעַס *and her rival provoked her deeply* 1 S 1$_{6}$.

Hi. $_{46.1.3}$ Pf. הִכְעִיס, הִכְעַסְתָּ, הִכְעִיסוּ (הִכְעִסוּנִי); impf. 3fs תַּכְעֶסְנָה, אַכְעִיסֵם, יַכְעִיסֻהוּ, תַּכְעִיסוּ; + waw וְהִכְעַסְתִּי; וַיַּכְעֵס, וַיַּכְעִיסוּ (וַיַּכְעִיסוּהוּ); ptc. Si מכעיס, מַכְעִיסִים (מַכְעִסִים); inf. הַכְעִיס (הַכְעִיסֵנִי, הַכְעִסֵנִי, הַכְעִיסוֹ)—**provoke (to anger), disturb** (Ezk 32$_{9}$), **offend, insult,** <SUBJ> '' *Y.* Dt 32$_{21}$ Ezk 32$_{9}$, עַם *people* Is 65$_{3}$ Jr 8$_{19}$ 25$_{6.7(Qr)}$, Israel 1 K 14$_{15}$ 4QPseud^{b} 5.1$_{11}$, Israelite(s) Dt 4$_{25}$ 9$_{18}$ 31$_{29}$ 32$_{16}$, Ephraim Ho 12$_{15}$, Judaean Jr 44$_{8}$, בַּיִת *house* of Israel Jr 11$_{17}$, בַּיִת *house* of Judah Jr 11$_{17}$ Ezk 8$_{17}$, שְׁאֵרִית *remnant* 2 K 21$_{15}$, Jerusalem Jer 44$_{3}$ Ezk 16$_{26}$, עִיר *city* Jr 44$_{3}$.

Ahab 1 K 16$_{33}$ 21$_{22}$, Ahaz 2 C 28$_{25}$, Ahaziah 1 K 22$_{54}$, Baasha 1 K 16$_{2.7.13}$, Elah 1 K 16$_{13}$, Jeroboam 1 K 14$_{9}$ 15$_{30}$, Manasseh 2 K 21$_{6}$||2 C 33$_{6}$ 2 K 23$_{26}$, Omri 1 K 16$_{26}$, Sanballat Ne 3$_{37}$, Tobiah Ne 3$_{37}$.

אָב Israelite *father* Ps 78$_{58}$ 106$_{29}$, *father* Jr 7$_{18.19}$, אִשָּׁה *woman* Jr 7$_{18.19}$, צָרָה *rival-wife* 1 S 1$_{7}$, בֵּן Israelite *son* Jg 2$_{12}$ 2 K 17$_{11.17}$ Jr 32$_{30.32}$, Judaean *son* Jr 32$_{32}$, *son* Jr 7$_{18.19}$, מֶלֶךְ *king* 2 K 23$_{19}$, יֹשֵׁב *inhabitant* 2 K 22$_{17}$||2 C 34$_{25}$ Jr 25$_{6.7(Qr)}$; subj. not specified, Jr 32$_{29}$ Si 3$_{16}$.

<OBJ> '' *Y.* Dt 4$_{25}$ 9$_{18}$ 31$_{29}$ Jg 2$_{12}$ 1 K 14$_{9.15}$ 15$_{30}$ 16$_{2.7.13.26.33}$ 22$_{54}$ 2 K 17$_{11.17}$ 21$_{6(mss)}$||2 C 33$_{6}$ 2 K 21$_{15}$ 22$_{17}$||2 C 34$_{25}$ 2 K 23$_{19}$ (if ins.) 23$_{26}$ Is 65$_{3}$ Jr 7$_{18.19}$ 8$_{19}$ 11$_{17}$ 25$_{6.7}$ 32$_{29.30.32}$ 44$_{3.8}$ Ezk 8$_{17}$ 16$_{26}$ Ps 106$_{29(mss)}$ 2 C 28$_{25}$, אֱלֹהִים *God* Dt 4$_{25}$ 1 K 14$_{9}$ 15$_{30}$ 16$_{13.26.33}$ 22$_{54}$ Ps 78$_{58}$ 2 C 28$_{25}$, אֱלוֹהַּ *God* Dt 32$_{16}$, בֹּרֵא *creator* Si 3$_{16}$, Israelite(s) Dt 32$_{21}$, Hannah 1 S 1$_{7}$, לֵב *heart* Ezk 32$_{9}$.

<PREP> לְ introducing object, + אֱלֹהִים *God* 4QPseud^{b} 5.1$_{11}$ ([לא]לוהיכה), Levi 4QapJoseph^{b} 1$_{14}$, Judah 4QapJoseph^{b} 1$_{14}$, Benjamin 4QapJoseph^{b} 1$_{14}$.

בְּ of instrument, *by (means of), with*, + גּוֹי *nation* Dt 32$_{21}$, הֶבֶל *image* 1 K 16$_{13.26}$, פְּסִיל *image* Jr 8$_{19}$, בָּמָה *high place* Ps 78$_{58}$, מַעֲשֶׂה *deed* Dt 31$_{29}$ 1 K 16$_{7}$ 2 K 22$_{17}$||2 C 34$_{25}$ Jr 25$_{6.7}$ 32$_{30}$ 44$_{8}$, מַעֲלָל *deed* Ps 106$_{29}$, דָּבָר *word* 4QapJoseph^{b} 1$_{14}$, תּוֹעֵבָה *abominable practice* Dt 32$_{16}$, חַטָּאת *sin* 1 K 16$_{2}$, כַּעַס *anger* 1 K 15$_{30}$.

אֶל *because of*, + כַּעַס *anger* 1 K 21$_{22}$; עַל *upon, to*, + פָּנִים *face* Is 65$_{3}$; *because of*, + כַּעַס *anger* 2 K 23$_{26}$.

לְנֶגֶד *before*, + בֹּנֶה *builder* Ne 3$_{37}$.

<COLL> הִכְעִיס אֶפְרַיִם תַּמְרוּרִים *Ephraim has acted in a bitterly provocative manner* Ho 12$_{15}$.

Also 4QDibHam^{a} 26$_{7}$.*

⇒ כַּעַס *anger*, כַּעַשׂ *anger*.

כַּעַס $_{21.1.4}$ n.m. **anger**—כָּעַס; cstr. כַּעַס; sf. כַּעְסִי, כַּעַסְךָ, כַּעֲסוֹ (כַּעְסוֹ); pl. כְּעָסִים; see also כַּעַשׂ—**anger, irritation, provocation,** used of both divine and human **anger** (e.g. 1 S 1$_{6.16}$ 1 K 5$_{20}$ 2 K 23$_{26}$ Ezk 20$_{28}$), also of **grief** and **vexation** (e.g. Ps 6$_{8}$ 10$_{14}$); perh. **care*** (Ec 7$_{9}$).

<SUBJ> ידע ni. *be known* Pr 12$_{16}$, נוח *rest* Ec 7$_{9}$. <NOM CL> כַּעַס עִנְיָנוֹ *his occupation is a vexation* Ec 2$_{23}$, כַּעַס לְאָבִיו בֵּן כְּסִיל *a foolish son is a vexation to his father* Pr 17$_{25}$, בְּרֹב חָכְמָה רָב־כָּעַס *in greatness of wisdom is greatness of vexation* Ec 1$_{18}$, כַּעַס אֱוִיל כָּבֵד מִשְּׁנֵיהֶם *the provocation of a fool is heavier than both of them* Pr 27$_{3}$, טוֹב כַּעַס מִשְּׂחֹק *grief is better than laughter* Ec 7$_{3}$. <OBJ> ראה *see* Ps 10$_{14}$ (|| עָמָל *trouble*), גור *be afraid of* Dt 32$_{27}$, נתן *give* Ezk 20$_{28}$, פרר hi. *put an end to* Ps 85$_{5}$, סור hi. *remove* Ec 11$_{10}$.

<CSTR> כַּעַס אֱוִיל *provocation of a fool* Pr 27$_{3}$, כַּעַס קָרְבָּנָם *provocation of their offering* Ezk 20$_{28}$, כעס חמתו *vexation of his poison* 1QpHab 11$_{5}$; אֵשֶׁת ... כָּעַס *wife of ... vexation*, i.e. contentious wife Pr 21$_{19}$, רָב־כָּעַס *greatness of vexation* Ec 1$_{18}$, רֹב ... כַּעְסִי *greatness of ... my vexation* 1 S 1$_{16}$, כל כעסו *all his vexation* 4QpsEzek^{e} 6$_{3}$, כָּל־הַכְּעָסִים *all the provocations* 2 K 23$_{26}$.

<APP> תַּחֲרָה *contention* Si 34$_{29}$.

<PREP> בְּ of instrument, *by (means of), with*, + עשׁשׁ *be weak* Ps 31$_{10}$, כעס hi. *provoke to rage* 1 K 15$_{30}$; of accompaniment, *in, with*, + שׁתה ni. *be drunk* Si 34$_{29}$, בלע pi. *swallow* 1QpHab 11$_{5}$, פתח *open* mouth 4QapJoseph^{b} 1$_{21}$ ([בכעס]ם).

מִן of cause, *because of*, + עשׁשׁ *be weak* Ps 6$_{8}$ 1QH 5$_{34}$.

אֶל *because of*, + כעס hi. *provoke to rage* 1 K 21$_{22}$.

עַל *because of*, + חרה *burn* 2 K 23$_{26}$.

<COLL> וְכִעֲסַתָּה צָרָתָהּ גַּם־כַּעַס *and her rival provoked her deeply* 1 S 1$_6$. <SYN> עָמָל *trouble*.*

→ כעס *be vexed*.

[כער] 0.2 vb. **be dark—Pu.** 2 Ptc. Si מכוערין—**be ugly,** <SUBJ> אָדָם *human being* Si 11$_{2(A)}$, דָּבָר *word* Si 13$_{22}$. <PREP> בְּ *in, with*, + מַרְאֶה *appearance* Si 11$_{2(A)}$.

כַּעַשׂ 4 n.m. **vexation**—כָּעַשׂ; sf. כַּעְשִׂי, כַּעַשְׂךָ; see also כַּעַס—<SUBJ> שׁקל ni. *be weighed* Jb 6$_2$, הרג *slay* Jb 5$_2$. <OBJ> רבה hi. *increase* Jb 10$_{17}$. <PREP> מִן of cause, *because of*, + כהה *be dim* Jb 17$_7$.

→ כעס *be vexed*.

כַּף I 192.2.17 n.f. **hand**—כַּף; cstr. כַּף; sf. כַּפִּי, כַּפְּךָ, כַּפֶּךָ (כַּפֶּכָה), כַּפָּהּ; du. כַּפַּיִם; cstr. כַּפֵּי; sf. כַּפַּי, כַּפֶּיךָ (Q כפיכה), כַּפָּיו, כַּפֶּיהָ, כַּפֵּינוּ, כַּפֵּיהֶם (כַּפֵּימוֹ); pl. כַּפּוֹת; cstr. כַּפּוֹת; sf. כַּפֹּתָיו.

1a. usu. **hand, palm** (entire hand in e.g. Dt 25$_{12}$; כַּף יָד *palm of the hand* is *palm* as distinct from *hand*, but cf. 1 S 5$_4$), including hand of God (Is 62$_3$ Ps 119$_{109}$ [if em. כַּפִּי my soul is always in *my hand* to כַּפְּךָ *your hand*] Jb 13$_{21}$ 36$_{32}$), ocean current (Ps 98$_8$); at Ex 33$_{22}$ Is 33$_{15}$ Ps 129$_7$ 139$_5$, perh. כַּף II *skirt*.

b. in context of military victory or defeat, etc., and alw. preceded by prep. בְּ *into* or מִן *from* **power, domination, grip** (Jg 6$_{13.14}$ 1 S 4$_3$ 2 S 14$_{16}$ 19$_{10.10}$ 22$_{1.1}$||Ps 18$_{1.1[mss]}$ 2 K 16$_{7.7}$ 20$_6$||Is 38$_6$ Jr 12$_7$ 15$_{21}$ Mc 4$_{10}$ Hb 2$_9$ Ps 71$_4$ Pr 6$_3$ Ezr 8$_{31}$ 2 C 30$_6$ 32$_{11}$ 11QT 59$_{11}$).

c. foot of animal (Lv 11$_{27}$).

d. perh. fingerless **stump** of hand (2 K 9$_{35}$).*

e. sole of foot, human (Dt 2$_5$ 11$_{24}$ 28$_{35.56.65}$ Jos 1$_3$ 3$_{13}$ 4$_{18}$ 2 S 14$_{25}$ 1 K 5$_{17(Qr)}$ 2 K 19$_{24}$||Is 37$_{25}$ Is 1$_6$ 60$_{14}$ Ml 3$_{21}$ Jb 2$_7$ Dn 10$_{10[mss]}$ 4QCrypt 2.1$_5$) 4QJub^h 32$_{18}$ 4Q418 88$_6$, divine (Ezk 1$_7$ 43$_7$ perh. 1 K 5$_{17[Kt]}$), animal (Gn 8$_9$ Ezk 1$_7$).*

<SUBJ> כרת pass. *be cut (off)* 1 S 5$_4$, פרשׂ pass. *be extended* 1 K 8$_{54}$, נתק ni. *be drawn out* of water Jos 4$_{18}$, גאל ni. *be defiled* Is 59$_3$, עבר *pass*, i.e. be freed, from Ps 81$_7$ (or em. עבד *serve*, i.e. labour), נוח *rest* Jos 3$_{13}$, עשׂה *make* Pr 10$_4$ (if em. עָשָׂה a pauper *employs* a deceitful hand to עָשָׂה a deceitful hand *makes* a pauper), יטב hi. *do well* Mc 7$_3$ (or em.; see Nom. Cl.), תמך *hold* Is 33$_{15}$ Pr 31$_{19}$, דרך *tread* Dt 11$_{24}$ Jos 1$_3$.

<NOM CL> הֲכַף זֶבַח וְצַלְמֻנָּע עַתָּה בְּיָדֶךָ *is the hand of Zebah and Zalmunna now in your hand?* Jg 8$_6$ (mss בְּיָדֶיךָ *in your hands*) 8$_{15}$ (בְּיָדְךָ; or em. in both הַאַף *are* they *really?*), כַּף רַגְלֵיהֶם כְּכַף רֶגֶל עֵגֶל *the sole(s) of their feet were as the sole of a calf's foot* Ezk 1$_7$, עַל־הָרַע כַּפַּיִם לְהֵיטִיב appar. *their hands are on evil to do (it) well* Mc 7$_3$ (or em. לְהָרַע כַּפֵּיהֶם הֵיטִיבוּ *to do evil they make good*, i.e. skilful, *their hands*).

<OBJ> שׂים *place* 2 K 4$_{34}$ Jb 29$_9$ 40$_{32}$, שׁית *place* Ps 139$_5$, יצג hi. *place* Dt 28$_{56}$, שׂכך *surround* Moses *with* Ex 33$_{22}$, נשׂא *raise* Ps 63$_5$ 119$_{48}$ Lm 2$_{19}$ Lm 3$_{41}$ (if em. אֶל raise our hearts *together with* or *upon* our hands to אַל raise our hearts, *not* our hands) appar. Si 40$_{14}$ (but perh. כַּף *rock*), מצא *find* 2 K 9$_{35}$, סור hi. *remove* Ex 33$_{23}$, נער *shake*, i.e. remove Is 33$_{15}$, רחק hi. *remove* Jb 13$_{21}$ (or em. || אֵימָה *fear* to אַמָּה *forearm*, or em. אֶכֶף *pressure*), מלא pi. *fill* hand with, i.e. take handful of Lv 9$_{17}$ Ps 129$_7$.

פרשׂ *extend* in intercession Ex 9$_{29.33}$ 1 K 8$_{22.38}$||2 C 6$_{12.29}$ Is 1$_{15}$ (pi.) Ps 44$_{21}$ Jb 11$_{13}$ Ezr 9$_5$ 2 C 6$_{13}$ Si 48$_{20}$ 4QWiles 3$_3$ ([פ]רוש) 4QRitPur 42.2$_6$ (הפרוש כפי[ם] appar. *one who is extended of hands*) 11QPs^a 24$_3$, perh. in anguish Jr 4$_{31}$ (pi.), in charitable giving Pr 31$_{20}$, שׁטח pi. *extend* in intercession Ps 88$_{10}$.

מחא *strike*, i.e. clap Is 55$_{12}$ Ps 98$_8$, ספק *strike*, i.e. clap, Nm 24$_{10}$ Jb 27$_{23}$ (שׂפק) Lm 2$_{15}$, נכה hi. *strike*, i.e. clap 2 K 11$_{12}$ Ezk 21$_{19.22}$ 22$_{13}$, תקע *strike*, i.e. clap Na 3$_{19}$ Ps 47$_2$, specif. in gesture of pledge Pr 6$_1$ 17$_{18}$ 22$_{26}$.

עשׂה *employ* hands Pr 10$_4$ (or em.; see Subj.) 31$_{13}$, יטב hi. *make good* Mc 7$_3$ (if em.; see Nom. Cl.), קצץ *cut off* Dt 25$_{12}$, נקב *pierce* 2 K 18$_{21}$||Is 36$_6$, בקע *split* Ezk 29$_7$ (if em. כָּתֵף *shoulder*), רחץ *wash* in innocence Ps 26$_6$ 73$_{13}$, ברר hi. *clean* 11QPs^a Si 51$_{20}$ 1QH 16$_{10}$ 4QVisSam 2$_1$, זכך hi. *clean* Jb 9$_{30}$ (unless בְּבֹר כַּפָּי = *in the purity of my hands*).

<CSTR> כַּף־אֱלֹהָיִךְ *hand of your God* Is 62$_3$, כַּף מִדְיָן *hand of Midian* Jg 6$_{13}$ (כַּף־) 6$_{14}$, פְּלִשְׁתִּים *of (the) Philistines* 2 S 19$_{10}$, פַּרְעֹה *of Pharaoh* Gn 40$_{11.21}$, שָׁאוּל *of Saul* 2 S 22$_1$||Ps 18$_{1(mss)}$ (22$_{1[mss]}$||18$_1$ יַד *hand of*), כַּף זֶבַח וְצַלְמֻנָּע *hand(s) of Zebah and Zalmunna* Jg 8$_{6.15}$, כַּפֵּי אַהֲרֹן

hands of Aaron Ex 29$_{24}$||Lv 8$_{27}$.

כַּף אִישׁ *hand of a man* 1 K 18$_{44}$, הָאִישׁ *of the man* 2 S 14$_{16}$, כַּף־רֵעֶךָ *the hand of your neighbour* Pr 6$_3$, כַּפֵּי בָנָיו *hands of his* (Aaron's) *sons* Ex 29$_{24}$||Lv 8$_{27}$, כַּף מֶלֶךְ *hand of the king of* 2 K 16$_7$ (מֶלֶךְ־) 16$_7$ 20$_6$||Is 38$_6$ (מֶלֶךְ־) 2 C 30$_6$ (if em. מַלְכֵי *kings of*) 32$_{11}$, כַּף הַכֹּהֵן *hand of the priest* Lv 14$_{15.18.26.29}$, כַּפֵּי הַנָּזִיר *hands of the Nazirite* Nm 6$_{19}$.

כַּף אוֹיֵב וְאוֹרֵב *hand of the enemy and ambush* Ezr 8$_{31}$, כָּל־אֹיְבָיו *of all his enemies* 2 S 22$_1$||Ps 18$_1$, אֹיְבֶיהָ *of her enemies* Jr 12$_7$, אֹיְבַיִךְ *of your enemies* Mc 4$_{10}$, אֹיְבֵינוּ *of our enemies* 1 S 4$_3$ 2 S 19$_{10}$ (ms ins. כָּל־ *all* our enemies), עָרִצִים *of tyrants* Jr 15$_{21}$, מְעַוֵּל וְחוֹמֵץ *of the wrongdoer and oppressor* Ps 71$_4$, כַּף־רְמִיָּה *hand of deceit* Pr 10$_4$, רָע *of evil* Hb 2$_9$.

כַּף־רֶגֶל *sole of (the) foot* Is 1$_6$, מִדְרַךְ כַּף־רָגֶל *a place of,* i.e. for, *the sole of the foot* Dt 2$_5$, מדרוך כף [רגל בני אדם] any *place for the foot of a human being* 4QJub^h 32$_{18}$, כַּף רֶגֶל עֵגֶל *sole of the foot of a calf* Ezk 1$_7$, כַּף רַגְלְךָ *sole of your* (sg.) *foot* Dt 28$_{35.65}$ (כַּף־רַגְלֶךָ) 4Q418 88$_6$ (לכף רגלכה), כַּף רַגְלוֹ *sole of his foot* 2 S 14$_{25}$ Jb 2$_7$, כַּף־רַגְלָהּ *sole of her foot* Gn 8$_9$ Dt 28$_{56}$, כַּף־רַגְלְכֶם *sole of your* (pl.) *foot* Dt 11$_{24}$ Jos 1$_3$, כַּף רַגְלֵיהֶם *sole(s) of their feet* Ezk 1$_7$.

כַּפּוֹת רַגְלֵי הַכֹּהֲנִים *soles of the feet of the priests* Jos 3$_{13}$ 4$_{18}$, כַּפּוֹת רגלו *soles of his feet* (i.e. רַגְלָו) 1 K 5$_{17(Kt)}$ 4Q Crypt 2.1$_5$ (כפות רגליו), כַּפּוֹת רַגְלַי *soles of my feet* 1 K 5$_{17(Qr)}$ Ezk 43$_7$ (רַגְלַי) Dn 10$_{10(mss)}$, כַּפּוֹת רַגְלַיִךְ *soles of your* (fem. pl.) *feet* Is 60$_{14}$, כַּפּוֹת רַגְלֵיכֶם *soles of your* (masc. pl.) *feet* Ml 3$_{21}$, כַּף־פְּעָמַי *sole(s) of my feet* 2 K 19$_{24}$||Is 37$_{25}$.

כַּפּוֹת הַיָּדַיִם *the palms of the hands* 2 K 9$_{35}$, כַּפּוֹת יָדַי *palms of my hands* Dn 10$_{10}$, כַּפּוֹת יָדָיו *his palms* 1 S 5$_4$.

נִקְיֹן כַּפַּי *innocence of my hands* Gn 20$_5$, נְקִי כַפַּיִם *innocence of hands* Ps 24$_4$, בור כפים *purity of hands* 4QBéat 3.2$_3$, בור כפיו *purity of his hands* 1QS 9$_{15}$, בֹּר כַּפֶּיךָ *purity of your hands* Jb 22$_{30}$, בֹּר כַּפָּי *purity of my hands* Jb 9$_{30}$ (if כַּף is not obj.).

כָּל־יְגִיעַ כַּפָּיִם *all the labour of (the) hands* Hg 1$_{11}$, יְגִיעַ כַּפֶּיךָ *the labour of your hands* Ps 128$_2$ Jb 10$_3$, כַּפַּי *of my hands* Gn 31$_{42}$, פְּרִי כַפֶּיהָ *fruit of (the labour of) her hands,* i.e. earnings Pr 31$_{16}$, עמל כפים *(fruit of the) labour of hands* 1QS 9$_{22}$ (+ הוֹן *wealth*), כול משלח כפים *every extending of hands,* i.e. each enterprise 1QS 9$_{23}$ (=4QS^e 1.1$_1$ (משלוח), פֹּעַל כַּפָּיו *deed(s) of his hands* Ps 9$_{17}$, תְּבוּנַת *skill of* Ps 78$_{72(mss)}$, מַשְׂאַת כַּפַּי *raising of my hands* Ps 141$_2$.

מְלֹא כַף־קֶמַח *handful of meal* 1 K 17$_{12}$, מְלֹא כַף נָחַת *handful of rest* Ec 4$_6$, שְׁתֵּי כַּפּוֹת *two hands of* 1 S 5$_4$, כָּל־כַּף *every hand* Ezk 29$_7$ (if em. כָּתֵף *shoulder*).

<ADJ> כַּפּוֹ הַשְּׂמָאלִית *his left hand* Lv 14$_{16.27}$, כַּף הַכֹּהֵן הַשְּׂמָאלִית *the priest's left hand* Lv 14$_{15.26}$.

<PREP> לְ of benefit, *to, for* perh. 4Q418 88$_6$, + היה *be* rest Dt 28$_{65}$, מצא *find* rest Gn 8$_9$.

בְּ of place, *in(to), on(to)* Is 28$_4$ (or em. בְּכַפּוֹ *in his hand* to בְּכִפָּה *on a branch*) 59$_6$ Jon 3$_8$ Ps 7$_4$ 119$_{109}$ Jb 16$_{17}$ 1 C 12$_{18}$, + היה *be* Ex 4$_4$ Is 62$_3$, מצא ni. *be found* Jr 2$_{34}$ (if em. כָּנָף *wing,* i.e. hem), בוא *come* 2 K 18$_{21}$||Is 36$_6$ Pr 6$_3$, נתן *give,* i.e. place Jg 6$_{13}$ Jr 12$_7$, שׂים *place* soul, i.e. take risk Jg 12$_3$ 1 S 19$_5$ 28$_{21}$ Jb 13$_{14}$, לקח *take* stakes 2 S 18$_{14}$, תפשׂ *hold* Ezk 21$_{16}$ 29$_{7(Qr)}$, רצץ *be broken* perh. Ezk 29$_7$ (Qr); of instrument, *by (means of), with,* + חרב hi. *dry* 2 K 19$_{24}$||Is 37$_{25}$, תפשׂ *hold* Ezk 29$_{7(Kt)}$, ni. *be held* Ezk 21$_{29}$ (or em. בַּכַּף *by the hand* to בָּהֶם *by them*), perh. נכה hi. *strike,* i.e. clap Ezk 6$_{11}$; דבק בְּ *cling to* Jb 31$_7$.

כְּ *as* 1 K 18$_{44}$ Ezk 1$_7$.

מִן of direction, *from* 2 C 30$_6$, + ישׁע hi. *save* Jg 6$_{14}$ 1 S 4$_3$ 2 K 16$_{7.7}$, נצל ni. *be rescued* Hb 2$_9$, hi. *rescue* 2 S 14$_{16}$ 19$_{10}$ 22$_{1.1}$||Ps 18$_{1.1(mss)}$ 2 K 20$_6$||Is 38$_6$ Ezr 8$_{31}$ 2 C 32$_{11}$, מלט pi. *rescue* 2 S 19$_{10}$, פלט pi. *rescue* Ps 71$_4$, גאל *redeem* Mc 4$_{10}$, פדה *redeem* Jr 15$_{21}$ 11QT 59$_{11}$.

מִכַּף רַגְלוֹ וְעַד־קָדְקֳדוֹ *from the sole of his foot up to his pate,* + היה *be* 2 S 14$_{25}$, נכה hi. *strike* with infection Dt 28$_{35}$ (רַגְלְךָ ... קָדְקֳדֶךָ) Jb 2$_{7(Qr)}$; מִכַּף־רֶגֶל וְעַד־רֹאשׁ *from the sole of the foot up to the head* Is 1$_6$, ... אל ישא ואל יתן כ[י] אם מכף לכף *let him not receive and let him not give,* i.e. let him not trade ..., *except from hand to hand,* perh. for cash CD 13$_{15}$.

מִן of instrument, *by (means of), with,* + נטע *plant* Pr 31$_{16}$.

אֶל *into,* + רדה *scrape* honey Jg 14$_9$, *against,* + נכה hi. *strike,* i.e. clap Ezk 21$_{19.22}$; *together with* or *upon* Lm 3$_{41}$ (or em. עַל *upon* or אַל *not*).

עַל *over, upon* Lv 14$_{16.17.18.27.28.29}$, + הלך *go,* i.e. move Lv 11$_{27}$, כסה pi. *cover* Jb 36$_{32}$, שׂים *place* 2 K 4$_{34}$, נשׂא *raise* Ps 91$_{12}$ Lm 3$_{41}$ (if em. אֶל *together with* or *upon*),

נטף *drip* myrrh Ca 5_{5}, יצק *pour* oil Lv $14_{15.26}$, נוע hi. *shake*, i.e. move, Daniel Dn 10_{10}, חקק *engrave* Is 49_{16}; *into* hand or *upon* palm, + נתן *give*, i.e. place Gn $40_{11.21}$ Lv $8_{27.27}$ Nm 5_{18} 6_{19}, שׂים *place* Ex $29_{24.24}$, שׁקל *weigh*, i.e. pay, silver 2 S 18_{12}; *at, before*, + שׁחה htpal. *bow down* Is 60_{14}.

מֵעַל *from (upon)*, + לקח *take* Lv 8_{28}.

תַּחַת *under*, + היה *be* ashes Ml 3_{21}, נתן *give*, i.e. place 1 K 5_{17}.

<COLL> כַּף || יָד *hand* Is 62_{3} Jr 15_{21} Ps 71_{4} Pr 10_{4} $31_{19.20}$ 11QT 59_{11}, פֶּה *mouth* 2 K 4_{34}, עַיִן *eye* 2 K 4_{34} Is 33_{15}, אֹזֶן *ear* Is 33_{15}, אֶצְבַּע *finger* Is 59_{3}, רֶגֶל *foot* Ezk 6_{11}, שְׁכֶם *shoulder* Ps 81_{7}, לֵב *heart* Jb 11_{13} 4QBéat 3.2_{3} (+), שֵׁן *tooth* Jb 13_{14}, ראשׁ *head* Lm 2_{15}; [עצ]מותיו וכפיו *his bones and his hands* 4QWays[a] $1a2_{6}$.

2. ladle, spoon (or perh. **saucer, dish** as cultic objects), (Ex 25_{29}||37_{16} Nm 4_{7} 7_{14+15t} 1 K 7_{50}||2 C 4_{22} 2 K 25_{14}||Jr 52_{18} Jr 52_{19} 2 C 24_{14}).*

<NOM CL> הַכַּפּוֹת ... זָהָב סָגוּר *the ladles ... were of pure gold* 1 K 7_{50}||2 C 4_{22}, עֲשָׂרָה עֲשָׂרָה הַכַּף *ten (shekels) was (the weight of) of each ladle* Nm 7_{86}, קָרְבָּנוֹ ... כַּף אַחַת *his offering was ... one ladle* Nm $7_{14.20}$ (if em. הִקְרִיב אֶת־קָרְבָּנוֹ *he presented his offering*, one ladle) 7_{26+9t}, כַּפּוֹת זָהָב שְׁתֵּים עֶשְׂרֵה perh. *the gold ladles were twelve* Nm 7_{84} (see also Coll.). <OBJ> עשׂה *make* Ex 25_{29}||37_{16} 2 C 24_{14}, נתן *give*, i.e. place Nm 4_{7}, לקח *take* 2 K 25_{14}||Jr 52_{18} Jr 52_{19}.

<CSTR> כַּפּוֹת זָהָב *ladles of gold* Nm $7_{84.86}$; זְהַב הַכַּפּוֹת *gold of the ladles*, or *saucers* Nm 7_{86}. <APP> קָרְבָּן *offering* Nm 7_{20} (or em.; see Nom. Cl.), כְּלִי *vessel* 2 C 24_{14}, אֲשֶׁר זָהָב זָהָב *whatever was of gold* Jr 52_{19}. <ADJ> כַּף אַחַת עֲשָׂרָה זָהָב מְלֵאָה קְטֹרֶת *one ladle*, or *saucer*, *of ten (shekels of) gold, full of incense* Nm 7_{14+11t}, כַּפּוֹת זָהָב ... מְלֵאֹת קְטֹרֶת *gold ladles*, or *saucers*, *full of incense* Nm 7_{86}. <PREP> בְּ of instrument, *by (means of), with*, + נסך ho. *be poured out* in sacrifice Ex 25_{29}||37_{16}, שׁרת pi. *minister* 2 K 25_{14}||Jr 52_{18}. <COLL> כַּפּוֹת זָהָב שְׁתֵּים עֶשְׂרֵה *twelve golden ladles*, or *saucers* Nm 7_{86} (see also Nom. Cl.).

3. socket of hip joint (or perh. ball-shaped end of thigh bone) (e.g. Gn $32_{26.26.33.33}$), <SUBJ> יקע *be dislocated* Gn 32_{26}. <CSTR> כַּף הַיָּרֵךְ *socket of the hip joint* Gn 32_{33}, כַּף־יֶרֶךְ *socket of hip joint of* Gn $32_{26.33}$, כַּף־יְרֵכוֹ *socket of his hip joint* Gn 32_{26}, כפות הירך *sockets of the hip joint* 4QBibPar 1_{13}. <PREP> בְּ *against*, + נגע *touch* Gn $32_{26.33}$; עַל *over, upon* Gn 32_{33} 4QBibPar 1_{13}. <COLL> שתי כפות *two sockets of the* hip joint 4QBibPar 1_{13}.*

4. hollow of sling, <CSTR> כַּף הַקֶּלַע *hollow of the sling* 1 S 25_{29}. <PREP> בְּתוֹךְ appar. *from out of*, + קלע pi. *sling* 1 S 25_{29}.

5. handle of bolt (or perh. as §4, **hollow** into which bolt slides), <CSTR> כַּפּוֹת הַמַּנְעוּל *handles of the bolt* Ca 5_{5}.*

6. perh. **wing, flank** of army, <CSTR> גלול כפיים perh. *an encircling of flanks*, i.e. a pincer movement 1QM 9_{10} (גלול may be גְּלוֹל cstr. or גָּלוֹל, i.e. inf. of גלל *roll*; AHL גְּלִיל, i.e. pass. ptc. cstr. of גלל or cstr. of גָּלִיל *circle*; or em. כָּנָף *wing*).

7. handful, <OBJ> perh. נקה pi. *empty* 4Q417 2.1_{24}. <CSTR> כפי נחלתו *the handfuls of its inheritance* 4Q417 2.1_{24} (unless כְּפִי *in accordance with*), מְלֹא כַף־קֶמַח *fullness of a handful of meal* 1 K 17_{12}, מְלֹא כַף נָחַת *fullness of a handful of rest* Ec 4_{6}.*

8. basin of drain, [ה]מים הקריבין לכף הביב *the waters that are approaching the basin of the drain* 3QTr 9_{12} (others הקרובין לכף *that are near to the edge* [כַּף]; לכפר נבו ב near *to Kefar-nebo at*).*

Also 4QparaKings 104_{2}. <SYN> §1 יָד *hand*, פֶּה *mouth*, עַיִן *eye*, אֹזֶן *ear*, אֶצְבַּע *finger*, רֶגֶל *foot*, שְׁכֶם *shoulder*, לֵב *heart*, שֵׁן *tooth*, ראשׁ *head*.*

→ כפף *bend*.

* [כַּף] II $_{4}$ n.f. **skirt**—sf. כַּפּוֹ, כַּפֶּכָה, כַּפִּי; pl. sf. כַּפָּיו—unless כַּף I *hand* in all four, <SUBJ> תמך *hold* Is 33_{15}. <OBJ> שׁית *place* Ps 139_{5}, שׂכך *surround* Moses *with* Ex 33_{22}, נער *shake*, i.e. remove Is 33_{15}, מלא pi. *fill* Ps 129_{7}.

כֵּף I $_{2}$ n.m. **rock**—pl. כֵּפִים—**rock** or **mountain top**,* <APP> עָרוּץ *slope* Jb 30_{6}. <PREP> בְּ of place, *in, at*, + שׁכן *dwell* Jb 30_{6}, עלה *go up* Jr 4_{29}.

[כַּף] III n.[m.] **edge,** [ה]מים הקרובין לכף הביב *the waters that are near to the edge of the drain* 3QTr 9_{11} (others הקריבין לכף *that are approaching the basin* [כַּף]; לכפר נבו ב near *to Kefar-nebo at*).*

[כִּפָּא] 0.0.1 pl.n. **Kippa,** בנחל כפא *in the wadi (of) Kippa* (perh. Wadi Qumran), 3QTr 5_{12}.*

כפה 1.0.1 vb. **subdue—Qal** 1.0.1 Pf. Q כפיתה; impf. יִכְפֶּה־—**subdue, overturn,** <SUBJ> אֱלֹהִים *God* 4QapPs^b 31_5, מַתָּן *gift* Pr 21_{14} (or em. יִכְבֶּה/יְכַבֶּה *extinguishes* or יְכַפֵּר *averts*). <OBJ> אַף *anger* Pr 21_{14} (or em.; see Subj.). <PREP> לְ introducing object, + שׂנא ptc. *one who hates* 4QapPs^b 31_5; לְנֶגֶד *before,* + עַיִן *eye* 4QapPs^b 31_5 (עיני[ך]).

Pi. extinguish (as by-form of כבה pi.), Pr 21_{14} (if em.).*

כַּפָּה 4.0.1 n.f. **branch** of tree—כַּפָּה; sf. כִּפָּתוֹ; pl. cstr. כַּפֹּת (Lv 23_{40}); sf. Q כפותיו—usu. of palm tree, <SUBJ> עשׂה *do* Is 19_{15} (|| רֹאשׁ *head;* :: אַגְמוֹן *reed,* זָנָב *tail*), רען pa'lal *flourish* Jb 15_{32} (+ זְמוֹרָה *branch* or תִּמֹרָה *palm tree,* if em. תְּמוּרָה *exchange*). <OBJ> כרת hi. *cut off* Is 9_{13} (|| רֹאשׁ; :: זָנָב, אַגְמוֹן), לקח *take* Lv 23_{40} (|| עָנָף *branch*). <CSTR> כַּפֹּת תְּמָרִים *branches of palm trees* Lv 23_{40}. Also 4Qps Hod 2_5. <PREP> בְּ of place, *on* Is 28_4 (if em. בְּכַפּוֹ *in his hand* to בְּכִפָּה *on a branch*). <SYN> רֹאשׁ *head,* עָנָף *branch.* <ANT> אַגְמוֹן *reed,* זָנָב *tail.*

⇒ כפף *bend.*

כְּפוֹר I 9 n.m. **bowl**—pl. cstr. כְּפוֹרֵי (כְּפֹרֵי)—made of silver or gold, <CSTR> כְּפוֹרֵי כֶסֶף *bowls of silver* Ezr 1_{10}, כְּפוֹרֵי הַכֶּסֶף *the bowls of silver* 1 C 28_{17}, כְּפוֹרֵי זָהָב *bowls of gold* Ezr 1_{10} 8_{27} (כְּפֹרֵי), כְּפוֹרֵי הַזָּהָב *the bowls of gold* 1 C 28_{17}. <APP> כלין כופרין *vessels, (namely) bowls,* i.e. serving vessels 3QTr 10_{11} (unless כְּפֻרֵי *tarred* or *expiatory*). <PREP> לְ of benefit, *to, for* 1 C $28_{17.17}$; of possession, *(belonging) to, of* 1 C $28_{17.17}$. <COLL> בְּמִשְׁקָל לִכְפוֹר וּכְפוֹר *by the weight of a bowl and a bowl,* i.e. by the weight of each bowl 1 C $28_{17.17}$.*

כְּפוֹר II 3.2 n.m. **hoar frost**—כְּפֹר—<OBJ> שׁכן *settle* Si $43_{19(B)}$, ילד *bear child* Jb 38_{29}, שׁפך *pour out* Si $43_{19(Bmg)}$ (B שׁכן *dwell*), פזר pi. *scatter* Ps 147_{16}. <CSTR> כְּפֹר שָׁמַיִם *hoar frost of heaven* Jb 38_{29}. <PREP> כְּ *as,* + חספס pualal *be crisp* Ex 16_{14}; עַל *upon* Si 3_{15}.

⇒ כפר *cover.*

[כִּפּוּר], see כֹּפֶר *atonement.*

כְּפִי 11.1.6 prep. **in accordance with**—sf. כְּפִיךָ—lit. *according to the mouth of,* **1.** as prep., **in accordance with, in proportion to;** also **as** (Jb 33_6).

a. with verb, טמא *be impure* CD 12_{16}, יצא *go out* 1QM 2_8, עמד hi. *position* 2 C 31_2, נתן *give* Nm $7_{5.7.8}$ 35_8, לקט *gather* Ex 16_{21} (Gnz לְפִי *in accordance with,* as $16_{16.18}$), שׁוב hi. *take back,* i.e. repay Lv 25_{52}, יכח hi. *reprove* CD 20_4, יפע hi. *display* deeds CD 20_6, עשׂה *do* Nm 6_{21} 1QSa 1_{22}, כתב *write,* i.e. register CD 13_{12}.

b. with noun, עֲבוֹדָה *service* Nm $7_{5.7.8}$ 2 C 31_2, אֹכֶל *(need for) food* Ex 16_{21} (Gnz לְפִי), שָׁנָה *year* Lv 25_{52}, נֶדֶר *vow* Nm 6_{21} (mss נֵזֶר *Nazirite vow*), תְּעוּדָה *decree* of war 1QM 2_8, נַחֲלָה *inheritance* Nm 35_8 CD 13_{12}, מִדְרָשׁ *interpretation* of Torah CD 20_6, טֻמְאָה *impurity* CD 12_{16}, מַעַל *unfaithfulness* CD 20_4, מַעֲשֶׂה *deed* 1QSa 1_{22}.

c. in nom. cl., הֶן־אֲנִי כְפִיךָ לָאֵל *behold, I am like you in respect of God* Jb 33_6, כי יש אוהב כפי עת *for there is one who loves in accordance with the time,* i.e. only if it suits them Si 6_8. <COLL> כְּפִי ... כֵּן *in accordance with ... thus* Nm 6_{21}.

2. as conj., **in such a way that, so that,** הַקְּרָנוֹת אֲשֶׁר־זֵרוּ אֶת־יְהוּדָה כְּפִי־אִישׁ לֹא־נָשָׂא רֹאשׁוֹ these are *the horns that have scattered Judah in such a way that no one could hold his head up* Zc 2_4 (or del.).

3. כְּפִי אֲשֶׁר **because,** נָתַתִּי אֶתְכֶם נִבְזִים ... כְּפִי אֲשֶׁר אֵינְכֶם שֹׁמְרִים *I have made you despised ... because you do not keep* my ways Ml 2_9 (or del. אֲשֶׁר, leaving כְּפִי alone as conj., *because*).

⇒ כְּ *as.*

כָּפִיס 1.0.3 n.m. **beam**—cstr. Q כפיס—**beam, rafter,** <SUBJ> היה *be* 1QpHab 10_1 (+ בגזל *in robbery*), ענה *answer,* i.e. respond Hb 2_{11}. <OBJ> שׂים *place* 1QH 6_{26} (+ סוֹד *foundation*). <CSTR> כפיס עיצה *beam of its wood* 1QpHab 10_1 (+ אֶבֶן *stone*). <PREP> כְּ *as,* + זוע htpalp. *be moved* 1QH 6_{36} ([יזדעזע]).

כְּפִיר I 31.1.4 n.m. **young lion**—pl. כְּפִירִים (כְּפִרִים); sf. Q כפירכה, כְּפִירַיִךְ, Q כפיריו—**(young) lion,*** unless **tawny lion.***

<SUBJ> היה *be* Ezk 19$_{3.6}$, רוש *be poor* Ps 34$_{11}$, רעב *be hungry* Ps 34$_{11}$, דמה ni. *consider oneself like* Ezk 32$_{2}$, רבץ *crouch* Is 11$_{6}$ (or em. מרא *graze*), נתן *give*, i.e. raise voice Am 3$_{4}$, הגה *growl* Is 31$_{4}$, שׁאג *roar* Jg 14$_{5}$ Jr 2$_{15}$ Ps 104$_{21}$, נכה hi. *strike* 4QpNah 3.1$_{5}$. <NOM CL> כפיריו הם גדוליו *his lions are his great ones* 4QpNah 3.1$_{10}$. <OBJ> שׂים *place*, i.e. make Ezk 19$_{5}$, רמס *tread* Ps 91$_{13}$, אכל *eat*, i.e. devour Na 2$_{14}$.

<CSTR> כְּפִיר גּוֹיִם *young lion of the nations* Ezk 32$_{2}$, כְּפִיר אֲרָיוֹת *young of lions* Jg 14$_{5}$, כפיר החרון *the lion of wrath* 4QpHos^{b} 2$_{2}$ 4QpNah 3.1$_{5.6}$; פְּנֵי־כְפִיר *face of a young lion* Ezk 41$_{19}$, פי כפירים *mouth of lions* 1QH 5$_{9}$, שִׁנֵּי כְפִירִים *teeth of young lions* Jb 4$_{10}$, מַלְתְּעוֹת כְּפִירִים *jawbones of the young lions* Ps 58$_{7}$, חַיַּת *appetite of* Jb 38$_{39}$, שַׁאֲגַת *roar of* Zc 11$_{3}$, כָּל־כְּפִרֶיהָ *all its young lions* Ezk 38$_{13}$.

<PREP> לְ of benefit, *to, for* Na 2$_{12}$; *with*, + שׂחק *play* Si 47$_{3}$; נבט לְ hi. *look at* Ps 74$_{20}$ (if em. לַבְּרִית look *for the covenant* to לַכְּפִירִים *at the young lions*, i.e. the infidels).*

כְּ *as* Ho 5$_{14}$ Pr 19$_{12}$ 20$_{2}$, + היה *be* Mc 5$_{7}$ (|| אַרְיֵה *lion*), בטח *have confidence* Pr 28$_{1}$, ישׁב *sit* Ps 17$_{12}$, עזב *forsake* Jr 25$_{38}$, שׁאג *roar* Is 5$_{29}$ Jr 51$_{38}$.

מִן of direction, *from*, + שׁוב hi. *rescue* Ps 35$_{17}$.

עַל *concerning* 4QpNah 3.1$_{5.6}$.

בְּתוֹךְ *among*, + רבץ *couch* Ezk 19$_{2}$.

<COLL> כְּפִיר גּוֹיִם נִדְמֵיתָ *you considered yourself like a lion of the nations* Ezk 32$_{9}$. <SYN> אַרְיֵה *lion*.

[כְּפִיר] II $_{1}$ n.m. **copper vessel**—pl. sf. כְּפִרֶיהָ—<SUBJ> אמר *say* Ezk 38$_{13}$. <CSTR> כָּל־כְּפִרֶיהָ *all of its copper vessels* Ezk 38$_{13}$.*

כְּפִירָה $_{4}$ pl.n. **Chephirah,** Hivite city allocated to Benjamin, <SUBJ> היה *be* Jos 18$_{26}$. <NOM CL> ... עָרֵיהֶם הַכְּפִירָה *their cities were ... Chephirah* Jos 9$_{17}$. <CSTR> אַנְשֵׁי ... כְּפִירָה *men of ... Chephirah* Ne 7$_{29}$, בְּנֵי ... כְּפִירָה *the sons of ... Chephirah* Ezr 2$_{25}$. <APP> עִיר *city* Jos 18$_{26}$.

⇒ כְּפִירִים *Chephirim.*

כְּפִירִים $_{1}$ pl.n. **Chephirim,** appar. ident. with Chephirah, <PREP> בְּ of place, *in, at*, + יעד ni. *have appointment* Ne 6$_{2}$ (or em. כְּפָרִים *villages*).

⇒ כְּפִירָה *Chephirah.*

כפל $_{5.0.2}$ vb. **double—Qal** $_{4.0.2}$ Impf. Q יכפלו; + waw וְכָפַלְתָּ; ptc. Q כופלים, pass. כָּפוּל—**1. be double,** <SUBJ> מַעֲשֶׂה *work* of God 4Q392 1$_{7}$.

2. double (over), fold, <SUBJ> Moses Ex 26$_{9}$; subj. not specified, 1QpHab 7$_{15}$. <OBJ> יְרִיעָה *curtain* Ex 26$_{9}$. <PREP> עַל *upon* 1QpHab 7$_{15}$; אֶל־מוּל פְּנֵי *at the front of*, + אֹהֶל *tent* Ex 26$_{9}$.

3. pass., **be folded,** of breastpiece, <COLL> רָבוּעַ יִהְיֶה כָּפוּל *a square it is to be, folded* Ex 28$_{16}$, רָבוּעַ הָיָה כָּפוּל עָשׂוּ אֶת־הַחֹשֶׁן *a square it was, they made the breastpiece folded* Ex 39$_{9}$ (Sam עָשָׂה *he made*), זֶרֶת רָחְבּוֹ כָּפוּל *a span was its width, folded* Ex 39$_{9}$ (Sam lacks כָּפוּל).

Ni. $_{1}$ Impf. 3fs תִּכָּפֵל—**be doubled, be used a second time,** <SUBJ> חֶרֶב *sword* Ezk 21$_{19}$ (or em. שׁכל pi. let the sword *bereave*; + שְׁלִישִׁתָה use it *a third time*; or em. וְשֻׁלְּשָׁה *and let it be used a third time*).

⇒ כֶּפֶל *double.*

[כֶּפֶל] $_{3.1}$ n.m. **double**—cstr. כֶּפֶל; du. כִּפְלַיִם (du. except at Jb 41$_{5}$)—usu. **double (amount),** Jb 11$_{6}$ 41$_{5}$ Si 26$_{1}$; perh. **equivalent (amount),** Is 40$_{2}$. <NOM CL> מספר ימיו כפלים *the number of his days is double* Si 26$_{1}$, כִּי־כִפְלַיִם לְתוּשִׁיָּה *for there is double to understanding* Jb 11$_{6}$ (or em. כַּפְּלָאִים *as wonders* of his success, or פְּלָאִים/פְּלָיִם for *wonders* are for his working, or כְּפוּלִים *folded*, i.e. hidden, for his understanding, or rd. כִּפְלַיִם יַשֶּׁה *he exacts double*).* <OBJ> לקח *take* Is 40$_{2}$. <CSTR> כֶּפֶל רִסְנוֹ *double of his jaw*, appar. his two rows of teeth Jb 41$_{5}$ (or em. סִרְיֹנוֹ *of his armour*, i.e. second coat of mail). <PREP> בְּ of place, *in(to)*, + בוא *come* Jb 41$_{5}$.

Also 4QpsEzek^{c} 2$_{2}$ (כ[לפים]).

⇒ כפל *be double.*

כפן $_{1}$ vb. **be hungry—Qal** $_{1}$ Pf. כָּפְנָה—<SUBJ> גֶּפֶן *vine* Ezk 17$_{7}$ (mss כנף *thrust*). <OBJ> שֹׁרֶשׁ *root* Ezk 17$_{7}$. <PREP> עַל *upon*, + נֶשֶׁר *eagle* Ezk 17$_{7}$.

⇒ כָּפָן *hunger.*

כָּפָן $_{2}$ n.m. **hunger,** <ADJ> גַּלְמוּד *barren*, i.e. hard Jb 30$_{3}$. <PREP> לְ *at*, + שׂחק *laugh* Jb 5$_{22}$ (|| שֹׁד *destruction*); בְּ *because of*, + ערק *gnaw* Jb 30$_{3}$ (|| חֶסֶר *lack*). <SYN> חֶסֶר *lack*, שֹׁד *destruction*. ⇒ כפן *be hungry.*

כפף 5.1 vb. **bend—Qal** 4 Pf. כָּפַף; impv. Si כֹּיף; ptc. pass. כְּפוּפִים; inf. כֹּף—**bend, bend down, be bowed,** <SUBJ> אָדָם *human being* Is 58$_{5}$, נֶפֶשׁ *soul* Ps 57$_{7}$, כֹּל *everyone* Ps 145$_{14}$; subj. not specified, Ps 146$_{8}$ Si 30$_{12}$. <OBJ> רֹאשׁ *head* Is 58$_{5}$ Si 30$_{12}$. <PREP> בְּ of time, *in, at,* + נְעֻרוֹת *youth* Si 30$_{12}$.

Ni. 1 Impf. אִכַּף—**bow oneself down,** <SUBJ> worshipper Mc 6$_{6}$. <PREP> לְ of direction, *to,* + אֱלֹהִים *God* Mc 6$_{6}$.

→ כַּף I *palm (of hand),* כִּפָּה *branch.*

כפר 101.3.50 vb. **cover—Qal** 1.0.1 + waw וְכָפַרְתָּ; ptc. כופר—**1. cover over,** <SUBJ> Noah Gn 6$_{14}$. <OBJ> תֵּבָה *ark* Gn 6$_{14}$. <PREP> בְּ of instrument, *by (means of), with,* + כֹּפֶר *asphalt* Gn 6$_{14}$. <COLL> וְכָפַרְתָּ אֹתָהּ מִבַּיִת וּמִחוּץ *and you shall cover it inside and outside* with asphalt Gn 6$_{14}$.

2. make atonement, <SUBJ> כֹּהֵן *priest* 4QTohB^{c} 1$_{3}$. <PREP> בְּ of instrument, *by means of, with,* + דָּם *blood* 4QTohB^{c} 1$_{3}$.

Pi. 92.3.44 Pf. כִּפֶּר, 2ms Q כפרת (כִּפַּרְתָּה), כִּפַּרְתֶּם; impf. יְכַפֵּר (יְכַפְּרֶנָּה), 3fs Si תכפר, 2ms תְּכַפֵּר (תְּכַפְּרֵם), אֲכַפֵּר (אֲכַפְּרָה); + waw וַיְכַפֵּר, וְכִפֵּר, וְכִפַּרְתֶּם, וְכִפֶּר, Q ויכפרו; impv. כַּפֵּר; inf. כַּפֵּר (כַּפְּרָה, כַּפְּרֵךְ, כַּפְּרִי)—**atone (for), make expiation (for), make amends (for), free** (of sin), **purify, effect ransom (for);*** with God as subj., sometimes perh. **forgive** sin; also **cover** face (Gn 32$_{21}$), i.e. please, appease; **avert** anger (Pr 16$_{14}$ 21$_{14}$ [if em.]), disaster (Is 47$_{11}$).*

<SUBJ> יי *Y.* Dt 21$_{8}$=11QT 63$_{6}$ Dt 32$_{43}$ Jr 18$_{23}$ Ezk 16$_{63}$ 2 C 30$_{18}$ GnzPs 1$_{13}$ (+ סלח *pardon,* מחל *remit*), אֱלֹהִים *God* Ps 65$_{4}$ 78$_{38}$ 79$_{9}$, אֵל *God* 1QH 4$_{37}$ perh. 17$_{12}$ 1QS 2$_{8}$ 11$_{14}$ 4QRitPur 29.7$_{9(mg)}$ ([אל]) CD 2$_{5}$ 3$_{18}$ 4$_{6.9.10}$ 20$_{34}$, Israelite(s) Ezk 45$_{20}$, Aaron Ex 30$_{10.10}$ Lv 9$_{7.7}$ 16$_{6+8t}$ Nm 8$_{19.21}$ 17$_{11.12}$ 1 C 6$_{34}$ Si 43$_{16}$, David 2 S 21$_{3}$, Eleazar Lv 10$_{17}$, Ithamar Lv 10$_{17}$, Jacob Gn 32$_{21}$, Moses Ex 29$_{36.37}$ 32$_{30}$ Lv 8$_{15}$ Nm 8$_{12}$ 4QDibHam^{a} 1.2$_{9}$, Phinehas Nm 25$_{13}$ Si 45$_{231}$, מַטֶּה *tribe* 11QT 22$_{15}$.

אִישׁ *man* Pr 16$_{14}$ 1QS 5$_{6}$ 1QSa 1$_{3}$ (אנושי ... לכפ[ר]) perh. 4QTohB^{c} 1$_{7}$ ([י]כפר), בֵּן *son* Nm 8$_{19}$, of Israel 11QT 21$_{8}$ (בני יש[ראל]), בֶּן־אָדָם *son of human being, mortal* Ezk 43$_{20}$, בַּת *daughter* of Chaldaeans Is 47$_{11}$, כֹּהֵן *priest* Lv 4$_{20.26.31.35}$ 5$_{6.10.13.16.18.26}$ 7$_{7}$ 12$_{7.8}$ 14$_{18.19.20.31.53}$ 15$_{15.30}$ 16$_{32.33.33.33}$ 19$_{22}$ Nm 5$_{8}$ 6$_{11}$ 15$_{25.28.28}$ Ezk 43$_{26}$ 2 C 29$_{24}$ perh. 4QTohB^{c} 1$_{7}$ ([י]כפר) 11QT 16$_{14}$ 21$_{8}$ (הכוהנ[ים]) 22$_{15}$ 26$_{7.9}$ (both [הכוהן]), לֵוִי *Levite* 11QT 21$_{8}$ 22$_{15}$, מָשִׁיחַ *messiah* CD 14$_{19}$ ([מש]יח), נָשִׂיא *prince* 11QT 21$_{8}$, עֵצָה *council* 1QS 8$_{6.10(mg)}$, עֵד *witness* 1QS 8$_{6.10(mg)}$, בָּחִיר *chosen one* 1QS 8$_{6.10(mg)}$, טָהוֹר *pure one* 4QShirShabb^{a} 1.1$_{16}$, צְדָקָה *righteousness* Si 3$_{30}$, דָּם *blood* Lv 17$_{11.11}$, מַתָּן *gift* Pr 21$_{14}$ (if em. כפה *subdue*), רֵיחַ rest-giving *smell*, perh. 4QSD 7.2$_{9}$, אֵלֶּה *these* 1QS 9$_{4}$ 1QM 2$_{5}$; subj. not specified, Ex 30$_{15.16}$ Lv 1$_{4}$ 6$_{23}$ 8$_{34}$ 14$_{21.29}$ 16$_{10.27.34}$ 23$_{28}$ Nm 28$_{22.30}$ 29$_{5}$ 31$_{50}$ Ezk 45$_{15.17}$ Dn 9$_{24}$ Ne 10$_{34}$ 4QJub^{f} 32$_{13}$ ([לכ]פר) 11QMelch 2$_{8}$.

<OBJ> אֲדָמָה *land* Dt 32$_{43}$, מִקְדָּשׁ *sanctuary* Lv 16$_{33}$, קֹדֶשׁ *holy place* Lv 16$_{20}$, בַּיִת *house*, i.e. temple Ezk 45$_{20}$, אֹהֶל *tent* of meeting Lv 16$_{20.33}$, מִזְבֵּחַ *altar* Lv 16$_{20.33}$ Ezk 43$_{20}$, חֵמָה *anger* Pr 16$_{14}$, אַף *anger* Pr 21$_{14}$ (if em. כפה *subdue*), הֹוָה *disaster* Is 47$_{11}$, חַטָּאת *sin* Si 3$_{30}$, עָוֹן *iniquity* Ps 78$_{38}$ Dn 9$_{24}$ 1QH 4$_{37}$ 1QS 2$_{8}$ CD 14$_{19}$, פֶּשַׁע *transgression* Ps 65$_{4}$, אַשְׁמָה *guilt* 4QBark^{a} 1.1$_{4}$ ([א]שמתם), רָצוֹן *will* 4QShirShabb^{a} 1.1$_{16}$, פָּנִים *face* Gn 32$_{21}$.

<PREP> לְ of benefit, *for, on behalf of,* or introducing object 4QBapt 2.1$_{3}$, + Israel Dt 21$_{8}$=11QT 63$_{6}$, עַם *people* Dt 21$_{8}$=11QT 63$_{6}$, Jerusalem Ezk 16$_{63}$, נדב htp. ptc. *volunteer* 1QS 5$_{6}$, רָצוֹן *acceptance* 4QOrd^{b} 2.2$_{4}$; *in respect of, for,* + פֶּשַׁע *transgression* 4QOrd^{a} 1.2$_{2}$, כֹּל *everything* Ezk 16$_{63}$; *during,* + דּוֹר *generation* Ex 30$_{10}$.

בְּ of place, time, *in, among,* + קֹדֶשׁ *holy place* Lv 6$_{23}$ 16$_{17.27}$, יוֹם *day* 11QMelch 2$_{8}$ ([י]ו[ם]) 11QT 21$_{8}$ (ב[יום]) 22$_{15}$; of instrument, *by (means of), with* 4QTohB^{c} 1$_{4}$ 4QOrd^{b} 2.2$_{4}$, + מִנְחָה *cereal offering* Gn 32$_{21}$, אָשָׁם *guilt offering* Lv 7$_{7}$, פַּר *bull* 11QT 16$_{14}$, אַיִל *ram* of guilt offering Lv 5$_{16}$, *ram* of atonement Nm 5$_{8}$, שָׂעִיר *goat* 11QT^{b} 22$_{3}$ (שעיר] ... לכפ[ר בו) 11QT 26$_{9}$, נֶפֶשׁ *soul*, i.e. life Lv 17$_{11}$, מַיִם *water* 4QBark^{a} 1.3$_{3}$ ([במ]ים), מָה *what?* 2 S 21$_{3}$; of accompaniment, *with, in,* + רָז *mystery* CD 3$_{18}$, אַהֲבָה *love* GnzPs 1$_{13}$.

מִן of direction, *from,* + טֻמְאָה *uncleanness* Lv 14$_{19}$, אַשְׁמָה *wickedness* 11QT 18$_{7}$ ([וכפר] ... מכול אשמת[ם]); of agent, *by (means of),* + דָּם *blood* Ex 30$_{10}$; of cause, *because of,* + טֻמְאָה *uncleanness* Lv 16$_{16}$, חַטָּאת *sin* Lv 4$_{26}$ 5$_{6.10}$ 16$_{34}$, פֶּשַׁע *transgression* Lv 16$_{16}$, זוֹב *discharge* Lv

$15_{15.30}$.

עַל *upon, over,* + קֶרֶן *horn* Ex 30_{10}, שָׂעִיר *he-goat* Lv 16_{10}; *for, on behalf of,* + Israel Ne 10_{34} 1 C 6_{34} 2 C 29_{24} 4QPrFêtes^{b} 7_{1} ([ע]ל) 30_{1} (לכפר [על]יו ע[ל]), עַם *people* Lv $16_{30.33}$ Nm 17_{12} Ezk 45_{15} 4QMyst^{a} 55_{5} 11QT 16_{14} ([על כל עם]) 18_{7} ([וכפר]) $26_{7.9}$ 32_{6}, עֵדָה *congregation* Lv 4_{20} 10_{17} Nm 15_{25} 17_{11} 11QT^{b} 22_{3} (לכפ[ר]), Aaron Lv 8_{34}, אָדָם *human being* Lv 1_{4}, אִישׁ *man* Lv 19_{22} Nm 5_{8} 4QJub^{f} 32_{13} (לכ[פר]), אִשָּׁה *woman* Lv $12_{7.8}$ 15_{30}, בֵּן *son* Lv 8_{34} 11QMelch 2_{8}, Israelite *son* Lv 16_{34} 23_{28} Nm 8_{19} 25_{13} $28_{22.30}$ 29_{5} Si $45_{16.23}$, נָשִׂיא *prince* Lv 4_{26}, כֹּהֵן *priest* Lv 16_{33}, לֵוִי *Levite* Nm $8_{12.21}$, נָזִיר *Nazirite* Nm 6_{11}.

צרע pu. ptc. *one whose skin is diseased* Lv $14_{18.20.21.29}$, זוב ptc. *one who has a discharge* Lv 15_{15}, טָמֵא *impure one* 4QTohB^{c} 1_{7} ([י]כפר הוא על טמ[א]), טהר pi. ptc. *one who is cleansed* Lv $14_{19.31}$, אֶרֶץ *land* 4QSD 7.2_{9} (ה[א]רץ), בַּיִת *house* Lv 14_{53}, קֹדֶשׁ *holy place* Lv 16_{16}, מִזְבֵּחַ *altar* Ex $29_{36.37}$ 30_{10} Lv 8_{15} 16_{18}, תִּירוֹשׁ *new wine* 11QT 21_{8}, יִצְהָר *new oil* 11QT 22_{15} (יצ[הר]), חַטָּאת *sin* Lv 4_{35} Ps 79_{9}, עָוֹן *iniquity* Jr 18_{23} CD 4_{9}, אַשְׁמָה *guilt* 1QS 9_{4}, מַעַל *unfaithfulness* 1QS 9_{4}, פֶּשַׁע *transgression* GnzPs 1_{13}, שְׁגָגָה *error* perh. 1QMyst 6_{2} ([י]כפר על שגג[ ]), נֶפֶשׁ *soul, life* Ex $30_{15.16}$ Lv $4_{31.35}$ $5_{6.10.13.16.18.26}$ 17_{11} Nm $15_{28.28}$ 31_{50}.

בַּעַד *for, on behalf of* 1QDM 24_{1} (לכפ[ר]) 4QM^{a} 1_{4}, + עַם *people* Lv $9_{7.7}$ 16_{24}, עֵדָה *congregation* 1QM 2_{5} 4QapMos^{a} 1.2_{6} (וכ[פר]), בַּיִת *house* Lv $16_{6.11.17}$ Ezk 45_{17}, Aaron Lv 9_{7} $16_{6.11.17.24}$, שׁוב ptc. *one who repents* 4QShirShabb^{a} 1.1_{16} CD 2_{5}, perh. רִאשׁוֹן *first one* CD 4_{6} (שונים) 4_{10}, חזק hi. ptc. *one who holds* ordinances CD 20_{34}, אֶרֶץ *land* 1QS $8_{6.10(mg)}$ 1QSa 1_{3} (לכפ[ר בעד האר]ץ), חַטָּאת *sin* Ex 32_{30} 4QDibHam^{a} 1.2_{9}, עָוֹן *iniquity* 1QS 11_{14} CD 3_{18}, אַשְׁמָה *guilt* 1QH 17_{12} (בע[ד אשמה]) fr. 2_{13}, מַעַל *unfaithfulness* 1QH 17_{12} (בע[ד ... מעל]), כֹּל *everyone* 2 C 30_{18}.

לִפְנֵי *before,* + ״י *Y.* Lv 10_{17} $14_{18.29.31}$ $15_{15.30}$ 23_{28} Nm 15_{28} 31_{50}.

<COLL> שִׁבְעַת יָמִים תְּכַפֵּר *seven days you shall make atonement* for the altar Ex 29_{37}, כן יכפר אל בעדם *thus will God atone for them* CD 4_{10}.

כפר ‖ סלח ni. *be forgiven* Lv $4_{20.26.31.35}$ $5_{10.13.16.18.26}$ Nm $15_{25.28}$, טהר *be clean* Lv $12_{7.8}$ $14_{20.53}$, טהר pi. *cleanse* Nm 8_{21} Ezk 43_{26}; + טהר pi. *cleanse* 1QS 11_{14}, סלח *pardon* 1QS 2_{8}.

Also 1QMyst 6_{3} 4QRitMar 2_{6} 4QDibHam^{a} 11_{3}.

<SYN> סלח ni. *be forgiven,* טהר *be clean,* pi. *cleanse.*

Pu. $_{7.0.5}$ Pf. כֻּפַּר (כופר); impf. יְכֻפַּר (Q יכופר), 3fs תְּכֻפַּר (תכופר)—**be atoned for,** <SUBJ> דָּם *blood(guilt)* 11QT 63_{7}, בְּרִית *covenant* Is 28_{18}, חַטָּאת *sin* Is 6_{7} 1QS 3_{8}, עָוֹן *iniquity* Is 22_{14} 27_{9} Pr 16_{6} 1QS 3_{6}; subj. impersonal, Ex 29_{33} Nm 35_{33} 11QT 17_{2}.

<PREP> לְ of benefit, *to, for* 1QDM 4_{3} (ויכ[ופר]), + אֶרֶץ *land* Nm 35_{33}, Israelite(s) Is 22_{14} 11QT 63_{7}, עַם *people* 11QT 63_{7}, דָּם *blood* Nm 35_{33}; בְּ of time, *in, on,* + יוֹם *day* 1QDM 3_{11}; of instrument, *by (means of), with,* + חֶסֶד *loyalty* Pr 16_{6}, אֱמֶת *truth* Pr 16_{6}, בָּשָׂר *flesh* Ex 29_{33}, רוּחַ *spirit* 1QS 3_{8}, לֶחֶם *bread* Ex 29_{33}, זֹאת *this* Is 27_{9}; עַל *for, on behalf of* 11QT 17_{2}.

Hi. $_{0.0.1}$ Pf. Q הכפרתה—perh. **make atonement,** 4QPrFêtes^{c} 54_{2}.

Htp. $_{1}$ Impf. יִתְכַּפֵּר—**be atoned for,** <SUBJ> עָוֹן *iniquity* of house of Eli 1 S 3_{14}. <PREP> בְּ of instrument, *by (means of),* + זֶבַח *sacrifice* 1 S 3_{14}, מִנְחָה *cereal offering* 1 S 3_{14}; עַד *until,* + עוֹלָם *eternity* 1 S 3_{14}.

Ntp. $_{1}$ Pf. נִכַּפֵּר—**be atoned for,** <SUBJ> דָּם *blood,* i.e. guilt of innocent blood Dt 21_{8}. <PREP> לְ of benefit, *to, for,* + עַם *people* Dt 21_{8}.*

⇒ כְּפוֹר *hoar frost,* כֹּפֶר I *ransom,* כֹּפֶר II *asphalt,* כֹּפֶר IV *henna,* כִּפֻּר *atonement,* כַּפֹּרֶת *cover.*

כָּפָר $_{1.0.1}$ n.m. **village**—pl. כְּפָרִים—<PREP> בְּ of place, *in, at* 1 C 27_{25} 5/6ḤevBA 46_{1}, + יעד ni. *meet* Ne 6_{2} (if em.).*

[כִּפֻּר] $_{8.0.20}$ n.m. **atonement**—Q כפור; pl. כִּפֻּרִים (Q כפורים); cstr. Q כפורי—usu. pl. (sing. only at 4QBapt 4_{3}), **atonement;** sometimes perh. **rite of atonement** (e.g. 1QS 3_{4}); **redemption.**

<NOM CL> [אין כפורים] *there is no atonement* 4QJub^{f} 33_{13}.

<CSTR> כפורי ניחוח *atonement of pleasing odour,* i.e. pleasing atonement 1QS 3_{11}, כפורי רצון perh. *atonement of,* i.e. that brings, *acceptance* 4QOrd^{b} 13_{2}, [כפור רצ[ונ perh. *atonement of acceptance* 4QBapt 4_{3}, כפורי רצונכה *atonement of your acceptance* 4QRitPur 1.12_{3} (כפו[רי)

(רצונכה) 1.12_{14} (כפורן[י] רצונכ[ה]); חַטַּאת הַכִּפֻּרִים *sin offering of the atonement* Ex 30_{10} Nm 29_{11} 11QT $25_{14.15}$, אֵיל *ram of* Nm 5_{8}, כֶּסֶף *the silver of*, i.e. for, Ex 30_{16},* יוֹם *the day of* Lv $23_{27.28}$ 25_{9} 1QpHab 11_{7} (הכפורים) 1QLitPr 2_{6} (כפורים) 4QOtot 7_{2} 4QMishA 4.3_{7} (both הכפורים) 4.4_{3} ([הכפ]ורים) 4.5_{6} 4.6_{1} 4QMishB^{a} 2.2_{2} (all three הכפורים) 2.2_{6} ([יום ה]כפורים) 4QPrFêtes^{b} 2_{2} (יום] כפורי[ם) 11QPs^{a} 27_{8} (ים הכפורים) 11Q Melch 2_{7} (י[ום] [הכפ]ורים) 11QT 25_{11} (כפורים), [חוק כפור]ן *statute of atonement* 4QBapt 12_{3}.

<PREP> לְ *to, for, as* 4QRitPur 29.7_{21} 4QOrd^{b} 13_{2}; בְּ of instrument, *by (means of), with*, + זכה ni. *be purified* 1QS 3_{4}, טהר ni. *be purified* perh. 4QRitPur 1.12_{3} ([בכפו]ר[י]), רצה ni. *be accepted* 1QS 3_{11} (or בְּ *on account of*), קדשׁ pi. *sanctify* ([בכול] כפורן[י]); עַל *on behalf of, for*, + עשׂה *do*, i.e. offer sacrifice Ex 29_{36}.

Also 4QRitPur 39.2_{1} ([כפורי]ם) 4QOrd^{b} 6_{1} ([כ]פורים).*

כֹּפֶר I $_{13.0.6}$ n.m. **ransom**—Q כופר; cstr. כֹּפֶר; sf. כָּפְרְךָ, כָּפְרוֹ, Q כופרם—**ransom, redemption payment** (Ex 21_{30} 30_{12} Nm $35_{31.32}$ Is 43_{3} Ps 49_{8} Jb 33_{24} 36_{18} Pr 6_{35} 13_{8} 21_{18} 4QJub^{d} 21_{20}); **bribe** (1 S 12_{3} Am 5_{12} 1QH 15_{24}), <SUBJ> שׁית ho. *be imposed* Ex 21_{30}, נטה hi. *turn aside* Jb 36_{18}. <NOM CL> כֹּפֶר נֶפֶשׁ־אִישׁ עָשְׁרוֹ *his riches are the ransom of a man's life* Pr 13_{8}, כֹּפֶר לַצַּדִּיק רָשָׁע *the wicked one is a ransom for the righteous* Pr 21_{18}. <OBJ> מצא *find* Jb 33_{24}, נתן *give* Ex 30_{12} Ps 49_{8}, לקח *take* Nm $35_{31.32}$ 1 S 12_{3} Am 5_{12} 1QH 15_{24} 4QJub^{d} 21_{20} (לו תקח ש]וחד וכופר] *you are not to take a bribe or a ransom*).

<CSTR> כֹּפֶר נֶפֶשׁ *ransom of*, i.e. for, *a life* Pr 13_{8}, כֹּפֶר נַפְשׁוֹ *redemption payment of*, i.e. for, *his life* Ex 30_{12} 4QOrd^{a} 1.2_{6};* רָב־כֹּפֶר *greatness of the ransom* Jb 36_{18}, כָּל־כֹּפֶר *every bribe* Pr 6_{35} (or em. לְכֹפֶר *as a ransom*; + שֹׁחַד *bribe*). <PREP> לְ *as*, + נשׂא *raise*, i.e. accept Pr 6_{35} (if em.). <COLL> נָתַתִּי כָפְרְךָ מִצְרַיִם *I have given Egypt as your ransom* Is 43_{3}, נתתה רשעים [כ]ופרנו *you have given the wicked as our ransom* 1QLitPr 3.1_{5}, כסף הערכים אשר נתנו איש כפר נפשו *the money of valuation that a man gives as a ransom for his life* 4QOrd^{a} 1.2_{6}.

Also 1QLitPr 4_{4} perh. 4QpIsa^{c} 14_{5} (כפרם).*

⇒ כפר *cover*.

כֹּפֶר II $_{1}$ n.m. **bitumen, asphalt** for Noah's ark, <PREP> בְּ of instrument, *by (means of), with*, + כפר *cover* Gn 6_{14}.*

⇒ כפר *cover*.

כֹּפֶר III $_{1}$ n.m. **village**, <CSTR> כֹּפֶר הַפְּרָזִי *village of the open country*, i.e. without fortified wall 1 S 6_{18}. <PREP> עַד *until* 1 S 6_{18} (+ מֵעִיר מִבְצָר *from the fortified city*).*

כֹּפֶר IV $_{3}$ n.m. **henna**—pl. כְּפָרִים—**henna** (or perh. **cyprus**) **blossom**, <NOM CL> כְּפָרִים עִם־נְרָדִים *henna blossoms are with the nard* Ca 4_{13}. <CSTR> אֶשְׁכֹּל הַכֹּפֶר *the cluster of henna blossom* Ca 1_{14}. <PREP> בְּ of place, *in, among*, + לין *spend night* Ca 7_{12} (or כֹּפֶר III *village*).*

כְּפַר הָעַמֹּנִי $_{1}$ pl.n. **Chephar-ammoni**, town in Benjamin, <SUBJ> היה *be* Jos 18_{24}. <APP> עִיר *city* Jos 18_{24}.

⇒ כָּפָר *village* + עַמּוֹנִי *Ammonite*.

[כֹּפְרִי] I adj. **tarred**, כלין כופרין *tarred vessels* 3QTr 10_{11} (unless כְּפוֹר *bowl* or כִּפֻּרִי *expiatory*).

[כִּפֻּרִי] II adj. **expiatory**, כלין כופרין *expiatory vessels* 3QTr 10_{11} (unless כְּפוֹר *bowl* or כֹּפְרִי *tarred*).*

כַּפֹּרֶת $_{26.0.2}$ n.f. **cover, lid** of ark of covenant, as base for cherubim (Ex 25_{17}), **mercy seat, propitiatory** upon which ritual of day of atonement was performed (Lv 16_{13}).

<NOM CL> הַכַּפֹּרֶת אֲשֶׁר עַל־אֲרֹן הָעֵדֻת *the cover that is over the ark of the testimony* Ex 30_{6}, [ה]כפרת אשר עליו זהב טהור *the cover that is upon it is pure gold* 11QT 3_{9}, הכפרת אשר מלמע]לה שתים אמ[ות *the cover that is above is two cubits* 11QT 7_{9}. <OBJ> עשׂה *make* Ex 25_{17}||37_{6} 31_{7}||35_{12}, נתן *give*, i.e. place Ex 25_{21} 26_{34} 40_{20}, בוא hi. *bring* Ex 39_{35}, כסה pi. *cover* Lv 16_{13}.

<CSTR> כַּפֹּרֶת זָהָב *cover of gold* Ex 25_{17}; בֵּית הַכַּפֹּרֶת *house of the mercy seat*, i.e. holy of holies 1 C 28_{11},* קְצוֹת הַכַּפֹּרֶת *ends of the cover* Ex 25_{18}||37_{7}.

<PREP> מִן of direction, *from*, + עשׂה *make* Ex 25_{19}||37_{9}; אֶל *to*, + היה *be* Ex 25_{20}||37_{9}; אֶל־פְּנֵי *in front of*, + Lv 16_{2}; עַל *upon, over*, + ראה ni. *appear* Lv 16_{2}, סכך *cover* Ex

25$_{20}$, נזה hi. *sprinkle* Lv 16$_{15}$; עַל־פְּנֵי *in front of*, + נזה hi. *sprinkle* Lv 16$_{14}$; מֵעַל *(from) upon*, + דבר pi. *speak* Ex 25$_{22}$ Nm 7$_{89}$; לִפְנֵי *before*, + נתן *give*, i.e. place Ex 30$_6$, נזה hi. *sprinkle* Lv 16$_{14.15}$.*
→ כפר *cover*.

כפשׁ 1 vb. **bend—Hi.** 1 Pf. הִכְפִּישַׁנִי—**(cause to) bend, make cower, trample,** <SUBJ> ״ Y. Lm 3$_{16}$. <OBJ> worshipper Lm 3$_{16}$. <PREP> בְּ of place, *in*, + אֵפֶר *ashes* Lm 3$_{16}$.*

כַּפְתֹּר I 18 n.m. **knob**—כַּפְתֹּר; pl. sf. כַּפְתֹּרֶיהָ, כַּפְתֹּרֵיהֶם—**knob, ornament,** on tabernacle lampstand (Ex 25$_{31.33.33.34.35.35.35.36}$||37$_{17.19.19.20.21.21.21.22}$); **capital** of pillar (Am 9$_1$ Zp 2$_{14}$).

<SUBJ> היה *be* Ex 25$_{31}$||37$_{17}$ Ex 25$_{36}$||37$_{22}$. <NOM CL> כַּפְתֹּר תַּחַת שְׁנֵי הַקָּנִים *the knob is under two of the branches* of the lampstand Ex 25$_{35.35.35}$||37$_{21.21.21}$. <OBJ> נכה hi. *strike* Am 9$_1$ (unless subj., with הַכַּפְתּוֹר vocative).*

<PREP> בְּ of place, *in*, + לין *spend night* Zp 2$_{14}$. <COLL> שְׁלֹשָׁה גְבִעִים מְשֻׁקָּדִים ... כַּפְתֹּר וָפֶרַח *three cups shaped like almonds ... (with) the ornament and flower* Ex 25$_{33.33}$||37$_{19.19}$, בַּמְּנֹרָה אַרְבָּעָה גְבִעִים מְשֻׁקָּדִים כַּפְתֹּרֶיהָ *on the lampstand were four cups shaped like almonds (with) its ornaments* Ex 25$_{34}$||37$_{20}$.

כַּפְתּוֹר II 3 pl.n. **Caphtor,** appar. **Crete** (unless **Cappadocia**), assoc. with Philistines, <CSTR> אִי כַּפְתּוֹר *island of Caphtor* Jr 47$_4$. <PREP> מִן of direction, *from*, + יצא *go out* Dt 2$_{23}$, עלה hi. *bring up* Am 9$_7$.*
→ כַּפְתֹּרִי *Caphtorite.*

[כַּפְתֹּרִי] 3 gent. **Caphtorite**—pl. כַּפְתֹּרִים—alw. in pl., **Caphtorites, Cretans,** <SUBJ> יצא *go out* Dt 2$_{23}$. <OBJ> ילד *give birth (to)* Gn 10$_{14}$||1 C 1$_{12}$.
→ כַּפְתּוֹר *Caphtor.*

כַּר I 13 n.m. **ram**—pl. כָּרִים—(young) **ram** (Dt 32$_{14}$ 1 S 15$_9$ 2 K 3$_4$ Is 16$_1$ 34$_6$ Jr 51$_{40}$ Ezk 27$_{21}$ 39$_{18}$ Am 6$_4$); **battering ram** (Ezk 4$_2$ 21$_{27.27}$), <OBJ> שׂים *place* Ezk 4$_2$ 21$_{27.27}$, שׁוב hi. *bring back* 2 K 3$_4$, שׁלח *send* Is 16$_1$, אכל *eat* Am 6$_4$. <CSTR> יְקַר כָּרִים *preciousness of rams* Ps 37$_{20}$, חֵלֶב *fat of* Dt 32$_{14}$, דַּם *blood of* Is 34$_6$. <PREP> בְּ *in, with*, + סחר *trade* Ezk 21$_{27}$; כְּ *as* Jr 51$_{40}$; עַל *upon*, + חמל *have pity*, i.e. spare 1 S 15$_9$. <COLL> מֵאָה־אֶלֶף כָּרִים *one hundred thousand rams* 2 K 3$_4$, אֵילִים כָּרִים וְעַתּוּדִים *lambs, rams and (male) goats* Ezk 39$_{18}$.

כַּר II 2 n.m. **pasture**—pl. כָּרִים—<SUBJ> לבשׁ *be clothed with* Ps 65$_{14}$, רחב ni. *be spacious* Is 30$_{23}$. <COLL> יִרְעֶה מִקְנֶיךָ ... כַּר נִרְחָב *your cattle will graze ... (in) spacious pastures* Is 30$_{23}$.

[כַּר] III 1 n.m. **saddle-basket**—cstr. כַּר—<CSTR> כַּר הַגָּמָל *saddle-basket of the camel* Gn 31$_{34}$. <PREP> בְּ *in*, + שׂים *place* Gn 31$_{34}$.

כֹּר 8.0.2 n.m. **cor**—pl. כֹּרִים (Q כורין)—measure of dry or liquid capacity (1 K 5$_{2.2.25.25}$ Ezk 45$_{14}$ 2 C 2$_{9.9}$ 27$_5$), <OBJ> נתן *give* 1 K 5$_{25.25}$ 2 C 27$_5$, שׁלח *send* MurEpBarC$^b_3$, בוא hi. MurEpBarC$^b_3$ (תבו), שׁקל *weigh* Mur 24 2$_{17}$ (כ[ורין]; + סְאָה *seah*) 4$_{16}$, מדד *measure* Mur 24 5$_{12}$ (כ[ו]ין]; + לֶתֶךְ *lethech*).

<CSTR> כֹּר סֹלֶת *cors of flour* 1 K 5$_2$, כֹּר קֶמַח *cors of meal* 1 K 5$_2$, כֹּר חִטִּים *cors of wheat* 1 K 5$_{25}$, כֹּר שֶׁמֶן *cors of oil* 1 K 5$_{25}$. <APP> חִטָּה *wheat* 2 C 2$_9$ 27$_5$ Mur 24 2$_{17}$ (כ[ורין]) 4$_{16}$ 5$_{12}$ (כ[ו]ין]) MurEpBarC$^b_3$ (חנ[טי]ן), שְׂעֹרָה *barley* 2 C 2$_9$. <PREP> מִן of direction, *from* Ezk 45$_{14}$.

<COLL> שלו[שת כור]ין *three cors* Mur 24 5$_{12}$, ארבעת כ[ור]ין *four cors* Mur 24 2$_{17}$, חמשת כורין *five cors* MurEpBarC$^b_3$, ששת כורין *six cors* Mur 24 4$_{16}$, עֶשְׂרִים כֹּר *twenty cors* 1 K 5$_{25}$, שְׁלֹשִׁים כֹּר *thirty cors* 1 K 5$_2$, שִׁשִּׁים כֹּר *sixty cors* 1 K 5$_2$, עֲשֶׂרֶת אֲלָפִים כֹּרִים *ten thousand cors* 2 C 27$_5$, עֶשְׂרִים אֶלֶף כֹּר *twenty thousand cors* 1 K 5$_{25}$, כֹּרִים עֶשְׂרִים אֶלֶף *twenty thousand cors* 2 C 2$_{9.9}$.

כרבל 1 vb. **wrap—Pu.** 1 Ptc. מְכֻרְבָּל—**be wrapped,** <SUBJ> David 1 C 15$_{27}$. <PREP> בְּ *in, with*, + מְעִיל *robe* of linen 1 C 15$_{27}$.

כרה I 15.1.4 vb. **dig—Qal** 14.0.4 Pf. כָּרָה, כָּרִיתָ, כָּרִיתִי, כָּרוּ (כָּרוּהָ); impf. יִכְרֶה, Q נכרה; + waw וַיִּכְרוּ; ptc. כֹּרֶה; inf. Q כרות—**dig, excavate;** also **open** ears (Ps 40$_7$); perh. **pierce** limbs (Ps 22$_{17}$ [unless כרה IV *bind* or V *shrivel*]);

perh. **make deep** thoughts (4Q424 3$_{6}$).

<SUBJ> ′י *Y.* Ps 40$_{7}$, אֱלֹהִים *God* Ps 40$_{7}$, Asa 2 C 16$_{14}$, Jacob Gn 50$_{5}$, אִישׁ *man* Ex 21$_{33}$ Jr 18$_{20.22}$ Pr 16$_{27}$ 4Q424 3$_{6}$ (unless כרה II), נָדִיב *noble* Nm 21$_{18}$=CD 6$_{3}$ (|| חפר *dig*), עֶבֶד *servant* of Isaac Gn 26$_{35}$, יֹשֵׁב *inhabitant* Jr 18$_{20.22}$, זֵד *arrogant one* Ps 119$_{85}$, רָשָׁע *wicked one* Ps 7$_{16}$, עֵדָה *company* of evil ones Ps 22$_{17(mss)}$ (or em. אָסְרוּ *they bound*), בוא ptc. *one who comes* CD 6$_{9}$, לָבִא *lion* Ps 57$_{7}$; subj. not specified, Pr 26$_{27}$.

<OBJ> בְּאֵר *well* Gn 26$_{25}$ Nm 21$_{18}$=CD 6$_{3}$ CD 6$_{9}$, בֹּר *pit* Ex 21$_{33}$ Ps 7$_{16}$, שׁוּחָה *pit* Jr 18$_{20.22}$, שִׁיחָה pit Ps 57$_{7}$ 119$_{85}$, שַׁחַת *pit* Pr 26$_{27}$, קֶבֶר *grave* Gn 50$_{5}$ 2 C 16$_{14}$, דֶּרֶךְ *path* 4Q418 55$_{3}$, רָעָה *evil* Pr 16$_{27}$, אֹזֶן *ear* Ps 40$_{7}$, יָד *hand* Ps 22$_{17(mss)}$ (or em. אָסְרוּ), רֶגֶל *foot* Ps 22$_{17(mss)}$, מַחֲשָׁבָה *thought* 4Q424 3$_{6}$ (unless כרה II).

<PREP> לְ of benefit, *to, for,* + Asa 2 C 16$_{14}$, Jacob Gn 50$_{5}$, worshipper Ps 40$_{7}$ 119$_{85}$, נֶפֶשׁ *soul* Jr 18$_{20}$; בְּ of place, *in, at,* + אֶרֶץ *land* Gn 50$_{5}$; of instrument, *by (means of), with,* + מְחֹקְקָה *statute* CD 6$_{9}$, מְחֹקֵק *staff* Nm 21$_{18}$ CD 6$_{9}$, מִשְׁעֶנֶת *staff* Nm 21$_{18}$; of accompaniment, *with, in,* + עָמָל *toil* 4Q418 55$_{3}$; *at the command of,* + מְחֹקֵק *lawgiver* CD 6$_{3}$; לִפְנֵי *before,* + worshipper Ps 57$_{7}$.

<SYN> חפר *dig*.

Ni. 1.1 Pf. Si נכרה; impf. יִכָּרֶה—**be dug,** <SUBJ> שַׁחַת *pit* Ps 94$_{13}$, מִקְוֶה *reservoir* Si 50$_{3}$. <PREP> לְ of benefit, *to, for,* + רָשָׁע *wicked one* Ps 94$_{13}$; בְּ of time, *in, on,* + דּוֹר *generation* Si 50$_{3}$.*

⇒ כָּרָה *cistern*, מִכְרֶה *pit*.

כרה II 4.0.1 vb. **purchase—Qal** 4 Impf. תִּכְרוּ, יִכְרוּ; + waw וָאֶכְּרֶהָ, וַיִּכְרֶה; inf. Q כרות—**purchase, haggle;** perh. **acquire** (4Q424 3$_{6}$), <SUBJ> Israelite(s) Dt 2$_{6}$, Hosea Ho 3$_{2}$, friends of Job Jb 6$_{27}$, אִישׁ *man* 4Q424 3$_{6}$ (unless כרה I), מֶלֶךְ *king* of Israel 2 K 6$_{23}$ (unless כרה III *give feast*), חַבָּר *partner* Jb 40$_{30}$ (unless כרה III). <OBJ> אִשָּׁה *woman* Ho 3$_{2}$, מַיִם *water* Dt 2$_{6}$, כֵּרָה *feast* 2 K 6$_{23}$ (unless כרה III), מַחֲשָׁבָה *thought* 4Q424 3$_{6}$ (unless כרה I). <PREP> לְ of benefit, *to, for,* + Hosea Ho 3$_{2}$; בְּ of exchange, *for,* + כֶּסֶף fifteen *silver* pieces Ho 3$_{2}$; עַל *over,* + רֵעַ *friend* Jb 6$_{27}$, Leviathan Jb 40$_{30}$; מֵאֵת *(from) with,* + Edomites Dt 2$_{6}$.*

כרה III 2 vb. **feast—Qal** 2 Impf. יִכְרוּ; + waw וַיִּכְרֶה—**1. give (feast)** (2 K 6$_{23}$, unless כרה II *purchase*). **2. feast, feed** (Jb 40$_{30}$, unless כרה II *purchase*).

<SUBJ> מֶלֶךְ *king* of Israel 2 K 6$_{23}$, חַבָּר trading *partner* Jb 40$_{30}$. <OBJ> כֵּרָה *feast* 2 K 6$_{23}$. <PREP> לְ of benefit, *to, for,* + אֵלֶּה *these* (men) 2 K 6$_{23}$; עַל feed *on* Leviathan Jb 40$_{30}$.

Hi. 1 Inf. mss לְהַכְרוֹת—**invite to eat,** <SUBJ> עַם *people* 2 S 3$_{35(mss)}$ (L ברה hi. *feed*). <OBJ> דָּוִד *David* 2 S 3$_{35}$ (mss), לֶחֶם *food* 3$_{25(mss)}$ (second object).*

⇒ כֵּרָה *feast*.

כרה IV 1 vb. perh. **bind—Qal** 1 Pf. mss כָּרוּ (i.e. כָּרוּ, unless כָּרוּ, from כור; L כָּאֲרִי)—**bind,** <SUBJ> עֵדָה *company* of evil ones Ps 22$_{17(mss)}$ (or em. אָסְרוּ *they bound*). <OBJ> יָד *hand* Ps 22$_{17(mss)}$, רֶגֶל *foot* Ps 22$_{17(mss)}$.*

כרה V 1 vb. **be short—Qal** 1 Pf. mss כָּרוּ (i.e. כָּרוּ, unless כָּרוּ, from כור; L כָּאֲרִי)—**shrivel,** <SUBJ> יָד *hand* Ps 22$_{17(mss)}$, רֶגֶל *foot* Ps 22$_{17(mss)}$.*

[כָּרָה] 1 n.f. **cistern**—pl. cstr. כְּרֹת—<SUBJ> היה *be* Zp 2$_{6}$. <CSTR> כְּרֹת רֹעִים *cisterns of shepherds* Zp 2$_{6}$.*

⇒ כרה I *dig*.

כֵּרָה 1 n.f. **feast**—<OBJ> כרה *give (feast)* or *purchase* 2 K 6$_{23}$.*

⇒ כרה III *feast*.

כְּרוּב I 91.0.5 n.m. **cherub**—Q כרב; pl. כְּרוּבִים (כְּרֻבִים); cstr. Q כרובי; sf. Q כרוביהם—heavenly guardian of throne of Y., etc. (e.g. Gn 3$_{24}$ 1 S 4$_{4}$ 2 S 22$_{11}$||Ps 18$_{11}$ 2 K 19$_{15}$ ||Is 37$_{16}$ 1 C 13$_{6}$); image of cherub, made of gold or olive wood (e.g. Ex 25$_{18}$ Nm 7$_{89}$ 1 K 6$_{23}$ 2 C 3$_{7}$ 1 C 28$_{18}$).

<SUBJ> היה *be* Ex 25$_{20}$||37$_{9}$ 2 C 5$_{8}$, עשׂה pass. *be made* Ezk 41$_{18.20.25}$ (all three + תִּמֹרָה *palm tree*), עמד *stand* Ezk 10$_{3}$, הלך *go* Ezk 10$_{16}$, רמם ni. *rise up* Ezk 10$_{15}$, נפל *fall* 4QShirShabb^{f} 20.2$_{7}$ (ה[כרו]בים), סכך *cover* 1 K 8$_{7}$ Ezk 28$_{14.16}$ 1 C 28$_{18}$, כסה pi. *cover* 2 C 5$_{8}$, נשׂא *raise* Ezk 10$_{16.19}$ 11$_{22}$, רמם ni. *be lifted up* 4QShirShabb^{f} 20.2$_{7}$ (ה[כרו]בים), שׁלח *stretch out* Ezk 10$_{7}$, פרשׂ *spread out* 1 K 8$_{7}$ 1 C 28$_{18}$, ברך pi. *bless* 4QShirShabb^{d} 1.2$_{15}$ (+ אוֹפָן *wheel*) 4QShir

Shabb^{f} 20.2$_{7}$ (הֹ[כרו]בים ובו[ר]כו), אבד pi. *destroy* Ezk 28$_{16}$ (if em. וָאַבֶּדְךָ to וְאִבַּדְךָ or וַיְאַבֶּדְךָ).

<NOM CL> כְּרֻבִים מַעֲשֵׂה חֹשֵׁב *cherubim are the work of an artisan* Ex 26$_{1}$, אַתְּ־כְּרוּב *you are the cherub* Ezk 28$_{14}$ (or em. אֵת *with*), כְּרוּבִים הֵמָּה *they were the cherubim* Ezk 10$_{20}$, כֵּן הַכְּרוּב הַשֵּׁנִי *so was the second cherub* 1 K 6$_{26}$, עֶשֶׂר בָּאַמָּה הַכְּרוּב הַשֵּׁנִי *ten cubits was (the measurement of) the second cherub* 1 K 6$_{25}$, עַל־הַמִּסְגְּרוֹת ... כְּרוּבִים *upon the edges ... were the cherubim* 1 K 7$_{29}$, הַכְּרֻבִים אֲשֶׁר עַל־אֲרוֹן הָעֵדֻת *the cherubim that were upon the ark of the testimony* Ex 25$_{22}$.

<OBJ> נתן *give*, i.e. place 1 K 6$_{27}$, שׁכן hi. *position* Gn 3$_{24}$, עלה hi. *bring up* 2 C 3$_{14}$, פתח pi. *engrave* 1 K 7$_{36}$ 2 C 3$_{7}$, קלע *carve* 1 K 6$_{35}$, עשׂה *make* Ex 25$_{18.19.19.19}$‖37$_{7.8.8.8}$ 1 K 6$_{23}$‖2 C 3$_{10}$, צפה pi. *overlay* 1 K 6$_{28}$.

<CSTR> כרובי קודש *cherubim of holiness*, i.e. holy cherubim 4QShirShabb^{f} 20.2$_{3}$ (+ אוֹפַן *wheel*) 4QShir^{b} 41$_{2}$, קוֹמַת הַכְּרוּב *height of the cherub* 1 K 6$_{26}$, מִקְלְעוֹת הַכְּרוּבִים *wood-carvings of the cherubim* 1 K 6$_{29.32}$, רֹאשׁ הַכְּרֻבִים *head of the cherubim* Ezk 10$_{1}$, פְּנֵי הַכְּרוּב *face of the cherub* Ezk 10$_{14}$, פְּנֵי הַכְּרֻבִים *faces of the cherubim* Ex 25$_{20}$‖37$_{9}$, כְּנַף הַכְּרוּב *wing of the cherub* 1 K 6$_{24.24}$‖2 C 3$_{11}$ 1 K 6$_{27}$ 2 C 3$_{12.12}$, כַּנְפֵי הַכְּרֻבִים *wings of the cherubim* 1 K 6$_{27}$‖2 C 3$_{13}$ 8$_{6}$‖2 C 5$_{7}$ Ezk 10$_{5}$ (הַכְּרוּבִים) 2 C 3$_{11}$, רקיע הכרובים *firmament of the cherubim* 4QShirShabb^{f} 20.2$_{8}$, שְׁנֵי הַכְּרֻבִים *the two cherubim* Ex 25$_{22}$ Nm 7$_{89}$ 1 K 6$_{25}$.

<APP> מִמְשַׁח *anointed one* Ezk 28$_{14}$, זָהָב *gold* Ex 25$_{18}$, אַחֵר *other* 2 C 3$_{11.12}$.

<PREP> לְ of direction, *to* Ezk 41$_{18}$, + ראה ni. *appear* Ezk 10$_{8}$; of possession, *(belonging) to, of* 1 K 6$_{25}$ Ezk 41$_{18}$.

עַל *upon*, + עמד *stand* Ezk 10$_{18}$, רום *arise* Ezk 10$_{4}$, ירד hi. *bring down* 1 K 6$_{32}$, רכב *ride* 2 S 22$_{11}$‖Ps 18$_{11}$; מֵעַל *(from) upon*, + עלה ni. *be gone up* Ezk 9$_{3}$.

אֵצֶל *beside* Ezk 10$_{9.9.9}$.

אֵת *with*, + נתן *give*, i.e. place Ezk 28$_{14}$ (if em.).

בֵּין *between* Ezk 10$_{7}$ 41$_{18}$; מִבֵּין *(from) among*, + דבר pi. *speak* Ex 25$_{22}$ Nm 7$_{89}$; מִבֵּינוֹת לְ *(from) among* Ezk 10$_{6}$, + מלא pi. *fill* Ezk 10$_{2}$, שׁלח *stretch out* Ezk 10$_{7}$; אֶל־תַּחַת לְ *beneath* Ezk 10$_{2}$.

<COLL> כְּרוּב אֶחָד *one cherub* Ex 25$_{19.19}$‖37$_{8.8}$ 1 K 6$_{24}$ Ezk 10$_{9.9}$ 2 C 3$_{11.12.12}$ (or em. אַחֵר *other*), שְׁנַיִם כְּרֻבִים *two cherubim* Ex 25$_{18}$ 11QT 7$_{10}$, הַכְּרוּב הַשֵּׁנִי *the second cherub* 1 K 6$_{25.26}$.

יַעֲשֶׂה אֹתָהּ כְּרֻבִים *he shall make it (with) cherubim* Ex 26$_{31}$‖36$_{35}$, כְּרֻבִים ... תַּעֲשֶׂה אֹתָם *(with) cherubim ... you shall make them* Ex 26$_{1}$‖36$_{8}$.

י׳ יֹשֵׁב הַכְּרֻבִים *Y. who sits (above)*, i.e. is enthroned above, *the cherubim* 1 C 13$_{6}$, sim. Ps 99$_{1}$, י׳ צְבָאוֹת יֹשֵׁב הַכְּרֻבִים *Y. of hosts who sits (above)*, i.e. is enthroned above, *the cherubim* 1 S 4$_{4}$ 2 S 6$_{2}$, י׳ אֱלֹהֵי יִשְׂרָאֵל יֹשֵׁב הַכְּרֻבִים *Y. God of Israel who sits (above)*, i.e. is enthroned above, *the cherubim* 2 K 19$_{15}$, י׳ צְבָאוֹת אֱלֹהֵי יִשְׂרָאֵל יֹשֵׁב הַכְּרֻבִים *Y. of hosts, the God of Israel who sits (above)*, i.e. is enthroned above, *the cherubim* Is 37$_{16}$, ... רֹעֵה יִשְׂרָאֵל יֹשֵׁב הַכְּרֻבִים *the Shepherd of Israel ... who sits (above)*, i.e. is enthroned above, *the cherubim* Ps 80$_{2}$.

תַּבְנִית הַמֶּרְכָּבָה הַכְּרֻבִים זָהָב *the plan of the golden chariot (for) the cherubim* 1 C 28$_{18}$.*

Also 4QpsEzek^{e} 16$_{2}$.

כְּרוּב II $_{2}$ pl.n. **Cherub,** in Babylonia, <APP> Tel-melah Ezr 2$_{59}$‖Ne 7$_{61}$. <PREP> מִן of direction, *from*, + עלה *go up* Ezr 2$_{59}$‖Ne 7$_{61}$.

כָּרִי $_{2}$ gent. **Carite**—הַכָּרִי—collectively, of bodyguards of Athaliah, <OBJ> לקח *take* 2 K 11$_{19}$. <PREP> לְ of possession, *(belonging) to, of*, + לקח *take* 2 K 11$_{4}$.

כְּרִית $_{2}$ pl.n. **Cherith,** eastern tributary of River Jordan, <CSTR> נַחַל כְּרִית *brook of Cherith* 1 K 17$_{3.5}$.

כְּרִיתוּת $_{4}$ n.f. **divorce**—כְּרִיתֻת; sf. כְּרִיתֻתֶיהָ—<CSTR> סֵפֶר כְּרִיתֻת *document of divorce* Dt 24$_{1.3}$ Is 50$_{1}$ (כְּרִיתוּת), סֵפֶר כְּרִיתֻתֶיהָ *her document of divorce* Jr 3$_{8}$.*

⇒ כרת *cut*.

כַּרְכֹּב $_{2}$ n.m. **edge**—cstr. כַּרְכֹּב; sf. כַּרְכֻּבּוֹ—<CSTR> כַּרְכֹּב מִזְבֵּחַ *border of the altar* Ex 27$_{5}$. <PREP> תַּחַת *under* Ex 38$_{4}$, + נתן *give*, i.e. place Ex 27$_{5}$.

[כִּרְכּוּר] $_{0.0.1}$ n.[m.] perh. **circuit,** 4QpsHistB 1$_{4}$.

כַּרְכֹּם $_{1}$ n.m. **saffron**—<APP> פְּרִי *fruit* Ca 4$_{14}$.

כַּרְכְּמִישׁ 3 pl.n. **Carchemish**—כַּרְכְּמִשׁ—city on west bank of middle Euphrates, <PREP> בְּ of place, *in, at,* + היה *be* Jr 46$_{2}$, לחם ni. *fight* 2 C 35$_{20}$; כְּ *as* Is 10$_{9}$.

כַּרְכַּס 1 pr.n.m. **Carcas,** eunuch in court of Ahasuerus, <SUBJ> שׁרת pi. *minister* Est 1$_{10}$. <APP> Mehuman Est 1$_{10}$. <PREP> לְ of direction, *to,* + אמר *say* Est 1$_{10}$.

כִּרְכָּרָה 1 n.f. **dromedary**—pl. כִּרְכָּרוֹת—<PREP> בְּ *upon,* + בוא hi. *bring* Is 66$_{20}$ (|| סוּס *horse,* פֶּרֶד *mule*). <SYN> סוּס *horse,* פֶּרֶד *mule.*
⇒ כרר *turn.*

כֶּרֶם I 91.1.4.10 n.m. **vineyard**—כֶּרֶם; sf. כַּרְמִי, כַּרְמְךָ, כַּרְמוֹ; pl. כְּרָמִים; cstr. כַּרְמֵי; sf. כְּרָמֶיהָ, כְּרָמֵינוּ, כַּרְמֵיכֶם.*

<SUBJ> היה *be* 1 K 21$_{1}$ Is 5$_{1}$ Jr 35$_{9}$ Ca 8$_{11}$, קנה ni. *be bought* Jr 32$_{15}$, בער pu. *be grazed* or *be destroyed* Si 36$_{30}$ (+ באין גדר *without a wall*).

<NOM CL> כֶּרֶם י׳ צְבָאוֹת בֵּית יִשְׂרָאֵל *the vineyard of Y. of hosts is the house of Israel* Is 5$_{7}$, כְּרָמֵינוּ סְמָדַר *our vineyards are in blossom* Ca 2$_{15}$, כְּרָמֵינוּ לַאֲחֵרִים *our vineyards belong to others* Ne 5$_{5}$, כַּרְמִי שֶׁלִּי לְפָנָי *my vineyard, which is mine, is before me* Ca 8$_{12}$.

<OBJ> זרע *sow* Dt 22$_{9}$ 4QMMT B$_{78}$ (כ]רמו]), נטע *plant* Gn 9$_{20}$ Dt 6$_{11}$ 20$_{6}$ 28$_{30.39}$ Jos 24$_{13}$ (|| זַיִת *olive-grove*) 2 K 19$_{29}$||Is 37$_{10}$ Is 65$_{21}$ Jr 31$_{5}$ 35$_{7}$ Ezk 28$_{26}$ Am 5$_{11}$ 9$_{14}$ Zp 1$_{13}$ Ps 107$_{37}$ Pr 31$_{16}$ Ec 2$_{4}$, נתן *give* 1 S 22$_{7}$ 1 K 21$_{2.2.6.6.6.7}$ Jr 39$_{10}$ Ho 2$_{17}$ 4QConfess 2$_{9}$ (|| זַיִת), *give,* i.e. rent Ca 8$_{11}$.

בער hi. *allow to be grazed* Ex 22$_{4}$, בצר *gather grapes* Dt 24$_{21}$ Jg 9$_{27}$, זמר *prune* Lv 25$_{3.4}$, עלל po. *glean* Lv 19$_{10}$, לקשׁ pi. *glean* Jb 24$_{6}$, לקח *take* 1 S 8$_{14}$ (|| זַיִת; + שָׂדֶה *field*) 2 K 5$_{26}$ (|| זַיִת), ירשׁ *take possession* 1 K 21$_{15}$ Ne 9$_{25}$ (|| זַיִת), נטר *keep* Ca 1$_{6.6}$, שׁוב hi. *bring back,* i.e. restore Ne 5$_{11}$, חמד *desire* 11QT 57$_{21}$ (|| שָׂדֶה *field,* + הוֹן *wealth,* בַּיִת *house,* חמד pass. ptc. *desirable thing*).

ערב *mortgage* Ne 5$_{3}$, אכל *eat,* i.e. devour Am 4$_{9}$, שׁחת pi. *ruin* Jr 12$_{10}$, בער pi. *destroy* Is 3$_{14}$, חבל pi. *destroy* Ca 2$_{15}$, חרב hi. *destroy* Am 4$_{9}$ (if em.), עשׂר *confiscate one tenth* 1 S 8$_{15}$.

<CSTR> כֶּרֶם י׳ צְבָאוֹת *the vineyard of Y. of hosts* Is 5$_{7}$, כַּרְמֵי עֵין גֶּדִי *vineyards of Engedi* Ca 1$_{14}$, תִּמְנָתָה *of Timnath* Jg 14$_{5}$, כרם יחועלי *vineyard of Jehueli* Samaria ost. 55$_{1}$ 60$_{1}$ (יחועל[י]), הת[ל] *of the ruin* Samaria ost. 20$_{2}$ 53$_{2}$ 54$_{1}$ 58$_{2}$ 61$_{1}$ 72$_{1}$ 73$_{2}$ (כר]ם התל]), כֶּרֶם נָבוֹת *vineyard of Naboth* 1 K 21$_{7.15.16.18}$, אָדָם *of a human being* Pr 24$_{30}$.

כֶּרֶם רֵעֶךָ *vineyard of your neighbour* Dt 23$_{25}$, רָשָׁע *of wicked one* Jb 24$_{6}$ (or *wealthy one,* or em. עָשִׁיר *wealthy one*),* זַיִת *of olive(s)* Jg 15$_{5}$, חֶמֶר *of wine* Is 27$_{2(mss)}$, חֶמֶד *of beauty* Is 27$_{2}$, כַּרְמֵי־חֶמֶד *vineyards of beauty* Am 5$_{11}$.

אֶרֶץ ... כְּרָמִים *land of ... vineyards* 2 K 18$_{32}$||Is 36$_{17}$, צִמְדֵּי־כֶרֶם *acres of vineyard* Is 5$_{10}$, דֶּרֶךְ כְּרָמִים *way of vineyards* Jb 24$_{18}$, מִשְׁעוֹל הַכְּרָמִים *narrow path of,* i.e. between, *the vineyards* Nm 22$_{24}$, מַטָּעֵי כֶרֶם *planting of vineyards* Mc 1$_{6}$, נטעי כר[ם] *plantings of the vineyard* 4QD^{a} 6.4$_{2}$.

פֶּרֶט כַּרְמְךָ *fallen grapes of your vineyard* Lv 19$_{10}$, עללות הכ[רם] *gleanings of the vineyard* 4QD^{a} 6.3$_{4}$ 4QD^{e} 3.2$_{12}$ ([עול]לות), יין כרם *wine of the vineyard* Samaria ost. perh. 20$_{2}$ (י[י]ן) 53$_{2}$ 54$_{1}$ 72$_{1}$ 73$_{2}$ ([כר]ם), תְּבוּאַת הַכָּרֶם *produce of the vineyard* Dt 22$_{9}$ 4Q418 103.2$_{9}$ (תבוא[ת] ה[כרם]), פרי כר[ם *fruit of the vineyard* 4QapPs^{b} 1$_{6}$, מֵיטַב כַּרְמוֹ *best of his vineyard* Ex 22$_{4}$, נַחֲלַת ... כֶּרֶם *inheritance of ... the vineyard* Nm 16$_{14}$, הַרְבּוֹת ... כַּרְמֵיכֶם *the multitude of ... your vineyards* Am 4$_{9}$ (or em. הֶחֱרַבְתִּי *I have destroyed*), כָּל־כְּרָמִים *all the vineyards* Am 5$_{17}$.

<ADJ> טוֹב *good* 1 S 8$_{14}$ 1 K 21$_{2}$.

<PREP> לְ of direction, *to,* + שׁכם hi. *rise early* Ca 7$_{13}$, ענה pi. *sing* Is 27$_{2}$; of benefit, *to, for,* + עשׂה *do* Ex 23$_{11}$ Is 5$_{4.5}$; *concerning,* + שׁיר *sing* Is 5$_{1}$.

בְּ of place, *in, at* 1 K 21$_{18}$ Am 5$_{17}$ Ca 1$_{14}$ 1 C 27$_{27}$, + נטע *plant* 4QpsHod^{c} 2$_{3}$, יתר ni. *be left over* Is 1$_{8}$, בוא *enter* Dt 23$_{25}$, עבר *pass through* Nm 20$_{17}$ (+ שָׂדֶה), נטה *turn aside* Nm 21$_{22}$ (+ שָׂדֶה), ארב *lie in wait* Jg 21$_{20}$, רנן pu. *be joyful* Is 16$_{10}$.

מִן of direction, *from* Samaria ost. 20$_{2}$, + יצא *go out* Jg 21$_{21}$.

אֶל *to,* + ירד *go down* 1 K 21$_{16}$; עַל *upon,* + עבר *pass by* Pr 24$_{30}$; *over, in charge of* 1 C 27$_{27}$; בֵּין *between,* + שׁפט *judge* Is 5$_{3}$ (+ worshipper); עַד *unto, until,* + בוא *come* Jg 14$_{5}$, בער hi. *burn* Jg 15$_{5}$.

<COLL> לָוִינוּ כֶסֶף לְמִדַּת הַמֶּלֶךְ ... וּכְרָמֵינוּ *we have borrowed silver for the tax of the king ... (upon) our vineyards* Ne 5$_{4}$.

<SYN> זַיִת *olive-grove,* שָׂדֶה *field.*
⇒ כֹּרֵם *vinedresser.*

[כֶּרֶם] II 1 pl.n. **Cherem,** town in hill country of Judah, appar. ident. with 'En Karim 7 km W of Jerusalem, <NOM CL> בָּהָר ... כֶּרֶם *in the mountain(s) was ... Cherem* Jos 15$_{59}$ (if ins. כֶּרֶם *Cherem*). <APP> עִיר *city* Jos 15$_{59}$.
⇒ בֵּית הַכֶּרֶם *Beth-haccherem.*

כֹּרֵם 5 n.m. **vinedresser**—pl. כֹּרְמִים; sf. כֹּרְמֵיכֶם—<SUBJ> היה *be* 2 C 26$_{10}$, ילל hi. *wail* Jl 1$_{11}$. <NOM CL> ... בְּנֵי נֵכָר כֹּרְמֵיכֶם *sons of foreigners shall be ... your vinedressers* Is 61$_{5}$. <PREP> לְ *as,* + שׁאר hi. *leave over* 2 K 25$_{12}$||Jr 52$_{16}$.*
⇒ כֶּרֶם *vineyard.*

כַּרְמִי I 8.0.0.2 pr.n.m. **Carmi, 1.** son of Reuben, <NOM CL> בְּנֵי רְאוּבֵן ... וְכַרְמִי *the sons of Reuben were ... and Carmi* Gn 46$_{9}$, sim. Ex 6$_{14}$||1 C 5$_{3}$. <PREP> לְ of possession, *(belonging) to, of* Nm 26$_{6}$.

2. son of Zabdi and father of Achan, <NOM CL> בְּנֵי יְהוּדָה ... וְכַרְמִי *the sons of Judah were ... and Carmi* 1 C 4$_{1}$. <CSTR> בֶּן־כַּרְמִי *son of Carmi* Jos 7$_{1.18}$, בְּנֵי כַּרְמִי *sons of Carmi* 1 C 2$_{7}$.

3. Seal 477$_{1}$ (Lachish 8th/7th cent.).

4. Seal 568$_{2}$ (T. Beit Mirsim? 7th/6th cent.), <CSTR> בן כרמי *son of Carmi* Seal 568$_{2}$ (T. Beit Mirsim? 7th/6th cent.).
⇒ כַּרְמִי II *Carmite.*

כַּרְמִי II 1 gent. **Carmite,** collective, of descendants of Carmi son of Reuben, <CSTR> מִשְׁפַּחַת הַכַּרְמִי *family of the Carmites* Nm 26$_{6}$.
⇒ כַּרְמִי I *Carmi.*

כַּרְמִיל 3 n.m. **crimson**—<APP> אַרְגְּוָן *purple* 2 C 2$_{6}$. <PREP> בְּ of instrument, i.e. material, *in, with,* + עשׂה *make* 2 C 2$_{6.13}$. <COLL> וַיַּעַשׂ אֶת־הַפָּרֹכֶת ... כַּרְמִיל *and he made the curtain of ... crimson* 2 C 3$_{14}$.

כַּרְמֶל I 13 n.m. **orchard**—sf. כַּרְמִלּוֹ—**1. orchard, cultivated field,* garden** of fruit trees and vines (Is 10$_{18}$ Is 16$_{10}$ 29$_{17.17}$ 32$_{15.15.16}$ Jr 4$_{26}$ 48$_{33}$ 2 C 26$_{10}$). **2. plantation** of trees, or **fruitful land** in general (2 K 19$_{23}$||Is 37$_{24}$ Jr 2$_{7}$ Mc 7$_{14}$).

<SUBJ> חשׁב ni. *be reckoned* Is 29$_{17}$ 32$_{15}$. <NOM CL> הִנֵּה הַכַּרְמֶל מִדְבָּר *behold, the orchard was a steppe* Jr 4$_{26}$. <OBJ> כלה pi. *destroy* Is 10$_{18}$. <CSTR> אֶרֶץ הַכַּרְמֶל *the land of the garden,* i.e. of fruitfulness Jr 2$_{7}$, יַעַר כַּרְמִלּוֹ *the forest of its plantation* 2 K 19$_{23}$||Is 37$_{24}$. <PREP> לְ of direction, *to,* + שׁוב *go back* Is 29$_{17}$; *as,* + היה *be* Is 32$_{15}$; בְּ of place, *in, at,* + היה *be* 2 C 26$_{10}$, ישׁב *dwell* Is 32$_{16}$; מִן of direction, *from,* + אסף ni. *be taken away* Is 16$_{10}$ Jr 48$_{33}$; בְּתוֹךְ *within,* + שׁכן *dwell* Mc 7$_{14}$ (if not כַּרְמֶל II *Carmel*).*

כַּרְמֶל II 7.0.2 pl.n. **Carmel**—+ ה- of direction כַּרְמֶ֫לָה (הַכַּרְמֶ֫לָה)—**1.** הַכַּרְמֶל—mountain ridge S of Haifa (Jos 12$_{22}$ 19$_{26}$ 1 K 18$_{19.20.42}$ 2 K 2$_{25}$ 4$_{25}$ Is 33$_{9}$ 35$_{2}$ Jr 46$_{18}$ 50$_{19}$ Am 1$_{2}$ 9$_{3}$ Mc 7$_{14}$ Na 1$_{4}$ Ca 7$_{6}$).

<SUBJ> אמל pu. *waste away* Na 1$_{4}$, נער *dry out* Is 33$_{9}$. <CSTR> הַר הַכַּרְמֶל *the mountain of Carmel* 1 K 18$_{19.20}$ 2 K 2$_{25}$ 4$_{25}$, רֹאשׁ הַכַּרְמֶל *head,* i.e. top, *of Carmel* 1 K 18$_{42}$ Am 1$_{2}$ 9$_{3}$ 4Q418 161$_{10}$ (ש[ראו]), הֲדַר הַכַּרְמֶל *glory of Carmel* Is 35$_{2}$. <PREP> לְ of direction, *to* 4QpIsa^{c} 21$_{21}$3; of possession, *(belonging) to, of* Jos 12$_{22}$; בְּ of place, *in, at,* + פגע *reach* Jos 19$_{26}$; כְּ *as* Jr 46$_{18}$ Ca 7$_{6}$; בְּתוֹךְ *within* Mc 7$_{14}$ (if not כַּרְמֶל I *plantation*). <COLL> רָעָה הַכַּרְמֶל *he shall pasture on Carmel* Jr 50$_{19}$.*

2. place in Judah, appar. Kh. el-Kirmil, 12 km S of Hebron, <NOM CL> בָּהָר ... כַּרְמֶל *in the mountain(s) were ... Carmel* Jos 15$_{55}$. <PREP> בְּ of place, *in, at* 1 S 25$_{2}$, + היה *be* 1 S 25$_{7}$, גזז *shear sheep* 1 S 25$_{2}$. <COLL> הַכַּרְמֶ֫לָה (with ה- of direction), *to, into,* + בוא *come* 1 S 15$_{12}$ 25$_{40}$, עלה *go up* 1 S 25$_{5}$.*
⇒ כַּרְמְלִי *Carmelite.*

כַּרְמֶל III 3 n.m. **fresh ears (of cereal)**—prior to drying for making bread, <OBJ> בוא hi. *bring* 2 K 4$_{42}$, אכל *eat* Lv 23$_{14}$. <CSTR> כַּרְמֶל בְּצִקְלֹון *fresh ears of,* i.e. from, *a garden* 2 K 4$_{42}$ (if em. כַּרְמֶל בְּצִקְלֹנוֹ perh. *fresh ears in his bag;* or em. בְּצִקְלֹון כַּרְמִלּוֹ *plants of his orchard,* i.e. כַּרְמֶל I), גֶּרֶשׂ כַּרְמֶל *grits of fresh ears* Lv 2$_{14}$.*

כַּרְמְלִי 7 gent. **Carmelite**—fem. כַּרְמְלִית—<APP> Abigail 1 S 27$_{3}$ 30$_{5}$ 2$_{2}$ 3$_{3}$ 1 C 3$_{1}$, Hezro 2 S 23$_{35}$||1 C 11$_{37}$.
⇒ כַּרְמֶל II *Carmel.*

כְּרָן 2 pr.n.m. **Cheran,** son of Dishon the Horite, <CSTR>

בְּנֵי דִישׁוֹן ... וּכְרָן *the sons of Dishon were ... and Cheran* 1 C 1$_{41}$. <APP> בֵּן *son* Gn 36$_{26}$.

כרסם $_1$ vb. **tear—Pi.** $_1$ Impf. יְכַרְסְמֶנָּה—**tear off,** <SUBJ> חֲזִיר *wild boar* Ps 80$_{14}$. <OBJ> גֶּפֶן *vine* Ps 80$_{14}$.

כרע $_{36.0.1}$ vb. **bow—Qal** $_{31.0.1}$ Pf. כָּרַע, כָּרְעוּ; impf. יִכְרַע, יִכְרְעוּ (יִכְרָעוּן), תִּכְרְעוּ, תִּכְרַעְנָה, נִכְרְעָה; + waw וַיִּכְרַע, וַיִּכְרְעוּ, וָאֶכְרְעָה, וַתִּכְרַע; ptc. כֹּרֵעַ, כֹּרְעִים, Q כורעי, כֹּרְעוֹת; inf. כְּרֹעַ—**1. bow down, crouch, fall to one's knees, collapse.**

<SUBJ> Bel Is 46$_{1.2}$ (‖ קרס *bend over*), Nebo Is 46$_2$ (‖ קרס), Israel Nm 24$_9$ (‖ שׁכב *lie down*), Ezra Ezr 9$_5$, Joram 2 K 9$_{24}$, Judah Gn 49$_9$ (‖ רבץ *lie down*), Mordecai Est 3$_{2.5}$ (both ‖ שׁחה htpal. *worship*), Sisera Jg 5$_{27}$ (‖ נפל *fall*, שׁכב) 5$_{27.27}$ (both ‖ נפל), Solomon 1 K 8$_{54}$, אִשָּׁה *woman* 1 S 4$_{19}$ (+ ילד *bear child*), בֵּן Israelite *son* 2 C 7$_3$, כַּלָּה *daughter-in-law* 1 S 4$_{19}$ (+ ילד *bear child*).

מֶלֶךְ *king* 2 C 29$_{29}$, שַׂר *commander* 2 K 1$_{13}$, עֶבֶד *servant* Est 3$_2$ (‖ שׁחה htpal. *worship*), worshipper Ps 95$_6$ (‖ שׁחה htpal.), חקק ptc. as noun, *one who decrees* Is 10$_4$ (‖ נפל), יָעֵל *mountain goat* Jb 39$_3$, אַיָּלָה *doe* Jb 39$_3$, צִי *demon* Ps 72$_9$ (or em. צָרָיו *his foes*), בֶּרֶךְ *knee* 1 K 19$_{18}$ Is 45$_{23}$, הֵמָּה *they* Ps 20$_9$ (‖ נפל), אַחֵר *other one* Jb 31$_{10}$, כֹּל *everyone* Jg 7$_{5.6}$ Is 65$_{12}$ Ps 22$_{30}$ 2 C 29$_{29}$.

<PREP> לְ of direction, *to*, יי *Y.* Is 45$_{23}$, בַּעַל *Baal* 1 K 19$_{18}$, טֶבַח *slaughter* Is 65$_{12}$; בְּ *in*, + רֶכֶב *chariot* 2 K 9$_{24}$; עַל *upon, over*, + אִשָּׁה *woman* Jb 31$_{10}$, בֶּרֶךְ *knee* Jg 7$_{5.6}$ 1 K 8$_{54}$ 2 K 1$_{13}$ Ezr 9$_5$, רִצְפָּה *pavement* 2 C 7$_3$; תַּחַת *under*, + אַסִּיר *prisoner* Is 10$_4$.

<COLL> וַיִּכְרְעוּ אַפַּיִם אַרְצָה *and they bowed down with their faces to the ground* 2 C 7$_3$.

<SYN> רבץ *lie down*, שׁכב *lie down*, נפל *fall*, שׁחה htpal. *worship*.

2. ptc. as noun, **feeble one, prostrate one,** <OBJ> אמץ pi. *strengthen* Jb 4$_4$. <CSTR> כורעי עפר *prostrate ones of*, i.e. in, *the dust* 1QM 11$_{13}$; יד כורעי *hand of prostrate ones of* 1QM 11$_{13}$. <APP> בֶּרֶךְ *knee* Jb 4$_4$.

Hi. $_5$ Pf. הִכְרִיעַ, הִכְרַעְתָּנִי; impf. תַּכְרִיעַ; impv. הַכְרִיעֵנִי; inf. הַכְרֵעַ—**cause to bow down, throw into misery,** <SUBJ> יי *Y.* 2 S 22$_{40}$‖Ps 18$_{40}$ Ps 17$_{13}$, אֱלֹהִים *God* Ps 78$_{31}$, בַּת *daughter* Jg 11$_{35}$. <OBJ> Jephthah Jg 11$_{35}$, בָּחוּר *youthful one* of Israel Ps 78$_{31}$, אֹיֵב *enemy* Ps 17$_{13}$, קום ptc. *one who rises up*, i.e. adversary 2 S 22$_{40}$‖Ps 18$_{40}$. <PREP> תַּחַת *under*, + worshipper 2 S 22$_{40}$‖Ps 18$_{40}$.*

→ כֶּרַע *leg*.

[כֶּרַע] $_{9.0.3}$ n.[f.] **leg—**du. כְּרָעַיִם (כְּרָעַיִם); pl. sf. כְּרָעָיו—of passover lamb (Ex 12$_9$) or other sacrificial beast, of locust (Lv 21$_{11}$), of savaged beast (Am 3$_{12}$), <NOM CL> לוֹ כְרָעַיִם מִמַּעַל לְרַגְלָיו *it has jumping-legs above its feet* Lv 11$_{21(Qr)}$, var. 11QT 48$_5$. <OBJ> רחץ *wash* Ex 29$_{17}$ Lv 1$_{9.13}$ 8$_{21}$ 9$_{14}$, pi. 11QT 34$_{11}$ (+ קֶרֶב *innards*), נצל hi. *rescue* Am 3$_{12}$. <CSTR> שְׁתֵּי כְרָעַיִם *two legs* Am 3$_{12}$. <PREP> עַל *with* Ex 12$_9$ Lv 4$_{11}$, + שׂרף *burn* 11QT 16$_{12}$ (ישר[ו]פוהו [על ... כרעיו). <COLL> [ש]תי הכרעים *the two legs* 11QT 24$_4$.

→ כרע *bow down*.

כַּרְפַּס $_1$ n.[m.] **linen,** <SUBJ> אחז pass. *be held* by cords Est 1$_6$ (if em. חוּר כַּרְפַּס *white of linen* to כַּרְפַּס חוּר *linen of white*). <CSTR> חוּר כַּרְפַּס *white of linen* Est 1$_6$ (or em.).

כרר $_3$ vb. **turn—Pilp.** $_3$ Ptc. מְכַרְכֵּר—**dance** or **play** (with hands), i.e. **clap,*** <SUBJ> David 2 S 6$_{14.16}$ (‖ פזז pi. *leap*). <PREP> בְּ *with*, + עֹז *might* 2 S 6$_{14}$; לִפְנֵי *before*, + יי *Y.* 2 S 6$_{14.16}$.

<SYN> פזז pi. *leap*.

→ כִּכָּר *talent*, כִּרְכָּרוֹת *dromedary*.

כָּרֵשׂ $_{1.1}$ n.f. **stomach—**sf. כְּרֵשׂוֹ—<SUBJ> אכל *eat* Si 36$_{23}$ (Bmg) (B גַּרְגֶּרֶת *throat*). <OBJ> מלא pi. *fill* Jr 51$_{34}$.

[כַּרְשׁוֹן] $_{0.0.0.1}$ pr.n.m. **Carshon,** appar. father of Eleadah papMurPalimp^{b}3.

כַּרְשְׁנָא $_1$ pr.n.m. **Carshena,** prince at court of King Ahasuerus, <NOM CL> הַקָּרֹב אֵלָיו כַּרְשְׁנָא *the one(s) who were near to him were Carshena* ... Est 1$_{14}$ (or em. הִקְרִיב *he brought near*). <OBJ> קרב hi. *bring near* Est 1$_{14}$ (if em.).

כרת $_{288.6.53}$ vb. **cut—Qal** $_{135.2.17}$ Pf. כָּרַת (כְּרָתוֹ), כָּרַתִּי,

כְּרָתוּ, כָּרַתְנוּ; impf. יִכְרֹת (Q יכרות), 3fs תִּכְרָת־, 2ms
תִּכְרֹת (Q תכרות), אֶכְרֹת (אֶכְרוֹת, Qr אֶכְרָת־, אֶכְרְתָה),
נִכְרְתָה, נִכְרָת־) נִכְרֹת, (תכרותון Q, תִּכְרְתוּן) תִּכְרְתוּ, יִכְרְתוּ,
(וַיִּכְרָת־) וַיִּכְרֹת; וְכָרְתוּ, וְכָרַתָּ, וְכָרַתִּי, וְכָרַת + waw; (נִכְרְתָה־נּוּ),
3fs וַתִּכְרֹת, 2ms וַתִּכְרָת־ (Q ותכרות), וַיִּכְרְתוּ (וַיִּכְרְתֵהוּ),
וַתִּכְרְתוּ; impv. כְּרֹת (כְּרָת־, כִּרְתָה), כִּרְתוּ; ptc. כֹּרֵת (Q
כורת), כֹּרְתִים, כֹּרְתֵי, pass. כָּרוּת (כְּרוּת); inf. כָּרוֹת (כְּרֹת),
כְּרֹת (כְּרָת־, כְּרוֹת, כָּרְתִי.

1. make covenant; without object, **make covenant*** (1 S 11_2 [mss add obj.] 20_{16} 22_8 Is 57_8 Si $44_{18[Bmg]}$); **give** word (Hg 2_5); **inscribe** statute (Si 44_{20}).

<SUBJ> יי Y. Gn 15_{18} Ex 24_8 $34_{10.27}$=4QD[f] 4.2_3 Dt 4_{23} $5_{2.3}$ 9_9 28_{69} $29_{11.24}$ 31_{16} 1 K 8_9||2 C 5_{10} 1 K 8_{21}||2 C 6_{11} 2 K $17_{15.35.38}$ Is 61_8 Jr 11_{10} $31_{31.32.33}$ 32_{40} 34_{13} Ezk 34_{25} 37_{26} Ho 2_{20} Hg 2_5 Ps 89_4 105_9||1 C 16_{16} Ne 9_8 2 C 7_{18} 21_7 Si $44_{18(Bmg)}$ 4QJub[a] 1_5 4QapJoseph[b] 3_9 perh. 4QapJoshua[a] 14_4, appar. Y. 4QD[f] 4.2_2 11QT 29_{10}, אֲדֹנָי *Adonai* 4QDibHam[a] 3.2_{13}, אֱלֹהִים *God* Dt 5_2 $29_{11.24}$ 2 K 17_{15} Is 55_3 Ps 105_9||1 C 16_{16} Ne 9_8 4QapJoshua[a] 22.14 (כורת[ה]) perh. 4QapPs[b] 69_8, אֵל *God* 1QM 13_7 (כ]רתה]), Ephraim Ho 12_2, Israel 2 S 3_{21} Ho 10_4, Israelites Ex 23_{32} $34_{12.15}$ Dt 7_2 Jg 2_2 4QapPent 2_3 11QT $24_{.12}$, returning exiles Ne 10_1, עַם *people* of Jerusalem Jr 34_{15}, קָהָל *assembly* Ezr 10_3 2 C 23_3.

Abimelech Gn $21_{27.32}$ 26_{28}, Abraham Gn $21_{27.32}$ Si 44_{20}, Ahab 1 K 20_{34}, Ahuzzath Gn 26_{28}, David 1 S 18_3 23_{18} 2 S $3_{12.13}$ 5_3||1 C 11_3, Hezekiah 2 C 29_{10}, Hiram 1 K 5_{26}, Jacob Gn 31_{44}, Jehoiada 2 K 11_4 (+ שׁבע hi. *adjure*) 11_{17}||2 C 23_{16}, Job Jb 31_1, Jonathan 1 S 18_3 22_8 23_{18}, Joshua Jos $9_{6.15}$ 24_{25}, Josiah 2 K 23_3||2 C 34_{31} Laban Gn 31_{44}, Michael 4QZedek 1_6 (מ]יכ[אל), Moses Dt $28_{69.69}$ 29_{13} CD 15_8, Nahash 1 S $11_{1.2}$, Phicol Gn 26_{28}, Solomon 1 K 5_{26}, appar. Zechariah Zc 11_{10}, Zedekiah Jr 34_8.

אִישׁ *man* of Israel Jos $9_{6.7.11.16}$, of mockery Is 28_{15}, who violates covenant Jr 34_{18}, בֵּן *son* 1 S 22_8, Is 57_8, זֶרַע *offspring* Is 57_8, מֶלֶךְ *king* 1 K 20_{34} 2 K 23_3||2 C 34_{31} Jr 34_8 Ezk 17_{13}, מֹשֵׁל *ruler* Is 28_{15}, שַׂר *prince* Jr 34_{15}, חָסִיד *devotee* Ps 50_5, אוֹיֵב *enemy* Ps 83_6, מְשַׂנֵּא *enemy* Ps 83_6, Leviathan Jb 40_{28}.

<OBJ> בְּרִית *covenant* Gn 15_{18} $21_{27.32}$ 26_{28} 31_{44} Ex 23_{32} 24_8 $34_{10.12.15.27}$=4QD[f] 4.2_3 Dt 4_{23} $5_{2.3}$ 7_2 9_9 $29_{11.13.24}$ 31_{16} Jos $9_{6.7.11.15.16}$ 24_{25} Jg 2_2 1 S $11_{1.2(mss)}$ 18_3 23_{18} 2 S $3_{12.13.21}$ 5_3||1 C 11_3 1 K 5_{26} 8_{21}||2 C 6_{11} 1 K 20_{34} 2 K $11_{4.17}$||2 C $23_{3.16}$ 2 K $17_{15.35.38}$ 23_3||2 C 34_{31} Is 28_{15} 55_3 61_8 Jr 11_{10} $31_{31.32.33}$ 32_{40} $34_{8.13.15.18}$ Ezk 17_{13} 34_{25} Ho 2_{20} 10_4 12_2 Zc 11_{10} Ps 50_5 83_6 89_4 Jb 31_1 40_{28} Ezr 10_3 Ne 9_8 2 C 21_7 29_{10} 1QM 13_7 (כ]רתה]) 4QJub[a] 1_5 ([ברית]) 4QD[f] 4.2_2 4QapPent 2_3 ([ברית]) 4QpsEzek[d] 1.2_2 (כ]רתי]) 4QapPs[b] 69_8 4QBark[a] 3.2_2 4QZedek 1_6 (ב]רי[ת]) 4QDibHam[a] 3.2_{13} 11QT 2_4 (ב]רי[ת]) 2_{12} ([ברית]) 29_{10} CD 15_8, אֲמָנָה *covenant* Ne 10_1, דָּבָר *word* of covenant Hg 2_5, חֹק *statute* Si 44_{20}.

<PREP> לְ of benefit, *for* Israelites Ho 2_{20}, שָׁלוֹם *peace* 4QBark[a] 3.2_2; reintroducing subject, + Abraham Si 44_{20}, זֶרַע *offspring* Is 57_8; *with* perh. 4QapJoshua[a] 14_4 4QBark[a] 3.2_2, + יי *Y.* 2 C 29_{10}, אֱלֹהִים *God* Ezr 10_3 2 C 29_{10}, *gods* Ex 23_{32}, גּוֹי *nation* Dt 7_2, עַם *people* Jos 24_{25}, Israelites 4QapPs[b] 69_8, צֹאן *flock* of Israel Ezk 34_{25}, Ben-hadad 1 K 20_{34}, David 2 C 7_{18} 21_7, אִישׁ *man* of Jabesh-gilead 1 S $11_{1.2}$, בֵּן *son* of Israel Jr 32_{40} Ezk 37_{26}, אָב *father* 2 C 21_7 1QM 13_7 (כ]רתה]), שַׂר *prince*, i.e. captain, of guard 2 K 11_4, זָקֵן *elder* 2 S 5_3||1 C 11_3, יֹשֵׁב *inhabitant* Ex 23_{32} $34_{12.15}$ Jos $9_{6.7.11.15}$ (+ עשׂה שָׁלוֹם *make peace*) 9_{16} Jg 2_2 4QapPent 2_3 ([ליושב]) 11QT $24_{.12}$ (both [ליושב]), בָּחִיר *elect* Ps 89_4, אָבֵל *mourner* Is 61_8, צָמֵא *thirsty one* Is 55_3, עַיִן *eye* Jb 31_1.

בְּ of place/time, *at, in, on,* + Beer-sheba Gn 21_{32}, Bethel 11QT 29_{10}, Hebron 2 S 5_3||1 C 11_3, Horeb Dt 5_2 28_{69} 4QDibHam[a] 3.2_{13} ([בחו]רב]), אֶרֶץ *land* of Moab Dt 28_{69}, בַּיִת *house*, i.e. temple Jr 34_{15} 2 C 23_3, בָּשָׂר *flesh* Si 44_{20}, יוֹם *day* Ho 2_{20}; of instrument, *by (means of)*, or accompaniment, *with,* + אוֹת *sign* Si 44_{18}.

מִן appar. *with* foreign gods Is 57_8 (or em. מִן to עִם or כרה *buy* from).

עַל of instrument, *by (means of)*, or accompaniment, *with,* + זֶבַח *sacrifice* Ps 50_5; *against,* + אֱלֹהִים *God* Ps 83_6; perh. *in accordance with* or *concerning,* + דָּבָר *word*, i.e. commandment Ex 24_8.

עַל־פִּי *in accordance with,* + *word*, i.e. commandment Ex 34_{27} (Gnz מִשְׁפָּט *judgment* for דָּבָר).

אֵת *with,* + Israel Ex 34_{27}, Israelites Dt 5_3 4QDibHam[a] 3.2_{13}, בַּיִת *house* of Israel Jr $31_{31.33}$, of Judah Jr 31_{31}, עַם *people* Dt 31_{16} Jr 34_8 Hg 2_5 Zc 11_{10}, Abra(ha)m Gn 15_{18} Ps 105_9||1 C 16_{16}, Moses Ex 34_{27}, David 2 S 3_{21}, Abner 2 S $3_{12.13}$, Joshua and Zerubbabel Hg 2_5, אָב *father*, i.e.

ancestor, of Israel Dt 5$_{3}$ 2 K 17$_{15}$ Jr 11$_{10}$ 31$_{32}$ 34$_{13}$, בֵּן *son* of Israel Dt 28$_{69.69}$ 2 K 17$_{35.38}$ Jr 31$_{33(mss)}$, זֶרַע *offspring* Ezk 17$_{13}$ (מִזֶּרַע *one of the offspring of*), מָוֶת *death* Is 28$_{15}$.

עִם *with* MasJub 2$_{6}$, + עַם *people* Ex 24$_{8}$, Israelites Dt 4$_{23}$ 5$_{2}$ 9$_{9}$ 29$_{11}$ CD 15$_{8}$ 4QD[f] 4.2$_{3}$, בַּיִת *house* 1 S 20$_{16}$ 4QD[f] 4.2$_{2}$ ([את בית]), Assyria Ho 12$_{2}$, Abraham 4QapJoshua[a] 22.2$_{4}$ (כ[רת]ה) 4QpsEzek[d] 1.2$_{2}$ (כ[רתי ע]ם), Isaac Gn 26$_{28}$ 4QpsEzek[d] 1.2$_{2}$ ([כ]רתי ... יצח[ק]), Jacob 4QapJoseph[b] 3$_{9}$ 4QpsEzek[d] 1.2$_{2}$ ([כ]רתי ... [עם יעקוב]) 11QT 29$_{10}$, Job Jb 40$_{28}$ Ne 9$_{8}$, Moses 4QD[f] 4.2$_{3}$, Noah Si 44$_{18}$ (Bmg), Zedekiah 4QZedek 1$_{6}$, אָב *father*, i.e. ancestor, of Israel Dt 29$_{24}$ 1 K 8$_{21}$, בֵּן *son* of Jesse 1 S 22$_{8}$, of Israel 1 K 8$_{9}$||2 C 5$_{10}$ 2 C 6$_{11}$, מֶלֶךְ *king* 2 C 23$_{3}$, עוֹף *bird* Ho 2$_{20}$, חַיָּה *beast* Ho 2$_{20}$, רֶמֶשׂ *creeping thing* Ho 2$_{20}$.

בֵּין *between* Y., Jehoiada and people 2 K 11$_{17}$||2 C 23$_{16}$, Y. and Moses 4QJub[a] 1$_{5}$.

לִפְנֵי *before*, + ׳׳י *Y.* 1 S 23$_{18}$ 2 S 5$_{3}$||1 C 11$_{3}$ 2 K 23$_{3}$||2 C 34$_{31}$ Jr 34$_{15.18}$; לְעֵינֵי *before, in the sight of*, + קָהָל *assembly* 4QZedek 1$_{6}$.

<COLL> כרת + noun used adverbially, יוֹם *day* 4QJub[a] 1$_{5}$ (היום *today*).

2a. active, **cut down** tree or part of tree, sacred image; **cut off** foreskin, head, part of garment; **split** calf sacrificed in covenant (Jr 34$_{18}$), **tear** garment (2 S 10$_{4}$ ||1 C 19$_{4}$); perh. **take, remove** vine (Nm 13$_{23.24}$), **destroy** human being (perh. Jr 11$_{19}$ 50$_{16}$).

<SUBJ> ׳׳י *Y.* Is 18$_{5}$, עַם *people* Jg 9$_{49}$ 2 S 20$_{22}$, בַּיִת *house* of Israel and Judah Jr 11$_{19}$, Israelite(s) Ex 34$_{13}$ Dt 20$_{19.20}$ 11QT 2$_{7}$, Philistines 1 S 31$_{9}$, Sidonians 1 K 5$_{20}$, Abimelech Jg 9$_{48}$, Asa 1 K 15$_{13}$||2 C 15$_{16}$, David 1 S 17$_{51}$ 24$_{5.6.12}$, Gideon Jg 6$_{25.26.30}$, Hanun 2 S 10$_{4}$||1 C 19$_{4}$, Hezekiah 2 K 18$_{4}$, Hiram 2 C 2$_{15}$, Josiah 2 K 23$_{14}$, Sennacherib 2 K 19$_{23}$||Is 37$_{24}$, Zipporah Ex 4$_{25}$, אִישׁ *man* Nm 13$_{23}$ Jg 9$_{49}$ 1 K 5$_{20}$ Jr 22$_{7}$ 34$_{18}$, בֵּן *son* of Israel Nm 13$_{24}$, מֶלֶךְ *king* 2 K 23$_{14}$, עֶבֶד *servant* 2 C 2$_{7.15}$, חָרָשׁ *artisan* Is 44$_{14}$ perh. Jr 10$_{3}$, מַשְׁחִית *destroyer* Jr 22$_{7}$, זָר *stranger* Ezk 31$_{12}$, עָרִיץ *tyrant* Ezk 31$_{12}$, enemies of Jerusalem Jr 6$_{6}$, of Egypt Jr 46$_{23}$, of Babylon Jr 50$_{16}$, אֲשֶׁר *one who* encounters another in wood Dt 19$_{5}$; subj. not specified, Is 14$_{8}$ 2 C 2$_{9}$ (לַחֹטְבִים לְכֹרְתֵי הָעֵצִים *to the hewers, to the cutters of wood*).

<OBJ> אֲשֵׁרָה *Asherah* Ex 34$_{13}$ Jg 6$_{25.26.30}$ 2 K 18$_{4}$ 23$_{14}$ (אשריה[מה]), מִפְלֶצֶת *image* 1 K 15$_{13}$||2 C 15$_{16}$, עֵגֶל *calf* Jr 34$_{18}$, אֶשְׁכּוֹל *cluster* Nm 13$_{23.24}$, זַלְזַל *shoot* Is 18$_{5}$, זְמוֹרָה *branch* Nm 13$_{23}$, עֵץ *tree* Dt 19$_{5}$ 20$_{19.20}$ 1 K 5$_{20}$||2 C 2$_{7}$ Jr 10$_{3}$ perh. 11$_{19}$ 2 C 2$_{9}$ (כֹּרְתֵי הָעֵצִים *cutters of trees*) 2$_{15}$, עֵצָה *tree* Jr 6$_{6}$, שׂוֹכָה *branch* Jg 9$_{48.49}$ (if em. שׂוֹכֹה *his branch*, i.e. שׂוֹךְ, to שׂוֹכָתוֹ in same sense), אֶרֶז *cedar* 1 K 5$_{20}$ Is 44$_{14}$ Jr 22$_{7}$ Ezk 31$_{12}$, קוֹמָה *stature*, i.e. tallest, of cedars 2 K 19$_{23}$||Is 37$_{24}$, יַעַר *forest* Jr 46$_{23}$, כָּנָף *hem* 1 S 24$_{5.6.12}$, מַדְוֶה *garment* 2 S 10$_{4}$||1 C 19$_{4}$, רֹאשׁ *head* 1 S 17$_{51}$ 31$_{9}$ 2 S 20$_{22}$, עָרְלָה *foreskin* Ex 4$_{25}$, perh. Jeremiah Jr 11$_{19}$, זוֹרֵעַ *sower* Jr 50$_{16}$.

<PREP> לְ of benefit, *to, for*, + Solomon 1 K 5$_{20}$, חָרָשׁ *artisan* Is 44$_{14}$; split *into*, + שְׁנַיִם *two (parts)* Jr 34$_{18}$; בְּ of instrument, *by (means of), with*, + חֶרֶב *sword* 1 S 17$_{51}$, מַזְמֵרָה *pruning hook* Is 18$_{5}$; *in*, חֲצִי *half* 2 S 10$_{4}$||1 C 19$_{4}$; מִן of direction, remove/destroy *from*, + אֶרֶץ *land* Jr 11$_{19}$, Babylon Jr 50$_{16}$, שָׁם *there* Nm 13$_{23.24}$; עַד *unto*, + שֵׁת *buttock* 2 S 10$_{4}$, מִפְשָׂעָה *buttock* 1 C 19$_{4}$.

b. passive, **be cut off, <SUBJ>** רֹאשׁ *head* of image 1 S 5$_{4}$, כַּף *palm* 1 S 5$_{4}$. **<PREP>** אֶל *at, by*, + מִפְתָּן *threshold* 1 S 5$_{4}$.

c. passive ptc. as noun, **one who is mutilated**, i.e. genitally deformed, whether person or beast, **<SUBJ>** בוא *come* into assembly of Y. Dt 23$_{2}$ 4QMMT B$_{39}$ (כר[ו]ת). **<OBJ>** קרב hi. *bring forward* in offering Lv 22$_{24}$. **<CSTR>** כְּרוּת שָׁפְכָה *one mutilated of penis* Dt 23$_{2}$ 4QMMT B$_{39}$ (כר[ו]ת).

Also 4QHymnPr 1$_{6}$.

Ni. $_{72.4.27}$ Pf. נִכְרַת (נִכְרֶת), נִכְרְתָה (נִכְרֶתָה), נִכְרַתָּ, נִכְרְתוּ (נִכְרֶתוּ); impf. יִכָּרֵת (יִכָּרֶת־), 3fs תִּכָּרֵת, יִכָּרְתוּ (יִכָּרֵתוּ, יִכָּרֵתוּן); + waw וְנִכְרַת, וְנִכְרְתָה, וְנִכְרַתָּ, וְנִכְרְתוּ; Q ויכרת; ptc. Q נִכְרָתִים (CD 3$_{1}$); inf. הִכָּרֵת—**1. be cut off, be removed, be destroyed** (perh. sometimes, **be excommunicated**), **be blocked,*** of waters of Jordan (Jos 3$_{13.16}$ 4$_{7}$), perh. **be chewed** (Nm 11$_{33}$), appar. **be abrogated,*** of covenant (Si 50$_{24}$).

<SUBJ> Jacob 4QJub[h] 37$_{23}$ ([הכרת]), perh. Israel Ho 8$_{4}$ (or del. כרת ni.), Edomites Ob$_{10}$, בָּשָׂר *flesh*, i.e. living being Gn 9$_{11}$, i.e. quails' meat Nm 11$_{33}$, זֶרַע *offspring* Ps 37$_{28}$, אַחֲרִית *posterity* Ps 37$_{38}$ (|| שׁמד ni. *be destroyed*), יֶתֶר *remnant* of people Zc 14$_{2}$, מִשְׁפָּחָה *family* CD 3$_{1}$, בַּיִת *house* 4QD[a] 10.1$_{10}$, נֶפֶשׁ *soul*, i.e. human being Gn 17$_{14}$

Ex 12$_{15.19}$ 31$_{14}$ Lv 7$_{20.21.25.27}$ 18$_{29}$ 19$_{8}$ 22$_{3}$ 23$_{29}$ Nm 9$_{13}$ 15$_{30.31}$ 19$_{13.20}$ 4QpsJub^{a} 2.1$_{1}$ ([הנ]פש) 11QT 25$_{12}$, אִישׁ *man* Ex 30$_{33.38}$ Lv 17$_{4.9}$ 20$_{17.18}$ 1 K 2$_{4}$ 8$_{25}$||2 C 6$_{16}$ 1 K 9$_{5}$ ||2 C 7$_{18}$ Jr 33$_{17.18}$ 35$_{19}$ Ob$_{9}$ 11QT 27$_{7}$ 59$_{17}$, זָכוּר *male* CD 3$_{6}$, אִשָּׁה *woman* Lv 20$_{18}$, בֵּן *son* 4QJub^{h} 37$_{23}$ ([ונכ]רתים) CD 3$_{1}$, of Israel 4QJub^{c} 2$_{27}$ ([בני ישראל]), אָחוֹת *sister* Lv 20$_{17}$, נָטִיל *weigher* of silver Zp 1$_{11}$ (|| דמה ni. *be destroyed*), שֹׁקֵד *watcher* Is 29$_{20}$, מֶלֶךְ *king* CD 3$_{9}$ (|| אבד *perish*), מָשִׁיחַ *anointed one* Dn 9$_{26}$, אוֹיֵב *enemy* Mc 5$_{8}$ 1QH 6$_{34}$ ([נ]כרתו [אויבים]) perh. 4QapPs^{b} 28$_{3}$, צַר *adversary* 11Q Ps^{a} 22$_{10}$ (|| פזר htp. *be scattered*), צֹרֵר *adversary* Is 11$_{13}$ (+ סור *depart*), רָשָׁע *evildoer* Ps 37$_{34}$ Pr 2$_{22}$ 4QpPs^{a} 1.3$_{12}$ ([ר]שעי; || שמד ni. *be destroyed*), מֵרַע *evildoer* Ps 37$_{9}$, מרה hi. ptc. *one who rebels* 4QpPs^{a} 1.2$_{4}$, עָרִיץ *terrible one* 4Qp Ps^{a} 1.3$_{12}$, אכל ptc. *one who eats* meat with blood Lv 17$_{14}$, חזק hi. ptc. *one who holds* spindle 2 S 3$_{29}$, ישב ptc. *one who sits* 4QCommGenA 5$_{2}$ ([י]כרת), בוא ptc. *one who enters* covenant 1QS 2$_{16}$, חָסֵר *one who lacks* wealth 2 S 3$_{29}$, קלל pu. ptc. *one who is cursed* Ps 37$_{22}$ 4QpPs^{a} 1.3$_{12}$ ([מלול]לו), סור ptc. *one who departs* from Y. Jr 17$_{13}$ (Qr) (if em. כתב ni. *be inscribed*), זוב ptc. *one who has a discharge* 2 S 3$_{29}$, מְצֹרָע *leper* 2 S 3$_{29}$, נפל ptc. *one who falls* by sword 2 S 3$_{29}$, חֹטֵב *hewer* of wood Jos 9$_{23}$, שֹׁאֵב *drawer* of water Jos 9$_{23}$, עשה ptc. *one who does* work 4QJub^{c} 2$_{27}$, worshipper 4QapPs^{b} 33$_{9}$ ([א]כרת).

אֶרֶץ *land* Gn 41$_{36}$, מָעוֹן *dwelling place* Zp 3$_{7}$, מַיִם *waters* Jos 3$_{13}$ 4$_{7.7}$ (or del.), ירד ptc. *what goes down*, i.e. water Jos 3$_{16}$, עֵץ *tree* Jb 14$_{7}$, אֹכֶל *food* Jl 1$_{16}$, עָסִיס *new wine* Jl 1$_{5}$, קֶשֶׁת *bow* Zc 9$_{10}$, לָשׁוֹן perverse *tongue* Pr 10$_{31}$, פֶּה *mouth*, i.e. portion Zc 13$_{8}$ (|| גוע *expire*, :: יתר ni. *remain*).

אוֹת *sign* Is 55$_{13}$, מַשָּׂא *burden* Is 22$_{25}$ (|| אפס *cease*, כלה *be ended*), שִׂמְחָה *rejoicing* Jl 1$_{16}$, גִּיל *rejoicing* Jl 1$_{16}$, תִּקְוָה *hope* Pr 23$_{18}$ 24$_{14}$, אֱמוּנָה *faithfulness* Jr 7$_{28}$ (|| אבד *perish*), חֶסֶד *loyalty* Si 40$_{17(M)}$ (B מוט ni. *be shaken*), שֶׁקֶר *falsehood* 11QPs^{a} 22$_{7}$, עָוֶל *unrighteousness* 11QPs^{a} 22$_{7}$, בְּלִיַּעַל *worthlessness* Na 2$_{1}$ (or em. בָּךְ *in you* to בֶּן *son of* worthlessness; || כלה *be ended* [if em. כֻּלֹּה *all of it*, i.e. worthlessness]), בְּרִית *covenant* Si 50$_{24}$, שֵׁם *name* Is 48$_{19}$ (|| שמד ni.) 55$_{13}$ 56$_{5}$ Ru 4$_{10}$ Si 41$_{11}$, מַחֲצִית *half* of people 11QT 58$_{11}$, כֹּל *everyone* 4QHalakhah^{a} 13$_{5}$ CD 20$_{26}$.

<PREP> לְ of benefit, *to, for*, + David 1 K 2$_{4}$ 8$_{25}$||2 C 6$_{16}$ 1 K 9$_{5}$||2 C 7$_{18}$ Jr 33$_{17}$, Jonadab Jr 35$_{19}$, Simeon Si 50$_{24}$, זֶרַע Simeon's *offspring* Si 50$_{24}$, מֶלֶךְ *king* 11QT 59$_{17}$, כֹּהֵן *priest* Jr 33$_{18}$; לְעוֹלָם *for ever* Ob$_{10}$ 4QJub^{c} 2$_{27}$ ([לע]ו[ל]ם).

בְּ of place, *in*, + מִדְבָּר *steppe* CD 3$_{6}$; of time, *in, during*, or instrument, *by (means of)*, + רָעָב *famine* Gn 41$_{36}$, מִלְחָמָה *battle* 1QH 6$_{34}$ ([נ]כרתו), perh. שְׁרִירוּת *stubbornness* CD 3$_{1}$, אַף *anger* CD 3$_{9}$; בְּלֹא *without* 4QAdmonPar 2.3$_{7}$.

מִן of direction, *from*, + Israel Ex 12$_{15}$ Nm 19$_{13}$, Gibeonites Jos 9$_{23}$, Zion 11QPs^{a} 22$_{7}$, עֵדָה *congregation* Ex 12$_{19}$, עַם *people* Gn 17$_{14}$ Ex 30$_{33.38}$ Lv 7$_{20.21.25.27}$ 17$_{9}$ 19$_{8}$ 23$_{29}$ Nm 9$_{13}$ 11QT 25$_{12}$, בַּיִת *house* of Joab 2 S 3$_{29}$, אֱלֹהִים *God* Jl 1$_{16}$, יָד *hand* 4QD^{a} 10.1$_{10}$, עִיר *city* Zc 14$_{2}$, הַר *mountain* of Esau Ob$_{9}$, אֶרֶץ *land* Pr 2$_{22}$ 4QJub^{c} 2$_{27}$ ([הא]רץ), עִיר *city* 11QT 58$_{11}$, פֶּה *mouth* Jr 7$_{28}$ Jl 1$_{5}$, שִׂמְחָה *rejoicing* 4QapPs^{b} 33$_{9}$ ([א]כרת); of instrument, *by (means of)*, + מַיִם *waters* Gn 9$_{11}$.

עַל perh. *on account of, on behalf of* 4QHalakhah^{a} 2$_{2}$ 13$_{3}$ (ע[ליו]).

מִקֶּרֶב *from (among)*, + עַם *people* Ex 31$_{14}$ Lv 17$_{4}$ 18$_{29}$ Lv 20$_{18}$ Nm 15$_{30}$ 4QpsJub^{a} 2.1$_{1}$ ([מקרב ע]מיה); מִתּוֹךְ *from (among)*, + בֵּן *son* 1QS 2$_{16}$, עַם *people* 4QHalakhah^{a} 2$_{2}$ (ע[מו]) 11QT 27$_{12}$, עֵדָה *congregation* 4QpPs^{a} 3.4$_{18}$ (|| אבד *perish*), קָהָל *assembly* Nm 19$_{20}$, מַחֲנֶה *camp* CD 20$_{26}$; מִלִּפְנֵי *from (standing) in front of*, + יי *Y.* Lv 22$_{3}$ 1 K 8$_{25}$ ||2 C 6$_{16}$ Is 48$_{19}$ Jr 33$_{18}$; מֵעַל *from (sitting) upon*, + כִּסֵּא *throne* 1 K 2$_{4}$ 9$_{5}$; מֵעִם *from (with)*, + אָח *brother* Ru 4$_{10}$.

מִפְּנֵי *in front of* or *on account of*, + אֲרוֹן *ark* Jos 4$_{7}$; לְעֵינֵי *in the sight of*, + בֵּן *son* of people Lv 20$_{17}$; נֶגֶד *in front of*, + עַיִן *eye* Jl 1$_{16}$.

<COLL> הִכָּרֵת תִּכָּרֵת *it must be cut off* Nm 15$_{31}$, תַּמּוּ נִכְרָתוּ the waters *were completely blocked* Jos 3$_{16}$; כרת ni. + adverb, סָבִיב *round about* 11QPs^{a} 22$_{10}$.

2. appar. **be covenanted,** (of covenant) **be made,** באות עולם נכרת עמו *with an eternal sign it was covenanted to him* (Noah) Si 44$_{18(B)}$ (Bmg; B כרת Y. *entered into covenant with him*), <PREP> עִם *with*, + Abraham 4Qps Jub^{a} 1$_{4}$.

Also 1Q25 15$_{2}$ 4QHalakhah^{a} 7$_{6}$ ([הכ]רת).

<SYN> §1 אפס *cease*, כלה *be ended*, אבד *perish*, גוע *expire*, דמה ni. *be destroyed*, שמד ni. *be destroyed*, פזר htp.

be scattered. <ANT> §1 יתר ni. *remain*.

Pu. 2 Pf. כֹּרְתָה, כָּרַּת (unless both qal pass.)—**be cut down, be cut off,** <SUBJ> אֲשֵׁרָה *Asherah* Jg 6$_{28}$ (|| נתץ pu. *be torn down*), שֹׁר *navel cord* Ezk 16$_{4}$ (+ רחץ pu. *be washed*). <PREP> בְּ of time, *at, on*, + יוֹם *day* of birth Ezk 16$_{4}$. <SYN> נתץ pu. *be torn down*.

Hi. 78.0.9 Pf. הִכְרִיתוֹ, הִכְרַתִּי, הִכְרִית; impf. יַכְרִית (Q יכריתנה), יַכְרֵת, 3fs תַּכְרִיתֵךְ, 2ms תַּכְרִית (Q תכרת), וְהִכְרַתִּי, וְהִכְרִיתָה + waw; (נַכְרִיתֶנָּה) נַכְרִית, תַּכְרִית, תַּכְרִיתוּ, אַכְרִית (וְאַכְרִיתָה) וָאַכְרִית, וַיַּכְרֵת; וְהִכְרִיתוֹ, (וְהִכְרַתִּיו, וְהִכְרַתִּיךָ); inf. הַכְרִית (הַכְרִיתוֹ, הַכְרִיתֵךְ)—**cut off, remove, destroy.***

<SUBJ> ׳י *Y.* Lv 17$_{10}$ 20$_{3.5.6}$ 26$_{30}$ (|| שׁמד hi. *destroy*) Dt 12$_{29}$ 19$_{1}$ 1 S 2$_{33}$ 20$_{15}$ 2 S 7$_{9}$||1 C 17$_{8}$ 1 K 9$_{7}$ 14$_{10.14}$ 2 K 9$_{8}$ Is 9$_{13}$ 14$_{22}$ 48$_{9}$ Jr 44$_{11}$ 51$_{62}$ Ezk 14$_{8.13.17.19.21}$ 21$_{8.9}$ 25$_{7}$ (|| אבד hi. *destroy*, שׁמד hi. *destroy*) 25$_{13.16}$ (|| אבד hi. *destroy*) 29$_{8}$ 30$_{15}$ 35$_{7}$ Am 1$_{5.8}$ 2$_{3}$ Mc 5$_{9.10.11.12}$ Na 1$_{14}$ 2$_{14}$ Zp 1$_{3.4}$ 3$_{6}$ Zc 9$_{6.10}$ 13$_{2}$ Ml 2$_{12}$ Ps 12$_{4}$ 34$_{17}$ 109$_{15}$ (mss ni.), appar. Y. 11QT 59$_{15}$, אֱלֹהִים *God* Dt 12$_{29}$ 19$_{1}$, אֵל *God* 1QH 4$_{20.26}$ 4QJub^{d} 21$_{22}$ ((והכריתכ[ה])), Assyria Is 10$_{7}$ (|| שׁמד hi. *destroy*), Edom Ob$_{14}$, Canaanites Jos 7$_{9}$, expatriate inhabitants of Judah Jr 44$_{7.8}$ (or del.), enemies of Moab Jr 48$_{2}$.

Aaron Nm 4$_{18}$, Moses perh. Ex 8$_{5}$ Nm 4$_{18}$, perh. Pharaoh Ezk 17$_{17}$, Joshua Jos 11$_{21}$ (|| חרם hi. *exterminate*) 23$_{4}$, Saul 1 S 28$_{9}$, David 1 S 20$_{15}$ 24$_{22}$ (|| שׁמד hi. *destroy*) perh. Ps 101$_{8}$, Joab 1 K 11$_{16}$, Jezebel 1 K 18$_{4}$, Ahab 1 K 18$_{5}$, Obadiah 1 K 18$_{5}$, appar. Elijah 1 K 21$_{21}$, Jehu 2 C 22$_{7}$, מֶלֶךְ *king* 1 K 14$_{14}$, בֵּן *son* of Israel Jg 4$_{24}$, יֹשֵׁב *inhabitant* of Canaan Jos 7$_{9}$, בְּהֵמָה *beast* perh. 4QapPent 10.2$_{7}$, חַיָּה *beast* Lv 26$_{22}$ (|| שׁכל pi. *bereave*), חֶרֶב *sword* Na 3$_{15}$, אַף *anger* 1QM 1$_{4}$ (|| שׁמד hi. *destroy*), מָוֶת *death* Jr 9$_{20}$, appar. יוֹם *day* Jr 47$_{4}$; subj. not specified, Ps 109$_{13}$.

<OBJ> Isaac 4QJub^{d} 21$_{22}$ ((והכריתכ[ה])), גּוֹי *nation* Dt 12$_{29}$ 19$_{1}$ Jos 23$_{4}$ Is 10$_{7}$ Zp 3$_{6}$, לְאֹם *nation* 4QBark^{a} 1.2$_{2}$, Israel 1 K 9$_{7}$, Moab Jr 48$_{2}$, Ammonites Ezk 25$_{7}$ (|| אבד hi. *destroy*), Anakim Jos 11$_{21}$, Cherethites Ezk 25$_{16}$ (|| אבד hi.), שֵׁבֶט *tribe* Nm 4$_{18}$, Judah Jr 44$_{11}$, Nineveh Na 3$_{15}$ (|| אכל *eat*, i.e. destroy), עִיר *city* Mc 5$_{10}$ (+ הרס *tear down*), הָמוֹן *multitude* Ezk 30$_{15}$, שְׁאָר *remnant* Is 14$_{22}$ Zp 1$_{4}$, שָׂרִיד *remnant* Jr 47$_{4}$, אַחֲרִית *posterity* Ps 109$_{13}$, בַּיִת *house* of Jacob Is 48$_{9}$, of Ahab 2 C 22$_{7}$, *house* of Jeroboam 1 K 14$_{14}$, Jabin Jg 4$_{24}$, מֶלֶךְ *king* Jg 4$_{24}$, שֹׁפֵט *judge* Am 2$_{3}$, תמך ptc. *one who holds* sceptre Am 1$_{5.8}$, נָבִיא *prophet* 1 K 18$_{4}$, נגשׁ hi. ptc. *one who brings near* sacrifice Ml 2$_{12}$, צַדִּיק *righteous one* Ezk 21$_{8.9}$, פָּלִיט *fugitive* Ob$_{14}$, רָשָׁע *wicked one* Ezk 21$_{8.9}$, אוֹב *medium* 1 S 28$_{9}$, יִדְּעֹנִי *familiar spirit* 1 S 28$_{9}$, אוֹיֵב *enemy* 1 S 20$_{15}$ 2 S 7$_{9}$||1 C 17$_{8}$.

אָדָם *human being* Ezk 14$_{13.17.19.21}$ 25$_{13}$ 29$_{8}$ Zp 1$_{3}$, אִישׁ *man* Lv 20$_{3.5}$ 1 S 2$_{33}$ Jr 44$_{7}$ Ezk 14$_{8}$ 1QH 4$_{20}$, נֶפֶשׁ *soul*, i.e. person Lv 17$_{10}$ 20$_{6}$ Ezk 17$_{17}$, זָכָר *male* 1 K 11$_{16}$, אִשָּׁה *woman* Jr 44$_{7}$, עֹלֵל *child* Jr 9$_{20}$ 44$_{7}$ (עֹלֵל), יֹנֵק *child* Jr 44$_{7}$, זֶרַע *offspring* 1 S 24$_{22}$ 4QJub^{d} 21$_{22}$ (והכריתכ[ה ... ואת [זרעכה]) 11QT 59$_{15}$, נִין *descendant* Is 14$_{22}$, נֶכֶד *descendant* Is 14$_{22}$, יֹשֵׁב *inhabitant* Am 1$_{5.8}$, עבר ptc. *one who passes* Ezk 35$_{7}$, *violates* 1QH 4$_{26}$, שׁוּב ptc. *one who goes back* Ezk 35$_{7}$, עור ptc. *one who awakes* Ml 2$_{12}$ (or em. עֵד *witness*), ענה ptc. *one who answers* Ml 2$_{12}$, שׁתן hi. ptc. *one who urinates*, i.e. male 1 K 14$_{10}$ 21$_{21}$ 2 K 9$_{8}$, עָצוּר *fettered* 1 K 14$_{10}$ 21$_{21}$ 2 K 9$_{8}$, עָזוּב *free* 1 K 14$_{10}$ 21$_{21}$ 2 K 9$_{8}$, פעל ptc. *one who does* evil Ps 101$_{8}$, זנה ptc. *one prostituting oneself* Lv 20$_{5}$.

רֶכֶב *chariot* Zc 9$_{10}$, בְּהֵמָה *beast* Lv 26$_{22}$ (+ מעט hi. *diminish*) Ezk 14$_{13.17.19.21}$ 25$_{13}$ 29$_{8}$, סוּס *horse* Mc 5$_{9}$, צְפַרְדֵּעַ *frog* Ex 8$_{5}$, טֶרֶף *prey* Na 2$_{14}$, פֶּסֶל *image* Mc 5$_{12}$ Na 1$_{14}$, מַצֵּבָה *pillar* Mc 5$_{12}$, מַסֵּכָה *cast image* Na 1$_{14}$, חַמָּן *incense altar* Lv 26$_{30}$ (|| שׁמד hi. *destroy*), חֶסֶד *loyalty* 1 S 20$_{15}$, גָּאוֹן *pride* Zc 9$_{6}$, כֶּשֶׁף *sorcery* Mc 5$_{11}$, ראשׁ *head* Is 9$_{13}$, שָׂפָה *lip* Ps 12$_{4}$, לָשׁוֹן *tongue* Ps 12$_{4}$, זָנָב *tail* Is 9$_{13}$, קֶרֶן *horn* 1QM 1$_{4}$, מָקוֹם *place* Jr 51$_{62}$, זֵכֶר *memory* Ps 34$_{17}$ 109$_{15}$, שֵׁם *name* Jos 7$_{9}$ Is 14$_{22}$ Zp 1$_{4}$ Zc 13$_{2}$ (|| עבר hi. *cause to pass*).

<PREP> לְ of benefit, *to, for*, + Eli 1 S 2$_{33}$; of possession, *of, (belonging) to*, + יְהוּדִי *Judahite* Jr 44$_{7.8}$, Babylon Is 14$_{22}$, Sidon Jr 47$_{4}$, Tyre Jr 47$_{4}$, Ahab 1 K 21$_{21}$ 2 K 9$_{8}$, Jeroboam 1 K 14$_{10}$, אִישׁ *man* Ml 2$_{12}$; of direction, *to*, + עוֹלָם *eternity* 11QT 59$_{15}$.

בְּ of accompaniment, *with, in*, + מִשְׁפָּט *judgment* 1QH 4$_{20}$ (במ[שפ]ט) 4$_{26}$.

מִן of direction, *from*, + אֶרֶץ *earth* Jos 7$_{9}$ Ezk 29$_{8}$ Na 2$_{14}$ Ps 34$_{17}$ 109$_{15}$ 4QJub^{d} 21$_{22}$ ((והכריתכ[ה מן הארץ])), *land* 1 S 28$_{9}$ Ezk 14$_{13.17.19}$ Zc 13$_{2}$, אֲדָמָה *land* of Israel Ezk 21$_{8.9}$, הַר *mountain* Jos 11$_{21.21.21}$ Ezk 35$_{7}$, מָקוֹם *place* Zp 1$_{4}$, בִּקְעָה *valley* Am 1$_{5}$, Israel Is 9$_{13}$, Ephraim Zc 9$_{10}$, Edom Ezk 25$_{13}$, Egypt Ezk 29$_{8}$, עִיר *city* Ps 101$_{8}$, Anab Jos 11$_{21}$, Ashdod Am 1$_{8}$, Ashkelon Am 1$_{8}$, Beth-eden Am 1$_{5}$,

Debir Jos 11$_{21}$, Hebron Jos 11$_{21}$, Jerusalem Ezk 14$_{21}$ Zc 9$_{10}$, Pharaoh Ex 8$_{5}$, עַם *people* Ezk 25$_{7}$, בַּיִת *house* Ex 8$_{5}$, אֹהֶל *tent* Ml 2$_{12}$, חוּץ *street* Jr 9$_{20}$, יָד *hand* Mc 5$_{11}$; partitive, *any of*, + בְּהֵמָה *beast* 1 K 18$_{5}$; *from being, so as not to be*, + גּוֹי *nation* Jr 48$_{2}$.

מֵעִם *from (with)*, + מִזְבֵּחַ *altar* 1 S 2$_{33}$, בַּיִת *house* 1 S 20$_{15}$; מִקֶּרֶב *from (among)*, + עַם *people* Lv 17$_{10}$ 20$_{3.5.6}$ Mc 5$_{9.12}$, Moab Am 2$_{3}$; מִתּוֹךְ *from (among)*, + עַם *people* Ezk 14$_{8}$, Judah Jr 44$_{7}$, לֵוִי *Levite* Nm 4$_{18}$; מִפְּנֵי *from (before)*, + David 2 S 7$_{9}$||1 C 17$_{8}$; מֵעַל פְּנֵי *from (upon the face of)*, + אֲדָמָה *land* 1 K 9$_{7}$ Zp 1$_{3}$; מִתַּחַת *from beneath*, + שָׁמַיִם *heaven* 4QJub[d] 21$_{22}$ (והכריתכ]ה ... מ]תחת).

עַד *unto*, + עוֹלָם *eternity* 1 S 20$_{15}$.

<COLL> כרת hi. + adverb, עוֹד *again* perh. 4Q446 1$_{2}$. Also 4QparaKings 11$_{2}$.

<SYN> אבד hi. *destroy*, שׁמד hi. *destroy*, אכל *eat*, i.e. destroy, חרם hi. *exterminate*, עבר hi. *cause to pass*, הרס *tear down*, שׁכל pi. *bereave*.

Ho. 1 Pf. הָכְרַת—**be cut off, be ended,** <SUBJ> מִנְחָה *cereal offering* Jl 1$_{9}$ (+ שׁדד pu. *be devastated*), נֶסֶךְ *oblation* Jl 1$_{9}$. <PREP> מִן of direction, *from*, + בַּיִת *house* of Y. Jl 1$_{9}$.*

→ כְּרִיתוּת *divorce*, כְּרֻתָה *beam*.

כְּרֻתוֹת 3 n.f. **beam**—כְּרֻתֹת; cstr. כְּרֻתוֹת—<NOM CL> כְּרֻתוֹת אֲרָזִים עַל־הָעַמּוּדִים *beams of cedar were upon the pillars* 1 K 7$_{2}$. <CSTR> כְּרֻתֹת אֲרָזִים *beams of cedar* 1 K 6$_{36}$ 7$_{2}$ (כְּרֻתוֹת) 7$_{12}$; טוּר כְּרֻתוֹת *row of beams of* 1 K 6$_{36}$ 7$_{12}$.*

→ כרת *cut*.

כְּרֵתִי 10 gent. **Cherethite**—pl. כְּרֵתִים—collective (perh. in ref. to **Caphtorites, Cretans**), assoc. with Philistines, <SUBJ> עבר *pass by* 2 S 15$_{18}$, יצא *go out* 2 S 20$_{7.7}$, ירד *go down* 1 K 1$_{38}$, הלך hi. *bring* 1 K 1$_{38}$, רכב hi. *cause to ride* 1 K 1$_{38.44}$. <OBJ> שׁלח *send* 1 K 1$_{44}$, כרת hi. *destroy* Ezk 25$_{16}$. <CSTR> גּוֹי כְּרֵתִים *nation of the Cherethites* Zp 2$_{5}$, נֶגֶב הַכְּרֵתִי *Negeb of the Cherethites* 1 S 30$_{14}$, כָּל־הַכְּרֵתִי *all the Cherethites* 2 S 15$_{18}$. <PREP> עַל *over, in charge of* 2 S 8$_{18}$ (ms)||1 C 18$_{17}$ 2 S 20$_{23(Qr)}$. Also 2 S 8$_{18}$.*

כֶּשֶׂב 13.0.1 n.m. **sheep**—pl. כְּשָׂבִים—more commonly כֶּבֶשׂ, <SUBJ> ילד ni. *be born* Lv 22$_{27}$ (|| שׁוֹר *ox*, עֵז *goat*). <OBJ> פרד hi. *separate* Gn 30$_{40}$, קרב hi. *bring near*, i.e. offer Lv 3$_{7.7}$, שׁחט *slaughter* Lv 17$_{3}$ 4QMMT B$_{28}$ (|| שׁוֹר *ox*, עֵז *goat*). <CSTR> שֶׂה כְשָׂבִים *sheep of the sheep*, i.e. the lambs Dt 14$_{4}$, חֵלֶב־הַכֶּשֶׂב *fat of the sheep* Lv 4$_{35}$ 7$_{23}$, בְּכוֹר כֶּשֶׂב *firstborn of a sheep* Nm 18$_{17}$. <PREP> בְּ of accompaniment, *with, in* Gn 30$_{33}$, + סור hi. *remove* Gn 30$_{32.35}$; *among* Lv 22$_{19}$; מִן partitive, *some of, (any)one of* Lv 1$_{10}$. <SYN> שׁוֹר *ox*, עֵז *goat*.*

→ כִּשְׂבָּה *ewe*.

כִּשְׂבָּה 1 n.f. **ewe**—<OBJ> בוא hi. *bring* Lv 5$_{6}$. <APP> אָשָׁם *guilt offering* Lv 5$_{6}$.*

→ כֶּשֶׂב *sheep*.

כֶּשֶׂד 1 pr.n.m. **Chesed,** son of Abraham's brother Nahor, <OBJ> ילד *bear child* Gn 22$_{22}$. <APP> בֵּן *son* Gn 22$_{22}$.

[כַּשְׂדִּי] 69.0.1.1 gent. **Chaldaean**—pl. כַּשְׂדִּים—alw. pl., usu. of inhabitants of Chaldaea; also of Babylonian sage, astrologer (Dn 2$_{2.4}$), <SUBJ> היה *be* 2 K 25$_{25}$, שׁמע *hear* Jr 37$_{5}$, מצא ni. *be found* Jr 41$_{3}$, בוא *come* Jr 32$_{29}$, הלך *go* Jr 37$_{9.9}$, עלה *go up* Jr 37$_{5}$, שׁוב *go back* Jr 37$_{8}$, רכב *ride* Ezk 23$_{23}$, שׂים *place*, i.e. form, groups Jb 1$_{17}$, פשׁט *make raid* Jb 1$_{17}$, לקח *take* Jb 1$_{17}$, לכד *capture* Jr 37$_{8}$, שׁבר pi. *shatter* 2 K 25$_{13}$||Jr 52$_{17}$, נכה hi. *strike* Jb 1$_{17}$, נתץ *tear down* Jr 39$_{8}$, שׂרף *burn* Jr 32$_{29}$ 37$_{8}$ 39$_{8}$, יצת hi. *set on fire* Jr 32$_{29}$, צור *besiege* Jr 21$_{4.9}$ 37$_{5}$, לחם ni. *fight* Jr 32$_{29}$ 37$_{8}$, דבר pi. *speak* Dn 2$_{4}$.

<NOM CL> זְרֹעוֹ כַּשְׂדִּים *his arm is (against) the Chaldaeans* Is 48$_{14}$ (or em. זֶרַע *seed of* the Chaldaeans), כַּשְׂדִּים עַל־הָעִיר סָבִיב *the Chaldaeans were round about the city* 2 K 25$_{4}$||Jr 52$_{7}$.

<OBJ> אסף *gather* Jr 21$_{4}$, קום hi. *raise* Hb 1$_{6}$, בוא hi. *bring* Ezk 23$_{23}$, ירד hi. *bring down* Is 43$_{14}$, עבד *serve* Jr 40$_{9}$, לחם ni. *fight* Jr 21$_{4}$ 32$_{5}$ 33$_{5}$, נכה hi. *strike* 2 K 25$_{25}$ Jr 41$_{3}$.

<CSTR> אֶרֶץ כַּשְׂדִּים *land of the Chaldaeans* Is 23$_{13}$ Jr 24$_{5}$ 25$_{12}$ 50$_{1.8.25.45}$ 51$_{4.54}$ Ezk 1$_{3}$ 12$_{13}$, מַלְכוּת *kingdom of* Dn 9$_{1}$, אוּר *Ur of* Gn 11$_{28.31}$ 15$_{7}$ Ne 9$_{7}$ 4QCommGenA 2$_{9}$, זֶרַע *seed of* Is 48$_{14}$ (if em.), בַּת־כַּשְׂדִּים *daughter of the Chaldaeans* Is 47$_{1.5}$, מֶלֶךְ כַּשְׂדִּים *king of the Chaldaeans* 2 C 36$_{17(Qr)}$, עַבְדֵי הַכַּשְׂדִּים *servants of the Chaldaeans* 2 K

25$_{24}$, חֵיל גְּדוּדֵי כַשְׂדִּים *bands of the Chaldaeans* 2 K 24$_{2}$, חֵיל *army of* 2 K 25$_{5}$||Jr 52$_{8}$ 2 K 25$_{10}$||Jr 39$_{5}$ 52$_{14}$ Jr 35$_{11}$ 37$_{10.11}$, גְּאוֹן *pride of* Is 13$_{19}$, צַלְמֵי *images of* Ezk 23$_{14(Qr)}$, יַד *hand of* Jr 22$_{25}$ 32$_{4.24.25.28.43}$ 38$_{18}$ 43$_{3}$, ידי *hands of* perh. Lachish ost. 6$_{7}$, לְשׁוֹן *tongue*, i.e. language, *of* Dn 1$_{4}$.

<PREP> לְ of direction, *to*, + קרא *call* Dn 2$_{2}$; מִן of direction, *from*, + ברח *flee* Is 48$_{20}$; אֶל *to*, + יצא *go out* Jr 38$_{2}$, hi. *bring out* Jr 38$_{23}$, נפל *fall*, i.e. surrender Jr 37$_{13}$ 38$_{19}$; עַל *upon* Jr 50$_{35}$, + נפל *fall*, i.e. surrender Jr 21$_{9}$ 37$_{14}$; לִפְנֵי *before*, + עמד *stand* Jr 40$_{10}$; מִפְּנֵי *on account of*, + ירא *be afraid* 2 K 25$_{26}$ Jr 41$_{18}$, בוא *come* Jr 41$_{18}$.

⇒ כַּשְׂדִּים *Chaldaea*.

כַּשְׂדִּים 7 pl.n. **Chaldaea**—+ ה- of direction כַּשְׂדִּימָה—<SUBJ> היה *be* Jr 50$_{10}$. <NOM CL> כַּשְׂדִּים אֶרֶץ מוֹלַדְתָּם *Chaldaea is the land of their birth* Ezk 23$_{15}$. <OBJ> שׁלל *plunder* Jr 50$_{10}$. <CSTR> יֹשְׁבֵי כַשְׂדִּים *inhabitants of Chaldaea* Jr 51$_{24.35}$. <COLL> כַּשְׂדִּימָה (with ה- of direction), *at, in, to, into*, + בוא hi. *bring* Ezk 11$_{24}$, רבה hi. *multiply* Ezk 16$_{29}$, שׁלח *send* Ezk 23$_{16}$.

⇒ כַּשְׂדִּי *Chaldaean*.

כשׁה 1 vb. **be sated—Qal** 1 Pf. כָּשִׂיתָ—**be sated, be gorged with food,** <SUBJ> Jeshurun Dt 32$_{15}$ (|| שׁמן *be fat*, עבה *be thick*). <SYN> שׁמן *be fat*, עבה *be thick*.

[כשׁח] vb. **be lame—Qal, be disabled,** <SUBJ> יָמִין *right hand* Ps 137$_{5}$ (if em. תִּשְׁכַּח *may* my right hand *forget* to תִּכְשַׁח *may* my right hand *be disabled*).

[כָּשַׁי] 0.0.0.1 pr.n.m. **Cashai**—<PREP> לְ of possession, *(belonging) to, of* Seal 494$_{1}$ (7th cent.).

כַּשִּׁיל 1 n.m. **axe**—<PREP> בְּ of instrument, *by (means of), with*, + הלם *break in pieces* Ps 74$_{6}$ (|| כֵּילָף *crowbar*). <SYN> כֵּילָף *crowbar*.

⇒ כשׁל *stumble*.

[כַּשִּׁיר] adj. **skilful**—used as noun, **skilful (player),** הִנְּךָ לָהֶם כַּשִּׁיר עֲגָבִים *behold, you are to them a skilful player of love songs* Ezk 33$_{32}$ (if em. כְּשִׁיר *as a song* of love; or em. כְּשָׁר *as one who sings*).*

כשׁל 62.7.24 vb. **stumble—Qal** 29.3.12 Pf. כָּשַׁל, כָּשְׁלָה, כָּשְׁלְתָּ, כָּשְׁלוּ (כָּשֵׁלוּ), כָּשַׁלְנוּ; impf. Q יכשול, 2ms Q תכשל, יִכְשְׁלוּ (Q יכשולו), Q אכשול; + waw וְכָשַׁל, וְכָשַׁלְתָּ, וְכָשְׁלוּ; ptc. כּוֹשֵׁל, Q כושלים, Q כושלי, כּוֹשְׁלוֹת; inf. כָּשׁוֹל—**1. stumble, stagger, totter;** of strength, **fail** (Ps 31$_{11}$ Ne 4$_{4}$ GnzPs 1$_{26}$), <SUBJ> Jerusalem Is 3$_{8}$, Israel Ho 14$_{2}$, עַם *people* Is 28$_{13}$ Jr 6$_{21}$, הָמוֹן *multitude* Jr 46$_{16}$ (if em.), Judah Ho 5$_{5}$, Israelite(s) Is 59$_{10}$, שֵׁבֶט *tribe* Ps 105$_{37}$, אִישׁ *man* Lv 26$_{37}$ Si 41$_{2}$ 1QH 16$_{5}$ 1QSa 2$_{7}$, נַעַר *youth* Lm 5$_{13}$, עֶבֶד *servant* 1QH 17$_{23}$ (+ חטא *sin*), כֹּהֵן *priest* Ho 4$_{5}$, נָבִיא *prophet* Ho 4$_{5}$, גִּבּוֹר *warrior* Jr 46$_{6.12}$ (both || נפל *fall*), רַב *great one* Is 8$_{15}$ (|| נפל), קַל *swift one* Jr 46$_{6}$ (|| נפל), פָּרָשׁ *rider* Na 3$_{3}$, מַשְׂכִּיל *instructor* 1QS 11$_{12}$, דּוֹרֵשׁ *seeker* 4QpNah 3.2$_{6}$.

אָסִיר *prisoner* Ps 107$_{12}$, זָדוֹן *arrogant one* Jr 50$_{32}$ (|| נפל), צַר *adversary* Ps 27$_{2}$, אוֹיֵב *enemy* Ps 27$_{2}$, עֹזֵר *helper* Is 31$_{3}$, שִׂיב ptc. *grey-haired one* Si 42$_{9(M)}$, בֶּרֶךְ *knee* Is 35$_{3}$ Ps 109$_{24}$ 2QapProph 1$_{10}$ ([יכ]שלון), כֹּחַ *strength* Ps 31$_{11}$ Ne 4$_{4}$ GnzPs 1$_{26}$, אֱמֶת *truth* Is 59$_{14}$, כֹּל *everyone* 2 C 28$_{15}$; subj. not specified, Is 5$_{27}$ 40$_{30}$ 46$_{16}$ (|| נפל) Jb 4$_{4}$ Si 14$_{9}$ 4Q416 2.2$_{16}$.

<PREP> בְּ of place/time, *in, at*, + צָהֳרַיִם *noontime* Is 59$_{10}$, רְחוֹב *square* of town Is 59$_{14}$; of cause, *on account of, with* perh. 4Q415 11$_{9}$, + עָוֹן *iniquity* Ho 14$_{2}$ Ps 31$_{11}$ 1QS 11$_{12}$, עֵצָה *counsel* 4QpNah 3.2$_{6}$, עֵץ *wood*, i.e. load of wood Lm 5$_{13}$, דָּבָר *word* 1QH 17$_{23}$; of accompaniment, *with, in*, + מִשְׁפָּט *judgment* 1QH 16$_{5}$ (בכול מ[שפט]).

בְּ *against* Is 5$_{27}$, + אָח *brother* Lv 26$_{37}$, גִּבּוֹר *warrior* Jr 46$_{12}$, גְּוִיָּה *body* Na 3$_{3}$ 4QpNah 3.2$_{6}$, צוּר *rock* Is 8$_{15}$, אֶבֶן *stone* Is 8$_{15}$, מִכְשׁוֹל *obstacle* Jr 6$_{21}$.

מִן *because of*, + צוֹם *fasting* Ps 109$_{24}$.

עַל־יַד *beside*, + נָהָר *river* Jr 46$_{6}$.

עִם *with*, + Israel Ho 5$_{5}$, Ephraim Ho 5$_{5}$, כֹּהֵן *priest* Ho 4$_{5}$.

<COLL> כָּשַׁלְתָּ הַיּוֹם *you have stumbled today* Ho 4$_{5}$, כָּשַׁל גַּם־נָבִיא ... לָיְלָה *the prophet has also stumbled ... at night* Ho 4$_{5}$.

2. ptc. as noun, **one who stumbles,** <OBJ> קרא *call* 1QM 14$_{5}$, רום hi. *raise* 4QHod^{a} 7.1$_{17}$ 7.2$_{8}$. <CSTR> כושלי ארץ *stumbling ones of the earth* 4QHod^{a} 7.2$_{8}$; רוח כושלים *spirit of the stumbling ones* 1QH 8$_{36}$. <SYN> נפל *fall*.

Ni. 23.4.2 Pf. נִכְשַׁל, נִכְשְׁלוּ; impf. יִכָּשֶׁל־, 2ms תִּכָּשֵׁל,

יִכָּשְׁלוּ (יִכָּשֵׁלוּ), Si תכשלו; + waw וְנִכְשְׁלוּ; ptc. נִכְשָׁל, נִכְשָׁלִים; inf. הִכָּשְׁלָם (בְּכָשְׁלוֹ)—**1. be tottering, be cast out, be thrown to the ground, stumble,** <SUBJ> Israel Ho 5$_{5}$, עַם *people* Is 63$_{13}$ Jr 18$_{15(mss)}$ 31$_{9}$, Ephraim Ho 5$_{5}$, אִישׁ *man* Si 37$_{12(D)}$, בֵּן *son* Pr 4$_{12}$ Dn 11$_{14}$ Si 4$_{22}$, בָּחוּר *youth* Is 40$_{30}$, מֶלֶךְ *king* Dn 11$_{19}$, כֹּהֵן *priest* Jr 6$_{15}$ 8$_{12}$, נָבִיא *prophet* Jr 6$_{15}$ 8$_{12}$, אַדִּיר *noble one* Na 2$_{6}$ (or em. לֹא יִכָּשְׁלוּ *they will not stumble*), גִּבּוֹר *mighty one* CD 2$_{17}$ (‖ תעה *go astray*), רַב *great one* Dn 11$_{33.34.41}$, worshipper Si 30$_{21}$ 37$_{12(B)}$ 1QSb 2$_{26}$ ([תכשו]ל), רָשָׁע *wicked one* Ezk 33$_{12}$ Pr 4$_{19}$ 24$_{16}$, אוֹיֵב *enemy* Ps 9$_{4}$ Pr 24$_{17}$, פֹּשֵׁעַ *transgressor* Ho 14$_{10}$, רדף ptc. *pursuer* Jr 20$_{11}$, שׂכל hi. ptc. *one who has insight* Dn 11$_{35}$; subj. not specified, Si 41$_{9}$.

<PREP> לְ of agent, *by (means of)*, + מִכְשׁוֹל *obstacle* Si 4$_{22}$; of benefit, *to, for*, + שִׂמְחָה *joy* Si 41$_{9}$.

בְּ of place, *in, at*, + דֶּרֶךְ *way* Jr 18$_{15(mss)}$ 31$_{9.9}$ Ho 14$_{10}$, הֲלִיכָה *way* Na 2$_{6}$; of instrument, *by (means of), with*, + חֶרֶב *sword* Dn 11$_{33}$; *because of*, + רִשְׁעָה *wickedness* Ezk 33$_{12}$, עָוֹן *iniquity* Ho 5$_{5}$ Si 30$_{21}$, רָעָה *evil* Pr 24$_{16}$, פֶּשַׁע *transgression* 4QPrFêtes^{c} 12.1$_{5}$, מַחֲשָׁבָה *thought* CD 2$_{17}$, עַיִן *eye* of prostitution CD 2$_{17}$, מָה *what?* Pr 4$_{19}$.

<COLL> נכשלו בם מלנפנים עד הנה *they stumbled because of them from of old until now* CD 2$_{17}$.

2. ptc. as adj. or noun, **feeble (one), tottering (one),** <SUBJ> היה *be* Zc 12$_{8}$, אזר *gird on* 1 S 2$_{4}$. <SYN> תעה *go astray*.

Pi. $_{1}$ Impf. תְּכַשְּׁלִי—**cause to stumble,** <SUBJ> הַר *mountain of Israel* Ezk 36$_{14(Kt)}$ (Qr שׁכל pi. *make childless*) 36$_{15(mss)}$. <OBJ> גּוֹי *nation* Ezk 36$_{14.15(mss)}$.

Hi. $_{8.2.10}$ Pf. הִכְשִׁיל, Q הכשלתה, הִכְשַׁלְתֶּם; impf. יַכְשִׁילְךָ, תַּכְשִׁלִי, יַכְשִׁילוּ; + waw וַיַּכְשִׁילוּהוּ (וַיַּכְשִׁלוּם), Q ותכשילהו; ptc. Q מכשלת, מכשילים; inf. הַכְשִׁיל (הַכְשִׁילוֹ), Q לכשילם)—**cause to stumble, make unsteady, make feeble, overthrow,** <SUBJ> 'י *Y.* Jr 18$_{15}$ (if em.) Lm 1$_{14}$ perh. 4QparaKings 104$_{4}$, אֱלֹהִים *God* 2 C 25$_{8.8}$, *gods* 2 C 28$_{23}$, שָׁוְא *false god* Jr 18$_{15}$ (or em. וָאַכְשִׁלֵם *and I caused them to stumble*), הַר *mountain* of Israel Ezk 36$_{15}$, אִישׁ *man* 1QH 5$_{36}$ (‖ כלה pi. *destroy*), בֵּן *son* of Belial 4QMidrEschat^{a} 3$_{8}$ (+ כלה pi. *destroy*) 3$_{8}$, כֹּהֵן *priest* Ml 2$_{8}$ 1QpHab 11$_{8}$, רַע *evil one* Pr 4$_{16(Qr)}$, פעל ptc. *one who practises iniquity* Ps 64$_{9}$, זֹנָה *prostitute* (fem.) 4QWiles 1$_{14}$ ([הזונ]ה), רוּחַ *spirit* 1QS 3$_{24}$, תִּירוֹשׁ *wine* Si 34$_{25}$, עֵצָה *counsel* Si 30$_{21(Bmg)}$ (B כשל ni.), נֶגַע *plague* 1QH 5$_{28}$ (להכשי[ל]).

<OBJ> אֱלֹהִים *God* Ps 64$_{9}$, Israelites 1QpHab 11$_{8}$ 4QMidrEschat^{a} 3$_{8}$, עַם *people* Jr 18$_{15}$, גּוֹי *nation* Ezk 36$_{15}$, אִישׁ *man* 4QWiles 1$_{14}$, בֵּן *son* 1QS 3$_{24}$ 4QMidrEschat^{a} 3$_{8}$ ([בנ]י) 4QMidrEschat^{b} 9$_{7}$, Ahaz 2 C 28$_{23}$, מֶלֶךְ *king* 2 C 25$_{8}$, רַב *great one* Ml 2$_{8}$ Si 34$_{25}$, worshipper Si 30$_{21(Bmg)}$, רוּחַ *spirit* 1QH 5$_{28}$ (להכשי[ל רוח]) 5$_{36}$, כֹּחַ *strength* Lm 1$_{14}$.

<PREP> לְ introducing object, + Israel 2 C 28$_{23}$.

בְּ of place, time, *in, at, among*, + עַם *people* perh. 4QparaKings 104$_{4}$, דֶּרֶךְ *way* Jr 18$_{15}$, יוֹם *day* 1QpHab 11$_{8}$; of instrument, *by (means of), with*, + תּוֹרָה *instruction* Ml 2$_{8}$; בְּלֹא *without*, + דַּעַת *knowledge* 4QBéat 7.2$_{4}$ (בלו[א [דעת]).

לִפְנֵי *before*, + אוֹיֵב *enemy* 2 C 25$_{8}$.

<COLL> וַיַּכְשִׁילוּהוּ עָלֵימוֹ לְשׁוֹנָם *and they will cause him to stumble by their tongue* Ps 64$_{9}$.

Also 4QDibHam^{a} 1.6$_{17}$.

<SYN> כלה pi. *destroy*.

Ho. $_{1}$ Ptc. מֻכְשָׁלִים—**be overthrown,** <SUBJ> אִישׁ *man* of Judah Jr 18$_{23}$, יֹשֵׁב *inhabitant* of Jerusalem Jr 18$_{23}$. <PREP> לִפְנֵי *before*, + 'י *Y.* Jr 18$_{23}$.*

⇒ כָּשִׁיל *axe*, כִּשָּׁלוֹן *stumbling*, מִכְשׁוֹל *obstacle*, מַכְשֵׁלָה *ruin*.

כִּשָּׁלוֹן $_{1.1.1}$ n.m. **stumbling**—cstr. Si כשלון; sf. Q כשלוני—<SUBJ> היה *be* 1QH 9$_{25}$ (+ לִגְבוּרָה *as might*). <CSTR> כשלון ברכים *stumbling of knees*, i.e. weak knees Si 25$_{22}$. <PREP> לִפְנֵי *before* Pr 16$_{18}$ (‖ שֶׁבֶר *destruction*). <SYN> שֶׁבֶר *destruction*.*

⇒ כשל *stumble*.

כשף $_{6.0.1}$ vb. **practise sorcery—Pi.** $_{6.0.1}$ Pf. כִּשֵּׁף; ptc. מְכַשֵּׁף, מְכַשֵּׁפָה, מְכַשְּׁפִים—**1. practise sorcery,** <SUBJ> Manasseh 2 C 33$_{6}$ (‖ ענן po. *practise soothsaying*, נחשׁ pi. *practise divination*). <SYN> ענן po. *practise soothsaying*, נחשׁ pi. *practise divination*.

2. ptc. as noun, **sorcerer,** <SUBJ> מצא ni. *be found* Dt 18$_{10}$=11QT 60$_{18}$ (‖ מְעוֹנֵן *soothsayer*, מְנַחֵשׁ *diviner*). <OBJ> חיה pi. *preserve alive* Ex 22$_{17}$. <PREP> לְ of direction, *to*, + קרא *call* Ex 7$_{11}$ (‖ חָכָם *wise one*) Dn 2$_{2}$ (‖ כַּשְׂדִּי *Chaldaean, astrologer*, חַרְטֹם *magician*, אַשָּׁף *conjuror*); בְּ *against*, +

מהר pi. *be swift* Ml 3$_{5}$. <SYN> חָכָם *wise one*, מְעוֹנֵן *soothsayer*, מְנַחֵשׁ *diviner*.*
⇒ כַּשָּׁף *sorcerer*, כֶּשֶׁף *sorcery*.

כַּשָּׁף 1 n.m. **sorcerer**—pl. sf. כַּשָּׁפֵיהֶם—<PREP> אֶל *to*, + שׁמע *hear* Jr 27$_{9}$ (|| קֹסֵם *diviner*, מְעוֹנֵן *soothsayer*). <SYN> קֹסֵם *diviner*, מְעוֹנֵן *soothsayer*.*
⇒ כשׁף *practise sorcery*.

כֶּשֶׁף 6 n.m. **sorcery**—pl. כְּשָׁפִים; sf. כְּשָׁפַיִךְ, כְּשָׁפֶיהָ—<NOM CL> כְּשָׁפֶיהָ הָרַבִּים Jezebel's *sorceries are many* 2 K 9$_{22}$. <OBJ> כרת hi. *destroy* Mc 5$_{11}$. <CSTR> בַּעֲלַת כְּשָׁפִים *mistress of sorcery* Na 3$_{4}$, רֹב כְּשָׁפַיִךְ *greatness of your sorceries* Is 47$_{9.12}$. <PREP> בְּ of instrument, *by (means of), with*, + מכר *sell* Na 3$_{4}$.*
⇒ כשׁף *practise sorcery*.

כשׁר 3.1 vb. **be proper—Qal** 2.1 Pf. כָּשֵׁר; impf. יִכְשַׁר, Si 2ms תכשר—**be advantageous, be pleasing, succeed,** <SUBJ> worshipper Si 13$_{4}$, דָּבָר *thing* Est 8$_{5}$, זֶה *this action* Ec 11$_{6}$. <PREP> לְ of benefit, *to, for*, + עָשִׁיר *rich one* Si 13$_{4}$; לִפְנֵי *before*, + מֶלֶךְ *king* Est 8$_{5}$.

Hi. 1 Inf. הַכְשֵׁיר—**make advantageous,** <COLL> יִתְרוֹן הַכְשֵׁיר חָכְמָה *wisdom is an advantage for success* Ec 10$_{10}$ (or em. הַכְשֵׁיר to כִּשְׁרוֹן *skill*).*
⇒ כֹּשֶׁר *propriety*, כִּשְׁרוֹן *skill*.

[כֹּשֶׁר] 0.0.3 n.[m.] **propriety**—cstr. Q כושר—**propriety, rightness,** <NOM CL> עלי אין כשר לה[תלות] *for me there is no rightness*, i.e. it is not right for me, *to hang myself* 4QTobit^{e} 1.2$_{3}$. <CSTR> כושר מבינות *propriety of understanding* 4Q417 2.1$_{11}$; הוכח הכשר *rebuke of propriety*, i.e. proper rebuke 4Q417 1.1$_{2}$. <PREP> בְּ of accompaniment, *with, in* 4Q417 2.1$_{11}$; introducing object, + ראה *see* 4Q 418 77$_{2}$ ([בכוש]ר).

כִּשְׁרוֹן 3 n.m. **skill, skilfulness** (Ec 2$_{21}$ 4$_{4}$); **success** or **profit** (Ec 5$_{10}$), <NOM CL> מַה־כִּשְׁרוֹן לִבְעָלֶיהָ *what profit is there to its owners?* or *what does the success of its owners amount to?* Ec 5$_{10}$. <OBJ> ראה *see* Ec 4$_{4}$. <PREP> בְּ of instrument, *by (means of), with* Ec 2$_{21}$ (|| חָכְמָה *wisdom*, דַּעַת *knowledge*). <SYN> חָכְמָה *wisdom*, דַּעַת *knowledge*.*
⇒ כשׁר *be proper*.

כתב 225.1.130.6 vb. **write—Qal** 207.1.121.6 Pf. כָּתַב, כָּתַבְתָּ (כָּתָבְתָּ), כָּתַבְתִּי, כָּתְבוּ; impf. יִכְתֹּב (Q יכתוב, Q יִכְתְּבֵם, Q יכתובהו, יכתבהו), 2ms תִּכְתֹּב, אֶכְתֹּב (אֶכְתָּב־, אֶכְתֲּבֶנָּה), יִכְתְּבוּ (Q יכתובו), תִּכְתְּבוּ (Q תכתובו); + waw וְכָתַב (Q וכתבו, וְכָתַבְתָּ (וּכְתַבְתָּם), וְכָתַבְתִּי, Q וכתבוהו; וַיִּכְתֹּב (Kt וָאֶכְתֹּב, וַתִּכְתֹּב, 3fs וַיִּכְתְּבֵם, ויכתוב Q, וַיִּכְתָּב־), וַיִּכְתְּבוּ (וַיִּכְתְּבוּהָ), וָאֶכְתָּב־ Qr, ואכתוב־; impv. כְּתֹב (כָּתְבֵם) כָּתְבָה, כִּתְבוּ, (כָּתְבֵם, כָּתְבָה, כתוב Kt, כְּתָב־); ptc. כֹּתֵב, כֹּתְבִים, pass. כָּתוּב, כְּתוּבָה, כְּתוּבִים (כְּתֻבִים), כְּתוּבוֹת; inf. abs. כָּתוֹב, cstr. כְּתֹב (כְּתוֹב; כָּתְבוֹ)—**write, record, enrol, register** (appar. intrans. at 1QS 9$_{2}$), **sign** (Jr 32$_{12}$), **incise, engrave** (Ex 39$_{30}$); sometimes followed by words written (e.g. 1QS 5$_{15.17}$ 8$_{14}$ 1QM 3$_{2}$ 4$_{1}$ 6$_{2}$ 9$_{15}$ 4QMidrEschat^{a} 3$_{12}$ CD 1$_{13}$ 5$_{1}$ 7$_{19}$ 11$_{18}$ 19$_{1}$).

<SUBJ> ׳י *Y.* Ex 24$_{12}$ 34$_{1}$ Dt 4$_{13}$ 5$_{22}$ 10$_{2.4}$ 2 K 17$_{37}$ Jr 31$_{33}$ Ps 87$_{6}$, אֱלֹהִים *God* Ho 8$_{12(Qr)}$, אֵל Jb 13$_{26}$, Israel Dt 6$_{9}$, Israelite(s) Dt 11$_{20}$ 27$_{3.8}$ Ne 10$_{1}$ 1QM 3$_{2+14t}$ 4$_{1+12t}$ 5$_{1}$ 6$_{2.2.3}$ 9$_{15}$ 11QT 48$_{9}$ 56$_{20}$, עַם *people* Ezr 4$_{6}$, יַחַד *community* 1QS 5$_{23}$, רַב pl. *many* 4QD^{e} 7.1$_{10}$ ([הרבים] ... וכתו[בוהו]; =1QS 7$_{21}$ ni.).

Baruch Jr 36$_{4.6.17.18.27.32}$ 45$_{1}$, Bezalel Ex 39$_{30}$, Bishlam Ezr 4$_{7.7}$, David 2 S 11$_{14.15}$ 11QPs^{a} 27$_{4}$, Eleazar MurEp Beth-Mashiko$_{9}$, Eliashib Arad ost. 1$_{3}$ 7$_{5}$, Enoch 4Qps Jub^{c} 2$_{4}$ ([ח]נוך), Esther Est 8$_{8}$ (+ חתם *seal*) 9$_{29}$, Habakkuk Hb 2$_{2}$ 1QpHab 7$_{1}$, Haman Est 8$_{5}$, Hezekiah 2 C 30$_{1}$, Isaiah Is 8$_{1}$ 30$_{8}$ (|| חקק *engrave*) 2 C 26$_{22}$, Jehu 2 K 10$_{1.6}$, Jeremiah Jr 22$_{30}$ 30$_{2}$ 32$_{10}$ 36$_{2.28.29}$ 51$_{60}$, Jezebel 1 K 21$_{8.9}$, Jonathan MurEpJonathan$_{11}$ ([כת]בה), Joseph (son of Simeon) 5/6ḤevBA 44$_{30}$, Joshua Dt 31$_{19}$ Jos 8$_{32}$ 24$_{26}$, Joshua (son of Eleazar) MurEpBeth-Mashiko$_{8}$, Koheleth Ec 12$_{10(mss)}$, Masabbalah 5/6ḤevBA 44$_{28}$, Mithredath Ezr 4$_{7.7}$, Mordecai Est 8$_{8.10}$ (both + חתם *seal*) 9$_{20.23.29}$, Moses Ex 17$_{14}$ 24$_{4}$ 34$_{27.28}$ Nm 17$_{17.18}$ 33$_{2}$ Dt 31$_{9.19.22}$ 31$_{24}$ Jos 8$_{32}$ 4QZedek 3$_{6}$ 4QDibHam^{a} 1.3$_{12}$, Oholiab Ex 39$_{30}$, Niklah Mur 24 4$_{20}$ Samuel 1 S 10$_{25}$, Saphun 5/6ḤevBA 44$_{29}$, Sennacherib 2 C 32$_{17}$, Shemaiah 1 C 24$_{6}$, Tabeel Ezr 4$_{7.7}$, Tobiah 4QTobit^{e} 4$_{4}$, Uriah Kh. el-Qom tomb inscr. 3$_{1}$.

מֶלֶךְ *king* Dt 17$_{18}$, כֹּהֵן *priest* Nm 5$_{23}$, אִישׁ *man* Dt 24$_{1.3}$ Jos 18$_{4.6.8.8.9}$ Jb 31$_{35}$ 1QS 6$_{20.22}$ 9$_{2}$, בֵּן *son* Pr 3$_{3}$ 7$_{3}$ 11Q

Ps^{a} 27$_{4}$ Mur 24 4$_{20}$ MurEpBeth-Mashiko$_{8.9}$ 5/6ḤevBA 44$_{28.29}$, *son* of human being Ezk 24$_{2}$ 37$_{16.16.20}$ 43$_{11}$, נַעַר *youth* Jg 8$_{14}$ Is 10$_{19}$, חָכָם *wise one* Pr 22$_{20}$, מְבַקֵּר *examiner* 1QS 6$_{20.22}$ CD 9$_{18}$, עֶבֶד *servant* 4QDibHam^{a} 1.3$_{12}$ Lachish ost. 4$_{3}$ 40$_{5}$, עֵד *witness* Jr 32$_{12}$, רִיב *adversary* Jb 31$_{35}$, כְּנָת *associate* Ezr 4$_{7.7}$, נָבִיא *prophet* 4QDibHam^{a} 1.3$_{12}$, הִיא *it* Jos 10$_{13}$, זֶה *this one* Is 44$_{5}$; subj. not specified, 1QSa 1$_{21}$ 4QMMT C$_{26}$.

Subj. of pass., Israel 1 C 9$_{1}$, אִישׁ *man* Nm 11$_{26}$, בֵּן *son* 2 C 24$_{27}$, רֵעַ *neighbour* 1QS 6$_{26}$, כֹּהֵן *priest* 1QS 7$_{2}$, ראשׁ *family head* Ne 12$_{22.23}$, לוּחַ *tablet* Ex 31$_{18}$ 32$_{15.15}$ Dt 9$_{10}$, מְגִלָּה *scroll* Ezk 2$_{10}$, סֵפֶר *book* 4Q417 2.1$_{15}$, נִשְׁתְּוָן *letter* Ezr 4$_{7}$, דָּבָר *word* Dt 28$_{58}$ 2 K 23$_{3.24}$ Jr 51$_{60}$ Ec 12$_{10}$ 2 C 34$_{31}$ CD 7$_{10}$ 19$_{7}$, *act, deed* 1 K 11$_{41}$||2 C 9$_{29}$ 1 K 14$_{19.29}$ ||2 C 12$_{15}$ 1 K 15$_{7}$||2 C 13$_{22}$ 1 K 15$_{23}$||2 C 16$_{11}$ 1 K 15$_{31}$ 16$_{5.14.20.27}$ 22$_{39.46}$||2 C 20$_{34}$ 2 K 1$_{18}$ 8$_{23}$ 10$_{34}$ 12$_{20}$ 13$_{8.12}$ 14$_{15}$ ||2 C 25$_{26}$ 2 K 14$_{18.28}$ 15$_{6+6t}$ 16$_{19}$||2 C 28$_{26}$ 2 K 20$_{20}$||2 C 32$_{32}$ 2 K 21$_{17}$||2 C 33$_{19}$ 2 K 21$_{25}$ 23$_{28}$||2 C 35$_{26}$ 2 K 24$_{5}$ ||2 C 36$_{8}$ Est 10$_{2}$ 1 C 29$_{29}$ 2 C 27$_{7}$ 35$_{27}$ 4QMMT B$_{38}$.

עֵדוּת *testimony* 1 K 2$_{3}$, מִצְוָה *commandment* Dt 30$_{10}$ 1 K 2$_{3}$, מִשְׁפָּט *judgment* 1 K 2$_{3}$ Ps 149$_{9}$ CD 5$_{10}$, חֹק *statute* Dt 30$_{10}$ 1 K 2$_{3}$, מַשָּׂא *burden* 2 C 24$_{27}$, שְׁבֻעָה *oath* Dn 9$_{11}$, אָלָה *curse* Dt 29$_{19.20}$ Dn 9$_{11}$ 2 C 34$_{24}$ 4QSD 10$_{5}$ ([אלות]), קְלָלָה *curse* Dt 29$_{26}$, קֶשֶׁת *bow* 2 S 1$_{18}$, קִינָה *lamentation* Ezk 2$_{10}$ 2 C 35$_{25}$, הִי *woe* Ezk 2$_{10}$, הֶגֶה *groaning* Ezk 2$_{10}$.

חֳלִי *sickness* Dt 28$_{61}$, מַכָּה *wound* Dt 28$_{61}$, חַטָּאת *sin* of Judah Jr 17$_{1}$ (|| חרשׁ *engrave*), יְסוֹד *foundation* 2 C 24$_{27}$, תֹּכֶן *rank* 1QS 6$_{10}$, כָּבוֹד *glory* 4QTanḥ 8$_{13}$, הוֹן *wealth* perh. 4QTohD 1$_{2}$, אֵלֶּה *these* 1 C 4$_{41}$, כֹּל *all* Jos 1$_{8}$ 8$_{34}$ 23$_{6}$ 2 K 22$_{13}$||2 C 34$_{21}$ Is 4$_{3}$ Jr 25$_{13}$ Dn 12$_{1}$ 1 C 16$_{40}$ 4QMidr Eschat^{b} 10$_{12}$ 4QD^{e} 7.2$_{14}$ ([כ]תוב) 4Q DibHam^{a} 1.6$_{14}$ 5/6 ḤevBA 44$_{26}$; subj. impersonal, Jos 8$_{31}$ 1 K 21$_{11}$ 2 K 14$_{6}$ ||2 C 25$_{4}$ 2 K 23$_{21}$ Jr 32$_{44}$ Ps 40$_{8}$ Est 6$_{2}$ Dn 9$_{13}$ Ezr 3$_{2.4}$ Ne 8$_{14.15}$ 10$_{35.37}$ 13$_{1}$ 2 C 23$_{18}$ 30$_{5.18}$ 31$_{3}$ 35$_{12}$ 2QJuridical 1$_{3}$ 4QMMT B$_{66.70}$ ([כת]וב) B$_{76.77}$ C$_{6}$ ([כתו]ב) C$_{11.12.21}$ Si 48$_{10}$; impersonal subj. consisting of words quoted, Is 65$_{6}$ Ne 6$_{6}$ 7$_{5}$ 1QS 5$_{15.17}$ 8$_{14}$ 4QMidrEschat^{a} 3$_{2.12.15.16}$ 4$_{3}$ 4QMidrEschat^{b} 9$_{1.3.13}$ 10$_{7}$ 4QJub^{f} 33$_{12}$ ([כ]ת[וב]) 4QSD 2$_{3}$ 4QD^{a} 11$_{3.5.5a}$ 4QMMT B$_{27}$ C$_{12}$ ([כתו]ב) 11QMelch 2$_{9.19}$ (הכ]תו[ב) 2$_{23}$ CD 1$_{13}$ 5$_{1}$ 7$_{19}$ 9$_{5}$ 11$_{18.20}$ 19$_{1}$ (ככ as abbreviation of כאשׁר כתוב *as it is written*), perh. also (quotation lacking in fragments) 4QpIsa^{c} 1$_{2}$ ([כ]תוב) 4.2$_{18}$ 47$_{2}$ ([כתו]ב) 4QpIsa^{e} 1$_{2}$ 4QMidrEschat^{b} 8$_{11}$ 4Q178 3$_{2}$ 4Q Ages^{a} 5$_{2}$ ([כת]וב) 5$_{5}$ 4QCat 1$_{4}$ ([כ]תוב) 4QCitJub 1$_{9}$ 4Q CommGenA 3$_{1}$ 4QSD 2$_{2}$ 4QapJerB 8$_{2}$ 15$_{1}$ ([כשר כת]וב) 4QpsEzek^{e} 62.2$_{4}$ ([כתו]ב); subj. not specified, 4QSD 1.1$_{7}$ CD 13$_{12}$.

<OBJ> דָּבָר *word* Ex 24$_{4}$ 34$_{1.27.28}$ Dt 4$_{13}$ 5$_{22}$ 6$_{9}$ 10$_{2.4}$ 11$_{20}$ 27$_{3.8}$ 31$_{24}$ Jos 24$_{26}$ Jr 30$_{2}$ 36$_{2.4.17.27.28.32}$ 45$_{1}$ Est 9$_{20}$, מַאֲמָר *word*, i.e. signature 5/6ḤevBA 44$_{28.29.30}$, תּוֹרָה *law* Ex 24$_{12}$ Dt 31$_{9}$ Jos 8$_{32}$ 2 K 17$_{37}$ Jr 31$_{33}$ Ho 8$_{12}$ Pr 7$_{3}$ 11QT 56$_{20}$, מִצְוָה *commandment* Ex 24$_{12}$ 2 K 17$_{37}$ Pr 7$_{3}$, חֹק *statute* 2 K 17$_{37}$, מִשְׁפָּט *judgment* 2 K 17$_{37}$, חָזוֹן *vision* Hb 2$_{2}$ (|| באר pi. *record carefully*), שִׁיר *song* 11QPs^{a} 27$_{4}$, שִׁירָה *song* Dt 31$_{19.22}$, תְּהִלָּה *praise* 4QTobit^{e} 6$_{4}$ 11QPs^{a} 27$_{4}$, אָלָה *curse* Nm 5$_{23}$.

כְּתֹבֶת *writing* 11QT 48$_{9}$, אִגֶּרֶת *letter* 2 C 30$_{1}$, סֵפֶר *letter* 2 S 11$_{14}$ 1 K 21$_{8}$ 2 K 10$_{1.6}$ 2 C 32$_{17}$, *document*, i.e. bill of divorce Dt 24$_{1.3}$, *indictment* Jb 31$_{35}$, שִׂטְנָה *accusation* Ezr 4$_{6}$, מִכְתָּב *inscription* Ex 39$_{30}$, מִשְׁנֶה *copy* of law Dt 17$_{18}$ Jos 8$_{32}$, מְגִלָּה *scroll* Jr 36$_{6}$, אוֹת *sign*, i.e. description, of land Jos 18$_{4.8.9}$, פֵּרוּשׁ *list* of names 1QM 4$_{11.13}$, שְׁלִישִׁים *thirty* sayings Pr 22$_{20}$, הוֹן *wealth* 1QS 6$_{20}$, מְלָאכָה *(earnings from) work* 1QS 6$_{20}$.

אֶרֶץ *land* Jos 18$_{6.8}$, מוֹצָא *place of departure* Nm 33$_{2}$, עַם *people* Ps 87$_{6}$, שְׁאָר *remnant* Is 10$_{19}$, אִישׁ *man* Jr 22$_{30}$ 1QS 5$_{23}$ 6$_{22}$ 4QD^{e} 7.1$_{10}$ ([האי]שׁ ... וכתו[בוהו]; =1QS 7$_{21}$ ni.), אָדוֹן *lord* Lachish ost. 6$_{8}$, שַׂר *prince*, i.e. official Jg 8$_{14}$, זָקֵן *elder* Jg 8$_{14}$, יסף ni. ptc. *one who joins* CD 13$_{12}$, מִשְׁפָּחָה *family* 1QSa 1$_{21}$, חֶסֶד *loyalty* Pr 3$_{3}$, אֱמֶת *reliability* Pr 3$_{3}$, רָעָה *evil* Jr 51$_{60}$, מְרֹר *bitter thing* Jb 13$_{26}$, מַחֲלֹקֶת *division* of priesthood 1 C 24$_{6}$, שֵׁם *name* Nm 17$_{17.18}$ Ezk 24$_{2}$ Arad ost. 1$_{3}$ 1QM 5$_{1}$, בוא ptc. *thing to come* 1QpHab 7$_{1}$, זֹאת *this* Ex 17$_{14}$, כֹּל *everything* Arad ost. 40$_{5}$, the preceding letter MurEpBeth-Mashiko$_{8.9}$ MurEpJonathan$_{11}$ ([כת]בה) Mur 48$_{7}$; obj. not specified, Is 30$_{8}$ CD 9$_{18}$ Kh. el-Qom tomb inscr. 3$_{1}$.

<PREP> לְ of direction, *(in) to*, + יַחַד *community* 1QS 9$_{2}$; of benefit, *to, for*, + Israelite(s) Dt 31$_{19}$ 2 K 17$_{37}$, Ephraim Ho 8$_{12}$, Ezekiel Ezk 24$_{2}$, Jeremiah Jr 30$_{2}$, Moses Ex 34$_{27}$, מֶלֶךְ *king* Dt 17$_{18}$=11QT 56$_{20}$, אִשָּׁה *wife* Dt 24$_{1.3}$, worshipper Pr 22$_{20}$, שׁמר ptc. *one who keeps* 4Q417 2.1$_{15}$, חַיִּים *life* Is 4$_{3}$, ירה hi. inf. as noun *instruction* Ex 24$_{12}$.

לְ *according to*, + מַסָּע *departure point* Nm 33$_{2}$, עִיר *city*

Jos 18$_{9}$, חֵלֶק *share* Jos 18$_{9}$; *concerning*, + זָכָר *male* CD 5$_{10}$.

בְּ of instrument, *by (means of), with*, + יָד *hand* 1QS 6$_{20}$ CD 19$_{7}$, אֶצְבַּע *finger* of God Ex 31$_{18}$ Dt 9$_{10}$, חֶרֶט אֱנוֹשׁ *stylus of human being*, i.e. in common script Is 8$_{1}$, עֵט *stylus* Jr 17$_{1}$, דְּיוֹ *ink* Jr 36$_{18}$, שֵׁם *name* 1 C 4$_{41}$; of agent, *by*, + Jeremiah 4QpIsa^{c} 1$_{2}$ ([כ]תוב ... בירמ[יה]).

בְּ of place, *in, on*, + oneself 11QT 48$_{9}$, תּוֹרָה *law* 1 K 2$_{3}$ Dn 9$_{11.13}$ Ezr 3$_{2}$ Ne 8$_{14}$ 10$_{35.37}$ 1 C 16$_{40}$ 2 C 23$_{18}$ 25$_{4}$ 31$_{3}$ 35$_{26}$, סֵפֶר *book* Ex 17$_{14}$ Nm 5$_{23}$ Dt 28$_{58.61}$ 29$_{19.20.26}$ 30$_{10}$ 31$_{24}$ Jos 1$_{8}$ 8$_{31.34}$ 23$_{6}$ 24$_{26}$ 1 S 10$_{25}$ 2 S 11$_{15}$ 2 K 14$_{6}$ Jr 25$_{13}$ Dn 12$_{1}$ Ne 7$_{5}$ 13$_{1}$ 2 C 35$_{12}$ 1QS 7$_{2}$ 2QJuridical 1$_{3}$ 4QMidr Eschat^{a} 3$_{2.15.16}$ 4$_{3}$ 4QMidrEschat^{b} 8$_{11}$ 9$_{1}$ ([בספר]) 9$_{13}$ 4Q Cat 1$_{4}$ ([כ]תוב) 4QSD 10$_{5}$ 4QMMT C$_{6}$ ([כתו]ב בספר]) C$_{11.21}$ ([בס]פר) 4QDibHam^{a} 1.6$_{14}$, *letter* 1 K 21$_{9.11}$, אִגֶּרֶת *letter* Ne 6$_{6}$, מְגִלָּה *scroll* Ps 40$_{8}$, לוּחַ *tablet* 4QMidrEschat^{b} 10$_{12}$, דָּבָר *word* 2 C 12$_{15}$ 20$_{34}$ 4QZedek 3$_{6}$ (unless בדברו *when he spoke*) CD 7$_{10}$, שִׁיר *song* 11QMelch 2$_{9}$, מִדְרָשׁ *midrash* 2 C 13$_{22}$, חֶשְׁבּוֹן *account* 1QS 6$_{20}$, חָזוֹן *vision* 2 C 32$_{32}$, תִּשְׁבָּחָה *praise* 4QTobit^{e} 6$_{4}$, סֶרֶךְ *rule* 1QS 5$_{23}$ 6$_{22}$ 1QSa 1$_{21}$, שֵׁם *name* 1 K 21$_{8}$ Est 8$_{8.10}$, תֹּכֶן *rank* 1QS 9$_{2}$ 4Q D^{e} 7.1$_{10}$ ([וכתו]בוהו בתוכנו]; =1QS 7$_{21}$ ni.), מָקוֹם *place* 4Q D^{a} 11$_{5.5a}$CD 13$_{12}$; *on*, + שַׁעַר *gate* Dt 6$_{9}$ 11$_{20}$, יוֹם *day* Dt 31$_{22}$; introducing object, + סֵפֶר *document*, i.e. title deed Jr 32$_{10.12.44}$.

כְּ *according to*, + כֹּל *all* 4QZedek 3$_{6}$ ([ככ]ל).

מִן *on*, + עֵבֶר *side* Ex 32$_{15}$, זֶה *this* side Ex 32$_{15.15}$; *at*, + פֶּה *mouth*, i.e. dictation Jr 36$_{4.6.27.32}$ 45$_{1}$.

אֶל *to, for, in* 4QMMT C$_{26}$ Lachish ost. 6$_{8}$, + Jews Est 9$_{23}$, Gideon Jg 8$_{14}$, Joab 2 S 11$_{14}$, אָדוֹן *lord* Arad ost. 40$_{5}$ ([כתבת]י), שַׂר *prince* 2 K 10$_{6}$, זָקֵן *elder* 2 K 10$_{6}$, אֹמֵן *guardian* 2 K 10$_{6}$, סֵפֶר *book* Jr 30$_{2}$ 51$_{60}$, מְגִלָּה *scroll* Jr 36$_{2}$ Ezk 2$_{10}$; *concerning*, + Babylon Jr 51$_{60}$.

עַל *upon, on, in* 1QM 5$_{1}$, + דֶּלֶת *door* Lachish ost. 4$_{3}$, מְזוּזָה *door-post* Dt 6$_{9}$ 11$_{20}$, צִיץ *flower*, i.e. rosette of crown Ex 39$_{30}$, עֵץ *stick* Ezk 37$_{16.16.20}$, אֶבֶן *stone* Dt 27$_{3.8}$ Jos 8$_{32}$, מַטֶּה *staff* Nm 17$_{17.18}$, חֲצוֹצְרָה *trumpet* 1QM 3$_{2+12t}$, אוֹת *ensign* 1QM 3$_{13.15.5}$ ([ע]ל) 4$_{1+11t}$, לַהַב *point* of spear 1QM 6$_{2}$, זֶרֶק *javelin* 1QM 6$_{3}$, שֶׁלֶט *dart* 1QM 6$_{2}$, מָגֵן *shield* 1QM 9$_{15}$, לֵב *heart* Jr 31$_{33}$.

לוּחַ *tablet* Ex 34$_{1.28}$ Dt 4$_{13}$ 5$_{22}$ 10$_{2.4}$ Is 30$_{8}$ Pr 3$_{3}$ 7$_{3}$, גִּלָּיוֹן *tablet* Is 8$_{1}$, מְגִלָּה *scroll* Jr 36$_{4.28.29.32}$, סֵפֶר *book* Dt 17$_{18}$ =11QT 56$_{20}$ Jos 10$_{13}$ 18$_{9}$ 2 S 1$_{18}$ 1 K 11$_{41}$ 14$_{19.29}$ 15$_{7.23}$ ||2 C 16$_{11}$ 1 K 15$_{31}$ 16$_{5.14.20.27}$ 22$_{39.46}$ 2 K 1$_{18}$ 8$_{23}$ 10$_{34}$ 12$_{20}$ 13$_{8.12}$ 14$_{15}$||2 C 25$_{26}$ 2 K 14$_{18.28}$ 15$_{6+6t}$ 16$_{19}$||2 C 28$_{26}$ 2 K 20$_{20}$ 21$_{17.25}$ 23$_{3.21.24.28}$ 24$_{5}$||2 C 36$_{8}$ Jr 45$_{1}$ Est 10$_{2}$ Ne 12$_{23}$ 1 C 9$_{1}$ 2 C 27$_{7}$ 34$_{21.24.31}$ 35$_{27}$, *document* Jr 36$_{18}$, דָּבָר *word*, i.e. chronicle 1 C 29$_{29.29.29}$ 2 C 9$_{29}$ 33$_{19}$, מִדְרָשׁ *midrash* 2 C 24$_{27}$, נְבוּאָה *prophecy* 2 C 9$_{29}$, חָזוֹן *vision* 2 C 9$_{29}$, קִינָה *lament* 2 C 35$_{25}$.

עַל *concerning* 4QpIsa^{c} 1$_{2}$ ([כ]תוב) 4QMidrEschat^{b} 8$_{11}$ 9$_{3}$ 10$_{7}$ 4QCat 1$_{4}$ ([כ]תוב) 11QMelch 2$_{23}$, + עַם *people* 2 K 22$_{13}$ 4QMidrEschat^{a} 3$_{16}$, Israel 4QD^{a} 11$_{3}$, Jews Est 8$_{8}$, Judah 2 K 22$_{13}$, Josiah 2 K 22$_{13}$, Melchizedek 11QMelch 2$_{9}$, פַּרְעֹה *Pharaoh* 4QAges^{a} 5$_{5}$, נָשִׂיא *prince* CD 5$_{1}$, שמע hi. ptc. *one who announces* 11QMelch 2$_{19}$ (משמי[ע] ... הכ[תו]ב), worshipper Ps 40$_{8}$, אֶרֶץ *land* 4QAges^{a} 5$_{2}$ ([כר]וב על הא[רץ]), עֵת *time* CD 1$_{13}$.

עַל *according to*, + מִדְרָשׁ *interpretation* 4QD^{e} 7.2$_{14}$ ([כ]תוב); *by*, + פֶּה *mouth*, i.e. command of Y. Nm 33$_{2}$; *against*, + Job Jb 13$_{26}$; *to*, + Artaxerxes Ezr 4$_{7}$, Ephraim 2 C 30$_{1}$, Manasseh 2 C 30$_{1}$; *on behalf of*, + נֶפֶשׁ *soul*, i.e. self Mur 24 4$_{20}$ ([ע]ל).

מִקְצָת *some of*, + מַעֲשֶׂה *precept* of the law 4QMMT C$_{26}$; עִם *with*, + סֶרֶךְ *order* 1QM 4$_{11}$; אֵת *with*, + תֹּקֶף *authority* Est 9$_{29}$; לְעֵינֵי *before*, + בַּיִת *house* of Israel Ezk 43$_{11}$.

כְּפִי *according to*, + נַחֲלָה *inheritance* CD 13$_{12}$; לְפִי *according to*, + '' Y. Is 65$_{6}$, נַחֲלָה *inheritance* Jos 18$_{4}$; לִפְנֵי *before*, + אֵל *God* 4Q417 2.1$_{15}$, אִישׁ *man* 1QS 6$_{10}$, בֵּן *son* of Israel Jos 8$_{32}$, מֶלֶךְ *king* 1 C 24$_{6}$, Eliashib Arad ost. 7$_{5}$, אֲשֶׁר *one who* 1QS 6$_{26}$; אַחֲרֵי *after* 4QTohD 1$_{2}$.

<COLL> כְּתֹב זֹאת זִכָּרוֹן בַּסֵּפֶר *write this as a memorial in the book* Ex 17$_{14}$, תִּכְתְּבוּ אֶת־הָאָרֶץ שִׁבְעָה חֲלָקִים *you shall describe the land in seven portions* Jos 18$_{6}$, זֶה יִכְתֹּב יָדוֹ *this one will write on his hand* Is 44$_{5}$, הִיא כְתוּבָה פָּנִים וְאָחוֹר *it*, i.e. the scroll, *was written on the front and on the back* Ezk 2$_{10}$, הדבר כתוב עברה *the matter is written (concerning) a pregnant (animal)* 4QMMT B$_{38}$, כָּתוּב יֹשֶׁר דִּבְרֵי אֱמֶת *the words of truth were written uprightly* Ec 12$_{10}$, הַנִּשְׁתְּוָן כָּתוּב אֲרָמִית *the letter was written in Aramaic* Ezr 4$_{7}$, אין כתוב כי אם *nothing is written except*, i.e. only the following is written CD 9$_{5}$.

כתב + adverb, אַחַר *afterwards* 1QS 9$_{2}$; pass., + adverb, כֵּן *thus* 1QS 5$_{15}$ 11$_{18}$ 2QJuridical 1$_{3}$ 4QCitJub 1$_{9}$, שֵׁנִית *second (time)* 4QJub^{f} 33$_{12}$ ([כ]ת[וב]).

Also 4QpIsa^c 2$_5$ ([כ]תוב) 4.1$_1$ 4QapPs^b 70$_1$ 4QProph 1$_5$ 4QM^c 1$_{14}$ 4QM^f 8$_3$ ([י]כתובו) 18$_1$ 4QM^g 6$_3$. <SYN> חקק *engrave*, חרשׁ *engrave*, באר pi. *record carefully*.

Ni. $_{17.0.8}$ Pf. Q נכתבו; impf. יִכָּתֵב, 3fs תִּכָּתֵב, יִכָּתְבוּ (יִכָּתְבוּן); + waw וַיִּכָּתֵב; ptc. נִכְתָּב—**be written, be recorded, be inscribed,** <SUBJ> Isaac CD 3$_3$, Jacob CD 3$_3$, אִישׁ *man* 1QS 7$_{21}$ (=4QD^e 7.1$_{10}$ qal) 8$_{19}$ 4QS^d 1.2$_2$ (ולהכתב; =1QS 5$_{20}$ וכתבם *and they shall write them*, i.e. qal) CD 14$_4$ 19$_{35}$ (+ חשׁב ni. *be reckoned*), בֵּן *son* of Israel CD 14$_4$, כֹּהֵן *priest* CD 14$_4$, לֵוִי *Levite* CD 14$_4$, נָבִיא *prophet* Ezk 13$_9$, צֹרֵר *adversary* Ps 69$_{29}$, סור ptc. *one who departs* from Y. Jr 17$_{13(Qr)}$ (or em. כלם ni. *be put to shame* or כרת ni. *be cut off* or כבת ni. *be humbled*), גֵּר *sojourner* CD 14$_4$, מִשְׁקָל *weight* Ezr 8$_{34}$, סֵפֶר *book* of remembrance Ml 3$_{16}$ CD 20$_{19}$, כְּתָב *document*, i.e. edict Est 8$_8$, מִלָּה *word* Jb 19$_{23}$ (|| חקק ho. *be inscribed*), דָּבָר *matter* 4QD^a 11$_{16}$, זֹאת *this* Ps 102$_{19}$, כֹּל *all* Ps 139$_{16}$; subj. impersonal, Est 1$_{19}$ 2$_{23}$ 3$_{9.12.12}$ 8$_5$ 9$_{32}$.

<PREP> לְ of benefit, *to, for*, + דּוֹר *generation* Ps 102$_{19}$, יַחַד *community* 4QS^d 3.1$_3$; בְּ of place, *in*, + סֵפֶר *book* Est 2$_{23}$ 9$_{32}$, כְּתָב *document*, i.e. register Ezk 13$_9$ CD 19$_{35}$, תּוֹרָה *law* 4QTohB^c 2$_3$ ([בת]ורה), דָּת *law* Est 1$_{19}$, סֶרֶךְ *rule* 4QS^d 1.2$_2$ (ולהכתב; =1QS 5$_{20}$ וכתבם *and they shall write them*, i.e. qal), perh. אֶרֶץ *land* or *underworld* Jr 17$_{13}$ (unless כתב בְּ ni. *be signed over to* underworld; or em.); *according to*, + שֵׁם *name* Est 3$_{12}$ 8$_8$ CD 14$_4$, תֹּכֶן *rank* 1QS 7$_{21}$ (=4QD^e 7.1$_{10}$ qal) 8$_{19}$; כְּ *as*, + חֶרֶת *ink* 4QD^a 11$_{16}$, כֹּל *all* Est 3$_{12}$ 8$_9$; מִן of time, *from*, + יוֹם *day* CD 19$_{35}$; עַל *upon, in*, + סֵפֶר *book* Ps 139$_{16}$; עַל פְּנֵי *by*, + מְבַקֵּר *overseer* 4QD^a 11$_{16}$; עִם *with*, + צַדִּיק *righteous one* Ps 69$_{29}$; לִפְנֵי *before*, + י׳ Y. Ml 3$_{16}$, רֵעַ *neighbour* 4QS^d 1.2$_2$ (ולהכתב; =1QS 5$_{20}$ וכתבם *and they shall write them*, i.e. qal); אַחַר *after*, + אָח *brother* CD 14$_4$.

<COLL> ויכתבו אוהבים לאל *and they were recorded as friends of God* CD 3$_3$. <SYN> חקק ho. *be inscribed*.

Pi. $_1$ Pf. כִּתְּבוּ; ptc. מְכַתְּבִים—**keep writing,** <SUBJ> מְכַתֵּב *writer* Is 10$_1$. <OBJ> עָמָל *distress* Is 10$_1$.

Hi. $_{0.0.1}$ Inf. Q הכתיב—**dictate,** <SUBJ> מַלְאָךְ *angel* 4QJub^a 1$_{27}$ ([מלאך]). <PREP> לְ of direction, *to*, + Moses 4QJub^a 1$_{27}$ ([למשה]); מִן *from*, + רֵאשִׁית *beginning* 4QJub^a 1$_{27}$ ([מן ראשית]).*

⇒ כְּתָב *document*, כְּתֹבֶת *tattooing*, מִכְתָּב *inscription*.

כְּתָב $_{17.4.4}$ n.m. **writing**—cstr. כְּתָב; sf. כְּתָבָהּ, כְּתָבָם—**register, enrolment** (Ezk 13$_9$ Ezr 2$_{62}$||Ne 7$_{64}$ CD 19$_{35}$), **script, character, writing** (Est 1$_{22}$ 3$_{12}$ 8$_{8.9}$ Ezr 4$_7$), **letter, royal edict, written document** (Est 3$_{14}$ 4$_8$ 8$_{8.13}$ 9$_{27}$ Dn 10$_{21}$ 1 C 28$_{19}$ 2 C 2$_{10}$ 35$_4$ Mur 29 verso$_3$ ([ה[כ]תבין])), <SUBJ> כתב pass. *be written* Ezr 4$_7$, חרת pass. *be engraved* Si 45$_{11}$, ni. *be written* Est 8$_8$, חתם ni. *be sealed* Est 8$_8$, שׁוב hi. *be revoked* Est 8$_8$. <OBJ> בקשׁ pi. *seek* Ezr 2$_{62}$|| Ne 7$_{64}$, שׁאל *request* Mur 29 verso$_3$ (ה[כ]תבין).

<CSTR> כתב ימיניך *writing of your right hand* 1QPrLit 3.2$_7$ (|| מַעֲשֶׂה *work*), כְּתָב בֵּית־יִשְׂרָאֵל *register of the house of Israel* Ezk 13$_9$, כְּתָב הַדָּת *script of the decree* Est 4$_8$, הַנִּשְׁתְּוָן *of the letter* Ezr 4$_7$, כְּתָב אֱמֶת *writing of truth* Dn 10$_{21}$; פַּתְשֶׁגֶן הַכְּתָב *copy of the document* Est 3$_{14}$ 4$_8$ 8$_{13}$, משנא הכתב *copy of the document* 3QTr 12$_{11}$. <ADJ> זֶה *this* 3QTr 12$_{11}$ (הזא), זוֹ *this* 5/6ḤevBA 44$_{25}$ ([הכ[תב]).

<PREP> בְּ *in* 1 C 28$_{19}$ 2 C 35$_4$ Si 42$_7$ 45$_{11}$, + רשׁם pass. *be inscribed* Dn 10$_{21}$, כתב ni. *be written* Ezk 13$_9$ CD 19$_{35}$, נוח hi. *set* Si 39$_{32}$, נשׂא *raise*, i.e. compose, proverb Si 44$_5$, אמר *say*, i.e. answer 2 C 2$_{10}$; of instrument, *by (means of), with*, + חדשׁ pi. *renew* 1QLitPr 3.2$_7$; כְּ *as* Est 1$_{22}$ 3$_{12}$ 8$_{9.9}$ 9$_{27}$; אַחֲרֵי *after*, + רדף *follow* 5/6ḤevBA 44$_{25}$ (אח[רי] הכ[תב)

<SYN> מַעֲשֶׂה *work*.*

⇒ כתב *write*.

כְּתֹבֶת $_{1.0.1}$ n.f. **writing—incision** of a tattoo, <OBJ> נתן *give*, i.e. place Lv 19$_{28}$, כתב *write* 11QT 48$_9$. <CSTR> כְּתֹבֶת קַעֲקַע *writing*, i.e. incision, *of a tattoo* Lv 19$_{28}$ 11QT 48$_9$.*

⇒ כתב *write*.

[כִּתִּי] $_{8.0.35.11}$ gent. **Kittite**—Q כתיי; pl. כִּתִּים (כִּתִּיִּים, Q כתיאים)—member of **Kittim,** nation descended from Japheth (Gn 10$_4$||1 C 1$_7$), perh. settled in Cyprus; at Qumran prob. in ref. to Romans, **1.** as collective singular noun, **Kittim,** <CSTR> גדודי כתיי *troops of the Kittim* 1QM 1$_2$.

2. as plur. noun, **Kittites, Kittim,** <SUBJ> הלך *go* 1QpHab 3$_4$, בוא *come* Dn 11$_{30}$ 1QpHab 3$_9$, נפל *fall* 1QM 1$_9$, דושׁ *trample* 1QpHab 3$_9$, אכל *devour* 1QpHab 3$_9$, כמר *be hot* 1QpHab 3$_9$ ([יכמ[רו]), דבר pi. *speak* 1QpHab 3$_9$,

רעע hi. *do evil* 1QpHab 3_{4}, אבד pi. *destroy* 1QpHab 2_{12} 6_{10}, כתת *crush* 1QpHab 3_{1} (unless לכות is inf. cstr. hi. of נכה hi. *strike*) 4QpIsa^a 8_{3} ([הכ]תיאים אש[ר] יכת[ו]), ho. *be crushed* 1QM 18_{2}, בזז *plunder* 1QpHab 3_{1}, נתן ni. *be given* 4QpIsa^a 8_{8} ([ינת]נו), רחם pi. *have compassion* 1QpHab 6_{10}.

<NOM CL> בְּנֵי יָוָן ... כִּתִּים *the sons of Javan were ... Kittim* Gn 10_{4}||1 C 1_{7}. <OBJ> חרם hi. *destroy* perh. 1QM 18_{4} ([כ]תיים), הרג *kill* perh. 4QMishC^a 3.2 ([כת]יתים).

<CSTR> מלך הכתיים *king of the Kittim* 1QM 15_{2} 4QApocWeeks 1_{6} (מל[ך] כתיים), מושלי הכתיאים *rulers of the Kittim* 1QpHab $4_{5.10}$ 4QpNah 3.1_{3} (כתיים), גבורי כתיים *warriors of the Kittim* 1QM 19_{10} (ג[בורי]) 4QpIsa^a 8_{5} ([כת]יאים), חיל הכתיים *army of the Kittim* 1QM 17_{14} 1QpHab 9_{7} (הכתיאים), חללי כתיים *slain ones of the Kittim* 1QM 16_{8} 19_{13} ([ח]ללי כתי[ים]) 4QM^g 5_{6} ([ח]לל[י]), מחני *camps of* 1QM 16_{3}, מלחמת *war of* 4QpIsa^a 8_{7} (כתיאים), מערכת *battle line of* 1QM 16_{6} 17_{12} ([מע]רכת) 4QM^a 13_{5} (כתיאים), אִיֵּי כִתִּיִּים *coastlands of the Kittim* Jr 2_{10} Ezk 27_{6} (Qr), אֶרֶץ כִּתִּים *land of the Kittim* Is 23_{1}, ממשלת כתיים *dominion of the Kittim* 1QM 1_{6} 1QpHab 2_{14} (הכתיאים), יַד כִּתִּים *hand*, i.e. power, *of the Kittim* Nm 24_{24}.

<APP> צִי *ship* Dn 11_{30}.

<PREP> לְ of direction, *to*, + נתן *give* Arad ost. 1_{2} 2_{1} 4_{1} 7_{2} 8_{1} (כת[י]ם) 10_{2} ([כת]ים) 11_{2} 14_{2}; of benefit, *to, for*, + עשׂה *make* Arad ost. 5_{6} ([כ]ת[ים]); בְּ *against* 1QM 1_{12} 11_{11} 4QM^a 10.2_{8} (בכתיא[ים]) $10.2_{10.12}$, + נצח htp. *be directed* 1QM 16_{9} 17_{15} (מ[תנצח]ת בכ[תיים]).

עִם *with, against*, + סדר pi. *arrange* 4QM^a 11.2_{19} (כתי[אים]).

עַל *concerning* 1QpHab 2_{12} $3_{4.9}$ 6_{10} 4QpIsa^a 8_{3} ([על] [הכ]תיאים) 8_{8} ([על ה]כתיאים).

<COLL> כִּתִּים קוּמִי עֲבֹרִי *arise, pass over to the Kittim* Is 23_{12}(Qr), הכתיאים אשר פחדם ואמתם על כול הגואים *the Kittim, whose fear and dread are upon all the nations* 1QpHab 3_{4}.

2. as sing. noun, an individual **Kittite,** <CSTR> יד הכתי *hand of the Kittite* Arad ost. 17_{9}. Also 1QM 1_{4} 1QpHab 6_{1} 1QpPs 9_{4} ([כ]תיאים) 4QM^g 8_{3} 4QMishC^a 1_{5} (כתי[אים]) Arad ost. 10_{5}.

כִּתִּים, see כִּתִּי *Kittite*.

כָּתִית 5.0.1 adj. **beaten**—used attributively of שֶׁמֶן *oil* Ex 27_{20}||Lv 24_{2} Ex 29_{40}||Nm 28_{5} 1 K 5_{25} 11QT 21_{15}.*

⇒ כתת *crush*.

[כֹּתֶל] 1.0.2 n.[m.] **wall**—Q כותל; sf. כָּתְלֵנוּ—<PREP> בְּ of place, *in* CD 12_{17}; אַחַר *behind*, + עמד *stand* Ca 2_{9}.

Also 4QapMes 8_{1}.

כִּתְלִישׁ 1 pl.n. **Chitlish,** town in lowland of Judah, <NOM CL> בַּשְּׁפֵלָה ... כִּתְלִישׁ *in the lowland were ... Chitlish* Jos 15_{39}. <APP> עִיר *city* Jos 15_{39}.

כתם 1 vb. **be stained—Ni.** 1 Ptc. נִכְתָּם—<SUBJ> עָוֹן *iniquity* Jr 2_{22}. <PREP> לִפְנֵי *before*, + ״ *Y.* Jr 2_{22}.

⇒ מִכְתָּם *inscription*.

כֶּתֶם 9.1.3 n.m. **gold**—כֶּתֶם—<SUBJ> שׁנא *be changed* Lm 4_{1}, <NOM CL> רֹאשׁוֹ כֶּתֶם פָּז *his head was of pure gold* Ca 5_{11}.

<CSTR> כֶּתֶם אוֹפִיר *gold of Ophir* Is 13_{12} Ps 45_{10} Jb 28_{16} 4QM^a 11.1_{18} (אופירים), אוּפָז *of Uphaz* Dn 10_{5}; חֲלִי־כָתֶם *ornament of gold* Pr 25_{12}, בגדי כתם *robes of gold* Si 6_{29}, פז כת[ם] perh. *pure gold of gold* 4QM^h 6_{8}. <APP> עֲדִי *adornment* 4QapLam^a 1.2_{11}. <ADJ> טוֹב *good*, i.e. pure Lm 4_{1} 4QapLam^a 1.2_{11}, טָהוֹר *pure* Jb 28_{19}, פָּז *pure* Ca 5_{11}.

<PREP> לְ of direction, *to*, + אמר *say* Jb 31_{24}; בְּ *in*, + חגר pass. *be girded* Dn 10_{5}, סלה pu. *be valued* Jb $28_{16.19}$, נצב ni. *stand* Ps 45_{10}; מִן of comparison, *(more) than*, + יקר hi. *make rare* Is 13_{12}.

Also 4QHod^a 7.1_{10}.

כֻּתֹּנֶת 29.1.2 n.f. **tunic**—cstr. כְּתֹנֶת (Q כתונת); sf. כֻּתָּנְתִּי, כֻּתָּנְתּוֹ, כֻּתָּנְתֶּךָ; pl. כֻּתֳּנֹת (כָּתְנֹת); cstr. כָּתְנוֹת (כָּתְנֹת); sf. כֻּתָּנֹתָם*—long shirt-like **tunic** for both men and women (e.g. Gn 3_{21} 37_{3} 2 S 13_{8} 15_{32} Jb 30_{18} Ca 5_{3}), **tunic** for priests (e.g. Ex $28_{4.29}$ Lv $8_{7.13}$ 16_{4} Ezr 2_{69}||Ne 7_{69}), official **tunic** (Is 22_{21}).

<SUBJ> קרע pass. *be torn* 2 S 15_{32}. <NOM CL> עָלֶיהָ כְּתֹנֶת פַּסִּים perh. *upon her was tunic of*, i.e. reaching to, *the soles* of the feet 2 S 13_{18}.

<OBJ> עשׂה *make* Gn 3_{21} 37_{3} Ex 28_{40}||39_{27}, פאר pi. *beautify* Si 45_{8}, שׁבץ pi. *weave in patterns* Ex $28_{4.39}$, נתן

give Ezr 2$_{69}$||Ne 7$_{69}$ Ne 7$_{71}$, *give*, i.e. place Lv 8$_{7}$, לבשׁ *put on* Lv 16$_{4}$ (+ מִכְנָסַיִם *breeches*) 1QM 7$_{10}$ (|| מִכְנָסַיִם, בֶּגֶד *garment*) 4QOrd^{a} 2$_{7}$, hi. *clothe* Ex 29$_{5.8}$ 40$_{14}$ Lv 8$_{13}$ Is 22$_{21}$, לקח *take* Gn 37$_{31}$, פשׁט *take off* Ca 5$_{3}$, hi. *strip* Gn 37$_{23.23}$, קרע *tear* 2 S 13$_{19}$, שׁלח pi. *send away* Gn 37$_{32}$, טבל *dip* Gn 37$_{31}$, נכר hi. *recognise* Gn 37$_{32.33}$.

<CSTR> כְּתֹנֶת יוֹסֵף *tunic of Joseph* Gn 37$_{31}$, בְּנִי *of my son* Gn 37$_{33}$, בִּנְךָ *of your son* Gn 37$_{32}$, כתונת אשה *tunic of a woman* 4QOrd^{a} 2$_{7}$, כָּתְנֹת כֹּהֲנִים *tunics of the priests* Ezr 2$_{69}$||Ne 7$_{69}$ (כָּתְנוֹת) Ne 7$_{71}$, כָּתְנוֹת עוֹר *tunics of skin* Gn 3$_{21}$, כְּתֹנֶת־בַּד *tunic of linen* Lv 16$_{4}$ 1QM 7$_{10}$ (כתונת), כְּתֹנֶת פַּסִּים perh. *a tunic of*, i.e. reaching to, *the soles* of the feet Gn 37$_{3.23.32}$ 2 S 13$_{18.19}$ (הַפַּסִּים); פִּי כָתָּנְתִּי *mouth*, i.e. collar, *of my tunic* Jb 30$_{18}$.

<APP> כָּבוֹד *glory* Si 45$_{8}$, עֹז *strength* Si 45$_{8}$. **<PREP>** בְּ *in*, + נשׂא *raise* Lv 10$_{5}$. **<COLL>** כָּתְנֹת כֹּהֲנִים שִׁשִּׁים וְשִׁבְעָה *sixty-seven tunics of the priests* Ne 7$_{71}$, כָּתְנֹת כֹּהֲנִים מֵאָה *one hundred tunics of the priests* Ezr 2$_{69}$, כָּתְנוֹת כֹּהֲנִים שְׁלֹשִׁים וַחֲמֵשׁ מֵאוֹת *five hundred and thirty tunics of the priests* Ne 7$_{69}$. **<SYN>** מִכְנָסַיִם *breeches*, בֶּגֶד *garment*.*

כָּתֵף 67.0.0.1 n.f. **side, shoulder**—cstr. כֶּתֶף; sf. כְּתֵפִי, כְּתֵפָיו; pl. כְּתֵפֹת (כְּתֵפוֹת); cstr. כִּתְפֹת (כִּתְפוֹת); sf. כְּתֵפָם (כְּתֵיפָיו)—**1. side, wall*** of court of tabernacle (Ex 27$_{14.15}$||38$_{14.15}$), temple (1 K 6$_{8}$ 7$_{39.39.39}$ 2 K 11$_{11.11}$||2 C 23$_{10.10}$ Ezk 47$_{1.2}$ 2 C 4$_{10}$), gate of temple (Ezk 40$_{18.40.40.41.44.44.48}$ [if em.] 46$_{19}$), entrance of temple (Ezk 41$_{2.3}$ [if em.]), porch of temple (Ezk 41$_{26}$), perh. rock or crypt (Siloam royal steward tomb inscr. 2 [unless כָּתֵף = *slope*, as §3]).

<NOM CL> וְכִתְפוֹת הַפֶּתַח חָמֵשׁ אַמּוֹת מִפּוֹ וְחָמֵשׁ אַמּוֹת מִפּוֹ *and the walls of the entrance were five cubits on the one side and five cubits on the other* Ezk 41$_{2}$, וְכִתְפוֹת הַפֶּתַח שֶׁבַע אַמּוֹת מִפּוֹ וְשֶׁבַע אַמּוֹת מִפּוֹ *and the walls of the entrance were seven cubits on the one side and seven cubits on the other* Ezk 41$_{3}$ (if em. רֹחַב *width of* the entrance and ins. מִפּוֹ), וְכִתְפוֹת הַשַּׁעַר שָׁלֹשׁ אַמּוֹת מִפּוֹ וְשָׁלֹשׁ אַמּוֹת (וְשֶׁבַע אַמּוֹת מִפּוֹ) מִפּוֹ *and the walls of the gate were three cubits on the one side and three cubits on the other* Ezk 40$_{48}$ (if ins. וְכִתְפוֹת הַשַּׁעַר). **<CSTR>** כתף הצר *side of the rock* Siloam royal steward tomb inscr. 2 (or em. הצרח *of the crypt*), כֶּתֶף הַבַּיִת *side of the house* 1 K 6$_{8}$ 7$_{39.39.39}$ 2 K 11$_{11.11}$||2 C 23$_{10.10}$ Ezk 47$_{1}$ (or em. הַכָּתֵף *the side* and del. הַבַּיִת) 2 C 4$_{10}$ (if em. מִכֶּתֶף הַיְמָנִית *on the side of the southern one* to מִכֶּתֶף הַבַּיִת הַיְמָנִית *on the southern side of the temple*), הַשַּׁעַר *of the gate* Ezk 40$_{41}$ (הַשָּׁעַר) 46$_{19}$, הַשְּׁעָרִים *of the gates* Ezk 40$_{18}$, שַׁעַר *of the gate of* Ezk 40$_{44.44}$, הַיְמָנִית *of the south side* 2 C 4$_{10}$ (or em.), כִּתְפוֹת הַפֶּתַח *sides of the entrance* Ezk 41$_{2.3}$ (if em.), הָאוּלָם *of the porch* Ezk 41$_{26}$, הַשַּׁעַר *of the gate* Ezk 40$_{48}$ (if em.). **<ADJ>** שֵׁנִי *second* Ex 27$_{15}$||38$_{15}$, אַחֵר *other* Ezk 40$_{40}$, יְמָנִי *southern* 1 K 6$_{8}$ 7$_{39}$ 2 K 11$_{11}$||2 C 23$_{10}$ Ezk 47$_{1.2}$ 2 C 4$_{10}$ (if em.), שְׂמָאלִי *northern* 2 K 11$_{11}$ ||2 C 23$_{10}$. **<PREP>** לְ *at, on, by* Ex 27$_{14}$ 27$_{15}$||38$_{15}$ Ezk 40$_{41}$; בְּ *at, on, by* Siloam royal steward tomb inscr. 2 (חדן[ר] בכתף *a [grave] chamber is at the side of* the rock/crypt); מִן of direction, *from*, + ירד *go down* Ezk 47$_{1}$ (if em. מִתַּחַת מִכֶּתֶף *from beneath the side of* to מִן־הַכָּתֵף *from the side*), פכה pi. perh. *gush* Ezk 47$_{2}$, עמד *stand* 2 K 11$_{11}$||2 C 23$_{10}$; *at, on*, + נתן *give*, i.e. place, sea 1 K 7$_{39}$ (or del. נתן); אֶל *at, on, by* Ex 38$_{14}$ 1 K 6$_{8}$ Ezk 40$_{18.40.40.44.44}$ 41$_{26}$; עַל *at, on, by* Ezk 46$_{19}$, + נתן *give*, i.e. place, laver stands 1 K 7$_{39.39}$; עַד *unto*, + עמד *stand* 2 K 11$_{11}$||2 C 23$_{10}$.

2. shoulder, back,* of person (Nm 7$_{9}$ Jg 16$_{3}$ 1 S 17$_{6}$ Is 46$_{7}$ 49$_{22}$ Ezk 12$_{6.7.12}$ 24$_{4}$ 29$_{7.18}$ Zc 7$_{11}$ Jb 31$_{22}$ Ne 9$_{29}$ 1 C 15$_{15}$ 2 C 35$_{3}$), of beast (Is 30$_{6}$ Ezk 24$_{4}$ 34$_{21}$), **<SUBJ>** מרט pass. *be rubbed*, i.e. chafed Ezk 29$_{18}$ (|| רֹאשׁ *head*), סרר *be stubborn* Zc 7$_{11}$ (|| אֹזֶן *ear*) Ne 9$_{29}$ (|| עֹרֶף *neck*), נפל *fall*, i.e. be dislocated Jb 31$_{22}$ (|| אֶזְרֹעַ *arm*). **<OBJ>** נתן *give*, i.e. turn Zc 7$_{11}$ Ne 9$_{29}$, אסף *gather* Ezk 24$_{4}$ (|| יָרֵךְ *thigh*), בקע *split* Ezk 29$_{7}$ (or em. כַּף).

<CSTR> כָּל־כָּתֵף *every shoulder* Ezk 29$_{7}$ (or em.) 29$_{18}$. **<APP>** נֵתַח *piece* of meat Ezk 24$_{4}$. **<PREP>** בְּ perh. of place, *on* 2 C 35$_{3}$ (מַשָּׂא בַּכָּתֵף *carrying on the shoulder*), + נשׂא *raise*, i.e. carry, cultic furniture Nm 7$_{9}$ 1 C 15$_{15}$ (or em. בִּכְתֵפָם *on their shoulder* to כַּכָּתוּב *as it is written*); of instrument, *by (means of), with*, + הדף *push* Ezk 34$_{21}$ (|| צַד *side*, קֶרֶן *horn*); אֶל *upon*, + נשׂא *raise*, i.e. carry Ezk 12$_{12}$; עַל *upon*, + שׂים *place* city gates Jg 16$_{3}$; עַל *upon*, + נשׂא *raise*, i.e. carry Is 30$_{6}$ (|| דַּבֶּשֶׁת *hump*) Is 46$_{7}$ Ezk 12$_{6.7}$, ni. *be raised*, i.e. carried Is 49$_{22}$; בֵּין *between, across** 1 S 17$_{6}$ (unless כָּתֵף II *weapon*).

3. slope, hill,* usu. in descriptions of boundaries (Nm 34$_{11}$ Jos 15$_{8.10.11}$ 18$_{12.13.16.18.19}$), but also at Is 11$_{14}$ Ezk 25$_{9}$ perh. Dt 33$_{12}$, **<OBJ>** פתח *open* Ezk 25$_{9}$.

<CSTR> כֶּתֶף יָם־כִּנֶּרֶת *slope of the Sea of Chinnereth* Nm

34$_{11}$, הַיְבוּסִי *of the Jebusite(s)* Jos 15$_8$ 18$_{16}$, הַר־יְעָרִים *of Mount Jearim* Jos 15$_{10}$, מוֹאָב *of Moab* Ezk 25$_9$, עֶקְרוֹן *of Ekron* Jos 15$_{11}$, יְרִיחוֹ *of Jericho* Jos 18$_{12}$, לוּזָה *of Luz* Jos 18$_{13}$ (or del.), מוּל־הָעֲרָבָה *of,* at, *the front of the Arabah* Jos 18$_{18}$ (or em. בֵּית־עֲרָבָה slope of *Beth-arabah*), בֵּית־חָגְלָה *of Beth-hoglah* Jos 18$_{19}$.

<APP> כָּתֵף פְּלִשְׁתִּים appar. *(the) slope (of the) Philistines* Is 11$_{14}$ (or em. כָּתֵף *the slope of*). <PREP> בְּ *against,* + עוּף *fly* Is 11$_{14}$; אֶל *to,* + יצא *go out* Jos 15$_{11}$, עבר *pass* Jos 15$_{10}$ 18$_{13}$ (or del. אֶל־כֶּתֶף לוּזָה *to the slope of Luz*) 18$_{18.19}$ (or del. עבר, thus ירד *go down*), עלה *go up* Jos 15$_8$ 18$_{12}$, ירד *go down* Jos 18$_{16.19}$ (if em.); עַל *against,* + מחה *strike,* i.e. reach Nm 34$_{11}$; perh. בֵּין *between,* + שׁכן *dwell* among Benjamin's slopes Dt 33$_{12}$ (unless subj. is Benjamin, as §2, or כָּתֵף II *weapon*).*

4. shoulder piece* of ephod (Ex 28$_{7.12}$||39$_{4.7}$ 28$_{12}$ 28$_{18.20}$||39$_{25.27}$), <SUBJ> היה *be* Ex 28$_7$, חבר *be joined* to ends of ephod Ex 28$_{7.12}$||39$_{4.7}$. <OBJ> עשׂה *make* Ex 39$_4$. <CSTR> כִּתְפֹת הָאֵפֹד *the shoulder pieces of the ephod* Ex 28$_{12.25.27}$||39$_{7.18.20}$ (28$_{25.27}$ כִּתְפוֹת), שְׁתֵּי כְתֵפֹת *two shoulder pieces* Ex 28$_7$ 28$_{27}$||39$_{20}$. <PREP> עַל *upon,* + שׂים *place* stones of remembrance Ex 28$_{12}$||39$_7$, נשׂא *raise,* i.e. carry, names Ex 28$_{12}$; *to,* + נתן *give,* i.e. attach, (part of) breastplate Ex 28$_{25}$||39$_{18}$, rings of breastplate Ex 28$_{27}$||39$_{20}$.

5. bracket, cross piece at bottom of laver stand (1 K 7$_{30.30.31}$ [if em.] 7$_{34}$), <SUBJ> יצק pass. *be cast* 1 K 7$_{30}$ (or del.).

<NOM CL> וְאַרְבָּעָה פַעֲמֹתָיו כְּתֵפֹת לָהֶם *and its four feet had brackets* 1 K 7$_{30}$ (or em. וְאַרְבַּע פַּעֲמֹתֶיהָ in agreement with מְכוֹנָה *laver stand*), מִתַּחַת לַכִּיֹּר הַכְּתֵפֹת *the brackets were under the laver* 1 K 7$_{30}$ (or em. מִתַּחַת לַכִּיֹּרוֹת *under the lavers* and/or del. הַכְּתֵפֹת), וְאַרְבַּע כְּתֵפוֹת אֶל אַרְבַּע פִּנּוֹת הַמְּכֹנָה *and four brackets were at,* or *ran to, the four corners of the laver stand* 1 K 7$_{34}$ (mss עַל *at*).

<PREP> מִבֵּית *inside* 1 K 7$_{31}$ (if em. מִבֵּית לַכֹּתֶרֶת *inside the crown* to כְּתֵפֹת inside the *brackets*).*

⇒ §2 יָרֵךְ *thigh,* אֶזְרֹעַ *arm,* עֹרֶף *neck,* רֹאשׁ *head,* קֶרֶן *horn,* אֹזֶן *ear,* דַּבֶּשֶׁת *hump,* צַד *side.*

* [כָּתֵף] II 2 n.[m.] **weapon**—pl. cstr. כְּתֵיפָיו, כְּתֵפָיו—(unless כָּתֵף I *shoulder, slope*), וְכִידוֹן נְחֹשֶׁת בֵּין כְּתֵיפָיו *and a bronze javelin was among his weapons* 1 S 17$_6$, וּבֵין כְּתֵפָיו שָׁכֵן *and among his weapons* Benjamin *dwells* Dt 33$_{12}$, יִשְׂאוּ כְּתֹף וְכִנּוֹר *they raise themselves up like a sword,* i.e. in a sword dance, *with a harp* Jb 21$_{12}$ (unless *they raise [a sound] like tambourine and harp* [mss יִשְׂאוּ בְּתֹף *they take a tambourine*]).

כְּתֹף 1 n.m. **timbrel**—<OBJ> נשׂא *raise,* i.e. play Jb 21$_{12}$ (|| כִּנּוֹר *lyre*). <SYN> כִּנּוֹר *lyre.*

כתר I 1 vb. **be patient with—Pi.** 1 Impv. כַּתַּר—<SUBJ> Job Jb 36$_2$. <PREP> לְ of benefit, *to, for,* + Elihu Jb 36$_2$.

כתר II 4 vb. **surround—Pi.** 2 Pf. כִּתְּרוּ (כִּתְּרוּנִי)—<SUBJ> אִישׁ *man* of Israel Jg 20$_{43}$ (|| רדף hi. *pursue,* דרך hi. *overtake*), אַבִּיר *strong one* Ps 22$_{13}$. <OBJ> Benjaminite Jg 20$_{43}$, worshipper Ps 22$_{13}$. <SYN> רדף hi. *pursue,* דרך hi. *overtake.*

Hi. 2 Impf. יַכְתִּיר; ptc. מַכְתִּיר—**surround,** <SUBJ> צַדִּיק *righteous one* Ps 142$_8$, רָשָׁע *wicked one* Hb 1$_4$. <OBJ> צַדִּיק *righteous one* Hb 1$_4$, worshipper Ps 142$_8$.

כתר III 1 vb. **be crowned—Hi.** 1 Impf. יַכְתִּרוּ—**be crowned,** <SUBJ> עָרוּם *shrewd one* Pr 14$_8$. <COLL> עֲרוּמִים יַכְתִּרוּ דָעַת *the shrewd will be crowned with knowledge* Pr 14$_8$.

⇒ כֶּתֶר *crown,* כֹּתֶרֶת *capital.*

כֶּתֶר 3.0.1 n.m. **crown**—cstr. כֶּתֶר—**crown, turban,** of Persian king and queen (Est 1$_{11}$ 2$_{17}$), **decoration,** on head of horse (Est 6$_8$), <SUBJ> נתן ni. *be given,* i.e. be placed Est 6$_8$. <OBJ> שׂים *place* Est 2$_{17}$. <CSTR> כֶּתֶר מַלְכוּת *crown of the kingdom* Est 1$_{11}$ 2$_{17}$ 6$_8$, כתר צדק[ק] *crown of righteousness* 4QPrFêtes[c] 97.2$_2$. <PREP> בְּ of accompaniment, *with, in,* + בוא hi. *bring* Est 1$_{11}$.

⇒ כתר III *be crowned.*

כֹּתֶרֶת 24 n.f. **capital**—כּוֹתֶרֶת; pl. כֹּתָרוֹת (כֹּתָרֹת)—**capital** of column (e.g. 1 K 7$_{16.16.17.17}$ 2 K 25$_{17.17}$||Jr 52$_{22.22}$ 2 C 4$_{12.13}$), round **crown piece** on stand for laver (1 K 7$_{31}$), <NOM CL> כֹּתָרֹת ... מַעֲשֵׂה שׁוֹשָׁן *the capitals were ... the work of lilies,* i.e. they were constructed of lily-work 1 K 7$_{19}$, קוֹמַת הַכֹּתֶרֶת שָׁלֹשׁ אַמָּה *the height of the capital* *was three cubits* 2 K 25$_{17}$||Jr 52$_{22}$, חָמֵשׁ אַמּוֹת קוֹמַת הַכֹּתֶרֶת *five cubits was the height of the capital* 1 K 7$_{16.16}$, כֹּתָרֹת עַל־שְׁנֵי הָעַמּוּדִים *the capitals were upon the two pillars* 1 K 7$_{20}$, כֹּתֶרֶת עָלָיו *the capital was upon it* 2 K 25$_{17}$||Jr 52$_{22}$, כֹּתָרֹת ... גַּם־מִמַּעַל מִלְּעֻמַּת הַבֶּטֶן *the capitals were ... also above that which was beside the network* 1 K 7$_{20}$. <OBJ> עשׂה *make* 1 K 7$_{16}$ 2 C 4$_{12}$, כסה pi. *cover* 1 K 7$_{18}$.

<CSTR> גֻּלֹּת הַכֹּתָרֹת *the bowls of the capitals* 1 K 7$_{41.41.42}$ ||2 C 4$_{12.13}$ (both גֻּלּוֹת הַכֹּתָרוֹת), קוֹמַת הַכֹּתֶרֶת *height of the capital* 1 K 7$_{16.16}$ 2 K 25$_{17}$||Jr 52$_{22}$, שְׁתֵּי כֹתָרֹת *two capitals* 1 K 7$_{16}$. <ADJ> נְחֹשֶׁת *bronze* 2 K 25$_{17}$||Jr 52$_{22}$. <PREP> לְ of benefit, *to, for* 1 K 7$_{17.17.17}$, + עשׂה *do* 1 K 7$_{18}$; עַל *upon* 1 K 7$_{20}$ 2 K 25$_{17}$||Jr 52$_{22}$; מִבֵּית לְ *within* 1 K 7$_{31}$. <COLL> הַכֹּתֶרֶת הָאֶחָת *the first capital* 1 K 7$_{16}$, הַכֹּתֶרֶת הַשֵּׁנִית *the second capital* 1 K 7$_{16.18.20}$.

→ כתר III *be crowned.*

כתשׁ 1 vb. **pound—Qal** 1 Impf. 2ms תִּכְתּוֹשׁ—<SUBJ> worshipper Pr 27$_{22}$. <OBJ> אֱוִיל *foolish one* Pr 27$_{22}$. <PREP> בְּ of place, *in*, + מַכְתֵּשׁ *mortar* Pr 27$_{22}$; of instrument, *by (means of), with*, + עֱלִי *pestle* Pr 27$_{22}$.

→ מַכְתֵּשׁ *mortar.*

כתת 17.0.3 vb. **crush—Qal** 5.0.2 Impf. אֶכּוֹת; + waw וְכַתּוֹתִי; impv. כֹּתּוּ; ptc. pass. כָּתוּת; inf. cstr. Q כות—**beat, crush, hammer,** <SUBJ> ״ *Y.* Ps 89$_{24}$, Moses Dt 9$_{21}$, Kittim 1QpHab 3$_{1}$ (unless לכות is inf. cstr. hi. of נכה hi. *strike*; || בזז *plunder*) 4QpIsa^{a} 8$_{3}$ ([הכ]תיאים אש[ר] [יכתו]); subj. of pass., מעך pass. animal with *crushed* testicles Lv 22$_{24}$, נֵבֶל *storage jar* Is 30$_{14}$; subj. not specified, Jl 4$_{10}$. <OBJ> צַר *adversary* Ps 89$_{24}$, עִיר *city* 1QpHab 3$_{1}$, בַּיִת *house* of Israel 4QpIsa^{a} 8$_{3}$ ([הכ]תיאים), עָנָו *humble one* 4QpIsa^{a} 8$_{3}$ ([הכ]תיאים), עֵגֶל *calf* Dt 9$_{21}$, אֵת *blade* Jl 4$_{10}$, מַזְמֵרָה *vine-knife* Jl 4$_{10}$. <PREP> לְ *into*, + חֶרֶב *sword* Jl 4$_{10}$, רֹמַח *lance* Jl 4$_{10}$; מִפְּנֵי *(from) before*, + David Ps 89$_{24}$. <SYN> בזז *plunder*.

Pi. 5 Pf. כִּתְּתוּ, כִּתַּת—**beat, hammer into pieces,** <SUBJ> עַם *people* Is 2$_{4}$||Mc 4$_{3}$, גּוֹי *nation* Is 2$_{4}$||Mc 4$_{3}$, Hezekiah 2 K 18$_{4}$, Josiah 2 C 34$_{7}$, רֹעֶה *shepherd* Zc 11$_{6}$. <OBJ> אֶרֶץ *earth* Zc 11$_{6}$, פָּסִיל *idol* 2 C 34$_{7}$, נָחָשׁ *serpent* 2 K 18$_{4}$, חֶרֶב *sword* Is 2$_{4}$||Mc 4$_{3}$, חֲנִית *spear* Is 2$_{4}$||Mc 4$_{3}$. <PREP> לְ *into*, + אֵת *blade* Is 2$_{4}$||Mc 4$_{3}$, מַזְמֵרָה *vine-knife* Is 2$_{4}$||Mc 4$_{3}$.

Pu. 1 Pf. כֻּתְּתוּ—**be pushed against,** <SUBJ> גּוֹי *nation* 2 C 15$_{6}$, עִיר *city* 2 C 15$_{6}$. <PREP> בְּ *against*, + גּוֹי *nation* 2 C 15$_{6}$, עִיר *city* 2 C 15$_{6}$.

Hi. 2 + waw וַיַּכְּתוּ (וַיַּכְּתוּם)—**disperse,** <SUBJ> Amalekite Nm 14$_{45}$ (|| נכה hi. *strike*), Amorite Dt 1$_{44}$, Canaanite Nm 14$_{45}$ (|| נכה hi.). <OBJ> Israelite(s) Dt 1$_{44}$, בֵּן Israelite *son* Nm 14$_{45}$. <PREP> בְּ of place, *in, at*, + Seir Dt 1$_{44}$; עַד *until, as far as*, + Hormah Nm 14$_{45}$ Dt 1$_{44}$.

Ho. 4.0.1 Impf. יֻכַּתּוּ, יֻכַּת—**be beaten, be crushed, be hammered to pieces, be dispersed,** <SUBJ> Kittim 1QM 18$_{2}$, פָּסִיל *image* Mc 1$_{7}$, גִּבּוֹר *warrior* Jr 46$_{5}$, שָׁכֵן *inhabitant* Jb 4$_{20}$, שַׁעַר *gate* Is 24$_{12}$. <PREP> לְ of direction, *to*, + עֶרֶב *evening* Jb 4$_{20}$; מִן of direction, *from*, + בֹּקֶר *morning* Jb 4$_{20}$. <COLL> שְׁאִיָּה יֻכַּת שָׁעַר *the gate is beaten into ruin* Is 24$_{12}$.*

→ כָּתִית *beaten*, מְכִתָּה *fragment.*

ל

לְ †18687.†c.640.†c.6000.†926 prep. **to**—**a.** vocalized לֶאֱ׳, לַאֲ׳, לָאֳ׳, א, ה, ח, or ע (exceptions are לֵאלֹהִים, לֵאלֹהָיו, etc., לַאדֹנָי/לַי״); **b.** לִגְ׳ before any other consonant; **c. usu.** לָ before tone syllable, לָהֵמָּה, לָהֶן (לָהֵן, לָהֵנָּה); **d.** before a definite noun, לַ, לָ, or לֶ, i.e. with the vowel of the article ה; **e.** with sf., לִי, לְךָ (לְכָה), לָךְ (לֵכִי), לוֹ (לֹא, לְמוֹ), לָהּ (לָה), לָנוּ, לָכֶם (לכמה Q), לכן Q (לָכֵנָה), לָהֶם (לָמוֹ), Q להמה), Q להן.

1. of possession, **of,** p. 479a
2. of direction, **to, towards,** p. 480b
3. **as,**
    - **a. (so) as (to be), into,** p. 481a
    - **b. in the function/capacity of,** p. 481a
    - **c.** היה לְ **be as, become,** p. 481a
4. of place, **at, by,** p. 481b
5. of purpose,
    - **a. for (the purpose of),** p. 481b
    - **b. (in order) to,** p. 482a
    - **c. in order to obtain,** p. 482a
6. **about, in relation to,** p. 482a
7. of benefit, **to, for,** p. 482b
8. לְ + 'reflexive' suffix, p. 483a
9. **in accordance with,** p. 483a
10. **namely, even,** p. 483b
11. **amounting to,** p. 483b
12. introducing object, p. 483b
13. of agent, **by** p. 484a
14. of cause, **on account of,** p. 484a
15. of accompaniment, **with,** p. 484a
16. of instrument, **by (means of),** p. 484a
17. **in the estimation of,** p. 484a
18. **against,** p. 484a
19. לְלֹא **without,** p. 484a
20. perh. asseverative, **indeed,** p. 484a
21. perh. vocative, **O,** p. 484b
22. perh. of direction, **from, since,** p. 484b
23. לְ + inf. cstr. not expressing purpose, p. 484b

1. of possession, **of,* (belonging) to, pertaining to,** e.g. הַנִּשְׁאָרִים לְאַחְאָב *who were left of Ahab* 2 K 10_{17}, הַיּשְׁבִים לְדָוִד עַל־כִּסְאוֹ *whoever sit, of David, upon his throne* Jr 13_{13}, וּמִשְׁנֵהוּ כִלְאָב לַאֲבִיגַיִל *and his second was Chileab, belonging to,* i.e. whose mother was, *Abigail* 2 S $3_{3(Qr)}$, כָּל־רֹאשׁ לָחֳלִי *every head belongs to illness* Is 1_5, מִי אֲשֶׁר לְדָוִד *whoever belongs to David* 2 S 20_{11}, זֶבַח פֶּסַח הוּא לַי״ *it is Y.'s passover sacrifice* Ex 12_{27}, תְּרוּמָתָם לַי״ *Y.'s heave offerings from them* Ex 29_{28}, מַדּוּעַ אָדֹם לִלְבוּשֶׁךָ *why are your garments red?* Is 63_2, עֹד מִי־לְךָ פֹּה *do you have anyone else here?* Gn 19_{12}, כָּל־אֲשֶׁר־לוֹ *everything that he has* Gn 24_{36}, לִי־הֵם *they are mine* Gn 48_5, קֹדֶשׁ הִיא לָכֶם *it is your holiness* Ex 31_{14}, וְזֶה־לְּךָ *and this is yours* Nm 18_{11}, צַר־לִי עָלֶיךָ *distress is mine regarding you* 2 S 1_{26}, אוֹי לָנוּ *woe is ours* 1 S 4_7, הַמִּשְׁפָּט לֵאלֹהִים הוּא *the judgment belongs to God* Dt 1_{17}, שָׁלוֹם לַנַּעַר לְאַבְשָׁלוֹם *is there peace to,* i.e. does it go well with, *the lad, with Absalom?* 2 S 18_{29}, כִּי תְּשַׁע מֵאוֹת רֶכֶב בַּרְזֶל לוֹ *for he had 900 iron chariots* Jg 4_3, וְרֹאשׁ לוֹ חָפוּי *and his head was covered* 2 S 15_{30}, הָיְתָה־לִּי עֶדְנָה *can I have pleasure?* Gn 18_{12}, וַיְהִי לוֹ צֹאן רַבּוֹת *and he had large flocks* Gn 30_{43}, לֹא יִהְיֶה לְךָ *you are not to have* other gods Ex 20_3, לוֹ יִהְיֶה *it will be his* Lv 7_7, זֶה־יִהְיֶה לְךָ *this will be yours* Nm 18_9, וְכָל־יֶשׁ־לוֹ *and everything that he had* Gn 39_4.

כֹּל אֲשֶׁר אֵין־לוֹ סְנַפִּיר *whatever does not have fins* Lv 11_{12}, אַנְשֵׁי מָוֶת לַאדֹנִי הַמֶּלֶךְ *my lord the king's dead men* 2 S 19_{29}, רָעָב לַלֶּחֶם *a famine of bread* Am 8_{11}, אֶחָד לְמֵאָה הַקָּטָן וְהַגָּדוֹל לְאָלֶף *one, the smaller, pertained to,* i.e. was in charge of, *a hundred, the greater to a thousand* 1 C 12_{15}, אַתָּה ... הָאֱלֹהִים ... לְכֹל מַמְלְכוֹת הָאָרֶץ *you are ... God ... of all the kingdoms of the earth* 2 K 19_{15}, וְהוּא כֹהֵן לְאֵל עֶלְיוֹן *and he was priest of God Most High* Gn 14_{18}.

שְׁלֹמִית ... לְמַטֵּה דָן *Shelomith ... of the tribe of Dan* Lv 24_{11}, וְנָשִׂיא לִבְנֵי דָן *and the prince of the Danites* Nm 2_{25}, אֵל אֱלֹהֵי הָרוּחֹת לְכָל־בָּשָׂר *God, the God of the spirits of all flesh* Nm 16_{22}, מֶלֶךְ לְמוֹאָב *king of Moab* Nm 22_4, שְׁנֵי עֲבָדִים לְשִׁמְעִי *two servants of Shimei* 1 K 2_{39}, שָׂרֵי הַנִּצָּבִים

לִשְׁלֹמֹה *overseers of Solomon* 1 K 5_{30}, הַמֵּת לְיָרָבְעָם *the dead of Jeroboam* 1 K 14_{11}, סֵפֶר דִּבְרֵי הַיָּמִים לְמַלְכֵי יִשְׂרָאֵל *the chronicles of the monarchs of Israel* 1 K 14_{19}, ... בַּעְשָׁא לְבֵית יִשָּׂשכָר *Baasha ... of the house of Issachar* 1 K 15_{27}.

נָבִיא לַי׳ *a prophet of Y.* 1 K 18_{22}, מַעְבָּרֹת לְאַרְנוֹן *fords of the Arnon* Is 16_{2}, אֹרַח לַצַּדִּיק *path of the righteous* Is 26_{7}, מִכְתָּב לְחִזְקִיָּהוּ *a writing of Hezekiah* Is 38_{9}, תְּפִלָּה לַחֲבַקּוּק *a prayer of Habakkuk* Hb 3_{1}, מִזְמוֹר לְדָוִד *a psalm of David* Ps 3_{1}, מִזְמוֹר לְאָסָף *a psalm of Asaph* Ps 73_{1}, זֶבַח הַשְּׁלָמִים אֲשֶׁר לָעָם *the peace offerings of the people* Lv 9_{18}, וּמִנְחָתָם וְנִסְכֵּיהֶם לַפָּרִים לָאֵילִם וְלַכְּבָשִׂים *and with the cereal offerings and drink offerings pertaining to the bulls, the rams, and the lambs* Nm 29_{18}, אַהֲבָתֵךְ לִי *your love of me* 2 S 1_{26}, לָמָּה־לִּי רֹב־זִבְחֵיכֶם *for what benefit of mine is the abundance of your sacrifices?* Is 1_{11}, מַה־לָּנוּ חֵלֶק בְּדָוִד *what is our share in David?* 1 K 12_{16}, אֶלֶף לַמַּטֶּה אֶלֶף לַמַּטֶּה *a thousand belonging to each tribe* Nm 31_{4}, אַל לַמְלָכִים *it does not pertain to kings*, i.e. kings should not Pr 31_{4}, הֶחָזוֹן ... לְיָמִים רַבִּים *the vision ... pertains to many days (hence)* Ezk 12_{27}, אוֹת הִוא לְעֹלָם *it is a sign pertaining to eternity*, i.e. an eternal sign Ex 31_{17}.

וַיִּהְיוּ גֹזְזִים לְאַבְשָׁלוֹם *and Absalom had sheep shearers* 2 S 13_{23}, וְשָׂפָה אַחַת לְכֻלָּם *and they have all one language* Gn 11_{6}, וּלְרִבְקָה אָח *and Rebekah had a brother* Gn 24_{29}, הַחֵפֶץ לַי׳ *has Y. delighted?* 1 S 15_{22}, בְּגִבְּתוֹן אֲשֶׁר לַפְּלִשְׁתִּים *at Gibbethon which belongs to the Philistines* 1 K 15_{27}, רִיב לַי׳ *Y. has an indictment* Jr 25_{31}, לְמַהֵר שָׁלָל חָשׁ בַּז *belonging to Maher-shalal-hash-baz* Is 8_{1}, לַמְנַצֵּחַ *to the choirmaster* Ps 4_{1}, לְדָוִד *of David* Ps 11_{1}, לִבְנֵי־קֹרַח *of the sons of Korah* Ps 42_{1}, לְאָסָף *of Asaph* Ps 75_{1}, בְּאֶחָד לַחֹדֶשׁ *on the first day of the month* Gn 8_{13}, בַּחֹדֶשׁ הַשְּׁלִישִׁי לְצֵאת *in the third month of the exodus* Ex 19_{1}, בִּשְׁנַת שְׁתַּיִם לְאָסָא *in the second year of Asa* 1 K 15_{25}, וַיּוֹצִיאוּ ... אֶל־מִחוּץ לַמַּחֲנֶה *and they brought (him) ... to (the) outside (of) the camp* Lv 24_{23}.

לֹא יָדַעְנוּ מֶה־הָיָה לוֹ *we do not know what became to him*, i.e. has become of him Ex 32_{1}, קֹדֶשׁ קָדָשִׁים תִּהְיֶה לָכֶם *it will be your holy of holies* Ex 30_{36}, וִהְיִיתֶם לִי קְדֹשִׁים *and you will be my holy ones* Lv 20_{26}, צֹרְרִים הֵם לָכֶם *they have been your enemies* Nm 25_{18}, וְנָסַב לָכֶם הַגְּבוּל *and your border will turn* Nm 34_{3}, קָצִין תִּהְיֶה־לָּנוּ *you will be our ruler* Is 3_{6}.

2. of direction, **to, towards,** e.g. וַתִּתֵּן גַּם־לְאִישָׁהּ *and she gave also to her husband* Gn 3_{6}, וּלְאָדָם אָמַר *and to Adam he said* Gn 3_{17}, וַיִּשְׁקֹל אַבְרָהָם לְעֶפְרֹן *and Abraham weighed out to Ephron* Gn 23_{16}, וְנִזְבְּחוּ לַי׳ *that we may sacrifice to Y.* Ex 3_{18}, תַּקְרִיב רֵיחַ־נִיחֹחַ לַי׳ *you will offer a pleasing odour to Y.* Lv 6_{14}, אֲשֶׁר יִדֹּר קָרְבָּנוֹ לַי׳ *who vows his offering to Y.* Nm 6_{21}, מִיּוֹם לְיוֹם *from day to day* Est 3_{7}, אֲשֶׁר־יַקְרִיבוּ לַי׳ *which they offer to Y.* Nm 18_{15}.

הַנִּצְמָדִים לְבַעַל פְּעוֹר *who have joined themselves to Baal Peor* Nm 25_{5}, עַד אֲשֶׁר־יָנִיחַ י׳ לַאֲחֵיכֶם *until Y. gives rest to your brothers* Dt 3_{20}, אֲשֶׁר נִשְׁבַּע לַאֲבֹתֶיךָ *which he swore to your fathers* Dt 7_{12}, יוֹרוּ מִשְׁפָּטֶיךָ לְיַעֲקֹב *they will teach your judgments to Jacob* Dt 33_{10}, וַיַּעֲלֶה עוֹלָה לַי׳ *and he offered a whole burnt offering to Y.* 1 S 7_{9}, ... יֵעָזְבוּ ... לְעֵיט ... וּלְבֶהֱמַת הָאָרֶץ *they will be left ... to the birds ... and to the beasts of the land* Is 18_{6}, וּמָנִיתִי אֶתְכֶם לַחֶרֶב *and I will destine you to the sword* Is 65_{12}, וְהָעָם נִחָם לְבִנְיָמִן *and the people had compassion towards Benjamin* Jg 21_{15}, לְשִׁמְךָ וּלְזִכְרְךָ תַּאֲוַת־נָפֶשׁ *the desire of (our) soul is towards your name and your memory* Is 26_{8}.

וַיָּבֵא ... לַי׳ *and he brought ... to Y.* Gn 4_{3}, שַׁלְּחֻנִי לַאדֹנִי *send me to my master* Gn 24_{54}, הִנְנִי הוֹלֵךְ לְעַמִּי *behold, I am going to my people* Nm 24_{14}, וְשַׁבְתֶּם אִישׁ לִירֻשָּׁתוֹ *and each of you will return to his possession* Dt 3_{20}, וַיְהִי דְבַר־שְׁמוּאֵל לְכָל־יִשְׂרָאֵל *and the word of Samuel came to all Israel* 1 S 4_{1}, וַיִּפֹּל לְאַפָּיו *and he fell on his face* 1 S 20_{41}, וְנִבַּט לָאָרֶץ *and if one looks to the land* Is 5_{30}, נִגְדַּעְתָּ לָאָרֶץ *you are cut down to the ground* Is 14_{12}, וְכָל־פְּסִילֵי אֱלֹהֶיהָ שִׁבַּר לָאָרֶץ *and all the images of its gods he has shattered to the ground* Is 21_{9}, הִנִּיחַ לָאָרֶץ *he will cast down to the earth* Is 28_{2}, לְבוּל עֵץ אֶסְגּוֹד *shall I bow down to a block of wood?* Is 44_{19}.

שְׂאוּ לַשָּׁמַיִם עֵינֵיכֶם *lift your eyes to the heavens* Is 51_{6}, שָׁחָה לֶעָפָר נַפְשֵׁנוּ *our soul is bowed down to the dust* Ps 44_{26}, יָשׁוּב הַשָּׂדֶה לַאֲשֶׁר קָנָהוּ מֵאִתּוֹ *the field will return to the one from whom it was bought* Lv 27_{24}, ... וַיִּקַּח ... עֹלָה ... לֵאלֹהִים *and he took ... a burnt offering ... to God* Ex 18_{12}, דָּבְקָה לָאָרֶץ בִּטְנֵנוּ *our body cleaves to the ground* Ps 44_{26}, לֹא יִמְנַע טוֹב לַהֹלְכִים בְּתָמִים *he will not withhold good to those who walk in innocence* Ps 84_{12}, גָּמְלוּ לָהֶם רָעָה *they repaid evil to themselves* Is 3_{9}, אִישׁ לְאֹהָלָיו *each to his tent* 2 S 20_{1}, כַּאֲשֶׁר־שֵׁמַע לְמִצְרָיִם *when the report comes to*

Egypt Is 23$_{5}$, עֵין י׳ אֶל־יְרֵאָיו לַמְיַחֲלִים לְחַסְדּוֹ *the eye of Y. is towards those who fear him, towards those who await his loyalty* Ps 33$_{18}$.

3a. (so) as (to be), into, e.g. וּנְתַתִּיךָ לְגוֹיִם *and I will make you into nations* Gn 17$_{6}$, לְךָ נְתַתִּים ... לְחָק־עוֹלָם *I have given them to you ... as an everlasting decree* Nm 18$_{11}$, וּמְשַׁחְתּוֹ לְנָגִיד *and you will anoint him as a ruler* 1 S 9$_{16}$, כֹּחוֹ לֵאלֹהוֹ *his strength is as his god* Hb 1$_{11}$, וַיְצַוֵּהוּ י׳ לְנָגִיד *and Y. has appointed him as a ruler* 1 S 13$_{14}$, ... הִשְׁאִיר לְכֹרְמִים *he left (them) ... as vinedressers* 2 K 25$_{12}$, וְהִכָּהוּ לְשִׁבְעָה נְחָלִים *and he will strike it so as to become seven streams* Is 11$_{15}$, לָשׂוּם הָאָרֶץ לְשַׁמָּה *to make the land into a desolation* Is 13$_{9}$, הַשֶּׁמֶשׁ יֵהָפֵךְ לְחֹשֶׁךְ *the sun will be turned into darkness* Jl 3$_{4}$, וָאָקִים מִבְּנֵיכֶם לִנְבִיאִים *and I raised up some of your sons as prophets* Am 2$_{11}$, הַהֹפְכִים לְלַעֲנָה מִשְׁפָּט *who turn justice into wormwood* Am 5$_{7}$, דְּמֵה־לְךָ דוֹדִי לִצְבִי אוֹ לְעֹפֶר הָאַיָּלִים *liken yourself, my beloved, to a gazelle or to a young stag* Ca 2$_{17}$, אֵלֶּה תַּעֲשׂוּ ... לְעֹלֹתֵיכֶם וּלְמִנְחֹתֵיכֶם וּלְנִסְכֵּיכֶם וּלְשַׁלְמֵיכֶם *these you are to prepare ... (so) as (to be) your burnt offerings, your cereal offerings, your drink offerings, and your peace offerings* Nm 29$_{39}$, וְאֶעֶשְׂךָ לְגוֹי גָּדוֹל *and I will turn you into a great nation* Gn 12$_{2}$, וַיַּחַץ אֶת־הָעָם ... לִשְׁנֵי מַחֲנוֹת *and he divided the people into two groups* Gn 32$_{8}$.

3b. in the function of, in the capacity of, e.g. וַיִּתְיַצֵּב ... לְשָׂטָן *and he took his stand as an adversary* Nm 22$_{22}$, יָצָאתִי לְשָׂטָן *I have come out as,* i.e. in the capacity of, *an adversary* Nm 22$_{32}$, וּקְשַׁרְתָּם לְאוֹת *and you will bind (them) as a sign* Dt 6$_{8}$, אֲשֶׁר עֹמֵד לְנֵס עַמִּים *which stands as a signal to the nations* Is 11$_{10}$, ... וְהִתְנַחֲלוּם לַעֲבָדִים *and they will possess them ... as slaves* Is 14$_{2}$, וַיִּכְבִּישׁוּם לַעֲבָדִים וְלִשְׁפָחוֹת *they brought them into subjection as male and female servants* Jer 34$_{11}$(Kt).

3c. היה לְ **be as,** i.e. **become, turn into,** e.g. ... וַיְהִי לְנֶפֶשׁ חַיָּה *and he became a living soul* Gn 2$_{7}$, עֶבֶד עֲבָדִים יִהְיֶה לְאֶחָיו *a servant of servants he will be to his brothers* Gn 9$_{25}$, וְהָיִיתִי לָהֶם לֵאלֹהִים *and I will be their God* Gn 17$_{8}$, הָיִיתִי לִשְׁנֵי מַחֲנוֹת *I have become two companies* Gn 32$_{11}$, וְהָיָה הָאֹכֶל לְפִקָּדוֹן לָאָרֶץ *and the food will be a store for the land* Gn 41$_{36}$, יִהְיֶה־לְּעָם *he will become a people* Gn 48$_{19}$, וְהָיָה לְאַהֲרֹן ... לְחָק־עוֹלָם *and it will become for Aaron ... an eternal duty* Ex 29$_{28}$, וַתְּהִי אֲרָם לְדָוִד לַעֲבָדִים *and Aram became David's servants* 2 S 8$_{6}$, יְהִי־נָא דְּבַר אֲדֹנִי ... לִמְנוּחָה *may my lord the king's word become ... a comfort* 2 S 14$_{17}$.

4. of place, **at, by, on, along, over,** e.g. ... מְרִיתֶם לְמֵי מְרִיבָה *you rebelled at the waters of Meribah* Nm 20$_{24}$, תָּשִׁית לְרֹאשׁוֹ עֲטֶרֶת פָּז *you put on his head a crown of fine gold* Ps 21$_{4}$, הִרְכַּבְתָּ אֱנוֹשׁ לְרֹאשֵׁנוּ *you made men ride over our head(s)* Ps 66$_{12}$, וְיַעֲקֹב הָלַךְ לְדַרְכּוֹ *and Jacob went on his way* Gn 32$_{2}$, תִּהְיֶיןָ לְרֹאשׁ יוֹסֵף *they will be on Joseph's head* Gn 49$_{26}$, וַיַּעַמְדוּ ... לַמִּזְבֵּחַ וְלַבָּיִת *and they stood ... by the altar and by the temple* 2 K 11$_{11}$, וַיַּעֲמֹד לַמֶּלֶךְ appar. *and he stood by the king* 1 K 20$_{38}$, אִישׁ לְפֶתַח אָהֳלוֹ *each at the entrance of his tent* Nm 11$_{10}$.

וְעָמַדְתִּי לְיַד־אָבִי *and I shall stand at the hand of,* i.e. beside, *my father* 1 S 19$_{3}$, וַתֵּשֶׁב לִימִינוֹ *and she sat at his right hand* 1 K 2$_{19}$, לְמִכְמָשׂ יַפְקִיד כֵּלָיו *at Michmash he stores his baggage* Is 10$_{28}$, לְיַד־שְׁעָרִים לְפִי־קָרֶת wisdom cries *beside the gates at the entrance of the portals* Pr 8$_{3}$, וְהַשֹּׁעֲרִים לְשַׁעַר וָשָׁעַר *and the gatekeepers were at each gate* 2 C 35$_{15}$, הִתְקַדְּשׁוּ לְמָחָר *consecrate yourselves for tomorrow* Nm 11$_{18}$, לַמּוֹעֵד *at the appointed time* Jos 8$_{14}$.

וְהֵם עַל־הַמַּפְתֵּחַ וְלַבֹּקֶר לַבֹּקֶר *and they were in charge of opening up each morning* 1 C 9$_{27}$, וַיְהִי לִתְשׁוּבַת הַשָּׁנָה לְעֵת צֵאת *and it happened at the return of the year, the time when* kings *go forth* 2 S 11$_{1}$, מִקֵּץ יָמִים לַיָּמִים *at the end of each year* 2 S 14$_{26}$, אַחַת לְשָׁלֹשׁ שָׁנִים *once every three years* 1 K 10$_{22}$, לִשְׁלֹשֶׁת הַיָּמִים *within three days* Ezr 10$_{9}$, לְעֵת תָּמוּט רַגְלָם *at the time when their foot will slip* Dt 32$_{35}$, וּמַה־תַּעֲשׂוּ לְיוֹם פְּקֻדָּה *and what will you do on the day of visitation?* Is 10$_{3}$, לַיָּמִים אֲשֶׁר *in the days when ...* Ezk 22$_{14}$, לַיּוֹם אֲשֶׁר אֲנִי עֹשֶׂה *on the day when I make ...* Ml 3$_{17}$.

מִנֶּגֶב לְמַעֲלֵה עַקְרַבִּים *south of the ascent of Akrabbim* Nm 34$_{4}$, וּפֶתַח אֶחָד לַדָּרוֹם *and one door towards the south* Ezk 41$_{11}$, לַקָּדִים *to the east* Ezk 41$_{14}$, לַצָּפוֹן *on the north* Ezk 42$_{4}$, כַּאֲשֶׁר מִשְׁפָּטֶיךָ לָאָרֶץ *when your judgments are on the earth* Is 26$_{9}$, רָאִיתִי הֶהָמוֹן הַגָּדוֹל לִשְׁלֹחַ ... יוֹאָב *I saw a large crowd at Joab's sending,* i.e. when Joab sent, the king's servant 2 S 18$_{29}$, חֶמְאָה וּדְבַשׁ יֹאכֵל לְדַעְתּוֹ מָאוֹס בָּרָע *one,* i.e. people, *will be eating curds and honey at his knowing,* i.e. when he knows, *(how) to reject evil* Is 7$_{15}$.

5. of purpose, **a. for (the purpose of), to be used for,** followed by noun, e.g. קְחוּ ... שׁוֹר וָאַיִל לִשְׁלָמִים *take ...*

an ox and a ram for peace offerings Lv 9_{3}, וְעָשִׂיתָ מַעֲקֶה לְגַגֶּךָ *and you are to make a parapet for your roof* Dt 22_{8}, סֹלֶת בְּלוּלָה בַשֶּׁמֶן לְמִנְחָה *flour mixed with oil for a cereal offering* Nm 7_{79}, וְעָשִׂיתָ ... חֲמִשָּׁה בְרִיחִם לְקַרְשֵׁי צֶלַע־הַמִּשְׁכָּן *and you are to make ... five bars for the frames of the side of the tabernacle* Ex 26_{26} י׳ לְהוֹשִׁיעֵנִי *Y. is for saving me,* i.e. Y. is to save me Is 38_{20}.

5b. followed by infinitive construct, **(in order) to, so as to,** e.g. וַיְשַׁלְּחֵהוּ ... לַעֲבֹד *and he sent him out ... to work the ground* Gn 3_{23}, וַיְשַׁלַּח אֶת־הַיּוֹנָה ... לִרְאוֹת *and he sent the dove ... to see* Gn 8_{8}, וּרְאִיתִיהָ לִזְכֹּר *and I will look upon it to remember* Gn 9_{16}, וַיֵּצְאוּ לָלֶכֶת *and they went out to go* Gn 12_{5}, וְאַבְרָהָם הֹלֵךְ עִמָּם לְשַׁלְּחָם *and Abraham went with them to set them on the way* Gn 18_{16}, וַיֵּלֶךְ עֵשָׂו ... לָצוּד *and Esau went ... to hunt* Gn 27_{5}, וָאֵרֵד לְהַצִּילוֹ *and I have come down to rescue him* Ex 3_{8}, וַיָּבֹא אַהֲרֹן ... לֶאֱכָל־לֶחֶם *and Aaron came ... to eat bread* Ex 18_{12}.

וַיֵּצֵא לִקְרַאת י׳ *and he went out to meet,* i.e. against, *Y.* Nm 21_{23}, אַתֶּם עֹבְרִים ... לְרִשְׁתָּהּ *you are coming over to possess it* Dt 11_{11}, אֲשֶׁר־יִבְחַר לְשַׁכֵּן שְׁמוֹ שָׁם *where he chose to make his name dwell* Dt 14_{23}, וַיִּשְׁלַח שָׁאוּל ... לָקַחַת אֶת־דָּוִד *and Saul sent ... to take David* 1 S 19_{14}, וַיָּטֶל שָׁאוּל ... לְהַכֹּתוֹ *and Saul cast ... to strike him* 1 S 20_{33}, הוּא־יָרָה הַחֵצִי לְהַעֲבִרוֹ *he shot the arrows to go beyond him* 1 S 20_{36}, וַיָּקָם הַמֶּלֶךְ לִקְרָאתָהּ *and the king rose to meet her* 1 K 2_{19}, וַיִּגַּשׁ ... לְהָדְפָהּ *and he approached ... to push her away* 2 K 4_{27}, הוֹי הַמַּעֲמִיקִים ... לַסְתִּר עֵצָה *woe to those who make things deep ... to hide counsel* Is 29_{15}, אִשָּׁה ... לֹא תִקָּח ... לְגַלּוֹת עֶרְוָתָהּ *a woman ... you are not to take ... so as to uncover her nakedness* Lv 18_{18}.

5c. in order to obtain, followed by noun, e.g. ... וַיַּעֲלוּ לַמִּשְׁפָּט *and they went up for judgment* Jg 4_{5}.

6. about, concerning, with regard to, in respect of, as for, in relation to, e.g. מִי אֵלֶּה לָּךְ *what are these in relation to you?* Gn 33_{5} 2 S 16_{2}, כָּל־הַכָּתוּב לַחַיִּים *all who are recorded in respect of life* Is 4_{3}, לָמָּה זֶּה תִּשְׁאַל לִשְׁמִי *why do you ask (about) my name* Gn 32_{30}, וְשָׁמְרוּ ... לְכֹל עֲבֹדַת הָאֹהֶל *and they will attend ... with regard to all the service of the tent* Nm 18_{4}, קְחוּ ... צֵידָה לַדֶּרֶךְ *take ... provision in respect of the journey* Jos 9_{11}.

וַיִּשְׁאֲלוּ־לוֹ לְשָׁלוֹם *and they asked him about his welfare* Jg 18_{15}, מַה־נַּעֲשֶׂה ... לְנָשִׁים *what shall we do about wives?* Jg 21_{7}, וַיִּדְרֹשׁ לָאִשָּׁה *and he enquired after the woman* 2 S 11_{3}, וַיִּגְדַּל הַמֶּלֶךְ שְׁלֹמֹה ... לְעֹשֶׁר וּלְחָכְמָה *and King Solomon exceeded ... in respect of riches and wisdom* 1 K 10_{23}, כִּי־שָׁלַח אֵלַי לְנָשַׁי *for he sent to me for my wives* 1 K 20_{7}, נָקֵל לַצֵּל *it is easy with regard to the shadow* 2 K 20_{10}, וְיִסְּרוֹ לַמִּשְׁפָּט *and he instructs him about justice* Is 28_{26}, כָּל־עֵץ נֶחְמָד לְמַרְאֶה *every tree that is pleasant in respect of sight* Gn 2_{9}.

יְחַזְּקוּ ... לְכֹל אֲשֶׁר־יִמָּצֵא ... בֶּדֶק *they repaired* holes in the temple *(in respect of) wherever a breach was found* 2 K 12_{6}, וּלְיִשְׁמָעֵאל *as for Ishmael* Gn 17_{20}, וְלַנְּקֵבָה *and as for a female* Lv 27_{6}, לִנְדָרֶיהָ וּלְאִסַּר נַפְשָׁהּ *concerning her vows or her pledge of herself* Nm 30_{13}, לַנְּבִאִים *concerning the prophets* Jr 23_{9}, לְמִצְרַיִם *concerning Egypt* Jr 46_{2}, לֹא־יָקוּם עֵד אֶחָד בְּאִישׁ לְכָל־עָוֹן וּלְכָל־חַטָּאת *a single witness may not take the stand against someone in respect of any iniquity or any sin* Dt 19_{15}, וְכִצְבָאִים ... לְמַהֵר *and (they were) like gazelles ... in respect of speed* 1 C 12_{9}, כְּסוּפוֹת ... לַחֲלֹף *like whirlwinds ... in respect of changing,* i.e. in the way that one quickly replaces another Is 21_{1}.

7. of benefit, **to (the advantage/disadvantage of), for (the benefit, use, of), to be used by, on behalf of,** e.g. לֹא תִקַּח אִשָּׁה לִבְנִי *do not take a wife for my son* Gn 24_{37}, וַיִּבֶן ... לְפַרְעֹה *and they,* lit. one, *built ... for Pharaoh* Ex 1_{11}, פָּרַח מַטֵּה־אַהֲרֹן לְבֵית לֵוִי *Aaron's rod budded for the house of Levi* Nm 17_{23}, וְלָאָרֶץ לֹא יְכֻפַּר *and no atonement can be made for the land* Nm 35_{33}, קַח־נָא לְאַחֶיךָ *take now for your brothers* 1 S 17_{17}, וַיָּשֶׂם כִּסֵּא לְאֵם הַמֶּלֶךְ *and he set up a throne for the king's mother* 1 K 2_{19}, שְׁמֹר לְעַבְדְּךָ דָוִד *keep for your servant David* 1 K 8_{25}, וְעָשִׂינוּ לַי׳ *and we shall perform (sacrifice) for Y.* Ex 10_{25}, כָּל־אֲשֶׁר עָשָׂה י׳ לְפַרְעֹה *all that Y. did to Pharaoh* Ex 18_{8}, וְלָאָרֶץ לֹא יְכֻפַּר לַדָּם אֲשֶׁר שֻׁפַּךְ *as for the land, no expiation can be made for the blood shed on it* Nm 35_{33}, וְכֵן תַּעֲשֶׂה לַחֲמֹרוֹ *and you will do the same with his ass* Dt 22_{3}, בְּכוֹר אֲשֶׁר יְבֻכַּר לַי׳ *the firstborn who is (already) a firstling to Y.* Lv 27_{26}, וַתֵּלֶד שָׂרָה ... בֵן לַאדֹנִי *and Sarah bore ... a son to my master* Gn 24_{36}, וַיֵּרַע לְמֹשֶׁה *and it went ill for Moses* Ps 106_{36}, הוּא לָךְ כְּסוּת עֵינַיִם *it is for you a covering of the eyes* Gn 20_{16}, תּוֹרָה אַחַת לָהֶם *one (and the same) law for them* Lv 7_{7}, הַחֲמוֹרִים לְבֵית הַמֶּלֶךְ *the asses are for the king's house* 2 S

16$_{2}$, וַתִּקַּח־לוֹ אִמּוֹ אִשָּׁה *and his mother took a wife for him* Gn 21$_{21}$, הַבְּהֵמָה בָּזַזְנוּ לָנוּ *the cattle we kept as spoil for ourselves* Dt 2$_{35}$, אֶסְפָה־לִּי שִׁבְעִים אִישׁ *gather for me seventy men* Nm 11$_{16}$, וְהֵפַרְתָּה לִי *and you will thwart for me* the counsel of Ahithophel 2 S 15$_{34}$ *it was better for us in Egypt* Nm 11$_{18}$, זֶבַח ... לְכָל־הַמִּשְׁפָּחָה *sacrifice ... for the whole family* 1 S 20$_{6}$, צַר־לִי הַמָּקוֹם *the place is too narrow for me* Is 49$_{20}$, עֲצֻרָה־לָנוּ *forbidden to us* 1 S 21$_{6}$.

8. לְ + 'reflexive' suffix, restating subject, e.g. לֶךְ־לְךָ מֵאַרְצְךָ *go from your country* Gn 12$_{1}$, הַכֶּר־לְךָ מָה עִמָּדִי *point out what I have* Gn 31$_{32}$, קַח־לְךָ *take* Gn 31$_{32}$, עֲשֵׂה לְךָ *make* Nm 21$_{8}$, וְעָבַר לָכֶם *cross* Nm 32$_{21}$, פְּנוּ וּסְעוּ לָכֶם *turn and set out* Dt 1$_{7}$, הָבוּ לָכֶם *give* Dt 1$_{13}$, הִשָּׁמְרוּ לָכֶם *take heed* Dt 4$_{23}$, שׁוּבוּ לָכֶם לְאָהֳלֵיכֶם *return to your tents* Dt 5$_{30}$, פְּסָל־לְךָ *hew* Dt 10$_{1}$, שִׁבְעָה שָׁבֻעֹת תִּסְפָּר־לָךְ *you are to count seven weeks* Dt 16$_{9}$, חַג הַסֻּכֹּת תַּעֲשֶׂה לְךָ *keep the feast of booths* Dt 16$_{13}$, שָׁלוֹשׁ עָרִים תַּבְדִּיל לָךְ *separate three cities* Dt 19$_{2}$, וְיָסַפְתָּ לְךָ *and you shall add* Dt 19$_{9}$, הָכִינוּ לָכֶם *prepare* Jos 1$_{11}$, קֻם־לָךְ *get up* Jos 7$_{10}$, נְטֵה לְךָ *turn aside* 2 S 2$_{21}$, וּפָנִיתָ לְּךָ קֵדְמָה *turn eastwards* 1 K 17$_{3}$, שַׁאֲלִי־לָךְ *borrow* 2 K 4$_{3}$, הָרֶם לָךְ *pick it up* 2 K 6$_{7}$, חִדְלוּ לָכֶם *cease* Is 2$_{22}$, אַל תִּבְטְחוּ לָכֶם אֶל־דִּבְרֵי הַשֶּׁקֶר *trust not in false words* Jr 7$_{4}$, לָמָּה חָרָה לָךְ *why are you angry?* Gn 4$_{6}$, וַיֵּצֶר לוֹ *and he was distressed* Gn 32$_{8}$, וַיָּשֶׁת־לוֹ עֲדָרִים לְבַדּוֹ *and he set his flocks apart* Gn 30$_{40}$, לֹא תַעֲשׂוּ לָכֶם *you are not to make for yourselves* Ex 20$_{23}$, מָהֹר יִמְהָרֶנָּה לּוֹ *he will surely pay a brideprice for her* Ex 22$_{15}$, עַד מְלֹאת לוֹ *until there is completed* Lv 25$_{30}$, וַיָּשִׂימוּ לָהֶם אֶת־פֶּסֶל מִיכָה *and they set up Micah's image* Jg 18$_{31}$, בִּנְקוֹר לָכֶם כָּל־עֵין יָמִין *by putting out all your right eyes* 1 S 11$_{2}$, בִּקֵּשׁ י׳ לוֹ *Y. has sought* 1 S 13$_{14}$, וְלֹא יִחַם לוֹ *and he could not get warm* 1 K 1$_{1}$, וְנָס לוֹ מִפְּנֵי־חֶרֶב *and he will flee from the sword* Is 31$_{8}$, וַתִּבְטַח לְךָ עַל־מִצְרַיִם *and you trusted in Egypt* Is 36$_{9}$, נַפְשָׁהּ מָרָה־לָהּ *her soul is bitter* 2 K 4$_{27}$.

9. in accordance with, corresponding to, e.g. אַל־לְאֶרֶךְ אַפְּךָ תִּקָּחֵנִי *do not take me away in (accordance with) your forbearance* Jr 15$_{15}$, וְלֹא־לְמַרְאֵה עֵינָיו יִשְׁפּוֹט *and he will not judge (merely) in accordance with what he sees* Is 11$_{3}$, לְמִשְׁפְּחֹתֵיהֶם יָצְאוּ *they went out according to their families* Gn 8$_{19}$, לְדֹרֹתָם *according to their generations* Gn 17$_{9}$, לְמִינֵהוּ *according to its kind* Lv 11$_{16}$, לְצִבְאֹתָם *by their companies* Nm 2$_{22}$, לִשְׁבָטָיו *by his tribes* Nm 24$_{2}$, לְמֵאוֹת וְלַאֲלָפִים *by hundreds and thousands* 1 S 29$_{2}$, לְעִיר וָעִיר *city by city* 2 C 19$_{5}$, לַעֲבוֹדָה וַעֲבוֹדָה *in every kind of work* 2 C 34$_{13}$, צַו לָצָו קַו לָקָו *precept upon precept, line upon line* Is 28$_{10}$.

10. specifying or emphasizing, **namely, even, that is to say,** e.g. פֶּן יְבֻלַּע לַמֶּלֶךְ *lest the king be swallowed up* 2 S 17$_{16}$, לְרֵיחַ שְׁמָנֶיךָ טוֹבִים *your anointing oils are fragrant* Ca 1$_{3}$, נָתַתִּי לְךָ אֶת־מִשְׁמֶרֶת תְּרוּמֹתָי לְכָל־קָדְשֵׁי בְנֵי יִשְׂרָאֵל *I have entrusted to you the safekeeping of my gifts, namely all the holy offerings of the Israelites* Nm 18$_{8}$, וְהָיוּ בָּתֵּי יְרוּשָׁלַםִ ... כִּמְקוֹם הַתֹּפֶת ... לְכָל־הַבָּתִּים *and the houses of Jerusalem will become ... like the place of Topheth —that is to say, all the houses* that burned incense Jr 19$_{13}$, וְהָרַג מְלָכִים עֲצוּמִים: לְסִיחוֹן ... וּלְעוֹג *and killed mighty kings, even Sihon ... and Og* Ps 135$_{11}$, וָאַבְדִּילָה ... שְׁנֵים עָשָׂר לְשֵׁרֵבְיָה חֲשַׁבְיָה *and I separated ... twelve, namely Sherebiah, Hashabiah* and ten others Ezr 8$_{24}$, כָּל־הַתְּלָאָה אֲשֶׁר־מְצָאַתְנוּ לִמְלָכֵינוּ לְשָׂרֵינוּ ... וּלְכָל־עַמֶּךָ *all the distress that has found us, that is to say, our kings, our princes, ... and all your people* Ne 9$_{32}$.

11. amounting to, e.g. זָהָב טוֹב לְכִכָּרִים שֵׁשׁ מֵאוֹת *fine gold, amounting to 600 (talents)* 2 C 3$_{8}$, וּמִשְׁקָל לְמִסְמְרוֹת לִשְׁקָלִים חֲמִשִּׁים זָהָב *and the weight of the nails amounted to fifty gold (shekels)* 2 C 3$_{9}$, וּכְלֵי־כֶסֶף מֵאָה לְכִכָּרִים *and silver vessels, (worth) a hundred (talents), amounting to (?) talents* Ezr 8$_{26}$,

12. introducing object, e.g. וְנָשָׂאתִי לְכָל־הַמָּקוֹם *I will forgive the whole place* Gn 18$_{26}$, וַיִּשַּׁק יַעֲקֹב לְרָחֵל *Jacob kissed Rachel* Gn 29$_{11}$, לוּ ... יָבִינוּ לְאַחֲרִיתָם *if only ... they would consider their end* Dt 32$_{29}$, הָרְגוּ לְאַבְנֵר *they slew Abner* 2 S 3$_{30}$, אֹהֵב הָיָה חִירָם לְדָוִד *Hiram always loved David* 1 K 5$_{15}$, וַיִּשְׁאַל הַמֶּלֶךְ לָאִשָּׁה *and the king questioned the woman* 2 K 8$_{6}$, הוֹי הָאֹמְרִים לָרַע טוֹב *woe to those who call evil good* Is 5$_{20}$, וַתִּמְצָא ... יָדִי לְחֵיל הָעַמִּים *and my hand has found ... the wealth of nations* Is 10$_{14}$, כַּמַּיִם לַיָּם מְכַסִּים *as the waters cover the sea* Is 11$_{9}$, וַהֲצִיקוֹתִי לַאֲרִיאֵל *and I will distress Ariel* Is 29$_{2}$, וַיִּקַּח ... לְיִרְמְיָהוּ *and he took ... Jeremiah* Jr 40$_{2}$, וַיְקַנְאוּ לְמֹשֶׁה *and they envied Moses* Ps 106$_{16}$, וּפֶן־תִּדְרֹשׁ לֵאלֹהֵיהֶם *and lest you ask their gods* Dt 12$_{30}$, כִּי חָלָה לְטוֹב *for he awaits good* Mc 1$_{12}$.

13. in passive constructions, of agent, **by (the agency of),** e.g. נִדְרַשְׁתִּי לְלוֹא שָׁאָלוּ *I was (ready to be) sought by those who did not ask* Is 65_{1}, אַתֶּם נִטְמְאִים לְכָל־גִּלּוּלֵיכֶם *you are polluted by all your images* Ezk 20_{31}, ... וְנִבְחַר מָוֶת לְכֹל הַשְּׁאֵרִית *and death will be preferred ... by all the remnant* Jr 8_{3}, וְלֹא־יֵרָאֶה לְךָ שְׂאֹר *and there is no leaven to be seen by you,* i.e. you are to have no leaven Dt 16_{4}, בְּפִשְׁתֵּי הָעֵץ הָעֲרֻכוֹת לָהּ *in the stalks of flax that had been arranged by her* Jos 2_{6}.

14. of cause, **on account of, for (the sake of), because of, at (the news of),** e.g. לִבִּי לְמוֹאָב יִזְעָק *my heart cries out for Moab* Is 15_{5}, יְיֵלִיל מוֹאָב לְמוֹאָב *Moab will howl for Moab* Is 16_{7}, לַאֲשִׁישֵׁי קִיר־חֲרֶשֶׂת תֶּהְגּוּ *moan for the raisin cakes of Kir-haresheth* Is 16_{7}, מֵעַי לְמוֹאָב ... יֶהֱמוּ *my bowels sound for ... Moab* Is 16_{11}, אַל־תִּבְכּוּ לְמֵת *do not weep for the dead* Jr 22_{10}, נָסוּ לְקֹלָם *they fled at their cry* Nm 16_{34}, לְאַט־לִי *deal gently for my sake* with the lad 2 S 18_{5}.

15. of accompaniment, **with, in (a state of),** e.g. ... אִם נֶעֶשְׂתָה לִשְׁגָגָה *if ... it is done in error* Nm 15_{24}, וְאִישׁ מָשַׁךְ בַּקֶּשֶׁת לְתֻמּוֹ *and a man drew a bow in his innocence,* i.e. at random 1 K 22_{34}, לָבֶטַח *in safety* Lv 26_{5}, לָרֹב *in abundance* 1 C 29_{21}.

16. of instrument, **by (means of), with, through,** e.g. וַיַּחֲלֹשׁ יְהוֹשֻׁעַ אֶת־עֲמָלֵק ... לְפִי־חָרֶב *Joshua defeated Amalek ... with the edge of the sword* Ex 17_{13}, לְשֵׁמַע־אֹזֶן שְׁמַעְתִּיךָ *through the hearing of the ear have I heard of you* Jb 42_{5}.

17. in the estimation of, before, e.g. מָרְדֳּכַי ... גָּדוֹל לַיְּהוּדִים *Mordecai ... was great in the estimation of the Jews* Est 10_{3}, וָאֶהְיֶה תָמִים לוֹ *and I was blameless before him* 2 S 22_{24}.

18. against, e.g. חָטָאנוּ לַי׳ *we have sinned against Y.* Dt 1_{41}, זֹמֵם רָשָׁע לַצַּדִּיק *the wicked plots against the righteous* Ps 37_{12}.

19. לְלֹא **without,** e.g. וְיָמִים רַבִּים לְיִשְׂרָאֵל לְלֹא אֱלֹהֵי אֱמֶת *and Israel had many days without the true God* 2 C 15_{3}.

20. perh. asseverative, emphatic, **indeed,*** e.g. לֶאֱמֶת יוֹצִיא מִשְׁפָּט *indeed he will produce justice* Is 42_{3}, כִּי־אָדָם לְעָמָל יוּלָּד *for it is indeed humankind who engender trouble* Jb 5_{7} (if em. יוּלַּד *is born* to trouble), יֹלֵד כְּסִיל לְתוּגָה לוֹ *whoever begets a fool, trouble is indeed theirs* Pr 17_{21} (or em. תּוּגָה, without לְ), לְגַבֵּי חֹמֶר גַּבֵּיכֶם *indeed, your answers are answers of clay* Jb 13_{12}, הֲלִיכוֹת עוֹלָם לְהִתְחַתֵּאנָה *eternal orbits were indeed shattered* Hb 3_{6} (if em. לוֹ: תַּחַת אָוֶן eternal orbits bow down *to him; instead of iniquity*), כִּי לַי׳ מָגִנֵּנוּ וְלִקְדוֹשׁ יִשְׂרָאֵל מַלְכֵּנוּ *for indeed Y. is our shield and indeed the holy one of Israel is our king* Ps 89_{19} (or del. לְ both times), בַּת־עַמִּי לְאַכְזָר *the daughter of my people is indeed cruel* Lm 4_{3}.

21. perh. vocative, **O,*** e.g. הוי למות מה מר זכרך *alas, O death, how bitter is your memory* Si $41_{1(Bmg)}$, האח למות כי טוב חקיך *aha, O death, how good is your decree* Si $41_{2(B)}$, לָרֹכֵב בִּשְׁמֵי שְׁמֵי־קֶדֶם *O rider in the highest ancient heavens* Ps 68_{34}.

22. perh. of direction, **from, since,*** י׳ לַמַּבּוּל יָשָׁב וַיֵּשֶׁב י׳ מֶלֶךְ לְעוֹלָם *Y. has sat enthroned since the flood and Y. has sat as king from eternity* Ps 29_{10}.

23. לְ + infinitive construct not expressing purpose (contrast §3b).

23a. following modal or auxiliary verb, etc., e.g. הוֹאַלְתִּי לְדַבֵּר *I have undertaken to speak* Gn 18_{27}, לֹא־יָכֹל יוֹסֵף לְהִתְאַפֵּק *Joseph could not control himself* Gn 45_{1}, בֹּשֵׁשׁ מֹשֶׁה לָרֶדֶת *Moses delayed coming down* Ex 32_{1}, יִהְיֶה לְבָעֵר קָיִן *Kain shall be for burning* Nm 24_{22}, כַּאֲשֶׁר דִּמִּיתִי לַעֲשׂוֹת לָהֶם *as I thought to do to them* Nm 33_{56}, וְשָׁמַרְתָּ אֶת־מִצְוֹת י׳ ... לָלֶכֶת בִּדְרָכָיו *and you shall keep the commandments of Y., ... walking in his ways* Dt 8_{6}, חָשַׁק י׳ לְאַהֲבָה אוֹתָם *Y. had a desire to love them* Dt 10_{15}, וְלֹא־אָבָה הָאִישׁ לָלוּן *the man did not want to lodge* Jg 19_{10}, כִּי־כָלְתָה ... לְהָמִית *for it was determined ... to put him to death* 1 S 20_{33}, וַיַּחְמֹל לָקַחַת *and he refrained from taking* 2 S 12_{4}, וַיֹּאמֶר לְהַכּוֹת *and he said you should have struck* 2 K 13_{19}, וַיְקַו לַעֲשׂוֹת עֲנָבִים *and he expected it to yield grapes* Is 5_{2}, חָדַלְנוּ לְקַטֵּר *we ceased to burn incense* Jr 44_{18}.

23b. with verb of quantity or quality, וַתֹּסֶף לָלֶדֶת *and she bore again* Gn 4_{2}, וְיָסַף עוֹד לְהַנִּיחוֹ *and he will again abandon him* Nm 32_{15}, לֹא אוֹסִיף לְהוֹרִישׁ *I shall no longer drive out* Jg 2_{21}, לֹא תָשׁוּב לָלֶכֶת *you will not again go* 1 K 13_{17}, וַתָּרַע לַעֲשׂוֹת *and you have done evil* 1 K 14_{9}, הִקְשִׁיתָ לִשְׁאוֹל *you have asked a hard thing* 2 K 2_{10}, הֱטִיבֹתָ לַעֲשׂוֹת הַיָּשָׁר *you have done well in doing right* 2 K 10_{30}, כַּאֲשֶׁר־תַּמּוּ ... לָמוּת *when they were entirely ... dead* Dt

2$_{16}$, הִרְבָּה לַעֲשׂוֹת הָרַע *he did much evil* 2 K 21$_{6}$, כִּי־יַרְבֶּה לִסְלוֹחַ *for he will abundantly pardon* Is55$_{7}$, הֵיטַבְתָּ לִרְאוֹת *you have seen well* Jr 1$_{12}$, הַרְבּוּ לִפְשֹׁעַ *multiply sinning* Am 4$_{4}$.

23c. expressing ability, sufficiency, אֵין אִישׁ בָּאָרֶץ לָבוֹא עָלֵינוּ *there is no one in the land (able) to come in to us* Gn 19$_{31}$, כֵּן אֲדֹנִי הַמֶּלֶךְ לִשְׁמֹעַ הַטּוֹב *thus is my lord the king able to discern good* 2 S 14$_{17}$, הָאֱלֹהִים אָנִי לְהָמִית וּלְהַחֲיוֹת *am I God, able to give death or life?* 2 K 5$_{7}$, ... חָלָה לָמוּת *he was sick (enough) ... to die* 2 K 20$_{1}$, אֲשֶׁר־הוּא רָשָׁע לָמוּת *who is wicked enough to die* Nm 35$_{31}$, וְהָיָה לָנוּס שָׁמָּה כָּל־רֹצֵחַ *and any manslayer will be able to flee there* Dt 19$_{3}$, וּבַמֶּה תֵּאָסֵר לְעַנּוֹתֶךָ *and with what you might be bound that one could subdue you* Jg 16$_{6}$.

23d. functioning as participle, noun, etc. and not expressing purpose, e.g. וְהִנֵּה דְבַר־י׳ אֵלָיו לֵאמֹר *and behold the word of Y. came to him, saying* Gn 15$_{4}$, הַנִּצֶּבֶת עִמְּכָה בָּזֶה לְהִתְפַּלֵּל *who was standing by you here, praying* 1 S 1$_{26}$, לְהַקְשִׁיב מֵחֵלֶב אֵילִים *to listen is better than the fat of rams* 1 S 15$_{22}$, וַתַּעֲשֶׂה ... מַסֵּכוֹת לְהַכְעִיסֵנִי *and you made ... images, provoking me* 1 K 14$_{9}$, עוֹד הַיּוֹם בְּנֹב לַעֲמֹד *again today there is standing*, i.e. he will stop, *at Nob* Is 10$_{32}$, לִכְרָת־לוֹ אֲרָזִים *cutting cedars for himself* Is 44$_{14}$ (or em. הָלַךְ לִכְרָת *he has come to cut* or כָּרַת *he has cut* or יִכְרָת־ *he cuts*).

23e. introducing object clause,e.g. מָה י׳ ... שֹׁאֵל מֵעִמָּךְ כִּי אִם־לְיִרְאָה ... לָלֶכֶת ... וּלְאַהֲבָה *what does Y. ... ask of you except to fear ..., to go ..., and to love?* Dt 10$_{12}$.

*[לָא] n.[m.] **strength**, יֶשׁ־לָא לְיָדִי *there is strength to my hand*, i.e. I can Gn 31$_{29}$ (if em. יֶשׁ־לְאֵל יָדִי, i.e. אֵל II *strength*) Mc 2$_{1}$ (יָדָם *their hand*) Si 5$_{1}$ 14$_{11}$ (אם יש ... לא לידך *if there is ... strength to your hand*), אֵין לָא לְיָדֶךָ *there is no strength to your hand*, i.e. you cannot Dt 28$_{32}$ (if em. אֵין לְאֵל יָדֶךָ in same sense; mss יָדֶיךָ *your hands*) Ne 5$_{5}$ (יָדֵנוּ *our hand*; mss יָדֵינוּ *our hands*) 4QapLam[a] 1.1$_{2}$ (יָדֵנוּ), בִּהְיוֹת לָא לְיָדֶיךָ לַעֲשׂוֹת *when your hands have the strength to act*, i.e. when you can Pr 3$_{27(Qr)}$ (if em. לְאֵל יָדְךָ [Qr] in same sense).

⇒ לאה *be strong*.

*[לֵא] I adj. **hesitant**—לֵא(י)ם עַתָּה הֱיִיתֶם *now you have become hesitant* Jb 6$_{21}$ (if em. Kt לֹא *nothing*; Qr לוֹ *to him*; or em. לְאַל *as nothing*, or לִי *mine*).

⇒ לאה *be weary*.

לֹא I +5196.+173.+1092.9 negative part. **no(t)**—לוֹא, לֹה (Dt 3$_{11}$ [mss לֹא]), Q לוֹ).

1. followed by perfect:

a. introducing statement, p. 486a

b. in statements of consequence or cause, וְלֹא, בְּלֹא **so that not, seeing that not**, p. 486b

c. וְלֹא, בְּלֹא **but not**, p. 486b

d. in question, p. 486b

אִם־לֹא, הֲלֹא, אֵיךְ לֹא, מַדּוּעַ לֹא, לָמָּה לֹא, מִי לֹא, without introductory particle

e. in protasis, p. 487a

הִנֵּה לֹא, אֲשֶׁר־לֹא, אִם־לֹא

f. in apodosis, p. 487b

לוּלֵא, לוּ, אִם

g. with infinitive absolute and perfect, p. 487b

2. followed by imperfect:

a. in statement or assurance, p. 487b

b. in statements of consequence or purpose, p. 487b

לְמַעַן אֲשֶׁר לֹא, לְמַעַן לֹא, שֶׁלֹּא, אֲשֶׁר לֹא, וְלֹא, בְּשֶׁל שֶׁלֹּא, בְּלֹא

c. וְלֹא **but not**, p. 488a

d. in prohibition, p. 488b

e. אֲשֶׁר לֹא **not**, in prohibition in Qumran texts, p. 488b

f. in refusal or denial (1st person), p. 489a

g. in question, p. 489a

הֲלֹא, מָה לֹא, מַדּוּעַ לֹא, לָמָה/לָמָּה לֹא, עַד־מָתַי לֹא, עַד־אָנָה לֹא, כַּמָּה לֹא, מִי לֹא, without introductory particle

h. in protasis, p. 489b

אֲשֶׁר לֹא, אוּלַי לֹא, אִם־לֹא

i. in apodosis, p. 489b

לֹא with אִם, הִנֵּה, כִּי, לוּ, אֲשֶׁר, and הֲלֹא

j. with infinitive absolute and imperfect, p. 490a

3. followed by participle, p. 490a

4. with infinitive, p. 490b

5. followed by nominal clause, p. 490b
6. not followed by verb or nominal clause:
 a. noun or preposition, p. 491b
 b. **לֹא** with preposition and noun, p. 492a
 c. **לֹא** with preposition, p. 492a
 d. **בְּלֹא** **without, with non-, for non-, when it is not,** p. 492a
 e. adjective or adverb, p. 492a
7. **one that is not, has not,** p. 492b
8. as noun, **nothing,** p. 492b
9. as interjection, **no,** p. 492b
10. **הֲלֹא** modifying an entire clause, p. 492b
11. **וְלֹא** modifying an entire clause, p. 493a
12. Miscellaneous collocations:
 a. emphasis of negation not on verb; elliptical structures, p. 493a
 b. verb follows **לֹא** but not immediately, p. 493b
 c. **לֹא** plus verb combined with positive verb, p. 493b
 d. **אִם לֹא** in oaths, etc., p. 494a
 e. **לֹא ... כִּי**, p. 494a
 f. **לֹא ... עַד אֲשֶׁר**, **לֹא ... עַד**, etc., p. 494a
 g. **לֹא כִּי**, p. 494a
 h. Specific elliptical combinations, **אִם־לֹא**, **וָלֹא**, **אִם־לֹא**, p. 494b
 i. **לֹא ... כִּי אִם**, p. 494b
 j. **אִם־לֹא כִּי**, p. 494b
 k. **בְּטֶרֶם לֹא**, p. 494b
 l. Ketiv/Qere, p. 495a

לֹא is sometimes separated from the verb (many examples in Coll., §§1-2) and/or is associated with more than one verb, e.g. לֹא חֲמוֹר אֶחָד מֵהֶם נָשָׂאתִי *I have not taken one ass from them* Nm 16_{15}, לֹא בְמוֹתוֹ יִקַּח הַכֹּל *in his death he will not take anything* Ps 49_{18} (§2).

1. followed by perfect, **a.** usu. introducing factual statement of negative character, e.g. לֹא הִמְטִיר י׳ אֱלֹהִים *Y. God had not caused it to rain* Gn 2_{5}, לֹא יָדַעְתִּי *I do not know* Gn 4_{9}, עֶרְוַת אֲבִיהֶם לֹא רָאוּ *they did not see the nakedness of their father* Gen 9_{23}, Lachish ost. 2_{6} 3_{8} 6_{14} (ל[א] ה[י]ה *there was not*) Arad ost. 40_{8} ([לא נתן] *he did not give*) 40_{12} (י[לא נתת] *I did not give*), לֹא־טוֹב *it is not good* Gn 2_{18} Pr 17_{26} 18_{5} 25_{27} 28_{21}, כְּעֵגֶל לֹא לֻמָּד *like a calf that has not been trained* Jr 31_{18}.

1b. in statements implying consequence or cause, (1) **וְלֹא** **so that not, seeing that not,** e.g. כִּי הָיָה רְכוּשָׁם רָב וְלֹא יָכְלוּ לָשֶׁבֶת יַחְדָּו *for their possessions were great so that they could not live together* Gn 13_{6}, עַתָּה יָדַעְתִּי כִּי־יְרֵא אֱלֹהִים אַתָּה וְלֹא חָשַׂכְתָּ אֶת־בִּנְךָ *now I know that you fear God, seeing that you have not withheld your* only *son* Gn 22_{12}, Gn 35_{5} 36_{7} Nm 25_{11} Dt 3_{26} 1 S 14_{45} 2 K 11_{2}||2 C 22_{11}.

(2) **בְּלֹא** **so that not, seeing that not, unless,** נצר ק[ו]דש ... סותר בלוא נחשב ובלא נודע *the shoot of holiness ... (which) has been hidden so that it is not esteemed or known* 1QH 8_{10}, מה אזום בלוא חפצתה *how can I devise unless you have desired it* 1QH 10_{5}, 1QH $10_{6.6.7.7.19}$ 12_{34} 18_{19} 4QMyst[a] 8_{5} 4Q417 2.2_{14}.

1c. in adversative clauses, (1) **וְלֹא** **but not,** e.g. וָאֲדַבֵּר אֲלֵיכֶם וְלֹא שְׁמַעְתֶּם *and I spoke to you but you did not listen* Dt 1_{43}, Dt 1_{45} Jos 24_{10} Jg 2_{2} 6_{10} 8_{20} $11_{17.28}$ 12_{2} 19_{25} 1 S 9_{4} 13_{8} 22_{17} 23_{14} 31_{4}||1 C 10_{4} 2 S 13_{25} 17_{20} 22_{42}||Ps 18_{42} 2 S 23_{16}||1 C 11_{18} 1 K 22_{50} 2 K 2_{17} 8_{19}||2 C 21_{7} 2 K 14_{11}||2 C 25_{20} 2 K 17_{40} Is 7_{1} $65_{12.12}$ Jr 3_{7} $7_{13.13}$ 13_{11} 17_{23} $25_{3.4.7}$ 29_{11} 34_{14} $35_{14.15.17.17}$ 36_{31} 37_{14} 40_{14} 42_{21} 44_{5} 51_{9} Ezk $12_{2.2}$ Am $4_{6.8.9.10.11}$ Jon 1_{13} Zc 1_{4} $7_{13.13}$ Ca $3_{1.2}$ $5_{6.6}$ Ec 7_{28} Est 1_{17} Ezr 2_{62} Ne 9_{30} 1 C 27_{24} 2 C $24_{5.19.25}$ 33_{10}.

(2) **בְּלֹא** **but not,** ראה בלא הכיר *he has seen but not recognized* 1QH 8_{13}, ויחשוב בלא האמין *and he has considered but not believed* 1QH 8_{14}.

1d. in question, preceded by interrogative, (1) לָמָּה לֹא *why not?*, לָמָּה לֹא־הִגַּדְתָּ לִּי כִּי אִשְׁתְּךָ הִוא *why did you not tell me that she was your wife?* Gn 12_{18}, Gn 31_{27} 1 S 26_{15} 2 S 7_{7}||1 C 17_{6} 2 S 16_{17} 19_{26} Jr 29_{27}.

(2) **מַדּוּעַ לֹא** *why not?*, מַדּוּעַ לֹא כִלִּיתֶם חָקְכֶם לִלְבֹּן *why have you not completed your prescribed amount for making bricks?* Ex 5_{14}, Lv 10_{17} Nm 12_{8} Jg 11_{26} 1 S 20_{27} 2 S 11_{10} 18_{11} 1 K 2_{43} Jr 8_{22} Jb 24_{1}.

(3) **אֵיךְ לֹא** *how not?*, אֵיךְ לֹא יָרֵאתָ *how did you not fear?* 2 S 1_{14}, also Jr 49_{25}.

(4) **הֲלֹא** *did not?*, etc., e.g. הֲלֹא הוּא אָמַר־לִי *did he not say to me?* Gn 20_{5}, הֲלוֹא יָדַעְתָּ *do you not know?* Is 40_{28},

הֲלֹא שָׁלֹחַ שָׁלַחְתִּי אֵלֶיךָ *have I not sent to you?* Nm 22$_{37}$, Gn 27$_{36}$ 29$_{25}$ 44$_{15}$ Nm 12$_{2}$ 23$_{26}$ Jos 1$_{9}$ Jg 4$_{6.14}$ 6$_{14}$ 9$_{28}$ (if em. עִבְדוּ *serve* to עָבְדוּ *they served*) 10$_{11}$ (if ins. הוֹשַׁעְתִּי *have I* not *delivered?*) 15$_{11}$ 1 S 20$_{30}$ 2 S 2$_{26}$ 11$_{20}$ 19$_{23}$ 1 K 1$_{11.13}$ 18$_{13}$ 22$_{18}$‖2 C 18$_{17}$ 2 K 2$_{18}$ 4$_{28}$ 5$_{26}$ (if em. לֹא to הֲלֹא) 19$_{25}$‖Is 37$_{26}$ Is 40$_{21.21}$ Jr 13$_{21}$ 33$_{24}$ Ezk 12$_{9}$ 17$_{12}$ Zc 1$_{6}$ 4$_{5.13}$ Ml 2$_{10}$ Ps 14$_{4}$‖53$_{5}$ Jb 1$_{10}$ Pr 22$_{20}$ Ru 2$_{8.9}$ Si 46$_{4}$ 1QMyst 1.1$_{8.9}$ 4Q418 55$_{12}$ 4Q469 2$_{2}$.

(5) אִם־לֹא *did not?*, etc., e.g. אִם־לֹא בָכִיתִי לִקְשֵׁה־יוֹם עָגְמָה נַפְשִׁי לָאֶבְיוֹן *did I not weep for one whose day was hard, did not my soul grieve for the poor?* Jb 30$_{25}$, וְאִם לוֹא הַשְּׂחֹק הָיָה לְךָ יִשְׂרָאֵל *and was not Israel a derision to you?* Jr 48$_{27}$, הֲלוֹא יָדַעְתָּ אִם־לֹא שָׁמַעְתָּ *do you not know?, have you not heard?* Is 40$_{28}$, perh. אם לוא שמעתמה *have you not heard?* 4Q418 55$_{8}$, perh. ואם לא ירא *did he not fear?* Ḥorvat ʿUza bowl inscr.$_{4(Cross)}$.

(6) מִי לֹא *who not?*, מִי לֹא־יָדַע *who does not know?* Jb 12$_{9}$, עַל־מִי לֹא־עָבְרָה רָעָתְךָ *upon whom has your evil not come?* Na 3$_{19}$.

(7) without introductory particle, e.g. וְלֹא־הָיָה דְבָרִי רִאשׁוֹן *and was not my word the first?* 2 S 19$_{44}$, לֹא־לִבִּי הָלַךְ *did not my heart go?* 2 K 5$_{26}$ (or em. הֲלֹא, as §1d4), לא ידעתה קרא ספר *do you not know (how) to read a letter?* Lachish ost. 3$_{8}$.

1e. in protasis of conditional sentence, (1) אִם־לֹא *if not*, e.g. אִם־לֹא הֲבִיאֹתִיו אֵלֶיךָ ... וְחָטָאתִי לְךָ *if I have not brought him to you ... then I shall be guilty before you* Gn 43$_{9}$, perh. אִם־לֹא שָׁלַח יָדוֹ ... וְלָקַח בְּעָלָיו *if he has not extended his hand ... then its owner must take* Ex 22$_{10}$, ושב ... אם לא הלך עוד בשגגה *... and he is to return ... if he has not again walked in error* 4QS^{d} 3.1$_{1}$ (sim. 1QS 8$_{26}$), [ו]אם לוא השיגה ידו[ה די ... ו]המירה *and if her hand does not reach the sufficiency of*, i.e., if she cannot afford, a sheep ..., *then she is to exchange* the sheep 4QD^{a} 6.2$_{12(mg)}$, [ו]שלם האונס אם לא דבר א[מת] *and the oppressor will pay if he did not speak the truth* 4QD^{e} 6.3$_{14}$, [ו]אם לוא נגע בו [וטהור] *and if he did not touch it, then he will be pure* 4QTohC 1$_{5}$, Lv 25$_{28}$ Nm 5$_{19.19.28}$ Dt 21$_{14}$ 22$_{2}$=11QT 64$_{15}$ Jr 33$_{25}$ Jb 31$_{20}$ Pr 3$_{30}$ 4QD^{b} 7$_{5}$ 4QTohA 1.2$_{8}$ 4QTohC 1$_{5}$ CD 9$_{16}$.

(2) אֲשֶׁר־לֹא *if not*, e.g. אֲשֶׁר לֹא צָדָה ... וְשַׂמְתִּי לְךָ מָקוֹם *if he did not lie in wait ... then I shall appoint for you a place* Ex 21$_{13}$, אֲשֶׁר־לֹא־גָזַלְתִּי אָז אָשִׁיב perh. *if I have not stolen, then do I repay?* Ps 69$_{5}$.

(3) הִנֵּה לֹא *if not*, e.g. הִנֵּה לֹא־פָשָׂה הַנֶּתֶק ... וְהִתְגַּלָּח *if the itch has not spread ... then he will shave himself* Lv 13$_{32}$, Lv 13$_{5.6.34.53.55}$ 14$_{48}$.

1f. in apodosis of conditional sentence introduced by (1) אִם לֹא *if not, though not*, e.g. אִם־שׁוֹב תָּשׁוּב בְּשָׁלוֹם לֹא־דִבֶּר י׳ בִּי *if you indeed return in peace, Y. has not spoken through me* 1 K 22$_{28}$‖2 C 18$_{27}$, ואם ינוח לא נחה לו *and even though he rests*, i.e. stops, *he has found no (real) rest* Si 34$_{4}$.

(2) לוּ לֹא *if not*, לוּ חָפֵץ י׳ לַהֲמִיתֵנוּ לֹא־לָקַח מִיָּדֵנוּ עֹלָה *if Y. wished to kill us, he would not have taken from our hands a burnt offering* Jg 13$_{23}$.

(3) לוּלֵא *if not*, לוּלֵא חֲרַשְׁתֶּם בְּעֶגְלָתִי לֹא מְצָאתֶם חִידָתִי *if you had not ploughed with my heifer, you would not have found (the meaning of) my riddle* Jg 14$_{18}$.

1g. לֹא with infinitive absolute and perfect, e.g. הַצֵּל לֹא־הִצַּלְתָּ אֶת־עַמֶּךָ *you have by no means delivered your people* Ex 5$_{23}$, כי אם דמה יצוא [לא יצא] *unless her blood has indeed not issued* 4QD^{e} 4$_{4}$ (unless impf., יֵצֵא, as §2i), Nm 22$_{37}$ Jos 17$_{13}$ Jg 1$_{28}$.

2. followed by imperfect, **a.** usu. in factual or descriptive statement or assurance, e.g. וְלֹא יִתְבֹּשָׁשׁוּ *and they were not ashamed* Gn 2$_{25}$, עָרֵל זָכָר אֲשֶׁר לֹא־יִמּוֹל אֶת־בְּשַׂר עָרְלָתוֹ *an uncircumcised male who is not circumcised in the flesh of his foreskin* Gn 17$_{14}$, לֹא־אֹסִף לְקַלֵּל עוֹד אֶת־הָאֲדָמָה *I shall never again curse the ground* Gn 8$_{21}$, ולו[ן י]שוב [עוד] *and he is to return no more* 4QD^{a} 10.2$_{1}$, כי לא נראה את עזקה *for we cannot see Azekah* Lachish ost. 4$_{12}$.

2b. in statements of consequence or purpose:

(1) וְלֹא or ... וְ ... לֹא **so that not, lest**, e.g. וְלֹא תֹאמַר אֲנִי הֶעֱשַׁרְתִּי אֶת־אַבְרָם *so that you may not say, I have made Abram rich* Gn 14$_{23}$, הַרְבָּה אַרְבֶּה אֶת־זַרְעֵךְ וְלֹא יִסָּפֵר מֵרֹב *I shall indeed multiply your seed so that it cannot be counted for multitude* Gn 16$_{10}$, Gn 9$_{11.11}$ 14$_{23}$ 41$_{36}$ Ex 28$_{32}$‖39$_{23}$ 28$_{35.43}$ 30$_{12.20.21}$ 39$_{21}$ Lv 8$_{35}$ 10$_{6.9}$ 14$_{36}$ 15$_{31}$ 16$_{2.13}$ 18$_{21.28.30}$ 19$_{29}$ 20$_{14.22}$ 21$_{12.15.23}$ 22$_{2.9}$ Nm 1$_{53}$ 5$_{3}$ 8$_{19}$ 11$_{17}$ 14$_{42}$ 17$_{25}$ 18$_{3.5.32}$ 27$_{17}$ 35$_{12}$ Dt 14$_{2}$ 17$_{17}$ 18$_{16}$ 19$_{10}$ 22$_{8}$ 23$_{15}$ 24$_{15}$ 25$_{6}$ Jos 9$_{20}$ 20$_{9}$ 22$_{27}$ Jg 21$_{17}$ 1 S 5$_{11}$ 20$_{14}$ (or em. לֻא *would that* you do) 29$_{4.7}$ 2 S 13$_{25}$ 14$_{11}$ 21$_{17}$ 2 S 22$_{39}$

‖Ps 18_{39} 1 K 14_{2} 18_{44} 2 K 18_{32} Jr 11_{21} 25_{6} 37_{20} Ezk 3_{25} 18_{30} 44_{19} Jon 1_{6} 3_{9} Ml 1_{10} 3_{11} Jb 19_{8} Pr 8_{29} Ru 2_{22} 4_{10} Lm 3_{7} Est 1_{19} 9_{27} 2 C $19_{10.10}$ 23_{19} 24_{20} 1QS 5_{26} 11QT 45_{13} $46_{10.15}$ CD 9_{8} 12_{22} 15_{4}.

(2) **אֲשֶׁר לֹא so that not, lest,** e.g. אֲשֶׁר לֹא יִשְׁמְעוּ אִישׁ שְׂפַת רֵעֵהוּ *so that one may not hear*, i.e. understand, *the speech of one's neighbour* Gn 11_{7}, אַשְׁבִּיעֲךָ ... אֲשֶׁר לֹא־תִקַּח אִשָּׁה *I adjure you ... not to take a wife* Gn 24_{3}, אֲנִי מַשְׁבִּעֶךָ אֲשֶׁר לֹא־תְדַבֵּר אֵלַי רַק־אֱמֶת *I adjure you not to speak to me anything but the truth* 1 K 22_{16}‖2 C 18_{15}, Ex 20_{26} Ec 7_{21} Si 50_{24} 4QTohA 1.1_{6} (בעבור אשר ל[ו]א) 4QpsMos^{e} 1_{9} (למען אשר לא [יוכ]ל[ו] *so that they may not be consumed*) 11QT $48_{15.16}$ 57_{11} 58_{9} 62_{16} CD $12_{7.9}$.

(3) **שֶׁלֹּא so that not, lest,** שֶׁלֹּא יִמְצָא הָאָדָם *so that a human being may not find* Ec 7_{14}, also Si $30_{34.36}$ MurEp-Beth-Mashiko$_{6}$.

(4) **לְמַעַן לֹא, לְמַעַן אֲשֶׁר לֹא so that not, lest,** לְמַעַן לֹא־יִשָּׁמַע קוֹלוֹ *so that his voice may not be heard* Ezk 19_{9}, עשה אתה בי משפט למען לא נבדו ענוים ורשים *make judgment for me so that the humble and poor do not die* 4QapJoseph^{b} 1_{17}, והשארתי מהם פליטים למען אשר לא [יוכ]ל[ו] בחמתי *and I shall let some of them remain as survivors so that they cannot prevail against my anger* 4QpsMos^{e} 1_{9} (PC [יכ]ל[ו] so that they *are not destroyed* by), also Dt 20_{18} (לְמַעַן אֲשֶׁר לֹא) Ezk 14_{11} 25_{10} 26_{20} Zc 12_{7} Ps $119_{11.80}$ 125_{3} Si 38_{8} 45_{26}.

(5) **בְּלֹא so that not, with the result that not,** נְגֹאֲלוּ בַּדָּם בְּלֹא יוּכְלוּ יִגְּעוּ בִּלְבֻשֵׁיהֶם *they were defiled with blood so that no one could touch their garments* Lm 4_{14}.

(6) **בְּשֶׁל שֶׁלֹּא so that not,*** [לבני] הכוהנ[ים] ראו להזהיר ... בשל שלוא י[היו] מסיא[י]ם את העם עוון *it is fitting for the (sons of the) priests to be careful ... so that they do not cause the people to bear iniquity* 4QMMT B_{12}.

2c. וְלֹא in adversative clause, **but not,** e.g. אוֹ נוֹדַע כִּי שׁוֹר נַגָּח הוּא ... וְלֹא יִשְׁמְרֶנּוּ *or if it was known that the ox was in the habit of goring ... but he did not keep it in* Ex 21_{36}, וַאֲכַלְתֶּם וְלֹא תִשְׂבָּעוּ *and you will eat but not be satisfied* Lv 26_{26}, Dt 21_{18} $28_{30.30.31.31.41}$ 1 S 2_{25} Is 41_{12} Jr 1_{19} $7_{27.27}$ 11_{11} Ezk 26_{21} Ho $2_{9.9}$ $4_{10.10}$ 5_{6} Am $5_{11.11}$ 8_{12} Mc 3_{4} $6_{14.14.15.15.15}$ Hb $1_{2.2}$ Zp $1_{13.13}$ Ps 22_{3} $115_{5.5.6.6.7.7}$ $135_{16.16.17}$ Jb $14_{21.21}$ $19_{7.16}$ 30_{20} 35_{12} Pr $1_{28.28}$ 21_{13} Ec 8_{17} 4QpsEzek^{b} 1.2_{4}.

2d. in prohibition, instruction, or plea (2nd or 3rd person; distinction from §2a not alw. clear) followed by imperfect (rarely, jussive: Gn 24_{8} Dt 13_{1}), e.g. לֹא תֹאכְלוּ מִכֹּל עֵץ הַגָּן *you are not to eat of any tree in the garden* Gn 3_{1}, כָּל־מְלָאכָה לֹא־יֵעָשֶׂה *no work is to be done* Ex 12_{16}, לוא יומת כיא צדיק הואה *he is not to die, for he is righteous* 4QapMos^{a} 1.1_{6}, ולא תשלח *and do not send* Arad ost. 16_{10} (others ישלח and *he will* not *send*), ולא תדהם perh. *and be not idle* Meṣad Ḥashavyahu ost. 1_{14}, מעשה אשר לוא יעשה עוד *a deed that should not be done again* 4QMyst^{a} 3a.2_{6}, Gn 2_{17} $3_{3.3.17}$ 9_{4} 24_{37} $28_{1.6}$ Ex $5_{7.8.19}$ 12_{10} $13_{3.7.7}$ $19_{13.13}$ 20_{3} 22_{17} 23_{1} $24_{2.2}$ 25_{15} $29_{33.34}$ 30_{9} 34_{3} 35_{3} Lv 1_{17} $2_{11.11.13}$ 3_{17} $4_{2.13.22.27}$ $5_{11.11.17}$ $6_{5.6.10.16.23}$ $7_{15.19.23.24.26}$ 8_{33} $10_{6.7}$ 11_{4} $12_{4.4}$ $13_{11.33}$ 16_{29} $17_{12.12.14}$ 18_{3} 19_{4} $20_{19.23.25}$ 21_{1} 22_{6} 23_{3} 25_{4} $26_{1.1.1}$ 27_{10} Nm $1_{49.49}$ 4_{15} $5_{15.15}$ 6_{3} $8_{25.26}$ 9_{12} 10_{7} 18_{4} 20_{20} $22_{12.12}$ $28_{18.25}$ $29_{1.7.12.35}$ 30_{3} $35_{30.31.32.33.34}$ $36_{7.9}$ Dt 1_{17} 3_{22} $4_{2.2}$ 5_{7} $6_{14.16}$ 7_{2} 10_{16} 12_{4} $13_{1.1}$=11QT $54_{6.6}$ Dt $13_{16.17}$=11QT $55_{10.10}$ Dt 14_{1} 15_{2} 16_{3} $17_{1.11.15.16.16.17.17.17}$=11QT $56_{7.15.15.16.18.18.19}$ Dt $18_{1.2.9.10}$=11QT $60_{16.17}$ Dt 18_{22}=11QT 61_{4} Dt $19_{13.14.15.21}$=11QT 61_{11} Dt 20_{1}=11QT 61_{13} Dt $20_{16.19.19}$ $21_{16.23.23}$=11QT $64_{11.12}$ Dt 22_{1}=11QT 64_{13} Dt $22_{6.8}$ =11QT $65_{4.6}$ Dt $22_{26.29}$=11QT $66_{6.11}$ Dt $23_{1.1}$=11QT $66_{11.12}$ Dt 24_{4} 25_{3} 27_{5} $31_{8.8}$ Jos $6_{10.10.10}$ 20_{5} $23_{7.7.7.7}$ Jg 2_{2} 6_{10} 13_{14} 19_{24} 1 S 12_{21} 14_{34} 15_{3} 20_{15} 22_{5} $29_{4.9}$ 30_{23} 2 S 5_{23}‖1 C 14_{14} 2 S 21_{17} 1 K $2_{6.36}$ 3_{27} $11_{2.2}$ $12_{24.24}$‖2 C $11_{4.4}$ 1 K $13_{9.17}$ $18_{23.25}$ 20_{8} 22_{31}‖2 C 18_{30} 2 K 2_{16} $4_{28.29.29}$ 6_{22} 9_{3} 10_{19} $14_{6.6}$‖2 C $25_{4.4}$ 2 K 17_{12} 18_{36}‖Is 36_{21} Is 1_{13} 3_{7} $8_{12.12.12}$ $30_{10.10}$ Jr 11_{21} 13_{1} $16_{2.8}$ $17_{22.22}$ 23_{38} 25_{6} $35_{6.7.7.7.7}$ 43_{2} Ezk $3_{9.9}$ 18_{13} 20_{39} 24_{16} 42_{14} 44_{2} $46_{2.9.18}$ Ho $3_{3.3}$ Am 2_{12} $5_{5.5}$ $7_{13.16.16}$ Ml 2_{16} Ps $81_{10.10}$ Jb 38_{11} Pr 22_{24} Ru $2_{8.15.16}$ Lm 1_{10} Ezr 9_{12} Ne 7_{3} 13_{1} 1 C 17_{4} 22_{8} 28_{3} 2 C 8_{11} 23_{14} 28_{13} Si $4_{4.5}$ 7_{30} 9_{13} 11_{33} $34_{16(Bmg)}$ 1QS $2_{8.8.9.23.23}$ $3_{1.2}$ $5_{16.16.18}$ $6_{16.20}$ 7_{2+5t} $8_{23.23.25}$ $9_{1.9}$ 1QSa 1_{9} 4QSD 7.1_{8} 4QD^{a} 6.1_{9} 11_{6} 4QD^{e} 6.4_{18} (=CD 10_{7} אַל *not*) 4QD^{f} 3_{5} 4QapMos^{a} 1.1_{6} 4QWays^{a} 1a.2_{1} 11QT 2_{8} (ל[ו]א) $2_{9.11}$ $17_{11.16}$ $20_{12.13}$ 25_{9} $27_{6.9}$ 32_{14} 35_{12} 37_{11} 39_{7} $43_{4.11.15.17}$ 45_{4+7t} $47_{8.9.13.14.17}$ 48_{6+7t} 51_{6+7t} 52_{1+14t} $53_{6.15}$ 57_{14+6t} $58_{11.18.20}$ 62_{13} $63_{14.15}$ 66_{12+5t} CD $5_{2.9}$ $7_{1.3}$ $9_{2.2.9}$ 11_{23} 12_{4} $20_{13.30}$.

2e. אֲשֶׁר לֹא *not*, in prohibition, in Qumran texts* (cf. §4a), e.g. אשר לוא ילך איש בשרירות לבו *a man is not to* go in the stubbornness of his heart 1QS 5_{4}, אשר לא יוכיח איש ולא יתרובב *a man is not to reprove or to enter dispute* 4QS[d] 3.2_{1} (=1QS 9_{16} אשר לא with inf., as §4a), also 1QS $5_{4.14.15}$ (אשר לוא יוכל *one must not eat*; perh. = 4QS[d] 1.1_{8} ואל יוכל in same sense) 5_{16} 8_{25}.

2f. in refusal or denial (1st person), e.g. לֹא נֵלֵךְ *we shall not go* Jg 20_{8}, לֹא אָשׁוּב עִמָּךְ *I shall not return with you* 1 S 15_{26}, Jg 20_{8} 1 S 24_{11} 28_{23} 30_{22} 1 K $13_{8.8.8.16.16}$ $21_{4.6}$ 2 K 10_{5} Is 3_{7} $7_{12.12}$ Jr $2_{20.31}$ $6_{16.17}$ 22_{21} 35_{6} Am $5_{21.22.23}$ Zc 11_{9} Jb 32_{21} Ne 6_{11} 1QS $10_{19.20.20.21.21}$ 4QD[a] 11_{4} 4QpsEzek[c] 3.2_{2} 11QT $59_{6.6}$.

2g. in question, usu. preceded by interrogative particle, (1) לָמָה/לָמֶה לֹא *why not?*, לָמֶה לֹא תֹאכְלִי *why do you not eat?* 1 S 1_{8}, also 1 S 6_{3} Jb 3_{11}.

(2) מַדּוּעַ לֹא *why not?*, מַדּוּעַ לֹא־יִבְעַר הַסְּנֶה *why does the bush not burn?* Ex 3_{3}, also Jb 21_{4} Ne 2_{3}.

(3) מֶה לֹא *why not?*, מֶה לֹא־תִשָּׂא פִשְׁעִי *why do you not pardon my transgression?* Jb 7_{21}.

(4) הֲלֹא *do not?*, etc. (or in a clause introduced by interrogative -הֲ), e.g. הֲלוֹא תֵדְעוּ הֲלוֹא תִשְׁמָעוּ *do you not know?, did you not hear?* Is 40_{21}, הַאַף תִּסְפֶּה וְלֹא־תִשָּׂא לַמָּקוֹם *will you also destroy and not spare the place?* Gn 18_{24}, הֲשֹׁפֵט כָּל־הָאָרֶץ לֹא יַעֲשֶׂה מִשְׁפָּט *will the judge of all the earth not do justice?* Gn 18_{25}, הַדְּרָכַי לֹא יִתָּכְנוּ *are my ways not right?* Ezk $18_{29(mss)}$, Nm 12_{14} Jg 5_{30} 1 S 26_{14} 2 S 3_{38} 13_{4} 2 K 5_{12} 6_{11} Is 8_{19} $40_{21.21}$ 43_{19} 48_{6} Jr 5_{29} 9_{8} 13_{12} 18_{6} 38_{15} Ezk 13_{12} 24_{19} 34_{2} 37_{18} Am 8_{8} Ob$_{5.5}$ Mc 2_{7} Ps 85_{7} $94_{9.9.10}$ Jb 11_{2} Ru 3_{1} Ezr 9_{14} 2 C 20_{12} 32_{13} Si 32_{18} 4Q392 1_{8} 4QapPs[b] $13_{2.2}$ 4QapMes 2.2_{4} Lachish ost. 6_{8}.

(5) כַּמָּה לֹא *for how long not?*, i.e. how long until?, כַּמָּה לֹא־תִשְׁעֶה מִמֶּנִּי *how long until you look away from me?* Jb 7_{19}.

(6) עַד־אָנָה לֹא *for how long not?*, i.e. how long until?, עַד־אָנָה לֹא־יַאֲמִינוּ בִי *for how long will they not believe in me?* Nm 14_{11}, עַד־אָנָה לֹא תִשְׁקֹטִי *how long until you are quiet?* Jr 47_{6}.

(7) עַד־מָתַי לֹא *for how long not?*, i.e. how long until?, עַד־מָתַי לֹא־תֹאמַר *how long will you not say?* 2 S 2_{26}, עַד־מָתַי לֹא יוּכְלוּ נִקָּיֹן *how long will they be incapable of innocence?* Ho 8_{5}, עַד־מָתַי אַתָּה לֹא־תְרַחֵם *for how long will you not show mercy?* Zc 1_{12}.

(8) מִי לֹא *who not?*, מִי לֹא יִרָאֲךָ *who will not fear you?* Jr 10_{7}, אַרְיֵה שָׁאָג מִי לֹא יִירָא אֲדֹנָי י׳ דִּבֶּר מִי לֹא יִנָּבֵא *the lion roars, who is not afraid?; my Lord Y. has spoken, who will not prophesy?* Am 3_{8}, עַל־מִי לֹא־יָקוּם אוֹרֵהוּ *over whom does his light not rise?* Jb 25_{3}.

(9) without interrogative particle, e.g. וְלֹא יִסְקְלֻנוּ *and will they not stone us?* Ex 8_{22}, וְלֹא־אָז אֶשְׁלַח אֵלֶיךָ *shall I not then send to you?* 1 S 29_{12}, Ho 10_{9} Jon 4_{11}.

2h. in protasis of conditional sentence, (1) אִם־לֹא *if not, although not*,* e.g. אִם־לֹא יִתְּנוּ לָךְ וְהָיִיתָ נָקִי מֵאָלָתִי *if they will not give (her) to you, then you will be free of my oath* Gn 24_{41}, ואם לא ימצא נאמן *or if he would not be found faithful* 4QpsJub[a] 2.2_{8}, ואם לוא לא תשיג ידו *and if his hand does not reach*, i.e. if he is unable 4Q418 126.2_{13}, אם לא [יפחדו] ... [ישפוט] י׳ *if they do not fear, ... Y. will judge* 11QPsAp[a] 2_{9}, Gn 24_{8} 34_{17} 42_{37} $44_{23.32}$ Ex $4_{8.8.9.9}$ 13_{13} 21_{11} 22_{7} 34_{20} 40_{37} Lv $5_{1.7.11}$ 12_{8} 17_{16} $25_{30.54}$ $26_{14.18.23.27}$ $27_{20.27}$ Nm 19_{12} $32_{23.30}$ 33_{55} Dt 11_{28} 20_{12}=11QT 62_{8} Dt 24_{1} 25_{7} $28_{15.58}$ Jos 2_{14} 7_{12} Jg 4_{8} 14_{13} 1 S 12_{15} Is 7_{9} Jr 12_{17} 13_{17} 17_{27} 22_{5} 26_{4} 38_{18} Zc 14_{18} Ml $2_{2.2}$ Ps 7_{13} 59_{16} $127_{1.1}$ $137_{6.6}$ Jb 36_{12} Pr $4_{16.16}$ Ru 3_{13} 4_{4} Ca 1_{8} Si $11_{10.10}$ 1QS 7_{8} 4QCommGenA 3_{5} 4QSD 1.2_{5} perh. 4QpsEzek[c] 2_{9} 4Q418 126.2_{13} 11QT 43_{13} 50_{7} CD 6_{14}.

(2) אוּלַי לֹא *suppose that not*, אוּלַי לֹא־תֹאבֶה הָאִשָּׁה לָלֶכֶת *suppose that the woman is not willing to go* Gn 24_{5}, sim. Gn 24_{39}.

(3) אֲשֶׁר לֹא *if*, e.g. אֲשֶׁר לֹא־יַעֲלֶה ... וְלֹא עֲלֵיהֶם יִהְיֶה הַגָּשֶׁם *if any one does not go up ... there will be no rain upon them* Zc 14_{17}.

2i. in apodosis of conditional sentence introduced by (1) אִם *if, though*, e.g. אִם־אַחֶרֶת יִקַּח־לוֹ שְׁאֵרָהּ ... לֹא יִגְרָע *if he takes another (wife) to himself, he will not diminish ... her food* Ex 21_{10}, אם ישבע לוא [י]עמוד *if he swears, it will not stand* 4QJub[h] 35_{15}, perh. ואם תחסור לוא *and if you lack, do not* 4Q417 1.1_{19} (unless לוא = *[then] borrow*), אם קראתי אתה [ול]א אתננה *if I have read it (once), I do not do it again* Lachish ost. 3_{12} (others ואחר *then afterwards I can repeat it*), Ex 21_{21} $22_{14.24}$ 40_{37} Lv 7_{18} 27_{20} Nm 19_{12} 22_{18} 24_{13} $30_{6.13}$ Dt 24_{12} Jos 7_{12} Jg 4_{8} 13_{16} perh. 1 S 20_{14} (or em. וְלֻא *and if*) 2 S $18_{3.3}$ 1 K 1_{52} 2_{4} 13_{8} 2 K 2_{10} Is 7_{9} Jr 49_{9} Am 5_{22} Zc 14_{18} Ps 27_{3} 50_{12} 66_{1} Jb $9_{3.15.16}$ 16_{6} 34_{32} Pr 3_{24} $4_{12.16}$ Ec 8_{17} Si 9_{13} $11_{10.10.\ 10(B).\ 10(B)}$ ([ול]א) $12_{15.15.16}$ 16_{21} 4QD[a] 10.1_{1} 11QT $53_{11.12.21}$

59_{17} CD 6_{14} 9_{12}.

(2) הִנֵּה *if*, e.g. הִנֵּה פָּשָׂה הַנֶּתֶק בָּעוֹר לֹא־יְבַקֵּר הַכֹּהֵן *if the itch has spread in the skin, the priest will not seek* the yellow hair Lv 13_{36}.

(3) כִּי *if*, e.g. כִּי תֶחְדַּל לִנְדֹּר לֹא־יִהְיֶה בְךָ חֵטְא *if you refrain from vowing, there will be no sin in you* Dt 23_{23}, Dt 13_4=11QT 54_{10} Jr 38_{15} Ps 23_4 (גַּם כִּי *even though*).

(4) לוּ *if*, לוּ אָנֹכִי שֹׁקֵל עַל־כַּפַּי אֶלֶף כֶּסֶף לֹא־אֶשְׁלַח יָדִי *if I were to weigh out in my hand a thousand pieces of silver, I would not put forth my hand* against the king's son 2 S $18_{12(Qr)}$ (Kt לא I am *not* weighing).

(5) אֲשֶׁר *if, when*, e.g. וַאֲשֶׁר שָׁכַב לֹא־יוֹסִיף לָקוּם perh. *and if he lies down he will not arise again* Ps 41_9, אֲשֶׁר לֹא־יַעֲלֶה ... וְלֹא עֲלֵיהֶם יִהְיֶה הַגָּשֶׁם *if any one does not go up ... there will be no rain upon them* Zc 14_{17}.

(6) without introductory particle, e.g. דָּבָר גָּדוֹל הַנָּבִיא דִּבֶּר הֲלוֹא תַעֲשֶׂה *if the prophet had spoken a great thing, would you not have done (it)?* 2 K 5_{13} (or ins. אִם *if*).

2j. לֹא with infinitive absolute and imperfect, (1) לֹא before inf. abs., e.g. לֹא־מוֹת תְּמֻתוּן *you will certainly not die* Gn 3_4, 2 K $8_{10(Kt)}$ Jr 3_1 38_{15} Am 9_8 Ps 49_8; (2) לֹא after inf. abs., e.g. הַרְחֵק לֹא־תַרְחִיקוּ לָלֶכֶת *you are not to go a great distance* Ex 8_{24}, Ex 34_7 Lv 7_{24} Nm 14_{18} $23_{25.25}$ Dt 21_{14} Jg 15_{13} 1 K 3_{27} Is 30_{19} Jr 8_{12} 11_{12} 13_{12} 23_{32} 30_{11} 46_{28} Ezk 20_{32} Am 3_5 Na 1_3.

3. followed by participle, **a.** לֹא, e.g. לֹא מְבַקֵּשׁ רָעָתוֹ *he was not seeking his harm* Nm 35_{23}, לֹא נְבוֹנִים הֵמָּה *they do not understand* Jr 4_{22}, לא נכון *it is not certain* 1QH 4_{18}, יָדֶךָ לֹא־אֲסֻרוֹת *your hands were not bound* 2 S 3_{34}, בְּאֶרֶץ לֹא זְרוּעָה *in a land not sown* Jr 2_2, also Dt 4_{42} $19_{4.6}$ Jos 20_5 2 S $18_{12(Kt)}$ 1 K 10_{21} Is 33_1 Jr 18_{15} Ezk 4_{14} 16_{16} 22_{24} Zp 2_1 3_5 Ps 38_{15} $78_{8.37}$ Jb 12_3 13_2 Ezr $4_{2(Kt)}$ Si 15_{20} 4Q416 5_2 5/6ḤevEp 12_4 CD 9_{11}.

3b. הֲלֹא **is not?**, etc., e.g. הֲלוֹא דָוִד מִסְתַּתֵּר עִמָּנוּ *is not David hiding with us?* 1 S 23_{19}, הֲלוֹא־הֵם כְּתֻבִים *are they not written?* 1 K 11_{41}‖2 C 9_{29} 2 C $25_{26(mss)}$, Gn 37_{13} Jos 10_{13} 1 S 26_1 2 S 11_{10} 1 K 14_{29}‖2 C 12_{15} 1 K $15_{7.23.31}$ $16_{5.14.20.27}$ $22_{39.46}$ 2 K 1_{18} 8_{23} 10_{34} 12_{20} $13_{8.12}$ 14_{15} 14_{18}‖2 C 25_{26} 2 K 14_{28} $15_{6.21.36}$ 16_{19} 20_{20} $21_{17.25}$ 23_{28} 24_5 Is 57_{11} Jr 23_{24} Ps 54_2 Pr 26_{19} Est 10_2 Si 42_{22} 4QpsEzek[a] 3_3.

3c. בְּלֹא **without, not,** e.g. אָכְלוּ אֶת־הַפֶּסַח בְּלֹא כַכָּתוּב *they ate the passover not as prescribed* 2 C 30_{18}, בלוא נכון perh. *not being what is right* 4QBéat 11_2.

3d. בְּשֶׁלֹּא **while not,** בשלא עושה *while not doing*, i.e. cultivating, *(it)* Mur 24 2_{11}.

4. with infinitive,* **a.** לֹא, לֹא לְהַזְכִּיר בְּשֵׁם י׳ *one must not mention the name of Y.* Am 6_{10}, לֹא־לָכֶם וָלָנוּ לִבְנוֹת *it is not for you and for us to build* Ezr 4_3, לֹא לְהַשְׁחִית לְכָלָה *so as not to destroy completely* 2 C 12_{12}, ואמלא לשר להש[ב את בגד] עב[דה] perh. *and if it is not for the official*, i.e. if you do not feel obliged, *to return the garment of his servant*, then have pity upon me Meṣad Ḥashavyahu ost. 1_{12} (unless ואמלא *and if not*, i.e. if I am not innocent, or *and I shall pay* or *and I shall appeal* or *then I shall be vindicated*), ושלוא לזרוע שדו perh. *and no one is to sow their field* 4QMMT B_{78} (cf. §2d, unless construction is כתוב ... ש- *it is written ... that*), ולא לסור מחוקי אמתו *and no one is to turn from the statutes of his truth* 1QS 1_{15}, ואשר לוא להוכיח ולהתרובב *and one is not to reprove or to enter dispute* (cf. §2d) 1QS 9_{16}, ואם לו ליוסף מן החי[ות] *or if there is not to be added from the living (hairs)* 4QD[a] 6.1_{11} (ליוסף appar. error for inf. לְהוֹסִף or, as §2g1, impf. יוֹסִף); also Jg 1_{19} Jr $4_{11.11}$ 1 C 5_1 15_2 2 C 20_{17} 26_{18} Si 11_{29} 1QH 7_{15} ([לוא]) 10_{15} 12_{24} fr. 2_{12} fr. 5_{14} 1QS $1_{6.13.14.14.17}$ 3_{10} 4QTohB[a] 2_4 4Q392 1_2 4QMMT B_{77} 4Q416 2.4_7 perh. 4QMyst[a] $3a.2_4$ CD 2_{16} 7_2.

4b. הֲלֹא **is it not?**, e.g. הֲלוֹא לָכֶם לָדַעַת *is it not for you to know?* Mc 3_1 2 C 13_5, הֲלוֹא טוֹב לָנוּ שׁוּב *is it not better for us to go back?* Nm 14_3.

4c. בְּלֹא (1) **without,** בְּלֹא רְאוֹת *without seeing* Nm 35_{23}, בלוא הוכח *without reproaching* 4Q417 1_2.

(2) **so that not,** ותוסף לשונם כחרב אל תערה בלו[א כר]תה נפש עבדכה *their tongue is drawn in as a sword into its sheath, so that it might not cut off the soul of your servant* 1QH 5_{15}.

4d. אֲשֶׁר לֹא perh. **so that not,** אשר לא להכיחו עדותיך *that your testimonies might not reprove him* 4QapJoseph[b] 1_{28}.

5. followed by nominal clause, **a.** לֹא, e.g. לֹא מְרַגְּלִים אַתֶּם *you are not spies* Gn 42_{34}, לֹא מִזַּרְעֲךָ הוּא *he is not of your offspring* Gn 17_{12}, לֹא כַנָּשִׁים הַמִּצְרִיֹּת הָעִבְרִיֹּת *the Hebrew women are not like the Egyptian women* Ex 1_{19}, לֹא־אֲדֹנִים לָאֵלֶּה *there are no masters to these*, i.e. they have no masters 1 K 22$_{17}$||2 C 18$_{16}$, וְהוּא לֹא־אֹיֵב לוֹ *and he was not an enemy to him* Nm 35 $_{23}$, לֹא־רוּחַ בָּם *there is no spirit in them* Jr 10$_{14}$, לא רמיה [ב]מזמת לבכה *there is no deceit in the purpose of your heart* 1QH 4$_{21}$, אין משכלה בארצכם [ו]לוא מחלה *there are no miscarriages in your land nor sickness* 11QBer 1$_{11}$, דְּבָרָיו לֹא בְהַשְׂכֵּיל *his words are without insight* Jb 34$_{35}$, לֹא כָזֹאת בִּירוּשָׁלָםִ *there had been nothing like this in Jerusalem* 2 C 30$_{26}$, כִּי לֹא מִמּוֹצָא וּמִמַּעֲרָב וְלֹא מִמִּדְבַּר הָרִים *for not from east or from west and not from the steppe is there lifting up* Ps 75$_{7(mss)}$ (or em. twice לֻא *if only* there were; L מִמִּדְבַּר and not *from the steppe of* mountains), לֹא־בִישִׁישִׁים חָכְמָה *wisdom is not (found) among the aged* Jb 12$_{11}$ (if em. : לוֹ *for itself.* Wisdom is found among the aged),* לֹא בְקָרוֹב בְּנוֹת בָּתִּים *the building of houses is not (as) near* Ezk 11$_{3}$, שָׁכְרוּ וְלֹא־יַיִן *they become drunk but there was no wine* Is 29$_{9}$, לא לכל טוב תענוג *not in every good thing is there delight* Si 37$_{28}$, לֹא עֹזֵר לָמוֹ perh. *may they have no helper* Jb 30$_{13}$ (or em. עֹצֵר *there is no one restraining them*),* Gn 17$_{12}$ Ex 4$_{10}$ 16$_{8}$ Nm 17$_{5}$ 23$_{19.23.23}$ Dt 11$_{10}$ 17$_{15}$=11QT 56$_{15}$ Dt 20$_{15}$=11QT 62$_{12}$ Dt 20$_{20}$ 30$_{12.13}$ perh. 32$_{5.20.31.47}$ Jg 19$_{12}$ 1 S 15$_{29}$ 2 S 18$_{20}$ 21$_{2}$ 1 K 8$_{41}$||2 C 6$_{32}$ 1 K 9$_{20}$||2 C 8$_{7}$ 1 K 12$_{16}$||2 C 10$_{16}$ 1 K 19$_{11.11.12}$ 20$_{28}$ 22$_{33}$ 2 K 6$_{19.19}$ 19$_{18}$||Is 37$_{19}$ Is 8$_{23}$ 22$_{2}$ 27$_{11}$ 31$_{3}$ 53$_{2}$ 55$_{8.8}$ Jr 2$_{11.19}$ 5$_{10}$ 10$_{16.23.23}$ 16$_{20}$ 48$_{33}$ 49$_{31.31}$ 51$_{17.19}$ Ezk 7$_{11}$ 21$_{31}$ Ho 1$_{9}$ 2$_{1.4.4}$ 8$_{6}$ Am 7$_{14.14}$ 8$_{11.11}$ Mc 2$_{10}$ Hb 1$_{14}$ Zc 8$_{11}$ 13$_{5}$ Ps 5$_{5}$ 22$_{3}$ 92$_{16}$ Jb 18$_{17.19}$ 21$_{9.16}$ 28$_{14}$ 29$_{12}$ 33$_{9}$ 36$_{4.16}$ 38$_{26}$ 41$_{3}$ (if em. לִי הוּא *he is mine* to לֹא הוּא *he is not*, i.e there is not such a one)* Pr 27$_{24}$ 30$_{2}$ Ec 9$_{11.11.11.11.11}$ Ezr 10$_{13.13}$ 1 C 11$_{20(Kt)}$ 15$_{13}$ 29$_{1}$ 2 C 20$_{15}$ Si 3$_{10}$ 14$_{12}$ 37$_{28}$ 39$_{20}$ 1QH 4$_{18.30.30.31}$ 7$_{11}$ fr. 2$_{7}$ 1QM 11$_{5}$ 4QHalakhah^{a} 13$_{6}$ 4QD^{a} 6.2$_{2}$ 4QM^{a} 11.1$_{14}$ CD 5$_{16}$.

Sometimes וְלֹא *and not* introduces an additional predicate in a nominal clause, e.g. אַתָּה אָדָם וְלֹא־אֵל *you are a human being and not a god* Ezk 28$_{2.9}$, Gn 20$_{12}$ (אַךְ לֹא *but not*) Is 22$_{2}$ 31$_{3}$ 53$_{2.2}$ Jr 23$_{23}$ Ho 11$_{9}$ Am 5$_{18.20.20}$ Ps 22$_{7}$ Jb 18$_{19}$ Ezr 10$_{13}$.

5b. הֲלֹא **is not?**, etc., e.g. הֲלוֹא־אִישׁ אַתָּה *are you not a man?* 1 S 26$_{15}$, הֲלֹא כָל־הָאָרֶץ לְפָנֶיךָ *is not all the land before you?* Gn 13$_{9}$, הֲלוֹא זֶה אֲשֶׁר *is not this the one that?* Gn 44$_{5}$, הֲלוֹא כֹה דְבָרִי כָּאֵשׁ *is not my word thus: like fire?* Jr 23$_{29}$ (or em. כֹּוֶה does not my word *burn*, as §3b), הֲלוֹא־הִיא הַדַּעַת אֹתִי *is not that to know me?* Jr 22$_{16}$, Gn 19$_{20}$ 34$_{23}$ 40$_{8}$ Ex 14$_{12}$ Nm 22$_{30}$ Dt 3$_{11}$ 11$_{30}$ 32$_{6}$ Jg 9$_{38}$ 15$_{2}$ 1 S 9$_{20.21}$ 17$_{8.29}$ 20$_{37}$ 21$_{12}$ 29$_{3.5}$ 2 S 11$_{3}$ 15$_{35}$ 19$_{14}$ 2 K 6$_{32}$ 18$_{22}$||Is 36$_{7}$ Is 10$_{8.9}$ 44$_{20}$ 45$_{21}$ 51$_{9.10}$ 57$_{4}$ 58$_{6}$ Jr 5$_{3}$ 14$_{22}$ Ezk 21$_{5}$ Am 5$_{20}$ 9$_{7}$ Jon 4$_{2}$ Mc 3$_{11}$ Hb 1$_{12}$ Zc 3$_{2}$ Ml 1$_{2}$ 2$_{10}$ Jb 4$_{6}$ 7$_{1}$ 10$_{20}$ 22$_{5.12}$ Ru 3$_{2}$ 1 C 21$_{3}$.

5c. אִם־לֹא **or (is) not?**, e.g. הֲלֹא כְּכַרְכְּמִישׁ כַּלְנוֹ אִם־לֹא כְאַרְפַּד חֲמָת *is not Calno like Carchemish, or is not Hamath like Arpad?* Is 10$_{9}$, הַאַתָּה זֶה בְּנִי עֵשָׂו אִם־לֹא *are you my son Isaac or not?* Gn 27$_{21}$, sim. Gn 37$_{32}$ 42$_{16}$.

6. לֹא followed by noun, preposition, adjective, relative particle (used attibutively), **not, non-, im-, un-, without** (cf. §7), or (used predicatively) as negative existential particle, **there is not**, etc., or, in ref. to an elided, or indefinite, subj., **it is not, that is not**, etc.

6a. לֹא with following noun (sometimes לֹא qualifies the second element in a construct phrase), e.g. לֹא אֱלֹהַ *a non-god* Dt 32$_{17(L)}$, לֹא דָבָר *a non-thing* Am 6$_{13}$ (or em. לֹא דְבָר *Lo-debar*), בֹּקֶר לֹא עָבוֹת *a morning without clouds* 2 S 23$_{4}$, גּוֹיִם לֹא מְעָט *nations not a few* Is 10$_{7}$, לֹא־עֵת *it is not time* Gn 29$_{7}$, תוהו לא דרך *a chaos (where) there is not way* CD 1$_{15}$, var. 4QD^{a} 11$_{11}$, לֹא־חָמָס עָשָׂה *he practised non-violence* Is 53$_{9}$, חֶרֶב לֹא־אִישׁ *a sword not of a man* Is 31$_{8}$ 1QM 11$_{11}$, var. 1QM 11$_{12}$, איש לא הון *a man without wealth* Si 8$_{2(A\ erased)}$ (Amg לוֹ *to him*, i.e. who has).

לוא להפצי רבים *it is not according to the interest of the many* 1QS 6$_{11}$, לֹא־כַדָּת *it is not according to the law* Est 4$_{16}$, לוֹא אֲלֵיכֶם appar. *it is not for you* Lm 1$_{12}$ (or em. לְכוּ *go* or לְוָא *woe*), לֹא יֵשׁ־בֵּינֵינוּ מוֹכִיחַ *there is no arbitrator between us* Jb 9$_{33}$; (mss לוּ *if only* there were), אֲשֶׁר לֹא־בְרָע : אָלָה a generation *that will not be accompanied by evil. A curse* Ps 10$_{6}$ (or em. אֲשֶׁר לֹא כֹרַע אֵלֵךְ *[with] an unstumbling footstep shall I proceed*, as §6b), הֲלוֹא־עוֹד מְעַט מִזְעָר *is there not still a little while?* Is 29$_{17}$, הֲלֹא אַהֲרֹן אָחִיךָ הַלֵּוִי *is there not Aaron, your brother, the Levite?* Ex 4$_{14}$, הֲלוֹא אֶת־הַדְּבָרִים *are they not the words?* Zc 7$_{7}$ (or em. אֵלֶּה *these are*).

Lv 11$_{21(Kt)}$ 25$_{30(Kt)}$ Nm 20$_{5}$ Dt 11$_{2}$ 1 S 12$_{17}$ (הֲלוֹא) 2 K 4$_{23.23}$ Is 10$_{15}$ 29$_{9}$ 30$_{1.1.5.5}$ 31$_{8}$ 44$_{19.19}$ 51$_{21}$ Jr 5$_{12.19}$ 6$_{20}$ 29$_{11}$ 39$_{16}$ 44$_{27}$ Ezk 7$_{7.11.11.11}$ 16$_{61}$ Am 9$_{4}$ Mc 1$_{5.5}$ (both הֲלוֹא) Hb 2$_{13}$=1QpHab 10$_{6}$ Hg 1$_{2}$ Zc 4$_{6.6}$ 14$_{7.7}$ Ps 56$_{9}$ (הֲלֹא)

59$_{4.4}$ 107$_{40}$ 139$_{16(Kt)}$ Jb 9$_{32}$ 10$_{22}$ 12$_{24}$ 16$_{17}$ 22$_{16}$ 26$_{2.2.3}$ 34$_{20.24}$ 36$_{19.26}$ 38$_{26}$ 39$_{16}$ Pr 19$_{7(Kt)}$ 1 C 2$_{30.32}$ 2 C 13$_{9}$ 15$_{3.3.3}$ 26$_{18}$ 35$_{21}$ Si 9$_{8}$ 36$_{31(B)}$ (Bmg, C, D אין לו *there is not to him* for לא *without*) 1QH 4$_{38}$ 8$_{34}$ 15$_{12}$ 1QM 11$_{5}$ 1QS 6$_{1.12}$ 7$_{8.11}$ 1QSb 4$_{24}$ 4QD^{e} 7.1$_{13}$ 4QD^{h} 6$_{1}$ 4QMyst^{a} 3a.2$_{4}$ 4QapPs^{b} 10$_{3}$ 4QpsEzek^{c} 2$_{8.9}$ ([ול]א) 4QShirShabb^{f} 23.1$_{10}$ 4Q418 69.2$_{3}$ (הלא) 4QHod^{a} 7.2$_{19}$ 4QPseud^{b} 5.1$_{4.8}$ perh. 4QOrd^{b} 4$_{5}$ 4QShir^{b} 18.2$_{5}$ CD 9$_{3.10}$.

6b. לא with preposition and noun, e.g. לֹא לְעֶזְרָה לוֹ *it was not to him for help*, i.e. it was no help to him 2 C 28$_{21}$, לוא במשפט *not with justice*, i.e. unjustly 1QS 7$_{18}$ 4QD^{a} 7.2$_{9}$ ([לו במפש]פט) CD 14$_{22}$, כול מאומה אשר לוא במחיר *anything that is not for a price* 1QS 5$_{17}$, לֹא מִלִּבִּי *it is not from my heart* Nm 16$_{28}$.

6c. לא with preposition, אֶרֶץ לֹא לָהֶם *a land that is not theirs* Gn 15$_{13}$.

6d. בְּלֹא **without, with non-, for non-, when it is not**, etc. (i.e. בְּ of accompaniment, price, etc.), e.g. בְּלֹא־אֵיבָה *without enmity* Nm 35$_{22}$, בלוא מש[פט] *without justice* 4QMyst^{a} 7$_{5}$, בְּלֹא־אֵל *with a non-god* Dt 32$_{21}$, בְּלֹא עֶת־נִדָּתָהּ *when it is not the time of her impurity* Lv 15$_{25}$, בְּלוֹא לְשָׂבְעָה *(for that which is) without satiety* Is 55$_{2}$, Dt 32$_{21}$ Is 55$_{1.1.2}$ Jr 5$_{7}$ 22$_{13.13}$ Ezk 22$_{29}$ Ps 17$_{1}$ 44$_{13}$ Jb 8$_{11}$ 15$_{32}$ 30$_{28}$ 34$_{20}$ Pr 13$_{23}$ 16$_{8}$ 19$_{2}$ Ec 7$_{17}$ 10$_{11}$ Lm 1$_{6}$ 1 C 12$_{18.34}$ 2 C 21$_{20}$ Si 25$_{18}$ 30$_{24.38}$ 35$_{4.19}$ 37$_{31}$ 51$_{25}$ 1QH 1$_{8.22}$ 4$_{7}$ 7$_{18}$ ([בל]וא) 10$_{2.6.9}$ 11$_{18}$ 1QS 11$_{17}$ 1QMyst 1.2$_{6.6}$ 4QMyst^{c} 2b$_{3.3}$ 4Q416 2.3$_{20}$ 4Q418 126.2$_{5}$ 4QHod^{a} 7.2$_{2}$ Mur 22 1$_{5}$ GnzPs 3$_{3}$.

6e. לא with following attributive or predicative adjective (or participle as adjective) or adverb, e.g. לֹא־כֵן *it is not so/let it not be so* Gn 48$_{18}$ Ex 10$_{11}$, *not so* Nm 12$_{7}$ Dt 18$_{14}$ 2 S 18$_{14}$ (or em. לָכֵן *therefore*) 20$_{21}$ 23$_{5}$ Ps 1$_{4}$ Jb 9$_{35}$, לא כל בשת נאוה לבוש *not every shame(ful thing) is deserving of feeling ashamed* Si 41$_{16(M)}$, לא נאוה *unseemly* Si 10$_{18}$ 14$_{3.3}$, לֹא־טוֹב *not good* Ex 18$_{17}$ 1 S 26$_{16}$ 29$_{6}$ 2 S 17$_{7}$ (טוֹבָה) 1 K 19$_{4}$ Is 65$_{2}$ Ezk 18$_{18}$ 20$_{25}$ 36$_{31}$ (all three טוֹבִים) Ps 36$_{5}$ Pr 16$_{29}$ 19$_{2}$ 20$_{23}$ Ne 5$_{9}$ 1QH 15$_{18}$ Lachish ost. 6$_{6}$ (לא טבם), לֹא טָהוֹר *impure* Gn 7$_{2}$ (טְהֹרָה) 1 S 20$_{26}$ 2 C 30$_{17}$, לֹא נָכוֹן *not right* Ex 8$_{22}$ Ps 78$_{37}$, לֹא קָרוֹב *not near* Nm 24$_{17}$ Dt 22$_{2}$=11QT 64$_{14}$, Gn 15$_{16}$ Dt 30$_{11.11}$ 32$_{6}$ 1 S 2$_{24}$ 2 S 20$_{21}$ 1 K 7$_{31}$ 2 K 7$_{9}$ 17$_{9}$ Is 16$_{6.14}$ Jr 8$_{6}$ 23$_{10}$ 48$_{30.30}$ 51$_{5}$ Ho 13$_{13}$ Am 9$_{4}$ Ps 43$_{1}$ Jb 15$_{32}$ 26$_{2}$ 41$_{2}$ Pr 17$_{7}$ 19$_{10}$ 26$_{1}$ 30$_{25.26}$ Si 42$_{21(B)}$ 1QS 4$_{18}$.

7. לֹא as substantivized relative particle, **one who is not, one who has not**, etc. (cf. §6a), e.g. נִדְרַשְׁתִּי לְלוֹא שָׁאָלוּ נִמְצֵאתִי לְלֹא בִקְשֻׁנִי *I was sought by those who did not ask, I was found by those who did not seek me* Is 65$_{1}$, מֶה־עָזַרְתָּ לְלֹא־כֹחַ *how have you helped one who is without strength* Jb 26$_{2}$, [חומת] עוז ללוא תתזעזע *a strong wall that shall not be shaken* 1QH 6$_{27}$, בריחי עוז ללוא ישבורו *strong bars that shall not be broken* 1QH 6$_{28}$, עם לא בינות *a people that has not understanding* 1QH 2$_{19}$, וְאַחֲרֵי לֹא־יוֹעִלוּ הָלָכוּ *and they went after that which does not profit* Jr 2$_{8}$, מָה אֶקֹּב לֹא קַבֹּה אֵל וּמָה אֶזְעֹם לֹא זָעַם י׳ *how can I curse one whom God has not cursed and how can I denounce one whom Y. has not denounced* Nm 23$_{8}$, הוֹי הַמַּרְבֶּה לֹּא־לוֹ *woe to whoever multiplies that which is not his* Hb 2$_{6}$, וְהָיוּ כְּלוֹא הָיוּ *and they will be as those who had never been* Ob$_{16}$, מה אדבר בלא נודע ואשמיעה בלא סופר *what shall I speak concerning that which is not known, or declare concerning that which has not been told* 1QH 1$_{23}$, דרך לא טוב *a way that is not good* 1QH 15$_{18}$, Jr 2$_{11}$ Jb 26$_{2.3}$ 39$_{16}$ 1QH 5$_{37}$ 7$_{9}$ 4QSD 2$_{4}$ ([לוא]) 2$_{4}$ 4QMyst^{c} 2b$_{5}$ 4Q418 69.2$_{5.5}$.

8. as noun, **nothing**, e.g. עַתָּה הֱיִיתֶם לֹא *now you have become nothing* Jb 6$_{21(Kt)}$ (Qr לוֹ *to him*, or em. לְאַל *as nothing*, or לִי turned *against me*; or לְאִים *hesitant*); אִם־קָרָאתִי וַיַּעֲנֵנִי לֹא *when I call, he answers me nothing* Jb 9$_{16}$ (if em. וַיַּעֲנֵנִי לֹא־ *he answers*, I do *not* trust; or em. וְלֹא־יַעֲנֵנִי *he does not answer me*), נִבְזֶה וְלֹא חֲשַׁבְנֻהוּ perh. *we reckoned him despised and nothing*, i.e. a worthless nothing Is 53$_{3}$, מְרַדֵּף אֲמָרִים לֹא־הֵמָּה *one who pursues words, which are nothing* Pr 19$_{7(Kt)}$ (Qr לוֹ that are *his*; or em. לֹא־יִמָּלֵט *will not escape* or לֹא־יִחְיֶה *will not survive*).*

9. as interjection, **no, it is not so**, etc., e.g. לֹא־אֲדֹנִי שְׁמָעֵנִי *no, my lord, hear me* Gn 23$_{11}$ (or em. לֻא *if only*), Gn 42$_{10}$ Nm 22$_{30}$ Jg 12$_{5}$ 1 S 1$_{15}$ Hg 2$_{12}$ Zc 4$_{5.13}$ Jb 23$_{6}$ (or em. לֹא אַף־הוּא *no, but he* to לֻא אַף־הוּא *if only he indeed* or לֹא אַכְזָר הוּא *he is not so cruel*).*

10. הֲלֹא **is it not the case that?, surely,** modifying an entire clause or sentence, e.g. הֲלוֹא אִם־תֵּיטִיב שְׂאֵת *surely, if you do well, there will be acceptance* Gn 4$_{7}$, הֲלוֹא אִם־קָטֹן אַתָּה בְּעֵינֶיךָ רֹאשׁ שִׁבְטֵי יִשְׂרָאֵל אָתָּה *surely, even though you be small in your own eyes, you are (nonetheless) head of* the tribes of Israel 1 S 15_{17}, הֲלֹא כַּאֲשֶׁר עָשִׂיתִי ... כֵּן אֶעֱשֶׂה *is it not the case that just as I have done ... so shall I do?* Is 10_{11}, הֲלוֹא כִּי אָנֹכִי צִוִּיתִי אֶתְכֶם חִזְקוּ *is it not the case that because I have commanded you, (you are to) be strong?* 2 S 13_{28}, הֲלֹא דַּרְכֵיכֶם לֹא יִתָּכֵנוּ *surely it is your ways that are not just* Ezk 18_{25}, אֶשְׁמְעָה מַה־יְדַבֵּר י׳ הֲלֹא כִּי יְדַבֵּר שָׁלוֹם *let me hear what Y. speaks; is it not the case that he speaks peace?* Ps 85_{9} (if em. הָאֵל י׳ what *God* speaks, *Y.* , for he speaks), הֲלוֹא אִם־שָׁלוֹם וֶאֱמֶת יִהְיֶה בְיָמָי *surely there will be peace and security in my days* 2 K 20_{19}, הַלְיָרְשֵׁנוּ קְרָאתֶם לָנוּ הֲלֹא appar. *surely you have not called us to rob us?* Jg 14_{15} (mss הֲלֹם you have called us *hither?*), Dt 31_{17} 1 S 10_{1} 2 S 10_{3}‖1 C 19_{3} Is 28_{25} 4Q418 $69.2_{12.14}$ 81_{6}.

11. appar. וְלֹא **is it not the case that?, surely,** וְלֹא אִם־עוֹדֶנִּי חָי וְלֹא־תַעֲשֶׂה *surely, if I am still alive, surely, you will do* 1 S 20_{14} (or em. הֲלֹא אִם to וְלֹא אִם *surely, if* or וְאִם לֹא *and if* I am *not* still alive, or וְלֹא *and if* and the second וְלֹא to הֲלֹא or וָלֹא).

12. Miscellaneous collocations, **a.** לֹא (also הֲלֹא and בְּלֹא) negating a word other than a verb, with a verb preceding, e.g. וְהֵבֵאתִי עָלַי קְלָלָה וְלֹא בְרָכָה *and I shall bring a curse upon myself and not a blessing* Gn 27_{12}, יַרְשִׁיעֲךָ פִיךָ וְלֹא־אָנִי *your own mouth condemns you, and not I* Jb 15_{6}, וַיִּפְנוּ אֵלַי עֹרֶף וְלֹא פָנִים *and they turned to me (their) back and not (their) face* Jr 32_{33}, בטח בשמכה הגדול ולוא בחרב וחנית *he trusted in your great name and not in sword or spear* 1QM 11_{2}, הושעתנו ... בעבור רחמיכה ולוא כמעשינו *you have saved us ... on account of your compassion, and not according to our deeds* 1QM 11_{4}, וַיַּעֲשֶׂה הָרַע ... רַק לֹא כְאָבִיו *... and he did evil ... only not like his father* 2 K 3_{2}, וַאֲעַנֶּה אֶת־זֶרַע דָּוִד ... אַךְ לֹא כָל־הַיָּמִים *and I shall afflict the seed of David ... but not always* 1 K $11_{39(L)}$, יָשׁוּבוּ לֹא עָל appar. *they turn (but) not upwards* or *not (to) Al* or *to Not-Al* Ho 7_{16} (or em. to לִבְלִיַּעַל *to worthlessness* or לַבַּעַל *to Baal*),* הַעַל אֲדֹנֶיךָ ... שְׁלָחַנִי אֲדֹנִי ... הֲלֹא עַל־הָאֲנָשִׁים *is it to your lord ... that my lord has sent me ...?; is it not to the men* sitting on the wall? 2 K 18_{27} ‖Is 36_{12}, הַאֹתִי הֵם מַכְעִסִים ... הֲלוֹא אֹתָם *is it me whom they provoke? ... is it not themselves?* Jr 7_{19}, וְנִשְׁמַר שָׁם לֹא אַחַת וְלֹא שְׁתָּיִם *and he saved himself there not (just) once or twice* 2 K 6_{10}, Ex 3_{19} (or em. לֹא *not* with a mighty hand to אִם לֹא *if not*, i.e. unless it be, with) 4_{11} (הֲלֹא) 33_{16} (הֲלוֹא) Nm 12_{8} Jos $22_{26.26.28.28}$ $24_{12.12}$ 1 S 29_{4} (הֲלוֹא) 2 S 16_{19} (הֲלוֹא) 2 K 14_{3} 17_{2} Is 42_{24} (הֲלוֹא) $45_{13.13}$ $48_{1.1.7.10}$ Jr 2_{27} 7_{24} 15_{13} 17_{11} 18_{17} 21_{10} 23_{16} Ezk 3_{6} 20_{44} Ho 6_{6} 8_{4} Ps $100_{3(Kt)}$ (unless לֹא II *indeed*) $115_{1.1.17}$ Jb 4_{21} 19_{27} 32_{13} 34_{33} Pr 27_{2} 31_{12} Ec 5_{9} 10_{17} Lm 3_{2} Dn $8_{22.24}$ $11_{4.4.20.20}$ 1 C 21_{17} (or em. וּבְעַמְּךָ לֹא לְמַגֵּפָה appar. *and against your people, let not [your hand be] for striking* to וּבָעָם כְּלָא לַמַּגֵּפָה *but against the people restrain the striking*) 2 C 17_{4} 21_{20} 25_{2} 30_{19} Si 35_{12} 11QT $59_{20.21}$.

12b. לֹא negating a word other than a verb, with a verb following, e.g. לֹא יוֹם אֶחָד תֹּאכְלוּן *you shall eat not just one day* Nm 11_{19}, לֹא אֶת־אֲבֹתֵינוּ כָּרַת י׳ אֶת־הַבְּרִית הַזֹּאת כִּי אִתָּנוּ *it was not with our fathers that Y. made this covenant but with us* Dt 5_{3}, לֹא בְצִדְקָתְךָ י׳ אֱלֹהֶיךָ נֹתֵן לְךָ אֶת־הָאָרֶץ הַטּוֹבָה הַזֹּאת *it is not on account of your righteousness that Y. your God is giving you this good land* Dt 9_{6}, לֹא עַל־הַלֶּחֶם לְבַדּוֹ יִחְיֶה הָאָדָם *a human being lives not by bread alone* Dt 8_{3}, לֹא אֲשֶׁר יִרְאֶה הָאָדָם *not that which a human being sees* 1 S 16_{7} (mss כַּאֲשֶׁר not *as* a human being sees), לֹא בְּחֶרֶב וּבַחֲנִית יְהוֹשִׁיעַ י׳ *Y. saves not with sword or spear* 1 S 17_{47}, אֶרֶץ אֲשֶׁר לֹא בְמִסְכֵּנֻת תֹּאכַל־בָּהּ לֶחֶם *a land in which you shall eat bread without scarcity* Dt 8_{9}, לֹא־חָמָס עָשָׂה *he did no violence*, i.e. acted non-violently Is 53_{9}, לֹא־תֹהוּ בְרָאָהּ *not (as) chaos did he create it* Is 45_{18}, לֹא־אֱלֹהִים שְׁלָחוֹ *it was not God who sent him* Ne 6_{12}, לֹא־אוֹיֵב יְחָרְפֵנִי *it is not an enemy (who) reproaches me* Ps 55_{13}, לא לרבים היא נְכוֹחָה *not by many is it* (discipline) *understood* Si $6_{22(A)}$, לֹא־עַתָּה יֵבוֹשׁ יַעֲקֹב *Jacob will not now*, i.e. no more, *be ashamed* Is 29_{22}, לֹא צָר וּמַלְאָךְ פָּנָיו הוֹשִׁיעָם *not a messenger or an angel but his own presence saved them* Is $63_{9(Kt)}$ (if em. Qr לוֹ צָר וּמַלְאַךְ *he was afflicted and an angel of* his presence saved them), Nm 16_{29} Dt 7_{7} $9_{5.6}$ 29_{13} 32_{27} 2 S 23_{6} Is $28_{27.28}$ 43_{22} 48_{16} $52_{3.12.12}$ $57_{16.16}$ Jr 2_{34} 20_{3} 31_{32} Ezk 3_{5} 6_{10} 14_{23} 17_{17} $36_{22.32}$ Ml 2_{15} (or em. וְלֹא אֶחָד עָשָׂה *and has not one [God] made?* to אֵל one *God* made or הֲלֹא *surely*, one [god] made)* Ps 9_{19} $44_{4.7}$ 50_{8} $103_{9.9.10.10}$ 115_{17} $147_{10.10}$ Jb 7_{16} 12_{25} 13_{16} 14_{4} 20_{9} 22_{7} 30_{24} 32_{9} $34_{23.35}$ Ec 4_{12} 5_{19} 7_{10} 10_{10} Est 1_{16} Dn 9_{18} 2 C 19_{6} 30_{5} 32_{25} Si 14_{12} 30_{26}.

12c. לֹא negating a verb combined with a verb that is not negated, e.g. הַאַף תִּסְפֶּה וְלֹא־תִשָּׂא לַמָּקוֹם *will you also destroy and not spare the place?* Gn 18_{24}, וְנִחְיֶה וְלֹא

נָמוּת *so that we may live and not die* Gn 42$_{2}$, Gn 40$_{23}$ 43$_{8}$ 47$_{19}$ Lv 6$_{5.6}$ Nm 4$_{19}$ 9$_{22}$ Jg 14$_{16}$ 1 S 1$_{11}$ 2 K 18$_{32}$ 20$_{1}$||Is 38$_{1}$ Is 17$_{10}$ 41$_{9}$ 54$_{4}$ Ezk 18$_{28}$ 33$_{15}$ Ps 89$_{49}$ 118$_{17}$ 119$_{60}$ Ca 3$_{4}$ 4QD^{e} 7.1$_{13}$ GnzPs 2$_{8}$.

12d. אִם לֹא in oaths, etc., (thus may Y. do to me) **if** (I do) **not, truly, I swear that,** etc.,* e.g. ... אִם לֹא אֶת־דְּמֵי רָאִיתִי *truly, I have seen ... the blood of* Naboth 2 K 9$_{26}$, כֹּה יַעֲשֶׂה־לִּי אֱלֹהִים וְכֹה יוֹסִיף אִם־לֹא שַׂר־צָבָא תִּהְיֶה *thus may God do to me and thus may he continue (to do) if you do not become commander of the army* 2 S 19$_{14}$, אִם־לֹא מִדְּאָגָה מִדָּבָר עָשִׂינוּ אֶת־זֹאת *truly, we did this out of concern for the matter* Jos 22$_{24}$, אִם־לֹא אֶל־בֵּית־אָבִי תֵּלֵךְ *I swear that you will go to my father's house* Gn 24$_{38}$ (Sam כִּי אִם *instead* for אִם־לֹא), Nm 14$_{28.35}$ Jos 14$_{9}$ Jg 11$_{10}$ 1 K 20$_{23.25}$ Is 5$_{9}$ 8$_{20}$ 14$_{24}$ perh. Jr 15$_{11.11}$ 22$_{6}$ 42$_{5}$ 49$_{20.20}$ 50$_{45.45}$ Ezk 3$_{6}$ 5$_{11}$ 17$_{16.19}$ 20$_{33}$ 33$_{27}$ 34$_{8}$ 35$_{6}$ (lacking in mss) 36$_{5.7}$ 38$_{19}$ Ml 3$_{10}$ Ps 131$_{2}$ Jb 1$_{11}$ 2$_{5}$ 17$_{2}$ 22$_{20}$ 31$_{36}$; also אִם־אָנִי לֹא־אֶעֱבֹר ... וְאִם־אַתָּה לֹא־תַעֲבֹר *I swear that I shall not cross ... and you swear that you will not cross* Gn 31$_{52}$.

12e. לֹא ... כִּי not ... but, e.g. לֹא־עָלֵינוּ תְלֻנֹּתֵיכֶם כִּי עַל־י״ *your murmurings are not against us but against Y.* Ex 16$_{8}$, 1 S 8$_{7}$ Is 43$_{22}$ 1 C 29$_{1}$ 2 C 19$_{6}$ 20$_{15}$ Si 30$_{26}$ perh. 4QapJoseph^{c} 1$_{6}$= 4QapJoseph^{b} 19$_{4}$ CD 8$_{14}$ 19$_{27}$.

12f. לֹא ... עַד, לֹא ... עַד אֲשֶׁר, etc.

(1) **not ... until,** e.g. לֹא יַשְׁאִירוּ מִמֶּנּוּ עַד־בֹּקֶר *they are to leave none of it until morning* Nm 9$_{12}$, לֹא נִטֶּה יָמִין וּשְׂמֹאול עַד אֲשֶׁר־נַעֲבֹר גְּבוּלֶךָ *we shall not turn right or left until we cross your border* Nm 20$_{17}$, לֹא אֹכַל עַד אִם־דִּבַּרְתִּי *I shall not eat until I have spoken* Gn 24$_{33}$, Gn 28$_{15}$ 29$_{8}$ Lv 22$_{4}$ 23$_{14.14}$ 25$_{30}$ Nm 6$_{5}$ Jos 7$_{13}$ 8$_{26}$ 22$_{3}$ 1 S 9$_{13}$ 15$_{35}$ 16$_{11}$ 2 S 6$_{23}$ 22$_{38}$||Ps 18$_{38}$ 1 K 10$_{7}$||2 C 9$_{6}$ 1 K 10$_{12}$ 17$_{14}$ Is 42$_{4}$ 62$_{1}$ Jr 30$_{24}$ 35$_{14}$ 44$_{10}$ Ezk 21$_{32}$ 24$_{13}$ Jb 14$_{12}$ (עַד ... לֹא) Ca 3$_{4}$ Ne 4$_{5}$ 8$_{17}$ 13$_{19}$ 1 C 28$_{20}$ 2 C 15$_{19}$ Si 32$_{21}$ (עד ... לא) 32$_{21}$ CD 3$_{19}$ 6$_{10}$.

(2) **not ... even,** e.g. לֹא־אֶתֵּן לָכֶם מֵאַרְצָם עַד מִדְרַךְ כַּף־רָגֶל *I shall not give you of their land even a treading place for the sole of a foot* Dt 2$_{5}$, לֹא נִשְׁאַר עַד־אֶחָד *not even one was left* Jg 4$_{16}$.

12g. לֹא כִּי rather, instead, לֹא כִּי צָחָקְתְּ *instead you did laugh* Gn 18$_{15}$, 19$_{2}$ 42$_{12}$ Jos 5$_{14}$ 24$_{21}$ Jg 15$_{13}$ 1 S 2$_{16(Qr)}$ 10$_{19(mss)}$ (L לוֹ כִּי *to him, but*) 12$_{12}$ 2 S 16$_{18}$ 24$_{24}$ 1 K 2$_{30}$ 3$_{22.22.23}$ perh. 11$_{22}$ (mss לוֹ כִּי) 2 K 20$_{10}$ Is 30$_{16}$ perh. Jr 2$_{25}$ 42$_{14}$ 1 C 21$_{24}$.

12h. specific elliptical combinations, (1) וְלֹא **if not, in that case, at least,** וָלֹא יֵלֶךְ־נָא אִתָּנוּ אַמְנוֹן אָחִי *if not, let Amnon my brother go with us* 2 S 13$_{26}$, וָלֹא יֻתַּן־נָא לְעַבְדְּךָ *if not, let there be given to your servant* 2 K 5$_{17}$ (or em. in both וְלֹא *and if only*).

(2) אִם־לֹא **if not,** e.g. עַתָּה תִתֵּן וְאִם־לֹא לָקַחְתִּי בְחָזְקָה *now you must give (it); and if not, I shall take (it) by force* 1 S 2$_{16}$, אֵרְדָה־נָּא וְאֶרְאֶה הַכְּצַעֲקָתָהּ ... עָשׂוּ כָּלָה וְאִם־לֹא אֵדָעָה *I shall see whether ... they have done altogether according to its cry; and if not, I shall know* Gn 18$_{21}$, אם [יהיו נמ]נים אלה ואו[ף] אם לוא *if these can be counted, and even if not* 4QpsJub^{a} 2.1$_{7}$, sim. Gn 24$_{49}$ 1 S 6$_{9}$ Zc 11$_{12}$ Jb 9$_{24}$ 24$_{25}$ Si 12$_{2}$.

(3) אִם־לֹא **or not,** e.g. לָדַעַת הַהִצְלִיחַ י״ דַּרְכּוֹ אִם־לֹא *to know whether Y. would prosper his way or not* Gn 24$_{21}$, תִרְאֶה הֲיִקְרְךָ דְבָרִי אִם־לֹא *you will see whether my word will meet you,* i.e. it will happen to you, *or not* Nm 11$_{23}$, Ex 16$_{4}$ Dt 8$_{2}$ Jg 2$_{22}$ 4QapPs^{b} 69$_{7}$ ([ואם [לא]).

12i. לֹא ... כִּי אִם not ... unless, not ... except, not ... but rather, etc. (see כִּי *for*, §15), e.g. לֹא אֲשַׁלֵּחֲךָ כִּי אִם־בֵּרַכְתָּנִי *I shall not let you go unless you bless me* Gn 32$_{27}$, [ה]ארץ לו תוכל ל[הטהר מדם אדם כי אם בדם שפכוה] *the earth cannot be purified from the blood of a human being except through the blood of the one who shed it* 4QJub^{d} 21$_{19}$, [ל]וא אלך כי אם [שלחני] *I shall not go unless he sends me* 4QJub^{g} 27$_{6}$, וְלֹא־יָדַע אִתּוֹ מְאוּמָה כִּי אִם־הַלֶּחֶם *and he did not know anything with him,* i.e. he was not concerned about anything, *except the food* Gn 39$_{6}$, לוא לבן אדם דרך ... כי אם ברוח יצר אל *a human being has no perfection of way ... except by the spirit which God has formed for him* 1QH 4$_{31}$, לֹא יִירָשְׁךָ זֶה כִּי־אִם אֲשֶׁר יֵצֵא *this one will not be your heir, but rather the one who comes out* Gn 15$_{4}$, לֹא־הָיוּ לוֹ בָּנִים כִּי אִם־בָּנוֹת *he had no sons, but (only) daughters* Nm 26$_{33}$, 4QCommGenA 2$_{6}$ perh. 4QMyst^{a} 3a.2$_{6}$ 4QShir^{a} 1$_{7}$ ([כי א[ם]) CD 5$_{15}$.

12j. אִם־לֹא כִּי unless, אֵיכָה יִרְדֹּף אֶחָד אֶלֶף ... אִם־לֹא כִּי־צוּרָם מְכָרָם *how could one pursue a thousand ... unless their rock had sold them?* Dt 32$_{30}$.

12k. בְּטֶרֶם לֹא before, בְּטֶרֶם לֹא־יָבוֹא *before it comes* Zp 2$_{2}$ (or del.) 2$_{2}$, בְּטֶרֶם לֹא תִדַּחֲקוּ *before you are crushed*

Zp 2₂ (if em. בְּטֶרֶם לֶדֶת חֹק *before the birth, i.e. issue, of a statute*).

12l. Ketiv/Qere, Kt לא/Qr לוֹ *to him* Ex 21$_8$ Lv 11$_{21}$ 25$_{30}$ 1 S 2$_3$ 2 S 16$_{18}$ 2 K 8$_{10}$ Is 9$_2$ (or em. הַגּוֹי לוֹ *his nation* to הַגִּילָה *the joy*) 49$_5$ 63$_9$ Ps 100$_3$ 139$_{16}$ Jb 6$_{21}$ 13$_{15}$ 41$_4$ Pr 19$_7$ 26$_2$ Ezr 4$_2$ 1 C 11$_{20}$; Kt לוֹ/Qr לֹא 1 S 2$_{16}$ 20$_2$; Kt לא/Qr לוּ *if* 2 S 18$_{12}$.*

⇒ לֹא עַמִּי *Lo-ammi*, לֹא רֻחָמָה *Lo-ruhamah*, לוֹ דְבָר *Lo-debar.*

*[לְאֹ] II $_{27}$ part. **indeed,** perh. to be vocalized לֶא, לְא, or לָא, as original variant, or later misunderstanding, of emphatic לְ or of לוּ/לְא *indeed* (but all examples may be לֹא *not*), e.g. וְלֹא־לְמַרְאֵה עֵינָיו יִשְׁפּוֹט וְלֹא־לְמִשְׁמַע אָזְנָיו יוֹכִיחַ *and strictly in accordance with what his eyes see will he judge and strictly in accordance with what his ears hear will he decide* Is 11$_3$, לֹא־נָבִיא אָנֹכִי וְלֹא בֶן־נָבִיא אָנֹכִי *I am indeed a prophet but not the son of a prophet*, i.e. not a member of a prophetic guild Am 7$_{14}$, הֵן נִזְבַּח ... לְעֵינֵיהֶם וְלֹא יִסְקְלֻנוּ *if we sacrifice ... in their presence, they will surely stone us* Ex 8$_{22}$, כִּי אִם־יָדֹעַ אֵדַע כִּי־כָלְתָה הָרָעָה ... וְלֹא אֹתָהּ אַגִּיד לָךְ *for if I really knew that evil had been determined ... I would indeed tell you it* 1 S 20$_9$, כִּי עַתָּה לֹא־רָבְתָה מַכָּה בַּפְּלִשְׁתִּים *for now the defeat of the Philistines would have indeed been great* 1 S 14$_{30}$, הוּא־עָשָׂנוּ ולא אֲנַחְנוּ עַמּוֹ וְצֹאן מַרְעִיתוֹ *he made us and indeed we are his people, the sheep of his flock* Ps 100$_{3(Kt)}$ (Qr לוֹ we are *his*), 2 K 5$_{26}$ Jr 17$_8$ Ezk 11$_3$ 16$_{47.56}$ Ho 2$_{4.4}$ 4$_{14}$ Am 1$_2$ Jon 4$_{11}$ Jb 2$_{10}$ 8$_{12}$ 11$_{11}$ 13$_{15}$ 14$_{16}$ 21$_{29}$ 23$_{17}$ 33$_{14}$ Ps 105$_{28}$ Lm 3$_{36.38}$.*

לֶא, see לֹא II *indeed*, לוּ *if.*

לֹא דְבָר, see לוֹ דְבָר *Lo-debar.*

לאה I $_{19.1}$ vb. **be weary—Qal** $_3$ Impf. 2ms תִּלְאֶה, Si תלאו; + waw 3fs Sam ותלא, 2ms וַתֵּלֶא, וַיִּלְאוּ—**be weary, be impatient, be weak, dislike,** <SUBJ> Israelites Si 43$_{30(Bmg)}$ (:: חלף כֹּחַ hi. *renew strength*), David 1 S 17$_{39}$ (if em. וַיֹּאֶל *and he was willing* to וַיֵּלֶא *and he was [too] weary*), Agur Pr 30$_{1.1}$ (if em. in both לְאִיתִיאֵל *to Ithiel* to לָאִיתִי אֵל *I am weary, O God*, or לָאֶה אֶת־[הָ]אֵל *one who has wearied himself with God*), Job Jb 4$_{2.5}$ (|| בהל ni. *be dismayed*), אִישׁ *man* of Sodom Gn 19$_{11}$, גֶּבֶר *man* Pr 30$_{1.1}$ (if em.), בֵּן *son* Pr 30$_{1.1}$ (if em.), אֶרֶץ *land* Gn 47$_{13(Sam)}$ (MT וַתֵּלַהּ *and it languished*, from להה), עַיִן *eye* Jb 17$_2$ (if em. תָּלַן עֵינִי *my eye dwells* to תִּלְאֶן עֵינַי *my eyes are weary* [or em. תִּכְלֶן עֵינַי *my eyes fail*). <PREP> בְּ of cause, *on account of*, + מרה hi. inf. *rebelliousness* Jb 17$_2$ (if em.); אֵת *with*, + אֵל *God* Pr 30$_{1.1}$ (if em.); מִפְּנֵי *on account of*, + רָעָב *famine* Gn 47$_{13(Sam)}$. <COLL> וַיִּלְאוּ לִמְצֹא *and they became too weak to find* the entrance Gn 19$_{11}$. <SYN> בהל ni. *be dismayed.* <ANT> חלף כֹּחַ hi. *renew strength.*

Ni. $_{10}$ Pf. נִלְאָה, נִלְאֵית, נִלְאֵיתִי, נִלְאוּ; + waw וְנִלְאֵיתִי, וְנִלְאוּ—**be weary, be unable, weary oneself, languish,** <SUBJ> Y. Is 1$_{14}$ Jr 15$_6$, Jeremiah Jr 6$_{11}$ 20$_9$, Babylon Is 47$_{13}$, Moab Is 16$_{12}$ (1QIsa[a] בוא *come*), Egypt Ex 7$_{28}$, אִישׁ *man* Jr 9$_4$, עָצֵל *sluggard* Pr 26$_{15}$, נַחֲלָה *inheritance* Ps 68$_{10}$. <PREP> בְּ of instrument, *by (means of), with*, + רֹב *multitude* of counsels Is 47$_{13}$; עַל *upon*, + בָּמָה *high place* Is 16$_{12}$. <COLL> לאה ni. *be too weary/be unable* to, + inf. cstr. of שׁתה *drink* Ex 7$_{18}$, נשׂא *raise*, i.e. endure Is 1$_{14}$, כול hi. *contain* Jr 6$_{11}$ 20$_9$ (pilp.), נחם ni. *repent* Jr 15$_6$, שׁוב *go back* Jr 9$_4$ (if em. הַעֲוֵה נִלְאוּ: שִׁבְתְּךָ *they wear themselves out doing evil; your dwelling place is* among, to הֶעֱווּ וְנִלְאוּ שֻׁב: תֹּךְ *they do evil and are too weary to turn back; oppression is* among), hi. *take back* Pr 26$_{15}$.

Hi. $_6$ Pf. הֶלְאֵיתִךָ, הֶלְאָת, הֶלְאָנִי; impf. תַּלְאוּ; + waw וַיַּלְאוּךָ; inf. הַלְאוֹת—**weary, wear out,** <SUBJ> Y. Mc 6$_3$ Jb 16$_7$, בַּיִת *house* of David Is 7$_{13.13}$, appar. עִיר *city* Ezk 24$_{12}$ (or del. תְּאֻנִים הֶלְאָת *she has wearied [me or herself] with toil*), רַגְלִי *one on foot* Jr 12$_5$. <OBJ> אֱלֹהִים *God* Is 7$_{13}$, אִישׁ *man* Is 7$_{13}$, Jeremiah Jr 12$_5$, Job Jb 16$_7$, עַם *people* Mc 6$_3$.*

⇒ תְּלָאָה *weariness.*

*לאה II vb. **be strong—Qal, 1. be strong,** לָאִיתִי אֵל וָאֻכָל *I am strong (with) strength and I succeed* Pr 30$_1$ (if em. לְאִיתִיאֵל *to Ithiel*).

2. ptc. לָא as noun, **victor,** sometimes as part of divine title, Shaddai **the omnipotent,** אִם לֹא יָשׁוּב חַרְבּוֹ יִלְטוֹשׁ קַשְׁתּוֹ דָרַךְ וַיְכוֹנְנֶהָ *O that the victor would again sharpen his sword, bend his bow, and prepare it* Ps 7$_{13}$ (if em. לֹא if one does *not* go back), מַדּוּעַ מִשַּׁדַּי לֹא־נִצְפְּנוּ עִתִּים *why are the times hidden by Shaddai the omnipotent?* Jb 24$_{1}$ (if em. לֹא why are times *not* concealed by Shaddai?), וְאֵל הֵרַךְ לִבִּי וְשַׁדַּי הִבְהִילָנִי כִּי־לֹא *for God has made my heart weak and Shaddai has terrified me since he is the omnipotent* Jb 23$_{16}$ (if em. הִבְהִילָנִי: כִּי־לֹא *terrified me; for* I have *not* been destroyed), הֵן לֹא בְיָדָם טוּבָם *behold, the omnipotent—from his hands is their prosperity* Jb 21$_{16}$ (if em. לֹא בְיָדָם *not in their hand*), שַׁדַּי לֹא מְצָאנֻהוּ שַׂגִּיא־כֹחַ *Shaddai the omnipotent we have found (to be) great of strength* Jb 37$_{23}$ (if em. ־לֹא we have *not* found him), לֹא יִרְאֶה כָּל־חַכְמֵי־לֵב *the victor sees all who are wise of heart* Jb 37$_{24}$ (if em. ־לֹא the wise of heart do *not* see), וְלֹא עָרַךְ אֵלַי מִלִּין *but the omnipotent has prepared arguments for me* Jb 32$_{14}$ (if em. ־לֹא he did *not* prepare a case against me), הֵן יִקְטְלֵנִי לֹא אֲיַחֵל *though the omnipotent kill me, I shall hope* Jb 13$_{15}$ (if em. לֹא [Kt] I shall *not* or I shall *indeed* hope; Qr לוֹ hope *in him*), מִי־יִתֵּן טָהוֹר מִטָּמֵא לֹא אֶחָד *who can make the impure pure? Only the omnipotent one* Jb 14$_{4}$ (if em. לֹא *no* one), עָשִׁיר יִשְׁכַּב וְלֹא יֵאָסֵף *while a rich one sleeps the omnipotent one gathers (him in)* Jb 27$_{19}$ (if em. וְלֹא יֵאָסֵף *he is not gathered*), כִּי־בְאַחַת יְדַבֶּר־אֵל וּבִשְׁתַּיִם לֹא יְשׁוּרֶנָּה *for God speaks once and a second time the omnipotent considers it* Jb 33$_{14}$ (if em. לֹא he does *not* consider it), הֶן־אֵל כַּבִּיר וְלֹא יִמְאָס *behold, God, the aged one, the victor who is contemptuous* Jb 36$_{5}$ (if em. לֹא though God is great he is *not* contemptuous); also Ps 22$_{30}$ 27$_{13}$ 15$_{7}$ 85$_{7}$ 100$_{3}$ (if em. לֹא in all five).

⇒ לָא *strength.*

לֵאָה I $_{34.0.2}$ pr.n.f. **Leah,** Laban's older daughter and Jacob's first wife, mother of six sons and a daughter (Dinah), <SUBJ> שׂנא pass. *be hated* Gn 29$_{31.32}$, חשׁב ni. *be considered* alien 31$_{14}$, יצא *go out* 30$_{16}$, נגשׁ *approach* 33$_{7}$, קרא *meet* 30$_{16}$, הרה *conceive* 29$_{32}$ 30$_{17.19}$, ילד *give birth (to)* 29$_{32}$ 30$_{17.19.20}$ 34$_{1}$ 46$_{15}$, קרא *call*, i.e. name 29$_{32}$ 30$_{11.13.18.20}$, אמר *say* 29$_{32}$ 30$_{11.13.14.16.18.19}$ 31$_{14}$, ענה *answer* 31$_{14}$, ידה hi. *give thanks* 29$_{32}$, ראה *see* 30$_{9}$, ידע *know* 31$_{4}$, עמד *stand*, i.e. cease, giving birth 29$_{32}$ 30$_{9}$, לקח *take* 30$_{9}$, נתן *give* 30$_{9.14.18}$, שׂכר *hire* 30$_{16}$, שׁחה htpal. *bow down* 33$_{7}$, בנה *build* Ru 4$_{11}$.

<NOM CL> הִיא לֵאָה *she was Leah* Gn 29$_{25(Qr)}$, שֵׁם הַגְּדֹלָה לֵאָה *the name of the older one was Leah* 29$_{16}$.

<OBJ> לקח *take* Gn 29$_{23}$, בוא hi. *bring* 29$_{23}$, שׂים *place* 33$_{2}$, אהב *love* 29$_{32}$, אשׁר pi. *pronounce happy* 30$_{13}$, זבד *endow* 30$_{20}$, זבל *honour* 30$_{20}$, מכר *sell* 31$_{14}$, קבר *bury* 49$_{31}$.

<CSTR> שִׁפְחַת לֵאָה *female servant of Leah* Gn 30$_{10.12}$ 35$_{26}$, בְּנֵי *sons of* 35$_{23}$ 46$_{15}$, ־בַּת *daughter of* 34$_{1}$, עֵינֵי *eyes of* 29$_{17}$, אֹהֶל *tent of* 31$_{33.33}$, כלי דמ]ע[לאה דמע סירא perh. *vessels of Leah's tribute, Sira's tribute* 3QTr 11$_{14}$ (unless *vessel of Aloe resin, vessel of white-pine resin*; others כלי דמ]ע[אחד ... לאה ... סורא *liquid ... degenerate;* עשׂר *eleven votive vessels*).*

<APP> אֵם *mother* Gn 30$_{14}$=4QRP[b] 4b.1$_{9}$ ([א]מו]), בַּת *daughter* Gn 29$_{23.24}$ 46$_{18}$.

<PREP> לְ of direction, *to*, + נתן *give* Gn 29$_{24.32}$ 46$_{18}$, קרא *call* 31$_{4}$, אמר *say* 31$_{4}$; of possession, *of, (belonging) to* 31$_{14}$; כְּ *as* Ru 4$_{11}$; מִן of comparison, *(more) than*, + אהב *love* 29$_{30}$; אֶל *to*, + בוא *come* for sex 29$_{23}$ 30$_{16}$, hi. *bring* mandrakes 30$_{14}$=4QRp[b] 4b.1$_{9}$ ([ויבא]), לוה ni. *be joined* Gn 29$_{32}$, אמר *say* 30$_{14}$, שׁמע *listen* 30$_{17}$; עַל *among*, + חצה *divide* 33$_{1}$; עִם *with*, + שׁכב *lie* 30$_{14.16}$.*

לֵאָה II, see אַלְוָא *aloe.*

לְאוֹם, see לְאֹם *nation.*

לָאט, see לָט *secrecy* and לוט *wrap.*

לְאַט, see אַט *gentleness.*

לָאֵל $_{1}$ pr.n.m. **Lael,** Gershonite, father of Eliasaph, <CSTR> בֶּן־לָאֵל *son of Lael* Nm 3$_{24}$.

⇒ אֵל *God.*

לְאֹם $_{38.0.6}$ n.m. **nation**—לְאוֹם; sf. לְאוּמִּי; pl. לְאֻמִּים (לְאוּמִּים)—**nation, people,** used collectively, as subj. of pl. verb (Is 51$_{4}$ Pr 11$_{26}$); in ref. to Israel (Gn 25$_{23}$ Is 51$_{4}$), <SUBJ> אמץ *be strong* Gn 25$_{23}$, יעף *be weary* Jr 51$_{58}$=Hb 2$_{13}$ (|| עַם *people*), פרד ni. *be divided* Gn 25$_{23}$ (|| גּוֹי *nation*), אסף ni. *be gathered* Is 43$_{9}$ (|| גּוֹי), שׁחה htpal. *bow down* Gn 27$_{29}$ (|| עַם), עבד *serve* 1QSb 5$_{28}$ (ל[א]ומים),

שׁאה ni. *roar* Is 17_{13} (lacking in mss), המה *make a noise* Ps 65_8 (if em. הֲמוֹן *tumult of* nations), אזן hi. *hear* Is 51_4 (|| עַם), קשׁב hi. *pay attention* Is 34_1 (|| גּוֹי, + אֶרֶץ *earth*, תֵּבֵל *world*) 49_1 (|| אִי *island*), ידע *know* 1QH 6_{12} (|| גּוֹי), שׂמח *rejoice* Ps 67_5 (+ עַם), רנן pi. *exult* Ps 67_5, הלל pi. *praise* Ps 148_{11} (+ אֶרֶץ), זעם *curse* Pr 24_{24} (|| עַם), קבב *curse* Pr 11_{26}, חלף hi. *renew* Is 41_1 (or em. יַחֲלִיפוּ כֹחַ *let them renew their strength* to יַחֵלוּ לְתוֹכַחְתִּי *let them wait for my rebuke* or יִקְרְבוּ וְיֶאֱתָיוּן *let them approach and come*; + אִי), הגה *plot* Ps 2_1 (|| גּוֹי).

<OBJ> שׁלח pi. *send away* Ps 44_3 (|| גּוֹי *nation*), נתן *give* Is 43_4 (|| אָדָם *humankind*), כסה pi. *cover* Is 60_2 (|| אֶרֶץ *earth*), נחה hi. *guide* Ps 67_5, דין *judge* Ps 9_9 (|| תֵּבֵל *world*), רעע hi. *harm* Ps 44_3 (or em. תָּרַע *you harm*, to תָּרֹעַ *you crush*), דבר hi. *subdue* Ps 47_4 (|| עַם), כרת hi. *cut off* 4QBark^a 1.1_2 (+ גּוֹי).

<CSTR> אֶפֶס לְאֹם *lack of a people* Pr 14_{28} (|| עַם *people*), שְׁאוֹן לְאֻמִּים *roar of nations* Is 17_{12} (|| עַם), עֲדַת *assembly of* Ps 7_8, הֲמוֹן *tumult of* Ps 65_8 (or del. or em. הֲמוֹן to יֶהֱמוּן nations *make a noise*), עֲמַל *(reward of) toil of* Ps 105_{44} (|| גּוֹי *nation*), חֶסֶד *reproach of* Pr 14_{34} (or em. חֶסֶר *lack of*; + גּוֹי), עֵד לְאוּמִּים *witness of nations* Is 55_4 (or em. לְעַמִּים *to peoples*), מְצַוֵּה לְאֻמִּים *commander of peoples* Is 55_4 (or em. מְצַוֵּה *commander* for peoples [אֻמָּה]), שְׁנֵי לְאֻמִּים *two nations* Gn 25_{23}, כָּל־לְאֻמִּים *all nations* Ps 148_{11} 1QH 6_{12} (כול לאומים) 1QMyst 1.1_9 (פי כול לאומים *mouth of all nations*) 1QSb 5_{28} ([כול לא]ומים) 4QapLam^a 2_5 (שרתי כל לאומ[ים] *princess of all nations*) 4QMyst^a 10_5 (לכול [לא]ומים).

<PREP> לְ of benefit, *to, for* perh. 4QMyst^a 10_5 (לכול [לא]ומים); בְּ of place, *among* Is 43_9, + שׂים *place*, i.e. make, a shaking of the head Ps $44_{15(mss)}$ (L בַּל־אֻמִּים appar. *not peoples*, from אֻמָּה; || גּוֹי *nation*), זמר pi. *praise* Ps $57_{10(mss)}$||$108_{4(mss)}$ (L בַּל־אֻמִּים; || עַם *people*), עשׂה *do*, i.e. declare, reproof Ps $149_{7(mss)}$ (L בַּל־אֻמִּים; || גּוֹי); מִן of comparison, *(more) than*, + אמץ *be strong* Gn 25_{23}; בְּתוֹךְ *among*, + עזב *forsake* 4QBark^a 1.2_8 ([עזב]ם; + גּוֹי).

<COLL> לְאֻמִּים בָּאָרֶץ *(the) peoples in*, i.e. *of the earth* Ps 67_5.

Also 4QpIsa^c 50_2 (לאומי[ם]) perh. 4Q410 2_2 4QM^h 3_3 (ל[אומו]).

<SYN> גּוֹי *nation*, עַם *people*, אִי *island*, אָדָם *humankind*, אֶרֶץ *earth*, תֵּבֵל *world*.*

לְאֻמִּים 1 pr.n.m. **Leummim**, son of Dedan, <SUBJ> היה *be* son Gn 25_3 (or del.).

לֹא עַמִּי 2 pr.n.m. **Lo-ammi**, 'not my people', name given by Y. to son of Gomer and Hosea (Ho 1_9) and applied to Israel (Ho 2_{25}), <OBJ> קרא *call* name Ho 1_9 (+ כִּי אַתֶּם לֹא עַמִּי *for you are not my people*). <PREP> לְ of direction, *to*, + אמר *say* 2_{25} (+ עַמִּי־אַתָּה say to Lo-ammi, *You are my people*).

⇒ לֹא *not* + עַם *people*.

[לֹא רֻחָמָה] 3 pr.n.f. **Lo-ruhamah**—לֹא רֻחָמָה—'unpitied', name given by Y. to daughter of Gomer and Hosea (Ho $1_{6.8}$) and applied to Israel (Ho 2_{25}), <OBJ> קרא *call* name Ho 1_6 (+ כִּי לֹא אוֹסִיף עוֹד אֲרַחֵם *for I shall no longer pity*), גמל *wean* 1_8, רחם pi. *pity* 2_{25}.

⇒ לֹא *not* + רחם *pity*.

לֵב 599.58.166.1 n.m. **heart**—לֶב־; cstr. לֵב (לֶב־); sf. לִבִּי, לִבְּךָ (לִבֶּךָ, Q לבכה), לִבֵּךְ, לִבּוֹ, לִבָּהּ, לִבֵּנוּ, לִבְּכֶם (Q לבכמה), לִבָּם (Q לבמה), לִבָּן (לִבְּהֶן); pl. לִבּוֹת; cstr. לִבּוֹת; sf. לִבּוֹתָם (לִבֹּתָם).

Distinctions among these meanings oft. unclear; a physical sense (§4) is oft. possible in §§1-3. לֵב with possessive suffix (especially לִבִּי) may oft. refer to the whole person. Appar. not different in meaning from לֵבָב.

1. mind, thinking, intention, understanding, p. 498a
- **a.** thought, reason, knowledge, counsel, p. 498a
- **b.** wisdom, common sense, p. 498a
- **c.** attention, memory, p. 498a
- **d.** ability, skill, p. 498b

2. feelings, p. 498b
- **a.** joy, p. 498b
- **b.** pain, grief, sadness, p. 498b
- **c.** weakness, anxiety, fear, p. 498b
- **d.** courage, strength, p. 498b
- **e.** irritation, anger, p. 498b

1. mind, thinking, intention, understanding, in ref. to primarily intellectual processes of human beings or of cities, nations, etc. spoken of in human terms (e.g. Is 40$_2$ 47$_{7.10}$ Jr 3$_{10}$ 4$_{14}$ 48$_{29}$ Ob$_3$ Zp 3$_{14}$ 2 C 30$_{12}$) or of Y. (e.g. 1QH 4$_{18.21.24}$ 6$_{7.21}$ 4QBark^a 1.2$_{11}$) or of another deity (Ezk 28$_{2.6}$, perh. 11$_{21}$ [or em.]), as responsible for, representative of, or identified with the following.

a. thought, reason, knowledge, counsel, of human beings, Gn 17$_{17}$ 24$_{45}$ 27$_{41}$ 31$_{20}$ Ex 31$_6$ 35$_{34}$ 36$_2$ Dt 29$_3$ Jg 16$_{17.18.18}$ 1 S 1$_{13}$ 27$_1$ 2 S 15$_6$ 1 K 12$_{26.33[Qr]}$ Is 6$_{10}$ 32$_6$ 33$_{18}$ 44$_{19}$ 47$_{10}$ 51$_7$ Jr 23$_{16}$ 24$_7$ Ezk 13$_2$ (or em.) 13$_{17}$ Ho 4$_{11}$ Ob$_3$ Zc 12$_5$ Ps 10$_{6.11.13}$ 14$_1$||53$_2$ 19$_{15}$ 27$_8$ 35$_{25}$ 41$_7$ 49$_4$ 64$_7$ 74$_8$ 119$_{11.32.70}$ 140$_3$ Jb 8$_{10}$ 17$_4$ Pr 6$_{18}$ 10$_{20}$ 12$_{20}$ 14$_{10}$ 15$_{28}$ 16$_{1.9}$ 18$_2$ 19$_{21}$ 20$_5$ 22$_{15}$ 23$_{12.19.33}$ 24$_2$ 25$_3$ 28$_{26}$ Ec 1$_{16}$ 2$_{1.3.3.15.15}$ 3$_{11}$ (or em.) 3$_{17.18}$ 5$_1$ 7$_{4.4.22.25}$ 8$_5$ 10$_{2.2}$ Lm 3$_{65}$ Est 6$_6$ Ne 5$_7$ 6$_8$ Si 6$_{37}$ 12$_{16}$ 19$_2$ 35$_{16}$ 36$_5$ 37$_{14}$ 1QH 4$_{13}$ 6$_{22}$ 10$_{31}$ 11$_2$ 12$_{34}$ 18$_{24.26.28}$ 1QS 10$_{24}$ 11$_{16}$ 4QapPs^b 69$_3$ 4Q416 2.3$_{13}$ 4Q418 8$_{12}$ 4QHod^a 8$_1$ 4QShir^b 63.3$_2$ 11QPs^a 26$_{12}$ CD 1$_{11}$; of Y., Gn 8$_{21}$ Jr 7$_{31}$ Ps 33$_{11}$ Jb 36$_5$ 1QH 4$_{21}$.

b. wisdom, common sense, 1 K 3$_{9.12}$ 5$_9$ 10$_{24}$||2 C 9$_{23}$ Is 44$_{18}$ Jr 5$_{21}$ Ho 7$_{11}$ Jb 12$_{24}$ 37$_{24}$ Ps 90$_{12}$ (if em.) Pr 2$_{2.10}$ 6$_{32}$ 7$_7$ 8$_5$ 9$_{4.16}$ 10$_{8.13.21}$ 11$_{12.29}$ 12$_{11}$ (or em.; see Cstr.) 14$_{33}$ 15$_{14.21.32}$ 16$_{21.23}$ 17$_{16.18}$ 18$_{15}$ 19$_8$ 23$_{15}$ 24$_{30}$ Ec 1$_{16}$ 10$_3$ Si 3$_{29}$ 6$_{20}$ 16$_{23}$ 36$_{24[B]}$ 45$_{26}$ 50$_{27}$ 51$_{20}$ 1QH 14$_8$ 1QS 2$_3$ 4QapPs^b 1$_2$ 4Q418 81$_{20}$ 4Q424 3$_{6.6}$ 4QUnidA 2$_2$ GnzPs 4$_{7.19}$.

c. attention, memory, of human beings, Ex 7$_{23}$ 9$_{21}$ 1 S 4$_{20}$ 9$_{20}$ 25$_{25}$ 2 S 13$_{20}$ 18$_{3.3.33}$ 19$_{20}$ 1 K 8$_{47}$ 2 K 5$_{26}$ Is 42$_{25}$ 46$_8$ 47$_7$ 57$_{1.11}$ 65$_{17}$ Jr 3$_{16}$ 12$_{11}$ 17$_1$ 31$_{21.33}$ Ezk 40$_4$ 44$_{5.5}$ Ml 2$_{2.2}$ Ps 31$_{13}$ (or em.) 48$_{14}$ 62$_{11}$ Jb 1$_8$ 2$_3$ Pr 3$_3$ (or del.) 6$_{21}$ 7$_3$ 22$_{17}$ 23$_{26}$ 24$_{32}$ 27$_{23}$ Ec 1$_{13.17}$ 7$_{2.21}$ 8$_{9.16}$ 9$_1$ Lm 3$_{21}$ Dn 10$_{12}$ Si 6$_{32}$ 11$_5$ 12$_{11}$ 14$_{21}$ 16$_{20.24}$ 35$_{12}$ 38$_{20.26}$ 50$_{28}$ 4QBark^c 1.1$_5$ 4QBéat 14.2$_{18}$ Arad ost. 40$_4$; of Y., 1 K 9$_3$ ||2 C 7$_{16}$ Is 41$_{22}$ Jr 44$_{21}$ Jb 7$_{17}$.

d. ability, skill (Ex 28$_3$ 31$_6$ 35$_{10.25.26.35}$ 36$_{1.2.8}$).

2. feelings of human beings (e.g. Gn 34$_3$ 50$_{21}$ Jg 5$_9$ 19$_3$ 2 S 14$_1$ 19$_8$ Is 40$_2$ Jr 20$_9$ Ho 2$_{16}$ Ml 3$_{24.24}$ Ps 45$_2$ Ru 2$_{13}$ Ca 5$_2$ 2 C 30$_{22}$ Si 7$_{35}$ 8$_{19}$ 25$_{13}$ 30$_{23}$) or of Y. (Gn 6$_6$ Ho 11$_8$).

Especially as sensitive to:

a. joy, Ex 4$_{14}$ Jg 16$_{25}$ 18$_{20}$ 19$_{6.22}$ 1 S 2$_1$ 25$_{36}$ 2 S 13$_{28}$ 1 K 8$_{66}$||2 C 7$_{10}$ 1 K 21$_7$ Is 24$_7$ 65$_{14}$ 66$_{14}$ Zc 10$_{7.7}$ Ps 4$_8$ 13$_6$ 16$_9$ 19$_9$ 28$_7$ 33$_{21}$ 84$_3$ 105$_3$||1 C 16$_{10}$ Ps 119$_{111}$ Pr 15$_{13.15.30}$ 17$_{22}$ 23$_{15}$ 24$_{17}$ 27$_{9.11}$ Ru 3$_7$ Ca 3$_{11}$ Ec 2$_{10.10}$ 5$_{19}$ 7$_3$ 9$_7$ 11$_9$ Lm 5$_{15}$ Est 1$_{10}$ 5$_9$ Si 33$_{13}$ 34$_{28}$ 39$_{35}$ 40$_{20.26}$ 48$_{10}$ 11QPs^a 51$_{15}$ 1QH 10$_{31}$ 4QBark^d 7$_2$.

b. pain, grief, sadness, Ex 9$_{14}$ Is 15$_5$ 65$_{14}$ Jr 8$_{18}$ 23$_9$ Ezk 13$_{22}$ (if em.) Ps 13$_3$ 38$_9$ (or em.) 55$_5$ Pr 13$_{12}$ 14$_{13}$ 15$_{13}$ 25$_{20.20}$ (if em.) Ec 2$_{20.23}$ Lm 1$_{20.22}$ 2$_{18}$ (or em.) 2$_{19}$ 5$_{17}$ Ne 2$_2$ 1QH 5$_{31}$ 7$_5$ 10$_{33}$ fr. 4$_{13}$ 4QDibHam^a 1.6$_5$ 4QPr Fêtes^b 39$_1$ Lachish ost. 3$_6$.

c. weakness, anxiety, fear, Gn 42$_{28}$ 45$_{26}$ Dt 28$_{65}$ Jos 14$_8$ 1 S 4$_{13}$ 28$_5$ 2 K 6$_{11}$ Is 35$_4$ 57$_{15}$ 61$_1$ Jr 4$_{9.9}$ 48$_{41.41}$ 49$_{22.22}$ Ezk 13$_{22}$ 21$_{12.20}$ Na 2$_{11}$ Ps 10$_{17}$ 22$_{15}$ 27$_3$ 34$_{19}$ 40$_{13}$ 51$_{19}$ 61$_3$ 69$_{21}$ 102$_5$ 107$_{12}$ 119$_{161}$ 143$_4$ 147$_3$ 37$_1$ Jb 23$_{16}$ Pr 12$_{25}$ Ec 2$_{22}$ 1 S 17$_{32}$ Si 48$_{19}$ 1QH 8$_{32}$ 1QM 8$_{10}$ 11$_9$ 14$_6$ 4Q Wiles 2$_4$ 4QJub^h 35$_{14}$ 4QDiscourse 2.2$_7$ 4QBark^c 1.1$_{1.4}$ 1QH 2$_{9.28}$ 4QM^a 11.2$_{15}$ 11QPs^a 24$_{16}$ GnzPs 4$_1$.

d. courage, strength, of human beings, 2 S 7$_{27}$ 17$_{10}$ Is 46$_{12}$ (or em.) Ezk 22$_{14}$ Am 2$_{16}$ Ps 27$_{14}$ 76$_6$ 1QM 18$_{13}$ 4Q Discourse 2.2$_8$ 4QapPs^b 48$_9$ 4QRedInk 2$_2$ 4QDibHam^a 4$_{12}$ 11QPs^a 19$_{13}$ CD 20$_{33}$; of lion, 2 S 17$_{10}$; specif. as sustainable by food, Gn 18$_5$ Jg 19$_5$.

e. irritation, anger, Ezk 32$_9$ Ps 39$_4$ Pr 19$_3$ Ec 11$_{10}$.

f. contempt, 2 S 6$_{16}$||1 C 15$_{29}$ Pr 5$_{12}$.

g. jealousy, Pr 23$_{17}$.

h. conscience, 1 S 24$_4$ 25$_{31}$ 2 S 24$_{10}$.

3. will, inclination, disposition, personality, of human beings, Gn 6$_5$ 8$_{21}$ Ex 25$_2$ 35$_{5.21.22.29}$ 36$_2$ Nm 16$_{28}$

24$_{13}$ 32$_{7.9}$ Jg 5$_{15.16}$ 9$_3$ 1 S 10$_{9.26}$ 1 K 11$_3$ 18$_{37}$ 2 K 12$_5$ Is 29$_{13}$ 44$_{20}$ 57$_{17}$ 59$_{13}$ Jr 11$_{20}$ 12$_3$ 17$_{5.10}$ 20$_{12}$ 22$_{17}$ 32$_{39}$ Ezk 6$_9$ 11$_{19.19.19.21}$ 14$_{3.4.5.7}$ 18$_{31}$ 20$_{16}$ 28$_2$ 33$_{31}$ 36$_{26.26.26}$ Ho 7$_{6.14}$ Ps 7$_{10}$ 12$_{3.3}$ 17$_3$ 21$_3$ 26$_2$ 28$_7$ 33$_{15}$ 36$_2$ 37$_{4.31}$ 40$_{11}$ 44$_{19.22}$ 57$_8$||108$_2$ 57$_8$ 58$_3$ (or em.) 66$_{18}$ 78$_{8.37}$ 83$_6$ 105$_{25}$ 112$_{7.8}$ 119$_{36.112}$ 141$_4$ Jb 11$_{13}$ 15$_{12}$ 31$_{7.9.27}$ Pr 3$_1$ 4$_{4.23}$ 7$_{10.25}$ 14$_{30}$ 15$_{11}$ 17$_3$ 21$_{1.2}$ 23$_7$ 24$_{12}$ 26$_{25}$ perh. 27$_{19}$ 31$_{11}$ Ec 7$_{7.26}$ 8$_{11}$ Est 7$_5$ Dn 1$_8$ Ezr 6$_{22}$ 7$_{27}$ Ne 2$_{12}$ 3$_{38}$ 7$_5$ 1 C 12$_{34.34.39}$ 2 C 7$_{11}$ 12$_{14}$ 24$_4$ 29$_{31}$ 30$_{12}$ Si 4$_{17}$ 5$_2$ 8$_{1.2}$ 9$_9$ 10$_{12}$ 13$_{25.26}$ 14$_{1.3}$ 42$_{18}$ 45$_{23}$ 46$_{11}$ 1QH 4$_{14}$ 5$_{26.31}$ 7$_{13}$ 8$_{37}$ 17$_{22}$ 1QM 10$_5$ 1QS 2$_{11}$ 4QpIsa^c 23.2$_{13}$ 4QMidrEschat^b 9$_9$ 4Q183 1.2$_4$ 4Q Myst^a 3a.2$_{14}$ 8$_6$ 4QJub^h 37$_{21.21}$ 4QBark^a 1.2$_{10}$ 4Q Bark^d 2.i$_{14}$ 4QPrayer^d 1.1$_3$ 4QM^a 11.2$_{12}$ 4QM^h 2$_4$ 4Q Dib Ham^a 1.2$_{13}$ 4QapMes 2.2$_4$ 4QBéat 5$_5$ 11QT 58$_{20}$ 59$_{24}$ MurEpBarC^b$_6$ GnzPs 3$_7$; of Y., 2 S 7$_{21}$||1 C 7$_{19}$ (or em.) Is 63$_4$ Jr 3$_{15}$ 7$_{31}$ 19$_5$ 23$_{20}$ 30$_{24}$ 32$_{35}$ 34$_{21}$ Jb 34$_{14}$ Lm 3$_{33}$.

לֵב characterized as loyal, devoted (e.g. Jg 16$_{15}$ 2 S 15$_{13}$ 1 K 8$_{23}$||2 C 6$_{14}$ 1 K 12$_{27}$ 2 K 23$_3$ Is 38$_3$ Jr 3$_{10}$ 24$_7$ Zp 3$_{14}$ Ps 9$_2$ 119$_{2.10.34.58.69.145}$ 138$_1$ Pr 3$_5$ 1 C 28$_9$ 29$_9$ 2 C 6$_{38}$ Si 7$_{29}$ 47$_8$ 49$_3$ 1QH 15$_{10}$ 16$_{7.17}$ 1QS 5$_9$ 4Q417 1.1$_9$ 4QDib Ham^a 1.2$_{13}$ 4QBéat 3.2$_4$ 4QUnidC 1$_4$ CD 1$_{10}$ 15$_{9.12}$), upright, pure (e.g. Ps 7$_{11}$ 11$_2$ 32$_{11}$ 36$_{11}$ 51$_{12}$ 64$_{11}$ 94$_{15}$ 97$_{11}$ 119$_{80}$ 125$_4$ Jb 33$_3$ Pr 20$_9$ 22$_{11}$ 4QBark^c 1.1$_{10}$ 4QBéat 3.2$_1$), lowly (Si 11$_{5[B]}$), stubborn, hard (e.g. Ex 4$_{21}$ 7$_{3.13.14.22}$ 8$_{11.15.28}$ 9$_{7.12.34.35}$ 10$_{1.1.20.27}$ 11$_{10}$ 14$_{4.8.17}$ perh. Dt 29$_{18}$ Jos 11$_{20}$ 1 S 6$_6$ Is 63$_{17}$ Jr 3$_{17}$ 5$_{23}$ 7$_{24}$ 9$_{13}$ 11$_8$ 13$_{10}$ 16$_{12}$ 18$_{12}$ 23$_{17}$ Ezk 2$_4$ 3$_7$ Zc 7$_{12}$ Ps 81$_{13}$ Pr 28$_{14}$ Si 3$_{26.26}$ 16$_{15}$ 1QH 4$_{15}$ 16$_7$ perh. 1QS 1$_6$ 2$_{14}$ 2$_{26}$ 3$_3$ 4$_{11}$ 5$_4$ 7$_{19.24}$9$_{10}$ 4Q D^a 5.2$_{11}$ 4QConfess 2$_{3.5}$ 4QParGenEx 3$_{7.11}$ CD 2$_{18}$ 3$_{5.12}$ 8$_{8.19}$ 19$_{20.33}$ 20$_{10}$), evil, godless (e.g. Jr 4$_{14}$ Jb 36$_{13}$ Pr 26$_{23}$ Ec 9$_3$ 11$_9$ Si 10$_{13}$ 38$_{10}$ 4QAdmon 1$_3$ 4Q469 2$_3$ 4Q Sap^b 2$_7$), perverse, deceitful (e.g. Ps 101$_{4[mss]}$ Pr 6$_{14}$ 11$_{20}$ 12$_8$ 14$_{14}$ 17$_{20}$ Jr 14$_{14}$ 17$_9$ 23$_{26.26}$ Ho 10$_2$ Si 36$_{25}$ 1QH 7$_{27}$ 4QWiles 1$_2$ 4QapPs^b 85$_3$ 4QBark^a 1.2$_4$ 4QBéat 3.2$_3$ 5$_6$ 7.2$_6$), uncircumcised (Jr 9$_{25}$ Ezk 44$_{7.9}$ 1QpHab 11$_{13}$ 4QWiles 2$_5$), hostile (e.g. appar. Jr 51$_1$ Ps 55$_{22}$), foolish (e.g. Pr 12$_{23}$ 15$_7$ 4Q418 69.2$_{4.8}$ 205$_2$ 4QsapDidB 1$_8$), arrogant, proud (e.g. Jr 48$_{29}$ 49$_{16}$||Ob$_3$ 2 K 14$_{10}$||2 C 25$_{19}$ Ezk 28$_{2.17}$ Ho 13$_6$ Ps 131$_1$ Pr 16$_5$ 18$_{12}$ 21$_4$ 2 C 17$_6$ 26$_{16}$ 32$_{25.26}$ Si 11$_{30}$ 16$_{10}$ 1QpHab 8$_{10}$ 4QBark^c 1.2$_3$).

4. physical **heart, chest** of human being, Ex 28$_{29.30.31}$ 1 S 25$_{37}$ 2 S 18$_{14}$ 2 K 9$_{24}$ Is 1$_5$ 57$_{15}$ Jr 4$_{19.19}$ Ho 13$_8$ Na 2$_8$ Ps 37$_{15}$ 45$_6$ Ca 8$_6$, perh. Jr 48$_{36.36}$ Ps 38$_{11}$ 109$_{22}$; of Leviathan, Jb 41$_{16}$.

5. middle, depth, height, of sea, Ex 15$_8$ Ezk 27$_{4.25.26.27}$ 28$_{2.8}$ Ps 46$_3$ Pr 23$_{34}$ 30$_{19}$; heaven (Dt 4$_{11}$); terebinth, 2 S 18$_{14}$.

<SUBJ> היה *be* Jr 5$_{23}$ 48$_{41}$ 49$_{22}$ 1 S 4$_{13}$ (+ חָרֵד *trembling*) 2 S 15$_{13}$ (or em. לֵב־ *heart of* to כָּל־ *every*) 1 K 9$_3$ ||2 C 7$_{16}$ (|| עַיִן *eye*) Ps 22$_{15}$ (+ כַּדּוֹנַג *like wax*) 119$_{80}$ (+ תָּמִים *blameless*) Lm 5$_{17}$ (+ דָּוֶה *faint*; || עַיִן) Ne 3$_{38}$ 4QJub^h 37$_{21.21}$, גבה *be high* Ezk 28$_{2.17}$ Ps 131$_1$ (|| עַיִן) Pr 18$_{12}$ 2 C 17$_6$ 26$_{16}$ 32$_{25}$, רום *be high* Ho 13$_6$ 1QpHab 8$_{10}$, חסר *be lacking* Ec 10$_3$, אנשׁ pass. *be weak* Jr 17$_9$ (or em. אֱנוֹשׁ *human being*), דוה *be faint* Lachish ost. 3$_6$ (unless דָּוֶה *faint*, used predicatively), עטף *be faint* Ps 61$_3$, מוג *melt* Ezk 21$_{20}$, ni. *melt* Ezk 21$_{20(Gnz)}$ Si 48$_{19}$ ([נ]מוגו), מסס *melt* intrans. 1QH 2$_{28}$, ni. *melt* Ezk 21$_{12}$ (|| רוּחַ *spirit*, יָד *hand*, + בֶּרֶךְ *knee*) Na 2$_{11}$ (+ בֶּרֶךְ) Ps 22$_{15}$ 1QM 11$_9$ 14$_6$ 4QM^a 11.2$_{15}$, נגר ni. *be poured out* 1QH 8$_{32}$ (|| בָּשָׂר *flesh*), פוג *be numb* Gn 45$_{26}$, שׁמם htpo. *be appalled* Ps 143$_4$ (|| רוּחַ), חרד *tremble* 1 S 28$_5$ Jb 37$_1$, נוע htpol. *tremble* 4QDiscourse 2.2$_7$ (|| קֶרֶב *inside*), ירא *fear* Ps 27$_3$ (יִירָא my heart does not *fear*; mss אִירָא appar. *I shall* not *fear*, O my heart), פחד *fear* Ps 119$_{161}$, חיל *writhe* Ps 55$_5$, pol. *be brought to trembling* Ps 109$_{22}$ (if em. חלל *be pierced*), סער ni. *be troubled* 2 K 6$_{11}$, פעם ni. *be disturbed* 4QJub^h 35$_{14}$ ([לבוי פעם]), כנע ni. *be humbled* 4QDib Ham^a 1.6$_5$, זעף *be angry* Pr 19$_3$, קנא pi. *envy* Pr 23$_{17}$ (+ שָׂפָה *lip*), חמם *be hot* Ps 39$_4$, יבשׁ *be dry* Ps 102$_5$ (or del. יבשׁ, leaving לֵב as subj. of נכה ho. *be struck*), טפשׁ *be fat* Ps 119$_{70}$.

עמד *stand* Ezk 22$_{14}$ (|| יָד *hand*), מהר pi. *make haste* Ec 5$_1$ (+ פֶּה *mouth*), הלך *go* 2 K 5$_{26}$ Ezk 11$_{21}$ 20$_{16}$ 33$_{31}$ (or del. הלך, and read אַחֲרֵי בִּצְעָם לִבָּם *their heart is [on] their gain*) Jb 31$_7$ (+ אָשֻׁר *step*, עַיִן *eye*, כַּף *hand*), יצא *go out*, i.e. fail Gn 42$_{28}$, עזב *forsake* Ps 40$_{13}$, נפל *fall* 1 S 17$_{32}$, שׁבר ni. *be broken* Jr 23$_9$ (+ עֶצֶם *bone*) Ps 51$_{19}$ (or del. שׁבר ni.), דכה ni. *be crushed* Ps 51$_{19}$ (|| רוּחַ *spirit*) 4Q Wiles 2$_4$ 4QBark^c 1.1$_1$, כאב *be in pain* Pr 14$_{13}$, גלה htp. *be revealed* Pr 18$_2$ (or em. הוֹלֵלוֹת *folly of* his heart), פתה *be enticed* Jb 31$_{27}$, ni. Jb 31$_9$ (+ יָד, פֶּה *mouth*), pu. *be deceived* 1QH 8$_{37}$ ([פות[ה]), הפך ni. *be turned over* Ho 11$_8$ (+ נִחוּם *compassion*) Lm 1$_{20}$, שׁוב *go back* 1 K 12$_{27}$, סור *de-*

part Jr 17$_5$ Ezk 6$_9$ (or del. סור) Ps 101$_{4(mss)}$ Si 10$_{12}$ (if em. מלבו he departs *from his heart* to לבו *his heart* departs), שׂטה *stray* Pr 7$_{25}$, סוג ni. *go back* Ps 44$_{19}$ (+ אֲשֶׁר), סרר *be stubborn* Jr 5$_{23}$, מרה *be rebellious* Jr 5$_{23}$, חזק *be strong(-willed)* Ex 7$_{13.22}$ 8$_{15}$ 9$_{35}$, אמץ hi. *show courage* Ps 27$_{14}$, עזז *be strong* CD 20$_{33}$, תקף *be strong* 11QPs^a 19$_{13}$, כון ni. *be firm* Ps 57$_8$||108$_2$ 57$_8$ 78$_{37}$ 112$_7$ 4Q UnidC 1$_4$, יצק pass. *be cast*, i.e. hard Jb 41$_{16}$, כבד *be heavy* Ex 9$_7$, טחח *be covered* Is 44$_{18}$ (|| עַיִן *eye*), מלא *be full* Ec 8$_{11}$ 9$_3$ Si 10$_{13}$ ([לבנו]), *fill* Est 7$_5$ (or em. מְלָאוֹ whose heart *has filled him* to מְלֵא who *has filled* his heart, or מָלֵא whose heart *is full*), ni. *be filled* Si 4$_{17}$ (unless ימלא = he *fills* his heart, i.e. מלא pi.), נטה *turn* (intrans.) Jg 9$_3$, hi. *turn*, i.e. lead astray Is 44$_{20}$, נדב *be generous* Ex 25$_2$ 35$_{29}$ Si 45$_{23}$, לקח *take* Jb 15$_{12}$ (+ עַיִן *eye*), pu. *be taken* Ho 10$_2$ (if em. חלק *be smooth*).

חלק *be smooth* Ho 10$_2$ (or em. pu. *be divided* or לקח pu. *be taken*), תלל ho. *be deceived* Is 44$_{20}$, נשׁא ni. *be deceived* Si 46$_{11}$ (unless נשׂא ni. *be raised*; or em. שׂנה *prostitute oneself*), טוב *be good*, i.e. be glad Jg 16$_{25}$ 1 S 25$_{36}$ 2 S 13$_{28}$ Est 1$_{10}$, יטב *be good*, i.e. glad Jg 18$_{20}$ 19$_6$ 1 K 21$_7$ Ru 3$_7$ Ec 7$_3$ 11$_9$ (if em. hi.), *gladden* Pr 15$_{13}$ 17$_{22}$ (|| רוּחַ *spirit*) Ec 11$_9$ (or em.), שׂמח *rejoice* Zc 10$_7$ Ps 16$_9$ (|| כָּבוֹד *glory* [mss כָּבֵד *liver*], + בָּשָׂר *flesh*) 33$_{21}$ 105$_3$||1 C 16$_{10}$ Pr 23$_{15}$, גיל *rejoice* Zc 10$_7$ Ps 13$_6$ Pr 24$_{17}$, שׂישׂ *rejoice* Is 66$_{14}$ (+ עֶצֶם *bone*) 1QH 10$_{30}$ (+ נֶפֶשׁ *soul*), עלץ *exult* 1 S 2$_1$ (|| קֶרֶן *horn*), עלז *exult* Ps 28$_7$ (or em. בָּשָׂר my *flesh* exults), רנן pi. *exult* Ps 84$_3$ (||בָּשָׂר), רחשׁ *be astir* Ps 45$_2$.*

עשׂה *do* Is 32$_6$ (1QIsa^a חשׁב *reckon*), קנה *acquire* Pr 18$_{15}$ (|| אֹזֶן *ear*), נשׂא *raise*, i.e. stir Ex 35$_{21.26}$ 36$_2$ 2 K 14$_{10}$ ||2 C 25$_{19}$, ni. *be raised* Si 46$_{11}$ (unless נשׁא ni. *be deceived*; or em. שׂנה *prostitute oneself*), הלל htpol. *act madly* 1QH 10$_{33}$, perh. אחז *hold* Ec 2$_3$, נכה hi. *strike* 1 S 24$_6$ 2 S 24$_{10}$, ho. *be struck* Ps 102$_5$, סחר pealal *palpitate* Ps 38$_{11}$ (+ כֹּחַ), חלל *be pierced* Ps 109$_{22}$ (or em. חִיל pol. *be pierced*), חשׁב *reckon* 1QIsa^a 32$_6$, pi. *plan* Pr 16$_9$, חרשׁ *devise* Pr 6$_{18}$, אמר *say* Ps 27$_8$, דבר pi. *speak* Ps 41$_7$ Pr 23$_{33}$ (|| עַיִן *eye*), נגד hi. *tell* Si 37$_{14}$, הגה *meditate* Is 33$_{18}$ Pr 15$_{28}$ (:: פֶּה *mouth*) 24$_2$ (|| שָׂפָה *lip*), המה *make a noise* Jr 4$_{19}$ 48$_{36.36}$ 1QH 5$_{31}$ 7$_5$ fr. 4$_{13}$, קרא *call* Pr 12$_{23}$, זעק *cry* Is 15$_5$, צעק *cry* Lm 2$_{18}$ (or em. צָעַק לִבָּם אֶל־אֲדֹנָי *their heart cries to my Lord*, to צַעֲקִי לָךְ מָלֵא אֲדֹנָי *my cry to you is full, O my Lord*), עור *be awake* Ca 5$_2$, ראה *see* Ec 1$_{16}$ 8$_{16}$, שׁמע *hear* 1 K 3$_9$, ידע *know* Dt 29$_3$ Jr 24$_7$ Pr 14$_{10}$ Ec 1$_{17.17}$ 7$_{22.25}$ (or del. ידע; mss בְּלִבִּי *with my heart*) 8$_{5.16}$, בין ni. *be intelligent* 1 K 3$_{12}$ Pr 14$_{33}$ (+ בְּקֶרֶב *inside*) 15$_{14}$ 18$_{15}$, hi. *understand* Dn 10$_{12}$ Si 3$_{29}$ 36$_{24(B)}$ 1QH 18$_{20}$ ([יבין]), שׂכל hi. *be intelligent* Is 44$_{18}$ (|| עַיִן *eye*), *make wise* Pr 16$_{23}$, חכם *be wise* Pr 23$_{15}$.

שׁנה pi. *change* Si 13$_{25}$, נצר *keep* Pr 3$_1$, נהג *guide* Ec 2$_3$, מלך ni. *take counsel* Ne 5$_7$, אבה *consent* Si 14$_1$, נתן *give* Si 36$_{25}$, תור *explore* Ec 7$_{25}$ (mss בְּלִבִּי *with my heart*), בקשׁ pi. *seek* Pr 15$_{14}$ Ec 7$_{25}$, דרשׁ *seek* Ec 1$_{13}$ 2 C 12$_{14}$ 4QpIsa^c 23.2$_{13}$, בטח *trust* Ps 28$_7$ 112$_7$ (pass.) Pr 31$_{11}$, pass., סמך pass. *be supported* Ps 112$_8$ 4QBark^d 2.1$_{14}$, פתח ni. *be opened* 1QH 10$_{31}$, נאץ *spurn* Pr 5$_{12}$, זנה *prostitute oneself* Ezk 6$_9$ 11QT 59$_{14}$, שׂנה *prostitute oneself* Si 46$_{11}$ (if em. נשׂא ni. *be raised* or נשׁא ni. *be deceived*),* שׁכב *lie down* Ec 2$_{23}$, אבד *die* Jr 4$_{9.9}$, מות *die* 1 S 25$_{37}$.

<NOM CL> יֹשֶׁר־לִבִּי אֲמָרָי *my words are the uprightness of my heart* Jb 33$_3$, כָּל־שֵׁרִית יִשְׂרָאֵל לֵב אֶחָד *all the rest of Israel were (of) a single mind* 1 C 12$_{39}$ (mss שְׁאֵרִית), קְרָב־לִבּוֹ appar. *his heart is war* Ps 55$_{22}$ (or em. בְּלִבּוֹ war is *in his heart*), חַיֵּי בְשָׂרִים לֵב מַרְפֵּא *a mind of health is the life of the flesh* Pr 14$_{30}$, פַּלְגֵי־מַיִם לֶב־מֶלֶךְ *the heart of the king is channels of water* Pr 21$_1$, חֲרָמִים לִבָּהּ *her heart is nets* Ec 7$_{26}$, לֶב־אָיִן *there is no heart*, i.e. desire Pr 17$_{16}$, אֵין לֵב *there is no heart*, i.e. wisdom Jr 5$_{21}$ Ho 7$_{11}$ 4QapPs^b 1$_2$.

לִבִּי שָׂמֵחַ *my heart was joyful* Ec 2$_{10}$, כָּבֵד לֵב פַּרְעֹה *Pharaoh's heart is heavy*, i.e. obdurate Ex 7$_{14}$, עָקֹב הַלֵּב *the heart is devious* Jr 17$_9$ (or em. עָמֹק *deep*), לִבִּי דַוָּי *my heart is sick* Jr 8$_{18}$ Lm 1$_{22}$, לֵב עָמֹק *(the) heart is deep* Ps 64$_7$ (+ קֶרֶב *inside*), כֵּן לֵב־הָאָדָם לָאָדָם *so is the heart of a human to a human* Pr 27$_{19}$ (+ פָּנִים *face*), לֵב כְּסִילִים לֹא־כֵן *the heart of fools is not so*, or, *upright* Pr 15$_7$.

לִבִּי לְחוֹקְקֵי יִשְׂרָאֵל *my heart is for the commanders of Israel* Jg 5$_9$, לֵב חָכָם לִימִינוֹ *the heart of a sage is to his right* Ec 10$_2$, לֵב כְּסִיל לִשְׂמֹאלוֹ *the heart of a fool is to his left* Ec 10$_2$, לֵב חֲכָמִים בְּבֵית אֵבֶל *the heart of the wise is in the house of mourning* Ec 7$_4$, לֵב כְּסִילִים בְּבֵית שִׂמְחָה *the heart of fools is in the house of joy* Ec 7$_4$, לֵב רְשָׁעִים כִּמְעָט *the heart of the wicked is as a small thing* Pr 10$_{20}$ (or em. כְּמָעָה *as a grain*), לִבּוֹ כְּלֵב הָאַרְיֵה *his heart is like the heart of a lion* 2 S 17_{10}, לִבְּךָ אֵין אִתִּי *your heart is not with me* Jg 16_{15}, לִבּוֹ בַּל־עִמָּךְ *his heart is not with you* Pr 23_{7}, לֵב הַמֶּלֶךְ עַל־אַבְשָׁלוֹם *the heart of the king was for Absalom* 2 S 14_{1}, אֵין ... לִבְּךָ כִּי אִם־עַל־בִּצְעֶךָ *your heart ... is only for your unjust gain* Jr 22_{17} (‖ עַיִן *eye*).

<OBJ> מצא *find* 2 S 7_{27} (+ אֹזֶן *ear*), ברא *create* Ps 51_{12} (‖ רוּחַ *spirit*), עשׂה *make* Ezk 18_{31} (‖ רוּחַ), יצר *form* Ps 33_{15} (+ מַעֲשֶׂה *deed*), בוא hi. *bring* Pr 23_{12} (‖ אֹזֶן *ear*), קרב pi. *bring near* Ho 7_{6} (unless קֵרְבוּ כַתַּנּוּר לִבָּם = *they approach, their heart is like an oven*; or em. קָדַח their heart *blazes* like an oven).

נתן *give* Dt 28_{65} 29_{3} (‖ עַיִן *eye*, אֹזֶן *ear*) 1 K $3_{9.12}$ Jr 24_{7} 32_{39} (‖ דֶּרֶךְ *way* [or em. רוּחַ *spirit*]) Ezk 11_{19} (‖ רוּחַ) 11_{19} 36_{26} (‖ רוּחַ) 36_{26} 2 C 30_{12} 4Q183 1.2_{4} 4QDibHam[a] 18_{2} ([נ]תתה), *apply* Pr 23_{26} (+ עַיִן) Ec $1_{13.17}$ $7_{21.25}$ (if ins. נתן) $8_{9.16}$ $9_{1(\text{mss})}$ Dn 10_{12} Si 12_{11}, *cause to be* Ezk $28_{2.6}$, שׂים *place* heart, i.e. pay attention Ex 9_{21} 1 S 9_{20} 25_{25} (mss אֶל־ take *to* heart for אֶת־) 2 S $18_{3.3}$ (lacking in mss) Is 41_{22} Ezk 40_{4} 44_{5} (both + עַיִן, אֹזֶן) 44_{5} Jb 1_{8} 2_{3} 34_{14} (+ רוּחַ, נְשָׁמָה *breath*) Si 6_{32} (‖ אֹזֶן) 14_{21} $16_{20.24}$ 4QBark[c] 1.1_{10} 4QBéat 14.2_{18}, *cause to be* Zc 7_{12}, שׁית *place* heart, i.e. pay attention Ex 7_{23} 1 S 4_{20} 2 S 13_{20} (mss אֶל־ for אֶת־) Jr 31_{21} Ps 62_{11} Jb 7_{17} Pr 22_{17} (‖ אֹזֶן) 24_{32} 27_{23} Si $38_{20(\text{Bmg}).26}$, *cause to be* Ps 48_{14}.

שׁוב hi. *direct* Ml $3_{24.24}$ Si $38_{20(\text{B})}$ 48_{10} 4QapPs[b] 15_{1}, נטה *direct* Ps 119_{112} (if em. hi.; ‖ אֹזֶן *ear*), hi. *direct* 1 K 11_{3} Ps 119_{36} 141_{4} Pr 2_{2} (or em.) Si 9_{9} Arad ost. 40$_{4}$ ([ל]בה), סבב hi. *direct* 1 K 18_{37} Ezr 6_{22}, הפך *direct* Ps 105_{25}, *give* 1 S 10_{9}, סוג hi. *remove* 4QM[a] 11.2_{15}, נשׂא *raise*, i.e. turn away Si 7_{35}, רום hi. *raise* 1QM 14_{6}, אשׁר pi. *direct* Pr 23_{19}, פקד *command* 4QBark[c] 1.1_{5} (‖ כִּלְיָה *kidney*), יסר *discipline* 1QH 17_{22} ([יסר]תה), שׂכל hi. *make wise* 4QHod[b] 12_{2} ([לבי]), שׁגה hi. *lead astray* Si 8_{2} ([י]שג הל[ב]), עקב *trick* 4Q418 8_{12}.

גלה pi. *reveal* Si 8_{19} 1QH 12_{34} (+ פֶּה *mouth*) 18_{24}, פתח *open* 1QS 11_{16}, שׁפך *pour* Lm 2_{19}, מלא pi. *fill* Est 7_{5} (if em. qal *fill*, with לב as subj.) Si 4_{17} (unless ימלא his heart *is filled*, i.e. ni.), לקח *take* Ho 4_{11}, קנה *acquire* Pr 15_{32} (or em. קוֹנֶה לֵב *acquires understanding* to אֹהֵב נַפְשׁוֹ *loves one's soul*) 19_{8} (+ תְּבוּנָה *understanding*) Si 51_{20}, סור hi. *remove* Ezk 11_{19} 36_{26} Jb 12_{24}, מנע *withhold* Ec 2_{10}, גנב *steal*, i.e. win over Gn 31_{20} 2 S 15_{6} (pi.), צפן *hide* Jb 17_{4}, ערב *give in pledge* Jr 30_{21}, נגד hi. *tell*, i.e. reveal Jg $16_{17.18.18}$, סעד *sustain* Gn 18_{5} Jg 19_{5}, גבר hi. *strengthen* 4QDiscourse 2.2_{8}, חזק pi. *strengthen* 4QBark[c] 1.1_{1} 4QM[a] 11.2_{15} ([ו]ל[ב]) 4QDibHam[a] 4_{12}, specif. *harden* Ex 4_{21} 9_{12} $10_{20.27}$ 11_{10} $14_{4.8.17}$ Jos 11_{20} 4QParGenEx $3_{7.11}$ (ויחזק), כבד hi. *make heavy*, i.e. harden Ex $8_{11.28}$ 9_{34} $10_{1.1}$ 1 S 6_{6} (pi.), קשׁה hi. *harden* Ex 7_{3} Pr 28_{14} Si 16_{15}, קשׁח hi. *harden* Is 63_{17}, שׁמן hi. *cover in fat* Is 6_{10} (‖ עַיִן *eye*, אֹזֶן *ear*), כון hi. *establish* Ps 10_{17} (or em. תָּכִין *you will establish* to הֶגְיוֹן *meditation of* their heart; ‖ אֹזֶן) 78_{8} (mss בין hi. *cause* heart *to understand*) Jb 11_{13} Pr 8_{5} (if em. בין hi.) 2 C 12_{14} 1QH 7_{13} 4QBéat 3.2_{4}, רחב *widen* Ps 119_{32}, רחק pi. *distance* Is 29_{13} (+ שָׂפָה *lip*, פֶּה *mouth*), מגן pi. *hand over* 1QM 18_{13}.

כנע hi. *humble* Ps 107_{12} (or em. ni. *be humbled*, of לֵב), נוא hi. *discourage* Nm $32_{7(\text{Qr}).9}$ 4QM[h] 2_{4}, מסה hi. *melt* Jos 14_{8}, מסס hi. *melt* 1QM 8_{10}, כאה hi. *discourage* Ezk 13_{22} (or em. כאב hi. *hurt*), רכך hi. *weaken* Jb 23_{16}, פוג pi. *weaken* Si 30_{23} (‖ נֶפֶשׁ *soul*), יאשׁ pi. *cause to despair* Ec 2_{20}, חלה hi. *make ill* Pr 13_{12}, כעס hi. *anger* Ezk 32_{9}, שׁבר *break* Ezk 6_{9} (if em. נִשְׁבַּרְתִּי אֶת־ appar. *I was broken by* to וְשָׁבַרְתִּי אֶת־ *and I shall break*) Ps 69_{21} (or em. pi. *shatter*), אבד pi. *destroy* Ec 7_{7} (4QQoh[a] עוה pi. *pervert*), כלה pi. *destroy* Pr 25_{20} (if ins. מְכַלֶּה לִבּוֹ grief *destroys his heart*).

יטב hi. *gladden* Jg 19_{22}, שׂמח pi. *gladden* Pr 15_{30} (‖ עֶצֶם *bone*) 27_{9} (+ נֶפֶשׁ *soul*) 27_{11} 11QPs[a] Si 51_{15}, גיל hi. *gladden* Si $40_{26(\text{Segal})}$ ([יג]ילו), עליץ hi. *gladden* Si 40_{20}, חיה hi. *revive* Is 57_{15} (‖ רוּחַ *spirit*), כבס pi. *wash* Jr 4_{14}, טהר pi. *purify* Si 38_{10}, זכה pi. *purify* Pr 20_{9}, צרף *refine* Ps $26_{2(\text{Qr})}$ (‖ כִּלְיָה *kidney*) 4Q416 2.3_{13}, בחן *test* Jr 11_{20} (‖ כִּלְיָה) 12_{3} Ps 7_{10} (‖ כִּלְיָה) 17_{3} Pr 17_{3} 4QMyst[a] 3a.2_{14} 4QM[a] 11.2_{12} (=1QM 16_{15} לְבָב), תמם hi. *perfect* Si 49_{3} 4QBéat 3.2_{8}, חקר *search* Jr 17_{10} (‖ כִּלְיָה) Si 42_{18} (‖ תְּהוֹם *abyss*), ראה *see* Jr 20_{12} (‖ כִּלְיָה), בין hi. *cause to understand* Ps $10_{17(\text{ms})}$ $78_{8(\text{mss})}$ Pr 8_{5} (or em. כון hi. *establish*) Si 6_{37}, פתר *interpret* Si 50_{27} (unless פִּתּוּר = *interpretation of* their heart), אור hi. *enlighten* 1QS 2_{3}, תכן *measure* Pr 21_{2} 24_{12}, נצר *keep* Pr 4_{23}, פחז hi. *make reckless* Si $19_{2(\text{Segal})}$ ([יפח]יזו).

<CSTR> לֵב אֱלֹהִים *heart of a god* Ezk 28_{2}, אַבְשָׁלוֹם *of Absalom* 2 S 18_{14}, אַמְנוֹן *of Amnon* 2 S 13_{28} (לֵב־), דָּוִד *of*

David 1 S 24$_6$ 2 S 24$_{10}$ (both לֵב־), יוֹאָשׁ *of Joash* 2 C 24$_4$, לָבָן *of Laban* Gn 31$_{20}$, נָבָל *of Nabal* 1 S 25$_{36}$, שְׁלֹמֹה *of Solomon* 2 C 7$_{11}$.

לֵב־אִישׁ *heart of a man* 2 K 12$_5$ Pr 12$_{25}$ 18$_{12}$ (לֵב־) 19$_{21}$ 20$_5$, הָאִישׁ *of the man*, i.e. people, *of* Israel 2 S 15$_{13}$ (or em. כָּל־אִישׁ *every man of*), לֵב אַנְשֵׁי *heart of the men of* 2 S 15$_6$ 4QMidrEschat^b 9$_9$, אִשָּׁה *of a woman* Jr 48$_{41}$ 49$_{22}$, לב אנוש *heart of a person* Si 13$_{25}$ 37$_{14}$, לֵב הָאָדָם *the heart of humankind* Gn 8$_{21}$ Pr 27$_{19}$ (לֵב־), אָדָם *of a human being* 1 S 17$_{32}$ (לֵב־) Pr 16$_9$, לֵב בְּנֵי־הָאָדָם *the heart of human beings* Ec 8$_{11}$ 9$_3$, לִבּוֹת בְּנֵי־אָדָם *hearts of human beings* Pr 15$_{11}$, לֵב בְּנֵי יִשְׂרָאֵל *heart of the Israelites* Nm 32$_{7.9}$, בָּנִים *of the sons* Ml 3$_{24}$, אָבוֹת *of the fathers* Ml 3$_{24}$ (לֵב־) Si 48$_{10}$, לֵב־נַעַר *heart of a lad* Pr 22$_{15}$, לֵב הָעָם *heart of the people* Jos 14$_8$ 1 K 12$_{27}$ Is 6$_{10}$ (לֵב־) Ne 3$_{38(mss)}$, לב עמו *heart of his people* 4QM^a 11.2$_{12}$ (=1QM 16$_{15}$ לְבָב), לֵב עַמִּים *heart(s) of peoples* Ezk 32$_9$.

לֵב הַמֶּלֶךְ *heart of the king* 2 S 14$_1$ Jr 4$_9$ (לֵב־) Pr 21$_1$ (לֶב־מֶלֶךְ) Est 1$_{10}$ (לֵב־) Ezr 7$_{27}$, מֶלֶךְ־ *of the king of* 2 K 6$_{11}$ Ezr 6$_{22}$, מְלָכִים *of kings* Pr 25$_3$, הַשָּׂרִים *of the princes* Jr 4$_9$, ל[ב נ]דיבים *heart of nobles* Si 8$_2$, לֵב פַּרְעֹה *heart of Pharaoh* Ex 7$_{3.13.14.22}$ 8$_{15}$ (both לֵב־) 9$_{7.12.35}$ 10$_{20.27}$ 11$_{10}$ 14$_4$ (לֵב־) 14$_8$ Si 16$_{15}$, רָאשֵׁי *of the chiefs of* Jb 12$_{24}$, לֵב הַנְּבִאִים *heart(s) of the prophets* Jr 23$_{26}$, הַכֹּהֵן *of the priest* Jg 18$_{20}$, כָּל־הַלְוִיִּם *of all the Levites* 2 C 30$_{22}$.

לֵב בַּעְלָהּ *heart of her husband* Pr 31$_{11}$, לב עבדכה *heart of your servant* 1QH 14$_8$ 1QS 11$_{16}$=4QSi 1$_3$ (עבדך) Lachish ost. 3$_6$ ([ע[בדך]]), לֵב עֲבָדֶיךָ *heart(s) of your servants* 2 S 19$_8$, עֲבָדָיו *of his servants* Ex 10$_1$, שִׁפְחָתֶךָ *of your female servant* Ru 2$_{13}$, לב רעו *heart of his neighbour* 4Q Myst^a 6.2$_{12}$.

לב גבורים *heart of the warriors* 1QM 18$_{13}$, לֵב גִּבּוֹרֵי *heart of the warriors of* Jr 48$_{41}$ 49$_{22}$, לב אויב *heart of the enemy* 1QM 8$_{10}$, לֵב אוֹיְבֵי *heart(s) of the enemies of* Ps 45$_6$, לֵב קָמָי *the heart(s) of my opponents* (cipher for כַּשְׂדִּים *Chaldaea*) Jr 51$_1$.

לֵב חָכָם *heart of a wise one* Pr 16$_{23}$ Ec 8$_5$ 10$_2$ Si 3$_{29}$, כָּל־חֲכַם *of every wise one of* Ex 31$_6$, חֲכָמִים *of sages* Ec 7$_4$, צַדִּיק *of a righteous one* Ezk 13$_{22}$ (לֵב־) Pr 15$_{28}$, רְשָׁעִים *of wicked ones* Pr 10$_{20}$, כְּסִיל *of a fool* Ec 10$_2$, כְּסִילִים *of fools* Pr 12$_{23}$ 15$_7$ Ec 7$_4$, לב נבל *heart of a fool* Si 36$_5$ (+ מַחֲשָׁבָה *thought*), גאה *of a proud one* Si 11$_{30}$, ערל perh. *of an uncircumcised one* 4QWiles 2$_5$ (unless *an uncircumcised heart*), לֵב־חֹרְשֵׁי *heart of devisors of* Pr 12$_{20}$, לֵב מְבַקְשֵׁי *heart of those who seek* Y. Ps 105$_3$||1 C 16$_{10}$ (11QPs^a לב מבקש *heart of one who seeks*), נִדְכָּאִים *of contrite ones* Is 57$_{15}$ (|| רוּחַ *spirit*).

לֵב יְרוּשָׁלַםִ *heart of Jerusalem* Is 40$_2$, מִצְרַיִם *of Egypt* Ex 14$_{17}$, הָאַרְיֵה *of a lion* 2 S 17$_{10}$, הַשָּׁמַיִם *of heaven* Dt 4$_{11}$ (Sam לְבַב *heart*; or del. לֵב), לֶב־יָם *heart of the sea* Ex 15$_8$ Pr 23$_{34}$ 30$_{19}$, לֵב יַמִּים *heart of (the) seas* Ezk 27$_{4.25}$ (לֵב־) 27$_{26.27}$ 28$_{2.8}$ Ps 46$_3$, הָאֵלָה *of the terebinth* 2 S 18$_{14}$, שִׁקּוּצֵיהֶם *of their abominations* Ezk 11$_{21}$ (or em. אֵלֶּה אַחֲרֵי *these* went *after* their abominations),* לב מרמה *heart of deceit* 4QBéat 3.2$_3$ ([ל]ב) 5$_6$, אשמה *of wickedness* 4QSap^b 2$_7$, יגון *of grief* 4QPrFêtes^b 39$_1$, לֵב הָאֶבֶן *heart of stone* Ezk 11$_{19}$ 36$_{26}$ 1QH 18$_{20}$ ([האבן]) 18$_{26.28}$ ([האבן]), בָּשָׂר *of flesh* Ezk 11$_{19}$ 36$_{26}$, לב עפר *heart of dust* 1QH 18$_{24}$, אשמה *of guilt* 1QS 1$_6$, לֵב מַרְפֵּא *heart of health* Pr 14$_{30}$, חָכְמָה *of wisdom* Ps 90$_{12}$ (if em. לְבַב *heart of*).

יִשְׁרֵי־לֵב *the upright of heart* Ps 7$_{11}$ 11$_2$ 32$_{11}$ 36$_{11}$ 64$_{11}$ 94$_{15}$ 97$_{11}$, טְהָר־ *one who is pure of* Pr 22$_{11(Qr)}$, חֲכַם־ *one who is wise of* Ex 28$_{3(ms, Sam)}$ 31$_6$ 35$_{10}$ 36$_{1.2.8}$ Pr 10$_8$ 11$_{29}$ 16$_{21}$, חַכְמַת־ *woman who is wise of* Ex 35$_{25}$, חַכְמֵי־ *those who are wise of* Ex 28$_3$ 31$_{8(Sam)}$ Jb 37$_{24}$ 4Q418 81$_{20}$ 4Q UnidA 2$_2$, נְדִיב *one who is generous of* Ex 35$_5$ (לִבּוֹ *of his heart*) 35$_{22}$ 2 C 29$_{31}$, נדיבי לב *those who are generous of heart* 1QM 10$_5$, יֹשְׁבֵי לֵב *inhabitants of the heart of* Jr 51$_1$, שִׂמְחֵי־לֵב *those who are joyful of heart* Is 24$_7$, מְשַׂמְּחֵי־לֵב *those who gladden the heart* Ps 19$_9$ (|| עַיִן *eye*), טוֹבֵי לֵב *(feeling) good of heart* 1 K 8$_{66}$||2 C 7$_{10}$ Est 5$_9$ (טוֹב־), שפלי *lowly ones of* Si 11$_{5(B)}$, נְצֻרַת *woman who is guarded of* heart, perh. wily Pr 7$_{10}$ (or em. נִצֶּרֶת לֹט *one who keeps frankincense*),* נִמְהֲרֵי־ *those who are anxious of* Is 35$_4$, נִשְׁבְּרֵי־ *those who are broken of* Is 61$_1$ Ps 34$_{19}$ (|| רוּחַ *spirit*) 147$_3$ (שְׁבוּרֵי) GnzPs 4$_1$.

גְּבַהּ־לֵב *one who is exalted of heart* Pr 16$_5$ (Gnz גֹּבַע *exultation of* heart), רְחַב־ *one who is wide*, i.e. proud, *of* Pr 21$_4$ (Gnz רחב appar. *width of*; || עַיִן *eye*), אַמִּיץ לִבּוֹ *one who is mighty of (his) heart* Am 2$_{16}$, אַבִּירֵי לֵב *the mighty of heart* Is 46$_{12}$ (or em. אֹבְדֵי *ones dying of*) Ps 76$_6$ (or em. כָּל־בַּעֲרֵי *all who are brutish of* heart) 4QapPs^b 48$_9$ ([אבירי]), חִזְקֵי־לֵב *the strong of heart* Ezk 2$_4$ (|| פָּנִים *face*), קְשֵׁי־ *the hard of* Ezk 3$_7$ (|| מֵצַח *forehead*).

עָרֵל לֵב *one who is uncircumcised of heart* Ezk 44$_{9}$ (|| בָּשָׂר *flesh*, i.e. penis), עַרְלֵי־ *those who are uncircumcised of* Jr 9$_{25}$ Ezk 44$_{7}$ (|| בָּשָׂר), חַנְפֵי־ *those who are irreligious of* Jb 36$_{13}$, עִקֵּשׁ *one who is perverted of* Pr 17$_{20}$ (+ לָשׁוֹן *tongue*), עִקְּשֵׁי־ *the perverted of* Pr 11$_{20}$, נַעֲוֵה־ *one who is perverted of* Pr 12$_{8}$ (or em. נַעֲוֵה to נַעֲבֵה *one who is dense of*), נעוי לב *those who are perverse of* 1QH 7$_{27}$ 18$_{28}$ ([נעוי] [לב]), סוּג *one who is faithless of* Pr 14$_{14}$, חֲסַר־ *one who is lacking (of)* Pr 6$_{32}$ 7$_{7}$ 9$_{4.16}$ (both + פֶּתִי *simple one*) 10$_{13.21}$ (or em. בַּחֲסַר־לֵב die *as one who is lacking of heart* to בְּחֶסֶר die *in want*) 11$_{12}$ (+ תְּבוּנָה *understanding*) 12$_{11}$ (or em. חֲסַר־לֵב to חָסֵר *lacking*) 15$_{21}$ (+ תְּבוּנָה) 17$_{18}$ 24$_{30}$ Si 6$_{20}$, חסרי לב *those who are lacking (of) heart* Si 16$_{23}$ (if em. חסדי *loyalties*, or *those who are devout, of* heart), אוילי *those who are foolish of* 1QH 1$_{37}$ ([או]ילי) 4Q418 58$_{1}$ ([לב]) 69.2$_{4.8}$ 204$_{2}$ 4QsapDidB 1$_{8}$, שמן *one who is fat of* 4Q424 3$_{6}$, נמהרי *those who are swift of* 1QH 2$_{9}$, מארבי לב perh. *ambushers of the heart* 4Q158$_{2}$.

קִירוֹת לִבִּי *walls of my heart* Jr 4$_{19}$ (+ מֵעֶה *innard[s]*), סְגוֹר לִבָּם *enclosure of their heart* Ho 13$_{8}$, לוּחַ לִבָּם *tablet of their heart* Jr 17$_{1}$, לִבֶּךָ *of your heart* Pr 3$_{3}$ (or del.; + גַּרְגֶּרֶת *throat*) 7$_{3}$ (+ אֶצְבַּע *finger*), עורלת לבו *foreskin of his heart* 1QpHab 11$_{13}$, [לבנו] *of our heart* 4QDibHam^{a} 4$_{11}$, ערלות לבם *foreskins of their heart* 4QBark^{a} 1.2$_{4}$,* עקבת לב *traces*, i.e. signs, *of* a good *heart* Si 13$_{26}$.

גלולי לבו *idols of his heart* 1QS 2$_{11}$, [רש]עת לבו *wickedness of his heart* 4QMyst^{c} 7$_{3}$, הוות לבם *wickedness of their heart* 1QH 5$_{26.31}$ ([הוות]), שרירות לב *stubbornness*, or *thinking, of a heart of* 1QS 1$_{6}$, שְׁרִרוּת לִבִּי *stubbornness*, or *thinking, of my heart* Dt 29$_{18}$ 1QS 2$_{14}$ (שרירות),* לִבּוֹ *of his heart* Jr 16$_{12}$ 18$_{12}$ 23$_{17}$ 1QS 2$_{26}$ 3$_{3}$ 5$_{4}$ 7$_{19.24}$ 4QD^{a} 5.2$_{11}$ 4QConfess 2$_{3.5}$ CD 8$_{8}$ 19$_{20}$ (all ten שרירות), לִבָּם *of their heart* Jr 3$_{17}$ 7$_{24}$ 9$_{13}$ 11$_{8}$ (שְׁרִירוּת; + אֹזֶן *ear*) 13$_{10}$ Ps 81$_{13}$ (שְׁרִירוּת) 1QH 4$_{15}$ 1QS 9$_{10}$ 2QVerdict 2$_{4}$ CD 2$_{18}$ 3$_{5.12}$ 8$_{19}$ 19$_{33}$ 20$_{10}$ (all nine שרירות), מרמת לב *deceit of heart* 4QBéat 7.2$_{6}$, תַּרְמִית לִבָּם *deceit of their hearts* Jr 14$_{14(Qr)}$ 23$_{26}$ (תַּרְמִת), גבה לב *exaltation of heart* 4QBark^{c} 1.2$_{3}$ (|| עַיִן *eye*), גֹּבַהּ לִבּוֹ *exaltation of his heart* 2 C 32$_{26}$, רֻם לִבּוֹ *haughtiness of his heart* Jr 48$_{29}$, זְדוֹן לִבֶּךָ *presumptuousness of your heart* Jr 49$_{16}$||Ob$_{3}$ (לִבְּךָ), זדון לבם *presumptuousness of their heart* Si 16$_{10}$, עול לבה perh. *iniquity of her heart* 4QWiles 1$_{2}$ (|| כִּלְיָה *kidney*), נעוות ל[בי] *perversity of my heart* 1QH 17$_{19}$, [נעוות] לבו *perversity of his heart* 1QH 17$_{26}$, חנופות לבמה *profaneness of their heart* 4Q469 2$_{3}$.

טוּב לֵב *goodness of heart* Is 65$_{14}$ Pr 15$_{15}$ (if em. טוֹב־ *good* heart), שְׂשׂוֹן לִבִּי *joy of my heart* Ps 119$_{111}$, מְשׂוֹשׂ לִבֵּנוּ *joy of our heart* Lm 5$_{15}$, שמחת לב *joy of heart* Si 34$_{28(B)}$, שִׂמְחַת לִבּוֹ *joy of his heart* Ca 3$_{11}$ Ec 5$_{19}$, גיל לבי *rejoicing of my heart* 4QBark^{d} 7$_{2}$, רֹעַ לֵב *sadness of heart* Ne 2$_{2}$, כְּאֵב לֵב *pain of heart* Is 65$_{14}$ (|| רוּחַ *spirit*), עַצְּבַת־לֵב *pain of heart* Pr 15$_{13}$, כובוד לב *heaviness of heart* 1QS 4$_{11}$ 4QSap^{b} 24$_{2}$ ([כ]בוד), נַהֲמַת לִבִּי *groaning of my heart* Ps 38$_{9}$ (or em. לָבִיא *of a lion*), מ[כת] לב *wound of the heart* Si 25$_{13(Segal)}$, שבר לבי *fracture of my heart* 11QPs^{a} 24$_{16}$, שנות לב *sleep of the heart of* Si 33$_{13}$, נצח לב perh. *purification of the heart of* 4QMidrEschat^{b} 9$_{9}$.

חָכְמַת־לֵב *wisdom of heart* Ex 35$_{35}$ Si 45$_{26}$, חכמת לבו *wisdom of his heart* 4Q424 3$_{6}$, דעת לבו *knowledge of his heart* 11QPs^{a} 26$_{12}$, לבי *of my heart* 1QS 10$_{24}$ 4QHod^{a} 8$_{1}$, הגו לבו *meditation of his heart* 1QH 11$_{2}$, דֶּרֶךְ לִבּוֹ *way of his heart* Is 57$_{17}$ 4QBark^{a} 1.2$_{11}$ CD 1$_{11}$, דרך לבכה *way of your heart* 1QH 4$_{18.21.24}$ 6$_{7.21}$, דַּרְכֵי לִבְּךָ *ways of your heart* Ec 11$_{9}$ (|| עַיִן *eye*), יֵצֶר לֵב *inclination of the heart of* Gn 8$_{21}$, יצר לבנ[ו] *inclination of our heart* 4QMyst^{a} 8$_{6}$, לבם *of their heart* 4QAdmon 1$_{3}$, עצת לבו *counsel of his heart* 11QT 58$_{20}$, מחשבת לבכה *thought of your heart* 1QH 4$_{13}$, מַחְשְׁבֹת לִבּוֹ *thoughts of its heart* Gn 6$_{5}$ (+ יֵצֶר *inclination of*) Ps 33$_{11}$ (מַחְשְׁבוֹת), מזמת לבכה *plan of your heart* 1QH 4$_{21}$, מְזִמּוֹת לִבּוֹ *plans of his heart* Jr 23$_{20}$ 30$_{24}$, חֲזוֹן לִבָּם *vision of their heart* Jr 23$_{16}$ (+ פֶּה *mouth*).

מַעַרְכֵי־לֵב *arrangements of the heart* Pr 16$_{1}$ (+ לָשׁוֹן *tongue*), פתור לבן *interpretation of their heart* Si 50$_{27}$ (unless לבן obj. of פתר *interpret*), חִקְקֵי־לֵב *decrees of (the) heart* Jg 5$_{15}$, חִקְרֵי־ *searchings of* Jg 5$_{15(mss).16}$, תַּעֲלֻמוֹת לֵב *secrets of the heart* Ps 44$_{22}$, הֶגְיוֹן לִבִּי *meditation of my heart* Ps 19$_{15}$, לִבָּם *of their heart* Ps 10$_{17}$ (if em. תָּכִין *you establish* their heart), הָגוּת לִבִּי *meditation of my heart* Ps 49$_{4}$.

תַּאֲוַת לִבּוֹ *desire of his heart* Ps 21$_{3}$ (+ שָׂפָה *lip*), רַעְיוֹן לִבּוֹ *striving of the heart* Ec 2$_{22}$, מִשְׁאֲלֹת לִבֶּךָ *requests of your heart* Ps 37$_{4}$, משאלות לבי *requests of my heart* Gnz Ps 3$_{7}$, מִכְשׁוֹל לֵב *stumbling of heart* 1 S 25$_{31}$, מְגִנַּת־לֵב perh. *covering*, i.e. dullness, *of heart* Lm 3$_{65}$, יֹשֶׁר־לִבִּי

uprightness of my heart Jb 33$_{3}$, רֹחַב לֵב *width of heart* 1 K 5$_{9}$, כֹּחַ לֵב *strength of heart* Jb 36$_{5}$, צור לב *strength of heart* 4QRedInk 2$_{2}$.

כָּל־לֵב *all the heart* 2 K 23$_{3}$ (|| נֶפֶשׁ *soul*) Zp 3$_{14}$ Ps 119$_{2.10(mss).34.58.69.145}$ 1 C 12$_{34(mss)}$ Si 39$_{35}$ 1QH 15$_{10}$ (כול; || נֶפֶשׁ) 1QS 5$_{9}$ (כול; || נֶפֶשׁ) 4QS^{c} 1.1$_{1}$ (כול ל[ב]) 4QDibHam^{a} 1.2$_{13}$ (כול; || נֶפֶשׁ), CD 15$_{9.12}$ (both || נֶפֶשׁ), כָּל־לִבִּי *all my heart* Jr 32$_{41}$ (|| נֶפֶשׁ) Ps 9$_{2}$ 119$_{10}$ 138$_{1}$ GnzPs 4$_{19}$, כָּל־לִבְּךָ *all your heart* Pr 3$_{5}$, כל לבו *all his heart* Si 47$_{8}$, כָּל־לִבָּהּ *all her heart* Jr 3$_{10}$, כָּל־לִבָּם *all their heart* 1 K 8$_{23}$ ||2 C 6$_{14}$ Jr 24$_{7}$ 2 C 6$_{38}$.

<ADJ> אַחֵר *another* 1 S 10$_{9}$ Jr 32$_{39}$ Ezk 11$_{19}$ (if em. אֶחָד *one* in both) 4QBark^{a} 1.2$_{10}$ (א[ח]ר), שָׁלֵם *whole* Is 38$_{3}$ 1 C 28$_{9}$ 29$_{9}$ 1QH 16$_{7.17}$ CD 1$_{10}$,* אֶחָד *one* Jr 32$_{39}$ (or em.) Ezk 11$_{19}$ (or em.) Ps 83$_{6}$ (if em. יַחְדָּו *together*) 1 C 12$_{39}$ 2 C 30$_{12}$ 4Q183 1.2$_{4}$, יָחַד *united* Ps 83$_{6}$ (if em. יַחְדָּו), חָדָשׁ *new* Jr 32$_{39}$ (if em. אֶחָד) Ezk 11$_{19(mss)}$ 18$_{31}$ 36$_{26}$, טוֹב *good*, i.e. happy Pr 15$_{15}$ (if em. טוּב־ *goodness of* heart) Ec 9$_{7}$ Si 33$_{13}$ 4QpsEzek^{a} 4$_{2}$, שָׂמֵחַ *glad* Pr 15$_{13}$ 17$_{22}$, חָכָם *wise* 1 K 3$_{12}$, טָהוֹר *pure* Ps 51$_{12}$ 4QBark^{c} 1.1$_{10}$ 4QBéat 3.2$_{1}$, רַע *evil, sad* Jr 3$_{17}$ 7$_{24}$ 9$_{13(mss)}$ 11$_{8}$ 16$_{12}$ 18$_{12}$ Pr 25$_{20}$ 26$_{23}$ 4QConfess 2$_{3}$ (הר[ע]) 2$_{5}$, כָּבֵד *heavy* Si 3$_{26.27}$, עִקֵּשׁ *perverted* Ps 101$_{4(mss)}$, עָקֹב *deceitful* Si 36$_{25}$, עָרֵל *uncircumcised* perh. 4QWiles 2$_{5}$ (unless לב ערל = *heart of an uncircumcised one*), קָטָן *small* Si 14$_{3}$, רַגָּז *quaking* Dt 28$_{65}$.

<PREP> נָאוֶה לְ *fitting for* Si 14$_{3}$.

בְּ of place, *in(to)* 2 S 18$_{14}$ Is 51$_{7}$ 63$_{4}$ Jr 23$_{26}$ Ezk 27$_{4}$ Ps 37$_{31}$ 45$_{6}$ 55$_{22}$ (if ins. בְּ) Pr 6$_{14}$ 12$_{25}$ 26$_{25}$ (+ קוֹל *voice*) 30$_{19}$ 4QapPs^{b} 85$_{3}$ 4QPrFêtes^{b} 39$_{1}$ GnzPs 4$_{19}$, perh. 4QpsEzek^{a} 32$_{1}$ 4QWays^{b} 4$_{2}$ 6QD 5$_{5}$, + היה *be* Jr 20$_{9}$ (or del. בְּלִבִּי *in my heart*), בוא *come* Ps 37$_{15}$ Pr 2$_{10}$ (+ נֶפֶשׁ *soul*), נוח *rest* Pr 14$_{33}$, נתן *give*, i.e. place Ex 31$_{6}$ 35$_{34}$ 36$_{2}$ 1 K 10$_{24}$||2 C 9$_{23}$ Ps 4$_{8}$ Ec 3$_{11}$ (or em. בְּלִבָּם *in their mind* to בָּם *in them* or בּוֹ *in it*)* Ezr 7$_{27}$ 1QH 14$_{8}$, שׁית *place* Ps 13$_{3}$ (|| נֶפֶשׁ *soul*), שׂים *place* 4QPrayer^{d} 1.1$_{3}$ (בל[ב]) 4QShir^{b} 63.3$_{2}$, נטע *plant* 4QDibHam^{a} 1.2$_{13}$, צפן *store* Ps 119$_{11}$, אמר *say* Gn 17$_{17}$ 27$_{41}$ 1 K 12$_{26}$ Is 47$_{10}$ Ob$_{3}$ Zc 12$_{5}$ Ps 10$_{6.11.13}$ 14$_{1}$||53$_{2}$ 35$_{25}$ 74$_{8}$ Ec 2$_{1.15}$ 3$_{17.18}$ Est 6$_{6}$, דבר pi. *speak* Ec 2$_{15}$, חשׁב *think* Ps 140$_{3}$ Si 12$_{16}$, יחל pi. *hope* 4QapMes 2.2$_{4}$, חקק *engrave* 1QH 18$_{28}$, תור *explore* Ec 2$_{3}$, שׂמח *rejoice* Ex 4$_{14}$ (Sam לֵבָב), ראה *see* Ps 66$_{18}$, פעל *do* Ps 58$_{3}$ (or em. בְּלֵב *in [your] heart* to כֻּלְּכֶם *all of you*), רבה hi. *increase* GnzPs 4$_{7}$, קפא *congeal* Ex 15$_{8}$, בזה *despise* 2 S 6$_{16}$||1 C 15$_{29}$, מלא ni. *be filled* Ezk 27$_{25}$, כבד *be heavy* Ezk 27$_{25}$, מוט *shake* Ps 46$_{3}$, תקע *thrust* 2 S 18$_{14}$, שׁבר *break* Ezk 27$_{26}$, נפל *fall* Ezk 27$_{27}$, מות *die* Ezk 28$_{8}$, ישׁב *sit* Ezk 28$_{2}$, קשׁר pass. *be bound* Pr 22$_{15}$, שׁכב *lie down* Pr 23$_{34}$ (or em. רכב *ride*).

בְּ of accompaniment, *with* 4QDibHam^{a} 1.2$_{13}$ 4QBéat 3.2$_{1}$, + הלך *go* 1 K 8$_{23}$||2 C 6$_{14}$ Is 38$_{3}$ (htp.; + אֱמֶת *truth*) 1QS 1$_{6}$, בוא *come* Ps 90$_{12}$ (if em. וְנָבִא לְבַב *that we may bring a heart of* to וְנָבֹא בְּלֵב *that we may come with a heart of*), שׁוב *go back* Jr 3$_{10}$ 24$_{7}$ 2 C 6$_{38}$ 1QH 16$_{17}$ 1QS 5$_{9}$ CD 15$_{9}$ (לשו[ב]) 15$_{12}$, נדב htp. *volunteer* 1 C 29$_{9}$.

בְּ of instrument, *by (means of), with*, + שׁמר *keep* 2 K 23$_{3}$ Ps 119$_{34}$, נצר *keep* Ps 119$_{69}$, פחד *fear* Si 7$_{29}$, נטע *plant* Jr 32$_{41}$ (|| נֶפֶשׁ *soul*, + אֱמֶת *truth*), דבר pi. *speak* Ps 12$_{3.3}$ (+ שָׂפָה *lip*), קרא *cry* Ps 119$_{145}$, זעק *cry* Ho 7$_{14}$, צעק *cry* Lm 2$_{18}$ (if ins. בְּ), רנן hi. *exult* Si 39$_{35}$, חלה pi. *entreat* Ps 119$_{58}$, ידה hi. *give thanks* Ps 9$_{2}$ 138$_{1}$, עלז *exult* Zp 3$_{14}$, דרשׁ *seek* Ps 119$_{2.10}$ 4QS^{c} 1.1$_{1}$ (לדרוש ... בכול ל[ב]) 4QBéat 5$_{5}$ CD 1$_{10}$, בטח *trust* Pr 3$_{5}$, עבד *serve* 1 C 28$_{9}$ (|| נֶפֶשׁ *soul*) 1QH 16$_{7}$ (+ אֱמֶת *truth*), אהב *love* Si 47$_{8}$, בחר *choose* 1QH 15$_{10}$, שׁתה *drink* Ec 9$_{7}$, עדר *help* 1 C 12$_{34.34}$ (mss עזר *help*).

בְּ of cause, *on account of*, + תפשׂ *seize* Ezk 14$_{5}$; *with regard to* Ps 125$_{4}$; נגע בְּ *touch* 1 S 10$_{26}$ (4QSam^{a} לֵבָב *heart*), בטח בְּ *trust in* Pr 28$_{26}$ (+ חָכְמָה *wisdom*).

כְּ *as* 2 S 17$_{10}$, + היה *be* Jr 48$_{41}$ 49$_{22}$; *as though it were*, + נתן *give* Ezk 28$_{2.6}$ 4QBark^{a} 1.2$_{10}$; *in accordance with, after*, + נתן *give* shepherds Jr 3$_{15}$, עשׂה *do* 2 S 7$_{21}$||1 C 17$_{19}$ (or em. at 1 C וְכַלְבְּךָ for the sake of your servant, *even your dog*).

מִן of direction, *from* Nm 16$_{28}$, + יצא *go out* 2 K 9$_{24}$, hi. *take out* Jb 8$_{10}$ Si 35$_{16}$, סור *depart* Si 10$_{12}$ (or em. מִן, leaving לֵב as subj. of סור), hi. *remove* anger Ec 11$_{10}$ (|| בָּשָׂר *flesh*), מושׁ *depart* 4Q417 1.1$_{9}$; perh. of instrument, *by (means of), with* Ezk 13$_{2}$ (or em. לִנְבִיאֵי מִלִּבָּם appar. *to those who prophesy by their own heart* to אֲלֵיהֶם *to them*), נבא htp. *prophesy* Ezk 13$_{17}$, בדא *devise* 1 K 12$_{33(Qr)}$ (Kt מלבד he devised *on his own*) Ne 6$_{8}$ (mss ברא *create*), הגה po. *utter* Is 59$_{13}$, ענה pi. *afflict* Lm 3$_{33}$, עשׂה *do* Nm 24$_{13}$; perh. of agent, *by*, + שׁכח ni. *be forgot–*

ten Ps 31$_{13}$ (or em. כְּמֵת מִלֵּב I am forgotten by the heart *like one who is dead* to כְּכֶלֶב מֵת I am forgotten *like a dead dog*).

אֶל *in, to, right to*, + עצב htp. *be grieved* Gn 6$_6$, אמר *say* Gn 8$_{21}$ 1 S 27$_1$, דבר pi. *speak* Gn 24$_{45}$ 1 S 1$_{13(ms)}$, שׂים *place* 1 S 25$_{25(mss)}$ 2 S 13$_{33}$ 19$_{20}$, שׁית *place* 1 S 4$_{20(ms)}$ 2 S 13$_{20(mss)}$, נתן *give*, i.e. place Ec 7$_2$ 9$_1$ Ne 2$_{12}$ 7$_5$, שׁוב hi. *turn* 1 K 8$_{47}$ Is 44$_{19}$ Lm 3$_{21}$ (or em. שׂים *place*), הלך *go* Ezk 11$_{21}$ (or em. אֶל־לֵב to אֵלֶּה אַחֲרֵי *these* go *after*), עלה hi. *take up* Ezk 14$_{4.7}$ (or em. עַל *to* in both), שׁלח *send* Ex 9$_{14}$ (Sam עַל *against*); יעץ אֶל ni. *take counsel with* 4QapPs^b 69$_3$ ([נ]ועץ).

עַל *upon, to, in, into* Si 11$_5$, + היה *be* Ex 28$_{30}$, בוא *come* 2 C 7$_{11}$, שׁוב hi. *bring (back)* Is 46$_8$, עלה *go up* 2 K 12$_5$ Is 65$_{17}$ Jr 3$_{16}$ 7$_{31}$ 19$_5$ 32$_{35}$ 44$_{21}$ Si 35$_{12}$, hi. *take up* Ezk 14$_3$, נגע *reach* Jr 4$_{18(mss)}$, שׁוב *go back* Si 8$_1$ (ל[בו]), נשׂא *raise*, i.e. carry Ex 28$_{29.30}$, שׂים *place* Is 42$_{25}$ 47$_7$ 57$_{1.11}$ Jr 12$_{11}$ Ml 2$_{2.2}$ Ca 8$_6$ (+ זְרוֹעַ *arm*) Dn 1$_8$, שׁית *place* 1 S 4$_{20(mss)}$, נתן *give*, i.e. place Si 50$_{28}$, קשׁר *bind* Pr 6$_{21}$ (|| גַּרְגֶּרֶת *throat*), דבר pi. *speak* Gn 34$_3$ 50$_{21}$ Jg 19$_3$ 1 S 1$_{13}$ 2 S 19$_8$ Is 40$_2$ Ho 2$_{16}$ Ru 2$_{13}$ 2 C 30$_{22}$,* כתב *write* Jr 31$_{33}$, שׁיר *sing* Pr 25$_{20}$; *against*, + שׁלח *send* Ex 9$_{14(Sam)}$; חזק על pi. perh. *strengthen* 4QBark^c 1.1$_4$.

אֵת *by, through*, + שׁבר ni. *be broken* Ezk 6$_9$ (or em. qal *break*, with אֵת as object-marker).

עִם *with*, + היה *be* 2 C 24$_4$, דבר pi. *speak* Ec 1$_{16}$, יעץ *take counsel* 1QH 6$_{22}$.

בְּתוֹךְ *inside*, + כסה pi. *hide* Ps 40$_{11}$.

בְּקֶרֶב *inside* Ps 36$_2$.

עַד *unto*, + בער *burn* Dt 4$_{11}$ (Sam לֵבָב *heart*; or del. לֵב), נגע *reach* Jr 4$_{18}$.

בַּעַד *for the sake of* 4QsapDidB 1$_2$.

אַחֲרֵי *after*, + הלך *go* Si 5$_2$ (|| עַיִן *eye*).

<COLL> בְּלֵב וָלֵב *with a double heart* Ps 12$_3$ 1QH 4$_{14}$ 4QBéat 5$_5$ (בלב ול[ב]), בְּלֹא־לֵב וָלֵב *without a double heart*, i.e. whole-heartedly 1 C 12$_{34}$ (mss בְּכָל־ *with all [their]* heart), לב[לדעת] *a heart to know* 4QDibHam^a 18$_2$, נוֹעֲצוּ לֵב יַחְדָּו appar. *they take counsel together (with a single heart)* Ps 83$_6$ (or em. יַחְדָּו to יֶחְדּוּ *they rejoice* or אֶחָד with *one* heart, or יָחַד with a *united* heart), יחפצו לבו appar. *the desire (in) their heart* MurEpBarC^b$_6$, כְּלָיוֹת וָלֵב *kidneys and heart* Jr 11$_{20}$ 20$_{12}$.

Also 1QH fr. 5$_{11}$ 1QH^b 1$_{11}$ 2QapMoses 2$_1$ 4QapJoshua^a 6.2$_3$ 4QMyst^a 45$_1$ 4QErr 1$_{10}$ 4QapPent 9$_3$ 4Q423 6$_2$ 4QHod^b 7$_6$ 12$_2$ 4QSap^b 6$_5$ 4QPrFêtes^c 294$_1$ 4QBéat 14.1$_{15}$ 14.2$_{10}$ 6QapSam-Kgs 32$_2$.

<SYN> עַיִן *eye*,* אֹזֶן *ear*, שָׂפָה *lip*, פָּנִים *face*, מֵצַח *forehead*, גַּרְגֶּרֶת *throat*, יָד *hand*, קֶרֶן *horn*, עֶצֶם *bone*, כִּלְיָה *kidney*, כָּבֵד *liver* (mss), קֶרֶב *inside*, רוּחַ *spirit*, נֶפֶשׁ *soul*, בָּשָׂר *flesh*, דֶּרֶךְ *way*, תְּהוֹם *abyss*, כָּבוֹד *glory*.

<ANT> פֶּה *mouth*.*

⇒ לֵבָב *heart*, לבב *think*.

לְבֹא חֲמָת, see לְבוֹא חֲמָת *Lebo-hamath*.

[לֶבֶא] 1 n.[m.] **lion**—pl. לְבָאִם—<SUBJ> להט *devour* or *bewitch* Ps 57$_5$ (or em. לעט *devour*). <PREP> בְּתוֹךְ *among*, + שׁכב *lie down* Ps 57$_5$ (or em. נַפְשִׁי בְּתוֹךְ *my soul is among* lions to וְיוֹשַׁע נַפְשִׁי מִתּוֹךְ *and may he save my soul from [among]* lions and/or לְבָאִים *lions* to כְּלָבִים *dogs*).

⇒ לָבִיא *lion*.

[לְבָאָה] 1 n.f. **lion** (fem.)—pl. sf. לְבְאֹתָיו—<PREP> לְ of benefit, *for*, + חנק pi. *strangle* Na 2$_{13}$ (=4QpNah 3.1$_4$ לביותיו, from לְבִיָּה *lion* (fem.); + אַרְיֵה *lion*).

⇒ לָבִיא *lion*.

לְבָאוֹת 1 pl.n. **Lebaoth,** Simeonite town in southern Judah, appar. ident. with Beth-lebaoth at Jos 19$_6$ and Beth-biri at 1 C 4$_{31}$, <SUBJ> היה *be* Jos 15$_{32}$.

לבב I 3 vb. **think—Ni.** 1 Impf. יִלָּבֵב—**gain understanding,** or perh. **lack understanding,** וְאִישׁ נָבוּב יִלָּבֵב *and a hollow man will gain*, or *lack, understanding* Jb 11$_{12}$ (or em. וְאִישׁ נָבוּב יְלַבְּבוֹ *and a man is an offspring that* a donkey *produces*, from לבב III *sprout*).

Pi. 2 Pf. לִבַּבְתִּינִי (לִבַּבְתִּנִי)—**seduce, infatuate,** <SUBJ> אָחוֹת *sister* Ca 4$_{9.9}$, כַּלָּה *bride* Ca 4$_{9.9}$. <OBJ> male lover Ca 4$_{9.9}$. <PREP> בְּ of instrument, *by (means of), with*, בְּאַחַד מֵעֵינַיִךְ בְּאַחַד עֲנָק מִצַּוְּרֹנָיִךְ *with one (flash) of your eyes, with one bead of your necklace*.*

⇒ לֵב *heart*, לֵבָב *heart*.

לבב II $_{2}$ vb. **bake—Pi.** $_{1}$ Impf. 3fs תְּלַבֵּב; + waw 3fs וַתְּלַבֵּב—**bake,** <SUBJ> Tamar 2 S $13_{6.8}$ (+ לוש *knead,* בשל pi. *cook*), אָחוֹת *sister* 13_{6}. <OBJ> לְבִבָה *cake* 13_{6}. <PREP> לְעֵינֵי *before (the eyes of)* Amnon $13_{6.8}$.

→ לְבִבָה *cake.*

* [**לבב**] III vb. **sprout—Pi. cause to sprout, produce,** וְאִישׁ נָבוּב יְלַבְּבוֹ עָיִר *and a man is an offspring that* a donkey *produces* Jb 11_{12} (if em. וְאִישׁ נָבוּב יִלָּבֵב וְעַיִר *and a hollow[ed] man will gain,* or *lacks,understanding; and a donkey*).

לֵבָב $_{252.9.96.1}$ n.m. **heart**—cstr. לְבַב; sf. לְבָבִי, לְבָבְךָ, (לְבָבֵךְ, Q לבבכה), לְבָבוֹ, לְבָבֵךְ (I לבבה), לְבָבָהּ (לְבָבָהּ), לְבַבְכֶם (Q לבבכמה), לְבָבָם (לבבמה), לְבָבֵנוּ; pl. לְבָבוֹת; sf. mss לְבָבֵינוּ, לִבְבֵהֶן.

Distinctions among these meanings oft. unclear; a physical sense (§4) is oft. possible in §§1-3. לֵבָב with possessive suffix (especially לְבָבִי) may oft. refer to the whole person. Appar. not different in meaning from לֵב.

1. mind, thinking, intention, understanding, in ref. to primarily intellectual processes of human beings, as responsible for, representative of, or identified with the following.

a. thought, reason, knowledge, counsel, Gn 31_{20} Dt 7_{17} $8_{5.17}$ 9_{4} 18_{21}=11QT 61_{2} Dt 29_{18} Jos 23_{14} 1 S 9_{19} 1 K 2_{44} 10_{2}‖2 C 9_{1} Is 6_{10} 10_{7} 14_{13} 32_{4} 47_{8} 49_{21} Jr 5_{24} 13_{22} Ezk 38_{10} Ho 7_{2} Zp 1_{12} 2_{15} Zc 7_{10} 8_{17} Ps 4_{5} $73_{7.21}$ 77_{7} 78_{18} 139_{23} Jb 9_{13} 17_{11} Ec 9_{3} Si $37_{13.17}$ 43_{18} 1QH 2_{18} 4_{10} 5_{9} 8_{37} 11_{21} fr. 4_{12} 1QS 2_{13} 4_{2} $11_{3.5}$ 4QCryptA 1.1-2_{1} 4QMyst[c] $2a_{2}$ 4QapJoseph[b] $3_{3.5}$ 8_{4} perh. 4QpsEzek[a] 19_{2} 4Qsap HymnA 1.1_{4} 4QShir[b] 18.2_{8} 63.2_{3} 11QPs[a] 18_{5}.

b. wisdom, common sense of human beings, Ps 90_{12} (or em.) Jb 12_{3} $34_{10.34}$ Si 50_{23}; of Y, Jb 9_{4}.

c. attention, memory, Dt 4_{39} 6_{6} 11_{18} 30_{1} 32_{46} 1 S 21_{13} Jr 51_{50} Ezk 3_{10} Hg $1_{5.7}$ $2_{15.18.18}$ Jb 22_{22} Pr 4_{21} 1 C 22_{19} 2 C 6_{37} 4Q418 55_{4}.

2. feelings (e.g. Ps 62_{9} 1QH 5_{33}), especially as sensitive to **a.** joy, Ex $4_{14(Sam)}$ Dt 28_{47} Jg 19_{9} Is 30_{29} 60_{5} Jr 15_{16} Ezk 36_{5} Ps 104_{15} 2 C 32_{6} Si $30_{16[B].22}$ 4Q185 1.2_{12} 4QBark[d] 2.1_{15}. **b.** pain, grief, sadness, Dt 15_{10} 1 S 1_{8} 1 K 8_{38} Ps 25_{17} Si 38_{18} 1QH 7_{3} 4QShir[a] 1_{6}. **c.** weakness, anxiety, fear, Lv 26_{36} Dt 1_{28} $20_{3.8.8.8}$=11QT $62_{3.4.4}$ Dt $28_{28.67}$ Jos 2_{11} 5_{1} 7_{5} Is 1_{5} $7_{2.2.4}$ 13_{7} 19_{1} 21_{4} Jr 51_{46} Ps 73_{26} 109_{16} 2 C 13_{7} 1QH 2_{6} 4_{33} fr. 4_{14} 1QM 1_{14} $10_{3.6}$ 4Q185 1.1_{15} 4QpsEzek[c] 3.2_{5} 4QWays[b] 9_{2}. **d.** courage, strength, Ps 31_{25} 73_{26} perh. 84_{6} Dn 11_{25} 1QM 16_{14} 4QDibHam[a] 1.6_{9}; specif. as sustainable by food, Jg 19_{8} Ps 22_{27}. **e.** anger, Dt 19_{6}. **f.** hatred, Lv 19_{17}. **g.** desire, Pr 6_{25} Kuntillet 'Ajrud add. inscr. 2. **h.** conscience, Jb 27_{6}.

3. will, inclination, disposition, personality, of human beings, Nm 15_{39} Dt 4_{9} 8_{2} 11_{16} 17_{17}=11QT 56_{19} Dt 29_{17} $30_{14.17}$ Jos 14_{7} 24_{23} 1 S 7_{3} 4QSam[a] 10_{26} $14_{7.7}$ 16_{7} 2 S 7_{3}‖1 C 17_{2} 2 S 19_{15} 1 K $8_{17.18.18.39.39}$‖2 C $6_{7.8.8.30.30}$ 1 K $11_{2.4.9}$ Is 10_{7} Jr 32_{40} Ps 15_{2} 20_{5} perh. 69_{33} 86_{11} perh. 104_{15} (or em.) Jb 1_{5} Lm 3_{41} Dn 11_{28} Ezr 7_{10} Ne 9_{8} 1 C 12_{18} 22_{7} $28_{2.9}$ $29_{17.18.18}$ 2 C 1_{11} 15_{15} 29_{10} 32_{31} Si $37_{12.12}$ 1QS 4_{23} 5_{4} 10_{21} 4QBer[f] 1_{6} 4QparaKings 104_{1} 4Q415 2.2_{1} 4Q417 2.1_{27} 4QBark[c] 1.2_{1} 4QDibHam[a] 1.5_{13}; of Y., 1 S 2_{35} 13_{14} 2 K 10_{30}.

לֵבָב *heart* characterized as loyal, devoted (Dt 4_{29} 5_{29} 6_{5} 10_{12} 11_{13} 13_{4}=11QT 54_{13} Dt 26_{16} $30_{2.6.10}$ Jos 22_{5} 1 S 7_{3} $12_{20.24}$ 1 K 2_{4} $8_{48.58.61}$ $11_{4.4}$ 14_{8} $15_{3.3.14}$‖2 C 15_{17} 2 K $10_{15.15.15.31}$ 20_{3} 23_{45} Jr 29_{13} Jl 2_{12} Ps 86_{12} 111_{1} 1 C 29_{18} 2 C 11_{16} 15_{12} 16_{9} $19_{3.9}$ 20_{33} 22_{9} 25_{2} 30_{19} 31_{21} 34_{31} 4Qps Ezek[c] 3.2_{1} 1Qs 4_{2} 4QMMT C_{15} 4QShir[b] 48_{5} 11QPs[a] 22_{12} 11QT 59_{10} GnzPs 1_{9}), upright, pure (Gn $20_{5.6}$ Dt 9_{5}=CD 8_{14}=19_{27} 1 K 3_{6} 9_{4} Ps 24_{4} $73_{1.13}$ 78_{72} 101_{2} 119_{7} 1 C 29_{17} 2 C 29_{34} 1QS 11_{2} 4QD[a] 5.1c-d_{2}), penitent (2 K 22_{19}‖2 C 34_{27} Jl 2_{13}=4QD[a] 11_{5}a), stubborn, hard (Dt 2_{30} 15_{7} 1 S 6_{6} Ps 95_{8} 2 C 36_{13} 1QM 14_{7}), evil, worthless (Dt 15_{9} 1 S 17_{28} Ps 28_{3} 95_{10} Dn 11_{27}), perverse (Ps 101_{4} 1QS 11_{9}), uncircumcised (Lv 26_{41} Dt 10_{16} $30_{6.6}$ Jr 4_{4} 1QS 5_{26}), arrogant, proud (Dt 8_{14} 17_{20} Is 9_{8} 10_{12} Ezk $28_{5.6}$ Ps 101_{5} Dn 8_{25} 11_{12} 1QS 4_{9} 1QDM 2_{2} 4QWiles 2_{6} 4QpsEzek[a] 13.2_{1} 4Q psMos[d] 1.2_{6} 4QShir[b] 43_{8} 11QT 57_{14}).

4. physical **heart, chest,** Na 2_{8} 4QBark[d] 2.1_{3}.

5. middle of sea, Jon 2_{4} 4QBibPar 14.1_{7}; cedar, Ezk 31_{10}.

<SUBJ> היה *be* Dt 5_{29} 1 K 8_{61} 11_{4} $15_{4.14}$‖2 C 15_{17} (all four + שָׁלֵם *whole*) 1 C 12_{18} (+ לְיַחַד *for unity*) 4Qpara Kings 104_{1}, חיה *live* Ps 22_{27} 69_{33}, יטב *be good,* i.e. cheerful Jg 19_{9}, אמן ni. *be faithful* Ne 9_{8}, רעע *be bad,* i.e.

sad 1 S 1_{8}, grudging Dt 15_{10}, hi. *do evil* Dn 11_{27}, חמץ htp. *be embittered* Ps 73_{21} (+ כִּלְיָה *kidney*), חמם *be hot* Dt 19_{6}, גבה *be high* Ezk 28_{5}, רום *be high* Dt 8_{14} 17_{20} Ezk 31_{10} Dn 11_{12} 1QDM 2_{2} (לב[בכה]) 4QpsEzek[a] 13.2_{1} 4QpsMos[d] 1.2_{6} 11QT 57_{14}, רחב *be wide* Is 60_{5}, פתה *be enticed* Dt 11_{16}, אמץ hi. *exhibit strength* Ps 31_{25}, כבד ni. *be honoured* 4QMyst[c] $2a_{2}$, כאה ni. *be broken* Ps $109_{16(Gnz)}$, כנע ni. *be humbled* Lv 26_{41}, רכך *be weak* Dt 20_{3} Is 7_{4} Jr 51_{46} 1QM 10_{3}, מסס ni. *be melted* Dt 20_{8} =11QT 62_{4} Jos 2_{11} 5_{1} (both + רוּחַ *spirit*) 7_{5} Is 13_{7} (|| יָד *hand*) 19_{1} 1QH 4_{33} fr. 4_{14}, hi. *melt* Dt $20_{8(Sam)}$, שׁמם hi. *be appalled* 1QH 7_{3} 18_{20} (ל[בבי]), כלה *fail* Ps 73_{26} (|| שְׁאֵר *flesh*).

פנה *turn* (intrans.) Dt 29_{17} 30_{17}, נטה *turn* (intrans.) 1 K 11_{9}, סור *depart* Dt 17_{17} Ps 101_{4} (mss לֵב *heart*), תעה *stray* Is 21_{4}, המה *murmur* Si $43_{18(B)}$, תמה hi. *wonder* Si $43_{18(M)}$, נוע *tremble* Is $7_{2.2}$, ערץ *tremble* 4Q185 1.1_{15}, ידע *know* 1 K 2_{44} (or del.) Is 32_{4} (|| לָשׁוֹן *tongue*) perh. 4QpsEzek[a] 19_{2}, בין *understand* Is 6_{10} (+ לֵב *heart*, עַיִן *eye*, אֹזֶן *ear* [1QIsa[a], mss וּבִלְבָבוֹ *and with his heart*]) 32_{4}, hi. perh. *teach* 4QapJoseph[b] 3_{3}, חשׁב *think* Is 10_{7}, למד perh. pi. *teach* 4QapJoseph[b] 3_{5}, עלץ *exult* 4QBark[d] 2.1_{15}, חרף *reproach* Jb 27_{6}.

<NOM CL> עקר תחבולות לבב *the source of guidance is the heart* Si $37_{17(Bmg, D)}$ (B עקרת *sources of*), לְבָבִי עִם־לְבָבְךָ *my heart is (upright) with your heart* 2 K 10_{15}, לִי לֵבָב כְּמוֹכֶם *I have a heart like you* Jb 12_{3}, לְבָבוֹ עַל־בְּרִית קֹדֶשׁ *his heart will be against the holy covenant* Dn 11_{28}, עִם־לְבָבָם שָׁלֵם אֵלָיו appar. *with those whose heart is wholly directed to him* 2 C 16_{9}, רַךְ־לְבָבְךָ *your heart was tender* 2 K 22_{19}||2 C 34_{27}, כָּל־לֵבָב דַּוָּי *every heart is faint* Is 1_{5} (|| רֹאשׁ *head*).

<OBJ> בוא hi. *bring* Ps 90_{12} (or em. וְנָבֵא לְבַב *that we may bring a heart of* to וְנָבֹא בְּלֵב *that we may come with a heart of*), מצא *find* Ne 9_{8}, נתן *give* 1 C 29_{19}, *apply* 1 C 22_{19} (|| נֶפֶשׁ *soul*) 2 C 11_{16}, *cause to be* Ezk 28_{6}, שׂים *place*, i.e. apply Dt 32_{46} Hg $1_{5.7}$ (or del.) $2_{15.18.18}$ (or del.), כון hi. *apply* 1 S 7_{3} Ezr 7_{10} 2 C 19_{3} 20_{33} 30_{19}, *make firm* 1 C 29_{18}, נשׂא *raise* Lm 3_{41}, נטה hi. *direct* Jos 24_{23} 2 S 19_{15} (mss qal *turn* intrans., with לֵבָב as subj.) 1 K 8_{58} $11_{2.4}$, סור hi. *divert* 11QT 56_{19}.

עור *rouse* Dn 11_{25} (|| כֹּחַ *strength*), פחד pi. *frighten* 1QS 4_{2}, קשׁה hi. *harden* Ps 95_{8}, כבד pi. *make heavy*, i.e. harden 1 S 6_{6} (+ לֵב *heart*), אמץ pi. *strengthen* 1QM 1_{14} (ל[בבב]), i.e. harden Dt 2_{30} (|| רוּחַ *spirit*) 15_{7} (|| יָד *hand*) 2 C 36_{13} (|| עֹרֶף *neck*), חזק pi. *strengthen* 1QM 16_{14} 4QWays[b] 9_{2} 4QDibHam[a] 1.6_{9}, מסס hi. *melt* Dt 1_{28} 1QH 2_{6} 1QM 1_{14}, שׁפך *pour* Ps 62_{9}, פתח *open* 1QH fr. 4_{12}, שׁמם hi. *make desolate* 4QShir[a] 1_{6}, גנב *steal* heart, i.e. deceive Gn 31_{26}, מול *circumcise* Dt $30_{6.6}$, קרע *tear* Jl 2_{13}=4QD[a] 11_{5a} (:: בֶּגֶד *garment*).

דרשׁ *search* 1 C 28_{9} (+ יֵצֶר *purpose*), בחן *test* 1 C 29_{17} 1QM 16_{15} (ל[ב]ב; =4QM[a] 11.2_{12} לב), ידע *know* 1 K $8_{39.39}$||2 C $6_{30.30}$ Ps 139_{23} (|| שַׂרְעַפִּים *thoughts*), זכה pi. *purify* Ps 73_{13} (|| כַּף *hand*), יחד pi. *unite* Ps 86_{11} (or em. חדה *rejoice*, with לֵבָב as subj.), סעד *sustain* Jg 19_{8} Ps 104_{15} (or em.; see Cstr.), שׂמח pi. *gladden* Ps 104_{15} (+ פָּנִים *face*).

<CSTR> לְבַב אָסָא *heart of Asa* 1 K 15_{14}||2 C 15_{17}, דָּוִד *of David* 1 K 8_{17}||2 C 6_{7} (דָּוִיד) 1 K 11_{4} (דָּוִיד) 15_{3}, מִצְרַיִם *of Egypt* Is 19_{1}, מֶלֶךְ־אַשּׁוּר *of the king of Assyria* Is 10_{12}, אֶחָיו *of his brothers* Dt 20_{8}, כָּל־אִישׁ־יְהוּדָה *of every man of Judah* 2 S 19_{15}, גבר *of a man* 1QS 4_{23}, אֱנוֹשׁ *of a human being* Is 13_{7} Ps $104_{15.15}$ (both לְבַב־; or em. לְבָבוֹ *his heart*), בְּנֵי הָאָדָם *of human beings* 2 C 6_{30}, כָּל־בְּנֵי הָאָדָם *of all human beings* 1 K 8_{39}||2 C $6_{30(mss)}$, ל[בב בני אור] *heart of the sons of light* 1QM 1_{14}, לְבַב־הָעָם *heart of the people* Jos 7_{5}, לְבַב עַמְּךָ *heart of your people* 1 C 29_{18}, עַמּוֹ *of his people* Is 7_{2} 1QM 16_{15} (ל[ב]ב; =4QM[a] 11.2_{12} לֵב *heart*), לבב נִמְהָרִים *of the hasty* Is 32_{4} 1QH 8_{37} ([נמה]רים), [מ]שכילים *heart of the intelligent* 4QWays[a] 2_{9}, [נגו]עים *of stricken ones* 4QWays[b] 9_{2}, לְבַב זַרְעֶךָ *heart of your seed*, i.e. descendants Dt 30_{6}.

לְבַב חָכְמָה *heart of wisdom* Ps 90_{12} (or em. לֵב *heart*), לבב קושי *heart of stubbornness* 1QM 14_{7}, לבב ים *heart of (the) sea* 4QBibPar 14.1_{7}, לְבַב יַמִּים *heart of (the) seas* Jon 2_{4} (or del.).

אַנְשֵׁי לֵבָב *men of heart*, i.e. reason Jb $34_{10.34}$ 4QCryptA 1.1–2_{1}, חֲכַם *one who is wise of* Jb 9_{4} (|| כֹּחַ *strength*), בַּר־ *one who is pure of* Ps 24_{4} (|| כַּף *hand*), בָּרֵי *those who are pure of* Ps 73_{1}, יִשְׁרֵי *those who are upright of* 2 C 29_{34} 4QD[a] 5.1c-d_{2}, רַךְ הַלֵּבָב *the one who is weak of heart* Dt 20_{8}=11QT 62_{3} 2 C 13_{7} (רַךְ־לֵבָב), נִכְאֵה לֵבָב *one who is broken of heart* Ps 109_{16} (Gnz וְנִכְאָה *and* their heart *is broken*), מסי לבב *those who are melted of heart* 1QM 10_{6}, רְחַב לֵבָב *one who is wide of heart*, i.e. arrogant Ps 101_{5} (|| עַיִן *eye*), עַם־תֹּעֵי לֵבָב *a people (consisting) of those who stray of*, i.e. in, *(their) heart* Ps 95_{10} (ms עַד appar. *while* they stray in their heart), חסרי לבב *those lacking (of) heart* 11QPs[a] 18_{5}.

[עור]ל[ת] לבבו *foreskin of his heart* 1QS 5_{26}, עָרְלַת לְבַבְכֶם *foreskin of your heart* Dt 10_{16} (+ עֹרֶף *neck*) Jr $4_{4(\text{mss})}$, עָרְלוֹת *foreskins of* Jr 4_{4},* צוּר־לְבָבִי *rock of my heart* Ps 73_{26}.

עצת לבב *counsel of the heart* Si $37_{13(\text{B})}$, לבבך *of your heart* Si $37_{13(\text{D})}$, לבבו *of his heart* Si $37_{13(\text{Bmg})}$, מַשְׂכִּיּוֹת לֵבָב *imaginations of (the) heart* Ps 73_{7} (or em. בְּשֻׂכַּיִת *in the arrangement of*), מחשבת לבב *thought of the heart* 4QShir[b] 63.2_{3}, [מח]שבת כול לבב *thought of every heart* 4QShir[b] 22_{4}, יֵצֶר מַחְשְׁבוֹת לְבַב *imagination of the thoughts of the heart of* 1 C 29_{18}, מזמ[ות ל]בבם *plans of their heart* 11QMelch 3_{8}, מוֹרָשֵׁי לְבָבִי *desires*, or *veins*, *of my heart* Jb 17_{11} (or em. מֵיתְרֵי *cords of*).*

חכמת לבב *wisdom of heart* Si 50_{23}, תָּם־לֵבָב *integrity of heart* 1 K 9_{4}, לְבָבִי *of my heart* Gn 20_{5} (|| כַּף *hand*) Ps 101_{2}, לְבָבוֹ *of his heart* (תֹּם; + כַּף *hand*, תְּבוּנָה *understanding*), לְבָבְךָ *of your heart* Gn 20_{6}, יִשְׁרַת לֵבָב *uprightness of heart* 1 K 3_{6}, יֹשֶׁר לֵבָב *uprightness of heart* Ps 119_{7}, לְבָבִי *of my heart* 1 C 29_{17} 1QS 11_{2} (ישור), לְבָבְךָ *of your heart* Dt 9_{5}=CD 8_{14}=19_{27}, אורת לבבי *light of my heart* 1QS 11_{3}, טוּב לֵבָב *goodness of heart* Dt 28_{47} Si $30_{15(\text{B})}$ (Bmg שאר *of flesh*), ט[וב לב]בם *goodness of their heart* 4QDibHam[c] 131_{9}, שִׂמְחַת לֵבָב *joy of heart* Is 30_{29} Jr 15_{16} (לְבָבִי *my heart*) Ezk 36_{5} (כָּל־לֵבָב *of all the heart*) Si 30_{22} 4Q185 1.2_{12} (|| עַיִם *eye*).

פַּחַד לְבָבְךָ *fear of your heart* Dt 28_{67}, תִּמְהוֹן לֵבָב *confusion of heart* Dt 28_{28} 4QpsEzek[c] 3.2_{5}, נֶגַע לְבָבוֹ *affliction of his heart* 1 K 8_{38}, צָרוֹת לְבָבִי *troubles of my heart* Ps 25_{17}, נעוות לבבי *perversity of my heart* 1QS 11_{9}, רע לבב *sadness of heart* Si 38_{18}, רֹעַ לְבָבֶךָ *evil of your heart* 1 S 17_{28}, [קו]שי לבב *stubbornness of heart* 4QM[f] 1_{6}, גֹּדֶל לֵבָב *greatness*, i.e. arrogance, *of heart* Is 9_{8} 10_{12} (לֵבָב), רום לבב *haughtiness of heart* 1QS 4_{9} 4QWiles 2_{6}, זדון לבם *presumptuousness of their heart* 4QShir[b] 43_{8}.

כָּל־לֵבָב *every heart* Is 1_{5} Ezk 36_{5} Ps 111_{1} 4QShir[b] 22_{4} (כול), כָּל־לְבַב *every heart of* Is 13_{7}, כָּל־לְבָבִי *all my heart* Ps 86_{12} 1QH 14_{26} ([כול לב[בי]) 11QPs[a] 22_{12} (כול), כָּל־לְבָבְךָ *all your* (sg.) *heart* Dt 4_{29} 6_{5} (|| מְאֹד *might*) 10_{12} 26_{16} $30_{2.6.10}$ (all seven || נֶפֶשׁ) 4QMMT C_{15}, כָּל־לְבָבוֹ *all his heart* 1 K 14_{8} 2 K 10_{31} 23_{25} (|| מְאֹד, נֶפֶשׁ) 2 C 22_{9} 30_{19} 31_{21} 34_{31} (|| נֶפֶשׁ), כָּל־לְבַבְכֶם *all your* (pl.) *heart* Dt 11_{13} (4QDeut[k] כול) 13_{4}=11QT 54_{13} (כול) Jos 22_{5} 23_{14} (all four || נֶפֶשׁ) 1 S 7_{3} $12_{20.24}$ Jr 29_{13} Jl 2_{12}, כָּל־לְבָבָם *all their heart* 1 K 2_{4} 8_{48} 2 C 15_{12} (all three || נֶפֶשׁ) 15_{15} (+ רָצוֹן *desire*) 4QpsEzek[c] 3.2_{1} 11QT 59_{10} (כול; || נֶפֶשׁ), כָּל־לְבָבוֹת *all hearts* 1 C 28_{9}.

<ADJ> שָׁלֵם *whole* 2 K 20_{3} 1 C 29_{19} 2 C 19_{9} 25_{2}, עִקֵּשׁ *perverted* Ps 101_{4}, עָרֵל *uncircumcised* Lv 26_{41}, זֶה *this* Dt 5_{29} (לְבָבָם זֶה *this heart of theirs*).

<PREP> לְ of direction, *to*, + אמר *say* Ho 7_{2}; ראה לְ *see* or *look into* 1 S 16_{7} (or em. בְּ look *at* or *into*; :: עַיִן *eye*).

בְּ of place, *in(to)* Dt 8_{2} 30_{14} (|| פֶּה *mouth*) 1 S 2_{35} (mss כְּ *in accordance with*; || נֶפֶשׁ *soul*) 9_{19} 14_{7} 2 S 7_{3}||1 C 17_{2} 2 K 10_{30} (+ עַיִן *eye*) Is 10_{7} Ps 28_{3} 84_{6} Ec 9_{3} 2 C 32_{31} Si $37_{12(\text{Bmg, D})}$ 1QS 11_{5} 4QShir[b] 48_{5}, perh. 1Q38 $1_{1.1}$ 4QparaKings 12_{3} 4QWays[a] 2_{9} 4Q418 204_{2}, + היה *be* 4Q418 55_{4}, בוא *come* 1QH 11_{21} (|| עֶצֶם *bone*) 4QBark[d] 2.1_{3} ([תבוא]), hi. *bring* Lv 26_{36}, שׁלך hi. *throw* Jon 2_{4}, שׂים *place* 1 S 21_{13} Jb 22_{22} 1QH 2_{18} 4QBark[c] 1.2_{1}, נתן *give*, i.e. place Jr 32_{40} 4QsapHymnA 1.1_{4} 4QShir[b] 48.2_{1} ([ב]לב[בי]), צפן *store* Jb 10_{13}, שמר *keep* 1QS 10_{21}, לקח *take* into Ezk 3_{10}, ריב *contend* 1QS 4_{23}.

אמר *say* Dt 7_{17} 8_{17} 9_{4} 18_{21}=11QT 61_{2} Is 14_{13} 47_{8} 49_{21} Jr 5_{24} 13_{22} Zp 1_{12} 2_{15} Ps 4_{5}, דבר *speak* Ps 15_{2}, ברך pi. *bless*, i.e. curse Jb 1_{5}, htp. *bless oneself* Dt 29_{18} 1QS 2_{13}, חשב *think* Zc 7_{10} 8_{17}, שׂנא *hate* Lv 19_{17}, שׂמח *rejoice* Ex $4_{14(\text{Sam})}$, שׁנן (pi.) *sharpen*, appar. engrave, or enunciate, law 1QH 4_{10}, קום hi. *establish* plans 4QBer[f] 1_{6}, אמץ pi. *strengthen* secret of truth 1QH 5_{9}, ישׁר pi. perh. *rectify* works of iniquity 4QHod[f] 3_{1}, פתח *open* wide place 1QH 5_{33}, אור hi. *cause to shine* into 1QS 4_{2} 4QShir[b] 18.2_{8}.

בְּ of instrument, *by (means of), with*, + שׁוּב *go back* Dt 30_{10} 1 S 7_{3} 1 K 8_{48} 2 K 23_{25} Jl 2_{12} 4QMMT C_{15} 11QT 59_{10}, מוּשׁ hi. *depart* 4Q415 2.2_{2}, שׁמר *keep* Dt 26_{16} 2 C 34_{31}, דרשׁ *seek* Dt 4_{29} Jr 29_{13} (+ or del. דרשׁ, leaving בְּ governed by בקשׁ pi. *seek*) 2 C 15_{12} 22_{9} 31_{21} 1QH 14_{26} (בכול לב[בי אדרש]ך), אהב *love* Dt 6_{5} 13_{4}=11QT 54_{13} Dt

30$_{6}$ GnzPs 1$_{9}$, עבד *serve* Dt 10$_{12}$ 11$_{13}$ Jos 22$_{5}$ 1 S 12$_{20.24}$ 4QpsEzek^{c} 3.2$_{1}$, שׁמע *hear*, i.e. obey Dt 30$_{2}$, ברך pi. *bless* 11QPs^{a} 22$_{12}$, עשׂה *do* Dt 26$_{16}$ 2 C 19$_{9}$ 25$_{2}$, ידה hi. *give thanks* Ps 86$_{12}$ 111$_{1}$, שׁבע ni. *swear* 2 C 15$_{15}$, בין *understand* Is 6$_{10(mss)}$ 4QapJoseph^{b} 8$_{4}$, ידע *know* Jos 23$_{14}$, נסה pi. *test* Ps 78$_{18}$, חמד *desire* Pr 6$_{25}$, גדל hi. *magnify oneself* Dn 8$_{25}$.

בְּ of accompaniment, *in, with,* הלך *go* 1 K 2$_{4}$ 14$_{8}$ 2 K 10$_{31}$ 20$_{3}$ (htp.); נגע בְּ *touch* heart 4QSam^{a} 1 S 10$_{26}$ (MT לֵב *heart*).

כְּ *as* Si 37$_{12(Bmg[erased]).12}$, + היה *be* 1 K 11$_{4}$ 15$_{3}$, מסס ni. *be melted* Dt 20$_{8}$=11QT 62$_{4}$ (Sam and perh. 11QT hi. *cause to melt*); *in accordance with, after* 1 S 13$_{14}$ 14$_{7}$ perh. 4QapMos^{c} 5$_{3}$, + עשׂה *do* 1 S 2$_{35(mss)}$, נתן *give* Ps 20$_{5}$ Kuntillet ʻAjrud add. inscr. 2.

מִן of direction, *from,* + סור *depart* Dt 4$_{9}$; אֶל *to,* + שׁוב hi. *take back* Dt 4$_{39}$ 30$_{1}$=4QMMT C$_{15}$ ([והשיבות]ה אל ל[בב]ך) 2 C 6$_{37}$ 4QDibHam^{a} 1.5$_{13}$; עַל *upon, to,* + היה *be* Dt 6$_{6}$, שׁוב hi. *take back* Dt 4$_{39(Sam)}$ 30$_{1(Sam\ mss)}$, שׂים *place* Dt 11$_{18}$ (‖ נֶפֶשׁ *soul,* + יָד *hand,* עַיִן *eye*), תפף po. *beat* Na 2$_{8}$; *to,* + עלה *go up* Jr 51$_{50}$ Ezk 38$_{10}$, דבר pi. *speak* 2 C 32$_{6}$.

אֵת *with,* הֲיֵשׁ אֶת־לְבָבְךָ יָשָׁר appar. *is there an upright one with your heart?* 2 K 10$_{15}$ (or em. יָשָׁר to יֹשֶׁר *uprightness* or הֲיֵשׁ אֶת־לְבָבְךָ to הֲיֵשׁ לְבָבְךָ עִם־לְבָבִי *is your heart* upright *with my heart?*); עִם *with, in* Jos 14$_{7}$ 2 K 10$_{15}$ (if ins. עִם־לְבָבִי *with my heart*) 10$_{15}$ 2 C 29$_{10}$ Si 37$_{12(B)}$, + היה *be* Dt 15$_{9}$ Jos 14$_{7(mss)}$ 1 K 8$_{17.18.18}$‖2 C 6$_{7.8.8}$ 1 K 10$_{2}$‖2 C 9$_{1}$ 1 C 22$_{7}$ 28$_{2}$ (if ins. היה) 2 C 1$_{11}$ 4QSela 8.2$_{4}$ ([ויהיה עם לבבו]), ידע *know* Dt 8$_{5}$, שׂיח *meditate* Ps 77$_{7}$ (or move עִם־לְבָבִי to end of preceding verse); בְּתוֹךְ *within,* + שׁמר *keep* Pr 4$_{21}$ (+ עַיִן *eye*); אַחַר *after,* + תעה *stray* 1QS 5$_{4}$ (‖ עַיִן *eye* + יֵצֶר *imagination*); אַחֲרֵי *after,* + תור *go about* Nm 15$_{39}$ (‖ עַיִן *eye*) 4Q417 2.1$_{27}$ ([אחר]י; ‖ עַיִן).

Also 4QUnid 4$_{5}$ 4QAdmonPar 3.2$_{4}$ 4QapJoseph^{a} 3$_{4}$ 4QparaKings 82$_{1}$ 4Q392 2$_{1}$ (ל[בבי]) 4Q416 8$_{1}$ 4Q418 236$_{3}$ 4Q423 7$_{7}$ 4QRitMar 158$_{3}$ 4QShir^{b} 43$_{7}$ 4QBéat 23.2$_{2}$.

<SYN> יָד *hand,* כַּף *hand,* עַיִן *eye,* פֶּה *mouth,* לָשׁוֹן *tongue,* עֹרֶף *neck,* רֹאשׁ *head,* עֶצֶם *bone,* נֶפֶשׁ *soul,* רוּחַ *spirit,* שְׁאֵר *flesh,* כֹּחַ *strength,* מְאֹד *might,* שַׂרְעַפִּים *thoughts.*

<ANT> עַיִן *eye,* בֶּגֶד *garment.**

⇒ לֵב *heart.*

[לְבִבָה] 3 n.f. **cake**—pl. לְבִבוֹת—<OBJ> לבב pi. *bake* 2 S 13$_{6}$, בשׁל pi. *cook* 13$_{8}$, עשׂה *make* 13$_{10}$, לקח *take* 13$_{10}$, בוא hi. *bring* 13$_{10}$. <CSTR> שְׁתֵּי לְבִבוֹת *two cakes* 13$_{10}$.

⇒ לבב *bake.*

לְבַד 156.2.18 adv. and prep. **alone; besides**—לְבַד; sf. לְבַדִּי, לְבַדְּךָ (לְבַדֶּךָ), לְבַדּוֹ, לְבַדָּהּ, לְבַדְּכֶם, לְבַדָּם, לְבַדְּהֶן (לְבַדָּנָה).

1. לְבַד alone, only, by oneself, by itself, on one's own, on its own, etc.

a. without sf., **(1)** qualifying noun as subject of verb: noun, אִשָּׁה *wife* Zc 12$_{12.12.13.13.14}$, מִשְׁפָּחָה *family* Zc 12$_{12.12.12.13.13.14}$, אֵבֶר *limb* 11QT 24$_{8}$ (ארביה), אֲשֶׁר *that which* 11QT 14$_{11}$; verb, היה *be* 11QT 24$_{8}$ ([יהי]ו), ספד *mourn* Zc 12$_{12+10t}$, עשׂה ni. *be done* 11QT 14$_{11}$.

(2) qualifying noun as object of verb: noun, עוֹלָה *burnt offering* 11QT 24$_{10+6t}$, יְרִיעָה *curtain* Ex 26$_{9.9}$‖36$_{16.16}$, זֶה *this* Ec 7$_{29}$, כֹּל *everyone* who licks Jg 7$_{5}$; verb, מצא *find* Ec 7$_{29}$, חבר *join* Ex 26$_{9.9}$‖36$_{16.16}$, יצג hi. *place* Jg 7$_{5}$, עשׂה *make*, i.e. offer 11QT 24$_{10+6t}$.

(3) qualifying noun in nom. cl., שהם סלעים ארבע לב[ד] sixteen denars, *which are only four sela'im* 5/6Ḥev BA 44$_{21}$.

b. with sf., **(1)** qualifying noun as subject of verb: Y. 1 K 8$_{39}$ ‖2 C 6$_{30}$ Is 2$_{11.17}$ 44$_{24}$ 63$_{3}$ Ps 72$_{18}$ 136$_{4}$ Jb 9$_{8}$, Ahab 1 K 18$_{6}$, Amnon 2 S 13$_{32.33}$, Ben Sira Si 30$_{26}$, Daniel Dn 10$_{7.8}$, Eglon Jg 3$_{20}$, Elijah 1 K 18$_{22}$ 19$_{10.14}$, Jacob Gn 32$_{25}$, Job Jb 31$_{17}$, Judah Jr 17$_{4}$ (if em. וּבְךָ *even through your own fault* to לְבַדְּךָ *on your own*) Moses Ex 18$_{14.18}$ 24$_{18}$ Nm 11$_{14.17}$ Dt 1$_{9.12}$, Obadiah 1 K 18$_{6}$, Zion Is 49$_{21}$, אָדָם *human being* Gn 2$_{18}$, אִישׁ *man* Dt 22$_{25}$=11QT 66$_{5}$ 2 S 18$_{26}$ Ezk 14$_{16.18}$, אִשָּׁה *woman* 11QT 57$_{18}$, בֵּן *son* Gn 42$_{38}$ Pr 9$_{12}$, יֶלֶד *child* Gn 44$_{20}$, מַלְאָךְ *messenger* Jb 1$_{15}$, יֹשֵׁב *inhabitant* of Jerusalem Is 5$_{8}$, שֵׁבֶט *tribe* 1 K 12$_{20}$ 2 K 17$_{18}$, שֵׁם *name* of Y. Ps 148$_{13}$, זֶה *this (one)* 1 K 14$_{13}$ Jb 1$_{16.17.19}$, food Ex 12$_{16}$.

(2) qualifying subject nouns in clauses with these verbs, היה *be* Gn 2$_{18}$ 1 K 12$_{20}$ 11QT 57$_{18}$, יתר ni. *remain*

Gn 32$_{25}$ 44$_{20}$ 1 K 18$_{22}$ 19$_{10.14}$, שׁאר ni. *remain* Gn 42$_{38}$ 2 K 17$_{18}$ Is 49$_{21}$ Dn 10$_{8}$, ישׁב *sit* Ex 18$_{14}$ Jg 3$_{20}$, ho. *be accommodated* Is 5$_{8}$, שׂגב ni. *be exalted* Is 2$_{11.17}$ Ps 148$_{13}$, נשׂא *raise* Nm 11$_{14.17}$ Dt 1$_{9.12}$ Pr 9$_{12}$, נטה *extend* heavens Is 44$_{24}$ Jb 9$_{8}$, שׁמט *release* Jr 17$_{4}$ (if em.), ראה *see* Dn 10$_{7}$, ידע *know* 1 K 8$_{39}$‖2 C 6$_{30}$, עשׂה *do* Ex 18$_{18}$ Ps 72$_{18}$ 136$_{4}$ (ms lacks לְבַדּוֹ), ni. *be prepared* Ex 12$_{16}$, עלם *conceal* Si 30$_{26}$ (or em. עמל *toil*), הלך *go* 1 K 18$_{6.6}$, בוא *come* 1 K 14$_{13}$, דרך *tread* Is 63$_{3}$, רוץ *run* 2 S 18$_{24.25}$ 18$_{26}$, נגשׁ ni. *draw near* Ex 24$_{2}$, אכל *eat* Jb 31$_{17}$, נצל ni. *be delivered* Ezk 14$_{16.18}$, מלט ni. *escape* Jb 1$_{15.16.17.19}$, מות *die* Dt 22$_{25}$ 2 S 13$_{32.33}$, ho. *be put to death* 11QT 66$_{5}$.

(3) qualifying subject of nom. cl., Y. 2 K 19$_{15.19}$‖Is 37$_{16.20}$ Ps 83$_{19}$ (if em.; see §1b[5]) 86$_{10}$ Ne 9$_{6}$, David 1 S 21$_{2}$ (+ וְאִישׁ אֵין אִתָּךְ *and there is no one with you*), Aram-zoba, etc. 2 S 10$_{8}$, אִישׁ *man* 2 S 18$_{25}$, מֶלֶךְ *king* 1 C 19$_{9}$, עבד ptc. *worshipper* 2 K 10$_{23}$, יוֹנָה *dove* Ca 6$_{9}$ (if em. בָּרָה *pure* to לְבַדָּהּ), שַׂלְמָה *garment* Ex 22$_{26}$ (Sam שִׂמְלָה *garment*), שְׁנַיִם *two* 1 K 11$_{29}$ (or del. לְבַדָּם *they alone*).

(4) qualifying object of verb; noun: Y. 1 S 7$_{3.4}$, Sheba 2 S 20$_{21}$, מֶלֶךְ *king* 2 S 17$_{2}$ 11QT 57$_{7}$, עֵדֶר *flock* Gn 32$_{17}$, כִּבְשָׂה *ewe-lamb* Gn 21$_{28.29}$, חָצוֹר *Hazor* Jos 11$_{13}$; verb: נתן *give* Gn 32$_{17}$ 2 S 20$_{21}$, נצב hi. *place* Gn 21$_{28.29}$, עזב *leave* 11QT 57$_{7}$, עבד *serve* 1 S 7$_{3.4}$, נכה hi. *strike* 2 S 17$_{2}$, שׂרף *burn* Jos 11$_{13}$.

(5) qualifying noun (or suffix), יִהְיוּ־לְךָ לְבַדֶּךָ *let them be yours alone* Pr 5$_{17}$, לָהֶם לְבַדָּם נִתְּנָה הָאָרֶץ *to them alone the land was given* Jb 15$_{19}$, וַיָּשֶׁת־לוֹ עֲדָרִים לְבַדּוֹ *and he placed flocks for himself alone* Gn 30$_{40}$, וַיָּשִׂימוּ לוֹ לְבַדּוֹ וְלָהֶם לְבַדָּם וְלַמִּצְרִים ... לְבַדָּם *and they placed*, i.e. gave, food, *to him by himself and to them by themselves and to the Egyptians ... by themselves* Gn 43$_{32}$, זֹבֵחַ ... בִּלְתִּי לַי׳ לְבַדּוֹ *whoever sacrifices ... except to Y. alone* Ex 22$_{19}$ (lacking in Sam), לְךָ לְבַדְּךָ חָטָאתִי *against you alone have I sinned* Ps 51$_{6}$.

טַל יִהְיֶה עַל־הַגִּזָּה לְבַדָּהּ *there will be dew on the fleece alone* Jg 6$_{37}$ (sim. 6$_{39.40}$), לֹא עַל־הַמֶּלֶךְ לְבַדּוֹ עָוְתָה וַשְׁתִּי *not against the king alone has Vashti done wrong* Est 1$_{16}$, לֹא עַל־הַלֶּחֶם לְבַדּוֹ יִחְיֶה הָאָדָם *a human being will not live by bread alone* Dt 8$_{3}$, לֹא אִתְּכֶם לְבַדְּכֶם אָנֹכִי כֹּרֵת אֶת־הַבְּרִית הַזֹּאת *it is not with you alone that I make this covenant* Dt 29$_{13}$, לֹא תִּלָּחֲמוּ ... כִּי אִם־אֶת־מֶלֶךְ יִשְׂרָאֵל לְבַדּוֹ *you will not fight ... except with the king of Israel alone* 1 K 22$_{31}$‖2 C 18$_{30}$, וַיִּבֶז בְּעֵינָיו לִשְׁלֹחַ יָד בְּמָרְדֳּכַי לְבַדּוֹ *and it was despicable to him to lay hands on Mordecai alone* Est 3$_{6(mss)}$ (if em. וַיִּבֶז *and he despised*; L לִשְׁלֹחַ), perh. הממשלה לבדו עמו *government is with him alone* 4QNarr C 1$_{9(WA)}$ (unless עמו = *his people* alone; others לכדו *they captured*).

(6) qualifying person indicated by pronominal suffix of noun, אַזְכִּיר צִדְקָתְךָ לְבַדֶּךָ *I will mention your righteousness, yours alone* Ps 71$_{16}$, שִׁמְךָ י׳ לְבַדֶּךָ עֶלְיוֹן *your name, yours alone, is Y, most high* over all the earth Ps 83$_{19}$ (or em. ‸י׳ your name, yours alone, *is Y.*; you alone are most high).

(7) qualifying second element (*nomen rectum*) of a construct phrase, אַדְמַת הַכֹּהֲנִים לְבַדָּם *the land of the priests, theirs alone* Gn 47$_{26}$.

2. לְבַד as prep., **besides, apart from,** followed by noun, מִמְכָּר *sale* Dt 18$_{8}$=11QT 60$_{15}$ (or em. לְבַד מִן, as §4); with verb, אכל *eat* Dt 18$_{8}$ (or em.).

3. לְבַד בְּ **only, alone,** לְבַד־בְּךָ נַזְכִּיר שְׁמֶךָ ... י׳ *Y. ..., you alone, we mention your name*, i.e. we mention only your name Is 26$_{13}$ (or em. לְבַדְּךָ *you alone* [and] your name do we mention, as §1b[3]).

4. לְבַד מִן as prep. **besides, apart from, except,** qualifying noun (or pronom. sf. in ref. to noun), David, Hezekiah, and Josiah Si 49$_{4}$, Benjamin Jg 20$_{17}$, טַף *children* Ex 12$_{37}$, אִישׁ *man* 1 K 10$_{15}$‖2 C 9$_{14}$ (or em. אֳנִי *fleet* or עֹנֶשׁ *fine*), שַׂר *officer* 1 K 5$_{30}$, סֹחֵר *trader* 2 C 9$_{14}$, יֹשֵׁב *inhabitant* Jg 20$_{15}$, אַיָּל *deer* 1 K 5$_{3}$, צְבִי *gazelle* 1 K 5$_{3}$, יַחְמוּר *roebuck* 1 K 5$_{3}$, בַּרְבּוּר *goose* 1 K 5$_{3}$, חֵלֶב *fat* 11QT 16$_{13}$, נֶדֶר *votive offering* Nm 29$_{39}$, נְדָבָה *freewill offering* Nm 29$_{39}$ 11QT 29$_{5}$, עוֹלָה *burnt offering* 11QT 25$_{7}$ (לבד מעול[ת]), חַטָּאת *sin offering* 11QT 25$_{14}$, שַׂהֲרוֹן *crescent* Jg 8$_{26}$, נְטִיפָה *pendant* Jg 8$_{26}$, בֶּגֶד *garment* Jg 8$_{26}$, עֲנָק *necklace* Jg 8$_{26}$, מֶכֶר *price* Dt 18$_{8}$ (if em. לְבַד מִמְּכָרָיו *apart from [the proceeds of] the sale of it*, as §2, to לְבַד מִמְּכָרָיו in same sense), מִסְחָר *merchandise* 1 K 10$_{15}$ (or em. סַחַר *traffic*), אֶרֶץ *land* Jos 17$_{5}$, עִיר *city* Dt 3$_{5}$, חַטָּאת *sin* 2 K 21$_{16}$.

Qualifying nouns in clauses with these verbs, היה *be* Jg 8$_{26}$ 1 K 5$_{3.30}$ 10$_{15}$, פקד ho. *be mustered* Jg 20$_{15.17}$, נסע *set out* Ex 12$_{37}$, נפל *fall* Jos 17$_{5}$, עשׂה *do* Nm 29$_{39}$, לכד

capture Dt 3$_{5}$, שׁפך *pour* blood 2 K 21$_{16}$, שׁחת hi. *act corruptly* Si 49$_{4}$, אכל *eat* Dt 18$_{8}$ (if em.), שׂרף *burn* 11QT 16$_{13}$, קרב hi. *present* offering 11QT 25$_{7}$ (... והקו]רבתמה [לבד מעול]ת) 25$_{14}$ 29$_{5}$ ([ויקריבו]).

5. לְבַד עַל as prep. **besides, apart from,** חִזְּקוּ בִידֵיהֶם בִּכְלֵי־כֶסֶף ... וּבַמִּגְדָּנוֹת לְבַד עַל־כָּל־הִתְנַדֵּב *they strengthened their hands with silver vessels ... and with choice things apart from everything that was freely offered* Ezr 1$_{6}$ (or em. לָרֹב עַל *in abundance*, i.e. in addition, *to*).

6a. מִלְּבַד as prep. **besides, apart from, except,** qualifying pronom. sf. in ref. to Y., Dt 4$_{35}$ (אֵין עוֹד מִלְבַדּוֹ *there is none other apart from him*); qualifying noun, אִשָּׁה *wife* Gn 46$_{26}$, בֵּן *son* 1 C 3$_{9}$, עֶבֶד *servant* Ezr 2$_{65}$||Ne 7$_{67}$, אָמָה *female servant* Ezr 2$_{65}$||Ne 7$_{67}$, מות ptc. *dead one* Nm 17$_{14}$, אַיִל *ram* Nm 5$_{8}$, רָעָב *famine* Gn 26$_{1}$, שַׁבָּת *sabbath* Lv 23$_{38}$, יוֹם *day* 4QNarrD 2$_{4}$, מַתָּנָה *gift* Lv 23$_{38}$, נֶדֶר *votive offering* Lv 23$_{38}$, נְדָבָה *freewill offering* Lv 23$_{38}$, עֹלָה *burnt offering* Lv 9$_{17}$ Nm 28$_{23.31}$ 29$_{6+9t}$ 11QT 14$_{13}$, מִנְחָה *cereal offering* Nm 28$_{31}$ 29$_{6+9t}$, נֶסֶךְ *drink offering* Nm 29$_{6+9t}$, חַטָּאת *sin offering* Nm 29$_{11}$, בְּרִית *covenant* Dt 28$_{69}$, מִזְבֵּחַ *altar* Jos 22$_{29}$, אֵלֶּה *these* Dn 11$_{4}$, אֲשֶׁר *that which* Nm 6$_{21}$ 1 K 10$_{13}$||2 C 9$_{12}$, *those whom* 2 C 17$_{19}$, כֹּל *everyone* 2 C 31$_{16}$ (if em. מִלְּבַד הִתְיַחְשָׂם *apart from enrolling them* to מִלְּבַד כֹּל כְּדֵי הִתְיַחְשָׂם *besides everyone according to their enrolment*).

Qualifying nouns in clauses with these verbs, היה *be* Gn 26$_{1}$ Nm 17$_{14}$, קטר hi. *burn* Lv 9$_{17}$, עשׂה *do*, i.e. prepare, offering Nm 28$_{23.31}$ 29$_{6}$, קרב hi. *present* offering Nm 29$_{11+8t}$, צוה pi. *command* Dt 28$_{69}$, נדר *vow* Nm 6$_{21}$, בנה *build* Jos 22$_{29}$, נתן *give* 1 K 10$_{13}$||2 C 9$_{12}$ 2 C 31$_{16}$.

6b. מִלְּבַד as adv., **alone, on one's own,** , with verb, אֲשֶׁר־בָּדָא מלבד *which he had made up himself* 1 K 12$_{33(Kt)}$ (Qr מִלִּבּוֹ *from his [own] heart*).

7. לְבַד מֵאֲשֶׁר, conj., **unless,** אַחַת דָּתוֹ לְהָמִית לְבַד מֵאֲשֶׁר יוֹשִׁיט־לוֹ הַמֶּלֶךְ *the law concerning them was unequivocal, to kill (them) unless the king extended his sceptre to them* Est 4$_{11}$.

[לַבָּה] 1 n.f. **flame**—cstr. לַבַּת—<CSTR> לַבַּת־אֵשׁ *flame of fire* Ex 3$_{2}$ (Sam להבת *flame of*). <PREP> בְּ of place, *in*, + ראה ni. *appear* Ex 3$_{2}$.

[לְבָה] 1 n.f. **spirit**—sf. לִבָּתֵךְ—**spirit** or **anger,** מָה אֲמֻלָה לִבָּתֵךְ *how enfeebled is your spirit* Ezk 16$_{30}$ (or em. אֲמַלֵא/אִמָּלֵא how *I am filled* with anger against you, or מַה־לִּי וְלִבְרִיתֵךְ *what do I have to do with your covenant?*, or מַה־לִּי בְּרִית לְבִתֵּךְ *what is your daughter's covenant to me?*).*

לְבוֹא חֲמָת 7 pl.n. **Lebo-hamath**—לְבוֹא־, לְבֹא חֲמָת—on northern border of Israel, perh. El-Lebwe, 80 km N of Damascus (unless לְ *at* + בּוֹא *the entrance of* + חֲמָת *Hamath*), <CSTR> דֶּרֶךְ־חֶתְלֹן לְבוֹא־חֲמָת חֲצַר עֵינָן *the way of Hethlon, Lebo-hamath, Hazar-enon* Ezk 48$_{1}$. <PREP> עַד *unto* Jos 13$_{5}$ 1 C 13$_{5}$ (+ מִן־שִׁיחוֹר מִצְרַיִם *from Shihor of Egypt* unto Lebo-hamath), + ישׁב *dwell* Jg 3$_{3}$; עַד־נֹכַח *unto opposite* Ezk 47$_{20}$; ה- of direction, + תור *explore* Nm 13$_{21(Sam)}$ (MT lacks ה-), תאה pi. *mark out* Nm 34$_{8(Sam)}$ (MT lacks ה-).

לְבוֹנָה I 21.1.7 n.f. **frankincense**—לְבֹנָה; sf. לְבֹנָתָהּ—ingredient of incense (Ex 30$_{34}$), offered with cereal offering (Lv 2$_{1.2.15.16}$ 6$_{8}$ Si 50$_{9}$ CD 11$_{19}$ 11QT 20$_{10}$), placed with bread of presence (Lv 24$_{7}$ 11QT 8$_{10.12}$), as ingredient of perfume (Ca 3$_{6}$) or as cleansing or deodorizing agent (CD 11$_{4}$).

<SUBJ> היה *be* Lv 24$_{7}$ 11QT 8$_{10}$ ([והיתה]; both + לַלֶּחֶם לְאַזְכָּרָה אִשֶּׁה לי׳ *to the bread as a token offering, an offering by fire to Y.*), בוא *come* Jr 6$_{20}$ (or em. hi. *bring* frankincense; || קָנֶה *[fragrant] reed*) 11QT 38$_{8}$ ([הבאה]). <NOM CL> לְבוֹנָה בְּיָדָם *frankincense was in their hand* Jr 41$_{5}$ (|| מִנְחָה *grain offering*). <OBJ> בוא hi. *bring* Jr 6$_{20}$ (if em.) 17$_{26}$ (|| מִנְחָה *cereal offering*, זֶבַח *sacrifice*, עוֹלָה *burnt offering*, + תּוֹדָה *thank offering*), קרב pi. *present* 11QT 20$_{10}$, שׁלח *send* CD 11$_{19}$ (|| עוֹלָה *burnt offering*, מִנְחָה, עֵץ *wood*), לקח *take* Ex 30$_{34}$ (+ נָטָף *stacte*, שְׁחֵלֶת *onycha*, חֶלְבְּנָה *galbanum*, סַם *spice*), נתן *give*, i.e. place Lv 2$_{1}$ 5$_{11}$ 24$_{7}$ Nm 5$_{15}$ Ne 13$_{5}$ (|| מִנְחָה, + כְּלִי *vessel*, מַעֲשֵׂר *tithe*) 11QT 8$_{12}$, שׂים *place* Lv 2$_{15}$, נשׂא *raise* Is 60$_{6}$ (|| זָהָב *gold*), רום hi. *raise* Lv 6$_{8}$, זכר hi. *offer as token offering* Is 66$_{3}$ (|| מִנְחָה).

<CSTR> גִּבְעַת הַלְּבוֹנָה *hill of frankincense* Ca 4$_{6}$ (|| מֹר *myrrh*), עֲצֵי לְבוֹנָה *trees of frankincense* Ca 4$_{14}$ (+ אֲהָל *aloe*, מֹר *myrrh*, + קִנָּמוֹן *cinnamon*, נֵרְדְּ *nard*, כֹּפֶר *henna*,

כַּרְכֹּם *saffron*, קָנֶה *[fragrant] reed*), כְּרֵיחַ לְבֹנָה the scent of your clothes is *like the smell of frankincense* Ca 4$_{11}$ (if em. לְבָנוֹן like the smell of *Lebanon*; Gnz מִכָּל־בְּשָׂמִים is *of all spices*), אש לבונה *fire of frankincense* Si 50$_9$ (+ מִנְחָה *grain offering*), כָּל־הַלְּבֹנָה *all the frankincense* Lv 6$_8$, כָּל־לְבֹנָתָהּ *all its frankincense* Lv 2$_{2.16}$. <ADJ> זַךְ *pure* Ex 30$_{34}$ Lv 24$_7$, זאת *this* 11QT 8$_{10}$.

<PREP> לְ *to, for* 4QOrd[b] 12$_2$; בְּ of instrument, *by (means of), with*, + יגע hi. *weary* Is 43$_{23}$ (|| מִנְחָה *grain offering*), שׁוף pass. *be rubbed* CD 11$_4$ (|| מַיִם *water*); כְּ *as* Ho 14$_7$ (if em. לְבָנוֹן like *Mount Lebanon*); עַל *in addition to*, + קמץ *take handful* of fine flour and oil Lv 2$_2$, קטר hi. *burn* token offering Lv 2$_{16}$; *in charge of*, + מנה pu. *be appointed* 1 C 9$_{29}$ (|| בֹּשֶׂם *spice*, שֶׁמֶן *oil*, יַיִן *wine*, סֹלֶת *fine flour*, + כְּלִי *vessel*); אֵת *with*, + שׁוב hi. *bring back* vessels Ne 13$_9$ (|| מִנְחָה). <COLL> מְקֻטֶּרֶת מוֹר לְבוֹנָה *burned in myrrh and frankincense* Ca 3$_6$ (or em. מִקְטֹרֶת rising up *from the smoke of* myrrh).*

<SYN> קָנֶה *(fragrant) reed*, בֹּשֶׂם *spice*, שֶׁמֶן *oil*, יַיִן *wine*, סֹלֶת *fine flour*, זָהָב *gold*, מֹר *myrrh*, מִנְחָה *cereal offering*, זֶבַח *sacrifice*, עוֹלָה *burnt offering*, עֵץ *wood*, מַיִם *water*.

לְבוֹנָה II 3 pl.n. **Lebonah, 1.** perh. El-Lubbān, 5 km NW of Shiloh, מְסִלָּה הָעֹלָה ... מִנֶּגֶב לִלְבוֹנָה *the highway that goes up ... to the south of Lebonah* Jg 21$_{19}$. **2.** station of exodus in Sinai peninsula, perh. ident. with *Laban* at Dt 1$_1$, <PREP> בְּ of place, *at*, + חנה *encamp* Nm 33$_{20(Sam)}$ (MT לִבְנָה *Libnah*); מִן of direction, *from*, + נסע *set out* Nm 33$_{21(Sam)}$ (MT לִבְנָה).*

לָבוּשׁ, see לבשׁ *dress*.

לְבוּשׁ 31.0.2 n.m. **garment**—cstr. לְבוּשׁ; sf. לְבוּשִׁי, לְבוּשְׁךָ, לְבוּשׁוֹ (לְבֻשׁוֹ), לְבוּשָׁהּ, לְבוּשְׁכֶן, לְבוּשָׁם; pl. sf. masc. לְבוּשֵׁיכֶן (2 S 1$_{24}$ [mss לבושיכם]), לְבֻשֵׁיהֶן—**garment, clothing,** of man (e.g. Gn 49$_{11}$ Ml 2$_{16}$), woman (e.g. Ps 45$_{14}$ Pr 31$_{22.25}$), warrior (2 S 20$_8$), worshipper (2 K 10$_{22}$), king (e.g. Est 6$_8$ 8$_{15}$); skin of Leviathan (Jb 41$_5$).

<SUBJ> חפשׂ htp. *disguise oneself*, i.e. perh. be disfigured Jb 30$_{18}$. <NOM CL> מַדּוּעַ אָדֹם לְבוּשֶׁךָ *why is your garment red?* Is 63$_2$ (if em. לִלְבוּשֶׁךָ perh. why the red *of your garment?*; || בֶּגֶד *garment*), עֹז־וְהָדָר לְבוּשָׁהּ *strength and honour are her clothing* Pr 31$_{25}$, תְּכֵלֶת וְאַרְגָּמָן לְבוּשָׁם *their clothing was blue and purple* Jr 10$_9$, שֵׁשׁ וְאַרְגָּמָן לְבוּשָׁהּ *her clothing is fine linen and purple* Pr 31$_{22}$, לְבוּשִׁי שָׂק *my clothing was sackcloth* Ps 35$_{13}$, מִמִּשְׁבְּצוֹת זָהָב לְבוּשָׁהּ *her clothing is of settings of gold* Ps 45$_{14}$ (or em. בְּמִשְׁבְּצוֹת *in settings of* or וּמִשְׁבֶּצֶת *and woven in* gold), [הוא] ... לבוש *it is ... a garment* 4QD[f] 3$_{10}$.

<OBJ> לבשׁ *wear* Est 5$_1$ (if ins. לְבוּשׁ), נשׂא *raise*, i.e. wear 4QapLam[a] 1.2$_{11}$ (הלבו[שים]), נתן *give* Est 6$_9$ (|| סוס *horse*), *turn into* sackcloth Ps 69$_{12}$, לקח *take* Est 6$_{10.11}$ (both || סוס), שׂים *place*, i.e. cause (cloud) to be Jb 38$_9$ (|| חֲתֻלָּה *swaddling band*), בוא hi. *bring* Est 6$_8$ (|| סוס), יצא hi. *take out* 2 K 10$_{22}$, כבס pi. *wash* Gn 49$_{11}$ (|| סוּת *robe*).

<CSTR> לבוש צמר ופשתים *garment of wool and linen* 4QD[f] 3$_{10}$, לְבוּשׁ שָׂק *garment of sackcloth* Est 4$_2$, מַלְכוּת *of kingship* Est 5$_1$ (if ins. לְבוּשׁ) 6$_8$ 8$_{15}$ (+ תְּכֵלֶת וָחוּר *of blue and white*); פְּנֵי לְבוּשׁוֹ *(sur)face of his garment* Jb 41$_5$; נושאי הלבו[שים] *wearers of the garments* 4QapLam[a] 1.2$_{11}$ (erased). <APP> מַד *robe* 2 S 20$_8$, כִּלְאַיִם *two kinds* 4QD[f] 3$_{10}$ ([כלאים]).

<PREP> לְ perh. of possession, *of, (belonging) to* Is 63$_2$ (or em.; see Nom. Cl.); *for, as* Pr 27$_{26}$; בְּ of accompaniment, *with, (dressed) in*, + הדר pass. *be (made) glorious* Is 63$_1$ (unless הדר = *be adorned* by [i.e. בְּ of instrument]; + בֶּגֶד *garment*), בוא *come* Est 4$_2$, יצא *go out* Est 8$_{15}$; of instrument, *by (means of), in*, + לבשׁ *be dressed* Est 6$_8$; נגע בְּ *touch* Lm 4$_{14}$; כְּ *as*, + היה *be* 4Q418 103.2$_7$ (unless לבו[ש] = *one who is dressed*), כסה pi. *cover* Ps 104$_6$, יצב htp. *stand* Jb 38$_{14}$ (or em. צבע ni./htp. *be dyed* as though it were; + חֹמֶר *clay*); *as though they were*, + חלף hi. *change* Ps 102$_{27}$ (+ בֶּגֶד).

עַל *over, upon*, + עלה hi. *take up* ornaments 2 S 1$_{24}$; כסה pi. appar. *spread* violence Ml 2$_{16}$; *(in exchange) for*, + נפל hi. *cause* lots *to fall* Ps 22$_{19}$ (+ בֶּגֶד); *concerning*, + כתב pass. *be written* 4QMMT B$_{77}$ ([כתוב]); בְּלִי *without* or *for lack of*, + הלך pi. *go* naked Jb 24$_{10}$; מִבְּלִי *without* or *for lack of*, + לין *spend night* naked Jb 24$_7$ (+ כְּסוּת *covering*), אבד *die* Jb 31$_{19}$ (+ כְּסוּת).

<COLL> יוֹאָב חָגוּר ... לְבֻשׁוֹ *Joab was girded ... with his garment* 2 S 20$_8$.

Also perh. 3QTr 3$_9$ (others לכושי *pine*).

<SYN> בֶּגֶד *garment*, חֲתֻלָּה *swaddling band*, סוּת *robe*,

סוס *horse*.
⇒ לבשׁ *dress*.

לבט 3.0.2 vb. **ruin—Ni.** 3.0.2 Impf. יִלָּבֵט; + waw וילבטו; inf. Q הלבט—**be ruined,** <SUBJ> אִישׁ *man* 1QH 2_{19}, אֱוִיל *fool* Pr 10_8 (or em. וֶאֱוִיל שְׂפָתַיִם יִלָּבֵט *and a fool of lips will be ruined* to וֶאֱוִיל שְׁבָטִים יֵדָע *and a fool will experience blows*) 10_{10} (or em. וֶאֱוִיל שְׂפָתַיִם יִלָּבֵט to וּמוֹכִיחַ יַעֲשֶׂה שָׁלוֹם *and one who reproves will make peace*), עַם *people* Ho 4_{14} 1QH 4_7. <PREP> בְּ of cause, *on account of*, + מִשְׁגֶּה *error* 1QH 2_{19}, בִּינָה lack of *understanding* 1QH 4_7 (בְּלֹא *without*).

לָבִיא 11.0.1 n.[m.] **lion**—pl. Q לביאים—<SUBJ> הלך *go* Na 2_{12} (=4QpNah 3.1_1 אריה לבוא *a lion* went *to enter*), המם hi. *roar* Is 30_6 (if em. מֵהֶם *from them* to מֵהֵם *roars*; || לַיִשׁ *lion*), ידע *know* Is 56_{11} (if em. הַכְּלָבִים *the dogs* to הַלְּבָאִם *the lions*), יעד ho. *be appointed* for children of guilt 1QH 5_7 (|| אֲרִי *lion*). <NOM CL> לָבִיא ... מֵהֶם *a lion(ess) ... is from them* Is 30_6 (or em.), הַלְּבָאִם עַזֵּי־נֶפֶשׁ *the lions are strong of appetite* Is 56_{11} (if em.).

<CSTR> בְּנֵי לָבִיא *sons of a lion(ess)* Jb 4_{11} (+ לַיִשׁ *lion*), מְתַלְּעוֹת *fangs of* Jl 1_6 (+ אַרְיֵה *lion*), נַהֲמַת *groaning of* Ps 38_9 (if em. לִבִּי *of my heart* to לָבִיא *of a lion*). <APP> אַרְיֵה לָבִיא ... גּוּר אַרְיֵה *a lion, a lion(ess) ..., a lion's cub* Na 2_{12} (=4QpNah 3.1_1 ארי לבוא ... גור אריה *a lion* went *to enter ..., a lion's cub*), לביאים ... אריות *lions ... lions* 1QH 5_7.

<PREP> לְ of benefit, *for*, + צוד *hunt* prey Jb 38_{39} (+ כְּפִיר *[young] lion*); כְּ *as* Is 5_{29} (+ כְּפִיר), + כרע *crouch* Gn 49_9 (+ אַרְיֵה *lion*) Nm 24_9 (+ אֲרִי *lion*), רבץ *lie down* Gn 49_9, שׁכב *lie down* Nm 24_9, קום *arise* Nm 23_{24} (|| אֲרִי), שׁכן *dwell* Dt 33_{20}, טרף *tear* Dt 33_{20}, אכל *eat* Ho 13_8 (or em. וְאֹכְלֵם שָׁם כְּלָבִיא *and I shall eat them there like a lion* to וַאֲכָלוּם שָׁם כְּלָבִים *and there dogs will eat them*); בְּתוֹךְ *among*, + נתן *give*, i.e. place, worshipper 1QH 5_7.

<COLL> לָבִיא וָלַיִשׁ *a lion(ess) and a lion* Is 30_6.
<SYN> אֲרִי *lion*, לַיִשׁ *lion*.*
⇒ לָבֵא *lion*, לְבָאָה *lion* (fem.), לְבִיָּא *lion* (fem.), לְבִיָּה *lion* (fem.).

לְבִיָּא 1 n.f. **lion** (fem.), <NOM CL> מָה אִמְּךָ לְבִיָּא בֵּין אֲרָיוֹת *what a lioness was your mother among lions* Ezk 19_2.
⇒ לָבִיא *lion(ess)*.

לְבִיָּה 4.0.1 n.f. **lion** (fem.)—pl. sf. Q לביותיו—<PREP> לְ of benefit, *for*, + חנק pi. *strangle* 4QpNah 3.1_4 (=Na 2_{13} לְבִאֹתָיו, from לְבָאָה *lion* [fem.]; + אַרְיֵה *lion*).* <PREP> כְּ *as*, + כרע *stoop* Gn $49_{9(Sam)}$ (MT לָבִיא *lion*; + אַרְיֵה *lion*) Nm $24_{9(Sam)}$ (MT לָבִיא; + אֲרִי *lion*), רבץ *lie down* Gn $49_{9(Sam)}$ (MT לָבִיא), שׁכב *lie down* Nm $24_{9(Sam)}$ (MT לָבִיא), קום *rise* Nm $23_{24(Sam)}$ (MT לָבִיא; || אֲרִי *lion*), שׁכן *dwell* Dt $33_{20(Sam)}$ (MT לָבִיא), טרף *tear* Dt $33_{20(Sam)}$ (MT לָבִיא).
<SYN> אֲרִי *lion*.
⇒ לָבִיא *lion(ess)*.

לֻבִים, see לוּבִים *Libyans*.

[לָבָם] pr.n.[m.] **Labam,** Seal 89 (Beirut, 7th cent.; others לבן *Laban*).

לבן I 5.0.1 vb. **be white—Pi. whiten,** <SUBJ> שׂכל hi. ptc. *wise one* Dn 11_{35} (if em. hi. *be white*). <PREP> עַד *unto*, + עֵת *time* Dn 11_{35} (if em.).
Pu. 0.0.1 Ptc. מלובן—**be whitened,** <SUBJ> בַּרְזֶל *iron* 1QM 5_{11} (+ ברר pass. *be purified*, טָהוֹר *pure*). <PREP> כְּ *as*, + מַרְאָה *mirror* 1QM 5_{11}.
Hi. 4 Pf. הִלְבִּינוּ; impf. אַלְבִּין, יַלְבִּינוּ; inf. לַלְבֵּן—**1. be white,** <SUBJ> worshipper Ps 51_9 (+ טהר *be pure*), שָׂרִיג *tendril* Jl 1_7, חֵטְא *sin* Is 1_{18}. <PREP> כְּ *as*, + שֶׁלֶג *snow* Is 1_{18}; מִן of comparison, *(more) than*, + שֶׁלֶג *snow* Ps 51_9.
2. whiten, <SUBJ> שׂכל hi. ptc. *wise one* Dn 11_{35} (or em. pi. *whiten*; || ברר pi. *purify*, + צרף *refine*).
<SYN> ברר pi. *purify*.
Htp. 1 Impf. יִתְלַבְּנוּ—**whiten oneself,** <SUBJ> רַב pl. *many* Dn 12_{10} (|| ברר htp. *behave purely*, צרף ni. *be refined*).
<SYN> ברר htp. *behave purely*, צרף ni. *be refined*.
⇒ לָבָן *white*, לֹבֶן *whiteness*, לְבָנָה *moon*.

לבן II 3 vb. **make bricks—Qal** 3 Impf. נִלְבְּנָה; inf. לִלְבֹּן—**make bricks,** <SUBJ> אִישׁ *man* Gn 11_3 (+ שׂרף

burn), עַם *people* Ex 5$_{7}$, שֹׁטֵר *officer*, i.e. Israelite foreman Ex 5$_{14}$. <OBJ> לְבֵנָה *brick* Gn 11$_{3}$ Ex 5$_{7}$. <PREP> כְּ *as*, + תְּמוֹל שִׁלְשֹׁם *yesterday and the day before*, i.e. previously Ex 5$_{7.14}$.

→ לְבֵנָה *brick*, מַלְבֵּן *brick mould*.

לָבָן I $_{29.0.4}$ adj. **white**—cstr. לְבֶן־; fem. לְבָנָה; pl. masc. לְבָנִים, fem. לְבָנוֹת (לְבָנֹת)—usu. **white; also bare, treeless** (5/6ḤevBA 44$_{12.15}$).*

1. attributively, of בַּהֶרֶת *spot* Lv 13$_{4.19.24}$ (both + אֲדַמְדָּם *reddish*) 13$_{24.38.39}$ (+ כֵּהֶה *dull*), נֶגַע *wound* Lv 13$_{42}$ (+ אֲדַמְדָּם), שְׂאֵת *swelling* Lv 13$_{10.19.43}$, שֵׂעָר *hair* Lv 13$_{10.21.26}$, פְּצָלָה *strip* Gn 30$_{37}$, סוּס *horse* Zc 1$_{8}$ (both || אָדֹם *red*, שָׂרֹק *sorrel*, אָמֹץ *dappled* [if ins.], שָׁחֹר *black* [if ins.]) 6$_{3}$ (|| אָדֹם, אָמֹץ, שָׁחֹר, בָּרֹד *dappled*), שֶׁלֶג *snow* Jr 18$_{14}$ (if em. לְבָנוֹן snow of *Lebanon*), עָפָר *dust* (as white, i.e. lacking trees) 5/6ḤevBA 44$_{12.15}$, בַּרְזֶל *iron* 1QM 5$_{10}$, שֵׁשׁ *byssus* 1QM 7$_{10}$. <COLL> לְבֶן־שִׁנַּיִם מֵחָלָב *one white/whiter of teeth than milk* Gn 49$_{12}$ (:: חַכְלִילִי *dark* of eyes).

2. predicatively, of מָן *manna* Ex 16$_{31}$ (in nom. cl.), בֶּגֶד *garment* Ec 9$_{8}$ (with היה *be*), שֵׂעָר *hair* Lv 13$_{3.4.20}$ (all three + הפך *be turned*) 13$_{25}$ (+ הפך ni. *be turned*), נֶגַע *wound* Lv 13$_{13}$ (+ הפך) 13$_{17}$ (הפך לְ ni. *be turned*), בָּשָׂר *flesh* Lv 13$_{16}$ (הפך לְ ni.).

3. as noun, **white(ness)**, <SUBJ> יצא *go out* Zc 6$_{6}$. <NOM CL> כֹּל אֲשֶׁר־לָבָן בּוֹ *everyone in which there was white* Gn 30$_{35}$, מַחְשֹׂף הַלָּבָן אֲשֶׁר עַל־הַמַּקְלוֹת *stripping of the white that was upon the rods* Gn 30$_{37}$.*

<SYN> אָדֹם *red*, שָׂרֹק *sorrel*; אָמֹץ *dappled*, בָּרֹד *dappled*, שָׁחֹר *black*. <ANT> חַכְלִילִי *dark*.

→ לבן *be white*.

לָבָן II $_{54.0.3}$ pr.n.m. **Laban, 1.** son of Bethuel, brother of Rebekah, and father of Leah and Rachel.

<SUBJ> בוא *come* Gn 24$_{29}$ 30$_{27}$ 31$_{33.33}$, hi. *bring* 29$_{13.23}$, יצא *go out* 31$_{33}$, הלך *go* 31$_{19}$ 32$_{1}$, שׁוב *go back* 32$_{1}$, עבר *pass* 31$_{51}$, רוץ *run* 24$_{29}$ 29$_{13}$, רדף *pursue* 31$_{22}$, דלק *pursue* 31$_{36}$, דבק hi. *overtake* 31$_{22}$, נשׂג hi. *overtake* 31$_{25}$, קרא *meet* 29$_{13}$, שׁלח pi. *send* 30$_{25}$ 31$_{26.36}$ 4QTNaph 1$_{2}$, נהג *lead* 1$_{7}$, שׁכם hi. *rise early* Gn 32$_{1}$, ראה *see* 24$_{29}$, שׁמע *hear* 24$_{29}$ 29$_{13}$, אמר *say* 24$_{29.29.50}$ 29$_{14.15.19.26}$ 30$_{27.27.34}$ 31$_{26.43.48.48.51}$, דבר pi. *speak* 24$_{50}$ 31$_{24.26}$, ענה *answer* 24$_{50}$ 31$_{43}$, קרא *call*, i.e. name 31$_{47}$ perh. 31$_{48}$, ברך pi. *bless* 32$_{1}$, ידע *know* 30$_{25.27}$, נכר *recognize* 31$_{31}$, נתן *give* 29$_{19.24.26(Sam).26.29}$ 30$_{25.27.27.27.34}$ 46$_{18.25}$ 4QTNaph 1$_{2}$, יהב *give* Gn 29$_{21}$, לקח *take* 29$_{22}$ 31$_{22.31}$, סור hi. *remove* 30$_{34}$, עשׂה *do* 29$_{22.25}$ 31$_{12.43}$, שׂים *place* 30$_{34}$ 31$_{36}$, שׁמר ni. *take care* 31$_{24.26}$, מצא *find* 30$_{27}$ 31$_{31.33.34.34.35}$, חבק pi. *embrace* 29$_{13}$, נשׁק pi. *kiss* 29$_{13}$ 31$_{26}$ 32$_{1}$, בקשׁ pi. *seek* 31$_{36}$, חפשׂ *search* 31$_{33(Sam).33}$, חבשׁ *bind* 31$_{33(Sam mss).33(Sam mss)}$, אסף *gather* 29$_{22}$, פרק *redeem* 4QTNaph 1$_{2}$, רמה pi. *deceive* Gn 29$_{25}$, גזל *rob* 31$_{31}$, כרת *cut*, i.e. make, covenant 31$_{43}$, נחשׁ pi. *divine* 30$_{27}$, גזז *shear* 31$_{19}$, משׁשׁ pi. *feel* 31$_{34.36}$, תקע *pitch* tent 31$_{25}$, חלף hi. *change* 31$_{36}$, יכל *be able* 24$_{50}$.

<NOM CL> שְׁמוֹ לָבָן *his name was Laban* Gn 24$_{29}$.

<OBJ> ידע *know* Gn 29$_{5.5}$, עבד *serve* 29$_{15}$ 30$_{25.27}$ 31$_{36}$, ברך pi. *bless* 30$_{27}$, נטשׁ *(give) leave* 31$_{26}$.

<CSTR> בְּנֵי־לָבָן *sons of Laban* Gn 31$_{1}$, אֲחוֹת *sister of* 25$_{20}$, בַּת־ *daughter of* 29$_{10}$, בְּנוֹת *daughters of* 28$_{2}$, לֵב *heart of* 31$_{20}$, פְּנֵי *face of* 31$_{2}$, צֹאן *flock of* 29$_{10.10}$ 30$_{36.40.40}$.

<APP> אָח *brother* Gn 27$_{43}$ 28$_{2.5}$ 29$_{10.10.10}$, בֵּן *son* 28$_{5}$ 29$_{5}$.

<ADJ> אֲרַמִּי *Aramaean* Gn 25$_{20}$ 31$_{20.24}$.

<PREP> לְ of direction, + אמר *say* Gn 31$_{24.31.36}$, ספר pi. *tell* 29$_{13}$, נגד hi. *tell* 29$_{15}$ 31$_{20.26}$, ho. *be told* 31$_{22}$, לקח *take* 31$_{31}$; of possession, *of, (belonging) to* 29$_{16}$ 31$_{43}$, + היה *be* 30$_{27.42}$; of benefit, *for*, + נכר hi. *recognize* 31$_{31}$; בְּ *against*, + ריב *strive* 31$_{36}$; אֶל *to*, + בוא *come* 31$_{24}$ 4QT Naph 1$_{7}$, hi. *bring* Gn 31$_{36}$, הלך *go* 28$_{5}$, עבר *pass* 31$_{51}$, אמר *say* 29$_{21.25}$ 30$_{25.27}$ 31$_{26}$; עִם *with* 31$_{36}$, + גור *sojourn* 32$_{5}$, ישׁב *dwell* 29$_{14.19}$, עבד *serve* 29$_{25.26}$; בֵּין *between* 31$_{48}$, + היה *be* 31$_{43}$, שׂים *place* 30$_{34}$, ירה *throw*, i.e. place 31$_{51}$, שׁפט *judge* Gn 31$_{51}$.*

2. Seal 89 (Beirut, 7th cent.; others לבם *Labam*).

לָבָן III $_{1}$ pl.n. **Laban,** station of exodus in Sinai peninsula, perh. ident. with Libnah at Nm 33$_{20.21}$, <PREP> בֵּין *between* Dt 1$_{1}$.

לַבֵּן $_{1}$ perh. pr.n.[m.] **Labben,** Philistine or Edomite adversary of David, <CSTR> עַל־מוּת לַבֵּן *on the death of Labben* Ps 9$_{1(mss)}$ (unless לַבֵּן = *of the son* or *of Ben*; L

עַלְמוּת perh. *sotto voce* or *lute* or *melody*).

[לֹבֶן] $_{0.1}$ n.[m.] **whiteness**—sf. Si לבנו (לבנה)—of snow, <CSTR> תור לבנו *form*, i.e. beauty, *of its whiteness* Si 43$_{18(M)}$ (B תואר לבנה).
→ לבן *be white*.

לִבְנָה $_{18}$ pl.n. **Libnah, 1.** town in Judah, perh. T. Bornāṭ, 27 km NW of Hebron, <SUBJ> היה *be* Jos 15$_{42}$, פשׁע *rebel* 2 K 8$_{22}$‖2 C 21$_{10}$. <OBJ> נתן *give* Jos 10$_{29}$ 21$_{13}$‖1 C 6$_{42}$ (+ מִגְרָשׁ *pasture land*), appar. נכה hi. *strike* Jos 10$_{29}$. <CSTR> מֶלֶךְ לִבְנָה *king of Libnah* Jos 12$_{15}$. <PREP> לְ of benefit, *to, for*, + עשׂה *do* Jos 10$_{32.39}$; בְּ of place, *in*, + שׁאר hi. *leave* Jos 10$_{29}$; מִן of direction, place, *from* 2 K 23$_{31}$ 24$_{18}$ Jr 52$_{1}$, + עבר *pass* Jos 10$_{31}$; עַל *against*, + לחם ni. *fight* Jos 10$_{29(mss)}$ 2 K 19$_{8}$‖Is 37$_{8}$; עִם *with*, + לחם ni. *fight* Jos 10$_{29}$. <COLL> וַיַּעֲבֹר ... מִמַּקֵּדָה לִבְנָה *and he passed ... from Makkedah to Libnah* Jos 10$_{29}$.

2. station of exodus in Sinai peninsula, perh. ident. with *Laban* at Dt 1$_{1}$, <PREP> בְּ of place, *at*, + חנה *encamp* Nm 33$_{20}$ (Sam לְבוֹנָה *Lebonah*); מִן of direction, *from*, + נסע *set out* Nm 33$_{21}$ (Sam לְבוֹנָה).

לִבְנֶה $_{2}$ n.[m.] **storax, storax tree** (*styrax officinalis*) or **poplar** (*populus alba*), <CSTR> מַקַּל לִבְנֶה *rod of storax tree* Gn 30$_{37}$ (+ לוּז *almond*, עַרְמוֹן *plane*), כְּרֵיחַ לִבְנֶה the scent of your clothes is *like the smell of storax* Ca 4$_{11}$ (if em. לְבָנוֹן like the smell of *Lebanon*; Gnz מִכָּל־בְּשָׂמִים is *of all spices*). <PREP> כְּ *as* Ho 14$_{7}$ (if em. לְבָנוֹן; or em. לְבֹנָה like *frankincense*), + נכה hi. *strike* root Ho 14$_{6}$ (if em. לְבָנוֹן; or em. נכה hi. to נטה hi. *extend* or ירה hi. *throw*); תַּחַת *under*, + קטר pi. *burn incense* Ho 4$_{13}$ (+ אַלּוֹן *oak*, אֵלָה *terebinth*).

לְבָנָה I $_{3}$ n.f. **moon,** <SUBJ> חפר *be ashamed* Is 24$_{23}$ (or em. לְבֵנָה *brick*; :: חַמָּה *sun*). <CSTR> אוֹר־הַלְּבָנָה *light of the moon* Is 30$_{26}$ (:: חַמָּה). <PREP> כְּ *as* Ca 6$_{10}$ (:: חַמָּה).*
<ANT> ‖ חַמָּה *sun*.
→ לבן *be white*.

לְבָנָה II $_{2}$ pr.n.m. **Lebanah,** ancestor of the Nethinim of the time of Zerubbabel, <CSTR> בְּנֵי־לְבָנָה *sons of Lebanah* Ezr 2$_{45}$‖Ne 7$_{48}$.

לְבֵנָה $_{12.0.3}$ n.f. **brick**—cstr. לִבְנַת; pl. לְבֵנִים; cstr. Q לבני; sf. לִבְנֵיכֶם—**brick, tile,** perh. **paving stone** (Ex 24$_{10}$) or **precious stone, jewel(lery)*** (Ex 24$_{10}$ 4QShirShabb[f] 19$_{6.6}$ 11QShirShabb c$_{3}$ f$_{3.4}$).

<SUBJ> היה *be* Gn 11$_{3}$ (+ לְאָבֶן *as stone*; ‖ חֵמָר *bitumen*), חפר *be ashamed* Is 24$_{23}$ (if em. לְבָנָה *moon*), נפל *fall* Is 9$_{9}$ (+ גָּזִית *hewn stone*). <OBJ> לבן *make (bricks)* Gn 11$_{3}$ Ex 5$_{7}$, עשׂה *make* Ex 5$_{16}$, שׂרף *burn* Gn 11$_{3}$, לקח *take* Ezk 4$_{1}$, נתן *give*, i.e. place Ezk 4$_{1}$. <CSTR> לִבְנַת הַסַּפִּיר *paving of sapphire* Ex 24$_{10}$, לבני כבודם *bricks*, or *jewels*, *of their glory*, i.e. their glorious bricks 4QShirShabb[f] 19$_{6}$ (לבני [כ]בודם) 11QShirShabb f$_{4}$ (ל[בני]), לב[נ]י הוד והדר[ר] *bricks*, or *jewels*, *of splendour and majesty* 4QShirShabb[f] 19$_{6}$; מַתְכֹּנֶת הַלְּבֵנִים *quota of the bricks* Ex 5$_{8}$, תֹּכֶן לְבֵנִים *quota of bricks* Ex 5$_{18}$ (Sam הַלְּבֵנִים *of the bricks*), מַעֲשֵׂה לִבְנַת *work of paving* or *jewel(lery) of* sapphire Ex 24$_{10}$, מעשי לבני *work of bricks* or *jewels of* 4QShirShabb[f] 19$_{6}$ (ל[בנ]י) 11QShirShabb f$_{3}$ ([לב]ני). <PREP> בְּ of instrument, *by (means of), with*, + מרר pi. *make* life *bitter* Ex 1$_{14}$ (‖ חֹמֶר *mortar*); מִן partitive *(any) of*, + גרע *diminish* Ex 5$_{19}$; עַל *upon*, + קטר pi. *burn incense* Is 65$_{3}$ (1QIsa[a] וינקו ידים על האבנים perh. *and penises empty themselves into the vaginas*),* חקק *engrave* Ezk 4$_{1}$; סָבִיב לְ *around*, + חקק pu. *be engraved* 4QShirShabb[f] 19$_{5}$.*

Also 11QShirShabb c$_{3}$.
<SYN> חֹמֶר *mortar*, חֵמָר *bitumen*.
→ לבן *make bricks*.

לְבֹנָה, see לְבוֹנָה I *frankincense*.

לְבָנוֹן $_{71.2.7}$ pl.n. **Lebanon**—+ ה- of direction לְבָנוֹנָה—mountain range and assoc. territory on northern border of Israel, usu. with article (הַלְּבָנוֹן), as northern border (e.g. Dt 11$_{24}$ Jos 1$_{4}$), dwelling place of Hivites (Jg 3$_{3}$), place of cedars (Jg 9$_{15}$ 1 K 5$_{13.20}$ 2 K 14$_{9}$2 C 25$_{18}$ Is 2$_{13}$ 14$_{8}$ Jr 22$_{23}$ Ezk 17$_{3}$ 27$_{5}$ 31$_{3}$ Zc 11$_{1}$ Ps 29$_{5}$ 92$_{13}$ 104$_{16}$ Ca 5$_{15}$ Ezr 3$_{7}$ 2 C 2$_{7}$ Si 50$_{12}$), of other trees (Is 60$_{13}$ 2 C 2$_{7}$), of thistles (2 K 14$_{9}$); in name of part of Solomon's palace, בֵּית יַעַר הַלְּבָנוֹן *House of the Forest of Lebanon* (1 K 7$_{2}$ 10$_{17.21}$‖2 C 9$_{16.20}$).

<SUBJ> נפל *fall* Is 10$_{34}$ (+ יַעַר *forest*), שׁוב *turn*, i.e. be changed Is 29$_{17}$ (+ לַכַּרְמֶל *into a plantation*), חפר hi. *be ashamed* Is 33$_{9}$ (+ כַּרְמֶל *Carmel*, שָׁרוֹן *Sharon*, בָּשָׁן *Bashan*), קמל *decay* Is 33$_{9}$, מצא ni. *be found* Zc 10$_{10}$ (if וּלְבָנוֹן *and Lebanon* is moved to before לֹא יִמָּצֵא and *it will not be found*), פתח *open* doors Zc 11$_{1}$ (+ בָּשָׁן), חשׁב ni. *be reckoned* perh. 4QpIsa^{c} 21$_{2}$ (הל[ב]נון). <NOM CL> הלבנון הוא עצת היחד *Lebanon is the council of the community* 1QpHab 12$_{3}$, זֹאת הָאָרֶץ הַנִּשְׁאֶרֶת ... וְכָל־הַלְּבָנוֹן *this is the land that remains ... and all Lebanon* Jos 13$_{5}$, לְבָנוֹן אֵין דֵּי בָּעֵר *Lebanon is not a sufficiency of*, i.e. sufficient for, *burning* Is 40$_{16}$. <OBJ> ראה *see* Dt 3$_{25}$, קדר hi. *darken*, i.e. cause to mourn Ezk 31$_{15}$, רקד hi. *cause to skip* Ps 29$_{6}$ (+ שִׂרְיֹן *Sirion*), perh. עלה *go up* Jr 22$_{20}$ (+ בָּשָׁן *Bashan*, עֲבָרִים *Abarim*).

<CSTR> רֹאשׁ הַלְּבָנוֹן *head*, i.e. summit, *of Lebanon* Jr 22$_{6}$ (+ גִּלְעָד *Gilead*), בִּקְעַת *valley of* Jos 11$_{17}$ 12$_{7}$, הַר *mountain of* Jg 3$_{3}$, יַרְכְּתֵי *recesses of* 2 K 19$_{23}$||Is 37$_{24}$ (לְבָנוֹן), אַרְזֵי *cedars of* Jg 9$_{15}$ Is 2$_{13}$ 14$_{8}$ (לְבָנוֹן) Ps 29$_{5}$ 104$_{16}$ (לְבָנוֹן) 4QBer^{a} 5$_{5}$ ([לבנון]), עֲצֵי *trees/wood of* Ca 3$_{9}$ 2 C 2$_{7}$ (לְבָנוֹן), אֶרֶץ גִּלְעָד וּלְבָנוֹן *land of Gilead and Lebanon* Zc 10$_{10}$ (or move וּלְבָנוֹן *and Lebanon* to before לֹא יִמָּצֵא and *it will not be found*), אֶרֶץ הַכְּנַעֲנִי וְהַלְּבָנוֹן *the land of the Canaanite(s) and Lebanon* Dt 1$_{7}$, בֵּית יַעַר הַלְּבָנוֹן *House of the Forest of Lebanon* 1 K 7$_{2}$ 10$_{17.21}$||2 C 9$_{16.20}$, פֶּרַח לְבָנוֹן *bud of Lebanon* Na 1$_{4}$ (+ כַּרְמֶל *Carmel*, בָּשָׁן *Bashan*) Si 50$_{8}$ (לבנון) 4QpNah 1$_{7}$, רֵיחַ *scent of* Ca 4$_{11}$ (or em. לִבְנֶה *storax* or לְבֹנָה *frankincense*), שֶׁלֶג *snow of* Jr 18$_{14}$ (or em. לָבָן *white* snow), יַיִן *wine of* Ho 14$_{8}$, מִגְדַּל הַלְּבָנוֹן *the tower of Lebanon* Ca 7$_{5}$ (+ חֶשְׁבּוֹן *Heshbon*), חֲמַס *violence of* Hb 2$_{17}$, כְּבוֹד *glory of* Is 35$_{2}$ (+ שָׁרוֹן *Sharon*) 60$_{13}$, מִבְחַר וְטוֹב־לְבָנוֹן *the choice and goodness of Lebanon* Ezk 31$_{16}$ (+ עֵדֶן *Eden*), כָּל־הַלְּבָנוֹן *all Lebanon* Jos 13$_{5}$.

<ADJ> זֶה *this* Jos 1$_{4}$ (or del. הַזֶּה *this*).

<PREP> בְּ of place, *in* 1 K 5$_{13}$ 2 K 14$_{9.9.9}$||2 C 25$_{18.18.18}$ Ezk 31$_{3}$ Ps 92$_{13}$ Si 50$_{12}$, + היה *be* 1 K 5$_{28}$, בנה *build* 1 K 9$_{19}$||2 C 8$_{6}$, ישׁב *dwell* Jr 22$_{23}$; כְּ *as* Ho 14$_{7}$ (or em. לִבְנֶה *storax* or לְבֹנָה *frankincense*) Ca 5$_{15}$, + נכה hi. *strike* root Ho 14$_{6}$ (or em. לִבְנֶה and/or נטה hi. *extend* or ירה hi. *throw*), ציץ hi. *flourish* Ps 72$_{16}$ (if em. כַּלְּבָנוֹן פִּרְיוֹ וְיָצִיצוּ *its fruit is like Lebanon, and they will flourish* to כַּלְּבָנוֹן פִּרְיוֹ יָצִיץ *his fruit will flourish like Lebanon*).

מִן *from* Dt 11$_{24}$ (or ins. עַד from the steppe and *unto* Lebanon) Jos 1$_{4}$ 13$_{6}$ 1 K 5$_{20}$ 2 C 2$_{15}$ perh. 4QpsEzek^{a} 5$_{3}$ ([מן]), + בוא *come* Ca 4$_{8.8}$, hi. *bring* Ezr 3$_{7}$ 4QSela 8.2$_{6}$ ([מ]לבנון), ירד hi. *take down* 1 K 5$_{23}$, נזל *flow* Ca 4$_{15}$, לקח *take* Ezk 27$_{5}$ (+ שְׂנִיר *Senir*, בָּשָׁן *Bashan*, אִיֵּי כִתִּים *isles of the Kittim*), שׁלח *send* 2 C 2$_{7}$; אֶל *to*, + בוא *come* Ezk 17$_{3}$; עַד *unto* Dt 11$_{24}$ (if ins. עַד); אֶל־מוּל *towards* Jos 9$_{1}$; ה- of direction, *to*, + שׁלח *send* 1 K 5$_{28}$.*

Also 4QIsa^{c} 8$_{4}$ 4QpNah 1$_{7}$ 4QPseud^{a} 1$_{1}$.

לִבְנִי I 5 pr.n.m. **Libni, 1.** Levite, son of Gershon/m, <NOM CL> בְּנֵי גֵרְשׁוֹן לִבְנִי *the sons of Gershon were Libni* Ex 6$_{17}$, לְגֵרְשׁוֹם לִבְנִי בְנוֹ *belonging to Gershom was Libni, his son* 1 C 6$_{5}$. <APP> בֵּן *son* 1 C 6$_{5}$. <COLL> אֵלֶּה שְׁמוֹת בְּנֵי־גֵרְשׁוֹן ... לִבְנִי *these are the names of the sons of Gershon ... Libni* Nm 3$_{18}$ 1 C 6$_{2}$ (גֵּרְשׁוֹם *Gershom*).

2. Levite, son of Mahli and descendant of Merari, <NOM CL> בְּנֵי מְרָרִי ... לִבְנִי *the sons of Merari were ... Libni* 1 C 6$_{14}$. <APP> בֵּן *son* 1 C 6$_{14}$.

→ לִבְנִי *Libnite*.

לִבְנִי II 2 gent. **Libnite,** of descendants of Libni son of Gershon, <CSTR> מִשְׁפַּחַת הַלִּבְנִי *family of the Libnite(s)* Nm 3$_{21}$ 26$_{58}$.

→ לִבְנִי *Libni*.

לִבְנָת, see שִׁיחוֹר לִבְנָת *Shihor-libnath*.

לֵב קָמָי, see לֵב *heart*, Cstr.

לבשׁ 112.6.13 vb. **dress—Qal** 76.2.12 Pf. לָבַשׁ (לָבֵשׁ), לָבְשָׁה, לָבַשְׁתָּ, לָבַשְׁתִּי, לָבְשׁוּ; impf. יִלְבַּשׁ (יִלְבָּשׁ), 2ms תִּלְבַּשׁ (תִּלְבָּשׁ, Si תלבשנה), תִּלְבְּשִׁי (תִּלְבָּשִׁי), אֶלְבָּשֶׁנָּה, יִלְבְּשׁוּ (יִלְבָּשׁוּ, Q ילבשוה), 3fpl תִּלְבַּשְׁןָ, תִּלְבָּשׁוּ, נִלְבַּשׁ; + waw וְלָבַשׁ (וּלְבֵשָׁם), וְלָבְשׁוּ; וַיִּלְבַּשׁ (וַיִּלְבָּשֵׁנִי, וַיִּלְבָּשֵׁם), 3fs וַתִּלְבַּשׁ, וַיִּלְבְּשׁוּ; impv. לְבַשׁ, לִבְשִׁי, לִבְשׁוּ; ptc. Si לובש, לְבֻשִׁים (Q לובשים), לָבוּשׁ (לָבֻשׁ), לְבוּשׁ (לְבֻשׁ), לְבוּשֵׁי (לְבֻשֵׁי); inf. לְבֹשׁ, לָבוֹשׁ (Q לבוש).

1. dress (oneself) in, wear; rarely, without object, **dress oneself, dress up** (Jb 27$_{17}$ Hg 1$_{6}$ perh. Est 5$_{1}$).

<SUBJ> Y. Is 59$_{17.17}$ (|| עטה *wrap*) Ps 93$_{1.1}$ (|| אזר htp.

gird oneself) 104_1, Israelite Dt 22_{11}, Egyptians Jr 46_4, Aaron Lv $16_{4.4.23}$ (:: פשט *strip*) 16_{24}, Esther Est 5_1, Jacob Gn 28_{20} (|| אכל *eat*), Jehoshaphat 1 K 22_{30}||2 C 18_{29}, Job Jb 29_{14} 40_{10} (|| עטה), Mordecai Est 4_1, Saul 1 S 28_8, Tamar Gn 38_{19}, אִישׁ *man* Jon 3_5 4QSD 7.14 (י[ל]בש), גֶּבֶר *man* Dt 22_5 4QOrd^{a} 2_7, אִשָּׁה *woman* 2 S 14_2 Is 4_1 (|| אכל), בֵּן *son* Ezk $44_{17.19}$ (+ פשט) Si $6_{31(A)}$ (|| עטר pi. *wear as crown*) $40_{3(Bmg)}$, בַּת *daughter* 2 S 13_{18}, כֹּהֵן *priest* Ex 29_{30} Lv $6_{3.3}$ (יִלְבַּשׁ *he will wear* breeches; mss יִהְיוּ breeches *will be*) 6_4 (:: פשט) 16_{32} 21_{10} Ezk 42_{14} $44_{17.19}$ Ps 132_9=2 C 6_{41} 1QM 7_{10} 4QTohB^{b} 1_9 11QT 15_{16}, לֵוִי *Levite* Ezk $44_{17.19}$, נָבִיא *prophet* Zc 13_4, מֶלֶךְ *king* Est. 6_8, נָשִׂיא *prince* Ezk 7_{27} 26_{16} (:: פשט, סור hi. *remove*), רֹעֶה *shepherd* Ezk 34_3 (|| אכל *eat*), צַדִּיק *righteous one* Jb 27_{17}, גדל hi. ptc. *one who magnifies oneself* Ps 35_{26}, שָׂטָן ptc. *adversary* Ps 109_{29} (+ עטה), שׂנא ptc. *one who hates* Jb 8_{22}, רָשָׁע *wicked one* Ps 109_{18}, female lover Ca 5_3 (+ פשט), worshipper 1QH 5_{31}, זְרוֹעַ *arm* of Y. Is 51_9, בָּשָׂר *flesh* Jb 7_5, עַם *people* Hg 1_6 (|| אכל *eat*, שתה *drink*), Zion Is 49_{18} 52_1, כַּר *pasture* Ps 65_{14} (or em. הַר *mountain*), מִקְוֶה *pool* Si 43_{20}, Jerusalem Is 52_1 Jr 4_{30} (|| עדה *adorn oneself*), עִיר *city* Is 52_1; subj. not specified, Zp 1_8.

<OBJ> בֶּגֶד *garment* Gn 28_{20} 38_{19} Ex 29_{30} Lv 6_4 $16_{23.24.32.32}$ 21_{10} 1 S 28_8 2 S 14_2 1 K 22_{30}||2 C 18_{29} Is 52_1 59_{17} Ezk 42_{14} $44_{17.19}$ Si $6_{31(A)}$ (בגדי כבוד תלבשנה *[like] garments of honour will you wear it*) 1QM 7_{10} 11QT 15_{16} 40_1 ([הבגדים]), מַד *garment* Lv 6_3, שִׂמְלָה *garment* Dt 22_5 Is 4_1, לְבוּשׁ *garment* Est 5_1 (if ins. לְבוּשׁ), תִּלְבֹּשֶׁת *clothing* Is 59_{17} (or del. תִּלְבֹּשֶׁת), מַלְבּוּשׁ *clothing* Zp 1_8 Est 5_1 (if ins. מַלְבּוּשׁ), כְּתֹנֶת *tunic* Lv $16_{4.4}$ Ca 5_3 1QM 7_{10} 4QOrd^{a} 2_7, אַדֶּרֶת *cloak* Zc 13_4, מְעִיל *robe* 2 S 13_{18} (or em. מְעִילִים *robes* to מֵעוֹלָם *from of old*), מִכְנָסַיִם *breeches* Lv 6_3 16_4 1QM 7_{10}, אַבְנֵט *girdle* Lv 16_4, מִצְנֶפֶת *turban* Lv 16_4, סִרְיֹן *armour* Jr 46_4.

בַּד *linen* Lv 6_3 (מִדּוֹ בַד *his garment, linen*, Sam מַדֵּי בַד *garments of linen*), צֶמֶר *wool* Ezk 34_3, שַׁעַטְנֵז *mixed fabric* Dt 22_{11}, שָׁנִי *scarlet* Jr 4_{30}, שַׂק *sackcloth* Jon 3_5 Est 4_1.

עָפָר *dust* Si $40_{3(Bmg)}$, אֵפֶר *ashes* Est 4_1 Si $40_{3(Bmg)}$, עֹז *strength* Is 51_9 52_1 Ps 93_1, גֵּאוּת *majesty* Ps 93_1, הוֹד *splendour* Ps 104_1 Jb 40_{10}, הָדָר *honour* Ps 104_1 Jb 40_{10}, חָכְמָה *wisdom* Si $6_{31(A)}$, צֶדֶק *righteousness* Ps 132_9 Jb 29_{14}, צְדָקָה *righteousness* Is 59_{17}, תְּשׁוּעָה *salvation* 2 C 6_{41}, בֹּשֶׁת *shame* Ps 35_{26} Jb 8_{22}, כְּלִמָּה *shame* Ps 35_{26} 109_{29}, שְׁמָמָה *devastation* Ezk 7_{24}, חֲרָדָה *trembling* or *loincloth* Ezk 26_{16} (or em. חֲרָדוֹת to חֲגֹרוֹת *loincloths* or קְדֹרוּת *darkness*), קְדֹרוּת *darkness* Ezk 26_{16} (if em.) 1QH 5_{31}, קְלָלָה *curse* Ps 109_{18}, צֹאן *flock* Ps 65_{14} (or em. הַצֹּאן *the flock* to חָצִיר *grass*), רִמָּה *maggot* Jb 7_5, גּוּשׁ *scab* or clod Jb $7_{5(Qr)}$, מַיִם *water* Si 43_{20}, כֹּל *everyone* Is 49_{18}.

<PREP> בְּ of instrument, *by (means of), with, in*, + בֶּגֶד *garment* 4QSD 7.14 (י[ל]בש), לְבוּשׁ *garment* Est 6_8; כְּ *as though it* (etc.) *were*, + עֲדִי *ornament* Is 49_{18} (or del. כָּעֲדִי), שִׁרְיָן *armour* Is 59_{17} Si 43_{20}, מַד *garment* Ps 109_{18}, מְעִיל *robe* 4QapPs^{b} 15_{10}; מִן of direction, *from*, + עוֹלָם *eternity* 2 S 13_{18} (if em. מְעִילִים wear *robes*); עַל *upon*, + בָּשָׂר *flesh* Lv 6_3 (יִלְבַּשׁ *he will wear* breeches; mss יִהְיוּ breeches *will be*).

<COLL> וַתִּלְבַּשׁ אֶסְתֵּר מַלְכוּת perh. *and Esther dressed royally* Est 5_1 (or ins. לְבוּשׁ wore *garment of* royalty or מַלְבּוּשׁ wore *clothing of* royalty), אֵיכָכָה אֶלְבָּשֶׁנָּה *how can I wear it?* Ca 5_3, שִׁבְעַת יָמִים יִלְבָּשָׁם הַכֹּהֵן *seven days the priest is to wear them* Ex 29_{30}.

2. clothe, envelop, <SUBJ> רוּחַ *spirit* Jg 6_{34} 1 C 12_{19} 2 C 24_{20}, צֶדֶק *righteousness* Jb 29_{14}. <OBJ> Amasai 1 C 12_{19}, Gideon Jg 6_{34}, Job Jb 29_{14}, Zechariah 2 C 24_{20}, בֵּן *son* 2 C 24_{20}, כֹּהֵן *priest* 2 C 24_{20}.

3. pass. **be dressed (in), wear. a.** ptc. abs., <SUBJ> אִישׁ *man* 1 S 17_5 Ezk $9_{2.3}$ Dn 10_5 (+ חגר pass. *be girded*) 11QT 35_6, Joshua Zc 3_3 (+ היה *be*), בַּיִת *household* Pr 31_{21}. <COLL> לבש pass. *be dressed (in)* with item of clothing, etc., בֶּגֶד *garment* Zc 3_3 11QT 35_6 ([בג]די), בַּד *linen* Ezk $9_{2.3}$ Dn 10_5, שָׁנִי *scarlet* Pr 31_{21} (or em. שְׁנַיִם *twofold*), שִׁרְיוֹן *armour* 1 S 17_5, קַשְׂקֶשֶׂת *scale armour* 1 S 17_5.

b. ptc. cstr., <SUBJ> אִישׁ *man* Ezk 9_{11} $10_{2.6}$ Dn $12_{6.7}$, מֶלֶךְ *king* Is 14_{19}, פֶּחָה *governor* Ezk 23_{12}, סָגָן *prefect* Ezk 23_{12}, קָרוֹב appar. *warrior* Ezk $23_{6.12}$, פָּרָשׁ *rider* Ezk 38_{14}, מְאַהֵב *lover* Ezk 23_6, אַשּׁוּר *Assyria* Ezk 23_6, סוּס *horse* Ezk 38_{14}. <COLL> לְבוּשׁ הֲרֻגִים *one dressed of*, i.e. like, *(the) slain* Is 14_{19}, לְבֻשׁ הַבַּדִּים *the one dressed of*, i.e. in, *linen* Ezk 9_{11} $10_{2.6.7}$ (+ חָפְנֵי *hands of* those dressed in) Dn $12_{6.7}$ (both לְבוּשׁ), לְבֻשֵׁי תְכֵלֶת *those dressed of*, i.e. in, *purple* Ezk 23_6, מִכְלוֹל *of perfection* Ezk 23_{12} 38_4, ראשי לבושי פלא *heads of those dressed of*, i.e. in, *wonder*

4QShirShabb[f] 23.2₁₀.

Also 4QD[b] 7₁₃ ([לְ[ב]וּ[שׁ]) 4QapJoseph[b] 2₁₀ 4QpsMos[d] 63₁ 4Q418 105₁.

<SYN> §1 עטה *wrap*, אזר htp. *gird oneself*, עדה *adorn oneself*, עטר pi. *wear as crown*, אכל *eat*; שׁתה *drink*.

<ANT> פשׁט *strip*, סור hi. *remove*.

Pu. 4 Ptc. מְלֻבָּשִׁים—**be dressed (in), wear,** <SUBJ> Jehoshaphat 1 K 22₁₀‖2 C 18₉, אִישׁ *man* 1 K 22₁₀‖2 C 18₉, מֶלֶךְ *king* 1 K 22₁₀‖2 C 18₉, כֹּהֵן *priest* Ezr 3₁₀, לֵוִי *Levite* 2 C 5₁₂, מְשֹׁרֵר *singer* 2 C 5₁₂. <COLL> לבשׁ pu. *be dressed (in)* with item of clothing, etc., בֶּגֶד *garment* 1 K 22₁₀‖2 C 18₉, בּוּץ *byssus* Ezr 3₁₀ (if ins. בּוּץ) 2 C 5₁₂, שַׁעַטְנֵז *mixed fabric* 4Q418 103.2₇ (כלובן[שׁ בשׁעטנז] perh. *as one dressed in mixed fabric*), צֶמֶר *wool* 4Q418 103.2₇, פִּשְׁתִּים *flax* 4Q418 103.2₇.

Hi. 32.3.1 Pf. הִלְבִּישׁוּ, הִלְבִּישָׁה, הִלְבִּישַׁנִי, Q הלבשתני; impf. Si ילבשׁ, 3fs תַּלְבִּישׁ, 2ms תַּלְבִּישׁ (תַּלְבִּישֵׁנִי), אַלְבִּישׁ; + waw וַיַּלְבֵּשׁ; וְהִלְבִּישׁוּ, וְהִלְבַּשְׁתִּיו, (וְהִלְבַּשְׁתָּם) וְהִלְבַּשְׁתָּ (וַיַּלְבִּשֵׁם); Si וילבישׁהו, 3fs וַתַּלְבֵּשׁ, וְאַלְבִּישֵׁךְ, וַיַּלְבִּשֵׁהוּ (וַיַּלְבִּשׁוּם); ptc. מַלְבִּשְׁכֶם; impv. הַלְבֵּשׁ; inf. הַלְבִּישׁ.

1. dress another **(with),** <SUBJ> Y. Gn 3₂₁ Is 22₂₁ (‖ חזק pi. *strengthen*, i.e. bind, with girdle) 50₃ (+ שׂים *place*) 61₁₀ (‖ יעט *cover* [or em. עטה *wrap* or hi. *envelop*]) Ezk 16₁₀ (‖ נעל *provide shoes*, חבשׁ *bind*, כסה pi. *cover*) Ps 132₁₆.₁₈ Jb 10₁₁ (‖ סכך po. *weave*) Si 45₇ (‖ אזר pi. *gird*) 45₈ (‖ פאר pi. *adorn*) perh. 4QBark[e] 5₃, Haman Est 6₁₁ (+ רכב hi. *cause to ride*), Job Jb 39₁₉, Joshua Jos 3₄ (or em. וְהַלְבֵּשׁ אֹתְךָ *and dress yourself* to וְהִלְבִּשׁוּ אֹתוֹ *and they dressed him* or וַיַּלְבִּשׁוּ אֹתוֹ *and let them dress him*), Moses Ex 28₄₁ 29₅‖Lv 8₇ Ex 29₈‖Lv 8₁₃ (+ חגר *gird*) Ex 40₁₃.₁₄ Nm 20₂₆.₂₈, Rebekah Gn 27₁₅.₁₆, Saul 1 S 17₃₈ (+ נתן *give*, i.e. place) 17₃₈ 2 S 1₂₄, אִישׁ *man* Est 6₉ (if em. וְהִלְבִּישׁוּ *and let them dress* to וְהִלְבִּישׁוֹ *and let him dress him*) 2 C 28₁₅.₁₅ (‖ נעל hi. *provide shoes*, אכל hi. *feed*, שׁקה hi. *give to drink*, סוך *anoint*), פַּרְעֹה *Pharaoh* Gn 41₄₂ 4QJub[h] 40₇ ((וילבשׁ[הו])), שַׂר *prince* Est 6₉ (or em.), פַּרְתְּם *noble* Est 6₉ (or em.), מַלְאָךְ *angel* Zc 3₄ (or del.), עֹמֵד *attendant* Zc 3₅ (or del. לבשׁ hi.), נוּמָה *drowsiness* Pr 23₂₁; subj. not specified, Est 4₄.

<OBJ> (1) person, etc., dressed, Aaron Ex 28₄₁ 29₅‖Lv 8₇ Ex 40₁₃ Si 45₇.₈, Adam Gn 3₂₁, David 1 S 17₃₈.₃₈, Eleazar Nm 20₂₆.₂₈ (both :: פשׁט hi. *strip*), Eliakim Is 22₂₁, Jacob Gn 27₁₅, Job Jb 10₁₁, Joseph Gn 41₄₂ 4QJub[h] 40₇ ((וילבשׁ[הו])), Joshua Zc 3₄.₅ (or del. לבשׁ hi.), Mordecai Est 4₄ 6₁₁, אִישׁ *man* Est 6₉, אִשָּׁה *wife* Gn 3₂₁, בֵּן *son* Gn 27₁₅ Ex 28₄₁ 29₈‖Lv 8₁₃ Ex 40₁₄ Nm 20₂₆.₂₈ Is 22₂₁, בַּת *daughter* 2 S 1₂₄, אָח *brother* Ex 28₄₁, עֶבֶד *servant* Is 22₂₁, כֹּהֵן *priest* Ps 132₁₆, worshipper Is 61₁₀ 4QBark[e] 5₃, אוֹיֵב *enemy* Ps 132₁₈, צַוָּאר *neck* Jb 39₁₉, מַעֲרֹם *nakedness*, i.e. naked one 2 C 28₁₅, שָׁמַיִם *heaven* Is 50₃.

(2) item of clothing, בֶּגֶד *garment* Gn 41₄₂ Ex 40₁₃ Nm 20₂₆.₂₈ Is 61₁₀ Zc 3₅ (or del.) 4QJub[h] 40₇ ((וילבשׁ[הו])), מַד *garment* 1 S 17₃₈, כְּתֹנֶת *tunic* Ex 28₄₁ 29₅ 29₈‖Lv 8₁₃ Ex 40₁₄ Is 22₂₁, מְעִיל *robe* Ex 29₅‖Lv 8₇, מַחֲלָצָה *robe* Zc 3₄, אַבְנֵט *girdle* Ex 28₄₁, מִגְבָּעָה *head band* Ex 28₄₁, חֹשֶׁן *breastpiece* Ex 29₅, אֵפֹד *ephod* Ex 29₅, שִׁרְיוֹן *armour* 1 S 17₃₈, פַּעֲמוֹן *bell* Si 45₇₍B₎ (Bmg תעופה perh. *magnificence*), עוֹר *skin* Gn 27₁₆ Jb 10₁₁, בָּשָׂר *flesh* Jb 10₁₁, שָׁנִי *scarlet* 2 S 1₂₄, רִקְמָה *embroidered cloth* Ezk 16₁₀, קֶרַע *rag* Pr 23₂₁, קַדְרוּת *darkness* Is 50₃, יֶשַׁע *salvation* Ps 132₁₆, בֹּשֶׁת *shame* Ps 132₁₈, רַעְמָה perh. *mane* Jb 39₁₉, כָּלִיל *perfection* of glory Si 45₈, רוּחַ *spirit* of salvation 4QBark[e] 5₃.

<PREP> מִן of instrument, *(by) means of, with, in* 2 C 28₁₅; עַל *upon*, + יָד *hand* Gn 27₁₆, חֶלְקָה *smoothness*, i.e. smooth part, of neck Gn 27₁₆.

Also 4QPrayer[c] 7₃ ((ה]לבשׁתה[)).

<SYN> כסה pi. *cover*, יעט *cover*, חזק pi. *strengthen*, חבשׁ *bind*, אזר pi. *gird*, נעל *provide shoes*, סכך *weave together*, פאר pi. *adorn*, אכל hi. *feed*, שׁקה hi. *give to drink*, סוך *anoint*. <ANT> פשׁט hi. *strip*.

2. ptc. as noun, **wardrobe attendant,** מַעֲמַד מְשָׁרְתָיו וּמַלְבִּישָׁיו *the position of his servants and his wardrobe attendants* 1 K 10₅₍Qr₎ (if em. וּמַלְבֻּשֵׁיהֶם *and their garments*).

Htp. 0.1 Inf. התלבשׁו—**dress oneself (in), wear,** <SUBJ> Simeon Si 50₁₁ (+ בֶּגֶד in *garment*; עטה *wrap*). <SYN> עטה *wrap*.*

⇒ לְבוּשׁ *garment*, מַלְבּוּשׁ *garment*, תִּלְבֹּשֶׁת *garment*.

לְבֵשׁ, see לבשׁ *put on (a garment)*, Qal §3.

לֹג 5.0.0.3 n.m. **log**—cstr. לֹג; pl. Q לגין—unit of liquid measure, perh. a sixth of a litre, <OBJ> לקח *take* Lv

14$_{10.12.21.24}$, נוף hi. *wave* Lv 14$_{12.24}$. <CSTR> לֹג שֶׁמֶן *log of oil* Lv 14$_{10(Sam)}$ (לג שמן אחד) 14$_{21}$, לֹג הַשֶּׁמֶן *the log of oil* Lv 14$_{12.15.24}$; הן 1 וחצי הלג ורבעת הלג *1 hin and three quarters of a log* Susa inscribed measure 1, [רבע]ת הלג *quarter of a log* Susa inscribed measure 2. <APP> שֶׁמֶן *oil* Lv 14$_{10}$. <ADJ> אֶחָד *one* Lv 14$_{10}$. <PREP> בְּ *consisting of,* כלי דמע בלגין *tribute vessels consisting of logs* 3QTr 1$_{9}$ (unless בלגין = *sandalwood* or *in flasks* or *at the breastplate* or *master of nations*);* מִן partitive, *(some) of,* + לקח *take* Lv 14$_{15}$.

[לְגוֹס] 0.0.1 perh. pr.n.[m.] **Legos,** appar. invented as sequence within writing exercise, 4QNames$_{6}$ (or em. [ב]לגוס *Bilgos*).*

[לְגֵין] *flask,* see לֹג, Prep.

[לְגִין] *breastplate,* see לֹג, Prep.

לֹד 4 pl.n. **Lod,** town in Benjamin established by Shemed (1 C 8$_{12}$; mss Shemer), perh. El-Ludd, 18 km SE of Jaffa, alw. assoc. with Ono (אוֹנוֹ), <NOM CL> בְּנֵי בִנְיָמִן ... לֹד *the sons of Benjamin were ... Lod* Ne 11$_{35}$ (or em. מִבְּנֵי *of the sons of*). <OBJ> בנה *build* 1 C 8$_{12}$ (+ בַּת *daughter,* i.e. village). <CSTR> בְּנֵי־לֹד *sons of Lod* Ezr 2$_{33}$||Ne 7$_{37}$ (or em. אַנְשֵׁי *men of*).

לִדְבִר 1 pl.n. **Lidbir,** town in Gilead assigned to Gad, perh. T. el-Ḥamme, 35 km E of Shechem, appar. ident. with (or em. to) לוֹ דְבָר *Lo-debar* at 2 S 9$_{4.5}$ 17$_{27}$, <CSTR> גְּבוּל לִדְבִר *border of Lidbir* Jos 13$_{26}$ (unless גְּבוּל לְ- *border of* + דְּבִ[י]ר *Debir*).

לֵדָה 4 n.f. **birth,** <CSTR> אֵשֶׁת לֵדָה *woman of,* who is about to give, *birth* Jr 13$_{21}$. <PREP> לְ *for (the purpose of),* כֹּחַ אַיִן לְלֵדָה *there is no strength for (giving) birth* 2 K 19$_{3}$||Is 37$_{3}$ (or em. לַיֹּלֵדָה *to the woman giving birth* there is no strength); מִן privative, *without, so there is not,* יִתְעוֹפֵף כְּבוֹדָם מִלֵּדָה וּמִבֶּטֶן וּמֵהֵרָיוֹן *their glory will fly away without birth or womb or conception* Ho 9$_{11}$.

⇒ ילד *give birth.*

לֹה, see לֹא *not.*

להב vb. 0.0.1 **Qal** 0.0.1 Ptc. לוהבת—**blaze,** <SUBJ> אֵשׁ *fire* 1QIsa^{a} 5$_{24}$ (unless אש לוהבת = *fire of flames,* i.e. לֶהָבָה).

לַהַב 12.0.8 n.m. **flame, blade**—cstr. לַהַב; pl. לְהָבִים; cstr. לַהֲבֵי—**1. flame,** <SUBJ> יצא *go out* from mouth of Leviathan Jb 41$_{13}$, עלה *go up* from altar Jg 13$_{20}$. <NOM CL> להבי ג[פ]רית סודו *flames of brimstone are his foundation* 4QBéat 15$_{6}$. <CSTR> לַהַב אֵשׁ *flame of fire* Is 29$_{6}$ (+ סוּפָה *whirlwind,* סְעָרָה *whirlwind,* רַעַם *thunder,* רַעַשׁ *earthquake,* קוֹל *noise*) 30$_{30}$ (|| זַעַף *anger,* + נֶפֶץ *cloudburst,* זֶרֶם *storm,* אֶבֶן hail *stone*) Jl 2$_{5}$, לַהֲבֵי־אֵשׁ *flames of fire* Is 66$_{15}$ (+ חֵמָה *anger*) 4QShirShabb^{f} 15.2$_{3}$ 4QPrayer^{e} 3$_{1}$ 4QSap^{b} 1.2$_{4}$ CD 2$_{5}$, להבי ג[פ]רית *flames of brimstone* 4QBéat 15$_{6}$, לַהַב הַמִּזְבֵּחַ *flame of the altar* Jg 13$_{20}$; קוֹל לַהַב *sound of a flame* Jl 2$_{5}$, פְּנֵי לְהָבִים *faces of flames* Is 13$_{8}$, מראי להבי *appearance of flames of* 4QShirShabb^{f} 15.2$_{3}$. <PREP> בְּ of place, *in* 4QPrayer^{e} 3$_{1}$ 4QSap^{b} 1.2$_{4}$, + עלה *go up* Jg 13$_{20}$; of instrument, *by (means of), through,* + פקד ni. *be visited* or *be reminded* Is 29$_{6}$, ראה hi. *show* Is 30$_{30}$; perh. of accompaniment, *with,* + שׁוב hi. *take back,* i.e. express, anger Is 66$_{15}$.

2. flash of sword (distinctions among §§2-4 uncertain), <CSTR> לַהַב חֶרֶב *flash of sword* Na 3$_{3}$ (|| בָּרָק *flash*).

3. blade of sword, <PREP> אַחַר *after,* + בוא *enter* Jg 3$_{22}$ (+ נִצָּב *hilt*); בַּעַד *behind,* + סגר *close* Jg 3$_{22}$ (or em. נִצָּב).

4. point of spear (Jb 39$_{23}$), <SUBJ> רנה *rattle* Jb 39$_{23}$ (or em. רנן *exult*). <CSTR> לַהַב חֲנִית וְכִידוֹן *point of spear and javelin* Jb 39$_{23}$.

Also 1QH 5$_{84}$ 4QBark^{a} 1.2$_{13}$ 4QNarrA 1$_{8}$.*

<SYN> §1 זַעַף *anger;* §2 בָּרָק *flash.*

[לַהֹב] 0.0.6 n.[m.] **point, flame**—Q לוהב (להוב); cstr. Q להוב—**1. point** of spear, distinction from לַהַב not alw. clear in unpointed texts, <NOM CL> הלוהב ברזל לבן מאיר *the point shall be white shining iron* 1QM 5$_{10}$ (+ סֶגֶר *socket*), הלוהב חצי האמה *the point shall be half a cubit* 1QM 5$_{7}$ (+ סֶגֶר). <CSTR> להוב הזרק *point of the javelin* 1QM 6$_{2}$; תוך הלהב *centre of the point* 1QM 5$_{10}$. <PREP>

עַל *upon*, + כתב *write* 1QM 6_{2}.

2. perh. **flash** of (point of) spear, <NOM CL> להוב חנית כאש *the flash of the spear is like fire* 1QH 2_{26}.

3. flame, <CSTR> שביבי להוב *flashes of flame* 1QH 3_{30}.*

לֶהָבָה 20.2.5 **flame, point**—cstr. לַהֶבֶת; pl. לֶהָבוֹת (perh. Q לוהבת); cstr. לַהֲבוֹת—**1. flame,** <SUBJ> היה *be* Ob 1_{8} (+ בַּיִת *house* of Joseph; || אֵשׁ *fire*), יצא *go out* Nm 21_{28} Jr 48_{45} (both || אֵשׁ), להט pi. *set ablaze* Jl 1_{19} 2_{3} Ps 83_{15} (all three || אֵשׁ) 106_{18} (+ אֵשׁ), אכל *eat* Nm 21_{28}, בער *burn* Is 43_{2} (+ אֵשׁ), שׂרף *burn* Si $16_{6(B)}$ (A, Bmg יוקדת אש *fire is kindled*), כבה *be extinguished* Ezk 21_{3} (+ אֵשׁ). <OBJ> חצב *divide* Ps 29_{7}. <CSTR> לַהֶבֶת שַׁלְהֶבֶת *flame of flame* Ezk 21_{3}, לַהֶבֶת־אֵשׁ *flame of fire* Ex $3_{2(Sam)}$ (MT לַבַּת־ *flame of*) 4QpsJub^{b} 1_{2} 4QShirShabb^{d} 1.2_{9}, לַהֲבוֹת אֵשׁ *flames of fire* Ps 29_{7} 4QpsHod^{c} 3_{9} ([להב]ת/ות]); מאזרי להב[ת/ות] *those who gird themselves of*, i.e. with, *flames of* 4QpsHod^{c} 3_{9}, יַד לֶהָבָה *hand*, i.e. power, *of flame* Is 47_{14} (+ אֵשׁ *fire*), אֵשׁ לֶהָבָה *fire of flame*, i.e. flaming fire Is 4_{5} Ho 7_{6} Lm 2_{3} 4Q185 1.1_{9} 4QpsHod^{c} 3_{6}, לַהֲבוֹת *of flames* 1QIsa^{a} 5_{24} (לוהבת) Ps 105_{32}, בדני להבת *forms of flame of* 4QShirShabb^{d} 1.2_{9}. <PREP> לְ introducing predicate, + היה *be* Is 10_{17} (+ קָדוֹשׁ *holy one*; || אֵשׁ *fire*); בְּ of place, *in* 4QpsJub^{b} 1_{2}, + ראה ni. *appear* Ex $3_{2(Sam)}$; of cause, *on account of*, + כשׁל ni. *stumble* Dn 11_{33} (|| חֶרֶב *sword*, + בִּזָּה *booty*, שְׁבִי *captivity*); of instrument, *by (means of)*, + צרב ni. *be scorched* Ezk 21_{3}; כְּ *as*, + נשׂק hi. *burn* Si 43_{21}. <COLL> חֲשַׁשׁ לֶהָבָה יִרְפֶּה *dried grass sinks (in) the flame* Is 5_{24} (1QIsa^{a} ואש לוהבת ירפה perh. *and (in) fire of flames*, or *and blazing fire* [i.e. להב *blaze*], *it* [chaff] *grows weak*; + לְשׁוֹן אֵשׁ *tongue of fire*).

2. point of spear, <NOM CL> לַהֶבֶת חֲנִיתוֹ שֵׁשׁ־מֵאוֹת שְׁקָלִים בַּרְזֶל *the point of his spear was six hundred shekels of iron* 1 S 17_{7} (+ חֵץ *arrow* [Kt]/עֵץ *wood* [Qr], i.e. shaft).*

Also 4QpsHod^{c} 3_{7}.

<SYN> §1 אֵשׁ *fire*, חֶרֶב *sword*.

[לְהָבִי] 2 gent. **Lehabite**—pl. לְהָבִים—in ref. to a people of Egyptian ancestry, <OBJ> ילד *give birth (to)* Gn 10_{13}||1 C 1_{11}.

לַהַג 1 n.[m.] **study,** <NOM CL> לַהַג הַרְבֵּה יְגִעַת בָּשָׂר *much study is a weariness of the flesh* Ec 12_{12} (or הַג *reckoning* with לְ- introducing subject/predicate of nom. cl.;* + עֲשׂוֹת סְפָרִים *the making of books* or *casting of accounts*).

[לַהַד] 1 pr.n.m. **Lahad**—לַהַד—son of Jahath and brother of Ahumai, descendant of Judah, <OBJ> ילד hi. *beget* 1 C 4_{2}.

להה 1.2 vb. **be mad—Htpalp.** 1.2 Ptc. מִתְלַהְלֵהַּ—ptc. as noun, **fool**, perh. specif. **madman, maniac** (Pr 26_{18}), **irreligious one** (Si $35_{14.15}$), <SUBJ> ירה *throw*, i.e. shoot Pr 26_{18}, יקשׁ ni. *be ensnared* Si $35_{14.15}$. <PREP> כְּ *as* Pr 26_{18}.

להה 1 vb. **languish—Qal** 1 + waw 3fs וַתֵּלַהּ—<SUBJ> אֶרֶץ *land* Gn 47_{13} (Sam ותלא *it was weary*). <PREP> מִפְּנֵי *on account of*, + רָעָב *famine* Gn 47_{13}.

להט I 10.2 vb. **blaze—Qal** 1.1 Ptc. לֹהֵט, Si, Q לוהטת—**blaze,** <SUBJ> אֵשׁ *fire* Ps 104_{4} (or em. לַהַט *burning* to וְלַהַט *and flame*) Si 3_{30}.

Pi. 9.1 Pf. לִהֲטָה; impf. 3fs תְּלַהֵט; + waw וְלִהַט; 3fs וַתְּלַהֵט (וַתְּלַהֲטֵהוּ)—**set ablaze, burn,** <SUBJ> אִשָּׁה *woman* Si 9_{8}, אֵשׁ *fire* Dt 32_{22} (|| אכל *devour*, + קדח *be kindled*, יקד *burn*) Ps 97_{3}, לֶהָבָה *flame* Jl 1_{19} 2_{3} (both || אכל) Ps 83_{15} 106_{18} (both || בער *burn*), נֶפֶשׁ *breath* Jb 41_{13}, חֵמָה *anger* Is 42_{25} (+ בער), אַף *anger* Is 42_{25}, יוֹם *day* Ml 3_{19} (+ בער *burn*). <OBJ> אֹהֵב *lover* Si 9_{8}, Israel Is 42_{25}, צַר *enemy* Ps 97_{3}, זֵד *presumptuous one* Ml 3_{19}, רָשָׁע *wicked one* Ps 106_{18}, עשׂה ptc. *one who does* evil Ml 3_{19}, עֵץ *tree* Jl 1_{19}, הַר *mountain* Ps 83_{15}, מוֹסָד *foundation* Dt 32_{22}, גַּחֶלֶת *coal* Jb 41_{13}. <PREP> בְּ of instrument, *by (means of), with*, + אֵשׁ *fire* Si 9_{8}. <COLL> + adverb סָבִיב *round about* Ps 97_{3}.

Also perh. 4QapJoseph^{a} 2_{3} 4QPrFêtes^{c} 146_{4} (unless לַהַט *flame* in both).*

<SYN> אכל *devour*, בער *burn*.

⇒ לַהַט *flame*.

להט II 1 vb. perh. **devour—Qal** 1 Ptc. לֹהֲטִים—**devour** or **bewitch** (unless להט I *blaze*), <SUBJ> לָבִא *lion* Ps

57_5. <OBJ> בֵּן *son* of human being Ps 57_5 (or em. לעט *devour*).*

→ לַהַט II *enchantment*, לָט *secret*.

[לַ֫הַט] I $_{1.0.1}$ n.[m.] **flame, blade**—cstr. לַ֫הַט—**1.** perh. **blade,** <SUBJ> שׁמר *keep*, i.e. guard, way to tree of life Gn 3_{24}. <OBJ> שׁכן hi. *place* Gn 3_{24} (+ כְּרוּב *cherub*). <CSTR> לַהַט הַחֶרֶב *blade of the sword* Gn 3_{24}.

2. flame, <OBJ> עשׂה *make* Ps 104_4 (if em. אֵשׁ לֹהֵט *blazing fire* to אֵשׁ וָלַהַט *fire and flame*). <CSTR> להט אש *flame of fire* 1QH 8_{12} (+ רָז *mystery*, רוּחַ *spirit*). <PREP> בְּ of instrument, *by (means of), with*, + שׂכך *surround* 1QH 8_{12}.*

Also perh. 4QapJoseph[a] 2_3 4QPrFêtes[c] 146_4 (unless להט *blaze* in both).

→ להט *blaze*.

[לַ֫הַט] II $_4$ n.[m.] **enchantment**—sf. לַהֲטֵיהֶם—<PREP> בְּ of instrument, *by (means of, with*, + עשׂה *do*, i.e. work wonders Ex $7_{11.22(Sam)}$ $8_{3(Sam).14(Sam)}$ (MT לָט *enchantment* in all three).

להם $_2$ vb. **swallow—Htp.** $_2$ ptc. מִתְלַהֲמִים—ptc. as noun, **delicacies,** <PREP> כְּ *as*, דִּבְרֵי נִרְגָּן כְּמִתְלַהֲמִים *the words of a gossip are as delicacies* Pr 18_8=26_{22} (or em. כְּמַמְתַקִּים *as sweet things*, or מַכֹּת הֹלְמִים *the strokes of those who hammer*).

לָהֵן $_2$ conj. **therefore,** הֲלָהֵן תְּשַׂבֵּרְנָה ... הֲלָהֵן תֵּעָגֵנָה *would you therefore wait ... would you therefore shut yourselves off?* Ru 1_{13} (unless in both לָהֵן = לָהֶם *on account of them*).

[לַהֲקָה] $_1$ n.f. **seniority**—cstr. לַהֲקַת—**1. company (of elders). 2. old age**(if em.).

<OBJ> ראה *see* 1 S 19_{20} (or em.), בוז *despise* Pr 30_{17} (if em.). <CSTR> לַהֲקַת הַנְּבִיאִים *the company of the prophets* 1 S 19_{20} (or em. קְהִלַּת *assembly of*), לַהֲקַת אֵם *old age of a mother* Pr 30_{17} (if em. לִיקֲּהַת *obedience of* [or em. זִקְנַת *old age of*]).*

לוּ $_{22}$ conj. **if**—לוּא, mss לֻא, Sam לוי—**1.** usu. **if only, had, were,** introducing irreal condition.

a. with perfect in protasis and with apodosis in:

(1) perfect, לוּ הַחֲיִתֶם אוֹתָם לֹא הָרַגְתִּי אֶתְכֶם *if you had kept them alive, I would not kill you* Jg 8_{19}, לֹא שָׁמַרְתָּ אֶת־מִצְוַת י׳ ... כִּי עַתָּה הֵכִין י׳ אֶת־מַמְלַכְתְּךָ *if you had kept the commandment of Y., ... Y. would now have established your kingdom* 1 S 13_{13} (if em. לֹא you did *not* keep),* לוּא אָכֹל אָכַל ... כִּי עַתָּה לֹא־רָבְתָה מַכָּה perh. *had* the people *indeed eaten, ... would not the defeat now have been greater?* 1 S 14_{30} (mss לוֹא, לֻא *not*).

(2) imperfect, לוּ חָכְמוּ יַשְׂכִּילוּ זֹאת *if they were wise, they would understand this* Dt 32_{29}, לֹא־הִגַּדְתָּ לִּי וָאֲשַׁלֵּחֲךָ בְּשִׂמְחָה *if you had told me, I would have sent you away with joy* Gn 31_{27} (if em. לֹא *not*).

(3) וַיְהִי *it would have been*, לוּא הִקְשַׁבְתָּ לְמִצְוֹתָי וַיְהִי כַנָּהָר שְׁלוֹמֶךָ *if only you had listened to my commandments, your peace would have been like a river* Is 48_{18}.

b. with imperfect in both protasis and apodosis, לוּ חַיָּה רָעָה אַעֲבִיר בָּאָרֶץ ... אִם־בָּנִים ... יַצִּילוּ *if I caused wild beasts to pass through the land, ...* these three men *would surely not save ... sons* or daughters, but would only save themselves Ezk 14_{15} (or em. אוֹ *or [if]*), לֹא־אוֹיֵב יְחָרְפֵנִי וְאֶשָּׂא *if it were an enemy who had reproached me, then I could have endured it* Ps 55_{13} (if em. לֹא *not*), לוּ שָׁקוֹל יִשָּׁקֵל כַּעְשִׂי ... כִּי־עַתָּה מֵחוֹל יַמִּים יִכְבָּד *if my anger were weighed ... it would now be heavier than the sand of the seas* Jb 6_2, כִּי לֹא־תַחְפֹּץ זֶבַח וְאֶתֵּנָה *if he desires a sacrifice, I shall give* Ps 51_{18} (if em. לֹא you do *not* desire), Ps 81_{14} (if em.; see §1c[2]).

c. with participle in protasis and with apodosis in:

(1) perfect, לוּ חָפֵץ י׳ לַהֲמִיתֵנוּ לֹא־לָקַח *had Y. wished to kill us, he would not have accepted* a burnt offering Jg 13_{23}.

(2) imperfect, לוּ אָנֹכִי שֹׁקֵל עַל־כַּפַּי אֶלֶף כֶּסֶף לֹא־אֶשְׁלַח יָדִי *had I weighed in my hand a thousand pieces of silver, I would not put forth my hand* 2 S $18_{12(Qr)}$ (Kt לא), לוּ עַמִּי שֹׁמֵעַ לִי ... כִּמְעַט אוֹיְבֵיהֶם אַכְנִיעַ *if only my people would listen to me, ... I would quickly subdue their enemies* Ps 81_{14} (or em. שֹׁמֵעַ to יִשְׁמַע in same sense).

(3) היה *be* + participle, לוּ אִישׁ הֹלֵךְ ... וְהָיָה מַטִּיף *were a man to go about* and tell lies, ... *he would be (considered) preacher* Mc 2_{11} (or em. הָלַךְ in same sense).

d. with nom. cl. in both protasis and apodosis: לוּ אַבְשָׁלוֹם חַי וְכֻלָּנוּ ... מֵתִים כִּי־אָז יָשָׁר בְּעֵינֶיךָ *if Absalom were alive and all of us ... dead, then that would be right in your eyes* 2 S $19_{7(Qr)}$ (Kt ל א), כִּי לֹא מִמּוֹצָא וּמִמַּעֲרָב וְלֹא מִמִּדְבַּר הָרִים כִּי אֱלֹהִים שֹׁפֵט *for if only there were lifting up from east or from west or from the steppe, then God would be judge* Ps $75_{7(mss)}$ (if em. twice לֹא there is *no* lifting up; L מִמִּדְבַּר and not *from the steppe of* mountains).

e. with nom. cl. in protasis, and with apodosis in:

(1) perfect, לוּ יֶשׁ־חֶרֶב בְּיָדִי כִּי עַתָּה הֲרַגְתִּיךָ *were there a sword in my hand, I would kill you now* Nm 22_{29}.

(2) imperfect, לוּ־יֵשׁ נַפְשְׁכֶם תַּחַת נַפְשִׁי אַחְבִּירָה עֲלֵיכֶם בְּמִלִּים *if you were in my place, I could join words together against you* Jb 16_4.

2. introducing supposition, **a. supposing, what if?, perhaps,** לוּ יִשְׂטְמֵנוּ יוֹסֵף *supposing Joseph holds it against us?* Gn 50_{15}. **b. in case,** מְשַׁחֲרֵי לַטָּרֶף עֲרָבָה לוֹ לֶחֶם לַנְּעָרִים *going early for prey to the steppe, in case there is food for the young ones* Jb 24_5 (if em. לַטֶּרֶף עֲרָבָה לוֹ לֶחֶם going early *for prey; the steppe is for him food*).*

3. as exclamation, **if only, would that,** perh. sometimes, **indeed*** (perh. also em. refs. under לֹא II *indeed* to לֹא in this sense).

לוּ יִשְׁמָעֵאל יִחְיֶה לְפָנֶיךָ *would that Ishmael might live/ Ishmael indeed lives in your presence* Gn 17_{18} (Sam לוי; or em. זֶה *this* is Ishmael, who lives in your presence), לוּ שְׁמָעֵנִי *if only you would hear me* 23_5 (if em. לֵאמֹר לוֹ: *saying to him:* to לוּ : לֵאמֹר *saying, If only*) 23_{13} (Sam לִי *to me*), sim. 23_{11} (if em. לֹא אֲדֹנִי *no, my lord* to לוּ אֲדֹנִי *if only my lord* would hear me) 23_{15} (if em. לֵאמֹר לוֹ:),* לוּ יְהִי כִדְבָרֶךָ *if only it were,* or *it is indeed, according to your word* 30_{34}, לוּ־מַתְנוּ בְּאֶרֶץ מִצְרַיִם *would that we had died in the land of Egypt* Nm 14_2, Nm 14_2 20_3 (Sam לוי) Jos 7_7 Is 63_{19} 1 S $20_{14.14}$* Jb 9_{33} Ru 2_{13} (if em. לֹא *not* in all four) Is 64_4 (if ins. לוּ before פָּגַעְתָּ *you met*).

* **[לָוָא]** interj. **woe,** לָוָא אֲלֵיכֶם *woe to you* Lm 1_{12} (if em. לוֹא *is it nothing* to you?).

לוֹא, see לֹא *not*.

לוּא, see לוּ *if*.

לוֹא דְבָר, see לוֹ דְבָר *Lo-debar*.

[לוּב] 0.0.1 pr.n.m. perh. **Libya,** <SUBJ> נפל *fall* Ezk 30_5 (if em. כּוּב *Cub*; + כּוּשׁ *Ethiopia*, לוּד *Lud*, פּוּט *Put*). <NOM CL> לוב בסעדך *Libya was (as) your support* 4QpsEzek[a] 9.2_6.

Also perh. 4QpsEzek[d] 12.2_2.

[לוּבִי] 4 gent. perh. **Libyan**—pl. לוּבִים (לֻבִים)—<SUBJ> היה *be* Na 3_9 (+ בְּעֶזְרָתֵךְ *as your help*) 2 C 16_8 (+ לְחַיִל *as an army*), בוא *come* 2 C 12_3. <NOM CL> לֻבִים ... בְּמִצְעָדָיו *the Libyans ... shall be in his steps*, i.e. in his wake Dn 11_{43}. <APP> עָם *people* 2 C 12_3. <COLL> + כּוּשׁ *Ethiopia* Na 3_9, כּוּשִׁי *Ethiopian* Dn 11_{43} 2 C 12_3 16_8, פּוּט *Put* Na 3_9, מִצְרַיִם *Egypt* Na 3_9 Dn 11_{43}, סֻכִּיִּים *Sukkim* 2 C 12_3.

לוּד 5.0.1 pr.n.m. **Lud, 1.** son of Shem, <NOM CL> בְּנֵי שֵׁם ... וְלוּד *the sons of Shem were ... and Lud* Gn 10_{22} ||1 C 1_{17}.

2. nation, appar. descended from §1 (unless from לוּדִים *Ludim*), prob. in N Africa, but perh. ident. with Lydia, <SUBJ> היה *be* Ezk 27_{10} (+ בְּחֵילֵךְ *in your army*), תלה pi. *hang* Ezk 27_{10}, נתן *give* Ezk 27_{10}, נפל *fall* Ezk 30_5. <CSTR> בני לוד *sons of Lud* 1QM 2_{10}. <APP> גּוֹי *nation* Is 66_{19}, אִישׁ *man* Ezk 27_{10}. <PREP> אֶל *to*, + שׁלח pi. *send* Is 66_{19}. <COLL> + תַּרְשִׁישׁ *Tarshish* Is 66_{19}, פּוּל *Pul* Is 66_{19} (or em. פּוּט *Put*), כּוּשׁ *Ethiopia* Ezk 30_5, כּוּב *Cub* Ezk 30_5 (or em. כּוּב to לוּב *Libya*), פָּרַס *Persia* Ezk 27_{10}.

לוֹ דְבָר 3 pl.n. **Lo-debar**—לֹא דְבָר; mss לוֹא דְבָר—town in Gilead assigned to Gad, appar. near Mahanaim, perh. T. el-Ḥamme, 35 km E of Shechem, <CSTR> גְּבוּל לוֹ דְבָר *border of Lo-debar* Jos 13_{26} (if em. לִדְבִר border *of Debir* or border of *Lidbir*). <PREP> לְ *concerning*, + שׂמח *rejoice* Am 6_{13} (if em. לְלֹא דָבָר appar. *at nothing*); בְּ of place, *in* 2 S 9_4; מִן of direction, *from* 2 S $9_{4(mss)}$ 17_{27}, + לקח *take* Mephibosheth 2 S 9_5.

[לוּדִי] 3 gent. **Lydian**—pl. לוּדִים (Kt לודיים [1 C 1_{11}])—in ref. to people of Egyptian ancestry, <SUBJ> יצא *go* *out* Jr 46_9 (+ פּוּט *Put*, כּוּשׁ *Ethiopia*), דרך *tread*, i.e. bend, bow Jr 46_9, תפשׂ *hold* Jr 46_9 (or del. תפשׂ). <OBJ> ילד *beget* Gn 10_{13}||1 C 1_{11}. <APP> גִּבּוֹר *warrior* Jr 46_9.

לוה I $_{14.3.1}$ vb. **borrow—Qal** $_5$ Pf. לָוִינוּ; impf. 2ms תִּלְוֶה; ptc. לֹוֶה—**borrow,** <SUBJ> Israel(ites) Dt 28_{12} Ne 5_4 4Q414 1.1_{21}, רָשָׁע *wicked one* Ps 37_{21} (+ חנן *be gracious*, נתן *give*; :: שׁלם pi. *repay*), עֶבֶד *servant* Pr 22_7 (עֶבֶד לֹוֶה *one who borrows is a servant* to the lender). <OBJ> כֶּסֶף *money* Ne 5_4, הוֹן *wealth* 4Q414 1.1_{21}. <PREP> לְ *for (the purpose of)*, + מִדָּה *tribute* Ne 5_4, מַחְסוֹר *need* 4Q414 1.1_{21}. <COLL> לָוִינוּ כֶסֶף ... שְׂדֹתֵינוּ וּכְרָמֵינוּ *we have borrowed money ... (against the security of) our fields and vineyards)* Ne 5_4, כַּמַּלְוֶה כַּלֹּוֶה *as the lender, so is the borrower* Is 24_2. <ANT> שׁלם pi. *repay*.

Hi. $_{9.3}$ Pf. Si הלוית; impf. יַלְוְךָ, 2ms תַּלְוֶה (תַּלְוֶנּוּ); + waw וְהִלְוִיתָ; ptc. מַלְוֶה, cstr. מַלְוֵה—**lend (to),** <SUBJ> Israelite Ex 22_{24} (+ נשׁא *be a creditor*) Dt $28_{12.44}$, אִישׁ *man* Ps 112_5 (|| חנן *be compassionate*) Pr 22_7, בֵּן *son* perh. Si 8_{12}, גֵּר *sojourner* Dt 28_{44}, צַדִּיק *righteous one* Ps 37_{26} (|| חנן), חנן ptc. *one who is compassionate* to the poor Pr 19_{17}, נתן ptc. *one who gives* to the poor Si $32_{3(\text{Bmg})}$. <OBJ> ״ *Y.* Pr 19_{17} Si $32_{3(\text{Bmg})}$ (see Coll.), Israelite Dt 28_{44}, אִישׁ *man* Si 8_{12}, עַם *people* Ex 22_{24} (or em. אָח *brother*), גּוֹי *nation* Dt 28_{12}, גֵּר *sojourner* Dt 28_{44}, עָנִי *poor person* Ex 22_{24}. <COLL> מַלְוֵה ״ *lender of*, i.e. to, *Y.* Pr 19_{17} Si $32_{13(\text{Bmg})}$, כַּמַּלְוֶה כַּלֹּוֶה *as the lender, so is the borrower* Is 24_2 (+ נשׁא *be a creditor*). <SYN> חנן *be compassionate*.*

לוה II $_{12.1.10}$ vb. **accompany—Qal** $_{1.1}$ Impf. יִלְוֶנּוּ, Si ילוך—**accompany, stay with,** <SUBJ> שֵׁם *name* Si 41_{12}, טוֹב *good* Ec 8_{15}. <OBJ> אָדָם *human being* Ec 8_{15} (+ יְמֵי חַיָּיו *the days of their life* [mss מִסְפַּר *the number of* (the days of)]), בֵּן *son* perh. Si 41_{12}. <PREP> בְּ of accompaniment, *with, in,* or *in exchange for*, + עָמָל *toil* Ec 8_{15}; מִן of comparison, *(more) than,* + אֶלֶף *thousand* Si 41_{12} (אלפי אוצרות *thousands of treasures*).

Ni. $_{11.0.10}$ Pf. נִלְוָה, Q נלוו, ונלויתי; impf. יִלָּוֶה, יִלָּווּ; + waw וְנִלְווּ, וְנִלְוָה; ptc. perh. Q נלוה, נִלְוִים; inf. Q בהלוות—**join, join oneself** to, **associate, be associated** with, **ally oneself** with, of husband to wife (Gn 29_{34}), Levites to house of Aaron (Nm $18_{2.4}$), other tribes to Joseph (4QapJoseph^b 1_{20}), foreigners to (religion of) Israel (Is 14_1 $56_{3.6}$ Zc 2_{15} Est 9_{27} CD 4_3 1QS 5_6 4QpNah 3.2_9), insincere sympathizers to Israel (Dn 11_{34}), Israel to Y. (Jr 50_5 11QPs^a 22_7), one nation to another (Ps 83_9), perh. Samuel to God (4QVisSam 7_2); appar. of converts to Jewish parties: Ephraim to Israel (4QpNah 3.4_1), house of Peleg to Manasseh (4QpNah 3.4_1).

<SUBJ> Assyria Ps 83_9, גּוֹי *nation* Zc 2_{15}, מַטֶּה *tribe* of Levi Nm $18_{2.4}$, שֵׁבֶט *tribe* Nm $18_{2.4}$, בַּיִת *house* of Peleg 4QpNah 3.4_1, עַם *people* 4QpNah 3.2_9 (unless גֵּר *sojourner* is subj.), אִישׁ *husband* Gn 29_{34}, אָח *brother* Nm $18_{2.4}$ 4QapJoseph^b 1_{20}, בֵּן *son* of Israel Jr 50_5, Judah Jr 50_5 (or del. בֵּן), foreigner Is 56_3 (+ בדל hi. *separate*) 56_6, גֵּר *sojourner* Is 14_1 (+ ספח ni. *join oneself*) perh. 4QpNah 3.2_9, פֶּתִי *simple one* 4QpNah 3.3_5, יָדִיד *beloved one* 11QPs^a 22_7, רָשָׁע *evildoer* 4QpNah 3.4_1, רַב pl. *many* Dn 11_{34}, adherents to Jewish religion Est 9_{27}; subj. not specified, CD 4_3 1QS 5_6=4QS^b 5_6=4QS^d 1.1_5 (4QS^b [המתנדב]). <PREP> לְ *to* 4QVisSam $7_{2(\text{mg})}$ (+ גרתי עמו *I sojourned with him*); בְּ of place/time, *in, on,* + יוֹם *day* Zc 2_{15}; of instrument, *by (means of), with,* + חֲלַקְלַקּוֹת *flattery* Dn 11_{34}; אֶל *to*, + Y. Is 56_3 Jr 50_5 Zc 2_{15} 11QPs^a 22_7, Leah Gn 29_{34}; עַל *to* 1Q25 12_3, + Y. Is 56_6, Aaron Nm $18_{2.4}$, appar. נדב htp. ptc. *one who devotes himself* 1QS 5_6=4QS^b 5_6=4QS^d 1.1_5, Israel Is 14_1 4QpNah 3.3_5 ([י]שראל), Manasseh 4QpNah 3.4_1, עַם *people* Dn 11_{34}, יְהוּדִי *Jew* Est 9_{27}; עִם *with*, + Edom, Ishmaelites, Moab, Hagrites, Gebal, Ammon, Amalek, Philistia and inhabitants of Tyre Ps 83_9, Joseph 4QapJoseph^b 1_{20}, כֹּהֵן *priest* CD 4_3, גֵּר *sojourner* 4QpNah 3.2_9 (unless גֵּר is subj.); perh. עַד *unto* 4QWays^a 2_2. <COLL> + noun used adverbially, בְּרִית *(in a) covenant* Jr 50_5.*

Also 1QH $17_{19(\text{AHL})}$ (נלויתי; Licht נלאיתי *I have* not *wearied myself*) 4QHod^f 1_1 4Q448 C$_{7(\text{WA})}$ נלוים ([]מלחמת *joining for war*; Eshel, Eshel, Yardeni ל[]ום[] [מלחמהו] *for the day of war*).

לוז $_{5.1.4}$ vb. **depart; be devious—Qal** $_1$ Impf. יָלֻזוּ—**depart,** <SUBJ> appar. תּוּשִׁיָּה *prudence* Pr 3_{21}, מְזִמָּה *discretion* Pr 3_{21} (ms יזלו, perh. יֵזַלּוּ *let them not be despised*, i.e. זלל ni.; + נצר *keep*). <PREP> מִן of direction, *from*, +

עַיִן *eye* Pr 3$_{21}$.

Ni. $_{3.1.1}$ Pf. Si נלוז; + waw Q וילוזו; ptc. נָלוֹז; cstr. נְלוֹז; pl. נְלוֹזִים—**1. depart, stray,** <SUBJ> אִישׁ *man* Si 34$_8$ (+ נמצא תמים *he is found blameless*). <PREP> אַחַר *after*, + מָמוֹן *wealth* Si 34$_8$.

2. be devious, <SUBJ> אִישׁ *man* Pr 2$_{15}$ (or del. following בְּ *in* to make מַעְגָּל *track* subj.); subj. not expressed, Pr 3$_{32}$ 14$_2$. <PREP> בְּ of place, *in*, + מַעְגָּל *track* Pr 2$_{15}$ (or em.). <COLL> תּוֹעֲבַת י׳ נָלוֹז *a devious person is an abomination of*, i.e. to, Y. Pr 3$_{32}$ (+ יָשָׁר *upright*), נְלוֹז דְּרָכָיו *one devious of*, i.e. in, *one's ways* Pr 14$_2$ (+ יֹשֶׁר *uprightness*).

Also 4QpHos[a] 1$_5$.

Hi. $_{1.0.3}$ Impf. Q יַלִּיזוּ, יליז; + waw Q ויליזו; inf. abs. Q הליז—**1.** perh. **allow to depart,** <SUBJ> בֵּן *son* Pr 4$_{21}$ (+ שׁמר *keep*). <OBJ> דָּבָר *word* Pr 4$_{21}$. <PREP> מִן of direction, *from*, + עַיִן *eye* Pr 4$_{21}$.

2. pervert, <SUBJ> אִישׁ *man* 4Q424 1$_{9.9}$. <OBJ> מִשְׁפָּט *judgment* 4Q424 1$_9$. <PREP> בְּ of instrument, *by (means of), with*, + שָׂפָה *lip* 4Q424 1$_9$.

3. mock, <SUBJ> אכל ptc. *one who eats* 1QH 5$_{24}$ (כלי[או]; + גדל עָקֵב hi. *raise heel*). <PREP> בְּ of instrument, *by (means of), with*, + שָׂפָה *lip* 1QH 5$_{24}$; עַל *against* worshipper 1QH 5$_{24}$.*

→ לָזוּת *perversity*, לוז *perversity*, נָלוֹז *perversity*.

[לוֹז] $_{0.0.1}$ n.[m.] **perversity**—cstr. Q לוז—<CSTR> איש לוז שפתים *man of perversity of lips* 4Q424 1$_8$.

→ לוז *depart, be devious*.

לוּז I $_1$ n.[m.] **almond (tree)** (*amygdalus communis*), <CSTR> מַקֵּל ... לוּז *rod of ... almond* Gn 30$_{37}$ (+ לִבְנֶה *storax*, עַרְמוֹן *plane*).

לוּז II $_8$ pl.n. **Luz**—+ ה- of direction לוּזָה—**1.** former name of Bethel (Gn 28$_{19}$ 35$_6$ 48$_6$ Jos 18$_{13}$ Jg 1$_{23}$), but also distinguished from Bethel (Jos 16$_2$), <NOM CL> לוּז שֵׁם־הָעִיר לָרִאשֹׁנָה *Luz was the name of the city at first* Gn 28$_{19}$, sim. Jg 1$_{23}$, לוּזָה אֲשֶׁר בְּאֶרֶץ כְּנַעַן *to Luz which is in the land of Canaan* Gn 35$_6$, sim. 48$_6$. <CSTR> כֶּתֶף לוּזָה towards *the slope of Luz* Jos 18$_{13}$ (or del.). <PREP> בְּ of place *in*, + ראה ni. *appear* Gn 48$_3$; ה- of location, *to(wards) Luz*, + בוא *come* Gn 35$_6$, יצא *go out* Jos 16$_2$, עבר *pass* Jos 18$_{13}$.

2. town in Hittite territory, perh. El-Luwēze, 19 km SE of Sidon, <OBJ> קרא *call*, i.e. name Jg 1$_{26}$.

לוּחַ $_{43.0.5}$ n.m. **tablet**—cstr. לוּחַ; pl. לֻחֹת (לֻחוֹת, Q לוחות); du. לֻחֹתַיִם; cstr. לֻחֹת (לֻחוֹת, לוּחֹת, Q לוחות)—**1.** wooden or stone **tablet** for writing; specif. tablet of heart (Jr 17$_1$ Pr 3$_3$ 7$_3$), <SUBJ> היה *be* in the ark of the covenant Dt 10$_5$, כתב pass. *be written* Ex 31$_{18}$ 32$_{15}$ Dt 9$_{10}$. <NOM CL> הַלֻּחֹת מַעֲשֵׂה אֱלֹהִים הֵמָּה *the tablets were the work of God* Ex 32$_{16}$, שְׁנֵי לֻחֹת הָעֵדֻת בְּיָדוֹ *the two tablets of the testimony were in his hand* Ex 32$_{15}$, sim. 34$_{29}$ Dt 10$_3$, שְׁנֵי לֻחֹת הַבְּרִית עַל שְׁתֵּי יָדָי *the two tablets of the covenant were in my two hands* Dt 9$_{15}$, אֵין בָּאָרוֹן רַק שְׁנֵי לֻחוֹת הָאֲבָנִים *there was nothing in the ark except the two tablets of stone* 1 K 8$_9$‖2 C 5$_{10}$ (הַלֻּחוֹת *the tablets*). <OBJ> נתן *give* Ex 24$_{12}$ 31$_{18.18}$ Dt 5$_{22}$ 9$_{10.11.11}$ 10$_4$, *place* 2 C 5$_{10}$, לקח *take* Ex 34$_4$ Dt 9$_{9.9.17}$ 4QJub[a] prologue (ל]ק[חת [לחות]), תפשׂ *hold* Dt 9$_{17}$, פסל *hew* Ex 34$_{1.4}$ Dt 10$_{1.3}$, שׁלך hi. *throw* Ex 32$_{19}$ Dt 9$_{17}$, שׁבר pi. *break* Ex 32$_{19}$ 34$_1$ Dt 9$_{17}$ 10$_2$, שׂים *place* Dt 10$_{2.5}$, נוח hi. *place* 1 K 8$_9$, פתח *open* 4QapMes 7.5$_8$ ([לוחות]; others [קברות] *graves*). <CSTR> לֻחֹת אֶבֶן *tablets of stone* Ex 24$_{12}$ (הָאֶבֶן) 31$_{18}$, אֲבָנִים *of stone* (pl.) Ex 34$_{1.4.4}$ Dt 4$_{13}$ 5$_{22}$ 9$_{9.10}$ (both לוּחֹת הָאֲבָנִים) 9$_{11}$ (לֻחֹת הָאֲבָנִים lacking in Sam) 10$_1$ (לוּחֹת) 10$_3$ 1 K 8$_9$ (לֻחוֹת הָאֲבָנִים), לֻחֹת הָעֵדֻת *tablets of the testimony* Ex 31$_{18}$ 32$_{15}$ 34$_{29}$, הַבְּרִית *of the covenant* Dt 9$_9$ (לוּחֹת) 9$_{11}$ (לֻחוֹת) 9$_{15}$ 2 K 8$_9$‖2 C 5$_{10}$ (if ins.), לוּחַ לִבָּם *tablet of their heart* Jr 17$_1$ (+ קֶרֶן *horn* of altar), לִבֶּךָ *of your heart* Pr 3$_3$ (or del.; + גַּרְגְּרֹת *throat*) 7$_3$ (+ אֶצְבַּע *finger*), לוחות עולם *tablets of eternity* 4QRitPur 12$_4$ (others ליחות *liquids of*). <ADJ> רִאשׁוֹן *first* Ex 34$_1$ Dt 10$_2$. <PREP> בְּ of place, *on* 4QRitPur 12$_4$, + כתב pass. *be written* 4QMidrEschat[b] 10$_{12}$; introducing object, + תפשׂ *take hold of* Dt 9$_{17}$; עַל *upon* Dt 9$_{10}$, + היה *be* Ex 34$_1$ Dt 10$_2$, כתב *write* Ex 34$_{1.28}$ Dt 4$_{13}$ 5$_{22}$ 10$_{2.4}$ Is 30$_8$ (‖ סֵפֶר *book*) Hb 2$_2$ Pr 3$_3$ 7$_3$, חרשׁ pass. *be engraved* Jr 17$_1$, חרת pass. *be engraved* Ex 32$_{16}$, באר pi. *clarify* Hb 2$_2$. <COLL> שְׁנֵי הַלֻּחֹת *the two tablets* Dt 9$_{17}$ 10$_3$ 2 C 5$_{10}$, שְׁנֵי לֻחֹת *two tablets of* Ex 31$_{18}$ 32$_{15}$ 34$_{1.4.4.29}$ Dt 4$_{13}$ 5$_{22}$ 9$_{10.11.15}$ 10$_{1.3}$ 1 K 8$_9$.

2. wooden **board, plank** of altar (Ex 27$_8$‖38$_7$), door (Ca 8$_9$), boat (Ezk 27$_5$), <OBJ> בנה *build* Ezk 27$_5$, צור

enclose with Ca 89 (|| טִירָה *battlement*). <CSTR> לוחות [העו]ץ *boards of wood* 11QT 73, לוּחַ אֶרֶז *plank of cedar* Ca 89, נְבוּב לֻחֹת *hollow one of boards*, i.e. (altar) hollow with boards Ex 278||387, כָּל־לֻחֹתַיִם appar. *both the planks* Ezk 275 (or em. כָּל־לֻחֹתַיִךְ *all your planks*).

3. bronze **plate** of washstand in Solomon's temple (1 K 736), object in slaughterhouse (11QT 341), <CSTR> לוח נחו[שת] *plate of bronze* 11QT 341. <PREP> בְּ of place, *on* 11QT 341; עַל *upon*, + פתח pi. *engrave* 1 K 736.*

Also 11QT 71.

<SYN> §1 סֵפֶר *book*; §2 טִירָה *battlement*.

לוּחִית 2.0.1 pl.n. **Luhith**—לֻחִית (Kt לוחות)—in Moab, perh. Eḏ-Ḏubāb, 15 km E of southern end of Dead Sea, <CSTR> מַעֲלֵה הַלּוּחִית *ascent of Luhith* Is 155 Jr 485(Qr) (הַלֻּחִית). <PREP> מִן of direction, *from* 5/6ḤevBA 445.

לוֹחֵשׁ or more probably הַלּוֹחֵשׁ 2 pr.n.m. **Hallohesh,** family head at time of Nehemiah, father of Shallum, <NOM CL> רָאשֵׁי הָעָם ... הַלּוֹחֵשׁ *the chiefs of the people were ... Hallohesh* Ne 1025. <CSTR> בֶּן־הַלּוֹחֵשׁ *son of Hallohesh* Ne 312.

לוט 4 vb. **wrap—Qal** 3 Pf. לָאט; ptc. לוֹטָה, לוֹט—**1. wrap, cover,** <SUBJ> מֶלֶךְ *king* 2 S 195, לוֹט *covering* Is 257 (or em. pass. *be spread*). <OBJ> פָּנִים *face* 2 S 195. <PREP> עַל *over*, + עַם *people* Is 257 (or em.).

2. pass. **be wrapped, be covered,** <SUBJ> חֶרֶב *sword* 1 S 2110, לוֹט *covering* Is 257 (if em. הַלּוֹט הַלּוֹט *the covering that covers* to הַלּוֹט הַלּוּט *the covering that is spread*). <PREP> בְּ of instrument, *by (means of), with, in*, + שִׂמְלָה *garment* 1 S 2110; עַל *over*, + עַם *people* Is 257.

Hi. 1 + waw וַיָּלֶט—**wrap,** <SUBJ> Elijah 1 K 1913. <OBJ> פָּנִים *face* 1 K 1913. <PREP> בְּ of instrument, *by (means of), with, in*, + אַדֶּרֶת *cloak* 1 K 1913.

→ לוֹט *covering*.

לוֹט I 1 n.m. **covering,** וּבִלַּע ... פְּנֵי־הַלּוֹט הַלּוֹט עַל־כָּל־הָעַמִּים *and he will destroy ... the (surface of) the covering that covers (over) all the peoples* Is 257 (or em. הַלּוֹט *that covers* to הַלּוּט *that is wrapped*).

→ לוט *wrap*.

לוֹט II 33.1 pr.n.m. **Lot,** son of Haran, nephew of Abram, father of Moab and Ammon (Gn 1936 Dt 29 Ps 839), <SUBJ> הלך *go* Gn 1131 124.5, בוא *come* Gn 1131 125 1918.23, יצא *go out* Gn 1131 125 196.14, hi. *take out* Gn 196.12, עלה *go up* Gn 1930, מלט ni. *escape* Gn 1915.18, נגשׁ *draw near* Gn 196, נסע *journey* Gn 1311, אהל *pitch tent* Gn 1312, ישׁב *dwell* Gn 1131 1312 1929.30, *sit* Gn 191, קום *rise* Gn 191.15, עמד *stand* Gn 1915, קרא *meet* Gn 191, שׁחה htpal. *bow down* Gn 191, רכשׁ *acquire* Gn 125, עשׂה *make* Gn 191, i.e. acquire, persons Gn 125, אפה *bake* Gn 191, אמר *say* Gn 191.6.18, דבר *speak* Gn 1914.18, ראה *see* Gn 1310 191, נבט hi. *look* Gn 1915, לקח *take* Gn 1915, פרד ni. *separate oneself* Gn 138.14, בחר *choose* Gn 1311, פצר *urge* Gn 191, מהה htpalp. *hesitate* Gn 1915, מהר pi. *hurry* Gn 1918, נשׂא *lift* eyes Gn 1310, יכל *be able* Gn 1918, ירא *be afraid* Gn 1930, מות *die* Gn 1918. <NOM CL> לוט עִמּוֹ *Lot was with him* Gn 131. <OBJ> ילד hi. *beget* Gn 1127, דבק *overtake* Gn 1918, בוא hi. *bring* Gn 1910, יצא hi. *bring out* Gn 1915, שׁלח pi. *send* Gn 1929, לקח *take* Gn 1131 125 1412, שׁוב hi. *bring back* Gn 1416, נוח hi. *set down* Gn 1915. <CSTR> בְּנֵי־לוֹט *sons*, i.e. descendants, *of Lot* Dt 29.19 Ps 839, בְּנוֹת־ *daughters of* Gn 1936, מִקְנֵה־ *cattle of* Gn 137, מגורי *sojourning place of* Si 168. <APP> אִישׁ *man* Gn 199, בֵּן *son* Gn 1131 125 1412. <PREP> לְ of possession, *(belonging) to, of* Gn 196.12, + היה *be* Gn 135; of direction, *to*, + אמר *say* Gn 195; פצר בְּ *press upon* Gn 199, אוץ בְּ hi. *be impatient with* Gn 1915; אֶל *to*, + אמר *say* Gn 138 1912.18, קרא *call* Gn 195, סור *turn aside* Gn 191, בוא *come* Gn 195; עִם *with* Gn 1930, + עשׂה *do* Gn 1918; בֵּין *between* Lot and Abram Gn 138 (+ Abram); לִפְנֵי *in front of* Gn 138; אַחֲרֵי *behind*, + סגר *shut* Gn 196, נבט hi. *look* Gn 1915.

לוֹטָן 7 pr.n.m. **Lotan,** Horite chief, son of Seir, brother of Timna, father of Hori and Heman, <NOM CL> בְּנֵי שֵׂעִיר לוֹטָן *the sons of Seir were Lotan* 1 C 138. <CSTR> בְּנֵי־לוֹטָן *sons of Lotan* Gn 3622||1 C 139 (בְּנֵי לוֹטָן), אֲחוֹת *sister of* Gn 3622||1 C 139. <APP> אַלּוּף *chief* Gn 3629. <COLL> אֵלֶּה בְנֵי־שֵׂעִיר ... לוֹטָן *these are the sons of Seir: ... Lotan* Gn 3620, אֵלֶּה אַלּוּפֵי הַחֹרִי ... לוֹטָן *these are the chiefs of the Horites: ... Lotan* Gn 3629.

לֵוִי I $_{58.1.23.5}$ pr.n.m. **Levi, 1.** son of Jacob and Leah, father of Gershon, Kohath and Merari, <SUBJ> בוא *come* Gn 34$_{25}$, אמר *say* CD 4$_{15}$, לקח *take* Gn 34$_{25}$, עכר *trouble* Gn 34$_{30}$, באשׁ hi. *make* Jacob *odious* Gn 34$_{30}$, הרג *kill* Gn 34$_{25}$, אגד *bind* 5QRègle 2$_7$. <NOM CL> בְּנֵי לֵאָה ... לֵוִי *the sons of Leah were ... Levi* Gn 35$_{23}$, שִׁמְעוֹן וְלֵוִי אַחִים *Simeon and Levi are brothers* Gn 49$_5$. <OBJ> קרא *call*, i.e. name Gn 29$_{34}$, ילד hi. *beget* 4QpsJub[a] 2.2$_{11}$ 4QpsJub[b] 7$_4$ ([הוליד]). <CSTR> בֶּן־לֵוִי *son of Levi* Nm 16$_1$ Ezr 8$_{18}$ 1 C 6$_{23.28.32}$, בְּנֵי *sons of* Gn 46$_{11}$ Ex 6$_{16}$ 1 C 5$_{27}$ 6$_1$ 4QapJoseph[b] 17$_2$ ([לו]י), חַיֵּי *life of* Ex 6$_{16}$, יְמֵי ... לו[י] *days of ... Levi* 4QpsJub[a] 2.2$_{12}$. <APP> בֵּן *son* 1 C 6$_{23}$ CD 4$_{15}$, אָח *brother* Gn 34$_{25}$, יָדִיד *beloved one* 4QapJoshua[b] 1$_2$, דּוֹר *generation* 4QpsJub[a] 2.2$_{11}$ ([דו]ר) 4QpsJub[b] 7$_4$. <PREP> לְ of direction, *to*, + נתן *give*, i.e. allow 5QRègle 2$_7$; of benefit, *to, for* 4QapJoseph[b] 12$_1$ ([לל]וי); introducing object, + כעס hi. *anger* 4QapJoseph[b] 1$_{14}$; אֶל *to*, + אמר *say* Gn 34$_{30}$. <COLL> אֵלֶּה שְׁמוֹת בְּנֵי יִשְׂרָאֵל ... לֵוִי *these are the names of the sons of Israel: ... Levi* Ex 1$_2$, sim. 1 C 2$_1$.

2. tribe descended from preceding, <SUBJ> ירא *fear* Ml 2$_4$, עמד *stand* Dt 27$_{12}$, ברך pi. *bless* Dt 27$_{12}$, perh. קרב hi. *present* 4QRP[c] 23$_{10}$. <OBJ> פקד *number* 1 C 21$_6$. <CSTR> מַטֵּה לֵוִי *tribe of Levi* Nm 1$_{49}$ 3$_6$ 17$_{18}$ 18$_2$ Si 45$_6$ CD 10$_5$, שֵׁבֶט *tribe of* Dt 18$_1$, בֵּית *house of* Ex 2$_1$ Nm 17$_{23}$ Zc 12$_{13}$, בְּנֵי *sons of* Ex 32$_{26.28}$ Nm 3$_{15.17}$ 4$_2$ 16$_{7.8.10}$ 18$_{21}$ Dt 21$_5$=11QT 63$_3$ Dt 31$_9$ Jos 21$_{10}$ 1 K 12$_{31}$ Ezk 40$_{46}$ Ml 3$_3$ Ezr 8$_{15}$ Ne 10$_{40}$ 12$_{23}$ 1 C 9$_{18}$ 12$_{27}$ 23$_{6.24.27}$ 24$_{20}$ 1QM 1$_2$ 1QSa 1$_{22}$ 4QOrd[a] 5$_2$ ([לוי]) 4QApocWeeks$_5$ 5QRègle 2$_8$ ([בני]) 11QT 22$_4$, בַּת *daughter of* Ex 2$_1$ Nm 26$_{59}$, מִשְׁפַּחַת *families of* Nm 26$_{58}$, שַׁעַר *gate of* Ezk 48$_{31}$ 11QT 39$_{15.16}$ 40$_{14.15}$ 44$_5$, שם ... לוי *name of ... Levi* 1QM 5$_1$. <APP> בֵּן *son* 11QT 39$_{12}$. <PREP> לְ of benefit, *for*, + ילד *give birth* Nm 26$_{59}$; of direction, *to*, + נתן *give* Ml 2$_4$; perh. *concerning*, + אמר *say* Dt 33$_8$ 4QTestim$_{14}$, דבר pi. *speak* Dt 10$_9$; of possession, *(belonging) to, of* 1 C 27$_{17}$, + היה *be* Dt 10$_9$; אֵת *with*, + היה *be* Ml 2$_4$.

3. father of Jose, <CSTR> בן לוי *son of Levi* Kfar Birim inscr. **4.** <NOM CL> לוי חיב קרקס perh. *Levi is indebted of*, i.e. to, *Karkas* Frey 1286$_{19(AHL)}$. **5.** Frey 1285$_{23}$. **6.** Frey 1285$_{24}$. **7.** Frey 1286$_{18}$. Also 3QTJud 6$_2$ perh. 4QapJoseph[a] 7$_1$ ([לו]י).

⇒ לֵוִי *Levite*.*

לֵוִי II $_{296.0.36.2}$ gent. **Levite**—pl. לְוִיִּם (Q לויים, Q לויאים); sf. לְוִיֶּנוּ—one belonging to tribe of Levi (e.g. Ex 4$_{14}$ 6$_{25}$ Nm 1$_{47}$), usu. as cultic functionary, sometimes distinguished from כֹּהֵן *priest* (see §2, Coll.), sometimes appar. not (see §2, App.).

1. in sing., of individual Levite or used collectively or generically of Levites in general (without article: Ex 6$_{19}$ Nm 3$_{20.32}$ 18$_{23}$ 26$_{57}$ Dt 10$_8$ Jos 13$_{14.33}$ Ml 2$_8$ Ps 135$_{20}$ 1 C 6$_4$ 23$_{14}$ 24$_6$; with article: Dt 12$_{12.18.19}$ 14$_{27.29}$ 16$_{11.14}$ 18$_6$ 26$_{11.12.13}$); pl. (as §2) in mss of Ezr 10$_{15}$ and in Sam of Nm 3$_{32}$ 26$_{57}$.

<SUBJ> היה *be* Jg 17$_{13}$ 19$_1$, יאל hi. *be willing* Jg 17$_{11}$, ישׁב *dwell* Jg 17$_{11}$, גור *sojourn* Dt 18$_6$ Jg 19$_1$, לין *pass night* Jg 20$_4$, הלך *go* Jg 17$_{10}$ (or del.), בוא *come* Dt 14$_{29}$ 18$_6$=11QT 60$_{12}$ Jg 20$_4$, יצא *go out* Ex 4$_{14}$, שׁלח pi. *send* Jg 20$_4$, נשׂא *raise* Nm 18$_{23}$, אחז *hold* Jg 20$_4$, נתן *give* 2 C 31$_{14}$, נחל *inherit* Nm 18$_{23}$, אמר *say* Jg 20$_4$, דבר pi. *speak* Ex 4$_{14}$, ענה *answer* Jg 20$_4$, ראה *see* Ex 4$_{14}$, קרא *meet* Ex 4$_{14}$, שׂמח *rejoice* Dt 12$_{12}$ 16$_{11.14}$ 26$_{11}$, אכל *eat* Dt 12$_{18}$ 14$_{29}$ 26$_{12}$, שׂבע *be satisfied* Dt 14$_{29}$ 26$_{12}$, עבד *serve* Nm 18$_{23}$, עזר *help* Ezr 10$_{15}$, שׁרת pi. *minister* Dt 18$_6$, כהן pi. *act as priest* Jg 17$_{13}$, עשׂה *make* Kfar Birim inscr., נתח pi. *cut up* Jg 20$_4$.

<NOM CL> הוּא לֵוִי *he was a Levite* Jg 17$_7$, לֵוִי אָנֹכִי *I am a Levite* Jg 17$_9$, הַלֵּוִי אֲשֶׁר בִּשְׁעָרֶיךָ *the Levite who is within your gates* Dt 12$_{18}$ 14$_{27}$ 16$_{11}$, sim. Dt 12$_{12}$ 16$_{14}$, הַלֵּוִי ... אֲשֶׁר בְּקִרְבֶּךָ *the Levite ... who is among you* Dt 26$_{11}$, עֲלֵיהֶם נָגִיד כָּנַנְיָהוּ הַלֵּוִי *over them as a leader was Chananiah the Levite* 2 C 31$_{12(L\ Qr)}$, וְקוֹרֵא ... הַלֵּוִי ... עַל נִדְבוֹת הָאֱלֹהִים *and Kore ... the Levite ... was over the freewill offerings of God* 2 C 31$_{14}$.

<OBJ> עזב *forsake* Dt 12$_{19}$ 14$_{27}$, הרג *kill* Jg 20$_4$.

<CSTR> יַד הַלֵּוִי *hand of the Levite* Jg 17$_{12}$, קוֹל *voice of* Jg 18$_3$, שֵׁבֶט הַלֵּוִי *tribe of the Levites* Dt 10$_8$ Jos 13$_{14.33}$ 1 C 23$_{14}$, מִשְׁפְּחֹת *families of* Ex 6$_{19}$ Nm 3$_{20}$ 1 C 6$_4$, בֵּית *house of* Jg 18$_{15}$ (בֵּית־) Ps 135$_{20}$, נְשִׂיאֵי *leaders of* Nm 3$_{32}$, פְּקוּדֵי *mustered ones of* Nm 26$_{57}$, בְּרִית *covenant of* Ml 2$_8$.

<APP> Aaron Ex 4$_{14}$, Chananiah 2 C 31$_{12}$, Jahaziel 2 C 20$_{14}$, Jose Kfar Birim inscr., Kore 2 C 31$_{14}$, Shabbethai Ezr 10$_{15}$, אִישׁ *man* Jg 19$_1$ 20$_{4.4}$, בֵּן *son* 2 C 20$_{14}$

31_{14} Kfar Birim inscr., אָח *brother* Ex 4_{14}, נַעַר *lad* Jg $18_{3.15}$, שֹׁעֵר *porter* 2 C 31_{14}.

<PREP> לְ of direction, *to*, + נתן *give* Dt $26_{12.13}$; of possession, *(belonging) to, of* Dt 12_{12} 14_{27}; of benefit, *for*, + לקח *take* Jg 19_1; מִן partitive, *from (among)* 1 C 24_6; עַל *upon*, + היה *be* 2 C 20_{14}; *against*, + קום *rise* Jg 20_4; introducing object, + סבב *surround* Jg 20_4.

<COLL> גֵּר‖לֵוִי *sojourner* Dt 16_{14} $26_{11.12.13}$, + גֵּר Dt 14_{29} 16_{11}; ‖ יָתוֹם *orphan* Dt 16_{14} $26_{12.13}$, + יָתוֹם Dt 14_{29} 16_{11}; ‖ אַלְמָנָה *widow* Dt 16_{14} $26_{12.13}$, + אַלְמָנָה Dt 14_{29} 16_{11}; + Israelite(s) Dt $12_{12.18}$ $16_{11.14}$ 26_{11}, בֵּן *son* Dt $12_{12.18}$ $16_{11.14}$, בַּת *daughter* Dt $12_{12.18}$ $16_{11.14}$, עֶבֶד *servant* Dt $12_{12.18}$ $16_{11.14}$, אָמָה *female servant* Dt $12_{12.18}$ $16_{11.14}$.

2. in plural, <SUBJ> היה *be* Nm $3_{12.45}$ $8_{11.14}$ Ezk 44_{10} Ne 13_{22}, פקד ni. *be appointed* Ne 7_1, ho. *be appointed* 2 C 34_{12}, hotp. *be mustered* Nm 1_{47} 2_{33}, ספר ni. *be numbered* 1 C 23_2, יחשׂ htp. *enrol oneself* 2 C 31_{17}, קרא ni. *be invited* 1QSa 2_1, כלם ni. *be ashamed* 2 C 30_{15}.

הלך *go* Ne 10_{29} 2 C 11_{14}, בוא *come* Nm $8_{15.22.24}$ Ezk 44_{15} Ne 10_{29} 13_{22} 2 C 23_2 29_{12}, hi. *bring* Ezr 8_{30} Ne 10_{35} 2 C 24_6 30_{15}, יצא *go out* Ezk 44_{15} 2 C 24_5 1QM 7_{14}, hi. *take out* 2 C $29_{5.16}$, נגשׁ *approach* Ezk 44_{10}, hi. *present* CD 3_{21}, קרב *approach* Ezk 44_{15}, hi. *present* Ezk 44_{15} 2 C 35_{11}, עבר *pass* 1QS 2_{20}, רחק *be distant* Ezk 44_{10}, תעה *stray* Ezk 48_{11}, עזב *leave* 2 C 11_{14}, ברח *flee* Ne 13_{10}, מהר pi. *hurry* 2 C 24_5, נקף hi. *surround* 2 C 23_7.

עמד *stand* Dt 18_7=11QT 60_{14} Ezk $44_{10.15}$ Ezr $3_{10(mss)}$ Ne 12_{44} 2 C 7_6 29_{26} 30_{15} $35_{3.10}$ 1QM 15_4, hi. appar. *position oneself* Ezr 3_{10}, *appoint* 1 C 15_{17}, יצב htp. *position oneself* 2 C 11_{13}, עלה *go up* Ne 12_1 2 C 34_{30}, hi. *bring up* 1 K 8_4 Ne 10_{39} 1 C $15_{11.14}$ 2 C 5_5, *offer burnt offering* 2 C 23_{18}, קום *arise* Ezr 1_5 2 C 20_{19} 29_{12} 30_{27}, hi. *raise* Nm 1_{51}, נשׂא *raise* Nm 1_{50} Dt 31_{25} Jos 3_3 8_{33} 2 S 15_{24} Ezk 44_{10} 1 C $15_{2.26.27}$ 23_{26} 2 C 5_4, שׁמר *keep* Nm 1_{53} $31_{30.47}$ Ezk $44_{10.15}$=CD 3_{21} Ne 13_{22}, שׂים *place* 1 S 6_{15}, יצק hi. appar. *place* 2 S 15_{24} (or em. יצג *place*), נוח hi. *place* Ezk 44_{15}.

נתן *give* Nm 18_{26} 2 C 35_{11}, *place* 2 C 35_3, pass. *be given* Nm $3_{9.9}$ 8_{19} 18_6 1 C 6_{33}, לקח *take* Nm 18_{26}, קבל pi. *receive* Ezr 8_{30} 2 C 29_{16}, עשׂר pi. *receive tithe* Ne $10_{38.39}$, סור hi. *remove* 2 C 35_{11}, רוץ hi. *take quickly* 2 C 35_{11}, ירד hi. *take down* Nm 1_{51} 1 S 6_{15}, אסף *gather* 2 C 29_{12} 34_9, ni. *be gathered* Ne 8_{13}, קבץ *gather* 2 C 24_5.

שׁמע *hear* 2 C 29_5, אמר *say* Dt $27_{9.14}$ Ne $8_{9.11}$ 9_5 1QM 13_1 18_5 (ה[לויי]ם) 1QS 2_{11}, דבר pi. *speak* Dt 27_9, ספר pi. *relate* 1QS 1_{22}, נגד hi. *tell* Dt 17_9, ירה hi. *teach* Dt 24_8, בין hi. *be skilful* 2 C 34_{12}, *teach* Ne $8_{7.9}$ 2 C $35_{3(Qr)}$, שׂכל hi. *be skilful* 2 C 30_{22}, *consider* Ne 8_{13}, ענה *answer* Dt 27_{14} 1QM 13_1 18_5 (ה[לויי]ם), perh. *sing* Ezr 3_{10}, ברך pi. *bless* 2 C 30_{27} 1QM 13_1 18_5 (ה[לויי]ם) 1QS 1_{19}, perh. Jos 8_{33}, זעם *curse* 1QM 13_1, קלל pi. *curse* 1QS 2_4, הלל pi. *praise* Ezr 3_{10} 1 C 16_4 2 C 8_{14} 20_{19} 29_{30} 30_{21}, ידה hi. *give thanks* Ezr 3_{10} 1 C 16_4, htp. 2 C 30_{22}, זכר hi. *invoke* 1 C 16_4, שׁבע ni. *swear* Ezr 10_5, חשׁה hi. *silence* Ne 8_{11}, שׂמח *rejoice* 2 C 30_{25}, כתב pass. *be written* Ne 12_{22}, רוע hi. *sound* trumpet 1QM 8_9 16_7 (יריע[ו]) 4QM^c 1_9 (הל[ויים] מר[י]עים ...).

כון hi. *prepare* 2 C $35_{3.14.15}$, עבד *serve* Nm $8_{15.19.22}$ 18_6 2 C 35_3, שׁרת pi. *minister* Nm 1_{50} Jr 33_{22} Ezk 43_{19} $44_{10.15}$ 1 C 15_2 2 C 8_{14}, כהן pi. *act as priest* Ezk 44_{10}, קדשׁ pi. *sanctify* Ezk 44_{15} Ne 13_{22} 2 C 29_5, hi. *sanctify* Ne 12_{47} 2 C 30_{17} 11QT 60_6, htp. *sanctify oneself* 1 C $15_{12.14}$ 2 C $29_{5.12.34}$ 30_{15} 35_3, קדד *bow down* 2 C 29_{30}, שׁחה htpal. *worship* 2 C 29_{30}, סמך *rest* hands upon Nm 8_{12}, נפל hi. *cause to fall*, i.e. cast, lots Ne 10_{35}, זבח pi. *sacrifice* 2 C 30_{22}, שׁחט *slay* Ezk 44_{10} Ezr 6_{20} 2 C $35_{3.11}$, פשׁט hi. *strip*, i.e. flay 2 C 35_{11}, כפר pi. *make atonement* Nm 8_{19}, רום hi. *raise*, i.e. offer Nm 18_{26}, בער pi. *burn* Ne 10_{35}, בשׁל pi. *boil* 2 C 35_{11}, מסס hi. *cause to melt* 1QM 8_9.

בדל ni. *separate oneself* Ezr 9_1, חטא htp. *purify oneself from sin* Nm 8_{21}, טהר pi. *purify* Ne 12_{30} 2 C 29_{12}, htp. *purify oneself* Ezr 6_{20} (or del. לֵוִי) Ne 12_{30} 13_{22}, כבס pi. *wash* Nm 8_{21}, גלח pi. *shave* Ezk 44_{15}, כסם *trim hair* 44_{15}, שׁלח pi. *send*, i.e. grow, hair 44_{15}, לבשׁ *dress oneself* 44_{15}, pu. *be dressed* 2 C 5_{12}, חגר *gird oneself* Ezk 44_{15}, כרבל pu. *be robed* 1 C 15_{27}, פשׁט *strip* Ezk 44_{15}.

ישׁב *dwell* Nm 35_2 Jos 14_4 Ezr 2_{70}‖Ne 7_{72} Ne 11_3‖1 C 9_2, חנה *encamp* Nm $1_{50.53}$, אכל *eat* Dt $18_{1.7}$ 2 C 30_{22} (or em. אכל to כלה pi. *complete* festival), שׁתה *drink* 11QT 21_4 ([י]שׁתו), עשׂה *do* Ezk 44_{10} Ezr 10_5 Ne 12_{27} 13_{10} 2 C 23_8 35_{18}, חלל hi. *begin* Ezr 3_8, יסף hi. *add* 1QS 2_{11}, נצח pi. *oversee* Ezr 3_8, עזר *help* Ezr $10_{15(mss)}$, חזק *be strong* 2 C 31_4, pi. *strengthen*, i.e. help 2 C 29_{34}, hi. *repair* wall Ne 3_{17}, *take hold of*, i.e. join with Ne 10_{29}.

<NOM CL> שֹׁטְרִים הַלְוִיִּם *the Levites are officers* 2 C 19$_{11}$, הלוים שנים *the Levites will be second* CD 14$_{4.5}$, הַלְוִיִּם יֵשׁוּעַ בִּנּוּי ... *the Levites were Jeshua, Binnui* ... Ne 12$_{8}$, כָּל־הַלְוִיִּם ... מָאתַיִם שְׁמֹנִים וְאַרְבָּעָה *all the Levites were ... two hundred and eighty-four* Ne 11$_{18}$, הַלְוִיִּם בְּכָל־עָרֵי יְהוּדָה *the Levites were in all the cities of Judah* Ne 11$_{20}$, הַלְוִיִּם אֲשֶׁר בְּכָל־יִשְׂרָאֵל *the Levites who were in all Israel* 2 C 11$_{13}$, הַלְוִיִּם בִּמְלַאכְתָּ *the Levites are at (their) service* 2 C 13$_{10}$, הַלְוִיִּם יִשְׁרֵי לֵבָב ... מֵהַכֹּהֲנִים *the Levites were more upright of heart ... than the priests* 2 C 29$_{34}$, וְעִמָּהֶם יוֹזָבָד ... וְנוֹעַדְיָה ... הַלְוִיִּם *and with them were Jozabad ... and Noadiah ... the Levites* Ezr 8$_{33}$, וְעִמָּהֶם הַלְוִיִּם שְׁמַעְיָהוּ וּנְתַנְיָהוּ *and with them were the Levites Shemaiah and Nethaniah* 2 C 17$_{8}$, הל[ויי]ם אשר אתו *the Levites who are with him* 1QM 18$_{5}$, עַל־הֶחָתוּם ... לְוִיֵּנוּ *upon the sealed copy are ... our Levites* Ne 10$_{1}$, var. 10$_{2}$ (הַחֲתוּמִים *the sealed copies* [or em. הַחוֹתְמִים with *those who sealed* or אֵלֶּה הַחוֹתְמִים *these are the ones who sealed*), הַלְוִיִּם אֲחֵיהֶם עַל־אוֹצְרוֹת *the Levites, their brothers were in charge of the treasuries of* the temple 1 C 26$_{20}$ (if em. אֲחִיָּה *Ahijah* to אֲחֵיהֶם *their brothers*), הַלְוִיִּם עַל־שְׁחִיטַת הַפְּסָחִים *the Levites were in charge of the passover sacrifices* 2 C 30$_{17}$, לַמִּזְרָח הַלְוִיִּם שִׁשָּׁה appar. *at the east were six Levites* 1 C 26$_{17}$ (or em. לַמִּזְרָחָה לַיּוֹם שִׁשָּׁה *at the east there were six each day*), אֵלֶּה ... הַלְוִיִּם *these are ... the Levites* Ne 12$_{1}$, הֵם הַלְוִיִּם וְהָיוּ עַל *they were (the) Levites and they were in charge of* 1 C 9$_{26}$ (or em. וּמִן־הַלְוִיִּם יִהְיוּ *and some of the Levites were*).

<OBJ> בוא hi. *bring* Ne 12$_{27}$ 2 C 29$_{4}$, קרב hi. *present* Nm 8$_{9.10}$, פקד *muster* Nm 4$_{46}$, hi. *appoint* Nm 1$_{50}$, אסף *gather* 1 C 15$_{4}$ 23$_{2}$ 2 C 29$_{4}$, קבץ *gather* 2 C 24$_{5}$ 2 C 23$_{2}$, עמד hi. *position* Nm 8$_{13}$ 2 C 29$_{25}$, *appoint* Ezr 3$_{8}$ 2 C 8$_{14}$, נתן *give* Nm 3$_{9}$ 8$_{19}$, *cause to be* Ezk 44$_{10}$, חלק *apportion* 2 C 23$_{18}$, לקח *take* Nm 3$_{12.41.45}$ 8$_{6.18}$ 18$_{6}$, בקשׁ pi. *seek* Ne 12$_{27}$, נדח hi. *banish* 2 C 13$_{9}$, נוף hi. *wave (in offering)* Nm 8$_{11.13.15.21}$, בדל hi. *separate* Nm 8$_{14}$, טהר pi. *purify* Nm 8$_{15.21}$, צוה pi. *command* Dt 24$_{8}$ 31$_{25}$, שׁבע hi. *adjure* Ezr 10$_{5}$, רבה hi. *multiply* Jr 33$_{21}$, עזר *help* 1 C 15$_{26}$.

<CSTR> אֲבוֹת הַלְוִיִּם *(houses of the) fathers of the Levites* Ex 6$_{25}$ Jos 21$_{1}$, מִשְׁפְּחוֹת *families of* Jos 21$_{20}$ (מִשְׁפְּחוֹת ...) 21$_{27}$ (מִשְׁפְּחֹת) 21$_{34}$ (מִשְׁפְּחוֹת ...) 21$_{40}$, מַחְלְקוֹת ... *divisions of* 1 C 28$_{13.21}$ 2 C 31$_{2}$, בְּנֵי *sons of* 1 C 15$_{15}$ 24$_{30}$ 11QT 44$_{14}$ (מבני *from the sons of* corrected to מן *from*), רָאשֵׁי *chiefs of* Ne 11$_{16}$ 12$_{24}$ 1QM 2$_{2}$, שַׂר־ *chief of* 1 C 15$_{22}$, שָׂרֵי *princes of* Ezr 8$_{29}$ 10$_{5}$ (both ... שָׂרֵי) 1 C 15$_{16}$ 2 C 35$_{9}$, פְּקִיד *overseer of* Ne 11$_{22}$, פְּקוּדֵי *mustered ones of* Nm 3$_{39}$, פְּדוּיֵי *redeemed of* Nm 3$_{49}$, בֶּהֱמַת *beasts of* Nm 3$_{41.45}$, מַחֲנֵה *camp of* Nm 2$_{17}$, עָרֵי *cities of* Lv 25$_{32.33}$ Jos 21$_{41}$,* גְּבוּל *border of* Ezk 48$_{12}$, מַעֲלֵה *staircase of* Ne 9$_{4}$, אֲחֻזַּת *property of* Ezk 48$_{22}$, מְנָת *portion of* 2 C 31$_{4}$, מְנָיוֹת *portions of* Ne 13$_{5}$ (if em. מִצְוַת *commandment of*) 13$_{10}$, עולת הלויים *burnt offering of the Levites* 11QT 23$_{9}$ ([הלויים]) 24$_{11}$, עֲבֹדַת הַלְוִיִּם *work of the Levites* Ex 38$_{21}$ Ezr 8$_{20}$, מִצְוַת *commandment of* Ne 13$_{5}$ (or em.), בְּרִית *covenant of* Ne 13$_{29}$, יַד *hand of* 2 C 30$_{16}$, *control of* 2 C 23$_{18}$ 24$_{11}$, כָּל־הַלְוִיִּם *all the Levites* 2 S 15$_{24}$ Ne 11$_{18}$ 1 C 15$_{27}$ 2 C 30$_{22}$ (+ לֵב *heart of* all).

<APP> Adonijah 2 C 17$_{8}$, Amminadab 1 C 15$_{11}$, Asahel 2 C 17$_{8}$, Asaiah 1 C 15$_{11}$, Azariah 2 C 29$_{12}$, Bani Ne 9$_{5}$, Eden 2 C 29$_{12}$, Eliel 1 C 15$_{11}$, Hashabneiah Ne 9$_{5}$, Hodiah Ne 9$_{5}$, Jahath 2 C 34$_{12}$, Jehonathan 2 C 17$_{8}$, Jehuel 2 C 29$_{12}$, Jeshua Ne 9$_{5}$, Jeuel 2 C 29$_{12}$, Joah 2 C 29$_{12}$, Joel 1 C 15$_{11}$ 2 C 29$_{12}$, Jozabad Ezr 8$_{33}$, Kadmiel Ne 9$_{5}$, Kish 2 C 29$_{12}$, Mahath 2 C 29$_{12}$, Mattaniah 2 C 29$_{12}$, Meshullam Ezr 10$_{15(mss)}$ 2 C 34$_{12}$, Nethaniah 2 C 17$_{8}$, Noadiah Ezr 8$_{33}$, Obadiah 2 C 34$_{12}$, Pethahiah Ne 9$_{5}$, Rehum Ne 3$_{17}$, Shabbethai Ezr 10$_{15}$, Shebaniah Ne 9$_{5}$, Shemaiah 1 C 15$_{11}$ 2 C 17$_{8}$ 29$_{12}$, Shemiramoth 2 C 17$_{8}$, Sherebiah Ne 9$_{5}$, Shimei 2 C 29$_{12}$, Shimri 2 C 29$_{12}$, Tob-adonijah 2 C 17$_{8}$, Tobijah 2 C 17$_{8}$, Uriel 1 C 15$_{11}$, Uzziel 2 C 29$_{12}$, Zebadiah 2 C 17$_{8}$, Zechariah 2 C 29$_{12}$.

אִישׁ *man* Ne 11$_{20}$ 13$_{30}$, אָח *brother* Nm 18$_{6}$ Dt 18$_{7}$=11QT 60$_{14}$ Ezr 3$_{9}$ 1 C 6$_{33}$ 26$_{20}$ (if em. אֲחִיָּה *Ahijah* to אֲחֵיהֶם *their brothers*) 2 C 29$_{34}$ 35$_{15}$, בֵּן *son* Jos 21$_{20.34}$ Ezk 44$_{15}$ Ezr 3$_{10}$ 8$_{33}$ Ne 3$_{17}$ 2 C 29$_{12}$, כֹּהֵן *priest* Dt 17$_{9.18}$ 18$_{1}$ 24$_{8}$ 27$_{9}$ Jos 3$_{3}$ 8$_{33}$ Is 66$_{21}$ (mss add וְ *and* Levites in all three) Jr 33$_{18.21}$ Ezk 43$_{19}$ 44$_{15}$ 2 C 5$_{5}$ 23$_{18}$ 30$_{27}$ (mss add וְ in all three), perh. Ezr 10$_{5}$ Ne 10$_{29.35}$ 11$_{20}$, שׁרת pi. ptc. *minister* Jr 33$_{21}$ Ezk 45$_{5}$, שׁיר pol. ptc. *singer* 2 C 5$_{12}$, שׁמר ptc. *keeper* 2 C 34$_{9}$, שֵׁבֶט *tribe* Dt 18$_{1}$, מַחֲלֹקֶת *division* Ne 11$_{36}$.

<ADJ> קָדוֹשׁ *holy* 2 C 35$_{3}$.

<PREP> לְ of direction, *to*, + נתן *give* Nm 18$_{24.26}$ 31$_{30.47}$ 35$_{2.2.4.6.7.8}$ Jos 14$_{3.4}$ 21$_{3.8}$ 1 C 6$_{49}$ 11QT 22$_{12}$ 58$_{13}$,

רום hi. *raise*, i.e. contribute 2 C $35_{8.9}$, בוא hi. *bring* Ne 10_{38}, אמר *say* Ne 13_{22} 1 C 15_{11} 2 C 24_5 $29_{4.30}$ 35_3, קרא *call* 1 C 15_{11}; of possession, *of, (belonging) to* Jos 18_7 Jr 33_{18} Ezk 48_{13} (if em. -הַ *the* to -לַ *to the* Levites) 1 C $9_{33.34}$ 15_{12} $24_{6.31}$ 2 C $23_{4.6}$ 31_2 35_5 1QDM 1_3 (ללו[י]ים), + היה *be* Lv 25_{32} Dt 18_1 Ezk 45_{51}; of benefit, *to, for* Ne 12_{44} perh. 4QM^d 1_3 11QT 60_6, + היה *be* 11QT 22_{10}, עשׂה *do* Nm $8_{20.22.26}$, חשׁב ni. *be reckoned* Nm $18_{26.30}$, perh. קדשׁ hi. *sanctify* portions Ne 12_{47}, perh. עמד hi. *establish* duties Ne 13_{30}; *concerning* Nm 8_{24}, + צוה pi. *command* Nm 8_{20}; *as, in order to be*, + לקח *take* Is 66_{21}.

בְּ partitive, *(from) among* 2 C 31_{19}; בחר בְּ *choose* 1 C 15_2; כְּ *as*, + שׁרת pi. *minister* Dt 18_7=11QT 60_{14}; מִן of direction, *from*, + גאל *redeem* Lv 25_{33}; partitive, *(one) of, (some) of, (from) among* Jos 21_4 Ezr 3_{12} $7_{7.7}$ 10_{23} Ne 11_{15}||1 C 9_{14} Ne 11_{36} 13_{13} 1 C 9_{31} 2 C 34_{13} 1QM 7_{14} 4QM^h 4_5 ([ה]לוים) 11QT 44_{14} (מבני *from the sons of* corrected to מן) 57_{12} CD 13_3, + עמד hi. *appoint* 2 C 19_8, נתן *give*, i.e. appoint 1 C 16_4.

אֶל *to*, + בוא *come* Dt 17_9, נתן *give* Nm $7_{5.6}$ Ezk 43_{19}, דבר pi. *speak* Nm 18_{26}, אמר *say* Nm 18_{26}; עַל *upon*, + עלה *go up*, i.e. clothe (of garment) Ezk 44_{15}, סמך *lay* hands Nm 8_{10}; *on behalf of, for*, + כפר pi. *make atonement* Nm $8_{12.21}$; *concerning* Nm 8_{22} Ne 12_{44} 2 C 8_{15}; דרשׁ עַל *inquire of* 2 C 24_6 31_9; עדף עַל *be additional to* Nm 3_{46}.

אֵת *with* Jr 33_{21}; עִם *with*, + היה *be* Ne 10_{39}; מִתּוֹךְ *from among*, + כרת hi. *cut off* Nm 4_{18}; לִפְנֵי *before* 1QM 7_{15}, + עמד *stand* 11QT 61_8; מִלִּפְנֵי *in the presence of*, + כתב *write* king's law Dt 17_{18}; נֶגֶד *opposite*, + עמד *stand* Jos 8_{33}; אַחַר *after*, + עשׂה *do* 11QT 24_{11}.

<COLL> שבעה לויים *seven Levites* 1QM 7_{14}, הַלְוִיִּם שִׁשָּׁה *six Levites* 1 C 26_{17} (or em. לַמִּזְרָח הַלְוִיִּם שִׁשָּׁה appar. *at the east were six Levites* to לַמִּזְרָחָה לַיּוֹם שִׁשָּׁה *at the east there were six each day*).

לֵוִי || כֹּהֵן *priest* (in addition to refs. from App.) 1 K 8_4 Ezr 1_5 2_{70}||Ne 7_{72} Ezr $3_{8.10.12}$ 6_{20} (or del. כֹּהֵן) 7_7 $8_{29.30}$ 9_1 Ne 8_{13} 10_1 11_3||1 C 9_2 $12_{1.30.44.44}$ $13_{29(ms).30}$ 1 C 13_2 $15_{11.14}$ 23_2 $24_{6.31}$ $28_{13.21}$ 2 C 7_6 $8_{14.15}$ 11_{13} $13_{9.10}$ 19_8 23_4 24_5 $29_{4.26}$ $30_{15.21.25}$ $31_{2.2.4.9.17.19}$ 34_{30} $35_{8.10.11.18}$ 1QM 7_{15} 1QS 1_{19} 2_{11} CD 3_{21}, + כֹּהֵן Ne 8_9 10_{39} $13_{5.13}$ 2 C 23_6 $29_{34.34}$ 30_{16} 35_{14} 1QM 8_9 4QM^d 1_2 11QT $22_{10.12}$ 58_{13} 61_8.

|| נָתִין *temple servant* Ezr 2_{70}||Ne 7_{72} Ezr 7_7 8_{20} (+) 10_{29} 11_3||1 C 9_2, שֹׁעֵר *porter* Ezr 2_{70}||Ne 7_{72} Ezr 7_7 Ne 7_1 10_{29} 13_5 1 C 9_{26} 2 C 8_{14} 23_4 34_{13} 35_{15} (all five +), || מְשֹׁרֵר *singer* Ezr 2_{70}||Ne 7_{72} Ezr 7_7 Ne 7_1 10_{29} $13_{5.10}$ 1 C 9_{33} 15_{27} 2 C 35_{15} (all three +), שַׂר *prince* Ne 10_1 1 C 23_2 (+), שֹׁפֵט *judge* Dt 17_9 (+) 11QT 61_8.

|| יִשְׂרָאֵל *Israel* Ezr 2_{70}||Ne 7_{72} Ezr 10_5 Ne 11_3||1 C 9_2 Ne 11_{20} 2 C 35_{18} (both +); + יְהוּדָה *Judah* 2 C 35_{18}; || עַם *people* Ne 10_{35} 2 C 35_8 1QM 8_9 16_7, + עַם Ezr 2_{70}||Ne 7_{72} Ezr 9_1 Ne 10_{29} 2 C 34_{30}, + קָהָל *assembly* 2 C 30_{22}.

+ אִישׁ *man* 2 C 34_{30} 1QM 15_4, בֵּן *son* of Aaron 1 C 15_4 2 C $13_{9.10}$, of Zadok CD 3_{21}, of Israel CD $14_{4.5}$, ראשׁ *head* of ancestral house Ezr 1_5 2 C 19_8 23_2, שֹׁטֵר *officer* 2 C 34_{13} 1QM $7_{14.16}$, זָקֵן *elder* 1QM 13_1, סֹפֵר *scribe* 2 C 34_{13}, יֹשֵׁב *inhabitant* 2 C 30_{25} 34_{30} 35_{18}, גֵּר *sojourner* 2 C 30_{25} CD $14_{4.5}$.*

Also 4QM^b 1_{11} 4QM^g 8_1 (לויא[י]ם) Kfar Alma inscr. (הלו[י]).

<SYN> §1 גֵּר *sojourner*, יָתוֹם *orphan*, אַלְמָנָה *widow*; §2 כֹּהֵן *priest*, נָתִין *temple servant*, שֹׁעֵר *porter*, מְשֹׁרֵר *singer*, שַׂר *prince*, שֹׁפֵט *judge*, יִשְׂרָאֵל *Israel*, עַם *people*.

⇒ לֵוִי *Levi*.

[לִוְיָה] 2 n.f. **garland**—cstr. לִוְיַת—adorning head, <NOM CL> לִוְיַת חֵן הֵם לְרֹאשֶׁךָ *they* (instruction and teaching) *are a garland of grace for your head* Pr 1_9 (+ עֲנָק *necklace*), לִוְיַת כְּסִילִים אִוֶּלֶת *the garland of fools is folly* Pr 14_{24} (if em.; see Cstr.). <OBJ> נתן *give*, i.e. place Pr 4_9 (+ עֲטָרָה *crown*). <CSTR> לִוְיַת חֵן *garland of grace* Pr 1_9 4_9, לִוְיַת כְּסִילִים *garland of fools* Pr 14_{24} (if em. אִוֶּלֶת *folly of*).

לִוְיָתָן 6.0.1 n.m. **Leviathan**—sea creature, whether primaeval, fantastic, or simply huge, <OBJ> יצר *form* Ps 104_{26}, עור pol. *rouse* Jb 3_8, משׁך *draw* Jb 40_{25}, נתן *give* as food Ps 74_{14}. <CSTR> רָאשֵׁי לִוְיָתָן *heads of Leviathan* Ps 74_{14} (|| תַּנִּין perh. *serpent*). <APP> נָחָשׁ בָּרִחַ *swift (?) serpent* Is 27_1, נָחָשׁ עֲקַלָּתוֹן *writhing serpent* Is 27_1. <PREP> בְּ of instrument, *by (means of), with*, + שׂחק pi. *make sport* Ps 104_{26}; עַל *upon*, + פקד *visit*, i.e. bring, punishment Is $27_{1.1}$ (+ תַּנִּין). Also 4QapPs^a 3_1. <SYN> תַּנִּין perh. *serpent*.*

[לוּל] 1 n.[m.] **step**—pl. לוּלִים—between storeys of temple, <PREP> בְּ of instrument, *by (means of), with*, + עלה *go up* 1 K 6₈.

לוּלֵא 14 conj. **unless**—לוּלֵי—**1.** as unreal conditional particle, **if not, had not,** etc., **unless.**

a. with perfect in protasis and with apodosis in perfect, לוּלֵא הִתְמַהְמָהְנוּ כִּי־עַתָּה שַׁבְנוּ זֶה פַעֲמָיִם *if we had not delayed, we could now have returned twice* Gn 43₁₀, לוּלֵא חֲרַשְׁתֶּם בְּעֶגְלָתִי לֹא מְצָאתֶם חִידָתִי *if you had not ploughed with my heifer, you would not have found out my riddle* Jg 14₁₈, לוּלֵי מִהַרְתְּ ... כִּי אִם־נוֹתַר לְנָבָל *had you not made haste, ... there would surely not have remained* any-one *to Nabal* 1 S 25₃₄ (mss לוּלֵא), לוּלֵי י׳ ... הוֹתִיר לָנוּ שָׂרִיד כִּמְעָט כִּסְדֹם הָיִינוּ *if Y. ... had not left us a few survivors, we would soon have been as Sodom* Is 1₉; also Gn 31₄₂ Nm 22₃₃ (if em. אוּלַי *perhaps*) 2 S 2₂₇ (mss לוּלֵי).

b. with imperfect in protasis and with apodosis in **(1)** perfect, אָמַרְתִּי אַפְאֵיהֶם ... לוּלֵי כַּעַס אוֹיֵב אָגוּר *I might have said, I shall destroy them, ... did I not fear the anger of the enemy* Dt 32₂₇ (mss לוּלֵא); **(2)** waw consecutive + imperfect, וַיֹּאמֶר לְהַשְׁמִידָם לוּלֵי מֹשֶׁה ... עָמַד בַּפֶּרֶץ לְפָנָיו *he would have commanded their destruction had Moses not ... stood in the breach before him* Ps 106₂₃.

c. with participle in protasis and with apodosis in imperfect, לוּלֵי פְּנֵי יְהוֹשָׁפָט ... אֲנִי נֹשֵׂא אִם־אַבִּיט אֵלֶיךָ *if I did not have regard for Jehoshaphat, ... I would not look at you* 2 K 3₁₄.

d. with nominal clause in protasis and with apodosis in perfect, לוּלֵי י׳ עֶזְרָתָה לִּי כִּמְעַט שָׁכְנָה דוּמָה נַפְשִׁי *were Y. not my help my soul would soon have dwelt in silence* Ps 94₁₇, לוּלֵי תוֹרָתְךָ שַׁעֲשֻׁעָי אָז אָבַדְתִּי בְעָנְיִי *were your law not my delight, I should have perished in my affliction* Ps 119₉₂.

2. perh. as emphatic adverb, **indeed** (unless as §1, but with apodosis omitted), לוּלֵא הֶאֱמַנְתִּי לִרְאוֹת בְּטוּב־י׳ בְּאֶרֶץ חַיִּים *I indeed believed I would see the goodness of Y. in the land of the living* Ps 27₁₃ (mss lack לוּלֵא; or em. לוֹ : לֹא uttering violence *to himself*; I did *not* believe).*

3. לוּלֵי שֶׁ- **except that, unless,** ... לוּלֵי י׳ שֶׁהָיָה לָנוּ לוּלֵי י׳ שֶׁהָיָה לָנוּ ... אֲזַי חַיִּים בְּלָעוּנוּ *if Y. had not been on our side, ... if Y. had not been on our side, ... then they would have swallowed us alive* Ps 124₁.

Also perh. 4QPrQuot 205₁ (לולהי).

[לוּלָב] 0.0.1 n.[m.] **lulab,** palm-branch used for festive purposes, 4QRitMar 99₂ ([לולבי[ם).

לולהי, see לוּלֵא *if not.*

לון I 14.0.3 vb. **murmur—Ni.** 8.0.2 Impf. Q ילון, Kt תלונו; + waw וַיִּלֹּנוּ (Kt וילונו)—**murmur,** perh. **rebel,** <SUBJ> עַם *people* Ex 15₂₄, עֵדָה *congregation* Ex 16₂(Qr) Nm 16₁₁(Kt) 17₆ Jos 9₁₈, Korah Nm 16₁₁(Kt), אִישׁ *man* Nm 14₃₆(Kt) 1QS 7₁₇.₁₇, בֵּן *son* of Israel Ex 16₇(Kt) Nm 14₂; subj. not specified, 4QDᵉ 7.1₁₃ ([אשר ילו[ן] *[one] who murmurs)*. <PREP> בְּ of place, + מִדְבָּר *steppe* Ex 16₂(Qr); מִן *on,* + מָחֳרָת *next day* Nm 17₆; עַל *against,* + Aaron Ex 16₂(Qr).₇(Kt) Nm 14₂ 16₁₁(Kt) 17₆, Moses Ex 15₂₄ 16₂(Qr).₇(Kt) Nm 14₂.₃₆(Kt) 17₆, אָב *father* 4QDᵉ 7.1₁₃ ([ילו[ן]), נָשִׂיא *prince* Jos 9₁₈, רֵעַ *neighbour* 1QS 7₁₇, יְסוֹד *secret counsel* 1QS 7₁₇; appar. אֵת *with,* + עֵדָה *congregation* Nm 14₃₆(Kt).

Hi. 10.0.1 Pf. הֲלִינֹתֶם; impf. Qr תַּלִּינוּ; + waw וַיָּלֶן, Qr וַיַּלִּינוּ; ptc. מַלִּינִים (מַלִּינִם)—**1. murmur; growl** (Ps 59₁, if em. לין hi. *pass night*), <SUBJ> עַם *people* Ex 17₃, עֵדָה *congregation* Ex 16₂(Kt) Nm 14₂₇.₂₇.₂₉ 16₁₁(Qr), Korah Nm 16₁₁(Qr), אִישׁ *man* 1QH 5₂₅ (+ סרר *rebel*), בֵּן *son* of Israel Ex 16₇(Qr).₈ Nm 17₂₀, evildoer Ps 59₁₆ (if em. וַיָּלִינוּ if they are not satisfied *and pass the night* to וַיַּלִּינוּ *then they growl;* + יֶהֱמוּ כַכָּלֶב *they are noisy like a dog*). <OBJ> תְּלֻנָּה *murmuring* Ex 16₈ Nm 14₂₇ 17₂₀. <PREP> בְּ of place, + מִדְבָּר *steppe* Ex 16₂(Kt); עַל *against,* + Y. Ex 16₈ Nm 14₂₇.₂₇.₂₉ 16₁₁(Qr), Aaron Ex 16₂(Kt).₇(Qr) 17₂₀, Moses Ex 16₂(Kt).₇(Qr) 17₃.₂₀. <COLL> + adverb סָבִיב *round about* 1QH 5₂₅.

2. cause to murmur, <SUBJ> אִישׁ *man* Nm 14₃₆(Qr). <OBJ> עֵדָה *congregation* Nm 14₃₆(Qr). <PREP> עַל *against,* + Moses Nm 14₃₆(Qr).*

⇒ תְּלֻנָּה *murmuring.*

לון II, see לין *pass night.*

לוע, see לעע I *be rash*, II *swallow*.

לוש 5 vb. **knead—Qal** 5 + waw Qr וַתָּלָשׁ (Kt ותלוש); impv. לוּשִׁי; ptc. לָשׁוֹת; inf. לוּשׁ—**knead,** <SUBJ> Sarah Gn 18$_6$ (+ עשׂה *make* cakes), Tamar 2 S 13$_8$ (+ לבב pi. *bake*, בשׁל pi. *cook* cakes), אִשָּׁה *woman* 1 S 28$_{24}$ (+ אפה *bake* unleavened bread) Jr 7$_{18}$ (+ עשׂה), אֹפֶה *baker* Ho 7$_4$. <OBJ> בָּצֵק *dough* 2 S 13$_8$ Jr 7$_{18}$ Ho 7$_4$, קֶמַח *flour* Gn 18$_6$ 1 S 28$_{24}$.

[לוּשׁ], see לַיִשׁ III *Laish*.

[לָז], see הַלָּז *that*.

[לָזֶה], see הַלָּזֶה *that*.

[לֵזוּ], see הַלֵּזוּ *that*.

[לָזוּת] 1 n.f. **perversity**—cstr. לְזוּת—<OBJ> רחק hi. *distance* Pr 4$_{24}$ (∥ עִקְּשׁוּת *crookedness*). <CSTR> לְזוּת שְׂפָתַיִם *perversity of lips* Pr 4$_{24}$. <SYN> עִקְּשׁוּת *crookedness*.
⇒ לוז *depart*.*

לַח 6.0.3 adj. **moist**—לַח, לַחִים—**moist, fresh,** attributively of עֵנָב *grape* Nm 6$_3$ (:: יָבֵשׁ *dry*), עֵץ *tree* Ezk 17$_{24}$ 21$_3$ (both :: יָבֵשׁ) 1QH 3$_{29}$ 8$_{19}$ ([עץ]), יֶתֶר *cord* Jg 16$_{7.8}$ (both + אֲשֶׁר לֹא־חֹרָבוּ *that have not been dried*), מַקֵּל *rod* Gn 30$_{37}$, דֶּמַע *tribute* 3QTr 11$_{14}$ (לאח; others לֵאָה I *Leah* or II *aloe*). Also 4QBapt 1.1$_2$. <ANT> יָבֵשׁ *dry*.
⇒ לֵחַ *moisture*, לֵחָה *liquid*.*

[לֵחַ] 1.1 n.m. **moisture**—sf. לֵחֹה, 3fs Si לחה—**moisture** of tree (Jr 11$_{19}$ [if em.; see Prep.]), of tear from eye (Si 34$_{13}$), **freshness, vigour,** or perh. **smoothness** (of skin)* of person (Dt 34$_7$ Is 51$_{14}$ [if em.; see Subj.] Zp 1$_{17}$ [if em.; see Subj.] Ps 104$_{14}$ [if em.; see Obj.]), <SUBJ> נוס *flee*, i.e. flow,* or נסס *be dry* Dt 34$_7$ Si 34$_{13}$, שׁפך pu. *be poured out* Zp 1$_{17}$ (if em. לְחֻמָם *their flesh* to לֵחָם *their vigour*), חסר *be lacking* Is 51$_{14}$ (if em. לַחְמוֹ *his bread* to לֵחוֹ/לֵחֹמוֹ *his vigour*). <OBJ> יצא hi. *bring out* Ps 104$_{14}$ (if em. לֶחֶם *bread* to לֵחַ *freshness*). <PREP> בְּ of accompaniment, *with, in (a state of)*, + שׁחת hi. *destroy* Jr 11$_{19}$ (if em. בְּלַחְמוֹ *with its bread*, i.e. fruit, to בְּלֵחוֹ *in its vigour*).
⇒ לַח *moist*.*

[לֵחָה] 0.0.4 n.f. **liquid**—Q לחה; cstr. Q לחת—<NOM CL> לחת המוצקות והמקבל מהמה כהם לחה אחת *liquid of the streams*, i.e. poured out, *and in the receptacle for them*, i.e. the outpourings, *are (regarded as) the same liquid* 4QMMT B$_{57}$. <CSTR> לחת טל *liquid of dew* 4QTohA 2.2$_5$, מים *of water* 11QT 49$_{12}$, perh. לחת מי נדה *liquid of water of impurity* 4QTohB^c 1$_5$ (WA, EW ק]לחת] *pot of*), לחת המוצקות והמקבל *liquid of the streams*, i.e. poured out, *and of the receptacle* 4QMMT B$_{57}$, perh. ליחות עולם *liquids of eternity* 4QRitPur 12$_4$ (Baillet לוחות *tablets*); לחת ... תגאולת *defilement of ... moisture of* 11QT 49$_{12}$. <PREP> בְּ perh. of instrument, *by (means of)* 4QRitPur 12$_4$ (Baillet בלוחות *on tablets of*); מִן partitive, *from, (some) of*, + אכל *eat* 4QTohA 2.2$_5$. <ADJ> אֶחָד *one* 4QMMT B$_{58}$.
⇒ לַח *moist*.*

[לְחוּם] I 2 n.[m.] **flesh**—sf. לְחוּמוֹ, לְחֻמָם—**flesh, body, bowel(s),** <SUBJ> המה *make a noise* or *waste away* Jb 6$_7$ (if em. הֵמָּה כִּדְוֵי לַחְמִי *they are like the sickness of my food* to הֹמֶה כִּדְוַי לְחֻמִי *my bowels growl with*, or *waste away like, an echo*), שׁפך pu. *be poured out* Zp 1$_{17}$ (or em. לְחֻמָם *their flesh* to לֵחָם *their vigour*, or רַחֲמֵהֶם *their bowels*; ∥ דָּם *blood*). <NOM CL> שֹׁרֶשׁ רְתָמִים לְחוּמָם *their flesh is the root of broom* Jb 30$_4$ (if em. לַחְמָם *their food*). <PREP> בְּ of place, *on(to)*, + מטר hi. *rain* Jb 20$_{23}$ (unless לחום II *warfare*; or em. עָלֵימוֹ בִּלְחוּמוֹ *upon him, on his flesh* to עָלָיו מַבֵּל חֲמוֹ rain *upon him the fire of his wrath* or em. בִּלְחוּמוֹ to בְּלַחְמוֹ *as his bread* or חֲבָלִים *pains* or בַּלָּהוֹת *terrors*; + חֲרוֹן אַפּוֹ *the burning of his anger*). <SYN> דָּם *blood*.*

* **[לְחוּם]** II 1 n.[m.] **warfare**—sf. לְחוּמוֹ—**warfare** or **anger,** <PREP> בְּ of accompaniment, *in (a state of), with,* + מטר hi. *rain* Jb 20$_{23}$ (unless לחום I *flesh*; + חֲרוֹן אַפּוֹ *his fierce anger*).
⇒ לחם I *fight*.

לְחִי I $_{20.1.2}$ n.f. **jaw**—לְחִי; cstr. לְחִי; sf. לֶחֱיוֹ, לֶחֱיָהּ; du. לְחָיַיִם; cstr. לְחָיֵי; sf. לְחָיַי (לְחָיָי), לְחָיַיִךְ, לְחָיָו, לְחָיֵיהֶם—**1. jaw(bone)** of ass (Jg $15_{15.16.16.17}$), of Leviathan (Jb 40_{26}), of human being (e.g. Is 30_{28} Ezk 38_4), <OBJ> מצא *find* Jg 15_{15}, שׁלך hi. *throw* Jg 15_{17}, נקב *pierce* Jb 40_{26} (+ אַף *nose*). <CSTR> לְחִי חֲמוֹר *the jawbone of an ass* Jg $15_{15.16.16}$ (both הַחֲמוֹר), לְחָיֵי עַמִּים *jaws of (the) peoples* Is 30_{28}. <ADJ> טְרִיָּה *fresh* Jg 15_{15}. <PREP> בְּ of place, *in*, + נתן *give*, i.e. place, hooks Ezk 29_4 38_4; of instrument, *by (means of), with*, + חמר *flay* Jg 15_{16} (if em. חֲמוֹר חֲמֹרָתָיִם *a heap, two heaps* to חָמוֹר חֲמַרְתִּים *I have utterly flayed them*), נכה hi. *strike* Jg 15_{16} (or em.) 15_{16}; עַל *upon* Is 30_{28}, + רום hi. *raise* yoke Ho 11_4 (or em. עֹל *yoke* to עָל raise *suckling* to face, as §2a). <COLL> כָּל־הַיּוֹם לֹחֵם יִלְחָצֵנִי *all day long he oppresses*, i.e. slanders, *me with both jaws* Ps 56_2 (if em. לֹחֵם *a warrior* oppresses me).*

2. cheek, a. of human being (perh. at Ca 5_{13} לְחִי IV *hip*), <SUBJ> נאה pilel *be comely* Ca 1_{10} (|| צַוָּאר *neck*). <NOM CL> לְחָיָו כַּעֲרוּגַת הַבֹּשֶׂם *his cheeks are like a bed of spices* Ca 5_{13} (mss כַּעֲרוּגֹת *as beds of*). <OBJ> נתן *give*, i.e. offer, for striking Is 50_6 (|| גֵּו *back*, + פָּנִים *face*) Lm 3_{30}, נכה hi. *strike* Ps 3_8 (as second obj.; first obj. אֹיֵב *enemy*; or em. לְחִי to חִנָּם strike those who, *without cause*, + שֵׁן *tooth*) Jb 16_{10}. <PREP> עַל *upon* Lm 1_2 4QapLam^a 2_9, + נכה hi. *strike* 1 K 22_{24}||2 C 18_{23} Mc 4_{14}, ירד *go down* (of tear) Si 32_{18}.

b. of sacrificial beast, due to priest (Dt 18_3 11QT 20_{16} 22_{10}), <SUBJ> היה *be* appar. 11QT 22_{10}. <OBJ> נתן *give* Dt 18_3 (or em. חֲלָבִים *fat parts*; || זְרוֹעַ *shoulder*, קֵבָה *stomach*), רום hi. *raise*, i.e. offer 11QT 20_{16} ([לחיים]) 22_{10}, נוף hi. *wave* 11QT 20_{16}. <APP> תְּרוּמָה *offering* 11QT 20_{16} ([תו]נופה ... [לחיים]), תְּנוּפָה *wave offering* 11QT 20_{16}.*

<SYN> §2a צַוָּאר *neck*, גֵּו *back*; §2b זְרוֹעַ *shoulder*, קֵבָה *stomach*.

[לְחִי] II $_5$ pl.n. **Lehi**—לֶחִי—in lowland area of Judah, near Philistine territory, <CSTR> רָמַת לֶחִי *Ramath-lehi* Jg 15_{17}. <PREP> בְּ of place, *in* Jg $15_{19.19}$, + נטשׁ ni. *be spread out* Jg 15_9; עַד *unto*, + בוא *come* Jg 15_{14}; ה- of direction, *to, at Lehi*, + אסף ni. *be gathered* 2 S 23_{11} (if em. לַחַיָּה *into a troop* to לֶחֱיָה *to Lehi*).

[לְחִי] III n.[m.] **curse**, <PREP> בְּ of instrument, *by (means of), with*, + שׁוב hi. *bring back* Dn 11_{18} (if em. בִּלְתִּי *but rather* to בְּלֶחִי *with a curse*).

* **[לְחִי] IV** n.[m.] **hip, buttock** (unless לְחִי I *cheek*), <NOM CL> לְחָיָו כַּעֲרוּגַת הַבֹּשֶׂם *his hips are like a bed of spices* Ca 5_{13} (and exchange 5_{13} with 5_{16}).

→ לַח *moist*.

לְחַי רֹאִי, see בְּאֵר לַחַי רֹאִי *Beer-lahai-roi*.

לְחִית, see לוּחִית *Luhith*.

לחך $_{6.0.2}$ vb. **lick—Qal** $_1$ Inf. לְחֹךְ—**lick up, eat,** <SUBJ> שׁוֹר *ox* Nm 22_4. <OBJ> יֶרֶק *grass* Nm 22_4.

Pi. $_{5.0.1}$ Pf. לִחֲכָה; impf. יְלַחֲכוּ (יְלַחֲכוּ)—**lick (up), eat,** <SUBJ> מֶלֶךְ *king* Is 49_{23} (+ שׁחה htpal. *bow down*), שָׂרָה *princess* Is 49_{23}, אֹיֵב *enemy* Ps 72_9 (+ כרע *kneel*), מְעַנֶּה *oppressor* 1QM 1_{15} ([ילחכו])=4QM^b 1_7, גּוֹי *nation* Mc 7_{17}, קָהָל *congregation* Nm 22_4, אֵשׁ *fire* 1 K 18_{38} (+ אכל *eat*) Am 5_6 (if em. יִצְלַח כָּאֵשׁ lest *he sweep upon* the house of Joseph *like fire* to יְלַחֵךְ אֵשׁ lest *a fire lick* the house of Joseph).* <OBJ> רֶגֶל *foot* 4QM^b 1_7, מַיִם *water* 1 K 18_{38}, עָפָר *dust* Is 49_{23} Mc 7_{17} Ps 72_9 1QM 1_{15} ([ילחכו]), סָבִיב *surrounding (area)* Nm 22_4, בַּיִת *house* of Joseph Am 5_6 (if em.). <PREP> כְּ *as*, + נָחָשׁ *snake* Mc 7_{17}, זחל ptc. *crawling thing* Mc 7_{17}.*

Also 1Q25 6_3.

לחם I $_{171.2.10}$ vb. **fight—Qal** $_5$ Impv. לְחַם; ptc. לֹחֵם, לֹחֲמִים, לֹחֲמַי—**1. fight,** לְחַם אֶת־לֹחֲמָי ... יי *O Y. ..., fight (with) my adversaries* Ps 35_1 (|| ריב *strive*). **2.** ptc. as noun, **adversary, warrior,** לְחַם אֶת־לֹחֲמָי ... יי *O Y. ..., fight (with) my adversaries* Ps 35_1, כָּל־הַיּוֹם לֹחֵם יִלְחָצֵנִי appar. *all the day an adversary oppresses me* Ps 56_2 (or em. לְחָיִם *[with] both jaws* he oppresses me), כִּי־רַבִּים לֹחֲמִים לִי *for many are my adversaries* Ps 56_3. **3.** pass., **be embattled, be battered,*** מְזֵי רָעָב לְחֻמֵי רֶשֶׁף *(they will be) squeezed by famine, battered by plague* Dt 32_{24} (unless לחם II *eat*). <SYN> §1 ריב *strive*.

Ni. $_{167.2.10}$ Pf. נִלְחַם (נִלְחָם) נִלְחֲמוּ (נִלְחֲמוּ), נִלְחַמְתִּי; impf. יִלָּחֵם (יִלָּחֶם), 3fs תִּלָּחֵם, תִּלָּחֲמוּ (תִּלָּחֲמוּן), נִלָּחֵם (נִלָּחֲמָה); + waw וְנִלְחַם, וְנִלְחַמְתָּ, וְנִלְחַמְתִּי, וְנִלְחֲמוּ, וְנִלְחַמְתֶּם, וְנִלְחַמְנוּ; וַיִּלָּחֶם, וַיִּלָּחֲמוּ (וַיִּלָּחֲמוּנִי); impv. הִלָּחֵם (הִלָּחֶם), הִלָּחֲמוּ; ptc. נִלְחָם, נִלְחָמִים; inf. הִלָּחֵם (הִלָּחֶם, הִלָּחֲמוֹ, Q ללחם), נִלְחֹם, **fight, wage war, enter battle,** <SUBJ> Y. Ex 14$_{14.25}$ Dt 1$_{30}$ 3$_{22}$ 20$_4$ Jos 10$_{14.42}$ 23$_{3.10}$ Is 30$_{32}$ (or em. נִלְחַם *he has fought* to נָחֹלוּ dances *have been danced*) 63$_{10}$ Jr 21$_5$ Zc 14$_{3.3}$ Ne 4$_{14}$ 2 C 20$_{29}$ 32$_8$ Si 4$_{28}$ 1QM 10$_4$ 11$_8$ perh. 11$_{17}$ 4QPrayer^m 1.2$_1$, divine being Dn 10$_{20}$, Abimelech Jg 9$_{45.52}$, Balak Nm 22$_{11}$ Jos 24$_9$ Jg 11$_{25.25}$, Ben-hadad 1 K 20$_1$, David 1 S 17$_{33}$ 18$_{17}$ 19$_8$ 23$_5$ 29$_8$ 2 S 8$_{10}$||1 C 18$_{10}$ 2 S 12$_{29}$ 21$_{15}$ Si 47$_6$, Gaal Jg 9$_{38.39}$, Gideon Jg 8$_1$, Goliath 1 S 17$_{10}$, Hazael 2 K 12$_{18}$, Jehoash/Joash 2 K 13$_{12}$ 14$_{15}$, Jehoshaphat 1 K 22$_{46}$ 2 C 20$_{17}$, Jephthah Jg 11$_{6.8.9.32}$ 12$_{1.4}$, Jeroboam (son of Nebat) 1 K 14$_{19}$, Jeroboam (son of J[eh]oash) 2 K 14$_{28}$, Joab 2 S 12$_{26.27}$, Johanan Jr 41$_{12}$, J(eh)oram 2 K 8$_{29}$||2 C 22$_6$ 2 K 9$_{15}$, Joshua Ex 17$_{9.10}$ Jos 10$_{29.31.34.36.38}$ Si 46$_3$ (נל[חם]), Josiah 2 C 35$_{22.22}$, Jotham 2 C 27$_5$, Nebuchadrezzar Jr 21$_2$ 34$_1$, Neco 2 C 35$_{20}$, Pekah 2 K 16$_5$ Is 7$_1$, Rehoboam 1 K 12$_{21.24}$||2 C 11$_{1.4}$, Rezin 2 K 16$_5$ Is 7$_1$, Sanballat Ne 4$_2$, Saul 1 S 14$_{47}$ 15$_{18}$ 1 S 17$_{19}$, Sihon Nm 21$_{23.26}$ Jg 11$_{20}$, Sisera 1 S 12$_9$, Tirhakah 2 K 19$_9$||Is 37$_9$, Tobiah Ne 4$_2$, Uzziah 2 C 26$_6$.

Israel(ites) Dt 1$_{41.42}$ 20$_{10}$=11QT 62$_6$ Dt 20$_{19}$ Jos 10$_{25.34.36}$ 2 S 11$_{20}$ Jr 21$_4$ 32$_5$ 2 C 11$_4$ 4QpsEzek^c 2$_7$ 4QM^h 1$_3$, Benjamin 1 K 12$_{24}$||2 C 11$_4$, Judah Jg 1$_{3.5}$ Zc 14$_{14}$ 2 C 20$_{17}$, Simeon Jg 1$_3$, Amalekites Ex 17$_8$, Ammonites Ne 4$_2$, Amorites Jos 24$_{8.11}$, Arabs Ne 4$_2$, Aram 2 S 10$_{17}$||1 C 19$_{17}$, Ashdodites Ne 4$_2$, Assyrians 4QpIsa^a 5$_{11}$, Canaanite(s) Nm 21$_1$ Jos 24$_{11}$, Chaldaeans Jr 32$_{24.29}$ 37$_{8.10}$, Girgashites Jos 24$_{11}$, Hittites Jos 24$_{11}$, Hivites Jos 24$_{11}$, Jebusites Jos 24$_{11}$, Perizzites Jos 24$_{11}$, Philistines 1 S 4$_{9.10}$ 12$_9$ 13$_5$ 23$_1$ 28$_{1.15}$ 31$_1$||1 C 10$_1$, עַם *people* Ex 1$_{10}$ 2 S 2$_{28}$ 1 K 12$_{24}$ Jr 1$_{19}$ 15$_{20}$ 34$_1$ Ne 4$_8$, עֵדָה *congregation* 1QM 2$_{10.11.11.12.12.13}$, בַּיִת *house* 1 K 12$_{21}$||2 C 11$_1$ 1 K 12$_{24}$ Zc 10$_5$, עִיר *city* Is 19$_2$, מַמְלָכָה *kingdom* Is 19$_2$ Jr 34$_1$ 2 C 17$_{10}$, גֹּלָה *exiles* 1QM 1$_2$.

אִישׁ *man* Jg 10$_{18}$ 12$_3$ 1 S 17$_{9.10.19}$ 2 S 11$_{17}$ Is 19$_2$ 4QpsEzek^c 2$_7$, אָב *father* Jg 9$_{17}$, בֵּן *son* Nm 22$_{11}$ Jos 19$_{47}$ 24$_9$ Jg 1$_{8.9}$ 10$_9$ 11$_{4.5}$ 2 K 16$_5$ Is 7$_1$ Jr 41$_{12}$ 2 C 13$_{12}$ 1QM 1$_{2.11}$, אָח *brother* Jg 1$_3$, מֶלֶךְ *king* Nm 21$_{1.26}$ 22$_{11}$ Jos 9$_2$ 10$_5$ 11$_5$ 24$_9$ Jg 5$_{19.19}$ 11$_{12.27}$ 1 S 8$_{20}$ 12$_9$ 2 K 3$_{21}$ 6$_8$ 8$_{29}$ 9$_{15}$ 12$_{18}$ 16$_5$ 19$_{8.9}$||Is 37$_{8.9}$ Is 7$_1$ Jr 1$_{19}$ 21$_2$ 34$_1$ Dn 11$_{11}$ 2 C 11$_4$ 20$_{17}$ 35$_{20}$, שַׂר *prince* 1 S 12$_9$ 1 K 22$_{31.32}$||2 C 18$_{30.31}$ 2 K 10$_3$ Jr 1$_{19}$ 41$_{12}$, אָדוֹן *lord* 1 S 25$_{28}$, בַּעַל *lord* Jos 24$_{11}$, תַּרְתָּן *commander* Is 20$_1$, סָגָן *ruler* Ne 4$_8$, חֹר *noble* Ne 4$_8$, גִּבּוֹר *warrior* Jr 51$_{30}$, עֶבֶד *servant* 1 S 17$_{32}$ 2 S 21$_{15}$ 1 K 20$_{23.25}$, כֹּהֵן *priest* Jr 1$_{19}$, זָקֵן *elder* Jg 11$_6$, אֹהֵב *friend* Si 37$_5$, אֹיֵב *enemy* Jr 34$_{22}$, בקשׁ pi. ptc. *one who seeks* life Jr 34$_{22}$, רָשָׁע *wicked one* Ps 109$_3$, בחר pass. ptc. *chosen one* 1 K 12$_{21}$||2 C 11$_1$, יֹשֵׁב *inhabitant* 2 C 20$_{17}$, חַיִל *army* Jr 34$_{1.7.22}$, גּוֹרָל *lot* 1QM 1$_{11}$, כּוֹכָב *star* Jg 5$_{20.20}$, מִי *who?* Jg 1$_1$; subj. not specified, Jr 33$_5$.

<OBJ> מִלְחָמָה *war* 1 S 8$_{20}$ 18$_{17}$ 25$_{28}$ 2 C 32$_8$ Si 46$_3$ 4QM^h 1$_3$, worshipper Ps 109$_3$.

<PREP> לְ *for, on behalf of,* + Israel(ites) Ex 14$_{25}$ Dt 1$_{30}$ 3$_{22}$ 20$_4$ Jos 10$_{14.42}$ 23$_{3.10}$ 1QM 10$_4$, עַם *people* Ex 14$_{14}$ Ne 4$_{14}$, בֵּן *son* Si 4$_{28}$, חֹר *noble* Ne 4$_{14}$, סָגָן *ruler* Ne 4$_{14}$, גְּבוּרָה *might* 1QM 1$_{11}$.

בְּ of place/time, *in, at, on,* + Carchemish 2 C 35$_{20}$, Keilah 1 S 23$_1$, Rephidim Ex 17$_8$, Taanach Jg 5$_{19}$, מִישׁוֹר *plain* 1 K 20$_{23.25}$, בִּקְעָה *valley* 2 C 35$_{22}$, יוֹם *day* Zc 14$_3$, שָׁנָה *year* 1QM 2$_{10.11.11.12.12.13}$, appar. זֹאת *this (battle)* 2 C 20$_{17}$; of instrument, *by (means of), with,* + כְּלִי *weapon* Jr 21$_4$, יָד *hand* Jr 21$_5$, זְרוֹעַ *arm* Jr 21$_5$; of accompaniment, *with,* + אַף *anger* Jr 21$_5$, חֵמָה *anger* Jr 21$_5$, קֶצֶף *anger* Jr 21$_5$, קוֹל *voice* 1QM 1$_{11}$, תְּרוּעָה *shout* 1QM 1$_{11}$.

בְּ *against* 1QM 11$_{17}$ 4QPrayer^m 1.2$_1$, + Abimelech Jg 9$_{39}$, Adoni-bezek Jg 1$_5$, Hadadezer 2 S 8$_{10}$||1 C 18$_{10}$, Jephthah Jg 11$_{27}$ 12$_3$, Neco 2 C 35$_{22}$, Saul 1 S 28$_{15}$, Israel(ites) Nm 21$_{1.23}$ Jos 24$_{9.11}$ Jg 11$_{20(mss).25}$ 1 S 12$_9$ 28$_1$ 31$_1$||1 C 10$_1$ 2 K 6$_8$, Benjamin Jg 10$_9$, Judah Jg 10$_9$, Amalekites Ex 17$_{9.10}$ 1 S 15$_{18}$, Aram-naharaim 1QM 2$_{10}$, Assyria Is 30$_{32}$ (or em. נִלְחַם *he has fought* against to נָחֹלוּ dances *have been danced* over), Canaanites Jg 1$_{1.3.9}$, Edom 1 S 14$_{47}$, Egypt(ians) Ex 1$_{10}$ 14$_{25}$, Hul 1QM 2$_{11}$, Mesha 1QM 2$_{11}$, Midian Jg 8$_1$, Moab 1 S 14$_{47}$ 2 K 3$_{21}$, Persia 1QM 2$_{12}$, Philistines 1 S 14$_{47}$ 19$_8$ 23$_5$ 2 C 26$_6$, Ashdod Is 20$_1$, Jerusalem Jg 1$_8$ Zc 14$_{14}$ Ne 4$_2$, Lachish Jos 10$_{31}$, Rabbah 2 S 12$_{26.27.29}$, Samaria 1 K 20$_1$, Togar 1QM 2$_{11}$, Uz 1QM 2$_{11}$, עַם *people* Nm 22$_{11}$ Jg 9$_{38}$ Is 63$_{10}$,

גּוֹי *nation* Zc 14$_{3}$, מַמְלָכָה *kingdom* Is 19$_{2}$, עִיר *city* Jg 9$_{45}$ Is 19$_{2}$, אֶרֶץ *land* Jg 11$_{12}$ 4QPrEnosh 2$_{2}$ (בכול אר[צות]), בַּיִת *house* Jg 10$_{9}$, בֵּן *son* Jg 10$_{18}$ 11$_{6.8.9.32}$ 12$_{1}$ 1 S 14$_{47}$ 1QM 1$_{2}$ 2$_{10.11.11.12.12.13}$, אָח *brother* Is 19$_{2}$, מֶלֶךְ *king* Nm 21$_{26}$ 1 S 14$_{47}$ 2 C 35$_{22}$ 1QM 1$_{4}$, רֵעַ *friend* Is 19$_{2}$ 4QpsEzek[c] 2$_{7}$, אֹיֵב *enemy* 1 S 14$_{47}$ 29$_{8}$ 1QM 11$_{8}$, חַיִל *army* 1QM 1$_{2}$, גְּדוּד *troop* 1QM 1$_{2}$, מַרְשִׁיעַ *wicked one* 1QM 1$_{2}$, קַדְמֹנִי *easterner* 1QM 2$_{12}$, רוּחַ *spirit* 4QPrayer[d] 1.1$_{4}$, מִגְדָּל *tower* Jg 9$_{52}$.

כְּ *according to*, + כֹּל *everything* Dt 1$_{30.41}$.

מִן of direction, *from*, + שָׁמַיִם *heaven* Jg 5$_{20}$, מְסִלָּה *path* Jg 5$_{20}$.

אֶל *against*, + Jeremiah Jr 1$_{19}$ 15$_{20}$, Chaldaeans Jr 33$_{5(mss)}$.

עַל *against*, + Israel(ites) Jr 21$_{2}$, Debir Jos 10$_{38}$, Eglon Jos 10$_{34}$, Gath 2 K 12$_{18}$, Hebron Jos 10$_{36}$, Gibeon Jos 10$_{5}$, Jerusalem Is 7$_{1}$ Jr 34$_{1.7}$, Libnah Jos 10$_{29(mss)}$ 2 K 19$_{8}$||Is 37$_{8}$, עִיר *city* Dt 20$_{10}$=11QT 62$_{6}$ Dt 20$_{19}$ Jr 32$_{24.29}$ 34$_{1.7.22}$ 37$_{8}$.

עַל *for, on behalf of*, + אִשָּׁה *wife* Ne 4$_{8}$, בַּת *daughter* Ne 4$_{8}$, בֵּן *son* Ne 4$_{8}$, אָח *brother* Ne 4$_{8}$, בַּעַל *lord* Jg 9$_{17}$, בַּיִת *house* 2 K 10$_{3}$ Ne 4$_{8}$.

עִם *against*, 4QS[z] 3$_{5}$ + Y. 2 C 13$_{12}$, Amaziah 2 K 13$_{12}$ 14$_{15}$, David 2 S 10$_{17}$||1 C 19$_{17}$, Ishmael Jr 41$_{12}$, Jehoshaphat 2 C 17$_{10}$, Joshua Jos 9$_{2}$, Sisera Jg 5$_{20}$, Israel(ites) Ex 17$_{8}$ Jos 9$_{2}$ 11$_{5}$ Jg 11$_{4.5.20}$ 1 S 13$_{5}$ 2 C 11$_{1}$, Philistine(s) 1 S 17$_{19.32.33}$, Leshem Jos 19$_{47}$, Libnah Jos 10$_{29}$ (mss עַל *against*), בֵּן *son* 1 K 12$_{24}$ Jr 41$_{12}$, אָח *brother* 1 K 12$_{24}$||2 C 11$_{4}$, מֶלֶךְ *king* 2 K 13$_{12}$ 14$_{15}$ Dn 11$_{11}$ 2 C 27$_{5}$, שַׂר *commander* Dn 10$_{20}$, בַּיִת *house* 1 K 12$_{21}$, אֹיֵב *enemy* Dt 20$_{4}$ 2 C 20$_{29}$ 1QM 10$_{4}$, זָר *stranger* Si 37$_{5}$.

אֵת *against*, + Israel(ites) Jos 24$_{8}$ 1 K 20$_{23.25}$ Jr 21$_{5}$ 37$_{10}$, Ephraim Jg 12$_{4}$, Chaldaeans Jr 21$_{5}$ 32$_{5}$ 33$_{5}$ (mss אֶל *against*), Philistines 2 S 21$_{15}$, Goliath 1 S 17$_{9}$, Hazael 2 K 8$_{29}$||2 C 22$_{6}$ 2 K 9$_{15}$, Joab 2 S 11$_{17}$, מֶלֶךְ *king* 1 K 22$_{31}$||2 C 18$_{30}$ 2 K 8$_{29}$||2 C 22$_{6}$ 2 K 9$_{15}$ 19$_{9}$||Is 37$_{9}$ Jr 21$_{5}$, אֹיֵב *enemy* Jos 10$_{25}$ (אוֹתָם), קָטֹן *small one* 1 K 22$_{31}$||2 C 18$_{30}$, גָּדוֹל *great one* 1 K 22$_{31}$||2 C 18$_{30}$.

<COLL> with adverb or adverbial expression: פֶּה אֶחָד *(with) one mouth*, i.e. with one accord Jos 9$_{2}$, יַחַד *together* 1 S 17$_{10}$ 1QM 1$_{11}$, חִנָּם *gratuitously* Ps 109$_{3}$, כֹּל הַיּוֹם *all day* Jg 9$_{45}$, סָבִיב *round about* 1 S 14$_{47}$.

לחם ni. + חנה *encamp* Jos 10$_{5.31.34}$, צור *besiege* 1 K 20$_{1}$, נכה hi. *strike, defeat* Jos 19$_{47}$ Jg 1$_{5.8}$ 12$_{4}$ 1 S 17$_{9}$ 19$_{8}$ 23$_{5}$ 2 S 8$_{10}$||1 C 18$_{10}$, לכד *capture* Jos 10$_{38}$ 19$_{47}$ Jg 1$_{8}$ 9$_{45}$ 2 S 12$_{26.27.29}$ 2 K 12$_{18}$ Is 20$_{1}$ Jr 34$_{22}$ 37$_{8}$, ריב *strive* Jg 11$_{25}$, עזר *help* 2 C 32$_{8}$, כנע hi. *subdue* Si 47$_{6}$, חזק *be strong*, i.e. prevail 2 C 27$_{5}$, hi. *hold* shield Si 37$_{5}$, יכל *prevail* Jr 1$_{19}$ 15$_{20}$, צלח hi. *succeed* Jr 32$_{5}$ 2 C 13$_{12}$.

Also 1QSb 3$_{7}$ 1Q36 2$_{6}$.

⇒ לְחוּם II *warfare*, לֶחֶם II *war*, מִלְחָמָה *war*, לָחֵם *warrior*.

לחם II $_{6}$ vb. **eat—Qal** $_{6}$ Pf. לָחֲמוּ; impf. 2ms תִּלְחַם, אֶלְחַם; impv. לַחֲמוּ; ptc. לֹחֲמֵי; inf. לְחוֹם—**1. eat, destroy,** <SUBJ> רָשָׁע *wicked one* Pr 4$_{17}$, רַע *evil one* Pr 4$_{17}$, חֲסַר *one lacking* sense Pr 9$_{5}$ (|| שׁתה *drink*), חֵץ *arrow* Dt 32$_{24(Sam)}$, worshipper Ps 141$_{4}$; subj. not specified, Ob 7 (if em. לַחְמְךָ *your bread* to לֹחֲמֶיךָ *those who eat with you*) Pr 23$_{1.6}$. <OBJ> מָזֶה *one weakened* by hunger Dt 32$_{24(Sam)}$, לֶחֶם *bread* Pr 4$_{17}$ 23$_{6}$ (mss lack לֶחֶם). <PREP> בְּ partitive, *(some) of*, + לֶחֶם *bread* Pr 9$_{5}$, מַנְעַמִּים *delicacies* Ps 141$_{4}$; אֵת *with*, + מֹשֵׁל *ruler* Pr 23$_{1}$, רַע *one evil* of eye Pr 23$_{6(mss)}$.

2. pass., **be devoured,** מְזֵי רָעָב לְחֻמֵי רֶשֶׁף *(they will be) emaciated by famine, devoured by plague* Dt 32$_{24}$ (unless לחם I *fight*; Sam מזה רעב לחמו *on account of this, famine is his bread*).

<SYN> §1 שׁתה *drink*.*

⇒ לֶחֶם I *bread*.

לָחֵם $_{1}$ n.[m.] perh. **warrior,** אָז לָחֵם שְׁעָרִים perh. *was then a warrior (at) the gates?* Jg 5$_{8}$ (or em. מֵאָז לֹא לָהֶם שְׂעָרִים *unknown to them from of old* (from שׂער III *be acquainted*) or אָז לֶחֶם שְׂעֹרִים *when they had barley bread* or אָזַל לֶחֶם שְׂעֹרִים *the barley bread was exhausted* or אָז לְחָמֵשׁ עָרִים *then for five cities* no shield was seen).

⇒ לחם I *fight*.

לֶחֶם I $_{297.12.40.6}$ n.m. (f. at Gn 49$_{20}$ 1 S 10$_{4}$)* **bread**—לָחֶם; cstr. לֶחֶם; sf. לַחְמִי, לַחְמְךָ לַחְמֶךָ (לחמכה Q), לַחְמָם, לַחְמְכֶם, לַחְמֵנוּ, לַחְמָהּ, לַחְמוֹ.

1. bread, as distinct from other foods, sometimes specif. **loaf of bread** (e.g. Lv 23$_{17}$ 1 S 10$_{4}$ 17$_{17}$ 21$_{4}$ 25$_{18}$

2 S 16$_{1}$ 1 K 14$_{3}$ 2 K 4$_{42}$ Lachish ost. 9$_{3}$ Arad ost. 2$_{4}$ 3$_{7}$ 6$_{4}$ 10$_{3}$), Gn 25$_{34}$ 27$_{17}$ 45$_{23}$ Lv 26$_{26.26}$ Jos 9$_{12}$ Jg 7$_{13}$ 8$_{5}$ 1 S 2$_{36.36}$ 10$_{3}$ 21$_{5.7}$ 25$_{11}$ 2 S 6$_{19}$ 16$_{1.2}$ 1 K 17$_{6.6.11}$ Is 44$_{15.19}$ Jr 37$_{21.21}$ Ezk 4$_{9.16.17}$ Hg 2$_{21}$ Ps 104$_{15}$ Pr 6$_{26}$ 28$_{21}$ Ru 2$_{14}$ 1 C 16$_{3}$ Arad ost. 1$_{8}$ 5$_{6}$ 12$_{6}$, as distinct from other forms of cereal produce, Lv 23$_{14}$;* placed on table in sanctuary, Ex 25$_{30}$ 35$_{13}$ 39$_{36}$ 40$_{23}$ Lv 24$_{7}$ Nm 4$_{7}$ 1 S 21$_{5.7.7}$ 22$_{13}$ 1 K 7$_{48}$||2 C 4$_{19}$ Ne 10$_{34}$ 1 C 9$_{32}$ 23$_{29}$ 2 C 13$_{11}$ 11QT 8$_{10.12.13}$; used in ritual for institution of priests, Ex 29$_{2.23.23.32.34}$ Lv 8$_{26.31.32}$ 11QT 15$_{3a.10.12}$; perh. eaten in sacrificial meal, Ex 18$_{12}$ Ezk 44$_{3}$; eaten unleavened at passover, Dt 16$_{3}$; presented as offering of first fruits, Lv 23$_{17.18.20}$ Nm 15$_{19}$ 2 K 4$_{42.42}$ 1QS 6$_{5.6}$ 4QHalakhah^{a} 5$_{6}$ 11QT 18$_{14.14}$ 19$_{6.7.12}$.

2. although distinction from preceding oft. uncertain, **food** in general.

a. including bread, as part of staple diet* or as main constituent of meal, Gn 3$_{19}$ 14$_{18}$ 18$_{5}$ 21$_{14}$ 28$_{20}$ 31$_{54.54}$ 37$_{25}$ 39$_{6}$ 43$_{25.31.32}$ 49$_{20}$ Ex 2$_{20}$ 16$_{3}$ 23$_{25}$ 34$_{28}$ Lv 26$_{5.26}$ Nm 21$_{5.5}$ Dt 8$_{3.9}$ 9$_{9.18}$ 10$_{18}$ 23$_{5}$ 29$_{5}$ Jos 9$_{5}$ Jg 8$_{6.15}$ 13$_{16}$ 19$_{5.19}$ 1 S 9$_{7}$ 14$_{24.24.28}$ 16$_{20}$ 20$_{24.34}$ 28$_{20.22}$ 30$_{11.12}$ 2 S 3$_{29.35.35}$ 9$_{7.10.10}$ 12$_{17.20.21}$ 13$_{5}$ 1 K 5$_{2.23}$ 13$_{8.9.15.16.17.18.19.22.22.23}$ 18$_{4.13}$ 21$_{4.5.7}$ 22$_{27}$||2 C 18$_{26}$ 2 K 4$_{8.8}$ 6$_{22}$ 18$_{32}$||Is 36$_{17}$ 2 K 25$_{3.29}$||Jr 52$_{6.33}$ Is 3$_{1.7}$ 4$_{1}$ 21$_{14}$ 33$_{16}$ 51$_{14}$ (or em.; see Subj.) 55$_{2.10}$ 58$_{7.10(mss)}$ Jr 5$_{17}$ 38$_{9}$ 41$_{1}$ 42$_{14}$ 44$_{17}$ Ezk 4$_{13.15.16}$ 5$_{16}$ 12$_{18.19}$ 14$_{13}$ 16$_{19.49}$ 18$_{7.16}$ 48$_{18}$ Ho 9$_{4.4}$ (if em.; see Nom. Cl.) Am 4$_{6}$ 7$_{12}$ 8$_{11}$=4QpsEzek^{c} 2$_{9}$ Ob$_{7}$ (or em.; see Coll.) Ps 14$_{4}$||53$_{5}$ 37$_{25}$ 41$_{10}$ 78$_{20}$ 102$_{5.10}$ 104$_{14}$ (or em.; see Obj.) 105$_{16}$ 132$_{15}$ 136$_{25}$ 146$_{7}$ Jb 3$_{24}$ 6$_{7}$ (or em.; see Cstr.) 15$_{23}$ 20$_{14}$ 22$_{7}$ 27$_{14}$ 28$_{5}$ 33$_{20}$ 42$_{11}$ Pr 9$_{5.17}$ 12$_{9.11}$ 20$_{13}$ 22$_{9}$ 23$_{3.6}$ (mss lack לֶחֶם) 25$_{21}$ (or del. לֶחֶם) 28$_{3.19}$ 30$_{8.22}$ 31$_{14.27}$ Ru 1$_{6}$ Ec 9$_{7}$ 11$_{1}$ Lm 1$_{11}$ 4$_{4}$ 5$_{6.9}$ Dn 10$_{3}$ Ezr 10$_{6}$ Ne 5$_{15}$ 13$_{2}$ 1 C 12$_{41}$ Si 9$_{16}$ 14$_{10.10}$ 15$_{3}$ 34$_{12.23.24}$ 48$_{2}$ 1QH 5$_{23}$ 1QS 6$_{25}$ 1QSa 2$_{19.19.20.21}$ 4QSD 1.1$_{5.8.10}$ 4QD^{e} 3.2$_{19}$ 4QTohA 1.2$_{7}$ 4Q416 2.2$_{18.20}$.

Offered in sacrifice, Lv 3$_{11.16}$ 7$_{13}$ 21$_{6.8.17.21.22}$ 22$_{25}$ Nm 28$_{2.24}$ Ezk 44$_{7}$ Ml 1$_{7}$ 4QJub^{d} 2$_{19}$ 4QOrd^{c} 1.1$_{6.9}$; as livelihood of priestly families, Lv 22$_{7.11.13}$ Si 45$_{20}$ 4QHalakhah^{a} 11$_{1.2}$.

As payment for work (1 S 2$_{5}$ Ps 127$_{2}$), for prostitution (Ho 2$_{7}$ Pr 6$_{26}$ [§1]), gained by wickedness (Pr 4$_{17}$ 28$_{21}$ [§1]), deceit (Pr 20$_{17}$), assoc. with mourning (Ezk 24$_{17.22}$ [if em. in both; see Cstr.] Jr 16$_{7}$ [if em.; see Obj.] Ho 9$_{4}$), distress (Is 30$_{20}$ 1QH 5$_{33}$); Canaanites as food for conquering Israelites (Nm 14$_{9}$); body as food for maggots, 1QS 11$_{21}$.

b. food other than bread, Ps 42$_{4}$ 80$_{6}$ Jb 30$_{4}$ (or em.; see Nom. Cl.) Pr 27$_{27.27}$, specif. manna, Ex 16$_{4.8.12.15.22.29.32}$ Ps 78$_{25}$ 105$_{40}$ Ne 9$_{15}$).

c. flesh of sacrificial victims, Si 7$_{31}$.

d. food of animals, **fodder,** Is 65$_{25}$ Ps 147$_{9}$ Jb 24$_{5}$ Pr 6$_{8}$ 30$_{25}$.

e. fruit of tree, Jr 11$_{19}$ (or em.; see Prep.).

3. meal, 1 S 20$_{27}$ Ec 10$_{19}$ Si 41$_{19}$ (unless לֶחֶם II *war*); perh. Gn 31$_{54}$ 43$_{25}$ 2 K 25$_{29}$||Jr 52$_{33}$ Jr 41$_{1}$ Jb 42$_{11}$ (if in all six אכל לֶחֶם = 'eat a meal').*

4. food allowance, 1 K 11$_{18}$ Ne 5$_{14.18}$.

4. grain for producing bread, Is 28$_{28}$ 30$_{23}$, representative of food in general (distinction from §2a unclear), Gn 41$_{54.55}$ 47$_{12.13.15.17.17.19}$.

<SUBJ> היה *be* Gn 41$_{54}$ Nm 4$_{7}$ 1 S 21$_{7.7}$ 2 S 9$_{10}$ 1 K 5$_{2}$ 2 K 25$_{3}$||Jr 52$_{6}$ Ps 42$_{4}$ (+ דִּמְעָה *tears*) 11QT 8$_{13}$, נעם *be pleasant* Pr 9$_{17}$, ערב *be sweet* Pr 20$_{17}$, גאל pu. *be defiled* Ml 1$_{7}$ (or em. לֵחֹה/לְחָמוֹ *his vigour*), נתן ni. *be given* Is 33$_{16}$, סור ho. *be removed* 1 S 21$_{7}$, הפך ni. *be turned* Jb 20$_{14}$ 1QH 5$_{35}$ ([לְ]חמי), אפה ni. *be baked* Lv 23$_{17}$, דקק ho. *be crushed* Is 28$_{28}$, חסר *be lacking* Is 51$_{14}$, תמם *be finished* Jr 37$_{21}$, אזל *go*, i.e. be finished 1 S 9$_{7}$, בוא *come* 4QHalakhah^{a} 5$_{6}$, יצא *go out* Jb 28$_{5}$, סעד *sustain* Ps 104$_{15}$.

<NOM CL> הוּא הַלֶּחֶם *it is the bread* Ex 16$_{16}$, var. Pr 23$_{3}$, לַחְמוֹ הוּא *it is his food* Lv 22$_{7}$, לַחְמֵנוּ הֵם *they are our bread* Nm 14$_{9}$, יֵשׁ ... לֶחֶם *there is ... bread* Jg 19$_{19}$ 1 S 21$_{5}$, אֵין לֶחֶם (and vars.) *there is no bread* Gn 47$_{13}$ Nm 21$_{5}$ 1 S 21$_{5}$ Is 3$_{7}$ Jr 38$_{9}$ Pr 28$_{2}$, לֹא לַחֲכָמִים לֶחֶם *bread is not to the wise* Ec 9$_{11}$, עֲרָבָה לוֹ לֶחֶם appar. *the steppe is food for him* Jb 24$_{5}$ (or em. עֲרָבָה לוֹ לֶחֶם *the steppe; in case there is food*), שֹׁרֶשׁ רְתָמִים לַחְמָם perh. *the root of broom is their food* Jb 30$_{4}$ (or em. לְחֻמָּם *to warm themselves* or לְחוּמָם *their flesh*), עָפָר לַחְמוֹ *dust is his food* Is 65$_{25}$, לחם רמה מדורו perh. *his home is the food of maggots* 1QS 11$_{21}$, שְׁמֵנָה לַחְמוֹ *his food is fat* Gn 49$_{20}$ (Sam שָׁמֵן, i.e. masc.; or em. שֶׁמְּנָה Asher. *who rations* his bread),* כֹּל לֶחֶם צֵידָם יָבֵשׁ *all the food of their provisions was dry* Jos 9$_{5}$,

לַחְמָם לְנַפְשָׁם *their bread shall be for themselves* Ho 9_{4}, הַלֶּחֶם אֲשֶׁר בְּסַל הַמִּלֻּאִים *the bread that is in the basket of ordination* Lv 8_{31}, כְּלֶחֶם אוֹנִים לַחְמָם *their bread is like the bread of mourners* Ho 9_{4} (if em. לָהֶם *to them* to לַחְמָם), הַשֻּׁלְחָן אֲשֶׁר עָלָיו לֶחֶם הַפָּנִים *the table upon which is the bread of the presence* 1 K 7_{48} (∥2 C 4_{19} הַשֻּׁלְחָנוֹת וַעֲלֵיהֶם לֶחֶם הַפָּנִים *the tables, and upon them was the bread of the presence*), עֲלֵיהֶם מָאתַיִם לֶחֶם *upon them were two hundred loaves of bread* 2 S 16_{1}, זֶה לַחְמֵנוּ חָם *this bread of ours was hot* Jos 9_{12}.

<OBJ> אכל *eat* Gn 3_{19} $31_{54.54}$ 37_{25} 39_{6} $43_{25.32}$ Ex 2_{20} 16_{3} 18_{12} 29_{32} 34_{28} Lv 8_{31} 21_{22} 23_{14} 26_{5} Dt 8_{9} $9_{9.18}$ $14_{24.28}$ 16_{3} 20_{34} 28_{20} 29_{5} $30_{11.12}$ 2 S $9_{7.10.10}$ 12_{21} $16_{2(Qr)}$ 1 K $13_{8.9.15.16.17.18.19.22.22.23}$ $21_{4.5.7}$ 2 K $4_{8.8}$ 25_{29}∥Jr 52_{33} Is 4_{1} Jr 5_{17} 41_{1} Ezk 4_{13} (or del.) 4_{16} $12_{18.19}$ $24_{17.22}$ 44_{3} Am 7_{12} Ob 7 (if ins. אכל) Ps 14_{4}∥53_{5} 41_{10} 78_{25} 102_{5} 127_{2} Jb 42_{11} Pr 31_{27} Ec 9_{7} Dn 10_{3} Ezr 10_{6} Ne 5_{14} 1QH 5_{23}, hi. *feed* Ex 16_{32} 1 K 22_{27}∥2 C 18_{26} Ps 80_{6} Pr 25_{21} (or del. לֶחֶם) Si 15_{3} 4QHalakhah^{a} 11_{1} ([ואכל]ה) 11_{3} (לוא יאכלו את [לחם]) 4QD^{e} 3.2_{19} 4QOrd^{c} $1.1_{6.9}$ 11QT 19_{7} ([יואכלו]), ברה *eat* 2 S 12_{17}, hi. *feed* 2 S 3_{35} (mss כרה hi. *invite to eat*) 13_{5}, לחם *eat* Pr 4_{17} 23_{6} (or del.), טרף hi. *feed* Pr 30_{8}, כול pilp. *provide* Gn 47_{12} 1 K $18_{4.13}$, טעם *taste* 1 S 14_{24} 2 S 3_{35}.

נתן *give* Gn 25_{34} 28_{20} 47_{17} Ex $16_{8.15.29}$ Dt 10_{18} Jg $8_{6.15}$ 1 S 10_{4} 22_{13} 30_{11} 1 K 5_{23} 11_{18} (if em. וְלֶחֶם אָמַר לוֹ he gave him a house *and food he commanded for him* to וְלֶחֶם וַיֹּאמֶר לוֹ שֵׁב עִמָּדִי a house *and food and said to him, Stay with me*) Is $30_{20.23}$ 55_{10} Ezk 16_{19} $18_{7.16}$ Ho 2_{7} Ps 78_{20} 136_{25} 146_{7} 147_{9} Ru 1_{6} Ne 9_{15} Lachish ost. 9_{3} Arad ost. 2_{4} 10_{3} ([נתן] ... ל[ח]ם) 12_{6} ([ותן א]ת הלחם), *place* Gn 27_{17} Ex 25_{30} 1 S 21_{4}, יהב *give* Gn 47_{15}, פוק hi. *provide* Is $58_{10(mss)}$, בוא hi. *bring* Ex 39_{36} Lv 23_{17} 1 K $17_{6.6}$ 2 K 4_{42} Pr 31_{14} Lm 5_{9} 1 C 12_{41} (Gnz לָהֶם *to them*) 11QT 18_{14} 19_{12}, שׁוב hi. *bring back* Lv 26_{26}, יצא hi. *bring out* Gn 14_{18} Ps 104_{14} (or em. לֶחֶם *food* to לֵחַ *freshness*),* פרס *share* Is 58_{7} Jr 16_{7} (if em. לָהֶם *to them*) Lm 4_{4} (if em. לָהֶם or ins. לֶחֶם), שׂים *place* Gn 43_{31} 1 S 21_{7} 2 S 12_{20} 2 K 6_{22}, נגע *touch* 4QTohA 1.2_{7}, שׁלח pi. *send away*, i.e. cast, bread onto waters Ec 11_{1}, לקח *take* Gn 21_{14} Ex 29_{2} 1 S 17_{17} $25_{11.18}$ 1 K 14_{3}, לקט *gather* Ex 16_{22}, סור hi. *remove* 11QT 8_{12} ([הלחם]), בקשׁ pi. *seek* Ps 37_{25} Lm 1_{11} Ne 5_{18}, שׁאל *ask for* Lm 4_{4}, מצא *find* Ec 11_{1}, מנע *withhold* Jb 22_{7}, חסר *lack* Ezk 4_{17} 4Q416 2.2_{20}.

אפה *bake* Lv 26_{26} Is $44_{15.19}$, עשׂה *make* Gn 27_{17} Ex 35_{13} Nm 28_{24} Ezk 4_{15} Arad ost. 1_{8} 5_{6} ([לעשת]), *prepare* meal Ec 10_{19}, כון hi. *prepare* Pr 6_{8} 30_{25}, ערך *arrange* 11QT 8_{12} ([ובעורככה]), קרב hi. *bring near*, i.e. offer Lv $21_{6.8.17.21}$ 22_{25} Nm 28_{2} Ezk 44_{7}, נגשׁ hi. *bring near*, i.e. offer Ml 1_{7}, קטר hi. *burn as* Lv $3_{11.16}$ 4QJub^{d} 21_{9} (ל[חם]), ראה *see* Ex 16_{32}, ידע *know* Gn 39_{6}, מטר hi. *rain* Ex 16_{4}, רבה hi. *increase* Si 14_{10}, נשׂא *raise* Gn 45_{23}, ברך pi. *bless* Ex 23_{25}, זהם pi. *abhor* Jb 33_{20}, ספר *count* Arad ost. 3_{7}.

<CSTR> לֶחֶם אֱלֹהֶיךָ *bread of your God* Lv 21_{8}, אֱלֹהֵיהֶם *of their God* Lv 21_{6}, אֱלֹהֵיכֶם *of your God* Lv 22_{25}, אֱלֹהָיו *of his God* Lv $21_{17.21.22}$ (lacking in Sam), אַבִּירִים *of mighty ones* Ps 78_{25} Si 7_{31} (אברים appar. flesh *of bulls*, unless *of limbs [of sacrifices]*), אֲנָשִׁים *of men* Ezk $24_{17.22}$ (or em. אוֹנִים *of distress* or *of mourners* in both), לחם אישה *her husband's bread* 4QHalakhah^{a} 11_{1}, לֶחֶם־שְׁלֹמֹה *Solomon's food* 1 K 5_{2}, לֶחֶם אָבִיהָ *food of her father* Lv 22_{13}, הַפֶּחָה *of the governor* Ne $5_{14.18}$, רַע *of one who is evil of* eye Pr 23_{6} (mss lack לֶחֶם), בֵּיתֶךָ *of your household* Pr 27_{27}, בֵּיתִי *of my household* 1 K 5_{23}, לחם רמה *food of maggots* 1QS 11_{21}.

לֶחֶם שָׁמַיִם *bread of heaven* Ps 105_{40}, הַפָּנִים *of the presence* Ex 25_{30} (פָּנִים) 35_{13} 39_{36} 1 S 21_{7} 1 K 7_{48}∥2 C 4_{19},* הַמַּעֲרֶכֶת *of the array*, i.e. bread displayed on altar Ne 10_{34} 1 C 9_{32} (הַמַּעֲרָכֶת) 23_{29}, לֶחֶם הַתָּמִיד *the bread of continuity* Nm 4_{7} 2 K 25_{29} (unless וְאָכַל לֶחֶם תָּמִיד = *and he ate food always*),* שְׂעֹרִים *of barley* Jg 5_{8} (if em. לָחֶם שְׁעָרִים *a warrior was [at] the gates*) 7_{13} 2 K 4_{42}, לחם חטים *bread of wheat* 11QT 18_{14}, לֶחֶם מַצּוֹת *bread (consisting) of unleavened bread* Ex 29_{2} 4QD^{e} $3.2a_{1}$ (ל[ח]ם [המצ]ות), שֶׁמֶן *of*, i.e. with, *oil* Ex 29_{23} Lv 8_{26}, חֹם *of heat* 1 S 21_{7} (or em. חֹם to חַם *hot* bread), חֹל *of profaneness* 1 S 21_{5}, קֹדֶשׁ *of holiness* 1 S 21_{5} 4QHalakhah^{a} 11_{3} ([לחם הקודש]), ל[חם אשה] *bread of a fire offering* 4QJub^{d} 21_{9}, לֶחֶם אִשֶּׁה *bread of a fire offering* Lv $3_{11.16}$ Nm 28_{24} (אִשֶּׁה), לַחְמִי אִשַּׁי *food(s) of my fire offerings* Nm 28_{2} (if em. לַחְמִי לְאִשַּׁי *my food as my fire offerings*), לֶחֶם תְּנוּפָה *bread of waving*, i.e. to be waved Lv 23_{17}, הַבִּכּוּרִים *of the firstfruits* Lv 23_{20} 2 K 4_{42} (בִּכּוּרִים) 4QHalakhah^{a} 5_{6} 11QT 19_{5} ([לחם ה]בכורים) 19_{12}, הָאָרֶץ *of the earth* Nm

15_{19} 4QD[e] 3.2_{19} ([הארץ]).

לֶחֶם עֳנִי *bread of affliction* Dt 16_{3}, צַר *of distress* 1 K $22_{27(mss)}$ Is 30_{20} (צָר; or em. מִצָּר bread *instead of distress*), אוֹנִים *of distress(es)* or *of mourners* Ezk $24_{17.22}$ (if em. אֲנָשִׁים *of men* in both) Ho 9_{4}, לחם אנחה *bread of sighing* 1QH 5_{33}, לֶחֶם דִּמְעָה *bread of tears* Ps 80_{6}, הָעֲצָבִים *of toils* Ps 127_{2}, עַצְלוּת *of idleness* Pr 31_{27}, רֶשַׁע *of wickedness* Pr 4_{17}, שֶׁקֶר *of falsehood* Pr 20_{17}, כְּזָבִים *of lies* Pr 23_{3}, סְתָרִים *of secrecy* Pr 9_{17}, חֲמֻדוֹת *of preciousness* Dn 10_{3}, לחם שכל *bread of wisdom* Si 15_{3}, לֶחֶם צֵידָם *bread of their provisions* Jos 9_{5}, חֻקִּי *of my prescription* Ps 30_{8}, יוֹמָיִם *of*, i.e. sufficient for, *two days* Ex 16_{29}, מִשְׁנֶה *of*, i.e. consisting of, *a double (amount)* Ex 16_{22}.

כִּכַּר לֶחֶם *loaf of bread* Ex 29_{23} 1 S 2_{36} (לָחֶם) Jr 37_{21} Pr 6_{26} (לָחֶם) 1 C 16_{3}, כִּכְּרוֹת *loaves of* Jg 8_{5} 1 S 10_{3}, חַלַּת לֶחֶם *loaf of bread* Ex 29_{23}||Lv 8_{26}=11QT 15_{10} (לֶחֶם שֶׁמֶן *of bread of oil*) 2 S 6_{19}, חַלֹּת לֶחֶם *loaves of bread* Lv 7_{13} 11QT 18_{14} ([חלות]) 18_{15} ([חלות לחם]), צְלִיל לֶחֶם *loaf of bread of* barley Jg $7_{13(Qr)}$, פַּת־לֶחֶם *morsel of bread* Gn 18_{5} Jg 19_{5} 1 S 2_{36} (לָחֶם) 28_{22} 1 K 17_{11} Pr 28_{21}, פְּתוֹתֵי *morsels of* Ezk 13_{19}, ראשית הלחם *first fruits of bread* 1QS $6_{5.6}$ 1QSa $2_{19.19}$ (both רשת), עֵרֶךְ לֶחֶם *array of bread* Ex 40_{23}, מַעֲרֶכֶת *array of* 2 C 13_{11}, מַטֵּה־לֶחֶם *staff of*, i.e. for holding, *bread* Lv 26_{26} Ezk 4_{16} 5_{16} (לָחֶם) 14_{13} (לָחֶם) Ps 105_{16} Si 48_{2}, מִשְׁעַן־לֶחֶם *staff of bread* Is 3_{1}, סלי לחם *baskets of bread* 11QT $15_{3a.12}$, מוסר לחם *discipline of food* Si 34_{12}, חֲמוֹר לֶחֶם *ass of*, i.e. laden with, *bread* (unless name of weight)* 1 S 16_{20}.

חֲסַר־לָחֶם *one lacking*, i.e. in need, *of bread* 2 S 3_{29} Pr 12_{9}, נֹתְנֵי לַחְמִי *givers of my bread* Ho 2_{7}, מְבַקֶּשׁ־לָחֶם *seeker of bread* Ps 37_{25}, אוֹכֵל לַחְמִי *eater of my bread* Ps 41_{10}, [או]כלי לחמי *eaters of my bread* 1QH 5_{23}, אֹכְלֵי לַחְמְךָ *eaters of your bread* Ob$_{7}$ (ins. אֹכְלֵי), אֹכְלֵי לֶחֶם *eaters of bread of* Ps 127_{2}, בעלי לחמך *owners of your bread*, i.e. your table companions Si 9_{16}, אֶרֶץ לֶחֶם *land of bread* 2 K 18_{32}||Is 36_{17}, חֹסֶר לֶחֶם *lack of bread* Am 4_{6}, שִׂבְעַת־לֶחֶם *satisfaction*, i.e. plenty, *of bread* Ezk 16_{49}, בְּלוֹ לֶחֶם *gift of bread* Ne 5_{15} (if em. בְּלֶחֶם *some bread* to בְּלוֹ לֶחֶם *a gift of bread*), דְּוֵי לַחְמִי *sickness of my food* Jb 6_{7} (or em. הֵמָּה כִּדְוֵי לַחְמִי *they are like the sickness of my food*, appar. food that is loathsome to me, to זָהֲמָה חֵמָה כִדְוֵי לְחֶמְיָ כְּדֵי לַחְמִי my soul *loathes them as food* or

my bowels growl with, or *waste away like*, *an echo*),* שְׁתֵּי־לֶחֶם *two loaves* 1 S 10_{4}, מחצית לחמו *half his bread* 4QSD $1.1_{5.6}$ ([מחצית לחמו]) $1.1_{8.10}$, רביעית לחמו *a quarter of his food* 1QS 6_{25}, כָּל־הַלֶּחֶם *all the bread* Jr 37_{21}, כֹּל לֶחֶם *all the bread of* Jos 9_{5}.

<APP> אִשֶּׁה *fire offering* Lv $3_{11.16}$ 21_{6}, קָרְבָּן *offering* Nm 28_{2}, עֲבֹדָה temple *service* Ne 10_{34}, מִנְחָה *offering* 11QT 18_{14} 19_{12}, נִיחוֹחַ *rest giving (fragrance)* 4QJub[d] 21_{9} ([ניחוח] ל[חם]), חֵלֶב *fat* Ezk 44_{7}, דָּם *blood* Ezk 44_{7}, חַלָּה *loaf* Lv $23_{17(Sam)}$ 11QT 18_{14} ([חלות]), מַצָּה *unleavened bread* Dt 16_{3}, מַאֲכָל *food* 1 C 12_{41} (Gnz לָהֶם bring *to them* for לֶחֶם bring *food*), תְּבוּאָה *produce* Is 30_{23}, בִּכּוּרִים *firstfruits* 11QT 18_{14} 19_{6}, קֶמַח *flour* 1 C 12_{41}, דְּבֵלָה *fig* 1 C 12_{41}, צִמּוּק *raisin* 1 C 12_{41}, יַיִן *wine* 1 C 12_{41}, שֶׁמֶן *oil* 1 C 12_{41}, בָּקָר *oxen* 1 C 12_{41}, צֹאן *sheep* 1 C 12_{41}, לַחַץ *oppression* 1 K 22_{27}||2 C 18_{26}.

<ADJ> חָמֵץ *leavened* Lv 7_{13}, חַם *hot* 1 S 21_{7} (if em. חֹם bread of *heat*), חָדָשׁ *new* 11QT 19_{7}, זֶה *this* Jos 9_{12} (זֶה לַחְמֵנוּ *this bread of ours*) 1 S 17_{17} 11QT 8_{13}, קְלֹקֵל *vile* Nm 21_{5}.

<PREP> לְ of possession, *of, (belonging) to*, + היה *be* Lv 24_{7} 11QT 8_{10}; *in respect of, in connection with* 2 S $16_{2(Kt)}$ Am 8_{11}=4QpsEzek[c] 2_{9} 1 C 23_{29}; *(sufficient) for* Pr $27_{27.27}$; *as*, + היה *be* Ezk 48_{18}, עשׂה *make* into Ezk 4_{9}; *for (the purpose of obtaining)*, + נתן *give* money Ne 10_{34}, + צעק *cry out* Gn 41_{55}, נדד *wander* Jb 15_{23}; רעב לְ *be hungry for* Jr 42_{14}.

בְּ of instrument, *by (means of), with*, + נהל pi. *refresh* Gn 47_{17}, קדם pi. *meet* Dt 23_{5} Is 21_{14} Ne 13_{2}; of accompaniment, *with* perh. 4QMyst[a] 87_{2}, + אכל *eat* ashes Ps $102_{10(mss)}$, שחת hi. *destroy* tree Jr 11_{19} (or em. בְּלַחְמוֹ *with its fruit* to בְּלֵחוֹ *in its moisture*); of price, *(in exchange) for*, + קנה *buy* people and land Gn 47_{19}, שׂכר ni. *hire oneself out* 1 S 2_{5}, שׁקל *weigh* silver Is 55_{2} (בְּלוֹא־לֶחֶם *for what is not bread*); partitive, *some, any*, + אכל *eat* Lv 22_{11} Jg 13_{16} Pr 9_{5} 1QH 5_{33} 4QHalakhah[a] 11_{2}, יתר ni. *remain* Lv 8_{32}, לקח *take* Ne 5_{15} (or em. בְּלֶחֶם *some bread* to בְּלוֹ לֶחֶם *a gift of bread*); *against*, + שׁלח *send*, i.e. stretch out, hand 1QSa 2_{20} ([וישלח]) 2_{21} (ישל[ח]); קוץ בְּ *abhor* Nm 21_{5}.

כְּ *as (though they were)*, + אכל *eat* ashes Ps 102_{10}; מִן partitive, *some, any*, + אכל *eat* Lv 22_{13} Nm 15_{19} Ru 2_{14},

יתר ni. *remain* Ex 29$_{34}$, נתן *give* Pr 22$_{9}$; אֶל *to*, + בוא *come* 1 S 20$_{27}$; *at* meal, + ישׁב *sit* 1 S 20$_{24(Qr)}$, נטה hi. *stretch* elbow Si 41$_{19(B)}$ (unless לֶחֶם II *war*); נגע אֶל *touch* Hg 2$_{12}$; עַל *upon*, + עיט *rush* Si 14$_{10}$, נתן *give*, i.e. place 11QT 8$_{12}$; *in addition to*, + קרב hi. *present* sacrificial beasts Lv 23$_{18}$, נוף hi. *wave* sacrificial beasts Lv 23$_{20}$ 11QT 19$_{5}$ ([על לחם]); *in charge of* 1 C 9$_{32}$; *at* meal, + ישׁב *sit* 1 S 20$_{24(Kt)}$, נטה hi. *stretch* elbow Si 41$_{19(M)}$; *by (means of)*, + חיה *live* Dt 8$_{3}$; עַל *in respect of* Si 34$_{23.24}$; עִם *with*, + אכל *eat* 11QT 19$_{6}$ ([ואכלום ... עם]); לִפְנֵי *before*, + בוא *come* Jb 3$_{24}$.

<COLL> לֶחֶם מִן־הַשָּׁמַיִם *bread from heaven* Ex 16$_{4}$ Ps 105$_{40(mss)}$ Ne 9$_{15}$ (both מִשָּׁמַיִם), לחם חדש אביבות ומלילות *new bread, whether made of new or unripened ears of corn* 11QT 19$_{7}$,* לֶחֶם וָמַיִם *bread and water* 1 K 18$_{4.13}$ Ezk 4$_{17}$, לֶחֶם וָיַיִן *bread and wine* Gn 14$_{18}$ (וְיַיִן) Jg 19$_{19}$ Ne 5$_{15}$, לַחְמְךָ perh. *(those who eat) your bread* Ob$_{7}$ (or ins. אֹכְלֵי *eaters of*, or em. לֹחֲמֶיךָ *those who eat with you*), ונענש במה את מחצית לחמו *and he shall be punished in them*, i.e. at that time, *with half his bread* 4QSD 1.1$_{5}$ ([ונענש]) 1.1$_{6}$ ([א]ת מחצית לחמו) 1.1$_{8}$ ([ונענש]) 1.1$_{10}$.

לֶחֶם ... שְׁתַּיִם *two ... loaves* Lv 23$_{17}$, שְׁתֵּי־לֶחֶם *two loaves* 1 S 10$_{4}$, 3 [לח]ם *three loaves* Arad ost. 6$_{4}$ (others 300 [לח]ם *three hundred loaves*), חֲמִשָּׁה־לֶחֶם *five loaves* 1 S 21$_{4}$, עֲשָׂרָה לֶחֶם *ten loaves* 1 S 17$_{17}$ 1 K 14$_{3}$, 10 לחם *10 loaves* Lachish ost. 9$_{3}$, עֶשְׂרִים־לֶחֶם *twenty loaves of* barley 2 K 4$_{42}$, מָאתַיִם לֶחֶם *two hundred loaves* 1 S 25$_{18}$ 2 S 16$_{1}$, [לח]ם [מא]תים *two hundred loaves* Arad ost. 10$_{3}$, לחם 300 *300 loaves* Arad ost. 2$_{4}$.

תִּשְׂבְּעוּ־לָחֶם *you will be satisfied with bread* Ex 16$_{12}$, sim. Ex 16$_{8}$ Jr 44$_{17}$ Jb 27$_{14}$ Pr 12$_{11}$ 20$_{13}$ 28$_{19}$ 30$_{22}$ Lm 5$_{6}$, אֶבְיוֹנֶיהָ אַשְׂבִּיעַ לָחֶם *her paupers I shall satisfy with food* Ps 132$_{15}$, sim. 4Q416 2.2$_{18}$.

לֶחֶם || מַאֲכָל *food* Hg 2$_{12}$ Jb 33$_{20}$ Pr 6$_{8}$, מָזוֹן *food* Gn 45$_{23}$, נָזִיד *pottage* Gn 25$_{34}$ Hg 2$_{12}$, קָצִיר *harvest* Jr 5$_{17}$, בָּשָׂר *flesh* Ex 16$_{3}$ (+) 16$_{8.12}$ 29$_{32.34}$ Lv 8$_{31}$ (all three +) 8$_{32}$ 1 K 17$_{6.6}$ Dn 10$_{3}$ (+), שְׁאֵר *flesh* Ps 78$_{20}$, טִבְחָה *slaughter*, i.e. meat 1 S 25$_{11}$, רָקִיק *wafer* Ex 29$_{2.23}$ Lv 8$_{26}$ 1 C 23$_{29}$ (all three +), חַלָּה *loaf* Ex 29$_{2.23}$ Lv 8$_{26}$, נִקֻּד *biscuit* 1 K 14$_{3}$, בַּר *grain* Gn 45$_{23}$, קָלִי *parched grain* Lv 23$_{14}$ 1 S 17$_{17}$ 25$_{18}$ (both +), כַּרְמֶל *fresh grain* Lv 23$_{14}$, חִטָּה *wheat* Arad ost. 3$_{7}$, שְׂעֹרָה *barley* Ezk 13$_{19}$, זֶרַע *seed* Is 55$_{10}$, צמוק *raisin* 1 S 25$_{18}$ 2 S 16$_{1}$, דְּבֵלָה *fig* 1 S 25$_{18}$, קַיִץ *summer fruit* 2 S 16$_{1.2}$, מַטְעָם *delicacy* Gn 27$_{17}$ Pr 23$_{6}$ (+).

לֶחֶם || יַיִן *wine* Gn 14$_{18}$ Dt 29$_{5}$ Jg 19$_{19}$ 1 S 10$_{3}$ 25$_{18}$ 2 S 16$_{1.2}$ (all four +) Hg 2$_{12}$ Pr 4$_{17}$ 9$_{5}$ Ec 9$_{7}$ 10$_{19}$ Dn 10$_{3}$ (all four +) Ne 5$_{15}$ Si 34$_{12}$ Arad ost 2$_{4}$ (+), תִּירוֹשׁ *new wine* 2 K 18$_{32}$||Is 36$_{17}$ 1QS 6$_{5.6}$, שֵׁכָר *strong drink* Dt 29$_{5}$, שִׁקּוּי *drink* Ho 2$_{7}$ Ps 102$_{10}$, מַיִם *water* Gn 21$_{14}$ (+) Ex 23$_{25}$ 34$_{28}$ Nm 21$_{5}$ Dt 9$_{9.18}$ 23$_{5}$ 1 S 25$_{11}$ 30$_{11}$ (+) 30$_{12}$ 1 K 13$_{8.9.16.17.18.19.22.22}$ 18$_{4.13}$ 22$_{27}$||2 C 18$_{26}$ 2 K 6$_{22}$ Is 3$_{1}$ 21$_{14}$ (+) 30$_{20}$ 33$_{16}$ (+) Ezk 4$_{17}$ 12$_{18.19}$ Ho 2$_{7}$ Am 8$_{11}$=4QpsEzek^{c} 2$_{9}$ Jb 3$_{24}$ 22$_{7}$ Pr 9$_{17}$ (all three +) 25$_{21}$ (or del.) Ezr 10$_{6}$ Ne 9$_{15}$ 13$_{2}$ Si 15$_{3}$.

לֶחֶם || בֶּגֶד *garment* Gn 28$_{20}$, שִׂמְלָה *garment* Dt 10$_{18}$ Is 3$_{7}$ 4$_{1}$, חֶרֶב *sword* 1 S 22$_{13}$, בַּיִת *house* 1 K 11$_{18}$, כֶּרֶם *vineyard* 2 K 18$_{32}$||Is 36$_{17}$, עֹשֶׁר *wealth* Pr 30$_{8}$ (+) Ec 9$_{11}$, שָׂבְעָה *satisfaction* Is 55$_{2}$.

לֶחֶם + בִּרְיָה *food* 2 S 13$_{5}$, אֹכֶל *food* Lm 1$_{11}$, צַיִד *provisions* Ps 132$_{15}$, צֵידָה *provisions* Ps 78$_{25}$, שְׂלָו *quails* Ps 105$_{40}$, גְּדִי *kid* 1 S 10$_{3}$, צֹאן *sheep* 1 S 25$_{18}$, מַצָּה *unleavened bread* Lv 8$_{26}$ 1 C 23$_{29}$, סֹלֶת *flour* Ezk 16$_{19}$ 1 C 23$_{29}$, דָּגָן *grain* 2 K 18$_{32}$||Is 36$_{17}$, דְּבַשׁ *honey* Ezk 16$_{19}$, זַיִת *olive* 2 K 18$_{32}$, שֶׁמֶן *oil* Ho 2$_{7}$ Hg 2$_{12}$ Ezk 16$_{19}$, יִצְהָר *fresh oil* 2 K 18$_{32}$, צֶמֶר *wool* Ho 2$_{7}$, פֵּשֶׁת *flax* Ho 2$_{7}$, כֶּסֶף *silver* Ec 10$_{19}$, רֵישׁ *poverty* Pr 30$_{8}$, דִּמְעָה *tear* Ps 80$_{6}$.*

Also 4QpIsa^{e} 5$_{6}$ 4QCommGenC 8$_{3}$ 4QD^{e} 4$_{19}$ 4Q417 19$_{5}$ 4Q418 87$_{3}$ 4Q423 1.1$_{9}$.

<SYN> מַאֲכָל *food*, מָזוֹן *food*, נָזִיד *pottage*, מַטְעָם *delicacy*, קָצִיר *harvest*, בָּשָׂר *flesh*, שְׁאֵר *flesh*, טִבְחָה *slaughter*, i.e. meat, רָקִיק *wafer*, חַלָּה *loaf*, נִקֻּד *biscuit*, בַּר *grain*, קָלִי *parched grain*, כַּרְמֶל *fresh grain*, זֶרַע *seed*, חִטָּה *wheat*, שְׂעֹרָה *barley* , צִמּוּק *raisin*, דְּבֵלָה *fig*, קַיִץ *summer fruit*, יַיִן *wine*, שֵׁכָר *strong drink*, מַיִם *water*, בֶּגֶד *garment*, שִׂמְלָה *garment*, עֹשֶׁר *riches*, שָׂבְעָה *satisfaction*, חֶרֶב *sword*, בַּיִת *house*, כֶּרֶם *vineyard*.

→ לחם II *eat*.

[לֶחֶם] II $_{0.2}$ n.[m.] **war, fighting**—<CSTR> כלי לחם *weapons of war* Si 12$_{5}$. <PREP> עַל *of, concerning*, ... בוש ממטה אציל על לחם *be ashamed ... of fighting [against] someone with whom you dine* Si 41$_{19}$ (unless *be ashamed ... of stretching out your elbow at a meal*, i.e. לֶחֶם I).*

→ לחם I *fight*.

לַחְמִי 1 pr.n.m. **Lahmi,** brother of Goliath, <OBJ> נכה hi. *strike* 1 C 20_{5}. <APP> אָח *brother* 1 C 20_{5}.

לַחְמָם, see לַחְמָס *Lahmas.*

לַחְמָס 1 pl.n. **Lahmas,** town in the lowland of Judah, perh. Kh. el-Laḥm, 18 km WNW of Hebron, <NOM CL> בַּשְּׁפֵלָה ... לַחְמָס *in the lowland was ... Lahmas* Jos 15_{40} (mss לַחְמָם *Lahmam*). <APP> עִיר *city* Jos 15_{40}.

לחץ 19.0.1 vb. **squeeze—Qal** 18 Pf. לָחַץ, לָחֲצוּ; impf. יִלְחָצֵנִי, 2ms תִּלְחַץ (תִּלְחָצֶנּוּ, Sam תִּלְחָצוּ); + waw וְלָחֲצוּ, וּלְחַצְתֶּם; 3fs וַתִּלָּחֵץ, וַיִּלְחֲצוּ (וַיִּלְחָצוּם); ptc. לֹחֲצִים (לֹחֲצָיו), לֹחֲצֵיהֶם, לֹחֲצֵיכֶם)—**1. press, squeeze, push,** <SUBJ> Amorites Jg 1_{34}, זָקֵן *elder* 2 K 6_{32}, אָתוֹן *female ass* Nm 22_{25}. <OBJ> בֵּן *son* of Dan Jg 1_{34}, מַלְאָךְ *messenger* 2 K 6_{32}, רֶגֶל *foot* Nm 22_{25}. <PREP> בְּ of instrument, *by (means of), with,* + דֶּלֶת *door* 2 K 6_{32}; אֶל *to,* i.e. against, + קִיר *wall* Nm 22_{25}; ־ה- of direction, *towards,* + הַר *mountain* Jg 1_{34}.

2. oppress,* <SUBJ> Israel(ites) Ex 22_{20} (+ ינה hi. *oppress*) 23_{9}, Amalekites Jg 10_{12}, Egyptians Ex 3_{9}, Maonites Jg 10_{12} (or em. מָעוֹן *Maon* to מִדְיָן *Midian*), Sidonians Jg 10_{12}, Hazael 2 K 13_{22}, Jabin Jg 4_{3}, מֶלֶךְ *king* Jg 4_{3} 2 K $13_{4.22}$, לֹחֵם *warrior* Ps 56_{2} (or em. לֹחֵם to לְחֵם a person [אֱנוֹשׁ] oppresses me *[with] both jaws* or יִלְחָצֵנִי *oppresses me* to הִצִּילֵנִי *Y. has saved me;* + שׁאף *trample*), אוֹיֵב *enemy* Ps 106_{42}, אֱנוֹשׁ *human being* Ps 56_{2} (if em.), psalmist Ps 7_{5} (if em. וָאֲחַלְּצָה *and I plundered* to וָאֶלְחֲצָה *and I oppressed*), מַמְלָכָה *kingdom* 1 S 10_{18}, גּוֹי *nation* Am 6_{14}; subj. not specified, Nm 24_{8} (if em. חִצָּיו *his arrows* to לֹחֲצָיו *those who oppress him*) Jg 2_{18} (|| דחק *oppress*) 6_{9} Is 19_{20} Jr 30_{20}. <OBJ> Israel Nm 24_{8} (if em.; see Subj.) Jg 2_{18} 10_{12} 2 K $13_{4.22}$, Jacob, i.e. Israel Nm 24_{8} (if em.; see Subj.) Jr 30_{20}, בֵּן *son* of Israel Ex 3_{9} Jg 4_{3} 6_{9}, בַּיִת *house* of Israel Am 6_{14}, עַם *people* 1 S 10_{18} Ps 106_{42}, גֵּר *sojourner* Ex 22_{20} 23_{9}, צֹרֵר *enemy* Ps 7_{5} (if em.; see Subj.), psalmist Ps 56_{2}. <PREP> בְּ of instrument, *by (means of), with,* + חָזְקָה *strength* Jg 4_{3}; מִן of direction, *from,* + Lebohamath Am 6_{14}; עַד *unto,* + נַחַל *wadi* Am 6_{14}. <COLL> הַלַּחַץ אֲשֶׁר מִצְרַיִם לֹחֲצִים אֹתָם *the oppression with which the Egyptians oppress them* Ex 3_{9}; לחץ + adverb or noun used adverbially, רֵיקָם *without cause* Ps 7_{5} (if em.; see Subj.), יוֹם *day* 2 K 13_{22} Ps 56_{2}, שָׁנָה *year* Jg 4_{3}.

<SYN> דחק *oppress.*

Ni. 1.0.1 Pf. Q נחלץ; + waw 3fs וַתִּלָּחֵץ—**1. press oneself, be squeezed,** <SUBJ> אָתוֹן *female ass* Nm 22_{25}. <PREP> אֶל *to,* i.e. against, + קִיר *wall* Nm 22_{25}.

2. be forced, be under duress, <SUBJ> קָרוֹב *one who approaches* CD 5_{15}.*

⇒ לַחַץ *oppression.*

לַחַץ 12.0.1 n.m. **oppression**—לַחַץ; cstr. לַחַץ; sf. לַחֲצֵנוּ—**oppression, distress,** in ref. to scanty rations of bread and water (1 K 22_{27}||2 C 18_{26} Is 30_{20}), <OBJ> ראה *see* Ex 3_{9} Dt 26_{7} (|| עֳנִי *misery,* עָמָל *trouble*) 2 K 13_{4} 4QDibHam[a] 1.6_{12} (|| עָמָל), שׁכח *forget* Ps 44_{25} (|| עֳנִי), אכל hi. *feed* 1 K 22_{27}||2 C 18_{26}, נתן *give* Is 30_{20}. <CSTR> לַחַץ אוֹיֵב *oppression of the enemy* Ps 42_{10} 43_{2}, יִשְׂרָאֵל *of Israel* 2 K 13_{4}, לֶחֶם לַחַץ וּמַיִם לַחַץ *bread of oppression and water of oppression* 1 K 22_{27}||Is 30_{20}||2 C 18_{26} (Is צַר *of distress;* or em. מִצַּר/מִלַּחַץ *instead of distress/oppression*).* <PREP> בְּ of cause, *on account of,* + הלך *go* as a mourner Ps 42_{10}, htp. *go about* Ps 43_{2}; of instrument, *by (means of), with,* + גלה *uncover* ear Jb 36_{15} (+ עֳנִי *affliction*). <COLL> הַלַּחַץ אֲשֶׁר מִצְרַיִם לֹחֲצִים אֹתָם *the oppression with which the Egyptians oppress them* Ex 3_{9}.

<SYN> עֳנִי *misery,* עָמָל *trouble.**

⇒ לחץ *squeeze.*

לחשׁ 3 vb. **whisper—Pi.** 1 Ptc. מְלַחֲשִׁים—**1. whisper (prayers)** <SUBJ> Israelites 4QDibHam[a] 1.5_{17} (ל[ל]חש). <PREP> בְּ of time, *in, during,* + צָקוֹן *oppression* 4QDibHam[a] 1.5_{17} (ל[ל]חש).

2. ptc. as noun, snake **charmer,** <CSTR> קוֹל מְלַחֲשִׁים *voice of the charmers* Ps 58_{6} (+ חבר *charm*).

Htp. 2 Impf. יִתְלַחֲשׁוּ; ptc. מִתְלַחֲשִׁים—**whisper together,** <SUBJ> עֶבֶד *servant* 2 S 12_{19}, שׂנא ptc. *one who hates* Ps 41_{8} (+ חשׁב *plan*). <PREP> עַל *concerning,* + psalmist Ps 41_{8}. <COLL> + adverb, יַחַד *together* Ps 41_{8}.

⇒ לַחַשׁ *whisper.*

לַחַשׁ I 5.1 n.[m.] **whisper**—לַחַשׁ; pl. לְחָשִׁים—**1. whisper,** perh. of prayer (Is 26_{16}), of enemy (Si 12_{18}), <OBJ> צוק

pour out Is 26_{16} (or em. חָלַשְׁנוּ *we were weak*). <CSTR> רוב הלחש *abundance of whisper*, i.e. much whispering Si 12_{18}.

2. charm(s), charming, of snakes (Jr 8_{17} Ec 10_{11}), in ref. to magic (Is 3_3), <NOM CL> אֵין־לָהֶם לָחַשׁ *they* (snakes) *have no charming*, i.e. cannot be charmed Jr 8_{17}. <CSTR> נְבוֹן לָחַשׁ *one intelligent (in the use) of*, i.e. expert in, *charming* Is 3_3 (|| חֶרֶשׁ *sorcery*), דברי לחש *words of the spell* 11QPsAp^a 1_2 ([דברי לחש]) 4_4 (דברי ל[חש]). <PREP> בְּלוֹא *without*, + נשך *bite* Ec 10_{11}.

3. amulet, perh. of conch shells, <OBJ> סור hi. *remove* Is 3_{20}.

<SYN> §2 חֶרֶשׁ *sorcery*.
→ לחשׁ *whisper*.

לַחַשׁ II 0.0.0.1 pr.n.[m.] **Lahash,** <PREP> לְ of possession, *(belonging) to, of* Seal 251 (8th/7th cent.).

לָט 7 n.[m.] **secrecy**—לָאט; sf. לָטֵיהֶם—**1. secrecy,** <PREP> בְּ of accompaniment, *with, in,* + בוא *come* Jg 4_{21} Ru 3_7, דבר pi. *speak* 1 S 18_{22}, כרת *cut* skirt of robe 1 S 24_5.

2. magic spell, enchantment, <PREP> בְּ of instrument, *by (means of), with,* + עשׂה *do* Ex 7_{22} $8_{3.14}$ (Sam לַהַט *enchantment* in all three).

לֹט 2 n.[m.] **myrrh,** gum perh. of a species of cistus, <OBJ> ירד hi. *bring down* Gn 43_{11} (|| נְכֹאת *ladanum,* + צֳרִי *balm,* דְּבַשׁ *honey,* בָּטְנָה *pistachio,* שָׁקֵד *almond*), נשׂא *bear* Gn 37_{25} (|| צֳרִי, נְכֹאת). <APP> מִנְחָה *present* Gn 43_{11}. <COLL> נְכֹאת וָלֹט *ladanum and myrrh* Gn 43_{11}, צֳרִי וָלֹט *balm and myrrh* Gn 37_{25}.

<SYN> נְכֹאת *ladanum,* צֳרִי *balm.*

לְטָאָה 1.0.1 n.f. **lizard,** unclean beast, <OBJ> טמא pi. *declare unclean* 11QT 50_{20}. <NOM CL> זֶה לָכֶם הַטָּמֵא בַּשֶּׁרֶץ ... וְהַלְּטָאָה *this is what is unclean for you among the swarming things ... and the lizard* Lv 11_{30}. <APP> שֶׁרֶץ *swarming thing* 11QT 50_{20}.

לְטוּשִׁים 1 pr.n.m. **Letushim,** son of Dedan and appar. ancestor of north Arabian people, <SUBJ> היה *be* Gn 25_3 (or em. לֹטְשִׁים *smiths*).

לטשׁ 5.1 vb. **sharpen**—**Qal** 4.1 Impf. יִלְטוֹשׁ; ptc. לֹטֵשׁ (Si לוטשׁ); inf. לְטוֹשׁ—**sharpen, whet,** <SUBJ> perh. אֱלֹהִים *God* Ps 7_{13} (|| דרך *tread*, i.e. bend, bow, כון pol. *prepare*, i.e. string, bow), Israel 1 S 13_{20}, אִישׁ *each* 1 S 13_{20}, צַר *enemy* Jb 16_9 (+ חרק *gnash* teeth). <OBJ> מַחֲרֶשֶׁת *ploughshare* 1 S 13_{20}, אֵת *blade* 1 S 13_{20}, קַרְדֹּם *axe* 1 S 13_{20}, חֶרֶב *sword* Ps 7_{13}, עַיִן *eye* Jb 16_9. <PREP> לְ *against*, + Job Jb 16_9.

2. ptc. as noun, **forger, smith, sharpener,** <SUBJ> היה *be* Gn 25_3 (if em. לְטוּשִׁים *Letushim* to לֹטְשִׁים *smiths*). <OBJ> ילד *bear* Gn 4_{22} (or em.; see Cstr.). <CSTR> לֹטֵשׁ כָּל־חֹרֵשׁ appar. *sharpener*, i.e. instructor, *of every artisan* Gn 4_{22} (or em. אֲבִי כָּל־לֹטֵשׁ *the ancestor of every smith*); מעשה לוטשׁ *work of the smith* Si 34_{26}. <APP> Tubal-cain Gn 4_{22} (or em.; see Cstr.), Asshurim Gn 25_3 (if em.; see Subj.).

<SYN> §1 דרך *tread*, i.e. bend, bow, כון pol. *prepare*, i.e. string, bow.

Pu. 1 Ptc. מְלֻטָּשׁ—**be sharpened,** <SUBJ> תַּעַר *razor* Ps 52_4.

[לָיָה] 3 n.f. **spiral (border)**—pl. לֹיוֹת—of metal decorations of bases of lavers in Solomon's temple, <NOM CL> מִתַּחַת לָאֲרָיוֹת וְלַבָּקָר לֹיוֹת *below the lions and the oxen were spiral borders* 1 K 7_{29}, מַעֲבַר אִישׁ לֹיוֹת *at the side of each were spiral borders* 1 K 7_{30}. <OBJ> פתח pi. *engrave* 1 K 7_{36}. <APP> מַעֲשֵׂה מוֹרָד perh. *plated work* 1 K 7_{29}.

לַיִל 8 n.m. **night**—לָיִל; cstr. לֵיל—<NOM CL> לֵיל שִׁמֻּרִים הוּא לַי׳ *it is a night of watching to Y.* Ex 12_{42}. <CSTR> לֵיל שִׁמֻּרִים *a night of watching* <PREP> בְּ of time, *in* perh. 4Q PrQuot 146_1 (בליל[י]), + שׁדד pu. *be devastated* Is $15_{1.1}$, רנן *cry out* Lm $2_{19(Kt)}$, כבה *be extinguished* Pr $31_{18(Kt)}$; כְּ *as* Is 16_3 30_{29}; מִן partitive, *of,* מַה־מִּלַּיִל *what (is left) of the night?* 1QIsa^a 21_{11} Is 21_{11}.*

לַיְלָה 227.1.57 n.m. **night**—לָיְלָה; pl. לֵילוֹת; cstr. לֵילוֹת—<SUBJ> היה *be* Jr 33_{20} (if em.; see Coll.) Ps 104_{20} Jb 3_7 Ne 4_{16}, אמר *say* Jb 3_3, חוה pi. *declare* Ps 19_3, חדה *rejoice* Jb 3_6 (or em. יחד *be joined*), אתה *come* Is 21_{12}, בוא *come* Jb 3_6, שׁבת *cease* Gn 8_{22}, אבד *perish* Jb 3_3, סגר *close* Ps 139_{11} (if em.; see Nom. Cl.), אור hi. *give light* Ps 139_{12} (11QPs^a אזר *girdle*), נקר pi. *bore* bones Jb 30_{17}.

לַיְלָה

<NOM CL> לַיְלָה אוֹר night is light Ps 139$_{11}$ (or em. אוֹר to יִסְגֹּר it closes), לֹא־יוֹם וְלֹא־לָיְלָה it is not day and not night Zc 14$_{7}$, הוּא־הַלַּיְלָה הַזֶּה לַי׳ this same night is, i.e. belongs, to Y. Ex 12$_{42}$, לְךָ לַיְלָה yours is the night Ps 74$_{16}$, לַיְלָה לָכֶם מֵחָזוֹן night shall be to you without vision Mc 3$_{6}$, הלילה לנו רוש ממשל חו[שך] the night is for us the beginning of the rule of darkness 4QPrQuot 33.10$_{19}$.

<OBJ> ברא create Jr 33$_{25}$ (if em. בְּרִיתִי יוֹמָם my covenant is by day to בָּרָאתִי יוֹם I have created day), מנה pi. appoint Jb 7$_{3}$ (or em. pu.), שׂים place, i.e. cause to be, day Jb 17$_{12}$, קרא call Gn 1$_{5}$ (לַחֹשֶׁךְ קָרָא לָיְלָה he called the darkness night), לקח take Jb 3$_{6}$, שׁאף long for Jb 36$_{20}$, אור hi. illuminate Ex 14$_{20}$ (or em. יָאֵר it illuminated the night, to יַעַבְרוּ they passed the night, or יָאַר he cast a spell upon the night) Ps 105$_{39}$.

<CSTR> לֵילוֹת עָמָל nights of misery Jb 7$_{3}$, לילות השנה nights of the year 1QS 6$_{7}$; בִּן־לַיְלָה son of a night, i.e. within a night Jon 4$_{10.10}$, שׁוֹדְדֵי לַיְלָה plunderers of, i.e. in, the night Ob$_{5}$, דגלי לילה battalions of the night 4QPrQuot 29.8$_{11}$ ([ד]גלי) 29.8$_{19}$, רְסִיסֵי לָיְלָה (dew) drops of the night Ca 5$_{2}$, שינת לילה sleep of the night Si 40$_{5}$, תּוֹךְ הַלַּיְלָה middle of the night 1 K 3$_{20}$, חֲצֹת middle of Ex 11$_{4}$ Ps 119$_{62}$ (חֲצוֹת לַיְלָה) Jb 34$_{20}$ (חֲצוֹת־לָיְלָה), חֲצִי half of, i.e. midnight Ex 12$_{29}$ Jg 16$_{3.3}$ Ru 3$_{8}$, אִישׁוֹן לַיְלָה pupil, i.e. very middle, of the night Pr 7$_{9}$ 4QWiles 1$_{6}$ (אישני לילן[ה]), תועפות לילה eminence, i.e. depths, of night 4QWiles 1$_{4}$, קֵץ ... אַרְבָּעִים לָיְלָה the end of ... forty nights Dt 9$_{11}$, מֶמְשֶׁלֶת הַלַּיְלָה dominion of the night Gn 1$_{16}$, בוא ... לילה coming of ... night 1QS 10$_{10}$ 1QM 14$_{13}$ (ב[ו]א), מוצא לילה going out, i.e. end, of the night 1QH 12$_{7}$ 4QMyst^{a} 5$_{4}$, מועד לילה set time of night 1QH 12$_{6}$, מועדי ... לילה set times of ... night 4QParGenEx 2$_{12}$ (מ[ו]עדי) 4QPrQuot 33.10$_{21}$ (מועד[י]) 51$_{10}$.

חֲלוֹם הַלַּיְלָה dream of, i.e. in, the night Gn 20$_{3}$ 31$_{24}$ 1 K 3$_{5}$, מראה הלי[לה] vision of, i.e. in, the night 4QJub^{h} 32$_{21}$, חֲזוֹן לַיְלָה vision of, i.e. in, the night Is 29$_{7}$, חִזָּיוֹן vision of Jb 20$_{8}$ (לָיְלָה) 33$_{15}$, חֶזְיֹנוֹת visions of Jb 4$_{13}$ (לָיְלָה), מַרְאֹת visions of Gn 46$_{2}$ (הַלַּיְלָה), מִקְרֵה־ accident of Dt 23$_{11}$ (לָיְלָה) 11QT 45$_{7}$, פַּחַד dread of Ps 91$_{5}$=11QPsAp^{a} 5$_{7}$ (לָיְלָה), גְּנֻבְתִי לָיְלָה (thing) stolen of, i.e. by, night Gn 31$_{39}$, גורלות לילה lots of night 4QPrQuot 1.3$_{15}$, שלישית כול לילות a third of all the nights of 1QS 6$_{7}$.

כֹּל הַלַּיְלָה all the night 2 S 2$_{29}$, כָּל־הַלַּיְלָה Ex 14$_{21}$ Lv 6$_{2}$ Nm 11$_{32}$ Jos 10$_{9}$ Jg 16$_{2.2}$ 19$_{25}$ 1 S 31$_{12}$ 2 S 2$_{32}$ Is 62$_{6}$ Ho 7$_{6}$ Ps 78$_{14}$ (mss lack כָּל־), כָּל־הַלָּיְלָה all the night Ex 10$_{13}$ 14$_{20}$ 1 S 15$_{11}$ (both הַלָּיְלָה) 19$_{24}$ 28$_{20}$ 2 S 4$_{7}$ (both הַלָּיְלָה), כָּל־לַיְלָה every night Ps 6$_{7}$, כָּל־הַלֵּילוֹת all the nights Is 21$_{8}$, כול לילות all the nights of 1QS 6$_{7}$.

<APP> שִׁמֻּרִים watching Ex 12$_{42}$, יוֹם day Lv 8$_{35}$, בְּרִית covenant Jr 33$_{20}$.

<ADJ> אֶחָד one Gn 40$_{5}$ 41$_{11}$, זֶה this Ex 12$_{8.12.42}$ 4QPrQuot 76$_{3}$, הוּא that Gn 19$_{33.35}$ 26$_{24}$ 30$_{16}$ 32$_{14.22.23}$ Nm 14$_{1}$ Jos 8$_{9.13}$ Jg 6$_{25.40}$ 7$_{9}$ 1 S 19$_{10}$ 28$_{25}$ 2 S 2$_{29}$ 7$_{4}$||1 C 17$_{3}$ 2 K 19$_{35}$ Jb 3$_{6.7}$ Est 6$_{1}$ 2 C 1$_{7}$ 1QM 19$_{9}$ (ל[י]לה) 4QM^{a} 1$_{10}$ (ל[י]לה ההואה).

<PREP> לְ of direction, to, + חוה pi. declare Ps 19$_{3}$, בוא enter 4QAstrCrypt 1.2$_{11}$ (ת[בוא ללילה]) 1.2$_{13}$ (ת[בוא]) 1.2$_{14}$; concerning 4QPrQuot 64$_{4}$.

בְּ of time, in, on, by Ps 42$_{9}$ 90$_{4}$ 136$_{9}$ Ca 3$_{8}$ 1QM 19$_{9}$ ([ב]ל[י]לה) 4QOrdo 1$_{1}$ (בל[ילה]) 2$_{2.4}$, + היה be Jg 6$_{25}$ 7$_{9}$ 2 S 7$_{4}$||1 C 17$_{3}$ 2 K 19$_{35}$ Jb 24$_{14}$ 4QM^{a} 1$_{10}$ (ב[לי]לה), ראה see Ec 8$_{16}$, ni. appear Gn 26$_{24}$ 2 C 1$_{7}$ 7$_{12}$, בוא come Jr 49$_{9}$, הלך go Jos 8$_{13}$ 1 S 28$_{25}$, עלה go up Jr 6$_{5}$, עבר pass Ex 12$_{12}$ Is 28$_{19}$, סור turn aside Ne 9$_{19}$, לין lodge Gn 32$_{14.22}$ Jos 8$_{9}$, שׁכב lie Gn 30$_{16}$ Ec 2$_{23}$, חלם dream Gn 40$_{5}$ 41$_{11}$, קום rise Gn 32$_{23}$, עמד stand Ps 134$_{1}$, מלט ni. escape 1 S 19$_{10}$, נדד flee Est 6$_{1}$, אסף ni. be gathered 4QM^{b} 1$_{8}$, עשׂה do Jg 6$_{40}$, נתן give Jb 35$_{10}$, אוה pi. desire Is 26$_{9}$, בקשׁ pi. seek Ca 3$_{1}$, שׁקה hi. give to drink Gn 19$_{33.35}$, אכל eat Ex 12$_{8}$ 11QT 17$_{8}$, consume Gn 31$_{40}$, נגד hi. tell Ps 92$_{3}$, שׂיח converse Ps 77$_{7}$, זכר remember Ps 119$_{55}$, בכה weep Nm 14$_{1}$ Lm 1$_{2}$, רנן cry out Lm 2$_{19(Qr)}$, צעק cry out Ps 88$_{2}$, שׁדד pu. be devastated 1QIsa^{a} 15$_{1.1}$, כבה be extinguished Pr 31$_{18(Qr)}$, שׁלך ho. be cast out Jr 36$_{30}$, נכה hi. strike Ps 121$_{6}$, שׂחה hi. cause to swim, i.e. drench Ps 6$_{7}$; מֹשֵׁל בְּ rule over Gn 1$_{18}$ 4QJub^{a} 2$_{8}$.

כְּ as (in), משׁשׁ pi. grope Jb 5$_{14}$.

מִן partitive, of, מַה־מִּלַּיְלָה what (is left) of the night? Is 21$_{11}$.

עַד unto, + שׁלם hi. bring to an end Is 38$_{12.13}$, עלה hi. cause to go up, i.e. offer 2 C 35$_{14}$.

בֵּין between, + בדל hi. separate Gn 1$_{14}$ (+ יוֹם day).

<COLL> :: יוֹם day Gn 1$_{5.14.16.18}$ 7$_{4.12}$ 31$_{39.40}$ Ex 10$_{13}$ 24$_{18}$ 34$_{28}$ Nm 11$_{32}$ Dt 9$_{9.11.18.25}$ 10$_{10}$ 1 S 19$_{24}$ 30$_{12}$ 1 K 8$_{29}$

19$_{8}$ Is 27$_{3}$ 28$_{19}$ 62$_{6}$ Jr 33$_{20}$ 36$_{30}$ Jon 2$_{1}$ Zc 14$_{7}$ Ps 19$_{3.3}$ 74$_{16}$ 136$_{9}$ Jb 2$_{13}$ 3$_{3}$ Ec 8$_{16}$ Ne 4$_{16}$ 4QJub^{a} 2$_{8}$ 4QCommGenA 1$_{6}$ 4QParGenEx 2$_{8.12}$ GnzPs 4$_{10}$; + יוֹם Is 38$_{12.13}$ Ho 4$_{5}$ Ps 77$_{3}$ 88$_{2}$ 90$_{4}$ Jb 17$_{12}$.

:: יוֹמָם *by day* Ex 13$_{21.22}$ 40$_{38}$ Nm 14$_{14}$ Dt 1$_{33}$ Jg 6$_{27}$ 1 S 25$_{16}$ 2 S 21$_{10}$ Is 4$_{5}$ 21$_{8}$ Jr 31$_{35}$ Ps 22$_{3}$ 78$_{14}$ 91$_{5}$ Ne 9$_{12}$ 1QM 14$_{13}$ 4Q392 1$_{6}$; + יוֹמָם Ps 42$_{9}$ 121$_{6}$ Jb 5$_{14}$ Ne 9$_{19}$.

יוֹמָם וָלַיְלָה *by day and by night* Ex 13$_{21}$ Lv 8$_{35}$ Nm 9$_{21}$ (or em. יוֹם וָלַיְלָה *by day and by night*) Jos 1$_{8}$ 1 K 8$_{59}$ Is 60$_{11}$ Jr 8$_{23}$ 16$_{13}$ 33$_{20.25}$ (or em. both יוֹם וָלַיְלָה *day and night*) Ps 1$_{2}$ 32$_{4}$ 42$_{4}$ 55$_{11}$ Lm 2$_{18}$ Ne 1$_{6}$ 4$_{3}$ 1 C 9$_{33}$ 2 C 6$_{20}$ 1QH 8$_{30}$ 10$_{15}$ ([ול]ילה) 1QS 6$_{6}$ 4QsapDidA 1$_{10}$ (ולילה[ה]) 4Q417 1.1$_{22}$ 4QPrFêtes^{b} 41$_{2}$ 11QT 57$_{10}$.

יוֹם וָלַיְלָה *by day and by night* Gn 8$_{22}$ Nm 9$_{21}$ (if em. יוֹמָם וָלַיְלָה).

לַיְלָה וְיוֹמָם *by night and by day* Dt 28$_{66}$ Is 34$_{10}$ Jr 14$_{17}$.

לַיְלָה וָיוֹם *by night and by day* 1 K 8$_{29}$ Is 27$_{3}$ Est 4$_{16}$ 4QPrQuot 218$_{4}$.

:: בֹּקֶר *morning* Is 21$_{12}$ Ps 92$_{3}$; + בֹּקֶר *morning* Ho 7$_{6}$ Am 5$_{8}$ 1QM 14$_{13}$, אוֹר *light* Jb 24$_{14}$, נֶשֶׁף *twilight* Pr 7$_{9}$, עֶרֶב *evening* Pr 7$_{9}$ 1QM 14$_{13}$, אֲפֵלָה *darkness* Pr 7$_{9}$, יֶרַח *month* Jb 7$_{3}$.

לַיְלָה אֶחָד *one night* Gn 40$_{5}$ 41$_{11}$, שְׁלֹשָׁה לֵילוֹת *three nights* 1 S 30$_{12}$ Jon 2$_{1}$, שִׁבְעַת לֵילוֹת *seven nights* Jb 2$_{13}$, אַרְבָּעִים לַיְלָה *forty nights* Gn 7$_{4.12}$ Ex 24$_{18}$ 34$_{28}$ Dt 9$_{9.11.18.25}$ (הַלַּיְלָה) 10$_{10}$ 1 K 19$_{8}$ 4QCommGenA 1$_{6}$ 4QParGenEx 2$_{8}$ (אר[עים]).

לֵילוֹת/לַיְלָה used adverbially, (1) *for* a specified number of, *nights*, + היה *be* Gn 7$_{12}$ Ex 24$_{18}$ 34$_{28}$ Jon 2$_{1}$ 4QCommGenA 1$_{6}$ 4QParGenEx 2$_{8}$, ישׁב *sit*, i.e. remain Dt 9$_{9}$ Jb 2$_{13}$, עמד *stand*, i.e. remain Dt 10$_{10}$, נפל htp. *prostrate oneself* Dt 9$_{18}$, הלך *go* 1 K 19$_{8}$, אכל *eat* 1 S 30$_{12}$, שׁתה *drink* 1 S 30$_{12}$, מטר hi. *rain* Gn 7$_{4}$.

(2) *by night, in the night*, + היה *be* Ex 40$_{38}$ 1 S 25$_{16}$ 1 K 8$_{29}$||2 C 6$_{20}$ 1 K 8$_{59}$ Jr 33$_{20}$ (or em.; see above) Ps 42$_{4}$ 11QT 57$_{10}$, ישׁב *sit*, i.e. remain Lv 8$_{35}$, עמד *stand* GnzPs 4$_{10}$, קום *rise* Ex 12$_{30}$ Jg 9$_{32.34}$ 2 K 7$_{12}$ 8$_{21}$||2 C 21$_{9}$ Ne 2$_{12}$, בוא *come* Nm 22$_{20}$ 1 S 26$_{7}$ 28$_{8}$ 2 K 6$_{14}$ Ne 6$_{10}$, יצא *go out* Ex 12$_{41(Sam)}$ Jr 39$_{4}$ 52$_{7}$ Ne 2$_{13}$, hi. *bring out* Dt 16$_{1}$, נסע *set out* Nm 9$_{21}$, הלך *go* Ex 13$_{21.21}$ Nm 14$_{14}$ Dt 1$_{33}$, עלה *go up* Ne 2$_{15}$, ירד *go down* Nm 11$_{9}$ 1 S 14$_{36}$ Jr 14$_{17}$, hi. *cause to go down* Lm 2$_{18}$, מושׁ *depart* Ex 13$_{22}$, נוח *rest* 2 S 21$_{10}$, פקד *visit* Ps 17$_{3}$, קרא *call* Ex 12$_{31}$ Ps 22$_{3}$, שׁלח *send* Jos 8$_{3}$ נחה hi. *lead* Ps 78$_{14(mss)}$ Ne 9$_{12}$, דרשׁ *seek*, i.e. study 1QS 6$_{6}$, נתן *give* Jr 31$_{35}$, עמד hi. *set up* Ne 4$_{3}$, סבב *surround* Jg 20$_{5}$ Ps 55$_{11}$, עבד *serve* other gods Jr 16$_{13}$, עשׂה *do* Jg 6$_{27}$, ברא *create* Is 4$_{5}$, נצר *watch* Is 27$_{3}$, אכל *eat* Est 4$_{16}$, שׁתה *drink* Est 4$_{16}$, גנב *steal* Jb 27$_{20}$, חלק ni. *be divided* Gn 14$_{15}$, פתח pass. *be open* 1 K 8$_{29}$||2 C 6$_{20}$, סגר ni. *be shut* Is 60$_{11}$, כסה pi. *cover* Nm 9$_{16}$, נגר ni. *be poured*, i.e. stretched out Ps 77$_{3}$, הפך *overturn* Jb 34$_{25}$, פחד *fear* Dt 28$_{66}$, כבד *be heavy* Ps 32$_{4}$, יסר pi. *instruct* Ps 16$_{7}$, הגה *meditate* Jos 1$_{8}$ Ps 1$_{2}$ perh. 4Q418 43$_{4}$, פלל htp. *pray* Ne 1$_{6}$, בכה *weep* Jr 8$_{23}$, הסס *be silent* 1QH 10$_{15}$ ([ל]ילה), כשׁל *stumble* Ho 4$_{5}$ (or del.), עטף htp. *be faint* 1QH 8$_{29}$, כבה *be extinguished* Is 34$_{10}$, מות *die* 1 K 3$_{19}$; without verb, 1 C 9$_{33}$ 4Q392 1$_{6}$.

(3) *into, so as to be*, + חשׁך hi. *darken* day Am 5$_{8}$.

הַלַּיְלָה used adverbially, (1) *tonight*, + היה *be* Ru 1$_{12}$, בוא *come* Gn 19$_{5}$ Jos 2$_{2}$, לין *lodge* Nm 22$_{8}$ Jos 4$_{3}$ 2 S 17$_{16}$ 19$_{8}$ Ru 3$_{13}$, ישׁב *sit*, i.e. remain Nm 22$_{19}$, שׁכב *lie down* Gn 30$_{15}$, רדף *pursue* 2 S 17$_{1}$, שׁקה hi. *give to drink* Gn 19$_{34}$, דבר pi. *speak* 1 S 15$_{16}$, רום htpol. *extol* 4QPrQuot 5.11$_{3}$, מלט pi. *deliver* 1 S 19$_{11}$, זרה *winnow* Ru 3$_{2}$.

(2) *that night, by night, in the night*, + ראה *see* Zc 1$_{8}$, נגשׁ hi. *bring near* 1 S 14$_{34}$, יצא *go out* 2 K 25$_{4(mss)}$, ברח *flee* 2 K 25$_{4(mss)}$.

(3) *for the* specified number of *nights*, + נפל htp. *prostrate oneself* Dt 9$_{25}$.

כָּל־הַלַּיְלָה used adverbially, *all the night*, + קום *rise* Nm 11$_{32}$, נהג pi. *drive* Ex 10$_{13}$, הלך *go* 1 S 31$_{12}$ 2 S 2$_{29.32}$ 4$_{7}$, hi. *drive* Ex 14$_{21}$, נחה hi. *lead* Ps 78$_{14}$ (mss lack כָּל־), עלה *go up* Jos 10$_{9}$, קרב *draw near* Ex 14$_{20}$, ארב *wait in ambush* Jg 16$_{2}$ (or em. כָּל־הַיּוֹם *all day*), נפל *fall*, i.e. lie, naked 1 S 19$_{24}$, חשׁה *be silent* Is 62$_{6}$, חרשׁ htp. *keep still* Jg 16$_{2}$, עלל htp. *abuse* Jg 19$_{25}$, זעק *cry* 1 S 15$_{11}$, אכל *eat* 1 S 28$_{20}$, ישׁן *smoke* Ho 7$_{6}$; without verb Lv 6$_{2}$.

כָּל־הַלֵּילוֹת used adverbially, *all the nights*, + נצב ni. *stand* Is 21$_{8}$.

וַתָּקָם בְּעוֹד לַיְלָה *she rises when it is still night* Pr 31$_{15}$.

Also Si 38$_{27}$ (ליל[ה]) 1QMyst 13$_{4}$ (ליל[ה]) 4QpHos^{b} 3$_{2}$ 4QapPs^{b} 1$_{5}$ 4QM^{a} 8.1$_{11}$ 4QPrQuot 1.3$_{19}$ 15.6$_{9}$ 18.5$_{1}$ 29.8$_{4.23}$ 33.10$_{7}$ 39.13$_{2}$ 42$_{2.5}$ ([ה]ל[י]לה) 42$_{6}$ ([ל]ילה) 56.1$_{5}$ 61$_{2}$ 64$_{5}$ 86$_{4}$ (הליל[ה]) 136$_{2}$ 4QShir^{b} 52.3$_{6\text{-}8(vertical)}$ (ליל[ ]).

<ANT> יוֹם *day*, יוֹמָם *by day*, בֹּקֶר *morning*.*

לִילִית $_{1.0.1}$ pr.n.f. **Lilith**—pl. Q ליליות—demon;* perh. at Is 34$_{14}$ **nightjar,*** <SUBJ> רגע hi. *rest* Is 34$_{14}$ (+ שָׂעִיר *goat-demon*), שׁכן *dwell* Jb 18$_{15}$ (if em. מִבְּלִי־לוֹ *what is none of his*), מצא *find* Is 34$_{14}$. <OBJ> פחד pi. *frighten* 4Q Shir^a 1$_5$ (+ רוּחַ *spirit*, אֹחַ *owl* or *hyena*)=4QShir^b 10$_1$ ([לפחד] ... לילי[ת]), בהל pi. *terrify* 4QShir^a 1$_5$ ([לב]הל) =4QShir^b 10$_1$ ([לבהל] ... לילי[ת]). <CSTR> [נגע] ... [הלילית] *affliction of the Liliths* 11QPsAp^a 1$_4$.

לין $_{71.4.1.2}$ vb. **lodge—Qal** $_{69.3.1}$ Pf. לָנוּ, לָן; impf. יָלִין, 3fs תָּלִין (תָּלַן), 2ms תָּלִין (תָּלַן), תְּלִינִי, אָלִין, יָלִינוּ (יָלִינוּ) Jb 24$_7$), וַיָּלִינוּ, וַיָּלֶן, וַיָּלִינוּ (נָלִינָה) נָלִין, תָּלִינוּ; + waw 3fs וְלָנָה, 1cpl וְלַנּוּ; impv. לִין, לִינִי, לִינוּ; ptc. Si לָן, לָנִים; inf. לוּן (לִין)—**1. lodge, spend the night** (distinction from §§2-3 not alw. clear; perh. at Lv 19$_3$ 2 S 17$_8$ Jr 4$_{14}$ hi. *cause to remain [overnight]*), <SUBJ> Asaiah Arad ost. 40$_{11}$ ([א]שׁ[יה]ו), David 2 S 12$_{16}$ (+ שׁכב *lie down*) 17$_{16}$, Elijah 1 K 19$_9$, Ezra Ezr 10$_6$ (if em. וַיֵּלֶךְ *and he went*), Jacob Gn 28$_{11}$ 31$_{54}$ 32$_{14.22}$, Joshua Jos 3$_1$ 8$_{9.13}$ (if em. וַיֵּלֶךְ), Naomi Ru 1$_{16}$, Ruth Ru 1$_{16}$ 3$_{13}$, עַם *people* Jos 6$_{11}$ Is 65$_4$ (+ ישׁב *sit*), מַלְאָךְ *angel* Gn 19$_2$ (+ סור *turn aside*) 19$_2$, אִישׁ Gn 24$_{54}$ Jos 4$_3$ Jg 18$_2$ 19$_{4.6.7.9.9.10.20}$ 20$_4$ 2 S 19$_8$ Ne 4$_{16}$, בֵּן *son* of Israel Jos 3$_1$, אָב *father* 2 S 17$_8$, אָח *brother* Gn 31$_{54}$, חָתָן *son-in-law* Jg 19$_6$, נַעַר *lad* Jg 19$_{4.9.11}$ (+ סור) 19$_{13.15}$ (+ סור) 19$_{15}$ Ne 4$_{16}$, עֶבֶד *servant* Gn 24$_{23.25.54}$, פִּלֶגֶשׁ *secondary wife* Jg 19$_9$ 20$_4$, זָקֵן *elder* Nm 22$_8$, אָדוֹן *master* Jg 19$_{11.13.15.15}$, לֵוִי *Levite* Jg 19$_4$ 20$_4$, מְשָׁרֵת *minister* Jl 1$_{13}$ (+ בוא *come*), שֹׁעֵר *porter* 1 C 9$_{27}$, psalmist Ps 55$_8$, enemy Ps 59$_{16}$ (or em. וַיָּלִינוּ *and they lodge* to יַלִּינוּ *they murmur*), אֶבְיוֹן *poor one* Jb 24$_7$, עָנִי *afflicted one* Jb 24$_7$, אמן ni. ptc. *faithful one* Si 20$_4$, גֵּר *sojourner* Jb 31$_{32}$, דּוֹד *beloved* Ca 7$_{12}$, רֹכֵל *merchant* Ne 13$_{20.21}$, מֹכֵר *seller* Ne 13$_{20.21}$, אֹרֵחַ *traveller* Jg 19$_{20}$ Jr 14$_8$ (+ נטה *turn aside*), אֹרְחָה *caravan* Is 21$_{13}$, רְאֵם *wild ox* Jb 39$_9$, קָאַת perh. *pelican* Zp 2$_{14}$ (+ רבץ *lie down*), קִפֹּד perh. *bustard* Zp 2$_{14}$, בְּכִי *weeping* Ps 30$_6$; subj. not specified, Pr 19$_{23}$ (or em.; see Coll.) Si 34$_{20}$ ([י]לין).

<PREP> בְּ of place, time, *in*, *on*, + Gibeah Jg 19$_{13.15}$, Ramah Jg 19$_{13}$, עִיר *city* Jg 19$_{11}$, כָּפָר *village* Ca 7$_{12}$, מַחֲנֶה *camp* Gn 32$_{22}$ Jos 6$_{11}$, מָלוֹן *lodging place* Jos 4$_3$, בַּיִת *house* Arad ost. 40$_{11}$ ([בביתי]), רְחוֹב *square* Gn 19$_2$ Jg 19$_{20}$, חוּץ *street* Jb 31$_{32}$, הַר *mountain* Gn 31$_{54}$, מִדְבָּר *steppe* Ps 55$_8$, עֲרָבָה *steppe* 2 S 17$_{16}$, עֲבָרָה *ford* 2 S 17$_{16(mss)}$, יַעַר *forest* Is 21$_{13}$, נָצוּר *secret place* Is 65$_4$ (or em. בַּנְּצוּרִים *in the secret places* to בֵּין צוּרִים *among the rocks*), כַּפְתּוֹר *capital* Zp 2$_{14}$, שַׂק *sackcloth* Jl 1$_{13}$, לַיְלָה *night* Gn 32$_{14.22}$ Jos 8$_{9.13}$ (if em.; see Subj.), עֶרֶב *evening* Ps 30$_6$; בַּאֲשֶׁר תָּלִינִי אָלִין *where you lodge I will lodge* Ru 1$_{16}$.

עַל *beside, at*, + אֵבוּס *trough* Jb 39$_9$.

עִם *with*, + בְּתוּלָה *young woman* Si 20$_4$.

אֵת *with*, + David 2 S 19$_8$, עַם *people* 2 S 17$_8$.

נֶגֶד *in front of*, + חוֹמָה *wall* Ne 13$_{21}$.

עַד *until*, + בֹּקֶר *morning* Si 34$_{20}$ ([י]לין).

בְּתוֹךְ *within, among*, + Jerusalem Ne 4$_{16}$, עַם *people* Jos 8$_9$, עֵמֶק *valley* Jos 8$_{13}$ (if em.; see Subj.).

בֵּין *among*, + צוּר *rock* Is 65$_4$ (if em.; see above).

מִחוּץ לְ *outside*, + Jerusalem Ne 13$_{20}$.

סָבִיב *around*, + בַּיִת *house* 1 C 9$_{27}$.

<COLL> מָקוֹם לָלוּן *place (in which) to spend the night* Gn 24$_{25}$, var. 24$_{23}$.

+ adv. שָׁם *there* Gn 28$_{11}$ 32$_{14}$ Jos 3$_1$ Jg 18$_2$ 19$_{4.7}$ 1 K 19$_9$ Ezr 10$_6$ (if em.; see Subj.), פֹּה *here* Nm 22$_8$ Jg 19$_9$, מַדּוּעַ *why* Ne 13$_{21}$; + noun or adjective used adverbially, הַלַּיְלָה *tonight* Nm 22$_8$ Jos 4$_3$ 2 S 17$_{16}$ 19$_8$ Ru 3$_{13}$, עָרוֹם *naked* Jb 24$_7$, שָׂבֵעַ *satisfied* Pr 19$_{23}$ (or em. שָׂבֵעַ יָלִין *he spends the night satisfied* to יֹשֵׁב עֶלְיוֹן *one who dwells [with] the Most High*); פַּעַם וּשְׁתָּיִם *once or twice* Ne 13$_{20}$.

2. remain (overnight), <SUBJ> נְבֵלָה *corpse* Dt 21$_{23}$ =11QT 64$_{11}$, בָּשָׂר *flesh* Dt 16$_4$, חֵלֶב *fat* Ex 23$_{18}$, זֶבַח *sacrifice* Ex 34$_{25}$, פְּעֻלָּה *wages* Lv 19$_{13}$, טַל *dew* Jb 29$_{19}$. <PREP> לְ of time, *until*, + בֹּקֶר *morning* Ex 34$_{25}$ Dt 16$_4$; בְּ of place, *on*, + קָצִיר *branch* Jb 29$_{19}$; עַל *upon*, + עֵץ *tree* Dt 21$_{23}$; אֵת *with*, + Israelite Lv 19$_{13}$; עַד *until*, + בֹּקֶר *morning* Ex 23$_{18}$ Lv 19$_{13}$.

3. dwell, remain, <SUBJ> אָדָם *human being* Ps 49$_{13}$ (or em. בין *understand*), סָכָל *fool* Si 51$_{23}$, עַיִן *eye* Jb 17$_2$ (or em. לאה *be weary*), אֹזֶן *ear* Pr 15$_{31}$, נֶפֶשׁ *soul* Ps 25$_{13}$, צְרוֹר *bundle* of myrrh Ca 1$_{13}$, עֹז *strength* Jb 41$_{14}$, צֶדֶק *righteousness* Is 1$_{21}$, מַחֲשָׁבָה *thought* Jr 4$_{14}$, אָלָה *curse* Zc 5$_4$, מְשׁוּגָה *error* Jb 19$_4$, אָשָׁם *guilt* Pr 14$_9$ (if em. אֱוִלִים יָלִיץ *wickedness mocks fools* to אָהֳלֵי לֵצִים *the tents of fools* are wickedness; בְּאֹהֶל/בְּבָתֵּי אֱוִלִים יָלִין *in the tent/houses of* *fools* guilt *dwells*). <PREP> בְּ of place, *in*, + אֹהֶל *tent* Pr 14$_{9}$ (if em.; see Subj.), בַּיִת *house* Pr 14$_{9}$ (if em.) Si 51$_{23}$, צַוָּאר *neck* Jb 41$_{14}$, קִרְיָה *city* Is 1$_{21}$, טוֹב *good* Ps 25$_{13}$, יְקָר *honour* Ps 49$_{13}$; אֵת *with*, + Job Jb 19$_{4}$; בְּקֶרֶב *within, among*, + Israel Jr 4$_{14}$, חָכָם *wise one* Pr 15$_{31}$; בְּתוֹךְ *within*, + בַּיִת *house* Zc 5$_{4}$; בֵּין *between*, + שַׁד *breast* Ca 1$_{13}$. <COLL> + adv. עַד־מָתַי *how long?* Jr 4$_{14}$.

Htpol. 2.1.1 Impf. יִתְלוֹנָן (יִתְלֹנָן); impv. Q התלוננו—**dwell, abide,** <SUBJ> אֱנוֹשׁ *person* Si 14$_{26}$ (+ ישים קנו *he places his nest*), נֶשֶׁר *eagle* Jb 39$_{28}$ (|| שׁכן *dwell*); subj. not specified, Ps 91$_{1}$=11QPsAp[a] 3$_{4}$ ([יתלונן]; or em. רנן htpol. *shout (for joy)* || ישׁב *dwell*). <PREP> בְּ of place, *in*, + צֵל *shadow* Ps 91$_{1}$=11QPsAp[a] 3$_{4}$ ([בצ]ל ... [יתלונן]), עָנָף *branches* Si 14$_{26}$; עַל *upon*, + שֵׁן *tooth*, i.e. crag, of rock Jb 39$_{28}$, מְצוּדָה *stronghold* Jb 39$_{28}$. <COLL> + adverb or noun used adverbially, יַחַד *together* 4QMidrEschat[b] 11$_{3}$, סֶלַע *(upon the) rock* Jb 39$_{28}$.

<SYN> ישׁב *dwell*, שׁכן *dwell*.*

→ מָלוֹן *lodging place*, מְלוּנָה *lodge*.

ליץ 28.11.17 vb. **scorn—Qal** 17.10.3 Pf. + waw וְלַצְתָּ; ptc. לֵץ, לֵצִים—**1. scorn, scoff,** <SUBJ> subj. not specified, Pr 9$_{12}$ (:: חכם *be wise*) 5QapMal 1$_{2}$. <PREP> בְּ *at*, or introducing object, + בְּהֵמָה *beast* 5QapMal 1$_{2}$.

2. ptc. used as noun, **scorner, scoffer,*** <SUBJ> שׁמע *hear* Pr 13$_{1}$, שׁמר *keep* Si 35$_{18.18(B)}$ (|| זֵד *presumptuous one*), שׂנא *hate* Pr 9$_{8}$ (:: חָכָם *wise one*), אהב *love* Pr 15$_{12}$, חמד *delight in* Pr 1$_{22}$ (|| כְּסִיל *fool*, פֶּתִי *simple one*), בקשׁ pi. *seek* Pr 14$_{6}$ (:: בין ni. ptc. *understanding one*), לקח *take* Si 35$_{18(Bmg, E)}$, הלך *go* Pr 15$_{12}$, חרק *gnash* 1QH 2$_{11}$, כלה *come to an end* Is 29$_{20}$ (|| עָרִיץ *tyrant*).

<NOM CL> לֵץ הַיַּיִן *wine is a scoffer* Pr 20$_{1(L)}$ (mss הַיָּיִן; || המה ptc. *boisterous one*), לֵץ שְׁמוֹ *scoffer is his name* Pr 21$_{24}$ (+ זֵד *presumptuous one*), תוֹעֲבַת לְאָדָם לֵץ *a scoffer is an abomination to humans* Pr 24$_{9}$.

<OBJ> יסר *discipline* Pr 9$_{7}$ (+ רָשָׁע *wicked one*), יכח hi. *reprove* Pr 9$_{8}$, נכה hi. *strike* Pr 19$_{25}$ (+ בין ni. ptc. *understanding one*, פֶּתִי *simple one*), ענשׁ *punish* Pr 21$_{11}$ (+ פֶּתִי, חָכָם *wise one*), גרשׁ pi. *drive out* Pr 22$_{10}$, ישׁב hi. *seat* Si 8$_{11}$.

<CSTR> מוֹשַׁב לֵצִים *seat of scorners* Ps 1$_{1}$ (|| חַטָּא *sinner*), בית לצים *house of scorners* Si 11$_{30}$, מצות *strife of* Si 34$_{26}$, ריב *contention of* Si 34$_{26}$, מכת לץ *wound of a scorner* Si 3$_{28}$, [ש]מחת *joy of* 4Q418 100$_{1}$.

<PREP> לְ of direction, *to(wards)*, + ליץ hi. *be scornful* Pr 3$_{34}$ (or em. אִם־לַלֵּצִים *surely to scorners* to עִם־לֵצִים *with scorners*); of benefit, *to, for*, + כון ni. *be prepared* Pr 19$_{29}$ (+ כְּסִיל *fool*); אֶל *to, with*, + יעץ *counsel* a way Si 37$_{7(B)}$, חבר *join together* Si 13$_{1}$; מִן of direction, *from* Si 15$_{8}$ (+ אנשי כזב *men of falsehood*); מִפְּנֵי *from before*, + זוח *be moved* Si 8$_{11}$.

<SYN> §2 כְּסִיל *fool*, פֶּתִי *simple one*, זֵד *presumptuous one*, עָרִיץ *tyrant*, המה ptc. *boisterous one*, חַטָּא *sinner*.

<ANT> §1 חכם *be wise*.

Hi. 9.1.14 Pf. הֱלִיצֻנִי; impf. יָלִיץ (Q יליאצו; unless both Qal); ptc. מֵלִיץ, מְלִיצֵי, מְלִיצַי, מְלִיצֶיךָ, Si מְלִיצָיו; inf. Q הליץ—**1. scorn, deride, mock,** <SUBJ> Y. Pr 3$_{34}$ (+ נתן חֵן *show favour*), זֵד *presumptuous one* Ps 119$_{51}$, עֵד *witness* Pr 19$_{28}$, זוֹנָה *prostitute* 4QWiles 1$_{2}$ ([זונ]ה), אָשָׁם *wickedness* Pr 14$_{9}$ (or em. אֱוִלִים יָלִיץ אָשָׁם *wickedness mocks fools* to אָהֳלֵי לֵצִים *the tents of fools* are wickedness; בְּאֹהֶל/בְּבָתֵּי אֱוִלִים יָלִין *in the tent/houses of fools* wickedness *dwells*). <OBJ> psalmist Ps 119$_{51}$, אֱוִיל *fool* Pr 14$_{9}$ (or em.; see Subj.), מִשְׁפָּט *justice* Pr 19$_{28}$. <PREP> לְ of direction, *to(wards)*, + לֵץ *scorner* Pr 3$_{34}$ (or em. אִם־לַלֵּצִים *surely to scorners* to עִם־לֵצִים *with scorners*).

2. ptc. used as noun, **interpreter*** (Gn 42$_{23}$ 1QH 18$_{12}$), **spokesman, mediator** (Is 43$_{27}$ Jb 16$_{20}$ 33$_{23}$ 1QH 2$_{13.14.31}$ 4$_{7.9}$ 6$_{13}$ fr. 2$_{6}$ 4QpPs[a] 1.1$_{19}$ 4QDiscourse 7$_{2}$ 4QHod[a] 7.2$_{16}$), **envoy** (2 C 32$_{31}$), **official** (Si 10$_{2}$), <SUBJ> פשׁע *transgress* Is 43$_{27}$ (+ אָב *father*), תעה hi. *lead astray* 1QH 4$_{7}$ ([התעו]ם), אמר *say* Jb 33$_{23}$, נגד hi. *tell* Jb 33$_{23}$, חנן *be gracious* Jb 33$_{23}$, מצא *find* Jb 33$_{23}$. <NOM CL> המה מליצי כזב *they are mediators of lies* 1QH 4$_{9}$ (|| חֹזֶה *seer*), הַמֵּלִיץ בֵּינֹתָם *an interpreter was between them* Gn 42$_{23}$, מְלִיצַי רֵעָי *(it is) my spokesman* Jb 16$_{20}$ (if em. מְלִיצַי *my spokesmen*; + עֵד *witness*, שָׂהֵד *witness*), מליצי דעת עם כול צעודו *the mediators of knowledge are with all his steps* 1QH fr. 2$_{6}$, אִם־יֵשׁ עָלָיו ... מֵלִיץ *if he has ... a mediator* Jb 33$_{23}$, אין מליץ *there is no mediator* 1QH 6$_{13}$ 4QHod[a] 7.2$_{16}$, כְּשׁוֹפֵט עַם כֵּן מְלִיצָיו *as the judge of the people, so are its officials* Si 10$_{2}$. <OBJ> שׂים *place*, i.e. appoint 1QH 2$_{13}$. <CSTR> מְלִיצֵי שָׂרֵי *envoys of the princes of* Babylon 2 C 32$_{31}$, מליץ דעת *mediator of knowledge* 1QH 2$_{13}$ 4QpPs[a]

1.1$_{19}$, מליצי דעת *mediators of knowledge* 1QH fr. 2$_{6}$, מליצי תעות *mediators of error* 1QH 2$_{14}$, כזב *of lies* 1QH 2$_{31}$ 4$_{9}$, רמיה *of deceit* 1QH 4$_{7}$; קנאת מליצי *jealousy of the mediators of* 1QH 2$_{31}$. <APP> רֵעַ *cry* Jb 16$_{20}$, מַלְאָךְ *messenger* Jb 33$_{23}$. <ADJ> אֶחָד *one* Jb 33$_{23}$. <PREP> לְ of benefit, *to, for,* + היה *be* 1QH 2$_{14}$; שׁמע לְ *listen to* 4QpPs^a 1.1$_{19}$ (שמ[עו]); *as,* + חקק *engrave* on tongue 1QH 18$_{12}$; בְּ *in (the matter of),* + עזב *forsake* 2 C 32$_{31}$. <COLL> מליץ לעמך *a mediator for your people* 4QDiscourse 7$_{2}$, מליץ באלה *an interpreter in,* i.e. of, *these (things)* 1QH 18$_{12}$.

Also 4QLeqeṭ 1$_{6}$ (ילאצו) 4QapPent 1$_{7}$ (מליץ).

<SYN> חֹזֶה *seer.*

Pol. $_{1}$ Ptc. לֹצְצִים—ptc. used as noun, **scoffer,** <PREP> אֵת *with,* + משׁך *stretch out* hand Ho 7$_{5}$ (or em. מָשַׁךְ יָדוֹ *he stretched out his hand* to מָשַׁךְ יֵינוֹ *he mixed his wine*).

Htpol. $_{1}$ Impf. תִּתְלוֹצָצוּ—**scoff,** <SUBJ> אִישׁ *man* Is 28$_{22}$.*

⇒ לָצוֹן *scorning,* מְלִיצָה *satire.*

לַיִשׁ I $_{3}$ n.m. **lion,** <SUBJ> שׁוב *go back* Pr 30$_{30}$, המם hi. *roar* Is 30$_{6}$ (if em.; see Nom. Cl.), אבד *perish* Jb 4$_{11}$ (+ לָבִיא *lion*). <NOM CL> לַיִשׁ מֵהֶם *a lion is from them* Is 30$_{6}$ (or em. מֵהֶם to מֹהֵם *roars;* ‖ לָבִיא *lion*), לַיִשׁ גִּבּוֹר בַּבְּהֵמָה *a lion is a mighty one among beasts* Pr 30$_{30}$. <COLL> לָבִיא וָלַיִשׁ *a female lion and a lion* Is 30$_{6}$.

<SYN> לָבִיא *female lion.*

לַיִשׁ II $_{4}$ pl.n. **Laish**—+ ה- of direction לַיְשָׁה—city in extreme north of Canaan, conquered and renamed Dan by tribe of Dan, T. el-Qāḍī, 42 km E of Tyre, appar. ident. with Leshem at Jos 19$_{47}$, <NOM CL> לַיִשׁ שֵׁם־הָעִיר לָרִאשֹׁנָה *Laish was the name of the city at first* Jg 18$_{29}$. <OBJ> רגל pi. *spy out* Jg 18$_{14}$. <APP> אֶרֶץ *land* Jg 18$_{14}$. <PREP> עַל *to,* + בוא *come* Jg 18$_{27}$ (mss אֶל *to,* mss עַד *unto*); ה- of direction, *to* Laish, + בוא *come* Jg 18$_{7}$.

לַיִשׁ III $_{2}$ pr.n.m. **Laish,** father of Michal's second husband, Paltiel, <CSTR> בֶּן־לַיִשׁ *son of Laish* 1 S 25$_{44}$ (mss לוש *of Lush*) 2 S 3$_{15(Qr)}$ (Kt לוש).

לַיְשָׁה $_{1}$ pl.n. **Laishah,** perh. El-ʿĪsāwīye, 3 km NE of Jerusalem, הַקְשִׁיבִי לַיְשָׁה *attend, O Laishah* Is 10$_{30}$.

לכד $_{121.2.6}$ vb. **capture**—**Qal** $_{83.1.3}$ Pf. לָכַד (לָכֵד), לָכַדְתִּי, לְכָדֻנוּ; impf. יִלְכּוֹד (יִלְכְּדֶנָּה, יִלְכְּדֶנּוּ), 3fs Q תלכוד וְלָכַד + waw ;(יִלְכְּדֻנוּ, יִלְכְּדוּ) יִלְכְּדוּ, אֶלְכֹּד, (תִּלְכְּדוֹ) (וַיִּלְכְּדָהּ, וַיִּלְכָּד־) וַיִּלְכֹּד ;(וּלְכָדָהּ) וּלְכָדוּהָ, (וּלְכָדָהּ), לָכְדָה, impv. ;וַנִּלְכֹּד, (וַיִּלְכְּדָהּ, וַיִּלְכְּדוּהָ, וַיִּלְכְּדֻהוּ) וַיִּלְכְּדוּ לִכְדוּ; ptc. לֹכֵד (Si לוכד); inf. abs. לָכוֹד; cstr. לָכְדֵנִי (Q לכודני), לָכְדָה.

1. capture, seize, catch, ensnare, <SUBJ> Y. Jb 5$_{13}$, Abijah 2 C 13$_{19}$, Abimelech Jg 9$_{45.50}$, Asa 2 C 15$_{8}$ 17$_{2}$, David 2 S 5$_{7}$‖1 C 11$_{5}$ 2 S 8$_{4}$‖1 C 18$_{4}$ 2 S 12$_{28.29}$, Gideon Jg 8$_{12.14}$, Hazael 2 K 12$_{18}$, Jair Nm 32$_{41}$, Joab 2 S 12$_{26.27.28}$, Joshua Jos 10$_{1.28.35.37.39.42}$ 11$_{10.12.17}$, Nobah Nm 32$_{42}$, Othniel Jos 15$_{17}$ Jg 1$_{13}$, Samson Jg 15$_{4}$, Saul 1 S 14$_{47}$, Shalmaneser 2 K 18$_{9(mss).10}$, Shishak 2 C 12$_{4}$, Assyrians 2 C 32$_{18}$, Chaldaeans Jr 37$_{8}$ Hb 1$_{10}$, Ephraim Jg 7$_{24}$, Gilead Jg 12$_{5}$, Israel(ites) Nm 21$_{32}$ Dt 2$_{34}$ 2$_{35}$ 3$_{4}$ Jos 10$_{32.35.37.39(mss)}$, Judah Jg 1$_{18}$, Philistines 2 C 28$_{18}$, עַם *people* Jos 6$_{20}$, גּוֹי *nation* Hb 1$_{10}$, אִישׁ *man* Jos 6$_{20}$ Jg 7$_{24.25}$, אָב *father* Ne 9$_{25}$ 2 C 17$_{2}$, בֵּן *son* Nm 32$_{39.41}$ Jos 15$_{17}$ 19$_{47}$ Jg 1$_{8.13}$ 3$_{28}$, אָח *brother* Jos 15$_{17}$ Jg 1$_{13}$, מֶלֶךְ *king* 1 K 9$_{16}$ 2 K 12$_{18}$ 17$_{6}$ 18$_{10}$ Jr 32$_{3.28}$ 38$_{3}$ Dn 11$_{15.18}$ 2 C 12$_{4}$, פַּרְעֹה *Pharaoh* 1 K 9$_{16}$, שַׂר *commander* 2 C 33$_{11}$, תַּרְתָּן *commander* Is 20$_{1}$, רָשָׁע *wicked one* Jr 5$_{26}$, אוֹיֵב *enemy* Jr 34$_{22}$, חַיִל *army* Jr 34$_{22}$, גְּדוּד *troop* Jr 18$_{22}$, אֹרֵב *ambush* Jos 8$_{19.21}$, בקשׁ pi. ptc. *one who seeks* life Jr 34$_{22}$, perh. דרשׁ ptc. *one who seeks* 4QBark^d 2.1$_{2}$, אֲשֶׁר *the one who* Jos 15$_{16}$ Jg 1$_{12}$, כְּפִיר *(young) lion* Am 3$_{4}$, פַּח *trap* Am 3$_{5.5}$, רֶשֶׁת *net* Ps 35$_{8}$ 1QH 1$_{29}$, עָוֹן *iniquity* Pr 5$_{22}$; subj. not specified, Jr 32$_{24}$ Pr 16$_{32}$ 2 C 22$_{9}$ Si 37$_{11}$ $_{(Bmg, D)}$.

<OBJ> Ai Jos 10$_{1}$, Aijalon 2 C 28$_{18}$, Ashdod Is 20$_{1}$, Ashkelon Jg 1$_{18}$, Bethel 2 C 13$_{19}$, Beth-shemesh 2 C 28$_{18}$, Debir Jos 10$_{39}$, Eglon Jos 10$_{35}$, Ekron Jg 1$_{18}$, Ephron 2 C 13$_{19(Kt)}$ (Qr Ephrain), Gath 2 K 12$_{18}$, Gaza Jg 1$_{18}$, Gederoth 2 C 28$_{18}$, Gezer 1 K 9$_{16}$, Gilead Nm 32$_{39}$, Gimzo 2 C 28$_{18}$, Hazor Jos 11$_{10}$, Hebron Jos 10$_{37}$, Jashanah 2 C 13$_{19}$, Jazer Nm 21$_{32}$ (if em. וַיִּלְכְּדוּ בְּנֹתֶיהָ *and they captured its villages* to וַיִּלְכְּדוּהָ וּבְנֹתֶיהָ *and they captured it and its villages*), Jerusalem Jg 1$_{8}$, Kenath Nm 32$_{42}$, Kiriath-sepher Jos 15$_{16.17}$ Jg 1$_{12.13}$, Lachish Jos 10$_{32}$, Leshem Jos 19$_{47}$, Makkedah Jos 10$_{28}$, Rabbah 2 S 12$_{29}$, Samaria 2 K 17$_{6}$ 18$_{9(mss).10}$, Soco 2 C 28$_{18}$, Thebez Jg 9$_{50}$, Timnah 2 C 28$_{18}$, עִיר *city* Dt 2$_{34.35}$ 3$_{5}$ Jos 6$_{20}$ 8$_{19.21}$ 10$_{39}$

11$_{12}$ Jg 9$_{45}$ 2 S 12$_{26.27.28.28}$ Jr 32$_{3.24.28}$ 34$_{22}$ 37$_{8}$ 38$_{3}$ Pr 16$_{32}$ Dn 11$_{15}$ Ne 9$_{25}$ 2 C 12$_{4}$ 13$_{19}$ 15$_{8}$ 17$_{2}$ 32$_{18}$, בַּת *daughter*, i.e. village Nm 21$_{32}$ 32$_{42}$ 2 C 13$_{19.19.19}$ 28$_{18.18.18}$, חַוָּה *tent village* Nm 32$_{41}$, מְצוּדָה *stronghold* 2 S 5$_{7}$||1 C 11$_{5}$, מִבְצָר *fortress* Hb 1$_{10}$, אֶרֶץ *land* Jos 10$_{42}$, אֲדָמָה *land* Ne 9$_{25}$, מֶמְשָׁלָה *kingdom* 4QNarrC 1$_{9}$ (unless read לבדו *him alone*), גְּבוּל *border* Jg 1$_{18.18.18}$, מַעְבָּרָה *ford* Jg 3$_{28}$ 12$_{5}$, מַיִם *water* Jg 7$_{24.24}$, Jordan Jg 7$_{24.24}$, מְלוּכָה *kingship* 1 S 14$_{47}$.

Ahaziah 2 C 22$_{9}$, Jeremiah Jr 18$_{22}$, Manasseh 2 C 33$_{11}$, Nebuchadrezzar Jr 32$_{38}$, Oreb Jg 7$_{25}$, Zalmunna Jg 8$_{12}$, Zebah Jg 8$_{12}$, Zeeb Jg 7$_{25}$, מֶלֶךְ *king* Jos 10$_{39.42}$ 11$_{12.17}$ Jg 8$_{12}$, שַׂר *prince* Jg 7$_{25}$, פָּרָשׁ *cavalry officer* 2 S 8$_{4}$||1 C 18$_{4}$, אִישׁ *man* 2 S 8$_{4}$||1 C 18$_{4}$ Jr 5$_{26}$, נַעַר *lad* Jg 8$_{14}$, worshipper 4QBark^{d} 2.1$_{2}$, חָכָם *wise one* Jb 5$_{13}$, בקשׁ pi. ptc. *one who seeks* life Ps 35$_{8}$, רָשָׁע *wicked one* Pr 5$_{22}$, רֶגֶל *foot* 1QH 2$_{29}$, רַב pl. *many* Dn 11$_{18}$, שׁוּעָל *fox* Jg 15$_{4}$, רֶכֶב *chariot* 1 C 18$_{4}$.

<PREP> לְ *against*, + Ephraim Jg 12$_{5}$, Midian Jg 7$_{24}$, Moab Jg 3$_{28}$.

בְּ of time, place, *on, in*, + יוֹם *day* Jos 10$_{28.32.35}$, עֹרֶם *craftiness* Jb 5$_{13}$; of instrument, *by (means of), with* + חוֹחַ *fetter* 2 C 33$_{11}$.

מִן of direction, *from*, + Hadadezer 2 S 8$_{4}$||1 C 18$_{4}$, Jeroboam 2 C 13$_{19}$, מֶלֶךְ *king* 2 S 8$_{4}$||1 C18$_{4}$, בֵּן *son* 2 S 8$_{4}$; of place, *from*, i.e. in, + הַר *hill-country* 2 C 15$_{8}$; *from among*, + אִישׁ *man* Jg 8$_{14}$, of time, *at*, + קָצֶה *end* of three years 2 K 18$_{10}$.

עִם *with* perh. 4QNarrC 1$_{9}$.

עַד *as far as*, + Beth-barah Jg 7$_{24.24}$.

<COLL> + חנה *encamp* Jg 9$_{50}$ 2 S 12$_{28}$, צור *besiege* 2 K 18$_{10}$, שׁפך סוֹלְלָה *throw up siegeworks* Dn 11$_{15}$, צבר עָפָר *heap up earth* Hb 1$_{10}$, לחם ni. *fight* Jos 10$_{35.37.39}$ 19$_{47}$ Jg 1$_{8}$ 9$_{45}$ 2 S 12$_{26.27.29}$ 2 K 12$_{18}$ Is 20$_{1}$ Jr 34$_{22}$ 37$_{8}$, נתן בְּיַד *give into hand of* Jr 32$_{3.28}$, ni. *be given into hand of* Jr 32$_{24}$ 38$_{3}$, תמך ni. *be caught* Pr 5$_{22}$.

+ חרם hi. *destroy* Dt 2$_{34}$ Jos 10$_{1.28.35.37.39}$ 11$_{12}$, נכה hi. *smite* Jos 10$_{28.32.35.37.39}$ 11$_{12.17}$ 15$_{16}$ 19$_{47}$ Jg 1$_{8.12}$, מות hi. *kill* Jos 11$_{17}$, שׂרף *burn* 1 K 9$_{16}$ Jr 34$_{22}$ 37$_{8}$, + שׁלח pi. *send*, i.e. set, on fire Jg 1$_{8}$, ירשׁ *possess* Jos 19$_{47}$ Ne 9$_{25}$, hi. *dispossess* Nm 32$_{39}$, טמן *hide* trap Jr 18$_{22}$, אסר *bind* 2 C 33$_{11}$.

+ noun used adverbially, פַּעַם (at) one *time* Jos 10$_{42}$.

inf. abs. used with impf. of verb, Am 3$_{5}$.

2. take by lot, <SUBJ> Y. Jos 7$_{14.14.14}$, Joshua Jos 7$_{17}$ (or em. לכד ni. *be taken*). <OBJ> שֵׁבֶט *tribe* Jos 7$_{14}$, מִשְׁפָּחָה *family* Jos 7$_{14.17}$ (or em.; see Subj.), בַּיִת *house* Jos 7$_{14}$.

Also 4QSap^{b} 14$_{2}$.

Ni. 36.1.3 Pf. נִלְכַּד, נִלְכְּדָה, נִלְכַּדְתְּ, נִלְכַּדְתְּ; impf. יִלָּכֵד, יִלָּכְדוּ (יִלָּכְדוּ) יִלָּכְדוּן, תִּלָּכְדִי, תלכד Q, 2ms Si, תִּלָּכֵד 3fs, (יִלָּכֵד Q ילכדו); + waw וְנִלְכְּדָה, וְנִלְכְּדוּ (וְנִלְכְּדוּ); וַיִּלָּכֵד, 3fs וַתִּלָּכֵד, וַיִּלָּכְדוּ (וַיִּלָּכְדוּ); ptc. נִלְכָּד—**1. be captured, caught, ensnared,** <SUBJ> Moab Jr 48$_{7}$, Babylon Jr 50$_{2.9.24}$ 51$_{31}$, Jerusalem Jr 38$_{28.28}$ (lacking in mss), Kiriathaim Jr 48$_{1}$, Samaria 2 K 18$_{10}$, Sheshach Jr 51$_{41}$, עִיר *city* 1 K 16$_{18}$ Jr 51$_{31}$ Zc 14$_{2}$, אִישׁ *man* Jr 6$_{11}$, אִשָּׁה *woman* Jr 6$_{11}$, בֵּן *son* Pr 6$_{2}$ Si 9$_{3}$, גִּבּוֹר *warrior* Jr 51$_{56}$, זָקֵן *elder* Jr 6$_{11}$, מָלֵא *one full* of days, i.e. aged Jr 6$_{11}$, עַם *people* Is 28$_{13}$, רַב pl. *many* Is 8$_{15}$, עלה ptc. *one who goes up* from pit Is 24$_{18}$ Jr 48$_{44}$, חָכָם *wise one* Jr 8$_{9}$, מבין hi. ptc. *understanding one* 4Q525 14.2$_{27}$, צַדִּיק *righteous one* Jb 36$_{8}$, מָשִׁיחַ *anointed one* Lm 4$_{20}$, שֹׁרֵר *enemy* Ps 59$_{13}$, חוֹטֵא *sinner* Ec 7$_{26}$, בגד ptc. *treacherous one* Pr 11$_{6}$, רֶגֶל *foot* Ps 9$_{16}$ 1QH 8$_{34}$ (רג[ל]י), זֶרַע *seed*, i.e. descendants 4QJub^{a} 1$_{10}$, רוּחַ *breath* of nostril Lm 4$_{20}$.

<PREP> בְּ of instrument/place, *by (means of), with, in*, + אִשָּׁה *woman* Ec 7$_{26}$, פַּח *trap* Is 24$_{18}$ Jr 48$_{44}$, לְקָה *trap* Si 9$_{3}$, רֶשֶׁת *net* Ps 9$_{16}$, שְׁחִית *pit* Lm 4$_{20}$, חֶבֶל *rope* Jb 36$_{8}$, כֶּבֶל *fetters* 1QH 8$_{34}$, גָּאוֹן *pride* Ps 59$_{13}$, אֹמֶר *word* Pr 6$_{2}$, שָׂפָה *lip* 4Q525 14.2$_{27}$, הַוָּה *bluster* Pr 11$_{6}$.

מִן of direction, *from*, + שָׁם *there* Jr 50$_{9}$, קָצֶה *end* Jr 51$_{31}$, *by*, + אָלָה *curse* Ps 59$_{13}$, כַּחַשׁ *lying* Ps 59$_{13}$.

<COLL> || תפשׂ ni. *be seized* Jr 48$_{7}$ 51$_{41}$, יקשׁ ni. *be ensnared* Is 8$_{15}$ 28$_{13}$ Pr 6$_{2}$, אסר pass. *be bound* Jb 36$_{8}$, שׁבר ni. *be broken* Is 8$_{15}$ 28$_{13}$, חתת *be shattered* Jr 8$_{9}$ 50$_{2}$, בושׁ hi. *be put to shame* Jr 8$_{9}$ 48$_{1}$ 50$_{2}$, נפל *fall* Is 8$_{15}$.

+ יקשׁ *set a snare* Jr 50$_{24}$, חתת pi. *be shattered* Jr 51$_{56}$, שׁסס ni. *be plundered* Zc 14$_{2}$, שׁגל ni. *be ravished* Zc 14$_{2}$(Kt), נפל *fall* 4QJub^{a} 1$_{10}$, יצא בַּגּוֹלָה *go into exile* Jr 48$_{7}$.

:: מלט ni. *escape* Ec 7$_{26}$.

2. be taken by lot, <SUBJ> Achan Jos 7$_{18}$, Jonathan 1 S 14$_{41.42}$, Saul 1 S 10$_{21}$ 14$_{41}$, Zabdi Jos 7$_{17}$, בֵּן *son* Jos 7$_{18}$ 1 S 10$_{21}$, מִשְׁפָּחָה *family* Jos 7$_{17}$ (if em. qal) 1 S 10$_{21}$, שֵׁבֶט *tribe* Jos 7$_{16}$ 1 S 10$_{20}$; subj. not specified, Jos 7$_{15}$. <PREP> בְּ of accompaniment, *with*, + חֵרֶם *devoted object* Jos 7$_{15}$. <COLL> :: יצא *go out*, i.e. be cleared 1 S 14$_{41}$.

<SYN> §1 תפשׂ ni. *be seized,* יקשׁ ni. *be ensnared,* אסר pass. *be bound,* שׁבר ni. *be broken,* חתת *be shattered,* בושׁ hi. *be put to shame,* נפל *fall.*

<ANT> §1 מלט ni. *escape;* §2 יצא *go out,* i.e. be cleared.

Htp. 2 Impf. יִתְלַכָּדוּ (יִתְלַכְּדוּ)—**grasp one another, be compacted together,** of frozen water (Jb 37$_{30}$), of scales of Leviathan (Jb 41$_{9}$), <SUBJ> פָּנִים *face* of deep Jb 38$_{30}$, מָגֵן *shield,* i.e. scale Jb 41$_{9}$ (|| דבק pu. *be joined*), אִישׁ *each one* Jb 41$_{9}$. <COLL> || חבא htp. *keep oneself hidden* Jb 37$_{30}$; :: פרד htp. *be separated* Jb 41$_{9}$.

<SYN> דבק pu. *be joined.*

<ANT> פרד htp. *be separated.*

→ לֶכֶד *capture,* מַלְכֹּדֶת *snare.*

[לֶכֶד] 1 n.[m.] **capture**—לֶכֶד—**capture, being caught,** <PREP> מִן privative, *from,* + שׁמר *keep* Pr 3$_{26}$.

→ לכד *capture.*

לֵכָה 1 pr.n.m. **Lecah,** son of Er and great-grandson of Judah (unless name of town founded by Er), <CSTR> אֲבִי לֵכָה *father of Lecah* 1 C 4$_{21}$.

[לְכוּשִׁי] 0.0.1 adj. **pine,** of the Aleppo pine, used attributively of דֶּמַע *resin* 3QTr 3$_{9}$ (כלי דמע לכושי *vessels of resin of pine;* or rd. לבושי vessels of tribute, *my garments,* or ולבוהשין tribute vessels *and garments*).*

לָכִישׁ 24.0.0.1 pl.n. **Lachish**—I לכשׁ; + ה- of direction לָכִישָׁה—city of Judah, perh. T. ed-Duwēr, 26 km WNW of Hebron, <NOM CL> לָכִישׁ ... בַּשְּׁפֵלָה *in the lowland was ... Lachish* Jos 15$_{39}$. <OBJ> בנה *build* 2 C 11$_{9}$, נתן *give* Jos 10$_{32}$, עזר *help* Jos 10$_{33}$. <CSTR> מֶלֶךְ־לָכִישׁ *king of Lachish* Jos 10$_{3.5.23}$ 12$_{11}$ (both מֶלֶךְ לָכִישׁ), יוֹשֶׁבֶת לָכִישׁ *inhabitant of Lachish* Mc 1$_{13}$, משאת לכשׁ *signals of Lachish* Lachish ost. 4$_{10}$. <PREP> לְ of benefit, *to,* + עשׂה *do* Jos 10$_{35}$; בְּ of place, *in,* + ישׁב *dwell* Ne 11$_{30}$; מִן of direction, *from,* + שׁלח *send* 2 K 18$_{17}$||Is 36$_{2}$, עבר *pass* Jos 10$_{34}$, נסע *depart* 2 K 19$_{8}$||Is 37$_{8}$; אֶל *to,* + יתר ni. *remain* Jr 34$_{7}$; עַל *against* 2 C 32$_{9}$; ה- of direction, *to(wards),* + עבר *pass* Jos 10$_{31}$, נוס *flee* 2 K 14$_{19}$||2 C 25$_{27}$, שׁלח *send* 2 K 14$_{19}$||2 C 25$_{27}$ 2 K 18$_{14}$.

[לָכֵם], see לָכֵן *therefore.*

לָכֵן 200.2 adv. **therefore**—Si לכם—**1. therefore, thus, so, in that case,*** or **and, now then, granted,** introducing a following fact, idea, etc.*

a. followed by verb היה *be* 1 S 27$_{6}$ Is 5$_{24}$ 30$_{13}$ Jr 23$_{12}$ Ho 13$_{3}$ Mc 2$_{5}$ Zp 2$_{9}$, ישׁב *dwell* Jr 50$_{39}$, בוא *come* Jr 7$_{32}$ 16$_{14}$ 19$_{6}$ 23$_{7}$ 48$_{12}$ 49$_{2}$ 51$_{47.52}$, hi. *bring* Nm 20$_{12}$ 1 K 14$_{10}$ Ezk 28$_{7}$, יצא *go out* Ezk 21$_{9}$, עלה hi. *take up* Is 8$_{7}$, ירד *go down* 2 K 1$_{6.16}$, גלה *be exiled* Is 5$_{13}$ Am 6$_{7}$, שׁוב *go back* Ho 2$_{11}$ Ps 73$_{10(Qr)}$, hi. *take back* Ps 73$_{10(Kt)}$, רום *be exalted* Is 30$_{18}$, קום hi. *raise up* Si 45$_{24}$, שׁלח pi. *send* Is 10$_{16}$, פקד *visit* Is 26$_{14}$, חכה pi. *wait* Is 30$_{18}$ Zp 3$_{8}$.

אמר *say* Ex 6$_{6}$ Nm 25$_{12}$ 2 K 1$_{4}$ 19$_{32}$||Is 37$_{33}$ 2 K 21$_{12}$ Is 10$_{24}$ 28$_{16}$ 29$_{22}$ 30$_{12}$ 65$_{13}$ Jr 5$_{14}$ 6$_{21}$ 7$_{20}$ 9$_{6.14}$ 11$_{11.21.22}$ 14$_{15}$ 15$_{19}$ 18$_{13}$ 22$_{18}$ 23$_{2.15.38}$ 25$_{8}$ 28$_{16}$ 29$_{32}$ 32$_{28.36}$ 34$_{17}$ 35$_{17.19}$ 36$_{30}$ 44$_{11}$ 50$_{18}$ 51$_{36}$ Ezk 5$_{7.8}$ 11$_{7.16.17}$ 12$_{23.28}$ 13$_{8.13.20}$ 14$_{6}$ 15$_{6}$ 17$_{19}$ 20$_{30}$ 21$_{29}$ 22$_{19}$ 23$_{22.35}$ 24$_{6.9}$ 25$_{13.16}$ 26$_{3}$ 28$_{6}$ 29$_{8.19}$ 30$_{22}$ 31$_{10}$ 33$_{25}$ 34$_{20}$ 36$_{5.7.22}$ 39$_{25}$ Am 3$_{11}$ 5$_{16}$ 7$_{17}$ Mc 2$_{3}$ Zc 1$_{16}$ Jb 32$_{10}$, דבר pi. *speak* Ezk 14$_{4}$ 20$_{27}$, נגד hi. *tell* Jb 42$_{3}$, קרא *call* Is 30$_{7}$, שׁבע ni. *swear* 1 S 3$_{14}$, נבא ni. *prophesy* Ezk 11$_{4}$ 36$_{3.6}$ 37$_{12}$ 38$_{14}$, שׁמע *hear* 1 K 22$_{19}$||2 C 18$_{18}$ (or em. לֹא כֵן *it is not so*) Is 28$_{14}$ 51$_{21}$ Jr 6$_{18}$ 42$_{15}$ 44$_{26}$ 49$_{20}$ 50$_{45}$ Ezk 16$_{35}$ 34$_{7.9}$ 36$_{4}$ Ps 78$_{21}$ Jb 34$_{10}$, חזה *see* Ezk 13$_{23}$, ידע *know* 1 S 28$_{2}$ Is 52$_{6.6}$ (or del.), hi. *cause to know* Jr 16$_{21}$, נכר hi. *recognize* Jb 34$_{25}$, ירא *fear* Jb 37$_{24}$, ילל hi. *wail* Is 16$_{7}$, דמם *be silent* Am 5$_{13}$, שׂמח *rejoice* Ps 16$_{9}$, אהב *love* Ps 119$_{119}$, פתה pi. *entice* Ho 2$_{16}$.

עשׂה *do* Ezk 35$_{6.11}$ Am 4$_{12}$, בנה *build* Am 5$_{11}$, חלק pi. *divide* Is 53$_{12}$, נתן *give* Is 7$_{14}$ Jr 8$_{10}$ 18$_{21}$ Ezk 23$_{9}$ 25$_{4}$ Mc 1$_{14}$ (or em. לָכֵן תִּתְּנִי *therefore you will give* to לָךְ נִתְּנוּ *to you they gave*) 5$_{2}$, שׂים *place* 1 S 28$_{2}$, אסף *gather* 2 K 22$_{20}$, קבץ pi. *gather* Ezk 16$_{37}$, ירשׁ *possess* Is 61$_{7}$, פתח *open* Ezk 25$_{9}$, רחב *make wide* Is 5$_{14}$, רעה *pasture* Zc 11$_{7}$ (or em. לָכֵן עֲנִיֵּי *therefore the afflicted ones of* to לִכְנַעֲנִיֵּי *to the traders of*), שׁפט *judge* Ezk 18$_{30}$, ריב *contend* Jr 2$_{9}$, נקם ho. *be avenged* Gn 4$_{15}$ (or em. לֹא כֵן), כפר pu. *be atoned* Is 27$_{9}$, שׁכב *lie down* Gn 30$_{15}$, נפל *fall* Jr 6$_{15}$ 8$_{12}$ 49$_{26}$ 50$_{30}$, אכל *eat* Ezk 5$_{10}$ 36$_{14}$, ni. *be devoured* Jr 30$_{16}$ (or em. לָכֵן כָּל־ *therefore all* to וְכָל־ *and all*), יסף *add* Is 29$_{14}$ (if em. hi.), hi. *add* Jg 10$_{13}$ Is 29$_{14}$ (or em. qal), גרע *diminish* Ezk 5$_{11}$, ספק *strike* Ezk 21$_{17}$, נטה *stretch* hand Ezk 25$_{7}$, שׁוך

hedge up Ho 2_{8}, אצל ni. *be set aside* Si 46_{8}, חרשׁ ni. *be ploughed* Mc 3_{12}, ענק *be a necklace* Ps 73_{6}.

b. introducing nom. cl., לָכֵן נְאֻם־י׳ *therefore (the following is) an oracle of Y.* 1 S 2_{30}, var. Is 1_{24}, לָכֵן הִנְנִי עַל־הַנְּבִאִים *therefore, behold, I am against the prophets* Jr 23_{30}, לָכֵן הִנְנִי אֵלַיִךְ *therefore, behold, I am against you* Ezk 29_{10}, לָכֵן הִנְנִי *therefore, here am I* Jr 23_{39}, לָכֵן לַיְלָה לָכֶם מֵחָזוֹן *therefore it shall be night to you, without vision* Mc 3_{6}.

<COLL> following verb is pf., 1 S 3_{14} 27_{6} 2 K 14 19_{32} ||Is 37_{33} 2 K 21_{12} Is $5_{13.14}$ 10_{24} 26_{14} 28_{16} 29_{22} $30_{7.12}$ 65_{13} Jr 5_{14} 6_{21} 7_{20} $9_{6.14}$ $11_{11.21.22}$ 14_{15} 15_{19} 18_{13} 22_{18} $23_{2.15.38}$ 25_{8} 28_{16} 29_{32} $32_{28.36}$ 34_{17} $35_{17.19}$ 36_{30} 44_{11} 50_{18} 51_{36} Ezk $5_{7.8}$ 11_{7} $13_{8.13.20}$ 15_{6} 17_{19} 21_{29} 22_{19} $23_{9.22.35}$ $24_{6.9}$ $25_{7.13.16}$ 26_{3} 28_{6} $29_{8.19}$ 30_{22} 31_{10} 34_{20} $36_{5.7}$ 39_{25} Am 3_{11} $5_{11.16}$ 7_{17} Mc 2_{3} Zc 1_{16} Ps 16_{9} 73_{6} 78_{21} 119_{119} Jb 32_{10} 37_{24} 42_{3} Si 45_{24} 46_{8}; pf. + waw consecutive Ezk 35_{11}; impf. Gn 4_{15} 30_{15} Nm 20_{12} Jg 10_{13} 2 K $1_{6.16}$ 22_{20} Is 5_{24} 7_{14} 10_{16} 16_{7} 27_{9} $30_{13.18.18}$ 52_{6} 53_{12} 61_{7} Jr 2_{9} 6_{15} $8_{10.12}$ 23_{12} 30_{16} 49_{26} $50_{30.39}$ Ezk $5_{10.11}$ 13_{23} 18_{30} 21_{9} 35_{6} 36_{14} Ho 2_{11} 13_{3} Am 4_{12} 5_{13} 6_{7} Mc 1_{14} (or em.; see §1a) 2_{5} 3_{12} 5_{2} Zp 2_{9} Ps 73_{10} Jb 34_{25}; impf. + waw consecutive Zc 11_{7}; impv. Ex 6_{6} Nm 25_{12} 1 S $28_{2.2}$ 1 K 22_{19}||2 C 18_{18} Is 28_{14} 51_{21} Jr 6_{18} 18_{21} 42_{15} 44_{26} 49_{20} 50_{45} Ezk $11_{4.16.17}$ $12_{23.28}$ $14_{4.6}$ 16_{35} $20_{27.30}$ 21_{17} 33_{25} $34_{7.9}$ $36_{3.4.6.22}$ 37_{12} 38_{14} Zp 3_{8} Ps $16_{9(mss)}$ Jb 34_{10}; ptc. 1 K 14_{10} Is 8_{7} 29_{14} Jr 7_{32} $16_{14.21}$ 19_{6} 23_{7} 48_{12} 49_{2} $51_{47.52}$ Ezk 16_{37} $25_{4.9}$ 28_{7} Ho $2_{8.16}$.

יַעַן ... לָכֵן *because ... therefore* Nm 20_{12} 2 K 21_{12} (יַעַן אֲשֶׁר) 22_{20} Is 8_{7} 29_{14} (both יַעַן כִּי) 30_{13} Jr 23_{39} Ezk 5_{8} 13_{23} 16_{37} 21_{9} (יַעַן אֲשֶׁר) $25_{4.7.9.13.16}$ 26_{3} (יַעַן אֲשֶׁר) 28_{7} 29_{10} $35_{6.11}$ $36_{3.4}$ (יַעַן בְּיַעַן *because and by the cause [that]*; mss וּבְיַעַן) $36_{7.14}$.

לָכֵן כֹּה אָמַר י׳ (and vars.) *therefore thus has Y. said* 2 K 14 19_{32}||Is 37_{33} 2 K 21_{12} Is 10_{24} 28_{16} 30_{12} 65_{13} Jr 5_{14} 6_{21} 7_{20} $9_{6.14}$ $11_{11.21.22}$ 14_{15} 15_{19} 18_{13} 22_{18} $23_{2.15.38}$ 25_{8} 28_{16} 29_{32} $32_{28.36}$ 34_{17} $35_{17.19}$ 36_{30} 44_{11} 50_{18} 51_{36} Ezk $5_{7.8}$ 11_{7} $13_{8.13.20}$ 15_{6} 17_{19} 21_{29} 22_{19} $23_{22.35}$ $24_{6.9}$ $25_{13.16}$ 26_{3} 28_{6} $29_{8.19}$ 30_{22} 31_{10} 34_{20} $36_{5.7}$ 39_{25} Am 3_{11} 5_{16} 7_{17} Mc 2_{3} Zc 1_{16}.

לָכֵן שְׁמַע דְּבַר־י׳ (and vars.) *therefore hear the word of Y.* 1 K 22_{19}||2 C 18_{18} Is 28_{14} Jr 42_{15} 44_{26} Ezk 16_{35} $34_{7.9}$ 36_{4}, לָכֵן שִׁמְעוּ עֲצַת־י׳ *therefore hear the counsel of Y.* Jr 49_{20} 50_{45}, לָכֵן חַי־אָנִי נְאֻם אֲדֹנָי י׳ *therefore, as I live, (it is an) oracle of the Lord Y.* Ezk 5_{11} $35_{6.11}$ Zp 2_{9}, לָכֵן הִנֵּה־יָמִים בָּאִים *therefore, behold the days are coming* Jr 7_{32} 16_{14} 19_{6} 23_{7} 48_{12} 49_{2} 51_{47} (both הִנֵּה יָמִים) 51_{52}.

2. surely, assuredly (distinction from §1 not alw. clear), **a.** followed by verb, ידע *know* 1 S 28_{2}, למד pi. *teach* Jr 2_{33}, שׁבע ni. *swear* Jr 5_{2} (mss אָכֵן *indeed*), שׁוב *go back* Jg 11_{8} (or em. לֹא כֵן *not so*), שׁוב hi. *reply* Jb 20_{2}, דושׁ *thresh* Jg 8_{7}, יעד ni. *gather together* Nm 16_{11} (if em. עֲדָתְךָ הַנֹּעָדִים you and all *your company are the ones who have gathered together* to עֲדָתְכָה נֹעָדִים you and all *your company have gathered together*).

b. introducing nom. cl. לָכֵן אַתָּה וְכָל־עֲדָתְךָ הַנֹּעָדִים עַל־י׳ *surely you and all your company are the ones who have gathered together against Y.* Nm 16_{11} (or em.; see §2a).

<COLL> following verb is pf., Jg 11_{8} Jr 2_{33}; pf. + waw consecutive Jg 8_{7}; impf. 1 S 28_{2} Jr 5_{2} Jb 20_{2}; ptc. Nm 16_{11}.

Also perh. MasUnid2_{2} (אלכן; unless Aramaic) scrap$_{1}$ ([ ]לכן).

⇒ לְ *for* + כֵּן *thus*.

[לְלָאָה] 13 n.f. **loop**—cstr. לֻלְאֹת—on edges of curtains of tabernacle, for the hooks that joined them together, <SUBJ> קבל hi. *correspond* Ex 26_{5}||36_{12}. <OBJ> עשׂה *make* Ex $26_{4.5.5.10.10}$||$36_{11.12.12.17.17}$. <CSTR> לֻלְאֹת תְּכֵלֶת *loops of blue* Ex 26_{4}||36_{11}. <APP> אִשָּׁה *each one* Ex 26_{5}, אֶחָד *one* Ex 36_{12}. <PREP> בְּ of direction, *into*, + בוא hi. *bring* Ex 26_{11}. <COLL> חֲמִשִּׁים לֻלָאֹת *fifty loops* Ex $26_{5.5.10.10}$||$36_{12.12.17.17}$.

[לם], see מַרְבֶּה *increase*.

למד 86.10.26 vb. **learn**—**Qal** 24.4.5 Pf. לָמַד, לָמַדְתִּי, לָמְדוּ; impf. יִלְמַד, 3fs Si תלמד, 2ms תִּלְמַד (Si תלמוד), אֶלְמַד (אֶלְמְדָה), יִלְמְדוּ (יִלְמְדוּן), תִּלְמְדוּ; + waw וְלָמְדוּ, וּלְמַדְתֶּם; וַיִּלְמַד, וַיִּלְמְדוּ; impv. לִמְדוּ; ptc. pass. לִמּוּדֵי; inf. abs. לָמֹד; cstr. Q בְּ למוד (לָמְדִי)—**1. learn,** <SUBJ> Agur Pr 30_{3} (or em. לֹא־לִמַּדְתִּי *I have not learned* to אֵל לִמַּד אֹתִי *God taught me*; + ידע *know*), Ben Sira Si 51_{15}, Israel(ites) Dt 5_{1} 14_{23} 18_{9}=11QT 60_{16} Is 1_{17} (:: חדל *cease*), בַּיִת *house* of Israel Jr 10_{2}, עַם *people* Dt 4_{10} 31_{12} (|| שׁמע *hear*) Is 2_{4}=Mc 4_{3}, גּוֹי *nation* Is 2_{4}=Mc 4_{3}, אִישׁ *man* Dt 31_{12}, אִשָּׁה *woman* Dt 31_{12} Si 9_{1}, אָב *father* Ps 106_{35}, בֵּן *son* Dt 31_{13} (+ שׁמע

hear) Pr 30_3 Si 8_8, טַף *children* Dt 31_{12}, מֶלֶךְ *king* Dt 17_{19}, גֵּר *sojourner* Dt 31_{12}, יֹשֵׁב *inhabitant* Is 26_9 GnzPs 2_{16}, שָׁכֵן *neighbour* Jr $12_{16.16}$, רֹגֵן *murmurer* Is 29_{24} (|| ידע *know*), חבר ptc. *one who associates* Si 13_1, עבד ptc. *worshipper* GnzPs 1_8, רָשָׁע *wicked one* Is 26_{10}, psalmist Ps $119_{7.71.73}$ (+ בין hi. *cause to understand*), מַשְׂכִּיל *instructor* 1QS 9_{13}, גּוּר *cub* Ezk $19_{3.6}$.

<OBJ> מִצְוָה *commandment* Ps 119_{71}, חק *statute* Dt 5_1 Ps 119_{71}, מִשְׁפָּט *ordinance* Dt 5_1 Ps 119_7, לֶקַח *instruction* Is 29_{24} Si 8_8, חָכְמָה *wisdom* Pr 30_3 Si 51_{15}, שֵׂכֶל *insight* 1QS 9_{13}, בִּינָה *understanding* 4QapPs^b 76_{13} (unless pi.), דֶּרֶךְ *way* Jr 10_2 (if em. אֶל־ *concerning* way, to אֶת־ object marker) 12_{16} Si 13_1, חק *statute* 1QS 9_{13}, שִׁיר *song* GnzPs 1_8, מִלְחָמָה *war* Is 2_4=Mc 4_3, צֶדֶק *righteousness* Is $26_{9.10}$, מַעֲשֶׂה *deed* Ps 106_{35}, רָעָה *evil* Si 9_1.

<PREP> מִן of time, *from, since,* + נְעוּרִים *youth* Si 51_{15}; of direction, instrument, *from, by means of* + worshipper GnzPs 2_{16}, חִידָה *riddle* Si 8_8, שִׂיחָה *meditation* Si 8_8; אֶל *concerning,* + דֶּרֶךְ *way* Jr 10_2 (or em. אֶל־ to אֶת־ object marker or אֵל *God,* in app. to ״ *Y.*);* עַל *concerning, against,* + בֵּן *son* Si 9_1.

<COLL> + inf. cstr. (e.g. למד לִשְׁמֹר *learn to keep* Dt 17_{19}) of ירא *fear* Dt 4_{10} 14_{23} 17_{19} 31_{13}, עשׂה *do* Dt 17_{19} 18_9 =11QT 60_{16}, שׁמר *keep* Dt 17_{19}; + inf. abs. יטב hi. *do good* Is 1_{17}, טרף *tear* prey Ezk $19_{3.6}$; + adverb, עוֹד *again* Is 2_4 =Mc 4_3; inf. cstr. + finite form of למד Jr 12_{16}.

2. pass. be trained, <SUBJ> אִישׁ *man* 1 C 5_{18}, בֵּן *son* 1 C 5_{18}. <COLL> לְמוּדֵי מִלְחָמָה *trained of,* i.e. in, *war* 1 C 5_{18} (+ נשׂא *carry* shield and sword, דרך *tread,* i.e. bend, the bow).

<SYN> §1 שׁמע *hear,* ידע *know.*

<ANT> §1 חדל *cease.*

Ni. be trained, <SUBJ> עַיִר *male ass* Jb 11_{12} (if em. ילד ni. *be born*).

Pi. 57.6.17 Pf. לִמַּד, Si למדה, לִמַּדְתִּי, לִמַּדְתָּ, לִמַּדְתַּנִי, לִמְּדוּ (לִמְּדוּם), Q למדוהו (4QpsJub^c 2_1 corrected to למדנוהו), impf. יְלַמֵּד (יְלַמֶּד־, Q ילמדהו, Si ילמדנה), 3fs תְּלַמְּדֵנִי, 2ms תְּלַמְּדֵנִי (תְּלַמְּדֵנוּ, Q תלמדו, תְּלַמְּדֵם), אֲלַמְּדָה (אֲלַמֶּדְכֶם, Q אלמדכמה, אֲלַמְּדֵם), יְלַמְּדוּ (יְלַמֵּדוּן, Q ילמדוכה); + waw וְלִמַּדְתֶּם; וַיְלַמְּדֵהוּ (וַיְלַמְּדָהּ, Q וילמדנו), וַיְלַמְּדוּ; impv. לַמְּדֵנִי (לַמְּדָהּ, לַמֵּדְנָה); ptc. מְלַמֵּד (מְלַמֶּדְךָ, מְלַמְּדַי); inf. abs. לַמֵּד; cstr. לַמֵּד (לַמְּדָם)—**1. teach, train (in);** without explicit obj., **practise** battle song* (2 S 1_{18} [if em.] Ps 60_1).

<SUBJ> Y. Jg 3_2 2 S 22_{35}||Ps 18_{35} Is 48_{17} (+ דרך hi. *lead*) Jr $32_{33.33}$ Ps 25_4 (|| ידע hi. *cause to know*) $25_{5.9}$ (both + דרך hi.) 71_{17} 94_{10} (+ יסר *discipline*) 94_{12} (+ יסר pi. *discipline*) 119_{12+8t} 132_{12} 143_{10} (+ נחה hi. *lead*) 144_1 Pr 30_3 (if em. לֹא־לָמַדְתִּי *I have not learned* to אֵל לִמַּד אֹתִי *God taught me*) Si $15_{20(B)}$ 1QH 2_{17} 1QM 14_6 11QPs^a 24_8 (+ בין hi. *cause to understand*).

Amorites Dt 20_{18}=11QT 62_{16}, Canaanites Dt 20_{18} =11QT 62_{16}, Hittites Dt 20_{18}=11QT 62_{16}, Hivites Dt 20_{18} =11QT 62_{16}, Israel(ites) Dt 11_{19} Jr 2_{33} 9_4 13_{21} 31_{34} 1QSa 1_7 ([יל]מדהו), Jebusites Dt 20_{18}=11QT 62_{16}, Perizzites Dt 20_{18}=11QT 62_{16}, Aaron Si 45_{17}, Adonijah 2 C $17_{9.9}$, Asahel 2 C $17_{9.9}$, Ben-hail 2 C $17_{7.9.9}$, Elishama 2 C $17_{9.9}$, Ezra Ezr 7_{10}, Jehonathan 2 C $17_{9.9}$, Jehoram 2 C $17_{9.9}$, Joseph 4QapJoseph^b 1_{27}, Koheleth Ec 12_9, Micaiah 2 C $17_{7.9.9}$, Moses Dt $4_{1.5.14}$ 5_{31} 6_1 31_{19} (+ שׂים *place* in mouth) 31_{22} Si 45_5 perh. 1QM 10_2, Nethanel 2 C $17_{7.9.9}$, Nethaniah 2 C $17_{9.9}$, Obadiah 2 C $17_{7.9.9}$, Shemaiah 2 C $17_{9.9}$, Shemiramoth 2 C $17_{9.9}$, Tobadonijah 2 C $17_{9.9}$, Tobijah 2 C $17_{9.9}$, Zebadiah 2 C $17_{9.9}$, Zechariah 2 C $17_{7.9.9}$.

עַם *people* Dt 4_{10}, אִישׁ *man* Jr 9_4 31_{34}, אִשָּׁה *woman* Jr 9_{19}, אָב *father* Jr 9_{13}, בֵּן *son* of Judah 2 S 1_{18} (if em. וַיֹּאמֶר לְלַמֵּד בְּנֵי־יְהוּדָה קָשֶׁת appar. *and he said to teach the sons of Judah the bow* to וַיֹּאמֶר לְלַמֵּד בְּנֵי־יְהוּדָה *and he said, It is for the sons of Judah to practise*; or em. קָשֶׁת to קֹשֶׁט *truth,* i.e. teach accurately, or to קֶשֶׁב *attention,* i.e. teach attentively, or קִינוֹת teach *laments* or קִינַת שָׁאוּל *lament over Saul*).

שָׁכֵן *neighbour* Jr 12_{16}, שַׂר *prince* 2 C 17_7, משׁל ptc. *one who rules* Si 15_{10}, כֹּהֵן *priest* 2 C $17_{9.9}$, לֵוִי *Levite* 2 C $17_{9.9}$, נָבִיא *prophet* 4QapPs^b 69_4 (+ שׂכל hi. *instruct*), psalmist Ps 34_{12} 51_{15}, מַשְׂכִּיל *instructor* 1QS 3_{13} (|| בין hi. *cause to understand*), מְבַקֵּר *examiner* CD 15_{14} ([וילמד]), מִי *who* Is 40_{14} (|| בין hi.) 40_{14} (or del.; || ידע hi. *cause to know*), חָכְמוֹת *wisdom* Si 4_{11}, צוּר *rock* Ps 144_1; subj. not specified, Ps 60_1 Jb 21_{22} Dn 1_4.

<OBJ> (1) person, etc., taught, Y. Is $40_{14.14}$, Israel(ites) Dt $4_{1.5.14}$ 5_{31} 6_1 20_{18}=11QT 62_{16} Is 48_{17} Jr 9_{13} 32_{33} 1QM 10_4 4QapPs^b 69_4, עַם *people* Jr 12_{16} Ec 12_9 Si 45_{17}, Agur

Pr 30$_3$ (if em.; see Subj.), Enoch 4QpsJub^c 2$_1$ ([ח]נוך), אָדָם *human being* Ps 94$_{10}$, גֶּבֶר *man* Ps 94$_{12}$ Pr 30$_3$ (if em.; see Subj.) 1QH 2$_{17}$, בֵּן *son* Dt 4$_{10}$ 11$_{19}$ 2 S 1$_{18}$ Ps 34$_{12}$ 132$_{12}$ Pr 30$_3$ (if em.; see Subj.) Si 4$_{11}$ 1QS 3$_{13}$ 4QapPs^b 42$_1$ ([ת]למד), of Israel Dt 31$_{19.22}$ Dn 1$_4$ Si 45$_{17}$, בַּת *daughter* Jr 9$_{19}$, אָח *brother* Jr 31$_{34}$, יֶלֶד *child* Dn 1$_4$, רֵעַ *neighbour* Jr 31$_{34}$, רְעוּת *female neighbour* Jr 9$_{19}$, אַלּוּף *friend* Jr 13$_{21}$, אֶזְרָח *native* 1QSa 1$_7$ ([יל]מדהו), psalmist Ps 25$_{4.5}$ 71$_{17}$ 119$_{12+8t}$ 143$_{10}$ 11QPs^a 24$_8$, דּוֹר *generation* Jg 3$_2$, עָנָו *humble one* Ps 25$_9$, רַע fem. pl. *evil women* Jr 2$_{33}$, פֹּשֵׁעַ *transgressor* Ps 51$_{15}$, שׁוּב ptc. *one who goes back* CD 15$_{14}$ (וי[ל]מד), יָד *hand* 1 S 22$_{35}$||Ps 18$_{35}$ Ps 144$_1$ 4QapJoseph^b 2$_4$ (ל[מד]), לָשׁוֹן *tongue* Jr 9$_4$.

(2) thing taught, תּוֹרָה *law* 4QapJoseph^b 1$_{27}$ (תור[תך]), מִצְוָה *commandment* Dt 5$_{31}$ 6$_1$, חֹק *statute* Dt 4$_{5.14}$ 5$_{31}$ 6$_1$ 119$_{12+6t}$ Ezr 7$_{10}$ Si 45$_{5.17}$ 4QapJoseph^b 1$_{27}$, מִשְׁפָּט *ordinance* Dt 4$_{5.14}$ 5$_{31}$ 6$_1$ Ps 119$_{108}$ Ezr 7$_{10}$ Si 45$_{5.17}$ 11QPs^a 24$_8$, עֵדָה *testimony* Ps 132$_{12}$ Si 45$_5$, דָּבָר *word* Dt 11$_{19}$, סֵפֶר *book*, i.e. literature Dn 1$_4$, שִׁירָה *song* Dt 31$_{19.22}$, נְהִי *lament* Jr 9$_{19}$, קִינָה *dirge* Jr 9$_{19}$, מִכְתָּם *Miktam* Ps 60$_1$, דַּעַת *knowledge* Is 40$_{14}$ Ps 94$_{10}$ 119$_{66}$ Jb 21$_{22}$ Ec 12$_9$, יִרְאָה *fear* of Y. Ps 34$_{12}$, חָכְמָה *wisdom* Pr 30$_3$ (if em.; see Subj.) Si 15$_{10}$ 4QdivProv 1$_1$, בִּינָה *understanding* 1QH 2$_{17}$ 4QapJoseph^b 2$_4$ (unless qal), טוּב *goodness*, i.e. quality, of discernment Ps 119$_{66}$, שֶׁקֶר *lie* Si 15$_{20}$, קֶשֶׁת *bow* 2 S 1$_{18}$ (or em.; see Subj.), מִלְחָמָה *war* Jg 3$_2$ 1QM 14$_6$, אֹרַח *way* Ps 25$_4$, דֶּרֶךְ *way* Jr 2$_{33}$ Ps 25$_9$ 51$_{15}$, לָשׁוֹן *tongue*, i.e. language Dn 1$_4$.

<PREP> לְ *for (the purpose of)*, + מִלְחָמָה *war* 2 S 22$_{35}$ ||Ps 18$_{35}$ 4QapJoseph^b 2$_4$ (ל[מד]), קְרָב *war* Ps 144$_1$; introducing object, + אֵל *God* Jb 21$_{22}$, יִשְׂרָאֵל *Israel* Si 45$_5$, יַעֲקֹב *Jacob* Si 45$_{5(Bmg)}$, אָדָם *human being* Ps 94$_{10(mss)}$, אִישׁ *man* Si 15$_{20(B)}$, פֹּשֵׁעַ *transgressor* 4QapJoseph^b 1$_{27}$, עזב ptc. *one who forsakes* 4QapJoseph^b 1$_{27}$; בְּ of place, *in, among*, + עִיר *city* 2 C 17$_7$, יִשְׂרָאֵל *Israel* Ezr 7$_{10}$ Si 45$_{5(B)}$, יְהוּדָה *Judah* 2 C 17$_9$, עַם *people* 2 C 17$_9$; *concerning, in*, or introducing object, perh. 4QS^z 1$_5$, + אֹרַח *path* Is 40$_{14}$, סֵפֶר *book* 1QSa 1$_7$ ([יל]מדהו), תּוֹלֵדוֹת *nature* 1QS 3$_{13}$; אֶל *to*, + יָד *hand* 4QM^a 8.1$_4$ (ב[ידי]ם); מִן of time, *from, since*, + נְעוּרִים *youth* Ps 71$_{17}$ 1QSa 1$_7$ (מן נעו[ריו יל]מדהו); of direction, instrument, *from, by (means of)*, + תּוֹרָה *law* Ps 94$_{12}$; עַד *until, as long as*, + שָׁנָה *year* CD 15$_{14}$ (וי[ל]מד).

<COLL> + inf. cstr. (e.g. לְלַמֵּד אֶתְכֶם לַעֲשׂוֹת *to teach you to do* Dt 6$_1$), עשׂה *do* Dt 4$_1$ 6$_1$ 20$_{18}$=11QT 62$_{16}$ Ps 143$_{10}$, יעל hi. *profit* Is 48$_{17}$, דבר pi. *speak* Jr 9$_4$, שׁבע ni. *swear* Jr 12$_{16}$; + adverb, עוֹד *again* Jr 31$_{34}$ Ec 12$_9$, מֵאָז *from of old* 1QM 10$_2$.

לַמֵּד אֹתָם הַשְׁכֵּם וְלַמֵּד *teaching them, rising early and teaching*, i.e. persistently teaching them Jr 32$_{33}$.

2. ptc. used as noun, **teacher, <CSTR>** כָּל־מְלַמְּדַי *all my teachers* Ps 119$_{99}$. **<PREP>** לְ of direction, *to*, + נטה hi. *incline* ear Pr 5$_{13}$ (|| מוֹרֶה *teacher*), נתן *give* Si 51$_{17}$; מִן of comparison, *(more) than*, + שׂכל hi. *be prudent* Ps 119$_{99}$.

3. know, have sex with, אֲבִיאֲךָ אֶל־בֵּית אִמִּי תְּלַמְּדֵנִי *I would bring you to my mother's house, you would have sex with me* Ca 8$_2$ (unless תְּלַמְּדֵנִי = the house of my mother [who] *taught me*, as §1; or em. תֵּלְדֵנִי who *gave birth to me*).*

Also 4QBark^e 4.1$_1$ 4QM^h 4$_7$ (מלמדים, unless pu.).

<SYN> §1 ידע hi. *cause to know*, בין hi. *cause to understand*; §2 מוֹרֶה *teacher*.

Pu. 5.0.4 Pf. לֻמַּד; ptc. מְלֻמְּדֵי, מְלֻמָּדָה—**be taught, trained, skilled, <SUBJ>** גִּבּוֹר *warrior* Ca 3$_8$ (|| אחז pass. *be held*), אָח *brother* 1 C 25$_7$, חַרְטֹם *magician* 4QMyst^b 1a.2-b$_1$ ([החר]טמים), עֵגֶל *calf* Jr 31$_{18}$, עֶגְלָה *heifer* Ho 10$_{11}$, מִצְוָה *commandment* Is 29$_{13}$. **<COLL>** מְלֻמְּדֵי מִלְחָמָה *trained of*, i.e. in, *war* Ca 3$_8$ 1QM 6$_{12}$, מְלֻמְּדֵי־שִׁיר *trained of*, i.e. in, song 1 C 25$_7$, מלומדי רכב *skilled of*, i.e. in, *riding* 1QM 6$_{13}$, מלומדי חוק *trained of*, i.e. in, *statutes* 1QM 19$_{10}$ (+ שׂכל hi. *be wise*), מלמדי פשע *skilled of*, i.e. in, *transgression* 4QMyst^b 1a.2-b$_1$.

<SYN> אחז pass. *be held*.*

⇒ לִמֵּד *taught*, מַלְמָד *ox-goad*, תַּלְמִיד *scholar*.

[לָמֶד] 0.0.1 n.[m.] **lamedh,** the Hebrew letter, **<PREP>** בְּ of instrument, *by*, [יש]בע וגם באלף ולמד וגם באלף ודלת *he should swear neither by Aleph and Lamedh*, i.e. אֵל *God, nor by Aleph and Daleth*, i.e. אֲדֹ(נָי) *Adonai* CD 15$_1$.

[לִמֻּד] 6.1.5 adj. **taught**—cstr. לִמֻּד; sf. Q למודו; pl. לִמֻּדִים; cstr. לִמֻּדֵי (לִמּוּדֵי); sf. לִמֻּדַי, Q למודיך (Q למודיכה)—used as noun, **1. one used to, <SUBJ>** יכל *be able* Jr 13$_{23}$, יטב hi. *do good* Jr 13$_{23}$. **<CSTR>** לִמֻּד מִדְבָּר *one used to the steppe* Jr 2$_{24}$ (or em.; see App.), לִמֻּדֵי הָרֵעַ *ones used to* *doing evil* Jr 13$_{23}$. <APP> פֶּרֶא *wild ass* Jr 2$_{24}$ (or em. פֶּרֶה לִמֻּד מִדְבָּר *a wild ass used to the steppe* to פֹּרְצָה לַמִּדְבָּר *bursting out into the steppe*).

2. pupil, apprentice, student,* <NOM CL> כָּל־בָּנַיִךְ לִמּוּדֵי י׳ *all your sons will be pupils of Y.* Is 54$_{13}$. <CSTR> לִמּוּדֵי י׳ *pupils of Y.* Is 54$_{13}$, אל *of God* CD 20$_{4}$; לְשׁוֹן לִמּוּדִים *tongue of the pupils* Is 50$_{4}$. <PREP> לְ introducing object, + אזן hi. appar. *cause to hear* 1QH 8$_{36}$ ([להאזין]); בְּ of place, *among* perh. 4QHod^{b} 7$_{7}$, + חתם *seal* teaching Is 8$_{16}$; כְּ *as* 1QH 7$_{10}$ perh. 4QHod^{b} [כלמודן]יכה, + שׁמע *hear* Is 50$_{4}$; בְּתוֹךְ *among*, + נפל *fall* CD 20$_{4}$.

3. thing taught, teaching, <OBJ> שׁמע *hear* Si 51$_{28}$ 4QBark^{a} 1.2$_{4}$. <PREP> בְּ *in (accordance with)*, + כון hi. *establish* heart 1QH 7$_{14}$ ([בל]מודכיה; + אֱמֶת *truth*).

⇒ למד *teach.*

לָמָה 178.10.2 interrog. adv. **why?**—לָ֫מָּה usu. before א, ה, ע, alw. before יהוה, and at Ps 42$_{10}$ 43$_{2}$, also לָמָּה (Jb 7$_{20}$), לָמֶה (1 S 1$_{8.8.8}$)—as interrog. adv., **why?, for what reason?**; sometimes perh. as negative final conj., **lest*** (e.g. Gn 27$_{45}$ 47$_{19}$ Ex 22$_{12}$ 1 S 19$_{17}$ Ec 5$_{5}$ 7$_{16.17}$ Ca 1$_{7}$ Dn 1$_{10}$ Si 8$_{1}$ 12$_{5.12.12}$ 30$_{12}$ 37$_{8}$ 1QDM 2$_{4}$).

1a. with following verb, היה *be* Jg 21$_{3}$ 2 S 19$_{12.13.36}$ Jr 14$_{8.9}$ 15$_{18}$ 27$_{17}$ Ca 1$_{7}$ 1 C 21$_{3}$, הלך *go* Nm 22$_{37}$ 2 S 13$_{26}$ 15$_{19}$ 16$_{17}$ 19$_{26}$ Ps 42$_{10}$ (or em. htp.) Ru 1$_{11}$, htp. *go about* Ps 42$_{10}$ (if em. qal) 43$_{2}$, בוא *come* 2 S 14$_{32}$ Dn 10$_{20}$ 2 C 32$_{4}$, hi. *bring* Nm 14$_{3}$ 20$_{4}$ 1 S 21$_{15}$, יצא *go out* 1 S 17$_{8}$, hi. *bring out* Jb 10$_{18}$, עלה *go up* Jg 12$_{3}$ 15$_{10}$, hi. *bring up* Nm 20$_{5}$ 21$_{5}$, רום *be high* 1QDM 2$_{4}$, עזב *leave* Ps 22$_{2}$, עבר *transgress* 2 C 24$_{20}$, hi. *cause to cross* Jos 7$_{7}$, רדף *pursue* Jb 19$_{22}$, שׁוב *go back* Si 8$_{1}$, hi. *bring back* Ps 74$_{11}$, סור *turn aside* 1 S 6$_{3}$, נגשׁ ni. *draw near* 2 S 11$_{21}$, עמד *stand* Gn 24$_{31}$ Ps 10$_{1}$, ישׁב *sit* Jg 5$_{16}$, *dwell* 1 S 27$_{5}$, גור *sojourn* Jg 5$_{17}$ (mss lack לָמָּה).

אמר *say* Gn 12$_{19}$ Ex 32$_{12}$ Is 40$_{27}$ Jl 2$_{17}$ Ps 79$_{10}$ 115$_{2}$, דבר pi. *speak* Gn 44$_{7}$ 1 S 9$_{21}$ 2 S 19$_{30}$ Jr 2$_{29}$ (if em. ריב *strive*), נגד hi. *tell* Gn 12$_{18}$, בקשׁ pi. *seek* 1 C 21$_{3}$ Si 12$_{12}$, דרשׁ *seek* 2 C 25$_{15}$, שׁאל *ask* 1 S 28$_{16}$ 1 K 2$_{22}$, קלל pi. *curse* 2 S 16$_{9}$, גער *rebuke* Jr 29$_{27}$, רוע hi. *shout* Mc 4$_{9}$, קרא *call*, i.e. name Ru 1$_{21}$, שׁמע *hear* 1 S 15$_{19}$ 24$_{10}$, ראה *see* Dn 1$_{10}$, hi. *show* Hb 1$_{3}$, htp. *look at one another* Gn 42$_{1}$, נבט hi. *look at* Hb 1$_{13}$, רצד pi. *watch stealthily* Ps 68$_{17}$, חשׁב *think* 2 S 14$_{13}$, בכה *weep* 1 S 1$_{8}$, שׁמר *keep* 1 S 26$_{15}$, ירא *fear* Ps 49$_{6}$, מצא *find* Nm 11$_{11}$ Jg 6$_{13}$, שׁגה *go astray* Pr 5$_{20}$, תעה hi. *lead astray* Is 63$_{17}$, קשׁר *conspire* 1 S 22$_{13}$, רמה pi. *deceive* Gn 29$_{25}$ Jos 9$_{22}$ 1 S 19$_{17}$ 28$_{12}$, חבא ni. *hide oneself* Gn 31$_{27}$, סתר hi. *hide* face Ps 44$_{25}$ Jb 13$_{24}$, גנב *steal* Gn 31$_{30}$.

גרע ni. *be diminished* Nm 9$_{7}$ 27$_{4}$, חרשׁ hi. *be silent* 2 S 19$_{11}$, שׁבת *cease* Ne 6$_{3}$, ישׁן *sleep* Ps 44$_{24}$, יצת hi. *set fire* 2 S 14$_{31}$, חרה *be angry* Gn 4$_{6}$, *burn* Ex 32$_{11}$, קצף *be angry* Ec 5$_{5}$, רגז hi. *enrage* 1 S 28$_{15}$, רגשׁ *rage* Ps 2$_{1}$, קבל hi. *oppose* Si 12$_{5}$, ריב *strive* Jr 2$_{29}$ (or em. דבר *speak*), גרה htp. *fight* 2 K 14$_{10}$||2 C 25$_{19}$, בעט *kick* 1 S 2$_{29}$, הדף Si 12$_{12}$, נפל *fall* Gn 4$_{6}$ Si 8$_{1}$, נכה hi. *strike* Ex 2$_{13}$ 2 S 2$_{22}$ Jr 40$_{15}$ 2 C 25$_{16}$, נגף *strike* 1 S 4$_{3}$, נקשׁ htp. *strike* 1 S 28$_{9}$, מות *die* Gn 47$_{15.19}$ Dt 5$_{25}$ Jr 27$_{13}$ Ezk 18$_{31}$ 33$_{11}$ Jb 3$_{11}$ Ec 7$_{17}$, hi. *put to death* 1 S 19$_{17}$, ho. *be put to death* 1 S 20$_{32}$, שׁכל *be bereaved* Gn 27$_{45}$, שׁמם htpo. *ruin oneself* Ec 7$_{16}$.

נתן *give* Jb 3$_{20}$, שׂים *place* Jb 7$_{20}$, לקח *take* Pr 22$_{27}$ (or del.), נשׂא *bear* Si 11$_{33}$, עשׂה *do* Ex 5$_{15}$ 1 S 2$_{23}$ Jr 44$_{7}$ Lachish ost. 6$_{9}$ ([למ]ה), רבה hi. *increase* Si 11$_{10}$, חטא *sin* 1 S 19$_{5}$, רעע *be bad* 1 S 1$_{8}$, hi. *do evil* Gn 43$_{6}$ Ex 5$_{22}$ Nm 11$_{11}$, גמל *repay* 2 S 19$_{37}$, שׁלם pi. *repay* Gn 44$_{4}$, פרע hi. *cause to refrain* Ex 5$_{4}$, נוא hi. *restrain* Nm 32$_{7(Qr)}$, כבד pi. *make heavy*, i.e. harden, heart 1 S 6$_{6}$, *honour* 1Q26 1$_{5}$, קרע *tear* 2 K 5$_{8}$, פרץ *break down* Ps 80$_{13}$, זנח *reject* Ps 42$_{10}$ (if em. שׁכח *forget*) 43$_{2}$ 74$_{1}$ 88$_{15}$, שׁכח *forget* Ps 42$_{10}$ (or em. זנח *reject*) Lm 5$_{20}$, אכל *eat* 1 S 1$_{8}$, שׁקה hi. *give to drink* appar. Si 30$_{12(B)}$ (but prob. error for קשׁה *be hard*; Bmg קשׁה hi. *harden*, שׁקה hi.), בלע pi. *swallow* 2 S 20$_{19}$, צום *fast* Is 58$_{3}$, בנה *build* 2 S 7$_{7}$||1 C 17$_{6}$, חפץ *delight* 2 S 24$_{3}$, חכם *be wise* Ec 2$_{15}$, שׁקל *weigh* Is 55$_{2}$.

b. in nom. cl., לָמָּה לִּי חַיִּים *what use will life be to me?* Gn 27$_{46}$, לָמָּה־לִּי רֹב־זִבְחֵיכֶם *what use to me is the multitude of your sacrifices?* Is 1$_{11}$, כֹּחַ יְדֵיהֶם לָמָּה לִּי *the strength of their hands, what use is it to me?* Jb 30$_{2}$.

2. לָמָּה זֶּה **a.** with following verb, בוא hi. *bring* 1 S 20$_{8}$, עלה hi. *bring up* Ex 17$_{3}$, ירד *go down* 1 S 17$_{28}$, יצא *go out* Nm 11$_{20}$ Jr 20$_{18}$, עזב *leave* Ex 2$_{20}$, רדף *pursue* 1 S 26$_{18}$, רוץ *run* 2 S 18$_{22}$, עבר *transgress* Nm 14$_{41}$, נפל *fall* Jos 7$_{10}$ Si 37$_{8}$, צחק *laugh* Gn 18$_{13}$, שׁאל *ask* Gn 32$_{30}$ Jg 13$_{18}$, שׁלח *send* Ex 5$_{22}$, pi. *send* 2 S 3$_{24}$, מצא *find* Gn 33$_{15}$, צום *fast* 2 S 12$_{23}$ (mss lack זֶּה), חרה *be angry* 2 S 19$_{43}$, יגע *be weary* Jb

9$_{29}$, הבל *act vainly* Jb 27$_{12}$, נכר htp. *act as a stranger* 1 K 14$_6$.

b. in nom. cl., אִם־כֵּן לָמָּה זֶּה אָנֹכִי *if (it is) so, why am I?*, i.e. why do I live? Gn 25$_{22}$, לָמָּה־זֶּה לִי בְּכֹרָה *what is the use of a birthright to me?* Gn 25$_{32}$, sim. Jr 6$_{20}$ (לְבוֹנָה *frankincense*), לָמָּה־זֶּה לָכֶם יוֹם י׳ *what is the day of Y. to you?* Am 5$_{18}$, לָמָּה־זֶּה מְחִיר בְּיַד־כְּסִיל *what use is money in the hand of a fool?* Pr 17$_{16}$, זה למה זה *what is the purpose of this?* Si 39$_{21}$.

→ לְ *for* + מָה *what?*

לְמוֹ 4 prep. **as, for, over**—alternative form of לְ *to*— יֵשְׁבוּ בַסֻּכָּה לְמוֹ־אָרֶב *they* (lions) *remain in a thicket (used) as a lair* Jb 38$_{40}$, אִם־יִרְבּוּ בָנָיו לְמוֹ־חָרֶב *if his sons increase (they are destined) for the sword* Jb 27$_{14}$, וְיִדְּמוּ לְמוֹ עֲצָתִי *and they would be silent for*, i.e. listen to, *my advice* Jb 29$_{21}$ (mss לְמוֹעֲצָתִי *for my advice*, i.e. לְ *for* + מוֹעֵצָה *advice*), יָדִי שַׂמְתִּי לְמוֹ־פִי *my hand I have placed over my mouth* Jb 40$_4$.

→ לְ *to*.

לְמוֹאל, see מול *front*.

לְמוֹאֵל, see לְמוּאֵל *Lemuel*.

לְמוּאֵל 2 pr.n.m. **Lemuel**—לְמוֹאֵל—perh. king of Massa (Pr 31$_1$, if em. מֶלֶךְ מַשָּׂא appar. *[the] king; an oracle* which his mother taught him, to מֶלֶךְ מַשָּׂא *king of Massa*), <OBJ> יסר pi. *teach* Pr 31$_1$. <CSTR> דִּבְרֵי לְמוּאֵל *the words of Lemuel* Pr 31$_1$. <APP> מֶלֶךְ *king* Pr 31$_1$. <COLL> as vocative, *O Lemuel* Pr 31$_4$ (or del.).*

לִמּוּד, see לִמֵּד *taught*.

לֶמֶךְ 11.0.1 pr.n.m. **Lamech**—לָמֶךְ—**1.** Cainite, son of Methushael, and husband of Adah and Zillah, <SUBJ> אמר *say* Gn 4$_{23}$, לקח *take* wife Gn 4$_{19}$, הרג *kill* Gn 4$_{23}$, נקם ho. *be avenged* Gn 4$_{24}$. <OBJ> ילד *beget* Gn 4$_{18}$. <CSTR> נְשֵׁי לֶמֶךְ *wives of Lamech* Gn 4$_{23}$.

2. Sethite, son of Methuselah, <SUBJ> חיה *live* Gn 5$_{28.30}$, ראה *see* 1QNoah 3$_4$, ילד hi. *beget* Gn 5$_{28.30}$, מות *die* Gn 5$_{31}$. <OBJ> ילד hi. *beget* Gn 5$_{25.26}$. <CSTR> יְמֵי־לֶמֶךְ *days of Lamech* Gn 5$_{31}$. <COLL> חֲנוֹךְ מְתוּשֶׁלַח לָמֶךְ *Enoch, Methuselah, Lamech* 1 C 1$_3$.

לְמַעַן 272.10.51 prep. **for the sake of**—sf. לְמַעַנְךָ, לְמַעֲנִי (לְמַעֲנֵךְ Dn 9$_{19}$), Si למענו (Si למענהו), לְמַעַנְכֶם—**1.** as prep., **for the sake of, on account of,** before noun, or with suffix in ref. to noun, Y. 2 K 19$_{34}$||Is 37$_{35}$ Is 43$_{25}$ 48$_{11.11}$ 49$_7$ Is 55$_5$ Dn 9$_{17.19}$ Si 43$_{14(Bmg, M).26(B)}$ 1QH 6$_{10}$ fr. 4$_{16}$ 4QBark^a 1.3$_2$ 4QDibHam^a 1.6$_3$ perh. 4$_{17}$, Israel Dt 32$_6$ Is 43$_{14}$ 45$_4$, Jacob Is 45$_4$, David 1 K 11$_{12.13.32.34}$ 15$_4$ 2 K 8$_{19}$ 19$_{34}$||Is 37$_{35}$, אָב *father* 1 K 11$_{12}$, אָח *brother* Ps 122$_8$, עֶבֶד *servant* 1 K 11$_{13.32.34}$ 2 K 8$_{19}$ 19$_{34}$||Is 37$_{35}$ Is 45$_4$ Is 63$_{17}$ 65$_8$, צַדִּיק *righteous one* Gn 18$_{24}$, בָּחִיר *elect* Is 45$_4$, רָשׁ *poor one* 4Q416 2.4$_{10}$, אוֹיֵב *enemy* Ps 69$_{19}$, צֹרֵר *enemy* Ps 8$_3$, שׁוֹרֵר *enemy* Ps 5$_9$ 27$_{11}$ (or em. שִׁירָה *song*), טרף ptc. *one who tears* Jb 18$_4$, יָד *hand* 2 C 6$_{32}$ (or ins. כִּי יִשְׁמְעוּ אֶת־שִׁמְךָ *for they will hear of your* great *name* and your hand), זְרוֹעַ *arm* 2 C 6$_{32}$ (or ins. כִּי יִשְׁמְעוּ אֶת־שִׁמְךָ *for they will hear of your* great *name* and your arm), שַׁד *breast* Ezk 23$_{21}$ (or em. לְמַעַן to לְמַעֵךְ *to squeeze*, or לְמֹעַךְ *to be squeezed*), Jerusalem 1 K 11$_{13.32}$ Is 62$_1$, Zion Is 62$_1$, עִיר *city* 1 K 11$_{32}$, בַּיִת *house* of Y. Ps 122$_9$, of Israel Ezk 36$_{22.32}$, עַם *people* 4QapJoshua^a 22.1$_3$, חַיִּים *life* Dt 30$_6$ 4Q416 2.3$_{19}$, מְחָיָה *recovery* Si 38$_{14}$, בָּרָק *lightning* Ezk 21$_{33}$ (or em. מְרוּטָּה לְהָכִיל לְמַעַן בָּרָק appar. *polished, in order to make it devour for the sake of lightning* to מְרוּטָה לְכָלָה לְמַעַן בָּרֹק *polished for destruction in order to flash*, as §2a), טוּב *good* Ps 25$_7$, שֵׁם *name* 1 K 8$_{41}$||2 C 6$_{32}$ Is 48$_9$ 66$_5$ Jr 14$_{7.21}$ Ezk 20$_{9.14.22.44}$ Ps 23$_3$ 25$_{11}$ 31$_4$ 79$_9$ 106$_8$ 109$_{21}$ 143$_{11}$ 1QM 18$_8$ 4QM^g 10$_2$ 4QConfess 1.2$_{11}$, כָּבוֹד *glory* 1QH 11$_{10}$ 4Q416 2.3$_{18}$ 4QShir^b 28$_2$, בְּרִית *covenant* 2 K 13$_{23}$ 2 C 21$_7$ 1QM 18$_8$ (למען ב]ריתכה) 4QDibHam^a 1.2$_9$, צֶדֶק *righteousness* Is 42$_{21}$, תּוֹרָה *law* Ps 130$_4$ (if em. תִּוָּרֵא *that you may be feared*, as §2a, to תּוֹרָתֶךָ for the sake of *your law*), חֶסֶד *loyalty* Ps 6$_5$ 44$_{27}$ 4QBark^a 1.2$_4$, מִשְׁפָּט *judgment* Ps 48$_{12}$ 97$_8$, בֹּשֶׁת *shame* Jr 7$_{19}$, אַשְׁמָה *guilt* 1QH 5$_{25}$, זאת *this* 1 K 11$_{39}$.

לְמַעַן before verb, היה *be* 1 K 11$_{32.32}$, פגע *befall* 1QH 4$_{16}$, חפץ *be pleased* Is 42$_{21}$, גיל *rejoice* Ps 48$_{12}$ 97$_8$, חשה *be silent* Is 62$_1$, שׁקט *be silent* Is 62$_1$, עבר htp. *be angry* Dt 32$_6$, כעס hi. *anger* Jr 7$_{19}$, ארך hi. *delay* anger Is 48$_9$, אחר pi. *delay* Dn 9$_{19}$, זכר *remember* Ps 25$_7$, אהב *love* Dt 30$_6$,

חוס *pity* 4QDibHam^a 1.2$_9$, נשׂא *forgive* Gn 18_{24}, סלח *pardon* Ps 25_{11}, מחה *blot out* transgressions Is 43_{25}, סתר pi. *conceal* 1QH 5_{25}, אור hi. *cause* face *to shine* Dn 9_{17}, בוא *come* 1 K 8_{41}||2 C 6_{32}, שׁוב *go back* Is 63_{17}, פנה *turn* 2 K 13_{23}, שׁלח pi. *send* Is 43_{14}, רוץ *run* Is 55_5, נחה *lead* Ps 5_9 27_{11}, hi. *lead* Ps 23_3 31_4, נהל pi. *lead* Ps 31_4 (or em. נחם pi. *comfort*), עזב ni. *be abandoned* Jb 18_4, דבר pi. *speak* Ps 122_8, קרא *call* Is 45_4, שׁחה htpal. *prostrate oneself* Is 49_7, בקשׁ pi. *seek* Ps 122_9, פרע *let loose* Si $43_{14(M)}$, ברא *create* Si $43_{14(Bmg)}$, עשׂה *do* 1 K 11_{12} Is $48_{11.11}$ 65_8 Jr 14_7 Ezk $20_{9.14.22.44}$ $36_{22.32}$ 109_{21} 1QH 6_{10} ([עשׂ]תה) 1QM 18_8, נתן *give* 1 K $11_{13.13}$ 15_4, שׁית *place* 1 K 11_{34}, שׂים *place* 4QShir^b 28_2 (ש[מתה]), יסד pi. *found* Ps 8_3, גנן *protect* 2 K 19_{34}||Is 37_{35}, ישׁע hi. *save* 2 K 19_{34}||Is 37_{35} Ps 6_5 106_8, נצל hi. *save* Ps 79_9, פדה *ransom* Ps 44_{27} 69_{19}, כפר pi. *make atonement* Ps 79_9, טהר pi. *purify* 1QH 11_{10} 4QDibHam^a 1.6$_3$ (ות[ט]הרנו), חיה pi. *keep alive* Ps 143_{11} (or em. נחם pi. *comfort*), ענה pi. *afflict* 1 K 11_{39}, שׁחת hi. *destroy* 2 K 8_{19} 2 C 21_7, נדה pi. *exclude* Is 66_5, נאץ *spurn* Jr 14_{21}, צלח *succeed* Si 38_{14} $43_{27(B)}$, פתח *open* 1QM 18_8 ([למע]ן), perh. אכל hi. *cause to devour* Ezk 21_{33} (or em. מְרוּטָה לְהָכִיל לְמַעַן בָּרָק appar. *polished, in order to make it devour for the sake of lightning* to מְרוּטָה לְכָלָה לְמַעַן בְּרֹק *polished for destruction in order to flash*, as §2a), עשׂה pi. *press* Ezk 23_{21} (or em.; see above).

2. as conj., **in order that, so that, a.** with inf. cstr. of היה *be* 1 K 11_{36} Jr 44_8 Ezk 21_{15} (הֱיֵה), בוא hi. *bring* Gn 18_{19} Dt 6_{23}, רחק hi. *make distant* Jr 27_{10} Jl 4_6, נדח hi. *banish* Jr 27_{15}, גרשׁ *expel* Ezk 36_5 (מִגְרָשָׁהּ), סור *turn aside* Pr 15_{24}, ספר pi. *tell* Ex 9_{16}, ידע *know* Jos 4_{24} Jg 3_2 (or del. ידע) 1 K 8_{60} Ezk 38_{16} Mc 6_5 Si 46_6 ([דע]ת) 46_{10} 4QParGenEx 2_8 3_7 4QDibHam^a 1.2$_{10}$, hi. *cause to know* Dt 8_3, ירא *fear* Jos 4_{24} (if em. יְרָאתֶם *you have feared* to יִרְאָתָם so that *they may fear*), ראה *see* 1 S 17_{28}, hi. *show* Ezk 40_4, נבט hi. *look* Hb 2_{15} 1QH 4_{11}, עשׂה *do* Gn 50_{20} Jr 7_{10} (or em. עשׂה to שׁנה *change*), נתן *give* Dt 2_{30} Jr 43_3 Mc 6_{16} 2 C 25_{20}, שׁית *place* Ex 10_1, קום hi. *raise up*, i.e. establish Dt 8_{18} 9_5 29_{12} 1 K 12_{15}||2 C 10_{15} 2 K 23_{24} Jr 11_5, נצל hi. *deliver* Gn 37_{22}, ענה pi. *afflict* Ex 1_{11} Dt $8_{2.16}$, בחן *test* 4QBark^a 1.2$_7$, נסה pi. *test* Dt 8_{16} Jg 2_{22}, כחשׁ pi. *deceive* Zc 13_4, כעס hi. *anger* 2 K 22_{17} Jr 7_{18} $25_{7(Qr)}$ 32_{29} 2 C 34_{25}, חטא *cause to sin* Jr 32_{35}, גבר hi. *be mighty* 1QH 5_{15}, רבה *be many* Ex 11_9, hi. *increase* Dt 17_{16}=11QT 56_{16} 4QParGenEx 3_{11}, רחב hi. *make wide* Am 1_{13}, יסף *add* Is 30_1, טהר pi. *purify* Ezk 39_{12}, טמא pi. *defile* Lv 20_3, חלל pi. *profane* Am 2_7, ספה *sweep away* Dt 29_{18} 1QpHab 11_{14}, אבד hi. *destroy* 2 K 10_{19}, חרם hi. *destroy* Jos 11_{20}, שׁמד hi. *destroy* Jos 11_{20}, כרת hi. *cut off* Jr 44_8, זבח *sacrifice* 1 S 15_{15}, טבח *slaughter* Ezk 21_{15}, שׁפך *shed* blood Ezk $22_{6.9.12}$, בצע *extort* Ezk 22_{27}, רגע hi. *give rest* Jr 50_{34} (הִרְגִּיעַ), תפשׂ *hold* Ezk 14_5, מוג *melt* Ezk 21_{20} (לָמוּג; or em. הָמוֹג, i.e. ni.), ברק *flash* Ezk 21_{33} (if em. בָּרָק for the sake of *lightning* to בְּרֹק in order to *flash*), דבק hi. *cause to adhere* CD 1_{16}, יתר hi. *cause to remain* CD 2_{11}.

b. with impf. of היה *be* Ex 13_9 Dt 31_{19} Jos 4_6 4QparaKings 104_2 4QM^h 4_7, חיה *live* Dt 4_1 5_{33} 8_1 16_{20} 30_{19} Jr 35_7 Am 5_{14} 6QapSamKgs 27_1 (למען ת[חיה]), 11QT 51_{15}, יטב *be well* Gn 12_{13} Dt 5_{29} 6_{18} $12_{25.28}$ 22_7=11QT 65_5 Jr 7_{23} 11QT 53_6, חכם *be wise* Pr 19_{20}, שׂכל hi. *be prosperous* Jos 1_7, *make prosper* Dt 29_8 1 K 2_3, צלח *succeed* Si $43_{26(Bmg)}$, גדל *be great* Zc 12_7, חזק *be strong* Dt 11_8 Ezr 9_{12} 2 C 31_4, רבה *be many* Dt 11_{21}, ארך hi. *be long* Ex 20_{12}||Dt 5_{16} Dt 25_{15}, *prolong* Dt 4_{40} 11_9 17_{20}, נוח *rest* Ex 23_{12} Dt 5_{14}, עמד *stand* Jr 32_{14}, שׁבת *cease* Si $38_{8(B)}$, הלך *go* Is 28_{13} Ezk 11_{20} Pr 2_{20}, שׁוב *go back* Dt 13_{18} Jr 36_3 11QT 55_{11}, רוץ *run* Hb 2_2, שׁלח *send*, i.e. stretch, hand Ps 125_3, ישׁע ni. *be saved* Jr 4_{14}, חלץ ni. *be delivered* Ps 60_7 108_7, צדק *be vindicated* Is 43_{26} Ps 51_6 Jb 40_8 4QConfess 1.2$_{2.8}$, תפשׂ ni. *be caught* 1QH 4_{19}.

ראה *see* Ex 16_{32} Is 5_{19} 41_{20}, ספר *count* 4QD^a 6.1$_9$, pi. *tell* Ex 10_2 Ezk 12_{16} Ps 9_{15} 48_{14} 4QDibHam^a 1.6$_9$, ברך pi. *bless* Gn 27_{25} Dt 14_{29} 23_{21} 24_{19}, זמר pi. *praise* Ps 30_{13}, שׂמח *rejoice* Si 35_2, עלז *exult* Jr 51_{39} (or em. עלף *swoon*), בושׁ *be ashamed* Is 44_9 Ps 119_{80}, חרף pi. *reproach* Ne 6_{13}, שׁמע *hear* Nm 27_{20} Dt 31_{12}, ni. *be heard* Ezk 19_9, ידע *know* Ex $8_{6.18}$ 9_{29} 11_7 Lv 23_{43} Dt 29_5 1 K 8_{43}||2 C 6_{33} Is 43_{10} $45_{3.6}$ Jr 44_{29} Ps 78_6 Jb 19_{29} 1QH 4_{32} 4QPrQuot 51_{14}, אמן hi. *believe* Ex 4_5, ירא *fear* Dt 6_2 1 K 8_{40} Ne 6_{13} 2 C 6_{31}, ni. *be feared* Ps 130_4 (or em. תִּוָּרֵא that *you may be feared* to תּוֹרָתֶךָ for the sake of *your law*, as §1), זכר *remember* Nm 15_{40} Dt 16_3 Ezk 16_{63} 4QAdmon 1.1$_7$ (ל[מען]), ni. *be remembered* Is 23_{16} Ezk 25_{10}, למד *learn* Dt 14_{23} 17_{19} 31_{12} 119_{71}, שׁמר *keep* Jos 1_8 Ps 119_{101} 4QJub^c 2_7 (ל[מ]ע[ן] ו[ישמר]ו), נסה pi. *test* Ex 16_4, שׁכח *forget* Si $38_{8(Bmg)}$ 45_{26},

תעה *go astray* Ezk 14$_{11}$, שׁגג *sin unintentionally* 11QT 35$_{13}$, חטא *sin* Ps 119$_{11}$.

קום hi. *raise up*, i.e. establish 1 K 2$_4$, מצא *find* Ex 33$_{13}$ Jr 10$_{18}$ (or em. יִמְצָאוּ that *they might find* to יִמָּצְאוּ that *they might be found* or יֶאְשָׁמוּ that *they might be held guilty*; or לְמַעַן יִמְצָאוּ *that they might be found* to לְמָנְעָם מִצֵּאת *to keep them from going out*), לכד *capture* 2 C 32$_{18}$, ירשׁ *possess* Nm 36$_8$ Am 9$_{12}$ 1 C 28$_8$ 4QpsEzek^a 3$_3$, ישׁב *be inhabited* Ezk 26$_{20}$ (or em. שׁוב *go back*), ינק *suck* Is 66$_{11}$, מצץ *drain out* Is 66$_{11}$, חסר *lack* Ezk 4$_{17}$, חרב *be desolate* Ezk 6$_6$, ישׁם *be desolate* Ezk 12$_{19}$, שׁמם hi. *make desolate* Ezk 20$_{26}$, אבד *perish* 4QapJoseph^b 1$_{17}$, כרת ni. *be cut off* Ho 8$_4$ Ob$_9$, מחץ *shatter* Ps 68$_{24}$ (or em. מחץ ni. *be shattered*, or רחץ *wash*, or מצה ni. *be dragged*), נשׂא *carry* Ezk 16$_{54}$, שׁלם *be complete* Si 7$_{32}$, חמם *be warm* Ezk 24$_{11}$.

c. with pf. of ירא *fear* Jos 4$_{24}$ (or em.; see §2a), כעס hi. *anger* Jr 25$_{7(Kt)}$ (Qr §2a), ברא *create* Si 42$_{14(B)}$ (Bmg, M §1).

d. with pass. ptc. of שׂכר *hire* Ne 6$_{13}$ (or del.).

3. לְמַעַן אֲשֶׁר **in order to, in order that, so that,** with impf. of יטב *be well* Jr 42$_6$, גבה *be high* Ezk 31$_{14}$, בוא *come* Dt 27$_3$, hi. *bring* Lv 17$_5$, קרב *draw near* Nm 17$_5$, פוץ *be scattered* Ezk 46$_{18}$, צוה pi. *command* Gn 18$_{19}$, למד pi. *teach* Dt 20$_{18}$=11QT 62$_{15}$, ידע *know* Jos 3$_4$ Ezk 20$_{26}$, ראה *see* 2 S 13$_5$, לקח *take* Ezk 36$_{30}$, כלה *be destroyed* 4QpsMos^e 1$_9$ ([יוכ]ל[ו]).*

Also 4QPrayers^a 2$_2$ ([למען]) 4QapPent 1$_7$ ([ל]מען) 4QapJoshua^a 27$_1$ (ל[מען]) 4Q418 11$_1$ ([ל]מענ[ה]) 4QNarrF 1$_6$ 4QPrQuot 88$_3$ 4QPrFêtes^b 11$_3$ 4QPrFêtes^c 10.1$_1$ 147$_4$ (both [ל]מען) 11QT 13$_1$.

לְנֶגֶד, see נֶגֶד *in front of.*

[לֹעַ] $_1$ n.[m.] **throat**—sf. לֹעֲךָ—<PREP> בְּ of direction, *in(to)*, + שׂים *place* knife Pr 23$_2$.

⇒ לעע *swallow.*

לעב $_{1.1}$ vb. **deride—Hi.** $_1$ Ptc. מַלְעִבִים—**deride,** <SUBJ> עַם *people* 2 C 36$_{16}$ (+ בזה *despise*, תעע htpalp. *mock*). <PREP> בְּ introducing object, + מַלְאָךְ *messenger* 2 C 36$_{16}$.

Htp. $_{0.1}$ Impf. Si יתלעבך—**deride,** <SUBJ> בֵּן *son* Si 30$_{13(B)}$ (Bmg עלה htp. *raise oneself up*). <PREP> בְּ of instrument, *by (means of), with*, + אִוֶּלֶת *folly* Si 30$_{13(B)}$.

לעג $_{18.2.1}$ vb. **deride—Qal** $_{12.2}$ Pf. לָעֲגָה; impf. יִלְעַג (יִלְעָג), 3fs תִּלְעַג, 2ms תִּלְעַג, אֶלְעַג, יִלְעֲגוּ; + waw 2ms וַתִּלְעַג; ptc. לֹעֵג—**deride, mock (at),** <SUBJ> Y. Ps 2$_4$ (+ שׂחק *laugh*) 59$_9$ (|| שׂחק) Jb 9$_{23}$, בֵּן *son* Si 4$_1$ (+ דאב hi. *cause to languish*) Si 34$_{22(Bmg)}$, בְּתוּלָה *young woman* 2 K 19$_{21}$||Is 37$_{22}$ (|| בזה *despise*), Job Jb 11$_3$, אוֹיֵב *enemy* Ps 25$_2$ (if em. עלץ *exult* to לעג *mock*) 80$_7$, עֵד *witness* Ps 35$_{16}$ (if em. בְּחַנְפֵי לַעֲגֵי מָעוֹג appar. *as profane ones of mockers of a cake* to בְּהִנָּפְלִי/בְּחַנְפִי לָעֲגוּ לָעוֹג/לַעַג *when I fell over/when I limped they utterly mocked*), נָקִי *innocent one* Jb 22$_{19}$, עַיִן *eye* Pr 30$_{17}$ (+ בוז *despise*), חָכְמָה *wisdom* Pr 1$_{26}$ (+ שׂחק), כֹּל *everyone* Jr 20$_7$; subject not specified, Pr 17$_5$ (+ שׂמח *rejoice*). <PREP> לְ *at*, or introducing object, + Jeremiah Jr 20$_7$, Sennacherib 2 K 19$_{21}$||Is 37$_{22}$, מַת *man* Jb 22$_{19}$, אָב *father* Pr 30$_{17}$, מֶלֶךְ *king* 2 K 19$_{21}$||Is 37$_{22}$ Ps 2$_4$, רֹזֵן *ruler* Ps 2$_4$, worshipper Ps 25$_2$ (if em.; see Subj.) 80$_{7(mss)}$, גּוֹי *nation* Ps 59$_9$, רָשׁ *poor one* Pr 17$_5$, חַיִּים *life* Si 4$_1$, מַסָּה *despair* Jb 9$_{23}$; in ref. to subj. of לעג Ps 80$_7$; עַל *at*, or *introducing object*, + Ben Sira Si 34$_{22(Bmg)}$.

Also perh. 4QSap^a 1$_7$ ([ל]עג).

<SYN> שׂחק *laugh*, בזה *despise*.

Ni. $_1$ Ptc. cstr. נִלְעַג—**be incomprehensible,** in ref. to speaking a foreign language, ptc. used as noun, **incomprehensible one,** <OBJ> ראה *see* Is 33$_{19}$. <CSTR> נִלְעַג לָשׁוֹן *one incomprehensible of tongue* Is 33$_{19}$ (|| עֲמֵק *deep*, i.e. obscure, of speech; + אֵין בִּינָה *there is no understanding*). <APP> עַם *people* Is 33$_{19}$.

<SYN> עָמֵק *deep*.

Hi. $_{5.1.1}$ Impf. 2ms תַּלְעִיג, יַלְעִגוּ (Q ילעיגו); + waw וַיַּלְעִגוּ, וַיַּלְעֵג; ptc. מַלְעִגִים—**deride, mock (at),** <SUBJ> Israelites 2 C 30$_{10}$ (|| שׂחק hi. *laugh at*), Kittim 1QpHab 4$_2$ (|| בזה *despise*), Zophar Jb 21$_3$, Geshem Ne 2$_{19}$, Sanballat Ne 2$_{19}$ (|| בזה) 3$_{33}$, Tobiah Ne 2$_{19}$, בֵּן *son* Si 34$_{22(B)}$, עֶבֶד *servant* Ne 2$_{19}$, חֹרֹנִי *Horonite* Ne 2$_{19}$, עַמּוֹנִי *Ammonite* Ne 2$_{19}$, עַרְבִי *Arab* Ne 2$_{19}$, ראה ptc. *one who sees* Ps 22$_8$, שַׁאֲנָן *one at ease* Ps 123$_4$ (if em. הַלַּעַג *the derision* to הַלְעִיג *the deriding of* those at ease). <PREP> לְ *at*, or introducing object, + psalmist Ps 22$_8$; בְּ *at*, or introducing object, + רָץ *courier* 2 C 30$_{10}$; עַל *at*, or introducing object, + Ben Sira Si 34$_{22(B)}$, יְהוּדִי *Jew* Ne 3$_{33}$, רַב *great* *one* 1QpHab 4_{2}.

<SYN> שׂחק hi. *laugh at,* בזה *despise.*

→ לַעַג *derision,* לֹעַג *incomprehensibility,* לָעֵג *mocking.*

[לָעֵג] 1 adj. **mocking**—pl. cstr. לַעֲגֵי—used as noun, **mocker,** בְּחַנְפֵי לַעֲגֵי מָעוֹג appar. *as profane ones of mockers of a cake* Ps 35_{16} (or em. בְּחַנְפֵי to בְּהִנָּפְלִי/בְּחַנְפִי *when I fell over/when I limped* and/or לַעֲגֵי מָעוֹג to לַעֲגֵי מְעֻוָּג *mockers of a cripple* or עָגוּ מָעוֹג *they made a circle* or לָעֲגוּ לָעוֹג/לַעַג *they utterly mocked*).

→ לעג *deride.*

לַעַג 8.0.2 n.[m.] **derision, stammering**—cstr. לַעַג; sf. לַעְגָם; pl. cstr. לַעֲגֵי—**1a. derision, mockery,** <OBJ> שׁתה *drink* Jb 34_{7}. <PREP> בְּ of accompaniment, *with,* + שׂחק *laugh* 1QpHab 4_{6}. <COLL> לעג ... לגבורים *mockery for the mighty ones* 1QM 12_{7} (|| קֶלֶס *derision,* + בוז *contempt*).

1b. (object of) derision, mockery, <SUBJ> היה *be* Ps 79_{4} (|| קֶלֶס *derision,* חֶרְפָּה *reproach*). <OBJ> שׂים *place* Ps 44_{14} (|| חֶרְפָּה, קֶלֶס). <CSTR> הַלַּעַג הַשַּׁאֲנַנִּים appar. *the derision of those that are at ease* Ps 123_{4} (or em. הַלַּעַג לַשַּׁאֲנַנִּים *derision to those that are at ease,* or הַלְעִיג הַשַּׁאֲנַנִּים *the deriding of those that are at ease,* from לעג hi.; + בּוּז *contempt*). <PREP> לְ *as* or introducing predicate, + היה *be* Ezk 23_{32} (|| צְחֹק *laughingstock*) 36_{4} (|| בַּז *prey*). <COLL> לַעַג וָקֶלֶס *an object of mockery and derision* Ps 44_{14} 79_{4}.

2. pl. **stammering,*** <SUBJ> זול *cease* Ho 7_{16} (if em., see Nom. Cl.). <NOM CL> זוֹ לַעְגָּם *this is their stammering* Ho 7_{16} (or em. וְזָל לַעְגָּם *and their mockery will cease,* as §1a). <CSTR> לַעֲגֵי שָׂפָה *stammering of speech* Is 28_{11}=1QH 4_{16} (ל[וע]ג שפה; + לָשׁוֹן אַחֶרֶת *another tongue*). <PREP> בְּ of accompaniment, *with, in,* + דבר pi. *speak* Is 28_{11}=1QH 4_{16}.

<SYN> §1a קֶלֶס *derision;* §1b קֶלֶס *derision,* חֶרְפָּה *reproach,* צְחֹק *laughingstock,* בַּז *prey.*

→ לעג *deride.*

לַעְדָּה 1 pr.n.m. **Laadah,** Judahite, son of Shelah, and founder of Mareshah, <NOM CL> בְּנֵי שֵׁלָה ... וְלַעְדָּה *the sons of Shelah were ... and Laadah* 1 C 4_{21}. <APP> אָב *father* 1 C 4_{21}.

לַעְדָּן 7 pr.n.m. **Ladan, 1.** Levite, Gershonite and father of Jehiel, Zetham and Joel; perh. ident. with Libni at Ex 6_{17} Nm 3_{18} 1 C $6_{2.5}$, <NOM CL> לַגֵּרְשֻׁנִּי לַעְדָּן *of the Gershonites was Ladan* 1 C 23_{7}. <CSTR> בְּנֵי לַעְדָּן *sons of Ladan* 1 C 23_{8} 26_{21}. <PREP> לְ of possession, *(belonging) to, of* 1 C 23_{9} $26_{21.21}$. <APP> גֵּרְשֻׁנִּי *Gershonite* 1 C 26_{21}.

2. son of Tahan and father of Ammihud, descendant of Ephraim, <NOM CL> לַעְדָּן בְּנוֹ *Ladan was his son* 1 C 7_{26}.

לעז 1 vb. **speak a foreign language—Qal** 1 Ptc. לֹעֵז—**speak a foreign language, be foreign,** <SUBJ> עַם *people* Is 33_{19} (if em. נוֹעָז perh. *unintelligible* to לוֹעֵז *speaking a foreign language*) Ps 114_{1} (or em. לֹעֵז *foreign* to לְ־עָז *really strong,* i.e. barbaric).*

לעט 1 vb. **swallow—Qal, devour,** <SUBJ> לָבִא *lion* Ps 57_{5} (if em. להט *devour*). <OBJ> בֵּן *son* of human being Ps 57_{5} (if em.).

Hi. 1 Impv. הַלְעִיטֵנִי—**feed, allow to gulp down,** <SUBJ> Jacob Gn 25_{30}. <OBJ> Esau Gn 25_{30}. <PREP> מִן partitive, *(some) of,* + אָדֹם *red stuff* Gn 25_{30}.*

לָעִיר 2 pl.n. **Lair,** perh. Laḫiru, SE of Arbela, near Elamite border, unless לָעִיר *of the city of,* <CSTR> מֶלֶךְ לָעִיר *king of Lair* 2 K 19_{13}||Is 37_{13} (or em. לַעַשׁ *Laash*).

לְעֻמַּת 31.2.10 prep. **close by**—Q לעומת; sf. לְעֻמָּתוֹ, לְעֻמָּתָם (Q לעומתמה); pl. לְעֻמּוֹת—**1. close by, beside, alongside, parallel to, as well as,** followed by noun, or suffix in ref. to noun, David 2 S $16_{13.13}$ (mss + מִזֶּה *from there*), אִישׁ 4QM[a] 1_{12}, פָּנִים *face* Ezk 3_{8}, מֵצַח *forehead* Ezk 3_{8}, עָצֶה *spine* Lv 3_{9} 11QT 15_{8} 20_{7}, חַיָּה *living being* Ezk $1_{20.21}$ 3_{13}, כְּרוּב *cherub* Ezk 10_{19} 11_{22}, גְּבוּל *border* Ezk 48_{13}, מִסְגֶּרֶת *border* Ex 25_{27}||37_{14}, מַחְבֶּרֶת *joining* Ex 28_{27}||39_{20}, תְּרוּמָה *reserved land* Ezk 45_{6} $48_{18.18}$, לִשְׁכָּה *cell* Ezk 42_{7}, מוּסָד *foundation* 11QT 40_{10}, פִּנָּה *corner* 11QT 30_{6}, זֶה *this (one)* Ec 7_{14} Si $36_{14(Segal)}$ (לעומת [זה]) $42_{24(M)}$.

With verb, היה *be* Ex 25_{27}||37_{14} Ezk 48_{18}, נתן *give,* i.e. place Ex 28_{27}||39_{20} 45_{6}, *cause to be* Ezk $3_{8.8}$, סור hi. *remove* Lv 3_{9}, הלך *go* 2 S 16_{13}, נשׂא ni. *be lifted up* Ezk $1_{20.21}$, סקל pi. *throw stones* 2 S 16_{13}, עשׂה *make* Ec 7_{14}, 11QT 30_{6}

(וע[שיתה]), pass. *be made* 11QT 40$_{10}$ (וע[שום]).

2. corresponding to, agreeing with, according to, followed by noun, אָח *brother* 1 C 24$_{31.31}$ 26$_{12}$, קֶלַע *curtain* Ex 38$_{18}$, אֹרֶךְ *length* of gate Ezk 40$_{18}$, חֵלֶק *portion* Ezk 48$_{21}$, אֶחָד *one* portion Ezk 45$_{7}$, מִשְׁמָר *watch* Ne 12$_{24}$ 1 C 26$_{16}$, מִשְׁמֶרֶת *watch* 1 C 25$_{8(mss)}$, רַחֲמִים *compassion* 1QH 18$_{25}$ 4QAges[b] 1.2$_{3}$ (+ לְפִי *according to*).

With verb, נפל hi. *cast* lots 1 C 24$_{31}$ 25$_{8}$, נגשׁ hi. *bring near* 4QAges[b] 1.2$_{3}$, נצל hi. *deliver* 1QH 18$_{25}$ ([ותצילנו]).

<COLL> לְעֻמַּת כַּקָּטֹן כַּגָּדוֹל מֵבִין עִם־תַּלְמִיד *according to (this principle), as the small, so the great, teacher together with scholar* 1 C 25$_{8}$.

3. לעמת ככה **in accordance with this, accordingly,** + קום pi. *oblige* Mur 24 C$_{18}$. D$_{19}$ (לע[מת]), מרק *complete (transaction)* Mur 30 1$_{6}$ 2$_{24}$.

4. מִלְּעֻמַּת **close by,** + noun, בֶּטֶן *bulge* 1 K 7$_{20}$.

5. כְּלְעֻמַּת שֶׁ as conjunction, **as in accordance with (the way) that,** כְּלְעֻמַּת שֶׁבָּא כֵּן יֵלֵךְ *as in accordance with the way that he came, so shall he go* Ec 5$_{15}$ (if em. כָּל־עֻמַּת *just as*).

לַעֲנָה $_{8.1.5}$ n.f. **wormwood,** bitter plant, perh. *artemisia absinthium*, <NOM CL> יין ... לענה *wine is ... wormwood* Si 34$_{29}$ (|| ראשׁ *poison[ous plant]*, כְּאֵב *pain*, קָלוֹן *disgrace*), אין לענה לנגדו *there is no wormwood before him* 4QMyst[b] 6$_{5}$=7$_{2}$ (6$_{5}$ [א'ין]). <OBJ> אכל hi. *feed* Jr 9$_{14}$ 23$_{15}$ (both + מֵי־ ראשׁ *poisonous water*), רוה hi. *cause to drink* Lm 3$_{15}$ (|| מָרוֹר *bitter thing*), זכר *remember* Lm 3$_{19}$ (|| ראשׁ *poison[ous plant]*), פרה *bear fruit* Dt 29$_{17}$ 1QH 4$_{14}$ (both || ראשׁ). <APP> עֳנִי *affliction* Lm 3$_{19}$, מָרוּד *wandering* Lm 3$_{19}$. <PREP> לְ *into*, + הפך *turn* Am 5$_{7}$ (or em. לְמַעֲלָה *upside down*) 6$_{12}$ (|| ראשׁ *poison[ous plant]*); כְּ *as* Pr 5$_{4}$ (+ מַר *bitter*). <COLL> לַעֲנָה וָרֹאשׁ *wormwood and poison* Lm 3$_{19}$, ראשׁ וְלַעֲנָה *poison and wormwood* Dt 29$_{17}$.

Also 4QMyst[b] 2.1$_{5}$ 4QSD 9$_{3}$.

<SYN> ראשׁ *poison*, מָרוֹר *bitter thing*, כְּאֵב *pain*, קָלוֹן *disgrace*.

לעע I $_{2}$ vb. **be rash—Qal** $_{2}$ Pf. לָעוּ; impf. יָלַע—**1. be rash, speak rashly,** or perh. **gush,*** <SUBJ> אָדָם *person* Pr 20$_{25}$ (מוֹקֵשׁ אָדָם יָלַע קֹדֶשׁ *it is a snare for a person rashly to say, Holy;* + בקר pi. *enquire* after making vows), גּוֹי *nation* Ob$_{16}$ (unless לעע II *swallow*; or em. נוע *tremble*), דָּבָר *word* Jb 6$_{3}$.

לעע II $_{1.1}$ vb. **swallow—Qal** $_{1}$ Impf. 2ms Si תלע; + waw וְלָעוּ—**swallow, gulp down,** <SUBJ> בֵּן *son* Si 34$_{17}$, גּוֹי *nation* Ob$_{16}$ (unless לעע I *speak rashly;* or em. נוע *stumble;* || שׁתה *drink*). <SYN> שׁתה *drink*.

Pilp. lap up, <SUBJ> אֶפְרֹחַ *nestling* Jb 39$_{30}$ (if em. יְעַלְעוּ *they suck/wade through/shake*, i.e. עלע pi., to יְלַעְלְעוּ *they lap up*). <OBJ> דָּם *blood* Jb 39$_{30}$.*

⇒ לֹעַ *throat*.

[לַ֫עַשׁ] pl.n. **Laash,** region of Hamath, <CSTR> מֶלֶךְ לַעַשׁ *king of Laash* 2 K 19$_{13}$||Is 37$_{13}$ (if em. לָעִיר *Lair*).

לְפִי $_{16.1.1}$ prep. **according to**—sf. לְפִיהֶן—**according to, in proportion to, in accordance with;** with inf. cstr., לְפִי is sometimes a conjunction, **according as, when(ever)** (Nm 9$_{17}$ Jr 29$_{10}$).

Followed by noun or suffix in ref. to noun, טַף *children* Gn 47$_{12}$, פקד pass. ptc. *one numbered* Nm 26$_{54}$, רוּחַ *spirit* 4QTohD 1$_{5}$, זֶרַע *seed* Lv 27$_{16}$, אֹכֶל *food* (or אכל inf. *eating*) Ex 12$_{4}$ 16$_{16.18}$, דָּבָר *word* 1 K 17$_{1}$, נַחֲלָה *inheritance* Jos 18$_{4}$, שָׁנָה *year* Lv 25$_{51}$, חֶסֶד *loyalty* Ho 10$_{12}$, שֵׂכֶל *insight* Pr 12$_{8}$, מַהֲלָל *praise* Pr 27$_{21}$, צֹרֶךְ *need* Si 38$_{1(Bmg)}$, מִשְׁגָּה *error* CD 3$_{4}$ (if em. לִפְנֵי *before* to לְפִי), מלא inf. *being full*, i.e. complete Jr 29$_{10}$, רבב inf. *being many* Lv 25$_{16}$, מעט inf. *being few* Lv 25$_{16}$, עלה ni. inf. *being lifted up* Nm 9$_{17}$.

With verb, היה *be* Lv 27$_{16}$ 1 K 17$_{1}$, הלל pu. *be praised* Pr 12$_{8}$, כתב *write* Jos 18$_{4}$, רבה hi. *increase* Lv 25$_{16}$, מעט hi. *diminish* Lv 25$_{16}$, כול pilp. *provide* food Gn 47$_{12}$, כסס *determine* Ex 12$_{4}$, לקט *gather* Ex 16$_{16.18}$, קצר *reap* Ho 10$_{12}$, נתן ho. *be given* Nm 26$_{54}$, שׁוב hi. *give back* Lv 25$_{51}$, נסע *set out* Nm 9$_{17}$, פקד *visit* Jr 29$_{10}$, רעה *associate with* Si 38$_{1(Bmg, D)}$, ענשׁ *be punished* CD 3$_{4}$ (if em. לִפְנֵי *before* to לְפִי).

⇒ לְ *to* + פֶּה *mouth*.

לַפִּיד $_{13.0.1}$ n.m. **torch**—cstr. לַפִּיד; pl. לַפִּידִים (לַפִּדם), לַפִּדִים ,לַפִּידם); cstr. לַפִּידֵי—**1. torch,** <SUBJ> הלך *go* Jb 41$_{11}$ (+ כִּידוֹד *spark*), עבר *pass* Gn 15$_{17}$, אכל *devour* Zc

12$_6$. <NOM CL> לַפִּדִים בְּתוֹךְ הַכַּדִּים *torches were inside the jars* Jg 7$_{16}$. <OBJ> לקח *take* Jg 15$_4$, שׂים *place* Jg 15$_4$. <CSTR> לַפִּיד אֵשׁ *torch of fire* Gn 15$_{17}$ (|| תַּנּוּר *oven* of smoke) Zc 12$_6$ (|| כִּיּוֹר *pot* of fire) 1QM 11$_{10}$, לַפִּידֵי אֵשׁ *torches of fire* Dn 10$_6$ (+ בָּרָק *lightning*); מַרְאֵה הַלַּפִּדִים *appearance of the torches* Ezk 1$_{13}$ (or em. לַפִּדִים *of torches*; + גַּחֲלֵי־אֵשׁ *coals of fire*), אֵשׁ־לַפִּדוֹת *fire of torches* Na 2$_4$ (if em. אֵשׁ־פְּלָדוֹת perh. *fire of steel*). <ADJ> אֶחָד *one* Jg 15$_4$. <PREP> בְּ of place, *in*, + בער hi. *kindle* fire Jg 15$_5$; introducing object, + חזק hi. *hold* Jg 7$_{20}$; כְּ *as* Na 2$_5$ (+ בָּרָק *lightning*) Zc 12$_6$ Dn 10$_6$ 1QM 11$_{10}$, + בער *burn* Is 62$_1$ (+ נֹגַהּ *brightness*).

2. lightning, <OBJ> ראה *see* Ex 20$_{18}$ (|| קוֹל *sound*, i.e. thunder).

<SYN> §1 תַּנּוּר *oven*, כִּיּוֹר *pot*, §2 קוֹל *sound*, i.e. thunder.*

לַפִּידוֹת 1 pr.n.m. **Lappidoth,** husband of Deborah, <CSTR> אֵשֶׁת לַפִּידוֹת *wife of Lappidoth* Jg 4$_4$.*

[לִפְנַי] 1 adv. **in front**—לִפְנָי—הַבַּיִת הוּא הַהֵיכָל לִפְנָי perh. *the house, that is the hall in front* 1 K 6$_{17}$ (or em. לִפְנֵי to לִפְנֵי הַדְּבִיר *in front of the inner sanctuary*).

לִפְנֵי 1103.40.251.2 prep. **before**—sf. לְפָנַי (לְפָנַי), לְפָנֶיךָ (Q לפניכה), לְפָנָיו (Q לפנו, לפנוהי), לְפָנֶיהָ, לְפָנֵינוּ, לִפְנֵיכֶם, לִפְנֵיהֶם—**1.** לִפְנֵי **before, in front of, in the presence of,** usu. of place; also of time (e.g. Gn 13$_{10}$ 29$_{26}$ 36$_{31}$ Ex 10$_{14}$ Nm 13$_{22}$ Dt 4$_{32}$ Jos 10$_{14}$ 1 K 3$_{12}$ 14$_9$ 15$_3$ 16$_{25}$ 2 K 17$_2$ 23$_{25}$ Is 18$_5$ Am 1$_1$ Zc 8$_{10}$ Ml 3$_{23}$ Ec 1$_{16}$ 2 C 33$_{19}$ Si 38$_1$ 47$_{10}$ 48$_{25}$ 1QS 6$_{10}$ 11QT 17$_7$), seniority (e.g. 48$_{20}$ 1QS 6$_{11}$); sometimes **against** (e.g. Nm 16$_2$ Dt 31$_{21}$ Jos 1$_5$ Est 9$_2$ 2 C 13$_8$ 14$_9$ 20$_{12}$ Si 4$_{26}$ 8$_{11}$ 46$_3$).

a. followed by noun or suffix in ref. to noun, יי *Y.* Gn 7$_1$ 10$_{9.9}$ 17$_1$ 18$_{22}$ 24$_{40}$ 27$_7$ Ex 6$_{12.30}$ 16$_{9.33}$ 25$_{30}$ 27$_{21}$ 28$_{12.30.30.35.38}$ 29$_{11+5t}$ 30$_{8.16}$ 34$_{34}$ 40$_{23.25}$ Lv 1$_{3.5.11}$ 3$_{1.7.12}$ 4$_{4+8t}$ 5$_{26}$ 6$_{7.18}$ 7$_{30}$ 8$_{26.27.29}$ 9$_{2.4.5.21}$ 10$_{1.2.15.17.19}$ 12$_7$ 14$_{11+8t}$ 15$_{14.15.30}$ 16$_{7.10.13.30}$ 19$_{22}$ 23$_{11.20.28.40}$ 24$_{3.4.6.8}$ Nm 3$_{4.4}$ 5$_{16.18.25.30}$ 6$_{16.20}$ 7$_3$ 8$_{10.11.21}$ 10$_9$ 11$_{20}$ 14$_{37}$ 15$_{15.25.28}$ 16$_{7.16.17}$ 17$_{5.22}$ 18$_{19}$ 20$_3$ 26$_{61}$ 27$_{5.21}$ 31$_{50.54}$ 32$_{20+6t}$ Dt 1$_{45}$ 4$_{10}$ 6$_{25}$ 9$_{18.25}$ 10$_8$ 12$_{7.12.18.18}$ 14$_{23.26}$ 15$_{20}$ 16$_{11}$ 18$_7$ 19$_{17}$=11QT 61$_8$ Dt 24$_{4.13}$ 26$_{5.10.10.13}$ 27$_7$ 29$_{9.14}$ Jos 4$_{13}$ 6$_{8.26}$ 7$_{23}$ 18$_{6.8.10}$ 19$_{51}$ 22$_{27}$ Jg 6$_{18}$ 11$_{11}$ 20$_{26.26.28}$ 1 S 1$_{12.15.19}$ 2$_{28.30}$ 6$_{20}$ 7$_6$ 10$_{19.25}$ 11$_{15.15}$ 12$_7$ 15$_{33}$ 21$_8$ 23$_{18}$ 26$_{19}$ 2 S 5$_3$||1 C 11$_3$ 2 S 6$_{5+5t}$ 7$_{16(mss)}$ 7$_{18.26.29}$||1 C 17$_{16.24.27}$ 2 S 21$_9$ 1 K 2$_{4.45}$ 3$_6$ 8$_{23}$||2 C 6$_{14}$ 1 K 8$_{25}$ 8$_{25.28}$||2 C 6$_{16.19}$ 1 K 8$_{59}$ 8$_{62}$||2 C 7$_4$ 1 K 8$_{64.65}$ 9$_3$ 9$_4$||2 C 7$_{17}$ 1 K 9$_{25}$ 11$_{36}$ 17$_1$ 18$_{15}$ 19$_{11.11}$ 22$_{21}$||2 C 18$_{20}$ 2 K 3$_{14}$ 5$_{16}$ 16$_{14}$ 19$_{14}$||Is 37$_{14}$ 2 K 19$_{15}$ 20$_3$||Is 38$_3$ 2 K 22$_{19}$||2 C 34$_{27}$ 2 K 23$_3$||2 C 34$_{31}$ Is 23$_{18}$ 40$_{10}$ 43$_{10}$ 53$_2$ (or em. לְפָנָיו *before him* to לְפָנֵינוּ *before us*) 62$_{11}$ 65$_6$ 66$_{22.23}$ Jr 2$_{22}$ 7$_{10}$ 15$_{1.19}$ 18$_{23}$ 30$_{20}$ 31$_{36}$ 34$_{15.18}$ 35$_{19}$ 36$_{7.9}$ 42$_9$ 49$_{19}$ 50$_{44}$ Ezk 16$_{50}$ 22$_{30}$ 36$_{17}$ 41$_{22}$ 43$_{24}$ 44$_{15}$ 46$_{3.9}$ Ho 6$_2$ Jon 1$_2$ Hg 2$_{14}$ Ml 3$_{1.16}$ Ps 5$_{9(mss)}$ 18$_7$ (||2 S 22$_7$ lacks לְפָנָיו; del.) 19$_{15}$ 22$_{28.30}$ 41$_{13}$ 85$_{14}$ 88$_3$ 96$_6$||1 C 16$_{27}$ 96$_{13}$ 97$_3$ 98$_6$ 100$_2$ 102$_1$ 116$_9$ 119$_{169.170}$ 141$_2$ 142$_{3.3}$ 143$_2$ Jb 41$_2$ Pr 8$_{30}$ Lm 1$_{22}$ Dn 9$_{20}$ 10$_{12}$ Ezr 9$_{15.15}$ Ne 1$_6$ 9$_8$ 1 C 16$_{29}$ 17$_{25}$ 22$_{8.18}$ 23$_{13.31}$ 29$_{22}$ 2 C 1$_6$ 2$_3$ 6$_{24}$ 14$_{12}$ 20$_{9.13.18}$ 27$_6$ 29$_{11}$ 31$_{20}$ 33$_{12}$ 34$_{27}$ 2QapMoses 1$_4$ 4QMidrEschat[b] 3$_7$ 4QapPs[b] 24$_9$ ([ל]פניו) 31$_2$ ([יהו]ה) 8QHymn 2$_6$ 11QPs[a] 24$_7$ 26$_9$ 11QPsAp[a] 2$_6$ ([לפנ]ן) 2$_9$ ([לפני יה]וה) 11QT 15$_{12}$ ([ל]פני יה[וה]) 15$_{13.15}$ 20$_9$ (both [לפני יהוה]) 21$_{3.8}$ ([לפ]ני) 21$_{16}$ 22$_{14.16}$ 24$_9$ 25$_4$ ([ל]פני) 34$_{14}$ 53$_{8.10}$ 55$_{14}$ 56$_9$ 63$_8$ GnzPs 2$_{7.10.15}$ 3$_{2.11}$ 4$_{10.17}$.

appar. in ref. to Y., 1QpPs 9$_2$ 1QLitPr 3.2$_5$ 4QapPs[b] 33$_9$ 46$_{5.6}$ 4QMMT C$_{31}$ 4QShirShabb[f] 20.2$_7$ 4QPrFêtes[b] 20$_2$ ([לפני]כה) 4QPrFêtes[c] 1.1$_4$ ([לפניכ]ה) 131.2$_7$ 11QT 39$_6$ 52$_{9.16}$ 59$_{17}$ 60$_{11.14.19}$ 63$_3$ GnzPs 1$_{1.21}$.

אֱלֹהִים *God* Gn 6$_{11.13}$ 17$_{18}$ 48$_{15}$ Ex 18$_{12}$ Lv 23$_{28.40}$ Nm 10$_{9.10}$ Dt 4$_{10}$ 6$_{25}$ 12$_{7.12.18.18}$ 14$_{23.26}$ 15$_{20}$ 16$_{11}$ 24$_{13}$ 26$_{5.10.10.13}$ 27$_7$ 29$_{9.14}$ Jos 18$_6$ 24$_1$ Jg 21$_2$ 1 S 2$_{30}$ 6$_{20}$ 2 S 7$_{26.29}$||1 C 17$_{24.27}$ 1 K 8$_{23.25.28}$||2 C 6$_{14.16.19}$ 1 K 8$_{65}$ 11$_{36}$ 17$_1$ 2 K 22$_{19}$ ||2 C 34$_{27}$ Jr 7$_{10}$ 34$_{18}$ 35$_{19}$ 42$_9$ Ps 18$_7$ 50$_3$ 56$_{14}$ 61$_8$ 62$_9$ 68$_{4.5}$ 76$_8$ 79$_{11}$ 88$_3$ Ec 2$_{26.26}$ 5$_1$ 7$_{26}$ Dn 9$_{18.20}$ Ezr 8$_{21}$ 9$_{15.15}$ Ne 1$_{4.6}$ 9$_{8.32}$ 1 C 13$_{8.10}$ 16$_1$ 17$_{25}$ 29$_{15}$ 2 C 23$_5$ 6$_{24}$ 20$_9$ 27$_6$ 31$_{20}$ 34$_{27}$ Si 14$_{16}$ ([לפני]) 4QBibPar 10$_{10}$ 4Q185 1.2$_8$ 4Q392 1$_5$ 4QShir[b] 109$_2$ ([ל]פני אלוהים]) 11QT 55$_{14}$ 63$_8$, *god* 2 C 25$_{14}$, אֱלוֹהַּ *God* Hb 3$_5$ Jb 23$_4$ Ne 9$_{28}$ 4QapJoshua[a] 6.2$_2$, אֵל *God* Ps 102$_{29}$ 106$_{23}$ Jb 13$_{16}$ 35$_{14}$ Ne 9$_{32}$ Si 3$_{18}$ 1QH 1$_{24}$ 4$_{21}$ 7$_{14}$ 11$_{13}$ 15$_{25}$ 18$_{10}$ ([אלי]) 1QM 1$_9$ 2$_{2.5}$ 1QS 1$_{2.8.16}$ 3$_{11}$ 5$_{20}$ 11$_{17.21}$ 1QNoah 1$_4$ 4Q417 2.1$_{15}$ 4QPrQuot 1.3$_7$ ([א]ל) perh. 1.3$_{19}$ ([אל]) 4QRitPur 29.7$_6$ ([אל]) 11QPs[a] 27$_3$ CD 2$_{1.3}$ 20$_{28}$, אֲדֹנָי *my Lord* Is 40$_{10}$ Jr 2$_{22}$ Ezk 16$_{50}$ 44$_{15}$ Ps 86$_9$ 1QH 7$_{28.30.31}$ 16$_{14}$ 17$_{14}$ 4QDibHam[a] 1.3$_3$ 1.4$_7$ 5.2$_2$ ([לפניכ]ה) 4QDibHam[b] 124$_7$ ([לפנ]יכה) 4QDibHam[c] 124$_2$ ([עומד] [לפניכה]) 131$_{10}$ ([לפ]ניכה) 4QapMes 7.2$_4$ ([אדנ]י), שַׁדַּי

Shaddai Jb 35$_{14}$, עֶלְיוֹן *Most High* Si 50$_{16.17}$ 1QNoah 2$_{2}$ (לפ[ני]), גִּלּוּל *idol* Ezk 6$_{4.5}$ 8$_{11}$ 44$_{12}$ Si 30$_{18(B)}$, צֶלֶם *image* Ezk 16$_{18.19}$, מַלְאָךְ *angel* Nm 22$_{33}$ Jg 13$_{15}$ Zc 3$_{1.3.4}$ Ec 5$_{5}$ 4Q185 1.1$_{8}$.

Aaron Nm 3$_{6}$ 8$_{13.22}$ 9$_{6}$, Abigail 1 S 25$_{19}$, Abijah 2 C 13$_{15}$, Abijam 1 K 15$_{3}$, Abimelech Ps 34$_{1}$, Abner 2 S 2$_{14}$ 3$_{31}$, Abraham Gn 20$_{15}$, Absalom 2 S 15$_{1}$ 16$_{19}$, Achish 1 S 29$_{8}$, Adonijah 1 K 1$_{5.25}$, Ahab 1 K 16$_{30.33}$ 18$_{46}$, Ahasuerus Est 1$_{3.17.19}$, Ahimelech 1 C 24$_{6.31}$, Amnon 2 S 13$_{9}$, Artaxerxes Ne 2$_{1}$ (or em. לְפָנָיו *before him* [Artaxerxes] to לְפָנַי *before me* [Nehemiah]) 2$_{1}$, Asa 2 C 14$_{4.6.11}$ 15$_{2}$, Barak Jg 4$_{14.15}$, Cyrus perh. Is 41$_{2}$ 45$_{1.1.2}$, David 2 S 5$_{24}$ ||1 C 14$_{15}$ 2 S 5$_{20}$ 7$_{16}$ 11$_{13}$ 19$_{14}$ 1 K 2$_{26}$ 1 C 17$_{13}$ 24$_{31}$ 47$_{1}$ GnzPs 1$_{24}$, Ebed-melech Jr 39$_{16}$, Eleazar Nm 19$_{3}$ 27$_{2.19.21.22}$ 36$_{1}$ (if ins. וְלִפְנֵי אֶלְעָזָר *and before Eleazar*) Jos 17$_{4}$, Eli 1 S 3$_{1}$ 4QVisSam 1$_{3}$, Elihu Jb 33$_{5}$, Eliashib Arad ost. 7$_{6}$, Elisha 1 K 19$_{19}$ 2 K 4$_{12.38}$ 6$_{1}$ 8$_{9}$, Esther Est 4$_{5}$, Evil-merodach 2 K 25$_{29}$||Jr 52$_{33}$, Ezekiel Ezk 2$_{10}$ 8$_{1}$ 14$_{1}$ 20$_{1}$, Gehazi 2 K 5$_{23}$, Goliath 1 S 17$_{7}$, Haman Est 3$_{7}$ 5$_{14}$, Hananiah Jr 28$_{8}$, Hezekiah 2 K 18$_{5}$, Hoshea 2 K 17$_{2}$, Israel Gn 43$_{9}$ 4QM^{g} 1$_{0}$, Jacob Gn 27$_{20}$ 30$_{30}$ 32$_{4.17.21}$ 33$_{14}$, Jehoshaphat 1 K 22$_{10}$||2 C 18$_{9}$, Jehu 2 K 10$_{4}$, Jehoiada 2 C 24$_{14}$, Jephthah Jg 11$_{9}$, Jeremiah Jr 28$_{8}$ 40$_{4}$ 42$_{2}$, Jeroboam 1 K 14$_{9}$, Joab 2 S 2$_{14}$, Jonathan 1 S 14$_{13}$ 20$_{1}$, Joseph Gn 33$_{3}$ 41$_{43}$ 43$_{15.33}$ 44$_{14}$ 47$_{6}$ 50$_{18}$, Joshua (son of Nun) Jos 1$_{5}$ 17$_{4}$ Si 46$_{3}$, Joshua (priest) Zc 3$_{8.9}$, Josiah 2 K 23$_{25}$ 2 C 34$_{4}$, Koheleth Ec 1$_{16}$ 2$_{7.9}$, Laban Gn 30$_{33}$, Leah Gn 33$_{3}$, Lot Gn 13$_{9}$, Manasseh (son of Joseph) Gn 48$_{20}$, Manasseh (king) 2 K 21$_{11}$, Mordecai Est 6$_{11.13.13}$, Moses Ex 9$_{11}$ 17$_{6}$ 32$_{34}$ 33$_{19}$ Nm 9$_{6}$ 16$_{2}$ 27$_{2}$ 36$_{1}$ Dt 1$_{8.22.38}$ 2$_{31.33.36}$, Nebuchadnezzar Dn 1$_{18}$, Nehemiah Ne 2$_{1}$ (if em. לְפָנָיו *before him* to לְפָנַי *before me*) 5$_{15}$ 6$_{19}$, Omri 1 K 16$_{25}$, Rachel Gn 33$_{3}$, Rehoboam 1 K 12$_{8}$||2 C 10$_{8}$, Samuel 1 S 9$_{19.27}$ 10$_{8}$ 16$_{8.10}$ 19$_{24}$, Saul 1 S 9$_{12.24.24.27}$ 16$_{16.21.22}$ 17$_{57}$ 19$_{7}$ 23$_{24}$ 28$_{22.25}$, Solomon 1 K 3$_{12}$ (:: אַחֲרֵי *after*) 9$_{6}$||2 C 7$_{19}$ 10$_{8}$ ||2 C 9$_{7}$ 1 C 29$_{25}$ 2 C 1$_{12}$ (:: אַחֲרֵי) 10$_{6}$, Zadok 1 C 24$_{6.31}$, Zedekiah Jr 34$_{5}$, Zerah 2 C 14$_{9}$, Zerubbabel Zc 4$_{7}$.

Aramaeans 2 S 10$_{16}$||1 C 19$_{16}$ 1 C 19$_{14}$, Cherethites 2 S 20$_{8}$, Chaldaeans Jr 40$_{10}$ Ezk 23$_{24}$, Ethiopian(s) 2 C 14$_{9}$ Jr 39$_{16}$, Israel(ites) Gn Ex 21$_{1}$ 23$_{20.23.27.28}$ 33$_{2}$ Lv 26$_{7.8}$ Nm 10$_{33}$ Dt 7$_{2.23}$ 9$_{3.3}$ 11$_{26.32}$ 22$_{6}$=11QT 65$_{2}$ Dt 23$_{15}$ 28$_{7.7}$ 30$_{1.15.19}$ 31$_{3.3.5.8.21}$ Jos 10$_{10}$ 11$_{6}$ Jg 20$_{35}$ 1 S 7$_{10}$ 12$_{2.2}$ 18$_{16}$ 2 S 10$_{15.19}$||1 C 19$_{16.19}$ 1 K 9$_{6}$||2 C 7$_{19}$ 2 K 14$_{12}$||2 C 25$_{22}$ Is 55$_{12}$ 58$_{8}$ Jr 1$_{17}$ 9$_{12}$ 26$_{4}$ Ezk 8$_{11}$ Mc 2$_{13.13}$ Ps 105$_{17}$ Dn 9$_{10}$ 1QM 9$_{3}$ 10$_{2}$ (לפ[ני]ו) 4QPseud^{b} 5.1$_{11}$ 4QDibHam^{a} 6$_{11}$, Jews Jr 44$_{10}$ Est 9$_{2}$, Koa Ezk 23$_{24}$, Pelethites 2 S 20$_{8}$, Pekod Ezk 23$_{24}$, Philistine(s) 1 S 4$_{2.3.17}$ 17$_{41}$ 1 C 14$_{8}$, Shoa Ezk 23$_{24}$, Benjamin Jg 20$_{39}$ Ps 80$_{3}$ (ms lacks בִּנְיָמִין *Benjamin*), Ephraim Ps 80$_{3}$ (mss have לִבְנֵי *for the sons of* for לִפְנֵי), Manasseh Ps 80$_{3}$, Judah 1 S 18$_{16}$ 1 C 12$_{18}$ 2 C 13$_{13.15}$ 14$_{6.11}$.

עַם *people* Gn 23$_{12}$ Ex 13$_{22}$ Ex 17$_{5}$ 32$_{1.23}$ Nm 14$_{14.43}$ Dt 3$_{28}$ 10$_{11}$ 28$_{7.7}$ Jos 3$_{6.6.14}$ 4$_{11}$ 8$_{10.15}$ 24$_{12}$ Jg 18$_{21}$ 1 S 8$_{20}$ 18$_{13}$ 2 K 4$_{44}$ Jr 21$_{8}$ 33$_{24}$ Ezk 44$_{11}$ Jl 2$_{3.3}$ (both :: אַחֲרֵי *after*) 2$_{10}$ Mc 6$_{4}$ Ps 68$_{8}$ Ec 4$_{16}$ (or em. הָיָה לִפְנֵיהֶם to each who *was before them* to הָיוּ הַלְּפָנַי to all who were *those who were before me* or הָיָה לְפָנָיו *was before him* [child]) 1 C 22$_{18}$ 2 C 1$_{10}$ 1QM 17$_{15}$, קָהָל *assembly* Nm 14$_{5}$ (or del. קְהַל *assembly of*) Ne 8$_{2}$ 2 C 28$_{14}$ 29$_{23}$, עֵדָה *congregation* Nm 16$_{9}$ 27$_{2.17.19.22}$ 32$_{4}$ (or em. עֲדַת *congregation of* to בְּנֵי *sons of*) 35$_{12}$ Jos 18$_{1}$ 20$_{6.9}$ 1QSa 1$_{17}$, הָמוֹן *multitude* 2 C 20$_{12.17}$, חַיִל *army* Jl 2$_{11}$ Ne 3$_{34}$, צָבָא *army* 2 C 28$_{9}$, חָלוּץ pass. ptc. *one equipped for war* 2 C 20$_{21}$, מַמְלָכָה *kingdom* 2 C 13$_{8}$.

אָדָם *human being* Si 15$_{17}$ 16$_{14}$, אִישׁ *man* Gn 18$_{8}$ 24$_{33}$ 34$_{21}$ 43$_{14}$ Nm 16$_{2}$ Jos 7$_{4}$ 8$_{15}$ Jg 18$_{21}$ 20$_{42}$ 2 S 18$_{14}$ 20$_{8}$ 2 K 4$_{31}$ 5$_{15}$ Jr 49$_{5}$ Est 6$_{9}$ Dn 9$_{10}$ Ne 1$_{11}$ 2 C 13$_{7}$ 1QS 4$_{2}$ 6$_{4.11.26}$ 4QSD 1.1$_{7}$ ([איש]), אִשָּׁה *wife* 2 K 5$_{2}$, אָב *father* Gn 43$_{9}$ Nm 32$_{29}$ 1 S 20$_{1}$ 2 S 16$_{19}$ 1 K 2$_{26}$ Jr 44$_{10}$ Ne 9$_{11.35}$ 1 C 24$_{2}$ 2 C 10$_{6}$, אֵם *mother* 2 K 4$_{31}$ Pr 4$_{3}$, בֵּן *son* Gn 34$_{10}$ Nm 8$_{13.22}$ Dt 9$_{2}$ Jos 1$_{5}$ 17$_{4}$ Jg 20$_{32}$ 2 S 3$_{34}$ 16$_{19}$ 1 K 1$_{5}$ 16$_{30}$ 19$_{19}$ 2 K 17$_{2}$ 18$_{5}$ Jr 35$_{5}$ perh. Pr 23$_{1}$ Ne 9$_{24}$ 1 C 12$_{18}$ 24$_{6}$ 2 C 13$_{7}$ Si 8$_{11}$ 15$_{16}$ 34$_{16}$ 1QSa 2$_{3}$, of Israel Ex 13$_{21}$ Lv 18$_{27.28.30}$ Nm 14$_{43}$ 32$_{17}$ Dt 1$_{8.21.22.30.33}$ 2$_{33.36}$ 3$_{18}$ 4$_{44}$ Jos 3$_{11}$ 4$_{12}$ 8$_{32}$ 10$_{12}$ Jg 3$_{27}$ 4$_{23}$ 8$_{28}$, of Assyria Ezk 23$_{24}$, of Babylon Ezk 23$_{24}$, of man Ezk 4$_{1}$ 33$_{31}$, בַּת *daughter* 1 S 1$_{16}$, בְּכִירָה *firstborn daughter* Gn 29$_{26}$, אָח *brother* Gn 45$_{5.7}$ Dt 3$_{18}$ Jos 1$_{14}$ 2 S 13$_{9}$ Ne 3$_{34}$, יֶלֶד *child* Gn 33$_{3.3}$ Ec 4$_{16}$ (if em. לִפְנֵיהֶם *before them* to לְפָנָיו *before him*), עֶבֶד *servant* Gn 24$_{7.51}$ 33$_{14}$ Ex 7$_{10}$ 1 S 28$_{25}$ 2 S 2$_{17}$ 18$_{7.9}$ 1QH 16$_{14}$ GnzPs 1$_{24}$, שִׁפְחָה *female servant* Gn 33$_{3}$.

מֶלֶךְ *king* Jos 8$_{15}$ 2 S 14$_{33}$ 19$_{9.18.19}$ 24$_{4}$ 1 K 1$_{2.23.28.28.32}$ 3$_{16.22.24}$ 22$_{10.10}$||2 C 18$_{9.9}$ 2 K 21$_{11}$ 22$_{10}$||2 C 34$_{18}$ 2 K 25$_{29}$ ||Jr 52$_{33}$ Is 8$_{4}$ Jr 34$_{5}$ 36$_{22}$ 37$_{20}$ 38$_{26}$ 52$_{12}$ Ezk 28$_{17}$ 30$_{24}$ Ps 72$_{9}$ 98$_{6}$ Pr 22$_{29}$ Est 1$_{3.11.16.17.19}$ 2$_{9.17.23}$ 6$_{1}$ 7$_{9}$ 8$_{1.3.4.5.5}$ 9$_{11.25}$

Dn 1$_{5.19}$ 2$_{2}$ 11$_{16}$ Ezr 7$_{28}$ 9$_{9}$ Ne 2$_{1}$ (or em. לְפָנָיו *before him* to לְפָנָי *before me*) 2$_{1.5}$ 9$_{35}$ 1 C 24$_{6.31}$ 2 C 24$_{14}$ 29$_{23}$ 34$_{24}$ Si 7$_{5}$ 45$_{3}$ 4QShirShabb^{f} 23.2$_{8}$ ([מ]לך) 4Q476 1$_{6}$ 11QT 59$_{19}$, מֹשֵׁל *ruler* Si 4$_{27}$, רֹדֶה *ruler* 1QS 9$_{22}$, אָדוֹן *lord* Gn 47$_{18}$ 2 K 5$_{1}$ Jr 37$_{20}$, בַּעַל *lord* Jg 9$_{39}$, סֶרֶן *lord* of Philistines Jg 16$_{25}$, נָשִׂיא *prince* Nm 27$_{2}$ 36$_{1}$ Jos 17$_{4}$ 1QSb 5$_{22}$ 5$_{28}$ (לפ[ניכה]) 4QM^{g} 4$_{6}$, שַׂר *commander* Gn 40$_{9}$ Est 1$_{16}$ Dn 1$_{9}$ Ezr 7$_{28}$ 8$_{29}$ Ne 9$_{35}$ 12$_{36}$ 1 C 24$_{6}$ 2 C 28$_{14}$ Si 8$_{8}$, מְחֹקֵק *commander* Si 10$_{5}$, נָדִיב *noble* Pr 25$_{7}$ Si 38$_{3}$, גִּבּוֹר *warrior* 2 S 20$_{8}$, פַּרְעֹה *Pharaoh* Gn 41$_{46}$ 47$_{2.7}$ Ex 4$_{21}$ 7$_{10}$ 8$_{16}$ 9$_{10.13}$ 11$_{10}$, מֶלְצַר *steward* Dn 1$_{13}$, זָקֵן *elder* Ex 19$_{7}$ Dt 22$_{17}$ =11QT 65$_{13}$, שֹׁפֵט *judge* Dt 19$_{17}$=11QT 61$_{8}$ Dt 25$_{2}$ CD 15$_{3}$ ([לפני]), כֹּהֵן *priest* Nm 3$_{6}$ Lv 27$_{8.11}$ Nm 19$_{3}$ 27$_{2.19.21.22}$ 36$_{1}$ (if ins. וְלִפְנֵי ... הַכֹּהֵן) Dt 19$_{17}$=11QT 61$_{8}$ Jos 6$_{9.13}$ 17$_{4}$ Zc 3$_{8}$ Ne 9$_{35}$ 1 C 24$_{6}$ 26$_{19}$ 1QM 7$_{14}$ 1QSa 2$_{3.14}$ (ל[פניו]) 2$_{16}$ ([הכוהן]) 2$_{19}$ 4QTohB^{b} 1$_{3}$ ([הכהן] ... [ל]פניו) 11QT 23$_{11}$ 58$_{18}$, לֵוִי *Levite* Ezr 8$_{29}$ 2 C 19$_{11}$ 1QM 7$_{14}$ 11QT 61$_{8}$, נָבִיא *prophet* 1 S 10$_{5}$ 2 K 5$_{3}$ 42$_{2}$, מָשִׁיחַ *messiah* 1QSa 2$_{14.16}$ (both [מש]יח), worshipper Ps 5$_{9}$ 23$_{5}$ 57$_{7}$ 4QBark^{c} 1.1$_{4.4}$ 4QBark^{d} 2.1$_{12}$.

יֹעֵץ *counsellor* Ezr 7$_{28}$, עֵד *witness* 1QS 6$_{1}$ 9$_{3}$, יֹשֵׁב *inhabitant* Jos 8$_{15}$ Zc 12$_{8}$ Dn 9$_{10}$, זָר *stranger* Si 8$_{18}$, רֵעַ *neighbour* Pr 17$_{18}$ Si 34$_{18}$ 1QS 5$_{23}$ 7$_{12}$ 4QWays^{b} 1a.1$_{3}$ ([רע]הו) 2$_{2}$ ([רעהו]), lover Ezk 23$_{24}$ Ca 8$_{12}$, אֹיֵב *enemy* Lv 26$_{17.37}$ Nm 14$_{42}$ Dt 1$_{42}$ 28$_{25.25}$ Jos 7$_{8.12.12.13}$ Jg 2$_{14}$ 1 K 8$_{33.46}$||2 C 6$_{24.36}$ Jr 15$_{9}$ 18$_{17}$ 19$_{7}$ 49$_{37}$ Am 9$_{4}$ 2 C 25$_{8}$, שׂנא ptc. *one who hates* Ps 69$_{23}$, שֹׁבֶה *captor* 1 K 8$_{50}$ Ps 106$_{46}$ 2 C 30$_{9}$, רֹדֵף *pursuer* Lm 1$_{6}$, בקשׁ pi. ptc. *one who seeks* life Jr 49$_{37}$, בוא ptc. *one who comes* Dn 11$_{16}$, *one who enters* covenant 1QS 2$_{12}$, חזק hi. ptc. *one who grasps* commandments CD 3$_{16}$, מְבַקֵּר *examiner* 4QD^{a} 7.3$_{2}$ (ה[מבק]ר) 5QRègle 4$_{1}$ CD 15$_{11}$, יכח hi. ptc. *one who rebukes* 1QH 12$_{28}$, הֹרֵג *killer* Ezk 28$_{9}$, גֹּזֵז *shearer* Is 53$_{7}$, עִוֵּר *blind one* Lv 19$_{14}$ Is 42$_{16}$, גֹּאֵל *redeemer* Ps 19$_{15}$, גָּדוֹל *great one* Pr 18$_{16}$, צַדִּיק *righteous one* Ezk 3$_{20}$ Ec 9$_{1}$, חָכָם *wise one* Ec 9$_{1}$, perh. עָנָו *humble one* 4Q434 1.2$_{9}$, דַּל *poor one* GnzPs 3$_{17}$, קָדוֹשׁ *holy one* Hb 3$_{5}$ Si 50$_{17}$, רַחוּם *merciful one* Si 50$_{19}$, דַּכָּא *contrite one* Si 35$_{10}$, טוֹב *good one* Pr 14$_{19}$, רַע *wicked one* Jb 21$_{33}$, רָשָׁע *wicked one* Jb 21$_{8}$ (unless לִפְנֵיהֶם = *their predecessors*) 11QPs^{a} 24$_{5}$, חָשֹׁךְ *obscure one* Pr 22$_{29}$, בושׁ ptc. *ashamed one* Si 13$_{10}$, ידע ptc. *one who knows* Est 1$_{13}$, רֹפֵא *doctor* Si 38$_{15}$, עֹשֶׂה *maker* Si 38$_{15}$, לוֹקֵחַ *purchaser* Mur 30 1$_{6}$ 2$_{24}$, חַי *living one* Si 7$_{33}$ 42$_{8}$, רֹאשׁ *head* Nm 36$_{1}$ 1 C 24$_{6.31}$, רֶגֶל *foot* Est 8$_{3}$, בְּרִיאָה *creature* 4QD^{a} 10.2$_{9}$ ([לפני] ה[ב]ריאה).

בְּהֵמָה *beast* Lv 18$_{23}$, אַרְבֶּה *locust* Ex 10$_{14}$, עֵגֶל *calf* Ex 32$_{5}$, אַיִל *ram* Dn 8$_{4}$, צָפִיר *he-goat* Dn 8$_{7}$, מִקְנֶה *cattle* 1 S 30$_{20}$, לִוְיָתָן *Leviathan* Jb 41$_{2 (mss).14}$, חָצִיר *grass* Jb 8$_{12}$, גֶּפֶן *vine* Ps 80$_{10}$ (unless לְפָנֶיהָ = *her predecessors*).

Baal-zephon Ex 14$_{2.9}$, Jerusalem Is 52$_{12}$ Jr 1$_{17}$ 9$_{12}$, Mamre Gn 23$_{17}$, Medeba 1 C 19$_{7}$ (or em. מֵידְבָא *Medeba* to מֵי רַבָּה *sea of Rabba*), Migdol Nm 33$_{7}$, Nebo Nm 33$_{47}$, Pi-hahiroth Ex 14$_{2}$, Zoan Nm 13$_{22}$, עֲרָבָה *plain* Jos 8$_{14}$, גִּבְעָה *hill* Jb 15$_{7}$ Pr 8$_{25}$, אוּבָל *river* Dn 8$_{3.6}$, שִׁבֹּלֶת *stream* Si 4$_{26}$, מַעְיָן *spring* 1QH 12$_{28}$ ([לפני מעין]), צוּר *rock* Ps 19$_{15}$, עִיר *city* Jos 8$_{5.6.6}$, of Judah Jr 1$_{17}$ 9$_{12}$ 26$_{4}$, בַּיִת *house* 1 K 8$_{64}$||2 C 7$_{7}$ Ezk 9$_{6}$ 40$_{47}$ Ezr 10$_{1}$ 2 C 3$_{15}$ 20$_{9}$, מַחֲנֶה *camp* Ex 14$_{19}$ 2 C 14$_{12}$, אֹהֶל *tent* Ex 29$_{10}$ Lv 3$_{8.13}$ 4$_{14}$ Nm 3$_{7.38}$ 8$_{9}$ 18$_{2}$, מִשְׁכָּן *tabernacle* Lv 17$_{4}$ Nm 3$_{38}$ 7$_{3}$ Jos 22$_{29}$ 1 C 6$_{17}$ 16$_{39}$ 21$_{30}$ 2 C 1$_{5}$, הֵיכָל *temple* Jr 24$_{1}$, דְּבִיר *inner sanctuary* 1 K 6$_{17}$ (if em. הַהֵיכָל לִפְנֵי perh. *the hall in front* to הַהֵיכָל לִפְנֵי הַדְּבִיר *the hall in front of the inner sanctuary*) 6$_{20.21}$ 7$_{49}$|| 2 C 4$_{20}$, מִזְבֵּחַ *altar* Nm 7$_{10}$ Dt 26$_{4}$ 1 K 8$_{22.31}$||2 C 6$_{12.22}$ 2 K 11$_{18}$||2 C 23$_{17}$ 2 K 18$_{22}$||Is 36$_{7}$||2 C 32$_{12}$ Zc 14$_{20}$ 2 C 29$_{19}$ 11QPs^{a} 27$_{5}$, אֲרוֹן *ark* Ex 40$_{5}$ Jos 4$_{5}$ 6$_{4.6.7.8 (mss).13}$ 7$_{6}$ 1 S 5$_{3.4}$ 2 S 6$_{4}$ 1 K 3$_{15}$ 8$_{5}$||2 C 5$_{6}$ 1 C 15$_{24}$ 16$_{4.6.37.37}$, עֵדוּת *testimony* Ex 16$_{34}$ 30$_{36}$ Nm 17$_{19.25}$, כַּפֹּרֶת *mercy seat* Ex 30$_{6}$ (mss lack לִפְנֵי הַכַּפֹּרֶת) Lv 16$_{14.15}$, פָּרֹכֶת *curtain* Ex 30$_{6}$ 40$_{26}$, פֶּתַח *entrance* Ex 40$_{6}$, שַׁעַר *gate* Jos 7$_{5}$ perh. Est 4$_{6}$ Ne 8$_{1.3}$, רְחוֹב *square* Ne 8$_{3}$, חָצֵר *court* Ezk 40$_{19}$ Est 2$_{11}$ 2 C 20$_{5}$, מַעֲלָה *step* Ezk 40$_{22}$ (if em. עֹלָה *ascent* to מַעֲלָה) 40$_{26}$, עֹלָה *ascent* Ezk 40$_{22}$ (or em.), לִשְׁכָּה *chamber* Ezk 42$_{4.11}$, תָּא *chamber* Ezk 40$_{12}$, אוּלָם *porch* 2 C 8$_{12}$ 15$_{8}$, יָצוּעַ *couch* 4QVisSam 7$_{4}$, מִטָּה *couch* Ezk 23$_{41}$, מֶרְכָּבָה *chariot* 1 S 8$_{11}$, מוֹשָׁב *seat* 11QT 37$_{9}$, מַעֲרָכָה *battle-line* 1QM 16$_{13}$ 4QM^{c} 1$_{1}$, תֹּכֶן *measurement*, i.e. rank 1QS 6$_{10}$.

יוֹם *day* Jos 10$_{14}$ (:: אַחֲרֵי *after*) Zc 8$_{10}$, בֹּקֶר *morning* Si 47$_{10}$, שַׁבָּת *sabbath* Ne 13$_{19}$ perh. Meṣad Ḥashavyahu ost. 1$_{5}$ (unless שֶׁבֶת *cessation*), עֵת *time* 4QS^{e} 1.3$_{9}$ (= 1QS 9$_{13}$ לפי *according to*), קָרָה *cold* Ps 147$_{17}$, חֹם *heat* 1QH 8$_{25}$, חֹרֶב *heat* Si 43$_{3}$, קָצִיר *harvest* Is 18$_{5}$, אֵשׁ *fire* 4QHod^{a} 6$_{3}$ 4Q424 1$_{5}$, רַעַשׁ *earthquake* Am 1$_{1}$, רוּחַ *wind* Is 17$_{13}$ 1QH 7$_{23}$ 10$_{32}$ ([רוח]) fr. 3$_{6}$, סוּפָה *storm wind* Is 17$_{13}$, מָטָר *rain*

Si $40_{15(Bmg)}$ (B מִפְּנֵי *from before*), בָּרָד *hail* Si 35_{10}, קָמָה appar. *maturity* 2 K 19_{26}||Is 37_{27} (1QIsa[a] קדים *east wind*), יָרֵחַ *moon* Ps 72_{5}, קִנְאָה *jealousy* Pr 27_{4}, זַעַם *indignation* Na 1_{6}, גְּבוּרָה *might* 4QShir[b] 15_{4} (ל[פני]), לֶחֶם *bread* Jb 3_{24}, מִנְחָה *offering* 11QT 17_{7}, כָּבוֹד *glory* Pr 15_{33} 18_{12} Si 42_{17} 45_{25} 1QH 10_{11}, אַף *anger* 1QH 12_{18} (אפ[כה]) 12_{30}, חֵמָה *anger* 1QH 7_{29}, חָרוֹן *anger* Si $48_{10(Segal)}$ (לפנ[י חרון]), כִּשָּׁלוֹן *stumbling* Pr 16_{18}, נגע *stroke* 1QH 1_{32} 2_{7} (נג[ע]) 4_{36} 9_{12} fr. 1_{6}, שֶׁבֶר *breach* Pr 16_{18} 18_{12}, מִלְחָמָה *war* 1QH 7_{7}, מָוֶת *death* Gn $27_{7.10}$ 50_{16} Dt 33_{1} 1 C 22_{5} Si 11_{28}, פֹּעַל *deed* Si $37_{16(Bmg, D)}$, מִשְׁגֶּה *error* CD 3_{4} (or em. לִפְנֵי to לְפִי *according to*), צֹרֶךְ *need* Si 38_{1}, אֶחָד *one* 1 K 12_{30} CD $9_{19.19}$, שְׁנֵים עָשָׂר *twelve* 4QOrd[a] 2_{4}, מֵאָה *hundred* 2 K 4_{43}, רִאשׁוֹן *first one* Gn 32_{18}, רַב pl. *many* 1QS $6_{1.15}$ 13_{8} 4QSD 1.2_{5}, אֵלֶּה *these* 2 K 6_{22}.

b. **לִפְנֵי מִזֶּה before this,** with verb, עשׂה *make* Ne 13_{4}.

c. as conjunction, with inf. cstr. of היה *be* 1QS 3_{15} MasShirShabb 1_{6}, בוא *come* 1 S 9_{15} Ezk 33_{22} Jl 3_{4} Ml 3_{23} Si 48_{12}, שׁחת pi. *destroy* Gn 13_{10}, מלך *reign* Gn 36_{31}||1 C 1_{43}, גלע htp. *burst out* Pr 17_{14}, נפל *fall* 1QM 14_{3}, כנע ni. *humble oneself* 2 C 33_{19}, בנה ni. *be built* 4QNarrC 1_{18}, עשׂה *make* MasShirShabb 1_{5}, חנה pi. *have compassion* 1QH 1_{6} (חנ[ות]).

with verb, היה *be* Gn 10_{9} 30_{30} 34_{10} Ex 10_{14} 28_{38} 30_{16} Lv 26_{37} Nm 10_{10} 15_{15} 16_{16} 32_{22} Dt 4_{32} 24_{13} Jos 10_{14} 1 S 19_{7} 29_{8} 2 S 7_{26} 7_{29}||1 C 17_{27} 2 S 16_{19} 19_{14} 1 K 2_{45} 3_{12} 14_{9} 16_{33} 2 K $5_{1.2}$ 17_{2} 18_{5} 23_{25} Jr 28_{8} 31_{36} 33_{24} 34_{5} 39_{16} Ezk 33_{22} 36_{17} Ps 19_{15} 69_{23} Pr 4_{3} Ec 1_{16} $2_{7.9}$ 4_{16} 1 C 6_{17} 17_{13} 2 C 13_{13} 1QH 15_{25} 16_{15} (י[היה]) 17_{14} 4QBapt 2.1_{4} (ל[היות]) 4Q415 11_{6} 4Q418 167_{7} ([יהיה] ... לפנ[יו]), ni. *be* Zc 8_{10}, חיה *live* Gn 17_{18} Ho 6_{2} GnzPs 3_{2}.

עמד *stand* Gn 18_{22} 41_{46} 43_{15} Ex $9_{10.11}$ 17_{6} Lv 9_{5} 18_{23} Nm $27_{2.2.2.21}$ 35_{12} Dt 1_{38} 4_{10} 10_{8} 18_{7} $19_{17.17}$=11QT $61_{8.8}$ Dt 29_{14} Jos $20_{6.9}$ Jg 2_{14} 20_{28} 1 S 6_{20} $16_{21.22}$ 1 K $1_{2.28}$ $3_{15.16}$ 8_{22}||2 C 6_{12} 1 K 10_{8}||2 C 9_{7} 1 K 12_{8}||2 C 10_{8} 1 K 17_{1} 18_{15} 19_{11} 22_{21}||2 C 18_{20} 2 K 3_{14} 4_{12} $5_{15.16}$ 8_{9} 10_{4} Is 66_{22} Jr 7_{10} $15_{1.19}$ 18_{20} 35_{19} 40_{10} 52_{12} 49_{19} 50_{44} Ezk 8_{11} 22_{30} $44_{11.15}$ Na 1_{6} Zc $3_{1.3.4}$ Ps 76_{8} 106_{23} 147_{17} Pr 27_{4} Est 4_{5} (if em. hi.) 8_{4} 9_{2} Dn $1_{5.19}$ 2_{2} $8_{3.4.6.7}$ 11_{16} Ezr 9_{15} 2 C 10_{6} $20_{5.9.9.13}$ 29_{11} Si 4_{26} 1QH 4_{21} 12_{28} (י[עמוד לפני]) 18_{10} fr. 3_{6} 1QM 16_{13} 1QS 6_{15} 4Q178 1_{1} (לע[מ]וד) 4Q185 $1.1_{7.8}$ 4QapJoshua[a] $6.2_{2.2}$ 4QShirShabb[b] 2_{3} 4Q424 1_{5} 4QPseud[b] 5.1_{11} ([ע]מוד) 4QM[a] 10.2_{13} (ל[פני]) 4QM[c] 1_{1} 4QDibHam[a] 5.2_{2} 4QDibHam[b] 124_{7} 4QDibHam[c] 124_{2} ([עומד לפניכה]) 4QRitPur 29.7_{6} ([עומד]) 5QRègle 4_{1} (י[ע]מוד) 8QHymn 2_{6} (ע[ומדות]) 11QT $60_{11.14}$ 61_{8} GnzPs 4_{10}, hi. *position* Gn 47_{7} Lv 14_{11} $16_{7.10}$ (if em. יָעֳמַד־חַי the goat *was positioned alive* to יַעֲמִיד אֹתוֹ *he positioned it*) $27_{8.11}$ Nm 3_{6} $5_{16.18.30}$ $8_{13.13}$ $27_{19.19.22.22}$ Est 4_{5} (or em. qal) 2 C 33_{19} 1QH 7_{31} 9_{12} CD 15_{11} GnzPs 2_{10}, ho. *be positioned* Lv 16_{10} (or em.; see Hi.), יצב htp. *stand* Ex 8_{16} 9_{13} Dt 9_{2} Jos 1_{5} 24_{1} 1 S 10_{19} Jb 41_{2} Pr $22_{29.29}$ Si 8_{8} 38_{3} 46_{3} 47_{1} 1QH 7_{29} 10_{11} 11_{13} $12_{28.30}$ 16_{14} (ל[התיצב]) 1QS 11_{17} 11QPsAp[a] 2_{6} (התי[צבו]), נצב ni. *stand* Dt 29_{9}, hi. *position* Ps 41_{13} CD 2_{3}, קום *rise* Nm 16_{2} Jos $7_{12.13}$, htpol. *raise oneself up* 1QH fr. 1_{6} (ל[ה]תקוממ), ישׁב *sit, dwell* Gn 43_{33} Jg 20_{26} Jg 21_{2} 2 S 7_{18}||1 C 17_{16} 2 K 4_{38} 6_{1} Is 23_{18} Ezk 8_{1} 14_{1} 20_{1} 33_{31} Zc 3_{8} Ps 61_{8} 1QS 6_{4} 11_{21} 1QSa $2_{14.14.16}$ 4QDibHam[a] 1.4_{7}, hi. *cause to sit* Si 8_{11}, חנה *encamp* Ex $14_{2.2.9}$ Nm $33_{8.38}$ $33_{7.47}$ 1 C 19_{7}, שׁאר ni. *remain* Gn 47_{18}, שׁכב *lie down* 4QVisSam 1_{3} 7_{4}, אמן ni. *be established* 2 S 7_{16}, *be faithful* Ne 9_{8}, כון ni. *be established* 1 K 2_{45} Jr 30_{20} Ps 102_{29} 141_{2} Jb 21_{8} (unless לִפְנֵיהֶם = *their predecessors*) 1QLitPr 3.2_{5}, hi. *establish* 1 C 22_{5} 1QS 3_{15}, כלכל htp. *endure* Si $43_{3(B)}$, כול htpol. *withstand* Si $43_{3M)}$, גבה *be high* Pr 18_{12}, אמץ pi. *strengthen* 1QH 2_{7}, חזק pi. *strengthen* Si 45_{3} 1QH 1_{32} 7_{7}, *hold* 4QShirShabb[f] 23.2_{8}, hi. *be strong* 1QH 4_{36}, htp. *strengthen oneself* 2 C $13_{7.8}$ Si 42_{17}, גבר htp. *display arrogance* Si 38_{15}.

שׁחה htpal. *bow down* Gn 23_{12} Dt 26_{10} 1 S 1_{19} 2 S 14_{33} 2 K 18_{22}||Is 36_{7}||2 C 32_{12} Is 66_{23} Ezk 46_{3} Ps 22_{28} 86_{9} 2 C 25_{14} Si $50_{17.17}$ 11QT 39_{6} GnzPs 3_{17}, שׁחח *bow down* Pr 14_{19}, כרע *bow down* Ps 22_{30} 72_{9}, נפל *fall* Gn 44_{14} 50_{18} Lv $26_{7.8}$ Nm 14_{5} Jos 7_{6} 1 S $5_{3.3.4.4}$ 14_{13} 2 S 3_{34} 19_{19} Jr 36_{7} 37_{20} 42_{2} Est $6_{13.13}$ 8_{3} 2 C 20_{18} 1QM 1_{9} 4QShirShabb[f] 20.2_{7}, hi. *cause to fall* Jr 19_{7} 38_{26} 42_{9} Ezk 6_{4} Est 3_{7} Dn $9_{18.20}$ 1 C 24_{31}, htp. *prostrate oneself* Dt $9_{18.25}$ Ezr 10_{1}, ענה htp. *humble oneself* Dn 10_{12} Ezr 8_{21}, שׁפל hi. *abase* Pr 25_{7}, כשׁל hi. *cause to stumble* 2 C 25_{8}, ho. *be caused to stumble* Jr 18_{23}, נכה hi. *strike* Nm 32_{4} Dt 25_{2}, נגף *defeat* Jg 20_{35} 1 S 4_{3} 2 C 13_{15} $14_{11.11}$, ni. *be defeated* Lv 26_{17} Nm 14_{42} Dt 1_{42} $28_{7.25}$ Jg $20_{32.39}$ 1 S 4_{2} 7_{10} 2 S 2_{17} $10_{15.19}$||1 C $19_{16.19}$ 18_{7} 1 K 8_{33}||2 C 6_{24} 2 K 14_{12}||2 C 25_{22} 1QM 9_{3} 17_{15} (ל[נ]גפים) 6QapSamKgs 32_{2}, כבשׁ ni. *be subdued* Nm $32_{22.29}$ Jos 18_{1}

1 C 22$_{18.18}$, כנע ni. *be subdued* Jg 8$_{28}$, *humble oneself* 2 C 33$_{12}$ 34$_{27}$, hi. *subdue* Dt 9$_{3}$ Jg 4$_{23}$ Ne 9$_{24}$ 2 C 34$_{27}$, רדד *subdue* Is 45$_{1}$, המם *discomfit* Jos 10$_{10}$ Jg 4$_{15}$, חתת hi. *terrify* Jr 1$_{17}$ 49$_{37.37}$, ירא *fear* Ps 72$_{5}$, פחד *fear* 4QPseud[b] 5.1$_{1}$, נדח ni. *be thrust out* Jr 49$_{5}$, שׁחת ni. *be corrupt* Gn 6$_{11}$, שׁסף pi. *hew in pieces* 1 S 15$_{33}$, שׁבר *break* GnzPs 1$_{24}$, ni. *be broken* 2 C 14$_{12.12}$ 4QapJoseph[b] 2$_{12}$, pi. *break* 1 K 19$_{11}$, נתץ pi. *break down* 2 C 34$_{4}$, פרץ *break through* 2 S 5$_{20}$, פצח *break out* Is 55$_{12}$, בקע *split* Ne 9$_{11}$, שׁמם hi. *lay waste* CD 2$_{1}$, שׁבת hi. *bring to an end* Si 48$_{10}$ ([לפנ]י), הרג *kill* 2 K 11$_{18}$||2 C 23$_{17}$, יקע hi. *hang* 2 S 21$_{9}$.

אמר *say* Ex 6$_{30}$ Dt 26$_{5.13}$ 1 S 20$_{1}$ Ezk 28$_{9}$ Ec 5$_{5}$ Est 1$_{16}$ 7$_{9}$ Ne 3$_{34}$ 6$_{19}$, דבר pi. *speak* Ex 6$_{12}$ Nm 36$_{1.1}$ Jg 11$_{11}$ 1 K 3$_{22}$ Est 8$_{3}$ 1QS 6$_{10}$, נגד hi. *tell* Ps 142$_{3}$ Si 48$_{25}$, ענה *answer* Dt 31$_{21}$, ספר pi. *tell* CD 13$_{8}$, קרא *cry, proclaim* Gn 41$_{43}$ Ex 33$_{19}$ Jr 36$_{9}$ Est 6$_{11}$, *read* 2 K 24$_{10}$||2 C 34$_{18}$ Ne 8$_{3}$ 2 C 34$_{24}$, ni. *be proclaimed* Est 6$_{9}$, *be read* Est 6$_{1}$, צהל *shout for joy* GnzPs 1$_{21}$, שׁיר pol. *sing* 11QPs[a] 27$_{5}$, פלל htp. *pray* 1 S 1$_{12}$ 1 K 8$_{28}$ 2 K 19$_{15}$ Ne 1$_{4.6}$ 1 C 17$_{25}$ 2 C 6$_{24}$ 2QapMoses 1$_{4}$ GnzPs 2$_{7}$ 3$_{11}$ 4$_{17}$, חנן htp. *make supplication* 1 K 8$_{59}$ 9$_{3}$, נבא htp. *prophesy* 1 S 19$_{24}$ 1 K 22$_{10}$||2 C 18$_{9}$, ברך pi. *bless* Gn 27$_{7.7.10}$ Dt 33$_{1}$ 4QM[g] 1$_{0}$ ([וברכם]), אשׁר pi. *pronounce happy* Si 11$_{28}$, ידה hi. *give thanks* 4QBer[d] 1$_{6}$ (להוד[ות]), htp. *confess* CD 20$_{28}$, ארר pass. *be cursed* Jos 6$_{26}$ 1 S 26$_{19}$, צוה pi. *command* Gn 50$_{16}$, שׁבע ni. *swear* CD 15$_{3}$ ([שׁבע לפנת]), יכח hi. *reprove* 1QS[d] 1.2$_{6}$, מאן *refuse* Si 4$_{27}$, חזה *see* Am 1$_{1}$, ראה ni. *be seen* Dn 1$_{13}$, גלה pass. *be revealed* GnzPs 1$_{1}$, pi. *reveal* 1QNoah 2$_{2}$ ([גלון לפנ]י), זכר ni. *be remembered* Nm 10$_{9}$ 4QapPs[b] 50$_{3}$, hi. *cause to be remembered* Si 50$_{16}$, שׁאל *ask* Nm 27$_{21}$, שׁפט ni. *be judged* 4QOrd[a] 2$_{4}$, *plead* 1 S 12$_{7}$, נאק *groan* Ezk 30$_{24}$, גלה *uncover* ear 1 S 9$_{15}$, כתב *write* Jos 8$_{32}$ 1 C 24$_{6}$ 1QS 5$_{23}$ Arad ost. 7$_{6}$, pass. *be written* Is 65$_{6}$ 1QS 6$_{11.26}$ 4QSD 1.1$_{7}$ 4Q 417 2.1$_{15}$, ni. *be written* Ml 3$_{16}$ Est 2$_{23}$, חקק pass. *be engraved* 1QH 1$_{24}$, סרך *inscribe in order* 4QWays[b] 1a.1$_{3}$, כרת *cut* Is 18$_{5}$, i.e. make, covenant 1 S 23$_{18}$ 2 S 5$_{3}$||1 C 11$_{3}$ 2 K 23$_{3}$||2 C 34$_{31}$ Jr 34$_{15.18}$, חשׁב ni. *be reckoned* 4QDibHam[a] 1.3$_{3}$, רצה *be accepted* 1QS 3$_{11}$, אלם ni. *be dumb* Is 53$_{7}$, שׂחק pi. *make merry* 2 S 2$_{14}$ 6$_{5}$||1 C 13$_{8}$ 2 S 6$_{21}$ Pr 8$_{30}$, צחק pi. *make sport* Jg 16$_{25}$, גיל *rejoice* GnzPs 2$_{15}$, שׂמח *rejoice* Lv 23$_{40}$ Dt 12$_{12.18}$ 16$_{11}$ 27$_{7}$ 4QPrFêtes[c] 20$_{2}$ ([לפנ]כה) 11QT 21$_{8}$ (לפ[נ]י) 52$_{16}$, עלץ *exult* Ps 68$_{4}$ 4QShir[b] 109$_{2}$ ([ל]פני), עלז *exult* Ps 68$_{5}$, רנן *shout joyfully* Si 47$_{10}$ 50$_{19}$, pi. *shout joyfully* Ps 96$_{13}$ 1Q30 3$_{2}$, רוע hi. *shout* Ps 98$_{6}$, חצצר hi. *sound trumpet* 1 C 15$_{24}$, בכה *weep* Nm 11$_{20}$ Dt 1$_{45}$ 2 K 22$_{19}$||2 C 34$_{27}$, ספד *mourn* 2 S 3$_{31}$, רעה *associate with* Si 38$_{1}$.

בוא *come* Gn 6$_{13}$ Ex 28$_{30.35}$ 34$_{34}$ Lv 15$_{14}$ 1 S 18$_{13.16}$ 2 S 19$_{9}$ 20$_{8}$ 1 K 1$_{23.28.32}$ 8$_{31}$||2 C 6$_{22}$ Ezk 46$_{9}$ Ps 18$_{7}$ 79$_{11}$ 88$_{3}$ 100$_{2}$ 119$_{170}$ Jb 3$_{24}$ 13$_{16}$ Lm 1$_{22}$ Est 1$_{19}$ 8$_{1}$ 9$_{11.25}$ 1 C 16$_{29}$ 1QNoah 1$_{4}$ ([ותבוא]) 1QSa 1$_{17}$ 4QapPs[b] 24$_{9}$ (ל[פניו]) 11QT 58$_{18}$, hi. *bring* Lv 4$_{4.14}$ 14$_{23}$ Nm 7$_{3}$ 15$_{25}$ 31$_{54}$ 1 S 17$_{57}$ 1 K 3$_{24}$ Est 1$_{11.17}$ Dn 1$_{18}$ Ne 8$_{2}$ 2 C 24$_{14}$ 1QH 7$_{30}$ 1QS 6$_{1}$ 4QSD 1.2$_{5}$ ([והביאוה]) 4QM[g] 4$_{6}$, הלך *go* Gn 32$_{21}$ Ex 13$_{21}$ 14$_{19}$ 23$_{23}$ 32$_{1.23.34}$ Nm 14$_{14}$ Dt 1$_{30.33}$ 10$_{11}$ 31$_{8}$ Jos 3$_{6}$ 6$_{9.13}$ 1 S 17$_{7}$ 23$_{24}$ 2 S 6$_{4}$ 1 K 2$_{4}$ 3$_{6}$ 8$_{23}$||2 C 6$_{14}$ 1 K 8$_{25.25}$||2 C 6$_{16}$ 1 K 9$_{4}$||2 C 7$_{17}$ 1 K 12$_{30}$ Is 45$_{2}$ 52$_{12}$ 58$_{8}$ Am 9$_{4}$ Hb 3$_{5}$ Ps 97$_{3}$ Lm 1$_{6}$ 1 C 21$_{30}$ 1QS 7$_{12}$ 4QD[a] 10.2$_{9}$ ([הלך ... לפני]) 4QDibHam[a] 6$_{11}$ 11QPs[a] 26$_{9}$, pi. *go* Ps 85$_{14}$, htp. *go* Gn 17$_{1}$ 24$_{40}$ 48$_{15}$ 1 S 2$_{30}$ 12$_{2.2}$ 2 K 20$_{3}$||Is 38$_{3}$ Ps 56$_{14}$ 116$_{9}$ Est 2$_{11}$ 1QH 7$_{14}$ 1QS 1$_{8}$ 1QSb 5$_{22}$, יצא *go out* Nm 27$_{17}$ Jg 4$_{14}$ 9$_{39}$ 1 S 8$_{20}$ 18$_{13.16}$ 2 S 5$_{24}$||1 C 14$_{15}$ 2 S 24$_{4}$ Ps 68$_{8}$ 1 C 12$_{18}$ 14$_{8}$ 2 C 1$_{10}$ 14$_{9}$ 15$_{2}$ 20$_{17.21}$ 28$_{9}$ Si 16$_{14}$ 1QSa 1$_{17}$ ([לצאת]) 4Q185 1.2$_{8}$, hi. *bring out*, i.e. utter Ec 5$_{1}$, עלה *go up* Jos 8$_{10}$ 1 S 9$_{19}$ Is 53$_{2}$ Jon 1$_{2}$ Mc 2$_{13}$ 2 C 1$_{6}$, hi. *bring up* Ex 40$_{25}$, *offer* Jg 20$_{26}$ 2 S 6$_{17}$, ירד *go down* 1 S 10$_{8}$, עבר *pass* Gn 32$_{17}$ 33$_{3.14}$ Ex 17$_{5}$ Nm 32$_{21.27.29.32}$ Dt 3$_{18.28}$ 9$_{3}$ 31$_{3.3}$ Jos 1$_{14}$ 3$_{6.11}$ 4$_{5.11.12.13}$ 6$_{7}$ 1 S 9$_{27}$ 25$_{19}$ 2 K 4$_{31}$ Mc 2$_{13}$ 1QH 1$_{6}$ 1QS 1$_{16}$ 4QM[a] 1$_{9}$, pi. *cause to pass* 1 K 6$_{21}$, hi. *cause to pass* 1 S 16$_{8.10}$.

מושׁ hi. *depart* Ex 13$_{22}$, נסע *set out* Nm 10$_{33}$, נוס *flee* Dt 28$_{7.25}$ Jos 7$_{4}$ 8$_{5.6.6}$ 1 S 4$_{17}$ 1QH 12$_{18}$ ([ינוסו]), רוץ *run* 1 S 8$_{11}$ 2 S 15$_{1}$ 1 K 1$_{5}$ 18$_{46}$, רדף *pursue* Jos 7$_{5}$, צלח *rush* 2 S 19$_{18}$, שׁלח *send* Gn 24$_{7}$ 32$_{4}$ 45$_{5.7}$ Ex 23$_{20.28}$ 33$_{2}$ Dt 1$_{22}$ Jos 24$_{12}$ Mc 6$_{4}$ Ml 3$_{23}$ Ps 105$_{17}$ 1QSa 2$_{19}$ ([ישׁלח]), pi. *send* Ex 23$_{27}$, נחה hi. *lead* Pr 18$_{16}$, פוץ hi. *scatter* Jr 18$_{17}$, עזב *leave* 1 C 16$_{37.39}$ 2 C 28$_{14}$ 1QS 9$_{23}$, נטשׁ *leave* Pr 17$_{14}$, פרע *let go* 11QPs[a] 24$_{5}$, קרב *draw near* Ex 16$_{9}$ Nm 9$_{6.6}$ Jos 17$_{4.4.4}$ Ps 119$_{169}$, hi. *bring near, offer* Ex 29$_{10}$ Lv 1$_{3}$ 3$_{1.7.12}$ 6$_{7}$ 9$_{2}$ 10$_{1.19}$ 12$_{7}$ 17$_{4}$ Nm 3$_{4}$ 6$_{16}$ 7$_{3.10}$ 8$_{9.10}$ 16$_{17}$ 26$_{61}$ 27$_{5}$ Ezk 43$_{24}$ 1 C 16$_{1}$ 11QT 21$_{16}$ ([יקריבו]), נגשׁ *draw near* 1 C 19$_{14}$, hi. *bring near* 1 S 28$_{25.25}$ 2 C 29$_{23}$, הפך *turn* Jos 7$_{8}$, ni. *be turned* Jl 3$_{4}$, פנה *turn* Jos 7$_{12}$ Jg 20$_{42}$, pi. *prepare* Ml 3$_{1}$ Ps 80$_{10}$ (unless לְפָנֶיהָ = *her predecessors*), נטה *turn aside* Nm 22$_{33}$, hi.

incline Ezr 7$_{28}$ 9$_{9}$, ישט hi. *stretch* Si 34$_{18}$, שׁוב hi. *bring back* Nm 17$_{25}$, נהג *drive* 1 S 30$_{20}$, עור pol. *stir* Ps 80$_{3}$, דוץ *dance* Jb 41$_{14}$, כרר pilp. *dance* 2 S 6$_{14.16}$, רגז *quake* Jl 2$_{10}$, קרא *meet* Jos 8$_{14}$, ni. *be met* Dt 22$_{6}$=11QT 65$_{2}$ 2 S 18$_{9}$, קרה hi. *cause to occur* Gn 24$_{12}$ 27$_{20}$, יעד ni. *be assembled* 1 K 8$_{5}$||2 C 5$_{6}$ 1QSa 2$_{3}$, ho. *be placed* Jr 24$_{1}$, עצר ni. *be detained* 1 S 21$_{8}$, זרח *appear* 2 C 26$_{19}$, כחשׁ pi. *cringe* 4QapPs^{b} 33$_{9}$, מצא *find* Est 8$_{5}$ Si 3$_{18}$, ni. *be found* 4QS^{e} 1.3$_{9}$ ([הנ]מצא; = 1QS 9$_{13}$ לפי *according to*), יחל hi. *wait* 2 S 18$_{14}$, שׁנה pi. *change* Ps 34$_{1}$.

נשׂא *bear* Ex 28$_{12.30}$ Jos 3$_{14}$ 6$_{4.6.8.13}$ 1 S 2$_{28}$ 17$_{41}$ 1 K 2$_{26}$ 2 K 5$_{23}$ Is 8$_{4}$ Est 2$_{9.17}$, נתן *give, place* Gn 18$_{8}$ 29$_{26}$ 43$_{14}$ Ex 25$_{30}$ 30$_{6.36}$ 40$_{5.6}$ Lv 4$_{7}$ 16$_{13}$ 19$_{14}$ Dt 1$_{8.21}$ 2$_{31.33.36}$ 4$_{8}$ 7$_{2.23}$ 11$_{26.32}$ 23$_{15}$ 30$_{1.15.19}$ 31$_{5}$ Jos 10$_{12}$ 11$_{6}$ Jg 11$_{9}$ 1 S 1$_{16}$ 1 K 8$_{46}$ ||2 C 6$_{36}$ 1 K 8$_{50}$ 9$_{6}$||2 C 7$_{19}$ 2 K 4$_{43.44}$ Is 41$_{2}$ Jr 9$_{12}$ 15$_{9}$ 21$_{8}$ 26$_{4}$ 35$_{5}$ 44$_{10.10}$ Ezk 3$_{20}$ 4$_{1}$ 6$_{5}$ 16$_{18.19}$ 23$_{24}$ 28$_{17}$ Jl 2$_{11}$ Zc 3$_{9}$ Ps 106$_{46}$ Dn 1$_{9}$ 9$_{10}$ Ne 1$_{11}$ 9$_{35}$ 1 C 16$_{4}$ Si 7$_{33}$ 4Q434 1.2$_{9}$ 11QT 59$_{19}$, שׂים *place* Gn 48$_{20}$ Ex 19$_{7}$ 21$_{1}$ 40$_{26}$ Lv 24$_{6}$ Nm 16$_{7}$ Dt 4$_{44}$ Jg 18$_{21}$ 1 S 9$_{24}$ 28$_{22}$ 2 K 6$_{22}$ Is 42$_{16}$ Si 34$_{16}$ 1QS 2$_{12}$, pass. *be placed* 1 S 9$_{24}$, ho. *be placed* Gn 24$_{33(Qr)}$, ישׂם *place* Gn 24$_{33(Kt)}$, שׂית *place* Si 10$_{5}$, יצג hi. *place* Gn 43$_{9}$ 47$_{2}$, ho. *be placed* Si 30$_{18(B)}$, נוח *rest* 4Q392 1$_{5}$, hi. *place* Ex 16$_{33.34}$ Nm 17$_{19.22}$ Dt 26$_{4.10}$ Jg 6$_{18}$ 1 S 10$_{25}$, יצק *pour* 2 S 13$_{9}$, hi. *pour,* i.e. place Jos 7$_{23}$, ho. *be poured* Si 15$_{16}$, שׁפך *pour* 1 S 1$_{15}$ 7$_{6}$ Ps 62$_{9}$ 102$_{1}$ 142$_{3}$ 1 C 22$_{8}$ 4QPrFêtes^{c} 1.1$_{4}$ ([לפניכ]ה), סמך *lay* hands Lv 4$_{15}$, פרשׂ *spread* Dt 22$_{17}$ =11QT 65$_{13}$ 2 K 19$_{14}$||Is 37$_{14}$ Ezk 2$_{10}$, תפשׂ ni. *be caught* CD 9$_{19}$, נחל pi. *distribute* by lot Jos 19$_{51}$, ישׁר hi. *make straight* Ps 5$_{9}$ 1QS 4$_{2}$ 4QBark^{d} 2.1$_{12}$ (הוש[ו]ר), ערב *give in pledge* Pr 17$_{18}$, שׁקל *weigh* Ezr 8$_{29}$, מרק *complete* Mur 30 1$_{6}$ 2$_{24}$, יצר ni. *be formed* Is 43$_{10}$.

עשׂה *do* Ex 4$_{21}$ 11$_{10}$ Dt 6$_{25}$ Jg 13$_{15}$ 1 K 15$_{3}$ Ezk 16$_{50}$ Ne 9$_{28}$ 2 C 3$_{15}$ 31$_{20}$ Si 8$_{18}$ 1QS 1$_{2}$ 4QapMes 7.2$_{4}$ 11QPsAp^{a} 2$_{9}$ ([עושים לפני]) 11QT 37$_{9}$ (וע[ש]יתמה) 53$_{8}$ 55$_{14}$ 59$_{17}$ 63$_{8}$, ni. *be done* Lv 18$_{30}$, שׁמר *keep* Nm 3$_{7}$, נצר *keep* 4QBark^{c} 1.1$_{4}$, עבד *serve* Nm 8$_{22.22}$ Jos 22$_{27}$ 2 S 16$_{19.19}$, שׁרת pi. *minister* 1 S 3$_{1}$ Ezk 44$_{12}$ 1 C 6$_{17}$ 16$_{37}$ 1QM 2$_{2}$ 4QM^{h} 4$_{6}$ (וישר[תו לפני]ו) 11QT 15$_{15}$ ([לשרת לפני]) 56$_{9}$ 63$_{3}$ CD 9$_{19}$, מלך *reign* Gn 36$_{31}$||1 C 1$_{43}$, hi. *make king* 1 S 11$_{15}$, בנה *build* Ex 32$_{5}$ 2 C 8$_{12}$, ni. *be built* Nm 13$_{22}$, כרה *dig* Ps 57$_{7}$, אסם *store* Meṣad Ḥashavyahu ost. 1$_{5}$, חיל pol. *be brought to birth* Jb 15$_{7}$ Pr 8$_{25}$, נוף hi. *wave* Ex 29$_{24.26}$ Lv 7$_{30}$ 8$_{27.29}$ 9$_{21}$ 10$_{15}$ 14$_{12.24}$ 23$_{11.20}$ Nm 5$_{25}$ 6$_{20}$ 8$_{11.21}$ 11QT 15$_{12}$ ([ויניפו] ... [לפני]), נזה hi. *sprinkle* Lv 4$_{6.17}$ 14$_{16.27}$ 16$_{14.15}$, שׁלך hi. *cast* Ex 7$_{10}$ Jos 18$_{10}$, ירה *cast* Jos 18$_{6.8}$, שׁלל *plunder* 1QM 10$_{2}$ (לפנ[י]ו), קטר hi. *burn* Ex 29$_{25}$ Ex 30$_{8}$ Nm 17$_{5}$ 1 K 9$_{25}$ 1 C 23$_{13}$ 2 C 2$_{3.5}$ 11QT 34$_{14}$, בער pi. *burn* 2 C 4$_{20}$, pu. *burn* Jr 36$_{22}$, שׁחט *slaughter* Ex 29$_{11}$ Lv 1$_{5.11}$ 3$_{8.13}$ 4$_{4.15.24}$ Nm 19$_{3}$ 4QTohB^{b} 1$_{3}$ ([ל]פניו) 11QT 23$_{11}$, ni. *be slaughtered* Lv 6$_{18}$, זבח *sacrifice* Lv 9$_{4}$ 1 S 11$_{15}$ 1 K 8$_{62}$ ||2 C 7$_{4}$ 11QT 17$_{7}$ 53$_{10}$, אכל *eat* Ex 18$_{12}$ Dt 12$_{7.18}$ 14$_{23.26}$ 15$_{20}$ 2 S 11$_{13}$ 1 K 1$_{25}$ 2 K 25$_{29}$||Jr 52$_{33}$ Jl 2$_{3}$ Ps 50$_{3}$ 11QT 21$_{3}$ ([ואכלו]ם) 22$_{14}$ 52$_{9}$, קטר hi. *sacrifice* 4QMidrEschat^{b} 3$_{7}$, שׁתה *drink* 1 K 1$_{25}$ 1 C 29$_{22}$, ערך *arrange* Ex 27$_{21}$ 40$_{23}$ Lv 24$_{3.4.8}$ Ps 23$_{5}$ Jb 23$_{4}$ 33$_{5}$, pass. *be arranged* Ezk 23$_{41}$, סדר *arrange* 1QM 14$_{3}$, כפר pi. *make atonement* Lv 5$_{26}$ 10$_{17}$ 14$_{18.29.31}$ 15$_{15.30}$ 19$_{22}$ 23$_{28}$ Nm 15$_{28}$ 31$_{50}$ 11QT 22$_{16}$.

טהר *be pure* Lv 16$_{30}$, pi. *declare pure* 4QapPs^{b} 46$_{5}$, perh. htp. *purify oneself* 4QBapt 12$_{2}$ ([לפנ]יכה), צדק *be righteous* Ps 143$_{2}$ 1QH 7$_{28}$ (יצ[ד]ק) 11QPs^{a} 24$_{7}$, htp. *justify oneself* Si 7$_{5}$, יטב *be good* Est 5$_{14}$ Ne 2$_{5}$, כשׁר *be right* Est 8$_{5}$, מעט *be small* Ne 9$_{32}$, שׁקט *be quiet* 2 C 14$_{4}$, דשׁן htp. *satisfy oneself* 1QM 2$_{5}$, חטא *sin* Si 38$_{15}$, צנע pass. *be modest* Si 42$_{9(B)}$, ענשׁ *be punished* CD 3$_{4}$ (or em. לִפְנֵי to לְפִי *according to*), חלץ ni. *be equipped* Nm 32$_{17.20}$, נצח *flash* Si 35$_{10.10.10}$, פתח *open* Is 45$_{1}$ 4QMyst^{a} 3a.2$_{13}$ ([לפנ]יהם) CD 3$_{16}$, מסס ni. *melt* intrans. 4QHod^{a} 6$_{31}$, צלל *be dark* Ne 13$_{19}$, כתם ni. *be stained* Jr 2$_{22}$, יבשׁ *be dry,* i.e. wither Jb 8$_{12}$, נבל *wither* 1QH 8$_{25}$ 10$_{32}$, דעך ni. *be dried up* Si 40$_{15(Bmg)}$ (B מִפְּנֵי *from before*), גוע *expire* Nm 20$_{3}$, מות *die* Lv 10$_{2}$ Nm 3$_{4}$ 14$_{37}$ 1 C 13$_{10}$ 24$_{2}$.

2. מִלִּפְנֵי, **a. from before, from the presence of,** usu. of place; also of time (Ec 1$_{10}$ 1QS 1$_{25}$); with noun or suffix in ref. to noun, יי *Y.* Gn 4$_{16}$ 22$_{3}$ Lv 9$_{24}$ 10$_{2}$ 16$_{12}$ 22$_{3}$ Nm 17$_{11.24}$ 20$_{9}$ 1 S 21$_{7}$ 1 K 8$_{25}$||2 C 6$_{16}$ 1 K 21$_{29}$ Is 48$_{19}$ Jr 16$_{17}$ 18$_{23}$ 31$_{36}$ 33$_{18}$ Ezk 30$_{9}$ (or del.) Jon 1$_{3.3.10}$ Ps 17$_{2}$ 97$_{5}$ 1 C 16$_{30.33}$ 29$_{12}$ 2 C 19$_{2}$ 33$_{23}$ 4QpsEzek^{a} 16.1$_{2}$ 11QPs^{a} 24$_{14.15}$ (מלפ[נ]יכה) 11QPsAp^{a} 2$_{10}$ GnzPs 4$_{4.20}$, appar. in ref. to Y. 1QH fr. 2.1$_{15}$ 4QapPs^{b} 45$_{2}$ ([מלפנ]יך) 4QMMT C$_{28}$, אֱלֹהִים *God* 1 K 8$_{25}$||2 C 6$_{16}$ Ps 51$_{13}$ Ne 3$_{37}$ 2 C 34$_{27}$ perh. 4QConfess 1.2$_{7}$ 4QBéat 22$_{1}$ ([אלו]הים), אֱלוֹהַּ *God* Ps 114$_{7}$, אֵל *God* 1QH 1$_{25}$, אָדוֹן *lord* Ps 97$_{5}$ 114$_{7}$, עֶלְיוֹן *Most High* 11QPs^{a} 27$_{11}$, קָדוֹשׁ *holy one* Is 48$_{19}$, רום ptc. *high one* Is 57$_{16}$, נשׂא ni. ptc. *exalted one* Is 57$_{16}$, גֹּאֵל *re-*

deemer Is 48$_{19}$, מַלְאָךְ *angel* Nm 22$_{33(Sam)}$, Abraham Gn 23$_{4.8}$, David 2 S 7$_{15}$, Esau 4QTNaph 1$_{7}$, Elisha 2 K 5$_{27}$, Moses Ex 35$_{20}$ 36$_{3}$, Jeremiah 2 C 36$_{12}$, Israel(ites) Ex 23$_{28}$ Dt 9$_{4}$ 11$_{23}$ 28$_{31}$ 31$_{3}$ Jos 23$_{5.13}$ Ec 1$_{10}$ 1 C 19$_{18}$ 2 C 20$_{7}$ 11QT 60$_{20}$, עַם *people* 2 C 20$_{7}$, אָח *brother* 4QTNaph 1$_{7}$, רֵעַ *neighbour* 1QpHab 4$_{12}$, מֶלֶךְ *king* perh. 2 K 6$_{32}$ Est 1$_{19}$ 4$_{8}$ 7$_{6}$ 8$_{15}$, מַלְכָּה *queen* Est 7$_{6}$, פַּרְעֹה *Pharaoh* Gn 41$_{46}$ 47$_{10}$, שַׁלִּיט *ruler* Ec 10$_{5}$, כֹּהֵן *priest* Dt 17$_{18}$=11QT 56$_{21}$, לֵוִי *Levite* Dt 17$_{18}$, נָבִיא *prophet* 2 C 36$_{12}$, worshipper 4QBark^{d} 2.1$_{8}$ ([מלפ[נ]י]), זָקֵן *elder* Jos 23$_{5.13}$, שֹׁפֵט *judge* Jos 23$_{5.13}$, שֹׁטֵר *officer* Jos 23$_{5.13}$, עבר ptc. *one who passes* into covenant 1QS 1$_{25}$, בזה ni. ptc. *contemptible one* Dn 11$_{22}$, אֹיֵב *enemy* 1QH 3$_{7}$ ([מלפני אויב]), ראשׁ *head* Jos 23$_{5.13}$, בַּיִת *house* Ezr 10$_{6}$, אֹהֶל *tent* 2 C 1$_{13}$, מִזְבֵּחַ *altar* 1 K 8$_{54}$, שַׁעַר *gate* Ezk 40$_{19}$, יָצוּעַ *couch* 4Q392 1$_{9}$, כָּבוֹד *glory* 4QapMos^{c} 2.2$_{9}$ GnzPs 4$_{26}$, רַב pl. *many* 1QS 7$_{23}$ (unless מלפני *teachers of*, i.e. אלף pi. ptc.) 4QD^{a} 11$_{7}$.

With verb, היה *be* Ec 1$_{10}$, קום *rise* 1 K 8$_{54}$ Ezr 10$_{6}$, בוא *come* Jon 1$_{3}$ 2 C 1$_{13}$, יצא *go out* Gn 4$_{16}$ 41$_{46}$ 47$_{10}$ Ex 35$_{20}$ Lv 9$_{24}$ 10$_{2}$ Nm 17$_{11}$ 2 K 5$_{27}$ Ezk 30$_{9}$ (or del.) Ps 17$_{2}$ Ec 10$_{5}$ Est 1$_{19}$ 8$_{15}$ 1QS 7$_{23}$ (unless מלפני *teachers of*, i.e. אלף pi. ptc.) GnzPs 4$_{20}$, hi. *bring out* Nm 17$_{24}$, עבר *pass* 1QpHab 4$_{12}$, מושׁ *depart* Jr 31$_{36}$, נטה *turn aside* Nm 22$_{33(Sam)}$, ברח *flee* 4QTNaph 1$_{7}$, ירשׁ hi. *dispossess* Dt 11$_{23}$ Jos 23$_{5.13}$ 2 C 20$_{7}$ 11QT 60$_{20}$, גרשׁ pi. *drive out* Ex 23$_{28}$, הדף *thrust* Dt 9$_{4}$, נדף ni. *be driven* 4QapPs^{b} 46$_{8}$ ([מ]לפני); or qal *drive*), שׁלך hi. *cast* Ps 51$_{13}$, שׁטף ni. *be swept away* Dn 11$_{22}$, כרת ni. *be cut off* 1 K 8$_{25}$||2 C 6$_{16}$, שׁלח *send* 2 K 6$_{32}$, htp. *be sent* 4QD^{a} 11$_{7}$, בקשׁ pi. *seek* 4QMMT C$_{28}$, צוה pi. *command* GnzPs 4$_{5}$, נתן ni. *be given* 11QPs^{a} 27$_{11}$, שׁלם *be fulfilled* 11QPs^{a} 24$_{14}$, לקח *take* Ex 36$_{3}$ Lv 16$_{12}$ Nm 20$_{9}$, סור hi. *remove* 2 S 7$_{15}$, ho. *be removed* 1 S 21$_{7}$, אחז *seize* 4QBéat 22$_{1}$, גזל pass. *be seized* Dt 28$_{31}$, ברח *flee* Jon 1$_{3.10}$, נוס *flee* 1 C 19$_{18}$, בקשׁ pi. *seek* Est 4$_{8}$, אבד *perish* 4QpNah 1$_{8}$, שׁמד ni. *be destroyed* Is 48$_{19}$, hi. *destroy* Dt 31$_{3}$, מחה hi. *blot out* Jr 18$_{23}$, ni. *be blotted out* Ne 3$_{37}$, כרת ni. *be cut off* Lv 22$_{3}$ Jr 33$_{18}$, מסס ni. *melt* Ps 97$_{5}$, סתר ni. *be hidden* Jr 16$_{17}$, עדר ni. *be lacking* 1QH 1$_{25}$, רעד *tremble* 4QapMos^{c} 2.2$_{9}$, חיל *writhe* Ps 114$_{7.7}$ 1 C 16$_{30}$, עטף *be faint* Is 57$_{16}$, פחד *fear* 11QPsAp^{a} 2$_{10}$ ([יפחדו]), מדד *measure* Ezk 40$_{19}$, רנן pi. *shout joyfully* 1 C 16$_{33}$, קבר *bury* Gn 23$_{4.8}$, רבה hi. *multiply* 1QH 2.1$_{15}$ ([להר[בות]).

b. on account of, (because) of, followed by noun or suffix in ref. to noun, אֱלֹהִים *God* Ec 3$_{14}$ 8$_{12.13}$ 2 C 33$_{12}$, David 1 S 18$_{12}$, מֶלֶךְ *king* 1 S 8$_{18}$ Est 7$_{6}$ (or §2a), הָמוֹן *multitude* 2 C 32$_{7}$, לָשׁוֹן *tongue* 4QapLam^{b} 1$_{6}$, חֹרֶף *winter* 4QapLam^{a} 1.2$_{6}$.

with verb, כנע ni. *humble oneself* 1 K 21$_{29}$ 2 C 33$_{23.27.27}$ 34$_{27}$ 36$_{12}$ 4QapPs^{b} 45$_{2}$ ([מלפנ]יך), זעק *cry out* 1 S 8$_{18}$, ירא *be afraid* 1 S 18$_{12}$ Ec 3$_{14}$ 8$_{12.13}$, בעת ni. *be terrified* Est 7$_{6}$ (or §2a), חתת ni. *be terrified* 2 C 32$_{7}$, אחז *grasp* 4QapLam^{b} 1$_{6}$.

3. עַל־לִפְנֵי **to the front of,** with noun, אוּלָם *porch* Ezk 40$_{15}$ (mss עַד־לִפְנֵי *to the front of*).

4. עַד לִפְנֵי **to the front of,** with noun, אוּלָם *porch* Ezk 40$_{15(mss)}$, שַׁעַר *gate* Est 4$_{2}$.

with verb, בוא *come* Est 4$_{2}$.

5. כִּי אִם־לִפְנֵי **except before,** i.e. **until, unless,** followed by inf. cstr. of בוא *come*, i.e. set (of sun) 2 S 3$_{35}$, hi. *bring* 2 S 3$_{13}$.

With verb, ראה *see* 2 S 3$_{13}$, טעם *taste* 2 S 3$_{35}$.

Also 1QH fr. 4$_{9}$ fr. 11$_{7}$ 1QMyst 6$_{3}$ 1Q30 2$_{1}$ 1QH^{b} 1$_{3}$ 1Q39 1$_{3}$ 2Q29 3$_{1}$ 6QHymn 6$_{2}$ ([ל]פני) 4QpIsa^{a} 8$_{9}$ 4QpHos^{b} 33$_{2}$ ([לפנ]י) 4QpNah 1$_{10}$ 4QCommGenD 3$_{5}$ 4QD^{b} 8$_{2.3}$ 4QNid 4$_{4}$ 4QBer^{a} 13$_{3}$ 4QMyst^{a} 38$_{1}$ 4QapJoshua^{a} 1$_{1}$ 3.2$_{12}$ ([ל]פני) 4QapJoshua^{b} 13$_{1}$ 4QapPs^{b} 28$_{1}$ 4QparaKings 30$_{3}$ ([לפניכ[ה]) 4QpsEzek^{a} 45$_{2}$ ([מ]לפני) 4QpsEzek^{d} 2$_{2}$ ([מלפנ]י) 15$_{1}$ ([לפנ]י) 4QShirShabb^{b} 12$_{3}$ ([לפנ]י) 4Q408 11$_{2}$ ([מלפנ]) 4QBapt 4$_{1}$ ([ל]פניכה) 7.2$_{4}$ 4Q417 1.1$_{15}$ 4Q418 20$_{3}$ ([לפנ]י) 4QHod^{a} 8$_{4}$ 4QRitMar 47$_{2}$ 58$_{2}$ 87$_{2}$ ([ל]פני) 98$_{2}$ 4QPrFêtes^{b} 30$_{2}$ 4QPrFêtes^{c} 7$_{4}$ 21$_{1}$ 131.1$_{19}$ 191$_{2}$ 4QRitPur 28.7$_{3}$ 76$_{2}$ 4Q518 31$_{3}$ 5QRègle 2$_{9}$ 5Q19 1$_{2}$.

<ANT> אַחֲרֵי *after*.

לְפָנִים I $_{21.3.7}$ adv. **formerly, 1. formerly, in time past,** with verb, היה *be* Ne 13$_{5}$ 2 C 9$_{20}$, ישׁב *dwell* Dt 2$_{10.12.20}$, אמר *say* 1 S 9$_{9}$, קרא ni. *be called*, i.e. named 1 S 9$_{9}$, ראה ni. *be seen* 2 C 9$_{11}$, ידע *know* Jg 3$_{2}$ Jb 42$_{11}$, נתן *give*, i.e. place Ne 13$_{5}$, יסד *found* Ps 102$_{26}$.

In nom. cl., זֹאת לְפָנִים בְּיִשְׂרָאֵל *this was formerly (the custom) in Israel* Ru 4$_{7}$, מִן־חָם הַיֹּשְׁבִים שָׁם לְפָנִים *those who dwelt there formerly were of Ham* 1 C 4$_{40}$, חָצוֹר לְפָנִים הִיא רֹאשׁ כָּל־הַמַּמְלָכוֹת הָאֵלֶּה *Hazor was formerly the head of all these kingdoms* Jos 11$_{10}$, שֵׁם חֶבְרוֹן לְפָנִים קִרְיַת אַרְבַּע

the name of Hebron was formerly Kiriath-arba Jos 14_{15} Jg 1_{10}, sim. Jos 15_{15} Jg $1_{11.23}$.

2. firstly, with verb, ידע *know* Si 37_8, שׁמע *hear* 4Q Béat 14.2_{24} (:: אַחַר *afterwards*), בחר *test* Si 4_{17}, בקר pi. *examine* Si 11_7 (:: אַחַר), שׁלח *send*, i.e. stretch out, hand 1QSa 2_{20} ([ישלח]).

3. forwards, with verb היה *be* Jr 7_{24} (mss הלך *go*; :: לְאָחוֹר *backwards*).

4. as prep. = לִפְנֵי **before, in the presence of,** followed by noun, שֹׁפֵט *judge* CD 9_{10}.

5. מִלְּפָנִים **from of old,** with verb, נגד hi. *tell* Is 41_{26} (|| מֵרֹאשׁ *from the beginning*), כשׁל ni. *stumble* CD 2_{17} (+ עד הנה *until now*).

6. לְמִלְּפָנִים **formerly, from of old,** with verb עמד *stand* CD 3_{19} (+ עד הנה *until now*) 5_{17}, פקד *visit*, i.e. punish CD 5_{15} (למילפנים).

Also 4QpNah 3.1_8 (מלפנים).

<SYN> §4 מֵרֹאשׁ *from the beginning*.

<ANT> §2 אַחַר *afterwards*, §3 לְאָחוֹר *backwards*.

* [לְפָנִים] II 2 n.m. **predecessors** (or לִפְנֵי *before, in the presence of*), <NOM CL> זַרְעָם נָכוֹן לִפְנֵיהֶם עִמָּם וְצֶאֱצָאֵיהֶם לְעֵינֵיהֶם *their seed is established, their predecessors are with them, and their offspring are before them* Jb 21_8. <OBJ> פנה pi. *push aside* Ps 80_{10}.

לפף 1 vb. **cling—Pi.** Ptc. Q מלפפ[]—perh. **cling** or **wrap,** 4Q517 67_1 (.מלפפ).

לפת 3 vb. **twist—Qal** 1 + waw וַיִּלְפֹּת—**grasp,** perh. with twisting motion, <SUBJ> Samson Jg 16_{29}. <OBJ> עַמּוּד *pillar* Jg 16_{29}.

Ni. 2 Impf. יִלָּפְתוּ; + waw וַיִּלָּפֵת—**1. turn oneself over,** in bed, <SUBJ> אִישׁ *man* Ru 3_8.

2. intrans. **wind about, turn aside,** <SUBJ> אֹרַח *caravan* Jb 6_{18} (or em. אֹרְחָה *caravan*). <COLL> יִלָּפְתוּ אָרְחוֹת דַּרְכָּם *the caravans wind about* (or *turn aside from*) *their way* Jb 6_{18} (or em. pi. יְלַפְּתוּ *they wind* their way).

לֵץ, see ליץ *scorn*.

לָצוֹן 3.0.6 n.[m.] **scorning*** or **babbling,*** <OBJ> חמד *delight in* Pr 1_{22} (+ פֶּתִי *simplicity*). <CSTR> אִישׁ הלצון *man of scorning* CD 1_{14}, אַנְשֵׁי לָצוֹן *men of scorning* Is 28_{14} Pr 29_8 (+ חָכָם *wise one*) 4QpIsa[b] $2_{6.10}$ (both הלצון) 4QMidr Eschat[b] 8_7 (אנשי/איש] הלצון] *men/man of scorning*) 4Q Béat 22_8 CD 20_{11}.

⇒ ליץ *scorn*.

לֵצִים, see ליץ *scorn*.

[לָקָה] 0.1 n.f. **trap**—sf. לְקוֹתֶיהָ—<PREP> בְּ of instrument/place, *by (means of), with, in,* + לכד ni. *be captured* Si 9_3.

לַקּוּם 1 pl.n. **Lakkum,** town on northern border of Naphtali, <PREP> עַד *as far as*, + היה *be* Jos 19_{33}.

לקח 965.16.91.7 vb. **take—**

Qal
- **1a. take,** pp. 565a
  - **Subjects,** pp. 565a
  - **Objects,** pp. 567a
  - **Prepositions,** pp. 570b
  - **Collocations,** pp. 572b
- **1b.** ptc. used as noun, **purchaser,** pp. 573a
- **2. marry,** pp. 573a
- **3.** pass. **be taken,** pp. 574b

Niphal, pp. 574b
Pual, pp. 574b
Hophal, pp. 574b
Hithpael, pp. 574b

Qal 938.12.88.6 Pf. לָקַח (לָקֳח, קָח, לְקָחַנִי), I sf. 3ms (לְקַחְתָּנוּ), לָקַחַתְּ, לָקְחָה, (קָחָם, לְקָחָם, לְקָחָהּ, לקחה (לְקָחוּ) לָקְחוּ, (לְקַחְתִּיו, לְקַחְתִּיךָ, לְקָחְתִּי) לָקַחְתִּי, לְקַחַתְּ, יְקָחֶךָ, יְקָחֵךְ, יְקָחֵנִי, יִקָּח) יִקַּח impf. ;לָקַחְנוּ, לְקַחְתֶּם (תִּקָּחֵם, תִּקָּחֵךְ) תִּקַּח 3fs ,(יְקָחֶנָּה, יְקָחֶהָ, יְקָחֶנּוּ, יְקָחֵהוּ אֶקַּח, תִּקְחִי ,(תִּקָּחֶנָּה, תִּקָּחֶנּוּ, תִּקָּחֵנִי, תִּקָּח) תִּקַּח 2ms (תִּקָּחוּ) תִּקְחוּ, (יִקָּחוּ) יִקְחוּ, (אֶקָּחֵהוּ, אֶקָּחֵךְ, אֶקְחָה, אֶקָּח) וְלָקַחַתְּ, וְלָקְחָה, (וּלְקָחָהּ) וְלָקַח + waw ;(נִקְחָה) נִקַּח וְלָקְחוּ) וְלָקְחוּ, (וּלְקַחְתִּים, וּלְקַחְתִּיךָ) וְלָקַחְתִּי, וְלָקַחַתְּ, וַיִּקָּחֵהוּ, וַיִּקָּחֵנִי, וַיִּקָּח) וַיִּקַּח; וְלָקַחְנוּ, וּלְקַחְתֶּם, (וּלְקָחוּם

וַיִּקָּחֵם, וַיִּקָּחֶהָ), 3fs וַתִּקַּח (וַתִּקָּחֵנִי, וַתִּקָּחֵהוּ, וַתִּקָּחֶהָ, וַיִּקְחוּ, (וָאֶקָּחֵם, וָאֶקְחָה) וָאֶקַּח, וַתִּקְחִי, וַתִּקַּח 2ms, (וַתִּקָּחֵם קָחֶנָּה, קָחֶנּוּ, קְחָה, קַח) קַח; impv. וַנִּקַּח, (וַיִּקָּחוּם, וַיִּקָּחֵהוּ) קָחֵהוּ, קָחוּ) קְחוּ, (לְקְחִי) קְחִי, (לְקַח, קָחֶם־; ptc. לֹקֵחַ (Si, Q לוקח), לֹקְחִים, לֹקְחֵי; ptc. pass. לְקֻחִים; inf. abs. לָקוֹחַ (לָקֹחַ); cstr. קַחַת (קַחַת) לָקַחַת, קַחְתִּי, קַחְתֵּךְ, קַחְתּוֹ, קַחְתָּהּ).

1a. usu. **take,** also **receive** (e.g. Gn 4$_{11}$ 38$_{20}$ Ex 28$_{5}$ 36$_{3}$ Nm 34$_{14}$ Dt 9$_{9}$ Jos 13$_{8}$ Is 40$_{2}$), **accept** (Gn 21$_{30}$ 23$_{13}$ 32$_{10.11}$ Jg 13$_{23}$ 1 S 2$_{15}$ 2 K 5$_{15}$ Ps 6$_{10}$ Pr 10$_{8}$), **bring** (e.g. Gn 15$_{9.10}$ 27$_{9.13}$ Nm 19$_{2}$ 1 S 10$_{23}$ 20$_{31}$ 30$_{11}$ 1 K 7$_{13}$ 2 K 2$_{20}$), **place** (e.g. Jg 19$_{28}$ 2 S 13$_{19}$ Ezk 17$_{5}$ [or del.] Ps 75$_{3}$), **seize, capture** (e.g. Nm 21$_{25}$ Dt 3$_{4}$ Jos 11$_{16}$ 1 S 7$_{14}$ 2 S 8$_{1}$ 1 K 20$_{34}$ 2 K 13$_{25}$ 15$_{29}$ Jb 1$_{15}$), **acquire, obtain, purchase** (e.g. Pr 31$_{16}$ Ne 10$_{32}$ Si 8$_{9}$ 11QT 43$_{14}$), **captivate** (Pr 6$_{25}$ [unless אַל־תִּקָּחֲךָ *do not embolden yourself,* i.e. יקח pi.]); perh. **consider, understand** (4Q 418 77$_{2.4}$).

<SUBJ> Y. Gn 2$_{15.21.22}$ 5$_{24}$ 24$_{7}$ Ex 6$_{7}$ Lv 7$_{34}$ Nm 3$_{12}$ 8$_{16.18}$ 18$_{6}$ Dt 4$_{20}$ 10$_{17}$ 30$_{4}$ Jos 24$_{3}$ Jg 13$_{23}$ 2 S 7$_{8}$||1 C 17$_{7}$ 2 S 12$_{11}$ 22$_{17}$||Ps 18$_{17}$ 1 K 11$_{34.35.37}$ 19$_{4}$ 2 K 2$_{3.5}$ Is 47$_{3}$ 51$_{22}$ 66$_{21}$ Jr 3$_{14}$ 15$_{15}$ 25$_{9}$ 33$_{26}$ 43$_{10}$ 44$_{12}$ Ezk 16$_{61}$ (if em. בְּקַחְתֵּךְ *when you take* to בְּקַחְתִּי *when I take*) 17$_{22}$ 24$_{16.25}$ 36$_{24}$ 37$_{19.21}$ Ho 2$_{11}$ 11$_{3}$ 13$_{11}$ 14$_{3}$ Am 7$_{15}$ 9$_{3}$ Jon 4$_{3}$ Hg 2$_{23}$ Ml 2$_{13}$ Ps 6$_{10}$ 49$_{16}$ 50$_{9}$ 51$_{13}$ 68$_{19}$ 73$_{24}$ 75$_{3}$ 78$_{70}$ Jb 1$_{21}$ 12$_{20}$ 35$_{7}$ Si 32$_{14}$ 1QH 15$_{24}$ 4QparaKings 9$_{5}$ perh. 4QRitPur 48$_{6}$ (לקח[תנו]) 4QSela 8.2$_{3}$ ([יקח]) 11QPs^{a} 28$_{10}$, אֱלֹהִים *god* Dt 4$_{34}$.

Aaron Ex 7$_{9.19}$ 9$_{8.10}$ 12$_{32}$ 16$_{33}$ perh. 17$_{12}$ 32$_{4}$ Lv 9$_{2.15}$ 10$_{12}$ 16$_{5.7.12.14.18}$ Nm 1$_{17}$ 4$_{9.12}$ 17$_{11.12}$, Abigail 1 S 25$_{18}$, Abihu Lv 10$_{1}$, Abimelech, king of Gerar Gn 20$_{14}$ 21$_{30}$, Abimelech, son of Jerubaal Jg 9$_{43.48}$, Abiram Nm 16$_{1}$, Abishai 1 S 26$_{11}$ 2 S 20$_{6}$, Abner 1 S 17$_{57}$ 2 S 2$_{8}$, Abra(ha)m Gn 12$_{5.19}$ 14$_{21.23}$ 15$_{9.10}$ 17$_{23}$ 18$_{5.7.8}$ 21$_{14.27}$ 22$_{2.3.6.6.10.13}$ 4QpsJub^{a} 2.1$_{11}$ ([אבר]הם) perh. 4QComm GenA 2$_{12}$, Absalom 2 S 18$_{18}$, Achan Jos 7$_{1.21}$ Ahaz 2 K 16$_{8}$, Amraphel Gn 14$_{11.12}$, Aner Gn 14$_{24}$, Arioch Gn 14$_{11.12}$, Asa 1 K 15$_{18}$ 2 C 16$_{6}$, Asahel 2 S 2$_{21}$, Baanah 2 S 4$_{6.7}$, Balaam Nm 23$_{20}$, Balak Nm 22$_{41}$ 23$_{11.14.27.28}$, Barak Jg 4$_{6}$, Baruch Jr 36$_{14.14}$, Benaiah 1 K 1$_{33}$, Ben-hadad 2 K 13$_{25}$, Bezalel Ex 36$_{3}$, Boaz Ru 4$_{2}$, Chedorlaomer Gn 14$_{11.12}$, Coniah Lachish ost. 3$_{18}$, Dathan Nm 16$_{1}$, David 1 S 16$_{23}$ 17$_{17.18.40.49.51.54}$ 21$_{9.10.10}$ 25$_{25}$ 26$_{12}$ 27$_{9}$ 30$_{20}$ 2 S 8$_{1.7.8}$||1 C 18$_{1.7.8}$ 2 S 9$_{5}$ 12$_{30}$||1 C 20$_{2}$ 2 S 21$_{12}$ 1 C 21$_{23}$, Delilah Jg 16$_{12}$, Ebed-melech Jr 38$_{10.11.11}$, Ehud Jg 3$_{21}$, Elead 1 C 7$_{21}$, Eleazar Lv 10$_{12}$ Nm 17$_{4}$ 19$_{4}$ 31$_{51.54}$, Eliashib Arad ost. 3$_{8}$ 12$_{1}$ ([אלי]שב קח[ח]).

Elijah 1 K 17$_{19.23}$ 18$_{31}$ 2 K 2$_{8}$, Eliphaz Jb 42$_{8}$, Elisha 1 K 19$_{21}$ 2 K 2$_{14}$, Ephron Gn 23$_{13}$, Eshcol Gn 14$_{24}$, Esau Gn 33$_{10.11.11}$ 36$_{6}$, Ezer 1 C 7$_{21}$, Gehazi 2 K 4$_{29}$ 5$_{20.23.24.26.26}$, Gideon Jg 6$_{20.25.26.27}$ 7$_{8}$ (if em. וַיִּקְחוּ אֶת־צֵדָה הָעָם בְּיָדָם *and the people took provisions in their hands* to וַיִּקַּח אֶת־כַּדֵּי הָעָם מִיָּדָם *and he took the jars of the people from their hands*) 8$_{16.21}$, Hadad 1 K 11$_{18}$, Haman Est 6$_{10.11}$, Hananiah Jr 28$_{10}$, Hanun 2 S 10$_{4}$||1 C 19$_{4}$, Hazael 2 K 8$_{8.9.15}$, Hezekiah 2 K 19$_{14}$||Is 37$_{14}$, Hoshaiah Meṣad Ḥashavyahu ost. 1$_{8.9}$ (others Hashabiah in both), Hur perh. 17$_{12}$, Isaiah Is 8$_{1}$, Ish-bosheth 2 S 3$_{15}$, Ithamar Lv 10$_{12}$, Jael Jg 4$_{21}$, Jacob/Israel Gn 27$_{9.13.14.36.36}$ 28$_{11.18}$ 30$_{37}$ 31$_{1.45}$ 32$_{14.23.24}$ 48$_{22}$, Jair Dt 3$_{14}$, Japheth Gn 9$_{23}$, J(eh)oash 2 K 12$_{19}$ 13$_{15.15.18.18.25}$ 14$_{14}$, Jehoiada 2 K 11$_{4.19}$||2 C 23$_{1.20}$ 2 K 12$_{10}$, Jehoshaphat 2 K 3$_{15}$, Jehosheba 2 K 11$_{2}$||2 C 22$_{11}$, Jehudi Jr 36$_{21.21}$, Jerahmeel Jr 36$_{26}$.

Jeremiah Jr 13$_{4.6.7}$ 25$_{15.17}$ 32$_{11.14}$ 35$_{3}$ 36$_{2.28.32}$ 43$_{9}$, Jeroboam 1 K 11$_{31}$, Jesse 1 S 16$_{11.20}$, Jethro Ex 18$_{2.12}$, Joab 2 S 14$_{2}$ 18$_{14}$, Job Jb 2$_{8}$ 22$_{22}$ 38$_{20}$ 40$_{28}$, Jonathan, son of Saul 1 S 20$_{31}$, Jonathan, son of Kareah Jr 41$_{12.16}$ 43$_{5}$, Josiah 2 K 23$_{16}$, Joseph Gn 32$_{24}$ 43$_{18}$ 47$_{2}$ 48$_{1.9.13}$, Joseph (son of Ariston) MurEpBeth-Mashiko$_{3}$, Joshua Jos 7$_{24}$ 8$_{1.12}$ 11$_{16.23}$ 24$_{26}$, Korah Nm 16$_{1.6.17}$, Laban Gn 29$_{23}$ 31$_{23.32}$, Leah Gn 30$_{9}$, Levi Gn 34$_{25.26}$, Lot Gn 19$_{15}$, Magog Ezk 38$_{13}$, Mamre Gn 14$_{24}$, Manoah Jg 13$_{19}$, Moses Ex 4$_{9.9.17.20.20}$ 7$_{15}$ 9$_{8.10}$ 12$_{32}$ 13$_{19}$ 14$_{11}$ 17$_{5.5}$ 24$_{6.7.8}$ 28$_{9}$ 29$_{1+13t}$ 30$_{16.23.34}$ 32$_{20}$ 33$_{7}$ 34$_{4}$ 40$_{9.20}$ Lv 8$_{2+9t}$ 24$_{5}$ Nm 1$_{17}$ 3$_{41.45.47.47.49.50}$ 7$_{5.6}$ 8$_{6.8}$ 11$_{16}$ 12$_{1.1}$ 17$_{17}$ 20$_{8.9.25}$ 25$_{4}$ 27$_{18.22}$ 31$_{29.30.47.54}$ Dt 1$_{15.23}$ 9$_{9.21}$ 4QOrd^{a} 5$_{4}$ appar. 4QJub^{a} prologue ([ל]קח[ת]), Michal 1 S 19$_{13}$, Miriam Ex 15$_{20}$, Mordecai Est 2$_{7.15}$, Naaman 2 K 5$_{5}$, Nabal 1 S 25$_{11}$, Nadab Lv 10$_{1}$, Nahum Arad ost. 17$_{3}$, Naomi Ru 4$_{16}$, Nathan 1 K 1$_{33}$, Nebuchadnezzar Jr 27$_{20}$ 28$_{3}$, Nebuzaradan 2 K 25$_{20}$||Jr 52$_{26}$ Jr 39$_{12.14}$ 40$_{1}$ 4QpsEzek^{a} 16.1$_{5}$, Nebushazban Jr 39$_{14}$, Neco 2 K 23$_{34}$||2 C 36$_{4}$, Nergalsharezer Jr 39$_{14}$, Noah Gn 6$_{21}$ 7$_{2}$ 8$_{9.20}$, Obadiah 1 K 18$_{4}$, On Nm 16$_{1}$, Phineas Nm 25$_{7}$, Rachel Gn 30$_{15}$ 31$_{34}$, Rebekah Gn 24$_{65}$ 27$_{15.45}$, Rechab 2 S 4$_{6.7}$, Rizpah 2 S 21$_{10}$, Samson Jg 14$_{19}$ 15$_{4.6.15}$, Samuel 1 S 7$_{9.12}$ 9$_{22}$

10$_{1}$ 12$_{3.3.3.4}$ 16$_{2.13}$, Sarai Gn 16$_{3}$, Saul 1 S 9$_{3}$ 10$_{4}$ 11$_{7}$ 18$_{2}$ 31$_{4}$||1 C 10$_{4}$, Seraiah Jr 36$_{26}$, Selemiah Jr 36$_{26}$, Shem Gn 9$_{23}$, Shemaiah Lachish ost. 4$_{6}$, Shishak 1 K 14$_{26.26.26}$ ||2 C 12$_{9.9.9}$, Sihon Nm 21$_{26}$, Simeon Gn 34$_{25.26}$, Solomon 1 K 7$_{13}$, Tamar 2 S 13$_{8.9.10.19}$, Terah Gn 11$_{31}$, Tidal Gn 14$_{11.12}$, Tiglath-pileser 2 K 15$_{29}$, Zadok 1 K 1$_{33.39}$, Zechariah Zc 6$_{10.11}$ 11$_{7.10.13.15}$, Zedekiah Jr 37$_{17}$ 38$_{14}$, Ziba 2 S 19$_{31}$, Zipporah Ex 4$_{25}$.

אָדָם *human being* Gn 3$_{22}$ Is 44$_{15}$ 4QCreatA 1$_{9}$, אִישׁ *man, husband* Gn 24$_{22.61}$ 34$_{25}$ 43$_{15.15}$ Ex 12$_{3}$ 16$_{16}$ 36$_{3}$ Lv 10$_{1}$ Nm 13$_{20}$ 16$_{17.18}$ 17$_{24}$ 19$_{18}$ Dt 1$_{25}$ Jos 9$_{14}$ Jg 17$_{2}$ 18$_{17.18}$ 19$_{28.29}$ 20$_{10}$ 1 S 6$_{10}$ 30$_{11}$ 31$_{12.13}$ 2 S 12$_{4.4}$ 1 K 11$_{18}$ 2 K 2$_{20.20}$ 5$_{15.16.16}$ 6$_{2}$ 9$_{13}$ 11$_{9}$||2 C 23$_{8}$ 2 K 12$_{6}$ Jr 35$_{13}$ Ezk 8$_{3}$ (if em. אֵשׁ *fire* to אִישׁ *man*) 10$_{6.7}$ 18$_{8.13.17}$ Ps 49$_{18}$ Pr 7$_{20}$ Si 35$_{18}$ 1QS 5$_{16}$ 4QS^{z} 1$_{1}$ 11QT 51$_{17}$ CD 11$_{3}$, אִשָּׁה *woman, wife* Gn 3$_{6}$ 16$_{3}$ Ex 2$_{3.9}$ Lv 12$_{8}$ 15$_{29}$ Jos 2$_{4}$ Jg 4$_{21}$ 1 S 28$_{4}$ 2 S 17$_{19}$ 1 K 3$_{20}$ 14$_{3}$ 17$_{10.11.11}$ Pr 6$_{25}$ 31$_{16}$ 4QD^{e} 4$_{7}$, אָב *father* Dt 22$_{15}$=11QT 65$_{9}$ 1 S 24$_{12}$ 1 K 20$_{34}$, חֹתֵן *father-in-law* Ex 18$_{2.12}$, אֵם *mother* Dt 22$_{15}$=11QT 65$_{9}$ Jg 17$_{4}$, בֵּן *son* Gn 34$_{17.25.26.28}$ 46$_{6}$ Lv 10$_{1.12}$ Nm 4$_{9.12}$ 16$_{1}$ 25$_{7}$ Dt 3$_{14}$ Jos 7$_{1}$ Jg 4$_{6}$ 18$_{24.27}$ 1 S 8$_{3}$ 9$_{3}$ 17$_{17.18}$ 2 S 2$_{8}$ 4$_{6.7}$ 1 K 1$_{33}$ 19$_{21}$ 2 K 4$_{41}$ 6$_{2}$ 9$_{1.3}$ 13$_{25.25}$ Jr 2$_{30}$ 36$_{14.26}$ 41$_{12.16}$ 43$_{5}$ Ezk 23$_{10.25.26.29}$ Pr 2$_{1}$ 4$_{10}$ Si 8$_{9}$ 9$_{13}$ 16$_{24}$ 34$_{22}$ MurEpBeth-Mashiko$_{3}$ Lachish ost. 3$_{18}$ Meṣad Ḥashavyahu ost. 1$_{8.9}$, of Israel Ex 12$_{32}$ 16$_{16}$ 25$_{2.2.3}$ 27$_{20}$ Lv 9$_{3.5}$ 24$_{2}$ Nm 19$_{2.17}$ 31$_{11}$ 35$_{31.32}$ Jos 11$_{19}$, בֶּן־אָדָם *son of man, mortal* Ezk 3$_{10}$ 4$_{1.3.9}$ 5$_{1.1.1.2.3.4}$ 24$_{5}$ 37$_{16.16}$ 43$_{20.21}$ Si 40$_{6(Bmg)}$, חָתָן *son-in-law* Jg 15$_{6}$, בַּת *daughter* 2 S 21$_{10}$ 2 K 11$_{2}$||2 C 22$_{11}$, אָח *brother* Gn 27$_{35}$ 31$_{46}$ (or em. וַיִּלְקְטוּ *and they gathered*) 34$_{25.26}$ 37$_{24.31}$ 42$_{33.36}$ 43$_{11.12.13}$ 44$_{29}$ 45$_{18.19}$, אָחוֹת *sister* Ex 15$_{20}$ 2 K 11$_{2}$, נַעַר *lad* 1 S 2$_{16.16}$ 20$_{21}$ 2 S 4$_{12}$, בָּחוּר *youth* Ezk 23$_{25.26.29}$, בְּתוּלָה *young woman* Is 47$_{2}$ Jr 46$_{11}$.

מֶלֶךְ *king* Gn 14$_{11.12}$ Nm 21$_{26}$ Jg 5$_{19}$ 1 S 8$_{11.13.14.16}$ 2 S 8$_{8}$ 9$_{5}$ 20$_{3}$ 21$_{8}$ 1 K 7$_{13}$ 14$_{26}$||2 C 12$_{9}$ 1 K 22$_{3}$ 2 K 3$_{26.37}$ 6$_{13}$ 12$_{19}$ 13$_{15.15.18.18.25}$ 15$_{29}$ 18$_{32}$||Is 36$_{17}$ 2 K 24$_{7.12}$ Jr 17$_{23}$ 27$_{10}$ 28$_{3}$ 37$_{17}$ 38$_{14}$ Ezk 17$_{12.13.13}$ 2 C 16$_{6}$ 11QT 57$_{20}$, פַּרְעֹה *Pharaoh* Ex 14$_{6.7}$ 2 K 23$_{34}$, אָדוֹן *lord* Gn 39$_{20}$ Ex 21$_{10}$ 2 S 24$_{22}$ 2 K 5$_{20}$, בַּעַל *owner* Ex 22$_{10}$, נָשִׂיא *prince* Ezk 22$_{25}$ (if em. קֶשֶׁר נְבִיאֶיהָ *a conspiracy of her prophets* to אֲשֶׁר נְשִׂיאֶיהָ *whose princes*) 38$_{13}$ 46$_{18}$, שַׂר *commander* Gn 40$_{11}$ 2 S 2$_{8}$ 2 K 11$_{9}$ Jr 38$_{6}$ 41$_{12.16}$ 43$_{5}$ Lachish ost. 3$_{18}$, רַב *chief* 2 K 25$_{15.18.19.20}$||Jr 52$_{19.24.25.26}$ Jr 39$_{12.14}$ 40$_{1.2}$ 4QpsEzek^{a} 16.1$_{5}$, פֶּחָה *governor* Ezk 23$_{25.26.29}$ Ne 5$_{15}$, סָגָן *ruler* Ezk 23$_{25.26.29}$, עֶבֶד *servant* Gn 24$_{10.51}$ Jg 3$_{25}$ 1 K 9$_{28}$ ||2 C 8$_{18}$ 1 K 20$_{6.33}$ 22$_{3}$ 2 K 9$_{13}$, אָמָה *female servant* Ex 2$_{5}$, שֹׁפֵט *judge* 11QT 51$_{12}$, שֹׁטֵר *official* 11QT 51$_{12}$, כֹּהֵן *priest* Lv 4$_{5.25.30.34}$ 14$_{6+7t}$ Nm 5$_{17.17.25}$ 6$_{19}$ 17$_{4}$ 19$_{4.6}$ 25$_{7}$ 31$_{51.54}$ Dt 26$_{4}$ Jg 18$_{20}$ 1 S 2$_{14.15}$ 1 K 1$_{33.39}$ 2 K 12$_{6.8.9.10}$ Ezk 45$_{19}$ 1QpHab 8$_{12}$ 1QDM 3$_{12}$ ([י]קחו [הכוהנים]) 4$_{5}$ (ה[כוהן]) perh. 4QapMos^{a} 1.2$_{3.6}$ (יק[ח]) appar. 11QT 15$_{9}$ ([ויקחו]) 16$_{14}$ CD 16$_{14}$ (ה[כ]הנים), לֵוִי *Levite* Nm 8$_{8}$ 18$_{26.28}$ Dt 31$_{26}$ 2 C 23$_{8}$, נָבִיא *prophet* 1 K 1$_{33}$ 18$_{26}$ Jr 23$_{31}$ (or em. הָעֹלְקִים *who distort*) 28$_{10}$ Ezk 22$_{25}$ (or em.; see above), נְבִיאָה *prophet* (fem.) Ex 15$_{20}$, זבח ptc. *one who offers sacrifice* Zc 14$_{21}$, נָזִיר *Nazirite* Nm 6$_{18}$, קְדֵשָׁה *sacred woman* Gn 38$_{23}$, זָקֵן *elder* Ex 12$_{21.22}$ Dt 19$_{12}$ 21$_{3}$ 22$_{18}$=11QT 65$_{13}$ Jg 11$_{5}$ 2 K 10$_{6.7}$, אֹמֵן *guardian* 2 K 10$_{6.7}$, רֵעַ *friend* Gn 38$_{20}$ Jb 42$_{8}$, שָׁכֵן *neighbour* Ex 12$_{4}$, יֹשֵׁב *inhabitant* Jos 9$_{4}$ Jr 17$_{23}$ 35$_{13}$ 11QT 43$_{14}$, מַלְאָךְ *messenger* Jos 7$_{23}$ 1 S 19$_{14.20}$.

מְיַלֶּדֶת *midwife* Gn 38$_{28}$, אַלְמָנָה *widow* 1 K 17$_{10.11.11}$, זוֹנָה *prostitute* Is 23$_{16}$ Ezk 16$_{61}$ (or em.; see above), מְאַהֵב *lover* Ezk 16$_{39}$ 23$_{25.26.29}$, סֹחֵר *merchant* 1 K 10$_{28}$||2 C 1$_{16}$ (if em.; see below), נֹשֶׁה *creditor* 2 K 4$_{1}$ 4Q416 2.2$_{6}$, בֹּנֶה *builder* Ezk 27$_{5}$, אֹיֵב *enemy* Jr 20$_{5}$, חָכָם *wise one* Ex 28$_{5}$ Pr 10$_{8}$ 11$_{30}$ (or em. חָמָס *violence*) 21$_{11}$, חָרָשׁ *artisan* Is 44$_{14}$, יסר ptc. *one who disciplines* Pr 9$_{7}$, רֹעֶה *shepherd* Is 56$_{12}$, פעל ptc. *one who does* Mc 2$_{9}$ Ps 15$_{5}$, חשב ptc. *one who devises* iniquity Mc 2$_{9}$, דבר ptc. *one who speaks* Ps 15$_{5}$, הלך ptc. *one who goes* Ps 15$_{5}$, דרשׁ ptc. *one who seeks* Si 35$_{14.14}$, טהר htp. ptc. *one who is purified* Lv 14$_{10.21}$, זוב ptc. *one who has a discharge* Lv 15$_{14}$, רָעֵב *hungry one* Jb 5$_{5}$, רָשָׁע *wicked one* Pr 17$_{23}$, עָרִיץ *terrible one* Jb 27$_{13}$, זֵד *presumptuous one* Si 35$_{18(Bmg, E)}$, לֵץ *scorner* Si 35$_{18(Bmg, E)}$, כְּסִל *fool* Pr 8$_{10}$, פֶּתִי *simple one* Pr 8$_{10}$.

Amalekite(s) 1 S 30$_{16.18.19}$ 2 S 1$_{10}$, Aram 1 C 2$_{23}$, Chaldaeans 2 K 20$_{18}$||Is 39$_{7}$ 2 K 25$_{14}$||Jr 52$_{18}$ Ezk 23$_{25.26.29}$ Jb 1$_{17}$, Geshur 1 C 2$_{23}$, Ephraim Ho 10$_{6}$, Ethiopian Jr 38$_{10}$, Gad(ites) Jos 13$_{8}$ 18$_{7}$, Israel(ites) Ex 10$_{26}$ 21$_{14}$ 23$_{8}$ Lv 14$_{4.42.42}$ 23$_{40}$ 25$_{36}$ Nm 21$_{25}$ 34$_{18}$ Dt 3$_{4.8}$ 7$_{25}$ 15$_{17}$ 16$_{19}$ 22$_{6.7}$=11QT 65$_{4.5}$ Dt 24$_{19}$ 26$_{2}$ 29$_{7}$ Jos 3$_{12}$ 4$_{2}$ 6$_{18}$ 7$_{11}$ Jg 11$_{13.15}$ 1 S 4$_{3}$ 10$_{23}$ 2 S 18$_{17}$ 1 K 19$_{10}$ 2 K 7$_{13.14}$ 9$_{17}$ Jr 5$_{3}$ 20$_{10}$ 25$_{28}$ 32$_{33}$ 51$_{8}$ Ezk 22$_{12}$ 45$_{18}$ Ho 14$_{3}$ Am 5$_{11}$ 6$_{13}$ Pr 20$_{16}$ 22$_{25}$ 27$_{13}$ Ne 10$_{32}$ 11QT 2$_{9}$, Judah Jr 17$_{23}$, Koa Ezk

23$_{25.26.29}$, Pekod Ezk 23$_{25.26.29}$, Philistines 1 S 5$_{1.2.3}$ 6$_{7.8}$ 7$_{14}$, Reuben(ites) Jos 13$_{8}$ 18$_{7}$, Sabaeans Jb 1$_{15}$, Shoa Ezk 23$_{25.26.29}$, Temanite Jb 42$_{8}$, עַם *people* Ex 5$_{11}$ Jos 4$_{20}$ Jg 20$_{10}$ 1 S 14$_{32}$ 15$_{21}$ 2 K 14$_{21}$||2 C 26$_{1}$ 2 K 23$_{30}$||2 C 36$_{1}$ Is 14$_{2}$ Ezk 33$_{2}$, גּוֹי *nation* Jr 7$_{28}$, עֵדָה *congregation* Ex 12$_{3.5}$ 35$_{5}$ Nm 16$_{6.17}$ Jg 7$_{8}$ (unless em; see above), קָהָל *assembly* Ex 12$_{7}$, מִקְוֶה *collection*, i.e. company 1 K 10$_{28}$ ||2 C 1$_{16}$ (or em. וּמִקְוֵה [2 C וּמִקְוֵא] *and the company of* merchants, to וּמִקּוֹא *and from Kue*), חַיִל *army* Jr 39$_{5}$, מַטֶּה *tribe* Nm 34$_{14.15}$ Jos 18$_{7}$, בַּיִת *house* Ex 12$_{4}$, of Israel Ezk 36$_{30}$, Jerusalem/Zion Is 40$_{2}$ Ezk 16$_{16.17.18.20}$ 11QPs^{a} 22$_{13}$, Sidon Jl 4$_{5}$, Tyre Jl 4$_{5}$, עִיר *city* Ezk 22$_{12}$ Zp 3$_{2.7}$, אֲדָמָה *ground* Gn 4$_{11}$, גְּלִילָה *district* Jl 4$_{5}$.

יָד *hand* Am 9$_{2}$ Si 4$_{31(A)}$, אֹזֶן *ear* Jr 9$_{19}$ Jb 4$_{12}$, לֵב *heart* Jb 15$_{12}$ (מַה־יִּקָּחֲךָ לִבֶּךָ appar. *what has taken from you your mind?* unless *why has your heart emboldened you?*, i.e. יקח pi.),* רוּחַ *spirit* Ezk 3$_{14}$, לְבִיָּא *lion* (fem.) Ezk 19$_{2}$, נֶשֶׁר *eagle* Dt 32$_{11}$ Ezk 17$_{3.5.5}$ (or del.) 4QDibHam^{a} 6$_{8}$, שׁוֹט *scourge* Is 28$_{19}$, חֶרֶב *sword* Ezk 33$_{4.6}$, הֶבֶל *breath* Is 57$_{13}$, יַיִן *wine* Ho 4$_{11}$, תִּירוֹשׁ *new wine* Ho 4$_{11}$, מִסְפֵּד *mourning* Mc 1$_{11}$, אֹפֶל *darkness* Jb 3$_{6}$, בֶּצַע *extortion* Pr 1$_{19}$, אֶחָד *one* Gn 42$_{16}$ 1 S 26$_{22}$ 2 K 6$_{7}$ Is 6$_{6}$, חֲצִי *half* tribe of Manasseh Nm 34$_{14.15}$ Jos 18$_{7}$, רַב pl. *many* Ps 31$_{14}$, אַחֵר *another (one)* Ps 109$_{8}$, אֲשֶׁר *one who* 2 K 10$_{6.7}$ Ne 5$_{2.3}$ 4QD^{e} 7.1$_{11}$ ([אשר יקח]) 7.1$_{12}$ ([אשר]), כֹּל *all* Jos 11$_{19}$, מִי *who?* Dt 30$_{12.13}$; subj. not specified, Dt 27$_{25}$ Jg 14$_{11}$ 2 S 23$_{6}$ 1 K 3$_{24}$ 22$_{26}$||2 C 18$_{25}$ 2 K 20$_{7.7}$ 49$_{29}$ 51$_{26}$ Ezk 15$_{3}$ 30$_{4}$ Am 5$_{12}$ Jb 40$_{24}$ Pr 1$_{3}$ 22$_{27}$ (or em. יִקַּח *he will take* to יֻקַּח *it will be taken*, i.e. ho.) 24$_{32}$ Si 14$_{9}$ 4Q416 2.3$_{4}$ (לקח[תי]) 2.3$_{5}$ 4Q417 1.1$_{18}$ 4Q418 81$_{11}$ 4Q424 1$_{4.8}$.

<OBJ> אֱלֹהִים *god* Jg 18$_{24}$, Dagon 1 S 5$_{3}$, פֶּסֶל *graven image* Jg 18$_{17.18.20}$, מַסֵּכָה *molten image* Jg 18$_{17.18}$, תְּרָפִים *teraphim* Gn 31$_{34}$ Jg 18$_{17.18.20}$ 1 S 19$_{13}$, Aaron Lv 8$_{2}$ 20$_{25}$, Abiram Nm 16$_{1}$ (if em. וְדָתָן to דָּתָן), Abra(ha)m Gn 11$_{31}$ 24$_{7}$ Jos 24$_{3}$, Absalom 2 S 18$_{17}$, Achan Jos 7$_{24}$, Amos Am 7$_{15}$, Armoni 2 S 21$_{8}$, Azariah 2 K 14$_{21}$, Balaam Nm 22$_{41}$ 23$_{11.14.27.28}$, Baruch Jr 36$_{26}$, Ben-hadad 1 K 20$_{33}$, Benjamin Gn 42$_{36}$ 43$_{15}$, Dathan Nm 16$_{1}$ (if em. וְדָתָן to דָּתָן), David 1 S 17$_{31.57}$ 18$_{2}$ 19$_{14.20}$ 2 S 7$_{8}$||1 C 17$_{7}$ 2 S 22$_{17}$||Ps 18$_{17}$ Ps 78$_{70}$ 11QPs^{a} 28$_{10}$, Dinah Gn 34$_{26}$, Eleazar Nm 20$_{25}$, Elisha 2 K 6$_{13}$, Elishaphat 2 C 23$_{1}$, Enoch Gn 5$_{24}$, Ephraim Gn 48$_{13}$, Esther Est 2$_{7.15}$, Ezekiel Ezk 3$_{14}$ 8$_{3}$, Hadassah Est 2$_{7}$, Hagar Gn 16$_{3}$, Hiram 1 K 7$_{13}$, Hodaviah Lachish ost. 3$_{18}$, Isaac Gn 22$_{3}$ 4QpsJub^{a} 2.1$_{11}$, Ish-bosheth 2 S 2$_{8}$, Ishmael Gn 17$_{23}$, Jaazaniah Jr 35$_{3}$, Jacob Gn 27$_{45}$, Jehoahaz 2 K 23$_{30.34}$ ||2 C 36$_{1.4}$, Jehoiachin 2 K 24$_{12}$, Jephthah Jg 11$_{5}$, Jeremiah Jr 15$_{15}$ 37$_{17}$ 38$_{6.14}$ 39$_{12.14}$ 40$_{1}$, Jeroboam 1 K 11$_{37}$, Joash 2 K 11$_{2}$||2 C 22$_{11}$, Job Jb 3$_{6}$ 15$_{12}$, Joseph Gn 37$_{24}$ 39$_{20}$, Joshua Nm 27$_{18.22}$, Leah Gn 29$_{23}$, Lot Gn 11$_{31}$ 14$_{12}$, Maaseiah 2 C 23$_{1}$, Manasseh Gn 48$_{1.13}$, Mephibosheth 2 S 21$_{8}$, Micaiah 1 K 22$_{26}$||2 C 18$_{25}$, Michal 2 S 3$_{15}$, Nebuchadrezzar Jr 43$_{10}$, On Nm 16$_{1}$ (if em. וְדָתָן to דָּתָן), Rebekah Gn 24$_{61}$, Sarai Gn 11$_{31}$ 12$_{5}$, Saul 1 S 9$_{22}$ 10$_{23}$, Semachiah Lachish ost. 4$_{6}$, Seraiah 2 K 25$_{18.20}$||Jr 52$_{24.26}$, Simeon Gn 42$_{24}$, Uzziah 2 C 26$_{1}$, Zedekiah Jr 39$_{5}$, Zephaniah 2 K 25$_{18.20}$||Jr 52$_{24.26}$, Zerubbabel Hg 2$_{23}$, Zilpah Gn 30$_{9}$, Zipporah Ex 18$_{2}$.

אִישׁ *man* Gn 7$_{2}$ 43$_{18}$ 47$_{2}$ Ex 21$_{14}$ Nm 1$_{17}$ 11$_{16}$ 16$_{1}$ (or em. יקח hi. *be insolent*) 27$_{18}$ Dt 1$_{15.23}$ 19$_{12}$ 22$_{18}$=11QT 65$_{13}$ Jos 2$_{4}$ 3$_{12}$ 4$_{2}$ 8$_{12}$ Jg 4$_{6}$ 6$_{27}$ 20$_{10}$ 1 S 24$_{3}$ 1 K 11$_{18}$ 2 K 3$_{26}$ 11$_{9}$||2 C 23$_{8}$ 2 K 25$_{19.20}$||Jr 52$_{25.26}$ Jr 38$_{10.11}$ 41$_{12.16}$ Ezk 33$_{2}$ Ru 4$_{2}$ Lachish ost. 3$_{18}$, גֶּבֶר *man* Jr 41$_{16}$, אִשָּׁה *woman, wife* Gn 7$_{2}$ 19$_{15}$ 32$_{23.24}$ 36$_{6}$ Ex 4$_{20}$ 18$_{2}$ Dt 22$_{15}$=11QT 65$_{9}$ (unless obj. בָּתוּל *[token of] virginity*) Jg 15$_{6}$ 19$_{28}$ 2 S 3$_{15}$ 12$_{11}$ 14$_{2}$ 20$_{3}$ Jr 41$_{12}$ 43$_{5}$, פִּילֶגֶשׁ *secondary wife* Jg 19$_{28}$ 20$_{3}$, אָדָם *human being* Gn 2$_{15}$, אָב *father* Gn 45$_{18}$ Jos 24$_{3}$, אֵם *mother* Dt 22$_{6}$=11QT 65$_{4}$, בֵּן *son* Gn 11$_{31}$ 12$_{5}$ 14$_{12}$ 17$_{23}$ 18$_{7.8}$ 22$_{2.3}$ 36$_{6}$ 48$_{1.9}$ Ex 4$_{20}$ 18$_{2}$ Lv 8$_{2}$ 9$_{2.3}$ 12$_{8}$ 15$_{14.29}$ Nm 8$_{8.8}$ 20$_{25}$ 27$_{18}$ Dt 22$_{7}$=11QT 65$_{5}$ Jos 7$_{24}$ 1 S 8$_{11}$ 14$_{32}$ 20$_{31}$ 2 S 2$_{8}$ 9$_{5}$ 21$_{8}$ 1 K 3$_{20}$ 17$_{19}$ 2 K 3$_{27}$ 10$_{7}$ 11$_{2}$||2 C 22$_{11}$ 2 K 14$_{14}$ 23$_{30}$||2 C 36$_{1}$ Jr 3$_{14}$ 35$_{3}$ Ezk 16$_{20}$ 23$_{10.25}$ 24$_{25}$ 45$_{18}$ Hg 2$_{23}$ Pr 6$_{25}$ 2 C 23$_{1}$ 4QpsJub^{a} 2.1$_{11}$ 4QapMos^{a} 1.2$_{3}$ ([בן]) Lachish ost. 3$_{18}$, of Israel Ex 6$_{7}$ 14$_{11}$ Ezk 37$_{21}$, בַּת *daughter* Gn 19$_{15}$ 29$_{23}$ 34$_{17}$ 36$_{6}$ Lv 14$_{10}$ Jos 7$_{24}$ 1 S 8$_{13}$ Jr 43$_{5}$ Ezk 16$_{20}$ 23$_{10.25}$ 24$_{25}$ Est 2$_{7.15}$, i.e. village 1 C 2$_{23}$ 18$_{1}$, כַּלָּה *daughter-in-law* Gn 11$_{31}$, אָח *brother* Gn 31$_{23}$ 42$_{16}$ 43$_{13}$ Nm 18$_{6}$ Jr 35$_{3}$, יֶלֶד *child* Gn 32$_{23.24}$ Ex 2$_{9}$ 1 K 17$_{23}$ 2 K 4$_{1}$ Ru 4$_{16}$, טַף *children* Jr 41$_{12}$ 43$_{5}$, בָּחוּר *youth* 1 S 8$_{16}$, נַעַר *lad* Gn 22$_{3}$ 1 S 9$_{22}$ 16$_{11}$, נַעֲרָה *young woman* Est 2$_{7}$, בְּכוֹר *firstborn* Nm 8$_{16}$ 2 K 3$_{27}$, פִּטְרָה *that which first opens* womb Nm 8$_{16}$, יָלִיד *one born* Gn 17$_{23}$, יָחִיד *only one* Gn 22$_{2}$ 4QpsJub^{a} 2.1$_{11}$.

מֶלֶךְ *king* 2 K 24$_{12}$ Jr 43$_{10}$ Ezk 17$_{12}$ Ho 13$_{11}$, אָדוֹן *lord*

1 K 2$_{3.5}$, נָשִׂיא *prince* Nm 34$_{18}$, שַׂר *commander* 2 K 11$_{4.19}$ ||2 C 23$_{1.20}$ 2 K 25$_{19.20}$ Ezk 17$_{12}$, שָׁלִישׁ *officer* Ex 14$_{7}$, אַדִּיר *noble* 2 C 23$_{20}$, מֹשֵׁל *ruler* Jr 33$_{26}$ 2 C 23$_{20}$, רָץ *runner*, i.e. guard 2 K 11$_{19}$, גִּבּוֹר *warrior* Jr 41$_{16(mss)}$ 43$_{5(mss)}$, שֹׁמֵר *keeper* 2 K 25$_{18.20}$||Jr 52$_{24.26}$, עֶבֶד *servant* Gn 20$_{14}$ 1 S 8$_{16}$ 2 S 7$_{8}$||1 C 17$_{7}$ 2 S 10$_{4}$||1 C 19$_{4}$ 2 S 20$_{6}$ 1 K 1$_{33}$ 2 K 5$_{26}$ Jr 43$_{10}$ Hg 2$_{23}$ Ps 78$_{70}$, שִׁפְחָה *female servant* Gn 16$_{3}$ 20$_{14}$ 30$_{9}$ 32$_{23.24}$ 1 S 8$_{16}$ 2 K 5$_{26}$, סָרִיס *eunuch* 2 K 25$_{19}$||Jr 52$_{25}$ 41$_{16}$, מִקְנָה *purchase*, i.e. one purchased Gn 17$_{23}$, קִנְיָן *acquisition*, i.e. thing acquired Gn 36$_{6}$, זָקֵן *elder* Jg 8$_{16}$, כֹּהֵן *priest* Jg 18$_{24.27}$ 2 K 25$_{18.20}$||Jr 52$_{24.26}$, לֵוִי *Levite* Nm 3$_{12.41.45}$ 8$_{6.18}$ 18$_{6}$, נָבִיא *prophet* 1 K 18$_{4}$ 2 K 6$_{13}$ Jr 36$_{26}$ 38$_{14}$, psalmist Ps 49$_{16}$ 73$_{24}$, מְנַגֵּן *minstrel* 2 K 3$_{15}$, סֹפֵר *secretary* 2 K 25$_{19.20}$||Jr 52$_{25.26}$ Jr 36$_{26}$, רַכָּב *rider* 2 K 9$_{17}$, רֶכֶב appar. *rider* 2 K 7$_{14}$, שׁמע ptc. *one who hears* Ezk 33$_{4}$, זָכָר *male* Gn 17$_{23}$, רשׁע hi. ptc. *wicked one* Jg 14$_{11}$.

Ephraim Ho 11$_{3}$, Israel(ites) Dt 4$_{20}$ 30$_{4}$ Jos 7$_{24}$ 2 K 18$_{32}$||Is 36$_{17}$ Is 14$_{2}$ 28$_{19}$ Am 9$_{2.3}$, Judah 2 C 16$_{6}$, מִצְרִי *Egyptian* Gn 16$_{3}$ 1 S 30$_{11}$, עַם *people* Ex 14$_{6}$ Jos 8$_{1}$ Jg 9$_{43}$ 2 K 11$_{19}$, בַּיִת *house(hold)* Gn 45$_{18}$ Jr 35$_{3}$, of Israel Ezk 36$_{24}$, Carites 2 K 11$_{19}$, מִשְׁפָּחָה *family* Jr 25$_{9}$, שֵׁבֶט *tribe* Ezk 37$_{19}$, מַמְלָכָה *kingdom* Dt 3$_{4}$ 1 K 11$_{34}$, מְלוּכָה *kingdom* 1 K 11$_{35}$, גּוֹי *nation* Dt 4$_{34}$, שְׁאֵרִית *remainder* Jr 41$_{16}$ 43$_{5}$ 44$_{12}$, תּוֹלֵדָה *generation* 4Q418 77$_{2}$, Abel-beth-maacah 2 K 15$_{29}$, Gath 1 C 18$_{1}$, Havvoth-jair 1 C 2$_{23}$, Hazor 2 K 15$_{29}$, Ijon 2 K 15$_{29}$, Janoah 2 K 15$_{29}$, Karnaim Am 6$_{13}$, Kedesh 2 K 15$_{29}$, Kenath 1 C 2$_{23}$, Metheg-ammah 2 S 8$_{1}$, Ramoth-gilead 1 K 22$_{3}$, עִיר *city* Nm 21$_{25}$ Dt 3$_{4}$ 1 S 7$_{14}$ 1 K 20$_{34}$ 2 K 13$_{25.25}$ 1 C 2$_{23}$, חֶבֶל *territory* Dt 3$_{4.14}$, Galilee 2 K 15$_{29}$, Gilead 2 K 15$_{29}$, אֶרֶץ *land* Nm 21$_{26}$ Dt 3$_{8}$ 29$_{7}$ Jos 11$_{16.23}$ Jg 11$_{13.15}$ 2 K 15$_{29}$, הַר *hill-country* Jos 11$_{16}$, נֶגֶב *Negeb* Jos 11$_{16}$, שְׁפֵלָה *lowland* Jos 11$_{16}$, עֲרָבָה *plain* Jos 11$_{16}$.

עֶצֶם *bone* Ex 13$_{19}$ 1 S 31$_{13}$ 2 S 21$_{12}$ 2 K 23$_{16}$, צֵלָע *rib* Gn 2$_{22}$, לְחִי *jawbone* Jg 15$_{15}$, קֶרֶן *horn* 1 S 16$_{13}$ 1 K 1$_{39}$, רֹאשׁ *head* 1 S 17$_{54}$ 2 S 4$_{7.12}$ 2 K 10$_{6}$, i.e. best one Ex 30$_{23}$, i.e. chief Nm 25$_{4}$ (or em. רָאשֵׁי הָעָם *the chiefs of the people* to רִשְׁעֵי הָעָם *the wicked ones of the people* or הָרְשָׁעִים *the wicked ones*) Dt 1$_{15}$, לָשׁוֹן *tongue* Jr 23$_{31}$ (or em.; see Subj.), i.e. bar, of gold Jos 7$_{21.23.24}$, שְׁכֶם *shoulder* Gn 48$_{22}$, זְרוֹעַ *shoulder* Nm 6$_{19}$, חָזֶה *breast* Ex 29$_{26}$ Lv 7$_{34}$ 8$_{29}$, שׁוֹק *thigh* Ex 29$_{22.25}$ Lv 7$_{34}$ 8$_{25}$, דָּם *blood* Gn 4$_{11}$ Ex 24$_{6.8}$ 29$_{16}$ Lv 8$_{15}$, בָּשָׂר *flesh* Jg 6$_{20}$ 1 S 2$_{15}$, כִּלְיָה *kidney* Ex 29$_{13.22.25}$ Lv 8$_{16.25.28}$, אַלְיָה *fat tail* Ex 29$_{22.25}$ Lv 8$_{25.28}$, יֹתֶרֶת *appendage* Ex 29$_{13.22.25}$ Lv 8$_{16.25.28}$, שֵׂעָר *hair* Nm 6$_{18}$, לֵב *heart*, i.e. mind Ho 4$_{11}$, נֶפֶשׁ *soul*, i.e. person Gn 12$_{5}$ 36$_{6}$ Jr 43$_{5}$ Ezk 33$_{6}$, i.e. life 1 S 24$_{12}$ 1 K 19$_{4.10}$ Jon 4$_{3}$ Ps 31$_{14}$ Pr 1$_{19}$ 11$_{30}$ (or em.; see Subj.), נְשָׁמָה *breath*, i.e. life Si 9$_{13}$, רוּחַ *spirit* Ps 51$_{13}$, גְּוִיָּה *body* 1 S 31$_{12}$.

בָּקָר *cattle* Gn 20$_{14}$ 21$_{27}$ 34$_{28}$ Ex 12$_{32}$ Nm 7$_{6}$ 1 S 14$_{32}$ 15$_{21}$ 27$_{9}$ 30$_{20}$ 2 K 5$_{26}$ Jb 1$_{15}$ 11QT 43$_{14}$, מִקְנֶה *cattle* Gn 36$_{6}$ 46$_{6}$ Ezk 38$_{13}$ 1 C 7$_{21}$, פַּר *bull* Ex 29$_{1}$ Lv 8$_{2}$ Nm 8$_{8.8}$ Jg 6$_{25.26}$ 1 K 18$_{26}$ Ezk 43$_{21}$ 45$_{18}$ Ps 50$_{9}$ Jb 42$_{8}$ 4QapMos[a] 1.2$_{3}$ ([פר]), עֵגֶל *calf* Ex 32$_{20}$ Lv 9$_{2.3}$ Dt 9$_{21}$, עֶגְלָה *heifer* Gn 15$_{9}$ Dt 21$_{3}$ 1 S 16$_{2}$, פָּרָה *heifer* Nm 19$_{2}$ 1 S 6$_{10}$ MurEp Beth-Mashiko$_{3}$ 11QT 16$_{14}$, שׁוֹר *ox* Jos 7$_{24}$ 1 S 12$_{3}$, צֶמֶד *yoke* of oxen 1 S 11$_{7}$ 1 K 19$_{21}$, צֹאן *sheep* Gn 20$_{14}$ 21$_{27}$ 34$_{28}$ Ex 12$_{21.32}$ Jos 7$_{24}$ 1 S 14$_{32}$ 15$_{21}$ 25$_{18}$ 27$_{9}$ 30$_{20}$ 2 K 5$_{26}$ Jr 49$_{29}$ 11QT 43$_{14}$, שֶׂה *sheep* Ex 12$_{3}$, כֶּבֶשׂ *sheep* Lv 9$_{3}$ 14$_{10.12.24}$, אַיִל *ram* Gn 15$_{9}$ 22$_{13}$ Ex 29$_{1.15.19.31}$ Lv 8$_{2}$ 9$_{2}$ 16$_{5}$ Jb 42$_{8}$ 4QapMos[a] 1.2$_{3}$ ([איל]), *leader* Ezk 17$_{13}$, כִּבְשָׂה *ewe* Gn 21$_{30}$ Lv 14$_{10}$ 2 S 12$_{4}$, טָלֶה *lamb* 1 S 7$_{9}$, עַתּוּד *he-goat* Ps 50$_{9}$, שָׂעִיר *he-goat* Lv 9$_{3.15}$ 16$_{5.7}$ (1QDM 3$_{12}$ [י]קחו [הכוהנים ... השעירים]) 4QapMos[a] 1.2$_{6}$ ([יק[ח]ן), עֵז *she-goat* Gn 15$_{9}$, גְּדִי *kid* Gn 27$_{9}$ Jg 13$_{19}$, סוּס *horse* Est 6$_{10.11}$, חֲמוֹר *ass* Gn 34$_{28}$ 43$_{18}$ Jos 7$_{24}$ 1 S 8$_{16}$ 12$_{3}$ 16$_{20}$ 27$_{9}$, אָתוֹן *she-ass* Jb 1$_{15}$, גָּמָל *camel* Gn 24$_{10}$ 1 S 27$_{9}$ Jb 1$_{17}$, יוֹנָה *dove* Gn 8$_{9}$, תֹּר *turtledove* Gn 15$_{9}$ Lv 12$_{8}$ 15$_{14.29}$, גּוֹזָל *fledgling* Gn 15$_{9}$ Dt 32$_{11}$ 4QDibHam[a] 6$_{8}$ ([גוזליו]), צִפּוֹר *bird* Lv 14$_{4.6.51}$, בְּהֵמָה *beast* Gn 36$_{6}$ Nm 3$_{41.45}$, בְּהֵמוֹת *Behemoth* Jb 40$_{24}$, לִוְיָתָן *Leviathan* Jb 40$_{28}$.

בֶּגֶד *garment* Gn 27$_{15}$ Ex 29$_{5}$ Lv 8$_{2}$ Nm 4$_{9}$ 1 S 27$_{9}$ 2 K 5$_{26}$ 9$_{13}$ Ezk 16$_{18}$ Pr 20$_{16}$ 27$_{13}$ CD 11$_{3}$ Meṣad Ḥashavyahu ost. 1$_{8.9}$, שִׂמְלָה *garment* Gn 9$_{23}$, לְבוּשׁ *garment* Est 6$_{10.11}$, אַדֶּרֶת *cloak* Jos 7$_{21.23.24}$ 2 K 2$_{8.14}$, כְּתֹנֶת *robe* Gn 37$_{31}$ 2 S 13$_{19}$, אֵפוֹד *ephod* Jg 18$_{17.18.20}$, אֵזוֹר *girdle* Jr 13$_{4.6.7}$, שַׂק *sack* Jos 9$_{4}$ 2 S 21$_{10}$, בְּלוֹי *rag* Jr 38$_{11}$, קֶרַע *torn piece of cloth)* 1 K 11$_{31}$, חֲלִיפָה *change* of clothing 2 K 5$_{5}$, אַרְגָּמָן *purple (material)* Ex 28$_{5}$, תּוֹלֵעָה *scarlet (material)* Ex 28$_{5}$, שָׁנִי *scarlet (material)* Gn 38$_{28}$ Lv 14$_{4.6.51}$ Nm 19$_{6}$, תְּכֵלֶת *blue (material)* Ex 28$_{5}$, שֵׁשׁ *fine linen* Ex 28$_{5}$, מָסָךְ *cover* 2 S 17$_{19}$, מַכְבֵּר *cover* 2 K 8$_{15}$, יְרִיעָה *curtain* Jr 49$_{29}$, כּוֹס *purse* 4Q416 2.2$_{6}$, נֶזֶם *(nose) ring* Gn 24$_{22}$, צָמִיד

bracelet Gn 24$_{22}$, אֶצְעָדָה *bracelet* 2 S 1$_{10}$, שַׂהֲרֹון *crescent* Jg 8$_{21}$, צָעִיף *veil* Gn 24$_{65}$, נֵזֶר *crown* 2 S 1$_{10}$, עֲטָרָה *crown* 2 S 12$_{30}$||1 C 20$_{2}$, מַטֶּה *staff* Ex 4$_{17.20}$ 7$_{9.15.19}$ 17$_{5}$ Nm 17$_{17.24}$ 20$_{8.9}$, שֵׁבֶט *staff* 2 S 18$_{14}$, מִשְׁעֶנֶת *staff* 2 K 4$_{29}$, מַקֵּל *staff* Gn 30$_{37}$ 1 S 17$_{40}$ Zc 11$_{7.10}$.

עֵץ *wood* Gn 22$_{6}$ Lv 14$_{4.6.51}$ Nm 19$_{6}$ Ezk 37$_{16.16.19}$, כַּף *palm branch* Lv 23$_{40}$, עָנָף *bough* Lv 23$_{40}$, צַמֶּרֶת *top* of cedar Ezk 17$_{3}$, עֹמֶר *sheaf* Dt 24$_{19}$, קוֹץ *thorn* Jg 8$_{16}$ 2 S 23$_{6}$, בַּרְקָן *brier* Jg 8$_{16}$, עֲבֹת *cord* Jg 16$_{12}$, קוֹרָה *log* 2 K 6$_{2}$, אֶרֶז *cedar* Ezk 27$_{5}$, אַלּוֹן *oak* Is 44$_{14}$, תִּרְזָה *oak* Is 44$_{14}$, אֲגֻדָּה *bunch* of hyssop Ex 12$_{22}$, בֹּשֶׂם *spice* Ex 30$_{23}$, סַם *spice* Ex 30$_{34}$, צֳרִי *balm* Jr 46$_{11}$ 51$_{8}$, נָטָף *stacte* Ex 30$_{34}$, שְׁחֵלֶת *onycha* Ex 30$_{34}$, חֶלְבְּנָה *galbanum* Ex 30$_{34}$, לְבֹנָה *frankincense* Ex 30$_{34}$, קְטֹרֶת *incense* Lv 16$_{12}$, אֵזוֹב *hyssop* Lv 14$_{4.6.51}$ Nm 19$_{6.18}$, תֶּבֶן *straw* Ex 5$_{11}$.

אֶבֶן *stone* Gn 28$_{18}$ 31$_{45.46}$ (or em.; see Subj.) Ex 17$_{12}$ 28$_{9}$ Lv 14$_{42}$ Jos 4$_{20}$ 24$_{26}$ 1 S 7$_{12}$ 17$_{49}$ 1 K 18$_{31}$ Jr 43$_{9}$ 51$_{26}$, צֹר *flint* Ex 4$_{25}$, סֶלַע *rock* 4QSela 8.2$_{3}$ ([ויקח]), חֶרֶשׂ *potsherd* Jb 2$_{8}$, עָפָר *dust*, i.e. plaster Lv 14$_{42}$, אֵפֶר *ashes* 2 S 13$_{19}$, גַּחֶלֶת *coal* Lv 16$_{12}$, פִּיחַ *soot* Ex 9$_{8.10}$, זָהָב *gold* Ex 28$_{5}$ Nm 31$_{51.54}$ 1 K 9$_{28}$||2 C 8$_{18}$ 1 K 15$_{18}$ 2 K 5$_{5.26}$ 14$_{14}$ 16$_{8}$ 25$_{15}$||Jr 52$_{19}$ Jl 4$_{5}$ Zc 6$_{11}$, כֶּסֶף *money, silver* Gn 43$_{12.15}$ Ex 30$_{16}$ Nm 3$_{49.50}$ Jos 7$_{21.23.24}$ Jg 17$_{2.4}$ 1 K 15$_{18}$ 2 K 5$_{5.26}$ 12$_{8.9}$ 14$_{14}$ 16$_{8}$ 25$_{15}$||Jr 52$_{19}$ Jl 4$_{5}$ Zc 6$_{11}$ 11$_{13}$, נְחֹשֶׁת *bronze* 2 S 8$_{8}$||1 C 18$_{8}$, מַיִם *water* Ex 4$_{9}$ Nm 5$_{17}$ 1 S 25$_{11}$ 1 K 17$_{10}$, אֵשׁ *fire* Gn 22$_{6}$ Ezk 10$_{6.7}$, רִצְפָּה *burning coal* Is 6$_{6}$, רְכוּשׁ *possessions* Gn 12$_{5}$ 14$_{11.12.21}$ 46$_{6}$, קִנְיָן *property* Ezk 38$_{13}$, אוֹר *light* Jb 38$_{20}$, חֹשֶׁךְ *darkness* Jb 38$_{20}$.

לֶחֶם *bread* Gn 21$_{14}$ Ex 29$_{1}$ 2 S 10$_{4}$ 25$_{11.18}$ 1 K 14$_{3}$, מַצָּה *unleavened bread* Jg 6$_{20}$ 11QT 15$_{9}$ ([ויקחו מצה]), כִּכָּר *loaf* Ex 29$_{22.25}$, *talent* 1 K 9$_{28}$||2 C 8$_{18}$ 2 K 5$_{5.23}$, חַלָּה *cake* Ex 29$_{1}$ Lv 8$_{26.28}$ Nm 6$_{19}$ 11QT 15$_{9}$ ([ויקחו]), נִקֻּד *cake* 1 K 14$_{3}$, רָקִיק *wafer* Ex 29$_{1.22.25}$ Lv 8$_{26.28}$ Nm 6$_{19}$ 11QT 15$_{9}$ ([ויקחו] ... רקי[ק]), לְבִבָה *cake* 2 S 13$_{10}$, בָּצֵק *dough* 2 S 13$_{8}$, קֶמַח *flour* 1 S 28$_{24}$ 2 K 4$_{41}$ Arad ost. 12$_{1}$ ([קח]), סֹלֶת *fine flour* Lv 14$_{10.21}$ 24$_{5}$ Nm 8$_{8}$, קָלִי *parched grain* 1 S 17$_{17}$ 25$_{18}$, חִטָּה *wheat* 2 S 4$_{6}$ Ezk 4$_{9}$, שְׂעֹרָה *barley* Ezk 4$_{9}$, דֹּחַן *millet* Ezk 4$_{9}$, דָּגָן *grain* Ho 2$_{11}$ Ne 5$_{2.3}$ 11QT 43$_{14}$, שֶׁבֶר *grain* Ne 10$_{32}$, אֲלֻמָּה *sheaf* Jb 5$_{5}$ (if em.; see below), כֻּסֶּמֶת *spelt* Ezk 4$_{9}$, צִמּוּק *cluster of raisins* 1 S 25$_{18}$, דְּבֵלָה *fig cake* 1 S 25$_{18}$ 2 K 20$_{7}$, פּוֹל *beans* Ezk 4$_{9}$, עֲדָשָׁה *lentil* Ezk 4$_{9}$, חֶמְאָה *curd* Gn 18$_{8}$, חָלָב *milk* Gn 18$_{8}$, שֶׁמֶן *oil* Ex 27$_{20}$ 29$_{7}$ 40$_{9}$ Lv 8$_{2.10}$ 14$_{10.21.24}$ 24$_{2}$ Arad ost. 12$_{1}$ ([קח]) 17$_{3}$ 11QT 43$_{14}$, חֵלֶב *fat* Ex 29$_{13.22}$ Lv 8$_{16.25.28}$, יַיִן *wine* Is 56$_{12}$ 11QT 43$_{14}$, תִּירוֹשׁ *new wine* Ho 2$_{11}$.

קָצִיר *harvest* Jb 5$_{5}$ (unless em. וְאֶל־מִצִּנִּים יִקָּחֵהוּ appar. *and from out of thorns he takes it* to וַאֲלֻמִּים צְנֻמִים יִקַּח הוּא *and dried sheaves he takes*), אָכְלָה *food* Gn 14$_{11}$ 4QD^{e} 7.1$_{11}$ ([יקח]) 7.1$_{12}$, רַעֲבוֹן *(food for) famine* Gn 42$_{33}$, צֵדָה *provisions* Jg 7$_{8}$ (or em.; see Subj.) 20$_{10}$, פְּרִי *fruit* Lv 23$_{30}$, דּוּדָאִים *mandrakes* Gn 30$_{15}$, עֵנָב *grape* Gn 40$_{11}$, כֶּרֶם *vineyard* 1 S 8$_{14}$ 2 K 5$_{26}$, שָׂדֶה 1 S 8$_{14}$ Pr 31$_{16}$, זַיִת *olive grove* 1 S 8$_{14}$ 2 K 5$_{26}$, נָוֶה *pasture* 2 S 7$_{8}$, טִבְחָה *slaughter* 1 S 25$_{11}$, זֶבַח *sacrifice* Ex 18$_{12}$, עֹלָה *burnt offering* Ex 18$_{12}$ Jg 13$_{23}$, מִנְחָה *grain offering* Lv 10$_{12}$ 14$_{10}$ Nm 5$_{25}$ 8$_{8}$ Jg 13$_{19.23}$, תְּרוּמָה *contribution* Ex 25$_{2}$||35$_{5}$ 25$_{2.3}$ 36$_{3}$, מַעֲשֵׂר *tithe* Nm 18$_{26.28}$, אָשָׁם *guilt offering* Lv 14$_{21}$.

מַאֲכֶלֶת *knife* Gn 22$_{6.10}$ Jg 19$_{29}$, חֶרֶב *sword* Gn 34$_{25}$ Jg 3$_{21}$ 1 S 17$_{51}$ 21$_{9.10.10}$ 31$_{4}$||1 C 10$_{4}$ 1 K 3$_{24}$ Ezk 5$_{1.1}$, חֲנִית *spear* 1 S 26$_{11.12.22}$, רֹמַח *spear* Nm 25$_{7}$, קֶשֶׁת *bow* 2 K 13$_{15.15}$, חֵץ *arrow* 1 S 20$_{21}$ 2 K 13$_{15.15.18}$, קַרְדֹּם *axe* Jg 9$_{48}$, בַּרְזֶל *iron (axe)* 2 K 6$_{7}$, מַרְצֵעַ *awl* Dt 15$_{17}$, מָגֵן *shield* 1 K 14$_{26}$||2 C 12$_{9}$, שֶׁלֶט *shield* 2 S 8$_{7}$||1 C 18$_{7}$, יָתֵד *tent peg* Jg 4$_{21}$ Ezk 15$_{3}$, מוֹקֵשׁ *snare* Pr 22$_{25}$, רֵחַיִם *millstones* Is 47$_{2}$, חֵמֶת *skin bottle* Gn 21$_{14}$, נֵבֶל *skin bottle* 1 S 25$_{18}$, נֹאד *bottle* Jos 9$_{4}$, כּוֹס *cup* Is 51$_{22}$ Jr 25$_{15.17.28}$, קֻבַּעַת *cup* Is 51$_{22}$, בַּקְבֻּק *jar* 1 K 14$_{3}$, צְלֹחִית *jar* 2 K 2$_{20}$, צִנְצֶנֶת *jar* Ex 16$_{33}$, כַּד *jar* Jg 7$_{8}$ (if em.; see Subj.), צַפַּחַת *jar* 1 S 26$_{11.12}$, פַּךְ *vial* 1 S 10$_{1}$ 2 K 9$_{1.3}$, סַל *basket* Lv 8$_{2}$, טֶנֶא *basket* Dt 26$_{4}$, מִזְרָק *dish* 2 K 25$_{15}$||Jr 52$_{19}$ Jr 52$_{18}$, סַף *basin* Jr 52$_{19}$, מְנַקִּית *bowl* Jr 52$_{19}$, מַשְׂרֵת *pan* 2 S 13$_{9}$, כַּף *pan* 2 K 25$_{14}$||Jr 52$_{18}$ Jr 52$_{19}$, סִיר *pot* 2 K 25$_{14}$||Jr 52$_{18}$ Jr 52$_{19}$, כְּלִי *vessel* Nm 4$_{12}$ 31$_{51}$ 1 S 21$_{9}$ 2 K 14$_{14}$ 25$_{14}$||Jr 52$_{18}$ Jr 27$_{20}$ 28$_{3}$ 49$_{29}$ Ezk 16$_{17.39}$ 23$_{26}$ Zc 11$_{15}$ 4QpsEzek^{a} 16.1$_{5}$.

צְרוֹר *bag* of money Pr 7$_{20}$, שׁוֹפָר *ram's horn* Jg 7$_{8}$, כִּנּוֹר *lyre* 1 S 16$_{23}$ Is 23$_{16}$, תֹּף *timbrel* Ex 15$_{20}$, לַפִּיד *torch* Jg 15$_{4}$, מְנוֹרָה *lampstand* Jr 52$_{19}$, מַחְתָּה *censer* Lv 10$_{1}$ Nm 16$_{6.17.18}$ 17$_{4.11}$ 2 K 25$_{15}$||Jr 52$_{19}$, יָע *shovel* 2 K 25$_{14}$||Jr 52$_{18}$, מְזַמֶּרֶת *snuffer* 2 K 25$_{14}$||Jr 52$_{18}$, מַפְתֵּחַ *key* Jg 3$_{25}$, מִשְׁכָּב *bed* Pr 22$_{27}$ (or em.; see Subj.), מַצֵּבָה *pillar* 2 S 18$_{18}$, עַמּוּד *pillar* Jr 27$_{20}$, יָם *sea* Jr 27$_{20}$, מְכוֹנָה *stand* Jr 27$_{20}$, מוֹטָה *bar* of yoke Jr 28$_{10}$, לְבֵנָה *brick* Ezk 4$_{1}$, מַחֲבַת *plate* Ezk 4$_{3}$, מֹאזְנַיִם *scales* Ezk 5$_{1}$, רֶכֶב *chariot* Ex 14$_{7}$, עֲגָלָה *wagon* Gn 45$_{19}$ Nm 7$_{6}$ 1 S 6$_{7}$, אֲרוֹן *ark* 1 S 4$_{3}$ 5$_{1.2}$ 6$_{8}$

2 K 12$_{10}$, תֵּבָה *ark* Ex 2$_{3.5}$, אֹהֶל *tent* Ex 33$_{7}$ Jos 7$_{24}$ Jr 49$_{29}$.

בְּרָכָה *blessing* Gn 27$_{35.36}$ 33$_{11}$ Nm 23$_{20}$ (if em. בָּרֵךְ I received a command *to bless* to בְּרָכָה I received *a blessing*) 2 K 5$_{15}$, נֹעַם *pleasantness* Zc 11$_{10}$, הָדָר *glory* Mc 2$_{9}$, מָשׂוֹשׂ *joy* Ezk 24$_{25}$, רָצוֹן *acceptance* Ml 2$_{13}$, מָעוֹז *refuge* Ezk 24$_{25}$, קֹדֶשׁ *holiness* 2 K 12$_{19}$, מוּסָר *discipline* Jr 2$_{30}$ 5$_{3}$ 7$_{28}$ 17$_{23}$ 32$_{33}$ 35$_{13}$ Zp 3$_{2.7}$ Pr 1$_{3}$ 8$_{10}$ 24$_{32}$ Si 34$_{22}$ 35$_{14}$ 4Q469 2$_{2}$, טַעַם *taste*, i.e. discretion Jb 12$_{20}$, שֵׂכֶל *insight* Si 8$_{9}$ 16$_{24}$ 35$_{18(Bmg, E)}$, בִּינָה *understanding* 4Q418 177$_{4}$, חֹק *statute* 4Q424 1$_{4}$, מִשְׁפָּט *justice* 4Q418 228$_{3}$, perh. עָוֶל *injustice* 4QpsEzek^{a} 13.2$_{4}$, נָקָם *vengeance* Is 47$_{3}$, נְקָמָה *vengeance* Jr 20$_{10}$, בָּשְׁנָה *shame* Ho 10$_{6}$, חֶרְפָּה *shame* Ezk 36$_{30}$, קָלוֹן *dishonour* Pr 9$_{7}$, בְּכֹרָה *birthright* Gn 27$_{36}$, אָחֻז *selection* Nm 31$_{30.47}$, נַחֲלָה *inheritance* Nm 34$_{14.15}$ Jos 13$_{8}$ 18$_{7}$ 4Q417 1.1$_{18}$ 4Q418 81$_{11}$, חֵלֶק *portion* Gn 14$_{24}$ Si 14$_{9}$, פַּת *morsel* Gn 18$_{5}$ 1 K 17$_{11}$.

עֵדוּת *testimony* Ex 40$_{9}$, סֵפֶר *book* Ex 24$_{7}$ Dt 31$_{26}$ 2 K 19$_{14}$||Is 37$_{14}$ Jr 32$_{11.14}$, לוּחַ *tablet* Ex 34$_{4}$ Dt 9$_{9}$ 4QJub^{a} prologue ([ל]קחת לחות]), גִּלָּיוֹן *tablet* Is 8$_{1}$, מְגִלָּה *scroll* Jr 36$_{2.21.21.28.32}$, חָתוּם *sealed* deed Jr 32$_{11.14}$, גָּלוּי *opened (deed)* Jr 32$_{11.14}$ (if del. סֵפֶר), דָּבָר *word* Jr 9$_{19}$ Ho 14$_{3}$, אֹמֶר *word* Pr 2$_{1}$ 4$_{10}$, תְּפִלָּה *prayer* Ps 6$_{10}$, שֵׁמֶץ *whisper* Jb 4$_{12}$, דַּעַת *knowledge* Pr 21$_{11}$, תּוֹרָה *law* Jb 22$_{22}$, מִצְוָה *commandment* Dt 30$_{12.13}$ Pr 10$_{8}$ Si 35$_{18(Bmg, E)}$, לֶקַח *teaching* Si 35$_{14}$, חָזוֹן *vision* 11QPs^{a} 22$_{13}$.

מִנְחָה *present* Gn 33$_{10}$ 43$_{15}$ 2 K 8$_{8.9}$, בְּלוֹ *gift* Ne 5$_{15}$ (if em.; see Prep.), מַתָּנָה *gift* Ps 68$_{19}$, עֵרָבוֹן *pledge* Gn 38$_{20}$, שֹׁחַד *bribe* Ex 23$_{8}$ Dt 10$_{17}$ 16$_{19}$ 27$_{25}$ 1 S 8$_{3}$ Ezk 22$_{12}$ Ps 15$_{5}$ Pr 17$_{23}$ Si 35$_{18(B)}$ 11QT 51$_{12.17}$ 57$_{20}$, כֹּפֶר *ransom* Nm 35$_{31.32}$ 1 S 12$_{3}$ Am 5$_{12}$ 1QH 15$_{24}$, מַשְׂאֵת *exaction* Am 5$_{11}$, נֶשֶׁךְ *interest* Lv 25$_{36}$ Ezk 22$_{12}$, תַּרְבִּית *increase* Lv 25$_{36}$ Ezk 18$_{8.13.17}$ 22$_{12}$, בֶּצַע *gain* Jg 4$_{21}$, יְגִיעַ *gain* Jr 20$_{5}$ Ezk 23$_{29}$, הוֹן *wealth* 1QpHab 8$_{12}$ 4Q416 2.3$_{5}$ 4Q424 1$_{8}$, הָמוֹן *wealth* Ezk 30$_{4}$, חֹסֶן *wealth* Jr 20$_{5}$ Ezk 22$_{25}$, אוֹצָר *treasure* 1 K 14$_{26}$||2 C 12$_{9}$ 1 K 15$_{18}$ Jr 20$_{5}$, פְּקֻדָּה *store*, i.e. wealth Ps 109$_{8}$, יְקָר *precious object* Jr 20$_{5}$ Ezk 22$_{25}$, מַחְמָד *desirable thing* 1 K 20$_{6}$ Ezk 24$_{16.25}$, טוּב *good (thing)* 2 S 24$_{22}$ Ho 14$_{3}$, טוֹב *good (thing)* 2 K 8$_{9}$, מַקָּחָה *ware* Ne 10$_{32}$, שָׁלָל *spoil* Nm 31$_{11}$ 1 S 30$_{16}$, חֲלִיצָה *spoil* Jg 14$_{19}$ 2 S 2$_{21}$, מַלְקוֹחַ *booty* Nm 31$_{11}$.

מוֹעֵד *appointed time* Ps 75$_{3}$, עֲרֻבָּה *token* 1 S 17$_{18}$, עֹמֶר *omer* Ex 16$_{16}$, לֹג *log* Lv 14$_{10.21.24}$, אֵיפָה *ephah* 1 S 17$_{17}$, שֶׁקֶל *shekel* Nm 3$_{47}$ Jos 7$_{21.23}$, סְאָה *seah* 1 S 25$_{18}$, רֵאשִׁית *best (ones)* 1 S 15$_{21}$, מִבְחָר *choice (one)* Ezk 24$_{5}$, מַשָּׂא *load* 2 K 8$_{9}$ Ezk 24$_{25}$, עֶמְדָּה *standing place* Mc 1$_{11}$, מְלֹא *fullness* Ex 9$_{8}$ Lv 16$_{12}$, מִשְׁנֶה *double portion* Gn 43$_{15}$, כֶּפֶל *double* Is 40$_{2}$, חֲצִי *half* Ex 24$_{6}$, עִשָּׂרוֹן *tenth part* Lv 14$_{10.21}$, אֶחָד *one* Gn 2$_{21}$ Lv 12$_{8}$ Nm 31$_{30.47}$ 1 S 9$_{3}$ Jr 3$_{14}$ Ezk 19$_{5}$, שְׁנַיִם *two* Gn 7$_{2}$ 48$_{13}$ Jr 3$_{14}$, חָמֵשׁ *five* 2 K 7$_{13}$, שֶׁבַע *seven* Gn 7$_{2}$, שְׁלֹשִׁים *thirty* Zc 11$_{13}$, שְׁלִישִׁי *third (part)* Ezk 5$_{2}$, מְעַט *a little* Ezk 5$_{3}$ Si 40$_{6(Bmg)}$, מַה *what?* Jb 35$_{7}$, אֲשֶׁר *that which* Gn 34$_{28}$ Lv 9$_{5}$ Jg 18$_{27}$ 1 S 25$_{35}$ 2 K 5$_{20}$ 25$_{15}$||Jr 52$_{19}$, אַחֵר *another* Ex 21$_{10}$, זֶה *this* Gn 44$_{29}$, אֵלֶּה *these* Gn 15$_{10}$, כֹּל *everything, everyone* Gn 31$_{1}$ 1 S 2$_{14}$ 30$_{18.19}$ 2 S 19$_{31}$ 1 K 14$_{26}$||2 C 12$_{9}$ 2 K 24$_{7}$ Is 57$_{13}$ Ps 49$_{18}$, מְאוּם *anything* CD 16$_{14}$, מְאוּמָה *anything* 1 S 12$_{4}$ 2 K 5$_{20}$ 1QS 5$_{16}$ 11QT 2$_{9}$ ([מאומה]).

<PREP> לְ in ref. to subj., *to, for (oneself)* perh. 1QDM 1$_{21}$ ([לק]חו), + Y. Ex 6$_{7}$ Nm 3$_{41}$ 8$_{16}$ perh. 4QRitPur 48$_{6}$ ([לקח]תנו), אֱלֹהִים *god* Dt 4$_{34}$, Aaron Ex 9$_{8}$ Lv 9$_{2}$, Abram Gn 14$_{21}$ perh. 4QCommGenA 2$_{12}$, David 1 S 21$_{10}$ 1 C 21$_{23}$, Eliphaz Jb 42$_{8}$, Isaiah Is 8$_{1}$, Jacob Gn 30$_{37}$, Jeremiah Jr 36$_{2.28}$, Jeroboam 1 K 11$_{31}$, Job Jb 2$_{8}$, Korah Nm 16$_{6}$, Laban Gn 31$_{32}$, Mordecai Est 2$_{7.15}$, Moses Ex 9$_{8}$ 30$_{34}$ Nm 27$_{18}$, Noah Gn 6$_{21}$ 7$_{2}$, Zechariah Zc 11$_{7.15}$, בֵּן *son* Gn 6$_{2}$, בֶּן־אָדָם *son of man, mortal* Ezk 4$_{1.3.9}$ 5$_{1.1.1}$ 37$_{16.16}$ (if em. לְקַח *take* to קַח לְךָ *take for yourself*), אָח *brother* Gn 45$_{19}$, פַּרְעֹה *Pharaoh* Gn 12$_{19}$, אָדוֹן *lord* Ex 21$_{10}$, זָקֵן *elder* Ex 12$_{21}$, נַעַר *lad* 1 S 2$_{16}$, כֹּהֵן *priest* 2 K 12$_{6}$, קְדֵשָׁה *cult-prostitute* Gn 38$_{23}$, נֹשֶׁה *creditor* 2 K 4$_{1}$, רֵעַ *friend* Jb 42$_{8}$, זוב ptc. *one who has a discharge* Lv 15$_{14}$, יסר ptc. *one who disciplines* Pr 9$_{7}$, Amalekites 1 S 30$_{19}$, Israel(ites) Lv 23$_{40}$ Dt 7$_{25}$ 22$_{7}$=11QT 65$_{5}$ Am 6$_{13}$, עַם *people* Ex 5$_{11}$, עֵדָה *congregation* Ex 12$_{3}$ Nm 16$_{6}$.

לְ of benefit/direction, *to, for*, + Y. Gn 15$_{9.10}$ Ex 18$_{12}$, Elijah 1 K 17$_{10}$, Elisha 2 K 2$_{20}$ 3$_{15}$, Esau Gn 32$_{14}$, Isaac Gn 27$_{9}$, Rebekah Gn 27$_{13}$, אִשָּׁה *wife* Gn 45$_{19}$, אָח *brother* Gn 32$_{14}$ 1 S 17$_{17}$, טַף *children* Gn 45$_{19}$, מֶלֶךְ *king* 1 K 3$_{24}$, טהר htp. ptc. *one who is purified* Lv 14$_{4}$, טָמֵא *unclean one* Nm 19$_{17}$, Israel(ites) Dt 30$_{12.13}$, עַם *people* Jg 20$_{10}$, בַּיִת *house* Ex 12$_{3}$, נֶפֶשׁ *soul* Pr 22$_{25}$, חֲמוֹר *ass* Jos 9$_{4}$, מַכְאוֹב *pain* Jr 51$_{8}$, מַחְסוֹר *need* 4Q424 1$_{8}$, עוֹלָם *eternity* Mc 2$_{9}$.

לְ *as, for (the purpose of)*, + בַּת *daughter* Est 2$_{7.15}$, עֶבֶד *slave* Gn 43$_{18}$ 2 K 4$_{1}$ Jb 40$_{28}$, רַקָּחָה *female perfumer* 1 S

8$_{13}$, טַבָּחָה *female cook* 1 S 8$_{13}$, אֹפָה *female baker* 1 S 8$_{13}$, כֹּהֵן *priest* Is 66$_{21}$, לֵוִי *Levite* Is 66$_{21}$, עַם *people* Ex 6$_{7}$ 4QRitPur 48$_{6}$ ([לקח]תנו), חַטָּאת *sin offering* Lv 9$_{2.3}$ 12$_{8}$ 16$_{5}$ Nm 8$_{8}$, עֹלָה *burnt offering* Lv 9$_{2.3}$ 12$_{8}$ 16$_{5}$, מִנְחָה *grain offering* Lv 14$_{21}$, תְּנוּפָה *waving* Lv 14$_{21}$, פִּנָּה *corner* Jr 51$_{26}$, מוֹסָד *foundation* Jr 51$_{26}$.

לְ *according to*, + מִשְׁפָּחָה *family* Ex 12$_{21}$, בַּיִת *house(hold)* Nm 34$_{14}$, גֻּלְגֹּלֶת *skull*, i.e. person Ex 16$_{16}$ Nm 3$_{47}$, אֲשֶׁר *those who* Ex 16$_{16}$.

לְ *(in exchange) for*, + נֶפֶשׁ *soul*, i.e. life Nm 35$_{31.32}$, עֲלִילָה *deed* 1QH 15$_{24}$.

לְ *before*, + עַיִן *eye* 2 S 12$_{11}$.

לְ introducing object, + Azariah 2 C 23$_{1}$, Ishmael 2 C 23$_{1}$, Jeremiah Jr 40$_{2}$, בֵּן *son* 2 C 23$_{1}$.

בְּ of place, *in, among*, + אָדָם *human being* Ps 68$_{19}$, יָד *hand* Gn 22$_{6}$ 43$_{12.15}$ Ex 4$_{17.20}$ 7$_{15}$ 15$_{20}$ 17$_{5}$ 34$_{4}$ Nm 25$_{7}$ Dt 1$_{25}$ Jg 7$_{8}$ (or em.; see Subj.) 9$_{48}$ 1 S 16$_{2}$ 17$_{40}$ 21$_{9}$ 2 S 23$_{6}$ 1 K 14$_{3}$ 17$_{11}$ 2 K 4$_{29}$ 5$_{5}$ 8$_{8.9}$ 9$_{1}$ Jr 36$_{14.14}$ 38$_{10.11}$ 43$_{9}$ Pr 7$_{20}$, כַּף *hand* 2 S 18$_{14}$, יָמִין *right hand* Gn 48$_{13}$, שְׂמֹאל *left hand* Gn 48$_{13}$, לֵבָב *heart* Ezk 3$_{10}$, כְּלִי *vessel* Gn 43$_{11}$ Nm 5$_{17}$ 1 K 17$_{10}$, בְּרִית *covenant* 2 C 23$_{1}$.

בְּ of time, *on*, + יוֹם *day* Lv 15$_{14.29}$ 23$_{40}$ Ne 10$_{32}$, שַׁבָּת *sabbath* Ne 10$_{32}$, עֵת *time* Dt 3$_{8}$ Ho 2$_{11}$, מוֹעֵד *season* Ho 2$_{11}$, רִאשׁוֹן *first (month)* Ezk 45$_{18}$, אֶחָד *one*, i.e. first (day of month) Ezk 45$_{18}$.

בְּ of instrument, *by (means of), with*, + אֶצְבַּע *finger* Lv 4$_{25.30.34}$ Nm 19$_{4}$, יָד *hand* Dt 4$_{34}$, זְרוֹעַ *arm* Dt 4$_{34}$, עַיִן *eye* appar. Jb 40$_{24}$, עַפְעַף *eyelid* Pr 6$_{25}$, צִיצִת *lock* of hair Ezk 8$_{3}$, חֶרֶב *sword* Gn 48$_{22}$, קֶשֶׁת *bow* Gn 48$_{22}$, מַזְלֵג *fork* 1 S 2$_{15}$, מֶלְקָחַיִם *tongs* Is 6$_{6}$, מִלְחָמָה *war* Dt 4$_{34}$ Jos 11$_{19}$ 2 K 13$_{25}$, חָזְקָה *force* 1 S 2$_{16}$, מַסָּה *trial* Dt 4$_{34}$, אוֹת *sign* Dt 4$_{34}$, מוֹפֵת *wonder* Dt 4$_{34}$, מוֹרָא *terror* Dt 4$_{34}$, מַגֵּפָה *stroke* Ezk 24$_{16}$.

בְּ of accompaniment, *with, in*, + עֶבְרָה *wrath* Ho 13$_{11}$.

בְּ *according to*, + מִכְסָה *number* Ex 12$_{4}$, שֶׁקֶל *shekel* Nm 3$_{47.50}$.

בְּ *on account of, for*, + חַטָּאת *sin* Is 40$_{2}$, רָעָב *famine* Ne 5$_{3}$.

בְּ of price, *(in exchange) for*, + מְחִיר *price* 1 K 10$_{28}$||2 C 1$_{16}$, כֶּסֶף *money* 11QT 43$_{14}$.

בְּ partitive, *(some) of*, + לֶחֶם *bread* Ne 5$_{15}$ (or em. בְּלֶחֶם *some bread* to בְּלוֹ לֶחֶם *gift of bread* and wine), יַיִן *wine* Ne 5$_{15}$ (or em.; see above).

בְּ introducing object, + רָז *mystery* 4Q418 77$_{4}$.

כְּ *about*, + חָמֵשׁ *five* thousand men Jos 8$_{12}$.

כְּ *according to*, + מִסְפָּר *number* 1 K 18$_{31}$, כֹּל *all* Jos 11$_{23}$.

מִן of direction, time, *from, at* perh. 4QCreatA 1$_{9}$, + אֵל *God* 4Q417 1.1$_{18}$, שַׁדַּי *the Almighty* Jb 27$_{13}$, Abraham Gn 23$_{13}$, Heldai Zc 6$_{10}$, Jacob (son of Judah) MurEp Beth-Mashiko$_{3}$, Jonah Jon 4$_{3}$, אִישׁ *man* 1 S 2$_{15}$ 4QD^{e} 7.1$_{12}$ 4Q416 2.3$_{5}$, אָדָם *human being* Gn 2$_{22}$, דַּל *poor one* Am 5$_{11}$, psalmist Ps 51$_{13}$, Israel(ites) Mc 1$_{11}$, עַם *people* Ne 5$_{15}$ 10$_{32}$, בַּיִת *house* Gn 24$_{7}$ 34$_{26}$ 2 S 9$_{5}$ Ps 50$_{9}$, of Israel Ezk 24$_{25}$, מַטֶּה *tribe* Nm 34$_{18}$, אֶרֶץ *land* Gn 24$_{7}$ 45$_{19}$ Jg 11$_{5}$ 1 S 30$_{16}$, יְאֹר *Nile* Ex 4$_{9}$, יַרְדֵּן *Jordan* Jos 4$_{20}$, Berothai 2 S 8$_{8}$, Betah 2 S 8$_{8}$, Cun 1 C 18$_{8}$, Lebanon Ezk 27$_{5}$, Lo-debar 2 S 9$_{5}$, Kue 1 K 10$_{28}$||2 C 1$_{16}$ (if em. מִקְוֵה [2 C מִקְוֵא] appar. *company of* to מִקּוֹא *from Kue*), Paran 1 K 11$_{18}$, Shilo 1 S 4$_{3}$, Tibhath 1 C 18$_{8}$, Tyre 1 K 7$_{13}$, עִיר *city* 2 S 8$_{8}$ 2 K 25$_{19}$||Jr 52$_{25}$ Jr 3$_{14}$, יָד *hand* Gn 4$_{11}$ 21$_{30}$ 33$_{10}$ 38$_{20}$ 48$_{22}$ Ex 32$_{4}$ Nm 5$_{25}$ 21$_{26}$ Dt 3$_{8}$ 26$_{4}$ Jg 7$_{8}$ (if em.; see Subj.) 13$_{23}$ 1 S 10$_{4}$ 12$_{3.4}$ 25$_{35}$ 2 S 8$_{1}$||1 C 18$_{1}$ 1 K 11$_{34.35}$ 22$_{4}$ 2 K 5$_{20.24}$ 13$_{25.25}$ 19$_{14}$||Is 37$_{14}$ Is 40$_{2}$ 51$_{22}$ Jr 25$_{15.17.28}$ Ml 2$_{13}$ Jb 35$_{7}$ 4QpsEzek^{a} 13.2$_{4}$ 1QS 5$_{16}$ 4QD^{e} 4$_{7}$ 4QD^{f} 4.2$_{13}$ (=CD 16$_{14}$ מאת *from*) 4Q418 81$_{11}$ 97$_{2}$ 4QRedInk 3$_{4}$, חֵיק *bosom* 1 K 17$_{19}$ Pr 17$_{23}$, פֶּה *mouth* Jb 22$_{22}$, אַיִל *ram* Ex 29$_{22}$ Nm 6$_{19}$, סַל *basket* Lv 8$_{26}$ Nm 6$_{19}$, שָׁלָל *spoil* 1 S 15$_{21}$, אֹהֶל *tent* 1 K 1$_{39}$, לִשְׁכָּה *chamber* Jr 36$_{21}$, חָצֵר *court* Jr 39$_{14}$, מִכְלָה *enclosure* Ps 50$_{9}$ 78$_{70}$, נָוֶה *pasture* 2 S 7$_{8}$ ||1 C 17$_{7}$, קֶבֶר *grave* 2 K 23$_{16}$, קֵץ *end* Gn 16$_{3}$, דָּבָר *word* Jb 4$_{12}$, שְׁמִיעָה *tradition* Si 8$_{9}$, מַחֲצִית *half* Nm 31$_{29.30.47}$, מָקוֹם *place* Jr 13$_{7}$ 28$_{3}$, זֶה *this*, i.e. here Jr 38$_{10}$ Lachish ost. 3$_{18}$, שָׁם *there* Gn 27$_{9.45}$ Dt 19$_{12}$ 30$_{4}$ 1 S 10$_{23}$ 17$_{49}$ 2 S 14$_{2}$ 1 K 9$_{28}$||2 C 8$_{18}$ 2 K 6$_{2}$ Jr 13$_{6}$ 38$_{11}$ Ezk 5$_{3}$ Am 9$_{2}$ Arad ost. 17$_{3}$.

מִן partitive, *(some) of, from among*, + בֵּן *son* Jg 4$_{6}$ 2 K 20$_{18}$||Is 39$_{7}$, נַעַר *lad* 1 S 9$_{3}$, זָקֵן *elder* Ex 17$_{5}$, עֶבֶד *servant* Jg 6$_{27}$, זָקֵן *elder* Ru 4$_{2}$, Israel(ites) Dt 1$_{23}$ 1 S 24$_{3}$ Is 66$_{21}$, עַם *people* Jos 4$_{2}$ Ezk 33$_{6}$, גּוֹי *nation* Ezk 36$_{24}$, שֵׁבֶט *tribe* Jos 3$_{12}$ 4$_{2}$, זֶרַע *seed* Jr 33$_{26}$ Ezk 17$_{5.13}$, בְּהֵמָה *beast* Gn 7$_{2}$ 8$_{20}$, בָּקָר *cattle* 2 C 12$_{4}$, מִקְנֶה *cattle* Ex 10$_{26}$, צֹאן *sheep* 2 S 12$_{4}$, כֶּבֶשׂ *lamb* Ex 12$_{5}$, עֵז *she-goat* Ex 12$_{5}$, סוּס *horse* 2 K 7$_{13}$, עוֹף *birds* Gn 8$_{20}$, צֵלָע *rib* Gn 2$_{21}$, דָּם *blood* Ex 12$_{7}$

$29_{12.20.21}$ Lv $4_{5.25.30.34}$ $8_{23.30}$ $14_{14.25}$ $16_{14.18}$ Nm 19_4 Ezk 43_{20} 45_{19} 1QDM 4_2 (ל[קח] מן [דמו]), hair Ezk 5_4, שֶׁמֶן *oil* Ex 29_{21} Lv 8_{30} 14_{15}, פְּרִי *fruit* Gn 3_6 Nm 13_{20} Dt 1_{25}, רֵאשִׁית *first*, i.e. firstfruits Dt 26_2, זִמְרָה *choice produce* Gn 43_{11}, מַאֲכָל *food* Gn 6_{21}, צַיִד *provisions* Jos 9_{14}, זֶבַח *sacrifice* Lv 7_{34}, עֵץ *tree* Gn 3_{22} Ezk 15_3, אַלּוֹן *oak* Is 44_{15}, תִּרְזָה *oak* Is 44_{15}, אֹרֶן *laurel* Is 44_{15}, אֶרֶז *cedar* Is $44_{15(mss)}$, צַמֶּרֶת *top* of cedar Ezk 17_{22}, בֶּגֶד *garment* Ezk 16_{16}, חוּט *thread* Gn 14_{23}, שְׂרוֹךְ *sandal lace* Gn 14_{23}, חֵרֶם *devoted object* Jos 6_{18} $7_{1.11}$, סִיר *pot* Zc 14_{21}, אֶבֶן *stone* Gn 28_{11}, עָפָר *dust* Nm 5_{17} 19_{17}, מַיִם *water* Ex 4_9, לֹג *log* Lv 14_{15}, נַחֲלָה *inheritance* Ezk 46_{18}, בוא ptc. *that which comes* Gn 32_{14}, כֹּל *all* Gn 14_{23}.

מִן *against*, + Jeremiah Jr 20_{10}.

מֵאֵת *from*, + Jedaiah Zc 6_{10}, Naaman 2 K 5_{20}, Og Dt 3_4, Tobiah Zc 6_{10}, אִישׁ *man* Ex 25_3, אָב *father* 1 K 20_{34}, בֵּן *son* of Israel Lv 7_{34} 16_5 Nm 17_{24} $18_{26.28}$, אָח *brother* Gn 42_{24} Lv 25_{36}, בְּכוֹר *firstborn* Nm 3_{50}, מֶלֶךְ *king* Dt 3_4, בַּעַל *lord* 2 S 21_{12}, פָּקוּד *officer* Nm 31_{51}, שַׂר *commander* Nm $31_{51.54}$, נָשִׂיא *prince* Nm 7_5 17_{17}, רֹאשׁ *chief* Nm 7_5, עֶבֶד *servant* 2 K 5_{15}, מַכָּר *acquaintance* 2 K $12_{6.8}$, Aramaean 2 K 5_{20}, Israel(ite) 1 S 7_{14} CD 16_{14}, עַם *people* Dt 3_4 2 K 12_9, עֵדָה *congregation* Ex 35_5, גּוֹלָה *exiles* Zc 6_{10}, עדף ptc. *surplus one* Nm 34_9.

מֵעִם *from*, + Paltiel 2 S 3_{15}, אִישׁ *husband* 2 S 3_{15}, בֵּן *son* 2 S 3_{15}, פָּנִים *presence* Gn 44_{29}, מִזְבֵּחַ *altar* Ex 21_{14}.

מִקֶּרֶב *from among*, + גּוֹי *nation* Dt 4_{34}.

מֵעַל *from upon*, + עוֹלֵל *child* Mc 2_9, מִזְבֵּחַ *altar* Lv 16_{12} Is 6_6, רֹאשׁ *head* 2 S 12_{30}‖1 C 20_2 2 K $2_{3.5}$, צַוָּאר *neck* Jr 28_{10}, יָרֵךְ *thigh* Jg 3_{21}.

מֵאֵצֶל *from before*, + אִשָּׁה *woman* 1 K 3_{30}.

מִלִּפְנֵי *from before*, + Y. Lv 16_{12}, Moses Ex 36_3 Nm 20_9.

מִתַּחַת *from under* Pr 22_{27} (or em.; see Subj.).

אֶל־פְּנֵי *before*, + אֹהֶל *tent* Lv 9_5.

אֶל מִן *from out of*, + צֵן *thorn* Jb 5_5 (or em.; see Obj.).

מִקְצָה *from among*, + אָח *brother* Gn 47_2, עַם *people* Ezk 33_2.

מִתּוֹךְ *from among, from out of*, + בֵּן *son* of Israel Nm 3_{12} 8_6 18_6, אֹהֶל *tent* Jos 7_{23}.

מִבֵּין *from among*, + גּוֹי *nation* Ezk 37_{21}.

מֵעֵבֶר *from beyond*, + נָהָר *river* Jos 24_3.

מֵעֵבֶר לְ *beyond, on the opposite side of*, + Jordan Nm 34_{15} Jos 18_7.

מִבֵּינוֹת לְ *from between*, + גַּלְגַּל *wheel* Ezk 10_6, כְּרוּב *cherub* Ezk 10_6.

מֵאַחַר *from after*, + צֹאן *sheep* 2 S 7_8 11QPs[a] 28_{10}.

מֵאַחֲרֵי *from after*, + צֹאן *sheep* Am 7_{15} 1 C 17_7 (מִן־אַחֲרֵי).

אֶל *to*, + Israel (Jacob) Gn 48_9, Aaron Nm 19_2, David 1 S 30_{11}, Elisha 2 K 2_{20}, Moses Ex 27_{20} 24_2 Nm 19_2, Saul 1 S 20_{31}, Zedekiah Jr 38_{14}, מֶלֶךְ *king* Jr 38_{14}, Israel(ites) 2 S 4_3, אֹהֶל *tent* Nm 11_{16}, רֹאשׁ *head*, i.e. top Nm 23_{14}, אֶרֶץ *land* 2 K 18_{32}‖Is 36_{17}, גְּבוּל *border* Jb 38_{20}, מָבוֹא *entrance* Jr 38_{14}, מָקוֹם *place* Nm 23_{27}.

עַל *upon*, + אִישׁ *man* CD 11_3, רֹאשׁ *head* 2 S 13_{19}, זְרוֹעַ *arm* Ho 11_3, חֲמוֹר *ass* Jg 19_{28}.

עַל *beside*, + מַיִם *water* Ezk 17_5 (or del.).

עַל *for*, + יָד *hand* Gn 24_{22}.

עַל *against*, + נָקִי *innocent one* Ps 15_5.

עִם *with*, + Barak Jg 4_6, Benaiah 1 K 1_{33}, Hadad 1 K 11_{18}, Jehoida 2 C 23_1, Joseph Gn $47_{2(Sam)}$ 48_1, Joshua Jos 8_1, Laban Gn 31_{23}, Moses Ex 13_{19}, Nathan 1 K 1_{33}, Zadok 1 K 1_{33}, אִישׁ *man* 1 K 11_{18}, בֵּן *son* Jg 4_6 1 K 1_{33}, פַּרְעֹה *Pharaoh* Ex 14_6, כֹּהֵן *priest* 1 K 1_{33}, נָבִיא *prophet* 1 K 1_{33}, חֲצִי *half* tribe of Manasseh Jos 13_8, Israel(ites) Ho 14_3, עלם ni. ptc. *one who hides oneself* 4Q424 1_4.

אֵת *with*, + Aaron Lv 8_2, Moses Ex 17_5, Saul 1 S 9_3, בֵּן 1 S 9_3, of Israel 4QpsEzek[a] 16.1_5, מֶלֶךְ *king* 2 K 3_{26}, שַׂר *prince* 4QpsEzek[a] 16.1_5 ([השרים]), כֹּהֵן *priest* 4QpsEzek[a] 16.1_5.

תַּחַת *instead of*, + בְּכוֹר *firstborn* Nm $3_{12.41.45}$ 8_{18}.

<COLL> :: נתן *give* Gn 14_{21} Ho 13_{11} Jb 1_{21}; + נתן *give* Gn 3_6 15_{10} $18_{7.8}$ 20_{14} $21_{14.27}$ 23_{13} 30_9 38_{28} 39_{20} 48_{22} Ex 12_7 16_{33} $29_{12.20}$ 30_{16} 40_{20} Lv $4_{25.30.34}$ 7_{34} $8_{15.23}$ $14_{14.25}$ 15_{14} 16_{18} Nm 4_{12} 5_{17} $6_{18.19}$ $7_{5.6}$ 18_{28} Nm $31_{29.30.47}$ Dt 1_{15} 15_{17} 19_{12} 29_7 Jos 11_{23} Jg 14_{19} 15_6 17_4 1 S $2_{15.16}$ 6_8 8_{14} 10_4 25_{11} 2 S 12_{11} 20_3 1 K 11_{35} 15_{18} $17_{19.23}$ 18_{26} 19_{21} 2 K 12_{10} Jr 20_5 32_{14} 36_{32} 39_{14} Ezk $4_{1.3.9}$ 10_7 $16_{17.61}$ $17_{5.22}$ $18_{8.13}$ 33_2 43_{20} 45_{19} Jb 35_7 2 C 22_{11}.

‖ נשׂא *lift* Is 57_{13} Ezk 3_{14} 38_{13}; + נשׂא Dt 32_{11} Jr 49_{29} Ezk 8_3 38_{13}.

‖ לקט *gather* Gn 31_{46} (or em.; see Subj.); + לקט Ex 16_{16}.

‖ שׁמע *hear* Ezk 3_{10} Ps 6_{10}; + שׁמע Jr 9_{19} 17_{23} Si 16_{24}

34$_{22}$.

|| בזז *plunder* Jr 20$_{5}$.

|| שׁלל *spoil* Ezk 38$_{13}$.

+ גנב *steal* 2 K 11$_{2}$||2 C 22$_{11}$, סור hi. *remove* Jb 12$_{20}$, שׂים *place* Jb 22$_{22}$. שׂים לֵב *pay attention* Si 16$_{24}$, שׁית לֵב *pay attention* Pr 24$_{32}$, צפן *treasure* Pr 2$_{1}$.

+ adverb, עוֹד *again* Ezk 5$_{4}$ 36$_{30}$, אַחַר *afterwards* Ps 73$_{24}$, לָמָּה *why?* Pr 22$_{27}$ (or em.; see Subj.).

+ noun used adverbially, (1) take *to(wards), into*, שָׂדֶה *field* Nm 23$_{14}$, רֹאשׁ *head*, i.e. top Nm 23$_{28}$, כָּבוֹד *glory* Ps 73$_{24}$; (2) take *as*, תַּעַר *razor* Ezk 5$_{1}$; (3) הַיּוֹם *today* 2 K 2$_{3.5}$ 4QparaKings 9$_{5}$.

With inf. of another verb in purpose clause (e.g. לְקַחְתָּנוּ לָמוּת *you took us away to die* Ex 14$_{11}$), היה *be* 2 S 7$_{8}$||1 C 17$_{7}$, עשׂה *make* Ezk 27$_{5}$, עבד *serve* Ex 10$_{26}$, מות *die* Ex 14$_{11}$ 21$_{14}$, שׁפך *shed* blood Ezk 22$_{12}$, דרג htp. *scrape* Jb 2$_{8}$, נטה hi. *turn aside* justice Pr 17$_{23}$, נכה hi. *strike* Dt 27$_{25}$, קבב *curse* Nm 23$_{11}$, נחל *divide for inheritance* Nm 34$_{18}$.

1b. ptc. used as noun, **purchaser,** <CSTR> [רשי] הלוקח *right of the purchaser* Mur 30 2$_{22}$ (+ יֹרֵשׁ *heir*). <PREP> לְ of possession, *(belonging) to, of* Mur 22 2$_{11}$ 30 1$_{3}$ 2$_{15}$.

2. marry, take in, or, **for, marriage, sexual intercourse,*** etc., usu. of woman being taken by or for man; of man being taken by woman (Gn 30$_{15}$ Ezk 16$_{32}$); sometimes of person who arranges marriage (e.g. Gn 21$_{21}$ 34$_{4}$ 38$_{6}$ Ex 34$_{16}$ Dt 7$_{3}$ Jg 14$_{2.3}$ 1 S 25$_{40}$ Jr 29$_{6}$ Ne 10$_{31}$ 1 C 7$_{15}$ perh. 4QHalakhah^{a} 12$_{7}$), <SUBJ> Aaron Ex 6$_{23}$, Abimelech Gn 20$_{2.3}$, Abra(ha)m Gn 11$_{29}$ 25$_{1}$, Ahab 1 K 16$_{31}$, Ahimaaz 1 K 4$_{15}$, Amram Ex 6$_{20}$, Barzillai Ezr 2$_{61}$||Ne 7$_{63}$, Boaz Ru 4$_{13}$, Cain 11QJub 4$_{9}$, Caleb 1 C 2$_{19}$, David 1 S 25$_{39.40.43}$ 2 S 5$_{13}$ 11$_{4}$ 12$_{9.10}$ 1 C 14$_{3}$, Eleazar Ex 6$_{25}$, Esau Gn 26$_{34}$ 28$_{9}$ 36$_{2}$, Hamor Gn 34$_{4.21}$, Hezron 1 C 2$_{21}$, Hosea Ho 1$_{2.3}$, Isaac Gn 24$_{67}$ (+ וַתְּהִי לוֹ לְאִשָּׁה *and she was to him for a wife*) 25$_{20}$, Jacob Gn 27$_{46}$ 28$_{1.2.6}$ 31$_{50}$, Jeremiah Jr 16$_{2}$, Jehohanan Ne 6$_{18}$, Judah 38$_{2.6}$, Lamech Gn 4$_{19}$, Machir 1 C 7$_{15}$, Mered 1 C 4$_{18}$, Moses Nm 12$_{1.1}$, Nahor Gn 11$_{29}$, Rachel Gn 30$_{15}$, Rehoboam 2 C 11$_{18.20}$, Samson Jg 14$_{3.8}$, Shechem Gn 34$_{2.21}$, Solomon 1 K 7$_{8}$, 1 K 3$_{1}$.

אִישׁ *man* Ex 2$_{1}$ Lv 20$_{14.17.21}$ Dt 20$_{7.7}$ 22$_{13.14}$=11QT 65$_{7.8}$ Dt 23$_{1}$ 24$_{1.3.4.5.5}$ 25$_{7.8}$ Jg 19$_{1}$ 21$_{22}$ 4QD^{f} 3$_{13.15.15}$ 4QD^{h} 5$_{4}$ 4QOrd^{a} 2$_{8}$ 4QHalakhah^{a} 12$_{2.7}$ 11QT 66$_{11.12.14.15.16}$ perh. 66$_{17}$ CD 5$_{7}$, אִשָּׁה *woman* Ezk 16$_{32}$, אָב *father* Gn 34$_{4}$ Jg 14$_{2.3}$, אֵם *mother* Gn 21$_{21}$ Jg 14$_{2}$, בֵּן *son* Gn 6$_{2}$ 34$_{9.16}$ Ex 6$_{25}$ Lv 21$_{7.7}$ 1 K 16$_{31}$ Ezk 44$_{22.22}$ Ne 6$_{18}$, of Israel Lv 18$_{17.18}$ Jg 3$_{6}$, חָתָן *son-in-law* Gn 19$_{14}$, יָבָם *brother-in-law* Dt 25$_{5}$, יֶלֶד *child* Ho 1$_{2}$, מֶלֶךְ *king* Gn 20$_{2}$ 11QT 57$_{16.17}$, פַּרְעֹה *Pharaoh* Gn 12$_{19}$, עֶבֶד *servant* Gn 24$_{3.4.7.37.38.40.48}$, כֹּהֵן *priest* Lv 21$_{7.7.13.14.14}$ Jr 29$_{6.6}$ Ezk 44$_{22.22}$, לֵוִי *Levite* Jg 19$_{1}$ Ezk 44$_{22.22}$, נָבִיא *prophet* Jr 29$_{6.6}$, זָקֵן *old one* Gn 24$_{3.4.7}$ Jr 29$_{6.6}$, Israel(ites) Ex 34$_{16}$ Dt 7$_{3}$ 21$_{11}$=11QT 63$_{11}$ Ne 10$_{31}$ 11QT 2$_{14}$ ([ולק]חתה), עַם *people* Jr 29$_{6.6}$, נטף hi. *one who drips*, i.e. preaches CD 4$_{20}$, אַחֵר *another (one)* perh 11QT 62$_{2}$ ([י]קחנה]); subj. not specified, 4Q416 2.3$_{20.20}$ 4Q417 1.1$_{11}$ CD 7$_{6}$=19$_{3}$ 13$_{16}$ (ל[וק]ח).

<OBJ> Abigail 1 S 25$_{39.40}$, Adah Gn 36$_{2}$, Ahinoam 1 S 25$_{43}$, Basemath, daughter of Elon Gn 26$_{34}$, Basemath, daughter of Ishmael Gn 36$_{2}$, Basemath, daughter of Solomon 1 K 4$_{15}$, Bathsheba 2 S 11$_{4}$, Bithiah 1 C 4$_{18}$, Dinah Gn 34$_{2}$, Elisheba Ex 6$_{23}$, Ephrath 1 C 2$_{19}$, Gomer Ho 1$_{3}$, Jezebel 1 K 16$_{31}$, Jochebed Ex 6$_{20}$, Judith Gn 26$_{34}$, Maacah 2 C 11$_{20}$, Mahalath, daughter of Ishmael Gn 28$_{9}$, Mahalath, daughter of Jerimoth 2 C 11$_{18}$, Oholibamah Gn 36$_{2}$, Rebekah Gn 24$_{67}$, Ruth Ru 4$_{13}$, Sarai/Sarah Gn 12$_{19}$ 20$_{2}$, Shua Gn 38$_{2}$.

אִישׁ *husband* Gn 30$_{15}$, אִשָּׁה *woman, wife* Gn 4$_{19}$ 6$_{2}$ 11$_{29}$ 20$_{3}$ 21$_{21}$ 24$_{3.4.7.37.38.40}$ 25$_{1}$ 26$_{34}$ 27$_{46}$ 28$_{1.2.6.6}$ 31$_{50}$ 36$_{2}$ 38$_{6}$ Lv 18$_{18}$ 20$_{14.21}$ 21$_{7.7.13}$ Nm 12$_{1.1}$ Dt 20$_{7.7}$ 21$_{11}$=11QT 63$_{11}$ Dt 22$_{13.14}$=11QT 65$_{7.8}$ Dt 23$_{1}$ 24$_{1.3.4.5.5}$ 25$_{5}$ Jg 14$_{2.3.3.8}$ 19$_{1}$ 21$_{22}$ 2 S 5$_{13}$ 12$_{9.10}$ 1 K 16$_{31}$ Jr 16$_{2}$ 29$_{6.6}$ Ho 1$_{2}$ Ezr 2$_{61}$||Ne 7$_{63}$ 1 C 7$_{15}$ 14$_{3}$ 2 C 11$_{18}$ 4QHalakhah^{a} 12$_{2}$ 4QD^{h} 5$_{4}$ (אש[ה]) 4QMMT B$_{40}$ (ל[ו]קח[ים]) 4Q416 2.3$_{20}$ 11QT 57$_{16.17}$ perh 62$_{2}$ ([י]קחנה]) 66$_{11.12}$ CD 4$_{20}$ 7$_{6}$=19$_{3}$ 13$_{16}$ (ל[וק]ח אש[ה]), פִּילֶגֶשׁ *secondary wife* Jg 19$_{1}$ 2 S 5$_{13}$, אֵם *mother* Lv 20$_{14}$, בַּת *daughter* Gn 19$_{14}$ 24$_{48}$ 25$_{20}$ 26$_{34}$ 28$_{9}$ 34$_{2.9.16.21}$ 36$_{2}$ 38$_{2}$ Ex 2$_{1}$ 6$_{23}$ Lv 18$_{17}$ 20$_{17}$ Dt 7$_{3}$ Jg 3$_{6}$ 2 S 11$_{4}$ 1 K 3$_{1}$ 4$_{15}$ 7$_{8}$ 16$_{31}$ Ho 1$_{3}$ Ne 6$_{18}$ 10$_{31}$ 1 C 2$_{21}$ 4$_{18}$ 2 C 11$_{18(Qr)}$ (Kt בֵּן *son*) 11$_{20}$ 4QHalakhah^{a} 12$_{7}$ perh. 4QDibHam^{a} 1.3$_{16}$ 11QT 66$_{14.16}$ CD 5$_{7}$, אָחוֹת *sister* Gn 36$_{2}$ Ex 6$_{23}$ Lv 20$_{17}$ 11QJub 4$_{9}$ 11QT 66$_{14.15}$, יְבֶמֶת *sister-in-law* Dt 25$_{7.8}$, דּוֹדָה *aunt* Ex 6$_{20}$, אַלְמָנָה *widow* Lv 21$_{14}$ Ezk

44$_{22.22}$, גרשׁ ptc. pass. *divorced woman* Lv 21$_{14}$ Ezk 44$_{22}$, חָלָל *defiled one* Lv 21$_{14}$, זֹנָה *prostitute* Lv 21$_{14}$, בְּתוּלָה *young woman* Lv 21$_{14}$ Ezk 44$_{22}$ 4QOrd^{a} 2$_{8}$, זָר *stranger* Ezk 16$_{32}$, מוֹלָד *offspring* 4Q416 2.3$_{20}$ 4Q417 1.1$_{11}$, כֹּל *anyone* 4QD^{f} 3$_{13.15.15}$.

<PREP> לְ in ref. to subj., *to, for (oneself)*, + Aaron Ex 6$_{23}$, Abram Gn 11$_{29}$, Amram Ex 6$_{20}$, Caleb 1 C 2$_{19}$, David 1 S 25$_{39}$ 2 S 12$_{9}$, Eleazar Ex 6$_{25}$, Esau Gn 28$_{9}$, Hamor Gn 34$_{21}$, Hosea Ho 1$_{2}$, Isaac Gn 25$_{20}$, Jacob Gn 28$_{2.6.6}$, Jeremiah Jr 16$_{2}$, Lamech Gn 4$_{19}$, Nahor Gn 11$_{29}$, Shechem Gn 34$_{21}$, אִישׁ *man* Dt 24$_{3}$ Jg 19$_{1}$, בֵּן *son* Gn 34$_{9.16}$ Ex 6$_{25}$ Ezk 44$_{22}$, of Israel Jg 3$_{6}$, Israel(ites) Dt 21$_{11}$=11QT 63$_{11}$, יָבָם *brother-in-law* Dt 25$_{5}$, מֶלֶךְ *king* 11QT 57$_{16}$, כֹּהֵן *priest* Ezk 44$_{22}$, לֵוִי *Levite* Jg 19$_{1}$ Ezk 44$_{22}$.

לְ *as*, + אִשָּׁה *wife* Gn 12$_{19}$ 25$_{20}$ 28$_{9}$ 34$_{21}$ Ex 6$_{20.23}$ Dt 21$_{11}$ 24$_{3}$ 25$_{5}$ Jg 3$_{6}$ 14$_{2}$ 1 S 25$_{39.40}$ 2 S 12$_{9}$ 1 K 4$_{14}$ Ezk 44$_{22}$.

לְ of benefit, *to, for*, + David 1 S 25$_{40}$, Er Gn 38$_{6}$, Huppim 1 C 7$_{15}$, Isaac Gn 24$_{4}$, Samson Jg 14$_{2.3}$, Shechem Gn 34$_{4}$, Shuppim 1 C 7$_{15}$, בֵּן Gn 24$_{3.4.7.37.38.40.48}$ Ex 34$_{16}$ Dt 7$_{3}$ Jr 29$_{6}$ Ne 10$_{31}$ 11QT 2$_{14}$ (... [ולק]חתה [לבניכה]), נַעַר *lad* Gn 21$_{21}$, בְּכוֹר *firstborn* Gn 38$_{6}$.

בְּ of place, *in*, + Jerusalem 1 C 14$_{3}$.

בְּ of time, *in, during*, + חַיִּים *life* CD 4$_{20}$.

בְּ of instrument, *by (means of), with*, + מִלְחָמָה *war* Jg 21$_{22}$.

כְּ *according to*, + מִנְהָג *custom* CD 19$_{3}$.

מִן partitive, *(some) of, from among*, + בַּת *daughter* Gn 24$_{3.37}$ 27$_{45}$ 28$_{1.2.6}$ 36$_{2}$ Ex 6$_{25}$ 34$_{16}$ Ezr 2$_{61}$||Ne 7$_{63}$ 4QapJoshua^{a} 10$_{2}$ 11QT 2$_{14}$ ([ולק]חתה [מבנותיהם]), Philistines Jg 14$_{3}$, בַּיִת *house* Gn 24$_{40}$ Jg 19$_{1}$ 11QT 57$_{16}$, מִשְׁפָּחָה *family* Gn 24$_{40}$ 11QT 57$_{16}$, כֹּל *all* Gn 6$_{2}$.

מִן of direction, *from*, + אֶרֶץ *land* Gn 21$_{21}$, Jerusalem 2 S 5$_{13}$, שָׁם *there* Gn 24$_{7}$ 28$_{6}$.

אֶל *to*, + אָחוֹת *sister* Lv 18$_{18}$.

עַל *besides, (in addition) to*, + אִשָּׁה *wife* Gn 28$_{9}$ 11QT 57$_{17}$, בַּת *daughter* Gn 30$_{50}$.

אַחֲרֵי *after*, + Mahalath 2 C 11$_{20}$.

תַּחַת *instead of*, + אִישׁ *husband* Ezk 16$_{32}$.

<COLL> || בעל *marry* Dt 24$_{1}$ 11QT 65$_{7}$.

+ היה לו לְאִשָּׁה *be to him for a wife* Dt 24$_{4}$ 25$_{5}$ 1 S 25$_{43}$ 2 S 12$_{10}$ Ru 4$_{13}$.

+ יבם pi. *do duty of brother-in-law* Dt 25$_{5}$.

+ חתן htp. *become son-in-law* 1 K 3$_{1}$.

:: נתן *give* Gn 34$_{9.16.21}$ Dt 7$_{3}$ Jg 3$_{6}$ Jr 29$_{6}$ Ne 10$_{31}$; + נתן *give* Gn 16$_{3}$ 30$_{9}$.

+ ילד hi. *beget* CD 7$_{6}$=19$_{3}$.

+ adverb, עוֹד *again* 2 S 5$_{13}$ 1 C 14$_{3}$, אַחַר *afterwards* 4QD^{f} 3$_{15}$ (א[ח]ר).

3. pass. be taken, **<SUBJ>** subj. not specified, Pr 24$_{11}$. **<PREP>** לְ of direction, *to*, + מָוֶת *death* Pr 24$_{11}$.

Also 2Q27 1$_{3}$ 4QJub^{b} 1$_{1}$ ([ויק]ח) 4QCommGenB 2$_{4}$ 4QCommGenC 8$_{6}$ 4QD^{a} 12$_{9}$ ([יק]חנה) 14b$_{1}$ (לוק[ח]) 4QD^{e} 4$_{16}$ ([י]קחנה) 4QMyst^{b} 10$_{3}$ 4Q415 11$_{10}$ 4Q416 2.1$_{3}$ 2.2$_{3}$ ([תק]ח) 4Q417 1.1$_{15}$ 4Q418 33$_{1}$ 149$_{1}$ ([תק]ח) 202$_{1}$ 4Q423 14$_{2}$ 4QsapDidB 2-4.1$_{5}$ 4QBark^{e} 14$_{2}$ (לן [ק]ח) 4QNarrC 1$_{5}$ 4QRedInk 4$_{2}$ 5Q17 2$_{2}$ MasJub 1$_{3}$.

<SYN> §1 נשׂא *lift*, לקט *gather*, שׁמע *hear*, בזז *plunder*, שׁלל *spoil*.

<ANT> §§1, 2 נתן *give*.

Ni. 10.4.2.1 Pf. נִלְקַח (נִלְקָח), נִלְקָחָה; impf. Q ילקח, 3fs Q תלקח, אֶלָּקַח; + waw 3fs תִּלָּקַח; ptc. Si נלקח; inf. הִלָּקַח (הִלָּקְחוֹ)—**be taken (away),* removed, captured; be received, accepted** (4QPseud^{b} 5.1$_{8}$); **be obtained** (4QBéat 3.3$_{2}$), **<SUBJ>** Elijah 2 K 2$_{9}$ Si 48$_{9}$, Enoch Si 44$_{16}$ 49$_{14}$ (הניך appar. error for חנוך), Esther Est 2$_{8.16}$, אֲרוֹן *ark* 1 S 4$_{11.17.19.21.22}$, לֶחֶם *bread* 1 S 21$_{7}$, חֹק *statute* 4QPseud^{b} 5.1$_{8}$, perh. wisdom 4QBéat 3.3$_{2}$, הוּא *he* Ezk 33$_{6}$. **<PREP>** לְ of agent, *by*, + אֶחָד *one*; בְּ of time, *on*, + חֹדֶשׁ *month* Est 2$_{16}$; of instrument, *by (means of)*, + סְעָרָה *whirlwind* Si 48$_{9}$; *on account of*, + עָוֹן *iniquity* Ezk 33$_{6}$; of price, *(in exchange) for*, + זָהָב *gold* 4QBéat 3.3$_{2}$, כֶּסֶף *silver* 4QBéat 3.3$_{2}$ ([בכסף]); אֶל *to*, + Ahasuerus Est 2$_{16}$, מֶלֶךְ *king* Est 2$_{16}$, יָד *hand* Est 2$_{8}$, בַּיִת *house* Est 2$_{8.16}$; מֵעִם *from*, + Elisha 2 K 2$_{9}$. **<COLL>** הלקח אח perh. *what is taken by a brother*, i.e. a brother's share of an inheritance Si 14$_{14}$; לקח ni. + adverb, מַעְלָה *upwards* Si 48$_{9}$; noun used adverbially, פָּנִים *(into the) presence* Si 49$_{14}$.

Also Arad ost. 111$_{4}$.

Pu. 9.0.2 Pf. לֻקַּח (לֻקָּח), לֻקְּחָה, לֻקָּחְתְּ, Q לוקחתי, לֻקְּחוּ; + waw וְלֻקַּח; ptc. לֻקָּח—**be taken (from), derived (from)** (Jr 29$_{22}$), **captured,** **<SUBJ>** Adam Gn 3$_{19}$, Elijah 2 K 2$_{10}$, אָדָם *human being* Gn 3$_{23}$, בֵּן *son* Jr 48$_{46}$, בַּת *daughter* Jr 48$_{46}$, עֶבֶד *servant* Is 53$_{8}$, עַם *people* Is 52$_{5}$, worshipper 1QH 12_{24} ([לק]חתי) fr. 2_4, יֵצֶר creature 1QH 12_{27}, כֶּסֶף *silver* Jg 17_2, מֵאָה *hundred (pieces)* Jg 17_2, זֹאת *this (one)* Gn 2_{23}, impersonal Jr 29_{22}. <PREP> לְ *with respect to*, i.e. from, + אֵם *mother* Jg 17_2; בְּ of direction, place, *in(to)*, + שְׁבִי *captivity* Jr 48_{46}, שִׁבְיָה *captivity* Jr 48_{46}; מִן of direction, place, *from, out of*, + אִישׁ *man* Gn 2_{23}, exiles Jr 29_{22}, אֲדָמָה *ground* Gn 3_{19}, עָפָר *dust* 1QH 12_{24} ([לק]חתי) fr. 2_4, שָׁם *there* Gn 3_{23} 1QH 12_{27}; of cause, *on account of*, + עֹצֶר *oppression* Is 53_8, מִשְׁפָּט *judgment* Is 53_8; מֵאֵת *from*, + Elisha 2 K 2_{10}. <COLL> + adverb, חִנָּם *for nothing* Is 52_5; + noun used adverbially, קְלָלָה *(as a) curse* Jr 29_{22}.

Ho. $_6$ Impf. יֻקַּח (יֻקָּח); + waw 3fs וַתֻּקַּח—**be taken, brought,** <SUBJ> אִשָּׁה *woman* Gn 12_{15}, שְׁבִי *captives* Is 49_{25}, עֵץ *wood* Ezk 15_3, בַּרְזֶל *iron* Jb 28_2, מִשְׁכָּב *bed* Pr 22_{27} (יִקַּח *he will take* to יֻקַּח *it will be taken*), מַלְקוֹחַ *booty* Is 49_{24}, מְעַט *a little* water Gn 18_4. <PREP> מִן of direction, place, *from*, + גִּבּוֹר *mighty one* Is 49_{24}, עֵץ *wood* Ezk 15_3, עָפָר *dust* Jb 28_2; מִתַּחַת *from under* Pr 22_{27} (if em.; see Subj.). <COLL> + מלט ni. *escape* Is $49_{24.25}$; + inf. of purpose, עשׂה *make* Ezk 15_3; + adverb, לָמָּה *why?* Pr 22_{27} (if em.; see Subj.); + noun used adverbially, בַּיִת *(to the) house* Gn 12_{15}.

Htp. $_2$ Ptc. מִתְלַקַּחַת—**flash,** <SUBJ> אֵשׁ *fire* Ex 9_{24} Ezk 1_4. <PREP> בְּתוֹךְ *among*, + בָּרָד *hail* Ex 9_{24}.*

→ לֶקַח I *teaching*, לֶקַח II *acquisition*, מַלְקוֹחַ I *booty*, II *jaw*, מֶלְקָחַיִם *tongs*, מִקָּח *taking*, מַקָּחָה *ware*, לִקְחִי *Likhi*.

לֶקַח I $_{9.3.4}$ n.m. **teaching**—sf. לִקְחִי, לִקְחָהּ—**teaching, instruction, insight; persuasiveness** (Pr 7_{21} $16_{21.23}$ Si 51_{16}), <SUBJ> ערף *drip* Dt 32_2 (|| אִמְרָה *word*). <NOM CL> זַךְ לִקְחִי *my teaching is pure* Jb 11_4. <OBJ> למד *learn* Is 29_{24} (|| בִּינָה *understanding*) Si 8_8, יסף hi. *add* Pr 1_5 (|| תַּחְבֻּלָה *guidance*) 9_9 $16_{21.23}$ (+ פֶּה *mouth*, i.e. speech) 4QCryptA 3.2_5 (ה]וסיפו לק[ח]) 4Q418 81_{17} 4QBark^c 1.1_2, נתן *give* Pr 4_2 (+ תּוֹרָה *law*), לקח *take* Si $35_{14(B)}$ (+ מוּסָר *discipline*), נשׂא *take* Si $35_{14(Bmg)}$, מצא *find* Si $51_{16(11QPs^a)}$ (B דעה *knowledge*). <CSTR> רֹב לִקְחָהּ *abundance of her persuasiveness* Pr 7_{21}, דברו[י] לקח *words of teaching* 4Q424 1_7. <PREP> בְּ of instrument, *by (means of), with*, + נטה hi. *turn aside* Pr 7_{21} (|| חֵלֶק *smoothness*); introducing object, + שׂכל hi. *teach* 1QS 11_1.

Also perh. 4Q418 221_3.

<SYN> §1 אִמְרָה *word*, בִּינָה *understanding*, תַּחְבֻּלָה *guidance*.*

→ לקח *take*.

[לֶקַח] II $_{0.2}$ n.[m.] **acquisition**—sf. Si לקחו—**1. acquisition,** i.e. item received, <PREP> בושׁ על *be ashamed of* Si $42_{7(B)}$ (+ מַתַּת *gift*).

2. acceptance, <NOM CL> פועל רצונו לקחו *the one who does his will is his acceptance*, i.e. accepted by him Si $42_{15(B, M)}$ (Bmg לקח *is acceptance*).

→ לקח *take*.

לִקְחִי $_1$ pr.n.m. **Likhi,** Manassite, son of Shemida, <SUBJ> היה *be* 1 C 7_{19}. → לקח *take*.

לקט $_{37.0.5}$ vb. **gather—Qal** $_{14.0.4}$ Pf. לִקְטוּ (לָקְטוּ); impf. יִלְקְטוּ (יִלְקֹטוּן, Q ילקוטו, Q ילקטום), 3fs Q תלקוט, תְּלַקֵּטְהוּ; + waw Q ולקטם, וְלָקְטוּ ;וַיִּלְקְטוּ; impv. לִקְטוּ; inf. לְקֹט—**gather** manna (Ex 16_{4+8t} Nm 11_8), food (Ps 104_{28}), lilies (Ca 6_2), stones (Gn 31_{46}), **glean** (Ru 2_8 4QLeqeṭ $1_{2.5}$ $2_{2.3}$), <SUBJ> אִישׁ *man* Ex $16_{16.18}$ (both אִישׁ לְפִי אָכְלוֹ *each according to his eating*) 16_{21} (אִישׁ כְּפִי אָכְלוֹ *each according to his eating*) 4QLeqeṭ 2_3 ([אי]שׁ), עַם *people* Ex $16_{4.27}$ Nm 11_8, בֵּן *son* of Israel Ex 16_{16} (+ לקח *take*) $16_{17.18.21.22.26}$, בַּת *daughter* Ru 2_8, אָח *brother* Gn 31_{46} (|| לקח) 31_{46} (if em. וַיִּקְחוּ *and they took* to וַיִּלְקְטוּ *and they gathered*), דּוֹד *beloved* Ca 6_2, רבה hi. ptc. *one who increases* Ex 16_{17}, מעט hi. ptc. *one who diminishes* Ex 16_{17}, נֶפֶשׁ *soul*, i.e. person 4QD^b 6_7=4QD^e 3.2_{17}, מַעֲשֶׂה *work* Ps 104_{28}, כֹּל *everyone* 4QLeqeṭ 1_5 2_2 ([כול]ם). <OBJ> אֶבֶן *stone* Gn $31_{46.46}$ (if em.; see Subj.), לֶחֶם *bread* Ex $16_{4.21.22.26}$, שׁוֹשַׁן *lily* Ca 6_2, עֹמֶר *omer* Ex 16_{22}, סְאָה *seah* 4QD^b 6_7=4QD^e 3.2_{17} ([סאה]). <PREP> בְּ of place, שָׂדֶה *field* Ru 2_8; of time, *in*, + בֹּקֶר *morning* Ex $16_{21.22}$; of accompaniment, *in (a state of), with*, + טָהֳרָה *purity* 4QLeqeṭ 1_5 ([בטהרה]) 1_8 (ילק[טו]) 2_2 ([בטהרו]ה); מִן partitive, *(some) of*, + לֶחֶם *bread* Ex 16_{16}. <COLL> + noun used adverbially, דְּבַר יוֹם בְּיוֹמוֹ *the thing of a day for its day*, i.e. what is appropriate or due each day Ex 16_4, יוֹם יוֹם *each day* Ex 16_5, שֵׁשֶׁת יָמִים *six days* Ex 16_{26}.

Also 4QLeqeṭ 1_2 ([ילו]טנ[ה]) $1_{2.4}$ ([ילו]טנה).

<SYN> לקח *take.*

Pi. 21 Pf. לִקַּטְתְּ, לִקְּטָה, 3fs תְּלַקֵּט, 2ms תְּלַקֵּט, אֲלַקֲטָה; + waw וְלִקְטָה ;וַיְלַקֵּט, 3fs וַתְּלַקֵּט; ptc. מְלַקֵּט, מְלַקְּטִים; inf. לַקֵּט—**gather, glean,** <SUBJ> Joseph Gn 47$_{14}$, Ruth Ru 2$_{2+10t}$ (+ אסף *gather* at 2$_7$), בֵּן *son* Jr 7$_{18}$, of Israel Lv 23$_{22}$, נַעַר *lad* 1 S 20$_{38}$, מֶלֶךְ *king* Jg 1$_7$ (+ היה *be*), עֵדָה *congregation* Lv 19$_{9.10}$ (|| עלל po. *glean*), אֶחָד *one* 2 K 4$_{39.39}$; subj. not specified, Is 17$_5$ (|| אסף *gather*, + קצר *harvest*). <OBJ> לֶקֶט *gleaning* Lv 19$_9$ 23$_{22}$, פֶּרֶט *fallen grapes* Lv 19$_{10}$, אֹרָה *mallow* 2 K 4$_{39}$, פַּקֻּעֹת *gourds* 2 K 4$_{39}$, שִׁבֹּלֶת *ear of grain* Is 17$_5$, עֵץ *wood* Jr 7$_{18}$, כֶּסֶף *money* Gn 47$_{14}$, חֵץ *arrow* 1 S 20$_{38}$, מְלֹא *fullness* 2 K 4$_{39}$, אֲשֶׁר *that which* Ru 2$_{17.18}$. <PREP> בְּ of place, *in, among,* + שָׂדֶה *field* Ru 2$_{3.17}$, עֵמֶק *valley* Is 17$_5$, שִׁבֹּלֶת *ear of grain* Ru 2$_2$; of price, *(in exchange) for,* + שֶׁבֶר *grain* Gn 47$_{14}$; תַּחַת *under,* + שֻׁלְחָן *table* Jg 1$_7$; מִן of direction, *from,* + גֶּפֶן *vine* 2 K 4$_{39}$; בֵּין *among,* + עֹמֶר *sheaf* Ru 2$_{15}$; עַד *until,* + עֶרֶב *evening* Ru 2$_{17}$; אַחַר *after,* + אֲשֶׁר *one who* Ru 2$_2$; אַחֲרֵי *after,* + קֹצֵר *reaper* Ru 2$_3$. <COLL> + adverb, אֵיפֹה *where?* Ru 2$_{19}$; + noun used adverbially, הַיּוֹם *today* Ru 2$_{19}$.

<SYN> אסף *gather,* עלל po. *glean.*

Pu. 1 Impf. תְּלֻקְּטוּ—**be gathered,** <SUBJ> בֵּן *son* of Israel Is 27$_{12}$. <PREP> לְ *according to,* לְאַחַד אֶחָד *one by one* Is 27$_{12}$.

Htp. 1 + waw וַיִּתְלַקְּטוּ—**assemble** (intrans.), <SUBJ> אִישׁ *man* Jg 11$_3$. <PREP> אֶל *to,* i.e. around, + Jephthah Jg 11$_3$.*

⇒ לֶקֶט *gleaning,* יַלְקוּט *pouch.*

[לֶקֶט] 2.0.1 n.[m.] **gleaning**—cstr. לֶקֶט—**gleaning,** i.e. thing (that may be) gleaned, <NOM CL> כול הלקט [עד] סאה] *all the gleanings are up to a seah* 4QDa 6.3$_5$. <OBJ> לקט pi. *gather* Lv 19$_9$ 23$_{22}$. <CSTR> לֶקֶט קְצִירְךָ *gleaning of your harvest* Lv 19$_9$ 23$_{22}$, כול הלקט *all the gleanings* 4QDa 6.3$_5$.

⇒ לקט *gather.*

לקק 7 vb. **lick—Qal** 5 Pf. לָקְקוּ; impf. יָלֹק, יָלֹקּוּ; + waw וַיָּלֹקּוּ—**lick, lap,** <SUBJ> כֶּלֶב *dog* Jg 7$_5$ 1 K 21$_{19.19}$ 22$_{38}$, לָשׁוֹן *tongue* Ps 68$_{24}$ (if em. מֵאֹיְבִים מִנֵּהוּ appar. *from the enemies his portion* to דַּם אֹיְבִים תָּלֹק the tongue of your dog *will lick the blood of enemies*), אֲשֶׁר *one who* Jg 7$_5$. <OBJ> דָּם *blood* 1 K 21$_{19.19}$ 22$_{38}$ Ps 68$_{24}$ (if em.; see Subj.). <PREP> בְּ of instrument, *by (means of), with,* + לָשׁוֹן *tongue* Jg 7$_5$; מִן partitive, *(some) of,* + מַיִם *water* Jg 7$_5$. <COLL> מְקוֹם אֲשֶׁר לָקְקוּ הַכְּלָבִים *the place where the dogs licked* 1 K 21$_{19}$.

Pi. 2 Ptc. מְלַקְקִים—**lap,** <SUBJ> אִישׁ *man* Jg 7$_7$; subj. not specified, Jg 7$_6$. <PREP> בְּ of instrument, *by (means of), with,* + יָד *hand* Jg 7$_6$ (בְּיָדָם אֶל־פִּיהֶם *with,* i.e. by putting, *their hand to their mouth;* or em. בִּלְשׁוֹנָם *with their tongue*).

לִקְרַאת, see קרא II *meet,* Qal, Coll.

לקשׁ 1 vb. **glean—Qal** 1 Impf. יְלַקֵּשׁוּ—**glean,** <SUBJ> עָנִי *poor one* Jb 24$_6$ (+ קצר *reap*). <OBJ> כֶּרֶם *vineyard* Jb 24$_6$.

⇒ לֶקֶשׁ *crop.*

לֶקֶשׁ 2.0.0.1 n.[m.] **crop**—לֶקֶשׁ—**crop** of grass, of spring growth after latter rains, <SUBJ> עלה *go up,* i.e. grow Am 7$_1$. <NOM CL> הִנֵּה־לֶקֶשׁ אַחַר גִּזֵּי הַמֶּלֶךְ *behold it was the crop after the king's mowings* Am 7$_1$, perh. ירחו לקש *his two months are spring growth* Gezer calendar$_2$.

⇒ לקשׁ *glean.*

[לָשָׁד] 2 n.m. **cake, moisture**—cstr. לְשַׁד; sf. לְשַׁדִּי—**1. cake, delicacy,** <CSTR> טַעַם לְשַׁד הַשָּׁמֶן *taste of a cake of,* i.e. made with, *oil* Nm 11$_8$.

2. moisture, i.e. strength, vigour, <SUBJ> הפך ni. *be overturned* Ps 32$_4$ (or em. לְשֹׁנִי *my tongue*).

לָשׁוֹן 117.15.62 n.f. (sometimes m.) **tongue**—לָשׁוֹן; cstr. לְשׁוֹן (Si לשאון); sf. לְשׁוֹנִי, לְשׁוֹנְךָ, לְשׁוֹנֵךְ, לְשׁוֹנוֹ (לְשֹׁנוֹ), לְשׁוֹנָהּ, לְשׁוֹנֵנוּ (לְשֹׁנֵנוּ), לְשׁוֹנְכֶם, לְשׁוֹנָם; pl. לְשֹׁנוֹת; cstr. לְשֹׁנוֹת (Q לשונות), Q לשוני; sf. Si לשוניך, לְשֹׁנֹתָם.

1. tongue,* a. as organ of speech and song (but distinctions among §§1a, 2, and 3 oft. uncertain), Ex 4$_{10}$ Jos 10$_{21}$ 2 S 23$_2$ Is 32$_4$ 33$_{19}$ 35$_6$ 50$_4$ 57$_4$ 59$_3$ Jr 9$_{2.4.7}$ 18$_{18}$ 23$_{31}$ Ezk 3$_{5.6.26}$ 36$_3$ Ho 7$_{16}$ Mc 6$_{12}$ Ps 5$_{10}$ 10$_7$ 12$_{4.5}$ 15$_3$ =4QBéat 3.2$_1$ Ps 34$_{14}$ 35$_{28}$ 37$_{30}$ 39$_{2.4}$ 45$_2$ 50$_{19}$ 51$_{16}$ 52$_4$ 64$_{4.9}$ 66$_{17}$ (or em.; see תַּחַת, under Prep.) 73$_9$ 78$_{36}$ 119$_{172}$ 126$_2$ Jb 5$_{21}$ 6$_{30}$ 27$_4$ 29$_{10}$ 33$_2$ Pr 10$_{31}$ 16$_1$ 18$_{21}$ 31$_{26}$ Si 4$_{24}$

5$_{13.14.14}$ 37$_{18}$ 51$_{22}$ 1QH 1$_{28}$ 5$_{27}$ 7$_{10.11.13}$ 8$_{35}$ 11$_{4.34}$ 16$_{7}$ 17$_{17}$ 18$_{11}$ 1QS 10$_{8.22.23}$ 4Q185 1.3$_{13}$ 4QapJoseph^{b} 3$_{7}$ 4Q416 18$_{1}$ 4Q418 172$_{13}$ ([ובל]שונכה) 4QsapDidA 1$_{5}$ 4QsapDid B 6$_{4}$ 4QHod^{a} 7.1$_{14}$ 4QBark^{a} 6$_{2}$ (בלש[ון]) 4QBark^{c} 1.1$_{7}$ 4Q446 1$_{4}$, perh. 4QapJoseph^{b} 3$_{5}$ 4Q412 1$_{5}$ 4QHod^{a} 14$_{4}$ 4QparaKings 9$_{9}$ 4QRitPur 8.28$_{2}$ 4QShir^{b} 63.3$_{1}$.

b. as organ of drinking, Jg 7$_{5.6}$ (if ins. לָשׁוֹן) Is 41$_{17}$ Ps 22$_{16}$ Lm 4$_{4}$.

c. not, or not principally, as organ of speech, Zc 14$_{12}$ Ps 137$_{6}$ Jb 20$_{12}$ Ca 4$_{11}$ 1QH 5$_{31}$=4QHod^{c} 1.4$_{4}$.

d. tongue of dog, Ex 11$_{7}$ Ps 57$_{5}$ (if em. לָבִא *lion* to כֶּלֶב *dog*) 68$_{24}$.

e. tongue of lion, Ps 57$_{5}$ (or em.) 1QH 5$_{13.14(erased).14}$.

f. tongue of viper, Jb 20$_{16}$.

g. tongue of Leviathan, Jb 40$_{25}$.

h. tongue of Y., Is 30$_{27}$.

2. tongue representative of **(speaking) person,** Is 45$_{23}$ 54$_{17}$ Ps 31$_{21}$ (or del. לָשׁוֹן) Pr 28$_{23}$ perh. 4QPrQuot 4.7$_{4}$ 4QapJoshua^{b} 15$_{3}$.

3. words, speech, Is 3$_{8}$ Zp 3$_{13}$ Ps 52$_{6}$ 55$_{10}$ 71$_{24}$ 109$_{2}$ 120$_{2.3}$ 139$_{4}$ 140$_{4.12}$ Jb 15$_{5}$ Pr 6$_{17.24}$ 10$_{20}$ 12$_{18.19}$ 15$_{2.4}$ 17$_{4}$ 17$_{20}$ 21$_{6.23}$ 25$_{15.23}$ 26$_{28}$ Ec 10$_{11}$ Si 4$_{29}$ 8$_{3}$ 9$_{18}$ 25$_{19}$ (if em.; see Cstr.) 35$_{18}$ 36$_{28}$ 40$_{21}$ 51$_{2.6}$ 4QapLam^{b}$_{4.6}$ 4QD^{b} 5.3$_{3}$ (בל[שונו]) 4QHod^{a} 7.1$_{7}$ 4QBéat 14.2$_{26}$.

4. perh. **idiom, manner of speaking,** 4Q416 2.2$_{7}$.

5. (foreign) **language,** Gn 10$_{5.20.31}$ Dt 28$_{49}$ Is 28$_{11}$ 66$_{18}$ Jr 5$_{15}$ Zc 8$_{23}$ Est 1$_{22}$ 1$_{22}$ (or em.; see Cstr.) 3$_{12}$ 8$_{9.9}$ Dn 1$_{4}$ Ne 13$_{24}$ CD 14$_{10}$ 4QD^{a} 11$_{10}$ 4QNarr^{e} 3.1$_{8}$ perh. 4QMidr Eschat^{b} 10$_{11}$ 4QNarr^{e} 2$_{2}$ 4QRitPur 3.36$_{2}$.*

6. (mixing senses of §§2 and 5),* **people** speaking a language, **nation,** 1QMyst 1.1$_{10}$=4QMyst^{a} 1$_{2}$.

7. perh. **sense, meaning,** Is 28$_{11}$.*

8. bay of Dead Sea, Jos 15$_{2.5}$ 18$_{19}$, of sea of Egypt, Is 11$_{15}$.

9. ray of sun (or perh., as §1c, **tongue**),* Si 43$_{4}$.

10. flame of fire, Is 5$_{24}$ 1Q29 1$_{3}$ 2$_{3}$=4QapMos^{b} 1.2$_{1}$.

11. bar, ingot of gold, Jos 7$_{21.24}$.*

<SUBJ> נשׁת *be dry* Is 41$_{17}$, מקק ni. *decay* Zc 14$_{12}$, כרת ni. *be cut off* Pr 10$_{31}$, perh. אסף ni. *be gathered*, i.e. sheathed 1QH 5$_{14}$ (unless תּוסף is qal, *gather* sword) 8$_{35}$, דבק *cling* Ps 137$_{6}$ Jb 29$_{10}$ Lm 4$_{4}$ 1QH 5$_{31}$=4QHod^{c} 1.4$_{4}$, ho. *be stuck* Ps 22$_{16}$, חזק hi. *be strong* 1QMyst 1.1$_{10}$ =4QMyst^{a} 1$_{2}$ (מחזקת), מלא ni. *be full* Ps 126$_{2}$, מצא ni. *be found* Zp 3$_{13}$, לקק *lick* Ps 68$_{24}$ (if em. מֵאֹיְבִים מִנֵּהוּ appar. *from the enemies his portion* to דַּם אֹיְבִים תָּלֹק *will lick the blood of enemies*).

הלך *go* Ps 73$_{9}$ (or em. pi. *walk*), קום *arise* in judgment Is 54$_{17}$, בוא *come* Is 66$_{18}$, פנה *turn*, i.e. project, southward Jos 15$_{2}$, שׁלח pi. *send away* Si 37$_{18(Bmg, D)}$, פלט hi. *rescue* Si 5$_{13(C)}$, מהר pi. *hasten* Is 32$_{4}$, perh. רום hi. *raise* voice 1QH 8$_{35}$, perh. שׁמע hi. *announce* 1QH 18$_{11}$ (לה[שמיע]), perh. מלץ hi. *interpret* 1QH 18$_{11}$.

דבר pi. *speak* Is 32$_{4}$ Jr 9$_{4}$ Ps 12$_{4}$ 37$_{30}$ Jb 33$_{2}$ 4Q185 1.3$_{13}$, ספר pi. *relate* 1QS 10$_{23}$, הגה *utter* Is 59$_{3}$ Ps 35$_{28}$ 71$_{24}$ Jb 27$_{4}$, ענה *sing* Ps 119$_{172}$, רנן *exult* Is 35$_{6}$ Ps 51$_{16}$ 4QShir^{b} 63.3$_{1}$ (both pi.), ידה *praise* 4QRitPur 8.28$_{2}$ (לשונ[י]), שׁבע ni. *swear* Is 45$_{23}$, חשׁב *devise* Ps 52$_{4}$, צמד hi. *harness* deceit Ps 50$_{19}$, יטב hi. *improve* Pr 15$_{2}$ (or em. נטף *drip* or תֵּבַת *[is] an ark of* knowledge), ראה *see* Is 66$_{18}$, משׁל *rule* Si 37$_{18(B)}$, חיל pol. *engender* Pr 25$_{23}$, שׂנא *hate* Pr 26$_{28}$ (or em. יִשְׂנָא דַכָּיו *hates those it crushes* to יְנַשֵּׂא דָכְיוֹ *raises up its pounding* or יָבִיא שֶׁבֶר *brings destruction* or יַשִּׁיא בְעָלָיו/אֲדֹנָיו *deceives its possessor* or יִשְׂנָא בְעָלָיו/אֲדֹנָיו *hates its possessor*).

אכל *eat*, i.e. burn Is 5$_{24}$, גמר *burn* Si 43$_{4(M)}$ (ת[ג]מור [or em. תגמיר the tongue *is burnt*]; B תגמר, perh. pi., *burn*), שׁבר *break* Pr 25$_{15}$, הרג *kill* Jb 20$_{16}$.

<NOM CL> לְשׁוֹנָם ... אֶל־יי *their speech ... is against Y.* Is 3$_{8}$, לשון אדם מפלתו *the tongue of a person is their downfall* Si 5$_{13(A)}$, לְשׁוֹנָם חֶרֶב חַדָּה *their tongue is a sharp sword* Ps 57$_{5}$, חֵץ שָׁחֵט לְשׁוֹנָם *their tongue is a sharpened arrow* Jr 9$_{7(Qr)}$ (or em. לְשׁוֹנוֹ *his tongue;* Kt שׁוֹחֵט *destroying*), לְשׁוֹנָם רְמִיָּה בְּפִיהֶם *their tongue is deceit in their mouth* Mc 6$_{12}$, לְשׁוֹנִי עֵט סוֹפֵר מָהִיר *my tongue is the pen of a skilled scribe* Ps 45$_{2}$, כֶּסֶף נִבְחָר לְשׁוֹן צַדִּיק *the tongue of the righteous is choice silver* Pr 10$_{20}$ (or em. נִבְחָן *tested*), לְשׁוֹן חֲכָמִים מַרְפֵּא *the speech of the wise is healing* Pr 12$_{18}$, לְשׁוֹנוֹ כְּאֵשׁ אֹכָלֶת *his tongue is like a devouring fire* Is 30$_{27}$, משניהם לשון ברה *better than both of them* (flute and harp) *is pure speech* Si 40$_{21}$, עַד־אַרְגִּיעָה לְשׁוֹן שָׁקֶר *false speech is but for a moment* Pr 12$_{19}$, היש ... לשון *is there a (speaking) person?* 1QMyst 1.1$_{10}$=4QMyst^{a} 1$_{2}$.

<OBJ> שׁמר *keep* Pr 21$_{23}$ Si 35$_{18}$, נצר *keep* Ps 34$_{14}$, חלק hi. *make smooth*, i.e. flatter with, tongue Jr 23$_{31}$ (if em.

לקח *take*) Ps 5$_{10}$ Pr 28$_{23}$, חרץ *sharpen* Ex 11$_{7}$ Jos 10$_{21}$, שׁנן *sharpen* Ps 64$_{4}$ 140$_{4}$ 1QH 5$_{13}$, קרא *read* or *recite* 4QNarr^{e} 3.1$_{8}$ (ק[רא]), שׁמע *hear*, i.e. understand Dt 28$_{49}$, ראה *see* Jos 7$_{21}$, ידע *know* Jr 5$_{15}$, בחר *choose* Jb 15$_{5}$, אהב *love* Ps 52$_{6}$, שׂנא *hate* Pr 6$_{17}$, למד pi. *teach* Jr 9$_{4}$ Dn 1$_{4}$, נתן *give* Is 50$_{4}$, לקח *take* Jos 7$_{24}$ Jr 23$_{31}$ (or em. חלק hi. *make smooth*), קבץ pi. *gather* Is 66$_{18}$, רשׁע hi. *condemn* Is 54$_{17}$, מחץ *strike* Ps 68$_{24}$ (or em. חמץ *redden* or רחץ *wash* or מצה *tread*, with tongue or God as subj.),* חרם hi. *destroy* or *split* Is 11$_{15}$ (or em. חרב hi. *dry*), כרת hi. *cut off* Ps 12$_{4}$, פלג pi. *divide* Ps 55$_{10}$ (or em. פֶּלֶג *division* of tongue), בלע pi. *confuse* Ps 55$_{10}$ (or em.), כשׁל hi. *cause to stumble* Ps 64$_{9}$ (or em.; see עַל, under Prep.), ארך hi. *lengthen* Is 57$_{4}$, דרך hi. *tread*, i.e. bend, tongue into bow Jr 9$_{2}$ (or em. qal), שׁקע hi. *press down* Jb 40$_{25}$, דבק hi. *cause to adhere* Ezk 3$_{26}$.

יסד *establish* 4QD^{a} 11$_{10}$, גבר hi. *strengthen* 1QH 8$_{35}$, כון hi. *establish* 1QH 7$_{13}$ (ות]כן לבי ב[בריתכה ולשוני כלמודיך *and you have established my heart in your covenant and my tongue like [that of] your pupils*; or ולשוני introduces nom. cl., *my tongue is* like), perh. אסף *gather*, i.e. sheathe 1QH 5$_{14}$ (unless תוסף is ni. *be gathered*), פתח *open*, i.e. loosen 1QH 5$_{27}$ 4QBark^{c} 1.1$_{7}$ 4QShir^{b} 63.3$_{1}$.

<CSTR> לשון אדם *tongue of a person* Si 5$_{13}$, נצח perh. *of victory* 4QHod^{a} 7.1$_{14}$, יודע *of one who knows* 4Q185 1.3$_{13}$, לְשׁוֹן יוֹנֵק *tongue of (the) suckling* Lm 4$_{4}$, לִמּוּדִים *of pupils* Is 50$_{4}$, לְשׁוֹן אִלֵּם *tongue of a dumb one* Is 35$_{6}$ 4QBark^{a} 6$_{2}$ (בלשו[ן]), עִלְּגִים *of stammerers* Is 32$_{4}$, אֶפְעֶה *of a viper* Jb 20$_{16}$, כְּלָבֶיךָ *of your dogs* Ps 68$_{24}$.

לְשׁוֹן שָׁקֶר *speech of falsehood* Ps 109$_{2}$ Pr 6$_{17}$ (שָׁקֶר) 12$_{19}$ 21$_{6}$ (שֶׁקֶר) 26$_{28}$ (שֶׁקֶר) 1QH 5$_{27}$ (לְשׁוֹן = *tongue*), לשון שקרמה *the speech of their falsehood* 4QapLam$^{b}_{4}$, לשון גדופיהם *the speech of their reproaches* 4QapLam$^{b}_{6}$, לְשׁוֹן רְמִיָּה *speech of deceit* Ps 52$_{6(mss)}$ 120$_{2.3}$ (if em. in both; see App.), תַּרְמִית *of deceit* Zp 1$_{13}$, מִרְמָה *of deceit* Ps 52$_{6}$ Si 51$_{6}$, סֵתֶר *of secrecy* Pr 25$_{23}$, הַוּוֹת *of destruction* Pr 17$_{4}$, נָכְרִיָּה *of an alien woman* Pr 6$_{24}$ (if em.; see Adj.), צַדִּיק *of the righteous* Pr 10$_{20}$, חֲכָמִים *of the wise* Pr 12$_{18}$ 15$_{2}$, עֲרוּמִים *of the shrewd* Jb 15$_{5}$.

לשון הקודש *the language of holiness* 4QNarr^{e} 3.1$_{8}$, לְשֹׁנוֹת הַגּוֹיִם *languages of the nations* Zc 8$_{23}$, לְשׁוֹן עַם וָעָם *language of each people* Ne 13$_{24}$, לְשׁוֹן עַמּוֹ *language of his people* Est 1$_{22}$ (or em. כִּלְשׁוֹן עַמּוֹ speaking *according to the language of his people* to כִּלְשֹׁנוֹ עִמּוֹ speaking *with him according to his language* or כָּל־שֹׁוֶה עִמּוֹ speaking *absolutely plainly with him*), כַּשְׂדִּים *of (the) Chaldaeans* Dn 1$_{4}$.

לְשׁוֹן תַּהְפֻּכוֹת *tongue of perversity* Pr 10$_{31}$, [כו]ל לשוני דעת *all (speaking) persons (possessed) of knowledge* 4QPrQuot 4.7$_{4}$, לְשׁוֹן הַיָּם *bay of the sea* Jos 15$_{5}$ 18$_{19}$ (יָם־הַמֶּלַח *of the Dead Sea*) Is 11$_{15}$ (יָם־מִצְרַיִם *of the sea of Egypt*), לשון מאור *ray of the luminary* Si 43$_{4(Bmg, M)}$ (B לשאון), לְשׁוֹן אֵשׁ *flame of fire* Is 5$_{24}$ 1Q29 1$_{3}$ 2$_{3}$=4QapMos^{b} 1.2$_{1}$ (both לשונות אש), לְשׁוֹן זָהָב *bar of gold* Jos 7$_{21.24}$ (הַזָּהָב).

אִישׁ לָשׁוֹן *man of (unmeasured) speech* Ps 140$_{12}$ Si 8$_{3}$ 9$_{18}$, אשת *woman of* Si 25$_{20(Segal)}$ (if em. אשת [לשון]), בַּעַל הַלָּשׁוֹן *the possessor of speech*, i.e. snake charmer Ec 10$_{11}$, מַרְפֵּא לָשׁוֹן *healing of speech*, i.e. soothing words Pr 15$_{4}$ Si 36$_{28}$, חֶלְקַת *smoothness of* Pr 6$_{24}$ (or em. לָשׁוֹן alien *speech* to לְשׁוֹן *of speech of* alien woman), חצי לשון *arrows of* deceitful *speech* Si 51$_{6}$, פֶּלֶג לְשׁוֹנָם *division of their speech* Ps 55$_{10}$ (if em. פלג pi. *divide* speech), ומתקל לשון *offence of*, i.e. given by, *speech* 4QBéat 14.2$_{26}$.

שׁוֹט דבת לשון *lash of the spoken rumour* Si 51$_{2}$, שׁוֹט לָשׁוֹן *lash of (the) tongue* Jb 5$_{21}$ (or em. שׁוּט *wandering of*), מַעֲנֵה *answer of* Pr 16$_{1}$ Si 4$_{24}$ 1QH 7$_{11.13}$ 11$_{34}$ 16$_{7}$ 17$_{17}$, ד[ב]רי לשוני *the words of my tongue* 4QapJoseph^{b} 3$_{7}$, פרי לשון *fruit of the tongue (of)* 4Q416 18$_{1}$, []חק לשונכם perh. *statute of your tongue* 4QparaKings 9$_{9}$, זַעַם לְשׁוֹנָם *cursing*, or *stammering*, *of their tongue(s)* Ho 7$_{16}$,* שְׂפַת *edge of* Ezk 36$_{3}$, כְּבַד לָשׁוֹן *heavy of tongue* Ex 4$_{10}$ Ezk 3$_{5.6}$ (כִּבְדֵי; or del. in both), נִלְעַג *stammering of* Is 33$_{19}$, יַד־לָשׁוֹן *hand*, i.e. power, *of (the) tongue* Pr 18$_{21}$.

רִיב לְשֹׁנוֹת *contention of tongues*, i.e. speakers Ps 31$_{21}$ (or del. לְשֹׁנוֹת), שלוש לשונות *three flames of* 1Q29 2$_{3}$, כָּל־לָשׁוֹן *every tongue*, i.e. speaker Is 45$_{23}$ 54$_{17}$ perh. 4QapJoshua^{b} 15$_{3}$ (ובכו[ל]), כל לשון *every language* CD 14$_{10}$, כֹּל לְשֹׁנוֹת *all the languages of* Zc 8$_{23}$ 4QRitPur 3.36$_{2}$ (כול לשונות), [כו]ל לשוני *all tongues*, i.e. speakers, *of* 4QPrQuot 4.7$_{4}$.

<APP> רְמִיָּה *deceit* Ps 120$_{2.3}$ (or em. לָשׁוֹן רְמִיָּה *a tongue, deceit* to לְשׁוֹן רְמִיָּה *a tongue of deceit* in both).

<ADJ> אַחֵר *other* Is 28$_{11}$, אֶחָד *one* Jos 7$_{21}$, בַּר *pure* Si

40_{21}, רַךְ *soft* Pr 25_{15}, נָכְרִי *foreign* Pr 6_{24} (or em. לָשׁוֹן נָכְרִיָּה *alien speech* to לְשׁוֹן נָכְרִיָּה *speech of the alien woman*).

<PREP> לְ perh. of benefit, *to, for,* + שִׂים *place* doors *around* 4QsapDidA 1_5 ([שׂ]ים ... ללשונכה דלתי מ[גן] *place ... for your tongue doors of protection*); *in accordance with* Gn 10_5 (if ins. אֵלֶּה בְּנֵי יֶפֶת *these are the sons of Japheth* in accordance with) $10_{20.31}$, + פרד ni. *be separated* Gn 10_5 (or em.); of instrument, *by (means of), with,* + גבר hi. *be mighty* Ps 12_5 (or del. לְ, with לָשׁוֹן as obj. of גבר hi. *magnify*); of benefit, *to, for,* + יסף hi. *add* Ps 120_3 (if ins. לְ; ms. יֹסֵף ho. *be added*); בעל לְ pass. *be expert in (respect of)* CD 14_{10}.

בְּ of place, *in, on* Ps 139_4 Jb 6_{30} 1QS $10_{8.22}$ 4Q446 1_4, perh. 4Q418 172_{13} ([ובל]שונכה), + נתן *give*, i.e. place 1QH 11_4, ברא *create* breath 1QH 1_{28}, חקק *engrave* 1QH 18_{11}; of accompaniment, *with, in,* + היה *be* proud Si 4_{29}, יצא *go out* 4QapMos^{b} 1.2_1, סבב *surround* 4QapLam$^{b}{}_{4}$; of instrument, *by (means of), with* perh. 4QapJoshua^{b} 15_3 ([ובכ]ל) 4QHod^{a} 14_4 4QsapDidB 6_4 4QBark^{a} 6_2 (בלשו[ן]), + תמם *be destroyed* 1Q29 1_3, דבר pi. *speak* Is 28_{11} Ps 39_4 Ne $13_{24(mss)}$, ידה hi. *praise* Si 51_{22}, רום hi. *raise* voice 4QHod^{a} 7.1_{14}, עור pol. *rouse* 4QHod^{a} 7.1_7, כזב pi. *lie* Ps 78_{36}, רגל pi. *slander* Si 5_{14}, הפך ni. *be perverse* Pr 17_{20}, קלל ni. *be light*, perh. appear trivial 4QD^{b} 5.3_3 (בל[שונו]), לקק *lick* Jg $7_{5.6}$ (pi.; if ins. בִּלְשׁוֹנָם *with their tongue* and move בְּיָדָם אֶל־פִּיהֶם *with their hand to their mouth*), נכה hi. *strike* Jr 18_{18} (unless בַלָּשׁוֹן = let us strike Jeremiah *on his tongue*, i.e. בְּ of place; or em. בִּלְשׁוֹנוֹ in same sense), חטא *sin* Ps 39_2, פעל *do*, i.e. acquire, treasure Pr 21_6 (if em. פֹּעַל *deed of* to פֹּעֵל *one who does*).

כְּ *in accordance with*, + דבר pi. *speak* 4Q416 2.2_7, שׁלח *send* documents Est 1_{22}, דבר pi. *speak* Est 1_{22} (or em.; see Cstr.) Ne 13_{24}, כתב ni. *be written* Est 3_{12} $8_{9.9}$.

מִן of direction, *from* Jos 15_5, + היה *be* Jos 15_2, נצל hi. *deliver* Ps 120_2.

אֶל *at*, + היה *be* Jos 18_{19}; *by (means of), with,* + רגל *slander* Si 5_{14}.

עַל *upon* 2 S 23_2 Pr 31_{26}; *to*, + אזן hi. *listen* Pr 17_4; *by (means of), with,* + רגל *slander* Ps 15_3=4QBéat 3.2_1, כשׁל hi. *cause to stumble* Ps 64_9 (if em. וַיַּכְשִׁילוּהוּ עָלֵימוֹ לְשׁוֹנָם appar. *and they have caused it, their tongue, to stumble* to וַיַּכְשִׁילֵמוֹ עֲלֵי לְשׁוֹנָם *and he caused them to stumble with their tongue*).

תַּחַת *under* Ps 10_7 66_{17} (or em. וְרוֹמַם תַּחַת לְשׁוֹנִי *and praise was under my tongue* to וְרוֹמַמְתִּי מִתַּחַת לְשֹׂנְאָי *and I shall be exalted among all who hate me*) Ca 4_{11}, כחד hi. *hide* Jb 20_{12}.

בַּעַד *behind*, + סגר *close* 1QH $5_{14(erased)}$.

מִלִּפְנֵי *on account of*, + אחז *hold* (of terror) 4QapLam$^{b}{}_{6}$.

<COLL> דִּבְּרוּ אִתִּי לְשׁוֹן שָׁקֶר *they have spoken to me with false words* Ps 109_2 (ms דִּבֶּר *he has spoken*), [ו]לכול לשו[ן] למשפחותם] *and in respect of every language, according to their families* 4QD^{a} 10.1_3 (כל לשון *language of their clans* CD 14_{10} (רמ[ש]פחותם)), ומתקל לשון השמר מואדה appar. *and be very much on your guard against offensive speech* 4QBéat 14.2_{26}.

לָשׁוֹן ‖ פֶּה *mouth* Ex 4_{10} Is 57_4 Jr 9_7 (+) Zp 3_{13} (+) Zc 14_{12} (+) Ps 10_7 (+) 37_{30} 39_2 50_{19} 73_9 78_{36} 109_2 (+) 126_2 Jb 15_5 (+) 20_{12} (+) 33_2 (+) Pr 10_{31} (+) 15_2 21_{23} 26_{28} 31_{26} Si 9_{18} (+) 1QH 11_4 18_{11} 1QS 10_{23} 4QBark^{a} 6_2 (+; בלשו[ן]) 4QBark^{c} 1.1_7, שָׂפָה *lip* Is 28_{11} (+) 30_{27} 33_{19} (+) 59_3 Ezk $3_{5.6}$ Ps $12_{4.5}$ (both +) 34_{14} (+) 120_2 140_4 Jb 27_4 Pr 12_{19} 17_4 Ca 4_{11} (+) Si $51_{6.22}$ (both +) 1QH 1_{28} (+) $7_{11.13}$ (both +) 11_4 1QS 10_8 (+) 10_{22} 1QMyst 1.1_{10}=4QMyst^{a} 1_2 4QHod^{a} 7.1_{14} 14_4 4QShir^{b} 63.3_1 (+) 4QBéat 14.2_{26} (+), לֵב *heart* Pr 6_{17} (+) 10_{20} (+) 16_1 17_{20} (+) 1QH 7_{13} ([ל]בי) 4QBéat 3.2_1 (+), לֵבָב *heart* Is 32_4 Ps 15_3 (+), עַיִן *eye* Zc 14_{12} Pr 6_{17} (+), שֵׁן *tooth* Ps 57_5 1QH 5_{13} (+ שניהם *their teeth* for erased לשונם *their tongue*), בֶּרֶךְ *knee* Is 45_{23}, מַעֲלָל *deed* Is 3_8, מְלָאכָה *work* Si 4_{29}, כְּתָב *writing* Est 1_{22} 3_{12} $8_{9.9}$, סֵפֶר *writing* Dn 1_4, גּוֹי *nation* Is 66_{18}, עַם *people* 4QD^{a} 11_{10}.

לָשׁוֹן + חֵךְ *palate* Ezk 3_{26} Ps 137_6 Jb 6_{30} 29_{10} 33_2 Lm 4_4 1QH 5_{31}=4QHod^{c} 1.4_4, גָּרוֹן *throat* Ps 5_{10}, מַלְקוֹחַ *jaw* Ps 22_{16}, יָד *hand* Pr 6_{17} 4Q418 172_{13} ([ב]ידהה ... [ובל]שונכה), יָמִין *right hand* Ps 137_6, רֶגֶל *foot* Ps 68_{24} Pr 6_{17}, נֶפֶשׁ *soul* 4QpsEzek^{a} 10.1_6, דָּבָר *word* Ps 52_6 (or em. דֹּבֵר *speaker*) 1QH 1_{28} 4QapJoseph^{b} 3_5 ([ל]שונ[י]) 3_7 ([ד]ברי) 4QBark^{c} 1.1_7, סוֹד *secret* CD 14_{10}, חָמָס *violence* Ps 140_{12}, רוּחַ *wind* Pr 25_{23}, נָהָר *river* Is 11_{15}, לֶהָבָה *flame* Is 5_{24}.

Also 4QMidrEschat[b] 10_{11} 4QMyst[a] 66_1 ([ולשוננ[ת) 4QapJerB 8_6 4QNarr[e] 2_2 4Q408 9_2 4Q418 184_4 4Qsap DidB 1_5 2_3 4QRitMar 42_2 4QPrFêtes[c] 131.1_9 ([ל]שונו).

<SYN> פֶּה *mouth,* שָׂפָה *lip,* לֵב *heart,* לֵבָב *heart,* עַיִן *eye,* שֵׁן *tooth,* בֶּרֶךְ *knee,* מַעֲלָל *deed,* מְלָאכָה *work,* כְּתָב *writing,* סֵפֶר *writing,* גּוֹי *nation.*

→ לשן *slander.*

לִשְׁכָּה 47 n.f. **chamber**—+ ה- of direction לִשְׁכָּתָה; cstr. לִשְׁכַּת; pl. לְשָׁכוֹת (לְשָׁכֹת); cstr. לִשְׁכוֹת (לִשְׁכֹת)—**chamber, room, hall,** usu. part of a sanctuary; also of secretary's room in royal palace (Jr $36_{12.20.21}$), <SUBJ> היה *be* Ezk 45_5 (or em.; see Coll.), קצר pass. *be short* Ezk 42_5.

<NOM CL> לִשְׁכוֹת הַצָּפוֹן לִשְׁכוֹת הַדָּרוֹם ... לִשְׁכוֹת הַקֹּדֶשׁ *the chambers of the north (and) the chambers of the south ... are holy chambers* Ezk 42_{13}, הִנֵּה לְשָׁכוֹת ... לֶחָצֵר סָבִיב סָבִיב *behold there were chambers ... all around the court* Ezk 40_{17}, שְׁלֹשִׁים לְשָׁכוֹת אֶל־הָרִצְפָה *thirty chambers were on the pavement* Ezk 40_{17}, לִשְׁכָּה וּפִתְחָהּ בְּאֵילִים *a chamber and its entrance were next to the pillars* Ezk 40_{38}, מִחוּצָה לַשַּׁעַר הַפְּנִימִי לִשְׁכוֹת שָׁרִים בֶּחָצֵר הַפְּנִימִי *outside the inner gate were chambers of singers in the inner court* Ezk 40_{44} (or em. לְשָׁכוֹת שָׁרִים *chambers of singers* to לְשָׁכוֹת שְׁתַּיִם *two chambers*), זֹה הַלִּשְׁכָּה ... לַכֹּהֲנִים *this is the chamber ... for the priests* Ezk 40_{45}, הַלִּשְׁכָּה ... לַכֹּהֲנִים *the chamber ... is for the priests* Ezk 40_{46}, הַלְּשָׁכוֹת אֲשֶׁר לֶחָצֵר הַחִצוֹנָה *the chambers that were to the outer court* Ezk 42_8, הַלְּשָׁכוֹת אֲשֶׁר דֶּרֶךְ הַצָּפוֹן *the chambers that were toward the north* Ezk 42_{11}, var. 42_{12}, דֶּרֶךְ הַקָּדִים אֶל־פְּנֵי הַגִּזְרָה וְאֶל־פְּנֵי הַבִּנְיָן לְשָׁכוֹת *to the east opposite the space and opposite the building there were chambers* Ezk 42_{10}, לִשְׁכוֹת הַדָּרוֹם אֲשֶׁר אֶל־פְּנֵי הַגִּזְרָה *chambers of the south that were opposite the space* Ezk 42_{13}.

<OBJ> עשׂה *make,* i.e. prepare Ne 13_5, טהר pi. *cleanse* Ne 13_9, כון hi. *prepare* 2 C 31_{11}.

<CSTR> לִשְׁכַּת אֱלִישָׁמָע *chamber of Elishama* Jr $36_{20.21}$, גְּמַרְיָהוּ *of Gemariah* Jr 36_{10}, יְהוֹחָנָן *Jehohanan* Ezr 10_6 (mss יְהוֹנָתָן *of Jonathan*), מַעֲשֵׂיָהוּ *of Maaseiah* Jr 35_4, נְתַן־מֶלֶךְ *of Nathan-melech* 2 K 23_{11}, אִישׁ ... *of the man of* God Jr 35_4, בֶּן־ ... *of the son of* Jr $35_{4.4.10}$ Ezr 10_6, בְּנֵי חָנָן *of the sons of Hanan* Jr 35_4 (ms בֶּן־ *of the son of,* ms יָחָנָן *of Johanan*), הַסֹּפֵר ... *of the secretary* Jr $36_{10.12.20.21}$, הַשָּׂרִים *of the princes* Jr 35_4, הַסָּרִיס ... *of the eunuch* 2 K 23_{11}, שֹׁמֵר ... *of the keeper of* the threshold Jr 35_4, לִשְׁכוֹת שָׁרִים *chambers of singers* Ezk 40_{44} (or em.; see Nom. Cl.), לִשְׁכוֹת הַצָּפוֹן *the chambers of the north* Ezk 42_{13}, הַדָּרוֹם *of the south* Ezk 42_{13}, הַקֹּדֶשׁ *of holiness,* i.e. holy chambers Ezk 42_{13} 44_{19} (לִשְׁכֹת) 46_{19} (הַלְּשָׁכוֹת; or em. לִשְׁכוֹת), לִשְׁכוֹת בֵּית *the chambers of the house of* Ezr 8_{29} (הַלְּשָׁכוֹת) Ne 10_{39} 13_4 (if em. לִשְׁכַּת *the chamber of* to לִשְׁכֹּת); אֹרֶךְ הַלְּשָׁכוֹת *length of the chambers* Ezk 42_8, מַרְאֵה *appearance of* Ezk 42_{11}, פִּתְחֵי *entrances of* Ezk 42_{12}, אַחַת הַלְּשָׁכוֹת *one of the chambers* Jr 35_2, כָּל־הַלְּשָׁכוֹת *all the chambers* 1 C 28_{18} (‖ חָצֵר *court,* אוֹצָר *treasury*).

<ADJ> גָּדוֹל *great* Ne 13_5, עֶלְיוֹן *upper* Ezk 42_5, אֵלֶּה *these* Ezk 42_9.

<PREP> לְ *concerning* 1 C 28_{12}; בְּ of place, *in* 1 C 9_{33}, + קרא *read* Jr 36_{10}, פקד hi *deposit* Jr 36_{20}, נוח hi. *place* Ezk 44_{19}; בְּ *over,* + נתן pass. *be given,* i.e. appointed Ne 13_4; מִן of direction, *from,* + לקח *take* Jr 36_{21}, שׁלך hi. *throw* Ne 13_8; אֶל *to, at* 2 K 23_{11}, + הלך *go* Ezr 10_6, בוא hi. *bring* Jr $35_{2.4}$ Ezk 42_1 46_{19} Ne $10_{38.40}$, עלה hi. *bring up* Ne 10_{39}; עַל *to,* + ירד *go down* Jr 36_{12}; עַל *over, in charge of* 1 C 23_{28} (‖ חָצֵר *court*), + היה *be* 1 C 9_{26} (‖ אוֹצָר *treasury*); מִמַּעַל לְ *above* Jr 35_4; מִתַּחַת *below* Ezk 42_9; בֵּין *between* Ezk 41_{10}; לִפְנֵי *before* Ezk 42_4; אֶל־פְּנֵי *opposite* Ezk 42_7; לְעֻמַּת *corresponding to* Ezk 42_7; אֵצֶל *beside* Jr 35_4; ה- of direction, *to* the chamber, + בוא hi. *bring* 1 S 9_{22}.

<COLL> לְשָׁכוֹת שְׁתַּיִם *two chambers* Ezk 40_{44} (if em.; see Nom. Cl.), עֶשְׂרִים לְשָׁכֹת *twenty chambers* Ezk 45_5 (or em. עָרִים לָשָׁבֶת *cities to dwell in*), שְׁלֹשִׁים לְשָׁכוֹת *thirty chambers* Ezk 40_{17}; הַלְּשָׁכוֹת בֵּית י׳ used adverbially, *(in) the chambers of the house of Y.,* + שׁקל *weigh* Ezr 8_{29}.

<SYN> חָצֵר *court,* אוֹצָר *treasury.**

→ See also נִשְׁכָּה *room.*

לֶשֶׁם I 2 n.[m.] **jacinth,** or other (semi-)precious stone in Aaron's breastplate, perh. **pale carnelian,*** <NOM CL> הַטּוּר הַשְּׁלִישִׁי לֶשֶׁם שְׁבוֹ וְאַחְלָמָה *the third row is,* i.e. comprises, *a jacinth, an agate and an amethyst* Ex 28_{19}‖39_{12}.

לֶ֫שֶׁם II 2 pl.n. **Leshem,** city conquered and renamed Dan by tribe of Dan, appar. ident. with Laish at Jg 18$_{7.14.27.29}$, <OBJ> לכד *capture* Jos 19$_{47}$, נכה hi. *strike* Jos 19$_{47}$. <PREP> לְ introducing object, + קרא *call*, i.e. name Jos 19$_{47}$; עִם *with*, + לחם ni. *fight* Jos 19$_{47}$.

לשן 2 vb. **slander—Pi.,** see Hi.

Hi. 1 Impf. 2ms תַּלְשֵׁן—**slander,** <SUBJ> Israelite Pr 30$_{10}$ (Gnz תְּלַשֵּׁן, i.e. pi.). <OBJ> עֶבֶד *servant* Pr 30$_{10}$. <PREP> אֶל *to*, + אָדוֹן *master* Pr 30$_{10}$.

Po. 1 Ptc. Qr מְלָשְׁנִי, Kt מלושני—**slander,** <SUBJ> subj. not specified, Ps 101$_{5}$ (or em. מַלְשִׁין, i.e. hi.). <OBJ> רֵעַ *neighbour* Ps 101$_{5}$. <PREP> בְּ of accompaniment, *with*, + סֵתֶר *secrecy* Ps 101$_{5}$.

⇒ לָשׁוֹן *tongue*.

[לֶ֫שַׁע] 1 pl.n. **Lasha,** perh. in region of Dead Sea, <PREP> עַד *unto* Gn 10$_{19}$ (or em. בֶּלַע *Bela*).

לַשָּׁרוֹן 1 pl.n. **Lasharon,** in list of Canaanite kings defeated by Joshua, <CSTR> מֶלֶךְ לַשָּׁרוֹן *king of Lasharon* Jos 12$_{18}$.

לַת, see ילד *bear*.

[לֶ֫תֶךְ] 1.0.1 n.[m.] **lethech**—cstr. לֶתֶךְ—unit of dry measure, perh. half a homer, <SUBJ> מדד *weigh* Mur 24 E$_{12}$. <CSTR> לֶתֶךְ שְׂעֹרִים *lethech of barley* Ho 3$_{2}$. <PREP> בְּ of price, *(in exchange) for*, + כרה *buy* Ho 3$_{2}$, מכר *sell* Is 57$_{8}$ (if em. וַתִּכְרָת־לָךְ מֵהֶם perh. *and you cut*, i.e. made a covenant, *for yourself from them* to וְתִמְכְּרִי בְּכֹר וָלֶתֶךְ *and you sold for a kor and a lethech*).

Bibliography

AANLR	*Atti della Accademia Nazionale dei Lincei, Rome*
AB	Anchor Bible
ALUOS	*The Annual of Leeds University Oriental Society*
AOAT	Alter Orient und Altes Testament
ASTI	*Annual of the Swedish Theological Institute*
Barr	James Barr, *Comparative Philology and the Text of the Old Testament* (Oxford: Oxford University Press, 1968 [reprinted Winona Lake, IN: Eisenbrauns, 1987])
BASOR	*Bulletin of the American Schools of Oriental Research*
BethM	*Beth Mikra*
BETL	Bibliotheca ephemeridum theologicarum lovaniensium
Bib	*Biblica*
BWANT	Beiträge zur Wissenschaft vom Alten und Neuen Testament
BZ	*Biblische Zeitschrift*
BZAW	Beihefte zur *ZAW*
CBQ	*Catholic Biblical Quarterly*
CBQMS	*Catholic Biblical Quarterly*, Monograph Series
DJD	Discoveries in the Judaean Desert
DSD	*Dead Sea Discoveries*
HALAT	Ludwig Koehler *et al.* (eds.), *Hebräisches und aramäisches Lexikon zum Alten Testament* (5 vols.; Leiden: E.J. Brill, 1967–95)
HSS	Harvard Semitic Studies
HTR	*Harvard Theological Review*
HUCA	*Hebrew Union College Annual*
IEJ	*Israel Exploration Journal*
JBL	*Journal of Biblical Literature*
JCS	*Journal of Cuneiform Studies*
JNES	*Journal of Near Eastern Studies*
JNWSL	*Journal of Northwest Semitic Languages*
JQR	*Jewish Quarterly Review*
JSOTSup	*Journal for the Study of the Old Testament*, Supplement Series
JSS	*Journal of Semitic Studies*
JTS	*Journal of Theological Studies*
Lesh	*Lešonénu*
Kaltner	John Kaltner, *The Use of Arabic in Biblical Hebrew Lexicography* (CBQMS, 28; Washington, DC; The Catholic Biblical Association of America, 1996)
OBO	Orbis biblicus et orientalis
OTL	Old Testament Library
OTS	*Oudtestamentische Studiën*
PEQ	*Palestine Exploration Quarterly*
RB	*Revue biblique*
RicLing	*Ricerche linguistiche*
RQ	*Revue de Qumran*
SBLDS	Society of Biblical Literature Dissertation Series
SBLMS	Society of Biblical Literature Monograph Series
ScrHieros	Scripta Hierosolymitana
Stamm	J.J. Stamm, 'Hebräische Frauennamen', in *Hebräische Wortforschung: Festschrift zum 80. Geburtstag von Walter Baumgartner* (ed. G.W. Anderson *et al.*; VTSup, 16; Leiden: E.J. Brill, 1967), pp. 301-39
STDJ	Studies on the Texts of the Desert of Judah
Tarb	*Tarbiẕ*
TDOT	G.J. Botterweck and H. Ringgren (eds.), *Theo-*

logical Dictionary of the Old Testament (tr. John T. Willis *et al.*; Grand Rapids: Eerdmans, 1974–)

Thomas, *Lexicon* D. Winton Thomas, *A Hebrew and English Lexicon of the Old Testament*, revised edition (1970; unpublished)

TLOT Ernst Jenni and Claus Westermann (eds.), *Theologisches Handwörterbuch zum Alten Testament* (München: Chr. Kaiser, 1971–76)

UF *Ugarit-Forschungen*

VT *Vetus Testamentum*

VTSup *Vetus Testamentum*, Supplements

WBC Word Biblical Commentary

WO *Die Welt des Orients*

ZAW *Zeitschrift für die alttestamentliche Wissenschaft*

י

יאב *be willing*—Giovanni Garbini, 'Note semitiche II', *RicLing* 5 (1962), pp. 171-81 (180-81)

יָאוּשׁ *Jaush*—Martin Noth, 'Remarks on the Sixth Volume of Mari Texts', *JSS* 1 (1956), pp. 322-33 (326-27)

יאל I hi. *be willing* (1 S 17_{39})—Otto Eissfeldt, 'Zwei verkannte militär-technische Termini im Alten Testament', *VT* 5 (1955), pp. 232-38 (236-37)

יאל I *be pleased*—A.S. Kapelrud, 'יאל *y'l*', *TDOT*, V (1986), pp. 357-58

יאל II *be foolish*—A.S. Kapelrud, 'יאל *y'l*', *TDOT*, V (1986), pp. 357-58 (358)

יְאֹר *Nile*—H. Eising and J. Bergman, 'יְאֹר *ye'ōr*', *TDOT*, V (1986), pp. 359-63

יְבוּל *produce*—H.A. Hoffner, 'יבל *ybl*; יבול *yeḇûl*', *TDOT*, V (1986), pp. 364-67 (366-67)

יבל *bring*—H.A. Hoffner, 'יבל *ybl*; יבול *yeḇûl*', *TDOT*, V (1986), pp. 364-67

Qal ptc. *channel*—F. Nötscher, 'Entbehrliche Hapaxlegomena in Jesaia', *VT* 1 (1951), pp. 299-302 (299)

יבם I *marry sister-in-law*—E. Kutsch, 'יבם *ybm*; יָבָם *yāḇām*; יְבָמָה *yeḇāmâ*', *TDOT*, V (1986), pp. 367-73

יבם II *create* (cf. Ug. ybmt limm *creator* [fem.] *of peoples*)—Mitchell Dahood, 'Hebrew–Ugaritic Lexicography III', *Bib* 46 (1965), pp. 311-32 (313-14)

יָבָם *husband's brother*—E. Kutsch, 'יבם *ybm*; יָבָם *yāḇām*; יְבָמָה *yeḇāmâ*', *TDOT*, V (1986), pp. 367-73

יְבֶמֶת *sister-in-law*—E. Kutsch, 'יבם *ybm*; יָבָם *yāḇām*; יְבָמָה *yeḇāmâ*', *TDOT*, V (1986), pp. 367-73

יבשׁ I *be dry* (2 K 19_{26}||Is 37_{27} Jr 12_{13} 17_{13} Ps 37_{19})—Mitchell Dahood, 'Hebrew–Ugaritic Lexicography III', *Bib* 46 (1965), pp. 311-32 (314-15); H.D. Preuss, 'יָבֵשׁ *yāḇēš*; יַבָּשָׁה *yabbāšâ*; יַבֶּשֶׁת *yabbešeṯ*', *TDOT*, V (1986), pp. 373-79

יבשׁ II *be ashamed*—Thomas, *Lexicon*, X (1970), p. 37.

יָבֵשׁ I *dry*—H.D. Preuss, 'יָבֵשׁ *yāḇēš*; יַבָּשָׁה *yabbāšâ*; יַבֶּשֶׁת *yabbešeṯ*', *TDOT*, V (1986), pp. 373-79

יָבֵשׁ II *Jabesh*—H.D. Preuss, 'יָבֵשׁ *yāḇēš*; יַבָּשָׁה *yabbāšâ*; יַבֶּשֶׁת *yabbešeṯ*', *TDOT*, V (1986), pp. 373-79 (375-76)

יַבָּשָׁה *dry land*—H.D. Preuss, 'יָבֵשׁ *yāḇēš*; יַבָּשָׁה *yabbāšâ*; יַבֶּשֶׁת *yabbešeṯ*', *TDOT*, V (1986), pp. 373-79 (375)

יַבֶּשֶׁת *dry land*—H.D. Preuss, 'יָבֵשׁ *yāḇēš*; יַבָּשָׁה *yabbāšâ*; יַבֶּשֶׁת *yabbešeṯ*', *TDOT*, V (1986), pp. 373-79 (375)

יגה *be grieved*—S. Wagner, 'יָגָה *yāḡâ*; יָגוֹן *yāḡôn*; תּוּגָה *tûḡâ*', *TDOT*, V (1986), pp. 380-84

יָגוֹן *grief*—S. Wagner, 'יָגָה *yāḡâ*; יָגוֹן *yāḡôn*; תּוּגָה *tûḡâ*', *TDOT*, V (1986), pp. 380-84

יָגִיעַ *weary*—G.F. Hasel, 'יָגַע *yāga'*; יְגִיעַ *yegîa'*; יְגִיעָה *yegî'â*; יָגָע *yāḡā'*; יָגֵעַ *yāḡēa'*; יָגִיעַ *yāḡîa'*', *TDOT*, V (1986), pp. 385-93 (390)

יְגִיעַ *toil, product*—G.F. Hasel, 'יָגַע *yāga'*; יְגִיעַ *yegîa'*; יְגִיעָה *yegî'â*; יָגָע *yāḡā'*; יָגֵעַ *yāḡea'*; יָגִיעַ *yāḡîa'*', *TDOT*, V (1986), pp. 385-93 (390-91)

יְגִיעָה *wearying*—G.F. Hasel, 'יָגַע *yāga'*; יְגִיעַ *yegîa'*; יְגִיעָה *yegî'â*; יָגָע *yāḡā'*; יָגֵעַ *yāḡea'*; יָגִיעַ *yāḡîa'*', *TDOT*, V (1986), pp. 385-93 (390)

יגל *be afraid* (cf. Arab. wajila *be fearful*)—Thomas, *Lexicon*, X (1970), p. 42

יגן *beat* (cf. Arab. wajjana *beat*)—Thomas, *Lexicon*, X (1970), pp. 42-43

יגע *be weary*—G.F. Hasel, 'יָגַע *yāga'*; יְגִיעַ *yegîa'*; יְגִיעָה *yegî'â*; יָגָע *yāgā'*; יָגֵעַ *yāgēa'*; יָגִיעַ *yāgîa*'', *TDOT*, V (1986), pp. 385-93

pi. *torture* (cf. Arab. anja'a *hurt someone*)—H.L. Ginsberg, 'Lexicographical Notes', *ZAW* 51 (1933), pp. 308-309 (308); G.R. Driver, 'Studies in the Vocabulary of the Old Testament. VIII', *JTS* 36 (1935), pp. 293-301 (296-97); Barr, p. 328

יָגָע *gain*—G.F. Hasel, 'יָגַע *yāga'*; יְגִיעַ *yegîa'*; יְגִיעָה *yegî'â*; יָגָע *yāgā'*; יָגֵעַ *yāgēa'*; יָגִיעַ *yāgîa*'', *TDOT*, V (1986), pp. 385-93 (390)

יָגֵעַ *weary*—G.F. Hasel, 'יָגַע *yāga'*; יְגִיעַ *yegîa'*; יְגִיעָה *yegî'â*; יָגָע *yāgā'*; יָגֵעַ *yāgēa'*; יָגִיעַ *yāgîa*'', *TDOT*, V (1986), pp. 385-93

יָד I *hand*—Hans Walter Wolff, *Anthropology of the Old Testament* (tr. Margaret Kohl; London: SCM Press, 1974), pp. 59-60; J. Bergman, W. von Soden and P.R. Ackroyd, 'יָד *yād*; זְרוֹעַ *zerôa'*; יָמִין *yāmîn*; כַּף *kap*; אֶצְבַּע *'eṣba*'', *TDOT*, V (1986), pp. 393-426; A.S. van der Woude, 'יָד *yād* hand', *TLOT*, I (1997), pp. 497-502

Dt 15_2—Robert North, '*Yâd* in the Shemitta-Law', *VT* 4 (1954), pp. 196-99

Is 11_{11}—G.R. Driver, 'Hebrew Notes', *VT* 1 (1951), pp. 241-50 (242)

4QShir[b] 10_{12}—G. Wilhelm Nebe, 'Der Buchstabenname Yod als Ersatz des Tetragramms in 4 Q 511, Fragm. 10, Zeile 12?', *RQ* 12 (1986), pp. 283-84

arm—Aloysius Fitzgerald, 'Hebrew *yd* = "Love" and "Beloved"', *CBQ* 29 (1967), pp. 368-74 (373); J. Bergman, W. von Soden and P.R. Ackroyd, 'יָד *yād*; זְרוֹעַ *zerôa'*; יָמִין *yāmîn*; כַּף *kap*; אֶצְבַּע *'eṣba*'', *TDOT*, V (1986), pp. 393-426 (400); A.S. van der Woude, 'יָד *yād* hand', *TLOT*, II (1997), pp. 497-502 (499)

left hand—Mitchell Dahood, 'Hebrew–Ugaritic Lexicography III', *Bib* 46 (1965), pp. 311-32 (315); 'Congruity of Metaphors', in *Hebräische Wortforschung: Festschrift zum 80. Geburtstag von Walter Baumgartner* (ed. G.W. Anderson *et al.*; VTSup, 16; Leiden: E.J. Brill, 1967), pp. 40-49 (44-46); 'Comparative Philology Today and Yesterday' [Review of James Barr, *Comparative Philology and the Text of the Old Testament* (Oxford: Oxford University Press, 1968)], *Bib* 50 (1969), pp. 70-79 (72)

power—A.S. van der Woude, 'יָד *yād* hand', *TLOT*, II (1997), pp. 497-502 (500)

side—J. Bergman, W. von Soden and P.R. Ackroyd, 'יָד *yād*; זְרוֹעַ *zerôa'*; יָמִין *yāmîn*; כַּף *kap*; אֶצְבַּע *'eṣba*'', *TDOT*, V (1986), pp. 393-426 (400-401); A.S. van der Woude, 'יָד *yād* hand', *TLOT*, II (1997), pp. 497-502 (499)

portion—J. Bergman, W. von Soden and P.R. Ackroyd, 'יָד *yād*; זְרוֹעַ *zerôa'*; יָמִין *yāmîn*; כַּף *kap*; אֶצְבַּע *'eṣba*'', *TDOT*, V (1986), pp. 393-426 (401); A.S. van der Woude, 'יָד *yād* hand', *TLOT*, II (1997), pp. 497-502 (499)

monument—M. Delcor, 'Two Special Meanings of the Word יד in Biblical Hebrew', *JSS* 12 (1967), pp. 230-40 (230-34); O. Loretz, 'Stelen und Sohnespflicht im Totenkult Kanaans und Israel: *skn* (KTU 1.17 I 26) und *jd* (Jes 56,5)', *UF* 21 (1989), pp. 240-46; J. Bergman, W. von Soden and P.R. Ackroyd, 'יָד *yād*; זְרוֹעַ *zerôa'*; יָמִין *yāmîn*; כַּף *kap*; אֶצְבַּע *'eṣba*'', *TDOT*, V (1986), pp. 393-426 (401); A.S. van der Woude, 'יָד *yād* hand', *TLOT*, II (1997), pp. 497-502 (499)

peg—J. Bergman, W. von Soden and P.R. Ackroyd, 'יָד *yād*; זְרוֹעַ *zerôa'*; יָמִין *yāmîn*; כַּף *kap*; אֶצְבַּע *'eṣba*'', *TDOT*, V (1986), pp. 393-426 (401); A.S. van der Woude, 'יָד *yād* hand', *TLOT*, II (1997), pp. 497-502 (499)

axletree—J. Bergman, W. von Soden and P.R. Ackroyd, 'יָד *yād*; זְרוֹעַ *zerôa'*; יָמִין *yāmîn*; כַּף *kap*; אֶצְבַּע *'eṣba*'', *TDOT*, V (1986), pp. 393-426 (401)

armrest—J. Bergman, W. von Soden and P.R. Ackroyd, 'יָד *yād*; זְרוֹעַ *zerôa'*; יָמִין *yāmîn*; כַּף *kap*; אֶצְבַּע *'eṣba*'', *TDOT*, V (1986), pp. 393-426 (401); A.S. van der Woude, 'יָד *yād* hand', *TLOT*, II (1997), pp. 497-502 (499)

flock (cf. Arab. yad min ġanamin *flock*)—Joseph Reider, 'Contributions to the Scriptural Text', *HUCA* 24 (1952–53), pp. 85-106 (89)

descendant—Robert Gordis, 'A Note on *Yad*', *JBL* 62 (1943), pp. 341-44 (343-44)

בְּיָד רָמָה *with a high hand*—C.J. Labuschagne, 'The Meaning of *beyād rāmā* in the Old Testament', in *Von Kanaan bis Kerala: Festschrift für Prof. Mag. Dr. Dr. J.P.M. van der Ploeg O.P. zur Vollendung des siebzigsten Lebensjahres am 4. Juli 1979, berreicht von Kollegen, Freunden und Schülern* (ed. W.C. Delsman; AOAT, 211; Kevelaer/Neukirchen-Vluyn: Verlag Butzon & Bercker/Neukirchener Verlag, 1982), pp. 143-48; Gary A. Anderson, 'Intentional and Unintentional Sin in the Dead Sea Scrolls', in *Pomegranates and Golden Bells: Studies in Biblical, Jewish, and Near Eastern Ritual, Law, and Literature in Honor of Jacob Milgrom* (ed. David P. Wright, David Noel Freedman and Avi Hurvitz; Winona Lake, IN; Eisenbrauns, 1995), pp. 49-64 (50-54); A.S. van der Woude, 'יָד *yād* hand', *TLOT*, II (1997), pp. 497-502 (500)

מלא יָד *consecrate*—A.S. van der Woude, 'יָד *yād* hand', *TLOT*, II (1997), pp. 497-502 (500)

בְּיַד = בְּעַד—Robert Gordis, 'A Note on *Yad*', *JBL* 62 (1943), pp. 341-44 (341-43)

בְּיַד *from*—Mitchell Dahood, 'Qoheleth and Northwest Semitic Philology', *Bib* 43 (1962), pp. 349-65 (361)

עַל יַד *beside* (Jr 5$_{31}$)—G.R. Driver, 'Studies in the Vocabulary of the Old Testament. VIII', *JTS* 36 (1935), pp. 293-301 (298)

בֵּין יָדֶיךָ *between your hands*—Y. Avishur, 'Expressions of the Type *BYN YDYM* in the Bible and Semitic Languages', *UF* 12 (1980), pp. 125-33 (128-30)

יָד II *penis* (cf. Arab. wadda, Ugar. ydd *love*, Ugar. yd perh. *penis*)—M. Delcor, 'Two Special Meanings of the Word יד in Biblical Hebrew', *JSS* 12 (1967), pp. 230-40 (234-40); Matitiahu Tsevat, 'Some Biblical Notes', *HUCA* 24 (1952–53), pp. 107-14 (109-10); J. Bergman, W. von Soden and P.R. Ackroyd, 'יָד *yād*; זְרוֹעַ *zerôa'*; יָמִין *yāmîn*; כַּף *kap*; אֶצְבַּע *'eṣba''*, *TDOT*, V (1986), pp. 393-426 (402-403); A.S. van der Woude, 'יָד *yād* hand', *TLOT*, II (1997), pp. 497-502 (499)

יָד III *love*—Aloysius Fitzgerald, 'Hebrew *yd* = "Love" and "Beloved"', *CBQ* 29 (1967), pp. 368-74

ידה I *praise*—G. Mayer, J. Bergman and W. von Soden, 'ידה *ydh*; תּוֹדָה *tôḏâh*', *TDOT*, V (1986), pp. 427-443; C. Westermann, 'ידה *ydh* hi. to praise', *TLOT*, II (1997), pp. 502-508

Ps 74$_{19}$—Christopher T. Begg, 'The Covenantal Dove in Psalm lxxiv 19-20', *VT* 37 (1987), pp. 78-81 (78)

Ps 76$_{11}$—J.A. Emerton, 'A Neglected Solution of a Problem in Ps lxvi 11', *VT* 24 (1974), pp. 136-46 (145); John Gray, *The Biblical Doctrine of the Reign of God* (Edinburgh: T. & T. Clark, 1979), pp. 55-56; Mitchell Dahood, 'Love and Death at Ebla and their Biblical Reflections', in *Love and Death in the Ancient Near East: Essays in Honor of Marvin H. Pope* (ed. John H. Marks and Robert M. Good; Guilford, CN/Los Angeles, CA: Four Quarters Publishing Company/Western Academic Press, 1986), pp. 93-99 (95)

confess—G. Mayer, J. Bergman and W. von Soden, 'ידה *ydh*; תּוֹדָה *tôḏâh*', *TDOT*, V (1986), pp. 427-43 (439-443)

יָדָה *voice* (cf. Arab. dawiyyun *sound*)—H.L. Ginsberg, 'Lexicographical Notes', *ZAW* 51 (1933), pp. 308-309 (308); Barr, p. 328

יִדּוֹ *Iddo*—Aloysius Fitzgerald, 'Hebrew *yd* = "Love" and "Beloved"', *CBQ* 29 (1967), pp. 368-74 (374)

יַדַּי *Jaddai*—Aloysius Fitzgerald, 'Hebrew *yd* = "Love" and "Beloved"', *CBQ* 29 (1967), pp. 368-74 (374)

יָדִיד *beloved*—H.-J. Zobel, 'יָדִיד *yāḏîḏ*', *TDOT*, V (1986), pp. 444-48

יְדִידָה *Jedidah*—Stamm, p. 325

יְדִידֹת *love*—Gary A. Rendsburg, *Linguistic Evidence for the Northern Origin of Selected Psalms* (SBLMS, 43; Atlanta: Scholars Press, 1990), p. 32

ידע I *know*—J. Bergmann and G.J. Botterweck, 'יָדַע *yāḏa'*; דַּעַת *da'aṯ*; דֵּעַ *dēa'*; דֵּעָה *dē'â*; מוֹדָע *m ôḏā'*; מוֹדַעַת *môḏa'aṯ*; מַדָּע *maddā'*; מַנְדָּע *mandā'*', *TDOT*, V (1986), pp. 448-81; W. Schottroff, 'ידע *yd'* to perceive, know', *TLOT*, II (1997), pp. 508-21

Ps 71$_{15}$—G.R. Driver, 'Hebrew Notes', *VT* 1 (1951), pp. 241-50 (249)

recognize covenant partner—Herbert B. Huffmon, 'The Treaty Background of Hebrew *yāda'*', *BASOR* 181 (February, 1966), pp. 31-37 (34-37); Herbert B. Huffmon and Simon B. Parker, 'A Further Note on the Treaty Background of Hebrew *yāda'*', *BASOR* 184 (December, 1966), pp. 36-38

choose—Herbert B. Huffmon, 'The Treaty Background of Hebrew *yāda'*', *BASOR* 181 (February, 1966), pp. 31-

37 (35)

know good and evil—Elisha Qimron, 'Biblical Philology and the DSS', *Tarb* 58 (1989), pp. 297-315 (312)

ידע על *know about* (Jb 37$_{16}$)—Joseph Reider, 'Etymological Studies in Biblical Hebrew', *VT* 4 (1954), pp. 276-95 (293)

ni. *make oneself known*—J.H. Eaton, 'Some Misunderstood Hebrew Words for God's Self-Revelation', *The Bible Translator* 25 (1974), pp. 331-38 (333)

hi. *distinguish*—Elisha Qimron, 'Biblical Philology and the DSS', *Tarb* 58 (1989), pp. 297-315 (302-303)

ho. *be made known* (Ex 21$_{29}$)—W. Moran, Review of Albrecht Goetze, *The Laws of Eshnunna* (New Haven: American Schools of Oriental Research, 1956), *Bib* 38 (1957), pp. 216-21 (218)

ידע II *be quiet* (cf. Arab. wada'a *be quiet*)—D. Winton Thomas, 'The Root ידע in Hebrew, II', *JTS* 36 (1935), pp. 409-12; 'A Note on לא תדע in Proverbs v.6', *JTS* 37 (1936), pp. 59-60; 'More Notes on the Root ידע in Hebrew', *JTS* 38 (1937), pp. 404-405; 'Notes on בַּל־יָדְעָה in Proverbs 9$_{13}$', *JTS* ns 4 (1953), pp. 23-24; Barr, pp. 19-21, 328; Thomas, *Lexicon*, X (1970), pp. 139-49; J.A. Emerton, 'A Consideration of Some Alleged Meanings of *yd*'', *JSS* 15 (1970), pp. 145-80; 'A Further Consideration of D.W. Thomas's Theories about *yd*'', *VT* 41 (1991), pp. 145-63; 'The Work of David Winton Thomas as a Hebrew Scholar', *VT* 41 (1991), pp. 287-303 (300-301); J. Bergmann and G.J. Botterweck, 'יָדַע *yāḏa'*; דַּעַת *da'aṯ*; דֵּעַ *dēa'*; דֵּעָה *dē'â*; מוֹדָע *môḏā'*; מֹדַעַת *mōḏa'aṯ*; מַדָּע *maddā'*; מַנְדָּע *mandā*'', *TDOT*, V (1986), pp. 448-81 (450-51); W. Schottroff, 'ידע *yd'* to perceive, know', *TLOT*, II (1997), pp. 508-21 (509); W. Johnstone, '*yd'* II "be humbled, humiliated"?', *VT* 41 (1991), pp. 49-62; Kaltner, p. 106

Is 53$_{3}$—Peter R. Ackroyd, 'Meaning and Exegesis', in *Words and Meanings: Essays Presented to David Winton Thomas on his Retirement from the Regius Professorship of Hebrew in the University of Cambridge* (ed. Peter R. Ackroyd and Barnabas Lindars; Cambridge: Cambridge University Press, 1968), pp. 1-14 (11-14); Barr, p. 20

ידע III *care* (cf. Arab. istanda'a *be entrusted with*)—D.W. Thomas, 'A Note on וַיֵּדַע אֱלֹהִים in Exod. ii.25', *JTS* 49 (1948), pp. 143-44; Barr, pp. 22, 328; J. Bergmann and G.J. Botterweck, 'יָדַע *yāḏa'*; דַּעַת *da'aṯ*; דֵּעַ *dēa'*; דֵּעָה *dē'â*; מוֹדָע *môḏā'*; מֹדַעַת *mōḏa'aṯ*; מַדָּע *maddā'*; מַנְדָּע *mandā*'', *TDOT*, V (1986), pp. 448-81 (451)

ידע IV *punish* (cf. Arab. wada'a *be quiet*, specif. *be punished*)—D. Winton Thomas, 'Julius Fürst and the Hebrew Root ידע', *JTS* 42 (1941), pp. 64-65; 'Additional Notes on the Root ידע in Hebrew', *JTS* ns 15 (1964), pp. 54-57; J. Bergmann and G.J. Botterweck, 'יָדַע *yāḏa'*; דַּעַת *da'aṯ*; דֵּעַ *dēa'*; דֵּעָה *dē'â*; מוֹדָע *môḏā'*; מֹדַעַת *mōḏa'aṯ*; מַדָּע *maddā'*; מַנְדָּע *mandā*'', *TDOT*, V (1986), pp. 448-81 (452); W. Schottroff, 'ידע *yd'* to perceive, know', *TLOT*, II (1997), pp. 508-21 (509)

ידע VI *seek* (cf. Arab. da'ā *seek, ask after*)—D. Winton Thomas, 'Notes on Some Passages in the Book of Proverbs', *JTS* 38 (1937), pp. 400-403 (401); 'Textual and Philological Notes on Some Passages in the Book of Proverbs', in *Wisdom in Israel and the Ancient Near East: Festschrift H.H. Rowley* (ed. M. Noth and D.W. Thomas; VTSup, 3; Leiden: E.J. Brill, 1955), pp. 284-85; Barr, pp. 23-25; 'A Note on נוֹדַע in 1 Samuel ii.6', *JTS* ns 21 (1970), pp. 401-402; J. Bergmann and G.J. Botterweck, 'יָדַע *yāḏa'*; דַּעַת *da'aṯ*; דֵּעַ *dēa'*; דֵּעָה *dē'â*; מוֹדָע *môḏā'*; מֹדַעַת *mōḏa'aṯ*; מַדָּע *maddā'*; מַנְדָּע *mandā*'', *TDOT*, V (1986), pp. 448-81 (452); W. Schottroff, 'ידע *yd'* to perceive, know', *TLOT*, II (1997), pp. 508-21 (509)

ידע VII *leave* (cf. Arab. wadda'a *bid farewell*)—Barr, pp. 21-22, 328; J. Bergmann and G.J. Botterweck, 'יָדַע *yāḏa'*; דַּעַת *da'aṯ*; דֵּעַ *dēa'*; דֵּעָה *dē'â*; מוֹדָע *m ôḏā'*; מֹדַעַת *mōḏa'aṯ*; מַדָּע *maddā'*; מַנְדָּע *mandā*'', *TDOT*, V (1986), pp. 448-81 (451)

ידע VIII *call* (cf. Arab. da'ā *call*)—J. Bergmann and G.J. Botterweck, 'יָדַע *yāḏa'*; דַּעַת *da'aṯ*; דֵּעַ *dēa'*; דֵּעָה *dē'â*; מוֹדָע *môḏā'*; מֹדַעַת *mōḏa'aṯ*; מַדָּע *maddā'*; מַנְדָּע *mandā*'', *TDOT*, V (1986), pp. 448-81 (452)

ידע IX *tear down* (cf. Arab. dā'a *tear down, destroy*)—J. Bergmann and G.J. Botterweck, 'יָדַע *yāḏa'*; דַּעַת *da'aṯ*; דֵּעַ *dēa'*; דֵּעָה *dē'â*; מוֹדָע *môḏā'*; מֹדַעַת *mōḏa'aṯ*; מַדָּע *maddā'*; מַנְדָּע *mandā*'', *TDOT*, V (1986), pp. 448-81 (452); W. Schottroff, 'ידע *yd'* to perceive, know',

TLOT, II (1997), pp. 508-21 (509)

ידע X *leave alone* (cf. Arab. wada'a *be quiet*, specif. *leave alone, exempt*)—D.W. Thomas, 'Additional Notes on the Root ידע in Hebrew', *JTS* ns 15 (1964), pp. 54-57; Alfred Guillaume, 'The Arabic Background of the Book of Job', in *Promise and Fulfilment: Essays Presented to Professor S.H. Hooke in Celebration of his Ninetieth Birthday, 21st January 1964, by Members of the Society for Old Testament Study and Others* (ed. F.F. Bruce: Edinburgh: T. & T. Clark, 1963), pp. 106-27 (121); Lester L. Grabbe, *Comparative Philology and the Text of Job: A Study in Methodology* (SBLDS, 34; Missoula, MT: Scholars Press, 1977), pp. 105-107; J. Bergmann and G.J. Botterweck, 'יָדַע *yāḏa'*; דַּעַת *da'aṯ*; דֵּעַ *dēa'*; דֵּעָה *dē'â*; מוֹדָע *m ôḏā'*; מֹדַעַת *mōḏa'aṯ*; מַדָּע *maddā'*; מַנְדָּע *mandā''*, *TDOT*, V (1986), pp. 448-81 (451).

ידע XI *wrap up* (cf. Arab. mīda' *garment*)—H.H. Hirschberg, 'Some Additional Etymologies in Old Testament Lexicography', *VT* 11 (1961), pp. 371-85 (379); Barr, pp. 22, 328

ידע XII *reconcile* (cf. Arab. wāda'a *be reconciled*)—D.W. Thomas, 'Note on נוֹעֲדוּ in Amos iii.3', *JTS* ns 7 (1956), pp. 69-70; Barr, p. 328; J. Bergmann and G.J. Botterweck, 'יָדַע *yāḏa'*; דַּעַת *da'aṯ*; דֵּעַ *dēa'*; דֵּעָה *dē'â*; מוֹדָע *môḏā'*; מֹדַעַת *mōḏa'aṯ*; מַדָּע *maddā'*; מַנְדָּע *mandā''*, *TDOT*, V (1986), pp. 448-81 (451)

ידע XIII *deposit* (cf. Arab. istanda'a *deposit*)—Thomas, *Lexicon*, X (1970), pp. 139-49 (149)

יַדָּע *expert*—Elisha Qimron, 'Biblical Philology and the DSS', *Tarb* 58 (1989), pp. 297-315 (303-304)

יָהּ *Yah*—D.N. Freedmann, M.P. O'Connor and H. Ringgren, 'יהוה *YHWH*', *TDOT*, V (1986), pp. 500-521 (502)

'י *Yahweh*—Norman Walker, 'Yahwism and the Divine Name "Yhwh"', *ZAW*'70 (1958), pp. 262-65; H. Kosmala, 'The Name of God (YHWH and HU')', *ASTI* 2 (1963), pp. 103-106; Herbert H. Huffmon, 'Yahweh and Mari', in *Near Eastern Studies in Honor of William Foxwell Albright* (ed. Hans Goedicke; Baltimore: Johns Hopkins Press, 1971), pp. 283-85; Giovanni Garbini, *History and Ideology in Ancient Israel* (tr. John Bowden; London: SCM Press, 1988), pp. 56-58, 188-89; D.N. Freedman, M.P. O'Connor and H. Ringgren, 'יהוה *YHWH*', *TDOT*, V (1986), pp. 500-21; Stig I.L. Norin, *Sein Name allein ist hoch: das Jhw-haltige Suffix althebräischer Personennamen untersucht mit besonderer Berücksichtigung der alttestamentlichen Redaktionsgeschichte* (Coniectanea Biblica Old Testament Series, 24; Malmo: C.W.K. Gleerup, 1986); Ziony Zevit, 'Onomastic Gleanings from Recently Published Judahite Bullae', *IEJ* 38 (1988), pp. 227-34; E. Jenni, 'יהוה *yhwh* Yahweh', *TLOT*, II (1997), pp. 522-26

pronunciation—Peter Katz, 'יְהוָה = Jejā, יהיה = Jājā', *VT* 4 (1954), pp. 428-29; Steven T. Byington, 'יהוה and אדני', *JBL* 76 (1957), pp. 58-59; Ariel Alvarez Valdés, '¿El Dios de Israel era Yahvé o Jehová?', *Tierra Santa: La Revista de los Santos Lugares* 71 (1996), pp. 188-92

Ex 6_2—Karl Budde, 'Kleinigkeiten zur Genesis', *ZAW* 51 (1933), pp. 311-12

Ps 21_2—Mitchell Dahood, 'Comparative Philology Today and Tomorrow' [Review of James Barr, *Comparative Philology and the Text of the Old Testament* (Oxford: Oxford University Press, 1968)], *Bib* 50 (1969), pp. 70-79 (79)

אֵל 'י *Y., God*—Mitchell Dahood, 'Hebrew–Ugaritic Lexicography III', *Bib* 46 (1965), pp. 311-32 (317); 'Hebrew–Ugaritic Lexicography IV', *Biblica* 47 (1966), pp. 403-19 (410); 'Comparative Philology Today and Tomorrow' [Review of James Barr, *Comparative Philology and the Text of the Old Testament* (Oxford: Oxford University Press, 1968)], *Bib* 50 (1969), pp. 70-79 (72)

בְּעֵינֶיךָ אֲדֹנָי 'י *in the eyes of my Lord, Y.* (2 S 7_{19})—Francis I. Andersen, 'A Short Note on Construct *k* in Hebrew', *Bib* 50 (1969), pp. 68-69 (69)

יָהוּ *Yahu* (Hb 3_2)—Joseph Reider, 'Etymological Studies in Biblical Hebrew', *VT* 4 (1954), pp. 276-95 (284)

יְהוֹאָשׁ *Jehoash*—Martin Noth, 'Remarks on the Sixth Volume of Mari Texts', *JSS* 1 (1956), pp. 322-33 (326)

יְהוּדָה *Judah*—A.R. Millard, 'The Meaning of the Name Judah', *ZAW* 86 (1974), pp. 216-18; Manfred Görg, 'Juda—Namensdeutung in Tradition und Etymologie', in *Konsequente Traditionsgeschichte: Festschrift für Klaus Baltzer zum 65. Geburtstag* (ed. Rödiger Bartelmus, Thomas Krüger and Helmut Utzschneider; OBO, 126; Freiburg, Switzerland/Göttingen: Universitätsverlag/Vandenhoeck & Ruprecht, 1993), pp. 79-87; H.-J. Zobel, 'יְהוּדָה *yehûdâ*', *TDOT*, V (1986), pp. 482-99

יְהוּדִי *Jehudi*—Stamm, p. 322

יְהוּדִית *Judith*—Stamm, p. 322

יְהוֹחַיִל *Jehohail*—Ziony Zevit, 'Onomastic Gleanings from Recently Published Judahite Bullae', *IEJ* 38 (1988), pp. 227-34 (234)

יְהוֹסֵף *J(eh)oseph*—Scott C. Layton, 'Jehoseph in Ps 81,6', *Bib* 69 (1988), pp. 406-11

יְהוֹעַדָּן *Jehoaddan*—Stamm, p. 313

יָהִיר *proud*—Josua Blau, 'Etymologische Untersuchungen auf Grund des palästinischen Arabisch', *VT* 5 (1955), pp. 337-44 (342)

יַהֲלֹם *onyx*—John S. Harris, 'An Introduction to the Study of Personal Ornaments of Precious, Semi-Precious and Imitation Stones Used throughout Biblical History', *ALUOS* 4 (1962), pp. 49-83 (62-64)

יוֹאָשׁ *Joash*—Martin Noth, 'Remarks on the Sixth Volume of Mari Texts', *JSS* 1 (1956), pp. 322-33 (326)

יוֹבֵל *ram*—R.G. North, 'יוֹבֵל *yôḇēl*', *TDOT*, VI (1990), pp. 1-6

יוֹד *yod*—G. Wilhelm Nebe, 'Der Buchstabenname Yod als Ersatz des Tetragramms in 4 Q 511, Fragm. 10, Zeile 12?', *RQ* 12 (1986), pp. 283-84

יוֹם I *day*—W. von Soden, J. Bergman and M. Sæbø, 'יוֹם *yôm*; יוֹמָם *yômām*; יוֹם יהוה *yôm YHWH*', *TDOT*, VI (1990), pp. 7-32; E. Jenni, 'יוֹם *yôm* day', *TLOT*, II (1997), pp. 536-39

Jb 3_{8}—Lester L. Grabbe, *Comparative Philology and the Text of Job: A Study in Methodology* (SBLDS, 34; Missoula, MT: Scholars Press, 1977), pp. 35-38; E. Lipinski, 'לִוְיָתָן *liwyāṯān*', *TDOT*, VII (1995), pp. 504-509 (505-506)

Is 38_{10}—Mitchell Dahood, 'Textual Problems in Isaia', *CBQ* 22 (1960), pp. 400-409 (401)

עשׂה יָמִים *spend time* (Ec 6_{12})—C.L. Seow, 'Linguistic Evidence and the Dating of Qohelet', *JBL* 115 (1996), pp. 643-66 (658)

יוֹם י׳ *day of Y.* (Is 3_{14})—R. Althann, 'Consonantal *ym*: Ending or Noun in Isa 3,13; Jer 17,16; 1 Sam 6,19', *Bib* 63 (1982), pp. 560-65 (560-61)

יוֹם רָעָה *day of evil* (Jr 17_{16})—R. Althann, 'Consonantal *ym*: Ending or Noun in Isa 3,13; Jer 17,16; 1 Sam 6,19', *Bib* 63 (1982), pp. 560-65 (561-63)

אַחֲרִית הַיָּמִים *end of days*—Hans Kosmala, '"At the End of the Days"', *ASTI* 2 (1963), pp. 27-37.

חֲמֵשׁ יוֹם *five days* (1 S 6_{19})—R. Althann, 'Consonantal *ym*: Ending or Noun in Isa 3,13; Jer 17,16; 1 Sam 6,19', *Bib* 63 (1982), pp. 560-65 (563-65)

שֶׁבַע יוֹם *seven days* (1 S 6_{19})—R. Althann, 'Consonantal *ym*: Ending or Noun in Isa 3,13; Jer 17,16; 1 Sam 6,19', *Bib* 63 (1982), pp. 560-65 (563-65)

יוֹם II *storm* (cf. Akk. ūmu *storm [demon]*)—G.R. Driver, 'Isaiah i-xxxix: Textual and Linguistic Problems', *JSS* 13 (1968), pp. 36-57 (46-47); Jeffrey Niehaus, 'In the Wind of the Storm: Another Look at Genesis iii 8', *VT* 45 (1994), pp. 263-67

יוֹנָה I *dove*—G.R. Driver, 'Birds in the Old Testament: II. Birds in Life', *PEQ* 87 (1955), pp. 129-40 (129-30, 140); G.J. Botterweck and W. von Soden, 'יוֹנָה *yônâ*; תּוֹר *tôr* II; גּוֹזָל *gôzāl*; יְמִימָה *yemîmâ*', *TDOT*, VI (1990), pp. 32-40

יְוָנִי *Greek* (Hb 2_{5})—Joseph Reider, 'Etymological Studies in Biblical Hebrew', *VT* 4 (1954), pp. 276-95 (281)

יוֹסֵף *Joseph*—Scott C. Layton, 'Je(ho)seph in Ps 81,6', *Bib* 69 (1988), pp. 406-11

יוֹרֶה I *early rain*—Mitchell Dahood, 'Some Aphel Causatives in Ugaritic', *Bib* 38 (1957), pp. 62-73 (67-68)

יחד *be united*—H.-J. Fabry, 'יָחַד *yāḥaḏ*; יַחַד *yaḥaḏ*; יָחִיד *yāḥîḏ*; יַחְדָו *yaḥdāw*', *TDOT*, VI (1990), pp. 40-48

Gn 49_{6}—Wilfred G.E. Watson, 'Hebrew "To be Happy"—An Idiom Identified', *VT* 31 (1981), pp. 92-94

Jb 3_{6}—Lester L. Grabbe, *Comparative Philology and the Text of Job: A Study in Methodology* (SBLDS, 34; Missoula, MT: Scholars Press, 1977), pp. 32-35

יַחַד *unity*—J.C. de Moor, 'Lexical Remarks Concerning *yaḥad* and *yaḥdaw*', *VT* 7 (1957), pp. 350-55; H.-J. Fabry, 'יָחַד *yāḥaḏ*; יַחַד *yaḥaḏ*; יָחִיד *yāḥîḏ*; יַחְדָו *yaḥdāw*', *TDOT*, VI (1990), pp. 40-48 (44, 47-48)

community (cf. Ug. pqr yḥd *overseer of the community*; Greek ὅμιλος *crowd*, in ref. to Essenes)—Ralph Marcus, 'Philo, Josephus and the Dead Sea *Yaḥad*', *JBL* 71 (1952), pp. 207-209; Mitchell Dahood, 'Hebrew–

Ugaritic Lexicography III', *Bib* 46 (1965), pp. 311-32 (318)

together—H.-J. Fabry, 'יָחַד *yāḥad*; יַחַד *yaḥad*; יָחִיד *yāḥîd*; יַחְדָו *yaḥdāw*', *TDOT*, VI (1990), pp. 40-48 (45)

יַחְדָו *together*—J.C. de Moor, 'Lexical Remarks concerning *yaḥad* and *yaḥdaw*', *VT* 7 (1957), pp. 350-55; Kjell Aartun, 'Die hervorhebende Endung -*w*(V) an nordwestsemitischen Adverbien und Negationen', *UF* 5 (1973), pp. 1-5 (1-2); H.-J. Fabry, 'יָחַד *yāḥad*; יַחַד *yaḥad*; יָחִיד *yāḥîd*; יַחְדָו *yaḥdāw*', *TDOT*, VI (1990), pp. 40-48 (45)

Jr 31$_{13}$—M. Dahood, 'Comparative Philology Today and Yesterday' [Review of James Barr, *Comparative Philology and the Text of the Old Testament* (Oxford: Oxford University Press, 1968)], *Bib* 50 (1969), pp. 70-79 (78)

יָחִיד *only*—H.-J. Fabry, 'יָחַד *yāḥad*; יַחַד *yaḥad*; יָחִיד *yāḥîd*; יַחְדָו *yaḥdāw*', *TDOT*, VI (1990), pp. 40-48 (46)

יָחִיל *waiting*—C. Barth, 'יָחַל *yāḥal*; תּוֹחֶלֶת *tôḥelet*', *TDOT*, VI (1990), pp. 49-55 (49)

יחל I *wait*—C. Barth, 'יָחַל *yāḥal*; תּוֹחֶלֶת *tôḥelet*', *TDOT*, VI (1990), pp. 49-55; C. Westermann, 'יחל *yḥl* pi./hi. to wait', *TLOT*, II (1997), pp. 540-42

יחל II *be desperate* (cf. Arab. waḥila *sink into the mire, be uncertain*; Syr. 'ḥl *despair*)—Thomas, *Lexicon*, X (1970), pp. 218-19; G.R. Driver, 'Supposed Arabisms in the Old Testament', *JBL* 55 (1936), pp. 101-20 (112-13)

יחשׂ *be registered*—R. Mosis, 'יָחַשׂ *yāḥaś*', *TDOT*, VI (1990), pp. 55-59

יַחַשׂ *genealogical registration*—R. Mosis, 'יָחַשׂ *yāḥaś*', *TDOT*, VI (1990), pp. 55-59

יטב *be good*—H.J. Stoebe, 'טוֹב *ṭôb* good; יטב *yṭb* to be good; יָפֶה *yāpeh* pretty', *TLOT*, II (1997), pp. 486-95

Ec 11$_{9}$—Mitchell Dahood, 'Qoheleth and Northwest Semitic Philology', *Bib* 43 (1962), pp. 349-65 (363)

hi. *direct* one's way—H.J. Stoebe, 'טוֹב *ṭôb* good; יטב *yṭb* to be good; יָפֶה *yāpeh* pretty', *TLOT*, II (1997), pp. 486-95 (493)

יטשׁ *clash, dash* (cf. Arab. waṭasa *crush*, tawaṭṭasa *dash together*)—Thomas, *Lexicon*, X (1970), pp. 237-38

יַיִן *wine*—A. van Selms, 'The Etymology of *yayin*, "wine"', *JNWSL* 3 (1974), pp. 77-84; W. Dommershausen, 'יַיִן *yayin*', *TDOT*, VI (1990), pp. 59-64

Hb 2$_{5}$—Joseph Reider, 'Etymological Studies in Biblical Hebrew', *VT* 4 (1954), pp. 276-95 (281-82)

Ps 141$_{5}$—Gary A. Rendsburg, *Linguistic Evidence for the Northern Origin of Selected Psalms* (SBLMS, 43; Atlanta: Scholars Press, 1990), pp. 100-101

יכה *crouch* (cf. Arab. ittaqa'a/ittaqā *sit*)—Thomas, *Lexicon*, X (1970), p. 243

יכח *contend*—H.-J. Fabry, G. Mayer, 'יכח *ykḥ*; תּוֹכַחַת *tôkaḥat*; תּוֹכֵחָה *tôkēḥâ*', *TDOT*, VI (1990), pp. 64-71; G. Liedke, 'יכח *ykḥ* hi. to determine what is right', *TLOT*, II (1997), pp. 542-44

hi. *appoint*—Menaḥem Kister, 'Lexical Problems—Early and Late', *Tarb* 61 (1992), pp. 45-60 (46)

יָכִין *Jachin* (§5), M.J. Mulder, 'Die Bedeutung von Jachin und Boaz in 1 Kön. 7:21 (2 Chr. 3:17)', in *Tradition and Re-interpretation in Jewish and Early Christian Literature: Essays in Honour of Jürgen C.H. Lebram* (ed. J.W. van Henten; Studia Post-Biblica, 36; Leiden: E.J. Brill, 1986), pp. 19-26

יכל *be able*—H.-J. Fabry, H. Ringgren, J.A. Soggin, 'יָכֹל *yākōl*', *TDOT*, VI (1990), pp. 71-75

יְכָלְיָהוּ *Jecoliah*—Stamm, p. 311

ילד *give birth*—J. Schreiner and G.J. Botterweck, 'יָלַד *yālad*; יֶלֶד *yeled*; יַלְדָּה *yaldâ*; יַלְדוּת *yaledût*; יָלִיד *yālîd*; תּוֹלְדוֹת *tôledôt*', *TDOT*, VI (1990), pp. 76-81; J. Kühlewein, 'ילד *yld* to bear', *TLOT*, II (1997), pp. 544-46

pi. *beget*—Karl Budde, 'Kleinigkeiten zur Genesis', *ZAW* 51 (1933), pp. 311-12 (311)

hi. *beget* (Jb 5$_{7}$)—Mitchell Dahood, 'Hebrew–Ugaritic Lexicography III', *Bib* 46 (1965), pp. 311-32 (318)

יֶלֶד *child*—J. Schreiner and G.J. Botterweck, 'יָלַד *yālad*; יֶלֶד *yeled*; יַלְדָּה *yaldâ*; יַלְדוּת *yaledût*; יָלִיד *yālîd*; תּוֹלְדוֹת *tôledôt*', *TDOT*, VI (1990), pp. 76-81

יַלְדָּה *girl*—J. Schreiner and G.J. Botterweck, 'יָלַד *yālad*; יֶלֶד *yeled*; יַלְדָּה *yaldâ*; יַלְדוּת *yaledût*; יָלִיד *yālîd*; תּוֹלְדוֹת *tôledôt*', *TDOT*, VI (1990), pp. 76-81

יַלְדוּת *youth*—J. Schreiner and G.J. Botterweck, 'יָלַד *yālad*; יֶלֶד *yeled*; יַלְדָּה *yaldâ*; יַלְדוּת *yaledût*; יָלִיד *yālîd*; תּוֹלְדוֹת *tôledôt*', *TDOT*, VI (1990), pp. 76-81

יִלּוֹד *born*—J. Schreiner and G.J. Botterweck, 'יָלַד *yālad*; יֶלֶד *yeled*; יַלְדָּה *yaldâ*; יַלְדוּת *yaledût*; יָלִיד *yālîd*; תּוֹלְדוֹת

tôledôt', *TDOT*, VI (1990), pp. 76-81

יְלִיד *born*—J. Schreiner and G.J. Botterweck, 'יָלַד *yālad*; יֶלֶד *yeled*; יַלְדָּה *yaldâ*; יַלְדוּת *yaledût*; יָלִיד *yālîd*; תּוֹלְדוֹת *tôledôt*', *TDOT*, VI (1990), pp. 76-81

ילל *howl*—A. Baumann, 'ילל *yll*; יְלֵל *yelēl*; יְלָלָה *yelālâ*', *TDOT*, VI (1990) pp. 82-87

יְלֵל *howling*—A. Baumann, 'ילל *yll*; יְלֵל *yelēl*; יְלָלָה *yelālâ*', *TDOT*, VI (1990) pp. 82-87

יְלָלָה *howling*—A. Baumann, 'ילל *yll*; יְלֵל *yelēl*; יְלָלָה *yelālâ*', *TDOT*, VI (1990) pp. 82-87

יָם *sea*—H. Ringgren, 'יָם *yām*', *TDOT*, VI (1990), pp. 87-98

Ex 10₁₉—Greta Hort, 'The Plagues of Egypt', *ZAW 70* (1958), pp. 48-59 (51-52)

Is 57₂₀—Mitchell Dahood, 'Hebrew–Ugaritic Lexicography III', *Bib* 46 (1965), pp. 311-32 (319)

Jb 3₈—Lester L. Grabbe, *Comparative Philology and the Text of Job: A Study in Methodology* (SBLDS, 34; Missoula, MT: Scholars Press, 1977), pp. 35-38; E. Lipinski, 'לִוְיָתָן *liwyātān*', *TDOT*, VII (1995), pp. 504-509 (505-506)

Ps 106₇—Mitchell Dahood, 'Hebrew–Ugaritic Lexicography III', *Bib* 46 (1965), pp. 311-32 (318-19)

מִדְבַּר־יָם *steppe of the sea*—Benjamin Uffenheimer, 'The "Desert of the Sea" Pronouncement (Isaiah 21:1-10)', in *Pomegranates and Golden Bells: Studies in Biblical, Jewish, and Near Eastern Ritual, Law, and Literature in Honor of Jacob Milgrom* (ed. David P. Wright, David Noel Freedman and Avi Hurvitz; Winona Lake, IN: Eisenbrauns, 1995), pp. 677-88 (677-79)

רוּחַ־יָם *north wind*—Greta Hort, 'The Plagues of Egypt', *ZAW 70* (1958), pp. 48-59 (51-52)

pool—John Marco Allegro, *The Treasure of the Copper Scroll* (London: Routledge & Kegan Paul, 1960), pp. 161-62; Bargil Pixner, 'Unravelling the Copper Scroll Code: A Study on the Topography of 3Q15', *RQ* 11 (1983), pp. 323-61 (354)

יְמִימָה *Jemimah*—G.R. Driver, 'Birds in the Old Testament: II. Birds in Life', *PEQ* 87 (1955), pp. 129-40 (130, 140); Stamm, p. 330

יָמִין I *right* (Ex 10₁₉)—Greta Hort, 'The Plagues of Egypt', *ZAW 70* (1958), pp. 48-59 (51-52)

יָמִין IV *oath* (cf. Arab. yamīn)—L. Kopf, 'Arabische Etymologien und Parallelen zum Bibelwörterbuch', *VT* 9 (1959), pp. 247-87 (257-58)

יֵמִם *marsh fish*—G.R. Driver, 'Genesis xxxvi 24: Mules or Fishes?', *VT* 25 (1975), pp. 109-10; Kaltner, p. 73

ימן *go right*—H.-J. Fabry and J.A. Soggin, 'ימן יָמִין *yāmîn*; ימן *ymn* hiphil; יְמָנִי *yemānî*; יְמִינִי *yemînî*; יָמִינִי *yāmînî*; יִמְנָה *yimnâ*; תֵּימָן *têmān*', *TDOT*, VI (1990), pp. 99-104

יִמְנָה *Imnah*—H.-J. Fabry and J.A. Soggin, 'ימן יָמִין *yāmîn*; ימן hiphil; יְמָנִי *yemānî*; יְמִינִי *yemînî*; יָמִינִי *yāmînî*; יִמְנָה *yimnâ*; תֵּימָן *têmān*', *TDOT*, VI (1990), pp. 99-104

יְמָנִי *right*—H.-J. Fabry and J.A. Soggin, 'ימן יָמִין *yāmîn*; ימן hiphil; יְמָנִי *yemānî*; יְמִינִי *yemînî*; יָמִינִי *yāmînî*; יִמְנָה *yimnâ*; תֵּימָן *têmān*', *TDOT*, VI (1990), pp. 99-104

ימר *boast, exchange*—F. Nötscher, 'Entbehrliche Hapaxlegomena in Jesaia', *VT* 1 (1951), pp. 299-302 (299-300)

ינה *oppress*—Joseph Reider, 'Etymological Studies in Biblical Hebrew', *VT* 4 (1954), pp. 276-95 (281-82); A. van Selms, 'The Etymology of *yayin*, "wine"', *JNWSL* 3 (1974), pp. 77-84 (80-81); H. Ringgren, 'יָנָה *yānâ*', *TDOT*, VI (1990), pp. 104-106

ינק *suck*—H. Ringgren, 'יָנַק *yānaq*; יוֹנֵק *yônēq*; יוֹנֶקֶת *yôneqet*', *TDOT*, VI (1990), pp. 106-108

1QIsa[a] 65₃—Matitiahu Tsevat, 'Some Biblical Notes', *HUCA* 24 (1952–53), pp. 107-14 (109-10); Eduard Yechezkel Kutscher, *The Language and Linguistic Background of the Isaiah Scroll* (Jerusalem: Magnes Press, 1959), pp. 164, 183

יַנְשׁוּף *screech owl*—G.R. Driver, 'Birds in the Old Testament: I. Birds in Law', *PEQ* 87 (1955), pp. 5-20 (15, 20)

יסד *establish*—P. Humbert, 'Note sur yāsad et ses dérivés', in *Hebräische Wortforschung: Festschrift zum 80. Geburtstag von Walter Baumgartner* (ed. G.W. Anderson *et al.*; VTSup, 16; Leiden: E.J. Brill, 1967), pp. 135-42 (135-38); R. Mosis, 'יָסַד *yāsad*; יְסוֹד *yesôd*; יְסוּדָה *yesûdâ*; יְסֻד *yesud*; מוּסָד/מוּסָדָה *mûsād(â)*; מוֹסָד/מוֹסָדָה *môsād(â)*; מַסָּד *massād*', *TDOT*, VI (1990), pp. 109-21; W.H. Schmidt, 'יסד *ysd* to found', *TLOT*, II (1997), pp. 547-48

pi./pu. *re-establish*—A. Gelston, 'The Foundations of the Second Temple', *VT* 16 (1966), pp. 232-35

יְסַד *establishment*—P. Humbert, 'Note sur yāsad et ses dérivés', in *Hebräische Wortforschung: Festschrift zum*

80. Geburtstag von Walter Baumgartner (ed. G.W. Anderson *et al.*; VTSup, 16; Leiden: E.J. Brill, 1967), pp. 135-42 (139); R. Mosis, 'יָסַד *yāsaḏ*; יְסוֹד *yesôḏ*; יְסוּדָה *yesûḏâ*; יְסֻד *yesuḏ*; מוּסָדָה/מוּסָד *mûsāḏ(â)*; מוֹסָדָה/מוֹסָד *môsāḏ(â)*; מַסָּד *massāḏ*', *TDOT*, VI (1990), pp. 109-21

יְסוֹד *foundation*—P. Humbert, 'Note sur yāsad et ses dérivés', in *Hebräische Wortforschung: Festschrift zum 80. Geburtstag von Walter Baumgartner* (ed. G.W. Anderson, P.A.H. de Boer, G.R. Castellino, Henri Cazelles, E. Hammershaimb, H.G. May and W. Zimmerli; VTSup, 16; Leiden: E.J. Brill, 1967), pp. 135-42 (138-39); R. Mosis, 'יָסַד *yāsaḏ*; יְסוֹד *yesôḏ*; יְסוּדָה *yesûḏâ*; יְסֻד *yesuḏ*; מוּסָדָה/מוּסָד *mûsāḏ(â)*; מוֹסָדָה/מוֹסָד *môsāḏ(â)*; מַסָּד *massāḏ*, *TDOT*, VI (1990), pp. 109-21

Pr 12₃—Mitchell Dahood, 'Congruity of Metaphors', in *Hebräische Wortforschung: Festschrift zum 80. Geburtstag von Walter Baumgartner* (ed. G.W. Anderson *et al.*; VTSup, 16; Leiden: E.J. Brill, 1957), pp. 40-49 (43)

foundation of altar—Ziony Zevit, 'Philology, Archaeology, and a Terminus a Quo for P's *ḥaṭṭā't* Legislation', in *Pomegranates and Golden Bells: Studies in Biblical, Jewish, and Near Eastern Ritual, Law, and Literature in Honor of Jacob Milgrom* (ed. David P. Wright, David Noel Freedman and Avi Hurvitz; Winona Lake, IN: Eisenbrauns, 1995), pp. 29-38.

re-establishment—A. Gelston, 'The Foundations of the Second Temple', *VT* 16 (1966), pp. 232-35 (235)

thigh—W.F. Albright, in *Studies in Old Testament Prophecy* (ed. H.H. Rowley; Edinburgh: T. & T. Clark, 1950), p. 17; Barr, p. 328

יָסוּר *one who departs*—Mitchell Dahood, 'Hebrew–Ugaritic Lexicography III', *Bib* 46 (1965), pp. 311-32 (315)

יִסּוֹר *instruction, precept*—Jerome Murphy-O'Connor, 'A Literary Analysis of Damascus Document VI, 2—VIII, 3', *RB* 78 (1971), pp. 210-32 (221-23); Sidnie Ann White, 'A Comparison of the "A" and "B" Manuscripts of the Damascus Document', *RQ* 12 (1987), pp. 537-53 (40)

יסף *add*—G. André, 'יָסַף *yāsap*', *TDOT*, VI (1990), pp. 121-27

יסר I *discipline*—G.J. Botterweck and R.D. Branson, 'יָסַר *yāsar*; מוּסָר *mûsār*', *TDOT*, VI (1990), pp. 127-34; M. Sæbø, 'יסר *ysr* to chastise', *TLOT*, II (1997), pp. 548-51

pi. *discipline* (Jb 4₃)—M. Dahood, 'Comparative Philology Today and Yesterday' [Review of James Barr, *Comparative Philology and the Text of the Old Testament* (Oxford: Oxford University Press, 1968)], *Bib* 50 (1969), pp. 70-79 (76)

htp. *be instructed*—Jerome Murphy-O'Connor, 'A Literary Analysis of Damascus Document VI, 2—VIII, 3', *RB* 78 (1971), pp. 210-32 (221-23)

יסר II *be strong* (cf. Aram. אַשַּׁר *he strengthened*, Heb. אסר *bind*)—G.R. Driver, 'Studies in the Vocabulary of the Old Testament. VIII', *JTS* 36 (1935), pp. 293-301 (295-96); Barr, p. 328

יעד *appoint*—M. Görg, 'יָעַד *yā'aḏ*', *TDOT*, VI (1990), pp. 135-44; G. Sauer, 'יעד *y'd* to appoint', *TLOT*, II (1997), pp. 551-54

Jb 25₅—Markus Witte, *Philologische Notizen zu Hiob 21–27* (BZAW, 234; Berlin: W. de Gruyter, 1995), p. 128

יעל *profit*—H.D. Preuss, 'יעל *y'l*' *TDOT*, VI (1990), pp. 144-47; M. Sæbø, יעל *y'l* to be of use', *TLOT*, II (1997), pp. 554-56

יָעֵל II *Jael*—Stamm, p. 329

יַעֲלָא *Jaala*—Stamm, p. 329

יַעֲלָה *she-goat*—Mitchell Dahood, 'Hebrew–Ugaritic Lexicography III', *Bib* 46 (1965), pp. 311-32 (319)

יָעֵן *ostrich*—G.R. Driver, 'Birds in the Old Testament: II. Birds in Life', *PEQ* 87 (1955), pp. 129-40 (137-38)

bedouin—Thomas, *Lexicon*, X, p. 359

יַעַן I *because*—G.J. Thierry, 'Notes on Hebrew Grammar and Etymology', *OTS* 9 (1951), pp. 1-17 (11-13); M.J. Mulder, 'Die Partikel יַעַן', *OTS* 18 (1973), pp. 49-83

יַעֲנָה *desert/greed*—G.R. Driver, 'Birds in the Old Testament: I. Birds in Law', *PEQ* 87 (1955), pp. 5-20 (12-13, 20)

יעף I *be weary*—G.F. Hasel, 'יעף *y'p* I; יָעֵף *yā'ēp*; עיף *'yp*; עָיֵף *'āyēp*', *TDOT*, VI (1990), pp. 148-56

יָעֵף *weary*—G.F. Hasel, 'יעף *y'p* I; יָעֵף *yā'ēp*; עיף *'yp*; עָיֵף *'āyēp*', *TDOT*, VI (1990), pp. 148-56

יעץ *advise*—L. Ruppert, 'יָעַץ *yā'aṣ*; עֵצָה *'ēṣâ*; מוֹעֵצָה *mô'ēṣâ*', *TDOT*, VI (1990), pp. 156-85; H.-P. Stähli, 'יעץ *y'ṣ* to advise', *TLOT*, II (1997), pp. 556-59

יַעֲקֹב *Jacob*—H.-J. Zobel, 'יַעֲקוֹב/יַעֲקֹב *ya'aqōḇ/ya'aqôḇ*', *TDOT*, VI (1990) pp. 185-208

יַעֲקֹב־אֵל *Jacob-el*—D.N. Freedman, 'The Original Name of Jacob', *IEJ* 13 (1963), pp. 125-26; Mitchell Dahood, 'Hebrew–Ugaritic Lexicography III', *Bib* 46 (1965), pp. 311-32 (319)

יַעַר I *forest*—M.J. Mulder, 'יַעַר *ya'ar*', *TDOT*, VI (1990), pp. 208-17

Is 32_{19}—Joseph Reider, 'Contributions to the Scriptural Text', *HUCA* 24 (1952-53), pp. 85-106 (88-89)

Ps 132_6—A. Robinson, 'Do Ephrathah and Jaar Really Appear in Psalm 132_6?', *ZAW* 86 (1974), pp. 220-22

יפה *be beautiful*—C. Barth, 'יָפָה *yāpâ*; יָפֶה *yāpeh*; יְפִי *yepî*; יְפֵיפֶה *yepêpeh*', *TDOT*, VI (1990), pp. 218-20

יָפֶה *fair*—C. Barth, 'יָפָה *yāpâ*; יָפֶה *yāpeh*; יְפִי *yepî*; יְפֵיפֶה *yepêpeh*', *TDOT*, VI (1990), pp. 218-20

Ec 5_{17}—C.L. Seow, 'Linguistic Evidence and the Dating of Qohelet', *JBL* 115 (1996), pp. 643-66 (658)

יְפוּת *harmony*—Isaiah Sonne, 'Remarks on "Manual of Discipline", Col. vi, 6-7', *VT* 7 (1957), pp. 405-408

יָפֵחַ *witness* (cf. Ug. *yāpiḥu)—Mitchell Dahood, 'Hebrew–Ugaritic Lexicography III', *Bib* 46 (1965), pp. 311-32 (319); Dennis Pardee, '*Ypḥ* "Witness" in Hebrew and Ugaritic', *VT* 28 (1978), pp. 204-13

יְפִי *beauty*—C. Barth, 'יָפָה *yāpâ*; יָפֶה *yāpeh*; יְפִי *yepî*; יְפֵיפֶה *yepêpeh*', *TDOT*, VI (1990), pp. 218-220

יְפָיָהוּ *Jephaiah*—Eugenio Zolli, 'יפיהו',*Bib* 33 (1952), pp. 441-42

יפע *shine forth*—C. Barth, 'יָפַע *yāpa'*; יִפְעָה *yip'â*', *TDOT*, VI (1990), pp. 220-25; E. Jenni, 'יפע *yp'* to radiate', *TLOT*, II (1997), pp. 560-61

יִפְעָה *splendour*—C. Barth, 'יָפַע *yāpa'*; יִפְעָה *yip'â*', *TDOT*, VI (1990), pp. 220-25

arrogance (cf. Ug. yp' *be overweening*)—Theodore H. Gaster, 'Ezekiel xxviii.17', *ET* 62 (1950–51), p. 124

יפר *be many* (cf. Arab. wafara *be plentiful*; Ug. ypr *make to abound*)—I. Eitan, 'A Contribution to Isaiah Exegesis', *HUCA* 12–13 (1937–38), pp. 55-88 (61); Barr, pp. 286-87, 328

יצא I *go out*—H.D. Preuss, 'יָצָא *yāṣā'*; מוֹצָא *môṣā'*; תּוֹצָאוֹת *tôṣā'ôṯ*', *TDOT*, VI (1990), pp. 225-50

of refined metal—Raymond C. Van Leeuwen, 'A Technical Metallurgical Usage of יצא', *ZAW* 98 (1986), pp. 112-13

die—Menahem Kister, 'Notes on the Book of Ben-Sira', *Lesh* 47 (1983), pp. 125-46 (136); 'Additions to the Article "בשולי ספר בן־סירא"', *Lesh* 53 (1989), pp. 36-53 (49)

hi. *take out*—H.D. Preuss, 'יָצָא *yāṣā'*; מוֹצָא *môṣā'*; תּוֹצָאוֹת *tôṣā'ôṯ*', *TDOT*, VI (1990), pp. 225-50 (236-49)

Is 53_{10}—Mitchell Dahood, 'Textual Problems in Isa[a]', *CBQ* 22 (1960), pp. 400-409 (406)

lead out—Walter Gross, 'Die Herausführungsformel—Zum Verhältnis von Formel und Syntax', *ZAW* 86 (1974), pp. 424-53

cast into weapon—Raymond C. Van Leeuwen, 'A Technical Metallurgical Usage of יצא', *ZAW* 98 (1986), pp. 112-13

יצא II *be pure* (cf. Arab. waḍu'a)—G.R. Driver, 'Problems in the Hebrew Text of Proverbs', *Bib* 32 (1951), pp. 173-97 (190); 'Hebrew Notes', *VT* 1 (1951), pp. 241-50 (244); Barr, p. 166; Thomas, *Lexicon*, XI (1970), pp. 120, 328

יצג *place*—B. Johnson, 'יצג *yṣg*', *TDOT*, VI (1990), pp. 250-52; Michael S. Moore, *The Balaam Traditions: Their Character and Development* (SBLDS, 113; Atlanta: Scholars Press, 1990), p. 75

יצד *be firm* (cf. Arab. waṣada)—I. Eitan, 'A Contribution to Isaiah Exegesis', *HUCA* 12–13 (1937–38), pp. 55-88 (78); Barr, p. 328

יצה pi. *give last injunctions* (cf. Arab. waṣṣā *give parting charges, make a will*)—John Gray, *I and II Kings* (OTL; London: SCM Press, 3rd edn, 1977), pp. 99, 697; Barr, p. 328

יִצְהָר I *fresh oil*—H. Ringgren, 'יִצְהָר *yiṣhār*', *TDOT*, VI (1990), pp. 253-54

יָצוּעַ I *couch* (Gn 49_4)—Joseph Reider, 'Etymological Studies in Biblical Hebrew', *VT* 4 (1954), pp 276-95 (276); Mitchell Dahood, 'Hebrew–Ugaritic Lexicography III', *Bib* 46 (1965), pp. 311-32 (319); Manfred Oeming, *Das wahre Israel: die 'genealogische Vorhalle' 1 Chronik 1–9* (BWANT, 128; Stuttgart: Kohlhammer, 1990), pp. 137-38

יִצְחָק *Isaac*—Jan Heller, 'Jméno Jischak', *Krest'anská revue*

(Theologická Príloha) 4–5 (1955), pp. 102-104; P.-R. Berger, 'Die bisher ältesten keilschriftlichen Äquivalente zu zwei althebräischen Namen?', *UF* 1 (1969), pp. 216-17 (216)

פַּחַד יִצְחָק *thigh of Isaac*—Meir Malul, 'More on *Paḥad Yiṣḥāq* (Genesis xxxi 42, 53) and the Oath by the Thigh', *VT* 35 (1985), pp. 192-200

יְצִיאָה *outlet*—John Marco Allegro, *The Treasure of the Copper Scroll* (London: Routledge & Kegan Paul, 1960), pp. 159-60

יצע *extend*—Manfred Oeming, *Das wahre Israel: die 'genealogische Vorhalle' 1 Chronik 1–9* (BWANT, 128; Stuttgart: Kohlhammer, 1990), p. 138

יצק *pour out*—B. Johnson, 'יָצַק *yāṣaq*; צוּק *ṣûr*; יְצֻקָה *yeṣuqâ*; מָצוּק *māṣûq*', *TDOT*, VI (1990), pp. 254-57

יְצֻקָה *casting*—B. Johnson, 'יָצַק *yāṣaq*; צוּק *ṣûr*; יְצֻקָה *yeṣuqâ*; מָצוּק *māṣûq*', *TDOT*, VI (1990), pp. 254-57

יצר *form*—B. Otzen, 'יָצַר *yāṣar*; יֵצֶר *yēṣer*; צוּר *ṣûr*; צִיר *ṣîr*; צוּרָה *ṣûrâ*', *TDOT*, VI (1990), pp. 257-65; W.H. Schmidt, 'יצר *yṣr* to form', *TLOT*, II (1997), pp. 566-68

יֵצֶר I *formation*—B. Otzen, 'יָצַר *yāṣar*; יֵצֶר *yēṣer*; צוּר *ṣûr*; צִיר *ṣîr*; צוּרָה *ṣûrâ*', *TDOT*, VI (1990), pp. 257-65

creature—Elisha Qimron, 'Biblical Philology and the DSS', *Tarb* 58 (1989), pp. 297-315 (307)

imagination—Roland E. Murphy, '*Yēṣer* in the Qumran Literature', *Bib* 39 (1958), pp. 334-44; Hermann Lichtenberger, 'Zu Vorkommen und Bedeutung von יצר im Jubiläenbuch', *JSJ* 14 (1983), pp. 1-10; John J. Collins, *Jewish Wisdom in the Hellenistic Age* (OTL; Louisville, KY: Westminster/John Knox Press, 1997), pp. 81-83

יצת *kindle*—D.N. Freedman and J.R. Lundbom, 'יצת *yṣt*', *TDOT*, VI (1990), pp. 266-69

יֶקֶב *wine-vat*—M. Ottosson, 'יֶקֶב *yeqeḇ*', *TDOT*, VI (1990), pp. 269-70

יקד *be kindled*—D.N. Freedman and J.R. Lundbom, 'יָקַד *yāqaḏ*; יְקֹד *yeqōḏ*; מוֹקֵד *môqēḏ*', *TDOT*, VI (1990), pp. 271-74

יְקֹד *conflagration*—D.N. Freedman and J.R. Lundbom, 'יָקַד *yāqaḏ*; יְקֹד *yeqōḏ*; מוֹקֵד *môqēḏ*', *TDOT*, VI (1990), pp. 271-74

יָקוֹט *gossamer*—Joseph Reider, 'Etymological Studies in Biblical Hebrew', *VT* 4 (1954), pp. 276-95 (288-89); Lester L. Grabbe, *Comparative Philology and the Text of Job: A Study in Methodology* (SBLDS, 34; Missoula, MT: Scholars Press, 1977), pp. 58-60;

יָקוּשׁ/יָקוֹשׁ *(game) hunter*—Mitchell Dahood, 'Hebrew-Ugaritic Lexicography III', *Bib* 46 (1965), pp. 311-32 (321); H. Ringgren, 'יָקַשׁ *yāqaš*; יָקוֹשׁ *yāqôš*; מוֹקֵשׁ *môqēš*', *TDOT*, VI (1990), pp. 288-90

יקח *be shameless* (cf. Arab. waqiḥa)—G.R. Driver, 'Misreadings in the Old Testament', *WO* 1 (1947–52), pp. 234-38 (235); 'Hebrew Roots and Words', *WO* 1 (1947–52), pp. 406-15 (415); Barr, pp. 17-19, 271, 328

יַקִּיר *precious*—S. Wagner, 'יָקַר *yāqar*; יָקָר *yāqār*; יַקִּיר *yaqqîr*; יְקָר *yeqār*', *TDOT*, VI (1990), pp. 279-87

יקץ *awake*—G. Wallis, 'יקץ *yqṣ*; קיץ *qyṣ*', *TDOT*, VI (1990), pp. 274-79

יקר I *be precious*—S. Wagner, 'יָקַר *yāqar*; יָקָר *yāqār*; יַקִּיר *yaqqîr*; יְקָר *yeqār*' *TDOT*, VI (1990), pp. 279-87

hi. *make heavy* (cf. Arab. awqara *load*)—D. Winton Thomas, 'Notes on Some Passages in the Book of Proverbs', *JTS* 38 (1937), pp. 400-403 (402); Barr, p. 328

יקר II *split* (cf. Arab. waqara)—John Gray, *I and II Kings* (OTL; London: SCM Press, 3rd edn, 1977), p. 156; Barr, p. 329

יָקָר I *precious*—S. Wagner, 'יָקַר *yāqar*; יָקָר *yāqār*; יַקִּיר *yaqqîr*; יְקָר *yeqār*', *TDOT*, VI (1990), pp. 279-87

Pr 17_{27}—Mitchell Dahood, 'Congruity of Metaphors', in *Hebräische Wortforschung: Festschrift zum 80. Geburtstag von Walter Baumgartner* (ed. G.W. Anderson *et al.*; VTSup, 16; Leiden: E.J. Brill, 1957), pp. 40-49 (42)

יְקָר *preciousness*—S. Wagner, 'יָקַר *yāqar*; יָקָר *yāqār*; יַקִּיר *yaqqîr*; יְקָר *yeqār*', *TDOT*, VI (1990), pp. 279-87

יקשׁ *trap*—H. Ringgren, 'יָקַשׁ *yāqaš*; יָקוֹשׁ *yāqôš*; מוֹקֵשׁ *môqēš*', *TDOT*, VI (1990), pp. 288-90

ירא I *fear*—Bruna Costacurta, *La vita minacciata: il tema della paura nella bibbia ebraica* (Analecta biblica, 119; Rome: Editrice Pontificio Istituto Biblico), pp. 31-38, 258-59; H.F. Fuhs, 'יָרֵא *yārē*'; יִרְאָה *yir'â*; מוֹרָא *môrā*'', *TDOT*, VI (1990), pp. 290-315; C.H.J. van der Merwe, 'Is There Any Difference between ירא מן, ירא מפני, and ירא את?', *JNWSL* 18 (1992), pp. 177-83; H.-P.

Stähli, 'ירא yr' to fear', *TLOT*, II (1997), pp. 568-78

be afraid, fear (Qal, §1)—H.F. Fuhs, 'יָרֵא *yārē*'; יִרְאָה *yir'â*; מוֹרָא *môrā*'', *TDOT*, VI (1990), pp. 290-315 (295-96); H.-P. Stähli, 'ירא yr' to fear', *TLOT*, II (1997), pp. 568-78 (570-71)

fear Y. (Qal, §2)—H.F. Fuhs, 'יָרֵא *yārē*'; יִרְאָה *yir'â*; מוֹרָא *môrā*'', *TDOT*, VI (1990), pp. 290-315 (297-300); H.-P. Stähli, 'ירא *yr*' to fear', *TLOT*, II (1997), pp. 568-78 (571-78)

ni. *make oneself feared*—J.H. Eaton, 'Some Misunderstood Hebrew Words for God's Self-Revelation', *The Bible Translator* 25 (1974), pp. 331-38 (334)

נוֹרָא *feared*—H.F. Fuhs, 'יָרֵא *yārē*'; יִרְאָה *yir'â*; מוֹרָא *môrā*'', *TDOT*, VI (1990), pp. 290-315 (300-302); H.-P. Stähli, 'ירא yr' to fear', *TLOT*, II (1997), pp. 568-78 (571)

ירא II *drink deeply (of)*—Mitchell Dahood, 'Hebrew–Ugaritic Lexicography III', *Bib* 46 (1965), pp. 311-32 (321-22)

יִרְאָה *fear*—H.F. Fuhs, 'יָרֵא *yārē*'; יִרְאָה *yir'â*; מוֹרָא *môrā*'', *TDOT*, VI (1990), pp. 290-315 (311-14); H.-P. Stähli, 'ירא yr' to fear', *TLOT*, II (1997), pp. 568-78 (576)

one who fears—Mitchell Dahood, 'Hebrew–Ugaritic Lexicography III', *Bib* 46 (1965), pp. 311-32 (322-23)

יָרֵב *great*—G.R. Driver, 'Studies in the Vocabulary of the Old Testament. VIII', *JTS* 36 (1935), pp. 293-301 (295); Thomas, *Lexicon*, XI (1970), pp. 123, 335; Barr, p. 166

יְרֻבַּעַל *Jerubbaal*—Johannes C. de Moor, *The Rise of Yahwism: The Roots of Israelite Monotheism* (BETL, 91; Leuven: Leuven University Press, 1990), p. 201

ירד *go down*—G. Mayer, 'יָרַד *yārad*', *TDOT*, VI (1990), pp. 315-22

fall—G. Mayer, 'יָרַד *yārad*', *TDOT*, VI (1990), pp. 315-22 (317)

flow down—G. Mayer, 'יָרַד *yārad*', *TDOT*, VI (1990), pp. 315-22 (317-18)

go up (cf. Akk. [w]arādu, Arab. warada, Ug. yrd)—G.R. Driver, 'On עלה "went up country" and ירד "went down country"', *ZAW* 69 (1957), pp. 74-77; J.V. Kinnier Wilson, 'Hebrew and Akkadian Philological Notes', *JSS* 7 (1962), pp. 173-83 (173-75); Thomas, *Lexicon*, X (1970), p. 482; Barr, pp. 174-75

go south—G.R. Driver, 'On עלה "went up country" and ירד "went down country"', *ZAW* 69 (1957), pp. 74-77; Thomas, *Lexicon*, X (1970), p. 481; G. Mayer, 'יָרַד *yārad*', *TDOT*, VI (1990), pp. 315-22 (318)

roam—Thomas, *Lexicon*, X (1970), p. 481

be present—Thomas, *Lexicon*, X (1970), p. 481

hi. *cause to appear* (cf. Arab. awrada *bring, cause to be present*)—Thomas, *Lexicon*, X (1970), p. 489

יַרְדֵּן I *Jordan*—M. Görg, 'יַרְדֵּן *yardēn*', *TDOT*, VI (1990), pp. 322-30

name of town—Aaron Demsky, 'The Route of Jacob's Funeral Cortege and the Problem of *'Eber Hayyarden* (Genesis 50.10-11)', in *Minḥah le-Naḥum: Biblical and Other Studies Presented to Nahum M. Sarna in Honour of his 70th Birthday* (ed. Marc Brettler and Michael Fishbane; JSOTSup, 154; Sheffield: JSOT Press, 1993), pp. 54-63 (59-63)

יַרְדֵּן II *river*—Alfred Guillaume, 'The Arabic Background of the Book of Job', in *Promise and Fulfilment: Essays Presented to Professor S.H. Hooke in Celebration of his Ninetieth Birthday, 21st January 1964, by Members of the Society for Old Testament Study and Others* (ed. F.F. Bruce: Edinburgh: T. & T. Clark, 1963), pp. 106-27 (126)

ירה III *teach*—S. Wagner, 'יָרָה *yārâ* III; מוֹרֶה *môreh*', *TDOT*, VI (1990), pp. 339-47

lead—G.R. Driver, 'Hebrew Notes', *VT* 1 (1951), pp. 241-50 (249-50)

ho. *be taught*—Mitchell Dahood, *Psalms I: 51–100* (AB, 17; New York: Doubleday, 1968), p. 207; Christopher T. Begg, 'The Covenantal Dove in Psalm lxxiv 19-20', *VT* 37 (1987), pp. 78-81 (78)

ירה *be stupefied* (cf. Arab wariha *be afraid*)—Alfred Guillaume, *Hebrew and Arabic Lexicography*, I (Leiden: E.J. Brill, 1963), p. 27; Barr, pp. 6-7, 231; *HALAT*, II, p. 417a

יְרוּשָׁא *Jerusha*—Stamm, p. 327

יְרוּשָׁלַם *Jerusalem*—M. Tsevat, 'יְרוּשָׁלַם *yerûšālēm/yerûšālayim*', *TDOT*, VI (1990), pp. 347-55

יָרֵחַ *moon*—R.E. Clements, 'יָרֵחַ *yārēaḥ*; יֶרַח *yeraḥ*', *TDOT*, VI (1990), pp. 355-62

Jb 25₅—Joseph Reider, 'Contributions to the Scriptural Text', *HUCA* 24 (1952-53), pp. 85-106 (105); Markus

Witte, *Philologische Notizen zu Hiob 21–27* (BZAW, 234; Berlin: W. de Gruyter, 1995), pp. 127-28

יֶרַח I *month*—J.B. Segal, '"Yrḥ" in the Gezer "Calendar"', *JSS* 7 (1962), pp. 212-21; R.E. Clements, 'יָרֵחַ *yārēaḥ*; יֶרַח *yeraḥ*', *TDOT*, VI (1990), pp. 355-362

יָרִיב I *adversary*—Mitchell Dahood, 'Hebrew–Ugaritic Lexicography III', *Bib* 46 (1965), pp. 311-32 (323)

יְרִידָה *descent*—Al Wolters, 'The Fifth Cache of the Copper Scroll: "The Plastered Cistern of Manos"', *RQ* 13 (1988), pp. 167-76 (175-76)

יָרֵךְ *genitals*—Hans Walter Wolff, *Anthropology of the Old Testament* (tr. Margaret Kohl; London: SCM Press, 1974), p. 237; S.H. Smith, '"Heel" and "Thigh": The Concept of Sexuality in the Jacob–Esau Narratives', *VT* 40 (1990), pp. 464-73; Y. Ratzhabi, 'Biblical Euphemisms for Human Genitals', *BethM* 34 (1989–90), pp. 192-96 (193-94)

ירם *be high* (cf. Ug. *yrm*)—Mitchell Dahood, 'Hebrew–Ugaritic Lexicography III', *Bib* 46 (1965), pp. 311-32 (323-24)

ירע *tremble*—F. Nötscher, 'Entbehrliche Hapaxlegomena in Jesaia', *VT* 1 (1951), pp. 299-30 (299); Alfred Guillaume, 'A Note on the Roots ריע, ירע, and רעע in Hebrew', *JTS* ns 15 (1964), pp. 293-95; *HALAT*, II, p. 420a

ירק *spit*—D. Kellerman, 'יָרַק *yāraq*; יָרוֹק *yārôq*; יָרָק *yārāq*; יֶרֶק *yereq*; יֵרָקוֹן *yērāqôn*; יְרַקְרַק *yeraqraq*; יָרְקְעָם *yorqo'ām*; יַרְקוֹן *yarqôn*', *TDOT*, VI (1990), pp. 362-68

יָרָק *herbage*—D. Kellerman, 'יָרַק *yāraq*; יָרוֹק *yārôq*; יָרָק *yārāq*; יֶרֶק *yereq*; יֵרָקוֹן *yērāqôn*; יְרַקְרַק *yeraqraq*; יָרְקְעָם *yorqo'ām*; יַרְקוֹן *yarqôn*', *TDOT*, VI (1990), pp. 362-68

יֶרֶק *greenness*—D. Kellerman, 'יָרַק *yāraq*; יָרוֹק *yārôq*; יָרָק *yārāq*; יֶרֶק *yereq*; יֵרָקוֹן *yērāqôn*; יְרַקְרַק *yeraqraq*; יָרְקְעָם *yorqo'ām*; יַרְקוֹן *yarqôn*', *TDOT*, VI (1990), pp. 362-68

יַרְקוֹן *Jarkon*—D. Kellerman, 'יָרַק *yāraq*; יָרוֹק *yārôq*; יָרָק *yārāq*; יֶרֶק *yereq*; יֵרָקוֹן *yērāqôn*; יְרַקְרַק *yeraqraq*; יָרְקְעָם *yorqo'ām*; יַרְקוֹן *yarqôn*', *TDOT*, VI (1990), pp. 362-68

יֵרָקוֹן *sickness*—D. Kellerman, 'יָרַק *yāraq*; יָרוֹק *yārôq*; יָרָק *yārāq*; יֶרֶק *yereq*; יֵרָקוֹן *yērāqôn*; יְרַקְרַק *yeraqraq*; יָרְקְעָם *yorqo'ām*; יַרְקוֹן *yarqôn*', *TDOT*, VI (1990), pp. 362-68

יָרְקְעָם *Jorkeam*—D. Kellerman, 'יָרַק *yāraq*; יָרוֹק *yārôq*; יָרָק *yārāq*; יֶרֶק *yereq*; יֵרָקוֹן *yērāqôn*; יְרַקְרַק *yeraqraq*; יָרְקְעָם *yorqo'ām*; יַרְקוֹן *yarqôn*', *TDOT*, VI (1990), pp. 362-68

יְרַקְרַק *leaf* (cf. Arab. waraqatun)—Joseph Reider, 'Contributions to the Scriptural Text', *HUCA* 24 (1952–53), pp. 85-106 (100-101)

pale green—D. Kellerman, 'יָרַק *yāraq*; יָרוֹק *yārôq*; יָרָק *yārāq*; יֶרֶק *yereq*; יֵרָקוֹן *yērāqôn*; יְרַקְרַק *yeraqraq*; יָרְקְעָם *yorqo'ām*; יַרְקוֹן *yarqôn*', *TDOT*, VI (1990), pp. 362-368

ירשׁ *take possession*—N. Lohfink, 'יָרַשׁ *yāraš*; יְרֵשָׁה *yerēšâ*; יְרֻשָּׁה *yeruššâ*; מוֹרָשׁ *môrāš*; מוֹרָשָׁה *môrāšâ*', *TDOT*, VI (1990), pp. 368-96; H.H. Schmid, 'ירשׁ *yrš* to inherit', *TLOT*, II (1997), pp. 578-83

יְרֵשָׁה *possession*—N. Lohfink, 'יָרַשׁ *yāraš*; יְרֵשָׁה *yerēšâ*; יְרֻשָּׁה *yeruššâ*; מוֹרָשׁ *môrāš*; מוֹרָשָׁה *môrāšâ*', *TDOT*, VI (1990), pp. 368-96

יְרֻשָּׁה *possession*—N. Lohfink, 'יָרַשׁ *yāraš*; יְרֵשָׁה *yerēšâ*; יְרֻשָּׁה *yeruššâ*; מוֹרָשׁ *môrāš*; מוֹרָשָׁה *môrāšâ*', *TDOT*, VI (1990), pp. 368-96

יִשְׂרָאֵל *Israel*—Norman Walker, '"Israel"', *VT* 4 (1954), p. 434; Othniel Margalith, 'On the Origin and Antiquity of the Name »Israel«', *ZAW* 102 (1990), pp. 225-37; H.-J. Zobel, 'יִשְׂרָאֵל *yiśrā'ēl*', *TDOT*, VI (1990), pp. 397-420; G. Gerleman, 'יִשְׂרָאֵל *yiśrāʾēl* Israel', *TLOT*, III (1997), pp. 581-84

י' אֱלֹהֵי־יִשְׂרָאֵל *Y., the God of Israel*—H.-J. Zobel, 'יִשְׂרָאֵל *yiśrā'ēl*', *TDOT*, VI (1990), pp. 397-420 (413-14)

בְּנֵי־יִשְׂרָאֵל *sons of Israel*—H.-J. Zobel, 'יִשְׂרָאֵל *yiśrā'ēl*', *TDOT*, VI (1990), pp. 397-420 (401-404)

ישׁב *sit*—M. Görg, 'יָשַׁב *yāšaḇ*; מוֹשָׁב *môšāḇ*', *TDOT*, VI (1990), pp. 420-38

Ps 29$_{10}$—D.T. Tsumura, '"The Deluge" (*mabbûl*) in Psalm 29:10', *UF* 20 (1988), pp. 351-55

sit (down)—M. Görg, 'יָשַׁב *yāšaḇ*; מוֹשָׁב *môšāḇ*', *TDOT*, VI (1990), pp. 420-38 (424-26)

sit on throne—M. Görg, 'יָשַׁב *yāšaḇ*; מוֹשָׁב *môšāḇ*', *TDOT*, VI (1990), pp. 420-38 (430-31)

dwell, inhabit—M. Görg, 'יָשַׁב *yāšaḇ*; מוֹשָׁב *môšāḇ*', *TDOT*, VI (1990), pp. 420-38 (426-29)

settle—M. Görg, 'יָשַׁב *yāšaḇ*; מוֹשָׁב *môšāḇ*', *TDOT*, VI (1990), pp. 420-38 (426-29)

worship—L.H. Brockington, 'The Use of the Hebrew Verb יָשַׁב to Describe an Act in Religious Observance', in *Essays in honour of Griffithes Wheeler Thatcher*,

1863–1950 (ed. Evan Colin Briarcliffe MacLaurin; Sydney: Sydney University Press, 1967), pp. 119-25

hi. *settle* (Ps 103:9)—L. Kopf, 'Arabische Etymologien und Parallelen zum Bibelwörterbuch', *VT* 9 (1959), pp. 247-87 (258)

יְשׁוּעָה *salvation*—J.F.A. Sawyer, *Semantics in Biblical Research: New Methods of Defining Hebrew Words for Salvation* (Studies in Biblical Theology, II/24; London: SCM Press, 1972); 'A Historical Description of the Hebrew Root *YŠ*'', in *Hamito-Semitica* (ed. J. and T. Bynon; The Hague: Mouton, 1975), pp. 75-84; H.-J. Fabry and J.F. Sawyer, 'ישׁע *yš*'; הוֹשִׁיעַ *hôšîa'*; יְשׁוּעָה *yešû'â*; יֵשַׁע/יֶשַׁע *yēšaʻ/yešaʻ*; מוֹשָׁעוֹת *môšā'ôṯ*; תְּשׁוּעָה *tešû'â*', *TDOT*, VI (1990), pp. 441-63; E. Stolz, 'ישׁע *yš*' to help', *TLOT*, II (1997), pp. 584-87

Ps 53:7—Gary A. Rendsburg, *Linguistic Evidence for the Northern Origin of Selected Psalms* (SBLMS, 43; Atlanta: Scholars Press, 1990), p. 32

יְשׁוּעוֹת *saviour*—Mitchell Dahood, 'Hebrew–Ugaritic Lexicography III', *Bib* 46 (1965), pp. 311-32 (324)

יֶשַׁח *dysentery* (cf. Arab. šaḫāḫ *urine and excrement*)—A. Ehrman, 'A Note on Micah vi 14', *VT* 23 (1973), pp. 103-105

semen (cf. Arab. wasiḫa *be filthy*)—A.B. Ehrlich, *Randglossen zur hebräischen Bibel* (Leipzig: J.C. Hinrichs, 1908–14), V, p. 288; M. Pope, 'The Word שַׁחַת in Job 9:31', *JBL* 83 (1964), pp. 269-78 (270); Thomas, *Lexicon*, XI (1970), p. 329; Barr, p. 166

ישׁן II *be old*—Josua Blau, 'Über Homonyme und angeblich homonyme Wurzeln II', *VT* 7 (1957), pp. 98-102 (98-99)

יָשֵׁן I *sleeping*—J. Schüpphaus, 'יָשֵׁן *yāšēn*; יָשָׁן *yāšān*; שֵׁנָא *šēnā'*; שֵׁנָה *šēnâ*', *TDOT*, VI (1990), pp. 438-41

ישׁע *save*—J.F.A. Sawyer, *Hebrew Words for Salvation: New Methods of Defining Hebrw Words for Salvation* (Studies in Bibical Theology, II/24; London: SCM Press, 1972); 'A Historical Description of the Hebrew Root *YŠ*'', in *Hamito-Semitica* (ed. J. and T. Bynon; The Hague: Mouton, 1975), pp. 75-84; H.-J. Fabry and J.F. Sawyer, 'ישׁע *yš*'; הוֹשִׁיעַ *hôšîa'*; יְשׁוּעָה *yešû'â*; יֵשַׁע/יֶשַׁע *yēšaʻ/yešaʻ*; מוֹשָׁעוֹת *môšā'ôṯ*; תְּשׁוּעָה *tešû'â*', *TDOT*, VI (1990), pp. 441-63; E. Stolz, 'ישׁע *yš*' to help', *TLOT*, II (1997), pp. 584-87

Ps 118:25—Joseph A. Fitzmyer, 'Aramaic Evidence Affecting the Interpretation of *Hosanna* in the New Testament', in *Tradition and Interpretation in the New Testament: Essays in Honor of E. Earle Ellis for his 60th Birthday* (ed. Gerald F. Hawthorne and Otto Betz; Grand Rapids: Eerdmans, 1987), pp. 110-18

יֵשַׁע *salvation*—J.F.A. Sawyer, *Hebrew Words for Salvation: New Methods of Defining Hebrw Words for Salvation* (Studies in Bibical Theology, II/24; London: SCM Press, 1972); 'A Historical Description of the Hebrew Root *YŠ*'', in *Hamito-Semitica* (ed. J. and T. Bynon; The Hague: Mouton, 1975), pp. 75-84; H.-J. Fabry, J.F. Sawyer, 'ישׁע *yš*'; הוֹשִׁיעַ *hôšîa'*; יְשׁוּעָה *yešû'â*; יֵשַׁע/יֶשַׁע *yēšaʻ/yešaʻ*; מוֹשָׁעוֹת *môšā'ôṯ*; תְּשׁוּעָה *tešû'â*', *TDOT*, VI (1990), pp. 441-63; E. Stolz, 'ישׁע *yš*' to help', *TLOT*, II (1997), pp. 584-87

יָשְׁפֵה *jasper*—John S. Harris, 'An Introduction to the Study of Personal Ornaments of Precious, Semi-Precious and Imitation Stones Used throughout Biblical History', *ALUOS* 4 (1962), pp. 49-83 (65-66)

ישׁר *be straight*—L. Alonso Schökel, W. Mayer and H. Ringgren, 'יָשַׁר *yāšar*; יֹשֶׁר *yōšer*; יִשְׁרָה *yišrâ*; מִישׁוֹר *mîšôr*; מֵישָׁרִים *mêšārîm*', *TDOT*, VI (1990), pp. 463-72; G. Liedke, 'ישׁר *yšr* to be straight, right', *TLOT*, II (1997), pp. 588-90

יָשָׁר *straight*—L. Alonso Schökel, W. Mayer and H. Ringgren, 'יָשַׁר *yāšar*; יֹשֶׁר *yōšer*; יִשְׁרָה *yišrâ*; מִישׁוֹר *mîšôr*; מֵישָׁרִים *mêšārîm*', *TDOT*, VI (1990), pp. 463-72

יֹשֶׁר *uprightness*—L. Alonso Schökel, W. Mayer and H. Ringgren, 'יָשַׁר *yāšar*; יֹשֶׁר *yōšer*; יִשְׁרָה *yišrâ*; מִישׁוֹר *mîšôr*; מֵישָׁרִים *mêšārîm*', *TDOT*, VI (1990), pp. 463-72

יִשְׁרָה *uprightness*—L. Alonso Schökel, W. Mayer and H. Ringgren, 'יָשַׁר *yāšar*; יֹשֶׁר *yōšer*; יִשְׁרָה *yišrâ*; מִישׁוֹר *mîšôr*; מֵישָׁרִים *mêšārîm*', *TDOT*, VI (1990), pp. 463-72

יְשֻׁרוּן *Jeshurun*—M.J. Mulder, 'יְשֻׁרוּן *yešurûn*' *TDOT*, VI (1990), pp. 472-77

יָתֵד *peg* (Jg 5:26)—M. Dahood, 'Comparative Philology Today and Yesterday' [Review of James Barr, *Comparative Philology and the Text of the Old Testament* (Oxford: Oxford University Press, 1968)], *Bib* 50 (1969), pp. 70-79 (71-72)

יָתוֹם *orphan*—H. Ringgren, 'יָתוֹם *yāṯôm*', *TDOT*, VI (1990), pp. 477-81

יְתוּר *outcrop*—Gillis Gerleman, 'Rest und Überschuss: eine terminologische Studie', in *Travels in the World of the Old Testament: Studies Presented to Professor M.A. Beek on the Occasion of his 65th Birthday* (ed. M.S.H.G. Heerma van Voss, Ph. H.J. Houwink ten Cate and N.A. van Uchelen; Studia Semitica Neerlandica, 16; Assen: Van Gorcum, 1974), pp. 71-74 (74)

יתן II *give*—Mitchell Dahood, 'Hebrew–Ugaritic Lexicography III', *Bib* 46 (1965), pp. 311-32 (324-25)

יתר *exceed*—T. Kronholm, 'יָתַר *yāṯar* I; יֶתֶר *yeṯer* I; יוֹתֵר/יֹתֵר *yôṯēr/yōṯēr*; יֹתֶרֶת *yōṯereṯ*; יִתְרָה/יִתְרַת *yiṯrâ/yiṯraṯ*; יִתְרוֹן *yiṯrôn*; מוֹתָר *môṯār*; יַתִּיר/יַתִּירָה(א) *yattîr/yattîrâ(ā')*', *TDOT*, VI (1990), pp. 482-91

יוֹתֵר *donor*—Mitchell Dahood, 'Hebrew–Ugaritic Lexicography III', *Bib* 46 (1965), pp. 311-32 (324)

ni. *be enriched*—Mitchell Dahood, 'Hebrew–Ugaritic Lexicography III', *Bib* 46 (1965), pp. 311-32 (325)

יֶתֶר I *remnant*—T. Kronholm, 'יָתַר *yāṯar* I; יֶתֶר *yeṯer* I; יוֹתֵר/יֹתֵר *yôṯēr/yōṯēr*; יֹתֶרֶת *yōṯereṯ*; יִתְרָה/יִתְרַת *yiṯrâ/yiṯraṯ*; יִתְרוֹן *yiṯrôn*; מוֹתָר *môṯār*; יַתִּיר/יַתִּירָה(א) *yattîr/yattîrâ(ā')*', *TDOT*, VI (1990), pp. 482-91

totality—Gillis Gerleman, 'Rest und Überschuss: eine terminologische Studie', in *Travels in the World of the Old Testament: Studies Presented to Professor M.A. Beek on the Occasion of his 65th Birthday* (ed. M.S.H.G. Heerma van Voss, Ph. H.J. Houwink ten Cate and N.A. van Uchelen; Studia Semitica Neerlandica, 16; Assen: Van Gorcum, 1974), pp. 71-74

wealth—Mitchell Dahood, 'Hebrew–Ugaritic Lexicography III', *Bib* 46 (1965), pp. 311-32 (325)

יִתְרָה *abundance*—T. Kronholm, 'יָתַר *yāṯar* I; יֶתֶר *yeṯer* I; יוֹתֵר/יֹתֵר *yôṯēr/yōṯēr*; יֹתֶרֶת *yōṯereṯ*; יִתְרָה/יִתְרַת *yiṯrâ/yiṯraṯ*; יִתְרוֹן *yiṯrôn*; מוֹתָר *môṯār*; יַתִּיר/יַתִּירָה(א) *yattîr/yattîrâ(ā')*', *TDOT*, VI (1990), pp. 482-91

יִתְרוֹן *profit*—'T. Kronholm, יָתַר *yāṯar* I; יֶתֶר *yeṯer* I; יֹתֵר/יוֹתֵר *yôṯēr/yōṯēr*; יֹתֶרֶת *yō ṯereṯ*; יִתְרָה/יִתְרַת *yiṯrâ/yiṯraṯ*; יִתְרוֹן *yiṯrôn*; מוֹתָר *môṯār*; יַתִּיר/יַתִּירָה(א) *yattîr/yattîrâ(ā')*', *TDOT*, VI (1990), pp. 482-91; C.L. Seow, 'Linguistic Evidence and the Dating of Qohelet', *JBL* 115 (1996), pp. 643-66 (651, 659-60)

כ

כְּ *of*—Francis I. Andersen, 'A Short Note on Construct *k* in Hebrew', *Bib* 50 (1969), pp. 68-69 (69)

כאב *hurt, ruin*—R. Mosis, 'כאב *k'b*; כְּאֵב *ke'ēḇ*; מַכְאֹב *maḵ'ōḇ*', *TDOT*, VII (1995), pp. 7-12

כְּאֵב *pain*—R. Mosis, 'כסב *k'b*; כְּאֵב *ke'ēḇ*; מַכְאֹב *maḵ'ōḇ*', *TDOT*, VII (1995), pp. 7-12 (10)

כאר *bind*—K.-D. Schunck, 'כָּרָה *kārâ*; כֵּרָה *kērâ*; כְּרִית *kerîṯ*; מִכְרֶה *miḵreh*', *TDOT*, VII (1995), pp. 303-306 (305-306)

כאר po. *mutilate*—Thomas, *Lexicon*, XI (1970), p. 38

כבד *be heavy*—C. Dohmen and P. Stenmans, 'כָּבֵד *kāḇēḏ* I; כָּבֵד *kāḇēḏ* II; כֹּבֶד *kōḇeḏ*; כְּבוּדָּה *kebûddâ*; כְּבֵדֻת *kebēḏuṯ*', *TDOT*, VII (1995), pp. 13-22; C. Westermann, 'כבד *kbd* to be heavy', *TLOT*, II (1997), pp. 590-602

ni. *reveal one's glory*—J.H. Eaton, 'Some Misunderstood Hebrew Words for God's Self-Revelation', *The Bible Translator* 25 (1974), pp. 331-38 (337-38)

נִכְבָּד *honourable one*—C. Dohmen and P. Stenmans, 'כָּבֵד *kāḇēḏ* I; כָּבֵד *kāḇēḏ* II; כֹּבֶד *kōḇeḏ*; כְּבוּדָּה *kebûddâ*; כְּבֵדֻת *kebēḏuṯ*', *TDOT*, VII (1995), pp. 13-22 (21)

pi. *honour*—C. Dohmen and P. Stenmans, 'כָּבֵד *kāḇēḏ* I; כָּבֵד *kāḇēḏ* II; כֹּבֶד *kōḇeḏ*; כְּבוּדָּה *kebûddâ*; כְּבֵדֻת *kebēḏuṯ*', *TDOT*, VII (1995), pp. 13-22 (19-21); C. Westermann, 'כבד *kbd* to be heavy', *TLOT*, II (1997), pp. 590-602 (592-93, 595)

fête—Mitchell Dahood, 'Hebrew–Ugaritic Lexicography III', *Bib* 46 (1965), pp. 311-32 (326)

pu. *be enriched*—Mitchell Dahood, 'Hebrew–Ugaritic Lexicography III', *Bib* 46 (1965), pp. 311-32 (326)

hi. *make unresponsive*—C. Dohmen and P. Stenmans, 'כָּבֵד *kāḇēḏ* I; כָּבֵד *kāḇēḏ* II; כֹּבֶד *kōḇeḏ*; כְּבוּדָּה *kebûddâ*; כְּבֵדֻת *kebēḏuṯ*', *TDOT*, VII (1995), pp. 13-22 (20-21); C.

Westermann, 'כבד *kbd* to be heavy', *TLOT*, II (1997), pp. 590-602 (592)

htp. *be fêted*—Mitchell Dahood, 'Hebrew–Ugaritic Lexicography III', *Bib* 46 (1965), pp. 311-32 (326)

כָּבֵד I *heavy*—C. Dohmen and P. Stenmans, 'כָּבֵד *kāḇēḏ* I; כָּבֵד *kāḇēḏ* II; כֹּבֶד *kōḇeḏ*; כְּבוּדָּה *kᵉḇûddâ*; כְּבֵדֻת *kᵉḇēḏuṯ*', *TDOT*, VII (1995), pp. 13-22 (17-18); C. Westermann, 'כבד *kbd* to be heavy', *TLOT*, II (1997), pp. 590-602 (591-92)

כָּבֵד II *liver*—Hans Walter Wolff, *Anthropology of the Old Testament* (tr. Margaret Kohl; London: SCM Press, 1974), p. 64; C. Dohmen and P. Stenmans, 'כָּבֵד *kāḇēḏ* I; כָּבֵד *kāḇēḏ* II; כֹּבֶד *kōḇeḏ*; כְּבוּדָּה *kᵉḇûddâ*; כְּבֵדֻת *kᵉḇēḏuṯ*', *TDOT*, VII (1995), pp. 13-22 (13-14, 21-22); M. Weinfeld, 'כָּבוֹד *kāḇôḏ*', *TDOT*, VII (1995), pp. 22-38 (23-24); C. Westermann, 'כבד *kbd* to be heavy', *TLOT*, II (1997), pp. 590-602 (590-91)

as seat of human emotion—F. Nötscher, 'Heisst *Kābōd* auch „Seele"?', *VT* 2 (1952), pp. 358-62 (361); Mark S. Smith, 'The Heart and Innards in Israelite Texts: Notes from Anthropology and Psychobiology', *JBL* 117 (1998)

כֹּבֶד *heaviness*—C. Dohmen and P. Stenmans, 'כָּבֵד *kāḇēḏ* I; כָּבֵד *kāḇēḏ* II; כֹּבֶד *kōḇeḏ*; כְּבוּדָּה *kᵉḇûddâ*; כְּבֵדֻת *kᵉḇēḏuṯ*', *TDOT*, VII (1995), pp. 13-22 (22); C. Westermann, 'כבד *kbd* to be heavy', *TLOT*, II (1997), pp. 590-602 (591)

כְּבֵדֻת heaviness—C. Dohmen and P. Stenmans, 'כָּבֵד *kāḇēḏ* I; כָּבֵד *kāḇēḏ* II; כֹּבֶד *kōḇeḏ*; כְּבוּדָּה *kᵉḇûddâ*; כְּבֵדֻת *kᵉḇēḏuṯ*', *TDOT*, VII (1995), pp. 13-22 (22); C. Westermann, 'כבד *kbd* to be heavy', *TLOT*, II (1997), pp. 590-602 (591)

כבה *be extinguished*—A. Baumann, 'כָּבָה *kāḇâ*', *TDOT*, VII (1995), pp. 38-39

fall down (cf. Arab. kabā)—L. Kopf, 'Arabische Etymologien und Parallelen zum Bibelwörterbuch', *VT* 9 (1959), pp. 247-87 (259-60)

כָּבוֹד *glory*—M. Weinfeld, 'כָּבוֹד *kāḇôḏ*', *TDOT*, VII (1995), pp. 22-38; James K. Aitken, 'The Semantics of "Glory" in Ben Sira–Traces of Development in Post-Biblical Hebrew?', in *Proceedings of the Second Leiden Symposium (December 1997)* (provisional title; ed. T. Muraoka and J.F. Elwolde; STDJ; Leiden: E.J. Brill); C. Westermann, 'כבד *kbd* to be heavy', *TLOT*, II (1997), pp. 590-602 (593-602)

soul—F. Nötscher, 'Heisst *Kābōd* auch „Seele"?', *VT* 2 (1952), pp. 358-62

כְּבוּדָּה *glory*—C. Dohmen and P. Stenmans, 'כָּבֵד *kāḇēḏ* I; כָּבֵד *kāḇēḏ* II; כֹּבֶד *kōḇeḏ*; כְּבוּדָּה *kᵉḇûddâ*; כְּבֵדֻת *kᵉḇēḏuṯ*', *TDOT*, VII (1995), pp. 13-22 (22); C. Westermann, 'כבד *kbd* to be heavy', *TLOT*, II (1997), pp. 590-602 (593-94)

כַּבִּיר *aged one*—M. Dahood, Review of Jean Lévêque, *Job et son Dieu. Essai d'exégèse et de théologie biblique* (Paris: J. Gabalda, 1970), *Bib* 52 (1971), pp. 436-38 (438)

כבס *wash*—G. André, 'כָּבַס *kāḇas*', *TDOT*, VII (1995), pp. 40-42

כֹּבֵס *fuller*—G. André, 'כָּבַס *kāḇas*', *TDOT*, VII (1995), pp. 40-42 (41-42)

כבר pi. inf. *thoroughly*—Leo Hayman, 'A Note on Isa. 1:25', *JNES* 9 (1950), p. 21

כְּבָרָה I *sieve*—Joseph Reider, 'Contributions to the Scriptural Text', *HUCA* 24 (1952–53), pp. 85-106 (96)

כִּבְרָה II *stretch (of land)* (cf. Akk. kibr(āt)u *regions*; bēru *mile*)—Mordechai Cogan and Hayim Tadmor, *II Kings: A New Translation with Introduction and Commentary* (AB, 11; New York: Doubleday, 1988), p. 65

כֶּבֶשׂ *ram*—C. Dohmen, 'כֶּבֶשׂ *keḇeś*; כֶּשֶׂב *keśeḇ*; כִּבְשָׂה *kiḇśâ*; כִּשְׂבָּה *kiśbâ*; שֶׂה *śeh*', *TDOT*, VII (1995), pp. 43-52

כִּבְשָׂה *ewe lamb*—C. Dohmen, 'כֶּבֶשׂ *keḇeś*; כֶּשֶׂב *keśeḇ*; כִּבְשָׂה *kiḇśâ*; כִּשְׂבָּה *kiśbâ*; שֶׂה *śeh*', *TDOT*, VII (1995), pp. 43-52

כבשׁ *subdue*—Hans Walter Wolff, *Anthropology of the Old Testament* (tr. Margaret Kohl; London: SCM Press, 1974), p. 163; S. Wagner, 'כָּבַשׁ *kāḇaš*; כֶּבֶשׁ *keḇeš*; כִּבְשָׁן *kiḇšān*', *TDOT*, VII (1995), pp. 52-57

כֶּבֶשׁ *footstool*—S. Wagner, 'כָּבַשׁ *kāḇaš*; כֶּבֶשׁ *keḇeš*; כִּבְשָׁן *kiḇšān*', *TDOT*, VII (1995), pp. 52-57 (57)

כִּבְשָׁן *furnace*—S. Wagner, 'כָּבַשׁ *kāḇaš*; כֶּבֶשׁ *keḇeš*; כִּבְשָׁן *kiḇšān*', *TDOT*, VII (1995), pp. 52-57 (57)

כבת *humble* (cf. Arab. kabata)—G.R. Driver, 'Linguistic and Textual Problems: Jeremiah', *JQR* 28 (1937–38), pp. 97-129 (114)

כַּד *cup of fate*—Mitchell J. Dahood, 'Some Northwest-

Semitic Words in Job', *Biblica* 38 (1957), pp. 306-20 (316); Lester L. Grabbe, *Comparative Philology and the Text of Job: A Study in Methodology* (SBLDS, 34; Missoula, MT: Scholars Press, 1977), pp. 77-79

כַּדְכֹּד *agate*—John S. Harris, 'An Introduction to the Study of Personal Ornaments of Precious, Semi-Precious and Imitation Stones Used throughout Biblical History', *ALUOS* 4 (1962), pp. 49-83 (53-54)

כדם *bind* (cf. Arab. kadama *bite*, ukdima *be in bonds*)—Joseph Reider, 'Etymological Studies in Biblical Hebrew', *VT* 4 (1954), pp. 276-95 (279); A. Guillaume, 'The Meaning of כדמה in Ezek. XXVII. $_{32}$', *JTS* ns 13 (1962), pp. 324-25; Thomas, *Lexicon*, XI (1970), p. 88; Barr, p. 166

כהה I *be dim*—K.-D. Schunk, 'כָּהָה *kāhâ*; כֵּהֶה *kēheh*; כֵּהָה *kēhâ*', *TDOT*, VII (1995), pp. 58-59

כהה II *rebuke*—K.-D. Schunk, 'כָּהָה *kāhâ*; כֵּהֶה *kēheh*; כֵּהָה *kēhâ*', *TDOT*, VII (1995), pp. 58-59 (58)

כֵּהָה *lessening*—K.-D. Schunk, 'כָּהָה *kāhâ*; כֵּהֶה *kēheh*; כֵּהָה *kēhâ*', *TDOT*, VII (1995), pp. 58-59 (59)

כֵּהֶה *dim*—K.-D. Schunk, 'כָּהָה *kāhâ*; כֵּהֶה *kēheh*; כֵּהָה *kēhâ*', *TDOT*, VII (1995), pp. 58-59

כהן *act as priest*—J. Bergman, H. Ringgren and W. Dommershausen, 'כֹּהֵן *kōhēn*', *TDOT*, VII (1995), pp. 60-75 (66)

pi. *flaunt with pride* (cf. Syr. kahīnā *rich, happy, powerful*; kahīnūtā *fortune, abundance*)—G.R. Driver, 'Studies in the Vocabulary of the Old Testament. VIII', *JTS* 36 (1935), pp. 293-301 (295); Thomas, *Lexicon*, XI (1970), p. 106

כֹּהֵן *priest*—J. Bergman, H. Ringgren and W. Dommershausen, 'כֹּהֵן *kōhēn*', *TDOT*, VII (1995), pp. 60-75

collective—Norbert Lohfink, 'Zu Text und Form von Os 4,4-6', *Bib* 42 (1961), pp. 303-32 (305-308)

כְּהֻנָּה *priesthood* (1 S 2$_{36}$)—J. Bergman, H. Ringgren and W. Dommershausen, 'כֹּהֵן *kōhēn*', *TDOT*, VII (1995), pp. 60-75 (66)

כּוּךְ *crypt*—John Marco Allegro, *The Treasure of the Copper Scroll* (London: Routledge & Kegan Paul, 1960), pp. 168-169; Bargil Pixner, 'Unravelling the Copper Scroll Code: A Study on the Topography of 3Q15', *RQ* 11 (1983), pp. 323-61 (357-56); Al Wolters, 'The *Copper Scroll* and the Vocabulary of Mishnaic Hebrew', *RQ* 14 (1990), pp. 483-95 (489)

כּוֹכָב *star*—Sabatino Moscati, 'Sull'etimologia di כּוֹכָב', *Bib* 27 (1946), pp. 269-72; R.E. Clements, 'כּוֹכָב *kôkāb*', *TDOT*, VII (1995), pp. 75-85

כּוֹכְבֵי־אֵל *mighty stars*—Mitchell Dahood, 'Hebrew–Ugaritic Lexicography III', *Bib* 46 (1965), pp. 311-32 (326-27)

royal ensign (cf. Pers. kaukab / kaukaba)—John H. Hayes, *Amos, the Eighth-Century Prophet: His Times and his Preaching* (Nashville: Abingdon Press, 1988), pp. 176-77

כול *contain*—A. Baumann, 'כול *kwl*', *TDOT*, VII (1995), pp. 85-87

pilp. *measure*—Mitchell Dahood, 'Qoheleth and Northwest Semitic Philology', *Bib* 43 (1962), pp. 349-65 (359-60); Alexander Rofé, 'A Neglected Meaning of the Verb כול and the Text of 1QS VI:11–13', in *'Sha'arei Talmon': Studies in the Bible, Qumran, and the Ancient Near East Presented to Shemaryahu Talmon* (ed. Michael Fishbane and Emanuel Tov; Winona Lake, IN: Eisenbrauns, 1992), pp. 315-21; A. Baumann, 'כול *kwl*', *TDOT*, VII (1995), pp. 85-87

כון *be upright*—G.J. Thierry, 'Notes on Hebrew Grammar and Etymology', *OTS* 9 (1951), pp. 1-17 (3-4); K. Koch, 'כּוּן *kûn*; כֵּן *kēn*; מָכוֹן *mākôn*; מְכוֹנָה *mᵉkônâ*; תְּכוּנָה *tᵉkûnâ*', *TDOT*, VII (1995), pp. 89-101; E. Gerstenberger, 'כון *kûn* ni. to stand firm', *TLOT*, II (1997), pp. 602-606

pol. *ascertain* (cf. Ug. knn)—Mitchell Dahood, 'Hebrew–Ugaritic Lexicography III', *Bib* 46 (1965), pp. 311-32 (329)

כּוֹס I *cup*—G. Mayer, 'כּוֹס *kôs*', TDOT, VII (1995), pp. 101-104

כּוֹס II *tawny owl*—G.R. Driver, 'Birds in the Old Testament: I. Birds in Law', *PEQ* 87 (1955), pp. 5-20 (14, 20)

כּוֹשָׁרוֹת *prosperity*—A. van Selms, 'The Root *k-ṯ-r* and its Derivatives in Ugaritic Literature', *UF* 11 (1979), pp. 739-44 (743-44); Johannes C. de Moor, *The Rise of Yahwism: The Roots of Israelite Monotheism* (BETL, 91; Leuven: Leuven University Press, 1990), p. 119; C.L. Seow, 'Linguistic Evidence and the Dating of Qohelet', *JBL* 115 (1996), pp. 643-66 (652-53)

כזב pu. *be declared a liar*—M. Dahood, Review of Jean Lévêque, *Job et son Dieu. Essai d'exégèse et de théologie biblique* (Paris: J. Gabalda, 1970), *Bib* 52 (1971), pp. 436-38 (438)

כָּזְבִּי *Cozbi*—Stamm, p. 324

כָּזִיב II *menopause*—(cf. Arab. kaḏaba *fail* [of camel's milk], *be slow* [of camel])—Godfrey R. Driver, 'Problems of Interpretation in the Heptateuch', in *Mélanges bibliques rédigés en l'honneur de André Robert* (Travaux de l'Institut Catholique de Paris, 4; Paris: Bloud & Gay, 1957), pp. 66-76 (71-72); Thomas, *Lexicon*, XI (1970), p. 165

כֹּחַ III *suppuration* (cf. Arab. kayḥ *pus*)—Alfred Guillaume, 'The Arabic Background of the Book of Job', in *Promise and Fulfilment: Essays Presented to Professor S.H. Hooke in Celebration of his Ninetieth Birthday, 21st January 1964, by Members of the Society for Old Testament Study and Others* (ed. F.F. Bruce: Edinburgh: T. & T. Clark, 1963), pp. 106-27 (120)

כָּחֹל *blue*—A. Demsky, '"Dark Wine" from Judah', *IEJ* 22 (1972), pp. 233-34

כֹּחֵל *Kohel*—N. Avigad, 'Two Hebrew Inscriptions on Wine-Jars', *IEJ* 22 (1972), pp. 1-9

כחשׁ *deny*—Josua Blau, 'Über Homonyme und angeblich homonyme Wurzeln II', *VT* 7 (1957), pp. 98-102 (99)

ni. *cringe* (4QNonCanPs[b] 33_9)—William M. Schniedewind, 'A Qumran Fragment of the Ancient »Prayer of Manasseh«?', *ZAW* 108 (1996), pp. 105-107 (106-107)

כִּי I *that*—James Muilenberg, 'The Linguistic and Rhetorical Usages of the Particle כי in the Old Testament', *HUCA* 32 (1961), pp. 135-60; A. Schoors, 'The Particle כי', *OTS* 21 (1981), pp. 240-76; B.L. Bandstra, 'The Syntax of the Particle *Ky* in Biblical Hebrew and Ugaritic' (PhD dissertation; Yale University, 1982); W.T. Claassen, 'Speaker-Oriented Functions of *Kî* in Biblical Hebrew', *JNWSL* 11 (1983), pp. 29-44; Anneli Aejmelaeus, 'Function and Interpretation of כי in Biblical Hebrew', *JBL* 105 (1986), pp. 193-209; Menaḥem Ẓevi Kaddari, 'The Syntax of כי in the Language of Ben Sira', in *The Hebrew of the Dead Sea Scrolls and Ben Sira: Proceedings of a Symposium held at Leiden University, 11-14 December 1995* (ed. T. Muraoka and J.F. Elwolde; STDJ, 26; Leiden: E.J. Brill, 1997), pp. 87-91

who, which—A. Schoors, 'The Particle כי', *OTS* 21 (1981), pp. 240-76 (276)

if, when—Elisha Qimron and John Strugnell, *Qumran Cave 4. V: Miqṣat Ma'aśe ha-Torah* (DJD, 10; Oxford: Clarendon Press, 1994), pp. 78-79

indeed—G.R. Driver, '"Another Little Drink"—Isaiah 28: 1-22', in *Words and Meanings: Essays Presented to David Winton Thomas on his Retirement from the Regius Professorship of Hebrew in the University of Cambridge, 1968* (ed. Peter R. Ackroyd and Barnabas Lindars; Cambridge: Cambridge University Press, 1968), pp. 47-67 (61)

Ps 49_{16} 89_3—Mitchell Dahood, 'Hebrew–Ugaritic Lexicography III', *Bib* 46 (1965), pp. 311-32 (327)

Ps 76_{11}—John Gray, *The Biblical Doctrine of the Reign of God* (Edinburgh: T. & T. Clark, 1979), p. 56

Ec 5_6—Robert Gordis, *Koheleth—The Man and his World: A Study of Ecclesiastes* (New York: Schocken Books, 3rd edn, 1968), pp. 249-50

Lm 3_{22}—Thomas F. McDaniel, 'Philological Studies in Lamentations. II', *Bib* 49 (1968), pp. 199-217 (212-15)

Si 3_{16}—Menaḥem Ẓevi Kaddari, 'The Syntax of כי in the Language of Ben Sira', in *The Hebrew of the Dead Sea Scrolls and Ben Sira: Proceedings of a Symposium held at Leiden University, 11-14 December 1995* (ed. T. Muraoka and J.F. Elwolde; STDJ, 26; Leiden: E.J. Brill, 1997), pp. 87-91 (89-90)

how!—William F. Albright, 'The Refrain, «And God Saw Ki Tob» in Genesis', in *Mélanges bibliques rédigés en l'honneur de André Robert* (Travaux de l'Institut Catholique de Paris, 4; Paris: Bloud & Gay, 1957), pp. 22-26; James L. Kugel, 'The Adverbial Use of *kî ṭôb*', *JBL* 99 (1980), pp. 433-45; A. Schoors, 'The Particle כי', *OTS* 21 (1981), pp. 241-76 (273-75); J. Gerald Janzen, 'Kugel's Adverbial *kî ṭôb*: An Assessment', *JBL* 102 (1983), pp. 99-106

as—A. Schoors, 'The Particle כי', *OTS* 21 (1981), pp. 240-76 (275-76) *who?*—Mitchell Dahood, 'Interrogative *kî* in Psalm 90,11; Isaiah 36,19 and Hosea 13,9', *Bib* 60 (1979), pp. 573-74

כִּי אִם *indeed if* (Am 5_{22})—Meir Weiss, 'Concerning Amos' Repudiation of the Cult', in *Pomegranates and Golden Bells: Studies in Biblical, Jewish, and Near Eastern Ritual, Law, and Literature in Honor of Jacob Milgrom* (ed. David P. Wright, David Noel Freedman and Avi Hurvitz; Winona Lake, IN: Eisenbrauns, 1995), pp. 199-214 (204-206)

כִּי I *vulture* (cf. Arab. ki *pelican, ibis*)—Joseph Reider, 'Etymological Studies in Biblical Hebrew', *VT* 4 (1954), pp. 276-95 (294); G.R. Driver, 'Job 39:27-8: The *Ky*-Bird', *PEQ* 104 (1972), pp. 64-66; M.J. Dahood, 'Four Ugaritic Personal Names and Job $39_{5.26\text{-}27}$', *ZAW* 87 (1975), p. 220; Lester L. Grabbe, *Comparative Philology and the Text of Job: A Study in Methodology* (SBLDS, 34; Missoula, MT: Scholars Press, 1977), pp. 126-28; Kaltner, pp. 57-58

כִּי III *burn*—F. Nötscher, 'Entbehrliche Hapaxlegomena in Jesaia', *VT* 1 (1951), pp. 299-302 (300); A. Schoors, 'The Particle כי', *OTS* 21 (1981), pp. 240-76 (240)

כִּידוֹד *son* (cf. Ug. *kdd*)—Mitchell Dahood, 'Hebrew–Ugaritic Lexicography III', *Bib* 46 (1965), pp. 311-32 (327)

כִּידוֹן *sword*—G. Molin, 'What is a *Kidon*?', *JSS* 1 (1956), pp. 334-37; Thomas, *Lexicon*, XI (1970), p. 209; M. Heltzer, 'Akkadian *katinnu* and Hebrew *kîdōn* "sword"', *JCS* 41 (1989), pp. 65-68

כִּידָן *Spanish sword*—Russell Gmirkin, 'The War Scroll and Roman Weaponry Reconsidered', *DSD* 3 (1996), pp. 89-129 (120)

כִּיּוּן I *Kivvun*—Oswald Loretz, 'Die babylonischen Gottesnamen Sukkut und Kajjamānu in Amos 5,26', *ZAW* 101 (1989)

כִּיּוֹר *laver*—Heinrich Strauss, 'Eine neue Deutung der Amphora auf jüdischen Denkmälern der Antike', *ZAW* 72 (1960), pp. 66-69

כִּין *vagina*—H.H. Hirschberg, 'Some Additional Arabic Etymologies in Old Testament Lexicography', *VT* 11 (1961), pp. 373-85 (375-77); Barr, pp. 277, 329

כִּכָּר I *valley* (cf. Yemenite kurkūr)—Chaim Rabin, *Ancient West-Arabian* (London: Taylor's Foreign Press, 1951), p. 28; Barr, p. 100

כֹּל II *mallow*—Lester L. Grabbe, *Comparative Philology and the Text of Job: A Study in Methodology* (SBLDS, 34; Missoula, MT: Scholars Press, 1977), pp. 88-89

כֹּל III *measure*—Mitchell Dahood, 'Qoheleth and Northwest Semitic Philology', *Bib* 43 (1962), pp. 349-65 (359-60)

כלא *restrain*—J. Hausmann, 'כָּלָא *kālā*'; כֶּלֶא *kele*'; כְּלִיא *k^{e}lî*'; מִכְלָה *miklâ*', *TDOT*, VII (1995), pp. 143-45

כֶּלֶא I *confinement*—J. Hausmann, 'כָּלָא *kālā*'; כֶּלֶא *kele*'; כְּלִיא *k^{e}lî*'; מִכְלָה *miklâ*', *TDOT*, VII (1995), pp. 143-45 (143)

כֶּלֶא II *both* (cf. Ug. klat ydh *both his hands*, klatnm *in both hands*)—Mitchell Dahood, 'Hebrew–Ugaritic Lexicography III', *Bib* 46 (1965), pp. 311-32 (327-28)

כַּלָּב *hunter* (cf. Syr. kallāb)—G.R. Driver, 'Textual and Linguistic Problems of the Book of Psalms', *HTR* 29 (1936), pp. 171-95 (176); Barr, p. 329

כֶּלֶב I *dog*—Gilbert Brunet, 'L'hébreu *kèlèb*', *VT* 35 (1985), pp. 485-88; G.J. Botterweck, 'כֶּלֶב *keleb*', *TDOT*, VII (1995), pp. 146-57; Elaine Adler Goodfriend, 'Could *keleb* in Deuteronomy 23:19 Actually Refer to a Canine?', in *Pomegranates and Golden Bells: Studies in Biblical, Jewish, and Near Eastern Ritual, Law and Literature in Honor of Jacob Milgrom* (ed. David P. Wright, David Noel Freedman and Avi Hurvitz; Winona Lake, IN; Eisenbrauns, 1995), pp. 381-97 (388-92)

Ps $22_{17.21}$—G.J. Botterweck, 'כֶּלֶב *keleb*', *TDOT*, VII (1995), pp. 146-57 (156)

devotee—D. Winton Thomas, '*KELEBH* "Dog": Its Origins and Some Uses of It in the Old Testament', *VT* 10 (1960), pp. 410-27 (423-26); Gilbert Brunet, 'L'hébreu *kèlèb*', *VT* 35 (1985), pp. 485-88; Moshe A. Zipor, 'What Were the *k^{e}lābîm* in Fact?', *ZAW* 99 (1987), pp. 423-28; Elaine Adler Goodfriend, 'Could *keleb* in Deuteronomy 23:19 Actually Refer to a Canine?', in *Pomegranates and Golden Bells: Studies in Biblical, Jewish, and Near Eastern Ritual, Law, and Literature in Honor of Jacob Milgrom* (ed. David P. Wright, David Noel Freedman and Avi Hurvitz; Winona Lake, IN; Eisenbrauns, 1995), pp. 381-97

רֹאשׁ כֶּלֶב *dog-faced baboon*—D. Winton Thomas, '*KELEBH* "Dog": Its Origins and Some Uses of It in the Old Testament', *VT* 10 (1960), pp. 410-27 (417-23)

כֶּלֶב II *servant*—Othniel Margalith, '*Keleb*: Homonym or Metaphor?', *VT* 33 (1983), pp. 491-95 (494)

כלה pi. *destroy* (Ps 101$_5$)—Mitchell Dahood, 'Hebrew–Ugaritic Lexicography III', *Bib* 46 (1965), pp. 311-32 (328)

כלה *be complete*—F.J. Helfmeyer, 'כָּלָה *kālâ*', *TDOT*, VII (1995), pp. 157-164; G. Gerleman, 'כלה *klh* to be at an end', *TLOT*, II (1997), pp. 616-18

כלה אֶל/עַל *overtake*—L. Kopf, 'Arabische Etymologien und Parallelen zum Bibelwörterbuch', *VT* 9 (1959), pp. 247-87 (284)

pi. *complete*—F.J. Helfmeyer, 'כָּלָה *kālâ*', *TDOT*, VII (1995), pp. 157-164 (158-59, 162-63)

destroy—F.J. Helfmeyer, 'כָּלָה *kālâ*', *TDOT*, VII (1995), pp. 157-164 (160-61)

Ps 101$_5$—Mitchell Dahood, 'Hebrew–Ugaritic Lexicography III', *Bib* 46 (1965), pp. 311-32 (328)

pine—M. Dahood, Review of Robert de Langhe (ed.), *Le Psautier. Ses origines. Ses problèmes littéraires. Son influence* (Louvain: Publications Universitaires, 1961), *Bib* 44 (1963), pp. 104-106 (105); F.J. Helfmeyer, 'כָּלָה *kālâ*', *TDOT*, VII (1995), pp. 157-164 (163-64)

כָּלָה *end* (Na 1$_8$)—G.R. Driver, 'Studies in the Vocabulary of the Old Testament. VIII', *JTS* 36 (1935), pp. 293-301 (300-301)

כַּלָּה *bride*—Thomas, *Lexicon*, XI (1970), p. 295; J. Conrad, 'כַּלָּה *kallâ*', *TDOT*, VII pp. 164-69

כֶּלַח I *old age* or *vigour*—Mitchell J. Dahood, 'Northwest Semitic Philology and Job', in *The Bible in Current Catholic Thought* (ed. J.L. McKenzie; New York: Herder & Herder, 1962), pp. 55-74 (56); Lester L. Grabbe, *Comparative Philology and the Text of Job: A Study in Methodology* (SBLDS, 34; Missoula, MT: Scholars Press, 1977), pp. 43-46

כְּלִי *vessel*—K.-M. Beyse, ''כְּלִי *kelî*', *TDOT*, VII (1995), pp. 169-75

weapon—K.-M. Beyse, ''כְּלִי *kelî*', *TDOT*, VII (1995), pp. 169-75 (172)

(musical) instrument—K.-M. Beyse. ''כְּלִי *kelî*', *TDOT*, VII (1995), pp. 169-75 (175)

clothing, jewellery—K.-M. Beyse, ''כְּלִי *kelî*', *TDOT*, VII (1995), pp. 169-75 (173)

plan (Is 32$_7$)—K.-M. Beyse, ''כְּלִי *kelî*', *TDOT*, VII (1995), pp. 169-75 (172)

body (4Q416 2.2$_{21}$)—Daniel J. Harrington 'Ten Reasons Why the Qumran Wisdom Texts are Important', *DSD* 4 (1997), pp. 246-54 (252)

כְּלִיא *confinement*—J. Hausmann, 'כָּלָא *kālā'*; כֶּלֶא *kele'*; כְּלִיא *kelî'*; מִכְלָה *miklâ*', *TDOT*, VII (1995), pp. 143-45 (143)

כִּלְיָה *kidney*—Hans Walter Wolff, *Anthropology of the Old Testament* (tr. Margaret Kohl; London: SCM Press, 1974), pp. 65-66; D. Kellermann, 'כְּלָיוֹת *kelāyôt*', *TDOT*, VII (1995), pp. 175-78

כִּלְיוֹן *Chilion*—E. Lipinski, 'Peninna, Iti'el et l'athlète', *VT* 17 (1967), pp. 68-75 (68)

כָּלִיל I *whole offering*—O. Loretz, 'Die hebräische Opferterminus *KLJL* "Ganzopfer"', *UF* 7 (1975), pp. 569-60; A.S. Kapelrud, 'כָּלִיל *kālîl*', *TDOT*, VII (1995), pp. 182-85

כָּלִיל II *crown*—Thomas, *Lexicon*, XI (1970), pp. 295-96

כְּלִילָה *crown*—Thomas, *Lexicon*, XI (1970), p. 296

כלם I *humiliate*—S. Wagner, 'כלם *klm*; כְּלִמָּה; *kelimmâ*; כְּלִמּוּת *kelimmûṯ*', *TDOT*, VII (1995), pp. 185-96

כלם II *speak*—Joseph Reider, 'Etymological Studies in Biblical Hebrew', *VT* 4 (1954), pp. 276-95 (280); Barr, pp. 14-15; A.A. Macintosh, 'The Meaning of *mklym* in Judges xviii 7', *VT* 35 (1985), pp. 68-76; Kaltner, pp. 70-72

כְּלִמָּה I *insult* (Mc 2$_6$)—S. Wagner, 'כלם *klm*; כְּלִמָּה *kelimmâ*; כְּלִמּוּת *kelimmûṯ*', *TDOT*, VII (1995), pp. 185-96 (195)

כְּלִמָּה II *speech*—Joseph Reider, 'Etymological Studies in Biblical Hebrew', *VT* 4 (1954), pp. 276-95 (280); Barr, p. 15

כַּמְרִיר *darkness*—Lester L. Grabbe, *Comparative Philology and the Text of Job: A Study in Methodology* (SBLDS, 34; Missoula, MT: Scholars Press, 1977), pp. 29-31

כֵּן I *thus*—M.J. Mulder, 'Die Partikel כֵּן im Alten Testament', *OTS* 21 (1981), pp. 201-27

Is 52$_{14}$—Barr, pp. 284-85; E.Y. Kutscher, *The Language* *and Linguistic Background of the Isaiah Scroll (1QIsa*^{a}*)* (STDJ, 6; Leiden: E.J. Brill, 1974), p. 262

בְּכֵן *thereupon* (cf. Ug. bkm)—Mitchell Dahood, 'Qoheleth and Northwest Semitic Philology', *Bib* 43 (1962), pp. 349-65 (360)

עַל־כֵּן *therefore*, etc.—R. Frankena, 'Einige Bemerkungen zum Gebrauch des Adverbs *'al-ken* im Hebräischen', in *Studia biblica et semitica Theodoro Christiano Vriezen ... ab amicis, collegis, discipulis dedicata* (Wageningen: Veenman & Zonen, 1966), pp. 94-99; Hellmut Lenhard, 'Über den Unterschied zwischen לכן and על־כן', *ZAW* 95 (1983), pp. 269-72

כֵּן III *right*—K. Koch, 'כּוּן *kûn*; כֵּן *kēn*; מָכוֹן *māḵôn*; מְכוֹנָה *m*^{e}*ḵônâ*; תְּכוּנָה *t*^{e}*ḵûnâ*', *TDOT*, VII (1995), pp. 89-101 (91)

כֵּן IV *stand*—K. Koch, 'כּוּן *kûn*; כֵּן *kēn*; מָכוֹן *māḵôn*; מְכוֹנָה *m*^{e}*ḵônâ*; תְּכוּנָה *t*^{e}*ḵûnâ*', *TDOT*, VII (1995), pp. 89-101 (92)

כֵּן VI *position*—K. Koch, 'כּוּן *kûn*; כֵּן *kēn*; מָכוֹן *māḵôn*; מְכוֹנָה *m*^{e}*ḵônâ*; תְּכוּנָה *t*^{e}*ḵûnâ*', *TDOT*, VII (1995), pp. 89-101 (92)

כֵּנֶד *jug* (cf. Ug. knd)—Mitchell Dahood, 'Hebrew–Ugaritic Lexicography III', *Bib* 46 (1965), pp. 311-32 (328-29)

כנה *name*—H. Ringgren, 'כנה *knh*', *TDOT*, VII (1995), pp. 196-97

כַּנָּה *stock*—K. Koch, 'כּוּן *kûn*; כֵּן *kēn*; מָכוֹן *māḵôn*; מְכוֹנָה *m*^{e}*ḵônâ*; תְּכוּנָה *t*^{e}*ḵûnâ*', *TDOT*, VII (1995), pp. 89-101 (92)

כִּנּוֹר *lyre*—Mitchell Dahood, 'Hebrew–Ugaritic Lexicography III', *Bib* 46 (1965), pp. 311-32 (329); Edwin L. Brown, 'The Origin of the Constellation Name "Cynosura"', *Orientalia* 50 (1981), pp. 384-402 (387-88); M. Görg and G.J. Botterweck, 'כִּנּוֹר *kinnôr*', *TDOT*, VII (1995), pp. 197-204

כנע *be humble*—S. Wagner, 'כנע *kn'*', *TDOT*, VII (1995), pp. 197-204

כְּנַעַן I *Canaan* (person)—H.-J. Zobel, 'כְּנַעַן *k*^{e}*na'an*; כְּנַעֲנִי *k*^{e}*na'*^{a}*nî*', *TDOT*, VII (1995), pp. 211-28 (216)

כְּנַעַן II *Canaan* (place)—H.-J. Zobel, 'כְּנַעַן *k*^{e}*na'an*; כְּנַעֲנִי *k*^{e}*na'*^{a}*nî*', *TDOT*, VII (1995), pp. 211-28

כְּנַעֲנִי I *Canaanite*—H.-J. Zobel, 'כְּנַעַן *k*^{e}*na'an*; כְּנַעֲנִי *k*^{e}*na'*^{a}*nî*', *TDOT*, VII (1995), pp. 211-28 (224-28)

כָּנָף *wing*—W. Dommershausen, 'כָּנָף *kānāp*', *TDOT*, VII (1995), pp. 229-31; A.S. van der Woude, 'כָּנָף *kānāp* wing', *TLOT*, II (1997), pp. 618-20

פרשׂ כָּנָף *extend garment* (Ezk 16$_{8}$ Ru 3$_{9}$)—Karel van der Toorn, 'The Significance of the Veil in the Ancient Near East', in *Pomegranates and Golden Bells: Studies in Biblical, Jewish, and Near Eastern Ritual, Law, and Literature in Honor of Jacob Milgrom* (ed. David P. Wright, David Noel Freedman and Avi Hurvitz; Winona Lake, IN; Eisenbrauns, 1995), pp. 327-39 (334-35)

skirt—W. Dommershausen, 'כָּנָף *kānāp*', *TDOT*, VII (1995), pp. 229-31 (231); A.S. van der Woude, 'כָּנָף *kānāp* wing', *TLOT*, II (1997), pp. 618-20 (619-20)

כִּנֶּרֶת *Chinnereth*—M. Görg and G.J. Botterweck, 'כִּנּוֹר *kinnôr*', *TDOT*, VII (1995), pp. 197-204 (199-200)

כֶּסֶא *full moon*—H.-J. Fabry, 'כִּסֵּא *kissē*', *TDOT*, VII (1995), pp. 232-59 (232)

כִּסֵּא *throne*—H.-J. Fabry, 'כִּסֵּא *kissē*', *TDOT*, VII (1995), pp. 232-59

2 C 9$_{18}$—G.R. Driver, 'Studies in the Vocabulary of the Old Testament. VIII', *JTS* 36 (1935), pp. 293-301 (299-300)

כסה *cover*—H. Ringgren, 'כָּסָה *kāsâ*; כָּסוּי *kāsûy*; כְּסוּת *k*^{e}*sût*; מִכְסֶה *mikseh*; מְכַסֶּה *m*^{e}*ḵasseh*', *TDOT*, VII (1995), pp. 259-64

uncover—Mitchell Dahood, 'Hebrew–Ugaritic Lexicography III', *Bib* 46 (1965), pp. 311-32 (330)

cover (Jb 33$_{17}$)—Joseph Reider, 'Etymological Studies in Biblical Hebrew', *VT* 4 (1954), pp. 276-95 (292-93)

כסה על pi. *cover*—Bernard M. Levinson, 'Recovering the Lost Original Meaning of ולא תכסה עליו (Deuteronomy 13:9)', *JBL* 115 (1996), pp. 602-620 (607-609)

כָּסוּי *covering*—H. Ringgren, 'כָּסָה *kāsâ*; כָּסוּי *kāsûy*; כְּסוּת *k*^{e}*sût*; מִכְסֶה *mikseh*; מְכַסֶּה *m*^{e}*ḵasseh*', *TDOT*, VII (1995), pp. 259-64 (263-64)

כְּסוּת *covering*—H. Ringgren, 'כָּסָה *kāsâ*; כָּסוּי *kāsûy*; כְּסוּת *k*^{e}*sût*; מִכְסֶה *mikseh*; מְכַסֶּה *m*^{e}*ḵasseh*', *TDOT*, VII (1995), pp. 259-64 (263-64)

כִּסְיָה *rump*—Thomas, *Lexicon*, XI (1970), p. 377

כְּסִיל I *fool*—J. Schüpphaus, 'כסל *ksl*; כְּסִיל *k*^{e}*sîl*; כְּסִילוּת *k*^{e}*sîlût*; כֶּסֶל *kesel*; כִּסְלָה *kislâ*', *TDOT*, VII (1995), pp. 264-69; M. Sæbø, 'כְּסִיל *kesîl* fool', *TLOT*, II (1997), pp. 620-22 (620-21)

sluggish one—Thomas, *Lexicon*, XI (1970), p. 380

מְרַיִם כְּסִילִים *the desire of fools*—G.R. Driver, 'Note to D. Winton Thomas, "Notes on Some Passages in the Book of Proverbs"', *JTS* 38 (1937), pp. 400-403 (403)

כְּסִיל II *Orion*—J. Schüpphaus, 'כסל *ksl*; כְּסִיל *k^{e}sîl*; כְּסִילוּת *k^{e}sîlût*; כֶּסֶל *kesel*; כִּסְלָה *kislâ*', *TDOT*, VII (1995), pp. 264-69 (268-69); M. Sæbø, 'כְּסִיל *kesîl* fool', *TLOT*, II (1997), pp. 620-22 (620)

כְּסִילוּת *stupidity*—J. Schüpphaus, 'כסל *ksl*; כְּסִיל *k^{e}sîl*; כְּסִילוּת *k^{e}sîlût*; כֶּסֶל *kesel*; כִּסְלָה *kislâ*', *TDOT*, VII (1995), pp. 264-69 (265); M. Sæbø, 'כְּסִיל *kesîl* fool', *TLOT*, II (1997), pp. 620-22 (622)

כסל *be foolish*—J. Schüpphaus, 'כסל *ksl*; כְּסִיל *k^{e}sîl*; כְּסִילוּת *k^{e}sîlût*; כֶּסֶל *kesel*; כִּסְלָה *kislâ*', *TDOT*, VII (1995), pp. 264-69 (266); M. Sæbø, 'כְּסִיל *kesîl* fool', *TLOT*, II (1997), pp. 620-22 (620)

כֶּסֶל I *stupidity*—J. Schüpphaus, 'כסל *ksl*; כְּסִיל *k^{e}sîl*; כְּסִילוּת *k^{e}sîlût*; כֶּסֶל *kesel*; כִּסְלָה *kislâ*', *TDOT*, VII (1995), pp. 264-69 (266); M. Sæbø, 'כְּסִיל *kesîl* fool', *TLOT*, II (1997), pp. 620-22 (620)

כֶּסֶל II *thigh* (Jb 15_{27})—Mitchell Dahood, 'Hebrew–Ugaritic Lexicography III', *Bib* 46 (1965), pp. 311-32 (330); Review of Jean Lévêque, *Job et son Dieu. Essai d'exégèse et de théologie biblique* (Paris: J. Gabalda, 1970), *Bib* 52 (1971), pp. 436-38 (437); J.C. de Moor, 'The Anatomy of the Back', *UF* 12 (1980), pp. 425-26 (425); J. Schüpphaus, 'כסל *ksl*; כְּסִיל *k^{e}sîl*; כְּסִילוּת *k^{e}sîlût*; כֶּסֶל *kesel*; כִּסְלָה *kislâ*', *TDOT*, VII (1995), pp. 264-69; M. Sæbø, 'כְּסִיל *kesîl* fool', *TLOT*, II (1997), pp. 620-22 (620)

כִּסְלָה *stupidity*—J. Schüpphaus, 'כסל *ksl*; כְּסִיל *k^{e}sîl*; כְּסִילוּת *k^{e}sîlût*; כֶּסֶל *kesel*; כִּסְלָה *kislâ*', *TDOT*, VII (1995), pp. 264-69 (266); M. Sæbø, 'כְּסִיל *kesîl* fool', *TLOT*, II (1997), pp. 620-22 (620)

כַּסְלֻחִי *Casluhite*—Gary A. Rendsburg, 'Gen 10:13-14: An Authentic Hebrew Tradition Concerning the Origin of the Philistines', *JNWSL* 13 (1987), pp. 89-96

כסף II *be ashamed* (cf. Akk. kasāpu)—G.R. Driver, 'Problems and Solutions', *VT* 4 (1954), pp. 225-45 (242); Barr, p. 329

כֶּסֶף I *silver*—G. Mayer, 'כֶּסֶף *kesep*', *TDOT*, VII (1995), pp. 270-82 (273-77)

3QTr 9_{10}—Al Wolters, 'Notes on the Copper Scroll (3Q15)', *RQ* 12 (1987), pp. 589-96 (594-95)

כֶּסֶף עֹבֵר *usable silver*—Victor Avigdor Horowitz, '*kæsæp 'ober lassoḥer* (Genesis 23,16)', *ZAW* 108 (1996), pp. 12-19

כֶּסֶף II *disappointment*—G. Mayer, 'כֶּסֶף *kesep*', *TDOT*, VII (1995), pp. 270-82

כֶּסֶף III *food*—G.R. Driver, 'Linguistic and Textual Problems: Isaiah xl–lxvi', *JTS* 36 (1935), pp. 396-406 (404); 'Problems and Solutions', *VT* 4 (1954), pp. 225-45 (242); Barr, p. 153

כֹּסֶף *disappointment* (cf. Arab. kassafa *disappoint*)—G.R. Driver, 'Problems and Solutions', *VT* 4 (1954), pp. 225-45 (229); Kaltner, pp. 69-70

כעס *be angry*—N. Lohfink, 'כעס כָּעַס *kā'as*; כַּעַס *ka'as*', *TDOT*, VII (1995), pp. 282-88; F. Stolz, 'כעס *k's* to be angry', *TLOT*, II (1997), pp. 622-24

כַּעַס *anger*—N. Lohfink, 'כעס כָּעַס *kā'as*; כַּעַס *ka'as*', *TDOT*, VII (1995), pp. 282-88; F. Stolz, 'כעס *k's* to be angry', *TLOT*, II (1997), pp. 622-24

care (cf. Punic k's)—Mitchell Dahood, 'Hebrew–Ugaritic Lexicography III', *Bib* 46 (1965), pp. 311-32 (330)

כַּף I *hand*—J. Bergman, W. von Soden and P.R. Ackroyd, 'יָד *yāḏ*; זְרוֹעַ *zerôa'*; יָמִין *yāmîn*; כַּף *kap̄*; אֶצְבַּע *'eṣba'*', *TDOT*, V (1986), pp. 393-426 (403-405)

palm—J. Bergman, W. von Soden and P.R. Ackroyd, 'יָד *yāḏ*; זְרוֹעַ *zerôa'*; יָמִין *yāmîn*; כַּף *kap̄*; אֶצְבַּע *'eṣba'*', *TDOT*, V (1986), pp. 393-426 (403-404)

stump—J. Bergman, W. von Soden and P.R. Ackroyd, 'יָד *yāḏ*; זְרוֹעַ *zerôa'*; יָמִין *yāmîn*; כַּף *kap̄*; אֶצְבַּע *'eṣba'*', *TDOT*, V (1986), pp. 393-426 (404)

sole—J. Bergman, W. von Soden and P.R. Ackroyd, 'יָד *yāḏ*; זְרוֹעַ *zerôa'*; יָמִין *yāmîn*; כַּף *kap̄*; אֶצְבַּע *'eṣba'*', *TDOT*, V (1986), pp. 393-426 (405)

cultic utensil—Victor Avigdor Hurowitz, 'Solomon's Golden Vessels (1 Kings 7:48–50) and the Cult of the First Temple', in *Pomegranates and Golden Bells: Studies in Biblical, Jewish, and Near Eastern Ritual, Law, and Literature in Honor of Jacob Milgrom* (ed. David P. Wright, David Noel Freedman and Avi Hurvitz; Winona Lake, IN; Eisenbrauns, 1995), pp. 151-64 (157-

58); J. Bergman, W. von Soden and P.R. Ackroyd, 'יָד *yād*; זְרוֹעַ *zerôa'*; יָמִין *yāmîn*; כַּף *kap̄*; אֶצְבַּע *'eṣba''*, *TDOT*, V (1986), pp. 393-426 (404)

socket of hip—J. Bergman, W. von Soden and P.R. Ackroyd, 'יָד *yād*; זְרוֹעַ *zerôa'*; יָמִין *yāmîn*; כַּף *kap̄*; אֶצְבַּע *'eṣba''*, *TDOT*, V (1986), pp. 393-426 (405)

handle—J. Bergman, W. von Soden and P.R. Ackroyd, 'יָד *yād*; זְרוֹעַ *zerôa'*; יָמִין *yāmîn*; כַּף *kap̄*; אֶצְבַּע *'eṣba''*, *TDOT*, V (1986), pp. 393-426 (405)

handful—C.L. Seow, 'Linguistic Evidence and the Dating of Qohelet', *JBL* 115 (1996), pp. 643-66 (665); J. Bergman, W. von Soden and P.R. Ackroyd, 'יָד *yād*; זְרוֹעַ *zerôa'*; יָמִין *yāmîn*; כַּף *kap̄*; אֶצְבַּע *'eṣba''*, *TDOT*, V (1986), pp. 393-426 (404)

basin—John Marco Allegro, *The Treasure of the Copper Scroll* (London: Routledge & Kegan Paul, 1960), p. 158

כַּף II *skirt*—Meir Malul, 'כַּפִּי (Ex 33,22) and בְּחָפְנָיו (Prov 30,4): Hand or Skirt?', *ZAW* 109 (1997), pp. 356-68

כֵּף *mountain top* (cf. Arab. akāfīf *mountain tops*)—Alfred Guillaume, 'The Arabic Background of the Book of Job', in *Promise and Fulfilment: Essays Presented to Professor S.H. Hooke in Celebration of his Ninetieth Birthday, 21st January 1964, by Members of the Society for Old Testament Study and Others* (ed. F.F. Bruce: Edinburgh: T. & T. Clark, 1963), pp. 106-27 (119)

edge—Al Wolters, 'The *Copper Scroll* and the Vocabulary of Mishnaic Hebrew', *RQ* 14 (1990), pp. 483-95 (489)

כַּפָּא *Kippa*—John Marco Allegro, *The Treasure of the Copper Scroll* (London: Routledge & Kegan Paul, 1960), p. 144

כפה pi. *extinguish*—Mitchell Dahood, 'Hebrew–Ugaritic Lexicography III', *Bib* 46 (1965), pp. 311-32 (331)

כְּפוֹר I *bowl* (cf. Mari bît kuprim as part of treasury)—D.J. Wiseman, Review of M. Birot, *Textes administratifs de la salle 5 du palais* (Paris: Imprimerie Nationale, 1960), *JSS* 9 (1964), pp. 357-59 (358)

כלין כופרין *serving vessels*—Al Wolters, 'Notes on the Copper Scroll (3Q15)', *RQ* 12 (1987), pp. 589-96 (596)

כְּפִיר I *young lion* (cf. Arab. ğufr *young mountain goat*)—Joshua Blau, 'Etymologische Untersuchungen auf Grund des palästinischen Arabisch', *VT* 5 (1955), pp. 337-44 (342)

Ps 74$_{20}$—Christopher T. Begg, 'The Covenantal Dove in Psalm lxxiv 19-20', *VT* 37 (1987), pp. 78-81 (78)

tawny lion (cf. Eblaite kàpáru *copper*)—Mitchell Dahood, 'Love and Death at Ebla and their Biblical Reflections', in *Love and Death in the Ancient Near East: Essays in Honor of Marvin H. Pope* (ed. John H. Marks and Robert M. Good; Guilford, CN/Los Angeles, CA: Four Quarters Publishing Company/Western Academic Press, 1986), pp. 93-99 (95)

כְּפִיר II *copper vessel* (cf. Eblaite kàpáru *copper*)—Mitchell Dahood, 'Love and Death at Ebla and their Biblical Reflections', in *Love and Death in the Ancient Near East: Essays in Honor of Marvin H. Pope* (ed. John H. Marks and Robert M. Good; Guilford, CN/Los Angeles, CA: Four Quarters Publishing Company/Western Academic Press, 1986), pp. 93-99 (95)

כֶּפֶל *equivalent*—Gerhard von Rad, 'כִּפְלַיִם in Jes 40 $_2$ = Äquivalent?', *ZAW* 79 (1967), pp. 80-82

כפר *cover*—B. Lang, 'כִּפֶּר *kipper*; כַּפֹּרֶת *kappōreṯ*; כֹּפֶר *kōper*; כִּפֻּרִים *kippurîm*', *TDOT*, VII (1995), pp. 288-303 (293); F. Maass, 'כפר *kpr* pi. to atone', *TLOT*, II (1997), pp. 624-35

pi. *ransom*—Jacob Milgrom, 'The Literary Structure of Numbers 8:5–22 and the Levitic *Kippûr*', in *Perspectives on Language and Text: Essays and Poems in Honor of Francis I. Andersen's Sixtieth Birthday July 28, 1985* (ed. Edgar W. Conrad and Edward G. Newing; Winona Lake, IN: Eisenbrauns, 1987), pp. 205-209

atone—Matthew V. Khuzhivelil, 'Reconciliation in the Old Testament', *Bible Bhashyam* 9 (1983), pp. 168-78 (169-70)

כָּפָר *village*—F. Maass, 'כפר *kpr* pi. to atone', *TLOT*, II (1997), pp. 624-35 (626)

כֹּפֶר *atonement*—B. Lang, 'כִּפֶּר *kipper*; כַּפֹּרֶת *kappōreṯ*; כֹּפֶר *kōper*; כִּפֻּרִים *kippurîm*', *TDOT*, VII (1995), pp. 288-303 (297-99); F. Maass, 'כפר *kpr* pi. to atone', *TLOT*, II (1997), pp. 624-35 (625-26)

כִּפֻּרִים *atonement* (Ex 30$_{16}$), E.A. Speiser, 'Census and Ritual Expiation in Mari and Israel', *BASOR* 149 (February, 1959), pp. 17-25

כֹּפֶר I *ransom* (cf. Eblaite kàpáru *copper*)—Mitchell Dahood, 'Love and Death at Ebla and their Biblical Reflections', in *Love and Death in the Ancient Near East: Essays in Honor of Marvin H. Pope* (ed. John H. Marks and Robert M. Good; Guilford, CN/Los Angeles, CA: Four Quarters Publishing Company/Western Academic Press, 1986), pp. 93-99 (95); B. Lang, 'כִּפֶּר *kipper*; כַּפֹּרֶת *kappōreṯ*; כֹּפֶר *kōper*; כִּפֻּרִים *kippurîm*', *TDOT*, VII (1995), pp. 288-303 (301-302); F. Maass, 'כפר *kpr* pi. to atone', *TLOT*, II (1997), pp. 624-35 (626)

Ex 30_{12}—E.A. Speiser, 'Census and Ritual Expiation in Mari and Israel', *BASOR* 149 (February, 1959), pp. 17-25

כֹּפֶר II *bitumen*—F. Maass, 'כפר *kpr* pi. to atone', *TLOT*, II (1997), pp. 624-35 (626)

כֹּפֶר III village—F. Maass, 'כפר *kpr* pi. to atone', *TLOT*, II (1997), pp. 624-35 (626)

כֹּפֶר IV *henna* (cf. Ug. *kpr* perh. 'henna'; Eblaite kàpáru *copper*)—Mitchell Dahood, 'Love and Death at Ebla and their Biblical Reflections', in *Love and Death in the Ancient Near East: Essays in Honor of Marvin H. Pope* (ed. John H. Marks and Robert M. Good; Guilford, CN/Los Angeles, CA: Four Quarters Publishing Company/Western Academic Press, 1986), pp. 93-99 (95); Johannes C. de Moor, 'Ugaritic Smalltalk', *UF* 17 (1986), pp. 219-23 (220-21); F. Maass, 'כפר *kpr* pi. to atone', *TLOT*, II (1997), pp. 624-35 (626)

כֹּפְרִי I, II *tarred, expiatory*—Al Wolters, 'Notes on the Copper Scroll (3Q15)', *RQ* 12 (1987), pp. 589-96 (596)

כַּפֹּרֶת *cover*—Klaus Koch, 'Some Considerations on the Translation of *kappōret* in the Septuagint', in *Pomegranates and Golden Bells: Studies in Biblical, Jewish, and Near Eastern Ritual, Law, and Literature in Honor of Jacob Milgrom* (ed. David P. Wright, David Noel Freedman and Avi Hurvitz; Winona Lake, IN; Eisenbrauns, 1995), pp. 65-75

בֵּית־הַכַּפֹּרֶת *holy of holies*—Avi Hurvitz, 'Terms and Epithets Relating to the Jerusalem Temple Compound in the Book of Chronicles: The Linguistic Aspect', in *Pomegranates and Golden Bells: Studies in Biblical, Jewish, and Near Eastern Ritual, Law, and Literature in Honor of Jacob Milgrom* (ed. David P. Wright, David Noel Freedman and Avi Hurvitz; Winona Lake, IN; Eisenbrauns, 1995), pp. 165-83 (172-74)

כפשׁ hi. *trample*—Mitchell Dahood, 'Hebrew–Ugaritic Lexicography III', *Bib* 46 (1965), pp. 311-32 (331)

כַּפְתּוֹר I *capital* (Am 9_1)—Eberhard Ruprecht, 'Das Zepter Jahwes in den Berufsvisionen von Jeremia und Amos', *ZAW* 108 (1996), pp. 55-69 (67)

כַּפְתּוֹר II *Caphtor*—G.J. Thierry, 'Notes on Hebrew Grammar and Etymology', *OTS* 9 (1951), pp. 1-17 (14-15); G.A. Wainwright, 'Caphtor—Cappadocia', *VT* 6 (1956), pp. 199-210; John F. Brug, *A Literary and Archaeological Study of the Philistines* (BAR International Series, 265; Oxford: B.A.R., 1985), p. 8; Gary A. Rendsburg, 'Gen 10:13-14: An Authentic Hebrew Tradition Concerning the Origin of the Philistines', *JNWSL* 13 (1987), pp. 89-96

כרה I *dig*—K.-D. Schunk, 'כָּרָה *kārâ*; כֵּרָה *kērâ*; כְּרִית *kerîṯ*; מִכְרֶה *miḵreh*', *TDOT*, VII (1995), pp. 303-306 (304-305, 306)

כרה II *purchase*—K.-D. Schunk, 'כָּרָה *kārâ*; כֵּרָה *kērâ*; כְּרִית *kerîṯ*; מִכְרֶה *miḵreh*', *TDOT*, VII (1995), pp. 303-306 (305, 306)

כרה III *feast*—K.–D. Schunck, 'כָּרָה *kārâ*; כֵּרָה *kērâ*; כְּרִית *kerîṯ*; מִכְרֶה *miḵreh*', *TDOT*, VII (1995), pp. 303-306 (305)

כרה IV *bind*—K.–D. Schunck, 'כָּרָה *kārâ*; כֵּרָה *kērâ*; כְּרִית *kerîṯ*; מִכְרֶה *miḵreh*', *TDOT*, VII (1995), pp. 303-306 (305)

כרה V *be short* (cf. Akk. karû)—K.–D. Schunck, 'כָּרָה *kārâ*; כֵּרָה *kērâ*; כְּרִית *kerîṯ*; מִכְרֶה *miḵreh*', *TDOT*, VII (1995), pp. 303-306 (305-306)

כָּרָה *cistern*—K.-D. Schunk, 'כָּרָה *kārâ*; כֵּרָה *kērâ*; כְּרִית *kerîṯ*; מִכְרֶה *miḵreh*', *TDOT*, VII (1995), pp. 303-306 (304)

כֵּרָה *feast* (cf. Akk. kirētu)—Chaim Rabin, 'Etymological Miscellanea', in *Studies in the Bible* (ed. Chaim Rabin; ScrHieros, 8; Jerusalem: Magnes Press, 1961), pp. 384-400 (399); Barr, p. 102; John Gray, *I and II Kings: A Commentary* (OTL; London: SCM Press, 3rd edn, 1977), p. 517; K.–D. Schunck, 'כָּרָה *kārâ*; כֵּרָה *kērâ*; כְּרִית *kerîṯ*; מִכְרֶה *miḵreh*', *TDOT*, VII (1995), pp. 303-306 (305)

כְּרוּב I *cherub*—John Pairman Brown, 'Literary Contexts

of the Common Hebrew–Greek Vocabulary', *JSS* 13 (1968), pp. 163-91 (184-88); D.N. Freedman and M.P. O'Connor, 'כְּרוּב *kerûb*', *TDOT*, VII (1995), pp. 307-19

כְּרִיתוּת *divorce*—G.F. Hasel, 'כָּרַת *kārat*; כְּרֻתוֹת *kerutôt*; כְּרִיתֻת *kerîtut*', *TDOT*, VII (1995), pp. 339-52 (343); E. Kutsch, 'כרת *krt* to cut off', *TLOT*, II (1997), pp. 635-37 (635)

כֶּרֶם I *vineyard*—H.-P. Müller, 'כֶּרֶם *kerem*; כֹּרֵם *kōrem*; כַּרְמֶל *karmel*', *TDOT*, VII (1995), pp. 319-25

כֶּרֶם רָשָׁע *vineyard of a wealthy one*—Alfred Guillaume, 'The Arabic Background of the Book of Job', in *Promise and Fulfilment: Essays Presented to Professor S.H. Hooke in Celebration of his Ninetieth Birthday, 21st January 1964, by Members of the Society for Old Testament Study and Others* (ed. F.F. Bruce: Edinburgh: T. & T. Clark, 1963), pp. 106-27 (116)

pudenda—H.-P. Müller, 'כֶּרֶם *kerem*; כֹּרֵם *kōrem*; כַּרְמֶל *karmel*', *TDOT*, VII (1995), pp. 319-25 (324)

כֹּרֵם *vinedresser*—H.-P. Müller, 'כֶּרֶם *kerem*; כֹּרֵם *kōrem*; כַּרְמֶל *karmel*', *TDOT*, VII (1995), pp. 319-25 (320-23)

כַּרְמֶל I *orchard*—M.J. Mulder, 'כַּרְמֶל *karmel*', *TDOT*, VII (1995), pp. 325-336 (328-30)

cultivated field—Thomas, *Lexicon*, XI (1970), p. 460

כַּרְמֶל II *Carmel*—M.J. Mulder, 'כַּרְמֶל *karmel*', *TDOT*, VII (1995), pp. 325-336 (330-36)

כַּרְמֶל III *fresh ears*—G.R. Driver, *Canaanite Myths and Legends* (Edinburgh: T. & T. Clark, 1956), p. 164 n. 5; Barr, pp. 26, 294, 323; John Gray, *I and II Kings: A Commentary* (OTL; London: SCM Press, 3rd edn, 1977), pp. 501-502; Elisha Qimron, 'Biblical Philology and the DSS', *Tarb* 58 (1989), pp. 297-315 (308-10); M.J. Mulder, 'כַּרְמֶל *karmel*', *TDOT*, VII (1995), pp. 325-336 (328-30)

כָּרַע *bow*—H.-J. Fabry, 'כָּרַע *kāra'*', *TDOT*, VII (1995), pp. 336-39

כרר pilp. *play* (cf. Ug. krkr)—Y. Avishur, 'KRKR in Biblical Hebrew and in Ugaritic', *VT* 26 (1976), pp. 257-61

כרת *cut*—G.F. Hasel, 'כָּרַת *kārat*; כְּרֻתוֹת *kerutôt*; כְּרִיתֻת *kerîtut*', *TDOT*, VII (1995), pp. 339-52; E. Kutsch, 'כרת *krt* to cut off', *TLOT*, II (1997), pp. 635-37; Friedrich V. Reiterer, 'The Hebrew of Ben Sira Investigated on the Basis of his Use of כרת: A Syntactic, Semantic and Language-Historical Contribution', in *Proceedings of the Second Leiden Symposium (December 1997)* (provisional title; ed. T. Muraoka and J.F. Elwolde; STDJ; Leiden: E.J. Brill)

make covenant—J. Alberto Soggin, 'Akkadisch Tar *Berîti* und Hebräisch כרת ברית', *VT* 18 (1986), pp. 210-15 (214); G.F. Hasel, 'כָּרַת *kārat*; כְּרֻתוֹת *kerutôt*; כְּרִיתֻת *kerîtut*', *TDOT*, VII (1995), pp. 339-52 (349-52); E. Kutsch, 'כרת *krt* to cut off', *TLOT*, II (1997), pp. 635-37 (636-37)

ni. *be excommunicated*—G.F. Hasel, 'כָּרַת *kārat*; כְּרֻתוֹת *kerutôt*; כְּרִיתֻת *kerîtut*', *TDOT*, VII (1995), pp. 339-52 (347-49)

be abrogated (Si 50_{24})—J.F. Elwolde, 'Developments in Hebrew Vocabulary between Bible and Mishnah', in *The Hebrew of the Dead Sea Scrolls and Ben Sira: Proceedings of a Symposium held at Leiden University, 11-14 December 1995* (ed. T. Muraoka and J.F. Elwolde; STDJ, 26; Leiden: E.J. Brill, 1997), pp. 17-55 (33)

hi. *destroy*—G.F. Hasel, 'כָּרַת *kārat*; כְּרֻתוֹת *kerutôt*; כְּרִיתֻת *kerîtut*', *TDOT*, VII (1995), pp. 339-52 (344); E. Kutsch, 'כרת *krt* to cut off', *TLOT*, II (1997), pp. 635-37 (635-66)

כְּרֻתוֹת *beams*—G.F. Hasel, 'כָּרַת *kārat*; כְּרֻתוֹת *kerutôt*; כְּרִיתֻת *kerîtut*', *TDOT*, VII (1995), pp. 339-52 (343); E. Kutsch, 'כרת *krt* to cut off', *TLOT*, II (1997), pp. 635-37 (635)

כְּרֵתִי *Cherethite*—Celestina Milani, 'Contributo all'interpretazione del lessico Minoico', *Kadmos* 3 (1964), 8-24 (18-19); John F. Brug, *A Literary and Archaeological Study of the Philistines* (BAR International Series, 265; Oxford: B.A.R., 1985), p. 8

כֶּשֶׂב *lamb*—C. Dohmen, 'כֶּבֶשׂ *kebeś*; כֶּשֶׂב *keśeb*; כִּבְשָׂה *kibśâ*; כִּשְׂבָּה *kiśbâ*; שֶׂה *śeh*', *TDOT*, VII (1995), pp. 43-52

כִּשְׂבָּה *ewe lamb*—C. Dohmen, 'כֶּבֶשׂ *kebeś*; כֶּשֶׂב *keśeb*; כִּבְשָׂה *kibśâ*; כִּשְׂבָּה *kiśbâ*; שֶׂה *śeh*', *TDOT*, VII (1995), pp. 43-52

כַּשִּׁיר *skilful*—D. Kellermann, 'כָּשֵׁר *kāšēr*; כִּשְׁרוֹן *kišrôn*', *TDOT*, VII (1995) pp. 367-70 (370)

כִּשָּׁלוֹן *stumbling*—C. Barth, 'כָּשַׁל *kāšal*; מִכְשׁוֹל *mikšôl*; כִּשָּׁלוֹן *kiššālôn*; מַכְשֵׁלָה *makšēlâ*', *TDOT*, VII (1995), pp. 353-60

כשׁף *practise sorcery*—G. André, 'כָּשַׁף *kāšap*; כֶּשֶׁף *kešep*; כַּשָּׁף *kaššāp*; אַשָּׁף *'aššāp*; יִדְּעֹנִי *yiddeʿōnî*; לָחַשׁ *lāḥaš*; לַחַשׁ *laḥaš*; נָחַשׁ *nāḥaš*; נַחַשׁ *naḥaš*; עָנַן *'ānan* II; שָׁחַר *šāḥar* I', *TDOT*, VII (1995), pp. 360-66 (361, 364-65)

כַּשָּׁף *sorcerer*—G. André, 'כָּשַׁף *kāšap*; כֶּשֶׁף *kešep*; כַּשָּׁף *kaššāp*; אַשָּׁף *'aššāp*; יִדְּעֹנִי *yiddeʿōnî*; לָחַשׁ *lāḥaš*; לַחַשׁ *laḥaš*; נָחַשׁ *nāḥaš*; נַחַשׁ *naḥaš*; עָנַן *'ānan* II; שָׁחַר *šāḥar* I', *TDOT*, VII (1995), pp. 360-66

כֶּשֶׁף *sorcery*—G. André, 'כָּשַׁף *kāšap*; כֶּשֶׁף *kešep*; כַּשָּׁף *kaššāp*; אַשָּׁף *'aššāp*; יִדְּעֹנִי *yiddeʿōnî*; לָחַשׁ *lāḥaš*; לַחַשׁ *laḥaš*; נָחַשׁ *nāḥaš*; נַחַשׁ *naḥaš*; עָנַן *'ānan* II; שָׁחַר *šāḥar* I', *TDOT*, VII (1995), pp. 360-66

כשׁר *be proper*—C.L. Seow, 'Linguistic Evidence and the Dating of Qohelet', *JBL* 115 (1996), pp. 643-66 (652); D. Kellermann, 'כָּשֵׁר *kāšēr*; כִּשְׁרוֹן *kišrôn*', *TDOT*, VII (1995) pp. 367-70 (368-69)

כִּשְׁרוֹן *skill*—C.L. Seow, 'Linguistic Evidence and the Dating of Qohelet', *JBL* 115 (1996), pp. 643-66 (652); D. Kellermann, 'כָּשֵׁר *kāšēr*; כִּשְׁרוֹן *kišrôn*', *TDOT*, VII (1995) pp. 367-70 (368)

כתב *write*—H. Haag, 'כָּתַב *kāṯaḇ*; כְּתָב *keṯāḇ*; מִכְתָּב *miḵtāḇ*; כְּתֹבֶת *keṯōḇeṯ*', *TDOT*, VII (1995) pp. 371-82 (372-73)

כְּתָב *writing*—H. Haag, 'כָּתַב *kāṯaḇ*; כְּתָב *keṯāḇ*; מִכְתָּב *miḵtāḇ*; כְּתֹבֶת *keṯōḇeṯ*', *TDOT*, VII (1995) pp. 371-82 (381-82)

כְּתֹבֶת *writing*—H. Haag, 'כָּתַב *kāṯaḇ*; כְּתָב *keṯāḇ*; מִכְתָּב *miḵtāḇ*; כְּתֹבֶת *keṯōḇeṯ*', *TDOT*, VII (1995) pp. 371-82 (382)

כֻּתֹּנֶת *tunic*—H.-J. Fabry, 'כֻּתֹּנֶת *kuttōneṯ*', *TDOT*, VII (1995), pp. 383-87; F. Charles Fensham, 'A Cappadocian Parallel to Hebrew *Kutōnet*', *VT* 12 (1962), pp. 196-98

כָּתֵף I *side, shoulder*—H.-J. Zobel, 'כָּתֵף *kāṯēp*', *TDOT*, VII (1995), pp. 387-92

side, (side)wall—H.-J. Zobel, 'כָּתֵף *kāṯēp*', *TDOT*, VII (1995), pp. 387-92 (389)

shoulder, back—H.-J. Zobel, 'כָּתֵף *kāṯēp*', *TDOT*, VII (1995), pp. 387-92 (390)

בֵּין כְּתֵפָיו *between his shoulders*—Y. Avishur, 'Expressions of the Type *BYN YDYM* in the Bible and Semitic Languages', *UF* 12 (1980), pp. 125-33 (131-32)

slope, hill—Z. Kallai, 'Kateph—כתף', *IEJ* 15 (1965), pp. 176-77

shoulderpiece—H.-J. Zobel, 'כָּתֵף *kāṯēp*', *TDOT*, VII (1995), pp. 387-92 (389-90)

כָּתֵף II *weapon* (cf. Ug. ktp, a kind of weapon, Arab. katīf *broadsword*)—Roger T. O'Callaghan, *Orientalia* 21 (1952), pp. 42-43; G.R. Driver, *Canaanite Myths and Legends* (Edinburgh: T. & T. Clark, 1956), p. 145; Herbert Donner, 'Ugaritismen in der Psalmenforschung', *ZAW* 79 (1967), pp. 323-50 (348); Barr, p. 329

כתת *crush*—G. Warmuth, 'כתת *ktt*; כָּתִית *kāṯîṯ*', *TDOT*, VII (1995), pp. 392-94

ל

לְ *of*—Y. Yadin, 'A Further Note on the *Lamed* in the Samaria Ostraca', *IEJ* 18 (1968), pp. 50-51

indeed—Mitchell Dahood, 'Textual Problems in Isaia', *CBQ* 22 (1960), pp. 400-409 (406); William L. Moran, 'The Hebrew Language in its Northwest Semitic Background', in *The Bible and the Ancient Near East: Essays in Honor of William Foxwell Albright* (ed. G.E. Wright; New York: Doubleday, 1961), pp. 54-69 (60); A. Guillaume, 'The Arabic Background of the Book of Job', in *Promise and Fulfilment: Essays Presented to Professor S.H. Hooke in Celebration of his Ninetieth Birthday, 21st January 1964, by Members of the Society for Old Testament Study and Others* (ed. F.F. Bruce; Edinburgh: T. & T. Clark, 1963), pp. 106-27 (112); M. Dahood, 'Hebrew–Ugaritic Lexicography III', *Bib* 46 (1965), pp. 311-32 (318); Thomas F. McDaniel, 'Philological Studies in Lamentations. II', *Bib* 49 (1968), pp. 199-217 (206-208)

O!—William L. Moran, 'The Hebrew Language in its Northwest Semitic Background', in *The Bible and the Ancient Near East: Essays in Honor of William Foxwell Albright* (ed. G.E. Wright; Garden City, NY: Doubleday, 1961), pp. 54-69 (60-61); M. Dahood, 'Comparative Philology Today and Yesterday' [Review of James Barr, *Comparative Philology and the Text of the Old Testament* (Oxford: Oxford University Press, 1968)], *Bib* 50 (1969), pp. 70-79 (74)

from—Edmund F. Sutcliffe, 'A Note on *'Al, Le*, and *From*', *VT* 5 (1955), pp. 436-39; Mitchell Dahood, *Psalms I: 1–50* (AB, 16; Garden City, NY: Doubleday, 1966), p. 178

לָא *power* (cf. Ug. l'y *be strong*)—Wilfred G.E. Watson, 'Reclustering Hebrew *l'lyd-*', *Bib* 58 (1977), pp. 213-15; E. Lipinski, 'Peninna, Iti'el et l'athlète', *VT* 17 (1967), pp. 68-75 (74); Jan Joosten, 'Pseudo-Classicisms in Late Biblical Hebrew, in Ben Sira, and in Qumran Hebrew', in *The Hebrew of the Dead Sea Scrolls and Ben Sira: Proceedings of a Symposium held at Leiden University, 11-14 December 1997* (ed. T. Muraoka and J.F. Elwolde; STDJ, 26; Leiden: E.J. Brill, 1998)

לָא I *hesitant*—J. Reider, 'Etymological Studies in Biblical Hebrew', *VT* 4 (1954), 276-95 (288); S. Grill, 'Die alten Versionen und die Partikeln lo', lô, lû, lî', *BZ* 1 (1957), pp. 277-81 (279); David J.A. Clines, *Job 1–20* (WBC, 17; Dallas, TX: Word Books, 1989), p. 161

לֹא I *not*—Kjell Aartun, 'Die hervorhebende Endung -*w*(V) an nordwestsemitischen Adverbien und Negationen', *UF* 5 (1973), pp. 1-5 (3-5); W. Th. van Peursen, 'Negation in the Hebrew of Ben Sira', in *Proceedings of the Second Leiden Symposium (December 1997)* (provisional title; ed. T. Muraoka and J.F. Elwolde; STDJ; Leiden: E.J. Brill)

Jb 12_{12}—S. Grill, 'Die alten Versionen und die Partikeln lo', lô, lû, lî', *BZ* 1 (1957), pp. 277-81 (279); David J.A. Clines, *Job 1–20* (WBC, 17; Dallas, TX: Word Books, 1989), pp. 279, 295

Jb 30_{13}—Alfred Guillaume, 'The Arabic Background of the Book of Job', in *Promise and Fulfilment: Essays Presented to Professor S.H. Hooke in Celebration of his Ninetieth Birthday, 21st January 1964, by Members of the Society for Old Testament Study and Others* (ed. F.F. Bruce: Edinburgh: T. & T. Clark, 1963), pp. 106-27 (119)

Jb 41_{3}—S. Grill, 'Die alten Versionen und die Partikeln lo', lô, lû, lî', *BZ* 1 (1957), pp. 277-81 (280)

Ho 7_{16}—G.I. Davies, *Hosea* (New Century Bible; Grand Rapids: Eerdmans, 1992), p. 192

Ml 2_{15}—S. Grill, 'Die alten Versionen und die Partikeln lo', lô, lû, lî', *BZ* 1 (1957), pp. 277-81 (281)

בְּשֶׁל שֶׁלֹּא *so that not* (§2b6)—Elisha Qimron and John Strugnell, *Qumran Cave 4. V: Miqṣat Ma'aśe ha-Torah* (DJD, 10; Oxford: Clarendon Press, 1994), pp. 89-90

אֲשֶׁר לֹא *one is not to* (§2d)—Elisha Qimron, *The Hebrew of the Dead Sea Scrolls* (HSS, 29; Atlanta: Scholars Press, 1986), pp. 77-78; P. Wernberg-Møller, *The Manual of Discipline Translated and Annotated with an Introduction* (STDJ, 1; Leiden: E.J. Brill, 1957), p. 93

if *not* (§2g)—Gershon Brin, 'The Formula "If He Shall Not (Do)" and the Problem of Sanctions in Biblical Law', in *Pomegranates and Golden Bells: Studies in Biblical, Jewish, and Near Eastern Ritual, Law, and Literature in Honor of Jacob Milgrom* (ed. David P. Wright, David Noel Freedman and Avi Hurvitz; Winona Lake, IN; Eisenbrauns, 1995), pp. 341-62

if *not* in oaths (Coll., §4)—Gershon Brin, 'The Formula "If He Shall Not (Do)" and the Problem of Sanctions in Biblical Law', in *Pomegranates and Golden Bells: Studies in Biblical, Jewish, and Near Eastern Ritual, Law, and Literature in Honor of Jacob Milgrom* (ed. David P. Wright, David Noel Freedman and Avi Hurvitz; Winona Lake, IN; Eisenbrauns, 1995), pp. 341-62 (343)

one is not to (§4)—Elisha Qimron and John Strugnell, *Qumran Cave 4. V: Miqṣat Ma'aśe ha-Torah* (DJD, 10; Oxford: Clarendon Press, 1994), p. 80; Elisha Qimron, *The Hebrew of the Dead Sea Scrolls* (HSS, 29; Atlanta: Scholars Press, 1986), pp. 78-79; Johannes Renz and Wolfgang Röllig, *Handbuch der althebräischen Epigraphik. Band I: Die althebräischen Inschriften. Teil 1: Text und Commentar* (Darmstadt: Wissenschaftliche Buchgesellschaft, 1995), p. 319; Avi Hurvitz, 'Further Comments on the Linguistic Profile of Ben Sira: Syntactical Affinities with Late Biblical Hebrew', in *Proceedings of the Second Leiden Symposium (December 1997)* (provisional title; ed. T. Muraoka and J.F. Elwolde; STDJ; Leiden: E.J. Brill); Miguel Pérez Fernández, '4QMMT: Linguistic Analysis of Redactional Forms Related to Biblical and Rabbinic Language', in *Proceedings of the Second Leiden Symposium (December 1997)* (provisional title; ed. T. Muraoka and J.F. Elwolde; STDJ; Leiden: E.J. Brill)

nothing (§17)—Mitchell Dahood, 'Hebrew–Ugaritic Lexicography IV', *Biblica* 47 (1966), pp. 403-19 (408); David J.A. Clines, *Job 1–20* (WBC, 17; Dallas, TX: Word Books, 1989), pp. 161, 218

no! (Jb 23_6)—Joseph Reider, 'Contributions to the Scriptural Text', *HUCA* 24 (1952–53), pp. 85-106 (104); Markus Witte, *Philologische Notizen zu Hiob 21–27* (BZAW, 234; Berlin: W. de Gruyter, 1995), p. 66

לֻא II *indeed*—G.R. Driver, 'Amos vii. 14', *ET* 67 (1955-56), pp. 91-92; H. Neil Richardson, 'A Critical Note on Amos 7 $_{14}$', *JBL* 85 (1966), p. 89; Joe O. Lewis, 'An Asseverative לֻא in Psalm 100 $_3$?', *JBL* 86 (1967), p. 216; David Noel Freedman, 'Is Justice Blind? (Is 11,3 f.)', *Bib* 62 (1971), p. 536; C.F. Whitley, 'Some Remarks on *lû* and *lo*'', *ZAW* 87 (1975), pp. 202-204

לאה I *be weary*—Helmer Ringgren, 'לָאָה *lā'â*', *TDOT*, VII (1995), pp. 395-96

לאה II *be strong* (cf. Ug. l'y)—M. Dahood, Review of Y. Yadin, Y. Aharoni, R. Amiran, T. Dothan, I. Dunayevsky, J. Perrot and S. Angress, *Hazor II. An Account of the Second Season of Excavations, 1956* (Oxford: Oxford University Press, 1960), *Bib* 42 (1961), pp. 474-76 (475); *Psalms I: 1–50* (AB, 16; New York: Doubleday, 1966), pp. xxxvi, 46; E. Lipinski, 'Peninna, Iti'el et l'athlète', *VT* 17 (1967), pp. 68-75 (74); Barr, p. 329; M. Dahood, Review of Jean Lévêque, *Job et son Dieu. Essai d'exégèse et de théologie biblique* (Paris: J. Gabalda, 1970), *Bib* 52 (1971), pp. 436-38 (438); Review of Camillano Pio Fedrizzi, *Giobbe* (Rome: Marietti, 1972), *Bib* 55 (1974), pp. 287-88; David J.A. Clines, *Job 1–20* (WBC, 17; Dallas, TX: Word Books, 1989), pp. 282, 312-13

לֵאָה I *Leah*—M. Dahood, Review of Y. Yadin, Y. Aharoni, R. Amiran, T. Dothan, I. Dunayevsky, J. Perrot and S. Angress, *Hazor II. An Account of the Second Season of Excavations, 1956* (Oxford: Oxford University Press, 1960), *Bib* 42 (1961), pp. 474-76 (475); *Psalms I: 1–50* (AB, 16; New York: Doubleday, 1966), p. 46

3QTr 11_{14}—John Marco Allegro, *The Treasure of the Copper Scroll* (London: Routledge & Kegan Paul, 1960), p. 164.

לְאֹם *nation*—H.D. Preuss, 'לְאֹם *le'ōm*', *TDOT*, VII (1995), pp. 397-98

לֵב *heart*—F.H. von Meyenfeldt, *Het Hart (Lēb, Lēbāb) in het Oude Testament* (Leiden: E.J. Brill, 1950); Hans Walter Wolff, *Anthropology of the Old Testament* (tr. Margaret Kohl; London: SCM Press, 1974), pp. 40-58; H.-J. Fabry, 'לֵב *lēḇ*; לֵבָב *lēḇāḇ*', *TDOT*, VII (1995), pp. 399-437; F. Stolz, 'לֵב *lēb* heart', *TLOT*, II (1997), pp. 638-42

Ps 45_2—Robert North, 'Brain and Nerve in the Biblical Outlook', *Bib* 74 (1993), pp. 577-97 (592-97); J. Hoftijzer, 'Some Remarks on Psalm 45:2', in *Give Ear to my Words—Psalms and other Poetry in and around the Hebrew Bible: Essays in Honour of Professor N.A. van Uchelen* (ed. Janet Dyk; Amsterdam: Societas Hebraica Amstelodamensis, 1996), pp. 47-59

Ezk 11_{21}—H.-J. Fabry, 'לֵב *lēḇ*; לֵבָב *lēḇāḇ*', *TDOT*, VII (1995), pp. 399-437 (434)

Ec 3_{11}—H.-J. Fabry, 'לֵב *lēḇ*; לֵבָב *lēḇāḇ*', *TDOT*, VII (1995), pp. 399-437 (420-21)

Si 46_{11}—Menahem Kister, 'Notes on the Book of Ben-Sira', *Lesh* 47 (1983), pp. 125-46 (143)

נְצֻרַת לֵב *wily*—G.R. Driver, 'Hebrew Notes', *VT* 1 (1951), pp. 241-50 (250)

עָרְלַת לֵב *foreskin of heart*—H.-J. Fabry, 'לֵב *lēḇ*; לֵבָב *lēḇāḇ*', *TDOT*, VII (1995), pp. 399-437 (433-34, 437)

שְׁרִרוּת לֵב *stubbornness*, or *thinking*, *of heart*—Elisha Qimron, 'Biblical Philology and the DSS', *Tarb* 58 (1989), pp. 297-315 (313)

לֵב שָׁלֵם *whole heart*—H.-J. Fabry, 'לֵב *lēḇ*; לֵבָב *lēḇāḇ*', *TDOT*, VII (1995), pp. 399-437 (431-32)

דִּבֵּר עַל לֵב *spoke to the heart*—J.-M. Babut, *Les expressions idiomatiques de l'hébreu biblique* (Cahiers de la Revue Biblique, 33, Paris: Gabalda, 1995), pp. 84-87; H.-J. Fabry, 'לֵב *lēḇ*; לֵבָב *lēḇāḇ*', *TDOT*, VII (1995), pp. 399-437 (417-18)

לֵב *heart* || עַיִן *eye*—W.G.E. Watson, 'The Unnoticed Word Pair »eye(s)« // »heart«', *ZAW* 101 (1989), pp. 398-408

לבב I *think*—F. Stolz, 'לֵב *lēb* heart', *TLOT*, II (1997), pp. 638-42 (638)

לבב II *sprout* (cf. Aram. לבלב; Akk. lippu)—N.H. Tur-Sinai, *The Book of Job, A New Commentary* (Jerusalem: Kiryath Sepher, 1957)

עָרְלַת לֵבָב *foreskin of heart*—H.-J. Fabry, 'לֵב *lēḇ*; לֵבָב *lēḇāḇ*', *TDOT*, VII (1995), pp. 399-437 (433-34, 437)

מוֹרָשֵׁי לֵבָב *desires of the heart*—David J.A. Clines, *Job 1–20* (WBC, 17; Dallas, TX: Word Books, 1989), p. 374

לֵבָב *heart*—Hans Walter Wolff, *Anthropology of the Old Testament* (tr. Margaret Kohl; London: SCM Press, 1974), pp. 40-58; H.-J. Fabry, 'לֵב *lēḇ*; לֵבָב *lēḇāḇ*', *TDOT*, VII (1995), pp. 399-437

לִבָּה *spirit, anger*—G.R. Driver, 'Some Hebrew Words', *JTS* 29 (1928), pp. 390-96 (393); 'Studies in the Vocabulary of the Old Testament. III', *JTS* 32 (1931), pp. 361-66 (366)

לְבוֹנָה I *frankincense*—D. Kellermann, 'לְבֹנָה *leḇōnâ*', *TDOT*, VII (1995), pp. 441-47

לְבוֹנָה II *Lebonah*—D. Kellermann, 'לְבֹנָה *leḇōnâ*', *TDOT*, VII (1995), pp. 441-47 (446)

לְבִיא *lion* (fem.)—John Pairman Brown, 'From Divine Kingship to Dispersal of Power in the Mediterranean City-State', *ZAW* 105 (1993), pp. 62-86 (73)

לְבִיָּה *lion* (fem.) (4QpNah 3.1$_{4}$)—Elisha Qimron, *The Hebrew of the Dead Sea Scrolls* (HSS, 29; Atlanta: Scholars Press, 1986), p. 26

לָבָן I *white*—H. Ringgren, 'לבן *lbn*; לְבֵנָה *leḇēnâ*; לָבָן *lāḇān*; לְבָנָה *leḇānâ*', *TDOT*, VII (1995), pp. 438-41 (439-40)

bare—G.W. Nebe, 'Die hebräische Sprache der Naḥal Ḥever Dokumente 5/6Ḥev 44–46', in *The Hebrew of the Dead Sea Scrolls and Ben Sira: Proceedings of a Symposium held at Leiden University, 11–14 December 1995* (ed. T. Muraoka and J.F. Elwolde; STDJ, 26; Leiden: E.J. Brill, 1997), pp. 150-57 (152)

לָבָן II *Laban*—H. Ringgren, 'לבן *lbn*; לְבֵנָה *leḇēnâ*; לָבָן *lāḇān*; לְבָנָה *leḇānâ*', *TDOT*, VII (1995), pp. 438-41 (440)

לְבָנָה I *moon*—H. Ringgren, 'לבן *lbn*; לְבֵנָה *leḇēnâ*; לָבָן *lāḇān*; לְבָנָה *leḇānâ*', *TDOT*, VII (1995), pp. 438-41 (440)

לִבְנָה *precious stone*—Elisha Qimron, 'A Review Article of *Songs of the Sabbath Sacrifices* [sic]: *A Critical Edition*, by Carol Newsom', *HTR* 79 (1986), pp. 348-71 (357)

לְבֵנָה *brick*—John Pairman Brown, 'Literary Contexts of the Common Hebrew–Greek Vocabulary', *JSS* 13 (1968), pp. 163-91 (182-84); H. Ringgren, 'לבן *lbn*; לְבֵנָה *leḇēnâ*; לָבָן *lāḇān*; לְבָנָה *leḇānâ*', *TDOT*, VII (1995), pp. 438-41 (438-39)

Is 65$_{3}$—Matitiahu Tsevat, 'Some Biblical Notes', *HUCA* 24 (1952–53), pp. 107-14 (109-10); Mitchell Dahood, 'Textual Problems in Isaia', *CBQ* 22 (1960), pp. 400-409 (407-408); H. Ringgren, 'לבן *lbn*; לְבֵנָה *leḇēnâ*; לָבָן *lāḇān*; לְבָנָה *leḇānâ*', *TDOT*, VII (1995), pp. 438-41 (438-39)

לְבָנוֹן *Lebanon*—M.J. Mulder, 'לְבָנוֹן *leḇānôn*', *TDOT*, VII (1995), pp. 447-57

לבשׁ *dress*—J. Gamberoni and H.-J. Fabry, *TDOT*, VII (1995), 'לָבֵשׁ *lāḇēš*', pp. 457-68; E. Jenni, 'לבשׁ *lbš* to clothe oneself ', *TLOT*, II (1997), pp. 642-44

לֹג *log* (3QTr 1$_{9}$)—Bargil Pixner, 'Unravelling the Copper Scroll Code: A Study on the Topography of 3Q15', *RQ* 11 (1983), pp. 323-61 (343); Al Wolters, 'Notes on the Copper Scroll (3Q15)', *RQ* 12 (1987), pp. 589-96 (590-92); Manfred R. Lehmann, 'Identification of the Copper Scroll Based on its Technical Terms', *RQ* 5 (1964), pp. 97-105 (98-99); J.F. Elwolde, '3Q15: Its Linguistic Affiliation, with Lexicographical Comments', in *Proceedings of the International Symposium on the Copper Scroll, Manchester, September 1996* (ed. George J. Brooke and Philip R. Davies; JSPSup; Sheffield: Sheffield Academic Press, forthcoming)

לַהַב *flame*—J. Hausmann, 'לַהַב *lahaḇ*; לֶהָבָה *lehāḇâ*; שַׁלְהֶבֶת *šalheḇeṯ*', *TDOT*, VII (1995), pp. 469-73

לַהַב *flame*—J. Hausmann, 'לַהַב *lahaḇ*; לֶהָבָה *lehāḇâ*; שַׁלְהֶבֶת *šalheḇeṯ*', *TDOT*, VII (1995), pp. 469-73

לֶהָבָה *flame*—J. Hausmann, 'לַהַב *lahaḇ*; לֶהָבָה *lehāḇâ*; שַׁלְהֶבֶת *šalheḇeṯ*', *TDOT*, VII (1995), pp. 469-73

לַהַג *reckoning* (cf. Ugar. *hg*)—John Gray, *The Legacy of Canaan: The Ras Shamra Texts and their Relevance to the Old Testament* (VTSup, 5; Leiden: E.J. Brill, 2nd edn, 1965), pp. 275-76; Mitchell Dahood, 'Hebrew–Ugaritic Lexicography IV', *Biblica* 47 (1966), pp. 403-19 (408-409)

להט I *blaze*—J. Hausmann, 'לָהַט *lāhaṭ*; לַהַט *lahaṭ*', *TDOT*, VII (1995), pp. 473-74

להט II *devour/bewitch*—G.R. Driver, 'Studies in the Vocabulary of the Old Testament. IV', *JTS* 33 (1932), pp. 38-47 (39); A. Guillaume, 'The Hebrew Root להט', *JTS* 41 (1940), pp. 251-52; Kaltner, pp. 58-59; J. Hausmann, 'לָהַט *lāhaṭ*; לַהַט *lahaṭ*', *TDOT*, VII (1995), pp. 473-74 (473)

לַהַט *flame*—J. Hausmann, 'לָהַט *lāhaṭ*; לַהַט *lahaṭ*', *TDOT*, VII (1995), pp. 473-74

לַהֲקָה *company, old age* (cf. Ethiopic lehiq *elder*)—G.R. Driver, 'Some Hebrew Words', *JTS* 29 (1928), pp. 390-96 (394); D. Winton Thomas, 'A Note on לִיקֲהַת in Proverbs xxx. 17', *JTS* 42 (1941), pp. 154-55; Barr, pp. 25-26, 231-32, 267, 270

לוּ *indeed*—C.F. Whitley, 'Some Remarks on *lû* and *lo*'', *ZAW* 87 (1975), pp. 202-204

if only (Gn 23$_{6.11.13.15}$)—S. Grill, 'Die alten Versionen und die Partikeln lo', lô, lû, lî', *BZ* 1 (1957), pp. 277-81 (277-78)

1 S 13$_{13}$ 20$_{14}$—S. Grill, 'Die alten Versionen und die Partikeln lo', lô, lû, lî', *BZ* 1 (1957), pp. 277-81 (278)

in case (Jb 24$_{5}$)—Alfred Guillaume, 'The Arabic Background of the Book of Job', in *Promise and Fulfilment: Essays Presented to Professor S.H. Hooke in Celebration of his Ninetieth Birthday, 21st January 1964, by Members of the Society for Old Testament Study and Others* (ed. F.F. Bruce: Edinburgh: T. & T. Clark, 1963), pp. 106-27 (116)

לָוָא *woe* (cf. Amor. לִוְיָה *dirge*)—J. Reider, 'Etymological Studies in Biblical Hebrew', *VT* 4 (1954), 276-95 (295)

לוה I *borrow*—D. Kellermann, 'לָוָה II *lāwâ* II', *TDOT*, VII (1995), pp. 477-78

לוה II *accompany*—D. Kellermann, 'לָוָה I *lāwâ* I', *TDOT*, VII (1995), pp. 475-768

לוז *depart*—H. Ringgren, 'לוּז *lûz*; לָזוּת *lāzûṯ*', *TDOT*, VII (1995), pp. 478-79

לוּחַ *tablet*—A. Baumann, 'לוּחַ *lûaḥ*', *TDOT*, VII (1995), pp. 480-83

לֵוִי I *Levi*—Martin Noth, 'Remarks on the Sixth Volume of Mari Texts', *JSS* 1 (1956), pp. 322-33 (327); D. Kellermann, ''לֵוִי *lēwî*; לְוִיִּם *lewîyîm*', *TDOT*, VII (1985), pp. 483-503

לֵוִי II *Levite*—D. Kellermann, ''לֵוִי *lēwî*; לְוִיִּם *lewîyîm*', *TDOT*, VII (1985), pp. 483-503

עָרֵי הַלְוִיִּם *cities of the Levites*—D. Kellermann, ''לֵוִי *lēwî*; לְוִיִּם *lewîyîm*', *TDOT*, VII (1985), pp. 483-503 (494-96)

לִוְיָתָן *Leviathan*—H.H. Rowley (on G.R. Driver), 'The Istanbul Congress of Orientalists and the Old Testament', *VT* 1 (1951), pp. 313-18 (314); E. Lipinski, 'לִוְיָתָן *liwyāṯān*', *TDOT*, VII (1995), pp. 504-509; J.A. Emerton, 'Leviathan and *Ltn*: The Vocalization of the Ugaritic Word for the Dragon, *VT* 32 (1982), pp. 327-31; Stanley V. Udd, 'More on the Vocalization of *Ltn*', *VT* 33 (1983), pp. 509-10

לוּלֵא *unless* (Ps 27$_{13}$)—S. Grill, 'Die alten Versionen und die Partikeln lo', lô, lû, lî', *BZ* 1 (1957), pp. 277-81 (280)

לון I *murmur*—K.-D. Schunck, 'לוּן *lûn*; תְּלֻנּוֹת *telunnôṯ*', *TDOT*, VII (1995), pp. 509-12; R. Knierim, 'לון *lûn* to rebel', *TLOT*, II (1997), pp. 644-46

לָזוּת *perversity*—H. Ringgren, 'לוּז *lûz*; לָזוּת *lāzûṯ*', *TDOT*, VII (1995), pp. 478-79

לח *moist*—H.-J. Fabry, 'לַח *laḥ*; לֵחַ *lēaḥ*', *TDOT*, VII (1995), pp. 512-17

לֵחַ *moisture*—H.-J. Fabry, 'לַח *laḥ*; לֵחַ *lēaḥ*', *TDOT*, VII (1995), pp. 512-17

Jr 11$_{19}$—Mitchell Dahood, 'Hebrew–Ugaritic Lexicography IV', *Biblica* 47 (1966), pp. 403-19 (409)

smoothness—Jeffrey H. Tigay, 'לא נס לחה "He Had Not Become Wrinkled" (Deuteronomy 34,7)', in *Solving Riddles and Untying Knots: Biblical, Epigraphical, and Semitic Studies in Honor of Jonas C. Greenfield* (ed. Ziony Zevit, Seymour Gitin and Michael Sokoloff; Winona Lake, IN; Eisenbrauns, 1995), pp. 345-50

נָס לֵחַ *tears flow*—Menahem Kister, 'Some Notes on Biblical Expressions and Allusions and the Lexicography of Ben Sira', in *Proceedings of the Second Leiden Symposium (December 1997)* (provisional title; ed. T. Muraoka and J.F. Elwolde; STDJ; Leiden: E.J. Brill)

לֵחָה *liquid*—Elisha Qimron, '3. The Language', in *Qumran Cave 4. V: Miqṣat Ma'aśe ha-Torah* (ed. Elisha Qimron and John Strugnell; DJD, 10; Oxford: Clarendon Press, 1994), pp. 65-108 (92); H.-J. Fabry, 'לַח *laḥ*; לֵחַ *lēaḥ*', *TDOT*, VII (1995), pp. 512-17 (517)

לְחוּם I *flesh*—Lester L. Grabbe, *Comparative Philology and the Text of Job: A Study in Methodology* (SBLDS, 34; Missoula, MT: Scholars Press, 1977), pp. 76-77

לָחוּם II *warfare*—Lester L. Grabbe, *Comparative Philology and the Text of Job: A Study in Methodology* (SBLDS, 34; Missoula, MT: Scholars Press, 1977), pp. 76-77

לְחִי I *jaw*—H. Ringgren, 'לְחִי *leḥî*', *TDOT*, VII (1995), pp. 517-19

Ps 56_{2}—Mitchell Dahood, 'Hebrew–Ugaritic Lexicography IV', *Biblica* 47 (1966), pp. 403-19 (409)

לְחִי IV *hip, buttock* (cf. Greek ἰσχάς 'fig' > 'fresh, fruit' > 'buttock, hip')—Giovanni Garbini, 'Calchi lessicali greci nel «Cantico dei cantici»', *AANLR* 39 (1984), pp. 149-60 (158-59)

לחך *lick*—H. Ringgren, 'לָחַךְ *lāḥak̲*', *TDOT*, VII (1995), p. 520

pi. *lick* (Am 5_{6})—Joseph Reider, 'Contributions to the Scriptural Text', *HUCA* 24 (1952–53), pp. 85-106 (95)

לחם I *fight* (Dt 32_{24})—Jonas C. Greenfield, 'Smitten by Famine, Battered by Plague (Deuteronomy 32:24)', in *Love and Death in the Ancient Near East: Essays in Honor of Marvin H. Pope* (ed. John H. Marks and Robert M. Good; Guilford, CN/Los Angeles, CA: Four Quarters Publishing Company/Western Academic Press, 1986), pp. 151-52

לחם II *eat*—Gary A. Rendsburg, *Linguistic Evidence for the Northern Origin of Selected Psalms* (SBLMS, 43; Atlanta: Scholars Press, 1990), pp. 99-100

לֶחֶם I *bread*—W. Dommershausen and H.-J. Fabry, 'לֶחֶם *leḥem*', *TDOT*, VII (1995), pp. 521-29

as fem. noun—Stanley Gevirtz, 'Asher in the Blessing of Jacob (Genesis xlix 20)', *VT* 37 (1987), pp. 154-63 (161-62)

Gn 49_{20}—Stanley Gevirtz, 'Asher in the Blessing of Jacob (Genesis XLIX 20)', *VT* 37 (1987), pp. 154-63 (159)

Lv 23_{14}—Elisha Qimron, 'Biblical Philology and the DSS', *Tarb* 58 (1989), pp. 297-315 (308-10)

Jb 6_{7}—Klaus Berger, 'Die Bedeutung der wiederentdeckten Weisheitsschrift der Kairoer Geniza für das Alte Testament', *ZAW* 103 (1991), pp. 114-21 (118)

Ec 11_{1}—M. Dahood, 'Qoheleth and Recent Discoveries', *Bib* 39 (1958), pp. 302-18 (315-16); W. Dommershausen and H.-J. Fabry, 'לֶחֶם *leḥem*', *TDOT*, VII (1995), pp. 521-29 (524-25)

11QT 19_{7}—Elisha Qimron, 'Biblical Philology and the DSS', *Tarb* 58 (1989), pp. 297-315 (309-10)

לֶחֶם הַפָּנִים *bread of the presence*—W. Dommershausen and H.-J. Fabry, 'לֶחֶם *leḥem*', *TDOT*, VII (1995), pp. 521-29 (525-26)

לֶחֶם הַתָּמִיד *the bread of continuity*—W. Dommershausen and H.-J. Fabry, 'לֶחֶם *leḥem*', *TDOT*, VII (1995), pp. 521-29 (525-26)

food—Edward Ullendorff, 'The Contribution of South Semitics to Hebrew Lexicography', *VT* 6 (1956), pp. 190-98 (192); P. Swiggers, 'The Meaning of the Root *LḤM* "Food" in the Semitic Languages', *UF* 13 (1981), pp. 307-308; W. Dommershausen and H.-J. Fabry, 'לֶחֶם *leḥem*', *TDOT*, VII (1995), pp. 521-29 (521, 523-24)

Ps 104_{14}—Giuseppe Leonardi, 'Note su alcuni versetti del Salmo 104', *Bib* 49 (1968), pp. 238-43 (241)

אכל לֶחֶם *eat a meal*—W. Dommershausen and H.-J. Fabry, 'לֶחֶם *leḥem*', *TDOT*, VII (1995), pp. 521-29 (523)

לָחֶם II *war*—Menahem Kister, 'Some Notes on Biblical Expressions and Allusions and the Lexicography of Ben Sira', in *Proceedings of the Second Leiden Symposium (December 1997)* (provisional title; ed. T. Muraoka and J.F. Elwolde; STDJ; Leiden: E.J. Brill), n. 3

לחץ *squeeze*—J. Reindl, 'לָחַץ *lāḥaṣ*', *TDOT*, VII (1995), pp. 529-33

oppress—J. Reindl, 'לָחַץ *lāḥaṣ*', *TDOT*, VII (1995), pp. 529-33 (532)

לַחַץ *oppression*—J. Reindl, 'לָחַץ *lāḥaṣ*', *TDOT*, VII (1995), pp. 529-33 (533)

לֶחֶם לַחַץ וּמַיִם לַחַץ *bread and water of oppression*—L. Kopf, 'Arabische Etymologien und Parallelen zum Bibelwörterbuch', *VT* 9 (1959), pp. 247-87 (261)

לַיִל *night*—A. Stiglmair and H.-J. Fabry, 'לַיְלָה/לַיִל *layil/laylâ*', *TDOT*, VII (1995), pp. 533-42

לַיְלָה *night*—A. Stiglmair and H.-J. Fabry, 'לַיְלָה/לַיִל *layil/laylâ*', *TDOT*, VII (1995), pp. 533-42

לִילִית *Lilith*—G.R. Driver, 'Birds in the Old Testament: II. Birds in Life', *PEQ* 87 (1955), pp. 129-40 (135-36)

nightjar—G.R. Driver, 'Lilith', *PEQ* 91 (1959), pp. 55-57

לִין lodge—E.B. Oikonomou, לִין lîn; מָלוֹן mālôn; מְלוּנָה melûnâ', *TDOT*, VII (1995), pp. 543-46

לִיץ scorn—H. Neil Richardson, 'Some Notes on לִיץ and its Derivatives', *VT* 5 (1955), pp. 163-79; C. Barth, לִיץ *lyṣ*; לִיץ lîs; לֵץ lēṣ; לָצוֹן lāṣôn; מֵלִיץ mēlîṣ', *TDOT*, VII (1995), pp. 547-52

לֵץ scoffer—H. Neil Richardson, 'Some Notes on לִיץ and its Derivatives', *VT* 5 (1955), pp. 163-79 (170-73); C. Barth, לִיץ *lyṣ*; לִיץ lîs; לֵץ lēṣ; לָצוֹן lāṣôn; מֵלִיץ mēlîṣ', *TDOT*, VII (1995), pp. 547-52

מֵלִיץ interpreter—H. Neil Richardson, 'Some Notes on לִיץ and its Derivatives', *VT* 5 (1955), pp. 163-79 (167-69); C. Barth, לִיץ *lyṣ*; לִיץ lîs; לֵץ lēṣ; לָצוֹן lāṣôn; מֵלִיץ mēlîṣ', *TDOT*, VII (1995), pp. 547-52 (550-52)

לְכוּשִׁי pine—Al Wolters, 'Notes on the Copper Scroll (3Q15)', *RQ* 12 (1987), pp. 589-96 (593-94)

לָכֵן therefore—Hellmut Lenhard, 'Über den Unterschied zwischen לכן and על־כן', *ZAW* 95 (1983), pp. 269-72; K. Koch, כּוּן kûn; כֵּן kēn; מָכוֹן mākôn; מְכוֹנָה mekônâ; תְּכוּנָה tekûnâ', *TDOT*, VII (1995), pp. 89-101 (91)

and, now then—W. Eugene March, '*Lākēn*: Its Functions and Meanings', in *Rhetorical Criticism: Essays in Honor of James Muilenburg* (ed. Jared J. Jackson and Martin Kessler; Pittsburgh Theological Monograph Series, 1; Pittsburgh: Pickwick Press, 1974), pp. 256-84

לָמַד learn—Jonas C. Greenfield, 'Ugaritic *mdl* and its Cognates', *Bib* 45 (1964), pp. 527-34 (529-30)

Jr 10$_2$—Mitchell Dahood, 'Hebrew–Ugaritic Lexicography IV', *Biblica* 47 (1966), pp. 403-19 (410)

pi. *practise* battle song—Otto Eissfeldt, 'Zwei verkannte militär-technische Termini im Alten Testament', *VT* 5 (1955), pp. 232-38 (235)

know, have intercourse with (cf. Akk. *lamādu* know sexually)—Shalom M. Paul, 'Gleanings from the Biblical and Talmudic Lexica in Light of Akkadian', in *Minḥah le-Naḥum: Biblical and Other Studies Presented to Nahum M. Sarna in Honour of his 70th Birthday* (ed. Marc Brettler and Michael Fishbane; JSOTSup, 154; Sheffield: JSOT Press, 1993), pp. 242-56 (249-51)

לָמֻד pupil—Wilfred G.E. Watson, Review of Joseph Jensen, *The Use of Tôrâ by Isaiah: His Debate with the Wisdom Tradition* (Washington, DC: The Catholic Biblical Association of America, 1973), *Bib* 56 (1975), pp. 274-76 (275)

לָמָה lest (cf. Maltese li ma)—Richard S. Tomback, 'An Unrecognized Maltese West-Semitic Isogloss', *JNWSL* 12 (1984), pp. 121-23

לְמוּאֵל Lemuel (cf. Mari divine name *Lim*)—A. Jirku, 'Das n. pr. Lemu'el (Prov 31$_1$) und der Gott Lim', *ZAW* 66 (1954), p. 151

לְמַעַן for the sake of—H.A. Brongers, 'Die Partikel לְמַעַן in der biblisch-hebräischen Sprache', *OTS* 18 (1973), pp. 84-96

לָעַג stammering—Shalom M. Paul, 'Hosea 7:16: Gibberish Jabber', in *Pomegranates and Golden Bells: Studies in Biblical, Jewish, and Near Eastern Ritual, Law, and Literature in Honor of Jacob Milgrom* (ed. David P. Wright, David Noel Freedman and Avi Hurvitz; Winona Lake, IN; Eisenbrauns, 1995), pp. 707-12

לעז speak a foreign language (Ps 114$_1$)—Mitchell Dahood, 'Hebrew–Ugaritic Lexicography IV', *Biblica* 47 (1966), pp. 403-19 (411)

לעט hi. *feed*—Robert Alter, *Genesis: Translation and Commentary* (New York/London: W.W. Norton & Company, 1996), pp. xxiv-xxv

לעע I gush—M. Dahood, Review of Friedrich Horst, *Hiob* (Neukirchen Kreis Moers: Verlag der Buchhandlung des Erziehungsvereins, 1960), *Bib* 43 (1962), pp. 225-26 (225)

לעע II pilp. *lap up*—Lester L. Grabbe, *Comparative Philology and the Text of Job: A Study in Methodology* (SBLDS, 34; Missoula, MT: Scholars Press, 1977), pp. 128-30

לַפִּיד torch—S. Segert, 'Zur Etymologie von Lappīd »Fackel«', *ZAW* 74 (1962), pp. 323-24

לַפִּידוֹת Lappidoth—S. Segert, 'Zur Etymologie von Lappīd »Fackel«', *ZAW* 74 (1962), pp. 323-24

לִפְנֵי before (Ec 4$_{16}$)—Mitchell Dahood, 'Qoheleth and Northwest Semitic Philology', *Bib* 43 (1962), pp. 349-65 (357)

לְפָנִים II predecessors—Mitchell Dahood, 'Hebrew–Ugaritic Lexicography IV', *Biblica* 47 (1966), pp. 403-19 (411)

לָצוֹן scorning—C. Barth, לִיץ *lyṣ*; לִיץ lîs; לֵץ lēṣ; לָצוֹן lāṣôn; מֵלִיץ mēlîṣ', *TDOT*, VII (1995), pp. 547-52 (549-50)

Bibliography to Lamedh

babbling—H. Neil Richardson, 'Some Notes on לִיץ and its Derivatives', *VT* 5 (1955), pp. 163-79 (177-78); 'Two Addenda to "Some Notes on לִיץ and its Derivatives"', *VT* 5 (1955), pp. 434-36 (436)

לקח *take*—H. Seebass, 'לקח *lāqaḥ*', *TDOT*, VIII (1997), pp. 16-21; H.H. Schmid, 'לקח *lqḥ* to take', *TLOT*, II (1997), pp. 648-51

Nm 16_{1}—Barr, pp. 17-18; Jacob Milgrom, *Numbers: the Traditional Hebrew Text with the New JPS Translation* (The JPS Torah Commentary; Philadelphia: The Jewish Publication Society, 1990), p. 312; Baruch A. Levine, *Numbers 1–20: A New Translation with Introduction and Commentary* (AB, 4; New York: Doubleday, 1993), pp. 410-11

Jb 15_{12}—M. Dahood, 'Comparative Philology Today and Yesterday' [Review of James Barr, *Comparative Philology and the Text of the Old Testament* (Oxford: Oxford University Press, 1968)], *Bib* 50 (1969), pp. 70-79 (73)

marry—H. Seebass, 'לקח *lāqaḥ*', *TDOT*, VIII (1997), pp. 16-21 (19); H.H. Schmid, 'לקח *lqḥ* to take', *TLOT*, II (1997), pp. 648-51 (650)

ni. *be taken (away)*—H. Seebass, 'לקח *lāqaḥ*', *TDOT*, VIII (1997), pp. 16-21 (19-20); H.H. Schmid, 'לקח *lqḥ* to take', *TLOT*, II (1997), pp. 648-51 (649-50)

לֶקַח I *teaching*—H. Seebass, 'לפח *lāqaḥ*', *TDOT*, VIII (1997), pp. 16-21 (21); H.H. Schmid, 'לקח *lqḥ* to take', *TLOT*, II (1997), pp. 648-51 (651)

לָקַט *take*—H. Ringgren, 'לָקַט *lāqaṭ*', *TDOT*, VIII (1997), pp. 21-23

לָשׁוֹן *tongue*—B. Kedar-Kopfstein, 'לָשׁוֹן *lāšôn*', *TDOT*, VIII (1997), pp. 23-33 (27-28)

Ps 68_{24}—Joseph Reider, 'Contributions to the Scriptural Text', *HUCA* 24 (1952-53), pp. 85-106 (101); John Gray, *The Biblical Doctrine of the Reign of God* (Edinburgh: T. & T. Clark, 1979), p. 53

זַעַם לְשׁוֹנָם *stammering of their tongue*—Shalom M. Paul, 'Hosea 7:16: Gibberish Jabber', in *Pomegranates and Golden Bells: Studies in Biblical, Jewish, and Near Eastern Ritual, Law, and Literature in Honor of Jacob Milgrom* (ed. David P. Wright, David Noel Freedman and Avi Hurvitz; Winona Lake, IN; Eisenbrauns, 1995), pp. 707-12

(foreign) language—B. Kedar-Kopfstein, 'לָשׁוֹן *lā šôn*', *TDOT*, VIII (1997), pp. 23-33 (29-30)

people—Isaac Rabinowitz, 'The Authorship, Audience, and Date of the de Vaux Fragment of an Unknown Work', *JBL* 71 (1952), pp. 19-32 (29)

sense, meaning (+ לַעֲגֵי שָׂפָה *mocking speech*)—Vincent Tanghe, 'Dichtung und Ekel in Jesaja xxviii 7-13', *VT* 43 (1993), pp. 235-60 (239, 249-50, 258-60)

ray, tongue (Si 43_{4})—Menaḥem Kister, 'A Contribution to the Interpretation of Ben-Sira', *Tarb* 59 (1990), pp. 303-78 [360] [in Hebrew]); John Strugnell, 'Notes and Queries on the "Ben Sira Scroll from Masada", in A. Malamat (ed.), *W.F. Albright Volume=Eretz-Israel* 9 (Jerusalem: Israel Exploration Society, 1969), pp. 109-19 (117)

bar—B. Kedar-Kopfstein, 'לָשׁוֹן *lāšôn*', *TDOT*, VIII (1997), pp. 23-33 (28)

לִשְׁכָּה *chamber*—D. Kellermann, 'לִשְׁכָּה *liškâ*', *TDOT*, VIII (1997), pp. 33-38 (34)

לֶשֶׁם *pale carnelian*—John S. Harris, 'An Introduction to the Study of Personal Ornaments of Precious, Semi-Precious and Imitation Stones Used throughout Biblical History', *ALUOS* 4 (1962), pp. 49-83 (66)

ENGLISH–HEBREW INDEX